The Snettis Hoards

Volume I

Edited by Julia Farley and Jody Joy

With contributions from Ian Stead and Sophia Adams, Janet Ambers, Caroline Cartwright, Mike Cowell, Paul Craddock, John Davies, Michael de Bootman, Philip de Jersey, John Fenn, Eleanor Ghey, Marilyn Hockey, David Holman, Duncan Hook, Susan La Niece, Janet Lang, Alice Lyons, Peter Makey, Nigel Meeks, Aude Mongiatti, Peter Northover, Daniel O'Flynn, Sarah Percival, Alan Pipe, Matthew Ponting, Fleur Shearman and Tony Spence

The British Museum

Publication supported by:

Eyre Family Foundation

The Pennycress Trust

Publishers
The British Museum
Great Russell Street
London WC1B 3DG

Series editor
Sarah Faulks

The Snettisham Hoards
Edited by Julia Farley and Jody Joy

ISBN 9780861592258
ISSN 1747 3640
doi 10.48582/3xdb-ns12

Front cover: The torcs of Hoard L *in situ* in the hoard pit. Photograph taken during the British Museum excavations in 1990
Pg. iv: aerial shot of Snettisham village, 2023. Image © Rod Trevaskus
Pg. vi: close up view of torc fragment S.13 showing anthropomorphic decoration

Printed and bound in the UK by 4edge Ltd, Hockley

Further information about the Museum and its collection can be found at britishmuseum.org

Contents

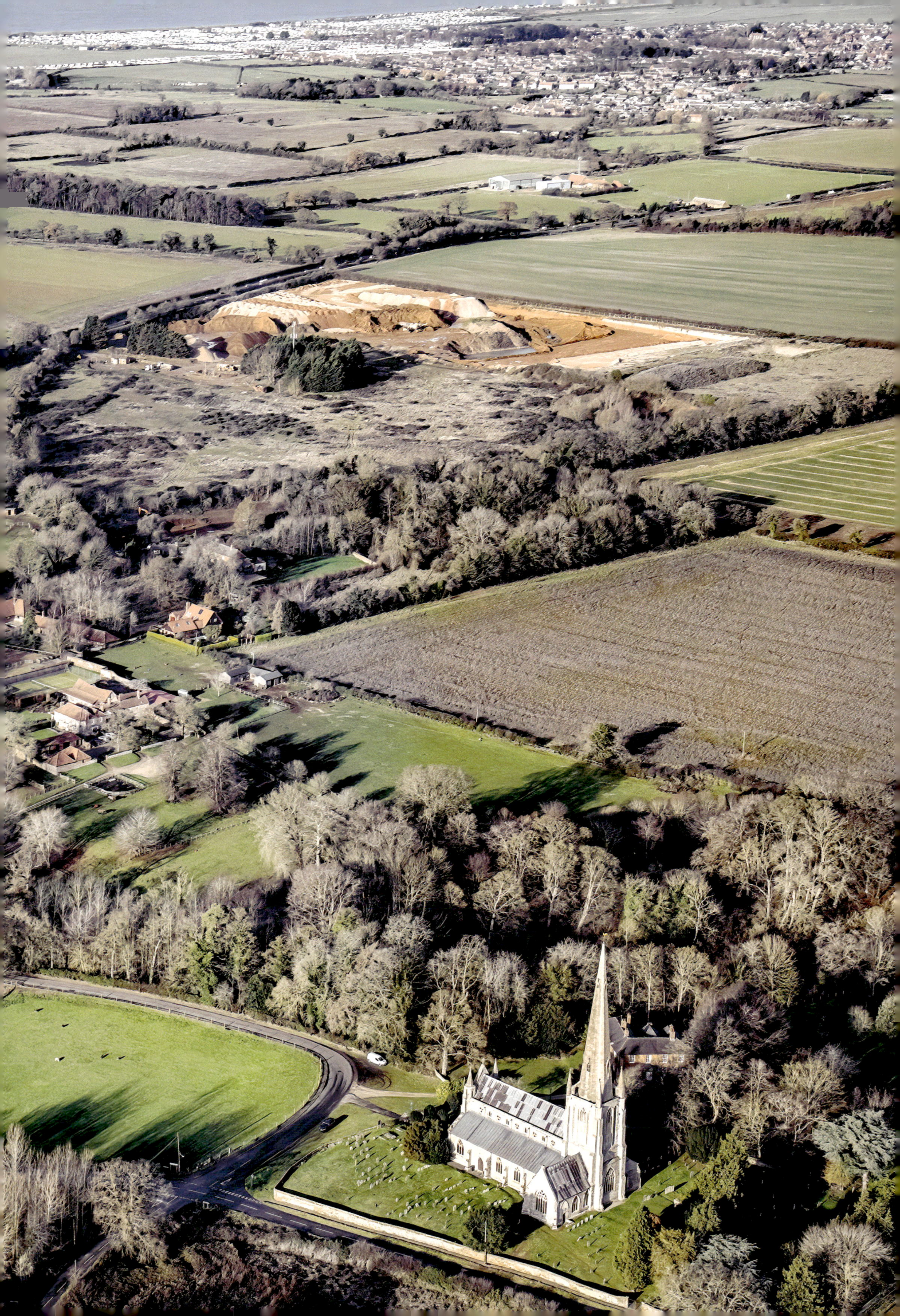

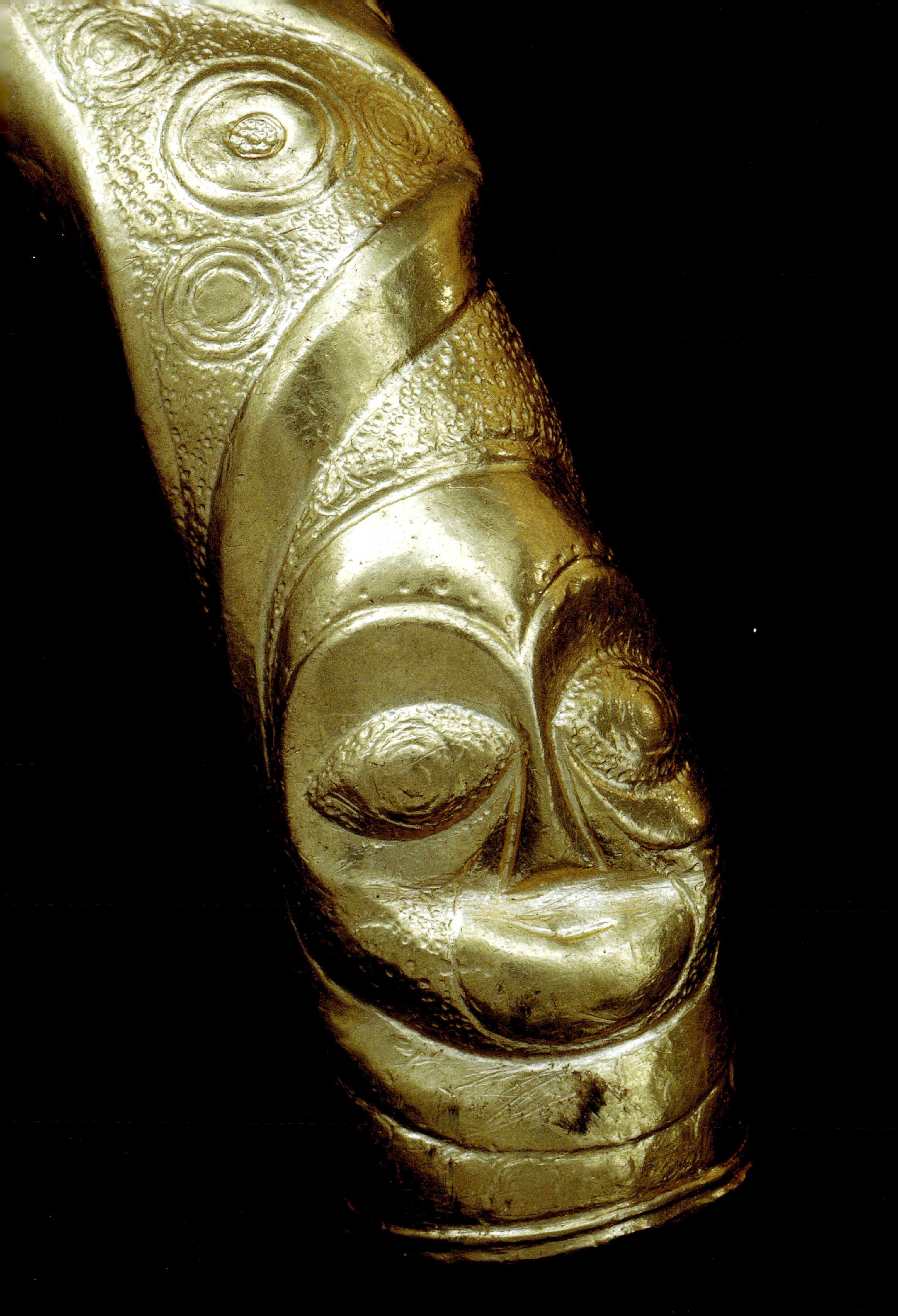

Acknowledgements

Snettisham has a long history. So many hours of human effort have been poured out in libation to this phenomenal site that it would be impossible to mention everyone who has left a mark on this volume. Nonetheless, as the editors, we have done our best here to attempt a list of thanks. We are so grateful to you all.

In some ways this book, of course, begins with those first finds at the site in the 1940s and 1950s. Everyone from the ploughmen and foremen who initially reported the finds, to the director of the Norfolk Lavender Company who called in Norwich Castle Museum (NCM), set the story in motion. The Curator of Archaeology at NCM, Roy Rainbird Clarke, led the first excavations. In the 1970s, Barbara Green from NCM carried out a survey at the site and in the 1980s the Norfolk Archaeological Unit (NAU, subsequently known as Norfolk Landscape Archaeology), who would go on to play a crucial role in the later digs, carried out a detailed fieldwalking exercise.

The British Museum (BM) project which ultimately led to this publication began with Dr Ian Stead. In 1990, when Cecil 'Charles' Hodder made the discoveries that would prompt the BM excavations, Stead was the Deputy Keeper of the Department of Prehistoric and Romano-British Antiquities. He went on to lead large-scale investigations of the site during three successive seasons in 1990, 1991 and 1992. The importance of his contribution to the story of Snettisham cannot be overstated.

Like any excavation, innumerable hands came together to run the digs at Snettisham. Stead's 1990–1 excavation team included BM staff members Tony Spence (Department of Prehistoric and Romano-British Antiquities), Dave Webb (Department of Photography) and Simon Dove (Department of Conservation). Tony Pacitto operated survey equipment and assisted in the direction of the excavations. Charles Hodder worked throughout as a full member of the team, lending his considerable skills as a detectorist. The core team also included Peter Makey, Ian Blomeley, Tim Compton and other volunteers, some provided by the NAU, where the main contacts were Andrew Rogerson and David Gurney. Derek Edwards dealt with air photography, while Dave Miller drove the bulldozer that towed the box scraper. Mike Cowell (from the BM Research Laboratory) organised an extensive phosphate survey. In the 1992 season, Neil O'Loughlin and Dave Webb supervised the trenches while Sheelagh Stead ran the finds shed. A rota of BM warders guarded the site around the clock to provide much needed security. The excavations were made possible by the support of Sir Stephen and Lady Lycett Green, the Trustees of the Ken Hill Estate, and the farm manager, John Austen. It is thanks to all these individuals, and many more besides, that we now have the archaeological records that enabled the publication of this book.

Following the completion of his fieldwork at Snettisham, Stead worked towards writing up his excavations and all the previous discoveries made at Ken Hill. He retired in 1996 but continued to work on the publication alongside various other projects until 2009. At this time, he had made significant progress in terms of drafting the catalogue, reporting on the excavations and history of discoveries, and compiling a gazetteer of other torcs from the British Isles. When he left the Museum, Dr Stead generously left us a copy of his work in progress. He also consented for his account of the excavations to be included in the finished book and it is presented here as Chapter 2. We extend our thanks to Dr Stead for bearing with us through the ups and downs of this project. None of it would have been possible without him.

Work on the Snettisham assemblages continued under one of the present editors, Jody Joy, then curator of the British and European Iron Age collections. The records made by Ralph Jackson and Duncan Hook at the time Hoard F came to the British Museum were particularly helpful in carrying out this work. We are also very grateful to Jody's volunteer Alice Thompson, who assisted him in weighing, measuring and recording the material. She is one of the few people in the world who has seen so many objects from the site. Ola O'Brien and other volunteers later assisted Julia in the same manner.

As specialist reports were commissioned, a wider group were brought together to publish the site. Alice Lyons picked up Val Rigby's work on the Roman pottery, while Sarah Percival took on the prehistoric pottery. Peter Makey, who had long remained guardian of the flint assemblage from the site, took on the lithics. Animal bone was covered by Alan Pipe from MOLA, and Sophia Adams and Derek Hamilton provided generous advice on the new programme of radiocarbon dating. Sophia also went on to complete a specialist report on the brooches. Michael de Bootman kindly allowed us to include information from his later geophysical surveys. Finds have continued almost down to the present, and we would like to thank later detectorists S. Brown, K. Elfleet and K. Jackson who undertook a survey of the wooded area, and Natasha Hutcheson and the team who investigated the Romano-Celtic temple site in 2004.

As this work was unfolding, the comprehensive scientific examination of the material in the British Museum's Department of Scientific Research was ably led by Nigel Meeks and later assisted and managed by Aude Mongiatti. This scientific analysis was a crucial part of the investigation of the assemblages from Snettisham and forms a core part of this book. Caroline Cartwright's work has been critical to our understanding of torc manufacture and she has been a very supportive presence throughout the course of the project. Many other members of the Department of Scientific Research at the British Museum also made significant contributions to the project over the years, including Janet Ambers, Paul Craddock, Duncan Hook, Susan La Niece, Janet Lang and Dan O Flynn. We also thank Carl Heron for steering the project through the final publication stages. Metalworker John Fenn worked with Nigel Meeks to help reveal the intricacies of wire torc manufacture, being very generous with his time and expertise. Peter Northover, with Oxford University student Emma Stone, analysed the composition of objects at Norwich Castle Museum, work begun at the instigation of the then curator, Barbara Green. Matthew Ponting carried out an analysis of some of the Snettisham coins, which he has kindly allowed us to reproduce here. Scientific knowledge and new analytical technologies are constantly evolving, and we thank Tess Machling and Roland Williamson for their suggestion to X-ray the Great Torc in 2016 as they began their important research into the construction of this object and other similar torus torcs.

Conservation work was also important in shaping our understanding of the Snettisham finds. With her wonderful piecing together of numerous small fragments of copper alloy, rather like an archaeological jigsaw, Fleur Shearman identified the copper alloy helmet from Hoard F. Marilyn Hockey also restored some of the decorated torcs, revealing the complicated ornament. Ian MacIntyre created a replica of the Great Torc which has been of enormous use for study and teaching, as well as understanding the manufacture of these complicated objects.

Many of the decorated torcs were beautifully drawn by British Museum illustrator Jim Farrant. After Jim retired, first Stephen Crummy and later Craig Williams picked up the project. Stephen brought his considerable enthusiasm, as well as some innovative techniques to record the helmet. Craig has been a stalwart, contributing his enormous artistic talent and a level of technical skill which we believe is unsurpassed. Craig is a brilliant colleague and friend and has been a vital contributor to the volume, providing many insights which have substantially improved this publication.

Photography of objects was undertaken by British Museum photographers David Agar, Kevin Lovelock, Ivor Kerslake and Saul Peckham. John Williams organised and facilitated the work. We are especially grateful to Kevin Lovelock for being such a good companion to Jody on trips to Norwich to photograph artefacts from Snettisham held at NCM. This was another key element of the project, and this publication would not have been possible without the access to the NCM collections provided by John Davies and Tim Pestell. For both the editors, it has been a highlight of our careers to work so closely with John and Tim, and we have each learnt a great deal about curating from both. Alongside John Davies, Amy Seaman also made an important contribution in terms of producing the catalogue of artefacts from Snettisham held at NCM, unravelling in the process several puzzles left over from Rainbird Clarke's original publication. Adrian Marsden is thanked for lively discussions about the coins.

As the publication progressed, remaining object photography and the enormous task of laying out the catalogue plates was taken on by the wonderful Rod Trevaskus. Rod brought order to a chaotic mass of photos, allowing the hoards and stray finds to be seen and understood in their entirety for, perhaps, the first time since they were in circulation in Iron Age Norfolk. He was also incredibly patient with the long process of editing and fine tuning. As his interest in the site grew, ever undaunted, Rod took to the skies and got his pilot's license. You can see one of his aerial photos of the site at the start of volume 1.

A word should also be said about the amazing Collections Care team at the Department of Britain, Europe and Prehistory at the BM for their work in wrangling the notoriously difficult Snettisham collection. A mere glance at the pages of the catalogue will confirm what a daunting task this is! Various people helped over the years, but we would particularly like to thank James Baker, Elena Jones, Jim

Peters and Sam Wyles. James showed incredible patience in terms of transporting items between departments. Elena Jones, Jim Peters and Sam Wyles also helped locate items hiding in plain sight. Registrars, including Marta Mroczek, supported the documentation of the finds. We would also like to thank Ben Roberts, who was the office mate and fellow curator to both editors at different times. Our colleague in the then Department of Coins and Medals, Ian Leins, was also very supportive, contributing invaluable advice and insights, particularly regarding Iron Age coinage. After Ian's departure from the BM, curator Eleanor Ghey ably took on the work of publishing the coins, dealing with this other very daunting assemblage with her characteristic scholarly flair, pragmatism and good humour. David Holman made a study of the potin coins, and Philip de Jersey has generously allowed us to reproduce here his work on Hoard P. Thanks for earlier work on the coins are due to Amanda Chadburn and Andrew Burnett.

Many other colleagues and former colleagues at the British Museum have provided advice, help and encouragement over the years, including: Silke Ackerman, Sophia Adams, Alexandra Baldwin, Sue Brunning, Ollie Cooke, Chris Entwistle, Richard Hobbs, Sonja Marzinzik, Ralph Jackson, Stuart Needham, Val Rigby, Naomi Speakman, Mansell Spratling, Gill Varndell, Neil Wilkin and the much-missed Ross Thomas. Roger Bland, Jill Cook, Leslie Webster and Jonathan Williams, as Keepers of the Department of Britain, Europe and Prehistory, provided valuable advice and support. A special word should be said here about our fondly remembered colleague Ralph Jackson, who was not only the first person at the British Museum to begin work on processing Hoard F, but also in his long and distinguished career supported and mentored both editors as they began theirs. Ralph helped make us the curators we are today.

Beyond the walls of the British Museum, many other colleagues across the UK and beyond have helped to shape the book you hold in your hands with their generous words of insight, encouragement and advice. They include Barbara Armbruster, Mary Cahill, Tim Champion, John Creighton, Mary Davis, Rose Ferraby, Duncan Garrow, Melanie Giles, Martin Goldberg, Chris Gosden, Colin Haselgrove, Jason Hawkes, Fraser Hunter, Yvonne Marshall, Vincent Megaw, Tom Moore, Niall Sharples, Alison Sheridan, Fraser Sturt, John Talbot and Julian Whitewright. We cannot thank you enough.

Throughout nearly all our time working in earnest on the project, the editors have been enormously fortunate to work with our editor at the British Museum, Sarah Faulks. Sarah has been the driving force behind the publication, providing just the right mix of friendly encouragement and cajoling necessary to keep such a large and unwieldy project moving. This book was decades in the making, and it exists now because of Sarah.

Another person we would like to single out for special thanks is JD Hill. Throughout the long history of the project, as Head of Research at the British Museum, JD has fought for the Snettisham publication, finding funding when it was needed and providing invaluable support and encouragement. He also has high standards. His comments on previous drafts were some of the most challenging to remedy, but they have also substantially benefitted the final product.

The same is true of our peer reviewers, Andrew Fitzpatrick, Adam Gwilt and Marcos Martinón-Torres, all of whom gave invaluable feedback on earlier drafts, significantly improving the book, and have been incredibly generous with their expertise. The editors are also extremely grateful to Rachel Tyson for her meticulous copyediting of the manuscript and to Nicola King for the magisterial index. All mistakes, of course, remain our own. The high production values of the publication have only been made possible through funding from the Eyre Family Foundation and The Pennycress Trust and we offer our thanks to both funders for their generosity.

So many others have been part of the Snettisham story over the last almost 80 years since the first finds were unearthed that it is not possible to name and thank them all here, but please know that we are incredibly grateful to everyone who has lent their time and energy to making this publication a reality.

All that is left for us as the editors to say is this: this book is for you. Whether you have been eagerly awaiting its publication for decades or have never heard of the site, as you hold this book in your hands or read it on your screen you, too, are now part of the story of Snettisham. This publication has been a long time in the making, involving many people, but it does not mark the end of work on the site. Rather, this is a new chapter. We hope that sharing the finds, and new discoveries about how they were made, worn, used and deposited, will allow other scholars to now take up the mantle. Snettisham, surely, still has many secrets left to tell. We look forward to learning all about them.

Julia Farley and Jody Joy
September 2024

Acknowledgements of individual authors

Julia Farley: Anyone who has spoken to me about Snettisham over the last decade will have heard me talk about The Curse. Whilst that is a story for another day, despite my protestations, there is in fact strong evidence that the publication is not actually cursed at all: the absolute gift that it has been to work with everyone who has contributed to this book, and especially my wonderful co-editors. I have learned so much from you both, and you have turned the many and various tribulations of Snettisham into a pleasure. Jody, I am in awe of your academic insight, deep knowledge of the Iron Age as well as your personal grit and determination to get the project over the line. Sarah, you are an absolute star, and it is thanks to your patience, compassion, dedication and motivation that this book exists. Thank you both.

Huge thanks are also due to my wonderful husband, Andy Merrills, who has patiently and lovingly supported me at every stage of working on the book.

Jody Joy: I have worked on this publication since 2009. Although I left the British Museum in 2014, Julia who took over from my role as Iron Age Curator generously allowed me to continue working with her on the book. Snettisham is unique, and researching and writing about the site and the finds has been a career highlight. I feel incredibly fortunate to have had the opportunity to spend so much time with many fantastically talented people making spectacular discoveries about some of the most fascinating objects I have ever encountered and I want to thank everyone who has made this book possible. At times the pressure to complete it has felt overwhelming, especially during a recent and prolonged period of ill health, but I have been fortunate to have worked with two phenomenal co-editors, Julia and Sarah, who shouldered a great deal of the burden for the project during my illness. Rarely in my life have I met two people so profoundly good at what they do. Julia is one of the most enthusiastic, driven and knowledgeable people I have ever met. Similarly, Sarah has been a constant source of support, as well as possessing the skill and expertise to consistently guide us along the best path to complete the book. They have been good friends in difficult times and I am hugely thankful to them both.

On a personal note, I wanted also to give special thanks to my friend and colleague Mansel Spratling. We have discussed the project many times over the past 15 years and he has always helped guide me in the right direction.

Finally, I am hugely indebted to my wife, Miriam, and my children, Florence and Samuel. Thank you for always being there.

Caroline Cartwright: Thanks are due to the team of colleagues who have been researching Snettisham over the decades for stimulating discussion and collaboration. For the author's fresh wood experiments in August 2018, thanks are due to the following for providing fresh shoots: Rebecca Stacey for willow and elder, Peter Williams for dogwood, Aude Mongiatti for hazel and Margaret Sax for field maple.

Mike Cowell: Thanks are due to Dr M.J. Hughes who took many of the soil samples and to Ms Fiona Lewis (on secondment from Bradford University) who carried out most of the subsequent chemical analyses.

John Davies: Thanks are offered to Amy Seaman for the time and effort she gave to the project and for being a joy to work with. Thanks are also due to Dr Adrian Marsden who undertook the initial identification of the 2003–9 coins.

Eleanor Ghey: Thanks are due to Tim Pestell, John Davies and Adrian Marsden at Norwich Castle Museum; Ian Leins, Richard Abdy, Amelia Dowler and Sam Moorhead at the British Museum for their input as well as Alberto Giannese, Julia Farley and Sarah Faulks. In addition, she would like to thank David Holman, John Talbot, John Sills, Philip Kinns, Marie-Christine Marcellesi and Rod Trevaskus. Thanks also are due to the British Numismatic Society for their permission to partly reproduce the text written by Philip de Jersey from P. de Jersey (2014), *Coin Hoards in Iron Age Britain* (British Numismatic Society Special Publication no. 12).

David Holman: The author would like to thank the staff of Norwich Castle Museum for facilitating access to Hoard C.

Alice Lyons: The author would like to thank Val Rigby (freelance specialist) for her initial work which forms the basis of the Roman pottery report and her comments on the final draft. Thanks are also extended to Julia Farley for her help with bringing this report to publication.

Nigel Meeks, Aude Mongiatti and Daniel O'Flynn: The completion of the scientific work is a tribute to many people at the British Museum across different departments over an extended period of time who have contributed to the Snettisham project. We thank the Friends of the British Museum who generously funded some of the laboratory facilities used in this project. Use of a digital optical microscope, analytical scanning electron microscopes and a high-powered digital radiography suite has been key to unravelling the range and practicalities of the metalsmithing traditions preserved within the fabric of the artefacts from Snettisham. We would also like to thank the following British Museum staff who, over the years, have contributed to the science and understanding of the Snettisham material, notably Paul Craddock, Janet Lang and Quanyu Wang as supporting metallurgists. Carl Heron as the current Director of Scientific Research is thanked for embracing the concluding years of the Snettisham scientific project. We are also grateful to the previous Keepers of the Department who have overseen and supported the research programme. The success of the scientific work is testament to all who have been involved.

Peter Northover: The author wishes to thank, first of all, Ms Emma Stone upon whose thesis for Part II of her BA Degree in Metallurgy and the Science of Materials Chapter 18 is based; thanks are also very much due to Professor Sir Peter Hirsch and the Department of Metallurgy and the Science of Materials in the University of Oxford for facilitating the project, and Chris Salter for unstinted assistance with the microprobe analysis. In Norfolk, thanks are due to the late Barbara Green, who instigated the project, and the late Tony Gregory and his amazing knowledge of the Iron Age material of Norfolk. The author would also like to acknowledge the late Jean-Pierre Mohen, then of the Musée des Antiquités Nationals, Saint-Germain-en-Laye, for making available for analysis important comparative material in France.

Fleur Shearman and Marilyn Hockey: Both authors would like to offer their thanks to conservators from the British Museum, notably Simon Dove, Ruth Goldstraw, Pippa Pearce, Penny Hill, Anna Gill, Ruth Scott and Duygu Camurçuoglu. The scientific investigation of the metals was also supported by Lorna Green and David Thickett from the Conservation Research section. Students from conservation internships also made a valuable contribution to the project. These included MSc/MA students from the Institute of Archaeology, University of London (UCL), and particularly He Huang, who carried out both investigation and XRF analyses on the fragmented torcs, under supervision from metals scientist Quanyu Wang. Naomi Hemuki of Westdean College contributed to the cleaning, reconstructing and re-packing of fragmentary torcs. Conservation students from the Sorbonne, Paris, also worked on the reconstruction of fragmentary torcs as part of student internships held at the British Museum over several years.

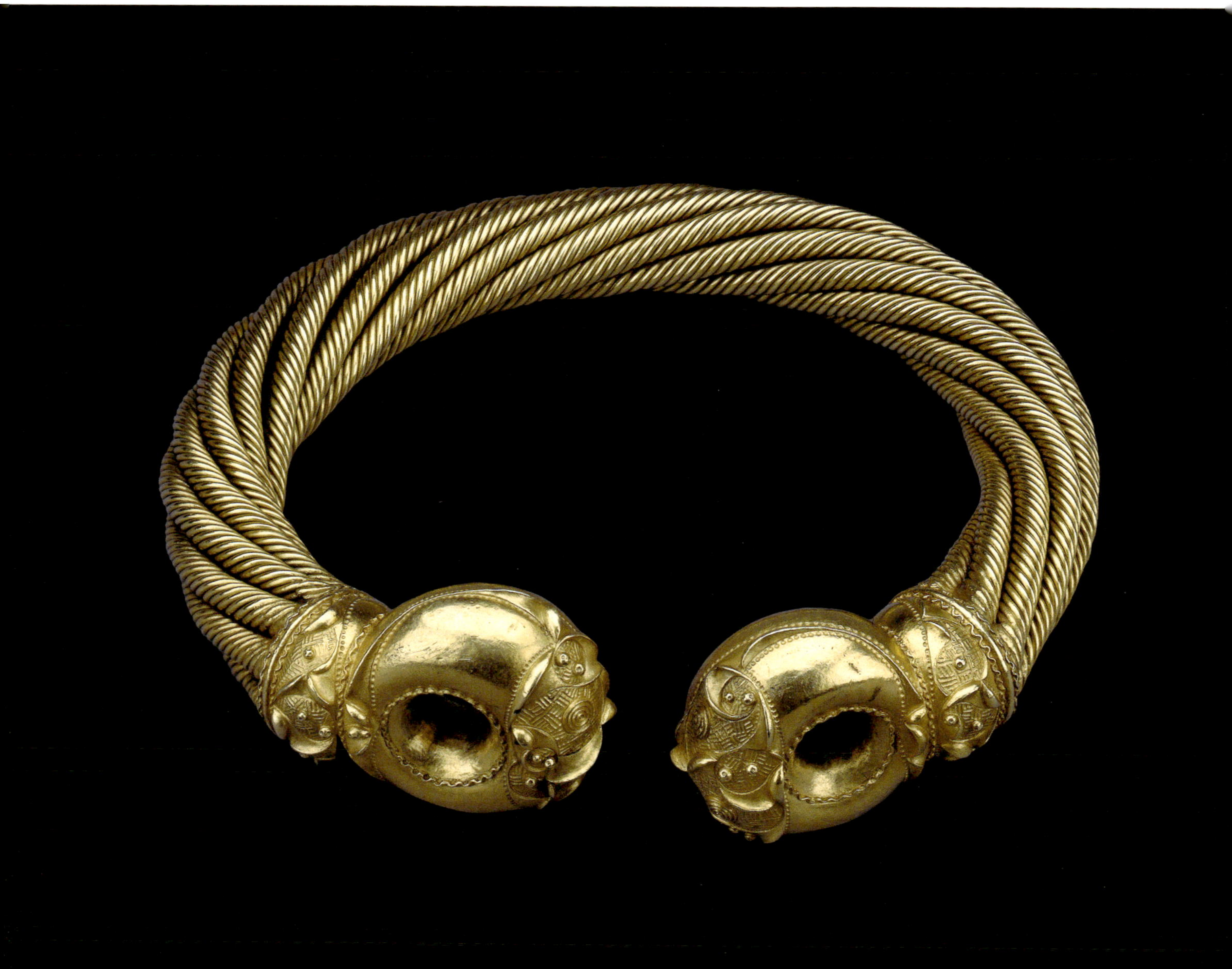

Figure 1.1 The Snettisham 'Great Torc', E.1a

Part I: The Site

Chapter 1
Introduction

Julia Farley and Jody Joy

For over 70 years, spectacular discoveries have been made on a wooded hillside near the village of Snettisham, on the north-west Norfolk coast (**Fig. 1.2**). The unprecedented number of precious metal objects found has led to the location, at Ken Hill (TF 682 349), becoming known as the 'gold field'. The finds, including gold, silver and copper alloy torcs, bracelets, rings and ingots, represent the largest assemblage of prehistoric jewellery from anywhere in Europe, and one of the densest concentrations anywhere of objects decorated with Celtic art. Collectively they have been referred to as the 'Snettisham Treasure', though in fact the deposits consist of at least 14 separate hoards. The objects were buried between around 350 BC and AD 200, spanning the Later Iron Age and Early Roman periods, but with a peak of activity around 60 BC.

The finds were all made in a relatively small area, today contained within part of a single field and an adjoining area of woodland (**Fig. 1.3**). In the Later Iron Age this was most likely an open-air natural site, although there is evidence for a field system which may be associated with the same period as the torc hoards. In the 1st or 2nd century AD, the area containing the hoards was partially enclosed by a large-scale ditch which surrounds an area of around 8 hectares, open on the downward-sloping south-west side. In this volume, 'the site' at Snettisham generally refers to this partially enclosed area.

The objects from Snettisham, particularly the so-called 'Great Torc' (**Fig. 1.1**), have become iconic, featuring in virtually every published discussion of ancient Britain or Celtic art (e.g. Stead 1985a; 1996; Moscati *et al.* 1991; James 1993; Jope 2000; Garrow and Gosden 2012; Farley and Hunter 2015). Yet, despite this renown, the site has never been fully published. This book is the first time that all the finds made between 1948 and 2009 have been brought together in a single volume. This includes early finds from the 1940s–70s, held by Norwich Castle Museum (NCM), the material from the British Museum (BM) excavations in 1990–2 (held by the BM), and finds made as part of metal-detector surveys between 2003 and 2009 (in the collections of NCM). The site has produced an astonishing range and quantity of objects: finds from the 'gold field' at Snettisham comprise over 80% of the corpus of such torcs and bracelets known from Britain.

The Snettisham torcs have been closely studied using cutting-edge scientific techniques, and the results of this extensive programme of investigation are presented here in full for the first time. This work has revealed fascinating new insights into how these objects were constructed and the materials used to create them, including organic components such as wooden cores which helped to maintain the integrity of coiled neck-ring wire 'ropes' during construction. Colour was evidently an important aspect of torc manufacture, and analysis has demonstrated the use of an extensive range of alloys as well as deliberate surface enrichment, and even mercury gilding, one of the earliest recorded instances of such techniques in Europe. Radiocarbon dating of organic components is combined here with new stylistic analyses to suggest that the use of torcs in Norfolk (and perhaps elsewhere in Britain) stretches back at least as far as the 3rd century BC and possibly the

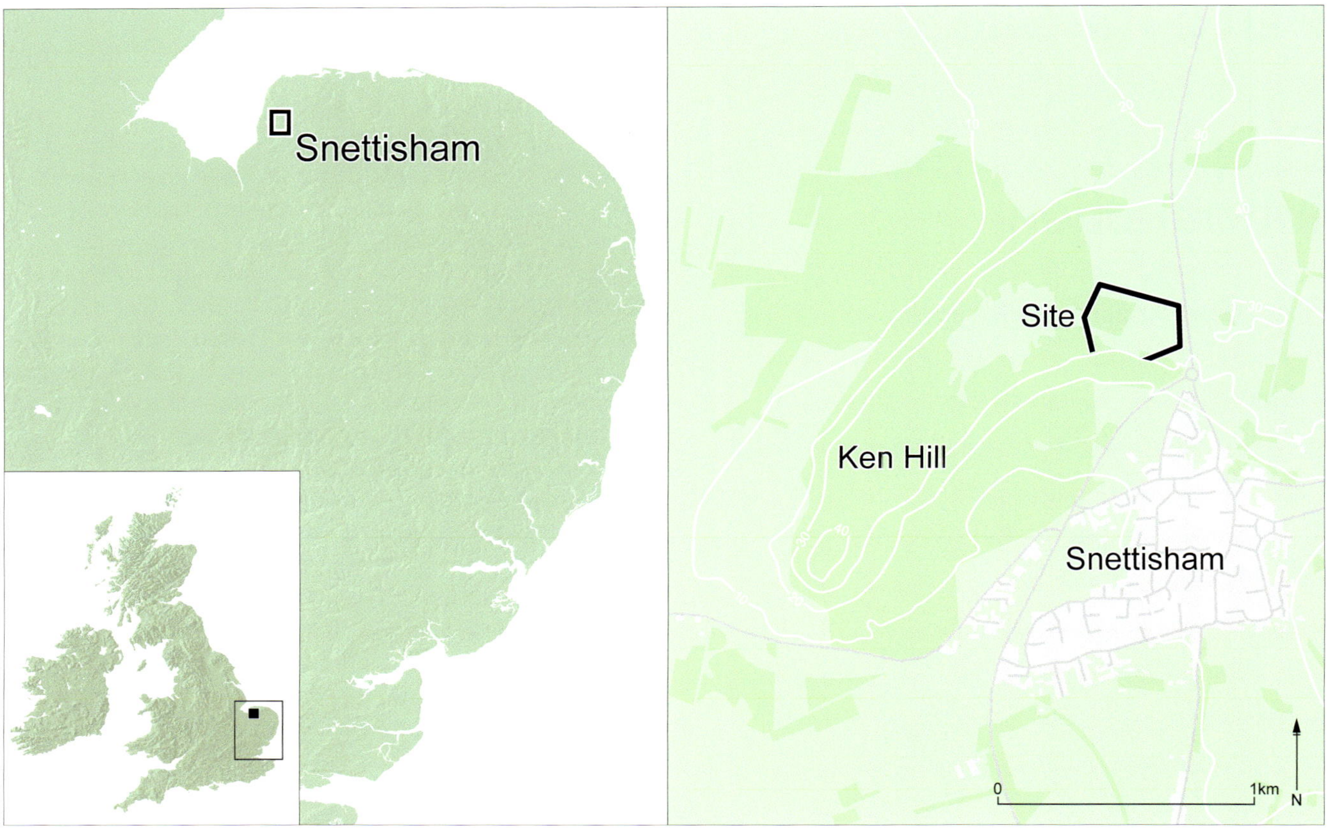

Figure 1.2 Location map showing Snettisham on the north-west Norfolk coast

4th century BC. This supports evidence from other more recent finds (such as the hoard of Middle Iron Age torcs from Leekfrith, Staffordshire, Farley *et al.* 2018) which challenge the previously widely held assumption that the use and manufacture of Iron Age precious metal torcs in Britain was largely restricted to the 1st century BC.

A major reason for the continued importance of Snettisham is that it represents one of the relatively few cases where Iron Age hoards have been recovered under conditions of modern archaeological excavation. In many cases the torcs seem to have been carefully arranged in the ground, being placed either one by one or in small groups to form stacked 'nests'. The meticulous recording carried out on site allows us to reconstruct the sequence of actions which created the hoards, including the order in which individual objects were placed into the pits. This has led to important new insights into hoarding practices, and the social role of the deposits at Snettisham. The 1990s excavations and an associated programme of radiocarbon dating also allow us to appreciate the wider pattern of activities at the site, spanning from the Neolithic to the Late Roman period.

The main period of hoarding, likely culminating around 60 BC, coincides with a major change in the region. From at least the 3rd century BC, precious metals worn in the form of bodily ornament such as torcs had played a central part in the construction and negotiation of identities in north-west Norfolk and beyond. After the mid-1st century BC, much of the significance and power once associated with torcs seems to have waned, most likely connected to the rise of a new form of precious metal object which played a key role in performing social authority: coinage. Following Gosden (2013), we argue here that this shift from a 'world of torcs' to a 'world of coins' is essential to understanding the exceptional finds from Snettisham.

Together, these new insights into the social significance of torcs, their dating and manufacture, as well as the processes which led up to their eventual deposition, allow us to come closer than ever before to understanding who the makers, wearers and depositors of these objects may have been. The results, presented here, have far-reaching implications in many spheres, from the study of Iron Age Britain, to deposition and ritual practices, and our understanding of Celtic art.

The discoveries and their significance

Chapter 4 gives a full chronological account of all known discoveries from the 'gold field' and adjacent woodland. The finds and main features are summarised in **Figure 1.3**. The hoards have traditionally been named alphabetically in order of discovery, and that terminology is kept here. Most of the hoards were discovered during two periods of activity or excavation, in 1948–50 and the early 1990s, but chance discoveries have also been made over the years by farmers and metal-detector users. Two archaeologists, Roy Rainbird Clarke and Ian Stead, both played an important role in investigating Ken Hill and their excavations form the basis for our knowledge of this hugely important site.

Early discoveries made between 1948 and 1950 (Hoards A, B, C, D and E) were reported by Brailsford (1951) and Rainbird Clarke (1950), the latter then Deputy Curator of Norwich Museums. Clarke subsequently oversaw the recovery and retention of the initial discoveries and conducted a small excavation, which was fully published

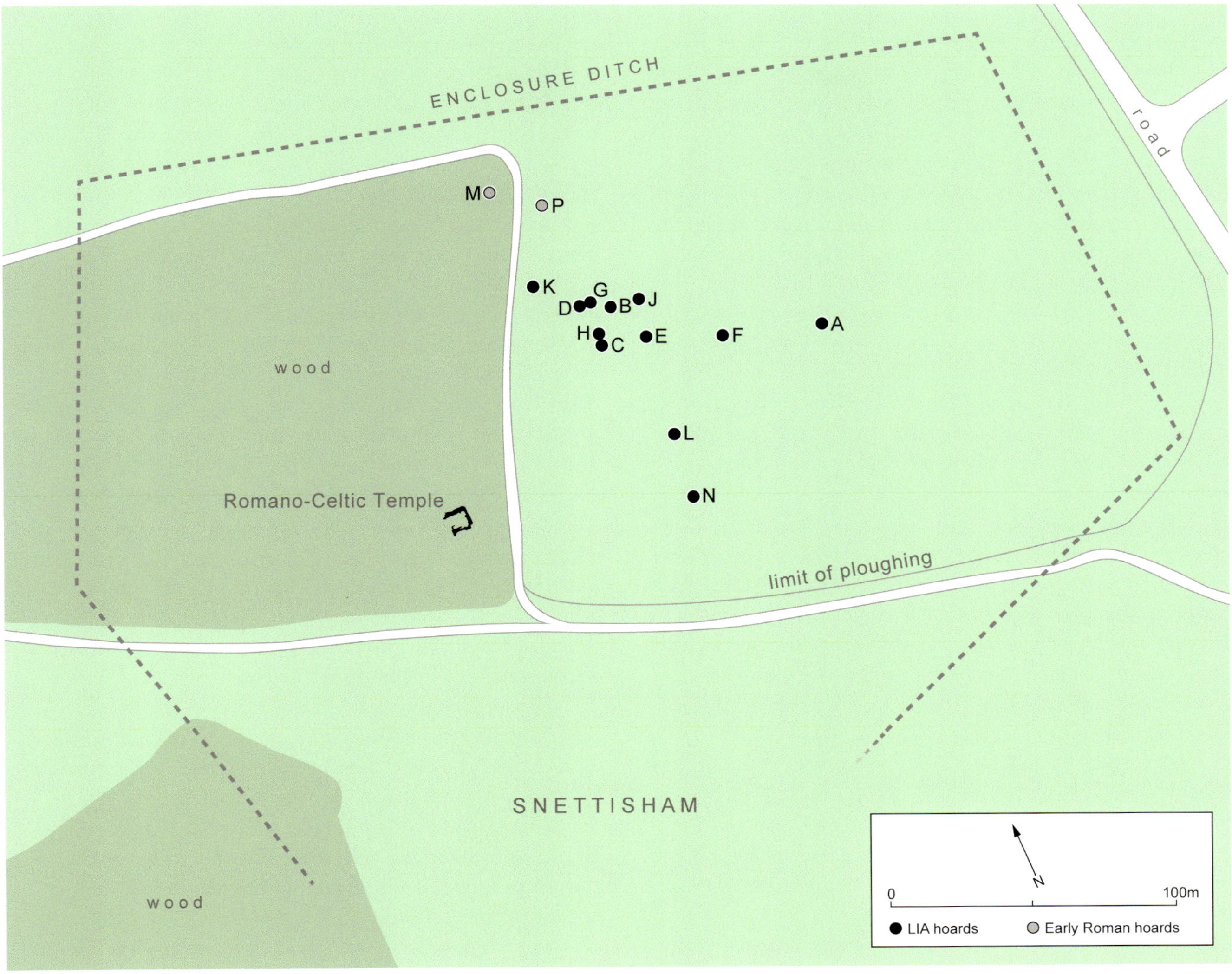

Figure 1.3 Overall map showing the key features and hoard findspots at Snettisham

(Clarke 1954). The legacy of his work is apparent in the displays of torcs and other artefacts at NCM.

A handful of subsequent single finds from the 1960s were reported by Burns (1971), but otherwise the next significant discoveries were made by metal-detecting in 1989–90. In late 1990, local detectorist Cecil 'Charles' Hodder uncovered Hoard F, nearly 600 artefacts contained within a fragmentary copper alloy vessel which was later revealed to be a helmet. Once the find was reported, Ian Stead, then Deputy Keeper of the Department of Prehistoric and Romano-British Antiquities at the British Museum, conducted large-scale investigations of the site during three successive seasons of excavations in 1990, 1991 and 1992. Torc Hoards G, H, J, K, and L and part of scattered coin Hoard N were uncovered during 1990. Between the 1990 and 1991 seasons of archaeological excavation, illicit detectorists raided the site, removing a large hoard of silver Iron Age coins contained within a silver bowl (Hoard P, or the 'Bowl Hoard'), and Hodder also uncovered a group of silver-copper alloy lumps which have become known as Hoard M. The 1991 and 1992 excavation seasons focused on extending the excavation area in the part of the field which had produced the hoards, as well as investigating wider evidence for activity across the site. Most importantly, the large polygonal ditch was revealed, partially enclosing an area of around 8 hectares, with the Iron Age hoards at the centre. Ceramic evidence suggests that this ditch dates to the Early Roman period, at least a century after the main period of deposition for the torc hoards.

After the BM excavations, there was something of a hiatus in discoveries. This changed in 2003, when metal detectorists S. Brown, K. Elfleet and K. Jackson (working with full permission and cooperation from the landowner) undertook a survey of the wooded area immediately adjacent to the hoard. Numerous finds were recovered, and processed as Treasure cases under the new 1996 Treasure Act (previous finds having been covered by the older Treasure Trove legislation). They were subsequently acquired by NCM.

The initial metal-detector survey (subsequent phases of which would continue until 2009) revealed the footings of a stone structure, which was investigated by Natasha Hutcheson in 2004 and revealed to be a rectilinear building, interpreted as a Romano-Celtic temple (Hutcheson 2011).

The scope, structure and arrangement of this book

The aim of this book is to produce the first full account of the discoveries at Snettisham, incorporating scientific analysis and detailed consideration and reinterpretation of the significance of the site.

An interim report on the first season of the BM excavations (which included Hoards F, G, H, J, K, L and N) was quickly published, appearing in *Antiquity* in 1991 (Stead 1991a). Subsequent discoveries elsewhere, in particular at Essendon, and Stead's pre-existing publication commitments (e.g. Stead 2006; Stead *et al.* 2006) delayed his full publication of Snettisham. Stead continued to work on the publication until 2009, and also published an updated interim report which included the 1991 and 1992 seasons (Stead 2014). He has kindly allowed his account of the excavations and discoveries to be reproduced here (Ch. 2), where it is presented largely in its original form. Stead also made his draft manuscript available to the present authors, for which we are grateful. This covered discoveries up to and including the BM excavations, but the scope of this volume has now been extended to include details of the 2003–9 metal-detecting.

The book is divided into three parts, spread across two volumes. Volume 1 contains Parts I and II (Chs 1–15). Part I gives an overview of the site and the excavations, while Part II focuses exclusively on the Later Iron Age and Early Roman hoards, including catalogues of the metalwork and coins and an exploration of their archaeological contexts, where known. Part III, in Volume 2, presents wider interpretation and discussions (Chs 16–24).

Part I begins with Stead's original account of the site and the BM 1990–2 excavations (Ch. 2). This is followed by a detailed analysis of the site location and its context in the wider landscape of north-west Norfolk (Ch. 3). Chapter 4 presents a detailed chronological account of the history of the discoveries from the 1940s to 2009.

The structural report on the excavations forms the second half of Part I. Chapter 5 presents the excavation methodology, geophysical and phosphate surveys, and an account of the areas and features investigated in each season of the 1990s excavations, along with the results of the two programmes of radiocarbon dating carried out on the excavated material. Chapters 6 to 10 present the site evidence in a phase-by-phase discussion, from the Early Neolithic to the post-medieval period. Specialist reports on non-metalwork finds, including lithics, pottery, ironworking debris and animal bone, are included in the relevant phase chapters.

Part II of the volume focuses on the Later Iron Age and Early Roman hoards, beginning with an introduction to the hoard evidence and summary of finds by hoard (Ch. 11). Chapter 12 presents the detailed stratigraphic information derived from the excavation of the hoards recovered by the BM in 1990, including plans and sections of the hoard pits.

The hoard finds are then presented. Chapter 13 gives the typology of torc and other artefact types used in the catalogue which follows (Ch. 14). The typology is an updated and revised version of Stead's (Stead 1991a). This is the first time that all Iron Age and Roman metalwork finds from the site have been treated together in this way, allowing a detailed consideration of the relationship between the collections housed at the BM (Hoards D, E, F, G, H, J, K, L and M, and other finds from the 1990s excavations) and NCM (Hoards A, B, C, stray finds from the 1960s–80s, and finds from the 2003–10 metal-detector surveys). The hoard and stray find Iron Age and Roman coins from both collections are covered in Chapter 15, along with a separate section on the (now lost) 'Bowl Hoard' (Hoard P).

Part III of the book (presented in Volume 2) offers detailed analyses, interpretation and discussion of the metalwork finds which make the site so exceptional. These include the ground-breaking conservation campaign (Ch. 16), which has allowed reconstruction and interpretation of several key objects, such as the helmet which contained Hoard F, and several crushed tubular torcs. Scientific analysis of the materials and techniques used to manufacture the torcs is presented in Chapter 17, accompanied in Chapter 18 by compositional analysis of the bronze objects. Environmental evidence from the objects themselves as well as a survey of the native species currently present in the surrounding area is offered in Chapter 19. Some of the torcs from Snettisham had long lives, with several likely to be more than a century old at the time they were buried, and many showing evidence for repair or deliberate fragmentation and recombination. This has been investigated using a number of techniques, including microscopic examination, and consideration of other signs of wear and repair. The results are presented in Chapter 20, which considers torc biographies and lifecycles.

Discussion chapters 21 to 24 bring together the contextual evidence from the site with the detailed analyses of the hoard objects to assess the significance of Snettisham. We focus on a number of questions including, 'Why Snettisham?' and 'What did the Snettisham hoards do?' The finds from Snettisham represent one of the greatest concentrations of decorated Iron Age metalwork anywhere in Europe, in particular objects decorated with Celtic art. The importance of this decoration is considered in Chapter 21, which presents not just detailed stylistic arguments, but also a consideration of what this art did, and how it transformed both object and wearer. Chapter 22 considers the relationships between people, objects and materials in Iron Age Norfolk. This includes a corpus of other known torcs from Iron Age Britain (an updated and expanded version of a gazetteer originally compiled by Stead).

Chapter 23 and the final conclusion Chapter 24 move beyond material culture to explore the place of Snettisham in its wider social and landscape context. Discussion focuses on the site, its changing significance over time, and the potential importance of its location. A key part of our approach is to ask not just why hoards were buried, but what these assemblages do. Above all, we conclude that, although the deposits are clearly related, it is not productive to view the Snettisham hoards in their entirety as a single 'treasure'. Each hoard is different, with different collection and depositional histories. Individual hoards 'did' something different. Repeatedly depositing artefacts at Snettisham, but with subtle differences in the composition and make-up of the hoards, was part of creating, negotiating and reinforcing social structures, as well as performing and creating social change. Specifically, we argue that hundreds of torcs were deliberately taken out of social circulation around 60 BC as part of a shift from a 'world of torcs' to a 'world of coins' (Gosden 2013).

Appendices provide supporting information. At the end of Part I, Appendix 1 provides a full list of contexts from the

1990–2 excavations and the find types represented, while Appendix 2 presents a report on unstratified flint. The other appendices are found at the end of Part III: Appendix 3 comprises a concordance with previously published finds listings, catalogues and numbering systems; and Appendices 4 and 5 give the results of compositional analyses of Iron Age gold alloy coins and selected gold and silver alloy objects from the NCM collections and comparative material.

Previous publications

The earlier finds from the site (Hoards A–E) were published by Brailsford (1951) and Rainbird Clarke (1950, 1954), with later finds described by Burns (1971), but there has been no previous attempt to bring discussion of these together with later phases of investigation at the site. Similarly, later finds have generally been published in isolation, such as Hutcheson's 2004 excavations (Hutcheson 2011) and the 2003–10 coin finds (Marsden 2011). This book brings these discussions together for the first time.

Stead has published two interim reports on the excavations at Snettisham. One (Stead 1991a) discussed the first season of the British Museum excavations (which included Hoards F, G, H, J, K, L and N). A second updated interim report included the 1991 and 1992 seasons (Stead 2014). In these reports, Stead outlined the events leading up to the 1990 excavation, and the approach taken by the archaeologists on site. He described the large fragmentary Hoard F (which had been lifted by Hodder) and reported key finds from the 'nested' torc deposits recovered by archaeological excavation (Hoards G, H, J, K and L). He had also begun to develop a typology for classifying the wide variety of torcs found at Snettisham (many of which are found nowhere else), including the distinctions between loop, cage, buffer and reel terminals. Much of the paper was taken up with discussion of the motivations for deposition, not least because this impacted on the legal status of the find. In 1990, Treasure Trove law was still in force (later superseded by the 1996 Treasure Act). Under Treasure Trove, a key determining aspect in the disposition and ownership of the find was whether it had been buried with the intention of recovery. Stead, comparing the hoards to known votive assemblages from watery deposits and sanctuary sites, argued that the Snettisham finds were different and represented a 'tribal treasury' which had been buried with the intention of retrieval (1991a, 462–3).

The 'tribal treasury' argument was challenged by Andrew Fitzpatrick (1992a), who suggested that a stronger case could be made for votive deposition, arguing that the modern division between ritual offerings (as gifts to the gods not intended to be disturbed) and savings hoards (destined for recovery and possibly recycling) may not have been relevant in the Iron Age.

Since the early 1990s, there have been major shifts in Iron Age studies. Of particular relevance here are the move towards votive interpretations of hoards and the development of object-focused theoretical perspectives which foreground the active role played by items such as the Snettisham torcs. The lack of a comprehensive publication of the Snettisham finds has impacted on how far this exceptional site has been incorporated into contemporary scholarship, but it has certainly appeared in the literature. In particular, Hutcheson (2003) has revisited the nested hoards of torcs published by Stead (1991a) to argue (like Fitzpatrick) for a votive interpretation. Hutcheson's approach included a consideration of whether colour might have been more important than metal content in determining the order of deposition. The site has of course also featured in innumerable other discussions of Celtic art and wider Iron Age society, and these works are referenced extensively in Part III of this volume.

Archive

Copies of the site archives of Rainbird Clarke's and Stead's excavations are held respectively at NCM and the BM. The objects from Snettisham are distributed between both institutions, with the current location of each object noted in the catalogue.

Note on find numbers, contexts and recording

As with any site which has been explored over many decades, a number of different recording and cataloguing systems have been used in previous publications. The various systems are summarised below.

Object catalogues

The metalwork finds are held by two museums and include discoveries made in a number of different phases of investigation (see Chs 2 and 4). As a result, no previous catalogue system covered all finds, and so in this book metal finds have been given new codes so that they can be unified under a single numbering system, divided by hoard (see Ch. 14). A full concordance with all known previous cataloguing systems is given in Appendix 3. For Hoards A–E, this includes correlation with the previous publication of the finds by Rainbird Clarke (1954), where two separate systems were used simultaneously, one numbering the finds by hoard, and one ordering them by object type. Hoards A–C are in NCM and so have NCM registration numbers. Hoards D and E are in the BM.

NCM registration numbers take the form of the year of acquisition, a stem number for the acquisition group, and then a specific object number, each separated by a full stop, e.g. the Snettisham Hoard A–C material was the 74th group of material acquired in 1949, and so all finds have the stem 1949.74. The first item registered, one of the tubular torcs from Hoard A, was assigned 1949.74.1, the second 1949.74.2, etc. Not all objects were given a specific object number, and so at present these are identified only by their stem. The 2003–9 material has not yet been registered, so does not have registration numbers. For the purposes of recording carried out for this catalogue, each individual object was assigned a raffle ticket with a unique number, and these tickets are, at the time of writing, stored with the objects. The raffle ticket numbers are included in the concordance table in Appendix 3, to assist future researchers wishing to identify specific objects from the catalogue.

BM registration numbers are more complicated, due to the multiple seasons of excavation and the distinction between Treasure Trove and non-Treasure Trove material. The relevant registration stems are listed at the end of

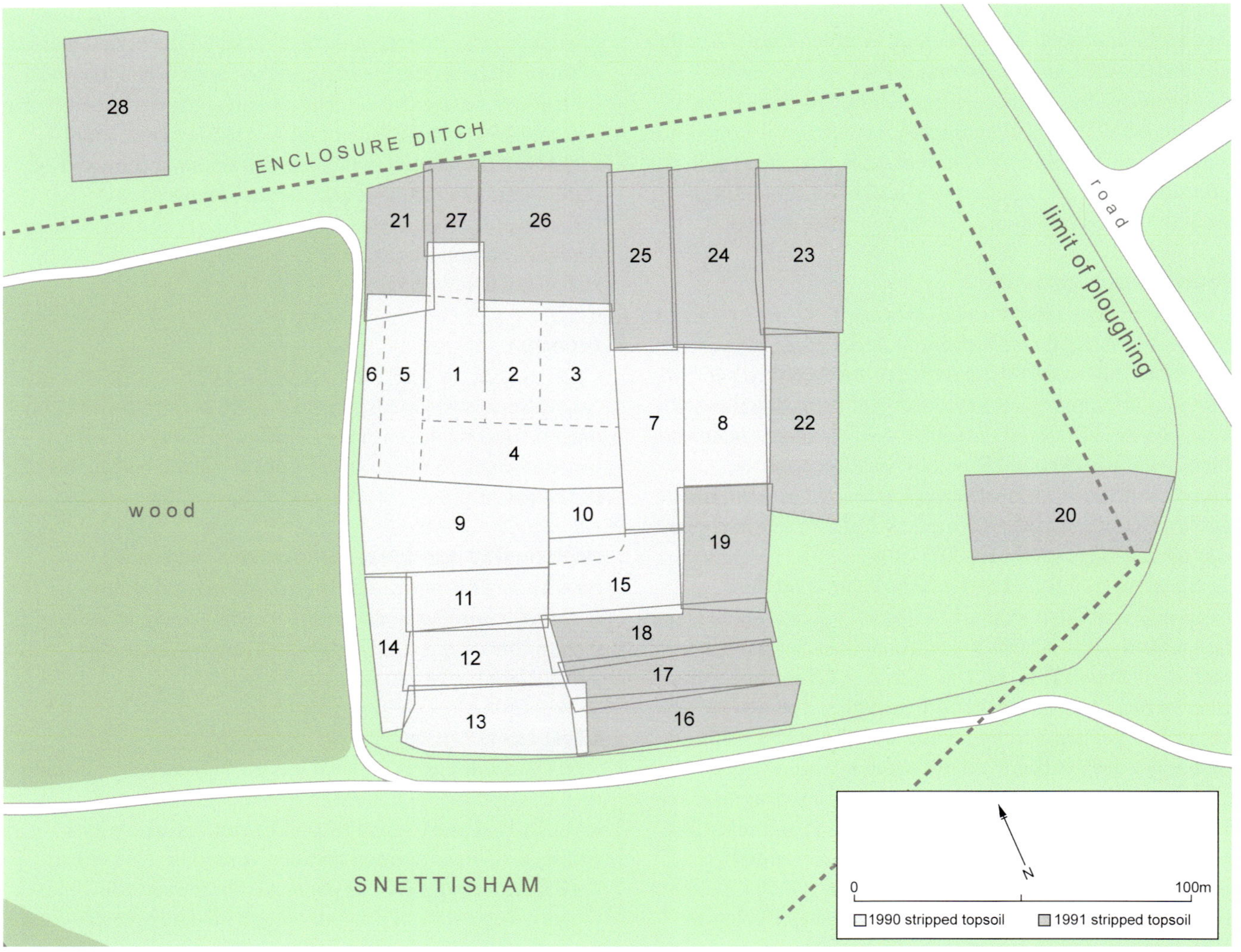

Figure 1.4 Map of the main stripped areas explored in 1990 (light grey) and 1991 (darker grey), numbered 1–28

Chapter 2, after the detailed phases of acquisition of BM material are explained.

The parts of Hoard F (and a small number of other stray finds) recovered by Hodder in 1990 were assigned numbers 1–526 by Ralph Jackson when they were brought into the BM. These numbers have been used in some previous publications (e.g. Cartwright *et al.* 2012; Garrow *et al.* 2009) and so they are included in the concordance as 'Jackson no.'. Objects from Hoard F found during the subsequent BM excavations were given four-letter site codes (see below) and do not have Jackson numbers. All of the Hoard F objects have now been given a single sequence of catalogue numbers, beginning 'F.' They are ordered by object type, beginning with interlinked/composite groups of objects, since it is not possible to determine a sequence of burial or recovery.

The objects in Hoards G, H, J, K and L were also assigned four-letter codes during the BM excavations. Sometimes multiple fragments of a single torc, especially those damaged by ploughing, were lifted separately, and given different codes. Here, each torc is simply given one number, starting with the hoard letter, with numbers assigned in the order in which the torcs were recovered. Hoard M (a group of six large amorphous silver-copper alloy lumps) was recovered during detecting by Hodder, and so was not assigned excavation codes.

Non-hoard finds have been made at the site since the 1960s through to 2009, and have been variously acquired by both the BM and NCM. Most were made during ploughing (1960s–70s: NCM) or metal-detecting (1989: NCM; 1990–2: BM; 2003–10: NCM). A very small number were stratified finds recovered during the BM excavations (1990–2: BM). All of these metal finds are here given a single number sequence, starting with the letter 'S.', though divided into earlier finds (Late Bronze Age to Earlier Iron Age), then torcs, ingots and similar finds which may represent scattered hoard material, and finally other finds less likely to derive from hoards.

Iron Age and Roman coins from the site are similarly unified in a single catalogue here for the first time. In Chapter 15 they are given a single numerical sequence, including the early Hoards (B and C) published by Rainbird Clarke (1954), the coins recovered from Hoards F and N during Hodder's detecting and the BM excavations, and the stray and excavation finds from both the BM excavations and the later detecting at the site. Coin Hoard P is now lost; the coins are discussed, but not given catalogue numbers.

For pottery, bone and lithics, only the finds from the BM excavations are published here. In these cases, the BM site codes (see below) have been used, rather than creating a new catalogue system.

The British Museum excavations

Three seasons of excavation were carried out at Snettisham by the BM in the early 1990s, following Hodder's discovery of Hoard F. These took place in November–December 1990, November 1991 and September–October 1992. In addition, a metal-detector survey was carried out in March 1992. The first season of excavation (1990) focused on the area which had produced the hoards. The second season in 1991 explored further south and east in the hoard field and also opened up slots across features to the north and east discovered by geophysical survey. The latter were revealed to be deep, V-cut linear ditches which formed the large polygonal enclosure partially surrounding the field. The subsequent season in 1992 focused on exploring this enclosure ditch, as well as areas of possible prehistoric activity in the southern part of the hoard field.

Each season of excavation was assigned a different two-letter code, which was used in various aspects of recording, all of which begin with 'S' for Snettisham. These are:

- SN (excavation November–December 1990)
- SE (special code given to finds from pottery-rich pit SN25, excavated in 1990)
- ST (excavation November 1991)
- SM (metal-detector survey March 1992)
- SA (excavation September–October 1992).

Find numbers

Finds from the BM excavations were assigned four-letter codes. The first two letters relate to the excavation season, and the second two letters are assigned in sequence, so the first find from 1990 was SN/AA, then SN/AB, SN/AC etc. SN/AZ is followed by SN/BA, and so on. These codes are equivalent to find numbers, assigned in the order of discovery, and do not necessarily relate to any particular context. Many finds, particularly non-hoard finds from 1990–1, were unstratified, being found in the topsoil or subsoil. Some four-letter codes were assigned to individual objects, while others refer to small groups of material recovered from the same area. For example, ST/EZ refers to a mixed group of material including pottery, bone, flint, charcoal and furnace debris, all recovered from a small area of a particular layer in feature ST35.

Feature and context numbers

In 1990 and 1991, features were given hybrid number and letter codes, using the first two letters for the excavation year and then numbers starting at 1 and assigned in sequence. The number codes have been used in this report where they refer to specific features other than hoard pits; for example SN23 is a Neolithic pit excavated in 1990, and ST35 is a section of the enclosure ditch linear excavated in 1991.

Large areas stripped by box scraper in 1990–1 were also assigned letter codes. For the avoidance of confusion, in this publication each stripped area has been assigned a number in the sequence in which they were opened. **Figure 1.4** shows the location of these areas within the field.

In 1992, hybrid letter–number codes were given to trenches, so Trench 5 in 1992 is given code SA5. Features and contexts within each trench were given numbers, e.g. SA5/1 (the topsoil across Trench 5); SA5/2 (the part of the enclosure ditch which runs across Trench 5). Sections of the ditches were given letters, and the layers/contexts within these sections were given numbers. So, for example, SA5/2, Section D, Layer 3 refers to the third layer down within Section D of the enclosure ditch in Trench 5 (Feature SA5/2). **Figure 4.1** summarises the areas investigated in 1991–2.

Note on spelling

In this book we use the spelling 'torc' rather than 'torque' following Clarke (1954) in the first report on the discoveries from Snettisham.

Abbreviations used

- ACBMG = Archaeological Ceramic Building Materials Group
- BM = British Museum
- CADB = Celtic Art Database
- CBM = Roman ceramic building material
- HER = Historic Environment Record
- HNER = Norfolk Historic Environment Record
- IARCH = Iron age and Roman Coin hoarding research project
- NCM = Norwich Castle Museum
- NMP = Norfolk National Mapping Programme
- PAS = Portable Antiquities Scheme
- PCRG = Prehistoric Ceramic Research Group
- PDR = Post Deverel-Rimbury
- SHARP = Sedgeford Historical and Archaeological Research Project
- TT = Treasure Trove

Chapter 2
Excavating at Snettisham

Ian Stead

Introduction

Snettisham, between King's Lynn and Hunstanton in Norfolk, has long been famous for its Iron Age gold torcs. The first discoveries were made when the field now known as the 'gold field' (TF 68153490), on the Ken Hill Estate, was ploughed rather deeper than usual for a cereal crop. Previously it had been used for the cultivation of lavender. On 12 November 1948 the ploughman unearthed three gold tubular torcs and part of another. He showed them to his foreman who identified them as bits of an old brass bedstead, so they were left out in the field. On the following day the ploughman found a second deposit, and the day after that he found a third. All the artefacts stayed in the field for about a week, until they attracted the attention of a director of the Norfolk Lavender Company, who called in the Norwich Castle Museum. The Keeper of Archaeology, Rainbird Clarke, immediately organised an archaeological excavation and soon located the sites of the three hoards, which he labelled in order of discovery, A, B and C. A series of trenches in the surrounding area revealed no more hoards, and no other remains contemporary with the hoards (Clarke 1954).

Two years later, in November 1950, the ploughman unearthed two more lots of gold artefacts, subsequently labelled Hoards D and E. In Hoard E was the magnificent Great Torc, a small British coin within it (see Ch. 15, Cat. no. 169), together with the terminal of another torc and a decorated bracelet; 'Hoard D' was a single torc, with a ring through one terminal (Clarke 1954). D and E may have been deposited with other artefacts but there was no excavation to investigate their sites. Subsequently, isolated torcs were found in 1964 (S.17 and S.31 in the vicinity of B–E; Burns 1971), in 1968 (S.16 deposited by a harrow on the track southwest of the hoards; Burns 1971) and in 1973 (S.18 about 130m north-west of Hoards B–E; unpublished). In the 1970s, Barbara Green from Norwich Castle Museum carried out a survey at the site with the involvement of the BBC. A detailed fieldwalking exercise by the Norfolk Archaeological Unit over the winter of 1983–4 produced no Late Iron Age artefacts in the area and it was generally assumed that the site had been thoroughly wrecked by ploughing.

Then, in 1989 local detectorist Cecil Hodder (known to his friends as Charles) was given permission to use his metal detector on the site and in the month after harvest he recovered some fragments of torcs (S.25, S.27 and S.28) and three British coins (Cat. nos 219, 234 and 259). Encouraged by these finds, he returned the following year to carry out a more thorough survey. On 25 August 1990 Hodder located Hoard F, a mass of fragmentary artefacts in gold, silver and copper alloy. He fully appreciated the significance of his find and tried to contact the Norfolk archaeologists, but it was the Bank Holiday weekend and nobody was available. Hodder decided to carry out the excavation himself. Hoard F weighed 9.2kg and had been deposited in a shallow pit, possibly within a copper-alloy helmet whose remains were in very poor condition.

The discovery of Hoard F showed that the site had not been completely destroyed and proved the need for an immediate archaeological investigation before treasure hunters were alerted. The location of the 1948/50 hoards had been plotted on Ordnance Survey maps, in a large open field adjoining a major road, making it an easy target for clandestine metal detectorists. Statutory protection, scheduling the site as an Ancient Monument, would not deter the more unscrupulous operators. The Trustees of the British Museum decided to launch their own investigation before the new discovery received publicity. The immediate aim was to attempt to recover any hoards still in the ground and the long-term goal was to investigate the archaeological context thoroughly.

The decision to search for hoards faced archaeologists with an unusual challenge which had to be met within a tight time schedule and accompanied by a high level of security. The obvious solution was to use metal detectors, but archaeological organisations have little experience in this field. Fortunately, my colleague Tony Pacitto was available to advise and participate and Charles Hodder was also keen to help. Several metal detectors, and a gradiometer for geophysical survey, were assembled and employed in experiments at Snettisham at the end of October 1990. A collection of copper alloy artefacts weighing about 1kg was buried as a 'hoard' and surface metal was scattered to test the reactions of various machines. Hodder's Tesoro metal detector and a borrowed Garrett machine met with the most success, but they seemed unable to distinguish between small shallow finds and the large deep 'hoard'. Gridded squares in the vicinity of the hoards were surveyed with a gradiometer but no pattern emerged, and when the same squares were surveyed with the metal detectors a considerable amount of superficial and recent metal was collected. Hoard F had been found after Hodder had dug a hole to check a fairly weak signal and then got a much louder response at the bottom of his excavation. So no signal from the metal detector could be dismissed lightly and a vast area had to be explored in a fairly short time. It was decided that the most effective way to distinguish between superficial metal and substantial hoards was to remove the plough soil and thus get nearer to the hoards.

A full-scale excavation started two weeks later, on 12 November 1990, and lasted for five weeks. Its resumption was delayed until November of the next year because of a crop of sugar beet, and then followed by a metal-detecting survey in the adjoining wood in March 1992. Subsequent excavations in September and October 1992 concentrated on the surrounding area in an attempt to find a context for the hoards. The various seasons of excavation are summarised in **Figure 4.1**.

The key members of the 1990–1 team (some of whom are shown in **Figure 2.1**) included three of the British Museum staff: the writer, Tony Spence from the Department of Prehistoric and Romano-British Antiquities, and Dave Webb, seconded from the Department of Photography. Simon Dove, Department of Conservation, made frequent visits and provided invaluable help. Tony Pacitto, adept at solving problems and skilled in electronics, operated a metal detector and gradiometer as well as assisting in the direction of the excavations. Charles Hodder made a vital contribution with his metal detector and worked throughout the excavations as a full member of the team but refusing to accept payment. The core team was completed by Peter Makey, Ian Blomeley, Tim Compton and other volunteers, some provided by the Norfolk Archaeological Unit. In Dave Miller we were fortunate to have an extremely skilful driver for the bulldozer that towed the box scraper. So good was he that later we persuaded him to participate in a similar excavation at Essendon in Hertfordshire, a long way from his base. In the 1992 season Neil O'Loughlin and Dave Webb supervised the sites and Sheelagh Stead ran the finds shed. The security problem was eased by a rota of British Museum warders who guarded the site round the clock for the entire length of the excavations. Everyone who worked on the site signed a paper disclaiming any reward under Treasure Trove regulations.

The project met with the full support of the Norfolk Archaeological Unit (subsequently Norfolk Landscape Archaeology) where our main contacts were Andrew Rogerson and David Gurney. Derek Edwards showed us the air photography cover and photographed the excavations from the air. Norwich Castle Museum gave access to detailed records plotting the previous discoveries of hoards and isolated torcs and facilitated subsequent research by lending artefacts to the British Museum. The operations would have been impossible without the support of Sir Stephen and Lady Lycett Green, the Trustees of the Ken Hill Estate, and the farm manager, John Austen.

Excavations 1990–1991

In an attempt to define targets at the start of the excavation Mike Cowell (British Museum Research Laboratory) organised an extensive phosphate survey that revealed an increase in phosphate levels in the wood to the west (where Romano-British pottery was found in animal burrows) but nothing significant in the immediate vicinity of the hoards (see Ch. 5). Meanwhile, the first aim of the excavators was to locate the pit for Hoard F, easily found because it had been accurately plotted by Hodder. Its re-excavation provided the opportunity to examine the carrstone rock and the depth of plough soil – an essential preliminary to the use of heavy machinery. In the second week of the excavation a large box scraper was used to strip the soil in shallow spits whilst a team of archaeologists watched as the soil entered the box, observed the scraped surface and examined the soil deposited on the spoil heap north-west of the stripped area. Metal detectors were used by Charles Hodder and Tony Pacitto to scan the stripped surface and anomalies were flagged and immediately investigated by other members of the team. Archaeological finds were plotted using an electronic distance meter operated by Tony Spence. The first area to be stripped (Area 1; see **Fig. 1.4** for locations of numbered stripped areas), about 60 by 20m, was in the vicinity of Hoards B and D and on the first day Hoard G was located. Three days later, and 11m away, Hoard H was found. The hoards were excavated successively and a routine was established: after the artefacts had been plotted, they were photographed by Dave Webb and lifted, taken to Ken Hill House to be shown to Sir Stephen and transported to Norwich to be secured in a safe at the Castle Museum. The days were short and very cold.

The box scraper was then used to extend the excavated area to the east (Areas 2–3), where Hoard J was discovered at

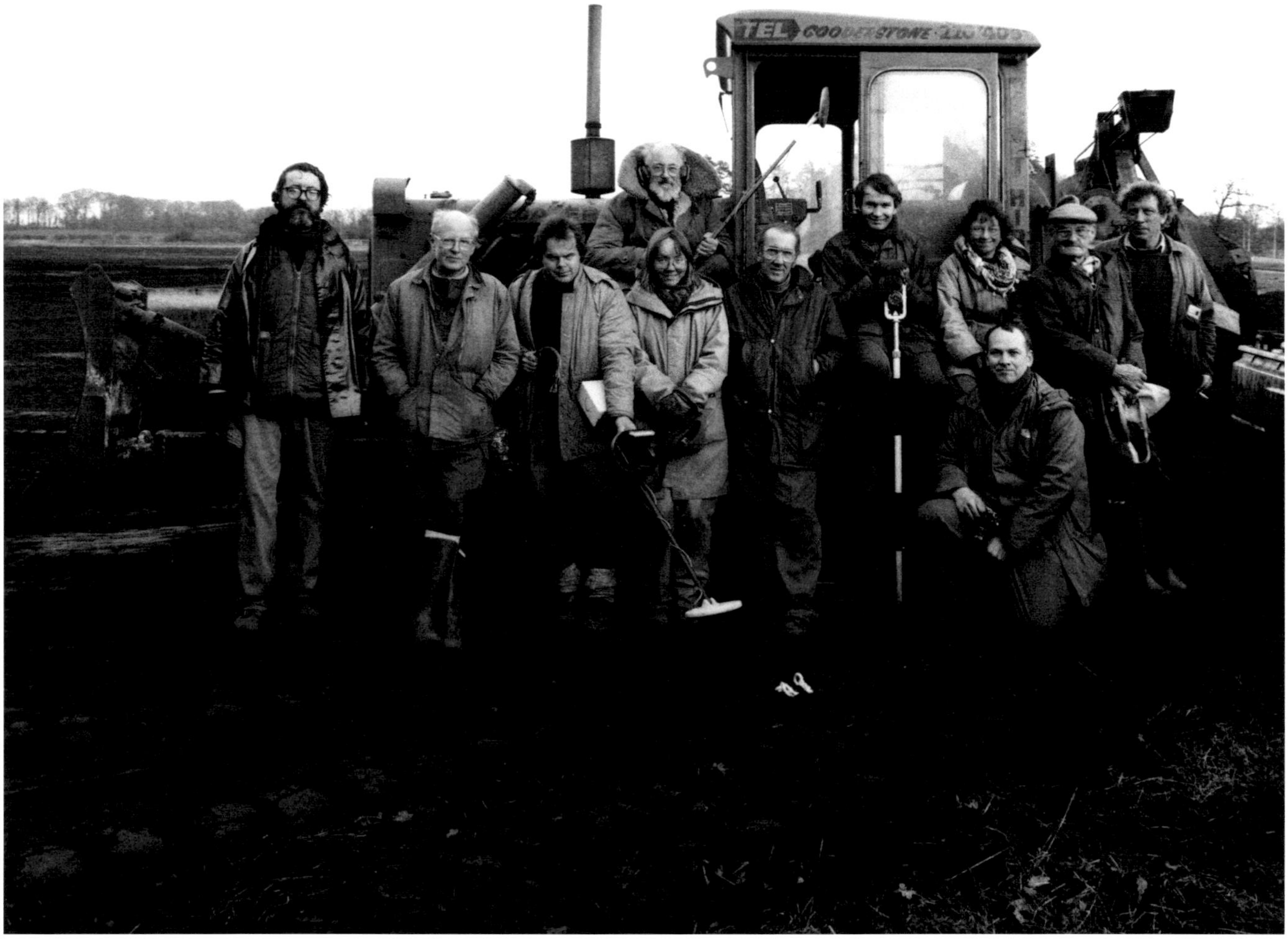

Figure 2.1 The 1990 excavation team on site. From left to right: Tim Compton, Ian Stead, Peter Makey, Tony Pacitto (back), Alice Lyons, Mike Hurn, Tony Spence, Pippa Smith, Dave Webb (front), Charles Hodder, Dave Miller

the beginning of the third week. Torcs from its upper layers had been damaged and scattered, with fragments being found to the north and south of undisturbed torcs in a shallow pit. The box scraper then removed plough soil to the south (Area 4), over the site of Hoard F and the presumed sites of Hoards C and E, and to the west as far as the track adjoining the wood (Area 5). There, only 7m from the track, Hoard K was found. Like Hoard J its upper torcs had been scattered by agricultural machinery in an even longer north to south line but the nucleus remained in a similar shallow pit.

Meanwhile the central part of the stripped area, amounting to just under 1,000 sq.m and including the sites of Hoards G, H and J and the assumed sites of Hoards B to E, was thoroughly excavated by hand in search of other archaeological features. Five small shallow pits were discovered and all had Neolithic finds (SN21, 23, 24, 28 and 29; see **Fig. 6.2**). This area was trowelled down to the natural rock but the only other finds were occasional prehistoric sherds in shallow sandy depressions (some undoubtedly animal burrows) and a few scattered Iron Age and Roman coins. The edge of one of Rainbird Clarke's trenches was almost certainly identified, cutting pit SN21. Another Neolithic pit was found when shovel-scraping in the stripped area to the east (SN27), as well as a pit containing a large quantity of Earlier Iron Age pottery (SN25).

At this stage, the start of the fourth week and the beginning of December, the area stripped by machine and scanned by metal detectors included the sites of most known hoards, but its boundary was only 4m beyond Hoard F and Hoard A was well outside it, some 30m further to the east. It seemed reasonable to expect other hoards to the east and perhaps to the south and north. The central area subjected to excavation with trowels (see Ch. 5, **Fig. 5.5**) had produced no Iron Age features and if it were to be extended in similar detail there was every chance that more Neolithic pits would be uncovered and the team would be diverted from its main objective. So it was decided to change tactics. The box scraper would continue to strip the upper part of the topsoil but there would be no intention of following this with shovel-scraping or trowelling. That way hoards could be located by the metal detectors leaving other archaeological features undisturbed.

Accordingly, more than 2,000 sq.m were stripped to the east of Hoard F but the area was devoid of coins and torc fragments. Two more Neolithic pits (SN26 and 30) were discovered when the box scraper went deeper than intended and the 1948 excavation for Hoard A was recognised and re-excavated but without further finds. Attention then turned to the area south of Hoards C and H (Area 9), where Iron Age coins had been found previously. Scattered Iron Age metalwork and some coins were discovered as well as worked flints, more here than elsewhere on the site: throughout these excavations Peter Makey ensured the recovery of flint from across the stripped areas of the site.

Towards the end of the fourth week it was decided that the area had been thoroughly checked for hoards and the excavation started to close down. But Pacitto was not entirely satisfied with the survey at the southern margin of the site. He took the metal detector out again and discovered Hoard L, the most impressive collection found on these excavations and 40m away from the nearest other hoard. The security warders returned, the huts were re-hired and the excavation was extended for a further week. The box scraper was then used to strip topsoil to the south and east of Hoard L (Areas 10–15), and though other coins and torc fragments were found there was no other hoard. Towards the end of the fifth week the site was backfilled under archaeological supervision and the area was again scanned with metal detectors. In all 1.2 hectares had been investigated. The excavation ended on 14 December.

Over the winter of 1990–1 Charles Hodder continued to work with his metal detector until the field was sown with sugar beet. Then he turned his attention to the adjoining wood. Even in winter the vegetation rendered most of the wood impenetrable as far as metal detectors were concerned but on an earlier occasion Hodder had managed to find an Iron Age coin (Icenian 'Bury', Cat. no. 275). In the north-east corner of the wood, in March 1991, he found Hoard M. Quite different from the others, it was a collection of six rough lumps of silver-copper alloy with a total weight of 6.6kg.

The British Museum project was resumed in November 1991, late in the year because it had to follow the sugar beet harvest. Again the box scraper was employed to strip the upper levels of topsoil, each spit was surveyed by the two metal detectorists and there was no intention of excavating areas by hand. To the south of the area cleared in 1990 (in Area 18) several Iron Age coins and fragments of a torc (S.24) were found, including a concentration of coins that was almost certainly a scattered hoard (Hoard N). To the east an outlying area (Area 20) (see **Figs 1.4, 4.1**) was stripped because torc fragments (S.25, S.27, S.28) and lumps of silver had been detected there by Hodder, but only a single torc fragment (S.52) was found. The main area was then extended to the north and then to the east and north-east.

In the north-west corner, to the east of Hoard M, in Area 21, an area of about 2,000m^2 had been 'salted' by clandestine metal detectorists: hundreds of small fragments of metal had been distributed in an attempt to deter other detectorists. The farm manager, John Austen, reported that he had disturbed metal detectorists working there earlier in the year and that they had marked out the area with flagged posts. There were very few archaeological finds when this area was stripped, the most interesting being fragments from a silver vessel (P.1–7). At the time the full significance of the vessel fragments was not appreciated but later it became apparent that the clandestine metal detectorists had made off with a hoard said to have been buried in a silver vessel (Hoard P, Ch. 15). In 1990 its site, 40m away from the nearest other hoard, had been covered by our main spoil heap. The final area excavated in 1991, Area 28, to the north of the wood where a torc had been discovered in 1973 (S.18), produced no other antiquities and brought the total area stripped in 1990 and 1991 to 2.5 hectares.

In March 1992 further work with our metal detectors in the north-east corner of the wood located a Roman coin (Cat. no. 479) and a fragment of a torc (S.78). The wood was the obvious place to look for more hoards but until the trees were felled there was no hope of carrying out a thorough excavation. The owners had no intention of felling trees in the foreseeable future.

Excavations in 1992

To the north of the Area 21, stripped in 1991, iron slag was scattered over part of the field. It had been noted in 1990, and indeed had been plotted in 1953 on maps in Norwich Castle Museum. But in 1991 it was obvious that the clandestine metal detectorists had dug into it. Their backfilled hole was investigated and a mass of iron slag located, the occasional sugar beet indicating that the disturbance was very recent. A trench excavated in 1991 (ST35) showed that the slag was in the filling of a Roman ditch (see Ch. 9), a discovery that prompted a re-examination of air photographs where its line was now quite obvious. Previously it had been confused with a relatively modern field boundary. The air photographs showed a sharp corner to the east, beyond which it continued to the south, parallel to the modern road. The filling of the ditch responded well to the gradiometer, so after tracking it with traverses an area survey was started in 1991, resumed in March and concluded in October 1992. A polygonal enclosure of about 8 hectares was defined (see **Fig. 9.1**).

Trench ST35 excavated in 1991 revealed a ditch with a steep-sided V-shaped profile and a narrow flat channel at the bottom. It was 1.8m deep below the present ground level and 2.8m wide at the base of the plough soil (see **Fig. 9.6**). The upper part was filled with a compact mass of slag and furnace debris that seemed to have been dumped from the south side. The gradiometer showed that the slag filling extended for about 20m: it was a deliberate filling, presumably to form a causeway. In the excavated section it extended to the plough soil and any original surface would have been destroyed. The deposition of the slag was dated by Roman pottery including a sherd of Oxford ware no earlier than AD 350 (ST/DN, also ST/DM; the coin Cat. no. 506 – was found towards the top of the slag). In the lower filling of the ditch, 0.4m from the bottom, were two joining sherds of 1st-century AD wheel-thrown coarse ware (ST/GE).

The initial section cut through the slag in the ditch filling (ST35) was towards the middle of a 320m length of ditch that formed the north side of the enclosure. At the west end the ditch turned to the south-west at an angle of 100° and at the east end it turned to the south at an angle of 107°. The east ditch, in the open field, was surveyed by gradiometer with little difficulty and a south-east corner was located, again with an angle of 107°. The south-east ditch then crossed the drive leading to Ken Hill House, and was actually detected under the surface of the drive. As it headed to the south it became less clear and eventually disappeared from the geophysical survey. The sharp north-west corner took the ditch into the wood where it was tracked by a series of traverses in relatively open areas. South of the wood, and south of the drive, it was re-located in grassland on a very different alignment having turned at an angle of 140° in the south-west corner of the wood. Only a short length of the west ditch, about 40m, could be surveyed before it passed into another wood where traverses eventually failed to locate it. But in that 40m length a very clear entrance was located, the only entrance discovered in the entire circuit. The area was subsequently stripped and excavated as Trench 5.

The gradiometer met with problems south of the drive, in an area of parkland, ploughed field, mixed wood and a poplar plantation. Here the plateau of the main site ended and the land sloped down as the carrstone gave way to clay. Complications were caused by other buried linear features, some of which were recent attempts at drainage and others perhaps periglacial; there were difficulties with undergrowth and close-set trees in the wood; and widespread remains of the wire netting originally erected to protect the poplars from rabbits. But there was no doubt that the south-east ditch went down the hill beyond the plateau, contrary to expectations that it would turn to follow the contours.

The gradiometer's attempts to locate a south ditch were unsuccessful though it did show a short length of apparent ditch aligned with the last point at which the south-east ditch had been identified. On excavation (Trench 3, feature SA3/2) it was found to contain a recent land-drain 1.3m below the present surface: the possibility that the land-drain had been inserted into the ancient ditch was considered but excavation to the east and west failed to locate it. An attempt was then made to clear remnants of the wire netting in order to track the south-east ditch but the second survey produced similar negative results. Trenching eventually narrowed its terminus down to within 5m (between Trenches 11 and 19): inevitably it was covered by a poplar tree. A trench in the wood (Trench 14) located the west ditch south-east of the entrance but there was no possibility of defining its southern terminal.

It seems that the polygonal enclosure was not ditched on the south side. The south-east ditch, and perhaps the south-west ditch too had not extended much beyond the edge of the carrstone, ending at a still active springline. The south side of the enclosure was open to what in antiquity would have been marshes bordering an inlet from the Wash.

The south-west entrance, the only entrance identified by the gradiometer survey was an obvious target for excavation (see **Figs 9.3–4**). An area 24 by 14m (Trench 5) was excavated to expose the entrance and areas on both sides of the ditch in the hope of locating a gateway and bank, perhaps in the form of post holes or a palisade trench. But the only archaeological features apart from the enclosure ditch were a recent ditch that crossed its line (SA5/4) and two shallow hollows (SA5/3 and SA5/5) no more than 0.1 to 0.15m deep, one with a couple of flint flakes and some Earlier Iron Age pottery (SA/BJ). There was a causeway 6m wide between the terminals of the ditch but no hint of metalling, hollow-way or wheel ruts. In the 5.5 to 6m excavated on either side of the ditch there was no trace of the structure of a bank. A 15m length of ditch north of the entrance was completely excavated to find dating evidence. Here the ditch was about 2.5m wide and 1.2m deep where it cut the carrstone, 1.5 to 1.6m deep below the present ground surface. In the middle filling (Layer 3), some 0.5 to 0.6m above the floor of the ditch, were large sherds from 1st to 2nd-century AD pots (SA/AL – projected on the section, see **Fig. 9.5a**; SA/AQ, SA/AU, SA/AV, and SA/BB; see Ch. 9, **Fig. 9.7** nos 3–8) and four 4th-century Roman coins (Cat. nos 473 and 478 – projected on the section, see **Fig. 9.5a**; and Cat. nos 471–2). In the primary silting, within 0.1m of the bottom, were many sherds from a Neronian/Flavian jar (SA/BQ; see **Fig. 9.7** no. 2) and one large sherd from a 2nd-century pot (SA/BM; see **Fig. 9.7** no. 1). The ditch had been allowed to silt from *c.* AD 100, and there was no evidence to suggest that its original excavation was any earlier: none of the other sections through the enclosure ditch produced anything to vary these conclusions (see Ch. 9).

The south-east ditch (explored in Trenches 1, 2, 6, 11 and 17) was similar to the others in depth and profile and again no evidence for a bank was located. Lengths of ditch amounting to 11m were cleared, producing less pottery but confirming the dating from the other side of the site, and including a greyware sherd in the primary filling (SA/BC). The most significant find was a brooch about 0.8m from the bottom of the ditch (S.244).

Two areas inside the enclosure were excavated in 1992 in an attempt to locate remains contemporary with the filling of the enclosure ditch, but none were found. The first, in grassland south of the modern drive (Trench 7), was selected because the gradiometer survey had suggested several ditches on two orientations. The excavation uncovered two ditches parallel with the drive (SA7/4 and SA7/5) and re-cut ditches on north–south orientations (SA7/3, SA7/6 and SA7/8). All were disturbed by animal burrows but they included prehistoric and a very few Romano-British sherds. The gradiometer showed that the parallel ditches continued alongside the drive to the eastern limits of the enclosure where a trench (Trench 17) proved that one of them (SA17/3) cut across the line of the filled enclosure ditch. This stratification and their alignment with the drive suggests that the parallel ditches were relatively modern field boundaries and drainage ditches and that the prehistoric and Roman sherds were residual in them. There were only three minor features undisturbed by modern ditches and animal burrows, two small pits 0.5m diameter cut 0.2m into the carrstone (one, SA7/10 with Earlier Iron Age sherds, SA/DM in the pit and SA/DL above; the other, SA7/12, without finds) and SA7/2, the base of an Earlier Iron Age pot with burnt stones in and around it (SA/CD).

The second excavation, Trench 12, an area of just over 300 sq.m in the field north of the drive, was sited towards the centre of the polygonal enclosure, in an area where 'Norfolk Wolf' staters had been found and where two apparent ditches had been located on the geophysical survey. The 'ditches' (SA12/2 and SA12/3) were not archaeological, perhaps they were periglacial, but several small, shallow pits (SA12/4–28) were also discovered. Some were certainly the remains of animal burrows but others seemed to be the result of human intervention: the bottoms of pits or perhaps post holes, nine of which produced prehistoric pottery. Shallow pits like these would be the sole surviving remains of hoard pits if the hoards had been completely removed but there were no fragments of metal so perhaps they relate to the possible settlement or midden activity attested by the sherds (see Ch. 7).

The occasional piece of *tegula* from the south-west part of the site and a fragment of flue tile from the wood to the west of the hoards suggested that there had been a Roman building somewhere in the vicinity (see Ch. 9).

One other trench (Trench 15) was excavated in 1992, in a field known as Bunting's Pasture, to the east of the 'gold field', on the east side of the road from King's Lynn to Hunstanton. In 1989 Charles Hodder had surveyed the field with his metal detector and discovered a pair of bronze artefacts ('drinking horn terminals', S.253–4). He identified the approximate site, near a spring, the area was again surveyed with metal detectors and a single trench was excavated. Nothing of any antiquity was found.

Treasure Trove

The Snettisham Treasure was discovered at a time when Treasure Trove regulations were still in force, regulations that were eventually superseded by the 1996 Treasure Act. Treasure Trove was a royal prerogative that gave the Crown the right to any gold or silver that had been hidden, provided that the owner was unknown and that he or she had hidden it with a view to recovering it (*animus revertendi*). In certain parts of the country the franchise for Treasure Trove had been assigned to other bodies. Where a find was suspected of being Treasure Trove the local coroner determined its fate, usually at an inquest and often with a jury: if the find was declared Treasure Trove the coroner seized it for the Crown or a franchisee, if not it was returned to the landowner. In recent times it became the practice for the Crown to offer Treasure Trove to a museum and for the museum to give the finder a reward amounting to the full market value of the artefacts in order to encourage the reporting of discoveries.

Treasure Trove was devised as a source of income for early medieval monarchs and was a very unsatisfactory way of protecting antiquities in the 20th century. It was part of common law, not statutory law, and there were problems with definition. Gold and silver usually occur as alloys and some artefacts, such as plated coins, have only a little precious metal. Many hoards had both a Treasure Trove and non-Treasure Trove component, so were split between two owners. To qualify as Treasure Trove artefacts had to have been deliberately hidden, so many single pieces (e.g. a ring or a coin) that could have been lost were not usually regarded as Treasure Trove. And the artefacts had to have been hidden with the intention of recovery, which was not always easy for an inquest to decide. The concept of *animus revertendi* was a potential problem with many Treasure Trove cases. Some hoards were undoubtedly buried for safety and intended to be recovered. But grave goods, for instance, were deliberately buried but would be expected to stay in the earth forever (though even grave goods in barrows were once regarded as the king's property, Bruce-Mitford 1950). Far more complex, because it depends on archaeological theory and fashion, is the argument that items of precious metal could have been buried as gifts for the gods. A famous case that used this argument, the Broighter Hoard (found in 1896, County Londonderry, Northern Ireland), was eventually brought to trial in the High Court of Justice in 1903 and declared Treasure Trove (Armstrong 1920). Acknowledging the difficulty in addressing the original intention behind deposition, the 1996 Treasure Act removed the *animus revertendi* requirement for most potential Treasure finds.

The first inquest on the Snettisham Treasure, held on 18 December 1948 at Hunstanton, decided that Hoard A was Treasure Trove, but not Hoards B and C which were held to include too little precious metal. The Treasure Trove items were the property of the Duchy of Lancaster, the franchisee, and were passed to Norwich Castle Museum; non-Treasure Trove items were donated to the same museum by the landowner. The gold objects from Hoards A and B found during Rainbird Clarke's excavation were seized by the coroner without an inquest. Hoard D was declared Treasure Trove at an inquest at Hunstanton on 23 November 1950. The following day Hoard E was discovered and seized by the coroner without an inquest. Hoards D and E were acquired by the British Museum who paid a reward of £1,850 to the finder, Tom Rout. Sir Stephen Lycett Green recalled that when the Great Torc (Hoard E) was found he took it across to Sandringham, where King George VI was in residence. The king asked to whom this magnificent object belonged, and Sir Stephen replied, 'To you, sire'. The king, of course, was also Duke of Lancaster. A version of this story, later denied by Sir Stephen, related that the king not only held the torc but also wore it on his neck.

Single Snettisham torcs declared Treasure Trove at inquests on 17 August 1964 (Dersingham), 18 September 1968 (Snettisham) and 20 August 1973 (Hunstanton) were passed to Norwich Castle Museum and the finders rewarded. An inquest on Charles Hodder's 1989 finds was held at King's Lynn on 14 December 1989 and both Treasure Trove and non-Treasure Trove items were acquired by Norwich Castle Museum. Hoard F and fragments found about that time were the subject of an inquest on 7 March 1991: the gold and silver items were declared Treasure Trove and the British Museum paid Hodder a reward; the non-Treasure Trove items were purchased from the Trustees of the Ken Hill Estate. The gold and silver items from the 1990 and 1991 excavations and Hodder's finds from those two years were declared Treasure Trove at inquests held at King's Lynn on 26 March 1991 and 20 February 1992. The Duchy of Lancaster gave these pieces to the British Museum but no reward was paid because all members of the excavation team, including Charles Hodder who refused to be treated differently, had signed papers disclaiming any right to a reward. The non-Treasure Trove items from 1990 and 1991 were purchased by the British Museum from the Trustees of the Ken Hill Estate.

Treasure Trove has a bearing on another aspect of this project. In 1993 it was decided to follow the Snettisham excavation by investigating the nearby site at Sedgeford, where part of a torc had been found in 1965 (BM 1968,1004.1; Brailsford 1971). The excavation was about to start when the landowner withdrew his consent on legal advice. He asked for half the value of any gold or silver found on his land. But if such gold or silver was declared Treasure Trove then it would belong to the Duchy of Lancaster and it was not the landowner's to sell. The British Museum could not accept this condition so the excavation was aborted. But a decade later, in 2004, when the 1996 Treasure Act gave the landowner a legitimate right to half the value of the Treasure, the Sedgeford site was surveyed by metal detectorists working for another organisation and the rest of the torc was found (BM 2005,1103.1; TAR 2004, 48–9, no. 35).

British Museum registration numbers

Treasure Trove complicated the way in which artefacts have been registered in the British Museum because registration numbers are assigned to a batch of artefacts acquired from a single source and recorded according to the month and year in which they are acquired. Thus 1991,0501.6 is the sixth item of the first batch of artefacts acquired in May 1991 by the then Department of Prehistoric and Romano-British Antiquities (sometimes given the prefix 'P' within museum documentation e.g. P. 1991,0501.6). As each batch is acquired from a single owner Treasure Trove (TT) and non-Treasure Trove (non-TT) items are recorded separately which results in 10 different registration batch numbers for Snettisham items in the Department of Britain, Europe and Prehistory (the successor of the Department of Prehistoric and Romano-British Antiquities) and a further eight numbers for items in the Department of Money and Medals (formerly Department of Coins and Medals):

- *Hoards D and E:*
  Objects: 1951,0402.1–4
  Coin: 1951,0507.1
- *Hoard F and other Hodder finds:*
  Objects: TT, 1991,0501.1–233; non-TT, 1991,0702.1–277
  Coins: TT, 1991,0904.1–15; non-TT, 1991,1016.1
- *1990 excavations:*
  Objects: TT, 1991,0407.1–66; non-TT, P1991,1101.1–5
  Coins: TT, 1991,1017.1–15; non-TT, 1991,1018.1–22
- *1990–1, Hodder's metal-detecting:*
  Objects: TT, 1992,1203.1–12; (see below for non-TT)
  Coins, TT, 1992,0803.1–4
- *1991 excavations:*
  Objects: TT, 1992,1202.1–9; non-TT, 1991,0409.1–30 (includes Hodder 1990–1)
  Coins: 2009,4213.1–105 (also used for 1992), 2018,4117.1–2
- *1992 excavations:*
  Objects: 1992,0210.1–6
- *Hodder's drinking horn terminals:*
  1993,0201.1–2

This helps to explain why the catalogue for Hoards G–L is not organised in order of registration but by a simple numerical sequence relating to the order in which artefacts in each hoard were removed from the ground.

Chapter 3
The Site and its Local Context

Julia Farley and Jody Joy, with a contribution by Tony Spence

Snettisham village is located between King's Lynn and Hunstanton, in north-west Norfolk. The 'gold field' is on a promontory known as Ken Hill, just to the north-west of the modern village (**Figs 3.1–2**). The form of the hill is rather like a curled finger pointing down from north to south, with its highest point at the southern 'fingertip' and the hoard field nestled on the sheltered lower slope towards the base of the 'finger'. Although very close to the coast, the site itself is on the inland side of the hill, overlooking the Ingol valley and the contemporary village of Snettisham.

Ken Hill is an outcrop of ferruginous sandstone, known locally as 'carrstone', a material which is widely used in north-west Norfolk as a building material. In its degraded state it forms a coarse ginger to dark-brown sand, which is very free draining, and of limited agricultural use. Ken Hill is an unusual feature in the region, where most of the coastal plain consists of flat, low-lying marshy ground: the Norfolk Fens. Today, it forms a promontory overlooking the Wash (the rectangular estuary and bay formed at the border between north-west Norfolk and Lincolnshire, running out into the North Sea, see **Fig. 1.2**).

Much of Norfolk is low-lying and is less than 60m (200ft) above current sea levels (**Fig. 3.8b**). The Snettisham promontory is a conspicuous feature in the surrounding landscape, visible from some way along the coast in either direction. It is part of the so-called 'western escarpment', which runs north–south at the fen edge. The highest point of the escarpment is just over 100m above present-day sea levels. The site at Snettisham sits towards the north-western edge of this ridge. The highest parts of the hoard field are around 35m above sea level, with the southern end of the hill rising to up to 42m. These characteristics have led researchers such as John Davies to speculate that Ken Hill was '…a special place with a unique strategic importance' (Davies 2008, 101).

The environment of Iron Age Norfolk was very different from today (Davies 2008, 87) and water tables were higher and river channels deeper (Wiltshire and Murphy 1999, 156). The coastline, rivers and estuaries of Norfolk offered natural routeways which facilitated contact with neighbouring regions, as well as further afield across the Wash to central and northern England, and across the North Sea to the continent (Davies 2008, 87). As such, the Snettisham promontory would have been a well-connected area in the Late Iron Age, at the northern end of navigable waterways running from inland Norfolk down to the Wash and ultimately out into the North Sea, and lying close to the path of the Icknield Way (a routeway with likely prehistoric origins linking north-west Norfolk to Suffolk and beyond). The Snettisham site is currently located slightly inland, but it was far closer to the sea during the Late Iron Age. From around 250 BC, continuing into the Roman period, sea levels rose to 1.5m above present-day levels with the Fenland coastline running as far south as a line roughly extending from Wisbech to Downham Market (Waller 1994, 75–9, fig. 5.22; Davies 2008, 87) (**Fig. 3.3**). Considering this marine transgression and factoring in the effects of modern-day drainage, during the Late Iron Age Ken Hill would have stood as a headland reaching out into the Wash, surrounded by water on three sides and probably accessible by boat at high tide. The southern, unenclosed, side of the hoard field

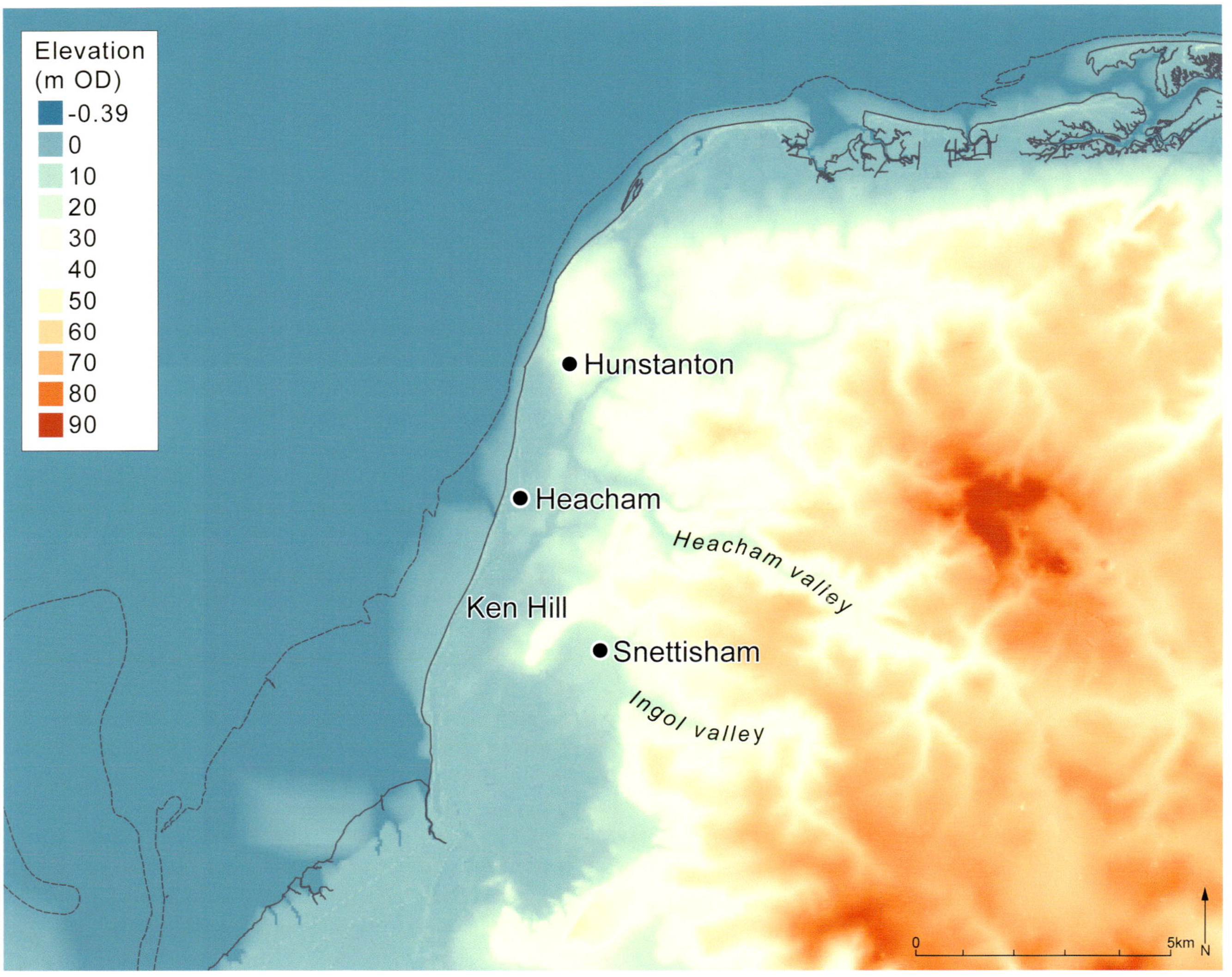

Figure 3.1 Elevation map showing the area around Snettisham. Ken Hill forms a promontory out into the Wash

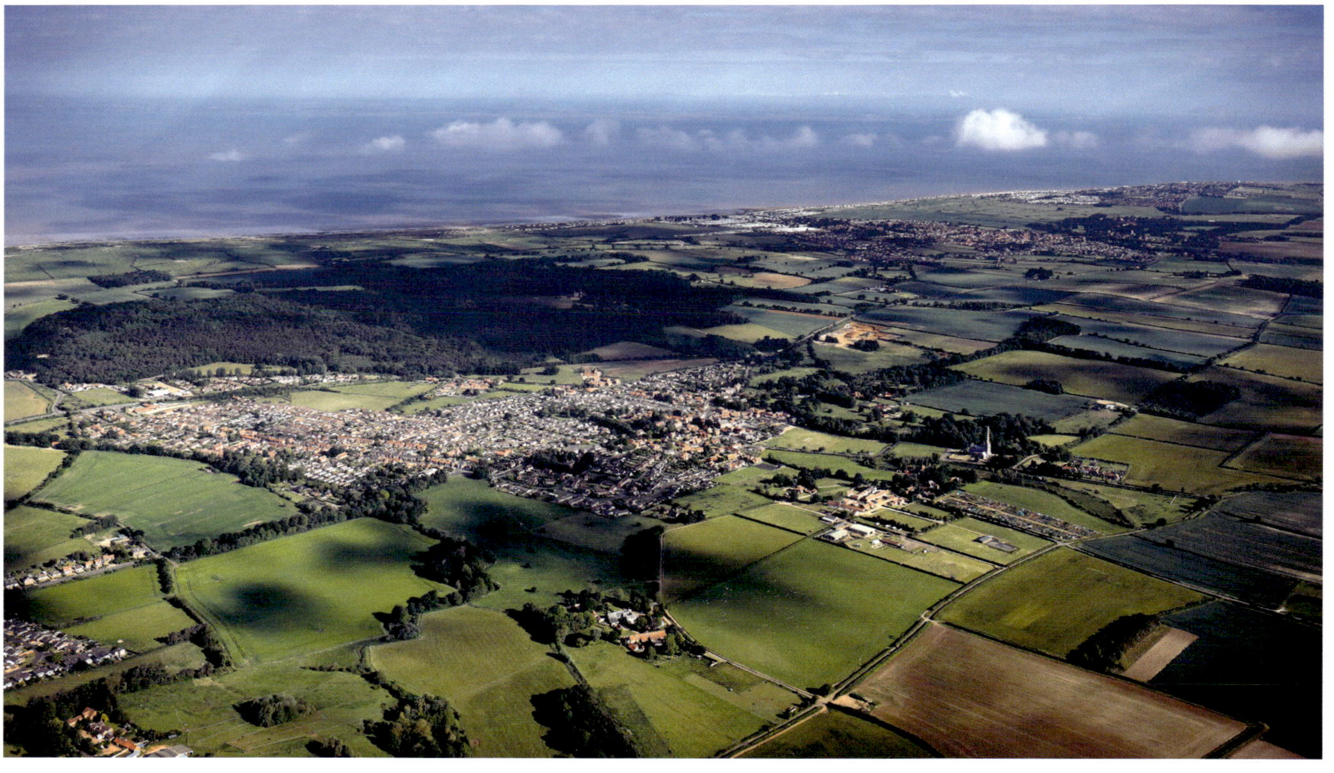

Figure 3.2 Aerial photograph showing the view north-west across Snettisham village towards the Wash. Ken Hill is the wooded promontory on the centre left; the 'gold field' lies on the lower slope of the hill, on the right-hand edge of the wooded area (image ©aeroengland.co.uk)

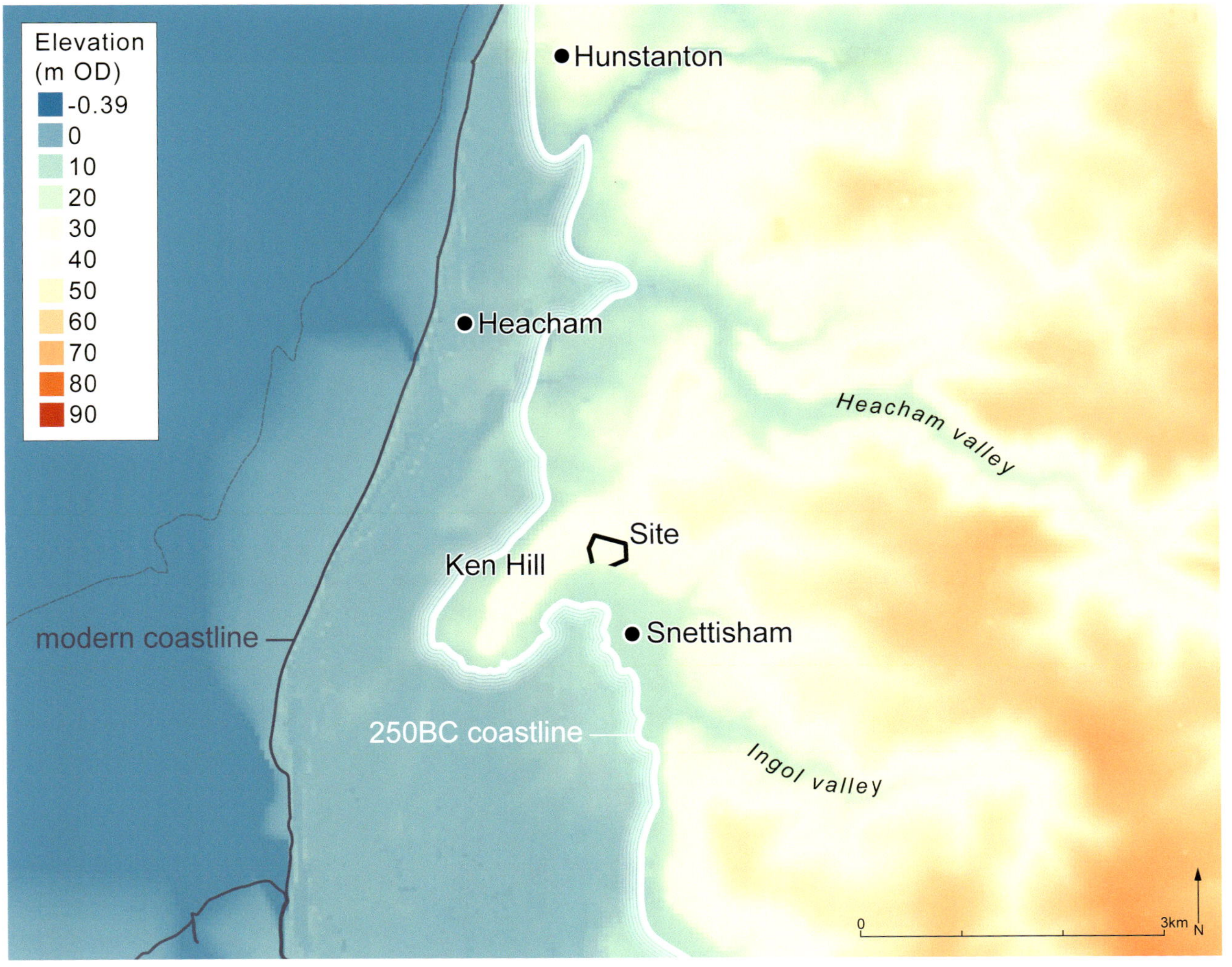

Figure 3.3 Map showing likely Late Iron Age sea levels in the area around Snettisham

would have been bordered by an inlet from the Wash. Today, the River Ingol runs just to the south of the Ken Hill promontory, rising from lime-rich springs in the chalk uplands near Shernborne, and flowing out into the Wash.

The hoard field is bounded on the east by the King's Lynn to Hunstanton Road, the A149, and to the south by the driveway to Ken Hill House (**Fig. 3.5**). To the west is a low, coniferous plantation, around which the field wraps to the north (**Figs 3.4–5**). Beyond it is a mature deciduous woodland. As the land slopes away to the south there is an open plantation of poplars, with the ground dropping away to a wide basin. Historically, the field is known to have been used for lavender cultivation, but at the time of the first season of the BM excavations (1990) the crop was sugar beet.

Today, the rest of the Ken Hill promontory is wooded, but this has not always been the case. Substantial woodland clearance had taken place in the region by the Late Bronze Age or Early Iron Age (Davies 2008, 138) and by the Late Iron Age much of Norfolk was intensively farmed (Davies 1996, 64–5), though the pattern was varied, and some regions were a patchwork of woodland, heathland and farmland, even within quite a small area (Hutcheson 2004, 4). The presence of a prehistoric field system covering what is now the hoard field shows that at least parts of the promontory were treeless/cleared perhaps as early as the Neolithic (see Ch. 5). Some features interpreted by Ian Stead and his team as tree bowls (such as the pit just to the west of Hoard F) indicate tree growth at the site, but this is difficult to date. In Faden's 1797 map of Norfolk, there is only a small area of woodland, 'Caen Hill Wood', shown at the north-eastern (inland) end of the promontory (**Fig. 3.6b**), though the rectilinear bounding of the woodland suggests this was either a planation or the remnant of once more extensive tree cover. By the time of the first Ordnance Survey (1885, **Fig. 3.6c**), the entire lower part of the promontory was wooded, as it remains today. Neither of these maps show any woodland coverage in the hoard field itself. Today, the western half of the hoard field is covered with a tree plantation. This is absent in pre-WWII photographs of the field, but the first half appears in 1946 aerial photographs, and by the time of 1988 aerial photography (**Fig. 3.6d**) it had reached its present extent. The newer trees in this plantation are believed to have been planted around 1960.

With the exception of these wooded areas, the land around Ken Hill today consists primarily of arable fields. From at least the 16th century, the area just to the south of the promontory (south-west of the village) was common land used for grazing and also as a rabbit warren (Whyte 2009, 91–124; Bailey 1988). This perhaps goes some way to explaining the heavy rabbit disturbance found throughout the site, which has unfortunately in some instances impacted upon our ability to reconstruct stratigraphic sequences.

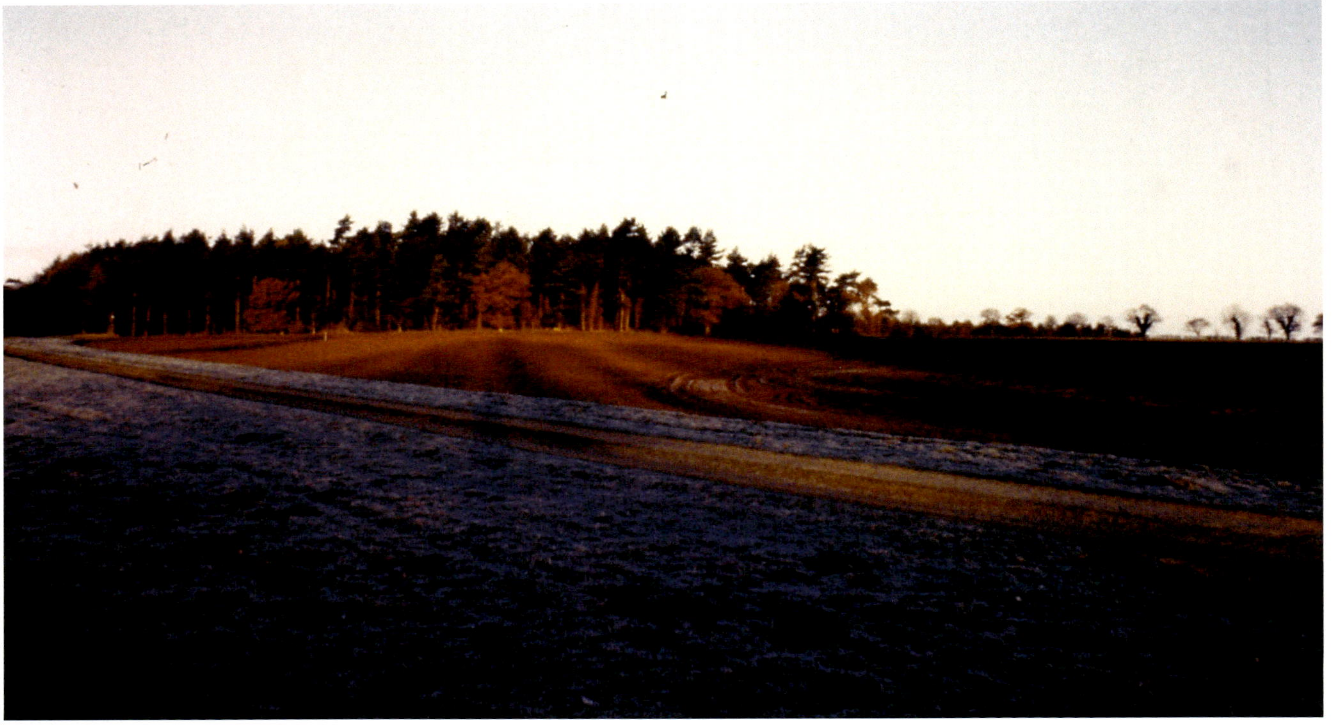

Figure 3.4 The 'gold field' in winter 1990. Image taken from south of the drive bordering the field, looking north-west, across the 'gold field' as the slope rises slightly towards the adjacent conifer plantation

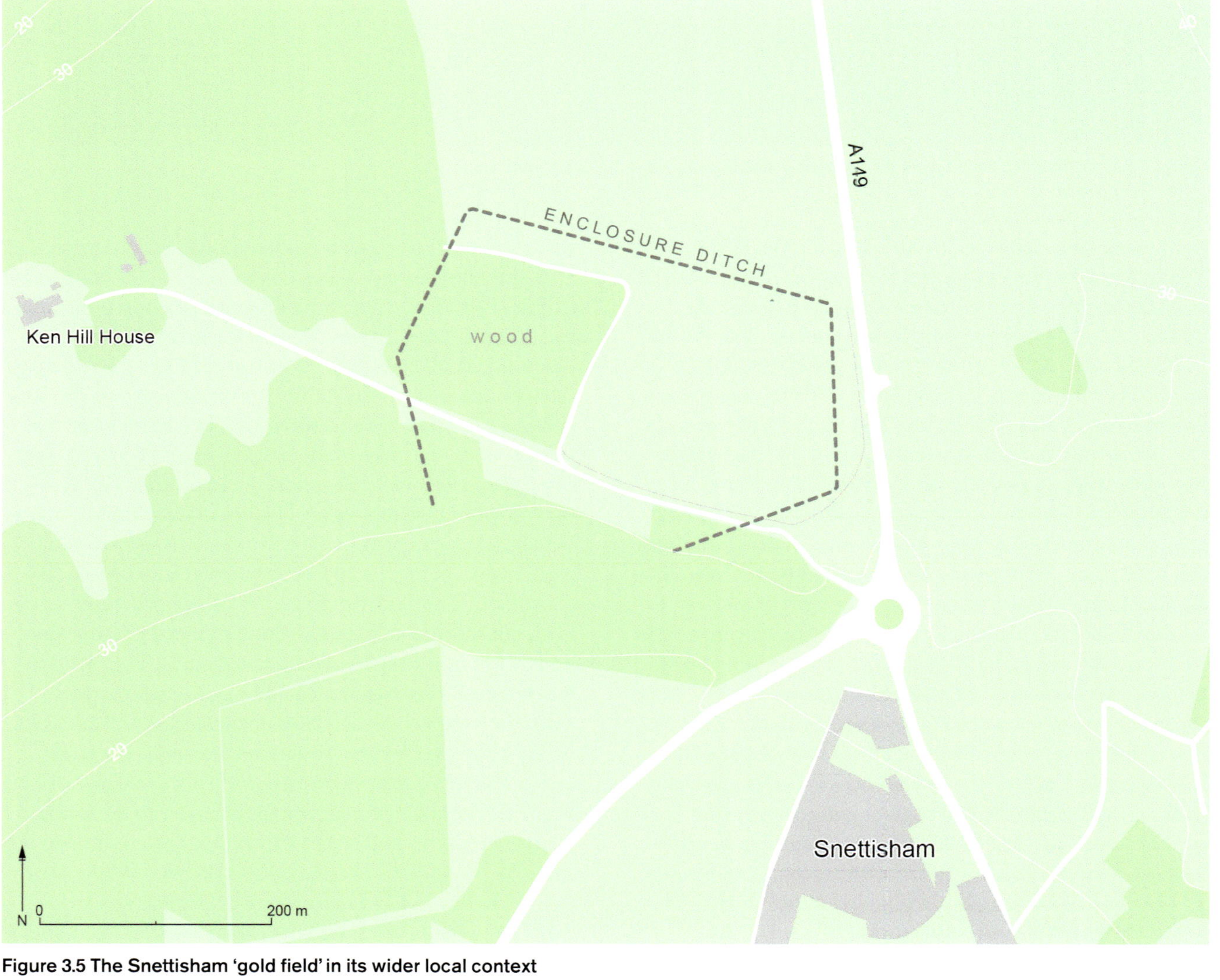

Figure 3.5 The Snettisham 'gold field' in its wider local context

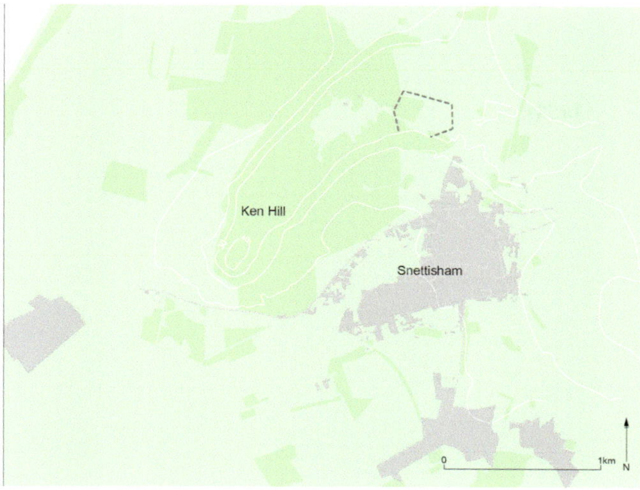

Figure 3.6a An outline of the current field boundaries

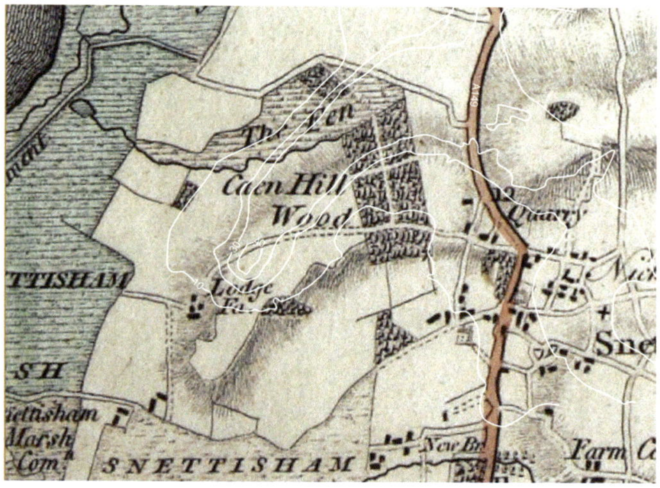

Figure 3.6b The area around Snettisham and Ken Hill in Faden's 1797 map of Norfolk

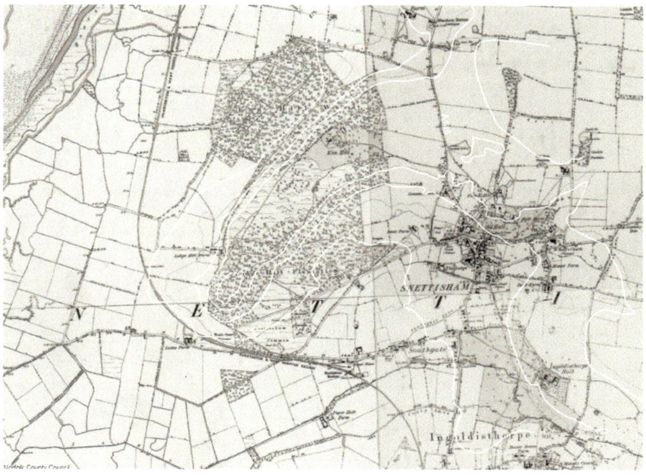

Figure 3.6c The area around Snettisham and Ken Hill in the first edition Ordnance Survey map (survey 1885, published 1886)

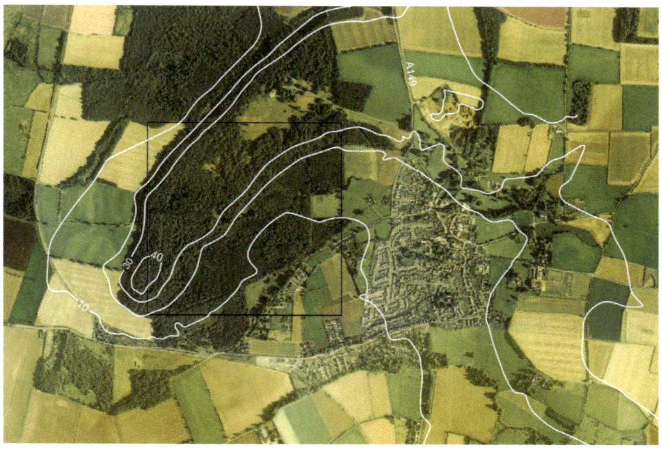

Figure 3.6d The area around Snettisham and Ken Hill in 1988 aerial photography carried out by BKS on behalf of Norfolk County Council. Image © Norfolk County Council

Until very recently, the landscape has been used to support a mix of farming with sport – the wood to the west and general layout of hedgerows and copses is testament to the pheasant shooting associated with Norfolk Estates of the last two centuries (indeed, a great many recent spent cartridge casings were recovered from the hoard field itself). With the Wash less than 3km to the west, wildfowling – particularly for winter geese – provided another important local pastime. Today, the area known as 'Wild Ken Hill', is a conservation area where practices such as sustainable agriculture and 'rewilding' are actively promoted.

The archaeology of Snettisham and immediate environs

The Norfolk Historic Environment Record (NHER) records widespread evidence for human occupation across multiple periods at Ken Hill (NHER 1487). This includes Mesolithic flakes and points, a Neolithic saddle quern and a possible working area used to produce Neolithic or Early Bronze Age stone artefacts. The ceramic and lithic evidence from the BM excavations supports the idea that there was Neolithic settlement in the immediate vicinity, with pits containing domestic or pre-midden material. There was a substantial amount of depositional activity in the area during the later Bronze Age; at least five and possibly six Bronze Age hoards have been recovered from the vicinity of Snettisham village, and indeed the site itself (Ch. 7, and see Lawson 2018).

In addition to the torc hoards at Ken Hill, there are also other nearby finds of Iron Age objects (**Fig. 3.7**). A copper alloy terret (rein-ring) decorated with punched dots and inlaid red glass enamel was discovered around 700m north-north-east of the hoard in *c.* 1971 (NHER 2779). It is on display in the Boudica Gallery at NCM (NWHCM: L1975.11). A pair of copper alloy objects decorated with birds' heads and thought to have been drinking horn terminals were also discovered by Charles Hodder in 1989 just to the east of the 'gold field', on the other side of the road from King's Lynn to Hunstanton (S.253–4; NHER 25249) (Gurney 1990). The findspot was investigated in 1992 by Stead and his team (Trench SA15) but other than revealing that the site was located near a spring, nothing of note was discovered (Ch. 5). A hoard of two local uninscribed Iron Age gold coins (*c.* 80–60 BC) was also discovered in the vicinity of Ingoldisthorpe in 1988 (IARCH-BD63EC; de Jersey 2014, no. 187).

Despite these finds, there is no definitive evidence for contemporary Iron Age settlement on Ken Hill itself. This does not mean that the site was isolated during the main period of deposition in the 2nd and 1st centuries BC, since

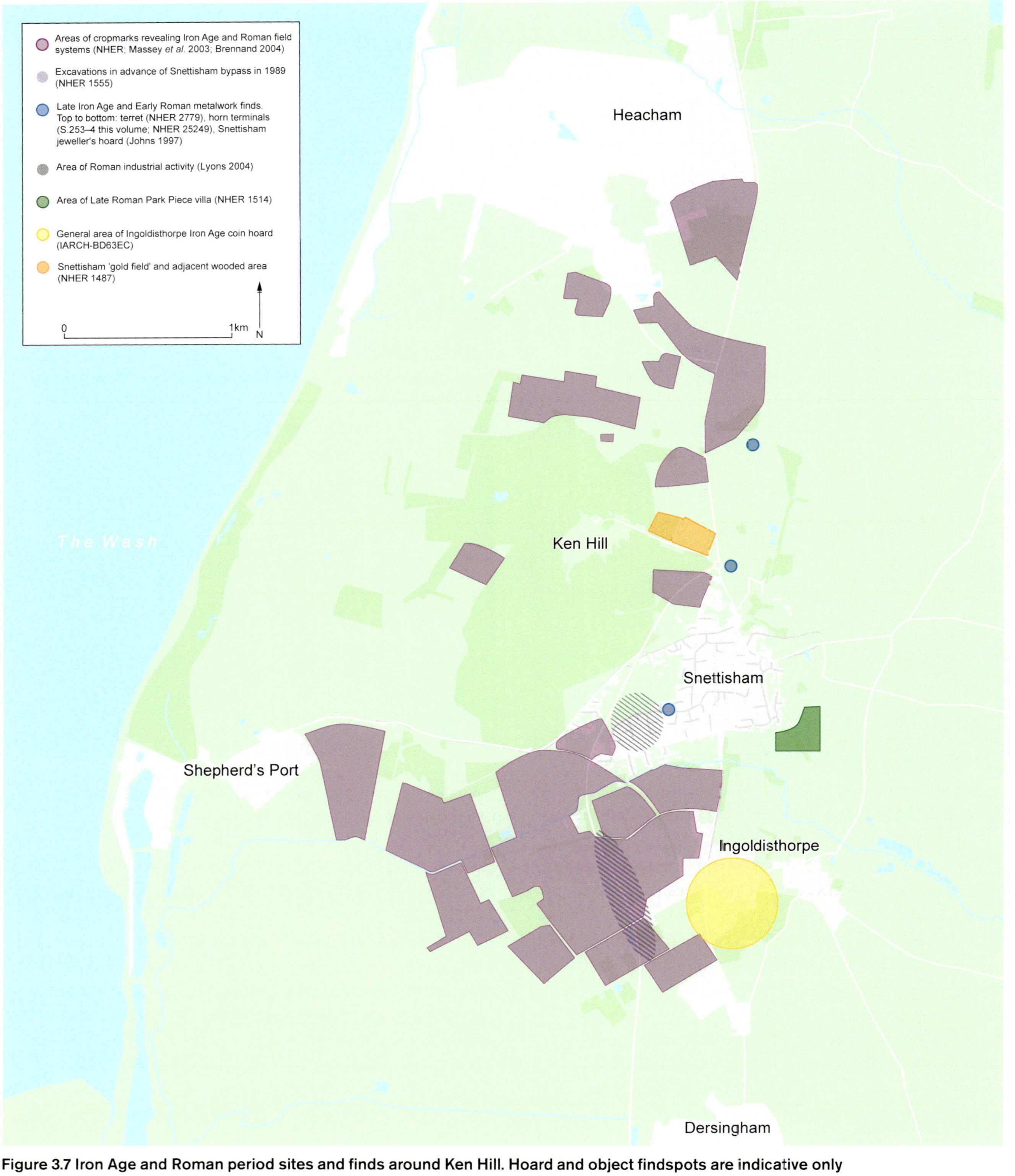

Figure 3.7 Iron Age and Roman period sites and finds around Ken Hill. Hoard and object findspots are indicative only

Iron Age settlement in Norfolk is often difficult to detect archaeologically. For instance, the primarily acidic soils means that bones, both animal and human, tend to be poorly preserved (Hill 2007, 28; Tremlett 2011, 34). No human remains were found at Snettisham, and the nearest site with evidence for funerary activity is the possible Iron Age cremation from Heacham (NHER 1401, found before 1911 and now lost). Pottery from the BM excavations provides evidence for likely feasting activities in the Late Bronze Age to Earlier Iron Age, and it is quite possible that many of the people visiting the site, especially in this period, lived nearby.

Aerial photography and geophysical survey has identified cropmarks representing extensive systems of fields, droveways and enclosures in the area around Snettisham (**Fig. 3.7**). These are part of a wider band of such cropmarks on this area of the north-west Norfolk coast, running north–south between Heacham and Dersingham. These farmsteads occupied the greensand belt, between the 10m and 35m OD contours, with the land sloping down towards the saltmarshes and fenland to the west, and rising up towards a chalk ridge in the east (Massey *et al.* 2003, 339; Brennand 2004). Massey *et al.* (*ibid.*) note that the field systems seem to have developed in a piecemeal manner. While there is no single overarching system of land division evident in these complex multi-phase cropmarks, general alignments of fields and droveways can be followed over distances of up to 1.5km. They propose that the east–west droveways may have provided seasonal transhumance routes for moving stock between the uplands and the saltmarsh.

Most of these field systems have not been excavated, and so they remain hard to date. One concentration of cropmarks in the Ingol valley just south of Ken Hill was explored in 1989 prior to the construction of the A149 Snettisham bypass (**Fig. 3.7**). This revealed an extensive Roman settlement with several phases of occupation and industrial activity, spanning from at least the 1st to 3rd centuries AD (Flitcroft 2001). It is possible some elements of the field system date back to the Iron Age, and there are certainly Late Iron Age finds distributed across the area of enclosures south of Snettisham village, including a strainer vessel spout now in King's Lynn Museum (NHER 34531; Albone *et al.* 2007, 65–7). This may have been the closest area of settlement to Ken Hill in the Late Iron Age, and if so the position of the hoard field on the lower slopes on the inland side of Ken Hill would have afforded views between the settlement and main area of depositional activity.

The field system revealed through geophysical survey in the 'gold field' at Snettisham (see Ch. 5) is most likely part of this wider agricultural landscape. In this case, it appears to be cut by the enclosure ditch which partially surrounds the area containing the hoards. Pottery finds from the BM 1990–2 excavations suggest that this ditch had begun to silt up from the mid-1st century to mid-2nd century AD, and there is no evidence that it was constructed significantly earlier. All that can be said for certain about the underlying field system is that it most likely pre-dates the enclosure of the hoard field. Overlaying de Bootman's geophysical survey data from the 'gold field' (Ch. 5) with the findspots of the Late Iron Age torc hoards (Ch. 8) suggests the tantalising possibility that the two may be contemporary, with the hoard findspots seeming to relate to the field system (see **Fig. 8.2a–b**).

Deposition was still happening up at Ken Hill in the 1st century AD (Hoard P dates to this period, and Hoard M most likely dates to the 1st or 2nd centuries AD). Nearby (**Fig. 3.7**), the Romano-British Snettisham jeweller's hoard (found during construction of a house in the village itself) was buried in the mid-2nd century AD (Johns 1997). This deposit consists of Roman coins and jewellery, including numerous finger-rings and bracelets. It also contained twisted gold wires with a very similar form to some of those from the Snettisham torcs. Metal analysis revealed these wires contained around 85% gold, which is the same as many of the artefacts from the 'gold field' (Ch. 17). Indeed, in her report on the Roman jeweller's hoard Catherine Johns concluded, '…it is difficult to escape the conclusion that some of this metal derives from Snettisham Iron Age hoard material' uncovered intentionally or otherwise in the Roman period (Johns 1997, 46). Johns (*ibid.*, 73) also speculated that the Roman jewellers may have been descendants of the craftspeople who made the Iron Age artefacts.

The area around Snettisham continued to remain important well into the Roman period; Late Roman, early medieval and medieval pottery has also been unearthed in surrounding areas, and the 'gold field' itself has produced evidence for Late Roman iron production. There is a Roman villa at Park Piece, on the other side of Snettisham village, less than 1.5km from the hoard field (**Fig. 3.7**, NHER 1514), where finds from excavations in 1931 suggest a main period of occupation in the 3rd to 4th centuries AD. As well as domestic material, these excavations uncovered evidence for iron processing, including hearths and large quantities of iron-smithing slag. Evidence for later Roman industrial activity was also revealed during excavations in Snettisham village (**Fig. 3.7**, Lyons 2004).

If evidence from the Snettisham jeweller's hoard hints at the disturbance and recovery of at least some Iron Age torc hoards in the Roman period, there may also have been later, unrecorded discoveries in the Ken Hill hoard field. A final note from the NHER describes a local legend current in the early 20th century that children were not allowed to play in the Ken Hill woods 'because there is gold in there'. This information was told to an E.B. Green by an old lady and was relayed to Rainbird Clarke sometime around 1950. It indicates a folk memory of discoveries that must precede the first recorded finds from the late 1940s.

The wider context: north-west Norfolk

The overall picture of north-west Norfolk in the Iron Age, particularly along the fen-edge, is a well-settled landscape dotted with small, unenclosed villages. Davies (1996, 73–5; 1999, 30–2; 2008 95–100) has also identified six enclosed medium-sized 'forts' located in the west of the county, each with earthworks enclosing 1.5 to 6 hectares, and dating from the 5th to 1st centuries BC. Warham Camp, Holkham, and South Creake are all within 30km of Snettisham on or near the north Norfolk coast; Narborough and Bawsey lie a similar distance inland to the south (**Fig. 3.8a–b**). Thetford Castle lies much further south. Although they are mostly at fairly low elevations, their topographic locations often appear significant: Holkham occupies a spit along the coastal marshes, and South Creake is situated at the edge of a plateau, with views of the sea to the north (Penn 2006, 22). Thetford Castle occupies a site of strategic importance, on a chalk rise overlooking fords where the Icknield Way crosses the Thet and Little Ouse rivers, and is enclosed by bivallate earthworks to the north, and a meander of the River Thet to the south. There is little evidence for intensive occupation or domestic activity at these sites, and Davies and others generally interpret them as having a special significance for their communities, perhaps as public spaces used for political, ceremonial or ritual events and gatherings (Davies 1996, 73–5; Penn 2006). Whilst none of these sites have depositional activity comparable to Snettisham, torcs and torc fragments have been found near Bawsey. The earthworks at Bawsey are undated, but Davies (2008, 99) argued that torcs and torc fragments found in the area suggested it was a site of 'some importance' in the Iron Age.

Aside from these large-scale enclosed sites, most settlement in Iron Age Norfolk appears to have been unenclosed, what J.D. Hill (1999, 190) has called a 'spurgy'

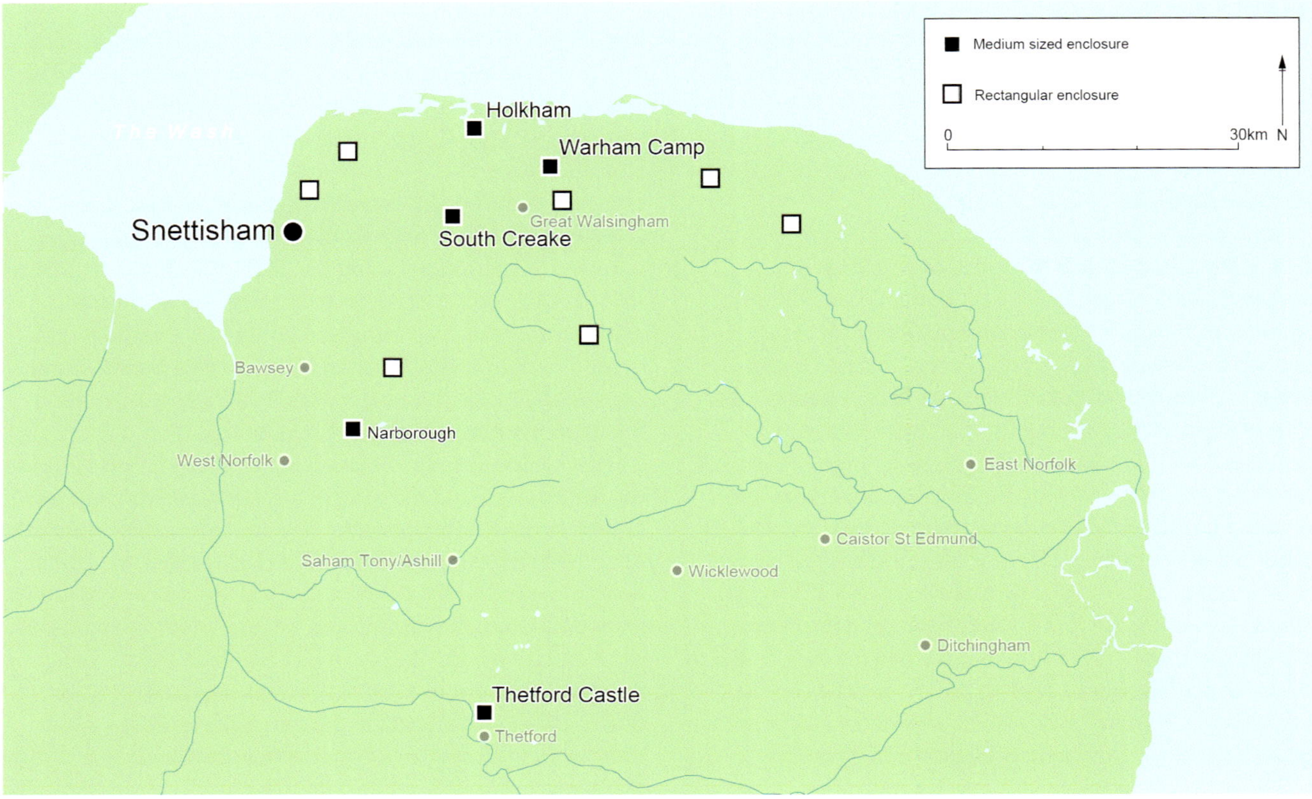

Figure 3.8a Iron Age fort sites in north-west Norfolk, in relation to Snettisham

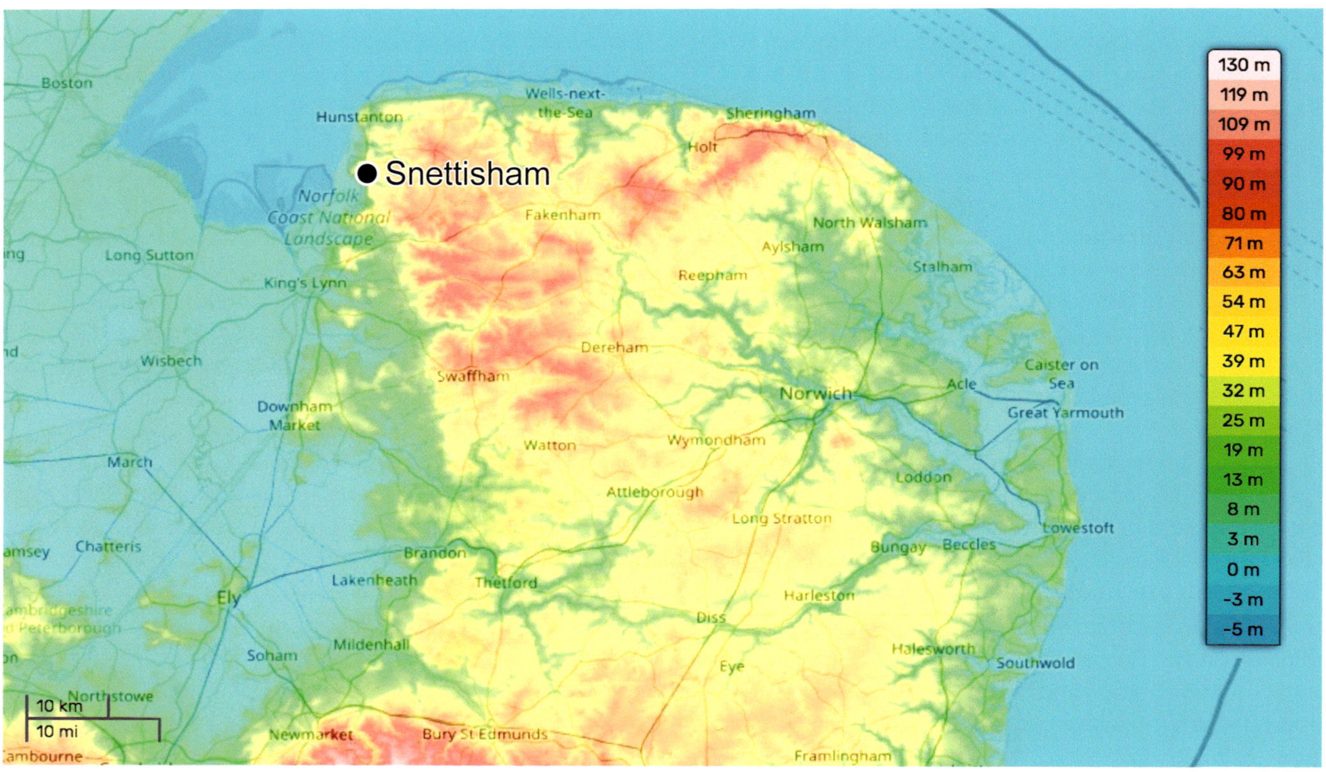

Figure 3.8b Topographic map of Norfolk

landscape with 'spreads of material and settlement components extending over large areas: relatively large, unenclosed, agglomerations of round-houses and other structures.' Davies (2008, 119–25) noted that some of these dense agglomerations of settlement (Caistor St Edmund, Saham Toney/Ashill and Thetford), whilst unenclosed, otherwise have a density and variety of finds and activity that can be compared to *oppida* sites in southern England, and may thus represent regional centres. Though others, such as Hill (1999), prefer to avoid the loaded term '*oppida*', there are clearly large, denser agglomerations of settlement in certain areas that appear to have hosted a variety of activities. Research by the Norfolk National Mapping Programme (NMP) has highlighted the presence of more Iron Age enclosures than has been previously recognised (Tremlett 2011, 27). These range from small sites which may

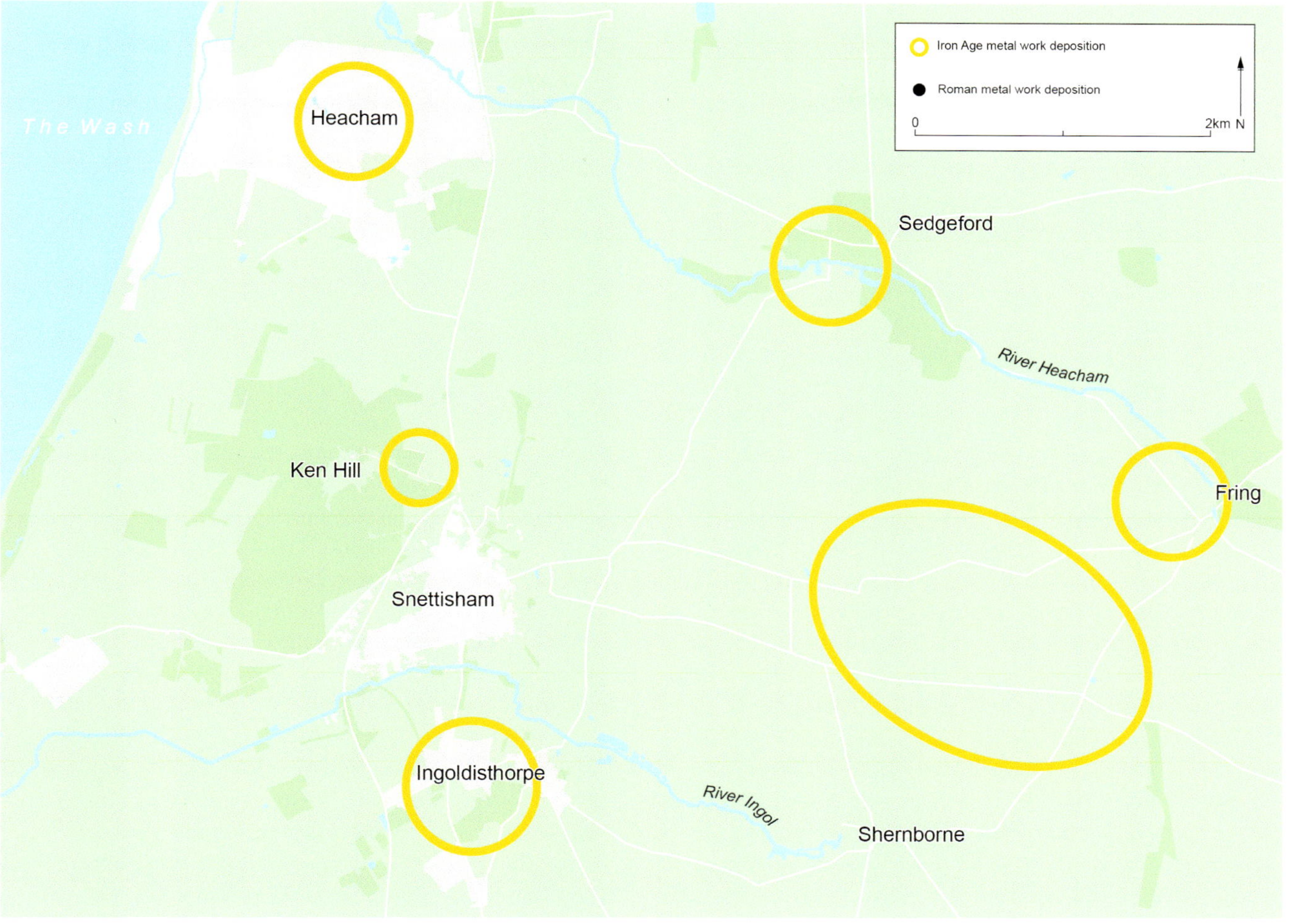

Figure 3.9 Sites in the vicinity of Snettisham with evidence for Iron Age and Early Roman metalwork deposition. Aside from the 'gold field' at Snettisham, the findspots shown here are indicative only

have had an agricultural function to large complexes of fields and enclosures up to a kilometre in extent that may represent 'enclosed components' of much larger open settlements (*ibid*., 29–30).

Snettisham is part of a spur of downland which appears to be another such dense agglomeration of intense activity (SHARP 2014, 48–9), stretching from Fring in the east to the Wash in the west, and bounded to north and south respectively by the Heacham and Ingol rivers (**Fig. 3.9**).

This wider area of activity in the immediate vicinity of Ken Hill can be divided into at least five sites with evidence for Late Iron Age coin hoard or metalwork deposition. Hoards have been found at Heacham, Ingoldisthorpe, Sedgeford and Fring and there have also been a cluster of finds to the east (**Fig. 3.9**).

Sedgeford (NHER 1609) lies inland, around 3km to the north-east. Here, a multi-phase site has been excavated over a number of years as part of the Sedgeford Historical and Archaeological Research Project ('SHARP'), a community archaeology project. This has produced evidence for possible Iron Age settlement and Late Iron Age ritual activity in the 1st centuries BC and AD. This is focused in several different areas. On a low hilltop just to the south of the River Heacham, a gold alloy torc of a type similar to those seen at Snettisham was recovered in two parts (one discovered in 1965 and the other in 2004, Moshenska 2004, 8–10; see Ch. 21), and metal-detector survey has revealed several concentrations of Iron Age and Roman metalwork. The excavation team interpret this spread as evidence of a large hilltop sanctuary site, perhaps associated with a cropmark complex of five or six nested rectilinear enclosure ditches that they liken to the Late Iron Age sanctuary and ritual centre at Fison Way, Thetford, Norfolk (SHARP 2014, 33–4). Further, perhaps related, Iron Age activity has been identified at the foot of the hill, just to the north, at a multi-period site known as the 'Boneyard' due to the presence of an early medieval cemetery (SHARP 2014, 37–45). Here, a hoard of 39 Gallo-Belgic E staters concealed in a cow bone was excavated in 2003 (IARCH Reid 2003, 21–4; Davies *et al*. 2004; Dennis and Faulkner 2004), located adjacent to a small ditched enclosure at the base of the valley (Moshenska 2004, 11–12). A number of other 'special deposits' dating to the Iron Age have been found in this area (SHARP 2014, 42–3). Immediately to the south of the enclosure, slightly upslope from the valley bottom, an intact horse burial associated with Iron Age pottery was found in close proximity to a large east–west ditch containing late 1st-century AD Roman fineware and imitation Gallo-Belgic pottery (Reid 2003, 21–4; Moshenska 2004, 11–12; Moshenska 2005). The scale of excavations at the Boneyard makes it hard to fully reconstruct the nature of the Late Iron Age activity, but it is likely that the landscape was settled, perhaps divided into small farmsteads. The small enclosure at the base of the valley, where the coins were deposited, may have been a ritual site contemporary with but smaller than the hoard field at Snettisham, and appears to have been within a site defined by linear ditches on a scale not dissimilar to those seen at Snettisham. Although their full extent and nature is unclear, the SHARP team (2014, 46) suggest that, 'The big ditches, probably with associated banks and perhaps palisades, would have been imposing features, designed to mark out certain spaces along the water's edge as sacred.'

There have been a number of Late Iron Age finds around 3.5–4.5km to the east of the Snettisham hoard field, along Fring Road and Bircham Road. Metal-detecting in 1988 recovered a crescentic copper alloy plate with inscribed and red glass enamel decoration (NHER 24432). It is recorded in the NHER as a possible shield mount, thought to date to the 1st century AD but, given harness fittings are far more common than shields and are frequently decorated with glass enamel and inscribed patterns, it more likely represents a fragment from a harness fitting, probably a terret. Based on the description of its decoration, it could date to the 1st century BC or the 1st century AD. A Late Iron Age brooch was discovered nearby in 1948 (NHER 1673), and two Iron Age pottery scatters were noted in 1987 (NHER 23701; NHER 23702). At least one Iron Age coin hoard has also been discovered in this general area, confusingly sometimes referred to simply as being from 'Snettisham' (de Jersey 2014, 308–10, no. 195, Shernborne I and II; Talbot 2017, 225, Shernborne A and B). Coin finds have been reported over a number of years and, like Ken Hill, this may also represent a site which saw multiple acts of deposition over the Late Iron Age and Early Roman periods (see Ch. 15).

Iron Age coin hoards have been found at Heacham (IARCH-126307; de Jersey 2014, no. 185) and Ingoldisthorpe (IARCH-BD63EC; de Jersey 2014, no. 187), both consisting of 1st-century BC uninscribed local gold coins. Two Iron Age coin hoards have also been found at Fring, slightly further to the east. One is a group of 170 Gallo-Belgic coins dating to the mid-1st century BC (IARCH-744618; de Jersey 2014, no. 183), the other is a mid-1st-century AD Icenian silver hoard (IARCH-B1844F; de Jersey 2014, no. 182; Chadburn 1990; Gurney and Chadburn 1991).

Even beyond the general environs of Snettisham, north-west Norfolk saw extensive metalwork deposition in the 1st centuries BC and AD. There are a number of torc finds from further afield, such as at North Creake, 15km east of Snettisham (see Ch. 22), and a hoard of harness fittings stylistically dated to *c.* 150–50 BC (Clarke 1951b) was found at Ringstead, around 6km to the north of the 'gold field'.

In a complicated and shifting world of relatively ephemeral settlement, fixed sites of activity with distinctive topographic locations (such as Thetford Castle, South Creake and Snettisham) may have acted as nodes, tethering communities to the landscape and taking on particularly important social, political and religious roles. Taken together, the evidence suggests a well-settled Late Iron Age and Roman landscape in north-west Norfolk, with major enclosed settlements to the south and west of Snettisham and probably smaller villages and their associated droveways and field systems in the immediate vicinity. This was an area which saw extensive metalwork deposition in the 1st centuries BC and AD, and most likely a regional centre. Ken Hill stood out as a significant landmark and has produced by far the most impressive hoard deposits, but many other nearby sites also saw deposition of Late Iron Age and Roman metalwork, suggesting a wider, closely interlinked, landscape of deposition.

Chapter 4
The History of Discoveries at Snettisham

Julia Farley and Jody Joy

This chapter presents an expanded and revised version of notes first prepared and made available to the authors by Dr Ian Stead.

This chapter summarises the history of discoveries at Snettisham, where finds have been made over a period of around 70 years, beginning in 1948. **Figure 4.1** summarises the finds and areas of investigation by date. Some of this information has already been presented in Chapter 2, but it is summarised here for the purpose of reporting a complete history in one place.

1940s–1960s: Hoards A–E and Rainbird Clarke's excavations

The first five hoards were found between 1948 and 1950, following a period of deep ploughing which disturbed the deposits (**Fig. 4.1**). Hoard A (a group of at least four tubular torcs, three of them largely complete, **Fig. 4.2**) was uncovered on 12 November 1948 by tractor driver Mr P.L. Williamson (Clarke 1954, 28–32). The next day his plough also unearthed Hoards B and C: groups of fragmented gold and copper alloy torcs, rings, ingots and, in the case of Hoard C, potin coins. The finds were reported by Mr Williamson to his foreman but were deemed as being of low importance, and they remained in a heap in the field, visible from the main road from Snettisham to Hunstanton, for about a week. Subsequently, Mr Linnaeus Chilvers, the owner of a local lavender cultivation company, asked to examine the finds. Unfortunately, when the objects were gathered for this purpose, some parts of Hoards B and C became intermixed (thus, in the catalogue, while some finds can be securely attributed to either Hoard B or Hoard C, others are grouped together and designated as 'Hoard B/C'). Mr Chilvers quickly recognised the remarkable nature of the assemblage and informed Ivan Thatcher, then President of the Norfolk Research Committee. Mr Thatcher passed on details of the discovery to Roy Rainbird Clarke, who was then both Deputy Curator of Norwich City Museums and Keeper of Archaeology at Norwich Castle Museum. Clarke first visited the site on 29 November, and collected additional fragments from the plough soil from the sites of each of the three hoards (Clarke 1954, 30). The artefacts were handed over to the coroner (Mr L.H. Atwood). At the coroner's inquest on 18 December, Hoard A was declared Treasure Trove and the gold torcs were held by the coroner on behalf of the Crown. Despite arguments made by Clarke that the finds should all be treated equally on the grounds of their archaeological significance, Hoards B and C were returned to the landowner.

In late December 1948, with assistance from the Norfolk Research Committee, Clarke conducted an excavation at the site (**Fig. 4.3**). The three hoards that had thus far been discovered were spread quite widely across the field, and Clarke determined that it was not practical to strip the entire area. He opted instead to investigate each of the hoard findspots and open a series of trenches across the intervening areas 'designed to ensure that the presence of any structures would be recognised' (Clarke 1954, 30). No structures or evidence of activity from any other period were discovered, but Clarke succeeded in locating more hoard finds *in situ*, including 12 gold coins from Hoard B (Cat. nos 1–12) and

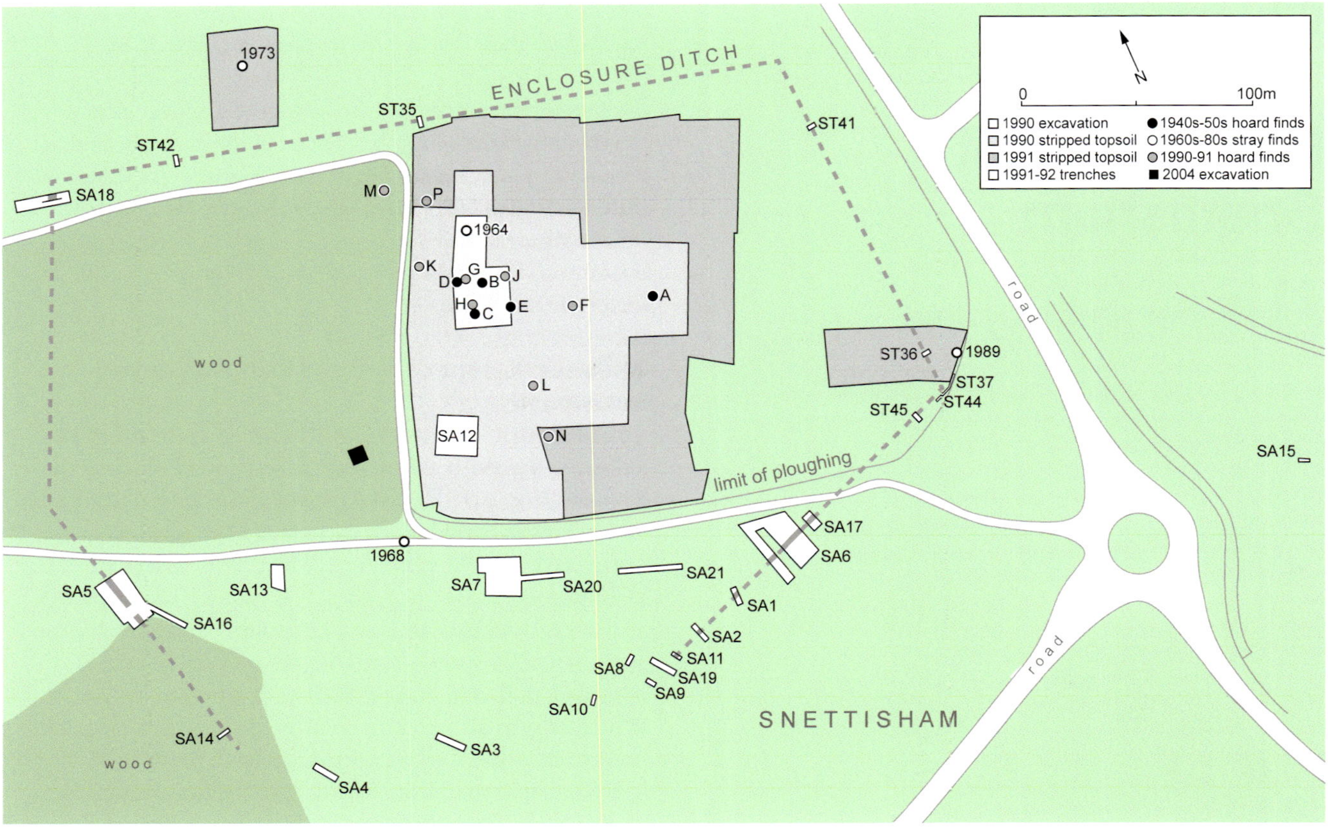

Figure 4.1 Findspots and areas of investigation by date

further gold torc fragments from Hoard A. The gold coins appeared to have been a discrete deposit. Clarke also found additional artefacts from Hoard B '... undisturbed beneath a stone adjacent to the gold coins' (*ibid*., 36): a 'group' of eight interlinked objects (rings B.1a–h). These items were seized by the coroner on behalf of the Crown as Treasure Trove, this time without an inquest.

After a valuation made at the BM, the tractor driver was awarded £400 for finding the torcs and the Norfolk Research Committee received £25 for the gold coins. The BM waived its claim to the material so the National Art Collections Fund presented the gold torcs from Hoard A to Norwich City Museums. They subsequently also purchased the gold coins from Hoard B and in May 1949 the landowner, Sir Stephen Lycett Green, donated the remainder of Hoards B and C to Norwich City Museums.

Clarke's excavations at the site (**Fig. 4.3**) indicated that Hoard A had been thoroughly dispersed by the plough over an area of 15 by 4 feet (Clarke 1954, 35). Owing to the presence of iron nails, Clarke (*ibid*., 35) suggested that Hoards B and C were originally contained in large wooden boxes, each around 3 feet square. It may well be that Clarke was misled by the nails as very many (most likely modern) nails were found in the plough soil during the excavations of 1990 and 1991 (Stead pers. comm.; Ch. 2); nails rarely appear to have been used in boxes in the Iron Age. As some of the artefacts, including the excavated gold coins from Hoard B, were found 'lying on edge', Clarke also suggested that within Hoards B and C some objects may have been contained within separate leather or textile bags, perhaps (based on the group of interlinked objects) grouped according to size rather than metal composition (*ibid*., 36).

The field was deep-ploughed again in the autumn of 1950. On 17 November, tractor driver Mr T.F. Rout discovered Hoard D when he noticed his plough had brought a torc to the surface in addition to a small ring. The torc was damaged by the plough and the ring was accidently broken by the police, who were called out to deal with the find. These artefacts were declared Treasure Trove at an inquest on 23 November. The next day, Mr Rout uncovered Hoard E, comprising perhaps the most iconic find from the site, the so-called 'Great Torc' (**Fig. 4.4**). A matching bracelet was linked to it by a broken gold alloy torc threaded through its terminals, and a gold coin (Cat. no. 169) was subsequently discovered within the ropes of the neck-ring. These items were declared Treasure Trove without inquest and Mr Rout was awarded £1,850 for his discoveries. Both hoards were deemed as being of national importance and so were acquired by the BM. Hoards D and E may originally have contained further artefacts but no archaeological excavations were carried out in this area until the 1990s.

In January 1952, Charles Lewton Brain investigated the wooded area adjacent to the 'gold field' where the torcs had been discovered and found a 'dump of mixed refuse' (NHER 1487). In addition to pottery dating to the Iron Age and Roman periods, Lewton Brain recovered oyster shells, wall plaster, coarse red brick *tesserae* and animal bones.

1960s–1970s: stray finds

At least three complete gold/silver alloy torcs and one terminal were recovered as stray finds during ploughing at Ken Hill in the 1960s and 70s (**Fig. 4.1**; Burns 1971). In March 1964, a complete torc (S.17) was discovered by a Mr Laud whilst drilling sugar beet. It was found in the same vicinity as Hoards B–E. In May of that year a fragmentary torc terminal (S.31) was also discovered nearby by Mr G.W. Button. An inquest was held at Dersingham on 15 August and both torcs were declared Treasure Trove and subsequently acquired by NCM (NCM 1965.30). On 29 February 1968, a further complete torc (S.16) was discovered on the edge of the field by Mr Dix, a farmworker. It was probably dragged by the harrow and thrown off when turning (Burns 1971, 228). This torc was declared Treasure Trove at an inquest on 18 September 1968 and is also at NCM (NCM 1969.55.3). A further torc (unpublished) (S.18) was discovered in 1973 about 130m north-west of where Hoards B–E were found. It was a surface find found in two pieces. Again, it was declared Treasure Trove and is now at NCM (NCM 1977.307). Finally, a note recorded by Tony Gregory in the NHER for Snettisham (NHER 1487), indicated that a further electrum loop terminal torc may have been discovered sometime in the late 1970s but was never officially reported.

1980s–1990s: Hoards F–P

Over the winter of 1983–4, the Norfolk Archaeological Unit conducted a detailed fieldwalking programme in the 'gold field' but uncovered no Late Iron Age artefacts, leading them to conclude that the site had been destroyed by ploughing (NHER 1487). This was assumed to be the case until 1989 when Charles Hodder was given permission to use his metal detector on the site after the field had been harvested. He discovered torc fragments (S.25, S.27, S.28) and coins (Cat. nos 219, 234 and 259). An inquest held at King's Lynn in December 1989 declared the torc fragments and a gold stater Treasure Trove; the other coins were declared not Treasure Trove. Both Treasure Trove and non-Treasure Trove items were acquired by NCM. Just to the east of the site, where Trench SA15 would later be located, Hodder also discovered two horn terminals (S.253–4) in 1989.

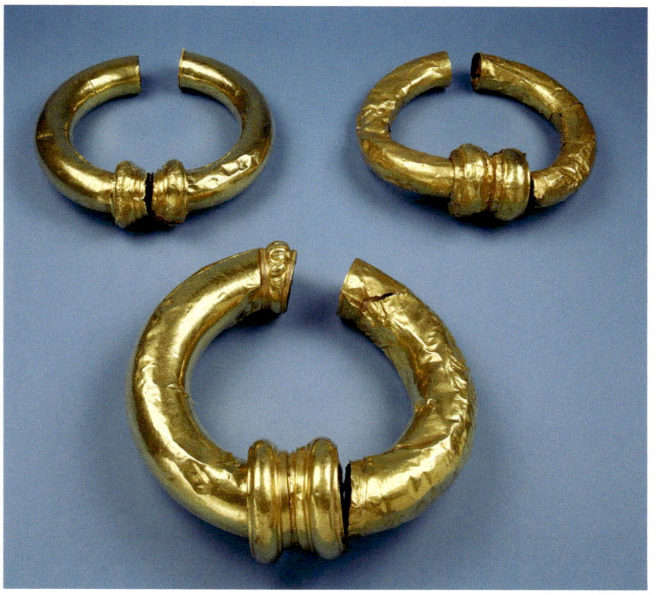

Figure 4.2 The three more or less complete tubular torcs from Hoard A, discovered in 1948 and subsequently restored (see Ch. 16). Norwich Castle Museum, 1949.74.1, 1949.74.2 and 1949.74.3

Hoard F

With permission from the landowner, Hodder returned the following year and on 25 August 1990 he discovered what later became known as Hoard F, comprising a huge quantity of fragmentary gold, silver and copper alloy artefacts, and nine gold coins, all originally contained within a copper

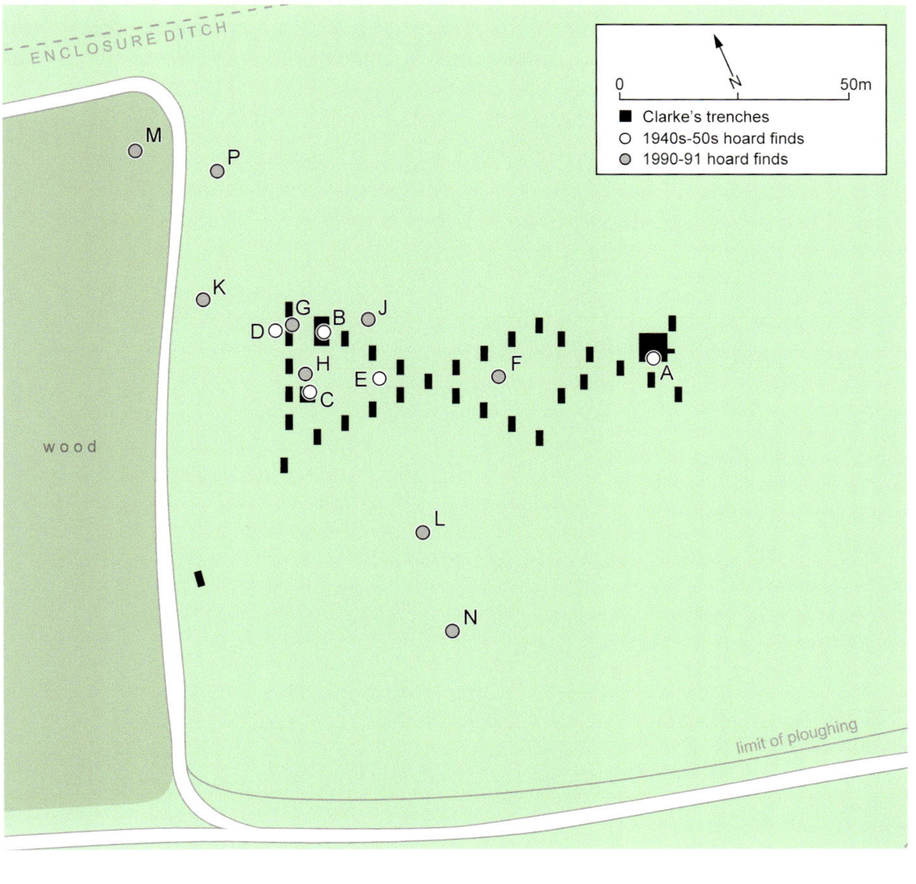

Figure 4.3 Clarke's 1948 excavations (after Clarke 1954)

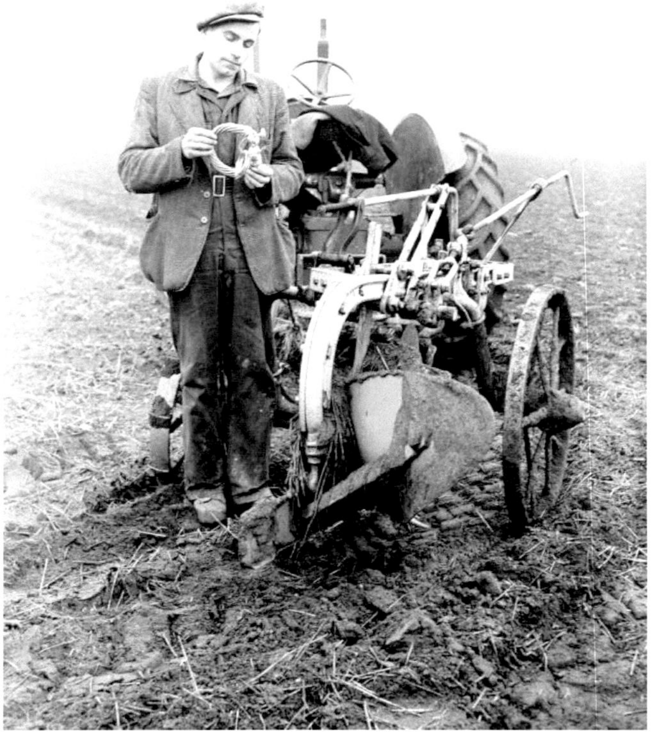

Figure 4.4 Tom Rout holding the Great Torc and other associated finds (Hoard E) shortly after its discovery in 1950 (image: *Eastern Daily Press*)

alloy helmet (Ch. 14). Hodder knew the find was significant but was unable to report it immediately to local archaeologists due to the timing, explaining 'with a discovery of this importance I would normally [have] contacted The Norfolk Archaeology Unit. As the day was the Saturday of August Bank Holiday weekend this may have caused problems, I therefore decided to excavate the treasure myself' (letter from Hodder dated 3 September 1990, NHER 1487).

Hodder made a rough plan of the discovery (see **Fig. 12.1**) and recorded his account in a letter (see Ch. 12), but there are no photographs of the hoard *in situ*. When the area was re-excavated by a team from the BM (Chs 2 and 12) they uncovered a pit about 0.3m below present ground level and 0.35m in diameter, which is believed to be the original hoard pit. There were no remains or stains of the copper alloy container on the wall or base of the pit but some of the original sides had been overcut. In one place a piece of multi-strand wire torc lay undisturbed against the pit wall. Other small fragments of torcs and tiny pieces of copper alloy sheet were also discovered in the surrounding area and by sieving the backfilled soil from Hodder's excavation.

Hoard F was sent to the BM shortly after its discovery. The hoard and the fragments found about that time were the subject of an inquest on 7 March 1991. The gold and silver items were declared Treasure Trove and the BM paid Hodder a reward. Non-Treasure Trove items were purchased by the BM from the Trustees of the Ken Hill Estate.

Hoards G–L

Torc hoards G, H, J, K and L, some of the most spectacular and intact deposits from the site, were discovered during the first season of BM excavations in 1990. A full account of these discoveries and the 1990–2 excavations is outlined elsewhere in this volume (Chs 2, 5–12). They differed from Hoard F in that they each consisted largely of complete torcs which had been placed into defined pits in the ground in a 'nested' arrangement. Hoard G had been disturbed by animal burrowing but, like Hoard H, it consisted of two distinct levels, an upper fill and a lower fill, divided by a layer of soil but seemingly filled in as a single episode. Hoard L, the most spectacular, also had two separate deposits, but in this case a small upper pit had seemingly been dug into the top of a backfilled larger pit. Nevertheless, the two deposits seem to reference one another and it is unlikely they were separated by a long interval. Hoards J and K had been severely truncated by ploughing, and only their lower torcs remained *in situ*. There was no evidence for separate deposits or multiple fills within these hoard pits.

Hoard M

Charles Hodder discovered Hoard M (a group of large amorphous lumps of silver-copper alloy) while metal-detecting in the north-east corner of the wood in March 1991. One of the first tasks of the BM excavations in November 1991 was to investigate this findspot, but no further finds were made and there was no evidence of a hoard pit or other context.

Hoard P

Hoard P comprised over 6,000 coins, many contained in a silver bowl, which was discovered by clandestine metal-detector users sometime after the BM's first season of excavations had been completed late in 1990. Unfortunately, the hoard was located under the main spoil heap and so had not been found by Stead and his team. Fragments of the silver bowl left behind by the metal-detector users were later located by Stead (Ch. 2, P.1–7). Stead described the circumstances of the discovery of the hoard and its later dispersal through the international antiquities trade in his account of the Salisbury Hoard. It is worth quoting this at length:

> ... I heard rumours that a coin hoard had been removed from the Gold Field about the time of our 1991 excavation. The informant had commented that our security had been inadequate, but I was quite confident that it had not been breached. I was told that I might get more information from Wobbly Dave who lived in Essex, drove a blue Cortina, and always had a pick-axe handle at the ready. He has earned his nickname because he would throw a wobbly if he was crossed. But my informant did not know how I could make contact, so sadly I was spared the experience. At the time I thought that the hoard, if there was a hoard, had probably come from another site.
>
> But I had to think again about 18 months later, in October 1993, when I was given some very precise information. The hoard had comprised 6,000 coins, and most of them had been to the USA and back. They had been found by a metal detectorist who had been looking for a torc, and he had been most disappointed with his 6,000 coins. The site was described

> precisely, by the track, adjoining the wood, half-way down the field. Most of the coins were silver, and they had been buried in a silver bowl; below it, as a separate deposit, were 500 gold coins and some curious ingots. My informant's description of the ingots matched exactly the unique ingots found at Essendon. Very few people knew about the Essendon ingots: this story sounded genuine. More impressive still was the mention of a silver bowl, which would have been extremely rare in the context of a Celtic coin hoard… (Stead 1998, 147–8).

Subsequently, several attempts have been made to piece together the possible contents of Hoard P from contemporary accounts and coin auction catalogue listings. This work is detailed further in Chapter 15.

2000s: Treasure finds and excavations in the wooded area

From 2003–6, with full permission and cooperation from the landowner, a group of metal-detector users, S. Brown, K. Elfleet and K. Jackson, undertook a survey of the wooded area immediately adjacent to the site of the 1990–2 excavations (**Fig. 4.1**). They used a mini digger to scrape off strips of topsoil and a metal detector to locate metal artefacts in the ground below the topsoil and from the bucket of the digger. Finds were recorded and plotted and a summary report produced by the finders. From 2005, Chris Berks of Chris Berks Archaeology aided recording and recovery of finds. All finds were initially reported to Andrew Rogerson at Norfolk Landscape Archaeology and metal artefacts were brought to the BM for the completion of Treasure reports undertaken by J.D. Hill, Eleanor Ghey, Ian Leins and Jody Joy (2003 T169, 2005 T487 and 2007 T697). A further Treasure find of several coins (2009 T666) was dealt with locally. The finds from these Treasure cases were acquired by NCM, and are included in the catalogue (Chs 14–15).

The 2003–9 Treasure finds represent at least three distinct periods of activity disturbed by recent agricultural activity, tree planting, as well as the action of tree roots. An antler cheekpiece (see Ch. 7) and miniature copper alloy socketed axe (S.9) most likely date to the Late Bronze Age or Earlier Iron Age (*c.* 1000–600 BC, see Ch. 7). Most finds date from the Later Iron Age and Early Roman period (*c.* 350 BC–AD 40/80, see Chs 8–9), including coins and fragments of torcs and copper alloy sheet, perhaps from metal vessels. Like the finds from the nearby 'gold field', these objects probably originated from hoards, in this instance disturbed by tree planting and tree roots. Finally, later Roman coins and pottery suggest a second period of Roman activity, a couple of hundred years later, perhaps related to the Romano-Celtic temple (see below), or other later Roman activity at the site (see Ch. 9).

Possible Romano-Celtic temple

Following the activities of the metal-detector users in 2004, which revealed the remains of a stone wall, an excavation was organised by Natasha Hutcheson at the request of the Norfolk County Council's Portable Antiquities Scheme Officer. A full account of the excavation is published elsewhere (Hutcheson 2011) but a summary is presented here and in Chapter 9. The excavations revealed the outline of a stone structure 6 x 6m in area, which Hutcheson interpreted as the remains of a small stone-built Romano-Celtic temple with a mosaic floor, painted plaster and a tiled roof (see **Fig. 9.2**). Hutcheson also postulated that the large enclosure ditch identified by Stead in his excavations (Ch. 2) demarcated a *temenos*, or sacred area, related to the temple (Hutcheson 2011, 45). According to Hutcheson, it was apparent from the outset of the excavation that the site had been severely disturbed. Some of this disturbance could be related to tree planting and the action of tree roots, or previous archaeological investigations such as the activities of Charles Lewton Brain in January 1952, who uncovered material perhaps also relating to the possible temple (see above) (NHER 1487). But Hutcheson believed these activities could not explain the level of destruction observed and she suggested the structure had been deliberately destroyed in the Late Roman period (Hutcheson 2011, 47).

Chapter 5
The Results of the 1990–1992 British Museum Excavations

Written and compiled by Julia Farley, with contributions by Tony Spence, Mike Cowell, Michael de Bootman and Sophia Adams

This structural report complements the narrative account of the BM excavations given by Stead in Chapter 2. The first section outlines the 1990–2 excavation methodology, while the second details the excavated archaeological features by year of discovery; a full list of contexts is included separately as Appendix 1.

The 1990–2 excavations, in particular the mid-winter 1990 excavations of the hoards, were carried out under challenging, semi-salvage operating conditions on a difficult geology. The hoards were vulnerable to theft (as indeed shown by the subsequent illicit detecting on the site resulting in the loss of Hoard P), and so it was not possible to carry out a full large-scale area investigation of the kind more commonly seen in modern development-funded archaeology. The report presented here is very closely based on the detailed notes recorded on site by the excavation team.

The results of a soil phosphate survey from 1991 are presented at the end of this chapter, as well as the results of two geophysical surveys carried out between 2006 and 2009. Whilst geophysical survey was carried out in 1991–2 (**Fig. 5.6**) and informed the placement of trenches, the technology of survey equipment and data-processing software has improved dramatically in the intervening decades. Thus the new surveys reveal features which were not identified in the 1990s.

Two programmes of radiocarbon dating have been carried out on the material from the BM excavations, one as part of the University of Oxford 'Technologies of Enchantment' project (Garrow *et al.* 2009), and the other as part of the preparation of this report. The results of both are included at the end of this chapter, as **Tables 5.2–3**.
For the purposes of this volume, the activity at the site has been divided into 6 phases:

- Phase 1: Early Neolithic (*c.* 3650–3400 BC)
- Phase 2: Bronze Age to Earlier Iron Age (*c.* 2500–350 BC)
- Phase 3: Later Iron Age (*c.* 350–60 BC)
- Phase 4: Latest Iron Age/Early Roman (*c.* AD 1–200)
- Phase 5: Late Roman (*c.* AD 350–400)
- Phase 6: Medieval and post-medieval (*c.* AD 1100 onwards).

These are mentioned below, and a phase-by-phase account of activity at the site is presented in Chapters 6 to 10.

The methodology for the 1990–1992 excavations
Tony Spence

In the first two seasons of excavation (1990 and 1991) a systematic metal-detection survey was adopted, aiming to ensure areas were cleared to the base of the plough soil. In the third (1992) season, local trenches were excavated over features identified by magnetometer survey (**Fig. 5.6**) in an attempt to get better, *in situ* dating evidence.

The standard process was to, first, contour survey the field. This was undertaken using a Zeiss Elta 4 Total Station, with a baseline established about 8m from the east side of the conifer plantation, and arbitrarily given co-ordinates 5000E/5000N–5000E/5100N and heights determined with reference to a bench mark located north-east of the field on the A149, at 35.17m OD.

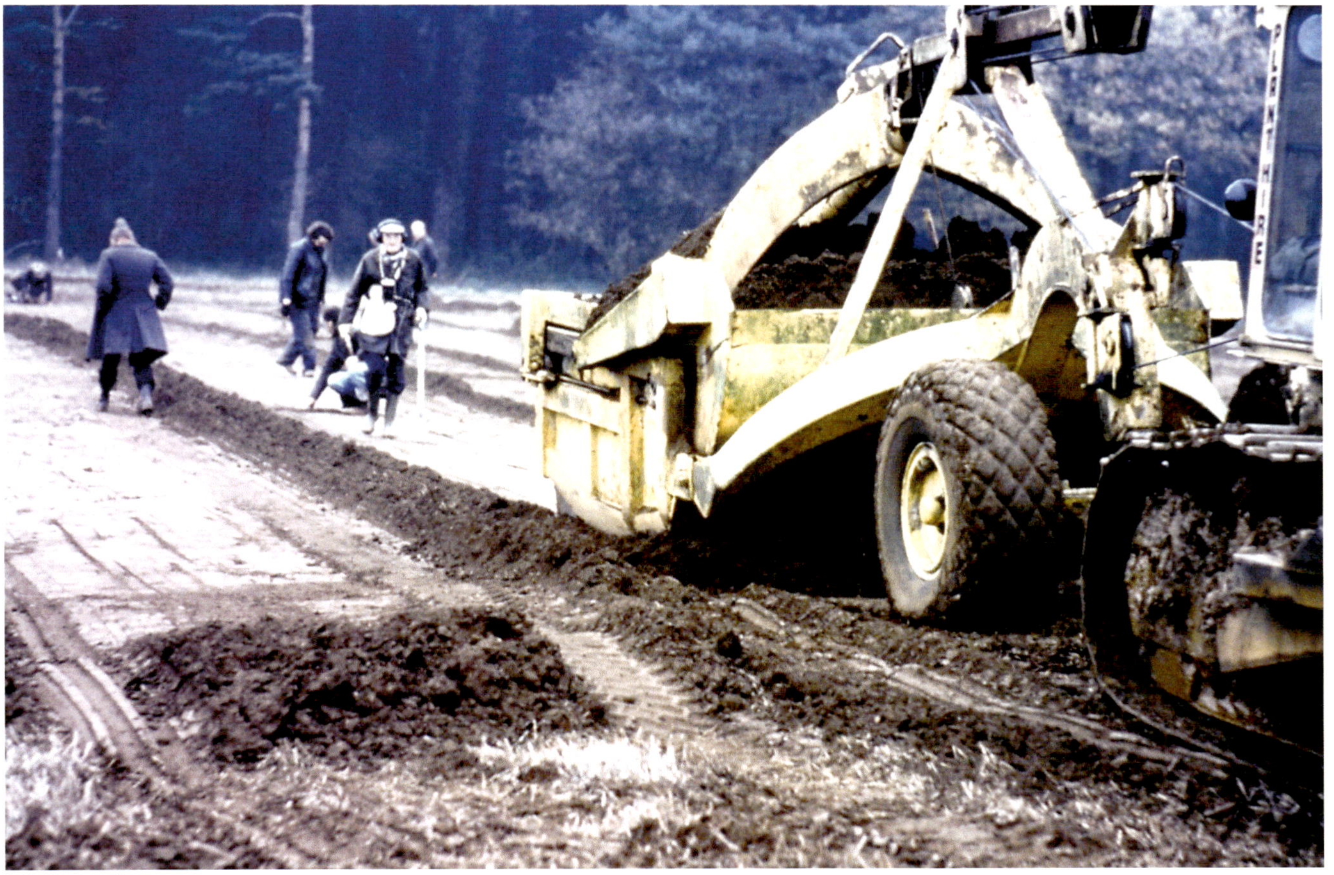

Figure 5.1 Metal-detecting surveys were carried out along transects created by the box scraper

For the subsequent metal-detector surveys, initially string lines were laid out across the field *c.* 2.5m apart, and the transects surveyed by up to three team members using a variety of metal detectors. Subsequently the lines created by the box scraper were used (**Fig. 5.1**). Any readings were marked with plastic garden tags and another member of the team would hand excavate to retrieve the reading (**Fig. 5.2**). To speed the process, hand-held detectors were given to the retrievers. If a reading produced an archaeologically significant item, the findspot would be surveyed using the Elta. Once a strip of say 25 x 50m had been cleared, a bulldozer pulling the box scraper would make another run, and remove about 5–7cm of soil. Two members of the team would follow the box, and two more, one on each side, look at what was being pulled up by the machine, and walk the spoil heap as it was dumped. With practice, the team was able to keep up a continuous process of detecting, excavating, recording and machining. Depending on the depth of the soil, up to six passes were required to get down to the base of the plough soil. The machine would then move to a new adjacent area, but dump the soil over the previously stripped area.

The team found that detection signals were made up to *c.* 12cm in depth, but there was huge variability (as would be expected) depending on size, orientation, metal type and soil condition. Generally, gold, lead and iron gave good signals, tin foil excellent, but base-metal coins, such as potins, were virtually undetectable.

Occasionally the detecting signals proved to be more significant than a stray find disturbed by the plough. Given that these were hoards of torcs *in situ*, after confirmation that there was something there, the location was protected by an upturned bucket, and machining continued around it. Once the area had been cleared, a small tent was positioned over it, and excavation commenced. For Hoards J, K and L this happened over weekends when the machine was not operating (**Fig. 5.3**).

At the close of the first season, and in the second and third, in specific magnetometer-surveyed locations, the base of the plough soil was cleaned to inspect archaeological features. The weathered surface of the carrstone is far from uniform in its natural state, and irregular sand-filled cracks occur; the stone itself is lying in thin beds dipping to the east which break up very easily. At this close to the surface the stone is soft, heavily weathered and easily dug into with the most basic of tools. Archaeological features were generally easy to spot, either through an admixture of humic soil in the sand, or evidence of localised burning. However, in the case of the *in situ* hoards, this was not the case; in Hoard L, the intermediate band of clean sand and carefully laid stone between the upper and lower pits gave all the appearance of natural.

Equipment on site consisted of a broad range from the complex to the mundane. The magnetometer surveys were at first hand-held in the usual manner, but after the second (1991) season, as the project broadened into wider landscape investigation, Tony Pacitto developed his 'chariot' (**Fig. 5.4**). This was a hand-drawn cart with the magnetometer mounted on it, which triggered a reading every metre. Squares 20 x 20m were set out, and bamboo canes placed as sighting lines at alternate metre points to ensure good coverage of the field. The Elta 4 proved versatile in

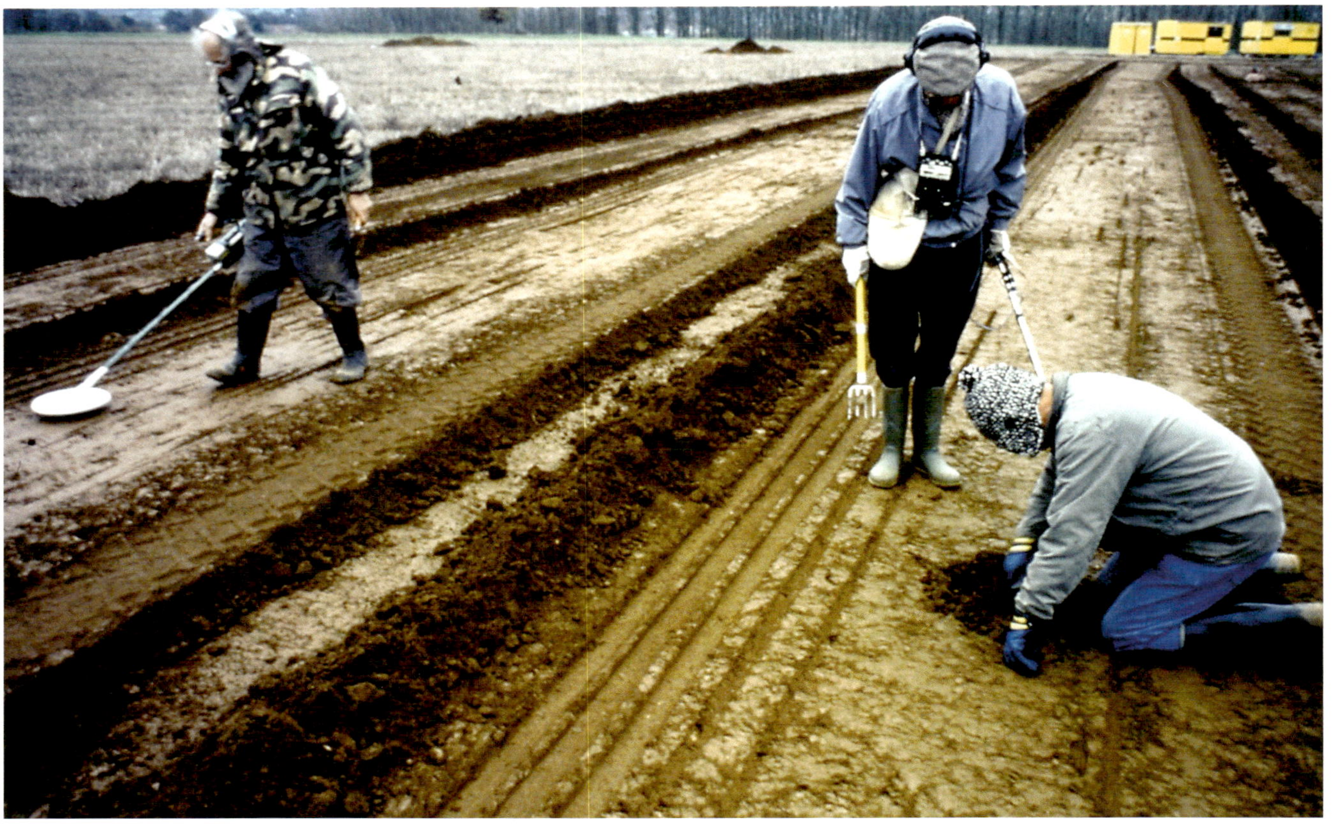

Figure 5.2 Readings from the detectors were investigated through hand excavation. Left to right: Tony Pacitto, Charles Hodder, Ian Stead

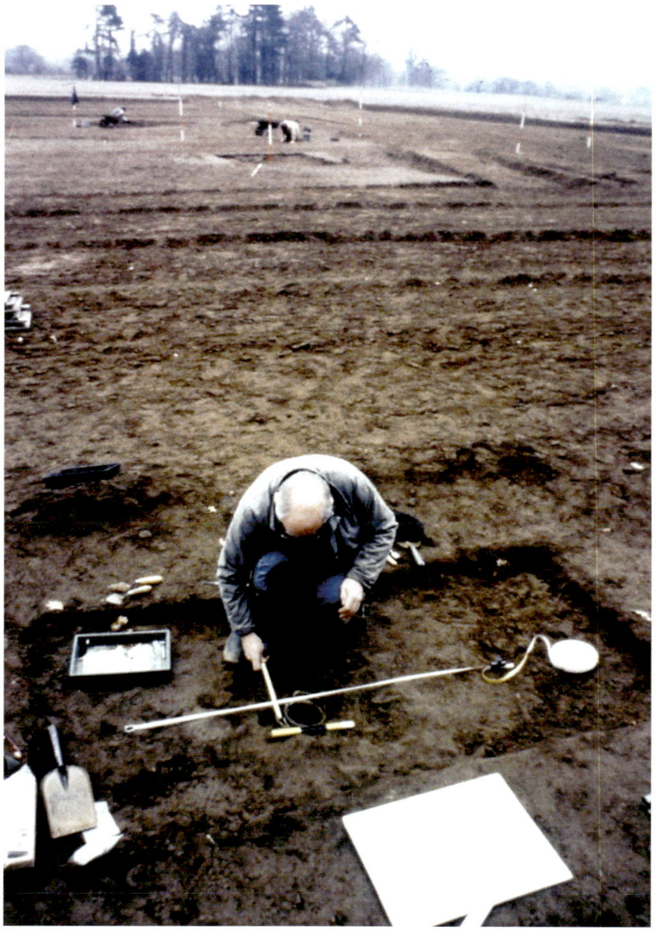

Figure 5.3 Ian Stead hand excavating *in situ* torcs in the Hoard K pit

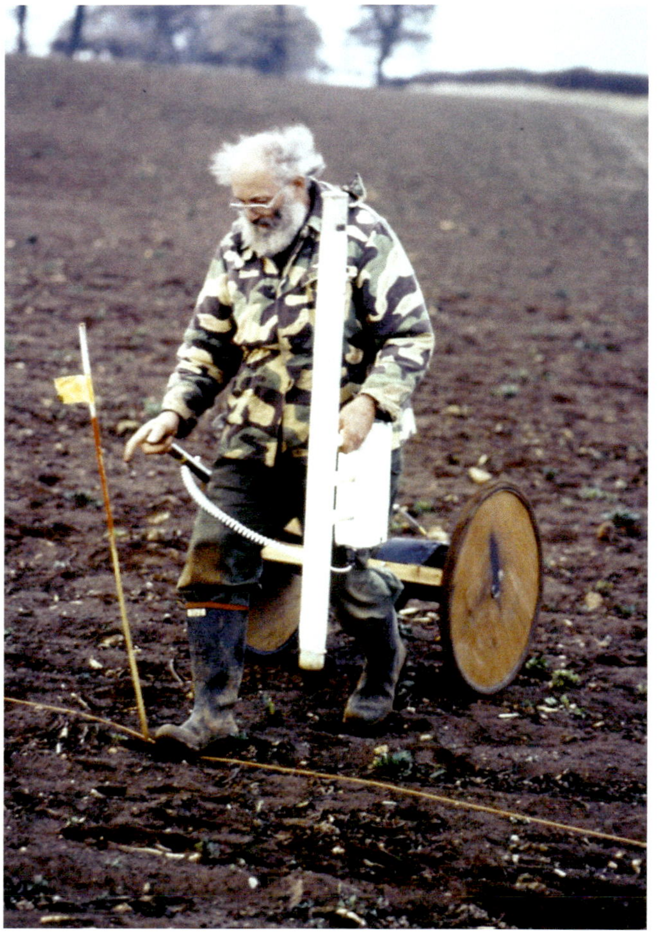

Figure 5.4 Tony Pacitto surveying in the hoard field with 'the chariot', a hand-drawn cart carrying the magnetometer. The turning of the wheels automatically triggered a reading to be taken every metre

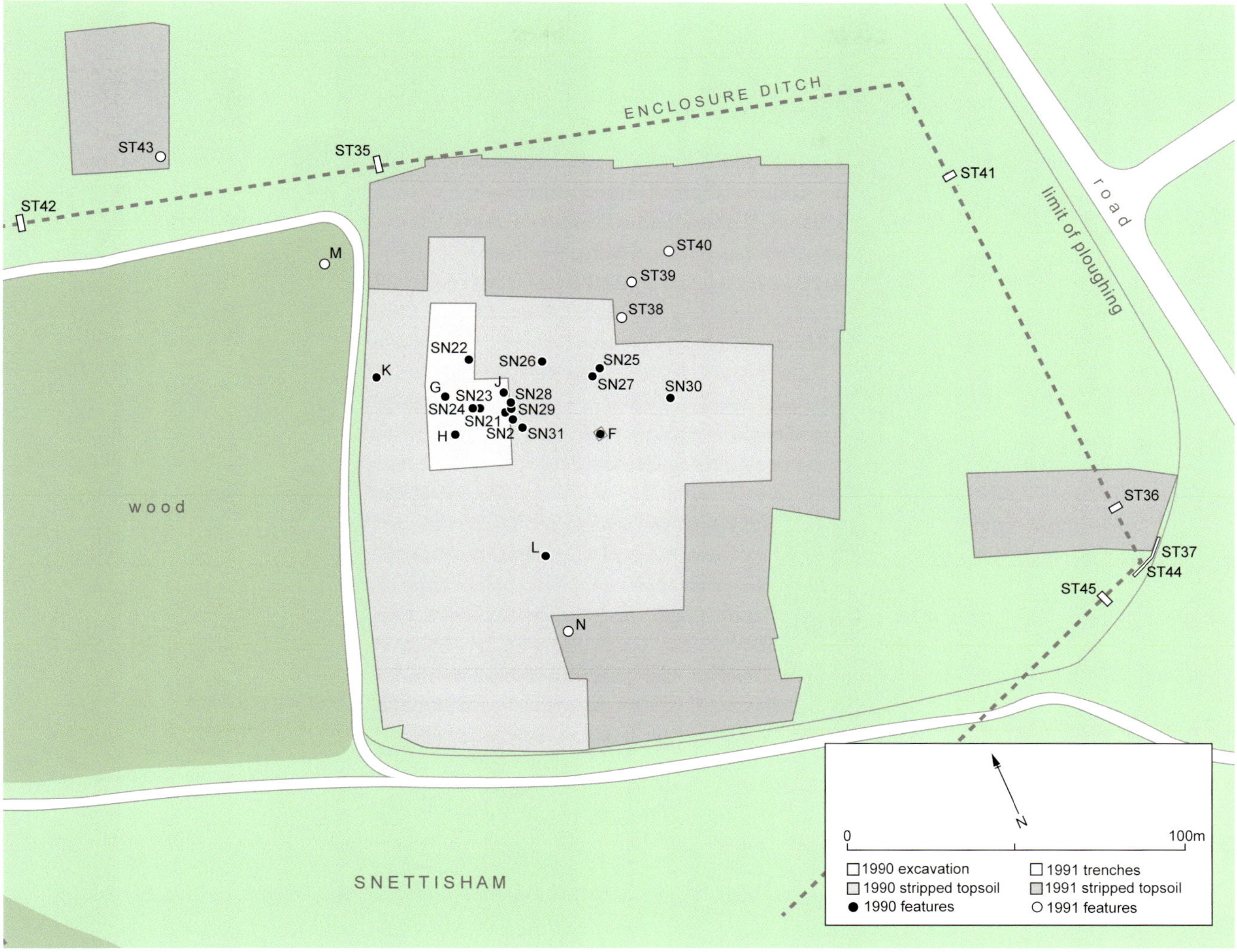

Figure 5.5 Plan showing locations of stripped areas and features investigated in 1990 and 1991

delivering accurate and speedy survey information, most of which could be plotted each tea break.

Excavation equipment varied from the bulldozer-drawn box scraper – which was key to enabling significant progress – to the usual hand-tools. Excavation of the hoards relied on a variety of hand equipment – plastic kitchen scoops proving particularly useful in removing soil but not damaging the metal. Paint and other brushes were not particularly helpful with the damp sand, tending to smear rather than remove. Metal detection relied on a variety of different equipment. The majority of the field survey relied on discriminating detectors with 20–40cm coils, and these were usually sufficient for identifying metal finds for recovery. A deep-seeking detector was also used for initial survey to check for the presence of deeper deposits. Over-ear headphones were essential, partly due to machining noise, but also helping against the cold. The hand-held devices were standard DIY-issue pipe and cable detectors, and particularly useful during the machining.

The 1990–1992 excavations

The 1990 season

As outlined above and in Chapters 1 and 2, in the 1990 excavation season large areas of the hoard field (Areas 1–15) were stripped using a box scraper and surveyed by metal detector. A number of Neolithic pits were revealed early on. Due to the challenges of excavating at the site, the limited time available, and the very real risk from illicit detectorists, a conscious effort was made to avoid disturbing further Neolithic material in order to focus on the Later Iron Age hoards.

Four kinds of features were excavated in 1990 (see **Fig. 5.5**): a series of Neolithic (Phase 1) pits (SN21, SN23, SN24, SN26, SN27, SN28, SN29, SN30); a pit (SN31) containing a very small amount of burnt bone which was radiocarbon dated to Phase 2 (**Table 5.3**); a slightly smaller pit containing a large quantity of Earlier Iron Age (Phase 2) pottery (SN25); and the Later Iron Age (Phase 3) metalwork hoard pits F, G, H, J, K and L. All of these features (except Hoard F, which was located and excavated by Charles Hodder, see Chs 2 and 4) were identified through topsoil clearance and metal-detecting in the main hoard field or the subsequent excavation carried out by hand across a smaller area. The archaeological features uncovered in this season of excavation are considered in more detail in the phase-by-phase discussions (Chs 6–8). Two (SN2 and SN22) were revealed to be natural and are not considered further. Note that not all SN numbers are included in the context listing since they were not originally applied exclusively to features. SN1–20 referred variously to stripped areas, hoard pits, pottery findspots etc. and for this reason were often duplications of other labelling systems.

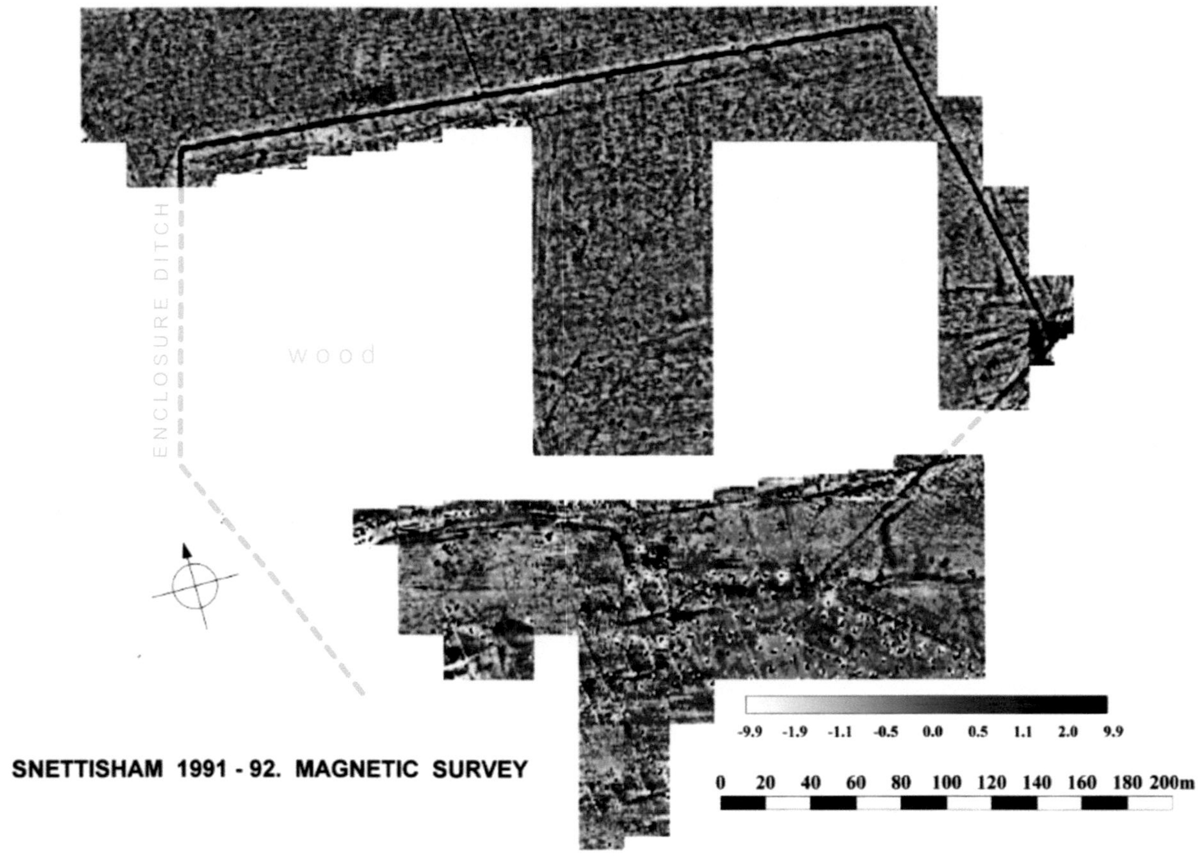

Figure 5.6 The results of gradiometer survey carried out during the BM 1991–2 excavation seasons, revealing the northern and eastern sides of the polygonal enclosure ditch

The 1991 season

Figure 5.5 shows the features and areas investigated in 1991. In March 1991, Charles Hodder had discovered Hoard M (a group of large amorphous lumps of silver-copper alloy, radiocarbon dated to Phase 4, see **Table 5.2**) in the north-east corner of the wood. One of the first tasks of the excavations in November 1991 was to investigate this findspot, but no further discoveries were made. As the find was made at the base of a pine tree, it was not possible to discern the limits or nature of any hoard pit, and indeed it is possible the finds had been re-deposited.

The area stripped of topsoil was extended in the main field to the south and east (Areas 16–19 and 22), leading to the discovery of Hoard N, a disturbed Iron Age coin hoard (Phase 3), in Area 18. The cleared areas were extended to the north (Areas 21 and 25–27), uncovering three flint concentrations and/or burnt areas likely associated with the same period of activity as the Neolithic pits (ST38, ST39, ST40, all in Area 25). An area to the north-west (Area 28, which had produced an Iron Age torc in 1973, S.18) was stripped but produced very few finds or features except a similar area of burning with a concentration of flint (ST43) that may likewise be associated with Neolithic activity. These features are considered further in the discussion of Phase 1 (Ch. 6).

The stripping of Area 21 also provided an opportunity to investigate a linear spread of furnace debris and slag, extending E–W for around 20m. This was in the vicinity of the area where Hoard P had earlier been stolen by illicit metal detectorists (see Chs 2, 4, 12 and 15). A gradiometer survey carried out in 1991 (see Ch. 2; **Fig. 5.6**) revealed that this was part of a large, polygonal enclosure ditch, almost completely surrounding the area which produced the hoards, though open to the south-west where the ground descends towards what would have been an inlet from the Wash.

Slots were dug through the northern part of the ditch in the area of the slag deposit (ST35), and to the east (ST36). A slit trench (ST37) was opened in an attempt to follow the path of the enclosure ditch to the south of ST36, but there was a very deep overburden in this area. Further slots were subsequently opened across the enclosure ditch to the north (ST42) and east (ST41). Another slot (ST44) was opened to the south of ST36 to investigate the path of the enclosure ditch, but found no features, despite excavation down to the natural carrstone. Slot ST45 was then dug to the west of ST36, revealing the turn of the enclosure ditch. The five 1991 slots (ST35, ST36, ST41, ST42 and ST45, see **Fig. 5.5**) are considered in the sections on Phases 4 and 5 (Ch. 9), alongside the enclosure ditch excavations from 1992.

The 1992 season

The 1992 season focused on providing a wider context for the hoards. A total of 21 trenches were opened over features identified by geophysical survey (see **Table 5.1** and **Fig. 5.7**). A trench-by-trench outline is given below, and a full list of contexts can be found in Appendix 1.

Trench	Description
SA1	Machine strip across enclosure ditch
SA2	Machine strip across enclosure ditch
SA3	Machine strip across modern field drain
SA4	Machine strip to check for enclosure ditch alignment (no features)
SA5	Machine strip across west side of enclosure ditch, including entranceway
SA6	Machine strip across enclosure ditch
SA7	Machine strip of area to south of main field
SA8	Hand-dug trench to check for enclosure ditch alignment (no features)
SA9	Hand-dug trench to check for enclosure ditch alignment (no features)
SA10	Hand-dug trench to check for enclosure ditch alignment (no features)
SA11	Hand-dug trench to check for enclosure ditch alignment (no features)
SA12	Machine strip to investigate ditch junction on gradiometer survey
SA13	Machine strip to investigate ditches to south of main field
SA14	Hand-dug trench to check for enclosure ditch alignment
SA15	Hand-dug trench at site where drinking horn terminals found (S.253–4), located over the main road, to east of main site
SA16	Machine strip extension of SA5 to investigate ditches to the east
SA17	Machine strip across enclosure ditch, east of SA6, to explore ditch junction
SA18	Machine strip across enclosure ditch and outer ditch to west
SA19	Machine strip to check for enclosure ditch alignment (no features)
SA20	Machine strip extension to east of SA7
SA21	Machine strip extension to east of SA7 and SA20

Table 5.1 Trenches opened in 1992

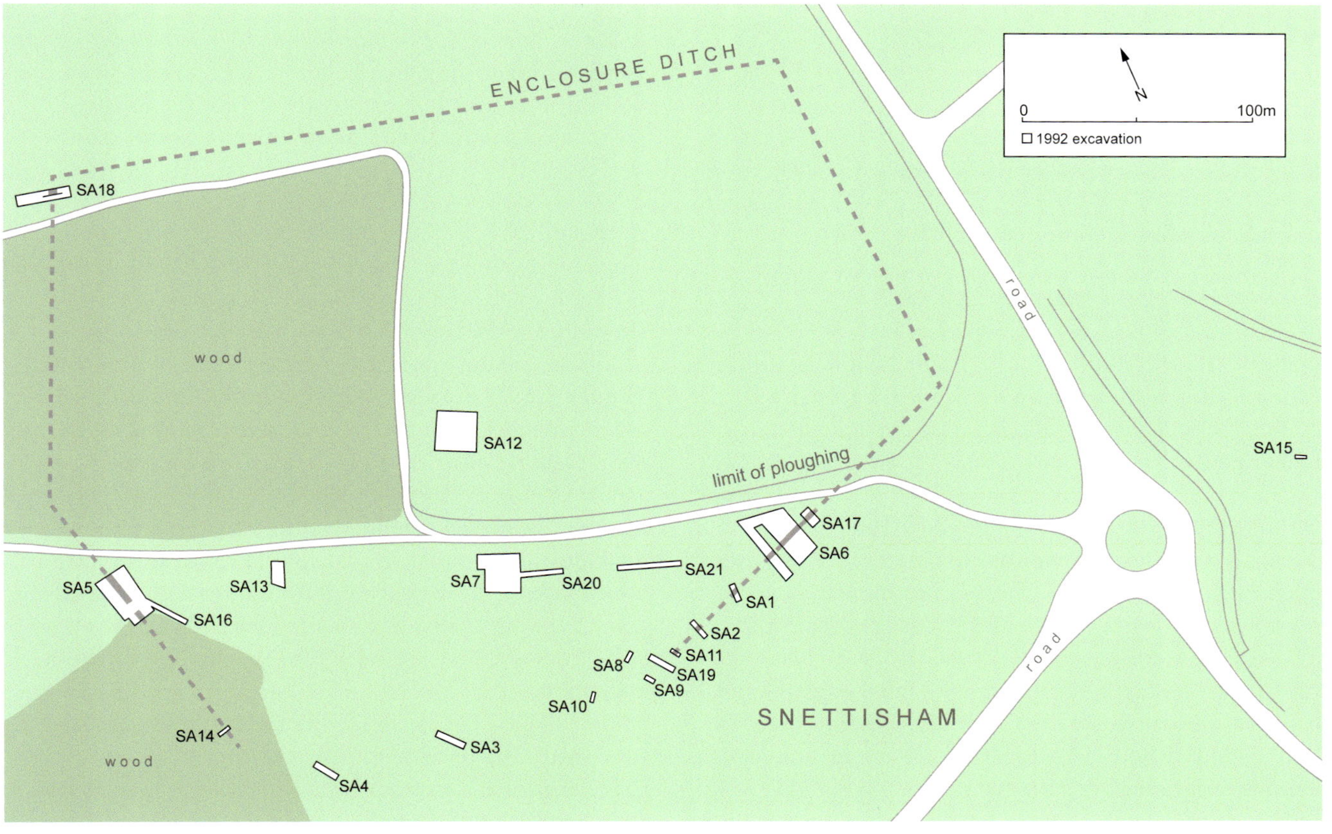

Figure 5.7 Plan showing locations of trenches excavated in 1992

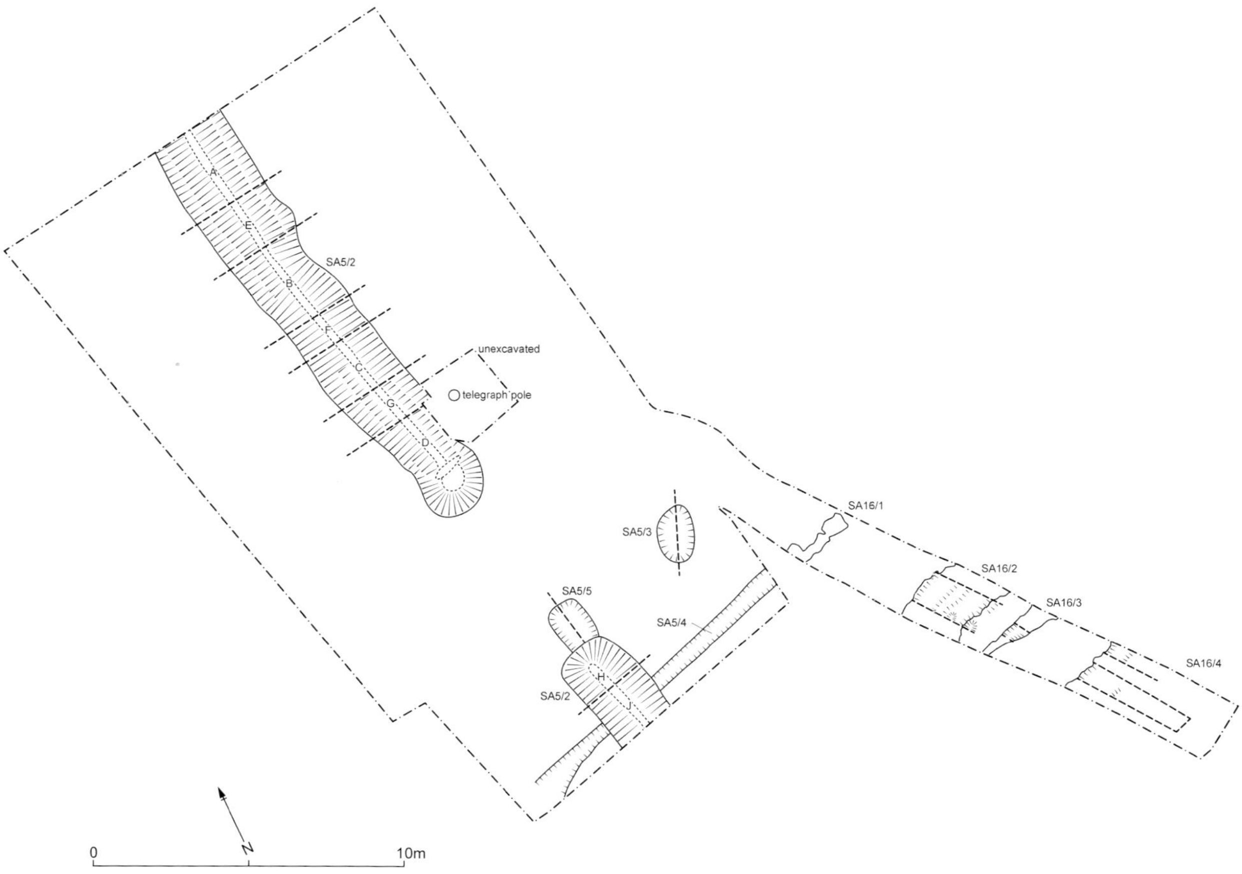

Figure 5.8 Plan of Trenches 5 and 16

SA1: machine strip across enclosure ditch
Trench 1 (2.5 x 7.5m, oriented approximately N–S), was opened up across the south-east side of the enclosure ditch, following the line from ST45 (excavated the previous year). Context SA1/1 was the plough soil, a uniform reddish sandy soil with gravel found across the trench. SA1/2, the enclosure ditch, is discussed in more detail in Chapter 9.

SA2: machine strip across enclosure ditch
Trench 2 (2.5 x 7.5m, oriented approximately N–S) was opened up to the south-west of Trench 1, following the line of the enclosure ditch. Context SA2/1 was the plough soil. SA2/2, the enclosure ditch, is discussed in more detail in Chapter 9.

SA3: machine strip across modern field drain
Trench 3 (2.5 x 15m, oriented approximately NW–SE) was opened up at the far south of the site, extrapolating a possible line of the enclosure ditch from Trenches 1 and 2. The same reddish-grey sandy topsoil with gravel and tree roots (SA3/1) was present. A ditch was uncovered (SA3/2), running approximately E–W across the trench, cut into hard, light yellowish-grey clayey soil. However, although on a similar alignment, this was not the enclosure ditch. At its base (*c.* 0.45m below the base of the topsoil) was a field drain of 18th or 19th-century origin.

SA4: machine strip to check for enclosure ditch alignment
Trench 4 (2.5 x 12m, oriented approximately NW–SE) was opened up to the west of Trench 3 in an attempt to locate the south-west edge of the enclosure ditch. However, no features could be discerned. The topsoil (SA4/1), about 0.3m in depth, lay directly over the yellowish-grey clayey sand covering the bottom of the trench. In the centre of Trench 4 this was overcut to a depth of 0.6m to confirm that it was natural.

SA5 and extension SA16: machine strip across west side of enclosure ditch, including entranceway
Trench 5 (24 x 14m, oriented approximately N–S) was opened up on the south-west side of the site to explore the section of the enclosure ditch which included an entrance or gateway, visible on the 1991 gradiometer survey. Features are shown in **Figure 5.8**. The same reddish-grey sandy subsoil (SA5/1) was present below the turf as in the other trenches to the east. The enclosure ditch (SA5/2) was clearly visible, with a sequence of four fills apparent in most of the excavated sections. This is discussed further in Chapter 9. The enclosure ditch was cut by a shallow linear ditch (SA5/4), which petered out to the west. This was most likely a vestigial trace associated with much more recent landscaping activity at the edge of the woodland or the track running along its perimeter.

Two shallow but apparently archaeological hollows were excavated (SA5/3 and SA5/5). Each was a shallow pit/depression filled with reddish sandy soil. There were no finds from SA5/5, and very few from SA5/3. These included both prehistoric and post-medieval pottery, as well as an iron knife fragment (S.353) from the very surface. Neither feature could be closely dated, though SA5/5 was cut by the enclosure ditch, so must pre-date this Phase 4 (Early Roman) feature. The inclusion of post-medieval pottery suggests that SA5/3 was later.

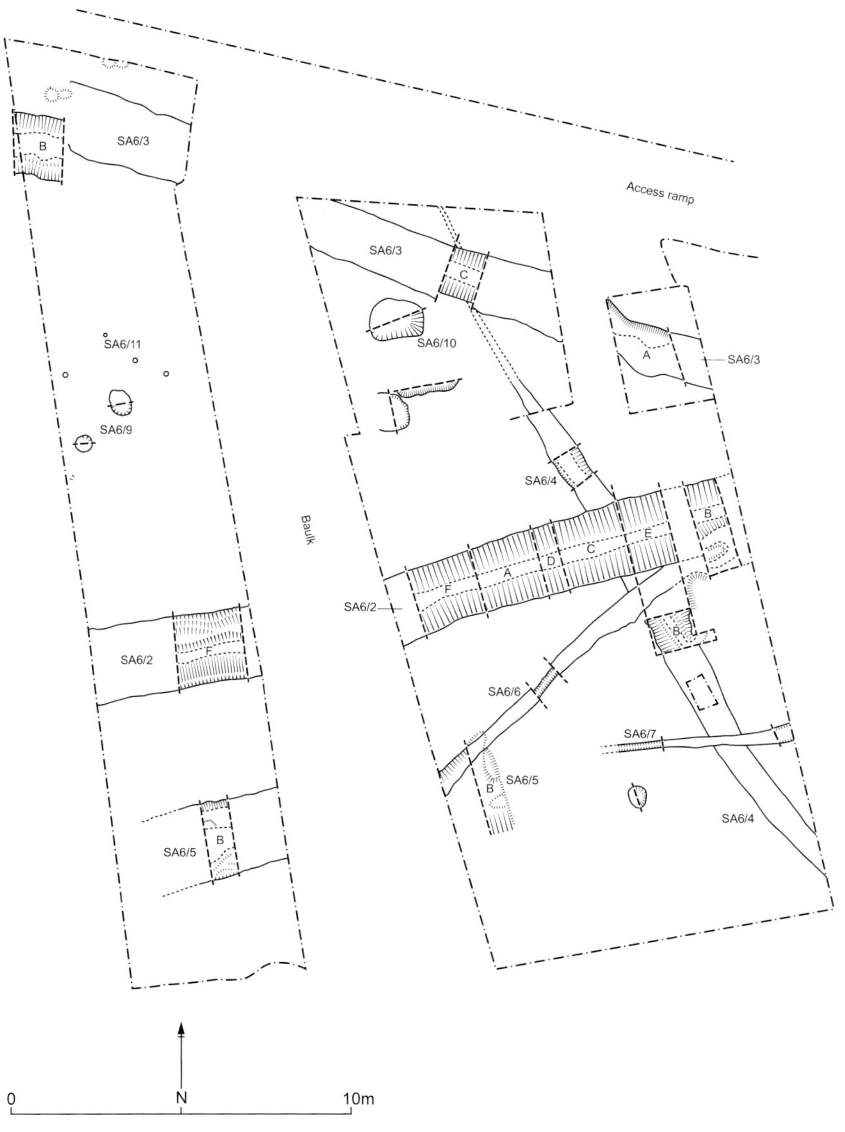

Figure 5.9 Plan of Trench 6

Trench 16 was a narrow slot measuring 2.5 x 25m, an extension of Trench 5 to the south-east to investigate ditches indicated by the gradiometer survey. Below the reddish sandy topsoil (SA16/1) three very shallow ditches (SA16/2, SA16/3, SA16/4) were cut on average 0.15m deep into the carrstone natural (0.25m), but with a deep overburden of up to 0.9m. They follow the curve of the contours, and may be part of later landscaping work. At least one, SA16/3, gave the appearance of a natural feature, and none produced any finds.

SA6 and extension SA17: machine strip across enclosure ditch

Trench 6 was opened up to explore the line of the enclosure ditch between Trench 1 and ST45. The original trench (10 x 25m, oriented N–S) was expanded by digging a parallel trench (5 x 25m) around 5m to the west and extending both up to the modern road. Features are shown in **Figure 5.9** (NB: SA6/8 was re-coded on site as SA6/3B). Beneath the plough soil (SA6/1), the enclosure ditch (SA6/2) was clearly visible, with a similar profile to that seen in Trenches 1, 2 and 5.

The enclosure ditch cut two natural features: SA6/4 and SA6/6. SA6/4 was a linear feature running N–S. The upper fill of reddish earth could be confused with an archaeological ditch, but below that was a deep, narrow crack filled with sand. It produced no finds and was certainly natural, a periglacial wedge. SA6/6 was another deep periglacial crevice cut by the enclosure ditch, with a light-coloured sandy fill. A number of other natural features were also uncovered: SA6/7, SA6/5 and SA6/10. SA6/7 was a similar narrow, U-shaped feature running straight across the trench E–W and ending abruptly. It was devoid of finds except for a copper alloy pin fragment (S.246) near the surface, which could be Romano-British, or part of a much later buckle. Like SA6/4, the deep filling of sand below the reddish upper fill showed that it was natural rather than archaeological. SA6/5 was an irregular hollow, broad and shallow with a flat base, cut no more than 0.2m into the carrstone. There were no significant finds, and it is likely that this feature was also natural. Small, shallow pit SA6/10 produced flints from the lower part of the feature but was otherwise lacking any finds. It could be closely dated and may be natural.

SA6/9 was a post hole which was found to contain modern nails and charcoal, suggesting a modern origin. The four small possible post holes SA6/11 were devoid of

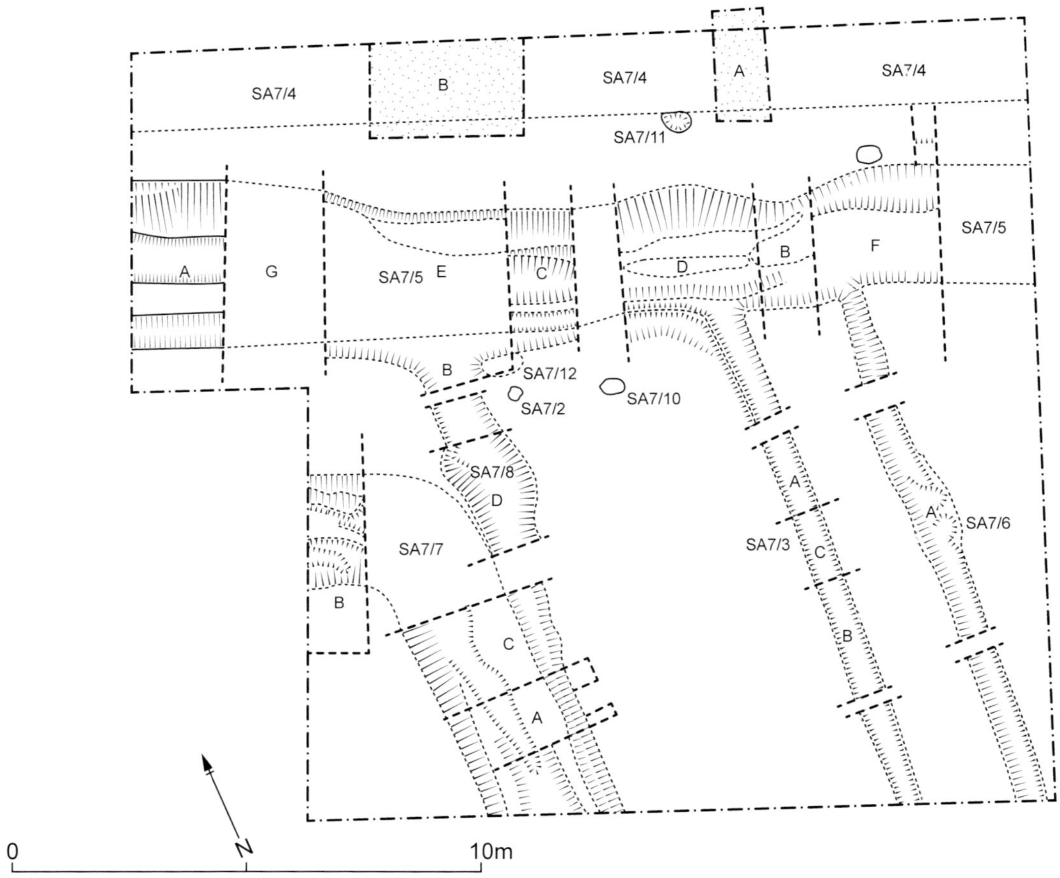

Figure 5.10 Plan of Trench 7

finds and may also be modern, including the possibility that they are animal burrows rather than human-made features.

SA6/3 was a very shallow ditch, almost without finds. A series of episodes of re-cutting (A, B and C) were evident, all following the same line. Trench 17, a machine strip 5 x 10m, oriented N–S, was opened up to the east of Trench 6 to investigate the relationship of ditch SA6/3 to the enclosure ditch, SA6/2. Below the topsoil (SA17/1), the enclosure ditch (SA17/2) was revealed, as well as the extension of ditch SA6/3 (SA17/3). A sondage trench was put in along the west end of the feature to help define stratigraphy, before taking the junction down in plan. The east section clearly showed a line of carrstone, demonstrating that ditch SA17/3 cut the enclosure ditch (SA17/2) (see **Fig. 9.5b**). Although in Trench 6 ditch SA6/3 produced residual Late Bronze Age and Earlier Iron Age pottery, the stratigraphy in Trench 17 clearly shows it to be post-Roman (and perhaps much more recent).

SA7 and eastern extensions SA20 and SA21: machine strip of area to south of main field

Trench 7 was a NE–SW machine strip, approximately 15 x 18m, opened up south of the modern road, close to the south-east corner of the wood adjoining the hoard field. Features are shown in **Figure 5.10** (NB: SA7/9 was re-coded, and SA7/13 was an extension of SA7/5). Below the reddish sandy topsoil directly below grass level (SA7/1) were a number of small pits, some of which produced Late Bronze Age and Earlier Iron Age pottery (SA7/2, SA7/10, SA7/11 and SA7/12). It is likely that some of these represent a distinct period of activity at the site (Phase 2), discussed in Chapter 7.

Two large ditches ran E–W across the north of Trench 7: SA7/4 and SA7/5 (which showed evidence for multiple phases of re-cutting). Whilst these E–W ditches produced prehistoric and Romano-British pottery, this was likely residual. SA7/4 and SA7/5 may be part of the same sequence of recent (Phase 6) E–W ditches seen to the east in Trenches 6 and 7 (SA6/3, SA17/3). SA17/3 cut the enclosure ditch, supporting the idea that these are later features. SA7/4 to the north ran parallel with the modern metalled road surface, and appeared to be traces of a pre-modern track, subsequently levelled up to form a raised base for the modern drive.

A number of the features in Trench 7 (SA7/3, SA7/6, SA7/7 and SA7/8) were shallow N–S gullies which joined SA7/5 at its southern edge. Each had a single fill of silty sand with inclusions of small stones. These features had been substantially disturbed by animal burrowing; ditch SA7/7 produced infant rabbit bones, most likely representing *in situ* deaths of this burrowing species (see Ch. 10).

It was not possible to ascertain the stratigraphic relationship between the E–W ditches (SA7/4, SA7/5) and N–S gullies (SA7/3, SA7/6, SA7/7, SA7/8). None of the N–S gullies could be dated, and it is likely they are natural, perhaps periglacial.

Trenches 20 and 21 were machine strip extensions (2.5 x 20m and 2.5 x 30m respectively) eastward from the centre of Trench 7 to locate any other N–S ditches comparable to those seen in Trench 7. No features were detected in Trench 20. In Trench 21, three ditches (SA21/2, SA21/3, SA21/4) were located at the east end of the trench, all running parallel N–S. These ditches were devoid of any finds and so could not be dated. Again, it is possible that they were of natural origin.

SA8: hand-dug trench to check for enclosure ditch alignment

Trench 8 was a hand-dug strip 3.2 x 1m, running broadly NE–SW, pursuing a possible turn of the enclosure ditch postulated from the geophysical survey. Context SA8/1 was ascribed to the build-up of sandy soil under the poplar wood to the south to a depth of approximately 0.75m before a sandy clay natural. The only feature located (SA8/2) was a narrow, shallow ditch running E–W, which produced no finds, most likely a fairly recent attempt at drainage (see also SA11/3, which may be a continuation of this drainage ditch to the east in Trench 11). To check that the natural had been reached below SA8/2, the trench was overcut at the base into grey clay, at one point revealing some surviving carrstone over the clay, presumably a remnant of natural, geological stratification (the same was seen in Trenches 10 and 11).

SA9: hand-dug trench to check for enclosure ditch alignment

Trench 9 was another hand-dug slot, 3.3 x 1.8m and running broadly NW–SE. It was opened across the projected line of the enclosure ditch, located in Trenches 1 and 2. Context code SA9/1 was assigned to the build-up of sandy soil in the poplar wood, ranging from 0.7m deep at the north side to 0.1m at the south side above the carrstone level. There was much evidence of rabbit activity in this hill wash. No features were located within the trench. It seemed likely that the enclosure ditch must end further north-east, and to this end Trench 11 was opened between Trench 2 and Trench 9 to look for the ditch terminus (see below).

SA10: hand-dug trench to check for enclosure ditch alignment

Trench 10, running broadly NE–SW and 2.7 x 0.9m, was opened in an attempt to locate the southern side of the enclosure ditch. Context SA10/1 was assigned to a build-up of sandy soil in the poplar wood, approximately 0.8m deep. By a depth of 1m there was no trace of the enclosure ditch, only an increasingly clayey natural. At the very north end of the trench, a small number of pieces of carrstone were found running E–W at a depth of 0.8m below the surface. They may form another modern drainage element or perhaps be natural periglacial features (see Trench 8 and 11).

SA11: hand-dug trench to check for enclosure ditch alignment

Trench 11 (1 x 5m, oriented NW–SE) was opened between Trench 2 and Trench 9 to look for the continuation, or possibly the terminus, of the enclosure ditch. SA11/1 was ascribed to the sandy topsoil. The natural took the form of weathered carrstone, with grey clay below. At a depth of about 1.3m, the lines of two ditches were visible. The main enclosure ditch (SA11/2) was cut by another (SA11/3) with a much stonier filling. SA11/3, running E–W, was on line with ditch SA8/2, and likely also related to recent drainage activity. The enclosure ditch was excavated to a depth of 1.4m, but the base was not reached.

SA12: machine strip to investigate ditch junction on gradiometer survey

Trench 12 was a square machine strip running NE–SW, measuring 20 x 20m. It was opened over Areas 11–12, where a number of Iron Age coins had been found in 1990 (Ch. 15, Cat. nos 223, 238, 246–50, 252–3, 273, 283), and to investigate a possible ditch junction seen on the gradiometer survey. Features are shown in **Figure 5.11**. Context SA12/1 was assigned to the topsoil. After scraping down to the natural surface, the outlines of two irregular, curving gullies (SA12/2 and SA12/3) were visible. Both of these were interpreted as natural features in 1992. However, Later geophysical survey (carried out in 2006–9, see below) revealed a series of enclosures across the hoard field, most likely part of a field system. Ditches associated with this series of enclosures should have been present in Trench 12, but were not observed during excavation. It is possible that these ditches are represented by SA12/2 and SA12/3 but that the nature of the re-deposited carrstone fills made it difficult to differentiate features from the natural. The geophysical survey also suggests that the field system may only have been revealed at substantial depth. Thus, an alternative explanation is that the challenging nature of the carrstone geology meant that the excavation did not go deep enough to encounter the ditches revealed by the later survey.

Feature SA12/6 was a possible hearth (see Ch. 7). The other features from the trench (SA12/4, SA12/5 and SA12/7 to SA12/28) were a series of small holes 0.13–0.27m in diameter, many of which produced Late Bronze Age to Earlier Iron Age pottery, as well as some flint (sherds: SA/JO, SA/JP, SA/KF, SA/KG, SA/KH, SA/KK, SA/KL, SA/KM, SA/KN, SA/KO; flints: SA/KG*, SA/KJ*, SA/KL, SA/KM*, SA/KN*, SA/KO*). These were tentatively recorded in the site notebooks as post holes, but are interpreted here as animal burrows; no certain ancient post hole was found at the site (Ian Stead pers. comm.). Other small circular features were planned (see **Fig. 5.11**), but not assigned numbers. No finds are recorded from these un-numbered features and it is likely that they too were animal burrows or natural hollows.

Despite the heavy burrowing disturbance, the relatively large quantities of pottery recovered suggest that this was an area of prehistoric activity pre-dating the Later Iron Age hoards immediately to the north. This is discussed in more detail in Chapter 7.

SA13: machine strip to investigate ditches to south of main field

Trench 13 (5 x 11m, oriented NE–SW), was opened to the south of the modern road, between Trench 5 and Trench 7 to investigate ditches curving south from the line of the drive, but hit a major recent disturbance to the north with a very sharp vertical edge. North of that was clear sand on top of carrstone. The disturbance was likely to be recent carrstone quarrying which here and to the west had created a ridge south of the track that branches off to the south of the drive. The track continues south-west, more or less through to the

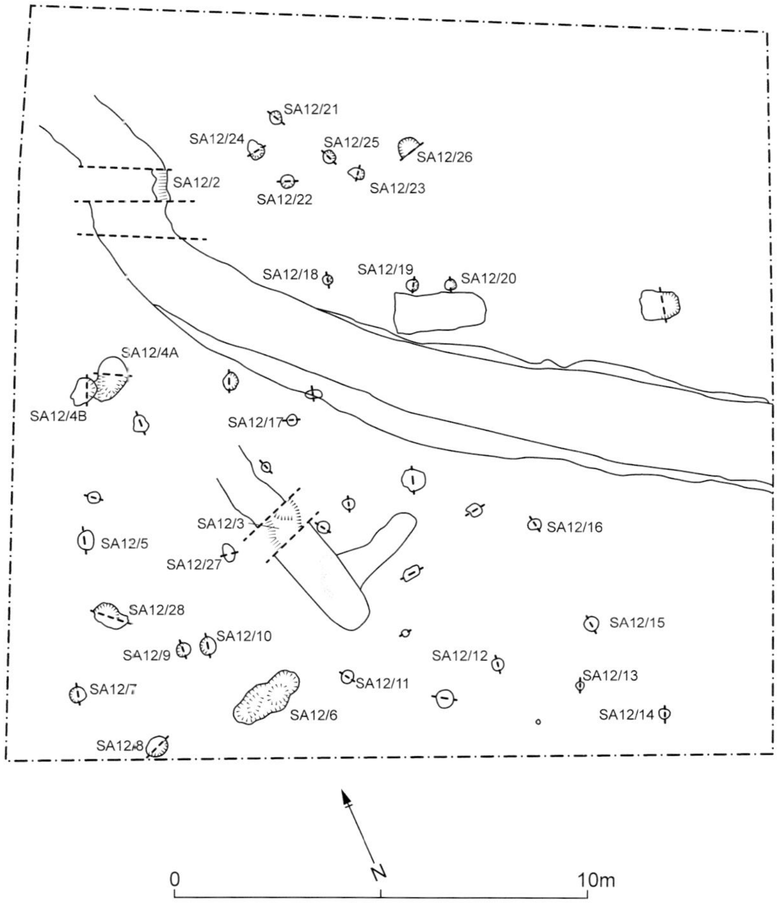

Figure 5.11 Plan of Trench 12

entrance of the enclosure (in Trench 5) and beyond that the track is bordered on its south side by two slight banks and ditches, possibly defining different parts of the wood.

SA14: hand-dug trench to check for enclosure ditch alignment

Trench 14 (1 x 6m, oriented E–W) was opened up to the south of Trench 5 along the projected line of the enclosure ditch on the south side of the entranceway. A ditch on this line (SA14/2) was revealed, which may be part of the enclosure ditch but did not have the distinctive V-shaped profile seen elsewhere. There was extensive evidence of rabbit disturbance.

SA15: hand-dug trench at site where drinking horn terminals found, located over the main road, to east of 'gold field'

Trench 15 (oriented NW–SE, 5 x 1.5m) was opened substantially to the east of the main site to explore the area where Charles Hodder had discovered two drinking horn terminals (S.253–4) in 1989. A substantial amount of post-medieval tile and building debris (SA15/2) was uncovered below the topsoil (SA15/1), concentrated at the west end, where it was around 0.6m deep. Below this there was natural carrstone at both ends of the trench from 0.6–0.7m below the surface. In the central part of the trench was a tree bowl with sandy fill (SA15/3) to a depth of around 1.8m, below which the natural carrstone began. No ancient features were observed.

For SA16 see SA5

For SA17 see SA6

SA18: machine strip across enclosure ditch and outer ditch to west

Trench 18 (oriented E–W, 5 x 20m) was opened across the north-west corner of the enclosure ditch to investigate a small ditch just outside the enclosure, to the west. Features are shown in **Figures 5.12–13**. The enclosure ditch in this section (SA18/2) ran roughly N–S, and was similar in profile to elsewhere but with a broader base. The second ditch (SA18/3) was approximately 1m in width, running SW–NE. It was shallow and devoid of any finds and so could not be dated.

SA19: machine strip to check for enclosure ditch alignment

Trench 19 (2.5 x 12m, oriented N–S) was opened up between Trench 9 and Trench 11 in an attempt to find the terminus of the enclosure ditch (which was seen in Trench 11 but not present in Trench 9). Context SA19/1 was given to the topsoil. There was a fairly level natural outcrop of carrstone boulders (with one very large boulder removed) at a depth of 1.0–1.1m below the hill wash. No features were located. This suggests that the terminus of the enclosure ditch lay under a poplar tree just to the north, between Trenches 19 and 11.

For SA20 and SA21 see SA7

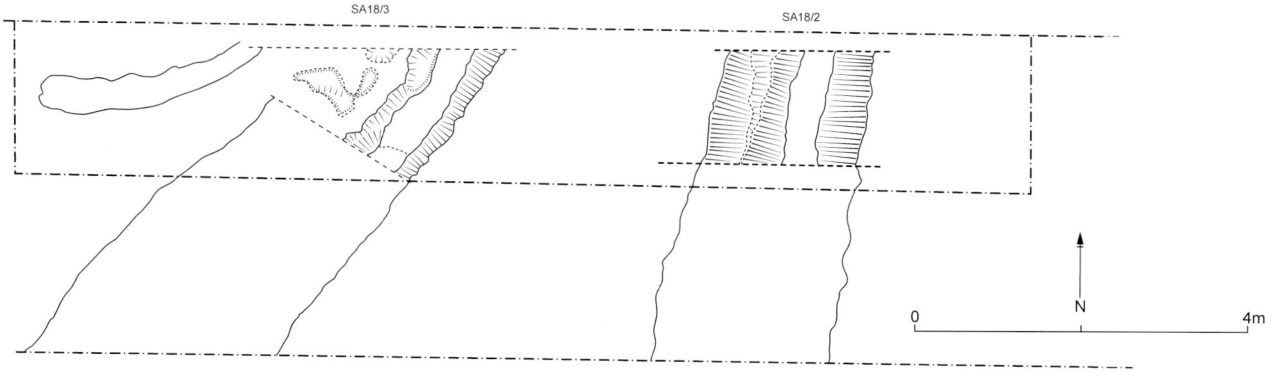

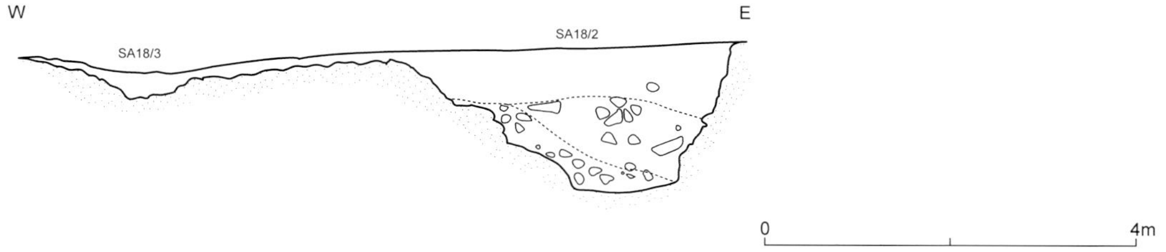

Figures 5.12–5.13 Plan of Trench 18 (above); section through ditch SA18/2 and SA18/3 (below)

Soil phosphate survey, 1991

Mike Cowell

In support of other physical survey techniques being used on the site during Ian Stead's 1990–1 excavations, a soil phosphate survey was carried out. Enriched levels of phosphate in soils are a characteristic feature of human occupation and the aim of the survey was to seek evidence for any settlement that had been established at or nearby the location of the hoards. Initially, samples were taken only over the 'gold field', as this was the first to be excavated and stripped, but the survey was subsequently extended into parts of the adjacent woodland.

Sampling and analysis

The soil coverage at Snettisham is relatively shallow and consists of about 50cm of sandy topsoil that overlays and grades into a ferruginous, cemented sand layer called carrstone. Since any evidence of enriched phosphate will lie within the topsoil, and the field has been ploughed, it was considered advisable to sample at two depths, at about 10cm and 40cm, in case there had been some disturbance of the stratigraphy or leaching of phosphate. A sampling grid was laid out at 10m intervals based on the site reference point (5000E/5000N) and covered, in extent, approximately 150m in the N–S direction and 230m in the E–W direction. This included most of the open field where many of the hoards were found and extended into part of the woodland to the west. Owing to the location of trees, it was not possible to sample at exactly 10m intervals in the woodland and some points had to be omitted due to such obstructions. Sampling was carried out rapidly using a Dutch auger that was turned to the appropriate, and approximate, depth and the soil sample extracted from near the point of the auger. Samples of about 20–30cm of soil were collected from each location, and depth, and stored in self-sealed plastic bags.

The soil samples were analysed in the Department of Scientific Research at the BM using a standard colorimetric procedure (molybdenum blue method) that has been applied to other soil surveys, including Grimes Graves (Craddock *et al.* 1985; Hughes *et al.* 2012). Briefly, this involved taking a sub-sample of 1g of each soil, adding 10ml of hydrochloric acid (2 molar) and heating these on a water bath to near boiling point for about 1 hour to release the phosphate. After cooling, an aliquot of 0.5ml was taken from each of the sample solutions, transferred to 20 or 25ml flasks and diluted colorimetric reagent was added. Standard solutions with known amounts of phosphate were treated in the same way. The intensity of the blue colour that developed, which is proportional to the concentration of phosphate in the solution, was then measured in a colorimetric cell in the wavelength range 700–900nm. The results are reported in parts per 100,000 of phosphorus ($pp10^5$ of P or mg of P per 100g of soil). The analytical errors, precision and accuracy, are expected to be in the range ±15–25%.

Results and discussion

A preliminary examination of the data showed phosphate concentrations in the range about 50–600 $pp10^5$, with the highest values very localised. Where the concentrations are high, whatever the sampling depth, the samples collected at the deeper location (about 40cm) had much higher concentrations. For this reason, and as a greater coverage of analyses was available for this depth, the discussion of results is confined to the data obtained for the 40cm samples. The relevant phosphate concentrations are tabulated in **Figure 5.14**, which shows the value at each grid point sampled. In addition, a contour chart has been prepared (**Fig. 5.15**) from the grid data which has been overlaid to show the relationship to the wooded area and hoard findspots.

As can be seen from **Figures 5.14–15**, much of the open field area has soil phosphate concentrations in the range 30–100 $pp10^5$. Although the 'natural' level of phosphate varies between different soil types so that a single figure for 'background' cannot be quoted, the range up to 100 $pp10^5$ seems to be typical. Such values are similar to the background levels observed from surveys at the Neolithic

Easting

	4900	4910	4920	4930	4940	4950	4960	4970	4980	4990	5000	5010	5020	5030	5040	5050	5060	5070	5080	5090	5100	5110	5120	5130
5200																								
5190																								
5180																								
5170																								
5160																								
5150																								
5140																								
5130											45	45	40	40										
5120											45	75	70	30										
5110						45	35	40	40	60	60	65	62	60										
5100						50	30	45	55	65	80	70	80	55	60	60	50	35	55	45	40			
5090						40	40	55	65	50	85	65	70	45	60	75	50	50	70	40	30			
5080						50	70	50	45	40	80	70	75	65	70	65	40	65	70	30	30			
5070						50	212	130				60	50	45	70	75	99	80	70	60	30			
5060					83	272	181	213	233	243	60	110	80	115	80	99	85	75	75	75	70			
5050			269	240	299	335	238	359	254	30	100	90	85	90	90	80	90	60	65	45	60			
5040			156	232	261	384	272	429	299	275	95	105	105	105	75	75	70	70	60	100	70			
5030			218	203	335	465	429	632	264	32	105	105	80	60	70	80	55	75	65	70	70			
5020			45	50	125	295	585	435	145	115	100	110		90	80	65	50	65	70	40	65			
5010			60	70	80	280	375	525	420	150	90	55	50	80	80	85	70	70	75	65	35			
5000					65	160	635	445	345	130	75	50	70	55	50	50	50		35	20	20			
4990					60	45	340	355	365	265	45	65	50	55	45	60	65	55	50	40	30			
4980					166	217	344	351	339	286	75	70	50	55	55	55	40	50	45	40	45			
4970					37	40	90	175	95	57	80	80	80	85	80	60	55	55	50	40	40			
4960								95	105	90	95	85	85	70	75	65	65	65	50	50	65			
4950					35	68	149	97	82	40	100	90	85	90	90	80	90	60	65	45	60			
4940					40	113	57	46	79	65	60	110	80	115	80	100	85	75	75	75	70			
4930					32	37	51	84	79	54														
4920							103		110		124													
4910																								
4900							192				17													
4890																								
4880							45		24		12													
4870																								
4860							60		52															
4850																								
4840																								

Northing

Figure 5.14 Soil phosphate concentrations (parts per 100,000) of samples taken at 40cm depth (© Mike Cowell)

flint mines at Grimes Graves (see above). Samples with 100–200 pp10^5 may be an indication of slight evidence of human occupation. From the contours in **Figure 5.15** it can be seen that there are some areas to the west of the open field with values in that range and also a few isolated points elsewhere. Most of the values within that range in the open field are probably due to spread from the much higher values within the wood. It should also be noted, from **Figure 5.14**, that many of those in the range 100–200 pp10^5 are only just over 100 pp10^5.

The area with the highest phosphate levels is in the wood just west of the hoard field, where levels as high as 600 pp10^5 have been found. Several lines of evidence indicate that this phosphate is associated with human occupation. First, the soil cover is visually much darker than either the soils further west in the wood, where the phosphate levels are much lower, or in the open field. Sherds of Romano-British pottery were found in the soil in this part of the wood (Ch. 9); some were found at 4960E/5010N during the soil sampling, together with fragments of bone. The high phosphate area

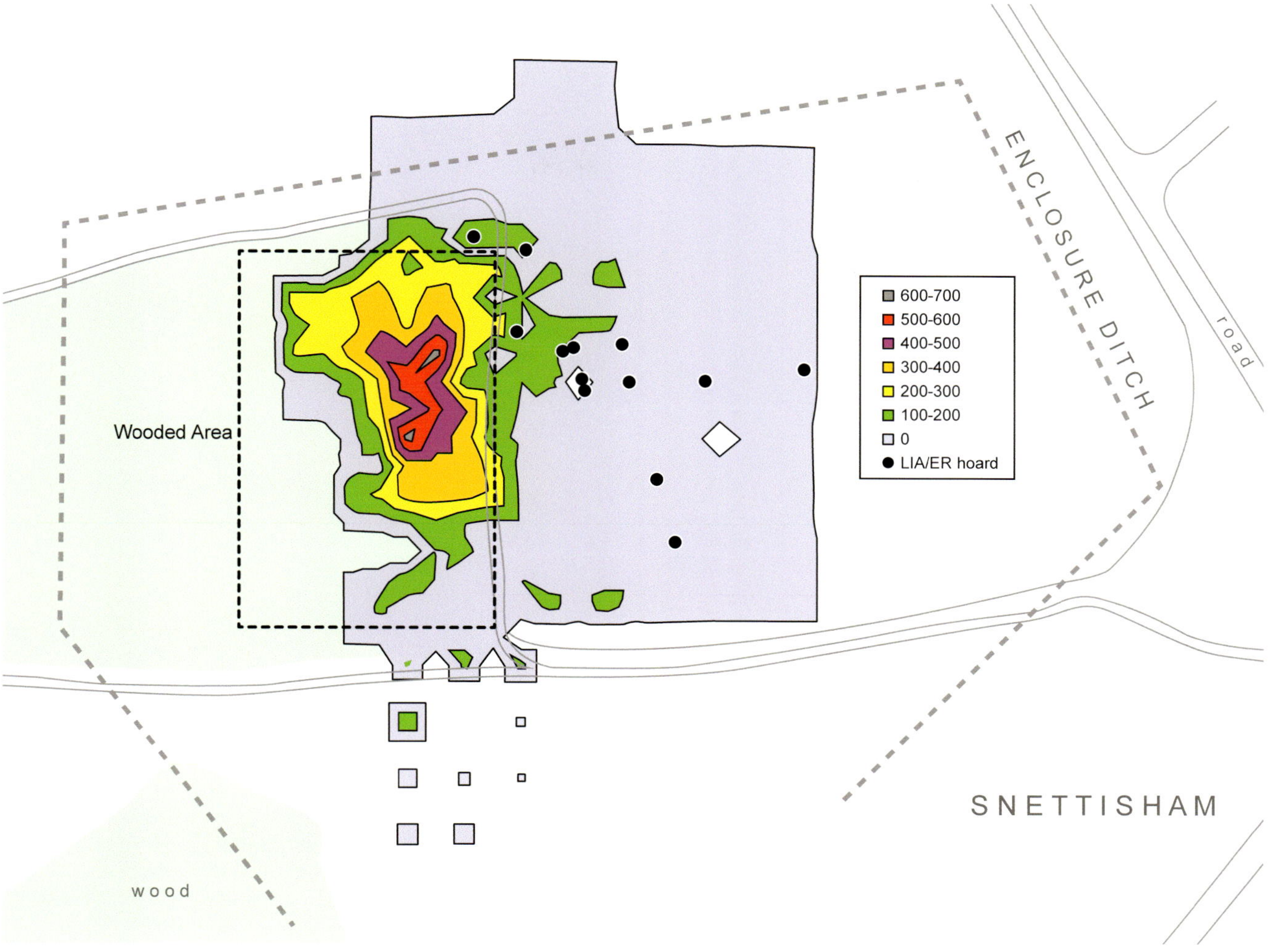

Figure 5.15 Contour chart of soil phosphate distribution, values in parts per 100,000 taken at 40cm depth

also has a dense nettle cover, often indicative of rich, disturbed soils, that thins out in other areas of the woodland. Although there seem to be two foci for the highest levels of phosphate, at about 4970E/5030N and 4960E/5000N about 30m apart, this may not necessarily reflect two separate areas of occupation as the level in the zone between them is within the measurement errors of the peak levels. The overall extent of intensive occupation within the sampled area seems to be about 80m N–S and 50m E–W, i.e. an area of approximately 4,000m².

From the phosphate alone, it is not possible to determine the date of this occupation; this can only be determined by excavation and the establishment of a datable context. The association with Romano-British pottery suggests that it may date to that period (Ch. 9), although the wooded area also produced the densest concentration of Phase 2 (Late Bronze Age to Earlier Iron Age) metalwork finds, and thus it is also possible that this higher phosphate concentration relates to Phase 2 midden-generating activity (Ch. 7).

Conclusions

The phosphate survey found no evidence for human occupation in the 'gold field'. But, there are very high levels of phosphate in the adjacent woodland, indicating an area of intensive occupation over about 4,000m². Association with Romano-British pottery suggests that it may date from this period, although an earlier or later date is also possible.

Geophysical survey, 2006–2009

Michael de Bootman

In late October 2006, the writer undertook a fluxgate gradiometer survey of the Ken Hill 'gold field'. A ground penetrating radar survey was later carried out by Ralph Potter, University of East London, in June 2009, with the data processing being undertaken by Dr Tim Dennis, University of Essex. The locations of the two survey areas are shown in **Figure 5.16**.

Methodology

Fluxgate gradiometer

A grid of forty 30 x 30m data squares, including partials, covering 3.5 hectares was established using standard survey practice and referenced to known points within the landscape. A Bartington 601 dual fluxgate gradiometer was used, and data was collected in a zig-zag format from each square along 2m transects with readings recorded every 0.25m.

Ground penetrating radar

A grid of three 20 x 60m data squares covering 0.54 hectares was established, and geo-referenced with differential GPS (Global Positioning System), with the co-ordinates being post-processed. A Mala X3M tow-system with a shielded 500MHz antenna and a data-recording 150mm distance

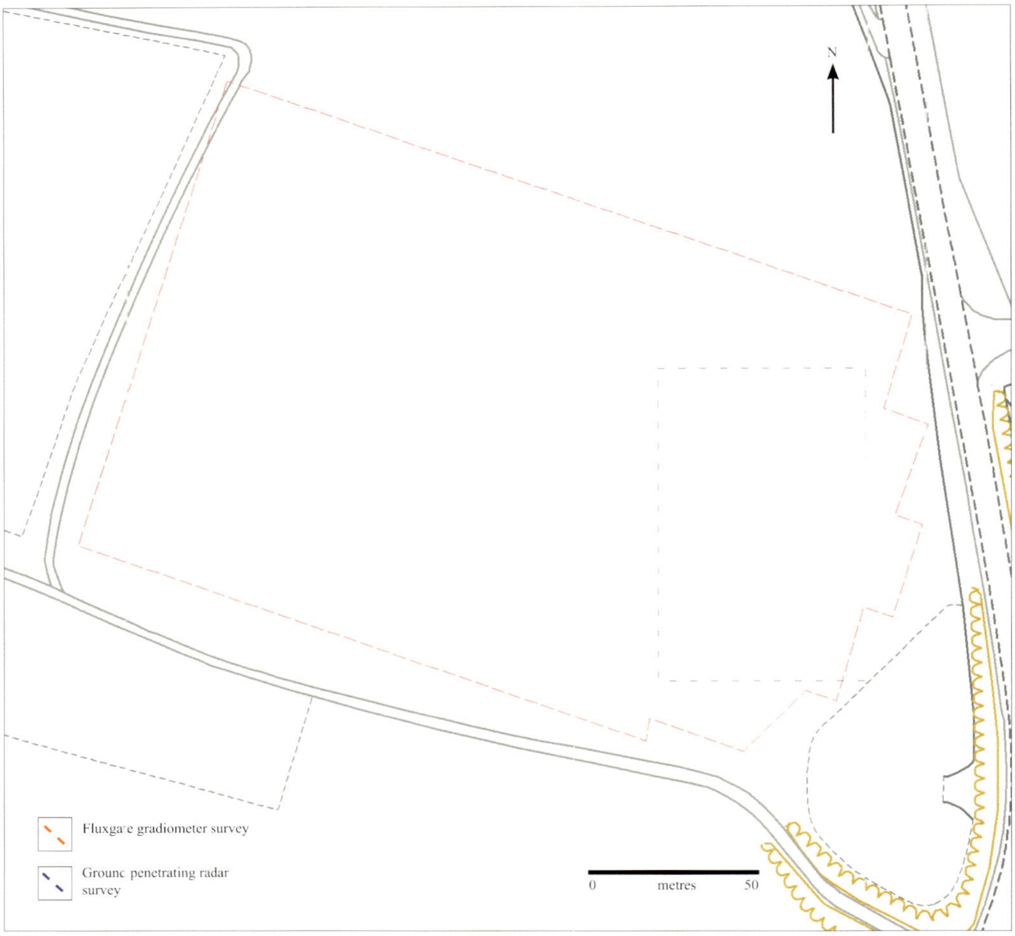

Figure 5.16 Location of fluxgate gradiometer (2006) and ground penetrating radar (2009) surveys

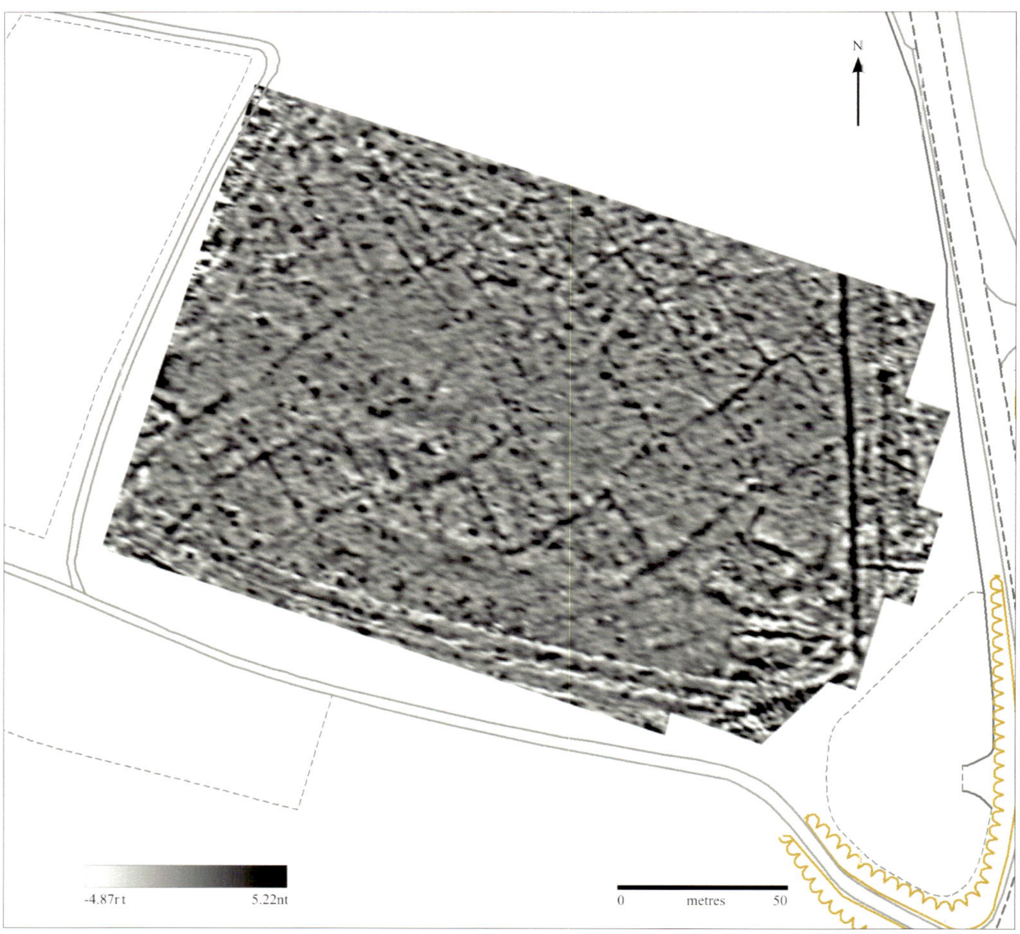

Figure 5.17 Fluxgate gradiometer survey – processed results

wheel was used. The data was collected in a zig-zag format along 0.5m transects, with readings being recorded every 0.05m. Averaging was achieved by 'stacking' four readings at each measurement point with a depth setting of 3.00m.

Processing

Rectification, mapping and interpretation of the processed data were undertaken using mapinfo 10.

Fluxgate gradiometer (**Fig. 5.16**)

The data, initially processed in 2006, has been re-processed using the latest Geoscan Geoplot software version 4. Numerous processing steps were required on the raw data that included:

- Despike which removed random/spurious 'iron spikes'
- Clip to limit the data to specified maximum and minimum values
- Destagger to correct displacement of anomalies caused by alternate zig-zag traverses
- Zero-mean traverse to set the background mean of each traverse within the data square to zero and remove the effect of striping
- Low-pass filter to remove high frequency, small-scale spatial details and enhance large weaker features
- Interpolate to increase the data points in the survey to create a smoother appearance.

Ground penetrating radar (GPR) (**Fig. 5.19a–d**)

The data processing was undertaken by Dr Tim Dennis using bespoke-written software. All data from the survey block were loaded into what amounts to a three-dimensional array, with processing (filtering) operations available in space (XY) and time (T) dimensions. Stages used on the Snettisham datasets were:

- Along-track mean level subtraction at each time sample value
- Adaptive Gain Equalisation – this calculates the RMS (root mean square) value of the signal on each depth/timeslice. The resulting profile is smoothed with a Gaussian filter and used to normalise the RMS value on all depth/timeslices to a constant value. This is an effective way to accommodate the wide dynamic signal range GPR systems produce, from the large-amplitude signals at near-zero delay due to direct transmit-receiver antenna coupling to the smallest components at maximum time delay
- Rectification – the raw signals are bidirectional but structures are clearer if the signal magnitude is used instead. Here zero amplitude is rendered as black, with white used for maximum (after clipping)
- Spatial Filter – a small level of Gaussian low-pass filtering is applied in the along-track direction on depth/timeslice images for further noise reduction before scaling to equal resolution in both spatial dimensions. The result is 400 sequential 0.75m depth/timeslices in a .png format. The sub-blocks were then laid out into a composite as individual frames. The sequence can then be converted and viewed as a video animation.

Interpretation

The fluxgate gradiometer survey produced responses that included negative and positive linears, and positive areas/points. Linears that are entirely positive in polarity normally relate to infilled cut features whose fillings are magnetically enhanced in comparison with surrounding matrices. Such features may be ancient ditches, former field boundaries or the results of ploughing activity. Some may even be of natural origin. Similarly, positive areas or points may indicate either pits of an archaeological nature, or naturally occurring depressions in the ground.

There are a few linear responses in the dataset that are completely negative in polarity. These are probably evidence of ploughing activities where a slight bank of soil has built up, producing a lower magnetic magnitude relative to the background topsoil.

Three groups or types of positive features were identified in the fluxgate gradiometer survey (**Fig. 5.18**). These include numerous small positive areas/points, and two sets of positive linears. **Figure 8.2a–b** shows these in relation to the hoard findspots and other excavated features.

One set of positive linears (**Fig. 5.18** – positive linear 1) criss-crossed the majority of the survey area, representing a network of SE/NW by NE/SW rectilinear ditched enclosures. The other group of positive linears were located on the eastern side of the field (**Fig. 5.18** – positive linear 2). The strongest responses (**Fig. 5.17**) clearly represent the east side and south-east corner of the polygonal enclosure identified in the BM excavations. Other similar linears running parallel and at right angles in close proximity may be contemporary.

The ground penetrating radar survey was sited parallel to the enclosure ditch at a location where the fluxgate gradiometer survey indicated it bisected the criss-crossing positive linears, in order to investigate the relationship between these features.

The accompanying data confirmed the results from the fluxgate gradiometer survey, showing the enclosure ditch (**Fig. 5.19d**: low amplitude reflection 2), and the criss-crossing ditches (**Fig. 5.19d**: low amplitude reflection 1). The ditches show as black, indicating absence of signal reflection; elsewhere the signals are unstructured and noise-like. The likely explanation for this is that the 'natural' background soil structure is gravel-like, possibly containing many larger stones. In the ditches the backfill is more uniform with few reflection centres, for example alluvium. Only three of the 400 depth slices are illustrated. **Figure 5.19a** shows the depth at approximately 1.50m, where both the criss-crossing features and the enclosure ditch are present, similarly **Figure 5.19b** illustrates the same at 1.80m, while **Figure 5.19c** at 2.20m shows the criss-crossing features, but does not contain the enclosure ditch. Given the relative depths of these features, the most likely scenario is that the enclosure ditch post-dates the much deeper field system ditches.

Conclusion

The results from Snettisham show a network of rectilinear ditched enclosures, represented by a series of positive linears criss-crossing the majority of the survey area (**Fig. 5.18** –

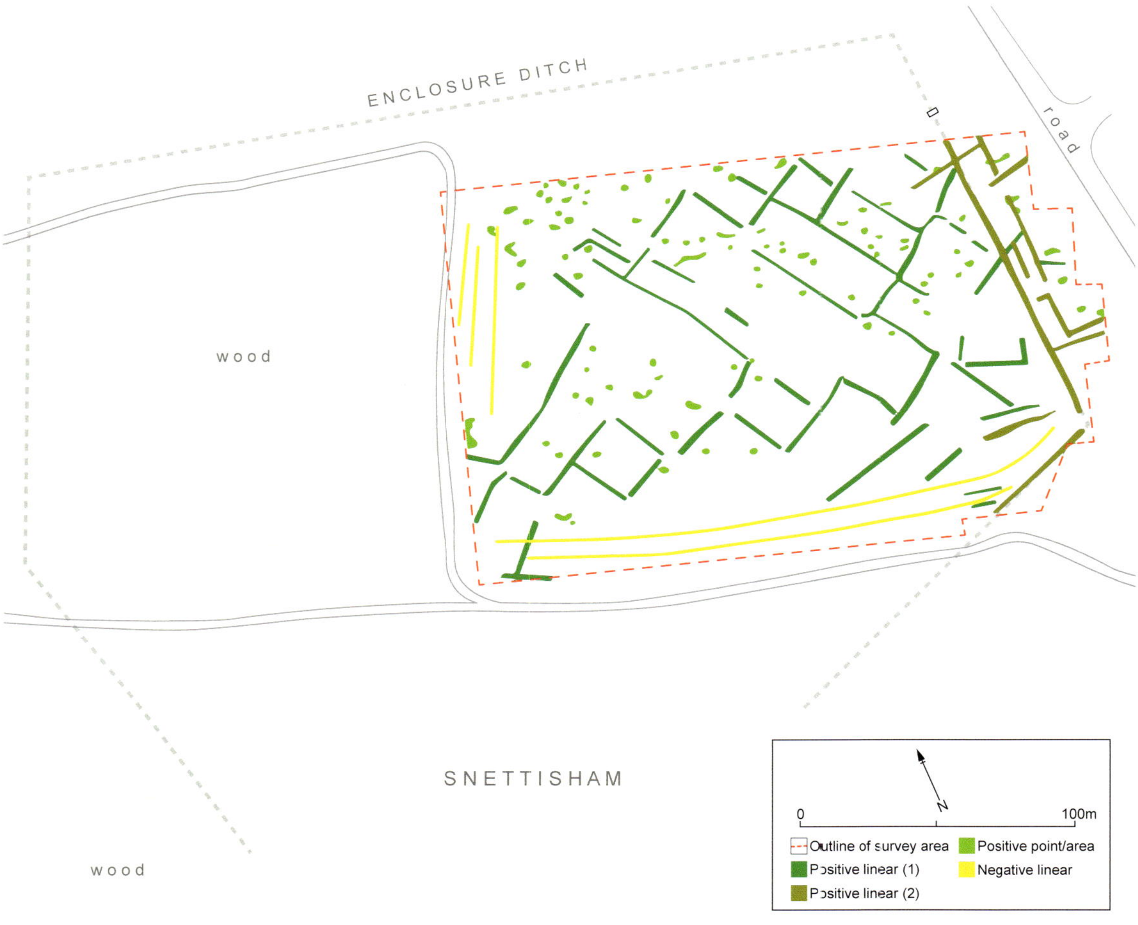

Figure 5.18 Fluxgate gradiometer survey – interpretation of processed results

positive linear 1) and also present in the ground penetrating radar data (**Fig. 5.19d** – low amplitude reflection 1).

Work by the Norfolk Air Photographic Interpretation team has interpreted extensive cropmarks to the north in the area of Heacham and south around Ingoldisthorpe and Dersingham as rectilinear field systems dating to the Iron Age or Roman period (see **Fig. 3.7**; Massey *et al.* 2003, 339–41; Brennand 2004; Albone *et al.* 2007, 91–3). The criss-crossing features identified in both geophysical surveys at Ken Hill are characteristically very similar to these cropmarks, and probably form part of the same landscape.

The polygonal enclosure ditch identified during the BM excavations is also evident in both geophysical survey datasets (**Fig. 5.18** – positive linear 1, **Fig. 5.19d** – low amplitude reflection 2). The ground penetrating radar depth slice at 2.20m (**Fig. 5.19c**) shows the criss-crossing features but not the enclosure ditch, indicating that the enclosure ditch is most likely a later feature.

The numerous positive areas/points are a little more enigmatic to interpret. They may be either archaeological or natural.

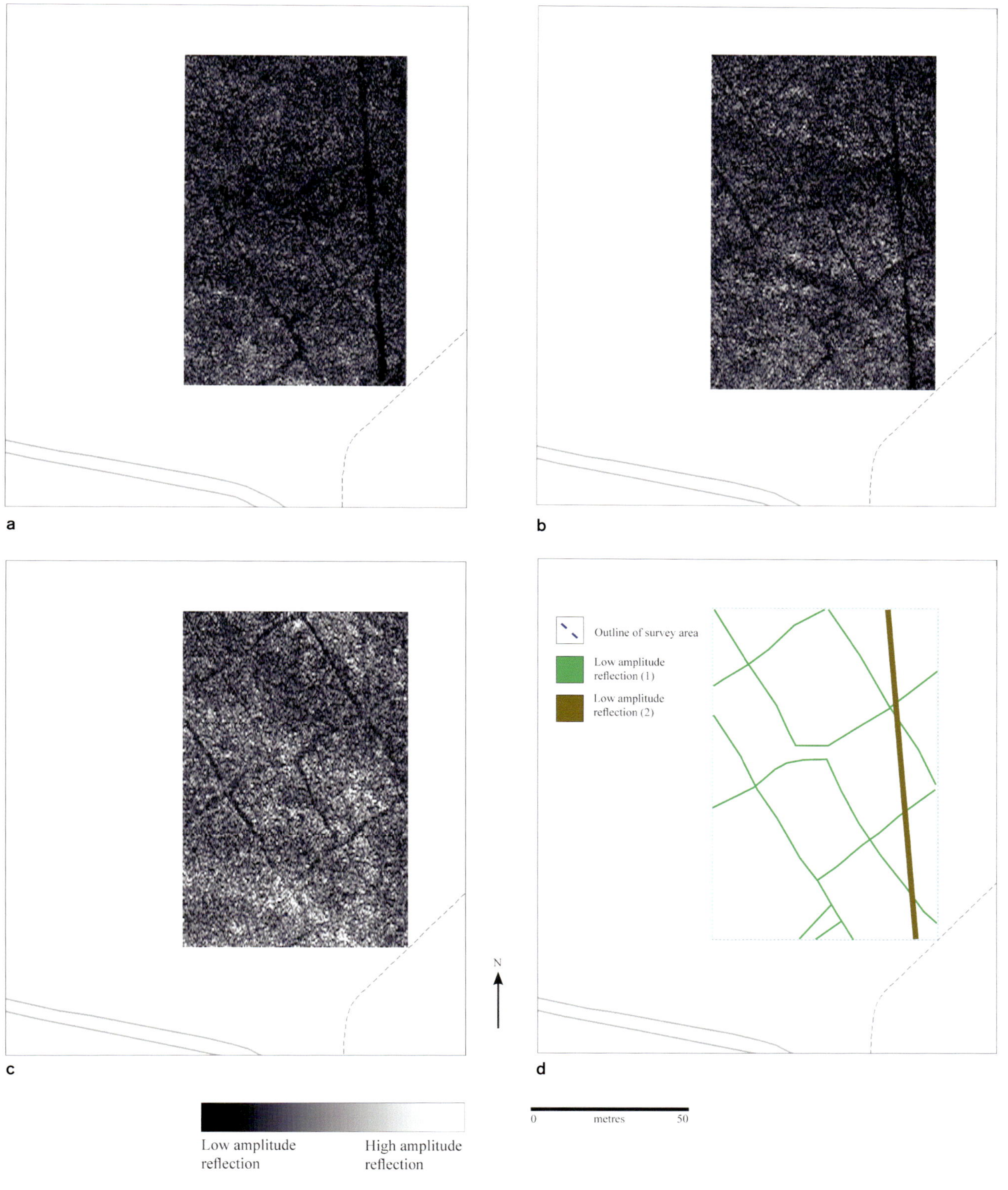

Figure 5.19a–d Ground penetrating radar – processed results and interpretation: a) Ground penetrating radar – processed depth slice 1.50m; b) Ground penetrating radar – processed depth slice 1.80m; c) Ground penetrating radar – processed depth slice 2.20m; d) Ground penetrating radar – consolidated interpretation between 1.50–2.20m (© Michael de Bootman)

Radiocarbon dating programme results

Julia Farley and Sophia Adams

Two programmes of radiocarbon dating have been carried out on the material from the BM excavations at Snettisham. Organic remains from the hoards, including charred wood cores from torcs, were sampled as part of the University of Oxford 'Technologies of Enchantment' project (**Table 5.2**; Garrow *et al.* 2009), which sought to create an improved framework for the absolute dating of Celtic art objects. There was very little organic material from the hoard pits, and so this aspect of the sampling programme was limited. Note that the dates given below vary slightly from those given in the 2009 volume, since an updated calibration curve has been used. A second programme of radiocarbon dating was undertaken by the BM as part of the preparation of this report (**Table 5.3**). This focused on stratified material from the 1991–2 excavations, in particular the enclosure ditch.

Object	CADB code	Sample description	Est. age of wood	Lab. no.	δ13C	Radiocarbon measurement BP	Calibrated date (95% confidence) IntCal20	Calibrated date (68% confidence) IntCal20
F.168	CA33	Field maple wood charcoal inside torc	< 10 yrs	OxA-18219	-26.56	2181 ± 29	370–120 cal BC	350–170 cal BC
L.6*	CA46	Lime wood fibre string bound around torc	<5 yrs	OxA-18222	-27.43	2175 ± 31	360–110 cal BC	350–170 cal BC
L.6*	CA35	Lime wood fibre string bound around torc	<5 yrs	OxA-18220	-28.22	2500 ± 31	780–510 cal BC	770–550 cal BC
M.1–M.5	CA47	Alder wood charcoal embedded within silver-copper alloy lumps from hoard	old	OxA-18223	-26.12	1931 ± 29	20–210 cal AD	30–130 cal AD

* Two samples were apparently taken from this repair to L.6: one from the torc itself, which had been heavily conserved, and another from a separate, untreated fragment. It is likely that the unexpectedly ancient date (780–510 cal BC) was affected by the conservation treatment, rendering it unreliable.

Failed samples:

F.167	CA32	Hazel wood charcoal inside torc	< 10 yrs	OxA	N/A	N/A	N/A	N/A
G.16*	CA34	Lime wood fibre string bound around torc	<5 yrs	OxA-18164	N/A	N/A	N/A	N/A

*Published as G.17 in Garrow *et al.* 2009

Table 5.2 Radiocarbon measurements and calibrated date ranges from the dating programme carried out as part of the University of Oxford 'Technologies of Enchantment' project (Garrow *et al.* 2009), which produced the Celtic Art Database (CADB). Measured at the Oxford Radiocarbon Accelerator Unit; dates were originally calibrated with reference to the IntCal09 calibration curve (Reimer *et al.* 2009) using the OxCal calibration program v.4.1.5 (Bronk Ramsey 2009). Dates have been recalibrated using the internationally agreed terrestrial calibration curve IntCal20 (Reimer *et al.* 2020) and the OxCal calibration program c.4.4.4 (Bronk Ramsey 2021). Results are rounded out to 10 years

Sample type	Species	Site code	Context	Lab. no.	δ13C	Radiocarbon measurement BP	Calibrated date (95% confi-dence) IntCal20	Calibrated date (68% confidence) IntCal20
Cremated bone	Mammal (species unknown)	SN/FE	SN31, pit	SU-ERC-89720 (GU53518)	-21.2	2868 ± 26	1130–930 cal BC	1110–1000 cal BC
Charcoal	*Carpinus betulus*, hornbeam (< 10 yrs old)	ST/DY	ST35, enclosure ditch, Layer 1	SU-ERC-89717 (GU53515)	-24.3	1653 ± 26	260–540 cal AD	370–530 cal AD
Animal bone	Large mammal (species unknown)	ST/DY	ST35, enclosure ditch, Layer 1	SU-ERC-89721 (GU53519)	-22.0	1656 ± 28	260–540 cal AD	360–440 cal AD
Charcoal	*Salix* sp., willow (< 10 yrs old)	ST/EZ	ST35, enclosure ditch, Layer 2	SU-ERC-89718 (GU53516)	-25.5	1669 ± 26	250–530 cal AD	360–420 cal AD
Animal bone	Large mammal (?Bos, ?tibia)	ST/EZ	ST35, enclosure ditch, Layer 2	SU-ERC-89722 (GU53520)	-22.0	1777 ± 28	210–360 cal AD	240–330 cal AD
Charcoal	*Salix* sp., willow; *Corylus avellana*, hazel (< 10 yrs old)	ST/HL	ST42, enclosure ditch, Layer 2	SU-ERC-89719 (GU53517)	-25.6	1702 ± 26	250–420 cal AD	260–410 cal AD
Animal bone	*Bos taurus*	SA/AK	SA5/2, enclosure ditch, Layer 2	SU-ERC-89723 (GU53522)	-21.9	1693 ± 26	250–420 cal AD	260–410 cal AD
Animal bone	*Bos taurus*	SA/CO	SA6/2, enclosure ditch, Layer 2	SU-ERC-89727 (GU53524)	-21.4	1811 ± 28	130–340 cal AD	210–320 cal AD
Animal bone	*Bos taurus*	SA/BT	SA6/2, enclosure ditch, Layer 3	SU-ERC-89728 (GU53525)	-21.1	1769 ± 28	220–370 cal AD	240–330 cal AD
Animal bone	*Bos taurus*	SA/AW	SA6/3, ditch	SU-ERC-89729 (GU53526)	-21.9	355 ± 27	1450–1640 cal AD	1470–1630 cal AD
Animal bone	Mammal (species unknown)	SA/GO	SA7/5, ditch	SU-ERC-89730 (GU53527)	-23.1	412 ± 26	1430–1620 cal AD	1440–1480 cal AD

Failed samples:

Sample type	Species	Site code	Context	Lab. no.
Animal bone	Mammal (species unknown)	ST/GC	ST42, enclosure ditch, Layer 1	GU53521
Animal bone	?*Bos taurus*	SA/AV	SA5/2, enclosure ditch, Layer 3	GU53523

Table 5.3 Radiocarbon measurements and calibrated date ranges from the BM excavations dating programme. Measured at the Scottish Universities Environmental Research Centre (SUERC). Detailed descriptions of the methods employed by the SUERC Radiocarbon Laboratory can be found in Dunbar *et al.* (2016). Dates were calibrated with reference to the IntCal13 calibration curve (Reimer *et al.* 2013) using the OxCal calibration program v.4.3.2 (Bronk Ramsey 2009). Dates have been recalibrated using the internationally agreed terrestrial calibration curve IntCal20 (Reimer *at al.* 2020) and the OxCal calibration program c.4.4.4 (Bronk Ramsey 2021). Results are rounded out to 10 years

Chapter 6
Phase 1: Early Neolithic (*c.* 3650–3400 BC)

Julia Farley and Jody Joy, with contributions by Sarah Percival and Peter Makey

The earliest evidence from excavations at the site dates to the Early Neolithic period, comprising a cluster of pits containing Neolithic pottery, and various scatters of worked flint, as well as stray finds of other stone objects, primarily a small number of polished stone axes.

This chapter presents the evidence from excavation, and specialist reports on the Neolithic pottery, flint, and other stone objects. There were no organic finds from Neolithic features, and thus it was not possible to carry out radiocarbon dating. The dating suggested for this phase (*c.* 3650–3400 BC) is based on comparison of the ceramics from the pit cluster at Snettisham with a better-dated assemblage from Kilverstone, Norfolk.

Early Neolithic features

Figures 6.1–2 and **Table 6.1** detail the Phase 1 features at the site. Eight pits were revealed which contained Early Neolithic pottery and stone artefacts. Seven were in Areas 1 to 3 (the immediate vicinity of the hoards), and one, SN30, is an outlier slightly to the east. The other features are shallow areas of burning or flint concentrations in Areas 25 and 28.

The distribution shown in **Figure 6.1** includes all Phase 1 features observed during the excavations, but it is most likely incomplete as the excavators attempted to leave Neolithic material undisturbed where possible (see Ch. 2). After several pits (SN21, SN23, SN24, SN28, SN29) were uncovered in the central area subjected to excavation by hand in 1990 (within Areas 1 and 2, **Fig. 5.5**) it was decided to avoid stripping to this depth with the box scraper. The other Neolithic pits from that season were found when shovel-scraping (SN27) or when the box scraper went deeper than intended (SN26 and SN30).

Features dated to Phase 1

NB: Descriptions of pit fills were not recorded, nor was large-scale flotation of soil samples carried out, although small soil samples from some pits were retained.

SN21: Shallow circular pit (its edge cut by one of Rainbird Clarke's trenches), 1.00 by 0.95m, no more than 0.1m deep below the stripped surface (**Fig. 6.2**). Neolithic sherds: SN/FQ, SN/RK; flints SN/MK* (NB: Not all flint from the site was retained, and those objects marked with * had not been located at the time of publication), SN/RK.

SN23: Shallow circular pit, 1.0 by 0.9m, 0.18m deep (**Fig. 6.2**). Neolithic sherds: SN/RL; flints: SN/ML*, SN/RL.

SN24: Shallow circular pit, 1.05m diameter, 0.2m deep; only 0.25m from SN23 (**Fig. 6.2**). Neolithic sherds: SN/RM, SN/MM; flints: SN/MM, SN/RM.

SN26: Pit, 0.9 by 0.6m, 0.2m deep, with many cobbles (some broken) and several sherds (**Figs 6.2–3**). Neolithic sherds: SN/QJ; cobble samples: SN/QO.

SN27: Circular pit, 0.7m diameter, 0.12m deep (**Fig. 6.2**). Neolithic sherds: SN/QP.

SN28: Pit, 1.2 by 1m, 0.15m deep (**Fig. 6.2**). Neolithic sherds: SN/OD, SN/RG; flints: SN/OD, SN/RG.

SN29: Pit, 1.2 by 1m, 0.2m deep (**Fig. 6.2**). Neolithic sherds: SN/NP, SN/RJ; flints: SN/NP, SN/RJ.

SN30: Shallow pit, 0.7 by 0.5m, 0.18m deep (**Fig. 6.2**). Neolithic sherds: SN/MV, SN/NA; flints: SN/MV, SN/NA; Neolithic polished stone axe: SN/NB*.

Ex. year	Area	Feature	Type
1990	Area 2	SN21	Pit
1990	Area 1	SN23	Pit
1990	Area 1	SN24	Pit
1990	Area 3	SN26	Pit
1990	Area 3	SN27	Pit
1990	Area 2	SN28	Pit
1990	Area 2	SN29	Pit
1990	Area 7	SN30	Pit
1991	Area 25	ST38	Burnt area and flint concentration
1991	Area 25	ST39	Flint concentration
1991	Area 25	ST40	Burnt area and flint concentration
1991	Area 28	ST43	Burnt area and flint concentration

Table 6.1 Phase 1 features

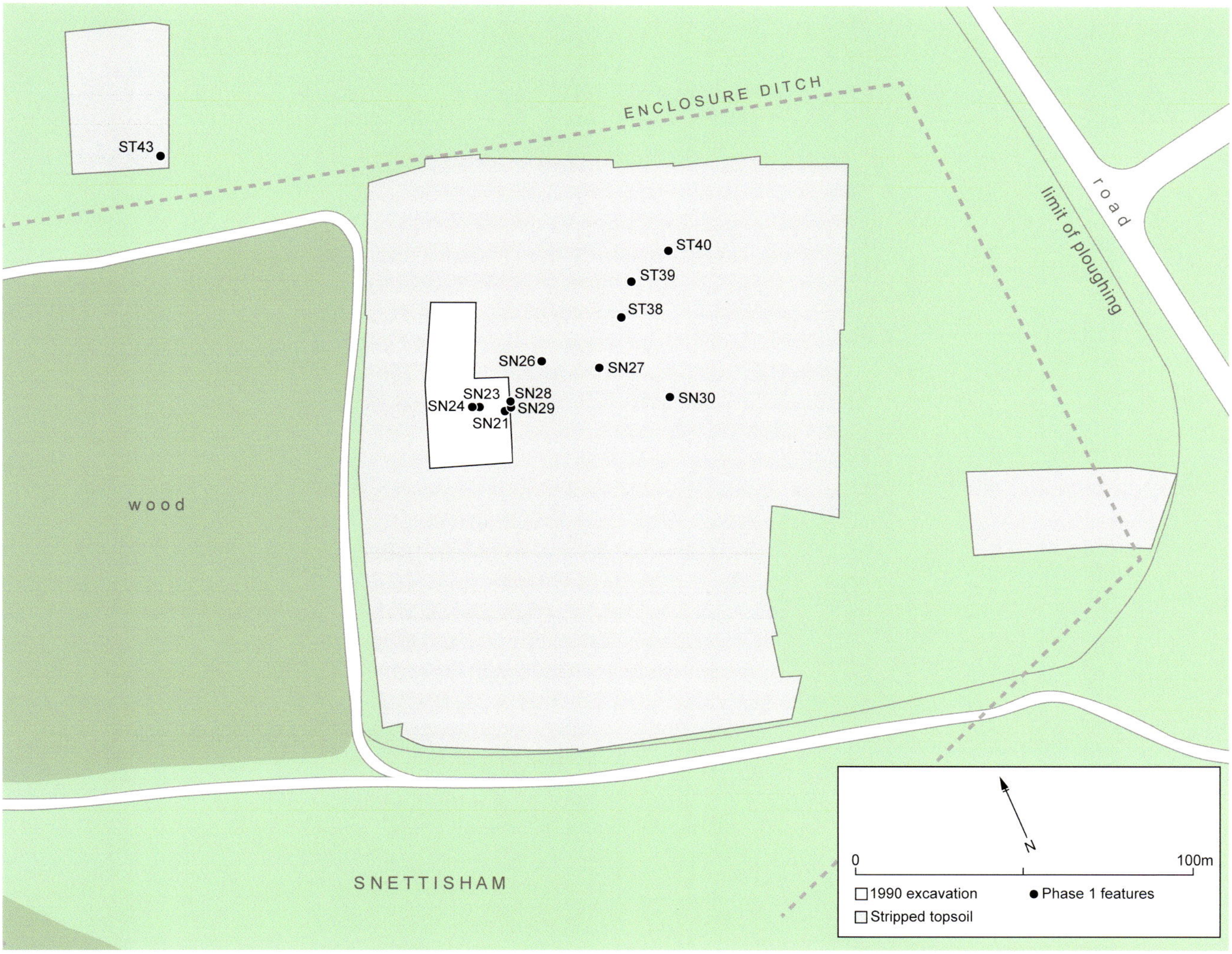

Figure 6.1 Plan showing locations of Phase 1 features

ST38: Circular burnt area, 1.3m in diameter, no more than 2–3cm deep, with flint concentration within and around it. Flints: ST/EP, ST/EQ (from feature), and ST/EO (immediately to the west of burnt area).

ST39: Flint concentration. Flints: ST/ER. Described by Peter Makey (below) as resembling 'the fill of a small ploughed-out pit or post hole'. He suggests that the flints may represent 'the remains of a knapping event from which material had been removed for use'.

ST40: Burnt area, 0.25m in diameter, 0.14m deep, and flint concentration. Flints: ST/ES. Peter Makey (below) suggests that the flint concentration represents 'a spread of material that was being intentionally crushed to provide flint temper for prehistoric pottery production'.

ST43: Burnt area, 0.25m in diameter, 0.08m deep, and flint concentration. Flints: ST/HT.

In addition to these Phase 1 features, Neolithic flint tools and flakes (see below) also appeared as residual finds in later

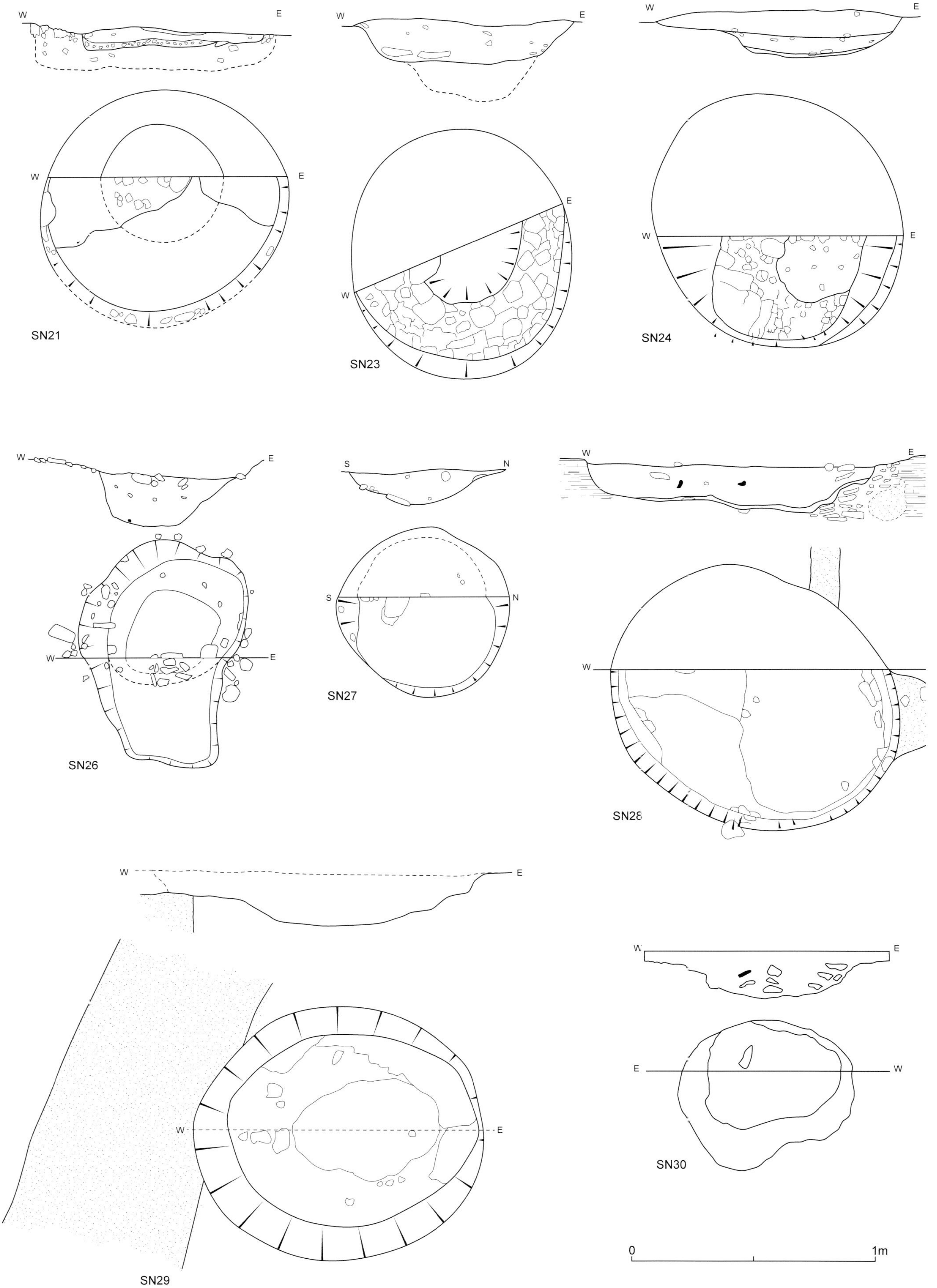

Figure 6.2 Phase 1 feature plans and sections (SN21, SN23, SN24, SN26, SN27, SN28, SN29, SN30)

features, including Hoard pits F, H and L (Phase 3) and the enclosure ditch (Phases 4–5). A complete Neolithic polished stone axe ST/GR , and fragment ST/ET were recovered from the topsoil of Area 21 in 1991. Another axe fragment SA/CZ was a residual find in modern ditch SA7/5 (see below).

Early Neolithic pottery

Sarah Percival

A total of 3,061 sherds of prehistoric pottery weighing 16,197g were collected from the British Museum excavations at Ken Hill, Snettisham. The assemblage includes a mix of Early Neolithic, Later Neolithic to Early Bronze Age and Post Deverel-Rimbury pottery recovered from pits, enclosure and other ditches and from cleaning around the areas surrounding the hoards. The pottery is poorly preserved with a mean sherd weight of 5g, with most sherds being small and abraded.

This section presents the Phase 1 material (earlier Neolithic), whilst Chapter 7 presents the Phase 2 material (Bronze Age to Earlier Iron Age pottery, as well as a handful of later Neolithic sherds) and Chapter 8 presents the small quantity of Phase 3 material (Late Iron Age pottery).

Methodology

The assemblage was analysed in accordance with the guidelines for analysis and publication recommended by the Prehistoric Ceramic Research Group (PCRG 2010). The total assemblage was studied and a full catalogue prepared (in archive, held by the British Museum). The sherds were examined using a binocular microscope (x10 magnification) and were divided into fabric groups defined on the basis of inclusion types. Vessel form was recorded and the sherds were counted and weighed to the nearest whole gram. Decoration, condition, food residues and sooting were also noted.

Earlier Neolithic pottery

The earlier Neolithic assemblage comprises 426 sherds weighing 2,307g, a little over half of which was recovered from pits excavated during the 1990 season (SN21, SN23, SN24, SN26, SN27, SN28, SN29 and SN30). The remainder was collected during cleaning of the stripped surfaces mostly from areas investigated in 1990 with smaller quantities recovered in 1991 and 1992 (**Table 6.2**).

The earlier Neolithic pottery is predominantly flint tempered, with fabrics containing flint forming 94% of the total assemblage by weight. The fine to coarse flint-tempered fabrics match those identified locally at Spong Hill and tend to form a continuum rather than falling into distinct fabric types (Healy 1988, 64). The remainder of the sherds are sandy or occasionally vacuous with sparse sub-angular voids perhaps representing lost chalk inclusions. Flint fabrics are widely used throughout the earlier Neolithic in East Anglia and form the major component of contemporary local assemblages from Spong Hill, Broome Heath and Kilverstone (Longworth 1960, 228; Wainwright 1972; Garrow *et al.* 2006, 29).

The assemblage includes rims from 22 vessels in a range of open and bag-shaped, round-based bowl forms. The vessels have shallow-moulded shoulder ledges with externally thickened, flattened, folded or rolled rims. A little less than 40% of the sherds have smoothed surfaces and less than 1% are burnished. The majority of the vessels are undecorated. Two have incised or channelled decoration forming a herringbone motif comparable to Mildenhall Ware vessels found at Kilverstone (Garrow *et al.* 2006, fig. 2.30, P121, P128) and Spong Hill (Healy 1988, fig. 71, P136). One bowl has slashes along the rim top, a decorative trait again found within Mildenhall Ware assemblages such as Spong Hill and Kilverstone (Healy 1988, fig. 67, P85; Garrow *et al.* 2006).

A little over half of the Neolithic pottery came from a cluster of seven pits in Areas 1 to 3 (SN21, SN23, SN24, SN26, SN27, SN28 and SN29, all in the area of the metalwork hoards) and isolated outlier pit or hollow SN30 (to the east, in Area 7). There may well have been other Neolithic pits in the area, but after the first few were discovered, a conscious effort was made to avoid disturbing more, since the main focus of the 1990 excavations was the Later Iron Age metalwork hoards. The pit assemblages have a small mean sherd weight of a little over 5g and contained 35 burnt or heavily burnt sherds alongside fresh and un-burnt pieces. The high degree of fragmentation and lack of complete or semi-complete profiles for the numerous vessels represented suggest that individual pots were already broken up, mixed and dispersed before deposition. The presence of burnt and fresh sherds is also consistent with the infilling of the pits with domestic debris from pre-pit or midden material (Healy 2013, 23; Garrow 2006). The small size of the sherds prohibited extensive re-fitting; however, conjoining sherds were noted between SN21 and SN28 suggesting that these pits in the cluster had been filled with material from the same source.

The Neolithic bowl is similar to the assemblages found at Kilverstone (Garrow *et al.* 2006, fig. 2.28) and Spong Hill (Healy 1988) being a mix of undecorated bowl and Mildenhall Ware. Plain and Mildenhall-style bowl are frequently found together in pit assemblages (Healy 1988; Garrow *et al.* 2006; Longworth 1960) and the pit cluster and isolated pit found during the 1990s excavations form a further example of pit deposition of curated occupation debris.

The remainder of the sherds were recovered from the cleaning of stripped surfaces. This context of recovery is more unusual as, as Healy notes, Early Neolithic bowl was absent from subsoil layers at Spong Hill and is rare in similar deposits elsewhere in the region (Healy 2013, 13). It is possible that these sherds were displaced from natural features or tree bowls comparable to midden deposits excavated at Colney where a large assemblage of pot and flint survived in the base of a natural hollow (Whitmore 2004).

Plain Bowl and Mildenhall Ware were current during the same broad period beginning in southern England between 3855–3730 cal BC (68% probability) and ending *c.* 3355–3210 cal BC (68% probability: Whittle *et al.* 2011, 762). The pit clusters at Kilverstone, which produced extremely similar vessels, were radiocarbon dated to 3650–3400 cal BC (Garrow *et al.* 2006, fig. 2.49) and a similar date range is suggested here.

Feature phase	Ex. year	Area	Feature	Feature type	Find code	Quantity	Weight (g)
1	1990	Area 1	SN23	Pit	SN/RL	17	55
			SN24	Pit	SN/MM	4	15
					SN/RM	3	5
		Area 2	SN21	Pit	SN/FQ	31	221
					SN/RK	3	6
			SN26	Pit	SN/QJ	23	57
			SN27	Pit	SN/QP	19	45
			SN28	Pit	SN/OD	6	31
					SN/RG	46	364
			SN29	Pit	SN/NP	4	17
					SN/RJ	50	124
		Area 7	SN30	Pit	SN/MV	6	22
					SN/NA	30	352
Unphased	1990	Area 1	Topsoil/subsoil SN/JB SN/KC		SN/BJ	29	95
					14	14	
					3	4	
		Area 2	Topsoil/subsoil SN/RN		SN/OC	3	14
					16	94	
		Area 4	Topsoil/subsoil SN/KU SN/ND		SN/KR	2	64
					9	27	
					1	9	
		Area 7	Topsoil/subsoil		SN/MS	3	14
	1991	Area 16	Topsoil/subsoil ST/AT		ST/AG	8	32
					86	583	
	1992	Trench 5	SA5/1	Topsoil/subsoil	SA/AC	10	43
Total						**426**	**2,307**

Table 6.2 Quantity and weight of Early Neolithic pottery by feature

Neolithic flint

Peter Makey

The flint totals 4,891 pieces plus an estimated 13,000 small spalls (these being predominately flakes less than 2mm in maximum length) from feature ST40 (burnt area and flint concentration in Area 25).

The assemblage contains remarkably few retouched pieces but a large proportion of cores. Plough damage is evident on a very large proportion of the pieces; many have also been burnt both during prehistory and more recently. Nearly all the pieces have been knapped by the application of hard hammerstones, many of which are present in the assemblage. There is a small degree of bipolar percussion evident in the fieldwalked material. There does not appear to be a great deal of correlation between the debitage and the suite of retouched implements. Intriguingly, the distribution of cores does not always correlate with increased abundance of flint debitage.

The four-letter codes used here (e.g. ST/FC) generally refer to mixed groups of material recovered from the same area (see Ch. 1 for full explanation of these codes). In this chapter, the flint is first summarised by artefact type, and then a more detailed account of flint from Neolithic features is included, as well as flint redeposited in Bronze Age and Iron Age features. Unstratified flint, and flint redeposited in later features, is included in Appendix 2.

Artefact types represented

L = length; W = width; D = depth

Cores

Many of the cores are ad hoc chunks or lumps with multiple irregular flake removals. Most of the cores have been worked to exhaustion. Cores were distributed throughout the area though there are slight 'hot spots'. On the cores traces of flake removal scars predominate over blade and bladelet scars in these areas. The incidence of cores is not proportionate with regard to the incidence of debitage. Group ST/FC from Area 26 contained an irregular single-platformed flake core (dimensions: L 104mm, W 44mm, D 37mm; 142g) that had been split in two in antiquity; the pieces perfectly conjoined. That particular core had a very heavily battered platform and punctiform bulbs. It is probable that it had been used as an anvil. The distribution of keeled cores is variable, with clusters appearing in some areas (e.g. Area 23). Core rejuvenation flakes are found in small numbers and are predominately plunging forms.

Hammerstones

Spherical and sub-spherical flints have been used as hammerstones. In some instances (e.g. group SA/CT from Trench 7) the pieces have also been used as anvils on which pieces of flint have rested during knapping. Hinged flakes and punctiform platforms are quite common.

Scrapers

A variety of forms are present and, due to the nature of the assemblage, when they occur they tend to be an admixture from different periods. A fine sub-circular extended end scraper manufactured on fine grained, olive-grey-coloured (Munsell (1991) 5Y 3/3) till flint was recovered from SA/CP. The piece measures 32mm in length and 35mm in width and is notable for possessing a multi-faceted platform, a pronounced bulb of percussion and extensive edge use wear. A fine convex extended end/horseshoe scraper from SA/BZ has most of the dorsal surface covered with cortex and an offset bulb of percussion. The implement has been extensively used. Broad 'horseshoe' extended end forms are rare, and outnumbered by scrapers made on cores. Double-sided scrapers are a rare form (one was present in Area 28 topsoil). Long end forms are notably scarce. These are defined here as scrapers manufactured on the proximal or distal ends of elongate flakes or blades with lengths measuring more than twice their breadth. Despite their relative scarcity a fine long end scraper came from SA/CQ.

A particularly rare typological form, the denticulate scraper, is present in the Ken Hill assemblages; examples come from Area 28 (ST/HS), topsoil in Area 24 and general topsoil; unfortunately all are unstratified. Scrapers have been manufactured on the coarse-grained flint available on site and finer till flint available from East Anglia. There is a slight bias in raw material selectivity with smaller end and extended end forms being made on finer flint. These are some of the few period-diagnostic pieces that probably represent a later Neolithic phase of activity.

Burins and gravers

Burins are of three main types; firstly, those intentionally manufactured by the removal of burinating spalls (e.g. SA/DQ from Trench 12) and secondly, ad hoc varieties formed by minimal retouching, typically on a spur of a hinged flake. The final varieties are un-retouched examples/gravers, where a flake facet has been utilised. In rare instances other support forms have been used; in SA/DU (from Trench 7) a burin was manufactured on a spurred projection from a core platform removal (rejuvenation flake).

A fine 'classic' dihedral burin was recovered from Trench 12 topsoil (SA/DS). Area 27 (ST/HM) produced a burin that had been manufactured on the point of a broad/broken flake. Two of the four gravers from Area 26 (ST/FC) are broad-hinged flakes on which use wear is clear on a spur resultant from the hinged termination.

Piercers

The piercers are predominantly defined by minimal retouch; in some instances (e.g. Area 14) a flake facet has been used without recourse to retouching. Two piercers from Area 26 (ST/FC) have been fashioned on fragments of cores and examples from SA/CU (Trench 7) and fieldwalking have been manufactured on core rejuvenation flakes. A piercer manufactured by slightly concave retouch on the left-hand side of a spur formed by the breakage of a broad flake was present in Area 21 (ST/HP).

Awls

The low number of awls is intriguing considering the high number of burins and piercers. Area 19 (ST/BN) contained a large flake that was shaped on its dorsal and ventral surface to form an awl. Manufactured on a dark olive flint, two finely worked and utilised examples comes from Area 26 (ST/EV & ST/HF)

Spurred pieces

Area 26 (ST/FC) contained a spurred flake; another example comes from the topsoil in Area 14. One of the best examples comes from the general unstratified assemblage: a flake with a projection defined by single notching of opposed margins.

Serrated pieces

A crude blade from Area 21 (ST/HP) possesses very fine edge serrations (<0.3mm depth, <0.2mm spacing) along a 35mm edge.

Notched pieces

Single, double and triple-notched pieces are present in proportionally large numbers. Many of the notches have been manufactured in an ad hoc fashion on chunks and chunky flakes. The number of notches on a flake/chunk varies but is predominately between two and three. The notches are mainly formed by retouching. An unstratified notch from Area 15 had been manufactured on a long end, flake scraper (catalogued as a notch). In some instances (Area 21, ST/HP), notches are shallow (<3mm) despite being extensively retouched.

Denticulates

Despite a large number of notched pieces in the assemblage, denticulates are quite rare. A fine example of a denticulate was found in Area 23 (ST/DR).

Laurel leaves

A fine though fragmentary laurel leaf was recovered from general fieldwalking. This piece is 30mm wide with a transverse snap fracture. Another example was present in Area 25 (ST/EO near feature ST38): a possible basal fragment from a large laurel leaf point. These probably represent an Early Neolithic phase on the site.

Fabricators

This is a relatively rare tool with predominately Neolithic associations. Area 28 topsoil produced a slightly curved rod-like fabricator of bi-convex section. Measuring 62mm in length by 20mm in width, the piece is heavily flaked and has characteristic tip abrasion on one end; such pieces have known Grooved Ware associations, for example at Carnaby Top, site 12, East Yorkshire (Manby 1974, 29, fig. 10.9). The fabricator from Area 26 (ST/FD) is a chunky double-edged blade with abrasion; the example from ST/FC, also in Area 26, is a rather crude stubby flake example. Area 24 (ST/DW) produced a large elongated battered piece that is probably a fabricator or a pick.

Knives

Knives are present in the assemblage from fieldwalking north and east of the wood and the topsoil in Area 28. These are both crude haphazard examples. Topsoil in Area 28 contained a proximal fragment from a very fine broad (29mm wide) double-edged flake knife with straight side retouch and heavy dorsal cortex. Two flake knives come from Area 26, one from ST/FC and one from ST/FD. One of the examples from ST/FC is a rather unusual flake knife with straight left-hand-side retouch on the side of a triangular-shaped flake support with a large hinged termination. The ventral proximal surface has had the bulb removed by flaking. This context also produced a plano-convex knife that resembles a tip fragment but is in fact intact. The example from ST/FD is crude, sub-oval in plan with retouch on both lateral margins and transverse ventral, distal retouch. A fragmentary flake knife with extensive edge use was recovered during fieldwalking in Area 27. The piece was a trancheform cortical flake with some resemblance to a transverse arrowhead. ST/EO (Area 25), contained an 'old looking' right-hand-side (semi-convex) flake knife. A fine single-edged flake knife with slight backing and dorsal blade scars comes from SA/DQ (Trench 12). An atypical knife was recovered from SA/BX in Trench 6. The knife is manufactured on the ventral surface of a large (length 50mm, width 44mm) crested, sub-ovate coarse-grained, light olive-grey-coloured raw material (Munsell 5Y 6/1) and possesses a cortical butt. Resembling a Neolithic 'horseshoe scraper', the ventral face has convex, invasive scalar flaking (17° edge angle) running from the distal to the right-hand margin.

Sickle

An irregular tertiary flake of fine-grained moderate yellowish-brown flint (Munsell 10YR 5/4) has a curved/crescentic edge defined by a small area of invasive flaking; the distal face of the implement possesses use wear and a high gloss that is consistent with the piece being used as a sickle.

Arrowheads

Unusually rare; there are far more flakes associated with the production of arrowheads than extant examples. It is possible that a couple of the miscellaneous retouched flakes from fieldwalking were initially intended to be large leaf arrowheads that failed during manufacture, one of the best examples being from Area 27. The finest example of an arrowhead is a slender minimally retouched piece manufactured on a blade and measuring 48mm (SN/NP) found during the 1990 excavations (Pit SN29). Area 26 fieldwalking produced a fine example of an unfinished oblique arrowhead of Clark's (1934) class G. The tip is missing due to post-depositional damage. Another example was present in the topsoil assemblage from Area 28. The piece appears to have failed during manufacture with an oblique distal breakage. Subsequently the piece was re-used as there is cutting wear on one margin extending to the breakage. Area 25, feature ST38, ST/EQ produced a burnt fragment of a large leaf arrowhead. Such pieces have primarily Early to Middle Neolithic associations. An unusual form of arrowhead was recovered from the general unstratified assemblage. The piece is a blade-like flake (length 40mm, width 20mm) with multiple dorsal bladelet, scars, and its proximal end has been invasively flaked to form a point. The distal end appears to have been snapped and the distal left-hand margin has three very small notches (1 x 1mm). The right-hand margin has another very small notch. These are probably notches to aid in binding the arrowhead to a shaft.

Axes

There is more evidence for axe manufacture and usage than intact and fragmentary axes. A highly polished flake from a polished flint axe was present in Area 20 (ST/CU), made on local pale yellowish-brown (Munsell 10YR 6/2) coarse-grained flint. The flake has been intentionally removed, probably to improve the surface appearance of the axe. After removal the flake has been lightly used in a cutting motion. The utilisation wear cuts through the polish. Trench 7, Feature 5, contained a polished green stone axe fragment (SA/CZ). There are pieces in the assemblage that look like they come from the finishing of flint flake axes (ST/HP, Area 21).

Microliths

Note: the location of retouch on microliths has been classified in relation to the point/tip rather than the bulb of percussion.

A small microlith (24mm long) was recovered from SA/AJ (Trench 5); the piece has right hand-side retouch and is in an unusually fresh state. The point of this piece has been fashioned on the distal as is usual for such pieces. An edge-blunted point with oblique distal right-hand-side retouch was present in the topsoil assemblage from Area 14. These represent evidence of later Mesolithic activity on the site. Micro-bladelets of possible Mesolithic aspect are present in small numbers.

Shouldered blades

Area 21 (ST/HP) contained a shouldered (left-hand side) blade with slight left-hand retouch and oblique left-hand distal retouch. Fieldwalking in Area 20 (ST/AS) produced a piercer that had been manufactured on a shouldered flake. These are normally pre-Neolithic although it is possible that they could be Early Neolithic.

Spurred pieces

Area 28 contained a spur manufactured on a discoidal core. The spur being defined by a slight marginal retouch of a flaking facet that forms a triangular projection.

Discussion

Since all the lithics were recovered in the stripped areas, the apparent lack of retouched material represents a genuine spatial distributional trait that has not been created by archaeological recovery sample bias. There is a restricted typological range of tools, with scrapers being in an unusually low proportion, whereas notches, burins and awls are present in numbers that are pro-rate a factor of ten times what might be expected. The notches show evidence of wood-working and may relate to woodland clearance in the Neolithic. The notched pieces appear to have been used to work wood; limited macro-wear suggests that some pieces may have been used as a kind of 'spoke shave', perhaps even used for the fashioning of wooden arrow shafts. However, it is of note that arrowheads are scarce, yet the debitage is indicative of the manufacture of both Early Neolithic leaf forms and later Neolithic oblique forms; Early Bronze Age barb-and-tang forms are absent. Burning is present throughout the assemblage and it relates to more than one functional cause. Interestingly, the distribution of cores does not always correlate with increased abundance of flint debitage and there are instances where beach-derived raw material was being used.

There are elements of Mesolithic and later Neolithic flint-working but the assemblage appears to be predominantly Early to Middle Neolithic. The Bronze Age material has been completely dispersed by modern agriculture.

Flint from Neolithic features

Pit SN21 (Area 2)

SN/RK: This group contained three pieces: one broken primary flake, one secondary and one tertiary flake. The primary and secondary flakes are of coarse-grained flint and probably come from the same piece. The tertiary flake is made of fine-grained olive-grey till flint (Munsell 5Y 3/2). The pieces are very fresh and do not look residual. They are undatable.

Pit SN23 (Area 1)

SN/ML* (mislabelled on bag and flint as SN/NL): A single chunky tertiary flake with platform facets.

SN/RL: This group contained five pieces of flint: a keeled blade core with three platforms, two flakes and two broken blades. The material is not in a fresh state and looks like an admixed assemblage.

Pit SN24 (Area 1)

SN/MM: A single small flake (25mm long) with platform trimming and minimal cortex the piece has recent (probably excavation) damage.

SN/RM (mislabelled on bag as SN/RN): This group contained three pieces: a secondary flake, a tertiary flake and a medial fragment of a single-crested bladelet. All are made from the same, possibly even the same nodule of fine-grained olive-grey (Munsell 5Y 3/2) till flint. The pieces are very fresh and do not look residual. They are probably Neolithic.

Pit SN28 (Area 2)

SN/OD: Two flints consisting of a small tertiary flake and an edge utilised (left hand side) blade; which retains traces of a core platform.

SN/RG: Totalling 36 pieces, this is a very homogeneous assemblage that may result from as few as four separate nodules of flint. Flake debitage totals 27 pieces from the following stages of reduction:

Cortical primary flakes = 6 (average size 41 x 32mm)
Secondary flakes = 6 (average size 26 x 14mm)
Tertiary flakes = 15 (average size 29 x 22mm and 18 x 10mm)

The tertiary debitage is very interesting; all is in a very fresh state and olive-grey (Munsell 5Y 3/2) fine-grained till flint. Six small, sub-oval-shaped pieces of debitage. In addition to flakes the assemblage includes seven small bladelets (three broken) with one particularly fine example (length 36mm, width 10mm). There are no cores but a single plunging core rejuvenation flake is present. The only retouched piece is an almost totally corticated flake with two small areas of nondescript retouch. This flint assemblage is probably Early Neolithic.

Pit SN29 (Area 2)

SN/NP: fine rare example of a minimally retouched slender lanceolate leaf-shaped arrowhead that has been manufactured on a single crested tertiary blade of medium to fine grained, light brownish grey (Munsell (1991) 5YR 6/1) till flint. The piece is between Green's (1980, 71) size 2–3 and of form C; measuring 48mm in length and 17mm in breadth (at widest point). Minimally retouched on its distal-dorsal/ventral and proximal-ventral, the piece is in pristine condition and does not appear to have been used.

SN/RJ: A small flint assemblage amounting to 24 pieces. There is a high degree of consistency in the flint which is in a very fresh state with six pieces being broken. Primary, secondary and tertiary flakes are present but the dominant feature of the assemblage is the high proportion of bladelets (average length 38mm) and blades (average length 33mm). Un-retouched bladelets amount to six pieces (three broken) and blades, two pieces (one broken). The flake debitage amounts to nine pieces (five primary, two secondary, two tertiary) and two chippings. One of the flakes shows very fine platform-edge trimming. There are two edge-retouched pieces; one is a broad edge-retouched flake with fine right-hand-side marginal retouch, which exhibits slight traces of edge use wear. The other piece is a proximal blade fragment with left-hand retouch. One tertiary flake shows use wear. A fragment from a single-crested bladelet has a notch on its left-hand margin; it is not possible to ascertain if this is due to accidental attrition or intentional; possibly as part of micro-burin manufacture. Most interesting is a tanged bladelet with a small area of minimal edge retouch on the proximal left-hand side. These last two pieces are more characteristic of later Mesolithic flint assemblages rather than later Neolithic or Early Bronze Age assemblages; as such this feature could be one of the earliest of the Ken Hill assemblages. The assemblage could be Early Neolithic and possibly even Mesolithic.

Pit SN30 (Area 7)

SN/MV: A double crested plunging, tertiary blade (almost core rejuvenation) of Neolithic aspect. The piece is in a fresh condition.

SN/NA: A collection of 9 predominately fresh-looking pieces, comprising 8 flakes and 1 bladelet. Four of the flakes are notably broad and come from early stages of core reduction (knapping). Two broad flakes almost conjoin, it looks as though the assemblage is derived from three separate nodules of raw material. One flake has surface gloss that results from the piece having been in the proximity of burning.

(Also polished stone axe SN/NB*) Missing

Feature ST38 (Area 25)
Burnt area and flint concentration. Three flint concentrations are associated with this feature: ST/EP and EQ within the feature, defined by respective areas of burning, and ST/EO comprising a spread immediately to the west of the feature.

ST/EP: Two flints: a struck primary flake with a pebble cortex and broad (32mm) tertiary flake with two proximal notches. The piece does not appear to have been used.

ST/EQ: The focus of the concentration was a flint core or hammerstone (extensive burning precludes accurate identification) associated with two fragments, three large tertiary flakes, two chunks, 17 small tertiary flakes (average length <20mm, width 20mm) and 107 (3.5g) small spalls (<4mm). All of the flint has been heavily burnt, consistent with having been in a fire; the pieces are calcined white to light grey in colour. In addition to the debitage and cores there is a calcined (white) medial and end fragment from a large (Green 1980: size class 2) finely shaped edge-retouched, pointed, leaf arrowhead. The form of arrowhead is most frequently found in Early to Middle Neolithic assemblages.

ST/EO: The assemblage totals 33 pieces. Notable pieces include three notched pieces, a flake knife and a small circular side and a possible basal fragment from a large laurel leaf point. The knife looks more residual than the rest of the material from the same context. The scrapers are characteristic of later Neolithic and Beaker type flint assemblages. The laurel leaf point is perhaps indicative of an Early to Middle Neolithic date.

Feature ST39 (Area 25): flint concentration
ST/ER: A small concentration of 24 flints including six cores, two core rejuvenation flakes, one notched flake, five flakes, eight chippings and two hammerstones. The hammerstones consisted of a very heavily battered lump and a re-purposed burnt core fragments. The assemblage was associated with pottery, and burning. Despite the fact that three of the cores are undiagnostic globular flake cores there is a degree of uniformity in the material. The two core rejuvenation flakes are consistent with the cores and comprise one sub-pyramidal-shaped basal removal and a flake that was struck down the core face. The notched flake is a very crude example. The concentration was from a reasonably small area and looked as though it was from the fill of a small ploughed-out pit or post hole. It is intriguing that only five flakes were found in association with the cores and only one retouched piece. It looks as though this was the remains of a knapping event from which material had been removed for use.

Feature ST40 (Area 25)
Burnt soil and flint. A small circular feature measuring 25 by 25cm and 14cm deep contained a large amount of burnt flint and carrstone.

ST/ES: There is a large quantity of small burnt flint spalls in the 3–5mm size range. These total about 12,300 pieces (weight 300g). There are a further 62 burnt flint chunks/flakes measuring between 10 and 25mm and 28 pieces measuring 25 to 45mm. Three larger pieces consist of two burnt pebbles: one of sandstone, one of flint and a flint lump measuring 65mm in length. The only struck flint was a heavily burnt unclassifiable core fragment. The flint spalls are of various forms and no fragments of tools or conventional knapping debitage are present. It appears as though the pieces have been intentionally burnt and crushed. It is most probable that this represents a spread of material that was being intentionally crushed to provide flint temper for prehistoric pottery production.

Feature ST43
A small circular burnt patch 25cm wide and 8cm deep.

ST/HT: 14 flints composed of four flakes, nine chunks (1–2cm in length) and a single chipping (<1cm). All the pieces are calcined and archaeological.

Flint from Late Bronze Age to Earlier Iron Age features

Pit SN25 (Area 3)
SE/BZ: Found on the pit surface and probably a residual Neolithic piece. The single flint is a broad, secondary flake with traces of use wear on its ventral left and right-hand margins.

Flint from Late Iron Age features

Hoard H (Area 4)
SN/EB: Two flints found in the top fill of the hoard H. These comprised a broken secondary flake and a core rejuvenation flake (platform removal) with slight ventral-convex retouch. The flake has post depositional damage. Both pieces are of a later Neolithic character.

Unstratified and redeposited flint from Phase 4–5 features, including the enclosure ditch, is included in Appendix 2 with the other unstratified flint.

Neolithic stone objects
Peter Makey and Julia Farley

ST/GR: Neolithic polished stone axe
Complete, some light abrasions on surface, possibly due to agricultural damage. Slight chip to the cutting edge. Rough, greyish stone with dark, reddish ferritic inclusions. Curved on one face, slightly flatter on the other. Uncertain axe group.

Dimensions: Weight: 373.1g; length: 120mm; maximum width: 64mm

Context: Topsoil/subsoil (1991, Area 21)

SN/NB: Neolithic polished stone axe*
Complete
Context: Neolithic pit SN30 (1990, Area 7)

ST/ET: Neolithic polished stone axe fragment
Broken fragment, comprising the damaged blade end, with several large chips broken away from each face, broken in half across the centre. Fine, polished greyish stone, with some reddish areas of the surface possibly indicating heating. Axe IP group VI

Dimensions: Weight: 108.5g; maximum remaining length: 48mm; maximum width: 64mm

Context: Topsoil/subsoil (1991, Area 21)

SA/CZ: Flake from Neolithic polished stone axe [Axe IP group VI]
Epidotised greenstone. A thin (5.57mm) marginal medial surface flake. Does not look like a re-sharpening flake but there is a bulb from its removal. Some grinding marks are still visible on the ground surface

Dimensions: Weight: 8.28g; maximum remaining length: 34.5mm; maximum width: 28.6mm Colour: Nearest match light olive brown (Munsell 5YR 5/6)

Context: Ditch SA7/5, Section A East 2.40 North 12.60: 21cm below feature surface (1992, Trench 7).

SA/CH: Stone axe-hammer or mace head, unfinished. Manufactured from the local (on-site) carrstone, showing characteristic banding.

Colour: Moderate brown (Munsell 5YR 4/4)

The piece split during manufacture due to an inherent fracture in the raw material initiated by the drilling of hour-glass perforations. The tapering perforation on the upper face is 15mm deep and 13mm wide. The lower face (defined by a natural flatter surface) is 15mm wide at lip and 10mm wide at base, and 18mm deep. The perforations are offset with the lower face being 13mm from the edge of the axe. The hole is only 23mm from the back of the piece. Other than drilling, the stone is unmodified.

Dimensions: Length: 94mm; width 57mm; thickness: 44mm; weight: 314.4g

Context: Ditch SA7/6 (1992, Trench 7)

*Not located at time of publication

Discussion

The main evidence for Early Neolithic occupation at Ken Hill takes the form of a cluster of seven pits in the vicinity of the hoards, another outlying pit, and areas of burning and/or flint concentrations which are more widely distributed across the site. It should be noted that the proximity of the main Neolithic pit cluster to the Late Iron Age hoards is most likely due to recovery bias. This was the only area of the site which was fully investigated below the ploughsoil. After these pits were discovered, the excavators attempted to leave Neolithic material undisturbed where possible, so it is highly likely that further Neolithic pits remained undetected in other areas of the site. The Neolithic ceramic assemblage is overwhelmingly Early Neolithic, and the lithic assemblage is predominantly Early to Middle Neolithic. There is very little evidence for later Neolithic activity at the site, although some of the flint may date from this period. Lithic finds also suggest activity stretching back as far as the Mesolithic period, a possibility supported by earlier stray finds of Mesolithic flakes and points from the immediate vicinity (NHER 1487).

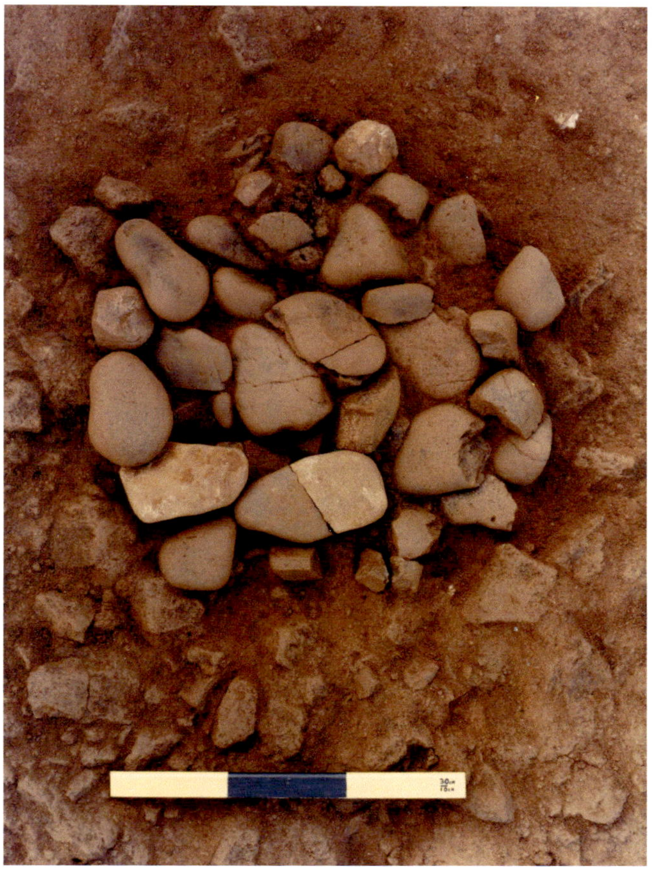

Figure 6.3 Pit SN26, showing the large deposit of cobbles

Early Neolithic pit-cluster sites are widespread across Norfolk, with well-studied examples at Spong Hill (33km from Snettisham; Healy 1988; 2013) and Kilverstone (55km from Snettisham; Garrow 2006, 40–58). As a coastal site on the northern fen-edge, Snettisham is something of a geographical outlier; most pit-cluster sites are located on light soils in inland river valleys, generally sited on relatively low-lying ground, just above the flood-plain of the nearest river (Garrow 2006, fig. 3.7, 26). Evidence varies, but generally suggests persistent use of these sites in the form of intermittent occupation events, rather than long periods of continuous settlement. Garrow (2006, 59) has suggested that such intermittent periods of occupation may have varied in length, from days or weeks (perhaps on a seasonal basis) to a few years.

Many activities are attested; Garrow (2006, 57) suggests that these were sites where: 'flint was knapped, pots used and broken, fires lit; cereals were processed and wild resources eaten, and we can probably assume that domestic animals were kept.' Where re-fitting of lithic material and re-joining of pottery has been attempted, as at Kilverstone, the evidence suggests that occupation debris was allowed to accumulate in a pre-pit context such as a midden, with joining sherds subject to different degrees of weathering and some re-fitting lithics showing burning or other modification while these features are absent in others (Healy 2013). Pits were subsequently dug in which to deposit the midden material, a process perhaps connected to abandonment of the site (Healy 1988, 106). At sites such as Spong Hill and

Kilverstone, series of intercutting pits suggest successive episodes of digging and infilling, supporting the argument that the pit clusters were created over discontinuous episodes of occupation (Healy 2013; Garrow *et al.* 2006).

Percival (above) suggests that the high degree of fragmentation and presence of both burnt and fresh sherds in the Phase 1 features at Snettisham is consistent with the infilling of these pits with domestic debris from pre-pit or midden material. Joining sherds were also found in two separate pits in the main cluster, supporting the argument that the pits were filled with material from a single source. Whilst most of the pit fills do not appear to have been internally structured, the large number of cobbles in pit SN26 (**Fig. 6.3**), may represent a placed deposit.

A small pit cluster such as that seen at Snettisham could have developed over a relatively short period. Garrow (2006, 59) has suggested that: 'The scale and longevity of… re-occupations may have varied significantly, from visits perhaps involving a handful of people and lasting a few days or weeks (generating two or three pits and relatively little material) to those which perhaps involved many more people, and lasted months or even years (generating 12 or 15 pits and large amounts).' While a short focus of activity of just 1–35 years (at 95% probability) is suggested for a pit site at St Osyth in Essex (Hamilton *et al.* 2007), elsewhere the extensive radiocarbon dating programmes necessary to narrow down use-life have not been carried out. Thus, at other sites, a longer timescale in the order of several centuries is also possible (Healy 2013, 16).

No organic material was found in the Neolithic pits at Snettisham, and so it was not possible to carry out radiocarbon dating for this phase. At Kilverstone, which has produced a very similar ceramic assemblage, the Early Neolithic pit clusters have been dated to *c.* 3650–3400 BC (Garrow *et al.* 2006, 72), and it is likely that the activity at Snettisham dates to around the same time.

Chapter 7
Phase 2: Bronze Age to Earlier Iron Age (*c.* 2500–350 BC)

Julia Farley and Jody Joy, with contributions by Sarah Percival, Alan Pipe and John Davies

There is little evidence for later Neolithic activity at Snettisham, and only very limited indications of an Early Bronze Age presence (comprising a very small number of pot sherds, including a few fragments of Beaker). After the Early Neolithic pit cluster, the next major phase of activity dates to the Late Bronze Age to Earlier Iron Age (*c.* 1100–350 BC). The main evidence comes from ceramic deposits in pit SN25 and other features, though there are also a handful of stray finds of metalwork and an antler bridle-bit from the wooded area to the west of the 'gold field' which can be stylistically dated to the Late Bronze Age or Earlier Iron Age.

This chapter presents the evidence from excavation, and specialist reports on the Bronze Age to Earlier Iron Age pottery and antler cheekpiece. A short summary of the metal finds is included, though the detailed catalogue entries for these objects are found alongside the other metalwork in Part II of this volume. The approach to the animal bone from the site is covered below, as this is the first phase which produced bone: a small amount of unidentified calcined bone from a pit with no other finds. The bone was radiocarbon dated to the Late Bronze Age, but otherwise dating for this period is based on ceramic evidence.

Bronze Age to Earlier Iron Age features

Figures 7.1–2 and **Table 7.1** detail the Phase 2 features at the site, excavated in 1990 and 1992. The only Phase 2 features from 1990 were pits SN31 and SN25. Pit SN25 was located to the east of the main concentration of metalwork hoards and contained a large quantity of Earlier Iron Age pottery. Pit SN31 was shallow and contained only a very small quantity of burnt bone (unidentified mammal, see below). The 1992 excavations revealed likely Phase 2 features in two areas: Trench 7 and Trench 12, both to the south of the hoards. In Trench 7, many features were heavily disturbed, but some certainly date to Phase 2. The trench as a whole produced a large quantity of Earlier Iron Age pottery, much of it residual in later ditch SA7/5, suggesting that the excavation of this ditch may have disturbed earlier features. Most of the relatively large number of features uncovered in Trench 12 were the remains of animal burrows, but one (SA12/6) is a possible hearth, and many produced Earlier Iron Age pottery.

Features likely dating to Phase 2:

SN25: Pit, 0.6 by 0.5m, 0.15m deep, containing a large quantity of pottery, likely dating to a single episode in the Earlier Iron Age. Sherds: SE/A–Z and SE/AA–BY. Flint: SE/BZ was recovered from the surface of the pit, likely residual. (The special two-letter code SE was assigned specifically to finds from this pit, although it was excavated in 1990, when most finds were assigned code SN. See Ch. 1).

SN31: Shallow pit with traces of burning, containing a small amount of calcined bone. Bone: SN/FE. The bone was radiocarbon dated to 1130–930 cal BC (at 95% probability, see **Table 5.3**).

SA7/2: Base of flint-gritted pot containing burnt stones, sitting in a small scoop in the natural. Burnt stones; pot base: SA/CD.

SA7/10: Pit, 0.5m in diameter, 0.2m deep, well defined except the south-west corner, which showed possible

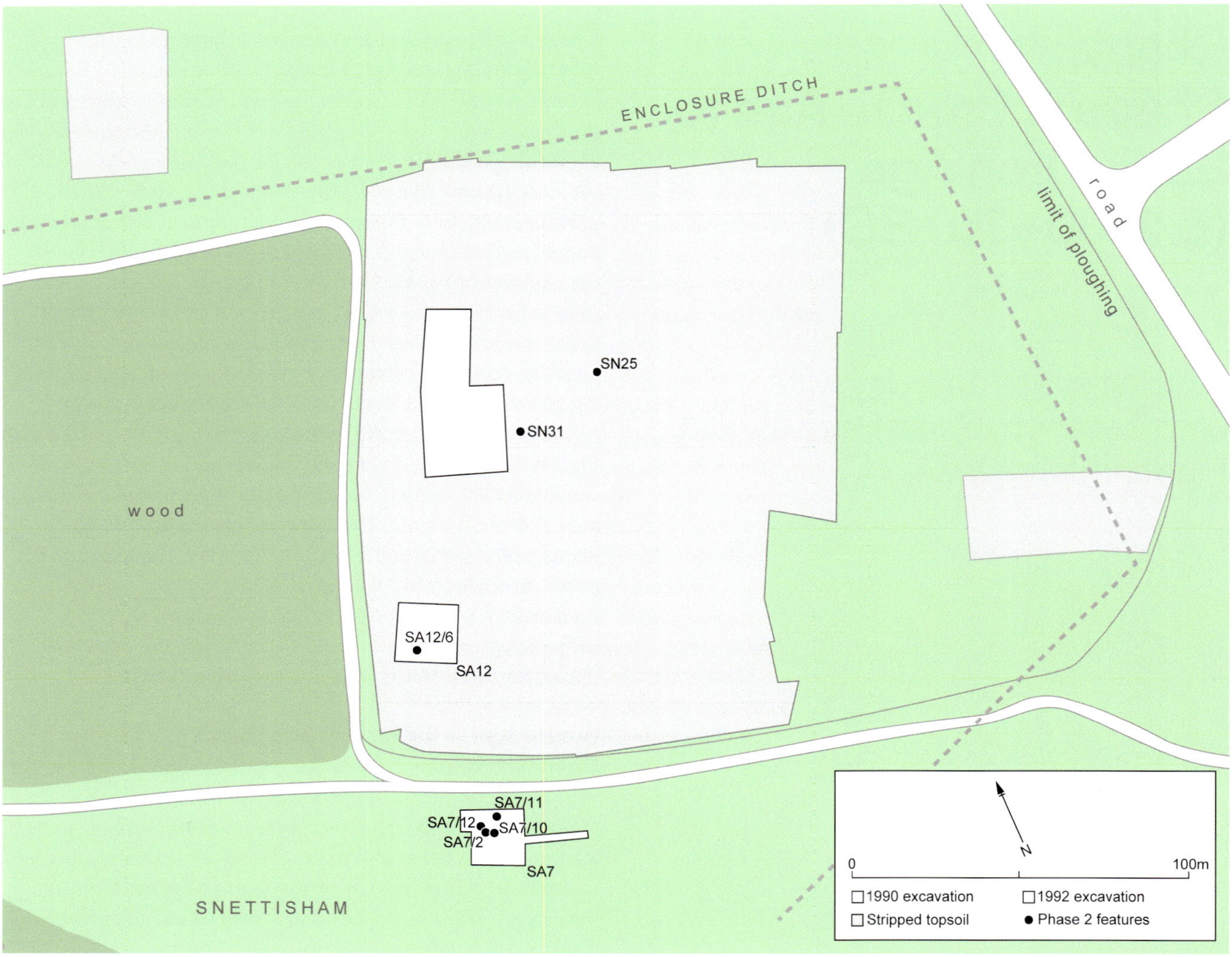

Figure 7.1 Plan showing locations of Phase 2 features

Figure 7.2 Phase 2 feature plans and sections (SN25, SA7/10 and SA7/11)

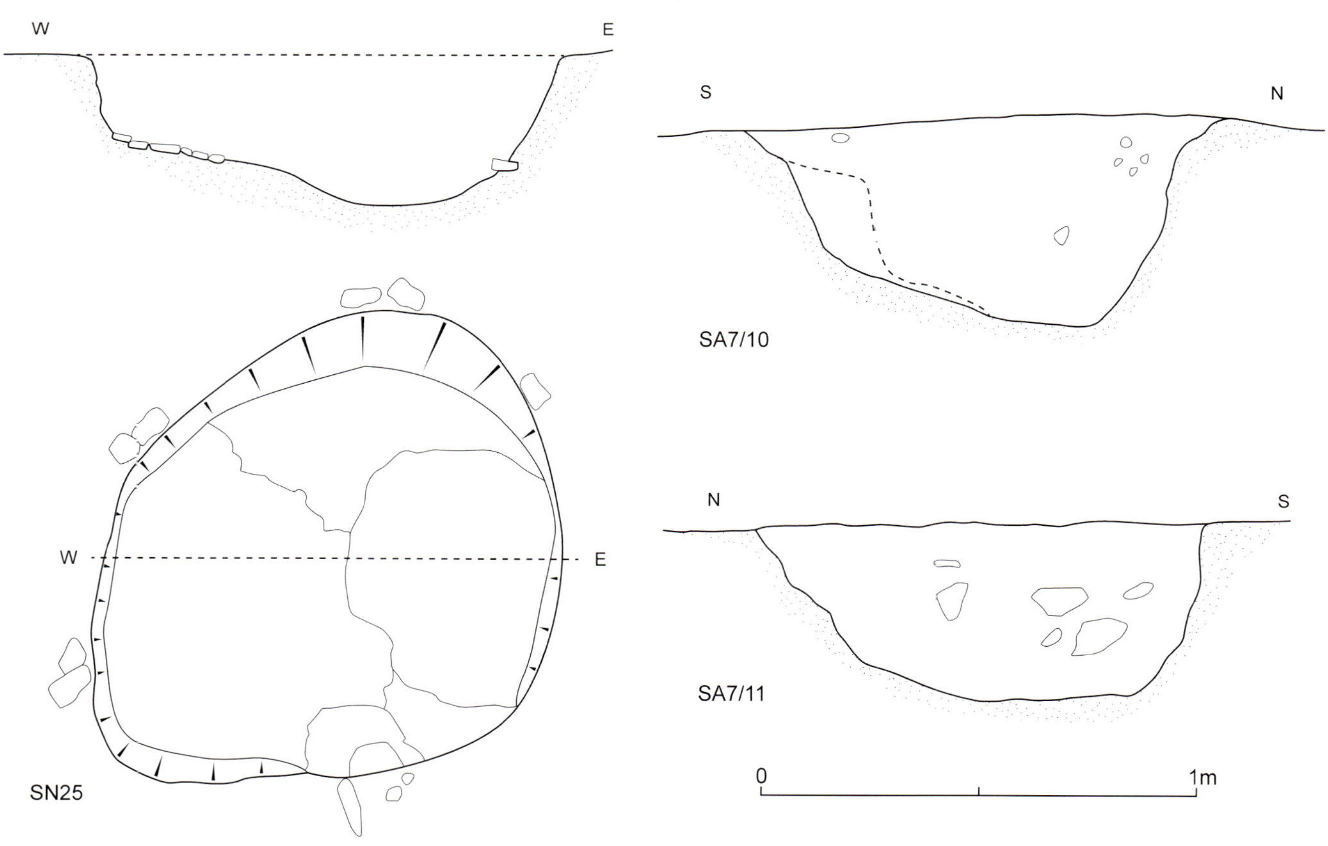

burrowing disturbance, containing flint, stones and pot sherds with a single fill. The bottom of the pit was greenish, weathered sand. Flints: SA/DL, SA/DM, SA/JL*; sherds: SA/DL, SA/DM, SA/JL.

SA7/11: Pit, 0.5–0.6m in diameter, 0.2–0.25m deep. Single fill of dark-grey ash, containing many burnt stones (size 2–10cm). The pit was steep sided with a flat base, somewhat disturbed by burrowing. Sherds: SA/JM, SA/JN; flints: SA/JM*, SA/JN*.

SA7/12: Pit, 0.5m in diameter, 0.3m deep. Steep sided, cut by much later ditch SA7/5. Contained burnt stone, although there was no sign of ash or charcoal, suggesting that the stones were heated elsewhere before deposition in the pit.

SA12/6: Possible hearth, approx. 0.45m in diameter, containing burnt material including stones, pot sherds and flint. Sherds: SA/KE; flints: SA/JT, SA/KE*.

Ex. year	Area	Feature	Type
1990	Area 3	SN25	Pit
1990	Area 1	SN31	Pit
1992	Trench 7	SA7/2	Scoop/hollow
1992	Trench 7	SA7/10	Pit
1992	Trench 7	SA7/11	Pit
1992	Trench 7	SA7/12	Pit
1992	Trench 12	SA12/6	?Hearth

Table 7.1 Phase 2 features

Later Neolithic to Earlier Iron Age Pottery

Sarah Percival

This section presents the Phase 2 pottery. For Methodology, see Chapter 6.

This pottery report uses the ceramic chronology 'Earliest Iron Age' spanning *c.* 800–600 BC, 'Early Iron Age' starting in *c.* 800 BC and continuing until 400/350 BC and Middle Iron Age *c.* 350–50 BC (Brudenell 2012). For the pottery this Earliest/Earlier Iron Age terminology is kept here.

The Phase 3 activity at Snettisham cannot be neatly divided into 'Middle' and 'Late' Iron Age (see Ch. 8). For that reason, in the rest of this volume the terms 'Earlier Iron Age' (*c.* 800–350 BC) and 'Later Iron Age' (from *c.* 350 BC) are generally used, to distinguish between Phase 2 (this chapter) and later activity.

Later Neolithic to Early Bronze Age pottery

A total of 35 Later Neolithic to Early Bronze Age sherds weighing 146g were collected from topsoil in Areas 1 and 4 (SN/BY, SN/KS, SN/NL, SN/HZ, SN/KA and SN/KS). The sherds are small with a mean sherd weight of just over 4g and are in poor condition. The assemblage includes three sherds of Beaker weighing 9g (SN/HZ, SN/KA and SN/KS) comprising a rim and body sherd in sandy, grog-tempered fabric with fingernail-impressed decoration and fingertip rustication, and an undecorated body sherd in similar fabric. These fabrics compare well with Beaker assemblages found locally, for example at Hockwold (Healy 1996, fig. 61). The decorated sherds find parallel with domestic Beaker found locally at Runcton Holme and Reffley Wood on the outskirts of King's Lynn (Gibson 1982, fig. R.H.1, 6; fig. REF.1, 5).

The Beaker sherds were found during cleaning of stripped surfaces. Though Beaker is frequently found in pits it is also common in preserved soil layers, having originally been deposited in surface accumulations of which only a portion was eventually incorporated into cut features (Healy 2012, 157). Healy dates the start of non-funerary use of Beaker in southern Britain to be around 2490–2200 cal BC (at 95% probability; Healy 2012, 158).

Post Deverel-Rimbury (PDR) pottery

The largest component of the prehistoric pottery assemblage is of Post Deverel-Rimbury type with 2,513 Later Bronze Age to Earlier Iron Age sherds weighing 13,217g recovered from three feature types. A total of 874 sherds (6,147g) came from pits and hollows, principally SN25 which contained 700 sherds (4,619g). A further 728 sherds (2,940g) came from ditches, whilst the later Romano-British enclosure ditch produced 42 re-deposited sherds (243g). The remainder came from cleaning and unstratified contexts which produced 823 sherds (3,711g). The condition of the sherds is generally poor and the assemblage has an average sherd weight of 5g.

The PDR pottery is chiefly made of flint-tempered fabrics which form 98% of the assemblage by weight and 96% by sherd count. The extensive use of flint as a tempering material is rather problematic for dating the pottery as the small and undiagnostic body sherds which form the bulk of the assemblage are hard to distinguish from Early Neolithic pottery in similar fabrics; however, the characteristic wiped and textured surfaces of the PDR sherds allow for some differentiation. Five flint-tempered fabrics were identified, showing a range of flint inclusion size and density, the most abundant fabric containing moderate to common medium flint pieces (fabric F1). Other fabrics within the PDR assemblage were present only in small quantities. These include a sandy fabric (4% by count, 2% by weight) and organic, grog and shell-tempered fabrics (each forming less than 1% of the assemblage). The range of fabrics is typical of PDR assemblages in the region, with the addition of crushed burnt flint being characteristic of Later Bronze Age and Earlier Iron Age ceramics from Norfolk, Suffolk and eastern parts of the fen edge in Cambridgeshire (Brudenell 2012, table 4.2). Flint is readily available in the alluvial gravels local to Snettisham and was heated, crushed and added to clay to produce the characteristic fabric. The other fabrics present also contain inclusions which could be sourced locally to the site. The shell-tempered fabric may derive from local Snettisham Clay deposits which contain an abundant shelly fauna (British Geological Survey online database), though the shell-tempered pots may have been imported to Snettisham from across the Wash in Lincolnshire where shell-tempered fabrics, made from fossil-rich Jurassic clays, predominated.

The pottery forms are described using a combination of vessel categories, including a division into fine and coarse wares, vessel type and form (following Brudenell 2012). Many rim and upper body sherds were too small to identify;

however, a minimum of 61 separate vessels were identified by rim count of which 43 could be identified to form. As with most PDR assemblages, coarse ware jars predominate making up over half of the identifiable vessels represented within the assemblage (**Table 7.2**) and around 70% of the overall assemblage by weight and count. Coarse ware body sherds typically have rough wiping, round vertical wiping or finger-textured surfaces. The most frequently occurring vessel form is the neutral or open jar with high, rounded shoulders and upright or out-turned neck (form F). These jars occur in a range of sizes with rim diameters between 90 and 260mm. Two examples have fingertip-impressed decoration to the rim top, four have smoothed surfaces and most roughly wiped surfaces.

With a similar body shape to the shouldered jar form F, form G jars also have a neutral or open profile, high slack or weakly defined shoulders and upright, hollowed or out-turned necks. Form G are the next most common jar form in the assemblage, with four examples recorded of which one has slashed decoration to the rim top.

A range of ovoid closed jar forms is also present (forms A, B, C and D). These vessels have restricted necks or rims and ovoid bodies with direct, upright or slightly everted rims. Two rims are decorated with fingertip impressions, one to the rim top and one to the rim edge. Rim diameters span 120mm to 160mm.

Fine vessels are mostly distinguished by the presence of finely smoothed or burnished surfaces. A little under 30% of the assemblage by weight is burnished (28% by sherd count). Fine jars are rare with only one example identified. Fine bowls are more common though still more poorly represented than coarse jars. Several of the fine bowls, identified from distinctive decorated body sherds with smoothed or burnished surfaces, are from bipartite bowls with pronounced rounded or angular shoulder and inward-sloping neck, beaded or rounded rims and incised double or triple bands of decoration on the neck (Type M, Brudenell 2012 fig. 5.15, 17). This distinctive form is present in Norfolk, north-west Suffolk, and the eastern tip of Cambridgeshire in Earliest and Earlier Iron Age assemblages (Brudenell 2012, 239). Rims from five fine round-bodied bowls with rounded bead or everted rims and smoothed surfaces were also recovered (form K).

The assemblage also includes rims from ten small, fine, undecorated cups. Thin and finely finished body sherds present in the remainder of the assemblage indicate that these vessels were fairly well represented. The cups have rim diameters of between 90mm and 110mm and are found in a range of forms which mimic the full-sized vessels (**Table 7.2**).

Base sherds are poorly represented in the assemblage with just 21 examples recorded. These bases often have grit adhering to the underside, a characteristic trait of PDR assemblages, perhaps associated with manufacture. The bases are mostly simple base angles though some are pinched out, thumbed or stepped. The assemblage includes one handle or lug (SN/EC) similar to examples found at Clay Farm, Cambridgeshire dated to the Earlier Iron Age (M. Brudenell pers. comm.).

Decoration is rare, occurring on only 2% of the total assemblage by count and 3% by weight. On coarse wares where present the decoration consists of fingertip or fingernail impressions to the rim top (SA/JN, SE/A, SE/AN, SE/BU) or edge (SA/GO and SA/GP), limited fingertip impressions to the shoulder (SA/GR) and at least one vessel with fingertip rustication all over (SE/U). Fingertip decoration to the rim and shoulder is fairly common within Norfolk PDR assemblages such as West Harling and Trowse with Newton (Clark and Fell 1953; Percival 2000). Vessels with all-over rustication are found in Earliest and Earlier Iron Age assemblages all over East Anglia though, as Brudenell notes, are limited to only a few examples per assemblage (Brudenell 2012, 249, fig. 6.25). Locally, rusticated vessels have been found at Beeston Quarry (Ashwin and Flitcroft 1999, 244, fig. 23, P34) and West Harling (Clark and Fell 1953, 18, fig. 12, no. 26). Fine wares in the region are also mostly undecorated with the exception of the bipartite bowls which have double or triple-incised bands, one with a row of line stabbed dots along the cordon (Ashwin and Bates 2000, fig. 149, P113).

Three sherds have red haematite coating (SN/EP, SN/JV and SN/BV). This distinctive Earlier Iron Age pottery is rare in East Anglia though it has been previously found in fieldwalked material at Ken Hill (NHER 1490) as well as on the Aylsham Bypass with distribution perhaps focused on sites around the Icknield Way (Brudenell 2012, fig. 6.22).

The context of recovery for the PDR pottery includes around one third collected from pits, principally SN25 which produced 27% of the total PDR assemblage by sherd count and 34% by weight including rims from four vessels: three fine round-bodied bowls and a coarse rim from a vessel with all-over fingertip rustication. Within the assemblage from SN25 three groups, recovered at different points in the fill (SE/A, SE/AN and SE/BU), contained conjoining sherds from the same fine bowl. The average sherd weight for the feature is 7g, slightly larger than the overall assemblage average. The presence of conjoining sherds across finds collection units in the pit indicates that the material within it was probably deposited together or at least from the same source, whilst the incorporation of at least three fine bowls might indicate that the assemblage derived from a specific event, perhaps associated with food consumption.

Aside from pit SN25 and the Romano-British enclosure ditches (see below), the only archaeological features which produced PDR sherds were in Trenches 7 and 12, both located immediately south of the area which produced the Later Iron Age metalwork hoards. Some of these features may represent prehistoric activity at the site, though the majority are likely modern disturbance and animal burrows which contained residual prehistoric sherds. The only possible prehistoric features were two small pits (SA7/10, SA7/11), a possible hearth (SA12/6), and a small scoop or hollow (SA7/2) which contained the base of a flint-gritted pot (SA/CD) with associated burnt stones found *in situ* in the pot. The sherds from this area of the site comprise a much broader mix of vessels to those found in pit SN25, perhaps suggesting a different origin.

Excavations on PDR sites such as Broom in Bedfordshire have drawn attention to the uneven distribution of artefacts across features, even when these include a number of formally similar pits. The large assemblage from pit SN25

Class	Type	Form	Description	Quantity	Weight (g)	Vessel count by rim
Coarse	Jar	F	Jars with high, rounded shoulders and upright or out-turned necks	13	82	13
		G	Jars with high slack or weakly defined shoulders and upright, hollowed or out-turned necks	4	11	4
		E	Bipartite jars with marked or angular shoulder inward-sloping necks	7	47	3
		C	Barrel-shaped jars	2	29	2
		D	Ovoid or slightly flared jars with no distinct neck	2	12	2
		A	Jars with round bodies, no distinct shoulder and short upright or everted necks	1	5	1
		B	Ellipsoid jars with no neck	138	1,226	2
		Uncertain		18	51	14
Fine	Bowl	K	Round-bodied bowls	6	82	5
		M	Bipartite bowls with a pronounced rounded or angular shoulder and inward-sloping neck	8	38	
	Cup	R	Hemispherical cup	3	4	3
		T	Round-bodied cup with everted rim	6	14	4
		W	Tripartite cup with angular shoulder	1	1	
		F	Jars with high, rounded shoulders and upright or out-turned necks	3	19	3
	Jar	E	Bipartite jars with marked or angular shoulder inward-sloping necks	1	33	1
		Uncertain		5	29	4

Table 7.2 Quantity, weight and number of vessels by rim count of PDR vessels by vessel form

and relative absence of other large assemblages from contemporary cut features is therefore fairly typical and perhaps suggests that the pot-rich pit lay near to the original artefact source and therefore received more material (Brudenell and Cooper 2008, 14). The mixed condition of the pottery and varying sherd size suggests that the pot was already fragmented before entering pit SN25, though no especially burnt sherds were recorded. It is possible that this feature represents a midden deposit, smaller than but related to the extensive pot and artefact-rich accumulations most commonly found in southern Britain which typically produce huge quantities of fragmented pottery (Waddington *et al.* 2019, 3) and one of a number of similar, though less artefact intense, deposits beginning to be identified in eastern England (cf. Brudenell and Cooper 2008).

The remainder of the PDR assemblage was recovered from cleaning of stripped surfaces and from the enclosure ditch and other later ditches. It perhaps represents material from middens originally accumulated in pits or natural hollows in the underlying carrstone and subsequently dispersed through subsoil and later features cut through it. The sherds from these features are generally smaller (average sherd weight 5g) and more abraded than those from pit SN25, consistent with having been subjected to additional movement and attrition in transit. The only enclosure ditch contexts to produce prehistoric pottery were Layers 1 and 2 (the upper layers) in SA6/2 and SA17/2 (adjacent in trenches in the south-east part of the site) and Layer 3 in SA5/2 (on the south-west side of the site). In several cases the PDR pottery was recovered from deposits which overlay contexts containing Roman pottery, clearly showing that this was re-deposited residual material. It may not be coincidental that the direction of deep ploughing on the site was from the north-west to the south-east. Several areas of prehistoric activity, including pit SN25, are to the north-west of the part of the enclosure ditch which includes SA6 and SA17. Indeed, there is a join between two sherds from the topsoil of Trench SA7 on the south side of the site (SA/BU) and layer 2 of the enclosure ditch in Trench SA6 which lays around 100m to the east (SA/BW), again suggesting a common source for these sherds.

The assemblage contains sherds with both Later Bronze Age and Earlier Iron Age traits. The thin-walled, plain closed ellipsoid and ovoid jars with finger-textured surfaces are typical of Later Bronze Age pottery in northern East Anglia (Percival 2000, 215). Assemblages with comparable Later Bronze Age vessels have been found at Trowse with Newton and Watton Road on the Norwich Southern Bypass (Ashwin and Bates 2000, fig. 138 and fig. 175). Brudenell suggests dating for these Later Bronze Age assemblages falls around *c.* 1100–800 BC (Brudenell 2012). The angular-shouldered vessels, both plain and in limited numbers with fingertip decoration to the shoulder and rim top, the fine bowls with incised decoration, the all-over rusticated jar and haematite-coated vessels are all more typical of the Earlier Iron Age, dated 800–350 BC, and found more widely across the county. The presence of this mixed-period assemblage mimics those found elsewhere in Norfolk, for example at Trowse and other sites (Percival 2000; Brudenell 2012, table 4.4), and suggests that activity at Ken Hill may have taken place over an extended period.

The pottery has size, condition and depositional traits which suggest that it was derived from midden material. The activity which generated the material disposed of in the middens is unknown but differences in assemblage composition between the pot in pit SN25 and that found in other contexts and the lack of conjoining sherds between

SN25 and other pot from across the site suggests that different activities might have been taking place. It is also likely that the middens may have been active for some time. Large middens found in southern England have been suggested as being the focus for and remains of 'conspicuous community feasts, exchange ceremonies, and funerary and life-cycle rites' with several demonstrating comparatively long periods of activity of 500 years or more, with use extended from the Late Bronze Age on into the Iron Age (Waddington *et al.* 2019). Midden deposits at Llanmaes in the Vale of Glamorgan began around the same time as those at Snettisham, in the Later Bronze Age to Earlier Iron Age transition (Gwilt *et al.* 2016), but continued to develop throughout the Iron Age, with significant quantities of Later Iron Age and Roman pottery being incorporated and trampled into the deposit (Gwilt, Lodwick and Deacon 2006; 2016; Waddington *et al.* 2019, 13). It is possible that at Ken Hill activity which began with generation and deposition of midden material in the Later Bronze Age to Earlier Iron Age found ultimate expression with the extensive metalwork deposits of the Later Iron Age.

Bronze Age to Earlier Iron Age animal bone

Alan Pipe, Museum of London Archaeology (MOLA)

Introduction

The identifiable animal bone and mollusc shell recovered from Snettisham was quantified, identified and interpreted according to context and phase. This section presents the overall methodology, summarises the findings, and presents the Phase 2 bone (there was no animal bone from Phase 1 features). Bone and mollusc shell from other phases are covered in Chapters 8–10.

Methodology

Animal bones from each context sample group were described and recorded directly onto an Excel spreadsheet in terms of species, skeletal element, body-side, fragmentation and modification as appropriate (full spreadsheet in archive, held by the British Museum). Identifications of species and skeletal element referred to the MOLA reference collections. Modifications such as tool marks and gnawing were described using MOLA osteology codes and conventions. In general, each bone fragment was recorded as an individual database entry, either as single or multiple records, at an appropriate level of identification, 'cattle-sized' or 'sheep-sized mammal', based on size and wall thickness. Fragments assigned to the 'cattle-sized' category probably derive from cattle or horse; fragments recorded as 'sheep-sized' mammal could derive from sheep, goat, pig or dog. Measurement of a complete, fully fused cattle metatarsal from ST/DY followed von den Driesch 1976; calculation of cattle estimated stature from this bone followed von den Driesch and Boessneck (1974). Identification of the mollusc shells followed Hayward, Nelson-Smith and Shields (1996). For each context, the chronological narrative gives a description of the bone group in terms of species-composition, skeletal element and modification. Where possible, any implications for diet, disposal and activity are discussed in the chronological narrative and thematic text sections. Interpretation of evidence for burning followed Lyman (1994, 386).

Preservation, quantification, composition and modification

A summary of the animal bone is given here, and specific identifications for stratified material are included in the relevant phase discussions. Bone preservation was generally very poor throughout, with the bulk of the bone group consisting of friable, unidentifiable fragments of unidentifiable mammal bone likely to indicate the prevailing poor preservation and aggressive soil chemistry. Identifiable bone derived from cattle *Bos taurus*, sheep/goat *Ovis aries/Capra hircus*, pig *Sus scrofa*, horse *Equus caballus* and dog *Canis lupus familiaris* with three fragments of infant rabbit *Oryctolagus cuniculus* from SA/DY (Phase 6) only. There was no recovery of goat *Capra hircus*, or of fish, amphibians, game, scavenger or commensal species. Recovery of the infant rabbit is very likely to represent an *in situ* death of this burrowing species which, as a Norman introduction into the British Isles, is likely to have implications for local stratigraphy.

For the identified bone fragments, surface damage was usually sufficient to prevent measurement and to obscure or remove tool marks or any other modification. With the exception of the fragile infant rabbit bones from SA/DY, it is striking that almost all the identifiable bone assemblage derives from the most solid and robust skeletal elements (tooth, vertebra, mandible, innominate acetabulum, astragalus, phalange, metacarpal and metatarsal) and is therefore likely to be an artefact of the prevailing preservation conditions rather than a true reflection of the originally deposited faunal assemblage. Definite interpretation of the pattern of exploitation: meat diet, waste disposal and deposition, is effectively precluded beyond that the basic characteristics of the assemblage in terms of species, skeletal element, age and modification are established, although it is possible that other, less resistant, species and skeletal elements were originally present. A total of 140 at least partially identifiable fragments were recorded. Butchery marks were recorded from SN/AA (unstratified find from the wood) and ST/DN (ST35, enclosure ditch, Layer 1, Phase 5) only; white calcined bone was recorded from SN/FE (Phase 2 pit) only; there was no evidence for working, gnawing, pathological change or any other modification.

The mollusc fauna (from unstratified contexts and upper layers of Phase 4–5 features) derives entirely from occasional shells of economically important species: common/flat oyster *Ostrea edulis*, common cockle *Cerastoderma edule* and common periwinkle *Littorina littorea*, all of which are commercially harvested from suitable habitats around the East Anglian coast.

Phase 2 bone

Area 1, SN31, pit:

SN/FE Pit fill produced fragments of unidentifiable mammal bone calcined white indicating a high combustion temperature of at least 700° Celsius, equivalent to a cremation pyre or well-oxygenated hardwood fire (Lyman

Cat. no.	Museum	Ex. year	Findspot	Object name
S.1	BM	1990	Area 21	Socketed axe
S.2	BM	1990–1	Not recorded	Sword chape
S.3	NCM	2003–9	Wood	Razor
S.4	NCM	2003–9	Wood	Arrowhead
S.5	NCM	2003–9	Wood	Spearhead
S.6	NCM	2003–9	Wood	Blade fragment; ?Spearhead
S.7	NCM	2003–9	Wood	?Blade fragment
S.8	NCM	2003–9	Wood	Unidentified object fragment
S.9	NCM	2003–9	Wood	Miniature axe
S.10	NCM	2003–9	Wood	Moustache mount

Table 7.3 Phase 2 metalwork finds from the site. See catalogue in Chapter 14 for full discussion

1994, 386). There were no tool marks or any other evidence for modification. This material was radiocarbon dated to 1130–930 cal BC (at 95% probability, see **Table 5.3**).

Late Bronze Age to Earlier Iron Age metalwork

For simplicity, all metalwork from the site is presented in Part II of this volume, as the vast majority appears to originate from Phase 3 and 4 hoards. Only 10 copper alloy objects (S.1–S.10, see **Table 7.3**) may date to Phase 2 (Late Bronze Age to Earlier Iron Age). All are metal-detected stray finds. Eight were made in 2003–9, from the wooded area to the west of the 'gold field', while the others were recovered during the 1990s excavation. Axe fragment S.1 was found during detecting in Area 21, just beyond the north-east corner of the woods, while the findspot for sword chape S.2 was not recorded.

Although representing stray finds from the site, therefore with no evidence to connect them as a group other than their probable date of manufacture, this is an unusual collection of artefacts. Only the razor and socketed axe fragments can be securely dated to the Late Bronze Age or Earliest Iron Age. The socketed axe fragment is too worn for closer identification, but the Snettisham razor is of the Wiesloch type and can be assigned to the Llyn Fawr metalwork phase (*c.* 800–600 BC). These are uncommon finds with O'Connor (2007, app.2) listing only 11 sites where Wiesloch-type razors have been found in Britain, including a find from the Channel Islands. The closest parallel to the Snettisham razor comes from the multi-period Salisbury Hoard (BM 2001,0702.7; O'Connor 2007, 77) where it was deposited alongside material dating to around 200 BC (see below; Stead 1998).

Miniature socketed axes and 'moustache' mounts are both most common as unstratified stray finds (Robinson 1995; Bliss 2020; Davey 2020), and so neither object type can be closely dated within the Bronze Age and Iron Age. Bliss (2020) catalogued around 150 miniature axes from Britain. Some have been excavated from long-lived midden deposits dating to the Late Bronze Age and Early Iron Age at Whitchurch and Potterne (Bliss 2020; Waddington and Sharples 2011), and hilltop settlements and shrines dating to the Late Iron Age (Farley 2011). It is possible that most miniature axes were manufactured in the Late Bronze Age or Early Iron Age with some re-deposited at Late Iron Age and Roman period shrines (Bliss 2020, 22). So-called 'moustache' mounts are widely distributed across southern England, and some have Middle to Late Bronze Age associations (Davey 2020). Both object types appear within the multi-period Salisbury Hoard (moustache mount: BM 1998,0901.201; miniature axes: BM 1998,0901.44, 1998,0901.80: Robinson 1995; Bliss 2020), which is thought to have been deposited around 200 BC (Stead 1998). Also of interest is the association between a torc fragment and five miniature axes as well as other artefacts dating to the Late Bronze Age and Early Iron Age in a hoard from Whitchurch, Hampshire (Treasure case 2011 T152; PAS (Portable Antiquities Scheme) ID: HAMP-8A11A7; Bliss 2020, 6, fig. 3).

It is difficult to draw firm conclusions about these unusual objects, and the significance of their presence at Snettisham. As already outlined, some miniature axes have been found at Late Iron Age and Roman period sites interpreted as shrines. The presence of a razor, moustache mount and miniature axes in the Salisbury Hoard and the occurrence of miniature axes in the same hoard as a torc fragment at Whitchurch is also potentially significant. Rather than representing casual losses, these objects were probably deliberate deposits. Although chronologically the date of manufacture for several of these objects was in the Late Bronze Age or Early Iron Age, they could have been re-deposited, possibly even curated, and then deposited, sometime during the Later Iron Age or Early Roman periods.

Antler bridle cheekpiece

Julia Farley and John Davies

Material: Antler
Dimensions: Weight: 46.47g; length: 142mm; diameter: 5–21mm
Description: Bridle-bit cheekpiece made from antler tine (**Fig. 7.3**). A rectangular slot has been pierced through the centre. Two rectangular sockets have been cut part way into the inner (concave) face of the tine, towards the ends. They run perpendicular to the central slot. On either side of the two outer sockets are two lines of three circular holes, drilled at right angles into the sockets.

This would originally have been one of a pair of bridle-bit cheekpieces, serving to join the three main elements of the bridle: headpiece, mouthpiece and reins (Britnell 1976,

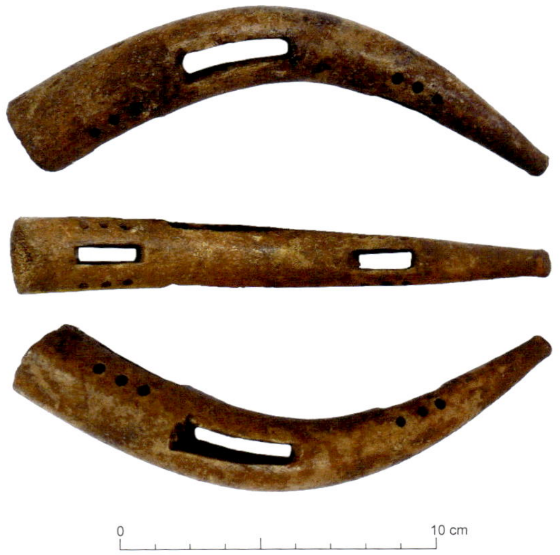

Figure 7.3 Late Bronze Age to Earlier Iron Age antler cheekpiece. Norwich Castle Museum, 2011.253

24, fig. 3A). The mouthpiece (either of bronze, or an organic material such as leather or rope) would have run through the central slots, joining the pair of cheekpieces and, on the outside, linking to the reins. The mouthpiece would have been held in position by Y-shaped headpiece straps on each side, with each arm of the 'Y' entering one of the partially pierced slots at the top and bottom of each cheekpiece. These headpiece straps were secured in place by wooden, bone or antler pegs, hammered through the circular holes.

Parallels

Antler cheekpieces have been recovered from many Iron Age sites, including Snailwell, Cambridgeshire (Lethbridge 1954, fig. 2); Glastonbury Lake Village, Somerset (Bulleid and Gray 1917, 440–54); Hunsbury Camp, Northamptonshire (BM 1896,0411.100–101); Auldhill, Portencross, North Ayrshire (Caldwell *et al.* 1998, 63–4); Potterne, Wiltshire (Seager Smith 2000, 230, fig. 93, nos 50–1); Denby, East Yorkshire (Rigby 2004, 172); and Viables Farm, Hampshire (Millett and Russell 1982, 82). But these are relatively simple artefacts, with fewer perforations or lacking the perpendicular arrangement of end sockets of the example from Snettisham.

Britnell (1976) identified a class of antler artefacts dating to the Bronze Age which more closely resemble the Snettisham cheekpiece. He published seven then-known examples from Britain (finds from Bledlow, Buckinghamshire; Ham Hill, Somerset; Hammersmith, London; Heathery Burn, Co. Durham; Sion Reach, Middlesex; and Washingborough, Lincolnshire). Additional similar examples have since been identified at the Late Bronze Age sites of Runnymede Bridge, Surrey (Longley 1980, 27–31) and Shinewater Marsh, East Sussex (BM 1997,1002.19). Longley (1980, 29–30) also classified this group and divided them into Class I, a distinctly British group provided with multiple peg holes on the two outermost sockets (examples from Ham Hill, Hammersmith, Sion Reach and Runnymede Bridge), and Class II (Bledlow, Heathery Burn, Washingborough, Runnymede Bridge and Shinewater Marsh), which are more varied and more closely paralleled on the continent. The find from Snettisham appears to fall into Longley's Class I.

Dating

On the continent, antler cheekpieces of this type have a long history, running back to the mid-second millennium BC (Britnell 1976, 28). British examples appear to date somewhat later. At Runnymede and Heathery Burn, the antler cheekpieces were found in association with Ewart Park-period metalwork, and Class I antler types are paralleled in metal bridle-bits from the Llyn Fawr period (Longley 1980, 30).

Conclusion

Taken together, this evidence suggests a likely date range around 800–600 BC for the Class I Snettisham example.

Discussion

There is little evidence for Late Neolithic or Early Bronze Age activity at Snettisham, despite the presence of a small number of Beaker sherds. However, the site seems to have taken on a special significance in the Late Bronze Age to Earlier Iron Age (*c.* 1100–350 BC).

There was clearly substantial Late Bronze Age depositional activity in the vicinity of the site, with at least five known Late Bronze Age hoards from the surrounding area of Snettisham and Shernborne parishes (Lawson 2018; NHER 1504, 1670, 1671, 1672, 1679, 17665, 25920, 28136; Treasure case 2006 T441, the latter found in the area of the site itself).

The small number of surviving features does not allow a detailed reconstruction of the nature of the Phase 2 activity at Snettisham. The majority of ceramics from this period were recovered from pit SN25 (to the east of the metalwork hoards) and Trenches 7 and 12 (immediately to the south). The latter had been heavily disturbed by animal burrowing and other recent activity; the only possible *in situ* deposits of Phase 2 material were two small pits (SA7/10, SA7/11), a possible hearth (SA12/6), and a small scoop or hollow (SA7/2) which contained the base of a flint-gritted pot with associated burnt stones.

Pit SN25 contained a large quantity of pottery, with larger sherds than elsewhere, including at least three fine bowls, and there are several cases of conjoining sherds from throughout the pit. Together, this suggests that the material was probably deposited in a single episode in the Earlier Iron Age, or derived from a single source. Percival (above) suggests that the material may represent a midden deposit from an event associated with food consumption.

The pits and burrows in Trenches 7 and 12 contained sherds representing a broader mix of vessel types to pit SN25, suggesting a different origin. This was a mixed-period assemblage encompassing the Late Bronze Age to Earlier Iron Age (*c.* 1100–350 BC), suggesting that activity may have taken place over an extended period of time. Percival (above) suggests that the composition of the assemblage implies midden material. Although the nature of the activity which generated these deposits cannot be ascertained with certainty, it is possible that it was associated with communal gatherings or feasting activities. The small number of non-ceramic finds from Ken Hill that can be securely dated to Phase 2 (the antler cheekpiece (see above), and metal finds S.1–S.10, where the findspot was record) are from the vicinity of the wooded area to the west, suggesting that activity in this period may have been concentrated away from the hoard field. The high levels of phosphate in the woods (Ch. 5) indicate an area of intensive activity or occupation over about 4,000m^2. This may be related to the Phase 2 midden-generating activity, although it is equally possible that it could be associated with the nearby Phase 4 Romano-Celtic temple (Ch. 9).

Although the evidence from Snettisham is on a much smaller scale, Percival draws parallels with large midden sites in south-central England (Waddington *et al.* 2019). Such long-lived Late Bronze Age to Early Iron Age midden sites are rare in eastern England, but Grandcourt Farm, Norfolk (Malone 2010), has a large number of pits with extensive evidence for Middle Iron Age structured deposits of pottery, brooches, amber, glass and shale, and may represent comparable activity in the vicinity of Snettisham (it lies around 18km to the south). Hargrave (2018, 154–5) argues that the depositional activity at Grandcourt Farm may be a forerunner to Snettisham, or at least 'a precursor to the general resurgence of metalwork deposition' in this part of north-west Norfolk in the Later Iron Age.

Chapter 8
Phase 3: Later Iron Age (*c.* 350–60 BC)

Julia Farley and Jody Joy, with contributions by Sarah Percival and Michael de Bootman

Phase 3 is the most intense period of depositional activity at Snettisham, including the burial of the bulk of the metalwork hoards, and all those containing torcs. Aside from the hoard pits themselves, there are no other features which can be securely attributed to this phase, although it is likely that the field system revealed through geophysical survey in 2006–9 (see Ch. 5 and **Fig. 8.2a–b**) was contemporary with the hoards.

A summary of the Phase 3 evidence is given in this chapter, alongside the short specialist report on the small quantity of Late Iron Age pottery from the BM excavations. The detailed stratigraphic information and the Phase 3 metalwork and coin catalogues are presented in Part II of this volume, which focuses exclusively on the Later Iron Age (Phase 3) and Early Roman (Phase 4) hoards.

Later Iron Age features

Table 8.1 lists the Phase 3 features from the 1990–2 excavations: torc hoards F, G, H, J, K, L and scattered coin hoard N. The torc hoards recovered in the 1940s–50s (A, B, C, D and E) also fall into this phase, and all the Phase 3 hoard findspots are shown in **Figure 8.1**. Most of the hoards were located in a fairly restricted area in the 'gold field'. Torc hoards B, C, D, E, G, H and J are all distributed in an area around 30–40m in diameter, with K just to the west, L and N 50–70m to the south, and F and A further east. A is the most isolated of the known hoards, around 70m from the main concentration.

The 'gold field' is situated on the lower slopes of the promontory of Ken Hill, a conspicuous feature in an otherwise low-lying landscape, which in the Iron Age would have reached out into the Wash. The hoard field itself is a plateau around 35m above sea level while, beyond, the southern terminal of Ken Hill rises up to a height of 42m. The hoard field is located on the sheltered inland side of the hill, sloping down towards what would have been an inlet from the Wash.

Hoards A to E were recovered during ploughing in the 1948–50, with additional finds made during subsequent excavations by Rainbird Clarke (Clarke 1954; Ch. 4). Hoard F was discovered by Charles Hodder whilst metal-detecting in August 1990, and it was this discovery which triggered the BM excavations. A narrative account of the excavation of the hoards is given by Stead (Ch. 2), and further excavation details are given in Part II of this volume.

The excavation methodology is described in Chapter 5. In summary, after Hoard F was recovered and recorded, a box scraper was brought onto site and used to strip the soil in

Table 8.1 Phase 3 features excavated 1990–2

Ex. year	Area	Feature	Type
1990	Area 4	Hoard F pit	Pit
1990	Area 1	Hoard G pit	Pit
1990	Area 1	Hoard H pit	Pit
1990	Area 2	Hoard J pit	Pit
1990	Area 6	Hoard K pit	Pit
1990	Area 9	Hoard L pit	Pit
1991	Area 18	Hoard N	Coin scatter

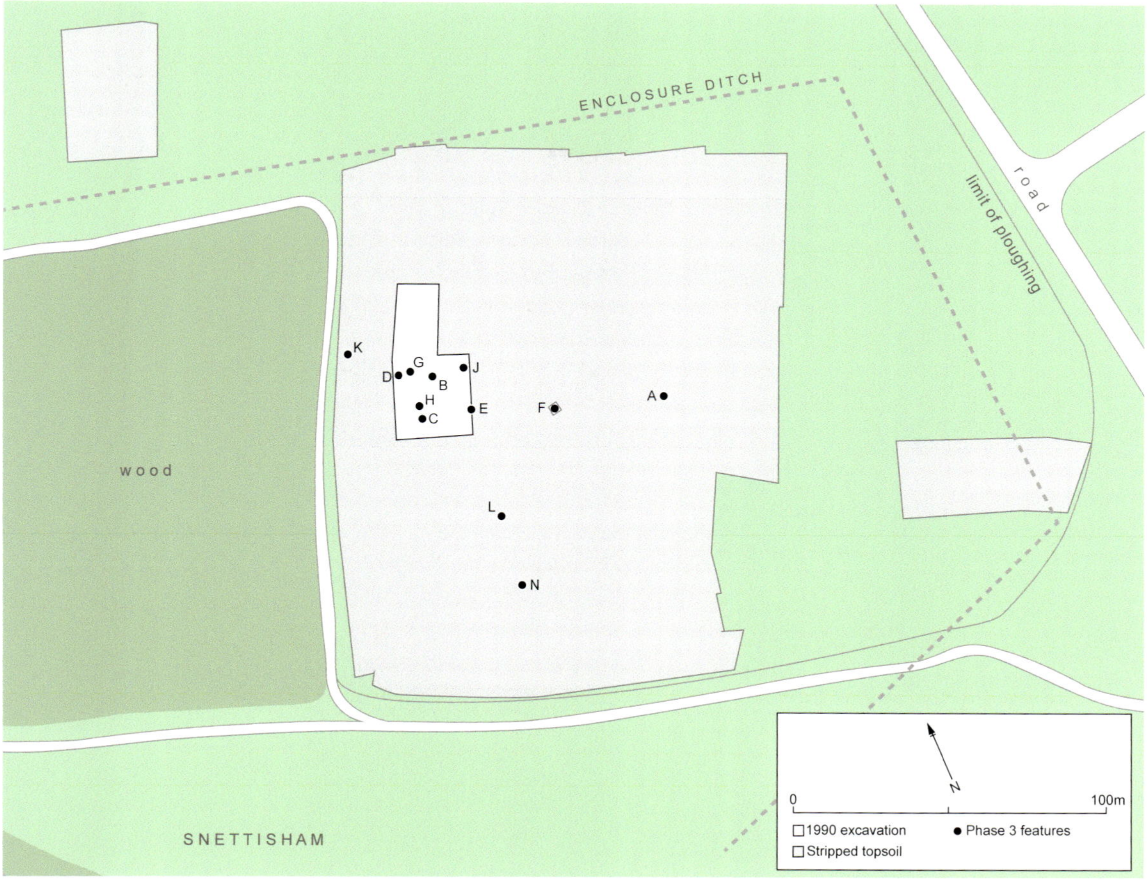

Figure 8.1 Location of Phase 3 features (Hoards A–L and N)

shallow spits. The sequence of stripping is shown in **Figure 1.4**. The first stripped areas were in the vicinity of known hoards, beginning with B and D, and the stripped area was gradually expanded to cover more of the field. This process was monitored by archaeologists, who also examined soil as it was deposited on the spoil heap. Hodder and Tony Pacitto used metal-detectors to scan the stripped surface, flagging any anomalies so that they could be investigated by the archaeologists. In this way, Hoards G to L were located; the coins forming Hoard N were also recovered by detecting. The hoard pits were excavated by hand, with the sequence of torcs carefully recorded as they were exposed and lifted (see Ch. 12).

Dating the hoards

Dating of the hoards (discussed more fully in Part II) is not straightforward. The majority of the Phase 3 hoards (A, D, G, H, J, K and L) contained only torcs and other ornaments/metalwork such as wrought rings of various sizes. Hoards B, C, E and F were torc hoards which also included coinage, and Hoard N was a dispersed coin hoard. The dating of the coins from Hoards B, C, E, F and N supports the idea that these hoards were more or less contemporary (Ch. 15). Hoard C contained potins, while the Hoard B, E, F and N coins are gold issues (F and N are Gallo-Belgic gold, B predominantly Gallo-Belgic gold with one insular gold quarter stater, and E a single insular gold quarter stater). The latest potins in Hoard C are dated by Holman (2016; Ch. 15) to *c.* 75/70–60/55 BC, with the composition of the assemblage suggesting that the hoard was deposited around 60 BC or shortly thereafter. The gold coins from Hoards B, E, F and N terminate with issues minted *c.* 80–60 BC (though note that some of these coins are relatively worn, and Sills tentatively dates the two insular gold issues from Hoards B and E to the period *c.* 60–50 BC, see Ch. 15). Gallo-Belgic E coins (the predominant gold coinage in circulation *c.* 60–50 BC) are, notably, absent from the hoards.

Organic material from two torcs was used to provide radiocarbon dates (**Table 5.2**; Garrow *et al.* 2009). The organic core (see Chs 17, 19) from one Hoard F torc fragment gave a date of 370–120 cal BC (at 95% probability). Given the associated coinage from Hoard F, some of the objects in the hoard were most likely over a century old at the time of burial. Likewise, two samples from an organic repair to torc L.6 were dated. One gave a surprisingly early date of 780–510 cal BC (at 95% probability), most likely an error, possibly due to conservation treatments (Garrow *et al.* 2009, 95). The other date (from an untreated fragment) was closely in line with the Hoard F sample, at 360–110 cal BC (at 95% probability). However, it is likely that the heavily repaired torc L.6 (like other very worn and damaged examples from Hoard L) was one of the older pieces in the hoard.

As no objects from the torc hoards can be securely dated to after *c.* 60 BC, this is taken as a likely terminal date for their deposition (see Ch. 22), and so for Phase 3. It is more difficult to establish the beginning of this phase. In terms of the types and styles of torcs represented, it is not possible to order the hoards chronologically. Aside from Hoard A, which contained exclusively large tubular torcs, the range of

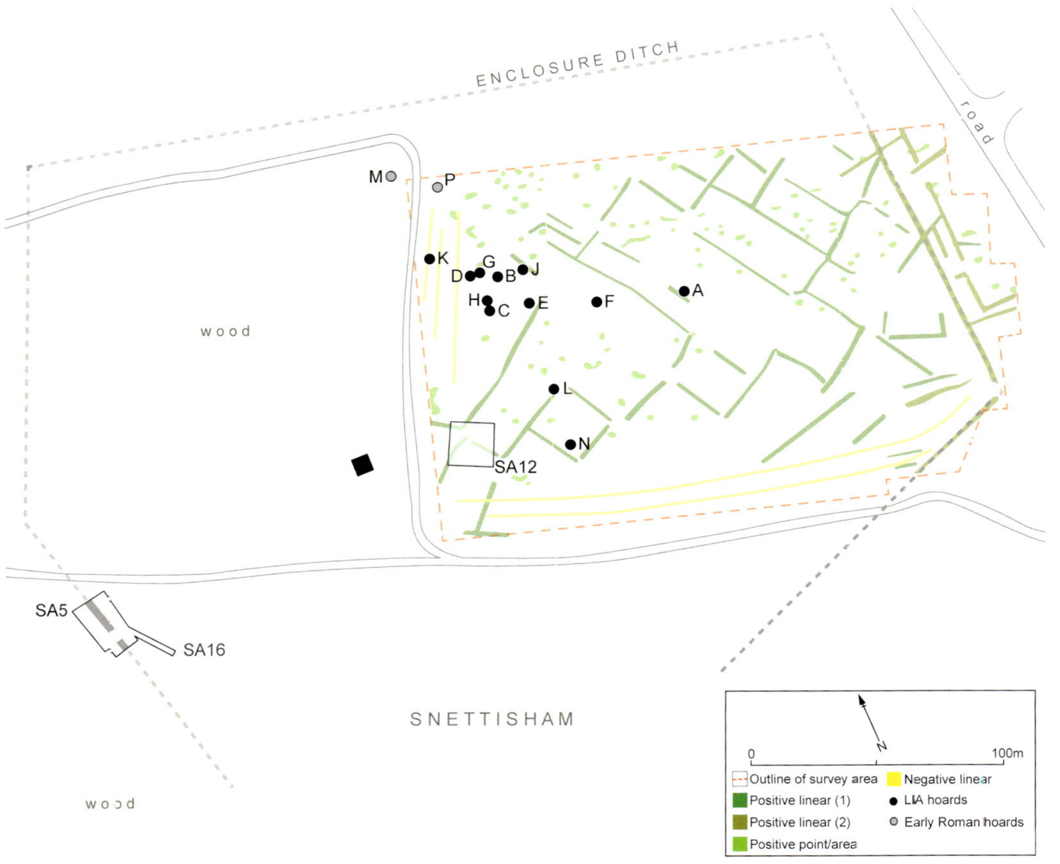

a)

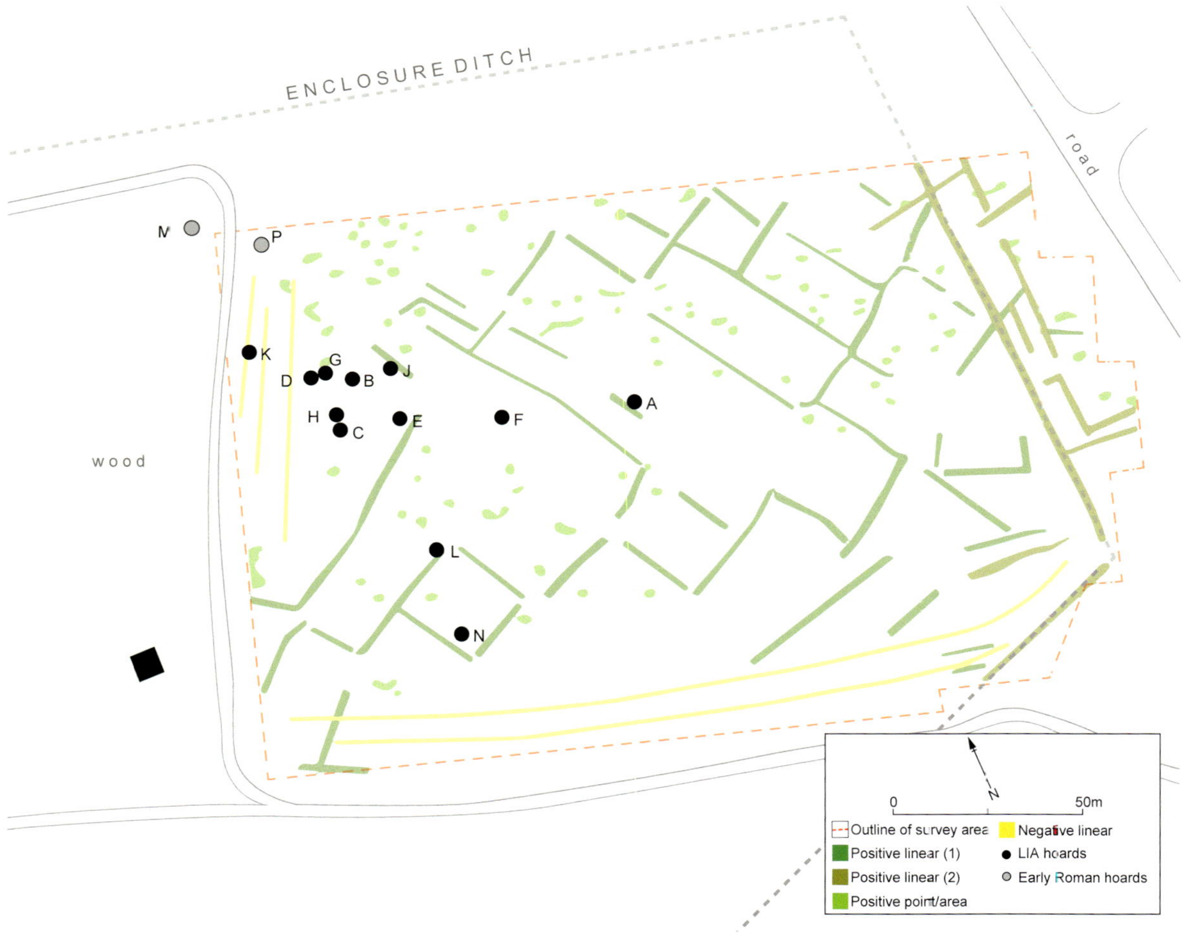

b)

Figure 8.2a–b Interpretation of processed results from fluxgate gradiometer survey in relation to (a) excavated features across the site including the entrance through to the enclosure ditch; (b) the hoard findspots

torcs contained within each hoard is broadly similar, and it is clear that many torcs were in circulation for a long time, perhaps many generations, before deposition (Ch. 20). Thus, the hoards could have been buried en masse over a relatively short length of time, or gradually over a much longer period. There could even have been decades between some of these deposits. Here, a date of *c.* 350 BC is cautiously offered as an indication of the earliest possible date of deposition for the hoards which cannot be given a *terminus post quem* through coinage (A, D, G, H, J, K and L), given the two radiocarbon dates of 370–110 cal BC for torcs with organic cores. Whilst gold and silver alloy torcs from Britain are generally stylistically dated to the 1st century BC (Ch. 22), it is likely, based on the radiocarbon dates from Snettisham and more recent finds such as the torc hoard from Leekfrith, Staffordshire (Farley *et al.* 2018) that such ornaments could well have been in production, use and circulation significantly earlier. However, the clustering of the latest dates for hoard coins in the mid-1st century BC (Hoards B, C, E, F and N) strongly suggests at the very least a peak of deposition at this time, even if some of the non-coin hoards could theoretically have been deposited significantly earlier. Whilst a cautious date range is given in this chapter for this phase of activity, the editors of this volume would advocate for a relatively narrow window of decades or even years for the deposition of the torc hoards, around or shortly after 60 BC.

Late Iron Age pottery

Sarah Percival

This section presents the Phase 3 pottery. For Methodology, see Chapter 6.

A small assemblage of 63 sherds of Late Iron Age pottery weighing 478g were collected, mostly as single or small numbers of sherds dispersed through unstratified contexts and a modern ditch (SA/HP, SA/HQ, SA/JK and SN/RD). A larger dump of 57 sherds, 389g, all from a single vessel in flint-tempered fabric, was recovered from Layer 1, the topmost fill of the Roman enclosure ditch (SA/BX). No diagnostic sherds survive. The small size of the sherds, which have a mean sherd weight of 6g, and the highly abraded condition suggest that they are re-deposited.

The only Phase 3 context to produce pottery was the fill of the Hoard K pit, which contained a small sherd of Earlier Iron Age pottery (SN/LH, 3g), almost certainly residual in this context.

The later prehistoric field system

Julia Farley, Jody Joy and Michael de Bootman

Geophysical survey carried out at Snettisham in 2006–9 (see Ch. 5) revealed a field system that may be contemporary with the Late Iron Age hoards. This is most likely part of a wider agricultural landscape; aerial photography and geophysical survey has identified cropmarks representing extensive systems of fields, droveways and enclosures along the area of the north-west Norfolk coast from Heacham to Dersingham (see **Fig. 3.7**). These farmsteads occupied the greensand belt, between the 10m and 35m OD contours, with the land sloping down towards the saltmarshes and fenland to the west, and rising up towards a chalk ridge in the east (Massey *et al.* 2003, 339; Brennand 2004). Massey *et al.* (*ibid.*) propose that the east–west droveways may have provided seasonal transhumance routes for moving stock between the uplands and the saltmarsh.

Most of these field systems have not been excavated, and so they remain hard to date, although they are generally assumed to be later prehistoric or early Roman. In the nearby Ingol valley, just to the south of Ken Hill, excavation of a similar field system revealed a Roman settlement with several phases of occupation and industrial activity, spanning from at least the 1st to 3rd centuries AD (Flitcroft 2001).

At Snettisham, some of the field system linears may have been encountered in Trench 12 in the 1992 excavations (see Ch. 5, **Fig. 5.11**), but no dateable material was found and they were interpreted at the time as natural features. Although geophysical survey was carried out in 1990–2, the technology available at the time was not sufficient to detect the features revealed in 2006–9, and thus the excavation team had little information to go on. Nevertheless, the work of de Bootman (Ch. 5) suggests that the field system is cut by the enclosure ditch which partially surrounds the area containing the hoards. Pottery finds from the BM 1990–2 excavations suggest that this ditch had begun to silt up from the mid-1st century to mid-2nd century AD, and there is no evidence that it was constructed significantly earlier (Ch. 9). Thus, the underlying field system most likely pre-dates the enclosure of the hoard field. It could be contemporary with Iron Age activity at the site, or even the Late Iron Age depositional activity. Overlaying de Bootman's geophysical survey data from the 'gold field' (Ch. 5) with the findspots of the Late Iron Age torc hoards (**Fig. 8.2a**) certainly suggests the tantalising possibility that the two may be contemporary, with the hoard findspots seeming to relate to the field system. Hoards B, C, D, E, G, H, K and J all appear to be contained within one rectilinear enclosure, clustered near the eastern corner (and possible entrance) to this defined area. Hoard F lies just to the east, around 20m beyond this possible entrance. Hoard A, around 30m east of Hoard F, and in a different enclosure, seems to be associated with a small linear feature. Hoards L and N appear at the north and south corners of a small square enclosed area just to the south of the main depositional area.

The field system may also have channelled movement across the site (**Fig. 8.2b**). Whilst we know very little about the way in which depositional activity and movement around the site was structured in the Late Iron Age (Phase 3), we can make some suggestions for the Early Roman period (Phase 4) (see **Fig. 8.2b**). The location of the entrance to the Phase 4 enclosure ditch and the siting of the possible Roman-Celtic temple structure indicate that people accessing the hoard field might have moved across the site from west to east, coming through the western entrance through the enclosure ditch and passing the square stone structure on their left. This route would lead straight to what appears to be a narrow entrance way in the field system (overlain by Trench SA12). This leads into the open area containing Hoard F. The small square enclosure containing Hoards L and N lies just to the right, and the enclosure containing most of the hoards is on the left. It is now hard to say whether this area, potentially a sacred precinct, extended further west or contained other features such as a shrine or grove.

Discussion

The most spectacular finds from the site date to the Later Iron Age, Phase 3 (*c.* 350–60 BC), the period which saw the deposition of the torc and coin hoards A, B, C, D, E, F, G, H, J, K, L and N. It is notable that some of these objects were ancient when they were deposited, their use perhaps even stretching back as far as the activities which led to the deposits of midden material at the site during Phase 2.

Aside from the hoard pits, no other features can be assigned to this period. The stray finds of metalwork and coins which date to this phase (see Part II, Chs 14–15) probably predominantly derive from hoard material dispersed by ploughing, other agricultural activity or animal burrowing.

The small quantities of Late Iron Age ceramics from the site are not sufficient to suggest any significant settlement activity, though it is likely that the enclosure or field system is contemporary with the Phase 3 hoards. Ken Hill was probably chosen as the location for these deposits due at least in part to its presence as a conspicuous natural feature in the landscape, perhaps one which had already become a focus for special activities in the Late Bronze Age and Earlier Iron Age (Phase 2, Ch. 7).

Whilst there are no hoards or features that can be securely dated to the second half of the first century BC, it is likely that depositional activity continued, albeit on a much smaller scale, between Phases 3 and 4. The analysis of stray finds of coins from the site (discussed in Ch. 15) suggests deposits of single coins and small hoards of local coinage over an extended period, with a slight peak around 10 BC, coinciding with the end of Norfolk Wolf B stater production (Talbot 2017, 100) and a wider peak in coin hoarding in East Anglia. The next major period of activity at the site falls in the 1st century AD.

Chapter 9
Phase 4: Latest Iron Age/ Early Roman (*c.* AD 1–200) and Phase 5: Late Roman (*c.* AD 350–400)

Julia Farley and Jody Joy, with contributions by Alice Lyons, Paul Craddock, Janet Lang, Caroline Cartwright and Alan Pipe

There was extensive activity at Snettisham in the Roman period, attested through both excavated features and stray finds. For the purposes of this volume, this is divided into two phases: Phase 4 comprises the Latest Iron Age and Early Roman period (*c.* AD 1–200), while Phase 5 falls in the Late Roman period (*c.* AD 350–400), when it seems that there was a significant change in the use of the site.

Phase 4 saw the deposition of two hoards: ingot hoard M (dated through radiocarbon dating) and the lost coin hoard P, dated through reconstruction of the coin composition. The activities identified through excavation which most likely fall into this phase are the digging of the large, polygonal, V-shaped ditch which partially encloses the 'gold field', and the construction of the stone-footed rectilinear structure in the wooded area to the west of hoards, excavated by Hutcheson in 2004 (Hutcheson 2011). The silting of the enclosure ditch is dated through analysis of the ceramic assemblage and radiocarbon dating of stratified bone, while the construction of the stone building is dated to the Romano-British period on the basis of analysis of the finds, which include coins and pottery.

Phase 5 saw the destruction of the stone structure (dated through a Late Roman coin found in a sealed destruction layer beneath a collapsed section of the wall) and the deliberate infilling of a stretch of the northern section of the enclosure ditch (dated through ceramic finds and radiocarbon dating of associated bone and charcoal).

This chapter presents detailed stratigraphic information on Phase 4–5 features from the 1990–2 BM excavations and summarises the results of the 2004 excavations in the wooded area to the west. It also includes specialist reports on finds from the BM excavation: Roman pottery, Roman ceramic building material, debris from iron production, the charcoal and animal bone from the enclosure ditch, and two shale objects that may date to the Romano-British period.

While short summaries of the two Phase 4 hoards are included below, the detailed catalogue entries for Roman-period metalwork and coins (both hoard and stray finds) are presented in Part II of this volume, which focuses on the Late Iron Age and Early Roman hoards.

Latest Iron Age and Roman features

Table 9.1 details the Phase 4–5 features excavated in 1990–2. **Figure 9.1** shows the location of these features on the site, alongside the Romano-British stone structure identified by Hutcheson (2011) during excavations in 2004 (plan shown in **Fig. 9.2**).

The Phase 4 hoards

Two hoards (M and P) date to Phase 4. Both were discovered by detectorists between the first and second seasons of the BM excavations (1990–1).

Hoard M, a group of six amorphous silver-copper alloy ingots, was found by Charles Hodder in March 1991, beneath a tree in the north-east corner of the wood. He reported the find to the BM team, but subsequent excavation of the findspot revealed no context for the hoard, nor any further finds. It is possible that they had been found in the field some time previously and re-deposited next to the tree. Charcoal lumps embedded in the ingots were

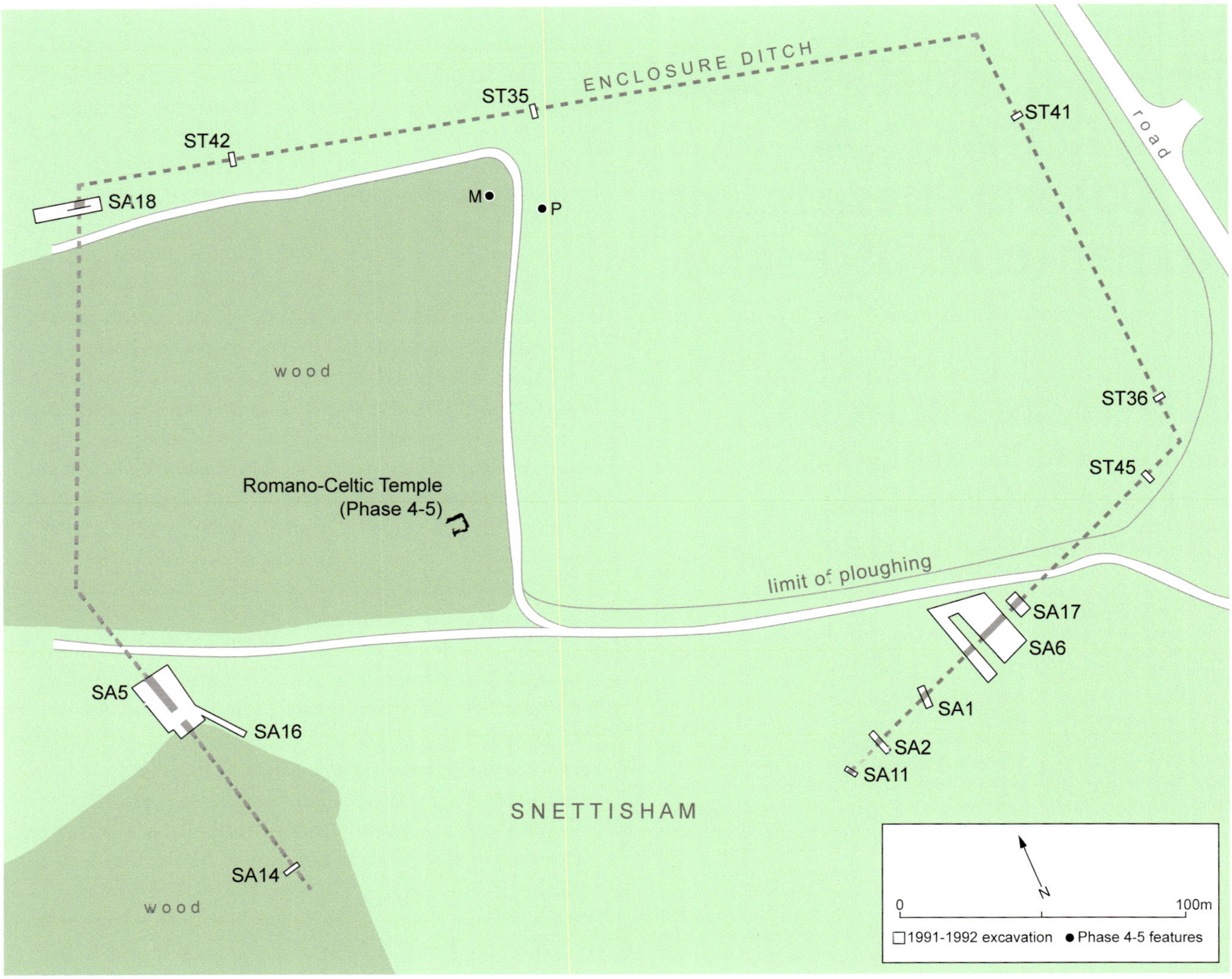

Figure 9.1 Plan showing location of Phase 4–5 features

Ex. year	Area	Feature	Type	Phase
1991	Wood	Hoard M	Metal-detector findspot	4
1990	?Area 21	Hoard P	Postulated metal-detector findspot	4
1991	Area 20	ST36	Enclosure ditch	4
1991	N/A	ST41	Enclosure ditch	4
1991	N/A	ST42	Enclosure ditch	4
1991	Area 20	ST45	Enclosure ditch	4
1992	Trench 1	SA1/2	Enclosure ditch	4
1992	Trench 2	SA2/2	Enclosure ditch	4
1992	Trench 5	SA5/2	Enclosure ditch	4
1992	Trench 6	SA6/2	Enclosure ditch	4
1992	Trench 11	SA11/2	Enclosure ditch	4
1992	Trench 17	SA17/2	Enclosure ditch	4
1992	Trench 18	SA18/2	Enclosure ditch	4
1992	Trench 14	SA14/2	?Enclosure ditch	?4
1991	Area 21	ST35	Enclosure ditch	4/5

Table 9.1 Phase 4–5 features from the 1990–2 excavations

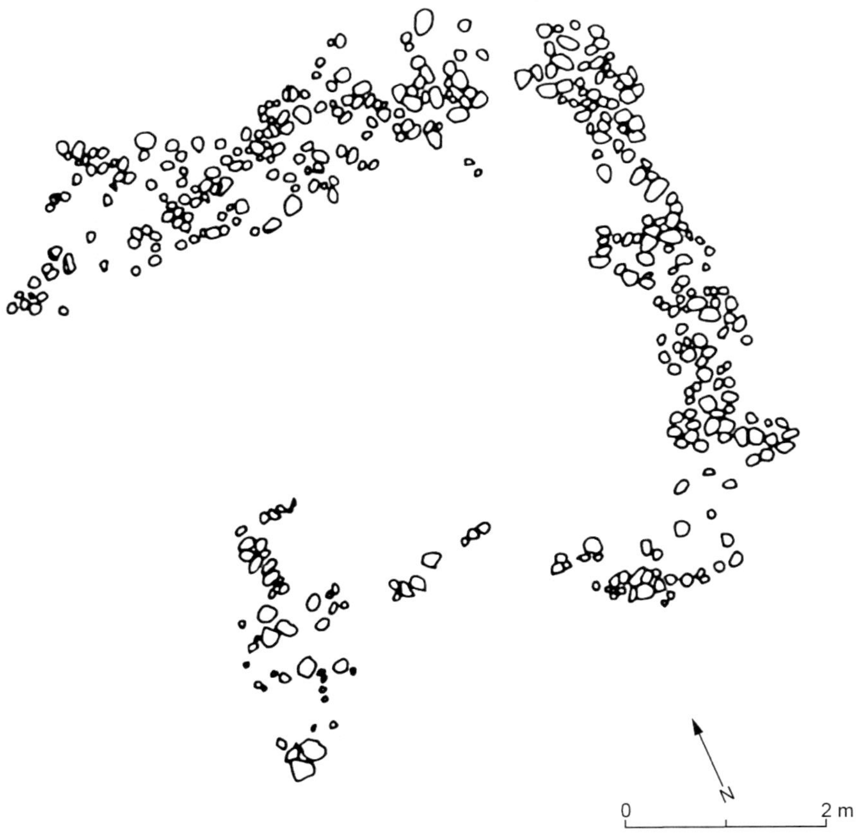

Figure 9.2 Plan of the square structure in the wood, after Hutcheson 2011

radiocarbon dated (**Table 5.2**; Garrow *et al.* 2009), giving a calibrated radiocarbon date of 20–210 cal AD (at 95% probability), with the bulk of the probability lying within the range 30–130 cal AD (at 68% confidence). It should be noted that the charcoal sampled was old alder wood, so the actual date of the hoard is likely to be somewhat later. Here it is assigned to Phase 4 (*c.* AD 1–200).

Hoard P, around 6,000 Iron Age silver coins buried in a silver bowl, along with other objects including precious metal ingots, was stolen by illicit detectorists operating on the site without permission. Stead (Ch. 2) suggests that it was located under the spoil heap of the 1990 excavations, in the north-west corner of the hoard field. Fragments from a silver vessel (P.1–7) were recovered from this area in 1991 when it was stripped in advance of archaeological excavation, most likely the last remnants of the hoard. Based on reconstruction of the coin assemblage from Celtic Coin Index records and contemporary sales catalogues (Ch. 15, Chadburn 2006; de Jersey 2014, no. 196.6; Talbot 2017, 223–4), it consisted predominantly of local silver issues, and was most likely deposited in the mid-1st century AD, probably around AD 60.

The full details of these hoard finds are given with the metalwork and coin catalogues in Part II of this volume.

Other features

Aside from the hoard findspots, there are two other archaeological features which likely date to Phases 4–5: the small rectilinear structure excavated by Hutcheson in 2004, and the enclosure ditch uncovered by Stead's excavations (Ch. 2).

Rectilinear structure

Excavations were carried out in the south-west corner of the wooded area just to the west of the 'gold field' in 2004 by Natasha Hutcheson, after metal detectorists surveying the site with permission of the landowner revealed the footings of a stone wall. Site conditions were extremely challenging, largely due to the extent of tree cover. An area of approximately 8 x 8m was cleared, revealing the outline of a square stone structure, *c.* 6 x 6m (**Fig. 9.2**, Hutcheson 2011). This small building was located directly opposite the entranceway to the polygonal enclosure (**Fig. 9.1**). Test pitting revealed no obvious stratigraphy within the interior. Trenches were opened to investigate the exterior of the structure, and two slots were dug across the walls. These revealed 'a shallow Carstone foundation built onto the natural Carstone geology' (*ibid.*, 43). Hutcheson proposed that the upper parts of the walls were most likely wooden.

Given the small scale of the excavation, a relatively large quantity of finds was recovered. This included an assemblage of small and abraded pottery sherds covering the period from the 3rd century BC to 3rd century AD (with a notable absence of Late Roman finewares), nine Iron Age and Roman coins, two small gold alloy lumps, animal bone and oyster shell. Structural debris included *tesserae*, fragments of dark-purple painted wall plaster, roof tiles, lumps of mortar, and other likely Romano-British-period ceramic building materials. Romano-British *tegulae* and a fragment of flue tile were also recovered from the wood as stray finds during the 1990–2 and earlier excavations (Chs 2, 4 and see below), supporting the idea that there was a structure in the vicinity.

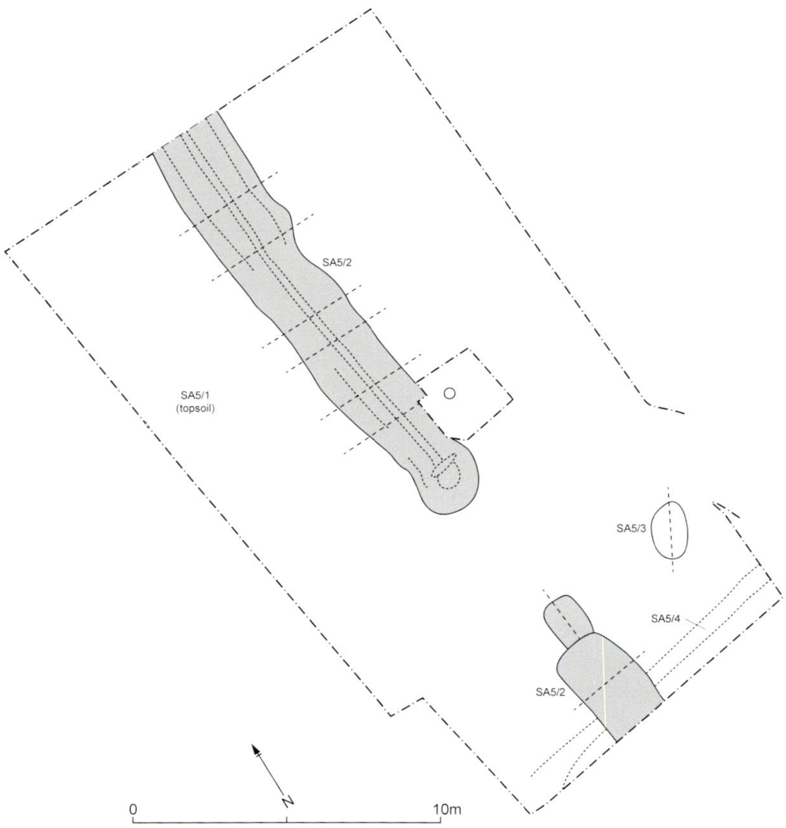

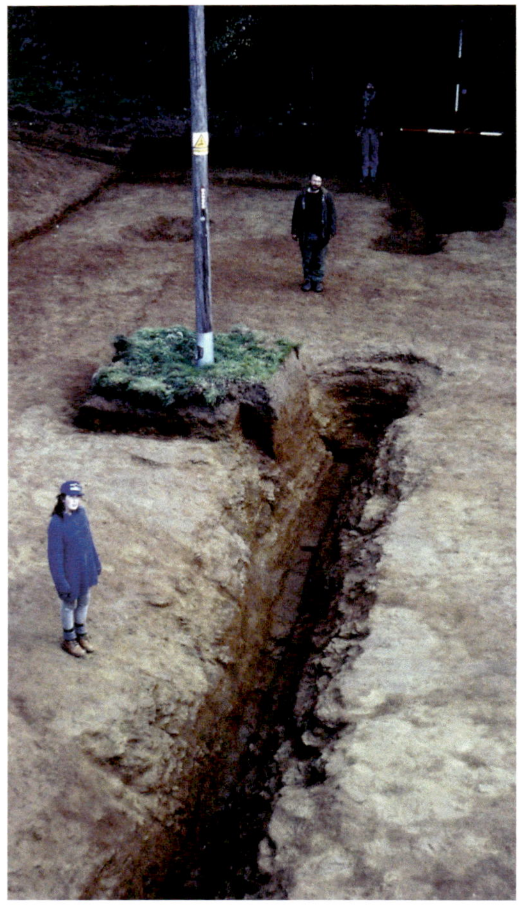

Figure 9.3 (above) Plan of the enclosure ditch entranceway in Trench 5

Figure 9.4 (right) Aerial view of the enclosure ditch entrance in Trench 5, looking south

Hutcheson (2011, 45) interpreted the square building as a Romano-Celtic temple with 'mosaic floor, painted plaster walls and a tiled roof'. Beyond the broad Romano-British date suggested by the structural evidence, the date of construction cannot be ascertained with certainty. However, the excavations uncovered a Late Roman coin dating to *c.* AD 350–360 under tumble from the north wall of the structure, providing a *terminus post quem* for the destruction of the building (Hutcheson 2011, 44). She posited that the structure might have been deliberately destroyed in the later 4th century, and it certainly appears that changes were taking place at the site around this time (see below).

The enclosure ditch

The main archaeological feature from Phases 4–5, uncovered in 1991–2, is the polygonal enclosure ditch which partially surrounds the hoard field on three sides (to the west, north and east, **Fig. 9.1**). The relevant trenches, slots and areas are listed in **Table 9.1**. The only entrance discovered was in Trench 5, in the south-west corner of the site (**Figs 9.3–4**). Despite attempts to uncover any southern side to the ditch, none could be located. On the south-west side, the ditch continued past the entrance and was seemingly identified in Trench 14 (though with a very different, shallower profile, see bottom right image in **Fig.**

Figure 9.5a Section through the enclosure ditch SA5/2

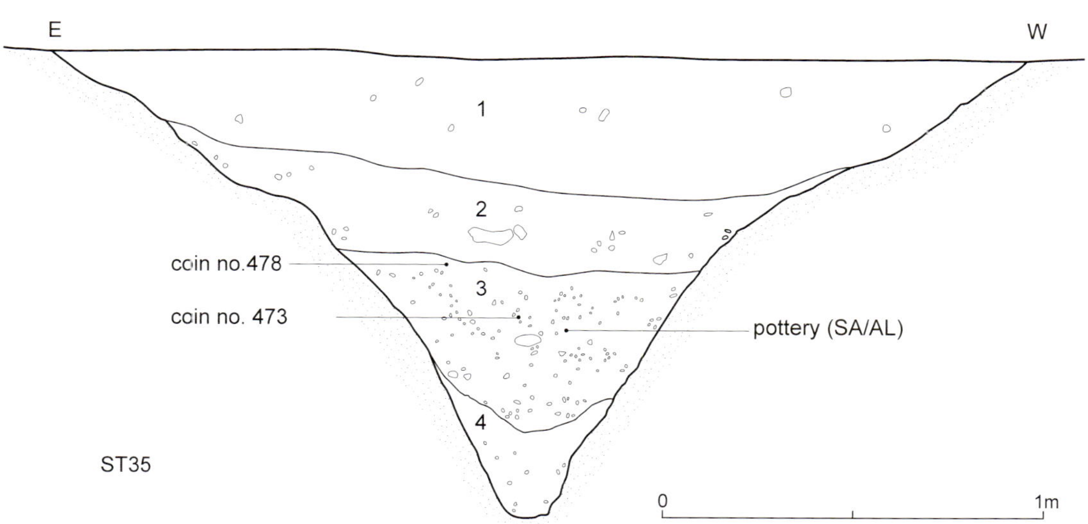

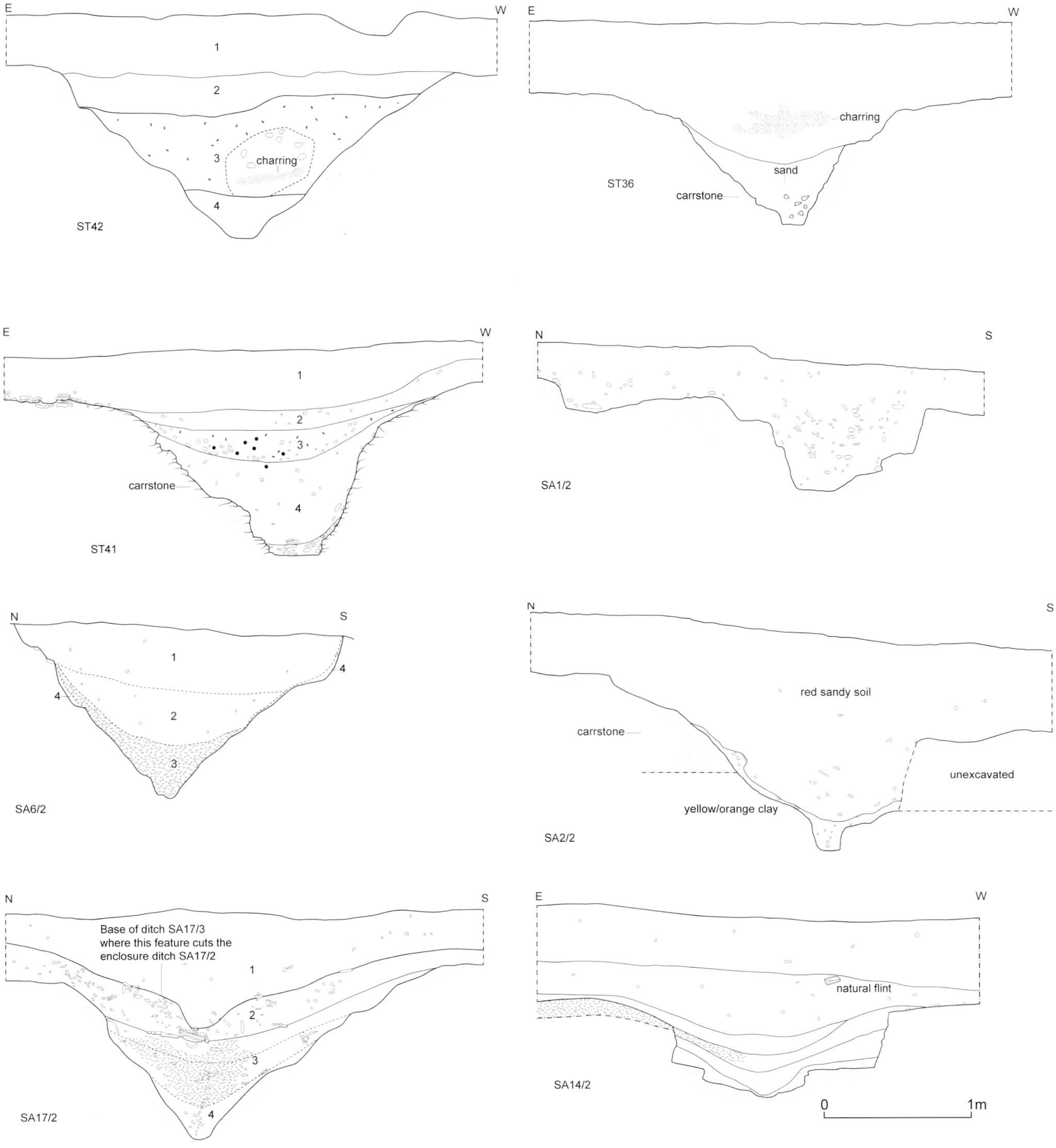

Figure 9.5b Sections through the enclosure ditch: ST36, ST41, ST42, SA1/2, SA2/2, SA6/2, SA17/2 and SA14/2

9.5b). It appeared to peter out around the edge of the carrstone, ending at the springline. To the south-east, the ditch extended downhill beyond the plateau, rather than following the contour line. Its terminus could not be precisely located, but most likely lay under a poplar tree directly between Trenches 11 and 19. All the evidence suggests that in antiquity the south side of the enclosure was open or bounded by a natural barrier (such as trees or hedges) which have left no archaeological trace. On this side, the land slopes down towards what would have been marshland, bordering an inlet from the Wash.

The enclosure ditch was about 2.3–2.8m wide at the base of the plough soil, and 1.5–1.8m below the present ground surface, cut around 1.2–1.4m deep into the carrstone. In most areas the ditch had a steep-sided, V-shaped profile with a narrow, flat channel at the bottom (**Fig. 9.5a–b**). **Figure 9.3** shows a plan of the entranceway in Trench 5, and a photograph is shown in **Figure 9.4**. A large area was stripped of topsoil, but there was no evidence of any gateway structure, post holes or a palisade trench, nor any metalling or wheel ruts in the 6m-wide causeway between the terminals of the ditch.

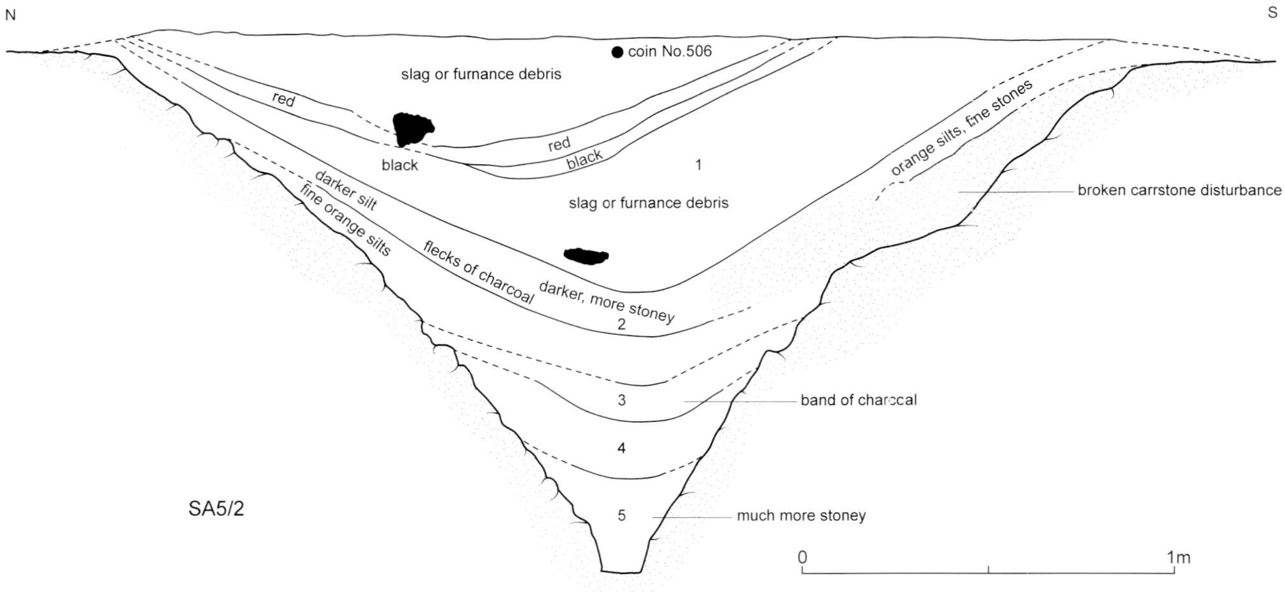

Figure 9.6 Section through the enclosure ditch at ST35

The function of the form of the deep, V-cut ditch is unclear. There is no surviving evidence for structures or a palisade, though it is possible that plants or light wooden structures could have been used to create a more imposing barrier. No surviving bank material was uncovered anywhere around the circumference, except in Trench 17. Here, the east section through the enclosure ditch (**Fig. 9.5b**) showed that in Layer 2 (see below) it had been infilled with quite large pieces of carrstone, perhaps from the levelling of a bank, in which case the bank must have been on the inside of the ditch. Otherwise, in most areas the sequence of silting and infilling seems to have been similar around the circuit.

Dating the enclosure ditch

Figure 9.5a–b shows sections through the enclosure ditch. Most areas, including trenches ST41, ST42, SA5, SA6 and SA17 (see **Fig. 9.5a** and left-hand side of **Fig. 9.5b**), were interpreted on-site as showing a sequence of four fills:

- Layer 1: Upper fill of reddish sandy soil with few pebbles. Roots often present
- Layer 2: Sandy soil with a higher frequency of stones, in some areas intermixed with grey or yellow sand
- Layer 3: Gravelly and coarse sandy fill
- Layer 4: Primary silting of the ditch: sandy, lighter in colour, few stones.

Towards the ends of the identified run of the ditch on the south side of the site, and in the south-east corner of the enclosure (Trenches ST36, ST45, SA1, SA2 and SA14), a shallower and simpler profile was recognised (right-hand-side of **Fig. 9.5b**). Only one other section, ST35 (**Fig. 9.6**), showed a significantly different pattern in the upper fill. The layers observed in ST35 were:

- Layer 1: Compact upper fill of slag and furnace debris, with lenses of charcoal
- Layer 2: Dark silty soil, stony, with flecks of charcoal, thin layer of fine orange silt at base. Carrstone rubble on the south side may be the remains of a slumped or levelled bank
- Layer 3: Gravelly and coarse dark sandy fill, no finds
- Layer 4: Primary silting of the ditch: orange sand, very few stones, Roman pot sherds ST/GE at the top of this layer
- Layer 5: Stony rubble, perhaps natural decayed carrstone.

Whilst ST35 Layers 3 and 4 are similar to those observed elsewhere, the unusual nature of Layers 1 and 2 suggest that in this area there was a phase of deliberate infilling towards the end of the Roman period (see below).

Table 9.2 lists finds from the enclosure ditch by layer (where this was recorded – the layer was not recorded for finds from ST45 and Trenches 1, 14 and 18 where, as discussed above, the stratigraphy was notably simpler). Where possible, stratified animal bone or charcoal was radiocarbon dated (see below and **Table 5.3**); a brief overview of the results is given in **Table 9.3**.

Residual flint occurred throughout. The only other find type from the primary silting (Layer 4) was a small quantity of Roman pottery (see below for full discussion). Some are types which cannot be closely dated within the Roman period (SA/AY; ST/FY). All of those which can be more closely dated are from the later 1st to mid-2nd century: ST/GE (*c.* AD 70–120); SA/BQ (*c.* AD 65–85); SA/BM (*c.* AD 90–160); SA/CA (late 1st to mid-2nd century). The latest may be ST/GB which has a potentially wide date range (mid-2nd to 4th century) though still beginning in the mid-2nd century AD. No datable organic remains were recovered from this primary silting layer, and so it was not possible to include this layer in the radiocarbon dating programme. Nevertheless, the Roman pottery from the mid-1st to mid-2nd centuries AD provides a *terminus post quem* for the silting of the ditch, and there is no evidence that it was constructed significantly earlier. There are some ceramic joins between layers 3 and 4, for example a Sandy Grey ware jar of a form dating to *c.* AD

Feature	Flint	Pre pot	RB pot	RB CBM	Animal bone	Charcoal	IA/RB metalwork	IA coin	RB coin	Furnace debris	Med/PM pot	Latest datable finds (AD)
ST36, Layer 1	-	-	x	-	-	-	-	-	-	-	x	Med/PM
ST41, Layer 1	x	-	-	-	-	-	-	-	-	-	x	Med/PM
ST42, Layer 1	x	-	-	-	x	-	-	-	-	-	-	Not closely datable
SA5/2, Layer 1	x	-	x	x	x	-	-	-	-	-	x	Med/PM
SA6/2, Layer 1	x	x	x	-	-	-	x (S.244)	-	-	-	-	mid-2nd C
SA17/2, Layer 1	x*	x	x	-	-	-	-	-	-	-	-	4th C
ST35, Layer 1	x	-	x	x	x	x	-	-	x (Cat. no. 506)	x	-	early 5th C
ST41, Layer 2	x	-	x	-	-	-	-	-	-	-	-	Not closely datable
ST42, Layer 2	-	-	x	-	-	x	-	-	-	-	-	Not closely datable
SA5/2, Layer 2	x	x	-	-	x	-	-	-	-	-	-	Not closely datable
SA6/2, Layer 2	x	x	-	x	x	-	-	-	-	-	-	Not closely datable
ST35, Layer 2	x	-	x	x	x	x	-	-	-	x	-	early 4th C
ST41, Layer 3	x	-	x	-	-	-	-	-	-	-	-	2nd C
SA5/2, Layer 3	x	x	x	x	x	-	-	-	x (Cat. nos 471, 472, 473, 478)	-	-	mid-2nd C (pot) 4th C (coins)
SA6/2, Layer 3	x	-	x	-	x	-	-	-	-	-	-	mid-2nd C
ST41, Layer 4	x	-	x	-	-	-	-	-	-	-	-	Not closely datable
ST42, Layer 4	-	-	x	-	-	-	-	-	-	-	-	Not closely datable
SA5/2, Layer 4	x	-	x	-	-	-	-	-	-	-	-	late 1st C–mid-2nd C
SA6/2, Layer 4	-	-	x	-	-	-	-	-	-	-	-	late 1st C–mid-2nd C
ST35, Layer 4	-	-	x	-	-	-	-	-	-	-	-	late 1st C–mid-2nd C

Table 9.2 Finds from enclosure ditch contexts by layer (contexts which produced no finds or where layer was not recorded, are omitted) (Abbreviations: CBM = ceramic building materials; IA = Iron Age; Med/PM = medieval or post-medieval; pot = pottery; Pre= Prehistoric; RB = Romano-British; * = flint not located at time of publication)

60–120 is represented in joining sherds from both SA/BQ (layer 4) and SA/BK (layer 3). This suggests that there was not a large gap of time between the primary silting and further gradual backfilling or silting of the ditches.

Layer 3 contained a far wider range of find types, predominantly Romano-British pottery dating from the mid-1st to 2nd centuries. Four 4th-century Roman coins (Cat. nos 471, 472, 473, 478) were found in level 3 of the enclosure ditch in Trench 5, see **Fig. 9.5a**, perhaps suggesting that the ditches were still open to this level at this time. This is supported by the only radiocarbon date from Layer 3 (SA/BT, **Table 9.3**), which suggests a 3rd to mid-4th-century date is most likely for the animal bone tested.

Layer 2 produced very little closely datable material, apart from Section ST35 which, as mentioned above, is an unusual case. Charcoal and animal bone gave radiocarbon dates spanning the mid-2nd to mid-5th centuries at the 95% confidence level, with a date range from the mid-3rd to early 5th century AD most likely. Whilst levels 3 and 4 are generally consistent with gradual silting of the ditch from the later-1st to mid-2nd centuries, Layer 2 shows signs of intentional backfilling in some areas. In Trench 17 there seems to be a dump of carrstone into the inner side of the

Sample type	Site code	Context	Date ranges at 95.4% probability
Charcoal	ST/DY	ST35, enclosure ditch, Layer 1	332–430 cal AD (92.1%); 493–510 cal AD (2.2%); 519–528 cal AD (1.1%)
Animal bone	ST/DY	ST35, enclosure ditch, Layer 1	263–275 cal AD (1.5%); 330–430 cal AD (90.8%); 494–510 cal AD (2.1%); 519–528 cal AD (1.0%)
Charcoal	ST/HL	ST42, enclosure ditch, Layer 2	255–302 cal AD (22.7%); 316–402 cal AD (72.7%)
Animal bone	SA/AK	SA5/2, enclosure ditch, Layer 2	257–297 cal AD (15.5%); 320–410 cal AD (79.9%)
Animal bone	SA/CO	SA6/2, enclosure ditch, Layer 2	128–258 cal AD (89.5%); 296–322 cal AD (5.9%)
Charcoal	ST/EZ	ST35, enclosure ditch, Layer 2	263–275 cal AD (2.7%); 330–423 cal AD (92.7%)
Animal bone	ST/EZ	ST35, enclosure ditch, Layer 2	140–198 cal AD (12.9%); 208–336 cal AD (82.5%)
Animal bone	SA/BT	SA6/2, enclosure ditch, Layer 3	141–197 cal AD (7.5%); 208–344 cal AD (87.9%)

Table 9.3 Radiocarbon dates from the enclosure ditch contexts by layer (for full details see Table 5.3)

ditch at the base of Layer 2, suggesting that an inner bank may have collapsed or been destroyed. The broken carrstone which makes up the south side of Layer 2 in ST35 may also be the remains of a slumped bank (although this could also have been caused by animal disturbance).

As well as the possible demolishing of the bank, ST35 was deliberately infilled with a large compact mass of slag and furnace debris, dumped from the south side (Layer 1, **Fig. 9.6**). This infilling was carried out along a stretch of ditch extending around 20m and was probably intended to provide a broad causeway giving entrance across the ditch on the north side. The top of this slag layer was truncated by the plough soil, so the surface of the causeway has not survived. The deposition of the slag was dated by Roman pottery, including sherds of Oxford ware dating no earlier than AD 350, and possibly as late as the early 5th century AD (ST/DN, ST/DY, ST/EZ). These were the latest fragments of Roman pottery from the site. An undated but most likely Roman coin (Cat. no. 506) was recovered from the top of the slag. Radiocarbon dates (**Tables 5.3**, **9.3**) support a date range of the mid-4th to mid-5th century AD for the infilling of the upper levels of the ditch in Trench ST35 (the charcoal dates should be considered more reliable than the heavily abraded animal bone, since the latter is more likely to be residual; all the charcoal samples for radiocarbon dating were identified by Caroline Cartwright (see below) as young roundwood <10 years old, and were found in the dumps of furnace debris). The date for the charcoal from ST/DY is cal AD 260–540 at 95% confidence, but the bulk of the probability is concentrated in the range 332–430 cal AD at 92.1% confidence).

Elsewhere, beyond ST35, the uppermost layer of the enclosure ditch (Layer 1) contained a very wide variety of finds including, in some cases, post-medieval pottery. In some areas it may have been disturbed by deep ploughing. The only other stratified metalwork came from this layer: a Late Iron Age brooch fragment from Layer 1 in SA6/2 (S.244). An Iron Age gold coin (Cat. no. 244) was also found in the upper fill of the enclosure ditch in ST45, most likely disturbed from the central area of the field.

It is notable that there is very little handmade Middle or Late Iron Age pottery from the enclosure ditch. Prehistoric pottery, presumably residual as it is highly abraded and, in some cases, overlies Roman pottery, was generally only recovered from the enclosure ditch in Trenches 6 and 17, and only in the upper Layers 1 and 2. These are slightly downhill from the main field, in the south-east corner of the site. The pottery in Layer 1 could have been introduced by deep ploughing (which ran NW to SE across the site), and that in Layer 2 perhaps through natural downhill spread of disturbed material. The only exception is an abraded Early Iron Age sherd (SA/AV) in Layer 3 in Trench 5, which must certainly be residual, since it occurs alongside 4th-century material (**Table 9.2**).

Overall, the evidence suggests that the enclosure was dug at the earliest in the mid-1st century, most likely after *c.* AD 100. Subsequent silting leading to the deposition of small quantities of mid-1st to mid-2nd-century AD Roman pottery towards the base of the ditch. There is relatively little evidence for 1st-century AD activity at the site, with small quantities of pottery, and only Hoards M (potentially) and P likely dating to this period. The enclosure ditch seems to have remained open as late as the 4th century AD, when it appears that in some areas there were deliberate attempts to backfill it. This is most noticeable in ST35, on the north side of the enclosure, where a dump of animal bone and furnace debris was used to create a new causeway across the ditch. Like the destruction of the square structure in the wooded area (Hutcheson 2011, 44) this deliberate infilling most likely dates to around the mid-4th to early 5th century AD. This points to deliberate re-purposing of the site around this time.

Roman pottery

Alice Lyons, based on an earlier report by Val Rigby

Introduction

A total of 267 Roman pottery sherds, weighing 4,045g (7.46 Estimated Vessel Equivalent (EVE)) were recovered during

Fabric number: description	Vessel forms	Count	Weight (g)	EVE	Weight (%)	EVE (%)
1: Sandy Grey wares	Beaker (folded), bowl, carinated jar, dish (flanged), flagon, jar (lid-seated), lid, storage jar, spindle whorl	220	3,151	5.67	77.90	76.00
2: Miscellaneous Coarse wares	Beaker, bowl, dish, flagon, jar, platter	23	261	0.85	6.45	11.39
3: Lower Nene Valley Grey ware	Flanged dish, necked jar	5	204	0.52	5.04	6.97
4: Colchester Colour-coated ware	Cup	1	1	0.00	0.02	0.00
5: Lower Nene Valley Colour-coat ware	Beaker, box lid, flagon, flanged dish, jar	10	173	0.33	4.28	4.42
6: Oxford Red-slipped ware	Bowl	2	19	0.00	0.47	0.00
7: Hadham Oxidised ware	Cordoned jar	2	13	0.02	0.32	0.28
8: Sandy Buff ware	Mortaria	2	153	0.07	3.78	0.94
9: Sandy Oxidised ware	Mortaria	1	49	0.00	1.22	0.00
10: Lower Nene Valley White ware	Mortaria	1	21	0.00	0.52	0.00
Total		**267**	**4,045**	**7.46**	**100.00**	**100.00**

Table 9.4 The Roman pottery assemblage, listed by fabric number

excavations at Ken Hill. This represents a minimum of 113 individual vessels. The majority of this pottery assemblage was recovered from the enclosure ditch, whose primary fills contain early to mid-Roman pottery. Latterly a large metalworking debris deposit, which contained diagnostically late (mid-4th +) Roman pottery, was laid to form a causeway across the enclosure.

In contrast to the large, well-preserved later prehistoric assemblage (see Chs 6–8) the Roman pottery is small and fragmentary. With the exception of the illustrated vessels, most pots are represented by just one worn sherd and even the more complete vessels show marked evidence of weathering. Generally, the assemblage is severely abraded with little or no original surface finish surviving, with an average sherd weight of 15g.

The abraded character of Roman pottery found at Snettisham has been noted previously (Flitcroft 2001, 65–6; Hutcheson 2011, 44) and indicates that this material has been exposed to significant post-depositional disturbance, probably during the middening process and possibly also by the plough; this pottery should therefore be considered residual or at least not deliberately deposited.

Methodology

The late Val Rigby undertook the initial analysis and wrote a draft report directly after excavations were completed in 1992; this work was reviewed and developed (at Val's request) by Alice Lyons in 2019.

The pottery was re-evaluated following the national guidelines (Barclay *et al.* 2016). The total assemblage was studied, and a catalogue was prepared (in archive). The sherds were examined using a hand lens (x10 magnification) and were divided into fabric groups defined based on inclusion types present. The sherds were counted and weighed to the nearest whole gram and recorded by context. Decoration, residues and abrasion were also noted. Vessel forms (jar, bowl) were also recorded although no overall typology was possible due to the fragmentary condition of the sherds. In lieu of a typology the most complete vessels from stratified deposits were selected for illustration to provide a visual characterisation of the assemblage. Parallels for fabrics and forms have been referenced from local excavations (Flitcroft 2001; Lyons 2004) and the National Roman Fabric Reference Collection (Tomber and Dore 1998). The BM curates the archive.

The pottery

A total of 10 broad fabrics were identified (**Table 9.4**).

Coarse wares

Fabric 1: Sandy Grey wares

The majority of the assemblage (80% by weight) comprises locally produced utilitarian Sandy Grey (reduced) wares. No kilns were found during this excavation, but local contemporary coarse ware manufacture has been previously recorded elsewhere in Snettisham village (Lyons 2004, 32–41). This fabric was mainly used for jar/bowl and storage jars, although a small number of beakers and flagons were identified, and also a complete conical spindle whorl. Within this broad group it was possible to isolate several distinctive subgroups (Fabrics 1a–1d), which are characterised briefly below (**Table 9.5**).

Fabric 1a: Early Roman Sandy Grey ware

These Early Roman jar/bowl forms combine handmade and wheel-throwing techniques with hand-shaped bases and wheel-finished shoulder, rim and external finish. The fabrics are fine, sandy and have a red/brown core and dark-grey to black surfaces. The firing temperature was low with damp smoke-producing fuel being added after the initial period of oxidation. Date: AD 70–120.

Fabric 1b: Black-slipped Sandy Grey ware

This fabric is similar to 1a, probably using the same local clay source. It was primarily used to produce necked jars, some of which were lid-seated, and also shallow dishes or platters and one example of a folded beaker. The wheel-thrown vessels were fired at a higher temperature, with a grey core and dark-grey to black surfaces. Date: AD 70–150.

Fabric 1c: Coarse Sandy Grey ware

Again, this fabric originated from the same local clay source, but was mainly used for the manufacture of large storage

Fabric number: description	Vessel forms	Count	Weight (g)	EVE
1: Sandy Grey wares	Beaker (folded), bowl, flagon, jar (lid-seated; carinated), lid, storage jar, spindle whorl	87	777	1.92
1a: Early Roman Sandy Grey ware	Bowl, necked jar	30	150	0.65
1b: Black-slipped Sandy Grey ware	Beaker (folded), necked jar (lid-seated), platter	37	404	1.23
1c: Coarse Sandy Grey ware	Dish (flanged), jar, storage jar	14	652	0.57
1d: Sandy Grey ware with argillaceous pellets	Beaker (carinated), dish, jar, necked bowl, lid	52	1168	1.30
Total		**220**	**3,151**	**5.67**

Table 9.5 The Sandy Grey ware fabrics, listed in numerical order

jars so the clay was heavily tempered with coarser sand, argillaceous pellets and carrstone fragments of between 1mm and 5mm. Date: 2nd century AD.

Fabric 1d: Sandy Grey ware with argillaceous pellets
This distinctive Sandy Grey ware fabric contains common argillaceous pellets as a natural component of the clay body. Most sherds are from a large necked bowl, but a carinated beaker, jar and dish/lid pieces were also found. These vessels are wheel-thrown and kiln-fired, with a light grey-buff core with darker blue-grey surfaces. This fabric has been previously identified in south Norfolk (Lyons and Tester 2014: VGW) and also to the north in Lincolnshire (Stead 1976, 136–53) which suggests a similar clay source was exploited along a large part of the English east coast. Date: early to mid-2nd century AD.

Fabric 2: Miscellaneous Coarse wares
Various undifferentiated reduced and oxidised wheel-thrown sand-tempered kiln-fired grey wares are included here. The sherds are too small and abraded for classification.

Fabric 3: Lower Nene Valley Grey ware (Perrin 1999, 78–87)
Sand-tempered white ware with pale blue-grey metallic surfaces, the exterior highly burnished in zones. Two vessels identified: a flanged dish with incised scroll on the flange and a large necked jar. Date: late 2nd to early 4th century AD.

Fine wares

Fine wares are poorly represented within the assemblage; notably no Gaulish samian (Tomber and Dore 1998, 25–41) was found. This absence, however, is typical of outlying minor settlements anywhere within Roman Britain as its consumption was concentrated at major foci where inhabitants had access to markets and surplus income to spend on luxury goods. In this particular case, it is also possible that scavengers removed any samian from accumulated rubbish for trimming and re-use before it was dumped on the site. The remaining fine ware assemblage, although small, proves a connectiveness beyond the local economy with a particularly strong affinity with the large Lower Nene Valley manufacturing centre located at *Durobrivae* (Water Newton near Peterborough), *c.* 60km south-west of Snettisham on the western fen edge.

Fabric 4: Colchester Colour-coated ware (Tomber and Dore 1998, COL CC 1, 132)
A smooth buff fabric with a buff-coloured slip produced in Colchester, Essex. Found in the form of a CAM 62 cup. Date: pre-AD 79 (pre-Flavian).

Fabric 5: Lower Nene Valley Colour-coated ware (Tomber and Dore 1998, LNV CC, 118)
This pale fabric consistently decorated with an iron-rich orange-brown slip was found in a range of vessel forms including beakers (late 2nd–mid-3rd century) and a flagon, lid, flanged dish and beaker (4th century). Date: late 2nd to 4th century AD.

Fabric 6: Oxford Red-slipped ware (Tomber and Dore 1998, OXF RS, 176)
This is a distinctive orange fabric, usually with a grey core and fine slip, often stamped and rouletted. Two bowl sherds were found, one stamped and one rouletted, probably from the same necked bowl (Young 1977, C78). Date: mid-4th century +.

Fabric 7: Hadham Oxidised ware (Tomber and Dore 1998, HAD OX, 151)
A bright orange fabric with slipped and burnished surfaces. One sherd was found from a cordoned jar. Date: mid-4th century +.

Mortaria

Mortaria are mixing bowls, lined with coarse grits (Tyers 1996, 117–35). Their presence here indicates the settlement that deposited this material had adopted Romanised kitchen wares and could afford to use these specialised and expensive vessels (de Bootman and Lyons 2021).

Fabric 8: Sandy Buff ware (Tomber and Dore 1998, COL WH, 133)
Beaded and flanged mortarium fragment. The sandy fabric is even-textured and brown-buff in colour. Only one worn example (two joining sherds) was found, for which no surface finish survives; traces of white and grey trituration grit only over the rim. Probably traded from Colchester rather than local to north Norfolk. Date: early to mid-2nd century (Hadrianic–Antonine).

Fabric 9: Sandy Oxidised ware
Bead and flanged mortarium fragment. The fabric is orange sandy ware with brown argillaceous inclusions. Worn, but with traces of a clear white slip under the flange. Probably of local manufacture as occasional white-slipped mortaria are known to be produced at Pentney (de Bootman and Lyons 2021). Date: 3rd–4th century AD.

Fabric 10: Lower Nene Valley White ware (Tomber and Dore 1998, LNV WH, 119)
One mortarium white ware body fragment, with slag trituration grits. Date: 3rd–4th century AD.

The illustrated catalogue of Romano-British forms **(Fig. 9.7)**
Vessels are wheel-thrown and kiln-fired unless stated otherwise.

1. Carinated beaker, rim only. Fabric 1d: Light-grey sandy texture with dark-grey argillaceous inclusions (?ironstone); severely abraded, no surface finish survives. AD 90–160. SA/BM 1; SA5/2, Section G, Layer 4.
2. Necked bowl, complete profile. Fabric 1a: Red-brown core, black surfaces, roughly smoothed finish. Almost complete vessel. Hand-shaped, wheel-finished and clamp-fired. A local product. AD 65–85. SA/BQ 1+ SA/AR+ SA/AY+ SA/BR. SA5/2, Sections B, C and F, Layers 1, 3 and 4.
3. Ring-necked flagon, three even rings. Fabric 2: Orange ware, no evidence of a cream slip. Complete neck circuit (5cm diameter) and a single handle. Probably local, no obvious identifying characteristics. AD 120–180. SA/BK 1. SA5/2, Section G, Layer 3.
4. Flat-based platter. Fabric 1b: dense stippled black argillaceous pellets, some fine white quartz sand: sandwich firing; grey core; red/brown under-surface; black slurry smoothed surface finish. Clamp-fired. A local product. AD 120+. SA/AU 1, SA5/2, Section B, Layer 3.
5. Necked jar, with slight shoulder groove. Fabric 1b: Unevenly fired; grey core; dark-grey surfaces with buff patches and a smoothed finish. A local product. Clamp-fired. AD 70–120. SA/AV 1, SA5/2, Section D, Layer 3.
6. Necked jar, with shoulder groove. Fabric 1b: light-grey-brown core; traces of dark-blue-grey surfaces; extremely abraded, no surface finish survives. Probably a local product. AD 70–120. SA/AV 2, SA5/2, Section D, Layer 3.
7. Wide-mouthed jar, with shoulder groove. Almost complete rim and base circuits but no complete profile. Fabric 1d: Light-grey sandy core with dark-grey argillaceous inclusions (?ironstone); darker grey surfaces; abraded, with traces of a burnished finish above the shoulder groove. AD 90–180. SA/AL and SA/AU, SA5/2, Sections A and B, Layer 3.
8. Necked storage jar, slight cordon at neck base and shoulder groove. Fabric 1c: Heavily tempered with coarse brown carrstone fragments between 1–5mm, plus black argillaceous and white quartz sand; sandwich firing, grey core, red-brown under-surface and surfaces with a black matt slurry finish. Rim certainly wheel-finished, but due to size and weight, the base and body were hand-shaped. Clamp-fired. A local product. AD 70–160. SA/AN and SA/AQ, SA5/2, Sections B and C, Layers 1 and 3
9. Bead and flange mortarium. Fabric 8: Buff even-textured sandy matrix; extremely abraded, with very worn interior, traces of grey and white flint trituration grits confined to the rim. Slightly burnt at the base. One rim and base. Colchester product. AD 120–160. SA/CN 1, Trench 6, topsoil.
10. Bead and flange mortarium. Flange fragment only. Fabric 9: Orange sandy matrix, cream surfaces. No evidence of trituration grit. Probably made at Pentney, Norfolk. SA/CN 2, Trench 6, topsoil.

The pottery in context

The majority of the stratified pottery assemblage was recovered from the enclosure ditch, whose primary fills contained pottery deposited in the Flavian to Antonine period (AD 70–160). A number of slots were excavated through this ditch, and most areas produced small amounts of stratified early to mid-Roman locally produced coarse ware pottery (ST35, ST36, ST41, ST42, SA5/2, SA6/2, SA17/2 and SA18/2). Similar small deposits of mid-Roman pottery were also recovered from ditch SA14/2, which may be an extension of the enclosure ditch to the south of SA5/2.

In one area in the north (ST35), a large deposit of waste metalworking debris (slag) had been laid over the enclosure ditch as 'hardcore' to form a causeway. This layer contained pottery diagnostic of the later Roman period (mid-4th to early 5th century), notably Lower Nene Valley Colour-coated and Oxford Red-slipped ware vessels.

The only other areas which produced Roman pottery from archaeological features were Trenches SA3 (likely residual in post-medieval ditch SA3/2), SA6 (ditch SA6/3 and pit SA6/10, neither of which could be closely dated), SA7 (ditches SA7/3, SA7/5, SA7/6, SA7/7) and SA12 (animal burrow/?post hole SA12/5). Apart from the well-preserved upper part of a cupped rim flagon found in SA3, the remainder of the Roman pottery found within these deposits was characterised as being locally produced coarse wares mostly comprising undiagnostic jar/bowl forms, with a small number of finer beaker fragments also found. Trenches SA7 and SA12 are otherwise notable for large quantities of prehistoric (mostly Early Iron Age) pottery, and none of the features could be securely dated as Roman.

The enclosure ditch
Roman pottery was recovered in small quantities from several of the slots excavated across the enclosure ditch (ST14, ST42, SA6, SA14, SA17 and SA18). The material excavated from SA5/2 has been chosen to describe in detail as it was the best-preserved group and is thought to be representative of the larger assemblage.

South-west enclosure ditch SA5/2
Section SA5/2 of the enclosure ditch had four distinct fills:

- Layer 1: sandy topsoil
- Layer 2: similar to level 1, but with intermixed yellow sand and higher frequency of stones
- Layer 3: a more gravelly and coarse sandy fill
- Layer 4: lighter, sandy fill with few stones, the primary silting of the ditch.

Pottery from the primary deposits (Layer 4) of the ditch comprise several sherds from grey (Fabric 1; 2 sherds, weighing 7g) and oxidised (Fabric 2; 2 sherds, weighing 15g) fine sand-tempered kiln-fired vessels of indeterminate closed forms which are unlikely to be earlier than 2nd century AD. Also found was the fragmentary remains of a carinated beaker (Fabric 1d; 2 sherds, weighing 15g) manufactured

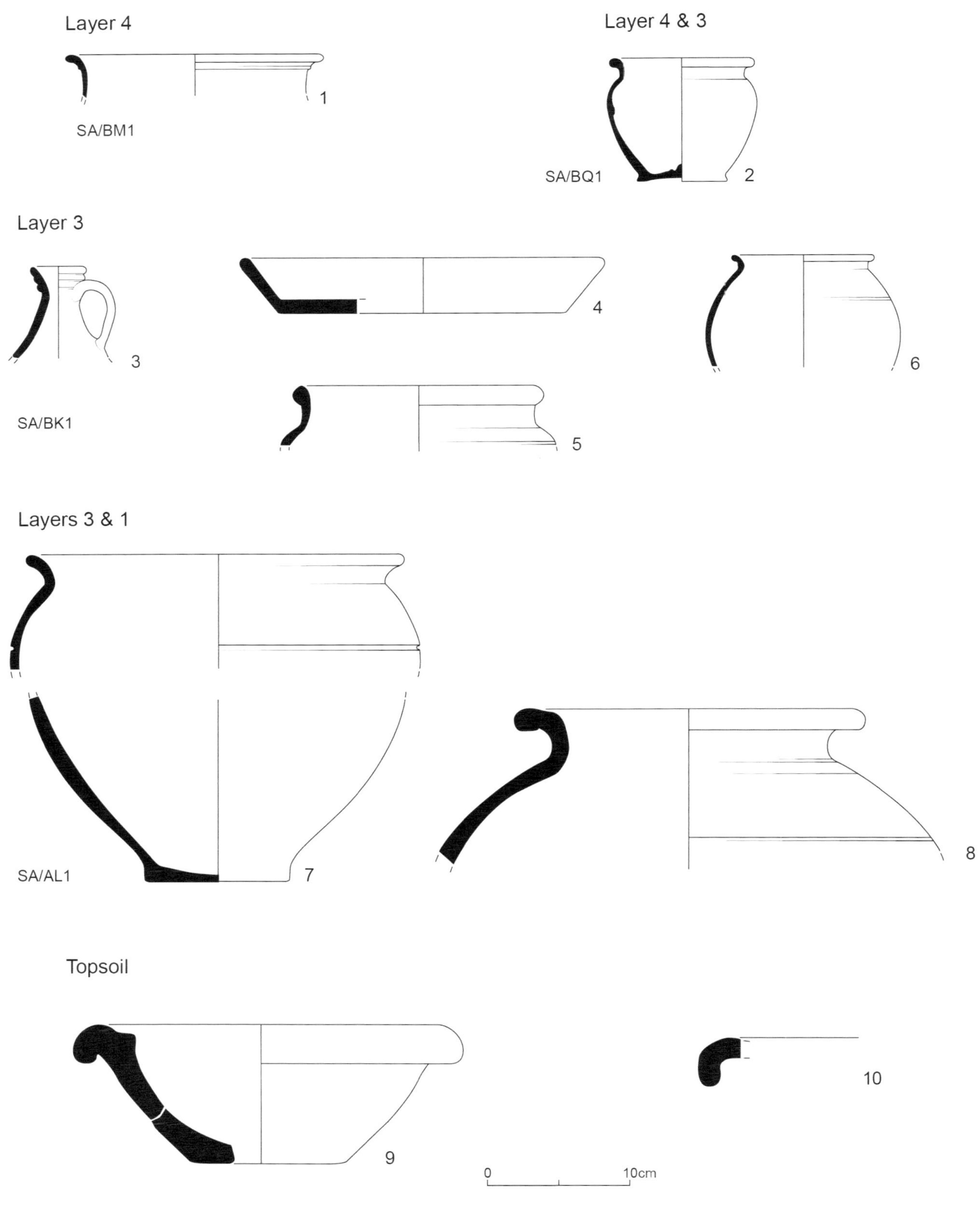

Figure 9.7 The catalogue of illustrated Romano-British pottery forms

between AD 90 and 160 (**Fig. 9.7.1**). A Lincolnshire source is suggested for this beaker as it is typical of the Dragonby/Roxby product range found at Old Winteringham and Winterton in Hadrianic–Antonine contexts (Stead 1976, 136–53). The earliest stratified vessel, however, is a hand-shaped and wheel-finished necked bowl in a local sandy fabric (Fabric 1a; 15 sherds, 99g) dating to AD 65-85 (**Fig. 9.7.2**). Joining sherds from this necked bowl, which together form a complete profile, were found in different slots in Layer 4, and also higher up in the stratigraphic sequence in Layer 3.

The most diagnostic pots were scattered along the ditch throughout Layers 3 and 1. Of these the most complete vessel is a fragmentary, but almost restorable to complete, large necked bowl which was also produced in the 2nd century AD (**Fig. 9.7.7**) (Fabric 1d; 6 sherds, 119g). Like the beaker found in Layer 4 (**Fig. 9.7.1**), the fabric of this vessel suggests it may also have its origins in north Lincolnshire. Despite most sherds being present, they have abraded fracture edges and little surface finish survives; they are in poor condition compared to some of the prehistoric vessels, suggesting that they were exposed to the weather for some time before deposition.

Although represented by only a few sherds, three other vessels were recovered in reasonably good condition. These comprise a very large storage jar with a rim diameter of 24cm (Fabric 1c; 3 sherds, weighing 436g) likely to date to the late 1st or early 2nd century, the complete neck and handle from a flagon (**Fig. 9.7.3**; Fabric 2; 1 sherds, 44g) and a deep platter (Fabric 1b; 6 sherds, 127g) both of 2nd-century date.

The weathered condition of the majority of Roman pottery sherds within the ditch can only be the result of a significant period of exposure after they were broken and before their final deposition. Fragments of the same vessel being present in consecutive layers within the ditch, such as the hand-shaped necked bowl (**Fig. 9.7.2**), suggests they were laid down fairly quickly before the different parts of the vessel became completely dispersed. One explanation for this pattern of deposition is that all the pottery was deposited within the ditch within a short time, possibly originating from an adjacent decaying midden which would explain both its weathered condition and the presence of related sherds in different layers within the ditch. Sadly, due to their residual nature, this pottery provides only a tentative *terminus ante quem* for the digging of the ditches. It is also worthy of note that no pottery datable to the 3rd or 4th centuries was identified in the lower enclosure ditch deposits (although a few highly abraded pieces were found in the uppermost layer, along with post-medieval fragments).

North enclosure ditch, feature ST35

This part of the enclosure ditch had an unusual section. The lower layers, 2–4, seem similar to those of the south-west enclosure ditch, with an underlying Layer 5 which may simply be natural weathered carrstone. However, the uppermost level, 1, was not the sandy topsoil seen in other areas of the enclosure ditch but consisted of a large quantity of slag, furnace debris and charcoal, probably deliberately laid as a causeway.

The pottery group from the ditch filling includes traded wares typical of supply to north Norfolk in the Late Roman period (Andrews 1985, 86). There are no obvious medieval or modern sherds. The most common source, probably due to its river connection, is the Lower Nene Valley potteries (Perrin 1999) with six colour-coated vessels, a white ware mortarium and two grey ware pots, a jar and a bowl. There is at least one bowl in Oxford Red-slipped ware which is unlikely to pre-date the mid-4th century. (At present the chronological evidence demonstrates that, excluding London, Oxford Red-slipped wares did not reach sites east of Watling Street in any quantity before the early 4th century).

All of these sherds were found stratified within or below the slag layer. They are single sherds, abraded and each representing a single pot. The presence of this diagnostically Late Roman pottery indicates that the slag surface cannot have been laid before AD 350.

Conclusion

This assemblage comprises two distinct groups of Roman pottery: one early to mid-Roman deposit related to the silting-up of the enclosure ditch, the second a Late Roman group associated with the construction of a new causeway into the enclosure. Although the quantity of material is small, and the condition of the pottery poor, enough survives to establish that both groups largely comprise locally made utilitarian coarse ware jar/bowl forms. In addition, the presence of non-local coarse wares (from Lincolnshire), traded domestic British fine wares (primarily from the Lower Nene Valley, also Essex, Oxfordshire and Hertfordshire) and specialist mixing bowls (mortaria from the Nene and Nar Valleys) demonstrate that the settlement that deposited this material had both the surplus wealth and the trade connections to acquire non-local wares, particularly so in the later Roman period.

Enough diagnostic material has survived, therefore, to make a significant contribution to the interpretation of the site and character of the nearby settlement that deposited this material.

Roman ceramic building material

Alice Lyons, based on an earlier report by Val Rigby

Introduction

A total of 11 Roman ceramic building material (CBM) fragments, weighing 707g, were recovered from the enclosure ditch and unstratified within the nearby woodland at Ken Hill. No complete examples were found, and the fragments have an average sherd weight of only 64g.

Methodology

The CBM was counted and weighed, identified by form and fabric type, any complete dimensions measured, and a catalogue prepared (in archive). Levels of abrasion, any evidence of re-use or burning were also recorded. This follows guidelines laid down by Archaeological Ceramic Building Materials Group (ACBMG 2002). The site archive is held by the BM.

The assemblage (Table 9.6)

The Roman tile was consistently made in a sandy orange/red fabric with occasional small flint (3–6mm) inclusions, consistent with local production.

Description	Fragment count	Weight (g)
Roof: *tegula*	2	272
Hypocaust: box flue	3	262
Roof: *imbrex*	3	154
Undiagnostic fragments	3	19
Total	**11**	**707**

Table 9.6 The CBM assemblage, listed in descending order of weight

Although no complete examples were found, some pieces could be identified, and these comprise roof tile: *tegula* and *imbrex*, also box tile: which would have been fixed into the wall to transport hot air as part of the hypocaust heating system.

Conclusion

The presence of this Roman tile indicates a substantial Roman dwelling once existed in the vicinity, but this material may have been transported some distance (for re-use or use as hardcore) from the location of this building.

Debris of iron production

Paul Craddock and Janet Lang

In one section of the polygonal enclosure ditch large quantities of slag and associated metallurgical debris had been dumped, presumably from nearby iron production.

Iron smelting by the direct or so-called bloomery process involved the reduction of the iron ore minerals to produce a solid lump of iron, the bloom, and large quantities of slag. The bloom formed in the hottest part of the furnace in the vicinity of the bellows pipes whereas the liquid slag drained to the bottom of the furnace from where it could be periodically tapped. As the bloom had never been molten it invariably contained quantities of slag together with unreduced ore and charcoal. To remove the majority of these the bloom was vigorously hammered at white heat to literally squeeze them out, the process known as bloom smithing. This process required the bloom to be frequently reheated on a hearth, which also produced a slag and fragments of the vitrified and slagged hearth lining. The refined bloom could then be made into the required artefacts by blacksmithing, hammering the iron at red heat, which also required frequent reheating on a hearth creating more slaggy material and fragments of the hearth.

The vast majority of the furnace debris from Snettisham came from ST35, a slot through the north side of the enclosure ditch in Area 21. Here, the section through the enclosure ditch was quite unlike that seen elsewhere. It appears that, rather than gradual silting, a stretch of around 20m of the ditch was deliberately backfilled with furnace debris and charcoal, perhaps to create an entranceway. Pottery recovered from immediately above and below this deposit suggest that this was done after the mid-4th century AD (see above).

Furnace debris was recovered from the upper fill, Layer 1 (ST/BX, ST/DH, ST/DO, ST/DP, ST/DX, ST/DY) and the fill immediately below, Layer 2 (ST/EZ). This material from the ditch comprised mainly fragments of slag together with some heavily slagged and vitrified rough clay material and a selection was made, concentrating on the slagged clay material as being more likely to be informative of the processes involved.

Fragments of slag and partially slagged and vitrified clay fragments are not uncommon finds on Iron Age and later sites, and are usually to be interpreted as the remains of blacksmithing. Here the considerable quantities of slag are suggestive of smelting. This is confirmed by the presence of tap slag as only the smelting process generated sufficient quantities of slag to require periodic draining. The slagged and partially vitrified clay pieces had the shape and appearance typical of hearth bottoms and are likely to be associated with bloom smithing operations, although some blacksmithing operations cannot be excluded.

Metal-detecting just to the south-east of ST35 produced several unstratified lumps of slaggy iron in the vicinity of the ditch (ST/GD). These were initially assumed to be fragments of failed blooms, but on metallographic examination were found to be of metal that had once been molten. Furthermore, they were not of the more familiar cast iron, iron with a little carbon, but instead were of almost pure iron with substantial traces of phosphorous. This would have lowered the melting point of the iron quite substantially; the full metallurgical description of these highly unusual and interesting pieces are published elsewhere (Lang *et al.* 2019). Whilst these pieces are unstratified, it is likely that they belong to the same Romano-British ironworking operations as the stratified material excavated from the ditch.

Cast iron was not intentionally produced until many centuries later. The primary product of the Romano-British smithing operations evidenced at Snettisham would have been a solid iron bloom formed near the bellows tubes in the centre of the furnace. The slaggy iron found during metal-detecting would have drained down as a component of the slag and it is very likely that the smiths were not aware of its existence.

As already noted, the low melting point was primarily due to the phosphorous content which would have been a component of the ore. Iron smelting slags with high phosphorous contents have been noted at other Roman iron smelting sites in Norfolk, including one at the nearby Station Road site in Snettisham (Chirikure and Painter 2002). At these sites the ore was identified as being composed of iron hydroxides, goethite and lepidocrocite, together with some iron oxide, hematite minerals in a sandy matrix. This is the highly ferruginous Norfolk carrstone, usually thought of as a decorative building stone, but which was certainly quarried for iron production in Roman times (Tylecote 1967).

The few pieces of slag collected from the ditch excavation were tested with a magnet but none contained metallic iron. This partly reflects the differing collecting strategies: the metal detectorists who recovered ST/GD were seeking metal, whereas the archaeologists were collecting process evidence, mainly the slagged and vitrified clay together with only a small selection of slag pieces that would have formed the bulk of the deposit.

The combined archaeological and metallurgical evidence suggests that here, as elsewhere in Late Roman

Taxon	Site code	Context
Salix sp., willow	ST/DH	ST35, enclosure ditch, Layer 1
Tilia sp., lime	ST/DO	ST35, enclosure ditch, Layer 1
Salix sp., willow; *Tilia* sp., lime; *Carpinus betulus*, hornbeam	ST/DQ	ST35, enclosure ditch, Layer 1
Carpinus betulus, hornbeam (< 10 years old)	ST/DY+	ST35, enclosure ditch, Layer 1
Castanea sativa, sweet chestnut	ST/DY	ST35, enclosure ditch, Layer 1
Corylus avellana, hazel	ST/DX	ST35, enclosure ditch, Layer 1
Corylus avellana, hazel	ST/EY	ST35, enclosure ditch, Layer 2
Salix sp., willow (< 10 years old)	ST/EZ+	ST35, enclosure ditch, Layer 2
Salix sp., willow; *Corylus avellana*, hazel (< 10 years old)	ST/HL+	ST42, enclosure ditch, Layer 2

Table 9.7 Charcoal from the enclosure ditch (samples marked with + were radiocarbon dated, see Tables 5.3, 9.3)

Norfolk, the phosphorous-rich ferruginous carrstone was being smelted to produce iron.

Charcoal from the enclosure ditch

Caroline Cartwright

Charcoal samples from eight contexts in the enclosure ditch were submitted for taxon identification using a variable pressure scanning electron microscope (see Chapter 19 for methodology). Some roundwood (branch or twig) fragments less than 10 years old were then selected for radiocarbon dating. **Table 9.7** provides the details, including three that yielded radiocarbon dates around the mid-3rd to early 5th or mid-6th century AD, with the probabilities concentrated in the mid-4th to mid-5th century AD (see **Tables 5.3, 9.3**). The charcoal fragments from enclosure ditch contexts appear to be associated with furnace debris (see above), so it is not surprising to find that the taxa selected included those renowned for yielding good charcoal for fuel (see **Table 19.3**). *Salix* sp. (willow), *Tilia* sp. (lime), *Carpinus betulus* (hornbeam) and *Corylus avellana* (hazel) feature prominently in the specimens that were radiocarbon dated; all of these taxa yielded roundwood less than 10 years old. In addition, charcoal fragments from a post-Roman introduced tree, *Castanea sativa* (sweet chestnut) (**Fig. 9.8**) were present in ST35, enclosure ditch Layer 1 (ST/DY). These were not submitted for radiocarbon dating, as there were younger fragments of hornbeam present from the same context.

Animal bone and mollusc shell from the enclosure ditch

Alan Pipe

This section presents the Phase 4–5 animal bone. For Methodology, see Chapter 7.

Area 21, ST35, enclosure ditch, Layer 1

ST/DN produced eight fragments of identifiable mammal bone: two of horse *Equus caballus* and six of cattle *Bos taurus*. Horse produced two fragments of worn adult mandibular (lower jaw) teeth. Cattle included single fragments of worn adult left-side upper premolar tooth with right-side humerus (upper fore-leg), radius and ulna (lower fore-leg), adult cervical (neck) vertebra and femur (upper hind-leg). The radius was fused at the proximal end indicating an animal in at least the second year; this bone had been chopped transversely. The femur had been knife-cut. There was no other evidence for modification.

ST/DX produced five fragments of identifiable mammal bone derived from horse *Equus caballus*; sheep/goat *Ovis aries/Capra hircus*; and dog *Canis lupus familiaris*. Horse included single fragments of innominate acetabulum (hip socket) and a complete fully fused first phalange (basal toe joint). Fusion on the phalange indicated an adult horse in at least the second year. Sheep/goat included two fragments of radius (lower fore-leg); dog included an unworn canine tooth.

ST/DY produced seven identifiable fragments of mammal bone. These comprised a fragment of adult ram *Ovis aries* skull and horncore; a fragment of horse *Equus caballus* innominate; and single fragments of cattle *Bos taurus* right-side juvenile mandible (lower jaw), left-side adult upper premolar tooth, left- and right-side adult upper molar teeth and a complete, fully fused metatarsal (hind-foot). Fusion of the metatarsal indicated an animal in at least the third year. Measurement of the metatarsal greatest length allowed calculation of an estimated 'withers' (shoulder) height of 1.180m, somewhat taller than the 300 BC Iron Age (1.08m) and Romano-British (1.12m) examples quoted by Davis (1987, 178). A sample from this material was radiocarbon dated to 260–540 cal AD (at 95% probability, see **Table 5.3**).

Area 21, ST35, enclosure ditch, Layer 2

ST/EY produced 33 fragments of identifiable mammal bone mainly including 'cattle-sized' mammal, with small numbers of cattle *Bos taurus*, horse *Equus caballus*, sheep/goat *Ovis aries/Capra hircus*, horse *Equus caballus* and dog *Canis lupus familiaris*. 'Cattle-sized' mammal included 20 fragments of vertebra and rib; cattle included single fragments of worn right-side upper premolar tooth and cervical (neck) vertebra; horse included worn single fragments of lumbar (lower back) vertebra and innominate (pelvis); sheep/goat included two worn adult right-side upper molar teeth, with single fragments of left- and right-side sub-adult mandible (lower jaw); and right-side

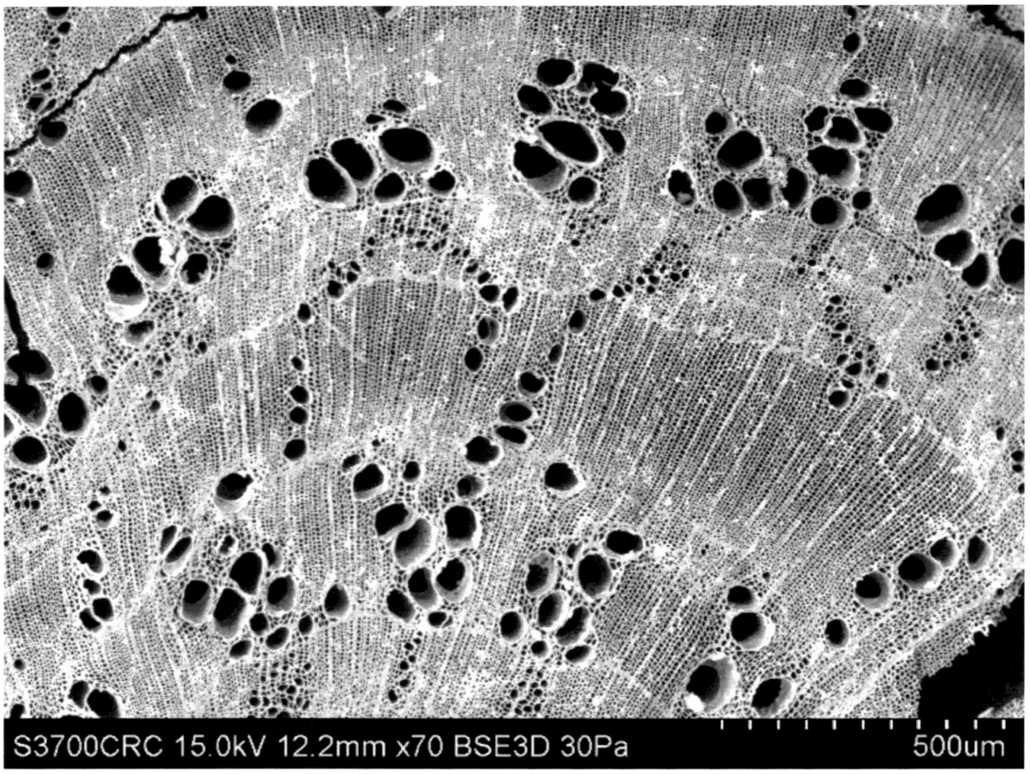

Figure 9.8 Variable pressure scanning electron microscope image of a transverse section of *Castanea sativa* (sweet chestnut) charcoal from ST35, enclosure ditch, Layer 1 (ST/DY). Image by C.R. Cartwright

astragalus ('ankle'); dog included single examples of right-side young adult mandible (lower jaw) and adult atlas (neck) vertebra and third metatarsal (hind-foot).

ST/EZ produced nine fragments of identifiable mammal bone, including cattle *Bos taurus*; sheep/goat *Ovis aries/Capra hircus*, horse *Equus caballus* and dog *Canis lupus familiaris*. Cattle included single fragments of sub-adult skull and ulna (lower fore-leg); sheep/goat included single fragments of adult incisor tooth and metacarpal (fore-foot); horse included single fragments of adult lumbar (lower back) vertebra and right-side femur (upper hind-leg), both probably from animals in at least the fourth year; dog included single fragments of adult left-side mandible (lower jaw), atlas (neck) vertebra and third metatarsal (hind-foot). There were no tool marks or any other evidence for modification. A sample from this material was radiocarbon dated to 210–360 cal AD (at 95% probability, see **Table 5.3**).

ST42, enclosure ditch, Layer 1

ST/GC produced unidentifiable fragments of mammal bone. An attempt to radiocarbon date this material failed (see **Table 5.3**).

Trench 5, SA5/2, enclosure ditch, Layer 1

SA/AJ produced a fragment of adult cattle *Bos taurus* left-side mandible (lower jaw). There were no tool marks or any other evidence for modification. In addition, this group included two valves (shells) of an economically important marine/estuarine bivalve mollusc species, common cockle *Cerastoderma edule*.

SA/AN produced a fragment of 'cattle-sized' long-bone mid-shaft. There were no tool marks or any other evidence for modification.

Trench 5, SA5/2, enclosure ditch, Layer 2

SA/AK included a fragment of cattle *Bos taurus* left-side humerus (upper fore-leg). There were no tool marks or any other evidence for modification. A sample from this material was radiocarbon dated to 250–420 cal AD (at 95% probability, see **Table 5.3**).

Trench 5, SA5/2, enclosure ditch, Layer 3

SA/AV produced 15 fragments of 'cattle-sized' tooth enamel. There were no tool marks or any other evidence for modification. An attempt to radiocarbon date this material failed (see **Table 5.3**).

Trench 6, SA6/2, enclosure ditch, Layer 2

SA/CO produced eight fragments of cattle *Bos taurus* tooth enamel with single worn adult right-side upper molar and lower third molar teeth. There were no tool marks or any other evidence for modification. A sample from this material was radiocarbon dated to 130–340 cal AD (at 95% probability, see **Table 5.3**).

Trench 6, SA6/2, enclosure ditch, Layer 3

SA/BT produced 11 fragments of cattle *Bos taurus* maxillary (upper) and mandibular (lower) premolar and molar teeth. Dental wear indicates all derived from adult, or at last sub-adult, animals with single left- and right-side mandibular third molars showing wear sufficient to indicate animals, probably the same individual, in at least the fifth year. There were no tool marks or any other evidence for modification. A sample from this material was radiocarbon dated to 220–370 cal AD (at 95% probability, see **Table 5.3**).

Trench 6, SA6/2, enclosure ditch, Layer ?

SA/BW produced only a single unidentifiable fragment of

'cattle-sized' long-bone mid-shaft. There were no tool marks or any other evidence for modification.

SA/CF included two fragments of adult horse *Equus caballus* maxillary (upper jaw) molar tooth. Both were worn, indicating adult animals. There were no tool marks or any other evidence for modification.

Trench 18, SA18/2, enclosure ditch (upper fill)

SA/JU included two shells of economically important marine/estuarine molluscs; single shells of common periwinkle *Littorina littorea* and common cockle *Cerastoderma edule*.

Possible Romano-British shale objects

SA/HW: Shale ?disc/?bead
Small section of a flat, circular shale pierced disc or bead. Flat on both sides, with sub-rectangular cross-section, tapering thinner on one side. Sharp breaks at both ends.
Dimensions: Weight: 0.6g; maximum length: 17mm; maximum thickness: 5mm; width: 10mm
Context: Ditch SA7/5, Section D (1992, Trench 7, Phase ?6)

SA/HC: Shale ?finger-ring/?bead
Flat, triangular piece of shale, with one corner sawn off, and saw marks indicating the beginnings of the removal of the second and, perhaps, third corners. Drilled through the centre with a large circular perforation. Most likely an early stage in the production of a finger-ring or thick, circular bead. Abraded surface with some chipping.
Dimensions: Weight: 22.8g; maximum remaining length: 57mm; thickness: 15mm; diameter of central hole: 16mm
Context: Topsoil/subsoil, over enclosure ditch SA17/2 (1992, Trench 17)

Whilst neither of these objects came from a datable context, similar simple shale beads and rings are known from Romano-British sites. See for example Tyrrell and Major (2015) and Crummy (1983, 49–50).

Discussion

Snettisham retained its importance into the earlier Roman period (Phase 4). Two hoards most likely date to the 1st and 2nd centuries AD: the large silver-copper alloy lumps of Hoard M and the now-lost silver coin hoard, Hoard P. The construction of the large polygonal enclosure ditch seems to have taken place around the late 1st to mid-2nd century AD. It was also most likely during Phase 4 that the square stone structure uncovered in the wooded area (Hutcheson 2011) was constructed. It has at least a special relationship to the enclosure, lying directly opposite the south-west entrance. Though there is no evidence that the structure itself was a focus for deposition of any kind, it stood between the entranceway and the area which produced the hoards. See discussion of movement around the site in this period in Chapter 8.

Hutcheson (2011) has interpreted this square structure as a Romano-Celtic temple, and that interpretation is followed here. Elsewhere in southern Britain, Romano-Celtic temples generally consist of two nested elements: an inner *cella* (5.1–16m across) and an outer ambulatory (8.5–22m across) (Lewis 1966, 1–56; Historic England 2018). They are often square in plan, as at Snettisham, but can also be rectangular, circular or polygonal. Many such sites sit within a larger walled or ditched enclosure defining the sacred precinct or *temenos*. There is no sign of an ambulatory at Snettisham, but this is paralleled at other sites. For example, at Hayling Island, off the Hampshire coast, there is no ambulatory around the *cella*, but it sits within a larger enclosure *c.* 40 x 43m (King and Soffe 2007). The high levels of phosphate in the wooded area (Ch. 5) indicate an area of intensive activity just north-west of the temple structure, over about 4,000m². Romano-British pottery was found in the same area, suggesting that this may have been contemporary with the temple, although it is equally possible that it might be associated with the midden-generating activity from Phase 2.

The polygonal *temenos* at Snettisham covers an area of around 8 hectares, partially enclosed by large V-cut ditches, 2.3–2.8m wide at the base of the plough soil, and 1.5–1.8m below the present ground surface. The south side was probably unenclosed, sloping down towards boggy ground and an inlet from the Wash. There are ditches on a similar scale potentially enclosing an area of Late Iron Age votive deposition at Sedgeford, just a few kilometres east of Snettisham (SHARP 2014, 37–47; Ch. 3), though the limited excavation and survey of these ditches do not allow a full reconstruction of their circuit. Elsewhere in southern England, there are other examples of Early Roman square temple structures sitting within a larger ditched *temenos* (Lewis 1966, 131–2). For example, at Harlow, Essex, a small square Romano-Celtic temple on a hilltop is surrounded by an oval enclosure ditch around the base of the hill, enclosing an area of around 4.9 hectares, while at Gosbecks, near Colchester, Essex, a square temple surrounded by a series of concentric ditched square enclosures sits within a *temenos* area of 2.65 hectares, defined by a walled and ditched boundary. Lewis (1966, 132) suggested that a 'non-defensive' ditch such as that seen at Gosbecks and Harlow might typically be the first stage in the enclosure of an Early Roman temple precinct, often being later replaced by a stone wall, though this did not occur at Snettisham or Harlow.

At Snettisham, it seems that the building of the Romano-Celtic temple and enclosure of the site was a way of bounding an existing sacred place which had been a site of deposition perhaps for several centuries. This is paralleled at other sites, including Hayling Island, where the Romano-Celtic temple seems to have succeeded an earlier Late Iron Age shrine (King and Soffe 2007). Hutcheson (2011; 2004, 90–2) has argued that in Early Roman Norfolk the building of Roman temples at sites which saw Late Iron Age deposition (such as Snettisham, North Creake and Fring) was a way of formalising a previously more fluid depositional landscape, and the transformation of the site at Ken Hill in the Early Roman period would certainly have redefined and perhaps overtly controlled the way in which the site was used and accessed. It is notable that the 'gold field' (the area which produced the Late Iron Age metalwork hoards), rather than the temple structure, sits at the centre of the *temenos*, suggesting that the main focus of the site may have remained a natural, open area perhaps with associated field system or enclosures (see Ch. 8). At other sites where the temple structure is not central within the *temenos*, it has been suggested that a grove or natural feature such as a spring might have formed the main ritual focus (Lewis 1966, 134–5), but there is no direct evidence for a grove at Snettisham in the Late Iron Age, especially given the presence of a field system which is cut by the Phase 4 enclosure ditch (Ch. 5).

The enclosure ditch seems to have silted gradually from at least the mid-2nd century AD. Subsequently, there seems to have been a change in the use of the site in the Late Roman period, Phase 5 (*c*. AD 350–400). At this time, it appears that the enclosure ditch was only partially infilled, but there may have been a deliberate attempt to level the inner bank in at least some areas (seen in Trench 17 and ST35). At the centre of the north side (around ST35), the enclosure ditch was completely infilled for a length of around 20m with slag and furnace debris, most likely to create a causeway across the ditch, suggesting a re-organisation of the layout and use of the site. Pottery finds and radiocarbon dates suggest this occurred from the mid-4th century AD. In the Late Roman period, it is evident that there were a range of industrial processes taking place in the immediate vicinity of Snettisham (see e.g. Lyons 2004), and it is likely that the ironworking which produced the furnace debris filling the north side of the enclosure ditch probably occurred nearby. The square stone structure in the woods was also most likely demolished at around this time, with a Roman coin dated AD 350–360 securely lodged under the rubble of the north wall (Hutcheson 2011, 44). This may have constituted a deliberate abandonment of the site; there is very little evidence for early medieval activity.

Chapter 10
Phase 6: Medieval and Post-Medieval (*c.* AD 1100 onwards)

Julia Farley and Jody Joy, with a contribution by Alan Pipe

There is very little evidence for activity at Ken Hill in the immediate post-Roman period. The next phase which can be identified through ceramic evidence is medieval, represented by green-glazed Grimston Ware. No excavated features can be securely assigned to the medieval period however, with excavated post-Roman evidence mainly comprising post-medieval agricultural, drainage and landscaping work.

This chapter gives a brief summary of medieval and later activity, since it impacts on the legibility of some of the earlier phases. For example, deep ploughing and animal burrowing from extensive rabbit activity at the site has caused disturbance to the hoard pits and other features. A summary of the medieval and post-medieval ceramics and metalwork is presented, although a full report on this material is outside the scope of the current volume. The specialist report on animal bone from Phase 6 contexts (or radiocarbon dated to Phase 6) is also included below.

Medieval and post-medieval features

Several of the trenches excavated in 1992 produced clear evidence of post-medieval activity, including possible field boundaries, landscaping features and drainage ditches (see **Table 10.1**). In the majority of cases, these were E–W drainage or landscaping ditches running south of the modern drive, more or less along the line of the contours as the site slopes away from the hoard field. Sections of a ditch immediately to the south of the drive were uncovered in Trenches 5, 6, 7 and 17. In the latter case this feature clearly cut the enclosure ditch. Radiocarbon dates from animal bone recovered from the E–W ditches SA6/3 and SA7/5 gave dates in the AD 1430–1640 range at 95% probability (**Table 5.3**), and natural gully SA7/7 contained infant rabbit bones likely evidence of modern disturbance. Slightly further south, down the slope, other E–W ditches were revealed in Trenches 8 and 11. These were on the same alignment and so are likely the same feature, or closely related. Slightly further south again, Trench 3 contained a modern drainage ditch, also running E–W, with an 18th to 19th-century ceramic field drain at its base. Carrstone quarrying was evidenced in Trench 13, also immediately to the south of the modern driveway.

Medieval and post-medieval ceramics and metalwork

Green-glazed Grimston Ware from the 12th to 14th centuries is well represented at the site. In addition, in 1989, a watching brief undertaken during construction of the A149 Snettisham bypass revealed a mass of unstratified Grimston Ware just to the south-east of the 'gold field' (NHER 25748).

Medieval metalwork from the BM excavations includes hooked tags and a copper alloy seal. Later finds include a small number of vessel fittings, lead weights and a 17th-century lead seal. Most were unstratified stray finds, though a crotal bell was discovered alongside 17th to 18th-century pot sherds in Trench 15, Feature SA15/2. It is notable that a very large number of 18th and 19th-century buttons were recovered during metal-detecting surveys of the hoard field, as well as a range of coins and tokens which are more varied than might normally be expected (E. Ghey pers. comm.). This suggests that there may have been dumps of more recent material at the site in the 18th to earlier 20th centuries, perhaps due to the use of night soil as fertiliser.

Ex. year	Area	Feature	Type	Phase
1992	Trench 3	SA3/2	Ditch	6
1992	Trench 5	SA5/3	Hollow	?6
1992	Trench 5	SA5/4	Ditch	6
1992	Trench 6	SA6/3A	Ditch	?6
1992	Trench 6	SA6/3B	Ditch	?6
1992	Trench 6	SA6/3C	Ditch	?6
1992	Trench 6	SA6/9	Post hole	6
1992	Trench 6	SA6/11	?Post hole/?animal burrow	?6
1992	Trench 7	SA7/4	Ditch	6
1992	Trench 7	SA7/5	Ditch	?6
1992	Trench 7	SA7/13 (extension to SA7/5)	Ditch	?6
1992	Trench 8	SA8/2	Ditch	6
1992	Trench 11	SA11/3	Ditch	6
1992	Trench 13	SA13/1	Recent disturbance	6
1992	Trench 15	SA15/2	Building debris	6
1992	Trench 16	SA16/2	Ditch	?6
1992	Trench 16	SA16/4	Ditch	?6
1992	Trench 17	SA17/3	Ditch	6

Table 10.1 Phase 6 features

Medieval and post-medieval animal bone

Alan Pipe, Museum of London Archaeology

This section presents the Phase 6 animal bone. For Methodology, see Chapter 7.

Trench 6, SA6/3, ditch

SA/AW included a fragment of fused left-side distal ('elbow') end of cattle *Bos taurus* humerus. There were no tool marks or any other evidence for modification. This material was radiocarbon dated to 1450–1640 cal AD (at 95% probability, see **Table 5.3**).

Trench 7, SA7/5, ditch

SA/GO produced unidentifiable fragments of unidentifiable mammal bone. This material was radiocarbon dated to 1430–1620 cal AD (at 95% probability, see **Table 5.3**).

Trench 7, SA7/7, natural feature (gully) (included here as the infant rabbit bones are likely evidence of modern disturbance)

SA/CT included a fragment of 'cattle-sized' long-bone mid-shaft. There were no tool marks or any other evidence for modification.

SA/DY included single fragments of cattle *Bos taurus* right-side proximal radius and ulna (lower fore-leg), possibly from the same animal. The radius was fused, indicating an animal in at least the second year. There were no tool marks or any other evidence for modification. In addition, there were single fragments of unfused infant right- and left-side rabbit *Oryctolagus cuniculus* radius and right-side femur (upper hind-leg).

Discussion

There is no evidence for immediate post-Roman activity at the site. Ceramic evidence suggests 12th to 14th-century occupation in the vicinity, although no excavated features could be securely dated to this period. The evidence from the 1990–2 excavations suggests that Phase 6 interventions at the site mainly consisted of post-medieval agricultural and drainage activity.

The disturbed state of many of the archaeological features across the site was due to animal burrowing (especially rabbits), and deep ploughing across the hoard field. The infant rabbit bones recovered from gully SA7/7 (see above) are further evidence for the widespread presence of this burrowing animal. From at least the 16th century, an area of common land just south of Ken Hill was used as a rabbit warren (Ch. 3), and there are numerous historical accounts of the problems caused on adjacent agricultural land around Snettisham by escaping rabbits (Whyte 2009, 91–124; Bailey 1988). Extensive disturbance was also noted in the wooded area to the west by Hutcheson (2011). She suggested that this could be due to deliberate destruction of the site and structure, but it is possible that it simply results from later agricultural, drainage, landscaping and animal activity.

Appendix 1
Full List of Contexts from the 1990–1992 Excavations, with Associated Artefacts, Ecofacts and Samples

This appendix provides a full list of contexts from the 1990–1992 excavations, with details of associated artefacts, ecofacts and samples.

Abbreviations

CBM: ceramic building materials
Ex.: excavation
IA: Iron Age
MD: metal detector
Med/PM: medieval or post-medieval
Pot: pottery
Pre: Prehistoric
RB: Romano-British

Ex. year	Area	Feature code	Feature type	Context	Flint	Other stone	RB pot	RB CBM	Pre pot	Animal bone	Charcoal	IA/RB metalwork	IA coin	RB coin	Furnace debris	Med/PM pot	Phase
1990	Area 1	N/A	Topsoil/subsoil	N/A	x	-	x	-	x	-	-	x	x	x	-	-	N/A
1990	Area 2	N/A	Topsoil/subsoil	N/A	-	-	-	-	x	-	-	x	x	x	-	-	N/A
1990	Area 3	N/A	Topsoil/subsoil	N/A	-	-	-	-	x	-	-	x	-	-	-	-	N/A
1990	Area 4	N/A	Topsoil/subsoil	N/A	x	-	-	-	x	-	-	x	x	-	-	-	N/A
1990	Area 5	N/A	Topsoil/subsoil	N/A	x	-	-	-	x	-	-	x	x	x	-	-	N/A
1990	Area 6	N/A	Topsoil/subsoil	N/A	-	-	-	-	x	-	-	-	-	-	-	-	N/A
1990	Area 7	N/A	Topsoil/subsoil	N/A	-	-	-	-	x	-	-	x	-	x	-	-	N/A
1990	Area 8	N/A	Topsoil/subsoil	N/A	-	-	-	-	-	-	-	-	-	-	-	-	N/A
1990	Area 9	N/A	Topsoil/subsoil	N/A	x	-	-	-	-	-	-	x	x	-	-	-	N/A
1990	Area 10	N/A	Topsoil/subsoil	N/A	-	-	-	-	-	-	-	-	x	-	-	-	N/A
1990	Area 11	N/A	Topsoil/subsoil	N/A	-	-	-	-	-	-	-	x	x	-	-	-	N/A
1990	Area 12	N/A	Topsoil/subsoil	N/A	x	-	-	-	x	-	-	x	x	-	-	-	N/A
1990	Area 13	N/A	Topsoil/subsoil	N/A	-	-	x	-	x	-	-	-	x	-	-	x	N/A
1990	Area 14	N/A	Topsoil/subsoil	N/A	-	-	-	-	-	x	-	x	x	-	-	-	N/A
1990	Area 15	N/A	Topsoil/subsoil	N/A	x	-	-	-	x	-	-	x	x	-	-	-	N/A
1990	Area 4	Hoard F pit	Pit	N/A	x	-	-	-	-	-	-	x	x	-	-	-	3
1990	Area 1	Hoard G pit	Pit	N/A	-	-	-	-	-	-	-	x	-	-	-		3
1990	Area 1	Hoard H pit	Pit	N/A	x	-	-	-	-	-	-	x	-	-	-	x	3
1990	Area 2	Hoard J pit	Pit	N/A	-	-	-	-	-		-	x	-	-	-	-	3
1990	Area 6	Hoard K pit	Pit	N/A	-	-	-	-	x	-	-	x	-	-	-	-	3
1990	Area 9	Hoard L pit	Pit	N/A	x	-	-	-	-	-	-	x	-	-	-	-	3
1990	Area 2	SN2	Natural feature (large magnetic anomaly)	N/A	-	-	-	-	-	-	-	-	-	-	-	-	N/A
1990	Area 2	SN21	Pit	N/A	x	-	-	-	x	-	-	x	-	-	-	-	1
1990	Area 1	SN22	Natural feature (gully)	N/A	-	-	-	-	x	-	-	-	-	-	-	-	N/A
1990	Area 1	SN23	Pit	N/A	x	-	-	-	x	-	-	-	-	-	-	-	1
1990	Area 1	SN24	Pit	N/A	x	-	-	-	x	-	-	-	-	-	-	-	1

Ex. year	Area	Feature code	Feature type	Context	Flint	Other stone	RB pot	RB CBM	Pre pot	Animal bone	Charcoal	IA/RB metalwork	IA coin	RB coin	Furnace debris	Med/PM pot	Phase
1990	Area 3	SN25	Pit	N/A	x	-	-	-	x	-	-	-	-	-	-	-	2
1990	Area 3	SN26	Pit	N/A	-	x	-	-	x	-	-	-	-	-	-	-	1
1990	Area 3	SN27	Pit	N/A	-	-	-	-	x	-	-	-	-	-	-	-	1
1990	Area 2	SN28	Pit	N/A	x	-	-	-	x	-	-	-	-	-	-	-	1
1990	Area 2	SN29	Pit	N/A	x	-	-	-	x	-	-	-	-	-	-	-	1
1990	Area 7	SN30	Pit	N/A	x	x	-	-	x	-	-	-	-	-	-	-	1
1990	Area 1	SN31	Pit	N/A	-	-	-	-	-	x	-	-	-	-	-	-	2
1991	Wood	Hoard M	MD findspot	N/A	-	-	-	-	-	-	-	x	-	-	-	-	4
1991	?Area 21	Hoard P	Postulated MD findspot	N/A	-	-	-	-	-	-	-	x	x	x	-	-	4
1991	Area 16	N/A	Topsoil/subsoil	N/A	x	-	-	-	x	-	-	x	x	-	-	-	N/A
1991	Area 17	N/A	Topsoil/subsoil	N/A	x	-	-	-	x	-	-	x	-	x	-	-	N/A
1991	Area 18	N/A	Topsoil/subsoil	N/A	x	-	x	-	x	-	-	x	x	x	-	-	N/A
1991	Area 19	N/A	Topsoil/subsoil	N/A	x	-	-	-	-	-	-	x	-	-	-	-	N/A
1991	Area 20	N/A	Topsoil/subsoil	N/A	x	-	x	-	-	x	-	x	x	x	-	x	N/A
1991	Area 21	N/A	Topsoil/subsoil	N/A	x	x	x	-	x	-	-	x	x	x	x	-	N/A
1991	Area 22	N/A	Topsoil/subsoil	N/A	x	-	-	-	-	-	-	-	-	x	-	-	N/A
1991	Area 23	N/A	Topsoil/subsoil	N/A	x	-	-	-	-	-	-	x	-	x	-	-	N/A
1991	Area 24	N/A	Topsoil/subsoil	N/A	x	-	-	-	x	-	-	x	x	x	-	-	N/A
1991	Area 25	N/A	Topsoil/subsoil	N/A	x	-	-	-	-	-	-	x	-	x	-	x	N/A
1991	Area 26	N/A	Topsoil/subsoil	N/A	x	-	-	-	x	-	-	x	x	x	-	-	N/A
1991	Area 27	N/A	Topsoil/subsoil	N/A	x	x	x	-	x	-	-	x	x	x	x	x	N/A
1991	Area 28	N/A	Topsoil/subsoil	N/A	x	-	-	-	-	-	-	-	-	-	-	x	N/A
1991	Area 21	ST35	Topsoil/subsoil	N/A	-	-	-	-	-	-	-	-	-	-	-	x	N/A
1991	Area 21	ST35	Enclosure ditch	Layer 1	x	-	x	x	-	x	x	-	-	x	x	-	4 to 5

Ex. year	Area	Feature code	Feature type	Context	Flint	Other stone	RB pot	RB CBM	Pre pot	Animal bone	Charcoal	IA/RB metalwork	IA coin	RB coin	Furnace debris	Med/PM pot	Phase
1991	Area 21	ST35	Enclosure ditch	Layer 2	x	-	x	x	-	x	x	-	-	-	x	-	4 to 5
1991	Area 21	ST35	Enclosure ditch	Layer 3	-	-	-	-	-	-	-	-	-	-	-	-	4
1991	Area 21	ST35	Enclosure ditch	Layer 4	-	-	x	-	-	-	-	-	-	-	-	-	4
1991	Area 21	ST35	Enclosure ditch	Layer 5	-	-	-	-	-	-	-	-	-	-	-	-	4
1991	Area 20	ST36	Enclosure ditch	Layer 1	-	-	x	-	-	-	-	-	-	-	-	x	4
1991	Area 20	ST36	Enclosure ditch	Layer 2	-	-	-	-	-	-	-	-	-	-	-	-	4
1991	Area 20	ST36	Enclosure ditch	Layer 3	-	-	-	-	-	-	-	-	-	-	-	-	4
1991	Area 20	ST36	Enclosure ditch	Layer 4	-	-	-	-	-	-	-	-	-	-	-	-	4
1991	Area 20	ST37	Topsoil/subsoil	N/A	-	-	-	-	-	-	-	-	-	-	-	x	N/A
1991	Area 25	ST38	Burnt area and flint concentration	N/A	x	-	-	-	-	-	-	-	-	-	-	-	1
1991	Area 25	ST39	Flint concentration	N/A	x	-	-	-	-	-	-	-	-	-	-	-	1
1991	Area 25	ST40	Burnt area and flint concentration	N/A	x	-	-	-	-	-	-	-	-	-	-	-	1
1991	Area 18	Hoard N	Coin scatter	N/A	-	-	-	-	-	-	-	-	x	-	-	-	3
1991	N/A	ST41	Enclosure ditch	Layer 1	x	-	-	-	-	-	-	-		-	-	x	4
1991	N/A	ST41	Enclosure ditch	Layer 2	x	-	x	-	-	-	-	-	-	-	-	-	4
1991	N/A	ST41	Enclosure ditch	Layer 3	x	-	x	-	-	-	-	-	-	-	-	-	4
1991	N/A	ST41	Enclosure ditch	Layer 4	x	-	x	-	-	-	-	-	-	-	-	-	4
1991	N/A	ST42	Enclosure ditch	Layer 1	x	-	-	-	-	x	-	-	-	-	-	-	4
1991	N/A	ST42	Enclosure ditch	Layer 2	-	-	x	-	-	-	x	-	-	-	-	-	4
1991	N/A	ST42	Enclosure ditch	Layer 3/4	-	-	x	-	-	-	-	-	-	-	-	-	4
1991	Area 28	ST43	Burnt area and flint concentration	N/A	x	-	-	-	-	-	-	-	-	-	-	-	1
1991	Area 20	ST44	Topsoil/subsoil	N/A	-	-	-	-	-	-	-	-	-	-	-	-	N/A

Ex. year	Area	Feature code	Feature type	Context	Flint	Other stone	RB pot	RB CBM	Pre pot	Animal bone	Charcoal	IA/RB metalwork	IA coin	RB coin	Furnace debris	Med/PM pot	Phase
1991	Area 20	ST45	Enclosure ditch	N/A	x	-	-	-	-	-	-	-	x	-	-	x	4
1992	Trench 1	SA1/1	Topsoil/subsoil	N/A	-	-	-	-	-	-	-	-	-	-	-	-	N/A
1992	Trench 1	SA1/2	Enclosure ditch	Layer 1	x	-	-	-	-	-	-	-	-	-	-	-	4
1992	Trench 1	SA1/2	Enclosure ditch	Layer 2A	-	-	-	-	-	-	-	-	-	-	-	-	4
1992	Trench 1	SA1/2	Enclosure ditch	Layer 2B	-	-	-	-	-	-	-	-	-	-	-	-	4
1992	Trench 1	SA1/2	Enclosure ditch	Layer 3	-	-	-	-	-	-	-	-	-	-	-	-	4
1992	Trench 1	SA1/2	Enclosure ditch	Layer 4	-	-	-	-	-	-	-	-	-	-	-	-	4
1992	Trench 2	SA2/1	Topsoil/subsoil	N/A	x	-	-	-	-	-	-	-	-	-	-	-	N/A
1992	Trench 2	SA2/2	Enclosure ditch	Layer 1	-	-	-	-	-	-	-	-	-	-	-	-	4
1992	Trench 2	SA2/2	Enclosure ditch	Layer ?2	-	-	-	-	-	-	-	-	-	-	-	-	4
1992	Trench 3	SA3/1	Topsoil/subsoil	N/A	x	-	-	x	-	-	-	-	-	-	-	-	N/A
1992	Trench 3	SA3/2	Ditch	N/A	x	-	x	-	-	-	-	-	-	-	-	x	6
1992	Trench 4	SA4/1	Topsoil/subsoil	N/A	-	-	-	-	-	-	-	-	-	-	-	-	N/A
1992	Trench 5	SA5/1	Topsoil/subsoil	N/A	x	-	-	-	x	-	-	-	-	-	-	x	N/A
1992	Trench 5	SA5/2	Enclosure ditch	Layer 1	x	-	x	x	-	x	-	-	-	-	-	x	4
1992	Trench 5	SA5/2	Enclosure ditch	Layer 2	x	-	-	-	x	x	-	-	-	-	-	-	4
1992	Trench 5	SA5/2	Enclosure ditch	Layer 3	x	-	x	x	x	x	-	-	-	x	-	-	4
1992	Trench 5	SA5/2	Enclosure ditch	Layer 4	x	-	x	-	-	-	-	-	-	-	-	-	4
1992	Trench 5	SA5/3	Hollow/pit	N/A	x	-	-	-	x	-	-	x	-	-	-	x	?6
1992	Trench 5	SA5/4	Ditch	N/A	-	-	-	-	-	-	-	-	-	-	-	-	6
1992	Trench 5	SA5/5	Hollow/pit	N/A	-	-	-	-	-	-	-	-	-	-	-	-	?pre-4

Ex. year	Area	Feature code	Feature type	Context	Flint	Other stone	RB pot	RB CBM	Pre pot	Animal bone	Charcoal	IA/RB metalwork	IA coin	RB coin	Furnace debris	Med/PM pot	Phase
1992	Trench 6	SA6/1	Topsoil/subsoil	N/A	x	-	x	-	-	-	-	-	-	-	-	-	N/A
1992	Trench 6	SA6/2	Enclosure ditch	Layer 1	x	-	x	-	x	-	-	x	-	-	-	-	4
1992	Trench 6	SA6/2	Enclosure ditch	Layer 2	x	-	-	x	x	x	-	-	-	-	-	-	4
1992	Trench 6	SA6/2	Enclosure ditch	Layer 3	x	-	x	-	-	x	-	-	-	-	-	-	4
1992	Trench 6	SA6/2	Enclosure ditch	Layer 4	-	-	x	-	-	-	-	-	-	-	-	-	4
1992	Trench 6	SA6/3A	Ditch	N/A	-	-	-	-	-	x	-	-	-	-	-	-	?6
1992	Trench 6	SA6/3B	Ditch	N/A	x	-	x	-	x	-	-	-	-	-	-	x	?6
1992	Trench 6	SA6/3C	Ditch	N/A	-	-	-	-	-	-	-	-	-	-	-	-	?6
1992	Trench 6	SA6/4	Natural feature (gully)	N/A	-	-	-	-	-	-	-	-	-	-	-	-	N/A
1992	Trench 6	SA6/5	Natural feature (scoop/ hollow)	N/A	-	-	-	-	-	-	-	-	-	-	-	-	N/A
1992	Trench 6	SA6/6	Natural feature (gully)	N/A	-	-	-	-	-	-	-	-	-	-	-	-	N/A
1992	Trench 6	SA6/7	Natural feature (gully)	N/A	-	-	-	-	-	-	-	x	-	-	-	-	N/A
1992	Trench 6	SA6/9	Post hole	N/A	-	-	-	-	-	-	-	-	-	-	-	-	6
1992	Trench 6	SA6/10	?Natural feature (pit/ hollow)	N/A	x	-	x	-	-	-	-	-	-	-	-	-	?N/A
1992	Trench 6	SA6/11	?Post hole/?animal burrow	N/A	-	-	-	-	-	-	-	-	-	-	-	-	?6
1992	Trench 7	SA7/1	Topsoil/subsoil	N/A	x	-	-	-	x	x	-	-	-	-	-	-	N/A
1992	Trench 7	SA7/2	Scoop/hollow	N/A	-	x	-	-	x	-	-	-	-	-	-	-	2
1992	Trench 7	SA7/3	Natural feature (gully)	N/A	x	-	x	-	x	-	-	-	-	-	-	-	?
1992	Trench 7	SA7/4	Ditch	N/A	x	-	-	-	x	-	-	-	-	-	-	-	6
1992	Trench 7	SA7/5	Ditch	N/A	x	x	x	-	x	x	-	x	-	-	-	-	?6

Ex. year	Area	Feature code	Feature type	Context	Flint	Other stone	RB pot	RB CBM	Pre pot	Animal bone	Charcoal	IA/RB metalwork	IA coin	RB coin	Furnace debris	Med/PM pot	Phase
1992	Trench 7	SA7/6	Natural feature (gully)	N/A	x	x	x	-	x	-	-	-	-	-	-	-	?
1992	Trench 7	SA7/7	Natural feature (gully)	N/A	x	-	x	-	x	x	-	-	-	-	-	x	?
1992	Trench 7	SA7/8	Natural feature (gully)	N/A	x	-	-	-	x	-	-	-	-	-	-	-	?
1992	Trench 7	SA7/10	Pit	N/A	x	-	-	-	x	-	-	-	-	-	-	-	2
1992	Trench 7	SA7/11	Pit	N/A	x	-	-	-	x	-	-	-	-	-	-	-	?2
1992	Trench 7	SA7/12	Pit	N/A	-	x	-	-	-	-	-	-	-	-	-	-	?2
1992	Trench 7	SA7/13	Ditch	N/A	x	-	-	-	x	-	-	-	-	-	-	-	?6
1992	Trench 8	SA8/1	Topsoil/subsoil	N/A	-	-	-	-	-	-	-	-	-	-	-	-	N/A
1992	Trench 8	SA8/2	Ditch	N/A	-	-	-	-	-	-	-	-	-	-	-	-	6
1992	Trench 9	SA9/1	Topsoil/subsoil	N/A	x	-	x	-	-	-	-	-	-	-	-	-	N/A
1992	Trench 10	SA10/1	Topsoil/subsoil	N/A	-	-	-	-	-	-	-	-	-	-	-	-	N/A
1992	Trench 11	SA11/1	Topsoil/subsoil	N/A	-	-	-	-	-	-	-	-	-	-	-	-	N/A
1992	Trench 11	SA11/2	Enclosure ditch	N/A	-	-	-	-	-	-	-	-	-	-	-	-	4
1992	Trench 11	SA11/3	Ditch	N/A	-	-	-	-	-	-	-	-	-	-	-	-	6
1992	Trench 12	SA12/1	Topsoil/subsoil	N/A	x	-	x	-	x	-	-	-	-	-	-	x	N/A
1992	Trench 12	SA12/2	Natural feature (gully)	N/A	x	-	-	-	x	-	-	-	-	-	-	-	N/A
1992	Trench 12	SA12/3	Natural feature (gully)	N/A	-	-	-	-	-	-	-	-	-	-	-	-	N/A
1992	Trench 12	SA12/4A	Animal burrow/?post hole	N/A	-	-	-	-	x	-	-	-	-	-	-	-	?
1992	Trench 12	SA12/4B	Animal burrow/?post hole	N/A	-	-	-	-	x	-	-	-	-	-	-	-	?
1992	Trench 12	SA12/5	Animal burrow/?post hole	N/A	-	-	x	-	x	-	-	-	-	-	-	-	?

Ex. year	Area	Feature code	Feature type	Context	Flint	Other stone	RB pot	RB CBM	Pre pot	Animal bone	Charcoal	IA/RB metalwork	IA coin	RB coin	Furnace debris	Med/PM pot	Phase
1992	Trench 12	SA12/6	?Hearth	N/A	x	-	-	-	x	-	-	-	-	-	-	-	?2
1992	Trench 12	SA12/7	Animal burrow/?post hole	N/A	-	-	-	-	-	-	-	-	-	-	-	-	?
1992	Trench 12	SA12/8	Animal burrow/?post hole	N/A	-	-	-	-	x	-	-	-	-	-	-	-	?
1992	Trench 12	SA12/9	Animal burrow/?post hole	N/A	x	-	-	-	x	-	-	-	-	-	-	-	?
1992	Trench 12	SA12/10	Animal burrow/?post hole	N/A	-	-	-	-	x	-	-	-	-	-	-	-	?
1992	Trench 12	SA12/11	Animal burrow/?post hole	N/A	-	-	-	-	-	-	-	-	-	-	-	-	?
1992	Trench 12	SA12/12	Animal burrow/?post hole	N/A	x	-	-	-	-	-	-	-	-	-	-	-	?
1992	Trench 12	SA12/13	Animal burrow/?post hole	N/A	-	-	-	-	-	-	-	-	-	-	-	-	?
1992	Trench 12	SA12/14	Animal burrow/?post hole	N/A	-	-	-	-	-	-	-	-	-	-	-	-	?
1992	Trench 12	SA12/15	Animal burrow/?post hole	N/A	-	-	-	-	x	-	-	-	-	-	-	-	?
1992	Trench 12	SA12/16	Animal burrow/?post hole	N/A	x	-	-	-	x	-	-	-	-	-	-	-	?
1992	Trench 12	SA12/17	Animal burrow/?post hole	N/A	-	-	-	-	-	-	-	-	-	-	-	-	?
1992	Trench 12	SA12/18	Animal burrow/?post hole	N/A	-	-	-	-	-	-	-	-	-	-	-	-	?
1992	Trench 12	SA12/19	Animal burrow/?post hole	N/A	-	-	-	-	-	-	-	-	-	-	-	-	?
1992	Trench 12	SA12/20	Animal burrow/?post hole	N/A	-	-	-	-	-	-	-	-	-	-	-	-	?
1992	Trench 12	SA12/21	Animal burrow/?post hole	N/A	-	-	-	-	-	-	-	-	-	-	-	-	?
1992	Trench 12	SA12/22	Animal burrow/?post hole	N/A	x	-	-	-	x	-	-	-	-	-	-	-	?
1992	Trench 12	SA12/23	Animal burrow/?post hole	N/A	-	-	-	-	-	-	-	-	-	-	-	-	?
1992	Trench 12	SA12/24	Animal burrow/?post hole	N/A	-	-	-	-	-	-	-	-	-	-	-	-	?
1992	Trench 12	SA12/25	Animal burrow/?post hole	N/A	-	-	-	-	-	-	-	-	-	-	-	-	?

Ex. year	Area	Feature code	Feature type	Context	Flint	Other stone	RB pot	RB CBM	Pre pot	Animal bone	Charcoal	IA/RB metalwork	IA coin	RB coin	Furnace debris	Med/PM pot	Phase
1992	Trench 12	SA12/26	Animal burrow/?post hole	N/A	x	-	-	-	x	-	-	-	-	-	-	-	?
1992	Trench 12	SA12/27	Animal burrow/?post hole	N/A	x	-	-	-	x	-	-	-	-	-	-	-	?
1992	Trench 12	SA12/28	Animal burrow/?post hole	N/A	-	-	-	-	-	-	-	-	-	-	-	-	?
1992	Trench 13	SA13/1	Recent disturbance	N/A	x	-	-	-	-	-	-	-	-	-	-	-	6
1992	Trench 14	SA14/1	Topsoil/subsoil	N/A	-	-	-	-	-	-	-	-	-	-	-	-	N/A
1992	Trench 14	SA14/2	?Enclosure ditch	N/A	x	-	x	-	-	-	-	-	-	-	-	-	?4
1992	Trench 15	SA15/1	Topsoil/subsoil	N/A	-	-	-	-	-	-	-	x	-	-	-	x	N/A
1992	Trench 15	SA15/2	Building debris	N/A	x	-	-	-	-	x	-	-	-	-	-	x	6
1992	Trench 15	SA15/3	Natural feature (tree bowl)	N/A	x	x	-	-	-	-	-	-	-	-	-	x	N/A
1992	Trench 16	SA16/1	Topsoil/subsoil	N/A	x	-	-	-	x	-	-	-	-	-	-	x	N/A
1992	Trench 16	SA16/2	Ditch	N/A	-	-	-	-	-	-	-	-	-	-	-	-	?6
1992	Trench 16	SA16/3	?Natural feature (Ditch/ gully)	N/A	-	-	-	-	-	-	-	-	-	-	-	-	N/A
1992	Trench 16	SA16/4	Ditch	N/A	-	-	-	-	-	-	-	-	-	-	-	-	?6
1992	Trench 17	SA17/1	Topsoil/subsoil	N/A	x	x	-	-	-	-	-	-	-	-	-	x	N/A
1992	Trench 17	SA17/2	Enclosure ditch	Layer 1	x	-	x	-	x	-	-	-	-	-	-	-	4
1992	Trench 17	SA17/2	Enclosure ditch	Layer 2	-	-	-	-	-	-	-	-	-	-	-	-	4
1992	Trench 17	SA17/2	Enclosure ditch	Layer 3	-	-	-	-	-	-	-	-	-	-	-	-	4
1992	Trench 17	SA17/2	Enclosure ditch	Layer 4	-	-	-	-	-	-	-	-	-	-	-	-	4
1992	Trench 17	SA17/3	Ditch	N/A	-	-	-	-	-	-	-	-	-	-	-	x	6
1992	Trench 18	SA18/1	Topsoil/subsoil	N/A	x	-	x	-	x	-	-	-	-	-	-	x	N/A

Ex. year	Area	Feature code	Feature type	Context	Flint	Other stone	RB pot	RB CBM	Pre pot	Animal bone	Charcoal	IA/RB metalwork	IA coin	RB coin	Furnace debris	Med/PM pot	Phase
1992	Trench 18	SA18/2	Enclosure ditch	N/A	x	-	x	-	-	x	-	-	-	-	-	x	4
1992	Trench 18	SA18/3	Ditch	N/A	-	-	-	-	-	-	-	-	-	-	-	-	?
1992	Trench 19	SA19/1	Topsoil/subsoil	N/A	x	-	-	-	x	-	-	-	-	-	-	-	N/A
1992	Trench 20	SA20/1	Topsoil/subsoil	N/A	x	-	-	-	-	-	-	-	-	-	-	x	N/A
1992	Trench 21	SA21/1	Topsoil/subsoil	N/A	x	-	-	-	-	-	-	-	-	-	-	x	N/A
1992	Trench 21	SA21/2	?Natural feature (Ditch/ gully)	N/A	-	-	-	-	-	-	-	-	-	-	-	-	?
1992	Trench 21	SA21/3	?Natural feature (Ditch/ gully)	N/A	-	-	-	-	-	-	-	-	-	-	-	-	?
1992	Trench 21	SA21/4	?Natural feature (Ditch/ gully)	N/A	-	-	-	-	-	-	-	-	-	-	-	-	?

Appendix 2
Unstratified Flint and Flint Redeposited in Later Features

Peter Makey

This appendix provides a full report of the unstratified flint and flint redeposited in later features at the site. See Chapter 6 for a summary of flint by artefact type as well as a more detailed account of flint from Neolithic features and flint redeposited in Bronze Age and Iron Age features.

Unstratified flint from general areas and fieldwalking 1990–1991

Areas 1–13: 1990 (SN) topsoil and fieldwalking

The flint assemblage recovered during general topsoil stripping during the 1990 season totals 1,043 pieces. This material is from the upper topsoil; once areas were defined, unstratified flint finds were allocated as unstratified in their respective coded areas. This general assemblage is, as might be expected, generally heavily damaged, with extensive evidence of plough damage. There is a surprisingly limited typological range of tools, retouched and utilised pieces amounting to 198 pieces and debitage totalling 845 pieces including cores. There are a few miscellaneous retouched pieces in the topsoil that may come from knives or scrapers. Period-diagnostic implements are scarce although the assemblage is predominately Neolithic.

In the area north-east of the wood, the debitage is very crude with almost 80% showing traces of very heavy battering although in terms of overall state the material looks slightly fresher. There is probably a degree of primary reduction in this area. Much of the discarded debitage here would have been highly suitable for the manufacture of tools such as scrapers. However, there is less selectivity with regard to the quality of the raw material.

SN/EC (in SN19, a pottery findspot to the east of this area) contained a broken flake of fine olive grey (Munsell 5Y 4/1) till flint. Probably Neolithic.

Area 14: 1990 (SN) topsoil and fieldwalking

The topsoil assemblage is nondescript but contains a high proportion of crude flake cores and debitage that is primarily composed of chunky tertiary flakes; only two heavily rolled blades are present. Two chunks are burnt. The cores are heavily battered and show some signs of anvil percussion. There is one fine opposed platform blade core that is also the only patinated example from this area. It is probable that this represents a later Mesolithic or Early Neolithic element. Four scrapers are present, which are all broad end forms. Two single-notched flakes, a spurred flake, a fine un-retouched piercer (defined by use wear) and a broad, flaked finely retouched piercer; SN/JB are present in the assemblage; but most notable is the presence of a small edge-blunted point microlith that is in fine condition. Overall, post-depositional damage is extensive.

Area 15: 1990 (SN) topsoil and fieldwalking

The unstratified material in this area is extensively plough-damaged although breakage is comparably low (<20%), the cores are heavily rolled. There are six small blades and an atypically large (length 56mm, width 18mm) double-crested, utilised blade.

There are probably two separate phases of Neolithic material, a wider variety of flaking techniques being evident. Notable examples of flaking styles are represented by a fragmentary bi-facially flaked piece and broken glossy trancheform flake. The flake gloss may be related to heat pre-treatment and this is possibly the bi-product of arrowhead manufacture. Evidence of fine platform edge trimming is present on a broken flake from SN/KX. The core rejuvenation flakes are a variety of forms but two examples retain traces of 'chisel-shaped' flake removals suitable for arrowhead manufacture. The scrapers are manufactured on thinner flakes than other areas despite the presence of flake debitage suitable for manufacturing scrapers. A piercer has been fashioned on a flake that is probably the bi-product of flake axe manufacture. Two trimmed flakes in the assemblage may be related to flake knife production.

SN/BC scraping over SN6, a pottery findspot to the west of the area investigated in 1990, produced a crude flake and a worn chunky cortical flake in association with abraded sherds of possible Later Bronze Age pottery.

SN/KC produced a primary flake and a blade that had macroscopic edge wear. The pieces are probably residual.

1991 (ST) Backfill from 1990 excavations

The backfill only contained 40 pieces of flint: 19 flakes/chunks/chippings, one blade, 16 cores, one hammerstone, a piece of battered natural and two miscellaneously retouched pieces. With regard to 1990 topsoil-stripping by box scraper and the area covered this indicates a high recovery rate.

1991 (ST) general fieldwalking

In the general fieldwalking assemblage from 1991 there is a great deal of variation in the degree of plough damage. The tertiary debitage contains a high proportion of blades and bladelets (>50%); they are scarce in the secondary debitage. This trend is also notable in ST/AS (Area 20, fieldwalking) which also contained a notched bladelet. The blade material is a mix of very fresh-looking material and occasional densely patinated (white) multi-crested blades.

The reduction sequence of debitage from the fieldwalking 1990 and 1991 compared:

1) North-east of wood (1990, SN)
Primary = 118 (67%); secondary = 53 (30%); tertiary = 4 (3%)
2) ST Fieldwalking (1991, ST)
Primary = 54 (39%); secondary = 64 (46%); tertiary =22 (15%)

Area 18: 1991 (ST) topsoil and fieldwalking

In group ST/BH the ratio of primary: secondary: tertiary, flakes is different and translates to primary 38%: secondary 41%: tertiary 21%. This material resembles a knapping cluster.

In group ST/BK the debitage is more blade-like.

Area 19: 1991 (ST) topsoil and fieldwalking

The assemblage from this area includes one very large patinated, single-crested flake (ST/BN) and a two-platformed blade core of Mesolithic character, although the majority of the material in this area is of Neolithic aspect.

(ST/BN) primary/cortical debitage is predominant in this group at 51%.

There is a great deal of uniformity in the raw material used to manufacture the scrapers in ST/BN.

Area 20: 1991 (ST) topsoil and fieldwalking

In this area there was a degree of chronologically related spatial patterning although quantification of this is difficult. The material is predominately Neolithic.

ST/BW contained a possible pick that was manufactured on a dark olive-grey flint with a light patina. The piece resembles a very heavily reworked core. The same context also contained a crude possible flake knife.

This assemblage is notable for including a flake from a polished flint axe, a retouched core rejuvenation flake (side platform removal) from a large fine core and a core in group ST/CU. The core is a particularly fine four-platformed blade type (removals, 30mm in length) which possesses two sets of opposed keeled platforms retaining an area of smooth nodular cortex.

Area 21: 1991 (ST) topsoil and fieldwalking

The flint assemblage in this area is predominately composed of crude unclassifiable cores, three of which have been burnt, and comparatively few rejuvenation flakes. Unusually there are no scrapers but a far wider typological range of retouched tools than most of the other areas. The ST/HP assemblage includes a small spherical, cortical flint nodule that has been used as a hammerstone. Probably of later Neolithic date, the assemblage is uniform, with flake debitage being predominately chunky with a high incidence of primary flakes. Traces of burning are limited. Notable pieces include a small utilised flake that possibly comes from the finishing of a flake axe, a possible flint sickle (ST/HP) and a shouldered blade with edge blunting.

Group ST/DY contained three burnt chunks, two primary flakes and a burnt flake with two small areas of nondescript retouch. The pieces are made of coarse-grained local flint and look residual.

Group ST/EY produced just four pieces, all undatable. These comprise three small chunks and a cortical primary flake.

Group ST/HP includes chunky debitage which is mainly from primary and secondary stages of reduction. Plough damage is very extensive on this material. There are four utilised flakes, four utilised blade fragments, a possible axe flake and a flaked flake that may be a bi-product of axe manufacture. The utilised flakes are broad and the blades comprise three medial and one distal fragment that has been snapped and comes from a broader blade that has been extensively rolled. The utilised blade fragments are notable since there is little evidence of blades in this area. In addition to this, one broad flake shows use wear that has not modified its edges. The miscellaneous and edge-retouched pieces are, with one exception, very crude. The retouched component includes a piercer, two single-notched flakes and a double-notched cortical flake worked on the ventral face. Further notable pieces include an invasively flaked, retouched fragment with heavy patina which possibly comes from the manufacture of a single-edged flake knife but has been classed as indeterminate. A retouched flake from this assemblage possesses a heavy use gloss and is probably an unusual flint sickle, and a crude flake has a very fine serrated edge. This assemblage also contains a shouldered (left-hand side) blade with slight marginal left-hand retouch and oblique left-hand distal retouch. This possibly represents a Mesolithic component of the assemblage, being reminiscent of an edge-blunted blade.

Area 22: 1991 (ST) topsoil and fieldwalking

Group ST/CR: the material from this area is a reasonably uniform mix of broad flakes and regular blade-like flakes with a high proportion of tertiary debitage (40%). Flakes range in length from 20 to 61mm, and in breadth from 12 to 33mm. Most of the raw material is a brownish-grey (Munsell 5YR 4/1) fine-grained till flint. Breakages amount to 18 pieces (17.4%); plough damage is variable and appears to be relatively recent. Only four of the pieces are burnt, two of which are cores. The cores are notably small and two have platforms that have been rejuvenated. There are only seven scrapers, all of which are small. One example is a small (30mm-long) patinated long end scraper with convex retouch on the proximal end of a small bladelet of Mesolithic character. Another crude end scraper is notable for having a pronounced hertzian bulb of percussion, consistent with an indirect knapping technique. There are three utilised pieces in this area, one of which has an old-looking patina. A notable inclusion is a shouldered blade (proximal, left-hand side) with slight right-hand edge retouch.

Area 23: 1991 (ST) topsoil and fieldwalking

There is a degree of conformity in this area with a high ratio (36%) of retouched implements; stylistically almost 70% of the flint is probably of contemporary date. The assemblage is consistent with Middle to later Neolithic flint assemblages. Fine-quality dark olive-grey flint was selected for the majority of the pieces and the quality of knapping is high. Of note is the occurrence of nine notched flakes, one piercer, a serrated-edged bladelet, a spurred flake and a denticulate flake. The notched pieces are crude and include pieces with one, two and four notches. In two instances these have been manufactured on discarded core rejuvenation flakes. In ST/CT there are 20 tertiary flakes which include small flakes and chippings consistent with a knapping assemblage. Of note are some flakes suitable for, or the bi-product of, the production of leaf-shaped arrowheads despite the paucity of such pieces in the collection.

Area 24: 1991 (ST) topsoil and fieldwalking

There is a large topsoil assemblage that has a large proportion of tertiary flakes (58 pieces; 37%) and fine blades and bladelets. Compared to other areas, evidence of burning is limited with only two pieces, a flake and a core, having been burnt. There is a great variation in the cores and the form of the scrapers, although the scrapers tend to be in the smaller size range (<30mm), more characteristic of later Neolithic assemblages. Early Neolithic material is represented by a small collection of patinated blades and core rejuvenation flakes in the topsoil. Notable pieces in the topsoil assemblage are two serrated-edged bladelets, and one serrated-edged blade. There is an unusual flake of oviform shape that is not retouched but has heavy abrasion around all of its lateral edges, consistent with its having been used as a knapping tool. A finely retouched flake scraper fragment looks as though the knapper's intention may have been to produce a leaf arrowhead.

A broad (width 42mm, length 6mm) flake of light olive-grey (Munsell 5Y 6/1) till flint with heavy invasive dorsal flaking may be related to flint axe production.

In group ST/DW there is proportionally a very high ratio (42%) of retouched tools and tertiary flakes; five pieces have been burnt. It is possible that some of the material is Early Neolithic. The Area 24 lithic suite is suggestive of settlement, with the assemblage i looking more 'domestic' than in other areas. Some of the debitage and miscellaneous retouched pieces look like the bi-product of knife manufacture. There is an unusually high proportion of notched flakes (six pieces), all of which appear to have been used. The use wear is consistent with wood-working. The assemblage is similar to adjacent Area H.

Area 25: 1991 (ST) topsoil and fieldwalking

Evidence of hard hammer technique is evident on material from this area; many pieces possess dorsal hinge terminations and dorsal flake and blade scars are frequent.

Most of the material is probably Neolithic although there is probably a small Beaker component exemplified by a small circular side and end scraper from ST/EO. The topsoil assemblage contained a trimmed blade that resembles a large backed blade microlith. The piece is atypical and may be a scarce indicator of a later Mesolithic, Early Neolithic phase of activity on the site. There is a comparative shortage of scrapers in this area although they are present in the topsoil (six examples). In Area 10 there is a noticeable increase in the incidence of macroscopic use wear.

ST/EM: Some of the scrapers here have faceted butts and are broader than many in the other areas. There is a concentration of piercers (four) and notched pieces (seven). Other notable pieces include a crude awl. A further three notched pieces and a flake knife were present in ST/EO. The knife looks more residual than the material from the same context. The bulk of the assemblage is probably Neolithic.

ST/EW: single find of a crude partly bifacially flaked leaf shaped arrowhead of Green's (1980) type.2Bm, with a shallow notch on its left-hand margin that has been formed from the ventral surface. The piece has been manufactured on medium grained olive grey (Munsell 5Y 4/1) till derived flint, with a small degree of dorsal cortex and has been slightly damaged. It appears as though the notch was to aid in hafting. The example is typical of Early to Middle Neolithic assemblages.

Area 26: 1991 (ST) topsoil and fieldwalking

The flint from this area is predominately of Early to Middle Neolithic character, consistent with Peterborough Ware assemblages, with a lesser component of material that looks earlier. Though small, this area appears to have a slightly more varied range of typological implement forms and the occurrence of three awls is noteworthy.

Damage is extensive with almost a quarter of the material being broken. There is a disparity with many of the broken pieces being proximal ends of pieces. Many of the flakes have hinge terminations. Plough damage is extensive on many of the flints. There is a difference in the colour of the raw material in this area where a slightly more grey-coloured flint predominates. Sixteen pieces including two core fragments have been burnt and the burning appears to be of ancient origin, related to possible domestic activities. There is an increase in the representation of blades and bladelets and a comparatively low proportion of scrapers; indeed, the fieldwalking assemblage from Area 26 only produced three scrapers. One of the scrapers (ST/HG) is notably atypical of the rest of the Ken Hill material, being a small (length 19mm, thickness 43mm) thin cortical scraper of circular form. The flakes are broad, often being over 30mm in width. Notable surface finds are a damaged, unfinished oblique arrowhead and a broken minimally retouched leaf arrowhead (ST/HH). The leaf arrowhead has minimal proximal retouch, although it possesses a fine invasive retouch on the proximal end of a single crested blade like flake. The tip has been broken since deposition. This piece has parallels in the Neolithic assemblage from Hurst Fen, Mildenhall, Suffolk (Clark *et al.* 1960, 220, fig. 13, F32).

The main characteristic of the Area 26 flint assemblages is the large proportion of cores and the comparative lack of associated flakes although over 50% of the flakes are from tertiary stages of core reduction and the presence of arrowheads and knives.

ST/EV contained a finely worked awl, manufactured on a core rejuvenation flake, a miscellaneously retouched chunk and two burnt core fragments. The flakes are mainly primary with pebble cortex.

ST/FB contained a large cortical triple-notched flake, a very large tabular core, and a rejuvenation flake from a three-platformed blade core with traces of flake removals of over 88mm in length.

ST/FC: In this group the flint is predominately of Middle Neolithic aspect with a slight increase in the incidence of dorsal blade scars. ST/FC contains seven blades. Notable pieces include an end scraper with three notches, three piercers, four gravers and a crude fabricator. All the gravers possess traces of heavy utilisation. ST/FC also contained the sole example of a tanged flake that had been manufactured on a plunging core rejuvenation flake. Non-retouched pieces of note include a split core and two hammerstones. One hammerstone is a small spherical (45mm diameter) flint nodule; the other is a small utilised gravel pebble that has received heavy repeated battering. A discoidal core fragment has received miscellaneous retouch.

This group contains a notable piece of non-prehistoric flintwork in the form of a small gun flint; probably from a pistol of 18th to 19th-century date. Rectangular in shape and made by the segmented blade technique, it measures 15 x 22 x 6.5mm with a straight snap fracture to both lateral margins and a hinged butt and a partial dorsal cortex. The gun flint is made of local greyish-brown fine-grained till flint (Munsell 5YR 3/2) with a dark yellowish-orange (Munsell 10YR 6/6) cortex. There is a slight trace of edge usage consistent with firing. The flint is not consistent with the products of the local Brandon gun flint factories.

ST/FD contained no cores despite having rejuvenation flakes. Rejuvenation flakes had in two instances been re-purposed; one being notched and one being used to manufacture a scraper. The debitage totalled 39 pieces including a blade and a bladelet. Notable pieces include a flake knife, a fabricator, a piercer, two denticulate flakes and a notch.

ST/HE was a single find spot for a flake knife or leaf point defined by fine, though minimal invasive parallel, bifacial retouch on proximal and distal ends.

ST/HF was a single find spot for a very fine awl with an elongate point retouched down both of its lateral margins and extensive edge use and tip abrasion.

ST/HG was a single find spot for a small circular scraper (as above).

ST/HH was a single find spot for a broken minimally retouched elongate leaf arrowhead.

Area 27: 1991 (ST) topsoil and fieldwalking

The material from this area is atypical of the Snettisham assemblage and is probably related to the admixture of Neolithic and Bronze Age flint. Four of the flakes bear a very dense white cortication/patination and there is a variation in raw material utilisation. Many of the flints show traces of hard hammer percussion. Almost 5% of the lithic material has been subjected to prehistoric burning. Twenty-one (un-retouched) blades are present in this area's assemblage which is higher than normal; furthermore, the blade material almost conjoins. It is possible that ploughing had only started to disperse material just prior to the excavations.

ST/GO: Crude debitage; mainly tertiary flakes but includes three blades and one bladelet. One of the five cores has been re-used as a hammerstone. One chunk suitable for manufacturing a scraper has been burnt. There is a single extended end scraper with a squared end and two single-notched flakes, one of which also possesses edge use wear.

ST/HM: Four of the scrapers have been manufactured on cores, one of which was a discoidal form. Another atypical feature of the scrapers in this area is an unusual tendency for the retouching having been applied to the bulbar end of flake supports. At least one of the miscellaneous retouched pieces looks like a failed attempt at manufacturing flake knives. A single-edged flake knife is present in the ST/HM assemblage. The implement has fine scalar retouch on its right-hand margin and bears an unusual patination. This piece may represent earlier Neolithic elements. Also in the ST/HM assemblage there is a flake with retouch along two margins, forming a point; it may be coincidental, however, as this implement is more of a later Mesolithic aspect.

Area 28: 1991 (ST) topsoil and fieldwalking

There is a slight variation in the flint raw material selected for knapping in this area; with olive-black (Munsell 5Y 2/1) flint being more frequent than the olive-grey (Munsell 5Y 4/1) that constitutes the bulk of the material. With one exception the cores are very irregular flake forms showing no overall consistency and heavy post-depositional damage. The one exception is a single platformed bladelet core that has been worked all round. This is possibly a Mesolithic piece. In the topsoil assemblage nearly 58% of debitage comes from tertiary stages of knapping and includes fine finishing/trimming flakes and three trancheform flakes that would be suitable for arrowhead production. There is a low incidence of burning with just two pieces being burnt. Some of the edge-retouched flakes in this area are very broad, one example from the topsoil being 58mm in width. Notable pieces from the topsoil include a crude piercer: a cortical flake that possesses a broad single notch (16mm width, 4mm depth), a spur manufactured on a flat core and a crude flake knife on a broad flake with heavy cortex. A second knife is represented by a proximal fragment of a very fine double-edged flake knife.

A fine, thin oval-plan, double-sided scraper of probable Neolithic date is present in the topsoil.

Another scraper is of unusual elongated-end form being manufactured on the end of a plunging core rejuvenation flake. The piece looks a bit like a fabricator but has use wear consistent with a scraper. The retouched pieces in Area 28 have a lower degree of visible edge use than those in other areas. Of most note is the presence of a failed (during manufacture) later Neolithic oblique arrowhead of Clark's (1934) class G and a heavily worked rod-like fabricator of bi-convex section.

ST/HS: Notable inclusions are three blades and two bladelets, a very crude notched flake, and 18 cores, three of which are burnt. The flakes are very chunky and crude. Eight scrapers are present; these are of varying typological forms but do include a rare denticulate scraper with three denticulations on its left-hand side and end, and right-hand side retouch.

Unstratified and re-deposited flint from 1991 (ST) slots through enclosure ditch

Feature ST41 (1991 slot through enclosure ditch)

ST41 topsoil: Twelve pieces of flint. Two cortical nodule fragments (not cores) show traces of bashing and minimal flake removals; one of which is partially patinated. There are three crude flake cores: two double platformed and one globular unclassifiable. A core fragment has been used as a hammerstone. The debitage is crude and totals three pieces: a cortical chipping, one secondary and one tertiary flake. The retouched component of the assemblage consists of just three pieces: two scrapers and an edge-retouched flake. One scraper is a convex end form on a cortical pebble; the other is a flake scraper with a small area of retouch and post-depositional damage. Both pieces have been used. The edge-retouched flake is a broad flake (30mm width) with a pronounced bulb, minimal retouch and a recent notch that is damage related rather than functional/intentional.

ST/FU (ST41, enclosure ditch, Layer 1): The assemblage comprises two un-retouched flakes: one primary and one secondary in sharp condition. Raw material is fine to medium-grained olive-grey (Munsell 5Y 4/1) and dark yellowish-orange (10 YR 6/6) till flint.

ST/FW (ST41, enclosure ditch, Layer 2): A secondary blade-like flake in very fresh condition with extensive platform crushing. Raw material is fine grained olive-grey (Munsell 5Y 4/1) till flint.

ST/FX (ST41, enclosure ditch, Layer 3): Contained two pieces: a core and a chunk. The core is keeled with three platforms and has been manufactured on a till pebble; olive-black (Munsell 5Y 2/1) with extensive dark yellowish-orange (Munsell 10YR 6/6) cortex. The core has 12 small flake removals (average 18 x 20mm). The material is very fresh.

ST/FY (ST41, enclosure ditch, Layer 4): A small tertiary flake with a fine-trimmed platform. Olive-grey (Munsell 5Y 4/1) flint.

Feature ST42 (1991 slot through enclosure ditch)

ST/FZ (ST42, enclosure ditch, Layer 1): The fill contained only 11 pieces, none of which are period-diagnostic although one piece is probably of an earlier date than the rest. Ten pieces are debitage and one piece is a single-notched flake. Four of the pieces of debitage are small, heavily burnt (calcined) chunks. The un-burnt debitage comprises a crude secondary flake, three tertiary flakes and a chunk, plus an older looking, totally white patinated and rolled flake. A tertiary flake has a shallow notch on its distal end (12mm length by 2mm depth).

ST/GA (ST42, enclosure ditch, Layer 1): The debitage is very crude and chunky, amounting to 24 pieces, plus one fine-crested flake. Eleven pieces of the debitage are burnt. In addition to this an unidentifiable flake core fragment, two pieces of carrstone and a piece of unworked natural flint have also been burnt. A piece of natural has battering. The sole diagnostic implement is a piercer manufactured on the convergence of two snap fractures. Most of the raw material is the coarse-grained flint often found on site. This is probably the crudest of the Ken Hill assemblages.

ST42 at 58cm depth: Below the upper fill the feature contained two pieces: a moderate brown (Munsell 5YR 4/4) chert flake with a slight quartzite cortex and small chunk of lightly burnt flint.

ST45: a broken edge retouched single crested bladelet with superficial resemblance to a microlith; the retouch is on the ventral right and side and is invasive/minimal. The piece is most probably Neolithic and is not in a fresh state.

Unstratified and re-deposited flint from 1992 (SA) excavations

The most noticeable feature of the SA (i.e. 1992) flint assemblages (mostly from the southern part of the site, where the 1992 trenches were opened) is the limited implement range.

There is a slight difference with regards to the raw material in SA, which tends to be light olive-grey or darker in colour, i.e. extremes. There are broader flakes, many hinged, and a mixture of very large and small squat flakes; pieces tend to be broader than they are long. In SA/AC the flakes are different being atypically large and blade-like. The retouched component is low but piercers and gravers are a feature. There is slight evidence for a limited degree of blade production (SA/DF); where present in the stratified contexts blades tend to be proximal and medial fragments (with a few exceptions such as assemblage SA/CJ) the distal ends tend to be missing. Assemblage SA/CJ appears to represent one or two knapping events for the production of blades/bladelets with two flakes conjoining a broken bladelet; a further two pieces nearly refit. Large blade material is present in SA/BY and SA/KA. In a few instances (e.g. SA/AS) cores are in association with debitage removed from them. In many instances (e.g. SA/EC) there are densely, patinated blades in assemblages of un-patinated material. In a few instances (e.g. SA/AV) there are exceptionally large flakes but by and large these are rare occurrences.

In at least one instance (SA/DF) it appears as though flint has been crushed and/or burnt, probably to provide temper for pottery. Occasionally the assemblages contain large natural cortical nodules of high-quality flint from which a single flake has been removed. A high degree of burning is evident in most of the sealed assemblages. This tends to be more evident on the chunks and chippings and as such is possibly related to the production of flint temper.

The overall incidence of edge utilisation is rare; notable exceptions are a large blade-like flake from SA/AC and two blades from SA/BY.

1992 Trench 1

SA/AA (Trench 1, Feature SA1/2, enclosure ditch): A collection of irregular flakes and three chunks, two of which are calcined (burnt). One flake has an old-looking patina. Retouch includes a graver on a thin flake and a crude piercer. The graver is defined by minimal retouch and use wear. Despite being from a sealed context this material does not look stratified.

1992 Trench 2

SA/AE (Trench 2 topsoil): Nondescript chunky material including a broad flake with utilisation and a very crude scraper manufactured on a previously rolled irregular flake.

1992 Trench 3

SA/AF (Trench 3 topsoil): Primary and secondary flakes; one with a very pronounced hinge termination and excavation damage.

1992 Trench 5

SA/AB (Trench 5, Feature SA5/2, Section A, Layer 1, enclosure ditch): Hinged flake, single-crested bladelet.

SA/AC (Trench 5 topsoil): Variable material includes four cores and a plunging rejuvenation flake. Debitage is a mix of primary, secondary and tertiary flakes, some with pronounced hinge terminations. The flakes are larger than most of the Ken Hill material and blade form. One broad flake (length 33mm, width 34mm) has heavy unidirectional ventral use wear. A flake with a single notch (dorsal, right-hand side) also has traces of use wear on the ventral right-hand side, opposed to the notch. A scraper has been manufactured on the ventral face of a core rejuvenation flake/platform removal.

SA/AH (Trench 5, Feature SA5/2, Section C, Layer 1, enclosure ditch): A collection of crude, irregular material containing a single-platformed core, two broken blades and most notably a 'classic' angle burin. A broken blade and two flakes have an old dense white-coloured patina.

SA/AJ (Trench 5, Feature SA5/2, Section B, Layer 1, enclosure ditch): Mainly small spall-like flakes and crude nondescript cortical flakes and chunks. The assemblage includes a very crude edge-retouched flake and microlith with right hand side retouch.

SA/AK (Trench 5, Feature SA5/2, Section A, Layer 2, enclosure ditch): Tertiary flake.

SA/AL (Trench 5, Feature SA5/2, Section A, Layer 3, enclosure ditch): Convex end and side (right) on a thin flake with a pronounced bulb.

SA/AN (Trench 5, Feature SA5/2, Section B, Layer 1, enclosure ditch): One flake is calcined and looks older. The material is very crude and includes an irregular cortical flake with use wear.

SA/AP (Trench 5, Feature SA5/2, Section C, Layer 1, enclosure ditch): Six nondescript flakes and a very crude flake scraper (right-hand side).

SA/AS (Trench 5, Feature SA5/2, Section D, Layer 1, enclosure ditch): A fresh-looking, fine, two-platformed blade/bladelet core of olive-grey till flint (Munsell 5Y 4/1) in association with a blade that may have come from the core.

SA/AU (Trench 5, Feature SA5/2, Section B, Layer 3, enclosure ditch): Four tertiary flakes.

SA/AV (Trench 5, Feature SA5/2, Section D, Layer 3, enclosure ditch): This assemblage contains the largest/broadest of all the flakes from Ken Hill, measuring 56mm in length by 73mm in width. The flake has an overall light-grey-coloured patination.

SA/AX (Trench 5, Feature SA5/2, Section E, Layer 1, enclosure ditch): Primary and secondary flakes plus a patinated bladelet, an irregular multi-platformed flake core and a crude discoidal core.

SA/AY (Trench 5, Feature SA5/2, Section B, Layer 4, enclosure ditch): Core platform removal with hertzian cone not related to associated tertiary flake.

SA/AZ (Trench 5, Feature SA5/2, Section H, Layer 1, enclosure ditch): Core; side platform removal has edge retouch.

SA/BA (Trench 5, Feature SA5/2, Section H, Layer 2, enclosure ditch): A broad flake has received transverse irregular distal retouch that cuts through a dense white old-looking patination.

SA/BJ (Trench 5, Feature SA5/3, hollow): Includes a very large (length 67mm, width 37mm) tertiary flake with dorsal hinge scars, a large core rejuvenation flake from the side of a platform and a convex extended end scraper (length 38mm, width 35mm).

SA/BK (Trench 5, Feature SA5/2, Section G, Layer 3, enclosure ditch): Contains two flakes, one of which is an atypically broad (length 44mm, width 52mm) tertiary flake, consistent with an Early Neolithic date.

SA/BP (Trench 5, Feature SA5/2, Section F, Layer 3, enclosure ditch): A broken flake and a tertiary bladelet (bladelet broken in excavation).

SA/BZ (Trench 5, Feature SA5/2, Section J, Layer 1, enclosure ditch): A tertiary flake, bladelet and a cortical extended end / horseshoe scraper.

1992 Trench 6

SA/AD (Trench 6 topsoil): Nondescript collection of irregular flakes and chunks includes four cores (one fragmentary) and most notably a core scraper with two areas of abrupt retouch on a flat tabular core.

SA/BD (Trench 6, Feature SA6/2, Section A, Layer 1, enclosure ditch): Includes an atypical very large (length 78mm, width 31mm) tertiary blade of locally derived coarse-grained flint.

SA/BS (Trench 6, Feature SA6/2, Section B, Layer 2, enclosure ditch): A fresh tertiary bladelet and blade-like flake.

SA/BT (Trench 6, Feature SA6/2, Section B, Layer 3, enclosure ditch): Core rejuvenation flake from the side of a platform and a tertiary flake.

SA/BW (Trench 6, Feature SA6/2, Section C, enclosure ditch): A broad flake and a tertiary flake with utilisation wear on right-hand side.

SA/BX (Trench 6, Feature SA6/2, Section F, Layer 1, enclosure ditch): One flake, a burnt chunk and an atypical flake knife, worked on the ventral surface of a large flake.

SA/CF (Trench 6, Feature SA6/2, Section D, enclosure ditch): A flake and a cortical blade.

SA/CG (Trench 6, Feature SA6/2, Section F, Layer 1, enclosure ditch): Two chunks and a broken flake. The flake looks suited to the manufacture of leaf-shaped arrowheads.

SA/CN (Trench 6 topsoil): Two pieces were calcined; these were a broad hinged flake and a small core platform removal. The remaining pieces were a finishing flake (flake removed near the end of tool production) and a fine extended end/horseshoe scraper. The scraper measures 33.3mm diameter and possesses traces of heavy edge use and ventral trimming.

SA/CO (Trench 6, Feature SA6/2, Section E, Layer 2, enclosure ditch): Includes a small (length 20mm), thin, cortical convex end scraper with almost knife-like retouch.

SA/CX (Trench 6 topsoil): A broken flake and a calcined flint hammerstone fragment.

SA/DW (Trench 6 topsoil): One irregular core plus chunks and flakes. Notable inclusions are a proximal medial fragment from a high-quality single-crested blade, another similar blade fragment (medial) and a fragment from a broad (22mm) blade that possesses an atypical old white patina and fine platform-edge trimming.

SA/EA (Trench 6, Feature SA6/3, Section B, ditch): Blade-like material; broken.

1992 Trench 7

SA/BY (Trench 7 topsoil): This appears to be the product of three separate knapping events, two of which were geared to the production of large blades and one geared to the production of flakes. There is a single multi-platformed core and a primary flake. One broad flake possesses double dorsal blade scars. Four pieces are totally patinated/corticated and a dense white in colour. These comprise two broad flakes, a broken single-crested blade and a denticulate blade. There is fine trimming evident on the platform edges. The notched piece is a single-crested tertiary flake with two small denticulations on the right-hand side, near the distal end. On the ventral surface opposite the denticulations there is a degree of use wear. A fine cortical blade manufactured on fine-grained brownish-black (Munsell 5 YR 2/1) till flint also shows traces of heavy edge use on its left-hand side.

SA/CC (Trench 7 topsoil): Two very broad flakes, one fine and one hinged.

SA/CH (Trench 7, Feature SA7/6, gully): Fifty-two pieces, mainly undiagnostic chunks and chippings although 20 small spalls are present. The chunks are calcined. There is a fragmentary core rejuvenation flake that has been removed from the side of a core. Two retouched implements are present in the assemblage: a single notch on a very large flake and a burin on a cortical flake. The notched flake has a single notch that is particularly well defined by fine retouch and possesses clear and heavy macroscopic traces of edge use. The burin is a classic example defined by a burin spall.

SA/CJ (Trench 7, Feature SA7/5, Section A, ditch): Three cores, two side platform rejuvenation flakes and a collection of small cortical flakes that includes between two and five re-fits onto a fine bladelet fragment (distal medial). The flint is a very uniform collection and also includes a nodule that has had an intentional flake removal.

SA/CK (Trench 7, Feature SA7/3, Section B, gully): The assemblage is an undatable collection of large chunky debitage and small flakes and spalls. Looks like knapping debitage from more than three separate events that has been incorporated into a later feature. It includes primary, secondary and tertiary flakes.

SA/CL (Trench 7, Feature SA7/3, Section A, gully): A nondescript collection of chunky debitage, including two cores and a single notch on a chunk. The material is extensively burnt.

SA/CM (Trench 7, Feature SA7/5, Section B, ditch): Irregular material includes a fragmentary core and a heavily battered chunky flake. There is a small unclassifiable retouched fragment from a scraper and a very chunky blade with edge retouch. One broad flake is atypical and possesses a dense white patination and dorsal blade scars. Two of the flakes have flaked dorsal surfaces.

SA/CP (Trench 7, Feature SA7/4, ditch): A pebble-slice flake, cortical core platform-edge removal and an extended end scraper.

SA/CQ (Trench 7, Feature SA7/5, Section A, ditch): A fine cortical long end scraper with heavy use wear and faceted butt with remnants of core platform.

SA/CR (Trench 7 topsoil): Material almost conjoins. There were probably three parent nodules; the debitage is from primary and secondary stages of reduction. Three of the flakes are heavily calcined (burnt). There are two retouched pieces: a piercer and a graver, the latter being manufactured on a minimally retouched spur of a broken flake.

SA/CS (Trench 7, Feature SA7/5, Section A, ditch): Mixed assemblage; although sealed there is no retouched component although there are two broken bladelet fragments and a heavily burnt core rejuvenation flake taken from the side of a core platform.

SA/CT (Trench 7, Feature SA7/7, ?ditch): Nondescript debitage but includes a large (75mm diameter) sub-spherical flint hammerstone/anvil; extensively battered, the piece has been used as both a hammerstone and an anvil.

SA/CU (Trench 7, Feature SA7/8, Section A, gully): Includes a large secondary flake and a piercer that has been manufactured on the platform of a core rejuvenation flake, via the application of both flake removal and retouch.

SA/CV (Trench 7, Feature SA7/8, Section B, gully): A single tertiary flake.

SA/CW (Trench 7, Feature SA7/6, gully): Mixed inconsistent, small debitage including spalls and two broader dished flakes, a fragment of a keeled flake core, two broken bladelets and a lump that had been battered.

SA/CY (Trench 7, Feature SA7/5, Section B, ditch): Hinged tertiary flake, with post-excavation damage.

SA/DB (Trench 7, Feature SA7/7, ?ditch): A nondescript mix of chippings, broad flakes and three broken crested blade-like flakes. There is a piercer on a chunk that is defined by minimal retouch on a projection.

SA/DC (Trench 7, Feature SA7/5, Section C, ditch): This assemblage is composed of crude flakes, chippings and spalls, many of which have been heavily burnt. The assemblage also includes a natural lump of flint with some battering. There are two blade fragments, and an older looking, patinated core rejuvenation flake, which was removed from the side of a core platform. There are no period-diagnostic pieces.

SA/DE (Trench 7, Feature SA7/6, gully): The material includes three core rejuvenation flakes. One of the rejuvenation flakes is plunging and comes from a bladelet core, one is unclassifiable and possesses a dense old patina and the third is atypically large (length 66mm) and comes from the side of a core platform. A piercer has been formed on a chunky flake by the application of slight retouch.

SA/DF (Trench 7, Feature SA7/8, gully): This assemblage is predominately composed of spalls and chunks, many of which have been burnt. Notable pieces include a broken blade and bladelet (proximal fragments) and a natural lump of flint that has been crushed. One broad broken flake has been utilised.

SA/DH (Trench 7, Feature SA7/5, Section A, ditch): Irregular squat flakes and a core rejuvenation flake from a broad-flake core.

SA/DK (Trench 7, Feature SA7/5, Section A, ditch): Two flakes and two cores. One of the cores is a large broad-flake variety manufactured on a large cortical nodule with a keeled platform.

SA/DL (Trench 7 topsoil): A single small broken tertiary spall.

SA/DM (Trench 7, Feature SA7/10, pit): Includes a broken double-crested blade with a dense white patina.

SA/DN (Trench 7, Feature SA7/6, gully): Irregular chunky flakes.

SA/DO (Trench 7, Feature SA7/5, Section C, ditch): The assemblage includes two primary flakes and is composed mainly of chippings and spalls. Despite being from a sealed context there is a great deal of inconsistency in the debitage. Only three retouched pieces are present: a retouched chunk, a single notch on the ventral of a broken, flaked flake and a denticulate flake. The denticulate flake has two small contiguous notches on the right-hand side of a broad-hinged flake with ancillary platform-edge retouch.

SA/DP (Trench 7, Feature SA7/5, Section C, ditch): Includes one core platform removal and small chunks and chippings, some of which have been burnt (calcined).

SA/DR (Trench 7, Feature SA7/3, gully): A single chunk.

SA/DT (Trench 7, Feature SA7/5, Section C, ditch): Crude material, heavily corticated.

SA/DU (Trench 7, Feature SA7/7, Section B, ?ditch): Looks like the reduction of three separate cores. The assemblage includes a fine edge-utilised blade and an unused burin that has been manufactured on a large core rejuvenation flake. The core rejuvenation flake support is a large platform removal from a fine class A1 flake core.

SA/DX (Trench 7, Feature SA7/8, gully): Chunky debitage with two cores; one large chunk was split during excavation. There is a miscellaneously retouched cortical flake worked on its ventral surface.

SA/DY (Trench 7, Feature SA7/7, Sections A and C, ?ditch): Nondescript chunky flakes, predominately cortical with extensive burning plus two cores (one a keeled fragment) and a fine distal medial blade fragment which has straight left-hand marginal edge retouch. Despite being from a sealed context the material looks of mixed date.

SA/DZ (Trench 7, Feature SA7/5, Section C, ditch): Debitage totals 43 pieces of which over 90% is from tertiary stages of core reduction and includes many small flakes, chunks, two spalls, a broken bladelet and broken large double-crested blade. The material includes a large irregular flake core with at least three platforms, a core platform removal from a smaller core and a slightly retouched side platform core rejuvenation flake. A very large (diameter 64mm) cortical 'pot lid'-type natural fractured flake has received very slight edge utilisation. Two more flakes and a blade have edge use. Only four pieces are burnt (all broken flakes). The raw material is mixed and includes a flaked gravel pebble.

SA/EB (Trench 7, Feature SA7/3, gully): Two tertiary flakes and a chunk.

SA/EC (Trench 7, Feature SA7/5, Section D, ditch): Crude material, mainly chunks with a small overall degree of burning. One of the pieces in the assemblage possesses a dense, old white patina; this is a proximal medial fragment of fine double-crested blade of Early Neolithic character. The assemblage also includes an edge-utilised chunk and blade. A piercer has been manufactured by very minimal retouching of the spur on a broken flake. A crude irregular cortical flake has a small degree of ventral, right-hand side retouch.

1992 Trench 12

SA/DG (Trench 12 topsoil): Very crude material with extensive recent damage, includes a miscellaneously retouched irregular chunky flake and a broad utilised flake, ventral.

SA/DS (Trench 12 topsoil): The cut contained a large assemblage of crude cores of various shapes and sizes, and associated primary knapping debitage of a primarily chunky character. This assemblage appears to be a primary core preparation site. Many of the pieces are of poor quality local raw material. There is a lump of natural from which a single flake has been removed and two cores have been re-purposed as hammerstones, in addition to a small hammerstone flake. There are proportionally few tertiary flakes, notably only four core rejuvenation flakes, which is not surprising viewing the state of the cores; however, the rejuvenation flakes are of a finer quality than the extant cores and appear to represent the reduction of lithic pieces that may have been used in other areas of the site. All the cores are flake forms; there are few blade scars and no blade debitage. Five pieces are burnt, including two core fragments.

Primary debitage = 30; secondary debitage = 16 pieces; tertiary debitage = 14.

The retouched component is small and includes an edge-retouched core fragment, a denticulate chunk, a crude core that has received a single notch, three scrapers, two small crude end forms, and one unclassifiable. The assemblage also includes a very fine dihedral burin.

SA/DQ (Trench 12 topsoil): Flake debitage is variable with hinged terminations, platform-edge battering and multiple dorsal flaking being present. A small core rejuvenation flake from the side of a platform is not consistent with the debitage. Another plunging rejuvenation flake from a small keeled flake core is retouched as a scraper, with convex retouch to the right-hand side near the striking platform. There is a crude edge-retouched blade (right-hand side), and an edge-utilised flake (broken). Two burins are present. One is formed by a burinating flake removal on the proximal right-hand side of a cortical flake, the other by minimal flaking of a tertiary flake with a hinged termination. A broad cortical flake has two areas of edge retouch. A crude broad (width 45mm) flake knife has been manufactured on a cortical flake with a very pronounced bulb of percussion. The piece has been slightly burnt. A somewhat finer example has fine straight invasive ventral right-hand side retouch with slight dorsal backing and dorsal blade scars. A fine single-crested tertiary blade may be contemporary with the flake knife

SA/KD (Trench 12, Feature SA 12/1 shovel scrape over feature): The scrape produced 20 struck flints; including four chunks, 14 flakes (some are broad) one fine crested blade and a broad edge retouched flake. The condition of this assemblage is variable with some pieces being very fresh looking whilst some are very abraded.

SA/KL (Trench 12, Feature SA 12/16, small pit or animal burrow): The feature contained three small nondescript flakes, one of which was broken and calcined and one had recent (post-prehistoric) edge damage in the form of a notch. The pieces are probably Later Neolithic.

1992 Trench 13

SA/DD (Trench 13 topsoil): Notable is the inclusion of a large cortical nodule (length 80mm, width 60mm) with a single flake removal and a small (length 29mm) pebble-derived battered core.

SA/JV (Trench 18, Feature SA 18/2, ditch, lower fill): A small collection of 15 pieces including one chunk, two chippings, ten flakes (2 of which are broken) a miscellaneously retouched flake and a core (single platformed). The pieces are crude and made of locally derived raw material. Most of the pieces are abraded and do not look consistent with a sealed prehistoric deposit. The core is partially flaked and possesses scars from eight small (average length of removals is 17mm) flake removals. The pieces are of a later Neolithic character.

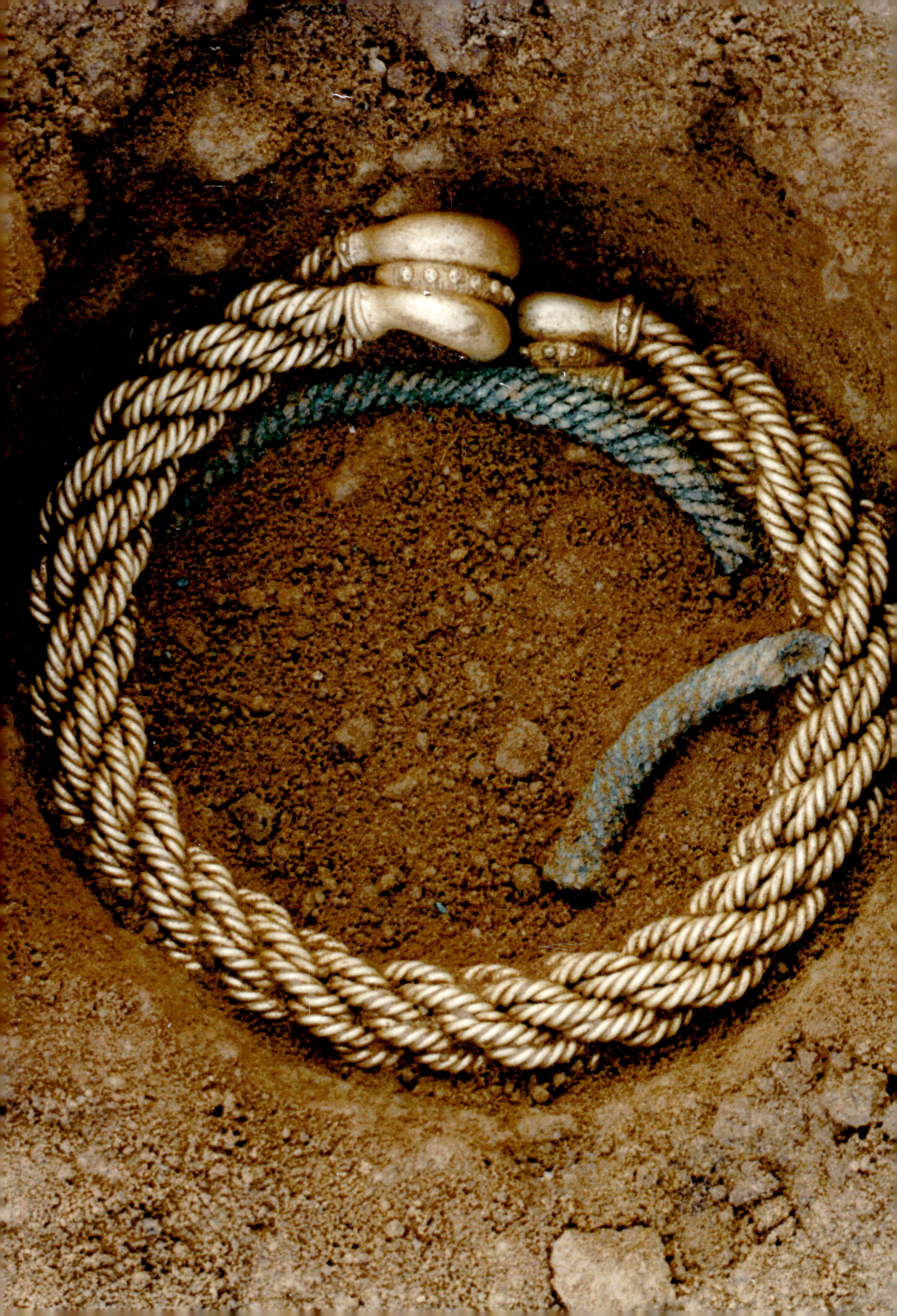

Part II: The Late Iron Age and Early Roman Hoards

Chapter 11
Introduction to Part II and Summary of Finds by Hoard and Type

Julia Farley and Jody Joy

Facing page: photograph of the top of the lower pit of Hoard H, showing torcs H.7 and H.8 *in situ*

This second section of the book focuses on the Phase 3 and 4 (Later Iron Age to early Roman) hoards and related stray finds, presenting hoard listings, archaeological contexts and full catalogues of the metalwork and coins. At least 14 securely attested hoards are known from Snettisham. Twelve are torc hoards (A, D, G, H, J, K, L), coin hoards (N), or mixed hoards of torcs and coins (B, C, E, F) from Phase 3. Two date to Phase 4 (ingot hoard M and large mixed coin/object hoard P).

The metalwork assemblage from Snettisham is one of the most exceptional from any Iron Age site in Europe. There are over 1,200 individual pieces in the catalogue (see Ch. 14 and **Table 11.1**), the majority of them torcs. More than 70 complete or near-complete torcs and bracelets have been recovered across the hoards and stray finds (tabulated in **Table 11.2**), with hundreds more represented by fragments. It is notable that none of the broken objects can be linked across hoards. Because many fragments may have derived from a single torc, it is difficult to estimate the precise number of objects. There are at least around 400 tubular and multi-strand torcs and bracelets represented (approximately 350 multi-strand and 50 tubular). The potential total number of torcs and bracelets is closer to 500 if groups of rod and wire fragments which likely derive from similar objects are included. The other significant and unusual group of objects present are simple metal rings, of which there are over 100 examples with at least 50% of the circuit present, and around another 40 smaller fragments.

This chapter summarises the nature and contents of each of the hoards, including information about date of discovery, current location and dating evidence from coins and radiocarbon dating (Gosden *et al.* 2009 see **Table 5.2**). The hoard entries below point to discussions elsewhere in this monograph. A historical account of the earlier discoveries (Hoards A to E) is given in Chapter 4, and detailed stratigraphic information on the hoards excavated by the BM in 1990–1 (including F, G, H, J, K, L, M and N) is presented in Chapter 12. At the end of the chapter, following the hoard-by-hoard breakdown, **Table 11.1** summarises the hoard and stray finds in the BM and NCM collections by object type.

Chapter 13 provides the metalwork typology developed for the study of the Snettisham hoard material. The detailed finds catalogues are found in Chapters 14 (objects) and 15 (coins). The Hoard F helmet (F.445) is a unique object which was the subject of a sustained and thorough conservation campaign, and thus it is singled out for more detailed treatment in the catalogue. Hoard P (a large coin hoard also known as the 'Bowl Hoard') was stolen from the site by illicit detectorists, and the results of attempts to reconstruct its contents are found in Chapter 15, though the coins are not included in the catalogue numbering. The catalogues are organised by hoard, with a final section covering stray finds of metalwork and coins from the site, many of which are probably dispersed hoard material. This is discussed in more detail in the catalogues themselves.

Late Iron Age (Phase 3) hoards

Hoard A: Hoard of tubular torcs

Location: NCM

Discovered by ploughing in 1948, with additional fragments recovered during Rainbird Clarke's 1948 excavations (Clarke 1954). See accounts of discovery in Chapters 2 and 4.

- Three near-complete gold alloy tubular torcs (A.1–3)
- At least one fragmentary gold alloy tubular torc (A.4–7)
- Perforated gritstone pebble (A.8)

Hoard B: Hoard of fragmentary multi-strand torcs/ bracelets, with rings, ingots and gold coins

Location: NCM

Discovered by ploughing in 1948, with coins and additional objects recovered during Rainbird Clarke's 1948 excavations (Clarke 1954). See accounts of discovery in Chapters 2 and 4.

Terminal date based on coinage: *c.* 80–60 BC (see Ch. 15)

Coins:

- Eleven gold Gallo-Belgic A and C staters and quarter staters (Cat. nos 1–11)
- One insular British Cf gold quarter stater (Cat. no. 12)

Objects:

One interlinked composite group (B.1a-h) and 27 individual objects and groups of fragments. Together these comprise:

Bracelets:

- Two gold/silver alloy loop terminal bracelets, one represented by fragments (B.8, B.12–13)

Torcs/bracelets:

- Three fragments of gold/silver alloy multi-strand loop terminal torcs/bracelets (B.1e, B.5, B.9)
- Two fragments from copper alloy multi-strand loop terminal torcs/bracelets (B.11, B.17)
- Six neck-ring/body fragments from gold/silver alloy multi-strand torcs or bracelets (B.1f, B.1g, B.2, B.3, B.4, B.7)
- One neck-ring/body fragment from a copper alloy multi-strand torc or bracelet (B.14)
- Two fragments or groups of fragments of gold/silver alloy wire likely from a multi-strand torc or bracelet (B.6, B.10)
- Four fragments of copper alloy wire likely from a multi-strand torc or bracelet (B.15, B.16, B.18, B.19)

Rings:

- Seven gold/silver alloy large rings (B.1a, B.1b, B.20 to B.24)
- Three gold/silver alloy small rings (B.1c, B.1h, B.25)
- One copper alloy small ring (B.1d)

Ingots:

- One gold/silver alloy linear ingot (B.26)
- One gold/silver alloy lump ingot (B.27)

Other finds:

- One copper alloy clamp (B.28)
- Five iron nails (published by Clarke 1954, but now considered most likely post-medieval) (B.29–33)

Hoard C: Hoard of fragmentary multi-strand torcs/ bracelets, with rings, and potin coins

Location: NCM

Discovered by ploughing in 1948, with additional fragments recovered during Rainbird Clarke's 1948 excavations (Clarke 1954). See accounts of discovery in Chapters 2 and 4. Terminal date based on potin coinage: *c.* 60/55 BC (see Ch. 15)

Coins:

- At least 155 potin coins (see Ch. 15)

Objects:

Torcs/bracelets:

- Two gold/silver alloy loop terminal multi-strand torcs/ bracelets, represented by fragments (C.7–18, C.20)
- Three copper alloy buffer terminal multi-strand torcs/ bracelets, represented by fragments (C.22, C.25–7, C.31)
- Two groups of neck-ring/body fragments of gold/silver alloy multi-strand torcs or bracelets (C.1–5, C.21)
- Five groups of neck-ring/body fragments of copper alloy multi-strand torcs or bracelets (C.23, C.24, C.28–30, C.34–6, C.43)
- Two fragments of gold/silver alloy wire or rod likely from a multi-strand torc or bracelet (C.6, C.19)
- Nine fragments or groups of fragments of copper alloy wire likely from a multi-strand torc or bracelet (C.32, C.33, C.37 to C.42, C.44)

Rings:

- Two gold/silver alloy large rings (C.45, C.46)
- One gold/silver alloy small ring (C.47)
- Two copper alloy small rings (C.48, C.49)

Other finds:

- One fragment of gold/silver alloy sheet (C.50)
- Two fragments of copper alloy sheet (C.55, C.56)
- One fragment of copper alloy strip or binding (C.54)
- Three copper alloy rivet heads (C.51 to C.53)
- Five iron nails (published by Clarke 1954, but now considered most likely post-medieval) (C.57 to 61)

Additional material possibly associated with Hoards B/C

Location: NCM

Some parts of Hoards B and C became intermixed shortly after their discovery. Thus, in the catalogue, some finds can be securely attributed to either Hoard B or Hoard C, but others are designated as 'Hoard B/C'). See Chapter 4.

Torcs:

- Three complete loop terminal copper alloy multi-strand torcs (B/C.9, B/C.10, B/C.11)
- One near-complete ring terminal copper alloy small multi-strand torc (B/C.47–9)

Bracelets:

- One complete loop terminal copper alloy multi-strand bracelet (B/C.12)

Torcs/bracelets:

- Four gold/silver alloy loop terminal multi-strand torcs/ bracelets, represented by fragments (B/C.1, B/C.2, B/C.5, B/C.7–8)
- Twelve copper alloy loop terminal multi-strand torcs/ bracelets, represented by fragments (B/C.13, B/C.14–15, B/C.16, B/C.19–22, B/C.24, B/C.25, B/C.26–34, B/C.35, B/C.36, B/C.37, B/C.50–53, B/C.54–5)
- Pair of neck-ring/body fragments from a gold/silver alloy multi-strand torc or bracelet (B/C.3–4)
- Ten neck-ring/body fragments or groups of fragments from copper alloy multi-strand torcs or bracelets (B/C.23,

B/C.42–3, B/C.44–5, B/C.56, B/C.57, B/C.58, B/C.59, B/C.60, B/C.62)
- One wire fragment likely from a gold/silver alloy multi-strand torc or bracelet (B/C.6)
- Eight wire fragments or groups of fragments likely from copper alloy multi-strand torcs or bracelets (B/C.17, B/C.18, B/C.38 to B/C.41, B/C.46, B/C.61, B/C.63)

Rings:
- Twelve copper alloy large rings or fragments of large rings (B/C.65 to B/C.76)
- One gold/silver alloy small ring (B/C.64)
- Seven copper alloy small rings (B/C.77 to B/C.83)

Ingots and lumps:
- One gold/silver alloy triangular ingot (B/C.84)
- Two gold/silver alloy linear ingots (B/C.85, B/C.86)
- One amorphous lump of gold/silver alloy (B/C.87)

Other finds:
- One copper alloy scale pan (B/C.88)
- One copper alloy fitting (B/C.90)
- Two joining fragments of copper alloy binding strip from the corner of a hide-shaped shield (B/C.89)
- One additional fragment of copper alloy binding strip (B/C.95)
- Five groups of fragments of copper alloy sheet (B/C.91 to B/C.94)
- One fragment of slag (B/C.96)

Hoard D: One composite group based around a complete multi-strand torc

Location: BM
Discovered by ploughing in 1950. See accounts of discovery in Chapters 2 and 4.
- One composite group formed of a gold/silver alloy multi-strand loop terminal torc (D.1a) and a silver alloy large ring (D.1b)

Hoard E: One composite group based around a complete multi-strand torc

Location: BM
Discovered by ploughing in 1950. See accounts of discovery in Chapters 2 and 4.
Terminal date based on coinage: *c.* 60 BC (see Ch. 15)

One composite group comprising:

Coins:
- One insular British Cf gold quarter stater coin (Cat no. 169)

Objects:
- One complete gold/silver alloy multi-strand torus terminal torc (E.1a), a gold/silver alloy multi-strand buffer terminal torc fragment (E.1b), and a gold/silver alloy sheet bracelet (E.1c)

Hoard F: Hoard of fragmentary multi-strand torcs/bracelets, with rings, ingots and gold coins. Many composite groups. Assemblage contained within a copper alloy helmet

Location: BM
Discovery: Located and lifted by Charles Hodder in August 1990. Findspot subsequently investigated by archaeologists during the 1990 BM excavations. See accounts in Chapters 2 and 4, and detailed report in Chapter 12.
Terminal date based on coinage: *c.* 80–60 BC (see Ch. 15)
Radiocarbon dating: The organic core from one Hoard F torc fragment (F.168) gave a date of 370–160 cal BC at 95.4% probability (**Table 5.2**; Garrow *et al.* 2009).

Coins:
- Nine gold Gallo-Belgic A and C staters and quarter staters (Cat. nos 170–178)

Objects:

Hoard F is the largest single object assemblage from Snettisham, containing 47 composite groups (F.1–F.44, F.56, F.62 and F.251, incorporating a total of 142 complete and fragmentary objects), and 396 single objects/fragments. There were no complete, undamaged torcs and bracelets in Hoard F, though there are a handful of near-complete examples, see **Table 11.2**. The copper alloy objects include some gilded pieces, see **Table 11.1**.

Overall, the assemblage comprised:

Torcs:
- Nineteen fragments (or groups of fragments) from gold/silver alloy multi-strand torcs with known terminal type (buffer: F.41 (part), F.71, F.92–3, F.106, F.115, F.118; cage: F.4a, F.98; loop: F.39 (part), F.78, F.80, F.444; ring: F.4b, F.5c, F.8a, F.68, F.117; torus: F.72; reel: F.119–20)
- Ten fragments (or groups of fragments) from copper alloy multi-strand torcs with known terminal type (buffer: F.162–5, F.168, F.169, F.187, F.202–3; loop: F.186, F.206, F.352–60; ring: F.185; torus: F.207)
- Nine neck-ring fragments (or groups of fragments) from gold/silver alloy multi-strand torcs (F.6a (part), F.74, F.77, F.79, F.96–7, F.99–104, F.109–11, F.112–13, and small torc F.116)
- Six neck-ring fragments (or groups of fragments) from copper alloy multi-strand torcs (F.166, F.167, F.189, F.190–6, F.197–8, F.201)
- Thirty-nine fragments (or groups of fragments) from gold/silver alloy tubular torcs (Type 1: F.1c, F.1d, F.2a, F.4f, F.5g, F.31b, F.33 (part), F.57, F.58. F.59; Type 2: F.63–6; Type 3: F.2g, F.2h, F.35 (part), F.47, F.48, F.60, F.62 (part); Type 4: F.6b, F.30a, F.42 (part), F.45, F.46, F.61; Type 5; F.31a, F.43 (part); Type 4/5: F.2e, F.19b, F.29a, F.32 (part), F.50 to F.56; Uncertain type: F.2c (part), F.49)

Bracelets:
- Two gold/silver alloy bracelets with loop terminals (F.7f, F.121)
- Two fragmentary copper alloy bracelets with loop terminals (F.208, F.209)

Torcs/bracelets:
- Thirty-seven fragments (or groups of fragments) from gold/silver alloy multi-strand torcs/bracelets with known terminal type (buffer: F.146; cage: F.7e, F.38 (part), F.85, F.86, F.95; loop: F.2f, F.3b, F.3h–i, F.4c, F.4d, F.4e, F.7c, F.9b, F.14a, F.17c, F.18h, F.24a, F.70, F.73, F.87, F.89, F.90, F.91, F.136, F.140; ring: F.3c, F.7d, F.7g (part), F.9a, F.10a, F.36 (part), F.40 (part), F.43 (part), F.82, F.105, F.107)
- Fourteen fragments (or groups of fragments) from copper alloy multi-strand torcs/bracelets with known terminal type (buffer: F.179, F.188, F.249; loop: F.3g, F.8b, F.16a–b, F.204–5, F.210, F.256–61, F.326–7, F.361, F.362–3; ring: F.15a; torus: F.351)
- Fifty-five neck-ring/body fragments (or groups of

fragments) from gold/silver alloy multi-strand torcs or bracelets (F.1e (part), F.2d, F.3e, F.5d (part), F.5f, F.6f, F.7g (part), F.9c, F.9d, F.11a–b, F.13b, F.17a, F.20b, F.21b, F.22a, F.29b, F.32 (part), F.34 (part), F.37 (part), F.42 (part), F.81, F.83, F.84, F.88, F.94, F.108, F.114, F.123 to F.131, F.132–3, F.134, F.135, F.137, F.138, F.139, F.141 to F.145, F.147–8, F.151, F.153, F.154–7, F.158 to F.161)
- Fifty-one neck-ring/body fragments (or groups of fragments) from copper alloy multi-strand torcs or bracelets (F.3f, F.13a, F.15b, F.23b, F.44 (part), F.171, F.172, F.173, F.174, F.175–8, F.180–84, F.199, F.200, F.211 to F.217, F.218–40, F.241, F.243 to F.248, F.250 to F.255, F.328–35, F.336–7, F.338 to F.344, F.345–6, F.347 to F.350, F.364–74, F.375, F.376)
- Seven wire fragments (or groups of fragments) likely from a gold/silver alloy multi-strand torc or bracelet (F.7b, F.69, F.75–6, F.122, F.149, F.150, F.152)
- Twenty-one wire fragments (or groups of fragments) likely from a copper alloy multi-strand torc or bracelet (F.170, F.242, F.262, F.263, F.264, F.265–6, F.267 to F.270, F.271–80, F.281, F.282, F.283–8, F.289–90, F.291, F.292–309, F.310–23, F.324, F.325, F.328)

Rings:
- Twenty-eight gold/silver alloy large rings or fragments of large rings (F.1a, F.1b, F.3a, F.5a, F.5b, F.6a (part), F.6d, F.7a, F.19a, F.20a, F.26a, F.28b, F.412 to F.419, F.421 to F.427, F.435
- Three copper alloy large rings or fragments of large rings (F.3d, F.409, F.428)
- Forty-nine gold/silver alloy small rings or fragments of small rings (F.6c, F.6e, F.6g, F.18b to F.18g and F.18j to F.18l, F.21a, F.22b, F.23a, F.24b, F.25a to F.25j, F.26b to F.26e, F.27a, F.27b, F.28a, F.386 to F.397, F.399, F.400, F.401, F.403)
- Seven copper alloy small rings or fragments of small rings (F.404 to F.408, F.410, F.411)
- Four fragments of gold/silver alloy large or small rings: (F.33 (part), F.398, F.402, F.420)

Ingots and lumps:
- Two gold/silver alloy linear ingots (F.438, F.439)
- One copper alloy linear ingot (F.440)
- One amorphous lump of gold/silver alloy (F.436–7)
- One group of small amorphous lumps of copper alloy (F.442)

Other finds:
- One fragmentary copper alloy helmet (F.445)
- Twenty-four Gold/silver alloy wire fragments (or groups of fragments) not obviously from a multi-strand torc/bracelet (F.1e (part), F.2b, F.2c (part), F.2i, F.5e, F.10b, F.12a, F.12b, F.17b, F.18a, F.29c, F.30b, F.33 (part), F.34 (part), F.35 (part), F.36 (part), F.38 (part), F.39 (part), F.40 (part), F.41 (part), F.43 (part), F.44 (part), F.62 (part), F.429)
- Five copper alloy wire fragments (or groups of fragments) not obviously from a multi-strand torc/bracelet (F.14b, F.430 to F.434)
- Four fragments or melted fragments of gold/silver alloy sheet (F.5d (part), F.34 (part), F.37 (part), F.43 (part))
- Two fragments or groups of fragments of copper alloy sheet (F.441, F.443)
- Seven fragments or groups of fragments of gold/silver alloy strip (F.18i, F.67, F.377 to F.381)
- Seven fragments or groups of fragments of copper alloy strip (F.8c, F.8d, F.8e, F.382 to F.385)

Hoard G: Hoard primarily composed of complete multi-strand torcs, with four large rings

Location: BM

Discovery: Located and excavated during the BM 1990 excavations. Split into two pits, one above the other. See detailed report in Chapter 12.

Upper pit (G.1 to G.10):
- Six complete or near-complete gold/silver alloy multi-strand torcs (ring terminal: G.1, G.9; loop terminal: G.3, G.4, G.5a, G.7). G.5a is part of a composite group also including 3 complete gold/silver alloy small rings: G.5b, G.5c and G.5d.
- Three complete or near-complete gilded copper alloy multi-strand torcs (buffer terminal: G.6, G.8, G.10)
- One fragmentary copper alloy multi-strand torc (buffer terminal: G.2)

Lower pit (G.11 to G.20):
- One complete gold/silver alloy multi-strand torc (ring terminal: G.11)
- Two complete or near-complete gilded copper alloy multi-strand torcs (buffer terminal: G.12, G.13)
- One complete or near-complete copper alloy multi-strand torc (buffer terminal: G.15)
- One fragmentary copper alloy multi-strand torc (buffer terminal: G.16)
- One complete or near-complete copper alloy small multi-strand torc (loop terminal: G.14)
- Three complete gold/silver alloy large rings (G.17 to G.19), and one in copper alloy (G.20)

Hoard H: Hoard primarily composed of complete multi-strand torcs

Location: BM

Discovery: Located and excavated during the BM 1990 excavations. Split into two pits, one above the other. See detailed report in Chapter 12.

Upper pit (H.1 to H.6):
- One composite group made of two complete gold/silver alloy multi-strand torcs twisted together (loop terminal: H.2a; ring terminal: H.2b)
- Three complete gold/silver alloy multi-strand torcs (hook terminal: H.3; loop terminal: H.5, H.6)
- Two complete or near-complete copper alloy multi-strand torcs (buffer terminal: H.1; ring terminal: H.4)

Lower pit (H.7 to H.11):
- One complete gold/silver alloy multi-strand torc (ring/torus terminal: H.7)
- Three complete copper alloy multi-strand torcs (buffer terminal: H.8, H.9, loop terminal: H.11)
- One complete gilded copper alloy multi-strand torc (buffer terminal: H.10)

Hoard J: Hoard primarily composed of complete multi-strand torcs

Location: BM

Discovery: Located and excavated during the BM 1990 excavations. See detailed report in Chapter 12.

- Two complete gold/silver alloy multi-strand torcs (ring terminal: J.6, J.7)
- Two fragmentary gold/silver alloy multi-strand torcs (loop terminal: J.1, J.2)
- Two fragmentary copper alloy multi-strand torcs (buffer terminal: J.3; unknown terminal type: J.4)
- A composite group consisting of two fragmentary gold/silver alloy multi-strand torcs (ring terminal J.5b; loop terminal J.5c) and one fragmentary copper alloy multi-strand torc (buffer terminal: J.5a)

Hoard K: Hoard primarily composed of complete multi-strand torcs

Location: BM
Discovery: Located and excavated during the BM 1990 excavations. See detailed report in Chapter 12.

- Two complete or near-complete copper alloy multi-strand torcs (ring terminal: K.1; loop terminal: K.4)
- Two fragmentary gilded copper alloy multi-strand torcs (unknown terminal type: K.2, K.3)
- Three complete gold/silver alloy multi-strand torcs (ring terminal: K.5, K.6. K.7)

Hoard L: Hoard primarily composed of complete multi-strand torcs

Location: BM
Discovery: Located and excavated during the BM 1990 excavations. Split into two pits, one above the other. See detailed report in Chapter 12, and step-by-step excavation images in Chapter 23 (**Figs 23.6–23.8**).
Radiocarbon dating: An untreated sample from an organic repair to torc L.6 gave a date of 370–160 cal BC at 93.8% probability (**Table 5.2**; Garrow *et al.* 2009).

Upper pit (L.1 to L.7):

- Five complete gold/silver alloy multi-strand torcs (loop terminal: L.2, L.4, L.7; ring terminal: L.3; torus terminal: L.1)
- One complete or near-complete gilded copper alloy multi-strand torc (buffer terminal: L.5)
- One complete copper alloy multi-strand torc (buffer terminal: L.6)

Lower pit (L.8 to L.21):

- Ten complete or near-complete gold/silver alloy multi-strand torcs (buffer terminal: L.11, L.12, L.13, L.17; ring terminal: L.18; torus terminal: L.10a, L.14, L.19a, L.20a, L.21a). Four of these are composite groups, incorporating other gold/silver alloy torc/bracelet and wire fragments as additions or repairs (L.10a-b, L.19a-f, L.20a-b and L.21a-b).
- Two fragments of gold/silver alloy multi-strand torcs (cage terminal: L.15; ring terminal: L.16)
- One complete or near-complete copper alloy multi-strand torc/bracelet (loop terminal: L.8)
- One fragment of gilded copper alloy multi-strand torc (loop terminal: L.9)

Hoard N: Dispersed gold coin hoard

Location: BM
Discovery: Recovered as scattered stray finds during metal-detecting survey carried out as part of the BM excavations in 1990 and 1991. See details in Chapter 12.
Terminal date based on coinage: *c.* 80–60 BC (see Ch. 15)

- Nine gold Gallo-Belgic A and C staters and quarter staters (Cat. nos 179–187)

Early Roman (Phase 4) hoards

Hoard M: Hoard of silver/copper alloy lumps

Location: BM
Discovery: Recovered by detectorist Charles Hodder March 1991. Subsequent excavation revealed no archaeological context. See details in Chapter 12.
Radiocarbon dating: Charcoal embedded in the amorphous lumps M.1–M.5 was radiocarbon dated (**Table 5.2**; Garrow *et al.* 2009), giving a calibrated date range of AD 1–130 (at the 95.4% confidence level). The charcoal sampled was old alder wood, so the actual date of the hoard is likely to be somewhat later.

- Five amorphous lumps of silver-copper alloy (M.1–M.5)
- One smaller lump of copper alloy (M.6)

Hoard P: Coin hoard contained within a silver bowl. Possibly accompanied by other objects including ingots

Location: Lost, although silver bowl fragments in the BM may be from this hoard.
Discovery: Stolen from the site by illicit metal detectorists sometime between the 1990 and 1991 excavation seasons. Subsequently dispersed in the trade, and thus its contents can only be partially reconstructed (see accounts of discovery in Chs 2, 4 and 12, and detailed reconstruction of contents in Ch. 15; see also Chadburn 2006, hoard no. 41). All finds lost/dispersed in the trade, except for fragments of the silver bowl.
Terminal date based on coinage: Early AD 60s (see Ch. 15)

Coins:

- *c.* 6,000 silver coins, predominantly local issues
- *c.* 90 to 500 gold coins

Objects:

- Silver bowl (fragments survive, see P.1–P.7)
- Three copper alloy brooches
- Multi-strand torc fragment
- Three 'saucer-shaped' ingots (1 gold alloy, 1 silver alloy, 1 copper alloy)

Table 11.1 Summary of the hoard and stray finds in both BM and NCM collections by object type

Object group	Object type	Gold/silver alloy	Copper alloy (or other materials, indicated in brackets)
MULTI-STRAND TORCS AND BRACELETS	*MULTI-STRAND TORCS/BRACELETS*		
	Buffer terminal torc/bracelet	F.146	C.22, C.25–7, C.31, F.179, F.188, F.249
	Cage terminal torc/bracelet	F.7e, F.38 (part), F.85, F.86, F.95	N/A
	Loop terminal torc/bracelet	B.1e, B.5, B.9, C.7–18, C.20, B/C.1, B/C.2, B/C.5, B/C.7–8, F.2f, F.3b, F.3h–i, F.4c, F.4d, F.4e, F.7c, F.9b, F.14a, F.17c, F.18h, F.24a, F.70, F.73, F.87, F.89, F.90, F.91, F.136, F.140, L.19c, S.11b	B.11, B.17, B/C.13, B/C.14–15, B/C.16, B/C.19–22, B/C.24, B/C.25, B/C.26–34, B/C.35, B/C.36, B/C.37, B/C.50–53, B/C.54–5, F.3g, F.8b, F.16a–b, F.204–5, F.210, F.256–61, F.326–7, F.361, F.362–3
	Ring terminal torc/bracelet	F.3c, F.7d, F.7g (part), F.9a, F.10a, F.36 (part), F.40 (part), F.43 (part), F.82, F.105, F.107	F.15a+, L.8
	Torus terminal torc/bracelet	N/A	F.351
	Neck-ring/body fragment with no terminal	B.1f, B.1g, B.2, B.3, B.4, B.7, C.1–5, C.21, B/C.3–4, F.1e (part), F.2d, F.3e, F.5d (part), F.5f, F.6f, F.7g (part), F.9c, F.9d, F.11a–b, F.13b, F.17a, F.20b, F.21b, F.22a, F.29b, F.32 (part), F.34 (part), F.37 (part), F.42 (part), F.81, F.83, F.84, F.88, F.94, F.108, F.114, F.123 to F.131, F.132–3, F.134, F.135, F.137, F.138, F.139, F.141 to F.145, F.147–8, F.151, F.153, F.154–7, F.158 to F.161, S.30, S.45, S.46 (part)	B.14, C.23, C.24, C.28–30, C.34–6, C.43, B/C.23, B/C.42–3, B/C.44–5, B/C.56, B/C.57, B/C.58, B/C.59, B/C.60, B/C.62, F.3f, F.13a+, F.15b, F.23b+, F.44 (part), F.171+, F.172+, F.173+, F.174+, F.175–8+, F.180–84+, F.199, F.200, F.211 to F.217, F.218–40, F.241, F.243 to F.248, F.250 to F.255, F.328–35, F.336–7, F.338 to F.344, F.345–6, F.347 to F.350, F.364–74, F.375, F.376
	Wire or rod fragments likely from a multi-strand torc or bracelet	B.6, B.10, C.6, C.19, B/C.6, F.7b, F.69, F.75–6, F.122, F.149, F.150, F.152, L.10b, S.41–4, S.47, S.49 to S.65, S.67, S.68	B.15, B.16, B.18, B.19, C.32, C.33, C.37 to C.42, C.44, B/C.17, B/C.18, B/C.38 to B/C.41, B/C.46, B/C.61 B/C.63,, F.170+, F.242, F.262, F.263, F.264, F.265–6, F.267 to F.270, F.271–80, F.281, F.282, F.283–8, F.289–90, F.291, F.292–309, F.310–23, F.324, F.325, F.328, S.81, S.82
	MULTI-STRAND TORCS		
	Buffer terminal torc	E.1b, F.41 (part), F.71, F.92–3, F.106, F.115, F.118, L.11, L.12, L.13, L.17, S.19, S.48	F.162–5+, F.168, F.169+, F.187, F.202–3, G.2, G.8+, G.10+, G.12+, G.13+, G.15, G.16, H.1, H.8, H.9, H.10+, J.3, J.5a, L.5+, L.6, S.79
	Cage terminal torc	F.4a, F.98, L.15	N/A
	Loop or Hook* terminal torc	D.1a, F.39 (part), F.78, F.80, F.444, G.3, G.4, G.5a, G.7, H.2a, H.3*, H.5, H.6, J.1, J.2/S.20, J.5c, L.2, L.4, L.7, S.18, S.21, S.23–9, S.31–40	B/C.9, B/C.10, B/C.11, F.186, F.206, F.352–60, G.6+, G.14, H.11, K.4, L.9+
	Ring terminal torc	F.4b, F.5c, F.8a, F.68, F.117, G.1, G.9, G.11, H.2b, H.7, J.5b, J.6, J.7, K.5, K.6, K.7, L.3, L.16, L.18, S.16, S.17	B/C.47–9, F.185, H.4, K.1
	Torus or Reel** terminal torc	E.1a, F.72, F.119–20**, L.1, L.10a, L.14, L.19a, L.20a, L.21a	F.207, S.77, S.78
	Neck-ring fragments with no terminal	F.6a (part), F.74, F.77, F.79, F.96–7, F.99–104, F.109–11, F.112–13, F.116, S.22	F.166+, F.167, F.189, F.190–6, F.197–8, F.201, J.4, K.2+, K.3+, S.80
	MULTI-STRAND BRACELETS		
	Loop or Hook* terminal bracelet	B.8, B.12–13, F.7f*, F.121	B/C.12, F.208, F.209
WIRE/ROD	Wire and rod fragments not obviously from a multi-strand torc/bracelet	F.1e (part), F.2b, F.2c (part), F.2i, F.5e, F.10b, F.12a, F.12b, F.17b+, F.18a, F.29c, F.30b, F.33 (part), F.34 (part), F.35 (part), F.36 (part), F.38 (part), F.39 (part), F.40 (part), F.41 (part), F.43 (part), F.44 (part), F.62 (part), F.429, L.19b, L.20b, S.66, S.125, S.132 to S.136 (parts), S.140 (part)	F.14b, F.430 to F.434, S.127, S.128, S.129

TUBULAR TORCS AND BRACELETS	TUBULAR BRACELETS		
	Annular tubular bracelet	E.1c	N/A
	TUBULAR TORCS		
	Type 1	F.1c, F.1d, F.2a, F.4f, F.5g, F.31b, F.33 (part), F.57, F.58. F.59, S.14	N/A
	Type 2	F.63–6	N/A
	Type 3	F.2g, F.2h, F.35 (part), F.47, F.48, F.60, F.62 (part)	N/A
	Type 4	F.6b, F.30a, F.42 (part), F.45, F.46, F.61, S.13	
	Type 5	F.31a, F.43 (part)	N/A
	Type 4/5	F.2e, F.19b, F.29a, F.32 (part), F.50 to F.56, S.11a	N/A
	Type 6	A.1, A.2, A.3, A.4–7	S.12 (iron core only)
	Tubular torc fragment of uncertain type	F.2c (part), F.49, L.19d	N/A
OTHER POSSIBLE TORC COMPONENTS		S.15, S.69	N/A
RINGS	Large ring	B.1a, B.1b, B.20 to B.24, C.45, C.46, D.1b, F.1a, F.1b, F.3a, F.5a, F.5b, F.6a (part), F.6d, F.7a, F.19a, F.20a, F.26a, F.28b, F.412 to F.419, F.421 to F.427, F.435, G.17 to G.19, S.84, S.85	B/C.65 to B/C.76, F.3d, F.409, F.428, G.20
	Small ring	B.1c, B.1h, B.25, C.47, B/C.64, F.6c, F.6e, F.6g, F.18b to F.18g and F.18j to F.18l, F.21a, F.22b, F.23a, F.24b, F.25a to F.25j, F.26b to F.26e, F.27a, F.27b, F.28a, F.386 to F.397, F.399, F.400, F.401, F.403, G.5b, G.5c, G.5d	B.1d, C.48, C.49, B/C.77 to B/C.83, F.404 to F.408, F.410, F.411
	Fragment from large or small ring	F.33 (part), F.398, F.402, F.420, S.86 to S.98	S.99, S.100
INGOTS AND LUMPS	Linear ingot	B.26, B/C.85, B/C.86, F.438, F.439, S.112 to S.116	F.440, S.117 to S.122
	Lump ingot	B.27, S.101, S.102, S.103	S.104, S.106 to S.111
	Triangular ingot	B/C.84	S.105
	Amorphous lump	B/C.87, F.436–7, S.46 (part), S.132 to S.136 (parts), S.137, S.138, S.141 to S.178	F.442, M.1 to M.6, S.140 (part), S.179 to S.233, S.234 (iron)
SHEET/STRIP	Sheet	C.50; F.5d (part), F.34 (part), F.37 (part), F.43 (part), P.1 to P.7, S.70 to S.75, S.139 (part), S.140 (part)	C.55, C.56, B/C.91 to B/C.94, F.441, F.443, S.308 to S.351
	Strip	F.18i, F.67, F.377 to F.381, L.19e, L.19f, L.21b, S.76	C.54, B/C.89, B/C.95, F.8c, F.8d, F.8e, F.382 to F.385, S.276 to S.306, S.307 (iron)
BA/EIA (PHASE 2) OBJECTS		N/A	S.1–10
BEADED AND ROD TORCS/ BRACELETS		N/A	S.83, S.235 to S.241
BROOCHES		S.242	S.243 to S.246
FINGER RINGS		N/A	S.247, S.248
BUTTONS/ RIVETS/RIVET HEADS		N/A	C.51 to C.53, S.249 to S.252, S.267 to S.275
FITTINGS/TOOLS		N/A	B/C.88, B/C.90, S.126, S.253 to S.266, S.352 to S.354
MAIL ARMOUR		N/A	S.355, S.356–9 (iron)
HELMET		N/A	F.445

OTHER/ UNIDENTIFIED		N/A	A.8 (stone), B.28, B/C.96 (slag), S.123, S.124, S.130, S.131, S.139 (part), S.360 to 365
NAILS (LIKELY POST-MEDIEVAL)		N/A	B.29 to 33 (iron), C.57 to 61 (iron)

Notes on **Table 11.1**:
*F.7f has one loop and one hook terminal. The only fully hook terminal object is H.3, which may be unfinished.
**The only reel terminal object is F.119–20.
+Gilded or possibly gilded (determined for British Museum objects only)
NB: A dash '–' is used to link groups which are likely to come from the same object. The word 'to' is used to link a run of separate objects in the same category. 'Part' is used to refer to individual components of fused composite groups which include multiple fragments. For simplicity, where multiple interpretations of a single object are possible, it has been assigned to the most likely identification for the purposes of this table.

Table 11.2 Listing of complete and near-complete torcs and bracelets from Snettisham by type (74 objects)

Object type	Cat. nos
Tubular torcs	A.1, A.2, A.3, F.63–F.65
Multi-strand bracelets	B.8, B/C.12, E.1c, F.7f, F.121, F.208, F.209
Multi-strand torc/bracelet	L.8
Multi-strand small torcs	B/C.47–B/C.49, F.116, G.14
Multi-strand torcs	B/C.9, B/C.10, B/C.11, B/C.50–B/C.51, D.1a, E.1a, F.186, F.201, G.1, G.3, G.4, G.5a, G.6, G.7, G.8, G.9, G.10, G.11, G.12, G.13, G.15, H.1, H.2a-b, H.3, H.4, H.5, H.6, H.7, H.8, H.9, H.10, H.11, J.6, J.7, K.1, K.4, K.5, K.6, K.7, L.1, L.2, L.3, L.4, L.5, L.6, L.7, L.10a, L.11, L.12, L.13, L.14, L.17, L.18, L.19a, L.20a, L.21a, S.16, S.17, S.18

Chapter 12
Excavation of the Hoards Recovered in 1990–1991

Julia Farley

These accounts are based closely on the contemporary excavation notes. Descriptions of pit fills are given where recorded. Small soil samples were taken from Hoard pits G, H, K and L. Some small metal fragments were discovered in these samples, but there was no visible evidence for surviving organic remains. Where possible, organic components from the hoards were radiocarbon dated. These instances (in Hoards F, L and M) are noted below.

Late Iron Age (Phase 3) hoards

Hoard F

Hoard F (finds F.1–F.443) was uncovered by detectorist Charles Hodder on 25 August 1990, a mass of gold/silver alloy and copper alloy torcs, bracelets and rings, many of them fragmentary. A stray fragment found just to the west (F.444) is also most likely from Hoard F, disturbed by ploughing. There were nine gold coins (Ch. 15, Cat. nos 170–178), five of them (Cat. nos 174–8) found within tubular torc fragment F.53, which had been folded closed at the ends, and four (Cat. nos 170–3) found within the hoard pit. All are Gallo-Belgic A or C types, most likely minted in the period 100–60 BC (see Ch. 15). The finds had been deposited at the base of a shallow pit in an inverted copper alloy helmet (F.445), which was highly fragmented at the time of discovery. The vast majority of these finds were recovered by Hodder, with some small fragments found during the subsequent excavation.

Radiocarbon dating of an organic core from torc F.168 gave a date of 370–120 cal BC (at 95% confidence; see Chapter 19 and **Table 5.2**).

Figure 12.1 shows a sketch of the hoard pit drawn by Hodder shortly after his discovery, from a letter dated 3 September 1990 (NHER 1487). This is the best-surviving record of the hoard *in situ*. Hodder recalled that the first finds were made around 11–12 inches (0.3m) below the surface, with the pit extending a further 12 inches into the ground. The relevant section of Hodder's letter is worth quoting at length:

> A faint detector sound led me to dig a small hole 11 inches deep, at this depth I observed two twisted strands of what appeared to be gold. This wire did not yield to a gentle pull, it was attached to something below.
>
> Further recovery was carried out only with a pointed piece of wood and my hands in order not to mark or damage any item.
>
> I found no trace of a container lid or cover, the hoard was quite compact, there were no air pockets, just sandy earth and lumps of sandstone.
>
> By the time I had recovered all the items the hole was 24 inches deep, on my way down with the digging a shape appeared around the hole side and I could see there had been a container or vessel. Small pieces [of] green natalic [?metallic] material remained stuck to the sides of the hole, I was able to preserve this shape down to the bottom of where the container had been.
>
> As much as possible of this thin copper sheet (?) was recovered but it was very brittle and I could not find any large pieces.
>
> The bottom of the hole was neat, appeared to be slightly smaller in diameter than the upper part of the container, also the bottom was flat and seemed deliberately made so, with

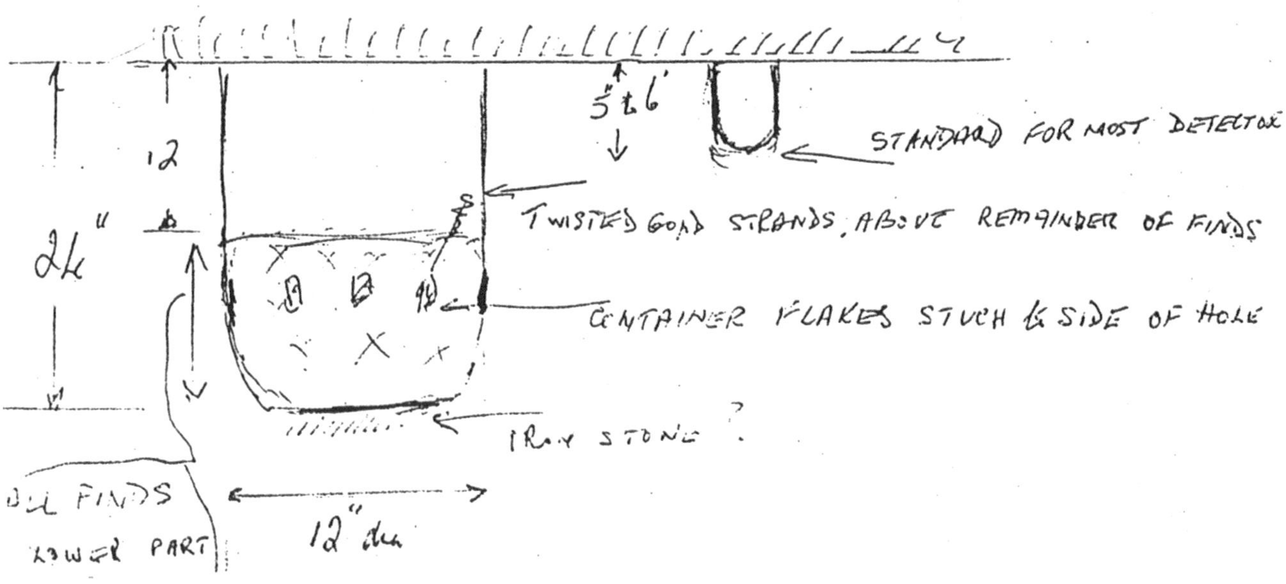

Figure 12.1 Sketch of Hoard F pit in section, made by Wing Commander Hodder shortly after he excavated the finds

> pieces of sandstone fitted together. If the archaeologists wish to see this no doubt I can uncover the hole, providing it is done before being ploughed. I do not know when it will be plowed [sic] again. I found no trace of the container bottom. In removing the items, which lasted over one hour, I left all the intreloched [?interlocked] items just as I found them.
>
> I returned home feeling very pleased with this fantastic collection of Iron Age craftsmanship, I shall be sorry when the archaeologist comes to collect them today, I will still have the satisfaction of knowing they will be in a display for all to see.
>
> The finds were washed in soapy water only, no other cleaning was carried out.
>
> When cleaning I found a short piece of damaged torc tube which rattled, on opening one end five gold coins came out.
>
> Extract from Hodder's letter dated 3 September 1990 (NHER 1487).

Hodder was confident that he had discovered the base of the original pit, with the description of the base as, 'flat and… deliberately made so, with pieces of sandstone fitted together', most likely a reference to the natural carrstone into which the pit was cut. The helmet (F.445) was highly fragmentary, but the suggestion from Hodder's account of the 'container', flakes of which were stuck to the side around the pit, is that it was at least partially complete when placed into the ground, and had been used to contain the hoard. This is discussed in more detail in the catalogue entry in Chapter 14, which outlines the conservation and reconstruction of the helmet. Hodder noted that he 'found no trace of the container bottom', and indeed it has not proved possible to reconstruct the crown of the helmet, so it is possible that the metal in this area was damaged or missing before deposition. In this case, rather than holding the hoard, the helmet might simply have been placed into the pit first, inverted. The other finds were largely fragmentary, with few complete objects, and over 40 composite assemblages formed from multiple fragments interlinked, looped, inserted or fused together (Chs 13, 20, 21).

The finds recovered by Hodder were eventually taken to the British Museum. Ralph Jackson, Romano-British Curator in the then Department of Prehistoric and Romano-British Antiquities, produced a catalogue of the finds in preparation for the Treasure Trove inquest. Metal analysis was undertaken by Duncan Hook of the British Museum Research Laboratories. Jackson listed 595 artefacts and a total of 501 numbers were assigned (as the sheet fragments were all assigned one number). The total weight of the artefacts was 9.1815kg, excluding the coins and vessel fragments. The preparatory work by Jackson and Hook was an invaluable aid to the preparation of the present volume, and the numbers assigned by Ralph Jackson are included in the concordance.

The area was subsequently investigated by Stead and his team. A 2m by 2m trench was opened up over the findspot of the hoard. Hodder's pit was easily located. As re-excavated it was 0.35m in diameter, with a base 0.52m below the modern ground level. It had been overcut, and there were no traces of the original sides. Although Hodder did not recover finds from the upper levels, when soil from the pit and surrounding surface was sieved, many small fragments were recovered. (These are F.153, F.212, F.213, F.214, F.226, F.282, F.306. F.307, F.316, F.322, F.324, F.338, F.340, F.344, F.352, F.382, F.411, F.421, F.432, F.441, F.442, F.443, and parts of the helmet F.445.) An additional torc fragment (F.444) was found just to the west of the other finds, 0.45–0.50m from the edge of the pit. This fragment was found at a depth of 0.26m, placing it towards the bottom of the plough soil (which was around 0.30m deep). Stead concluded that it had most likely been moved by ploughing, and it does seem likely that the top of Hoard F had been truncated in this way. This would explain Hodder's discovery of a small number of 'twisted gold strands' above the main hoard deposit which contained all the other finds (**Fig. 12.1**). Some of the stray finds from the surrounding area may also have originated in Hoard F.

The plan and profile (**Figs 12.2–4**) show the area disturbed by metal-detecting activity, Hodder's pit, and

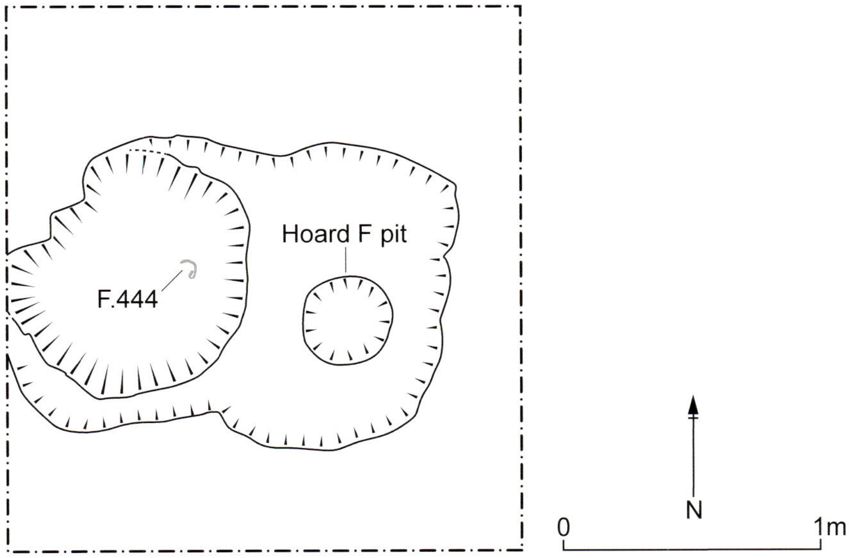

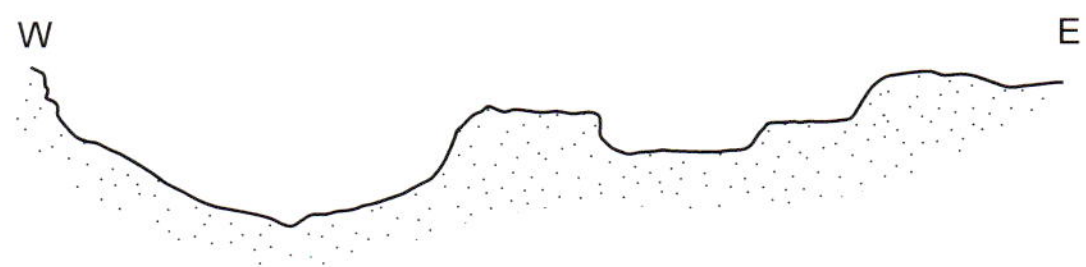

Figure 12.2 (top) Plan of Hoard F trench after excavation and removal of finds

Figure 12.3 (bottom) Sketch profile of Hoard F trench, after truncation of topsoil

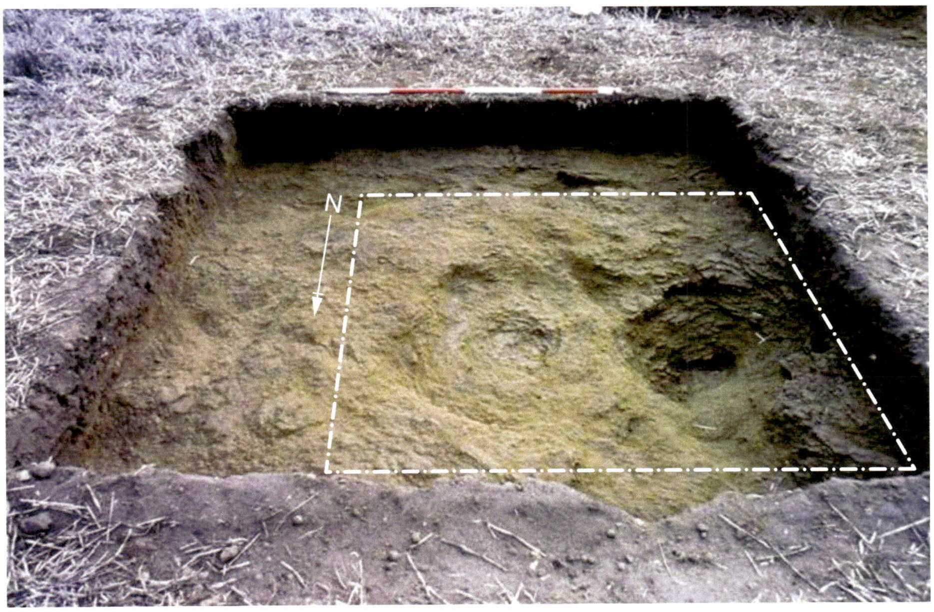

Figure 12.4 Photograph of the Hoard F trench (looking south). Taken after excavation, including extension of trench to the east and south

what Stead interpreted as a tree bowl, around 0.9m in diameter, just to the west. Aside from F.444, which was found at the base of the plough soil, there were no finds from this other hollow, so it does not seem likely to have been a hoard pit.

Hoard G

Hoard G was discovered by Hodder, using his metal detector, on 19 November 1990. Hodder lifted the uppermost torc, G.1, before it was recorded by archaeologists. Fragmentary copper alloy torc G.2, beneath, may also have been disturbed during the initial discovery. The pit was then exposed by the archaeologists, and the torcs planned *in situ* before further lifting.

Figures 12.7–10 show the torcs from the upper pit of Hoard G *in situ*. There was a great deal of overlapping of the torcs, most likely suggesting that G.8 and G.10 were deposited together; then G.9, G.6, and G.5, in turn; then G.3, G.4 and G.7 together, intertwined, with G.2 presumably placed on top followed by G.1 (**Fig. 12.11**). After G.1–G.10 had been removed, there was a fairly clear earth surface with only a small number of copper alloy fragments visible. However, Hodder's metal detector recorded a strong signal and so the base of the pit was further explored, revealing a second group of torcs beneath. These are shown in **Figures 12.12–16**. The most impressive torc in the hoard (G.11) was uppermost in this lower section of the pit. Immediately beneath were a group of copper alloy torcs (G.12–G.16)

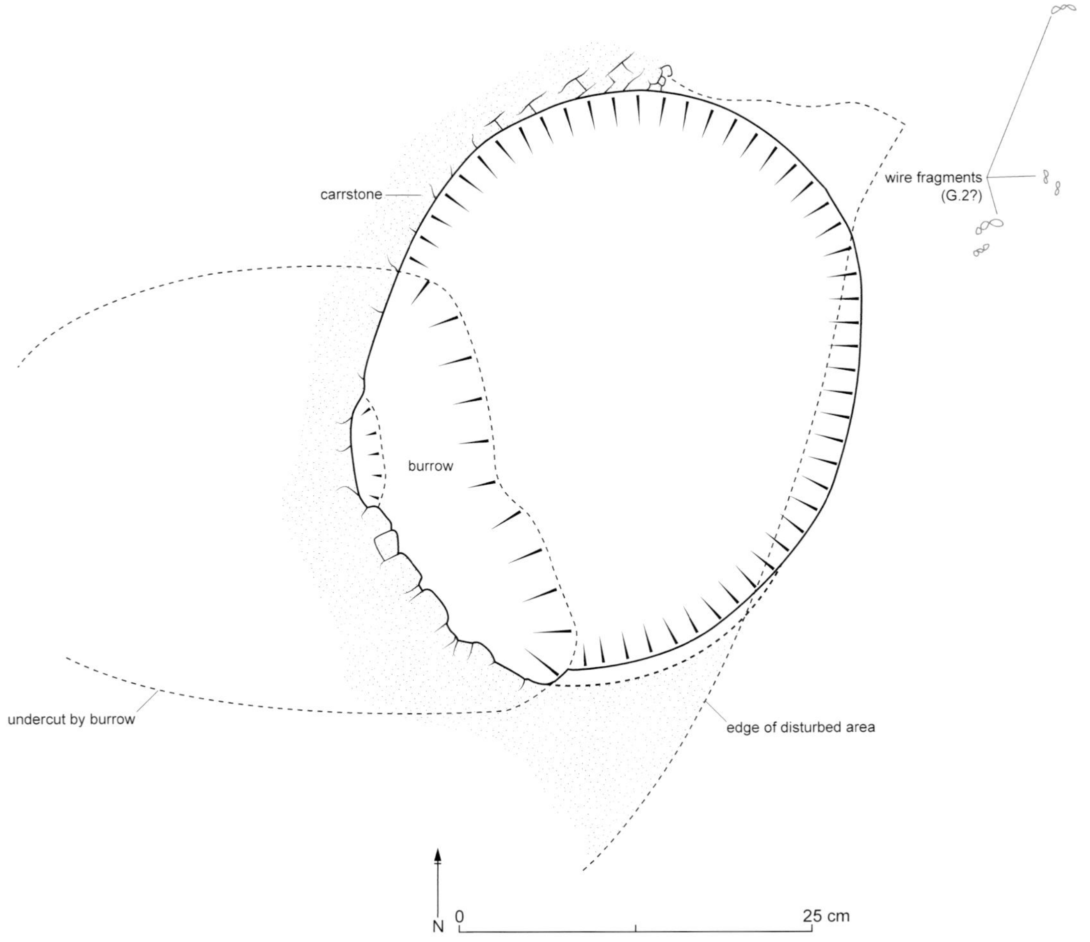

Figure 12.5 Plan of Hoard G pit after excavation and removal of artefacts

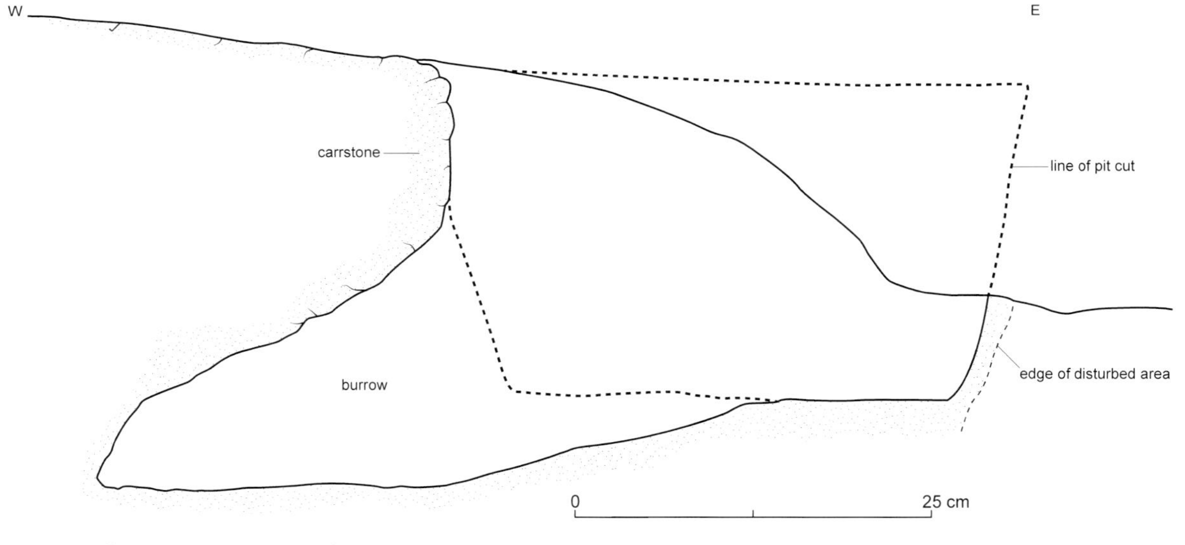

Figure 12.6 Section through Hoard G pit after excavation and removal of artefacts

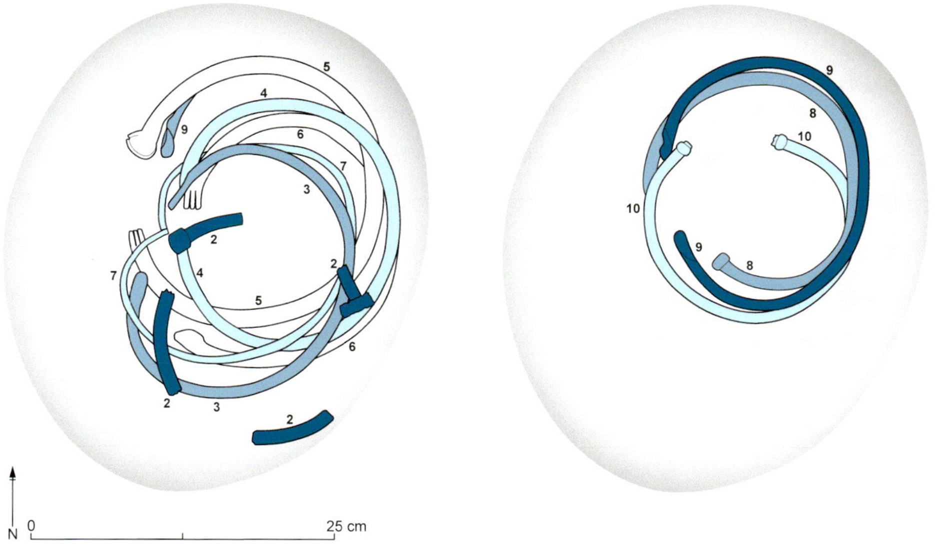

Figure 12.7 Hoard G upper pit torc overlay drawings, showing torcs G.2–G.10 (the uppermost torc, G.1, was removed before planning)

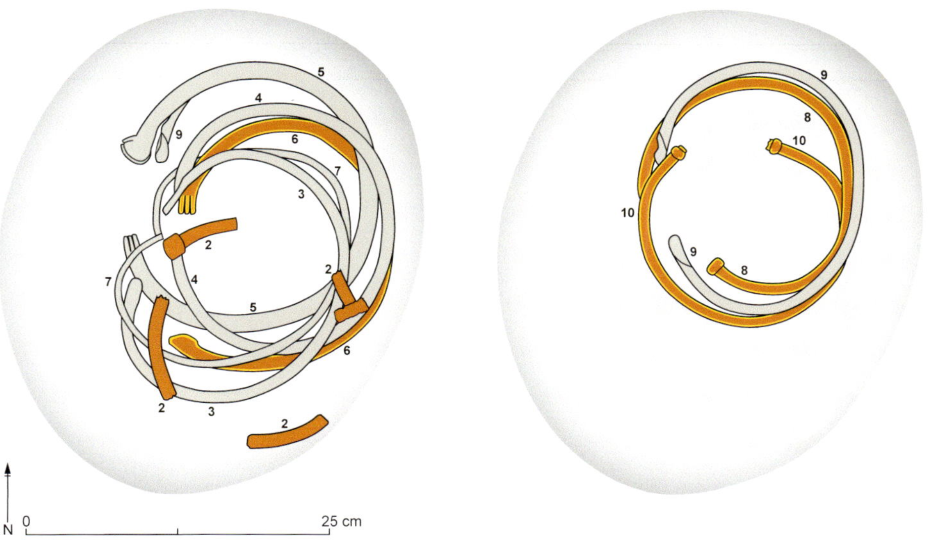

Figure 12.8 Hoard G upper pit torc overlay drawings, colour-coded according to surface metal content (for key see Fig. 23.5)

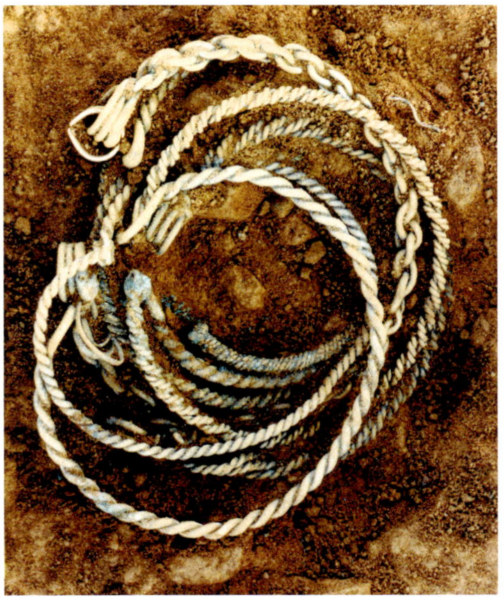

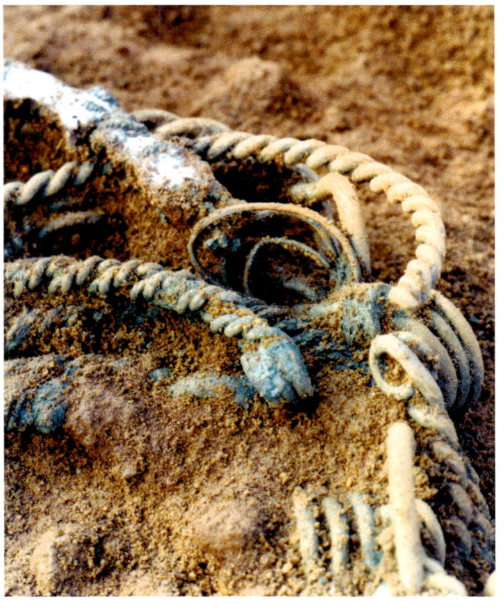

Figure 12.9 Photograph of the upper pit of Hoard G, showing torcs G.3–G.10 *in situ*

Figure 12.10 *In situ* detail photograph showing the complex interrelationship of torcs G.3–G.10

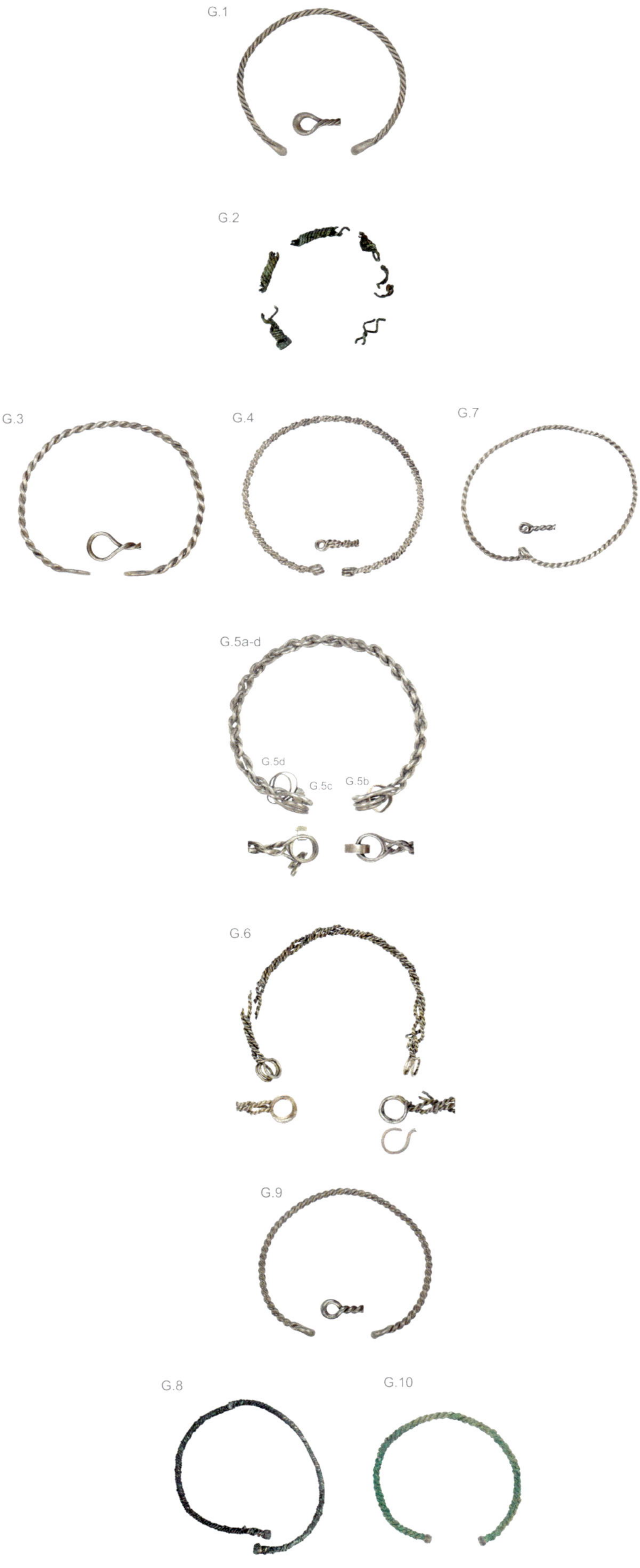

Figure 12.11 The order of deposition of torcs in the upper pit of Hoard G. The torcs at the bottom of the image were deposited first. Torcs displayed at the same level were deposited together

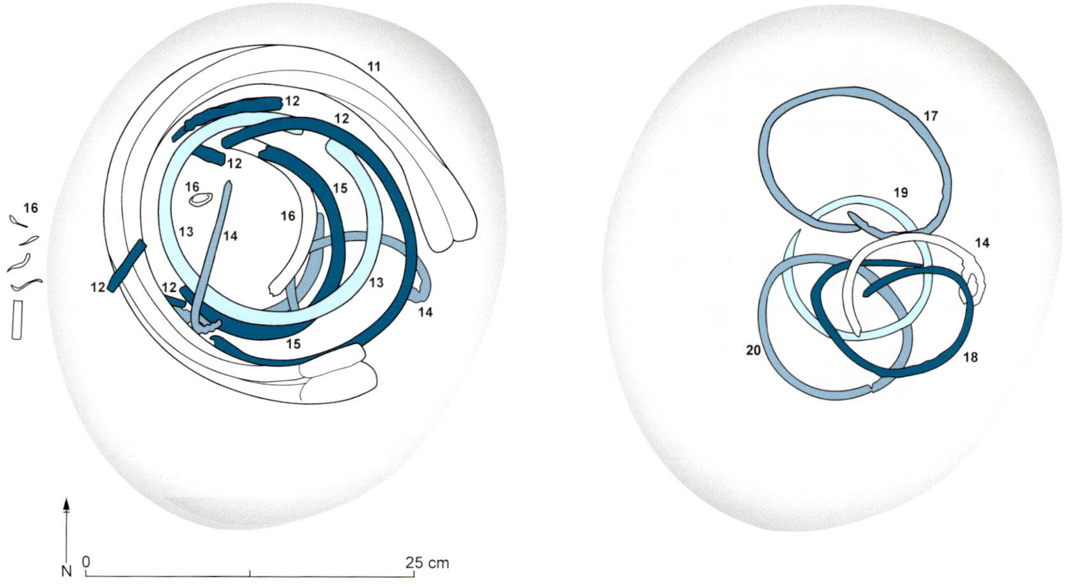

Figure 12.12 Hoard G lower pit torc overlay drawings, showing objects G.11–G.20

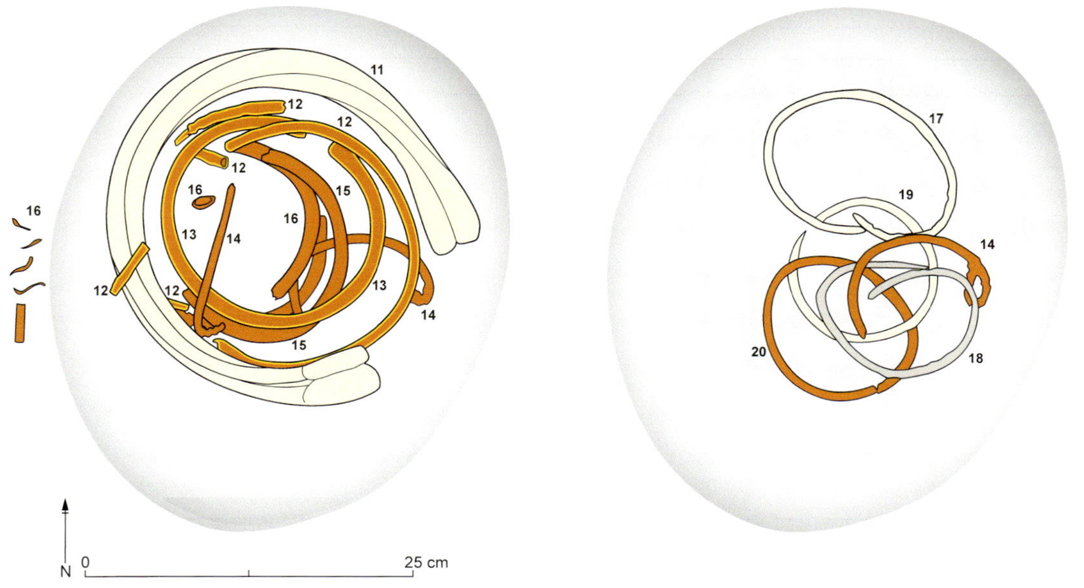

Figure 12.13 Hoard G lower pit torc overlay drawings, showing objects G.11–G.20, colour-coded according to surface metal content (for key see Fig. 23.5)

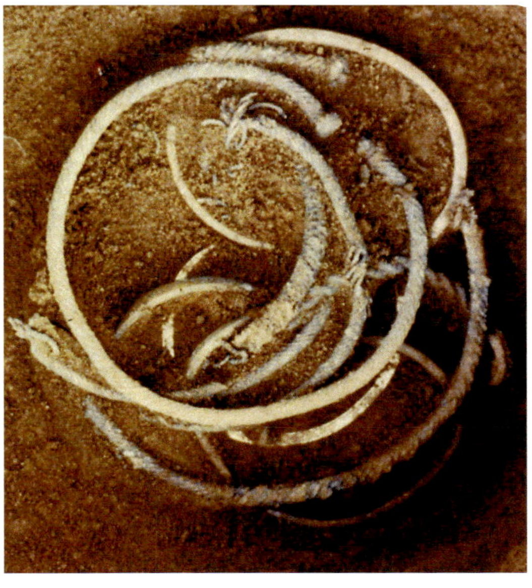

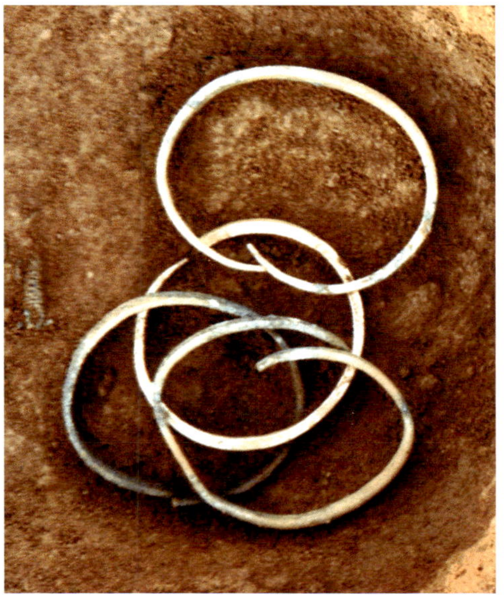

Figure 12.14 Photograph of the middle of the Hoard G lower pit, showing copper alloy torcs G.12–G.16 *in situ*, with large penannular rings G.17–G.20 beginning to be uncovered

Figure 12.15 Photograph of the bottom of the Hoard G lower pit, showing large penannular rings G.17–G.20 *in situ*

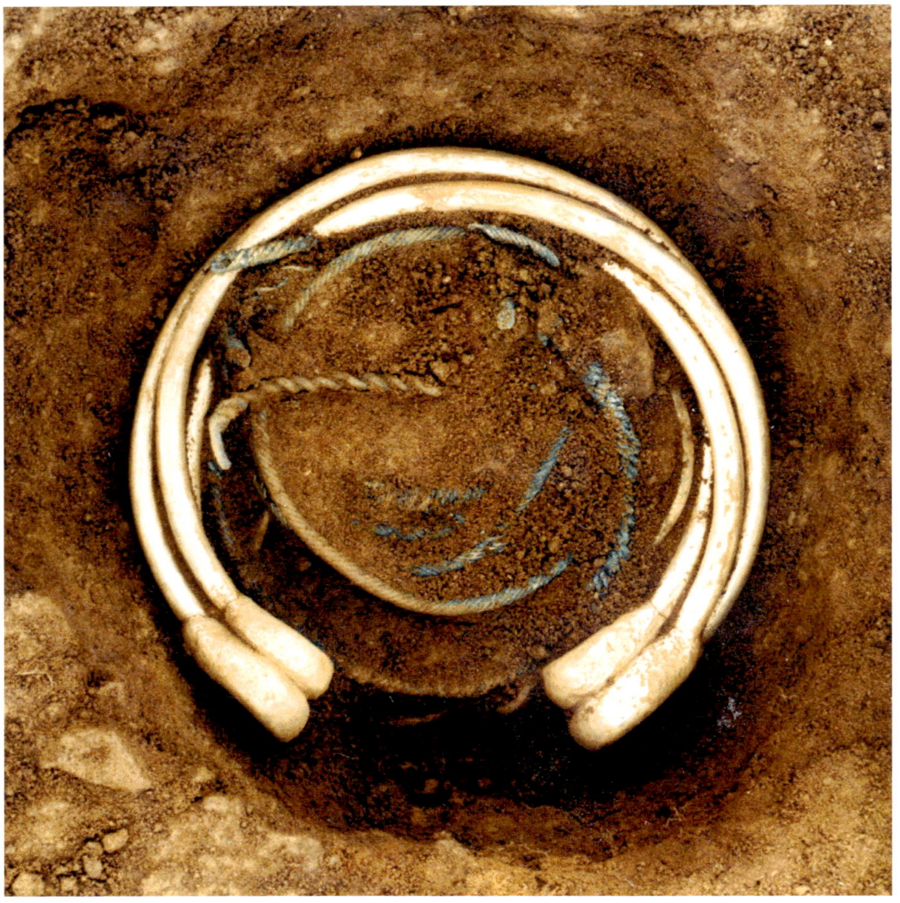

Figure 12.16 Photograph of the top of the lower pit of Hoard G, showing large gold/silver alloy torc G.11 *in situ*, with copper alloy torcs G.12–G.16 beginning to be uncovered

which were severely corroded and had been heavily disturbed by animal burrowing. These torcs were complex to interpret because of their poor level of preservation, and a full understanding was only possible after conservation work had been carried out (hence the slight differences here from Stead's interim report, Stead 1991a). There were torc fragments in disturbed ground up to 0.2m from the edge of the pit and also in the animal burrow itself, well below the surface of the carrstone. The majority of the damage seems to have been caused by animal burrowing, but not everything could be blamed on animal disturbance. G.13 is reasonably complete, but missing a terminal, the end of the neck-ring having been 'repaired' with an organic 'string'. G.16 is also missing a terminal and shows an organic repair, and in this case little enough of the torc survives to suggest that it may well have been incomplete when deposited. Two other torcs (G.14 and G.15) were each found in two main parts, and the angle of the pieces in the ground strongly suggests that they were deposited this way. The two pieces of G.15 were superimposed, one on top of the other, as if it was placed into the ground folded over on itself, whilst one part of G.14 was at the base of the pit and the other, projecting upwards, was at the top of the lower group. At the very base of the pit were a group of four large penannular rings (G.17–G.20) which were in good condition. Two were interlinked, and it is possible all four were placed as a group. **Figure 12.17** shows the order of deposition as far as it can be reconstructed.

Figures 12.5–6 show the plan and section of the pit after complete excavation and removal of the artefacts. The hoard pit was 0.27–0.34m across and 0.45m deep below the ground level, cut 0.18m into the carrstone. The section shows the heavy disturbance of the west side of the pit by animal burrowing. There is no evidence for two cuts, so it seems most likely that after the pit was dug, objects G.11–G.20 were deposited first, the pit was partially backfilled, and then torcs G.1–G.10 were placed into the pit before it was fully backfilled.

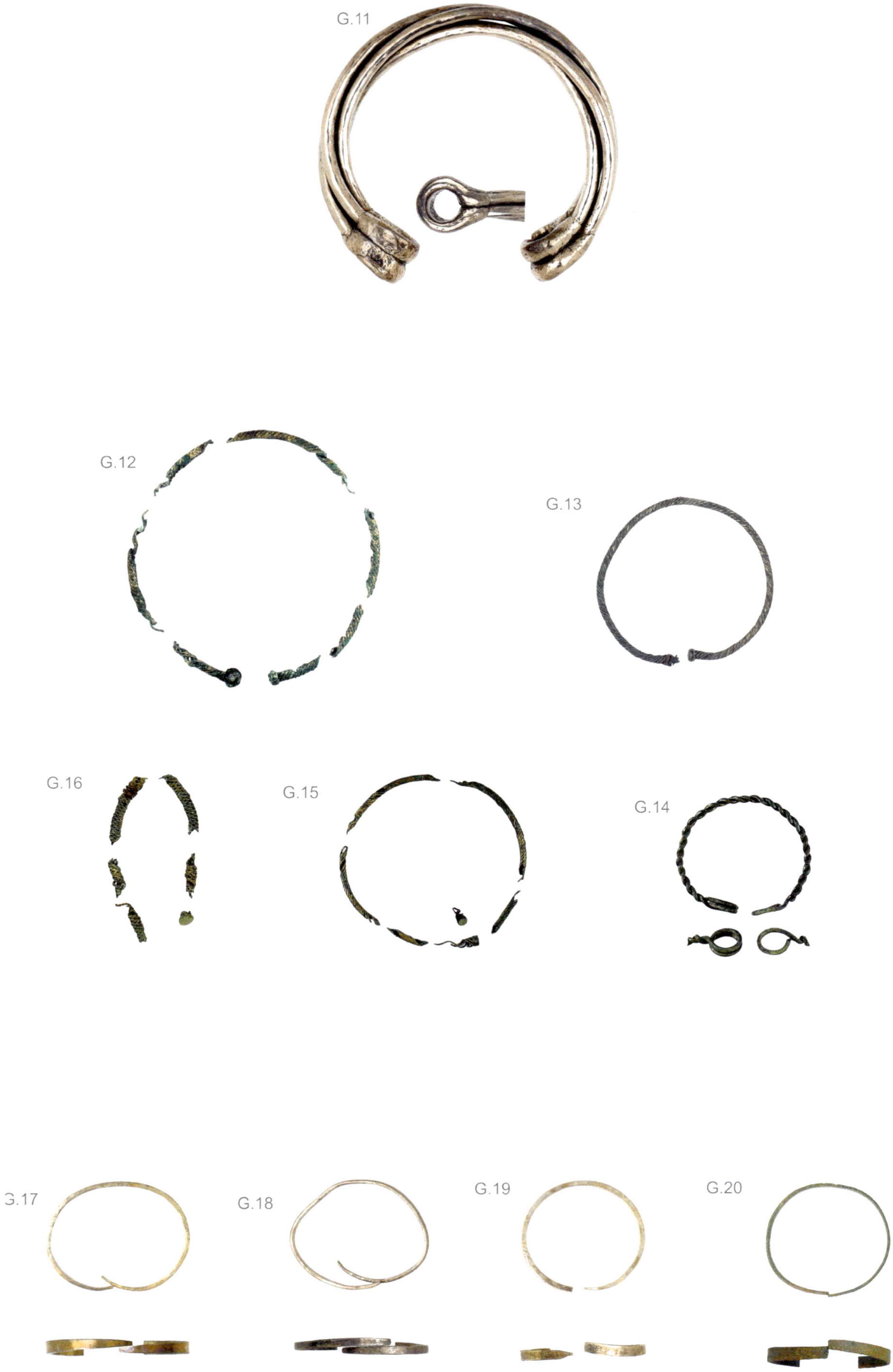

Figure 12.17 The order of deposition of torcs in the lower pit of Hoard G. The torcs at the bottom of the diagram were deposited first. Torcs displayed at the same level were deposited together, or their order of deposition cannot be discerned

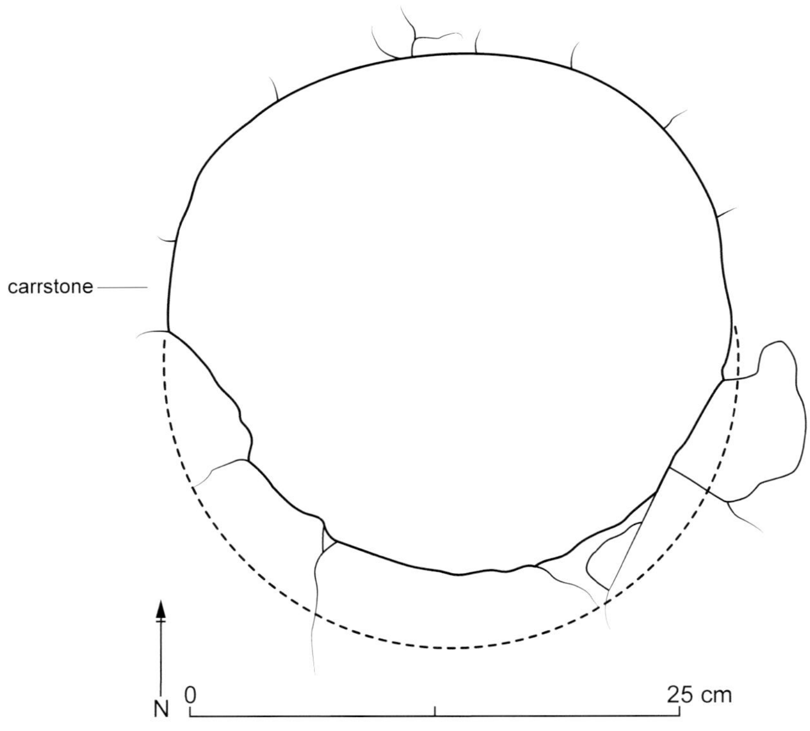

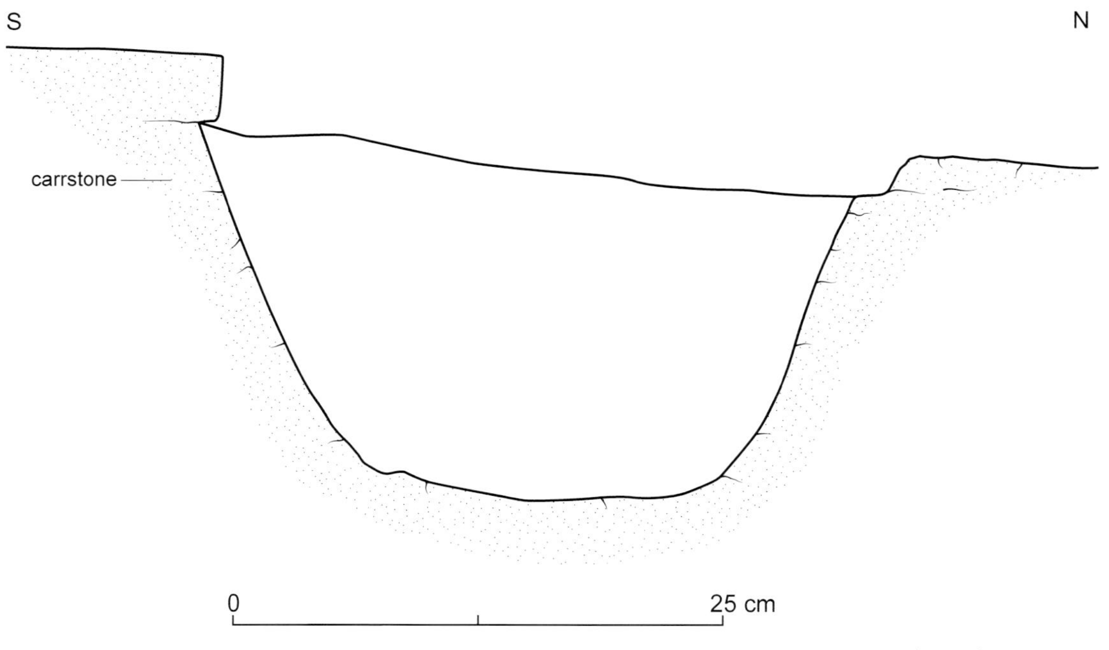

Figures 12.18 and 12.19 Plan of Hoard H pit after excavation and removal of the majority of the torcs (above) and section through Hoard H pit after excavation and removal of the artefacts (below)

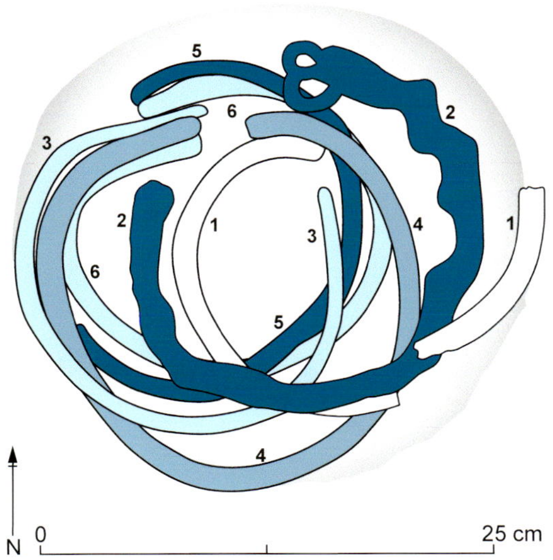

Figure 12.20 Hoard H upper pit torc overlay drawing, showing torcs H.1–H.6

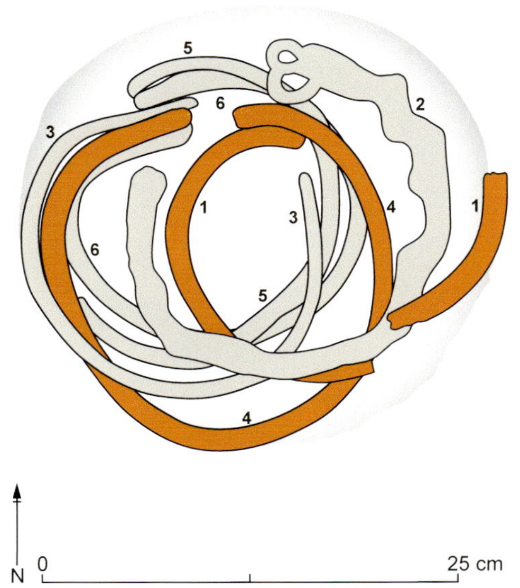

Figure 12.21 Hoard H upper pit torc overlay drawing, showing torcs H.1–H.6, colour-coded according to surface metal content (for key see Fig. 23.5)

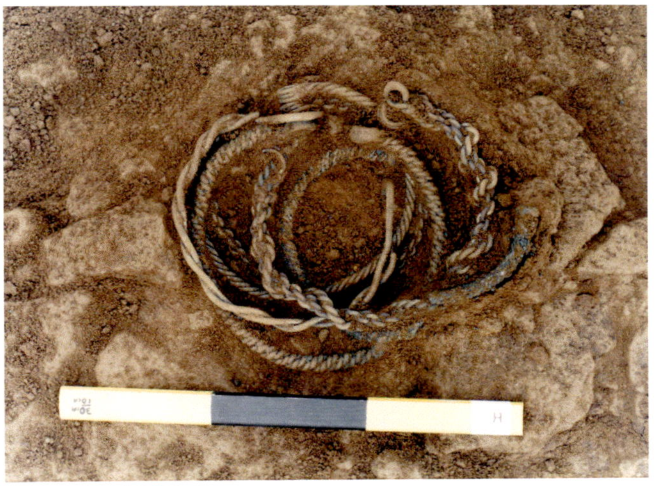

Figure 12.22 Photograph of the top of the upper pit of Hoard H, showing torcs H.1–H.6 *in situ*

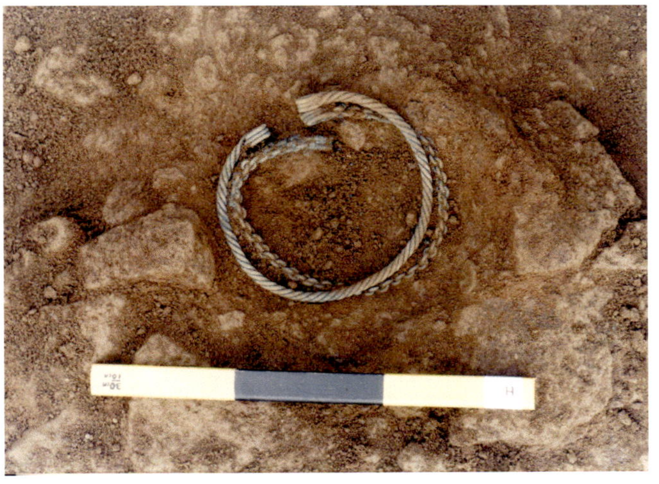

Figure 12.23 Photograph of the bottom of the upper pit of Hoard H, showing torcs H.5 and H.6 *in situ*

Hoard H

Hoard H was also discovered by Hodder during metal-detecting on 19 November 1990, but in this case it was undisturbed. **Figure 12.18** shows the plan of the pit before removal of the torcs nearest the base (H.9–H.11) and **Figure 12.19** shows the section of the pit after complete excavation and removal of all artefacts. The pit was 0.22m diameter at the top, and cut about 0.16m into the natural underlying rock. The sides of the pit sloped, giving a narrower base, around 0.15m in diameter.

Like Hoard G, there were two distinct levels in the pit. There were six torcs, H.1–H.6, in the upper deposit (**Figs 12.20–3**), with the lower four in this upper group seemingly placed one by one (H.6, H.5, H.4 and then H.3), followed by H.1 and H.2a-b being placed together. H.1 and H.4 are copper alloy torcs, whilst the remaining four are precious metal torcs with a silverish surface colour. H.2a-b is a composite group made from two separate torcs twisted together. **Figure 12.24** shows the order of deposition.

Five torcs comprise the lower deposit (**Figs 12.25–30**). As in Hoard G, the uppermost torc in the lower half of the pit (here H.7) was the most visually impressive of the group and the one with the highest gold content. H.7 had been compressed slightly by the person who deposited it, terminals overlapping to fit into the small pit. Once it was removed by the excavators, this compression was released and it sprang open, back to its original shape. Below H.7 were four copper alloy torcs (H.8–H.11). All were heavily corroded and H.8 and H.9 had broken, but they appear to have been more or less complete when deposited. H.11, the simplest torc of the group, had been placed at the base of the pit first, followed by H.9 and H.10 together, then H.8, and finally H.7 (**Fig. 12.31**). As with pit G, the suggestion is that a single pit was dug, the first group of torcs interred, a small amount of soil backfilled, and then the upper deposit laid. The evidence does not allow a clear estimation of the time that elapsed, except to say that there was no evidence for a period of silting, suggesting that the second hoard was most likely buried not long after the first.

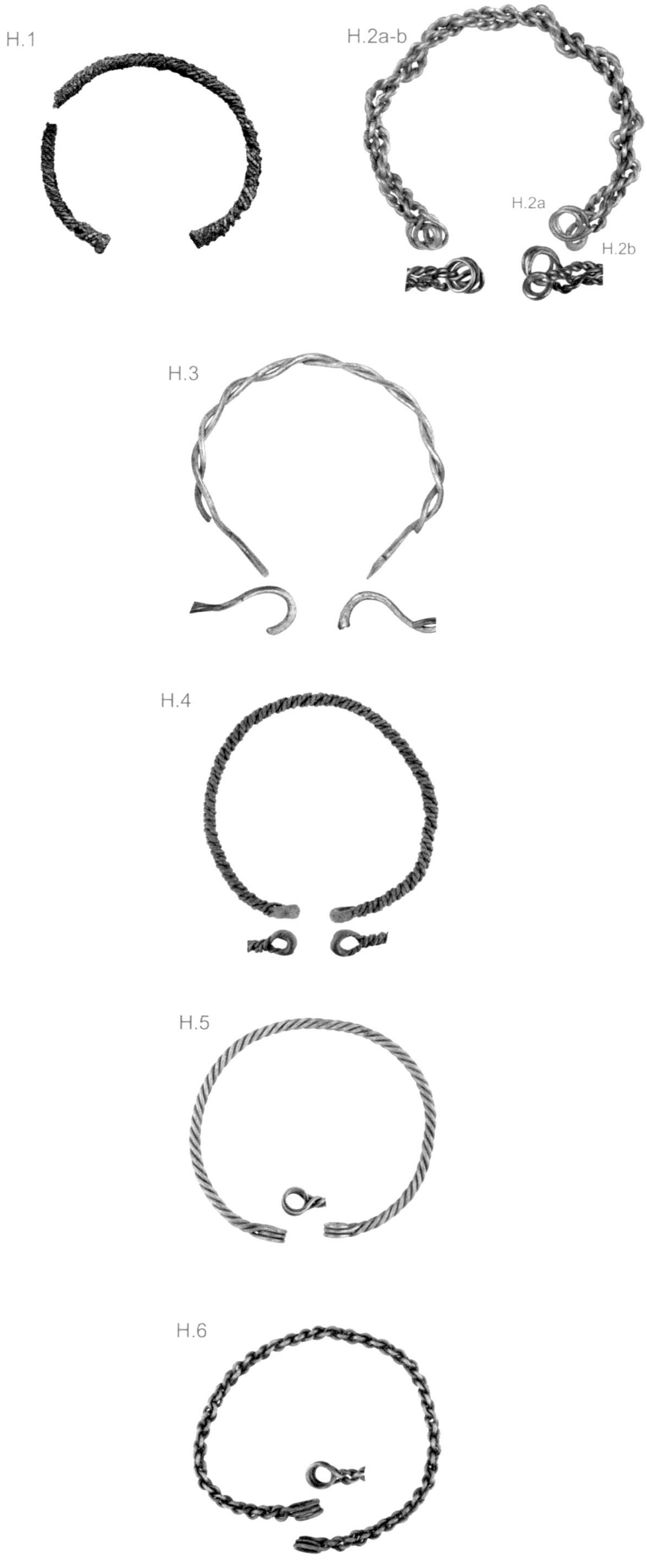

Figure 12.24 The order of deposition of torcs in the upper pit of Hoard H. The torcs at the bottom of the diagram were deposited first. Torcs displayed at the same level were deposited together

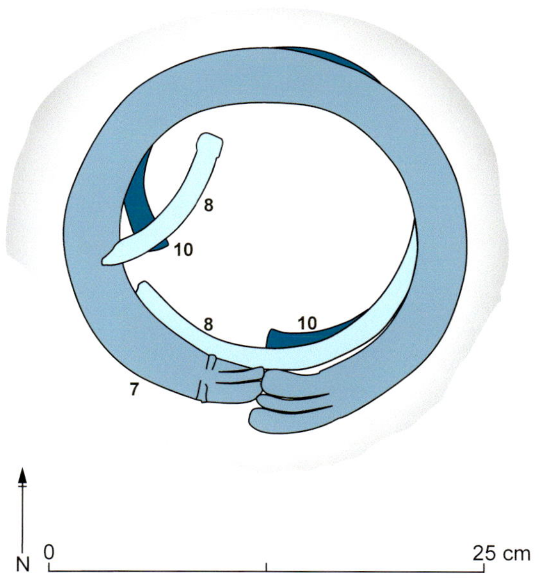

Figure 12.25 Hoard H lower pit torc overlay drawing, showing torcs H.7, H.8 and H.10

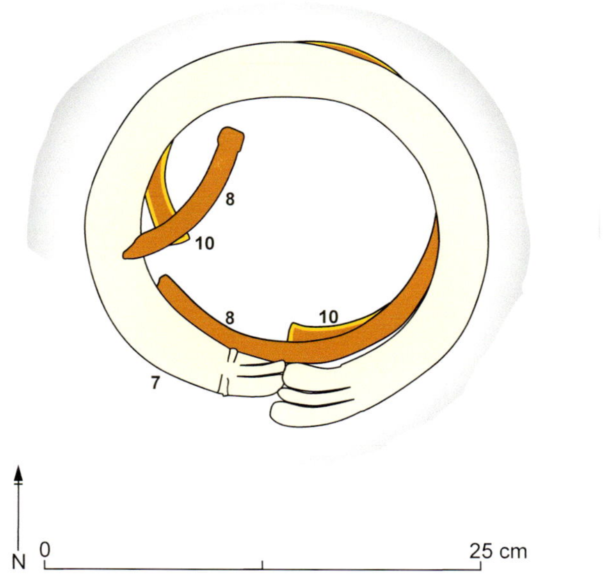

Figure 12.26 Hoard H lower pit torc overlay drawing, showing torcs H.7, H.8 and H.10, colour-coded according to surface metal content (for key see Fig. 23.5)

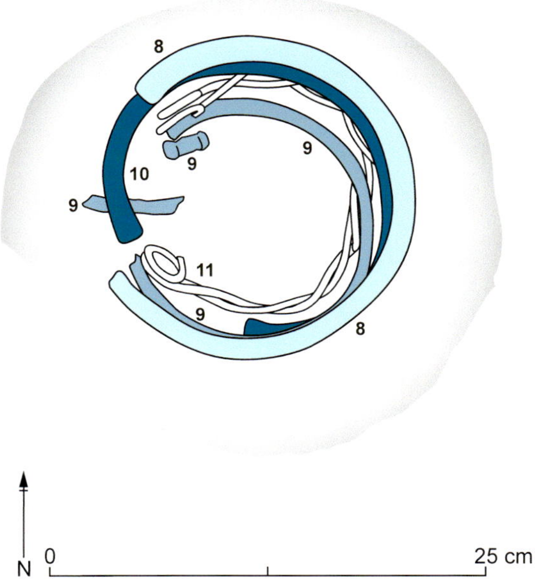

Figure 12.27 Hoard H lower pit torc overlay drawing, showing torcs H.8–H.11

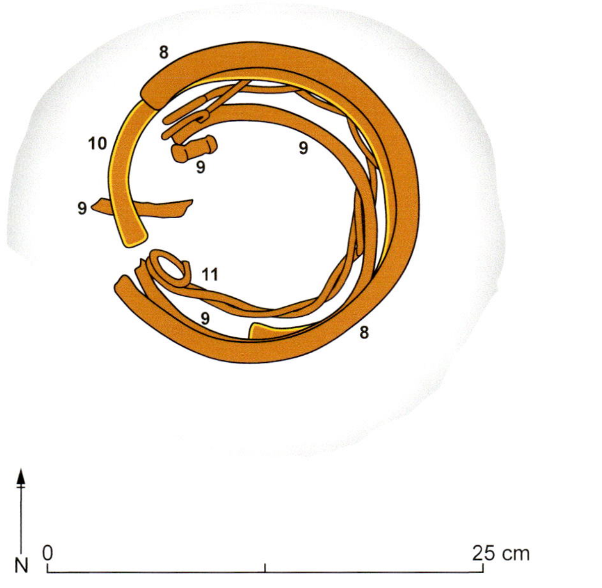

Figure 12.28 Hoard H lower pit torc overlay drawing, showing torcs H.8–H.11, colour-coded according to surface metal content (for key see Fig. 23.5)

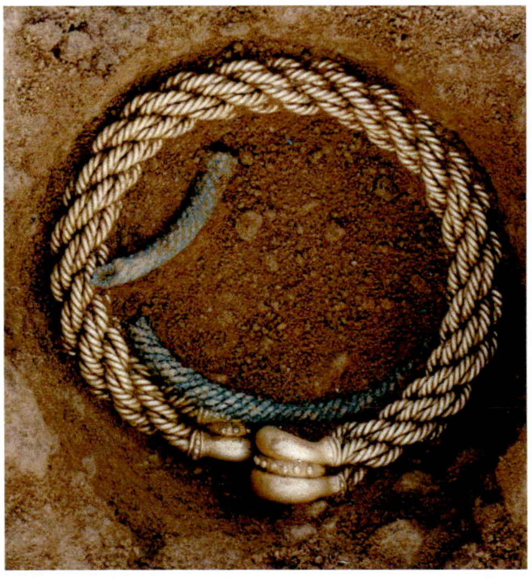

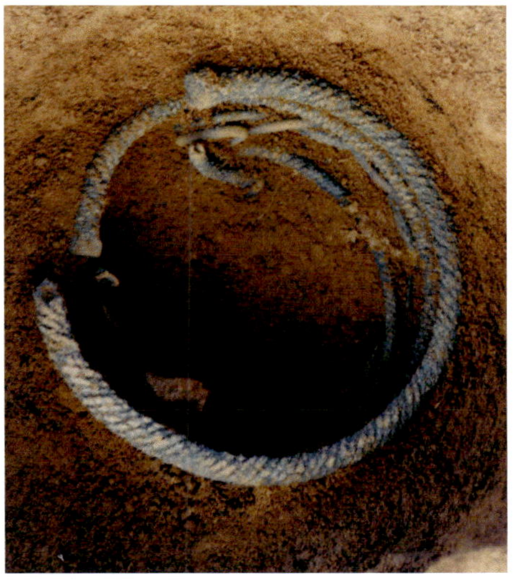

Figure 12.29 Photograph of the top of the lower pit of Hoard H, showing torcs H.7–H.8 *in situ*

Figure 12.30 Photograph of the bottom of the lower pit of Hoard H, showing torcs H.8–H.11 *in situ*

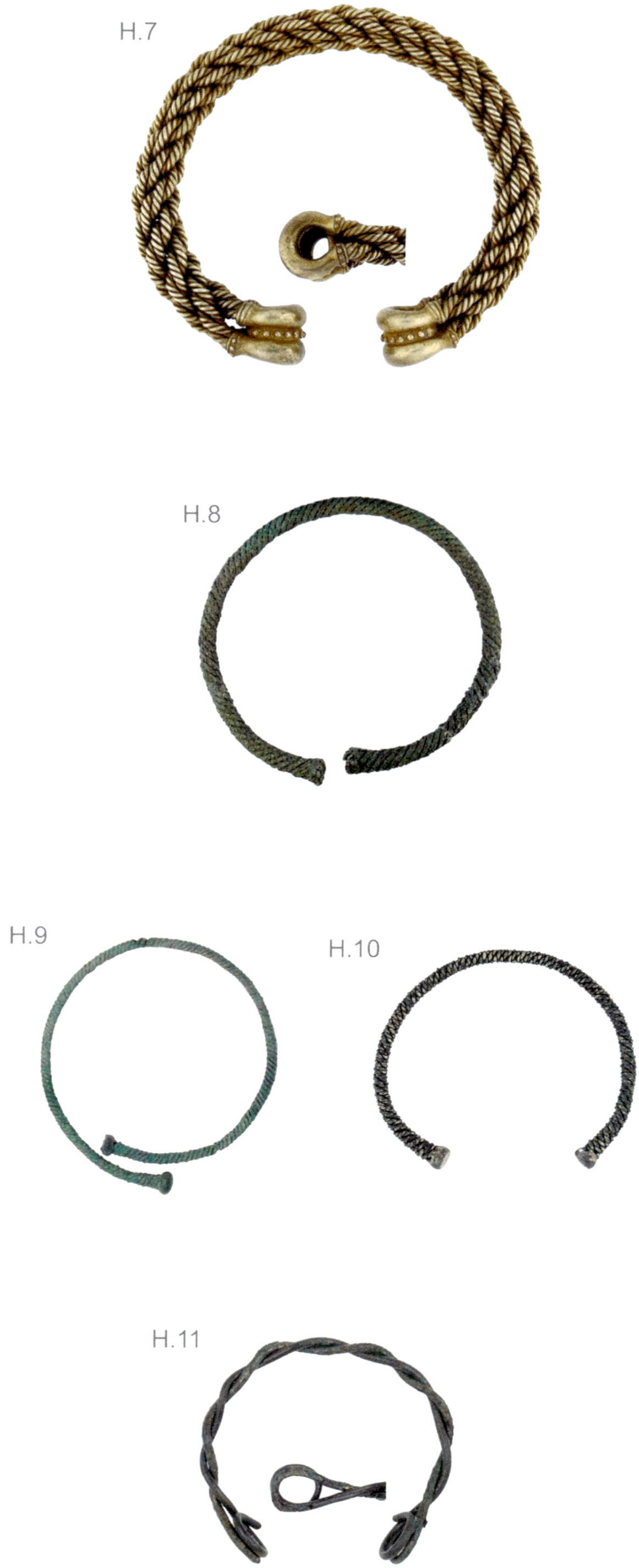

Figure 12.31 The order of deposition of torcs in the lower pit of Hoard H. The torcs at the bottom of the diagram were deposited first. Torcs displayed at the same level were deposited together

Hoard J

Hoard J was discovered by Hodder with his metal detector on 25 November 1990, and subsequently investigated by the excavation team. The hoard was in a very shallow pit, 0.22 by 0.24m, seemingly cut no larger than the torcs themselves (thus only the torcs were drawn, and the pit was not separately planned). Only one layer of torcs was apparent, though the hoard had been heavily disturbed and truncated at the top after being struck by agricultural machinery.

Torcs J.1–J.4 (two gold/silver alloy and two copper alloy) were very fragmented and had been scattered in a line to the north. The assignment of fragments to particular objects was not completed until after the conservation and cataloguing process. The torcs below J.1–J.4 were largely undisturbed (**Figs 12.32–6**). Gold/silver alloy torcs J.7 and then J.6 had been laid into the ground first, followed by composite group J.5a–c. This group comprised two gold/silver alloy torcs, each broken in half when buried, with a length of copper alloy torc threaded through their remaining terminals. The copper alloy torc J.5a had been bent before deposition and was probably not complete at the time of burial. **Figure 12.37** shows the order of deposition.

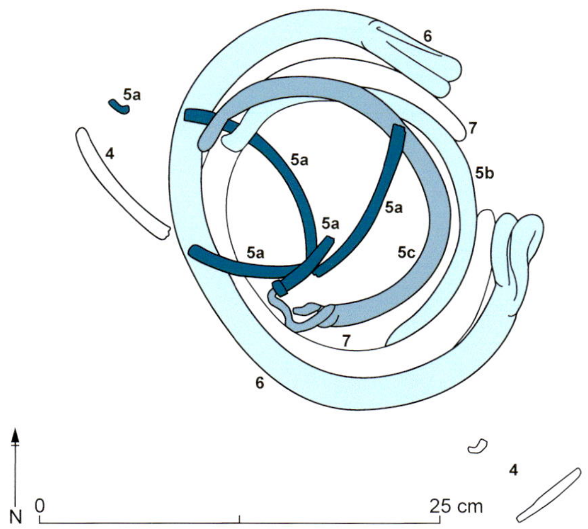

Figure 12.32 Hoard J torc overlay drawing (upper layers disturbed by north–south ploughing)

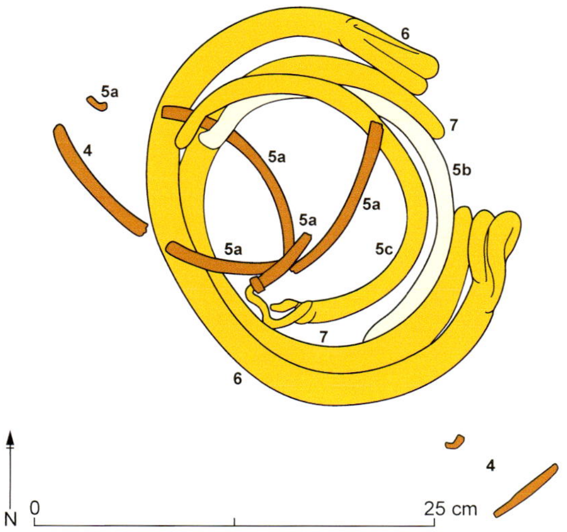

Figure 12.33 Hoard J torc overlay drawing, colour-coded according to surface metal content (for key see Fig. 23.5)

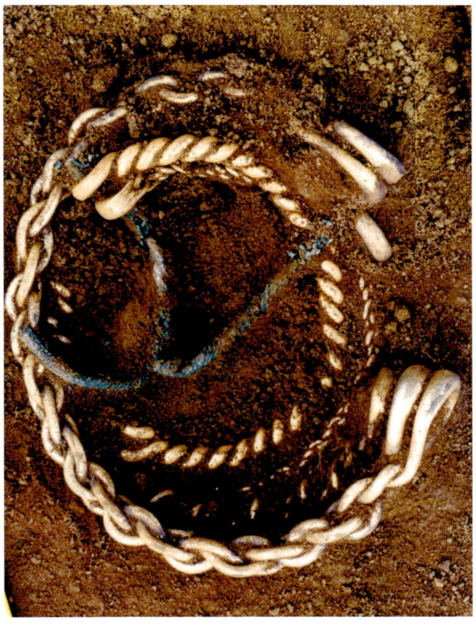

Figure 12.34 Photograph of Hoard J *in situ*, showing composite torc fragment group J.5a–c overlying complete torcs J.6 (uppermost) and J.7 (beneath)

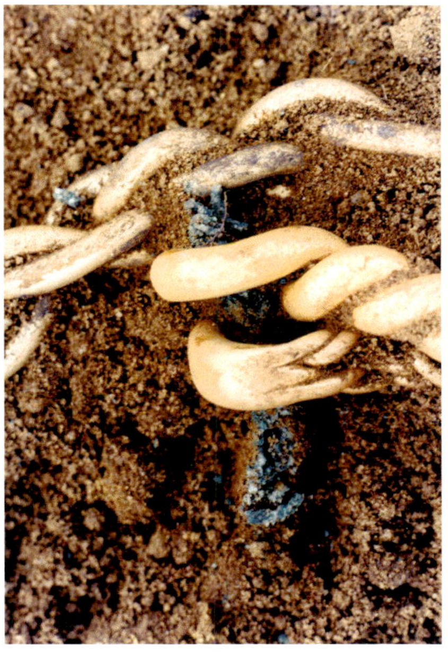

Figure 12.35 *In situ* detailed photograph showing the insertion of torc J.5a through the terminals of torcs J.5b and J.5c

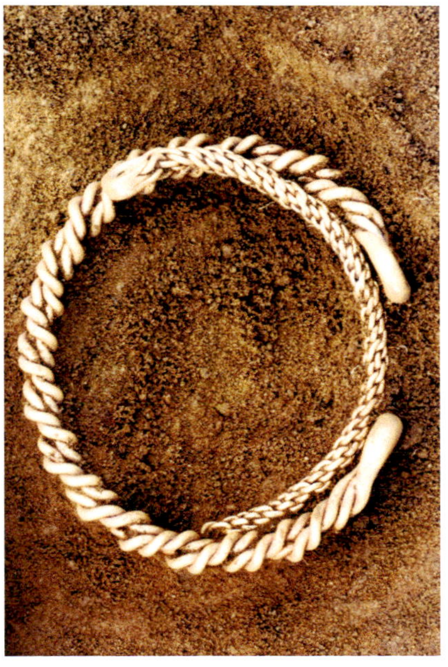

Figure 12.36 *In situ* photograph of torc fragment J.5b overlying torc J.7

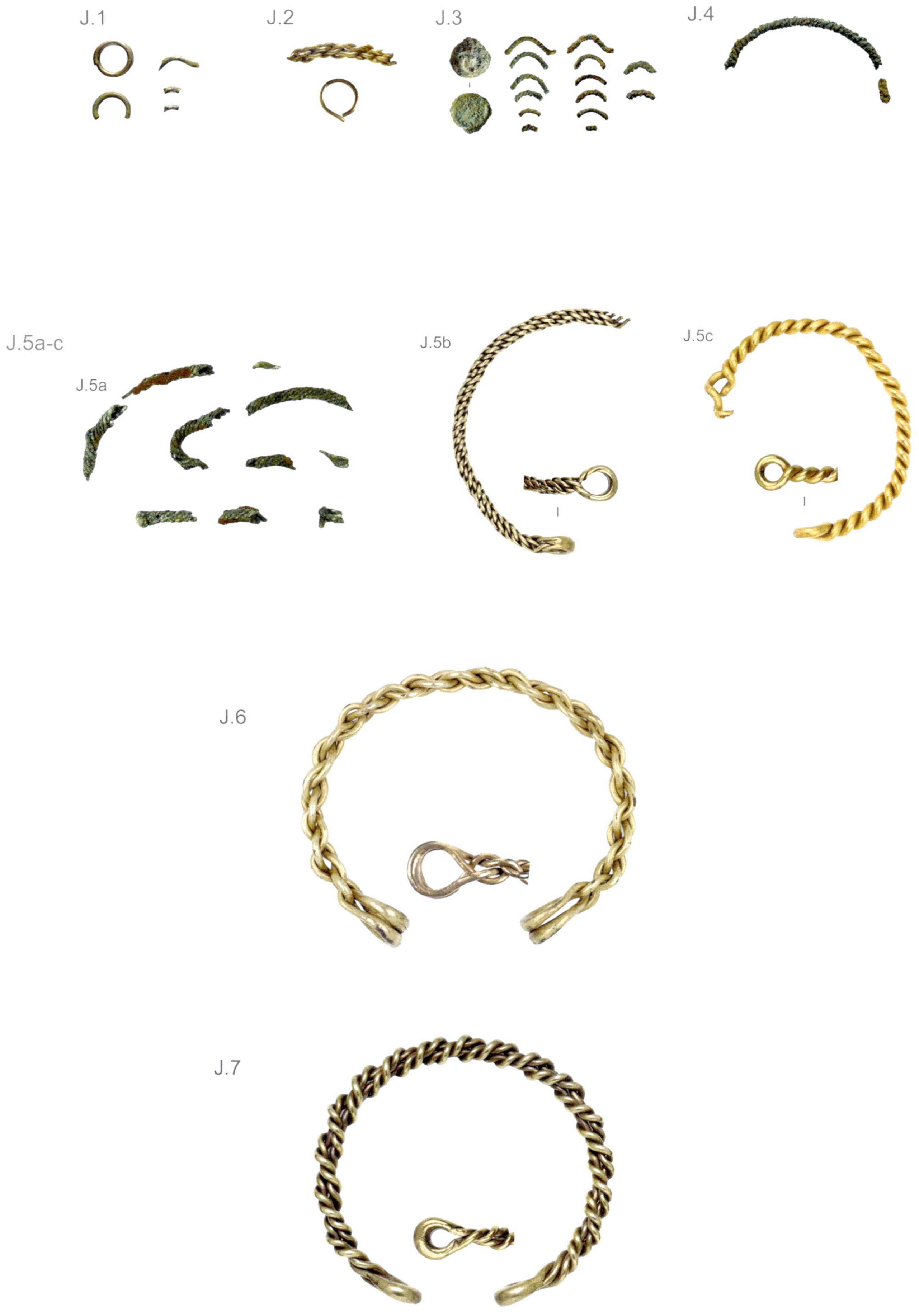

Figure 12.37 The order of deposition of torcs in Hoard J. The torcs at the bottom of the diagram were deposited first. Torcs displayed at the same level were deposited together, or their order of deposition cannot be discerned

Hoard K

Hoard K was found by Tony Pacitto with his metal detector on 1 December 1990. The first visible signs were the remains of four copper alloy torcs that had been hit by the plough and scattered along a 1.25m line running north–south across the hoard pit (**Figs 12.39–40, 12.41b**). These copper alloy torcs, K.1–K.4, were planned and recovered, allowing investigation of the pit. The pit survived to a depth of 0.13m in the carrstone bedrock, and was 0.21–0.24m in diameter at its surface (**Fig. 12.38**). Three complete gold/silver alloy torcs, K.5–K.7, were found *in situ* at the base of the pit (**Fig. 12.41a**). K.7 had been deposited first, with K.6 placed on top, followed by K.5 (**Fig. 12.42**).

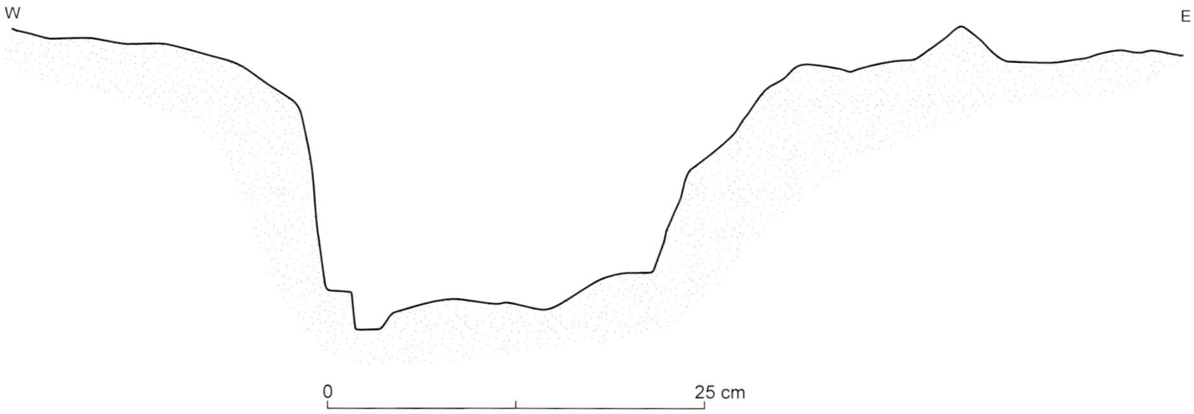

Figure 12.38 Section through Hoard K pit, after complete excavation and removal of artefacts

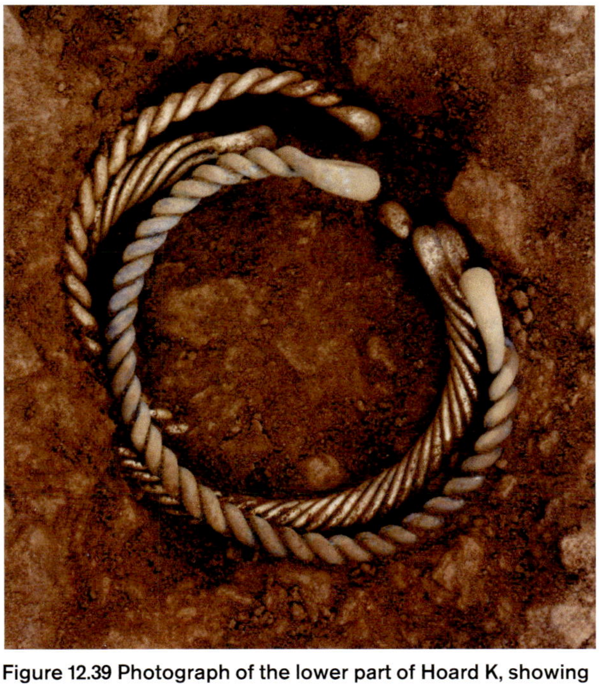

Figure 12.39 Photograph of the lower part of Hoard K, showing torcs K.5, K.6 and K.7 *in situ*

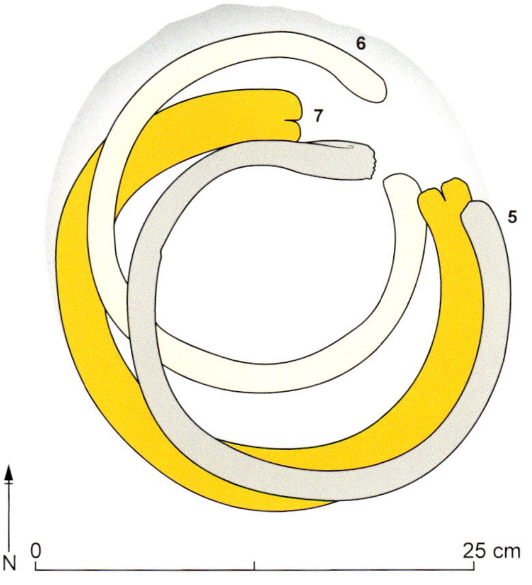

Figure 12.40 Hoard K torc overlay drawing, colour-coded according to surface metal content (for key see Fig. 23.5)

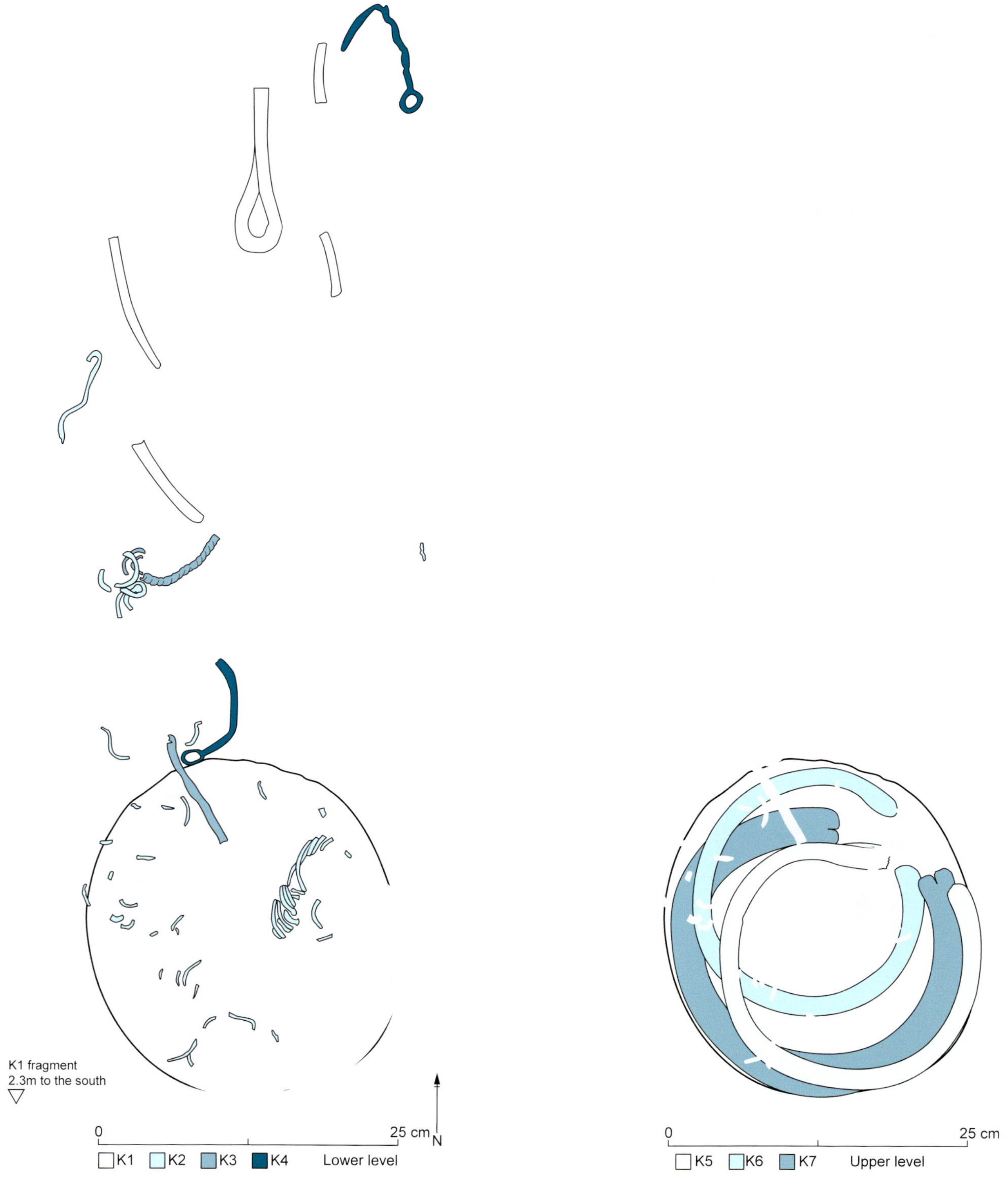

Figure 12.41a–b Hoard K torc overlay drawings showing torcs K.1–K.4 which were scattered by ploughing (a, left) and K.5–K.7 which were found undisturbed *in situ* at the base of the pit (b, right)

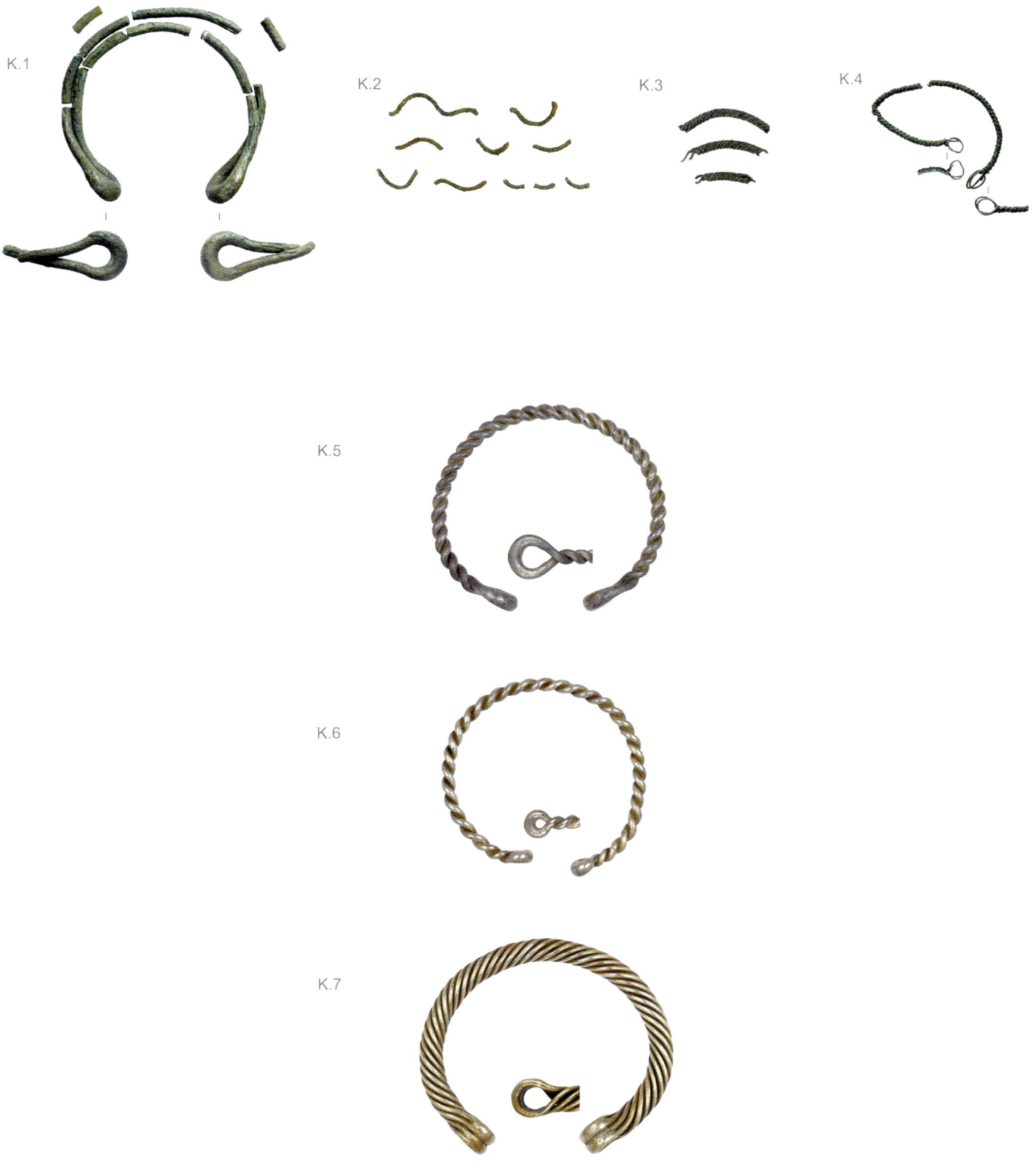

Figure 12.42 The order of deposition of torcs in Hoard K. The torcs at the bottom of the diagram were deposited first. The upper layer was disturbed by ploughing and the order of deposition of K.1–K.4 cannot be discerned

Hoard L

Hoard L, the best preserved of the hoards, was found by Pacitto with his metal detector on 6 December 1990. Initially it appeared to resemble the others excavated in 1990, an undisturbed 'nest' of seven torcs (L.1–L.7) buried in a small pit about 0.1m below the level of the carrstone. The torcs were most likely placed in the ground in sequence (L.7, L.6, L.5, L.4, L.3, L.2, and finally L.1, **Figs 12.45–7, 23.7**). Once these seven torcs had been removed, the metal detector continued to give a strong signal at the base of the pit. The base was further explored, revealing that L.1–L.7 were in the upper filling of a much larger pit, 0.35–0.45m across at the top, narrowing to 0.27–0.36m at the bottom, cut 0.33m deep below the level of the carrstone (**Figs 12.43–4**). Around 0.16–0.18m below L.7 was another group of 14 torcs, L.8–L.21, deposited in sequence from L.21, ending with L.8 (**Figs 12.48–50, 23.6**). Stead recorded in the excavation notes that it was unclear whether the upper torcs were in the filling of the main pit, contemporary with the lower torcs (separated by a layer of soil, comparable to that seen in Hoards G and H), or had been subsequently inserted in a small pit cut into the filling of the main pit. The site plans and sections clearly show two

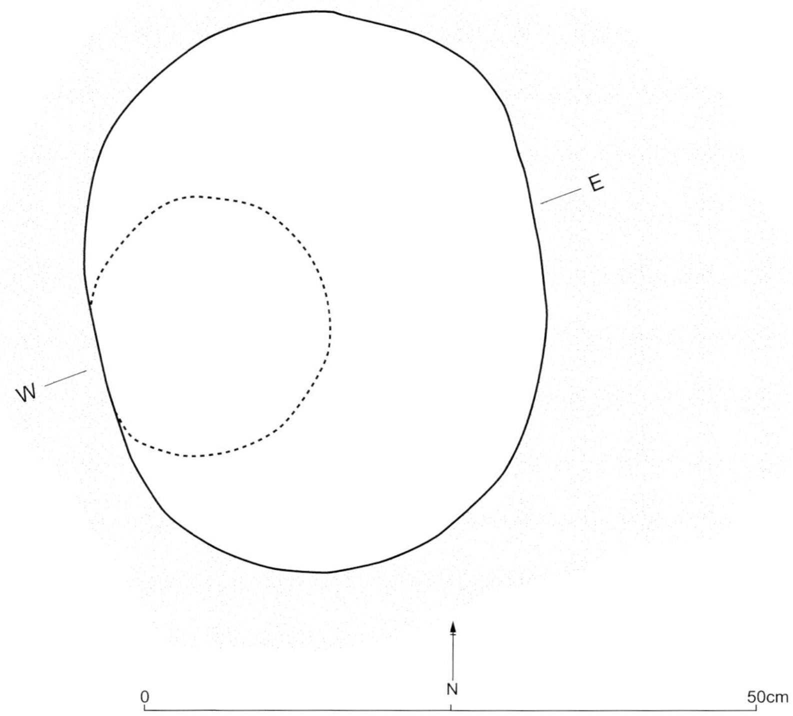

Figure 12.43 Plan of Hoard L pits (A: upper, and B: lower)

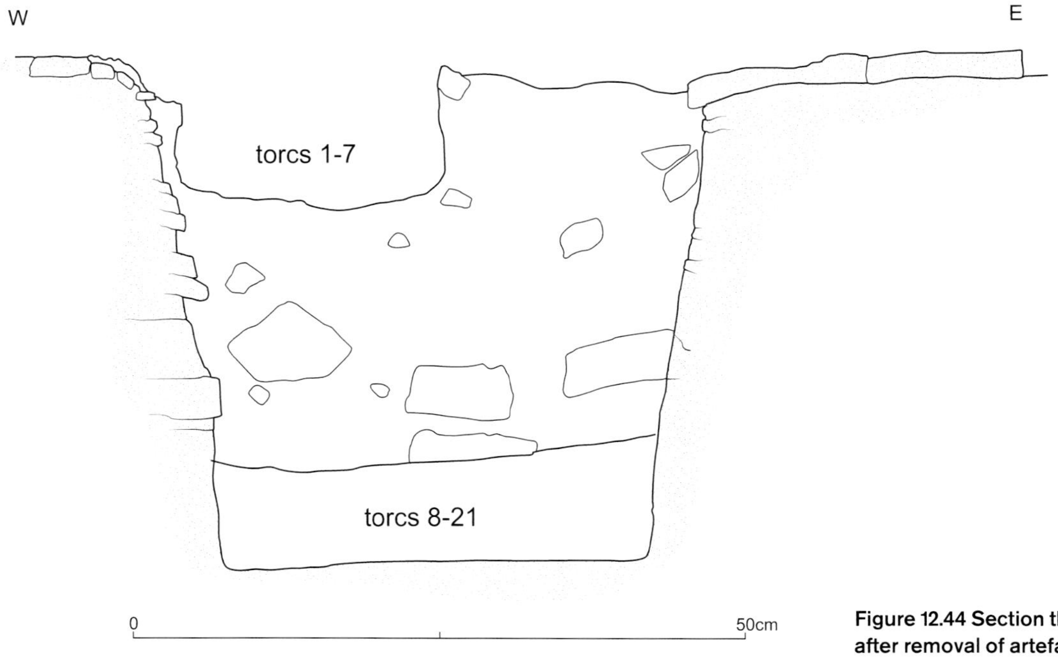

Figure 12.44 Section through Hoard L pit(s), after removal of artefacts

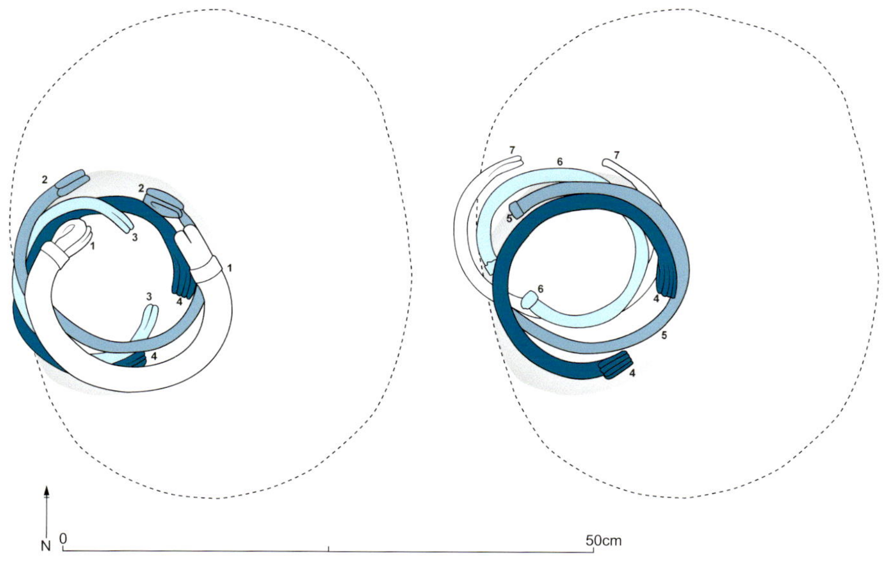

Figure 12.45 Hoard L upper pit torc overlay drawings, showing torcs L.1–L.7

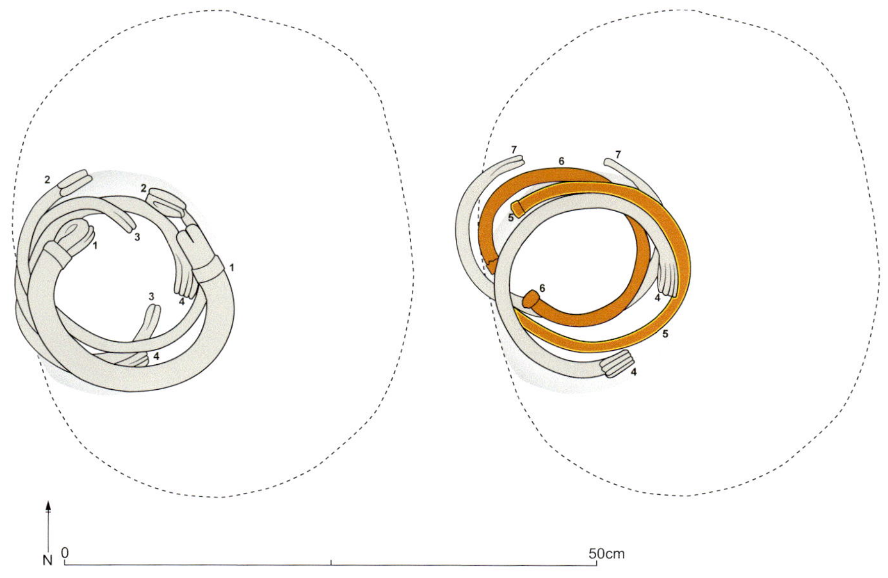

Figure 12.46 Hoard L upper pit torc overlay drawings, showing torcs L.1–L.7, colour-coded according to surface metal content (for key see Fig. 23.5)

Figure 12.47 The order of deposition of torcs in the upper pit of Hoard L. The torcs at the bottom of the diagram were deposited first

L.1

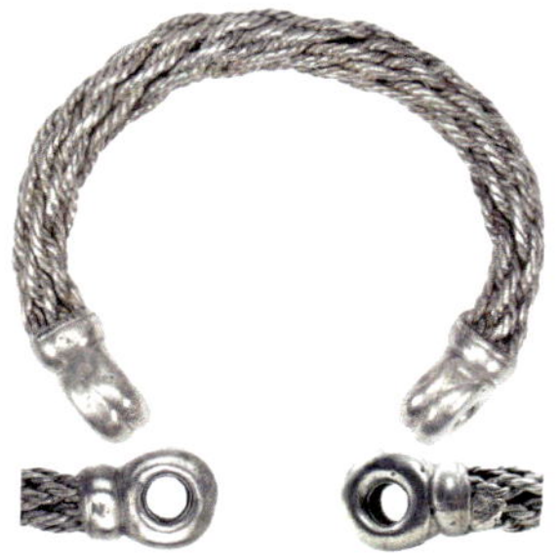

L.2

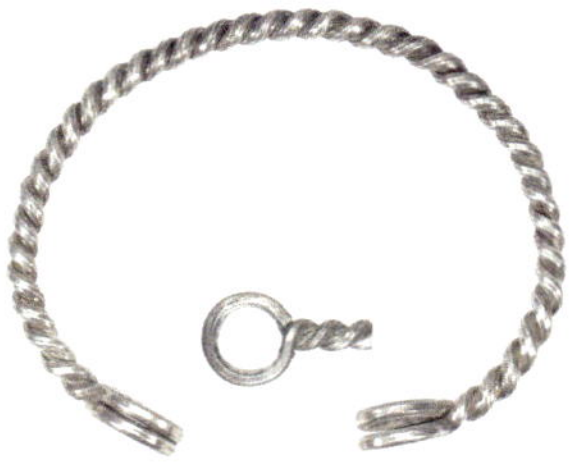

L.3

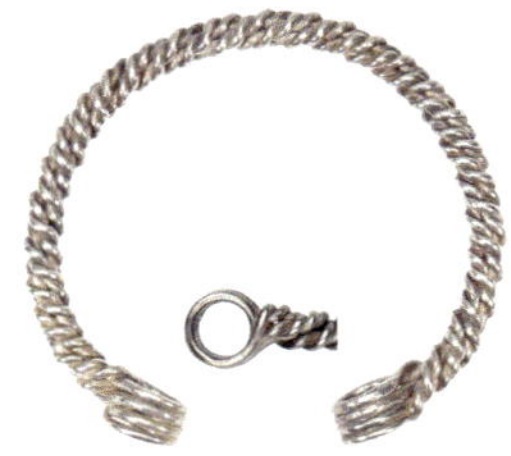

L.4

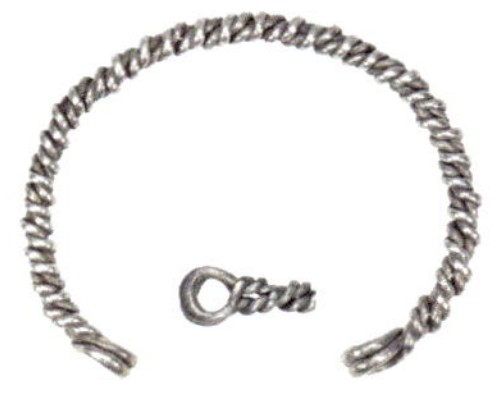

L.5

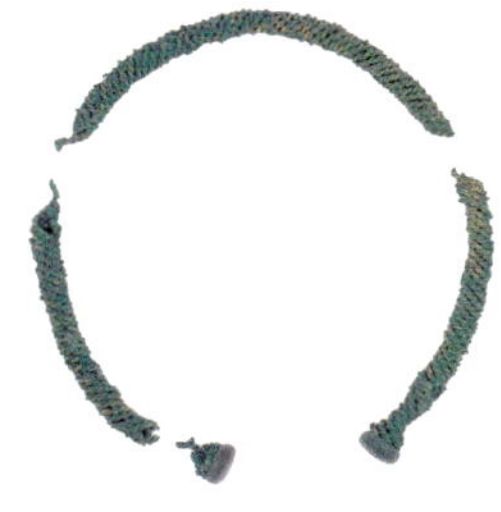

L.6

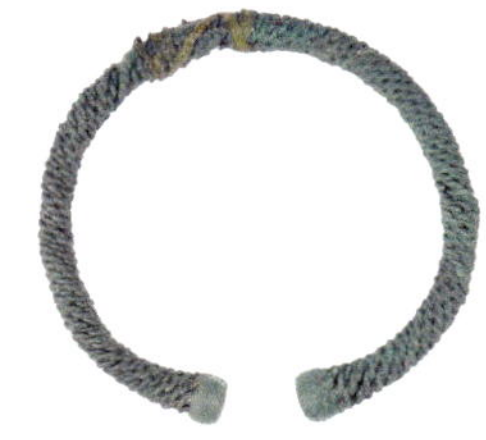

L.7

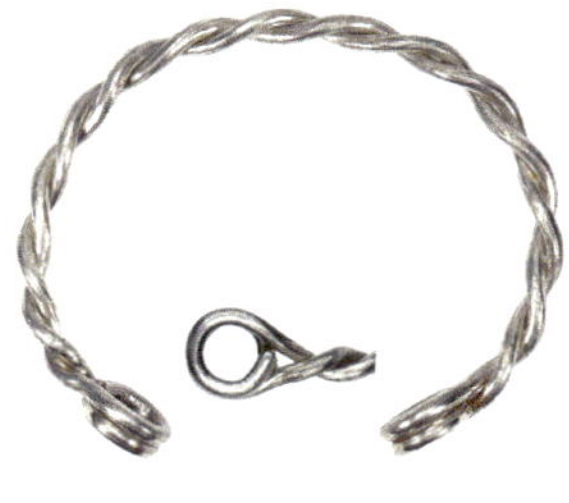

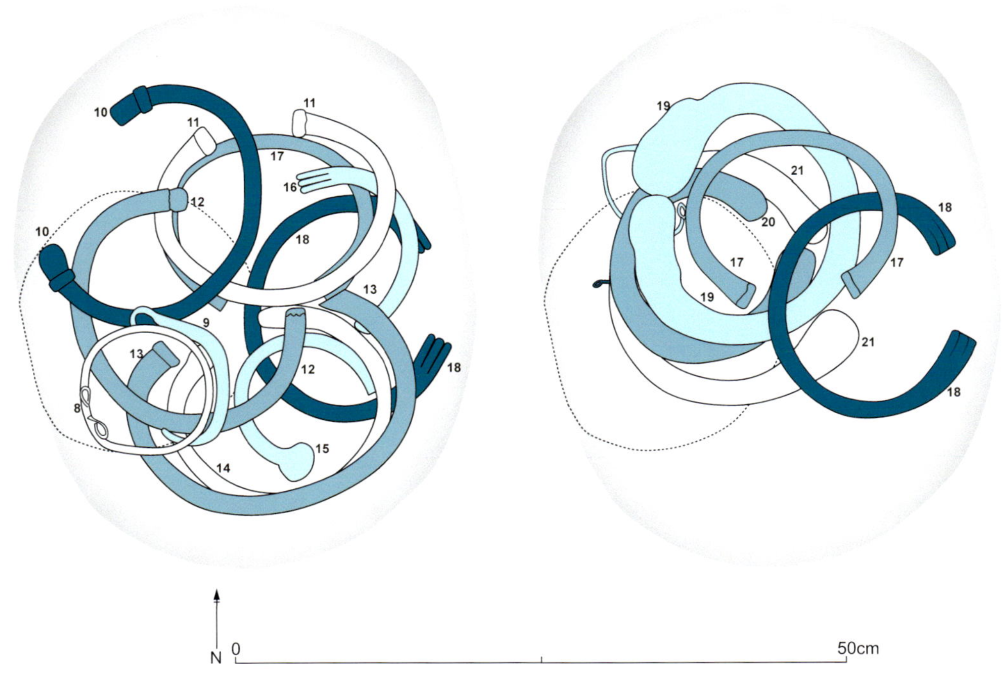

Figure 12.48 Hoard L lower pit torc overlay drawings, showing torcs L.8–L.21

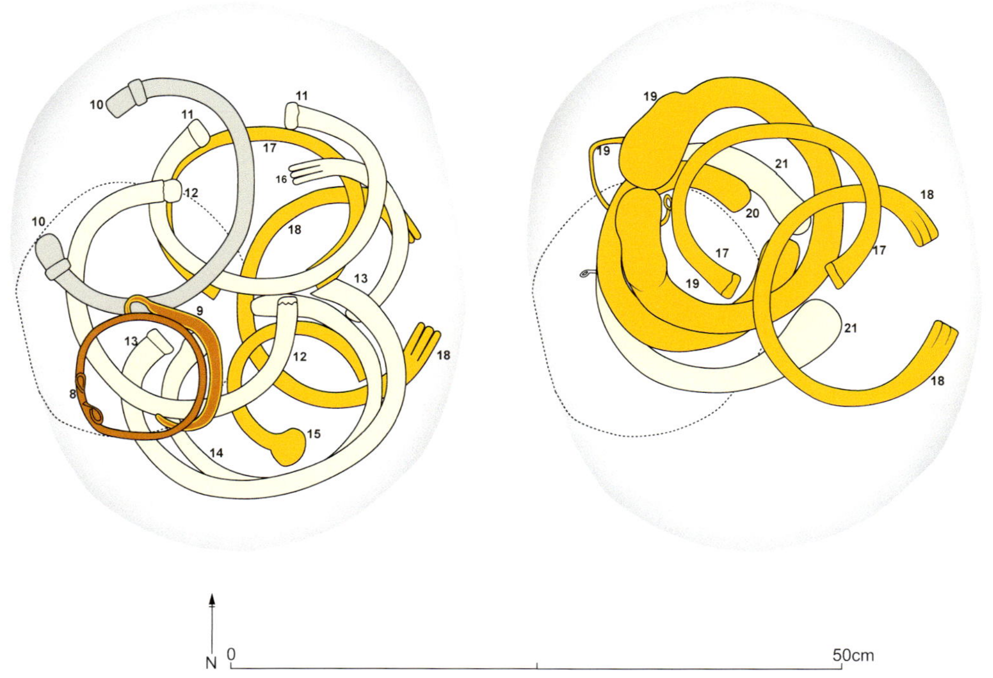

Figure 12.49 Hoard L lower pit torc overlay drawings, showing torcs L.8–L.21, colour-coded according to surface metal content (for key see Fig. 23.5)

separate cuts, with the smaller respecting the edge of the larger, and therefore it seems most likely that a second pit was dug into the first. This could have been either more or less immediately after the initial deposit had been made, or sometime later. Nonetheless, the two deposits seem to reference one another in a number of ways (see Chs 20 and 23–4), and must certainly have been closely related.

Radiocarbon dating of part of an organic repair from torc L.6 gave a date of 360–110 cal BC (at 95% confidence; see Ch. 19 and **Table 5.2**).

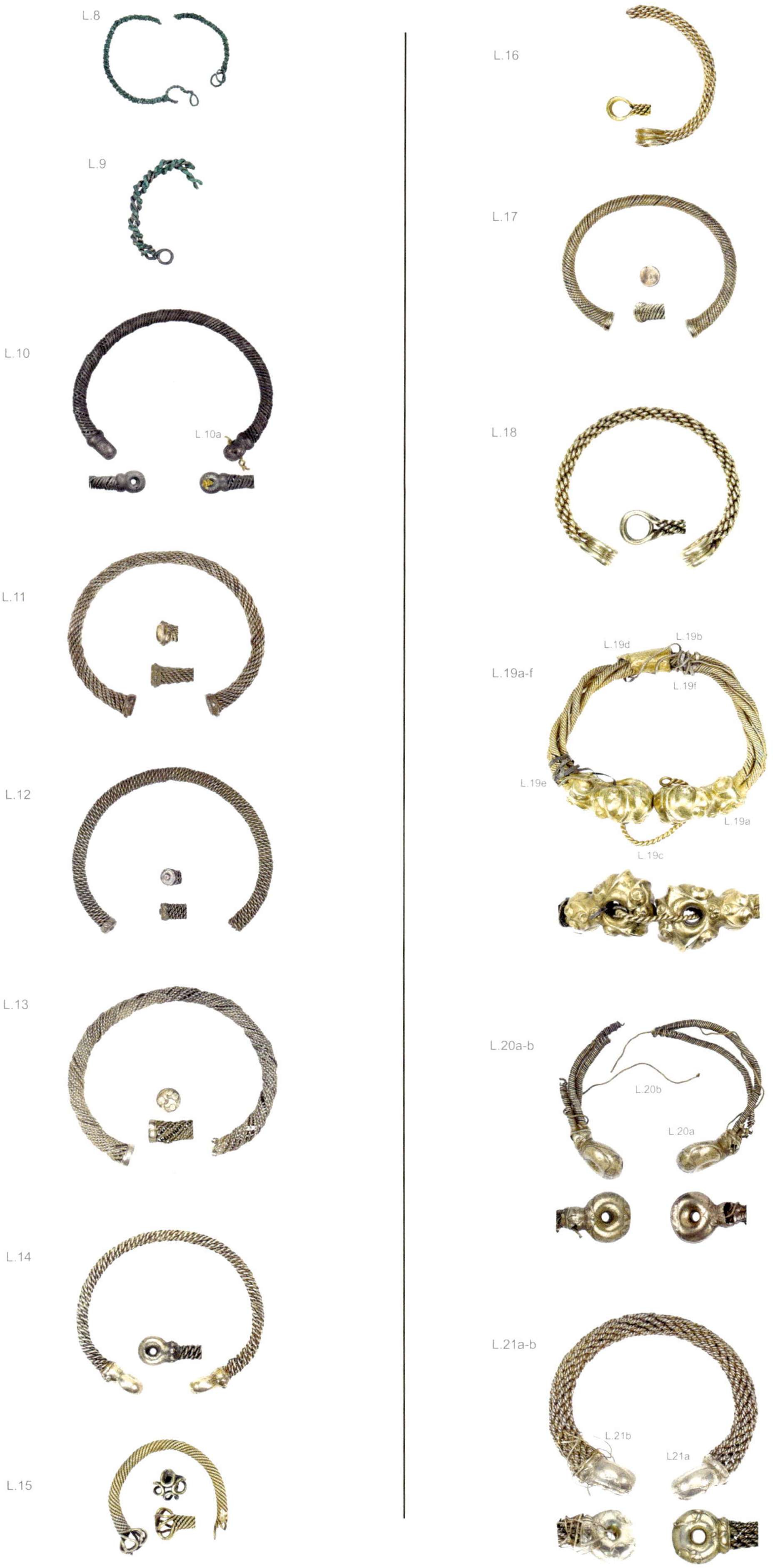

Figure 12.50 The order of deposition of torcs in the lower pit of Hoard L. The torcs on the right were deposited first, from bottom to top, followed by the torcs in the left column, from bottom to top

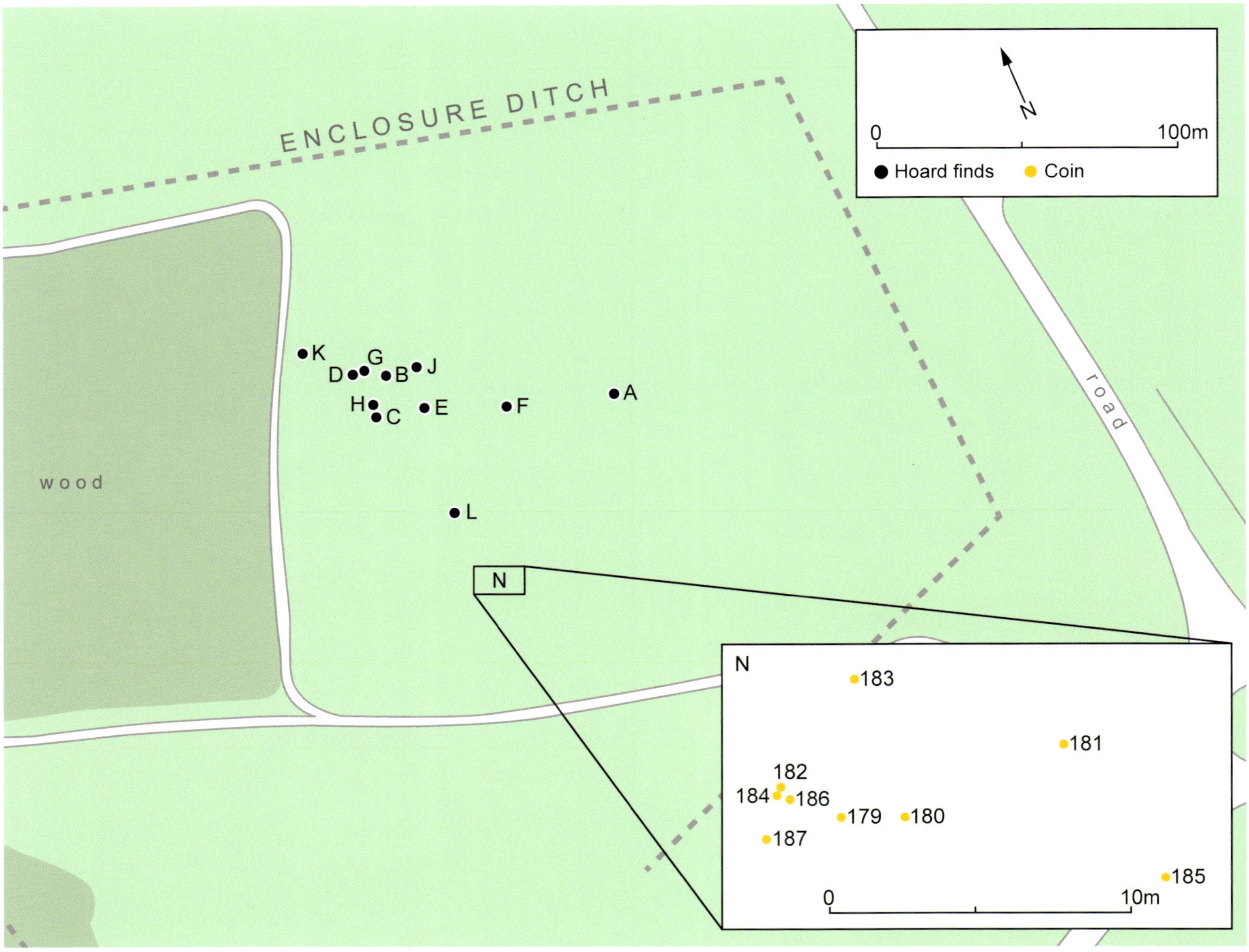

Figure 12.51 Distribution of coin scatter forming Hoard N (labelled with their coin catalogue numbers)

Hoard N

Hoard N was a scatter of metal-detected Gallo-Belgic A and C gold coins, assumed to be a dispersed hoard (**Fig. 12.51**). Four of them (Cat. nos 182, 184, 186 and 187), found on 12 November 1991, were virtually together but there was no hint of a pit. Two others had been found the previous day, 1.5m (Cat. no. 179) and 3.5m (Cat. no. 180) away from that spot. Three more, found 5m (Cat. no. 183), 9m (Cat. no. 181) and 12m (Cat. no. 185) away, were almost certainly from the same hoard (two of them were found the same two days but the third, Cat. no. 183, was found in 1990).

The hoard comprised:

- Five Gallo-Belgic A staters (Cat. nos 179–183)
- One Gallo-Belgic A quarter stater (Cat. no. 184)
- Two Gallo-Belgic C staters (Cat. nos 185–6)
- One worn Gallo-Belgic C quarter stater (Cat. no. 187).

All are Gallo-Belgic A or C types, most likely minted in the period 100–60 BC (see Ch. 15).

Early Roman (Phase 4) hoards

Hoard P

Hoard P, a large hoard of Iron Age coins buried in a silver bowl (hence often known as the 'Bowl Hoard'), was removed from the site illegally by illicit detectorists sometime between the 1990 and 1991 excavation seasons. Stead (Ch. 2) suggests that it was located under the spoil heap of the 1990 excavations, in the north-west corner of the hoard field. Fragments from a silver vessel (P.1–P.7) were recovered from this area in 1991 when it was stripped in advance of archaeological excavation, most likely the last remnants of the hoard.

According to Chadburn (2006, hoard 41, 'Hunstanton I'), the lowest part of the deposit consisted of 90 or more gold coins and three 'saucer-shaped ingots' (one gold alloy, one silver alloy, and one predominantly of copper). Above this base deposit was the silver bowl containing *c.* 6,000 coins, and above that were found three brooches and a torc fragment.

Reconstruction of the coin assemblage from Celtic Coin Index records and contemporary sales catalogues (Ch. 15, Chadburn 2006; de Jersey 2014, no. 196.6; Talbot 2017, 223–4) suggests that Hoard P was most likely deposited in the mid-1st century AD, perhaps around the early AD 60s. It consisted primarily of local East Anglian silver coinage.

Hoard M

The other Phase 4 assemblage, Hoard M, was found by Charles Hodder with his metal detector in March 1991, in the north-east corner of the wood. It consisted of six amorphous lumps of metal (five of silver/copper alloy, M.1–M.5, and one small piece of copper alloy, M.6) that had been heated in a furnace to a high temperature – but not sufficiently high to have made them fully liquid. M.1–M.5 were alloys of about 75% silver and 25% copper (suggesting that they were recycled artefacts rather than silver processed from ore) and weighed a total of 6.65kg; the largest lump alone (M.1) was 4.5kg.

The ingots or lumps were found within 2m of one another, one partly exposed on the ground and the others very close to the surface, at the foot of a tree in the corner of the wood. Subsequent excavation of the findspot revealed no features or additional finds. It is possible that they had been found in the field some time previously and re-deposited next to the tree.

Embedded charcoal lumps were radiocarbon dated (see **Table 5.2**; Garrow *et al.* 2009), providing a calibrated radiocarbon date of 20–210 cal AD at 95% confidence, and 30–130 cal AD at 68% confidence. The charcoal consisted of old alder wood, and so the age of the wood must also be taken into account when considering this date.

Chapter 13
Iron Age Metalwork Typology

Julia Farley and Jody Joy

This chapter provides an overview of the basic terminology and typology employed in relation to the Iron Age metalwork in this volume, particularly torcs, bracelets and rings. It is based in part on initial typological work carried out by Ian Stead (1991a). This typology forms the basis for the catalogue of the torc hoards and stray finds presented in the following chapter. The forms and functions of these objects are discussed in more detail in Chapter 22 and their decoration in Chapter 21.

Terminology

TORC – Penannular or annular personal ornament, large enough to be worn at the neck (i.e. an internal circumference of over *c.* 280mm). Formed of a wire or sheet-metal neck-ring, usually with prominent terminals.

BRACELET – Penannular or annular personal ornament, formed of wire or sheet metal, of a size most likely to have been worn at the wrist (i.e. an internal circumference of under *c.* 230mm).

TORC/BRACELET – Personal ornament fragment which could have belonged to either a torc or a bracelet.

The division of ornaments into 'torcs' and 'bracelets' is, of course, not entirely clear-cut. It is possible for example that some ornaments were worn higher up the arm, not just at the wrist. However, the size cut-offs used here have been chosen to reflect what appears to be a genuine ancient division between distinct groups of objects: larger ones (here referred to as torcs) above *c.* 280mm internal circumference, and smaller ones (here referred to as bracelets) below *c.* 230mm internal circumference.

Figure 13.1 shows the approximate internal diameters of all the torcs and bracelets from Snettisham which were complete and undistorted enough to allow a reliable measurement to be taken. Only four out of over 60 objects are clearly bracelet-sized, with the fragmentary F.208 and F.209 likely coming in at under 130mm in internal circumference, and the slightly larger B/C.12 and F.121 measuring 213mm and 201mm respectively. There are four other objects which are likely bracelets which do not feature in this graph as their circumferences are not easily measured. Tubular bracelet E.1c is not included in the figure due to its distorted shape, but would likely measure in at around 230mm, with this slightly larger opening probably reflecting the fact that its annular form does not allow it to be opened up to be taken on and off. B.8 and F.7f have been heavily distorted, and B.12–13 is too fragmentary to be certain of its original form, but from the fine nature of the wires a bracelet seems the most likely identification.

There is no object from Snettisham with an internal diameter between 230mm and 280mm. There are only three torcs between 230 and 330mm in internal circumference (B/C.47–8, G.14, F.116) all with internal diameters of just over 280mm (**Fig. 13.1**). These could potentially have been worn on a very slender neck or around the arm. They are referred to in the catalogue as 'small torcs'. All other complete or near-complete torcs have internal circumferences of over 330mm and are highly likely to be neck ornaments. However, as with the bracelets, for the torcs of a smaller size we cannot rule out the possibility that they were worn around the upper arm (see Ch. 22 for a full discussion of torc diameters).

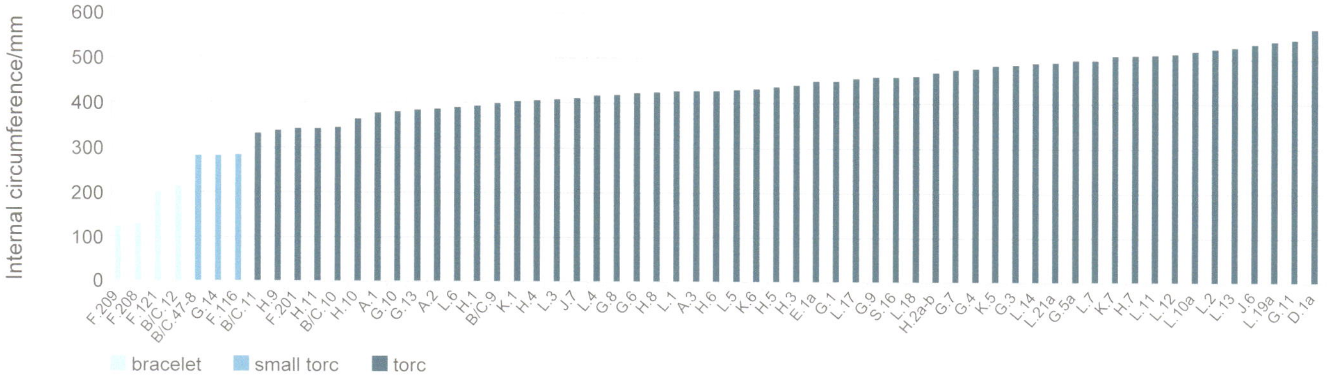

Figure 13.1 The internal diameters of the 61 most complete torcs and bracelets from Snettisham, ordered by size. Each bar represents one object; the height of the bar shows the diameter

NECK-RING – The main body of a torc, excluding terminals. Formed of wires or sheet metal.

BODY – The main circumference of a bracelet, excluding the terminals. Formed of wires or sheet metal.

TERMINAL – When complete, a penannular torc or bracelet has two terminals (see **Fig. 13.3** for detailed terminal typology). In some cases, these are formed from the wires or sheet metal which make up the neck-ring. On other torcs the terminals are separate components (of cast or sheet metal) which were cast or soldered onto the neck-rings. In such cases, the term *COLLAR* is used to describe the part of the terminal which accommodates the wires of the neck-ring (see **Fig. 13.5**). The construction of these separate terminals can be very complicated, comprising many different components (see Ch. 17).

WIRE – a single strand of metal which may be circular, faceted or (more rarely) square in cross-section. The basic building block of the neck-rings/bodies of multi-strand wire torcs and bracelets (see below). The term 'wire' is used for strands of metal 0.6–6.5mm in diameter.

ROD – a thick single strand of metal, similar in form to the definition for wire (above), but over 6.5mm in diameter.

Whilst the division between 'wire' and 'rod' is somewhat arbitrary, it is used because there does appear to be a qualitative difference between the fine-wire and more robust torcs. The frequencies of the various wire/rod diameters are shown in **Figure 13.2**. The most frequent wire diameters are 1.1–2.0mm, accounting for over 50% of objects and fragments. Above 6.5mm, the term rod is used. In practice, this refers to a small group of objects and fragments with rod diameters of 7.1–10.5mm. By number of catalogue entries, the most frequent rod diameters are 8.6–9.0mm. In part this reflects the fact that at least two torcs made from rod of this diameter have been cut into sections: see Cat. nos S.31–9 and S.41–4.

TWISTED WIRE – a single strand of wire (usually square in cross-section) which has been tightly twisted on itself to give a crimped appearance. Such twisting can be either right-slanting (Z-twist) or left-slanting (S-twist) (see below).

ROPE – multiple wires plied or coiled together. A torc neck-ring or bracelet body can be composed of a single rope, or a number of ropes which are themselves plied or coiled around one another, to form a *CABLE*. (See discussion of Stages in the neck-ring terminology section, below.)

RIBBON – a narrow strip or band of metal with flat cross-section.

Torc typology

The following typology is quite loose, based on the variety of different terminals and neck-ring/body constructions.

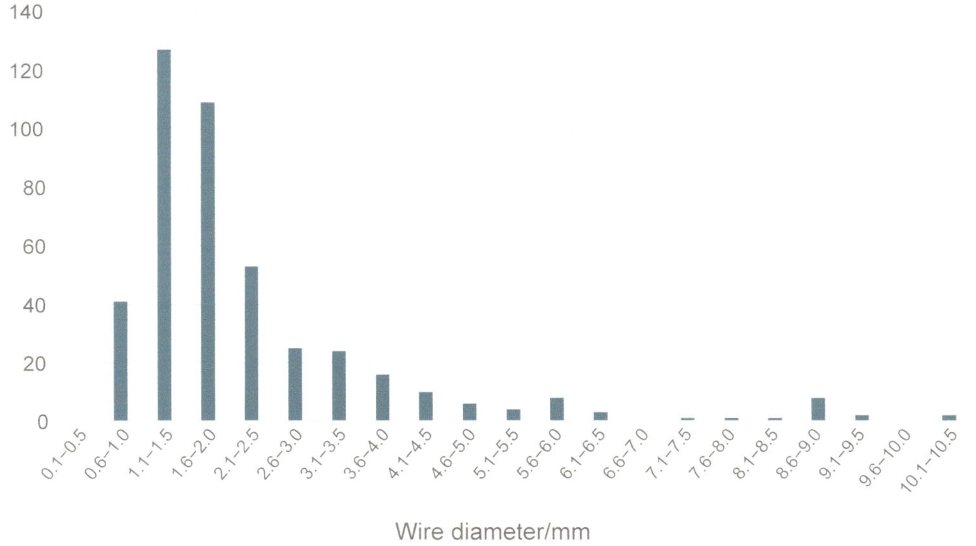

Figure 13.2 The frequency of wire diameters among all the multi-strand torcs and fragments from Snettisham with a reasonably identifiable neck-ring construction (n=441)

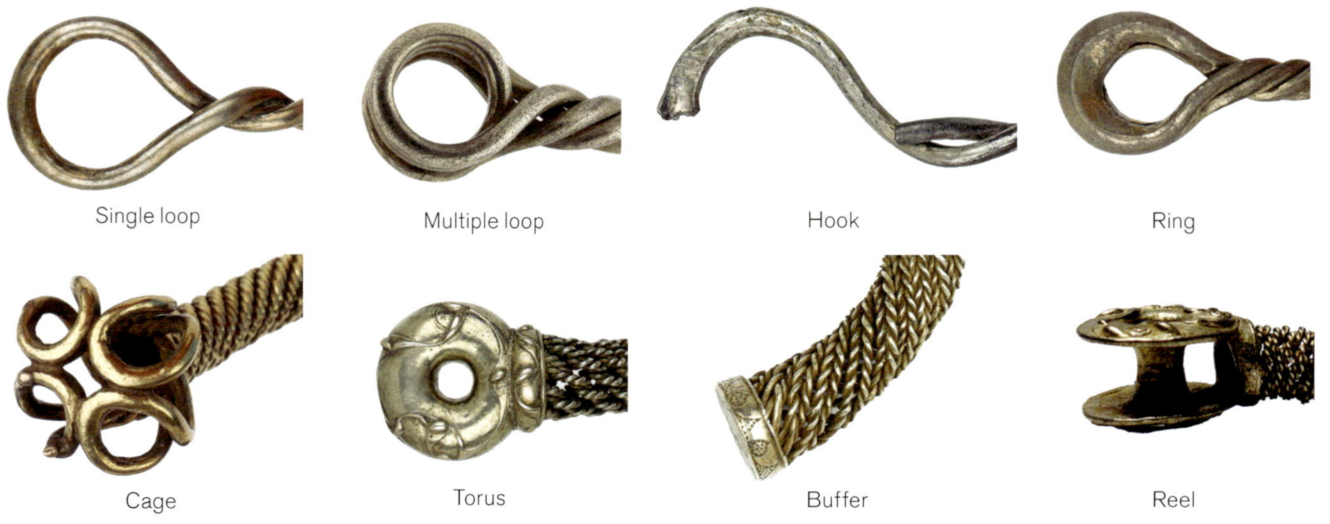

Figure 13.3 The main torc terminal types (images not to scale)

Whilst there are preferential pairings of neck-ring and terminal types (see below) the variety of combinations is such that a typology combining terminals and neck-rings would be unnecessarily complicated and cumbersome. Consequently, terminals and neck-rings are defined separately, meaning that terminal type and neck-ring type can be combined in multiple ways.

Neck-rings

TUBULAR – made of sheet metal formed into a tube, creating hollow, tubular neck-rings. Some tubular torcs have an iron core. Others may have been filled with an organic substance such as wax. Tubular torc types are further subdivided below.

MULTI-STRAND – the neck-rings/bodies of the majority of torcs and bracelets are comprised of multiple wires. The language and notation employed to discuss the arrangements of these wires (see below) has been adapted from that used to describe the structure of spun yarns in ancient textiles, including the Stage method developed by Dixon (1957) and the use of parenthetical notation outlined by Splitstoser (2012).

Figure 13.4 The terminology used to refer to parts of buffer terminals

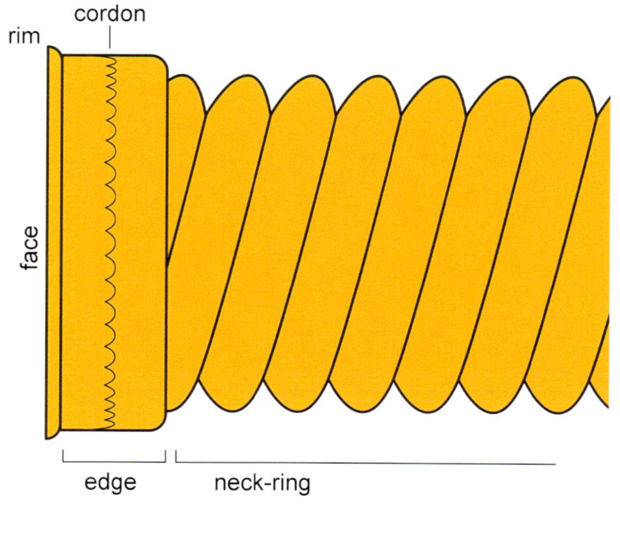

Terminals

Seven or eight principal types of torc and bracelet terminal can be identified (**Fig. 13.3**). Whilst there is huge variety in form, certain neck-ring/body constructions are more likely to be paired with specific terminal types. For example, tubular torcs and Stage 2 coiled torcs (see below) generally have buffer terminals.

BUFFER TERMINAL – Flat, circular terminals (see **Fig. 13.4** for terminology). Range from a very simple, plain facing, cast onto the end of the neck-ring, to something more ornate. The flat, circular face of the terminal can be decorated with inscribed or raised ornament, as can the edges. Terminals vary in thickness.

LOOP TERMINAL – Terminal formed of a SINGLE LOOP or MULTIPLE LOOPS. The loops are formed using the wires or ropes of the neck-ring, and are usually more or less circular in shape. Loop terminals range in size and thickness depending on the diameter of the wires/ropes of the neck-ring. The majority are annular, although some are penannular. In the latter case, where the loop is significantly incomplete, the terminal is referred to as a *HOOK TERMINAL*. This is very unusual, and may indicate a damaged or unfinished terminal (see e.g. H.3). Loop terminals are often continuous with the neck-ring wires so that a multi-strand torc can effectively be made from a single length of wire, bent back on itself at one terminal, with the ends of the wire meeting at the other. Manufacturing marks sometimes reveal soldered or hammered joins at the terminals to disguise the ends of the wire. The details of the loop terminal construction are described on a case-by-case basis in the catalogue.

RING TERMINAL – Similar to a loop terminal, but where the loop(s) has/have been thickened by hammering or the casting-on of additional metal. Generally this means that none of the ends of the neck-ring wires are visible. The central eye of the ring ranges from near-circular to teardrop-shaped. Decoration is sometimes applied by punching. If a ring terminal is made from a multiple-loop terminal, the joins between the loops may be soldered and decorated.

REEL TERMINAL – Cast terminals in the shape of a simple fly-fishing or cotton reel. The terminal attaches onto the neck-ring via a collar resembling a buffer terminal. This is unusual, with only one example recorded (F.119–F.120).

TORUS TERMINAL – Hollow, doughnut-shaped terminal, see **Figure 13.5** for terms used to refer to different elements of the terminals. Very often decorated with raised and inscribed ornament. Often attached to the neck-ring/body wires via a collar, as for reel terminals, above. These collars are often also decorated.

CAGE TERMINAL – Terminal formed from one or more wires (often extensions of the neck-ring wires), which are looped back on themselves to form a hollow, often more or less spherical, wire 'cage'. Additional decoration, such as soldered pellets, is sometimes added.

Of the multi-strand torcs and fragments from Snettisham, 184 objects had an identifiable terminal type. The proportions of each type are summarised in **Figure 13.6**. Torus and reel types have been grouped, as reel terminals are represented by only one torc. Likewise, only torc H.3 has two clear hook terminals, and so this has been grouped with loop terminals. Of terminals generally made from the neck-ring wires themselves with small additions (loop/hook, ring and cage), loop terminals are by far the most common, with cage the most unusual. In terms of the types where terminals are made as separate components, buffer terminals are more common than torus. Torus terminals are also generally the most complex in terms of construction.

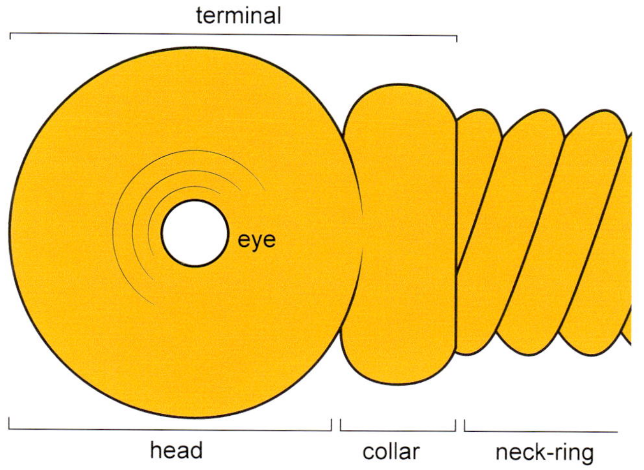

Figure 13.5 The terminology used to refer to parts of torus terminals

Tubular torc types

Tubular torcs are here divided into six types (**Fig. 13.7**). Type 1 have small, hollow buffer terminals (35–38mm in diameter) with no clasp, and narrow neck-rings (<10mm in cross-section). These are similar to Hautenauve's (2005) Type IIIa 'torque pénannulaire à corps massif et tampons sans fermoir', but with hollow (rather than solid) neck-rings. Hautenauve (2005, 99) classes them as a special group of 'filiforme' torcs, but here it is preferred to group them with tubular examples, since in all securely identified cases (i.e. where a terminal is present) the neck-rings are hollow. There are five certain examples from Snettisham, all fragments with only one terminal remaining (F.1c, F.1d, F.57, F.58, F.59). Most of the terminals are plain, but F.57 has curvilinear decoration. Other fragments of narrow tubular neck-rings (F.2a, F.4f, F.5g, F.31b, F.33, S.14) may be from Type 1 torcs. Most of the neck-rings are undecorated, but fragments F.31b and F.33 have punched or stippled decoration.

Type 2 (of which there is only one example at Snettisham, F.63–6) have small buffer terminals (approx. 30mm in diameter) fastened by a clasp, and a narrow neck-ring (around 10mm in cross-section). The example from Snettisham is in several pieces, and the neck-ring has an iron core. This type is similar to Hautenauve's (2005) Type IIIe 'corps creux, tampons à fermoir', though she classes this particular torc from Snettisham as a unique example of a 'torque tubulaire à double fermoir' (Hautenauve 2005, 98–9).

Type 3 have larger hollow buffer terminals (47–60mm in diameter), often decorated with stippling or other texturing. Several have a smaller bead or collar behind the main terminal, before narrowing into the neck-ring. There are six terminals of this type from Snettisham (F.2g, F.2h, F.35, F.47, F.48, F.60), some with a filler of sand or perhaps an organic material. No terminals of this type have surviving neck-rings, so the form and diameter of the neck-rings are uncertain, although it is possible that neck-ring fragment F.62 is from such a torc.

Type 4 (F.6b, F.30a, F.42, F.45, F.46, F.61, S.13) have hollow neck-rings of medium diameter (12–35mm), expanding towards flat buffer terminals which are simple

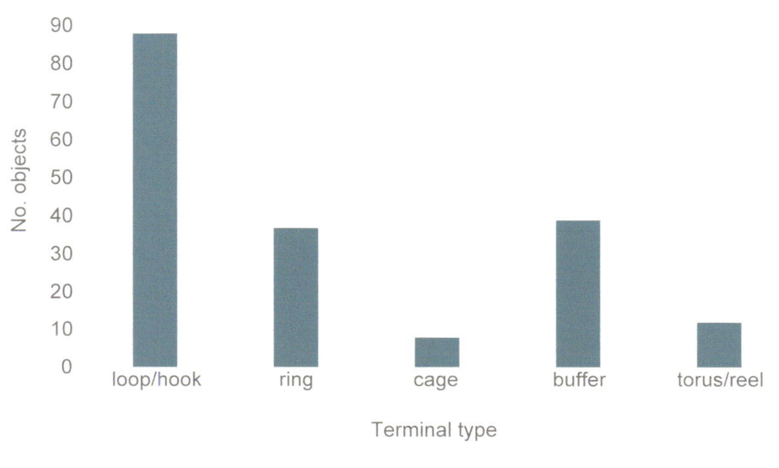

Figure 13.6 The frequency of terminal types among the multi-strand torcs, bracelets and fragments from Snettisham

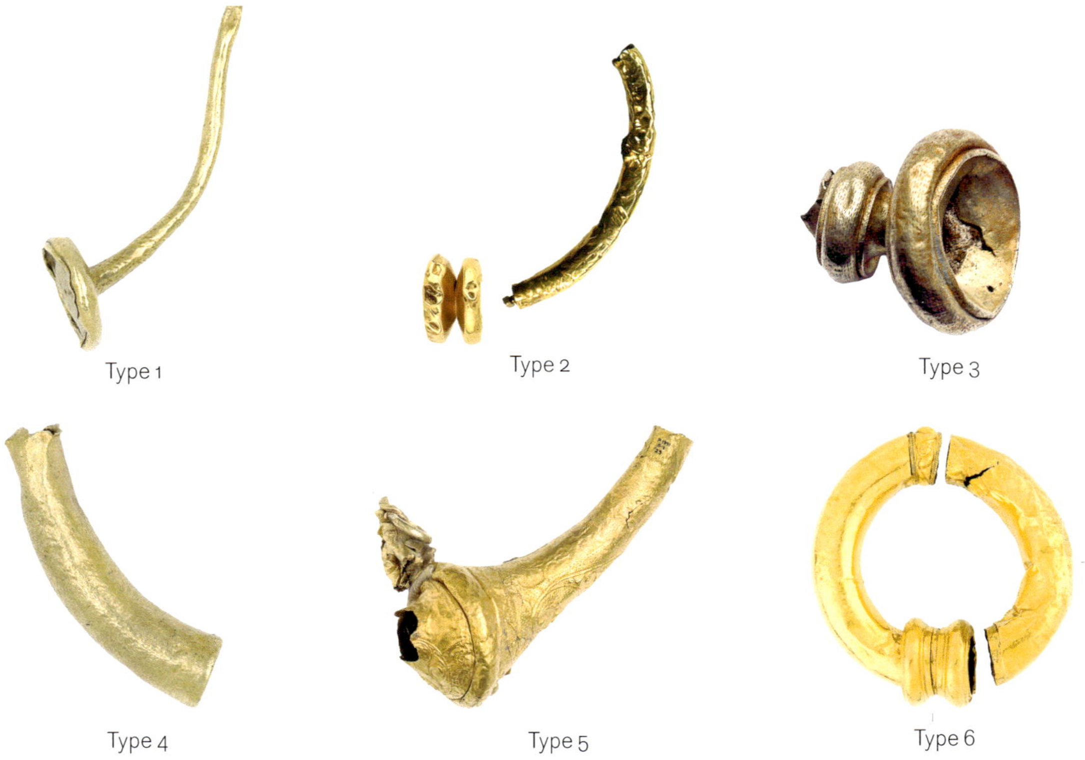

Figure 13.7 Tubular torc types (images not to scale)

'caps' to the ends of the neck-ring. Hautenauve (2005, 96–8) subdivides this group into 'torques tubulaires cylindriques' and 'torques tubulaires tronconiques' (the latter flaring more noticeably towards the terminals). Many of these torcs have intricate decoration.

Type 5 are hollow tubular torcs with large (*c.* 60mm), expanded buffer terminals, narrowing to a hollow neck-ring.

Figure 13.8 Staged construction of plied and cabled structures in yarn or wire

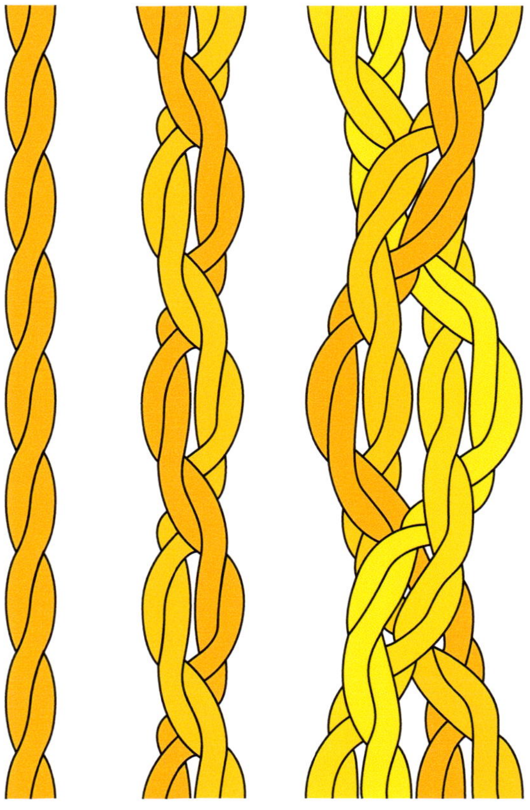

There are two examples from Snettisham, each comprising a single damaged terminal: F.31a and F.43. These are classed alone together by Hautenauve (2005) as 'torques tubulaires à extrémités en trompette'. Both terminals (which are from different torcs) are decorated with curvilinear designs. In both cases, the end of the terminal does not survive, so it is unclear if these torcs had clasps or fixings at the front.

Type 6 are the massive tubular torcs present in Snettisham Hoard A (A.1, A.2, A.3, A.4–A.7) and as stray find S.12 (of which only the iron core remains), with these finds representing between them a minimum number of five such torcs from the site. These are classed by Hautenauve (2005) as Type V 'torc tubulaire à fermoir dorsal et tampons articulés'.

Multi-strand neck-ring/body construction

An extraordinarily diverse range of multi-strand torc neck-ring and bracelet body constructions are represented at Snettisham. All are created by twisting/plying or coiling wires together (see below). Whilst in some cases this may create a visual effect similar to a plait or braid, there are no cases of actual braided wire neck-rings at Snettisham. In order to accurately codify the sheer variety of constructions present, it was necessary to develop a new terminology based on those used in textile literature for multi-strand yarns.

Dixon (1957, 135) used the Stage system to describe the observable features of complex yarn constructions (**Fig. 13.8**). A 'single-ply' yarn is Stage I, and two or more such yarns spun (plied) directly together constitute a Stage II yarn. Similarly, two or more Stage II yarns spun together create a Stage III yarn, and two or more Stage III elements combine to form a Stage IV yarn.

The same principles of construction can be found in multi-strand torc neck-rings and bracelet bodies. At Snettisham, the vast majority of these artefacts consist of

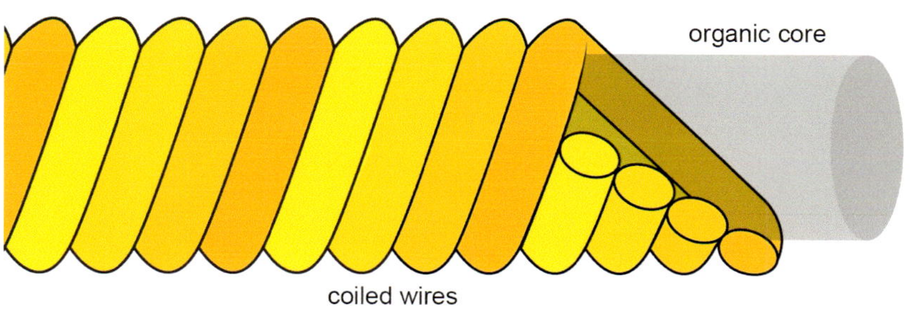

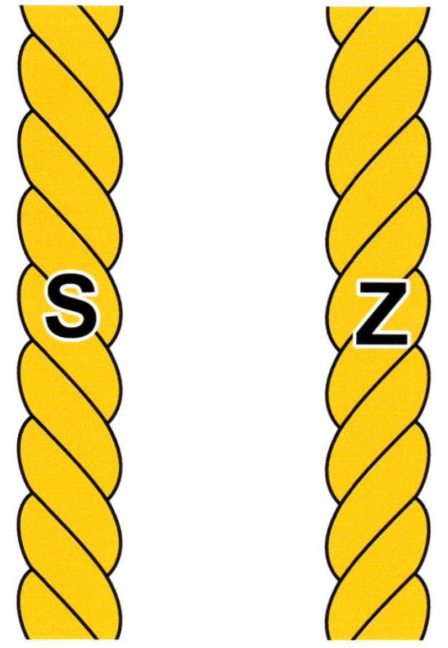

Figure 13.9 (above) Diagram of coiled wire neck-ring or rope construction

Figure 13.10 (right) S- and Z-twist, showing direction of slant in the torc wires

either a Stage II or Stage III structure. For the purposes of the catalogue, Stage I elements are referred to as *WIRES* or *STRANDS*, Stage II elements as *ROPES*, and Stage III and IV elements as *CABLES* (please note that this differs from the terminology employed by Dixon, 1957).

Despite numerous similarities, there are three key differences between the construction of wire torcs and spun yarns. First, in the case of textiles even a 'single-ply' (Stage I) yarn is formed from a bundle of plant or animal fibres which are usually spun either clockwise (Z-twist) or anti-clockwise (S-twist) (**Fig. 13.10**). This can vary even within a single yarn. This is not the case for wires. The majority of torc wires are not twisted on themselves, and most neck-rings consist of uniform wires. Second, in order to balance the twist in flexible fibres, a Stage II or III spun yarn will usually involve elements of both S-spin and Z-spin (for example two clockwise or Z-spun yarns will usually be plied together in the anti-clockwise S-twist direction). The twist in rigid torc wires does not need to be balanced in the same way, and S is by far the most common direction of twist (although sometimes combinations of S- and Z-twist are used to give particular braid-like effects, see below). For this reason, in the metalwork catalogue the direction of twist/plying for multi-strand torc and bracelet constructions is not stated unless it is Z. Third and finally, apart from braided and plaited yarn structures and some modern art yarns, in textiles threads are usually plied together (whether tightly or loosely) without any attempt to create space between the plies. In torc neck-rings, this is just one of two main techniques by which wires are arranged:

- *PLIED* – multiple wires (usually two) are twisted tightly or loosely together, as for yarns.
- *COILED* – multiple wires (usually three or more) are coiled around a flexible core (**Fig. 13.9**), possibly thin lengths of flexible wood or rope (see Ch. 19). Whilst on rare occasions this core is preserved, it is usually missing from the finished artefact, leaving a hollow void at the centre of a coiled tube. Yarns produced from plant or animal fibre would generally not be rigid enough to maintain a hollow core in this way.

Specific forms of multi-strand neck-ring construction were generally preferred for different terminal types. For example, the ropes of buffer terminal torcs are usually coiled, while torcs with loop terminals often have plied neck-rings.

Both PLYING and COILING can be either Z-twist or S-twist (**Fig. 13.10**), but the S direction predominates; just 11% of multi-strand Snettisham torcs and bracelets have a Z-twist element to their construction (though notably Hoards B and C have a higher proportion of Z-twist objects at 17%, see Ch. 20). S and Z are preferred here to the terms 'clockwise' and 'anti-clockwise', since the latter are relative terms which depend on the relationship between the maker and fibres or wires being twisted. In fibre spinning, and thus in textile-study terminology, 'clockwise' is used to denote Z-twist and 'anti-clockwise' denotes S-twist. However, this is based on the model of a spinner turning a spindle or similar tool which hangs away from them. If torc wires were instead clamped at the top and turned from below, then, from the perspective of the maker, a clockwise turn would be the direction to result in an S-twist. For the avoidance of confusion, we thus exclusively use the terms S-twist and Z-twist in the catalogue.

There are no clear-cut cases of Stage 1 (single wire) torcs or bracelets from Snettisham, although of course the narrow tubular torcs (Type 1 and Type 2, see above) have this appearance. There are a handful of cases where single solid wires may be from simple Stage I torc neck-rings (e.g. F.30b, S.67, S.68), but none of these have terminals attached, and they could equally be unused/unfinished wires or fragments from circular-section rings (such as F.1b, F.6a, F.6d and F7a).

Thus, the simplest wire torcs which can be securely identified as such have Stage II plied neck-rings (as **Fig. 13.11a**: two wires plied together into a single rope) or Stage II coiled neck-rings (as **Fig. 13.11b**: comprised of multiple wires coiled around a core, again creating a single rope). Stage III cable neck-rings consist of multiple plied ropes which are then themselves plied together (**Fig. 13.11c(i), (ii)**), or multiple coiled or plied ropes which are coiled together (**Figs 13.11d–e**). Wires which have been coiled at Stage II are not generally plied at Stage III. A very small number of torcs with Stage IV neck-rings were present at

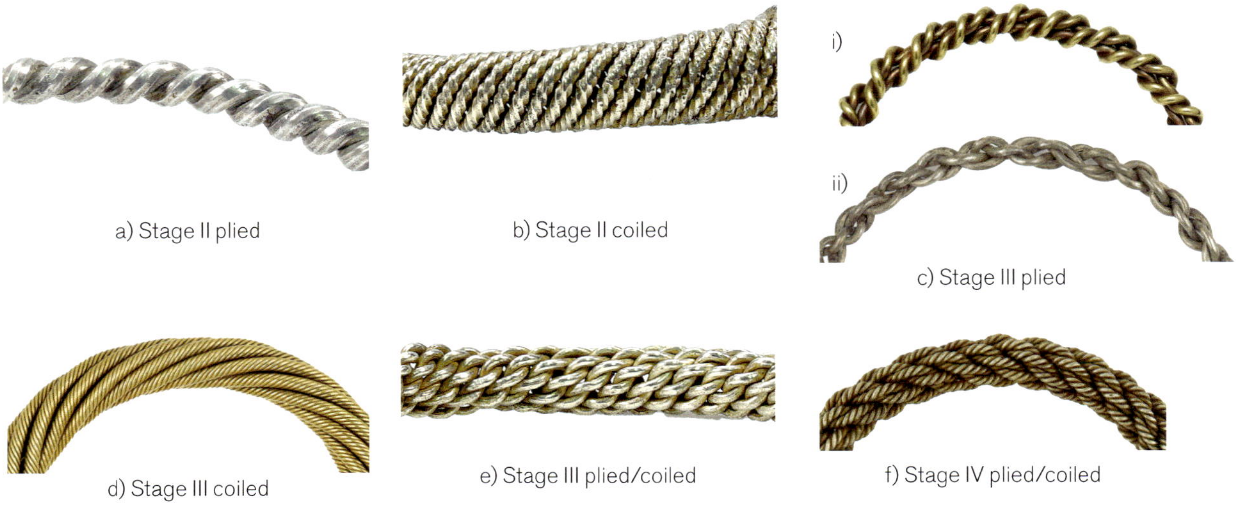

Figure 13.11 Neck-ring construction patterns seen in the Snettisham torcs (images not to scale)

Snettisham (F.119–F.120, H.7, L.1, L.21a, with B/C.62 and F.375 also possibly representing fragments of Stage IV objects). These combine two or more Stage III elements by plying or coiling to create complex cables (**Fig. 13.11f**).

To account for all possible arrangements of torc wires, the following notation has been developed (**Table 13.1**), based on the parenthetical notation employed for yarn by Splitstoser (2012). Because S-twist predominates, the direction of twist is not mentioned unless it is Z. Shaded information is included only for Stage III and IV neck-ring constructions. In the very rare cases of Stage IV neck-rings, an extra set of outer parentheses is also added, including **L**: the number of Stage III elements. The total number of wires in the neck-ring = **J** x **K** x **L**.

For example, the torcs in **Figure 13.11** can be described as follows:

13.11 (a) The rope of this Stage II neck-ring is made up of **2** wires which are **P**lied tightly together. The wires are **F**aceted in cross-section. The code for this structure is therefore **(2P)F**.

13.11 (b) The rope of this Stage II neck-ring is made up of **8** wires which are **C**oiled around a hollow core. The wires are **T**wisted. The code for this structure is therefore **(8C)T**.

13.11 (c)i) The cable of this Stage III neck-ring is made up of two Stage II plied ropes, each of which resembles the **(2P)** structure of **Figure 13.11a**. These **2** ropes are themselves **P**lied together. The wires are ci**R**cular in cross-section. The code for this structure is therefore **(2P(2P))R**. The total number of wires is 2x2=4.

13.11 (c)ii) This Stage III neck-ring is constructed in much the same way as that in **Figure 13.c(i)**, except that the **2** individual S-plied **(2P)** ropes are **P**lied together in the **Z**-twist direction, giving the code **(2PZ(2P))R**. The total number of wires is 2x2=4, as for **Figure 13.11c(i)**.

Note that in Stage III plied torc neck-rings, a purely S-twist construction (as in **Figure 13.11c(i)**) tends to give a more cramped and chaotic appearance, whereas introducing a stage of Z-twist (as in **Figure 13.11c(ii)**) creates a construction more akin to a balanced plied yarn, even resembling a braid.

13.11 (d) The cable of this Stage III neck-ring is made up of eight ropes, each of which resembles the **(8C)** structure seen in **Figure 13.11b**. These **8** Stage II coiled ropes are themselves **C**oiled together around a hollow core. All the wires are ci**R**cular in cross-section. This gives the code **(8C(8C))R**. The total number of wires is 8x8=64. Although the S-twist direction is used at each stage, the coiled ropes have a flatter profile than plied ropes, giving a smoother and more even structure than that seen in **Figure 13.11c(i)**.

13.11 (e) This Stage III cable is constructed from six Stage II ropes. Each rope resembles the **(2P)** structure of **Figure 13.11a**, except that they are plied together in the **Z**-twist direction, giving each rope the code **(2PZ)**. These **6** plied ropes are **C**oiled together S-twist. All the wires are ci**R**cular in cross-section, giving the full code **(6C(2PZ))R**. The total number of wires is 2x6=12. Note that the mixture of Z- and S-twist gives a more yarn-like structure than the uni-directional S-twist of **Figure 13.11d**.

13.11 (f) This is a Stage IV complex cable neck-ring. The basic Stage II components are sets of **3** wires **P**lied together with an S-twist **(3P)**. These are again **P**lied S-twist in sets of **3** to give Stage III elements with the code **(3P(3P))**. Finally, **4** of these Stage III elements are **C**oiled together in the opposite direction (**Z**-twist). All the wires are circular in cross-section, so the final code is **(4CZ(3P(3P)))**. The total number of wires is 4x3x3=36. As for **Figure 13.11e**, the combination of S- and Z-twist has created a pleasingly balanced yarn-like structure.

Around 350 identifiable multi-strand torcs/bracelets are represented at the site, compared to around 50 tubular torcs. Of the multi-strand objects, about 270 have enough surviving material for the neck-ring/body structure to be fully recorded. Around 70 of these are complete or near-complete, and the rest are fragments, the majority from Hoard F. Stage II neck-ring constructions are most common (73%), followed by Stage III (25.5%) and Stage IV (1.5%). Amongst the Stage II constructions, the most common by far was a simple plied structure (69%, the majority of them 2-ply), whilst coiled constructions accounted for the remaining 31%.

Wire diameter and neck-ring/body construction was clearly an element of overall multi-strand torc/bracelet design, and there are clear associations between more intricate neck-ring/body constructions, finer wire

(	K: No. Stage II elements (ropes), if a Stage III (cable) construction	Form of Stage III construction	(	J: No. Stage I elements (wires) in each Stage II element (rope)	Form of Stage II construction	)	)	Cross-section of Stage I elements (wires)
		C: Coiled			C: Coiled			Q: square
								R: circular
		P: Plied			P: Plied			F: faceted
								T: twisted

Table 13.1 Multi-strand neck-ring construction codes

diameters, and more complex or decorated terminal types (such as buffer, reel, and torus, which are the only types decorated with curvilinear La Tène-style motifs – Ch. 21). Curvilinear decoration appears on less than 1% of torcs/bracelets with Stage II constructions, around 12% of Stage III constructions, and 50% of the more complete Stage IV objects. Such decoration also appeared only on multi-strand torcs/bracelets with a wire diameter of 1.1–2.0mm and some tubular torcs. Ring and loop terminal torcs are more likely to be made of thicker wires or rods, and often show simpler neck-ring constructions.

Typology of other artefacts

Rings

Thick strips or bars of metal, most often wrought bars with rectangular cross-section, which are formed into a ring. These are broadly circular in plan, unless otherwise specified in the description. Terminals are often rounded or tapered, though sometimes broken or sharply cut. Four types are distinguished based on the position of the terminals:

- Penannular
- Abutted (terminals touching)
- Overlapping
- Spiral (terminals overlapping by more than half a turn).

Stead and Clarke (e.g. Clarke 1954, Stead 1991a) both interpreted these objects as 'ingot rings' (for smaller sizes) or 'ingot bracelets' (for larger sizes), suggesting that they were a stage in metalworking processes or intended for trade as a raw material, with a secondary function as items of dress (to be worn on fingers/toes or wrists, depending on size). The square or rectangular cross-section of many of the Snettisham rings could be seen to support the notion that they were not finished artefacts and may have been uncomfortable to wear.

We have deliberately avoided using the terms 'finger-ring', 'toe-ring' and 'bracelet' for these objects, as it is far from certain that they were intended to be worn in this way. Here we use 'ring' purely as a shape descriptor. Whilst we do not use the term 'ingot ring', it is, of course, entirely plausible that such artefacts were used as a stock of metal for recycling.

The rings at Snettisham come in a variety of sizes (**Figs 13.12, 13.13**). Whilst it is possible that some of these could have been worn on the body (on fingers, toes, wrists or ankles, or strung from other ornaments as part of composite groups, see below), the overall distribution of sizes does not support a neat division into functional categories. Were this the case, we would expect a clear binomial distribution of the diameters, with finger/toe-rings clustering at one end and bracelets at the other, and very few occupying the liminal zone of roughly 34–50mm in external diameter which would be very difficult to wear as either finger/toe-rings or bracelets.

In fact, all but the smallest of the Snettisham rings are too large to be finger-rings. Swift (2017) measured internal diameters of finger-rings from Roman burials of known age and sex, finding that rings buried with children were in the range 12–20mm (with a peak at 14mm), rings buried with adult men ranged from 16–22mm in internal diameter (peaking at 18mm), and those buried with adult women ranged from 13–20mm, with a peak at 17mm.

At Snettisham, there is a peak in frequency at around 20–34mm in external diameter, (internal diameters of roughly 17–31mm), accounting for 63 of the 99 measurable rings, with 53 of those above 24mm in external diameter (**Figs 13.12, 13.13**). The smallest could have been worn as finger-rings, but the trend towards larger sizes suggests that toe-rings are a more likely intended function if these were indeed worn on the body. There are 16 rings at 34.1-52mm in external diameter (approx. 35–49mm internally) most of which could not easily have been worn on fingers, toes or adult wrists. Finally, a long tail in the distribution accounts for 20 rings with varied external diameters from just over 52mm to 138mm.

In this volume, rings from Snettisham are classed by size: 'small' if they have an external diameter up to 34mm (giving an internal diameter of around 31mm). Such objects could have functioned as finger- or toe-rings. Above this, objects are categorised as 'large rings'. These sizes, as discussed, are too varied to indicate function.

Ingots

Linear ingots – straight metal bars, D-shaped to circular in section with rounded ends, making them somewhat cigar-shaped. They range in length from around 50–100mm.

Triangular ingots – metal lumps that have been created by melting material together in triangular-shaped crucibles, examples of which have been discovered on other Iron Age sites (e.g. Musson *et al.* 1991, 272–4).

Lump ingots – metal lumps without a distinguishing shape, but which appear to have been intentionally formed in some way, whether through casting or hammering. Generally sub-circular or oval in form, often hammered flat.

Amorphous lumps – unshaped lumps of metal. These range in size from very small examples to the substantial lumps of metal found in Hoard M. Possibly metalworking waste or a stage from metalworking processes, or unworked melted objects. These lumps sometimes include fragments of part-melted objects, see e.g. S.132–S.136.

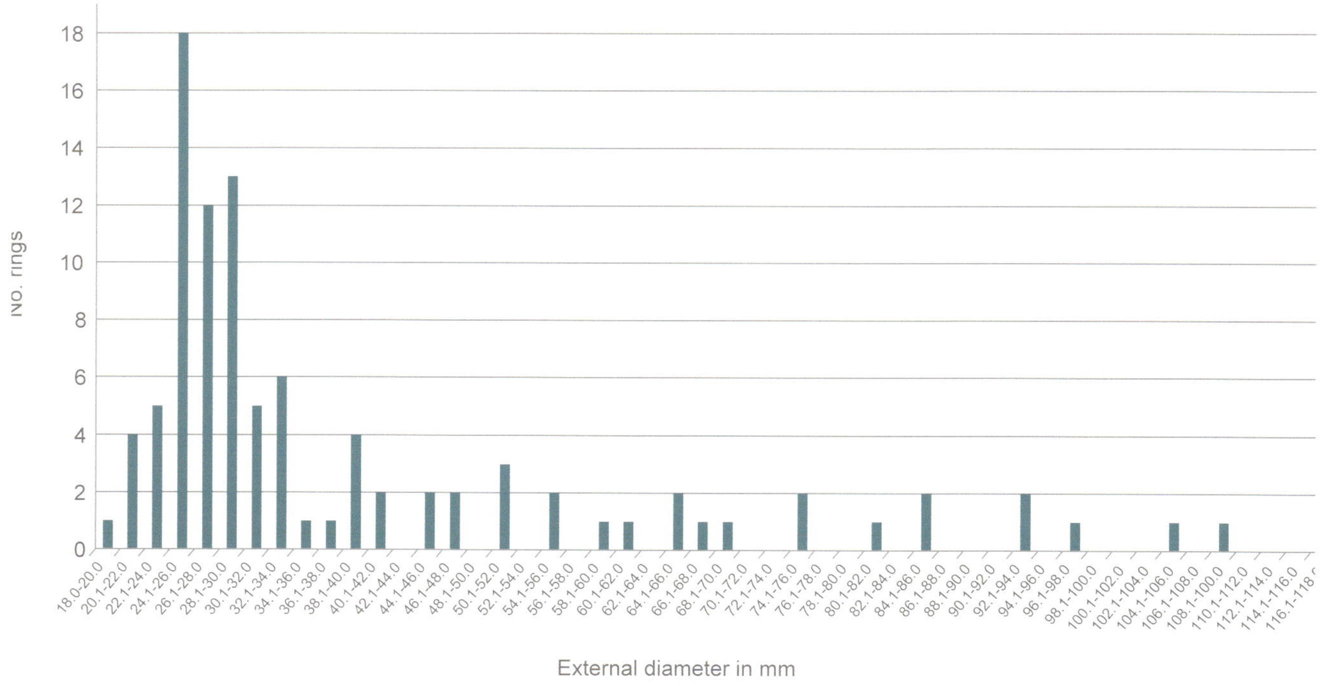

Figure 13.12 The external diameters of metal rings from Snettisham (internal diameters are generally around 3mm less than these values). This includes 98 of the 99 rings for which a reliable external diameter can be measured, omitting the outlier F.7a, which has a large external diameter of 13.8mm. Heavily distorted rings have been omitted, even if their circumference is complete, e.g. F.424 to F.427

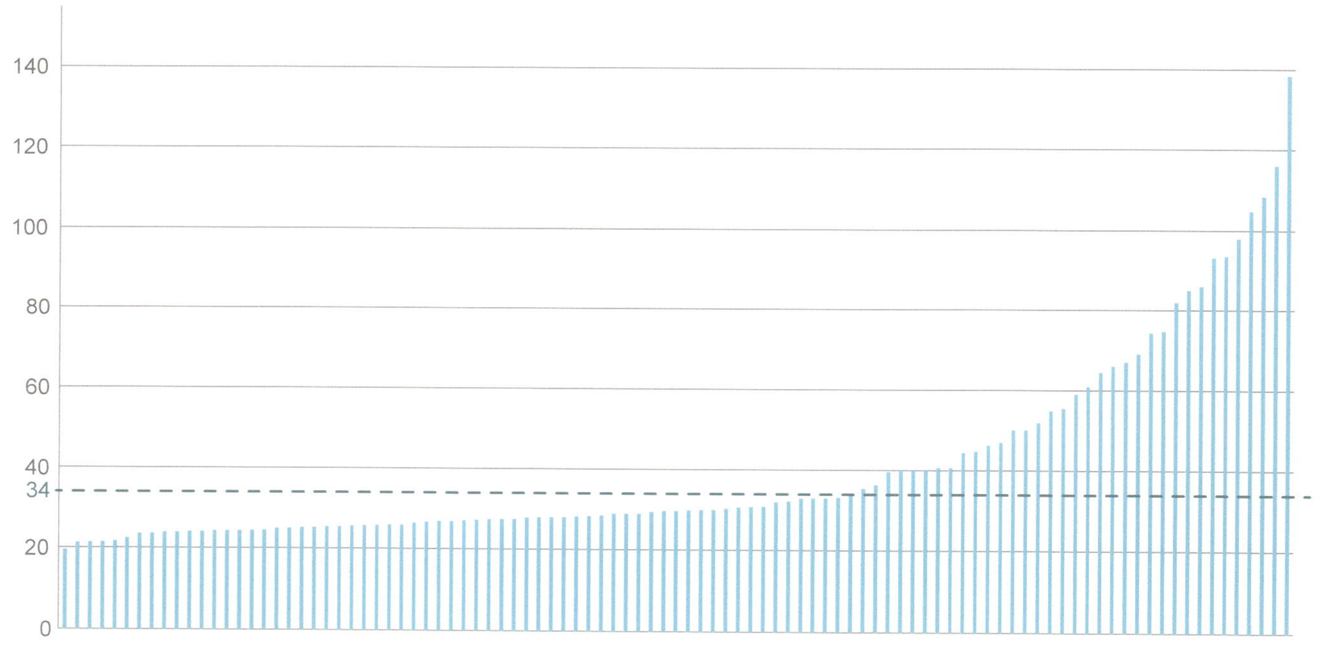

Figure 13.13 The external diameters of the 99 metal rings from Snettisham which were complete enough to allow a reliable measurement to be taken, ordered by size. Each bar represents one ring; the height of the bar shows the diameter. Heavily distorted rings have been omitted, as for Fig. 13.12

Linkage

Some artefacts, particularly within Hoard F, are linked. Collectively these are termed *COMPOSITE GROUPS*. In the catalogue, each composite group is covered under a single number. The different methods of linkage are defined as follows:

INTERLINKED – Where an artefact has been looped onto another, for example two rings, or a ring through the terminal of a torc.

INSERTED – Where one object has been inserted inside another and is either completely contained or partially protruding.

FUSED – Where an object has been attached to another by applying heat to partially melt the metal so fusing the two artefacts together.

PLIED/TWISTED – In one case (torcs H.2a and H.2b) two separate torcs have been twisted/plied together to make a single, composite torc.

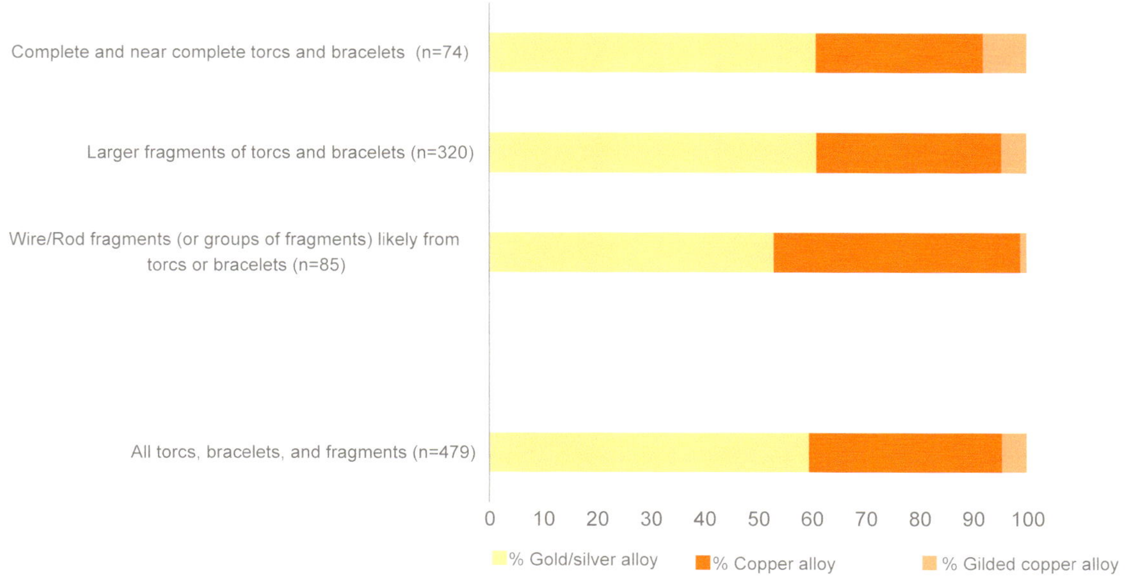

Figure 13.14 Relative proportions of different alloy types for torcs and bracelets from Snettisham, divided according to completeness of the objects

	Gold/silver alloy	Copper alloy	Gilded copper alloy (and possibly gilded)	Totals
Complete and near complete torcs and bracelets	44	23	7	**74**
Larger fragments of torcs and bracelets	195	110	15	**320**
Wire/Rod fragments (or groups of fragments) likely from torcs or bracelets	45	39	1	**85**
Totals	**284**	**172**	**23**	**479**

Table 13.2 Numbers of torcs, bracelets and related fragments from Snettisham, by alloy type

A note on alloys

In the catalogue, materials of the torcs are referred to as 'copper alloy' (for those torcs clearly exhibiting a greenish corrosion patina, some of which have been gilded) or 'gold/ silver alloy' (for torcs where visual analysis suggests that precious metal content predominates). Many of the latter are ternary alloys of gold, silver and copper, and the group includes base alloys in which copper is the dominant component. Metallurgy and alloy composition are discussed extensively in Chapters 17 and 18, and Appendices 4 and 5 include results from surface analysis. Torcs which have been analysed have been recorded as such in the catalogue to allow cross-referencing.

It appears that the proportions of torc and bracelet components present in gold/silver vs. copper alloys vary for complete objects compared to smaller fragments (see **Table 13.2** and **Fig. 13.14**). For complete/near-complete torcs and bracelets and larger fragments, around 60% are of gold/ silver alloy, whereas this falls to around 53% for fragments of wire/rod which likely derive from torcs or bracelets. This is likely due in large part to the fact that heavily corroded copper alloy objects are more likely to fragment post-deposition. (Although the counts in these figures group fragments which likely derive from the same object to avoid exacerbating this effect). However, although gilded copper alloy objects would be just as likely to fragment, a smaller proportion of fragmented pieces are gilded (or most likely gilded) compared to more complete objects (around 9% of complete or near-complete objects, around 5% of larger fragments, and 1% of wire fragments are likely gilded). This suggests that gilded torcs were less likely to be fragmented, or at least less likely to be deposited as fragments, than other copper alloy torcs. However, the results should be taken with caution since the data on gilding is only available for British Museum objects, and there has not been an exhaustive survey of all objects and fragments to check for traces of gilding. Thus this pattern could be an artefact of the sampling strategy rather than ancient depositional practices.

Chapter 14
Iron Age Hoards and other Metalwork

Julia Farley, Jody Joy and John Davies, with contributions by Nigel Meeks, Fleur Shearman and Sophia Adams

This chapter presents a full catalogue of the metalwork from the site, including both hoards and stray finds, bringing together the collections of both NCM and the BM. The majority of the finds are Later Iron Age (Phase 3), though Bronze Age to Earlier Iron Age (Phase 2) stray finds are included (S.1–10), as well as later Roman period (Phase 4–5) material from the site (Hoards M and P and a small number of stray finds). The Iron Age and Roman coins are covered in Chapter 15. The catalogue employs the typology and terminology set out in Chapter 13. This detailed catalogue is complemented by the summary of hoard contents given in Chapter 11. All finds are illustrated on the plates included in the catalogue, with the exception of stray finds of amorphous copper alloy lumps (S.141–S.234), and copper alloy sheet fragments with no original edges (S.340–S.351).

The hoards are presented first, in order of discovery (A, B, C, D, E, F, G, H, J, K, L, M, P), followed by stray finds and the very small number of non-hoard stratified finds from the 1990–2 excavations. The non-hoard finds are divided into two parts: Phase 2 finds, and Phase 3–4 (the latter further divided by find type).

The coins from the mixed torc/object hoards (B, C, E, F and P) and Hoard N (comprised exclusively of coins) are dealt with in Chapter 15, which covers hoard and stray finds of Iron Age and Roman coins.

Order and numbering

The material from Snettisham is complicated, and there is no single, simple way to group and order the finds. The approach taken in the catalogue has been designed to emphasise context (in terms of hoard groups, interlinked assemblages and order of recovery), rather than find type. In order to allow finds to also be studied and grouped by the object types they represent, a full listing by type is included at the end of Chapter 11.

Each object or fragment is given a number in the catalogue, starting with the hoard letter (or, in the case of stray and stratified finds, 'S.'). Composite groups of objects (where they have been linked, inserted or fused together, see Ch. 13) are given a single number. In cases of interlinking or insertion, where the individual elements of the composite group remain distinct and could (at least in theory) be separated, each component is given a part letter in the catalogue, e.g. D.1 is a composite group comprising torc D.1a and ring D.1b; wire fragment F.30b is inserted into the broken end of tubular torc fragment F.30a. Where fusing/melting has occurred, leaving the elements of the composite group permanently joined, they are treated under a single catalogue entry without part letters, e.g. F.32 is a fragment of tubular torc neck-ring fused onto part of a multi-strand torc/bracelet.

Hoards D and E each comprise a single composite group, listed under one number. For those hoards with multiple groups/objects where order of recovery or deposition cannot be ascertained (A, B, C, F, M, P), finds are ordered by object type, beginning with interlinked/composite groups. In the hoards subject to archaeological excavation (G, H, J, K and L), each find is given one number, assigned in the order in which the objects were recovered/lifted.

Other numbering and cataloguing systems that have previously been applied to the Snettisham material are explained in Chapter 1, and a full concordance is given in Appendix 3.

Abbreviations used in the object catalogue

- Wt = weight
- D(ext) = maximum external diameter of torc, bracelet or ring
- D(nr) = average diameter of torc neck-ring or bracelet body in cross-section
- D(cable) = maximum diameter of individual cable in cross-section (for Stage IV neck-rings, see Ch. 13)
- D(rope) = maximum diameter of individual rope in cross-section (for Stage III/IV neck-rings, see Ch. 13)
- D(wire) = maximum diameter of individual wires or rods in cross-section
- D(term) = maximum diameter of torc or bracelet terminal
- L = maximum length. When the object is distorted or bent, this is the maximum dimension of the object as seen
- W = maximum width (for square or rectangular-section rings, this is in cross-section)
- T = maximum thickness (for square or rectangular-section rings, this is in cross-section)
- MSCC = Multi-strand component construction code, e.g. '(2P)R' (see detailed typology in Ch. 13)
- [Analysed: see Ch.] = Object scientifically analysed, see chapter listed for further results and discussion. Due to the complexities of cross-referencing with Clarke (1954), in some cases for the material from NCM it has not been possible to precisely identify the components analysed (see Ch. 18 and Appendix 5).

Hoard A

Found in 1948, a group of three near-complete Type 6 tubular torcs (A.1–3), and broken fragments of one or more additional examples (A.4–7), as well as a perforated gritstone pebble (A.8). Unless otherwise stated, objects were recovered during ploughing. Some fragments were retrieved during subsequent excavations carried out by Rainbird Clarke (1954). References to Clarke's catalogue entries are included below, and a full concordance with Clarke's catalogue appears in Appendix 3.

All the Hoard A torcs had suffered plough damage and were in crumpled condition when discovered. A.1, A.2 and A.3 have undergone restoration and some reconstruction (Ch. 16). A.1 and A.3 both have buffer terminals which have been joined together by conservators. Originally these separate components would have been articulated to slot and connect together, creating annular torcs with front and rear/dorsal muffs. Possible methods of attachment for these and similar torcs are discussed below and shown in **Figures 21.8–10**, and also described by Hautenauve (2005, 84–5) and Eluère (1987).

A.1: Gold alloy and iron tubular torc (Pl. 14.1)
TUBULAR (TYPE 6)
NCM: 1949.74.2
Published reference: Clarke 1954, 37; pls i, ii; Tubular Torc 1
[Analysed: see Ch. 17]

A large hollow Type 6 tubular torc with iron plug (see **Figs 17.4a–e, 21.8**). The smooth, bright yellow body comprises two tubular sections, one of which (shown on the left-hand side of the plate) is attached to two joining front buffer terminals and a dorsal muff. The muff has a border comprising narrow bands of filigree in herringbone pattern. The central zone of the muff is in raised relief, which carries a repeated device of a circle and two lobes. Each of the buffer terminals has a smooth, rounded central zone bordered by narrow cordons on each side. The other half of the torc (shown on the right-hand side of the plate) has more surface damage. The inner face of the neck-ring carries a row of 33 ring punch-marks, each being approximately 4mm in diameter. There are additional rows of 10 punch-marks on either side, at the front (see View A in **Fig. 21.8**). Clarke (1954, 37) noted that parts of the torc originally had a filling of beeswax and sand.

Notes from scientific analysis (Nigel Meeks)
This is the largest of the tubular torcs. Each of the two tubular neck-ring sections is about 50mm in diameter, made of thin sheet gold (*c.* 0.15mm). The tubes have folds and kinks in the sheet from damage, although they do maintain their general curved tubular shape. One tube is separate from the other components, while the other has an elaborate decorated dorsal muff with filigree wire band at one end and both of the large, hollow sheet terminals attached at the other end.

The terminal attached directly to the tube is correctly positioned, with the recessed lip of the tube passing into the terminal. The other terminal has been inserted onto (into?) the first terminal and fixed with modern adhesive materials, unlike in the original published photograph in Clarke (1954) where the terminals are each on their own half tube. Where they are visible, the exposed ends of the sheet seem to be rather ragged. The terminals were seemingly only fixed mechanically onto the tubes; there is no evidence of soldering here.

The separate tubular half is of hollow gold sheet with no added wire/filigree or sheet decoration, although it does have a series of punch-marks. On the inner curvature of one tube surface, a linear series of 13 small (4mm) round ring punch-marks have been made by a single punch tool used repeatedly (**Fig. 14.1**) and these cross a small square ancient repair patch soldered into and flush with the tube (see **Fig. 20.1**). There is evidence in places of a seam along the length around the outer side of the tube (**Fig. 14.2**).

The decorated dorsal muff is made from sheet gold, probably by a combination of repoussé for the deep ornamental designs followed by chasing to outline and define the front surfaces of the decoration (**Fig. 14.3a–b**). The two techniques are often used in conjunction to create a finished piece. There are lines of dot-punched decoration within the chased lines adding sharp details to the overall design (**Fig. 14.4**).

Of particular interest is the filigree wire decoration running around both ends of the decorated zone. Optical microscopy and radiography of details of the filigree wires (see **Fig. 17.4c–e**) show they are made of two wire ropes, lying adjacent to each other and minimally soldered

A.1

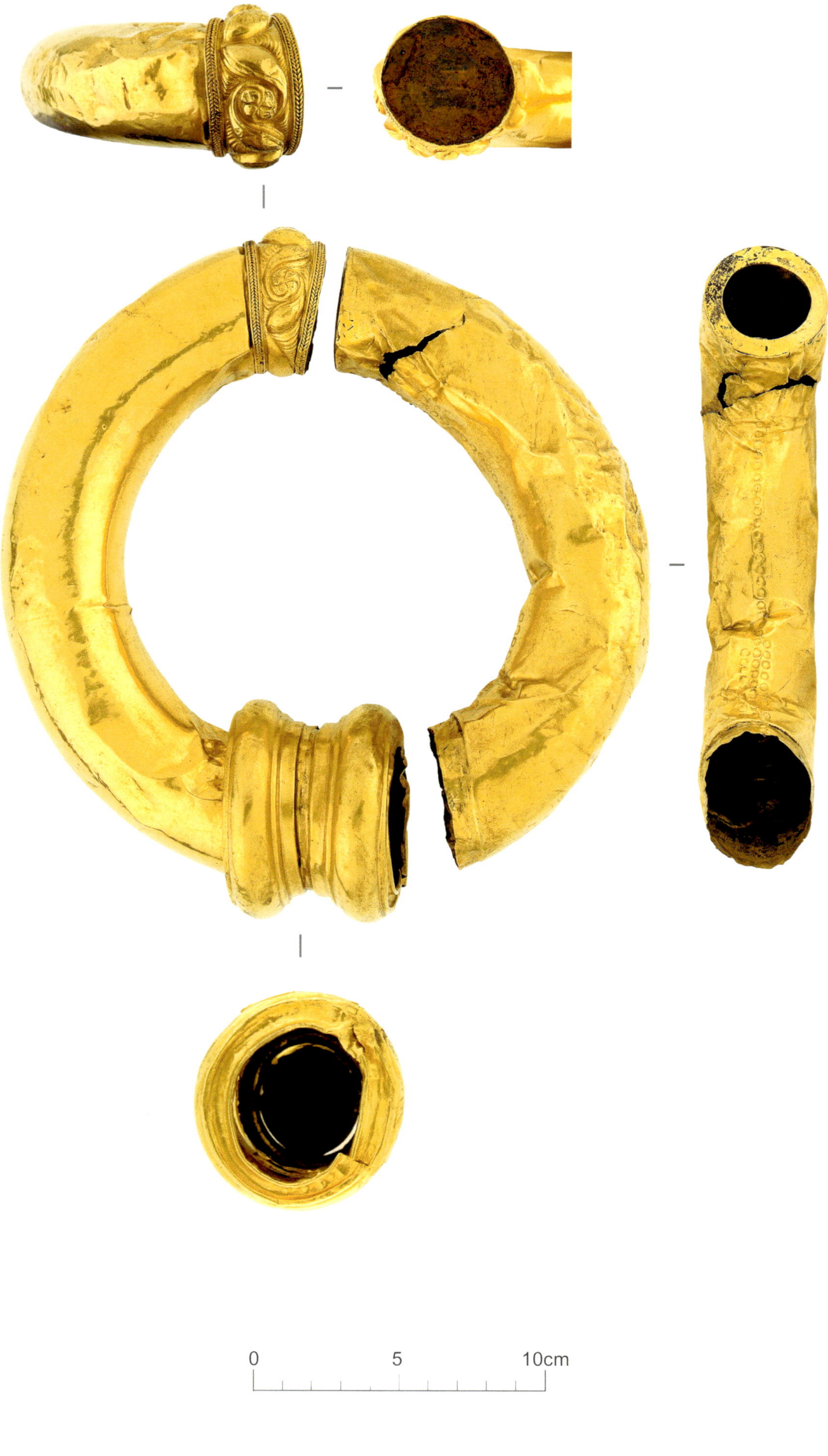

Plate 14.1

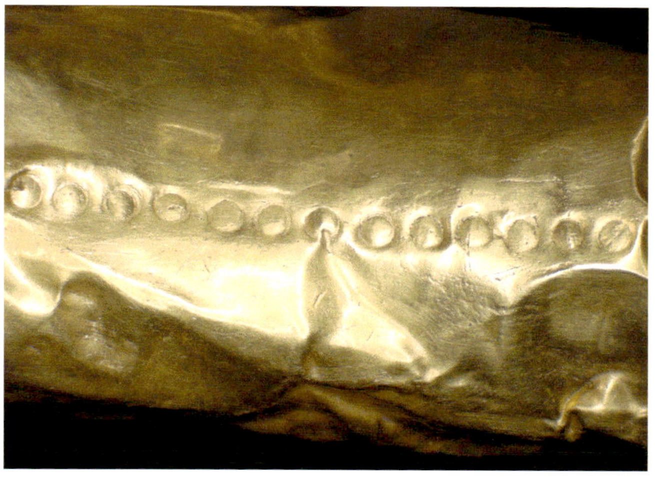

Figure 14.1 Line of circular punch marks that go over a soldered patch repair in A.1 (see also Fig. 20.1)

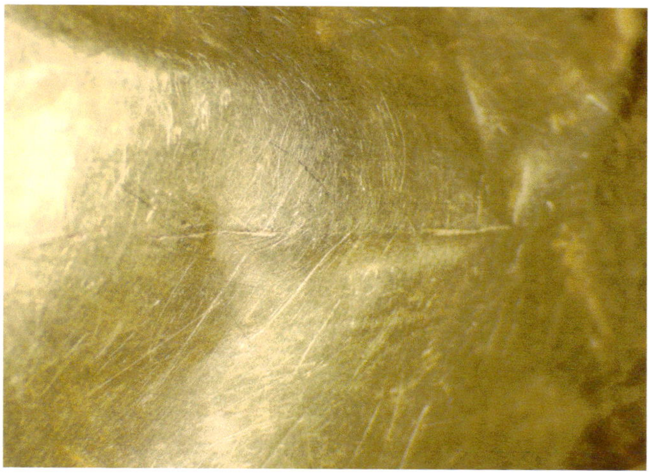

Figure 14.2 Seam on outer curve of the tube in A.1

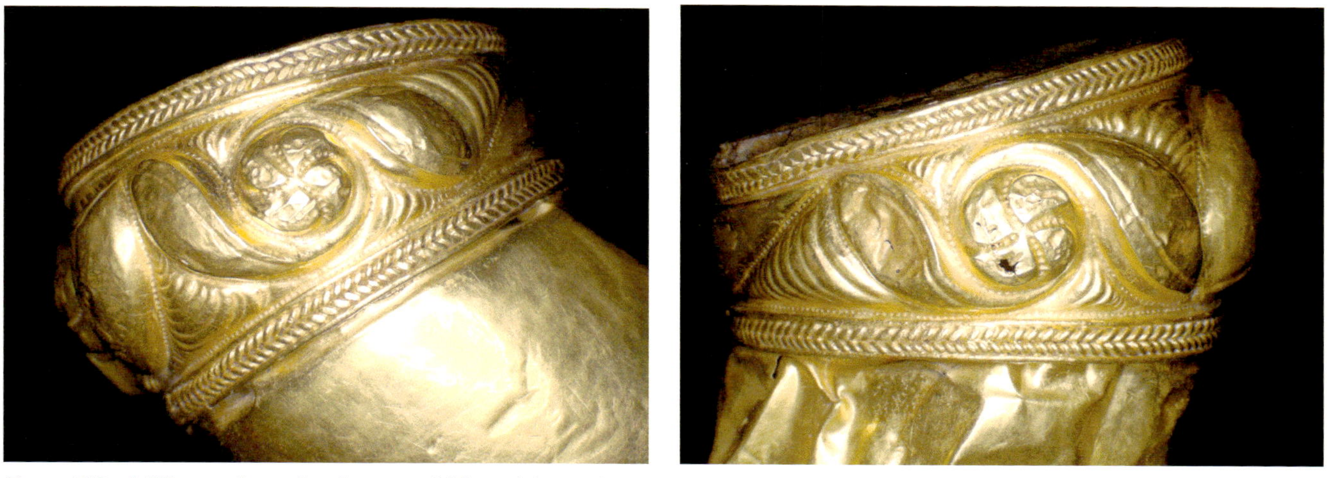

Figure 14.3a–b Filigree wire and and repouseé/chased decoration on one terminal in A.1

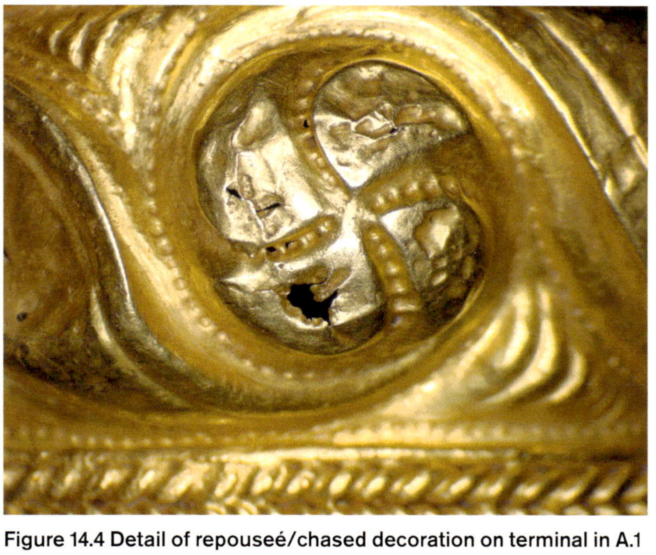

Figure 14.4 Detail of repouseé/chased decoration on terminal in A.1

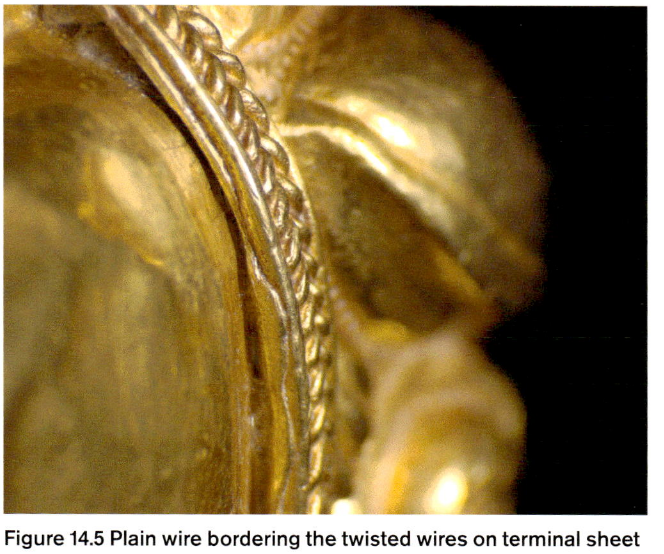

Figure 14.5 Plain wire bordering the twisted wires on terminal sheet with upturned edge in A.1

together and to the underlying sheet. Each rope is formed of a pair of wires twisted together. One of the pairs has been plied S-twist and the other Z-twist, giving the impression of a braid when they are viewed side by side. The plied wires are set between a parallel pair of wires of similar diameter to complete the design. This is clearly seen edge-on (**Fig. 14.5**). On one side of the terminal the soldered join between the ends of the filigree wires can be seen where the neatness loses its form (see **Fig. 17.4c**).

The torc has a unique rusted iron disc plug filling the whole end of the dorsal muff. At the centre of the plug the faint outlines of two rectangular rusted iron features are seen. Extending from behind the oblong pieces are two iron bars which meet and appear to be broken from an original longer rod-like attachment. The radiograph (see **Fig. 17.4b**) clearly shows a broken, curved iron bar (presumably iron) within the gold tube of which one end extends towards the iron disc plug within the terminal, although judging by the reverse curvature it is probably broken from an original fixing point on the back of the disc.

There is no residual filling material within the hollow tubes but there may well have been a lightweight filler surrounding the central iron rod. This would have served to support the thin torc walls to prevent major denting or collapse during use. The torc is dented, but displays little polishing and use wear (see Ch. 20).

Wt: 449.3g; D(ext): *c.* 218mm (side to side); *c.* 240mm (front to back, including terminals and dorsal muff); D(nr): 50.0mm; D(term): 78.0mm (front terminals), 57.0mm (dorsal muff)

A.2: Gold alloy tubular torc (Pl. 14.2)
TUBULAR (TYPE 6)
NCM: 1949.74.1
Published reference: Clarke 1954, 38; pls i, ii; Tubular Torc 2
[Analysed: see Ch. 17 and Appendix 5]

Large, hollow Type 6 tubular torc (see **Figs 17.5, 21.9**). The smooth and bright yellow tubular body is separated into two equal halves, each with a buffer terminal. Both of the buffer terminals are smooth, rounded and bordered by narrow cordons at the open end. One neck-ring section (shown on the left-hand side of the plate) carries a single line of seven circular punch-marks on the inner curve (see View B in **Fig. 21.9**). The second piece (on the right-hand side of the plate) has a narrow decorative ring at the rear, decorated with beaded wire. The inner curve of the tube carries a row of 14 ring punch-marks at the buffer terminal end (see View C in **Fig. 21.9**). There is also a single ring stamp at the rear, on the outside of the curve.

Notes from scientific analysis (Nigel Meeks)
A large tubular torc with beaded wire decoration. The torc is an example of a two piece, apparently circular, torc that does not fit together properly. With the terminal ends together there is a gap of some 25mm at the other ends of the tubes. There appears to be a missing component that would have joined the torc ends together, presumably a dorsal muff similar to that on torc A.1. An appropriate spacer piece is shown in the suggested reconstruction illustrated in **Figure 21.9**.

The tubes are made from thin sheet gold (0.15mm) and there is a seam running down the inner curve of the tube where the sides of the sheet overlap and are soldered together (**Fig. 14.6**). The tubes are relatively unmarked or damaged, compared to A.1 and A.3. However, the tube shown on the left-hand side of the plate (and **Fig. 21.9**) has a long brittle fracture crack running on the inner side of the ring, adjacent to a line of 14 small (2.5mm) round ring punch-marks. The punch-marks all seem to be from the same tool, and the last one in the line has two additional small dots punched within the ring (**Fig. 14.7**). At one point there is a fold in the tube sheet that partly covers the mark indicating that the punch-marks were made before the folding occurred, presumably during bending to adjust the curvature of the tube (**Fig. 14.8**). The other tube of this torc (shown on the right-hand side of the plate and **Fig. 21.9**) has seven similar ring punch-marks in a similar position near to the terminal.

The non-terminal end of the tube on the left-hand side of the plate is open and somewhat jagged; there is no obvious fixing or mount for attachment of the dorsal muff. The end of the other tube has a decorative beaded wire ring soldered onto the outside (see **Fig. 17.5**). The sheet had first been worked to form a lip and trough to allow the beaded wire to fit snugly,

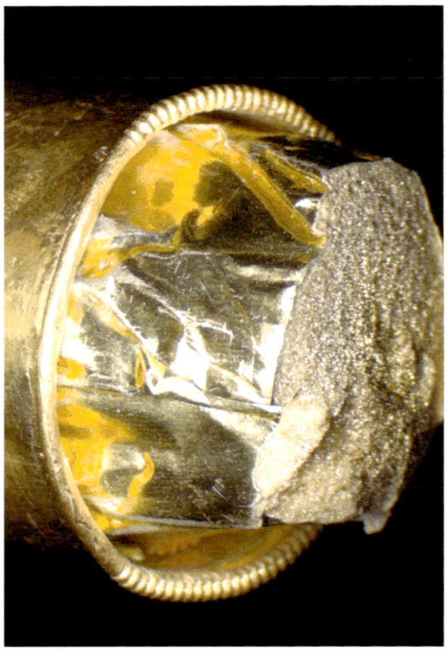

Figure 14.6. Soldered seam on inner curve in the tube of A.2

Figure 14.7 Fourteen punch marks and detail on A.2. Compare view b in Fig. 21.9

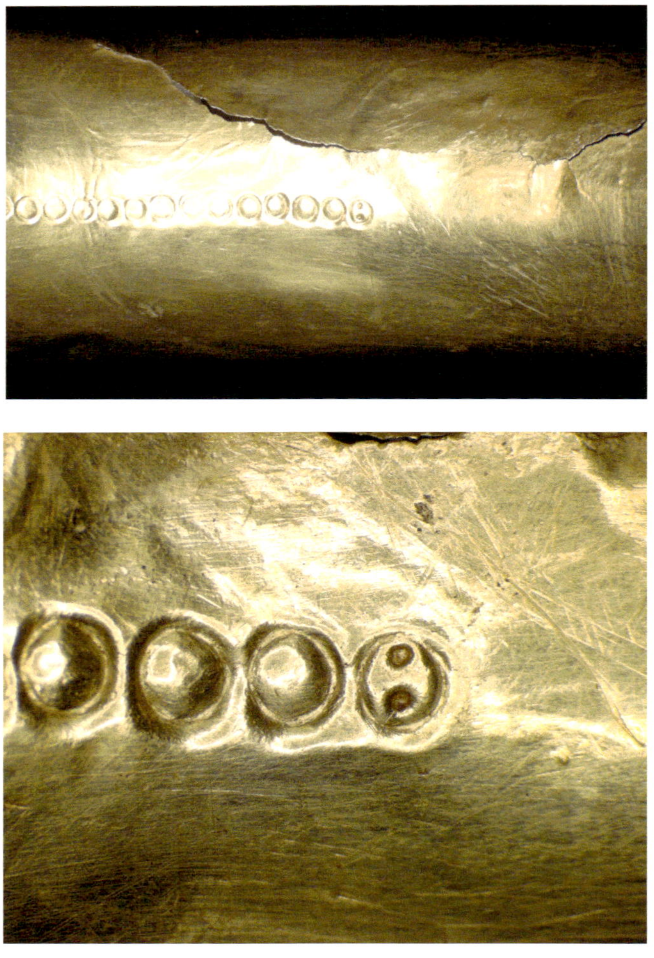

A.2

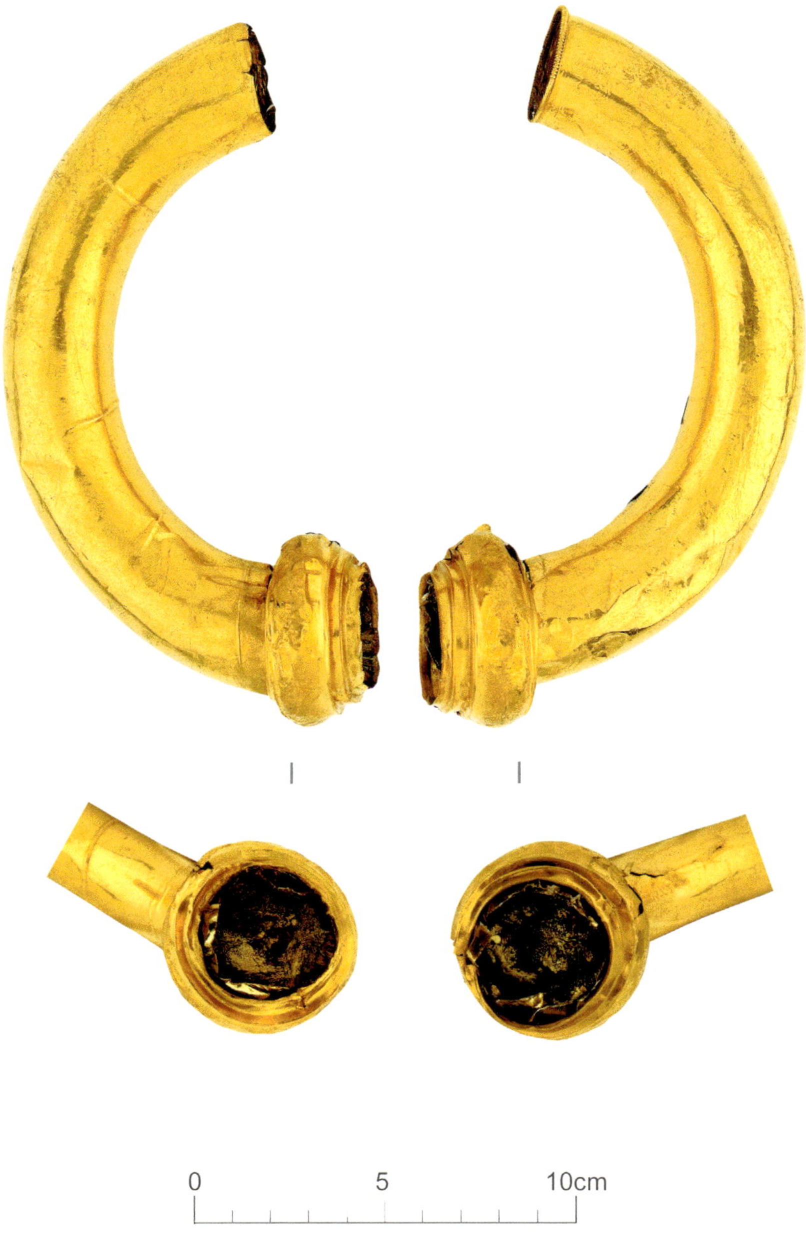

Plate 14.2

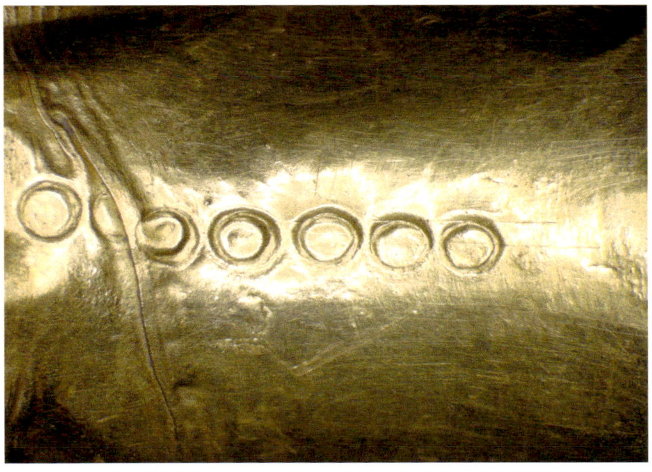

Figure 14.8. Circular punch marks along inner curve of tube and the kinked fold in the tube on A.2. Compare view c in Fig. 21.9. Note the brittle stress crack along the sheet tube

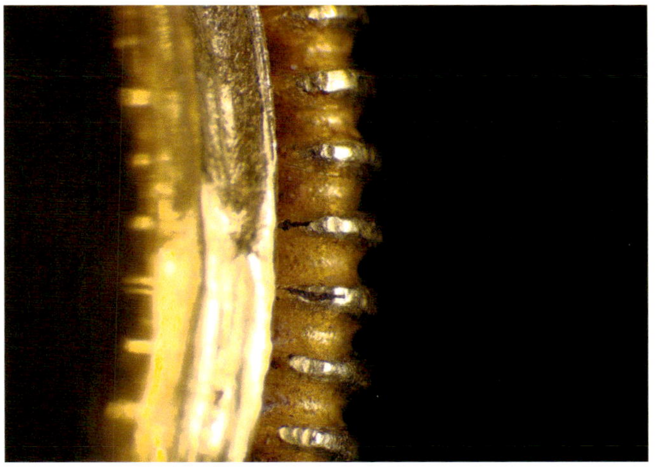

Figure 14.9 Circumferential groove just visible on centre bead of A.2

with the sheet wrapping round the wire a little from below (tube side), and into which it has been soldered, thus leaving a neat open-ended tube. Again, there is no internal fixing or material that might suggest the method of connecting the two tube ends together. The decorative wire is beaded only around two thirds of its length. The remaining wire is plain and clearly shows the original un-beaded wire diameter (see **Fig. 17.5**). The original wire was probably hammered into a round section. The plain wire is about 1.2mm in diameter, the beading is 1.5mm wide and bead spacing is 1.0mm. The plain region of the wire is on the inner curvature of the torc and may have been deliberately left smooth as this is the part of the torc that pressed on the neck during use, a plain wire being more comfortable than a beaded one.

The beaded wire is quite uniform in diameter and spacing showing a sophisticated use of a pre-formed beading tool (Whitfield 1998). There is clear evidence on some beads of the characteristic central circumferential groove that forms with the use of beading tools (**Fig. 14.9**). The metal is mechanically displaced and forced up into the rounded grooved tool and the circumferential groove forms where the two displaced sides meet. In this manner the beading is of similar workshop technology to much of the classical beaded wire commonly found on goldwork from the eastern Mediterranean and through into the medieval European periods (Whitfield 1998). The pre-formed beading tool used was clearly accurately made.

The two hollow terminals are of similar design to those of the other large torcs, and are of similar-thickness gold sheet to the tubes. The ends which attach to the tubes have a stepped flange design allowing them to be push-fitted onto the tubes with no evidence of soldering or other mechanical fixing to hold the terminals in place. The opposite open ends have exposed, rather rough or crudely finished sheet. It appears that a component is probably missing that covered these ends when fully assembled. Presumably the actual fittings to join the two halves of the torc were internal to the tubes, with the terminals seemingly acting as coverings for the joining mechanism, as evidenced by the part-remaining iron core in torc A.1. A possible joining mechanism is suggested in **Figure 21.9**.

Wt: 111.5g; D(ext): 187.0mm; D(nr): 32.0mm; D(term): 52.0mm

A.3: Gold alloy and iron tubular torc (Pl. 14.3)
TUBULAR (TYPE 6)
NCM: 1949.74.3
Published reference: Clarke 1954, 38–9; pls i, ii; Tubular Torc 3
[Analysed: see Ch. 17 and Appendix 5]

Large hollow Type 6 tubular torc (see **Fig. 21.10**). The smooth, bright yellow hollow tubular body is separated into two sections. One (shown on the left-hand side of the plate) is attached to two joining buffer terminals. As with torc A.2, both of the buffer terminals are smooth, rounded and bordered by narrow cordons on the sides which join the neck-ring and each other. The neck-ring section which is attached to the terminals has suffered more damage. It is also decorated: on the inner face is a row of 13 stamps (each stamp comprising four dots in a square). The three stamps nearest the terminal are flanked on either side by three more such stamps, giving a block of nine (see View D in **Fig. 21.10**). The second, separate neck-ring section (on the right-hand side of the plate) is plain and undecorated.

Notes from scientific analysis (Nigel Meeks)
This torc is another example of a two piece, apparently circular, tubular torc. It has two large hollow terminals of a stepped flange design similar to those of the other Hoard A torcs, which connect as loose push-fits onto the tubes with no evidence of soldering or other mechanical fixing to hold the terminals in place. They are now stuck together with modern glue. Presumably the ancient fixings were internal to the tubes, as evidenced by the part-remaining iron core in torc A.1; a mechanism suggested by Hautenauve (2005, 84–5) is depicted in **Figure 21.10**. The terminals seemingly act as coverings for the attachment. The tubes are quite marked and dented, and the one with the attached terminals is particularly crumpled and cracked showing the gold is in a work-hardened state. The terminals are of similar thickness gold sheet to the tubes.

On the tube not affixed to the terminals (on the right-hand side of the plate and **Fig. 21.10**), one end is of rather rough or crudely finished sheet with a slightly reduced

Figure 14.10 Flange for terminal fitting on A.3

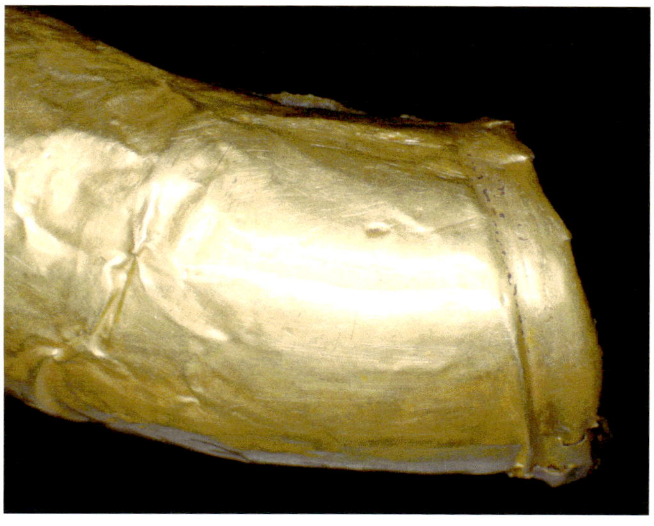

Figure 14.11 Ring support soldered to inside of tube on A.3. Compare view b-b on Fig. 21.10

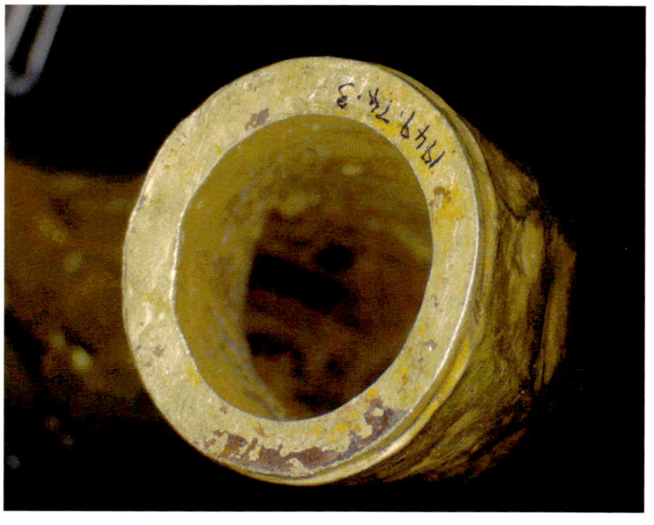

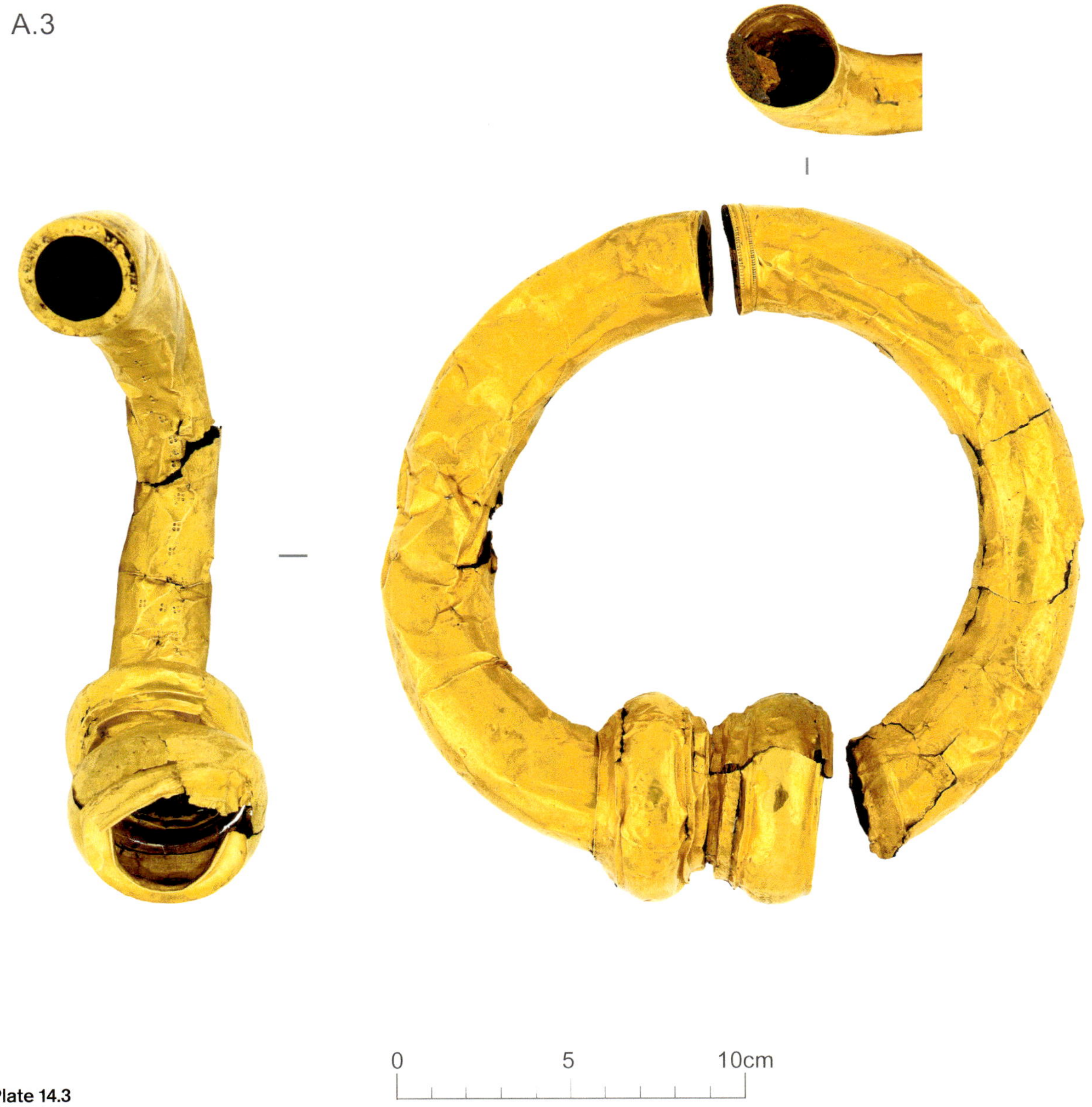

Plate 14.3

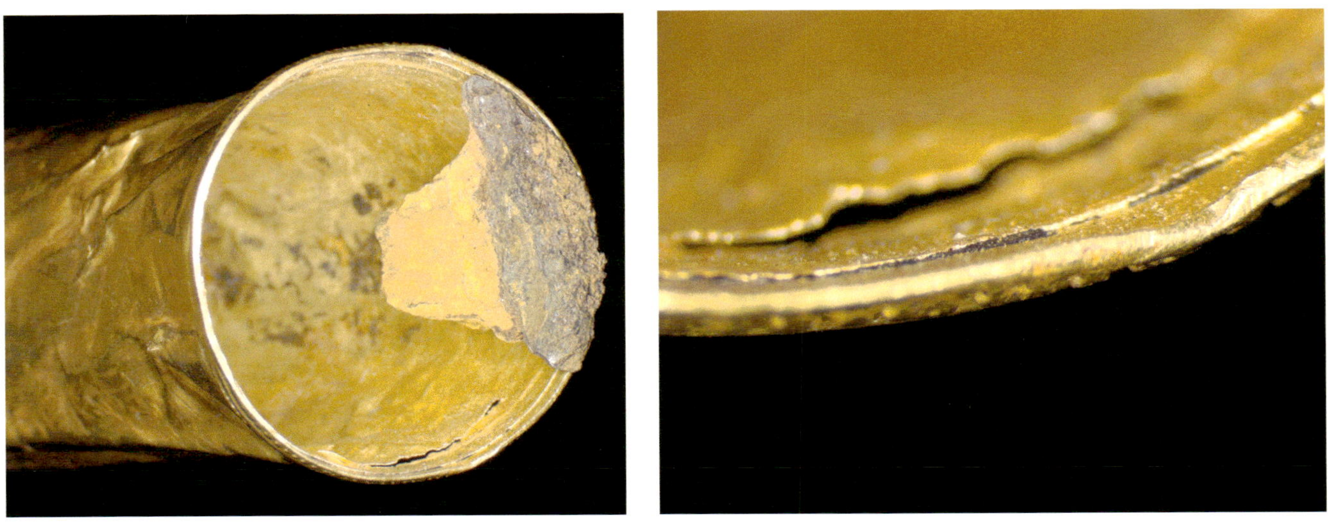

Figure 14.12 Thin sheet walls with band soldered to outside end of tube on A.3

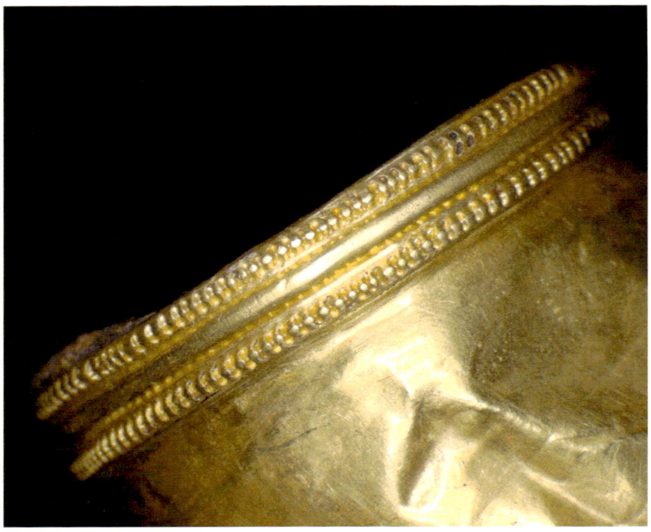
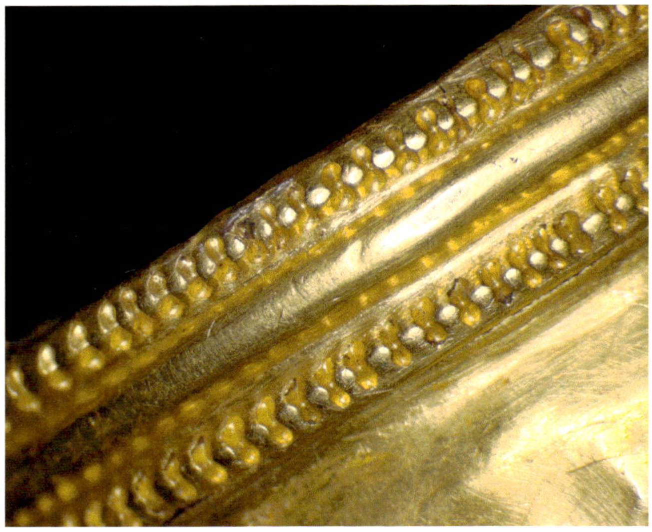

Figure 14.13 Decorative punched strip on A.3. Compare view c on Fig. 21.10

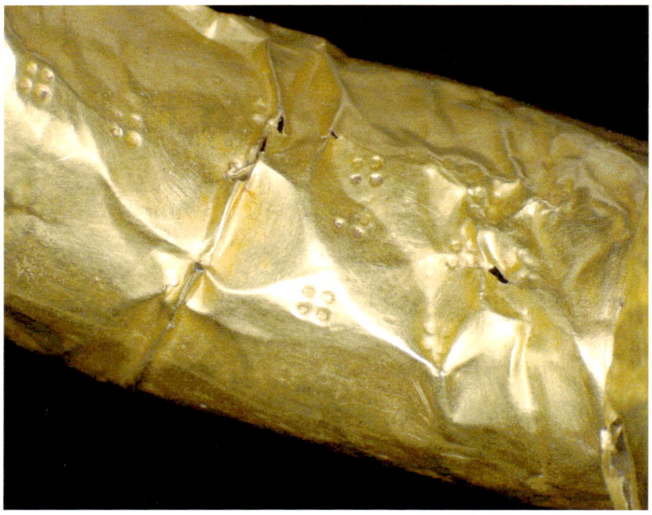
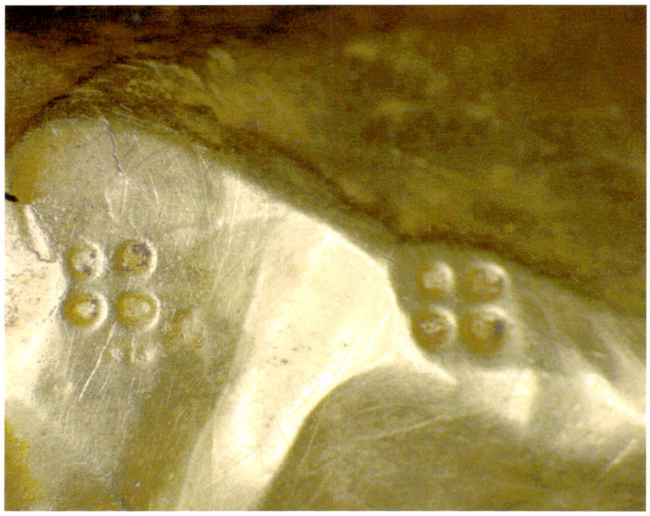

Figure 14.14 Punch marks on A.3. Compare view d on Fig. 21.10

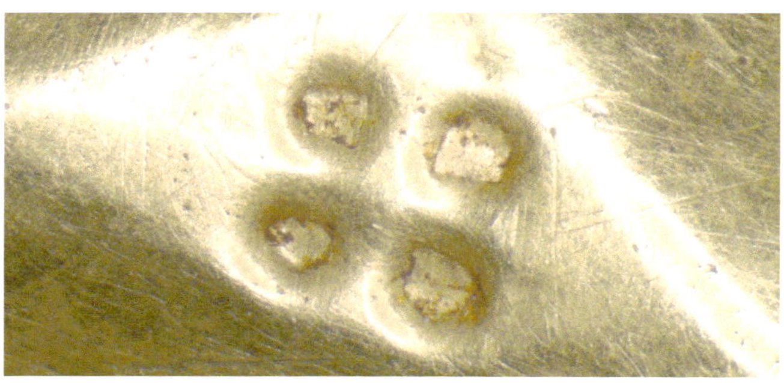

Figure 14.15 Detail of punch mark group on A.3

diameter flange: this is the end which would originally have fitted into the terminal (**Fig. 14.10**). At the other end of this tube, a decorative band of punched gold strip is soldered onto the outside of the thin tubular sheet (**Figs 14.12–13**). The decorative strip has two parallel rows of regular knobbly punched decoration separated by two grooves and a central rounded ridge (**Fig. 14.13**). The punched pattern has two alternating components: a rounded peg standing proud with two broad supporting sides and a recessed dumbbell or figure of eight between, the whole producing the appearance of a tyre-tread pattern. Essentially the dumbbell-shaped punch was struck down sequentially into the rounded ridge of gold, probably resting on a small domed stake, leaving the proud pegs between the punch-marks. It was most probable that the thick, decoratively punched strip was made before soldering onto the outside of the tube, rather than punching *in situ* as there are no signs of the punching showing on the inside of the tube (**Fig. 14.12**).

On the section of tubular neck-ring attached to the terminals (on the left-hand side of the plate and **Fig. 21.10**), a wide circular ring is soldered inside the other end of the tube, forming a neat, plain end, unlike the rough-cut ends of other torcs (**Fig. 14.11**). This ring supports the tube to keep its shape. Presumably this would butt against the corresponding interface with the other tube, or interlock via a mechanism like that suggested in **Figure 21.10**, using a clip similar to that listed below as part of A.4. On this tube there is a line of rounded punch-marks in groups of four (**Figs 14.14–15**). The spacing between the marks in each set of four is quite regular which suggests a single four-pronged punch rather than a single point punch being extremely carefully aligned to make the accurate groups. The inner corners of the quad punch-marks are pointed to near right-angles, facing the centre, while the outer edges are curved.

Wt: 139.6g; D(ext): 202.0mm; D(nr): 33.0mm; D(term): 61.0mm

A.4

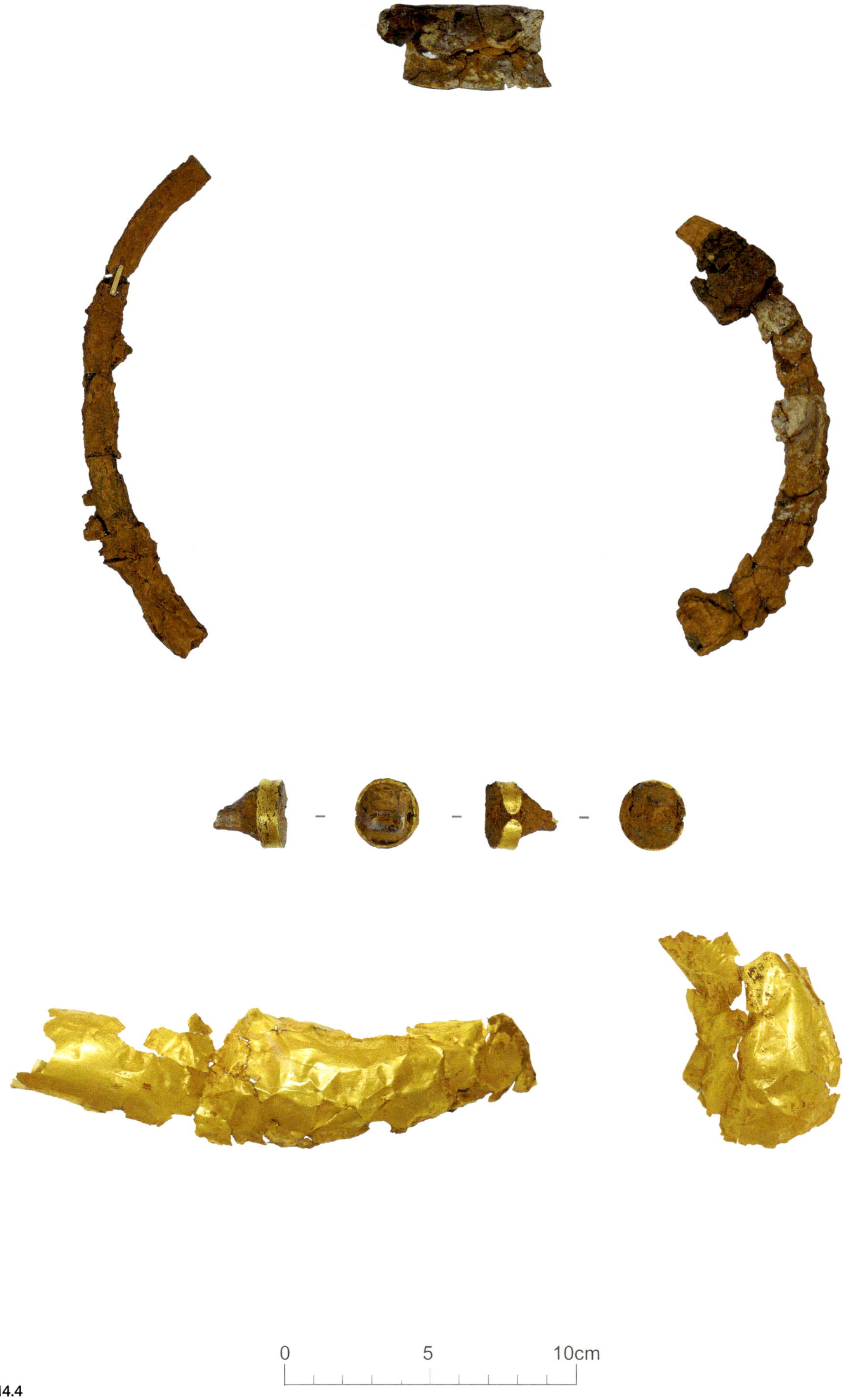

Plate 14.4

Remaining fragments of tubular torc(s) from Hoard A were all recorded by Clarke as 'A.4.' These pieces represent at least one additional torc, though some fragments could also have come from A.1–3 (see below). Here the key components are addressed separately (as A.4–7) for easier discussion and analysis.

A.4: Gold alloy and iron tubular torc fragments (Pl. 14.4)

TUBULAR (TYPE 6)
NCM: 1949.74.6
Published reference: Clarke 1954, 39; Tubular Torc 4
[Analysed: see Ch. 17 and Appendix 5]
Context details: Found during ploughing and Rainbird Clarke excavations.

Six fragments of one or more gold Type 6 tubular torc(s):

- A piece of organic core material (top of the plate) which once fitted onto one of the core rods.
- Two portions of the original curved iron torc core (second from top on the plate), both with rectangular section.
- Terminal of a clasp or fixing mechanism (second from bottom on the plate, and shown in **Fig. 14.16**), comprising an iron core with gold strip binding around the edge. The back of this iron terminal narrows into a shank, which has a rectangular-shaped section.
- Two sheet fragments (shown at the bottom of the plate) which are made from a very fine sheet gold. They are both very fragile, with torn edges. They retain a curved profile but their once-smooth surface has been damaged.

Notes from scientific analysis (Nigel Meeks)

The radiograph of the iron and gold torc component (**Fig. 14.16**) gives an insight into the construction of this possible clip device. It would seem reasonable to suggest that this clip may well have been on the end of an iron core rod, as part of the attachment between two tubular torc halves, as illustrated in **Figure 21.10**. Hautenauve (2005, 84–5) suggests a possible association between this clasp or clip and the narrowed end of the neck-ring section of A.3 (seen on the left-hand side of the A.3 plate), into which it fits. It might have been part of A.3 or another similar torc.

Measurements

Body fragment 1: 180 x 40mm; 13.0g
Body fragment 2: 80 x 50mm; 5.7g
Clasp terminal: Head diameter 23mm; iron shank section 11 x 4mm; 19.4g
Curved iron core fragment 1: 170mm long; 29.8g

Figure 14.16 X-radiograph of iron clip (part of A.4)

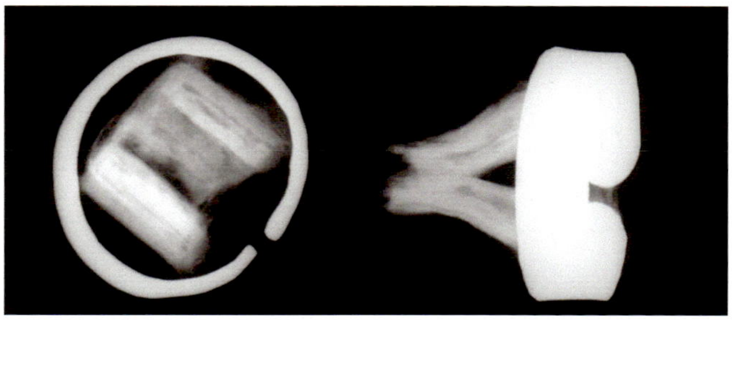

Curved iron core fragment 2: 150mm long; 51.2g
Core material fragment: 61.0mm long; 29.5mm diameter; 11.9g

A.5–6: Pair of gold alloy tubular torc terminals (Pl. 14.5)

TUBULAR (TYPE 6)
Published reference: Clarke 1954, 39; pl. i; Tubular Torc 4
[Analysed: see Ch. 17]

Damaged buffer terminals from Type 6 tubular torc in the style of those recorded in A.1–A.3 above. The terminals are smooth, rounded and bordered by narrow cordons at their open ends.

A.5: NCM: 1949.74.4 (Pl. 14.5)
Wt: 9.1g; D(nr): 27.0mm; D(term): 49.0mm; W: 21.5mm

A.6: NCM: 1949.74.5 (Pl. 14.5)
Wt: 9.5g; D(nr): 27.0mm; D(term): 47.0mm; W: 23.5mm

Notes from scientific analysis (Nigel Meeks)

Two sheet gold terminals about 0.15mm thick. Terminal A.5 is largely intact with only a few small missing pieces, but with some cracks through the sheet. It is essentially undistorted and thus retains its original shape. Terminal A.6 is somewhat distorted, cracked and broken with some fragments missing.

They are each constructed from a single piece of gold sheet, there being no evidence of a seam either inside or out. The inside surface is a mottled texture (**Fig. 14.17**), not burnished, as one might expect from hammering onto a metal stake, suggesting these components were possibly hammered onto a softer, more textured material such as antler or wood.

The outside surfaces of the terminals are well burnished and polished. The terminals have been shaped on a former of some kind. Various stress cracks are found in the work-hardened sheet which has led to the loss of material.

The terminal design is the same as the other hollow sheet terminals with two flanges each side. The tubular torc neck-rings fit into these without any other fixing. Each terminal has one inner lip folded inwards while the other remains pointing outwards.

Figure 14.17 Textured inside surface of torc terminal A.5

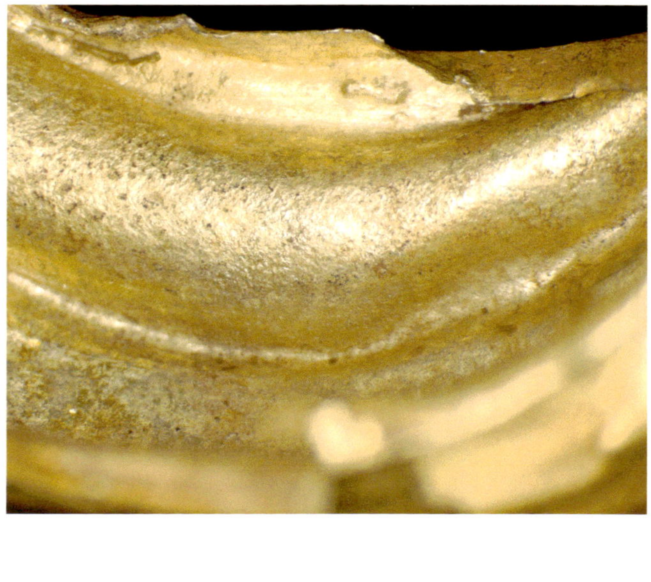

A.5

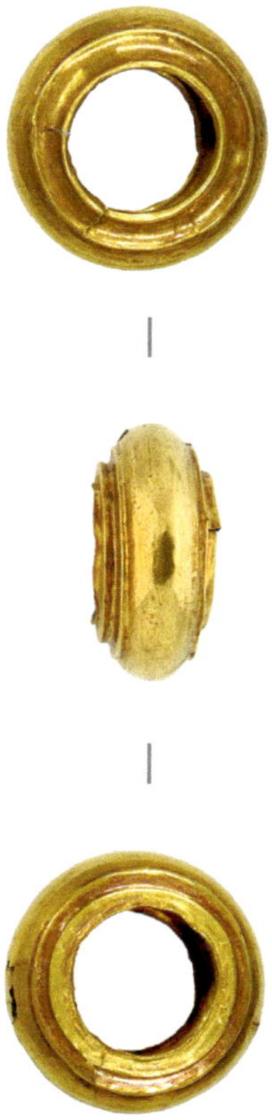

A.6

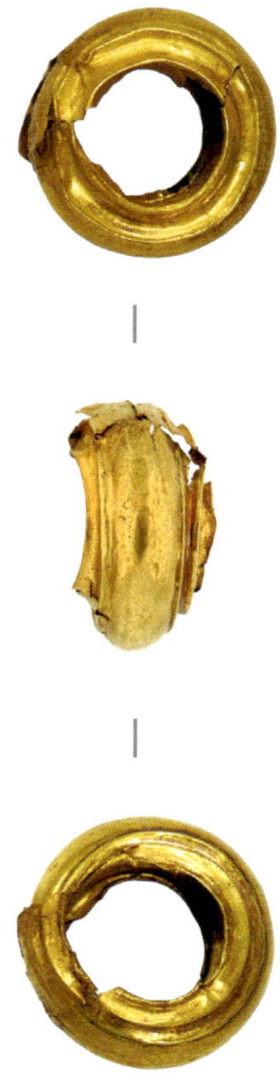

A.7

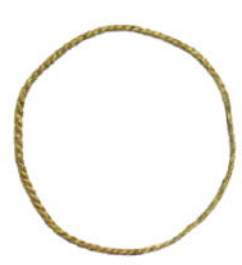

A.8

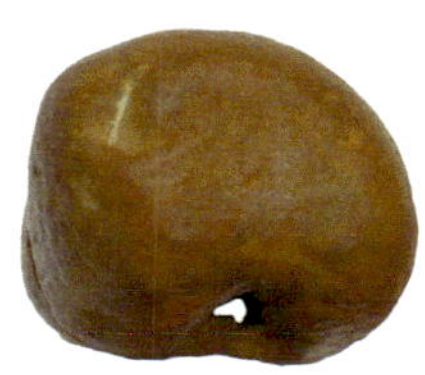

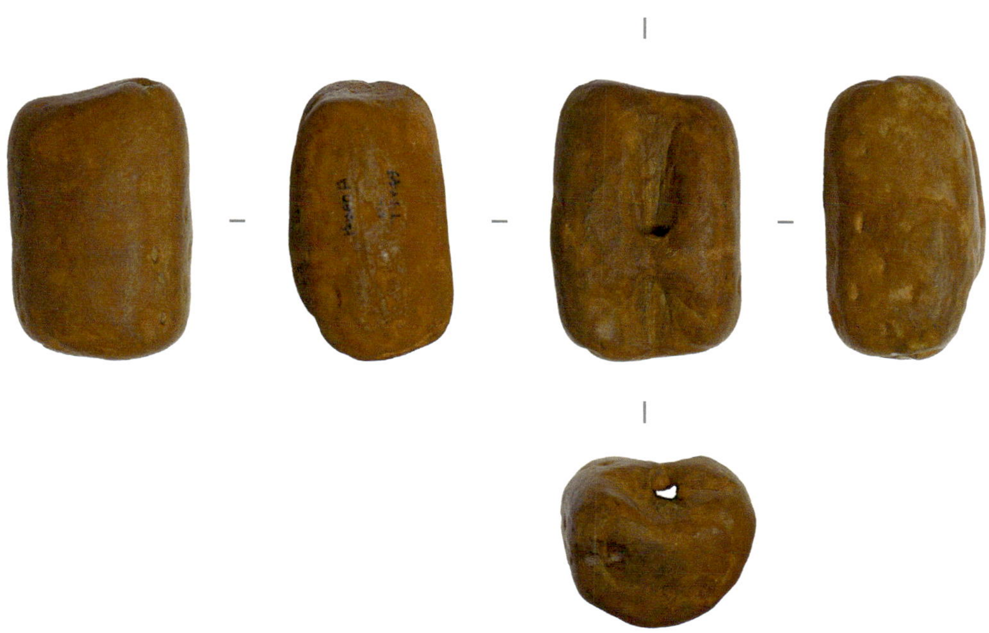

0 5 10cm

Plate 14.5

A.7: Gold alloy wire ring, likely a tubular torc component (Pl. 14.5)
?TUBULAR
NCM: 1949.74
Published reference: Clarke 1954, 39, pl. i; Tubular Torc 4
[Analysed: see Ch. 17]

Wire ring, made of two ropes soldered together, each formed from pairs of wires which have been plied together and then soldered. Most likely from a tubular torc. May be associated with the same fragmentary object as A.4–6; the ring circumference is the same as the inner circumference of terminals A.5–6. Alternatively, it could be an unused filigree wire decoration for soldering to a tubular torc, in the manner of the beaded wire on torc A.2; it is of similar wire diameter and ring circumference.

Notes from scientific analysis (Nigel Meeks)
The wires which make up A.7 are about 1mm thick individually, so the combined width of the two ropes lying parallel is about 2mm. The wires within each rope are soldered together, and the two adjacent ropes are also soldered together (see **Fig. 17.6**). Both ropes are plied in the same direction (S-twist). This gives an effect unlike the chevron design on the filigree wire of torc A.1 in which the adjacent clockwise and anti-clockwise twisted wires create a braid-like effect.

There is some evidence of diagonal lines on the wires that is indicative of strip twisting or block twisting (Oddy 1977). At the point where the original wire ends have looped round to meet and complete the ring, they have been intertwined and soldered together. This region also appears to have been hammered and filed to a compact oblong cross-section some 22mm long, unlike the rest of the ring where the wires remain in their original rounded section (**Fig. 14.18**).

The wires have a rough or lumpy surface texture that is symptomatic of excess solder having flowed over much of the wire when not fully molten. The solder between the twists of wire at their point of contact is dendritic, which is a common characteristic of solder. The adjacent pairs are soldered together where the wires touch, but not at every point of contact.

There are many flat points and well-worn surfaces on the exposed wires that reveal the core wire for EDX analysis. They seem to have been abraded after soldering which removed the surface solder in those places. At high magnification the surface of the solder shows the etched and meandering recrystallised grain boundaries with round porosity that commonly appear on ancient buried gold (**Fig. 14.19**).

Surface analyses were made of a few key regions where the twisted wires were soldered together. X-ray maps and also batch point analyses were also made in the same regions. The maps indicated some concentrations of silver and copper together, and point analyses confirmed that these corresponded to solder regions compared to lower values for wire regions. The results were somewhat variable due to effects of surface enrichment and burial. The following analyses appear to be reasonably representative of the wire and solder compositions in the region of the oblong section which has better geometry for analysis:

	Cu%	Ag%	Au%
Oblong region of ring			
Wires, mean:	0.6	13.8	85.6
Solder, mean:	2.2	22.0	75.8
Rounded twisted wire			
Wires, mean:	0.7	16.6	82.7
Solder, mean:	3.7	23.8	72.5

In both regions the solder appears to have significantly higher silver and copper content than the wire and hence has a lower melting point than the wire by some 50°C (see **Fig. 17.47a**). The solder is clearly made of an alloy with added copper. Gold with silver up to a content of about 25% (or more) could simply be natural silver-rich (alluvial) gold. Adding copper would lower the melting point further whilst maintaining the golden colour. The alloy composition of the wires is more like that seen in the gold sheet alloys of the BM collection (see **Table 17.2**) with higher gold than generally seen in the wires of the BM torcs. Conversely, the solder composition is more like the wire alloys of the BM torcs (see **Table 17.4**). This suggests a sound knowledge of the principles of alloying metallurgy, temperature characteristics and control for use on different types of object, components and solders.

Wt: 1.1g; D(term): 30.0mm; W: 1.8mm; T: 0.5mm

Figure 14.18 Wire ring. Detail of oblong section of soldered wires on A.7

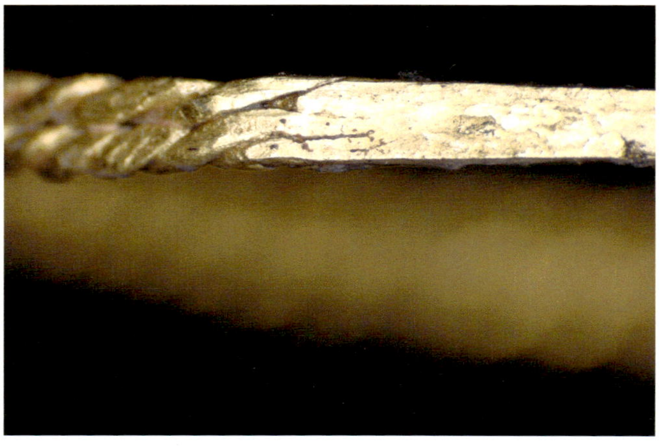

Figure 14.19 SEM detail of surface of gold wire ring (A.7) showing meandering recrystallised grain boundaries. Scale bar is 50µm

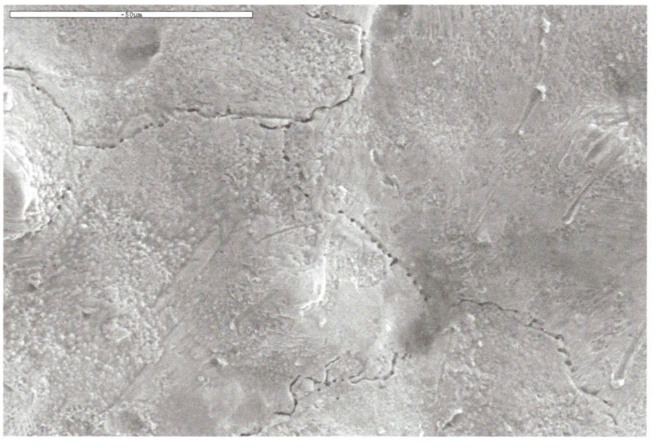

A.8: Gritstone pebble (Pl. 14.5)
NCM: 1949.74.7
Published reference: Clarke 1954, 39; fig. 6
Smooth, oval-shaped pebble with perforation. The channel running through the stone (D-shaped in cross-section) suggests it may have been used to shape or finish wires, but there is no categorical evidence for this.
Wt: 244.5g; L: 74.0mm; W: 50.0mm; T: 44.0mm

Hoard B

Found in 1948. Unless otherwise stated, objects were recovered during ploughing. Some fragments were retrieved during subsequent excavations carried out by Rainbird Clarke (1954), and this is noted in their entries; some excavated fragments are mentioned in Clarke's text and others were identified through information written on the objects themselves.

There is substantial confusion around the contents of Hoards B and C. This publication follows Clarke (1954) in assigning objects between these hoards. Clarke's published references are included in the catalogue entries, and a full concordance with Clarke's catalogue appears in Appendix 3. Where objects were not illustrated in Clarke's publication, the correspondence with Clarke's numbering was ascertained based on descriptions and cross-referencing with annotated photocopies taken by Peter Northover in the 1980s (copies of which are held in the BM archive). Some material from Hoards B and C became intermixed shortly after discovery (see Ch. 4) and cannot be securely assigned to either hoard. This material appears under catalogue section 'Hoard B/C'.

Clarke published five iron nails as coming from Hoard B, and another five from Hoard C. He suggested that these were the remains of wooden boxes which once contained the two hoards. However, such large, rectangular-section iron nails are not a well attested Iron Age find type, and nor are these examples obviously sets, being varied in size, shape and appearance. Subsequent metal-detector survey of the field in the 1990s revealed many hundreds of comparable iron nails in a dense spread across the entire site, a sample of which have been retained at the BM for future study (1990,0409.31). It thus seems most likely that the nails initially believed to be associated with Hoards B and C are in fact part of this wider, almost certainly post-medieval scatter, and became associated with the hoard material only by the coincidence of their proximity. Nevertheless, Clarke's nails are included here for completeness, as B.29–33, and C.57–61.

B.1a–h: Composite group (interlinked) (Pl. 14.6)
Torc fragments and rings B.1b–h were all looped onto large ring B.1a
Context details: Found during Clarke's excavations, Trench 2, beneath a stone, adjacent to the gold coins from Hoard B.

B.1a: Gold/silver alloy large ring (Pl. 14.6)
NCM: 1949.75.24
Published reference: Clarke 1954, 54, no. 14; pl. xii, in group; Hd. B No. 7
[Analysed: see Appendix 5]
Complete gold/silver alloy large ring with overlapping terminals, each with a flat, tapered end. Made from a strip with rectangular section, with pronounced ribs along the upper and lower edges of the external face.
Wt: 28.6g; D(ext): 55.0mm; W: 8.0mm; T: 6.0mm

B.1b: Gold/silver alloy large ring (Pl. 14.6)
NCM: 1949.75.17
Published reference: Clarke 1954, 54, no. 13; pl. xii, in group; Hd. B No. 6
[Analysed: see Appendix 5]
Complete gold/silver alloy penannular large ring. Made from a strip with rectangular section, with pronounced ribs along the upper and lower edges of the external face. The ends are tapered.
Wt: 14.0g; D(ext): 40.0mm; W: 5.5mm; T: 2.0mm

B.1c: Gold/silver alloy small ring (Pl. 14.6)
NCM: 1949.75.9
Published reference: Clarke 1954, 56, no. 12; pl. xii, in group; Hd. B No. 10
[Analysed: see Appendix 5]
Complete gold/silver alloy small spiral ring with around 1 3/4 turns, made from a strip with rectangular cross-section. Slightly tapered ends.
Wt: 9.5g; D(ext): 26.0mm; W: 6.0mm; T: 2.0mm

B.1d: Copper alloy small ring (Pl. 14.6)
NCM: 1949.75
Published reference: Clarke 1954, 55, no. 1; pl. xii, bottom right of group; Hd. B No. 12
[Analysed: see Ch. 18]
Copper alloy small penannular ring, made from a strip with rectangular cross-section. Broken at one end and slightly rounded at the other.
Wt: 6.2g; D(ext): 24.0mm; W: 5.0mm; T: 2.0mm

B.1e: Gold/silver alloy torc/bracelet (Pl. 14.6)
NCM: 1949.75.72
Published reference: Clarke 1954, 46, no. 1; pl. xii, top left of group; Hd. B No. 13
[Analysed: see Appendix 5]
Gold/silver alloy loop terminal fragment from multi-strand torc/bracelet, made from a single loop of circular-section wire, with some flattened/faceted areas along its length. Cut at one end, with multiple chisel marks, other end original.
Wt: 4.7g; D(wire): 3.2mm; D(term): 19.0mm

B.1f: Gold/silver alloy torc/bracelet (Pl. 14.6)
MSCC: (5C)R
NCM: 1949.75.37
Published reference: Clarke 1954, 46, no. 3; pl. xii, no. 3 and in group, centre right; Hd. B No. 15
[Analysed: see Appendix 5]
Fragment of gold/silver alloy multi-strand torc neck-ring or bracelet body, cut at both ends. Stage II construction of five circular-section wires coiled loosely together. The whole fragment has been bent into a rough penannular ring.
Wt: 6.2g; D(nr): 2.0mm; D(wire): 1.0mm; L: 40.0mm

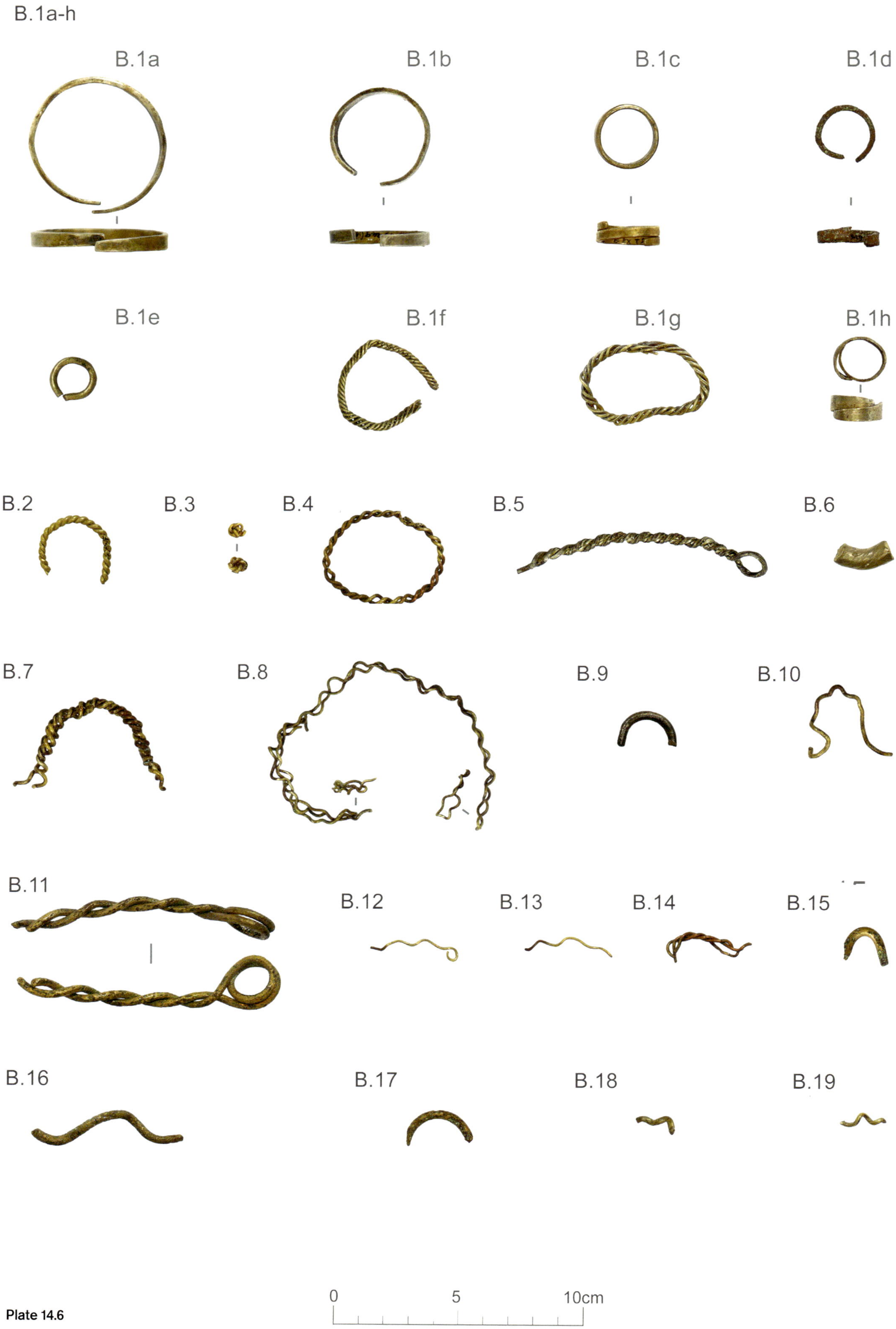
B.1a-h
B.1a
B.1b
B.1c
B.1d
B.1e
B.1f
B.1g
B.1h
B.2
B.3
B.4
B.5
B.6
B.7
B.8
B.9
B.10
B.11
B.12
B.13
B.14
B.15
B.16
B.17
B.18
B.19
0
5
10cm

Plate 14.6

B.1g: Gold/silver alloy torc/bracelet (Pl. 14.6)
MSCC: (4C)Q
NCM: 1949.75.40
Published reference: Clarke 1954, 46, no. 4; pl. xii, no. 4; Hd. B No. 16
[Analysed: see Appendix 5]
Fragment of gold/silver alloy multi-strand torc neck-ring or bracelet body, cut at both ends. Stage II construction of four square-section wires coiled loosely together. The whole fragment has been bent into a sub-oval ring, with the ends threaded together.
Wt: 10.1g; D(nr): 3.0mm; D(wire): 1.0mm; L: 52.0mm

B.1h: Gold/silver alloy small ring (Pl. 14.6)
NCM: 1949.75
Published reference: Clarke 1954, 56, no. 14; pl. xii, bottom left of group; Hd. B No. 11
[Analysed: see Appendix 5]
Complete gold/silver alloy small ring, made from a strip with rectangular cross-section. Overlapping ends, with tapered terminals.
Wt: 4.9g; D(ext): 21.5mm; W: 7.5mm; T: 1.3mm

B.2: Gold/silver alloy torc/bracelet (Pl. 14.6)
MSCC: (2P)R
NCM: 1949.75.38
Published reference: Clarke 1954, 46, no. 2; pl. xii, no. 2; Hd. B No. 14
[Analysed: see Appendix 5]
Fragment of gold/silver alloy multi-strand torc neck-ring or bracelet body, cut at both ends. Stage II construction of two circular-section wires plied tightly together. The whole fragment has been bent into a U-shape.
Wt: 4.4g; D(nr): 2.0mm; D(wire): 1.3mm; L: 29.0mm

B.3: Gold/silver alloy torc/bracelet (Pl. 14.6)
MSCC: (2P)R
NCM: 1949.75.48
Published reference: Clarke 1954, 47, no. 8; pl. ix; Hd. B No. 20
[Analysed: see Appendix 5]
Fragment of gold/silver alloy multi-strand torc neck-ring or bracelet body, cut at both ends. Stage II construction of two circular-section wires plied tightly together. The whole fragment has been bent into a tight, tiny coil.
Wt: 2.2g; D(nr): 5.0mm; D(wire): 1.2mm; L: 8.0mm

B.4: Gold/silver alloy torc/bracelet (Pl. 14.6)
MSCC: (?2P)R
NCM: 1949.75.41
Published reference: Clarke 1954, 47, no. 7; pl. xii; Hd. B No. 19
[Analysed: see Appendix 5]
Fragment of gold/silver alloy multi-strand torc neck-ring or bracelet body, cut at both ends. Stage II construction of two circular-section wires plied very loosely together. It is possible that a third original ply is now missing. The whole fragment has been bent into an oval ring, with the cut ends abutting.
Wt: 6.7g; D(nr): 2.0mm; D(wire): 1.0mm; L: 49.0mm

B.5: Gold/silver alloy torc/bracelet (Pl. 14.6)
MSCC: (2P)T
NCM: 1949.75.15
Published reference: Clarke 1954, 47, no. 14; pl. ix; Hd. B No. 21
[Analysed: see Appendix 5]
Fragment of gold/silver alloy multi-strand torc or bracelet, comprising one single-loop terminal and a length of neck-ring/body, cut at the other end. Stage II construction of two twisted square-section wires plied loosely together. The terminal is a continuous loop, with the wire having a faceted cross-section in this area, continuing into the square-section neck-ring wires. Possible evidence for a hammered join on the terminal.
Wt: 23.3g; D(nr): 2.0mm; D(wire): 2.4mm; D(term): 13.2mm; L: 99.0mm

B.6: Gold/silver alloy wire/?torc/?bracelet (Pl. 14.6)
MSCC: (?P)F
NCM: 1949.75
Published reference: Clarke 1954, 47, no. 15; pl. ix; Hd. B No. 22
[Analysed: see Appendix 5]
Context details: Found during Clarke's excavations, Trench 2.
Short length of gold/silver alloy faceted wire, cut at both ends. Most likely from multi-strand torc or bracelet; the wire is bent in a way which suggests it was originally part of a Stage II (or III) plied construction.
Wt: 12.1g; D(wire): 8.5mm; L: 24.0mm

B.7: Gold/silver alloy torc/bracelet (Pl. 14.6)
MSCC: (?3C)R
NCM: 1949.75.39
Published reference: Clarke 1954, 46, no. 5; Hd. B No. 17
[Analysed: see Appendix 5]
Fragment of gold/silver alloy multi-strand torc neck-ring or bracelet body, unevenly cut at both ends – the wires do not all end at the same point. Stage II construction of three circular-section wires coiled very loosely together. It is possible that additional original wires are now missing. The whole fragment has been bent into a rough U-shape.
Wt: 10.4g; D(nr): 5.0mm; D(wire): 1.7mm; L: 61.0mm

B.8: Gold/silver alloy bracelet (Pl. 14.6)
MSCC: (?3P)R
NCM: 1949.75.16
Published reference: Clarke 1954, 46, no. 6; pl. ix; Hd. B No. 18
[Analysed: see Appendix 5]
Gold/silver alloy multi-strand loop terminal bracelet, which has been almost entirely untwisted. Seemingly originally of Stage II construction, formed from three circular-section wires plied together. Two wires survive more or less intact, one is broken off only a short distance from the terminal. Terminals originally a continuous loop at each end, with ends of the wire meeting in the body of the bracelet.
Wt: 14.9g; D(nr): 5.0mm; D(wire): 1.0mm; L: 91.0mm

B.9: Gold/silver alloy torc/bracelet (Pl. 14.6)
NCM: 1949.75
Published reference: Clarke 1954, 47, no. 20; Hd. B No. 24
[Analysed: see Appendix 5]
Fragment of loop terminal, from gold/silver alloy multi-strand torc/bracelet. Made from circular-section wire, broken at one end, with flat, tapering terminal at the other.
Wt: 3.4g; D(wire): 3.9mm; L: 23.8mm

B.10: Gold/silver alloy wire/?torc/?bracelet (Pl. 14.6)
NCM: 1949.75
Bent/curving fragment of circular-section gold/silver alloy wire, cut at both ends. Most likely from a multi-strand torc neck-ring or bracelet body which has been untwisted.
Wt: 0.5g; D(wire): 1.0mm; L: 36.0mm

B.11: Copper alloy torc/bracelet (Pl. 14.6)
MSCC: (2P)R
NCM: 1949.75.30
Published reference: Clarke 1954, 47, no. 19; pl. ix; Hd. B No. 23
Fragment of copper alloy multi-strand torc or bracelet, comprising one continuous double-loop terminal and a length of neck-ring/body, cut at the other end. Stage II construction of two circular-section wires plied loosely together.
Wt: 19.2g; D(nr): 10.0mm; D(wire): 3.0mm; D(term): 22.0mm; L: 105.0mm

B.12–13: Gold/silver alloy wire/?bracelet (Pl. 14.6)
NCM: 1949.75
B.12 and B.13 are very similar in form and wire-diameter, and may be part of the same object.

B.12: Fragment of gold/silver alloy wire, broken at both ends, wavy or coiled in from. Possibly part of the body of a fine multi-strand bracelet.
Wt: 0.4g; D(wire): 0.8mm; L: 35.0mm

B.13: Fragment of gold/silver alloy wire, broken at both ends. Small loop at one end may be a terminal, the rest of the wire is wavy or coiled in from. Possibly the loop terminal and part of the body of a fine multi-strand bracelet.
Wt: 0.5g; D(wire): 0.8mm; L: 35.0mm

B.14: Copper alloy torc/bracelet (Pl. 14.6)
MSCC: (?3P)R
NCM: 1949.75
Fragment of copper alloy multi-strand torc neck-ring or bracelet body, broken at both ends. Stage II construction of two circular-section wires plied together. The ply is very loose, suggesting that there may originally have been one or more additional strands.
Wt: 1.5g; D(nr): 3.0mm; D(wire): 1.0mm; L: 36.0mm

B.15: Copper alloy wire/?torc/?bracelet (Pl. 14.6)
NCM: 1949.75
Published reference: Clarke 1954, 47, no. 20; Hd. B No. 24
[Analysed: see Ch. 18]
Curved fragment of circular-section copper alloy wire, broken at both ends. Perhaps part of a multi-strand torc or bracelet.
Wt: 3.4g; D(wire): 3.9mm; L: 19.3mm

B.16: Copper alloy wire/?torc/?bracelet (Pl. 14.6)
NCM: 1949.75
Published reference: Clarke 1954, 47, no. 21; Hd. B No. 25
[Analysed: see Ch. 18]
Curved fragment of circular-section copper alloy wire, cut at one end and broken at the other. Perhaps part of a multi-strand torc or bracelet.
Wt: 5.5g; D(wire): 3.2mm; L: 60.8mm

B.17: Copper alloy torc/bracelet (Pl. 14.6)
NCM: 1949.75
Published reference: Clarke 1954, 47, no. 20; Hd. B No. 24
[Analysed: see Ch. 18]
Context details: Found during Clarke's excavations, Trench 2.
Fragment of loop terminal, from copper alloy multi-strand torc/bracelet, broken at both ends. Made from circular-section wire.
Wt: 2.6g; D(ext): 27.0mm; D(wire): 3.0mm; W: 26.5mm

B.18: Copper alloy wire/?torc/?bracelet (Pl. 14.6)
NCM: 1949.75
Fragment of circular-section copper alloy wire, cut at both ends. Perhaps part of a multi-strand torc or bracelet; the curvature of the fragment suggests it was originally part of a coiled construction.
Wt: 0.7g; D(wire): 1.6mm; L: 15.5mm

B.19: Copper alloy wire/?torc/?bracelet (Pl. 14.6)
NCM: 1949.75
Fragment of circular-section copper alloy wire, cut at both ends. Perhaps part of a multi-strand torc or bracelet; the curvature of the fragment suggests it was originally part of a coiled construction.
Wt: 0.7g; D(wire): 1.5mm; L: 18.7mm

B.20: Gold/silver alloy large ring (Pl. 14.7)
NCM: 1949.75.13
Published reference: Clarke 1954, 54, no. 12; Hd. B No. 5
[Analysed: see Appendix 5]
Gold/silver alloy large penannular ring, made from a strip with rectangular cross-section. One blunt, slightly tapered terminal and one cut end.
Wt: 20.9g; D(ext): 98.0mm; W: 9.5mm; T: 1.8mm

B.21: Gold/silver alloy large ring in three parts (Pl. 14.7)
Published reference: Clarke 1954, 54, no. 11; Hd. B No. 3
Three joining sections of a single gold/silver alloy large ring, each fragment broken at both ends. Made from a strip with rectangular cross-section, with pronounced ribs along the upper and lower edges of the external face.
Context details: Found during Clarke's excavations, Trench 2.

Part 1: NCM: 1949.75.26
Wt: 12.2g; L: 71.2mm; W: 5.0mm; T: 3.3mm

Part 2: NCM: 1949.75
Wt: 5.2g; L: 40.5mm; W: 4.8mm; T: 2.7mm

Part 3: NCM: 1949.75
Wt: 3.4g; L: 27.4mm; W: 5.0mm; T: 2.8mm

B.22: Gold/silver alloy large ring in two parts (Pl. 14.7)
Published reference: Clarke 1954, 54, no. 11; Hd. B No. 3
Two joining sections of a single gold/silver alloy large ring. Made from a strip with rectangular cross-section, with pronounced ribs along the upper and lower edges of the external face.
Context details: Found during Clarke's excavations, Trench 2.

Part 1: NCM: 1949.75
One original, blunt terminal, the other end broken.
Wt: 6.2g; L: 49.4mm; W: 5.0mm; T: 2.5mm

Part 2: NCM: 1949.75
Broken at both ends.
Wt: 8.1g; L: 56.0mm; W: 5.4mm; T: 2.7mm

B.23: Gold/silver alloy large ring in two parts (Pl. 14.7)
Published reference: Clarke 1954, 54, no. 11; Hd. B No. 3
Two joining sections of a single gold/silver alloy large ring . Made from a strip with rectangular cross-section, with pronounced ribs along the upper and lower edges of the external face.
Context details: Found during Clarke's excavations, Trench 2.
Broken at both ends.

Part 1: NCM: 1949.75
Formed from two re-joined fragments, broken at both ends.
Wt: 12.0g; L: 71.5mm; W: 5.1mm; T: 2.8mm

Part 2: NCM: 1949.75
Wt: 10.0g; L: 65.2mm; W: 5.3mm; T: 2.7mm

B.24: Gold/silver alloy large ring in three parts (Pl. 14.7)
Published reference: Clarke 1954, 54, no. 15; Hd. B No. 4
[Analysed: see Appendix 5]
Three fragments, most likely from a single gold/silver alloy large penannular ring. Each made from a strip with rectangular cross-section, with pronounced ribs along the upper and lower edges of the external face.

Part 1: NCM: 1949.75.84
Broken at both ends.
Wt: 11.4g; L: 75.0mm; W: 5.0mm; T: 3.0mm

Part 2: NCM: 1949.75
Broken at both ends.
Wt: 13.9g; L: 81.5mm; W: 5.0mm; T: 3.0mm

Part 3: NCM: 1949.75
One original, tapered end, the other polished for metallography.
Wt: 9.0g; L: 63.0mm; W: 5.0mm; T: 3.0mm

B.25: Gold/silver alloy small ring (Pl. 14.7)
NCM: 1949.75.46
Published reference: Clarke 1954, 56, no. 11; pl. xii; Hd. B No. 9
[Analysed: see Appendix 5]
Context details: Found during Clarke's excavations, Trench 2.
Gold/silver alloy small ring, made from a strip with rectangular cross-section. Overlapping ends: one broken, the other slightly tapered.
Wt: 11.0g; D(ext): 25.0mm; W: 8.0mm; T: 2.0mm

B.26: Gold/silver alloy linear ingot (Pl. 14.7)
NCM: 1949.75.51
Published reference: Clarke 1954, 58 (cake), no. 2; pl. xiii, upper; Hd. B No. 2
Context details: Found during Clarke's excavations, Trench 2.
[Analysed: see Appendix 5]
Gold/silver alloy linear ingot. Rectangular in cross-section, with flattened top and bottom faces and flat, parallel long sides. The narrower ends are rounded, giving the ingot a sub-rectangular or oval shape in plan.
Wt: 19.2g; L: 29.0mm; W: 13.0mm; T: 4.0mm

B.27: Gold/silver alloy lump ingot (Pl. 14.7)
NCM: 1949.75
Published reference: Clarke 1954, 58 (cake), no. 1; pl. xiii, upper; Hd. B No. 1
Context details: Found during Clarke's excavations, Trench 2.
[Analysed: see Appendix 5]
Gold/silver alloy lump ingot, sub-circular in plan, hammered flat, with rounded edges. Clear hammer marks on each flat face.
Wt: 10.7g; L: 18.5mm; W: 16.5mm; T: 4.0mm

B.28: Copper alloy clamp (Pl. 14.7)
NCM: 1949.75.41
Published reference: Clarke 1954, 58 (Misc.), no. 1; pl. xiii, lower, Misc. 1; Hd. B No. 8
Context details: Found during Clarke's excavations, Trench 2.
[Analysed: see Ch. 18]
U-shaped copper alloy clamp, resembling a large staple. Rectangular in cross-section.
Wt: 1.1g; L: 25.0mm; T: 1.5mm

B.29–33: Five iron nails (likely post-medieval and not in fact directly associated with Hoard B)
Not pictured.
NCM: 1949.75
Published reference: Clarke 1954, 58 (Misc.), no. 3; Hd. B No. 26
Context details: Hoard B; Found during Rainbird Clarke excavations.

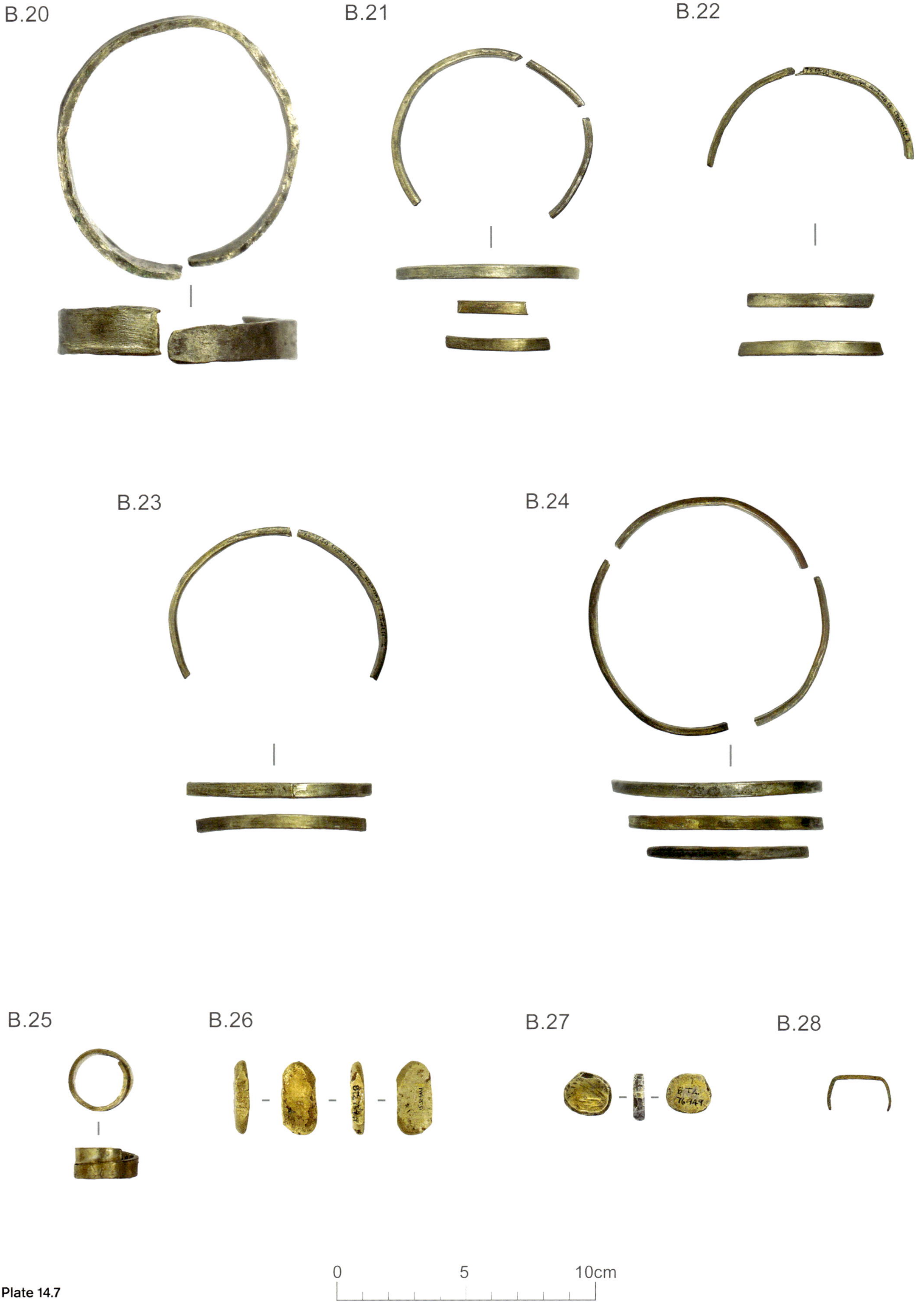

Plate 14.7

All are iron nails with rectangular-section shanks. B.29 and B.33 have circular heads.

B.29: Wt: 4.6g; D: 8.0mm (head); L: 48.0mm; W: 5.5mm; T: 5.0mm
B.30: Wt: 8.5g; L: 51.0mm; W: 10.5mm; T: 4.2mm
B.31: Wt: 7.0g; L: 66.0mm; W: 9.5mm; T: 5.0mm
B.32: Wt: 15.7g; L: 61.0mm; W: 12.0mm; T: 8.5mm
B.33: Wt: 1.4g; D: 5.5mm (head); L: 48.0mm; W: 3.0mm; T: 2.0mm

Hoard C

Found in 1948. Unless otherwise stated, objects were recovered during ploughing. Some fragments were retrieved during subsequent excavations carried out by Rainbird Clarke (1954), and this is noted in their entries; identification of excavated fragments is based on Clarke's text and information written on the objects themselves.

There is substantial confusion around the contents of Hoard B and C (see introduction to Hoard B catalogue).

Clarke published five iron nails as coming from Hoard C. These are now believed to be post-medieval (see introduction to Hoard B catalogue), but are included here for completeness as C.57–61.

C.1–5: Gold/silver alloy torc/bracelet (Pl. 14.8)

MSCC: (4C)R
NCM: 1949.75
Published reference: Clarke 1954, 47, no. 12; Hd. C No. 16
[Analysed: see Appendix 5, and Ch. 19 for identification of the wood]

Five fragments of gold/silver alloy multi-strand torc neck-ring or bracelet body, each cut or broken at both ends. Stage II construction of four circular-section wires coiled together around a hollow core.

C.1: Wt: 2.0g; D(nr): 4.0mm; D(wire): 1.0mm; L: 34.0mm
C.2: Wt: 1.8g; D(nr): 4.0mm; D(wire): 1.0mm; L: 30.0mm
C.3: Wt: 1.9g; D(nr): 4.0mm; D(wire): 1.0mm; L: 26.0mm
C.4: Wt: 1.4g; D(nr): 4.0mm; D(wire): 1.0mm; L: 19.0mm
C.5: Wt: 1.0g; D(nr): 4.0mm; D(wire): 1.0mm; L: 18.0mm

C.6: Gold/silver alloy rod/?torc/?bracelet (Pl. 14.8)

NCM: 1949.75.50
Published reference: Clarke 1954, 47, no. 9; pl. ix; Hd. C No. 12
[Analysed: see Appendix 5]
Curved fragment of circular-section gold/silver alloy rod, most likely from a multi-strand torc or bracelet. Cut at both ends.
Wt: 5.2g; D(wire): 7.0mm; L: 24.0mm

C.7–18: Gold/silver alloy rod/wire/?torc/?bracelet (Pl. 14.8)

NCM: 1949.75
[Analysed: see Appendix 5]

C.7–18 are short lengths of gold/silver alloy circular-section (or lightly faceted) rod/wire, which may originally have been part of a multi-strand torc or bracelet. The fragments are similar in form, and some may be from the same torc. Clear cut-marks show that the object, or objects, were deliberately broken up before deposition. C.14 and C.17 are likely fragments from loop terminals, the other fragments are either too short to identify (C.7, C.8, C.11, C.15, C.16, C.18) or display a curvature which suggests they are more likely to be from the neck-ring/body of a Stage II (or III) plied torc or bracelet (C.9, C.10, C.12, C.13).

C.7: Published reference: Clarke 1954, 47, no. 9; pl. ix; Hd. C No. 12
Cut at both ends, little survives.
Wt: 3.1g; D(wire): 7.0mm; L: 10.5mm

C.8: Published reference: Clarke 1954, 47, no. 9; pl. ix; Hd. C No. 12
Cut at both ends, little survives.
Wt: 3.5g; D(wire): 7.0mm; L: 14.0mm

C.9: Published reference: Clarke 1954, 47, no. 9; pl. ix; Hd. C No. 12
Context details: Found during Clarke's excavations, Trench 20.
Cut at both ends.
Wt: 10.1g; D(wire): 6.8mm; L: 20.0mm

C.10: Published reference: Clarke 1954, 47, no. 9; pl. ix; Hd. C No. 12
Cut at both ends.
Wt: 7.0g; D(wire): 6.5mm; L: 32.8mm

C.11: Published reference: Clarke 1954, 47, no. 9; pl. ix; Hd. C No. 12
Cut at both ends, little survives.
Wt: 3.3g; D(wire): 6.5mm; L: 8.5mm

C.12: Published reference: Clarke 1954, 47, no. 9; pl. ix; Hd. C No. 12
Cut at both ends, with multiple blows visible. The surface is damaged, suggesting the fragment has been hammered.
Wt: 7.6g; D(wire): 6.0mm; L: 20.0mm

C.13: Published reference: Clarke 1954, 47, no. 11; pl. ix; Hd. C No. 14
Cut at both ends.
Wt: 11.8g; D(wire): 6.0mm; L: 32.0mm

C.14: Published reference: Clarke 1954, 47, no. 10; Hd. C No. 13
Short, curved length of wire, most likely part of a loop terminal. Cut with a double-bladed implement at both ends, or possibly hammered until it broke.
Wt: 12.0g; D(wire): 6.0mm; L: 38.0mm

C.15: Published reference: Clarke 1954, 47, no. 9; pl. ix; Hd. C No. 12
Cut at both ends, little survives.

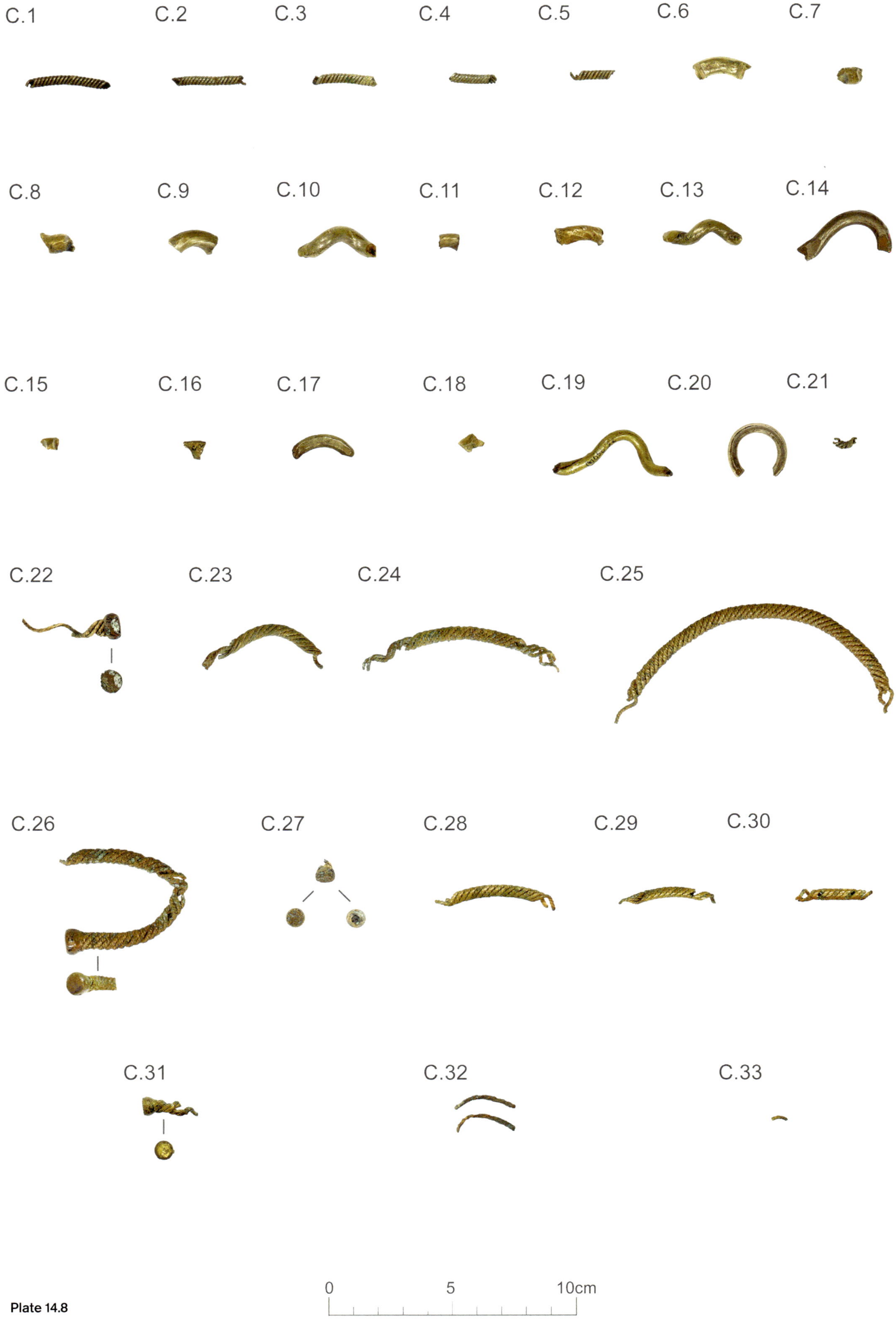
C.1
C.2
C.3
C.4
C.5
C.6
C.7
C.8
C.9
C.10
C.11
C.12
C.13
C.14
C.15
C.16
C.17
C.18
C.19
C.20
C.21
C.22
C.23
C.24
C.25
C.26
C.27
C.28
C.29
C.30
C.31
C.32
C.33
0
5
10cm

Plate 14.8

Wt: 1.2g; D(wire): 5.5mm; L: 8.3mm
C.16: Published reference: Clarke 1954, 47, no. 9; pl. ix; Hd. C No. 12
Cut at both ends, little survives.
Wt: 1.4g; D(wire): 5.0mm; L: 9.0mm; W: 7.2mm

C.17: Published reference: Clarke 1954, 58 (cake), no. 5; Hd. C No. 15
Curved length of wire, oval in cross-section at the ends, though hammered flat on the uncurved faces to give a squarish section. Cut at one end and slightly rounded at the other. Most likely from the loop terminal of a multi-strand torc.
Wt: 7.7g; D(wire): 5.0mm; L: 25.0mm

C.18: Published reference: Clarke 1954, 47, no. 9; pl. ix; Hd. C No. 12
Cut at both ends, little survives.
Wt: 1.1g; D(wire): 4.5mm; L: 10.5mm; W: 8.0mm

C.19: Gold/silver alloy wire/?torc/?bracelet (Pl. 14.8)
MSCC: (?C/P)R
NCM: 1949.75.36
Published reference: Clarke 1954, 47, no. 11; pl. ix; Hd. C No. 14
Short length of circular-section gold/silver alloy wire, cut at both ends. The curvature suggests it was either part of a loop terminal, or originally part of a Stage II coiled or plied torc neck-ring or bracelet body.
Wt: 10.6g; D(wire): 4.3mm; L: 48.2mm

C.20: Gold/silver alloy torc/bracelet (Pl. 14.8)
NCM: 1949.75
Published reference: Clarke 1954, 47, no. 11; pl. ix (this fragment not pictured); Hd. C No. 14
Curved length of circular-section gold/silver alloy wire, most likely part of the loop terminal from a multi-strand torc or bracelet. Cut at both ends.
Wt: 7.4g; D(wire): 3.8mm; D(term): 24.0mm

C.21: Gold/silver alloy torc/bracelet (Pl. 14.8)
MSCC: (??(4C))R
NCM: 1949.75
Published reference: Clarke 1954, 47, no. 12; Hd. C No. 16
[Analysed: see Appendix 5]
Fragment of gold/silver alloy multi-strand torc neck-ring or bracelet body, broken at both ends. What remains is a Stage II component of four circular-section wires coiled together. The curvature suggests it was most likely originally part of a larger Stage III plied or coiled construction.
Wt: 0.6g; D(rope): 4.0mm; D(wire): 1.0mm; L: 10.0mm

C.22: Copper alloy torc/bracelet (Pl. 14.8)
MSCC: (7C)T
NCM: 1949.75
Published reference: Clarke 1954, 52, no. 1; pl. xi, right; Hd. C No. 17
[Analysed: see Ch. 18, and see Ch. 19 for identification of the wood]
Fragment of copper alloy multi-strand torc or bracelet, comprising one buffer terminal and a short length of neck-ring/body, unevenly broken at the other end. Stage II construction of seven strands of twisted square-section wire coiled together around a hollow core. The buffer terminal is plain, slightly expanding towards the flat front face.
Wt: 3.1g; D(nr): 7.0mm; D(wire): 0.8mm; D(term): 9.7mm; L: 39.4mm

C.23: Copper alloy torc/bracelet (Pl. 14.8)
MSCC: (6C)[3T,3R, alternating]
NCM: 1949.75
Published reference: Clarke 1954, 47, no. 22; Hd. C No. 19
[Analysed: see Ch. 18]
Fragment of copper alloy multi-strand torc neck-ring or bracelet body, cut or broken at both ends. Stage II construction of six wires coiled together around a hollow core. Three are circular-section, three are twisted square-section wires, with the two types alternating.
Wt: 4.8g; D(nr): 5.0mm; D(wire): 1.5mm; L: 48.5mm

C.24: Copper alloy torc/bracelet (Pl. 14.8)
MSCC: (6C)T
NCM: 1949.75
Published reference: Clarke 1954, 47, no. 22; Hd. C No. 19
[Analysed: see Ch. 18]
Fragment of copper alloy multi-strand torc neck-ring or bracelet body, broken at both ends, with the wires ending at different points. Stage II construction of six twisted square-section wires coiled together around a hollow core.
Wt: 6.6g; D(nr): 6.0mm; D(wire): 1.4mm; L: 79.0mm

C.25–7: Copper alloy torc/bracelet (Pl. 14.8)
MSCC: (5C)T
[Analysed: see Ch. 18]
Three fragments of copper alloy multi-strand buffer terminal torc/bracelet with Stage II construction of five strands of twisted square-section wire coiled together around a hollow core. The buffer terminals are plain, slightly expanding towards the flat front face.

C.25: NCM: 1949.75.12
Published reference: Clarke 1954, 52, no. 2; pl. xi, right; Hd. C No. 18
Fragment of copper alloy multi-strand torc neck-ring or bracelet body, broken at both ends, with the wires ending at different points.
Wt: 17.2g; D(nr): 6.0mm; D(wire): 1.2mm; L: 112.5mm

C.26: NCM: 1949.75.54
Published reference: Clarke 1954, 52, no. 1; pl. xi, right; Hd. C No. 17
[Analysed: see Ch. 19 for identification of wood]
Fragment of copper alloy multi-strand torc or bracelet, comprising one buffer terminal and a short length of neck-ring/body, broken at the other end. The whole fragment has been bent into a rough U-shape, with significant damage to the neck-ring wires at the base of the 'U'.
Wt: 13.7g; D(nr): 6.0mm; D(wire): 1.2mm; D(term): 10.0mm; L: 51.0mm

C.27: NCM: 1949.75
[Analysed: see Ch. 19 for identification of wood]
Published reference: Clarke 1954, 52, no. 3 (left); pl. xi, right; Hd. C No. 20
Fragment of copper alloy multi-strand torc or bracelet, comprising one buffer terminal and a short length of neck-ring/body, unevenly broken at the other end.
Wt: 1.7g; D(nr): 6.2mm; D(wire): 1.0mm; D(term): 8.0mm; L: 8.8mm

C.28–30: Copper alloy torc/bracelet (Pl. 14.8)
MSCC: (5C)T
NCM: 1949.75
Published reference: Clarke 1954, 47, no. 22; Hd. C No. 19
[Analysed: see Ch. 18]
Three fragments of copper alloy multi-strand torc neck-ring or bracelet body, each cut or broken at both ends, with the wires ending at different points. Stage II construction of five twisted square-section wires coiled together around a hollow core. Very pronounced wear on interior surfaces.

C.28: Wt: 3.0g; D(nr): 4.0mm; D(wire): 1.1mm; L: 45.0mm

C.29: Wt: 2.4g; D(nr): 4.0mm; D(wire): 1.1mm; L: 39.0mm

C.30: Wt: 1.9g; D(nr): 4.0mm; D(wire): 1.1mm; L: 31.0mm
Fragment shows traces of an organic core.

C.31: Copper alloy torc/bracelet (Pl. 14.8)
MSCC: (3P(2P))Q
NCM: 1949.75.53
Published reference: Clarke 1954, 52, no. 3 (right); pl. xi, right; Hd. C No. 20
[Analysed: see Ch. 18, and Ch. 19 for identification of wood]
Fragment of copper alloy multi-strand torc or bracelet, comprising one simple buffer terminal with flat face and convex edge, and short length of neck-ring/body, broken at the other end. Stage III construction of three ropes plied together, each formed from two square-section wires plied together.
Wt: 2.8g; D(nr): 6.0mm; D(rope): 3.0mm; D(wire): 1.0mm; D(term): 8.0mm; L: 23.0mm

C.32: Copper alloy wire/?torc/?bracelet (Pl. 14.8)
MSCC: (?C)T
NCM: 1949.75
Two fragments of twisted copper alloy wire, each broken at both ends. Possibly originally part of a Stage II coiled torc or bracelet.
Wt: 0.9g; D(wire): 1.8mm; L: 23.8mm (max.)

C.33: Copper alloy wire/?torc/?bracelet (Pl. 14.8)
MSCC: (?P/C)T
NCM: 1949.75
Short length of twisted square-section copper alloy wire, cut or broken at both ends. The curvature suggests it was originally part of a Stage II coiled or plied multi-strand torc or bracelet.
Wt: 0.1g; D(wire): 1.5mm; L: 6.5mm

C.34–6: Copper alloy torc/bracelet (Pl. 14.9)
MSCC: (?C)T
NCM: 1949.75
These groups each comprise short lengths of twisted square-section copper alloy wire, of similar diameter. Each fragment is broken at both ends and coiled in a way which suggests it originally formed part of a Stage II coiled multi-strand torc or bracelet. They have been grouped according to the tightness of the coil, where the fragments are long enough for this to be discerned, but some or all of these fragments could be from the same object.

C.34: Thirty-seven fragments, tightly coiled. Wt: 9.1g (total); D(nr): *c.* 6.0mm; D(wire): 1.3mm; L: 44.0mm (max.)
C.35: Seventy-eight fragments, loosely coiled. In one case, two adjoining strands from the coil remain.
Wt: 20.6g (total); D(nr): *c.* 4.0–6.5mm; D(wire): 1.3mm; L: 42.0mm (max.)

C.36: Sixty-four short fragments.
Wt: 5.6g (total); D(wire): 1.3mm; L: 10.0mm (max.)

C.37: Copper alloy wire/?torc/?bracelet (Pl. 14.9)
MSCC: (?C)T
NCM: 1949.75
Short fragment of twisted square-section copper alloy wire, broken at both ends. The curvature suggests it may have originally been part of a Stage II coiled or plied multi-strand torc or bracelet.
Wt: 0.2g; D(wire): 1.0mm; L: 9.5mm

C.38: Copper alloy wire/?torc/?bracelet (Pl. 14.9)
MSCC: (?P/C)Q
NCM: 1949.75
Short fragment of square-section copper alloy wire, cut or broken at both ends. The curvature suggests it may have originally been part of a Stage II coiled or plied multi-strand torc or bracelet. Some splitting/laminating of the wire.
Wt: 0.2g; D(wire): 1.8mm; L: 11.5mm

C.39: Copper alloy wire/?torc/?bracelet (Pl. 14.9)
NCM: 1949.75
Short fragment of square-section copper alloy wire, broken at both ends. Perhaps originally part of a multi-strand torc neck-ring or bracelet body.
Wt: 0.1g; D(wire): 0.8mm; L: 8.5mm

C.40: Copper alloy wire/?torc/?bracelet (Pl. 14.9)
MSCC: (?P/C)R
NCM: 1949.75
Five fragments of circular-section copper alloy wire, cut or broken at both ends. The loose curvature suggests they may have originally been part of a Stage II coiled or plied multi-strand torc or bracelet.
Wt: 0.9g; D(wire): 1.5mm; L: 15.0mm (max.)

C.41: Copper alloy wire/?torc/?bracelet (Pl. 14.9)
MSCC: (?P/C)R
NCM: 1949.75
Two fragments of circular-section copper alloy wire, cut or broken at both ends. The tight curvature suggests they were

originally part of a Stage II coiled or plied multi-strand torc or bracelet.
Wt: 0.3g; D(wire): 1.2mm; L: 7.0mm (max.)

C.42: Copper alloy wire/?torc/?bracelet (Pl. 14.9)
MSCC: (?P/C)R
NCM: 1949.75
Two fragments of circular-section copper alloy wire, each broken at both ends. The curvature suggests they may originally have part of a Stage II coiled or plied multi-strand torc or bracelet.
Wt: 0.3g; D(wire): 1.2mm; L: 10.0mm (max.)

C.43: Copper alloy torc/bracelet (Pl. 14.9)
MSCC: (?C)R
NCM: 1949.75
Twenty-three fragments of circular-section copper alloy wire, each cut or broken at both ends and loosely coiled in a way which suggests it originally formed part of a Stage II coiled torc or bracelet.
Wt: 7.3g; D(wire): 1.2mm; L: 35.3mm (max.)

C.44: Copper alloy wire/?torc/?bracelet (Pl. 14.9)
NCM: 1949.75
Short length of circular-section copper alloy wire, cut or broken at both ends. Possibly from a multi-strand torc or bracelet.
Wt: 0.5g; D(wire): 2.0mm; L: 20.0mm

C.45: Gold/silver alloy large ring (Pl. 14.10)
NCM: 1949.75.51
Published reference: Clarke 1954, 58 (cake), no. 4; pl. xiii, upper; Hd. C No. 2
[Analysed: see Appendix 5]
Gold/silver alloy large ring made from a thick bar with cross-section varying from squarish to rectangular. Coiled into a tight, flattened spiral. Broken into three pieces at the tight bends where the spiral has been crushed flat. One end tapered, one flat, cut end.
Wt: 58.1g; L: 58.0mm; W: 9.0mm; T: 4.5mm

C.46: Gold/silver alloy large ring (Pl. 14.10)
NCM: 1949.75.41
Published reference: Clarke 1954, 54, no. 1; Hd. C No. 3
[Analysed: see Appendix 5]
Complete gold/silver alloy large ring (joined from three fragments), made from a strip with rectangular cross-section. Overlapping ends, each blunt, but slightly tapered.
Wt: 22.7g; D(ext): 40.0mm; W: 6.8mm; T: 3.2mm

C.47: Gold/silver alloy small ring (Pl. 14.10)
NCM: 1949.75.6
Published reference: Clarke 1954, 56, no. 15; pl. xii; Hd. C No. 6
[Analysed: see Appendix 5]
Complete gold/silver alloy small spiral ring, made from a strip with rectangular cross-section. Around two complete turns. Blunt, slightly tapered ends.
Wt: 12.0g; D(ext): 19.5mm; W: 3.5mm; T: 1.8mm

C.48: Copper alloy small ring (Pl. 14.10)
NCM: 1949.75
Published reference: Clarke 1954, 55, no. 2; Hd. C No. 4
[Analysed: see Ch. 18]
Complete copper alloy small ring (joined from three fragments), made from a strip with rectangular cross-section. Overlapping, slightly tapered ends.
Wt: 11.6g; D(ext): 33.0mm; W: 7.0mm; T: 2.5mm

C.49: Copper alloy small ring (Pl. 14.10)
NCM: 1949.75
Published reference: Clarke 1954, 55, no. 3; Hd. C No. 5
[Analysed: see Ch. 18]
Complete copper alloy small ring with overlapping tapered terminals, made from a strip with rectangular cross-section.
Wt: 11.4g; D(ext): 30.0mm; W: 5.2mm; T: 3.0mm

C.50: Gold/silver alloy sheet (Pl. 14.10)
NCM: 1949.75
Published reference: Clarke 1954, 58 (cake), no. 3; pl. xiii, upper, 3; Hd. C No. 11
[Analysed: see Appendix 5]
Small fragment of gold/silver alloy sheet, folded and hammered. Possibly originally part of a tubular torc or sheet terminal component.
Wt: 0.7g; L: 11.4mm; T: 1.8mm (max.), sheet *c.* 0.3mm

C.51: Copper alloy rivet head (Pl. 14.10)
NCM: 1949.75.57
Published reference: Clarke 1954, 57, no. 5; pl. xiii, lower; Hd. C No. 8
Hollow, circular, dome-shaped copper alloy rivet head or boss, with ragged outer edge. Made from thin sheet.
Wt: 0.9g; D(ext): 14.0mm

C.52: Copper alloy rivet head (Pl. 14.10)
NCM: 1949.75.58
Published reference: Clarke 1954, 57, no. 3; pl. xiii, lower; Hd. C No. 9
Hollow, circular, dome-shaped copper alloy rivet head with pierced central hole. Made from thin sheet.
Wt: 0.7g; D(ext): 12.0mm

C.53: Copper alloy rivet head (Pl. 14.10)
NCM: 1949.75.58
Published reference: Clarke 1954, 57, no. 3; pl. xiii, lower; Hd. C No. 9
Hollow, circular, dome-shaped copper alloy rivet head with raggedly broken outer edge. Made from thin sheet, with remains of circular-section shank protruding from centre on reverse.
Wt: 0.7g; D(ext): 10.0mm

C.54: Copper alloy binding strip/fitting (Pl. 14.10)
NCM: 1949.75.45
Published reference: Clarke 1954, 57, no. 2; pl. xiii, lower; Hd. C No. 7
[Analysed: see Ch. 18]
Arc of thin copper alloy U-shaped binding strip, or possibly section from the outer cover of an iron ring or fitting such as a bridle-bit side-link. Decorated on the exterior with two

C.34

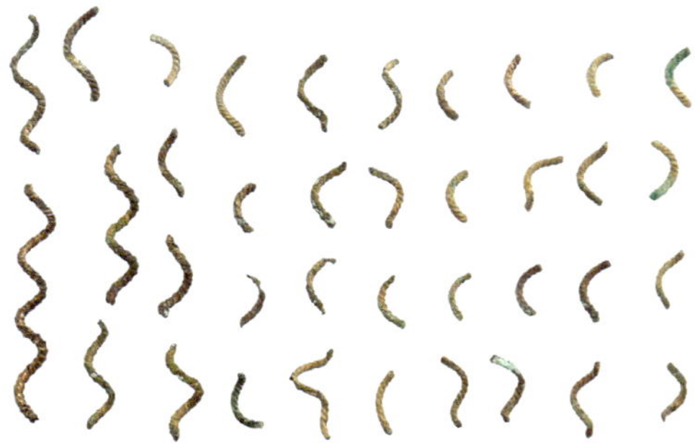

C.35

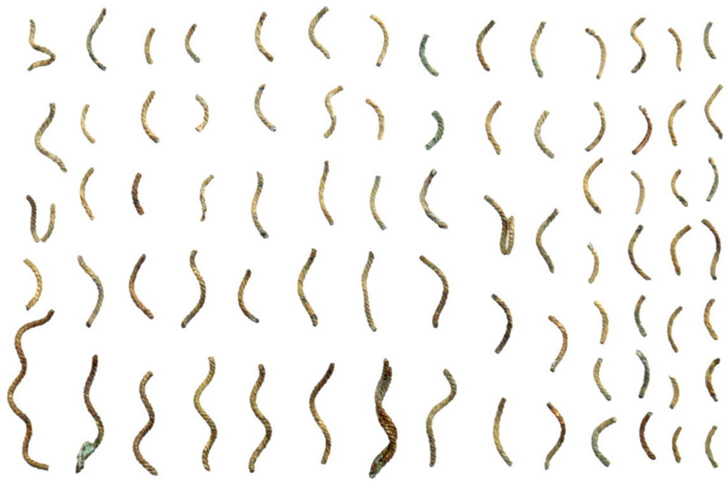

C.36

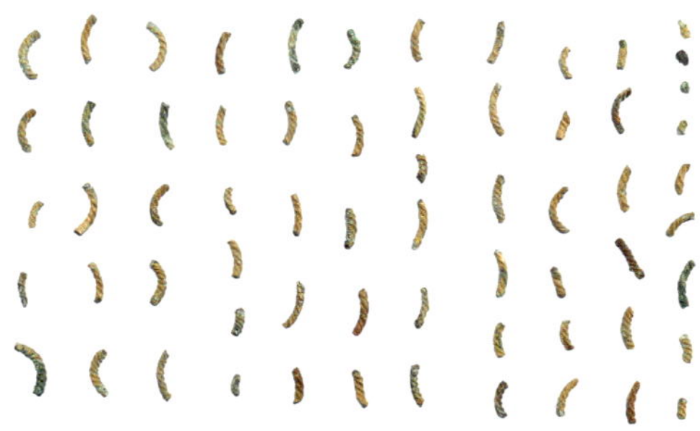

C.37

C.38

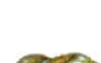

C.39

C.40

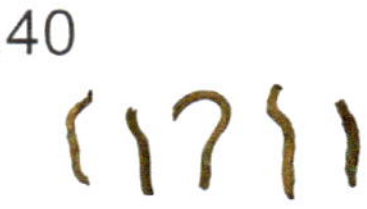

C.41

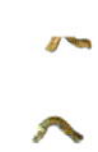

C.42

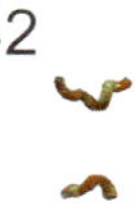

C.43

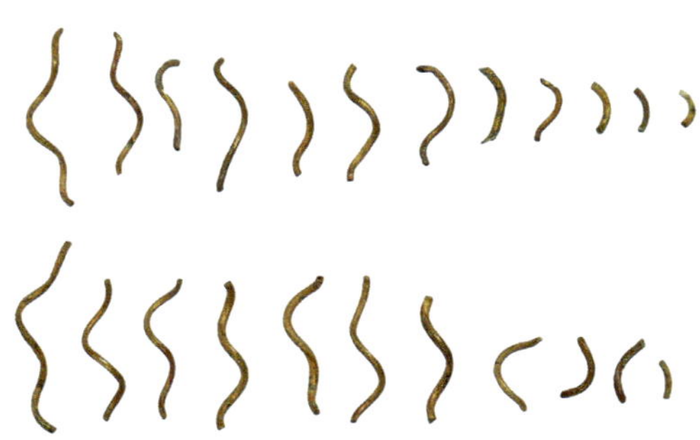

C.44

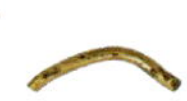

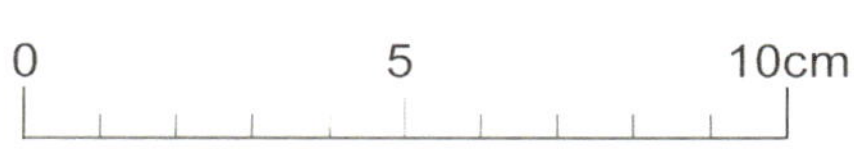

Plate 14.9

C.45

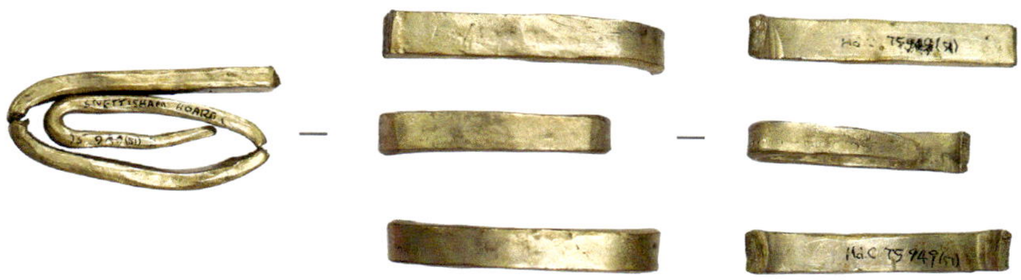

C.46

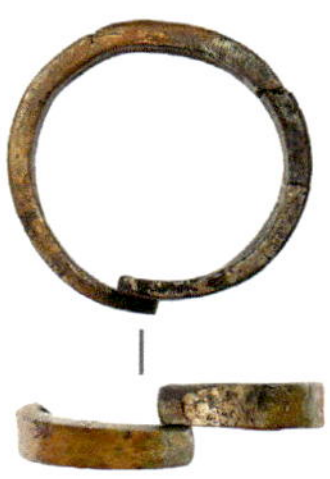

C.47

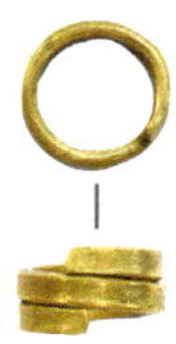

C.48

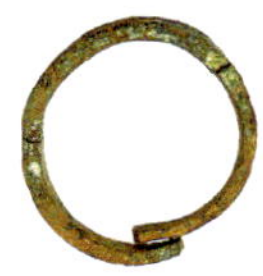

C.49

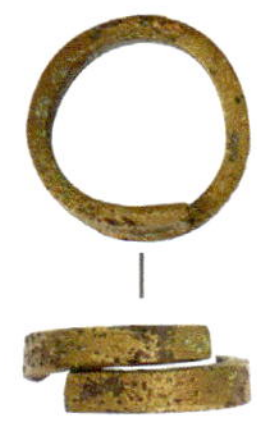

C.50

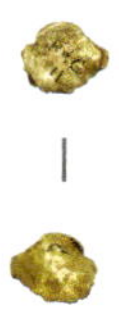

C.51

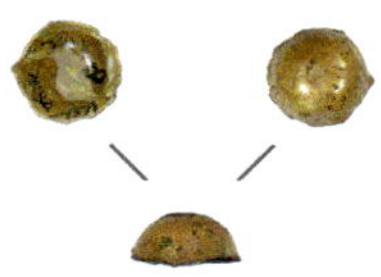

C.52

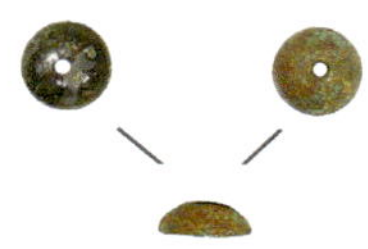

C.53

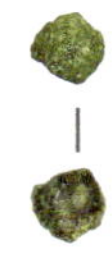

C.54

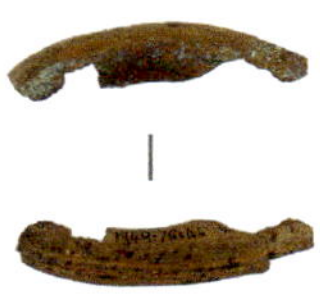

C.55

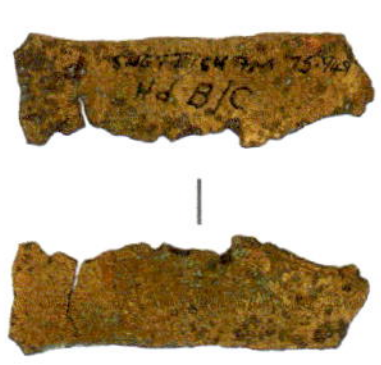

C.56

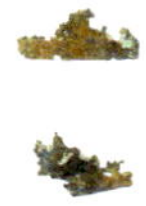

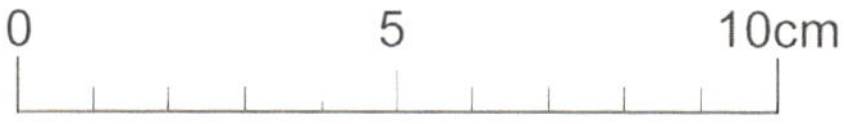

Plate 14.10

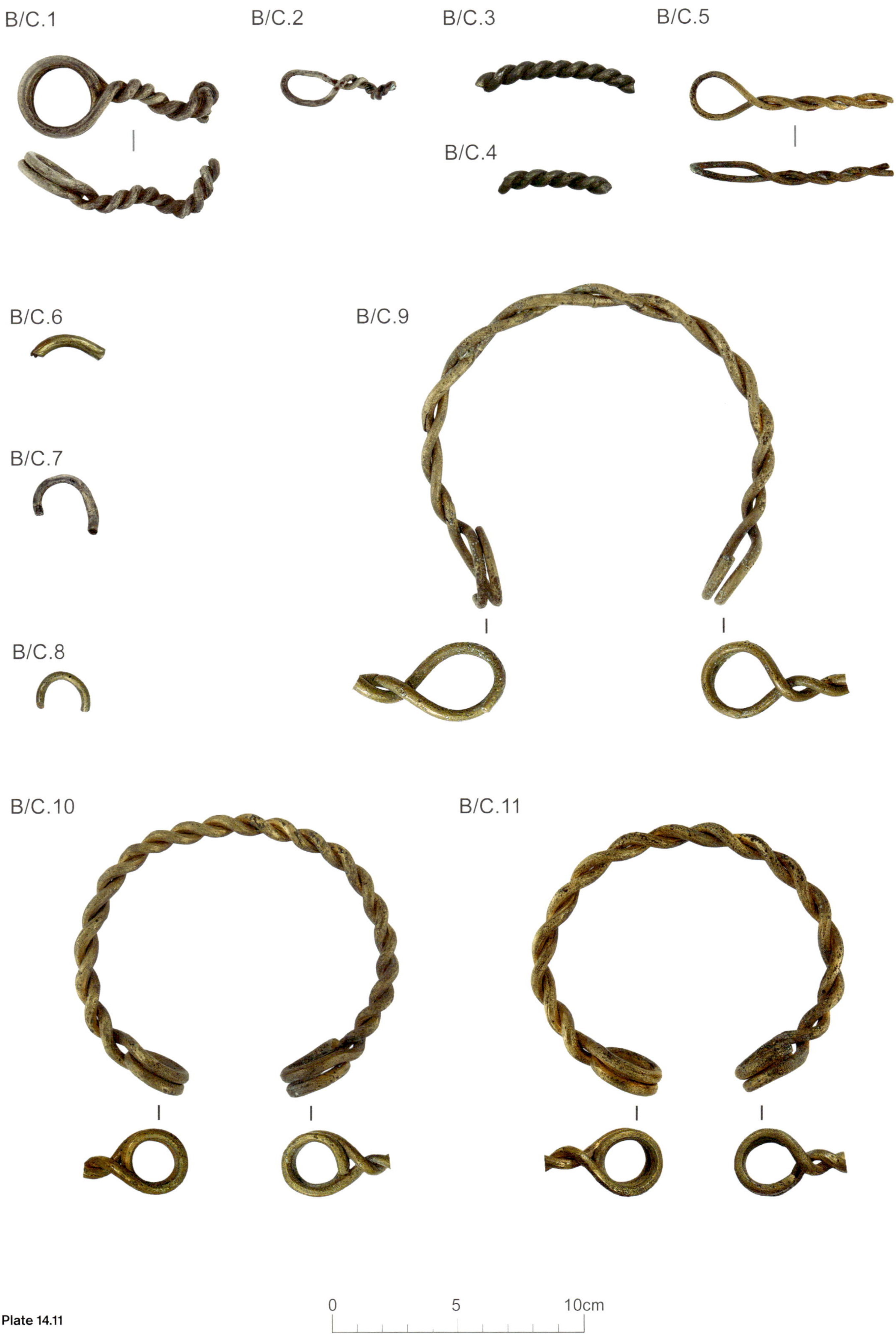

Plate 14.11

grooved lines down the centre, parallel to the curve of the arc.
Wt: 2.1g; L: 39.0mm; W: 8.0mm; T: 0.3mm

C.55: Copper alloy sheet (Pl. 14.10)
NCM: 1949.75
Published reference: Clarke 1954, 57, no. 6; Hd. C No. 10
Copper alloy sheet fragment with at least one curved original edge. Other edges probably broken.
Wt: 2.6g; L: 47.0mm; W: 14.8mm; T: 0.5mm

C.56: Copper alloy sheet (Pl. 14.10)
NCM: 1949.75
Published reference: Clarke 1954, 57, no. 6; Hd. C No. 10
Context details: Found during Clarke's excavations, Trench 20.
Two small copper alloy sheet fragments, each with one possible original straight edge.
Wt: 0.2g; L: 16.0mm (max.); T: 0.3mm

C.57–61: Five iron nails (likely post-medieval, see note in introduction to Hoard B catalogue)
Not pictured.
NCM: 1949.75
Published reference: Clarke 1954, 58 (Misc.), no. 4; fig. 9; Hd. C No. 1
Context details: Found during Clarke's excavations.
These nails were not seen at NCM; descriptions are based on a photocopy taken by Peter Northover in the 1980s (a copy of this image is held in the BM archive).

C.57-8: Iron nails with circular heads and rectangular-section shanks.
C.59-61: Iron nails with rectangular-section shanks.

Hoard B/C

Found in 1948. Material from Hoards B and C which became intermixed shortly after discovery and cannot be securely assigned to either hoard (see Ch. 4 and introduction to Hoard B catalogue).

B/C.1: Gold/silver alloy torc/bracelet (Pl. 14.11)
MSCC: (?2P(2P))R
NCM: 1949.75.49
Published reference: Clarke 1954, 47, no. 16; pl. ix; Hd. B/C No. 26
[Analysed: see Appendix 5]
Fragment of gold/silver alloy multi-strand torc or bracelet, comprising a double-loop terminal and a short length of neck-ring/body, cut at the other end. What remains of the neck-ring/body is a Stage II component formed from two circular-section wires plied tightly together. The wires are twisted in such a way as to suggest that they are more likely to have been part of a larger Stage III construction, perhaps a triple-loop terminal with (2P(2P))R neck-ring.
Wt: 38.2g; D(rope): 7.5mm; D(wire): 3.0mm; D(term): 27.2mm; L: 80.0mm

B/C.2: Gold/silver alloy torc/bracelet (Pl. 14.11)
MSCC: (?2P(2P))R
NCM: 1949.75
Published reference: Clarke 1954, 47, no. 18; pl. ix; Hd. B/C No. 28
[Analysed: see Appendix 5]
Fragment of gold/silver alloy multi-strand torc or bracelet, comprising a single-loop terminal and a short length of neck-ring/body, cut or broken at the other end. What remains of the neck-ring/body is a Stage II component formed from two circular-section wires plied together. The wires are twisted in such a way as to suggest that they are more likely to have been part of a larger Stage III construction, perhaps a double- or triple-loop terminal with (2P(2P))R neck-ring.
Wt: 6.3g; D(nr): *c.* 10.0mm; D(rope): 4.5mm; D(wire): 2.3mm; D(term): 24.0mm; L: 46.0mm

B/C.3–4: Gold/silver alloy torc/bracelet (Pl. 14.11)
MSCC: (2P)R
NCM: 1949.75
Published reference: Clarke 1954, 48, no. 47; pl. ix; Hd. B/C No. 53
[Analysed: see Appendix 5]

B/C.3 and B/C.4 are two joining fragments of the same gold/silver alloy torc neck-ring or bracelet body, with Stage II construction of two circular-section wires plied together.
B/C.3: Broken at both ends.
Wt: 17.0g; D(nr): 7.0mm; D(wire): 3.2mm; L: 60.0mm
B/C.4: Cut at one end and broken at the other (where it joins B/C.3).
Wt: 11.2g; D(nr): 7.0mm; D(wire): 3.2mm; L: 45.0mm

B/C.5: Gold/silver alloy torc/bracelet (Pl. 14.11)
MSCC: (2PZ)Q
NCM: 1949.75.29
Published reference: Clarke 1954, 48, no. 44; pl. ix; Hd. B/C No. 50
[Analysed: see Appendix 5]
Fragment of gold/silver alloy multi-strand torc or bracelet, comprising one single-loop terminal and a length of neck-ring/body, cut or broken at the other end. Stage II construction of two square-section wires plied together Z-twist. The wires are circular-section in the area of the terminal.
Wt: 9.9g; D(nr): 6.0mm; D(wire): 2.0mm; D(term): 20.0mm; L: 81.0mm

B/C.6: Gold/silver alloy wire/?torc/?bracelet (Pl. 14.11)
NCM: 1949.75
Published reference: Clarke 1954, 47, no. 17; pl. ix; Hd. B/C No. 27
[Analysed: see Appendix 5]
Curved fragment of circular cross-section gold/silver alloy wire, most likely from a multi-strand torc or bracelet. Cut at one end, original flat end at the other. Perhaps part of a loop terminal.
Wt: 6.2g; D(wire): 5.0mm; L: 30.0mm

B/C.7–8: Gold/silver alloy torc/bracelet (Pl. 14.11)
NCM: 1949.75
Published reference: Clarke 1954, 48, no. 36; pl. ix; Hd. B/C

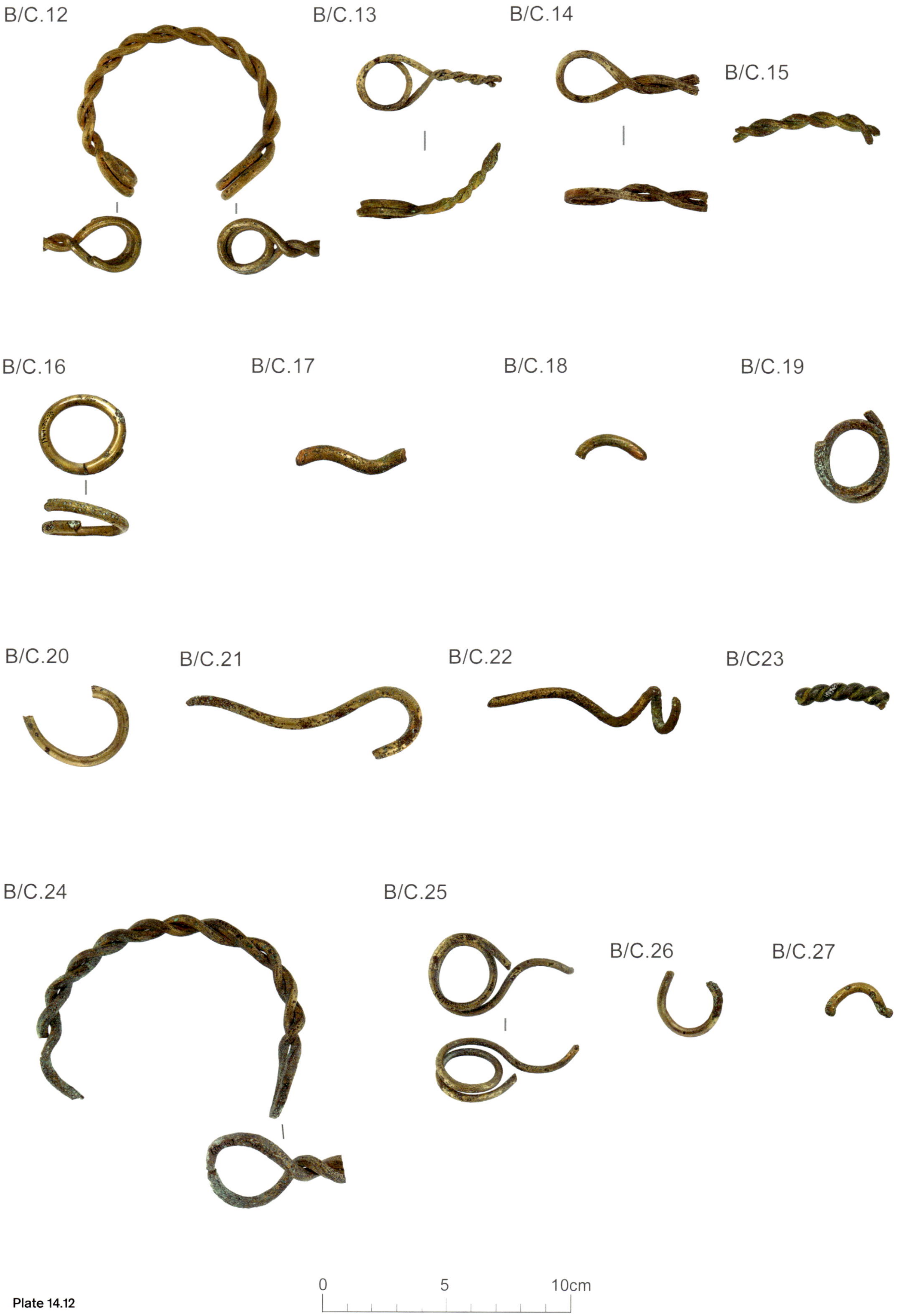

B/C.12
B/C.13
B/C.14
B/C.15
B/C.16
B/C.17
B/C.18
B/C.19
B/C.20
B/C.21
B/C.22
B/C23
B/C.24
B/C.25
B/C.26
B/C.27
0
5
10cm

Plate 14.12

No. 42
[Analysed: see Appendix 5]

B/C.7–8 are two joining fragments of the same loop terminal from a gold/silver alloy multi-strand torc or bracelet, and they are shown together in Clarke (1954). Each is a curved fragment of circular-section wire.

B/C.7: Broken both ends.
Wt: 5.4g; D(wire): 4.0mm; L: 30.0mm

B/C.8: Broken at one end, and flat at the other.
Wt: 3.6g; D(wire): 4.0mm; L: 22.0mm

B/C.9: Copper alloy torc (Pl. 14.11)
MSCC: (2PZ)R
NCM: 1949.75.9
Published reference: Clarke 1954, 48, no. 33; pl. viii; Hd. B/C No. 39

[Analysed: see Ch. 18]
Complete copper alloy multi-strand torc with double-loop terminals. Stage II neck-ring formed from two circular-section wires plied together Z-twist. Each open-loop terminal is formed from the ends of the two separate neck-ring wires, with each wire ending in a hook at each end.
Wt: 117.8g; D(ext): 144.5mm; D(nr): 8.8mm; D(wire): 4.0mm; D(term): 31.5mm

B/C.10: Copper alloy torc (Pl. 14.11)
MSCC: (2PZ)R
NCM: 1949.75.3
Published reference: Clarke 1954, 47, no. 31; pl. viii; Hd. B/C No. 37
[Analysed: see Ch. 18]
Complete copper alloy multi-strand torc with double-loop terminals and a Stage II neck-ring formed from two circular-section wires plied together Z-twist. One terminal is continuous with the neck-ring wires, while at the other each loop is open.
Wt: 130.6g; D(ext): 128.8mm; D(nr): 9.5mm; D(wire): 5.0mm; D(term): 26.5mm

B/C.11: Copper alloy torc (Pl. 14.11)
MSCC: (2PZ)F
NCM: 1949.75.7
Published reference: Clarke 1954, 48, no. 32; pl. viii; Hd. B/C No. 38
[Analysed: see Ch. 18]
Complete copper alloy multi-strand torc with double-loop terminals and a Stage II neck-ring formed from two slightly faceted wires plied together Z-twist. One terminal is continuous with the neck-ring wires, while at the other each loop is open.
Wt: 128.7g; D(ext): 124.5mm; D(nr): 9.5mm; D(wire): 5.0mm; D(term): 27.5mm

B/C.12: Copper alloy bracelet (Pl. 14.12)
MSCC: (2PZ)F
NCM: 1949.75.4
Published reference: Clarke 1954, 47, no. 30; pl. viii; Hd. B/C No. 36
[Analysed: see Ch. 18]
Complete copper alloy multi-strand bracelet with double-loop terminals and a Stage II neck-ring formed from two slightly faceted wires plied together Z-twist. One terminal is continuous with the neck-ring wires, while at the other each loop is open.
Wt: 50.4g; D(ext): 82.0mm; D(nr): 7.0mm; D(wire): 3.2mm; D(term): 23.0mm

B/C.13: Copper alloy torc/bracelet (Pl. 14.12)
MSCC: (2P)Q
NCM: 1949.75
Published reference: Clarke 1954, 48, no. 41; pl. ix; Hd. B/C No. 47
[Analysed: see Ch. 18]
Fragment of copper alloy multi-strand torc or bracelet, comprising one continuous double-loop terminal and a length of neck-ring/body, cut at the other end. The Stage II neck-ring is formed from two square-section wires plied together.
Wt: 10.2g; D(nr): 5.0mm; D(wire): 2.0mm; D(term): 25.0mm; L: 59.0mm

B/C.14–15: Copper alloy torc/bracelet (Pl. 14.12)
MSCC: (2PZ)Q
NCM: 1949.75
[Analysed: see Ch. 18]

B/C.14–15 are most likely from the same copper alloy multi-strand torc or bracelet, with Stage II neck-ring/body formed from two square-section wires plied together Z-twist.

B/C.14: Published reference: Clarke 1954, 48, no. 45; pl. ix; Hd. B/C No. 51
Fragment comprising one continuous single-loop terminal and a short length of neck-ring/body, cut at the other end.
Wt: 11.8g; D(nr): 7.0mm; D(wire): 2.8mm; D(term): 21.5mm; L: 58.0mm

B/C.15: Published reference: Clarke 1954, 48, no. 48; pl. ix; Hd. B/C No. 54
Fragment of torc neck-ring or bracelet body, cut at both ends.
Wt: 8.6g; D(nr): 7.0mm; D(wire): 2.8mm; L: 59.0mm

B/C.16: Copper alloy torc/bracelet (Pl. 14.12)
NCM: 1949.75.20
Published reference: Clarke 1954, 48, no. 38; pl. ix; Hd. B/C No. 44
[Analysed: see Ch. 18]
Copper alloy loop terminal fragment from multi-strand torc or bracelet. What remains is a single-loop of circular-section wire, broken at both ends. Probably originally part of at least a double-loop terminal.
Wt: 16.4g; D(ext): 35.0mm; D(wire): 5.0mm

B/C.17: Copper alloy wire/?torc/?bracelet (Pl. 14.12)
MSCC: (?2P)R
NCM: 1949.75

Published reference: Clarke 1954, 48, no. 40; pl. ix; Hd. B/C No. 46
[Analysed: see Ch. 18]
Short length of copper alloy circular-section wire, broken at one end, cut at the other. Curved in a way which suggests it originally formed part of a Stage II construction in a multi-strand torc or bracelet, most likely two such wires plied together.
Wt: 11.7g; D(wire): 5.8mm; L: 45.0mm

B/C.18: Copper alloy wire/?torc/?bracelet (Pl. 14.12)
NCM: 1949.75
Published reference: Clarke 1954, 48, no. 40; pl. ix; Hd. B/C No. 46
[Analysed: see Ch. 18]
Curved fragment of circular cross-section copper alloy wire, cut at one end and rounded at the other. Most likely from the loop terminal of a multi-strand torc or bracelet.
Wt: 6.3g; D(wire): 5.5mm; L: 29.0mm

B/C.19– 22: Copper alloy torc/bracelet (Pl. 14.12)
[Analysed: see Ch. 18]
B/C.19–22 are copper alloy wire fragments of similar diameter which could represent parts of the same loop-terminal multi-strand torc or bracelet.

B/C.19: NCM: 1949.75
Published reference: Clarke 1954, 48, no. 35; pl. ix; Hd. B/C No. 41
Part of a double-loop terminal, made from wire with a circular cross-section. Cut or broken at both ends. Wt: 20.3g; D(wire): 4.5mm; D(term): 31.0mm; L: 39.5mm

B/C.20: NCM: 1949.75
Published reference: Clarke 1954, 48, no. 39; pl. ix; Hd. B/C No. 45
Curved fragment of circular cross-section copper alloy wire, broken at both ends. Perhaps part of a loop terminal.
Wt: 11.2g; D(wire): 4.5mm; L: 43.0mm

B/C.21: NCM: 1949.75
Published reference: Clarke 1954, 48, no. 40; pl. ix (top left, mis-labelled in the plate as no. 42); Hd. B/C No. 46
Bent and curved fragment of circular cross-section copper alloy wire, perhaps part of a loop terminal and start of the neck-ring/body. Broken at one end and flat at the curved end which may form the terminal.
Wt: 19.2g; D(wire): 4.5mm; L: 95.0mm

B/C.22: NCM: 1949.75.20
Published reference: Clarke 1954, 48, no. 40; pl. ix; Hd. B/C No. 46
Distorted coil of circular-section copper alloy wire which may represent a damaged double-loop terminal. The wire extends as a single strand into what would have been the beginning of the neck-ring/body and is cut at the end.
Wt: 16.7g; D(wire): 4.5mm; L: 78.0mm

B/C.23: Copper alloy torc/bracelet (Pl. 14.12)
MSCC: (2P)R
NCM: 1949.75.47
Fragment of copper alloy multi-strand torc neck-ring or bracelet body, cut or broken at both ends. Stage II construction of two circular-section wires plied together.
Wt: 11.5g; D(nr): 7.0mm; D(wire): 4.4mm; L: 38.0mm

B/C.24: Copper alloy torc/bracelet (Pl. 14.12)
MSCC: (2PZ)Q
NCM: 1949.75.27
Published reference: Clarke 1954, 48, no. 43; pl. viii; Hd. B/C No. 49
[Analysed: see Ch. 18]
Fragment of copper alloy multi-strand torc or bracelet, comprising one single-loop terminal and a length of neck-ring/body, cut or broken at the other end, with one wire extending slightly further than the other. Stage II construction of two square-section wires plied together Z-twist. The terminal is an open loop, formed from the ends of the neck-ring wires, which abut at the very end of the terminal.
Wt: 55.5g; D(nr): 8.0mm; D(wire): 4.0mm; D(term): 30.5mm; L: 108.0mm

B/C.25: Copper alloy torc/bracelet (Pl. 14.12)
NCM: 1949.75.25
Published reference: Clarke 1954, 48, no. 37; pl. ix; Hd. B/C No. 43
[Analysed: see Ch. 18]
Part of a double-loop terminal from a multi-strand copper alloy torc or bracelet, made from wire with a circular cross-section. The wire extends as a single strand to form the beginning of the neck-ring, cut at the end.
Wt: 15.7g; D(wire): 4.0mm; D(term): 7.8mm; L: 59.0mm

B/C.26–31: Copper alloy torc/bracelet (Pls 14.12–14.13)
NCM: 1949.75
Published reference: Clarke 1954, 48, no. 40; pl. ix; Hd. B/C No. 46
[Analysed: see Ch. 18]
B/C.26–30 are all curved fragments of circular-section copper alloy wire, and may be part of the same multi-strand torc or bracelet; B/C.31 (and B/C.32–4) may also be part of the same object. B/C.26 is likely part of a loop terminal, while the other fragments are from the neck-ring/body.

B/C.26: Most likely part of a loop terminal. Broken at both ends.
Wt: 6.0g; D(wire): 3.8mm; D(term): 27.2mm; L: 27.0mm

B/C.27: Broken at both ends.
Wt: 3.7g; D(wire): 3.8mm; L: 27.5mm

B/C.28: Broken at both ends.
Wt: 3.5g; D(wire): 4.0mm; L: 23.8mm

B/C.29: Broken at both ends.
Wt: 4.0g; D(wire): 4.0mm; L: 18.6mm

B/C.30: Broken at one end and possibly cut at the other.
Wt: 2.2g; D(wire): 3.9mm; L: 18.8mm

B/C.31: Broken at both ends.
Wt: 14.3g; D(wire): 3.9mm; L: 98.0mm

B/C.32: Copper alloy wire/?torc/?bracelet (Pl. 14.13)
NCM: 1949.75
Published reference: Clarke 1954, 48, no. 40; pl. ix; Hd. B/C No. 46
[Analysed: see Ch. 18]
Curved fragment of circular cross-section copper alloy wire, perhaps part of a multi-strand torc or bracelet. Broken at one end and cut at the other.
Wt: 6.2g; D(wire): 4.0mm; L: 53.0mm

B/C.33: Copper alloy wire/?torc/?bracelet (Pl. 14.13)
NCM: 1949.75
Published reference: Clarke 1954, 48, no. 40; pl. ix; Hd. B/C No. 46
[Analysed: see Ch. 18]
Curved fragment of circular cross-section copper alloy wire, perhaps part of a multi-strand torc or bracelet. Broken at both ends.
Wt: 2.2g; D(wire): 4.0mm; L: 26.8mm

B/C.34: Copper alloy wire/?torc/?bracelet (Pl. 14.13)
NCM: 1949.75
Published reference: Clarke 1954, 48, no. 40; pl. ix; Hd. B/C No. 46
[Analysed: see Ch. 18]
Curved fragment of circular cross-section copper alloy wire, perhaps part of a multi-strand torc or bracelet. Broken at both ends.
Wt: 1.9g; D(wire): 3.7mm; L: 20.0mm

B/C.35: Copper alloy torc/bracelet (Pl. 14.13)
MSCC: (2PZ)R
NCM: 1949.75.28
Published reference: Clarke 1954, 48, no. 42; pl. ix; Hd. B/C No. 48
[Analysed: see Ch. 18]
Fragment of copper alloy multi-strand torc or bracelet, comprising one double-loop terminal and a length of neck-ring/body, broken at the other end. Stage II construction of two circular-section wires plied together Z-twist.
Wt: 20.1g; D(nr): 6.0mm; D(wire): 3.0mm; D(term): 20.0mm; L: 90.0mm

B/C.36: Copper alloy torc/bracelet (Pl. 14.13)
MSCC: (2PZ)F
NCM: 1949.75
Published reference: Clarke 1954, 48, no. 46; pl. ix; Hd. B/C No. 52
[Analysed: see Ch. 18]
Fragment of copper alloy multi-strand torc or bracelet, comprising one single-loop terminal and a short length of neck-ring/body, cut or broken at the other end. Stage II construction of two faceted wires plied together Z-twist.
Wt: 10.7g; D(nr): 9.0mm; D(wire): 3.0mm; D(term): 20.5mm; L: 46.0mm

B/C.37: Copper alloy torc/bracelet (Pl. 14.13)
NCM: 1949.75.22
Published reference: Clarke 1954, 48, no. 34; pl. ix; Hd. B/C No. 40
[Analysed: see Ch. 18]
Fragment of copper alloy circular-section wire formed into a ring, most likely the loop terminal from a multi-strand torc or bracelet.
Wt: 10.6g; D(ext): 41.0mm; D(wire): 3.3mm

B/C.38: Copper alloy wire/?torc/?bracelet (Pl. 14.13)
NCM: 1949.75
Published reference: Clarke 1954, 48, no. 40; pl. ix; Hd. B/C No. 46
[Analysed: see Ch. 18]
Curved fragment of circular cross-section copper alloy wire, perhaps part of a multi-strand torc or bracelet. Broken at both ends.
Wt: 2.7g; D(wire): 3.0mm; L: 42.5mm

B/C.39: Copper alloy wire/?torc/?bracelet (Pl. 14.13)
NCM: 1949.75
Published reference: Clarke 1954, 48, no. 40; pl. ix; Hd. B/C No. 46
[Analysed: see Ch. 18]
Curved fragment of circular cross-section copper alloy wire, perhaps part of a multi-strand torc or bracelet. Broken at both ends.
Wt: 2.0g; D(wire): 3.2mm; L: 23.8mm

B/C.40: Copper alloy wire/?torc/?bracelet (Pl. 14.13)
NCM: 1949.75
Published reference: Clarke 1954, 48, no. 40; pl. ix; Hd. B/C No. 46
[Analysed: see Ch. 18]
Curved fragment of circular cross-section copper alloy wire, perhaps part of a multi-strand torc or bracelet. Bent into a U-shape and cut at both ends.
Wt: 2.1g; D(wire): 3.0mm; L: 16.5mm

B/C.41: Copper alloy wire/?torc/?bracelet (Pl. 14.13)
MSCC: (?C)T
NCM: 1949.75
Published reference: Clarke 1954, 47, no. 29; pl. ix, upper right; Hd. B/C No. 35
[Analysed: see Ch. 18]
Nine fragments of twisted square-section copper alloy wire, probably from a multi-strand torc or bracelet, broken at both ends. The curvature suggests they were originally part of a Stage II coiled construction.
Wt: 19.3g (total); D(wire): 2.5mm; L: 82.0mm (max.)

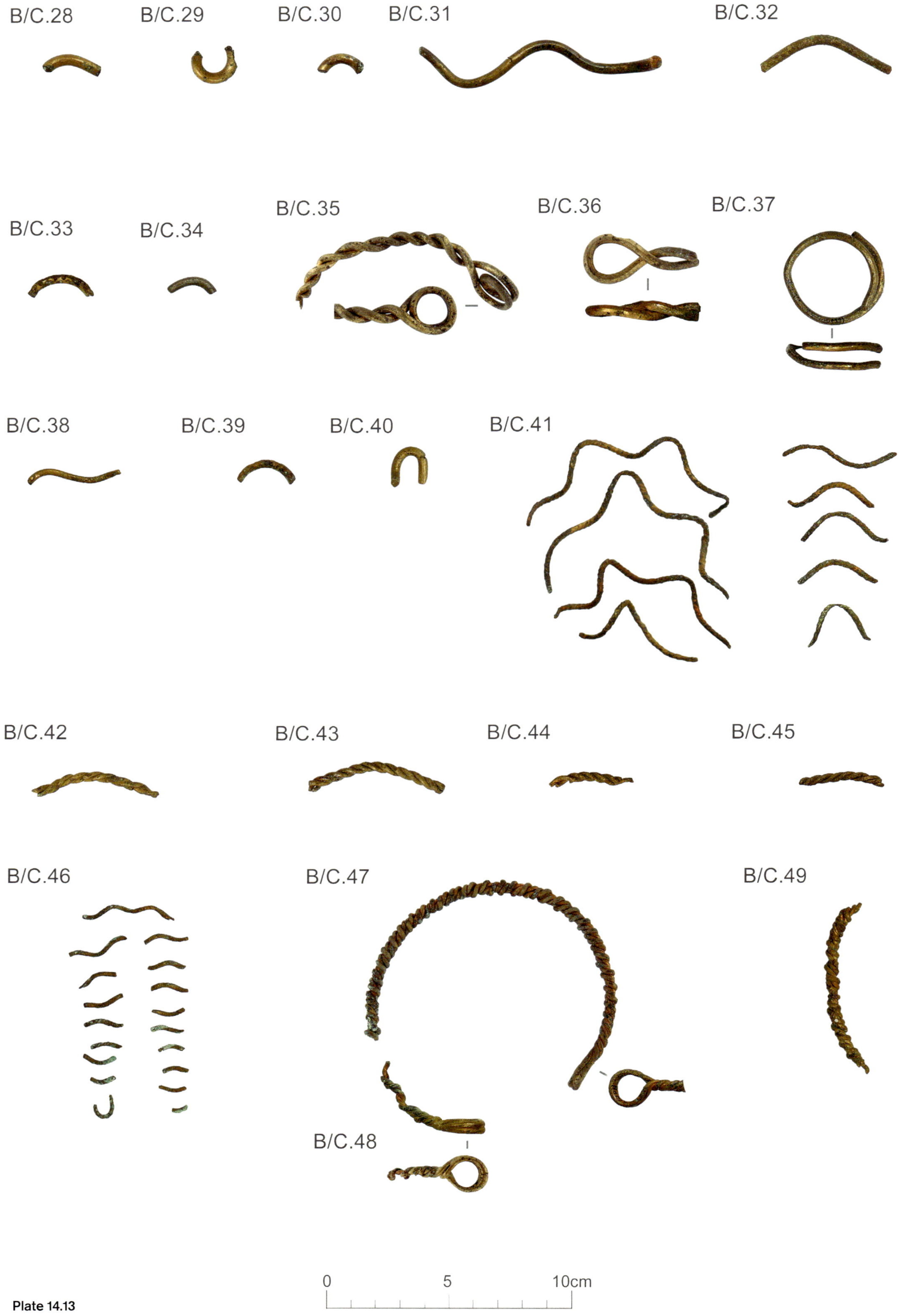
B/C.28
B/C.29
B/C.30
B/C.31
B/C.32
B/C.33
B/C.34
B/C.35
B/C.36
B/C.37
B/C.38
B/C.39
B/C.40
B/C.41
B/C.42
B/C.43
B/C.44
B/C.45
B/C.46
B/C.47
B/C.49
B/C.48
0
5
10cm

Plate 14.13

B/C.42–3: Copper alloy torc/bracelet (Pl. 14.13)
MSCC: (3PZ)R
Published reference: Clarke 1954, 47, no. 26; Hd. B/C No. 32
[Analysed: see Ch. 18]
B/C.42–3 are most likely from the same object. Each is a fragment of copper alloy multi-strand torc neck-ring or bracelet body, with Stage II construction of three circular-section wires plied together Z-twist.

B/C.42: NCM: 1949.75.37
Cut at both ends.
Wt: 5.4g; D(nr): 4.0mm; D(wire): 2.0mm; L: 55.2mm

B/C.43: NCM: 1949.75
Cut or broken at both ends.
Wt: 2.3g; D(nr): 3.0mm; D(wire): 1.8mm; L: 34.0mm

B/C.44–5: Copper alloy torc/bracelet (Pl. 14.13)
MSCC: (3P)R
Published reference: Clarke 1954, 47, no. 26; Hd. B/C No. 32
[Analysed: see Ch. 18]
B/C.44–5 are most likely from the same object. Each is a fragment of copper alloy multi-strand torc neck-ring or bracelet body, with Stage II construction of three circular-section wires plied together.

B/C.44: NCM: 1949.75.37
Cut at both ends.
Wt: 4.1g; D(nr): 4.0mm; D(wire): 1.8mm; L: 51.5mm

B/C.45: NCM: 1949.75
Cut or broken at both ends.
Wt: 2.0g; D(nr): 3.0mm; D(wire): 1.7mm; L: 34.0mm

B/C.46: Copper alloy wire/?torc/?bracelet (Pl. 14.13)
MSCC: (?P/C)R
NCM: 1949.75
Short lengths of circular-section copper alloy wire from a multi-strand torc or bracelet, each cut or broken at both ends. The curvature suggests they were originally part of a Stage II coiled or plied construction.
Wt: 5.4g (total); D(wire): 2.0mm; L: 37.0mm (max.)

B/C.47–9: Copper alloy small torc (Pl. 14.13)
MSCC: (2P(2P))R
[Analysed: see Ch. 18]
B/C.47–8 are part of the same copper alloy small multi-strand torc, with Stage III construction of two ropes plied together, each comprising two circular-section wires plied together. B/C.49 may be part of the same or a very similar object.

B/C.47: NCM: 1949.75.11
Published reference: Clarke 1954, 47, no. 23; pl. viii; pl. ix; Hd. B/C No. 29
Fragment comprising one double thickened/merged ring terminal and a short length of neck-ring, broken at the other end.
Wt: 29.2g; D(ext): 102.0mm; D(nr): 6.2mm; D(rope): 3.2mm; D(wire): 1.4mm; D(term): 15.8mm;

B/C.48: NCM: 1949.75.11
Published reference: Clarke 1954, 47, no. 23; pl. viii; pl. ix; Hd. B/C No. 29
Fragment comprising a double thickened/merged ring terminal and a short length of neck-ring, cut or broken at the other end.
Wt: 6.5g; D(nr): 5.0mm; D(rope): 3.0mm; D(wire): 1.4mm; D(term): 17.0mm; L: 50.0mm

B/C.49: NCM: 1949.75
Published reference: Clarke 1954, 47, no. 25; Hd. B/C No. 31
Fragment of torc neck-ring, cut or broken at each end.
Wt: 8.4g; D(nr): 5.5mm; D(rope): 3.1mm; D(wire): 1.4mm; L: 67.0mm

B/C.50–3: Copper alloy torc/bracelet (Pl. 14.14)
MSCC: (2P(2P))R
[Analysed: see Ch. 18]
B/C.50–53 may be from the same copper alloy multi-strand torc or bracelet, with loop terminals and Stage III construction of two ropes plied tightly together, each comprising two circular-section wires plied tightly together.

B/C.50: NCM: 1949.75.14
Published reference: Clarke 1954, 47, no. 24; pl. viii; Hd. B/C No. 30
Fragment comprising the crushed remains of a broken, double-loop terminal and most of the neck-ring/body, cut or broken at the other end.
Wt: 32.0g; D(ext): 99.0mm; D(nr): 5.0mm; D(rope): 2.8mm; D(wire): 1.3mm

B/C.51: NCM: 1949.75
Published reference: Clarke 1954, 47, no. 25; Hd. B/C No. 31
Fragment comprising a broken loop terminal and part of the neck-ring/body, cut or broken at the other end. Only one complete loop of the terminal remains, but it appears that part of a second loop may have been broken and bent away from the first.
Wt: 6.1g; D(nr): 5.0mm; D(rope): 2.0mm; D(wire): 1.2mm; D(term): 13.5mm; L: 58.0mm

B/C.52: NCM: 1949.75.31
Published reference: Clarke 1954, 47, no. 25; Hd. B/C No. 31
Seventeen fragments of worn copper alloy Stage III multi-strand torc neck-ring or bracelet body, all broken at both ends. Seven are Stage III components, on the other ten fragments only a Stage II element of the Stage III construction remains.
Wt: 23.5g (total); D(nr): 5.0mm; D(rope): 2.3mm; D(wire): 1.3mm; L: 55.0mm (max.)

B/C.53: NCM: 1949.75
Published reference: Clarke 1954, 47, no. 25; Hd. B/C No. 31
Three fragments of copper alloy multi-strand torc neck-ring or bracelet body, each cut or broken at each end. What remains are Stage II components, formed from two circular-section wires plied together. The fragments are curved in a way which suggests they originally formed part of a larger Stage III construction.

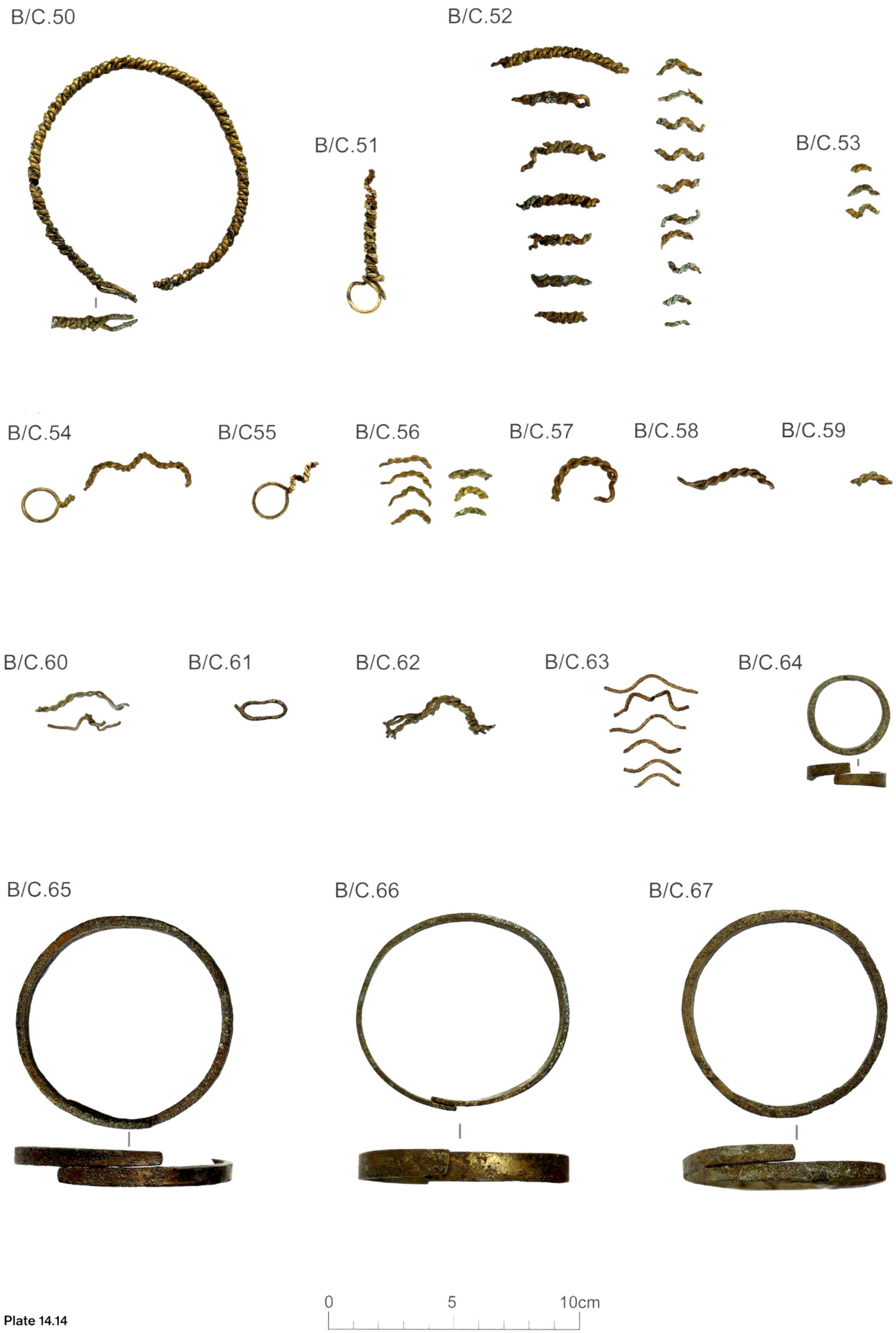
B/C.50
B/C.51
B/C.52
B/C.53
B/C.54
B/C55
B/C.56
B/C.57
B/C.58
B/C.59
B/C.60
B/C.61
B/C.62
B/C.63
B/C.64
B/C.65
B/C.66
B/C.67
0
5
10cm

Plate 14.14

Wt: 1.1g (total); D(rope): 1.9mm; D(wire): 1.1mm; L: 13.0mm (max.)

B/C.54–5: Copper alloy torc/bracelet (Pl. 14.14)
MSCC: (?3C(2P))R
Published reference: Clarke 1954, 47, no. 27; pl. ix, lower left (erroneously labelled as 'no. 29'); Hd. B/C No. 33
[Analysed: see Ch. 18]
B/C.54–5 are joining fragments of the same copper alloy multi-strand torc or bracelet with loop terminals. The two terminal fragments are shown joined in Clarke (1954). All that remains of the neck-ring/body is a Stage II component, comprising two circular-section wires plied together. The form suggests that the original construction was Stage III, formed from at least three such ropes coiled together.

B/C.54: NCM: 1949.75.12
Fragment comprising one half of a double-loop terminal with a short length of neck-ring/body, broken at the other end, and an additional (joining) fragment of neck-ring/body.
Wt: 3.1g; D(rope): 2.5mm; D(wire): 1.3mm; D(term): 12.0mm; L: 22.0mm, 43.0mm

B/C.55: NCM: 1949.75
Fragment comprising one half of a double-loop terminal with a short length of neck-ring/body, broken at the other end.
Wt: 1.5g; D(nr): 5.5mm; D(rope): 2.0mm; D(wire): 1.0mm; D(term): 14.0mm; L: 32.0mm

B/C.56: Copper alloy torc/bracelet (Pl. 14.14)
MSCC: (?C(2P))R
NCM: 1949.75
Published reference: Clarke 1954, 47, no. 25; Hd. B/C No. 31
[Analysed: see Ch. 18]
Seven fragments of copper alloy multi-strand torc neck-ring or bracelet body, cut or broken at each end. What remains are Stage II components, formed from two circular-section wires plied together. The fragments are curved in a way which suggests they originally formed part of a larger Stage III coiled construction.
Wt: 3.1g (total); D(rope): 2.3mm; D(wire): 1.0mm; L: 21.0mm (max.)

B/C.57: Copper alloy torc/bracelet (Pl. 14.14)
MSCC: (2P)R
NCM: 1949.75
Published reference: Clarke 1954, 47, no. 28; Hd. B/C No. 34
[Analysed: see Ch. 18]
Fragment of copper alloy multi-strand torc neck-ring or bracelet body, cut at both ends, with one wire extending further than the others. Stage II construction of two circular-section wires plied together. The whole fragment has been bent into a rough U-shape.
Wt: 2.7g; D(nr): 4.0mm; D(wire): 1.5mm; L: 28.0mm

B/C.58: Copper alloy torc/bracelet (Pl. 14.14)
MSCC: (?P(2P))R
NCM: 1949.75
Published reference: Clarke 1954, 47, no. 28; Hd. B/C No. 34
[Analysed: see Ch. 18]
Fragment of multi-strand copper alloy torc neck-ring or bracelet body, broken at both ends. What remains is a Stage II component of two circular-section wires plied together. This rope is curved and may originally have formed part of a Stage III plied construction.
Wt: 2.0g; D(rope): 3.5mm; D(wire): 1.5mm; L: 38.8mm

B/C.59: Copper alloy torc/bracelet (Pl. 14.14)
MSCC: (?C([1+1x2P]P))R
NCM: 1949.75
Published reference: Clarke 1954, 47, no. 28; Hd. B/C No. 34
[Analysed: see Ch. 18]
Fragment of multi-strand copper alloy torc neck-ring or bracelet body, broken at both ends. What remains is a Stage II/III component of two elements plied together. One is a circular-section wire, while the other is itself a Stage II component, formed from two narrow circular-section wires plied together. The whole fragment is curved and may originally have formed part of a more complex construction. The Stage II rope that forms one of the plies is most likely a joining section between two wires, since mixed-stage plies are not otherwise attested in the Snettisham assemblage or other Iron Age torcs.
Wt: 0.8g; D(rope): 3.0mm (whole rope); D(wire): 1.5mm (for single wire and the (2P)R ply); L: 17.0mm

B/C.60: Copper alloy torc/bracelet (Pl. 14.14)
MSCC: (?C(2P))R
NCM: 1949.75.24
[Analysed: see Ch. 18]
Published reference: Clarke 1954, 47, no. 25; Hd. B/C No. 31
Two fragments of copper alloy multi-strand torc neck-ring or bracelet body, broken at both ends. What remains are Stage II components of two circular-section wires plied together. These ropes are curved in a way which suggests they originally formed part of a Stage III coiled construction. Possibly deliberately untwisted.
Wt: 1.6g (total); D(rope): 2.8mm; D(wire): 1.0mm; L: 37.5mm (max.)

B/C.61: Copper alloy wire/?torc/?bracelet (Pl. 14.14)
NCM: 1949.75
Published reference: Clarke 1954, 47, no. 25; Hd. B/C No. 31
[Analysed: see Ch. 18]
Fragment of copper alloy circular-section wire bent into an oval loop, possibly a squashed loop terminal from a multi-strand torc or bracelet.
Wt: 0.9g; D(wire): 1.3mm; L: 21.5mm; W: 7.0mm

B/C.62: Copper alloy torc/bracelet (Pl. 14.14)
MSCC: (?C(3P(2P)))R
NCM: 1949.75
Published reference: Clarke 1954, 47, no. 25; Hd. B/C No. 31
[Analysed: see Ch. 18]
Fragment of copper alloy multi-strand torc neck-ring or bracelet body, cut or broken at both ends. What remains is a Stage III component formed from three ropes plied together,

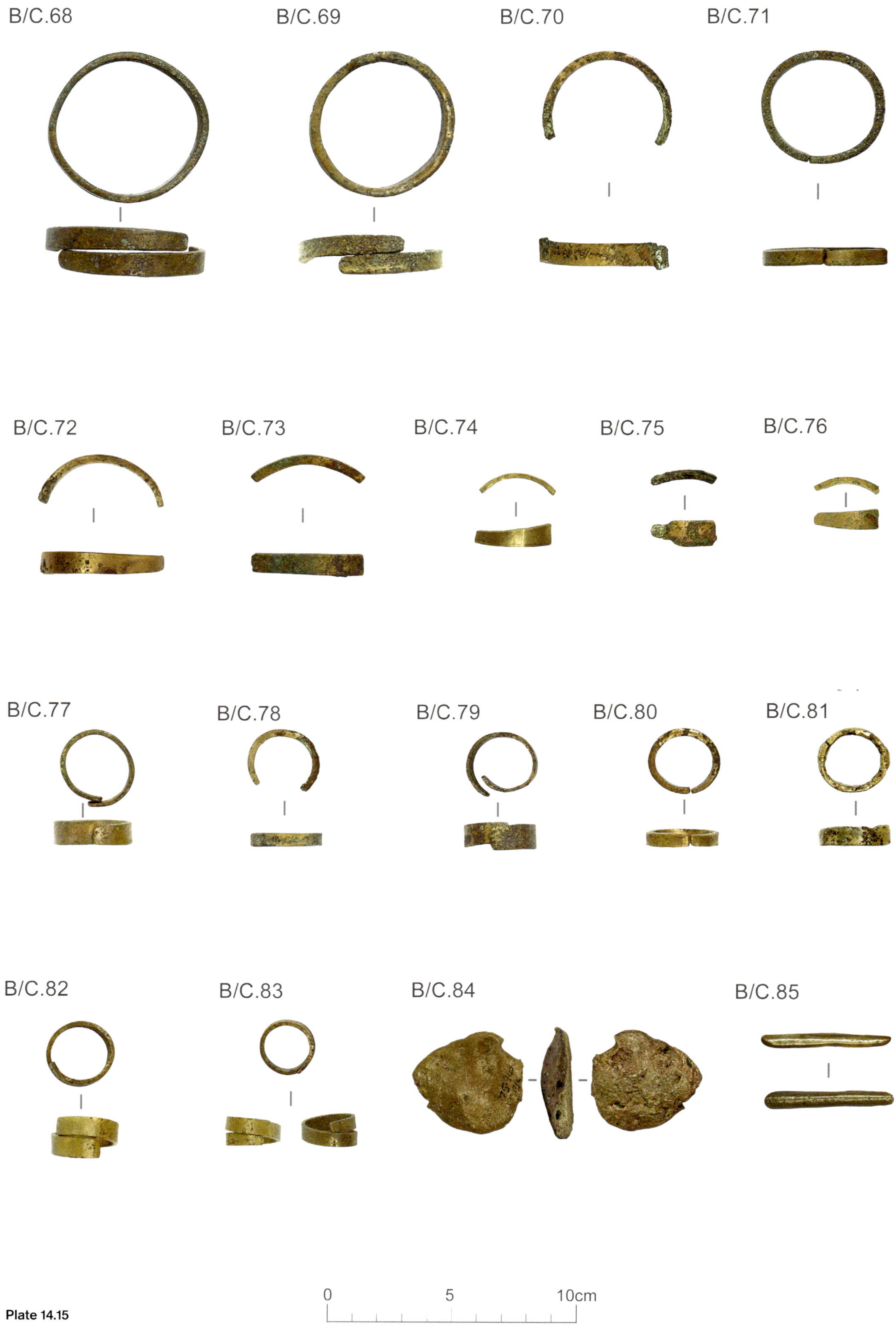
B/C.68
B/C.69
B/C.70
B/C.71
B/C.72
B/C.73
B/C.74
B/C.75
B/C.76
B/C.77
B/C.78
B/C.79
B/C.80
B/C.81
B/C.82
B/C.83
B/C.84
B/C.85
0
5
10cm

Plate 14.15

each of which consists of two circular-section wires plied together. The whole fragment is curved in a way which suggests that it may have originally formed part of a Stage IV construction. The wires have been partially untwisted at one end.
Wt: 3.6g; D(cable): 5.6mm; D(rope): 2.5mm; D(wire): 1.0mm; L: 45.0mm

B/C.63: Copper alloy wire/?torc/?bracelet (Pl. 14.14)
MSCC: (?C)T
NCM: 1949.75
Six fragments of copper alloy twisted wire, broken at both ends. Each is curved in a way which suggests it was originally part of a coiled construction in a multi-strand torc or bracelet.
Wt: 3.0g; D(wire): 1.3mm; L: 37.5mm (max.)

B/C.64: Gold/silver alloy small ring (Pl. 14.14)
NCM: 1949.75
Published reference: Clarke 1954, 55, no. 4; Hd. B/C No. 10 (rendered as Hd. C No. 10 in Clarke 1954, in error)
[Analysed: see Appendix 5]
Complete gold/silver alloy small ring with overlapping terminals, made from a strip with rectangular cross-section. Flat, slightly tapered ends.
Wt: 13.8g; D(ext): 33.0mm; W: 7.2mm; T: 2.8mm

B/C.65: Copper alloy large ring (Pl. 14.14)
NCM: 1949.75.23
Published reference: Clarke 1954, 54, no. 2; fig. 7; Hd. B/C No. 1
[Analysed: see Ch. 18]
Complete copper alloy large ring with overlapping terminals. Made from a strip with rectangular cross-section. Blunt, slightly rounded ends.
Wt: 54.8g; D(ext): 86.0mm; W: 3.8mm; T: 6.5mm

B/C.66: Copper alloy large ring (Pl. 14.14)
NCM: 1949.75.17
Published reference: Clarke 1954, 54, no. 4; fig. 7; Hd. B/C No. 3
[Analysed: see Ch. 18]
Complete copper alloy large ring with overlapping terminals. Made from a strip with rectangular cross-section. Blunt, slightly rounded ends.
Wt: 53.0g; D(ext): 85.0mm; W: 11.2mm; T: 2.0mm

B/C.67: Copper alloy large ring (Pl. 14.14)
NCM: 1949.75.21
Published reference: Clarke 1954, 54, no. 3; Hd. B/C No. 2
[Analysed: see Ch. 18]
Complete copper alloy large ring with overlapping terminals. Made from a strip with rectangular cross-section. Flat, slightly tapered ends.
Wt: 54.8g; D(ext): 82.0mm; W: 7.0mm; T: 4.0mm

B/C.68: Copper alloy large ring (Pl. 14.15)
NCM: 1949.75.10
Published reference: Clarke 1954, 54, no. 5; fig. 7; Hd. B/C No. 4
[Analysed: see Ch. 18]
Complete copper alloy large ring with overlapping terminals. Made from a strip with rectangular cross-section. Slightly rounded, tapered ends.
Wt: 53.6g; D(ext): 64.5mm; W: 9.5mm; T: 3.5mm

B/C.69: Copper alloy large ring (Pl. 14.15)
NCM: 1949.75.19
Published reference: Clarke 1954, 54, no. 6; Hd. B/C No. 5
[Analysed: see Ch. 18]
Complete copper alloy large ring with overlapping terminals. Made from a strip with rectangular cross-section. Flat, slightly tapered terminals.
Wt: 43.5g; D(ext): 59.0mm; W: 7.6mm; T: 4.0mm

B/C.70: Copper alloy large ring (Pl. 14.15)
NCM: 1949.75.48
Published reference: Clarke 1954, 54, no. 9; Hd. B/C No. 8
[Analysed: see Ch. 18]
Fragment of around two thirds of a large copper alloy ring, made from a strip with rectangular cross-section. Broken at both ends.
Wt: 22.7g; D(ext): 52.0mm; W: 9.0mm; T: 3.8mm

B/C.71: Copper alloy large ring (Pl. 14.15)
NCM: 1949.75.8
Published reference: Clarke 1954, 54, no. 7; Fig. 7; Hd. B/C No. 6
[Analysed: see Ch. 18]
Complete copper alloy large ring with flat, abutting terminals. Slightly oval in plan. Made from a strip with rectangular cross-section.
Wt: 25.7g; D(ext): 50.2mm; W: 6.8mm; T: 3.2mm

B/C.72: Copper alloy large ring (Pl. 14.15)
NCM: 1949.75
Published reference: Clarke 1954, 54, no. 8; Hd. B/C No. 7
[Analysed: see Ch. 18]
Fragment of around half of a copper alloy large ring, made from a strip with rectangular cross-section. One end cut/broken, one tapered original end.
Wt: 11.5g; L: 50.0mm; W: 8.0mm; T: 2.8mm

B/C.73: Copper alloy large ring (Pl. 14.15)
NCM: 1949.75
Published reference: Clarke 1954, 54, no. 10; Hd. B/C No. 9
[Analysed: see Ch. 18]
Fragment of a around a quarter of a copper alloy large ring, made from a strip with rectangular cross-section. Broken at one end, flat at the other.
Wt: 12.7g; L: 46.0mm; W: 8.0mm; T: 3.5mm

B/C.74: Copper alloy large ring (Pl. 14.15)
NCM: 1949.75
Published reference: Clarke 1954, 54, no. 10; Hd. B/C No. 9
[Analysed: see Ch. 18]
Small fragment of a copper alloy large ring, made from a

B/C.86

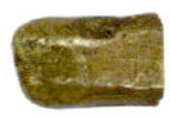

B/C.87

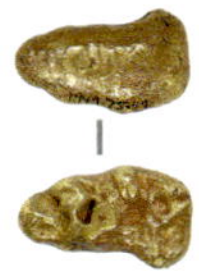

B/C.88

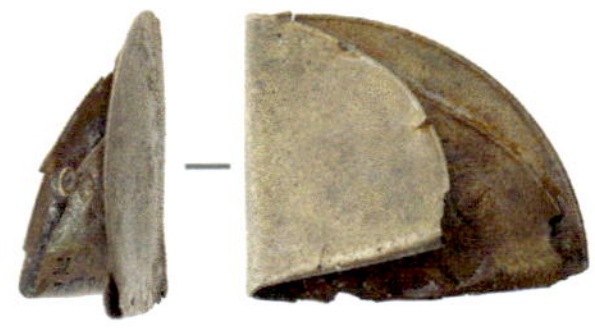

B/C.89

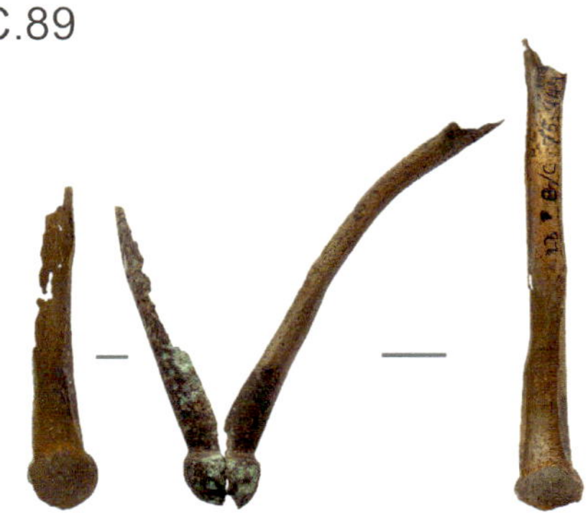

B/C90

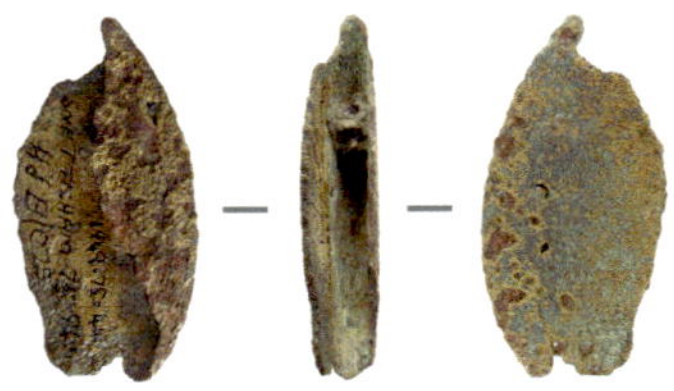

B/C.91

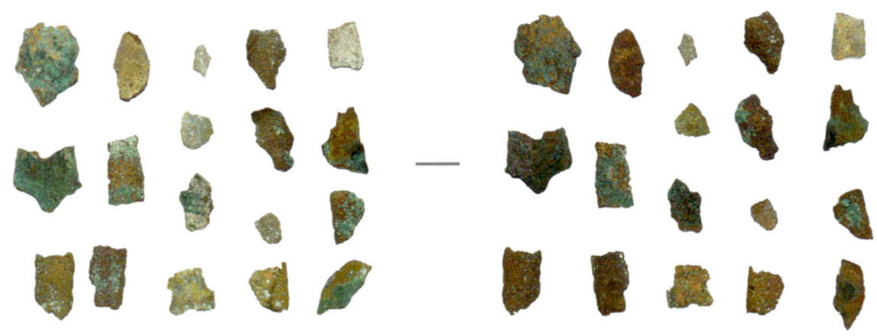

B/C.92

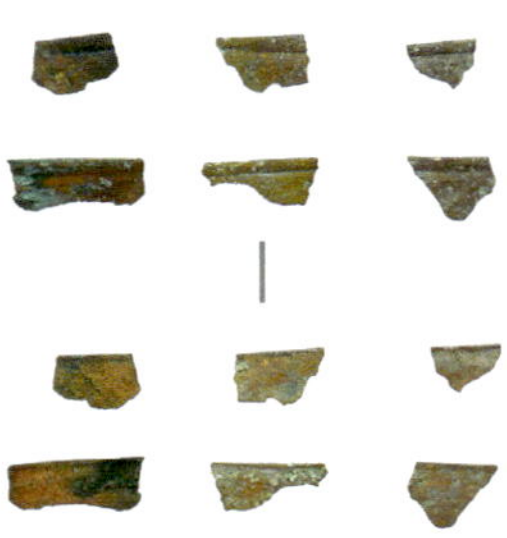

B/C.93

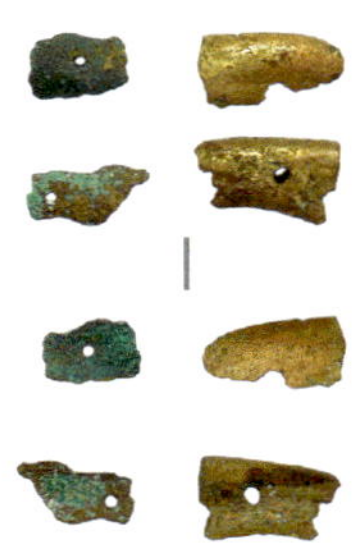

B/C.94

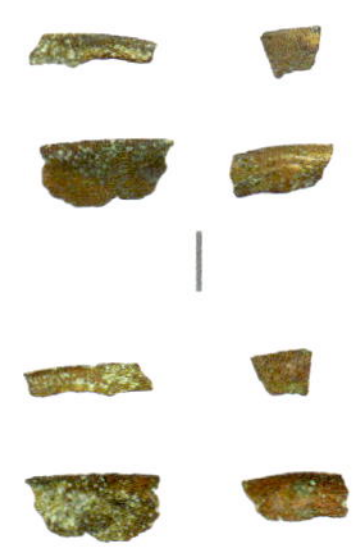

B/C.95

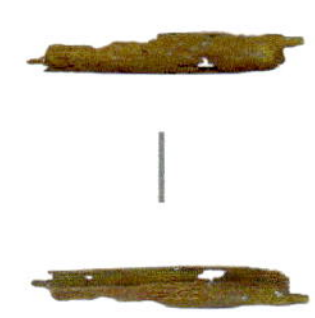

B/C.96

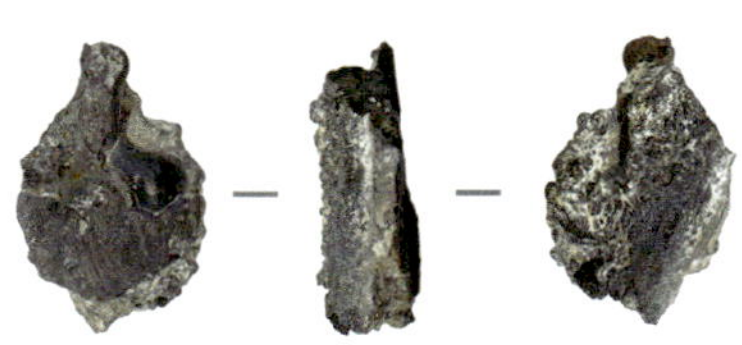

0 5 10cm

Plate 14.16

strip with rectangular cross-section. Broken at both ends.
Wt: 5.2g; L: 31.0mm; W: 8.5mm; T: 2.0mm

B/C.75: Copper alloy large ring (Pl. 14.15)
NCM: 1949.75
Published reference: Clarke 1954, 54, no. 10; Hd. B/C No. 9
[Analysed: see Ch. 18]
Small fragment of a copper alloy large ring, heavily corroded, made from a strip with rectangular cross-section. Tapers irregularly at one end, broken at the other.
Wt: 3.5g; L: 27.0mm; W: 9.0mm; T: 3.0mm

B/C.76: Copper alloy large ring (Pl. 14.15)
NCM: 1949.75
Published reference: Clarke 1954, 54, no. 10; Hd. B/C No. 9
[Analysed: see Ch. 18]
Small fragment of a copper alloy large ring, made from a strip with rectangular cross-section. Tapers towards one flat end, broken at the other.
Wt: 3.1g; L: 25.0mm; W: 7.0mm; T: 2.3mm

B/C.77: Copper alloy small ring (Pl. 14.15)
NCM: 1949.75.11
Published reference: Clarke 1954, 55, no. 5; Hd. B/C No. 11
[Analysed: see Ch. 18]
Complete copper alloy small ring with overlapping, slightly rounded terminals. Made from a strip with rectangular cross-section.
Wt: 12.6g; D(ext): 32.0mm; W: 9.0mm; T: 2.0mm

B/C.78: Copper alloy small ring (Pl. 14.15)
NCM: 1949.75.12
Published reference: Clarke 1954, 55, no. 6; Hd. B/C No. 12
Fragment of around two thirds of a copper alloy small ring, made from a strip with rectangular cross-section. Broken at one end, and one square, original terminal.
Wt: 7.3g; D(ext): 29.0mm; W: 6.2mm; T: 2.8mm

B/C.79: Copper alloy small ring (Pl. 14.15)
NCM: 1949.75.14
Published reference: Clarke 1954, 55, no. 8; Hd. B/C No. 14
[Analysed: see Ch. 18]
Complete copper alloy small ring with overlapping, slightly rounded terminals. Slightly distorted/oval in plan; made from a strip with rectangular cross-section.
Wt: 10.7g; D(ext): 29.0mm; W: 9.5mm; T: 2.0mm

B/C.80: Copper alloy small ring (Pl. 14.15)
NCM: 1949.75.16
Published reference: Clarke 1954, 55, no. 10; Hd. B/C No. 16
[Analysed: see Ch. 18]
Complete copper alloy small ring with slightly tapered, flat, abutting terminals. Made from a strip with rectangular cross-section.
Wt: 10.4g; D(ext): 29.0mm; W: 6.0mm; T: 3.0mm

B/C.81: Copper alloy small ring (Pl. 14.15)
NCM: 1949.75.17
Published reference: Clarke 1954, 56, no. 13; Hd. B/C No. 17
[Analysed: see Ch. 18]
Complete copper alloy small annular ring, made from a strip with rectangular cross-section. Hammered and part melted.
Wt: 10.6g; D(ext): 28.0mm; W: 6.5mm; T: 3.0mm

B/C.82: Copper alloy small ring (Pl. 14.15)
NCM: 1949.75.13
Published reference: Clarke 1954, 55, no. 7; Hd. B/C No. 13
[Analysed: see Ch. 18]
Complete copper alloy small ring with overlapping, slightly rounded terminals. Made from a strip with rectangular cross-section.
Wt: 12.7g; D(ext): 27.5mm; W: 7.5mm; T: 2.0mm

B/C.83: Copper alloy small ring (Pl. 14.15)
NCM: 1949.75.15
Published reference: Clarke 1954, 55, no. 9; pl. xii; Hd. B/C No. 15
[Analysed: see Ch. 18]
Complete copper alloy small spiral ring, made from a strip with rectangular cross-section. Around 1.6 turns; slightly tapered, flat ends.
Wt: 11.9g; D(ext): 22.5mm; W: 6.8mm; T: 2.0mm

B/C.84: Gold/silver alloy triangular ingot (Pl. 14.15)
NCM: 1949.75.193
Published reference: Clarke 1954, 58 (cake), no. 7; pl. xiii, upper; Hd. B/C No. 19
[Analysed: see Appendix 5]
Small triangular gold/silver alloy ingot with rounded corners, and slightly convex faces and sides. Irregular surface, smooth in some areas and pitted in others. From the base of a triangular crucible.
Wt: 50.8g; L: 44.0mm; T: 9.0mm

B/C.85: Gold/silver alloy linear ingot (Pl. 14.15)
NCM: 1949.75.52
Published reference: Clarke 1954, 58 (cake), no. 6; pl. xiii, upper; Hd. B/C No. 18
[Analysed: see Appendix 5]
Linear gold/silver alloy ingot with squarish cross-section and rounded ends. Slightly tapering towards one end.
Wt: 12.1g; L: 52.0mm; W: 6.0mm; T: 5.0mm

B/C.86: Gold/silver alloy linear ingot (Pl. 14.16)
NCM: 1949.75
Published reference: Clarke 1954, 58 (cake), no. 8; pl. xiii, upper; Hd. B/C No. 20
[Analysed: see Appendix 5]
Short length of linear gold/silver alloy ingot with flattened oval cross-section. Rounded at one end and cut at the other.
Wt: 11.6g; L: 20.0mm; W: 12.0mm; T: 11.0mm

B/C.87: Gold/silver alloy amorphous lump (Pl. 14.16)
NCM: 1949.75.49
Published reference: Clarke 1954, 58 (cake), no. 9; pl. xiii, upper; Hd. B/C No. 21
[Analysed: see Appendix 5]

Small, irregular gold/silver alloy lump or droplet. Irregular surface, smooth on one side, pitted on the other. Possibly waste from metalworking, or a melted object.
Wt: 12.9g; L: 23.0mm; W: 11.0mm; T: 7.0mm

B/C.88: Copper alloy scale pan (Pl. 14.16)
NCM: 1949.75.45
Published reference: Clarke 1954, 57, no. 4; pl. xiii, lower; fig. 8; Hd. B/C No. 22
[Analysed: see Ch. 18]
Disc of thin copper alloy sheet which has been folded into quarters. Slightly concave, with incised line around the circumference on both sides. There are three holes or fittings spaced equally around the edge of the disc. One is a small eyelet riveted onto the outside of the pan. The other two are small, pierced rivet holes, likely from similar eyelets. When complete, the object would thus presumably have had three small eyelets equally spaced around the edge.
Parallels: This object is most likely a scale pan for the accurate weighing out of small quantities of material. A ring through each of the eyelets would have allowed for its suspension on a steelyard balance. Such finds are more common from Roman and later contexts. See Crummy (1983, 99–100, fig. 104, 2508) for a similar Roman example from the mid-1st-century AD destruction levels at Colchester, and a detailed description of the functioning of a steelyard balance. A small and very simple scale pan was also recovered from a Roman site just to the south of Snettisham Village (Lyons 2004, 49, SF 84).

In the Roman period, steelyards of various sizes were used in weighing out of a wide variety of materials, from large commercial transactions in the order of kilograms, down to small quantities of spices or pharmaceuticals.

A decorated convex metal disc 106mm in diameter, and with three equally spaced holes around the circumference like the Snettisham pan, was recovered from the River Bann in Ireland (Raftery 1940). Raftery tentatively proposed that it might have been used as a balance pan (*ibid.*, 29). The decoration is La Tène in style, but the object cannot be closely dated.

Small equal-arm balance scales (with two arms rather than a single arm like a steelyard balance) are attested in Late Iron Age contexts both in Britain and on the continent, especially sites potentially associated with coin production, e.g. Verulamium (Wheeler and Wheeler 1936, 176–7). Various authors have proposed that these 'coin scales' might have been used to weigh out metals for alloying, or for checking the weights of metal pellets, coin blanks, or finished coins (Van Arsdell 1993; Wainwright and Spratling 1973, 115, 120).

In the context of Snettisham, it is possible that this scale pan was used for weighing out small quantities of metals for use in the mixing of different alloys for torc production, or to ascertain the weight of coins or ingots, but this remains speculative.
Wt: 17.3g; L: 40.0mm; approx. original diameter: *c.* 70mm

B/C.89 Copper alloy binding strip from hide-shaped shield (Pl. 14.16)
NCM: 1949.75.56
Published references: Clarke 1954, 57, no. 1; pl. xiii, lower; Hd. B/C No. 23. Stead (1991c, 24, 30, Type E No. 10)
[Analysed: see Ch. 18]
Two fragments of U-shaped copper alloy binding strip, each terminating in a knob at one end and broken at the other. The two fragments join at their knob terminals to give a V-shape, and would originally have formed the corner of a hide-shaped shield.
Parallels: Similar pieces of shield binding are known from Iron Age contexts across southern Britain (Stead 1991c, Type E, 30). A complete shield of this type was present in a burial at Mill Hill, Deal (Stead 1995b), while miniature shields in the same form were recovered from the Salisbury Hoard (Stead 1998).
Part 1: Wt: 3.5g; L: 68.0mm; W: 13.0mm; T: 0.2–0.3mm
Part 2: Wt: 5.0g; L: 86.0mm; W: 12.0mm; T: 0.2–0.3mm

B/C.90: Copper alloy fitting (Pl. 14.16)
NCM: 1949.75.44
Published reference: Clarke 1954, 58 (Misc.), no. 2; pl. xiii, lower, Misc. 2; Hd. B/C No. 25
[Analysed: see Ch. 18]
Curved section of hollow copper alloy sheet-metal fitting with heavily pitted surface.
Wt: 10.1g; L: 48.0mm; W: 23.0mm; T: 6.0mm

B/C.91: Copper alloy sheet (Pl. 14.16)
NCM: 1949.75
Published reference: Clarke 1954, 57, no. 7; Hd. B/C No. 24
[Analysed: see Ch. 18]
Eighteen fragments of heavily corroded copper alloy sheet, no original edges. The majority of the fragments are curved/distorted.
Wt: 6.7g; L: 19.0mm; T: 0.5mm

B/C.92: Copper alloy sheet (Pl. 14.16)
NCM: 1949.75
Published reference: Clarke 1954, 57, no. 7; Hd. B/C No. 24
[Analysed: see Ch. 18]
Six copper alloy sheet fragments, each with one original straight, thickened edge, with incised line.
Wt: 2.0g; L: 18.8mm (max.); T: 1.0mm (rim), 0.2–0.3mm (body)

B/C.93: Copper alloy sheet (Pl. 14.16)
NCM: 1949.75
Published reference: Clarke 1954, 57, no. 7; Hd. B/C No. 24
[Analysed: see Ch. 18]
Four fragments of slightly U-shaped copper alloy binding strip, each pierced through with a single, circular rivet hole.
Wt: 2.8g; L: 19.0mm (max.); T: 0.2–0.3mm

B/C.94: Copper alloy sheet (Pl. 14.16)
NCM: 1949.75
Published reference: Clarke 1954, 57, no. 7; Hd. B/C No. 24
[Analysed: see Ch. 18]
Four copper alloy sheet fragments, each with one possible original straight edge.
Wt: 1.1g; L: 17.8mm; T: 0.2–0.3mm

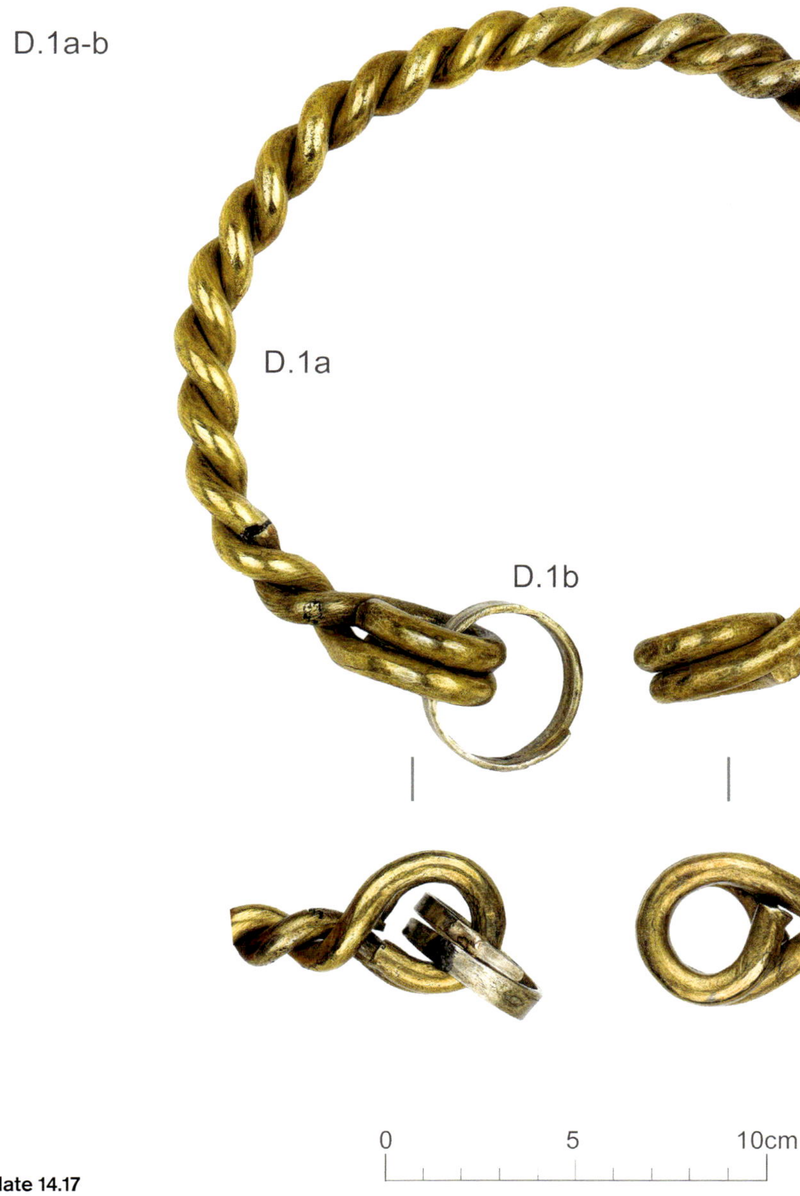

Plate 14.17

B/C.95: Copper alloy binding strip (Pl. 14.16)
NCM: 1949.75
Published reference: Clarke 1954, 57, no. 7; Hd. B/C No. 24
[Analysed: see Ch. 18]
Fragment of U-shaped copper alloy binding strip, broken on all edges.
Wt: 0.6g; L: 36.2mm; T: 0.2–0.3mm

B/C.96: Metalworking waste (slag) (Pl. 14.16)
NCM: 1949.75
Amorphous lump of metalworking waste, probably iron slag.
Wt: 13.4g; L: 38.0mm; W: 23.8mm; T: 11.8mm

Hoard D

Found during ploughing in 1950.

D.1a–b: Composite group (interlinked) (Pl. 14.17)
BM: 1951,0402.1
Large ring D.1b is looped through one of the terminals of torc D.1a.
Wt: 1060.8g (total for D.1a–b)
D.1a: Gold/silver alloy torc
Published reference: Clarke 1954, 47, no. 13; pl. x
MSCC: (2P)R
Gold/silver alloy multi-strand torc, with Stage II neck-ring formed from two thick circular-section rods plied tightly together. The rods are broken in several places and have been repaired using modern conservation methods. The double loop terminals are formed from the ends of the two neck-ring rods, with each rod terminating in an open loop at each end.
D(ext): 215.0mm; D(nr): 17.1mm; D(wire): 9.0mm; D(term): 39.7 and 40.3mm
D.1b: Gold/silver alloy large ring
Published reference: Clarke 1954, 47, no. 16; pl. x
Complete gold/silver alloy large ring with tapering terminals which overlap by around half a turn. Made from a strip with rectangular cross-section.
D(ext): 44.5mm; W: 10.0mm; T: 2.4mm

E.1a-c

E.1a

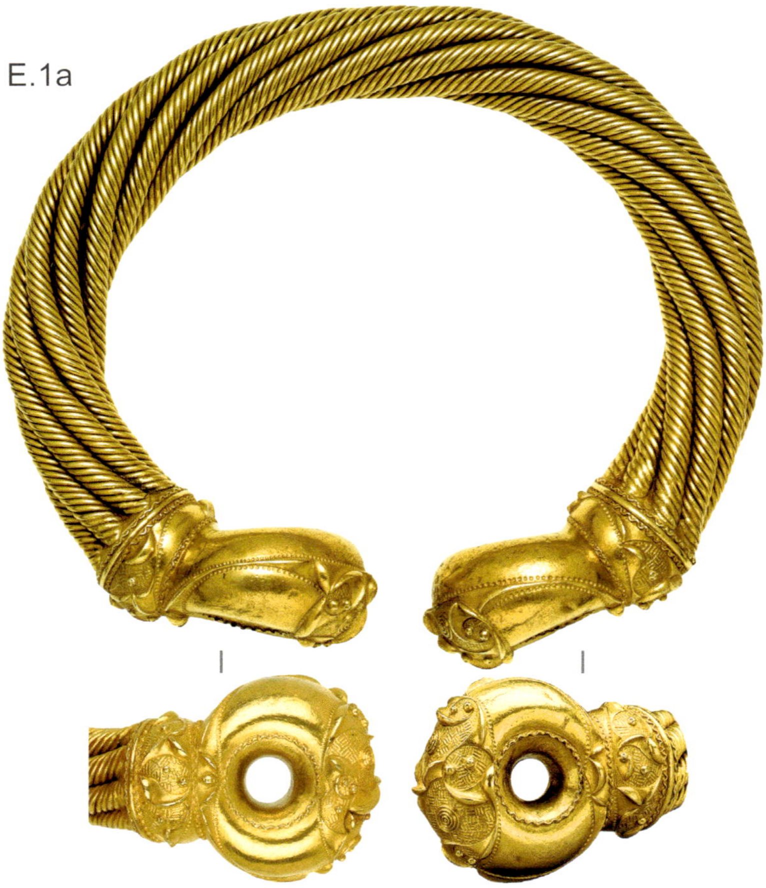

E.1b

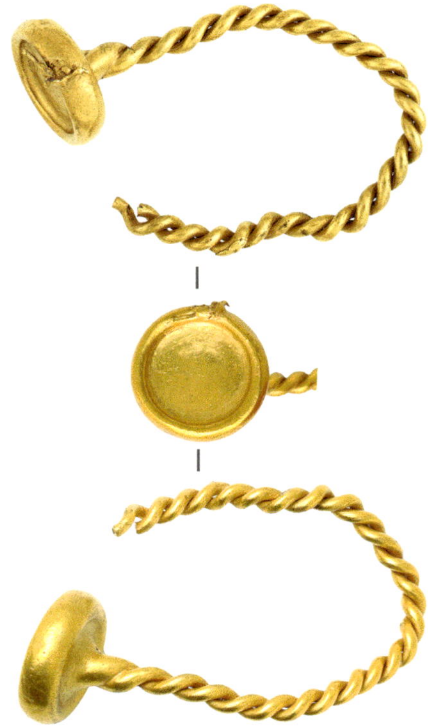

E.1c

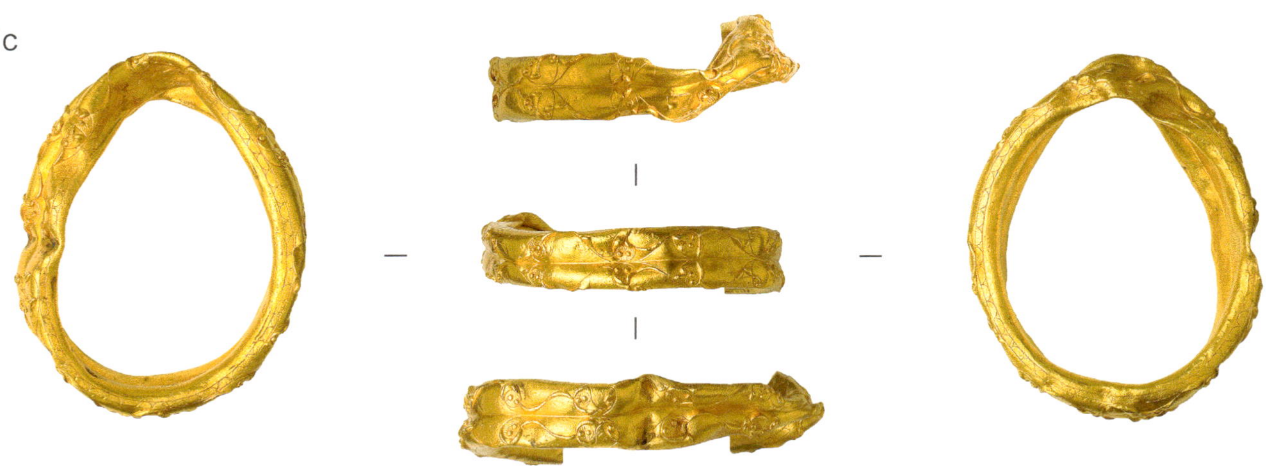

Plate 14.18

0 5 10cm

Hoard E

Found during ploughing in 1950.

E.1a–c: Composite group (interlinked, inserted) (Pl. 14.18)

When found, torc fragment E.1b was looped through the terminals of the 'Great Torc' E.1a, and bracelet E.1c was threaded onto E1.b (**Fig. 20.32** shows a reconstruction of the original grouping). The coin (Cat. no. 169) was found inserted into one of the terminals of the 'Great Torc'.

E.1a: Gold/silver alloy torc
MSCC: (8C(8C))R
BM: 1951,0402.2
[Analysed: see Ch. 17]
Gold/silver alloy multi-strand torc with complex ornamented torus terminals, known as the 'Great Torc' (see **Figs 17.57, 17.82–93, 17.95–7, 17.101, 20.2–3, 20.14, 21.14**). The major areas of decoration appear towards the front of each terminal, within an oval-shaped panel with tapering wings on either side. The collars are also decorated on their outer sides with similar designs. The decoration on each terminal is different but the patterns of both are made up of raised lobes framing hatched trumpet and circle motifs. Stage III neck-ring formed from eight ropes coiled together around a hollow core; each rope is formed from eight coiled circular-section wires. Total number of wires is 64. At least two wires are broken close to one of the terminals. See Chapter 17 for information on construction, and Chapter 21 for a full discussion of decoration.
Wt: 1084.0g; D(ext): 199.0mm; D(nr): 25mm at the back expanding to 30mm near the terminals; D(rope): 7.3mm; D(wire): 1.6mm; D(term): 56.3 and 56.5mm

E.1b: Gold/silver alloy torc
MSCC: (2P)R
BM: 1951,0402.3
Gold/silver alloy multi-strand torc fragment, comprising one buffer terminal and part of the neck-ring. Stage II construction of two thick, circular-section wires plied tightly together. Terminal has rounded edges and the face is dished within a raised rim. On the underside there is a rounded, raised rim, then a concentric concavity which rises in the centre towards the neck-ring strands. There are tiny fragments, including wire 1.4mm diameter, fused (with melted drops) on the face of the terminal and another slight accretion on one of the strands. The ends of the broken strands are quite different: one is a sharp break, whilst the other has a slightly raised rim, suggesting a stress fracture. Both are clearly ancient breaks, snapped off rather than cut. The whole fragment is bent into a U-shape to pass through the terminals of E.1a.
Wt: 124.0g; D(nr): 7.1mm; D(wire): 3.6mm; D(term): 36.3mm; L: 109.4mm

E.1c: Gold/silver alloy bracelet
BM: 1951,0402.4
Gold/silver alloy sheet bracelet, hollow (see **Fig. 21.40**). The exterior is ornamented in the same style as E.1a, with two opposing scrolls comprising hatched motifs linked by flowing raised lobe motifs. A line runs along the middle separating the two scrolls. The raised decoration is bordered on both sides by an inscribed pattern of joining semi-circles set within two parallel lines. A central indented line runs around the centre circumference of the interior. See Chapter 21 for a full discussion of decoration.
Wt: 111.0g; D(ext): 96.8mm; W: 17.4mm; T: 8.9mm

Hoard F

Found during detecting by Charles Hodder in 1990. Finds with Jackson numbers were recovered by Hodder; finds with BM site codes were located during the subsequent BM excavations. All found in the Hoard F pit unless otherwise stated.

F.1a–e: Composite group (interlinked) (Pl. 14.19)

Rings and torc/bracelet fragments F.1b–e are looped onto large ring F.1a (**Fig. 23.4**).

F.1a: Gold/silver alloy large ring
BM: 1991,0501.1; Jackson no.: 1a
Gold/silver alloy large penannular ring with one tapered terminal and one cut end. Made from a strip with rectangular cross-section.
Wt: 71.0g; D(ext): 67.0mm; W: 7.0mm; T: 4.0mm

F.1b: Gold/silver alloy large ring
BM: 1991,0501.2; Jackson no.: 1b
Complete gold/silver alloy large ring, with overlapping flat terminals. Made from wire with circular cross-section.
Wt: 69.9g; D(ext): 66.0mm; D(wire): 6.0mm

F.1c: Gold/silver alloy torc
TUBULAR (TYPE 1)
BM: 1991,0501.5; Jackson no.: 1c
Gold/silver alloy terminal from Type 1 tubular torc. Plain, with a slight rim around the circumference of the dished face. The remains of the narrow tubular neck-ring have been flattened and made into a loop, which protrudes on the reverse of the terminal.
Does not seem to be a pair to F.1d.
Wt: 18.0g; D(term): 35.0mm

F.1d: Gold/silver alloy torc
TUBULAR (TYPE 1)
BM: 1991,0501.3; Jackson no.: 1e
Gold/silver alloy terminal from Type 1 tubular torc. Plain with a prominent raised rim and slightly concave circle in the centre of the face. The remains of the narrow tubular neck-ring have been flattened and made into a loop, which protrudes on the reverse of the terminal.
Does not seem to be a pair to F.1c.
Wt: 20.0g; D(term): 37.0mm

F.1e: Gold/silver alloy torc/bracelet
MSCC: (2P)R/ (3P(2P))R
BM: 1991,0501.4; Jackson no.: 1d
Fragment of gold/silver alloy multi-strand torc neck-ring or bracelet body: three ropes, each of two wires plied together, have been loosely twisted together and arranged into a rough loop. It is not clear if this is a short section of Stage III neck-ring/body (3P(2P))R, or lengths of a Stage II (2P)R

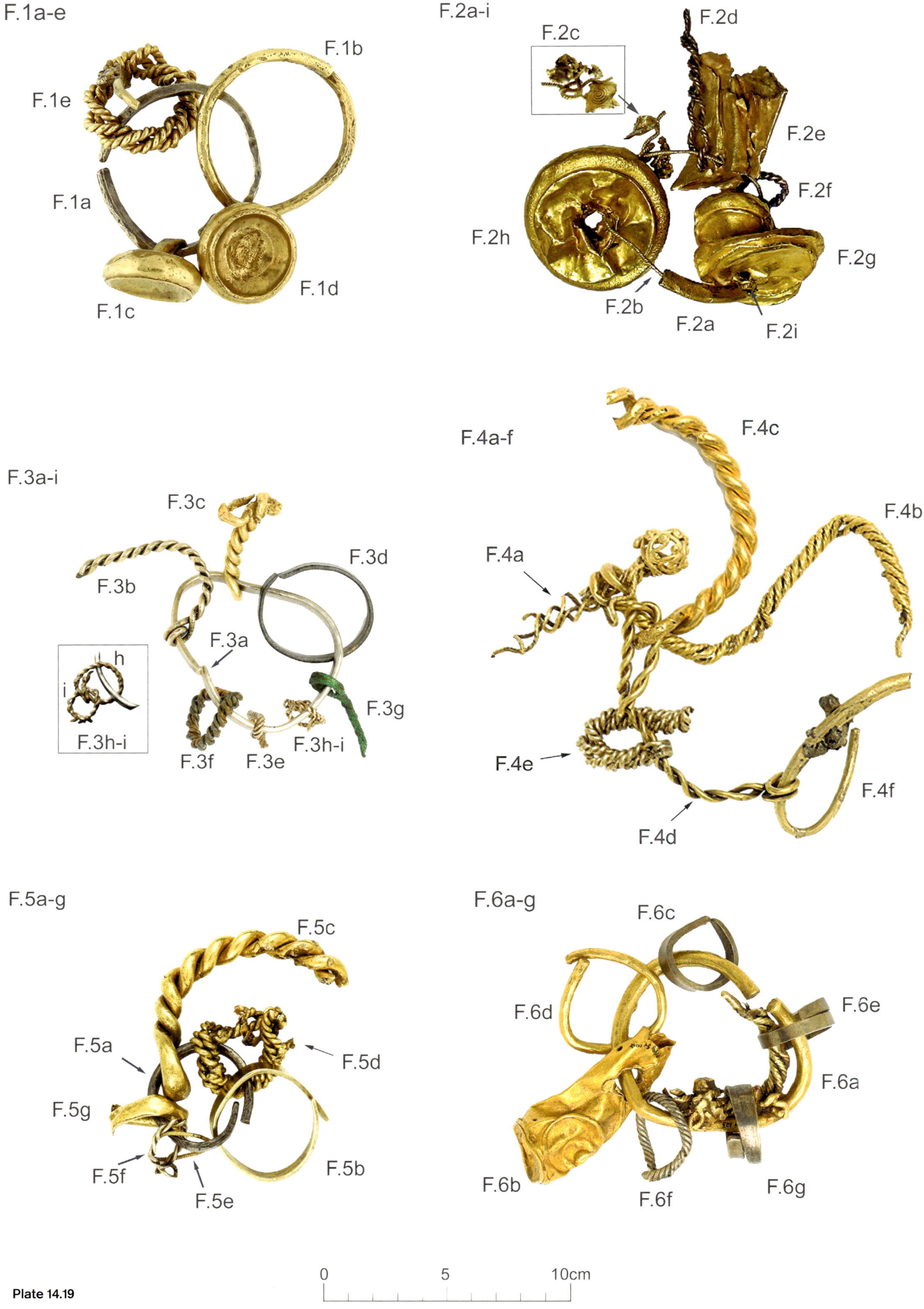
F.1a-e
F.1a
F.1b
F.1c
F.1d
F.1e
F.2a-i
F.2a
F.2b
F.2c
F.2d
F.2e
F.2f
F.2g
F.2h
F.2i
F.3a-i
F.3a
F.3b
F.3c
F.3d
F.3e
F.3f
F.3g
F.3h-i
h
i
F.3h-i
F.4a-f
F.4a
F.4b
F.4c
F.4d
F.4e
F.4f
F.5a-g
F.5a
F.5b
F.5c
F.5d
F.5e
F.5f
F.5g
F.6a-g
F.6a
F.6b
F.6c
F.6d
F.6e
F.6f
F.6g
0
5
10cm

Plate 14.19

neck-ring/body twisted together. A single additional strand of circular-section wire is fused onto one of the ropes.
Wt: 75.0g; D(ext): 48.0mm; D(nr): 13.0mm; D(rope): 5.0mm; D(wire): 2.2mm

F.2a–i: Composite group (interlinked) (Pl. 14.19)
Torc fragment F.2a is clamped over the join where the ends of wire loop F.2b meet. F.2c–i are looped onto this ring. Torc and wire fragments F.2c–i are looped onto F.2a–b. The components of F.2c are fused together. Tubular torc fragment F.2e is looped onto the wire through a pierced hole. Torc fragment F.2f is strung onto the wire through its loop terminal.
Wt: 135.0g (total for F.2a–i)

F.2a: Gold/silver alloy torc
TUBULAR (TYPE 1)
BM: 1991,0501.6; Jackson no.: 2a
Short length of neck-ring from gold/silver alloy Type 1 tubular torc.
L: 35.9mm

F.2b: Gold/silver alloy wire
BM: 1991,0501.6; Jackson no.: 2a
Length of gold/silver alloy twisted wire, bent into a loop.
D(ext): 66.6mm; D(wire): 1.5mm

F.2c: Gold/silver alloy torc
?TUBULAR
BM: 1991,0501.7; Jackson no.: 2b
Irregularly bent and looped length of gold/silver alloy twisted wire (similar to F.2a) with two small fused gold/silver alloy attachments: one an amorphous melted lump, the other a piece of sheet (probably from a tubular torc or torus torc terminal) with concentric circle decoration (see **Fig. 21.7**). There are similar concentric circle motifs on both tubular torcs such as S.13 and the torus terminals of the 'Great Torc', E.1a.
D(wire): 1.6mm; L: 29.9mm

F.2d: Gold/silver alloy torc/bracelet
MSCC: (3P)R
BM: 1991,0501.8; Jackson no.: 2c
Fragment of gold/silver alloy multi-strand torc neck-ring or bracelet body, broken at both ends: Stage II rope, formed from three circular-section strands of wire tightly plied together. The rope is folded in half and loosely twisted on itself.
D(nr): 2.6mm; D(wire): 1.1mm; L: 65.5mm

F.2e: Gold/silver alloy torc
TUBULAR (TYPE 4/5)
BM: 1991,0501.9; Jackson no.: 2d
Gold/silver alloy sheet fragment – a flattened section from the neck-ring of a Type 4 or 5 tubular torc. Roughly torn at both ends, pierced through near one end.
L: 56.0mm; T: 0.2mm

F.2f: Gold/silver alloy torc/bracelet
MSCC: (2P)R
BM: 1991,0501.10; Jackson no.: 2e
Fragment of gold/silver alloy multi-strand torc or bracelet, comprising one double-loop terminal (a continuous loop extending to form the two neck-ring/body wires), and a length of neck-ring/body, broken at the other end. Stage II construction of two circular-section wires plied tightly together. The whole fragment is coiled round into a loop.
D(ext): 20.2mm; D(nr): 3.2mm; D(wire): 1.7mm; D(term): 8.1mm

F.2g: Gold/silver alloy torc
TUBULAR (TYPE 3)
BM: 1991,0501.11; Jackson no.: 2f
Gold/silver alloy buffer terminal from Type 3 tubular torc; flattened, damaged and perforated through the centre of the terminal. Flat face with raised outer rim. Behind the terminal the neck-ring widens into a bead with concentric rim. Torn across at start of neck-ring.
Does not appear to be a pair to F.2h. Similar, although not the pair, to F.35, F.47 and F.48.
D(term): 55.0mm; L: 39.9mm

F.2h: Gold/silver alloy torc
TUBULAR (TYPE 3)
BM: 1991,0501.13; Jackson no.: 2g
Gold/silver alloy buffer terminal from Type 3 tubular torc; flattened, damaged and perforated through the centre of the terminal. Smooth, dished face with raised rim, and outer band around the edge textured with small tool marks. Torn across at start of neck-ring.
Does not appear to be a pair to F.2g.
D(term): 59.5mm; L: 23.6mm

F.2i: Gold/silver alloy wire
BM: 1991,0501.12; Jackson no.: 2h
Short length of gold/silver alloy circular-section wire, roughly formed into a small ring with overlapping ends.
D(ext): 9.0mm; D(wire): 1.4mm

F.3a–i: Composite group (interlinked) (Pl. 14.19)
Large ring and torc/bracelet fragments F.3b–h are looped onto large ring F.3a. F.3b, c and g are looped on through their terminals. Torc/bracelet fragment F.3i is looped onto F.3h (see **Fig. 20.29**).
Wt: 110.6g (total for F.3a–i)

F.3a: Gold/silver alloy large ring
BM: 1991,0501.120; Jackson no.: 3a
Complete gold/silver alloy large ring with slightly overlapping rounded, tapering terminals. Slightly irregular ovoid shape in plan. Made from a strip with rectangular cross-section.
Wt: 37.0g; D(ext): 74.3mm; W: 6.9mm; T: 3.0mm

F.3b: Gold/silver alloy torc/bracelet
MSCC: (2P)R
BM: 1991,0501.121; Jackson no.: 3b
Fragment of gold/silver alloy multi-strand torc or bracelet, comprising one double-loop terminal (a continuous loop extending to form the two neck-ring/body wires), and a length of neck-ring/body, broken at the other end. Stage II

construction of two circular-section wires plied tightly together.
Wt: 13.2g; D(nr): 4.6mm; D(wire): 2.5mm; D(term): 10.7mm; L: 56.8mm

F.3c: Gold/silver alloy torc/bracelet
MSCC: (2P)R
BM: 1991,0501.122; Jackson no.: 3c
Fragment of gold/silver alloy multi-strand torc or bracelet, comprising one ring terminal (formed from the two neck-ring/body wires, with additional metal added to thicken it), and a length of neck-ring/body, broken at the other end. Stage II construction of two circular-section wires plied tightly together. The broken end is a fused mass, as if the fragment has been partially melted.
Wt: 29.7g; D(ext): 54.0mm; D(nr): 7.1mm; D(wire): 3.5mm; D(term): 13.2mm

F.3d: Copper alloy large ring
BM: 1991,0702.10; Jackson no.: 3d
Copper alloy large ring with abutting terminals. Made from a strip with rectangular cross-section. One tapering, slightly rounded terminal and one cut end.
Wt: 14.0g; D(ext): 47.0mm; W: 6.4mm; T: 1.8mm

F.3e: Gold/silver alloy torc/bracelet
MSCC: (4PZ)R
BM: 1991,0501.123; Jackson no.: 3e
Fragment of gold/silver alloy multi-strand torc neck-ring or bracelet body, cut at both ends. Stage II construction of four circular-section wires plied together Z-twist. This rope is bent into an oval ring with overlapping ends, both of which are cut.
D(nr): 3.0mm; D(wire): 1.2mm; L: 27.4mm

F.3f: Copper alloy torc/bracelet
MSCC: (2P(2P))R
BM: 1991,0702.11; Jackson no.: 3f
Fragment of copper alloy multi-strand torc neck-ring or bracelet body, broken at both ends. Stage III construction with cable formed from two ropes plied together, each of which is made up of two circular-section wires which are themselves plied tightly together. The short length of cable is bent into a teardrop-shaped loop with touching ends.
Wt: 10.3g; D(nr): 5.8mm; D(rope): 3.0mm; D(wire): 1.6mm; L: 42.5mm

F.3g: Copper alloy torc/bracelet
MSCC: (4P)?Q
BM: 1991,0702.12; Jackson no.: 3g
Fragment of copper alloy multi-strand torc or bracelet, comprising one double-loop terminal (a continuous loop formed from a pair of wires doubled back on themselves, extending to form the four neck-ring/body wires), and a length of neck-ring/body, broken at the other end. Stage II construction of four wires plied together. The wires are not well preserved, but are possibly square in cross-section.
Wt: 3.3g; D(nr): 4.0mm; D(wire): 1.4mm; D(term): 15.4mm; L: 43.3mm

F.3h: Gold/silver alloy torc/bracelet
MSCC: (2PZ)Q
BM: 1991,0501.124; Jackson no.: 3h
Fragment of gold/silver alloy multi-strand torc or bracelet, comprising one loop terminal (a single continuous loop extending to form the two neck-ring/body wires), and a length of neck-ring/body, cut at the other end. Stage II construction of two square-section wires plied loosely together Z-twist. The fragment is bent into a ring with the cut ends overlapping with the terminal.
Probably part of the same original object as F.3i, with which it is interlinked.
D(ext): 20.1mm; D(nr): 2.3mm; D(wire): 1.4mm; D(term): 10.2mm

F.3i: Gold/silver alloy torc/bracelet
MSCC: (2PZ)Q
BM: 1991,0501.124; Jackson no.: 3h
Fragment of gold/silver alloy multi-strand torc neck-ring or bracelet body, cut at both ends. Stage II construction of two square-section wires plied loosely together Z-twist. The fragment is bent into a ring with the cut ends overlapping.
Probably part of the same original object as F.3h, with which it is interlinked.
D(ext): 13.4mm; D(nr): 2.3mm; D(wire): 1.4mm

F.4a–f: Composite group (interlinked) (Pl. 14.19)
Torc and bracelet fragments F.4a–f are interlinked in a complex way. F.4a passes through the terminal of F.4b. F.4b and a loop at the end of F.4d both pass through the terminal of F.4c. F.4d also passes through the terminal of F.4e. F.4f is looped through the terminal of F.4d.
Wt: 405.0g (total for F.4a–f)

F.4a: Gold/silver alloy torc
MSCC: (6C)T
BM: 1991,0501.46; Jackson no.: 53a
Fragment of gold/silver alloy multi-strand torc, comprising one terminal and length of Stage II neck-ring formed from six twisted wires coiled together. The neck-ring is very distorted and fragmentary, with clear evidence of wear of the internal faces of the wires, where they once touched and rubbed together. The wires are individually cut or broken away at different lengths. Elaborate cage terminal formed from the neck-ring wires, with involuted loops and additional applied scroll and pellet motifs. In the area of the terminal, the wires are circular, rather than square, in cross-section. Some evidence that the terminal has been part melted on one side.
D(wire): 1.5mm; D(term): 20.5mm; L: 91.9mm

F.4b: Gold/silver alloy torc
MSCC: (4C)T
BM: 1991,0501.47; Jackson no.: 53b
Fragment of gold/silver alloy multi-strand torc, comprising ring terminal and length of neck-ring, the wires being cut/broken to different lengths. Stage II construction of four twisted wires coiled together. The terminal is a pair of confronted, thickened circular-section rings, each a continuous loop extending to form a pair of square-section twisted wires. These two pairs form the four neck-ring

strands. The whole fragment is bent into an S-shape.
D(nr): 6.4mm; D(wire): 2.7mm; D(term): 16.7mm; L: 130.6mm

F.4c: Gold/silver alloy torc/bracelet
MSCC: (2P)R
BM: 1991,0501.48; Jackson no.: 53c
Fragment of gold/silver alloy multi-strand torc or bracelet, comprising one loop/ring terminal (a continuous, perhaps slightly thickened, loop extending to form the two neck-ring/body wires), and a length of neck-ring/body, broken at the other end. Stage II construction of two circular-section wires plied tightly together. The end of the terminal is partially melted, and small pellets of melted gold adhere to the neck-ring wires in several places.
D(nr): 10.1mm; D(wire): 5.1mm; D(term): 23.1mm; L: 106.9mm

F.4d: Gold/silver alloy torc/bracelet
MSCC: (2PZ)R
BM: 1991,0501.49; Jackson no.: 53d
Fragment of gold/silver alloy multi-strand torc or bracelet, comprising one double-loop terminal (a continuous loop extending to form the two neck-ring/body wires), and a length of neck-ring/body, broken at the other end. Stage II construction of two circular-section wires plied tightly together Z-twist. The broken end is bent back on itself to form a teardrop-shaped loop.
D(nr): 6.0mm; D(wire): 2.4mm; D(term): 15.3mm; L: 102.6mm

F.4e: Gold/silver alloy torc/bracelet
MSCC: (3P(2P))R
BM: 1991,0501.50; Jackson no.: 53e
Fragment of gold/silver alloy multi-strand torc or bracelet, comprising one triple-loop terminal and a length of Stage III neck-ring/body, cut at the other end. The cable is formed from three ropes plied together, each of which is made up of two circular-section wires which are themselves plied tightly together. The terminal consists of three loops, each a continuous loop extending to form the two wires of one of the ropes. The torc fragment is bent back on itself to form a U-shape.
D(nr): 8.7mm; D(wire): 2.1mm; D(term): 11.4mm; L: 50.8mm

F.4f: Gold/silver alloy torc
TUBULAR (TYPE 1)
BM: 1991,0501.51; Jackson no.: 53f
Fragment of gold/silver alloy Type 1 tubular torc neck-ring: a tube which tapers to a solid rod at the narrower end. Broken at both ends. A small melted mass with partially coalesced gold wire fragments is fused to the hollow end. The fragment has been bent back on itself, to form a loop.
D(nr): 7.2mm; L: 82.8mm; W: 28.3mm

F.5a–g: Composite group (interlinked) (Pl. 14.19)
Ring, torc/bracelet and wire fragments F.5b–g are looped onto large ring F.5a. F.5c is looped on through its terminal (see **Figs 17.1, 17.18, 20.30**).
Wt: 281.3g (total for F.5a–g)

F.5a: Gold/silver alloy large ring
BM: 1991,0501.53; Jackson no.: 55a
Gold/silver alloy large ring with overlapping terminals. Made from a strip with rectangular cross-section. One tapered terminal and one cut end.
D(ext): 44.8mm; L: 7.2mm; W: 3.7mm

F.5b: Gold/silver alloy large ring
BM: 1991,0501.54; Jackson no.: 55b
Gold/silver alloy large ring with overlapping terminals. Made from a strip with rectangular cross-section. One tapered terminal and one cut end.
D(ext): 50.2mm; L: 7.7mm; W: 2.0mm

F.5c: Gold/silver alloy torc
MSCC: (2P)R
BM: 1991,0501.55; Jackson no.: 55c
[Analysed: see Ch. 17]
Fragment of gold/silver alloy multi-strand torc, comprising one thickened ring terminal (formed from the ends of the neck-ring wires) and length of neck-ring, cut at the other end (see **Fig. 17.18a**). Stage II construction of two circular-section wires plied together. Flaws are visible on the terminal, and the neck-ring shows evidence of cracking, cut-marks or chisel blows, and melting.
D(nr): 11.8mm; D(wire): 5.9mm; D(term): 27.2mm; L: 90.6mm

F.5d: Gold/silver alloy torc/bracelet
MSCC: (4P(2P))R
BM: 1991,0501.56; Jackson no.: 55d
[Analysed: see Ch. 17]
Fragment of gold/silver alloy multi-strand torc neck-ring or bracelet body, broken at both ends and roughly shaped into a ring. Stage III construction with cable formed from four ropes plied loosely together, each of which is made up of two circular-section wires which are themselves plied tightly together. Gold sheet fragments and droplets are fused on in several places.
D(nr): 11.0mm; D(rope): 4.4mm; D(wire): 2.1mm; L: 43.9mm

F.5e: Gold/silver alloy wire
BM: 1991,0501.57; Jackson no.: 55e
[Analysed: see Ch. 17]
Short length of twisted gold/silver alloy wire, cut or broken at both ends and roughly shaped into a ring.
D(wire): 1.7mm; L: 28.1mm

F.5f: Gold/silver alloy torc/bracelet
MSCC: (2P)R
BM: 1991,0501.58; Jackson no.: 55f
[Analysed: see Ch. 17]
Fragment of gold/silver alloy multi-strand torc neck-ring or bracelet body, cut at both ends. Stage II construction of two circular-section wires plied loosely together. The fragment is bent into a ring with the cut ends overlapping.
D(nr): 3.0mm; D(wire): 1.4mm; L: 32.9mm

F.5g: Gold/silver alloy torc
TUBULAR (TYPE 1)

BM: 1991,0501.59; Jackson no.: 55g
Fragment of gold/silver alloy Type 1 tubular torc neck-ring, a hollow tube of thin sheet, broken at both ends. Distorted and roughly shaped into a ring.
D(nr): 9.0mm; L: 32.4mm

F.6a–g: Composite group (interlinked) (Pl. 14.19)
Rings and torc/bracelet fragments F.6b–g are looped onto large ring F.6a (see **Fig. 20.31**).
Wt: 211.6g (total for F.6a–g)

F.6a: Gold/silver alloy large ring; torc
MSCC: (4C)T
BM: 1991,0501.103; Jackson no.: 116a
Complete gold/silver alloy large penannular ring of solid circular cross-section, slightly bent out of shape, with flat-ended terminals. There is a melted cavity about half-way around the ring. There are globules and lumps of semi-coalesced gold fused to the object in several places, and a mass of part-melted fragments fused to one half of the inner surface. The major component of this fused mass is a fragment of gold/silver alloy torc neck-ring or bracelet body, comprising four twisted wires coiled together, melted and broken at the ends. Other fused fragments include twisted wires and a strand of circular-section wire.
D(ext): 74.7mm; D(wire): 5.6mm

F.6b: Gold/silver alloy torc
TUBULAR (TYPE 4)
BM: 1991,0501.104; Jackson no.: 116b
Terminal fragment of gold/silver alloy Type 4 tubular torc: torn, crushed and distorted (see **Fig. 21.22**). At the terminal, the exterior of the neck-ring is decorated with repoussé and chased ornament as well as punch-marks. Overall, the pattern is in the form of an elongated lyre; the background is stippled, but the raised motifs are predominantly plain, although some of the motifs, particularly the raised sections delineating the lyre, are laddered. The expanded terminal has a round, dished end-plate, with a repoussé circular 'segmented wreath' and a small central circular hole/perforation. There is a similar perforation through the neck-ring near its broken end, and another, smaller one just short of the terminal. A large ragged hole was also punched through the broken end of the neck-ring, probably to allow suspension. See Chapter 21 for a full discussion of decoration.
D(term): 25.1mm; L: 71.9mm

F.6c: Gold/silver alloy small ring
BM: 1991,0501.105; Jackson no.: 116c
Gold/silver alloy small penannular ring, made from a strip with rectangular cross-section. One tapering terminal and one cut end.
D(ext): 27.2mm; W: 9.8mm; T: 2.5mm

F.6d: Gold/silver alloy large ring
BM: 1991,0501.106; Jackson no.: 116d
Complete gold/silver alloy large ring of solid circular cross-section, with overlapping flat-ended terminals.
D(ext): 40.7mm; D(wire): 3.9mm

F.6e: Gold/silver alloy small ring
BM: 1991,0501.107; Jackson no.: 116e
Complete gold/silver alloy small spiral ring, made from a strip with rectangular cross-section. Neatly rounded tapering terminals, overlapping by just over half a turn.
D(ext): 27.5mm; W: 10.8mm; T: 1.8mm

F.6f: Gold/silver alloy torc/bracelet
MSCC: (5C)R
BM: 1991,0702.2; Jackson no.: 116f
Fragment of gold/silver alloy multi-strand torc neck-ring or bracelet body, cut or broken at both ends. Stage II construction of five circular-section wires coiled together. The fragment is bent into a ring, with the ends slightly overlapping.
D(nr): 3.7mm; L: 34.2mm

F.6g: Gold/silver alloy small ring
BM: 1991,0501.108; Jackson no.: 116g
Complete gold/silver alloy small spiral ring made from a strip with rectangular cross-section. One tapering terminal and one cut end, overlapping by around half a turn.
D(ext): 28.2mm; D(wire): 1.2mm; W: 12.0mm; T: 2.7mm

F.7a–g: Composite group (interlinked) (Pl. 14.20)
Torc/bracelet/wire fragments F.7b–g are looped onto large ring F.7a. All are looped through their terminals, except for F.7e, which is looped on as a ring (see **Fig. 23.3**).
Wt: 291.5g (total for F.7a–g)

F.7a: Gold/silver alloy large ring
BM: 1991,0702.3; Jackson no.: 117a
Gold/silver alloy large penannular ring of irregular, oval shape, formed from circular-section wire.
D(ext): 138.4mm; D(wire): 4.5mm

F.7b: Gold/silver alloy wire/?torc/?bracelet
MSCC: ?(2P)T
BM: 1991,0501.109; Jackson no.: 117b
Fragment of gold/silver alloy twisted wire, bent back and plied on itself, with a small loop at the fold. It may be from a multi-strand torc or bracelet, with Stage II neck-ring/body and simple loop terminal, but the use of twisted wire for the terminal portion would be unusual.
D(nr): 4.4mm; D(wire): 2.3mm; L: 58mm

F.7c: Gold/silver alloy torc/bracelet
MSCC: (2P)R
BM: 1991,0702.4; Jackson no.: 117c
Fragment of gold/silver alloy multi-strand torc or bracelet, comprising one double-loop terminal (a continuous loop extending to form the two neck-ring/body wires), and a length of neck-ring/body, broken at the other end. Stage II construction of two circular-section wires plied tightly together.
D(nr): 3.6mm; D(wire): 2.5mm; D(term): 17.8mm; L: 67.9mm

F.7d: Gold/silver alloy torc/bracelet
MSCC: (2P(2PZ))R
BM: 1991,0501.110; Jackson no.: 117d

Fragment of gold/silver alloy multi-strand torc or bracelet, comprising one thickened ring terminal, continuing into the paired ropes of the neck-ring/body. Stage III construction of two ropes plied loosely together, each of which is made up of two circular-section wires which are themselves plied tightly together Z-twist. Each of the ropes is cut/broken at a different point.
D(nr): 7.8mm; D(rope): 3.9mm; D(wire): 2.0mm; D(term): 18.8mm; L: 82.6mm

F.7e: Gold/silver alloy wire/?torc/bracelet
MSCC: (2P)T
BM: 1991,0501.111; Jackson no.: 117e
Fragment of gold/silver alloy twisted wire, cut or broken at both ends, bent/looped and plied back on itself. Possibly part of a multi-strand torc or bracelet, comprising a simple cage terminal and length of neck-ring/body with Stage II construction. The ?terminal is formed from the continuous, looped wire, folded into two involuted loops. The whole fragment is curled into a ring.
D(nr): 6.0mm; D(wire): 3.3mm; L: 64.5mm

F.7f: Gold/silver alloy bracelet
MSCC: (2P)R
BM: 1991,0501.112; Jackson no.: 117f
Broken gold/silver alloy multi-strand bracelet, Stage II body formed from two circular-section wires plied together. One of the wires is broken in the middle, and the whole is heavily bent and distorted. One terminal is a double-hook terminal formed from the two ends of the wire, and the other is a simple loop where the wire has been bent back on itself.
D(nr): 5.6mm; D(wire): 2.7mm; D(term): 13.5mm; L: 146.2mm

F.7g: Gold/silver alloy torc/bracelet
MSCC: (3P)2R+1T
BM: 1991,0501.113; Jackson no.: 117g
Fragment of gold/silver alloy multi-strand torc or bracelet, comprising one ring terminal and a length of neck-ring/body, cut or broken and part melted at the other end. Stage II construction formed from two circular-section and one (discontinuous) twisted wire, plied together. The thickened ring terminal is a continuous loop extending to become the pair of circular-section neck-ring/body wires. The end of the twisted wire is looped around the base of the terminal. There is a mass of semi-coalesced globules and plied paired wire fragments fused to the neck-ring.
D(nr): 7.5mm; D(wire): 3.3mm; D(term): 16.3mm; L: 78.9mm

F.8a–e: Composite group (interlinked) (Pl. 14.20)
Wire/strip and torc/bracelet fragments F.8b–e are looped through the terminal of F.8a. In the case of torc/bracelet fragment F.8b, the body of the loop rather than the terminal is used.
Wt: 19.3g (total for F.8a–e)

F.8a: Gold/silver alloy torc
MSCC: (2P(3P))R
BM: 1991,0702.62; Jackson no.: 262a
Fragment of gold/silver alloy multi-strand torc, comprising one thickened ring terminal, continuing into the paired ropes of the neck-ring/body, which are broken at slightly different points. Stage III construction of two ropes plied loosely together, each of which is made up of three circular-section wires which are themselves plied tightly together.
D(nr): 3.6mm; D(wire): 1.7mm; D(term): 21.8mm; L: 55.2mm

F.8b: Copper alloy torc/bracelet
MSCC: (2PZ)R
BM: 1991,0702.63; Jackson no.: 262b
Fragment of copper alloy multi-strand torc or bracelet, comprising a single-loop terminal (a continuous loop extending to form the two neck-ring/body wires) and length of neck-ring/body, broken at the other end. Stage II construction of two circular-section wires plied together Z-twist. The whole fragment is curved into a teardrop-shaped loop.
D(nr): 3.0mm; D(wire): 1.6mm; D(term): 6.4mm; L: 50.1mm

F.8c: Copper alloy wire/strip
BM: 1991,0702.64; Jackson no.: 262c
Fragment of copper alloy wire/strip with squarish cross-section, bent into a polygonal loop.
D(ext): 24mm; L: 24mm; T: 1.6mm

F.8d: Copper alloy wire/strip
BM: 1991,0702.65; Jackson no.: 262c
Fragment of copper alloy wire/strip with squarish cross-section, bent into a polygonal loop.
D(ext): 25.9mm; L: 25.9mm; T: 1.6mm

F.8e: Copper alloy wire/strip
BM: 1991,0702.66; Jackson no.: 262c
Fragment of copper alloy wire/strip with squarish cross-section, bent into a polygonal loop. One additional loose fragment.
D(ext): 25.2; 14.0mm; L: 25.2; 14.0mm; T: 1.6mm

F.9a–d: Composite group (interlinked) (Pl. 14.20)
Torc/bracelet fragments F.9a–d are believed to have been an interlinked group, as they were presented by the finder looped together on a piece of twine (though without written comment).

F.9a: Gold/silver alloy torc/bracelet
MSCC: (4P)T
BM: 1991,0501.125; Jackson no.: 4a
[Analysed: see Ch. 17]
Fragment of gold/silver alloy multi-strand torc or bracelet, comprising one thickened ring terminal: a continuous loop continuing into two pairs of neck-ring/body wires. These two pairs form the four neck-ring/body strands. Stage II construction, originally of four twisted strands plied together, though one strand is now missing, broken off at the terminal. The whole fragment is bent into a teardrop shape with crossed ends.
Wt: 10.9g; D(ext): 38.9mm; D(nr): 4.5mm; D(wire): 1.8mm; D(term): 9.6mm

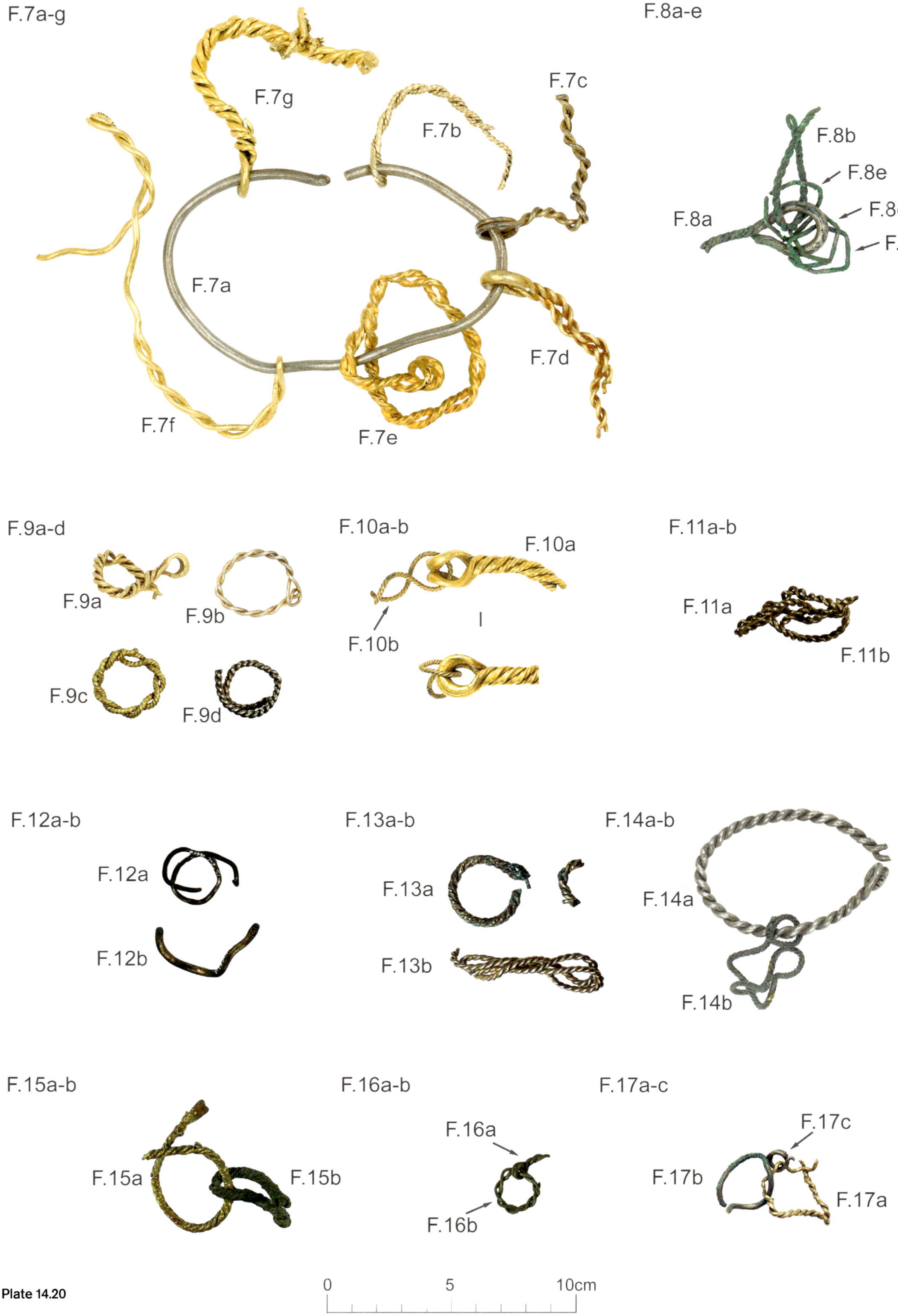

F.7a-g
F.7g
F.7b
F.7c
F.7a
F.7d
F.7f
F.7e
F.8a-e
F.8b
F.8e
F.8d
F.8a
F.8c
F.9a-d
F.9a
F.9b
F.9c
F.9d
F.10a-b
F.10a
F.10b
F.11a-b
F.11a
F.11b
F.12a-b
F.12a
F.12b
F.13a-b
F.13a
F.13b
F.14a-b
F.14a
F.14b
F.15a-b
F.15a
F.15b
F.16a-b
F.16a
F.16b
F.17a-c
F.17c
F.17b
F.17a
0
5
10cm

Plate 14.20

F.9b: Gold/silver alloy torc/bracelet
MSCC: (2P)R
BM: 1991,0501.126; Jackson no.: 4b
Fragment of gold/silver alloy multi-strand torc or bracelet, comprising one single-loop terminal (a continuous loop extending to form the two neck-ring/body wires), and a length of neck-ring/body, cut at the other end. Stage II construction of two circular-section wires plied tightly together. The whole fragment is bent into a circle, with the cut ends protruding through the terminal.
Wt: 4.4g; D(ext): 35.0mm; D(nr): 3.4mm; D(wire): 1.4mm; D(term): 8.0mm

F.9c: Gold/silver alloy torc/bracelet
MSCC: (2P)T
BM: 1991,0501.127; Jackson no.: 4c
[Analysed: see Ch. 17]
Fragment of gold/silver alloy multi-strand torc neck-ring or bracelet body, cut at both ends. Stage II construction of two twisted wires plied loosely together. The whole fragment is bent into a circle, with the cut ends overlapping.
Wt: 10.1g; D(ext): 29.3mm; D(nr): 4.8mm; D(wire): 2.2mm

F.9d: Gold/silver alloy torc/bracelet
MSCC: (2P)R
BM: 1991,0501.128; Jackson no.: 4d
[Analysed: see Ch. 17]
Fragment of gold/silver alloy multi-strand torc neck-ring or bracelet body, cut at both ends. Stage II construction of two circular-section wires plied tightly together. The whole fragment is bent into a circle, with the cut ends overlapping by around half a turn.
Wt: 6.4g; D(ext): 27.0mm; D(nr): 3.3mm; D(wire): 1.5mm

F.10a–b: Composite group (interlinked) (Pl. 14.20)
Wire fragment F.10b is looped through the terminal of torc fragment F.10a.
Wt: 34.5g (total for F.10a–b)

F.10a: Gold/silver alloy torc/bracelet
MSCC: (4P)T
BM: 1991,0501.40; Jackson no.: 46a
Fragment of gold/silver alloy multi-strand torc or bracelet comprising a ring/cage terminal, and a length of neck-ring/body, broken at the other end. Stage II construction of four twisted wires plied loosely together. The terminal is a pair of confronted, thickened circular-section rings, each a continuous loop extending to form a pair of square-section twisted wires. These two pairs form the four neck-ring strands.
D(nr): 7.6mm; D(wire): 3.2mm; D(term): 14.7mm; L: 57.7mm

F.10b: Gold/silver alloy wire
BM: 1991,0501.41; Jackson no.: 46b
Fragment of gold/silver alloy twisted wire, broken at both ends. Bent into a loose figure of eight.
D(wire): 2.0mm; L: 35.8mm

F.11a–b: Composite group (interlinked) (Pl. 14.20)
MSCC: (2PZ)R
Torc/bracelet fragments F. 11a and F.11b are interlinked, and probably originally formed part of the same object. Each is a fragment of gold/silver alloy multi-strand torc neck-ring or bracelet body, broken at both ends and bent into a crude ring. Stage II construction of two circular-section wires plied together Z-twist.
Wt: 12.2g (total for F.11a–b)

F.11a: Gold/silver alloy torc/bracelet
BM: 1991,0501.133; Jackson no.: 22a
[Analysed: see Ch. 17]
D(nr): 3.2mm; D(wire): 1.5mm; L: 51.6mm

F.11b: Gold/silver alloy torc/bracelet
BM: 1991,0501.133; Jackson no.: 22b
D(nr): 3.2mm; D(wire): 1.5mm; L: 35.2mm

F.12a–b: Composite group (interlinked) (Pl. 14.20)
Wire fragments F.12a and F.12b were originally interlinked.

F.12a: Gold/silver alloy wire
BM: 1991,0702.51; Jackson no.: 205a
Fragment of gold/silver alloy circular-section wire, broken at both ends. Roughly coiled into a loose two-turn spiral.
Wt: 3.1g; D(wire): 1.9mm; L: 31.5mm

F.12b: Gold/silver alloy wire
BM: 1991,0702.50; Jackson no.: 205b
Fragment of gold/silver alloy circular-section wire, bent and distorted, broken at both ends.
Wt: 3.8g; D(wire): 3.1mm; L: 41.9mm

F.13a–b: Composite group (interlinked) (Pl. 14.20)
Torc/bracelet fragments F.13a and F.13b were originally interlinked.

F.13a: Copper alloy torc/bracelet
MSCC: (4P)T
BM: 1991,0501.182; Jackson no.: 155a/b
Fragment of copper alloy, possibly gilded, multi-strand torc neck-ring or bracelet body, broken at both ends and bent into a crude ring. Stage II construction of four twisted wires plied together. Now in two parts.
Wt: 5.0g; D(nr): 3.7mm; D(wire): 1.4mm; L: 31.0mm

F.13b: Gold/silver alloy torc/bracelet
MSCC: (2P)R
BM: 1991,0501.182; Jackson no.: 155c
Fragment of gold/silver alloy multi-strand multi-strand torc neck-ring or bracelet body, broken at both ends and bent into a rough double figure-of-eight shape. Stage II construction of two circular-section wires plied together.
Wt: 8.4g; D(nr): 2.4mm; D(wire): 1.3mm; L: 56.2mm

F.14a–b: Composite group (interlinked) (Pl. 14.20)
The neck-ring/body of torc/bracelet fragment F.14a passes through loop at the end of wire fragment F.14b.
Wt: 34.7g (total for F.14a–b)

F.14a: Gold/silver alloy torc/bracelet
MSCC: (2P)R
BM: 1991,0501.209; Jackson no.: 214a
Fragment of gold/silver alloy multi-strand torc or bracelet comprising one double-loop terminal (a continuous loop extending to form the two neck-ring/body wires), and a length of neck-ring/body, broken at the other end. Stage II construction of two circular-section wires plied together. The whole fragment is curved into an oval loop.
D(nr): 5.5mm; D(wire): 2.6mm; D(term): 10.4mm; L: 79.1mm

F.14b: Copper alloy wire
BM: 1991,0702.9; Jackson no.: 214b
[Analysed: see Ch. 17]
Fragment of twisted copper alloy wire, broken at both ends (**Fig. 17.36**). Bent and distorted into an irregular shape with a loop at one end.
D(wire): 2.4mm; L: 39.5mm

F.15a–b: Composite group (interlinked) (Pl. 14.20)
Torc/bracelet fragments F.15a and F.15b are looped together.
Wt: 19.4g (total for F.15a–b)

F.15a: Copper alloy torc/bracelet
MSCC: (4P)T
BM: 1991,0702.137; Jackson no.: 257a
[Analysed: see Ch. 17]
Fragment of gilded copper alloy multi-strand torc or bracelet comprising one double-ring terminal and length of neck-ring/body, cut at the other end (see **Fig. 17.49**). Stage II construction of four twisted wires plied together. The terminal is a pair of circular-section loops, soldered together to form a single ring, which extends to form two pairs of square-section twisted wires. These two pairs form the four neck-ring strands. The terminal has been flattened and broken. The whole fragment has been bent into a ring with overlapping ends.
D(nr): 3.9mm; D(wire): 1.2mm; L: 53.5mm

F.15b: Copper alloy torc/bracelet
MSCC: (5C)T
BM: 1991,0702.138; Jackson no.: 257b
Fragment of copper alloy multi-strand torc neck-ring or bracelet body, cut at one end and broken at the other. Stage II construction of five twisted wires coiled together. The whole fragment has been bent to form a crude ring.
D(nr): 5.2mm; D(wire): 1.6mm; L: 41.1mm

F.16a–b: Composite group (interlinked) (Pl. 14.20)
Torc/bracelet fragment F.16b is looped through the terminal of torc/bracelet fragment F.16a. They probably originally formed part of the same object.
Wt: 2.8g (total for F.16a–b)

F.16a: Copper alloy torc/bracelet
MSCC: (2P)R
BM: 1991,0702.226; Jackson no.: 450a
Fragment of copper alloy multi-strand torc or bracelet, comprising one double-loop terminal (a continuous loop extending to form the two neck-ring/body wires), and a length of neck-ring/body, broken at the other end. Stage II construction of two circular-section wires plied loosely together.
D(nr): 3.0mm; D(wire): 1.3mm; D(term): 6.8mm; L: 18.5mm

F.16b: Copper alloy torc/bracelet
MSCC: (2P)R
BM: 1991,0702.227; Jackson no.: 450b
Fragment of copper alloy multi-strand torc neck-ring or bracelet body, cut at both ends. Stage II construction of two circular-section wires plied loosely together. The fragment is bent into a ring with overlapping ends.
D(nr): 3.6mm; D(wire): 1.3mm; L: 20.8mm

F.17a–c: Composite group (interlinked) (Pl. 14.20)
Wire F.17b and torc/bracelet fragment F.17c are looped onto torc/bracelet fragment F.17a.
Wt: 7.5g (total for F.17a–c)

F.17a: Gold/silver alloy torc/bracelet
MSCC: (2P)Q
BM: 1991,0501.216; Jackson no.: 286a
[Analysed: see Ch. 17]
Fragment of gold/silver alloy multi-strand torc neck-ring or bracelet body, cut at both ends. Stage II construction of two lightly twisted square-section wires plied together, one wire extending further than the other. The fragment is bent into an irregular ring with overlapping ends.
D(nr): 2.2mm; D(wire): 1.5mm; L: 30.5mm

F.17b: Gold/silver alloy wire
BM: 1991,0702.8; Jackson no.: 286b
[Analysed: see Ch. 17]
Fragment of gold/silver alloy circular-section wire, broken at both ends, bent into an irregular penannular ring. This precious metal alloy also shows traces of mercury gilding (see **Fig. 17.51a**).
D(wire): 2.0mm; L: 27.5mm

F.17c: Gold/silver alloy torc/bracelet
BM: 1991,0501.217; Jackson no.: 286c
Double-loop terminal from gold/silver alloy multi-strand torc or bracelet, formed from a continuous length of circular-section wire.
D(wire): 1.3mm; D(term): 8.4mm; L: 11.8mm

F.18a–l: Composite group (interlinked) (Pl. 14.21)
Rings, wire and torc/bracelet fragments F.18a–l were originally linked together in a chain: a to b, b to c etc. The only exception is the small fragment of strip, F.18i, which was attached to the torc fragment F.18h.
Wt: 127.7g (total for F.18a–l)

F.18a: Gold/silver alloy wire
BM: 1991,0501.62; Jackson no.: 59a
Fragment of gold/silver alloy twisted wire, spiralled into a ring. Broken at both ends.
D(ext): 28.6mm; W: 14.1mm; T: 2.5mm

F.18b: Gold/silver alloy small ring
BM: 1991,0501.63; Jackson no.: 59b
Complete gold/silver alloy small ring with overlapping tapered and roughly-rounded terminals. Made from a strip with rectangular cross-section.
D(ext): 25.7mm; W: 6.2mm; T: 2.8mm

F.18c: Gold/silver alloy small ring
BM: 1991,0501.64; Jackson no.: 59c
Gold/silver alloy small penannular ring made from a strip with squarish cross-section. One rounded and one cut end.
D(ext): 28.1mm; W: 5.1mm; T: 3.4mm

F.18d: Gold/silver alloy small ring
BM: 1991,0501.65; Jackson no.: 59d
Complete gold/silver alloy small ring with overlapping tapered, rounded terminals. Made from a strip with rectangular cross-section.
D(ext): 27.4mm; W: 13.0mm; T: 1.8mm

F.18e: Gold/silver alloy small ring
BM: 1991,0501.66; Jackson no.: 59e
Gold/silver alloy small penannular ring made from a strip with thick, rectangular cross-section. One tapered and one cut end.
D(ext): 21.7mm; W: 8.1mm; T: 3mm

F.18f: Gold/silver alloy small ring
BM: 1991,0501.67; Jackson no.: 59f
Gold/silver alloy small spiral ring made from a strip with squarish cross-section. Roughly cut ends, slightly distorted form.
D(ext): 33.1mm; W: 15.1mm; T: 2.1mm

F.18g: Gold/silver alloy small ring
BM: 1991,0501.68; Jackson no.: 59g
Complete gold/silver alloy small spiral ring with tapered, rounded terminals. Made from a strip with rectangular cross-section.
D(ext): 24.2mm; W: 12.6mm; T: 2.2mm

F.18h: Gold/silver alloy torc/bracelet
MSCC: (2P)R
BM: 1991,0501.69; Jackson no.: 59h
Fragment of gold/silver alloy multi-strand torc or bracelet, comprising a single-loop terminal (a continuous loop extending to form the two neck-ring/body wires) and a length of neck-ring/body, cut at the other end. Stage II construction of two circular-section wires plied together. The fragment is bent into a ring with the cut ends of the wires overlapping with the terminal.
D(ext): 25.8mm; D(nr): 4.6mm; D(wire): 2.7mm; D(term): 13.9mm

F.18i: Gold/silver alloy strip
BM: 1991,0501.69.a; Jackson no.: 59h
Small fragment of gold/silver alloy strip with rectangular cross-section, folded in half.
Wt: 0.3g; L: 31.0mm; W: 4.0mm; T: 0.1mm

F.18j: Gold/silver alloy small ring
BM: 1991,0501.70; Jackson no.: 59i
Gold/silver alloy small spiral ring made from a strip with rectangular cross-section. Both ends cut.
D(ext): 30.4mm; W: 6.0mm; T: 2.3mm

F.18k: Gold/silver alloy small ring
BM: 1991,0501.71; Jackson no.: 59j
Complete gold/silver alloy small spiral ring made from a strip with rectangular cross-section. Tapered, rounded terminals.
D(ext): 28.3mm; W: 17.0mm; T: 2mm

F.18l: Gold/silver alloy small ring
BM: 1991,0501.72; Jackson no.: 59k
Complete gold/silver alloy small ring with overlapping tapered, rounded terminals. Made from a strip with rectangular cross-section.
D(ext): 25.9mm; W: 10.2mm; T: 2.1mm

F.19a–b: Composite group (interlinked) (Pl. 14.21)
Ring F.19a and tubular torc fragment F.19b are interlinked. F.19b is looped over F.19a, with its ends hammered together to join the two.
Wt: 25.5g (total for F.19a–b)

F.19a: Gold/silver alloy large ring
BM: 1991,0501.160; Jackson no.: 96a
Complete gold/silver alloy large ring with overlapping tapered, rounded terminals. Made from a strip with rectangular cross-section.
D(ext): 40.0mm; W: 7.9mm; T: 2mm

F.19b: Gold/silver alloy torc
TUBULAR (TYPE 4/5)
BM: 1991,0501.161; Jackson no.: 96b
[Analysed: see Ch. 17]
Fragment of gold/silver alloy Type 4 or 5 tubular torc neck-ring, slightly tapered, with 'punch-textured' surface (see **Fig. 17.12a–c**). Broken at both ends and crushed flat.
L: 37.5mm; W: 24.9mm; T: 12.7mm

F.20a–b: Composite group (interlinked) (Pl. 14.21)
Ring F.20a and torc/bracelet fragment F.20b are interlinked.
Wt: 18.1g (total for F.20a–b)

F.20a: Gold/silver alloy large ring
BM: 1991,0702.29; Jackson no.: 128a
Gold/silver alloy large ring with overlapping terminals, made from a strip with rectangular cross-section. One rounded and one cut end.
D(ext): 46.4mm; W: 7.0mm; T: 1.9mm

F.20b: Gold/silver alloy torc/bracelet
MSCC: (2P)R
BM: 1991,0702.30; Jackson no.: 128b
Fragment of gold/silver alloy multi-strand torc neck-ring or bracelet body, cut at both ends. Stage II construction of two circular-section wires plied together. The fragment is bent

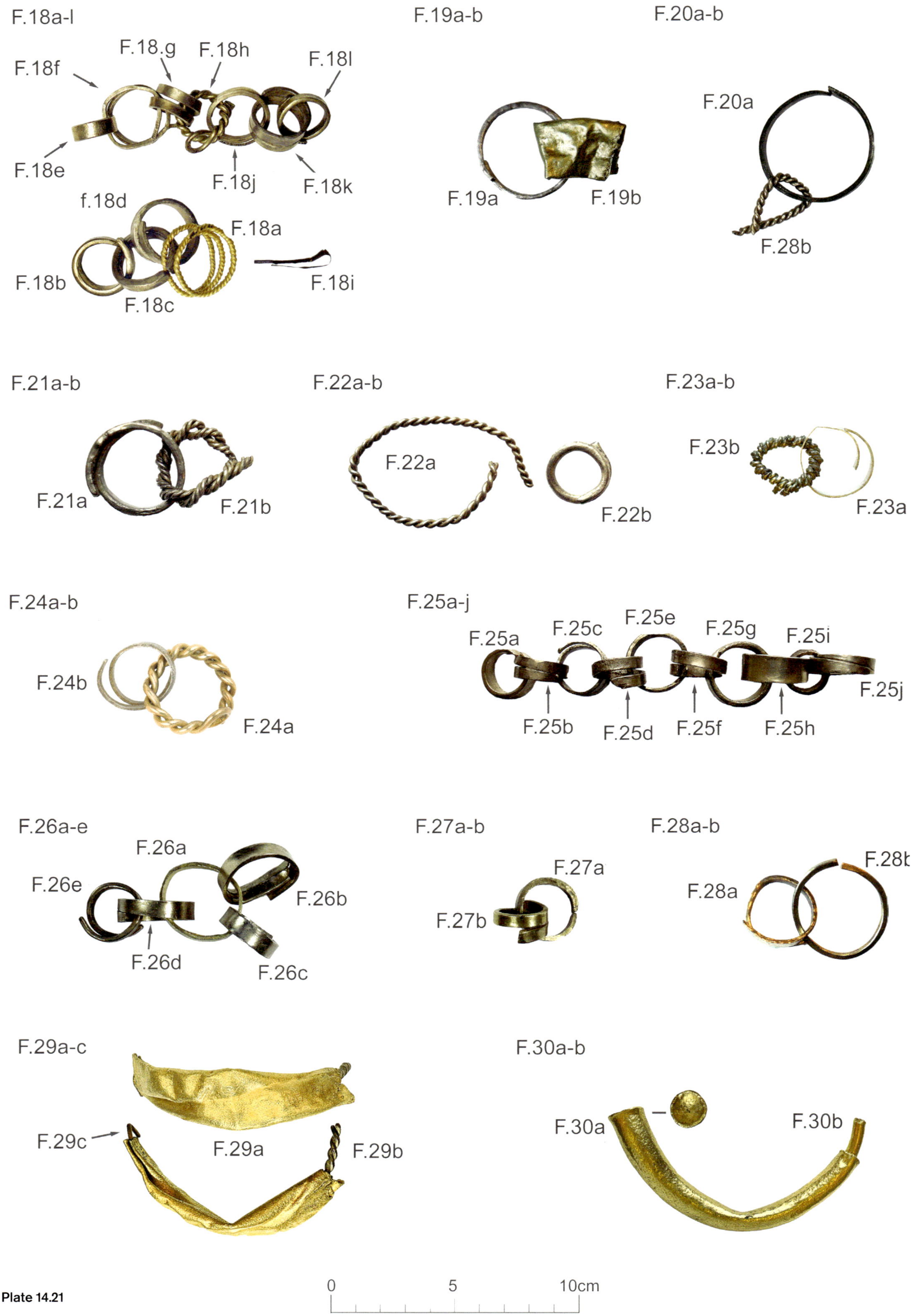

F.18a-l
F.18f
F.18.g
F.18h
F.18l
F.18e
F.18j
F.18k
f.18d
F.18a
F.18b
F.18c
F.18i
F.19a-b
F.19a
F.19b
F.20a-b
F.20a
F.28b
F.21a-b
F.21a
F.21b
F.22a-b
F.22a
F.22b
F.23a-b
F.23b
F.23a
F.24a-b
F.24b
F.24a
F.25a-j
F.25a
F.25c
F.25e
F.25g
F.25i
F.25j
F.25b
F.25d
F.25f
F.25h
F.26a-e
F.26a
F.26e
F.26b
F.26d
F.26c
F.27a-b
F.27a
F.27b
F.28a-b
F.28b
F.28a
F.29a-c
F.29c
F.29a
F.29b
F.30a-b
F.30a
F.30b
0
5
10cm

Plate 14.21

into a teardrop shape, with overlapping ends.
D(nr): 3.5mm; D(wire): 1.6mm; L: 35.4mm

F.21a–b: Composite group (interlinked) (Pl. 14.21)
Ring F.21a and torc/bracelet fragment F.21b are interlinked.

F.21a: Gold/silver alloy small ring
BM: 1991,0501.206; Jackson no.: 204a
Gold/silver alloy small ring with overlapping tapered, rounded terminals. Made from a strip with rectangular cross-section. The shape of the ring in plan is slightly irregular, and one edge shows signs of hammering.
Wt: 13.0g; D(ext): 28.5mm; T: 2.3mm

F.21b: Gold/silver alloy torc/bracelet
MSCC: (2P(2P))R
BM: 1991,0501.207; Jackson no.: 204b
[Analysed: see Ch. 17]
Fragment of gold/silver alloy multi-strand torc neck-ring or bracelet body with Stage III construction, broken at both ends. The cable is formed from two ropes plied loosely together, each of which is made up of two circular-section wires which are themselves plied together. The short length of cable is bent into a rough ring with slightly overlapping ends.
Wt: 6.2g; D(nr): 6.3mm; D(rope): 2.5mm; D(wire): 1.1mm; L: 39.2mm

F.22a–b: Composite group (interlinked) (Pl. 14.21)
Torc/bracelet fragment F.22a and ring F.22b were originally interlinked.

F.22a: Gold/silver alloy torc/bracelet
MSCC: (2P)R
BM: 1991,0501.148; Jackson no.: 82a
[Analysed: see Ch. 17]
Fragment of gold/silver alloy multi-strand torc neck-ring or bracelet body, cut at both ends. Stage II construction of two circular-section wires plied together. The fragment is bent into a rough oval shape, with the ends not quite overlapping.
Wt: 10.6g; D(nr): 3.6mm; D(wire): 1.7mm; L: 74.3mm

F.22b: Gold/silver alloy small ring/?torc
BM: 1991,0501.149; Jackson no.: 82b
Gold/silver alloy small ring, with flat terminals which overlap by almost half a turn. Made from circular-section wire. Possibly a double-loop terminal from a multi-strand torc.
Wt: 12.1g; D(ext): 27.3mm; D(wire): 4.0mm

F.23a–b: Composite group (interlinked) (Pl. 14.21)
Ring F.23a and torc/bracelet fragment F.23b are interlinked.
Wt: 13.4g (total for F.23a–b)

F.23a: Gold/silver alloy small ring
BM: 1991,0702.42; Jackson no.: 207a
Gold/silver alloy small ring with overlapping terminals. Made from a strip with rectangular cross-section. Slightly tapered, cut ends.
D(ext): 32.3mm; W: 5.0mm; T: 0.9mm

F.23b: Copper alloy torc/bracelet
MSCC: (2P(2P))R
BM: 1991,0702.43; Jackson no.: 207b
Fragment of copper alloy, possibly gilded, multi-strand torc neck-ring or bracelet body with Stage III construction, broken at both ends. The cable is formed from two ropes plied together, each of which is made up of two circular-section wires which are themselves plied together. Bent into a rough ring, with slightly overlapping ends.
D(ext): 30.7mm; D(nr): 6.3mm; D(rope): 2.2mm; D(wire): 1.1mm

F.24a–b: Composite group (interlinked) (Pl. 14.21)
Torc/bracelet fragment F.24a and ring F.24b are interlinked.
Wt: 29.0g (total for F.24a–b)

F.24a: Gold/silver alloy torc/bracelet
MSCC: (2P)R
BM: 1991,0501.130; Jackson no.: 20b
Fragment of gold/silver alloy multi-strand torc or bracelet, comprising a single-loop terminal (a continuous loop extending to form the two neck-ring/body wires) and a length of neck-ring/body, cut at the other end. Stage II construction of two circular-section wires plied loosely together. The fragment is bent into a ring, with the cut end just slightly passing through the loop terminal.
D(ext): 38.0mm; D(nr): 6.1mm; D(wire): 2.8mm; D(term): 12.9mm

F.24b: Gold/silver alloy small ring
BM: 1991,0501.131; Jackson no.: 20a
Gold/silver alloy small ring with overlapping terminals. Made from a strip with rectangular cross-section. One slightly tapered and one cut end (possibly a recent break).
D(ext): 30.0mm; W: 5.0mm; T: 1.3mm

F.25a–j: Composite group (interlinked) (Pl. 14.21)
Rings F.25a–j are linked together in a chain: a to b, b to c etc (**Fig. 23.2**).
Wt: 127.1g (total for F.25a–j)

F.25a: Gold/silver alloy small ring
BM: 1991,0501.14.a; Jackson no.: 5a
Complete gold/silver alloy small ring with overlapping rounded terminals. Made from a strip with rectangular cross-section.
D(ext): 24.4mm; W: 11.8mm; T: 2.4mm

F.25b: Gold/silver alloy small ring
BM: 1991,0501.14.b; Jackson no.: 5b
Gold/silver alloy small ring with overlapping terminals. Made from a strip with rectangular cross-section. One slightly tapered and one broken end.
D(ext): 25.5mm; W: 10.1mm; T: 2.2mm

F.25c: Gold/silver alloy small ring
BM: 1991,0501.14.c; Jackson no.: 5c
Complete gold/silver alloy small spiral ring made from a strip

with rectangular cross-section. Slightly rounded terminals.
D(ext): 24.5mm; W: 15.5mm; T: 1.5mm

F.25d: Gold/silver alloy small ring
BM: 1991,0501.14.d; Jackson no.: 5d
Gold/silver alloy small spiral ring made from a strip with rectangular cross-section. One slightly rounded and one broken terminal.
D(ext): 25.8mm; W: 14.6mm; T: 2.7mm

F.25e: Gold/silver alloy small ring
BM: 1991,0501.14.e; Jackson no.: 5e
Gold/silver alloy small ring with overlapping terminals. Made from a strip with rectangular cross-section. One tapered and one cut end.
D(ext): 29.7mm; W: 9.2mm; T: 2.0mm

F.25f: Gold/silver alloy small ring
BM: 1991,0501.14.f; Jackson no.: 5f
Complete gold/silver alloy small ring with overlapping slightly rounded terminals. Made from a strip with rectangular cross-section.
D(ext): 26.5mm; W: 12.5mm; T: 2.0mm

F.25g: Gold/silver alloy small ring
BM: 1991,0501.14.g; Jackson no.: 5g
Gold/silver alloy small ring with overlapping terminals, made from a strip with rectangular cross-section. One tapered and one cut end.
D(ext): 30.8mm; W: 13.2mm; T: 2.8mm

F.25h: Gold/silver alloy small ring
BM: 1991,0501.14.h; Jackson no.: 5h
Complete gold/silver alloy small penannular ring made from a strip with rectangular cross-section. Complete, slightly rounded terminals.
D(ext): 30.7mm; W: 13.3mm; T: 2.4mm

F.25i: Gold/silver alloy small ring
BM: 1991,0501.14.i; Jackson no.: 5i
Complete gold/silver alloy small penannular ring made from a strip with rectangular cross-section. Slightly rounded terminals.
D(ext): 21.4mm; W: 6.5mm; T: 1.7mm

F.25j: Gold/silver alloy small ring
BM: 1991,0501.14.j; Jackson no.: 5j
Complete gold/silver alloy small spiral ring made from a strip with rectangular cross-section. Tapering terminals.
D(ext): 29.9mm; W: 8.6mm; T: 2.0mm

F.26a–e: Composite group (interlinked) (Pl. 14.21)
Rings F.26a–e are an interlinked group. F.26b, F.26c and F.26d are interlinked with F.26a. F.26e is interlinked with F.26d.
Wt: 53.9g (total for F.26a–e)

F.26a: Gold/silver alloy large ring
BM: 1991,0501.140; Jackson no.: 58a
Complete gold/silver alloy large ring with overlapping tapered, slightly rounded terminals. Made from a strip with rectangular cross-section.
D(ext): 35.5mm; W: 13.0mm; T: 1.4mm

F.26b: Gold/silver alloy small ring
BM: 1991,0501.141; Jackson no.: 58b
Gold/silver alloy small ring with overlapping terminals. Made from a strip with rectangular cross-section. One uneven and one cut end.
D(ext): 30.9mm; W: 10.8mm; T: 1.7mm

F.26c: Gold/silver alloy small ring
BM: 1991,0501.142; Jackson no.: 58c
Gold/silver alloy small ring with abutted terminals. Made from a strip with rectangular cross-section. One tapered, rounded terminal and one cut end.
D(ext): 24.4mm; W: 9.0mm; T: 2.0mm

F.26d: Gold/silver alloy small ring
BM: 1991,0501.143; Jackson no.: 58d
Complete gold/silver alloy small ring with overlapping tapered, slightly rounded terminals. Made from a strip with rectangular cross-section.
D(ext): 29.7mm; W: 9.2mm; T: 1.6mm

F.26e: Gold/silver alloy small ring
BM: 1991,0702.7; Jackson no.: 58e
Complete gold/silver alloy small ring with overlapping tapered, roughly rounded terminals. Made from a strip with rectangular cross-section.
D(ext): 25.5mm; W: 10.6mm; T: 1.8mm

F.27a–b: Composite group (interlinked) (Pl. 14.21)
Rings F.27a and F.27b are interlinked.
Wt: 19.9g (total for F.27a–b)

F.27a: Gold/silver alloy small ring
BM: 1991,0501.139; Jackson no.: 51a
Gold/silver alloy small ring with abutted terminals, made from a strip with rectangular cross-section. Tapered ends, one rounded and one cut.
D(ext): 21.3mm; W: 11.2mm; T: 2.3mm

F.27b: Gold/silver alloy small ring
BM: 1991,0702.22; Jackson no.: 51b
Gold/silver alloy small spiral ring made from a strip with rectangular cross-section. One tapered, rounded terminal and one broad cut end.
D(ext): 25.3mm; W: 6.6mm; T: 2.5mm

F.28a–b: Composite group (interlinked) (Pl. 14.21)
Rings F.28a and F.28b are interlinked.
Wt: 22.5g (total for F.28a–b)

F.28a: Gold/silver alloy small ring
BM: 1991,0501.167; Jackson no.: 129a
Gold/silver alloy small ring with overlapping terminals. Made from a strip with rectangular cross-section. One rounded and one cut end.
D(ext): 29.5mm; W: 6.0mm; T: 1.6mm

F.28b: Gold/silver alloy large ring
BM: 1991,0501.168; Jackson no.: 129b
Gold/silver alloy large ring with flat, abutted terminals. Made from a strip with square cross-section.
D(ext): 40.7mm; W: 3.1mm; T: 2.4mm

F.29a–c: Composite group (inserted) (Pl. 14.21)
Torc/bracelet fragment F.29b and wire fragment F.29c are inserted into either end of tubular torc fragment F.29a.
Wt: 33.4g (total for F.29a–c)

F.29a: Gold/silver alloy torc
TUBULAR (TYPE 4/5)
BM: 1991,0501.135; Jackson no.: 25
Fragment of gold/silver alloy Type 4 or 5 tubular torc neck-ring, cut at both ends, flattened and bent. It has been hammered flat at the cut ends after the insertion of torc/wire fragments F.29b and c. The surface is covered in punched 'stipple' decoration.
Perhaps part of the same object as F.56.
L: 91.0mm; W: 19.8mm

F.29b: Gold/silver alloy torc/bracelet
MSCC: (2P)R
BM: 1991,0501.135; Jackson no.: 25
Fragment of gold/silver alloy multi-strand torc neck-ring or bracelet body, partly contained within F.29a, cut at visible end. Stage II construction of two circular-section wires plied together.
D(nr): 3.6mm; D(wire): 2.0mm

F.29c: Gold/silver alloy wire
BM: 1991,0501.135; Jackson no.: 25
Fragment of bent circular-section gold/silver alloy wire, partly contained within F.29a, cut at visible end.
D(wire): 1.5mm

F.30a–b: Composite group (inserted) (Pl. 14.21)
Wire/torc fragment F.30b is inserted into the broken end of the neck-ring of tubular torc fragment F.30a.
Wt: 82.0g (total for F.30a–b)

F.30a: Gold/silver alloy torc
TUBULAR (TYPE 4)
BM: 1991,0501.90; Jackson no.: 101
Fragment of gold/silver alloy Type 4 tubular torc comprising one flat, expanded buffer terminal and part of the plain, tapered neck-ring, cut at the other end. The inner face of the neck-ring has been hammered flat to hold in place inserted wire F.30b. The terminal has a plain, concave end-plate with small central hole, fused slightly unevenly to the tube end.
D(term): 15.5mm; L: 104.7mm

F.30b: Gold/silver alloy wire/?torc
BM: 1991,0501.90; Jackson no.: 101
Fragment of gold/silver alloy circular-section wire, possibly from a simple torc neck-ring. Partly contained within F.30a, broken at visible end.
D(wire): 5.3mm

F.31a–b: Composite group (inserted) (Pl. 14.22)
Tubular torc fragment F.31b was found inside crushed tubular torc fragment F.31a. A hole has been roughly punched through the terminal of F.31a, suggesting that this fragment was once part of (or intended to be part of) an interlinked group.

F.31a: Gold/silver alloy torc
TUBULAR (TYPE 5)
BM: 1991,0501.28; Jackson no.: 33
Fragment of gold/silver alloy Type 5 tubular torc, comprising buffer terminal and part of the neck-ring, formed of thin sheet (see **Fig. 21.36**). Flattened, torn, and badly distorted. The neck-ring is ornamented with decoration organised into rectangular, triangular and diamond-shaped zones, defined by parallel lines and chevrons. Various zones contain inscribed motifs including concentric circles but also curvilinear fin motifs. Backgrounds also differ and include dimples, regular dots and plain areas. The flat(ish) terminal is decorated in a different style. The overall pattern forms a rough lyre-shape with an opposing pair of swirls flanked by an arrangement of fin motifs and tendrils. The motifs are plain, and the background is stippled. Of note are the tendrils at each end of the pattern. A part-melted, coalesced mass of gold, incorporating gold/silver alloy twisted wire fragments, is fused to the end of the terminal. See Chapter 16 for details of the conservation process, and Chapter 21 for a full discussion of decoration.
Wt: 63.4g; D(term): 60.2mm; L: 107.8mm

F.31b: Gold/silver alloy torc
TUBULAR (TYPE 1)
BM: 1991,0501.28.a
Fragment of gold/silver alloy tubular torc neck-ring, probably from a Type 1 torc, cut or torn at both ends, and crushed flat at one end. Decorated with zig-zag lines of punched decoration running along the neck-ring, which delimit diamond-shaped zones (see Ch. 21 for discussion of decoration).
Wt: 4.9g; D(nr): 8.8mm; L: 60.3mm

F.32: Composite group (fused): Gold/silver alloy torc; torc/bracelet (Pl. 14.22)
TUBULAR (TYPE 4/5); MSCC: (2P)R
BM: 1991,0501.136; Jackson no.: 26
Fragment of gold/silver alloy Type 4 or 5 tubular torc neck-ring, distorted, and torn at both ends (see **Fig. 23.1**). Decorated with rows of punched dots, running parallel along the neck-ring (see **Fig. 21.6**). Several fragments are fused onto the middle of the tubular piece, including a part-melted fragment of gold/silver alloy multi-strand torc neck-ring or bracelet body (with Stage II construction of two circular-section wires plied together), and globules of melted gold/silver alloy.
Wt: 24.2g; L: 63.2mm; W: 11.8mm

F.33: Composite group (fused): Gold/silver alloy torc; strip/ ?small/large ring; wire (Pl. 14.22)
TUBULAR (TYPE 1)
BM: 1991,0501.165; Jackson no.: 102

F.31a-b

F.31a

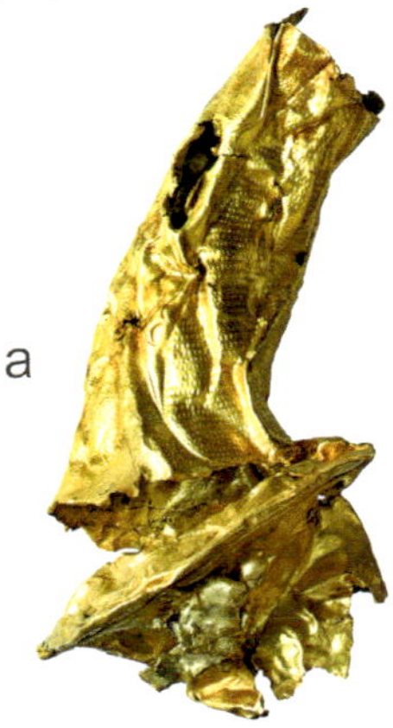

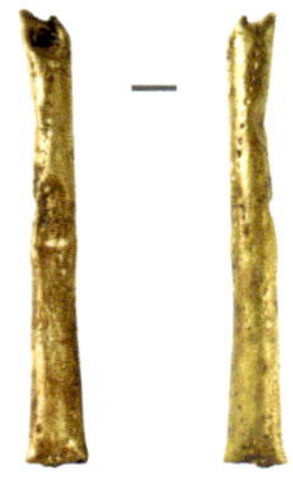

F.31b

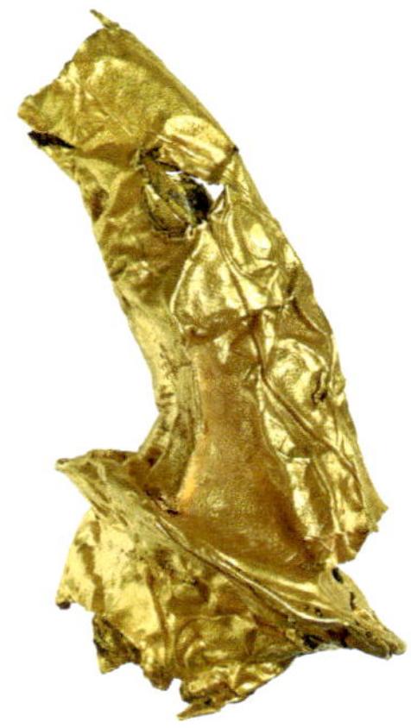

F.32

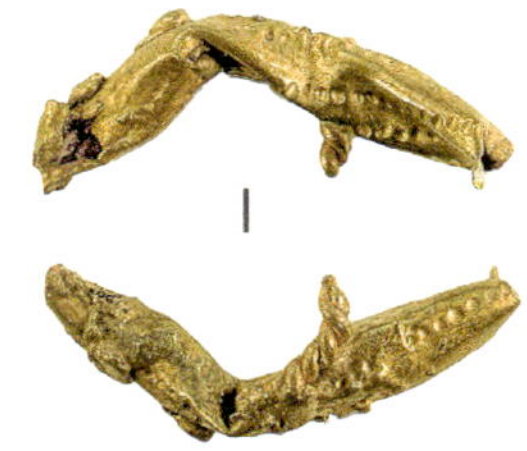

F.33

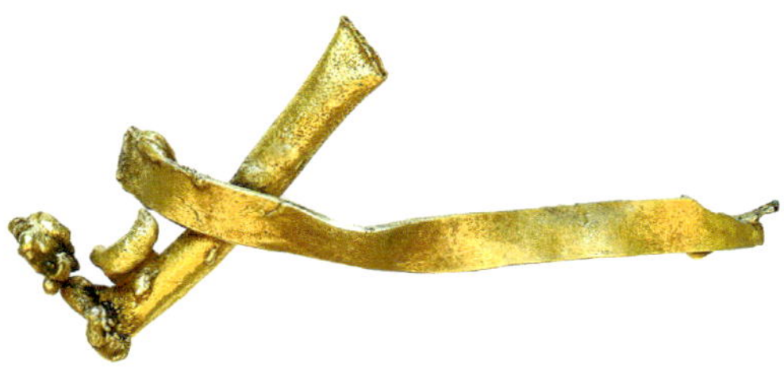

F.34

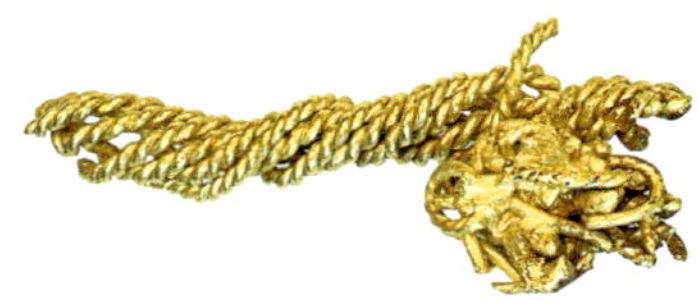

F.35

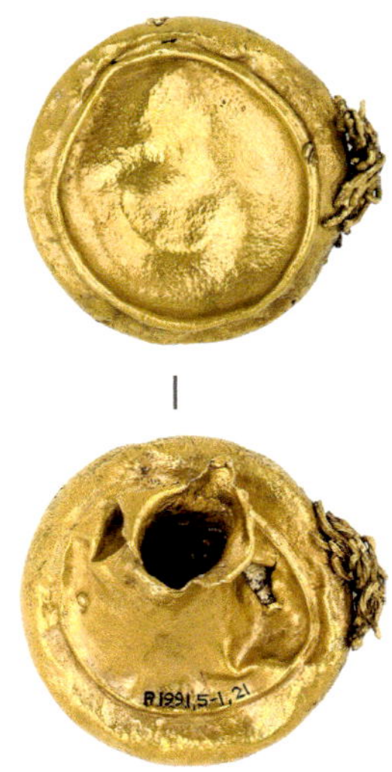

F.36

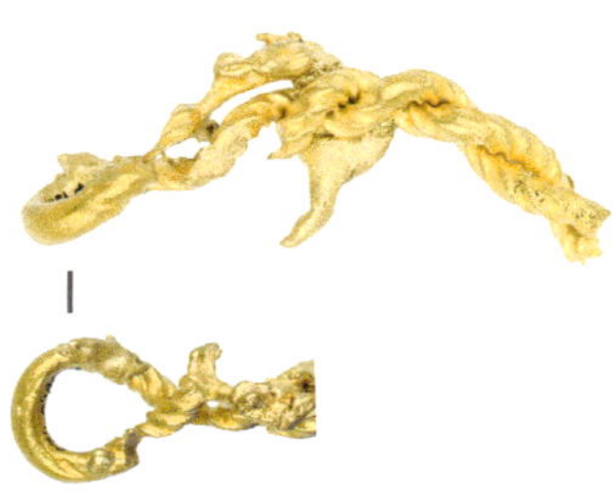

F.37

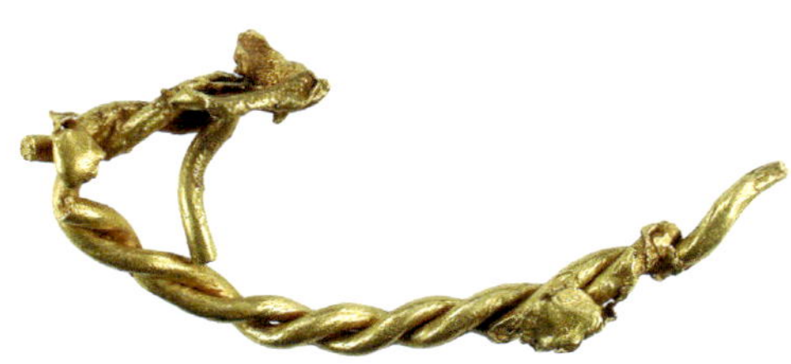

F.38

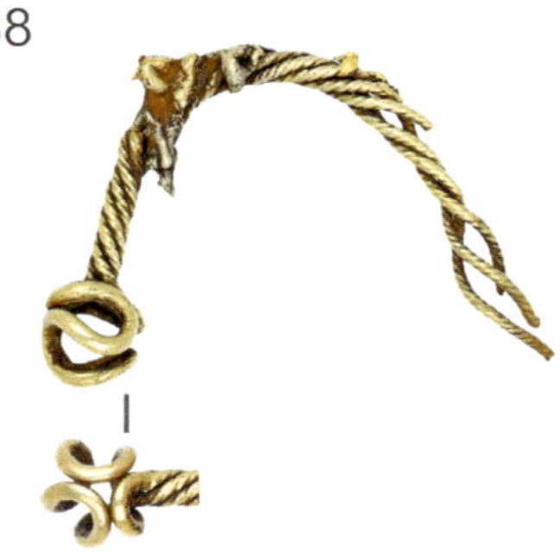

F.39

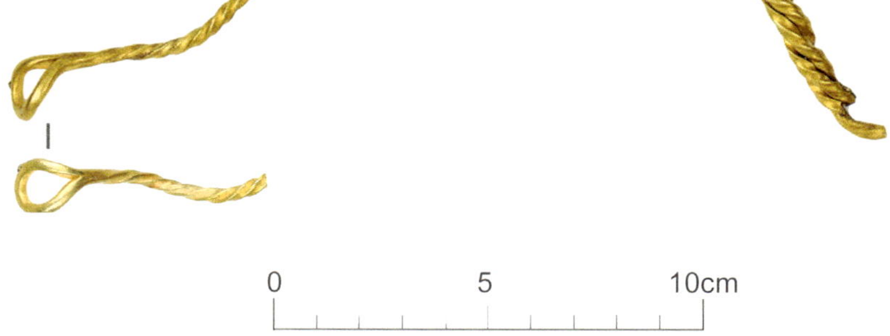

0 5 10cm

Plate 14.22

Fragment of gold/silver alloy strip (likely part of an uncoiled large/small ring), partially melted at both ends, fused to a fragment of gold/silver alloy narrow tubular torc neck-ring, probably from a Type 1 torc, broken/cut at both ends. The tubular torc fragment is decorated with punched 'stipple' texture. Other part-melted gold/silver alloy fragments also adhere to one end of the broken tubular torc, including a small piece of slender twisted wire.
Wt: 53.7g; L: 109.7mm (strip); 64.4mm (tubular torc fragment); W: 9.1mm (strip); 8.5mm (tubular torc fragment); T: 1.4mm (strip)

F.34: Composite group (fused): Gold/silver alloy torc/bracelet; wire; sheet (Pl. 14.22)
MSCC: (6C(2P))R
BM: 1991,0501.16; Jackson no.: 7
[Analysed: see Ch. 17]
Fragment of gold/silver alloy multi-strand torc neck-ring or bracelet body of Stage III construction, cut or broken at both ends. The cable is formed from six coiled ropes, each of which is made up of two plied circular-section wires. The whole fragment is bent and distorted, and near one end is a fused gold/silver alloy mass of plain and twisted wire fragments and sheet (see **Fig. 20.27**).
Wt: 58.4g; D(nr): 8.0mm; D(rope): 2.8mm; D(wire): 1.4mm; L: 79.0mm

F.35: Composite group (fused): Gold/silver alloy torc; wire (Pl. 14.22)
TUBULAR (TYPE 3)
BM: 1991,0501.21; Jackson no.: 13
[Analysed: see Ch. 17]
Large gold/silver alloy buffer terminal from Type 3 tubular torc, broken off at the neck-ring. Flat face with raised outer rim, textured with tool marks. On the reverse, a raised concentric ring divides this outer edge of the buffer terminal from the start of the neck-ring. A cluster of part-melted, fine, twisted gold/silver alloy wire fragments is fused to one side of the rim, and gold droplets are fused in several other places.
Similar, although not the pair, to F.2g, F.47 and F.48.
Wt: 52.3g; D(term): 57.8mm; L: 31.5mm

F.36: Composite group (fused): Gold/silver alloy torc/bracelet; ?wire (Pl. 14.22)
MSCC: (2P)TZ
BM: 1991,0501.23; Jackson no.: 18
Fragment of gold/silver alloy multi-strand torc/bracelet comprising one thickened ring terminal (continuous with the neck-ring/body wires) and length of neck-ring/body, broken at the other end. Stage II construction of two Z-twisted wires plied together. The whole fragment is bent, distorted, and part melted, and in the centre is a fused mass of gold/silver alloy droplets and ?wire.
Wt: 72.3g; D(nr): 12.2mm; D(wire): 5.1mm; D(term): 20.9mm; L: 81.5mm

F.37: Composite group (fused): Gold/silver alloy torc/bracelet; sheet (Pl. 14.22)
MSCC: (2P)R
BM: 1991,0501.24; Jackson no.: 19
[Analysed: see Ch. 17]
Fragment of gold/silver alloy multi-strand torc neck-ring or bracelet body, broken at both ends, at different lengths along each wire. Stage II construction of two circular-section wires plied together. The whole fragment is bent, distorted, and part melted. Fragments of gold/silver alloy sheet are fused to both ends.
Wt: 111.7g; D(nr): 8.8mm; D(wire): 4.3mm; L: 121.8mm

F.38: Composite group (fused): Gold/silver alloy torc/bracelet; ?wire (Pl. 14.22)
MSCC: (4C)T
BM: 1991,0501.43; Jackson no.: 48
Fragment of gold/silver alloy multi-strand torc/bracelet comprising one cage terminal and a length of neck-ring/body, with each wire broken at a different point. Stage II construction of four twisted wires coiled together. The cage terminal consists of a continuous length of circular-section wire, forming three involuted loops. This extends into two pairs of wires which form the neck-ring/body. The whole fragment is bent, distorted, and part melted, and in the centre is a fused mass of gold/silver alloy droplets and ?wire.
Wt: 30.2g; D(nr): 5.2mm; D(wire): 1.7mm; D(term): 16.3mm; L: 78.0mm

F.39: Composite group (fused): Gold/silver alloy torc; wire (Pl. 14.22)
MSCC: (3P)T
BM: 1991,0501.44; Jackson no.: 50
Fragment of gold/silver alloy multi-strand torc comprising most of the neck-ring and parts of both terminals, although pulled open so as to be almost straight. The Stage II construction of three twisted wires plied together. The more complete terminal consists of a single continuous circular-section loop which extends to form one of the neck-ring wires, probably originally part of a double- or triple-loop terminal. The other terminal is represented only by the broken neck of one loop. The neck-ring is bent, distorted, and part melted, two of the wires are incomplete, one having broken at the site of a possible casting flaw. Small globules of gold and twisted wire fragments are fused to the torc in several places.
Wt: 72.7g; D(nr): 8.3mm; D(wire): 3.6mm; D(term): 13.9mm; L: 204.0mm

F.40: Composite group (fused): Gold/silver alloy torc/bracelet; wire (Pl. 14.23)
MSCC: (2P)R
BM: 1991,0501.52; Jackson no.: 54
[Analysed: see Ch. 17]
Fragment of gold/silver alloy multi-strand torc/bracelet comprising one ring terminal (continuous with the neck-ring/body wires) and part of the neck-ring/body. Stage II construction of two circular-section wires plied together. The neck-ring/body is severely bent and distorted, with the wires pulled apart and melted at the broken end. Fragments of twisted and circular-section gold alloy wire are fused to the neck-ring in several places (see **Figs 17.2, 20.25**).
Wt: 373.7g; D(wire): 5.6mm; D(term): 36.7mm; L: 180.0mm

F.40

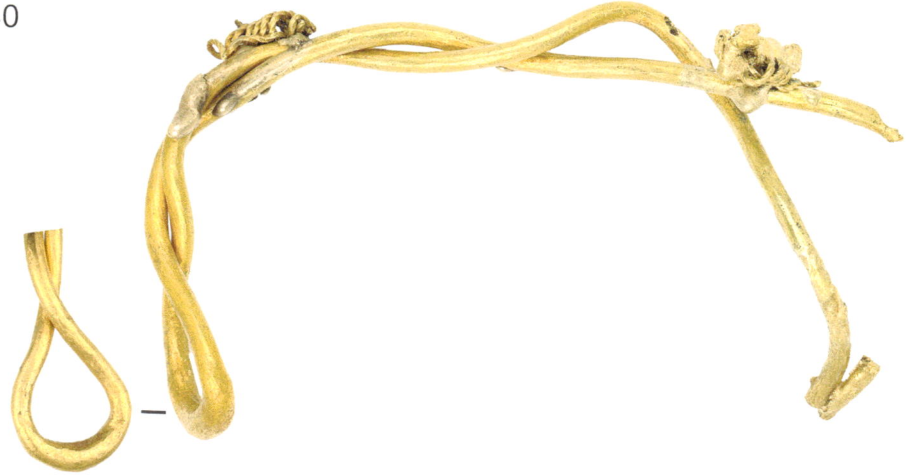

F.41

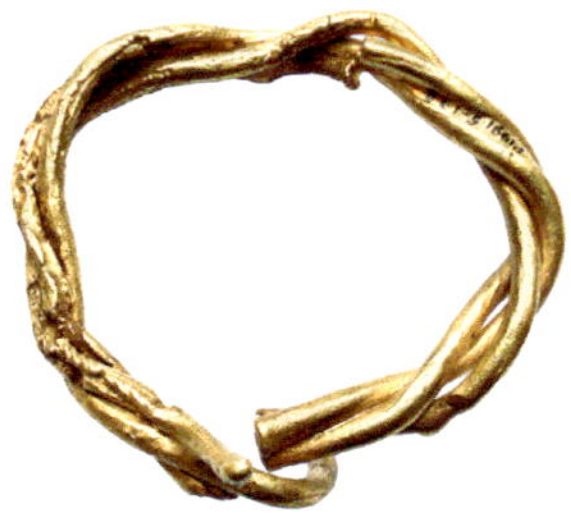

F.42

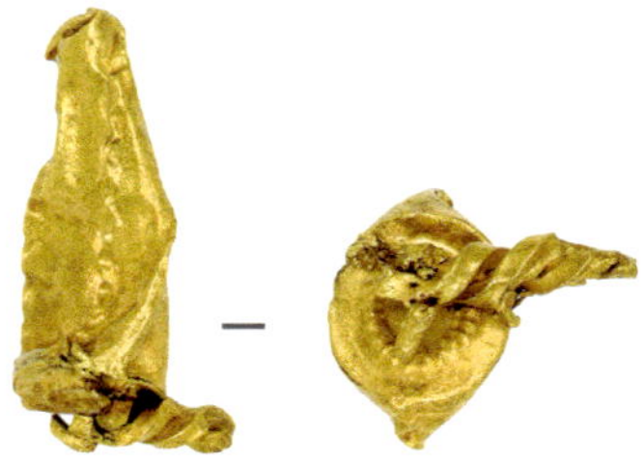

F.43

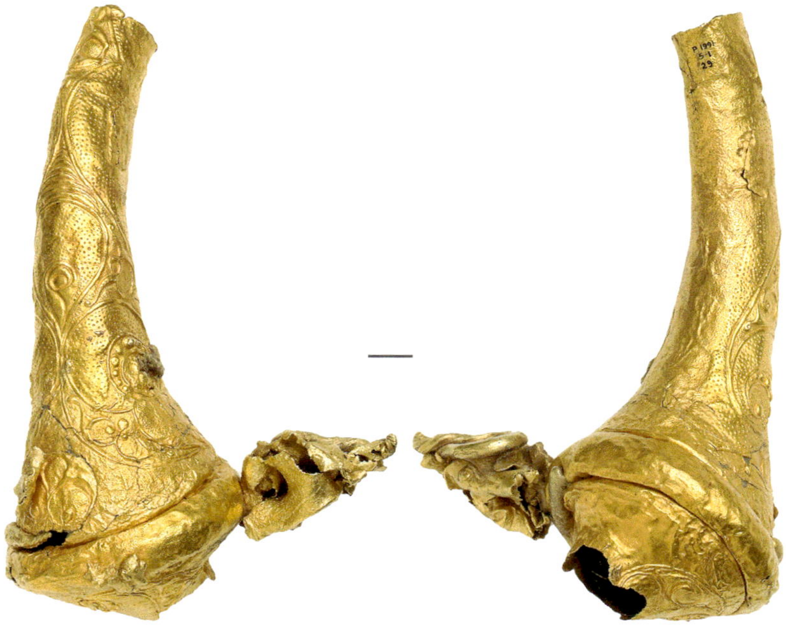

F.44

F.45

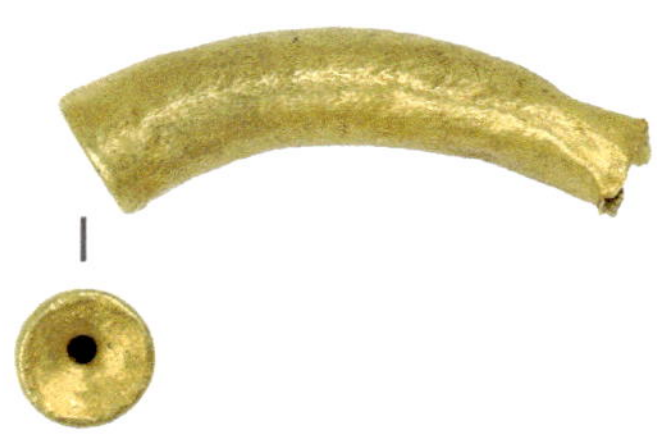

F.46

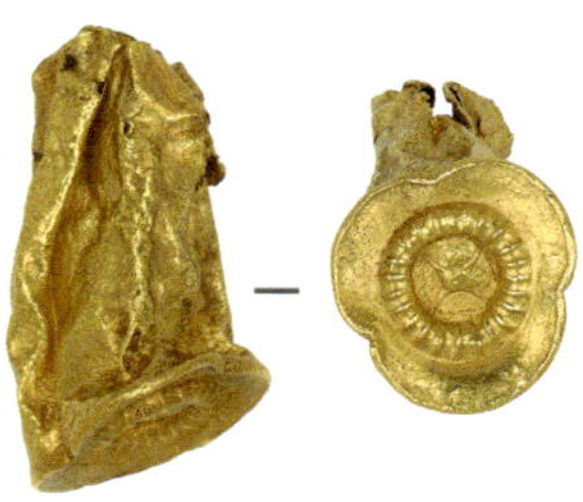

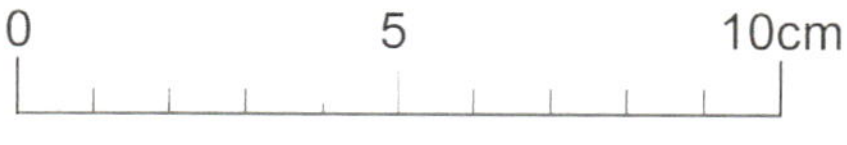

Plate 14.23

F.41: Composite group (fused): Gold/silver alloy torc (Pl. 14.23)
MSCC: (3P)R
BM: 1991,0501.78; Jackson no.: 66
Fragment of gold/silver alloy multi-strand torc neck-ring, coiled into a rough ring. Stage II construction of three circular-section wires plied together. One end is broken, distorted and part melted. The other end may be a simple form of buffer terminal: the lightly expanded flat ends of the three wires are fused together into a triple-lobed 'cap'. The wires are broken or partially melted in several places and a semi-coalesced strand of narrow twisted gold wire is fused to one of them near the broken end.
Wt: 116.2g; D(ext): 72.4mm; D(nr): 7.1mm; D(wire): 3.8mm

F.42: Composite group (fused): Gold/silver alloy torc (Pl. 14.23)
TUBULAR (TYPE 4); MSCC: (2P)Q
BM: 1991,0501.96; Jackson no.: 108
Fragment of a gold/silver alloy Type 4 tubular torc comprising flat buffer terminal and part of the lightly tapering neck-ring, torn at the other end (see **Figs 20.26**, **21.5**). The neck-ring has three crimped 'pie-crust' seams running parallel along its length, and a punch-textured or stippled surface. The expanded terminal has a round end-plate with a repoussé circular 'segmented wreath' motif. The object is badly crushed and distorted, especially at the broken end. Fragments of semi-coalesced metal fused to the end of the terminal include a section of Stage II multi-strand torc/bracelet neck-ring/body made up of two square-section gold/silver alloy wires twisted together, broken at both ends.
Wt: 35.8g; D(wire): 3.2mm; D(term): 24.5mm; L: 70.5 (total); 62.60mm (tubular torc fragment); 31.40mm (twisted wires)

F.43: Composite group (fused): Gold/silver alloy torc/bracelet; gold/silver alloy wire; gold/silver alloy sheet (Pl. 14.23)
TUBULAR (TYPE 5); MSCC: (2P)T
BM: 1991,0501.29; Jackson no.: 34
Fragment of decorated gold/silver alloy Type 5 tubular torc, comprising one damaged buffer terminal and part of the neck-ring (see **Figs 16.5–6**, **21.37**). The convex face of the terminal face is surrounded by a raised, rounded rim. Behind this, the tubular body narrows to form a tapering neck-ring, which is torn at the other end. When discovered the fragment was badly distorted, crushed and torn; shape now restored. It is elaborately decorated with decoration extending across the terminal and much of the neck-ring, comprising embossed curvilinear motifs on a punch-textured background. The torc was fabricated from several individual components. The face of the terminal is damaged, with some of the sheet missing, creating a hole. Part-melted material is fused on in this area, including fragments of gold/silver alloy sheet with embossed decoration (perhaps part of a tubular torc or bracelet), and the ring terminal of a multi-strand gold/silver alloy torc with Stage II neck-ring formed from two twisted wires plied together. Other gold/silver alloy wire and sheet fragments, as well as amorphous droplets, adhere to other areas. See Chapter 16 for details of the conservation process, and Chapter 21 for a full discussion of decoration. A hole has been roughly punched through the neck-ring near the broken end, suggesting that this fragment was once part of (or intended to be part of) an interlinked group. F.241 was found inside during conservation.
Wt: 119.1g; D(term): 63.2mm; L: 163.0mm

F.44: Composite group (fused): Copper alloy torc/bracelet (Pl. 14.23)
MSCC: (2PZ)R
BM: 1991,0407.46; Site code: SN/AJ
Context details: Hoard F pit; Excavated find, at edge of hoard pit.
Fragment of copper alloy multi-strand torc neck-ring or bracelet body, cut or broken at both ends. Stage II construction of two circular-section wires plied together Z-twist. Damaged and part melted, with small adhering fragments of gold twisted wire.
Wt: 0.9g; D(nr): 3.8mm; D(wire): 2.4mm; L: 23.5mm

F.45: Gold/silver alloy torc (Pl. 14.23)
TUBULAR (TYPE 4)
BM: 1991,0501.91; Jackson no.: 103
Fragment of gold/silver alloy Type 4 tubular torc, comprising a short section of hollow neck-ring, torn at one end, with buffer terminal at the other. The expanded terminal has a dished, circular end-plate, pierced by a small hole, a little off-centre. The surface of the neck-ring is textured with linear tool or punch-marks.
Wt: 33.0g; D(term): 18.3mm; L: 77.8mm

F.46: Gold/silver alloy torc (Pl. 14.23)
TUBULAR (TYPE 4)
BM: 1991,0501.98; Jackson no.: 110
Fragment of gold/silver alloy Type 4 tubular torc, comprising one terminal and a short length of tubular neck-ring, crushed and distorted (see **Fig. 21.24**). The neck-ring expands towards the flat trefoil-shaped buffer terminal, the end-plate of which is decorated with a repoussé circular 'segmented wreath' motif. Within the wreath is a repoussé four-armed star, creating four semi-circular arcs within the negative space inside the circular 'wreath'. These arcs are picked out with simple dot-punched stippled decoration. The neck-ring also has a punch-textured surface, and the broken end is very ragged. See Chapter 21 for a full discussion of decoration.
Wt: 27.7g; D(term): 34.4mm; L: 61.0mm

F.47: Gold/silver alloy torc (Pl. 14.24)
TUBULAR (TYPE 3)
BM: 1991,0501.20; Jackson no.: 12
Gold/silver alloy buffer terminal from Type 3 tubular torc, broken at start of neck-ring, with remains of sandy or organic infill visible at the break. The terminal has a flat centre with raised outer rim. Behind the terminal, the neck-ring widens into a bead with concentric rim. The external circumference of both the terminal and bead are decorated with stippling. A hole has been roughly punched through one side of the terminal, perhaps suggesting that it was

F.47

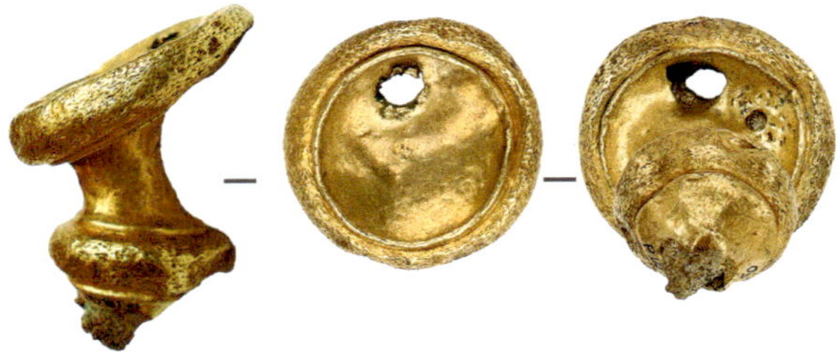

F.48

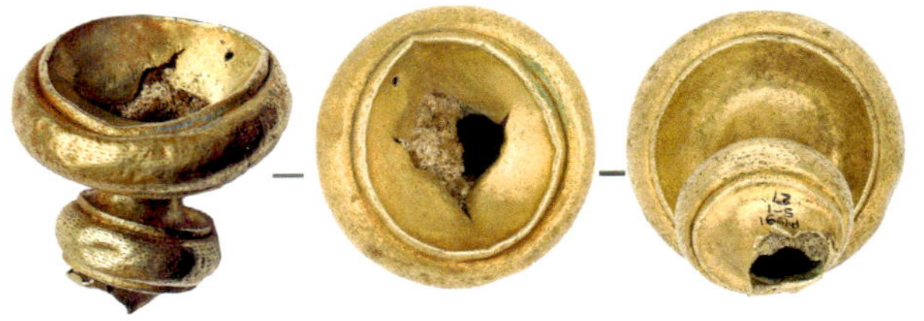

F.49

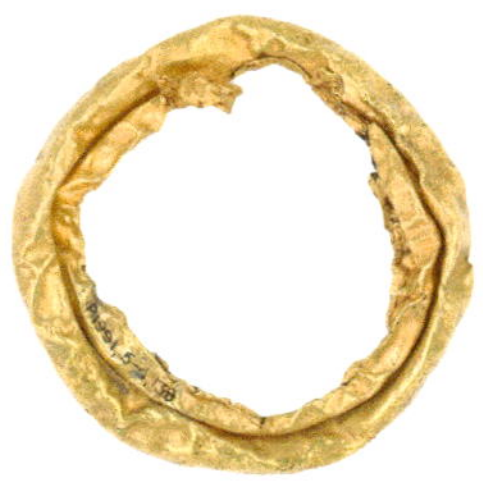

F.50

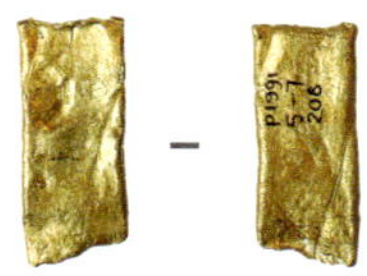

F.51

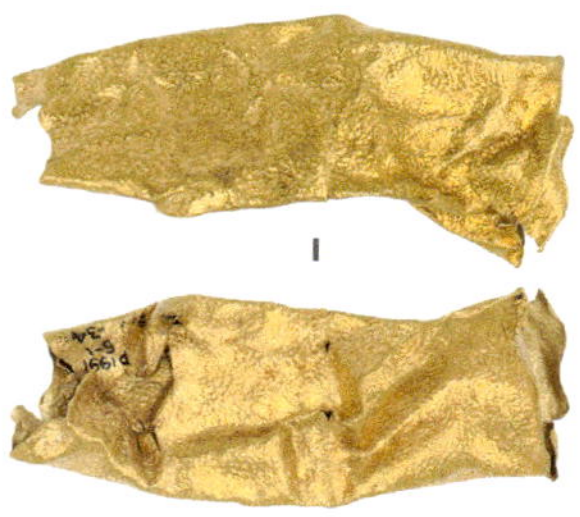

F.52

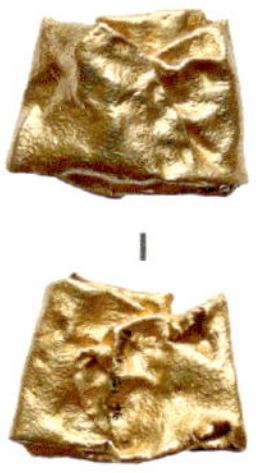

F.53

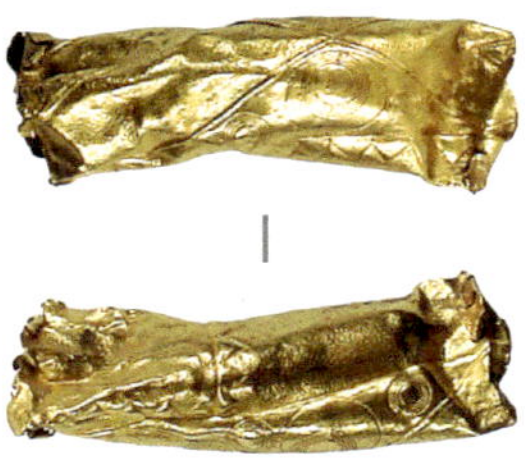

F.54

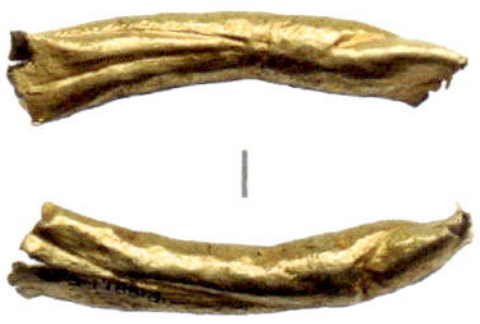

F.55

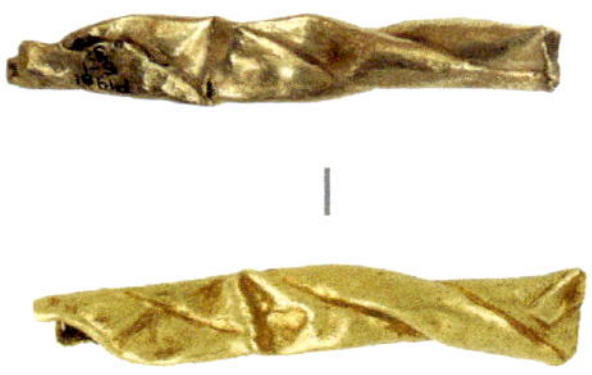

F.56

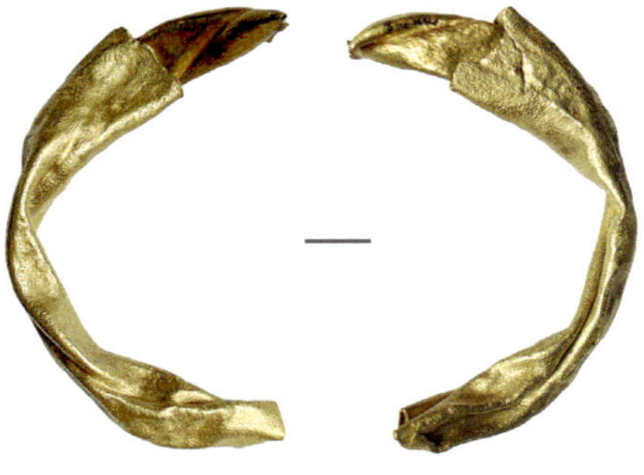

F.57

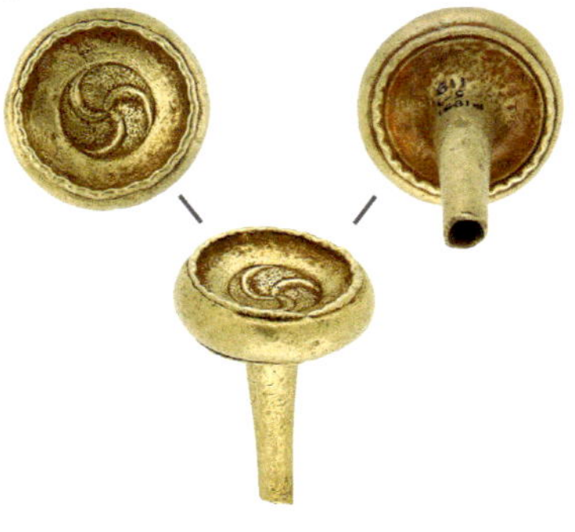

F.58

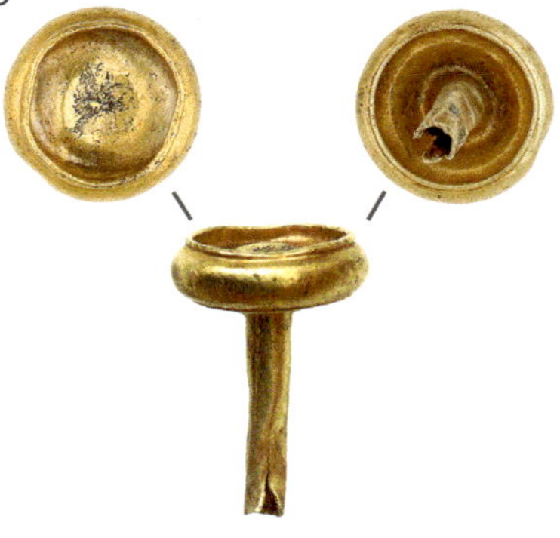

F.59

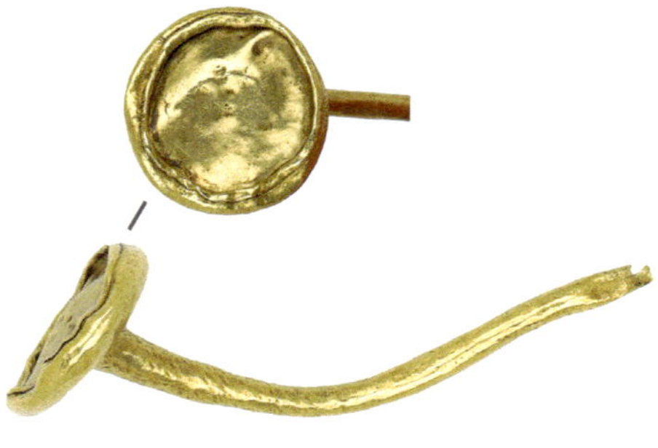

F.60

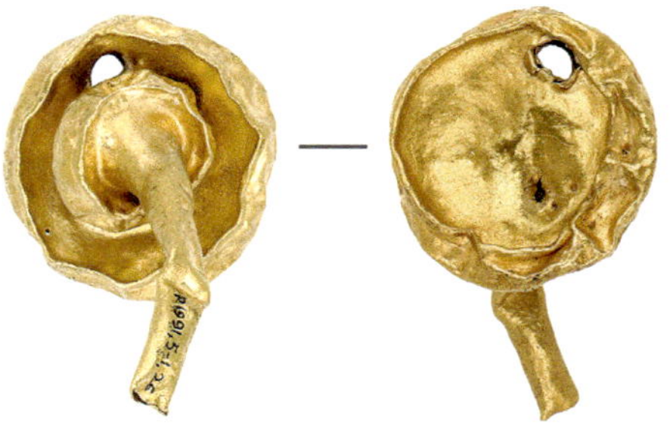

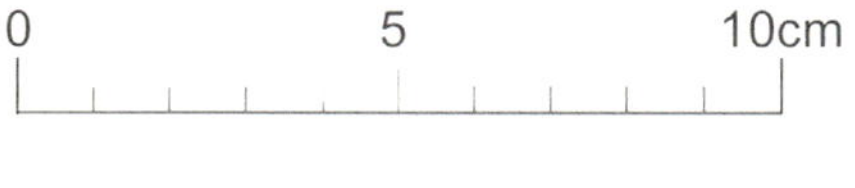

Plate 14.24

originally part of an interlinked group.
Similar, although not the pair, to F.2g and F.35. Possibly the pair to F.48.
Wt: 49.0g; D(term): 47.2mm; L: 62.2mm

F.48: Gold/silver alloy torc (Pl. 14.24)
TUBULAR (TYPE 3)
BM: 1991,0501.27; Jackson no.: 32
[Analysed: see Ch. 17]
Gold/silver alloy buffer terminal from Type 3 tubular torc, broken at start of neck-ring, with remains of sandy or organic infill visible at the break (see **Figs 17.7a, 17.8a–b, 17.13**). The terminal has a dished centre, indented and damaged, with raised outer rim. Behind the terminal the neck-ring widens into a bead with concentric rim. The external circumference of both the terminal and bead are decorated with stippling. This decoration is heavily worn. A hole punched roughly through the end of the terminal perhaps suggests that it was originally part of an interlinked group.
Similar, although not the pair, to F.2g and F.35. Possibly the pair to F.47.
Wt: 50.5g; D(term): 48.6mm; L: 44.5mm

F.49: Gold/silver alloy torc (Pl. 14.24)
TUBULAR
BM: 1991,0501.138; Jackson no.: 35
[Analysed: see Ch. 17]
Gold/silver alloy sheet ring, almost certainly the crushed and distorted buffer terminal section of a tubular torc, with the centre torn out.
Wt: 19.1g; D(ext): 60.2mm; T: 12.0mm

F.50: Gold/silver alloy torc (Pl. 14.24)
TUBULAR (TYPE 4/5)
BM: 1991,0501.208; Jackson no.: 209
Fragment of gold/silver alloy Type 4 or 5 tubular torc neck-ring, torn at both ends and hammered flat. The surface is decorated with broadly-spaced stippling or punch-marks.
Wt: 6.0g; L: 32.1mm; W: 13.3mm; T: 2.0mm

F.51: Gold/silver alloy torc (Pl. 14.24)
TUBULAR (TYPE 4/5)
BM: 1991,0501.34; Jackson no.: 40
[Analysed: see Ch. 17]
Fragment of gold/silver alloy Type 4 or 5 tubular torc neck-ring, broken or torn at both ends and flattened (see **Fig. 17.11**). Although badly crushed and distorted, punch-texture stippling is visible on the surface.
Wt: 14.5g; D(nr): 28.5mm; L: 73.8mm

F.52: Gold/silver alloy torc (Pl. 14.24)
TUBULAR (TYPE 4/5)
BM: 1991,0501.76; Jackson no.: 64
[Analysed: see Ch. 17]
Fragment of gold/silver alloy Type 4 or 5 tubular torc neck-ring, broken or torn at both ends (see **Fig. 20.23**). The surface is decorated with punch-textured stippling. The fragment has been flattened and folded/rolled up on itself, and there are at least two roughly made small holes in the gold sheet (though these do not pierce all the way through the object). Other similar pieces have been folded around e.g. a small ring.
Wt: 18.0g; L: 31.7mm; W: 25.7mm; T: 10.1mm

F.53: Gold/silver alloy torc (Pl. 14.24)
TUBULAR (TYPE 4/5)
BM: 1991,0501.118; Jackson no.: 307
[Analysed: see Ch. 17]
Fragment of gold/silver alloy Type 4 or 5 tubular torc neck-ring, broken or torn at both ends (see **Fig. 21.4**). When discovered it was pinched and hammered closed at both ends, though subsequently opened at one end by the finder. Elaborately decorated with punched and chased designs; zones of decoration are separated by simple double-grooved lines. One zone is quite simple, with punch-texture/stippling and a line of small, untextured triangles. Another is divided into diamond and triangular-shaped panels within which decorative motifs include concentric circles, crescents and punch-texturing. See Chapter 21 for a full discussion of decoration.
Contained five gold coins (Cat. nos 174–8).
Wt: 23.6g; L: 66.9mm; W: 18.7mm

F.54: Gold/silver alloy torc (Pl. 14.24)
TUBULAR (TYPE 4/5)
BM: 1991,0501.31; Jackson no.: 37
Fragment of gold/silver alloy Type 4 or 5 tubular torc neck-ring, broken or torn at both ends. Decorated with impressed lines, which delimit zones of punch-texture/stippling (see **Fig. 21.3**).
Similar to F.55, though not a joining piece.
Wt: 11.1g; L: 60.0mm

F.55: Gold/silver alloy torc (Pl. 14.24)
TUBULAR (TYPE 4/5)
BM: 1991,0501.32; Jackson no.: 38
[Analysed: see Ch. 17]
Fragment of gold/silver alloy Type 4 or 5 tubular torc neck-ring, broken or torn at both ends. Decorated with impressed lines, creating a spiral design or mock-twist, alternating plain and punch-textured/stippled zones (see Ch. 21 for discussion of decoration).
Similar to F.54, though not a joining piece.
Wt: 13.1g; D(nr): 13.9mm; L: 72.6mm

F.56: Composite group (inserted): Gold/silver alloy torc (Pl. 14.24)
TUBULAR (TYPE 4/5)
BM: 1991,0501.97; Jackson no.: 109
Two fragments of gold/silver alloy Type 4 or 5 tubular torc neck-ring: one inserted into the other, though most likely from the same object. Both are crushed and hammered flat. Punch-textured decoration; an impressed line/groove appears to slowly spiral around the neck-ring.
Perhaps part of the same object as F.29a.
Wt: 39.4g; L: 79.4mm; W: 17.8mm

F.57: Gold/silver alloy torc (Pl. 14.24)
TUBULAR (TYPE 1)
BM: 1991,0501.119; Jackson no.: 30

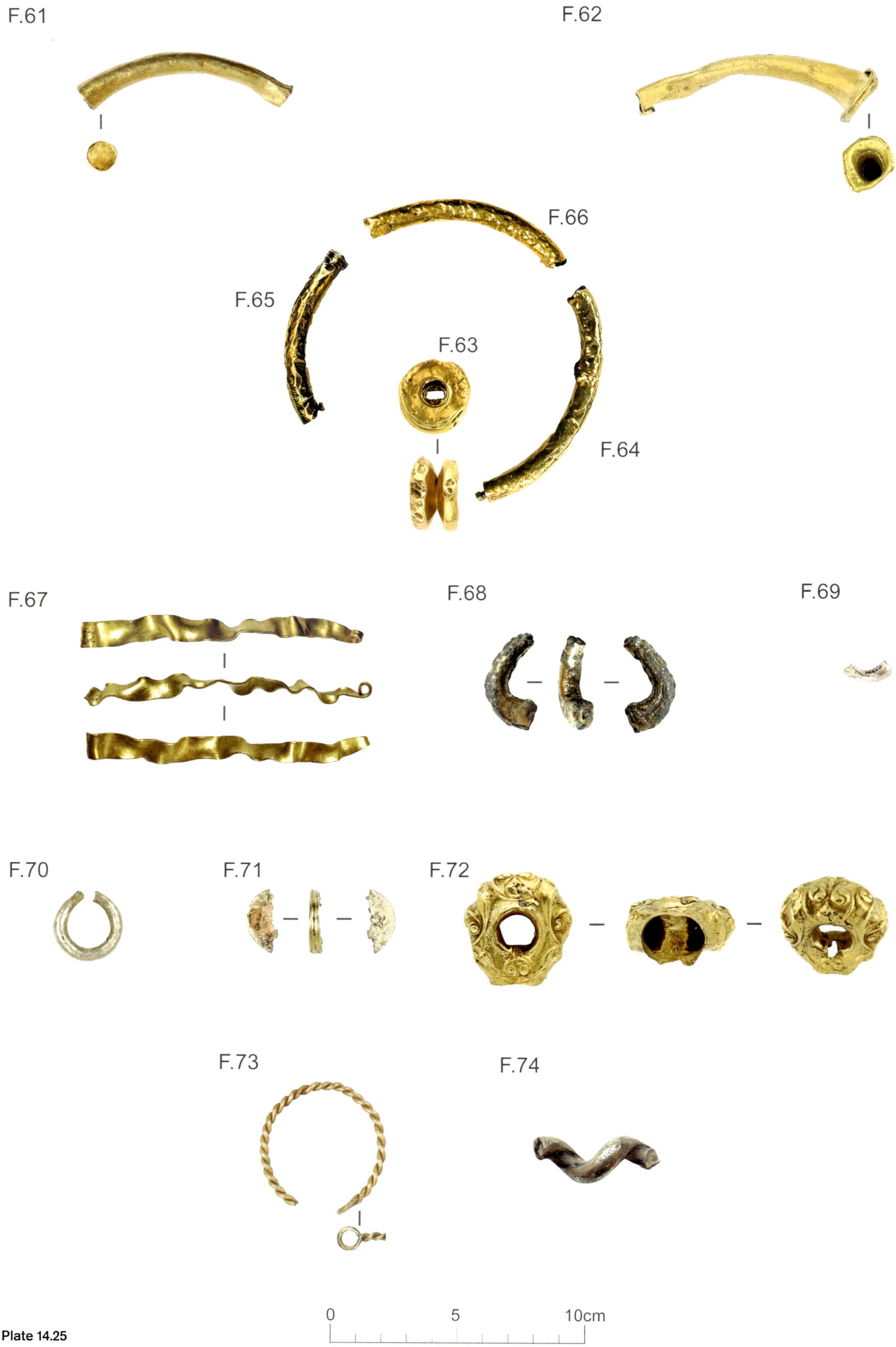

Plate 14.25

Fragment of gold/silver alloy Type 1 tubular torc, comprising a buffer terminal and length of neck-ring, cut or broken at the other end (see **Fig. 21.23**). The terminal has a 'pie-crust' crimped rim moulding around the circumference on the front, and the dished face has a central circular design of a triskele in relief against a stippled/punch-textured background. See Chapter 21 for a full discussion of decoration.
Wt: 42.5g; D(term): 34.0mm; L: 47.0mm

F.58: Gold/silver alloy torc (Pl. 14.24)
TUBULAR (TYPE 1)
BM: 1991,0501.25; Jackson no.: 29
Fragment of gold/silver alloy Type 1 tubular torc, comprising a buffer terminal and length of neck-ring, cut or broken at the other end. The terminal has a dished face and back, with simple raised circular rim around front and back circumference. The broken neck-ring has been hammered and bent. The neck-ring has clearly been constructed from a rolled length of sheet, and the seam is visible along one side.
Wt: 34.7g; D(nr): 8.5mm; D(term): 34.6mm; L: 51.5mm

F.59: Gold/silver alloy torc (Pl. 14.24)
TUBULAR (TYPE 1)
BM: 1991,0501.77; Jackson no.: 65
Fragment of gold/silver alloy Type 1 tubular torc, comprising a buffer terminal and length of neck-ring, roughly broken at the other end. The terminal is plain apart from simple rim moulding around the circumference on the front, and is slightly crushed, dented and distorted. The neck-ring is also distorted and hammered out of shape.
Wt: 48.0g; D(nr): 8.6mm; D(term): 37.9mm; L: 118.1mm

F.60: Gold/silver alloy torc (Pl. 14.24)
TUBULAR (TYPE 3)
BM: 1991,0501.26; Jackson no.: 31
Fragment of gold/silver alloy Type 3 tubular torc, comprising one terminal and a short length of tubular neck-ring, the whole severely crushed and distorted. The terminal is plain, with simple raised circular rim around front and back circumference. The neck-ring expands into a bead behind the terminal, with the same raised rim moulding. A hole punched through the edge of the terminal perhaps suggests that it was originally part of an interlinked group.
Wt: 60.4g; D(term): 49.1mm; L: 79.5mm

F.61: Gold/silver alloy torc (Pl. 14.25)
TUBULAR (TYPE 4)
BM: 1991,0501.164; Jackson no.: 100
Fragment of gold/silver alloy Type 4 tubular torc comprising a short section of hollow neck-ring, broken and slightly distorted at one end, expanding towards a buffer terminal at the other. The terminal has a dished, circular end-plate.
Wt: 19.5g; D(term): 12.0mm; L: 85.0mm

F.62: Composite group (fused): Gold/silver alloy torc; gold/silver alloy wire (Pl. 14.25)
TUBULAR (?TYPE 3);
BM: 1991,0501.30; Jackson no.: 36
[Analysed: see Ch. 17]
Fragment of gold/silver alloy tubular torc neck-ring, cut at one end, and expanding at the other towards the (missing) terminal (see **Fig. 17.7b**). At the terminal end, the fragment ends in an open trumpet-shape, with the edge being a rolled rim that probably marked the start of the buffer terminal, possibly a Type 3 form. In the interior at this end, a seam is visible around the circumference, showing that the flared terminal end was formed from a separate sheet component to the neck-ring. The fragment is partially crushed and distorted, and a short cut length of gold/silver alloy circular-section wire is fused to the broken end of the neck-ring.
Wt: 29.9g; L: 95.0mm

F.63–6: Gold/silver alloy and iron torc (Pl. 14.25)
TUBULAR (TYPE 2)
F.63–6 most likely represent a single torc, broken and incomplete. The T-shaped fastener of F.64 fits into the slot on F.63.

F.63: BM: 1991,0501.33; Jackson no.: 39
Fragment of gold/silver alloy Type 2 tubular torc, comprising a hollow double buffer terminal, which would have fastened to the narrow neck-ring by means of a central rectangular slot. Each terminal is a simple flat disc. The perimeter of each is badly dented, and the circular aperture in each outer face is torn. A packing material, possibly resin or beeswax, survives inside both terminals.
Wt: 14.2g; D(term): 29.8mm; T: 17.5mm

F.64: BM: 1991,0501.35; Jackson no.: 41
Fragment of gold/silver alloy Type 2 tubular torc neck-ring. One end terminates in a plate with a T-shaped projection/fastening. The other end is broken, revealing an iron core. Iron corrosion has burst through the gold sheet in places along the neck-ring. The surface is dented and hammered.
Wt: 17.2g; D(nr): 9.2mm; L: 94.3mm

F.65: BM: 1991,0501.36; Jackson no.: 42
[Analysed: see Ch. 17]
Fragment of gold/silver alloy Type 2 tubular torc neck-ring with degraded iron core visible inside. One end has a narrow gold collar soldered around the circumference of the neck-ring just behind the rim, with one neat and four rougher small circular holes beyond it. The other end also appears to be the original end of a section of neck-ring, but is more heavily damaged, with the sheet being torn. The surface is dented and hammered.
Wt: 9.3g; D(nr): 9.4mm; L: 71.4mm

F.66: BM: 1991,0501.134; Jackson no.: 24
Fragment of gold/silver alloy Type 2 tubular torc section of neck-ring with degraded iron core visible inside. One end has a narrow gold collar soldered around the circumference of the neck-ring just behind the rim, perhaps the end of a section of sheet forming the neck-ring. The other end is broken and partly crushed. The surface is dented and hammered.
May be part of the same torc as F.63–5.
Wt: 11.6g; D(nr): 9.0mm; L: 82.0mm

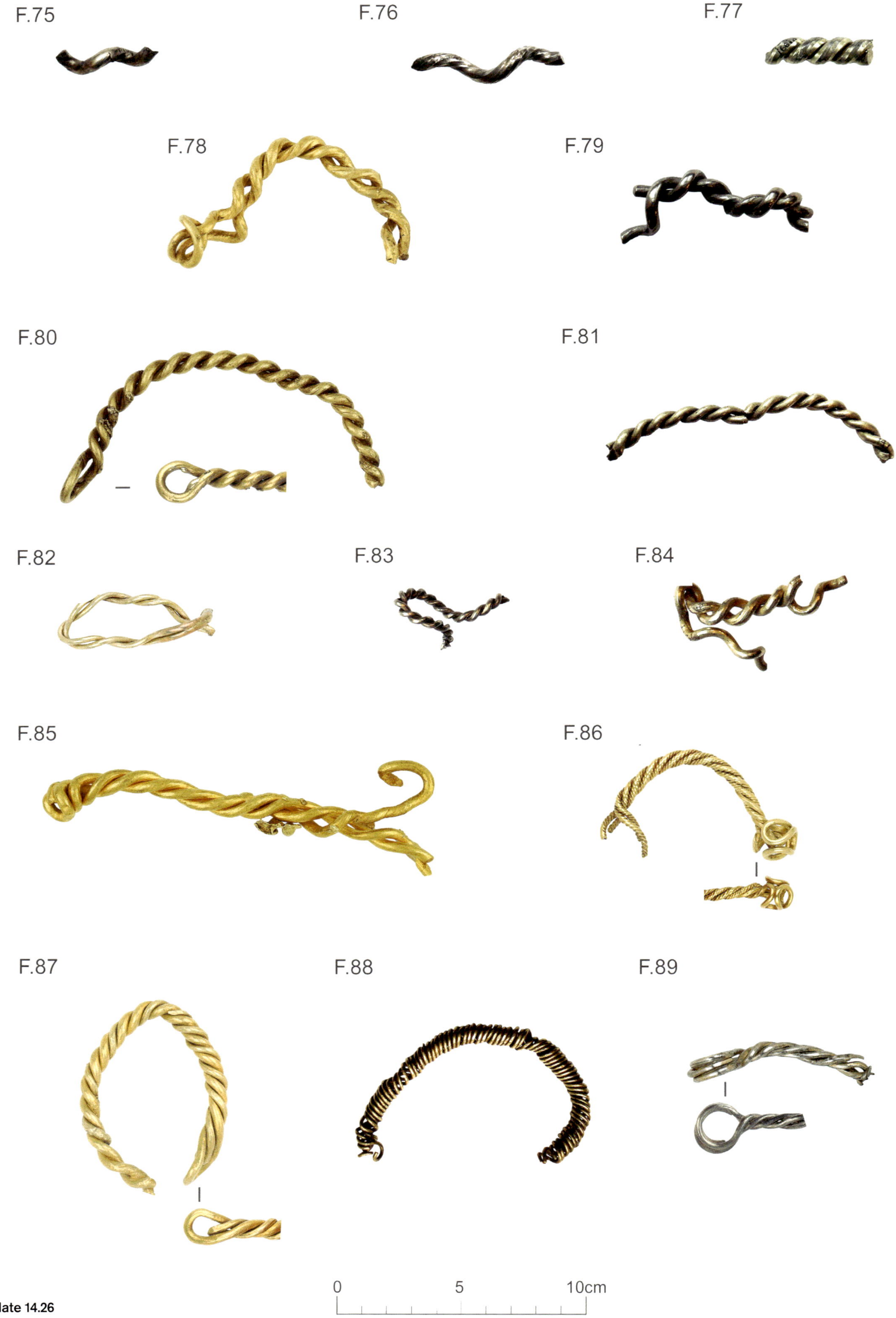
F.75
F.76
F.77
F.78
F.79
F.80
F.81
F.82
F.83
F.84
F.85
F.86
F.87
F.88
F.89
0
5
10cm

Plate 14.26

F.67: Gold/silver alloy strip/?torc (Pl. 14.25)
BM: 1991,0501.132; Jackson no.: 21
Gold/silver alloy strip with rectangular cross-section, distorted as if it has been tightly coiled or twisted and then flattened. Rolled into a small loop at one end, broken at the other. Possibly originally part of a ribbon torc.
Wt: 17.0g; L: 111.3mm; W: 10.6mm; T: 1.0mm

F.68: Gold/silver alloy torc (Pl. 14.25)
BM: 1991,0702.46; Jackson no.: 208
Fragment of gold/silver alloy multi-strand torc comprising around half of a ring terminal. Broken in antiquity, and flattened by hammering to give the terminal a squarish section. Broken across the centre of the ring, revealing a small squarish void in the core. One side is plain, the other most likely has some kind of simple, linear cast decoration, the design of which is obscured by corrosion products.
Wt: 21.7g; D(wire): 8.7mm; L: 38.3mm

F.69: Gold/silver alloy wire/?torc/?bracelet (Pl. 14.25)
BM: 1991,0702.47; Jackson no.: 308
Fragment of curved gold/silver alloy circular-section wire, cut at both ends. Most likely part of a loop terminal from a multi-strand torc/bracelet.
Wt: 3.8g; D(wire): 6.5mm; L: 19.6mm

F.70: Gold/silver alloy torc/bracelet (Pl. 14.25)
BM: 1991,0501.212; Jackson no.: 218
Loop terminal from a gold/silver alloy multi-strand torc or bracelet, formed from circular-section wire. The terminal is cut or broken at both ends, so it may once have been part of a double-loop terminal.
Wt: 14.4g; D(wire): 5.4mm; D(term): 27.5mm

F.71: Gold/silver alloy torc (Pl. 14.25)
BM: 1991,0501.183; Jackson no.: 156
Fragment of buffer terminal from gold/silver alloy multi-strand torc, comprising approximately half of the flat plain cast 'cap', broken down the middle to leave a semi-circular fragment. Two parallel cordons run around the edge circumference. On the reverse, small fragments of melted wire are visible, but it is not possible to discern the neck-ring construction.
Wt: 4.8g; L: 25.1mm; W: 10.9mm; T: 5.4mm

F.72: Gold/silver alloy torc (Pl. 14.25)
BM: 1991,0501.45; Jackson no.: 52
[Analysed: see Ch. 17]
Detached torus terminal from a gold/silver alloy multi-strand torc (see **Figs 17.100c–d, 21.31**). Very thin sheet, with elaborate relief decoration of curvilinear motifs set in a stippled/punch-decorated field, some suggestive of zoomorphic or anthropomorphic forms. The sheet is split along a join within the eye of the terminal, and there is dented and torn damage in several places. Small gold/silver alloy sheet fragments and semi-coalesced globules adhere in several places. See Chapter 17 for information on construction, and Chapter 21 for a full discussion of decoration.

Notes from scientific analysis (Nigel Meeks)
This is an individual terminal, hollow with thin walls. There are no broken wires attached to the terminal flange where it has broken away from the neck-ring. It has a deep relief design that appears to be chased into the metal, with features outlined with additional chased lines and circumferential chased lines at the edge of the central hole, similar to torc L.19a. The recessed areas between the main design features are covered in a dot-punched decoration to give texture to these areas. This is in contrast to torc terminals that have cast-in deep relief decoration, such as L.21a, in which the recessed areas are left plain and smooth. Looking inside the open terminal shows the thin nature of the metal and the relief decoration clearly shows as a negative impression in the metal from within, having been chased from the outside. This would not be the case if it had been cast. It would not be possible to produce the complex hollow doughnut form by raising the sheet terminal in one piece. A small linear slot, which looks like part of a lateral seam, is seen on the side of the terminal. This may be evidence of a solder seam joining two halves of the sheet terminal. There is no visible evidence of a separately added tubular core such as that described by Machling and Williamson (2016) for the Netherurd torc terminal. These observations confirm that the terminal is made from sheet, and it can be compared to the complete torc L.19a, which also has highly decorative and elaborate sheet gold terminals.
On both sides of the terminal there are splashes of molten gold similar to those seen on other objects in the fragmentary Hoard F.
Wt: 22.9g; D(term): 43.0mm; W: 44.0mm

F.73: Gold/silver alloy torc/bracelet (Pl. 14.25)
MSCC: (2P)R
BM: 1991,0501.89; Jackson no.: 77
Fragment of gold/silver alloy multi-strand torc or bracelet comprising one loop terminal (continuous with the neck-ring/body wires) and a short length of neck-ring/body, cut at the other end. Stage II construction of two circular-section wires plied together. The whole fragment is bent into a penannular ring, perhaps suggesting that it was originally part of an interlinked group.
Wt: 9.1g; D(ext): 49.3mm; D(nr): 3.7mm; D(wire): 1.9mm; D(term): 9.8mm

F.74: Gold/silver alloy torc (Pl. 14.25)
MSCC: ?(2P)R
BM: 1991,0501.151; Jackson no.: 84
Fragment of gold/silver alloy multi-strand torc neck-ring, consisting of a single circular-section rod, cut at both ends. It has clearly been plied with another rod to form a Stage II neck-ring.
Wt: 35.4g; D(wire): 8.9mm; L: 50.5mm

F.75–6: Gold/silver alloy torc (Pl. 14.26)
MSCC: (2P)F
Fragments of gold/silver alloy multi-strand torc, each comprising a single faceted wire, cut at both ends (see **Fig. 20.22**). Almost certainly part of a Stage II neck-ring formed

from two wires plied together. F.75 and F.76 are almost certainly part of the same torc.

F.75: BM: 1991,0501.173; Jackson no.: 134
Wt: 11.2g; D(wire): 6.0mm; L: 41.0mm

F.76: BM: 1991,0501.174; Jackson no.: 135
Stress cracks in several places.
Wt: 15.7g; D(wire): 5.8mm; L: 61.8mm

F.77: Gold/silver alloy torc (Pl. 14.26)
MSCC: (2P)F
BM: 1991,0501.210; Jackson no.: 215
Fragment of gold/silver alloy multi-strand torc neck-ring, cut at both ends (see **Fig. 20.20a–b**). Stage II construction of two faceted wires plied together. Stress cracks in several places.
Wt: 22.5g; D(nr): 10.5mm; D(wire): 5.6mm; L: 43.6mm; W: 13.3mm; T: 2.0mm

F.78: Gold/silver alloy torc (Pl. 14.26)
MSCC: (2P)F
BM: 1991,0501.37; Jackson no.: 43
Fragment of gold/silver alloy multi-strand torc comprising one double-loop terminal (continuous with the neck-ring wires) and part of the neck-ring, cut at the other end. Stage II construction of two faceted wires plied together. The terminal is very distorted, as if it has been deliberately untwisted, and there are tool marks on the neck-ring.
Wt: 115.0g; D(nr): 7.1mm; D(wire): 4.2mm; L: 97.2mm

F.79: Gold/silver alloy torc (Pl. 14.26)
MSCC: (?P(2P))R
BM: 1991,0501.152; Jackson no.: 85
Fragment of gold/silver alloy multi-strand torc neck-ring, cut at both ends. Stage II construction of two circular-section wires plied together. The wires are bent and distorted at the ends, and the whole fragment is curved in such a way as to suggest it originally formed part of a Stage III plied construction.
Wt: 37.9g; D(nr): 9.0mm; D(wire): 4.9mm; L: 77.8mm

F.80: Gold/silver alloy torc (Pl. 14.26)
MSCC: (2P)R
BM: 1991,0501.38; Jackson no.: 44
Fragment of gold/silver alloy multi-strand torc comprising one loop terminal (continuous with the neck-ring wires) and a length of the neck-ring, broken at the other end. Stage II construction of two circular-section wires plied together. Semi-coalesced fragments and small droplets of gold are fused to the terminal and neck-ring in many places.
Wt: 108.8g; D(nr): 7.0mm; D(wire): 4.2mm; D(term): 17.7mm; L: 130.9mm

F.81: Gold/silver alloy torc/bracelet (Pl. 14.26)
MSCC: (2P)R
BM: 1991,0501.147; Jackson no.: 81
Fragment of gold/silver alloy multi-strand torc neck-ring or bracelet body, broken at both ends, and bent/damaged in the middle of the fragment. The patina suggests the damage to the middle may be relatively recent. Stage II construction of two circular-section wires plied together.
Wt: 32.4g; D(nr): 7.1mm; D(wire): 3.5mm; L: 116.7mm

F.82: Gold/silver alloy torc/bracelet (Pl. 14.26)
MSCC: (2P)R
BM: 1991,0501.155; Jackson no.: 88
Fragment of gold/silver alloy multi-strand torc or bracelet, comprising a length of neck-ring/body, cut at one end, and part of one ring terminal (continuous with the neck-ring wires), now broken across the mid-point of the ring. Stage II construction of two circular-section wires plied together.
Wt: 16.5g; D(nr): 4.1mm; D(wire): 2.3mm; L: 63.6mm

F.83: Gold/silver alloy torc/bracelet (Pl. 14.26)
MSCC: (2P)R
BM: 1991,0501.159; Jackson no.: 95
Fragment of gold/silver alloy multi-strand torc neck-ring or bracelet body, cut at both ends and bent into a rough loop. Stage II construction of two circular-section wires plied together.
Wt: 10.3g; D(rope): 4.5mm; D(wire): 2.3mm; L: 46.6mm

F.84: Gold/silver alloy torc/bracelet (Pl. 14.26)
MSCC: (2P)R
BM: 1991,0501.158; Jackson no.: 94
[Analysed: see Ch. 17]
Fragment of gold/silver alloy multi-strand torc neck-ring or bracelet body, broken at both ends. Stage II construction of two circular-section wires plied together. The ends of the wires are bent and distorted, and one end has been hammered. One wire extends further than the other at each end.
Wt: 12.7g; D(wire): 2.7mm; L: 49.1mm

F.85: Gold/silver alloy torc/bracelet (Pl. 14.26)
MSCC: (3P)R
BM: 1991,0501.95; Jackson no.: 107
[Analysed: see Ch. 17]
Fragment of gold/silver alloy multi-strand torc or bracelet, broken at one end and with what is perhaps a simple or unfinished cage terminal at the other, formed from the continuous, involuted, folded end of two of the neck-ring wires. Stage II construction of three circular-section wires plied together. The whole fragment is bent straight, and the broken end is damaged and the wires pulled apart. Small globules and fragments of gold/silver alloy adhere to the object in several places.
Wt: 180.0g; D(nr): 7.9mm; D(wire): 4.3mm; D(term): 17.3mm; L: 157.0mm

F.86: Gold/silver alloy torc/bracelet (Pl. 14.26)
MSCC: (4C)T
BM: 1991,0501.42; Jackson no.: 47
Fragment of gold/silver alloy multi-strand torc or bracelet comprising one cage terminal and a length of neck-ring, broken at the other end. Stage II construction of four twisted wires coiled together around a hollow core, though one of the wires is untwisted (with simple square cross-section). The cage terminal is continuous with the neck-ring/body wires, though

in the area of the terminal the wires are circular in cross-section. One pair of the neck-ring wires join to form two involuted loops in the inside of the terminal. The other pair of wires are joined by a series of three involuted loops which create a more elaborate multi-lobed outer cage terminal.
Wt: 37.0g; D(nr): 6.4mm; D(wire): 2.6mm; D(term): 19.1mm; L: 79.7mm

F.87: Gold/silver alloy torc/bracelet (Pl. 14.26)
MSCC: (3P)R
BM: 1991,0501.93; Jackson no.: 105
Fragment of gold/silver alloy multi-strand torc or bracelet, comprising a single-loop terminal (continuous with two of the neck-ring/body wires) and a length of neck-ring/body, cut or broken and part melted at the other end. Stage II construction of three circular-section wires plied together, broken at different points along the remaining length. The whole fragment has been bent into a penannular ring, perhaps suggesting that it was originally part of an interlinked group. Globules of gold are fused to the neck-ring.
Wt: 94.2g; D(nr): 9.0mm; D(wire): 3.1mm; D(term): 15.0mm; L: 77.2mm

F.88: Gold/silver alloy torc/bracelet (Pl. 14.26)
MSCC: (4C)R
BM: 1991,0501.22; Jackson no.: 17
[Analysed: see Ch. 17]
Fragment of gold/silver alloy multi-strand torc neck-ring or bracelet body, broken at both ends, and bent (see **Figs 17.27–8, 20.8a–b**). Stage II construction of four circular-section wires coiled around a hollow core.
Wt: 38.2g; D(nr): 8.9mm; D(wire): 1.5mm; L: 95.1mm

F.89: Gold/silver alloy torc/bracelet (Pl. 14.26)
MSCC: (4P)R
BM: 1991,0501.101; Jackson no.: 113
[Analysed: see Ch. 17]
Fragment of gold/silver alloy multi-strand torc or bracelet, comprising one triple-loop terminal and a length of neck-ring/body, cut at the other end (see **Fig. 17.33d**). Stage II construction of four circular-section wires plied together. Two of the neck-ring/body wires terminate in open loops, the third terminal loop is continuous, formed from the two remaining wires.
Wt: 19.7g; D(nr): 5.8mm; D(wire): 2.7mm; D(term): 20.4mm; L: 75.4mm

F.90: Gold/silver alloy torc/bracelet (Pl. 14.27)
MSCC: (4P)T
BM: 1991,0501.157; Jackson no.: 91
Fragment of gold/silver alloy multi-strand torc or bracelet consisting of one double-loop terminal and a length of neck-ring/body, cut or broken at the other end. Stage II construction of four twisted wires plied together. Each loop is continuous, extending to form one pair of the neck-ring/body wires. The outer loop is of twisted wire, the inner loop is circular in cross-section.
Wt: 30.5g; D(nr): 6.3mm; D(wire): 3.0mm; D(term): 15.0mm; L: 79.0mm

F.91: Gold/silver alloy torc/bracelet (Pl. 14.27)
MSCC: (4P)T
BM: 1991,0501.100; Jackson no.: 112
Fragment of gold/silver alloy multi-strand torc or bracelet consisting of one double-loop terminal and a length of neck-ring/body, cut or broken at the other end, with one wire extending slightly further than the others. Stage II construction of four twisted wires plied together. Each loop is continuous, extending to form one pair of the neck-ring/body wires. The outer loop is of twisted wire (although smoothed or possibly part melted on the exterior on one side); the inner loop is circular in cross-section. The whole fragment is bent into an open, penannular ring, perhaps suggesting that it was originally part of an interlinked group.
Wt: 19.6g; D(nr): 4.9mm; D(wire): 1.8mm; D(term): 11.9mm; L: 65.9mm

F.92–3: Gold/silver alloy torc (Pl. 14.27)
MSCC: (5C)R
F.92 and F.93 were broken in antiquity but join.

F.92:
BM: 1991,0501.82; Jackson no.: 70
Fragment of gold/silver alloy multi-strand torc, comprising one buffer terminal and a length of neck-ring, broken at the other end (see **Fig. 21.28**). Stage II construction of five circular-section wires coiled together around a hollow core. The terminal is a very simple, small, flat buffer terminal, face decorated with a simple incised design of interlocked circle and hatched crescent in an enclosing circle. The motif is in the form of an armadillo (see Joy 2008, fig. 5.1). A simple indented cordon runs around the edge of the terminal. See Chapter 21 for a full discussion of decoration.
Wt: 25.1g; D(nr): 5.3mm; D(wire): 1.3mm; D(term): 6.8mm; L: 100.5mm

F.93:
BM: 1991,0501.83; Jackson no.: 71
[Analysed: see Ch. 17]
Fragment of gold/silver alloy multi-strand torc neck-ring, broken at both ends and bent into a rough ring, perhaps suggesting that it was originally part of an interlinked group. Stage II construction of five circular-section wires coiled together around a hollow core.
Wt: 20.2g; D(nr): 5.2mm; D(wire): 1.3mm; L: 67.5mm

F.94: Gold/silver alloy torc/bracelet (Pl. 14.27)
MSCC: (5C)T
BM: 1991,0501.17; Jackson no.: 8
[Analysed: see Ch. 17]
Fragment of gold/silver alloy multi-strand torc neck-ring or bracelet body, broken at both ends, and bent into a rough ring, perhaps suggesting that it was originally part of an interlinked group. Stage II construction of five twisted wires coiled around a hollow core.
Wt: 65.3g; D(nr): 9.6mm; D(wire): 2.2mm; L: 78.3mm

F.95: Gold/silver alloy torc/bracelet (Pl. 14.27)
MSCC: (6C)T
BM: 1991,0501.18; Jackson no.: 9

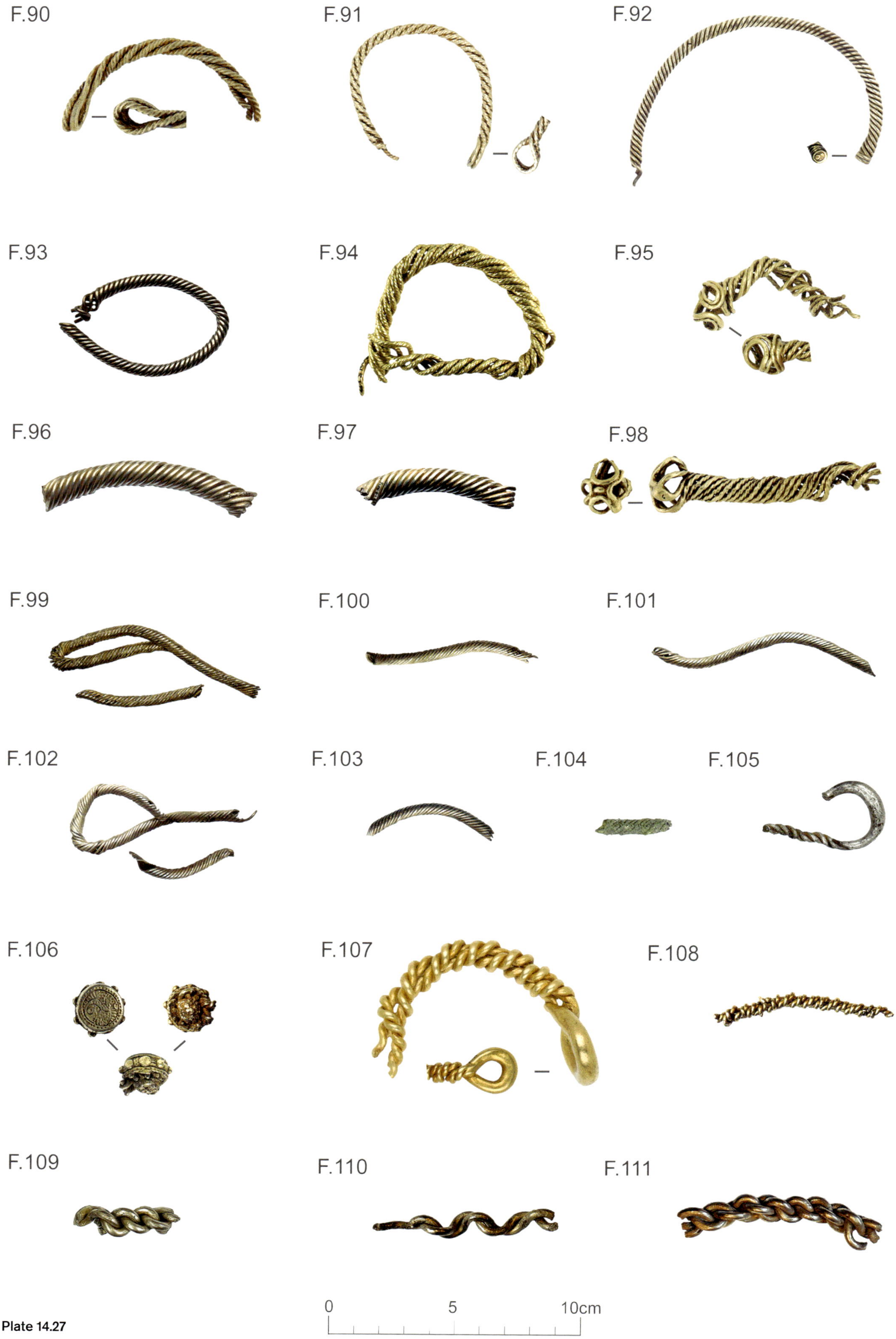
F.90
F.91
F.92
F.93
F.94
F.95
F.96
F.97
F.98
F.99
F.100
F.101
F.102
F.103
F.104
F.105
F.106
F.107
F.108
F.109
F.110
F.111
0
5
10cm

Plate 14.27

Fragment of gold/silver alloy multi-strand torc comprising a cage terminal and part of the neck-ring/body, broken at the other end, where the wires are bent and distorted. Stage II construction of six twisted wires coiled around a hollow core. The terminal is a continuous series of three involuted loops, executed in a pair of parallel wires, one twisted and one circular in cross-section. These loops extend to form two pairs of the neck-ring/body strands, the fifth strand is soldered to join one of these pairs.
Wt: 28.5g; D(nr): 9.0mm; D(wire): 1.7mm; L: 66.7mm

F.96–7: Gold/silver alloy torc (Pl. 14.27)
MSCC: (8C)R
Fragments of gold/silver alloy multi-strand torc neck-ring, each cut and crushed flat at both ends, most likely by snipping with a double-bladed tool (see **Fig. 20.17**). Stage II construction of eight circular-section wires coiled together around a hollow core. F.96 and F.97 are almost certainly broken parts of the same incomplete torc.

F.96:
BM: 1991,0501.84; Jackson no.: 72
Wt: 30.9g; D(nr): 10.0mm; D(wire): 1.8mm; L: 85.1mm

F.97:
BM: 1991,0501.85; Jackson no.: 73
[Analysed: see Ch. 17]
Wt: 20.7g; D(nr): 9.8mm; D(wire): 1.8mm; L: 63.7mm

F.98: Gold/silver alloy torc (Pl. 14.27)
MSCC: (8C)T
BM: 1991,0501.15; Jackson no.: 6
Fragment of gold/silver alloy multi-strand torc comprising a cage terminal and part of the neck-ring, broken at the other end, where the wires are bent and distorted. Stage II construction of eight twisted wires coiled around a hollow core. The terminal is formed from four confronted circular-section loops, each a continuation of one pair of the neck-ring wires. The small space at the centre of these four loops is filled with a fused globule of gold/silver alloy.
Wt: 55.3g; D(nr): 6.2mm; D(wire): 0.9mm; D(term): 13.9mm; L: 92.0mm

F.99–104: Gold/silver alloy torc(s) (Pl. 14.27)
MSCC: (9C)R
F.99–104 may be part of the same or very similar torcs.

F.99:
BM: 1991,0501.137; Jackson no.: 27
[Analysed: see Ch. 17]
Fragment of gold/silver alloy multi-strand torc neck-ring, broken at both ends. Stage II construction of nine circular-section wires coiled together around a hollow core (see **Fig. 17.33b–c**). Now in two parts, originally one piece coiled into an elongated loop, perhaps suggesting that it was once part of an interlinked group.
Wt: 15.5g; D(nr): 4.8mm; D(wire): 0.9mm; L: 84.1mm

F.100:
BM: 1991,0501.185; Jackson no.: 164

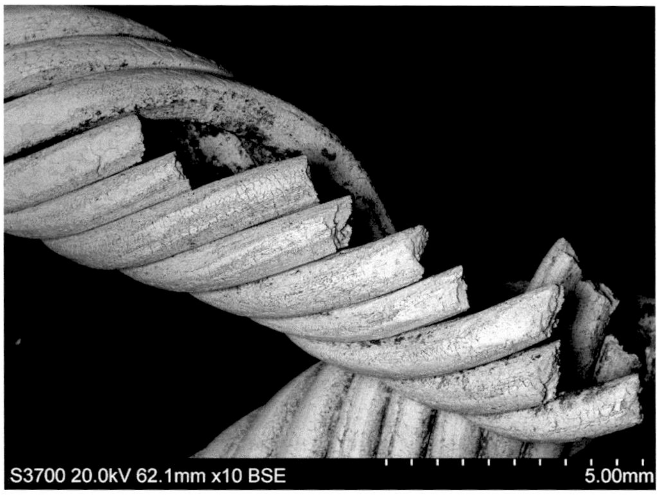

Figure 14.20 SEM detail showing extensive corrosion and cracking in F.102

Fragment of gold/silver alloy multi-strand torc neck-ring, broken at both ends. Stage II construction of nine circular-section wires coiled together around a hollow core.
Wt: 4.1g; D(nr): 4.4mm; D(wire): 1.0mm; L: 68.1mm

F.101:
BM: 1991,0501.186; Jackson no.: 165
Fragment of gold/silver alloy multi-strand torc neck-ring, broken at both ends. Stage II construction of nine circular-section wires coiled together around a hollow core.
Wt: 6.9g; D(nr): 4.4mm; D(wire): 1.0mm; L: 88.7mm

F.102:
BM: 1991,0501.187; Jackson no.: 166
[Analysed: see Ch. 17]
Fragment of gold/silver alloy multi-strand torc neck-ring, broken at both ends (see **Fig. 17.33a**). Stage II construction of nine circular-section wires coiled together around a hollow core. Now in several parts, originally one piece coiled into a rough loop, perhaps suggesting that it was once part of an interlinked group.

Notes from scientific analysis (Nigel Meeks)
Torc fragment F.102 is typical of the small torcs from Snettisham in terms of its wire construction. SEM images of the twisted wires of this fragmentary torc show the heavily cracked outer surface but also very smooth areas of polish from wear. The stress corrosion cracking and fractured wire ends show brittle failure of the entire multiple wire torc due to extensive corrosion after burial (**Figs 14.20, 17.33a**). The hollow centres of torcs such as this example are of great interest from the manufacturing viewpoint. The only way to tightly twist such wires and to additionally bend the assembled wires to the final curved shape without them collapsing onto each other was to wind them round a core or former (see Chs 17 and 19). The wires might also have been annealed on the former during winding to soften the metal and remove the springiness that would otherwise tend to untwist them. Annealing would allow very tight spiralling and the wires would then work-harden in their twisted form which would help prevent untwisting.
Wt: 16.9g; D(nr): 4.4mm; D(wire): 1.0mm; L: 74.2mm

F.103:
BM: 1991,0501.215; Jackson no.: 275
[Analysed: see Ch. 17]
Fragment of gold/silver alloy multi-strand torc neck-ring, broken at both ends. Stage II construction of nine circular-section wires coiled together around a hollow core.
Wt: 4.1g; D(nr): 4.6mm; D(wire): 0.9mm; L: 50.8mm

F.104:
BM: 1991,0702.182; Jackson no.: 360
Fragment of gold/silver alloy multi-strand torc neck-ring, cut at one end and broken at the other (perhaps recently). Stage II construction of nine circular-section wires coiled together around a hollow core.
Wt: 1.8g; D(nr): 4.8mm; D(wire): 0.6mm; L: 29.5mm

F.105: Gold/silver alloy torc/bracelet (Pl. 14.27)
MSCC: (?P(3PZ))R
BM: 1991,0501.211; Jackson no.: 217
Fragment of gold/silver alloy multi-strand torc, comprising part of one ring terminal and a short length of neck-ring, broken at the other end. What remains of the neck-ring is a Stage II component of three circular-section wires plied together Z-twist. These merge to form part of a thickened ring terminal. Based on the construction of other similar torcs, it is likely that the complete neck-ring had a Stage III construction, with several similar Stage II ropes plied together.
Wt: 13.8g; D(rope): 4.3mm; D(term): 27.1mm; L: 48.8mm

F.106: Gold/silver alloy torc (Pl. 14.27)
MSCC: (?C(2P))R
BM: 1991,0501.19; Jackson no.: 10
[Analysed: see Ch. 17]
Buffer terminal from gold/silver alloy multi-strand torc (see **Fig. 21.39**). Nine small dot-punched domed projections around the outside edge of the terminal are set in a basket-hatched field. On the face of the terminal, a ring of dots and an engraved circle encompass engraved La Tène-style designs: lobe and tendril motif, with dot-punched/stippled and basket-hatched trumpet voids. On the back, projecting wire stubs are all that remain of the Stage III neck-ring. This was most likely formed of a number of ropes twisted around a hollow core, with the one remaining rope formed from two circular-section wires plied together. See Chapter 21 for a full discussion of decoration.

Notes from scientific analysis (Nigel Meeks)
An individual cast terminal, with all the wires broken away from the back. There is an engraved and punched design on the front and the side of the terminal has nine cast-in round granules of which four are very worn down (see **Fig. 21.39**). The engraved decoration shows the sharp V-shaped grooves of the engraving tool and small miss-cuts where lines start, end or overlap. The dot decoration is punched with a single round-ended tool which was also used to chase a few extended dots.

The side view shows the cast-in rounded 'knobs' which also have punched dot decoration, and between the knobs are chased indentations alternating vertical and horizontal. A row of round punch-marks runs around the neck of the terminal. The broken ends of the wires from the torc show they are round-section, 2mm in diameter, and twisted in pairs. In the centre of the wires is a mass of metal which is the plug of the casting that flowed into the hollow space within the twisted wires of the torc. This is also seen in the back view.

The back view of the terminal shows that the neck-ring is made of eight pairs of twisted wires. The neck-ring probably looked similar to torc L.13, a springy and flexible coiled multi-strand torc.
Wt: 39.1g; D(term): 21.1mm; T: 15.9mm

F.107: Gold/silver alloy torc/bracelet (Pl. 14.27)
MSCC: (2P(2P))R
BM: 1991,0501.92; Jackson no.: 104
Fragment of gold/silver alloy multi-strand torc comprising one ring terminal and a short length of neck-ring/body, cut or broken at the other end. Stage III construction of two ropes plied together, each of which consists of two circular-section wires plied together. The terminal is a thickened ring which extends to form the two neck-ring ropes.
Wt: 148.9g; D(nr): 13.2mm; D(rope): 7.7mm; D(wire): 3.3mm; D(term): 28.8mm; L: 90.5mm

F.108: Gold/silver alloy torc/bracelet (Pl. 14.27)
MSCC: (2P(2P))R
BM: 1991,0501.154; Jackson no.: 87
[Analysed: see Ch. 17]
Fragment of gold/silver alloy multi-strand torc neck-ring or bracelet body, broken at both ends. Stage III construction of two ropes plied together, each of which consists of two circular-section wires plied together. One end is partially melted, and there is a small globule of gold and a fragment of part-melted wire fused to it.
Wt: 12.4g; D(nr): 6.0mm; D(rope): 2.9mm; D(wire): 1.5mm; L: 71.9mm

F.109–11: Gold/silver alloy torc (Pl. 14.27)
MSCC: (2PZ(2P))R
Fragments of gold/silver alloy multi-strand torc neck-ring, Stage III construction of two ropes plied together Z-twist, each of which is made up of two circular-section wires which are themselves plied tightly together. F.109–11 are most likely part of the same torc.

F.109: BM: 1991,0702.48; Jackson no.: 324
Fragment of neck-ring, cut at both ends.
Wt: 16.7g; D(nr): 12.0mm; D(rope): 6.5mm; D(wire): 3.5mm; L: 42.3mm

F.110: BM: 1991,0501.175; Jackson no.: 136
Fragment of neck-ring. What remains is just one Stage II rope of two circular-section wires which are plied together. One end is distorted, both are broken and show distress fractures around the break.
Wt: 13.6g; D(rope): 6.5mm; D(wire): 3.3mm; L: 73.4mm

F.111: BM: 1991,0501.176; Jackson no.: 137
Fragment of gold/silver alloy multi-strand torc neck-ring, cut at both ends.

Wt: 38.4g; D(nr): 12.4mm; D(rope): 6.5mm; D(wire): 3.3mm; L: 81.6mm

F.112–13: Gold/silver alloy torc (Pl. 14.28)
MSCC: (2PZ(4P))R
Fragments of gold/silver alloy multi-strand torc neck-ring, each broken at both ends. Stage III construction of two ropes loosely plied together Z-twist, each of which is made up of four circular-section wires plied together. F.112 and F.113 are most likely part of the same torc.

F.112: BM: 1991,0702.59; Jackson no.: 267
Wt: 11.0g; D(nr): 5.5mm; D(rope): 2.5mm; D(wire): 1.0mm; L: 97.5mm

F.113: BM: 1991,0501.184; Jackson no.: 157
Wt: 10.1g; D(nr): 6.0mm; D(rope): 3.0mm; D(wire): 1.0mm; L: 106.1mm

F.114: Gold/silver alloy torc/bracelet (Pl. 14.28)
MSCC: (3C(2P))R
BM: 1991,0501.39; Jackson no.: 45
Fragment of gold/silver alloy multi-strand torc neck-ring or bracelet body, raggedly cut/broken at both ends. Stage III construction of three ropes coiled around a hollow core, each rope formed of two circular-section wires plied together. The whole fragment is distorted and bent into a penannular loop.
Wt: 71.0g; D(nr): 8.4mm; D(rope): 4.2mm; D(wire): 1.9mm; L: 77.2mm

F.115: Gold/silver alloy torc (Pl. 14.28)
MSCC: (3P(6C))R
BM: 1991,0501.163; Jackson no.: 98
Fragment of gold/silver alloy multi-strand torc, comprising a buffer terminal and a very short length of the neck-ring (see **Fig. 21.21**). Stage III construction of three ropes plied together, each rope consisting of six circular-section wires coiled around a hollow core. The buffer terminal was cast onto the ends of the wires, and some of the metal has run down inside the hollow coils of the neck-ring ropes. The terminal has a plain, flat ended face. The edge is lightly convex, with a simple grooved moulding around the edge at the terminal end and a beaded moulding around the neck-ring end. The inner side of the edge is otherwise plain, while the outer side has six low circular bosses with trilobate divisions. See Chapter 21 for a full discussion of decoration.
Wt: 56.3g; D(nr): 16.5mm; D(rope): 8.5mm; D(wire): 1.7mm; D(term): 24.7mm; L: 30.4mm

F.116: Gold/silver alloy small torc (Pl. 14.28)
MSCC: (4CZ(2P))R
BM: 1991,0501.145; Jackson no.: 79
[Analysed: see Ch. 17]
Fragment of gold/silver alloy small multi-strand torc, comprising the majority of the neck-ring, cut at both ends where the terminals would have been (see **Figs 17.25, 17.29a–c, 20.4a–b, 20.19b**). Stage III construction of four ropes coiled together Z-twist, each of which consists of two circular-section wires plied together.
Wt: 22.1g; D(ext): 98.4mm; D(nr): 3.9mm; D(rope): 2.0mm; D(wire): 1.0mm

F.117: Gold/silver alloy torc (Pl. 14.28)
MSCC: (4P(2P))R
BM: 1991,0501.94; Jackson no.: 106
Fragment of gold/silver alloy multi-strand torc comprising one poorly-formed ring terminal, and a short length of neck-ring, broken and part melted at the other end. Stage III construction of four ropes plied together, each of which consists of two circular-section wires plied together. The thickened ring terminal is fused to the end of the neck-ring wires. It is either poorly cast or damaged by melting. Small globules of gold/silver alloy adhere to the whole object.
Wt: 147.0g; D(nr): 17.8mm; D(rope): 8.0mm; D(wire): 3.2mm; D(term): 40.8mm; L: 106.3mm

F.118: Gold/silver alloy torc (Pl. 14.28)
MSCC: (6C(2PZ))R
BM: 1991,0501.129; Jackson no.: 16
Fragment of gold/silver alloy multi-strand torc, comprising a simple cast-on buffer terminal and around half the neck-ring, cut at the other end. Stage III construction of six ropes coiled together, each of which consists of two circular-section wires plied together Z-twist. The terminal has a plain, flat face and two parallel grooved cordons around the edge.
Wt: 87.2g; D(nr): 10.3mm; D(rope): 3.0mm; D(wire): 1.6mm; D(term): 18.6mm; L: 148.7mm

F.119–20: Gold/silver alloy torc (Pl. 14.29)
MSCC: (5C(3P(2P)))R
[Analysed: see Ch. 17]
F.119 and F.120 are broken parts of the same incomplete torc (see **Figs 17.39–41, 17.43–5, 17.66, 21.17**). The break appears ancient (brittle/stress fracture). See Chapter 17 for information on construction, and Chapter 21 for a full discussion of decoration.

F.119:
BM: 1991,0501.81; Jackson no.: 69
Terminal of gold/silver alloy multi-strand torc, with the wires broken off at the start of the neck-ring. Little of the neck-ring remains, but it appears as F.120: Stage IV construction of five cables coiled together around a hollow core. Each cable consists of three ropes loosely plied together, and each rope is formed from two circular-section wires plied together. The reel terminal was cast onto the neck-ring and is decorated on both faces in relief with lobes, tendrils and bosses in a tripartite design repeated on each face. A simple indented line marks the rim. The hollow core of the reel is undecorated, and there is a plain collar where it meets the neck-ring.
Wt: 61.5g; D(term): 39.0mm; L: 43.0mm

F.120:
BM: 1991,0501.80; Jackson no.: 68
Fragment of gold/silver alloy multi-strand torc, comprising one reel terminal, and a damaged and broken length of neck-ring, as well as 16 additional wire fragments, now detached. Stage IV construction of five cables coiled

F.112

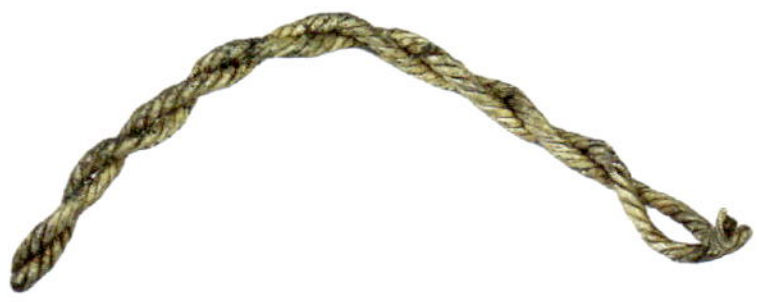

F.113

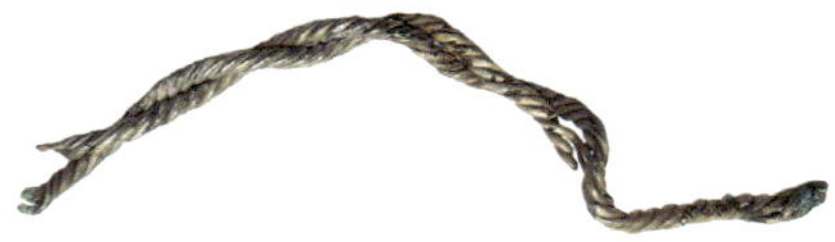

F.114

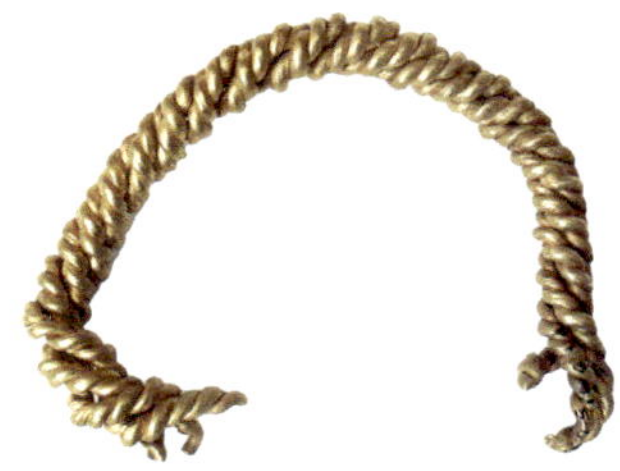

F.115

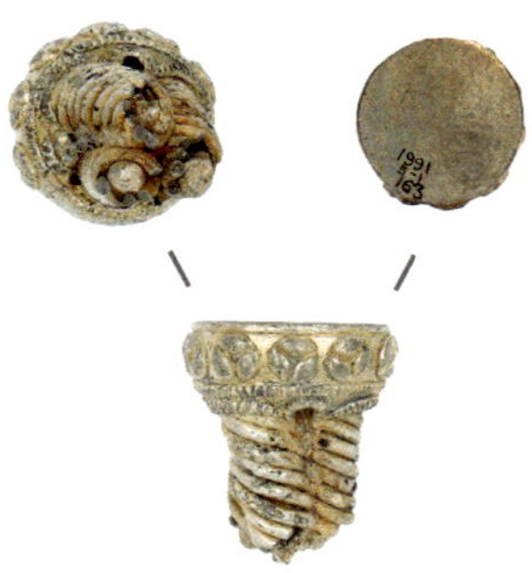

F.116

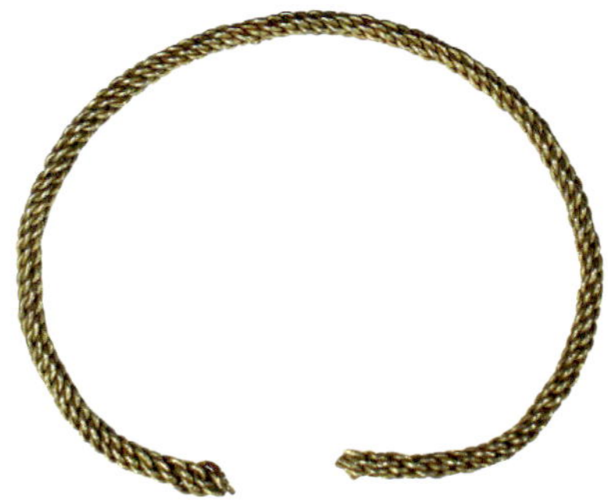

F.117

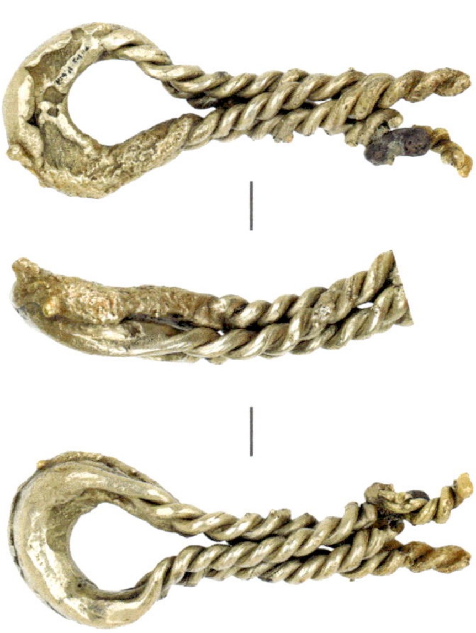

F.118

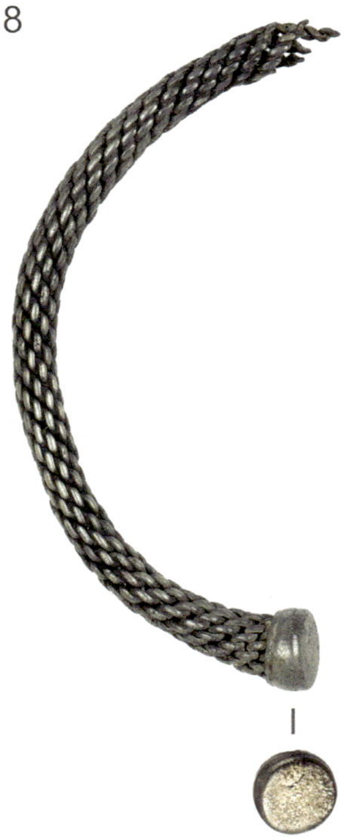

0 5 10cm

Plate 14.28

F.120

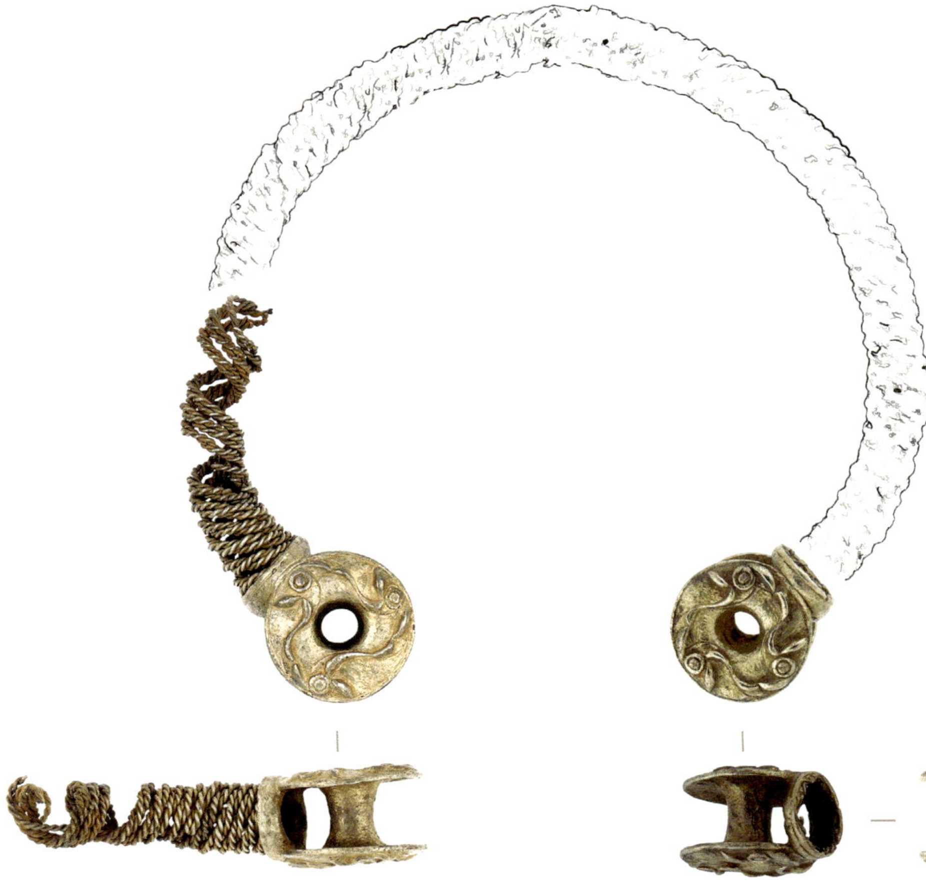

F.119

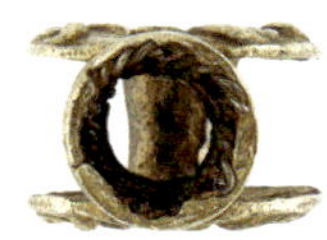

F.121

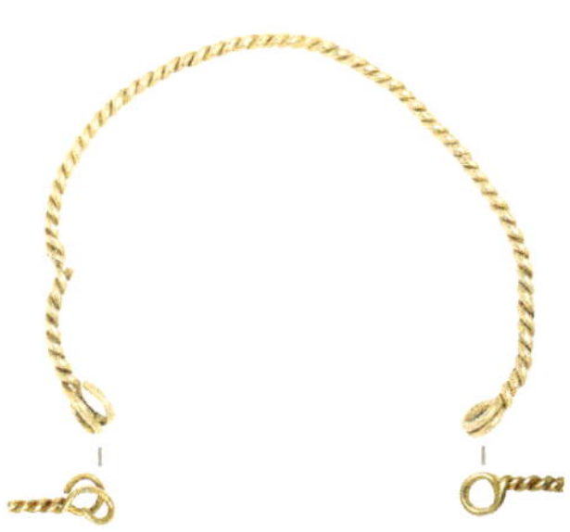

F.122

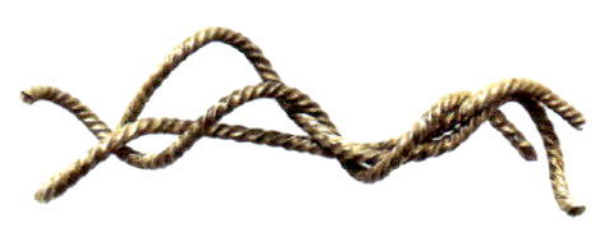

F.123

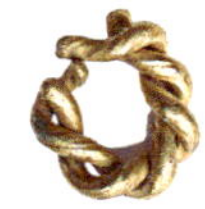

F.124

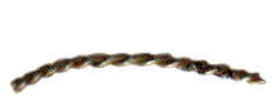

F.125

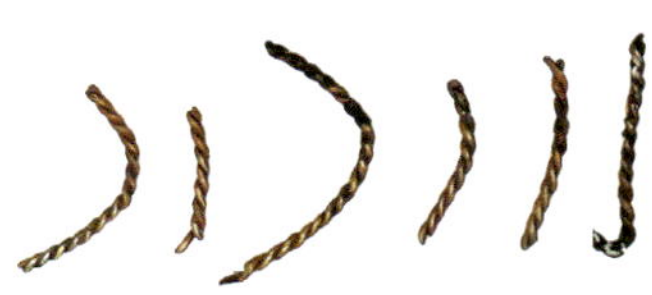

F.126

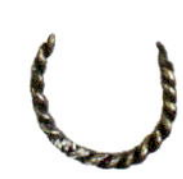

F.127

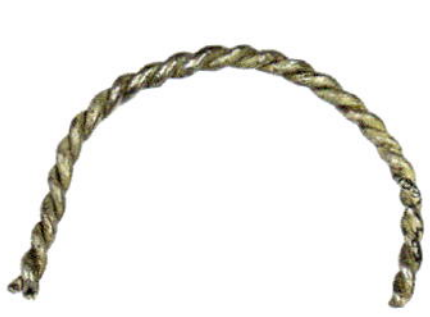

F.128

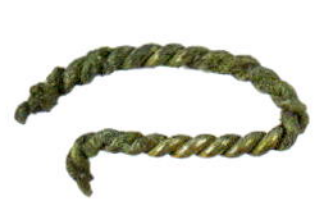

F.129

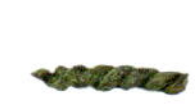

F.130

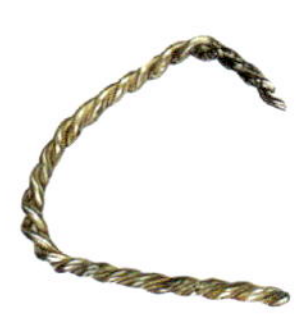

F.131

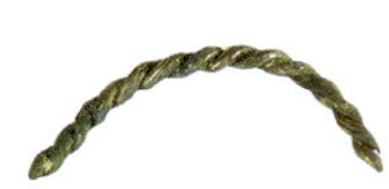

0 5 10cm

Plate 14.29

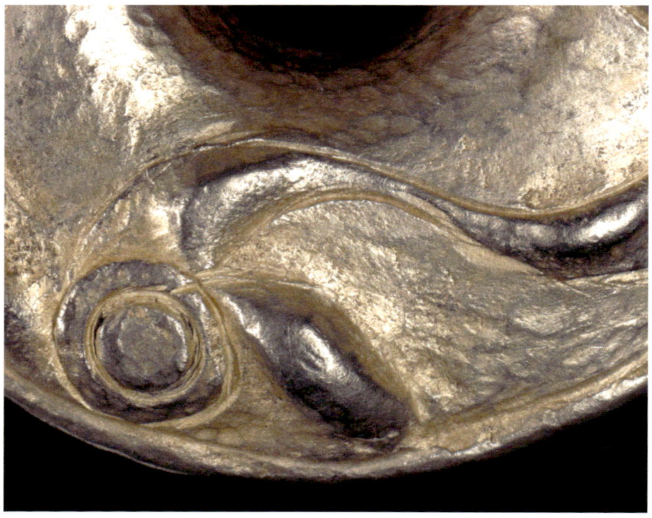

Figure 14.21 Detail of terminal showing engraved lines detailing cast features on F.120

together around a hollow core. Each cable consists of three ropes loosely plied together, and each rope is formed from two circular-section wires plied together. The reel terminal was cast onto the neck-ring and is decorated on both faces in relief with lobes, tendrils and bosses in a tripartite design repeated on each face. A simple indented line marks the rim. The hollow core of the reel is undecorated, and there is a plain collar where it meets the neck-ring.
Wt: 110.4g (main section); 9.5g (additional wire fragments); D(nr): 19.0mm; D(cable): 3.6mm; D(rope): 2.0mm; D(wire): 1.1mm; D(term): 39.3mm; L: 111.8mm

Notes from scientific analysis on F.119–20 (Nigel Meeks)
This reel terminal torc is in two parts, one (F.120) with a section of multi-strand wire neck-ring and the other (F.119) being just the second terminal which has completely broken away from the torc wires. The terminals are cast onto the wires. This is another example of a torc with a Stage IV neck-ring construction with very thin wires, and the design is very springy. In this case each pair of plied wires is tightly twisted to form the ropes, but the ropes and cables are not very tightly twisted together. This is clearly shown in the damaged part of the neck-ring in which the wires are stretched open. The open reel design, the broken wires, and the loose terminal all provide visible access to investigate the construction of the torc and allowed direct examination of the metal surfaces in the scanning electron microscope. Moreover, the broken wires provided samples for metallurgical mounting and polishing for microscopy and microanalysis to determine the true nature of the original alloy used and the metallurgical processes used in wire making and surface treatment (Ch. 17).

The wires form a very secure junction with the cast-on terminal as they enter at an extremely low angle and so a length of each wire curves around the inside of the terminal, forming a long joint (see **Fig. 17.66**). In this image two wire ends are also seen just piercing through the neck of the cast terminal. Looking inside the open reel of the terminal clearly shows the dribbles of solidified metal squeezing over and between the ends of the wires making a strong mechanical join even though the molten metal had not fully fused onto the wires at this point.

The terminals are different from most other terminals, not only because of the open reel design but also showing a deliberate overall surface texture that is unlike the smoother design of other torcs. The designs on the terminals are cast-in as part of the main terminal structure. The outlines of these decorative features were later engraved to define them more clearly (**Fig. 14.21**). The lines are sharply cut and well formed, and there is evidence of multiple cuts and marks where the tool has slipped or gone too far. These marks confirm the removal of metal by a pre-formed sharp metal engraving tool, rather than by the use of a chasing tool that displaces metal.
F.119 has broken away from the twisted wires at the base of the terminal neck but this again allows a clear view of the internal construction. The wires are cleanly broken suggesting brittle failure from stress corrosion of the wires in the ground. In this case the metal has gripped and fused to the outer sides of the shallow angle wires and has not flowed to fully encase them. This is probably a feature of the original clay core and clay plug that were moulded into the open inner regions to cover the wires to contain the molten metal on the terminal end.

F.121: Gold/silver alloy bracelet (Pl. 14.29)
MSCC: (2P)R
BM: 1991,0501.146; Jackson no.: 80
Gold/silver alloy multi-strand bracelet with simple Stage II body of two circular-section wires plied together, and double-loop terminals. One double loop is continuous, where the wire is bent back on itself, while the other terminal has open loops formed by the two ends of the single doubled-back wire. Complete, but bent open and slightly distorted, with one body wire broken at the point of the bend.
Wt: 6.2g; D(ext): 69.0mm; D(nr): 2.4mm; D(wire): 1.1mm; D(term): 6.6mm

F.122: Gold/silver alloy wire/?torc/?bracelet (Pl. 14.29)
MSCC: (?3P)T
BM: 1991,0501.153; Jackson no.: 86
[Analysed: see Ch. 17]
Fragments of gold/silver alloy wire, possibly from a torc or bracelet. Three lengths of twisted wire are very loosely and irregularly plied/wrapped together. All ends broken.
Wt: 11.0g; D(wire): 1.9mm; L: 74.0mm

F.123: Gold/silver alloy torc/bracelet (Pl. 14.29)
MSCC: (2P)R
BM: 1991,0501.79; Jackson no.: 67
Fragment of gold/silver alloy multi-strand torc neck-ring or bracelet body, broken at both ends and bent into a ring, perhaps suggesting that it was originally part of an interlinked group. Stage II construction of two circular-section wires plied together.
Wt: 18.0g; D(ext): 25.2mm; D(nr): 7.1mm; D(wire): 3.3mm

F.124: Gold/silver alloy torc/bracelet (Pl. 14.29)
MSCC: (2P)R
BM: 1991,0501.194; Jackson no.: 176
Fragment of gold/silver alloy multi-strand torc neck-ring or

bracelet body, cut or broken at both ends. Stage II construction of two circular-section wires plied together.
Wt: 0.6g; D(nr): 1.9mm; D(wire): 0.9mm; L: 33.4mm

F.125: Gold/silver alloy torc/bracelet (Pl. 14.29)
MSCC: (2P)R
BM: 1991,0702.70; Jackson no.: 269, 416–18, 420–1
Six non-joining fragments of gold/silver alloy multi-strand torc neck-ring or bracelet body, each broken at both ends, and some bent. Stage II construction of two circular-section wires plied together.
Wt: 3.2g; D(nr): 2.0mm; D(wire): 1.0mm; L: 32.1 mm (max.)

F.126: Gold/silver alloy torc/bracelet (Pl. 14.29)
MSCC: (2P)R
BM: 1991,0702.72; Jackson no.: 427
Fragment of gold/silver alloy multi-strand torc neck-ring or bracelet body, broken at both ends and bent into a rough U-shape. Stage II construction of two circular-section wires plied together.
Wt: 1.3g; D(nr): 2.2mm; D(wire): 1.1mm; L: 19.3mm

F.127: Gold/silver alloy torc/bracelet (Pl. 14.29)
MSCC: (2P)R
BM: 1991,0702.69; Jackson no.: 260
Fragment of gold/silver alloy multi-strand torc neck-ring or bracelet body, broken at one end and cut at the other, bent into a rough U-shape. Stage II construction of two circular-section wires plied together.
Wt: 5.1g; D(nr): 3.4mm; D(wire): 1.5mm; L: 53.5mm

F.128: Gold/silver alloy torc/bracelet (Pl. 14.29)
MSCC: (2P)R
BM: 1991,0702.204; Jackson no.: 383
Fragment of gold/silver alloy multi-strand torc neck-ring or bracelet body, broken at both ends. Stage II construction of two circular-section wires plied together. The whole fragment is bent into a loose U-shape.
Wt: 4.6g; D(nr): 2.7mm; D(wire): 1.5mm; L: 38.9mm

F.129: Gold/silver alloy torc/bracelet (Pl. 14.29)
MSCC: (2P)R
BM: 1991,0702.221; Jackson no.: 407
Fragment of gold/silver alloy multi-strand torc neck-ring or bracelet body, broken at both ends. Stage II construction of two circular-section wires plied together.
Wt: 1.0g; D(nr): 3.2mm; D(wire): 1.5mm; L: 20.1mm

F.130: Gold/silver alloy torc/bracelet (Pl. 14.29)
MSCC: (2P)R
BM: 1991,0702.68; Jackson no.: 259
Fragment of gold/silver alloy multi-strand torc neck-ring or bracelet body, broken at both ends and bent into a rough U-shape. Stage II construction of two circular-section wires plied together.
Wt: 4.2g; D(nr): 3.0mm; D(wire): 1.6mm; L: 37.2mm

F.131: Gold/silver alloy torc/bracelet (Pl. 14.29)
MSCC: (2P)R
BM: 1991,0702.219; Jackson no.: 399
Fragment of gold/silver alloy multi-strand torc neck-ring or bracelet body, broken at both ends. Stage II construction of two circular-section wires plied together.
Wt: 2.9g; D(nr): 3.3mm; D(wire): 1.6mm; L: 46.1mm

F.132–3: Gold/silver alloy torc/bracelet (Pl. 14.30)
MSCC: (2P)R
Fragments of gold/silver alloy multi-strand torc neck-ring or bracelet body, each broken at both ends and bent into a U-shape. Stage II construction of two circular-section wires plied together. F.132–3 are probably part of the same object.

F.132: BM: 1991,0501.180; Jackson no.: 146
Wt: 5.1g; D(nr): 3.2mm; D(wire): 1.7mm; L: 36.4mm

F.133: BM: 1991,0501.181; Jackson no.: 147
Wt: 4.5g; D(nr): 3.2mm; D(wire): 1.7mm; L: 41.2mm

F.134: Gold/silver alloy torc/bracelet (Pl. 14.30)
MSCC: (2P)R
BM: 1991,0702.205; Jackson no.: 384
Fragment of gold/silver alloy multi-strand torc neck-ring or bracelet body, broken at one end and cut at the other. Stage II construction of two circular-section wires plied together.
Wt: 1.8g; D(nr): 3.4mm; D(wire): 1.7mm; L: 34.8mm

F.135: Gold/silver alloy torc/bracelet (Pl. 14.30)
MSCC: (?P(2P))R
BM: 1991,0501.222; Jackson no.: 380
[Analysed: see Ch. 17]
Fragment of gold/silver alloy multi-strand torc neck-ring or bracelet body, broken at both ends and bent into a rough V-shape (see **Fig. 17.30a–c**). What remains is a Stage II component of two circular-section wires plied together. It is bent in a way which suggests it originally formed part of a Stage III plied construction.
Wt: 3.1g; D(nr): 3.5mm; D(wire): 1.8mm; L: 24.3mm

F.136: Gold/silver alloy torc/bracelet (Pl. 14.30)
MSCC: (2P)R
BM: 1991,0702.220; Jackson no.: 400
Fragment of gold/silver alloy multi-strand torc or bracelet, comprising a simple double-loop terminal (continuous with the neck-ring/body wires) and part of the neck-ring/body, broken at the other end. Stage II construction of two circular-section wires plied together.
Wt: 3.8g; D(nr): 3.6mm; D(wire): 1.9mm; D(term): 7.2mm; L: 28.8mm

F.137: Gold/silver alloy torc/bracelet (Pl. 14.30)
MSCC: (2P)R
BM: 1991,0702.212; Jackson no.: 392
Fragment of gold/silver alloy multi-strand torc neck-ring or bracelet body, broken at both ends (one break perhaps recent). Stage II construction of two circular-section wires plied together. The whole fragment is bent into a U-shape.
Wt: 4.2g; D(nr): 3.6mm; D(wire): 1.9mm; L: 37.8mm

F.138: Gold/silver alloy torc/bracelet (Pl. 14.30)
MSCC: (?C(2P))R

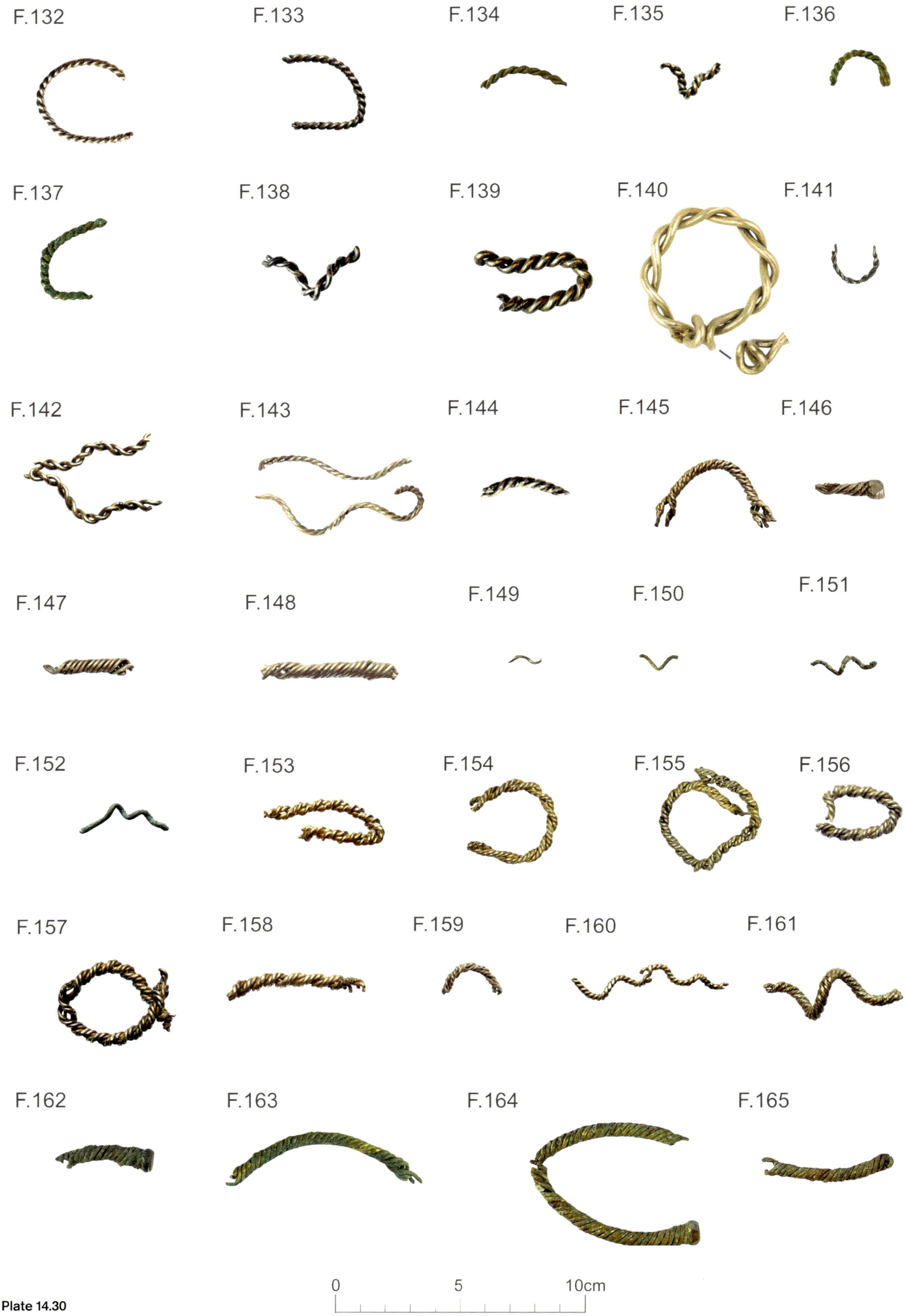
F.132
F.133
F.134
F.135
F.136
F.137
F.138
F.139
F.140
F.141
F.142
F.143
F.144
F.145
F.146
F.147
F.148
F.149
F.150
F.151
F.152
F.153
F.154
F.155
F.156
F.157
F.158
F.159
F.160
F.161
F.162
F.163
F.164
F.165
0
5
10cm

Plate 14.30

BM: 1991,0501.177; Jackson no.: 138
Fragment of gold/silver alloy multi-strand torc neck-ring or bracelet body, cut at one end and broken at the other (perhaps recently). What remains is a Stage II component of two circular-section wires plied together. It is bent in a way which suggests it originally formed part of a Stage III coiled construction.
Wt: 5.6g; D(nr): 4.5mm; D(wire): 2.3mm; L: 39.4mm

F.139: Gold/silver alloy torc/bracelet (Pl. 14.30)
MSCC: (2P)R
BM: 1991,0501.178; Jackson no.: 139
Fragment of gold/silver alloy multi-strand torc neck-ring or bracelet body, broken at both ends. Stage II construction of two circular-section wires plied together. The whole fragment is bent into a U-shape.
Wt: 26.5g; D(nr): 6.9mm; D(wire): 3.3mm; L: 47.9mm

F.140: Gold/silver alloy torc/bracelet (Pl. 14.30)
MSCC: (2P)R
BM: 1991,0501.102; Jackson no.: 115
Fragment of gold/silver alloy multi-strand torc or bracelet, comprising one terminal and a length of neck-ring/body broken at the other end and part melted. Stage II construction of two circular-section wires loosely plied together. The terminal is formed from the continuous looped end of the neck-ring/body wire, bent back on itself to form what is probably a damaged double loop or simple (perhaps unfinished) cage terminal. The whole fragment has been bent into a ring with the broken end just meeting the terminal, perhaps suggesting that it was originally part of an interlinked group.
Wt: 46.5g; D(ext): 58.4mm; D(nr): 8.7mm; D(wire): 3.5mm

F.141: Gold/silver alloy torc/bracelet (Pl. 14.30)
MSCC: (2PZ)R
BM: 1991,0702.71; Jackson no.: 419
Fragment of gold/silver alloy torc neck-ring or bracelet body, broken at both ends and bent into a rough U-shape. Stage II construction of two circular-section wires plied together Z-twist.
Wt: 0.8g; D(nr): 2.0mm; D(wire): 1.0mm; L: 19.0mm

F.142: Gold/silver alloy torc/bracelet (Pl. 14.30)
MSCC: (?P(2PZ))R
BM: 1991,0501.179; Jackson no.: 141
Fragment of gold/silver alloy multi-strand torc neck-ring or bracelet body, broken at both ends and with one wire broken in the middle. What remains is a Stage II component of two circular-section wires plied together Z-twist. It is bent in a way which suggests it originally formed part of a Stage III plied construction.
Wt: 11.6g; D(nr): 4.3mm; D(wire): 1.9mm; L: 55.5mm

F.143: Gold/silver alloy torc/bracelet (Pl. 14.30)
MSCC: (?C(3P))R
BM: 1991,0702.67; Jackson no.: 266, 271
Two joining fragments of gold/silver alloy torc neck-ring or bracelet body, broken at both ends. What remains are Stage II components of three circular-section wires plied together. The fragments are bent in a way which suggests they may have originally formed part of a Stage III coiled construction, though this is not certain.
Wt: 6.3g; D(rope): 2.6mm; D(wire): 1.2mm; L: 67.5 mm (max.)

F.144: Gold/silver alloy torc/bracelet (Pl. 14.30)
MSCC: (3P)2T+1R
BM: 1991,0501.188; Jackson no.: 168
Fragment of gold/silver alloy multi-strand torc neck-ring or bracelet body, broken at both ends. Stage II construction of two twisted and one circular-section wire plied together.
Wt: 4.2g; D(nr): 4.2mm; D(wire): 2.1mm; L: 35.5mm

F.145: Gold/silver alloy torc/bracelet (Pl. 14.30)
MSCC: (4P)T
BM: 1991,0501.190; Jackson no.: 170
Fragment of gold/silver alloy multi-strand torc neck-ring or bracelet body, broken at one end and cut at the other. Stage II construction of four twisted wires plied together. The wires are splayed out at each end.
Wt: 8.0g; D(nr): 4.4mm; D(wire): 1.7mm; L: 48.8mm

F.146: Gold/silver alloy torc/bracelet (Pl. 14.30)
MSCC: (6C)3R+3T
BM: 1991,0501.214; Jackson no.: 240
[Analysed: see Ch. 17]
Fragment of gold/silver alloy multi-strand torc or bracelet, comprising one buffer terminal, and part of the neck-ring/body, broken at the other end. Stage II construction of six wires coiled together around a hollow core; three of the wires are twisted and three are circular in cross-section. The terminal is a simple 'cap' to the wires, with inset face-plate with worn dot-punched decoration. Two crimped or 'pie-crust' cordons run around the edge circumference of the terminal. These mouldings are very worn; in one area they are completely worn away (**Figs 14.22**; see Ch. 21 for discussion of decoration).

Notes from scientific analysis (Nigel Meeks)
The twisted square-section wires are very heavily worn through prolonged use. The outer wire surfaces have been worn smooth such that some of the square sections are unrecognisable; however, some of the inner square corners have worn deeply into the adjacent wires through use of the torc over time. These heavy wear characteristics are seen on many torcs (see Ch. 20). In this case the small object may have been a bracelet, worn on the wrist, which would account for the extensive wear, being easily exposed to daily manual activities. The small terminal firmly fixed the coiled wires in place. In this case, the terminal looks like a sheet cap which has been moulded over the ends of the wires and probably soldered into position.
Wt: 4.5g; D(nr): 6.7mm; D(wire): 1.5mm; D(term): 8.6mm; L: 27.8mm

F.147–8: Gold/silver alloy torc/bracelet (Pl. 14.30)
MSCC: (6C)R
[Analysed: see Ch. 17]
Fragments of gold/silver alloy multi-strand torc neck-ring or

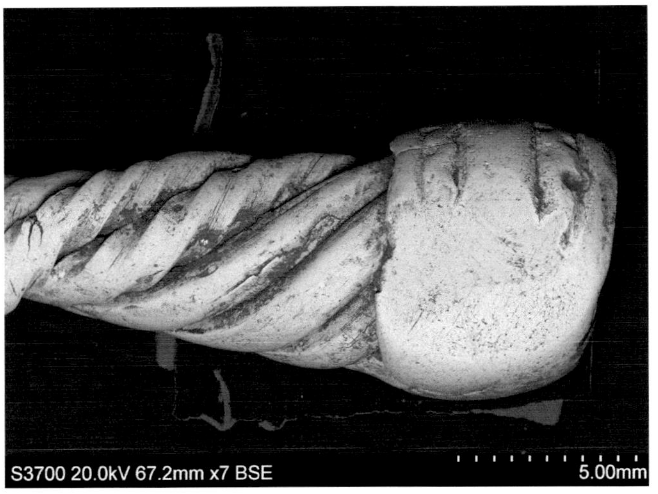

Figure 14.22 SEM detail showing the heavily worn twisted wires and terminal on F.146

bracelet body. Stage II construction of six circular-section wires coiled together around a hollow core. F.147 and F.148 are probably part of the same object.

F.147: BM: 1991,0501.221; Jackson no.: 353
Broken at both ends.
Wt: 3.8g; D(nr): 6.5mm; D(wire): 1.5mm; L: 36.5mm

F.148: BM: 1991,0501.86; Jackson no.: 74
Cut and distorted at both ends.
Wt: 8.4g; D(nr): 6.9mm; D(wire): 1.6mm; L: 55.4mm

F.149: Gold/silver alloy wire/?torc/?bracelet (Pl. 14.30)
MSCC: (?C)R
BM: 1991,0702.95; Jackson no.: 167
Fragment of gold/silver alloy multi-strand torc neck-ring or bracelet body, broken at both ends. The remaining fragment is a circular-section wire, coiled in such a way as to suggest it was originally part of a Stage II coiled construction.
Wt: 0.2g; D(wire): 0.9mm; L: 13.5mm

F.150: Gold/silver alloy wire/?torc/?bracelet (Pl. 14.30)
MSCC: (?C)T
BM: 1991,0702.96; Jackson no.: 175
Fragment of gold/silver alloy multi-strand torc neck-ring or bracelet body, broken at both ends. The remaining fragment is a twisted wire, coiled in such a way as to suggest it was originally part of a Stage II coiled construction.
Wt: 0.3g; D(wire): 1.4mm; L: 15.6mm

F.151: Gold/silver alloy torc/bracelet (Pl. 14.30)
MSCC: (?C)R
BM: 1991,0702.228.b; Jackson no.: 451
Fragment of gold/silver alloy multi-strand torc neck-ring or bracelet body, broken at both ends (one break perhaps recent). What remains are two circular-section wires, coiled together in a way which suggests they originally formed part of a Stage II coiled construction.
Wt: 0.8g; D(wire): 1.7mm; L: 26.4mm

F.152: Gold/silver alloy wire/?torc/?bracelet (Pl. 14.30)
MSCC: (?C)R
BM: 1991,0702.228.a; Jackson no.: 451
Fragment of gold/silver alloy multi-strand torc neck-ring or bracelet body, broken at both ends. The remaining fragment is a circular-section wire, coiled in such a way as to suggest it was originally part of a Stage II coiled construction.
Wt: 1.5g; D(wire): 2.1mm; L: 35.7mm

F.153: Gold/silver alloy torc/bracelet (Pl. 14.30)
MSCC: (2P(2P))R
BM: 1991,0407.44.a; Site code: SN/AD
Context details: Hoard F pit; Excavated find, surface trowelling.
[Analysed: see Ch. 17]

Fragment of a gold/silver alloy Stage III multi-strand torc neck-ring or bracelet body, broken at one end and cut at the other. The cable is formed from two ropes plied together, each of which is made up of two circular-section wires plied together. The fragment is bent into a narrow, rough U-shape. The fact that the fragment is bent into a loop (though open) perhaps suggests that it was originally part of an interlinked group.
Wt: 11.7g; D(nr): 6.0mm; D(rope): 3.3mm; D(wire): 1.5mm; L: 48.7mm

F.154–7: Gold/silver alloy torc/bracelet (Pl. 14.30)
MSCC: (2P(3P))R
F.154–7 may be broken parts of the same incomplete torc. (F.158 may be part of the same object, though the wire diameter is a little thicker)

F.154: BM: 1991,0501.144; Jackson no.: 78
[Analysed: see Ch. 17]
Fragment of a gold/silver alloy Stage III multi-strand torc neck-ring or bracelet body, cut at both ends (see **Fig. 17.21**). The cable is formed from two ropes plied together, each of which is made up of three circular-section wires plied together. The fragment is bent into a penannular ring, perhaps suggesting that it was originally part of an interlinked group.
Wt: 8.1g; D(nr): 5.5mm; D(rope): 2.9mm; D(wire): 0.9mm; L: 35.9mm

F.155: BM: 1991,0702.17; Jackson no.: 23
Fragment of a gold/silver alloy Stage III multi-strand torc neck-ring or bracelet body, broken at both ends. The cable is formed from two ropes plied together, each of which is made up of three circular-section wires plied together. The fragment is coiled into a rough ring with overlapping ends, perhaps suggesting that it was originally part of an interlinked group.
Wt: 12.3g; D(nr): 4.7mm; D(rope): 2.3mm; D(wire): 1.1mm; L: 42.7mm

F.156: BM: 1991,0501.87; Jackson no.: 75
[Analysed: see Ch. 17]
Fragment of a gold/silver alloy Stage III multi-strand torc neck-ring or bracelet body, cut at both ends (**Fig. 17.31a–d**).

The cable is formed from two ropes plied together, each of which is made up of three circular-section wires plied together. The fragment is bent into a rough penannular ring, perhaps suggesting that it was originally part of an interlinked group.
Wt: 9.5g; D(nr): 5.6mm; D(rope): 2.9mm; D(wire): 1.3mm; L: 35.0mm

F.157: BM: 1991,0501.88; Jackson no.: 76
Fragment of a gold/silver alloy Stage III multi-strand torc neck-ring or bracelet body, cut at both ends. The cable is formed from two ropes plied together, each of which is made up of three circular-section wires plied together. The fragment is bent into a rough ring with overlapping ends, perhaps suggesting that it was originally part of an interlinked group.
Wt: 18.5g; D(nr): 5.5mm; D(rope): 2.9mm; D(wire): 1.3mm; L: 47.1mm

F.158: Gold/silver alloy torc/bracelet (Pl. 14.30)
MSCC: (2P(3P))R
BM: 1991,0501.191; Jackson no.: 172
[Analysed: see Ch. 17]
Fragment of gold/silver alloy Stage III multi-strand torc neck-ring or bracelet body, broken at one end and cut at the other. The cable is formed from two ropes plied together, each of which consists of three circular-section wires plied together.
Wt: 8.2g; D(nr): 6.2mm; D(rope): 2.9mm; D(wire): 1.4mm; L: 55.1mm

F.159: Gold/silver alloy torc/bracelet (Pl. 14.30)
MSCC: (3P(2P))R
BM: 1991,0501.193; Jackson no.: 174
[Analysed: see Ch. 17]
Fragment of gold/silver alloy multi-strand Stage III torc neck-ring or bracelet body, broken at both ends. The cable is formed from three ropes plied together, each of which consists of two circular-section wires plied together. The whole fragment is curved into a shallow U-shape.
Wt: 1.9g; D(nr): 2.1mm; D(rope): 2.0mm; D(wire): 1.1mm; L: 24.6mm

F.160: Gold/silver alloy torc/bracelet (Pl. 14.30)
MSCC: (?C(2P))R
BM: 1991,0501.192; Jackson no.: 173
[Analysed: see Ch. 17]
Fragment of gold/silver alloy multi-strand torc neck-ring or bracelet body, broken at both ends (see **Fig. 17.26a–d**). What remains is a Stage II component, formed from two circular-section wires plied together. The whole is coiled, suggesting that it might once have been part of a Stage III coiled construction. One of the wires is broken in the centre of the fragment, but continues on both sides.
Wt: 5.0g; D(rope): 2.6mm; D(wire): 1.5mm; L: 62.6mm

F.161: Gold/silver alloy torc/bracelet (Pl. 14.30)
MSCC: (?C(4P))T
BM: 1991,0501.189; Jackson no.: 169
Fragment of gold/silver alloy multi-strand torc neck-ring or bracelet body, broken at one end and cut at the other. What remains is a Stage II component, formed from four twisted wires plied together. The whole is coiled, suggesting that it might once have been part of a Stage III coiled construction.
Wt: 11.0g; D(rope): 4.1mm; D(wire): 1.7mm; L: 55.6mm

F.162–5: Copper alloy torc (Pl. 14.30)
MSCC: (5C)3Q+2T
Fragments of copper alloy multi-strand torc, possibly gilded, with buffer terminals. The terminals are plain, with a simple grooved cordon around the edge. Stage II construction of five wires coiled together around a hollow core. Two of the wires are twisted and the other three are square-section. F.162–5 are most likely part of the same torc.

F.162: BM: 1991,0702.92; Jackson no.: 161
Fragment comprises one plain buffer terminal and a short length of neck-ring, broken at the other end.
Wt: 7.0g; D(nr): 6.5mm; D(wire): 1.4mm; D(term): 9.5mm; L: 39.3mm

F.163: BM: 1991,0702.94; Jackson no.: 163
Fragment of torc neck-ring, broken at both ends.
Wt: 9.1g; D(nr): 5.3mm; D(wire): 1.5mm; L: 78.5mm

F.164: BM: 1991,0702.123; Jackson no.: 243
Fragment comprises one buffer terminal and a short length of neck-ring, broken at the other end. The whole fragment is bent back on itself to form a U-shape, with wires very damaged/broken at the base of the 'U'.
Wt: 15.7g; D(nr): 5.5mm; D(wire): 1.2mm; D(term): 9.1mm; L: 68.3mm

F.165: BM: 1991,0702.135; Jackson no.: 255
Fragment of torc neck-ring, broken at both ends.
Wt: 5.3g; D(nr): 5.7mm; D(wire): 1.1mm; L: 52.2mm

F.166: Copper alloy torc (Pl. 14.31)
MSCC: (5C)T
BM: 1991,0702.132; Jackson no.: 251
[Analysed: Ch. 19 for identification of wood]
Fragment of copper alloy, possibly gilded, multi-strand torc neck-ring, broken at one end and cut at the other (see **Fig. 19.1c**). Stage II construction of five twisted wires coiled together. The fragment is bent into a U-shape, perhaps suggesting that it was originally part of an interlinked group. Damage at the centre of the tight bend reveals a carbonised wood core.
Wt: 10.4g; D(nr): 4.5mm; D(wire): 1.3mm; L: 60.6mm

F.167: Copper alloy torc (Pl. 14.31)
MSCC: (6C)T
BM: 1991,0702.122; Jackson no.: 242
[Analysed: see Ch. 17, and Ch. 19 for identification of wood]
Fragment of copper alloy multi-strand torc neck-ring, broken at one end and cut at the other with a double-bladed implement (see **Figs 17.55a–c, 19.1b**). Stage II construction of six twisted wires coiled together. Carbonised wood is visible within the core, emerging from the broken end.
Wt: 10.7g; D(nr): 6.4mm; D(wire): 1.4mm; L: 79.2mm

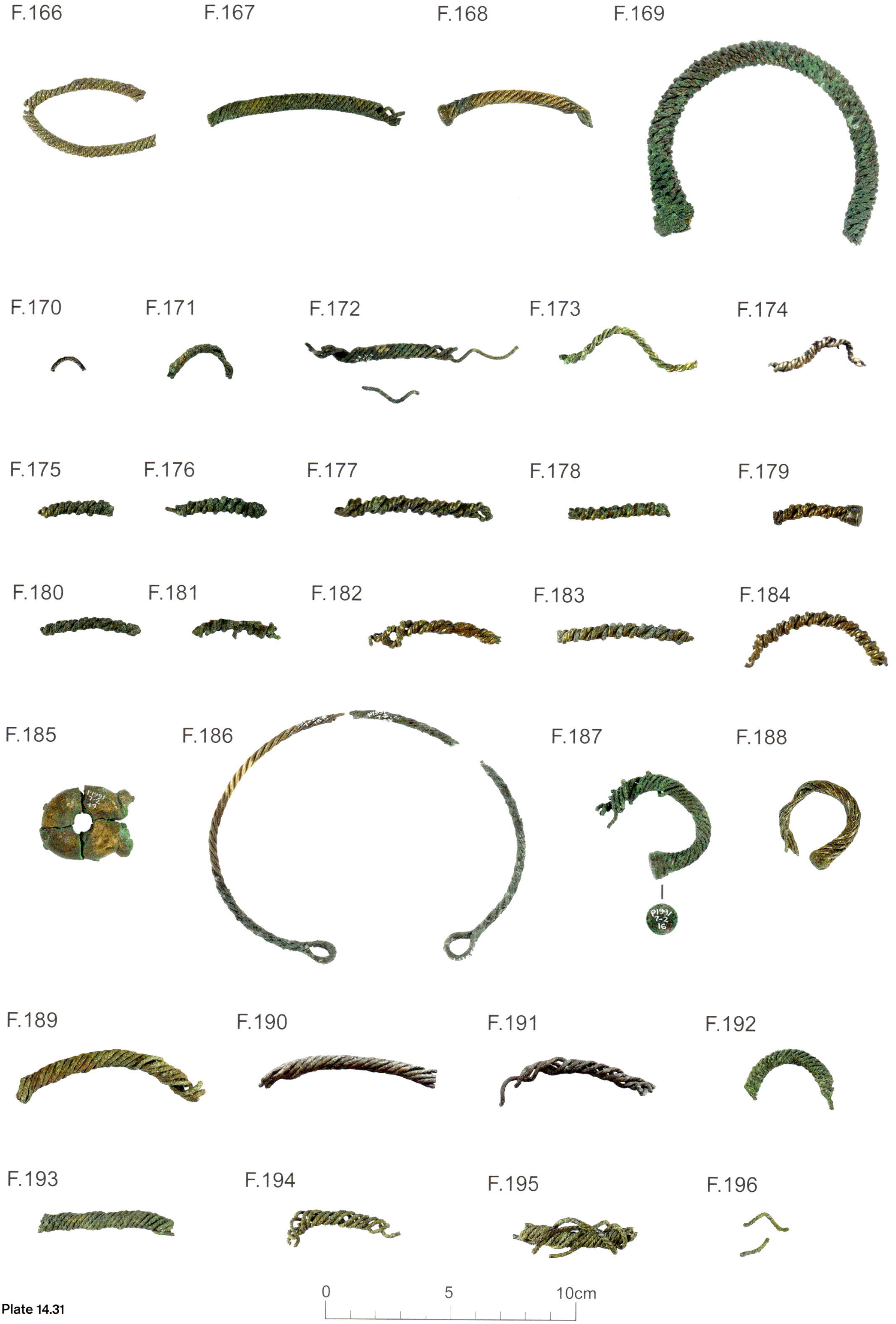
F.166
F.167
F.168
F.169
F.170
F.171
F.172
F.173
F.174
F.175
F.176
F.177
F.178
F.179
F.180
F.181
F.182
F.183
F.184
F.185
F.186
F.187
F.188
F.189
F.190
F.191
F.192
F.193
F.194
F.195
F.196
0
5
10cm

Plate 14.31

F.168: Copper alloy torc (Pl. 14.31)
MSCC: (6C)T
BM: 1991,0702.121; Jackson no.: 241
[Analysed: see Ch. 17, and Ch. 19 for identification of wood; Radiocarbon dated: See Table 5.2]
Fragment of copper alloy multi-strand torc comprising one plain buffer terminal and a short length of neck-ring, broken at the other end (see **Figs 17.35a–b**, **19.1a**). Stage II construction of six twisted wires coiled together. Carbonised wood is visible within the core, emerging from the broken end.
Wt: 9.3g; D(nr): 5.4mm; D(wire): 1.3mm; D(term): 8.8mm; L: 62.2mm

F.169: Copper alloy torc (Pl. 14.31)
MSCC: (6CZ(2PZ))R
BM: 1991,0702.61; Jackson no.: 302, 303
Fragment of copper alloy, possibly gilded, multi-strand Stage III torc, comprising a buffer terminal and length of neck-ring, cut at the other end with a double-bladed implement. The cable is formed from six ropes coiled together Z-twist around a hollow core, each rope consisting of two circular-section wires plied together, also Z-twist. The buffer terminal is badly corroded. The end appears to be plain and flat, the sides plain and convex, with two simple, grooved cordons around the edge.
Wt: 72.0g; D(nr): 9.6mm; D(rope): 3.0mm; D(wire): 1.4mm; D(term): 19.3mm; L: 92.5mm

F.170: Copper alloy wire/?torc/?bracelet (Pl. 14.31)
MSCC: (?C)T
BM: 1991,0702.274; Jackson no.: 501c
Fragment of copper alloy, possibly gilded, twisted wire, perhaps from a multi-strand torc or bracelet, broken at both ends. This wire curved in a way which suggests it might once have formed part of a Stage II coiled construction.
Wt: 0.4g; D(wire): 1.9mm; L: 14.5mm

F.171: Copper alloy torc/bracelet (Pl. 14.31)
MSCC: (4P)T
BM: 1991,0702.88; Jackson no.: 154
Fragment of copper alloy, possibly gilded, multi-strand torc neck-ring or bracelet body, broken at both ends and curved. Stage II construction of four twisted wires plied together.
Wt: 2.6g; D(nr): 3.3mm; D(wire): 1.5mm; L: 26.7mm

F.172: Copper alloy torc/bracelet (Pl. 14.31)
MSCC: (6C)T
BM: 1991,0702.14; Jackson no.: 92, 93
Fragment of copper alloy, possibly gilded, multi-strand torc neck-ring or bracelet body, broken at both ends, and a single additional broken wire fragment. Stage II construction of six twisted wires coiled together around a hollow core.
Wt: 6.4g; D(nr): 6.5mm; D(wire): 1.5mm; L: 85.1mm

F.173: Copper alloy torc/bracelet (Pl. 14.31)
MSCC: (?C(2P))R
BM: 1991,0702.140; Jackson no.: 263
Fragment of copper alloy, possibly gilded, multi-strand torc neck-ring or bracelet body, broken at both ends. What remains is a Stage II component, formed from two circular-section wires plied together. This is curved in a way which suggests it might once have formed part of a Stage III coiled construction.
Wt: 3.5g; D(rope): 3.5mm; D(wire): 1.7mm; L: 55.3mm

F.174: Copper alloy torc/bracelet (Pl. 14.31)
MSCC: (2P(3P))R
BM: 1991,0501.213; Jackson no.: 235
Fragment of copper alloy, possibly gilded, multi-strand torc neck-ring or bracelet body, broken at both ends, with each wire broken at different points. Stage III construction of two ropes plied together, each of which consists of three circular-section wires plied together.
Wt: 3.5g; D(nr): 4.5mm; D(rope): 2.4mm; D(wire): 1.1mm; L: 39.1mm

F.175–8: Copper alloy torc/bracelet (Pl. 14.31)
MSCC: (2P(2P))R
Fragments of copper alloy, possibly gilded, multi-strand torc neck-ring or bracelet body, each broken at both ends. Stage III construction of two ropes plied together, each rope made up of two circular-section wires plied together. F.175–8 may be from the same torc.

F.175: BM: 1991,0702.169; Jackson no.: 336
One break perhaps recent.
Wt: 3.5g; D(nr): 5.8mm; D(rope): 3.3mm; D(wire): 1.2mm; L: 30.9mm

F.176: BM: 1991,0702.161; Jackson no.: 328
Wt: 4.2g; D(nr): 6.5mm; D(rope): 3.0mm; D(wire): 1.4mm; L: 40.8mm

F.177: BM: 1991,0702.156; Jackson no.: 322
Wt: 11.2g; D(nr): 7.5mm; D(rope): 3.8mm; D(wire): 1.7mm; L: 63.5mm

F.178: BM: 1991,0702.158; Jackson no.: 325
Wt: 5.4g; D(nr): 5.6mm; D(rope): 3.0mm; D(wire): 1.8mm; L: 41.0mm

F.179: Copper alloy torc/bracelet (Pl. 14.31)
MSCC: (2P(2P+3P))R
BM: 1991,0702.117; Jackson no.: 236
[Analysed: see Ch. 17]
Fragment of copper alloy multi-strand torc or bracelet comprising one buffer terminal and a short length of neck-ring/body, broken at the other end (see **Fig. 17.69a–c**). The terminal has a plain face and pair of simple grooved cordons around the edge. Stage III construction of two ropes plied together. One rope is formed from two circular-section wires plied together, and the other from three circular-section wires plied together (one slightly finer than the others).
Wt: 6.3g; D(nr): 5.5mm; D(rope): 3.0mm; D(wire): 1.5mm; D(term): 7.9mm; L: 35.0mm

F.180–4: Copper alloy torc/bracelet (Pl. 14.31)
MSCC: (2P(2P))R

Fragments of gilded copper alloy multi-strand torc neck-ring or bracelet body, each broken at both ends (see **Figs 17.48a–b, 17.50a–b**). Stage III construction of two ropes plied together, each rope made up of two circular-section wires plied together. F.180–4 may be part of the same object.

F.180: BM: 1991,0702.164; Jackson no.: 331
Wt: 3.9g; D(nr): 5.4mm; D(rope): 3.0mm; D(wire): 1.4mm; L: 40.0mm

F.181: BM: 1991,0702.172; Jackson no.: 339
The fragment is heavily damaged, perhaps part melted.
Wt: 3.6g; D(nr): 5.8mm; D(rope): 3.3mm; D(wire): 1.9mm; L: 35.7mm

F.182: BM: 1991,0702.111; Jackson no.: 229
[Analysed: see Ch. 17]
The ropes are pulled apart at one end.
Wt: 6.7g; D(nr): 5.7mm; D(rope): 3.7mm; D(wire): 1.7mm; L: 53.2mm

F.183: BM: 1991,0702.112; Jackson no.: 230
Wt: 6.0g; D(nr): 6.0mm; D(rope): 3.0mm; D(wire): 1.2mm; L: 54.8mm

F.184: BM: 1991,0702.116; Jackson no.: 234
Wt: 8.4g; D(nr): 5.9mm; D(rope): 3.7mm; D(wire): 1.6mm; L: 57.3mm

F.185: Copper alloy torc (Pl. 14.31)
BM: 1991,0702.49; Jackson no.: 210–13
Four joining fragments of cast copper alloy ring/torus terminal from a torc (see **Fig. 21.16**). The outer edge is decorated with small cast raised circular dots and an inscribed design, now indistinct due to corrosion products, consisting of flowing fin motifs. There is a decorative cast moulding around the collar. Hammer blows are visible in several places, suggesting the terminal was deliberately broken up in antiquity. See Chapter 21 for a full discussion of decoration.
Wt: 75.6g; D(term): 32.0mm; L: 38.0mm; T: 13.0mm

F.186: Copper alloy torc (Pl. 14.31)
MSCC: (4P)R
BM: 1991,0702.54; Jackson no.: 391, 402, 404–5, 408–9
Copper alloy torc in several parts (re-joined from fragments). The torc has simple double-loop terminals. On both sides, the loops appear to be continuous, extending to form the two pairs of wires which form the neck-ring. Stage II construction of four circular-section wires plied together.
Wt: 20.5g; D(ext): 101.2mm (approx.); D(nr): 3.8mm; D(wire): 1.5mm; D(term): 11.3mm

F.187: Copper alloy torc (Pl. 14.31)
MSCC: (8C)T
BM: 1991,0702.16; Jackson no.: 15
Fragment of copper alloy multi-strand torc, comprising one buffer terminal and a length of neck-ring, with the wires irregularly broken and partly distorted at the other end. The terminal has a plain, slightly convex, face and pair of grooved cordons around the edge. Stage II construction of eight twisted wires coiled together. The whole fragment is bent into a U-shape.
Wt: 19.2g; D(nr): 7.8mm; D(wire): 1.8mm; D(term): 12.9mm; L: 47.9mm

F.188: Copper alloy torc/bracelet (Pl. 14.31)
MSCC: (7C)T
BM: 1991,0702.139; Jackson no.: 258
Fragment of copper alloy multi-strand torc or bracelet, comprising one plain, rounded buffer terminal and a short length of neck-ring/body, broken and ragged at the other end. Stage II construction of seven twisted wires coiled together around a hollow core. The fragment has been bent into a penannular ring, perhaps suggesting that it was originally part of an interlinked group, and the wires are heavily worn.
Wt: 8.4g; D(nr): 5.3mm; D(wire): 1.0mm; D(term): 8.7mm; L: 34.5mm

F.189: Copper alloy torc (Pl. 14.31)
MSCC: (6C)3R+3T
BM: 1991,0702.120; Jackson no.: 239
Fragment of copper alloy multi-strand torc neck-ring, broken at both ends. Stage II construction of six wires coiled together around a hollow core. Three of the wires are twisted, alternating with three circular-section wires.
Wt: 15.2g; D(nr): 7.7mm; D(wire): 1.6mm; L: 75.9mm

F.190–6: Copper alloy torc (Pl. 14.31)
MSCC: (6C)T
F.190–6 may be part of the same torc.

F.190:
BM: 1991,0702.124; Jackson no.: 244
Fragment of copper alloy multi-strand torc neck-ring, broken at one end and cut at the other with a double-bladed implement. Stage II construction of six twisted wires coiled together around a hollow core.
Wt: 10.4g; D(nr): 6.3mm; D(wire): 1.7mm; L: 71.1mm

F.191:
BM: 1991,0702.125; Jackson no.: 244
Fragment of copper alloy multi-strand torc neck-ring, broken at both ends. Stage II construction, probably originally of six twisted wires coiled together around a hollow core, but only four of these strands now remain.
Wt: 5.5g; D(wire): 1.7mm; L: 61.5mm

F.192:
BM: 1991,0702.126; Jackson no.: 245
Fragment of copper alloy multi-strand torc neck-ring, broken at both ends. Stage II construction of six twisted wires coiled together around a hollow core. The fragment is bent into a shallow U-shape.
Wt: 6.0g; D(nr): 5.7mm; D(wire): 1.5mm; L: 36.0mm

F.193:
BM: 1991,0702.128; Jackson no.: 247
Fragment of copper alloy multi-strand torc neck-ring, cut at

both ends with a double-bladed implement. Stage II construction of six twisted wires coiled together around a hollow core.
Wt: 7.1g; D(nr): 6.7mm; D(wire): 1.2mm; L: 54.8mm

F.194:
BM: 1991,0702.129; Jackson no.: 248
Fragment of copper alloy multi-strand torc neck-ring, broken at both ends. Stage II construction, probably originally of six twisted wires coiled together around a hollow core, but only four of these strands now remain.
Wt: 4.0g; D(wire): 1.4mm; L: 45.9mm

F.195:
BM: 1991,0702.131; Jackson no.: 250
Fragment of copper alloy multi-strand torc neck-ring, broken at both ends. Stage II construction of six twisted wires coiled together around a hollow core. Three additional twisted wires have been loosely wrapped around the outside, but may originally have been part of the same object.
Wt: 10.1g; D(nr): 7.1mm; D(wire): 1.3mm; L: 50.0mm

F.196:
BM: 1991,0702.134; Jackson no.: 253
Fragment of copper alloy multi-strand torc, comprising a short length of twisted wire, broken at both ends. The wire is coiled in such a way to suggest that it once formed part of a Stage II neck-ring formed from multiple twisted wires coiled together around a hollow core.
Wt: 0.6g; D(wire): 1.5mm; L: 18.2mm

F.197–8: Copper alloy torc (Pl. 14.32)
MSCC: (5C)T
Fragments of copper alloy multi-strand torc neck-ring, each broken at both ends. Stage II construction of five twisted wires coiled together around a hollow core. F.197–8 may be part of the same torc.

F.197: BM: 1991,0702.127; Jackson no.: 246
Wt: 3.7g; D(nr): 6.3mm; D(wire): 1.3mm; L: 32.0mm

F.198: BM: 1991,0702.130; Jackson no.: 249
One wire extends substantially further than the others.
Wt: 5.2g; D(nr): 6.4mm; D(wire): 1.5mm; L: 67.4mm

F.199: Copper alloy torc/bracelet (Pl. 14.32)
MSCC: (4C)T
BM: 1991,0702.136; Jackson no.: 256
[Analysed: see Ch. 19 for identification of wood]
Fragment of copper alloy multi-strand torc neck-ring or bracelet body, broken at both ends (see **Fig. 19.1d**). Stage II construction of four twisted wires coiled together. The whole fragment is bent back on itself to form a rough figure-of-eight shape, perhaps suggesting that it was originally part of an interlinked group. The wires are very corroded, with significant damage in some areas.
Wt: 9.8g; D(nr): 4.8mm; D(wire): 1.3mm; L: 55.0mm

F.200: Copper alloy torc/bracelet (Pl. 14.32)
MSCC: (5C)T
BM: 1991,0702.133; Jackson no.: 252
Fragment of copper alloy multi-strand torc neck-ring or bracelet body, broken at one end and cut at the other. The Stage II neck-ring is formed from five twisted wires coiled together around a hollow core. One end of the fragment is curved into a loop, perhaps suggesting that it was originally part of an interlinked group.
Wt: 12.4g; D(nr): 4.9mm; D(wire): 1.5mm; L: 56.8mm

F.201: Copper alloy torc (Pl. 14.32)
MSCC: (4C)R
BM: 1991,0702.18; Jackson no.: 28, 89, 171, 265
Fragments of copper alloy multi-strand torc neck-ring, now in two sections, re-joined from four fragments. The sections join to form a near-complete neck-ring, broken at both ends, but likely missing only its terminals. Stage II construction of four circular-section wires coiled together.
Wt: 24.0g; D(ext): 115.5mm; D(nr): 3.3mm; D(wire): 1.1mm

F.202–3: Copper alloy torc (Pl. 14.32)
MSCC: (4P(6C))T
F.202–3 are almost certainly from the same torc. Each fragment comprises one plain buffer terminal and a very small part of the neck-ring, broken at the other end. The terminals have plain faces, simple grooved rims and plain, convex edges. Very little of the Stage III neck-ring remains, but it was most likely formed from four ropes plied together, each of which was formed from six twisted wires coiled together.

F.202: BM: 1991,0702.1; Jackson no.: 11
Wt: 55.0g; D(wire): 1.9mm; D(term): 28.3mm; L: 27.7mm

F.203: BM: 1991,0702.13; Jackson no.: 99
Wt: 59.0g; D(wire): 1.8mm; D(term): 28.4mm; L: 28.3mm

F.204–5: Copper alloy torc/bracelet (Pl. 14.32)
MSCC: (?3C(2P))R
F.204–5 may be part of the same object.

F.204:
BM: 1991,0702.76; Jackson no.: 410
Fragment of copper alloy multi-strand torc or bracelet comprising a single loop (continuous with the neck-ring/body wires) of what was probably originally a double- or triple-loop terminal, and a short section of neck-ring/body, broken at the other end. All that remains of the neck-ring/body is a single rope formed from two circular-section wires plied together. This rope is coiled in a way which suggests that it was originally part of a Stage III construction of at least three such ropes coiled together around a hollow core.
Wt: 1.4g; D(rope): 2.8mm; D(wire): 1.5mm; D(term): 14.2mm; L: 27.5mm

F.205:
BM: 1991,0702.74; Jackson no.: 411–12, 423, 425, 428, 431, 436, 438, 439, 442–3, 447, 471
Thirteen non-joining fragments of copper alloy torc neck-ring or bracelet body, each broken at both ends. Stage II construction of two circular-section wires plied together. Most are bent or coiled as if they once have formed part of a

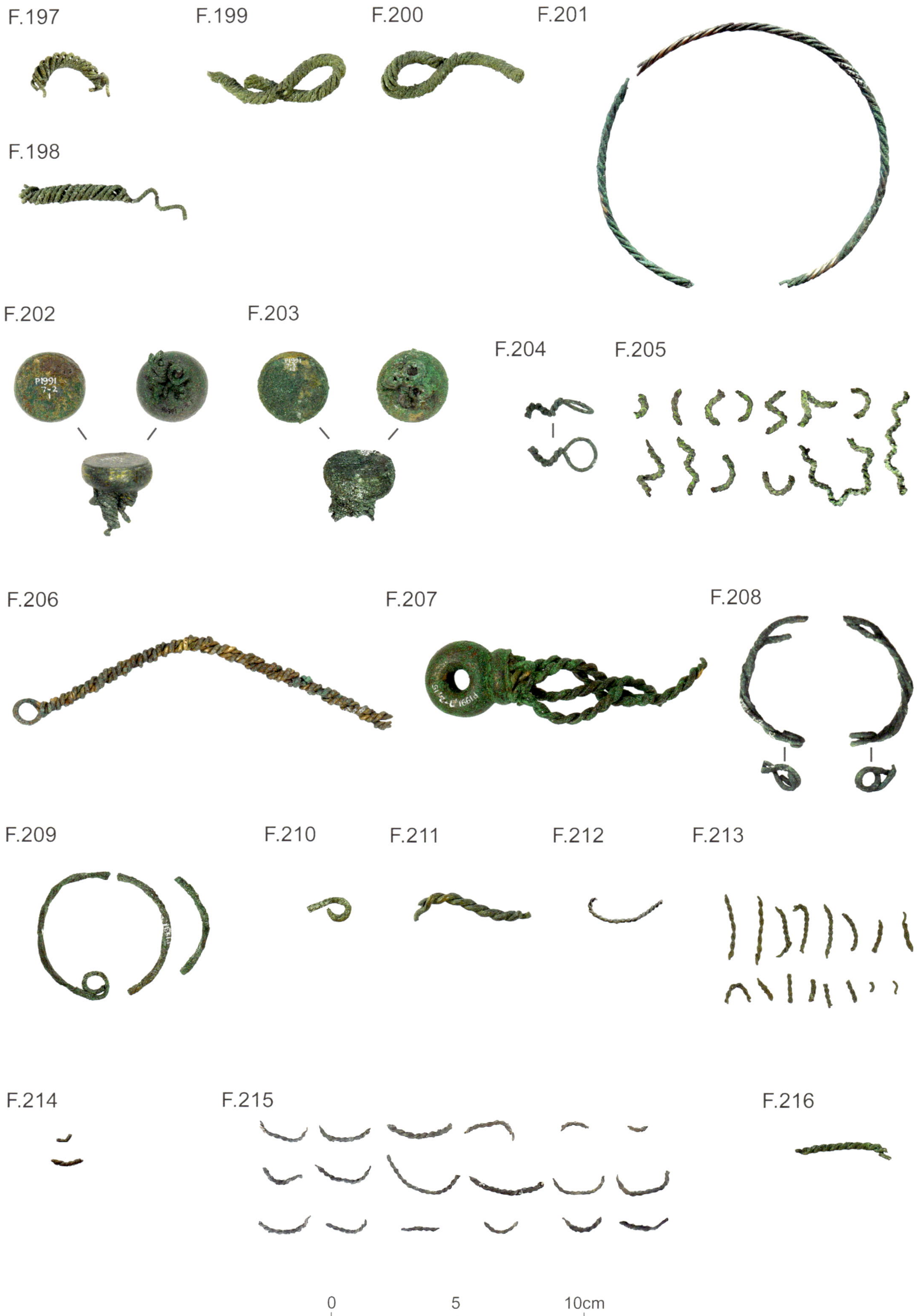
F.197
F.199
F.200
F.201
F.198
F.202
F.203
F.204
F.205
F.206
F.207
F.208
F.209
F.210
F.211
F.212
F.213
F.214
F.215
F.216
0
5
10cm

Plate 14.32

Stage III coiled construction.
Wt: 10.8g; D(nr): 2.6mm; D(wire): 1.4mm; L: 41.2 mm (max.)

F.206: Copper alloy torc (Pl. 14.32)
MSCC: (2P(2P))R
BM: 1991,0702.20; Jackson no.: 49
Fragment of copper alloy multi-strand torc, comprising one double-loop terminal and part of the neck-ring, cut at the other end. Stage III construction of two ropes plied together, each of which is formed from two circular-section wires plied together. Each terminal loop is continuous with a pair of wires which form one of the neck-ring ropes.
Wt: 24.0g; D(nr): 2.0mm; D(rope): 3.0mm; D(wire): 1.8mm; D(term): 11.2mm; L: 150.2mm

F.207: Copper alloy torc (Pl. 14.32)
MSCC: (7C(2P))R
BM: 1991,0702.15; Jackson no.: 14
Fragment of copper alloy multi-strand torc, comprising one plain cast torus terminal with simple collar and part of the neck-ring, irregularly broken at the other end. Stage III construction originally formed from seven ropes coiled together around a hollow core, each rope made up of two circular-section wires plied together. Only four ropes now survive.
Wt: 113.5g; D(rope): 5.0mm; D(wire): 2.4mm; D(term): 30.4mm; L: 112.1mm

F.208: Copper alloy bracelet (Pl. 14.32)
MSCC: (2P)T
BM: 1991,0702.52; Jackson no.: 342, 403
Copper alloy multi-strand bracelet in two pieces, reconstructed from fragments. Double-loop terminals: one is continuous, where the wire is bent back on itself, while the other terminal has open loops formed by the two ends of the single doubled-back wire. Stage II construction of two loosely twisted square-section wires loosely plied together. Very similar to F.209 but these pieces do not appear to be part of the same object.
Wt: 11.5g; D(nr): 6.0mm; D(wire): 2.3mm; D(term): 11.0mm; L: 53.0 mm (max.)

F.209: Copper alloy bracelet (Pl. 14.32)
MSCC: (2P)T
BM: 1991,0702.53; Jackson no.: 272–4, 340–1, 343–5
Three fragments of copper alloy multi-strand bracelet, reconstructed. The one remaining terminal is a single loop formed from the end of a body wire. Probably originally Stage II construction with two loosely twisted wires loosely plied together, though only one wire and a small part of the second now remains.
Very similar to F.208 but these pieces do not appear to be part of the same object.
Wt: 7.7g; D(wire): 2.6mm; L: 51.5 mm (max.)

F.210: Copper alloy torc/bracelet (Pl. 14.32)
BM: 1991,0702.224; Jackson no.: 448
Short length of circular-section copper alloy wire, ending in a loop. Perhaps part of the loop terminal of a multi-strand torc or bracelet.
Wt: 1.0g; D(wire): 2.5mm; D(term): 10.2mm; L: 17.5mm

F.211: Copper alloy torc/bracelet (Pl. 14.32)
MSCC: (2P)R
BM: 1991,0702.81; Jackson no.: 145
Fragment of copper alloy multi-strand torc neck-ring or bracelet body, broken at both ends and slightly bent/ distorted. Stage II construction of two circular-section wires plied together.
Wt: 4.9g; D(nr): 4.6mm; D(wire): 2.2mm; L: 46.3mm

F.212: Copper alloy torc/bracelet (Pl. 14.32)
MSCC: (2P)R
BM: 1991,0407.44.b; Site code: SN/AD
Context details: Hoard F pit; Excavated find, surface trowelling.
Fragment of copper alloy multi-strand torc neck-ring or bracelet body, broken at both ends and slightly curved. Stage II construction of two circular-section wires plied together.
Wt: 0.5g; D(nr): 2.1mm; D(wire): 0.7mm; L: 29.7mm

F.213: Copper alloy torc/bracelet (Pl. 14.32)
MSCC: (2P)R
BM: 1991,0407.45.f; Site code: SN/AE; SN/AF
Context details: Hoard F pit; Excavated find, surface trowelling/within hoard pit, down to 25cm.
Sixteen fragments of copper alloy multi-strand torc or bracelet, each consisting of a short length of neck-ring/body, broken at both ends. Stage II construction of two circular-section wires plied together. Most of the fragments are bent or curved. In three cases, only one wire remains.
Wt: 2.5g; D(nr): 1.6mm; D(wire): 0.7mm; L: 25.8 mm (max.)

F.214: Copper alloy torc/bracelet (Pl. 14.32)
MSCC: (2P)R
BM: 1991,0407.65.d; Site code: SN/AG
Context details: Hoard F pit; Excavated find, within hoard pit, down to bottom.
Two fragments of copper alloy multi-strand torc or bracelet, each consisting of a short length of neck-ring/body, broken at both ends. Stage II construction of two circular-section wires plied together. The fragments are slightly curved. In one case, only one wire remains.
Wt: 0.2g; D(nr): 1.9mm; D(wire): 0.9mm; L: 12.8 mm (max.)

F.215: Copper alloy torc/bracelet (Pl. 14.32)
MSCC: (?C(2P))R
BM: 1991,0702.73; Jackson no.: 268, 415, 422, 424, 426, 429, 430, 432–5, 437, 440–1, 445–6, 469–70
Eighteen non-joining fragments of copper alloy torc neck-ring or bracelet body, each broken at both ends; most are curved or bent. Stage II construction of two circular-section wires plied together. It is possible the curved fragments could be part of a larger Stage III coiled construction.
Wt: 6.1g; D(nr): 2.0mm; D(wire): 0.9mm; L: 30.3 mm (max.)

F.216: Copper alloy torc/bracelet (Pl. 14.32)
MSCC: (2P)R
BM: 1991,0702.213; Jackson no.: 393
Fragment of copper alloy multi-strand torc neck-ring or

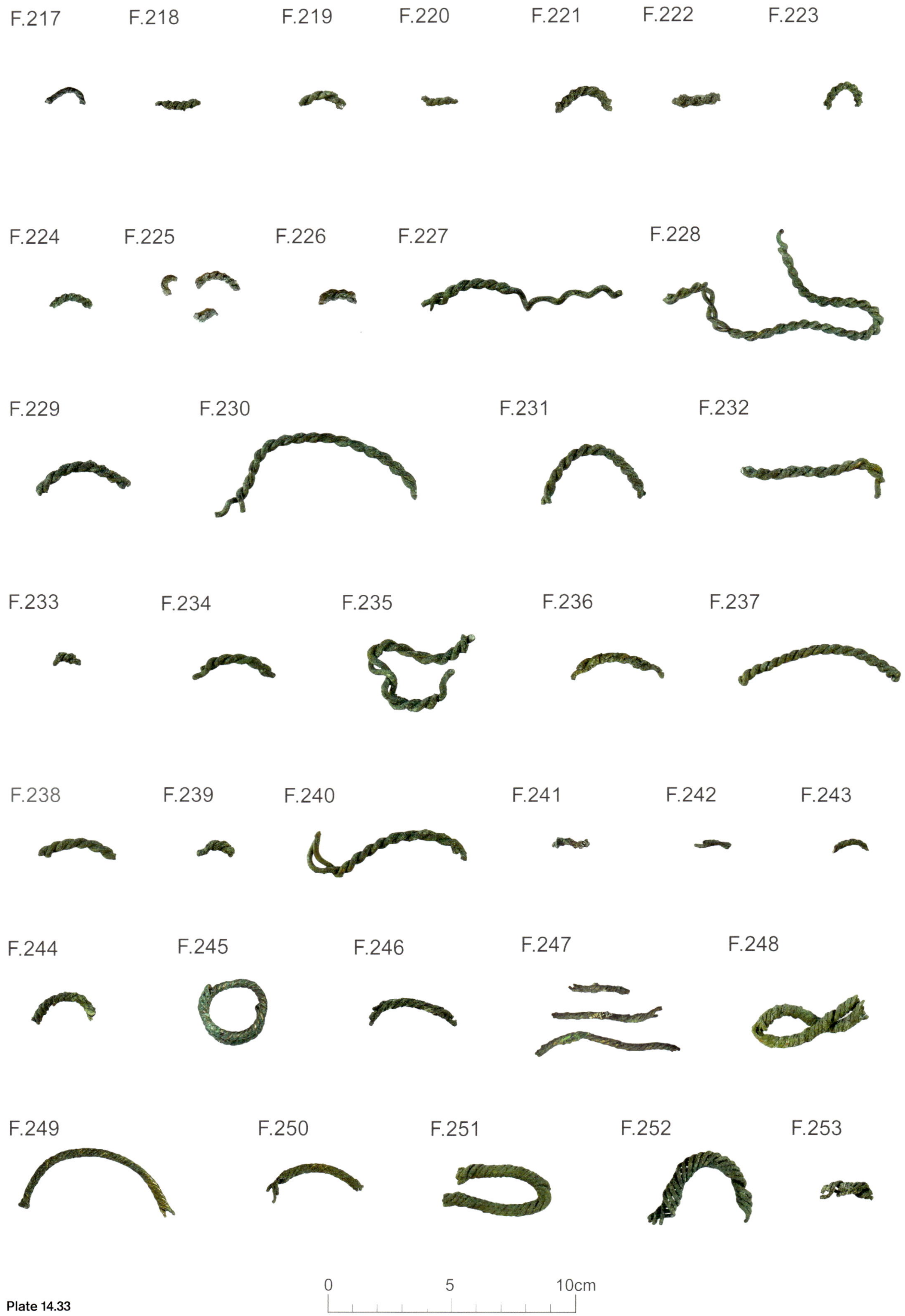
F.217
F.218
F.219
F.220
F.221
F.222
F.223
F.224
F.225
F.226
F.227
F.228
F.229
F.230
F.231
F.232
F.233
F.234
F.235
F.236
F.237
F.238
F.239
F.240
F.241
F.242
F.243
F.244
F.245
F.246
F.247
F.248
F.249
F.250
F.251
F.252
F.253
0
5
10cm

Plate 14.33

bracelet body, broken at both ends. Stage II construction of two circular-section wires plied together.
Wt: 1.7g; D(nr): 2.9mm; D(wire): 1.5mm; L: 38.3mm

F.217: Copper alloy torc/bracelet (Pl. 14.33)
MSCC: (?C)T
BM: 1991,0702.276; Site code: SN/AC
Context details: Hoard F pit; Excavated find, surface trowelling.
Fragment of copper alloy twisted wire, perhaps from a multi-strand torc or bracelet, broken at both ends. The wire is curved in a way which suggests it might once have formed part of a Stage II coiled construction.
Wt: 0.6g; D(wire): 2.4mm; L: 16.5mm

F.218–240: Copper alloy torc/bracelet (Pl. 14.33)
MSCC: (2P)R
Fragments of copper alloy multi-strand torc neck-ring or bracelet body, each broken at both ends. Stage II construction of two circular-section wires plied together. These fragments vary somewhat in diameter, but could potentially be part of the same original object, or similar objects.

F.218: BM: 1991,0702.209; Jackson no.: 388
Wt: 0.7g; D(nr): 4.0mm; D(wire): 1.9mm; L: 18.3mm

F.219: BM: 1991,0702.210; Jackson no.: 389
Wt: 1.0g; D(nr): 3.8mm; D(wire): 1.9mm; L: 19.2mm

F.220: BM: 1991,0702.217; Jackson no.: 397
Wt: 0.8g; D(nr): 3.4mm; D(wire): 1.9mm; L: 15.0mm

F.221: BM: 1991,0702.193; Jackson no.: 371
Wt: 1.4g; D(nr): 4.2mm; D(wire): 2.0mm; L: 23.3mm

F.222: BM: 1991,0702.195; Jackson no.: 373
Wt: 1.4g; D(nr): 4.8mm; D(wire): 2.0mm; L: 20.0mm

F.223: BM: 1991,0702.211; Jackson no.: 390
Fragment is curved into a U-shape.
Wt: 1.0g; D(nr): 3.4mm; D(wire): 2.0mm; L: 16.5mm

F.224: BM: 1991,0702.216; Jackson no.: 396
Fragment is curved.
Wt: 0.8g; D(nr): 3.4mm; D(wire): 2.0mm; L: 17.6mm

F.225: BM: 1991,0702.273; Jackson no.: 501b
Three curved fragments.
Wt: 1.7g; D(nr): 4.1mm; D(wire): 2.0mm; L: 18.1 mm (max.)

F.226: BM: 1991,0702.275; Site code: SN/AC
Context details: Hoard F pit; Excavated find, surface trowelling.
Fragment is curved.
Wt: 0.8g; D(nr): 4.7mm; D(wire): 2.0mm; L: 15.4mm

F.227: BM: 1991,0702.78; Jackson no.: 142
Fragment is bent. At one end, the wires are broken at different points, so one is more than twice as long as the other.
Wt: 5.3g; D(nr): 4.4mm; D(wire): 2.1mm; L: 81.0mm

F.228: BM: 1991,0702.77; Jackson no.: 140
Fragment is bent into a V-shape.
Wt: 14.0g; D(nr): 4.2mm; D(wire): 1.7mm; L: 89.6mm

F.229: BM: 1991,0702.190; Jackson no.: 368
Wt: 3.2g; D(nr): 4.4mm; D(wire): 2.1mm; L: 38.1mm

F.230: BM: 1991,0702.79; Jackson no.: 143
Fragment is slightly bent/distorted and partially untwisted at one end.
Wt: 8.7g; D(nr): 4.3mm; D(wire): 2.2mm; L: 81.9mm

F.231: BM: 1991,0702.185; Jackson no.: 363
Fragment is bent into a U-shape.
Wt: 4.5g; D(nr): 4.5mm; D(wire): 2.2mm; L: 42.8mm

F.232: BM: 1991,0702.186; Jackson no.: 364
Wt: 5.2g; D(nr): 4.7mm; D(wire): 2.2mm; L: 57.9mm

F.233: BM: 1991,0702.196; Jackson no.: 374
Wt: 0.5g; D(nr): 4.4mm; D(wire): 2.2mm; L: 11.8mm

F.234: BM: 1991,0702.189; Jackson no.: 367
Fragment is slightly curved.
Wt: 2.7g; D(nr): 4.4mm; D(wire): 2.3mm; L: 33.8mm

F.235: BM: 1991,0702.192; Jackson no.: 370
Fragment is bent and distorted into an irregular open loop.
Wt: 7.4g; D(nr): 4.3mm; D(wire): 2.3mm; L: 43.5mm

F.236: BM: 1991,0702.201; Jackson no.: 379
Wt: 2.8g; D(nr): 4.4mm; D(wire): 2.3mm; L: 37.8mm

F.237: BM: 1991,0702.187; Jackson no.: 365
Fragment is slightly curved.
Wt: 5.7g; D(nr): 4.4mm; D(wire): 2.4mm; L: 65.6mm

F.238: BM: 1991,0702.191; Jackson no.: 369
Fragment is slightly curved.
Wt: 2.5g; D(nr): 4.4mm; D(wire): 2.4mm; L: 31.6mm

F.239: BM: 1991,0702.197; Jackson no.: 375
Fragment is slightly curved.
Wt: 0.7g; D(nr): 4.6mm; D(wire): 2.4mm; L: 15.3mm

F.240: BM: 1991,0702.188; Jackson no.: 366
Fragment is curved. The wires are separated at one end, as if they have been pulled apart.
Wt: 6.2g; D(nr): 4.4mm; D(wire): 2.6mm; L: 64.8mm

F.241: Copper alloy torc/bracelet (Pl. 14.33)
Found inside F.43 during conservation.
MSCC: (?P(2P))R
BM: 1991,0702.19
Fragment of copper alloy multi-strand torc neck-ring or bracelet body, broken at both ends. Stage II construction of two circular-section wires plied together. The fragment is curved in a way which suggests it could have originally formed part of a Stage III plied construction.
Wt: 0.5g; D(nr): 3.1mm; D(wire): 2.0mm; L: 15.0mm

F.242: Copper alloy wire/?torc/?bracelet (Pl. 14.33)
MSCC: (?2P)R
BM: 1991,0702.223; Jackson no.: 444
Two lengths of circular-section copper alloy wire loosely plied together, broken at both ends. These may originally have formed part of a torc neck-ring or bracelet body with Stage II plied construction.
Wt: 0.4g; D(nr): 3.2mm; D(wire): 1.1mm; L: 15.5mm

F.243: Copper alloy torc/bracelet (Pl. 14.33)
MSCC: (3P)R
BM: 1991,0702.142; Jackson no.: 270
Fragment of copper alloy multi-strand torc neck-ring or bracelet body, broken at both ends. Stage II construction of three circular-section wires plied together.
Wt: 0.5g; D(nr): 2.8mm; D(wire): 0.8mm; L: 14.5mm

F.244: Copper alloy torc/bracelet (Pl. 14.33)
MSCC: (?C(3P))R
BM: 1991,0702.194; Jackson no.: 372
Fragment of copper alloy multi-strand torc neck-ring or bracelet body, broken at both ends. Stage II construction of three circular-section wires plied together. The fragment is curved in a way which suggests it could have originally formed part of a Stage III coiled construction.
Wt: 1.5g; D(nr): 3.6mm; D(wire): 1.4mm; L: 26.0mm

F.245: Copper alloy torc/bracelet (Pl. 14.33)
MSCC: (3P)R
BM: 1991,0702.57; Jackson no.: 261
Fragment of copper alloy multi-strand torc neck-ring or bracelet body, broken at both ends and bent into a ring, perhaps suggesting that it was originally part of an interlinked group. Stage II construction of three circular-section wires plied together.
Wt: 7.5g; D(ext): 28.8mm; D(nr): 3.8mm; D(wire): 2.1mm

F.246: Copper alloy torc/bracelet (Pl. 14.33)
MSCC: (4P)T
BM: 1991,0702.180; Jackson no.: 358
Fragment of copper alloy multi-strand torc neck-ring or bracelet body, broken at both ends. Stage II construction of four twisted wires plied together.
Wt: 2.1g; D(nr): 3.6mm; D(wire): 1.5mm; L: 35.4mm

F.247: Copper alloy torc/bracelet (Pl. 14.33)
MSCC: (4P)R
BM: 1991,0702.60; Jackson no.: 401, 406, 413
Three fragments of copper alloy torc neck-ring or bracelet body, with Stage II construction of four circular-section wires plied together. Each fragment is broken at both ends.
Wt: 5.5g; D(nr): 3.0mm; D(wire): 1.2mm; L: 57.4 mm (max.)

F.248: Copper alloy torc/bracelet (Pl. 14.33)
MSCC: (5C)3P+2T
BM: 1991,0702.175; Jackson no.: 352
Fragment of copper alloy multi-strand torc neck-ring or bracelet body, broken at both ends. Stage II construction of five wires coiled together around a hollow core. Two of the wires are twisted and the other three are circular-section. The whole fragment has been bent and twisted into a loop or rough figure of eight, perhaps suggesting that it was originally part of an interlinked group.
Wt: 10.7g; D(nr): 4.9mm; D(wire): 1.4mm; L: 47.3mm

F.249: Copper alloy torc/bracelet (Pl. 14.33)
MSCC: (5C)T
BM: 1991,0702.141; Jackson no.: 264
Fragment of copper alloy multi-strand torc or bracelet, comprising one plain, slightly expanded buffer terminal and a length of neck-ring/body, broken at the other end. Stage II construction of five twisted wires coiled together.
Wt: 4.7g; D(nr): 3.5mm; D(wire): 1.0mm; D(term): 4.8mm; L: 63.8mm

F.250: Copper alloy torc/bracelet (Pl. 14.33)
MSCC: (5C)T
BM: 1991,0702.181; Jackson no.: 359
[Analysed: see Ch. 17]
Fragment of copper alloy multi-strand torc neck-ring or bracelet body, broken at both ends and slightly curved (see **Figs 17.56, 20.28**). Stage II construction of five twisted wires coiled together around a hollow core. Very damaged at one end, and untwisted at the other.
Wt: 2.5g; D(nr): 3.6mm; D(wire): 1.6mm; L: 39.2mm

F.251: ?Composite group (inserted): Copper alloy torc/bracelet (Pl. 14.33)
MSCC: (5C)T
BM: 1991,0702.173; Jackson no.: 350
Fragment of copper alloy multi-strand torc neck-ring or bracelet body, broken at one end and cut at the other. Stage II construction of five twisted wires coiled together around a hollow core. An extra wire has been pushed into the central void. The whole fragment is bent into a narrow U-shape.
Wt: 10.8g; D(nr): 4.9mm; D(wire): 1.5mm; L: 44.3mm

F.252: Copper alloy torc/bracelet (Pl. 14.33)
MSCC: (?5C)T
BM: 1991,0702.174; Jackson no.: 351
Fragment of copper alloy multi-strand torc neck-ring or bracelet body, broken at both ends. Stage II construction of five twisted wires coiled together around a hollow core. The twist is loose, suggesting that one wire may be missing from the original construction. The whole fragment is bent into a U-shape.
Wt: 6.8g; D(nr): 6.7mm; D(wire): 1.5mm; L: 42.8mm

F.253: Copper alloy torc/bracelet (Pl. 14.33)
MSCC: (?5C)T
BM: 1991,0702.183; Jackson no.: 361
Fragment of copper alloy multi-strand torc neck-ring or bracelet body, broken at both ends. Stage II construction of five twisted wires coiled together around a hollow core. The twist is loose, suggesting that one wire may be missing from the original construction.
Wt: 2.0g; D(nr): 7.2mm; D(wire): 1.6mm; L: 22.8mm

F.254: Copper alloy torc/bracelet (Pl. 14.34)
MSCC: (?5C)T
BM: 1991,0702.176; Jackson no.: 354
Fragment of copper alloy multi-strand torc neck-ring or bracelet body, broken at both ends. Stage II construction of five twisted wires coiled together around a hollow core. The twist is loose, suggesting that one wire may be missing from the original construction.
Wt: 2.6g; D(nr): 6.8mm; D(wire): 2.2mm; L: 29.9mm

F.255: Copper alloy torc/bracelet (Pl. 14.34)
MSCC: (6C)R
BM: 1991,0702.58; Jackson no.: 254
Fragment of copper alloy multi-strand torc neck-ring or bracelet body, raggedly broken at both ends and bent into a U-shape. Stage II construction of six circular-section wires coiled around a hollow core.
Wt: 11.2g; D(nr): 4.5mm; D(wire): 1.2mm; L: 60.2mm

F.256–61: Copper alloy torc/bracelet (Pl. 14.34)
MSCC: (6C)T
Fragments of copper alloy multi-strand torc or bracelet with Stage II construction of six twisted wires coiled together around a hollow core. The diameters vary slightly, but these fragments could be part of the same or similar object(s).

F.256: BM: 1991,0702.184; Jackson no.: 362
Fragment comprising one simple loop terminal (continuous with two of the neck-ring wires) and a short length of neck-ring/body, broken at the other end. The fragment has been bent into a penannular ring, perhaps suggesting that it was originally part of an interlinked group.
Wt: 4.8g; D(nr): 5.2mm; D(wire): 1.2mm; D(term): 6.6mm; L: 25.5mm

F.257: BM: 1991,0702.178; Jackson no.: 356
Fragment broken at both ends and curved.
Wt: 3.4g; D(nr): 7.1mm; D(wire): 1.2mm; L: 28.1mm

F.258: BM: 1991,0702.179; Jackson no.: 357
Fragment broken at one end and cut at the other.
Wt: 3.6g; D(nr): 6.8mm; D(wire): 1.2mm; L: 29.9mm

F.259: BM: 1991,0702.23; Jackson no.: 114
Fragment cut at one end, broken at the other, and curved. Associated organic material (perhaps part of an original organic core or repair) also recovered.
Wt: 14.1g; D(nr): 5.7mm; D(wire): 1.4mm; L: 84.2mm

F.260: BM: 1991,0702.93; Jackson no.: 162
Fragment broken at both ends and curved.
Wt: 8.3g; D(nr): 6.9mm; D(wire): 1.5mm; L: 55.8mm

F.261: BM: 1991,0702.177; Jackson no.: 355
Fragment broken at both ends (very irregularly in one case) and curved.
Wt: 2.9g; D(nr): 7.3mm; D(wire): 1.5mm; L: 34.4mm

F.262: Copper alloy wire/?torc/?bracelet (Pl. 14.34)
MSCC: (??)R
BM: 1991,0702.154; Jackson no.: 301
Short fragment of circular-section copper alloy wire, broken at both ends. Bent in such a way as to suggest that it might originally have formed part of a Stage II construction in a multi-strand torc or bracelet.
Wt: 0.1g; D(wire): 0.8mm; L: 11.9mm

F.263: Copper alloy wire/?torc/?bracelet (Pl. 14.34)
MSCC: (??)R
BM: 1991,0702.153; Jackson no.: 300
Short fragment of circular-section copper alloy wire, broken at both ends. Curved in such a way as to suggest that it might originally have formed part of a Stage II construction in a multi-strand torc or bracelet.
Wt: 0.2g; D(wire): 1.1mm; L: 12.9mm

F.264: Copper alloy wire/?torc/?bracelet (Pl. 14.34)
MSCC: (??)R
BM: 1991,0702.248; Jackson no.: 474
Short fragment of circular-section copper alloy wire, broken at both ends. Curved in such a way as to suggest that it might originally have formed part of a Stage II construction in a multi-strand torc or bracelet.
Wt: 0.7g; D(wire): 2.3mm; L: 17.9mm

F.265–6: Copper alloy wire/?torc/?bracelet (Pl. 14.34)
MSCC: (??)Q
Short fragments of square-section copper alloy wire, each broken at both ends. Curved in such a way as to suggest that they might originally have formed part of a Stage II construction in a multi-strand torc or bracelet. The gauge of the wires is similar, although not identical, and these could originally have been part of the same object.

F.265: BM: 1991,0702.151; Jackson no.: 298
Wt: 0.1g; D(wire): 1.0mm; L: 5.2mm

F.266: BM: 1991,0702.152; Jackson no.: 299
Wt: 0.1g; D(wire): 1.1mm; L: 9.3mm

F.267: Copper alloy wire/?torc/?bracelet (Pl. 14.34)
MSCC: (??)R
BM: 1991,0702.233; Jackson no.: 456
Short fragment of circular-section copper alloy wire, broken at both ends. Curved in such a way as to suggest that it might originally have formed part of a Stage II construction in a multi-strand torc or bracelet.
Wt: 0.8g; D(wire): 2.3mm; L: 21.7mm

F.268: Copper alloy wire/?torc/?bracelet (Pl. 14.34)
MSCC: (??)R
BM: 1991,0702.263; Jackson no.: 489

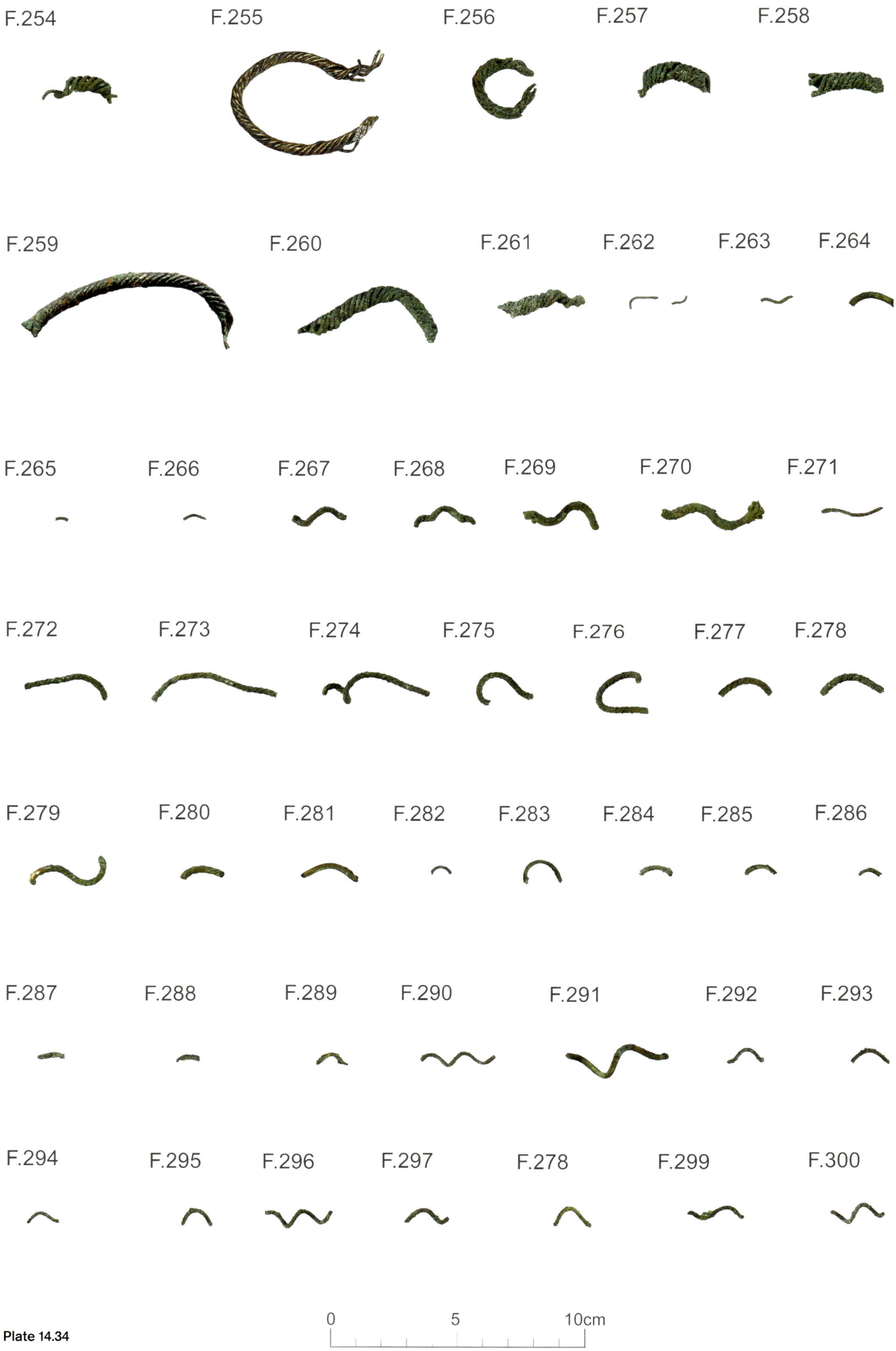
F.254
F.255
F.256
F.257
F.258
F.259
F.260
F.261
F.262
F.263
F.264
F.265
F.266
F.267
F.268
F.269
F.270
F.271
F.272
F.273
F.274
F.275
F.276
F.277
F.278
F.279
F.280
F.281
F.282
F.283
F.284
F.285
F.286
F.287
F.288
F.289
F.290
F.291
F.292
F.293
F.294
F.295
F.296
F.297
F.278
F.299
F.300
0
5
10cm

Plate 14.34

Short fragment of circular-section copper alloy wire, broken at both ends. Curved in such a way as to suggest that it might originally have formed part of a Stage II construction in a multi-strand torc or bracelet.
Wt: 0.9g; D(wire): 2.6mm; L: 24.3mm

F.269: Copper alloy wire/?torc/?bracelet (Pl. 14.34)
MSCC: (??)R
BM: 1991,0702.232; Jackson no.: 455
Short fragment of circular-section copper alloy wire, broken at both ends. Curved in such a way as to suggest that it might originally have formed part of a Stage II construction in a multi-strand torc or bracelet.
Wt: 3.0g; D(wire): 3.4mm; L: 30.0mm

F.270: Copper alloy wire/?torc/?bracelet (Pl. 14.34)
MSCC: (??)R
BM: 1991,0702.231; Jackson no.: 454
Short fragment of circular-section copper alloy wire, broken at both ends. Curved in such a way as to suggest that it might originally have formed part of a Stage II construction in a multi-strand torc or bracelet.
Wt: 4.3g; D(wire): 3.6mm; L: 40.4mm

F.271–80: Copper alloy wire/?torc/?bracelet (Pl. 14.34)
MSCC: (??)T
Short fragments of twisted copper alloy wire, broken at both ends unless otherwise stated. Curved in such a way as to suggest that they might originally have formed part of a Stage II construction in a multi-strand torc or bracelet. The wire gauges vary somewhat, but these fragments could originally have been part of the same or similar objects.
F.271: BM: 1991,0702.253; Jackson no.: 479
Wt: 0.3g; D(wire): 1.2mm; L: 24.2mm

F.272: BM: 1991,0702.238; Jackson no.: 461
Wt: 1.0g; D(wire): 2.2mm; L: 32.5mm

F.273: BM: 1991,0702.235; Jackson no.: 458
Wt: 1.7g; D(wire): 2.3mm; L: 49.3mm

F.274: BM: 1991,0702.237; Jackson no.: 460
Wt: 2.0g; D(wire): 2.4mm; L: 42.1mm

F.275: BM: 1991,0702.234; Jackson no.: 457
Wt: 1.6g; D(wire): 2.5mm; L: 22.9mm

F.276: BM: 1991,0702.236; Jackson no.: 459
Wt: 2.2g; D(wire): 2.5mm; L: 20.8mm

F.277: BM: 1991,0702.242; Jackson no.: 465
Wt: 1.0g; D(wire): 2.5mm; L: 21.1mm

F.278: BM: 1991,0702.230; Jackson no.: 453
Wt: 1.3g; D(wire): 2.7mm; L: 25.0mm

F.279: BM: 1991,0702.241; Jackson no.: 464
Wt: 1.6g; D(wire): 2.7mm; L: 30.9mm

F.280: BM: 1991,0702.240; Jackson no.: 463
Fragment is broken at one end and cut at the other.
Wt: 0.5g; D(wire): 2.8mm; L: 17.1mm

F.281: Copper alloy wire/?torc/?bracelet (Pl. 14.34)
MSCC: (?C)R
BM: 1991,0702.266; Jackson no.: 492
Short fragment of circular-section copper alloy wire, broken at both ends. Curved in such a way as to suggest that it might originally have formed part of a Stage II coiled construction in a multi-strand torc or bracelet.
Wt: 0.9g; D(wire): 2.2mm; L: 22.6mm

F.282: Copper alloy wire/?torc/?bracelet (Pl. 14.34)
MSCC: (?C)R
BM: 1991,0407.45.g; Site code: SN/AE; SN/AF
Context details: Hoard F pit; Excavated find, surface trowelling/within hoard pit, down to 25cm.
Short fragment of circular-section copper alloy wire, broken at both ends. Curved in such a way as to suggest that it might originally have formed part of a Stage II coiled construction in a multi-strand torc or bracelet.
Wt: 0.1g; D(wire): 0.9mm; L: 8.4mm

F.283–8: Copper alloy wire/?torc/?bracelet (Pl. 14.34)
MSCC: (?C)R
Short fragments of circular-section copper alloy wire, each broken at both ends. Curved in such a way as to suggest that they might originally have formed part of a Stage II coiled construction in a multi-strand torc or bracelet, or could possibly be part of a loop terminal. The wire gauges vary somewhat, but these fragments could originally have been part of the same or similar objects.
BM: 1991,0702.256; Jackson no.: 482
Wt: 0.4g; D(wire): 1.5mm; L: 15.4mm

F.284: BM: 1991,0702.264; Jackson no.: 490
Wt: 0.2g; D(wire): 1.5mm; L: 13.2mm

F.285: BM: 1991,0702.268; Jackson no.: 494
Wt: 0.2g; D(wire): 1.5mm; L: 12.5mm

F.286: BM: 1991,0702.270; Jackson no.: 496
Wt: 0.1g; D(wire): 1.5mm; L: 9.5mm

F.287: BM: 1991,0702.267; Jackson no.: 493
Wt: 0.1g; D(wire): 1.7mm; L: 10.7mm

F.288: BM: 1991,0702.269; Jackson no.: 495
Wt: 0.1g; D(wire): 2.0mm; L: 9.3mm

F.289–90: Copper alloy wire/?torc/?bracelet (Pl. 14.34)
MSCC: (?C)R

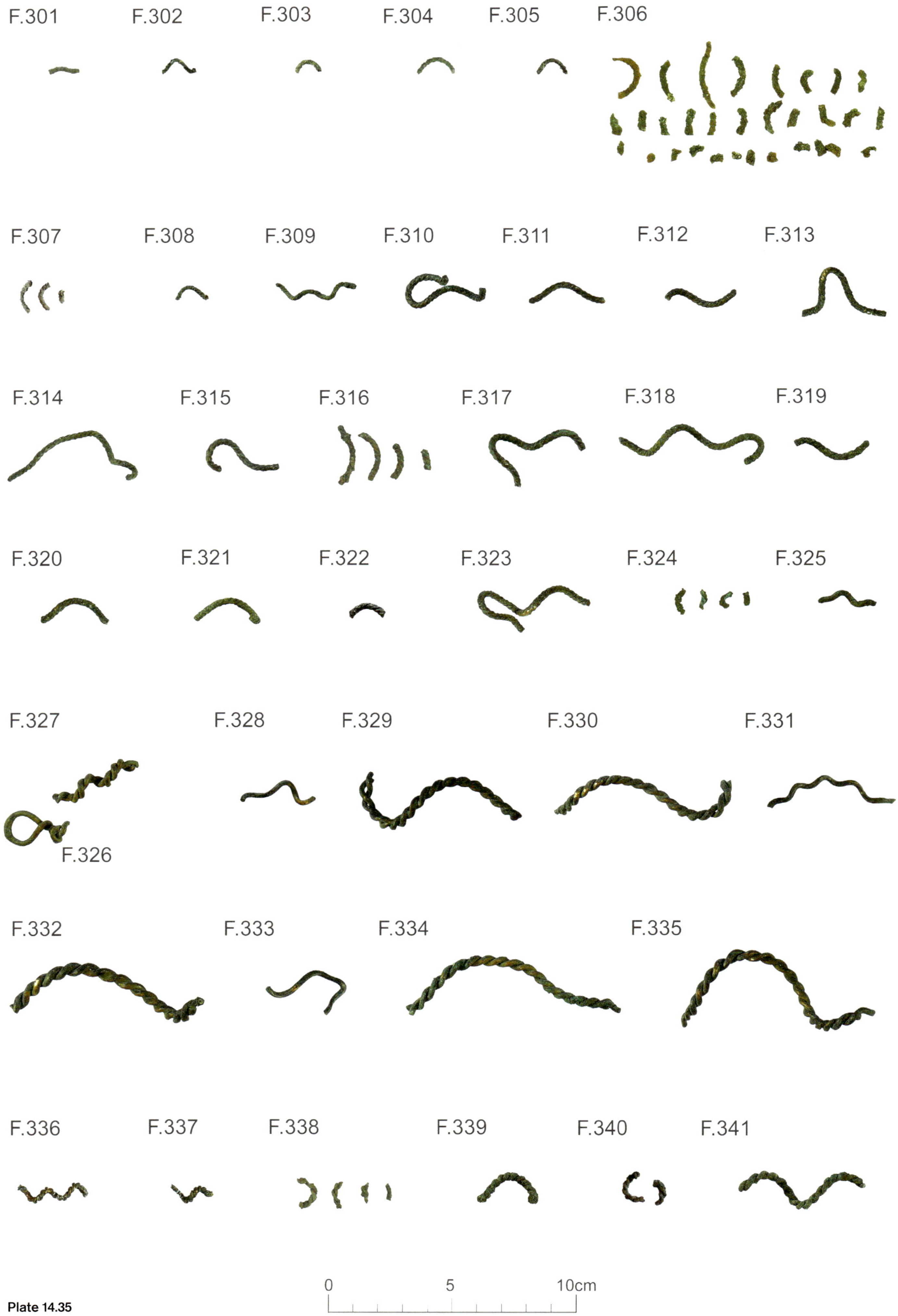
F.301
F.302
F.303
F.304
F.305
F.306
F.307
F.308
F.309
F.310
F.311
F.312
F.313
F.314
F.315
F.316
F.317
F.318
F.319
F.320
F.321
F.322
F.323
F.324
F.325
F.327
F.326
F.328
F.329
F.330
F.331
F.332
F.333
F.334
F.335
F.336
F.337
F.338
F.339
F.340
F.341
0
5
10cm

Plate 14.35

Short fragments of circular-section copper alloy wire, each broken at both ends. Curved in such a way as to suggest that they might originally have formed part of a Stage II coiled construction in a multi-strand torc or bracelet.

F.289: BM: 1991,0702.258; Jackson no.: 484
Wt: 0.2g; D(wire): 1.4mm; L: 12.3mm

F.290: BM: 1991,0702.250; Jackson no.: 476
Wt: 0.5g; D(wire): 1.6mm; L: 29.3mm

F.291: Copper alloy wire/?torc/?bracelet (Pl. 14.34)
MSCC: (?C)R
BM: 1991,0702.265; Jackson no.: 491
Short fragment of circular-section copper alloy wire, broken at both ends. Curved in such a way as to suggest that it might originally have formed part of a Stage II coiled construction in a multi-strand torc or bracelet.
Wt: 2.4g; D(wire): 2.4mm; L: 40.4mm

F.292–309: Copper alloy wire/?torc/?bracelet (Pls 14.34–5)
MSCC: (?C)T
Short fragments of copper alloy twisted wire, each broken at both ends. Curved in such a way as to suggest that they might originally have formed part of a Stage II coiled construction in a multi-strand torc or bracelet. There is some variation in gauge, but some of these fragments may have been part of the same original object(s).

F.292: BM: 1991,0702.247; Jackson no.: 473
Wt: 0.3g; D(wire): 1.4mm; L: 14.5mm

F.293: BM: 1991,0702.254; Jackson no.: 480
Wt: 0.3g; D(wire): 1.4mm; L: 15.2mm

F.294: BM: 1991,0702.260; Jackson no.: 486
Wt: 0.2g; D(wire): 1.4mm; L: 12.4mm

F.295: BM: 1991,0702.244; Jackson no.: 467
Wt: 0.3g; D(wire): 1.5mm; L: 12.1mm

F.296: BM: 1991,0702.251; Jackson no.: 477
Wt: 0.6g; D(wire): 1.5mm; L: 26.7mm

F.297: BM: 1991,0702.259; Jackson no.: 485
Wt: 0.3g; D(wire): 1.5mm; L: 17.7mm

F.298: BM: 1991,0702.243; Jackson no.: 466
Wt: 0.4g; D(wire): 1.6mm; L: 15.0mm

F.299: BM: 1991,0702.252; Jackson no.: 478
Wt: 0.4g; D(wire): 1.6mm; L: 22.5mm

F.300: BM: 1991,0702.245; Jackson no.: 468
Wt: 0.5g; D(wire): 1.7mm; L: 21.1mm

F.301: BM: 1991,0702.257; Jackson no.: 483
Wt: 0.2g; D(wire): 1.7mm; L: 12.2mm

F.302: BM: 1991,0702.261; Jackson no.: 487
Wt: 0.4g; D(wire): 1.7mm; L: 13.9mm

F.303: BM: 1991,0702.262; Jackson no.: 488
Wt: 0.2g; D(wire): 1.7mm; L: 10.7mm

F.304: BM: 1991,0702.249; Jackson no.: 475
Wt: 0.3g; D(wire): 1.8mm; L: 15.4mm

F.305: BM: 1991,0702.255; Jackson no.: 481
Wt: 0.3g; D(wire): 1.8mm; L: 12.3mm

F.306: BM: 1991,0407.45.d; Site code: SN/AE; SN/AF
Context details: Hoard F pit; Excavated find, surface trowelling/within hoard pit, down to 25cm.
Thirty-one fragments.
Wt: 2.4g; D(wire): 1.8mm; L: 27.8 mm (max.)

F.307: BM: 1991,0407.65.c; Site code: SN/AG
Context details: Hoard F pit; Excavated find, surface trowelling/within hoard pit, down to bottom.
Three fragments,
Wt: 0.4g; D(wire): 1.9mm; L: 13.4 mm (max.)

F.308: BM: 1991,0702.246; Jackson no.: 472
Wt: 0.3g; D(wire): 1.9mm; L: 13.6mm

F.309: BM: 1991,0702.239; Jackson no.: 462
Wt: 0.9g; D(wire): 2.0mm; L: 32.9mm

F.310–23: Copper alloy wire/?torc/?bracelet (Pl. 14.35)
MSCC: (?C)T
Short fragments of copper alloy twisted wire, broken at both ends. Curved in such a way as to suggest that they might originally have formed part of a Stage II coiled construction in a multi-strand torc or bracelet. F.310–23 are similar in gauge and may originally have been part of the same object.

F.310: BM: 1991,0702.90; Jackson no.: 159
Wt: 2.7g; D(wire): 2.3mm; L: 32.9mm

F.311: BM: 1991,0702.91; Jackson no.: 160
Wt: 2.3g; D(wire): 2.3mm; L: 30.5mm

F.312: BM: 1991,0702.89; Jackson no.: 158
Wt: 2.3g; D(wire): 2.4mm; L: 29.0mm

F.313: BM: 1991,0702.150; Jackson no.: 283
Wt: 2.5g; D(wire): 2.3mm; L: 34.0mm

F.314: BM: 1991,0702.147; Jackson no.: 280
Heavily distorted.
Wt: 2.4g; D(wire): 1.9mm; L: 52.5mm

F.315: BM: 1991,0702.148; Jackson no.: 281
Wt: 1.8g; D(wire): 2.5mm; L: 30.0mm

F.316: BM: 1991,0407.45.c; Site code: SN/AE; SN/AF
Context details: Hoard F pit; Excavated find, surface trowelling/within hoard pit, down to 25cm.
Four fragments.
Wt: 2.4g; D(wire): 2.5mm; L: 24.8 mm (max.)

F.317: BM: 1991,0702.145; Jackson no.: 278
Wt: 3.9g; D(wire): 2.6mm; L: 39.0mm

F.318: BM: 1991,0702.146; Jackson no.: 279
Wt: 3.6g; D(wire): 2.6mm; L: 57.4mm

F.319: BM: 1991,0702.149; Jackson no.: 282
Wt: 1.6g; D(wire): 2.6mm; L: 30.8mm

F.320: BM: 1991,0702.143; Jackson no.: 276
Wt: 1.4g; D(wire): 2.7mm; L: 27.7mm

F.321: BM: 1991,0702.229; Jackson no.: 452
Wt: 2.1g; D(wire): 2.7mm; L: 27.0mm

F.322: BM: 1991,0407.44.c; Site code: SN/AD
Context details: Hoard F pit; Excavated find from surface trowelling.
Wt: 0.6g; D(wire): 2.7mm; L: 14.5mm

F.323: BM: 1991,0702.144; Jackson no.: 277
Wt: 4.2g; D(wire): 2.8mm; L: 45.7mm

F.324: Copper alloy wire/?torc/?bracelet (Pl. 14.35)
MSCC: (?C)R
BM: 1991,0407.45.i; Site code: SN/AE; SN/AF
Context details: Hoard F pit; Excavated find, surface trowelling/within hoard pit, down to 25cm.
Four fragments of copper alloy circular-section wire, broken at both ends and very heavily corroded. Tightly curved in such a way as to suggest that they might originally have formed part of a Stage II coiled construction in a multi-strand torc or bracelet.
Wt: 0.6g; D(wire): 2.0mm; L: 10.6mm (max.)

F.325: Copper alloy wire/?torc/?bracelet (Pl. 14.35)
MSCC: (?P)R
BM: 1991,0702.198; Jackson no.: 376
Short fragment of copper alloy circular-section wire, broken at both ends. Curved in such a way as to suggest that it might originally have formed part of a Stage II plied construction in a multi-strand torc or bracelet.
Wt: 0.9g; D(wire): 2.4mm; L: 23.5mm

F.326–7: Copper alloy torc/bracelet (Pl. 14.35)
MSCC: (?2P(2P))R
F.326 and F.327 join.

F.326: BM: 1991,0702.202; Jackson no.: 381
Fragment of copper alloy multi-strand torc or bracelet, comprising a single-loop terminal (continuous with the neck-ring/body wires) and a short length of neck-ring/body, broken at the other end. What remains is a Stage II component, formed from two circular-section wires plied together. This is curved in a way which suggests it originally formed part of a Stage III construction, most likely of two such ropes plied together, with double-loop terminal.
Wt: 3.1g; D(rope): 3.8mm; D(wire): 1.8mm; D(term): 14.0mm; L: 26.6mm

F.327: BM: 1991,0702.203; Jackson no.: 382
Fragment of copper alloy multi-strand torc neck-ring or bracelet body, broken at both ends. What remains is a Stage II component, formed from two circular-section wires plied together. This is curved in a way which suggests it originally formed part of a Stage III construction, most likely of two such ropes plied together.
Wt: 3.5g; D(nr): 8.4mm; D(rope): 4.4mm; D(wire): 2.0mm; L: 37.4mm

F.328–35: Copper alloy wire/torc/bracelet (Pl. 14.35)
MSCC: (?C(2P))R
F.328–35 are very similar in gauge and construction and may originally have been part of the same object.

F.328: BM: 1991,0702.105; Jackson no.: 223
Short fragment of copper alloy circular-section wire, broken at both ends. Curved in such a way as to suggest that it might originally have formed part of a Stage II/III plied/coiled construction in a multi-strand torc or bracelet.
Wt: 1.3g; D(wire): 1.9mm; L: 30.4mm

F.329: BM: 1991,0702.101; Jackson no.: 219
Fragment of copper alloy multi-strand torc neck-ring or bracelet body, broken at both ends. What remains is a Stage II component of two circular-section wires plied together. It is loosely coiled, suggesting it may originally have been part of a Stage III coiled construction.
Wt: 7.2g; D(rope): 4.2mm; D(wire): 1.9mm; L: 65.5mm

F.330: BM: 1991,0702.102; Jackson no.: 220
Description as F.329.
Wt: 6.8g; D(rope): 3.9mm; D(wire): 1.9mm; L: 71.8mm

F.331: BM: 1991,0702.106; Jackson no.: 224
Description as F.328.
Wt: 2.1g; D(wire): 2.1mm; L: 56.3mm

F.332: BM: 1991,0702.107; Jackson no.: 225
Description as F.329.
Wt: 6.5g; D(rope): 4.3mm; D(wire): 2.1mm; L: 78.5mm

F.333: BM: 1991,0702.104; Jackson no.: 222
Description as F.328.
Wt: 1.9g; D(wire): 2.2mm; L: 32.8mm

F.334: BM: 1991,0702.100; Jackson no.: 216
Description as F.329.
Wt: 7.7g; D(rope): 4.3mm; D(wire): 2.3mm; L: 86.7mm

F.335: BM: 1991,0702.103; Jackson no.: 221
Description as F.329.
Wt: 8.4g; D(rope): 4.3mm; D(wire): 2.3mm; L: 78.3mm

F.336–7: Copper alloy torc/bracelet (Pl. 14.35)
MSCC: (?C(2P))R
Fragments of copper alloy multi-strand torc neck-ring or bracelet body, each broken at both ends. What remains are Stage II components of two circular-section wires plied together. They are loosely coiled, suggesting they may originally have been part of a Stage III coiled construction. F.336 and F.337 are possibly part of the same object. F.351 may also be associated.

F.336: BM: 1991,0702.86; Jackson no.: 152
Wt: 1.1g; D(nr): 6.5mm; D(wire): 1.1mm; L: 27.4mm

F.337: BM: 1991,0702.85; Jackson no.: 151
Wt: 1.4g; D(nr): 7.7mm; D(rope): 2.7mm; D(wire): 1.5mm; L: 16.7mm

F.338: Copper alloy torc/bracelet (Pl. 14.35)
MSCC: (?C(2P))R
BM: 1991,0407.45.e; Site code: SN/AE; SN/AF
Context details: Hoard F pit; Excavated find, surface trowelling/within hoard pit, down to 25cm.
Four fragments of copper alloy multi-strand torc neck-ring or bracelet body, broken at both ends and heavily corroded. What remains are Stage II components of two circular-section wires plied together. They are loosely coiled, suggesting they may originally have been part of a Stage III coiled construction.
Wt: 0.9g; D(rope): 2.6mm; D(wire): 1.3mm; L: 12.1 mm (max.)

F.339: Copper alloy torc/bracelet (Pl. 14.35)
MSCC: (?C(2P))R
BM: 1991,0702.200; Jackson no.: 378
Fragment of copper alloy multi-strand torc neck-ring or bracelet body, broken at both ends. What remains is a Stage II component of two circular-section wires plied together. It is loosely coiled, suggesting it may originally have been part of a Stage III coiled construction.
Wt: 2.0g; D(rope): 3.5mm; D(wire): 1.4mm; L: 24.7mm

F.340: Copper alloy torc/bracelet (Pl. 14.35)
MSCC: (?C(2P))R
BM: 1991,0407.65.b; Site code: SN/AG
Context details: Hoard F pit; Excavated find, within hoard pit, down to bottom.
Two fragments of copper alloy multi-strand torc neck-ring or bracelet body, broken at both ends. What remains are Stage II components of two circular-section wires plied together. They are loosely coiled, suggesting they may originally have been part of a Stage III coiled construction.
Wt: 0.9g; D(rope): 2.6mm; D(wire): 1.5mm; L: 12.7 mm (max.)

F.341: Copper alloy torc/bracelet (Pl. 14.35)
MSCC: (?C(2P))R
BM: 1991,0702.207; Jackson no.: 386
Fragment of copper alloy multi-strand torc neck-ring or bracelet body, broken at both ends. What remains is a Stage II component of two circular-section wires plied together. It is loosely coiled, suggesting it may originally have been part of a Stage III coiled construction.
Wt: 3.4g; D(nr): 16.3mm; D(rope): 3.7mm; D(wire): 1.6mm; L: 51.1mm

F.342: Copper alloy torc/bracelet (Pl. 14.36)
MSCC: (?C(2P))R
BM: 1991,0702.218; Jackson no.: 398
Fragment of copper alloy multi-strand torc neck-ring or bracelet body, broken at both ends. What remains is a Stage II component of two circular-section wires plied together. It is loosely coiled, suggesting it may originally have been part of a Stage III coiled construction.
Wt: 4.0g; D(rope): 3.4mm; D(wire): 1.7mm; L: 52.3mm

F.343: Copper alloy torc/bracelet (Pl. 14.36)
MSCC: (?C(2P))R
BM: 1991,0702.206; Jackson no.: 385
Fragment of copper alloy multi-strand torc neck-ring or bracelet body, broken at both ends. What remains is a Stage II component of two circular-section wires plied together. It is loosely coiled, suggesting it may originally have been part of a Stage III coiled construction.
Wt: 1.8g; D(rope): 3.9mm; D(wire): 1.8mm; L: 25.5mm

F.344: Copper alloy torc/bracelet (Pl. 14.36)
MSCC: (?C(2P))R
BM: 1991,0407.45.b; Site code: SN/AE; SN/AF
Context details: Hoard F pit; Excavated find, surface trowelling/within hoard pit, down to 25cm.
Three fragments of copper alloy multi-strand torc neck-ring or bracelet body, broken at both ends. What remains are Stage II components of two circular-section wires plied together. They are loosely coiled, suggesting they may originally have been part of a Stage III coiled construction.
Wt: 2.8g; D(rope): 4.1mm; D(wire): 1.9mm; L: 24.7mm (max.)

F.345–6: Copper alloy torc/bracelet (Pl. 14.36)
MSCC: (?C(2P))R
Fragments of copper alloy multi-strand torc neck-ring or bracelet body, each broken at both ends. What remains are Stage II components of two circular-section wires plied together. They are loosely coiled, suggesting they may originally have been part of a Stage III coiled construction. The gauges of F.345 ad F.346 are similar, and they may originally have been part of the same object.

F.345: BM: 1991,0702.214; Jackson no.: 394
Wt: 1.6g; D(rope): 3.5mm; D(wire): 2.0mm; L: 19.9mm

F.346: BM: 1991,0702.208; Jackson no.: 387
Wt: 1.4g; D(rope): 3.3mm; D(wire): 2.0mm; L: 23.8mm

F.347: Copper alloy torc/bracelet (Pl. 14.36)
MSCC: (?C(2P))R
BM: 1991,0702.199; Jackson no.: 377

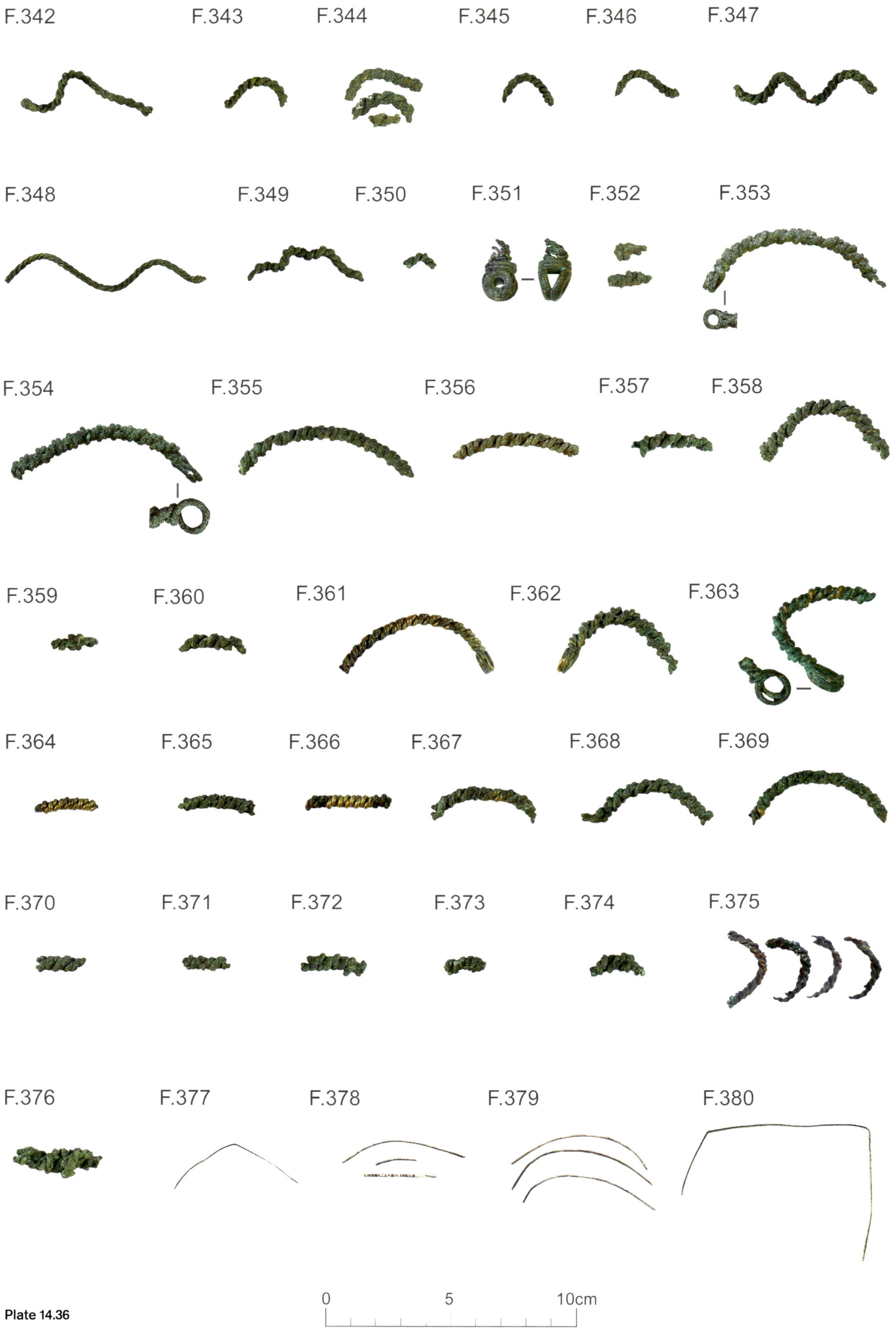
F.342
F.343
F.344
F.345
F.346
F.347
F.348
F.349
F.350
F.351
F.352
F.353
F.354
F.355
F.356
F.357
F.358
F.359
F.360
F.361
F.362
F.363
F.364
F.365
F.366
F.367
F.368
F.369
F.370
F.371
F.372
F.373
F.374
F.375
F.376
F.377
F.378
F.379
F.380
0
5
10cm

Plate 14.36

Fragment of copper alloy multi-strand torc neck-ring or bracelet body, broken at both ends and very damaged in the centre. What remains is a Stage II component of two circular-section wires plied together. It is loosely coiled, suggesting it may originally have been part of a Stage III coiled construction.
Wt: 4.3g; D(rope): 4.3mm; D(wire): 2.1mm; L: 57.2mm

F.348: Copper alloy torc/bracelet (Pl. 14.36)
MSCC: (?C(3P))R
BM: 1991,0702.222; Jackson no.: 414
Fragment of copper alloy multi-strand torc neck-ring or bracelet body, broken at both ends (one break perhaps recent). What remains is a Stage II component of three circular-section wires plied together. It is loosely coiled, suggesting it may originally have been part of a Stage III coiled construction.
Wt: 3.8g; D(rope): 2.5mm; D(wire): 1.4mm; L: 80.4mm

F.349: Copper alloy torc/bracelet (Pl. 14.36)
MSCC: (?P(2P))R
BM: 1991,0702.80; Jackson no.: 144
Fragment of copper alloy multi-strand torc neck-ring or bracelet body, broken at both ends. What remains is a Stage II component of two circular-section wires plied together. It is curved in a way which suggests it may originally have been part of a Stage III plied construction.
Wt: 4.7g; D(nr): 7.7mm; D(rope): 3.5mm; D(wire): 1.5mm; L: 46.1mm

F.350: Copper alloy torc/bracelet (Pl. 14.36)
MSCC: (?P(2P))R
BM: 1991,0702.215; Jackson no.: 395
Fragment of copper alloy multi-strand torc neck-ring or bracelet body, broken at both ends. What remains is a Stage II component of two circular-section wires plied together. It is curved in a way which suggests it may originally have been part of a Stage III plied construction.
Wt: 0.8g; D(rope): 3.3mm; D(wire): 1.7mm; L: 13.3mm

F.351: Copper alloy torc/bracelet (Pl. 14.36)
MSCC: (4C(2P))R
BM: 1991,0702.87; Jackson no.: 153
Fragment of copper alloy multi-strand torc or bracelet, comprising a torus terminal and short protruding fragments of neck-ring/body wires. The terminal is composed of two plano-convex discs with a small central perforation. At the neck-ring/body end, their bases rest on opposite edges of a buffer-terminal-like plate with grooved cordon around the edge, while their tops touch. Stage III construction of four ropes coiled around a hollow core, each rope formed from two circular-section wires plied together.
May be part of the same object as F.336–7.
Wt: 13.7g; D(nr): 9.3mm; D(rope): 2.7mm; D(wire): 1.1mm; D(term): 15.0mm; L: 27.5mm

F.352–60: Copper alloy torc (Pl. 14.36)
MSCC: (2P(2P))R
F.352–60 are most likely part of the same torc.

F.352: BM: 1991,0407.45.a; Site code: SN/AE; SN/AF
Context details: Hoard F pit; Excavated find, surface trowelling/within hoard pit, down to 25cm.
Two heavily corroded fragments of copper alloy Stage III multi-strand torc neck-ring, each broken at both ends. Cable formed from two ropes plied together, each of which is made up of two circular-section wires which are themselves plied together.
Wt: 2.8g; D(nr): 5.7mm; D(rope): 3.1mm; D(wire): 1.9mm; L: 17.9 mm (max.)

F.353: BM: 1991,0702.109; Jackson no.: 227
Fragment of copper alloy multi-strand Stage III torc, comprising one double-loop terminal (an open loop formed from the end of one of the neck-ring ropes) and a short length of neck-ring, broken at the other end. Cable formed from two ropes plied together, each of which is made up of two circular-section wires plied together.
Wt: 10.7g; D(nr): 6.0mm; D(rope): 3.1mm; D(wire): 2.1mm; D(term): 8.3mm; L: 74.0mm

F.354: BM: 1991,0702.110; Jackson no.: 228
Fragment of copper alloy multi-strand torc, comprising one double-loop terminal and a short length of neck-ring, broken at the other end. The Stage III neck-ring is formed from two ropes plied together. Each rope is formed from two circular-section wires plied together. Each terminal loop is continuous, extending to form one of the neck-ring ropes.
Wt: 12.4g; D(nr): 7.3mm; D(rope): 3.5mm; D(wire): 1.9mm; D(term): 16.0mm; L: 75.9mm

F.355: BM: 1991,0702.108; Jackson no.: 226
Fragment of copper alloy multi-strand Stage III torc neck-ring, broken at both ends. Cable formed from two ropes plied together, each of which is made up of two circular-section wires plied together.
Wt: 9.2g; D(nr): 5.3mm; D(rope): 3.0mm; D(wire): 1.8mm; L: 70.0mm

F.356: BM: 1991,0702.113; Jackson no.: 231
Description as F.355.
Wt: 5.6g; D(nr): 6.3mm; D(rope): 3.6mm; D(wire): 1.3mm; L: 50.3mm

F.357: BM: 1991,0702.114; Jackson no.: 232
Description as F.355.
Wt: 3.7g; D(nr): 6.1mm; D(rope): 3.0mm; D(wire): 1.6mm; L: 32.6mm

F.358: BM: 1991,0702.115; Jackson no.: 233
Description as F.355.
Wt: 8.9g; D(nr): 5.9mm; D(rope): 2.7mm; D(wire): 1.7mm; L: 52.0mm

F.359: BM: 1991,0702.118; Jackson no.: 237
Description as F.355.
Wt: 1.3g; D(nr): 6.2mm; D(rope): 4.0mm; D(wire): 2.0mm; L: 18.8mm

F.360: BM: 1991,0702.119; Jackson no.: 238
Description as F.355.
Wt: 2.8g; D(nr): 7.2mm; D(rope): 3.5mm; D(wire): 1.7mm; L: 27.7mm

F.361: Copper alloy torc/bracelet (Pl. 14.36)
MSCC: (2P(2P))R
BM: 1991,0702.84; Jackson no.: 150
[Analysed: see Ch. 17]
Fragment of copper alloy multi-strand torc or bracelet, comprising one triple-loop terminal and a length of Stage III neck-ring/body, broken at the other end (see **Figs 17.37–8, 17.54**). Cable formed from two ropes plied together, each rope made up of two circular-section wires plied together. One of the ropes forms a continuous single loop of the terminal, while the other forms a continuous double loop.
Wt: 10.2g; D(nr): 4.9mm; D(rope): 2.7mm; D(wire): 1.3mm; D(term): 8.8mm; L: 62.0mm

F.362–3: Copper alloy torc/bracelet (Pl. 14.36)
MSCC: (2P(2P))R
Fragments of copper alloy multi-strand torc or bracelet, each comprising one double-loop terminal and a length of Stage III neck-ring/body, broken at the other end. Cable formed from two ropes plied together, each rope made up of two circular-section wires plied together. Each rope forms one of the continuous terminal loops. The fragments are each bent into a U-shape. F.362–3 may be part of the same object.

F.362: BM: 1991,0702.160; Jackson no.: 327
Wt: 9.2g; D(nr): 6.7mm; D(rope): 3.1mm; D(wire): 1.2mm; D(term): 10.3mm; L: 48.5mm

F.363: BM: 1991,0702.82; Jackson no.: 148
Wt: 12.2g; D(nr): 5.7mm; D(rope): 3.2mm; D(wire): 1.7mm; D(term): 14.1mm; L: 44.2mm

F.364–74: Copper alloy torc/bracelet (Pl. 14.36)
MSCC: (2P(2P))R
Fragments of copper alloy multi-strand Stage III torc neck-ring or bracelet body, each broken at both ends. Cable formed from two ropes plied together, each of which is made up of two circular-section wires plied together. F.364–74 may be part of the same object.

F.364: BM: 1991,0702.162; Jackson no.: 329
Wt: 2.7g; D(nr): 4.8mm; D(rope): 2.6mm; D(wire): 1.0mm; L: 25.6mm

F.365: BM: 1991,0702.163; Jackson no.: 330
Wt: 3.2g; D(nr): 5.6mm; D(rope): 3.0mm; D(wire): 1.2mm; L: 30.8mm

F.366: BM: 1991,0702.83; Jackson no.: 149
Wt: 4.7g; D(nr): 5.1mm; D(rope): 2.6mm; D(wire): 1.3mm; L: 34.5mm

F.367: BM: 1991,0702.155; Jackson no.: 321
Wt: 5.1g; D(nr): 5.1mm; D(rope): 2.7mm; D(wire): 1.4mm; L: 42.1mm

F.368: BM: 1991,0702.159; Jackson no.: 326
One break may be recent. The other end is hammered and distorted.
Wt: 6.9g; D(nr): 6.0mm; D(rope): 3.1mm; D(wire): 1.4mm; L: 53.0mm

F.369: BM: 1991,0702.165; Jackson no.: 332
Wt: 7.5g; D(nr): 5.6mm; D(rope): 2.9mm; D(wire): 1.5mm; L: 55.5mm

F.370: BM: 1991,0702.166; Jackson no.: 333
Wt: 1.9g; D(nr): 6.3mm; D(rope): 3.6mm; D(wire): 1.7mm; L: 20.0mm

F.371: BM: 1991,0702.170; Jackson no.: 337
Wt: 1.6g; D(nr): 5.9mm; D(rope): 2.9mm; D(wire): 1.7mm; L: 19.0mm

F.372: BM: 1991,0702.167; Jackson no.: 334
Wt: 2.7g; D(nr): 6.4mm; D(rope): 3.5mm; D(wire): 1.8mm; L: 23.6mm

F.373: BM: 1991,0702.171; Jackson no.: 338
Wt: 1.7g; D(nr): 6.4mm; D(rope): 3.5mm; D(wire): 1.9mm; L: 17.0mm

F.374: BM: 1991,0702.168; Jackson no.: 335
Wt: 2.4g; D(nr): 8.0mm; D(rope): 3.5mm; D(wire): 2.0mm; L: 22.1mm

F.375: Copper alloy torc/bracelet (Pl. 14.36)
MSCC: (?C(3P(2P)))R
BM: 1991,0702.75; Jackson no.: 346, 347, 348, 349
Four non-joining fragments of copper alloy torc neck-ring or bracelet body, each broken at both ends. What remains are Stage III components with cable of three ropes plied together, each rope made up of two circular-section wires plied together. On two of the fragments, only two ropes survive. All the fragments are curved in a way which suggests they may originally have formed part of a Stage IV coiled construction. Very small additional individual wire fragments not photographed.
Wt: 5.7g; D(cable): 3.0mm; D(rope): 2.0mm; D(wire): 1.1mm; L: 30.7mm (max.)

F.376: Copper alloy torc/bracelet (Pl. 14.36)
MSCC: (3P(2P))R
BM: 1991,0702.157; Jackson no.: 323
Fragment of copper alloy multi-strand Stage III torc neck-ring or bracelet body, broken at both ends. Cable formed from three ropes plied together, each of which is made up of two circular-section wires plied together.
Wt: 6.1g; D(nr): 10.3mm; D(rope): 3.8mm; D(wire): 1.8mm; L: 35.3mm

F.377: Gold/silver alloy strip (Pl. 14.36)
BM: 1991,0501.195; Jackson no.: 179
Fragment of thin gold/silver alloy strip, rectangular in cross-section, broken at both ends.
Wt: 0.8g; L: 99.5mm; W: 1.2mm; T: 0.6mm

F.378: Gold/silver alloy strip (Pl. 14.36)
BM: 1991,0501.196; Jackson no.: 181
Three curved fragments of thin gold/silver alloy strip, rectangular in cross-section, broken at both ends and bent into a shallow V-shape. When found, these fragments were corroded together.
Wt: 0.6g; L: 49.1; 29.0; 17.0mm; W: 1.2mm; T: 0.6mm

F.379: Gold/silver alloy strip (Pl. 14.36)
BM: 1991,0501.197; Jackson no.: 182
Three curved fragments of thin gold/silver alloy strip, rectangular in cross-section, broken at both ends. When found, these fragments were corroded together.
Wt: 1.2g; L: 56.0; 54.0; 53.0mm; W: 1.2mm; T: 0.6mm

F.380: Gold/silver alloy strip (Pl. 14.36)
BM: 1991,0501.218; Jackson no.: 287
[Analysed: see Ch. 17]
Fragment of thin gold/silver alloy strip, rectangular in cross-section, broken at both ends and bent at approximately a right angle at two points to form a squarish U-shape.
Wt: 1.1g; L: 76.3mm; W: 1.4mm; T: 0.5mm

F.381: Gold/silver alloy strip (Pl. 14.37)
BM: 1991,0702.97; Jackson no.: 177
Fragment of thin gold/silver alloy strip, rectangular in cross-section, curved, and broken at both ends.
Wt: 0.3g; L: 47.7mm; W: 1.2mm; T: 0.4mm

F.382: Copper alloy strip (Pl. 14.37)
BM: 1991,0407.45.j; Site code: SN/AE; SN/AF
Context details: Hoard F pit; Excavated find, surface trowelling/within hoard pit, down to 25cm.
Four short lengths of copper alloy strip, rectangular in cross-section, each broken at both ends. One is bent into a shallow V-shape.
Wt: 0.5g; L: 30.5mm (max.); W: 1.4mm; T: 0.5mm

F.383: Copper alloy strip (Pl. 14.37)
BM: 1991,0702.98; Jackson no.: 178
Fragment of copper alloy strip with flat rectangular cross-section, curved, and broken at both ends.
Wt: 0.4g; L: 52.7mm; W: 1.2mm; T: 0.5mm

F.384: Copper alloy strip (Pl. 14.37)
BM: 1991,0702.55; Jackson no.: 285
Corroded/fused bundle of six thin copper alloy strips, each rectangular in cross-section, and broken at both ends. The bundle is bent at one end.
Wt: 2.9g; L: 77.5mm (max.); W: 1.4mm; T: 1.0mm

F.385: Copper alloy strip (Pl. 14.37)
BM: 1991,0702.56; Jackson no.: 284, 288–97, 497–8, 500
Fourteen non-joining fragments of thin copper alloy strip, each rectangular in cross-section, and broken at both ends. Most of the fragments are bent and distorted.
Wt: 5.1g; L: 89.9 mm (max.); W: 1.3mm; T: 0.9mm

F.386: Gold/silver alloy small ring (Pl. 14.37)
BM: 1991,0501.162; Jackson no.: 97
Complete gold/silver alloy small ring with overlapping tapered, rounded terminals. Made from a strip with rectangular cross-section.
Wt: 16.7g; D(ext): 25.1mm; W: 13.2mm; T: 2.3mm

F.387: Gold/silver alloy small ring (Pl. 14.37)
BM: 1991,0501.166; Jackson no.: 125
Complete gold/silver alloy small ring with overlapping terminals. Made from a strip with rectangular cross-section. One rounded terminal and one broken end.
Wt: 9.5g; D(ext): 24.2mm; W: 5.8mm; T: 1.9mm

F.388: Gold/silver alloy small ring (Pl. 14.37)
BM: 1991,0501.171; Jackson no.: 132
Complete gold/silver alloy small ring with overlapping tapered, rounded terminals. Made from a strip with rectangular cross-section.
Wt: 10.9g; D(ext): 25.3mm; W: 5.8mm; T: 1.8mm

F.389: Gold/silver alloy small ring (Pl. 14.37)
BM: 1991,0501.172; Jackson no.: 133
Complete gold/silver alloy small spiral ring made from a strip with rectangular cross-section. Tapered, rounded ends.
Wt: 11.2g; D(ext): 23.6mm; W: 10.8mm; T: 2.2mm

F.390: Gold/silver alloy small ring (Pl. 14.37)
BM: 1991,0501.202; Jackson no.: 194
Complete gold/silver alloy small ring with abutting, slightly tapered terminals. Made from a strip with rectangular cross-section.
Wt: 11.8g; L: 27.8mm; W: 7.3mm; T: 2.5mm

F.391: Gold/silver alloy small ring (Pl. 14.37)
BM: 1991,0501.203; Jackson no.: 200
Two joining fragments of gold/silver alloy small ring made from a strip with rectangular cross-section, each piece broken at both ends.
Wt: 7.7g; D(ext): 28.0mm; W: 7.8mm; T: 2.0mm

F.392: Gold/silver alloy small ring (Pl. 14.37)
BM: 1991,0702.28; Jackson no.: 127
Fragment of gold/silver alloy small ring made from a strip with rectangular cross-section, broken at both ends.
Wt: 4.1g; L: 24.0mm; W: 8.0mm; T: 2.1mm

F.393: Gold/silver alloy small ring (Pl. 14.37)
BM: 1991,0702.36; Jackson no.: 311
Fragment of gold/silver alloy small ring made from a strip with rectangular cross-section. One tapered, rounded terminal, and the other end broken.
Wt: 2.8g; L: 25.2mm; W: 7.7mm; T: 2.0mm

F.394: Gold/silver alloy small ring (Pl. 14.37)
BM: 1991,0702.38; Jackson no.: 313
Fragment of gold/silver alloy small ring made from a strip with rectangular cross-section. One cut terminal and one broken end.
Wt: 1.9g; L: 24.3mm; W: 4.9mm; T: 1.3mm

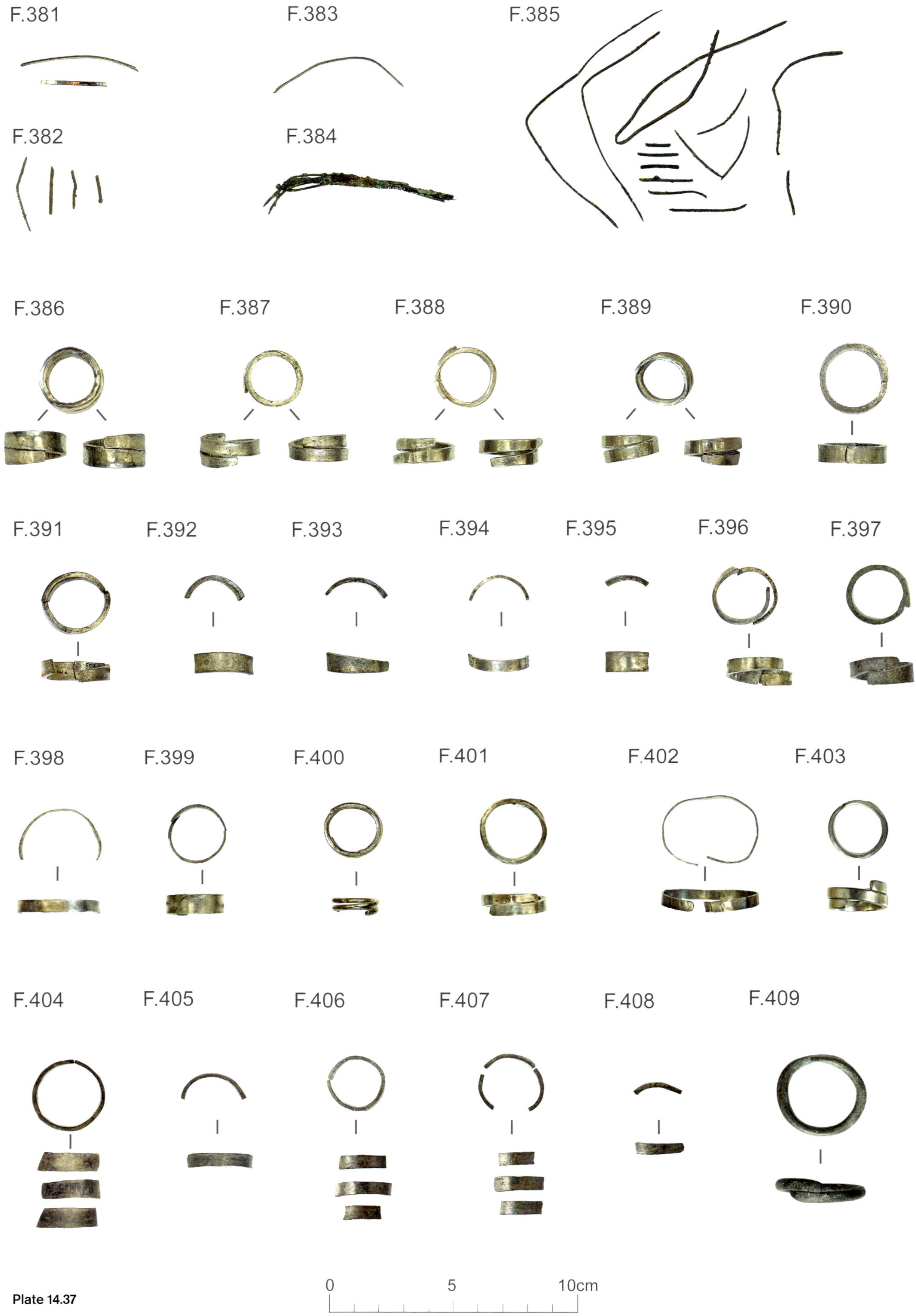
F.381
F.383
F.385
F.382
F.384
F.386
F.387
F.388
F.389
F.390
F.391
F.392
F.393
F.394
F.395
F.396
F.397
F.398
F.399
F.400
F.401
F.402
F.403
F.404
F.405
F.406
F.407
F.408
F.409
0
5
10cm

Plate 14.37

F.395: Gold/silver alloy small ring (Pl. 14.37)
BM: 1991,0702.39; Jackson no.: 314
Fragment of gold/silver alloy small ring made from a strip with rectangular cross-section. Broken at both ends.
Wt: 2.5g; L: 17.7mm; W: 8.3mm; T: 2.1mm

F.396: Gold/silver alloy small ring (Pl. 14.37)
BM: 1991,0702.32; Jackson no.: 191, 197
Two joining fragments of a complete gold/silver alloy small ring with overlapping rounded, tapering terminals. Made from a strip with rectangular cross-section.
Wt: 11.0g; D(ext): 26.8mm; W: 8.1mm; T: 2.1mm

F.397: Gold/silver alloy small ring (Pl. 14.37)
BM: 1991,0702.33; Jackson no.: 193
Gold/silver alloy small ring with overlapping terminals. Made from a strip with rectangular cross-section. One rounded terminal and one cut end.
Wt: 8.2g; D(ext): 26.0mm; W: 9.8mm; T: 2.3mm

F.398: Gold/silver alloy large/small ring (Pl. 14.37)
BM: 1991,0501.205; Jackson no.: 203
Fragment of gold/silver alloy ?large ring, broken at both ends. Made from a strip with rectangular cross-section. Possibly originally a small ring that has been distorted/ pulled open.
Wt: 2.6g; D(ext): 33.2mm; W: 4.9mm; T: 0.9mm

F.399: Gold/silver alloy small ring (Pl. 14.37)
BM: 1991,0702.34; Jackson no.: 198–9
Two joining fragments of gold/silver alloy small ring made from a strip with rectangular cross-section. One roughly rounded and one cut end.
Wt: 5.3g; D(ext): 23.7mm; W: 8.0mm; T: 1.1mm

F.400: Gold/silver alloy small ring/?torc (Pl. 14.37)
BM: 1991,0501.204; Jackson no.: 201
Complete gold/silver alloy small spiral ring with slightly tapered and rounded terminals. Made from a wire with oval cross-section. Possibly originally part of the loop terminal of a multi-strand torc.
Wt: 7.5g; D(ext): 24.0mm; W: 6.4mm; T: 2.5mm

F.401: Gold/silver alloy small ring (Pl. 14.37)
BM: 1991,0501.169; Jackson no.: 130
Complete gold/silver alloy small ring with overlapping tapered, roughly rounded terminals. Made from a strip with rectangular cross-section.
Wt: 10.5g; D(ext): 27.0mm; W: 6.0mm; T: 2.2mm

F.402: Gold/silver alloy large/small ring (Pl. 14.37)
BM: 1991,0501.170; Jackson no.: 131
Gold/silver alloy large penannular ring made from a strip with rectangular cross-section. Distorted into an open oval: possibly originally a small ring that has been pulled open. One slightly tapered, rounded terminal, and one cut end.
Wt: 4.0g; D(ext): 39.6mm; W: 4.7mm; T: 0.8mm

F.403: Gold/silver alloy small ring (Pl. 14.37)
BM: 1991,0501.73; Jackson no.: 61
Complete gold/silver alloy small spiral ring made from a strip with rectangular cross-section. Tapered, rounded terminals.
Wt: 12.3g; D(ext): 24.4mm; W: 9.8mm; T: 2.2mm

F.404: Copper alloy small ring (Pl. 14.37)
BM: 1991,0702.26; Jackson no.: 124, 195–6
Three joining fragments of a complete copper alloy small ring made from a strip with rectangular cross-section. Terminals overlap when the fragments are reassembled. Tapering, rounded ends.
Wt: 9.9g; L: 29.9 mm (max.); W: 9.0mm; T: 1.9mm

F.405: Copper alloy small ring (Pl. 14.37)
BM: 1991,0702.27; Jackson no.: 126
Fragment of copper alloy small ring made from a strip with rectangular cross-section. One rounded end, the other cut/ broken.
Wt: 2.6g; L: 26.4mm; W: 5.5mm; T: 1.6mm

F.406: Copper alloy small ring (Pl. 14.37)
BM: 1991,0702.37; Jackson no.: 312, 315, 319
Three joining fragments of copper alloy small ring made from a strip with rectangular cross-section. All ends broken.
Wt: 4.2g; L: 23.2 mm (max.); W: 5.5mm; T: 1.5mm

F.407: Copper alloy small ring (Pl. 14.37)
BM: 1991,0702.40; Jackson no.: 316, 318, 320
Three joining fragments of copper alloy small ring made from a strip with rectangular cross-section. All ends broken.
Wt: 3.9g; L: 20.5 mm (max.); W: 6.0mm; T: 1.6mm

F.408: Copper alloy small ring (Pl. 14.37)
BM: 1991,0702.41; Jackson no.: 317
Fragment of copper alloy small ring made from a strip with rectangular cross-section. One tapered, rounded terminal and one broken end (perhaps a recent break).
Wt: 1.4g; L: 19.8mm; W: 4.9mm; T: 2.4mm

F.409: Copper alloy large ring (Pl. 14.37)
BM: 1991,0702.44; Jackson no.: 202
Copper alloy large ring made from circular-section wire. The slightly overlapping terminals are flattened and roughly rounded.
Wt: 12.3g; D(ext): 36.4mm; D(wire): 4.9mm

F.410: Copper alloy small ring (Pl. 14.38)
BM: 1991,0702.35; Jackson no.: 310
Copper alloy small ring made from a strip with rectangular cross-section. Now bent in the centre, but originally with overlapping terminals. Tapered ends, one square-ended and one pointed.
Wt: 10.2g; L: 41.9mm; D(ext): 27.0mm; W: 11.1mm; T: 2.2mm

F.411: Copper alloy small ring (Pl. 14.38)
BM: 1991,0702.277; Site code: SN/AC
Context details: Hoard F pit; Excavated find, surface trowelling.

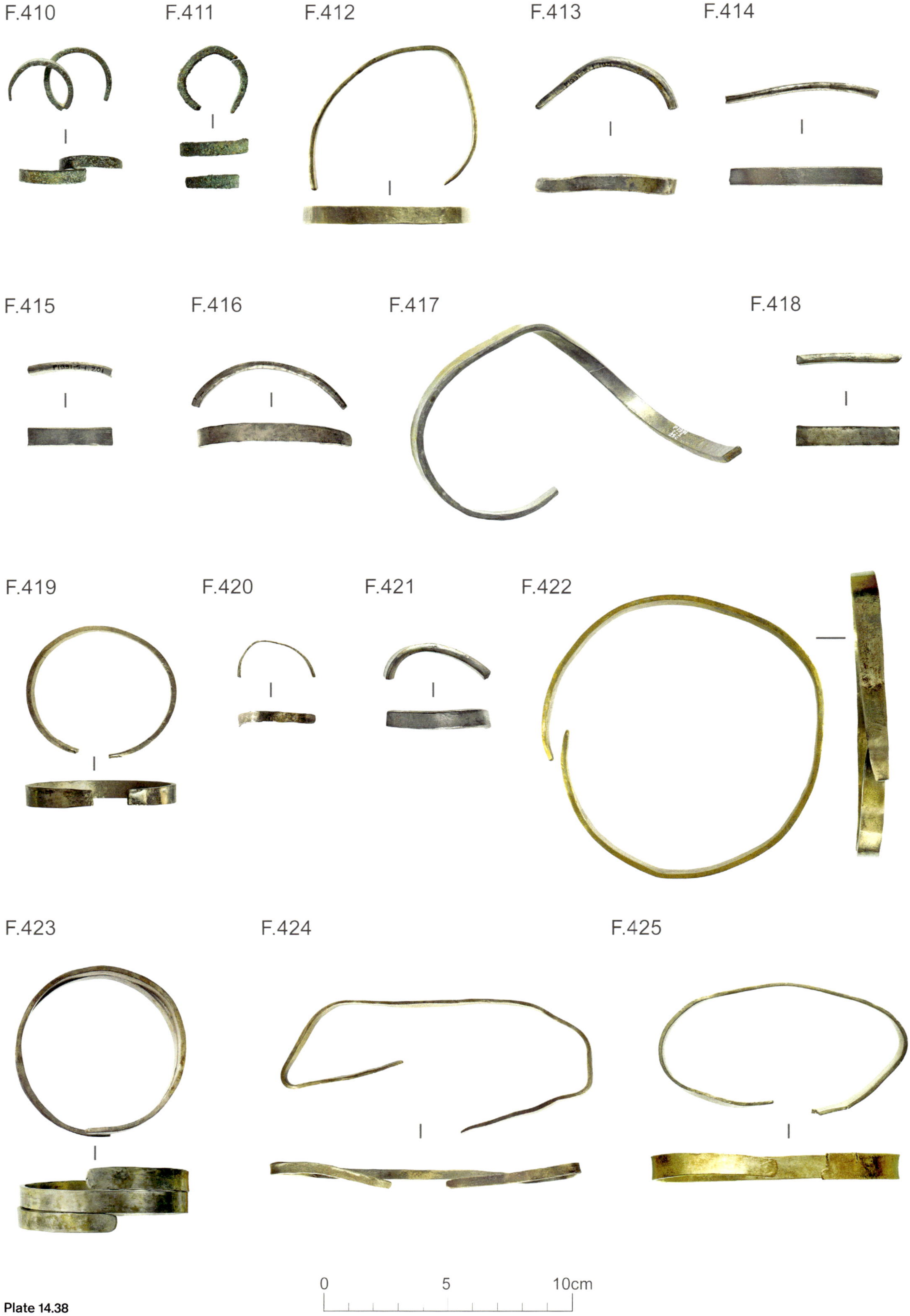
F.410
F.411
F.412
F.413
F.414
F.415
F.416
F.417
F.418
F.419
F.420
F.421
F.422
F.423
F.424
F.425
0
5
10cm

Plate 14.38

Two joining fragments of a copper alloy small penannular ring made from a strip with rectangular cross-section. One rounded, tapered terminal and one broken end. The break where the fragments join is recent.
Wt: 6.5g; D(ext): 27.9mm; W: 5.4mm; T: 3.5mm

F.412: Gold/silver alloy large ring (Pl. 14.38)
BM: 1991,0501.150; Jackson no.: 83
Gold/silver alloy large penannular ring made from a strip with rectangular cross-section. Bent and distorted. One tapered end with rounded terminal and the other, broader, end broken (perhaps a recent break).
Wt: 24.8g; L: 78.7mm; W: 7.7mm; T: 2.0mm

F.413: Gold/silver alloy ?large ring (Pl. 14.38)
BM: 1991,0501.199; Jackson no.: 187
Fragment of gold/silver alloy ?large ring made from a strip with rectangular cross-section. Original diameter uncertain as the object is distorted, pulled slightly straight. One tapered, slightly rounded terminal, broken at the other end.
Wt: 15.3g; L: 57.8mm; W: 7.0mm; T: 3.7mm

F.414: Gold/silver alloy ?large ring (Pl. 14.38)
BM: 1991,0501.200; Jackson no.: 188
Fragment of gold/silver alloy ?large ring made from a strip with rectangular cross-section. Original diameter uncertain as the object is distorted, pulled slightly straight. Broken at both ends.
Wt: 15.2g; L: 61.8mm; W: 7.7mm; T: 3.4mm

F.415: Gold/silver alloy ?large ring (Pl. 14.38)
BM: 1991,0501.201; Jackson no.: 190
Fragment of gold/silver alloy ?large ring made from a strip with rectangular cross-section. Original diameter uncertain as the object is distorted, pulled slightly straight. Broken at both ends.
Wt: 8.0g; L: 34.1mm; W: 7.6mm; T: 3.3mm

F.416: Gold/silver alloy large ring (Pl. 14.38)
BM: 1991,0702.24; Jackson no.: 122
Fragment of gold/silver alloy large ring made from a strip with rectangular cross-section. One tapered, rounded end, the other cut/broken.
Wt: 14.5g; L: 62.6mm; W: 8.0mm; T: 3.2mm

F.417: Gold/silver alloy large ring (Pl. 14.38)
BM: 1991,0702.25.a–c; Jackson no.: 123, 185–6
Three re-joined fragments of gold/silver alloy large ring made from a strip with rectangular cross-section. Bent and distorted out of shape. One tapered and roughly finished terminal, one end cut/broken.
Wt: 58.6g; L: 133.7mm; W: 8.0mm; T: 3.5mm

F.418: Gold/silver alloy large ring (Pl. 14.38)
BM: 1991,0702.31; Jackson no.: 189
Fragment of gold/silver alloy large ring made from a strip with rectangular cross-section. Broken at both ends.
Wt: 10.9g; L: 42.9mm; W: 8.3mm; T: 3.5mm

F.419: Gold/silver alloy large ring (Pl. 14.38)
BM: 1991,0501.219; Jackson no.: 304–6
Complete gold/silver alloy large penannular ring reconstructed from three fragments broken by finder. Made from a strip with rectangular cross-section. Tapered, roughly finished terminals.
Wt: 24.3g; D(ext): 60.9mm; W: 8.5mm; T: 2.0mm

F.420: Gold/silver alloy ?large ring (Pl. 14.38)
BM: 1991,0501.220; Jackson no.: 309
Fragment of gold/silver alloy ?large ring made from a strip with rectangular cross-section. Original diameter uncertain as the object is distorted, pulled slightly open. One rounded terminal, the other end broken, perhaps a recent break.
Wt: 1.7g; L: 31.7mm; W: 4.6mm; T: 1.3mm

F.421: Gold/silver alloy large ring (Pl. 14.38)
BM: 1991,0407.65.a; Site code: SN/AG
Context details: Hoard F pit; Excavated find, within hoard pit, down to bottom.
Fragment of gold/silver alloy large ring made from a strip with rectangular cross-section, broken at both ends.
Wt: 11.8g; L: 43.1mm; W: 7.7mm; T: 3.5mm

F.422: Gold/silver alloy large ring (Pl. 14.38)
BM: 1991,0501.61; Jackson no.: 57
Complete gold/silver alloy large ring with overlapping terminals. Made from a strip with rectangular cross-section. Tapered ends, one rounded, the other cut.
Wt: 92.0g; D(ext): 116.0mm; W: 10.3mm; T: 2.4mm

F.423: Gold/silver alloy large ring (Pl. 14.38)
BM: 1991,0501.117; Jackson no.: 192
Complete gold/silver alloy large spiral ring made from a strip with rectangular cross-section. Very slightly tapered, roughly rounded terminals.
Wt: 64.1g; D(ext): 69.0mm; W: 23.6mm; T: 2.1mm

F.424: Gold/silver alloy large ring (Pl. 14.38)
BM: 1991,0501.60; Jackson no.: 56
Complete gold/silver alloy large penannular ring made from a strip with rectangular cross-section, badly distorted. Tapered, rounded terminals.
Wt: 26.0g; L: 125.4mm; W: 4.4mm; T: 1.8mm

F.425: Gold/silver alloy large ring (Pl. 14.38)
BM: 1991,0501.99; Jackson no.: 111
Gold/silver alloy large penannular ring made from a strip with rectangular cross-section. Badly distorted, now oval in plan. One tapered, rounded terminal and one cut end.
Wt: 46.0g; L: 100.4mm; W: 10.1mm; T: 1.8mm

F.426: Gold/silver alloy large ring (Pl. 14.39)
BM: 1991,0501.115; Jackson no.: 121
Complete gold/silver alloy large penannular ring made from a strip with rectangular cross-section. Bent into an elongated oval, with inturned, tapered ends.
Wt: 51.1g; L: 119.6mm; W: 8.2mm; T: 2.8mm

F426

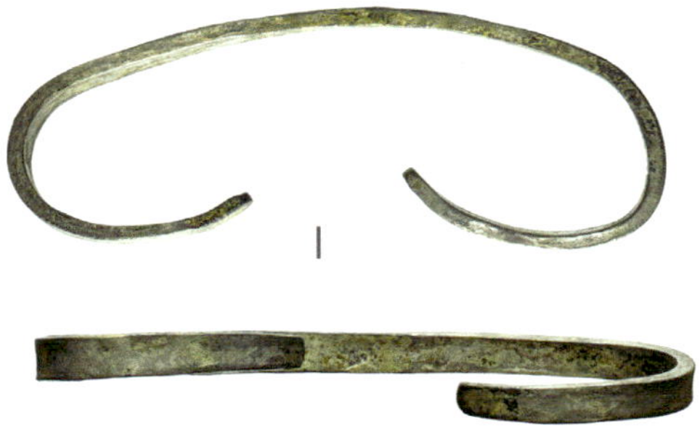

F.427

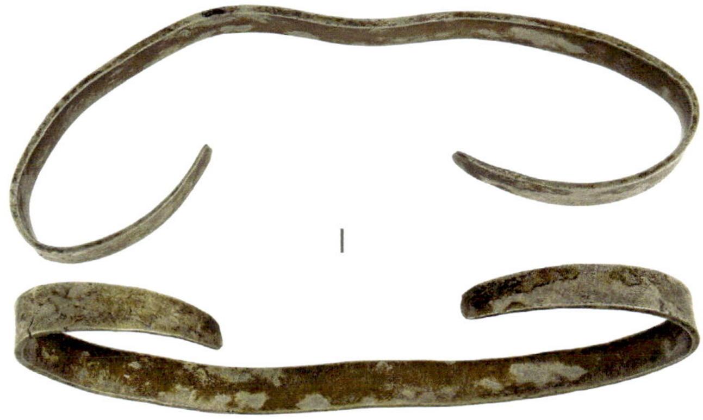

F.428

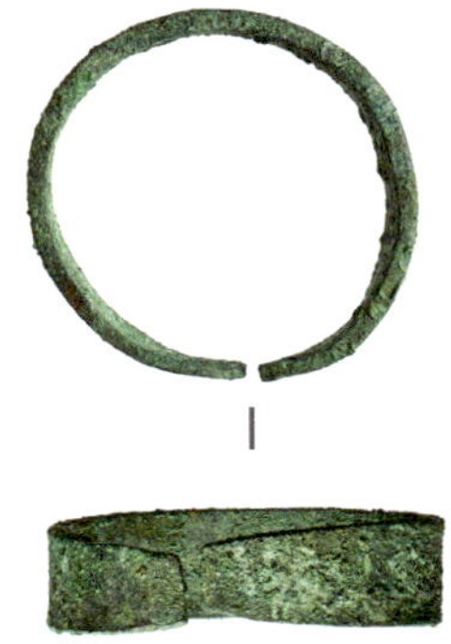

F.429

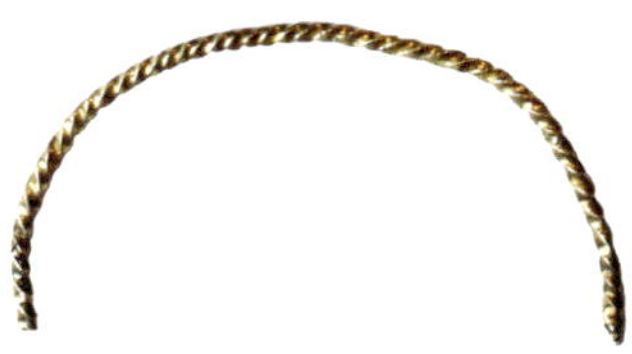

F.430

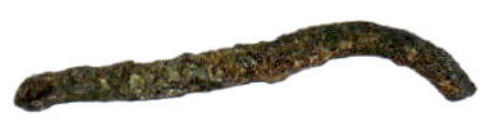

F.431

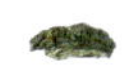

F.432

F.433

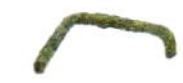

F.434

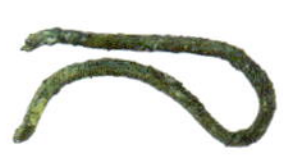

F.435

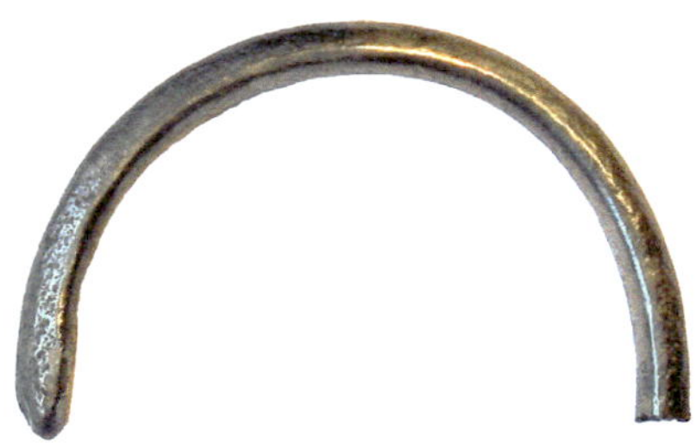

F.436

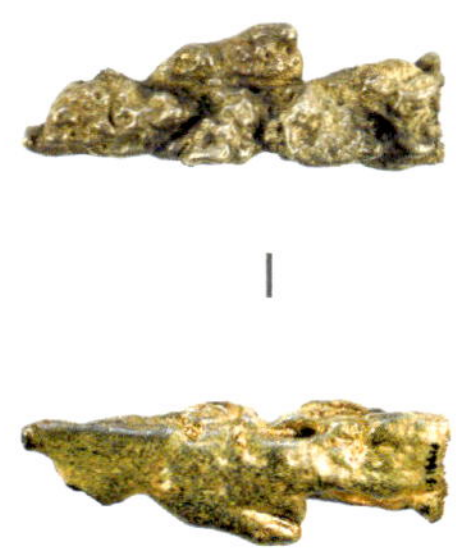

F.437

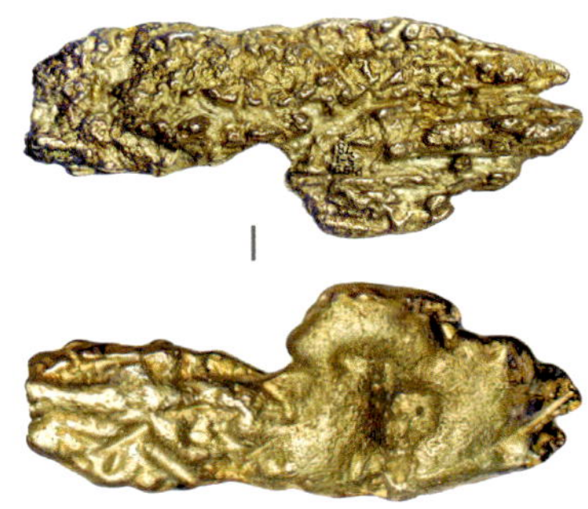

F.438

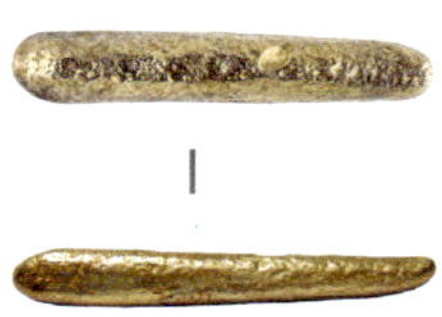

F.439

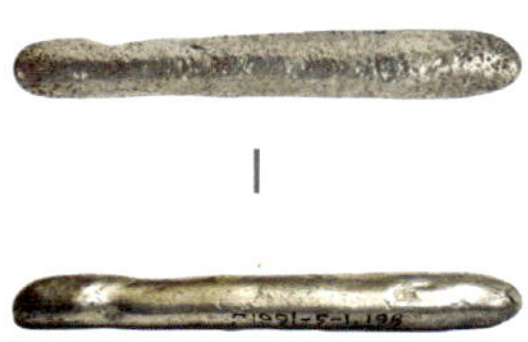

F.440

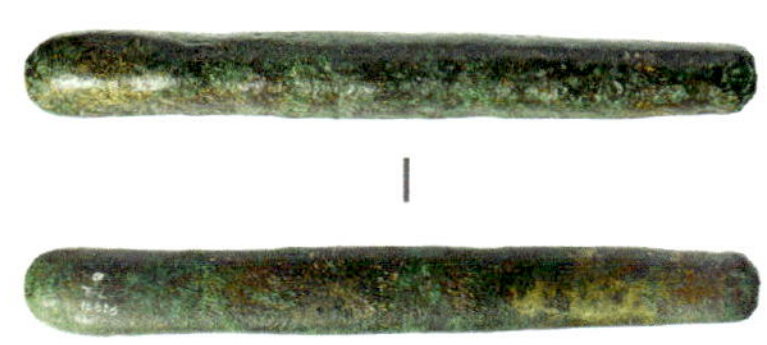

F.441

F.442

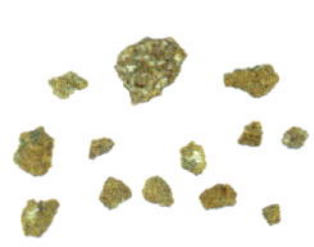

F.443

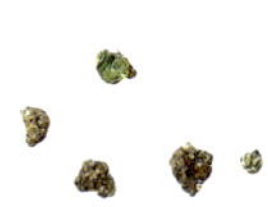

F.444

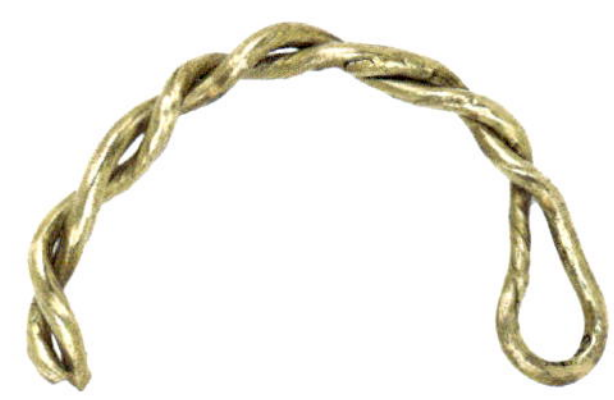

0 5 10cm

Plate 14.39

F.427: Gold/silver alloy large ring (Pl. 14.39)
BM: 1991,0501.116; Jackson no.: 184
Complete gold/silver alloy large penannular ring made from a strip with rectangular cross-section. Bent into an elongated oval, with inturned, tapered ends.
Wt: 70.3g; L: 166.0mm; W: 7.4mm; T: 2.3mm

F.428: Copper alloy large ring (Pl. 14.39)
BM: 1991,0702.21; Jackson no.: 60
Complete copper alloy large penannular ring made from a strip with rectangular cross-section. Tapering, cut terminals which do not quite touch.
Wt: 52.5g; D(ext): 55.6mm; W: 17.0mm; T: 3.5mm

F.429: Gold/silver alloy wire (Pl. 14.39)
BM: 1991,0501.156; Jackson no.: 90
[Analysed: see Ch. 17]
Fragment of twisted gold/silver wire, cut/broken at both ends (**Fig. 20.9a–c**).
Wt: 7.4g; D(wire): 2.9mm; L: 80.4mm

F.430: Copper alloy wire (Pl. 14.39)
BM: 1991,0702.45; Jackson no.: 206
Fragment of copper alloy wire with rough surface. Cross-section varies from circular to diamond-shaped. Bent and distorted, both ends broken.
Wt: 6.9g; D(wire): 5.2mm; L: 60.2mm

F.431: Copper alloy wire (Pl. 14.39)
BM: 1991,0702.99; Jackson no.: 180
Fragment of circular-section copper alloy wire, heavily corroded, broken at both ends.
Wt: 0.5g; L: 11.1mm; W: 4.2mm

F.432: Copper alloy wire (Pl. 14.39)
BM: 1991,0407.45.h; Site code: SN/AE; SN/AF
Context details: Hoard F pit; Excavated find, surface trowelling/within hoard pit, down to 25cm.
Fragment of copper alloy wire, square in cross-section and very slightly twisted, broken at both ends.
Wt: 0.2g; D(wire): 3.0mm; L: 6.9mm

F.433: Copper alloy wire (Pl. 14.39)
BM: 1991,0702.271; Jackson no.: 499
Fragment of circular-section copper alloy wire, broken at both ends. Bent at close to a right angle in two places.
Wt: 0.3g; D(wire): 1.5mm; L: 18.9mm

F.434: Copper alloy wire (Pl. 14.39)
BM: 1991,0702.225; Jackson no.: 449
Fragment of circular-section copper alloy wire, broken at both ends and bent into an irregular open loop.
Wt: 2.4g; D(wire): 2.0mm; L: 34.4mm

F.435: Copper alloy large ring/?ingot/?bracelet (Pl. 14.39)
BM: 1991,0702.5; Jackson no.: 118
Fragment comprising around half of acopper alloy large ring, perhaps an ingot or bracelet. Semi-circular in plan, with D-shaped cross-section. Broken or cut at one end, while the other has a finished, expanded, slightly rounded terminal.
Wt: 97.6g; L: 102.8mm; W: 12.0mm; T: 8.3mm

F.436–7: Gold/silver alloy lump (Pl. 14.39)
F.436–7 join.

F.436:
BM: 1991,0501.74; Jackson no.: 62
Irregular, flattish gold/silver alloy lump, one end broken. Fragments of slender, gold/silver alloy circular-section wire, semi-coalesced, project in several places.
Wt: 39.5g; L: 56.4mm; W: 20.4mm; T: 10.1mm

F.437:
BM: 1991,0501.75; Jackson no.: 63
Irregular, flattish gold/silver alloy lump, one end broken. At least two fragments of thin gold/silver-alloy twisted wire project from the main body of the lump.
Wt: 114.2g; L: 91.0mm; W: 37.5mm; T: 12.4mm

F.438: Gold/silver alloy linear ingot (Pl. 14.39)
BM: 1991,0501.114; Jackson no.: 120
Complete gold/silver alloy D-section linear ingot, with tapered, rounded ends.
Wt: 24.4g; L: 55.4mm; W: 9.7mm; T: 7.2mm

F.439: Gold/silver alloy linear ingot (Pl. 14.39)
BM: 1991,0501.198; Jackson no.: 183
Complete gold/silver alloy D-section linear ingot, slightly tapered, with rounded ends.
Wt: 22.0g; L: 66.5mm; W: 9.4mm; T: 6.3mm

F.440: Copper alloy linear ingot (Pl. 14.39)
BM: 1991,0702.6; Jackson no.: 119
Complete copper alloy D-section linear ingot, with tapered, rounded ends.
Wt: 63.8g; L: 96.1mm; W: 11.6mm; T: 10.8mm

F.441: Copper alloy sheet (Pl. 14.39)
BM: 1991,0407.45.k; Site code: SN/AE; SN/AF
Context details: Hoard F pit; Excavated find, surface trowelling/within hoard pit, down to 25cm.
Two small fragments of copper alloy sheet, fused together.
Wt: 0.1g; L: 7.0mm; T: 0.2mm

F.442: Copper alloy lump (Pl. 14.39)
BM: 1991,0407.45.l; Site code: SN/AE; SN/AF
Context details: Hoard F pit; Excavated find, surface trowelling/within hoard pit, down to 25cm.
Thirteen small, amorphous copper alloy lumps.
Wt: 0.9g; L: 10.0 mm (max.)

F.443: Copper alloy sheet/lump (Pl. 14.39)
BM: 1991,0407.65.e; Site code: SN/AG
Context details: Hoard F pit; Excavated find, within hoard pit, down to bottom.
Small fragments of copper alloy lumps or sheet.
Wt: 0.3g

F.444: Gold/silver alloy torc (Pl. 14.39)
MSCC: (2P)R
BM: 1991,0407.43; Site code: SN/AH
Context details: Near Hoard F. Most likely an outlier from the hoard, disturbed by ploughing.
Fragment of gold/silver alloy multi-strand torc, comprising a single-loop terminal (continuous with the neck-ring wires) and a length of neck-ring, cut and slightly melted at the other end. Stage II construction of two circular-section wires plied together. The loop terminal shows heavy cracking, and appears to have been partially untwisted.
Wt: 27.0g; D(nr): 7.0mm; D(wire): 3.6mm; D(term): 15.9mm; L: 76.8mm

The Hoard F helmet

Fleur Shearman and Julia Farley

F.445: Copper alloy helmet
BM: 1991,0702.272; Site Codes: SN/AC; SN/AJ; SN/AE; Jackson no.: 501a
Hoard F was deposited in what was originally thought to be a vessel or container made from copper alloy sheet. This was later re-identified as an unusual form of copper alloy helmet. It has subsequently been reconstructed from fragments including metal-detected finds and excavated finds (from both surface trowelling and within and around the edge of the Hoard F pit).

Discovery and identification

Hoard F was discovered during metal-detecting by Charles Hodder (see Chs 2, 4 and 12). In describing the specifics of retrieval, Hodder noted the presence of a copper alloy 'container or vessel' holding the hoard, though with no traces of a base. His account stated that the object was in a very fragmentary state, with no large pieces of copper alloy sheet surviving; he accompanied this with a sketch showing the precious metalwork held within a bowl-shaped object in a flat-bottomed pit (see Ch. 12; **Fig. 12.1**). Photographs taken by Hodder on site include several of the larger fragments of sheet, later integrated into the front of the helmet (see **Fig. 16.2**).

The findspot of Hoard F was subsequently investigated archaeologically, leading to the recovery of numerous further small copper alloy fragments from the vicinity of the metal-detected pit. At this stage the corroded and fragmentary sheet container was still categorised as a vessel; an understandable preliminary identification as the object was shattered into hundreds of small fragments and needed reassembly before it could be fully interpreted. The likelihood of a helmet in secondary usage as a container was unexpected in this context and the flat-bottom of the pit, and therefore by inference potentially the container, no doubt added to the assumption that it was a vessel.

Ralph Jackson and Ian Stead first recorded Hoard F when it entered the Museum (Chs 2, 12) (Stead and Jackson unpublished). Amongst the sheet fragments, they noted the presence of both hinges and perforated areas, features shared in common with Iron Age strainer bowls, such as the vessel from the Welwyn Garden City burial (Stead 1967) and in the later find from Chettle Park (BM 2009,8006.2) (see also Sealey 1999). A fragment later found to be the curved eyebrow arch of the helmet was initially interpreted as a distorted piece of the edge of the vessel.

The copper alloy sheet pieces were not further examined until 2007, when the copper alloy proportion of the metalwork was under review in advance of publication. Close examination of the fragments based on a visual assessment was progressed. Visual criteria used in categorisation were morphology and colour of corrosion, thickness of sheet and its curvature. Apart from a few broken torc strands the pieces of sheet were similar to each other; it was clear they were parts of the same object so work towards its reconstruction could begin. After the preliminary join-making, X-radiography of the object was carried out in the conservation laboratory (see below). This initial X-radiography suggested that the fragments may not in fact have originated from a vessel, but rather from a helmet. After discussion with the Iron Age curator (then Jody Joy) and Dr Stead, this identification was confirmed and the pieces formerly labelled as fragments of a vessel were reassigned as *militaria*.

The fragments which were subsequently reconstructed to form the helmet came from a variety of groups: the detected copper alloy sheet (Ralph Jackson no. 501), small fragments recovered during excavation of the Hoard F pit (site code SN/AC), and others retrieved from residues associated with copper alloy torcs from Hoard F (site codes SN/AE, SN/AJ). Some of the latter were identified during a review of all copper alloy sheet fragments from the site carried out in 2018. This survey included the reserve collections held in both NCM and the BM. Most could easily be discounted as stray finds of later medieval or post-medieval date, but three small diagnostic pieces of helmet were found from the context of the Hoard F pit. X-ray fluorescence analysis of a small sample of helmet fragments was also carried out in 2018 by Duncan Hook, using a Bruker ARTAX XRF spectrometer with a helium atmosphere, 50 kV X-ray tube voltage, 0.8 mA current, 0.6mm diameter collimator and 200s counting time.

At the time of writing, the surviving fragments of the Snettisham helmet have been reconstructed as far as possible with reversible adhesives and minimum use of gap fills to achieve a self-supporting structure. All joins were checked with the aid of a binocular microscope at magnifications of between x10 and x90. The methodology and ethical approaches for archaeological arms and armour are similar to approaches for archaeological conservation but benefit from specialised knowledge of this material by arms and armour conservators/restorers and close collaboration with colleagues in both British and European collections. For methodology of archaeological *militaria* conservation and reconstruction see Hockey and Shearman (2006) and Hockey *et al.* (2013).

Imaging the helmet

X-radiography proved to be a useful diagnostic tool in identifying the copper alloy fragments originating from the helmet. It was also used to record the fragments, as the technique is capable of producing images clarifying detail and construction elements not visible to the eye. Resultant

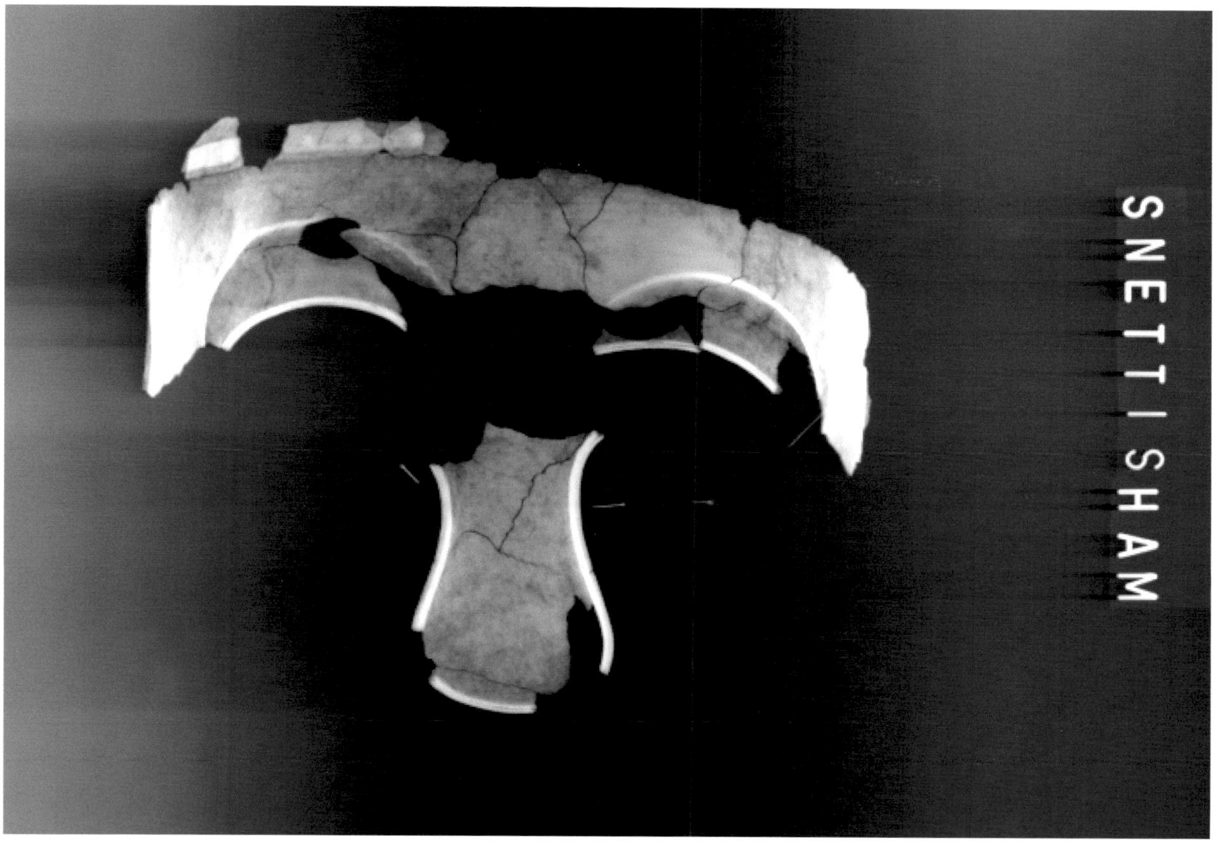

Figure 14.23 X-radiograph of the front of helmet after reconstruction

Figure 14.24 X-radiograph of layout of joining fragments from the back and sides of the helmet

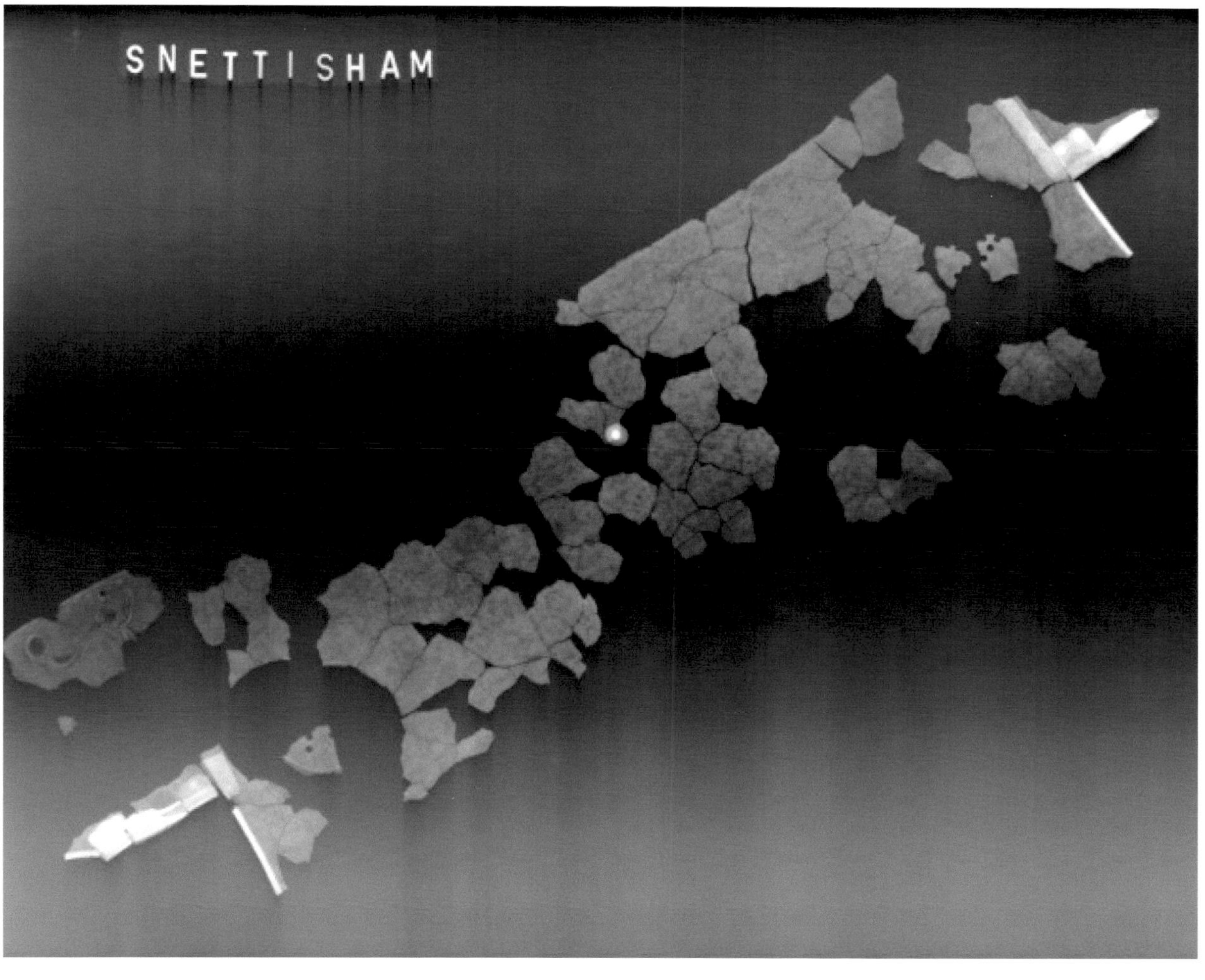

images can be interrogated for technical information which can also support joining and reconstruction (see Shearman and Dove 1997; Hockey *et al.* 2018).

The first helmet X-radiographs were taken with a Torrex X-radiography cabinet with film processing in the BM conservation laboratories. In 2014, a new digital capacity enabled a set of X-radiographs of the helmet to be produced in new facilities in the BM's World Conservation and Exhibitions Centre (WCEC) Weston Archaeology Suite (**Figs 14.23–4, 21.41a–b**). The move to digital capture meant images for conservation purposes were produced using a Euroteck cabinet with fixed source (Gulmay CP 225 kV X-radiography Generator and MP1 type2 Controller) in combination with a Carestream Industrex HPX-1 scanner and software. After digital capture, images created in Digital Images and Communications in Medicine (DCM) files were saved in .tiff and .jpeg format after enhancement or manipulation. A high resolution screen was used to evaluate the digital X-radiographs. Resultant images could be further manipulated and enhanced in Adobe Photoshop. The digital images had the advantage of being able to be manipulated, enlarged and shared electronically.

Investigation of the Snettisham hoards kept pace with current developments in imaging and CT scanning. In 2019, the helmet was photographed and scanned by Craig Williams, illustrator for the Department of Britain, Europe and Prehistory, at the BM, and a 3D model was created using photogrammetry software Agisoft Metashape (**Fig. 14.25**).

Study of the helmet is ongoing. Next steps will include 3D computer modelling in collaboration with archaeological illustrators and curators. The helmet would also benefit from non-contact laser scanning of internal surfaces for the production of a shaped support mount to enable non-contact study and even display. This would minimise the handling risk to the thin and corroded copper alloy of the helmet, making it easier for future researchers to continue exploring this fascinating object.

Description and condition

For the most part, only the lower part of the Snettisham Hoard F helmet can be reconstructed. Rather than being of a simple one-piece bowl construction, the crown seems to have been made separately, being riveted onto the lower section along a horizontal seam running around the helmet at brow level. Little of the crown survives, and no fragments of a knop or similar crown fitting were recovered, but the line of rivet fixings above the brow line can be clearly seen on the X-radiograph (**Fig. 14.23**).

At the front are two symmetrical eyebrow arches, which would once have continued down into a central nasal. The edges of these were finished with copper alloy binding strips. A detached nasal fragment remains, but does not join the brow section (**Figs 14.23**, **14.25**). The fragments reconstructed as a spoon-shaped nasal are reminiscent but distinctive from the form of the Corinthian-style helmet (cf. Bottini 1988, see discussion below). At the sides of the face, the helmet continues above eye level, with a horizontal copper-alloy-clad iron hinge on either side (**Figs 14.24–5, 14.28**) which appear to have originally held a strap. Behind the hinges, the body of the helmet descends sharply down towards the jaw line, and the vertical edges are finished with binding strips. The back of the helmet can be partially reconstructed: mostly it consists of plain copper alloy sheet, through holes have been intentionally pierced immediately behind the hinges, perhaps in the area of the ears. A rivet protrudes inwards from the centre back, presumably fixing an inner organic liner in place (see below).

Overall, around one third of the helmet is missing, including most of the crown and large areas of the lower edge of the back of the helmet. Recent breaks on corroded copper alloy are distinctive with sharp, clean (rather than corroded) cross-sections with distinctive break edges, while centuries-old breaks are often corroded over or still covered with compacted soil and greenish corrosion products of copper carbonates such as malachite (Scott 2002). Certain thick-walled diagnostic fragments (just under 2mm at their thickest points), located between nasal and brow and along the upper and lower edges of the helmet, showed evidence of recent 'fresh' breaks. It is probable that the broken-off sections of these diagnostic pieces were present but not recovered. In addition to missed fragments which were scattered in the spoil or not retrieved from the pit area, there was a degree of corrosion present on many broken cross-sections, suggesting that some parts of the helmet were likely broken or possibly missing in antiquity.

Features of the helmet

The methodical conservation work carried out on the helmet revealed a number of detailed aspects of its form and construction, including manufacturing evidence (in the form of hammer marks on the interior surface), edge bindings, hinges, perforated ear areas, decorative features and patches, crown construction, and additional rivet fastenings. These are explored in detail below.

Manufacturing evidence

Directional manufacture hammer strikes from beating out the copper alloy sheet which forms the helmet are visible to the eye. They appear particularly on the inner surfaces of the helmet where the metal surface is compacted by repeated strikes. Metallic areas are preserved on these inside surfaces towards the back of the helmet, which due to compaction has survived better than the corroded and blistered outer surfaces (**Fig. 14.27**).

Edge binding

The spoon-shaped nasal at the front of the helmet, the brow arches, and the lower helmet edging where it survives as fragments, are finished with a narrow U-shaped copper alloy edge strip, 3.5mm in width. This would appear to have been crimped in place to reinforce the edge of the helmet. Hammer marks also survive adjacent to the edge binding, indicating it was mechanically attached. Several additional short sections of straight edge binding survive. The lack of curvature suggests that these could have come from the edging of the damaged areas at the back of the helmet (along the neck-guard) or possibly the straight vertical-edged cheek.

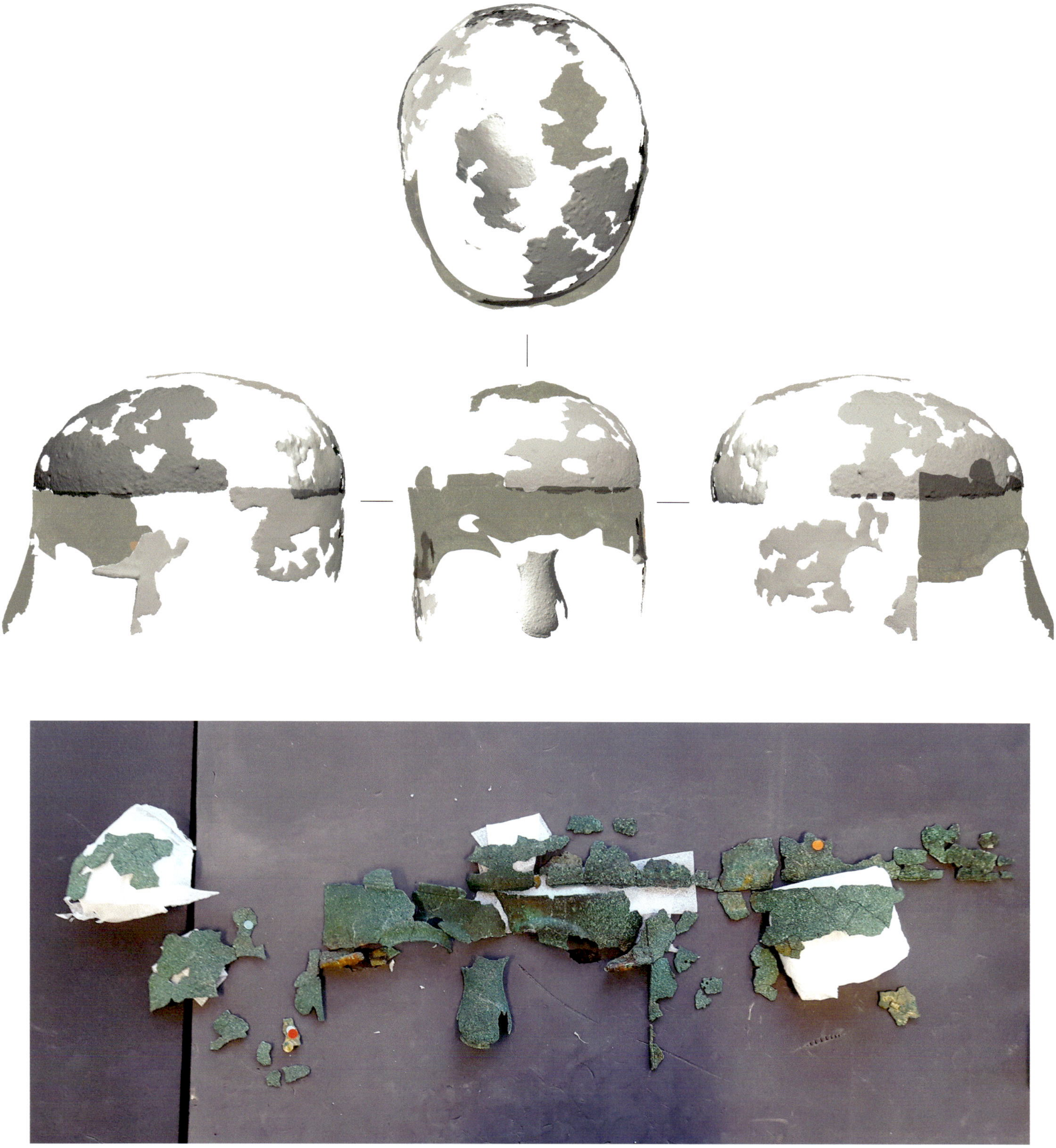

Figure 14.25 Digital reconstruction of the helmet by Craig Williams, made up of composite 3D scans using Agisoft Metashape photogrammetry software (above); photograph by Fleur Shearman of the main surviving areas of the helmet laid out (below)

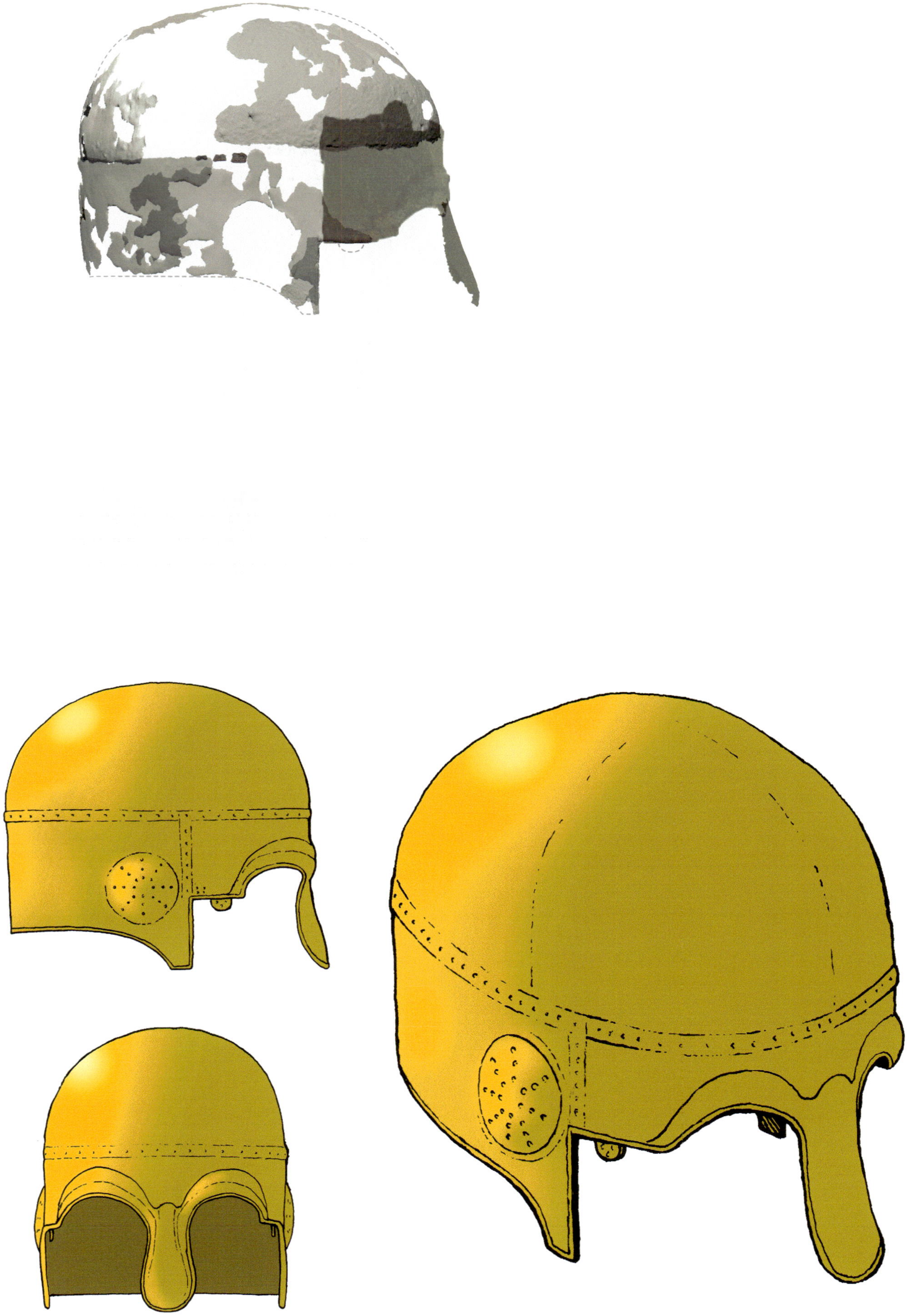

Figure 14.26 Digital reconstruction of the helmet by Craig Williams as detailed in Figure 14.25 (above). Simplified hypothetical reconstruction of the complete helmet, drawn by Craig Williams (below). It is not possible to accurately site the decorated fragments shown in Figures 14.29–30 and so they are not included here

Hinges

At the outer edges of the brow arches on each side of the helmet, a short, horizontal fitting bridges the gap between the brows and a vertical right angle where the helmet descends down towards the jaw. The placement of this vertical edge directly behind the brows suggests a closed-cap design, protecting ears, brow and temples.

The short horizontal element on either side of the brows is an articulated copper-alloy-clad iron hinge, with the copper alloy fixings in three parts (here labelled A, B and C, see **Fig. 14.28**), though on one side the component closest to the brow (C) is not present. Although traces of mineral-preserved leather do not survive, given the closed-cap design of the helmet, the function of the short hinges may simply be for a mobile chin strap. The central element (B) is a double layer of copper alloy sheet, in the shape of a half-moon or semi-circle (22mm in width, with a double thickness of 4mm), pierced by a single rivet. The gap between the two semi-circular sheets, allowing for an increase in volume through corrosion, represents the notional thickness of a missing material of approximately 2mm in thickness; most probably a pliable and strong leather. These semi-circular elements are currently positioned at right angles and facing inward on both sides of the helmet but are likely to be immobilised through corrosion rather than being in their original orientation.

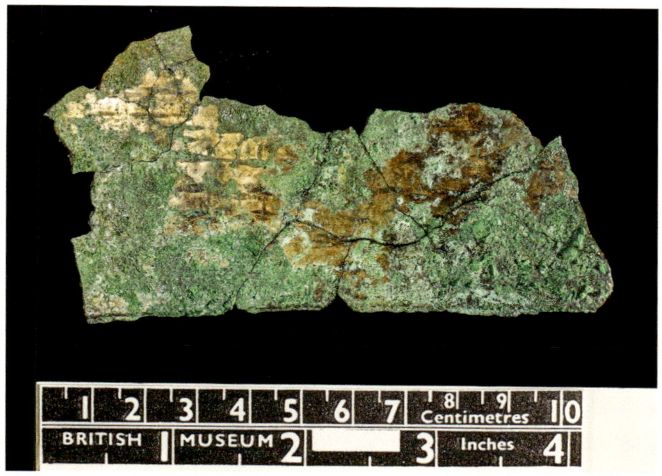

Figure 14.27 Manufacture hammer marks on inner surface of helmet

On either side of B are scallop-edged copper alloy sheet fittings (A and C), each riveted to the helmet body by either one or two flat-headed rivets. These scalloped fittings bridge the gaps between the central hinge and the brow on one side (C), and closed cap on the other (A), holding the iron hinge

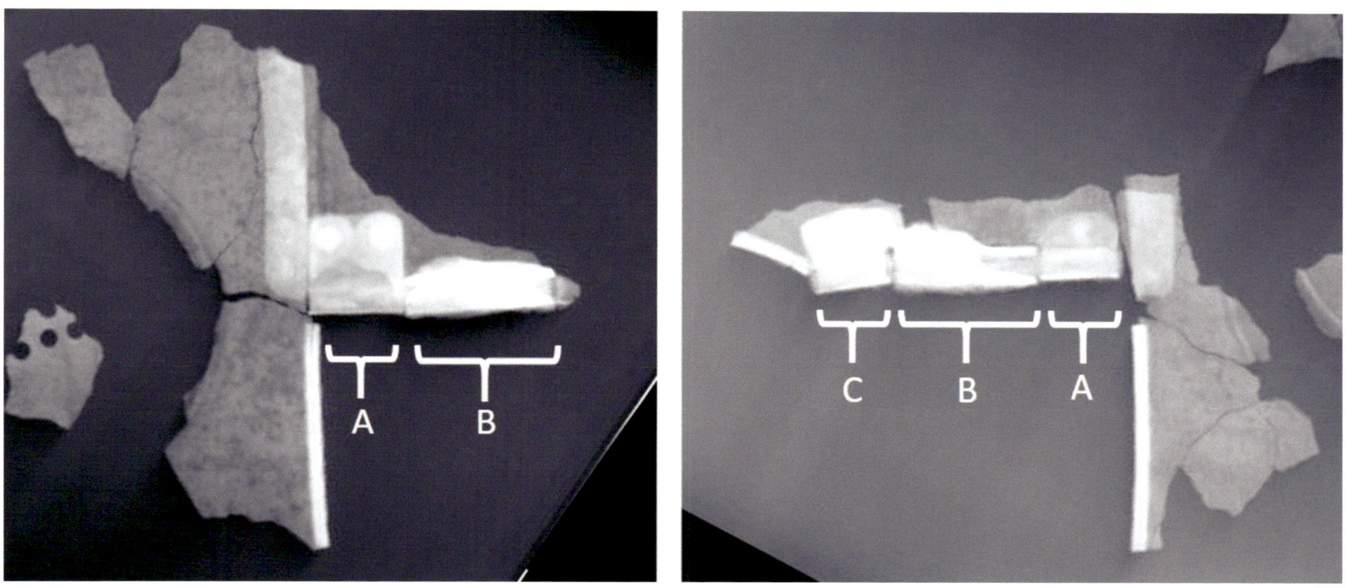

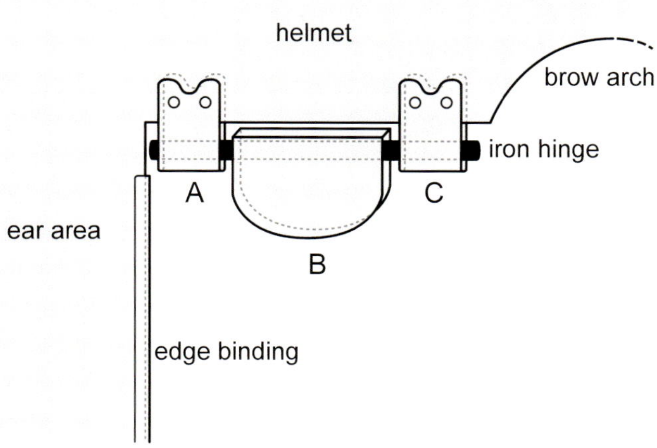

Figure 14.28 X-radiographs showing the hinge fittings in the cheek areas of the helmet (above, left and right); schematic drawing by Craig Williams showing a possible reconstruction of the hinge fitting (left). The central component (B) may have held a leather element such as a chin strap

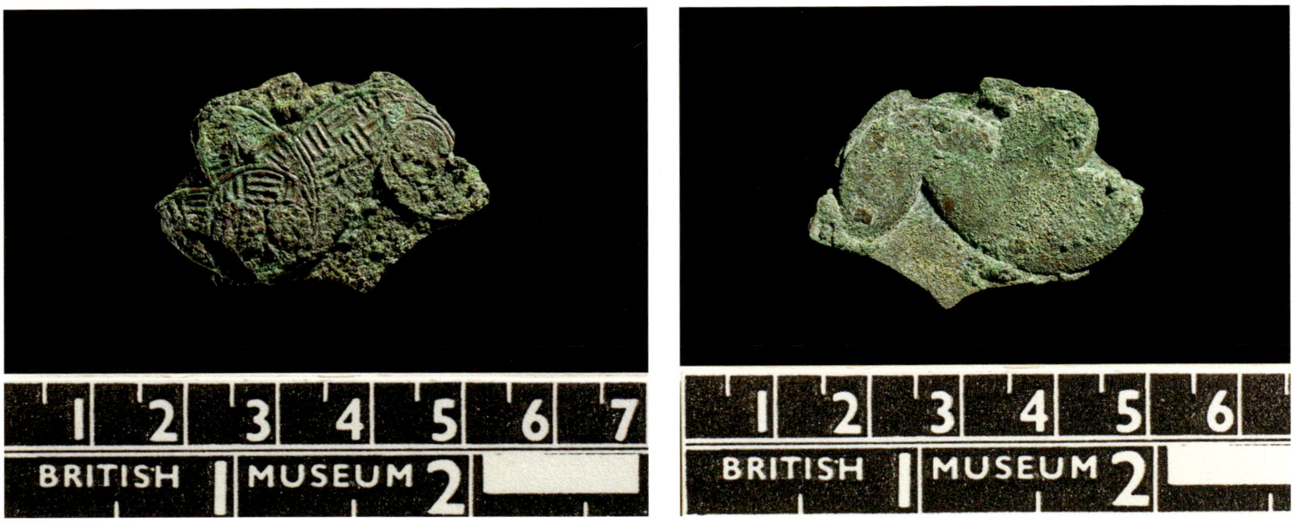

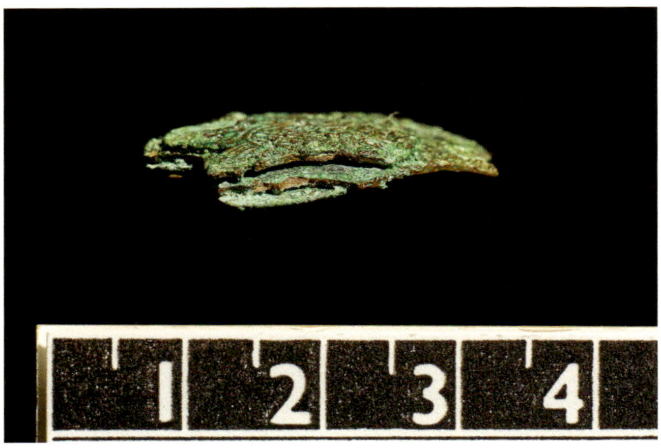

Figure 14.29 Front, back and side views of decorated patch from the helmet, showing the sandwiching of the helmet body fragment between a plain inner and decorated outer patch

in place. The riveting to the scalloped fittings is visible only in the X-radiography of this area (**Figs 14.24**, **14.28**). It is similar in appearance and size to the line of flat-headed rivets at brow level which secure the separate crown element.

Perforated ear areas

On opposing sides of the helmet, directly behind the vertical cheek edging, there are partially surviving areas of shallow circular repoussé, 50mm in diameter, with associated flat fragments, one of which joins to the feature and all of which are perforated with simple linear designs. A perforated area around the ears would enable the wearer to hear more clearly, while still offering more protection than the open ear form of helmet. The design of the perforations only partially survives but was clearly intended to be decorative, with simple patterns such as radiating lines which may have formed a star shape. Simple star-shaped perforated designs are also found on copper alloy sheet-metal vessels from the Iron Age, such as strainer bowls (see Stead 1967; Sealey 1999).

Decorative features and patches

Two copper alloy sheet fragments found in association with the helmet were decorated with curvilinear designs (see Ch. 21; **Figs 14.29–30**, **21.41**). X-radiography was particularly helpful in understanding these fragments.

The first (**Figs 14.29, 21.41a–b**) is a patch in the form of a lobed, S-shaped motif (see Ch. 21). This cannot be placed on the helmet reconstruction, but from the distinctive appearance of the corrosion it was clearly from the body of the helmet. Identically-shaped patches had been applied on either side of the sheet-metal body of the helmet, creating a triple-layer 'sandwich'. Examination of the digital X-radiograph shows that the appliqués had been placed over a pre-existent split in the thin metal of the helmet, and are therefore likely to be contemporaneous with manufacture. This kind of decorative repair as part of the manufacturing process is well attested in the Iron Age; for example, similar decorative patches were applied to defects in the copper alloy sheet sections of the Iron Age cauldrons from Chiseldon (Baldwin and Joy 2017, 37–64). The combined layers are 3mm in thickness, while the dimensions of the appliqués are 19 by 32mm. The the top layer of sheet (on the exterior of the helmet) was decorated with curvilinear designs delimited in so-called basket-weave hatching, while the opposing appliqué (on the inside of the helmet) was plain but copied its S-form. The patches were originally riveted neatly together through the helmet body at seven points, five of which still hold rivets. Not all of the fastening rivets on the corroded appliqué are visible to the naked eye, but they can be seen on the X-radiograph (see **Fig. 21.41a–b**).

The second piece of decorated copper alloy sheet (**Figs 14.30**, **21.41a–b**) is rectangular in plan with a shallow curve (63mm in length and 33.2mm in width). It is decorated with a repoussé reverse-S pattern with keeled roundel (see Ch. 21 for full discussion of decoration). One long edge is original; an incised line runs parallel to the surviving finished straight

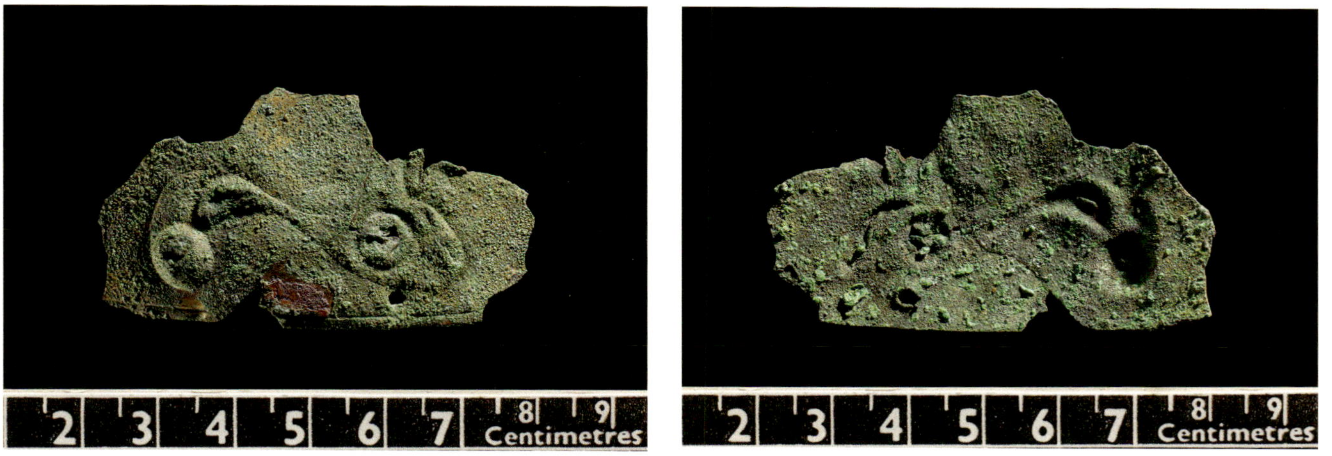

Figure 14.30 Front and back views of decorative sheet element, most likely from the helmet

edge. This edge is perforated in two areas along its length; one hole is undamaged and what is likely to be the siting for a second hole is torn across. No rivet fastenings survive in association with this fragment. The metal in this decorated fragment is of comparable width to the thinner areas of the helmet, typically just over 0.5mm, and its appearance is close but not identical. It is currently unplaced but may be a patch for the helmet or not directly associated with the object.

Crown construction

The body of the helmet curves gently towards a shallow, domed crown of thinner metal. The crown itself was made separately from the body, and riveted on. Running horizontally around the circumference of the helmet above the brow is an encircling overlap of sheet metal where these two components joined, secured with a line of small copper alloy disc-headed rivets. The helmet is fragmented around this circuit but most of the rivet overlap survives well. The crown, which would have been at the bottom of the hoard, was the most highly corroded area and survives only as multiple small fragments, some only a few millimetres in diameter. For this reason, its original appearance is currently unresolved. One fragment appears to show a shallow curvature at its broken edge which may be evidence for a missing addition such as a knop or other fitting; its placing within any restoration of the crown will be critical for its understanding.

Rivet fastenings and the helmet lining

Two separate rivets (not associated with double sheet fixings such as those seen around the crown) were recovered with the helmet. The first has a square head 8mm in width and has not as yet been located within the reconstruction. A fragment of corroded copper alloy sheet (1.8mm across) preserved at the top of the shank may be the remains of a retaining washer or associated with the helmet wall. Fibrous material preserved on the shank of this rivet suggests leather 2.5mm in thickness. If not from the helmet lining (see below), it is possibly part of a lost chin fastening.

The second rivet (**Fig. 14.31**) has a separate shank sleeve and circular disc head 8mm in diameter and can be securely placed by joins to the inner centre-back of the helmet. As it now protrudes from the surface into the interior of the helmet it would have certainly originally secured a liner with a thickness equivalent to the height of the shank of 2mm. Fibrous mineral-preserved organic remains were also present in the internal recessed surfaces of the circular repoussé areas around the ears, suggesting that a cap was present which extended to the temples and protected the ears. It is unlikely its inclusion to the light framework of the Snettisham helmet would afford significant additional protection to the head: the function suggested here is as a soft, padded liner. The fibrous mineralised material preserved in both areas by the agency of the copper alloy is characteristically turquoise in colour and under magnification resembles skin product or leather. Mineral-preserved fibres on the rivet shank were examined under magnification using a Kyowa binocular microscope. Structures closely resembling the fibre bundle structure from the corium of leather or skin product were noted. (Identification and interpretation were carried out in accordance with criteria set out by the Archaeological Leather Group (ALG) and using Leather Conservation Centre (LCC) samples and standards). The liner may have been exclusively of leather or skin product. If it was padded, woven textile does not seem to have been used, since no woven structures were noted. However, padded liners utilising a non-woven felted material remain a possibility. Scanning electron microscopy of the rivet and its degraded mineralised remains may resolve the suggested identification.

Parallels and date range

The Snettisham helmet has no exact parallels, and so cannot be closely dated stylistically. The latest datable objects from Hoard F are Gallo-Belgic coins minted 100–60 BC (Ch. 15), although some of the torcs may have been much older (Chs 8, 20 and 23). Stylistically, the decoration on the helmet is not dissimilar to other objects from Snettisham, but again this style is not closely datable (Ch. 21); objects with similar decoration are known from contexts spanning from the 3rd century BC to the 1st century AD.

Very few helmets are known from Iron Age Britain, and almost all are unusual in some way. If headdresses composed of bronze bands (such as the example from Mill Hill, Deal, Kent, see Stead 1995b) and other (probably ceremonial)

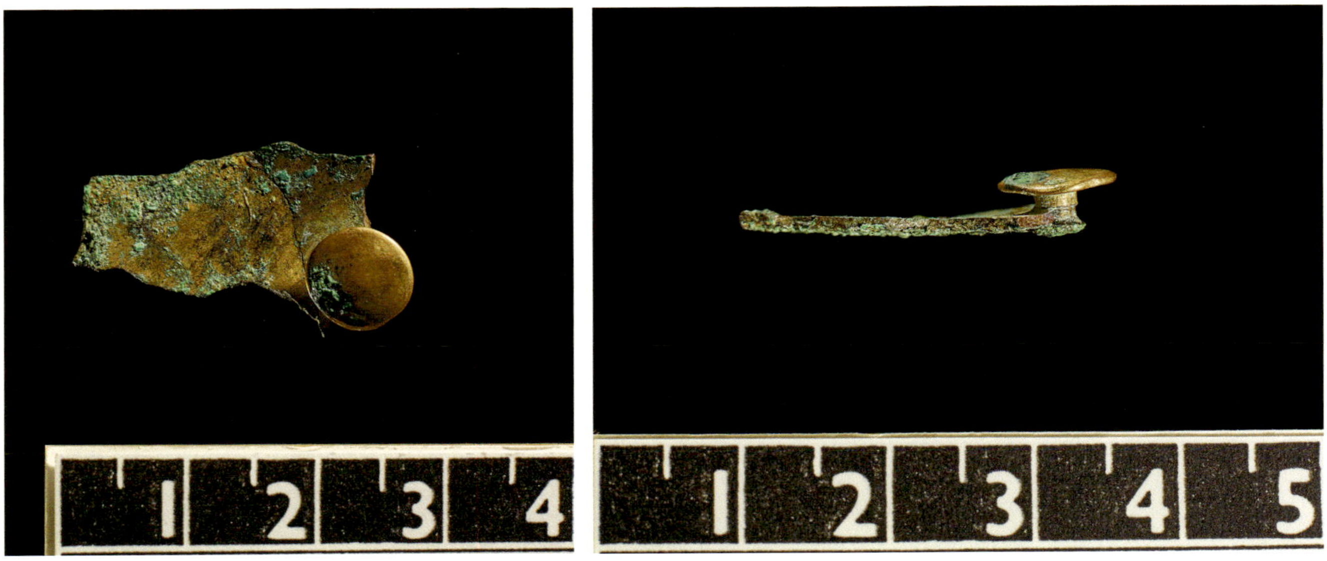

Figure 14.31 Side and front views of fragment from centre back of the helmet, pierced by a rivet

helmet-like headdresses identified by Stead (*ibid.*, 83–4; e.g. the find from Cerrig-y-Drudion, Conwy) are excluded, only three Late Iron Age helmets potentially contemporary with the Snettisham find are known from Britain. One is the unique horned helmet dredged from the Thames near Waterloo in central London (Jope 2000, 255; BM 1988,1004.1), which exhibits similar repoussé decorative elements to that seen on the decorated fragment from Snettisham (**Fig. 14.30**), stylistically dated to the 2nd or 1st centuries BC. There are also two 1st-century BC type helmets from Britain: one from a cremation burial at Bridge, near Canterbury, Kent (Farley *et al.* 2014) and one from an inhumation burial in North Bersted, Sussex (Taylor *et al.* 2014). The latter was ornamented with a spectacular openwork crest, decorated with La Tène-style motifs.

In this context, it is perhaps not surprising that the Snettisham helmet also seems to be unique. Unlike the helmets from Bridge and North Bersted, it does not fit into the standard array of continental forms, which are generally of simple bowl form with or without a neck-guard and knop, plume or ring as a central feature rising from the crown (Bottini 1988, 316; Brailsford 1975a; Feugère 1994; Pernet 2010). The nasal and brow ridges bear a superficial similarity to Chalcidian helmets (Bottini 1988, 137–50) and Corinthian-style helmets (Bottini 1988, 65–106). The former were in use in the Mediterranean world, particularly Greece and southern Italy, from the 5th to 4th centuries BC, and the latter from the 8th to 5th/4th centuries BC, although use and knowledge of the style may have persisted later, as attested by the appearance of a figure (perhaps Mars) wearing a similar helmet on the late 2nd-century BC 'Domitius Ahenobarbus relief' from Rome, now in the Louvre (see Bonanno 1976, 7–11). Nonetheless, the Snettisham helmet is distinct in form from both of these archaic and classical helmet types. It has a broader nasal than the Chalcidian helmet, and lacks the hinged cheekpieces and open ear areas of this style. Although having a closed-cap design which protects the ears and neck, it similarly lacks the closed, forward-reaching cheekpieces of the Corinthian-style helmet. Its two-part construction (with separate crown) is also unusual. With so few known helmets from Late Iron Age Britain, it is hard to say if unique examples like the Waterloo and Snettisham helmets are rare survivals from well-established traditions, or were designed and executed as one-off, singular pieces that would have marked the wearers out, perhaps both on the battlefield and in their communities. The fact that the helmet seems to have been deposited incomplete suggests that it may have been of some age by the time it was buried.

Hoard G (upper pit)

Recovered during the BM 1990 excavations. All finds from the upper Hoard G pit unless otherwise stated.

G.1: Gold/silver alloy torc (Pl. 14.40)
MSCC: (4P)R
BM: 1991,0407.1; Site code: SN/AQ
Gold/silver alloy torc with Stage II neck-ring formed from four circular-section wires plied together. Simple teardrop-shaped cast-on ring terminals, each extending into two pairs of wires which form the four neck-ring strands.
Wt: 101.2g; D(ext): 156.0mm; D(nr): 6.5mm; D(wire): 4.0mm; D(term): 21.2mm

G.2: Copper alloy torc (Pl. 14.40)
MSCC: (6C)T
BM: 1990,1101.23; Site code: SN/BP; SN/CD; SN/CE; SN/CF; SN/CG
Fragments of copper alloy multi-strand torc, comprising parts of the neck-ring, heavily fragmented, and one simple buffer terminal with a plain face and incised cordon around the edge. Many additional unjoined wire fragments. Originally the Stage II neck-ring was formed from six twisted wires coiled around a hollow core. Much of the damage is post-depositional, caused by animal burrowing. However, not all of the torc was recovered (one terminal is missing), so it is most likely that the torc was incomplete when it entered the ground.
Wt: 47.8g; D(nr): 13.8mm; D(wire): 2.0mm; D(term): 9.5mm

G.1

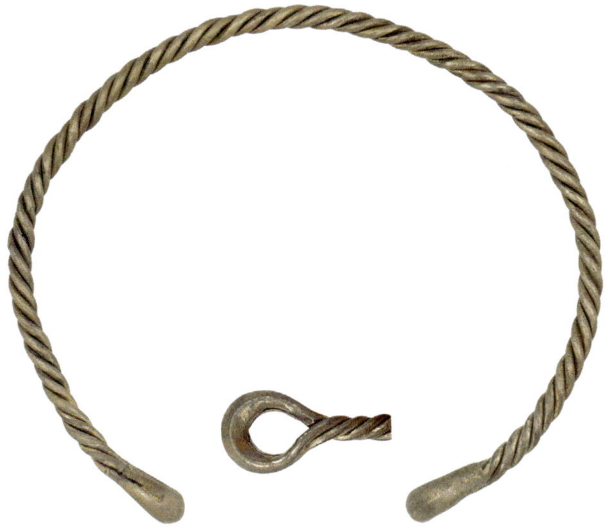

G.2

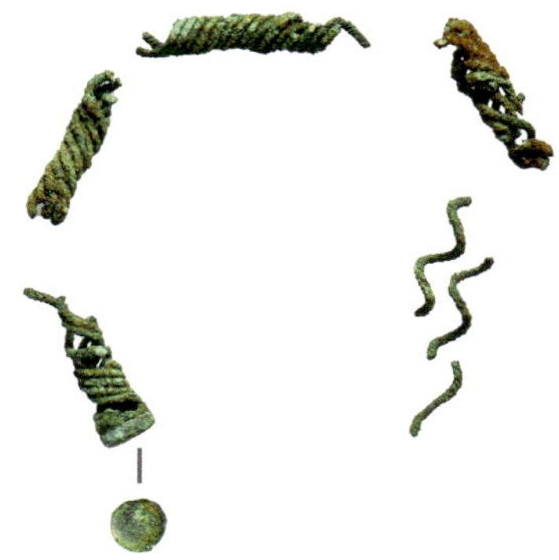

G.3

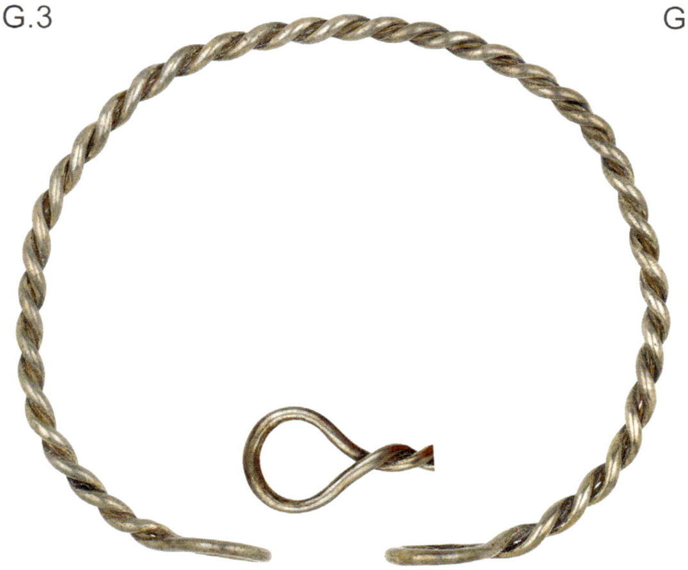

G.4

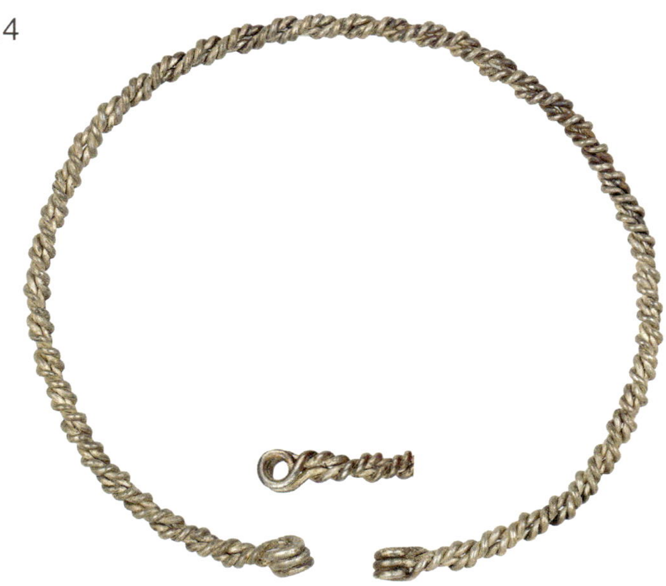

0 5 10cm

Plate 14.40

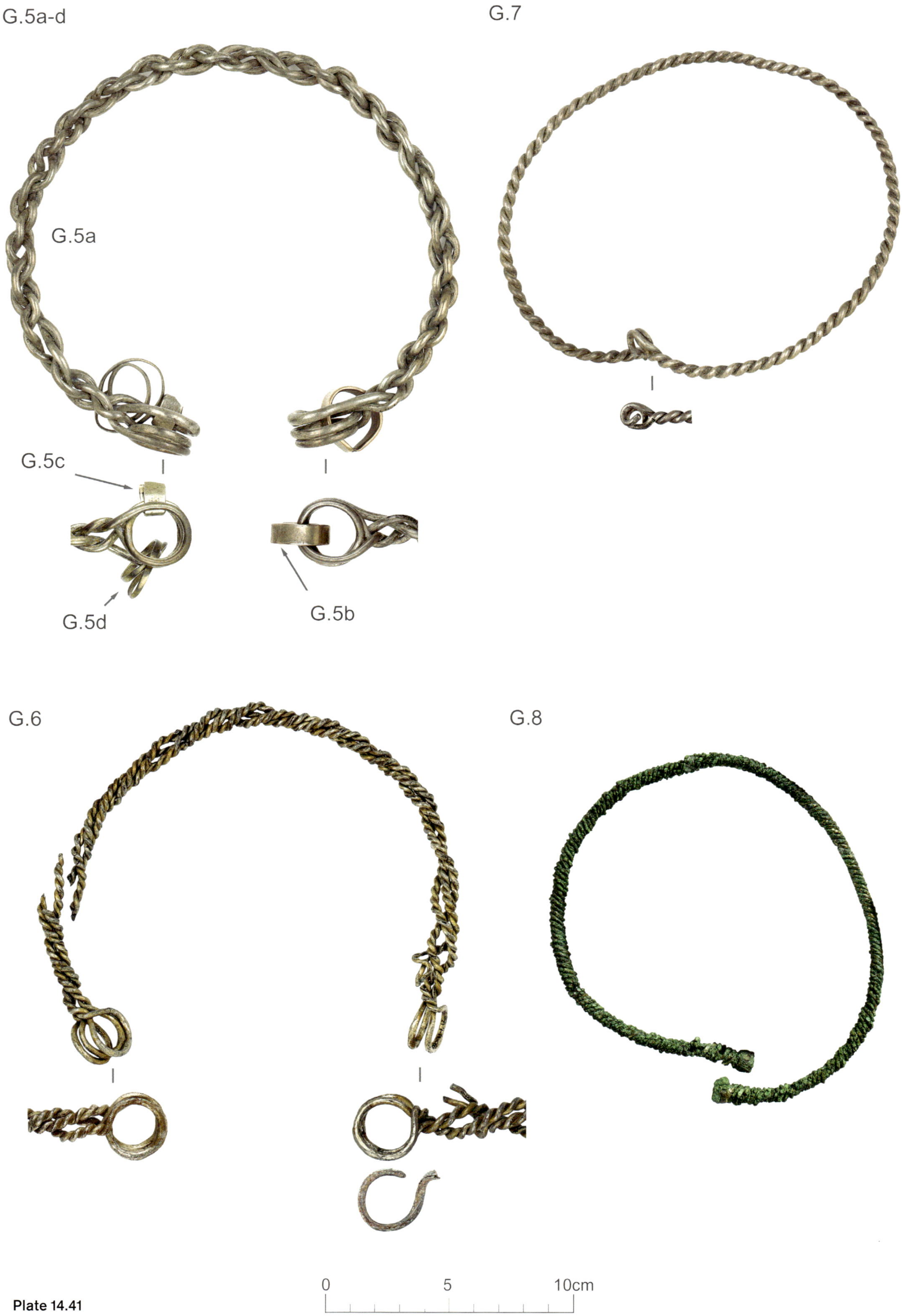

Plate 14.41

G.?2: Copper alloy torc (Pl. 14.40)
MSCC: ?(6C)T
BM: 1990,1101.24; Site code: SN/BO; SN/BQ; SN/CW; SN/DB; SN/DD; SN/DF; SN/DL; SN/DQ; SN/DT(ii); SN/FC; SN/FG; SN/GE; SN/GG; SN/JG
Context details: Found loose around top level of Hoard G, and in Hoard G upper pit.
Fragments of copper alloy twisted wire, each broken at both ends and coiled. Originally part of a coiled multi-strand torc neck-ring.
Not pictured.
Most likely part of torc G.2

G.3: Gold/silver alloy torc (Pl. 14.40)
MSCC: (2P)R
BM: 1991,0407.2; Site code: SN/CH
Gold/silver alloy multi-strand torc, with single-loop terminals and Stage II neck-ring of two circular-section wires plied together. Each terminal is a continuous loop, extending to form the two neck-ring wires. On one terminal, a soldered seam is visible in the interior where the wire ends must originally have joined.
Wt: 121.8g; D(ext): 170.0mm; D(nr): 7.5mm; D(wire): 3.8mm; D(term): 27.8mm

G.4: Gold/silver alloy torc (Pl. 14.40)
MSCC: (2P(2P))R
BM: 1991,0407.3; Site code: SN/CI
Gold/silver alloy multi-strand torc with small triple-loop terminals and Stage III neck-ring. The cable is formed from two ropes plied together, each of which is made up of two circular-section wires which are themselves plied together. The terminals are formed from the ends of the neck-ring wires: on each side, one of the ropes forms a continuous single loop, while the other forms a continuous double loop. Soldered areas obscure the joins of the wire ends.
Wt: 89.5g; D(ext): 167.0mm; D(nr): 7.3mm; D(rope): 3.8mm; D(wire): 2.1mm; D(term): 10.3mm

G.5a–d: Composite group (interlinked) (Pl. 14.41)
BM: 1991,0407.4; Site code: SN/CK
Ring G.5b is looped through one of the terminals of torc G.5a. Rings G.5c and G.5d are looped through the other terminal.
Wt: 233.1g (total for G.5a–d)

G.5a: Gold/silver alloy torc
MSCC: (2PZ(2P))R
Gold/silver alloy multi-strand torc with triple-loop terminals and Stage III neck-ring. The cable is formed from two ropes plied together Z-twist, each of which is made up of two circular-section wires which are themselves plied together. The terminals are formed from the ends of the neck-ring wires: on each side, one of the ropes forms a continuous single loop, while the other forms a continuous double loop. Soldered areas obscure the joins of the wire ends.
D(ext): 183.0mm; D(nr): 12.3mm; D(rope): 6.8mm; D(wire): 3.5mm; D(term): 27.8mm

G.5b: Gold/silver alloy small ring
Gold/silver alloy small ring with flat, abutting terminals. Made from a strip with rectangular cross-section.
D(ext): 24.6mm

G.5c: Gold/silver alloy small ring
Fragment of gold/silver alloy small ring made from a strip with rectangular cross-section. The cut ends are pinched together, giving the fragment a teardrop shape.
L: 16.5mm

G.5d: Gold/silver alloy small ring
Complete gold/silver alloy small spiral ring with rounded ends, made from a narrow strip with sub-rectangular cross-section.
D(ext): 33.8mm

G.6: Copper alloy torc (Pl. 14.41)
MSCC: (3P(2P))R
BM: 1990,1101.12; 1990,1101.14; Site code: SN/CL; SN/BR
[Analysed: see Ch. 17]
Silvered and gilded copper alloy multi-strand torc with triple-loop terminals and Stage III neck-ring. The surface treatment of this torc is very unusual (see Ch. 17, **Fig. 17.51b**). The cable is formed from three ropes plied together, each of which is made up of two circular-section wires which are themselves plied together. The terminals are formed from the ends of the neck-ring wires: on each side, each of the three ropes forms a continuous single loop. Soldered areas obscure the joins of the wire ends. Previously restored from fragments. One loop terminal remains separate.
Wt: 102.6g; D(ext): 170.0mm; D(nr): 17.8mm; D(rope): 5.9mm; D(wire): 3.1mm; D(term): 38.0mm

G.7: Gold/silver alloy torc (Pl. 14.41)
MSCC: (2P)R
BM: 1991,0407.5; Site code: SN/CM
Near-complete gold/silver alloy multi-strand torc, with one (slightly distorted) double-loop terminal and neck-ring. The other terminal appears to have been deliberately broken off. Stage II construction of two circular-section wires plied together. The remaining terminal has two open loops, each formed by the ends of one of the neck-ring wires.
Wt: 67.8g; D(ext): 162.0mm; D(nr): 5.2mm; D(wire): 2.9mm; D(term): 11.0mm

G.8: Copper alloy torc (Pl. 14.41)
MSCC: (4C)2T+2R
BM: 1990,1101.16; Site code: SN/CN
Gilded copper alloy multi-strand torc, heavily corroded, with overlapping buffer terminals with flat faces and rounded edges. Stage II neck-ring of four wires coiled together, alternating twisted and circular-section wires. Previously restored from fragments.
D(ext): 147.0mm; D(nr): 7.0mm; D(wire): 2.0mm; D(term): 10.0mm

G.9: Gold/silver alloy torc (Pl. 14.42)
MSCC: (2P)R
BM: 1991,0407.6; Site code: SN/CO
Gold/silver alloy multi-strand torc, with Stage II neck-ring formed of two circular-section wires plied together. The

G.9

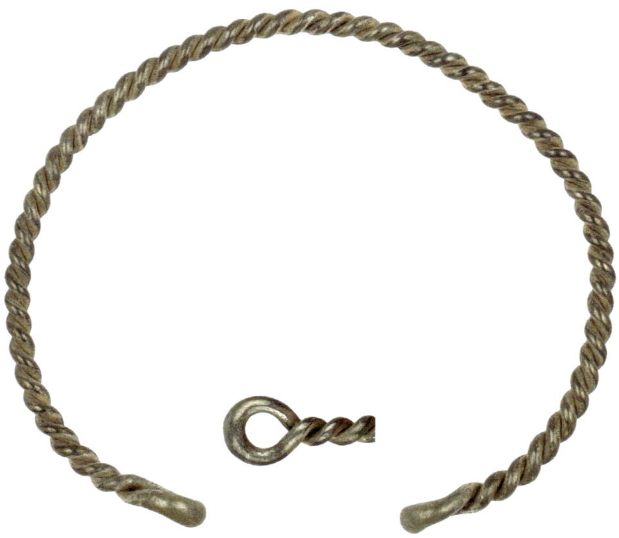

G.12

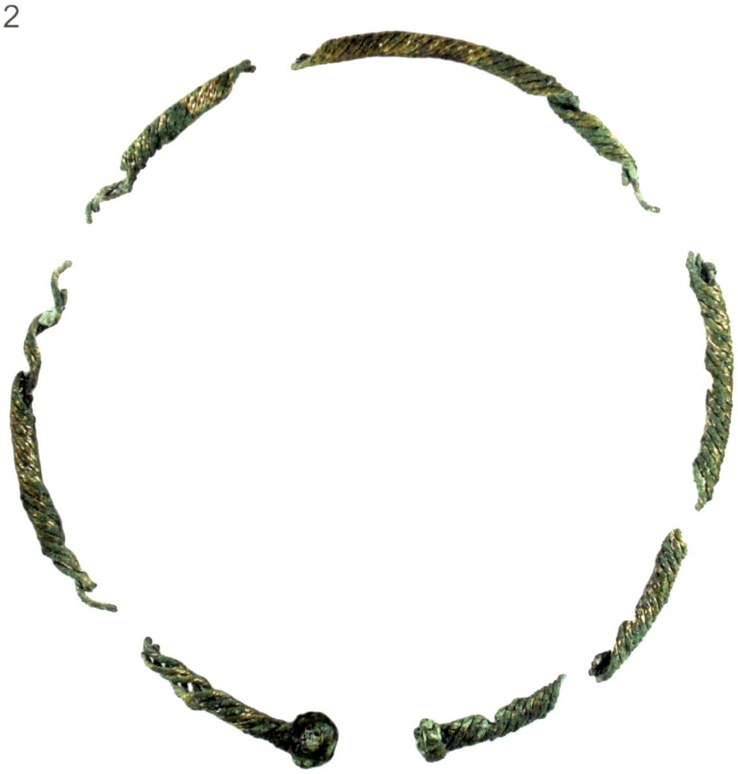

G.10

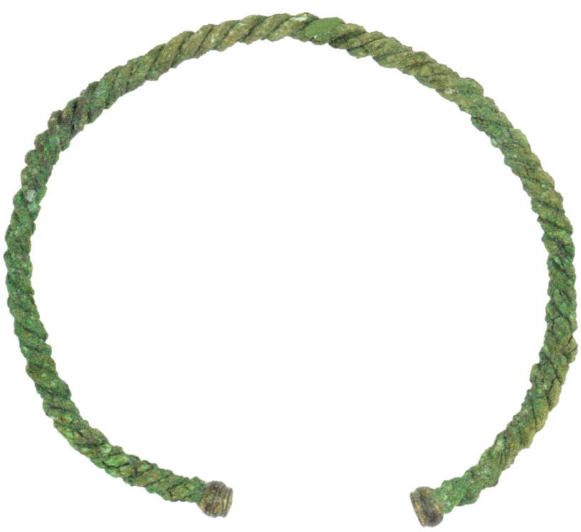

G.11

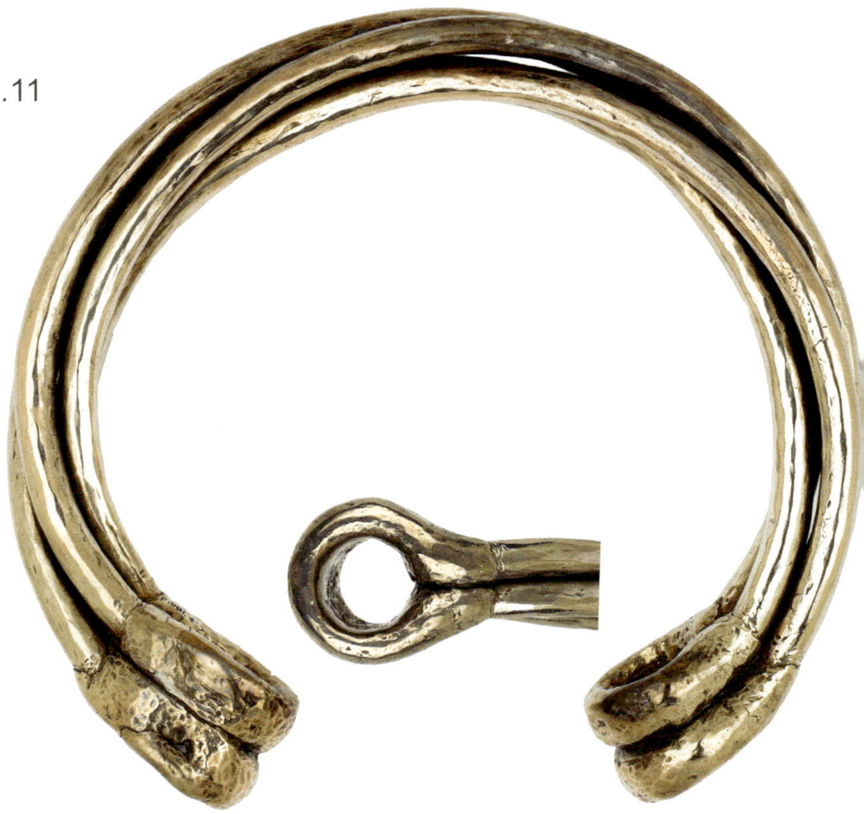

0 5 10cm

Plate 14.42

G.13

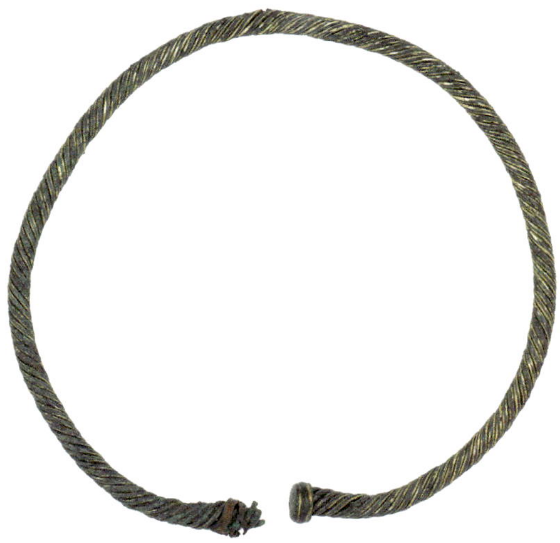

G.14

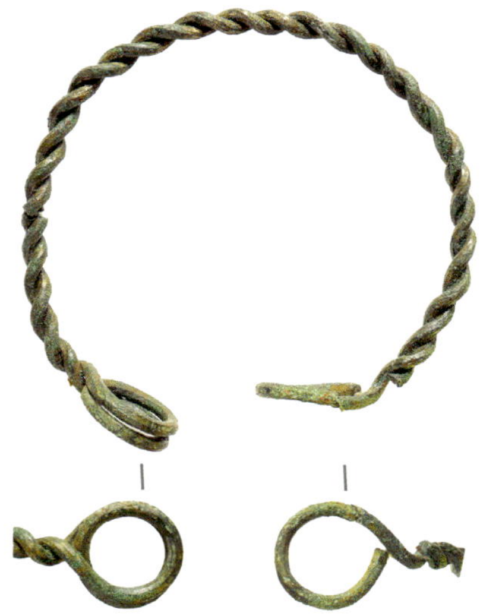

G.15

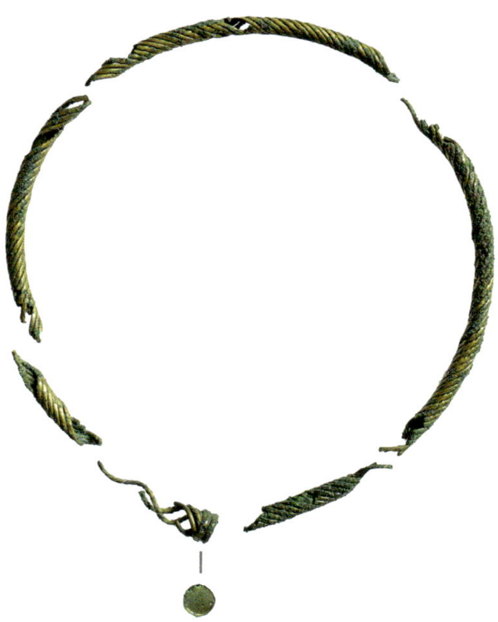

G.16

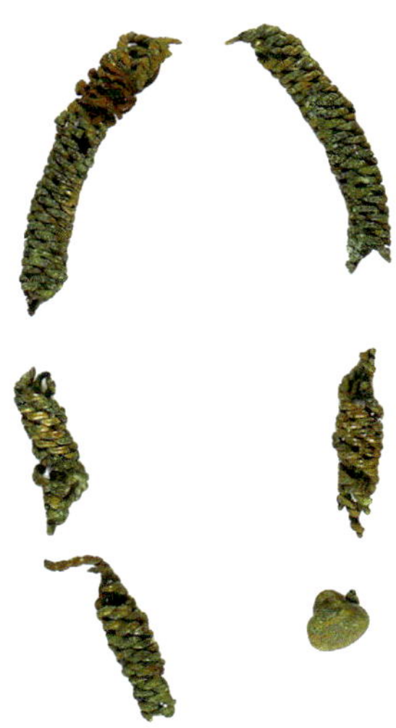

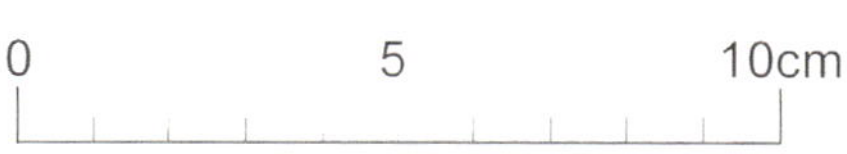

Plate 14.43

slightly thickened ring terminals are continuous loops formed from the ends of the neck-ring wires.
Wt: 110.9g; D(ext): 160.0mm; D(nr): 6.8mm; D(wire): 3.6mm; D(term): 18.6mm

G.10: Copper alloy torc (Pl. 14.42)
MSCC: (3C)R
BM: 1990,1101.17; Site code: SN/CP
Gilded copper alloy multi-strand torc, heavily corroded. Simple buffer terminals (of a different alloy and better preserved than the neck-ring) have rounded edges and projecting flat ends with cordon around the edge, giving a thistle-like shape. Stage II neck-ring of three circular-section wires coiled together. Previously restored from fragments.
D(ext): 136.6mm; D(nr): 7.9mm; D(wire): 3.5mm; D(term): 9.3mm

Hoard G (lower pit)

Recovered during the BM 1990 excavations. All finds from the lower Hoard G pit unless otherwise stated.

G.11: Gold/silver alloy torc (Pl. 14.42)
MSCC: (4P)R
BM: 1991,0407.7; Site code: SN/EA
Gold/silver alloy massive multi-strand torc. Stage II neck-ring made from four rods, plied around each other. They are only very slightly loosely plied, with each strand passing under or over the others only once. The bars are roughly finished with no attempt to remove hammer marks etc. The simple ring terminals are crudely formed, their surfaces covered with dents and imperfections, and very obvious joins where they have been cast onto the neck-ring. One terminal has an addition on the inside and at one edge. These could be from the wax model stage, but are more likely areas of additional metal which have been added to fix a flaw in the casting. On the outside, each terminal has the appearance of two adjoining loops with their ends meeting the four neck-ring wires, but there is no division inside the eye of the terminal; each is a single moulding.
Wt: 2395.0g; D(ext): 225.0mm; D(nr): 25.9mm; D(wire): 10.3mm; D(term): 44.2mm

G.12: Copper alloy torc (Pl. 14.42)
MSCC: (6C)T
BM: 1990,1101.19; Site code: SN/DW; SN/DY; SN/DZ; SN/FD; SN/FL; SN/FT; SN/GF
Copper alloy gilded multi-strand torc, heavily corroded, with simple buffer terminals, one very poorly preserved. Stage II neck-ring of six twisted wires coiled together. Previously restored from fragments, now in seven main parts with many additional loose fragments.
D(nr): 6.0mm; D(wire): 2.0mm; D(term): 13.0mm

G.13: Copper alloy torc (Pl. 14.43)
MSCC: (7C)Q
BM: 1990,1101.1; Site code: SN/FO
Copper alloy multi-strand torc, possibly gilded, with Stage II neck-ring formed from seven flat/rectangular-section wires coiled together. One simple buffer terminal, with slightly convex face and raised inner and outer cordons, survives. The other end of the neck-ring is bound with a strand of organic material, possibly used as a repair to secure the wires in place of the missing terminal. The torc is slightly distorted at the back where one of the strands is broken.
Wt: 52.1g; D(ext): 133.3mm; D(nr): 5.6mm; D(wire): 1.8mm; D(term): 10.1mm

G.14: Copper alloy small torc (Pl. 14.43)
MSCC: (2PZ)F
BM: 1990,1101.25; Site code: SN/DX; SN/GH
Near-complete copper alloy small multi-strand torc, with double-loop terminals, one of which is missing a loop (see **Fig. 20.33**). Stage II neck-ring of two faceted wires plied together Z-twist. The complete terminal is a continuous double-loop, extending into the neck-ring wires. Previously re-joined from fragments; the missing terminal loop could be due to post-depositional disturbance.
Wt: 47.0g; D(ext): 102.4mm; D(nr): 6.3mm; D(wire): 2.9mm; D(term): 22.9mm

G.?14: Copper alloy torc (Pl. 14.43)
MSCC: ?
BM: 1990,1101.26; Site code: SN/FO(ii)
Tiny fragments of copper alloy, heavily corroded.
Possibly part of the missing terminal from torc G.14, or one of the more heavily corroded torcs from the upper pit of Hoard G.
Not pictured
Wt: 0.7g

G.15: Copper alloy torc (Pl. 14.43)
MSCC: (8C)4T+4Q
BM: 1990,1101.27; Site code: SN/FU; SN/FW(i)
Copper alloy multi-strand torc with Stage II neck-ring formed from eight wires coiled together. Four of the wires (all adjoining) are flat/rectangular in section, and the other four are twisted. One simple buffer terminal with flat face and grooved cordon remains. The torc is heavily fragmented, largely due to post-depositional disturbance, but the fact that only one terminal has been recovered suggests that it could have been incomplete when it was deposited.
Wt: 27.0g; D(nr): 5.0mm; D(wire): 1.2mm; D(term): 8.3mm

G.?12/15: Copper alloy torc (Pl. 14.43)
BM: 1990,1101.28; Site code: SN/BS; SN/BT; SN/BV; SN/CD(ii); SN/CJ; SN/CX; SN/CY; SN/CZ; SN/DG; SN/DJ; SN/DK; SN/DN; SN/DP; SN/DU(i); SN/DV(i); SN/FB; SN/FH; SN/FI; SN/FM; SN/FN; SN/FV; SN/FW(ii); SN/GB; SN/GC; SN/HF
Context details: Found loose around and within Hoard G pit.
Fragments of copper alloy coiled twisted and square-section wire, all short sections, broken at both ends. Originally part of a coiled multi-strand torc neck-ring.
Most likely part of either torc G.12 or G.15.
Not pictured.

G.16: Copper alloy torc (Pl. 14.43)
MSCC: (5C(2P))R
BM: 1990,1101.29; Site code: SN/DA; SN/FX; SN/GU; SN/HB; SN/HC
[Analysed: see Ch. 19]
Fragmented copper alloy multi-strand torc with one

remaining simple buffer terminal with flat face. Stage III neck-ring of five coiled ropes, each of which is made up of two circular-section wires plied together. One of the neck-ring fragments has been bound with an organic string, perhaps a repair, identified as lime bast fibres (see Ch. 19, **Fig. 19.2**). The terminal is broken off from the torc to reveal a 'plug' which projected into the neck-ring and stubs of some of the neck-ring wires, showing that the terminal was cast on. The torc is heavily fragmented, with many unjoined fragments from throughout the lower half of the lower Hoard G pit: the terminal was below G.11, some of the strands about the level of G.17–G.20 and others in areas of disturbance (likely animal burrows) at the side of the pit. This fragmentation and scattering is most likely mainly due to post-depositional disturbance, but the torc was probably incomplete when it entered the ground.
Wt: 16.7g; D(nr): 8.2mm; D(rope): 2.0mm; D(wire): 1.0mm; D(term): 11.8mm

G.?16: Copper alloy torc (Pl. 14.43)
MSCC: (?5C(2P))R
BM: 1990,1101.13; Site code: SN/BU; SN/CL; SN/DI; SN/DS; SN/DT(i); SN/DU(ii); SN/DV(ii); SN/GI
Context details: Found loose around and within Hoard G pit.
Fragments of copper alloy circular-section wire, all short sections, broken at both ends. Curved in a way which suggests they were originally part of a plied and coiled Stage III construction in a multi-strand torc neck-ring.
Very likely part of torc G.16.
Not pictured

G.17: Gold/silver alloy large ring (Pl. 14.44)
BM: 1991,0407.8; Site code: SN/GQ
Complete gold/silver alloy large ring with overlapping, tapered terminals. Made from a strip with rectangular cross-section.
Wt: 108.0g; D(ext): 108.4mm; W: 11.5mm; T: 4.2mm

G.18: Gold/silver alloy large ring (Pl. 14.44)
BM: 1991,0407.9; Site code: SN/GR
Complete gold/silver alloy large ring with overlapping, tapered terminals. Made from a strip with rectangular cross-section.
Wt: 64.8g; D(ext): 104.8mm; W: 7.0mm; T: 3.4mm

G.19: Gold/silver alloy large ring (Pl. 14.44)
BM: 1991,0407.10; Site code: SN/GS
Gold/silver alloy large penannular ring made from a strip with rectangular cross-section. One terminal is flat and hardly tapering, the other tapers sharply, almost to a point.
Wt: 93.0g; D(ext): 93.2mm; W: 8.7mm; T: 4.5mm

G.20: Copper alloy large ring (Pl. 14.44)
BM: 1990,1101.2; Site code: SN/GT
Complete copper alloy large ring with flat, abutting terminals. Made from a strip with rectangular cross-section.
Wt: 49.2g; D(ext): 93.6mm; W: 7.8mm; T: 2.4mm

Hoard H (upper pit)

Recovered during the BM 1990 excavations. All finds from the upper Hoard H pit.

H.1: Copper alloy torc (Pl. 14.45)
MSCC: (6C)?R
BM: 1990,1101.18; Site code: SN/AW; SN/CR
Copper alloy multi-strand torc, heavily corroded, with simple flat buffer terminals with slightly rounded edges and Stage II neck-ring of six ?circular-section wires coiled together. Broken into three pieces when found, the damage perhaps due to large pieces of carrstone in the filling of the pit. Two of the fragments are now re-joined. Many additional unjoined fragments.
Wt: 121.2g; D(ext): 145.0mm; D(nr): 10.0mm; D(wire): 2.5mm; D(term): 14.5mm

H.2a–b: Composite group (plied/twisted) (Pl. 14.45)
BM: 1991,0407.11; Site code: SN/CS
Torcs H.2a and H.2b are plied/twisted together to make a composite torc.
Wt: 240.0g (total for H.2a and H.2b)

H.2a: Gold/silver alloy torc
MSCC: (2PZ(2P))R
Gold/silver alloy multi-strand torc with triple-loop terminals and Stage III neck-ring. The cable is formed from two ropes plied together Z-twist; each rope is made up of two circular-section wires which are themselves plied together. The terminals are formed from the ends of the neck-ring wires: on each side, one of the ropes forms a continuous single loop, while the other forms a continuous double loop. Soldered areas obscure the joins of the wire ends.
D(ext): 174.0mm; D(nr): 12.3mm; D(rope): 7.0mm; D(wire): 2.8mm; D(term): 23.2mm

H.2b: Gold/silver alloy torc
MSCC: (2P)R
Gold/silver alloy torc with Stage II neck-ring formed from two circular-section wires plied together. Simple thickened ring terminals, each a continuous ring extending into the two neck-ring strands.
D(ext): 174.0mm; D(nr): 8.6mm; D(wire): 3.8mm; D(term): 18.0mm

H.3: Gold/silver alloy torc (Pl. 14.45)
MSCC: (2P)R
BM: 1991,0407.12; Site code: SN/CT
Gold/silver alloy multi-strand torc with hook terminals and Stage II neck-ring of two circular-section wires plied very loosely together (see **Fig. 20.13**). At each terminal, one neck-ring wire ends sharply, while the other continues into a hook. The hooks have been hammered flat. The torc may be complete as it stands, though it is the only example of this terminal type. Alternatively, it may originally have had complete loop terminals, or it may be an incomplete ring terminal torc, where the additional metal has not yet been cast on.
Wt: 97.3g; D(ext): 157.0mm; D(nr): 8.4mm; D(wire): 4.2mm

G.17

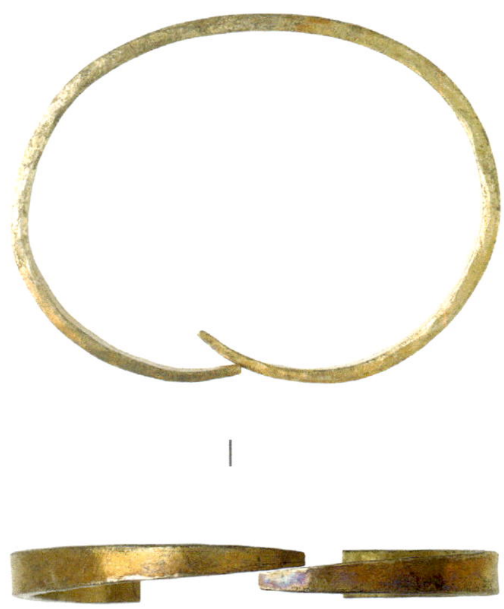

G.18

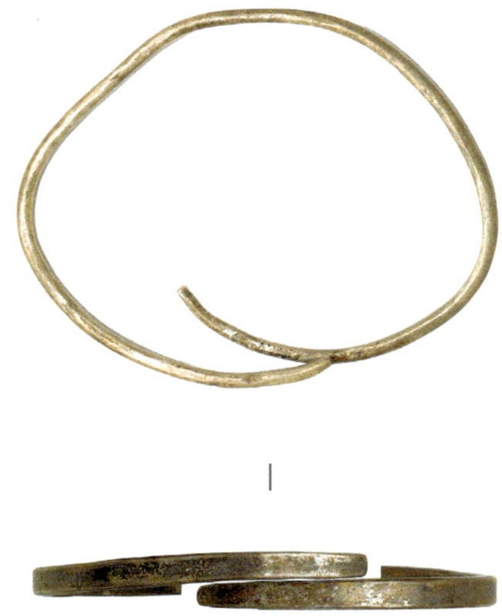

G.19

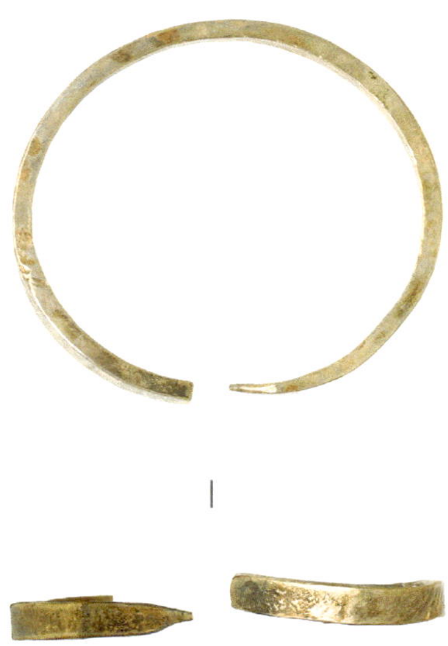

G.20

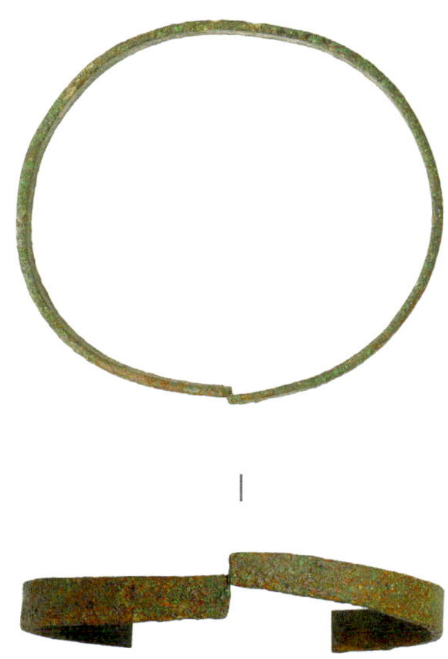

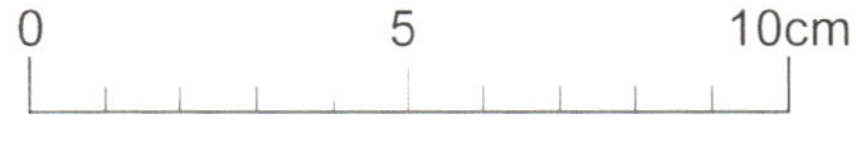

Plate 14.44

H.1

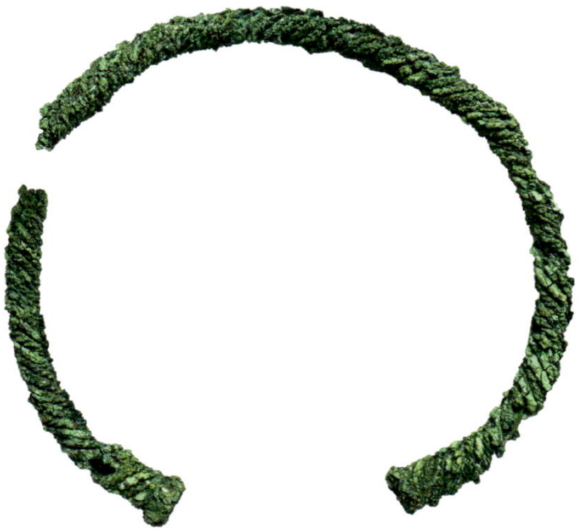

H.2a-b

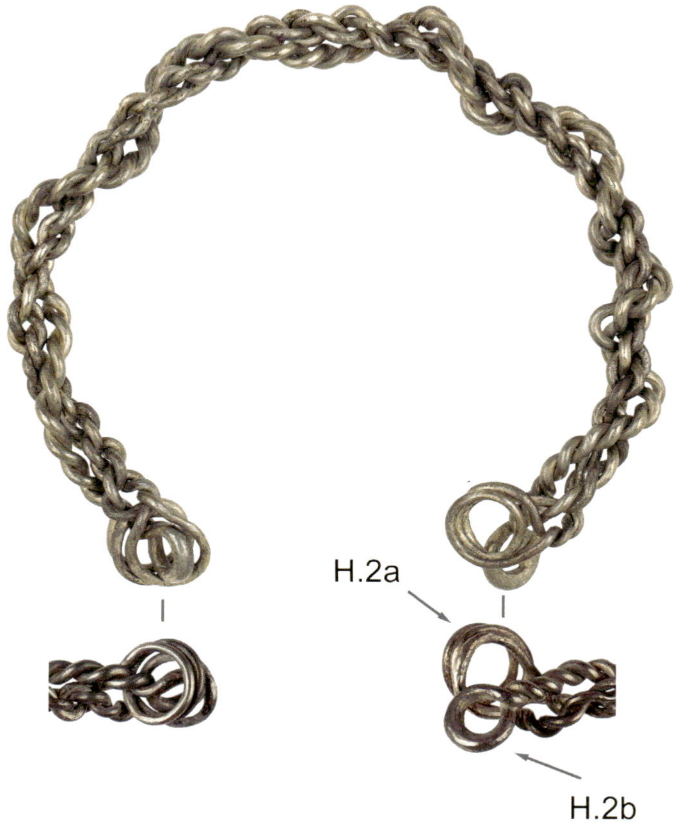

H.3

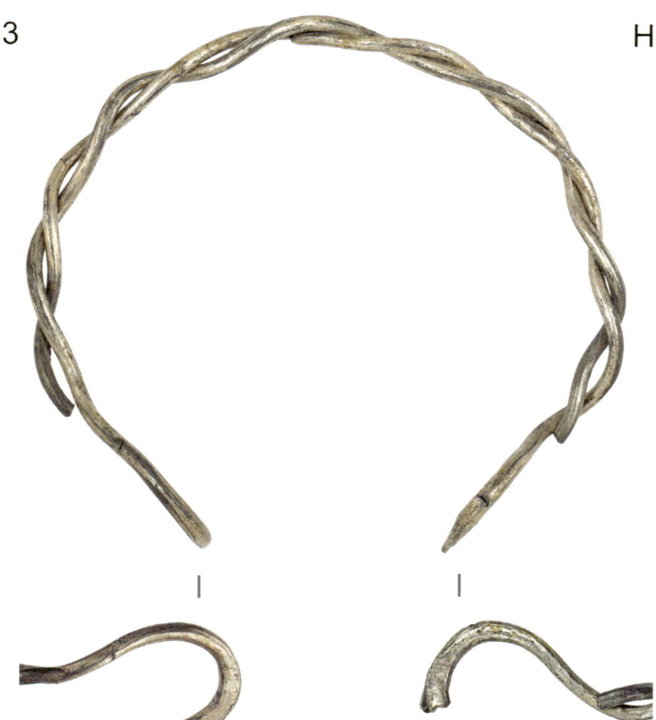

H.4

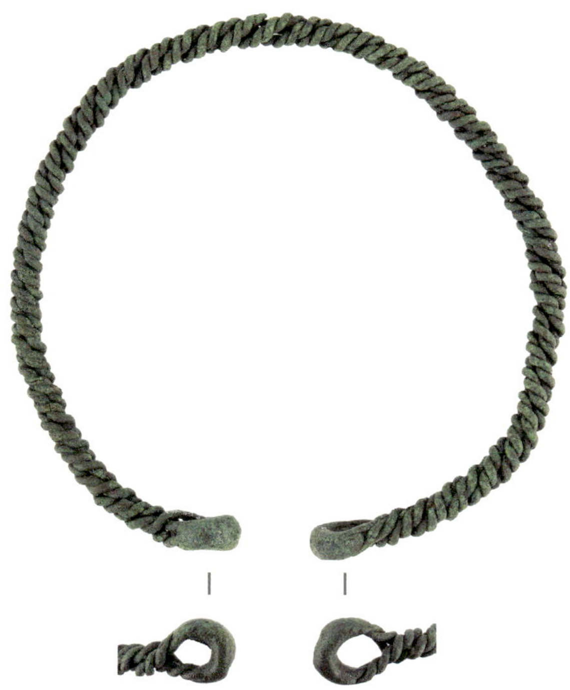

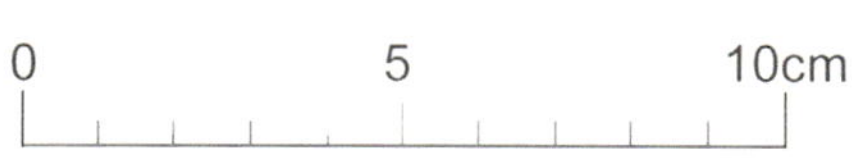

Plate 14.45

H.5

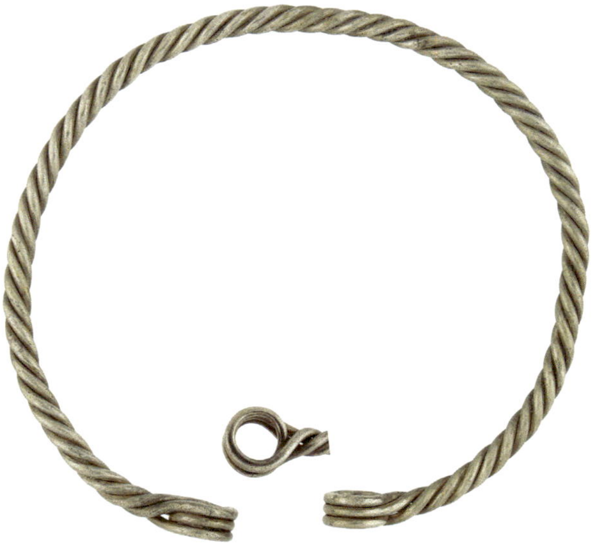

H.6

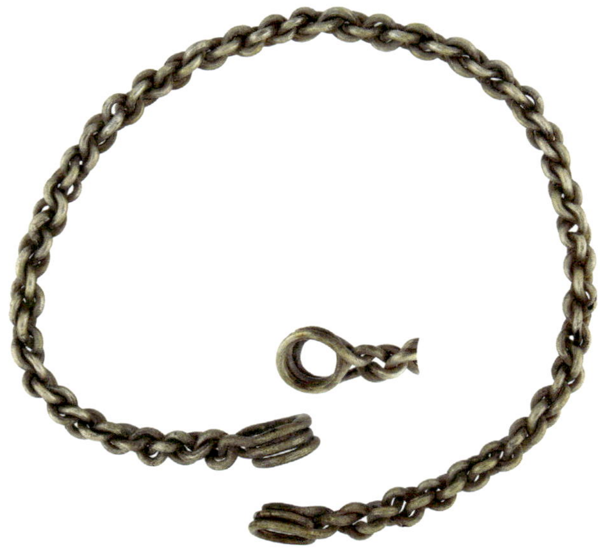

H.7

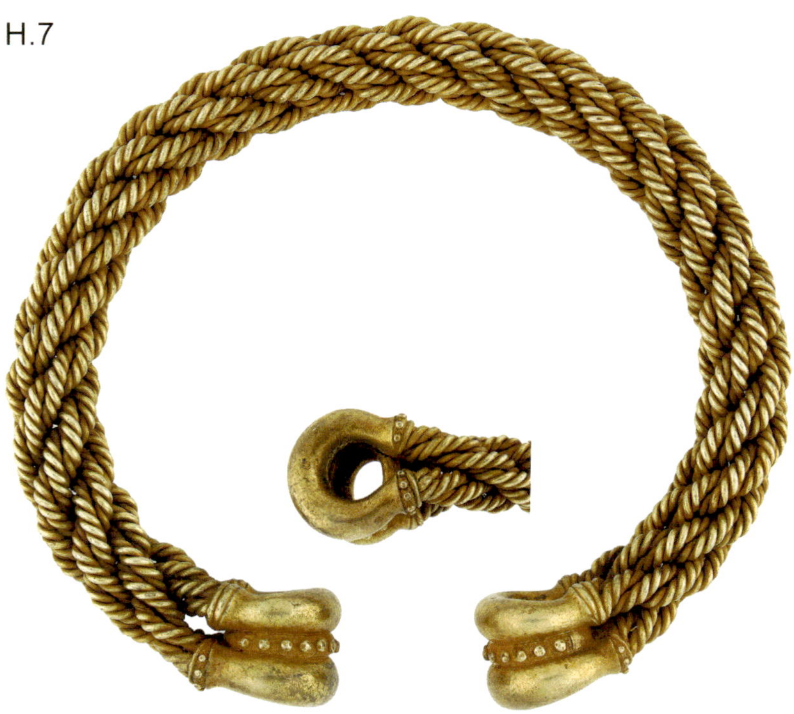

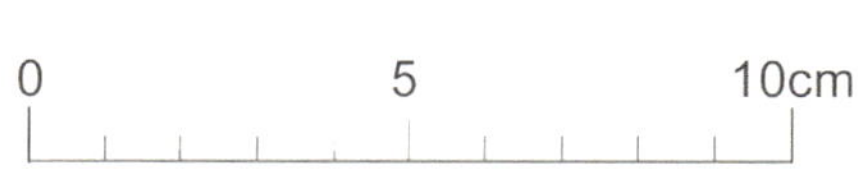

Plate 14.46

H.4: Copper alloy torc (Pl. 14.45)
MSCC: (3P(2P))R
BM: 1990,1101.3; Site code: SN/CU
Copper alloy multi-strand torc with ring terminals and Stage III neck-ring formed from three plied ropes, each of which is made up of two circular-section wires plied together. The ring terminals are cast onto the ends of the neck-ring wires. Each terminal forms a continuous loop, extending on one side into one of the ropes and on the other side into the remaining two ropes.
Wt: 186.6g; D(ext): 145.0mm; D(nr): 8.0mm; D(rope): 3.8mm; D(wire): 2.1mm; D(term): 19.0mm

H.5: Gold/silver alloy torc (Pl. 14.46)
MSCC: (4C)R
BM: 1991,0407.13; Site code: SN/CV
Gold/silver alloy multi-strand torc with triple-loop terminals and Stage II neck-ring of four circular-section wires coiled together. The terminals are formed from the ends of the neck-ring wires: on each side, one pair of neck-ring wires forms a continuous single loop, while the other forms a continuous double loop. Soldered or hammered areas obscure the joins of the wire ends.
Wt: 120.0g; D(ext): 153.0mm; D(nr): 7.0mm; D(wire): 3.1mm; D(term): 18.0mm

H.6: Gold/silver alloy torc (Pl. 14.46)
MSCC: (2P(2PZ))R
BM: 1991,0407.14; Site code: SN/DR
Gold/silver alloy multi-strand torc with triple-loop terminals and Stage III neck-ring. The cable is formed from two ropes plied together, each of which is made up of two circular-section wires which are themselves plied together Z-twist. The terminals are formed from the ends of the neck-ring wires: on each side, the wires of one rope form a continuous single loop, while the wires of the other form a continuous double loop. Soldered areas obscure the joins of the wire ends. The whole torc is slightly distorted, with the terminals slightly overlapping.
Wt: 119.1g; D(ext): 154.0mm; D(nr): 9.0mm; D(rope): 4.2mm; D(wire): 2.3mm; D(term): 18.0mm

Hoard H (lower pit)

Recovered during the BM 1990 excavations. All finds from the lower Hoard H pit.

H.7: Gold/silver alloy torc (Pl. 14.46)
MSCC: (4CZ(3P(3P)))R
BM: 1991,0407.15; Site code: SN/FJ
Gold/silver alloy multi-strand torc with complex ring terminals. Each cast terminal consists of a double ring, with the two rings joined by a central band decorated with raised knobs, each with three dots (see Ch. 21 for discussion of decoration). The same dotted knob motif decorates the front part of the join between the terminal and the neck-ring. The Stage IV neck-ring is made up of four cables coiled together Z-twist. Each cable comprises three ropes plied together, and each rope consists of three circular-section wires plied together. The torc was slightly compressed in the pit, springing back into shape when lifted.
Wt: 1208.3g; D(ext): 206.0mm; D(nr): 22.0mm; D(cable): 7.3mm; D(rope): 3.5mm; D(wire): 1.2mm; D(term): 36.0mm

H.8: Copper alloy torc (Pl. 14.47)
MSCC: (6C)?Q
BM: 1990,1101.4; Site code: SN/FK; SN/FZ
Copper alloy multi-strand torc with Stage II neck-ring formed from six wires coiled together. The wires are heavily corroded, but may be squarish in cross-section. Simple buffer terminals with flat faces and rounded edges. Previously restored from separate fragments.
Wt: 122.5g; D(ext): 152.0mm; D(nr): 8.6mm; D(wire): 2.3mm; D(term): 13.4mm

H.9: Copper alloy torc (Pl. 14.47)
MSCC: (4C)R
BM: 1990,1101.8; Site code: SN/FY; SN/GK; SN/GL
Copper alloy multi-strand torc with Stage II neck-ring formed from four circular-section wires coiled around an organic core. Slightly overlapping simple buffer terminals with flat faces and rounded edges. Previously restored from separate sections; a sample of the charcoal core was also retained.
Wt: 56.7g; D(ext): 119.0mm; D(nr): 5.7mm; D(wire): 1.6mm; D(term): 11.2mm

H.10: Copper alloy torc (Pl. 14.47)
MSCC: (4C(2P))R
BM: 1990,1101.5; Site code: SN/GO
Gilded copper alloy multi-strand torc with Stage III neck-ring and simple buffer terminals with flat faces and rounded edges. The cable is formed of four coiled ropes, each of which is made up of two circular-section wires plied together.
Wt: 96.3g; D(ext): 132.0mm; D(nr): 8.0mm; D(rope): 2.3mm; D(wire): 1.2mm; D(term): 14.0mm

H.11: Copper alloy torc (Pl. 14.47)
MSCC: (2P)R
BM: 1990,1101.6; Site code: SN/GP
Copper alloy multi-strand torc with double-loop terminals and Stage II neck-ring of two circular-section wires plied loosely together (see **Fig. 20.33**). Each double-loop terminal is made up of two open loops, each formed from the curved end of one of the neck-ring wires. One of the wires is significantly more corroded than the other, suggesting a possible difference in alloy or surface treatment.
Wt: 96.7g; D(ext): 127.0mm; D(nr): 9.0mm; D(wire): 4.6mm; D(term): 24.4mm

Hoard J

Recovered during the BM 1990 excavations. All finds from the Hoard J pit unless otherwise stated.

J.1: Gold/silver alloy torc (Pl. 14.48)
MSCC: ?
BM: 1991,0407.42; Site code: SN/GV; SN/GW; SN/GX; SN/GZ; SN/HG; SN/JX
Context details: Found in plough scatter around Hoard J.
Fragments from a gold/silver alloy multi-strand torc

H.8

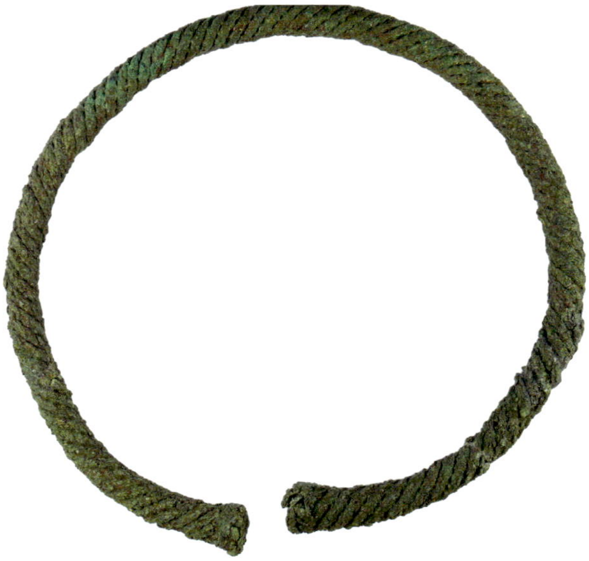

H.9

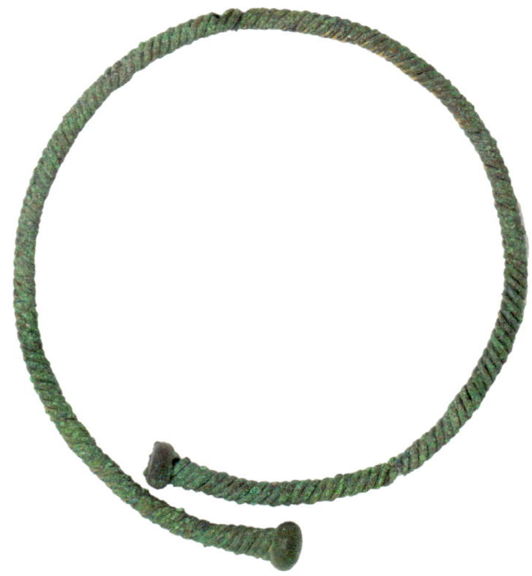

H.10

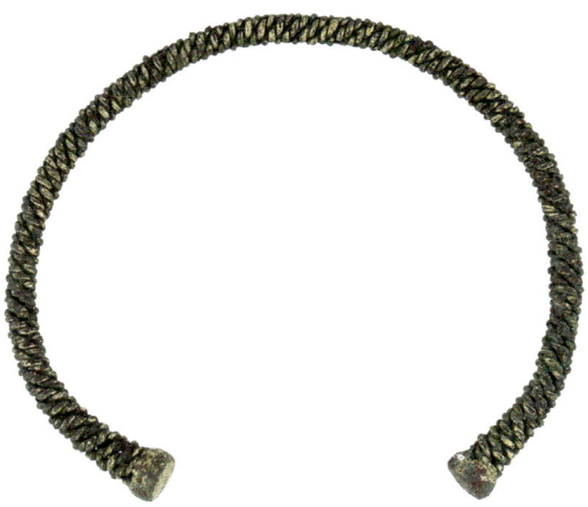

H.11

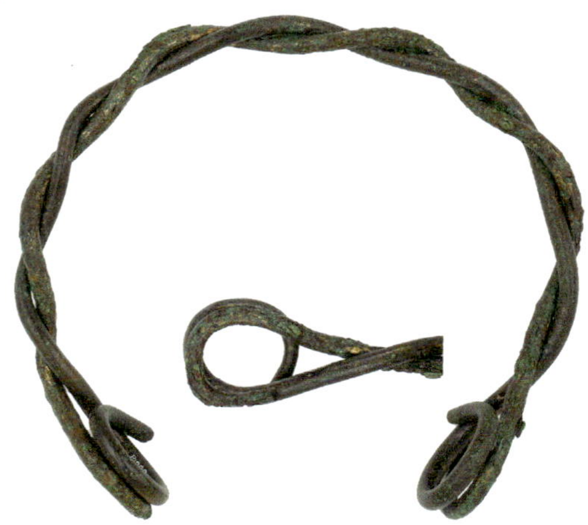

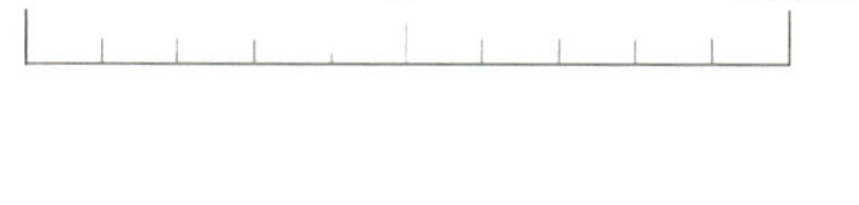

Plate 14.47

including the remains of a double-loop terminal, and additional wire fragments from the neck-ring. The torc is very fragmentary, and cannot be fully reconstructed, suggesting that it may not have been complete when it was deposited.
Possibly part of the same torc as S.54.
Wt: 12.8g (largest frags); D(wire): 3.8mm; D(term): 26.8mm; L: 29.0 mm (max.)

J.2: Gold/silver alloy torc (Pl. 14.48)
MSCC: (3P(2PZ))R
BM: 1991,0407.41; 1991,0407.55; Site code: SN/HA; SN/KZ
Context details: Found in plough scatter around Hoard J.
Fragments from a gold/silver alloy multi-strand torc including a short length of neck-ring, broken at both ends, and a single-loop terminal with one flat end and one broken end where it would most likely have continued into the neck-ring wires. Stage III construction of three ropes plied together, each of which is made up of two circular-section wires which are themselves plied together Z-twist. The torc is very fragmentary, and cannot be fully reconstructed, suggesting that it may not have been complete when it was deposited.
Probably part of the same torc as S.20
Wt: 20.6g; D(nr): 11.8mm; D(rope): 6.8mm; D(wire): 2.3mm; D(term): 23.2mm; L: 65.7 mm (max.)

J.3: Copper alloy torc (Pl. 14.48)
MSCC: (?C)T
BM: 1990,1101.30; Site code: SN/EV; SN/GY; SN/HD; SN/HL; SN/HR; SN/JC; SN/HE; SN/HH; SN/HJ; SN/HK; SN/HM
Context details: Found in plough scatter around Hoard J, and in Hoard J pit.
Fragments of a copper alloy multi-strand torc. Heavily fragmented, most likely disturbed by ploughing. All that remains are a single plain buffer terminal with one strand of the neck-ring protruding from the back, and a small number of twisted wire fragments, curved in a way which suggests they were once part of a coiled Stage II neck-ring. This partial recovery suggests that the torc was most likely incomplete when it entered the ground.
Wt: 36.1g; D(wire): 3.1mm; D(term): 22.2mm

J.4: Copper alloy torc (Pl. 14.48)
MSCC: (3P(2P))R
BM: 1990,1101.32; Site code: SN/HO; SN/JF; SN/JY
Two fragments of a copper alloy multi-strand torc neck-ring, each broken at both ends. Stage III construction of three plied ropes, each of which is formed from two circular-section wires plied together. The torc has been disturbed by ploughing, but the partial recovery suggests that it may not have been complete when it entered the ground.
Wt: 14.3g; D(nr): 5.7mm; D(rope): 2.8mm; D(wire): 1.5mm; L: 95.8 mm (max.)

J.5a–c: Composite group (interlinked) (Pl. 14.48)
The terminals of torc fragments J.5b and J.5c were originally looped onto copper alloy torc J.5a.

J.5a: Copper alloy torc
MSCC: (6C)T
BM: 1990,1101.31; Site code: SN/JD; SN/JL; SN/JM; SN/JN; SN/JE; SN/JK
Fragments of a copper alloy multi-strand torc. Heavily fragmented, most likely disturbed by ploughing. What remains are fragments of neck-ring, each broken at both ends, and one plain buffer terminal. Stage II construction of six twisted wires coiled around a hollow core. As far as can be reconstructed, the fragmentary torc has been tightly bent into a V-shape in at least one place. The partial recovery suggests that the torc was most likely incomplete when it entered the ground.
Wt: 12.4g; D(nr): 4.8mm; D(wire): 1.8mm; D(term): 7.3mm

J.5b: Gold/silver alloy torc
MSCC: (4CZ(2P))R
BM: 1991,0407.18; Site code: SN/JQ
Fragment of gold/silver alloy multi-strand torc, comprising a simple ring terminal, and a length of neck-ring, cut at the other end. Stage III construction of four ropes coiled together Z-twist, each of which is made up of two circular-section wires plied together. The ring terminal is cast onto the ends of the neck-ring wires. It forms a continuous loop, extending into the two pairs of ropes which form the four neck-ring ropes. All the neck-ring strands are sharply cut at the break, but the ends appear worn, suggesting the object may have been in circulation or use for some time between breakage and deposition.
Wt: 136.1g; D(nr): 9.8mm; D(rope): 4.6mm; D(wire): 2.0mm; D(term): 22.6mm; L: 153.0mm

J.5c: Gold/silver alloy torc
MSCC: (2P)R
BM: 1991,0407.17; Site code: SN/JP
Fragment of gold/silver alloy multi-strand torc comprising one loop terminal and a length of neck-ring, broken and distorted at the other end, with the wires pulled apart. Stage II construction of two circular-section wires plied together. The simple terminal is a continuous loop, extending to form the two neck-ring wires.
Wt: 298.1g; D(nr): 10.4mm; D(wire): 5.2mm; D(term): 22.7mm; L: 137.7mm

J.6: Gold/silver alloy torc (Pl. 14.49)
MSCC: (2CZ(2P))R
BM: 1991,0407.16; Site code: SN/JO
Gold/silver alloy multi-strand torc, with slightly thickened double-ring terminals. Stage III construction of two ropes coiled together Z-twist, each of which is made up of two circular-section wires plied together. The terminals are formed from the ends of the neck-ring wires: on each side, the two wires from each of the two ropes form a continuous loop; the thickened ends obscure the joins of the wires.
Wt: 518.0g; D(ext): 203.0mm; D(nr): 16.5mm; D(rope): 9.7mm; D(wire): 4.6mm; D(term): 36.0mm

J.7: Gold/silver alloy torc (Pl. 14.49)
MSCC: (2P(2P))R
BM: 1991,0407.19; Site code: SN/JR

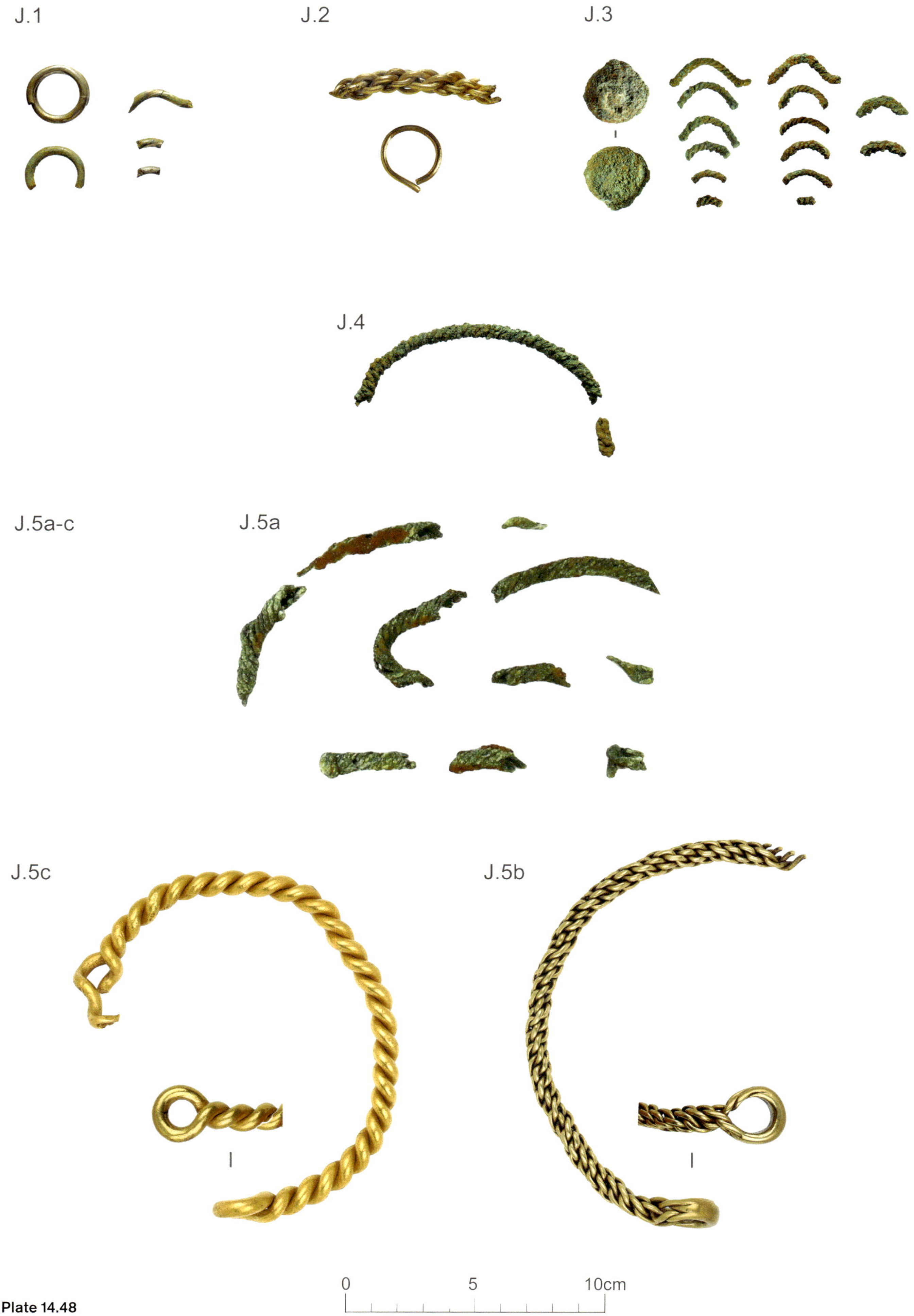

Plate 14.48

Gold/silver alloy multi-strand torc with ring terminals and Stage III neck-ring. The cable is formed of two ropes plied together, each of which is made up of two circular-section wires plied together. The ring terminals are cast onto the ends of the neck-ring wires. Each forms a continuous loop, extending into the two neck-ring ropes.
Wt: 469.3g; D(ext): 166.0mm; D(nr): 17.7mm; D(rope): 8.0mm; D(wire): 3.6mm; D(term): 26.5mm

J.?: Copper alloy torc
MSCC: ?
BM: 1990,1101.33; Site code: SN/HN
Fragments of wires from copper alloy multi-strand torc(s). Found in soil sample.
Possibly associated with Hoard J, but cannot be assigned to a particular torc.
Not pictured

Hoard K
Recovered during the BM 1990 excavations. All finds from the Hoard K pit.

K.1: Copper alloy torc (Pl. 14.50)
MSCC: (2P)R
BM: 1990,1101.34; Site code: SN/LA; SN/LB; SN/LC; SN/LD; SN/MC; SN/MD; SN/MF; SN/MH; ?ST/AC; ?ST/AJ
Copper alloy multi-strand torc with ring terminals, intentionally fragmented into at least 10 sections (see Ch. 16 for details of the conservation process). Possibly cast rather than forged, the Stage II neck-ring is formed from thick rods. These two rods cross only twice, once behind each terminal, and otherwise seem to lie parallel rather than being plied together. Simple, thickened ring terminals emerge from the ends of the rods, perhaps cast in one piece.
Wt: 369.5g; D(ext): 160.0 (approx)mm; D(nr): 15.7mm; D(wire): 7.8mm; D(term): 40.0mm

K.2: Copper alloy torc (Pl. 14.50)
MSCC: (?C)T+Q
BM: 1990,1101.35; Site code: SN/LE; SN/LG; SN/LJ; SN/LM; SN/LO; SN/LP; SN/LQ; SN/LR; SN/LS; SN/LT; SN/MA; SN/MB; SN/MG
Fragments of a gilded copper alloy multi-strand torc neck-ring, both terminals missing. The wire fragments have not been reconstructed, but suggest a Stage II coiled construction of a combination of twisted and square-section wires, some showing traces of gilding. Only a representative sample of the large number of wire fragments was photographed. The torc may have been near-complete when it was deposited, and have been disturbed by ploughing and burrowing animals.
D(wire): 3.2mm

K.3: Copper alloy torc (Pl. 14.50)
MSCC: (6C)T
BM: 1990,1101.36; Site code: SN/LF; SN/LK; SN/LN
Gilded copper alloy multi-strand torc neck-ring, reconstructed from fragments, now in three main sections, both terminals missing. One of the ends has been deliberately cut. Stage II construction of six twisted wires coiled around a hollow core. However, there is a highly unusual aspect to the construction: in one of the three sections, one of the six twisted wires is, in part, formed from two wires twisted together, i.e. (2P)R. This extends over only a very short length and could have been a way of joining two lengths of wire in an unobtrusive manner, since the plied construction closely resembles a single twisted wire at first glance. The torc may have been near-complete when it was deposited, and have been disturbed by ploughing and burrowing animals.
Wt: 28.7g; D(nr): 6.3mm; D(wire): 1.6mm

K.4: Copper alloy torc (Pl. 14.50)
MSCC: (3P(2P))R
BM: 1990,1101.37; Site code: SN/LL; SN/ME
Copper alloy multi-strand torc, with simple double-loop terminals and Stage III neck-ring. The cable is formed from three ropes plied together, each of which is made up of two circular-section wires plied together. One rope ends at each terminal, the other two form continuous loops (one of which is broken). The torc is complete but broken in two.
Wt: 25.3g; D(nr): 4.9mm; D(rope): 2.4mm; D(wire): 1.6mm; D(term): 15.3mm; L: 91.1mm

K.5: Gold/silver alloy torc (Pl. 14.51)
MSCC: (2PZ)R
BM: 1991,0407.20; Site code: SN/LV
Gold/silver alloy multi-strand torc with Stage II neck-ring formed from two circular-section wires plied together Z-twist. Simple ring terminals are formed from the thickened ends of the two neck-ring wires.
Wt: 402.0g; D(ext): 180.0mm; D(nr): 12.8mm; D(wire): 6.5mm; D(term): 36.4mm

K.6: Gold/silver alloy torc (Pl. 14.51)
MSCC: (2P)R
BM: 1991,0407.21; Site code: SN/LX
Gold/silver alloy multi-strand torc with Stage II neck-ring formed from two circular-section wires plied together. Simple ring terminals are formed from the thickened ends of the two neck-ring wires.
Wt: 358.0g; D(ext): 161.0mm; D(nr): 11.8mm; D(wire): 6.0mm; D(term): 23.2mm

K.7: Gold/silver alloy torc (Pl. 14.51)
MSCC: (8C)R
BM: 1991,0407.22; Site code: SN/LY
Gold/silver alloy multi-strand torc with ring terminals and Stage II neck-ring formed from eight circular-section wires coiled together around a hollow core. The terminals are merged double rings, cast onto the ends of the neck-ring wires, with a central groove between the two rings bearing a series of punched dots (see Ch. 21 for discussion of decoration).
Wt: 865.0g; D(ext): 199.0mm; D(nr): 18.7mm; D(wire): 4.5mm; D(term): 31.0mm

J.6

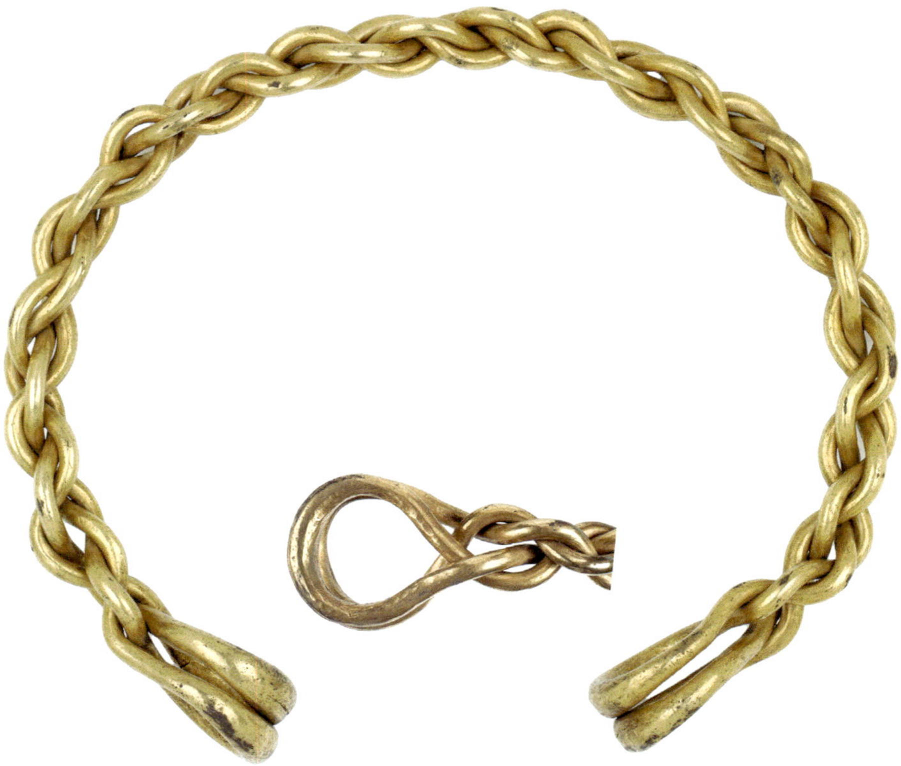

J.7

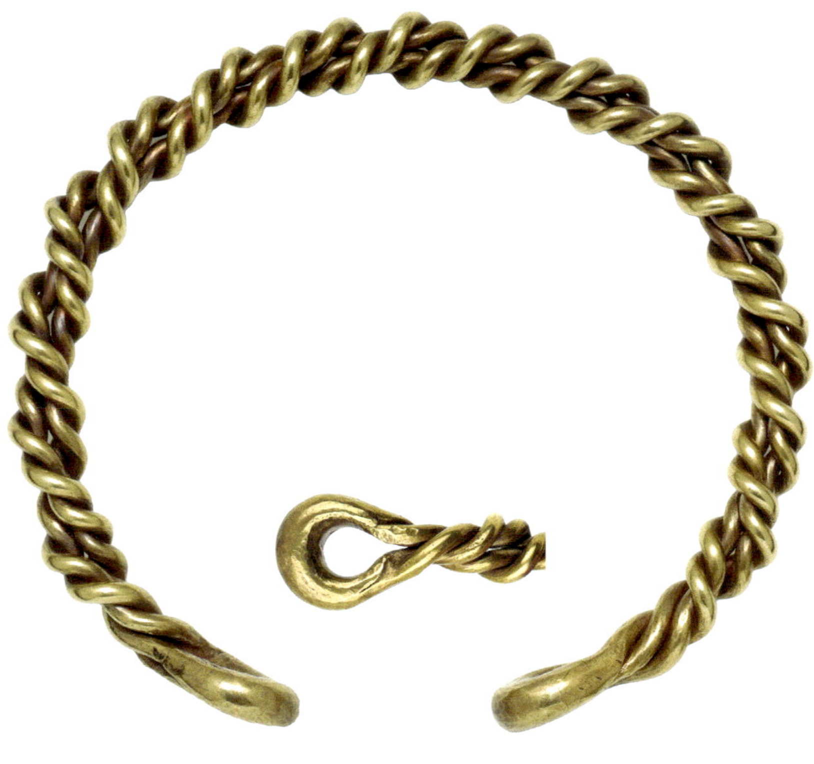

Plate 14.49

0 5 10cm

K.1

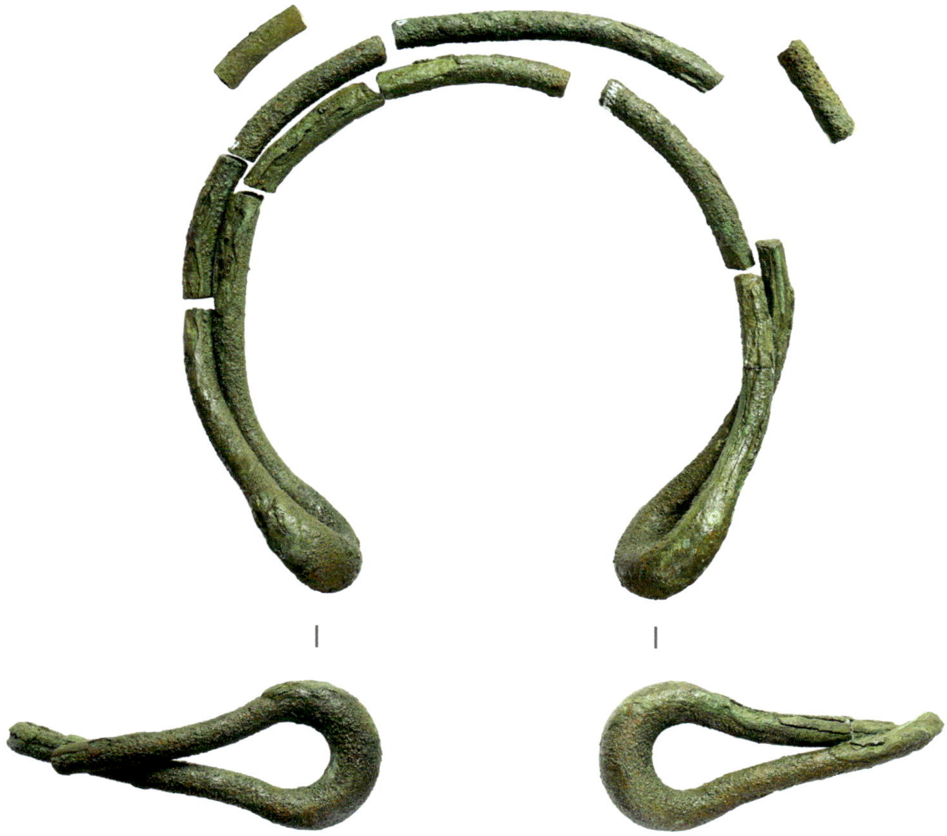

K.2

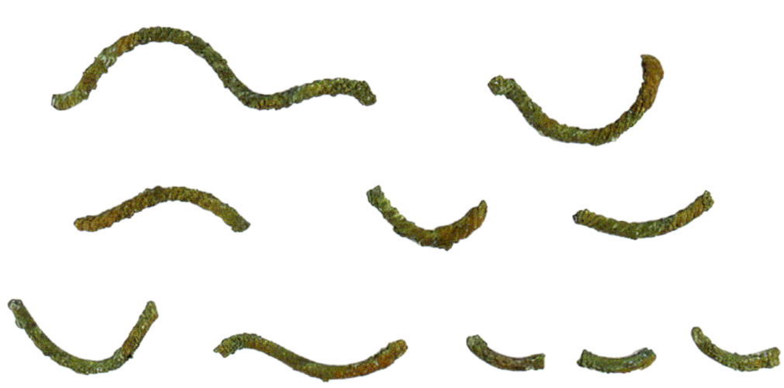

K.3

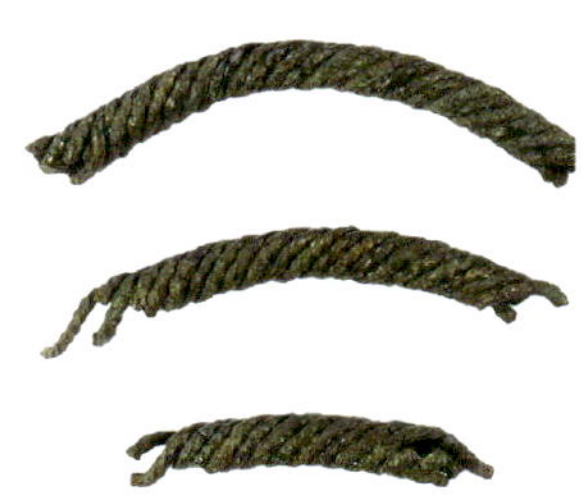

K.4

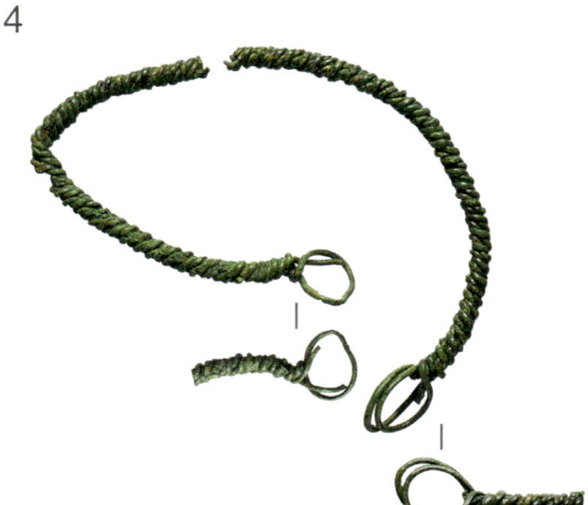

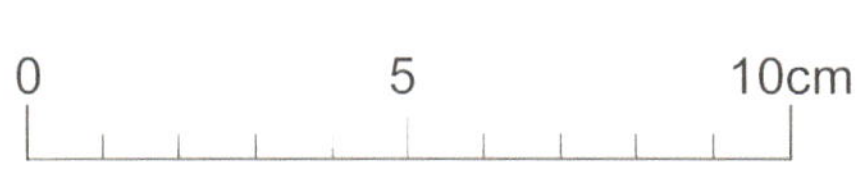

Plate 14.50

K.5

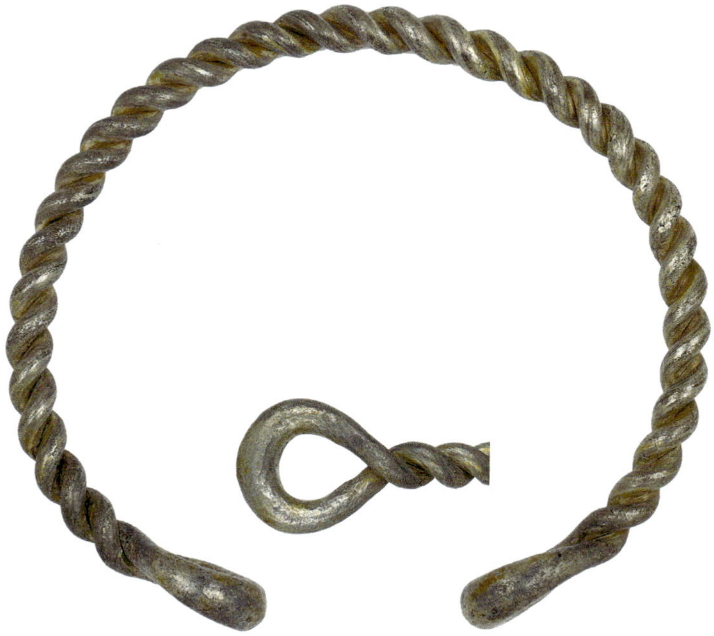

K.6

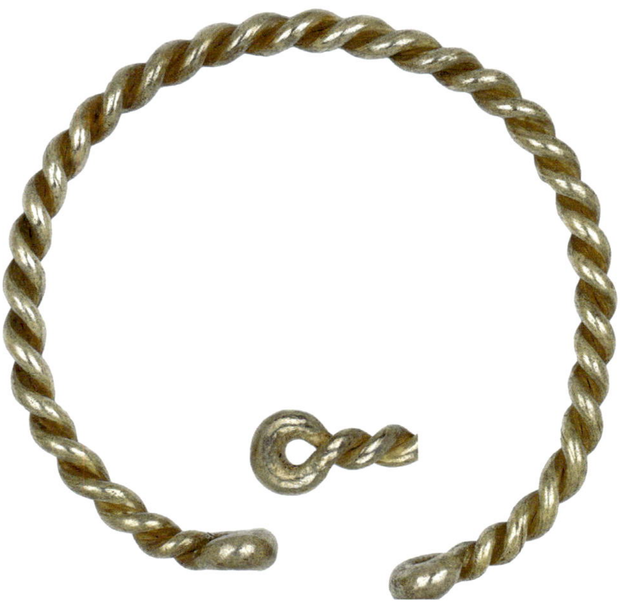

K.7

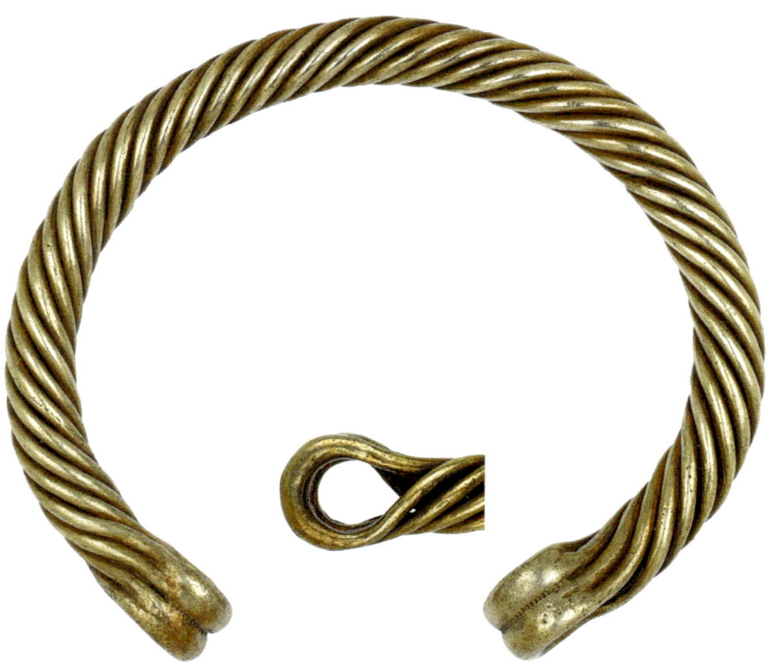

0 5 10cm

Plate 14.51

Hoard L (upper pit)

Recovered during the BM 1990 excavations. All finds from the upper Hoard L pit.

L.1: Gold/silver alloy torc (Pl. 14.52)
MSCC: (6C(2PZ(3P)))R
BM: 1991,0407.23; Site code: SN/NM
[Analysed: see Ch. 17]
Gold/silver alloy multi-strand torc with cast-on torus terminals (see **Figs 20.7a–b, 20.10, 23.8**). The Stage IV neck-ring is formed from six cables coiled together around a hollow core. Each cable is formed from two ropes loosely plied together Z-twist, and each rope consists of three circular-section wires plied together. The hollow terminals are very thin castings, open in the interior of the eye, and with some holes, cracks and patches (the latter notably on the torus of one terminal and the collar of the other). Each terminal has a groove running down the centre of the torus, as if dividing it into two adjacent rings. Towards the collar, this groove expands to a triangular or trumpet shape. Each collar has an inner cordon and in places where it meets the neck-ring the casting is incomplete and some wires can be seen within, and merging with, the collar.

Notes from scientific analysis (Nigel Meeks)
This torc has a complex Stage IV neck-ring construction, similar to L.21a. In this case, the overall appearance of the neck-ring wires is somewhat asymmetrical and is much less uniform. The wire ropes are quite loosely twisted together, and this has resulted in a very flexible neck-ring. The wires are highly polished and heavily worn on the outer sides and there is deep wear between wires that have rubbed together over a long period of use in antiquity (see **Fig. 20.7a–b**), with the open, flexible structure tending to exacerbate the wear between wires.

The terminals are of open torus form and have been cast onto the prepared wires. There is extensive evidence of metal flow and infilling of the gaps during casting and solidification around and between the wires. The castings are imperfect and there is a large cold-shut (a gap where the metal solidified before fully filling the mould) on one terminal which appears to have been repaired in antiquity with an additional cast-on plug (see **Fig. 20.10**). In addition, there are several regions where the wires penetrate through the casting as the wax model was too thin (**Figs 14.32–3**). One terminal is also loose on the wires and the wire has broken through, enlarging the hole (**Fig. 14.32**). There are file marks around the neck of the terminal that also cut into the exposed wires, probably used to add definition to the casting (**Fig. 14.32**).

This torc is also very similar in wear patterns to L.21a. One wire is broken, most likely a fatigue fracture due to constant flexing during use. The wires also show many linear facets in protected regions showing the wires were not originally finished to a particularly round section. There are deep linear grooves clearly visible on several wires, indicating possible folded strip origin.
Wt: 656.8g; D(ext): 184.0mm; D(nr): 24.2mm; D(cable): 9.5mm; D(rope): 5.4mm; D(wire): 2.1mm; D(term): 36.6mm

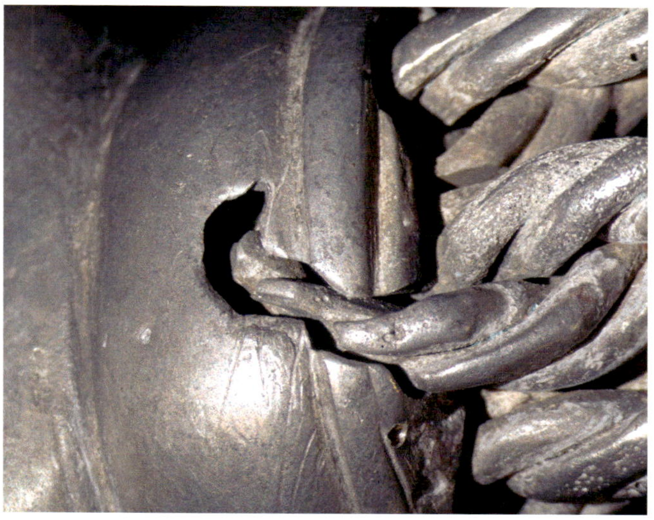

Figure 14.32 Detail of join where wires meet terminal, showing wire visible through hole in the collar on torc L.1

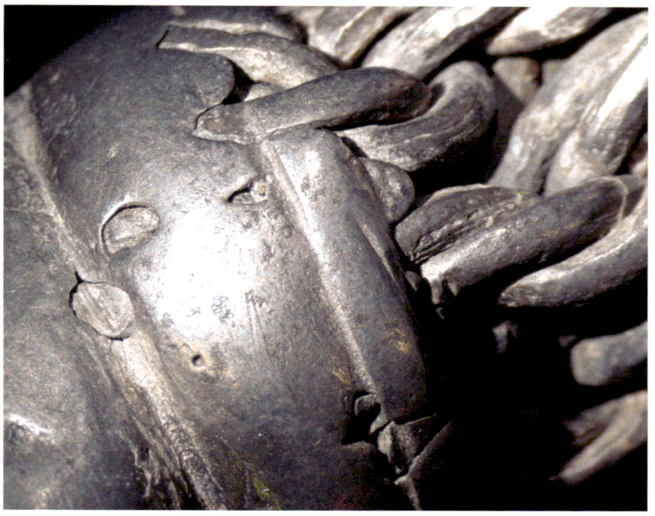

Figure 14.33 Detail of join where wires meet terminal, with wires exposed at the ends of the collar on torc L.1

L.2: Gold/silver alloy torc (Pl. 14.52)
MSCC: (2P)F
BM: 1991,0407.24; Site code: SN/NO
[Analysed: see Ch. 17]
Gold/silver alloy multi-strand torc with simple double-loop terminals and Stage II construction of two faceted rods plied together (see **Fig. 17.16**). Terminals are formed from the ends of the two neck-ring rods; each rod terminates in an open loop at each end, giving a double-loop terminal.

Notes from scientific analysis (Nigel Meeks)
The two thick rods which make up the torc are each heavily faceted, being octagonal along their entire length. The two rods are twisted together 19 full turns to create the neck-ring. This is probably as tightly twisted as can be achieved. The torc has double-loop non-fused terminals similar to torc L.7, and unlike the closed loops of e.g. G.1. The rod facets run parallel to each other, spiralling around with the neck-ring twists, which shows that the rods were not pre-twisted individually before the two rods were plied together as a pair, as can be seen on a few smaller square-section wire torcs (e.g. F.9a). They were simply twisted tightly together, producing a very uniform geometric pattern to the neck-ring.

L.1

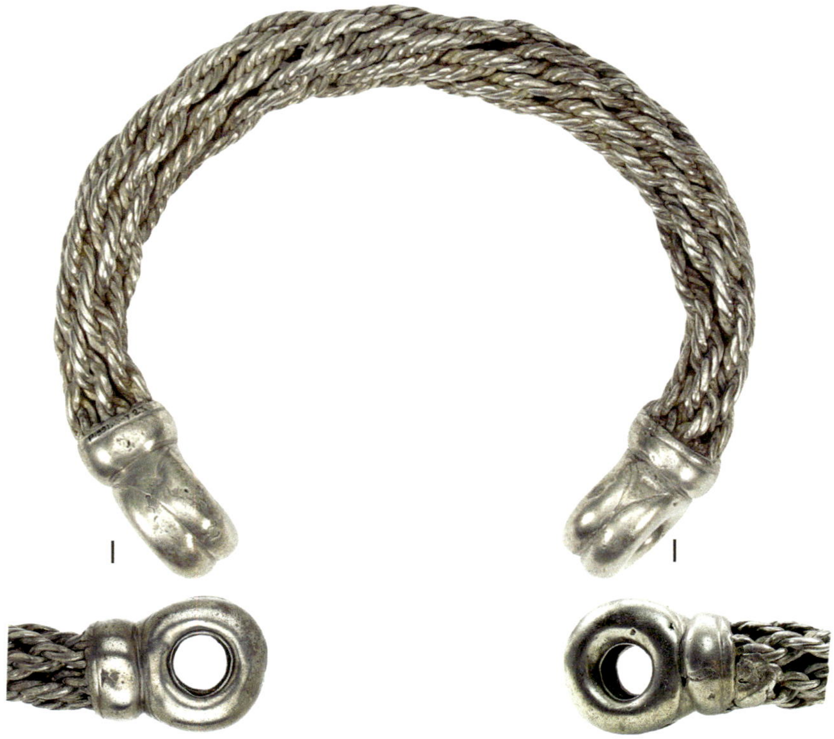

L.2

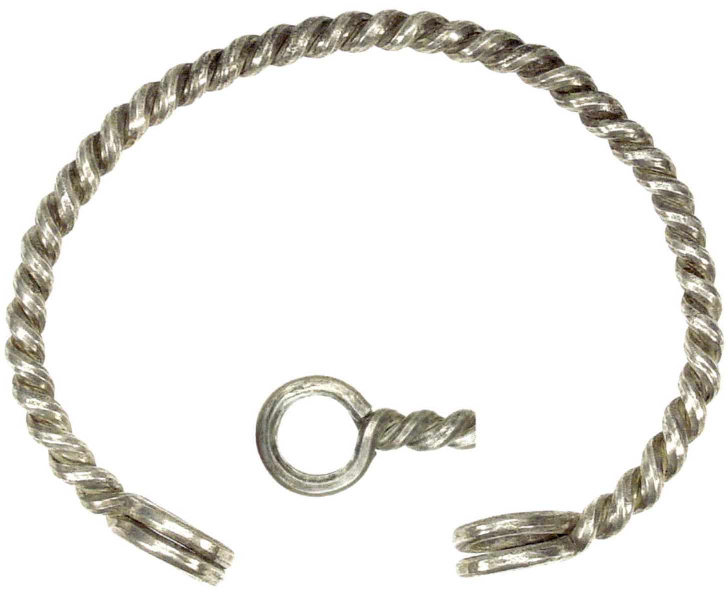

L.3

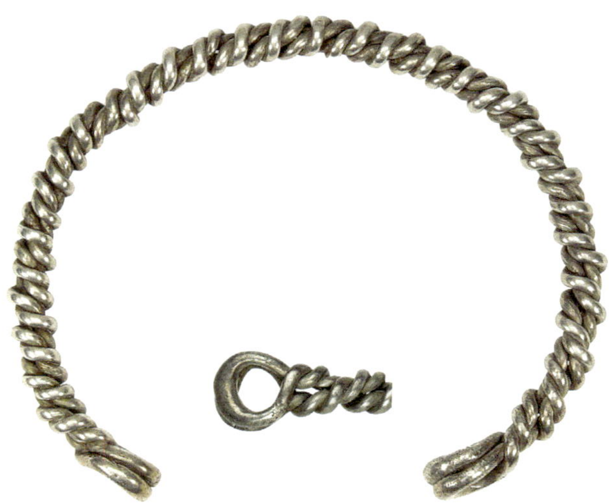

0 5 10cm

Plate 14.52

A second feature seen on L.2 are linear grooves and striations that run along the length of the rods, particularly in protected regions within the spirals; some are fine and others are coarser (**Fig. 14.34**). This has been seen on many wires and rods of various thicknesses (Ch. 17). These lines scratched into the metal surface have apparently not been deformed by hammering, suggesting that they are part of a finishing process on the wires after faceting and before making into the neck-ring. Either they were caused by filing or by abrading during smoothing the wires to their final shape. Nevertheless, the wires were most likely not pulled through a drawplate as such, as the true function of a drawplate is to produce successively thinner round-section wires (Whitfield 1990), and there is no evidence of this on the Snettisham torcs (see Ch. 17 for a full discussion of wire manufacture).
Wt: 318.0g; D(ext): 188.0mm; D(nr): 10.7mm; D(wire): 7.1mm; D(term): 32.5mm

L.3: Gold/silver alloy torc (Pl. 14.52)
MSCC: (2P(2P))R
BM: 1991,0407.25; Site code: SN/NR
[Analysed: see Ch. 17]
Gold/silver alloy multi-strand torc with double-ring terminals and Stage III neck-ring formed from two plied ropes, each of which is made up of two circular-section wires plied together. Each thickened ring terminal forms a continuous loop, extending into one of the two neck-ring ropes.

Notes from scientific analysis (Nigel Meeks)
Another variation on the theme of multi-strand thick wire torcs is exemplified by torc L.3. It comprises two Stage II components, each comprising two round-section wires plied together, with single-ring terminals. These two components are themselves twisted together, using mandrels through the two terminal loops at each end, to form a Stage III neck-ring. The resulting neck-ring is rather 'lumpy' or irregular because the overlapping wires do not lie comfortably together, and the effect is to produce a different texture to this torc compared to other more uniform types. On the loops of this torc the closing mechanism for completing the ring terminal was to cast-on extra metal. This is clearly seen in the plate, where much casting porosity is visible in the surface of the cast-on sections.
Wt: 202.6g; D(ext): 156.0mm; D(nr): 13.0mm; D(rope): 6.9mm; D(wire): 3.0mm; D(term): 21.2mm

L.4: Gold/silver alloy torc (Pl. 14.53)
MSCC: (3P(2P))R
BM: 1991,0407.26; Site code: SN/NW
[Analysed: see Ch. 17]
Gold/silver alloy multi-strand torc with quadruple-ring terminals and Stage III neck-ring formed from three plied ropes, each of which is made up of two circular-section wires plied together (see **Fig. 17.60a–b**). The terminals are formed from the ends of the neck-ring wires: on each side, the wires of one rope form a continuous double-loop, while the wires of the other two ropes each form continuous single loops, giving a total of four loops on each terminal.

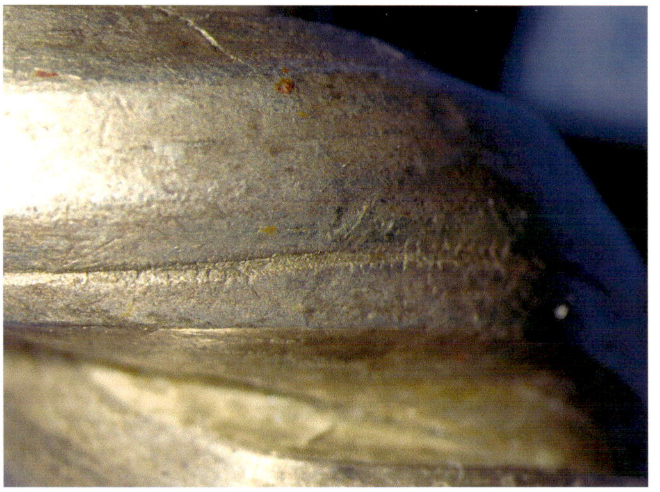
Figure 14.34 Fine striations visible in protected areas of the wires on torc L.2

Hammered overlap joins obscure the wire ends in the terminals.

Notes from scientific analysis (Nigel Meeks)
L.4 shows another variation on a similar Stage III construction to torc L.3, but with additional loop terminals, making four at each end. The wires are fairly round in section but retain evidence of many linear facets along their length and there is an overlap join on one of the loops where the ends of the wires are joined (see **Fig. 17.60a–b**). The exposed outer surfaces are polished from use wear while the recessed twists retain the angular linear facets.
Wt: 370.4g; D(ext): 162.0mm; D(nr): 14.7mm; D(rope): 7.5mm; D(wire): 3.1mm; D(term): 27.4mm

L.5: Copper alloy torc (Pl. 14.53)
MSCC: (5C(2P))R
BM: 1990,1101.10; Site code: SN/NY
Copper alloy multi-strand torc, possibly gilded, with simple buffer terminals and Stage III neck-ring formed from five ropes coiled around a hollow core, each of which is made up of two circular-section wires plied together. Reconstructed from fragments, now in four main pieces, with additional unjoined fragments.
Wt: 73.3g (four largest frags); D(ext): (approx.) 156.0mm; D(nr): 9.6mm; D(rope): 2.5mm; D(wire): 1.5mm; D(term): 14.3mm

L.6: Copper alloy torc (Pl. 14.53)
MSCC: (7C(2P))R
BM: 1990,1101.7; Site code: SN/NZ
[Analysed: see Ch. 17; Radiocarbon dated: See Table 5.2; See Ch. 16 for details of conservation work]
Copper alloy multi-strand torc with simple buffer terminals and Stage III neck-ring formed from seven ropes coiled around a hollow core, each of which is made up of two circular-section wires plied together (see **Figs 16.3–4**). The terminals have rounded edges and flat, undecorated ends. One terminal is more corroded than the other and the back of the torc, for a length of about 42mm, has been repaired by binding/wrapping with organic strip. Additional detached fragments of the binding strip are stored separately.

L.4

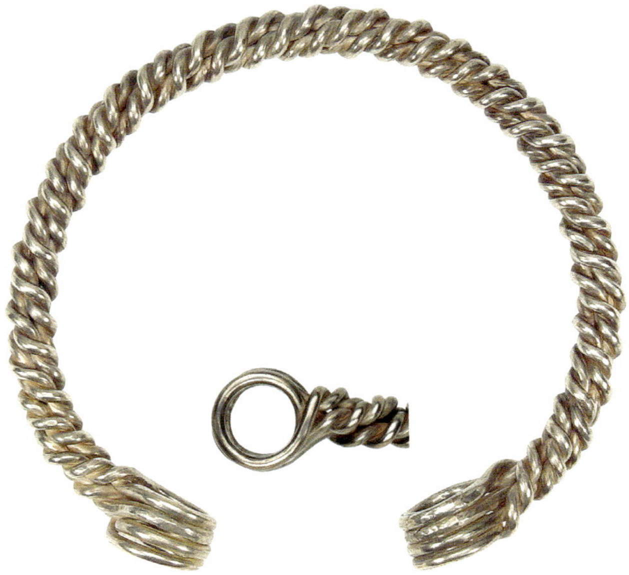

L.5

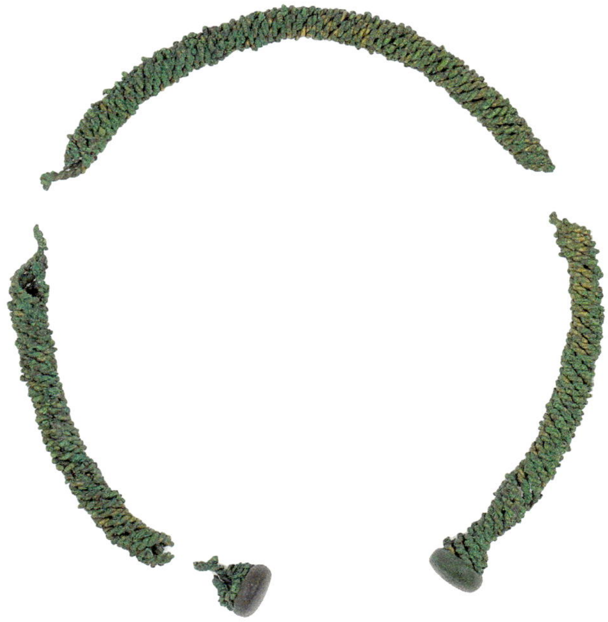

L.6

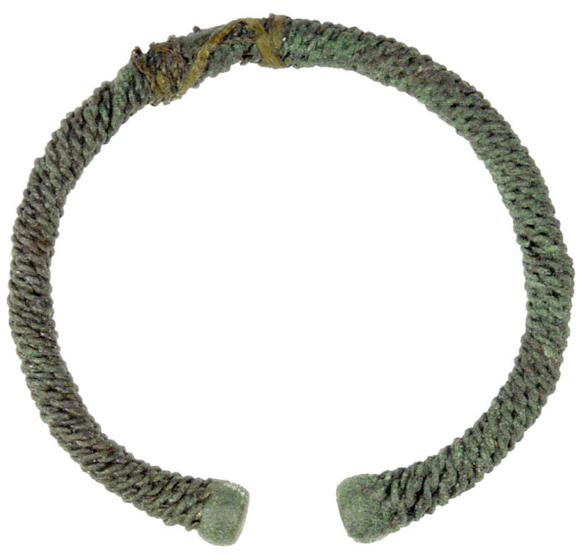

0 5 10cm

Plate 14.53

Notes from scientific analysis (Nigel Meeks)
The neck-ring is hollow in the centre which would make this copper alloy torc springy in the same manner as many of the gold alloy torcs. This is particularly important in this case as the terminals are only 25mm apart and it would need to be opened quite wide for putting on and taking off. The wires are heavily corroded with typical green copper corrosion products (and with what appears to be surface lacquer from conservation treatment). What makes this torc unique is the tightly wrapped organic material around the mid-point of the neck-ring, appearing as both a flat fibrous strip and as a plied string. This may originally have been added to repair or strengthen the torc at this point as there does appear to be some wire damage and thinning to the wires in this region. The organic material was identified by Caroline Cartwright (Ch. 19) as lime wood fibre string, and samples of this were radiocarbon dated (see **Table 5.2**).
Wt: 199.7g; D(ext): 149.1mm; D(nr): 12.5mm; D(rope): 3.6mm; D(wire): 2.5mm; D(term): 17.6mm

L.7: Gold/silver alloy torc (Pl. 14.54)
MSCC: (2P)R
BM: 1991,0407.27; Site code: SN/OA
[Analysed: see Ch. 17]
Gold/silver alloy multi-strand torc with simple double-loop terminals and Stage II neck-ring formed from two circular-section wires loosely plied together (see **Fig. 17.59a–b**). The terminals are formed from the ends of the two neck-ring wires; each terminates in an open loop at each end, giving a double-loop terminal.

Notes from scientific analysis (Nigel Meeks)
The two thick, round-section wires which make up the torc are twisted together with seven full turns to form the Stage II neck-ring. The length of each wire is about 65cm, hence a total of around 130cm of wire was required for the complete torc. The wires are not perfectly rounded and show a number of flat areas, indentations and hammer marks, particularly towards the terminals (see **Fig. 17.59a–b**). The main exposed wire regions have rounded and smooth high points from use wear, compared with the protected inner areas. Each torc wire has a round loop terminal with the wire end closing the loop and touching the wire, but not soldered or fused to it. With the wires twisted together, this gives a double-loop terminal.
Wt: 347.7g; D(ext): 184.0mm; D(nr): 12.8mm; D(wire): 6.2mm; D(term): 31.2mm

Hoard L (lower pit)

Recovered during the BM 1990 excavations. All finds from the lower Hoard L pit.

L.8: Copper alloy torc/bracelet (Pl. 14.54)
MSCC: (2P(2P))R
BM: 1990,1101.9; Site code: SN/OS; SN/OT
Copper alloy multi-strand torc/bracelet with damaged double-loop terminals, in two pieces. One terminal has only a single loop remaining, and the neck-ring/body wires have been partially untwisted, suggesting the terminal was intentionally removed. Stage III construction of two ropes plied together, each made up of two circular-section wires plied together. At the complete end, each rope forms a single continuous loop, giving the double-loop terminal. Whilst some damage has occurred post-deposition, the torc was most likely deposited without the missing terminal loop.
Wt: 37.4g; D(nr): 6.2mm; D(rope): 3.4mm; D(wire): 2.0mm; D(term): 14.5mm; L: 112.0 mm (max.)

L.9: Copper alloy torc (Pl. 14.54)
MSCC: (2P(2P))R
BM: 1990,1101.11; Site code: SN/OL; SN/OL; SN/OU
Gilded copper alloy fragment from multi-strand torc, comprising one double-loop terminal and a section of neck-ring, partially untwisted at the broken end. Stage III construction of two ropes plied together, each made up of two circular-section wires plied together. The double-loop terminal is continuous, formed from the ends of one of the neck-ring ropes. The other rope is broken, but would probably originally also have terminated in a continuous loop or double loop, giving a triple- or quadruple-ring terminal.
Wt: 32.0g; D(nr): 13.0mm; D(rope): 6.3mm; D(wire): 2.9mm; D(term): 15.4mm; L: 102.4mm

L.10a–b: Composite group (interlinked) (Pl. 14.54)
Wires L.10b are inserted through one terminal of torc L.10a
Wt: 202.3g (total for L.10a and L.10b)

L.10a: Gold/silver alloy torc
MSCC: (6C)2T+4Q
BM: 1991,0407.28; Site code: SN/OF
Gold/silver alloy multi-strand torc with torus terminals and Stage II neck-ring formed from six wires coiled together (see **Fig. 21.25**). Two of the wires (equally spaced between the other four) are twisted, and the others are squarish in section. One strand is broken, with a short length missing. The cast torus terminals have small central eyes and broad collars with a rounded edge. They seem to have been hollow castings. There are some small holes in one terminal and a larger one (possibly with core visible inside) in the other. There is very faint, heavily worn decoration on the terminals, incorporating shapes with hatched 'basket-weave' backgrounds. There was originally a triangular panel of similar ornament on the outside of each collar, now very faint. See Chapter 21 for a full discussion of decoration.
D(ext): 190.0mm; D(nr): 12.4mm; D(wire): 2.0mm; D(term): 22.5mm

L.10b: Gold/silver alloy torc/wire
MSCC: (?2P)T
BM: 1991,0407.28; Site code: SN/OG
Two lengths of gold/silver alloy twisted wire, each broken at both ends, plied loosely together.
D(wire): 2.2mm; L: 40.2mm

L.11: Gold/silver alloy torc (Pl. 14.55)
MSCC: (8CZ(2P))R
BM: 1991,0407.29; Site code: SN/OH
Gold/silver alloy multi-strand torc with buffer terminals and Stage III neck-ring (see **Fig. 21.19**). The cable is formed

L.7

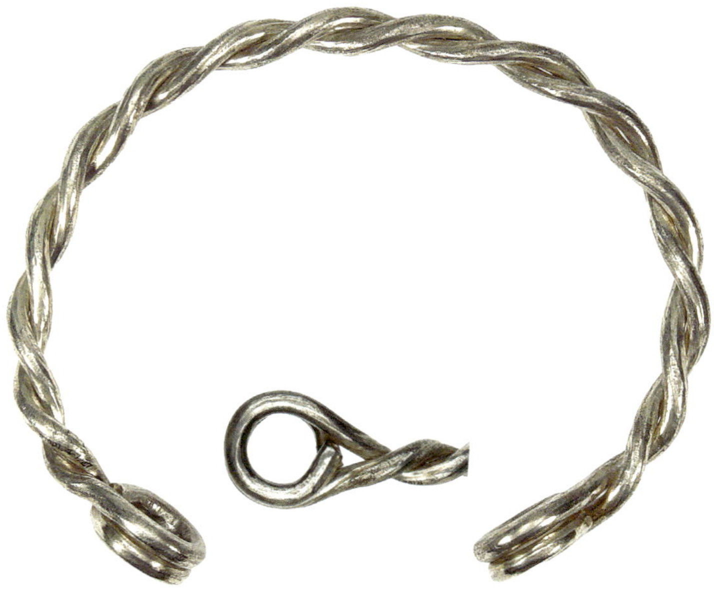

L.8

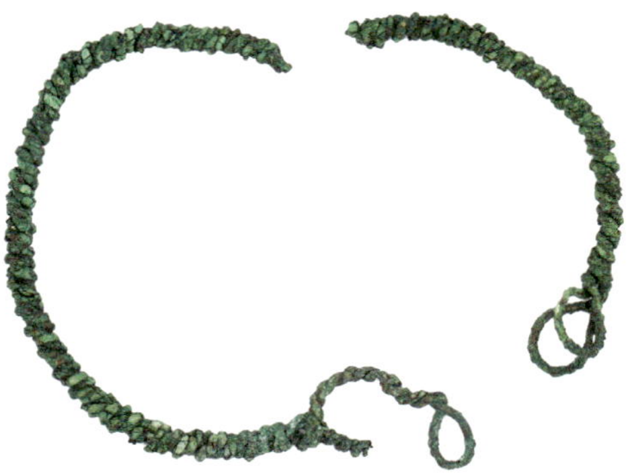

L.9

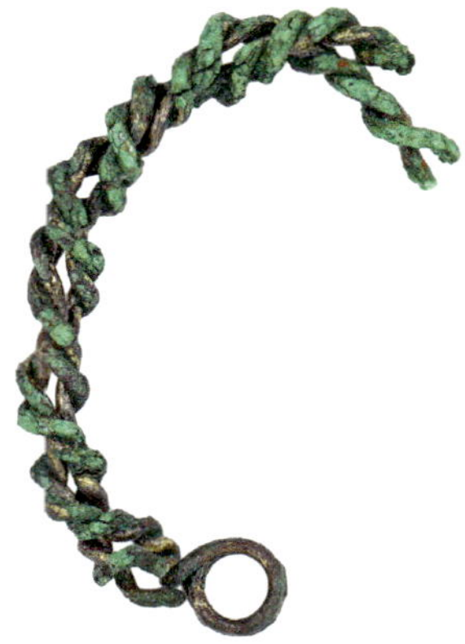

L.10a-b

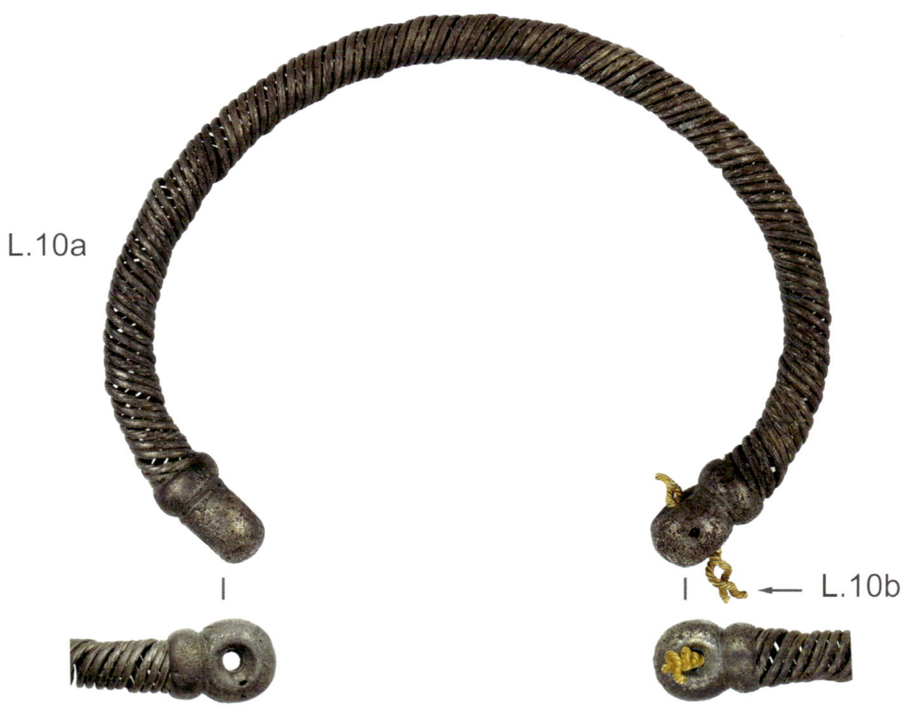

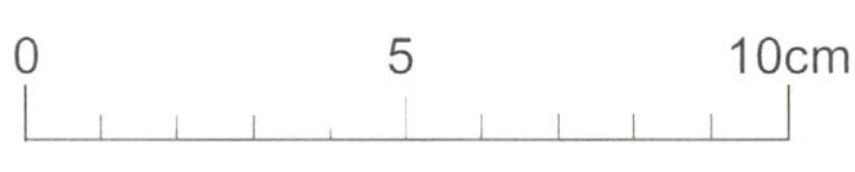

Plate 14.54

from eight ropes coiled Z-twist around a hollow core, each made up of two circular-section wires plied together. Originally in two fragments, now re-joined. Several neck-ring rope strands are broken over a length of about 25mm. The slightly flared buffer terminals have rounded edges with pronounced, raised cordons around the front faces and where they meet the neck-rings. The flat undecorated faces are deeply recessed. The edges of the terminals are decorated on the front in very high relief (rising to a maximum of about 2.5mm above the surface) with a three-part design: a central lobe and dot set between two swags with semi-circular terminals. The orientation of the lobe and dot motif differs from one terminal to the other. See Chapter 21 for a full discussion of decoration.
Wt: 282.4g; D(ext): 188.0mm; D(nr): 12.8mm; D(rope): 3.9mm; D(wire): 1.5mm; D(term): 23.9mm

L.12: Gold/silver alloy torc (Pl. 14.55)
MSCC: (8C(2P))R
BM: 1991,0407.30; Site code: SN/OW
Near-complete gold/silver alloy multi-strand torc with one remaining buffer terminal and Stage III neck-ring (see **Fig. 21.20**). The break at the point of the missing terminal is very clean. The cable is formed from eight ropes coiled around a hollow core, each made up of two circular-section wires plied together. The break is very clean. The remaining terminal has rounded edges with raised cordons around the front face and where it meets the neck-ring. It is decorated around the outside edge with a relief zig-zag design created from opposing leaf motifs. The fin motifs created in the negative space are textured with stippled hatching. The terminal face has a raised outer rim, and a raised central button with a slight depression in the centre. See Chapter 21 for a full discussion of decoration.
Wt: 269.6g; D(ext): 191.0mm; D(nr): 13.9mm; D(rope): 4.0mm; D(wire): 1.6mm; D(term): 17.6mm

L.13: Gold/silver alloy torc (Pl. 14.55)
MSCC: (14C(2P(Z)))R
BM: 1991,0407.31; Site code: SN/OY
[Analysed: see Ch. 17]
Near-complete gold/silver alloy multi-strand torc with one remaining buffer terminal and Stage III neck-ring (see **Figs 17.15, 17.104a–c, 21.29**). The cable is formed from 14 ropes coiled around a hollow core, each made up of two circular-section wires plied together. Half of these are plied Z-twist, and the other half S-twist; the two types are alternated, giving an unusual texture to the neck-ring which resembles a braided rope. Four of the ropes have broken away from the surviving buffer terminal and at the other end of the neck-ring. The edge of the terminal is slightly convex, with a cordon where it meets the neck-ring. The edge is decorated with pointillé outlines alternating teardrop and triangular shapes. The flat face has chased/engraved decoration in the form of mirror-style motifs delineated by regular basketry hatching. See Chapter 21 for a full discussion of decoration.

Notes from scientific analysis (Nigel Meeks)
This is another very springy and flexible coiled multi-strand torc with a simple cast cap-end buffer terminal. One

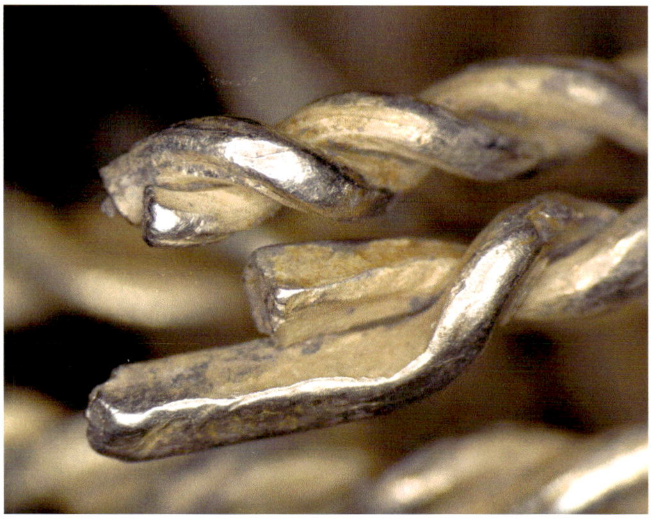

Figure 14.35 The exposed square-section wire ends on L.13

terminal is missing and the coiled neck-ring is showing signs of untwisting, and a little damage that probably occurred at the time the terminal was lost or removed. The buffer terminal has been decorated by engraving and chasing. What makes this torc unusual is the clever Stage III construction, where pairs of plied wires are assembled together with both S- and Z-twists. This gives a distinctive but subtle textural design to the torc, similar in appearance to the decorative filigree wires on tubular torc A.1.

While the overall appearance of this torc may look similar to that of torc L.17, the wires are very different. The coiled neck-ring comprises 14 ropes, each consisting of a pair of thin wires plied together. Each narrow wire is faceted. The facets are very uniform, and deep striations are also seen running along some wires and there are thin folds where the metal has smeared over due to hammering. The exposed outer wires are polished smooth from ancient use wear.

The ends of the wires are square in section where they are exposed at the damaged end (**Fig. 14.35**) and where they enter the terminal at the other end. This is clear proof that the original wires were made by hammering the stock alloy down to small dimension square-section wires and then the last stage of shaping was hammering along the square edges to produce the multiple facets that we commonly find on many of the Snettisham wires (see Ch. 17 for a full discussion of wire manufacture).

The buffer terminal appears to be cast, and is clearly fused to some of the neck-ring wires; there are file marks to clean up these joins. Other wires are loose in the terminal and have broken away.

The flat end of the buffer terminal has a beautifully engraved and chased design (**Figs 14.36**, **17.104a**). The main curved shapes have been defined using a sharp (metal) engraving tool that has left the characteristic V-shaped grooves of the tool's cutting edge as metal was cut away. The areas between have a recessed pattern of short lines created with a round-ended sharp chasing tool. Each line has tiny ridges left by the end of the tool showing the sequence of hammer blows used to move the tool through the metal. The ends of the tool marks show the splaying of the metal at the end of the last hammer stroke in those lines. It is probable

L.11

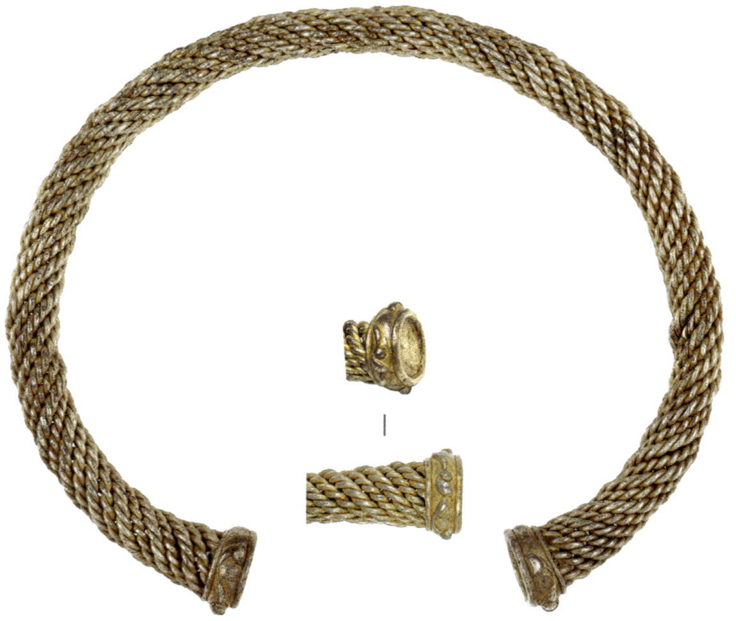

L.12

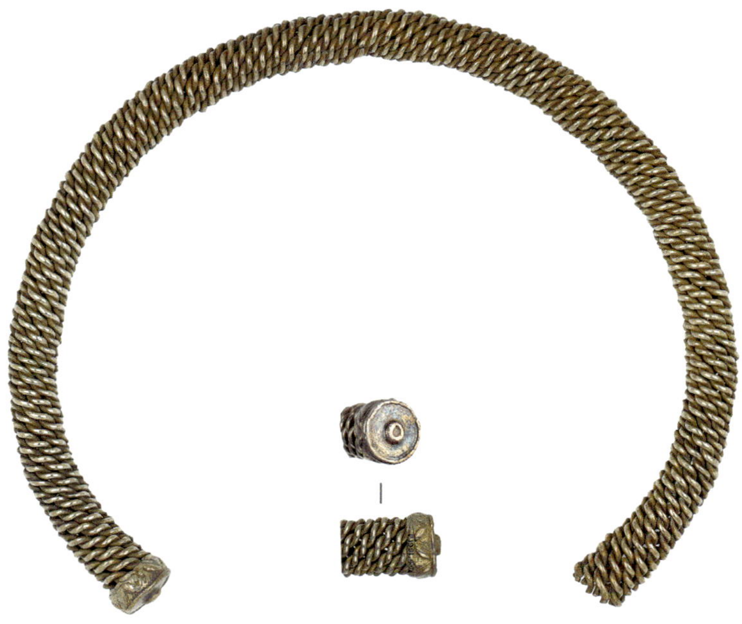

L.13

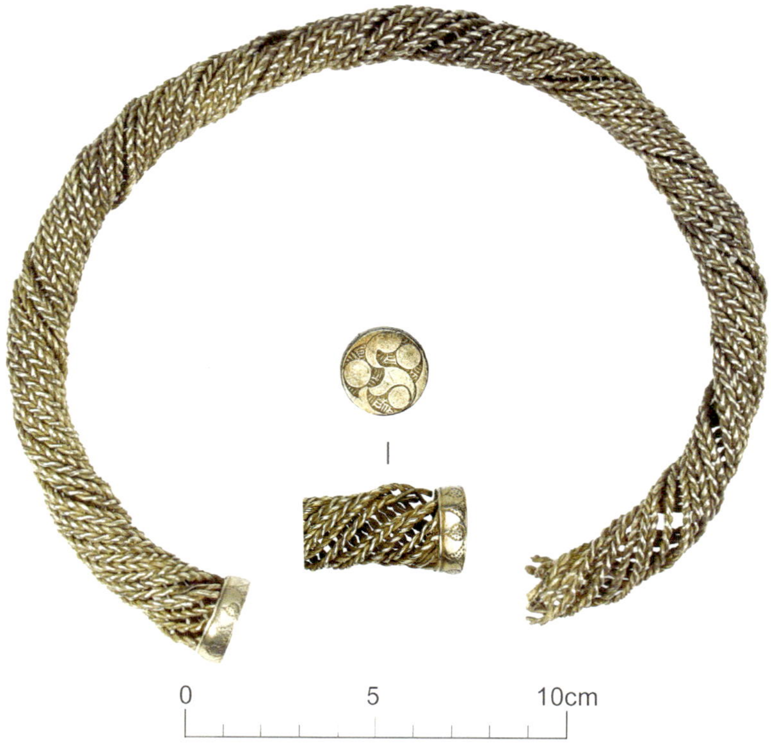

Plate 14.55

that metal was removed from the surface during the punching to create the recessed texture, as there is no evidence of raised ridges at the sides of the grooves from displaced metal or of polishing to remove them. So, the tool was essentially a combination chasing/engraving tool.

The outer edge of the terminal has a repeat geometrical pattern of teardrop and V-shapes formed by engraving the shape outlines and infilling with round punch-marks.
Wt: 237.4g; D(ext): 199.0mm; D(nr): 15.6mm; D(rope): 2.0mm; D(wire): 1.1mm; D(term): 23.3mm

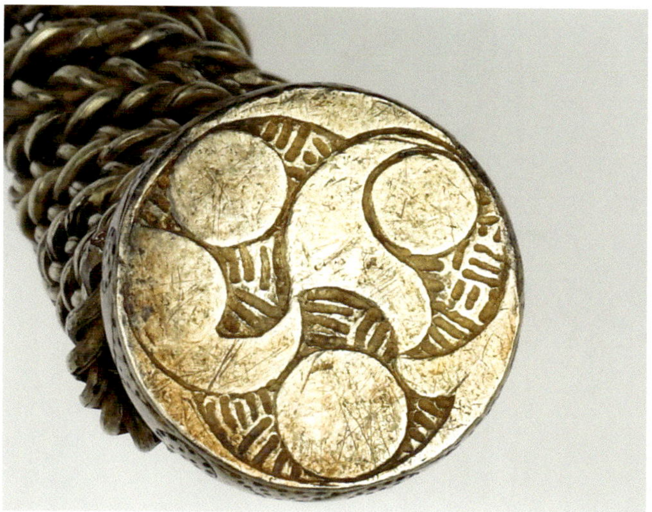

Figure 14.36 Detail of buffer terminal on L.13

Wt: 429.9g; D(ext): 179.0mm; D(nr): 11.3mm; D(rope): 4.1mm; D(wire): 2.1mm; D(term): 29.3mm

L.14: Gold/silver alloy torc (Pl. 14.56)
MSCC: (6C(2P))R
BM: 1991,0407.32; Site code: SN/PA
[Analysed: see Ch. 17]
Gold/silver alloy multi-strand torc with torus terminals and Stage III neck-ring. The cable is formed from six ropes coiled around a hollow core, each made up of two circular-section wires plied together. One of the simple cast torus terminals is now rather loose. The terminal heads seem to have been solid castings but the collars are hollow, each with a crude inner cordon. The collars are decorated with five raised, rounded dots on their outer edges, perhaps the heads of rivets mechanically affixing the terminals to the neck-ring (see Ch. 21 for discussion of decoration).

Notes from scientific analysis (Nigel Meeks)
This is a multi-strand torc, with Stage III neck-ring construction similar in overall appearance to e.g. L.18, but in this case with a completely different type of terminal: the torus terminals of L.14 are hollow castings attached to the prepared twisted wires of the neck-ring.
Six pairs of wires are coiled to form the neck-ring. They lie comfortably together, showing that the same number of turns was used for each plied pair. These circular-section wires show similar characteristics to other wires from the site, with uniform thickness, some evidence of linear faceting and smooth, polished outer exposed wires. But in this case there is a more prominent linear seam running along the wires. The seam runs along each wire with the twisting of the pairs. This seam must be a product of wire manufacture and possibly indicative of the use of a folded strip which has been made into round-section wire, albeit on a smaller scale than in the thick wire of torc S.31–9.
The wire neck-ring was prepared and assembled before the cast terminals were added. The terminals are simple. They are doughnut-shaped, hollow and have a wide neck that encapsulates the wire ends of the neck-ring. Unusually, compared to the other Snettisham torcs, there are five rivet heads on each terminal. Assuming these pass right into the terminals and are not simply a surface decoration, these would provide anchor points for the wires as a secure mechanical attachment.

Figure 14.37 shows a detail of the wires entering one terminal: there is no evidence of flow of metal onto the wires in this case. Other torcs, e.g. L.1, show metal flow. With this torc the terminals were therefore most likely cast separately and then added with the mechanical fixture. There is evidence of hammering to deform the neck edges to sit closer onto the wires.

L.15: Gold/silver alloy torc (Pl. 14.56)
MSCC: (8C)T
BM: 1991,0407.33; Site code: SN/PC
Fragment of gold/silver alloy multi-strand torc, comprising part of the neck-ring, broken and partly melted at one end, and a single surviving cage terminal. The terminal is formed from four confronted circular-section loops, each a continuation of one pair of the neck-ring wires, and also shows some evidence of melting. Stage II construction of eight twisted wires coiled around a hollow core.
Wt: 198.4g; D(nr): 11.0mm; D(wire): 2.6mm; D(term): 32.5mm; L: 112.0mm

L.16: Gold/silver alloy torc (Pl. 14.56)
MSCC: (6C(2PZ))R
BM: 1991,0407.34; Site code: SN/PE
[Analysed: see Ch. 17]
Fragment of gold/silver alloy multi-strand torc comprising one ring terminal and part of the Stage III neck-ring, cut at the other end (see **Figs 20.4b, 20.19a**; see Ch. 21 for discussion of decoration). The cable is formed from six ropes

Figure 14.37 Detail of join where wires meet terminal on torc L.14

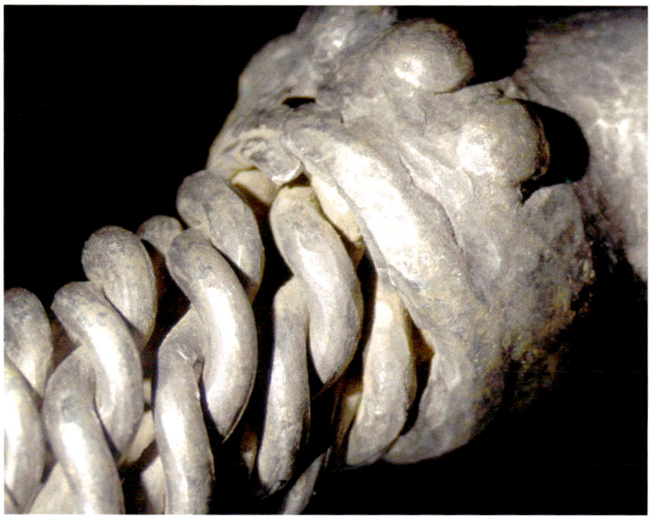

L.14

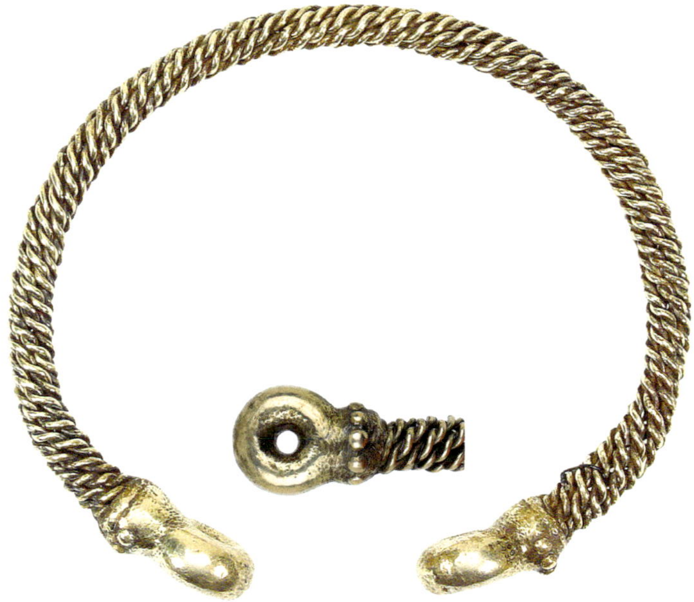

L.15

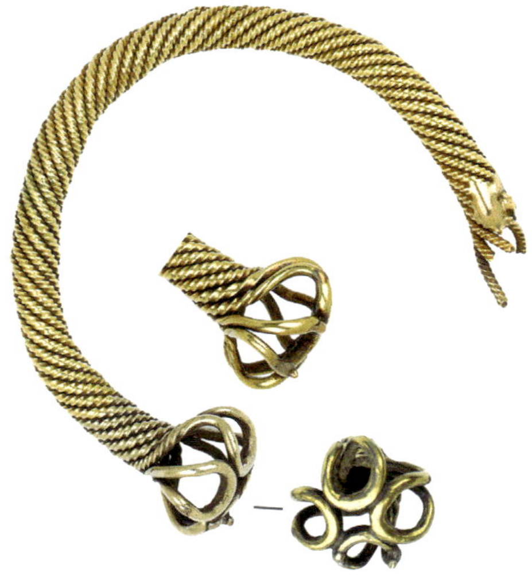

L.16

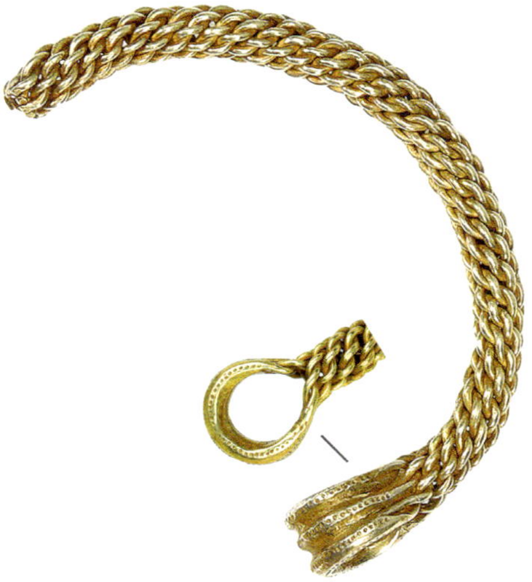

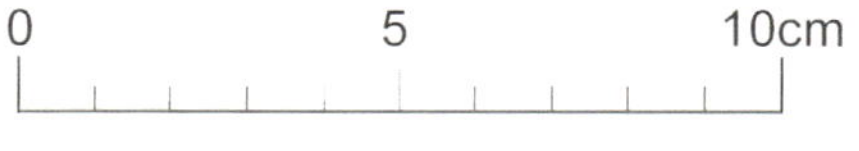

Plate 14.56

coiled together, each made up of two circular-section wires plied together Z-twist. The ring terminal is a merged triple loop, the three elements joined by applied sheet gold (see below). Each of the three loops is decorated round the circumference with a line of dots, and the outer loop has similar decoration on the outside. The ring terminals are continuous with the neck-ring wires, each of the three rings extending into two of the ropes.

Notes from scientific analysis (Nigel Meeks)
The Stage III neck-ring of this torc is formed from six ropes, each comprising two wires. The ropes were made in pairs: a long pair of wires was bent at the centre point around a mandrel to form an open loop, with the extended pairs then twisted together into two two-ply units, with another loop terminal made at the far end. Three identical such units, each with exactly the same number of twists, were themselves coiled together very neatly to form the complex multiple 12-wire torc. The adjacent twists fall comfortably together making a very elegant, uniform pattern. The final part of construction was to cover each three-loop terminal with a thin sheet of gold alloy, fold it around the loops and into the valleys between them, and hammer the sheet to tightly enclose the wires and to mechanically secure the loops together (**Fig. 14.38**). The terminals were finished by punching a dot decoration around each of the covered loops. The individual wires are of a fairly uniform round section but facets are again seen along their length – most clearly seen in the protected areas deeper into the twists. The outer exposed wires have been polished smooth by wear from use in antiquity. The SEM wire detail images (**Fig. 20.4b**) show the outer smoothness, linear facets, linear striations and deep groove, a thin folded overlap from hammering and wear indentations. The torc was clearly worn in antiquity.

The neck-ring wires have been cut through deliberately in antiquity with a straight cut from a chisel (**Fig. 20.19a**).
Wt: 174.6g; D(nr): 6.8mm; D(wire): 2.0mm; D(term): 24.7mm; L: 136.4mm

L.17: Gold/silver alloy torc (Pl. 14.57)
MSCC: (8C)T
BM: 1991,0407.35; Site code: SN/PG
[Analysed: see Ch. 17]
Gold/silver alloy multi-strand torc, with buffer terminals and Stage II neck-ring of eight twisted wires coiled around a hollow core (four of the strands are broken at different points towards the back) (see **Fig. 20.5a–c** and Ch. 21). The cast buffer terminals have plain, flat faces and are decorated around the edge with a crimped cordon. Some of the neck-ring strands have merged when the terminal was cast on.

Notes from scientific analysis (Nigel Meeks)
This torc is a very springy and flexible coiled multi-strand torc with a simple cast cap-end buffer terminal.
Individual wires are made from square-section wire that is quite tightly twisted on itself and this gives the characteristic uniform spiral geometrical texture or pattern. As the wire is twisted, the square-section corners effectively become ridges while the flat-section sides become concave valleys between

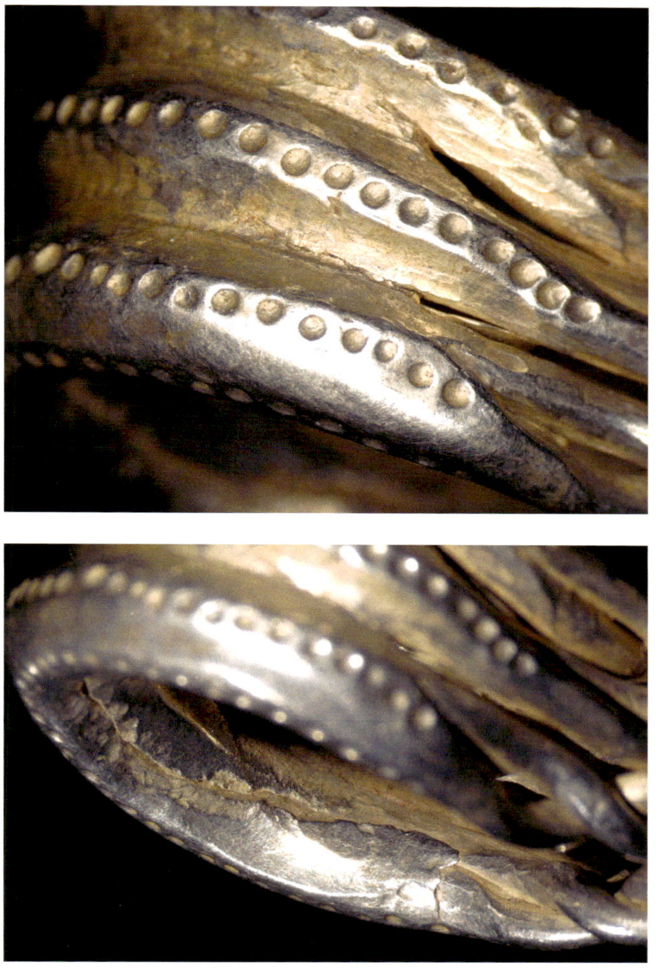

Figure 14.38 Detail of decoration and overlapping sheet on the terminals of L.16

the ridges. Eight such twisted wires were then coiled together, probably around a former to prevent them collapsing onto themselves during twisting and subsequent bending of the neck-ring into its shape (Chs 17, 19). Both of these mechanical operations were done before casting-on the terminals so that the wires could move relative to one another during bending. They were then permanently locked into the coiled and curved shape once the terminals were cast on.

The buffer terminals are plain on their flat ends but have a wavy cast-in pattern around the outer circumference, where they join the neck-ring. The assembled cap and wires are well fused and a little post-casting tooling was applied to clean up the terminal where the wires join at around 45 degrees.

Because the torc is so flexible there is a lot of wear between adjacent wires through extensive use in antiquity (see **Fig. 20.5a–c**), more than is seen on most torcs, yet overall the torc is in very good condition. This implies much careful wearing in antiquity, probably over some time to create the degree of wear. Some wires are broken but the majority are sound.
Wt: 216.0g; D(ext): 167.0mm; D(nr): 11.0mm; D(wire): 2.0mm; D(term): 20.1mm

L.18: Gold/silver alloy torc (Pl. 14.57)
MSCC: (4CZ(2P))R
BM: 1991,0407.36; Site code: SN/PJ
[Analysed: see Ch. 17]

L17

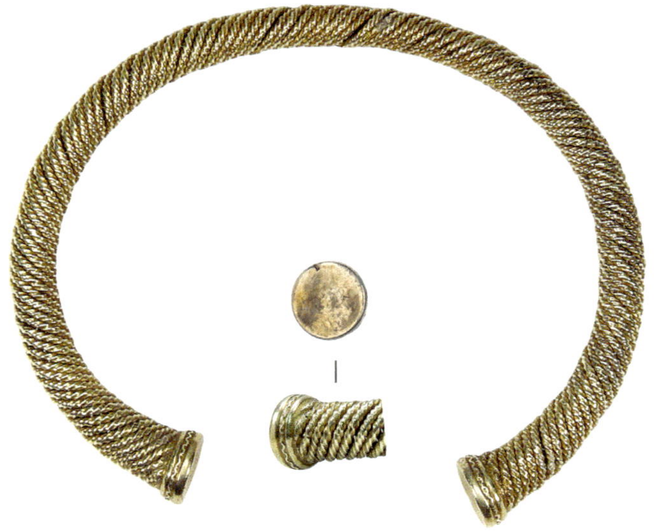

L.18

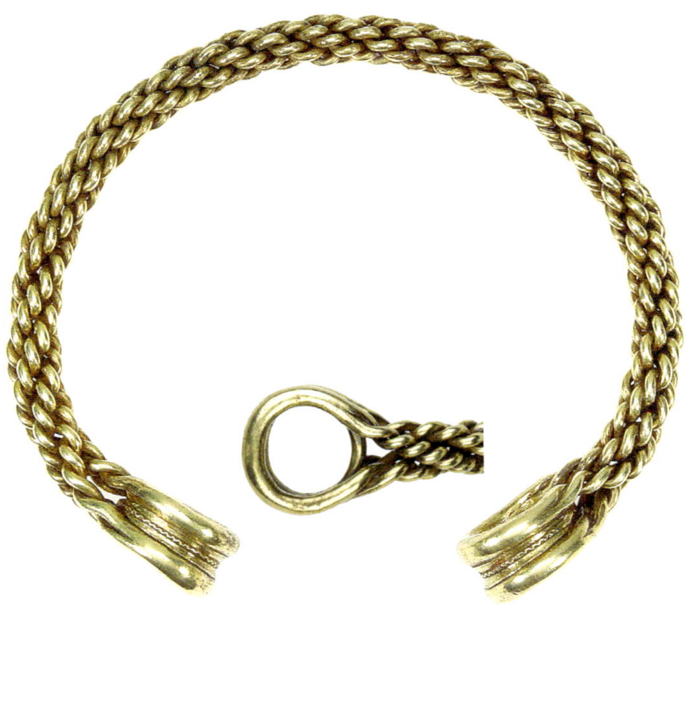

0 5 10cm

Plate 14.57

Gold/silver alloy multi-strand torc with Stage III neck-ring and double-ring terminals. The cable is formed of four ropes coiled together Z-twist, each made up of two circular-section wires plied together. The terminals are merged double rings with a wide (?soldered) ring between the two elements. The wide central ring is slightly concave and decorated with a central notched/crimped rib (see Ch. 21 for discussion of decoration). The outer rings are continuous with the neck-ring wires, each extending into two of the ropes.

Notes from scientific analysis (Nigel Meeks)
This torc shows similar construction to L.16, but with two rather than three components twisted together, giving eight wires in the finished torc neck-ring. The main difference in construction is that here there is a third loop inserted in the middle of each ring terminal as a spacer.

The loops each comprise two fused wires, from the original pair of round-section wires, formed into a single loop, probably hammered to mechanically fuse them together into one round-section loop – the seams between loop wires are seen in (**Fig. 14.39**). It is a possibility that some soldering was used to facilitate fusion of the loops together along with the third spacer loop as the complete joins are seamless and there is a fine stress corrosion crack at the join, typical of an ancient soldered joint. There are also some mechanical hammer marks inside of the joined loops. The pre-formed Stage II components with their fused loops would have been twisted together in the same manner as L.16, with the loops most likely used as 'handles' for twisting the neck-ring. In this case the identically sized Stage II components match precisely in their twisting to form an elegant, symmetrical pattern. The final step in their construction was to punch a dot decoration onto the centre-line of each ring terminal and then to engrave lines around punched decoration (**Fig. 14.41**). These lines overlap the dots and partly obscure them, giving the effect of a zig-zag.

The wires are highly polished on the outside, with use wear between wires where they rubbed together in use. Protected areas of the wires show linear facets (**Fig. 14.40**). Wt: 537.2g; D(ext): 177.0mm; D(nr): 15.1mm; D(rope): 6.8mm; D(wire): 2.9mm; D(term): 34.3mm

L.19a–f: Composite group (interlinked) (Pl. 14.58)
BM: 1991,0407.37; Site code: SN/PL
[Analysed: see Ch. 17]
Torc L.19a has been heavily repaired using additional metal objects and components. Wire L.19b runs around the torc from terminal to terminal, wrapped around the neck-ring wires. Torc/bracelet L.19c is inserted through the terminals, acting as a clasp and support. Gold sheet or tubular torc fragment L.19d forms a 'collar' around the back where the wires of the neck-ring are broken. Strips L.19e are wrapped around one of the terminals as a repair to fix it to the neck-ring, and strip L.19f is used for a repair at the back of the torc neck-ring, alongside L.19d.
L.19b is perhaps the latest repair to torc L.19a. One of the wires of L.19b starts within terminal B where it is hooked over the strands of torc/bracelet L.19c, then wraps over the strips of L.19e, round the strands of the torc neck-ring, over the gold sheet at the back of the neck-ring (L.19d) and hooks

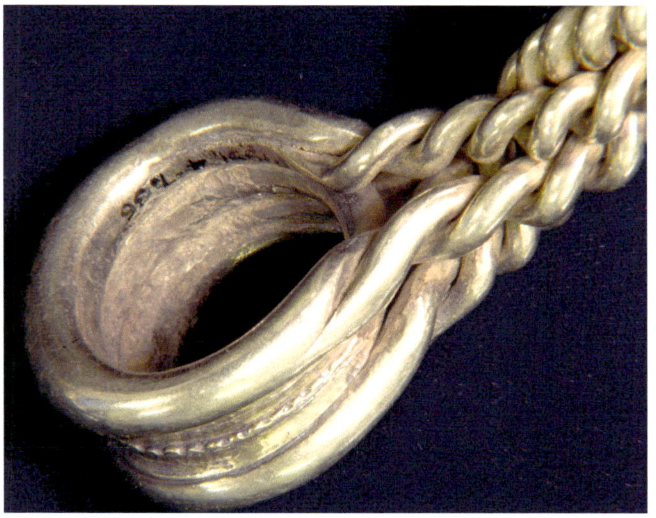

Figure 14.39 Detail showing fused terminals on L.18

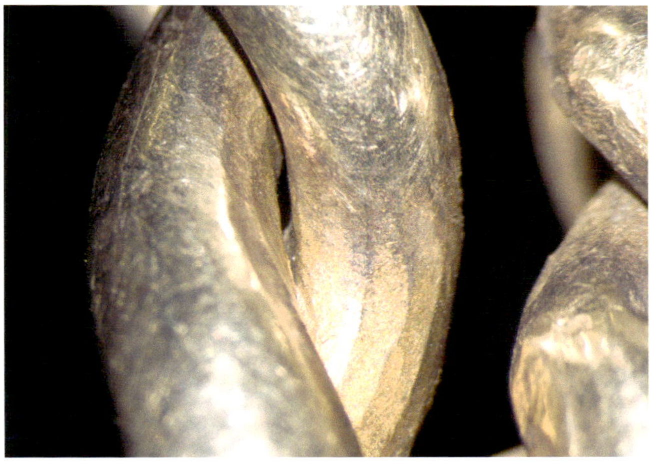

Figure 14.40 Detail showing faceted wires on L.18

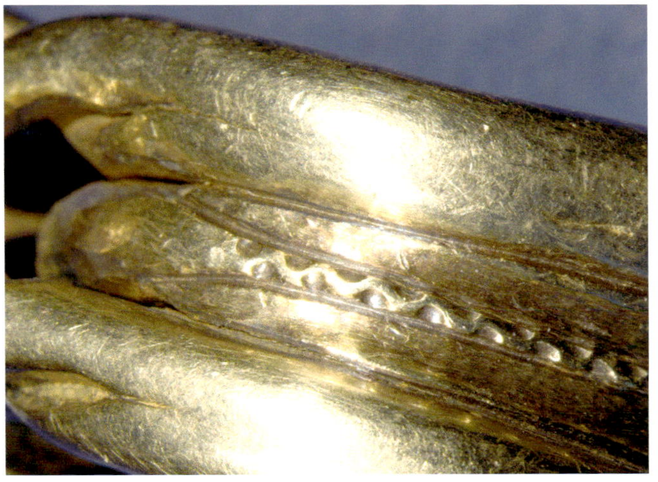

Figure 14.41 Detail showing chased and punched terminal decoration on L.18

under a piece of the same or very similar twisted strand. This second piece of L.19b is wrapped three times round the torc strands (and over the strip L.19f which repairs the back of the neck-ring). One end disappears amongst the strands and the other passes over gold sheet L.19d and ends amongst the strands on the other side.
Torc/bracelet fragment L.19c links the terminals of L.19, its own terminal passing through the perforation in terminal A

L.19a-f

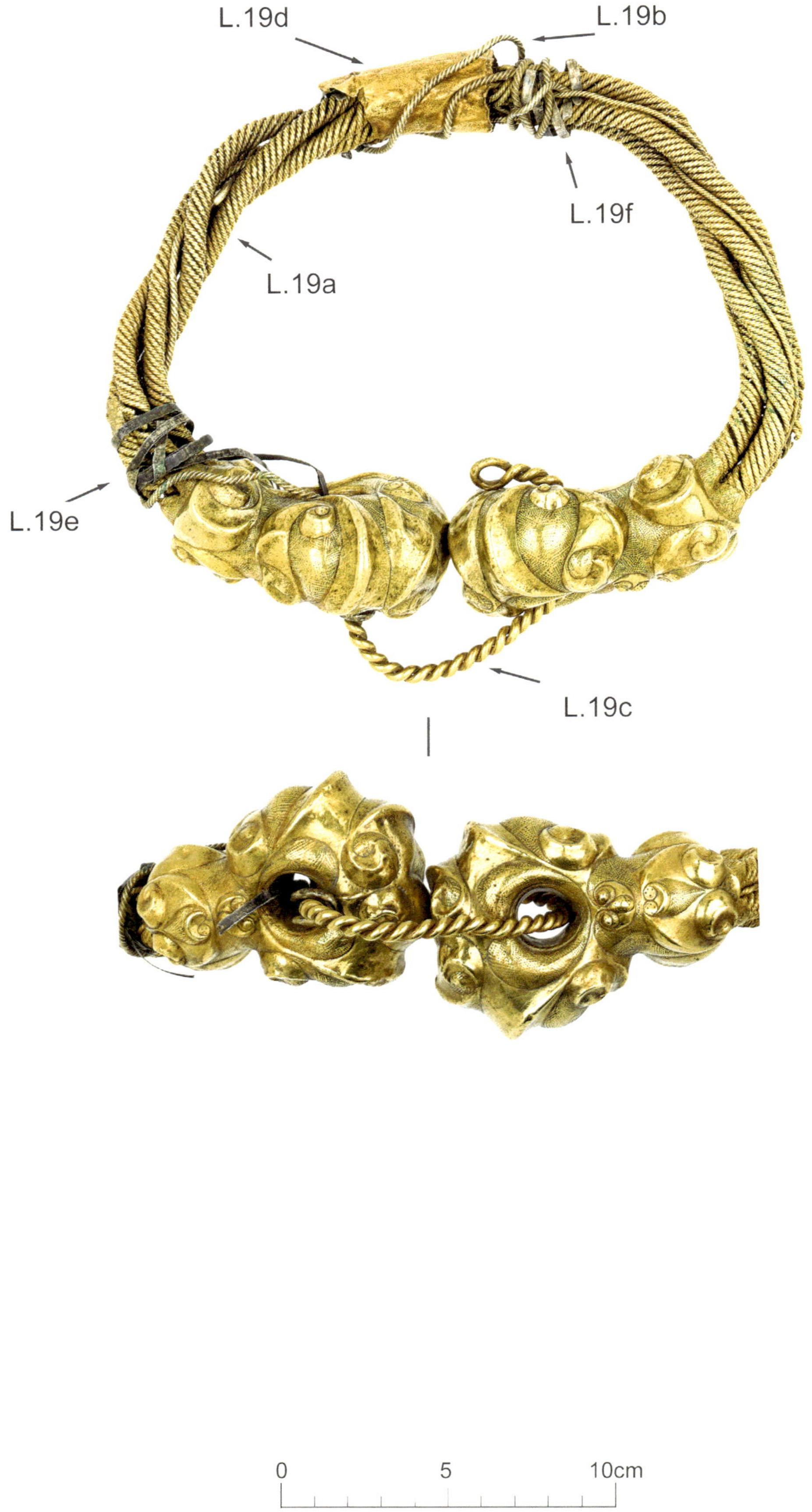

Plate 14.58

and its broken end stopping within terminal B.
Sheet gold 'collar' L.19d around the back of the neck-ring of torc L.19a covers strip L.19f and is covered by wire L.19b, suggesting a multi-phase or stage repair.
One strip of L.19e starts within the central hole of terminal B of torc L.19a and the other passes through this hole. Both are wrapped round the neck-ring wires adjoining the terminal and extend for about 25mm up the neck-ring.
Strip(s) L.19f are wrapped round the back of the neck-ring of torc L.19a at either side of the sheet 'collar' L.19d. One strip extends to 28mm from one end of the collar and the other stops on line with the other end of the collar. It may well be that they are linked under the collar.
Wt: 766.9g (total for L.19a–f)

L.19a: Gold/silver alloy torc
MSCC: (4C(4C))T
Gold/silver alloy multi-strand torc with sheet gold torus terminals. Sometimes known as 'The Grotesque Torc', or 'The Marriage Torc' (see **Figs 17.94a–b, 17.98–9, 17.100a–b, 17.101, 20.15–16, 21.30**). Complete, but much repaired in antiquity. The Stage III neck-ring is formed from four coiled ropes, each of which is made up of four coiled strands of twisted wire. The sheet gold terminals are shaped to grasp the ends of the four coiled cables (the sockets stippled like some of the decoration on the terminals). The terminals are decorated in high relief in the Plastic Style, including elements of zoomorphic decoration. There are several holes in the end of terminal A, and the neck-ring is completely broken at the back, where is has been repaired. See Chapter 17 for information on construction, and Chapter 21 for a full discussion of decoration.

Notes from scientific analysis (Nigel Meeks)
This torc is complex and has massive-looking terminals although it still has the overall main construction features of a multi-strand wire neck-ring. In this case the terminals are made from deeply embossed thin sheet gold, with better defined decoration than the sheet terminal F.72. The torc was extensively repaired in antiquity at a break in the middle of the neck-ring which is clearly visible in the X-radiograph (see **Fig. 20.16a–b**).

The neck-ring comprises four coiled ropes, each formed from multiple twisted square-section wire strands, giving a very even texture. The ropes are themselves loosely twisted together, with about three turns to form the completed neck-ring. The wire ends are soldered into the hollow sheet terminals. This combination makes a rather loose, flexible neck-ring compared to other more tightly twisted or coiled multi-strand examples.

The ends of all of the complete wire ropes enter just into the neck of the hollow terminals (see **Figs 17.98b, 17.99a–b, 17.101**, **20.16a–b**) and the terminal sheet has been pressed onto and around the wires which mechanically encloses them to hold them firmly. This reduces the otherwise open spaces between the terminal and wires. There is evidence of solder flow and heating on the wires as they enter the terminals. Unlike the cast terminal/wire interface on other torcs (e.g. L.21a) that are fairly solid and substantial, these have a more open structure as it was not possible to fill the spaces with solder. The overall mass of the terminals is actually minimised by the construction methods and produced a lighter weight, but still substantial, large torc.

The terminals have decorative designs and large deep features produced by hammering and chasing the sheet gold possibly in combination with repoussé, via the open neck (see **Fig. 17.100a–b**). Within some of the fields between the deep designs the surface has been textured in a punched dot pattern using a single round-ended punch (see **Fig. 17.100b**). The outlines of these areas have been defined by chasing lines around the perimeter. This is similar to terminal F.72.

The X-radiograph (see **Fig. 20.16a–b**) clearly shows that the neck-ring had been severed right through the middle region in antiquity. Possibly this was due to fatigue fracture with constant flexing and opening of the torc to fit around the neck. The repair must be ancient and is simply a collar of sheet gold (L.19d, possibly a tubular torc fragment) that has been wrapped around the broken wires and forming a double layer. There is no evidence of solder or any kind of more permanent repair either joining the wires together or joining the tubular sheet to the wires. The strips of silvery sheet and twisted single wires in the area (L.19b, e and f) might have some mechanical retaining purpose for the tubular sheet repair, but it is not a very substantial repair on its own that would allow further wearing of the torc. However, the broken torc or bracelet looping through the terminals (L.19c) may have been a securing 'clasp' to allow its use after the repair.

The surface of the sheet repair (L.19d) has been textured with fine dot-punched decoration similar to the terminal but done with a different punch.
D(ext): 210.0mm; D(nr): 19.0mm; D(rope): 11.4mm; D(wire): 1.7mm; D(term): 67.0mm

L.19b: Gold/silver alloy wire
Two lengths of gold/silver alloy twisted wire, of thicker gauge than the neck-ring wires of torc L.19a.
D(wire): 2.3mm

L.19c: Gold/silver alloy torc/bracelet
MSCC: (2P)R
Fragment of gold/silver alloy multi-strand torc or bracelet comprising one loop terminal (continuous with the neck-ring/body wires) and a length of neck-ring/body, broken at the other end. Stage II construction of two circular-section wires plied together.
D(ext): 78.0mm; D(nr): 4.8mm; D(wire): 2.5mm; D(term): 10.0mm

L.19d: Gold/silver alloy torc/sheet
?TUBULAR (?TYPE 4/5/6)
A length of sheet gold/silver alloy tube with no apparent join, possibly once part of a tubular torc. At one end there seem to be two very thin overlapping layers.
L: 55.0mm

L.19e: Gold/silver alloy strip
Two lengths of gold/silver alloy strip, with flat, rectangular cross-section.
W: 3.0mm; T: 0.2mm

L.20a-b

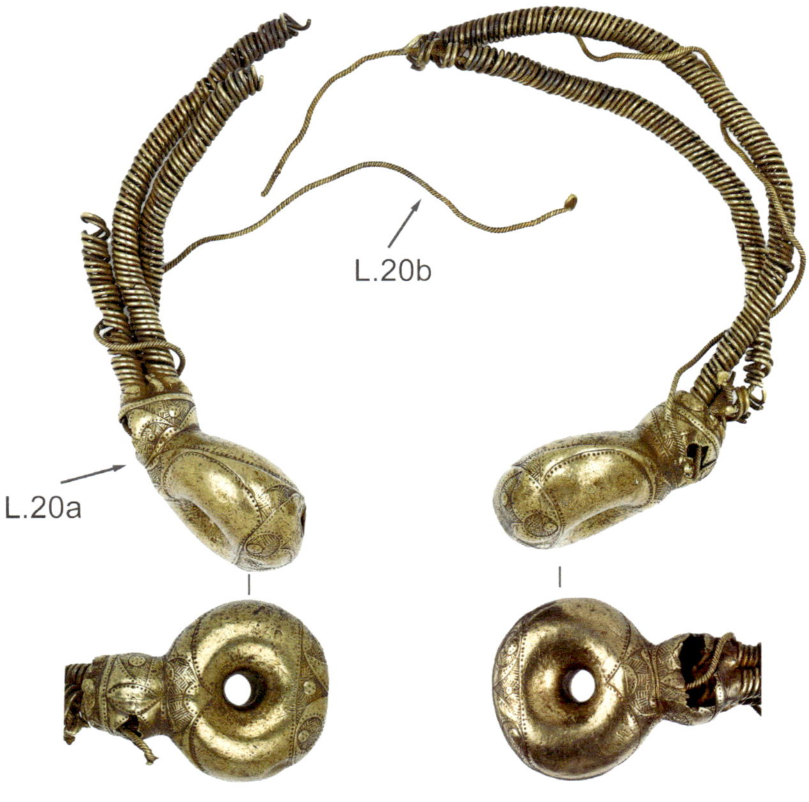

L.21a-b

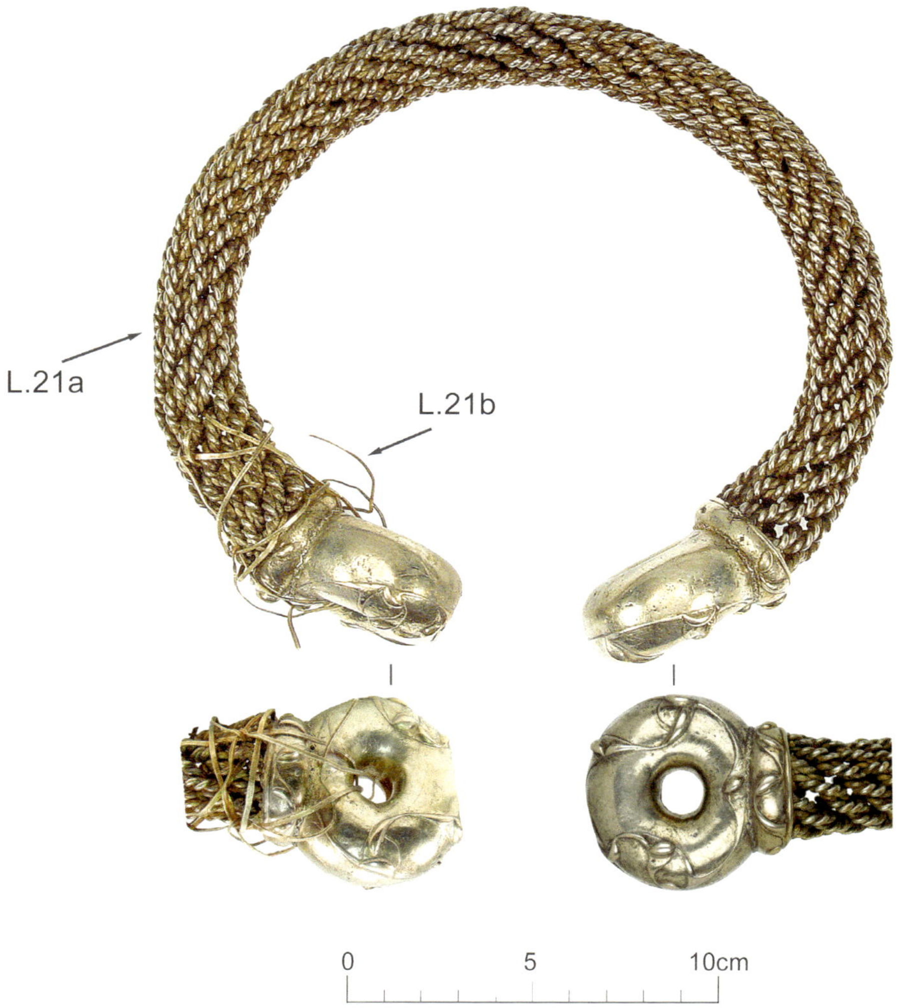

Plate 14.59

L.19f: Gold/silver alloy strip
Length(s) of gold/silver alloy strip, with flat, rectangular cross-section.
W: 3.0mm; T: 0.2mm

L.20a–b: Composite group (interlinked) (Pl. 14.59)
BM: 1991,0407.38; Site code: SN/PN
Broken torc L.20a has been repaired using twisted wires L.20b. One strand that starts in a hole in the side of the collar of terminal A is twisted once round all three coiled ropes and is then loose, terminating in a circular-section (not twisted) spiral about 5mm in diameter, like two coils of a brooch spring. Terminal B has been repaired with two lengths of twisted strand, one wrapped round one of the coiled ropes and hooked through a hole in the collar and the other passing through the other coiled rope. Even with these repairs, the torc is so broken that it is hard to imagine how it could have been worn.
Wt: 353.0g (total for L.20a–b)

L.20a: Gold/silver alloy torc
MSCC: (6C([2Px3]+[4Cx3]))R
Gold/silver alloy multi-strand torc in two halves (broken in antiquity), with torus terminals and Stage III neck-ring, now heavily damaged but probably originally comprising six ropes of two types coiled together, arranged alternately (see **Fig. 21.26**). The three more substantial ropes are formed from four wires coiled around a hollow core; each of the three smaller ropes has two strands twisted together. The ends of all six ropes survive in terminal A (the longest of the smaller ropes only 5mm long), but for the rest of the torc only the larger ropes now survive. The hollow, damaged torus terminals are probably of sheet construction. Each carries a La Tène-style incised design of triangular and other shapes infilled with random 'basket-weave' hatching and the occasional ring with dots, most of the shapes bordered by external lines of dots. The decoration is worn, especially on the ends. Decoration on the collars ends with a dotted cordon, beyond which the metal sheet is shaped to grasp each of the cables. The collar of terminal A is badly broken on the outside, with a hole about 20mm long and some 8mm wide, and the head has a large dent and a crack. Terminal B also has a hole through the collar (though not as big as that in A) and the end of the head is worn and dented, but not broken. The artefact looks much used and has been repaired in antiquity with a twisted piece of gold/silver alloy wire (L.20b) which is affixed to the base of each terminal. Both terminals also have small soldered or part-melted sheet fragments near the collar. See Chapter 21 for a full discussion of decoration.
D(ext): (approx.) 175.0mm; D(nr): 20.0mm; D(rope): 8.0 mm (max.); D(wire): 1.4mm; D(term): 49.5mm

L.20b: Gold/silver alloy wire
Three lengths of gold/silver alloy twisted wire used to repair torc L.20a.
D(wire): 1.8mm

L.21a–b: Composite group (interlinked) (Pl. 14.59)
BM: 1991,0407.39; Site code: SN/PO
[Analysed: see Ch. 17]
Strip L.21b is twisted around one of the terminals of torc L.21a, as a repair reattaching it to the neck-ring (**Fig. 14.42**).
Wt: 917.8g (total for L.21a–b)

L.21a: Gold/silver alloy torc
MSCC: (8C(2P(2P)))R
Gold/silver alloy multi-strand torc with Stage IV neck-ring and cast torus terminals (see **Figs 17.63–5, 17.68a–b, 20.6a–b, 20.11, 21.15, 23.8**). The neck-ring consists of eight cables coiled loosely together, each comprising two ropes plied together, each rope formed from two plied circular-section wires. One of the cables has broken near the terminal which is still securely attached. The other terminal has broken away from some (or all) of its neck-ring wires and has been crudely secured by a length of gold/silver alloy strip (L.21b). The terminals are flawed hollow castings and in parts the collar of one terminal does not completely cover the strands. The same terminal has three small holes and a large hole on the inside of the ring that are unlikely to be the result of damage and are probably casting flaws. Some small holes in more visible areas have very neat patches. The other (detached) terminal has a slightly smaller hole in the eye and a much larger hole at the end (up to 20mm long and 14mm wide), most likely a casting flaw. The collars are wider on the outside, and each has a plain cordon where it meets the head and a crimped cordon where it meets the neck-ring. There is high-relief ornament of lobes and triangular shapes on the collar and the head. See Chapter 17 for information on construction, and Chapter 21 for a full discussion of decoration.

Notes from scientific analysis (Nigel Meeks)
This is a multi-strand torc with Stage IV neck-ring construction, with the hollow terminals cast onto the prepared twisted wires of the neck-ring. It is similar to torc L.1. The torc has an entwined strip of rectangular-section wire (L.21b) wound round and through one terminal which serves no mechanical purpose, though it may have been intended to reinforce the join between neck-ring and terminal. The torus terminals were cast onto the neck-ring, and dribbling can be seen around the wires (see **Fig. 17.65**). There is a large cold-shut at the end of one terminal (**Figs 14.43, 17.68a–b**).

The overall appearance of the neck-ring wires is of a very symmetrical pattern, with the twists well aligned. The pairs of wires which form the ropes are tightly twisted together, as are the ropes and cables themselves, unlike the more loosely twisted torc L.1. Again, the wire characteristics make the neck-ring strong but flexible.

The outer regions of the wires are smooth and polished from wear (see **Fig. 20.6a–b**). The protected regions show many linear facets and a single groove and fine striations along the wires. Extreme mechanical wear is seen between many wires due to flexing and rubbing during extensive use in antiquity. A few wires are broken, particularly where they enter the terminals. In places the linear grooves are very deep and wide showing that the wire must have been originally folded from a strip. One unusual feature was noted on the surface of the worn outer wires – there is a

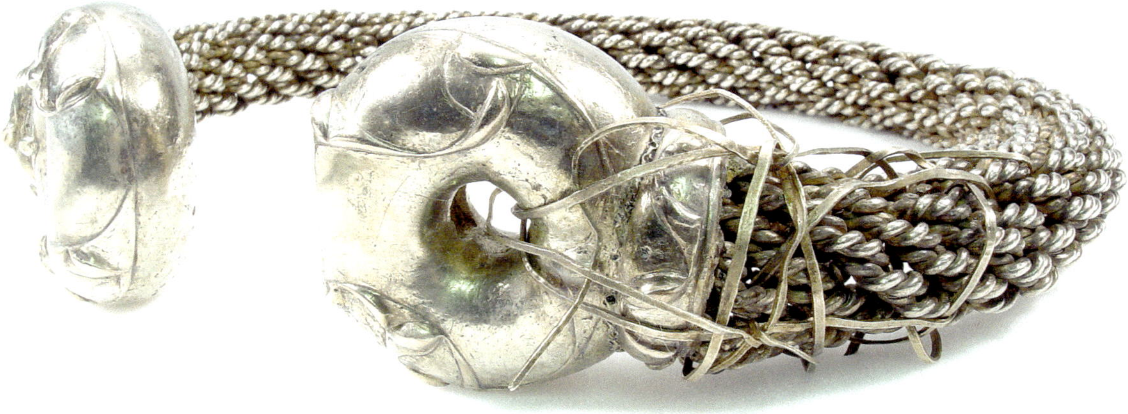

Figure 14.42 Detail showing looping of strip L.21b around the terminal of torc L.21a

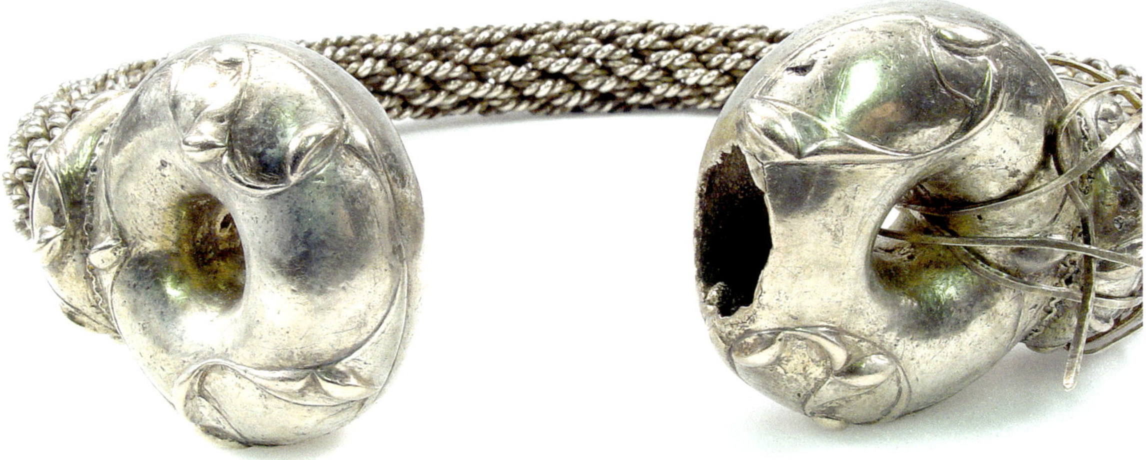

Figure 14.43 Detail showing terminal of L.21a with large cold-shut

colour difference between the worn centre areas of the curved wires and the surrounding surfaces. The worn centre is copper coloured and the outer edges more silver. This implies the surface layer is enriched in silver (depleted in copper), with the coppery-coloured core being exposed where this surface has worn away. This is typical of the silver-copper alloys that were investigated by sampling fragmentary pieces from Hoard F (Ch. 17), in which copper was found to be leached from the surface of these alloys by acidic pickling during manufacture. Therefore, by implication, this torc started as a silver/copper-rich alloy and the manufacturing process produced a more silvery colour.
D(ext): 199.0mm; D(nr): 21.1mm; D(cable): 5.9mm; D(rope): 4.0mm; D(wire): 2.0mm; D(term): 53.0mm

L.21b: Gold/silver alloy strip
Length of gold/silver alloy strip with flat rectangular cross-section, coiled/wrapped around the detached terminal of L.21a.
W: 1.0mm; T: 0.2mm

Hoard M

Recovered during detecting by Charles Hodder in 1991.
[Radiocarbon dated: see **Table 5.2**]

M.1: Silver-copper alloy lump (Pl. 14.60)
BM: 1992,1203.7
Large amorphous silver-copper alloy lump with charcoal inclusions.
Wt: 4482.0g; L: 245.0mm

M.2: Silver-copper alloy lump (Pl. 14.60)
BM: 1992,1203.8
Amorphous silver-copper alloy lump with charcoal inclusions.
Wt: 978.0g; L: 165.0mm

M.3: Silver-copper alloy lump (Pl. 14.60)
BM: 1992,1203.9
Amorphous silver-copper alloy lump with charcoal inclusions.
Wt: 767.0g; L: 123.0mm

M.4: Silver-copper alloy lump (Pl. 14.60)
BM: 1992,1203.10
Amorphous silver-copper alloy lump with charcoal inclusions.
Wt: 367.0g; L: 93.0mm

M.1

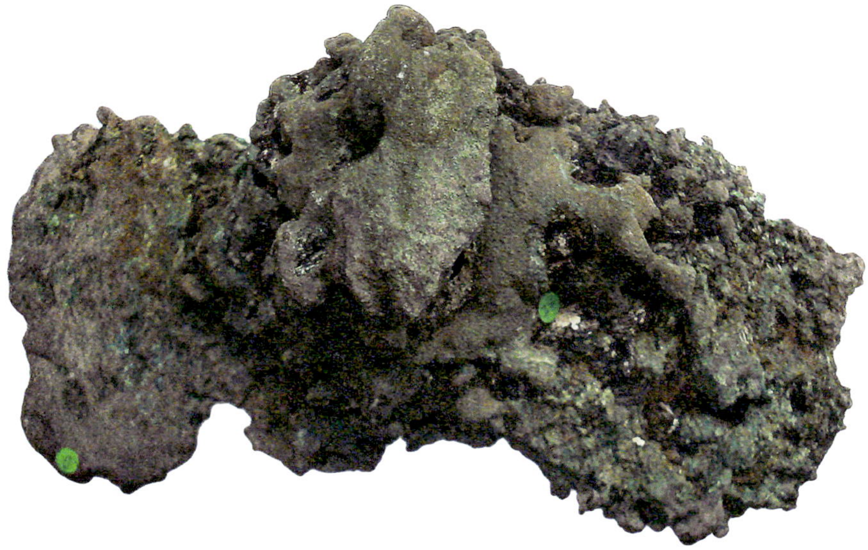

M.2

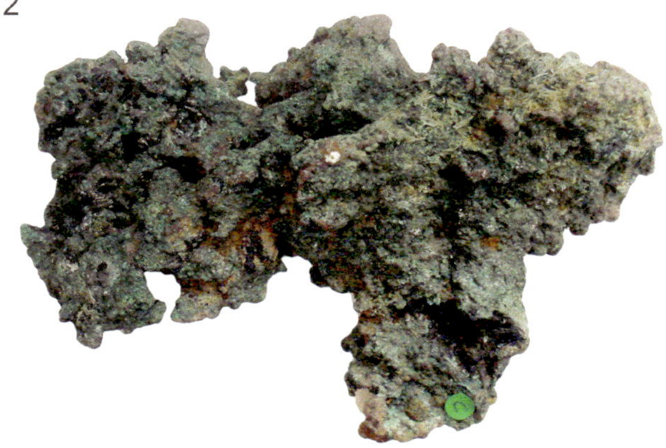

M.3

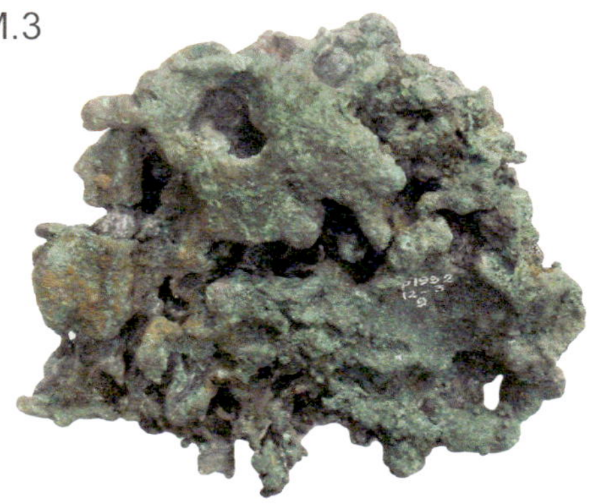

M.4

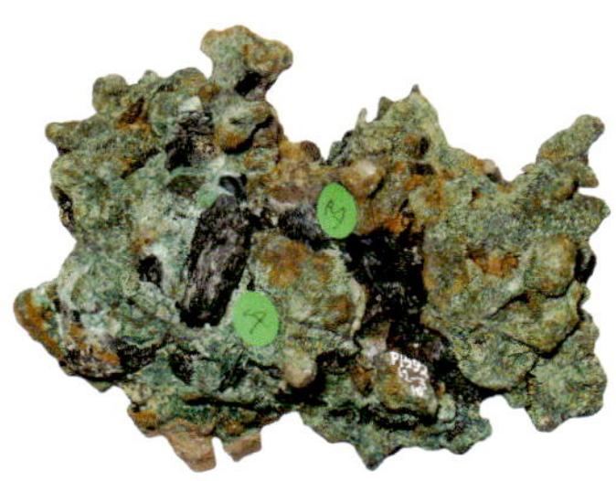

M.5

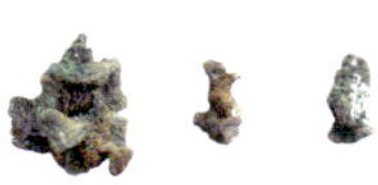

M.6

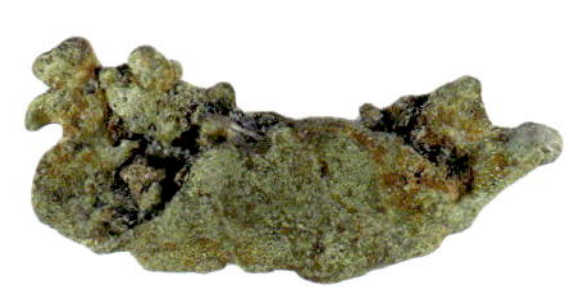

0 5 10cm

Plate 14.60

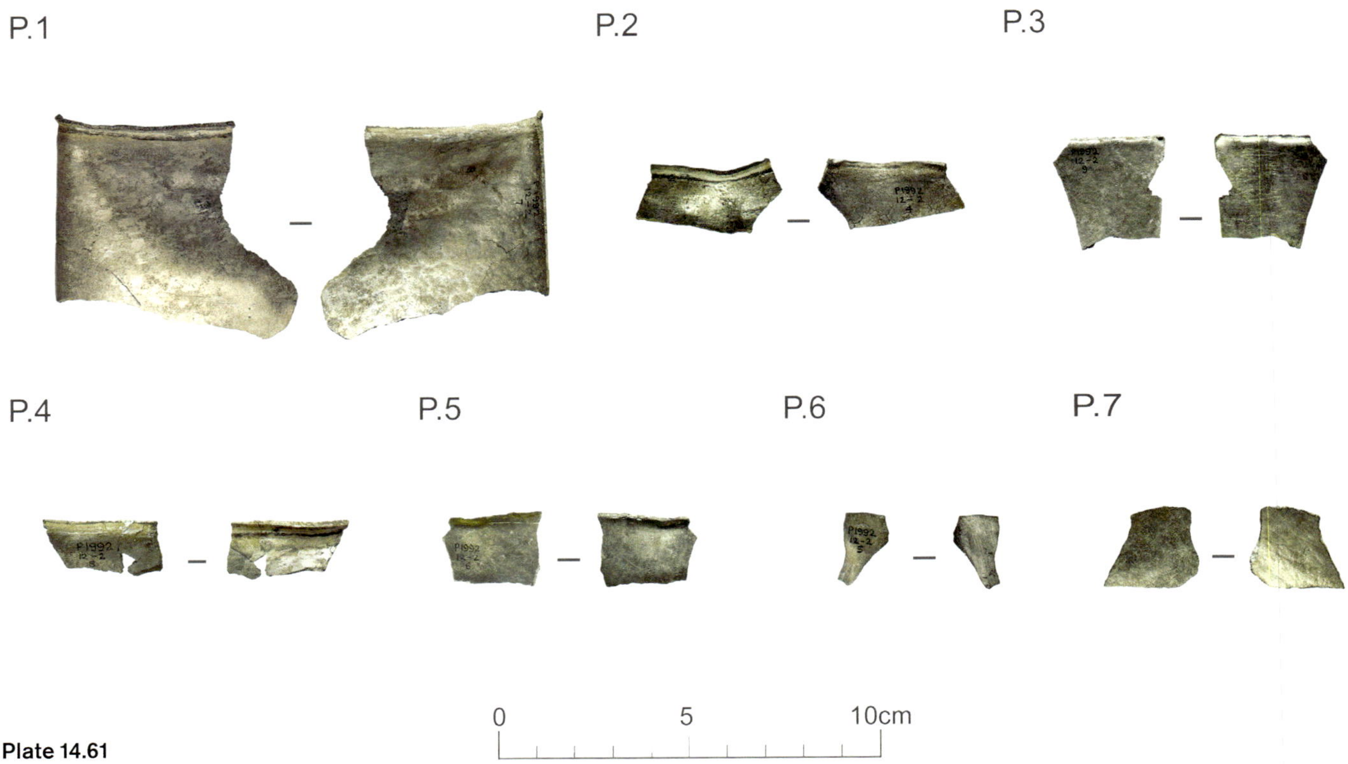

Plate 14.61

M.5: Silver-copper alloy lump (Pl. 14.60)
BM: 1992,1203.11
Three small amorphous silver-copper alloy lumps.
Wt: 8.0g; L: 20.5mm

M.6: Copper alloy lump (Pl. 14.60)
BM: 1991,0409.1
Amorphous copper alloy lump, possibly casting waste or a melted object.
Wt: 90.2g; L: 77.2mm; T: 18.0mm

Hoard P

Hoard P, composed predominantly of 1st-century AD local East Anglian silver coinage, was removed from the site by illicit metal detectorists between the 1990 and 1991 excavation seasons (Chs 2, 4, 12; see Ch. 15 for attempts to reconstruct the coin assemblage).

The hoard was reportedly found contained within a silver bowl. Seven non-joining fragments of silver vessel were recovered in or around the area thought to have produced the coin hoard during metal-detector surveys carried out as part of the 1991 (ST code) and 1992 (SM code) excavations. These finds are presented here as P.1–7.

P.1–7: Fragments of silver alloy vessel/bowl (Pl. 14.61)
Broken (non-joining) fragments of a silver alloy vessel, probably a bowl. Most likely the container which held the lost silver coin hoard, P. Simple raised copper alloy bowls are well known from Iron Age contexts, and a similar, although likely smaller, silver bowl was found in a mid-1st-century AD context at Hallaton, Leics. (Score 2011, 78, no. 30).

P.1: BM 1992,1202.7; Site code: ST/GT
Rim fragment from vessel. Body made from thin silver alloy sheet, with slightly thickened everted rim.
Wt: 23.0g; L: 81.3mm; T: 0.5mm (edge); T: 0.6mm (rim)

P.2: BM 1992,1202.4; Site code: ST/GQ
Rim fragment from vessel. Body made from thin silver alloy sheet, with slightly thickened everted rim.
Wt: 6.5g; L: 38.1mm; W: 18.1mm; T: 1.5mm (rim)

P.3: BM 1992,1202.9; Site code: ST/GW
Rim fragment from vessel. Body made from thin silver alloy sheet, with slightly thickened everted rim.
Wt: 5.2g; L: 36.8mm; W: 36.3mm; T: 0.4mm (edge); T: 0.7mm (rim)

P.4: BM 1992,1202.8; Site code: ST/GV
Rim fragment from vessel. Body made from thin silver alloy sheet, with slightly thickened everted rim. Now in two pieces and originally reconstructed from three pieces.
Wt: 4.9g; L: 31.0mm; W: 14.5mm; T: 0.9mm (edge); T: 2.0mm (rim)

P.5: BM 1992,1202.6; Site code: ST/GS
Rim fragment from vessel. Body made from thin silver alloy sheet, with slightly thickened everted rim.
Wt: 3.3g; L: 29.1mm; W: 22.0mm; T: 0.7mm (rim)

P.6: BM 1992,1202.5; Site code: ST/GQ
Fragment from vessel, body made from thin silver alloy sheet.
Wt: 0.4g; L: 20.8mm; W: 12.4mm; T: 0.2mm

P.7: BM 1992,0210.2; Site code: SM/AC
Context details: Metal-detected stray find March 1992.
Fragment from vessel, body made from thin silver alloy sheet.
Wt: 2.4g; L: 30.0mm; T: 0.8mm

Non-hoard metalwork finds

This catalogue covers non-hoard metalwork finds from across the site, and is divided into a number of sections:

Phase 2:

- S.1–S.10: Bronze Age to Earlier Iron Age (Phase 2) finds. See also Chapter 7 for further discussion of this material

Phases 3–4:

This section includes objects such as torcs and rings which may represent dispersed hoard material, alongside otherwise undiagnostic objects and fragments (such as ingots and sheet fragments) which find parallels in the hoards and thus may date to these phases of activity.

- S.11–S.83: Torcs, bracelets and related components contemporary with the hoards
    - S.11–S.76: Gold/silver alloy
    - S.77–S.83: Copper alloy
- S.84–S.100: Large/small rings
    - S.84–S.98: Gold/silver alloy
    - S.99–S.100: Copper alloy
- S.101–S.111: Lump and triangular ingots
    - S.101–S.103: Gold/silver alloy
    - S.104–S.111: Copper alloy
- S.112–S.122: Linear ingots
    - S.112–S.116: Gold/silver alloy
    - S.117–S.122: Copper alloy
- S.123–S.124: Unidentified objects: Possible ingots (copper alloy)
- S.125–S.129: Rod and wire
    - S.125–S.126: Gold/silver alloy
    - S.127–S.129: Copper alloy
- S.130–S.131: Metalworking waste (copper alloy casting sprues)
- S.132–S.140: Amorphous lumps: worked or incorporating part-melted objects and fused additions
    - S.132–S.138: Gold/silver alloy
    - S.139–S.140: Copper alloy
- S.141–S.234: Amorphous, unworked metal lumps (tabulated, not illustrated)
    - S.141–S.178: Gold/silver alloy
    - S.179–S.233: Copper alloys and lead alloys
    - S.234: Iron
- S.235–S.241: Possible beaded torc and bracelet fragments (copper alloy and iron)
- S.242–S.245: Brooches (silver and copper alloys) *(by Sophia Adams)*
- S.246–S.252: Other personal ornaments and fasteners (copper alloy)
- S.253–S.266: Fittings, mounts and strap fittings (copper alloy and iron)
- S.267–S.275: Rivets and rivet heads (copper alloy)
- S.276–S.286: Binding strips (copper alloy)
- S.287–S.307: Strip
    - S.287–S.306: Copper alloy
    - S.307: Iron
- S.308–S.339: Sheet fragments with original edges or other distinguishing features (copper alloy)
- S.340–S.351: Sheet fragments with no original edges or diagnostic features (copper alloy) (tabulated, not illustrated)
- S.352–S.354: Tools and implements (iron and copper alloy)
- S.355–S.359: Mail armour fragments and fitting (iron and copper alloy)
- S.360–S.365: Unidentified object fragments (copper alloy)

Almost all the finds dealt with in this section of the catalogue are stray finds recovered during agricultural activity or metal-detecting surveys at the site. There are three main phases of recovery (see also Chs 2 and 4):

- Torcs found during ploughing in the 1960s–70s (S.16–S.18 and S.31). These are held by NCM.
- Objects found in 1989–92 during Hodder's initial metal-detecting surveys of the 'gold field' and metal-detecting carried out as part of the 1990s excavation seasons. The majority of these are held by the BM, though a small group of 1989 finds are in NCM.
- Objects found during metal-detecting survey of the wooded area to the west of the 'gold field' in 2003–9. These are held by NCM.

The iron core from a tubular torc, S.12, was recovered in or shortly before 1999 (when it entered the collections of NCM), though no further information on the find circumstances could be found.

Only four objects, listed in **Table 14.1**, were discovered during archaeological excavation rather than detector survey. All were recovered during the 1992 season of the British Museum excavations. None of these objects, nor their contexts, can be closely dated. Brooch fragment S.244, identified by Sophia Adams, may date to 400–300 BC, but a post-150 BC date is also possible (see catalogue entry below). The knife, S.353, resembles Manning (1985) Type 1b, a Roman form most common in the 1st century AD.

This section of the catalogue combines the finds from across BM and NCM collections, allowing the identification of at least two fragmentary torcs which are split across the two museums (S.23–9 and S.31–9). In each catalogue entry, the museum and date of recovery are indicated, along with any details recorded about the method of discovery and location of the findspot. Objects for which the findspot was accurately recorded are plotted in **Figure 14.44**. At the time of writing, the 2003–9 material at NCM does not yet have full NCM registration numbers. In this case, each object was assigned a yellow raffle ticket during the study undertaken for this catalogue, based on the order of an original listing by John Davies and Amy Seaman. These raffle ticket numbers are given in the catalogue entries and also in the full concordance in Appendix 3.

In most cases, it is not possible to draw direct connections between these stray finds and the hoard material, though tubular torc core S.12 may be related to Hoard A, which has produced the only other comparable torcs from Snettisham. The upper part of Hoard J had been heavily truncated by ploughing, and it seems likely that S.20 is part of the same torc as J.2, and S.54 may be part of torc J.1. Similarly, many of the other fragmentary torcs, bracelets and rings (S.11–S.100) may also be scattered hoard material, in particular relating to the fragmentary Hoard F, which had clearly had its upper layers disturbed by ploughing. S.11a–b in particular are strong candidates for dispersed Hoard F material. However, no joins or direct connections have been identified at this time. The findspots of these objects, where

Cat. no.	Object	Trench	Feature	Feature Phase	Context details
S.244	Copper alloy bow brooch fragment	6	Enclosure ditch: SA6/2, section C	4	Layer 1, i.e. uppermost layer of ditch, cannot be considered a sealed context due to agricultural disturbance
S.246	Copper alloy strip, possibly pin from brooch or buckle	6	Natural feature (gully): SA6/7	N/A	Likely residual in a natural feature
S.286	Copper alloy U-shaped binding strip	7	Ditch: SA7/5, Section D	?6	Likely residual in a post-medieval feature
S.353	Iron knife	5	Hollow/Pit: SA5/3	?	From top 2–3cm of pit, i.e. cannot be considered a sealed context due to potential agricultural disturbance

Table 14.1 Non-hoard finds from archaeological excavation

recorded, are dispersed around the field rather than in a concentration which might suggest an additional hoard or hoards, though this cannot be ruled out.

Whilst the majority of the stray finds (torcs, rings, ingots, wire, S.11–S.129) have parallels in the torc hoards, suggesting they were part of the same phase and type of activity, other find types are present only in the dispersed material, especially that from the wooded area to the west of the site, surveyed in 2003–9. This includes metalworking debris in the form of casting sprues (S.130–S.131), and a large quantity of amorphous lumps of both gold/silver alloys (S.141–S.178) and copper and lead alloys (S.179–S.233) which may represent debris from metalworking or destructive processes such as the melting down of objects. Some of this material could be associated with later phases of activity at the site (Phases 4 and 5), but the presence of precious metal lumps suggests a likely association with the Phase 3 hoard activity. This argument is further strengthened by the fact that a small number of these lumps contain part-melted wire or gold sheet fragments likely from torcs (S.132–S.140).

Other find types are those that might be expected on an Iron Age and Roman site of this scale, including a small number of objects of personal adornment such as brooches, rings, buttons/fasteners (S.242–S.252), and beads that may be associated with one or more beaded torcs/bracelets (S.235–S.241), although this material is too corroded and fragmentary for secure identification. Various fittings and mounts (S.253–S.266) include a pair of zoomorphic copper alloy terminals, perhaps from drinking horns (S.253–4, found some way to the east, in the area of Trench 15), a terret (S.256–7) and a possible linch-pin terminal (S.255). There are two iron knives (S.352–S.353, not certainly ancient), and a small pair of copper alloy tweezers that are likewise hard to date closely (S.354).

Some of the stray finds clearly derive from larger objects, perhaps including metal vessels or vessels such as tankards with metal fittings. These include narrow strips of copper alloy sheet, some with rivet holes or extant rivets (S.287–S.307), a large number of copper alloy sheet fragments (S.308–S.351), nine copper alloy rivets and rivet heads (S.267–S.275), and fragments of U-shaped copper alloy binding strips (S.276–S.286). Some of this fragmentary material may also have derived from one or more shields. A corner binding from a hide-shaped shield was included in Hoard B/C (B/C.89) and the stray finds include another similar terminal (S.276).

Another set of material with martial associations amongst the stray finds is a small group of fragments derived from iron mail armour, or 'chain-mail' (S.356–9), likely dating from the Late Iron Age or Early Roman period. All the iron fragments come from the wooded area to the west of the 'gold field', and were recovered during the 2003–9 survey. Pre-conquest finds of mail armour are unusual in Britain. Perhaps the earliest example comes from a Middle Iron Age grave at Kirkburn in East Yorkshire (Stead 1991b, 224, figs 45, 81 and 127). There are more finds from Late Iron Age sites, including fragments of chain-mail from funerary contexts in 'chiefly' burials at Lexden (Essex, *c.* 20–15 BC, Laver 1927, 248; Foster 1986, 82–8), Folly Lane (St Albans/Verulamium, Herts, *c.* AD 50, Foster 1986; Niblett 1992, 923), and Baldock (Herts, late 1st century BC, Burleigh 1982). Other comparable mail armour finds come from the Stanwick Hoard (MacGregor 1962), the Late Iron Age/Early Roman Temple at Hayling Island (King, Soffe and Downey 1979, 7), and a placed deposit at the Roman temple at Ashwell (Jackson and Burleigh 2018, BM 2011,8012.40–3). The Folly Lane find was a complete tunic, whilst the mail armour from Baldock, Ashwell, and Stanwick had been deliberately fragmented in a manner seemingly similar to that seen at Snettisham. Over 140 fragments were present at Ashwell, and around 30 at Baldock, compared to just four at Snettisham. In some of these contexts, especially the high-status burials, the mail fragments may represent pre-conquest imports of Roman *lorica hamata* mail armour, perhaps as diplomatic gifts to indigenous elites. Whilst at present the Snettisham mail armour cannot be closely dated, the ring size of around 5mm is consistent with a date from the 3rd century BC to 3rd century AD (Wijnhoven 2022, 261–4).

S.355 (findspot not recorded) may represent a mail armour hook. These S-shaped 'dolphin' fittings were used in pairs to secure the shoulder flaps of mail armour from around the 3rd century BC to 1st century AD (Wijnhoven pers. comm.). Similar (although more elaborate) fittings have been found elsewhere in Britain, including in the Polden Hill Hoard (Brailsford 1975; BM 1846,0322.110–11), the Stanwick Hoard (BM 1847,0208.63, 2013,8037.1, 2018,8017.1), and at Hod Hill (1892,0901.543), Brough (BM 1874,0328.74), Camerton (Bristol Museum F684), Longthorpe (Bishop and Coulston 1993, 86), and Tooley Street (Southwark, BM 1905,1106.6) (see also Spratling 1972, nos 245–50).

Further research on the mail armour from Snettisham may uncover more details, or refine the dating, but this material certainly does not appear out of place at a Later

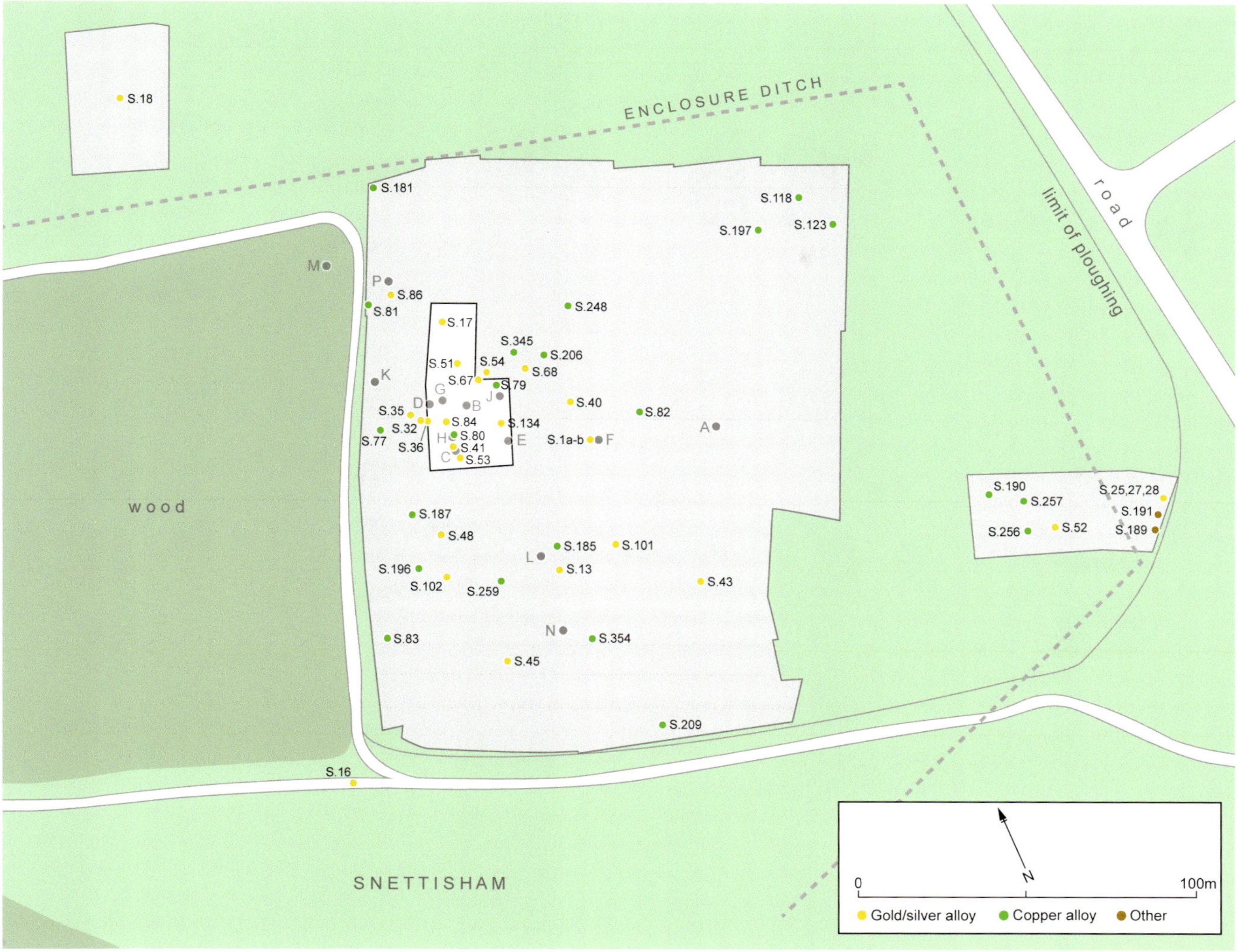

Figure 14.44 Distribution of stray finds

Iron Age and Early Roman temple site. In the absence of any other evidence, its presence alone is not enough to suggest a burial, but this remains a possibility.

Phase 2 Metalwork: Bronze Age and Earlier Iron Age finds

S.1: Copper alloy socketed axe fragment (Pl. 14.62)

BM: 1990,1101.42; Site code: SN/JZ
Findspot: Area 21
Context details: Metal-detected stray find from 1990 excavation.
Heavily worn and broken Late Bronze Age socketed axe fragment, comprising just the blade and part of the tip. Too worn for close identification.
Wt: 39.4g; L: 43.6mm; W: 35mm

S.2: Copper alloy sword chape (Pl. 14.62)

BM: 1991,0409.27; Site code: ST
Findspot: Not recorded
Context details: Metal-detected stray find Dec. 1990–April 1991.
Broken scabbard chape of simple semi-circular form, with the convex end defined by a bead. Flat on reverse, broken at the mouth. Probably the end of a Late Bronze Age bag-shaped dagger scabbard chape. cf. O'Connor (1980, 190–1, ref. 161), dating to *c.* 900–800 BC.
Wt: 6.3g; W: 30mm; T: 9.6mm

S.3: Copper alloy razor (Pl. 14.62)

NCM: yellow ticket no. 3
Findspot: Wooded area to west of main site
Context details: Metal-detected stray find 2003–9.
Terminal fragment from an Early Iron Age Hallstatt period razor. Moulded collar separates the perforated terminal from the body. Both arms are broken, leaving a V-shape fragment. Decorated on one side with three solid lines radiating away from the collar. This appears to be a Wiesloch-type razor, which can be assigned to the Llyn Fawr metalwork phase (*c.* 800–600 BC).

These razors are most common in Belgium and Britain (Jockenhövel 1980, 137–8, fig. 55). The closest parallel in Britain comes from the multi-period Salisbury Hoard (BM 2001,0702.7; O'Connor 2007) where it was deposited alongside Late Iron Age material (Stead 1998).
Wt: 1.8g; L: 20mm; W: 10mm; T: 2.5mm

S.4: Copper alloy arrowhead (Pl. 14.62)

NCM: yellow ticket no. 251
Findspot: Wooded area to west of main site
Context details: Metal-detected stray find 2003–9.

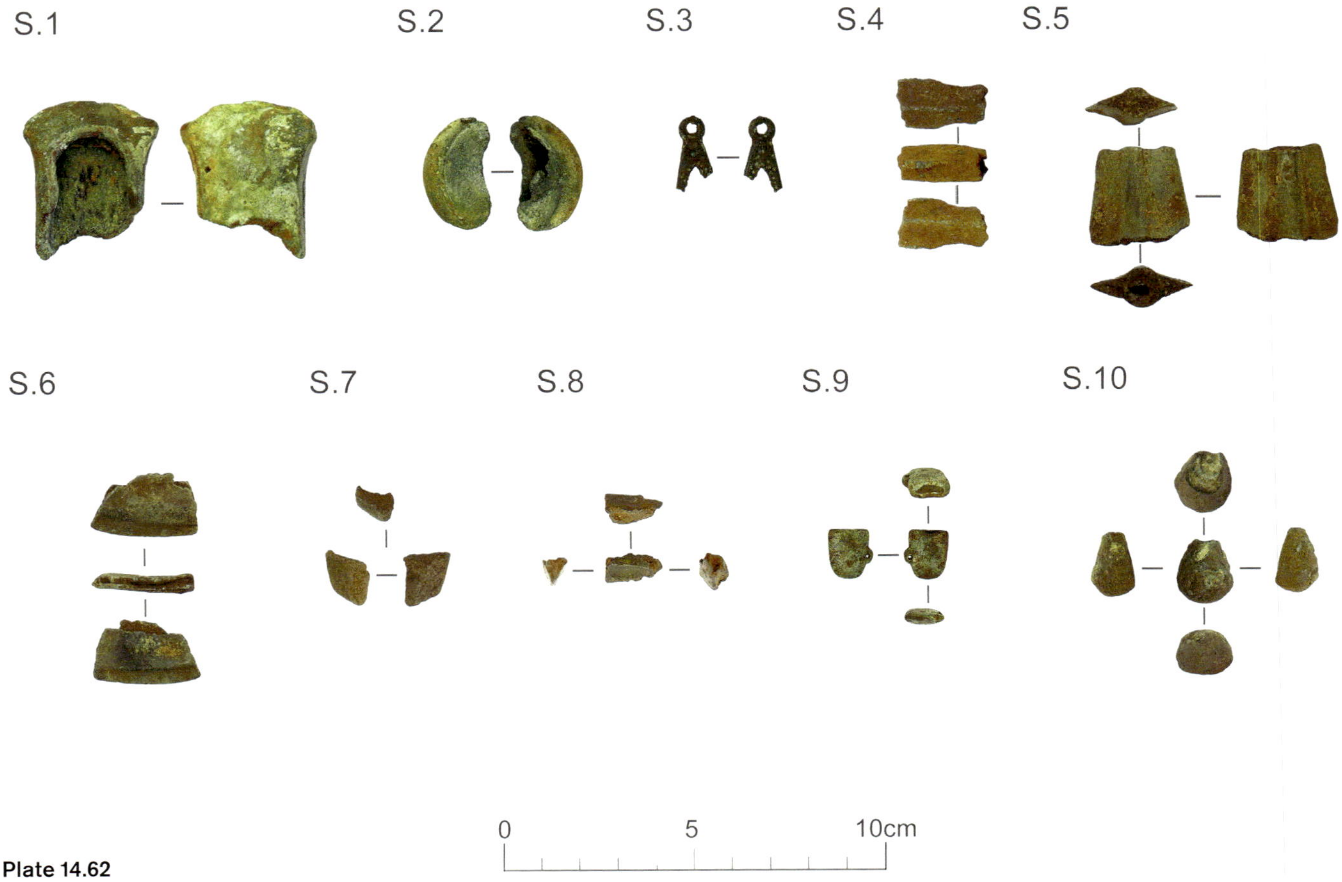

Plate 14.62

Broken Bronze Age copper alloy arrowhead, with raised central rib. The fragment comprises the base of the blade and the upper part of the socket; both the tip of the blade and the base of the socket are broken off.
Wt: 10.5g; L: 24mm; W: 14.6mm; T: 10.5mm

S.5: Copper alloy spearhead (Pl. 14.62)
NCM: yellow ticket no. 249
Findspot: Wooded area to west of main site
Context details: Metal-detected stray find 2003–9.
Short length of Bronze Age copper alloy spearhead, with raised central rib. Missing both tip and base, it is broken across the section of the blade on both ends, leaving a trapezoidal fragment from the body of the spearhead.
Wt: 18.4g; L: 24mm; W: 26.5mm; T: 10mm

S.6: Copper alloy blade fragment; ?spearhead (Pl. 14.62)
NCM: yellow ticket no. 250
Findspot: Wooded area to west of main site
Context details: Metal-detected stray find 2003–9.
Copper alloy blade fragment, with one straight sharp edge, and the rest raggedly torn. Possibly from a Bronze Age bladed implement such as a spearhead.
Wt: 6.2g; L: 28mm; W: 16.5mm; T: 4mm

S.7: Copper alloy ?blade fragment (Pl. 14.62)
NCM: yellow ticket no. 248
Findspot: Wooded area to west of main site
Context details: Metal-detected stray find 2003–9.
Undiagnostic copper alloy fragment, possibly from a Bronze Age bladed implement.
Wt: 4.3g; L: 18mm; W: 13mm; T: 9mm

S.8: Copper alloy unidentified object fragment (Pl. 14.62)
NCM: yellow ticket no. 89
Findspot: Wooded area to west of main site
Context details: Metal-detected stray find 2003–9.
Fragment of unidentified copper alloy object with one original edge. Triangular in cross-section. Possibly a broken fragment from the edge of a Bronze Age bladed object, though it is too worn and fragmentary to be closely identified.
Wt: 2.7g; L: 15mm; W: 7.4mm; T: 6.3mm

S.9: Copper alloy miniature axe (Pl. 14.62)
NCM: yellow ticket no. 2
Findspot: Wooded area to west of main site
Context details: Metal-detected stray find 2003–9.
Miniature copper alloy looped and socketed axe, with wide sub-rectangular socketed end, tapering towards a narrower, rounded blade. The integral loop is approximately half-way down one side.

Bliss (2020) has developed a typology for these miniature axes, but this example does not fit neatly into any of his categories, falling somewhere between his Class A ('symmetrical miniature axes with drooping blades, prominent side loops and sub-rectangular-section bodies, with little or no evidence of mouth mouldings' (Bliss 2020, 9))

and Class C1 ('Sub-rectangular miniature axes with elongated bodies … neatly made miniatures with either straight or inwardly-tapering sides which transition into rounded blades …, the side-loop on or close to the socket mouth' (*ibid.*, 12)). It lacks both the elongated body of Class C, and the distinctive 'drooping' form of Class A. Miniature socketed axes are most common as unstratified stray finds (Robinson 1995; Bliss 2020). Bliss's corpus comprises over 150 objects (more than four times the number catalogued 25 years earlier by Robinson), but the vast majority of these are metal-detected finds reported through the PAS. There are examples from more secure contexts. Two appear within the multi-period Salisbury Hoard (BM 1998,0901.44, 1998,0901.80; Robinson 1995; Bliss 2020), and they are also known from excavations at long-lived midden deposits such as Whitchurch (Warwickshire) and Potterne (Wiltshire), as well as Late Iron Age hilltop settlements and shrines (Farley 2011; Bliss 2020). They have been broadly dated anywhere from the Bronze Age to Roman period (Robinson 1995; Bliss 2020), but the comprehensive recent reappraisal by Bliss suggests that the few finds from stratified contexts would support a manufacturing date in the Late Bronze Age or Earliest Iron Age for most of these objects, though they seem in some cases to have been re-deposited at Late Iron Age and Roman period shrine sites (Bliss 2020, 22), as may indeed have occurred at Snettisham.
Wt: 2.6g; L: 13mm; W: 10mm (socket mouth); T: 4mm (max.)

S.10: Copper alloy 'moustache' mount (Pl. 14.62)
NCM: yellow ticket no. 10
Findspot: Wooded area to west of main site
Context details: Metal-detected stray find 2003–9.
Fitting taking the form of a tear-shaped lobe, decorated with two raised ribs. The rounded 'base' of the lobe, where it may have been attached to a larger object, is flat on one side, and hollow; this area now contains a mineralised accretion. The object narrows towards the other end of the lobe, where the tip has broken off.

This unusual fitting may be related to an enigmatic group of objects known as 'moustache mounts'. Davey (2020) has identified around 60 such 'UMO's ('Unidentified Moustache-shaped Objects'), distributed throughout southern England. They are most common as unstratified stray finds, and so cannot be closely dated. One appears in the multi-period Salisbury Hoard (BM 1998,0901.201), which includes Middle Bronze Age to Late Iron Age material. Elsewhere, they have come from sites producing more or less exclusively Bronze Age material (see e.g. PAS ID: SF9183 from Mildenhall, Suffolk) so a Middle to Late Bronze Age date is just as plausible as an Iron Age origin for these objects. There are a range of attachment mechanisms, from perforations to rivet holes, or sockets, though their function is not clear. A range of uses have been suggested, from decorative mounts to dagger pommels or chapes. Davey (2020) divides them into double-lobe and single-lobe types. His double-lobe forms are 'Dali' (e.g. PAS ID: HAMP-6F4C45), 'Pincer' (e.g. PAS ID: NMGW-AF1FCC), 'Kitchener' (e.g. PAS ID: NARC-6A4546), and 'Headphone' (e.g. PAS ID: HAMP-E8A481), while the single-lobe types are 'Shell' (e.g. PAS ID: WAW-83E1E3, SF-E76AB6 and SUSS-3AEC48) and 'Mussel' (e.g. PAS ID: SOM-7D864D). This fitting, if it is a moustache mount, most closely resembles a single-lobed 'Shell' type, missing its tip. Around 20 of these single-lobed, 'shell' type mounts are known, but their function is unclear (Davey 2020).
Wt: 9.7g; L: 17mm; W: 15mm; T: 12mm

Phase 3–4 Metalwork: Late Iron Age and Early Roman finds

Torcs, bracelets and related components contemporary with the hoards

Gold/silver alloy

S.11a–b: Fused composite group (Pl. 14.63)
Site code: SN/KD
Findspot: Area 3. Possible outlier from Hoard F?
Context details: Metal-detected stray find from 1990 excavation.
[Analysed: see Ch. 18]
Wt: 80.0g (Total weight for S.11a–b)

S.11a: Gold/silver alloy torc
TUBULAR (TYPE 4/5)
BM: 1991,0407.57
Gold/silver alloy Type 4 or 5 tubular torc fragment with lines of punched dotted decoration creating a line of elongated diamond shapes along the torc. Broken/torn at both ends and bent into a tight V-shape. Part melted, with numerous small fused additions. See Ch. 21 for discussion of decoration.
D(nr): 13.5mm; L: 66.7mm

S.11b: Gold/silver alloy torc/bracelet
MSCC: (2P)R
BM: 1991,0407.47
Fragment of gold/silver alloy multi-strand torc/bracelet comprising a single-loop terminal and part of the neck-ring/body. Stage II construction of two circular-section wires plied together. The terminal loop is continuous, extending to form the neck-ring wires. The wires are broken at the other end, and one is additionally broken in the middle. The whole fragment is bent, twisted and part melted, with small fused additions.
D(nr): 5.9mm; D(wire): 3.1mm; D(term): 18.0mm; L: 104.5mm

S.12: Iron tubular torc core (Pl. 14.63)
TUBULAR (TYPE 6)
NCM: 1999.44
Findspot: Not recorded. Possibly related to Hoard A, which has produced the only other comparable torcs from Snettisham.
Context details: Metal-detected stray find 1999.
Remains of the iron core of a large Type 6 tubular torc, in four parts; two have been glued together. The metal is rectangular in cross-section and when placed together the curved pieces form a roughly circular shape. There are the remains of a possible widened terminal on one of the

S.11a-b

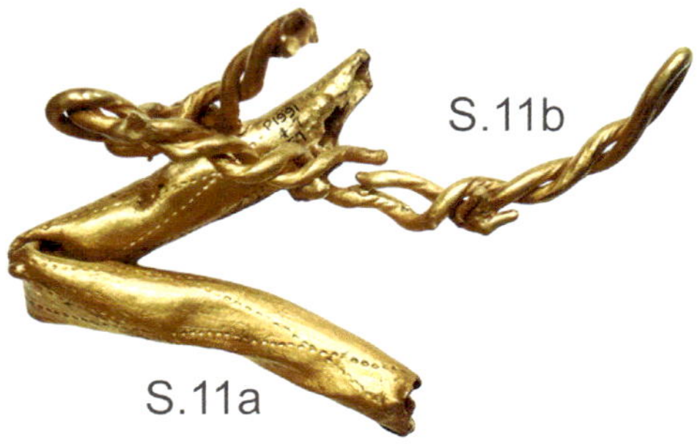

S.12

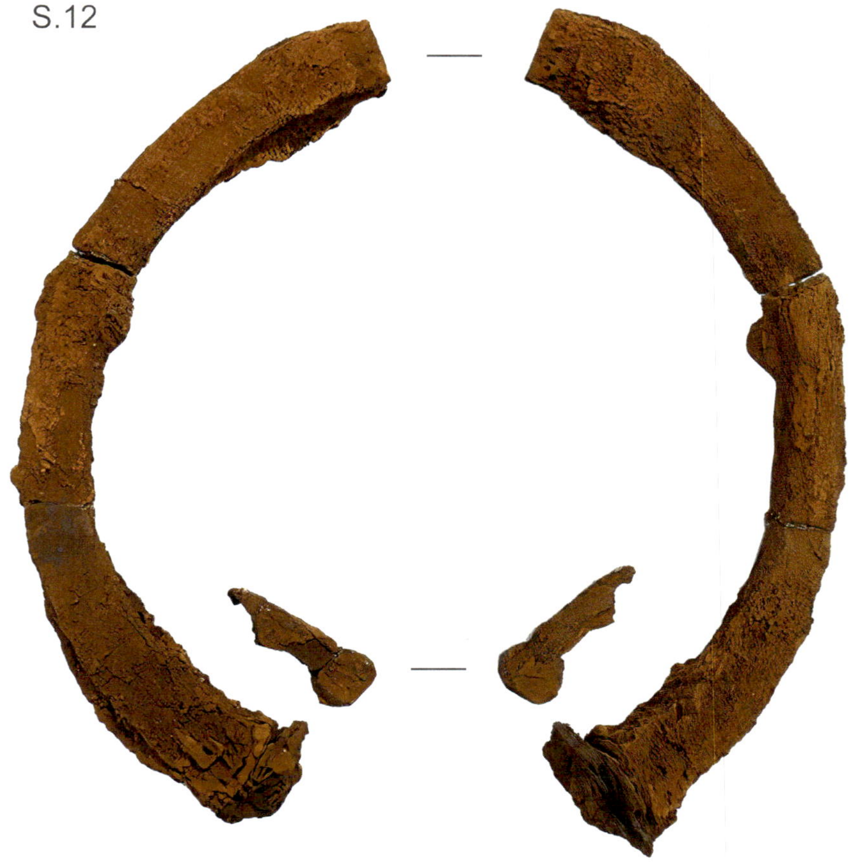

S.13

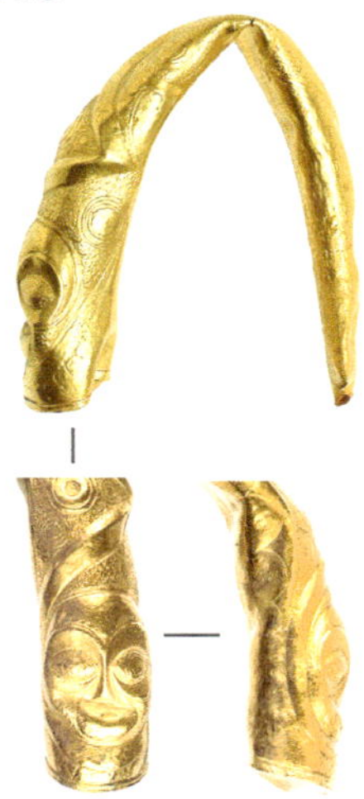

S.14

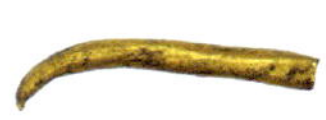

S.15

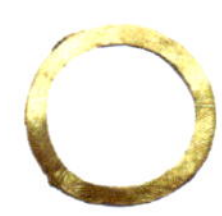

S.16

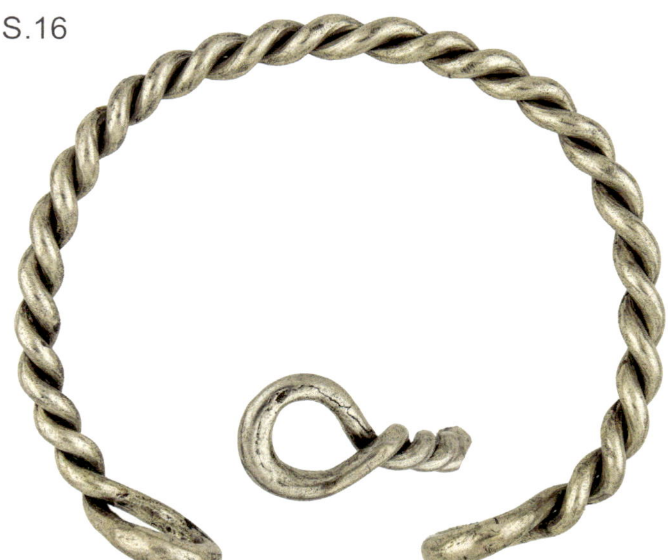

Plate 14.63

0 5 10cm

fragments, although the shape is too badly corroded to reconstruct.
Wt: 66.8g (total); D(term): 30.0mm (max.); L: 116.8mm (largest frag.); 160.0mm (two larger fragments, as they join); W: 14.0mm; T: 19.0mm

S.13: Gold/silver alloy torc (Pl. 14.63)
TUBULAR (TYPE 4)
BM: 1991,0407.40; Site code: SN/RO
Findspot: Area 15
Context details: Metal-detected stray find from 1990 excavation.
[Analysed: see Ch. 18]
Gold/silver alloy Type 4 tubular torc terminal, neck-ring broken at one end, and the whole fragment bent into a tight V-shape (see **Figs 17.9–10, 21.33**). The side of the terminal is decorated with raised and inscribed decoration. Near the terminal this decoration takes the form of a humanoid face with raised, lentoid-shaped eyes. Leading off from the face is a raised sinuous band. Decoration around this band comprises a series of concentric rings and areas of stippling. A double cordon around the edge marks the end of the terminal. The circular face of the buffer terminal is flat and undecorated. See Chapter 17 for further information on the manufacture, and Chapter 21 for discussion of the decoration.

Notes from scientific analysis (Nigel Meeks)
This tubular sheet terminal is relatively narrow and has been broken away from the rest of the neck-ring (the remainder of the object is missing). There is a kink in the tube about half-way along it where it has been folded. There is a soldered seam running along the interior length of the tube and the tubular terminal end is capped with a plain sheet with a circumferential ridge which is soldered in place. The embossed decoration is enhanced with details within the design that have been added by chased lines and punched dot decoration, for example the eyes (see **Figs 17.9–10**).

There is a transverse soldered seam joining two narrow parts of the tubular terminal. This might be the position of the point at which the sheet terminal was originally joined to the neck-ring to make the complete torc. The soldered area has been over-punched with a thin linear decoration to conceal the join (see **Fig. 17.10c**). The manufacture from multiple components is logical, as it would have been very difficult to make a complete thin tubular torc from a single piece of sheet.

The terminal also has an osmium-iridium inclusion in the sheet (**Fig. 14.45**). The presence of this hard metallic particle shows the gold was from an alluvial source and was not refined. The inclusion does not dissolve in molten gold so passes through to the hammered sheet (Ogden 1977; Meeks and Tite 1980).
Wt: 39.0g; D(term): 15.8mm; L: 65.4mm

S.14: Gold/silver alloy torc (Pl. 14.63)
TUBULAR (TYPE 1)
NCM: yellow ticket no. 34
Findspot: Wooded area to west of main site

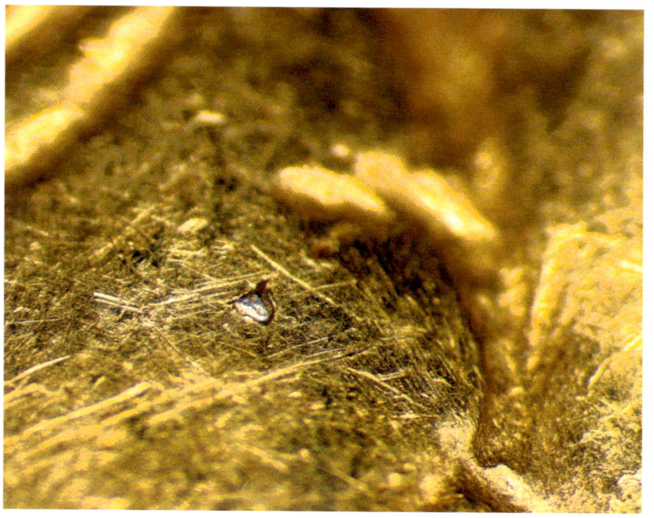

Figure 14.45 Detail of torc terminal S.13 showing the hard silvery coloured Os/Ir inclusion

Context details: Metal-detected stray find 2003–9.
Short length of gold/silver alloy tube, forming a hollow wire, broken at both ends. Bent and squeezed closed at one end. Possibly from the neck-ring of a Type 1 tubular torc.
Wt: 4.3g; D(nr): 5.0mm; L: 40.0mm

S.15: Gold/silver alloy ?torc (Pl. 14.63)
?TUBULAR (?TYPE 2/TYPE 6)
BM: 1992,1203.6
Findspot: Not recorded
Context details: Metal-detected stray find Dec. 1990–April 1991.
Thin circular gold/silver alloy ring, flat in cross-section. Probably a fragment or component from a tubular torc of Type 2 or Type 6 form.
Wt: 2.0g; D(ext): 25.5mm; T: 1.5mm

S.16: Gold/silver alloy torc (Pl. 14.63)
MSCC: (2P)R
NCM: 1969.55.3
Published reference: Burns 1971, 228–9
Findspot: South-west corner of the 'gold field', possibly thrown by the plough
Context details: Found during ploughing in 1968.
[Analysed: see Appendix 5 and Ch. 18]
Complete gold/silver alloy multi-strand torc (see **Fig. 17.61**). Slightly thickened ring terminals and Stage I neck-ring comprised of two thick wires, circular in cross-section, plied together.

Notes from scientific analysis (Nigel Meeks)
The torc is of a solid gold/silver alloy, a thick wire two-strand neck-ring design with simple ring terminals. The wire is essentially of circular-section form but there are still longitudinal facets remaining in the recessed regions showing that the hammered torc wires have had extensive polishing since their original twisting, either as a post-manufacture process or as use wear over a period of time. The torc could have been made from a single length of thick wire (about 140cm long), the centre point of this wire being bent double around a mandrel or rod to form one loop. With

S.17

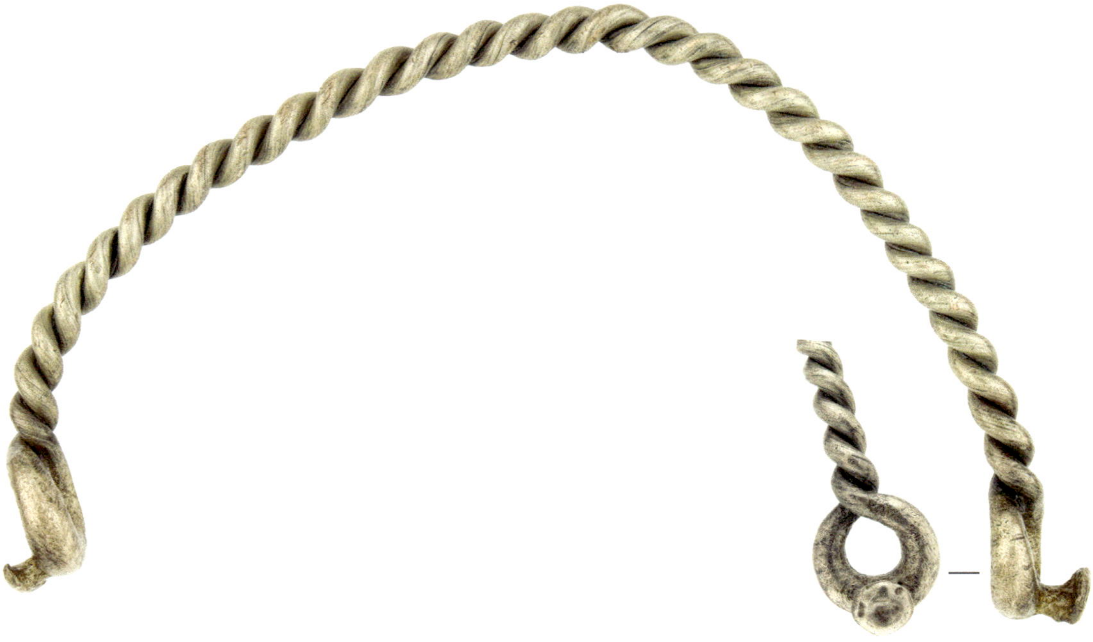

S.18

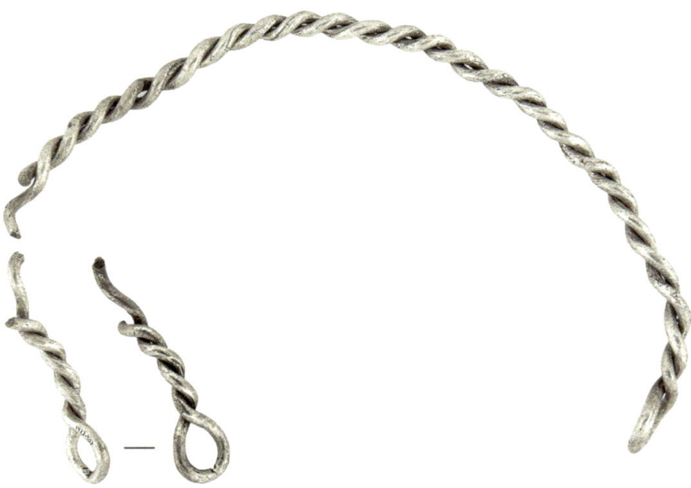

S.19

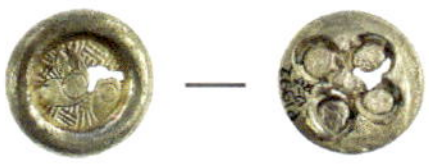

S.20

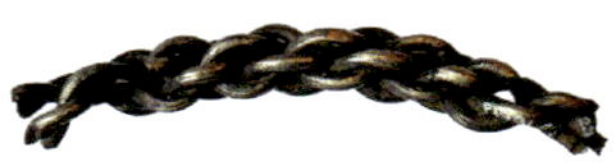

S.21

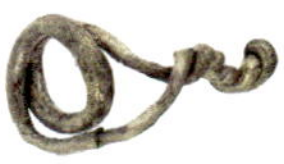

S.22

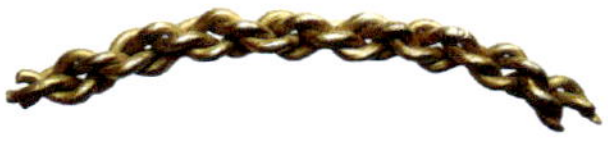

S.23

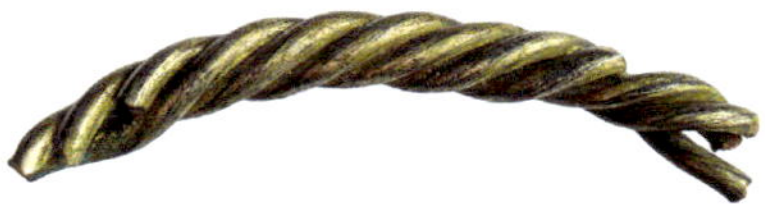

S.24

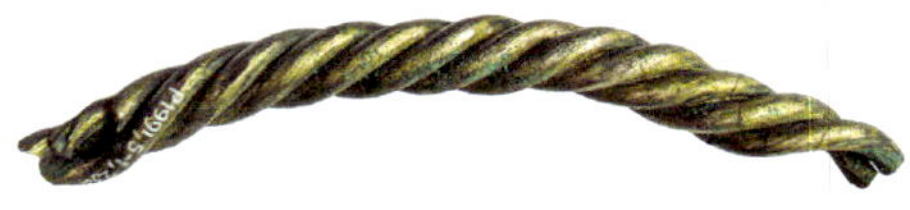

S.25

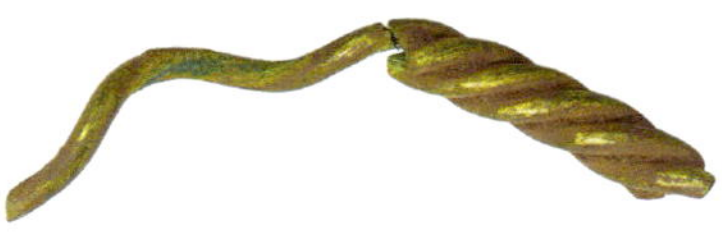

S.26

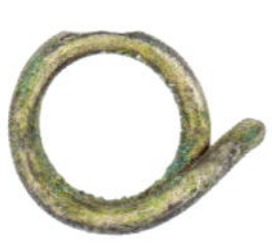

S.27

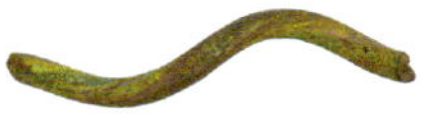

S.28

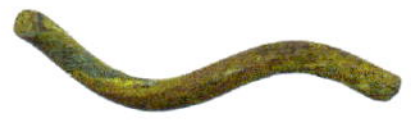

S.29

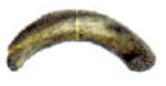

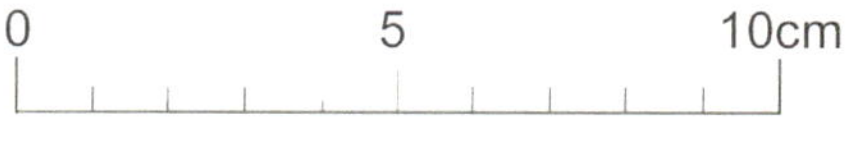

Plate 14.64

the wire ends firmly clamped, the mandrel could have been turned in a clockwise direction to twist the parallel wires together. This leaves the problem of finishing the other loop formed by bending the two wire ends around a mandrel and cutting to length – probably leaving an overlap to be fused, forged and filed.

However, both terminals both have a more bulbous thickness than the main wires and there is clear evidence of seams (see **Fig. 17.61a–b**). This might suggest that two wires were used rather than one and that both terminals needed to be closed by the addition of further metal. The thickening of the terminals may have been achieved by casting-on metal (this technology was used on many torcs in the form of complete cast terminals) then hammering to form the thicker terminals. Such a process would close, fuse, thicken and cover the cut ends of the wires. Similar evidence is found on the terminals on torc L.3. An additional parallel is the thickened terminals seen on the Ipswich torcs (Brailsford 1968; Brailsford and Stapley 1972) that have more refined ring terminals with elaborate cast embellishments on wire neck-rings of similar diameter.
Wt: 350.8g; D(ext): 170.0mm; D(nr): 11.8mm; D(wire): 5.4mm; D(term): 31.5mm

S.17: Gold/silver alloy torc (Pl. 14.64)
MSCC: (2P)R
NCM: 1965.30.1
Published reference: Burns 1971, 228–9
Findspot: Area 2
Context details: Found during ploughing in 1964.
[Analysed: see Appendix 5 and Ch. 18]
Gold/silver alloy multi-strand torc, complete, but bent outwards from its original form (see **Figs 17.62, 20.12**). Slightly thickened ring terminals, each with a knob-shaped protrusion on the exterior, at the very end of the ring, that looks integral. These flared knobs are most likely the remains of the sprues from casting-on additional material to the terminals to form the thickened rings (see Ch. 17 for more on casting-on of terminals). The Stage II neck-ring is comprised of two thick wires, circular in cross-section, plied together.
Wt: 624.0g; D(nr): 14.0mm; D(wire): 6.2mm; D(term): 40.0mm; L: 285.0mm

S.18: Gold/silver alloy torc (Pl. 14.64)
MSCC: (2P)R
NCM: 1977.307
Findspot: To north-west of 'gold field'
Context details: Found during ploughing in 1973.
[Analysed: see Appendix 5]
Complete gold/silver alloy multi-strand torc, broken close to one of the terminals, but the two fragments join. The whole torc has been stretched outwards slightly from its original form. This could be a result of deliberate breakage or simply plough damage. Simple single-loop terminals and Stage II neck-ring comprised of two wires, circular in cross-section, plied together.
Wt: 72.5g; 15.5g; D(ext): 180mm (reconstructed); D(nr): 8.0mm; D(wire): 3.1mm; D(term): 18.0mm

S.19: Gold/silver alloy torc (Pl. 14.64
MSCC: (4P(?5C))R
BM: 1992,1203.4
Findspot: Not recorded
Context details: Metal-detected stray find Dec. 1990–April 1991.
[Analysed: see Ch. 18]
Buffer terminal from a gold/silver alloy multi-strand torc (see **Figs 17.67a–c, 21.27**). Its flat face is decorated with keeled-roundel and circle motifs surrounded by three fin-shaped motifs filled with basket-hatching, enclosed by a raised rim. The terminal is flat on the reverse, with stubs of neck-ring wires protruding. The terminal appears to have been directly cast onto the neck-ring. Very little of the Stage III neck-ring survives, but where the wires have broken away at the back the beginnings of four ropes of circular-section strands are visible. It is not clear how many strands were coiled to make each rope, but it was most likely five or, perhaps, six. The four ropes were originally plied together.

Notes from scientific analysis (Nigel Meeks)
This single terminal is another example of an engraved buffer type. The fact that it has broken free from the torc wires except for a few short fragments allows study of the back, showing the details of the cast-on structures and the construction of the (now missing) neck-ring (see **Fig. 17.67b–c**). One of the wires from the back is seen protruding through to the front (see **Fig. 17.67a**).

The terminal is cast onto the wires and this is clearly seen on the back, which has four circular impressions of the original coiled ropes of the neck-ring. Each depression has a small fragment of the original wire fused into place. In the centre of each coil is a dimpled mound of the cast terminal metal that filled the wire coil to which it fused, or at least mechanically encapsulated, firmly holding the wires in place. Similarly, the outer edges of the coiled wires are firmly locked into position by the cast metal. The remaining wire fragments are broken (stress corrosion) showing that the coiled wires were originally firmly held to the terminal and have not simply fallen out. The wires appear to be round in cross-section, probably with flat facets, which can just be seen on some wires.

The oblique side view of the back of the terminal (see **Fig. 17.67c**) shows one coil of wires has five visible wire fragments (and possibly a sixth out of sight) tightly coiled together into a hollow spring-type spiral.

The coil was made by coiling all of the wires at the same time around a rod, organic core (Ch. 19), or mandrel, in order to allow the tight spiral to be made, and importantly to maintain the round hollow core by preventing the wires collapsing onto themselves during twisting. Four of these spiral forms were made for this torc. The nearest similar spiral construction is seen on the much larger torc L.19 in which the four coils were plied together with only a few turns between the terminals. It would seem reasonable to suppose that the coiled ropes of terminal S.20 were similarly twisted together. The number of turns of the four coils that can be safely put onto these hollow core torcs was limited by the diameters of the coiled components. Over-tightening would deform the torcs. Once damaged, it would be almost impossible to return them back to shape.

After the body of the neck-ring was made, the ends were clamped into their twisted form to prevent them untwisting. The ends were then squared off and prepared to receive moulding for the lost-wax terminal casting. The back of the terminal (see **Fig. 17.67b**) shows file marks where the casting was abraded to smooth it during finishing.
Wt: 6.1g; D(term): 19.0mm; T: 3.6mm

S.20: Gold/silver alloy torc (Pl. 14.64)
MSCC: (3P(2PZ))R
BM: 1991,0501.228
Jackson no.: 507
Findspot: Not recorded
Context details: Metal-detected stray find August 1990.
Fragment of gold/silver alloy multi-strand torc neck-ring, broken at both ends. Stage III construction of three ropes plied together, each of which is made up of two circular-section wires which are themselves plied together Z-twist.
Joining/related fragments: Probably part of the same torc as J.2 (which was disturbed by ploughing).
Wt: 19.0g; D(nr): 9.8mm; D(rope): 4.5mm; D(wire): 2.3mm; L: 78.3mm

S.21: Gold/silver alloy torc (Pl. 14.64)
MSCC: (?2P(2P))R
BM: 1992,1203.3
Findspot: Not recorded
Context details: Metal-detected stray find Dec. 1990–April 1991.
Fragment of gold/silver alloy multi-strand torc comprising a double-loop terminal and short length of neck-ring, broken at the other end. What survives of the neck-ring is a Stage II component of two circular-section wires plied together, but this is curved in a way which strongly suggests it originally formed part of a Stage III construction, probably of two such ropes plied together, giving a triple-loop terminal. The loop terminal is continuous with the neck-ring wires. There is some thickening of the wire at the terminal, and what may be a hammered overlap join. The whole terminal is quite distorted as if twisted or crushed.
Wt: 7.7g; D(rope): 4.0mm; D(wire): 2.1mm; D(term): 22.1mm; L: 35.4mm

S.22: Gold/silver alloy torc (Pl. 14.64)
MSCC: (2PZ(2P))R
BM: 1992,1203.2
Findspot: Not recorded
Context details: Metal-detected stray find Dec. 1990–April 1991.
Fragment of gold/silver alloy multi-strand torc neck-ring, cut at both ends. Stage III construction of two ropes plied together Z-twist, each of which is made up of two circular-section wires which are themselves plied tightly together.
Wt: 11.8g; D(nr): 7.1mm; D(rope): 3.8mm; D(wire): 1.8mm; L: 78.1mm

S.23–9: Gold/silver alloy torc (Pl. 14.64)
MSCC: (4P)R
This group of fragments, split between the BM and NCM collections, are probably part of the same torc. There are known joins between S.23 and S.29, and possible joins between S.25, S.27 and S.28.

S.23: BM: 1991,0501.231
Jackson no.: 510
Findspot: Not recorded
Context details: Metal-detected stray find August 1990.
Fragment of gold/silver alloy multi-strand torc neck-ring, broken at both ends. Stage II construction of four circular-section wires plied together.
Wt: 46.2g; D(nr): 9.5mm; D(wire): 3.9mm; L: 98.2mm

S.24: BM: 1991,0501.232
Jackson no.: 511
Findspot: Not recorded
Context details: Metal-detected stray find August 1990.
Fragment of gold/silver alloy multi-strand torc neck-ring, broken at both ends. Stage II construction of four circular-section wires plied together.
Wt: 46.2g; D(nr): 9.8mm; D(wire): 4.0mm; L: 116.4mm

S.25: NCM: 1990.204
Findspot: Area 20
Context details: Metal-detected stray find 1989.
Fragment of multi-strand gold/silver alloy torc, consisting of a short length of neck-ring broken at both ends. The Stage II construction consists of four circular-section wires plied together. Most of the wires are broken in roughly the same place, except for one wire which is more than twice as long as the other three.
Wt: 30.5g; D(nr): 9.5mm; D(wire): 4.0mm; L: 93.0mm

S.26: BM: 1991,0501.230
Jackson no.: 509
Findspot: Not recorded
Context details: Metal-detected stray find August 1990.
Fragment of gold/silver alloy multi-strand torc, comprising part of a double-loop terminal, formed from circular-section wire. Broken at both ends.
Wt: 13.5g; D(wire): 3.9mm; D(term): 27.3mm; L: 33.8mm

S.27: NCM: 1990.203b
Findspot: Area 20
Context details: Metal-detected stray find 1989.
Short length of circular-section wire, most likely a fragment from a gold/silver alloy multi-stand torc. The spiralling curvature suggests it was originally part of a Stage II coiled or plied neck-ring.
Wt: 6.6g; D(wire): 4.0mm; L: 54.0mm

S.28: NCM: 1990.203a
Findspot: Area 20
Context details: Metal-detected stray find 1989.
Short length of circular-section wire, broken at both ends, most likely a fragment from a gold/silver alloy multi-stand torc. The spiralling curvature suggests it was originally part of a Stage II coiled or plied neck-ring.
Wt: 6.5g; D(wire): 4.0mm; L: 51.0mm

S.29: BM: 1991,0501.229
Jackson no.: 508
Findspot: Not recorded
Context details: Metal-detected stray find August 1990.
Fragment of circular-section gold/silver alloy wire, broken at both ends. Bent in a way which suggests it once formed part of a Stage II multi-strand torc neck-ring.
Wt: 2.3g; D(wire): 4.3mm; L: 19.5mm

S.30: Gold/silver alloy torc/bracelet (Pl. 14.65)
MSCC: (3P)R
NCM: yellow ticket no. 93
Findspot: Wooded area to west of main site
Context details: Metal-detected stray find 2003–9.
Short fragment of gold/silver alloy multi-strand torc neck-ring or bracelet body, broken at both ends. Stage II construction of three circular-section wires plied together.
Wt: 7.6g; D(nr): 9.0mm; D(wire): 4.0mm; L: 26.0mm

S.31–9: Gold/silver alloy torc (Pl. 14.65)
MSCC: (2P)F
[Analysed: see Appendix 5 for S.31, and Ch. 18 for S.32 and S.34–9]
Fragments S.31–9, split between the BM and NCM collections, are probably part of the same torc (see **Figs 17.14, 17.17, 17.32**). S.40 may also be part of this object. There are joins between S.33, S.38 and S.39. All the breaks are torn in a way which may suggest plough damage, rather than deliberate fragmentation before deposition.

S.31: NCM: 1965.30.2.1
Published reference: Burns 1971, 228–9
Findspot: Area 3
Context details: Found during ploughing in 1964.
Single-loop terminal from a gold/silver alloy multi-strand torc, with a very short surviving length of neck-ring. The terminal looks to originally have been a double loop, but only one loop remains. The Stage II neck-ring was made up of two thick, faceted rods plied together. The loop fragment is broken at the neck-ring end (with a flat original terminal at the other), and the smaller fragment is broken at both ends.
Wt: 109.9g (total of 84.5g; 25.4g); D(wire): 9.0mm; D(term): 60.0mm; L: 61.5mm; 35.0mm

S.32: BM: 1991,0407.50; Site code: SN/AO
Findspot: Area 1
Context details: Metal-detected stray find from 1990 excavation.
Single-loop terminal from a gold/silver alloy multi-strand torc. The thick, faceted rod is broken at the neck-ring end, but the other end of the loop is an original flat terminal.
Wt: 89.1g; D(wire): 8.3mm; D(term): 42.3mm; L: 62.5mm

S.33: BM: 1991,0501.224
Jackson no.: 503
Findspot: Not recorded
Context details: Metal-detected stray find Dec. 1990–April 1991.
Single-loop terminal from a gold/silver alloy multi-strand torc. The thick, faceted rod is broken at the neck-ring end, but the other end of the loop is an original flat terminal.
Wt: 81.9g; D(wire): 8.7mm; D(term): 42.3mm; L: 58.0mm

S.34: BM: 1991,0501.226
Jackson no.: 505
Findspot: Not recorded
Context details: Metal-detected stray find Dec. 1990–April 1991.
Single-loop terminal from a gold/silver alloy multi-strand torc, formed from thick faceted rod. The fragment comprises around half of the loop, one flat original end, the other end broken.
Wt: 36.4g; D(wire): 8.7mm; L: 41.8mm

S.35: BM: 1991,0407.51; Site code: SN/KM
Findspot: Area 5
Context details: Metal-detected stray find from 1990 excavation.
Fragment of gold/silver alloy multi-strand torc neck-ring, broken at both ends. Stage II construction of two thick, faceted rods plied together.
Wt: 193.7g; D(nr): 16.6mm; D(wire): 9.0mm; L: 120.5mm

S.36: BM: 1991,0407.49; Site code: SN/AU
Findspot: Area 1
Context details: Metal-detected stray find from 1990 excavation.
Fragment of gold/silver alloy multi-strand torc neck-ring, broken at both ends. Stage II construction of two thick, faceted rods plied together.
Wt: 179.4g; D(nr): 16.1mm; D(wire): 8.9mm; L: 116.6mm

S.37: BM: 1992,1203.1
Findspot: Not recorded
Context details: Metal-detected stray find Dec. 1990–April 1991.
Fragment of gold/silver alloy multi-strand torc neck-ring, broken at both ends. Stage II construction of two thick, faceted rods plied together.
Wt: 105.7g; D(nr): 16.6mm; D(wire): 9.1mm; L: 77.4mm

S.38: BM: 1991,0501.223
Jackson no.: 502
Findspot: Not recorded
Context details: Metal-detected stray find Dec. 1990–April 1991.
Fragment of gold/silver alloy multi-strand torc neck-ring, broken at both ends. Stage II construction of two thick, faceted rods plied together.
Wt: 104.3g; D(nr): 16.8mm; D(wire): 8.8mm; L: 72.3mm

S.39: BM: 1991,0501.225
Jackson no.: 504
Findspot: Not recorded
Context details: Metal-detected stray find Dec. 1990–April 1991.
Fragment of gold/silver alloy multi-strand torc, comprising a short length of neck-ring, broken at both ends. All that remains is a length of thick, faceted rod, but it is bent in a

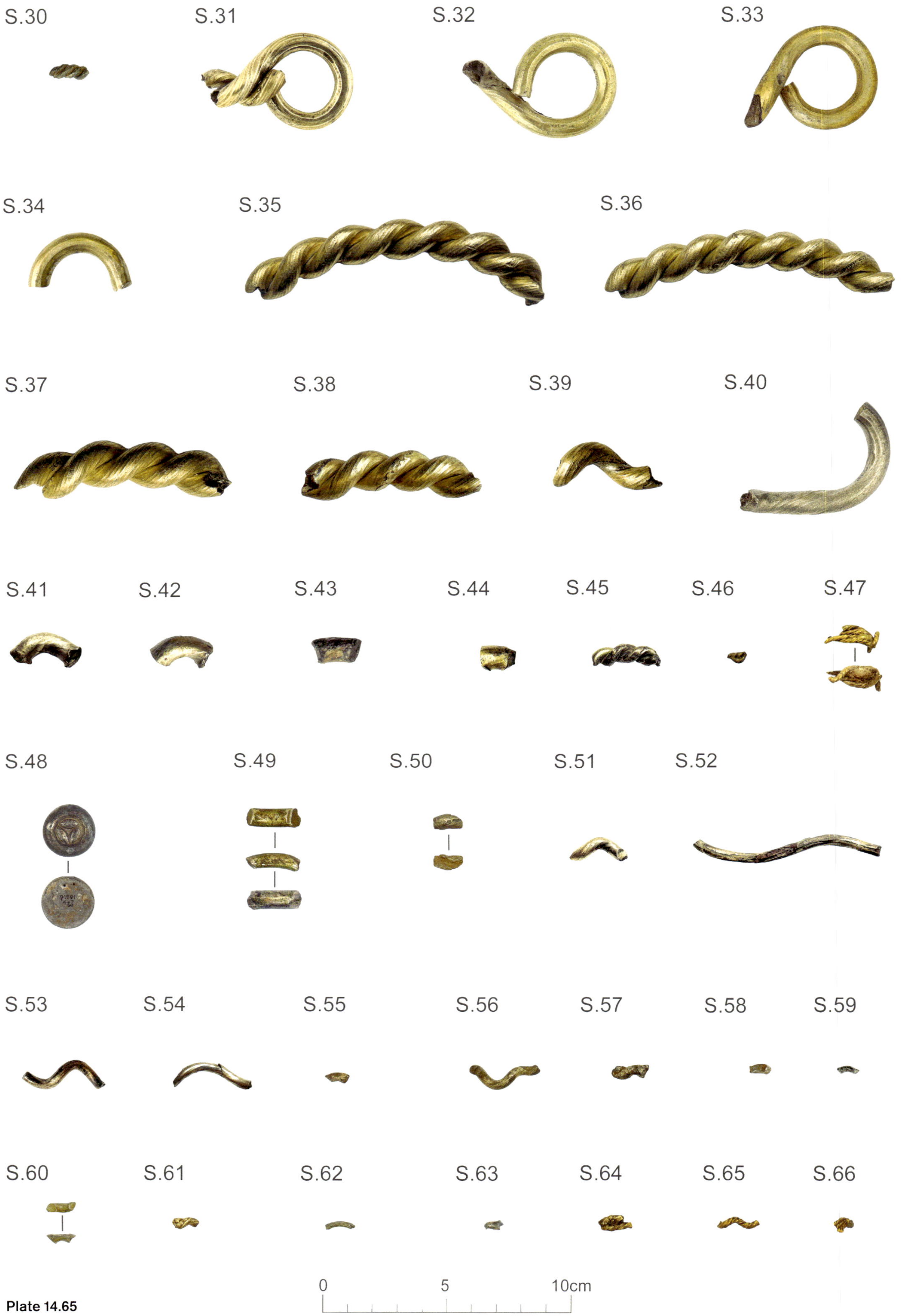
S.30
S.31
S.32
S.33
S.34
S.35
S.36
S.37
S.38
S.39
S.40
S.41
S.42
S.43
S.44
S.45
S.46
S.47
S.48
S.49
S.50
S.51
S.52
S.53
S.54
S.55
S.56
S.57
S.58
S.59
S.60
S.61
S.62
S.63
S.64
S.65
S.66
0
5
10cm

Plate 14.65

way which shows that it was originally part of a Stage II construction of two such rods plied together.
Wt: 31.5g; D(wire): 8.5mm; L: 41.9mm

Notes from scientific analysis (Nigel Meeks)
This particular fragmentary/broken multi-strand torc (S.31–9) has a very interesting physical form. There are a number of pieces (with different registration numbers) and they can all be joined into a single heavy torc. The torc was made from two of the thickest rods in the assemblage (9mm diameter) and also has the most facets (about 20). The torc rods are very tightly twisted together to form the neck-ring, probably as tight as it is possible to make them, and it would have required some force to achieve this.

The advantage of this torc from the examination point of view is that it is the brittle fractures to the neck-ring (seemingly without distortion from bending, and without deliberate cuts) make it possible to study the cross-section as well as the outer surface, revealing many of the manufacturing processes. At places along the length of the rods are thin overlapped seams or folds in the metal which are clearly thinned from hammering (see **Fig. 17.14c–d**). These are very clearly seen on one of the loop terminals and may well be from the edges of a deep single groove that is seen in the fractured ends of the rods (see **Fig. 17.14b**). This groove reaches to the very centre of the rod and appears at all of the breaks, suggesting that it runs the entire length of the rods, appearing at the surface as a single seam. There can be only one explanation in this case. The starting piece of metal for the rod must have been a thick flat strip of double width compared to its thickness that was subsequently folded along its length, possibly with a cut or chiselled centre-line groove to assist folding to double thickness. This folding would have produced a square rod for subsequent hammering and rounding to the desired thickness. This may seem to be an unnecessarily complicated process, compared to simply hammering a larger starting rod. However, the groove would actually facilitate the tight twisting of the thick pair of rods by allowing the individual twisting rods to slide internally (as well as over each other) rather than having to deform the very thick solid core metal. In this way the rods would twist more tightly and with less effort.

A similar seam is found on another gold torc fragment F.5c (see **Fig. 17.18a–b**) where the seam has opened very wide from the surface to reveal the deep groove to the centre of the thick wire. This process of using a folded strip to produce thick wires may be fairly common and could explain why a number of torc wires of various thickness have a continuous single line/groove/seam running along their lengths.

This seam is therefore unlike the double seam found on traditional hammered block-twist wires commonly seen on gold wire jewellery of the Greek period (Fitton 2009; Williams and Ogden 1994; Oddy 1977), although a similar hand hammering method was used.

The wires have a golden surface colour while the core is a pinkish colour. The colour difference indicates that the surface has been enriched in gold. Surface SEM-EDX analysis gave a typical composition of Au 63.7%, Ag 35.1, Cu 1.2%., whereas a small cleaned (shiny) area of the core gave values of about Au 30.9%, Ag 45.6%, Cu 23.5% putting the alloy into the silver-gold-copper alloy group of (see **Table 17.5**). This gives a very low melting point alloy (*c.* 810°C, see **Fig. 17.47a–b**). The matt, pink colour of the fractured surface of the fragments is due to re-deposited copper on the original fracture over time. The metallography and analysis of a polished section is illustrated (**Fig. 17.32a–b**), showing the thickness and microstructure of the enriched gold layer compared to the core alloy and enabling the method of enrichment/gilding of this apparently thin golden layer to be determined (Ch. 17).

S.40: Gold/silver alloy torc (Pl. 14.65)
BM: 1991,0407.66; Site code: SN/KE
Findspot: Area 3
Context details: Metal-detected stray find from 1990 excavation.
Single-loop terminal from a gold/silver alloy multi-strand torc. The thick, faceted rod is raggedly broken at the other end, as if wrenched apart from the neck-ring. The other end of the loop is an original flat terminal.
Joining/related fragments: Possibly part of the same torc as fragments S.31–9.
Wt: 51.7g; D(wire): 9.0mm; L: 60.6mm

S.41–4: Gold/silver alloy rod/?torc (Pl. 14.65)
MSCC: (?2P)R
S.41–4 are very similar and may be from the same torc (see **Fig. 20.21**). Each fragment consists of a short length of circular-section gold/silver alloy rod, cut at both ends, showing that this object was deliberately fragmented before deposition. Each rod fragment is bent in a way which suggests it once formed part of a Stage II torc neck-ring, probably made from two such rods plied together.

S.41: BM: 1991,0407.59; Site code: SN/KH
Findspot: Area 4
Context details: Metal-detected stray find from 1990 excavation.
Wt: 16.8g; D(wire): 8.6mm; L: 28.9mm

S.42: BM: 1992,1203.5
Findspot: Not recorded
Context details: Metal-detected stray find Dec. 1990–April 1991.
Wt: 13.8g; D(wire): 9.2mm; L: 25.5mm

S.43: BM: 1992,1202.2; Site code: ST/BM
Findspot: Area 19
Context details: Metal-detected stray find from 1991 excavation.
Wt: 10.3g; D(wire): 9.0mm; L: 20.1mm

S.44: BM: 1991,0501.233; Site code: SN/NJ
Findspot: Not recorded
Context details: Metal-detected stray find from 1990 excavation.
Wt: 11.9g; D(wire): 10.2mm; L: 14.5mm; T: 7.9mm

S.45: Gold/silver alloy torc/bracelet (Pl. 14.65)
MSCC: (2P)R
BM: 1991,0407.48; Site code: SN/RC
Findspot: Area 12
Context details: Metal-detected stray find from 1990 excavation.
Fragment of gold/silver alloy multi-strand torc or bracelet comprising part of neck-ring/body, cut at both ends. Stage II construction of two circular-section wires plied together.
Wt: 6.4g; D(nr): 8.1mm; D(wire): 4.5mm; L: 28.0mm

S.46: Gold/silver alloy lump; wire/?torc/?bracelet (Pl. 14.65)
NCM: yellow ticket no. 81
Findspot: Wooded area to west of main site
Context details: Metal-detected stray find 2003–9.
Amorphous lump of gold/silver alloy, incorporating a part-melted length of wire rope, formed from two wires plied together. This Stage II component may originally have been part of a multi-strand torc or bracelet.
Wt: 0.7g; D(wire): 1.0mm; L: 8.0mm; W: 5.0mm; T: 3.8mm

S.47: Gold/silver alloy wire/?torc/?bracelet (Pl. 14.65)
NCM: yellow ticket no. 73
Findspot: Wooded area to west of main site
Context details: Metal-detected stray find 2003–9.
Four curved lengths of twisted square-section gold/silver alloy wire, all broken and part melted. Now fused together with an additional lump of gold/silver alloy. The wires are curved in a way which suggests they originally formed part of a coiled component in a multi-strand torc or bracelet.
Wt: 3.2g; D(nr): 8.0mm; D(wire): 1.8mm; L: 22.0mm

S.48: Gold/silver alloy torc (Pl. 14.65)
BM: 1991,0407.60; Site code: SN/MY
Findspot: Area 9
Context details: Metal-detected stray find from 1990 excavation.
Buffer terminal, most likely originally from a gold/silver alloy multi-strand torc (see **Fig. 21.18**). Cast, and solid, it is unclear how the neck-ring would have been affixed. Flat on the back, the front is decorated with a raised rim around the circumference, and a simple tripartite relief design in the centre formed from three lentoid shapes joined end to end to form a triangle, giving a recessed central triangular motif in the negative space created between the lentoids.
Wt: 13.3g; D(term): 21.2mm; T: 6.9mm

S.49: Gold/silver alloy rod/?large ring/?torc (Pl. 14.65)
NCM: yellow ticket no. 30
Findspot: Wooded area to west of main site
Context details: Metal-detected stray find 2003–9.
Length of curved gold/silver alloy rod, possibly from a large ring or the loop terminal of a torc, cut at each end. Oval-shaped section; flatter on the inner face.
Wt: 10.1g; D(wire): 8.0mm; L: 22.0mm

S.50: Gold/silver alloy ?rod/?torc/?bracelet (Pl. 14.65)
NCM: yellow ticket no. 129B
Findspot: Wooded area to west of main site
Context details: Metal-detected stray find 2003–9.
Small fragment of gold/silver alloy faceted rod, whole circumference not preserved. Possibly part of a multi-strand torc or bracelet.
Wt: 0.8g; L: 12.0mm; W: 6.5mm; T: 2.0mm

S.51: Gold/silver alloy wire/?torc/?bracelet (Pl. 14.65)
MSCC: (?2P)R
BM: 1991,0407.53; Site code: SN/AX
Findspot: Area 1
Context details: Metal-detected stray find from 1990 excavation.
Short length of circular-section gold/silver alloy wire, cut at both ends. Bent in a way which suggests it once formed part of a Stage II torc neck-ring or bracelet body, probably made from two or three such wires plied together.
Wt: 5.3g; D(wire): 4.9mm; L: 23.2mm

S.52: Gold/silver alloy wire/?torc/?bracelet (Pl. 14.65)
MSCC: (?P)R
BM: 1992,1202.1; Site code: ST/BP
Findspot: Area 20
Context details: Metal-detected stray find from 1991 excavation.
Length of circular-section gold/silver alloy wire, broken at both ends. Bent in a way which suggests it once formed part of a loosely plied Stage II multi-strand torc neck-ring or bracelet body. Heavy corrosion and flaking along the surface.
Wt: 7.6g; D(wire): 4.2mm; L: 75.8mm

S.53: Gold/silver alloy wire/?torc/?bracelet (Pl. 14.65)
MSCC: (?P)R
BM: 1991,0407.52; Site code: SN/KF
Findspot: Area 4
Context details: Metal-detected stray find from 1990 excavation.
Length of circular-section gold/silver alloy wire, cut at both ends. Bent in a way which suggests it once formed part of a Stage II plied multi-strand torc neck-ring or bracelet body.
Wt: 6.1g; D(wire): 3.9mm; L: 33.6mm

S.54: Gold/silver alloy wire/?torc/?bracelet (Pl. 14.65)
MSCC: (?P)R
BM: 1991,0407.56; Site code: SN/EE
Findspot: Area 2
Context details: Metal-detected stray find from 1990 excavation.
Length of circular-section gold/silver alloy wire, cut at both ends. Bent in a way which suggests it once formed part of a Stage II plied multi-strand torc neck-ring or bracelet body. Fractured in the middle of the fragment, as if it has been deliberately bent/broken.

Joining/related fragments: Possibly part of torc J.1.
Wt: 3.7g; D(wire): 4.0mm; L: 31.5mm

S.55: Gold/silver alloy wire/?torc/?bracelet (Pl. 14.65)
NCM: yellow ticket no. 78
Findspot: Wooded area to west of main site
Context details: Metal-detected stray find 2003–9.
Short, curved fragment of gold/silver alloy circular-section wire. Possibly originally part of a multi-strand torc or bracelet.
Wt: 1.1g; D(wire): 4.0mm; L: 10.0mm

S.56: Gold/silver alloy wire/?torc/?bracelet (Pl. 14.65)
NCM: yellow ticket no. 142
Findspot: Wooded area to west of main site
Context details: Metal-detected stray find 2003–9.
Fragment of gold/silver alloy circular-section wire. Cut at both ends. Curved in a way which suggests it was originally part of a multi-strand torc or bracelet.
Wt: 3.1g; D(wire): 3.2mm; L: 28.5mm

S.57: Gold/silver alloy wire/?torc/?bracelet (Pl. 14.65)
NCM: yellow ticket no. 103
Findspot: Wooded area to west of main site
Context details: Metal-detected stray find 2003–9.
Short, curved fragment of gold/silver alloy circular-section wire. Cut or broken at both ends, and partially melted. Possibly originally part of a multi-strand torc or bracelet.
Wt: 1.4g; D(wire): 3.0mm; L: 15.0mm; W: 5.5mm

S.58: Gold/silver alloy wire/?torc/?bracelet (Pl. 14.65)
NCM: yellow ticket no. 91
Findspot: Wooded area to west of main site
Context details: Metal-detected stray find 2003–9.
Short, curved fragment of gold/silver alloy circular-section wire. Cut or broken at both ends, with evidence for hammering or perhaps partial melting. Possibly originally part of a multi-strand torc or bracelet.
Wt: 0.6g; D(wire): 3.0mm; L: 9.0mm

S.59: Gold/silver alloy wire/?torc/?bracelet (Pl. 14.65)
NCM: yellow ticket no. 95
Findspot: Wooded area to west of main site
Context details: Metal-detected stray find 2003–9.
Short, curved fragment of gold/silver alloy circular-section wire. Cut at both ends, with evidence for partial melting. Possibly originally part of a multi-strand torc or bracelet.
Wt: 0.6g; D(wire): 3.0mm; L: 9.0mm

S.60: Gold/silver alloy wire/?torc/?bracelet (Pl. 14.65)
NCM: yellow ticket no. 122
Findspot: Wooded area to west of main site
Context details: Metal-detected stray find 2003–9.
Short, curved fragment of gold/silver alloy circular-section wire. Cut at both ends. Possibly originally part of a multi-strand torc or bracelet.
Wt: 0.8g; D(wire): 2.7mm; L: 12.0mm

S.61: Gold/silver alloy torc/bracelet (Pl. 14.65)
NCM: yellow ticket no. 70
Findspot: Wooded area to west of main site
Context details: Metal-detected stray find 2003–9.
Fragment of gold/silver alloy circular-section wire, broken at both ends and partly melted. Curved in a way which suggests it originally formed part of a plied structure in a multi-strand torc or bracelet.
Wt: 1.0g; D(wire): 2.5mm; L: 11.0mm

S.62: Gold/silver alloy wire/?torc/bracelet (Pl. 14.65)
NCM: yellow ticket no. 50
Findspot: Wooded area to west of main site
Context details: Metal-detected stray find 2003–9.
Curved fragment of circular-section gold/silver alloy wire, possibly from a torc or bracelet.
Wt: 0.6g; D(wire): 2.0mm; L: 12.0mm

S.63: Gold/silver alloy wire/?torc/?bracelet (Pl. 14.65)
NCM: yellow ticket no. 112
Findspot: Wooded area to west of main site
Context details: Metal-detected stray find 2003–9.
Short, curved fragment of gold/silver alloy circular-section wire. Cut or broken at both ends. Possibly originally part of a multi-strand torc or bracelet.
Wt: 0.3g; D(wire): 2.0mm; L: 8.0mm

S.64: Gold/silver alloy wire/?torc/?bracelet (Pl. 14.65)
NCM: yellow ticket no. 28
Findspot: Wooded area to west of main site
Context details: Metal-detected stray find 2003–9.
Fragment of twisted square-section gold/silver alloy wire, possibly from a torc or bracelet. Folded back on itself, hammered, twisted and part melted. Possible additional adhering fragments.
Wt: 2.2g; D(wire): 4.0mm; L: 14.0mm

S.65: Gold/silver alloy wire/?torc/?bracelet (Pl. 14.65)
NCM: yellow ticket no. 144
Findspot: Wooded area to west of main site
Context details: Metal-detected stray find 2003–9.
Fragment of gold/silver alloy twisted square-section wire. Broken at both ends. Curved in a way which suggests it was originally part of a multi-strand torc or bracelet.
Wt: 1.1g; D(wire): 2.0mm; L: 17.0mm

S.66: Gold/silver alloy wire/amorphous lump (Pl. 14.65)
NCM: yellow ticket no. 68
Findspot: Wooded area to west of main site
Context details: Metal-detected stray find 2003–9.

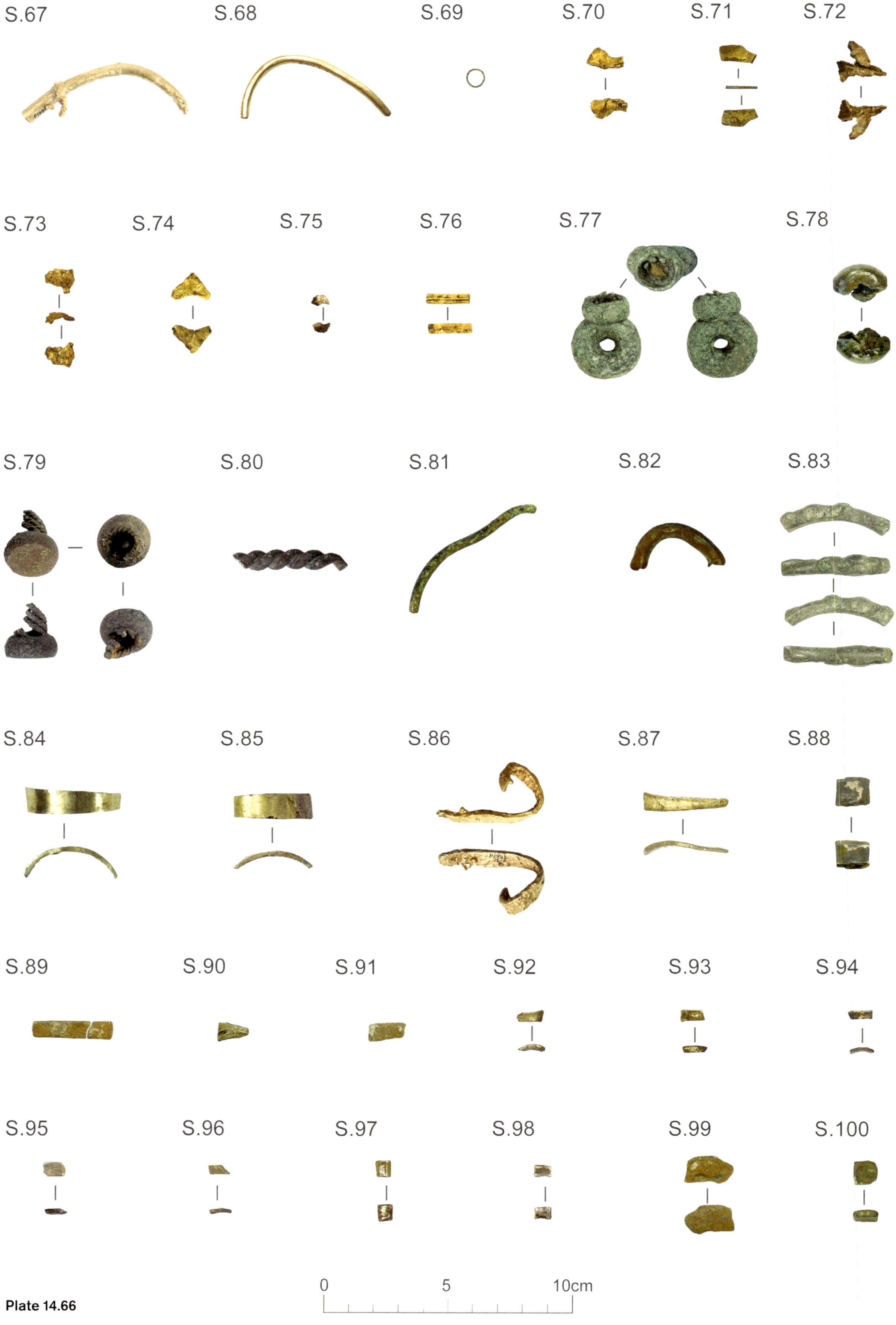
S.67
S.68
S.69
S.70
S.71
S.72
S.73
S.74
S.75
S.76
S.77
S.78
S.79
S.80
S.81
S.82
S.83
S.84
S.85
S.86
S.87
S.88
S.89
S.90
S.91
S.92
S.93
S.94
S.95
S.96
S.97
S.98
S.99
S.100
0
5
10cm

Plate 14.66

Amorphous lump of gold/silver alloy, formed from three part-melted lengths of twisted square-section wire.
Wt: 0.5g; D(wire): 1.0mm; L: 8.0mm; W: 5.0mm

S.67: Gold/silver alloy torc wire/?torc/?bracelet (Pl. 14.66)
BM: 1991,0407.58; Site code: SN/AP
Findspot: Area 1
Context details: Metal-detected stray find from 1990 excavation.
Gold/silver alloy thick circular-section wire, flat at one end and part melted at the other, possibly from a simple torc neck-ring or bracelet body. A short length of twisted square-section wire is fused onto it near the flat end.
Wt: 25.0g; D(wire): 6.1mm; 2.3mm (adhering twisted frag); L: 67.2mm; 11.4mm (adhering twisted fragment)

S.68: Gold/silver alloy wire/?torc/?bracelet (Pl. 14.66)
BM: 1991,0407.54; Site code: SN/JJ
Findspot: Area 2
Context details: Metal-detected stray find from 1990 excavation.
Gold/silver alloy circular-section wire, gently curved, broken at both ends. Possibly a simple torc neck-ring or bracelet body.
Wt: 12.5g; D(wire): 3.5mm; L: 60.9mm

S.69: Gold/silver alloy ring/?torc/?bracelet (Pl. 14.66)
NCM: yellow ticket no. 69
Findspot: Wooded area to west of main site
Context details: Metal-detected stray find 2003–9.
Small gold/silver alloy ring formed from fine, twisted square-section wire. Possibly a torc or bracelet component.
Wt: 0.1g; D(ext): 7.0mm; D(wire): 0.7mm

S.70: Gold/silver alloy sheet/?torc (Pl. 14.66)
NCM: yellow ticket no. 60
Findspot: Wooded area to west of main site
Context details: Metal-detected stray find 2003–9.
Fragment of gold/silver alloy sheet, folded and part melted. Possibly from a tubular torc.
Wt: 1.9g; L: 15.0mm; W: 9.0mm; T: 3.3mm

S.71: Gold/silver alloy sheet/?torc (Pl. 14.66)
NCM: yellow ticket no. 36
Findspot: Wooded area to west of main site
Context details: Metal-detected stray find 2003–9.
Small, clipped fragment of gold/silver alloy sheet. Possibly from a tubular torc.
Wt: 1.2g; L: 14.0mm; W: 7.0mm; T: 1.2mm

S.72: Gold/silver alloy sheet/?torc (Pl. 14.66)
NCM: yellow ticket no. 138
Findspot: Wooded area to west of main site
Context details: Metal-detected stray find 2003–9.
Torn and partially melted irregular fragment of gold/silver alloy sheet. Possibly from a tubular torc.
Wt: 1.1g; L: 20.0mm; W: 16.0mm; T: 3.0mm

S.73: Gold/silver alloy sheet/?torc (Pl. 14.66)
NCM: yellow ticket no. 64
Findspot: Wooded area to west of main site
Context details: Metal-detected stray find 2003–9.
Fragment of gold/silver alloy sheet, folded and torn. Possibly from a tubular torc.
Wt: 0.8g; L: 12.0mm; W: 9.0mm; T: 0.8mm

S.74: Gold/silver alloy sheet/?torc (Pl. 14.66)
NCM: yellow ticket no. 67
Findspot: Wooded area to west of main site
Context details: Metal-detected stray find 2003–9.
Fragment of gold/silver alloy sheet, folded and torn. Possibly from a tubular torc.
Wt: 0.3g; L: 16.0mm; W: 9.0mm; T: 0.2mm

S.75: Gold/silver alloy sheet/?torc (Pl. 14.66)
NCM: yellow ticket no. 158
Findspot: Wooded area to west of main site
Context details: Metal-detected stray find 2003–9.
Small fragment of gold/silver alloy sheet, torn, with no original edges. Possibly from a tubular torc.
Wt: 0.1g; L: 7.5mm; W: 5.5mm; T: 0.3mm

S.76: Gold/silver alloy strip /?torc (Pl. 14.66)
NCM: yellow ticket no. 66
Findspot: Wooded area to west of main site
Context details: Metal-detected stray find 2003–9.
Short fragment of gold/silver alloy strip with rectangular cross-section and raised, central, longitudinal rib on one side. Possibly a component from a tubular torc.
Wt: 0.6g; L: 18.0mm; W: 5.0mm; T: 0.5mm

Copper alloy
S.77: Copper alloy torc (Pl. 14.66)
MSCC: (?6C)R
BM: 1990,1101.21; Site code: SN/KP
Findspot: Area 5
Context details: Metal-detected stray find from 1990 excavation.
Fragment of copper alloy multi-strand torc, comprising a cast torus terminal, with plain head and simple collar. The remains of (?)six circular-section wires are preserved inside, suggesting a Stage II neck-ring formed from six wires coiled together around a hollow core.
Wt: 56.4g; D(term): 29.9mm; L: 35.6mm

S.78: Copper alloy torc (Pl. 14.66)
BM: 1992,0210.1; Site code: SM/AA
Findspot: Wooded area to west of main site
Context details: Metal-detected stray find March 1992. Re-deposited.
Fragment of thick copper alloy torus terminal, most likely from a multi-strand torc. Hollow interior and thick walls. Raggedly broken at the edges, only the very end of the head survives, not the collar where it would have attached to the neck-ring.
Wt: 11.2g; L: 21.9mm; T: 12.3mm

S.79: Copper alloy torc (Pl. 14.66)
MSCC: (7C)T
BM: 1990,1101.22; Site code: SN/EG
Findspot: Area 2
Context details: Metal-detected stray find from 1990 excavation.
Fragment of copper alloy multi-strand torc comprising one plain, slightly expanded buffer terminal with rounded edge and flat face, and a short length of neck-ring protruding from the back. The Stage II neck-ring is formed from seven twisted wires coiled together around a hollow core. A fragment of clay (?)mould remains attached to the inside of the neck-ring where it joins the terminal, perhaps from the casting process.
Wt: 24.2g; D(nr): 13.0mm; D(wire): 2.9mm; D(term): 21.3mm; L: 22.7mm

S.80: Copper alloy torc (Pl. 14.66)
MSCC: (2P)R
BM: 1990,1101.20; Site code: SN/AV
Findspot: Area 1
Context details: Metal-detected stray find from 1990 excavation.
Fragment of copper alloy multi-strand torc neck-ring, with clean flat breaks at both ends. Stage II construction of two circular-section wires plied together.
Wt: 11.4g; D(nr): 8.1mm; D(wire): 4.1mm; L: 46.0mm

S.81: Copper alloy wire/?torc/?bracelet (Pl. 14.66)
MSCC: (?P)R
BM: 1991,0409.22; Site code: ST/HD
Findspot: Area 21
Context details: Metal-detected stray find from 1991 excavation, most likely from 1990 backfill.
Length of copper alloy circular-section wire, broken at both ends. Bent in a way which suggests it may once have formed part of a loosely plied Stage II multi-strand torc neck-ring or bracelet body.
Wt: 7.1g; D(wire): 4.3mm; L: 66.0mm

S.82: Copper alloy wire/?torc/?bracelet (Pl. 14.66)
BM: 1990,1101.43; Site code: SN/MT
Findspot: Area 7
Context details: Metal-detected stray find from 1990 excavation.
Bent length of copper alloy circular-section wire, broken at both ends. Possibly part of the loop terminal from a multi-strand torc or bracelet.
Wt: 3.4g; D(wire): 3.9mm; L: 25.7mm

S.83: Copper alloy rod/?torc/?bracelet (Pl. 14.66)
BM: 1990,1101.48; Site code: SN/RF
Findspot: Area 14
Context details: Metal-detected stray find from 1990 excavation.
Curved section of copper alloy rod, broken at both ends, with relief zoomorphic decoration in the form of a stylised animal head with flaring nostrils (see discussion of decoration in Ch. 21, and **Fig. 21.31**). Surfaces partially hammered flat to give a squarish cross-section. Most likely part of a torc or bracelet.
The closest parallels are from north-east France, *c.* 350–250 BC, cf. Stead and Rigby (1999, 70–1, ML.1709).
Wt: 13.1g; D(wire): 6.8mm; L: 44.2mm

Large and small rings

Gold/silver alloy

S.84: Gold/silver alloy large ring (Pl. 14.66)
BM: 1991,0407.62; Site code: SN/CQ
Findspot: Area 1
Context details: Metal-detected stray find from 1990 excavation.
Fragment of gold/silver large ring, made from a strip with rectangular cross-section. Slightly tapering, broken at both ends.
Wt: 8.1g; L: 38.4mm; W: 10.2mm; T: 2.1mm

S.85: Gold/silver alloy large ring (Pl. 14.66)
BM: 1991,0501.227
Jackson no.: 506
Findspot: Not recorded
Context details: Metal-detected stray find August 1990.
Fragment of gold/silver alloy large ring, made from a strip with rectangular cross-section. Broken at both ends.
Wt: 6.8g; L: 31.7mm; W: 10.3mm; T: 2.0mm

S.86: Gold/silver alloy strip or ?large/?small ring (Pl. 14.66)
BM: 1992,1202.3; Site code: ST/FS
Findspot: Area 21
Context details: Metal-detected stray find from 1991 excavation, most likely from 1990 backfill.
Fragment of gold/silver alloy strip with rectangular cross-section, broken at both ends. Most likely a fragment of large or small ring that has been bent out of shape, and distorted by heat. Partially melted bubbling/globules all over the surface.
Wt: 11.4g; L: 43.1mm; W: 7.8mm; T: 2.1mm

S.87: Gold/silver alloy strip/?large/small ring (Pl. 14.66)
NCM: yellow ticket no. 31
Findspot: Wooded area to west of main site
Context details: Metal-detected stray find 2003–9.
Tapering length of gold/silver alloy strip with rectangular cross-section, possibly a fragment of large/small ring. Cut at both ends and slightly bent/distorted.
Wt: 3.5g; L: 34.0mm; W: 6.0mm; T: 2.0mm

S.88: Gold/silver alloy strip or ?large/?small ring (Pl. 14.66)
NCM: yellow ticket no. 124
Findspot: Wooded area to west of main site
Context details: Metal-detected stray find 2003–9.
Short fragment of gold/silver alloy strip with rectangular cross-section, possibly a fragment of large/small ring. Cut at both ends (the long sides of the fragments are the cut ends).
Wt: 3.0g; L: 14.0mm; W: 11.0mm; T: 2.5mm

S.89: Gold/silver alloy strip or ?large/?small ring (Pl. 14.66)
NCM: yellow ticket no. 32
Findspot: Wooded area to west of main site

Context details: Metal-detected stray find 2003–9.
Two joining fragments of a gold/silver alloy strip with rectangular cross-section, possibly a fragment of large/small ring. One broken end and one possible original flat terminal.
Wt: 2.6g; L: 33.0mm; W: 7.0mm; T: 1.2mm

S.90: Gold/silver alloy strip or ?large/?small ring (Pl. 14.66)
NCM: yellow ticket no. 52
Findspot: Wooded area to west of main site
Context details: Metal-detected stray find 2003–9.
Very short fragment of gold/silver alloy strip with rectangular cross-section, possibly a fragment of large/small ring. Cut at both ends, with clear tool marks (the long sides of the fragments are the cut ends).
Wt: 2.0g; L: 13.0mm; W: 7.0mm; T: 4.2mm

S.91: Gold/silver alloy strip or ?large/?small ring (Pl. 14.66)
NCM: yellow ticket no. 38
Findspot: Wooded area to west of main site
Context details: Metal-detected stray find 2003–9.
Short fragment of gold/silver alloy strip, with rectangular cross-section, possibly a fragment of large/small ring. Slightly tapered and broken at both ends.
Wt: 1.4g; L: 15.0mm; W: 6.0mm; T: 2.6mm

S.92: Gold/silver alloy strip or ?large/?small ring (Pl. 14.66)
NCM: yellow ticket no. 106
Findspot: Wooded area to west of main site
Context details: Metal-detected stray find 2003–9.
Short, curved fragment of gold/silver alloy strip with rectangular cross-section, possibly a fragment of large/small ring. Broken at both ends.
Wt: 0.8g; L: 11.0mm; W: 4.0mm; T: 1.6mm

S.93: Gold/silver alloy strip or ?large/?small ring (Pl. 14.66)
NCM: yellow ticket no. 99
Findspot: Wooded area to west of main site
Context details: Metal-detected stray find 2003–9.
Short, curved fragment of gold/silver alloy strip with rectangular cross-section, possibly a fragment of large/small ring. Cut at both ends.
Wt: 0.8g; L: 10.0mm; W: 4.0mm; T: 2.0mm

S.94: Gold/silver alloy strip or ?large/?small ring (Pl. 14.66)
NCM: yellow ticket no. 94
Findspot: Wooded area to west of main site
Context details: Metal-detected stray find 2003–9.
Short, curved fragment of gold/silver alloy strip with rectangular cross-section, possibly a fragment of large/small ring. Broken at both ends and partially melted.
Wt: 0.4g; L: 10.0mm; W: 3.0mm; T: 0.9mm

S.95: Gold/silver alloy strip or ?large/?small ring (Pl. 14.66)
NCM: yellow ticket no. 97
Findspot: Wooded area to west of main site
Context details: Metal-detected stray find 2003–9.
Short fragment of gold/silver alloy strip with rectangular cross-section, possibly a fragment of large/small ring. Cut or broken at both ends.
Wt: 0.6g; L: 9.0mm; W: 6.5mm; T: 1.8mm

S.96: Gold/silver alloy strip or ?large/?small ring (Pl. 14.66)
NCM: yellow ticket no. 77
Findspot: Wooded area to west of main site
Context details: Metal-detected stray find 2003–9.
Short, curved fragment of gold/silver alloy strip with rectangular cross-section, possibly a fragment of large/small ring. Broken at both ends.
Wt: 0.4g; L: 9.0mm; W: 4.0mm; T: 1.0mm

S.97: Gold/silver alloy strip or ?large/?small ring (Pl. 14.66)
NCM: yellow ticket no. 131
Findspot: Wooded area to west of main site
Context details: Metal-detected stray find 2003–9.
Very short fragment of gold/silver alloy strip with rectangular cross-section, possibly a fragment of large/small ring. Cut at both ends (the long sides of the fragments are the cut ends).
Wt: 0.7g; L: 7.0mm; W: 7.0mm; T: 2.0mm

S.98: Gold/silver alloy strip or ?large/?small ring (Pl. 14.66)
NCM: yellow ticket no. 98
Findspot: Wooded area to west of main site
Context details: Metal-detected stray find 2003–9.
Very short fragment of gold/silver alloy strip with rectangular cross-section, possibly a fragment of large/small ring. Cut at both ends (the long sides of the fragments are the cut ends).
Wt: 0.5g; L: 7.0mm; W: 5.0mm; T: 1.5mm

Copper alloy

S.99: Copper alloy strip or ?large/?small ring (Pl. 14.66)
NCM: yellow ticket no. 192
Findspot: Wooded area to west of main site
Context details: Metal-detected stray find 2003–9.
Short fragment of thick copper alloy strip, curved in cross-section, possibly a fragment of large/small ring. Broken at both ends.
Wt: 3.1g; L: 20.0mm; W: 10.0mm; T: 2.5mm

S.100: Copper alloy strip or ?large/?small ring (Pl. 14.66)
NCM: yellow ticket no. 42
Findspot: Wooded area to west of main site
Context details: Metal-detected stray find 2003–9.
Short fragment of copper alloy strip with rectangular cross-section, possibly a fragment of large/small ring. Broken at both ends.
Wt: 2.7g; L: 10.0mm; W: 10.0mm; T: 2.8mm

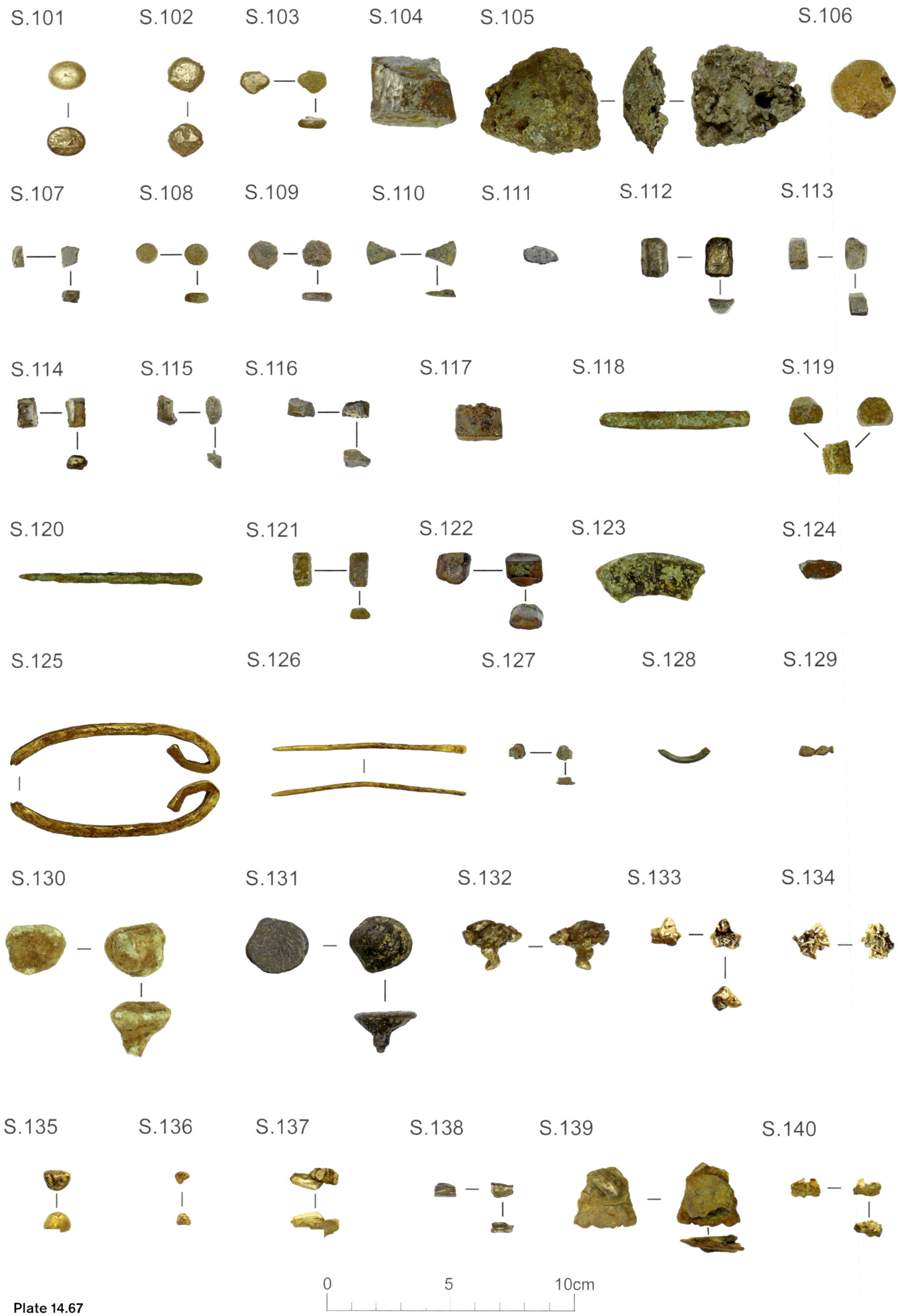
S.101
S.102
S.103
S.104
S.105
S.106
S.107
S.108
S.109
S.110
S.111
S.112
S.113
S.114
S.115
S.116
S.117
S.118
S.119
S.120
S.121
S.122
S.123
S.124
S.125
S.126
S.127
S.128
S.129
S.130
S.131
S.132
S.133
S.134
S.135
S.136
S.137
S.138
S.139
S.140
0
5
10cm

Plate 14.67

Lump and triangular ingots

Gold/silver alloy

S.101: Gold/silver alloy lump ingot (Pl. 14.67)
BM: 2009,4213.20; Site code: SN/PY
Findspot: Area 10
Context details: Metal-detected stray find from 1990 excavation.
Gold ingot or pellet, oval in plan. Slightly domed on one side and flat on the other. Possible coin blank.
Wt: 7.0g; L: 15.5mm

S.102: Gold/silver alloy lump ingot (Pl. 14.67)
BM: 2009,4213.21; Site code: SN/QA
Findspot: Area 11
Context details: Metal-detected stray find from 1990 excavation.
Gold ingot or pellet, roughly circular in plan. Flat but irregular surface on both sides. Possible coin blank.
Wt: 5.9g; D(ext): 14.5mm

S.103: Gold/silver alloy lump ingot (Pl. 14.67)
NCM: yellow ticket no. 135
Findspot: Wooded area to west of main site
Context details: Metal-detected stray find 2003–9.
Amorphous gold/silver alloy lump, hammered flat.
Wt: 3.3g; L: 12.0mm; W: 11.0mm; T: 4.0mm

Copper alloy:

S.104: ?Tin/Copper alloy lump ?ingot (Pl. 14.67)
BM: 1991,0409.28
Findspot: Not recorded
Context details: Metal-detected stray find Dec. 1990–April 1991.
Large ingot or lump of ?tin/copper, silverish in colour. Squarish in plan (broken at each end), with kite-shaped cross-section.
Wt: 115.1g; L: 34.0mm; W: 40.0mm; T: 20.0mm

S.105: Copper alloy triangular ingot with gold/silver alloy additions (Pl. 14.67)
NCM: yellow ticket no. 245
Findspot: Wooded area to west of main site
Context details: Metal-detected stray find 2003–9.
Small copper alloy ingot, from the base of a triangular crucible. Irregular top surface showing part-melted wire fragments and possibly small amounts of part-melted gold sheet.
Wt: 81.0g; L: 46.5mm; W: 42.3mm; T: 20.0mm

S.106: Copper alloy (?silver alloy/?lead alloy) lump ingot (Pl. 14.67)
BM: 1991,0409.4; Site code: ST/AK
Findspot: Area 17
Context details: Metal-detected stray find from 1991 excavation.
Thick, flattish ingot or lump of copper (or perhaps lead or silver) alloy, circular in plan, with irregular curved edges. Flat on one side, rougher on the other.
Wt: 30.3g; L: 26.2mm; T: 8.3mm

S.107: Copper alloy lump ingot (Pl. 14.67)
NCM: yellow ticket no. 47
Findspot: Wooded area to west of main site
Context details: Metal-detected stray find 2003–9.
Sub-cuboidal copper alloy fragment, hammered and broken.
Wt: 3.2g; L: 8.0mm; W: 7.0mm; T: 4.0mm

S.108: Copper alloy/lead alloy lump ingot (Pl. 14.67)
NCM: yellow ticket no. 195
Findspot: Wooded area to west of main site
Context details: Metal-detected stray find 2003–9.
Thick, flattened copper alloy disc.
Wt: 2.6g; D(ext): 9.0mm; T: 4.0mm

S.109: Copper alloy lump ingot (Pl. 14.67)
NCM: yellow ticket no. 143
Findspot: Wooded area to west of main site
Context details: Metal-detected stray find 2003–9.
Copper alloy lump hammered into a flat disc.
Wt: 2.1g; D(ext): 12.0mm; T: 4.0mm

S.110: Copper alloy lump ingot (Pl. 14.67)
NCM: yellow ticket no. 118
Findspot: Wooded area to west of main site
Context details: Metal-detected stray find 2003–9.
Fragment of broken, flat, copper alloy disc.
Wt: 1.3g; L: 12.0mm; W: 10.0mm; T: 3.5mm

S.111: Copper alloy lump ingot (Pl. 14.67)
NCM: yellow ticket no. 116
Findspot: Wooded area to west of main site
Context details: Metal-detected stray find 2003–9.
Fragment of broken, flat, copper alloy disc, roughly triangular in plan.
Wt: 1.0g; L: 14.0mm; W: 7.0mm; T: 1.8mm

Straight/bar ingots

Gold/silver alloy

S.112: Gold/silver alloy linear ingot (Pl. 14.67)
NCM: yellow ticket no. 141
Findspot: Wooded area to west of main site
Context details: Metal-detected stray find 2003–9.
Short section of gold/silver alloy linear ingot with trapezoidal cross-section, cut or broken at one end, with the original terminal intact at the other end.
Wt: 7.8g; L: 16.0mm; W: 11.0mm; T: 6.5mm

S.113: Gold/silver alloy linear ingot (Pl. 14.67)
NCM: yellow ticket no. 140
Findspot: Wooded area to west of main site
Context details: Metal-detected stray find 2003–9.
Short section of gold/silver alloy linear ingot with trapezoidal cross-section, cut or broken at both ends, possibly part of an ingot bar.
Wt: 5.9g; L: 13.0mm; W: 7.0mm; T: 6.5mm

S.114: Gold/silver alloy linear ingot (Pl. 14.67)
NCM: yellow ticket no. 110

Findspot: Wooded area to west of main site
Context details: Metal-detected stray find 2003–9.
Short section of gold/silver alloy rod with oval cross-section, cut at both ends, possibly part of a linear ingot.
Wt: 3.2g; D(wire): 12.0mm; L: 6.0mm

S.115: Gold/silver alloy linear ingot (Pl. 14.67)
NCM: yellow ticket no. 129A
Findspot: Wooded area to west of main site
Context details: Metal-detected stray find 2003–9.
Short section of gold/silver alloy rod with oval to D-shaped cross-section, cut at both ends, possibly part of a linear ingot.
Wt: 2.4g; L: 12.0mm; W: 7.0mm; T: 2.0mm

S.116: Gold/silver alloy linear ingot (Pl. 14.67)
NCM: yellow ticket no. 134
Findspot: Wooded area to west of main site
Context details: Metal-detected stray find 2003–9.
Short section of gold/silver alloy bar or rod, cut on three sides, possibly part of a linear ingot.
Wt: 2.1g; L: 11.0mm; W: 6.0mm; T: 5.0mm

Copper alloy

S.117: Copper alloy linear ingot (Pl. 14.67)
BM: 1990,1101.38; Site code: SN/AL
Findspot: Not recorded
Context details: Metal-detected stray find from 1990 excavation.
Length of copper alloy bar, rectangular in cross-section, cut/chiselled on one end, possibly part of a linear ingot.
Wt: 26.7g; L: 29.0mm; W: 23.4mm; T: 7.1mm

S.118: Copper alloy linear ingot (Pl. 14.67)
BM: 1991,0409.12; Site code: ST/DC
Findspot: Area 23
Context details: Metal-detected stray find from 1991 excavation.
Square-section copper alloy bar, tapering towards each end, possibly a linear ingot.
Wt: 17.9g; L: 60.5mm; W: 7.3mm; T: 6.8mm

S.119: Copper alloy linear ingot (Pl. 14.67)
NCM: yellow ticket no. 173
Findspot: Wooded area to west of main site
Context details: Metal-detected stray find 2003–9.
Short fragment of oval-section copper alloy rod, cut at both ends, possibly part of a linear ingot.
Wt: 7.7g; D(wire): 14.0mm; L: 10.0mm; T: 10.5mm

S.120: Copper alloy linear ingot/?wire (Pl. 14.67)
BM: 1991,0409.18; Site code: ST/EG
Findspot: Area 25
Context details: Metal-detected stray find from 1991 excavation.
Circular-section copper alloy wire, gradually tapering towards one pointed end, rounded at the other, possibly a linear ingot. Heavily corroded.
Wt: 7.1g; D(wire): 5.0mm; L: 73.8mm

S.121: Copper alloy linear ingot (Pl. 14.67)
NCM: yellow ticket no. 155
Findspot: Wooded area to west of main site
Context details: Metal-detected stray find 2003–9.
Short fragment of copper alloy bar with trapezoidal section, cut or broken at both ends, possibly part of a linear ingot.
Wt: 5.3g; L: 7.0mm; W: 14.0mm; T: 8.5mm

S.122: Copper alloy linear ingot (Pl. 14.67)
NCM: yellow ticket no. 153
Findspot: Wooded area to west of main site
Context details: Metal-detected stray find 2003–9.
Short fragment of oval-section copper alloy rod, chopped at both ends with a chisel, possibly part of a linear ingot.
Wt: 2.0g; L: 14.0mm; W: 10.0mm; T: 6.2mm

Other possible ingots

S.123: Copper alloy ?ingot/?fitting (Pl. 14.67)
BM: 1991,0409.13; Site code: ST/DE
Findspot: Area 23
Context details: Metal-detected stray find from 1991 excavation.
Flat copper alloy arc, rectangular in cross-section and broken at each end, perhaps an unusual ingot. Tool marks are clearly visible where the object has been hammered flat. Slightly flared outer edge.
Wt: 15.7g; L: 44.3mm; W: 17.4mm; T: 4.2mm

S.124: Copper alloy ?ingot/?fitting (Pl. 14.67)
BM: 1991,0409.6; Site code: ST/BG
Findspot: Area 18
Context details: Metal-detected stray find from 1991 excavation.
Short length of copper alloy rod or fragment from the flared edge of a larger object, approximately triangular in cross-section. Heavily corroded.
Perhaps part of a flat copper alloy object with flanged outer edge, similar to S.123.
Wt: 2.1g; L: 17.6mm; W: 8.4mm; T: 5.0mm

Rod and wire

Gold/silver alloy

S.125: Gold/silver alloy wire (Pl. 14.67)
NCM: yellow ticket no. 61
Findspot: Wooded area to west of main site
Context details: Metal-detected stray find 2003–9.
Fragment of thick, gold/silver alloy square-section wire, broken at one end and flat at the other, which is bent over. Clear evidence of folding and hammering on the corners. Possibly from an intermediate stage in wire production. See Chapter 17 for further discussion of wire making.
Wt: 25.9g; D(wire): 4.8mm; L: 8.1mm

S.126: Gold/silver alloy wire/?tool (Pl. 14.67)
NCM: yellow ticket no. 62
Findspot: Wooded area to west of main site
Context details: Metal-detected stray find 2003–9.
Worked fragment of heavily worn, twisted, square-section gold/silver alloy wire, slightly curved. Hammered flat at one end and worked to a point at the other, possibly for use as a fine tool of some kind.
Wt: 4.3g; D(wire): 1.7mm; L: 79.0mm; W: 3.0mm (flat end)

Copper alloy

S.127: Copper alloy rod (Pl. 14.67)
NCM: yellow ticket no. 198
Findspot: Wooded area to west of main site
Context details: Metal-detected stray find 2003–9.
Short fragment of copper alloy rod, one flat and one broken end; may have been hammered to flatten it into a disc.
Wt: 1.4g; D(ext): 7.0mm; L: 4.8mm

S.128: Copper alloy wire (Pl. 14.67)
NCM: yellow ticket no. 175
Findspot: Wooded area to west of main site
Context details: Metal-detected stray find 2003–9.
Curved copper alloy wire fragment with diamond-shaped cross-section, broken at both ends.
Wt: 1.2g; L: 21.0mm; W: 3.0mm

S.129: Copper alloy wire/strip (Pl. 14.67)
NCM: yellow ticket no. 29
Findspot: Wooded area to west of main site
Context details: Metal-detected stray find 2003–9.
Fragment of flat-section twisted copper alloy wire or strip.
Wt: 0.9g; D(wire): 4.0mm; L: 14.0mm

Metalworking waste

Copper alloy

S.130: Copper alloy casting sprue (Pl. 14.67)
BM: 1990,1101.49; Site code: SN/RR
Findspot: Not recorded
Context details: Metal-detected stray find from 1990 excavation, found during backfilling.
Copper alloy sprue from casting into a mould. Approximately conical in shape, broken off at narrow end.
Wt: 32.6g; L: 21.0mm; W: 24.7mm

S.131: Copper alloy casting sprue (Pl. 14.67)
NCM: yellow ticket no. 247
Findspot: Wooded area to west of main site
Context details: Metal-detected stray find 2003–9.
Conical copper alloy lump, most likely a broken-off sprue from casting into a mould.
Wt: 19.6g; D(ext): 23.2mm; L: 25.5mm; T: 15.4mm

Amorphous lumps: worked or incorporating part-melted objects and fused additions

Gold/silver alloy

S.132: Gold/silver alloy lump with incorporated wire (Pl. 14.67)
NCM: yellow ticket no. 63
Findspot: Wooded area to west of main site
Context details: Metal-detected stray find 2003–9.
Amorphous lump of gold/silver alloy, incorporating a part-melted length of gold/silver alloy wire.
Wt: 11.2g; D(wire): 2.8mm; L: 24.0mm; W: 19.0mm

S.133: Gold/silver alloy lump with incorporated wire (Pl. 14.67)
BM: 1992,1203.12
Findspot: Not recorded
Context details: Metal-detected stray find Dec. 1990–April 1991.
Partially melted lump of gold/silver alloy, with fused additions, including what may be a distorted strand of torc wire.
Wt: 5.1g; L: 12.5mm

S.134: Gold/silver alloy lump with incorporated wire (Pl. 14.67)
BM: 1991,0407.61; Site code: SN/JW
Findspot: Area 2; SN21 (This is a Neolithic pit, but a Rainbird Clarke trench cut the edge of this feature)
Context details: Metal-detected stray find from 1990 excavation.
Gold/silver alloy lump: including fused additions of short, part-melted twisted wire strands (see **Fig. 20.24**).
Wt: 4.9g; L: 16.3mm

S.135: Gold/silver alloy lump with incorporated wire (Pl. 14.67)
NCM: yellow ticket no. 72
Findspot: Wooded area to west of main site
Context details: Metal-detected stray find 2003–9.
Amorphous lump of gold/silver alloy, incorporating a part-melted length of twisted square-section wire.
Wt: 2.7g; D(wire): 1.6mm; L: 11.0mm; W: 8.0mm; T: 5.0mm

S.136: Gold/silver alloy lump with incorporated wire (Pl. 14.67)
NCM: yellow ticket no. 71
Findspot: Wooded area to west of main site
Context details: Metal-detected stray find 2003–9.
Amorphous lump of gold/silver alloy, incorporating a part-melted length of twisted square-section wire.
Wt: 0.8g; D(wire): 2.3mm; L: 6.0mm; W: 6.0mm; T: 3.8mm

S.137: Gold/silver alloy worked lump (Pl. 14.67)
NCM: yellow ticket no. 128
Findspot: Wooded area to west of main site
Context details: Metal-detected stray find 2003–9.
Amorphous gold/silver alloy lump, with some evidence of hammering.
Wt: 4.3g; L: 20.0mm; W: 12.0mm; T: 5.1mm

S.138: Gold/silver alloy worked lump (Pl. 14.67)
NCM: yellow ticket no. 85
Findspot: Wooded area to west of main site
Context details: Metal-detected stray find 2003–9.
Amorphous gold/silver alloy lump, showing evidence of being deliberately cut.
Wt: 1.5g; L: 10.0mm; W: 6.0mm; T: 4.5mm

Copper alloy

S.139: Copper alloy lump/?disc with incorporated gold/silver alloy additions (Pl. 14.67)
NCM: yellow ticket no. 74
Findspot: Wooded area to west of main site
Context details: Metal-detected stray find 2003–9.
Broken copper alloy disc, fused on one side to a thin,

amorphous gold/silver alloy lump or part-melted sheet fragment.
Wt: 10.3g; D(ext): 21.5mm (disc); L: 30.0mm; W: 28.0mm; T: 7.0mm

S.140: Copper alloy lump with incorporated gold/silver alloy wire and sheet (Pl. 14.67)
NCM: yellow ticket no. 130
Findspot: Wooded area to west of main site
Context details: Metal-detected stray find 2003–9.
Fragments of gold/silver alloy wire and sheet partially melted over an amorphous copper alloy lump.
Wt: 3.9g; L: 7.0mm; W: 12.0mm

S.141–S.234: Amorphous, unworked metal lumps **(Table 14.2)**
All were metal-detected stray finds, some made during the 1990s excavation seasons, others made in 2003–9. Groupings made by the finder were kept, hence some catalogue numbers for 2003–9 finds include multiple lumps.

The finds are ordered by metal (gold/silver alloy, followed by copper alloys, followed by iron), and within each metal group by weight.

For multiple groups, the weight given is the total, and the length the maximum dimension of the largest lump.

Possible beaded torc and bracelet fragments

Copper alloy and iron

S.235–6: Copper alloy and iron terminals, possibly from beaded ?torc/?bracelet (Pl. 14.68)
Findspot: Wooded area to west of main site
Context details: Metal-detected stray find 2003–9.
A pair of balustered/thistle-headed iron fittings with copper alloy plating, circular in cross-section. Possibly the terminals of a beaded torc or bracelet.
S.235: NCM: yellow ticket no. 4
Wt: 4.7g; D(ext): 10.0mm (bead); L: 21.0mm
S.236: NCM: yellow ticket no. 258
Wt: 6.5g; D(ext): 11.5mm; L: 19.2mm

S.237–9: Copper alloy beads possibly from ?torc/?bracelet (Pl. 14.68)
Findspot: Wooded area to west of main site
Context details: Metal-detected stray find 2003–9.
Three beads, possibly from the same beaded torc or bracelet.

S.237: NCM: yellow ticket no. *6*
Circular copper alloy bead with moulded collar at each end and square-shaped central perforation.
Wt: 4.1g; D(ext): 13.0mm (bead); L: 8.0mm

Cat. no.	Museum	Reg. no. or ticket no.	Site code	Findspot*	Discovery year	Material	Wt/g	L/mm (max.)	No. lumps (if multiple)
S.141	NCM	yellow ticket no. 113		Wood	2003–9	Gold/silver alloy	6.2	20.0	
S.142	NCM	yellow ticket no. 136		Wood	2003–9	Gold/silver alloy	3.9	12.0	
S.143	NCM	yellow ticket no. 82		Wood	2003–9	Gold/silver alloy	3.1	17.0	
S.144	NCM	yellow ticket no. 148		Wood	2003–9	Gold/silver alloy	3.1	11.0	
S.145	NCM	yellow ticket no. 108		Wood	2003–9	Gold/silver alloy	2.8	11.0	
S.146	NCM	yellow ticket no. 261		Wood	2003–9	Gold/silver alloy	2.6	16.5	
S.147	NCM	yellow ticket no. 92		Wood	2003–9	Gold/silver alloy	2.2	12.0	
S.148	NCM	yellow ticket no. 120		Wood	2003–9	Gold/silver alloy	1.8	11.0	
S.149	NCM	yellow ticket no. 125		Wood	2003–9	Gold/silver alloy	1.8	8.5	
S.150	NCM	yellow ticket no. 126		Wood	2003–9	Gold/silver alloy	1.8	11.0	
S.151	NCM	yellow ticket no. 149		Wood	2003–9	Gold/silver alloy	1.8	10.0	
S.152	NCM	yellow ticket no. 51		Wood	2003–9	Gold/silver alloy	1.6	11.0	
S.153	NCM	yellow ticket no. 35		Wood	2003–9	Gold/silver alloy	1.4	7.0	
S.154	NCM	yellow ticket no. 37		Wood	2003–9	Gold/silver alloy	1.3	12.0	
S.155	NCM	yellow ticket no. 65		Wood	2003–9	Gold/silver alloy	1.3	9.0	
S.156	NCM	yellow ticket no. 90		Wood	2003–9	Gold/silver alloy	1.3	9.0	

Table 14.2 Tabulated catalogue entries for amorphous, unworked metal lumps S.141–S.234. None are illustrated
* = 'Wood' denotes the wooded area to the west of the main site

Cat. no.	Museum	Reg. no. or ticket no.	Site code	Findspot*	Discovery year	Material	Wt/g	L/mm (max.)	No. lumps (if multiple)
S.157	NCM	yellow ticket no. 100		Wood	2003–9	Gold/silver alloy	1.3	10.0	
S.158	NCM	yellow ticket no. 109		Wood	2003–9	Gold/silver alloy	1.3	10.0	
S.159	NCM	yellow ticket no. 150		Wood	2003–9	Gold/silver alloy	1.3	11.0	
S.160	NCM	yellow ticket no. 104		Wood	2003–9	Gold/silver alloy	1.2	14.0	
S.161	NCM	yellow ticket no. 121		Wood	2003–9	Gold/silver alloy	1.2	12.0	
S.162	NCM	yellow ticket no. 152		Wood	2003–9	Gold/silver alloy	1.2	12.0	
S.163	NCM	yellow ticket no. 56		Wood	2003–9	Gold/silver alloy	1.1	11.0	
S.164	NCM	yellow ticket no. 87		Wood	2003–9	Gold/silver alloy	1.0	8.0	
S.165	NCM	yellow ticket no. 115		Wood	2003–9	Gold/silver alloy	1.0	7.0	
S.166	NCM	yellow ticket no. 123		Wood	2003–9	Gold/silver alloy	1.0	8.0	
S.167	NCM	yellow ticket no. 154		Wood	2003–9	Gold/silver alloy	1.0	9.0	
S.168	NCM	yellow ticket no. 80		Wood	2003–9	Gold/silver alloy	0.9	7.6	
S.169	NCM	yellow ticket no. 79		Wood	2003–9	Gold/silver alloy	0.8	6.0	
S.170	NCM	yellow ticket no. 114		Wood	2003–9	Gold/silver alloy	0.8	4.0	
S.171	NCM	yellow ticket no. 137		Wood	2003–9	Gold/silver alloy	0.8	11.0	
S.172	NCM	yellow ticket no. 101		Wood	2003–9	Gold/silver alloy	0.7	7.0	
S.173	NCM	yellow ticket no. 105		Wood	2003–9	Gold/silver alloy	0.7	6.0	
S.174	NCM	yellow ticket no. 151		Wood	2003–9	Gold/silver alloy	0.6	7.0	
S.175	NCM	yellow ticket no. 83		Wood	2003–9	Gold/silver alloy	0.5	8.0	
S.176	NCM	yellow ticket no. 107		Wood	2003–9	Gold/silver alloy	0.5	6.0	
S.177	NCM	yellow ticket no. 88		Wood	2003–9	Gold/silver alloy	0.4	5.0	
S.178	NCM	yellow ticket no. 117		Wood	2003–9	Gold/silver alloy	0.4	9.0	
S.179	BM	1991,0409.16	ST/DT	Area 24	1991	?Lead alloy	110.2	52.0	
S.180	NCM	yellow ticket no. 246		Wood	2003–9	Copper alloy	61.8	43.6	
S.181	BM	1991,0409.21	ST/GZ	Area 21	1991	Copper alloy	55.6	40.5	
S.182	NCM	yellow ticket no. 266		Wood	2003–9	Copper alloy	52.4	31.0	10
S.183	NCM	yellow ticket no. 200		Wood	2003–9	Copper alloy	34.3	29.0	12
S.184	NCM	yellow ticket no. 265		Wood	2003–9	Copper alloy; ?lead alloy	31.5	32.5	
S.185	BM	1990,1101.46	SN/OE	Area 9; near Hoard L	1990	Copper alloy	31.4	37.8	
S.186	NCM	yellow ticket no. 193		Wood	2003–9	Copper alloy	25.5	26.8	2
S.187	BM	1990,1101.44	SN/MX	Area 9	1990	Copper alloy	19.6	31.0	

Table 14.2 continued

Cat. no.	Museum	Reg. no. or ticket no.	Site code	Findspot*	Discovery year	Material	Wt/g	L/mm (max.)	No. lumps (if multiple)
S.188	NCM	yellow ticket no. 252		Wood	2003–9	Copper alloy	18.7	27.0	
S.189	BM	1991,0409.9	ST/CA	Area 20	1991	?Lead; ?silver alloy	18.4	39.2	
S.190	BM	1991,0409.2	ST/AA	Area 20	1991	Copper alloy	15.8	40.0	
S.191	BM	1991,0409.10	ST/CC	Area 20	1991	?Lead; ?silver alloy	15.0	32.9	
S.192	NCM	yellow ticket no. 264		Wood	2003–9	Copper alloy	14.3	23.8	
S.193	NCM	yellow ticket no. 197		Wood	2003–9	Lead alloy	14.3	35.0	
S.194	BM	1991,0409.7	ST/BL	Area 19	1991	Copper alloy	13.3	27.9	
S.195	BM	1990,1101.39	SN/BD	Area 1	1990	Copper alloy	11.7	28.9	
S.196	BM	1990,1101.45	SN/MZ	Area 9	1990	Copper alloy	11.0	21.8	
S.197	BM	1991,0409.17	ST/DV	Area 24	1991	Copper alloy	9.6	22.1	
S.198	NCM	yellow ticket no. 190		Wood	2003–9	Copper alloy	9.1	25.0	
S.199	BM	1991,0409.26		Not recorded	1990–1	Copper alloy	8.6	17.2	
S.200	NCM	yellow ticket no. 182		Wood	2003–9	Copper alloy	8.0	20.0	
S.201	NCM	yellow ticket no. 161		Wood	2003–9	Copper alloy	7.5	26.0	
S.202	NCM	yellow ticket no. 162		Wood	2003–9	Copper alloy	6.7	20.0	
S.203	NCM	yellow ticket no. 132		Wood	2003–9	Copper alloy	6.5	20.0	
S.204	NCM	yellow ticket no. 263		Wood	2003–9	Copper alloy; ?lead alloy	6.2	24.0	
S.205	NCM	yellow ticket no. 181		Wood	2003–9	Copper alloy	5.5	17.0	
S.206	BM	1990,1101.41	SN/EN	Area 2	1990	Copper alloy	5.5	26.0	
S.207	NCM	yellow ticket no. 86		Wood	2003–9	Copper alloy	4.7	17.0	
S.208	NCM	yellow ticket no. 84		Wood	2003–9	Copper alloy	3.3	17.0	
S.209	BM	1991,0409.3	ST/AE	Area 16	1991	Copper alloy	3.3	17.2	
S.210	NCM	yellow ticket no. 53		Wood	2003–9	Copper alloy	3.1	14.0	
S.211	NCM	yellow ticket no. 159		Wood	2003–9	Copper alloy	3.0	16.0	
S.212	BM	1991,0409.14	ST/DF	Not recorded	1991	Copper alloy	2.7	14.6	
S.213	NCM	yellow ticket no. 46		Wood	2003–9	Copper alloy; ?lead alloy	2.7	15.0	
S.214	NCM	yellow ticket no. 48		Wood	2003–9	Copper alloy	2.6	11.0	
S.215	NCM	yellow ticket no. 163		Wood	2003–9	Copper alloy	2.6	20.0	
S.216	NCM	yellow ticket no. 170		Wood	2003–9	Copper alloy	2.6	14.0	
S.217	NCM	yellow ticket no. 165		Wood	2003–9	Copper alloy	2.5	12.0	
S.218	NCM	yellow ticket no. 185		Wood	2003–9	Copper alloy	2.5	16.0	
S.219	NCM	yellow ticket no. 58		Wood	2003–9	Copper alloy	2.4	11.0	
S.220	NCM	yellow ticket no. 260		Wood	2003–9	Copper alloy	2.0	12.5	

Table 14.2 continued

Cat. no.	Museum	Reg. no. or ticket no.	Site code	Findspot*	Discovery year	Material	Wt/g	L/mm (max.)	No. lumps (if multiple)
S.221	NCM	yellow ticket no. 147		Wood	2003–9	Copper alloy	1.9	18.0	
S.222	NCM	yellow ticket no. 262		Wood	2003–9	Copper alloy	1.9	15.1	
S.223	NCM	yellow ticket no. 55		Wood	2003–9	Copper alloy	1.8	10.0	
S.224	NCM	yellow ticket no. 160		Wood	2003–9	Copper alloy	1.5	12.0	
S.225	NCM	yellow ticket no. 96		Wood	2003–9	Copper alloy	1.4	12.0	
S.226	NCM	yellow ticket no. 176		Wood	2003–9	Copper alloy	1.4	11.0	
S.227	NCM	yellow ticket no. 54		Wood	2003–9	Copper alloy	1.2	12.0	
S.228	NCM	yellow ticket no. 146		Wood	2003–9	Copper alloy	1.1	12.0	
S.229	NCM	yellow ticket no. 111		Wood	2003–9	Copper alloy	1.0	11.0	
S.230	NCM	yellow ticket no. 102		Wood	2003–9	Copper alloy	0.8	10.0	
S.231	NCM	yellow ticket no. 57		Wood	2003–9	Copper alloy	0.7	9.0	
S.232	NCM	yellow ticket no. 59		Wood	2003–9	Copper alloy	0.7	7.0	
S.233	NCM	yellow ticket no. 177		Wood	2003–9	Copper alloy	0.6	7.0	
S.234	NCM	yellow ticket no. 49		Wood	2003–9	Iron	3.1	20.0	

Table 14.2 continued

S.238: NCM: yellow ticket no. 7
Circular copper alloy bead with moulded collar at each end, threaded onto a short length of corroded iron bar.
Wt: 7.7g; D(ext): 12.0mm (bead); L: 20.0mm (including protruding iron bar)

S.239: NCM: yellow ticket no. 9
Hollow, hemispherical copper alloy bead with large, central circular perforation.
Wt: 4.5g; D(ext): 12.0mm (bead); L: 8.0mm

S.240: Iron bead possibly from ?torc/?bracelet (Pl. 14.68)
NCM: yellow ticket no. 8
Findspot: Wooded area to west of main site
Context details: Metal-detected stray find 2003–9.
Circular copper alloy bead with moulded collar at each end, threaded onto a short length of corroded iron bar. Probably from a beaded torc or bracelet.
Wt: 10.9g; D(ext): 20.0mm (bead); L: 12.0mm

S.241: Copper alloy ?bead possibly from ?torc/?bracelet (Pl. 14.68)
NCM: yellow ticket no. 5
Findspot: Wooded area to west of main site
Context details: Metal-detected stray find 2003–9.
Fragment of unidentified copper alloy object. Rectangular in cross-section at one end, waisted in the centre to give a circular section, and then flaring out to a small square cross-section at the other end. A very short length of circular-section rod appears to emerge at the square end. The flat sides of the rectangular-section area appear to have been cut, or perhaps hammered. May be a component from a beaded torc or bracelet that has been cut up or deliberately damaged.
Wt: 7.1g; D(ext): 10.0mm (bead); L: 15.0mm

Brooches
Sophia Adams

Silver and copper alloys

S.242: ?Silver alloy brooch spring (Pl. 14.68)
NCM: yellow ticket no. 157
Findspot: Wooded area to west of main site
Context details: Metal-detected stray find 2003–9.
Small fragment of a brooch spring made from circular-section wire, possibly a silver alloy. Three coils and the external chord survive. Broken where the inner coil meets the bow, and at the start of the first coil on the opposite side of the spring. Bilateral springs with external chords are a long-lasting feature of Iron Age brooches. Those with three or more coils on either side post-date *c.* 150 BC in England. The number of coils and the alloy suggest a date no earlier than *c.* 50 BC (Adams 2014; Adams 2020).
Wt: 4.6g; D(wire): 2.0mm; L: 24.0mm; W: 8.5mm (spring)

S.243: Copper alloy brooch (Pl. 14.68)
NCM: yellow ticket no. 11

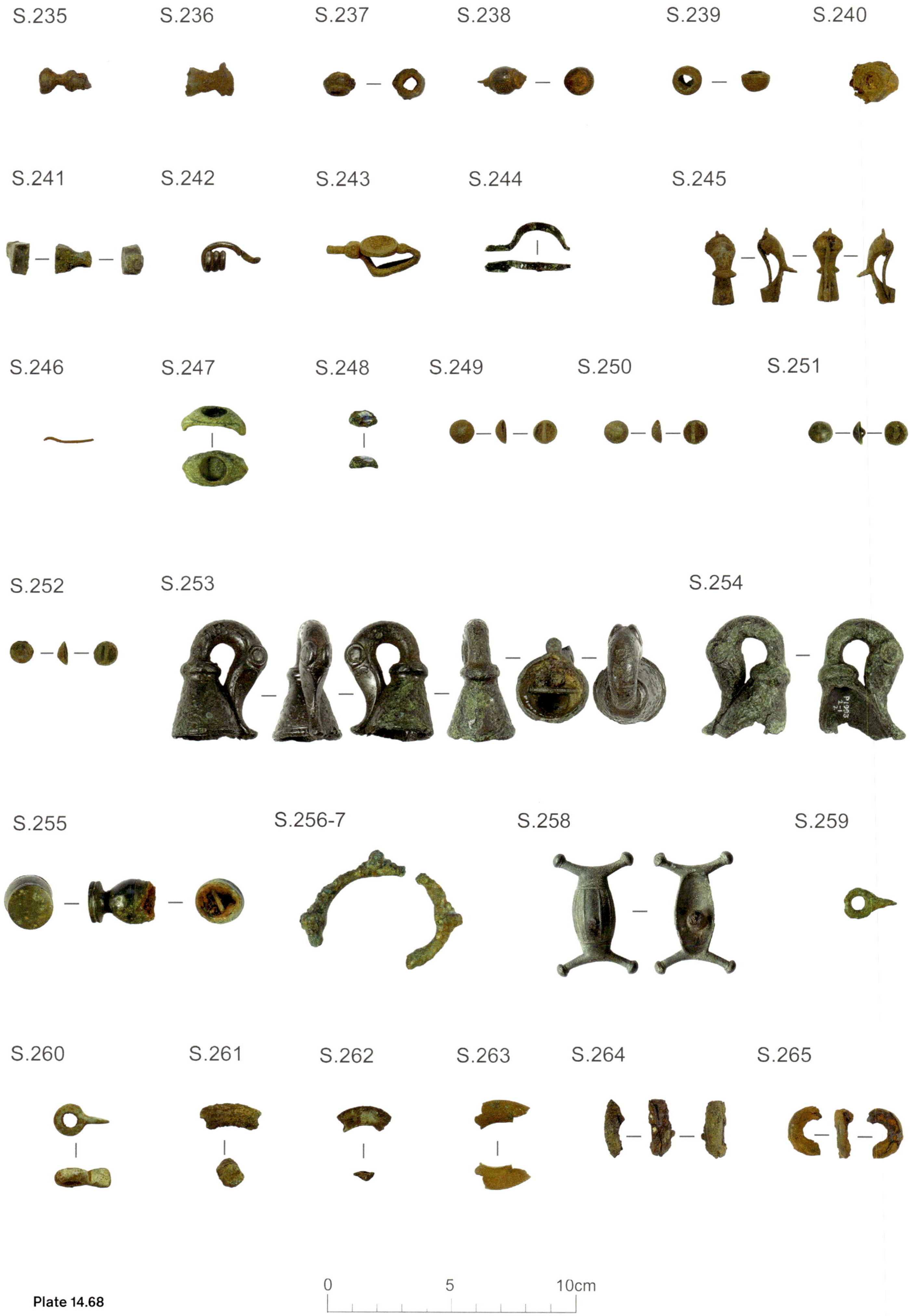
S.235
S.236
S.237
S.238
S.239
S.240
S.241
S.242
S.243
S.244
S.245
S.246
S.247
S.248
S.249
S.250
S.251
S.252
S.253
S.254
S.255
S.256-7
S.258
S.259
S.260
S.261
S.262
S.263
S.264
S.265
0
5
10cm

Plate 14.68

Findspot: Wooded area to west of main site
Context details: Metal-detected stray find 2003–9.
Copper alloy catch-plate and foot from a Middle Iron Age bow brooch. The reverted, sloped foot terminates in a dished, circular plate and a collar wrapped around the hip of the bow. The plate may originally have been inlaid with coral or glass. Very little of the plano-convex-section bow survives.
The shape, angle and attachment of the foot place this in Hull and Hawkes' Type 2Aa (1987) as further defined by Adams (2014) dating to *c.* 350–150 BC.
Wt: 8.1g; L: 38.0mm; W: 15.0mm (max.); T: 2.5mm (bow)

S.244: Copper alloy brooch (Pl. 14.68)
BM: 1992,0210.4; Site code: SA/BL
Findspot: Trench 6
Context details: Enclosure ditch: SA6/2, Section C, Layer 1
Copper alloy brooch with high arched, rectangular-section bow and long, wide catch-plate. The pin and spring are missing. The upper surface of the bow is decorated with a double row of punched dots. The foot is broken.
Although the high arched bow is often associated with Early Iron Age brooches it reappears during the later Iron Age combined with different foot and head forms. The cross-section of the early examples is circular or plano-convex, whereas the straight sides and rectangular cross-section of this example is more akin to later Iron Age brooches, as is the long catch-plate found on the reverted, attached foot forms of the 3B brooches. This could be an atypical variation on Hull and Hawkes' Type 1B brooches of 400–300 BC date but a post-150 BC date is also possible (Hull and Hawkes 1987; Mackreth 2011; Adams 2014).
Wt: 1.9g; L: 34.0mm; W: 2.9mm

S.245: Tinned copper alloy brooch (Pl. 14.68)
NCM: yellow ticket no. 267
Findspot: Wooded area to west of main site
Context details: Metal-detected stray find 2003–9.
Copper alloy Romano-British Almgren Type 101 brooch with white metal coating to the surface (tinning). Rounded trumpet-shaped head and fantail foot with perpendicular, semi-circular plate projecting from the centre of the brooch. Decoration (and tinning) is visible over these front features albeit in a worn condition: round dots on the upper part and across the top face of the plate. The fantail bears two, barely visible, small human faces in relief, one above the other. The sprung pin is mounted on the back of the brooch and rests in a triangular catch-plate.

A very close parallel is Mackreth's Almgren 101.1b brooch from Bottom Pond Farm, Owslebury 5550, pl. 133, *c.* AD 150–220 (Mackreth 2011, 192–3, pl. 133).
Wt: 6.2g; L: 30.5mm; W: 12.2mm (at head); T: 15.0mm (depth of whole brooch)

Other personal ornaments and fasteners

Copper alloy

S.246: Copper alloy strip/?brooch (Pl. 14.68)
BM: 1992,0210.5; Site code: SA/DV
Findspot: Trench 6
Context details: Ditch: SA6/7
Copper alloy rectangular-section strip, broken at both ends, with slight curve near one end. Possibly the pin from a penannular brooch or a buckle.
Wt: 0.2g; L: 20.0mm; W: 2.3mm; T: 1.0mm

S.247: Copper alloy finger-ring (Pl. 14.68)
BM: 1991,0409.15; Site code: ST/DG
Findspot: Not recorded
Context details: Metal-detected stray find from 1991 excavation, most likely from 1990 backfill.
Half of a large Roman finger-ring, with swollen recessed bezel in the centre. Missing the setting.
Henig Type II–III/Guiraud 2, AD 200–400 (Johns 1996, 42–4).
Wt: 5.9g; D(ext): 26.5mm; W: 14.1mm; T: 4.4mm

S.248: Copper alloy (and ?glass) ?finger-ring (Pl. 14.68)
BM: 1991,0409.19; Site code: ST/FO
Findspot: Area 26
Context details: Metal-detected stray find from 1991 excavation.
Heavily corroded finger-ring fragment, consisting of the area around the bezel, set with some blueish glass or enamel, poorly preserved. Possibly Roman in date.
Wt: 1.1g; L: 11.8mm; W: 7.4mm

S.249–52: Copper alloy buttons/fasteners (Pl. 14.68)
Findspot: Wooded area to west of main site
Context details: Metal-detected stray find 2003–9.
Four copper alloy buttons or fasteners, each comprising a shallow, hollow copper alloy dome, with bar on the underside. All four are near-identical and may be from the same object.

S.249: NCM: yellow ticket no. 17
Wt: 0.9g; D(ext): 10.0mm (head); T: 4.0mm

S.250: NCM: yellow ticket no. 16
Wt: 0.8g; D(ext): 10.0mm (head); T: 4.0mm

S.251: NCM: yellow ticket no. 18
Wt: 0.7g; D(ext): 10.0mm (head); T: 4.0mm

S.252: NCM: yellow ticket no. 19
Wt: 0.8g; D(ext): 10.0mm (head); T: 4.0mm

Fittings, mounts and strap fittings

Copper alloy and iron

S.253–4: Pair of zoomorphic copper alloy ?drinking horn terminals (Pl. 14.68)
Findspot: Trench 15, to east of main excavated area
Context details: Metal-detected stray finds 1989.
Two cast copper alloy conical terminals, each with a hollow internal socket and an end terminating in a loop in the form of a duck's head (or the head of a long-snouted animal) (see **Fig. 21.42**). The animal heads are sharply modelled in the

round and were cast by the lost-wax method. Possibly from drinking horns.

Such objects are rare, but cf. the bull-headed horn terminal from Needham, Norfolk, published by Davies (2011, 63–4).
See Chapter 21 for a full discussion of these objects.

S.253: BM: 1993,0201.1
Wt: 73.9g; D(ext): 29.5mm (base); L: 50.6mm

S.254: BM: 1993,0201.2
Wt: 51.4g; L: 50.0mm

S.255: Copper alloy linch-pin/fitting (Pl. 14.68)
BM: 1991,0409.24; Site code: ST/HX
Findspot: Not recorded
Context details: Metal-detected stray find from 1991 excavation.
Balustered copper alloy terminal with plain flat top and simple recessed line around circumference of the head. The form is very similar to vase-headed linch-pin terminals, cf. Palk (1992) Type IIA, nos 570–91, common from the later Iron Age to the Early Roman period. A copper alloy rivet runs across the socket, and some preserved wood remains in the interior. This suggests it may be a terminal fitted to a wooden rod rather than a linch-pin, which would be expected to have an iron (rather than wooden) shaft.
Wt: 33.9g; D(ext): 20.3mm; L: 27.4mm

S.256–7: Copper alloy terret (Pl. 14.68)
BM: 1991,0409.8; Site code: ST/BR; ST/BS
Findspot: Area 20
Context details: Metal-detected stray find from 1991 excavation.
Two broken fragments from a copper alloy terret ring, comprising most of the ring, although none of the strap bar is preserved. Very heavily corroded, and the break is clearly not recent. Three equally spaced sub-rectangular projections around the outer circumference, each flanked on either side by a slightly raised margin.
cf. Lewis's (2015, 91–5) 'terrets with triple projections' type, especially the 'triplets' sub-type (fig. 4.1(xiv)). Lewis dates this type to the mid-1st to 2nd centuries AD.
Wt: 26.9g (total); L: 49.1mm (max.)

S.258: Copper alloy and iron fitting (Pl. 14.68)
BM: 1991,0409.11; Site code: ST/CE
Findspot: Not recorded
Context details: Metal-detected stray find from 1991 excavation.
Very unusual copper alloy mount or fitting. The overall shape in plan is a capital 'I', where the vertical stem takes the form of a hollow sub-rectangular dome, swollen in the centre, and the top and bottom bars are projecting circular-section 'legs', each ending in a small spherical knob. The top of the central dome is decorated with a simple grid pattern in low relief. On the reverse, a corroded iron rivet would once have fixed the mount to a larger object, most likely organic.
Wt: 19.0g; L: 50.0mm; W: 32.7mm; T: 11.0mm

S.259: Copper alloy fitting (Pl. 14.68)
BM: 1990,1101.47; Site code: SN/PZ
Findspot: Area 11
Context details: Metal-detected stray find from 1990 excavation.
Small copper alloy ring with short broken-off length of shank, heavily corroded. Most likely part of a button and loop fastener. cf. Wild (1970), most similar to mid-1st-century AD examples, such as those from the Stanwick Hoard, e.g. MacGregor (1962) M.26–36.
Wt: 2.3g; L: 21.5mm; W: 12.8mm; T: 4.2mm

S.260: Copper alloy fitting (Pl. 14.68)
NCM: yellow ticket no. 139
Findspot: Wooded area to west of main site
Context details: Metal-detected stray find 2003–9.
Copper alloy fitting: small ring with a flat, projecting tang or shank or on one side.
Wt: 4.7g; D(ext): 14.0mm; L: 22.5mm; T: 7.5mm

S.261: Copper alloy rod/?strap fitting (Pl. 14.68)
NCM: yellow ticket no. 254
Findspot: Wooded area to west of main site
Context details: Metal-detected stray find 2003–9.
Curved fragment of circular-section copper alloy rod, broken at both ends and heavily corroded. Possibly part of a strap fitting.
Wt: 8.5g; D(ext): 8.8mm; L: 25.0mm

S.262: Copper alloy ?strap fitting (Pl. 14.68)
NCM: yellow ticket no. 188
Findspot: Wooded area to west of main site
Context details: Metal-detected stray find 2003–9.
Broken fragment of copper alloy object, perhaps part of a strap fitting. Curved in plan, flat on one side, with shallow triangular cross-section.
Wt: 2.6g; L: 22.0mm; W: 8.3mm; T: 3.0mm

S.263: Copper alloy strip/?strap fitting (Pl. 14.68)
NCM: yellow ticket no. 240
Findspot: Wooded area to west of main site
Context details: Metal-detected stray find 2003–9.

Curved fragment of U-shaped copper alloy strip, broken at both ends. Too shallow for a binding strip; possibly from the outer plating or sheath of a ring or harness/strap fitting.

Wt: 0.8g; L: 22.5mm; W: 9.5mm; T: 0.2mm (sheet); 5.5mm (total)

S.264: Copper alloy and iron strap fitting (Pl. 14.68)
NCM: yellow ticket no. 39
Findspot: Wooded area to west of main site
Context details: Metal-detected stray find 2003–9.
Small fragment of broken iron ring with oval cross-section; copper alloy sheet sheath on exterior face.
Wt: 2.8g; L: 23.6mm; W: 8.0mm; T: 6.5mm

S.265: Copper alloy and iron strap fitting (Pl. 14.68)
NCM: yellow ticket no. 26
Findspot: Wooded area to west of main site
Context details: Metal-detected stray find 2003–9.
Fragment of broken iron ring with circular cross-section; remains of copper alloy sheet sheath on exterior face.
Wt: 10.8g; L: 20.0mm; W: 19.0mm; T: 12.0mm

S.266: Copper alloy and iron sheet/?ring with rivets (Pl. 14.69)
NCM: yellow ticket no. 241
Findspot: Wooded area to west of main site
Context details: Metal-detected stray find 2003–9.
Fragment of thick iron sheet, or possibly part of the circuit of a small iron ring, heavily corroded. Pierced through by two circular-headed copper alloy rivets.
Wt: 2.5g; D(ext): 3.5mm (rivet heads); L: 20.5mm; W: 14.3mm; T: 6.2mm

Rivets and rivet heads

Copper alloy

S.267: Copper alloy mount/rivet (Pl. 14.69)
NCM: yellow ticket no. 168
Findspot: Wooded area to west of main site
Context details: Metal-detected stray find 2003–9.
S-shaped, raised copper alloy mount or rivet with single, square-section attachment pin at rear.
Wt: 1.8g; L: 20.0mm (mount); 10.0mm (pin); W: 11.0mm; T: 2.0mm (mount)

S.268: Copper alloy rivet (Pl. 14.69)
NCM: yellow ticket no. 20
Findspot: Wooded area to west of main site
Context details: Metal-detected stray find 2003–9.
Solid, domed copper alloy rivet head or terminal, with projecting circular-section shank. Incised decorative border around edge of domed head.
Wt: 5.8g; D(ext): 10.0mm (head); L: 17.0mm; W: 3.8mm (shank)

S.269: Copper alloy rivet head (Pl. 14.69)
NCM: yellow ticket no. 43
Findspot: Wooded area to west of main site
Context details: Metal-detected stray find 2003–9.
Solid, domed copper alloy rivet head with slightly projecting circular-section shank.
Wt: 2.8g; D(ext): 9.6mm (head); L: 7.0mm (total height, including shank); W: 2.8mm (shank); T: 6.0mm (head)

S.270: Copper alloy rivet head (Pl. 14.69)
NCM: yellow ticket no. 24
Findspot: Wooded area to west of main site
Context details: Metal-detected stray find 2003–9.
Shallow, hollow copper alloy domed rivet head, with central projecting shank on the reverse.
Wt: 1.8g; D(ext): 11.0mm (head); L: 5.3mm; W: 3.0mm (pin); T: 2.8mm (height of head)

S.271: Copper alloy rivet (Pl. 14.69)
NCM: yellow ticket no. 201
Findspot: Wooded area to west of main site
Context details: Metal-detected stray find 2003–9.
Copper alloy rivet with round, flat head and protruding circular-section shank.
Wt: 1.1g; D(ext): 10.5mm (head); L: 10.0mm; W: 2.0mm (shank)

S.272: Copper alloy rivet head (Pl. 14.69)
NCM: yellow ticket no. 23
Findspot: Wooded area to west of main site
Context details: Metal-detected stray find 2003–9.
Shallow, hollow copper alloy domed rivet head, with central projecting shank on the reverse.
Wt: 0.9g; D(ext): 9.0mm (head); L: 12.3mm; W: 1.0mm (pin); T: 4.0mm (height of head)

S.273: Copper alloy rivet head (Pl. 14.69)
NCM: yellow ticket no. 22
Findspot: Wooded area to west of main site
Context details: Metal-detected stray find 2003–9.
Shallow, hollow copper alloy domed rivet head, with central circular perforation.
Wt: 0.5g; D(ext): 12.0mm (head); T: 3.8mm (height of head)

S.274: Copper alloy rivet head (Pl. 14.69)
NCM: yellow ticket no. 25
Findspot: Wooded area to west of main site
Context details: Metal-detected stray find 2003–9.
Shallow, hollow copper alloy domed rivet head, with central projecting shank on the reverse.
Wt: 0.5g; D(ext): 10.0mm (head); L: 6.9mm; W: 1.0mm (pin); T: 3.8mm (height of head)

S.275: Copper alloy rivet head (Pl. 14.69)
NCM: yellow ticket no. 257
Findspot: Wooded area to west of main site
Context details: Metal-detected stray find 2003–9.
Small convex copper alloy dome, most likely a rivet head.
Wt: 0.2g; D(ext): 7.2mm; T: 1.7mm

Binding strips

Copper alloy

S.276: Copper alloy binding strip/?shield (Pl. 14.69)
NCM: yellow ticket no. 33
Findspot: Wooded area to west of main site
Context details: Metal-detected stray find 2003–9.
Bulbous terminal from a U-shaped copper alloy binding strip, broken at the other end. Probably one half of the terminal of the V-shaped corner of a hide-shaped shield binding.
Similar to the hide-shaped shield binding from Hoard B/C: B/C.89.
Wt: 1.7g; L: 30.0mm; W: 12.0mm; T: 4.2mm (total); *c.* 0.3mm (sheet)

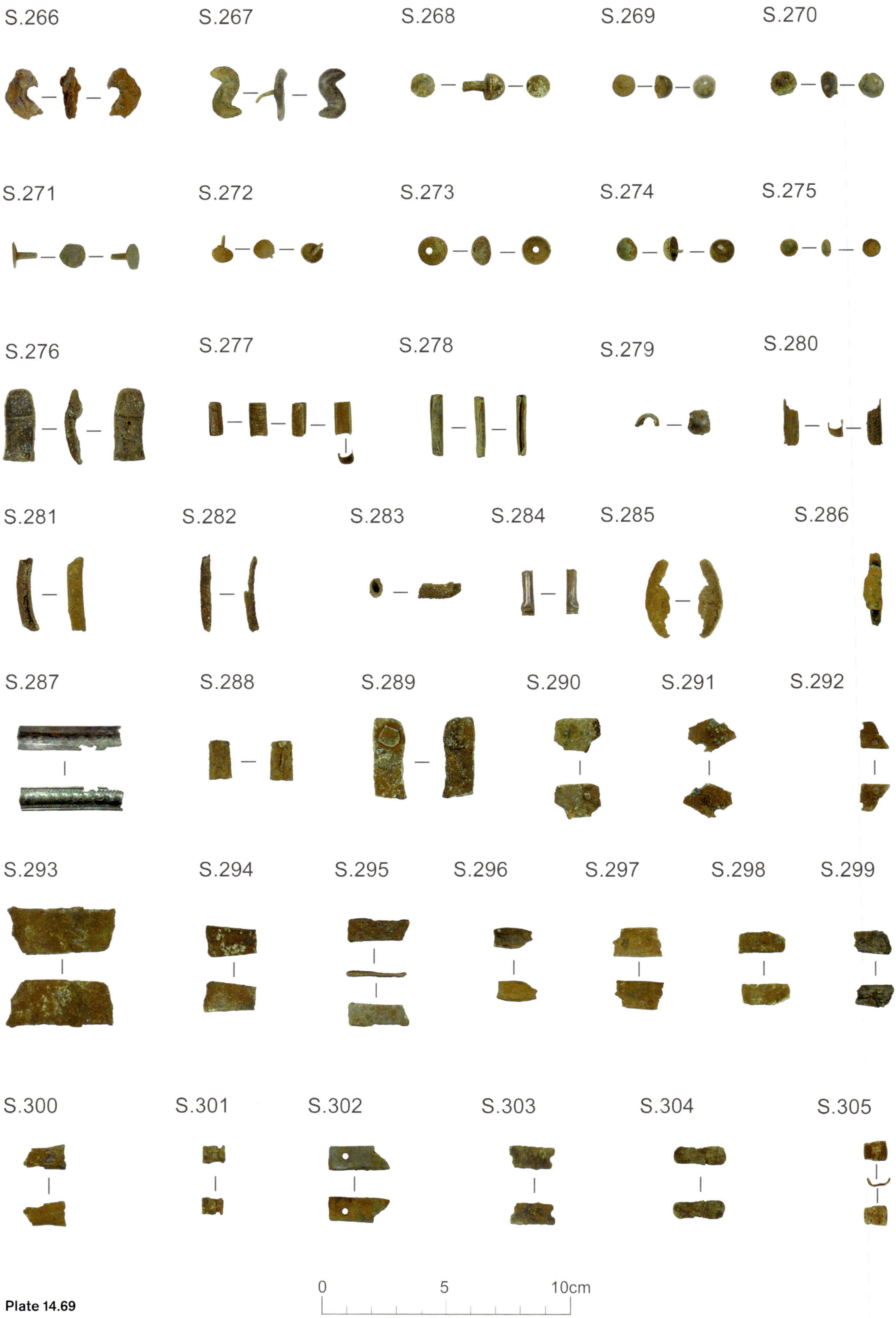
S.266
S.267
S.268
S.269
S.270
S.271
S.272
S.273
S.274
S.275
S.276
S.277
S.278
S.279
S.280
S.281
S.282
S.283
S.284
S.285
S.286
S.287
S.288
S.289
S.290
S.291
S.292
S.293
S.294
S.295
S.296
S.297
S.298
S.299
S.300
S.301
S.302
S.303
S.304
S.305
0
5
10cm

Plate 14.69

S.277: Copper alloy binding clamp (Pl. 14.69)
NCM: yellow ticket no. 244
Findspot: Wooded area to west of main site
Context details: Metal-detected stray find 2003–9.
U-shaped copper alloy binding clamp. Decorated on the exterior with incised transverse lines forming opposing curves that meet back-to-back in the centre of the clamp.
Wt: 1.2g; L: 14.5mm; W: 7.5mm; T: 0.3–0.5mm (sheet); 5.2mm (total)

S.278: Copper alloy ?binding clamp (Pl. 14.69)
NCM: yellow ticket no. 27
Findspot: Wooded area to west of main site
Context details: Metal-detected stray find 2003–9.
Short length of U-shaped copper alloy binding strip, squeezed almost closed. Perhaps a clamp as the terminals seem original, with simple incised decoration at each end.
Wt: 1.7g; L: 25.0mm; W: 4.2mm; T: 3.8mm

S.279: Copper alloy ?binding clamp (Pl. 14.69)
NCM: yellow ticket no. 40
Findspot: Wooded area to west of main site
Context details: Metal-detected stray find 2003–9.
Copper alloy fragment. Possible clamp from binding strip or fragment of bead.
Wt: 1.4g; D(ext): 10.0mm; W: 9.2mm; T: 2.0mm

S.280: Copper alloy binding strip (Pl. 14.69)
NCM: yellow ticket no. 186
Findspot: Wooded area to west of main site
Context details: Metal-detected stray find 2003–9.
Short fragment of U-shaped copper alloy binding strip, broken at both ends.
Wt: 4.7g; L: 19.0mm; W: 6.0mm; T: 4.0mm

S.281: Copper alloy binding strip (Pl. 14.69)
NCM: yellow ticket no. 169
Findspot: Wooded area to west of main site
Context details: Metal-detected stray find 2003–9.
Fragment of U-shaped copper alloy binding strip, broken at both ends.
Wt: 2.5g; D(ext): 8.0mm; L: 34.0mm; W: 8.0mm; T: 5.0mm

S.282: Copper alloy binding strip (Pl. 14.69)
NCM: yellow ticket no. 178
Findspot: Wooded area to west of main site
Context details: Metal-detected stray find 2003–9.
Crushed fragment of U-shaped copper alloy binding strip
Wt: 1.3g; L: 31.0mm; W: 5.0mm; T: 3.1mm

S.283: Copper alloy binding strip (Pl. 14.69)
NCM: yellow ticket no. 256
Findspot: Wooded area to west of main site
Context details: Metal-detected stray find 2003–9.
Length of U-shaped copper alloy binding strip, broken at both ends. Edges pinched together to form a narrow tube. Heavily corroded
Wt: 1.0g; L: 17.5mm; W: 6.0mm; T: 5.5mm

S.284: Copper alloy binding strip (Pl. 14.69)
NCM: yellow ticket no. 127
Findspot: Wooded area to west of main site
Context details: Metal-detected stray find 2003–9.
Fragment of U-shaped copper alloy binding strip, cut or broken at both ends.
Wt: 0.4g; L: 18.0mm; W: 4.0mm; T: 3.0mm

S.285: Copper alloy ?binding strip (Pl. 14.69)
NCM: yellow ticket no. 189
Findspot: Wooded area to west of main site
Context details: Metal-detected stray find 2003–9.
Broken fragment of copper alloy sheet, possibly part of a U-shaped binding strip.
Wt: 1.5g; L: 32.0mm; W: 10.0mm; T: 0.3mm (sheet); 3.0mm (total)

S.286: Copper alloy ?binding strip (Pl. 14.69)
BM: 1992,0210.6; Site code: SA/GM
Findspot: Trench 7
Context details: Ditch: SA7/5, Section D
Crushed fragment of U-shaped copper alloy binding strip, broken and heavily eroded at the edges.
Wt: 0.4g; L: 29.4mm; W: 1.2mm; T: 0.5mm

Strip

Copper alloy

S.287: Copper alloy decorative strip
BM: 1991,0409.20; Site code: ST/GM
Findspot: Area 27
Context details: Metal-detected stray find from 1991 excavation.
Copper alloy decorative strip with raised central rib, broken at both ends. The long flat sides are decorated with punched geometric decoration and the convex centre has less legible decoration.
Wt: 1.8g; L: 42.6mm; W: 10.0mm; T: 1.9mm

S.288: Copper alloy strip with ?rivet and adhering ?wire (Pl. 14.69)
NCM: yellow ticket no. 218
Findspot: Wooded area to west of main site
Context details: Metal-detected stray find 2003–9.
Fragment of copper alloy strip, broken at both ends. Pierced through by a small circular-headed rivet at one end. Adhering copper alloy wire fragment running down centre of strip.
Wt: 0.6g; L: 16.8mm; W: 9.0mm; T: 0.2–0.5mm (sheet); 1.5mm (rivet)

S.289: Copper alloy strip with rivet (Pl. 14.69)
NCM: yellow ticket no. 255
Findspot: Wooded area to west of main site
Context details: Metal-detected stray find 2003–9.
Fragment of copper alloy strip, broken at one end, and possibly both. Pierced through by a large-headed rivet, the head broken at the edges.
Wt: 3.3g; L: 33.5mm; W: 13.0mm; T: 0.8mm (strip), 1.8mm (including rivet)

S.290: Copper alloy strip with rivet (Pl. 14.69)
NCM: yellow ticket no. 212
Findspot: Wooded area to west of main site
Context details: Metal-detected stray find 2003–9.
Fragment of copper alloy strip, broken at both ends. Pierced through by one small circular-headed rivet.
Wt: 1.0g; L: 18.8mm; W: 13.8mm; T: 0.2mm

S.291: Copper alloy strip with rivet (Pl. 14.69)
NCM: yellow ticket no. 213
Findspot: Wooded area to west of main site
Context details: Metal-detected stray find 2003–9.
Fragment of copper alloy strip, broken at both ends. Pierced through by one small circular-headed rivet.
Wt: 0.7g; L: 19.5mm; W: 13.6mm; T: 0.2mm

S.292: Copper alloy strip with rivet (Pl. 14.69)
NCM: yellow ticket no. 217
Findspot: Wooded area to west of main site
Context details: Metal-detected stray find 2003–9.
Fragment of copper alloy strip, broken at both ends. Pierced through by one small circular-headed rivet.
Wt: 0.5g; D(ext): 4.0mm (rivet head); L: 15.0mm; W: 14.0mm; T: 0.2mm (sheet); 1.8mm (rivet)

S.293: Copper alloy strip (Pl. 14.69)
NCM: yellow ticket no. 205
Findspot: Wooded area to west of main site
Context details: Metal-detected stray find 2003–9.
Fragment of copper alloy strip, broken at both ends.
Wt: 2.5g; L: 43.0mm; W: 17.8mm; T: 0.5mm

S.294: Copper alloy strip ?with rivet (Pl. 14.69)
NCM: yellow ticket no. 208
Findspot: Wooded area to west of main site
Context details: Metal-detected stray find 2003–9.
Fragment of copper alloy strip, broken at both ends, slightly tapered. Possible remains of one small circular-headed rivet.
Wt: 2.5g; L: 23.0mm; W: 13.4mm; T: 1.0mm

S.295: Copper alloy strip (Pl. 14.69)
NCM: yellow ticket no. 167B
Findspot: Wooded area to west of main site
Context details: Metal-detected stray find 2003–9.
Short, rectangular length of copper alloy strip, broken at both ends.
Wt: 1.8g; L: 25.3mm; W: 9.5mm; T: 0.8mm

S.296: Copper alloy strip (Pl. 14.69)
NCM: yellow ticket no. 235
Findspot: Wooded area to west of main site
Context details: Metal-detected stray find 2003–9.
Fragment of thick copper alloy strip, slightly convex, and broken at both ends. Broken across a possible rivet hole at one end.
Wt: 1.1g; L: 16.2mm; W: 8.8mm; T: 1.0–1.5mm (sheet); 3.0mm (total)

S.297: Copper alloy strip (Pl. 14.69)
NCM: yellow ticket no. 209
Findspot: Wooded area to west of main site
Context details: Metal-detected stray find 2003–9.
Fragment of copper alloy strip, broken at both ends. Possible remains of the shank of one small rivet, where it pierced through the strip.
Wt: 1.0g; L: 20.0mm; W: 10.5mm; T: 0.5mm

S.298: Copper alloy strip (Pl. 14.69)
NCM: yellow ticket no. 184
Findspot: Wooded area to west of main site
Context details: Metal-detected stray find 2003–9.
Short fragment of thin copper alloy strip, broken at both ends.
Wt: 0.6g; L: 19.0mm; W: 8.0mm; T: 0.2mm

S.299: Copper alloy strip (Pl. 14.69)
NCM: yellow ticket no. 214
Findspot: Wooded area to west of main site
Context details: Metal-detected stray find 2003–9.
Fragment of copper alloy strip, slightly tapered, and broken at both ends. Formed from a rolled/folded piece of copper alloy sheet.
Wt: 0.6g; L: 16.8mm; W: 10.0mm; T: 1.6mm

S.300: Copper alloy strip (Pl. 14.69)
NCM: yellow ticket no. 219
Findspot: Wooded area to west of main site
Context details: Metal-detected stray find 2003–9.
Fragment of copper alloy strip, broken at both ends, slightly curved in cross-section.
Wt: 0.6g; L: 18.3mm; W: 10.5mm; T: 0.2–0.5mm (sheet); 2.8mm (total)

S.301: Copper alloy strip (Pl. 14.69)
NCM: yellow ticket no. 233
Findspot: Wooded area to west of main site
Context details: Metal-detected stray find 2003–9.
Short length of copper alloy strip, broken at both ends. Formed from a rolled/folded piece of copper alloy sheet.
Wt: 0.5g; L: 10.5mm; W: 8.5mm; T: 0.2mm (sheet); 1.8mm (total)

S.302: Copper alloy strip (Pl. 14.69)
NCM: yellow ticket no. 167A
Findspot: Wooded area to west of main site
Context details: Metal-detected stray find 2003–9.
Short, rectangular length of copper alloy strip, broken at both ends and perforated with small circular rivet hole.
Wt: 0.4g; L: 25.0mm; W: 10.5mm; T: 0.3mm

S.303: Copper alloy strip (Pl. 14.69)
NCM: yellow ticket no. 222
Findspot: Wooded area to west of main site
Context details: Metal-detected stray find 2003–9.
Fragment of copper alloy strip, broken across a large circular (?rivet) hole at both ends.
Wt: 0.4g; L: 18.5mm; W: 9.5mm; T: 0.2mm

S.304: Copper alloy strip (Pl. 14.69)
NCM: yellow ticket no. 236

Findspot: Wooded area to west of main site
Context details: Metal-detected stray find 2003–9.
Fragment of copper alloy strip, either very short strip or broken at both ends, but heavily worn along all edges.
Wt: 0.3g; L: 21.0mm; W: 7.6mm; T: 0.2mm

S.305: Copper alloy (?lead alloy) strip (Pl. 14.69)
NCM: yellow ticket no. 239
Findspot: Wooded area to west of main site
Context details: Metal-detected stray find 2003–9.
Fragment of shallow U-shaped copper alloy strip, broken at both ends. Tinned or leaded surface on one side.
Wt: 0.4g; L: 11.0mm; W: 9.5mm; T: 0.5mm

S.306: Copper alloy strip (Pl. 14.70)
NCM: yellow ticket no. 187
Findspot: Wooded area to west of main site
Context details: Metal-detected stray find 2003–9.
Short fragment of thin copper alloy strip. One original end, pierced with a circular rivet hole; broken at the other end.
Wt: 1.3g; L: 35.0mm; W: 15.0mm; T: 0.3mm

Iron

S.307: Iron strip (Pl. 14.70)
NCM: yellow ticket no. 45
Findspot: Wooded area to west of main site
Context details: Metal-detected stray find 2003–9.
Short fragment of iron strip with rectangular cross-section, broken at both ends.
Wt: 1.2g; L: 17.0mm; W: 7.0mm; T: 2.0mm

Sheet fragments with original edges or other distinguishing features

Copper alloy

S.308: Copper alloy sheet with rivet(s) (Pl. 14.70)
NCM: yellow ticket no. 207
Findspot: Wooded area to west of main site
Context details: Metal-detected stray find 2003–9.
Copper alloy sheet fragment with no original edges, torn and irregular in shape, pierced by one small circular-headed rivet, and possibly a second, though this area is obscured by corrosion.
Wt: 1.2g; L: 22.8mm; W: 13.0mm; T: 0.3mm

S.309: Copper alloy sheet with rivet (Pl. 14.70)
NCM: yellow ticket no. 215
Findspot: Wooded area to west of main site
Context details: Metal-detected stray find 2003–9.
Small, bent, copper alloy sheet fragment. One possible original edge, other edges torn and irregular. Possible remains of the shank of one small rivet, where it pierced through the strip.
Wt: 1.1g; L: 20.5mm; W: 15.5mm; T: 0.2–0.5mm

S.310: Copper alloy sheet with rivet (Pl. 14.70)
NCM: yellow ticket no. 206
Findspot: Wooded area to west of main site
Context details: Metal-detected stray find 2003–9.
Copper alloy sheet fragment with one possible original straight edge, other edges torn, pierced by a large circular-headed rivet.
Wt: 1.0g; D(ext): 7.0mm (rivet head); L: 27.0mm; W: 12.5mm; T: 0.2mm

S.311: Copper alloy sheet with rivets (Pl. 14.70)
NCM: yellow ticket no. 228
Findspot: Wooded area to west of main site
Context details: Metal-detected stray find 2003–9.
Three layers of copper alloy sheet riveted together with two small circular-headed rivets. The sheet fragments are torn and irregular. One of the rivets pierces only two of the three layers.
Wt: 1.0g; D(ext): 3.5mm (rivet heads); L: 16.5mm; W: 13.5mm; T: 0.2mm (sheet); 3.0mm (total)

S.312: Copper alloy sheet with rivets (Pl. 14.70)
NCM: yellow ticket no. 210
Findspot: Wooded area to west of main site
Context details: Metal-detected stray find 2003–9.
Copper alloy sheet object fragment, formed from two layers of sheet sandwiched together, one possible original edge, other edges torn and irregular. Pierced through by three small circular-headed rivets.
Wt: 0.9g; L: 15.0mm; W: 13.5mm; T: 1.8mm

S.313: Copper alloy sheet with rivet (Pl. 14.70)
NCM: yellow ticket no. 221
Findspot: Wooded area to west of main site
Context details: Metal-detected stray find 2003–9.
Three layers of copper alloy sheet riveted together with a small circular-headed rivet. The centre layer has no original edges, the outer layers are both small, square plates, possibly to reinforce the rivet.
Wt: 0.8g; L: 12.8mm; W: 12.0mm; T: 0.2mm (sheet); 3.0mm (total)

S.314: Copper alloy sheet with rivet (Pl. 14.70)
NCM: yellow ticket no. 230
Findspot: Wooded area to west of main site
Context details: Metal-detected stray find 2003–9.
Three layers of copper alloy sheet riveted together with a circular-headed rivet. The centre layer has no original edges, the outer layers are both small, square plates, possibly to reinforce the rivet.
Wt: 0.7g; D(ext): 4.5mm (rivet head); L: 10.8mm; W: 9.5mm; T: 0.2mm (sheet); 1.8mm (total)

S.315: Copper alloy sheet with rivet (Pl. 14.70)
NCM: yellow ticket no. 216
Findspot: Wooded area to west of main site
Context details: Metal-detected stray find 2003–9.
Small, roughly triangular, fragment of copper alloy sheet with one possible original straight edge, other edges broken. Pierced through by one circular-headed rivet.
Wt: 0.5g; D(ext): 6.0mm (rivet head); L: 17.0mm; W: 8.8mm; T: 0.2mm

S.316: Copper alloy; ?iron sheet with rivet (Pl. 14.70)
NCM: yellow ticket no. 224

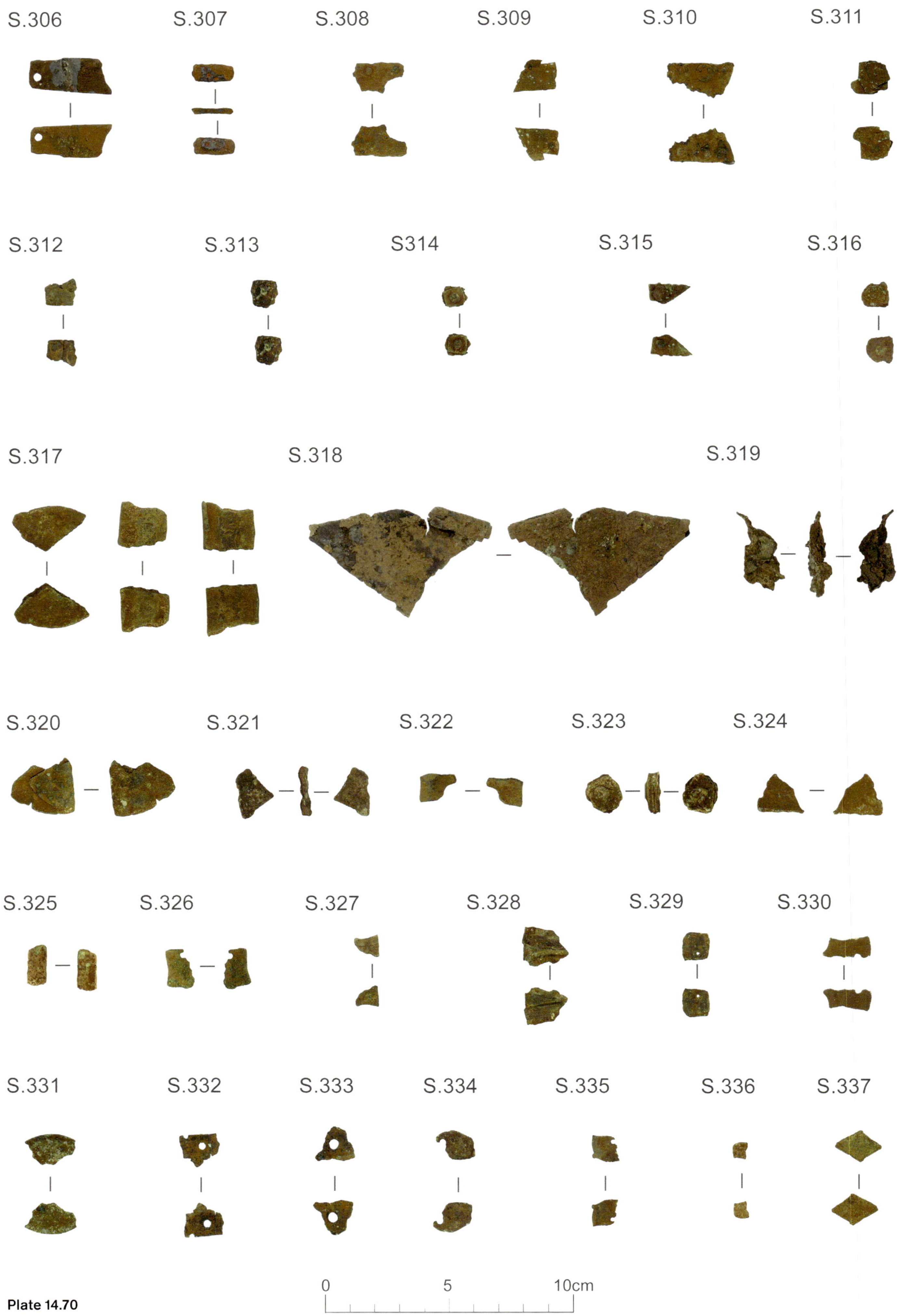
S.306
S.307
S.308
S.309
S.310
S.311
S.312
S.313
S314
S.315
S.316
S.317
S.318
S.319
S.320
S.321
S.322
S.323
S.324
S.325
S.326
S.327
S.328
S.329
S.330
S.331
S.332
S.333
S.334
S.335
S.336
S.337
0
5
10cm

Plate 14.70

Findspot: Wooded area to west of main site
Context details: Metal-detected stray find 2003–9.
Fragment of copper alloy sheet with no original edges, fixed to a second (?iron) sheet layer by a large circular-headed rivet.
Wt: 1.1g; D(ext): 9.0mm (rivet head); L: 12.3mm; W: 12.0mm; T: 2.3mm

S.317: Copper alloy (thick) sheet (Pl. 14.70)
NCM: yellow ticket no. 202
Findspot: Wooded area to west of main site
Context details: Metal-detected stray find 2003–9.
Three fragments of thick copper alloy sheet. Two appear to be short lengths from strips or bars. The other is triangular in plan, with one original curved edge and two torn or broken straight edges.
Wt: 28.7g (total); L: 21.4mm (max.)

S.318: Copper alloy sheet (Pl. 14.70)
NCM: yellow ticket no. 204
Findspot: Wooded area to west of main site
Context details: Metal-detected stray find 2003–9.
Copper alloy sheet fragment, triangular in plan. No original edges, although a short length of copper alloy strip is attached (possibly riveted) along part of one edge, suggesting it comes from a larger multi-component object, such as a vessel.
Wt: 7.3g; L: 74.0mm; W: 43.5mm; T: 0.5mm (sheet); 2.0mm (overlapping section)

S.319: Copper alloy sheet (Pl. 14.70)
NCM: yellow ticket no. 133
Findspot: Wooded area to west of main site
Context details: Metal-detected stray find 2003–9.
Copper alloy sheet fragment with irregular edges, heavily folded and possibly partially melted.
Wt: 5.9g; L: 35.0mm; W: 17.0mm

S.320: Copper alloy sheet (Pl. 14.70)
NCM: yellow ticket no. 253
Findspot: Wooded area to west of main site
Context details: Metal-detected stray find 2003–9.
Small, folded copper alloy sheet object fragment, with one original (though damaged) curved edge and other edges torn. The fragment is slightly dished, and may have come from a small circular object such as a spoon bowl or scale pan.
Wt: 5.3g; L: 27.0mm; W: 24.0mm; T: 3.5mm (folded)

S.321: Copper alloy sheet (Pl. 14.70)
NCM: yellow ticket no. 259
Findspot: Wooded area to west of main site
Context details: Metal-detected stray find 2003–9.
Fragment of thick, corroded, copper alloy sheet. Corrugated cross-section. One possible original edge, other edges torn. Approximately trapezoidal in plan.
Wt: 3.1g; L: 19.5mm; W: 20.5mm

S.322: Copper alloy sheet (Pl. 14.70)
NCM: yellow ticket no. 171
Findspot: Wooded area to west of main site
Context details: Metal-detected stray find 2003–9.
Thick fragment of broken copper alloy sheet, flat on one side, slightly convex on the other.
Wt: 3.0g; L: 18.0mm; W: 12.0mm; T: 3.0mm

S.323: Copper alloy sheet (Pl. 14.70)
NCM: yellow ticket no. 203
Findspot: Wooded area to west of main site
Context details: Metal-detected stray find 2003–9.
Fragment comprising three layers of thin copper alloy sheet riveted together.
Wt: 2.5g; L: 17.0mm; W: 12.0mm; T: 5.0mm

S.324: Copper alloy sheet (Pl. 14.70)
NCM: yellow ticket no. 242
Findspot: Wooded area to west of main site
Context details: Metal-detected stray find 2003–9.
Thick, slightly bent, roughly triangular, copper alloy sheet fragment, all sides broken.
Wt: 2.0g; L: 20.0mm; W: 17.0mm; T: 1.5mm

S.325: Copper alloy sheet (Pl. 14.70)
NCM: yellow ticket no. 237
Findspot: Wooded area to west of main site
Context details: Metal-detected stray find 2003–9.
Fragment of thick copper alloy sheet or strip, rectangular in plan with at least one original straight edge. Tinned or leaded surface on both sides.
Wt: 1.3g; L: 17.2mm; W: 8.5mm; T: 2.0mm

S.326: Copper alloy sheet (Pl. 14.70)
NCM: yellow ticket no. 231
Findspot: Wooded area to west of main site
Context details: Metal-detected stray find 2003–9.
Fragment of thick copper alloy sheet with at least one original, slightly curved, edge. Other edges broken. In one area, the edge break falls across a circular rivet hole.
Wt: 1.2g; L: 17.8mm; W: 12.5mm; T: 1.5mm

S.327: Copper alloy sheet (Pl. 14.70)
NCM: yellow ticket no. 164B
Findspot: Wooded area to west of main site
Context details: Metal-detected stray find 2003–9.
Thick, flat fragment of copper alloy sheet, roughly triangular in plan. Two broken edges, and one concave-curved original, thickened edge.
Wt: 1.1g; L: 12.0mm; W: 10.0mm; T: 1.6mm

S.328: Copper alloy sheet (Pl. 14.70)
NCM: yellow ticket no. 220
Findspot: Wooded area to west of main site
Context details: Metal-detected stray find 2003–9.
Copper alloy sheet object fragment with one possible original straight edge, other edges torn. Remains of part of a curved triangular or trumpet motif in repoussé.
Wt: 0.9g; L: 19.3mm; W: 15.5mm; T: 0.5mm (sheet); 1.6mm (total)

S.329: Copper alloy sheet (Pl. 14.70)
NCM: yellow ticket no. 223
Findspot: Wooded area to west of main site
Context details: Metal-detected stray find 2003–9.
Small, square copper alloy sheet fragment. Two or three original edges, possibly the terminal of a length of copper alloy strip. Pierced through near one edge with a small, circular rivet hole.
Wt: 0.7g; L: 14.0mm; W: 13.5mm; T: 0.2–0.5mm

S.330: Copper alloy sheet (Pl. 14.70)
NCM: yellow ticket no. 179
Findspot: Wooded area to west of main site
Context details: Metal-detected stray find 2003–9.
Fragment of thin copper alloy sheet with no original edges. Broken across a rivet hole at one point.
Wt: 0.5g; L: 20.0mm; W: 9.0mm; T: 0.5mm

S.331: Copper alloy sheet (Pl. 14.70)
NCM: yellow ticket no. 211
Findspot: Wooded area to west of main site
Context details: Metal-detected stray find 2003–9.
Small copper alloy sheet object fragment, roughly triangular in plan, with one original curved edge and two torn straight edges. The fragment is slightly dished, and may have come from a small circular object such as a spoon bowl or scale pan.
Wt: 0.5g; L: 20.5mm; W: 12.4mm; T: 0.3mm

S.332: Copper alloy sheet (Pl. 14.70)
NCM: yellow ticket no. 227
Findspot: Wooded area to west of main site
Context details: Metal-detected stray find 2003–9.
Bent and broken fragment of copper alloy sheet with one original straight edge and other edges torn and irregular. One complete and one torn circular rivet hole.
Wt: 0.5g; L: 17.0mm; W: 14.4mm; T: 0.2mm

S.333: Copper alloy sheet (Pl. 14.70)
NCM: yellow ticket no. 229
Findspot: Wooded area to west of main site
Context details: Metal-detected stray find 2003–9.
Small, roughly triangular fragment of copper alloy sheet, all edges torn. Pierced through just off-centre by a circular rivet hole.
Wt: 0.5g; D(ext): 4.0mm (rivet hole); L: 16.0mm; W: 15.2mm; T: 0.2mm

S.334: Copper alloy sheet (Pl. 14.70)
NCM: yellow ticket no. 232
Findspot: Wooded area to west of main site
Context details: Metal-detected stray find 2003–9.
Fragment of copper alloy sheet, irregular in form, with no original edges, highly polished on one side. In one area, the edge break falls across a circular rivet hole.
Wt: 0.5g; L: 17.4mm; W: 11.2mm; T: 0.4mm

S.335: Copper alloy sheet (Pl. 14.70)
NCM: yellow ticket no. 225
Findspot: Wooded area to west of main site
Context details: Metal-detected stray find 2003–9.
Copper alloy sheet fragment with one original curved edge with small (?decorative) projection, and two straight torn edges. One torn edge runs across a small circular rivet hole.
Wt: 0.4g; L: 14.9mm; W: 11.5mm; T: 0.2–0.5mm

S.336: Copper alloy sheet (Pl. 14.70)
NCM: yellow ticket no. 234
Findspot: Wooded area to west of main site
Context details: Metal-detected stray find 2003–9.
Fragment of copper alloy sheet, irregular in form, with areas of possible curved original edge. Suggestion of relief decoration on one side.
Wt: 0.4g; L: 8.0mm; W: 7.4mm; T: 1.0mm

S.337: Copper alloy sheet (Pl. 14.70)
NCM: yellow ticket no. 238
Findspot: Wooded area to west of main site
Context details: Metal-detected stray find 2003–9.
Small kite-shaped piece of copper alloy sheet, all edges seemingly original, with incised line around edge.
Wt: 0.4g; L: 18.5mm; W: 13.0mm; T: 0.2mm

S.338: Copper alloy sheet (Pl. 14.71)
NCM: yellow ticket no. 174
Findspot: Wooded area to west of main site
Context details: Metal-detected stray find 2003–9.
Fragments of thin copper alloy sheet. Torn, with one possible original edge. In the centre, the remains of what may be a rivet.
Wt: 0.3g; L: 11.0mm; W: 10.0mm; T: 0.3mm

S.339: Copper alloy sheet (Pl. 14.71)
NCM: yellow ticket no. 226
Findspot: Wooded area to west of main site
Context details: Metal-detected stray find 2003–9.
Small, clipped rectangle of copper alloy sheet. Pierced through just off-centre by a circular rivet hole.
Wt: 0.2g; L: 11.4mm; W: 8.0mm; T: 0.2mm

S.340–S.351: Sheet fragments with no original edges or diagnostic features (copper alloy) **(Table 14.3)**
Possibly from vessels or mounts. None could be associated with the helmet F.445.

All were metal-detected stray finds, some made during the 1990s excavation seasons, others made in 2003–9. Groupings made by the finder were kept, hence some catalogue numbers for 2003–9 finds include multiple fragments.

The finds are ordered by weight. For multiple groups, the weight given is the total, and the length is the maximum dimension of the largest fragment.

Tools and implements

Iron and copper alloy

S.352: Iron knife (Pl. 14.71)
BM: 1991,0409.23; Site code: ST/HV
Findspot: Area 21
Context details: Metal-detected stray find from 1991 excavation.

Cat. no.	Museum	Reg. no. or Ticket no.	Site code	Findspot*	Discovery year	Wt/g	L/mm (max.)	T/mm	No. fragments (if multiple)
S.340	NCM	yellow ticket no. 166		Wood	2003–9	7.1	23	0.3	14
S.341	NCM	yellow ticket no. 199		Wood	2003–9	4.1	19	0.2–3	19
S.342	NCM	yellow ticket no. 194		Wood	2003–9	2.7	23	0.3	3
S.343	NCM	yellow ticket no. 196		Wood	2003–9	2.5	29		3
S.344	NCM	yellow ticket no. 164A		Wood	2003–9	1.3	21	0.3	4
S.345	BM	1990,1101.40	SN/EF	Area 2	1990	1.3	35.2	0.3	
S.346	NCM	yellow ticket no. 172		Wood	2003–9	1.1	24	0.2	2
S.347	NCM	yellow ticket no. 180		Wood	2003–9	0.6	25	0.2	2
S.348	BM	1991,0409.25		Area 21	1991	0.5	17.4	0.8	
S.349	NCM	yellow ticket no. 119		Wood	2003–9	0.2	9	1	
S.350	NCM	yellow ticket no. 76		Wood	2003–9	0.1	30	0.8	
S.351	NCM	yellow ticket no. 191		Wood	2003–9	0.1	14	0.2	

Table 14.3 Tabulated catalogue entries for copper alloy sheet fragments with no original edges or diagnostic features. None are illustrated
* = 'Wood' denotes the wooded area to the west of the main site

Simple tanged iron knife with flat back and heavily corroded blade, missing the tip.
Not certainly ancient, but possibly the short, triangular form of Manning (1985) Type 16. A long-lived from, not closely datable.
Wt: 14.5g; L: 65.5mm; W: 21.4mm; T: 4.4mm

S.353: Iron knife (Pl. 14.71)
BM: 1992,0210.3; Site code: SA/BH
Findspot: Trench 5
Context details: Pit: SA5/3. From top 2–3cm of pit – i.e. may not necessarily relate to pit contents.
Simple iron knife with flat back and heavily corroded blade, missing the tip. The plate-tang is pierced to allow bone or wooden plates to be riveted on at either side to form the handle.
Not certainly ancient, but closest to Manning (1985) Type 1b, a Roman form most common in the 1st century AD.
Wt: 8.0g; L: 76.2mm; T: 3.9mm

S.354: Copper alloy tweezers (Pl. 14.71)
BM: 1991,0409.5; Site code: ST/AV
Findspot: Area 18
Context details: Metal-detected stray find from 1991 excavation.
Pair of simple copper alloy tweezers. Short, and probably broken at the ends, but the worn semi-circular terminals suggest they may have broken in antiquity and continued in use.
These are unusual in form, since they fuse to a single piece at the top, rather than being made from a single strip bent over to form a loop. Cf. Crummy (1983, 58–9); Crummy and Eckardt (2008, 48).
Wt: 1.7g; L: 33.7mm; W: 6.7mm; T: 1.3mm

Mail armour fragments and fitting

Copper alloy and iron
The authors are grateful to Dr Martijn Wijnhoven for his helpful insights on this material. Any mistakes remain the authors' own.

S.355: Copper alloy mail armour fitting (Pl. 14.71)
BM: 1990,1101.50
Findspot: Not recorded
Context details: Metal-detected stray find from 1990 excavation.
Flat copper alloy 'dolphin' fitting, broken at one end, pierced at the other. These flat S-shaped fittings are generally interpreted as fasteners from mail armour, although other uses are possible. Cf. Hod Hill I37 (Brailsford 1962; BM 1892,0901.543). Such fittings were used on both Iron Age and Early Roman mail armour from the 3rd century BC to the 1st century AD, for the purpose of fixing shoulder guards in place.
Wt: 7.5g; L: 50.0mm; W: 23.3mm; T: 1.3mm

S.356–9: Iron mail armour fragments (Pl. 14.71)
Findspot: Wooded area to west of main site
Context details: Metal-detected stray find 2003–9.
Four fragments of iron mail armour, apparently cut into small pieces. Rows of interconnected circular links are clearly defined. No joins found, but it is likely that these fragments were part of the same set of armour. Whilst at present this mail armour cannot be closely dated, the ring size of around 4–5mm is consistent with a date from the 3rd century BC to 3rd century AD (Wijnhoven 2022, 261-4).
D(ext): 4–5mm (each ring)

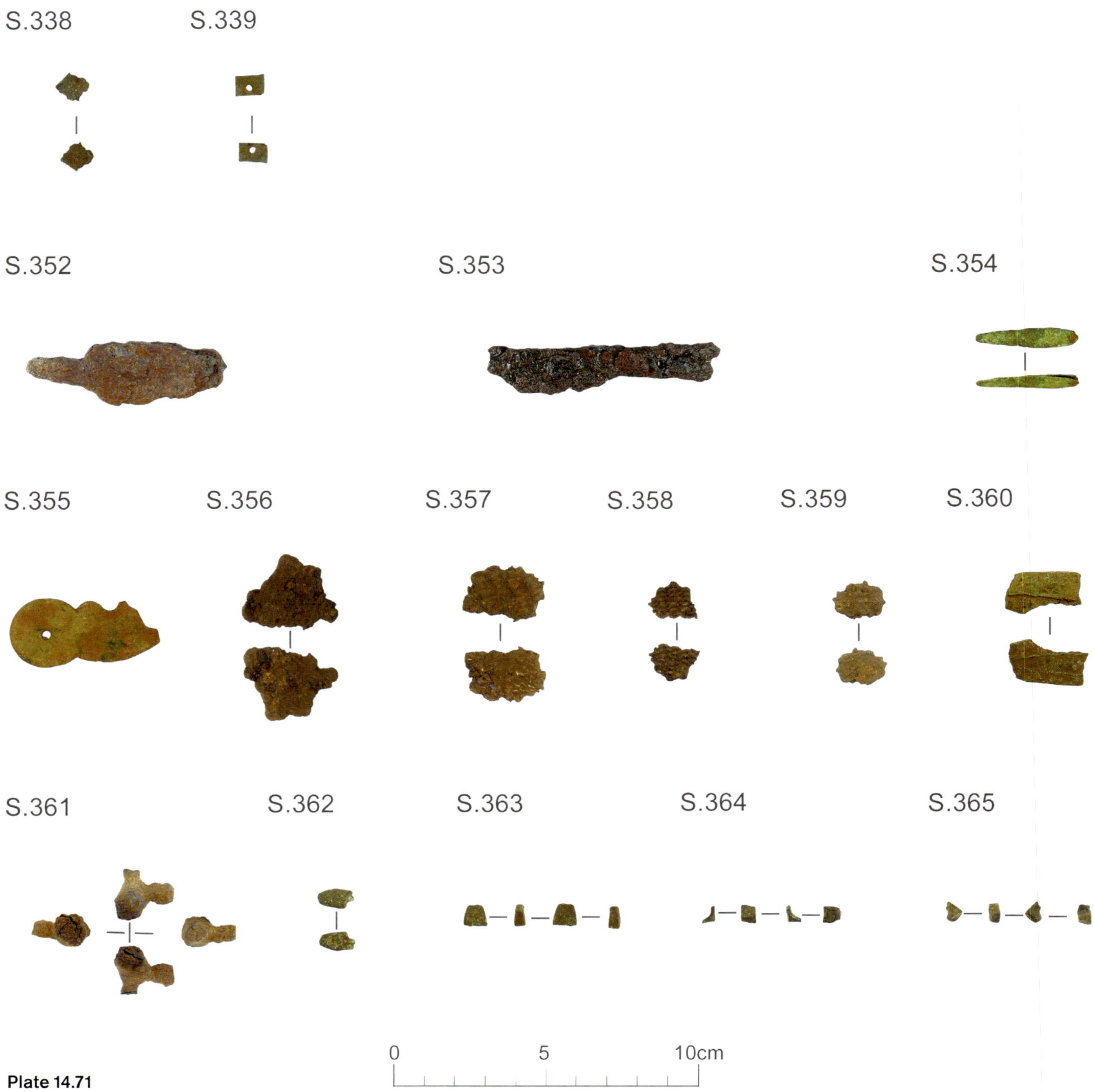

Plate 14.71

S.356: NCM: yellow ticket no. 12
Wt: 5.3g; L: 32.0mm; W: 30.0mm; T: 3.0mm

S.357: NCM: yellow ticket no. 13
Wt: 4.4g; L: 28.0mm; W: 20.0mm; T: 3.0mm

S.358: NCM: yellow ticket no. 14
Wt: 2.1g; L: 21.0mm; W: 15.0mm; T: 3.0mm

S.359: NCM: yellow ticket no. 15
Wt: 1.5g; L: 17.0mm; W: 13.0mm; T: 3.0mm

Unidentified object fragments

Copper alloy

S.360: Copper alloy unidentified object fragment (Pl. 14.71)
NCM: yellow ticket no. 183
Findspot: Wooded area to west of main site
Context details: Metal-detected stray find 2003–9.
Fragment of cast copper alloy object, curved in cross-section, approximately rectangular in plan, and broken on all sides.
Wt: 12.6g; L: 27.0mm; W: 12.0mm; T: 6.0mm

S.361: Copper alloy and iron unidentified object fragment (Pl. 14.71)
NCM: yellow ticket no. 75
Findspot: Wooded area to west of main site
Context details: Metal-detected stray find 2003–9.

Unidentifiable iron object fragment with copper alloy sheet plating.
Wt: 5.1g; L: 21.0mm; W: 17.0mm

S.362: Copper alloy unidentified object fragment (Pl. 14.71)
NCM: yellow ticket no. 44
Findspot: Wooded area to west of main site
Context details: Metal-detected stray find 2003–9.
Fragment of unidentified copper alloy object, circular in cross-section, slightly tapering at one end, broken at the other.
Wt: 2.0g; L: 12.0mm; W: 6.5mm; T: 5.0mm

S.363: Copper alloy unidentified object fragment (Pl. 14.71)
NCM: yellow ticket no. 243
Findspot: Wooded area to west of main site
Context details: Metal-detected stray find 2003–9.
Flat copper alloy fragment, roughly trapezoidal in plan and rectangular in cross-section. Broken at the wide base of the trapezium, other edges seem original, suggesting this may be the blunt tip of a larger object.
Wt: 1.4g; L: 8.5mm; W: 8.0mm; T: 4.0mm

S.364: Copper alloy unidentified object fragment (Pl. 14.71)
NCM: yellow ticket no. 41
Findspot: Wooded area to west of main site
Context details: Metal-detected stray find 2003–9.
Fragment of unidentified copper alloy object, corner of square or rectangular object with possible circular central hole.
Wt: 1.3g; L: 7.2mm; W: 6.0mm; T: 6.6mm

S.365: Copper alloy unidentified object fragment (Pl. 14.71)
NCM: yellow ticket no. 145
Findspot: Wooded area to west of main site
Context details: Metal-detected stray find 2003–9.
Fragment of unidentified copper alloy object, corner of square or rectangular object with possible circular central hole.
Wt: 0.9g; L: 7.0mm; W: 6.0mm; T: 3.5mm

Chapter 15
Iron Age and Roman Coins

Eleanor Ghey, John Davies, Philip de Jersey, David Holman and Julia Farley

This chapter is divided by period, beginning with the Iron Age coins, followed by Roman and later coins. The section on the Iron Age coins is by far the largest and is divided into a discussion of those from hoards (gold coins from Hoards B, E, F and N; a reassessment of potin coins from Hoard C; a reconstruction of the now-lost 'Bowl Hoard', Hoard P; and a discussion of the possibility of other coin hoards from the site) followed by single finds.

The coin catalogue at the end of this chapter is divided into three main parts, echoing the division of this discussion chapter:

- Part 1: Iron Age coins from Hoards B, C, E, F and N, and reconstructed listing of Iron Age coins from Hoard P
- Part 2: Iron Age single coin finds
- Part 3: Roman coins

The hoard coins were recovered as described for each hoard in Chapters 2, 4 and 12, mostly during ploughing in 1948–50 and Clarke's 1948 excavations, and the British Museum 1990–2 excavation seasons. The hoard coins included in the catalogue are in the British Museum collection, with the exception of the coins from Hoards B and C, which are in Norwich Castle Museum.

Single finds were recovered on multiple occasions. Charles Hodder's 1989 metal-detecting located three coins described in de Jersey (2014, 311) as 'Surface find III', now in Norwich Castle Museum. The British Museum excavations in 1990–2 produced numerous non-hoard coin finds (mostly stray finds made during metal-detector surveys of the stripped areas) which were acquired by the British Museum along with the rest of the excavation archive. Subsequent metal-detector finds were mostly made in the western area of the site between 2003 and 2009 (Treasure cases 2003 T169; 2005 T487; 2007 T695 and 2009 T666, also known as 'North-West Norfolk'; de Jersey 2014, 196.9). A preliminary listing of the latter (derived from the reports for HM Coroner prepared at the British Museum) appears in Marsden (2011, 57–8), although without images or full identifications. These metal-detected finds from 2003 onwards have been acquired by Norwich Castle Museum. At the time the Treasure cases were studied, little attention was paid to the Roman coins and it was not possible to view all these in Norwich, so their identification must in some cases remain tentative.

Iron Age coins
Eleanor Ghey

Part 1: The Hoards
Four of the torc hoards produced Iron Age coinage: Hoards B, C, E and F, summarised below. References are given to the hoard summaries published in de Jersey (2014, 314–17). A listing is also given in Sills (2003, 376–7), although some of the coins have since been reclassified in Sills 2017.

Hoard B (mixed coin/fragmentary torc hoard, coins shown in **Plate 15.1**) (de Jersey 2014, hoard no. 196.1; illustrated in Clarke 1954, pl. XIV):

- 9 gold Gallo-Belgic A and C staters and quarter staters
- 2 blank gold coins (stater and quarter stater)
- 1 British Insular Cf gold quarter stater

Period	Coin type	Hoard B	Hoard E	Hoard F	Hoard N
1 to 3 (200–80 BC)	GB A stater	2		1 (within helmet which contained F) 1 (cut, in torc fragment)	5 (1 cut and one reduced flan)
1 to 3 (200–80 BC)	GB A quarter stater	3		2 (in torc fragment)	1
4 (80–60 BC)	GB C stater	4		3 (within helmet which contained F) 2 (in torc fragment)	2
4 (80–60 BC)	GB C quarter stater				1
4 (80–60 BC)	Insular Cf quarter stater	1	1 (in torc terminal)		
uncertain	Stater	1 (hammered)			
uncertain	Quarter stater	1 (hammered)			
	Total	**12**	**1**	**9**	**9**

Table 15.1 Summary of the coin types represented in Hoards B, E, F and N, with their issue periods

Hoard C (mixed coin/fragmentary torc hoard) (de Jersey 2014, hoard no. 196.2; Dolley 1954). David Holman has studied the coins in Norwich Castle Museum and his reassessment is published below.

- 155 potin coins and 79 fragments (cast base-metal coins from south-east Britain)

Hoard E (composite group including the 'Great Torc', coins shown in **Plate 15.1**) (de Jersey 2014, hoard no. 196.3):

- 1 British Insular Cf quarter stater found in the torc terminal

Hoard F (mixed coin/fragmentary torc hoard, coin shown in **Plate 15.2**) (de Jersey 2014, hoard no. 196.4):

- 9 gold Gallo-Belgic A and C staters and quarter staters (5 of them found within a torc tube). One of the staters is a cut half.

There were also at least two other Iron Age coin hoards from the site. One is the posited scattered coin hoard, N (Chs 8 and 12), and the other the lost 'Bowl Hoard', P. Hoard P is discussed below in a separate section, based closely on catalogue entry no. 196.6 in de Jersey (2014), reproduced with kind permission from Philip de Jersey and the British Numismatic Society. This hoard was dispersed in trade and thus its reconstruction in the catalogue can only be hypothetical.

Hoard N (dispersed coin hoard, coins shown in **Plate 15.2**) (de Jersey 2014, hoard no. 196.5, without details):

- 9 gold Gallo-Belgic A and C staters and quarter staters

Hoard P (de Jersey 2014, hoard no. 196.6):

- Over 6,000 coins, predominantly local silver issues, found inside a metal container and possibly associated with a deposit of gold coins placed below it. The deposit seems to date to the final phase of local coinage.

The torc hoards and Hoard N

With the exception of the insular quarter staters found in Hoards B and E, the gold coins from the torc hoards are all Gallo-Belgic coins, Late Iron Age imports into Britain originating from the area of present-day north-eastern France and Belgium (see **Table 15.1**). Hoard N is of a similar character, despite apparently lacking other artefacts. The nine coins from Hoard N (cat. nos 179–87) consist of five Gallo-Belgic A staters (one of which has been cut, removing part of the flan) and one quarter stater, two Gallo-Belgic C staters and a worn Gallo-Belgic C quarter stater, identified by Sills (pers. comm.) as struck from the same flawed die as specimens recorded from findspots further south in Essex, Kent and West Sussex. It should be noted that Hoard N was dispersed and was identified on the basis of the proximity of the coins to each other (see Ch. 12).

A terminal date of 80–60 BC has previously been suggested for the latest coins in the torc hoards (e.g. Haselgrove 1995, 123), with the absence of Gallo-Belgic E coins, which were traditionally thought to have come into widespread circulation in Britain during the 50s BC, suggesting that the torc hoards were most likely to have been buried in the early to mid-1st century BC, around or before *c.* 60 BC. This is the period immediately before local coin production began (Ch. 23). The absolute dating of Iron Age coins continues to be a matter for debate and in the absence of consensus the most widely used dating is adopted here, with the proviso that it is likely to be subject to reinterpretation. The dating of the coins from Hoards B, E, F and N do suggest that these hoards are broadly contemporary, with the latest coin in Hoard F (Gallo-Belgic C) dating to Iron Age coin period 4, *c.* 80–60 BC (using periods from de Jersey after Haselgrove (de Jersey 2014, 11; Haselgrove 1993, 35)). It should be noted however that Sills (2017, 710) extends the latest possible dating of the Insular Cf quarter staters (of which there are two in the Snettisham mixed torc and coin hoards, one in Hoard B and one in Hoard E) into period 5 (*c.* 60–50 BC). Gallo-Belgic D and E are also thought by Sills to belong to period 5 but Gallo-Belgic E is notably absent from the Snettisham hoards. It is, however, one possibility suggested by Sills (2003, 376) on the basis of weight and metallurgy for the hammered-out stater in Hoard B (cat. no. 11), though an insular product may also be possible. The wear on the period 4 Gallo-Belgic C quarter stater from Hoard N (cat. no. 187) could also indicate a longer period between coin production and deposition in this hoard. A detailed summary of current debates on the dating of imported gold coinage in Britain cannot be given here, but increasingly archaeological evidence would seem to support the argument for pushing back the absolute chronology of particular Gaulish issues and lengthening use periods in general (see Haselgrove 2019). Therefore, given the challenges of dating this material and the apparent absence of Gallo-Belgic E, a terminal date of *c.* 60 BC would seem reasonable for the gold coinage in the torc hoards.

The treatment of these coins is also of interest. The 'hammered' coins in Hoard B (cat. nos 11–12) have been flattened on both sides so that a design is no longer visible. The stater is now 22mm in diameter (comparable in size to the other Gallo-Belgic A staters in the hoard) and the quarter stater 13mm (comparable with the Gallo-Belgic A quarter staters in the hoard). Clarke (1954, 59) mentions that the larger of these two blank coins was found sandwiched between the two staters, and the smaller between two quarter staters. It seems possible, therefore, that this modification was carried out for reasons unknown but related to their use as separating pieces in the deposit.

The quarter stater found in the terminal of the Great Torc in Hoard E (cat. no. 169) shows unusual patterns of wear, with many parallel scratches in the areas of low relief on the obverse in two directions, as well as wear to the higher relief areas. The cut stater from Hoard F (cat. no. 174) is extremely worn and has been cut straight in half, apparently along the hair bar with the 'face' portion surviving.

One of the Gallo-Belgic A staters from Hoard N (cat. no. 180) has had an irregularly shaped portion consisting of about one third of the flan removed by cutting from the edge and along the hair bar, although the remaining portion is approximately half a stater in weight. It is possible that this could relate to post-depositional damage but given the softness of gold it seems unlikely that such damage would not also have bent the coin. It may also be significant that the area of the obverse depicting the human head above the neck has been removed, leaving the cloak and elaborated hair.

Another coin from Hoard N (cat. no. 181) is much reduced in size around the edge of the flan so that the 'face' is also missing but this may be the result of wear, or striking on a small blank, as the edges are smooth. A central, circular area of the reverse is particularly worn. One other stater from Hoard N (cat. no. 179) has a bent flan and an indentation or peck-mark is visible on the interior of the fold in the area of the charioteer's hand. Another stater (cat. no. 182) appears to have a worn cut on the head perpendicular to the hair bar. This coin has a pitted surface, possibly from the action of heat or prolonged surface exposure.

Deliberate damage of coins prior to deposition in hoards has been noted elsewhere, although particularly in hoards containing South-Western British Iron Age coinage (see Bland *et al.* 2020, 246 for an overview). As well as the systematic cut-marks observed on South-Western staters, damage may take other forms, from the surface application of heat to the complete melting down of coins. Such pre-depositional treatment occurs on some but not all of the site finds discussed below and is mainly found in the earlier coins, suggesting it belongs to the earlier phases of deposition (or a phase of activity taking place prior to this) at the site and should be considered alongside the treatment of the other metalwork (deliberate fragmentation and combination of torc components is discussed in Ch. 20).

A reassessment of the coins in Snettisham Hoard C

David Holman

Hoard C is unique among the Snettisham hoard deposits in that it does not contain gold coins, but has as its principal component a sizeable quantity of base-metal potin coins, together with a large number of copper alloy torc fragments and rings. Potins are cast bronze coins, made in a tin-rich copper alloy which gives them a distinctive silvery appearance. They were produced in strips in moulds, each coin linked to the next by a runner channel, and as such each coin has sprues on one or both sides. The obverse depicts a stylised head of Apollo, while the reverse shows a stylised bull with the letters 'MA' above, ultimately derived from struck bronze coins of Massalia (Marseilles). Potins are traditionally associated with Kent, where they are most densely distributed, although they are found throughout south-east England and beyond. The first British potins, known as Kentish Primary or Thurrock potins, were likely produced from the mid-second century BC. Just over 30 of these types have been discovered at Snettisham, all of which are stray finds, discussed below (Cat. nos 368–401). Hoard C exclusively contains a later type known as Flat Linear potins, produced in the 1st century BC. There have been numerous attempts to classify the Flat Linear potin series, notably by Derek Allen (1938), who divided them into Classes I and II based on their flan sizes (large and small respectively). He later expanded this system, dividing Class I into types A–L, and the smaller Class II coins into types M–P (Allen 1971).

The national dataset of Flat Linear potin coins has since increased significantly in the seven decades since Hoard C was first published, which has enabled a much-enhanced understanding of these coins. This includes new potin hoards (such as one found during archaeological excavations close to the North Foreland in Thanet, Kent, in 1999), the reassessment of older hoards (such as the Birchington Hoard, also from Thanet), and large numbers of metal-detector finds. Work on this material led the current writer to develop a new classification system for the entire Flat Linear series (Holman 2016). This system replaces Allen's two classes (I and II) and 15 types (A–P), by splitting the series into seven groups (A–G), each of which can then be divided into subgroups, types, subtypes and variants. Coins of Allen's Class I fall within Groups A to F while those of Class II are all Group G, with his 51 varieties being reorganised and substantially expanded. Holman's groups are broadly chronological, with Group A being the earliest (production beginning in the second half of the 2nd century BC) and Group G the latest (with production of Flat Linear potins terminating around the middle of the 1st century BC). This refined classification demonstrates chronological changes in distribution, with increased spread of the coinage beyond Kent over time. Group A has an almost wholly Kentish distribution, while Groups F and G are scattered across the whole of south-east England and beyond, even as far away as Somerset and Yorkshire, and it is likely that some of these later potin types may have been produced in the North Thames region.

As a result of this work, it is now possible to undertake a reassessment of Hoard C together with a fully updated and expanded catalogue of the contents.

Previous work on Hoard C

The first catalogue of Hoard C, together with a report on the origin, distribution and manufacturing methods of potin coins, was published by Michael Dolley (Dolley 1954). His catalogue used an adapted version of the potin classification system originally devised by Robert Carson in his initial summary of the Sunbury hoard (Carson 1950). Dolley's catalogue includes 116 coins, but he made no attempt to include the fragments, which he thought represented probably another 29 coins, giving an estimated total of 145 coins. Other than Carson's system, the only pre-existing classification of the Flat Linear series available to Dolley was Allen's separation into Classes I and II (Allen 1938). All of the Hoard C coins fall within Class I, the larger and earlier class.

Dolley made the assumption that the potins were not current at the time of their burial, based on many of the gold coins from other hoards at the site being heavily worn and probably no longer current at the time of deposition (Dolley 1954, 74). It should however be borne in mind that a potin which looks worn from heavy use is more probably like that as a result of poor casting. Following on from this, he concurred with Allen's previous acceptance of an early date for the potins, although part of his reasoning was based on the appearance of apparent lettering on the reverse of one coin, which had been pointed out to him by Edward Robinson (*ibid.*, 77–8; 78, note 2). The coin in question is one of the earliest coins in the hoard (Cat. no. 14, below), but in fact, as Allen later realised, the supposed inscription is nothing more than flaws in the surface of the flan.

Dolley also argued that all Allen Class I potins circulated alongside each other, probably emanated from a common centre over a very short period of time and could be regarded as a single issue (*ibid.*, 82). The far more comprehensive dataset now available does not support this argument. Coins from archaeological excavations, as opposed to those in hoards, show that many of the earlier coins had apparently disappeared from circulation by the time Group F was in use. It can also be seen that the composition of the Flat Linear hoards is often very different from the surrounding single finds (Holman 2020, 36). It is now clear that production of the Flat Linear series extended over many years with production taking place at multiple locations, even outside the series' traditional Kentish homeland (Holman 2016). Dolley's statement that deterioration in style was not accompanied by a reduction in weight can also now not be sustained across the series as a whole.

As Dolley noted, the Snettisham hoard was well outside the normal circulation area of Flat Linear potins, the nearest other such coin known at that time having been found 70 miles away (Dolley 1954, 80). He assumed that the hoard coins had come from the Lower Thames region, at some date after *c.* 75 BC. That region, rather than east Kent, may well be right, but the date is probably several years too early, as will be discussed below.

Dolley thought that broken coins were proportionately more frequent among the less common types and that this might be a line of enquiry worth pursuing (*ibid.*, 82, note 2). The updated catalogue, which includes many of the previously unidentified broken coins, shows no evidence of any such bias, with many of the additional broken coins now seen to belong to Dolley's later and more common types. Owing to a discrepancy in some of the weights of coins listed by Dolley, it has not been possible to identify which coins 12 of Dolley's numbers refer to (Dolley catalogue numbers 1, 4, 20, 22, 25, 41, 65, 69, 71, 93, 96 and 108). Where there was uncertainty with matching Dolley's numbers to other objects this is indicated with a question mark in the updated catalogue.

In 1971, Allen published his classification of Flat Linear potins and converted Dolley's catalogue into his new system (Allen 1971, 149). As the range of known types was then much smaller, there was inevitably a far lesser degree of separation of the contents of the hoards than is possible today. Both men were correct in distinguishing between coins based on the direction of the head and bull on the obverse and reverse respectively, and whether the head contained an eye-ring with a central pellet or not, features which impact on both chronology and the linkage between different but clearly related types. Allen used 18 of the Hoard C coins as models for the drawings to accompany his 1971 paper (Allen types B, C3, C4, D3, E, F1, F6, GB3, H1, H2, H3, J3, J4, J7, L2, L3, L4, L6), although there are inaccuracies in some of the drawings.

The most recent summary of the hoard by Philip de Jersey (de Jersey 2014, 312–14; hoard no. 196.2) provides only an abbreviated listing based on Allen's classification, as the new system developed by the author (Holman 2016) was at that stage still in preparation. De Jersey included three separate alternative lists for the contents of Hoard C, one based on Allen (1971), one from records of the coins in the CCI, and one using details provided by the current writer which was different again, mainly because a larger number of coins could by then be identified (de Jersey 2014, 313, table 35). Only 98 Hoard C coins are currently recorded in the CCI and it has been found that a small number of errors occurred during recording. These errors are noted in the updated catalogue.

The composition of a selection of 20 coins from Hoard C has been analysed by Peter Northover, who noted that they varied not only typologically, but also in their metal content (Northover 1992, 262–3). However, as no weights are shown it is impossible to know which coins were tested (*ibid.*, 296–7).

A reassessment of Hoard C

Dolley's estimated total of 145 coins has until recently been accepted by other researchers, and was thought to be more or less correct on the current author's initial visit to Norwich Castle Museum in 2011. This total was derived from 129 coins – many complete, others partially reconstructed from fragments – which were possible to identify using Allen's 1971 system with some modification, and 122 unidentified fragments, of varying sizes, in 16 coin-tray compartments. On a further visit in 2014, using the author's new classification system for Flat Linear potins (Holman 2016), it was possible to improve the identifications. A further 26 coins were identified and, in some cases, partially reconstructed from 43 of the previously unidentified fragments. There are now 155 confirmed individual coins in the hoard, of which 143 have been identified to at least type

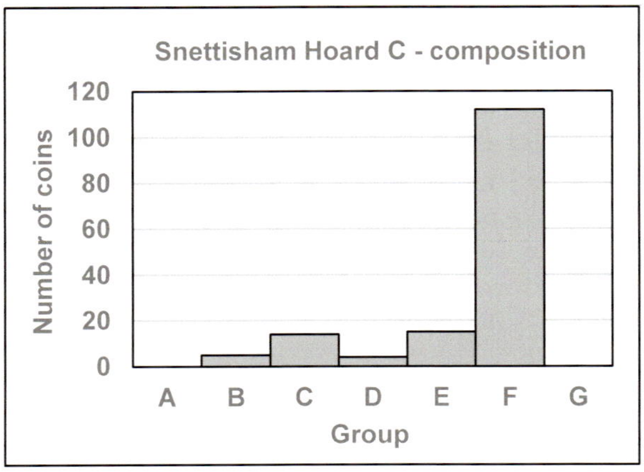

Group	Number	%
A	0	0
B	5	3.3
C	14	9.3
D	4	2.7
E	15	10.0
F	112	74.7
G	0	0
Uncertain	5	–

Figure 15.1 Group-level composition of Snettisham Hoard C (© David Holman)

level under Holman's classification, eight to group level and the other four within a group range. There remain a further 79 fragments, mostly very small, which cannot be associated with each other or any other coins. Based on the average weight of the complete coins in the hoard, these fragments could represent perhaps another eight coins, although in practice this is not possible to determine and some, perhaps even most, of these fragments are more likely to be part of known incomplete coins.

The group-level composition of Hoard C is shown in **Figure 15.1**. There are no Group A types, which are in any case extremely rare in the Flat Linear hoards, the only examples being one each in the Birchington and Thurnham hoards. Neither are there any Group G types as the hoard does not go late enough to include these. Three quarters of the hoard belongs to Group F, which comprises the latest element of the hoard, but there is a long tail back to Group B, the earliest coin present being type B2/2-1c, probably dating to the late 2nd century BC.

Hoard C contains a high number of coins which are stylistically relatively late within the range of Group F types present. Group F is dated by Holman to *c.* 75/70–60/55 BC, based on evidence from elsewhere (Holman 2016, 9–11). The latest phase of Group F (subgroup F4) is, however, absent. The evidence suggests that the hoard was deposited towards the latter stages of Group F, in which case a date of *c.* 60 BC or shortly after is likely. This is broadly contemporary with the suggested dates for the numerous gold hoards containing coins from the site, as discussed above. It could also be that the potins were buried after all the early gold hoards, but it is not possible to refine the dating to that level of accuracy.

Figure 15.2 shows Hoard C compared with four other selected Flat Linear hoards studied by the author. The chart shows the percentage of coins in each group (A to G, in chronological sequence) within each of these hoards. The earliest hoard shown is Birchington, Kent, which clearly peaks in Groups C and D before terminating very early in Group F. Although not shown here, the other Kentish hoards also terminate earlier than either Snettisham or a cluster of hoards from the lower Thames Valley, which include two large hoards illustrated here, Sunbury and Brentford I. The latest hoard shown is Takeley, Essex, the earliest coin in which is later than anything in the other hoards shown.

The closest typological, and thus chronological, comparisons to Snettisham can be found in the Thames Valley hoards, although the overall profile of Snettisham is later than either of these. The latest Flat Linear types in Hoard C are the same as those at Sunbury and Brentford, although the proportion of Group F is significantly higher at Snettisham (75%, as opposed to 49% for Sunbury and 58% for Brentford), which potentially indicates a later deposition date for Snettisham. Many of these coins fall within Dolley's type IIB1, which he noted as being in a much higher proportion at Snettisham than at Sunbury (Dolley 1954, 81).

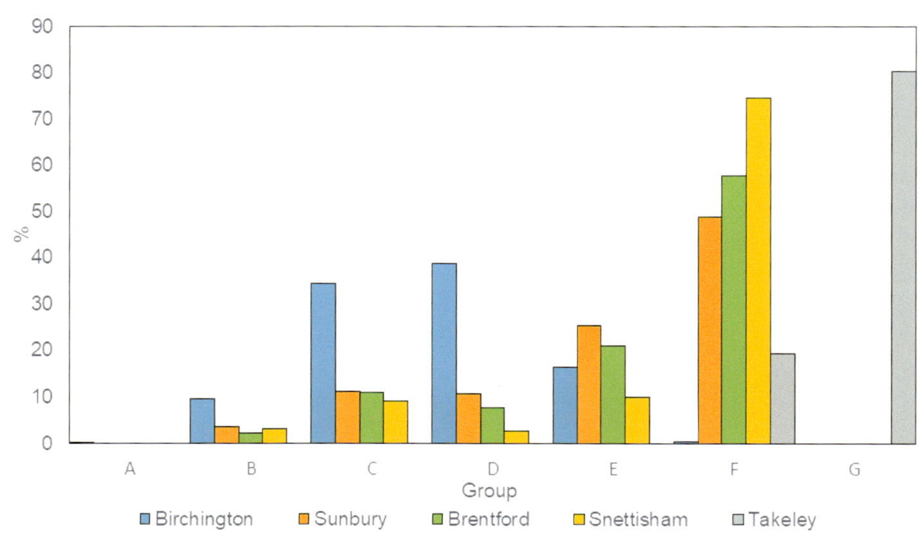

Figure 15.2 Comparison of Hoard C with selected Flat Linear potin hoards (© David Holman)

Although the number of identifiable coins from both hoards is now much greater, Dolley's observation remains essentially correct. The typologically latest type present in all three hoards is F3/3. Although the numbers are small, Snettisham has roughly double the proportion of this type than either of the Thames Valley hoards, again accentuating the later profile of Snettisham. Type F3/3 is absent from the other Thames Valley hoards as they are currently constituted although none are closed deposits and type F3/3, in any case scarce, may or may not have been present at the time of deposition.

Although we are looking at a narrow timeframe, the figures as we see them, with the noticeably higher proportion of Group F coins demonstrating an overall later profile, appear at face value to suggest that the deposition of Hoard C is unlikely to have taken place prior to the deposition of the Thames Valley hoards shown here. However, one other possibility for the differences between these hoards can be considered: differential rates of accumulation, assuming that the coins were not all removed from a circulating pool at around the same time. Analysis by the author of the Flat Linear potins from excavations in Canterbury has shown that virtually all of these belong to Groups F and, particularly, G. Significantly, there are no Group B potins from Canterbury despite them being common individual, stray finds in the surrounding area, which suggests they had ceased to circulate before the site was established sometime in the mid-1st century BC. If this argument is extended to the hoards, this could suggest that the earlier coins had been accumulated well before their eventual deposition and that their collection was not a single event. Hoards terminating at the same point, but with different typological distributions, may have been deposited within a very short period of time, the differences being the result of collection over an extended period rather than a snapshot of the circulating coinage at the time of deposition.

The origin of the potins deposited at Snettisham is less clear-cut than might at first appear. The automatic assumption would be Kent, but the composition of the hoard makes one hesitate and consider whether this was indeed the case. Some types in the hoard are rarely found in Kent, but they are known in much larger quantities from the Thames Valley hoards, for example type F1/3, which also appears among the few single finds from that area. There are only three recorded single finds of F1/3 from east Kent plus one in the Birchington hoard, although several examples have been noted in the as-yet uncatalogued Thurnham hoard. Where type F1/3, of which there are 12 examples at Snettisham, was produced is not possible to tell from the surviving evidence, but the possibility of it being a derivative issue originating in the Thames Valley, or at least somewhere other than east Kent, cannot be discounted. There are hints of derivative issues elsewhere in the Flat Linear series, in particular subgroup G4, which the evidence suggests was probably produced somewhere in the Essex/Hertfordshire region. Some other types present at Snettisham are completely absent from Kent on current evidence, but again they do appear in the Thames Valley hoards. This does not prove that those types were produced in the Thames Valley region, but the suspicion must remain that some of them may not be Kentish in origin, or at least not from the eastern part of the county. It can also be noted that type F2/1, the distribution of which is largely Kentish, is absent from Snettisham, although it is not inconceivable that this type, which is the likely immediate prototype of type F4/5, is slightly later.

Potin coins were produced in moulds, in strips of unknown length. Twenty of the coins in Hoard C have only one sprue, indicating that they were produced in the furthest depression in the mould. It has been possible to calculate the ratio of single-sprue coins as a proportion of the Birchington (8.2:1) and North Foreland (Kent) (8.9:1) hoards, but this is a trickier proposition with Snettisham because of the much greater number of incomplete coins. If it is assumed that this was the total number of single-sprue coins in the identified assemblage of 155, then a ratio of 7.75:1 is arrived at, which is not too far removed from the figure for Birchington. However, it may well be that the quantity of single-sprue coins in Hoard C was higher than can now be determined because a number of the identified coins do not include the relevant parts of the flan which contain the sprue and it is possible that the ratio is closer to 7:1. It can also be noted that at least two, and possibly up to five coins, have misaligned sprues, suggesting that they were the top coin in a strip. This very low number in comparison with the single-sprue coins might appear odd, but such a discrepancy has also been noted in the Thanet hoards. The reason is that coins from the top of the strip are generally hard to identify because the sprues, even if they survive, are often not long enough to determine that they are misaligned, and the resulting lack of evidence means that the number of coins noted as being from the top of a strip is probably a significant under-representation.

Most of the types present in Hoard C are known elsewhere although a few minor variants are otherwise so far unparalleled. The hoard contains one of only two known examples of type B3/2-5, and two of the three known examples of type C2/1-1.

The weight and diameter distribution are shown in **Figure 15.3** and their range and mean in **Figure 15.4**. As has previously been noted for the Birchington and North Foreland hoards, these show considerable variation, particularly in weight, demonstrating the difficulty of maintaining a standard weight for mould-cast coins, but the trend is for the weight and diameter to reduce over time (Holman 2020), a consequence of changes in the manufacturing process as noted by Van Arsdell (Van Arsdell 1989, 76–9). Although the range bars for Group F are of greater length than those for the other groups, this results from a combination of a much higher number of coins in Group F for which the data is available and a small number of unrepresentative outliers. The overall trend is clearly shown by the median reduction in both sets of data (**Table 15.2**). The reason for the differing totals is because the weights of incomplete coins have not been included, nor the diameters of those for which the data are unavailable because an insufficient amount of the coin survives to measure this.

Snettisham Hoards B and C were found by ploughing on consecutive days and were to some extent mixed up during recovery, and the totality of their individual contents cannot

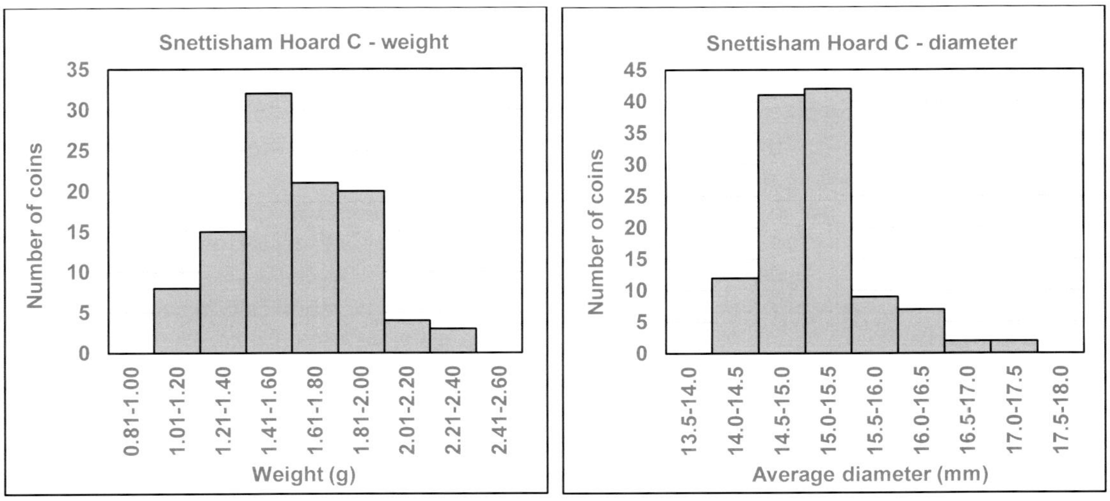

Figure 15.3 Weight and diameter distribution in Snettisham Hoard C (© David Holman)

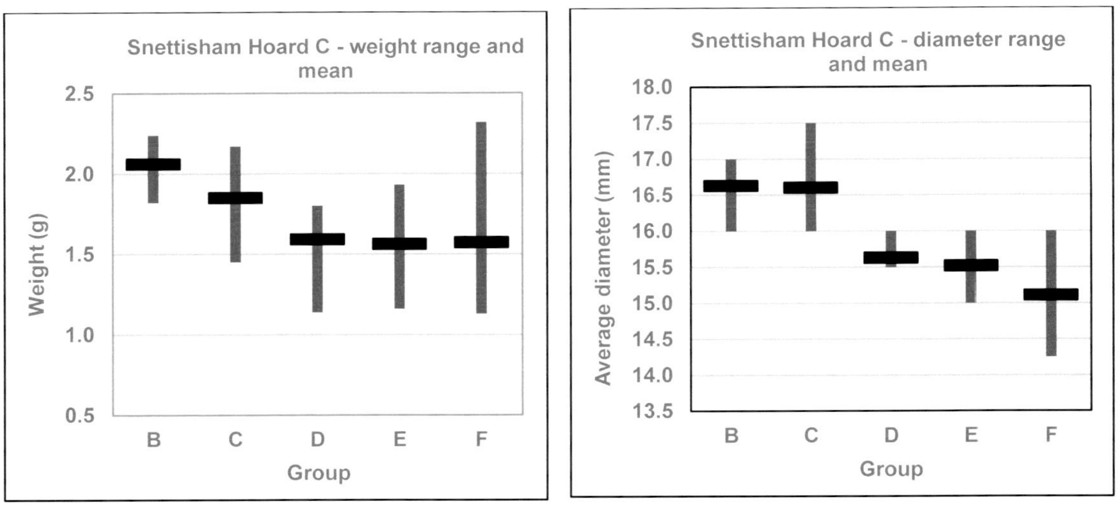

Figure 15.4 Weight and diameter range and mean, per group, in Snettisham Hoard C (© David Holman)

Group (weight – g)	Min.	Max.	Mean	Median	Number
B	1.82	2.24	2.06	2.11	3
C	1.45	2.17	1.85	1.87	8
D	1.14	1.80	1.59	1.70	4
E	1.16	1.93	1.56	1.60	11
F	1.13	2.32	1.57	1.53	77
Overall	1.13	2.32	1.61	1.57	103
Group (diameter – mm)					
B	16.00	17.00	16.63	16.75	4
C	16.00	17.50	16.60	16.50	10
D	15.50	16.00	15.63	15.50	4
E	15.00	16.00	15.52	15.50	13
F	14.25	16.00	15.11	15.00	84
Overall	14.25	17.50	15.35	15.25	115

Table 15.2 Summary of weight and average diameter data in Snettisham Hoard C

now be determined with certainty (Clarke 1954, 30–1). The potins presumably suffered a degree of fragmentation as a result of being hit by the plough. How many more, if any, tiny fragments of potin remain in the ground at Snettisham cannot be known, but it is possible that the hoard contained incomplete coins, and that what has been recovered is all there were. Limited evidence for the possible inclusion of incomplete coins in Flat Linear potin hoards can be seen elsewhere, although in several cases the circumstances of discovery render it uncertain. Only three Flat Linear hoards have been archaeologically excavated *in situ* and one of these (North Foreland) may have been disturbed in antiquity, with the status of the two incomplete and broken coins uncertain (Holman 2020, 31). Another, at Takeley, contains several incomplete coins which had conceivably entered the ground in that condition (Van Arsdell and Northover 2004; Holman 2022). However, the most significant indication that the phenomenon of the burial of fragmentary objects may have extended to potins can be seen in the Hillingdon hoard, discovered in 2020 and consisting entirely of Groups F and G, which included incomplete coins even at the undisturbed base of the deposit. (The writer expresses his thanks to HS2, Costain Skanska Joint Venture and Skanska Costain STRABAG Railways Joint Venture for allowing information about the Hillingdon hoard to be published here.) Apart from these, there are very few fragments in the Birchington hoard, although it is unknown if fragments were found but not retained at the time of discovery. There are numerous fragments in the Sunbury hoard, but their status is again uncertain. The Thurnham hoard contains many fragments but this hoard was disturbed by ploughing and the findspot is in an exceptionally flinty location, which is thought to be largely responsible for the shattered condition of the coins. That Hoard C contained fragmentary artefacts in addition to the coins, and also that Hoard F contained a large quantity of fragmentary material, lends weight to the notion that some of the coins themselves were also buried in an incomplete state, but again the circumstances of discovery make this impossible to confirm (Joy 2016, 244–7). In summary, this reappraisal of the potin coins from Hoard C shows that it contains a wide range of types across much of the Flat Linear series, with the earliest types probably dating to the late 2nd century BC and the latest suggesting a terminal date of *c.* 60 BC or shortly after.

Hoard P: The 'Bowl Hoard'

Philip de Jersey

This text is based closely on the catalogue entry, no. 196.6, in P. de Jersey (2014) *Coin Hoards in Iron Age Britain* (British Numismatic Society Special Publication no. 12).

The Bowl Hoard is, to date, probably the largest single hoard of British Iron Age coinage, and without a doubt one of the most important. The fact that it was illegally detected and then dispersed by two well-known dealers, before a complete record could be made of its contents, is a great loss not just to Iron Age numismatics but to our understanding of the conquest period in East Anglia and beyond.

As far as can be ascertained, the hoard was found in February 1991, by two detectorists searching without permission in the 'gold field' at Snettisham. The bulk of the coinage was reportedly contained within a metal bowl, apparently of silver. The bowl is said to have been 30cm in diameter at the rim, standing 20cm high. It was sold to a well-known coins and antiquities dealer and presumably on to a private collector.

Beneath the bowl there were 90 or more gold coins (a source reported 500 such coins to Ian Stead (Stead 1998, 147)), plus three saucer-shaped ingots: one in gold, one in silver alloy and one predominantly of copper (Chadburn 2006, hoard 41, 'Hunstanton I'). The ingots were apparently melted down after discovery. Above the bowl were three brooches and a torc fragment (*ibid.*). The hoard was said to have included so much material that it had to be dragged across the field. This may be hyperbole on the part of the finders – the maximum number of coins listed below would have weighed somewhere in the order of 12.5kg, hardly an enormous burden – but it is perhaps lent some support from the discovery of a number of fragments of silver bowl on the site during Ian Stead's excavations in November 1991 (P.1–7), which he suspected at the time were from a hoard (information from BM Department of Coins and Medals; Stead 1998, 146–8). It is tempting to suggest that these were lost as the hoard was removed from the field, and in this volume they are interpreted as likely being fragments from the Hoard P bowl.

There are rumours that the Bowl Hoard was located beneath one of the hoards which had been excavated by the British Museum in the autumn of 1990. However, this seems extremely unlikely, since the suggested terminal date of the Bowl Hoard in the mid-1st century AD appears to be many decades later than the deposition of the excavated hoards (none of which contain objects dating later than *c.* 60 BC). The bases of the hoard pits F, G, H, J, K and L were exhaustively investigated in 1990 by Stead's team. Stead hypothesised that the Bowl Hoard had been located beneath the 1990 spoil heap. This is in keeping with the locations of the fragments of silver bowl P.1–7 in the north-east corner of the field (Area 21) and a large pit dug by illicit detectorists in this area early in 1991 (see Chs 2, 4 and 12).

It is very difficult to obtain reliable figures for the precise number of coins contained in the hoard. Chadburn (2006, hoard 41) gives a total of *c.* 6,690, consisting of *c.* 6,600 silver coins in the bowl and the *c.* 90 gold said to have been found beneath it. Other sources have provided a total as high as *c.* 8,300, including *c.* 7,600 silver units and as many as *c.* 600 staters, 98 of which were 'in good gold', and 108 quarter staters. The gold content appears to have been significantly exaggerated in these figures (see group A in the list below), but it is difficult to be sure about the silver. The situation is further complicated by the existence of several parcels of coins which may or may not have been part of this hoard. Thus Chadburn (*ibid.*, hoard 45) lists as a separate deposit her 'Hunstanton II', a group consisting of at least 56 Norfolk Wolf staters and 100 silver units, while acknowledging that it may also have come from the 'gold field', and that it was found by the same detectorists as the Bowl Hoard. The group of 56 Norfolk Wolf staters was seized at Heathrow on the same occasion as 594 silver units allegedly from the Bowl Hoard; both groups were found not to be Treasure Trove in November 1994 and returned to Dolphin Coins. There are good numismatic and chronological reasons why the Norfolk Wolf staters and associated early Icenian silver should be considered as a separate deposit to the Bowl Hoard (Talbot 2017, 224), and so Chadburn's 'Hunstanton II' (de Jersey 2014, no. 196.7) is not included here.

Chadburn (*ibid.*, hoard 40) also lists a small 'Dersingham bypass' hoard which seems to be chronologically separate from the Bowl Hoard (de Jersey 2014, no. 196.8); this again is not included here, although it is not impossible that it might have been a parcel from the bigger hoard.

The impact of the Bowl Hoard on the coin trade was painfully evident by late 1991, by which time a huge quantity of Icenian silver was available from dealers throughout Britain, and abroad. Indeed, the hoard probably accounts for most of the unprovenanced Icenian silver still circulating in the trade, but in most cases it is impossible to trace these coins back to their source; many of the types involved are also relatively common as single finds, or have been sold from hoards legitimately dispersed since 1991.

No attempt has been made here to identify every possible Bowl Hoard coin in the Celtic Coin Index (CCI). There are however two groups of coins in the Index which can be more reliably associated with the find. In January 1995 a collector borrowed 1,135 silver coins (1,131 units and four half-units) from one of the dealers involved, and recorded these with the CCI (group B, below). The second, smaller group (425 coins, group C) consists almost entirely of coins which have been sold since 1991 with a Bowl Hoard provenance attached, or where some information exists to confirm an association with the hoard. On no account should this group be taken as a representative sample of the whole hoard: there is a marked bias towards inscribed North-Eastern types, for example, because of the interests of a particular collector.

These various groups total 1,673 coins with entries in the CCI, or about one quarter of the lower estimate for the entire hoard provided by Chadburn (above). There are many more coins in the CCI which must have come from the hoard – probably bringing the total recorded to at least 2,500 – and there is potential for more work in the future to identify them.

As far as can be reconstructed, the hoard consisted predominantly of later East Anglian coinage, alongside North-Eastern series coins and some North Thames issues. The silver component appears heavily biased towards the final local issues, e.g. Late Face Horse, Ecen and Anted (Talbot 2017, 223–4). Chadburn (2006, hoard 41) also suggests that there were 'at least three' Republican *denarii* in the hoard. Whilst precise dating is difficult due to the nature of the evidence, Talbot (2017, 109–10) suggests that the composition bears a strong similarity to 'revolt-period' hoards thought to have been buried in the early AD 60s, and this is the most likely date of deposition for Hoard P.

Coins from the three groups outlined above are listed in the catalogue section below (see pp. 379–93).

Other coin hoards from Snettisham

Eleanor Ghey

Two poorly provenanced coin hoards recorded by the Celtic Coin Index from trade are listed by de Jersey as being from Snettisham: 'Hunstanton II' (de Jersey 2014, 196.7) and 'Dersingham bypass' (*ibid.*, 196.8). Both contain uninscribed East Anglian gold and silver, with some North-Eastern coins possibly included in the former. Although it may be possible to disentangle these batches from the large number of coins potentially from the Bowl Hoard (P) on numismatic grounds, there seems little point in speculating further on their provenance, other than to note that there is likely to be further unreported material from the site at large.

Other hoards have been recorded as being from Snettisham parish but are not from this site and are therefore not listed in the catalogue in this volume. A hoard of 91 East Anglian 'Norfolk Wolf'-type staters and other local uninscribed staters, quarter staters and units now in the British Museum (registration numbers 1988,0403.1–43; 1989,0422.1–42; 1989,1120.1–6) is listed by Hobbs (2006, 39) and Sills (2003, 377) as a hoard from Snettisham found in 1987–9 (Gregory 1992, 50). De Jersey (2014, 308–10, no. 195) lists this hoard as Shernborne I and II (Talbot's Shernborne A (2017, 225)) but correctly notes their recorded findspot as within Snettisham parish. The coins were found spread over a 10 x 20m area, apparently deposited in two groups, with associated pottery. A find of 98 coins from the same site reported under the Treasure Act (Talbot's Shernborne B (2017, 226), with addenda) make this a much larger deposit and potentially extends the possible period of deposition into the final phase of East Anglian coinage. However, the presence of 28 Early Roman *denarii* (deposited after *c.* AD 138–41) from the same site (Treasure case 2014 T111) suggests that the site represents a long sequence of deposition of groups of coins and single coins similar to the pattern represented by the stray finds at the Snettisham excavation site, discussed below.

The Snettisham Jeweller's Hoard (Johns 1997) consisting of Roman coins and artefacts dated to after *c.* AD 154–61 was found within the village of Snettisham in 1985 and not at the hoard site, although it does provide further evidence of Roman period activity in the surrounding area (Ch. 3).

Part 2: The Iron Age single finds

The remaining catalogue (Part 2, cat. nos 188 to 414) presents 227 identifiable Greek and Iron Age coins ordered by production region and type. Of these, one (cat. no. 221) was excavated by Rainbird Clarke in 1948, and three (Cat. nos 219, 234 and 259) are from Hodder's 1989 detecting, all acquired by Norwich Castle Museum. Fifty-four are from the 1990–2 detecting and British Museum excavations at the site, though none were found in a stratified context (of these, 53 are in the BM while one (cat. no. 275) was retained by the finder). The other 169 coins derive from the assemblage metal-detected from 2003 onwards, and are now in Norwich Castle Museum.

Some of these coins have been published previously. De Jersey (2014, 315–16) gives partial details of further groups of coins under his listing for Hoard F, including seven that were found by Hodder around the time of the discovery of Hoard F in 1990 (cat. nos 197, 220, 239, 240, 362, 365 and 411), 26 coins (including a fused lump) found in the British Museum excavation that followed and a further 10 coins subsequently metal-detected by Hodder. He raises the question of possible association of the 33 coins from the first two groups with

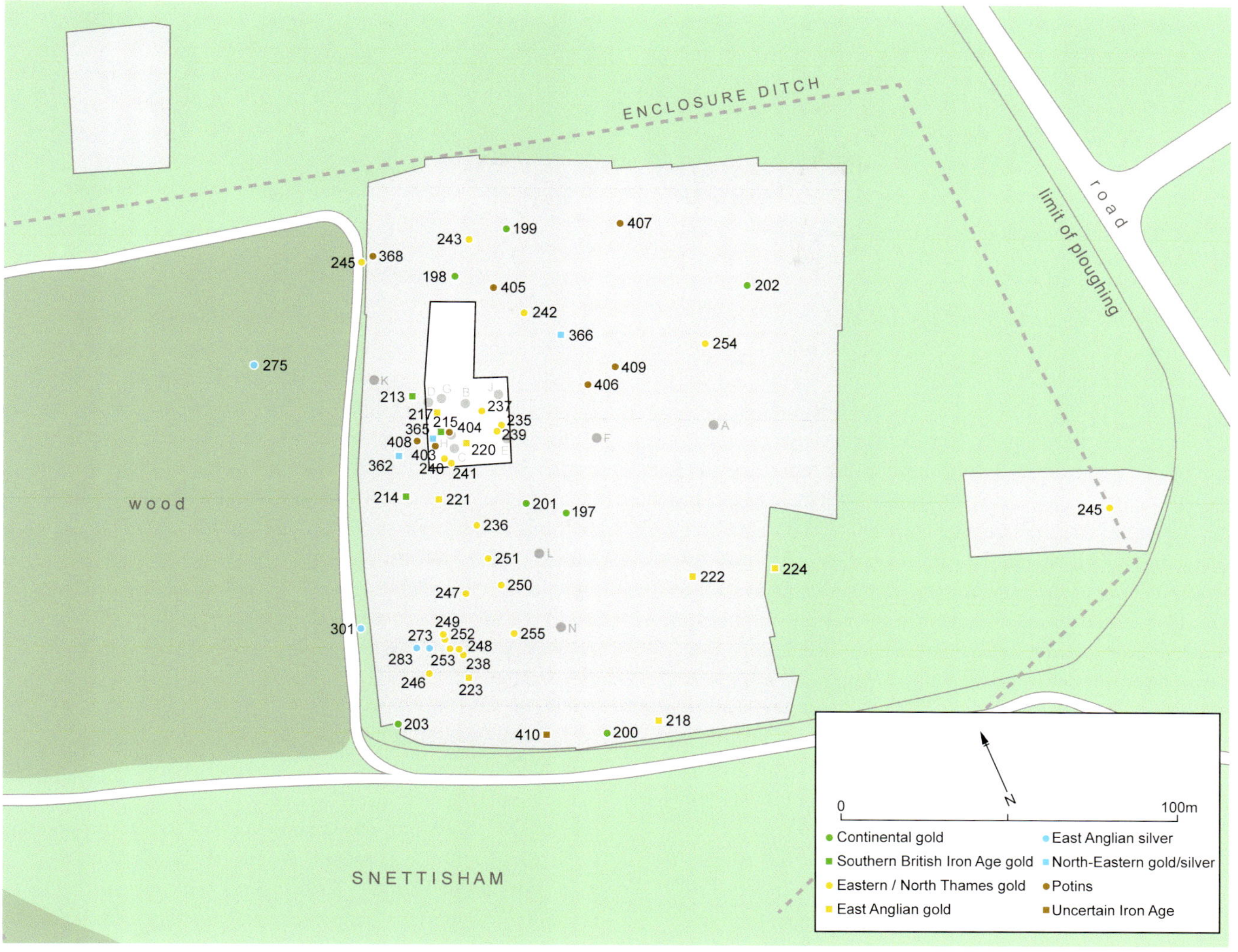

Figure 15.5 Distribution of single finds of Iron Age coins from the 'gold field' in relation to the hoards

Hoard F. Here, these coins have not been listed as they do not have a particular spatial relationship with Hoard F, merely being found in the same season. Further coins included below have not been published in earlier listings of material from the site and only 18 Iron Age coins from the excavation now in the British Museum were published by Hobbs (1996) with the provenance 'Snettisham Excavations 1988–91' (Hobbs 1996 nos 218–19, 249–52, 265–7, 272–8, 3187, 3545). The latter catalogue does not include imported coinage but many of the gold coins in the catalogue have since been identified by John Sills in his work on the continental and early British series (Sills 2003 and 2017).

The single finds span a wider chronological range than the hoard deposits, with all coin periods from 1 to 8 represented. This has significant implications for the interpretation of the site, particularly when considered alongside the assemblage of Roman coins discovered, as discussed below. Early imported coinage is present at the excavation site in the form of a plated Gaulish half stater, a Gallo-Belgic A stater and quarter stater and a Gallo-Belgic C stater (with the possible plated core of another) (cat. nos 197–201). As with the hoard assemblages, the continental gold is mostly worn and may have circulated for some time prior to deposition. Unlike the hoard coinage, the gold coins from the site span a longer chronological period, with a cluster in period 4 to 5 represented by early Southern / Eastern uninscribed coinage, followed by two plated copies of Gallo-Belgic E staters (traditionally attributed to period 5) and a North-Eastern stater and scyphate quarter stater (attributed to period 5 to 6). The proportion of plated coins from the site is higher than in the hoard coins. The wider metal-detected assemblage also contains a large group of local East Anglian silver units and fractions lacking from the excavated assemblage.

It can be seen that Snettisham attracted an unusual amount of non-local coinage, with British coins from the Southern, North-Eastern, Eastern and Kentish regions, the plated Gaulish stater and eight Greek coins from much further afield (including a 3rd-century BC bronze coin of Miletos with a previously unrecorded magistrate, Kleisipp[…] (cat. no. 195). The latter are likely to have had a long period of circulation and arrived in Britain around the same time as early continental Iron Age imports. The imported coinage may have travelled within Britain before finally reaching Snettisham, as is suggested by the wear and distribution of die-linked coins such as the Ca2 quarter stater (cat. no. 187, from Hoard N), for example (Sills pers. comm.). These networks connecting Snettisham with the Thames Valley area, Kent and Sussex may also be seen in the movement of potins discussed by Holman above.

Figure 15.5 shows the distribution of the single find Iron Age coins from the 'gold field' (including one discovered in

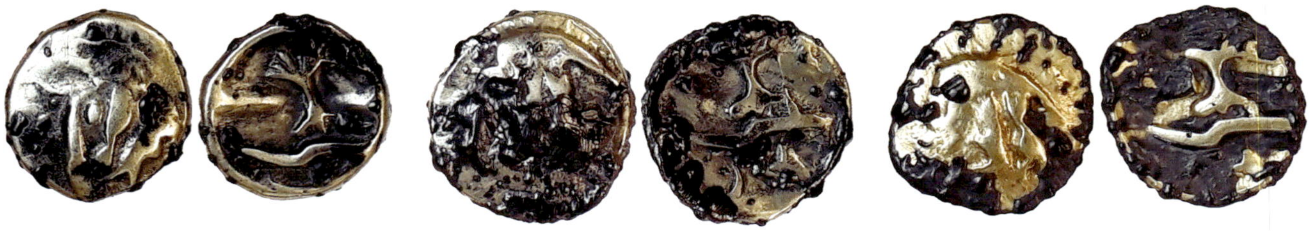

Figure 15.6 Gallo-Belgic D quarter staters (obverse and reverse) with deposit on the surface of the coin. Norwich Castle Museum, 2007.6, 2007.7 and 2007.8

1948, those from the British Museum 1990–2 excavations, and three from earlier metal-detecting by Hodder in 1989). Given that these finds lack stratigraphic context, it is difficult to assign meaning to their spatial distribution with confidence. It seems likely that the assemblage contains further dispersed hoards and some such potential groupings are discussed below. However, the overall impression is one of a large number of Iron Age coins scattered in and around the area of the torc hoards and in a radius of about 100m from the core area of the hoards (containing B, C, D, E, G, H). The post-2003 metal-detected material cannot be plotted but comes from an adjacent wooded area to the immediate west of the 'gold field' and appears to have had a similar density of distribution. The dispersed distribution of the coins could be the result of disturbance of deposits but the mixing of a variety of coin types would seem to suggest that many of the coins were individually deposited at the site rather than coming from hoards.

Any attempt to reconstruct hoards in the metal-detected assemblage must necessarily be speculative (and indeed incomplete, given the loss of coins from the site to illegal metal-detecting), but it is possible to suggest some potential groupings (see also Talbot 2017, 110). Among possible scattered smaller hoards within the deposit is a group of 23 'Norfolk Wolf'-type staters (*Ancient British Coins* (hereafter *ABC*) 1399: Cottam *et al.* 2010; cat. nos 234–55 and 259) and a further five found in the woodland (cat. nos 232–3 and 256–8). Coins of this type are distributed throughout the area of hoard deposition (see **Fig. 15.5**), but with a possible cluster of these staters and local silver coins about 30m from Hoard N.

The early British uninscribed gold coins from period 4 seem to be concentrated in an area about 20–30m radius from the location of Hoard C. The later East Anglian gold and most of the local silver seems to be concentrated more in the woodland area, possibly indicating a slight shift in the location of the later deposits, although later coins were still found in the main area of the hoards. A lump of what appears to be several silver East Anglian coins fused together (cat. no. 301) found about 10m away from Hoard N does seem to indicate a single deposit of coins in close physical association.

The metal-detected assemblage from the woodland contains a group of six British G quarter staters (*ABC* 2350; cat. nos 225–30), with two staters of the same class (*ABC* 2329; cat. nos 223–4) found in the excavation. The woodland assemblage also contains a group of six Gallo-Belgic D quarter staters that appear to have blobs of what may be molten silver or some other substance on their surface (cat. nos 204–8 and 210, **Fig. 15.6**). This has previously been noted by Talbot (2017, 110), who suggests that they are likely to have been part of the same deposit. It is not certain whether this is indicative of plated coins or evidence of pre-depositional treatment. Further analysis would be desirable. The same surface appearance can be seen on one of the Gallo-Belgic E coins from the site (cat. no. 203; the other, cat. no. 202, found almost 200m away, has almost entirely lost its plated surface). No analysis has been carried out on the plated coins, but the plated Insular Cf stater (cat. no. 213) found about 15m from Hoard B appears to have lost gold plate in the centre of its reverse, revealing a large circular patch of the underlying metal. The high proportion of such ancient forgeries from the site may suggest that they were deliberately selected for deposition in preference to genuine coins.

Another significant grouping consists of 34 'Kentish Primary' type potins (*ABC* 120, also known as the 'Thurrock' type, cat. nos 368–401) from the mid- to late 2nd century BC. The majority of these were found in the wooded area and probably represent a dispersed hoard. At least three potins (cat. nos 192–4) have since been reclassified by David Holman on the basis of their high weight and style as imported bronze units from the Greek colony of Massalia, the prototype on which Kentish Primary potins are based. These late 3rd to early 2nd-century BC coins were produced over a long period of time with a widespread distribution in southern coastal France and are likely to have reached Britain through long-distance networks along with the other Greek coins from the site. A number of the remaining Kentish Primary potins from the site are relatively high in weight but poorly preserved; they may benefit from further study after cleaning. Holman notes that:

> Of the certain potins, the more degraded varieties appear to be absent and they seem likely to be mostly, if not wholly from the earlier phases of the series.
>
> Kentish Primary potins are rare as stray finds in Norfolk and Marsden (2011) has noted that apart from Snettisham, the only other location in the county that has yielded them in any numbers is a site in the Waveney valley, a considerable distance away. The CCI and PAS databases between them list only four findspots of Kentish Primary potins (and only five findspots of Flat Linear potins). That so many have come from a small area at Snettisham, a location known for hoarding, suggests that many of them derive from a dispersed hoard of unknown size. Kentish Primary hoards are uncommon, only four certain ones being known: the very large Thurrock hoard (2,150 coins) and three much smaller hoards from Kent, all from near Folkestone (Folkestone (67 coins), Lyminge (77 coins) and Alkham (currently 235 coins). All of these hoards are larger than the putative Snettisham hoard. The distribution of single finds in addition to this cluster of hoards indicates a likely origin for the series in the east Kent region (Holman 2005, 36).

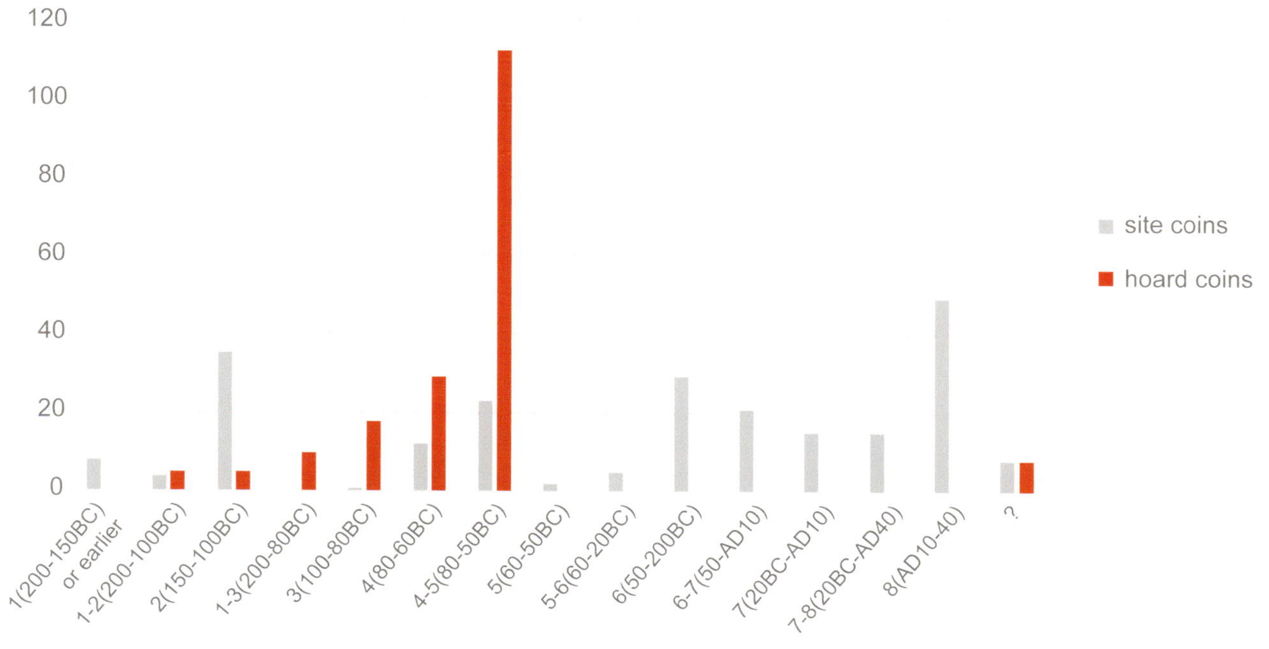

Figure 15.7 Number of Iron Age (and Greek) coins from the hoards and site by period of issue (excludes Hoard P)

Similar coins were in existence in the Paris Basin in the earlier 2nd century BC, although whether the British coins copied these, or were a separate development copying the prototype Massalia bronzes, which are also found in east Kent, has not been determined (Haselgrove 2006, 21). Although frustratingly elusive to confirm, what dating evidence there is for Kentish Primary potins also suggests an early date, probably starting no later than the mid-2nd century BC (*ibid.*, 19). They were probably superseded by the earliest Flat Linear potins by around 125 BC but that is far from certain and a later date is possible. Although these dates are much earlier than the principal Snettisham hoards, this does not preclude these coins having been deposited as a defined hoard at an early date. There is other earlier material from the site, as evidenced by radiocarbon dates obtained from organic remains associated with torcs in Hoards F and L, both of which gave dates no later than the 2nd century BC and quite possibly earlier [**Table 5.2**; Garrow *et al.* 2009]. However, Hoard F also included demonstrably later coins into the 1st century BC (see above). From this, the possibility that the Kentish Primary potins were also buried in this 'foreign' region at a date sometime after their period of issue should not be discounted.

Seven Flat Linear potins were also found at the excavation site during the 1990–2 excavations, and three of these were found in the area of Hoard C, perhaps outliers from this. David Holman has studied the eight potins from the site in the British Museum (seven Flat Linear and one Kentish Primary) and his identifications are included in the catalogue below. He writes:

This small sample broadly reflects the contents of Hoard C, with coins of [Holman's] Group F again forming the principal component (see above). Three of these coins – cat. nos 403–4 and 408 – were found less than 10 metres from the location of Hoard C and, given the circumstances of the original discovery, must be regarded as likely strays from the hoard although in the absence of proof they have been kept separate from the hoard catalogue. The others – cat. nos 405–7 and 409 – are well scattered and were found between 30 and 55 metres north-east of Hoard C. Despite the greater distance, it is possible that these also derive from Hoard C, perhaps as plough scatter, although it will never be possible to be certain. One further Flat Linear potin (type F3/3-2, cat. no. 402) was found *c.* 2003 although the location of this coin within the field is unknown.

Discussion

The evidence from the Iron Age coinage thus suggests that the site was not abandoned after the phase which saw the deposition of the torc hoards (Phase 3 of activity at Snettisham, *c.* 350–60 BC), but continued in use for wider forms of depositional activity (see Chs 8–9). Talbot (2017, 110) posited that, 'The evidence is not suggestive of continuous deposition of Icenian coinage, and hoarding appears to be concentrated in three main phases: before local production started [pre-*c.* 60 BC], the end of Norfolk Wolf B stater production [*c.* 20 BC] and the revolt period [*c.* AD 60, represented by Hoard P], the latter two coinciding with wider episodes of Icenian coinage hoarding.' On the basis of the coin evidence, the end of the first of these phases around 60 BC (i.e. coinage period 4, Phase 3 in this volume) could plausibly account for the deposition of the gold hoards (B, E, F and N), the potin hoard (C) and perhaps smaller gold deposits from the woodland assemblage (**Fig. 15.7**). The limited stratigraphic evidence available to us does not indicate a similar intensity of hoard deposition in the intervening period prior to the deposition of the Bowl Hoard P (around AD 60, Phase 4 in this volume) but rather deposition of single coins and small hoards over an extended period with a more local focus to the coinage. This later phase accounts for the majority of the silver coinage deposited at the site, which can be seen to come mainly from East Anglia (**Fig. 15.8**). With the exception of plated coins, the base-metal coins are generally earlier, consisting of potins and Greek imports.

Since Haselgrove (1987) drew attention to the practice of multiple deposition of Iron Age coins and coin hoards at a

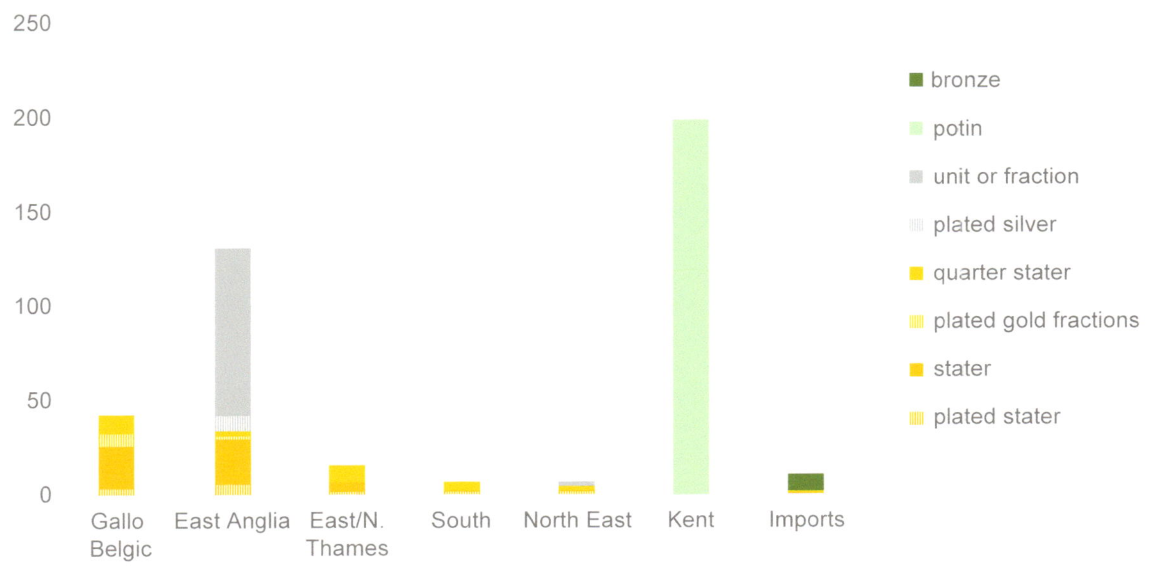

Figure 15.8 Number of Iron Age and Greek coins from the hoards and site by denomination and coin-producing region (excludes Hoard P)

single site, a number of such sites have undergone stratigraphic archaeological excavation. At Hallaton, Leicestershire (Leins 2007 and 2011), 14 distinct coin hoard deposits with similar composition were deposited in the entranceway to an enclosure in the mid-1st century AD; had the assemblage been ploughed out this patterning is unlikely to have been recognised in the numismatic record. The Roman temple sites at Wanborough, Surrey (Williams 2007), Harlow, Essex (Haselgrove 2005) and Hayling Island, Hampshire (King and Soffe 2001) all had earlier features that attracted Iron Age coin deposition, in hoards and as single finds. At other sites, such as Springhead, Kent (Andrews *et al.* 2011), Ashwell, Herts. (Jackson and Burleigh 2018) and Frensham, Surrey (Graham and Graham 2017), deposits of Iron Age coins are spatially separate from any Roman period foci, if they are present at all.

Comparative Norfolk sites that have undergone archaeological investigation are lacking. The assemblage from Fincham (de Jersey 2014, 285–90; Talbot 2017, 128) is also suggestive of cumulative deliberate deposition over an extended period of time, with the suggestive inclusion of coin blanks and droplets. However, that assemblage is predominantly silver and later in date, with the latest inscribed East Anglian types represented. The poorly understood assemblage from Welney (*ibid.*, 333–4) is more comparable to the early phase of hoarding at Snettisham, with Gallo-Belgic gold imports alongside uninscribed British gold. The assemblage from the 'Shernborne I and II' site discussed above also lacks archaeological investigation but appears to represent a concentrated deposit of similarly mixed Iron Age coinage with a long chronological range found adjacent to Early Roman coinage.

Part 3: Roman coins

The Roman coins are listed in Part 3 of the catalogue and derive from two groups:

- The 47 Roman coins from the British Museum excavations 1990–2 (registration numbers 1991,1018.12 to .19 and 2009,4213.28 to .66). None were found in securely stratified contexts, except for a group of four mid-4th-century AD coins found in the enclosure ditch in Trench 5 (cat. nos 471–3, 478; see **Fig. 9.5a**)
- The Roman coins metal-detected from the western area of the site between 2003 and 2007 (Treasure cases 2003 T169; 2005 T487 and 2007 T695), now in Norwich Castle Museum. These were not well-recorded at the time and are for the most part poorly preserved, although further identification may be possible in due course after cleaning.

The excavated and metal-detected assemblage contains a broad range of Roman coins (Part 3 of the catalogue), suggesting that the site was frequented to some extent throughout most of the Roman period. The 48 coins from the BM 1990–2 seasons contain two *denarii*, 31 1st to early 3rd-century *sestertii* and fractions, two 3rd-century radiates, nine 4th-century *nummi*, four 3rd to 4th-century base-metal coins and one further undated coin. The more recent metal-detected assemblage (from the wooded area to the west of the 'gold field') contains 35 further Roman coins and nine of uncertain date. This group is of broadly similar profile although it contains one Roman Republican *denarius* and two *nummi* of the Theodosian period. **Figure 15.9** shows the distribution of Roman coin finds in the 'gold field'. In terms of distribution, they are scattered more to the north of the area of dense Iron Age coin deposits with no obvious hoard deposits apart from the small cluster of four late Constantinian *nummi* from the enclosure ditch in Trench 5 (cat. nos 471–3, 478), the only securely stratified Roman coins.

When these assemblages are combined, there are 52 coins that can be put into a Reece period (one of the 21 periods of issue commonly used in analysis of Romano-British coinage, as set out by Reece (1968)) (**Fig. 15.10**), a number that is too small to make many significant conclusions, except to say that the bulk of the earlier coinage dates from the Flavian to the Antonine period (26 coins) and the later coinage peaks in the late 3rd century (9 radiates, including up to three of Carausius and some contemporary imitations) and the mid-4th century (14 mid- to late Constantinian *nummi* and contemporary copies). There are no clearly identifiable hoards within the group. The coins

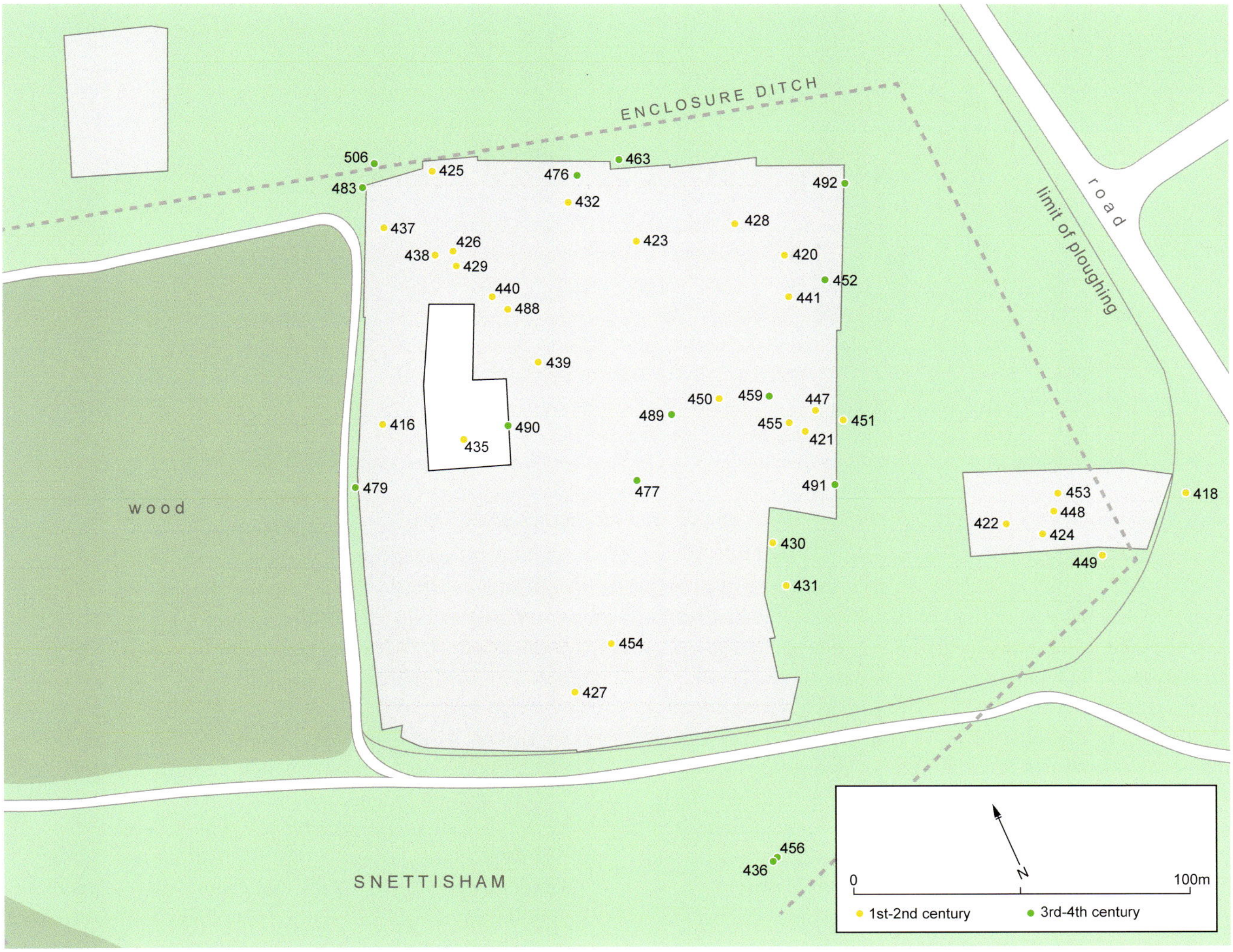

Figure 15.9 Distribution of Roman coins from the 'gold field'

that cannot be dated to a Reece period include three further Antonine coins (Reece periods 7 to 9).

Perhaps the most notable feature of the Roman assemblage is the lack of pre-Flavian coinage, represented only by a bronze of Nero and the Republican *denarius* of *c.* 81 BC. Although the inscribed East Anglian Iron Age units date to the first half of the 1st century AD, Roman coinage of this period is lacking, suggesting that the site had perhaps fallen out of use (at least in terms of coin deposition) by the period of the Roman conquest, or that only local coinage was deposited at that time. Talbot has suggested, regarding the absence of Republican *denarii*, it may be that Roman coins were being 'deliberately excluded from this highly important site [in the mid-first century AD], perhaps because they were viewed as

Figure 15.10 Roman coins from the site by their main period of production, compared to all Roman coinage from Norfolk listed on the PAS database (expressed per mill.)

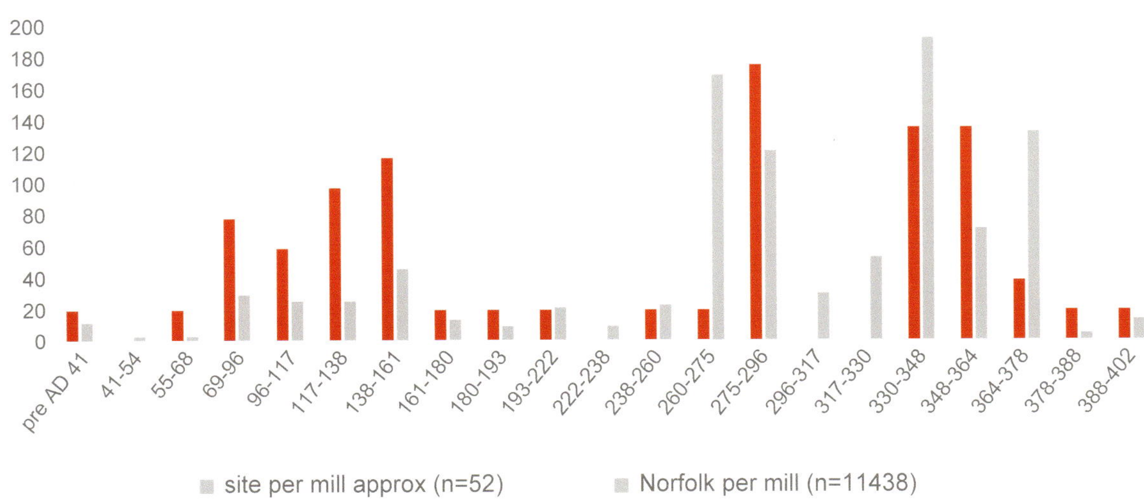

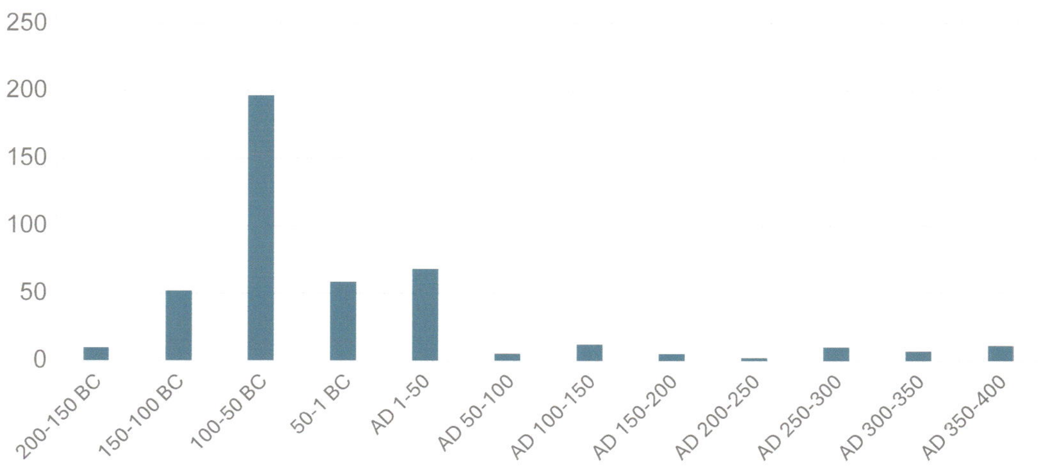

Figure 15.11 Approximate date of issue of Iron Age and Roman coins from Snettisham averaged over 50-year periods

being alien or barbarous' (Talbot 2017, 110). The absence of a clear understanding of the composition of Hoard P complicates this picture somewhat; it certainly seems that later and non-local inscribed coinage up to at least period 9 was present in this deposit (see de Jersey above). The presence of coinage at the site is more noticeable from the Flavian period, perhaps suggesting that this period of disuse was a temporary hiatus, though caution must be exercised in discussing a period of reduced supply. Antonine activity at the site could also be seen in the possible presence of recovered torc fragments in the Snettisham Jeweller's hoard (deposited after *c.* AD 154–61) (Ch. 3).

This nevertheless differs from the site at Hallaton, Leicestershire, where a phase of early gold coin deposition is followed by phases of 1st-century deposition of local silver, Eastern gold and a significant number of Roman Republican coins, with a Roman coin profile that is higher than the mean until the early 2nd century AD (Leins 2011, 43). It is also in marked contrast to Neronian hoard deposits from the southern part of the East Anglian coin-producing area that contained both *denarii* and local silver units, such as Eriswell (Kent and Burnett 1984) and Scole (Burnett 1986).

Later coins

It should be noted that the assemblage contains 42 medieval and later coins, tokens and medals (1991,1018.20 and .22; 2009,4213.67–96 and .105), spanning a range of dates from 1369 to 1988. Some of the items in this diverse assemblage could potentially have reached the site more recently, perhaps due to the spread of night soil or other material on the field from the settlement nearby (see Ch. 10 for discussion of post-medieval agricultural, drainage and landscaping work at the site).

The Snettisham coin assemblage: concluding remarks

Taken together, the Iron Age and Roman coin assemblages point to deposition of coinage at the site from the earliest period of Iron Age coin use in Britain through to the mid-1st century AD and beyond, with apparent peaks *c.* 60 BC (contemporary with at least some of the torc hoards), *c.* 20 BC, and from the pre-conquest period to *c.* AD 40, up to the final phase of Iron Age coin deposition represented by Hoard P, *c.* AD 60.

Despite the background pattern of continuity of use of the site for deposition represented by the single finds (a picture complicated by the apparent presence of scattered hoards within that assemblage), the hoard record suggests more sporadic moments of intense coin deposition at the site and notable absences should be considered. Gallo-Belgic E is not represented in the coin hoards and is only represented at the site as a whole by plated staters. Similarly, there is a lack of broadly contemporary local gold issues such as Norfolk Wolf A (*ABC* 1393), both of which are found in hoards from other North Norfolk sites (Talbot 2017, 111). The difficulty of providing absolute dating for the continental series in Britain has been alluded to above but the picture of more intense deposition of Gallo-Belgic C and D combined with the potin hoards points to a particular horizon of deposition around the end of Iron Age coin phase 4, *c.* 60 BC. This has been used to give a *terminus post quem* for the torc hoards (which contain a combination of coins of this phase and earlier examples with a potentially longer period of circulation prior to deposition). It is likely that the Greek coinage found at Snettisham reached Britain through the same long-distance networks as the continental Iron Age coinage and can therefore also be placed in this phase.

The bulk of the next phase of coin deposition involves Iron Age coinage of phases 6 to 8 (*c.* 50 BC to AD 40), perhaps the product of a longer period of more sporadic deposition of single finds with the exception of the suggested scattered hoard of Norfolk Wolf staters representing the peak around *c.* 20 BC. Whilst there are significant numbers of inscribed East Anglian silver coins found at the site, the Early Roman Imperial and Republican Roman *denarii* that were in circulation at the same time are notably absent (as noted by Talbot 2017, 110). Later inscribed Iron Age coinage from the Eastern (North Thames) region is also lacking from the assemblage. Given the presence of contemporary East Anglian coinage at the site this is perhaps surprising but may be a reflection of a wider change in orientation of regional networks in the early 1st century AD. This coinage reaches Suffolk in quantity but is rarely found in hoards from Norfolk, despite travelling far from its source (for example, the 79 coins of Cunobelin (period 8) found at Hallaton (Leins 2011, 39)). Apart from the potins, base metal coinage of Iron Age date is also lacking, in contrast to special deposits from sites in the North Thames area such as Ashwell (Jackson and Burleigh 2018), which unlike Snettisham is within the normal zone of distribution for this coinage. In general, the character of the Iron Age coinage from Snettisham in the period after 60 BC is more local, with fewer long-distance imports (North-Eastern coinage being an exception in its wider area of distribution (Bland *et al.* 2020, 242)).

The so-called 'Bowl hoard' (Hoard P), sadly, was perhaps key to understanding aspects of the nature and function of coin deposition at the site but its archaeological context and circumstances of deposition are now lost to us. It cannot be discussed with the same degree of confidence as the extant assemblage but de Jersey's tentative reconstruction of the hoard (see above and section in catalogue, below) paints a picture of a very mixed assemblage of material not normally hoarded together; both uninscribed and inscribed gold and silver, up to the latest phase of East Anglian and North-Eastern coinage issued around the conquest period (AD 40s) and potentially as late as *c.* AD 60, as found in the 'Revolt period' hoards of East Anglia (Talbot 2017, 125). If Hoard P did represent a single deposit, it is possible that it constitutes redeposited material from the site or elsewhere in the vicinity, some of which may have been originally deposited in the phases not well-represented in the excavated and metal-detected assemblage.

The number of Roman coins in the assemblage is relatively high in the later part of the 1st century and into the mid-2nd century (**Fig. 15.10**), making it possible to argue for some degree of continuity of use of the site for coin deposition. Further conclusions based on the Roman coins must remain tentative given the small number identified, but the relative lack of coinage in the Severan period might suggest little activity in this period, though in keeping with the general pattern for Norfolk and nationally. This apparent hiatus is more pronounced in the period *c.* AD 260–74, a time of plentiful supply of debased radiates. For the later Roman period (i.e. debased radiates and *nummi* from *c.* AD 274 to the end of the Roman period) the pattern of coinage at Snettisham is more in keeping with the general background pattern of coinage for Norfolk and no significant activity can be assumed. Certainly, when the Roman coin assemblage is taken as a whole, any equivalent intensity of deposition to that of the Iron Age is lacking (**Fig. 15.11**).

In terms of the significance of the Iron Age coin assemblage, the variety of non-local and imported coins (**Fig. 15.8**) as well as the long period of deposition of coinage seems to indicate a place of pre-eminent importance for the region and beyond. It can perhaps be compared to assemblages from southern coastal sites such as Hengistbury Head, Selsey and West Wittering that also display diverse assemblages and (in the case of Hengistbury) a long period of deposition (Bland *et al.* 2020, 245). Unlike Hengistbury, direct evidence for coin production is lacking and the presence of hoard groups combining coins and personal items speaks to the significance of Snettisham for individual and communal ritualised deposition rather than a role primarily associated with economic activities such as the production, exchange or decommissioning of coinage (although these activities need not be mutually exclusive).

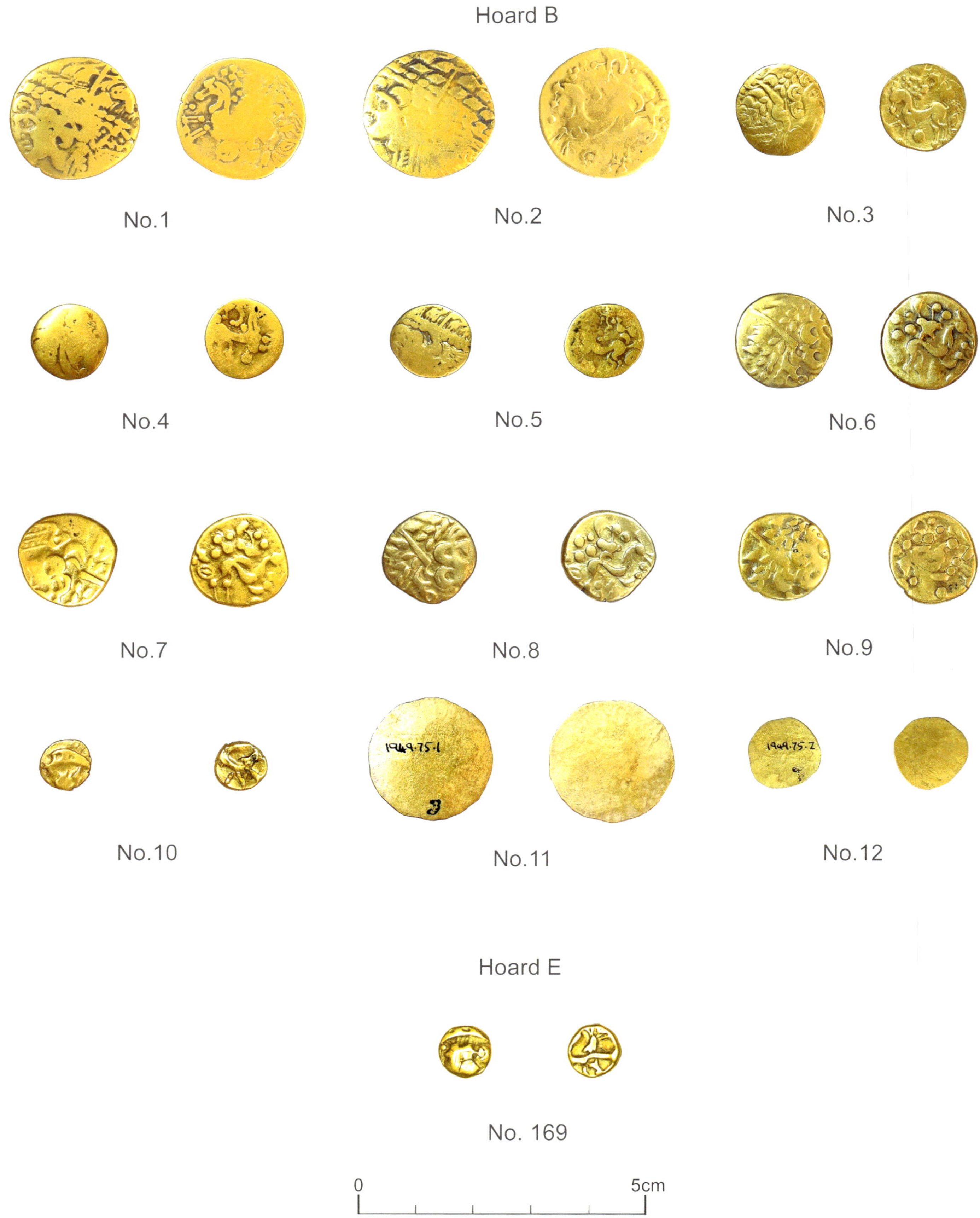

Plate 15.1 Iron Age Coins from Hoards B and E

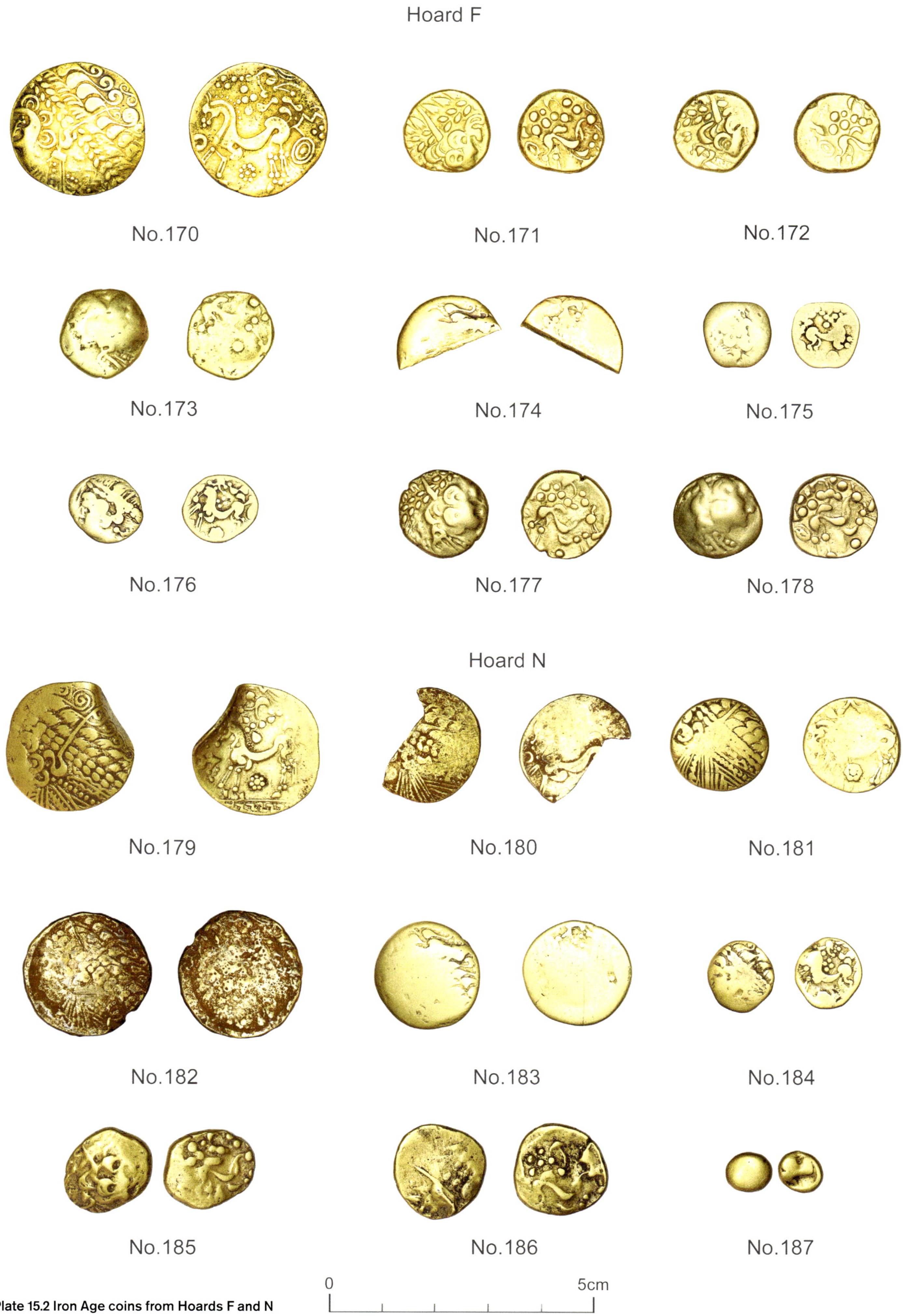

Plate 15.2 Iron Age coins from Hoards F and N

Catalogue of Coins

Notes

Eleanor Ghey

The catalogue uses *ABC* as the type reference for Iron Age coins, this being the most up-to-date work incorporating the numerous new types that have been discovered since the publication of Van Arsdell (1989) and Hobbs (1996). A full concordance of types is given in *ABC*.

For the Gallo-Belgic and early insular gold coinage, additional references to the typology used by Sills (2003 and 2017) is given. For East Anglian coinage, the terminology in Talbot 2017 is used.

Roman coins are phased by Reece periods (Reece 1968). The phasing used for the Iron Age coins is as below, taken from de Jersey 2014 (after Haselgrove 1993) and broadly consistent with *ABC*. Absolute chronology is a matter of debate and this is meant as a guide only. For the potins, Holman (2016, 11) gives approximate date ranges for subgroups:

Period 1 = 200–150 BC
Period 2 = 150–100 BC
Period 3 = 100–80 BC
Period 4 = 80–60 BC
Period 5 = 60–50 BC
Period 6 = 50–20 BC
Period 7 = 20 BC–AD 10
Period 8 = AD 10–40 very latest
Period 9 = AD 40–45
Period 10 = post-conquest

The majority of the NCM coins listed in Part II are from the 2003–9 Treasure cases (metal-detected in 2003–9, and processed as a number of different Treasure cases), though some identifications have been revised since the original cataloguing of the 2003–7 cases (reports submitted to HM Coroner in 2009 by the author and Ian Leins, with helpful assistance from Richard Abdy, Amelia Dowler and Sam Moorhead). The reference in the 'Reg. no.' column for these Treasure case coins (2003.1ff) is a reference number assigned during the cataloguing of these cases rather than their museum registration number. It was not possible to examine the 2009 T666 coins prior to publication and I am grateful to John Talbot for providing images and details of these. It was not always possible to match the Roman coins in NCM to their original identifications as they were not photographed at the time these Treasure reports were compiled and they could not all be re-examined.

Key to abbreviations used

ABC	*Ancient British Coinage* (Cottam *et al.* 2010)
Allen	Allen 1971
Axis	mould axis (for potins) expressed in degrees
BDW	Buckland, Dix and Wood
BMC	British Museum Catalogue (i.e. Hobbs 1996 for Iron Age coins, with volume no. for Roman coins)
BM reg. no.	British Museum Registration number
BN	Bibliothèque Nationale (Paris)
Boon	Boon 1988
CAN	Classical Numismatic Auction
CCI	Celtic Coin Index number
Clarke	Clarke 1954

CNG	Classical Numismatic Group	PSL	Priced Stock List
Cunetio	Besly and Bland 1983	RC	Reverse crossed
Denom.	Denomination	RP	Reverse parallel
Disc.	Discovery year and circumstances	Ref.	Reference
Dolley	Dolley 1954	*RIC*	*Roman Imperial Coinage* (followed by volume number)
DT	Delestrée and Tache 2002–8		
Exc.	Recovered during archaeological excavations	*RRC*	*Roman Republican Coinage* (Crawford 1974)
(i)	Irregular / imitation	Scheers	Scheers 1977
(in ex.)	inscription positioned below the exergual line on the reverse of a coin	SNC	Spink Numismatic Circular
		SNG	*Sylloge Nummorum Graecorum*
MBS	Mail Bid Sale	Strs	Presence of striations on potins (background patterning caused by use of an agent, probably wood, to smooth the mould prior to manufacture): C = crossed, P = parallel, O = obverse, R = reverse.
MD	Metal-detected		
NCM	Norwich Castle Museum		
NDA	No data available		
NFA	Numismatic Fine Arts		
OC	Obverse crossed	Unc.	Uncertain
OP	Obverse parallel	Wt	Weight in grammes

Part 1 IRON AGE COINS FROM THE HOARDS (Cat. nos 1–187)

Hoard B: Catalogue by Eleanor Ghey (Cat. nos 1–12; all in NCM)

All discovered during Rainbird Clarke's 1948 excavations (see Chs 2 and 4).

Gold staters and quarter staters

Cat. no.	NCM reg. no.	Obverse	Reverse	Denom.	*ABC*	Other refs[1]	Wt (g)	Period
1.	1949.76.1	Stylised head of Apollo, left	Stylised horse and chariot, left	stater	4	Ab1 Class 6; CCI 61.0297; Clarke no. 2	7.07	1–3
2.	1949.76.2	Stylised head of Apollo, left	Stylised horse and chariot, left	stater (possibly plated)	4	Ab1 Class 3b; CCI 61.0296; Clarke no. 1	5.38[2]	1–3
3.	1949.76.3	Stylised head of Apollo, right	Stylised horse, and chariot, left	quarter stater	28	Aa2 Class 3a; CCI 61.0289; Clarke no. 4	1.79	1–3
4.	1949.76.4	Stylised head of Apollo, right	Stylised horse, and chariot, right	quarter stater	28	Aa2 Class 5; CCI 61.0288; Clarke no. 6	1.52	1–3
5.	1949.76.6	Stylised head of Apollo, left	Stylised horse and chariot, left	quarter stater	31	Ab2 Class 3b; CCI 61.0303; Clarke no. 5	1.68	1–3
6.	1949.76.11	Stylised head of Apollo, right	Stylised horse, right	stater	13	Ca1 Class 3; CCI 61.0314; Clarke no. 8	6.23[3]	4
7.	1949.76.10	Stylised head of Apollo, right	Stylised horse, right	stater	13	Ca1 Class 3; CCI 61.0315; Clarke no. 10	6.48	4
8.	1949.76.8	Stylised head of Apollo, right	Stylised horse, right	stater	13	Ca1 Class 3; CCI 61.0316; Clarke no. 9	6.17[4]	4
9.	1949.76.9	Stylised head of Apollo, right	Stylised horse, right	stater	13	Ca1 Class 3; CCI 61.0317; Clarke no. 11	6.52[5]	4
10.	1949.76.12	Stylised animal	Abstract design	quarter stater	530	Insular Cf2 Class 1; CCI 61.0328; Clarke no. 12	1.50	4
11.	1949.75.1	Blank (hammered)	Blank (hammered)	stater	?	Uncertain type;[6] CCI 61.0286; Clarke no. 3	6.17	?
12.	1949.75.2	Blank (hammered)	Blank (hammered)	quarter stater	?	Uncertain type;[7] CCI 61.0285; Clarke no. 7	1.67	?

Hoard C: Catalogue by David Holman (Cat. nos 13–168)

All Flat Linear potins, in NCM. Types as per Holman 2016. All discovered during ploughing in 1948 (see Chs 2 and 4).

Cat. no.	Type	CCI no.	Dolley no.	Weight (g) * indicates incomplete coin	Circle diameter (mm)	Axis (degrees)	Strs	Comments
13.	B2/2-1c	61.0504		1.82	17.0	270		Allen E model (but there are no crescents in exergue)
14.	B2/4-1b	61.0503	46	2.11	16.5	90		Allen D3 model
15.	B3/2-4d	61.0491	9	1.73*	15.5–16.5	90		Chipped. Allen C3 model
16.	B3/2-5a	61.0492	8	2.24	17.0	90		Allen C4 model
17.	B2/2 or B3/2	–		0.59*	NDA	90		Fragment
18.	C2/1-1b	62.0152	10	2.17	16.5	270		Allen B model (eye pellet is a blemish in the flan, not part of design)
19.	C2/1-1	61.0511		1.81	16.5	270		
20.	C3/1-1a	61.0509		1.90	16.5	270		Allen F1 model
21.	C3/1-1	–		1.20*	NDA	270	RP	4 fragments; incomplete
22.	C3/1-2b	61.0524	2	1.87	16.5	90		Top of strip?
23.	C3/1-2b	61.0527		1.45	16.0	90	OP/RP	Striations very faint
24.	C3/1-2b	61.0528	3	1.87	17.5	270	OP/RP	Allen GB3 model
25.	C3/1-2b	61.0529	12?	1.78	16.5	90	OC/RC	
26.	C3/1-2d	61.0525		1.52*	16.0	90	OP/RP	Chipped. End of strip
27.	C3/1-2d	61.0526		1.93	16.5	90	OC/RC	
28.	C3/1-2d	–	11	1.66*	17.5	270	OP/RP	2 fragments; chipped.
29.	C3/1-2d	–		1.88*	NDA	90	RP	3 fragments; incomplete
30.	C3/1	–		0.94*	NDA	270	RP	2 fragments; incomplete
31.	C4/1-1b	–	21	1.55*	NDA	90	OP/RP	2 fragments; chipped
32.	D4/4-1b	61.0510	42	1.80	15.5	270		Allen F6 model
33.	D7/3-2b	61.0624	50	1.14	16.0	90		Weakly cast
34.	D7/3-2c	61.0608	48	1.71	15.5	90		
35.	D7/3-2d	61.0604	86	1.69	15.5	90		Appears to have been re-engraved
36.	E1/2-1b	–	6	1.39	15.5	90		2 fragments stuck together; complete
37.	E1/2-1b	–	5	1.73	16.0	90		
38.	E1/2-1	–		0.51*	NDA	90		Fragment
39.	E1/4-2a	61.0573	112	1.16	16.0	90		Allen J3 model. End of strip
40.	E1/4-2a	–	13	1.25*	16.0	90		2 fragments stuck together; chipped
41.	E1/4-2a or b	–	114?	1.51	15.5	90		2 fragments; complete
42.	E1/4-3a	61.0551	116	1.17	15.0	270		
43.	E2/2-1	61.0579	7	1.88	16.0	270		Obverse very weakly cast
44.	E3/3-2b	61.0585	97?	1.63	15.0–15.5	90		
45.	E3/4-1a	61.0557	45	1.93	15.5	270		Allen H1 model
46.	E3/4-2b	–	115?	1.40	NDA	270		5 fragments; complete. End of strip
47.	E3/4-2c	61.0576	43?	1.18*	15.0	270		Chipped, broken, repaired
48.	E3/4-2	–	44	1.60	15.5	270		3 fragments stuck together; complete
49.	E3/4-2	–		0.76*	15.5	270		Fragment. Reverse very weakly cast
50.	E4/4-2c	61.0577	113	1.76	15.0	90		Allen J4 model
51.	E1/4-3 or F1/3-1	61.0512		1.75	15.5	270		Reverse encrusted

Cat. no.	Type	CCI no.	Dolley no.	Weight (g) * indicates incomplete coin	Circle diameter (mm)	Axis (degrees)	Strs	Comments
52.	F1/3-2a	61.0571	54	1.16	15.0–15.5	270		
53.	F1/3-2a	61.0601	89	1.89	15.0	270		
54.	F1/3-2a	61.0606	56	1.29	15.5	270		
55.	F1/3-2a	61.0609	64	1.26	15.0–15.5	270		
56.	F1/3-2a	61.0621	60	1.42	14.0–15.0	270		
57.	F1/3-2a	61.0629	52	1.49	15.5	270		
58.	F1/3-2a	–		1.77*	NDA	270		5 fragments; chipped
59.	F1/3-2b	61.0598	53	1.43	14.5	270		End of strip
60.	F1/3-2b	61.0614	63	1.90	15.5	270		End of strip
61.	F1/3-4a	61.0572	62	1.53	15.0	270		Allen J7 model (but Allen's drawing is inaccurate)
62.	F1/3-4a	–	51	1.43	NDA	270		2 fragments; complete
63.	F1/3-4	–		1.14*	15.0–15.5	270		Chipped
64.	F2/2-2a	61.0639	15	1.79	15.0	90		
65.	F2/2-2a	61.0640	17	1.30	15.0–15.5	90		
66.	F2/2-2a	61.0641	16	1.79	15.0	90		
67.	F2/2-2a	61.0642	18	1.39	15.5	90		End of strip
68.	F2/2-2a	61.0643	19	1.56	15.5	90		End of strip
69.	F2/2-2a	61.0644	14	1.71	15.0–15.5	90		Allen L6 model
70.	F2/2-2a	–		1.47*	NDA	90		2 fragments; chipped
71.	F2/2-2	–		0.29*	NDA	90		Fragment
72.	F2/3-1c	61.0542	30	1.56	15.5	270		Weak obverse. End of strip
73.	F2/3-1c	61.0545	34	1.48	15.5	270		
74.	F2/3-1c	61.0547	32	1.83	16.0	270	OP	End of strip
75.	F2/3-1c?	–	38	1.67	NDA	90		4 fragments; complete
76.	F2/3-2a	61.0550	103	1.51	14.0–14.5	270		
77.	F2/3-2a	61.0586	85	1.76	14.5	270		Top of strip
78.	F2/3-2a	61.0587	27	1.18	14.5–15.0	270		
79.	F2/3-2a	61.0588	77	1.53	15.0	270		Broken and repaired
80.	F2/3-2a	61.0589	55	1.18	14.5	270		
81.	F2/3-2a	61.0590	88	2.26	15.0	270		Top of strip?
82.	F2/3-2a	61.0596	33	2.32	15.0	270		Irregular flan. Top of strip?
83.	F2/3-2a	61.0597	90	1.92	15.0	270		
84.	F2/3-2a	61.0603	101	1.31	15.0	270		
85.	F2/3-2a	61.0605	75	1.41	15.0	270		End of strip
86.	F2/3-2a	61.0607	83	1.94	15.0	270		Top of strip
87.	F2/3-2a	61.0610	92	2.04	14.5	270		Weakly cast
88.	F2/3-2a	61.0615	57	1.46	15.5	270		
89.	F2/3-2a	61.0627	91	1.94	15.0	270		End of strip
90.	F2/3-2a	–	76	1.27	15.0	270		End of strip
91.	F2/3-2a	–		0.91*	15.5	270		2 fragments; chipped
92.	F2/3-2a	–		1.11*	14.5	270		2 fragments; incomplete
93.	F2/3-2a	–		0.97*	NDA	270		3 fragments, 2 stuck together; incomplete
94.	F2/3-2a or b	–		0.61*	NDA	270		Fragment
95.	F1/3-2a or F2/3-2a	–		0.59*	NDA	270		2 fragments; incomplete
96.	F2/3-2b	61.0591		NDA	NDA	270		Obverse 61.0618 / reverse 61.0591
97.	F2/3-2b	61.0612	73	1.56	15.5	270		End of strip
98.	F2/3-2b	61.0613	95	1.62	15.0	270		

Cat. no.	Type	CCI no.	Dolley no.	Weight (g) * indicates incomplete coin(s)	Circle diameter (mm)	Axis (degrees)	Strs	Comments
99.	F2/3-2b	–	29	1.44	15.5	270		
100.	F2/3-2b	–		0.97*	15.5	270		Fragment.
101.	F2/3-1b or 2b	–		0.63*	NDA	270		2 fragments; incomplete
102.	F2/3-2c	61.0543	111?	1.71	15.5	270		
103.	F2/3-2c	61.0595	59	1.46	15.5	270		Allen L3 model
104.	F2/3-2c	61.0616	84	1.42	15.5	270		
105.	F2/3-2c	61.0618	58	1.57	15.5	270		Obverse 61.0631 / reverse 61.0618
106.	F2/3-2c	61.0620	39	1.81	15.5	270		
107.	F2/3-2c	61.0622	80	1.71	14.5	90		
108.	F2/3-2c	61.0623	98	1.82	15.0	90		
109.	F2/3-2c	61.0625	94	1.93	15.5	270		
110.	F2/3-2c	61.0626	68?	1.13	15.5	270		End of strip
111.	F2/3-2c	–	87	1.53*	15.5	270		Chipped. End of strip
112.	F2/3-2c	–		1.14*	15.5	270		Chipped. End of strip
113.	F2/3-2b or c	–		0.85*	15.5	270		Fragment
114.	F2/3-2d	61.0552	102	2.07	15.5	90		Obverse of unusual style
115.	F2/3-2d	61.0628	61	1.83	15.0	270		
116.	F2/3-2d	–	107	1.50	15.5	270		2 fragments; complete
117.	F2/3-2e	61.0549	79	1.34	15.0	90		
118.	F2/3-2e	61.0554	36	1.66	15.0	90		
119.	F2/3-2e?	61.0544	28	1.35	15.0	90		Weakly cast. Possibly a variant
120.	F2/3-2e?	61.0546	110	1.51	15.0–15.5	90		Corroded obverse
121.	F2/3-2e?	61.0592	31	1.44	14.5	90		End of strip
122.	F2/3-2f	61.0541	82	1.17	14.5	90		Holed (casting flaw).
123.	F2/3-2	–		1.33*	NDA	90		3 fragments stuck together; chipped. Obverse very weakly cast
124.	F2/3-2	–		0.80*	15.0	270		Fragment
125.	F2/3-2	–		1.05*	NDA	270		2 fragments; incomplete
126.	F2/3-2	–		0.92*	NDA	270		2 fragments; incomplete
127.	F2/3-2?	–		0.68*	NDA	270		Fragment
128.	F2/3-2?	–		0.56*	NDA	270		Fragment
129.	F2/3-1 or 2	–		0.65*	NDA	270		Fragment
130.	F2/3-4a	61.0583	105	1.24	15.0	270		Allen L2 model
131.	F2/3-4a	61.0617	24	1.94	15.5	90		
132.	F2/3-4c	61.0600	81	1.62	15.0	90		
133.	F2/3-7a	–		1.63*	15.5	270		Several fragments stuck together; chipped
134.	F2/3-8a	–	23	1.45	15.0	90		
135.	F2/3-9a	61.0599	66	1.59	15.0	90		End of strip
136.	F2/3-9a	61.0632	74	1.57	15.0	90		
137.	F2/3-9b	61.0593	70	1.29	15.0	90		End of strip
138.	F2/3-9b	61.0611	99	1.46	15.0	90		
139.	F2/3-9b	61.0631		NDA	NDA	90		Obverse 61.0630 / reverse 61.0631
140.	F2/3-10a	61.0548	26	1.31	15.0	90		Irregular flan
141.	F2/3-10a	61.0556	78	1.50	14.5	90		Allen H2 model
142.	F2/3-11a	61.0584	37	1.62	15.0	90		Allen L4 model
143.	F2/3-11a	61.0594	104	1.42	14.5–15.0	270		
144.	F2/3-11b	61.0540	100	1.96	15.0	90		

Cat. no.	Type	CCI no.	Dolley no.	Weight (g) * indicates incomplete coin	Circle diameter (mm)	Axis (degrees)	Strs	Comments
145.	F2/3-11c	61.0602	106	1.23	15.0	90		End of strip
146.	F2/3-11d	61.0553	49	1.68	15.0	90		
147.	F2/3-9 or 11	–		0.64*	NDA	90		Fragment
148.	F2/3	–		0.93*	NDA	90		3 fragments; incomplete
149.	F2/3	–		0.51*	NDA	270		2 fragments; incomplete
150.	F2/3	–		0.63*	NDA	270		2 fragments; incomplete
151.	F2/3	–		0.44*	NDA	270		Fragment
152.	F2/3	–		0.29*	NDA	270		Fragment
153.	F1/3 or F2/3	–		0.68*	NDA	270		Fragment
154.	F1/3 or F2/3	–		0.47*	NDA	270		Fragment
155.	F3/3-1a	61.0537	72	1.59	15.0	90		
156.	F3/3-1a	61.0538	35	1.49	15.5	90		Allen H3 model
157.	F3/3-1a	61.0539	109	1.38	15.0	90		
158.	F3/3-1a	61.0555	40	1.64	14.5	90		
159.	F3/3-2a	61.0619	67	1.76	14.5–15.0	90		
160.	F3/3-2a	61.0630	47	1.50	15.0	90		Reverse in CCI as 61.0630 but obverse not in CCI
161.	F	–		0.30*	NDA	Uncertain		2 fragments; incomplete
162.	F	–		0.24*	NDA	270		Fragment
163.	F	–		0.20*	NDA	Uncertain		Fragment
164.	D>F	–		0.94*	NDA	Uncertain		Fragment
165.	D>F	–		0.45*	NDA	270		Fragment
166.	D>F	–		0.71*	NDA	270		Fragment
167.	C>F	–		0.34*	NDA	Uncertain		Fragment
168.	*	–		12.20*	NDA	NDA	NDA	79 small fragments; unable to match

Hoard E: Catalogue by Eleanor Ghey (Cat. no. 169)

(In BM) Found within terminal of Great Torc, which was discovered during ploughing in 1950 (see Chs 2 and 4).

Southern British Insular Cf2 Class 1 gold quarter stater

Cat. no.	BM reg. no.	Obverse	Reverse	Denom.	*ABC*	Other refs	Wt (g)	Period
169.	1951,0507.1[8]	Stylised animal	Abstract design	quarter stater	530	Sills 2003, 376; 2017, 155. CCI 99.1801; Clarke no. 14	1.53	4

Hoard F: Catalogue by Eleanor Ghey (Cat. nos 170–8)

(All in BM) Found during metal-detecting by Charles Hodder in 1990 (see Chs 2, 4 and 12).

Presumably originally contained within the helmet which seems to have held all of Hoard F (F.445, see Ch. 12):

Gallo-Belgic gold staters

Cat. no.	BM reg. no.	Obverse	Reverse	Denom.	*ABC*	Other refs	Wt (g)	Period
170.	1991,0904.1	Stylised head of Apollo, left	Stylised chariot, left	stater (possible ancient forgery)[9]	4	Sills 2003 Gallo-Belgic Ab1 Class 2; CCI 99.1799	7.09	1–3
171.	1991,0904.2	Stylised head of Apollo, right	Stylised horse, right	stater	13	Sills 2003 Gallo-Belgic Ca1 Class 3; CCI 94.1701	6.58	4
172.	1991,0904.3	Stylised head of Apollo, right	Stylised horse, right	stater	13	Sills 2003 Gallo-Belgic Ca1 Class 3; CCI 94.1700[10]	6.66	4
173.	1991,0904.4	Stylised head of Apollo, right	Stylised horse, right	stater	13	Sills 2003 Gallo-Belgic Ca1 Class 3; CCI 94.1702	6.52	4

Found within tubular torc fragment (F.53):

Gallo-Belgic gold staters and quarter staters

Cat. no.	BM reg. no.	Obverse	Reverse	Denom.	*ABC*	Other refs	Wt (g)	Period
174.	1991,0904.5	Stylised head of Apollo, left	Stylised horse, left	stater (cut in half)	4	Sills 2003 Gallo-Belgic Ab1 Class 7; CCI 99 1798	3.38 (cut half)	1–3
175.	1991,0904.6	Stylised head of Apollo, right	Stylised horse, right	quarter stater	28	Sills 2003 Gallo-Belgic Aa2 Class 3b; CCI 99 1797	1.56	1–3
176.	1991,0904.7	Stylised head of Apollo, left	Stylised horse, left	quarter stater	31	Sills 2003 Gallo-Belgic Ab2 Class 3b; CCI 99.1800	1.69	1–3
177.	1991,0904.8	Stylised head of Apollo, right	Stylised horse, right	stater	13	Sills 2003 Gallo-Belgic Ca1 Class 3; CCI 94.1698	6.68	4
178.	1991,0904.9	Stylised head of Apollo, right	Stylised horse, right	stater	13	Sills 2003 Gallo-Belgic Ca1 Class 3; CCI 94.1699	6.65	4

Hoard N: Catalogue by Eleanor Ghey (Cat. nos 179–87)

(All in BM) Dispersed hoard excavated from topsoil/subsoil in 1990–1 (see Ch. 12).

Gallo-Belgic gold staters and quarter staters

Cat. no.	BM reg. no.	Obverse	Reverse	Disc.	Area	Site code	Denom.	*ABC*	Other refs	Wt (g)	Period
179.	2009,4213.1	Stylised head of Apollo, left	Stylised horse, left	1991	Area 18	ST/AY	stater	4	Sills 2003 Gallo-Belgic Ab1 Class 3b	7.51 Bent flan	1–3
180.	2009,4213.2	Stylised head of Apollo, left	Stylised horse, left	1991	Area 18	ST/AZ	stater	4	Sills 2003 Gallo-Belgic Ab1 Class 2	3.84 The coin has been cut, removing part of the flan	1–3
181.	2009,4213.3	Stylised head of Apollo, left	Stylised horse, left	1991	Area 18	ST/BA	stater	4	Sills 2003 Gallo-Belgic Ab1 Class 6	5.38 Flan reduced in size	1–3
182.	2009,4213.4	Stylised head of Apollo, left	Stylised horse, left	1991	Area 18	ST/BE	stater	4	Sills 2003 Gallo-Belgic Ab1	5.84	1–3
183.	1991,1017.1	Stylised head of Apollo, left	Stylised horse, left	1990	Area 15[11]	SN/RP	stater	4	Sills 2003 Gallo-Belgic Ab1 Class 7; CCI 99.1998	6.73	1–3
184.	2009,4213.5	Stylised head of Apollo, left	Stylised horse, left	1991	Area 18	ST/BD	quarter stater	31	Sills 2003 Gallo-Belgic Ab2 Class 3b	1.63	1–3
185.	2009,4213.6	Stylised head of Apollo, right	Stylised horse, right	1991	Area 18	ST/AX	stater	13	Sills 2003 Gallo-Belgic Ca1 Class 3	6.82	4
186.	2009,4213.7	Stylised head of Apollo, right	Stylised horse, right	1991	Area 18	ST/BC	stater	13	Sills 2003 Gallo-Belgic Ca1 Class 4	6.49	4
187.	2009,4213.8	Blank	Abstract design (very heavily worn)	1991	Area 18	ST/BB	quarter stater	–	Gallo-Belgic Ca2[12] Class 3	1.57	4

Hoard P: Catalogue by Philip de Jersey

In the sections which follow, coins from the three groups outlined in the main coins chapter, believed to come from the Bowl Hoard, are listed with their identifications in *Ancient British Coins* (*ABC*) (Cottam *et al.* 2010), CCI numbers and weights (where known). Coins in groups A and C are numbered individually and information sources (generally auction catalogues) given in each case. Coins in group B are simply listed by the number of each type. As noted above, the listings for Hoard P are drawn from those already published as Hoard no. 196.6, in P. de Jersey (2014) *Coin Hoards in Iron Age Britain* (British Numismatic Society Special Publication no. 12). They are reproduced here for completeness, though of course due to its theft and dispersal in the trade, the hoard can never be fully reconstructed. As such the coins are not included in the catalogue numbering for this volume; the item numbers below are from de Jersey 2014.

A) LIKELY GOLD CONTENT

The following figures are based on the records of the CCI and the summary by Chadburn (2006, hoard 41). Although most of the inscribed gold has resurfaced in the trade since the discovery of the hoard, the uninscribed gold is much harder to identify. Many of these coins are undoubtedly recorded in the CCI but scarcely any have a confirmed association with the hoard.

East Anglia, uninscribed gold

6+ Snettisham staters, including:

de Jersey no.	Denom.	*ABC*	CCI number	Wt (g)	Information source
1	stater	1402	05.0041	5.63	NFA MBS 28, 23.4.1992, lot 913
2	stater	1408	97.0445	-	Stacks, NY, 8.12.1993, lot 2043
3	stater	1411	93.0226	5.64	SNC April 1993, no. 1643
4	stater	1411	96.3128	5.68	Dolphin PSL 2, 1992, no. 30
5	stater	1411	97.0444	5.45	NFA MBS 28, 23.4.1992, lot 914
6	stater	1411	08.9533	5.42	Elsen 14.3.1992, lot 25

Some Snettisham quarters, possibly including:

de Jersey no.	Denom.	*ABC*	CCI number	Wt (g)	Information source
7	quarter stater	1462	93.0318	1.51	Rudd 1993 list 8, no. 23
8	quarter stater	1462	94.0585	1.15	Rudd 1994 list 10, no. 13
9	quarter stater	1462	94.0617	1.07	Cummings June 1993, H14
10	quarter stater	1462	94.105	-	BDW 1.6.1994, lot 709
11	quarter stater	1462	96.1185	1.08	Gainor, Toronto, 25.9.1994, lot 2
12	quarter stater	1462	96.3127	1.11	Vecchi 2, 12.9.1996, lot 1086
13	quarter stater	1462	97.0785	-	Galata autumn 1991, no. 198
14	quarter stater	1462	97.0786	-	Galata autumn 1991, no. 203
15	quarter stater	1462	03.115	1.14	NFA MBS 28, 23.4.1992, lot 926
16	quarter stater	1462	04.0688	1.10	Colonial Rare Coins, Nov. 1993, no. 2078
17	quarter stater	1462	10.2355	1.10	NFA MBS 28, 23.4.1992, lot 911
18	quarter stater	1462	10.2482	1.12	Grün 30.10.1992, lot 1
19	quarter stater	1465	91.0311	1.14	Vecchi 2, 12.9.1996, lot 957

47+ Freckenham staters, including:

de Jersey no.	Denom.	*ABC*	CCI number	Wt (g)	Information source
20	stater	Unc.[13]			
21	stater	Unc.			
22	stater	1441	93.0599	5.38	*SNC* Oct. 1993, no. 7011
23	stater (plated)	1441	94.1325	2.86	Private coll.
24	stater	1441	01.0206	5.22	Münzen und Medaillen 566, June 1993, no. 24
25	stater	1441	03.0138	5.39	CNG 11.6.1994, lot 517
26	stater	1444	10.2372	5.33	NFA 28, 23.4.1992, lot 884
27	stater	1447	92.1086	5.37	Rudd 1993 list 7, no. 9
28	stater	1447	93.0114	5.48	*SNC* May 1991, no. 2684

de Jersey no.	Denom.	*ABC*	CCI number	Wt (g)	Information source
29	stater (plated)	1447	93.0299	4.56	Rudd 1993 list 7, no. 10
30	stater	1447	94.0501	-	Private coll.
31	stater	1447	94.1025	5.38	BDW 1.6.1994, lot 680
32	stater	1447	99.0420	-	Dolphin 8, 1995/6, no. 34
33	stater	1447	08.9522	5.33	Kricheldorf 11.3.1992, lot 5
34	stater	1447	08.9523	-	Stacks, NY, 8.12.1993, lot 2041
35	stater	1447	08.9524	5.38	CNG 13.10.1992, lot 515
36	stater	1447	08.9525	-	Linzalone 19/1, spring 1996, no. 57
37	stater	1447	08.9526	-	Glendining 12.10.1992, lot 423
38	stater	1447	08.9527	-	Dolphin 10, winter 1996, no. 7
39	stater	1447	10.2376	-	Dolphin 6, 1995, no. 24
40	stater	1450	93.0190	-	Cummings March 1992, E11
41	stater	1450	93.0700	5.33	Private coll.
42	stater	1450	94.1022	5.37	BDW 1.6.1994, lot 676
43	stater	1450	94.1023	-	BDW 1.6.1994, lot 678
44	stater	1450	96.3043	5.34	Vecchi 2, 12.9.1996, lot 999
45	stater	1450	96.3044	5.35	Vecchi 2, 12.9.1996, lot 1000
46	stater	1450	97.1725	5.35	Glendining 12.10.1992, lot 422
47	stater	1450	99.0666	5.38	Lanz 26.11.1992, lot 19
48	stater	1450	08.8956	5.35	Münzen und Medaillen 547, Sept. 1991, no. 48
49	stater	1450	08.8957	5.38	Grün 9.11.1993, lot 88
50	stater	1450	08.8958	-	Stacks, NY, 8.12.1993, lot 2042
51	stater	1450	08.8959	-	Waddell 52, n.d., no. 1
52	stater	1450	08.8960	5.36	Münzen und Medaillen 554, May 1992, no. 65
53	stater	1450	08.8961	5.36	Kricheldorf 11.3.1992, lot 6
54	stater	1450	08.8963	5.37	Lanz 21.11.1991, lot 8
55	stater	1450	08.8964	-	Dolphin 2, 1992, no. 24
56	stater	1450	08.8965	5.39	Thirion, carnaval 1992, no. 2
57	stater	1450	08.8966	5.41	CNG 13.10.1992, lot 514
58	stater	1450	08.8967	5.35	Waddell 53, n.d., no. 1
59	stater (plated)	1450	10.2378	4.58	NFA 28, 23.4.1992, lot 885

31+ Irstead quarter staters, including:

de Jersey no.	Denom.	*ABC*	CCI number	Wt (g)	Information source
60	quarter stater	1471	93.0191	0.98	Cummings Feb. 1993, E27
61	quarter stater	1471	93.0395	1.04	Cummings June 1993, H23
62	quarter stater	1471	08.8983	1.03	Lanz 21.11.1991, lot 12
63	quarter stater	1471	08.8984	1.11	Münzen und Medaillen 549, Nov./Dec. 1991, no. 134
64	quarter stater	1474	95.0638	1.01	BDW 21.3.1995, lot 429 (ex Pheatt collection, bought 1991)
65	quarter stater	1474	95.3352	1.02	Private coll.
66	quarter stater	1474	95.3353	1.04	Private coll.
67	quarter stater	1474	08.8987	-	Cummings March 1992, E12
68	quarter stater	1474	08.8988	1.1	Christie's 13.10.1992, lot 111
69	quarter stater	1474	08.8989	1.0	Trenerry Nov./Dec. 1991, no. 81
70	quarter stater	1474	08.8990	1.1	Ponterio 20.1.1993, lot 72
71	quarter stater	1474	08.8992	1.04	CNG 13.10.1992, lot 516
72	quarter stater	1474	08.8994	-	Dolphin 2, 1992, no. 28
73	quarter stater	1474	08.8996	1.09	Lanz 21.11.1991, lot 9

de Jersey no.	Denom.	ABC	CCI number	Wt (g)	Information source
74	quarter stater	1474	08.8999	1.0	Berk 4.11.1992, lot 4
75	quarter stater	1474	08.9000	1.0	Berk 4.11.1992, lot 3
76	quarter stater	1474	0 8.9501	1.03	Berk 28.1.1993, lot 2
77	quarter stater	1474	08.9502	1.06	Münzen und Medaillen 549, Nov./Dec. 1991, no. 133
78	quarter stater	1474	08.9503	-	Cummings Sept. 1991, E17
79	quarter stater	1474	10.2341	-	Trenerry Oct. 1991, no. 94
80	quarter stater	1477	08.9518	1.03	Lanz 21.11.1991, lot 11
81	quarter stater	1477	08.9519	1.04	Münzen und M Medaillen 570, Nov./Dec. 1993, no. 211
82	quarter stater	1480	92.0978	1.13	*SNC* Dec. 1992, no. 7360
83	quarter stater	1480	92.1045	1.04	Rudd 1992 list 5, no. 17
84	quarter stater	1480	93.0077	1.10	*SNC* March 1992, no. 841
85	quarter stater	1480	94.0476	1.09	Rudd 1993 list 8, no. 24
86	quarter stater	1480	94.1027	-	BDW 1.6.1994, lot 682
87	quarter stater	1480	08.9506	1.11	Lanz 21.11.1991, lot 10
88	quarter stater	1480	08.9507	1.05	Münzen und Medaillen 547, Sept. 1991, no. 49
89	quarter stater	1480	08.9508	-	Galata autumn 1991, no. 208
90	quarter stater	1480	08.9509	1.05	CNG 2.9.1992, lot 910, 'near Tunbridge Wells' (catalogue note)

North Thames ('Trinovantes'), uninscribed gold[14]

de Jersey no.	Denom.	*ABC*	CCI number	Wt (g)	Information source
91	stater	2338	92.0495	5.91	Rudd 1992 list 5, no. 46
92	stater	2338	92.0671	5.88	Rudd 1993 list 7, no. 39

East Anglia, inscribed gold

18 ANTED(I) staters, including:

de Jersey no.	Denom.	*ABC*	CCI number	Wt (g)	Information source
93	stater	1639	92.0431	5.39	Superior 11.12.1992, lot 2001
94	stater	1639	92.0543	5.40	*SNC* Dec. 1992, no. 7362
95	stater	1639	93.0148	5.34	Ex Stack, lot 136 (Van Arsdell 1992, 80)
96	stater	1639	94.1028	5.40	BDW 1.6.1994, lot 683
97	stater	1639	96.3066	5.37	Vecchi 2, 12.9.1996, lot 1023
98	stater	1639	98.1239	5.36	Valued History 6, Sept. 1997, no. 16
99	stater	1639	99.0667	5.34	NFA MBS 28, 23.4.1992, lot 890
100	stater	1639	99.1877	5.49	Davissons 12, 18.11.1999, lot 567
101	stater	1639	00.1646	5.41	Leu 79, 31.10.2000, lot 12
102	stater	1639	08.8504	5.38	Lanz 21.11.1991, lot 15
103	stater	1639	08.8505	5.39	Münzen und Medaillen 547, Sept. 1991, no. 50
104	stater	1639	08.8508	-	Dolphin 5, 1994, no. 6010
105	stater	1639	08.8802	-	Stacks 8.12.1993, lot 2044

5 ECEN staters:

de Jersey no.	Denom.	*ABC*	CCI number	Wt (g)	Information source
106	stater	1651	92.0610	5.23	Ex Stack, lot 137
107	stater	1651	94.1188	5.37	Private coll.
108	stater	1651	98.0387	5.31	Triton 10.1.2006, lot 665
109	stater	1651	00.0379	5.35	NFA MBS 23.4.1992, lot 891
110	stater	1651	08.8803	-	Stacks 8.12.1993, lot 2045

3 ECE staters:

de Jersey no.	Denom.	*ABC*	CCI number	Wt (g)	Information source
111	stater	1654	92.0611	5.34	Private coll.
112	stater	1654	93.0147	5.35	Leu 79, 31.10.2000, lot 13
113	stater	1654	00.0380	5.36	NFA MBS 23.4.1992, lot 892

North-Eastern, inscribed gold
some VEP CORF staters, including:

de Jersey no.	Denom.	*ABC*	CCI number	Wt (g)	Information source
114	stater	1863	94.1185	4.97	Stacks 8.12.1993, lot 2047
115	stater	1854	94.1185	-	Private coll.

Chadburn (2006) dismissed reports of gold coins of Cunobelin in the hoard, but these rumours persist and seem to have some credibility. One classic type stater (*ABC* 2798, 5.50g) is recorded in the CCI from a usually reliable source (CCI 95.3387). However, it is unclear exactly how many were present, and whether they were predominantly staters or quarter staters.
Total (in CCI): 113 +

B) PARCEL OF 1135 SILVER COINS (CCI 95.1460–2594)[15]
Contents:
East Anglia, uninscribed silver

Number of coins	Denom.	Type	*ABC*	CCI numbers
2	unit	boar/horse A	1576	95.2001–2
11	unit	boar/horse B	1579	95.2003–13
47	unit	boar/horse C	1582	95.2014–60
74	unit	normal face/horse A	1564	95.2061–73, 2075–101, 2103–8, 2110–27, 2129–38
277	unit	normal face/horse B/C	1567	95.2074, 2102, 2109, 2128, 2139–411
12	unit	normal face/horse uncertain	1564/1567	95.2412–23
20	unit	early pattern/horse A	1588	95.1723, 2424–41, 2572
12	unit	early pattern/horse B	1591	95.2442–53
1	half-unit	early pattern/horse	1627	95.2591

East Anglia, inscribed silver

Number of coins	Denom.	Type	*ABC*	CCI numbers
153	unit	ANTED(I)	1642/1645	95.1604–18, 1620–1702, 1890, 1910, 1912, 1950, 1962, 1965, 1990–1, 1996, 2454–86, 2488–91, 2556, 2560–1, 2563–4, 2570, 2573, 2577, 2585
115	unit	ECEN	1657	95.1725, 1739–1819, 1821, 1823, 1825–6, 1831–4, 1843, 1868, 1878, 1881, 1919, 1930, 1953, 1968–9, 1972, 1986–7, 1992–5, 1998–2000, 2487, 2567, 2574, 2578–80
40	unit	ED(N)	1672	95.1619, 1703–21, 2492–511
14	unit	symbol	1678 / 1681	95.1724, 1726–38
146	unit	ECEN/ED(N)		95.1820, 1822, 1824, 1827–30, 1835–42, 1844–67, 1869–77, 1879–80, 1882–9, 1891–903, 1905–9, 1911, 1913–18, 1920–9, 1931–49, 1951–2, 1954–7, 1959–61, 1963–4, 1966–7, 1970–1, 1973–85, 1988, 2512–16
87	unit	ECE A	1660	95.1527–58, 1560–87, 2517–22, 2525–44, 2559

Number of coins	Denom.	Type	ABC	CCI numbers
88	unit	ECE B	1666	95.1460–526, 1559, 1602–3, 1997, 2523–4, 2557–8, 2562, 2565–6, 2568–9, 2571, 2575–6, 2581–2, 2584, 2586–7
25	unit	ECE B reversed	1669	95.1588–601, 2545–55
2	unit	AESV	1702	95.1722, 1904
1	unit	SAENV/ECEN mule[16]		95.1958
5	unit	pattern/horse unclassified		95.1989, 2583, 2588–90
1	half-unit	pattern/horse unclassified		95.2592

North-Eastern silver, uninscribed

Number of coins	Denom.	Type	ABC	CCI numbers
1	half-unit		1833	95.2593

North-Eastern silver, inscribed

Number of coins	Denom.	Type	ABC	CCI numbers
1	half-unit	VEP CORF	1902	95.2594

Total (in CCI): 1135 +

C) OTHER COINS IN THE CCI

East Anglia, uninscribed silver units[17]

de Jersey no.	Denom.	ABC	CCI number	Wt (g)	Information source
1	unit	1522	96.3060	1.15	Vecchi 2, 12.9.1996, lot 1017
2	unit	1522	96.3062	1.56	Vecchi 2, 12.9.1996, lot 1019
3	unit	1522	96.3063	1.10	Vecchi 2, 12.9.1996, lot 1020
4	unit	1522	01.0297	1.10	Private collection
5	unit	1531	97.0840	-	Private coll.ection
6	unit	1537	92.0557	1.20	Rudd 1992 list 3, no. 16
7	unit	1525	92.0486	0.91	Rudd 1992 list 5, no. 21
8	unit	1525	94.0608	1.22	Rudd 1994 list 11, no. 61
9	unit	1525	94.0609	1.38	Rudd 1994 list 11, no. 60
10	unit	1525	94.0610	1.32	Rudd 1994 list 11, no. 59
11	unit	1525	94.0611	1.00	Rudd 1993 list 9, no. 30
12	unit	1525	94.0614	1.47	Rudd 1994 list 13, no. 81
13	unit	1525	96.3049	1.37	Vecchi 2, 12.9.1996, lot 1006
14	unit	1525	96.3050	1.15	Vecchi 2, 12.9.1996, lot 1007
15	unit	1525	96.3051	1.28	Vecchi 2, 12.9.1996, lot 1008
16	unit	1525	96.3054	1.28	Vecchi 2, 12.9.1996, lot 1011
17	unit	1525	96.3056	1.22	Vecchi 2, 12.9.1996, lot 1013
18	unit	1525	96.3057	1.29	Vecchi 2, 12.9.1996, lot 1014
19	unit	1525	96.3058	1.23	Vecchi 2, 12.9.1996, lot 1015
20	unit	1525	96.3059	1.35	Vecchi 2, 12.9.1996, lot 1016
21	unit	1525	96.3061	1.36	Vecchi 2, 12.9.1996, lot 1018
22	unit	1525	97.0841	-	Private collection
23	unit	1525	01.0270	1.20	Private collection
24	unit	1525	01.0289	1.20	Private collection
25	unit (plated)	1525	01.0291	1.60	Private collection
26	unit	1510	96.3052	1.36	Vecchi 2, 12.9.1996, lot 1009
27	unit	1510	96.3053	1.38	Vecchi 2, 12.9.1996, lot 1010
28	unit	1561	96.3055	1.05	Vecchi 2, 12.9.1996, lot 1012
29	unit	1588	92.0334	1.14	Birmingham 1993 C388, ex Finney

de Jersey no.	Denom.	*ABC*	CCi number	Wt (g)	Information source
30	unit	1588	93.0302	1.14	Rudd 1993 list 7, no. 17
31	unit	1588	94.1554	1.18	SNC Dec. 1994, no. 7799
32	unit	1588	96.3065	1.20	Vecchi 2, 12.9.1996, lot 1022
33	unit	1588	97.0842	-	Private coll.
34	unit	1588	97.0843	-	Private coll.
35	unit	1591	95.1114	1.18	Private coll.
36	unit	1591	96.3064	1.13	Vecchi 2, 12.9.1996, lot 1021
37	unit	1591	97.0844	-	Private coll.
38	unit	1591	97.0845	-	Private coll.
39	unit	1591	09.4551	-	Berk 75, 28.1.1993, lot 64
40	unit	1591	09.4552	-	Berk 75, 28.1.1993, lot 65
41	unit	1591	09.4554	-	Berk 76, 21.4.1993, lot 132
42	unit	1591	09.4561	1.2	Berk 4.11.1992, lot 56
43	unit	1591	09.4562	-	Berk 4.8.1992, lot 63
44	unit	1591	09.4563	-	Berk 4.8.1992, lot 62
45	unit	1591	09.4566	-	CNA 14, 20.3.1991, lot 1259
46	unit	1591	09.4567	-	Cummings summer 1992, E14
47	unit	1591	09.5206	-	Trenerry summer 1991, no. 99
48	unit	1591	09.5207	-	Trenerry Feb./March 1992, no. 82
49	unit	1591	09.5208	-	Trenerry Xmas 1991, no. 93
50	unit	1591	09.5209	-	Trenerry Nov./Dec. 1991, no. 86
51	unit	1591	09.5299	-	Pegasi 78, 1993, no. 250
52	unit	1573	94.0533	1.13	Rudd 1993 list 9, no. 33
53	unit	1573	09.4571	-	Goodwin 86, summer 1991, no. 6
54	unit	1576	95.3359	1.07	Private coll.
55	unit	1576	95.3381	1.08	Private coll.
56	unit	1576	97.0846	-	Private coll.
57	unit	1579	94.0055	1.21	Private coll.
58	unit	1579	95.3358	1.17	Private coll.
59	unit	1579	95.3380	0.80	Private coll.
60	unit	1579	97.0847	-	Private coll.
61	unit	1579	97.0848	-	Private coll.
62	unit	1579	97.0849	-	Private coll.
63	unit	1579	97.0850	-	Private coll.
64	unit	1579	09.4581	-	Berk 75, 28.1.1993, lot 61
65	unit	1579	09.4586	-	Cummings March 1992, E14
66	unit	1582	94.0056	1.18	Private coll.
67	unit	1582	94.0057	1.20	Private coll.
68	unit	1582	94.0058	1.06	Private coll.
69	unit	1582	94.0481	-	Rudd (not in lists)
70	unit	1582	94.0511	-	Rudd (not in lists)
71	unit	1582	94.0512	1.15	Rudd 1994 list 10, no. 15
72	unit	1582	94.0513	-	Rudd (not in lists)
73	unit	1582	94.0514	1.16	Rudd 1993 list 9, no. 34
74	unit	1582	95.1112	1.20	Private coll.
75	unit	1582	95.3360	1.22	Private coll.
76	unit	1582	96.3047	0.99	Vecchi 2, 12.9.1996, lot 1004
77	unit	1582	97.0851	-	Private coll.
78	unit	1582	97.0852	-	Private coll.
79	unit	1582	97.0853	-	Private coll.
80	unit	1582	97.0854	-	Private coll.

de Jersey no.	Denom.	*ABC*	CCI number	Wt (g)	Information source
81	unit	1582	03.0360	1.22	Rudd 2003 Liz's list 5, no. 31
82	unit	1582	09.4591	-	Dolphin 2, 1992, no. 37
83	unit	1582	09.4592	-	Cummings Sept. 1991, E20
84	unit	1582	09.4595	-	Berk 75, 28.1.1993, lot 63
85	unit	1582	09.4596	=	Berk 75, 28.1.1993, lot 62
86	unit	1582	09.4598	0.93	NFA MBS 28, 23.4.1992, lot 887
87	unit	1582	09.4606	-	CNA 14, 20.3.1991, lot 1258
88	unit	1582	09.4608	1.20	Thirion autumn 1992, no. 3
89	unit	1582	09.5220	-	Trenerry Oct./Nov. 1992, no. 83
90	unit	1582	09.5221	-	Trenerry Oct. 1991, no. 96
91	unit	1582	09.5222	-	Trenerry Feb./March 1993, no. 64
92	unit	1582	09.5223		Trenerry summer 1993, no. 64
93	unit	1582	09.5224	-	Trenerry June 1993, no. 88
94	unit	1582	09.5226	-	Trenerry Xmas 1991, no. 86
95	unit	1582	09.5231	-	Trenerry March/April 1992, no. 97
96	unit	1582	09.5232	-	Trenerry Feb./March 1992, no. 77
97	unit	1582	09.5316	-	Stacks 8.12.1993, lot 2053
98	unit	1564	94.0515	1.18	Rudd 1993 list 9, no. 47
99	unit	1564	94.0518	-	Rudd 1994 list 10, no. 27
100	unit	1564	95.3361	1.20	Private coll.
101	unit	1564	95.3362	1.17	Private coll.
102	unit	1564	97.0856	-	Private coll.
103	unit	1567	94.0516	1.17	Rudd 1993 list 9, no. 46
104	unit	1567	94.0555	-	Rudd (not in lists)
105	unit	1567	94.0556	1.22	Rudd 1994 list 10, no. 26
106	unit	1567	94.0763	1.28	Rudd 1995 list 15, no. 29
107	unit	1567	95.0701	1.29	Private coll.
108	unit	1567	96.3087	1.27	Vecchi 2, 12.9.1996, lot 1044
109	unit	1567	96.3088	1.21	Vecchi 2, 12.9.1996, lot 1045
110	unit	1567	96.3089	1.25	Vecchi 2, 12.9.1996, lot 1046
111	unit	1567	97.0857	-	Private coll.
112	unit	1567	03.0251	1.25	Rudd 2003 list 69, no. 29
113	unit	1567	03.0642	1.28	Rudd 2003 list 72, no. 42

East Anglia, uninscribed silver half-units

de Jersey no.	Denom.	*ABC*	CCI number	Wt (g)	Information source
114	half-unit	Unc. boar/horse	93.0987	0.36	Birmingham 1993 C406, ex Finney
115	half-unit	1621	96.3106	0.62	Vecchi 2, 12.9.1996, lot 1064

East Anglia, silver units inscribed CAN DVRO

de Jersey no.	Denom.	*ABC*	CCI number	Wt (g)	Information source
116	unit	1630	94.0482	1.23	Rudd 1993 list 8, no. 26 (wrong rev. photo)
117	unit	1630	94.0525	1.16	Rudd 1993 list 9, no. 35
118	unit	1630	94.0545	-	Ritter 33, Dec. 1992, no. 304
119	unit	1630	95.1165	1.21	Private coll.
120	unit	1630	96.3048	1.20	Vecchi 2, 12.9.1996, lot 1005
121	unit	1630	97.0855	-	Private coll.
122	unit	1630	09.4618	-	Dolphin 2, 1992, no. 39
123	unit	1630	09.4622	1.24	CNA 25.3.1992, lot 1163
124	unit	1630	09.4623	-	Dolphin 5, 1994, no. 6028

East Anglia, silver units inscribed ANTED(I)

de Jersey no.	Denom.	*ABC*	CCI number	Wt (g)	Information source
125	unit	1642/1645	93.0400	1.01	Cummings June 1993, H29
126	unit	1642/1645	93.0668	1.15	Private coll.
127	unit	1642/1645	95.3403	1.10	Private coll.
128	unit	1642/1645	96.1202	1.17	Private coll.
129	unit	1642/1645	96.1210	1.13	Private coll.
130	unit	1642/1645	96.1211	1.25	Private coll.
131	unit	1642/1645	96.1213	1.19	Private coll.
132	unit	1642/1645	96.1221	1.20	Private coll.
133	unit	1642/1645	96.1228	1.25	Private coll.
134	unit	1642/1645	96.1229	1.14	Private coll.
135	unit	1642/1645	96.1230	1.17	Private coll.
136	unit	1642/1645	96.1231	1.29	Private coll.
137	unit	1642/1645	96.3067	1.22	Vecchi 2, 12.9.1996, lot 1024
138	unit	1642/1645	96.3068	1.16	Vecchi 2, 12.9.1996, lot 1025
139	unit	1642/1645	97.0858	-	Private coll.
140	unit	1642/1645	97.0859	-	Private coll.
141	unit	1642/1645	97.0860	-	Private coll.
142	unit	1642/1645	97.0861	-	Private coll.
143	unit	1642/1645	97.0862	-	Private coll.
144	unit	1642/1645	97.0863	-	Private coll.
145	unit	1642/1645	97.0864	-	Private coll.
146	unit	1642/1645	97.0884	-	Private coll.
147	unit	1642/1645	97.0887	-	Private coll.
148	unit	1642/1645	98.1382	1.18	Rudd 1998 list 36, no. 16
149	unit	1642/1645	98.1383	1.21	Rudd 1998 list 36, no. 17
150	unit	1642/1645	04.2407	1.20	Rudd 2004 Liz's list 14, no. 33

East Anglia, silver units inscribed ECEN

de Jersey no.	Denom.	*ABC*	CCI number	Wt (g)	Information source
151	unit	1657	93.0615	1.25	Private coll.
152	unit	1657	93.0677	1.23	Private coll.
153	unit	1657	94.0529	-	Rudd 1993 list 9, no. 39
154	unit	1657	94.0543	-	Rudd 1993 list 9, no. 38
155	unit	1657	94.0544	1.25	Rudd 1994 list 10, no. 19
156	unit	1657	94.0586	-	Rudd 1994 list 10, no. 20
157	unit	1657	96.1204	1.21	Private coll.
158	unit	1657	96.1205	1.18	Private coll.
159	unit	1657	96.1208	1.14	Private coll.
160	unit	1657	96.1215	1.29	Private coll.
161	unit	1657	96.1218	1.26	Private coll.
162	unit	1657	96.1225	1.12	Private coll.
163	unit	1657	96.3069	1.20	Vecchi 2, 12.9.1996, lot 1026
164	unit	1657	96.3070	1.14	Vecchi 2, 12.9.1996, lot 1027
165	unit	1657	96.3071	1.24	Vecchi 2, 12.9.1996, lot 1028
166	unit	1657	97.0865	-	Private coll.
167	unit	1657	97.0866	-	Private coll.
168	unit	1657	97.0867	-	Private coll.
169	unit	1657	97.0885	-	Private coll.
170	unit	1657	97.0886	-	Private coll.
171	unit	1657	98.1384	1.25	Rudd 1998 list 36, no. 19

de Jersey no.	Denom.	*ABC*	CCI number	Wt (g)	Information source
172	unit	1657	98.1385	1.16	Rudd 1998 list 36, no. 18
173	unit	1657	98.1390	1.26	Rudd 1998 list 36, no. 24
174	unit	1657	02.0088	1.25	Rudd 2002 list 62, no. 42

East Anglia, silver units inscribed ED(N)

de Jersey no.	Denom.	*ABC*	CCI number	Wt (g)	Information source
175	unit	1672/1675	94.0538	1.25	Rudd 1994 list 10, no. 21
176	unit	1672/1675	94.0549	1.25	Rudd 1993 list 9, no. 43
177	unit	1672/1675	94.0551	1.26	Rudd 1995 list 15, no. 55
178	unit	1672/1675	94.0552	1.27	Rudd 1994 list 13, no. 43
179	unit	1672/1675	94.0553	-	Rudd 1994 list 10, no. 23
180	unit	1672/1675	94.0554	1.21	Rudd 1994 list 10, no. 24
181	unit	1672/1675	96.1203	1.23	Private coll.
182	unit	1672/1675	96.1207	1.27	Private coll.
183	unit	1672/1675	96.1217	1.27	Private coll.
184	unit	1672/1675	96.1224	1.26	Private coll.
185	unit	1672/1675	98.1386	1.23	Rudd 1998 list 36, no. 20
186	unit	1672/1675	99.1591	1.24	Rudd 1999 list 47, no. 60

East Anglia, symbol type inscribed silver units

de Jersey no.	Denom.	*ABC*	CCI number	Wt (g)	Information source
187	unit	1678/1681	96.1227	1.18	Private coll.
188	unit	1678/1681	96.3074	0.77	Vecchi 2, 12.9.1996, lot 1031
189	unit	1678/1681	97.0874	-	Private coll.
190	unit	1678/1681	97.0875	-	Private coll.

East Anglia, silver units inscribed ECEN *or* ED(N)

de Jersey no.	Denom.	*ABC*	CCI number	Wt (g)	Information source
191	unit		94.0541	1.28	Rudd 1993 list 9, no. 37
192	unit		96.3073	1.27	Vecchi 2, 12.9.1996, lot 1030
193	unit		97.0871	-	Private coll.
194	unit		97.0872	-	Private coll.
195	unit		97.0873	-	Private coll.
196	unit		98.1387	1.21	Rudd 1998 list 36, no. 21

East Anglia, silver units inscribed ECE

de Jersey no.	Denom.	*ABC*	CCI number	Wt (g)	Information source
197	unit	1660	93.0678	1.26	Private coll.
198	unit	1660	93.1000	1.25	Birmingham, ex Finney, ex Dolphin
199	unit	1660	94.0540	1.21	Rudd 1993 list 9, no. 41
200	unit	1660	96.1206	1.15	Private coll.
201	unit	1660	96.1209	1.26	Private coll.
202	unit	1660	96.1226	1.26	Private coll.
203	unit	1660	96.3075	1.18	Vecchi 2, 12.9.1996, lot 1032
204	unit	1660	96.3076	1.20	Vecchi 2, 12.9.1996, lot 1033
205	unit	1660	96.3077	1.22	Vecchi 2, 12.9.1996, lot 1034
206	unit	1660	96.3078	1.22	Vecchi 2, 12.9.1996, lot 1035
207	unit	1660	97.0876	-	Private coll.
208	unit	1660	97.0877	-	Private coll.
209	unit	1660	01.0528	1.17	Rudd 2001 list 57, no. 64
210	unit	1660	01.1471	1.22	Rudd 2001 list 60, no. 47

de Jersey no.	Denom.	*ABC*	CCI number	Wt (g)	Information source
211	unit	1663/1666	93.0669	1.01	Private coll.
212	unit	1663/1666	94.0483	-	Rudd (not in lists)
213	unit	1663/1666	94.0539	1.18	Rudd 1993 list 9, no. 42
214	unit	1663/1666	94.0542	-	Rudd (not in lists)
215	unit	1663/1666	96.1212	1.27	Private coll.
216	unit	1663/1666	96.1214	1.22	Private coll.
217	unit	1663/1666	96.1216	1.21	Private coll.
218	unit	1663/1666	96.1219	1.26	Private coll.
219	unit	1663/1666	96.1220	1.23	Private coll.
220	unit	1663/1666	96.3072	1.46	Vecchi 2, 12.9.1996, lot 1029
221	unit	1663/1666	96.3079	1.24	Vecchi 2, 12.9.1996, lot 1036
222	unit	1663/1666	96.3080	1.20	Vecchi 2, 12.9.1996, lot 1037
223	unit	1663/1666	96.3081	1.27	Vecchi 2, 12.9.1996, lot 1038
224	unit	1663/1666	96.3082	1.23	Vecchi 2, 12.9.1996, lot 1039
225	unit	1663/1666	96.3083	1.24	Vecchi 2, 12.9.1996, lot 1040
226	unit	1663/1666	97.0878	-	Private coll.
227	unit	1663/1666	97.0879	-	Private coll.
228	unit	1663/1666	97.0880	-	Private coll.
229	unit	1663/1666	97.0881	-	Private coll.
230	unit	1663/1666	03.0173	1.23	Rudd 2003 Liz's list 4, no. 32
231	unit	1663/1666	03.0916	1.26	Rudd 2004 Liz's list 9, no. 34
232	unit	1663/1666	06.0566	1.25	Rudd 2007 list 91, no. 101
233	unit	1669	93.0679	1.19	Private coll.
234	unit	1669	94.0537	1.25	Rudd 1998 list 36, no. 25
235	unit	1669	96.1222	1.24	Private coll.
236	unit	1669	96.1223	1.21	Private coll.
237	unit	1669	96.3084	1.23	Vecchi 2, 12.9.1996, lot 1041

East Anglia, silver units inscribed SAENV

de Jersey no.	Denom.	*ABC*	CCI number	Wt (g)	Information source
238	unit	1699	93.0194	1.24	Cummings Feb. 1993, E32
239	unit	1699	95.1113	1.20	Private coll.
240	unit	1699	96.3085	1.10	Vecchi 2, 12.9.1996, lot 1042
241	unit	1699	97.0882	-	Private coll.
242	unit	1699	01.0268	1.20	Private coll.
243	unit	1699	01.0269	1.20	Private coll.
244	unit	1699	01.0529	1.24	Rudd 2001 list 57, no. 65

East Anglia, silver units inscribed AESV

de Jersey no.	Denom.	*ABC*	CCI number	Wt (g)	Information source
245	unit	1702	93.0193	1.21	Rudd 1993 list 9, no. 45
246	unit	1702	94.0532	-	Rudd (not in lists)
247	unit	1702	95.3363	1.26	Private coll.
248	unit	1702	95.3364	1.19	Private coll.
249	unit	1702	96.3086	1.31	Vecchi 2, 12.9.1996, lot 1043
250	unit	1702	05.0719	1.24	Rudd 2005 Liz's list 20, no. 35

East Anglia, uncertain pattern/horse silver units

de Jersey no.	Denom.	*ABC*	CCI number	Wt (g)	Information source
251	unit		95.1145	1.38	Private coll.
252	unit		97.0883	-	Private coll.

East Anglia, silver half-units inscribed ECEN, ECE *or* ED(N)[18]

de Jersey no.	Denom.	*ABC*	CCI number	Wt (g)	Information source
253	half-unit	1684–1693	93.0398	0.49	Cummings June 1993, H26
254	half-unit	1684–1693	93.0998	0.47	Birmingham 1993 C417, ex Finney
255	half-unit	1684–1693	93.0999	0.57	Birmingham 1993 C418, ex Finney
256	half-unit	1684–1693	94.0156	0.50	Private coll.
257	half-unit	1684–1693	94.0157	0.43	King's Lynn Museum
258	half-unit	1684–1693	94.0535	0.49	Rudd 1994 list 10, no. 25
259	half-unit	1684–1693	94.0536	0.47	Rudd 1998 list 33, no. 19
260	half-unit	1684–1693	95.1115	0.49	Private coll.
261	half-unit	1684–1693	95.1146	0.54	Private coll.
262	half-unit	1684–1693	95.3382	0.46	Private coll.
263	half-unit	1684–1693	97.0868	-	Private coll.
264	half-unit	1684–1693	97.0869	-	Private coll.
265	half-unit	1684–1693	97.0870	-	Private coll.
266	half-unit	1696	93.0996	0.54	Birmingham, ex Finney, ex Dolphin

North-Eastern, uninscribed silver units[19]

de Jersey no.	Denom.	*ABC*	CCI number	Wt (g)	Information source
267	unit	1779 or 1782	95.3355	1.20	Private coll.
268	unit	1779 or 1782	96.1284	0.77	Private coll.
269	unit	1779 or 1782	96.1286	1.04	Private coll.
270	unit	1779 or 1782	96.1287	0.94	Private coll.
271	unit	1779 or 1782	96.1288	1.12	Private coll.
272	unit	1779 or 1782	96.1289	1.31	Private coll.
273	unit	1779 or 1782	96.1291	1.09	Private coll.
274	unit	1779 or 1782	96.3092	1.45	Vecchi 2, 12.9.1996, lot 1050
275	unit	1779 or 1782	96.3093	1.49	Vecchi 2, 12.9.1996, lot 1051
276	unit	1779 or 1782	96.3094	1.05	Vecchi 2, 12.9.1996, lot 1052
277	unit	1779 or 1782	96.3095	0.72	Vecchi 2, 12.9.1996, lot 1053
278	unit	1779 or 1782	96.3096	1.18	Vecchi 2, 12.9.1996, lot 1054
279	unit	1779 or 1782	96.3098	1.31	Vecchi 2, 12.9.1996, lot 1056
280	unit	1779 or 1782	96.3100	0.95	Vecchi 2, 12.9.1996, lot 1058
281	unit	1779 or 1782	96.3101	1.00	Vecchi 2, 12.9.1996, lot 1059
282	unit	1779 or 1782	96.3105	1.26	Vecchi 2, 12.9.1996, lot 1063
283	unit	1785	96.3104	1.01	Vecchi 2, 12.9.1996, lot 1062
284	unit	1788	96.3102	1.44	Vecchi 2, 12.9.1996, lot 1060
285	unit	1791	96.3103	1.46	Vecchi 2, 12.9.1996, lot 1061
286	unit	1797	96.1285	1.60	Private coll.
287	unit	1797	96.1290	1.32	Private coll.
288	unit	1797	96.1292	1.40	Private coll.
289	unit	1797	96.1293	1.46	Private coll.
290	unit	1797	96.3097	0.95	Vecchi 2, 12.9.1996, lot 1055
291	unit	1797	96.3099	1.25	Vecchi 2, 12.9.1996, lot 1057
292	unit	1806	00.0195	1.08	Private coll.

North-Eastern, uninscribed silver half-units

de Jersey no.	Denom.	*ABC*	CCI number	Wt (g)	Information source
293	half-unit	1833	00.0159	0.39	Private coll.
294	half-unit	1833	07.0355	0.54	Private coll.

North-Eastern, silver units inscribed VEP, VEP CORF *or similar*

de Jersey no.	Denom.	*ABC*	CCI number	Wt (g)	Information source
295	unit	1866–1884	95.1116	1.01	Private coll.
296	unit	1866–1884	96.3111	1.25	Vecchi 2, 12.9.1996, lot 1070
297	unit	1866–1884	96.3112	1.27	Vecchi 2, 12.9.1996, lot 1071
298	unit	1866–1884	07.0254	1.36	Private coll.
299	unit	1866–1884	07.0255	0.87	Private coll.
300	unit	1866–1884	07.0260	1.02	Private coll.
301	unit	1866–1884	07.0261	0.96	Private coll.
302	unit	1866–1884	07.0262	1.00	Private coll.
303	unit	1866–1884	07.0266	1.24	Private coll.
304	unit	1866–1884	07.0270	1.16	Private coll.
305	unit	1866–1884	07.0295	1.29	Private coll.

North-Eastern, silver half-units inscribed VEP, VEP CORF *or similar*

de Jersey no.	Denom.	*ABC*	CCI number	Wt (g)	Information source
306	half-unit	1887–1908	95.1117	0.54	Private coll.
307	half-unit	1887–1908	96.3113	0.53	Vecchi 2, 12.9.1996, lot 1072
308	half-unit	1887–1908	96.3115	0.52	Vecchi 2, 12.9.1996, lot 1074
309	half-unit	1887–1908	00.0125	0.54	Private coll.
310	half-unit	1887–1908	07.0252	0.44	Private coll.
311	half-unit	1887–1908	07.0253	0.50	Private coll.
312	half-unit	1887–1908	07.0256	0.56	Private coll.
313	half-unit	1887–1908	07.0257	0.56	Private coll.
314	half-unit	1887–1908	07.0258	0.48	Private coll.
315	half-unit	1887–1908	07.0259	0.56	Private coll.
316	half-unit	1887–1908	07.0263	0.53	Private coll.
317	half-unit	1887–1908	07.0264	0.52	Private coll.
318	half-unit	1887–1908	07.0265	0.53	Private coll.
319	half-unit	1887–1908	07.0267	0.54	Private coll.
320	half-unit	1887–1908	07.0268	0.43	Private coll.
321	half-unit	1887–1908	07.0269	0.53	Private coll.
322	half-unit	1887–1908	07.0271	0.50	Private coll.
323	half-unit	1887–1908	07.0272	0.49	Private coll.
324	half-unit	1887–1908	07.0273	0.43	Private coll.
325	half-unit	1887–1908	07.0274	0.55	Private coll.
326	half-unit	1887–1908	07.0275	0.52	Private coll.
327	half-unit	1887–1908	07.0276	0.47	Private coll.
328	half-unit	1887–1908	07.0277	0.44	Private coll.
329	half-unit	1887–1908	07.0278	0.43	Private coll.
330	half-unit	1887–1908	07.0279	0.51	Private coll.
331	half-unit	1887–1908	07.0280	0.53	Private coll.
332	half-unit	1887–1908	07.0281	0.38	Private coll.
333	half-unit	1887–1908	07.0282	0.52	Private coll.
334	half-unit	1887–1908	07.0283	0.51	Private coll.
335	half-unit	1887–1908	07.0284	0.51	Private coll.
336	half-unit	1887–1908	07.0285	0.53	Private coll.
337	half-unit	1887–1908	07.0286	0.54	Private coll.
338	half-unit	1887–1908	07.0287	0.47	Private coll.
339	half-unit	1887–1908	07.0288	0.49	Private coll.
340	half-unit	1887–1908	07.0289	0.54	Private coll.
341	half-unit	1887–1908	07.0290	0.55	Private coll.

de Jersey no.	Denom.	*ABC*	CCI number	Wt (g)	Information source
342	half-unit	1887–1908	07.0291	0.50	Private coll.
343	half-unit	1887–1908	07.0292	0.42	Private coll.
344	half-unit	1887–1908	07.0293	0.54	Private coll.
345	half-unit	1887–1908	07.0294	0.37	Private coll.
346	half-unit	1887–1908	07.0296	0.47	Private coll.
347	half-unit	1887–1908	07.0297	0.48	Private coll.
348	half-unit	1887–1908	07.0298	0.43	Private coll.
349	half-unit	1887–1908	07.0299	0.50	Private coll.
350	half-unit	1887–1908	07.0300	0.59	Private coll.
351	half-unit	1887–1908	07.0301	0.38	Private coll.
352	half-unit	1887–1908	07.0302	0.52	Private coll.
353	half-unit	1887–1908	07.0303	0.45	Private coll.
354	half-unit	1887–1908	07.0304	0.51	Private coll.
355	half-unit	1887–1908	07.0305	0.53	Private coll.
356	half-unit	1887–1908	07.0306	0.48	Private coll.
357	half-unit	1887–1908	07.0307	0.49	Private coll.
358	half-unit	1887–1908	07.0308	0.50	Private coll.
359	half-unit	1887–1908	07.0309	0.39	Private coll.
360	half-unit	1887–1908	07.0310	0.55	Private coll.
361	half-unit	1887–1908	07.0311	0.57	Private coll.
362	half-unit	1887–1908	07.0312	0.53	Private coll.
363	half-unit	1887–1908	07.0313	0.52	Private coll.
364	half-unit	1887–1908	07.0314	0.50	Private coll.
365	half-unit	1887–1908	07.0315	0.42	Private coll.
366	half-unit	1887–1908	07.0316	0.57	Private coll.
367	half-unit	1887–1908	07.0317	0.53	Private coll.
368	half-unit	1887–1908	07.0318	0.50	Private coll.
369	half-unit	1887–1908	07.0319	0.58	Private coll.
370	half-unit	1887–1908	07.0320	0.51	Private coll.
371	half-unit	1887–1908	07.0321	0.60	Private coll.
372	half-unit	1887–1908	07.0322	0.58	Private coll.
373	half-unit	1887–1908	07.0323	0.54	Private coll.
374	half-unit	1887–1908	07.0324	0.46	Private coll.
375	half-unit	1887–1908	07.0325	0.55	Private coll.
376	half-unit	1887–1908	07.0326	0.52	Private coll.
377	half-unit	1887–1908	07.0327	0.52	Private coll.
378	half-unit	1887–1908	07.2302	-	Cummings summer 1992, E25
379	half-unit	1887–1908	07.2305	0.43	In trade (Gillis)
380	half-unit	1887–1908	07.2308	-	Trennery Xmas 1991, no. 105

North-Eastern, silver minims inscribed VEP CO

de Jersey no.	Denom.	*ABC*	CCI number	Wt (g)	Information source
381	minim	1914	93.0097	0.35	Private collection
382	minim	1914	93.0098	0.30	Private collection
383	minim	1914	93.0099	0.26	Private collection
384	minim	1914	94.0223	0.28	Private collection
385	minim	1914	96.3114	0.26	Vecchi 2, 12.9.1996, lot 1073

North-Eastern, silver units inscribed IISVP RASV

de Jersey no.	Denom.	*ABC*	CCI number	Wt (g)	Information source
386	unit	1920	96.3110	1.32	Vecchi 2, 12.9.1996, lot 1069
387	unit	1920	02.1177	1.32	BMC 3273
388	unit	1920	07.0245	1.07	Private coll.
389	unit	1920	07.0246	1.17	Private coll.
390	unit	1920	07.0247	1.35	Private coll.
391	unit	1920	07.0248	1.32	Private coll.
392	unit	1920	07.0249	1.29	Private coll.

North-Eastern, silver units inscribed AVN COST

de Jersey no.	Denom.	*ABC*	CCI number	Wt (g)	Information source
393	unit	1935–1941	93.0977	1.22	Cummings Xmas 1993, H48
394	unit	1935–1941	95.3354	1.15	Private coll.
395	unit	1935–1941	95.3356	1.30	Private coll.
396	unit	1935–1941	95.3357	1.04	Private coll.
397	unit	1935–1941	96.3108	1.16	Vecchi 2, 12.9.1996, lot 1066
398	unit	1935–1941	99.0874	1.12	Rudd 1999 list 46, no. 34
399	unit	1935–1941	99.1257	1.24	Rudd 1999 list 47, no. 46
400	unit	1935–1941	07.0214	1.08	Private coll.
401	unit	1935–1941	07.0215	0.98	Private coll.
402	unit	1935–1941	07.0216	0.93	Private coll.
403	unit	1935–1941	07.0217	1.28	Private coll.
404	unit	1935–1941	07.0218	1.31	Private coll.
405	unit	1935–1941	07.0219	1.28	Private coll.
406	unit	1935–1941	07.0220	-	Private coll.
407	unit	1935–1941	07.0221	0.87	Private coll.
408	unit	1935–1941	07.0222	1.00	Private coll.
409	unit	1935–1941	07.0223	1.20	Private coll.
410	unit	1950	92.0612	1.28	Private coll.

North-Eastern, silver half-units inscribed AVN COST

de Jersey no.	Denom.	*ABC*	CCI number	Wt (g)	Information source
411	half-unit	1953	96.3109	0.46	Vecchi 2, 12.9.1996, lot 1067
412	half-unit	1953	07.0235	0.52	Private coll.
413	half-unit	1953	07.0236	0.57	Private coll.
414	half-unit	1953	07.0237	0.49	Private coll.
415	half-unit	1953	07.0238	0.48	Private coll.
416	half-unit	1953	07.0239	0.58	Private coll.
417	half-unit	1953	07.0240	0.53	Private coll.
418	half-unit	1953	07.0241	0.53	Private coll.
419	half-unit	1953	07.0242	0.58	Private coll.
420	half-unit	1953	07.0243	0.54	Private coll.
421	half-unit	1953	07.0244	0.22	Private coll.

North-Eastern, silver unit inscribed LAT ISON

de Jersey no.	Denom.	ABC	CCI number	Wt (g)	Information source
422	unit	1959	07.0250	1.26	Private coll.

North-Eastern, silver half-unit inscribed LAT ISON

de Jersey no.	Denom.	*ABC*	CCI number	Wt (g)	Information source
423	half-unit	1968	07.0251	0.52	Private coll.

North Thames, uninscribed silver unit

de Jersey no.	Denom.	*ABC*	CCI number	Wt (g)	Information source
424	unit	2481	95.1148	1.36	Private coll.

Uncertain Iron Age silver fraction

de Jersey no.	Denom.	ABC	CCI number	Wt (g)	Information source
425	fraction		95.1147	0.07	Private coll.

Total: 425 +

Part 2 OTHER IRON AGE COINS FROM THE SITE (all unstratified topsoil/subsoil contexts unless stated): *Catalogue by Eleanor Ghey (NB catalogue numbering resumes from here)*

Greek coins: Cat. nos 188–95

Cat. no.	Museum	Reg. no.	Obverse	Reverse	Disc.	Area	Site code	Denom. / Mint	*ABC*	Other refs	Wt (g)	Date
188.	NCM	2005.1	Female head, left	Horse right, palm behind; before, three pellets above and one below	MD 2003–9	Woodland	N/A	Bronze / Carthage	N/A	*SNG* Copenhagen 118; Alexandropoulos 2007, 367, no. 18m	2.26	*c.* 400–350 BC
189.	NCM	2007.1	Female head, left	Horse right, palm behind	MD 2003–9	Woodland	N/A	Bronze / Carthage	N/A	Cf. Alexandropoulos 2007, 366, no. 18	2.32	*c.* 400–350 BC
190.	NCM	2005.2	Head of Apollo, laureate, left	[...] (in ex.) Bull, butting, right	MD 2003–9	Woodland	N/A	Bronze / Massalia	N/A	Cf. Feugère and Py 2011, 110ff, series MBM-28 or 33	5.43 (18mm diam.)	*c.* late 3rd to early 2nd century BC
191.	NCM	2007.3	Head, left	Bull, butting right?	MD 2003–9	Woodland	N/A	Bronze / probably Massalia or imitation	N/A	As above	4.82 (14mm diam.)	*c.* late 3rd to early 2nd century BC
192.	NCM	2003.5	Head, left	Bull butting right	MD 2003–9	Woodland	N/A	Bronze / probably Massalia or imitation[20]	N/A	As above	5.48	*c.* late 3rd to early 2nd century BC
193.	NCM	2003.6	Head, left	Bull butting right	MD 2003–9	Woodland	N/A	Bronze / probably Massalia or imitation	N/A	As above	5.67	*c.* late 3rd to early 2nd century BC
194.	NCM	2003.7	Head, left	Bull butting right	MD 2003–9	Woodland	N/A	Bronze / probably Massalia or imitation	N/A	As above	6.17	*c.* late 3rd to early 2nd century BC
195.	NCM	2007.2	Head of Apollo, right	Lion, right, looking back. Star above. ΚΛΕΙΣΙΠΠ in exergue. Monogram / N in right field	MD 2003–9	Woodland	N/A	Hemiobol / Miletos, magistrate 'Kleisipp[...]'[21]	N/A	Cf. Marcellesi 2004 9, p.173 or 35, p.179 for type	4.61	*c.* late 3rd to 2nd century BC

Imported continental Iron Age coinage

Gaul (Normandy) (Cat. nos 196–7)

Cat. no.	Museum	Reg. no.	Obverse	Reverse	Disc.	Area	Site code	Denom.	*ABC*	Other refs	Wt (g)	Period
196.	NCM	2007.4	Head, right, scroll below neck	Horse (and rider?), left	MD 2003–9	Woodland	N/A	stater (plated)	N/A	Uncertain, probably Normandy, cf. DT II series 242	5.09	1–2
197.	BM	1991,0904.13	Stylised head, right	Horse and charioteer, right; wheel below	MD 1990	Area 10	N/A (Jackson no. 523)	half stater (plated)	N/A	Sills 2003, 377; BN 10198 type; cf. DT I 101 type	2.44	1–2

Gallo-Belgic (Cat. nos 198–212)

Cat. no.	Museum	Reg. no.	Obverse	Reverse	Disc.	Area	Site code	Denom.	ABC	Other refs	Wt (g)	Period
198.	BM	1992,0803.1	Laureate head of Apollo, left	Horse, left	MD 1990–1	Area 27	N/A	stater	4	Sills 2003 Gallo-Belgic Ab Class 7[22]	6.86	1–2
199.	BM	1992,0803.2	Laureate head of Apollo, right	Horse, right	MD 1990–1	Area 26	N/A	quarter stater	28	Sills 2003 Gallo-Belgic Aa Class 4	1.73	1–2
200.	BM	1991,1017.3	Stylised head of Apollo, right	Stylised horse, right	MD 1990	Area 13	SN/RA	stater	13	Sills 2003 Gallo-Belgic Ca1 Class 3; CCI 99.1997	6.59	4
201.	BM	2009,4213.19	Stylised head of Apollo, right	Stylised horse, right	MD 1990–1	Area 9	N/A	stater (plated – core only)	Cf 13	Gallo-Belgic C	2.03	4
202.	BM	2009,4213.24	Illegible	Stylised horse, right	MD 1990–1	Area 23	N/A	stater (plated – core only)	Cf 16	Gallo-Belgic E	2.22	5
203.	BM	2009,4213.27	Die obliterated	Stylised horse, right	MD 1990–1	Area 14	N/A	stater (plated)	16	Gallo-Belgic E, Scheers Class II	4.07	5
204.	NCM	2007.5	Uncertain animal	Abstract design	MD 2003–9	Woodland	N/A	quarter stater (plated?)	40	Gallo-Belgic D	0.88[23]	4–5
205.	NCM	2007.6	Uncertain animal	Abstract design	MD 2003–9	Woodland	N/A	quarter stater (plated?)	40	Gallo-Belgic D	1.21	4–5
206.	NCM	2007.7	Uncertain animal	Abstract design	MD 2003–9	Woodland	N/A	quarter stater (plated?)	40	Gallo-Belgic D	1.10	4–5
207.	NCM	2007.8	Uncertain animal	Abstract design	MD 2003–9	Woodland	N/A	quarter stater (plated?)	40	Gallo-Belgic D	0.99	4–5
208.	NCM	2007.9	Uncertain animal	Abstract design	MD 2003–9	Woodland	N/A	quarter stater (plated?)	40	Gallo-Belgic D	0.94	4–5
209.	NCM	2007.10	Uncertain animal	Abstract design	MD 2003–9	Woodland	N/A	quarter stater	40	Gallo-Belgic D, Scheers Class III	1.46	4–5
210.	NCM	2007.11	Uncertain animal	Abstract design	MD 2003–9	Woodland	N/A	quarter stater (plated)	40	Gallo-Belgic D	0.81	4–5
211.	NCM	2005.19	Uncertain animal	Abstract design	MD 2003–9	Woodland	N/A	quarter stater	40	Gallo-Belgic D	1.44	4–5
212.	NCM	2005.20	Uncertain animal	Abstract design	MD 2003–9	Woodland	N/A	quarter stater (plated – core only)	40	Gallo-Belgic D	0.85g	4–5

British Iron Age Coinage

Southern British Iron Age (Cat. nos 213–16)

Cat. no.	Museum	Reg. no.	Obverse	Reverse	Disc.	Area	Site code	Denom.	*ABC*	Other refs	Wt (g)	Period
213.	BM	1991,1017.2	Stylised head of Apollo, right	Stylised horse, right	MD 1990	Area 5	SN/KQ	stater (plated)	515	Sills 2017, 153, Insular Cf1 Class 1; CCI 99.1996	6.29	4
214.	BM	1991,1017.6	Stylised head of Apollo, right	Stylised horse, left	MD 1990	Area 9	SN/MW	stater	482	Sills 2017, 102, British Ad1 Class 3; BMC 24 type; CCI 99.1993	6.44	4
215.	BM	1991,1017.4	Uncertain animal	Abstract design	MD 1990	Area 4	SN/KL	quarter stater	N/A	Sills 2017, 107, British Aa2 Class 1; CCI 95.3817	1.48	4
216.	NCM	2009.8	Uncertain animal	Abstract design	MD 2003–9	Woodland	N/A	quarter stater	N/A	Sills 2017, British Aa2 Class 2	1.51	4

Eastern British Iron Age / North Thames (Cat. nos 217–31)

Cat. no.	Museum	Reg. no.	Obverse	Reverse	Disc.	Area	Site code	Denom.	*ABC*	Other refs	Wt (g)	Period
217.	BM	1991,1017.5	Stylised head of Apollo, right	Stylised horse, left	MD 1990	Area 1	SN/HQ	stater	2430	Sills 2017, 416, British Ab1 Class 3; CCI 99.1994	6.36	4
218.	BM	2009,4213.9	Stylised head of Apollo, right	Stylised horse, left	MD 1991	Area 16	ST/AD	stater	2430	Sills 2017, 416, British Ab1 Class 3	6.43	4
219.	NCM	1990.204.2	Stylised head of Apollo, right	Stylised horse, left	MD 1989[24]	Area 9	N/A	stater	2430	Sills 2017, 416, British Ab1 Class 3; CCI 90.0005	6.35	4
220.	BM	1991,0904.12	Uncertain animal	Abstract design	MD 1990	Area 4	N/A (Jackson no. 524)	quarter stater	2448	Sills 2017, 418, British Ac2[25] Class 2; CCI 95.3818	1.21	4
221.	NCM	1949.76.13	Uncertain animal	Abstract design	Exc. 1948	Clarke's 'Site 33'; Area 9	N/A	quarter stater	2448	Sills 2017, 418, British Ac2[26] Class 2; CCI 61.0326; Clarke no. 13	1.26	4
222.	BM	1992,0803.3	Uncertain animal	Abstract design	MD Dec. 1990–1	Area 19	N/A	quarter stater	2448 var.	Sills 2017, 418, British Ab2 Class 3; CCI 15.0326	1.39	4–5
223.	BM	1991,1017.7	Stylised head of Apollo, right	Stylised horse, right	MD 1990	Area 12	SN/QG	stater	2329	Sills 2017, 426, British G1 Class 2a; CCI 99.1992	6.13	4–5
224.	BM	1992,0803.4	Stylised head of Apollo, right	Stylised horse, right	MD 1990–1	Just to the east of Area 19	N/A	stater	2329	Sills 2017, 426, British G1 Class 2a; CCI 15.0598	5.88	4–5
225.	NCM	2007.12	Uncertain animal	Horse, right	MD 2003–9	Woodland	N/A	quarter stater	2350	CCI 17.0279 Sills 2017, 428, British G2 Class 2a[27]	1.31	4–5
226.	NCM	2007.13	Uncertain animal	Horse, right	MD 2003–9	Woodland	N/A	quarter stater	2350	CCI 17.0284 Sills 2017, 428, British G2 Class 2a	0.96	4–5
227.	NCM	2007.14	Uncertain animal	Horse, right	MD 2003–9	Woodland	N/A	quarter stater	2350	CCI 17.0282 Sills 2017, 428, British G2 Class 2a	1.10	4–5
228.	NCM	2007.15	Uncertain animal	Horse, right	MD 2003–9	Woodland	N/A	quarter stater	2350	CCI 17.0281 Sills 2017, 428, British G2 Class 2a	0.76 (incomplete)	4–5
229.	NCM	2007.16	Uncertain animal	Horse, right	MD 2003–9	Woodland	N/A	quarter stater	2350	CCI 17.0280 Sills 2017, 428, British G2 Class 2a	1.05	4–5

Cat. no.	Museum	Reg. no.	Obverse	Reverse	Disc.	Area	Site code	Denom.	*ABC*	Other refs	Wt (g)	Period
230.	NCM	2007.37	Uncertain animal	Horse, right.	MD 2003–9	Woodland	N/A	quarter stater	2350	CCI 17.0283 Sills 2017, 428, British G2 Class 2a	0.64 (incomplete)	4–5
231.	NCM	2007.57	Crescents in wreath	[…] Horse, left, branch below	MD 2003–9	Woodland	N/A	stater (plated)	cf. 2392	Plated core of stater of Dubnovellaunos, BMC 2441	3.11	7

East Anglian British Iron Age (Norfolk and neighbouring counties)

Gold (Cat. nos 232–63)

Cat. no.	Museum	Reg. no.	Obverse	Reverse	Disc.	Area	Site code	Denom.	*ABC*	Other refs	Wt (g)	Period
232.	NCM	2005.21	Head, right	Wolf, left	MD 2003–9	Woodland	N/A	stater	1399		5.50	6
233.	NCM	2005.22	Head, right	Wolf, left	MD 2003–9	Woodland	N/A	stater	1399		5.49	6
234.	NCM	1990.203.1	Head, right	Wolf, left	MD 1989	Area 15	N/A	stater[28]	1399	CCI 90.0008	5.85	6
235.	BM	1991,1017.10	Head, right	Wolf, left	MD 1990	Area 2	SN/EQ	stater[29]	1399	BMC 218; CCI 97.0072	5.60	6
236.	BM	1991,1017.12	Head, right	Wolf, left	MD 1990	Area 9	SN/JH	stater	1399	BMC 219; CCI 97.0073	5.54	6
237.	BM	1991,1017.9	Head, right.	Wolf, left	MD 1990	Area 2	SN/ER	stater	1399	BMC 249; CCI 97.0102	5.72	6
238.	BM	1991,0904.15	Head, right	Wolf, left	MD 1990[30]	Area 12	SN/NH	stater	1399	BMC 251; CCI 97.0104	5.02	6
239.	BM	1991,1018.1	Head, right	Wolf, left	MD 1990	Area 1	SN/NG	stater[31]	1399	BMC 252; CCI 97.0105	5.05	6
240.	BM	1991,0904.14	Head, right	Wolf, left	MD 1990	Area 4	N/A (Jackson no. 522)	stater	1399	BMC 274; CCI 97.0127	4.91	6
241.	BM	1991,1017.8	Head, right	Wolf, left	MD 1990	Area 4	SN/KG	stater	1399	BMC 276; CCI 97.0129	5.47	6
242.	BM	1991,1017.11	Head, right	Wolf, left	MD 1990	Area 2	SN/EH	stater	1399	BMC 275; CCI 97.0128	5.19	6
243.	BM	2009,4213.11	Head, right	Wolf, left	MD 1991	Area 27	ST/GL	stater	1399	BMC 218 type	5.30	6
244.	BM	2009,4213.10	Head, right	Wolf, left	Exc. 1991, enclosure ditch, ST45	Area 20	ST/CQ	stater	1399	BMC 227 type	5.18	6
245.	BM	2009,4213.12	Head, right	Wolf, left	MD 1991	Area 21	ST/HA	stater	1399	BMC 227 type	4.95	6
246.	BM	1991,1018.2	Head, right	Wolf, left	MD 1990	Area 12	SN/QF	stater (plated)	1399	BMC 250; CCI 97.0103	3.72	6
247.	BM	1991,1018.5	Head, right	Wolf, left	MD 1990	Area 11	SN/QD	stater[32]	1399	BMC 265; CCI 97.0118	4.62	6
248.	BM	1991,1018.4	Head, right	Wolf, left	MD 1990	Area 12	SN/QV	stater	1399	BMC 266; CCI 97.0119	3.61	6
249.	BM	1991,1018.6	Head, right	Wolf, left	MD 1990	Area 12	SN/QX	stater	1399	BMC 267; CCI 97.0120	4.20	6
250.	BM	1991,1018.3	Head, right	Wolf, left	MD 1990	Area 11	SN/QE	stater[33]	1399	BMC 272; CCI 97.0125	4.63	6
251.	BM	1991,1018.8	Head, right	Wolf, left	MD 1990	Area 9	SN/NE	stater	1399	BMC 273; CCI 97.0126	4.23	6
252.	BM	1991,1018.7	Head, right	Wolf, left	MD 1990	Area 12	SN/QU	stater	1399	BMC 277; CCI 97.0130	4.09	6
253.	BM	1991,1018.9	Head, right	Wolf, left	MD 1990	Area 12	SN/QT	stater	1399	BMC 278; CCI 97.0131	4.25	6
254.	BM	2009,4213.14	Head, right	Wolf, left	MD 1991	Area 24	ST/EH	stater (plated)	1399	BMC 227 type	4.29	6
255.	BM	2009,4213.15	Head, right	Wolf, left	MD 1991	Area 12	ST/FA	stater (plated)	1399	BMC 227 type	3.97	6
256.	NCM	2007.18	Head, right	Wolf, left	MD 2003–9	Woodland	N/A	stater (base)	cf 1399	BMC 253 type	3.33	6
257.	NCM	2007.19	Head, right	Wolf, left	MD 2003–9	Woodland	N/A	stater (base)	cf 1399	BMC 253 type	3.40	6

Cat. no.	Museum	Reg. no.	Obverse	Reverse	Disc.	Area	Site code	Denom.	*ABC*	Other refs	Wt (g)	Period
258.	NCM	2007.20	Head, right	Wolf, left	MD 2003–9	Woodland	N/A	stater (base)	cf 1399	BMC 253 type	3.17	6
259.	NCM	1990.204.3	Head, right	Wolf, left	MD 1989[34]	Area 13	N/A	stater (plated copper alloy core)	cf 1399	CCI 90.0028	1.76	6
260.	NCM	2005.23	Lattice design	Horse, right; below, pellet in circle	MD 2003–9	Woodland	N/A	quarter stater	1480	Irstead type	1.02	7
261.	NCM	2005.24	Lattice design	Horse, right	MD 2003–9	Woodland	N/A	quarter stater? (plated copper alloy core)	Cf 1477 / 1480	Possible Irstead / Boar Horse C type	0.54	7
262.	NCM	2007.22	Wreath	Horse, right	MD 2003–9	Woodland	N/A	quarter stater	1462	Snettisham type	0.95	6–7
263.	NCM	2007.23	Wreath	Horse, right	MD 2003–9	Woodland	N/A	quarter stater	1462	Snettisham type	0.97	6–7

Silver (Cat. nos 264–361)

Cat. no.	Museum	Reg. no.	Obverse	Reverse	Disc.	Area	Site code	Denom.	*ABC*	Other refs	Wt (g)	Period
264.	NCM	2007.24	Head, left	Horse, left	MD 2003–9	Woodland	N/A	unit	1495	Bury A	1.20	6–7
265.	NCM	2007.25	Head, left	Horse, left	MD 2003–9	Woodland	N/A	unit	1495	Bury A	1.21	6–7
266.	NCM	2007.26	Head, left	Horse, left	MD 2003–9	Woodland	N/A	unit	1495	Bury A	1.18	6–7
267.	NCM	2007.27	Head, left	Horse, left	MD 2003–9	Woodland	N/A	unit	1495	Bury A	0.88	6–7
268.	NCM	2005.31	Head, left	Horse, left	MD 2003–9	Woodland	N/A	unit	1495	Bury A	0.84	6–7
269.	NCM	2007.28	Head, right	Horse, right	MD 2003–9	Woodland	N/A	unit	1501	Bury B	1.23	6–7
270.	NCM	2007.29	Head, right	Horse, right	MD 2003–9	Woodland	N/A	unit	1501	Bury B	1.17	6–7
271.	NCM	2007.30	Head, right	Horse, right	MD 2003–9	Woodland	N/A	unit	1501	Bury B	1.00	6–7
272.	NCM	2009.13	Head, right	Horse, right	MD 2003–9	Woodland	N/A	unit	1501	Bury B	1.36	6–7
273.	BM	1991,1017.13	Head, left	Horse, right	MD 1990	Area 12	SN/QW	unit	1519	Bury E	0.83 (incomplete)	6–7
274.	NCM	2005.32	Head, right?	Horse, left	MD 2003–9	Woodland	N/A	unit	uncertain	Uncertain Bury type [35]	0.49 (incomplete)	6–7
275.	N/A	Retained by finder	Head, left	Stylised horse, right, star above tail	MD 1991	Woodland	ST/KA	unit	1522	Large Flan A	not recorded	6–7
276.	NCM	2007.31	Head, right	Horse, right	MD 2003–9	Woodland	N/A	unit	1525	Large Flan C	1.28	6–7
277.	NCM	2007.32	Head, right	Horse, right	MD 2003–9	Woodland	N/A	unit	1525	Large Flan C	0.60	6–7
278.	NCM	2003.37	Head, bearded, right	Horse, right	MD 2003–9	Woodland	N/A	unit (plated)	1525	Large Flan C[36]	0.99	6–7
279.	NCM	2005.35	Head, right	Horse, right	MD 2003–9	Woodland	N/A	unit	1525	Large Flan C	0.92g	6–7
280.	NCM	2005.36	Head, right	Horse, right	MD 2003–9	Woodland	N/A	unit (plated)	1525	Large Flan C	0.81g	6–7
281.	NCM	2005.37	Head, right	Horse, right	MD 2003–9	Woodland	N/A	unit	1525	Large Flan C	1.24g	6–7
282.	NCM	2003.31	Head, right	Illegible (folded inwards)	MD 2003–9	Woodland	N/A	unit	Cf 1510 / 1525	Large Flan B or C	1.27	6–7
283.	BM	1991,1017.14	Head, right	Horse, right	MD 1990	Area 12	SN/QS	unit	1531	BMC 3545; Snettisham unit	0.95 (incomplete)	7

Cat. no.	Museum	Reg. no.	Obverse	Reverse	Disc.	Area	Site code	Denom.	*ABC*	Other refs	Wt (g)	Period
284.	NCM	2009.11	Head, right (unclear)	Horse, right	MD 2003–9	Woodland	N/A	unit	1531	Snettisham unit	0.66 (bent / folded flan)	7
285.	NCM	2003.29	Illegible	Horse, right	MD 2003–9	Woodland	N/A	unit	1537	Irstead A	1.06	7
286.	NCM	2005.33	Head, right	Horse, right	MD 2003–9	Woodland	N/A	unit	1537 var.[37]	Plouviez unit; BMC 3546 type	1.16	7
287.	NCM	2003.33	Illegible	Horse, right	MD 2003–9	Woodland	N/A	unit	1537 var.[38]	Plouviez unit; BMC 3546 type	1.07	7
288.	NCM	2003.22	Head right	Horse, left	MD 2003–9	Woodland	N/A	unit	Cf 1549/ 1558	Saham Toney unit	0.75	7
289.	NCM	2007.33	Head, right	Horse, right	MD 2003–9	Woodland	N/A	unit	1561	Saham Toney unit[39]	0.69	7
290.	NCM	2007.34	Head, right	Horse, right	MD 2003–9	Woodland	N/A	unit	1561	Saham Toney unit	0.70	7
291.	NCM	2007.35	Head, right	Horse, right	MD 2003–9	Woodland	N/A	unit	1567	Late Face Horse	0.96	8
292.	NCM	2007.36	Head, right	Horse, right	MD 2003–9	Woodland	N/A	unit	1567	Late Face Horse	0.92	8
293.	NCM	2005.38	Head right	Horse, right	MD 2003–9	Woodland	N/A	unit	Cf 1567	Late Face Horse type (folded)	1.24	8
294.	NCM	2005.39	Head right	Horse, right	MD 2003–9	Woodland	N/A	unit	1567	Late Face Horse	1.07	8
295.	NCM	2005.40	Head right	Horse, right	MD 2003–9	Woodland	N/A	unit	Cf 1567	Late Face Horse	0.82 (incomplete)	8
296.	NCM	2007. 38	Head, right	Horse, right	MD 2003–9	Woodland	N/A	unit (plated)	1564 / 7	Late Face Horse	0.65	8
297.	NCM	2005.34	Head, right?	Horse, right?	MD 2003–9	Woodland	N/A	unit	uncertain	Possibly Late Face Horse	0.67	8?
298.	NCM	2005.26	Boar, right	Horse, right	MD 2003–9	Woodland	N/A	unit	1570	Early Boar Horse	1.51	7
299.	NCM	2005.25	Boar, right	Horse, right; above, wheel	MD 2003–9	Woodland	N/A	unit	1573	Early Boar Horse	1.20	7
300.	NCM	2005.28	Boar, right	Horse, right; pellets in exergue	MD 2003–9	Woodland	N/A	unit	1576	Boar Horse B (A) type	1.15	7–8
301.	BM	1991,1017.15	Boar, right	Not visible	MD 1990	Area 14	SN/RE	fused lump of silver coins, including one unit	1576	One identifiable Boar Horse B (A) type	7.76 (total). In two fragments	7
302.	NCM	2005.29	Boar, right	Horse, right; below, star	MD 2003–9	Woodland	N/A	unit	1579	Boar Horse B type	1.18	7–8
303.	NCM	2003.36	Boar, right	Horse, right; below, star	MD 2003–9	Woodland	N/A	unit	1579	Boar Horse B type	1.12	7–8
304.	NCM	2003.23	Boar, right	Horse, right; below, cross	MD 2003–9	Woodland	N/A	unit (plated)	1579 var.	Boar Horse B[40]	1.27	7–8
305.	NCM	2003.15	Boar, right	Horse, right; below, star	MD 2003–9	Woodland	N/A	unit	1579	Boar Horse B	1.18	7–8
306.	NCM	2003.20	Boar, right	Horse, right; below, star	MD 2003–9	Woodland	N/A	unit	1579	Boar Horse B	1.34	7–8
307.	NCM	2007.39	Boar, right	Horse, right; below, star	MD 2003–9	Woodland	N/A	unit	1579	Boar Horse B	1.01	7–8

Cat. no.	Museum	Reg. no.	Obverse	Reverse	Disc.	Area	Site code	Denom.	*ABC*	Other refs	Wt (g)	Period
308.	NCM	2007.40	Boar, right	Horse, right; below, star	MD 2003–9	Woodland	N/A	unit	1579	Boar Horse B	0.98	7–8
309.	NCM	2009.12	Boar, right	Horse, right; below, star	MD 2003–9	Woodland	N/A	unit	1579	Boar Horse B	1.06	7–8
310.	NCM	2005.30	Boar, right?	Horse, right; star below	MD 2003–9	Woodland	N/A	unit	Cf 1579	Boar Horse B	0.65g (incomplete)	7–8
311.	NCM	2009.2	Boar, right	Horse, right	MD 2003–9	Woodland	N/A	unit	1582	Boar Horse C	0.58 (incomplete)	7–8
312.	NCM	2005.41	Crescents on crossed wreaths	Horse, right	MD 2003–9	Woodland	N/A	unit	1588	Early Pattern Horse A	1.16g	8
313.	NCM	2005.53	Four petals	Horse, left	MD 2003–9	Woodland	N/A	half unit	1606	Early Pattern Horse B	0.56g	7–8
314.	NCM	2003.14	Triangle with central pellet	Horse, right, wheel above	MD 2003–9	Woodland	N/A	half unit (plated)	1618	Snettisham and Plouviez type[41]	0.44	7
315.	NCM	2007.41	Boar, right	Horse, right	MD 2003–9	Woodland	N/A	half unit	1621?	Boar Horse B	0.28 (frag.)	7–8
316.	NCM	2007.42	Boar, right	Horse, right	MD 2003–9	Woodland	N/A	half unit	1621	Boar Horse B	0.50	7–8
317.	NCM	2009.10	Boar, right	Horse, right	MD 2003–9	Woodland	N/A	half unit (plated)	1621	Boar Horse B	0.38	7–8
318.	NCM	2003.24	Crescents on wreath	Horse, right. ANT[ED]	MD 2003–9	Woodland	N/A	unit	1642/5	Anted; BMC 3856 type	1.08	8
319.	NCM	2007.44	Crescents on wreath	Horse, right	MD 2003–9	Woodland	N/A	unit	Cf 1642/5	Anted	0.87	8
320.	NCM	2005.45	Crescents on wreath	Horse, right	MD 2003–9	Woodland	N/A	unit	cf 1642/5	Anted	0.78	8
321.	NCM	2005.46	Crescents on wreath	Horse, right	MD 2003–9	Woodland	N/A	unit	cf 1642/5	Anted	1.06	8
322.	NCM	2005.47	Crescents on wreath	Horse, right	MD 2003–9	Woodland	N/A	unit	cf 1642/5	Anted	1.09	8
323.	NCM	2003.32	Crescents on wreath	Horse, right. [ANTE]D	MD 2003–9	Woodland	N/A	unit	1645	Anted; Cf. BMC 3856	0.54	8
324.	NCM	2005.42	Crescents on wreath	Horse, right. ANTED	MD 2003–9	Woodland	N/A	unit	1645	Anted; BMC 3800 type	1.12	8
325.	NCM	2005.43	Crescents on wreath	Horse, right. [AN]TED	MD 2003–9	Woodland	N/A	unit	1645	Anted; BMC 3800 type	0.86	8
326.	NCM	2005.44	Crescents on wreath	Horse, right. [AN]TED	MD 2003–9	Woodland	N/A	unit	1645	Anted; BMC 3856 type	1.23	8
327.	NCM	2009.4	Crescents on wreath	Horse, right. [ANTE]D	MD 2003–9	Woodland	N/A	unit	1645	Anted	1.12	8
328.	NCM	2005.52	Crescents in lozenge	Horse, right. [A]NT[E]D	MD 2003–9	Woodland	N/A	half unit	1648	Anted	0.37	8
329.	NCM	2005.49	Crescents on wreath	Horse, right. [E]CE[N]	MD 2003–9	Woodland	N/A	unit	1657	Ecen	1.13	8
330.	NCM	2005.50	Crescents on wreath	Horse, right. [E]CEN	MD 2003–9	Woodland	N/A	unit	1657	Ecen	1.11	8
331.	NCM	2003.18	Crescents on wreath	Horse, right. [E] CEN	MD 2003–9	Woodland	N/A	unit	1657	Ecen	0.79	8
332.	NCM	2003.21	Crescents on wreath	Horse, right. ECEN	MD 2003–9D	Woodland	N/A	unit	1657	Ecen	1.12	8
333.	NCM	2005.48	Crescents on wreath	Horse, right	MD 2003–9	Woodland	N/A	unit	Cf 1657ff	Ecen	1.08	8

Cat. no.	Museum	Reg. no.	Obverse	Reverse	Disc.	Area	Site code	Denom.	*ABC*	Other refs	Wt (g)	Period
334.	NCM	2003.16	Crescents on wreath	Horse, right.	MD 2003–9	Woodland	N/A	unit	Cf 1657ff	Ecen	1.25	8
335.	NCM	2003.19	Crescents on wreath	Horse, right	MD 2003–9	Woodland	N/A	unit	Cf 1657ff	Ecen	0.80	8
336.	NCM	2003.25	Crescents on wreath	Horse, right	MD 2003–9	Woodland	N/A	unit	Cf 1657ff	Ecen	1.24	8
337.	NCM	2003.26	Crescents on wreath	Horse, right	MD 2003–9	Woodland	N/A	unit	Cf 1657ff	Ecen	0.99	8
338.	NCM	2003.27	Crescents on wreath	Horse, right	MD 2003–9	Woodland	N/A	unit	Cf 1657ff	Ecen	0.77	8
339.	NCM	2003.34	Crescents on wreath	Horse, right	MD 2003–9	Woodland	N/A	unit	Cf 1657ff	Ecen	0.77	8
340.	NCM	2007.45	Crescents on wreath	Horse, right. [E]CEN	MD 2003–9	Woodland	N/A	unit	1657	Ecen	1.13	8
341.	NCM	2009.3	Crescents on wreath	Horse, right. ECE[N]	MD 2003–9	Woodland	N/A	unit	1657	Ecen	0.99	8
342.	NCM	2009.5	Crescents on wreath	Horse, right. [ECE]N	MD 2003–9	Woodland	N/A	unit	1657	Ecen	1.14	8
343.	NCM	2007.46	Crescents on wreath	Horse, right. ECEN	MD 2003–9	Woodland	N/A	unit (plated?)	1657	Ecen	0.77	8
344.	NCM	2007.47	Crescents on wreath	Horse, right. ECE	MD 2003–9	Woodland	N/A	unit	1663	Ece B; BMC 4445 type	0.82	8
345.	NCM	2007.48	Crescents on wreath	Horse, right. ECE	MD 2003–9	Woodland	N/A	unit	1663 /6	Ece B; BMC 4431 / 4445 type	1.02	8
346.	NCM	2003.28	Crescents on wreath	Horse, right. ED[N]	MD 2003–9	Woodland	N/A	unit	1672	Ecen; BMC 4223ff	1.10	8
347.	NCM	2007.51	Crescents on wreath	Horse, right. (ECE[N]?)	MD 2003–9	Woodland	N/A	unit	Cf 1657ff	Ecen?	0.84	8
348.	NCM	2007.43	Crescents on wreath	Horse, right	MD 2003–9	Woodland	N/A	unit	uncertain	Uncertain inscribed	0.61	8
349.	NCM	2007.49	Crescents on wreath	Horse, right	MD 2003–9	Woodland	N/A	unit	uncertain	Uncertain inscribed	1.11	8
350.	NCM	2007.50	Crescents on wreath	Horse, right	MD 2003–9	Woodland	N/A	unit	uncertain	Uncertain inscribed	0.65	8
351.	NCM	2007.52	Crescents on wreath	Horse, right	MD 2003–9	Woodland	N/A	unit	uncertain	Uncertain inscribed	0.90	8
352.	NCM	2007.53	Crescents on wreath	Horse, right	MD 2003–9	Woodland	N/A	unit	uncertain	Uncertain inscribed	1.13	8
353.	NCM	2007.54	Crescents on wreath	Horse, right	MD 2003–9	Woodland	N/A	unit	uncertain	Uncertain inscribed	0.82	8
354.	NCM	2007.55	Crescents on wreath	Horse, right	MD 2003–9	Woodland	N/A	unit	uncertain	Uncertain inscribed	0.94	8
355.	NCM	2007.56	Crescents on wreath	Horse, right	MD 2003–9	Woodland	N/A	unit (plated)	uncertain	Uncertain inscribed	0.60 (incomplete)	8
356.	NCM	2003.30	Crescents on wreath	Horse, right	MD 2003–9	Woodland	N/A	unit	uncertain	Uncertain inscribed	0.77	8
357.	NCM	2003.17	Crescents on wreath	Horse, right	MD 2003–9	Woodland	N/A	unit	uncertain	Uncertain inscribed	1.08	8
358.	NCM	2003.35	Crescents on wreath	Horse, right	MD 2003–9	Woodland	N/A	unit	uncertain	Uncertain inscribed	0.53	8
359.	NCM	2003.13	Illegible	Horse, right?	MD 2003–9	Woodland	N/A	unit	uncertain	Uncertain	0.39 (incomplete)	?
360.	NCM	2005. 51	Illegible	Illegible	MD 2003–9	Woodland	N/A	unit	uncertain	Uncertain	1.12	?
361.	NCM	2005.27	Illegible	Horse, right	MD 2003–9	Woodland	N/A	unit or fraction	uncertain	Possibly Late Face Horse?	0.45	?

North-Eastern British Iron Age (Lincolnshire and neighbouring counties) (Cat. nos 362–7)

Cat. no.	Museum	Reg. no.	Obverse	Reverse	Disc.	Area	Site code	Denom.	*ABC*	Other refs	Wt (g)	Period
362.	BM	1991,0904.10	Head, right	Horse, right	MD 1990	Area 5	N/A (Jackson no. 526)	stater	1716	BMC 182 type; CCI 97.1735	6.09	5–6
363.	NCM	2007.17	Head, right	Horse, right	MD 2003–9	Woodland	N/A	stater (plated)	1719	Cf BMC 186 type	3.55	5–6
364.	NCM	2007.21	Stylised boar	Reversed S-shaped design	MD 2003–9	Woodland	N/A	quarter stater (scyphate)	1770 var.	BMC 3187 var. (reversed S)	0.59 (frag)	5–6
365.	BM	1991,0904.11	Stylised boar, right.	S-shaped design	MD 1990	Area 4	N/A (Jackson no. 521)	quarter stater (scyphate)	1770	BMC: 3187; CCI 96.1300	1.49	5–6
366.	BM	2009,4213.13	Boar, right	Horse, left	MD 1991	Area 26	ST/EL	silver unit	1782	BMC 3200 type	1.23 (incomplete)	6–8
367.	NCM	2009.7	Boar, right	Horse, right	MD 2003–9	Woodland	N/A	silver unit	1800		0.98 (incomplete)	6

British Iron Age Kent (potins) (Cat. nos 368–409)[42]

Cat. no.	Museum	Reg. no.	Obverse	Reverse	Disc.	Area	Site code	Denom.	*ABC*	Other refs	Wt (g)	Period
368.	BM	2009,4213.18	Head, left	Bull butting right	MD 1991	Area 21	ST/GU	potin	120	Kentish Primary (BMC 660 type)	3.55	2
369.	NCM	2003.1	Head, left	Bull butting right	MD 2003–9	Woodland	N/A	potin	cf 120	Kentish Primary	3.07	2
370.	NCM	2003.2	Head, left	Bull butting right	MD 2003–9	Woodland	N/A	potin	cf 120	Kentish Primary	4.84	2
371.	NCM	2003.3	Head, left	Bull butting right	MD 2003–9	Woodland	N/A	potin	cf 120	Kentish Primary	4.22	2
372.	NCM	2003.4	Head, left	Bull butting right	MD 2003–9	Woodland	N/A	potin	cf 120	Kentish Primary	4.03	2
373.	NCM	2003.8	Head, left	Bull butting right	MD 2003–9	Woodland	N/A	potin	cf 120	Kentish Primary	3.58	2
374.	NCM	2003.9	Head, left	Bull butting right	MD 2003–9	Woodland	N/A	potin	cf 120	Kentish Primary	4.10	2
375.	NCM	2003.10	Head, left	Bull butting right	MD 2003–9	Woodland	N/A	potin	cf 120	Kentish Primary	3.57	2
376.	NCM	2003.11	Head, left	Bull butting right	MD 2003–9	Woodland	N/A	potin	cf 120	Kentish Primary	3.39	2
377.	NCM	2003.12	Head, left	Bull butting right	MD 2003–9	Woodland	N/A	potin	cf 120	Kentish Primary	3.15 (incomplete)	2
378.	NCM	2005.3	Head, left	Bull butting right	MD 2003–9	Woodland	N/A	potin	cf 120	Kentish Primary	3.14	2
379.	NCM	2005.4	Head, left	Bull butting right	MD 2003–9	Woodland	N/A	potin	cf 120	Kentish Primary	3.34	2
380.	NCM	2005.5	Head, left	Bull butting right	MD 2003–9	Woodland	N/A	potin	cf 120	Kentish Primary	3.44	2
381.	NCM	2005.6	Head, left	Bull butting right	MD 2003–9	Woodland	N/A	potin	cf 120	Kentish Primary	3.65	2
382.	NCM	2005.7	Head, left	Bull butting right. MA above	MD 2003–9	Woodland	N/A	potin	cf 120	Kentish Primary	3.47	2

Cat. no.	Museum	Reg. no.	Obverse	Reverse	Disc.	Area	Site code	Denom.	*ABC*	Other refs	Wt (g)	Period
383.	NCM	2005.8	Head, left	Bull butting right	MD 2003–9	Woodland	N/A	potin	cf 120	Kentish Primary	2.05	2
384.	NCM	2005.9	Head, left	Bull butting right	MD 2003–9	Woodland	N/A	potin	cf 120	Kentish Primary	3.90	2
385.	NCM	2005.10	Head, left	Bull butting right (probably)	MD 2003–9	Woodland	N/A	potin	cf 120	Kentish Primary	2.80	2
386.	NCM	2005.11	Head, left	Bull butting right	MD 2003–9	Woodland	N/A	potin	cf 120	Kentish Primary	4.26	2
387.	NCM	2005.12	Head	Bull butting right	MD 2003–9	Woodland	N/A	potin	cf 120	Kentish Primary	3.79	2
388.	NCM	2005.13	Head, left	Bull butting right	MD 2003–9	Woodland	N/A	potin	cf 120	Kentish Primary	2.18 (incomplete)	2
389.	NCM	2005.14	Head	Bull butting right	MD 2003–9	Woodland	N/A	potin	cf 120	Kentish Primary	4.01	2
390.	NCM	2005.15	Head, left	Bull butting right	MD 2003–9	Woodland	N/A	potin	cf 120	Kentish Primary	3.38	2
391.	NCM	2005.16	Head, left	Bull butting right	MD 2003–9	Woodland	N/A	potin	cf 120	Kentish Primary	3.51	2
392.	NCM	2005.17	Head, left	Bull butting right	MD 2003–9	Woodland	N/A	potin	cf 120	Kentish Primary	3.93	2
393.	NCM	2005.18	Head	Bull butting right	MD 2003–9	Woodland	N/A	potin	cf 120	Kentish Primary	2.81	2
394.	NCM	2007.58	Head, left	Bull butting right	MD 2003–9	Woodland	N/A	potin	Cf 120	Kentish Primary	3.92	2
395.	NCM	2007.59	Head, left	Bull butting right	MD 2003–9	Woodland	N/A	potin	Cf 120	Kentish Primary	3.28	2
396.	NCM	2007.60	Head	Bull butting right	MD 2003–9	Woodland	N/A	potin	Cf 120	Kentish Primary	1.31	2
397.	NCM	2007.61	Head	Bull	MD 2003–9	Woodland	N/A	potin	Cf 120	Kentish Primary	2.72 (incomplete)	2
398.	NCM	2007.62	Head	Bull butting right	MD 2003–9	Woodland	N/A	potin	Cf 120	Kentish Primary	2.88 (incomplete)	2
399.	NCM	2007.63	Head, left	Bull	MD 2003–9	Woodland	N/A	potin	Cf 120	Kentish Primary	2.78 (incomplete)	2
400.	NCM	2007.64	Head	Bull	MD 2003–9	Woodland	N/A	potin	Cf 120	Kentish Primary	2.80 (incomplete)	2
401.	NCM	2009.1	Head, left	Bull, right. MA above	MD 2003–9	Woodland	N/A	potin	Cf 120	Kentish Primary	4.25	2
402.	NCM	2007.65	Head, right	Bull, left	MD 2003–9	Woodland	N/A	potin	cf 171	Flat Linear,[43] Holman F3/3-2 type	1.42	4–5
403.	BM	1991,1018.10	Stylised head, right	Stylised bull butting left	MD 1990	Area 1	SN/JS	potin	171	BMC 686 type; Holman F2/3-2c type[44]	1.58	4–5
404.	BM	1991,1018.11	Stylised head, right	Stylised bull butting right	Found on spoil heap 1990	?Area 4 (position on plan approximate)	SN/KJ	potin	165	BMC 705 type; Holman E3/4-2c type[45]	1.17	4
405.	BM	2009,4213.16	Stylised head, left	Stylised bull butting left	MD 1991	Area 26	ST/JB	potin	165	BMC 681 type; Holman D6/1-2 type	1.58	3

Cat. no.	Museum	Reg. no.	Obverse	Reverse	Disc.	Area	Site code	Denom.	*ABC*	Other refs	Wt (g)	Period
406.	BM	2009,4213.17	Stylised head, right	Stylised bull butting left	MD 1991	Area 3	ST/AU	potin	171	BMC 686 type; Holman F2/3-2a var.[46]	1.35 g	4–5
407.	BM	2009,4213.22	Stylised head, right	Stylised bull butting left	MD 1990–1	Area 25	N/A	potin	171	BMC 686 type; Holman F2/3-11b type	1.80	4–5
408.	BM	2009,4213.23	Stylised head, right	Stylised bull butting left	MD 1990–1	Area 4	N/A	potin	171	BMC 686 type; Holman F2/3-2b or c type	1.26 (incomplete)	4–5
409.	BM	2009,4213.25	Stylised head, left	Stylised bull butting right	MD 1990–1	Area 7	N/A	potin	150	BMC 711 type; Holman B3/2-3c type	1.64	2

Uncertain Iron Age coins (Cat. nos 410–14)

Cat. no.	Museum	Reg. no.	Obverse	Reverse	Disc.	Area	Site code	Denom.	*ABC*	Other refs	Wt (g)	Period
410.	BM	2009,4213.26	Illegible	Illegible	MD 1990–1	Area 13	N/A	Possible core of plated stater	uncertain		3.22	?
411.	BM	1991,1016.1	Illegible	Illegible	MD 1990	?Area 4 (findspot not plotted)	N/A (Jackson no. 525)	Possible core of plated stater	uncertain		1.21	?
412.	NCM	2003.39	Illegible	Illegible	MD 2003–9	Woodland	N/A	Possible core of plated quarter stater	uncertain	Possibly Insular Cf	0.87	?
413.	NCM	2009.6	Coin 1: Illegible. Coin 2: Boar, right	Coin 1: Illegible. Coin 2: Illegible	MD 2003–9	Woodland	N/A	Silver units, two fused together	uncertain	East Anglian or North-Eastern	0.92	?
414.	NCM	2009.9	Illegible	Illegible	MD 2003–9	Woodland	N/A	Possible core of plated silver unit	uncertain[47]		0.70	?

Part 3 ROMAN COINS FROM THE SITE (all unstratified topsoil/subsoil contexts unless stated) (Cat. nos 415–97)

Catalogue by Eleanor Ghey

Cat. no.	Museum	Reg. no.	Disc.	Area	Site code	Issuer	Obverse	Reverse	Ref.	Date (AD unless otherwise stated)	Wt (g)	Denom.	Reece period
415.	NCM	2007.66	MD 2003–9	Woodland	N/A	A. Postumius Albinus	Bust of Diana right	A·POST·A·F·S·N·ALBIN Sacrificial scene	*RRC* 372/1	81 BC	1.85	*denarius serratus*	1
416.	BM	1991,1018.12	MD 1990	Area 5	SN/ KN	Nero (possibly)	Head of emperor (Nero?) right	Seated figure (Securitas?), right	Uncertain	*c.* 54–68	6.70	*dupondius / as*	3
417.	NCM	2005.54	MD 2003–9	Woodland	N/A	Vespasian	[IMP] CAES VESP AVG [...] Head of Vespasian, laureate, right	Vespasian seated right	cf. *RIC* 2.1: 545, p.98	73	2.43	*denarius*	4
418.	BM	2009,4213.64	MD 1991	Area 20	ST/CB	Vespasian	[IMP CAES VESP] ASIAN AVG COS VIII Head of Vespasian, radiate, right; globe at point of bust	S C (in field) Pax standing left, sacrificing at altar and holding branch in left hand	*RIC* 2.1: 1143, p.142. Mint of Lugdunum	71	8.33	*dupondius*	4
419.	NCM	2005.55	MD 2003–9	Woodland	N/A	Domitian	IMP CAES DOMITIAN AVG GERM COS X[I] Head of Domitian, radiate, right, with aegis	[FIDEI] PVBLICAE Fides standing left	*RIC* 2.1: 289, p.285	85	7.87	*dupondius*	4
420.	BM	2009,4213.65	MD 1991	Area 23	ST/DK	Domitian (possibly)	Head (of Domitian?), right	Illegible	Uncertain	*c.* 69–96	3.74	*dupondius / as*	4?
421.	BM	2009,4213.66	MD 1991	Area 22	ST/CK	Trajan	[IMP CAES NER TRAIANO OPTIMO AVG GE]R DAC PARTHICO P M [TR P COS VI P P] Bust of Trajan, laureate, [draped], right	[IMP CAES NER TRAIANO OPTIMO AVG GE]R DAC PARTHICO P M [TR P COS VI P P]; PROVIDENTIA AVGVSTI S P Q R, S C (in field), Providentia standing left	*RIC* 2: 663, p.291	116–117	16.21	*sestertius*	5
422.	BM	2009,4213.36	MD 1991	Area 20	ST/BO	Trajan	Laureate head of Trajan, right	Illegible	Uncertain	98–117	15.90	*sestertius*	5
423.	BM	2009,4213.37	MD 1991	Area 25	ST/EK	Trajan	IMP CAES NERVAE TRAIANO AVG GER DAC [P M TR P COS VI P P] Bust of Trajan, radiate, draped, right	S P Q R OPTIMO PRINCIPI // VIA TRAIANA / S C Via Traiana reclining left on rocks, head right, holding wheel in right hand and branch in left hand	*RIC* 2: 641, p.289 (var.)	112–114 (?)	11.02	*dupondius*	5
424.	BM	2009,4213.39	MD 1991	Area 20	ST/BT	Hadrian	[IMP CAESAR TRA] IANVS HAD[RIANVS AVG] Laureate bust of Hadrian with right shoulder and chest bare, but drapery on his left shoulder, facing right	Illegible; // ADVENTVS AVG / S C (in ex.) Roma seated right, holding a vertical spear and clasping right hands with Hadrian, standing left	*RIC* 2.3, p.87 no. 158. BMC3: 1123 type	118	15.58 (loss on edge)	*sestertius*	6
425.	BM	2009,4213.38	MD 1991	Area 27	ST/GN	Hadrian	HADRIANVS AVGVSTVS Bust of Hadrian, laureate, right, drapery on left shoulder	COS [III] Roma, standing left, holding Victory and spear	*RIC* 2.3, p.123 no. 722; BMC3: 361 type	124–7	2.90	*denarius*	6
426.	BM	1991,1018.13	MD 1990	Area 1	SN/ BB	Hadrian (probably)	Head of emperor (Hadrian?), right	Illegible	Uncertain	117–138 (?)	5.66	*as* (probably)	?6

Cat. no.	Museum	Reg. no.	Disc.	Area	Site code	Issuer	Obverse	Reverse	Ref.	Date (AD unless otherwise stated)	Wt (g)	Denom.	Reece period
427.	BM	2009,4213.41	MD 1991	Area 17	ST/AL	Hadrian	Radiate (?) bust of Hadrian, right	Fortuna (?) seated left with rudder and cornucopiae.	Uncertain	117–138	4.82	*dupondius* (probably)	6
428.	BM	2009,4213.40	MD 1991	Area 24	ST/DU	Hadrian (possibly)	Head, right	Illegible	Uncertain	*c.* 100–200	18.23	*sestertius*	?6
429.	BM	1991,1018.15	MD 1990	Area 1	SN/BA	Antoninus Pius	[ANTONINVS AVG] PIVS P P TR P XVIII Radiate head of Antoninus Pius, right	[LIB]E[RTAS] COS IIII; S C (in field) Libertas standing right, holding pileus	*RIC* 3: 932, p.142; BMC4 1967, p.330 type	154–155	9.82	*dupondius*	7
430.	BM	2009,4213.29	MD 1992	Just east of stripped area	SM/AI	Antoninus Pius (possibly)	Laureate head, right	Uncertain standing female figure	Uncertain	*c.* 43–192	15.30	*sestertius*	?7
431.	BM	2009,4213.42	MD 1991	Just east of stripped area	ST/CJ	Antoninus Pius	Laureate head of Antoninus Pius, right	Uncertain standing figure	Uncertain	138–161	15.55	*sestertius*	7
432.	BM	2009,4213.44	MD 1991	Area 26	ST/FN	Antoninus Pius	DIVA FAVSTINA Bust of Faustina I, right	AED DIV FAVSTINAE Hexastyle temple; standing figure in temple	*RIC* 3: 343, p.69; BMC4 339, p.52 type	141–161	2.60	*denarius*	7
433.	NCM	2007.68	MD 2003–9	Woodland	N/A	Marcus Aurelius (as Caesar under Antoninus Pius)	AVRELIVS CAESAR AVG PII F Head of Marcus Aurelius, right	COS II Honos standing left	*RIC* 3: 429a; BMC 595 type	145–160	2.20	*denarius*	7
434.	NCM	2007.69	MD 2003–9	Woodland	N/A	Antoninus Pius	Head of emperor, right	Illegible. Standing figure	Uncertain	*c.* 138–161	5.78	*dupondius / as*	7
435.	BM	2009,4213.46	Stray find 1991, made during backfilling	?Area 4 (position on plan approximate)	ST/JA	Marcus Aurelius and Lucius Verus	DIVVS ANTON[INV]S Head of deified Antoninus Pius, bare, right	DIVO [PIO]; S C (in field), Column on base, surmounted by statue of Divus Antonius	*RIC* 3: 1269, p.315; BMC4: 880, p.526 type	*c.* 161–169	16.70	*sestertius*	8
436.	BM	2009,4213.28	MD 1992	South of 'gold field'	SA/JQ	Commodus (possibly)	Laureate, draped bust, right	Uncertain standing female figure	Uncertain	*c.* 138–211	19.51	*sestertius*	?9
437.	BM	2009,4213.47	MD 1991	Area 21	ST/GX	Uncertain Antonine emperor	Radiate head of Antonine emperor, right	Illegible	Uncertain	*c.* 138–192	4.61	*dupondius*	7–9
438.	BM	1991,1018.14	MD 1990	Area 1	SN/AY	Uncertain Antonine empress	Bust of uncertain Antonine empress, right	Illegible	Uncertain	*c.* 138–192	6.79	*dupondius / as* (possibly)	7–9
439.	BM	1991,1018.16	MD 1990	Area 2	SN/EM	Uncertain Antonine emperor	Head of uncertain Antonine emperor, right	Standing figure	Uncertain	*c.* 138–192	11.75	*sestertius* (probably)	7–9
440.	BM	2009,4213.43	MD 1991	Area 26	ST/FR	Uncertain Antonine emperor	Head (or bust) of uncertain Antonine emperor, laureate, right	Draped female figure standing left.	Uncertain	*c.* 138–192	17.48	*sestertius*	7–9
441.	BM	2009,4213.45	MD 1991	Area 23	ST/DJ	Uncertain Antonine empress	Draped bust of uncertain Antonine empress, right	Standing female figure	Uncertain	*c.* 138–192)	18.14	*sestertius*	7–9
442.	NCM	2007.67	MD 2003–9	Woodland	N/A	Julia Domna under Septimius Severus	IVLIA AVGVSTA Draped bust, right	FELICITAS Felicitas standing left	*RIC* 4: 551, p.167	196–211	2.44	*denarius*	10

Cat. no.	Museum	Reg. no.	Disc.	Area	Site code	Issuer	Obverse	Reverse	Ref.	Date (AD unless otherwise stated)	Wt (g)	Denom.	Reece period
443.	NCM	2007.70	MD 2003–9	Woodland	N/A	Uncertain	Head, right	Illegible	Uncertain		4.93	*dupondius / as*	1–11
444.	NCM	2007.71	MD 2003–9	Woodland	N/A	Uncertain	Head, right	Standing figure	Uncertain		6.10	*dupondius / as*	1–11
445.	NCM	2007.72	MD 2003–9	Woodland	N/A	Uncertain	Illegible	Illegible	Uncertain		3.89	*dupondius / as*	1–11
446.	NCM	2007.73	MD 2003–9	Woodland	N/A	Uncertain	Illegible	Illegible	Uncertain		5.82	*dupondius / as*	1–11
447.	BM	2009,4213.53	MD 1991	Area 22	ST/CD	Uncertain	Illegible	Illegible	Uncertain	*c.* 50–300	14.92	*sestertius*	1–11
448.	BM	2009,4213.56	MD 1991	Area 20	ST/BY	Uncertain	Radiate head, right	Illegible	Uncertain	*c.* 50–300	5.73	*dupondius*	1–11
449.	BM	2009,4213.58	MD 1991	Area 20	ST/BU	Uncertain	Radiate head, right	Standing figure.	Uncertain	*c.* 50–300	5.51	*dupondius / as*	1–11
450.	BM	2009,4213.54	MD 1991	Area 24	ST/DS	Uncertain	Illegible	Illegible	Uncertain	*c.* 50–300	6.93	*dupondius / as* (probably)	1–11
451.	BM	2009,4213.55	MD 1991	Area 22	ST/CO	Uncertain	Illegible	Uncertain standing figure	Uncertain	*c.* 50–300	6.89	*dupondius / as* (probably)	1–11
452.	BM	2009,4213.57	MD 1991	Area 23	ST/DD	Uncertain	Illegible	Illegible	Uncertain	*c.* 50–300	3.11	*dupondius / as* (possibly)	1–11
453.	BM	2009,4213.59	MD 1991	Area 20	ST/BZ	Uncertain	Head, right	Illegible	Uncertain	*c.* 50–300	5.83	*dupondius / as* (probably)	1–11
454.	BM	2009,4213.60	MD 1991	Area 18	ST/AW	Uncertain	Head, right	Uncertain figure, possibly Virtus standing right with spear and parazonium	Uncertain	*c.* 50–300	4.48	*dupondius / as*	1–11
455.	BM	2009,4213.61	MD 1991	Area 22	ST/CM	Uncertain	Head, right	Illegible	Uncertain	*c.* 50–300	4.53	*dupondius / as*	1–11
456.	BM	2009,4213.30	MD 1992	South of 'gold field'	SA/JR	Uncertain	Head, right	Illegible	Uncertain	*c.* 1–200	3.41	*dupondius / as*	1–11
457.	BM	2018,4117.1	MD 1990	N/A	N/A	Uncertain	Illegible	Illegible	Uncertain	*c.* 1–200	2.48 (incomplete)	*dupondius / as* (cut half)	1–11
458.	NCM	2007.83	MD 2003–9	Woodland	N/A	Valerian and Gallienus (joint reign)	Radiate of Valerian II as Caesar / D2 bust	IOVI CRESCENTI (Jupiter)	*Cunetio* 738; *RIC* 3: mint of Gaul	255	2.27	radiate	12
459.	BM	2009,4213.48	MD 1991	Area 22	ST/CL	Tetricus I	[...T]ETRIC[VS...] Radiate bust of Tetricus I, right	Standing female figure (Pax?)	Uncertain	271–274	1.77	radiate	13
460.	NCM	2007.81	MD 2003–9	Woodland	N/A	Carausius	Carausius (radiate, cuirassed, draped, right.) IMP C CAR[...]	Pax standing left holding vertical sceptre	Uncertain	*c.* 286–293	1.09	radiate	14
461.	NCM	2007.82	MD 2003–9	Woodland	N/A	Carausius	No details	No details	*RIC* 5.2: 12, p.464	*c.* 286–293	3.27	radiate	14
462.	NCM	2007.85	MD 2003–9	Woodland	N/A	Carausius?	No details	Female figure(s) standing left	Uncertain	*c.* 286–293	0.58 incomplete	radiate	14
463.	BM	2009,4213.49	MD 1991	Area 25	ST/EJ	Uncertain Allectus?	[IMP C A...] Radiate bust, right	Illegible (mintmark in exergue). Laetitia (?) standing left	Uncertain	*c.* 293–296	1.68 (incomplete)	radiate	14
464.	NCM	2007.84	MD 2003–9	Woodland	N/A	Victorinus	Illegible	Sol Invictus prototype	*Cunetio* 2958	*c.* 275–285	0.58	radiate (i)	14
465.	NCM	2007.79	MD 2003–9	Woodland	N/A	Irregular	Illegible	Standing female figure	Uncertain	*c.* 275–285	0.82	radiate (i)	14
466.	NCM	2007.80	MD 2003–9	Woodland	N/A	Irregular	Illegible	Standing figure	Uncertain	*c.* 275–285	0.14	radiate? (i) small module	14
467.	NCM	2005.60	MD 2003–9	Woodland	N/A	Irregular	Head, right	Standing figure	Irregular	*c.* 275–285	0.45	radiate (i)	14

Cat. no.	Museum	Reg. no.	Disc.	Area	Site code	Issuer	Obverse	Reverse	Ref	Date (AD unless otherwise stated)	Wt (g)	Denom.	Reece period
468.	NCM	2005.61	MD 2003–9	Woodland	N/A	Irregular	Head, right	Standing figure	Irregular	*c.* 275–285	0.85	radiate (i)	14
469.	NCM	2007.86	MD 2003–9	Woodland	N/A	House of Constantine	Constantinopolis	Victory standing left on prow	Irregular, cf. Boon 127	330–340	1.54	*nummus* (i)	17
470.	NCM	2005.57	MD 2003–9	Woodland	N/A	House of Constantine	Illegible	GLORIA EXERCITVS one standard	Uncertain mintmark	335–341	1.51	*nummus*	17
471.	BM	2009,4213.31	Exc. 1992	Enclosure ditch, Trench 5, SA5/2, Section G, Layer 3	SA/BG	Constans	[CON]STAN[...] Head (or bust), diademed, right	[VICTORIAE DD AVGGQ NN]; mintmark: Є //TRS, Two Victories	*RIC* 8: 197–9, p.152. Trier mint	347–348	0.52 (incomplete)	*nummus*	17
472.	BM	2009,4213.34	Exc. 1992	Enclosure ditch, Trench 5, SA5/2, Section B, Layer 3	SA/AT	Constans	[C]ONSTAN [...] Bust of Constans, right, draped and diademed	[VICTORIA]E DD NN AVGGQ N[N]; mintmark: D //[TR.], Two Victories	*RIC* 8: 193, p.152. Trier mint	347–348	0.60 (incomplete)	*nummus*	17
473.	BM	2009,4213.35	Exc. 1992	Enclosure ditch, Trench 5, SA5/2, Section B, Layer 3	SA/AO	Constans or Constantius II	CONS[...] Bust of emperor, right, draped and diademed	[VICTORIAE DD NN AVG] GQ NN; mintmark: branch// T[R.], Two Victories	*RIC* 8: 203–11, p.152. Trier mint	347–348	0.48 (incomplete)	*nummus*	17
474.	NCM	2005.58	MD 2003–9	Woodland	N/A	House of Constantine	Illegible, bust right	[VICTORIAE DD AVGG Q NN], M (in field). Two Victories	Mint of Trier	343–348	0.79	*nummus*	17
475.	NCM	2005.64	MD 2003–9	Woodland	N/A	House of Constantine	Illegible	Two Victories?	Irregular	347–348	0.52	*nummus* (i)	17
476.	BM	2009,4213.50	MD 1991	Area 27	ST/GK	Magnentius	A (behind bust); [DN] MAG[...] Draped, bare-headed bust of Magnentius, right	GLO[RIA ROMANORVM; mintmark // [T]R[.] crescent Soldier galloping right spearing fallen victim	*RIC* 8: 271, p.158. Trier mint	*c.* 350–351	1.62 (half)	*nummus* (cut half)	18
477.	BM	1991,1018.17	MD 1990	Area 7	SN/MU	Magnentius	Illegible. A behind head. Bust of Magnentius, bare-headed, right	Two Victories holding wreath inscribed VOT / V / MVLT / X surmounted by Chi-Rho	Uncertain	350–353	2.33	*nummus*	18
478.	BM	2009,4213.33	Exc. 1992	Enclosure ditch, Trench 5, SA5/2, Section B, Layer 3	SA/AM	Magnentius	DN [...] Draped bust of Magnentius, bare-headed, right	VICTORA (sic) DD NN AVG ET CAE[S] Two Victories with wreath inscribed VOT / [V] / VLT / [X]	Irregular	*c.* 351–353	1.23	*nummus* (i)	18
479.	BM	2009,4213.32	MD 1992	Woodland	SM/AD	House of Constantine	Draped and diademed bust, right	Soldier spearing fallen horseman	Irregular	*c.* 348–361	0.74	*nummus* (i)	18
480.	NCM	2005.62	MD 2003–9	Woodland	N/A	House of Constantine	Illegible	Soldier spearing fallen horseman	Irregular	*c.* 355–364	0.35	*nummus* (i)	18
481.	NCM	2005.63	MD 2003–9	Woodland	N/A	House of Constantine	Illegible	Soldier spearing fallen horseman	Irregular	*c.* 355–364	0.48	*nummus* (i)	18

Cat. no.	Museum	Reg. no.	Disc.	Area	Site code	Issuer	Obverse	Reverse	Ref.	Date (AD unless otherwise stated)	Wt (g)	Denom.	Reece period
482.	NCM	2003.40	MD 2003–9	Woodland	N/A	House of Constantine	Bust right, letter behind head	Soldier spearing fallen horseman	Irregular	*c.* 355–364	0.72	*nummus* (i)	18
483.	BM	2009,4213.51	MD 1991	Area 21	ST/GY	Valens	DN VALEN [S P F AVG] Diademed bust of Valens, right	GLORIA ROMANORVM; mintmark: [O] / F I//[...] Emperor advancing right, holding standard and dragging captive	*RIC* 9: 10b, p.44. Lyon mint	364–367	2.65	*nummus*	19
484.	NCM	2007.87	MD 2003–9	Woodland	N/A	House of Valentinian	Illegible	SECVRITAS REIPVBLICAE, Victory standing left. [O]F / [.]// [...]?	Uncertain	364–378	1.07	*nummus*	19
485.	NCM	2005.56	MD 2003–9	Woodland	N/A	Gratian	D N GRATIAN[VS...] AVG Bust, right	VOT XV / MVLT [X X] // LVG[S] Inscription in wreath	Lyon mint cf. *RIC* 9: p.48, no. 30a	378–383	1.57	*nummus*	20
486.	NCM	2007.88	MD	Woodland	N/A	Honorius	Illegible	VICTORIA AVGGG Victory advancing left	Western mint	393–5	1.06	*nummus*	21
487.	NCM	2005.59	MD 2003–9	Woodland	N/A	Uncertain	Illegible	Illegible (late)	Uncertain	*c.* 348–402	1.15	*nummus*	18–21?
488.	BM	2009,4213.52	MD 1991	Area 26	ST/FP	Uncertain	Illegible	Illegible	Uncertain	*c.* 296–400	3.23	*nummus* (probably)	15–21
489.	BM	1991,1018.18	MD 1990	Area 7	SN/MJ	Uncertain	Illegible	Illegible	Uncertain	*c.* 260–400	0.68	radiate or *nummus*	13–21
490.	BM	1991,1018.19	MD 1990	Area 2	SN/EJ	Uncertain	Illegible	Illegible	Uncertain	*c.* 260–400	0.36	radiate or *nummus*	13–21
491.	BM	2009,4213.62	MD 1991	Area 22	ST/CN	Uncertain	Illegible	Illegible	Uncertain	*c.* 260–400	1.63	radiate or *nummus*	13–21
492.	BM	2009,4213.63	MD 1991	Area 23	ST/DA	Uncertain	Illegible	Illegible	Uncertain	*c.* 260–400	0.96	radiate or *nummus*	13–21
493.	NCM	2007.74	MD 2003–9	Woodland	N/A	Uncertain	Illegible	Illegible	Uncertain	*c.* 260–400	0.90	radiate or *nummus*	13–21
494.	NCM	2007.75	MD 2003–9	Woodland	N/A	Uncertain	Illegible	Illegible	Uncertain	*c.* 260–400	0.21	radiate or *nummus*	13–21
495.	NCM	2007.76	MD 2003–9	Woodland	N/A	Uncertain	Illegible	Illegible	Uncertain	*c.* 260–400	0.48	radiate or *nummus*	13–21
496.	NCM	2007.77	MD 2003–9	Woodland	N/A	Uncertain	Illegible	Illegible	Uncertain	*c.* 260–400	0.58	radiate or *nummus*	13–21
497.	NCM	2007.78	MD 2003–9	Woodland	N/A	Uncertain	Illegible	Possibly falling horseman?	Uncertain	*c.* 260–400	0.41	radiate (i) or *nummus* (i) small module	13–21

UNCERTAIN IRON AGE OR ROMAN COINS (Cat. nos 498–507)

Cat. no.	Museum	Reg. no.	Disc.	Area	Site code	Obverse	Reverse	Description	Wt (g)
498.	NCM	2007.89	MD 2003–9	Woodland	N/A	Illegible	Illegible	Uncertain Roman or Iron Age	1.16
499.	NCM	2007.90	MD 2003–9	Woodland	N/A	Illegible	Illegible	Uncertain possibly Iron Age	1.77
500.	NCM	2007.91	MD 2003–9	Woodland	N/A	Illegible	Illegible	Uncertain possibly Roman	1.11
501.	NCM	2007.92	MD 2003–9	Woodland	N/A	Illegible	Illegible	Uncertain copper alloy coin	1.41
502.	NCM	2007.93	MD 2003–9	Woodland	N/A	Illegible	Illegible	Uncertain possibly Roman	0.42
503.	NCM	2007.94	MD 2003–9	Woodland	N/A	Illegible	Illegible	Roman fragment	1.01
504.	NCM	2007.95	MD 2003–9	Woodland	N/A	Illegible	Illegible	Silver or copper alloy coin fragment or droplet (not seen at NCM)	0.36
505.	NCM	2007.96	MD 2003–9	Woodland	N/A	Illegible	Illegible	Possible potin fragment	1.24
506.	BM	2018,4117.2	Exc. 1991	Area 21, enclosure ditch ST35, Layer 1	ST/EX	Illegible	Illegible	Uncertain Roman or Iron Age copper alloy coin with adhering organics (mineralised fern frond)	2.98
507.	NCM	2003.38	MD 2003–9	Woodland	N/A	Illegible	Illegible	Possible core of plated coin, but iron corrosion products visible	1.21

Notes

1 Classifications from Sills 2003 where applicable.

2 Published weights in CCI, Clarke 1954 and Sills 2003, 376 are 7.10g for Clarke 1 and 6.03g for Clarke no. 2. The weights in the text and the plates in Clarke 1954 do not correspond; the numbering used in this catalogue relates to plate XIV. That publication appears to be the source of the CCI weights. This coin, however, has the appearance of a plated copy, although surface analysis by Northover (1992, 281) indicated a (possibly anomalously) high gold content for the coin weighing 7.10, listed (*ibid.*) as coin 1 from the hoard. The discrepancy in the weights for cat. no. 2 cannot be explained (Northover also gives 6.03g and it therefore seems that they were not re-weighed for that analysis).

3 Weight recorded as 5.52 in Clarke 1954 and CCI.

4 Weight recorded as 6.51 in Clarke 1954 and CCI, as no. 11.

5 Weight recorded as 6.18 in Clarke 1954 and CCI, as no. 9.

6 Sills (2003, 376) describes this as hammered out and possibly GB Ab1 cl 7 or GB E Class 1–3, 60.2% fine Au.

7 Sills (*ibid.*) describes this as hammered out and probably GB A or B, 71.6% fine Au.

8 Listed in error in Sills 2003, 376 as at NCM, but the NCM coin (1951.93.2, CCI 61.0327 1.55g) is an electrotype of this coin. The coin has unusual patterns of wear on the obverse.

9 Described by Sills 2003, 157 and 377 as an insular copy or plated. No analysis has been carried out to confirm this.

10 Sills and de Jersey have weights for 1991,0904.2, .3 and .4 assigned to different coins. Image on CCI for 94.1702 matches coin .4 and 94.1700 coin .3 but weights reversed.

11 Listed with site finds and not Hoard N by de Jersey.

12 Eleanor Ghey is grateful to John Sills for identifying this coin. He notes that it is a very worn product from a flawed die shared with CCI 12.0278, 07.0350, 15.0310 and 15.0311, the last three with findspots in West Sussex, Essex and Kent respectively.

13 Suggested to be ABC 1414 or 1420, but likely candidates not identified in CCI.

14 This type would traditionally be described as a Whaddon Chase stater, but Sills suggests that it may be a derivative Trinovantian issue (see entry for *ABC* 2338).

15 Weights are provided at www.finds.org.uk/CCI.

16 Described by John Talbot (pers. comm.) as a 'hubbed, plated Saenu/Ecen mule' (a hubbed die is a die made from an existing coin, generally thought to be a forgery).

17 In addition to the coins listed here, Michael Trenerry offered three groups of boar/horse units, apparently all of *ABC* 1582 type, in his lists of July/August 1992 (lot 72, 10 coins), July/August 1995 (lot 92, six coins), and May/June 1996 (lot 102, 33 coins). The coins are illustrated in heaps and no attempt has been made here to identify individual coins, or to ascertain whether any are repeated through the lots. There are also many more *ABC* 1564/1567 coins from the Bowl Hoard identified in various auction catalogues of the early and mid-1990s, but at the time of compiling (in 2015) these had not yet been allotted CCI numbers and thus they are not included here. The same observation applies to the ECEN and ECE types, and to a lesser extent to AESV and SAENV.

18 Inscriptions generally off the flan.

19 Additional examples of North-Eastern silver from the Bowl Hoard, both inscribed and uninscribed, have now been identified in auction catalogues of the mid-1990s, but at the time of writing these had not yet been included in the CCI and consequently they are not listed here.

20 Coins 2003.5 to .7 initially listed as Kentish Primary potins but removed to this section on account of their high weight. Many of the Kentish Primary potins are corroded or require cleaning and identification must remain inconclusive.

21 With thanks to Philip Kinns and Marie-Christine Marcellesi for this identification of a previously unrecorded magistrate, perhaps Kleisipp[ides] or Kleisipp[os].

22 Sills 2003, 377 also lists an unreported Gallo-Belgic Ab1 Class 2 (plated?) stater sold by Freeman & Sear 14/1/1998 lot 12, 5.77g CCI 98.0232.

23 The surface of coins 2007.5–9 is covered with what appears to be melted silver (see **Fig. 15.6** and wider discussion of heating in Ch. 20). In some cases, it is unclear if this is an underlying core (as apparent for 2007.11) or overlying the surface. The metal is paler than that of 2007.10 and 2005.19. No analysis has been carried out. The similar treatment might suggest that the coins were originally deposited together. As far as it has been possible to make out detail these coins correspond to Sills 2017, 15 type 25 to 26.

24 De Jersey 2014, 311 surface find III no. 2. appears to be this coin. Listed by Sills 2003, 377 as seen at the BM in 1989.

25 Reclassified from Sills 2003, 377 British Ao quarter mint B.

26 Reclassified from Sills 2003, 377 British Ao quarter mint B. This is listed by de Jersey 2014, 311 as surface find I. It is noted as coming from site 33. The British Ab2 Class 3 type is Talbot's Ingoldisthorpe quarter and may be attributed to East Anglia; this coin is the one referred to by Talbot as from Hoard B (2017, 12).

27 This group of coins is listed by Sills without weights as CCI 17.0279–84. The attribution of CCI numbers to particular coins may be incorrect as renumbering has occurred and they have not been checked against the CCI card index.

28 Listed as part of surface find III by de Jersey 2014, 311. Misshapen flan.

29 Analysed (see Appendix 4).

30 This is the coin referred to in de Jersey 2014, 315 note 355.

31 Recorded in BMC as a plated forgery, though analysis (see Appendix 4) did not find evidence that the coin was plated.

32 Analysis (see Appendix 4) suggests this coin is base but not plated.

33 Analysis (see Appendix 4) suggests this coin is base but not plated.

34 De Jersey 2014, 311 surface find III no. 4. appears to be this coin. It is the 'uncertain plated stater' recorded with the same date of discovery as surface finds 2 and 3. Coin no. 5, a silver East Anglian unit, does not appear on the list provided by NCM for this group.

35 The obverse is unclear. There is a wheel with spokes terminating in pellets above the horse as commonly seen in B (horse right). Possibly Bury D, F or H?

36 Talbot die-group 2.

37 Pellet triad below horse.

38 Pellet triad below horse.

39 Talbot's reverse 1 (2017, 207).

40 Cross below horse?

41 Triangle obverse as Talbot 2017, 173 G and H.

42 Including identifications of the Flat Linear potins by David Holman.

43 This is the additional potin referred to by Holman in the text as one further Flat Linear potin of type F3/3-2 found *c.* 2003.

44 Listed by de Jersey (2014) under Hoard F, no. 41.

45 Listed by de Jersey (2014) under Hoard F, no. 42.

46 Variant with two lines on neck.

47 John Talbot tentatively identified this as probably the core of a plated East Anglian Early Pattern Horse A unit.

The Snettisham Hoards

Volume II

Edited by Julia Farley and Jody Joy

With contributions from Ian Stead and Sophia Adams, Janet Ambers, Caroline Cartwright, Mike Cowell, Paul Craddock, John Davies, Michael de Bootman, Philip de Jersey, John Fenn, Eleanor Ghey, Marilyn Hockey, David Holman, Duncan Hook, Susan La Niece, Janet Lang, Alice Lyons, Peter Makey, Nigel Meeks, Aude Mongiatti, Peter Northover, Daniel O'Flynn, Sarah Percival, Alan Pipe, Matthew Ponting, Fleur Shearman and Tony Spence

The British Museum

Publication supported by:

Eyre Family Foundation

The Pennycress Trust

Publishers
The British Museum
Great Russell Street
London WC1B 3DG

Series editor
Sarah Faulks

The Snettisham Hoards
Edited by Julia Farley and Jody Joy

ISBN 9780861592258
ISSN 1747 3640
doi 10.48582/3xdb-ns12

Front cover: Torc L.19a–f, from Hoard L. The torc terminals are decorated with Celtic art, and it has been heavily repaired
Pg. iv: close up view of the decorated torus terminal of torc L.21a
Pg. vi: close up view of the decorated buffer terminal of torc L.13

Printed and bound in the UK by 4edge Ltd, Hockley

Contents

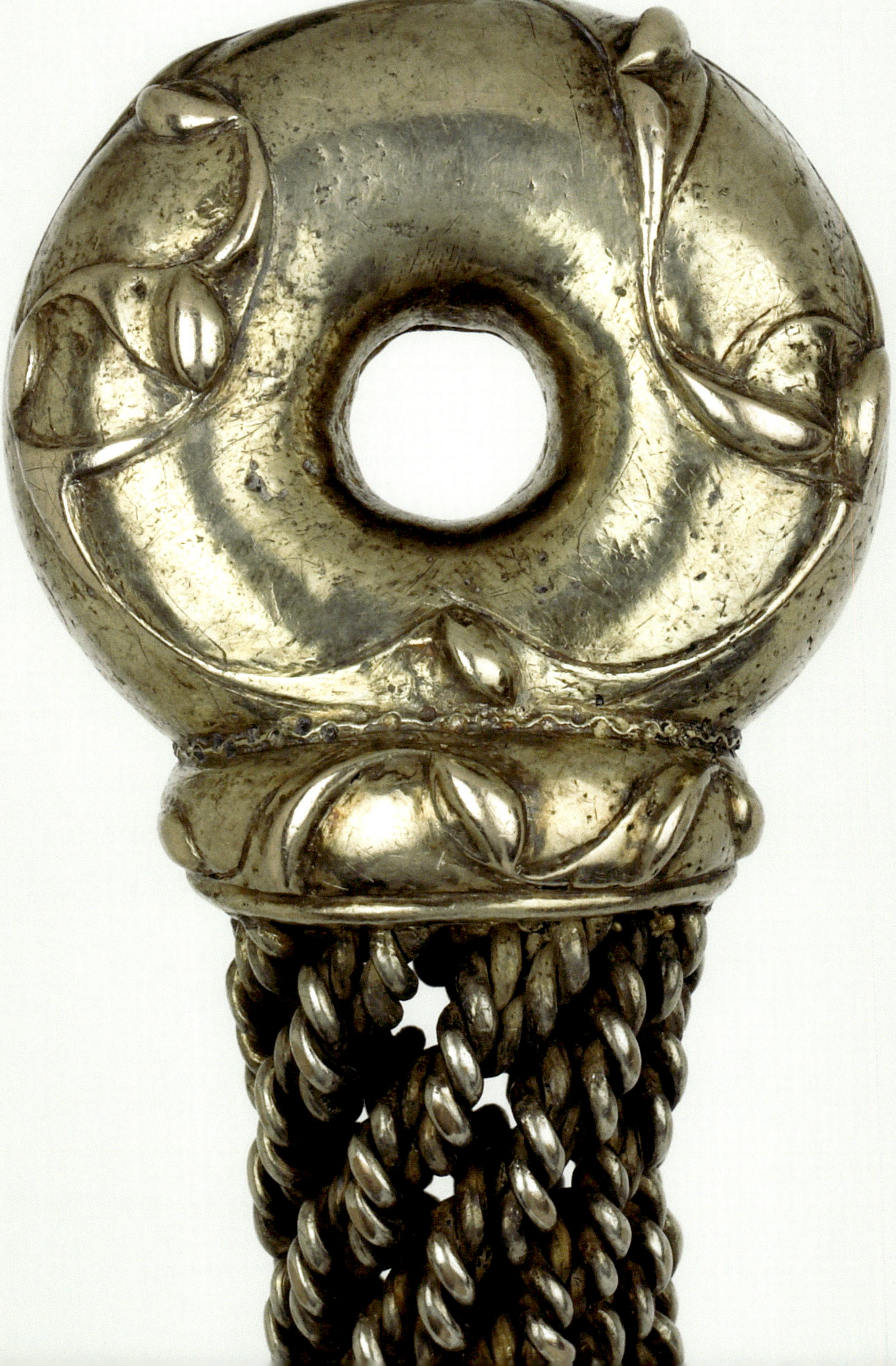

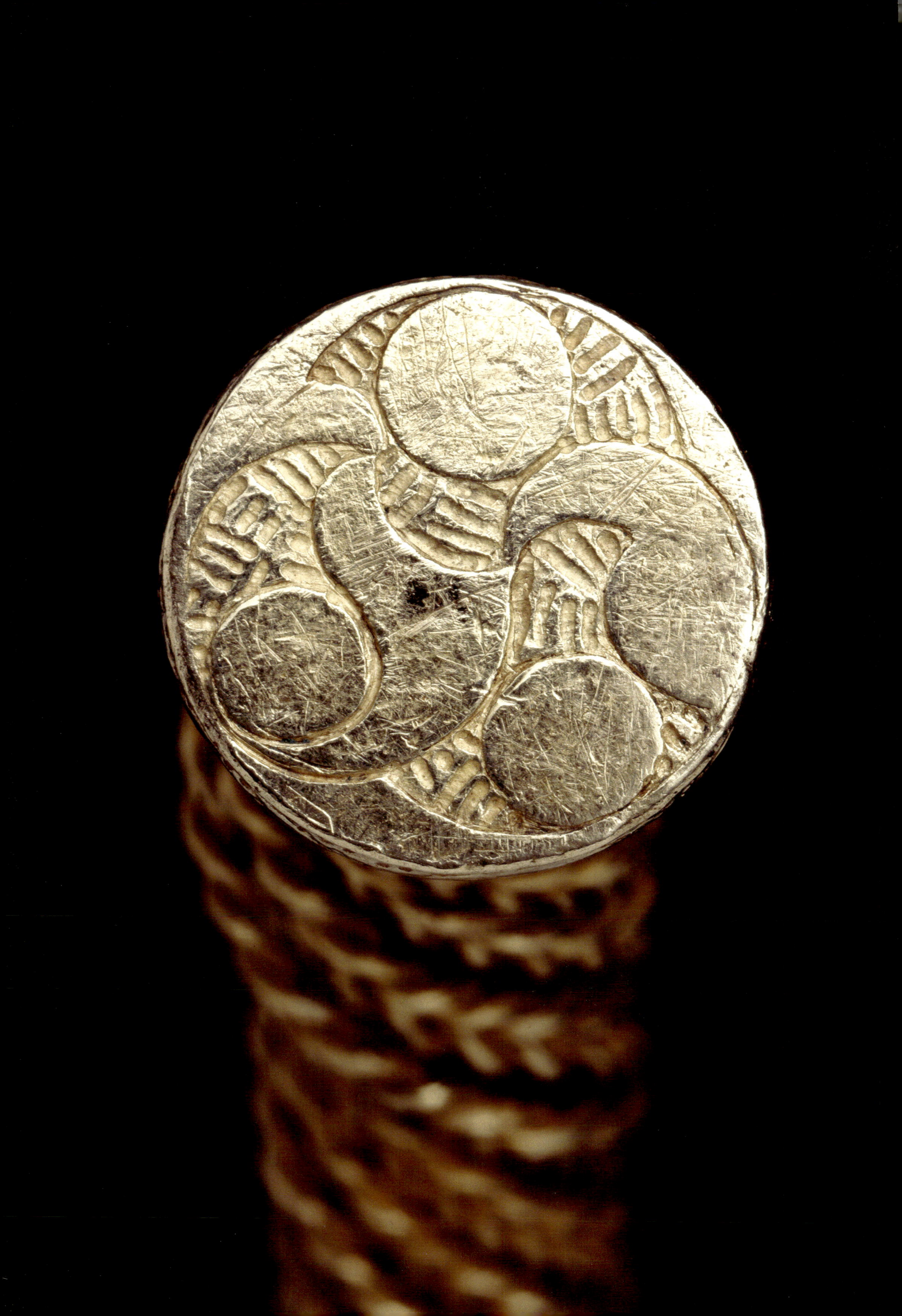

Part III: Discussion

Julia Farley and Jody Joy

Volume 1 of this book presented Parts I and II (Chs 1–15). Part I gave an overview of the site, the history of discoveries and the 1990–2 British Museum excavations, while Part II focused on the Later Iron Age and Early Roman hoards, including their archaeological context and detailed catalogues of both metalwork and coins. This volume, Volume 2 (Part III, Chs 16–24), moves from the detailed excavation reports and catalogues to consider the conservation and scientific analysis of the hoard objects, as well as exploring the wider significance of the site and finds.

Chapter 16 presents the ground-breaking conservation campaign, which has allowed the reconstruction and interpretation of several key objects, including the helmet which contained Hoard F, and several crushed tubular torcs. A comprehensive programme of scientific analysis was carried out to investigate the materials and techniques used to manufacture the torcs, and this is presented in Chapter 17, accompanied in Chapter 18 by a discussion of the compositional analyses of the bronze objects. Environmental evidence from charred wood preserved at the site is assessed in Chapter 19. Chapter 20 explores torc biographies and lifecycles through evidence for use, wear and repair of the Snettisham torcs, some of which are likely to have been more than a century old at the time they were buried, and many of which show evidence for repair or deliberate fragmentation and recombination. These analytical chapters are supported by appendices found at the end of Part III: Appendix 3 comprises a concordance with previously published finds listings, catalogues and numbering systems; and Appendices 4 and 5 give the results of compositional analyses of Iron Age gold alloy coins and selected gold and silver alloy objects from the NCM collections and comparative material.

Discussion chapters 21 to 24 investigate the wider significance of Snettisham in discussions of Celtic art, the social role of hoards and life in Iron Age Britain more generally. The finds from Snettisham represent one of the greatest concentrations of decorated Iron Age metalwork anywhere in Europe. The importance of this decoration is considered in Chapter 21, which presents not just detailed stylistic arguments, but also a consideration of what this art did, and how it transformed both object and wearer. Chapter 22 considers the relationships between people, objects and materials in Iron Age Norfolk. This includes a corpus of other known torcs from Iron Age Britain (an updated and expanded version of a gazetteer originally compiled by Ian Stead). Chapter 23 and the final conclusion, Chapter 24, move beyond material culture to explore the place of Snettisham in its wider social and landscape context. Discussion focuses on the site, its changing significance over time and the potential importance of its location. The editors argue that repeatedly depositing artefacts at Snettisham, with subtle differences in the composition and make-up of each of the hoards, was part of creating, negotiating and reinforcing social structures, as well as performing and creating social change. Specifically, we suggest that hundreds of torcs were deliberately taken out of social circulation around 60 BC as part of a shift from a 'world of torcs' to a 'world of coins' (Gosden 2013).

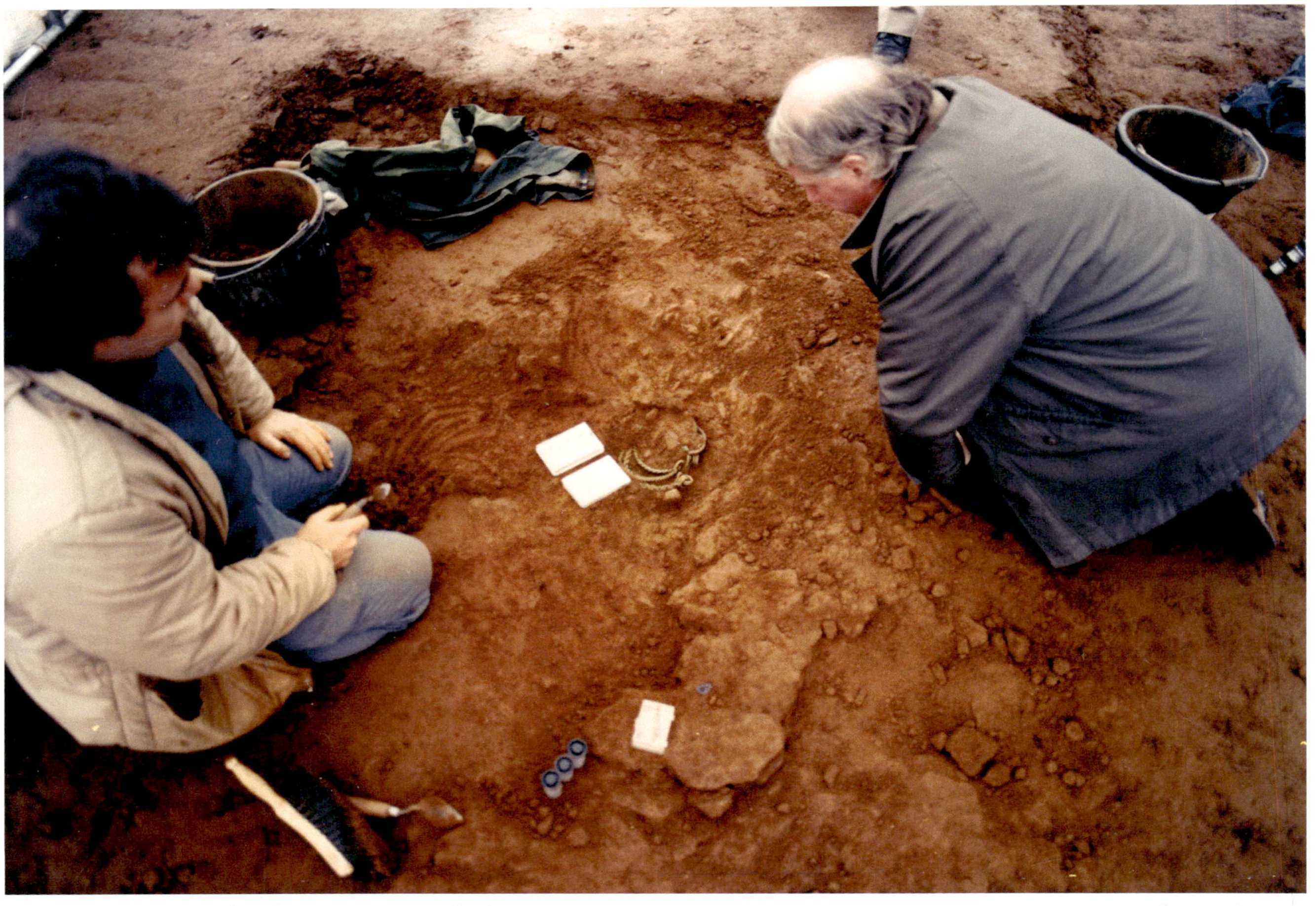

Figure 16.1 Simon Dove (right) and Peter Makey (left) lifting torcs from Hoard G, during the 1990s excavations at Snettisham (Ken Hill)

Chapter 16
Conservation of the Snettisham Torcs

Fleur Shearman and Marilyn Hockey

This chapter describes the role played by the discipline of archaeological conservation applied to the conservation and research of objects recovered from Snettisham. This work was largely carried out by metals conservators at the BM and has run in parallel with scientific investigation and archaeological research since the first discoveries at Ken Hill in the late 1940s. This chapter deals primarily with the torcs. For the reconstruction and investigation of the Hoard F helmet, see Chapter 14, entry for F.445 (pp. 266–274).

Since 1922 the BM had profited in having a designated Research Laboratory which housed the Science Department of analytical scientists working on fundamental questions of a material or technical nature. This allowed an integrated team of archaeologists, scientists, conservators and replica makers to work in close proximity. Conservation of the Snettisham artefacts benefitted by working with specialist mount-makers and designers both within and outside the Museum, leading to enhanced opportunities for public display and loan of the metalwork, enabling a wider sharing of the material outside London and Norwich.

Interventions 1949–1990

The hollow, tubular torcs which comprised Hoard A had most likely already suffered plough damage by the time of their discovery. Fragmentation and deformation can be seen in a black and white photograph taken before restoration (Clarke 1951c). Intentional dismantling before original deposition is a relevant factor for metalwork across the hoards (Ch. 20), but for the highly restored Hoard A, this cannot now be clearly and sequentially quantified. The extent of burial damage and resulting fragility of the torcs evidently led to the decision, in the years following their recovery, to carry out interventions in order to both strengthen and restore them to something approaching an authentic, original state.

It is recorded in the monthly reports of the Research Laboratory that they first assayed the Snettisham metalwork for bullion value in February 1949. The torcs from Snettisham were also investigated by scientists and material specialists in that year (Research Laboratory archive correspondence files, BM, Department of Scientific Research). It has not been possible to locate surviving documentation of the detail of early treatment interventions in the post-war period. In Rainbird Clarke's (1954) account of his excavations and discoveries at Snettisham, the sheet-metal torcs are illustrated in a restored state, reconstructed into complete torcs with location and reintegration of formerly detached elements. It is likely that then, as now, this was carried out by careful manual manipulation or controlled use of soft tools such as a horn hammer to remove dents. The reattachment and reinforcing of loose and damaged fragments and stabilisation of running or mobile cracks would be carried out to prevent further damage occurring (Plenderleith and Wernher 1971 [1956]; Hockey 2001). It is probable that this work was led or executed personally by Herbert Maryon (a specialist in metalwork and enamelling who worked as a technical attaché of the Research Laboratory at the BM between 1945 and 1963), in association with Moss and Plenderleith, also of the Research Laboratory (Plenderleith and Wernher 1971 [1956]; Maryon

2011 [1912]). A close collaboration was also maintained by Rainbird Clarke with colleagues in the Prehistory and Europe subsection of the Department of British and Medieval Antiquities at the Museum.

The Research Laboratory facility was also responsible for creating early replicas of museum artefacts in a variety of different materials. The Snettisham torcs benefitted from pioneering replica-making facilities in the form of electroforming tanks which had been installed in 1949 in the Research Laboratory and which enabled electroform replicas to be made. The replica of the Snettisham Great Torc was among the first such copies made by a combination of moulding, electroforming and fabrication likely carried out by specialists such as Baron Nimmo and his colleague Arthur Prescott. For metals, this procedure began with the creation of moulds using silicone rubber. This came under the care of skilled technicians as it involved a direct moulding from often fragile objects to create a master mould from which to make the electroform. The silicone moulds were then immersed in electrodeposition plating tanks. The copy made in copper by electrodeposition could then be gilded or silvered using cyanide salts, again by tank immersion. The complete replica of the Great Torc included neck wires made by Herbert Maryon.

Much of the applied conservation research for Snettisham would have been carried out in the Research Laboratory premises, as it had its own integrated conservation area with designated metals specialist technicians and, from the mid-1970s, conservators, a number of whom were trained as silversmiths. This practical underpinning knowledge proved particularly useful in solving questions of the technical manufacture and decoration of metals in dialogue with the materials scientists. Experimental wires, neck-rings and a range of terminal types were made to investigate the manufacture of these features of the torcs (see also Ch. 17).

The replica of the Great Torc was displayed in a 1972 exhibition commemorating the fiftieth anniversary of the Research Laboratory, held in the upper floor public galleries of the Department of Prehistoric and Romano-British Antiquities. This replica is still in use as a teaching aid for public outreach activities for families and academic research by archaeologists and metallurgists (see **Fig. 17.58**).

Conservation of material recovered during the 1990s excavations at Snettisham

On-site conservation

A site conservator, Simon Dove, was included in the team that excavated at Snettisham. After training at the Institute of Archaeology, Simon had been based in the Department of Prehistoric and Romano-British Antiquities. He played a full part in the archaeological excavations, as well as giving guidance on the lifting of vulnerable finds.

The role of a site conservator is to ensure safe retrieval of objects, to minimise loss of information and physical damage or disturbance and to ensure they are packed securely for transit. The conservator is also responsible for the continuity of archaeological recording of a contextual nature. At Snettisham, recovery of the stratified deposits of multiple, sometimes fragmentary, torcs from stacked pits was progressed after recording and planning relative positions within the layered deposits (Ch. 12). Each stage was documented by the site photographer.

In the case of the more fragmentary torcs, lifting would have been carried out by the site conservator. Limited use of consolidants and reinforcing materials is routine in these circumstances, in order to mitigate further damage and enable safe lifting to take place. In this case their use would have been carefully managed to avoid contamination of associated organic materials. Block lifting of associated groups of fragile objects was not pursued as an option at Snettisham for logistical reasons, as the deep pits would have been damaged by the soil disturbance necessary for extraction (**Fig. 16.1**).

Transfer to the BM and initial processing and recording

The recovered finds from the 1990–2 excavations were sent to the BM Department of Conservation. Dove received and assessed the recently excavated metalwork, leading a parallel and co-ordinated conservation campaign, providing an essential and meticulous link of continuity between the excavations, the old conservation laboratory based in the Department of Prehistoric and Romano-British Antiquities, and the Department of Conservation, which had been established in 1975. The team which processed over 300 torcs retrieved from the 1990s campaign included most of the metals specialists who worked in the conservation department. This included valuable work by conservation students from universities overseas, including the Sorbonne, as well as MA/MSc students from the Institute of Archaeology in London, who were on placement in the Metals Section at the time.

As team leader, Dove oversaw the multiple variations in treatment regimens required for the range of metals and states of preservation present across the different groups and hoards. He also supervised the methodical recording of treatments and the later transfer of these written records to computer archives in the later 1990s. Treatment records included technical observations made by conservators, which assisted with archaeological interpretation of the hoards.

The Snettisham torcs were subject to a number of conservation processes at the BM. The rest of this chapter explores four of these: corrosion removal; the recording and recovery of organic evidence and traces of gilding; reconstruction of fragmentary objects (primarily those subject to accidental breakage during burial or recovery); and investigative reshaping of decorated crushed gold objects.

Corrosion removal

Where the metal of the gold and silver torcs was alloyed with substantial amounts of copper, or where copper alloy objects were co-located with them in burial, the precious metal was often covered with the corrosion products of the baser copper metal. In terms of electro-chemical potential the baser copper metal will corrode in preference to the nobler metal. This was particularly true of Hoard F, where a copper alloy helmet (see Chs 12 and 14, F.445) had been used to contain gold, silver and copper alloy torc fragments. Both

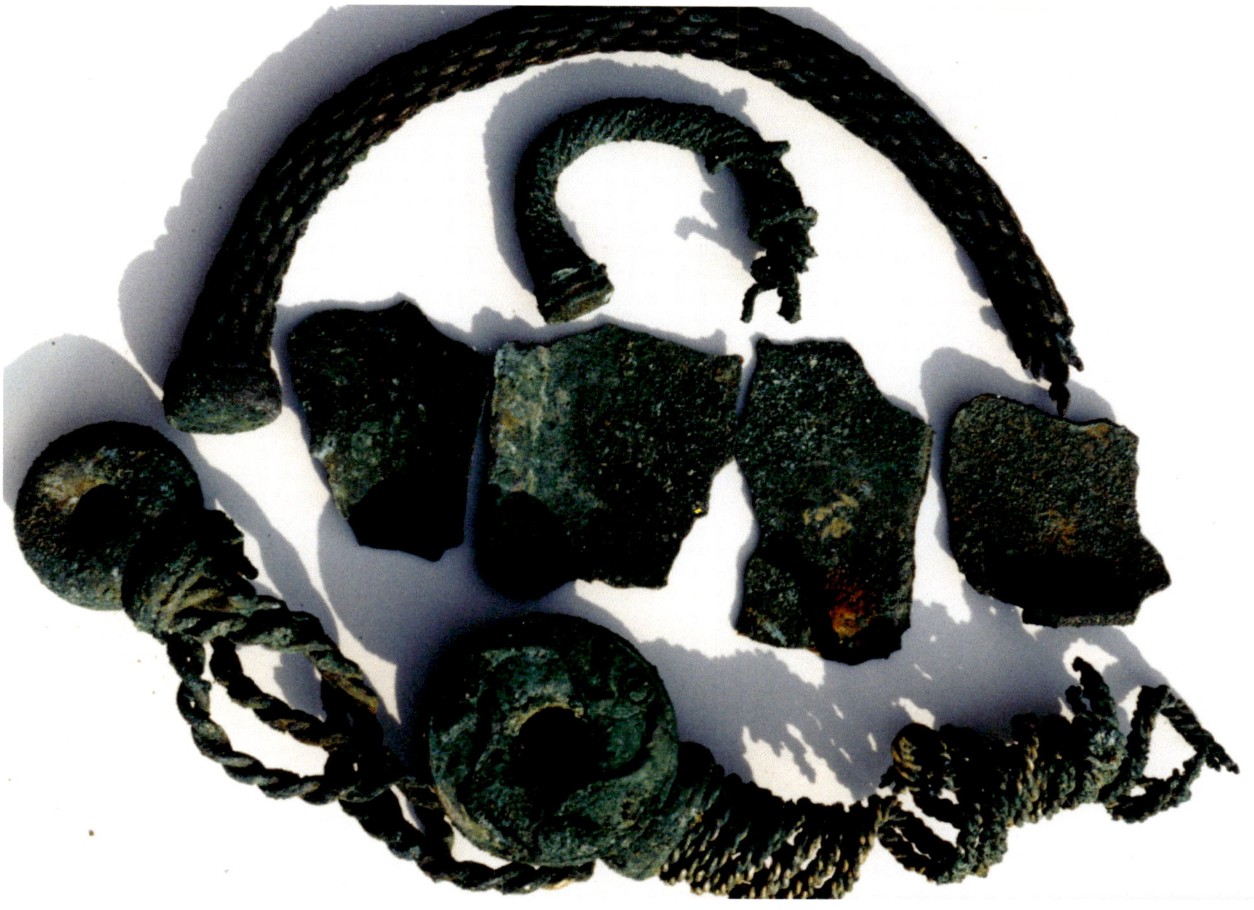

Figure 16.2 Helmet and torc fragments from Hoard F, photographed on site by Charles Hodder, showing green deposits of copper corrosion on surfaces

copper alloy and precious metal objects were comprehensively covered in green copper corrosion products at the time of recovery (**Fig. 16.2**).

Conservators bring their training and experience into play in deciding on appropriate choice of treatments and approaches to the retrieval of information. These decisions are acted upon after discussion with curators and scientists about the goals and direction of research. Corrosion removal is a relatively common procedure, but rigorous preliminary microscopic examination of surface and substrate is required to select the appropriate procedure, particularly if underlying polychromy or gilding is suspected (see Ch. 17).

It is a legitimate course of action to recover the original surface of corroded objects by the judicious use of dilute chemicals, where the substrate is suitable and providing their use is carefully managed and any residues neutralised or washed off (Cronyn 1990). The mild chemical reagents soften and loosen the copper corrosion products which can then be removed with wooden or metal tools. This process is carried out while working with a binocular microscope to avoid marking the surface, so that any original tool or wear marks can be assessed. It is also essential to restrict the use of chemicals to local and dilute applications, as early on in the conservation of the Snettisham torcs it was understood that there was a great variety of metal surface compositions, some of which were clearly the result of intentional treatments (see Ch. 17). As surface colour was clearly being manipulated for deliberate effect, it was essential that this evidence was not compromised by abrasive cleaning or polishing of the metal, which could have destroyed or damaged surviving evidence. Additionally, making joins to complete broken torcs would have hidden the metallurgy of the cross-section, where in many cases wires could clearly be seen to have enriched levels of silver and gold at their surfaces. Where technology studies took precedence over display criteria, such re-joining work was not progressed.

Gilding and organic evidence recovered during conservation

Corrosion products on the surface of objects was also found in some cases to be masking traces of gold leaf and mercury-amalgam gilding, used to embellish the silver and copper alloy torcs. This was uncovered during microscopic examination. In these instances, in order to avoid the risk of dislodging the gilding, corrosion could only be removed locally and incrementally under a binocular microscope, using small hand-tools such as small medical scalpels. Following examination and cleaning to reveal the decorative surfaces, many gilded fragments from broken copper alloy torcs were sorted and categorised by Institute of Archaeology MSc student He Huang, who then worked under BM metals scientist Dr Quanyu Wang in the X-ray fluorescence analysis (XRF) of the pre-sorted metalwork. (For results of analyses and technical discussion of gilding, see Ch. 17.)

Mineral-preserved organic remains are commonly found in association with archaeological metalwork where their

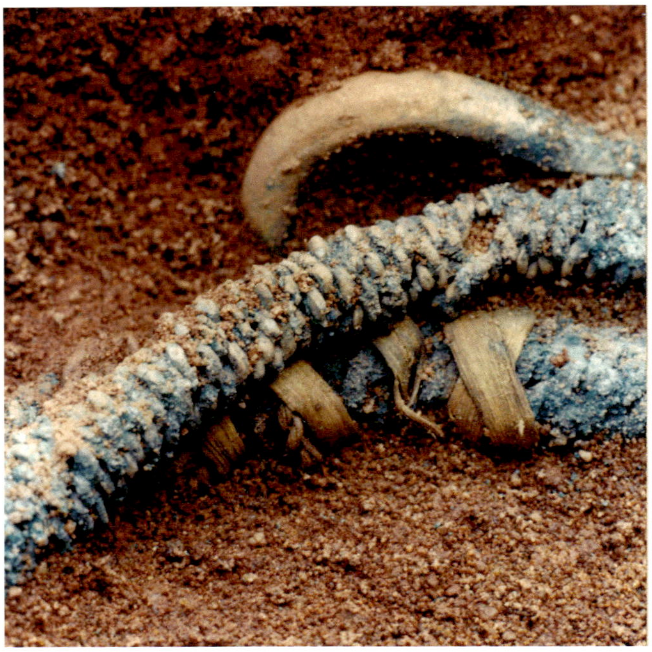

Figure 16.3 Detail of copper alloy torc L.6 *in situ* with original organic binding repair

exact form may be permanently captured or 'fossilised' in preserved or replaced form. Burning of wood to produce charcoal can also transform it to a stable form amenable to species identification. While undergoing microscopic investigation during the initial conservation process prior to corrosion removal and stabilisation, five torcs with charred organic remains in their terminals were revealed and conserved. Additionally, any other organic materials used, such as original repairs or attachments, were noted. Observations were logged by annotated drawings on conservation technical information records and drawn to the attention of materials scientists reviewing technological aspects of torc manufacture (see **Figs 17.55, 17.56, 19.1**). In order that these remains were amenable to taxonomic studies by scientists, consolidation with synthetic materials was kept to a minimum. (See Ch. 19 for identification and interpretation of organic materials found in association with the torcs.)

Fragmentation and reconstruction

The Snettisham hoards include a proportion of both fragmentary metal and melted pieces, for example those found in Hoard F. In these cases, it was important to distinguish between deliberate damage, resulting from human agency before burial, and post-deposition damage due to deteriorating physical condition. A timeline may be evident where deliberate pre-deposition damage and post-deposition damage occurs within the same objects, such as instances where inter-crystalline corrosion, developing through centuries of burial, causes tears and cracks exhibiting diagnostic granular edges, which run through ancient repairs or deliberate deformation.

Both copper alloy and silver alloy torcs had fragmented due to corrosion and a weakened structure, evidenced by a typical jagged break edge profile. Where it could be established that torcs had been subject to fragmentation as a consequence of corrosion and/or soil pressure during burial, they were, as far as possible, reconstructed using reversible adhesives. Where remedial work was helpful for illustrating original form and structure they were physically reconstructed and support mounts prepared.

There are two main goals in reassembly of fragmented objects: legibility and stability. While it is usual to attempt to return legibility to the original object and enable it to be studied and even appreciated as part of a museum display, more critically a corroded fragmentary object is always vulnerable to further damage. Natural corrosion processes during burial produce a weakened and transformed structure, prone to further disintegration and at risk from handling.

An example among the Snettisham torcs was L.6, a multi-strand copper alloy torc which had been broken and repaired by the time it was deposited. The plant fibre binding, wound round the damaged area of the torc in antiquity, can be clearly seen in a site photograph of the excavation of this hoard (**Fig. 16.3**; see Ch. 19 for identification and analysis).

The broken torc wires were still mobile, rendering the fragile organic binding extremely vulnerable. Neither the torc nor its repair had the physical strength to be self-supporting. After careful recovery by the site conservator and transfer to the conservation laboratory, the solution was to insert strands of fibreglass tissue, pre-soaked in adhesive, into the hollow core between the wires to give back its structural integrity and to immobilise both inorganic and organic elements (**Fig. 16.4a–b**).

The fibre binding was lightly consolidated to strengthen its weakened structure and an unconsolidated sample kept for identification purposes. The torc in a conserved condition could now be displayed as part of its contextual group, Hoard L. The display support mount lifted the binding clear of direct contact with any surface.

In addition to unintentional breakage, deliberate cutting up could also be recognised among the finds from Snettisham. A good example is a solid, plain, copper alloy torc K.1, which had intentionally been cut up into short sections (for more on the practice of cutting up, see Ch. 20). It would be inappropriate to reconstruct this torc even though it would have been quite feasible to reassemble it. The solution was to lay out the pieces in their relative position in a pre-cut mount so the torc could be physically supported but could be easily read as a complete object, making categorisation and cataloguing easier.

Investigative reshaping

Hoard F contained two crushed gold alloy tubular torc fragments, each consisting of a terminal and a short part of the hollow neck-ring (F.31a and F.43). Both were reshaped by metals conservator Marilyn Hockey in 2007 at the request of Ian Stead and Jody Joy. The torcs were first assessed for suitability in terms of their physical properties and the validity of the rationale for changing appearance by this route of intervention. Ethical investigative reshaping carried out at the BM had been described some years previously at an international metals conference (Hockey 2001) and had been explored in an earlier publication (Oddy 1992; see also Hockey 1989; 1993; 1999; 2001).

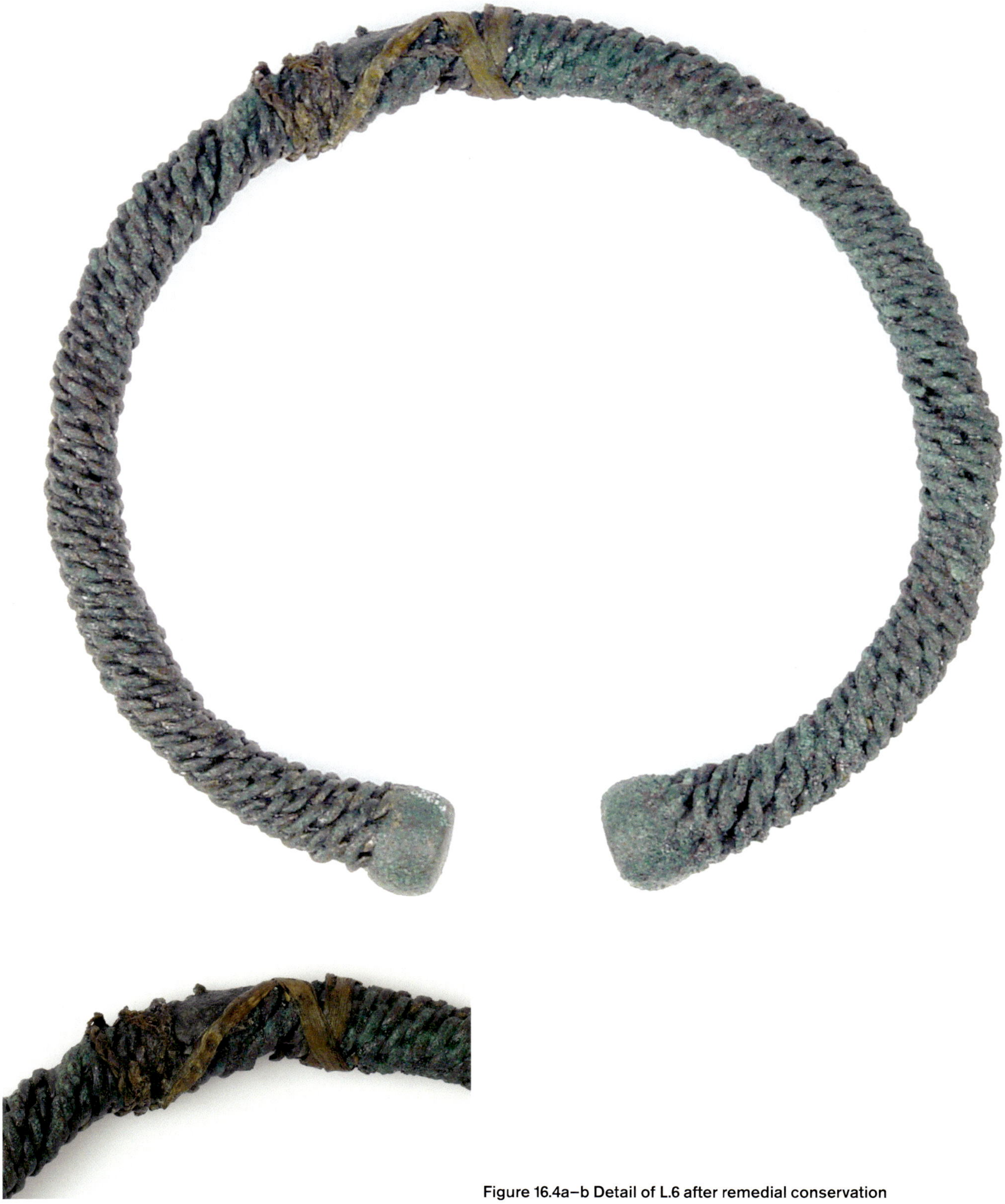

Figure 16.4a–b Detail of L.6 after remedial conservation

An essential corollary to the feasibility of the shaping process is the ethics of reshaping ancient metal. If it can be proven that the object was deliberately deformed or broken in antiquity it would be unlikely that it would be 'taken back' to an earlier albeit undamaged condition unless, as is the case with torcs F.31a and F.43, such work is considered essential to progress interpretation and scholarship (Oddy 1992; Hockey 2001). After detailed discussion with curators it was decided that as so few items from the hoards were decorated, and given that the decoration on these pieces was so unusual, the research potential of this reshaping work outweighed other ethical considerations, so long as the work was fully documented.

Alloy content is a critical point as reshaping of crushed gold metal may not be practically possible where silver or copper is also present as they can harden and embrittle the nobler metal, particularly where inter-crystalline corrosion has occurred. This is equally true of silver alloys with a high

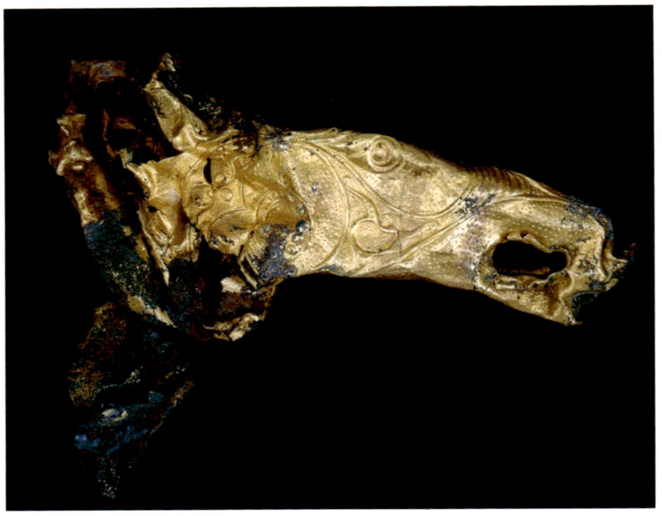

Figure 16.5 Hollow gold torc F.43, before investigative reshaping

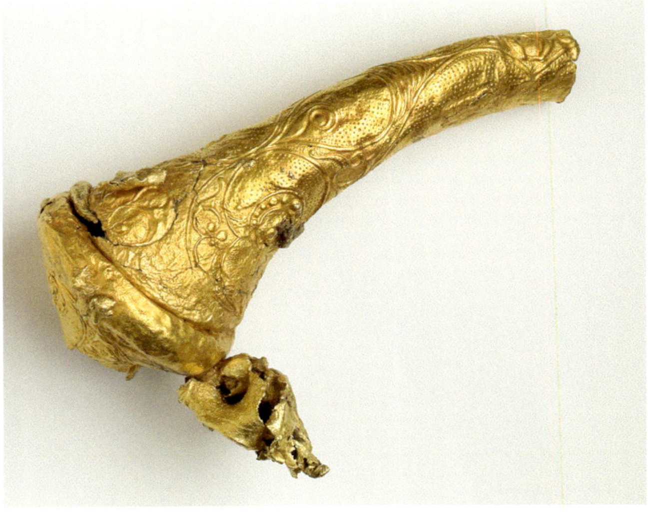

Figure 16.6 Hollow gold torc F.43, after investigative reshaping

copper content where the precious metal has been extended by alloying with a baser copper content. In the instance of the crushed gold torcs from Hoard F, a detailed condition assessment was undertaken by both the conservator and metallurgist Duncan Hook before any physical manipulation was progressed. This included metallurgical work to confirm the purity of the gold and therefore its amenability to reshaping.

The advantages of investigative and remedial reshaping fundamentally include bringing structural integrity and strength by restoring the original form and shape of the object (Hockey 2001). This is achieved by manual manipulation, bringing together breaks and unfolding creases by hand, while backing or bridging weak areas with the use of adhesives and lightweight backing materials such as nylon gossamer tissue. No hot working is used in this process. The use of heat in the reshaping or repair of archaeological gold is not necessary in circumstances such as those described here and carries risks which almost invariably contraindicate its use.

Torc F.43 was fully reshaped manually as described above. The fragment had self-evidently been deliberately flattened and pierced for suspension in antiquity. Molten pieces of other gold objects had then attached themselves to areas of the already flattened surface (**Fig. 16.5**). The rationale for reversing this ancient flattening was as mentioned above, to reveal the hidden decoration, which was the subject of speculation. Only after unfolding could the full design be seen for the first time (**Fig. 16.6**).

F.31a was investigated experimentally and partly opened out using the same methods as in F.43, to reveal the decoration and its original form. A new discovery was a hidden piece of another torc (F.31b) which was released from its trapped position inside the terminal.

Since the date of this work, non-invasive methods of imaging such as Computed Tomography (CT) scanning have been developed, which in some cases can be used to interrogate the hidden interiors as well as surfaces of objects (Fletcher 2017). These techniques remain challenging to use on gold alloys, due to X-ray absorption and scatter from the metal (see Ch. 17), but it is possible that such non-invasive imaging options might be possible on similar objects in the future. Reflectance Transformation Imaging (RTI) is also now routinely carried out in the Museum and elsewhere in the cultural heritage field to interrogate and resolve surfaces of objects.

Conclusions

The conservation of the Snettisham torcs at the BM involved an integrated team of archaeologists, curators, specialist material scientists, metals conservators and replica makers. This interdisciplinary team enabled the entire assemblage to be researched in depth over decades. The precious metal torcs from Snettisham, which are of the best of their group, occupied the majority of the efforts. On completion of the gold and silver torcs, the team could also turn to the fragmentary copper alloy and sheet-metal objects.

The approach was carefully tailored for each object, based on an assessment of structural integrity and degree of corrosion, biography (whether any damage was intentional or accidental), whether traces of organics or technological processes such as gilding survived, and the potential costs and benefits of more interventive processes such as reshaping. This fundamental work has enabled the hundreds of complete and fragmentary torcs from Snettisham to be catalogued, researched and, in many cases, displayed to the public.

Chapter 17
Technology and Manufacture of the Snettisham Torcs

Nigel Meeks, Aude Mongiatti, Daniel O'Flynn and John Fenn, with contributions by Janet Ambers, Caroline Cartwright, Duncan Hook and Susan La Niece

17.1 Introduction

This chapter deals with the technology and manufacture of the torcs from Snettisham. The number and variety of torcs from the site provide a unique opportunity to study Iron Age metalsmithing traditions. The technological history of an object is locked into the microstructure and composition of the metal and the tool marks from the goldsmith's handiwork are preserved in the surface. Varied colours, from golden through to silver, reflect the compositional range of the alloys used, and processes of surface enrichment and even gilding.

Building on a preliminary publication by Meeks *et al.* (2014), this chapter presents the first fully detailed publication of the comprehensive technological examination of the Snettisham metalwork. Further technical and scientific analyses that informed detailed descriptions of individual objects are presented in the catalogue, Chapter 14.

This chapter is divided into six main parts. The first, section 17.2, introduces the analytical techniques used, the range of objects sampled and the sampling methodology. Over a hundred objects were analysed, selected to be representative of wider patterns among the hoard material.

The main materials used in the construction of many of the torcs are gold sheet and wires and the composition and manufacture of these materials are investigated in detail in sections 17.3 and 17.4.

In terms of composition, the analysis showed four different alloy groups:

- High gold-silver with low copper alloys (used in both wires and sheet objects)
- Silver-gold-copper alloys (wires)
- High-copper and low-gold silver alloys (wires)
- Bronzes (wires)

The nature of these alloys reveals the skill and adaptability of Iron Age metalsmiths. The high-gold alloys used for sheet metal were carefully selected for maximum malleability and ductility, whilst the wide range of alloys used in wire manufacture seems to have been designed to take advantage of the compositions with the lowest possible melting temperatures.

Colour was clearly an important element in alloy selection too, and both wire and sheet components show distinct evidence for specific treatments such as surface enrichment of gold/silver content. Extensive experimental work on wire production, in partnership with accomplished metalsmith John Fenn (detailed on p. 433), has revolutionised our understanding of how this versatile material was manufactured in late Iron Age Britain. Fenn was able to produce extremely close replicas of the wires seen at Snettisham, demonstrating that they were produced by forging out square-section wire from an ingot or rod. Repeated cycles of hammering, annealing and pickling to create the wires resulted in the selective removal of much of the copper from the surface, while the gold and silver from the original copper-rich core phase both stayed in the surface layer, consequently enriching it in precious metals.

This transforms the surface colour, which becomes notably silvery/pale gold compared to the coppery-coloured core. Some of the gold sheet samples tested, and wires with a very thick enriched surface, in particular those with depleted silver as well as copper, may also have been treated by a chemical process akin to the 'parting process' used in gold refining.

These aspects of alloy composition, colour and surface treatment are discussed in section 17.5. Perhaps the most dramatic discovery is the use, on some bronze torc wires, of mercury gilding. This is the earliest documented use of this technique in Britain and speaks to the wide networks of trade and technological exchange in which goldsmiths and their communities must have been involved. The techniques observed at Snettisham suggest a preference for torcs in colours ranging from white, through pale or silvery greenish-gold, to yellow-gold. More reddish/copper-coloured alloys appear to have been avoided, though of course bronze objects appear in most of the hoards. The deployment of gilding, however, does suggest that yellow gold must have been a highly valued colour.

The final main section, 17.6, is a comprehensive study of the construction of multi-component torcs with details of the manufacture of large wire neck-rings and a focus on cast-on terminals and other forms of terminal construction. The range of objects at the site is extraordinary, with remarkable variation across certain standard elements of torc construction. Tubular torcs and a small number of unusual terminals were constructed from gold sheet. These complicated composite objects were soldered or mechanically attached together, some including decorative elements such as beaded wire and filigree, with tooled decoration including both simple punch-marks and high-relief repoussé designs embellished with punching and chasing. Multi-strand torcs also show great diversity, from the simplest two-wire neck-rings to complicated designs which combine wires in multiple stages to produce effects resembling cables or braids. The preservation of organic remains in some small bronze torcs demonstrates how wires were sometimes coiled around a wooden core to create a rope-like effect. Terminals are just as diverse, ranging from simple loops made from the ends of the neck-ring wires, to solid cast-on buffer and torus terminals, right through to complex composite terminals with both cast and sheet elements. The range of techniques and designs employed suggests a rich and varied metalworking tradition, revealing the incredible skill and depth of knowledge of the metalworkers who created these spectacular objects.

Finally, a short discussion and summary of the findings is presented in section 17.7.

A note on alloys

The terminology used around alloys in this chapter is different from the more general terms applied in the catalogue. There are well over a thousand metal objects and fragments from Snettisham, and the vast majority have not been subject to scientific analysis to determine their precise composition. For this reason, the catalogue uses only general terms based, in most cases, on visual examination of the objects. The term 'gold/silver alloy' is used for torcs where visual analysis suggests a significant precious metal content. The analytical work outlined in this chapter and in Chapter 18 (on samples prepared specifically for microscopy and analysis of uncorroded core metal) shows that most of these are ternary alloys of gold, silver and copper, and that this broad group includes some alloys in which copper is the dominant component. Thus, 'gold/silver alloy' as used in the catalogue, includes: high gold-silver/ low copper alloys, silver-gold-copper alloys, and high-copper/ low-gold silver alloys. For those objects where only a visual examination of their surface has been carried out, it is not possible to categorise them into these alloy groups because the surface colour is not necessarily indicative of the core alloy composition due to surface enrichment effects (detailed in sections below).

In the catalogue, the broad term 'copper alloy' is used for those objects and numerous fragments that clearly exhibit a greenish surface corrosion patina, common to such buried objects. Scientific analysis of a limited number of these (82 analysed in Ch. 18; Appendix 5) show they are all of bronze (i.e. the common and widespread alloy of copper and tin), which strongly suggests that the vast majority, if not all, of the 'copper alloy' objects in the Snettisham Hoards are bronzes. Analysis has also revealed that some of these bronze objects were originally gilded.

The binary distinction in the catalogue between copper alloy and precious metal objects is simplistic compared to the nuanced scientific analysis presented here. However, it does reflect what appears to be a genuine ancient distinction between bronzes and objects containing significant amounts of gold and silver (see Ch. 18).

17.2 Methods and sampling strategy

In order to investigate the goldsmithing manufacturing and decorative techniques used to create the Snettisham artefacts, a number of complete torcs were first studied non-invasively using radiography and microscopy, the majority of these from Hoard L (see **Table 17.1**). Most were also analysed non-destructively using X-ray fluorescence (XRF) on their surface to identify their alloy compositions. The initial results obtained from these non-invasive analyses were useful although limited: a wide range of alloys was identified, but due to potential surface effects, such as deliberate treatment and corrosion, surface analysis may not fully reflect the core metal. Similarly, the construction of torcs could be identified directly from artefacts but the making of individual components, such as sheets and wires, needed further investigation. The broken fragments of torcs, sheets and wires from Hoard F provided the perfect opportunity for selection, sampling and preparing small cut pieces for full compositional analysis and metallurgical examination, which would identify core alloy compositions, surface enrichment and details of sheet and wire making. The preliminary non-invasive binocular optical microscopy (OM) study provided an informed sampling strategy in terms of the range of components' colours, sizes and shapes and corresponding types of alloys.

From the wide range of torcs, wire components and fragments in the collection, representative examples of most types were examined for evidence of construction, and appropriate samples taken of these types from the fragmentary Hoard F for microscopy and analysis (**Table 17.1** gives a full listing of all objects analysed or sampled as

Catalogue number (this volume)	Registration number (BM unless otherwise noted; NCM = Norwich Castle Museum)	X-radiography	SEM imaging	Optical microscopy	Polished cross-section specimen number	SEM imaging of polished sample	SEM-EDX analysis	Optical microscopy of etched bronze sample
	Snettisham finds							
A.1	1949.74.2 (NCM)	x		x				
A.2	1949.74.1 (NCM)			x				
A.3	1949.74.3 (NCM)			x				
A.4	1949.74.6 (NCM)	x						
A.5	1949.74.4 (NCM)			x				
A.6	1949.74.5 (NCM)			x				
A.7	1949.74. (NCM)			x				
E.1a (Great Torc)	1951,0402.2	x	x	x				
F.5c	1991,0501.55			x				
F.5d	1991,0501.56			x	J1513	x	x	
F.5e	1991,0501.57			x	J1515	x	x	
F.5f	1991,0501.58			x	J1514	x	x	
F.9a	1991,0501.125		x	x	J1494	x	x	
F.9c	1991,0501.127		x	x	J1495	x	x	
F.9d	1991,0501.128		x	x	J1496	x	x	
F.11a	1991,0501.133		x	x	J1497	x	x	
F.14b	1991,0702.9		x	x	J1532	x	x	
F.15a	1991,0702.137		x	x				
F.17a	1991,0501.216		x	x	J1533	x	x	
F.17b	1991,0702.8		x		J1534	x	x	
F.19b	1991,0501.161		x	x	J1493	x	x	
F.21b	1991,0501.207		x	x	J1531	x	x	
F.22a	1991,0501.148		x	x	J1488	x	x	
F.34	1991,0501.16		x	x	J1503	x	x	
F.35	1991,0501.21			x				
F.37	1991,0501.24		x (of wire)	x	J1505	x	x	
F.40	1991,0501.52			x				
F.48	1991,0501.27		x	x	J1506	x	x	
F.49	1991,0501.138		x	x	J1501	x	x	
F.51	1991,0501.34		x	x	J1521	x	x	
F.52	1991,0501.76		x	x	J1509	x	x	
F.53	1991,0501.118				J1523	x	x	
F.55	1991,0501.32		x	x	J1507	x	x	
F.62	1991,0501.30		x	x	J1522	x	x	
F.65	1991,0501.36		x	x	J1508	x	x	
F.72	1991,0501.45		x	x				
F.84	1991,0501.158		x	x	J1492	x	x	
F.85	1991,0501.95		x	x	J1525	x	x	
F.88	1991,0501.22		x	x	J1504	x	x	
F.89	1991,0501.101		x	x	J1524	x	x	
F.93	1991,0501.83		x	x	J1510	x	x	
F.94	1991,0501.17		x	x	J1502	x	x	
F.97	1991,0501.85		x	x	J1511	x	x	

Table 17.1 Objects analysed as part of this study, and methods used

Catalogue number (this volume)	Registration number (BM unless otherwise noted; NCM = Norwich Castle Museum)	X-radiography	SEM imaging	Optical microscopy	Polished cross-section specimen number	SEM imaging of polished sample	SEM-EDX analysis	Optical microscopy of etched bronze sample
F.99	1991,0501.137		x	x	J1498	x	x	
F.102	1991,0501.187		x	x	J1538	x	x	
F.103	1991,0501.215		x	x	J1530	x	x	
F.106	1991,0501.19			x				
F.108	1991,0501.154		x	x	J1490	x	x	
F.116	1991,0501.145		x	x	J1500	x	x	
F.119–20	1991,0501,80–81		x	x	J1460	x	x	
F.122	1991,0501.153		x		J1491	x	x	
F.135	1991,0501.222		x	x	J1526	x	x	
F.146	1991,0501.214		x	x	J1529	x	x	
F.147	1991,0501.221		x	x	J1527	x	x	
F.148	1991,0501.86		x	x	J1512	x	x	
F.153	1991,0407.44.a			x	J1516	x	x	
F.154	1991,0501.144		x	x	J1499	x	x	
F.156	1991,0501.87		x	x	J1520	x	x	
F.158	1991,0501.191		x	x	J1537	x	x	
F.159	1991,0501.193		x	x	J1535	x	x	
F.160	1991,0501.192		x	x	J1536	x	x	
F.167	1991,0702.122		x	x				
F.168	1991,0702.121		x	x				
F.179	1991,0702.117		x	x				
F.182	1991,0702.111		x	x				
F.250	1991,0702.181				J1462	x	x	x
F.361	1991,0702.84		x	x	J1463T (transverse section) J1464L (longitudinal section)	x	x	x
F.380	1991,0501.218				J1528	x	x	
F.429	1991,0501.156		x	x	J1489	x	x	
G6	1990,1101.12; 1990,1101.14				J1022	x	x	
L.1	1991,0407.23			x				
L.2	1991,0407.24			x				
L.3	1991,0407.25			x				
L.4	1991,0407.26			x				
L.6	1990,1101.7			x				
L.7	1991,0407.27			x				
L.13	1991,0407.31			x				
L.14	1991,0407.32			x				
L.16	1991,0407.34		x	x				
L.17	1991,0407.35			x				
L.18	1991,0407.36			x				
L.19a (Grotesque Torc)	1991,0407.37	x	x	x				
L.21a	1991,0407.39			x				

Table 17.1 continued

Catalogue number (this volume)	Registration number (BM unless otherwise noted; NCM = Norwich Castle Museum)	X-radiography	SEM imaging	Optical microscopy	Polished cross-section specimen number	SEM imaging of polished sample	SEM-EDX analysis	Optical microscopy of etched bronze sample
S.11a	1991,0407.57		x	x	J1517	x	x	
S.11b	1991,0407.47			x	J1519	x	x	
S.13	1991,0407.40		x	x				
S.16	1969.55.3 (NCM)			x				
S.17	1965.30.1 (NCM			x				
S.19	1992,1203.4			x				
S.32	1991,0407.50					x	x	
S.34	1991,0501.226		x	x				
S.35	1991,0407.51		x	x				
S.36	1991,0407.49		x	x				
S.37	1992,1203.1		x	x		x	x	
S.38	1991,0501.223		x					
S.39	1991,0501.225		x	x				
	Sedgeford Torc							
N/A	2005,1103.1	x	x	x				
N/A	1968,1004.1	x		x				
	Newark Torc							
N/A	Newark and Sherwood Museum Service	x	x	x				

Table 17.1 continued

part of this study). This allowed the technological study of goldsmithing practices and the determination of alloy compositions and surface-enrichment processes. The technological study involved visual examination and photographic recording of complete and fragmentary torcs for their physical form and metalsmithing construction techniques. This was followed by detailed examination involving macro-imaging, digital optical microscopy and scanning electron microscopy with energy dispersive X-ray microanalysis (SEM-EDX) of objects and samples taken from fragments to unravel their metallurgical technology. This comprehensive approach provided visual and analytical evidence of the sophisticated metalworking techniques used by the Iron Age craftworkers. In addition, XRF surface analysis was carried out on various torcs that were not able to be sampled. XRF was the technique used for the original analytical survey of the excavated material and discovered the use of mercury gilding on some bronze objects (see below and Ch. 18 for more on mercury gilding): an early analytical study of sampled fragments from the collection of Snettisham material at Norwich Castle Museum for a BA dissertation provided the first clues to the potential range of alloys used (Stone 1987; Ch. 18; Appendix 5). High-voltage X-radiography was used on a few selected torcs and terminals to investigate internal structures and fabrication techniques. A series of experimental reconstructions of key goldsmithing processes allowed metallurgical characterisation of the goldsmithing technologies and workshop practices, and a comprehensive understanding of the metals and methods used.

Full details of the techniques and terminologies used in optical microscopy, scanning electron microscopy with microanalysis and X-radiography are given on pp. 475–7.

Sampling of fragmentary wires, sheet and terminals from Hoard F

It has been long recognised that the main techniques for constructing torcs and terminals in Iron Age Britain were a combination of thick and thin wire manufacture, casting of some terminals, creation of a variety of sheet components, and various punching, chasing, engraving and forming operations as appropriate for the individual objects (Brailsford and Stapley 1972; Clarke 1954), the range of which illustrates the extensive skill-set of the metalsmiths. All of these processes are represented at Snettisham, and Hoard F (an assorted collection of hundreds of fragments of broken, cut and damaged objects) is broadly representative of the range of terminal and neck-ring types, alloys, colours, and construction techniques. Because many artefacts from Hoard F are fragmentary, this provided the opportunity for selective sampling in order to carry out a full metallurgical and SEM-EDX examination and microanalytical survey of the wide range of wire types and colours. In addition, many of the fragments are small enough to allow direct observation of their surfaces in the large chamber SEM to

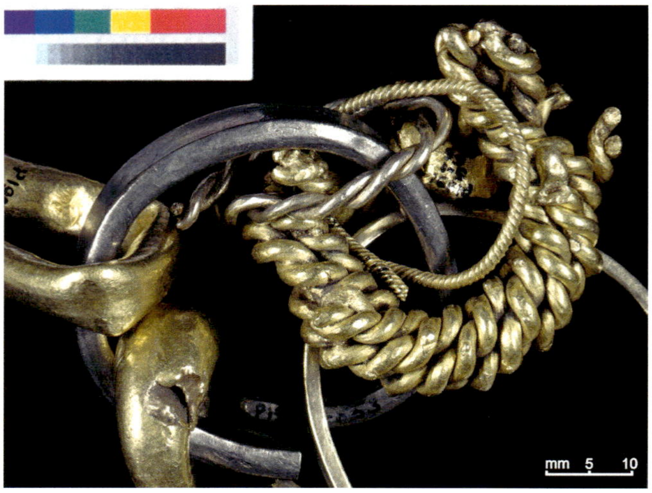

Figure 17.1 Example of an interlinked wire assemblage from Hoard F (F.5a–g) with several different wire types of gold and silver alloys (see also Fig. 17.18a–b)

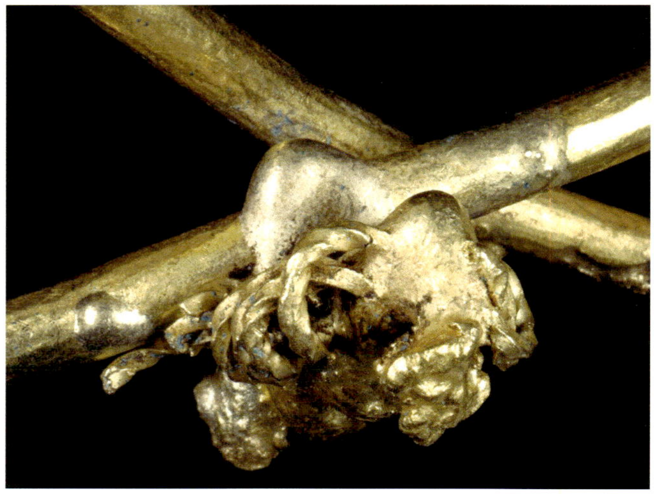

Figure 17.2 Fused mixed gold wires with solidified molten globules, Hoard F (F.40)

characterise surface textures, worked details and physical forms, corrosion and damage/cutting, and wear during use. Hoard F was therefore identified as ideal for the purpose of our scientific investigation into wide-ranging aspects of torc construction and manufacture without requiring damage to complete objects.

The fragmentary wires range between 0.6mm to just over 10mm in thickness and are of various forms: circular section with smooth surfaces, finely faceted circular section, heavily faceted 'polygonal' section, very thick multi-faceted 'circular' section, square section, twisted square section, and some heavily corroded wires whose forms cannot now be discerned. Multiple wires were often coiled or twisted/plied together to make multi-strand constructions (see the neck-ring construction typology section in Ch. 13). Additionally, there are composite groups of various mixed and seemingly unrelated torc and wire fragments interlinked together (**Fig. 17.1**), and also fused mixed wire assemblages with solidified molten globules on their surfaces (**Fig. 17.2**) (see also sections on these composite objects in Chs 20 and 23).

Binocular optical microscopy of the fragmentary mixed wire and sheet objects of Hoard F facilitated selection for sampling. In addition, digital imaging recorded the key characteristics of the sampled wire types that were representative of the whole range of gold, silver and bronze torcs and wires found within the Snettisham collection. As the colours of the wires and sheets are determined by the surface composition of the metal, it was essential to sample and mount them as polished cross-sections for microscopy and analysis, to characterise the full range of alloys used and compare the original core metal with the surface composition and microstructure and identify potential evidence of surface-enrichment processes.

In consultation with curators and following careful macroscopic and microscopic assessments of the fragments and artefacts from Hoard F, over 50 small samples *c.* 2mm long were cut through wire and sheet using a low-speed diamond saw (**Fig. 17.3a**). Samples were mounted in epoxy resin and cross-sections polished down to a final finish with 1 micron diamond paste (**Fig. 17.3b**). For SEM-EDX microscopy and analysis, the gold and silver alloy samples

Figure 17.3a–b a) Low speed diamond saw in action cutting a multi-strand thin wire sample (arrowed) from reel terminal torc F.120 (object in Fig. 17.39); b) Cut sample of tightly twisted multi-strand bronze torc/bracelet fragment F.361 (detail in Fig. 17.54a–e) mounted in transverse cross-section in the centre of a resin mount and polished ready for optical microscopy and SEM examination. The mount is 30mm in diameter

a

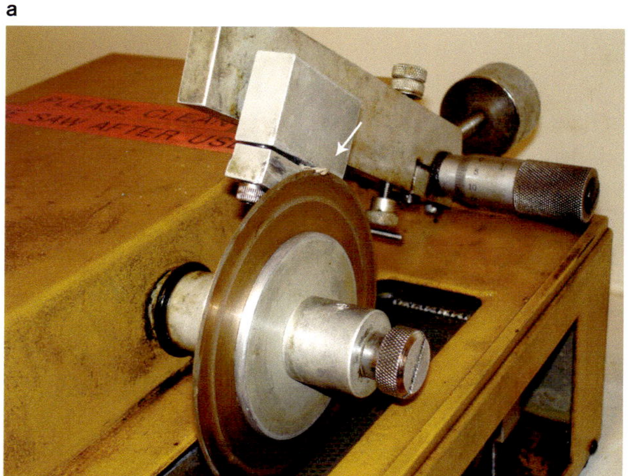

b

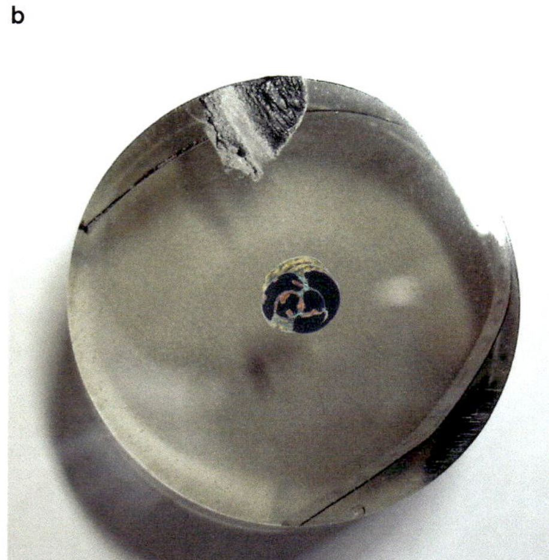

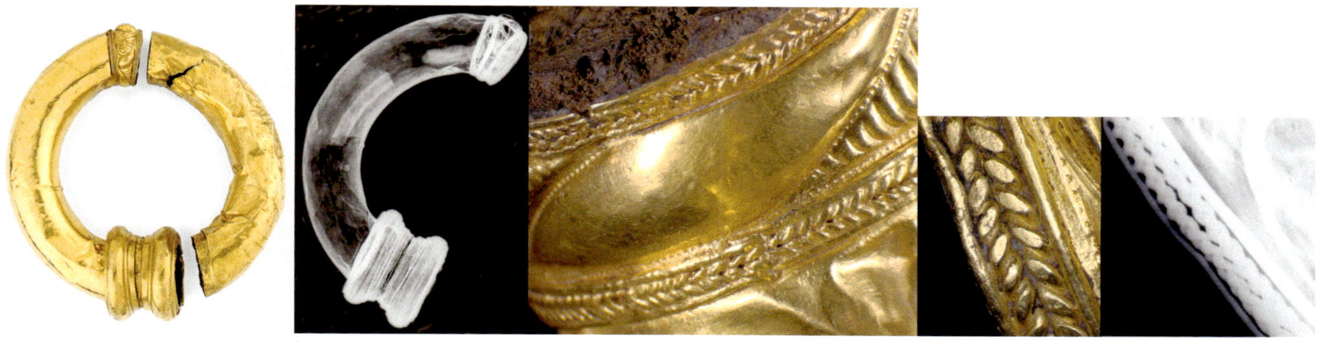

Figure 17.4a–e a) Large gold tubular torc A.1 (approx. diameter 240mm front to back including terminals); b) Film X-radiograph of torc A.1 showing the broken iron core inside (radiograph: J. Ambers); c, d) Photomicrographs and e) X-radiograph detail of the chased, punched and filigree wire decoration (Z- and S-twist adjacent pairs) on the rear join 'terminal' of torc A.1

were not etched (to avoid changing the composition), but the microstructures and different compositional phases were observed by SEM backscattered electron (BSE) imaging. Bronze samples from small fragmentary torcs were etched to show grain structures by optical microscopy. Gilded bronzes were examined by SEM-EDX in cross-section and directly on the object surface to identify the gilding method and illustrate wear in places where the gilding was worn through to the underlying bronze. In addition, some of the small multi-wire bronze torcs were mounted in section to study the trapped charred wood stem cores that were found *in situ* from surface examination (see p. 455).

The following sections examine the materials used in the objects from Snettisham: gold sheet (17.3) and wire (17.4), before going on to consider the wider significance of the alloy composition, surface treatments, and colours of these objects (17.5).

17.3 Gold sheet: composition, decoration and use in objects' manufacture

Some of the largest and most visually impressive objects from Snettisham, as well as the most ornately decorated, are torcs made from thin gold sheet. This section deals with the composition and manufacture of gold sheet torcs and torc components, with more detail also given in the relevant catalogue entries (Ch. 14).

The skill of working with sheet gold formed a parallel metalsmithing technology to that seen in the (more numerous) wire torcs. In particular, sheet-working techniques were used to construct large Type 6 tubular torcs (**Fig. 17.4a–e**, see typology in Ch. 13, especially **Fig. 13.5**) found predominantly in Hoards A and F, as well as terminals of various kinds.

In some cases sheet and wire components were combined in a single object: hollow sheet terminals such as F.72 (**Fig. 17.100c–d**) were joined to multi-strand wire neck-rings, as seen on the Grotesque Torc, L.19 (**Fig. 17.98a–c**.). The production of these torc terminals is discussed elsewhere in this chapter (see p. 471).

Construction and decoration of gold sheet objects

The elaborate decoration on many of the gold sheet torcs at Snettisham was created using a variety of techniques, chief among them chasing, punching and repoussé. These three techniques are types of plastic deformation, meaning that no metal is removed but the distortion is permanent and irreversible (Untracht 1982; Maryon 2011). Chasing deforms the metal sheet from the front side by hammering punches of various shapes across the surface to produce decorative patterns, while punching involves the impression of a single design, usually repeated more than once, by striking a punch with a hammer. Chasing is often applied in combination with repoussé, which entails deforming the metal from the back to create highly three-dimensional shapes and decoration. These techniques were applied in the manufacture of many of the tubular torcs and other sheet components, along with the introduction of other decorative elements such as filigree and beaded wire.

Type 6 tubular torcs

The large Type 6 tubular torcs such as those from Hoard A (Ch. 13, **Fig. 13.7**, and see catalogue entries in Ch. 14) were constructed from a number of sheet components. The terminals of the large Type 6 torcs are separate elements, with some showing evidence for repoussé as well as chased

Figure 17.5 Detail of the uniformly spaced, accurately made, beaded wire on the terminal of tubular torc A.2

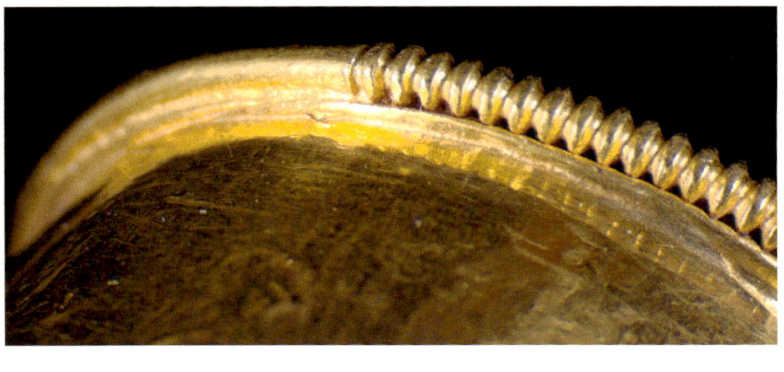

Figure 17.6 Detail of filigree wire (both S-twist adjacent pairs) on separate ring A.7, which is most likely from fragmented tubular torc A.4–6

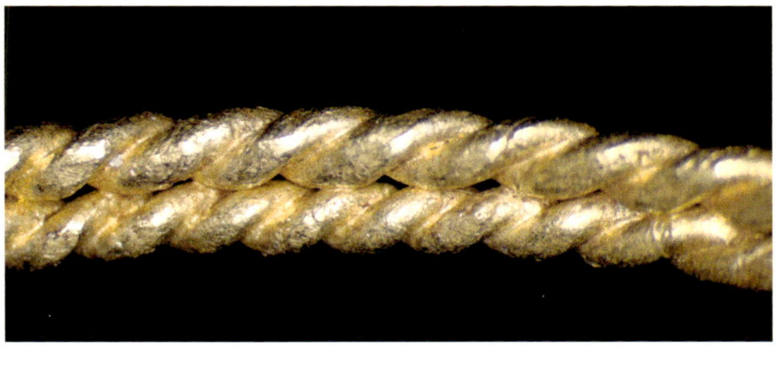

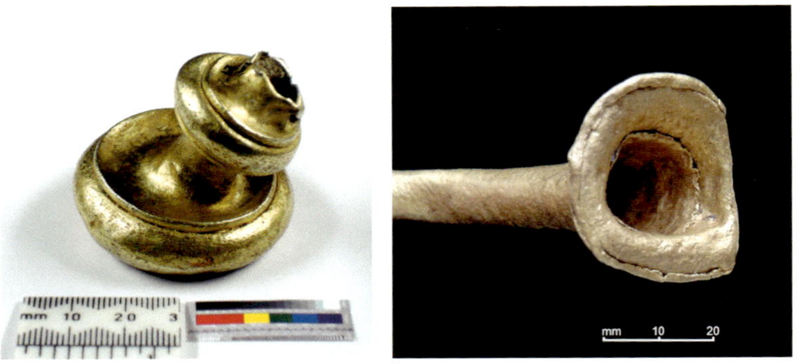

a b

Figure 17.7a–b a) Hollow terminal F.48 showing levels of construction, and b) hollow neck-ring F.62 from a similar terminal, showing the internal overlapping tubular sheet construction

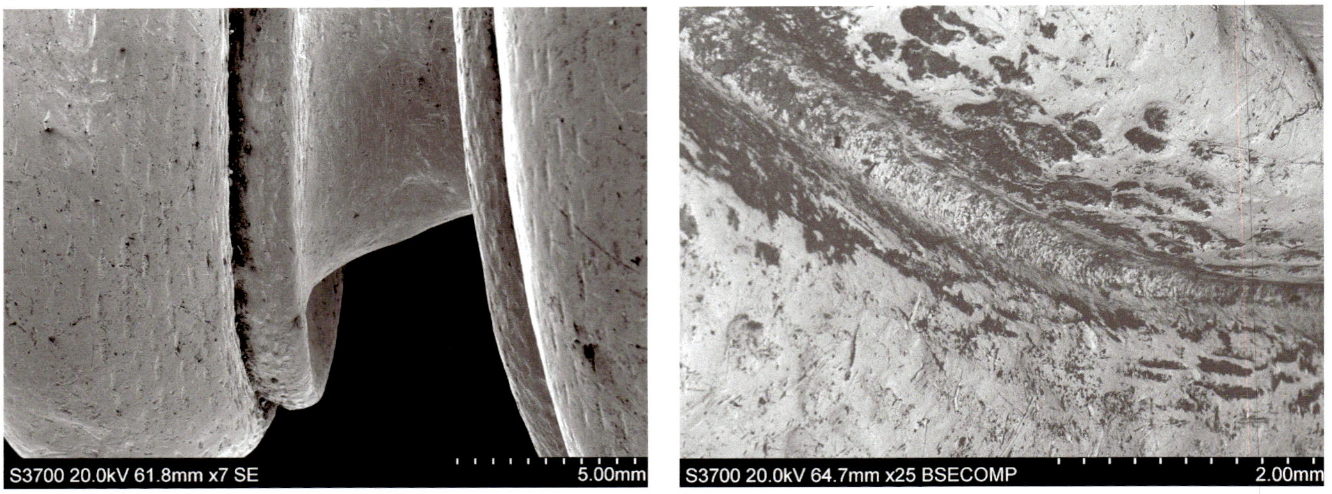

a b

Figure 17.8a–b SEM images of hollow terminal F.48: a) Secondary electron (SE) image of diagnostic tool marks for the shaping and decoration and b) BSE image of the characteristic dendritic surface structure of soldered areas between components. SEM image widths *c.* 15 and 5mm respectively

and punched decoration (e.g. **Fig. 17.4a–e**, and see Ch. 14). These terminals were affixed to the tubular neck-rings, which are made in two parts, each forming around half the circumference of the torc and joining at both the back and front of the neck (**Fig. 17.4a**). The large decorative terminals sit at the front of these torcs, and torc A.1 also has a decorative 'terminal' section at the rear join (**Fig. 17.4a**). The tubular neck-rings themselves were made from thin gold sheet supported by a central iron core (**Fig. 17.4b**), packed with lightweight filler material (now missing), perhaps a mixture of clay, sand and wax (Clarke 1954, 37). Decorative wirework was also incorporated into the tubular torc designs, with evidence for use of beaded wires (Williams and Ogden 1994; Whitfield 2004) on the neck-ring of A.2 (**Fig. 17.5** and Ch. 14), filigree on the rear connector of A.1 (**Fig. 17.4c–e**), and a separate ring (A.7) that may be part of broken tubular torc A.4–6 (**Fig. 17.6** and Ch. 14).

Detailed observations on construction from the scientific analysis of Hoard A are included in the catalogue entries in Chapter 14, where additional images of the object features and metalsmithing techniques described here can be found.

Figure 17.9 Anthropomorphic tubular face terminal S.13 with designs created by a combination of repoussé, chasing and punching

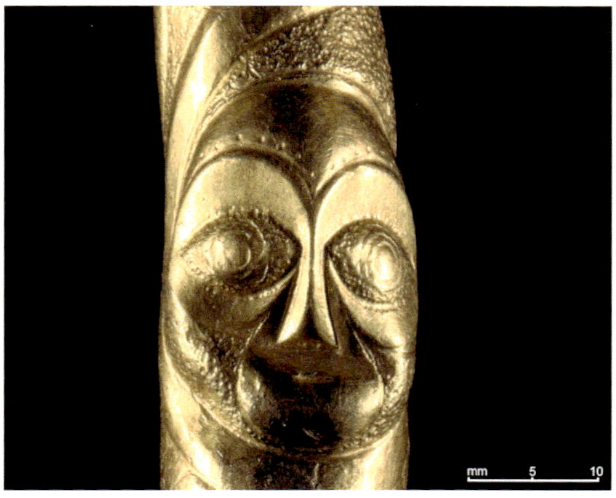

Other tubular torcs

Gold sheet was also used for other types of tubular torc. The manufacturing techniques used were varied and are discussed in more detail on a case-by-case basis in catalogue entries in Chapter 14.

Type 3 tubular torcs (see Ch. 13, **Fig. 13.7**) have multi-component terminals and narrow neck-rings, as seen on F.48, which is made of several pieces soldered together circumferentially to produce the terminal (**Fig. 17.7a**), and F.62, a hollow neck-ring flaring to a trumpet shape, which shows tube-in-tube assembly (**Fig. 17.7b**). Terminal F.48 has a finely punched decorative texture (**Fig. 17.8a**) and dendritic solder joining components (**Fig. 17.8b**).

Some sheet gold tubular torcs, for example the anthropomorphic face terminal S.13 (**Fig. 17.9**) from a Type 4 tubular torc, reveal diagnostic marks and patterns from hammering and shaping the decorative designs using the traditional goldworking techniques of repoussé, chasing and punching (Maryon 2011; Untracht 1982) to create the

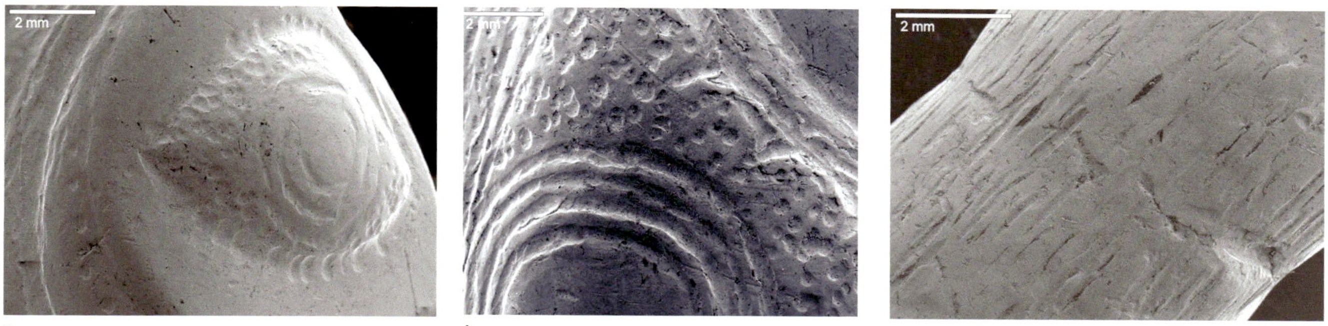

a b c

Figure 17.10a–c a) and b) SEM SE image details of the punched and chased design tool marks on the anthropomorphic terminal S.13; c) The linear punched marks cover a solder joint between two joined tubes, perpendicular to the lines of the punch-marks

elaborately detailed anthropomorphic decoration on the torc terminal (**Fig. 17.10a–c**).

Composition of gold sheet

Eleven small sheet torc fragments (one stray find and the others from Hoard F) provided samples for microscopy and analysis (**Table 17.2**). In two cases, samples of sheet are from torc fragments with recognisable terminals, e.g. F.48 (**Fig. 17.7a**), whereas other folded and squashed sheet samples are from less clear torc types, e.g. F.51 (**Fig. 17.11a**). The analysis of the uncorroded core within the cross-sections of the gold sheet samples gives the composition of the original gold alloy used to make the objects. Analysis of the near surface regions of the same cross-sections gives the composition of the surface of the object, which confers the perceived gold colour. Around half of these pieces showed evidence of surface enrichment in gold content compared to their core.

Overall, elemental analysis of the sheet samples showed that the alloys are composed mainly of gold (66–90 wt% Au with an average of 81 wt%) with some silver (8–32 wt% Ag with an average of 17 wt%) and very little copper (1–3 wt % Cu with an average of 2 wt%) (**Table 17.2**). The microstructures of these high-gold, low-copper alloys are composed of a homogeneous single phase which would have provided the required properties for the alloy to be hammered into thin sheet without cracking and further worked into tubular forms and terminals, while retaining sufficient stiffness in the finished objects. Comparison of gold-rich sheet core compositions with those of wires is shown in the ternary diagrams in **Fig. 17.46a–b**, with the sheet alloys being in the upper right region of the diagram, showing high gold and low copper contents. This suggests that alloy compositions for gold sheet were deliberately chosen over, and distinct from, the main alloys used for wire production, most likely for metalsmithing reasons, such as ductility, this being the paramount mechanical requirement for sheet gold production. The high-gold alloy would also be less susceptible to tarnishing and discolouration.

The compositions of the sheet surfaces in cross-section were compared to those of their core bulk (**Table 17.2**). Six of these eleven high-gold alloy samples show no difference in surface composition to the core and no surface microstructure to indicate enrichment. By comparison, the surfaces of the other five (sheet fragments F.19b, F.51, F.52, F.55 and terminal F.48) display different compositions to the cores, with more gold (87–95 wt% Au) and less silver and copper (4–18 wt% Ag and 0.5–2 wt% Cu). The surface enrichment of these sheets appears to be mainly on one surface only and the silver content is significantly reduced, more than might be expected from repeated routine annealing and pickling during the metal forming process (for explanation and discussion of these processes see pp. 431–2 below).

Fragments such as F.51 (**Fig. 17.11a–b**) and F.19b (**Fig. 17.12a**), both of which have very uniformly golden surfaces, are covered with textured punch-marks. Their cross-sections show surface enrichment mainly on one side with associated grain boundary corrosion and some loss of metal in these regions (**Fig. 17.11b–c**). The gold-enriched surface of the folded gold tubular torc sheet F.19b (**Fig. 17.12a–c**) is thicker, highly porous and more uniform in depth. This

Figure 17.11a–c a) Photomacrograph and b) SEM BSE image of a deliberately folded tubular torc neck-ring fragment with punched decoration (F.51); c) SEM BSE image section detail showing irregular surface enrichment (bright areas) on the lower side and grain boundary corrosion causing cracks in the metal. The sheet is 0.13mm thick

a b c

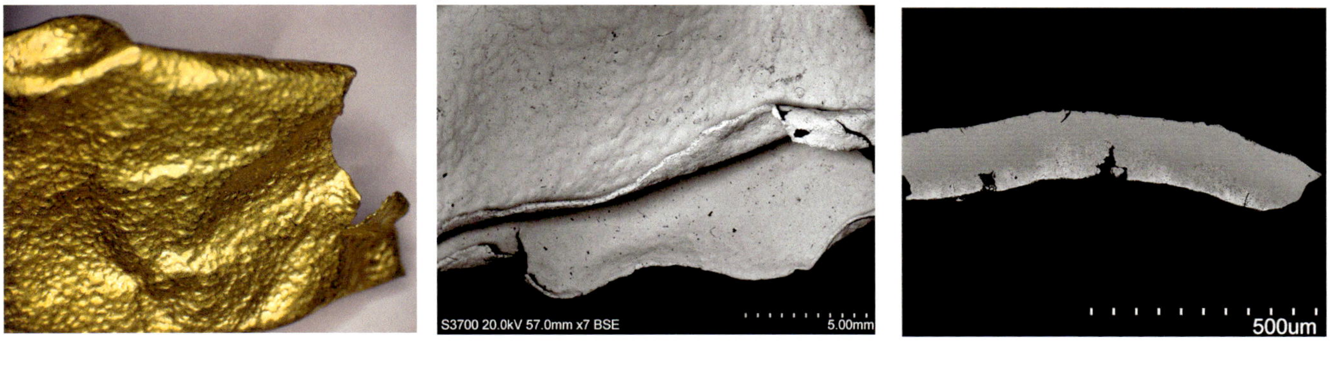

		Bulk composition (wt%)			Surface composition (wt%)		
Cat. no. BM reg. no. (Polished sample no.)	**Tubular torc type**	**Au**	**Ag**	**Cu**	**Au**	**Ag**	**Cu**
S.11b 1991,0407.47 (J1519)	4/5	83.7	14.1	2.2	no surface enrichment observed		
F.37 1991,0501.24 (J1505)	?	84.7	13.3	2.0	no surface enrichment observed		
F.48 1991,0501.27 (J1506)	3	66.1	31.6	2.3	81.9	17.5	0.6
F.62 1991,0501.30 (J1522)	?3	84.0	14.5	1.5	no surface enrichment observed		
F.55 1991,0501.32 (J1507)	4/5	78.5	20.1	1.4	90.1	8.2	1.7
F.51 1991,0501.34 (J1521)	4/5	81.8	15.6	2.6	86.7	11.0	2.3
F.65 1991,0501.36 (J1508)	2	76.5	20.5	3.0	no surface enrichment observed		
F.52 1991,0501.76 (J1509)	4/5	84.6	13.5	1.9	94.9	4.2	0.9
F.53 1991,0501.118 (J1523)	4/5	84.8	13.1	2.1	no surface enrichment observed		
F.49 1991,0501.138 (J1501)	1/2	90.4	8.4	1.2	no surface enrichment observed		
F.19b 1991,0501.161 (J1493)	4/5	76.9	20.5	2.6	93.9	5.6	0.5
mean		81.1	16.8	2.1	89.5	9.3	1.2
min		66.1	8.4	1.2	81.9	4.2	0.5
max		90.4	31.6	3.0	94.9	17.5	2.3

Table 17.2 SEM-EDX analyses of high-gold sheet from torcs (11 samples). Representative area analyses of the bulk compositions and enriched surfaces in polished sections

layer (see **Table 17.2** for composition) has many rounded areas of open porosity with grain boundary enrichment (**Fig. 17.12c**), showing that the surface-enrichment process was done following the hammering of the sheet and the construction of the object. The hammering process would have otherwise essentially squashed the porosity flat, as seen in the case of surface-enriched wires (see below and e.g. **Fig. 17.42**). The cross-section showing the surface microstructure of a sheet fragment from tubular torc terminal F.48 appears similar to sheets F.51 and F.19b (**Figs 17.11–13**). This sheet also measures *c.* 0.16mm thick with loss of surface material associated with grain boundary corrosion on one side, as well as variable thickness surface enrichment in these regions (**Fig. 17.13a–b**).

These observations raise the intriguing possibility of deliberate surface enrichment on one side of the sheet only. The Staffordshire Hoard of Anglo-Saxon gold and silver metalwork shows similar effects of surface enrichment on the objects (Blakelock 2016). Corrosion can be dismissed as the main cause here, because the sheet would be corroded equally on both sides.

One possible explanation for a single-sided surface enrichment could be gold parting using salt cementation, a process first used for purifying electrum (a natural gold-silver alloy), especially if carried out on the finished objects, where the outer surface might be exposed to greater chemical leaching than the interior. The microstructure of the sheet-metal samples from Snettisham looks very similar to that of refined gold foils found at the gold-refining site of Sardis (modern-day Turkey) and dated to the reign of the Lydian King Croesus (560–547 BC) (Ramage and Craddock 2000, figs 5.51–4, 146–9). During cementation, gold sheet pieces are heated for a long time to temperatures of several hundred degrees in a sealed 'parting vessel' with salt (sodium chloride) in a matrix of sand/clay and charcoal forming a reducing atmosphere (Ramage and Craddock 2000). This process removes silver as well as copper, and the surface analysis of sample F.19b could be interpreted in this manner (**Table**

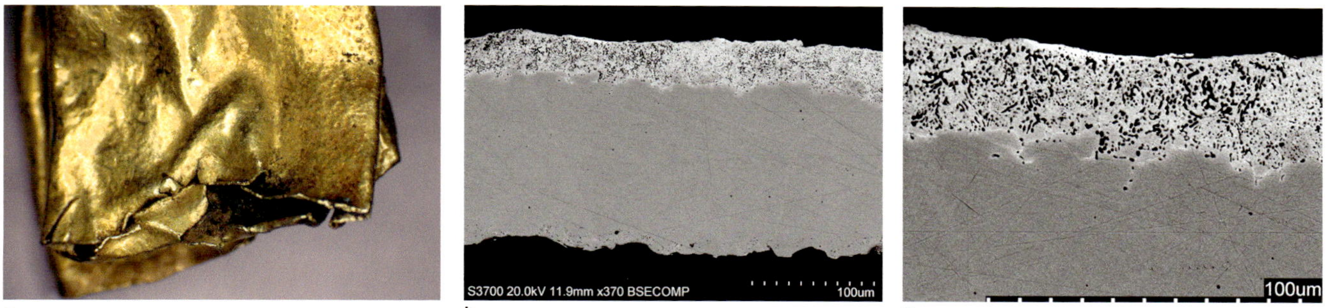

Figure 17.12a–c a) Folded gold torc sheet F.19b; b–c) SEM BSE images showing thick surface enrichment on one side, only 0.04mm thick, on a 0.17mm-thick sheet. Only the very surface of the porous gold-enriched layer has been polished. The porosity results from the loss of silver and copper within the alloy (Table 17.2)

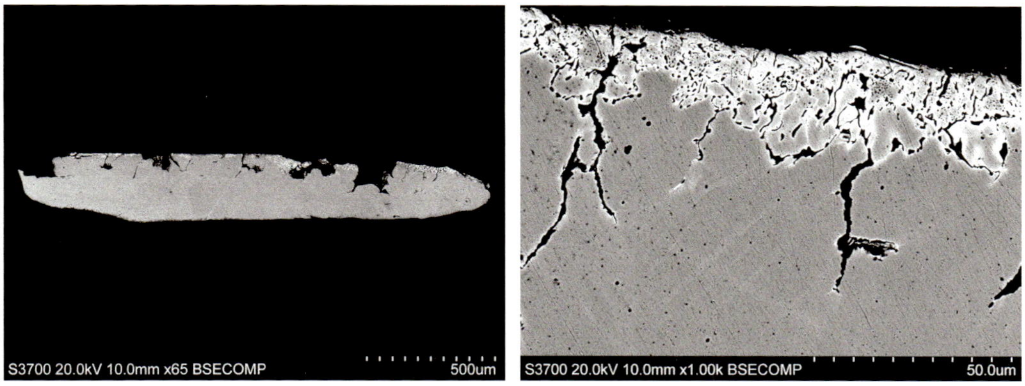

Figure 17.13a–b Terminal F.48 sheet cross-section: a) Note the loss of surface material associated with grain boundary corrosion and b) SEM BSE image detail showing the gold-enriched grain boundaries in the enriched zone on one surface

17.2). A similar method is mentioned in La Niece (1995), where gold alloy chisels from Ur (*c.* 2600 BC) are thought to have been surface enriched by a comparable process (Shalev 1993).

Although it is unlikely as the sole explanation, long-term corrosion also has to be considered as a factor for localised micro-enrichment, especially because the porosity in the enriched layer is not heavily burnished (i.e. not compressed by polishing). There is also grain boundary cracking and loss of surface material due to deeply penetrating corrosion in the samples of terminal F.48 and sheet F.51 (**Figs 17.11, 17.13**). The gold-enriched areas appear bright in the SEM BSE images and, deep down, corrosion cracks can be seen in the newly formed cracked surfaces, which would suggest corrosion is at least partly responsible for the loss of silver (Dugmore and DesForges 1979). Nevertheless, whilst some enrichment might be expected due to corrosion from the burial environment (with preferential loss of copper and, to a lesser extent, silver) or due to exposure to the skin during wear, the high level of surface enrichment observed here cannot be explained only by these two phenomena, especially as in many cases enrichment occurs on only one side of the sheet, even at the edge of fragments where both sides would have been equally exposed to the burial environment. In addition, half of the sheet samples with similar bulk compositions showed no surface enrichment, while coming from the same burial environment.

17.4 Wires: manufacture, experimental, gold/silver alloy groups, bronze, and torc case study

This section deals with the huge variety of wires found at Snettisham, their composition and manufacture. The vast majority of torcs from Snettisham are multi-strand types with wires of varying thicknesses and configurations as a major component of their construction. Wires are also used for filigree decoration on two of the large tubular torcs (**Figs 17.4c–e, 17.6**).

The sampled wires display a range of very different colours, from silvery to rich yellow-gold, and a variety of sections, from circular, to faceted, to square. Their outer colour is a feature of the composition of the surface, but, in many cases, it may not represent the composition of the original core metal because of surface enrichment, hence the need to sample the wires in full cross-section for metallography and analysis (see methods section, p. 420).

The wires found at Snettisham range from 0.6mm to just over 10mm in thickness. All have the physical evidence of mechanical deformation and faceting from being hammered from shorter, thicker primary rods/ingots, lengthening these into smaller diameter long wires. Evidence for this can be seen in the multiple faceting along the length of the wires (e.g. torc fragments S.34–S.39) and a seam and overlapping metal smears, visible in places on many wires (e.g. see **Figs 17.14–15**). All these features were created by repeated cycles of hammering (plus annealing and pickling – for explanation and discussion of these processes see pp. 431–2 below) during wire production and have been reproduced by experimental metalsmithing (see p. 433 and e.g. **Fig. 17.20a–b**). None of the wires show evidence of being drawn (i.e. no multiple linear striations from a draw-plate) (Untracht 1969).

The surface condition of the wires varies from smooth and uncorroded for the high-gold alloys to a number displaying severe stress corrosion cracks (Dugmore and DesForges 1979) with brittle and flaking surfaces caused by the residual stresses in the metal from twisting during

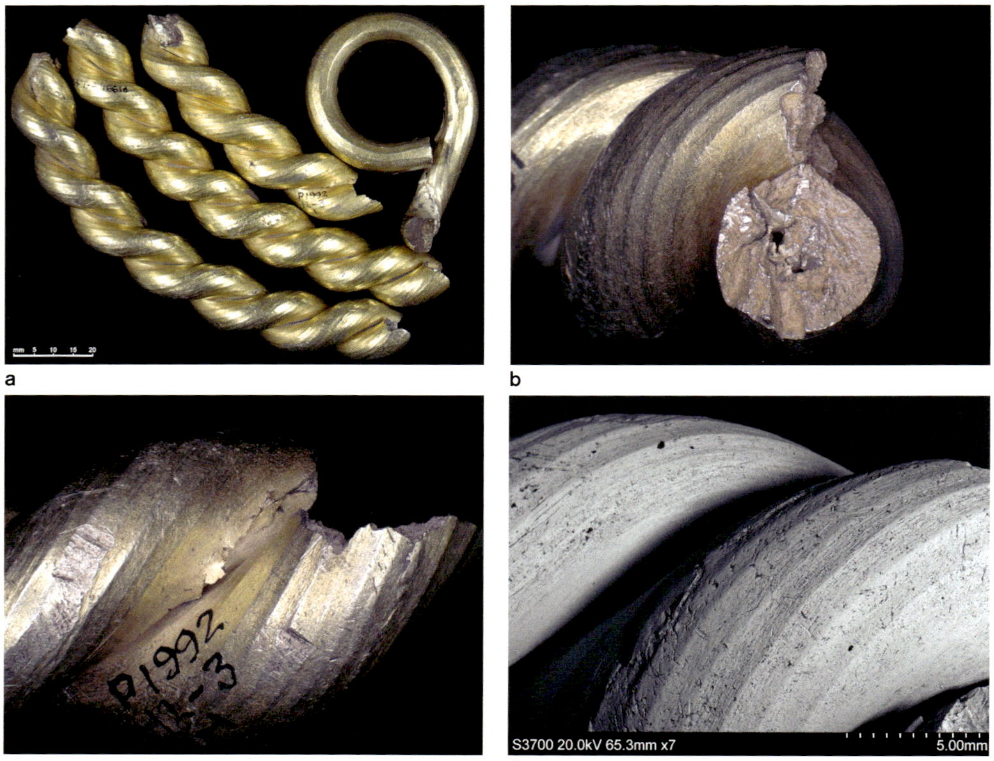

a b c d

Figure 17.14a–d Broken fragments from torc S.31–S.39. a) Photomacrograph (scale 20mm), b, c) photomicrographs and d) SEM BSE image of the thickest wire torc fragments with multiple parallel facets from hammering running down the full length of the wires. b) Note the split running half-way through the section of the fractured end from the surface to the centre, leaving a hole in the centre, and the thin overlapping folds of gold and more coppery-coloured sub-surface metal

manufacture and wear (**Figs 17.40d, 17.33a–b**). The effects on the wire surface are a direct result of the composition of the alloys used, in particular the alloys with low proportions of gold and silver, which are subject to corrosion during burial.

This section begins with general observations on the manufacture of wires, followed by a description of the extensive and illuminating experimental wire manufacture carried out by practising metalsmith John Fenn, and the application of the results to the interpretation of the material from Snettisham.

There is significant variation in the alloys used to produce the wires found at Snettisham, and thus the rest of this section is divided according to alloy composition. The core microstructures of the wires may be divided into four main alloy types based on the relative gold/silver/copper bulk concentrations (**Tables 17.4–6**): high gold-silver low copper alloys (p. 437), silver-gold-copper alloys (p. 439), high-copper low-gold silver alloys (p. 440), and copper alloys lacking any significant gold or silver content (p. 441).The high gold-silver with low copper alloys are a homogeneous solid solution (e.g. **Fig. 17.26a–d**) and, by contrast, both the silver-gold-copper and the silver with high-copper and low-gold alloys have finely dispersed two-phase eutectic microstructures (e.g. **Figs 17.29–30**).

The final part of this section draws together the various aspects of wire analysis and production to present a detailed discussion of the composition and manufacture of the wire elements of torc F.119–20.

Figure 17.15 Torc L.13 with thin wires, *c.* 2mm diameter, showing longitudinal faceting with a deep linear groove and smeared overlap metal from hammering

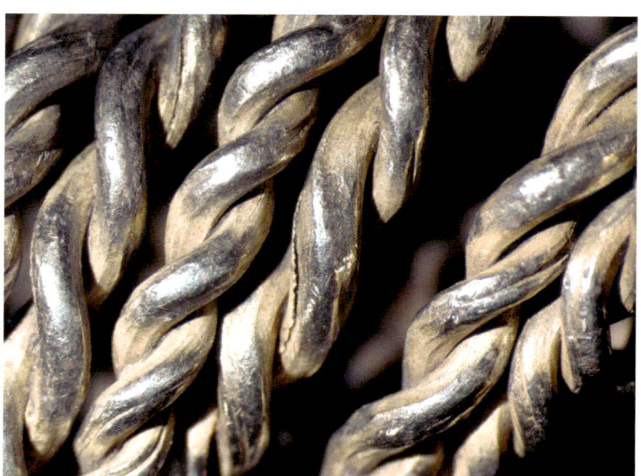

Manufacture of wires

Wires were produced in a variety of thicknesses and with varying cross-sections depending on the design requirement of the torcs. The examination of wires by microscopy, analysis and experimental wire forming allows us to interpret the manufacture and surface treatment of the wires. Making both thick and thin torc wires was a similar process, involving cycles of hammering a rod to reduce its diameter and elongate it into a thinner wire, followed by annealing to soften the metal, quenching, and then pickling to remove oxide discolouration. The cyclical process of hammering, annealing and pickling is halted once the desired wire thickness is achieved (Maryon 2011; Untracht 1982) and the wires can then be finally polished to a shiny smooth finish, as required. Some square-section wires were also twisted individually to give a spiral effect.

The process

Wire was started from a cast rod/billet or block of appropriate length and girth, which was hammered on an anvil (probably of iron) with frequent annealing, to elongate

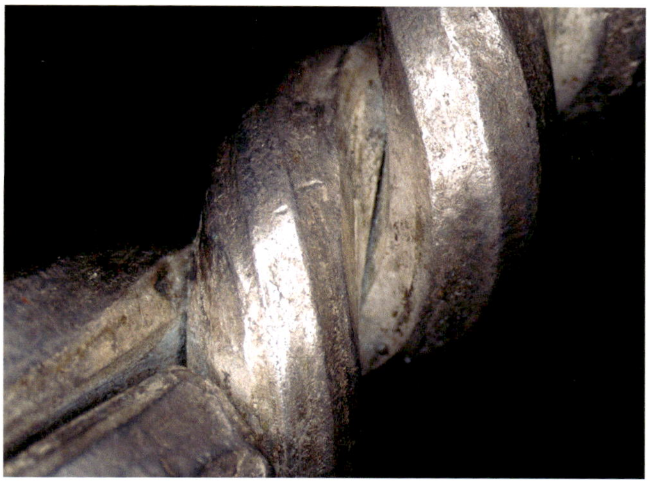

Figure 17.16 Detail of torc L.2, with neck-ring formed from tightly plied, thick, faceted rods, 7.1mm in diameter

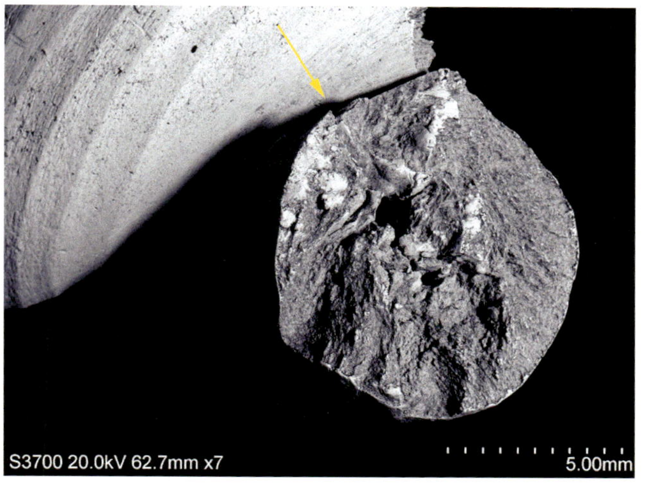

Figure 17.17 SEM BSE image of a broken fragment from torc S.31–S.39. Thick wire showing a groove extending from the surface (arrow) to the centre where it appears more as two holes (see also Fig. 17.14a–d). Note the linear hammered facets on the wire. The brighter areas at the edge of the fractured surface are where the thin gold-enriched surface layer has folded inwards when the wire broke

the metal to the required length and at the same time reduce the thickness. Hammering to the desired section diameter and form would be done in a sequence of repeat operations in which the thickness of the original square rod/wire was reduced in each hammering cycle by up to *c.* 40% (see experimental wire production section, p. 433).

An example of a small (5cm) cast linear ingot was found in Hoard B/C (B/C.85), and others in Hoard F (F.438–40). The size of the ingot used as a starting point likely varied depending on the desired final length and thickness of the wire. The thickest fragmentary torcs (such as S.31–S.39, with a wire diameter of around 9mm, **Figs 17.14, 17.32**) show that thick rod-like ingots must have been made as a starting point for those wires. At the other end of the scale, two multi-strand wire torcs/bracelets F.135 and F.156 with much narrower wire diameters (1.8mm and 1.3mm respectively) show evidence of residual dendritic cast microstructures (**Figs 17.30–1**), which is unexpected considering the extensive hammering thought to be necessary in preparing them. In these cases, it may suggest that relatively long, thin ingots were cast to reduce the amount of hammering required to produce the narrow wires.

Consultation with a practising metalsmith (see p. 433 below), suggested that even for producing round-section wires, it is far easier to first hammer square-section rods/wires. This was achieved by hammering along a length of the metal on an anvil, producing an oblong section, then turning through 90 degrees and repeating the hammering along the other side to square it up again and so forth. It is more efficient and quicker to work the wire this way than trying to hammer round-section wires directly by constantly rotating the ingot during hammering. This is also the case for the thinner wires and accounts for why so many wires of all thicknesses have either clear or residual evidence for longitudinal facets. Thus, thick wires with multiple linear facets, for example the octagonal-section wires of torc L.2 (**Fig. 17.16**), were made by hammering a square-section rod/wire along the apex corners onto an anvil thereby producing pairs of flat faces for each pass of the hammer along the rod. Hence, an octagonal rod/wire is easily produced from a square-section rod.

In the case of thick wire torc L.7 (**Fig. 17.59a–b**), the final wire is essentially of circular section. This required careful hammering with much rotation of the wire in the finishing process to remove the linear facet corners generated by initially hammering flat faces and thus create the roundness along the entire length. These facet corners were, however, not fully removed, as they appear in protected areas between twists. Some of the smoothing observed on the wires is therefore due to polishing of the finished torc and use wear (Ch. 20).

Many wires of varying thickness and section have an apparent single seam that runs along their length. This seam is clearly seen in the fractured ends of the thickest torc fragments, e.g. S.31–S.39 where the surface seam is in fact a crack along the length of the wire that reaches right to the centre of the wires, where it opens out forming a hole (**Fig. 17.17**). This feature is also seen on torc F.5c (**Fig. 17.18a–b**).

This crack was most likely formed by preparing a hammered strip of metal, then folding and hammering it along its entire length to double its thickness. The reason for this may be that it facilitated the twisting/plying together of thick wires (see section below on neck-ring construction, p. 454), as the overlapping internal folds would tend to slip over each other, avoiding the need for more effort to deform the thick solid core.

Annealing and surface enrichment of wires

During the process of hammering, the metal would gradually become brittle and less ductile, a process known as work hardening. The metal would therefore have required frequent annealing to prevent it cracking from over-hammering, as the wire reached its limit of plasticity. Annealing refers to heating some way above recrystallisation temperature (*c.* 350–400 °C) (in practical terms at dark red temperature *c.* 550–650 °C, **Table 17.3**). This reorganises and recrystallises the metal, releasing the accumulated internal stress and deformation of the crystal lattice, by re-forming new equiaxed grain boundaries. Without annealing, further hammering would increase stress between grains until fractures started propagating through

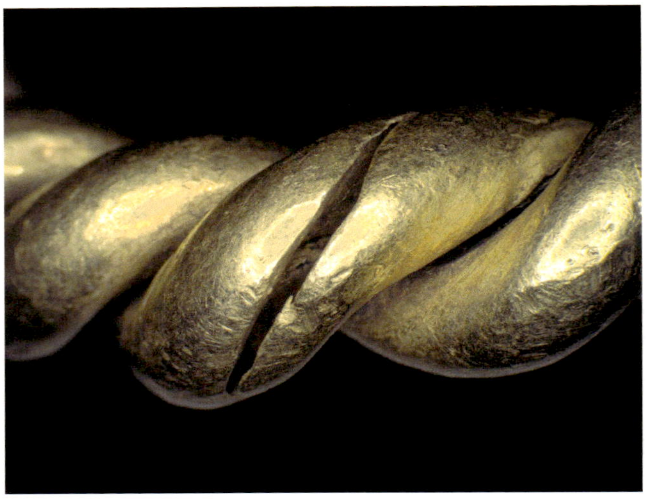

a

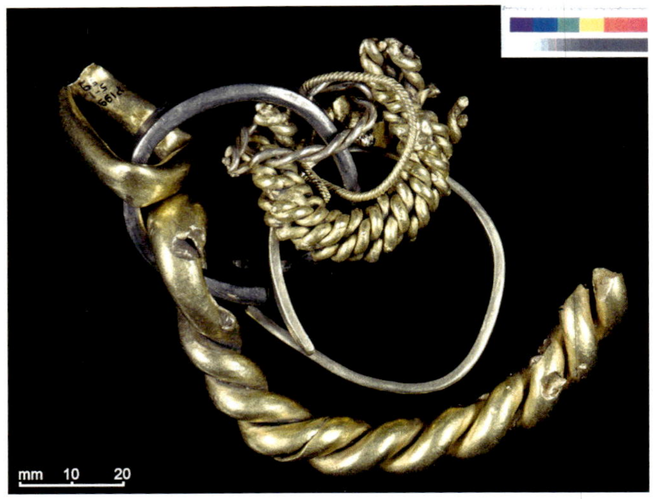

b

Figure 17.18a–b a) Detail of thick torc fragment F.5c (from mixed group in b) showing an exceptional deep groove into the core (see also Fig. 17.1)

the crystal lattice of the metal, ultimately leading to a break. No further elongation of cracked, hard and weakened metal could then be made, thus preventing the possibility of further reduction to thinner wires. Annealing softens the alloy, restoring its ductility, which is its ability to be hammered further to extend the wire length without cracking, and malleability, or ability to reduce its diameter while maintaining its rounded section shape. Annealing is particularly important for the less ductile and less malleable lower gold content alloys.

Quenching likely followed annealing to retain the microstructure resulting from high-temperature annealing; this would be achieved by plunging the hot metal into cold liquid. Pickling involves soaking the annealed metal piece in a mild acidic medium to remove surface oxidation, which would result in a clean, shiny/matt metal and microscopically porous surface. (Pliny in his *Natural History*, Book XXXIII, Chapter 20 (on metals) describes the method for annealing and pickling: '… the copper is first well hammered, after which it is subjected to the action of fire, and then cooled with a mixture of salt, vinegar, and alum. It is then cleansed of all extraneous substances, it being known by its brightness when it has been sufficiently purified.')

The precise details of the wire-making process likely varied depending on the alloy used. For example, gold-rich wires may have required less annealing, as they would have been less prone to stress cracking. In the case of wires with a higher copper content in their alloys, pickling in acid would have been necessary to remove the black copper oxide that forms on the wire surface during annealing.

The cyclical combination of hammering and annealing with pickling creates surface enrichment of gold and silver in the Snettisham wires, seen especially in the alloys with lower proportions of silver and gold in their core metal, i.e. the higher copper alloys lose much of the surface copper in this process (see **Figs 17.24, 17.43–4** element maps below). Essentially, this enrichment occurs as part of the wire-making process. The long and repetitive cycles of hammering, annealing and pickling would have progressively enriched the surface of the wire in gold and silver without any additional process and resulted in the variety of colours observed. The wires would transform from a red-coppery colour to a golden or pale gold-silvery one, depending on the original core composition. Some broken ends of wires clearly show the copper-rich core metal and the enriched golden surface (e.g. **Figs 17.43–4**). This phenomenon of surface enrichment in wires was duplicated in experimental wire production. It is considered in detail for different alloys below (p. 432) and summarised in the section on alloy composition, colours and surface treatments (p. 452).

Other tools for wire production

There is no evidence for drawn wires at Snettisham. The technique of wire-drawing was commonly used from around the 10th–11th centuries AD (Oddy 1977), although evidence for the technology may date back to as early as the Late Bronze Age period (Northover 1995b), and drawn iron wire has also been attested in Late Iron Age mail armour (Özşen and Willer, 2016).

It has been suggested that grooved anvils (also called swage blocks) could have been used to help shape the faceted wires and this has been described for the Ipswich torcs (Brailsford and Stapley 1972). Like many metalsmithing

Table 17.3 Annealing temperatures of common gold alloys

Alloy	Annealing temperature °C	Colour
Pure gold, 24 carat	200	Black heat
21–22 carat (alloy containing approx. 90% gold)	550–600	Very dark red
18 carat (alloy containing 75% gold)	550–600	Very dark red
14 carat (alloy containing 58% gold)	650	Dark red
Sterling silver (alloy containing 92.5% silver)	600–650	Dark red

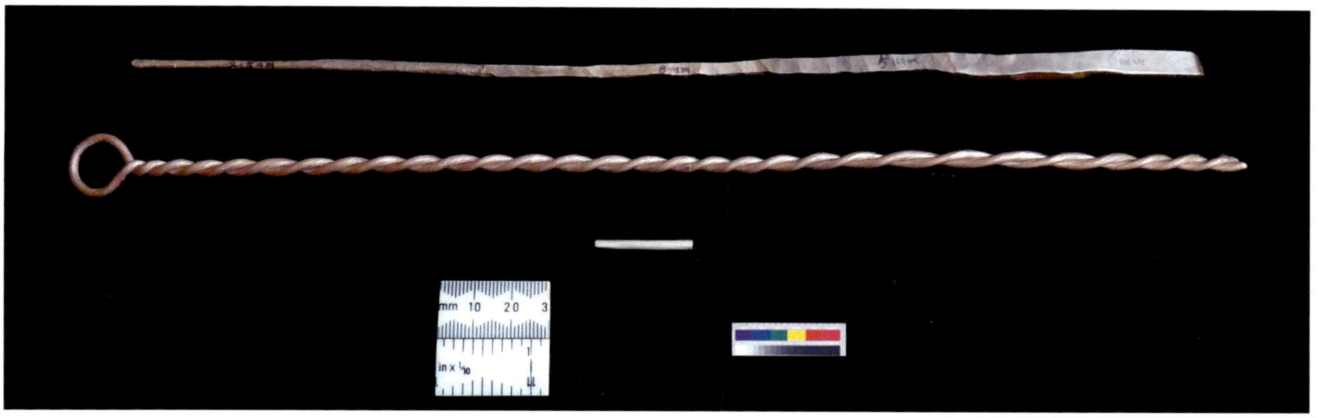

Figure 17.19 Experimental wires (John Fenn). Top is the stepped square-section copper rod, 6mm, 5mm, 3mm down to 2.5mm circular-section. Centre: plied 2.5mm circular-section wire with loop used for twisting with mandrel. Bottom: piece of the silver-copper alloy wire used for the enrichment test

processes, there are a number of ways of achieving the same result. The problem with the swage block hypothesis is that, in the whole collection of torcs and fragments from Snettisham, there are many different numbers of facets on many different thicknesses of wire and, hence, this would mean needing as many different accurately grooved swage block grooves to account for all of the variations found. This is not impossible as swage blocks are known from the Bronze Age (Bass 2005), but perhaps unlikely here. There remains the possibility that a few standard-sized swage block grooves may have been in use during part of the wire preparation process, but experiments in making hammered wire (see below) show that hammering alone adequately explains the mechanical features found on the Snettisham torc wires.

It has also been suggested anecdotally that the stone with a hole found at Snettisham (A.8) may have been used for drawing wire. Rainbird Clarke (1954, 39) noted that it seemed likely from the grooving on the pebble that 'metal has been drawn through the aperture', suggesting its use in the breaking down and reforming of tubular torcs into other ornaments. This is very possible, though the use of the pebble more specifically as a 'draw plate' is unlikely because the dimensions and geometry of the entry hole necessary for the mechanics of wire drawing are very precise (Changsun Moon and Naksoo Kim 2012). However, the stone could have served as a gauge to size wire; some sort of simple gauge would have had great practical use.

Bronze torc/bracelet fragment F.361 (**Figs 17.37–8**) has a group of very deep parallel grooves running lengthwise that cut into parts of the wires. These are relatively more prominent and numerous than on other torc wires. This raises the possibility that the wires may have been pulled through some form of final shaping perforation, with rough edges, or have been filed or scraped with a coarse and sharp instrument as part of the finishing process of the wire. But in this case, it seems to have caused surface damage rather than achieving a smooth finish. Other areas on the same wires are smoothly polished. The grooves look very sharp – more like cuts from a hard, metallic instrument rather than from a coarse stone instrument (**Fig. 17.38**). Examples of broadly similar striations on Iron Age silver rings are reported from the Palacio hoard in southern Spain (Murillo-Barroso *et al.* 2015) and tentatively interpreted as the result of a final potentially similar pulling process to even the diameter of the wires.

Experimental wire manufacture

John Fenn, practising metalsmith

As we have seen, the Snettisham wires have two common features: facets and smears run along the length of many wires of all diameters and, generally, the wires are surface enriched. Experiments were carried out to make reproduction wires for comparison and to record the sequence and timing of each step, and overall duration of processes.

Three experiments were carried out:

1. Hammering a square-section copper rod in stages to a round-section wire.
2. Making a uniform thickness 2.5mm circular-section wire and twisting/plying it into a two-ply structure.
3. Hammering, annealing and pickling a silver-copper alloy wire to test for surface enrichment.

Hammering a square section of copper rod

Using a square rod from the start is a most important practical finding in the procedure for efficiently making circular-section wires. It is far easier and quicker to elongate a square rod to a square wire than trying to maintain a circular-section wire continuously from the start while hammering. With every two passes of the hammer along the wire the square section is maintained. As the wire thins, turning the square edge-on and hammering along the square corners produces eight flat facets along the wire. Many of the Snettisham wires have evidence of long flats or facets from this hammering technique. When the rod reaches about 3mm square, round wire naturally starts to form during hammering.

Thus, the starting point for making 2.5mm *circular-section* wires were 6mm *square-section* 14cm-long rods. These would extend on hammering and annealing in stages to a length of 92cm, enough to make a simple Stage II torc neck-ring formed from a double length of the wire plied into a two-ply structure (**Fig. 17.19** middle) (details below). A 'stepped' experimental wire (**Fig. 17.19** top) shows a sequence of successive hammered stages from the thick starting rod (6mm, 5mm, 3mm, down to 2.5mm circular section). The

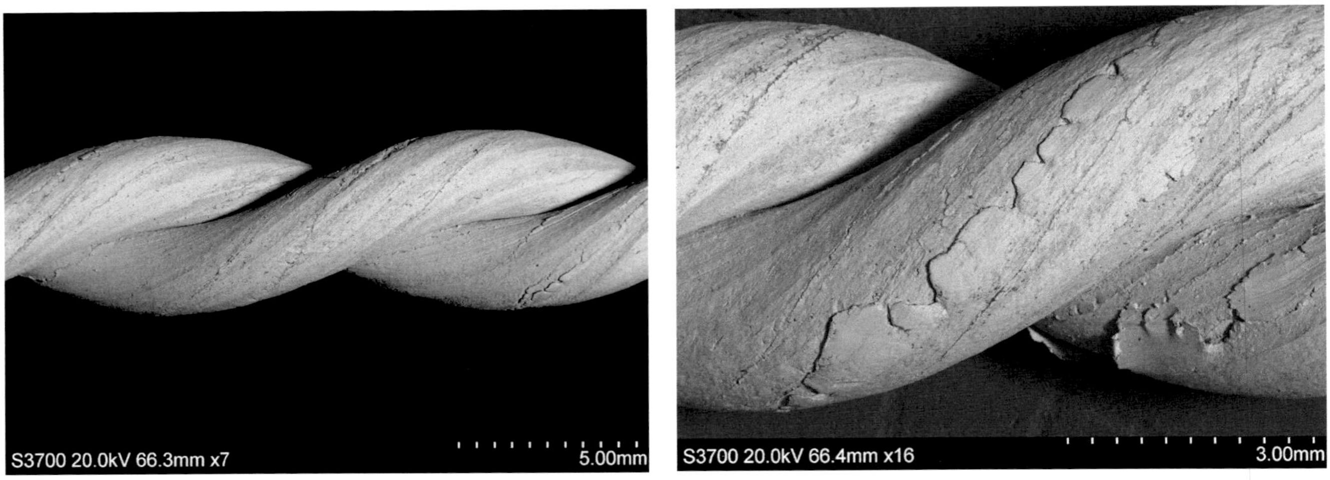

a b

Figure 17.20a–b SEM BSE images of experimental hammered and twisted wire. Note the facets along the wires and the flakes and smears that occur during hammering, reproducing those found on Snettisham wires (see also cross-section in Figure 17.22)

first hammered step reduced the thickness by 18%. After annealing, the next sequence reduced this to 3mm square (a reduction of 40%) without signs of overworking. It took 20 minutes to make the stepped example piece, including annealing.

Uniform thickness copper wire manufacture

Using a 1kg hammer with a transverse long convex face about 13mm wide, about three to five hammer blows a second were used on a copper alloy rod on a slightly convex anvil. The hammer was dragged slightly in the direction of elongation at each blow to increase the reduction by almost a quarter. The convex hammer face helped continuously spread the metal rod out lengthways from the impact point and rapidly facilitated elongation of the wire. By comparison, a flat hammer tends to spread the wire sideways only. No special care was needed during hammering while the metal was thick enough to maintain its square section without twisting. As the bar thinned to around 3mm square, the long unsupported length started to twist and deform, and a lozenge section developed. At this point, it took some skill to get back to the square section. This is the stage of hammering when circular-section wire naturally starts to form.

During hammering, the surface of the wire flaked or smeared (**Fig. 17.20**), a feature seen on many Snettisham wires (**Figs 17.21, 17.33**); these tend to split away when the wire is later twisted/plied. The wires were hammered along their length twice between most annealing steps that were done at red heat (*c.* 750 °C) and then quenched. The variable thickness of the wires was seen easily when annealing began, the thinner sections becoming red some time before thicker parts. Flaking may derive from the same square corners being retained throughout all the stages of reduction. Sharp corners are effectively unsupported and become stressed and vulnerable during the radical elongation. Possibly, knocking corners back or reducing sharpness might reduce flaking.

Times of hammering to make 92cm of 2.5mm diameter copper wire (annealing and quenching was carried out between each stage):

- First stage: Starting length 14cm, 6mm square. Hammering for 2 minutes, length now 17.2cm. Increase: 3.2cm.
- Second stage: Hammering for 4 minutes, length now 21.6cm. Increase: 4.4cm.
- Third stage: Hammering for 2 minutes, length now 28.6cm. Increase: 7cm.
- Fourth stage: Hammering for 3 minutes, length now 33cm. Increase: 4.4cm. The section began to become lozenge-shaped and was corrected with more hammering.
- Fifth stage: Hammering carefully for 7 minutes, length now 38cm. Increase: 5cm. The section, measured for the first time, is approximately 4 to 3.5mm square.
- Sixth stage: Hammering for 3 minutes, length now 43.8cm. Increase: 5.8cm. The metal section went out of square; a small planishing hammer was used to correct the whole length. This took 5–6 minutes, leaving the wire still 43.8cm long, and the section approximately 3mm square.
- Seventh stage: Using a large hammer for 6.5 minutes to give a length of 48.3cm. Increase: 4.5cm. Section still approximately 3mm square.
- Eighth stage: Hammering for 6 minutes, now 54.6cm long. Increase: 6.3cm
- Ninth stage: Hammering without annealing for 7 minutes, length 59.6cm. Increase: 5cm. The cross-section remains, curiously, still about 3mm square.
- Tenth stage: Last square section. Hammering with a large hammer for 11 minutes, length 68.6cm. Increase: 9cm. The section is now 3mm to 2.75mm square. To this stage it has taken 57 minutes of hammering, not including annealing. The whole time including annealing was 1 hour 43 minutes.
- Swaging: 1 hour using a flat hammer and a single grooved lower swage. Length now 89cm. After annealing, the wire was approximately 2.5 to 3mm diameter round and was stretched manually by 2.5cm to a length of 91.5cm. This wire demonstrates uneven thickness. A further 20 minutes was spent making adjustments and finishing.

Total time using a heavy cross-peen hammer to hammer out 91.5cm of approximately 2.5mm copper wire from 14cm rod, 6mm square was, in this attempt, 2 hours 20 minutes. The Snettisham Great Torc contains very approximately

19m of wire (64 individual strands of 1.6mm diameter and perhaps around 30cm in length). Therefore, based on this experimental work, a rough approximation for the time it may have taken to make the wires for the Great Torc, is about 50 hours in total, say one week for an individual, to hammer out 19 metres of wire (admittedly thinner than the test wire), although it is entirely feasible that a small group of workers might make the wire for a large torc in possibly less time.

The wire was finished by hammering with a flat-faced hammer and flat stake to achieve the best uniformity, and finally it was hammered into a simple bottom swage to facilitate the lengthening of the wire and some correction of the thickness. This took an hour to refine the form of the 92cm-long wire. It was then annealed followed by light corrective hammering on an anvil. Small sharps that appeared were occasionally smoothed with a stone.

For the first attempt at plying two strands of wire together, the experimental wire was first doubled back on itself and the two halves then twisted together without a final anneal, but this produced an uneven twist. While the thickness of the finished test wire appeared to be even, in fact it varied in thickness, which caused the uneven twist to develop, with the slightly thicker regions twisting less than the thinner ones. Thinking that this was due to unevenly work-hardened metal, the thicker wire region was annealed and twisted again – but this increased the problem.

For the second attempt, the wire was prepared for twisting by an even annealing, then lightly smoothed using a stone, papered and finally burnished with a steel tool to produce a bright finish. Twisting again using an iron bar in the loop (at the doubled wire centre) and straining back to tension the wires produced the plied wire in **Figure 17.19**. However, it still remained somewhat unevenly twisted after four or five additional turns, owing to the slightly variable wire thickness along the length (2.5–3.0mm). By chance, when the original straight wire was folded double before twisting, wires of similar thickness lay adjacent to each other. The importance of this is that if regions of thick and thin wire were alongside during twisting, the thinner wire would tend to wrap around the thicker rather than twisting uniformly together, thus producing a very uneven result. In this case similar thicknesses were adjacent on the final twisted wire, so this did not happen, and the result was a good representation of plied pairs of wires from Snettisham.

This practical difficulty in producing a uniform thickness of wire highlights the quality of the original Snettisham wires and the precision of the metalsmiths in producing so much wire of routine uniformity throughout the wire size ranges.

Silver wire enrichment experiment

It was suggested above that the silver/gold-rich surfaces of the Snettisham wires are the result of copper depletion during the pickling that followed multiple hammering and annealing/quenching stages during wire production. The relatively low number of hammering and annealing cycles taken to produce copper wire showed minimal oxide build-up. Therefore, in order to test the hypothesis of surface enrichment of a silver-copper-gold alloy by repeated

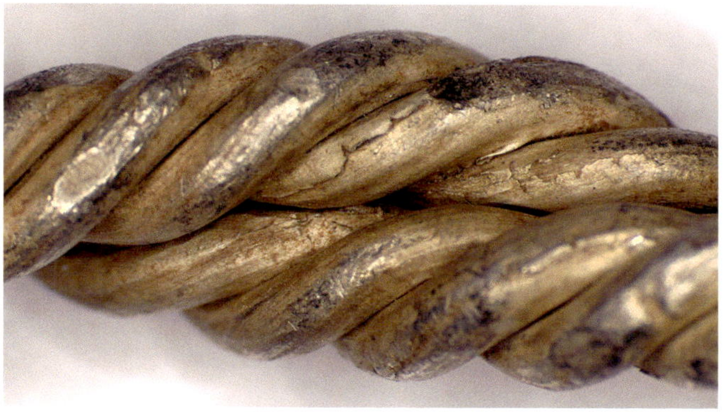

Figure 17.21 Snettisham torc/bracelet wire F.154 showing the smeared flaking caused by hammering the wire

hammering, annealing and pickling using a similar production sequence, we conducted the following experiment.

A representative alloy was made of approximately 70% silver and 30% copper, typical of the Snettisham high-copper silver alloys (see pp. 440, 446 **Table 17.6**), but without gold, and formed into a 5mm square-section rod. This was repeatedly hammered, annealed and quenched to produce wire with facets in the same manner as the copper wire test (above) to see if silver surface enrichment occurred.

At first the 5mm square rod elongated only 10mm at each stage. The alloy remained ductile to begin with, but, towards the end, it was difficult to maintain the perfect square section; then the hammering became more severe and less regular, the metal became stiffer and in fact less responsive to the bright red annealing temperature. It took approximately 13 two-minute hammering sequences to complete the wire from the rod.

Following each hammering stage, the first five annealing steps were done at dull red heat. However, to maximise the chance of producing a silver-rich surface by oxidising the copper, the remaining nine stages were annealed as hot as could be safely done on the thinning wire, at about bright red heat. After each annealing step, the wire was quenched in fairly strong acid pickle (240ml of vinegar to 17g of salt), and to further enrich the surface the last three stages involved boiling in the pickle, first for 5 minutes then for 8 minutes and, after the final hammering, for 17 minutes.

In all, the wire was made in 33 minutes and was 22.5cm long. As an indication of copper loss (and/or possibly silver loss) during the 13 hammering and pickling stages, the wire was weighed before and after the procedure. The total original weight was 12.46g with a loss of about 0.36g (approximately 3 wt%). Calculations show that this weight loss over the large surface area of the wire (1400 square millimetre surface area of 2mm diameter) would account for several microns depth loss of surface copper – essentially a silver-enriched layer of this thickness.

SEM microscopy of the sampled wire in cross-section confirms this very clearly. An enriched layer *c.* 6 microns thick was produced simply by these repeated cycles of hammering, annealing and pickling during the wire-making process (**Figs 17.22–3**).

The silver-rich layer is remarkably solid and uniform with only very fine residual porosity and has a clear continuity

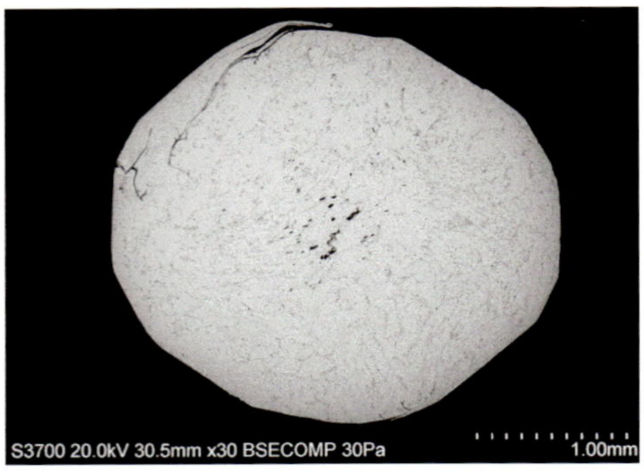

Figure 17.22 SEM BSE image of the cross-section of the experimentally made high-copper silver alloy wire. Note the multiple flat facets on the wire section and the smeared overlap. The copper-rich phase of the eutectic alloy is darker than the bright silver-rich phase

with the silver phase of the underlying core metal, just like the Snettisham wires (see below, pp. 443–7). The progressively enriched layer was clearly compacted from successive hammering phases, thus removing the porosity from the loss of copper of the two-phase alloy. The compressed microstructure shows no evidence of further dissolution of copper from the copper phase of the core alloy beneath. This suggests that the final 17-minute pickling carried out after the final hammering was unnecessary and that all of the enrichment was achieved during the dynamic phases of the wire-making process. Essentially, the silver layer had formed a passivating barrier between the pickling solution and the sub-surface core metal (**Fig. 17.23**).

The SEM-EDX elemental X-ray distribution maps of the cross-section illustrate the clear compositional change that occurred during the wire-making process, with the enrichment of silver on the surface because of the depletion of copper compared to the two-phase eutectic core alloy (**Fig. 17.24**).

In sum, the experimentally hammered high-copper silver alloy wire produced surface enrichment that formed progressively as a natural part of the dynamic wire manufacturing process through cycles of hammering, annealing (with oxidation of copper on the surface) and pickling (removal of copper oxide from the surface).

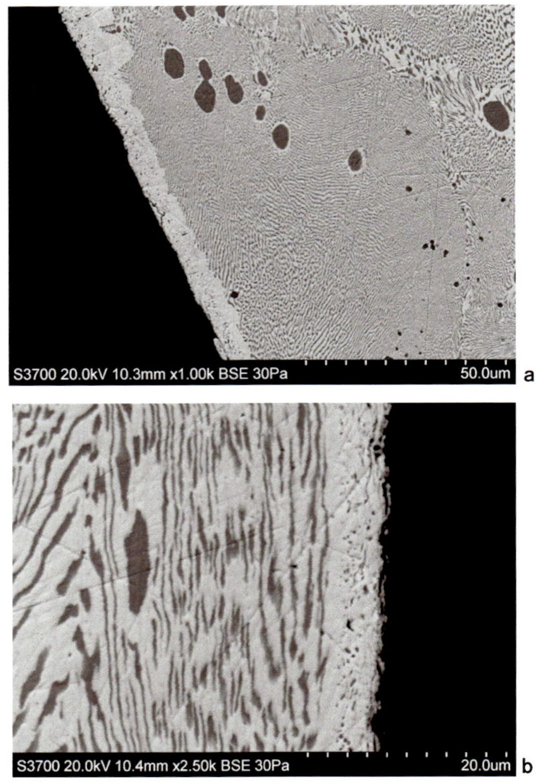

Figure 17.23a–b SEM BSE images at higher magnification of the experimentally made 70 wt% silver/30 wt% copper alloy wire. Details (a) x1000 and b) x2500) clearly show the 6-micron-thick surface-enriched layer that formed during the wire manufacturing process. Note the well-defined solid layer directly on the underlying core metal. The darker core phase is rich in copper. The brighter silver phase is continuous between the enriched surface layer and core phase

Repeated hammering to further extend the wire compresses the porosity left by the removal of copper oxide. Clearly, the composition of the wire alloy affects the amount of surface enrichment and thickness of the enriched layer; so do variations in the hammering/annealing cycles for any given wire. Overall, the experimentally surface-enriched wire looks very like the Snettisham wires of similar microstructure and composition (e.g. **Fig. 17.25**, F.116; and **Fig. 17.31**, F.156), the alloys of which also contain gold and

Figure 17.24a–b SEM-EDX elemental distribution maps for silver and copper acquired on the cross-section of experimentally made 70 wt% silver/30 wt% copper wire (see Fig. 17.23) for: a) silver, showing the silver-enriched surface layer, and b) copper, which is completely depleted from the surface. Note the eutectic core alloy showing both silver and copper. (NB: Colours are relative concentrations of the element in each image: yellow/orange higher and blue/green lower) (x1000, image width *c.* 125 microns)

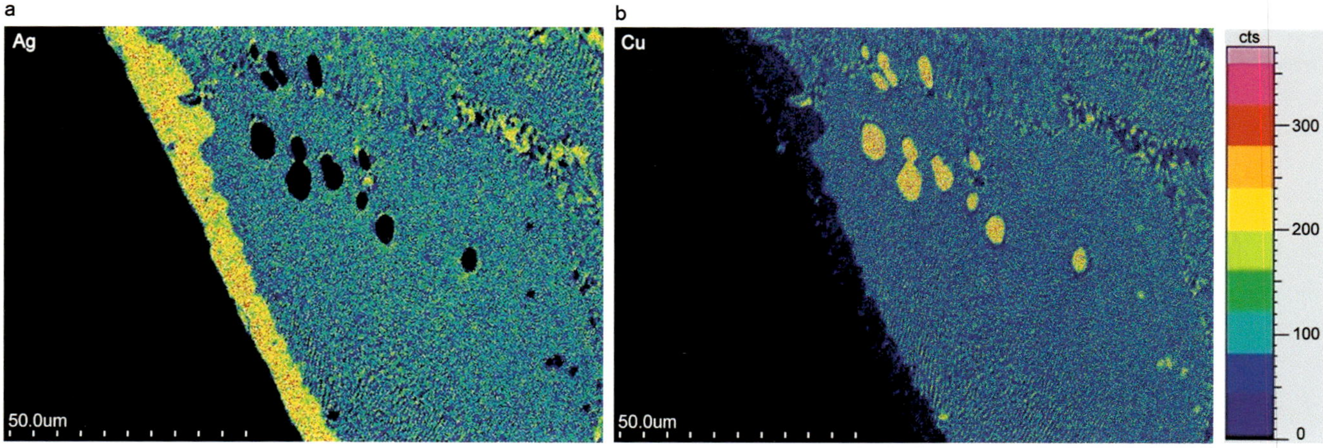

are enriched in gold and silver at the surface and depleted in copper (**Table 17.5**).

The following sections present microscopic and analytical observations from the Snettisham wires themselves and from polished specimens according to alloy composition, beginning with high gold-silver with low copper alloy wires (p. 437), and moving on to consider silver-gold-copper alloy wires (p. 439), high-copper and low-gold silver alloy wires (p. 440), and bronze wires (p. 441), finishing with a detailed case study on the wires of multi-strand torc F.119–20 (p. 443).

High gold-silver low copper alloy wires

Twelve wire samples have core alloys made of a homogeneous solid solution (e.g. **Fig. 17.26**) rich in gold and silver and poor in copper, with nine showing some gold enrichment on the surface. Nine samples have lower silver and copper concentrations in the enriched surface layer (**Table 17.4**), with some showing very similar microstructures to the enriched gold sheets (see p. 427), i.e. porosity and grain boundary corrosion. Perhaps corrosion during burial is superimposed on the effects of a putative 'refining' type of ancient surface treatment (Ramage and Craddock 2000; Blakelock 2016), as argued above for gold sheet.

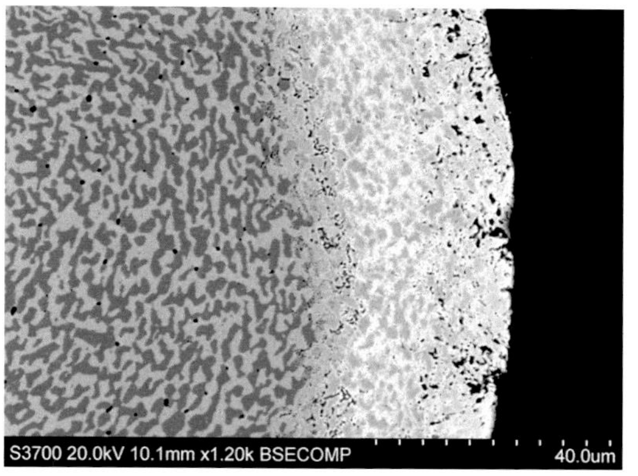

Figure 17.25 SEM BSE image of Snettisham torc wire F.116 with eutectic core and thick enriched surface

Torc/bracelet F.88 (**Fig. 17.27**) has the thickest gold-enriched surface layer of any of the sampled high gold-silver with low copper alloy wires, despite its low copper content and high gold and silver contents, which would make it difficult to surface enrich by the simple method of oxidising the copper during annealing and pickling (see above, pp.

		Bulk composition (wt%)			Surface composition (wt%)		
Cat. no. BM reg. no.	**Polished sample no.**	**Au**	**Ag**	**Cu**	**Au**	**Ag**	**Cu**
S.11a 1991,0407.57	J1517	79.8	16.7	3.5	85.3	12.1	2.6
F.34 1991,0501.16	J1503	73.9	22.8	3.3	75.6	21.6	2.8
F.94 1991,0501.17	J1502	71.3	24.6	4.1	81.6	16.8	1.6
F.88 1991,0501.22	J1504	51.7	42.4	5.9	79.0	20.7	0.3
F.5d 1991,0501.56	J1513	68.7	27.0	4.3	83.5	15.6	0.9
F.5e 1991,0501.57	J1515	73.4	23.7	2.9	85.6	12.1	2.3
F.85 1991,0501.95	J1525	94.0	5.4	0.6	no surface enrichment observed		
F.9a 1991,0501.125	J1494	57.2	37.1	5.7	77.1	22.2	0.7
F.9c 1991,0501.127	J1495	71.6	25.0	3.4	81.9	16.4	1.7
F.160 1991,0501.192	J1536	60.4	35.8	3.8	72.4	26.0	1.6
F.146 1991,0501.214	J1529	79.7	16.9	3.4	no surface enrichment observed		
F.17a 1991,0501.216	J1533	81.6	15.9	2.5	no surface enrichment observed		
mean		71.9	24.4	3.6	80.2	18.2	1.6
min		51.7	5.4	0.6	72.4	12.1	0.3
max		94.0	42.4	5.9	85.6	26.0	2.8

Table 17.4 SEM-EDX compositional analysis of high gold-silver with low copper alloys (12 wire samples). Representative area analyses of the bulk compositions and enriched surfaces in polished cross-sections. Compositional data plotted on Au/Ag/Cu ternary diagrams in Fig. 17.46

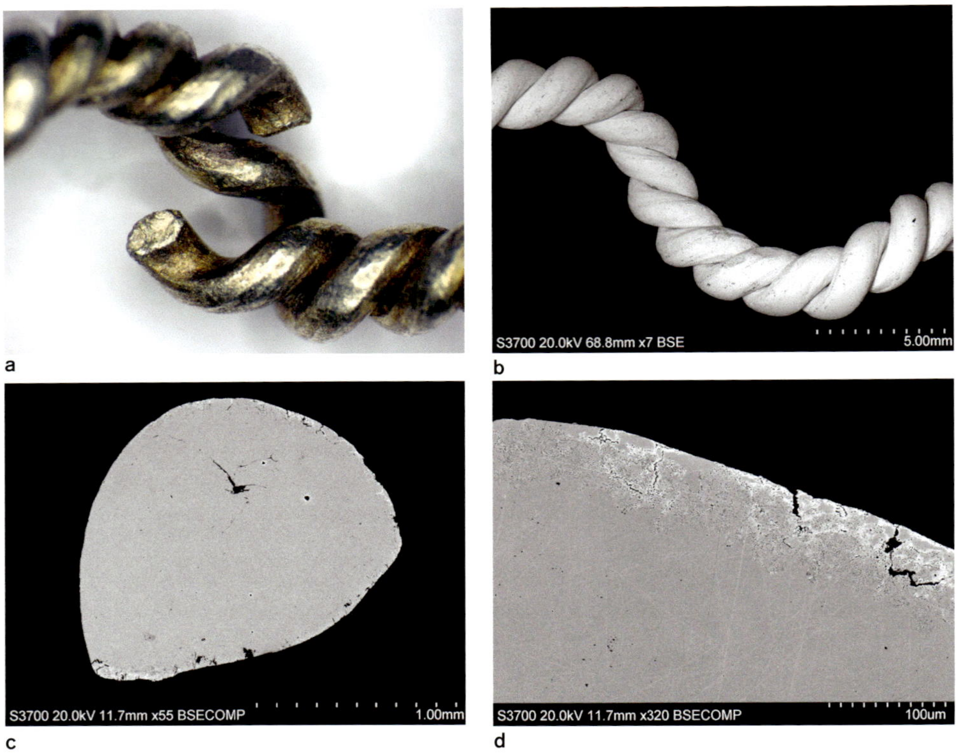

Figure 17.26a–d a) Photomicrograph and b) SEM BSE image of gold-coloured wire torc/bracelet F.160; c) and d) SEM BSE images of a cross-section showing the core alloy being a homogeneous single-phase solid solution with high gold and low copper contents, and the brighter surface area being gold enriched. Note the smoothly worn surface of the wire on the left side of the wire cross-section in c) from heavy wear that has worn away the gold-enriched surface, and the absence of the original gold-enriched surface lost in this region. Torcs were functional objects which experienced a great deal of use. The use wear traces seen on objects from Snettisham are discussed extensively in Chapter 20

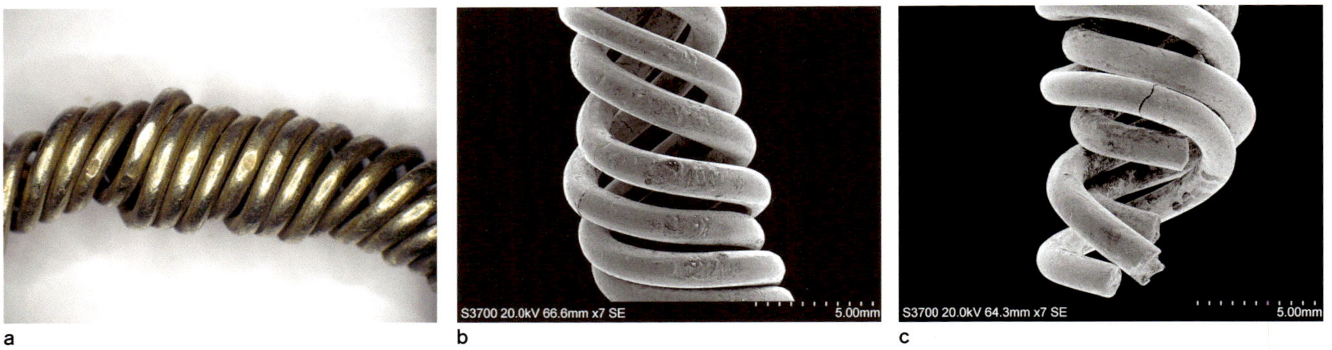

Figure 17.27a–c a) Torc/bracelet fragment F.88; SEM SE images of b) a slightly opened region showing its four coiled wires and c) the cracked and broken end

431–2). The torc is a pale gold-coloured, tightly coiled small diameter torc neck-ring or bracelet body section. It is fragmentary and appears to have been deliberately over-twisted, deformed and broken. It comprises four wires about 1.5mm thick and is similar to other small torcs.

A polished cross-section shows its extremely thick surface-enriched layer (up to 0.4mm), almost half the overall wire thickness (three quarters of the wire volume) (**Fig. 17.28**). This is in complete contrast to torc/bracelet F.160, which is of relatively similar core composition but with much thinner surface enrichment (**Table 17.4**; **Fig. 17.26**).

The core microstructure of the wires of F.88 is an extremely fine two-phase structure with a composition of 51.7 wt% Au, 42.4 wt% Ag, 5.9 wt% Cu, while the thick surface has lost around half of the silver as well as most of the copper (79.0 wt% Au, 20.7 wt% Ag, 0.3 wt% Cu) (**Table 17.4**). This is the thickest enrichment layer of any wire examined by far; the loss of around half of the silver in the enriched region suggests a potential enrichment process (La Niece 1995), beyond the simple removal of oxidised copper from the surface during wire manufacture. As argued above in the case of gold sheet, the microstructure of the enriched

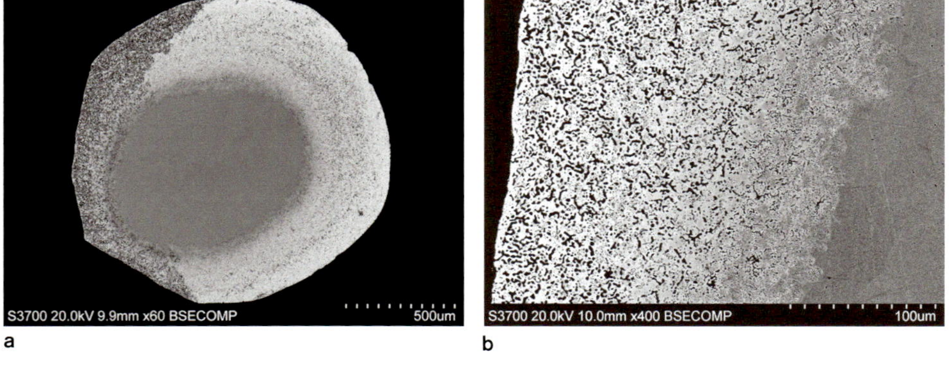

Figure 17.28a–b SEM BSE images of a) the extremely thick surface enrichment of torc/bracelet wire F.88 showing heavy wear as flat spots with corrosion penetrating these areas where the original protective burnished surface gold is missing, and b) of the thick gold-enriched surface with porosity, where the copper-rich phase has been depleted

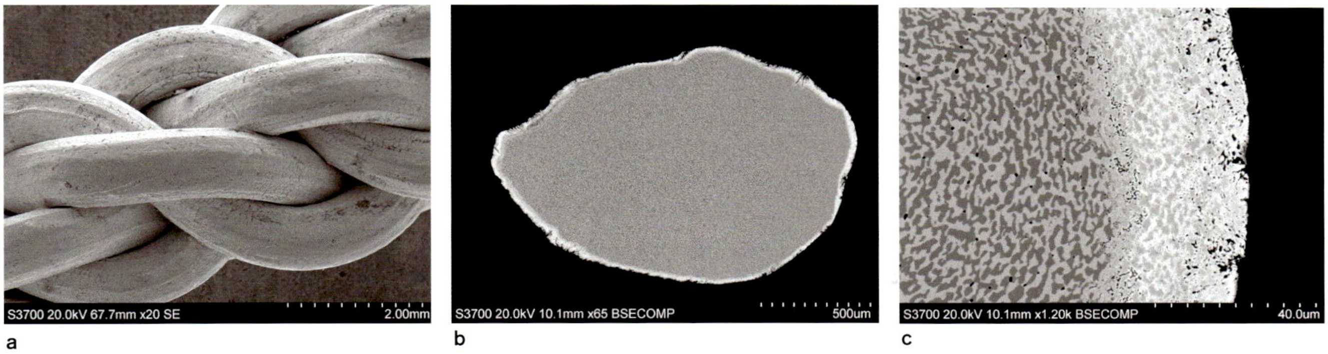

Figure 17.29a–c a) SEM SE image of torc F.116 plied wires with linear facets; b) SEM BSE image of the wire cross-section, showing the darker core and the brighter surface layer and the irregular profile of the wire due to hammered facets and wear; c) SEM BSE image of the two-phase core alloy with dark-grey copper-rich phases and medium-grey silver-rich phases (left) and of the thick bright gold-enriched layer (right)

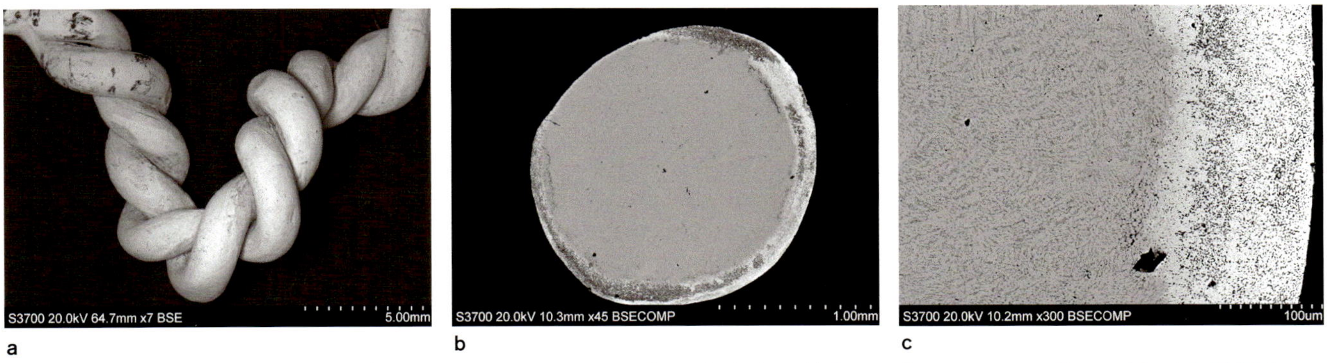

Figure 17.30a–c SEM BSE images of a) the torc/bracelet fragment F.135 plied wires; b) the medium-grey core alloy and the bright thick gold-enriched surface layer, showing variable corrosion within it and extensive wear through use (left of wire); c) the medium grey two-phase core alloy rich in copper and silver and the bright thick gold-enriched surface layer

layer, and in particular the porosity in the corroded region, is much like that of refined gold samples and material treated by salt parting (cementation) (Ramage and Craddock 2000, chapters 5, 9, 10). This type of process could also explain the thickness of the enriched zone in this case. In addition, such a salt parting process could have been carried out on a thick alloy rod *before* proceeding with the sequence of hammering to make the thin, elongated wire. A longer period of high-temperature chemical reactions would allow deeper penetration of the surface by leaching agents, leaving the metal porous for further reaction, compared with the hammering, annealing and pickling cycles, which would essentially compress and seal the porous surface during wire elongation, thus retarding or slowing further enrichment during these cycles (see p. 436).

Silver-gold-copper alloy wires

By comparison with the high gold-silver with low copper alloy wires, the majority of the sampled Snettisham wires are lower in gold (mean value of 24 wt% Au, see **Table 17.5**) and have a two-phase microstructure, which appears mottled light-grey and mid-grey on SEM BSE micrographs (**Figs 17.29–30**). These two-phase core alloys are essentially the result of the dominant silver-copper eutectic microstructure in which the light-grey phase of the SEM BSE images (e.g. **Fig. 17.29c**) is silver-rich while the dark-grey phase is copper-rich (**Tables 17.5–6**). Gold appears in solid solution in both phases, but is distributed non-uniformly between the two; there is more gold in the copper-rich phase than in the silver-rich one.

A most important feature of these lower-gold wires is that they typically show a thicker compacted enriched surface layer compared to the higher gold alloys. This is simply the result of the relative ease with which the deeper interconnecting honeycomb copper is accessible to oxidation during annealing and removal by pickling, and hence the development of thicker surface enrichment. This thickness is also an indicator of the large number of hammering/

Figure 17.31a–d a) Wire torc/bracelet F.156; b) SEM SE image of the plied 1.4mm-thick wires showing extensive stress corrosion cracks; c) and d) SEM BSE images of the cross-section showing the severe corrosion of the copper-rich phase of the core below the intact enriched surface layer. Note the residual dendritic core microstructure at high magnification

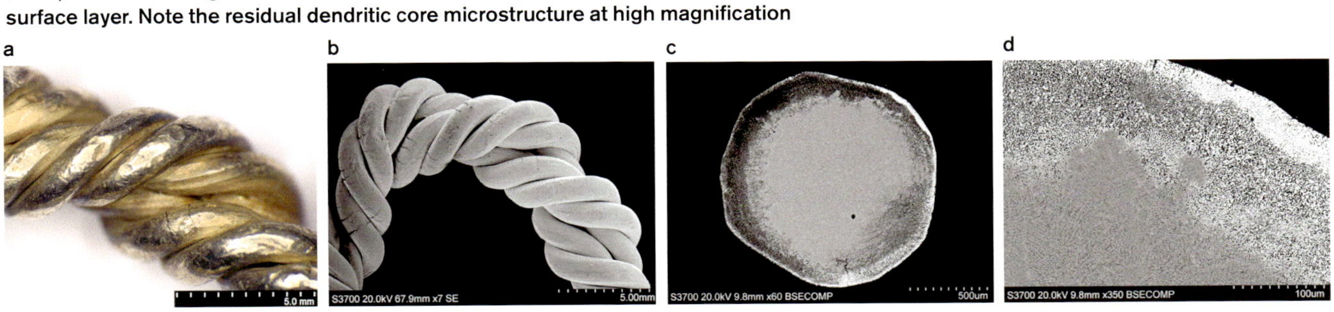

		Bulk composition (wt%)			Surface composition (wt%)		
Cat. no. BM reg. no.	Polished sample no.	Au	Ag	Cu	Au	Ag	Cu
F.153 1991,0407.44.a	J1516	30.2	49.6	20.2	58.6	39.7	1.7
F.5f 1991,0501.58	J1514	26.2	46.6	27.2	26.8	67.7	5.9
F.93 1991,0501.83	J1510	20.5	53.2	26.3	33.6	64.1	2.3
F.97 1991,0501.85	J1511	12.2	52.8	35.0	31.3	67.8	0.9
F.156 1991,0501.87	J1520	29.1	53.2	17.7	63.1	35.2	1.7
F.9d 1991,0501.128	J1496	26.3	50.9	22.8	43.3	53.3	3.4
F.11a 1991,0501.133	J1497	21.3	64.4	32.3	30.3	64.1	5.6
F.154 1991,0501.144	J1499	23.8	49.3	26.9	38.8	58.5	2.7
F.116 1991,0501.145	J1500	18.5	45.5	36.0	32.5	64.0	3.5
F.108 1991,0501.154	J1490	39.6	46.8	13.6	66.7	32.6	0.7
F.429 1991,0501.156	J1489	29.5	45.2	25.3	49.3	47.9	2.8
F.84 1991,0501.158	J1492	24.2	57.1	18.7	36.3	62.4	1.3
F.158 1991,0501.191	J1537	29.7	52.5	17.8	64.7	34.2	1.1
F.159 1991,0501.193	J1535	10.8	45.3	43.9	24.8	71.4	3.8
F.21b 1991,0501.207	J1531	20.4	43.5	36.1	45.0	52.0	3.0
F.147 1991,0501.221	J1527	16.4	51.0	32.6	35.2	58.0	6.8
F.135 1991,0501.222	J1526	27.2	58.4	14.4	48.1	47.3	4.6
S.32; S.37 1991,0407.50; 1992,1203.1	J1710 J1711	30.9	45.6	23.5	63.7 mean max 87.0	35.1	1.2
mean		24.2	50.6	26.1	44.0	53.1	2.9
min		10.8	43.5	13.6	24.8	32.6	0.7
max		39.6	64.4	43.9	66.7	71.4	6.8

Table 17.5 SEM-EDX analyses of silver-gold-copper alloys (18 wire samples). Representative area analyses of the bulk compositions and enriched surfaces in polished cross-sections. Compositional data plotted on Au/Ag/Cu ternary diagrams in Fig. 17.46

annealing/pickling cycles such wires have gone through. The thickness varies from several microns to over 100 microns. While many wires show a fairly solid metal interface between the thick surface layer and the core (**Fig. 17.29**), others have a corroded layer of variable thickness at the interface, where the copper-rich phase has preferentially been leached away during burial (**Figs 17.30–1**). The integrity of the structure is nonetheless maintained by the continuity of the uncorroded silver-rich phase network from the core to the enriched surface layer.

The thick wire torc S.31-9 has a very thin golden surface layer (up to *c.* 87 wt% Au) and the fractured ends of the core are pink-coppery coloured from corrosion of the copper phase of the core (*c.* 24 wt% Cu) (**Fig. 17.32**). Thus, this thickest faceted torc wire has the same overall microstructure, composition and enriched surface as the other thinner wire torcs, suggesting the same processes were used to make this one too.

High-copper and low-gold silver alloy wires

High-copper and low-gold silver alloy wires are generally more brittle than the high gold ones; they display severe stress corrosion cracks on their surface and large fractures from twisting and wear (**Fig. 17.33a**), as well as flaking of

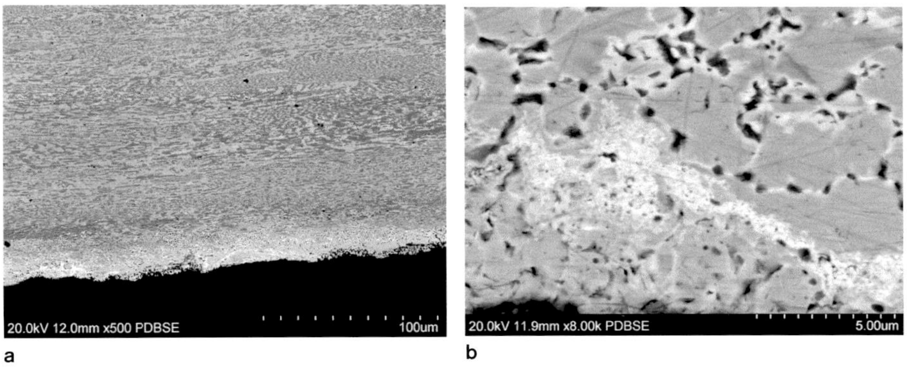

Figure 17.32a–b SEM BSE images of torc fragment from S.31–S.39 in polished cross-section: a) two-phase eutectic core and the diffuse surface enrichment on this thick wire; b) brighter fine very high-gold (87 wt% Au) grain boundary regions within the overall enriched surface layer

the enriched surface from the severely corroded core (**Fig. 17.33b** and also see the reel torc F.120 on p. 443). Sample F.89 was so friable that the surface had flaked and was even missing from the sampled section.

The cross-sections of eight such wires show that they are made of a two-phase core alloy rich in silver and copper and poor in gold (**Fig. 17.33c**). Their core composition ranges between 34 and 71 wt% for silver, 21 and 55 wt% for copper and very variable gold between 0.4 and 10 wt% (**Table 17.6**). The wire surfaces, on the other hand, contain more silver and gold, up to 92 wt% Ag and rather variable gold up to 22 wt% Au, and much reduced copper (between 1.3 and 9 wt% Cu). From these results, it appears that silver-copper wires were produced in a similar way to the gold-rich wires, through repeated cycles of hammering, annealing and pickling in acid. The surfaces of the wires have been enriched in precious metals, giving them a silvery colour. In these cases, the copper-rich phase has been largely removed and the porosity left behind was compressed by subsequent hammering (**Fig. 17.33d**).

Essentially, these results show that all of the gold-silver-copper alloy wires have a significant amount of surface enrichment, which gave the wires, and hence the torcs, a lighter, brighter and more golden appearance (depending on the alloy) after manufacture, compared to the basic starting alloys used to make them.

Bronze wires

In the Catalogue (Chapter 14), the broad term 'copper alloy' is used for those objects clearly exhibiting a greenish corrosion patina. In this Science Chapter, analysis shows that the sampled wires were of bronze (i.e. an alloy of copper and tin). Hence the projection that the vast majority, if not all of the green corroded Snettisham objects described as 'copper alloy' are also bronze. Essentially the Snettisham material predates the appearance of brass (i.e. an alloy of copper and zinc) in the Roman Period (Montero-Ruis and Perea 2007: Craddock *et al.* 2004).

There are only a few complete bronze torcs, such as L.6 (**Fig. 17.34**), although there are a large number of bronze torc wire fragments, with many being generally from smaller and thinner torcs than the range observed for gold and silver alloys. Many of the small, thin bronze wire torcs are in a heavily corroded state with much green copper corrosion on their surfaces, yet some are still smooth with bronze-coloured surfaces (**Fig. 17.35**). The workmanship in terms of consistent wire size and uniformly tight twisting of these torcs is similar to those of gold alloys.

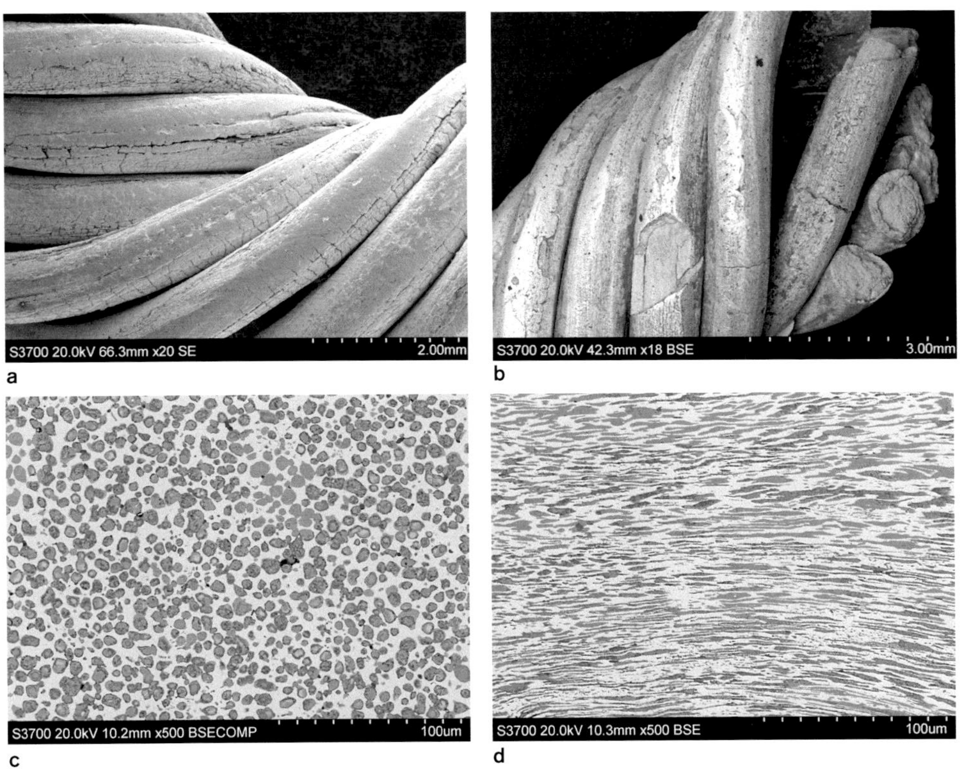

Figure 17.33a–d a) SEM SE image of the brittle and damaged coiled silver alloy wires with multiple stress corrosion cracks from torc F.102; SEM BSE images of b) the surface and broken ends of torc F.99 wires, showing the clear difference between the solid core and the corroded 'skin', which is flaking away; c) the transverse cross-section of a silver alloy wire from torc F.99, showing the two-phase core with a light-grey silver-rich phase and a dark-grey, partially corroded, copper-rich phase; d) the longitudinal section of a silver alloy wire from torc/bracelet F.89, showing the flattened, extended microstructure resulting from the hammering process

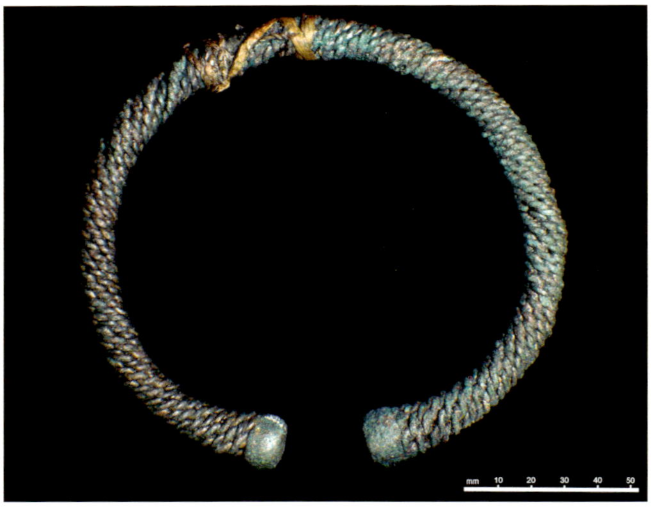

Figure 17.34 Bronze torc L.6, showing its heavily corroded surface and fibrous string wrapping (scale 50mm)

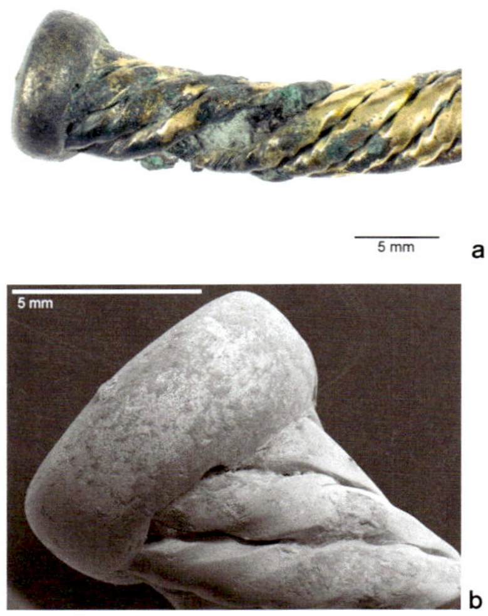

Figure 17.35a–b a) Torc F.168 with bronze wire surface exposed and only limited corrosion compared to many extensively corroded similar-sized torcs. Note the extreme wear on the wires; b) SEM BSE detail of torc F.168 showing the dendritic structure on the cast-on terminal surface

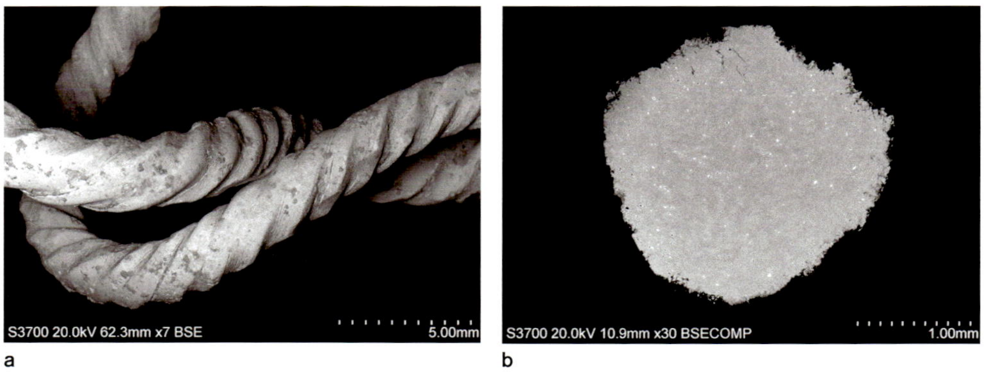

Figure 17.36a–b Bronze wire fragment F.14b. SEM BSE images of a) twisted square-section wire, which gives it a decorative 'spiral' appearance, and b) cross-section showing residual coring and sparse distribution of lead inclusions (white dots). The surface is uneven and pitted through corrosion, but the core remains uncorroded

Only a limited number of bronze wires from The British Museum Snettisham objects were sampled for metallography and analysis, because a further 82 similar bronze samples from the Norwich Castle Museum's Snettisham collection (plus a number of gold/silver alloys samples) were analysed independently by Stone (1987) (Ch. 18). The bronze alloys are typically low-tin bronze with small quantities of lead, nickel and/or arsenic (e.g. F.14b: 86 wt% Cu, 13 wt% Sn, 0.2 wt% Pb, 0.2 wt% Ni and 0.6 wt% As) and appear to be quite free of inclusions. Corrosion attacks quite deeply on the surface of this wire but the core remains uncorroded (**Fig. 17.36**).

Etched bronze cross-sections show annealed equiaxed grain structures, indicating that the hammered wires were most likely fully annealed to release the internal stress and crystalline deformation within the metal and hence soften it before the final coiling/plying. This was achieved in order to facilitate and maintain the tightly twisted final shape and prevent the torcs from springing open. Some areas have strained grains from the final twisting (**Fig. 17.37**). The addition of terminals by casting-on (see below, p. 458) would have provided heat to further anneal the metal.

Figure 17.37a–c Bronze torc/bracelet fragment F.361. Etched metallurgical polished cross-section under optical illumination showing the equiaxed grain structures, which form during recrystallisation of the bronze while heated during annealing, which releases the trapped stress from plastic deformation of the hammered and twisted wires (Bozzolo and Bernacki 2020). Note the parallel bands/lines within grains are annealed 'twinned' grain boundaries, some of which are deformed by the final mechanical deformation (twisting). Note the very deep channels on the wires in this are caused by the folding of the corners of the square-section wire during hammering. These are not the same as the parallel grooves discussed on the same bronze wire and shown in Figure 17.38

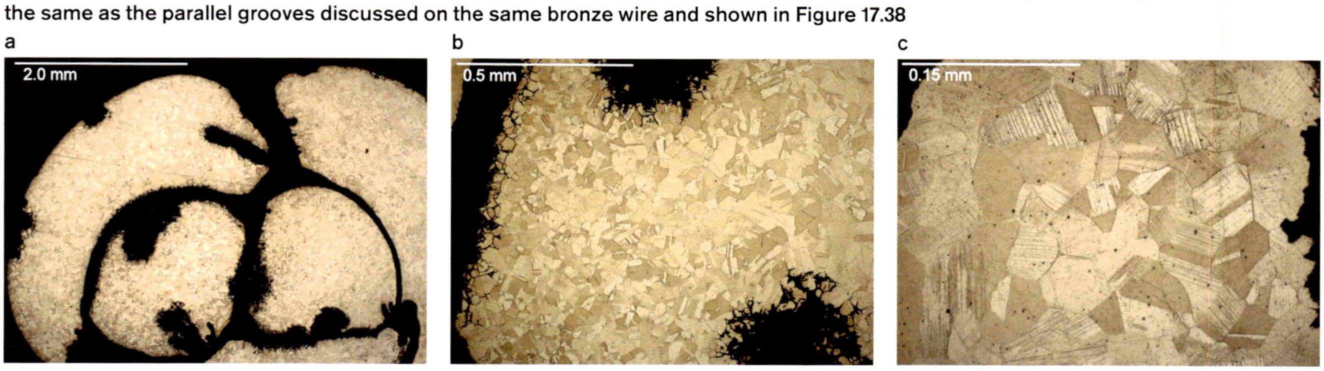

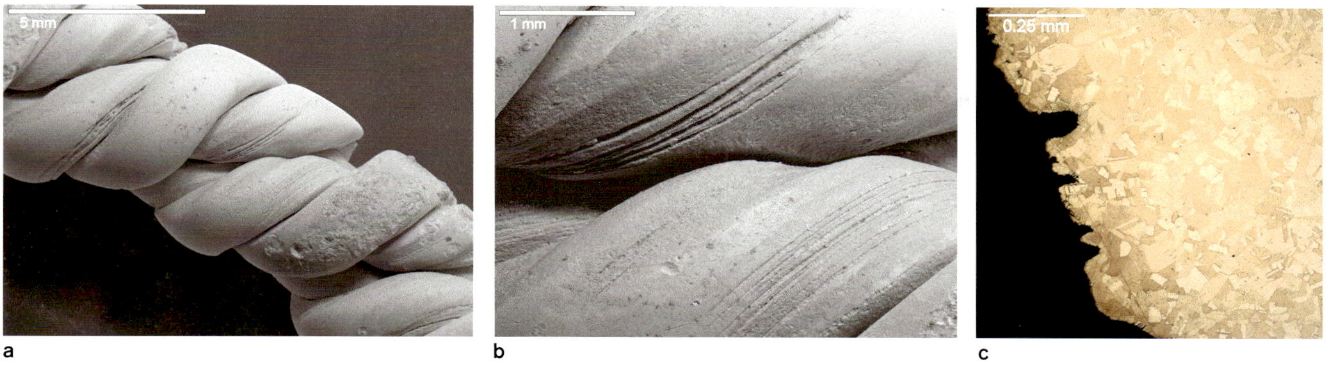

Figure 17.38a–c Bronze torc/bracelet fragment F.361. a, b) SEM BSE images showing the deep parallel score marks along the wire surfaces; c) Photomicrograph of the polished and etched cross-section of these deep score marks in the wire surface

Mercury gilding was observed on a number of bronze wires, and this is considered on p. 450.

Wire case study: Torc F.119–20

Of all the wires and torcs examined, the reel terminal torc F.119–20 exhibits most, if not all, of the characteristics of wire technology, metallography, composition, surface enrichment and corrosion that exemplify the Snettisham wire-based torc collections (**Fig. 17.39**). Hence, the detailed study of this torc provided optimal parameters for surface observation and sampling for full optical investigation and SEM-EDX analysis of the material.

The composition of the wires falls into the category of high-copper and low-gold silver alloys (p. 440, **Table 17.6**). The surface colour of the torc wires is light brown/golden and the original ancient fractured ends of the wire are bright red with cuprite corrosion and a golden rim (**Fig. 17.40a**). Examination in the SEM shows the wire surface to be in very poor condition: it is highly porous and deeply cracked circumferentially (**Fig. 17.40b–d**).

The polished cross-section of the wires shows a pink-coloured (copper-rich) uncorroded core metal, surrounded by a dark corrosion layer, and on the surface a thick silvery-golden layer (**Fig. 17.41a**). The SEM BSE images (**Fig. 17.41b–d**) show a homogeneous two-phase eutectic core alloy and a compressed thick surface-enriched layer, in which the silver and gold are doubled in concentration while the copper has depleted to one sixth of the core alloy value (**Table 17.7**).

It is interesting to note that the heavily hammered and elongated wire (**Fig. 17.41b–d**) shows no evidence of

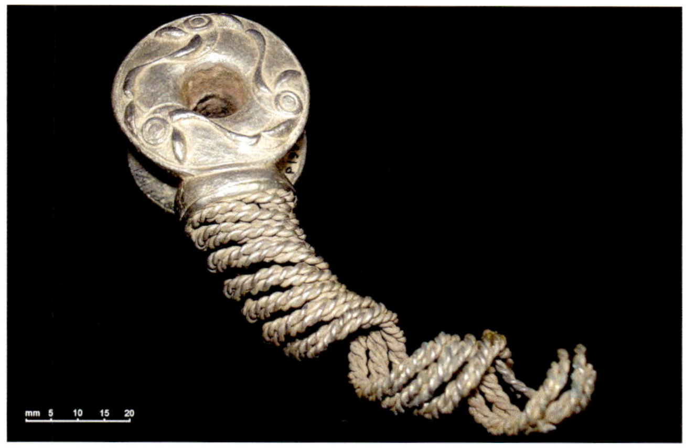

Figure 17.39 Reel terminal torc fragment F.120

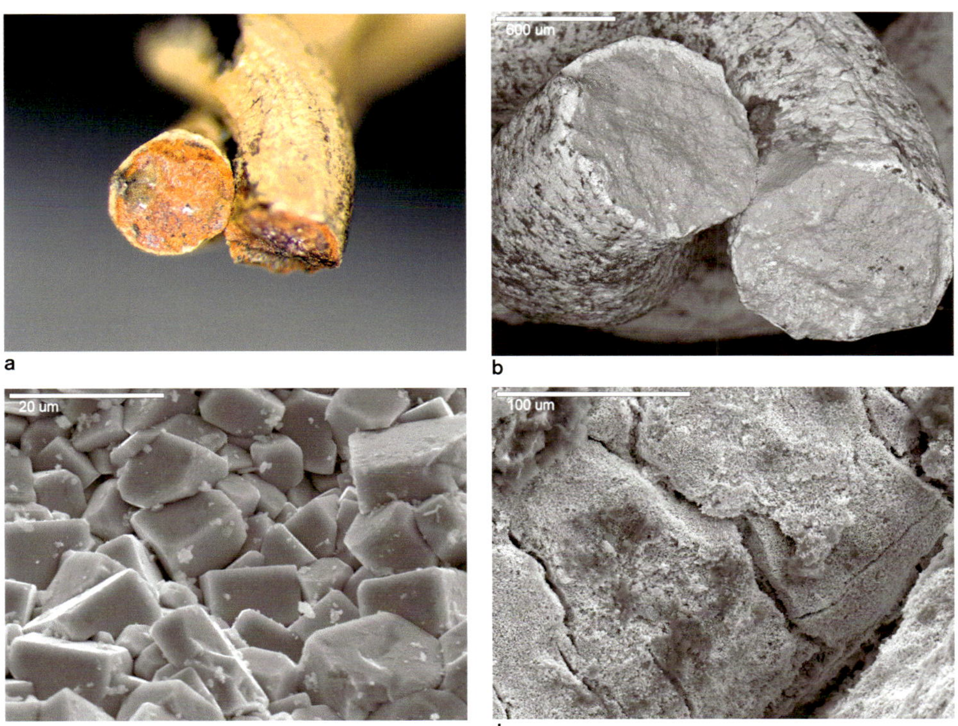

Figure 17.40a–d a) Optical micrograph of the ancient broken ends of the wires of reel terminal torc F.120 showing the bright red cuprite (copper oxide) crystals and the golden-coloured metallic surface; b) SEM BSE image of the same wires, which are about 1.2mm thick; c) SEM SE image at high magnification showing the cubic cuprite crystals; d) SEM SE image of the surface of the wire showing the fine porous surface and the deep tangential stress corrosion cracks into the metal

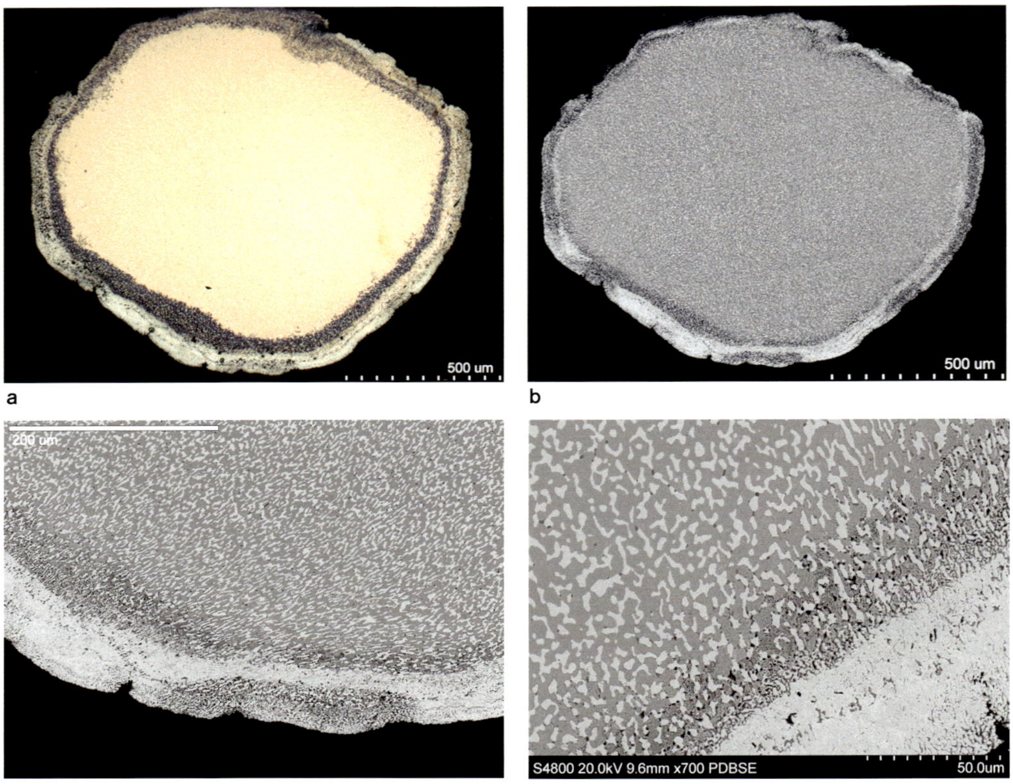

Figure 17.41a–d Reel terminal torc F.120. The optical polished cross-section of the wires (a) shows a pink-coloured (copper-rich) core metal, surrounded by a dark corrosion layer, and on the surface a thick, lighter silvery-golden layer (*c.* 70 microns thick). The flattened sides are facets from hammering. SEM BSE images (b–d) show a homogeneous two-phase core alloy and the compressed surface-enriched layer, *c.* 60 microns thick. The wire is around 1.2mm in cross-section

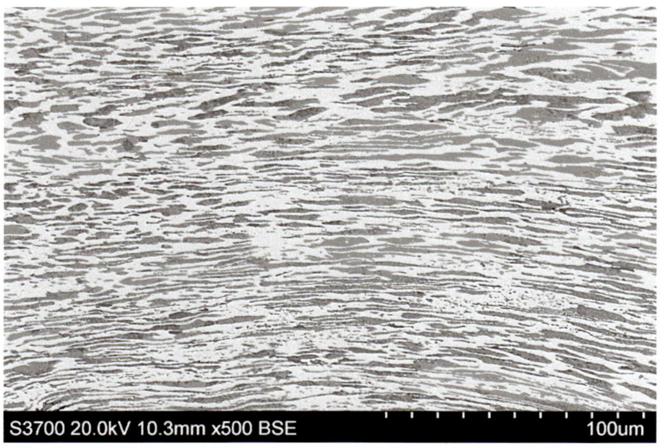

Figure 17.42 SEM BSE image of the longitudinal section of silver-copper-rich wire F.89, which has a similar core microstructure to F.120, showing the extreme phase elongation from deformation in the wire during hammering to lengthen it and reduce the diameter

deformation of the two-phase eutectic alloy core when seen in transverse section because the microstructure is uniformly compressed circumferentially during this process of hammering to elongate the wire and reduce its diameter. In contrast the longitudinal section microstructure shows extreme mechanical elongation of the two-phase core alloy, because the wire lengthens and the two phases are stretched linearly during hammering (**Fig. 17.42** shows this elongation in a similar torc wire).

SEM-EDX elemental mapping for gold, silver and copper of the neck-ring wires clearly shows that gold and silver are enriched in the surface layer and are uniformly distributed at lower levels in the core, while copper is very depleted in the surface layer and uniformly distributed at a high level in the core (**Figs 17.43–4**). There is a very clear boundary in the composition between the core and surface layer, with a corrosion layer in between. Oxygen shows its highest concentration where copper has oxidised (**Fig. 17.44e**), just below the gold/silver-enriched layer. This oxidation of copper took place during annealing at an elevated temperature (e.g. *c.* 550 °C, dull red heat). The two-phase microstructure and enriched surface layer of this wire (**Fig. 17.44** and at higher magnification in **Fig. 17.44**) is common to many of the silver wires with a high-copper and low-gold core composition (**Tables 17.6–7**). Gold is distributed throughout the core in both the silver-rich and copper-rich phases, but more gold is associated with the copper than with the silver. This was determined by the microanalysis of the different phases in the core (**Table 17.7** spectra 7 and 8) and observation of the changes in composition within the thick surface-enriched zone (**Fig. 17.45** and corresponding **Table 17.7**).

As discussed on pp. 435–6, the surface-enriched layer forms during an important part of the wire-making process, in which annealing the work-hardened wire (typically at *c.* 550–650 °C) causes the surface copper phase to become oxidised by heat, leaving black copper oxide on the wire surface. This copper oxide is then removed by pickling, leaving only gold and silver from the original copper-rich phase on the surface. Subsequent hammering to extend the wire further reduces the surface porosity left by the removal of the copper. It is this simple process that is key to the formation of enrichment in precious metal at the surface of the Snettisham wire work.

The following section brings together scientific discussions on alloy composition, surface treatments and colour for the material from Snettisham, combining the analyses of gold sheet and wires discussed in sections 17.3 and 17.4.

17.5 Alloy compositions, surface treatments and colours

This section covers the Snettisham sampled gold/silver alloy objects in the British Museum collections, bringing together

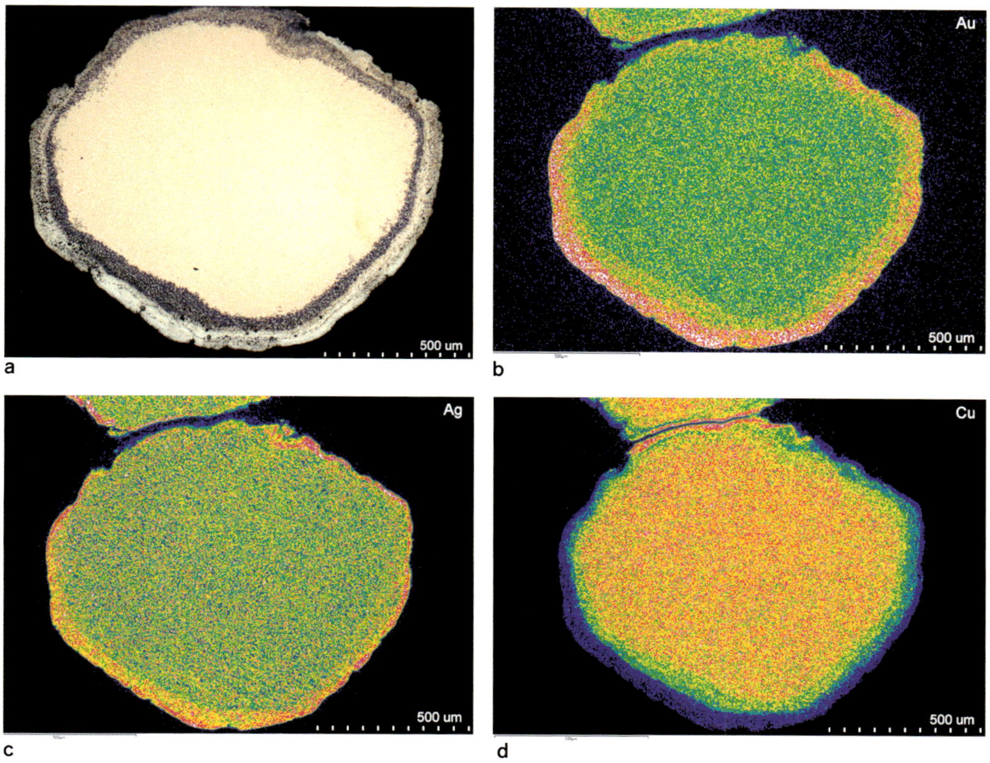

Figure 17.43a–d a) Optical metallographic image of the polished section of torc F.120 wire, showing the coppery-coloured core, the pale silver/gold surface layer, and a dark corrosion layer between. Elemental X-ray distribution maps for gold (b), silver (c) and copper (d) showing the copper-rich core and the gold/silver-enriched and copper-depleted surface. Core composition: Au 10.2 wt%, Ag 34.4 wt%, Cu 55.4 wt%; Surface layer composition: Au, 22.4 wt%, Ag 68.5 wt%, Cu, 9.2 wt% (Table 17.6)

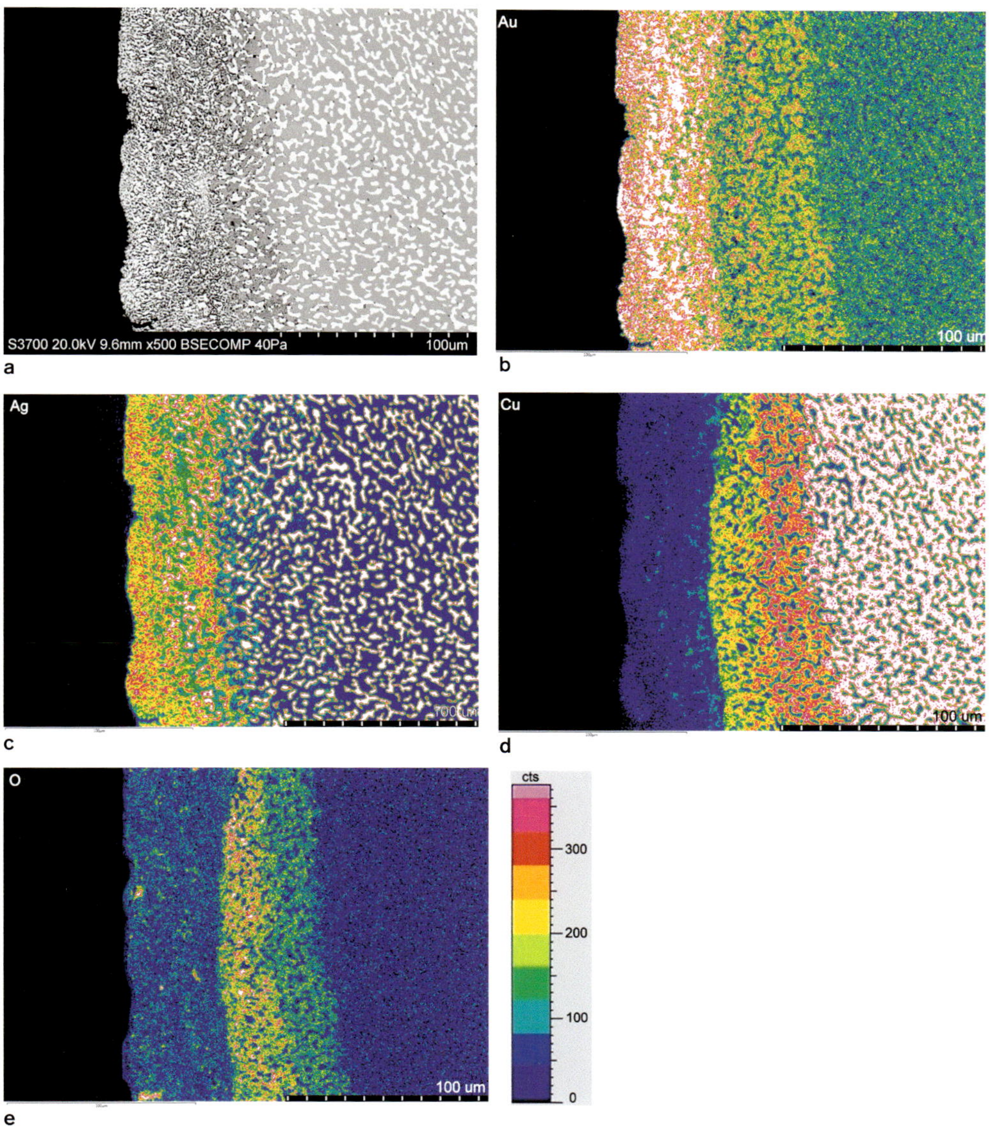

Figure 17.44a–e High magnification detail (x500, scale 100µm) of Fig. 17.44, showing a wire section from torc F.120: a) SEM BSE image showing the two-phase core microstructure to the right and the gold/silver-enriched surface layer to the left; elemental X-ray distribution maps of b) gold, c) silver, d) copper, and e) oxygen (image width *c.* 0.25mm). Colour scale shows relative element concentrations in each map

		Bulk composition (wt%)			Surface composition (wt%)		
Cat. no. BM reg. no.	**Polished sample no.**	**Au**	**Ag**	**Cu**	**Au**	**Ag**	**Cu**
F.120 1991,0501.80	J1460	10.2	34.4	55.4	22.4	68.5	9.2
F.148 1991,0501.86	J1512	8.5	70.7	20.8	11.9	86.8	1.3
F.89 1991,0501.101	J1524	5.7	58.4	35.9	no surface enrichment observed – flaked surface		
F.99 1991,0501.137	J1498	8.5	51.8	39.7	3.6	90.2	6.2
F.22a 1991,0501.148	J1488	8.1	67.4	24.5	14.2	83.0	2.8
F.102 1991,0501.187	J1538	6.8	44.2	49.0	12.7	80.4	6.9
F.103 1991,0501.215	J1530	6.5	48.7	44.8	4.5	88.8	6.7
F.380 1991,0501.218	J1528	0.4	57.7	41.9	0.8	91.8	7.4
mean		6.8	54.2	39.0	10.0	84.2	5.8
min		0.4	34.4	20.8	0.8	68.5	1.3
max		10.2	70.7	55.4	22.4	91.8	9.2

Table 17.6 SEM-EDX analyses of high-copper and low-gold silver alloys (8 wire samples). Representative area analyses of the bulk compositions and enriched surfaces on polished sections. Compositional data plotted on Au/Ag/Cu ternary diagrams in Fig. 17.46

Figure 17.45 SEM BSE image of torc F.120 wire, showing the areas and points of analyses from Table 17.7 (image width *c.* 0.25mm)

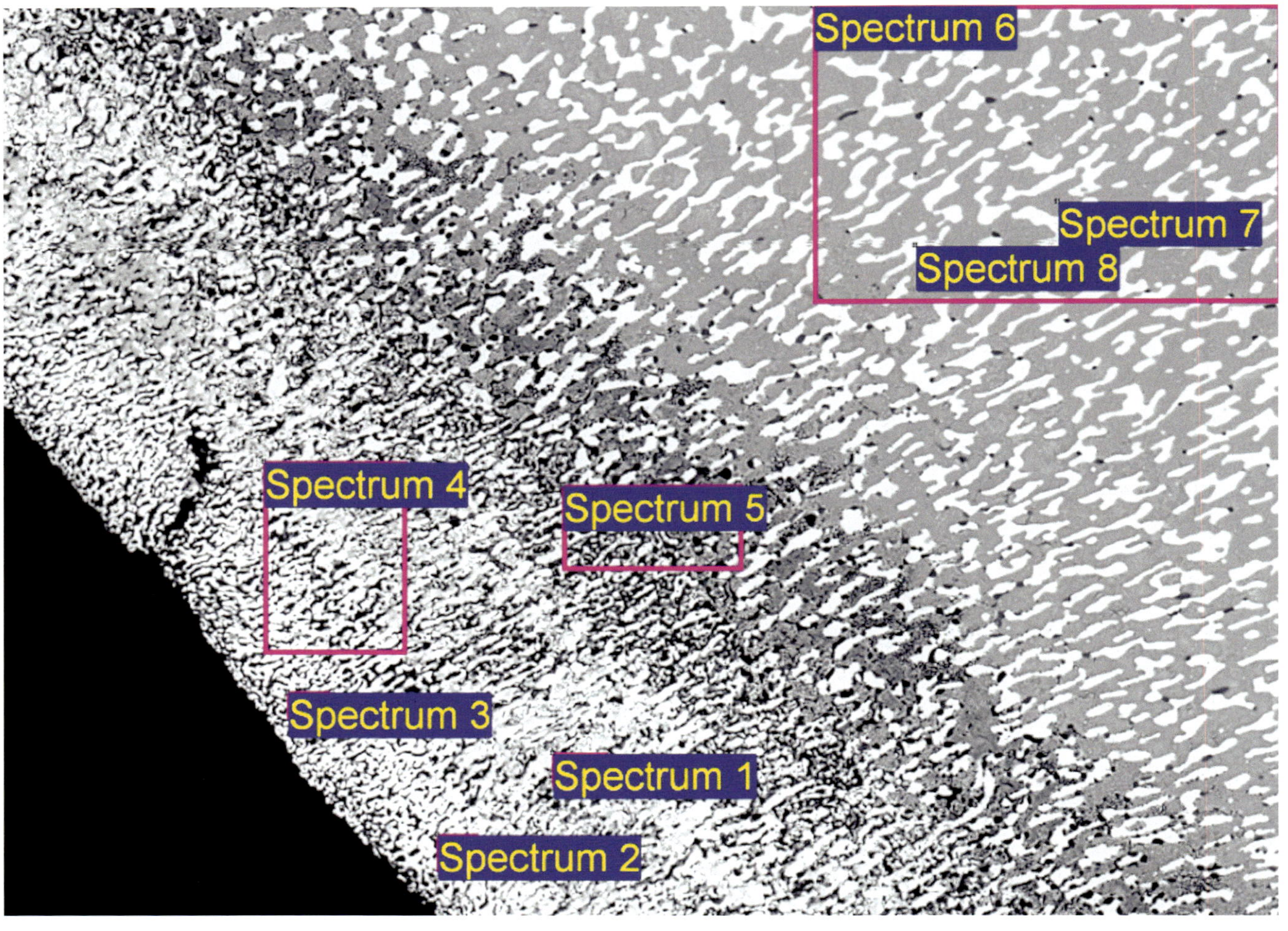

Spectrum	Polished section area	Cu %	Ag %	Au %
Spectrum 1	Enriched layer, small area	11.5	64.4	24.1
Spectrum 2	Enriched layer, small area	7.1	72.4	20.5
Spectrum 3	Enriched layer, small area	8.8	71.3	19.9
Spectrum 4	Enriched layer, larger area	9.2	65.9	24.9
Mean	Enriched layer	9.2	68.5	22.3
Spectrum 5	Corroded zone	42.2	43.0	14.8
Spectrum 6	Uncorroded core area	55.0	34.6	10.4
Spectrum 7	Copper-rich phase core	76.0	11.7	12.3
Spectrum 8	Silver-rich phase core	14.4	80.0	5.6

Table 17.7 SEM-EDX microanalyses of key areas of the polished cross-section from torc F.120 wire shown in Fig. 17.45

the discussions of gold sheet and wires in sections 17.3 and 17.4. It complements the analysis of the 82 bronze objects from Snettisham Hoards A, B and C in the collections of Norwich Castle Museum (see Ch. 18).

Alloy compositions

The core alloy compositions of all the sampled wires and sheet fragments (components from multi-strand and tubular torcs) are plotted in **Figure 17.46a**. This diagram emphasises in particular the grouping of the copper/silver-rich wires (p. 448) (< 50 wt% Au, **Tables 17.5–6** and **Fig. 17.46a** lower centre right), which include the silver-gold-copper alloys and high-copper and low-gold silver alloys, and the alignment of the gold-rich wires and sheets (> 50 wt% Au, **Tables 17.2, 17.4**) along the gold-silver axis (**Fig. 17.46a**, upper right). The surface analyses (in cross-section) of the same samples are plotted in **Figure 17.46b**. All the copper-rich core analyses now move to the right and align near the gold-silver axis. The comparison between the two diagrams shows a severe loss in copper from the surface layer of the copper-silver eutectic alloys, thus resulting in surfaces enriched in gold and silver. In contrast, most of the high gold-silver and low-copper wire alloys show only limited surface enrichment, in a similar way to the gold-rich sheet alloys.

Although objects from different Snettisham hoards have been analysed separately due to their present-day division between museums, objects from Hoard F (at the British Museum) (**Figure 17.46a)** show the same alloy similarities and distribution to the gold/silver objects analysed from Hoards A, B and C (at Norwich Castle Museum. Stone, 1987 (see **Fig. 18.1**). This suggests the probability of a very close origin of manufacture, or certainly a very closely related goldsmithing tradition, across the material in these separate hoards. It is likely that it was all drawn from a similar circulation pool, at around the same time.

It is interesting to note that, in the uncorroded core metal, gold is associated more in the copper-rich phase of the silver-copper eutectic than with the silver-rich phase (**Table 17.7** spectra 7 and 8). This would account for the high-gold enrichment when the copper is depleted from the wire surface. Simultaneous enrichment in precious metals and depletion in base metal was most likely achieved through the combination of mechanical and chemical processes described above.

With the sheet and wire core alloy compositions plotted on the temperature isothermal contour diagram, the groupings clearly show the melting ranges of the alloys used by the metalsmiths for fabricating the torcs (**Fig. 17.47**). These vary between 780 °C and 870 °C for the lower-gold alloys, and 950 °C and 1050 °C for the gold-rich alloys, the latter including both sheet and wire (**Tables 17.2, 17.4**). Thus, the former cluster around the lowest melting range of the isothermal diagram, because of the incorporation of a significant amount of copper into the alloys of lower gold content. It must have been known to the metalsmiths that mixtures of gold, silver and copper in this range of proportions produced molten alloys more easily. They appear to have been deliberately exploiting the low-melting characteristics of these gold-silver-copper alloys that we can now see by way of the ternary phase diagram (cf. Lyman 1973). This might be one of the most important characteristics for the Iron Age craftspeople, allowing much easier and fuel-efficient use of resources in melting the alloys. Perhaps this was a very important practical consideration in the production process of the majority of these alloys. Knowing also that the final metal colour of the torcs would change during manufacture, the initial metal mix (with high copper) was not so important viewed from the perspective of the final achieved gold/silver colour of the artefact.

In summary, metallography and SEM-EDX examination have shown that four main precious metal alloys were used in the manufacture of the objects examined:

1. The highest average gold alloys, mainly seen in sheet objects (**Table 17.2**, p. 428).
2. High gold-silver and low copper alloys used in wires (**Table 17.4**, p. 437).
3. Silver-gold-copper alloys used in wires (**Table 17.5**, p. 440).
4. High-copper and low-gold silver alloys used in wires (**Table 17.6**, p. 446).

The latter two types comprise the majority of the wires sampled. The main metallurgical reason that alloys rich in gold were used for sheet objects is that they are malleable and therefore more easily hammered into thin sheet than the silver/copper-rich alloys which work-harden more quickly.

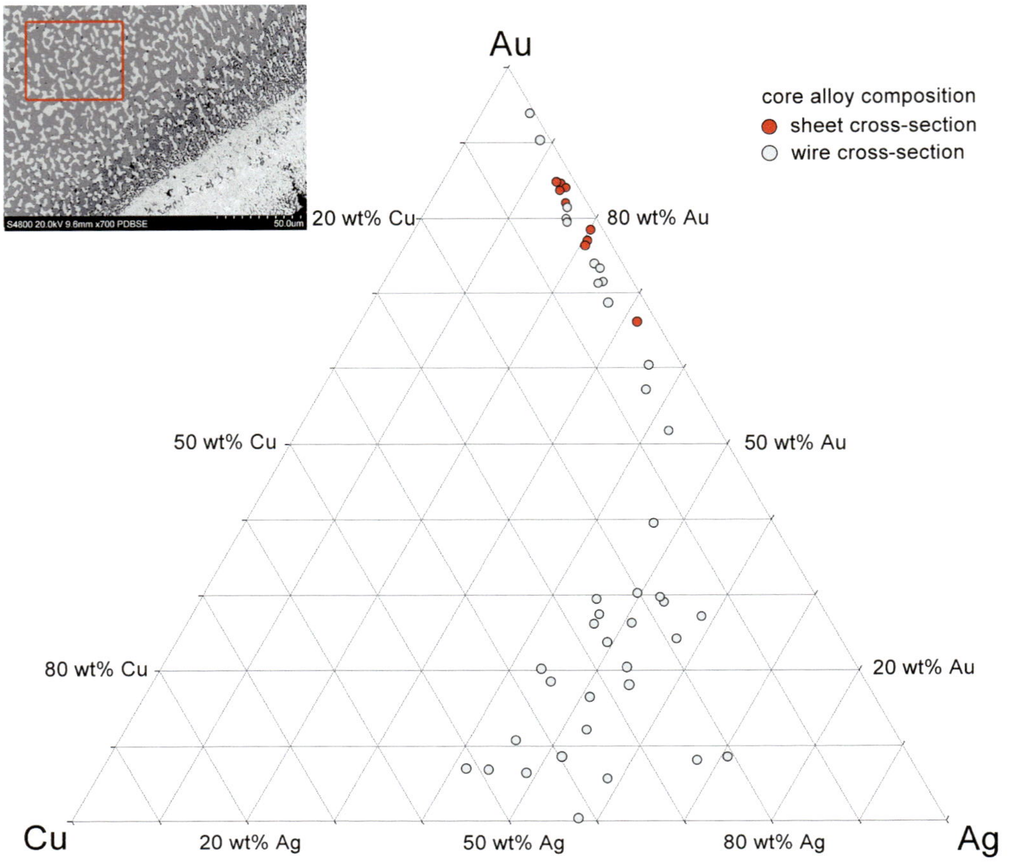

a

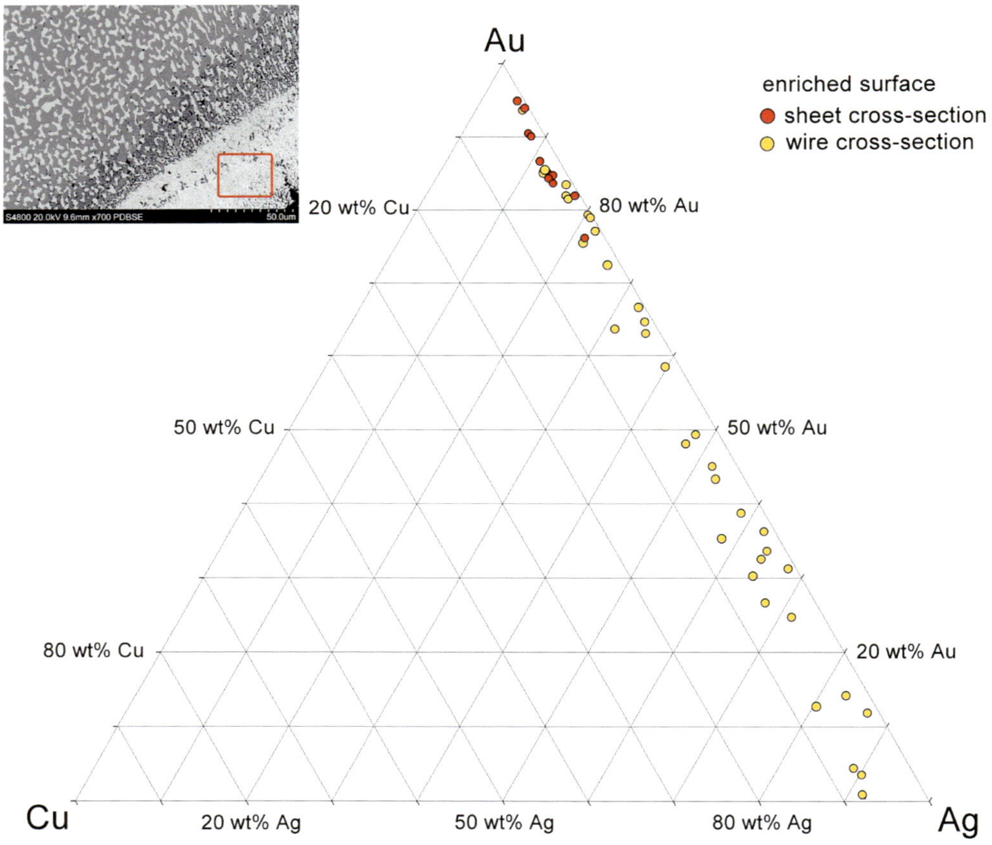

b

Figure 17.46a–b Gold-silver-copper ternary diagrams of a) the core compositions of 50 cross-sections showing the high gold-silver wires and sheet upper right, and the grouping of all the higher copper alloys lower centre; (b) the corresponding surface composition of the same samples. These clearly show the depletion in copper resulting in surfaces enriched in gold and silver for all of the copper-rich core samples. Inserted SEM BSE images are typical areas analysed in the core and surface layers

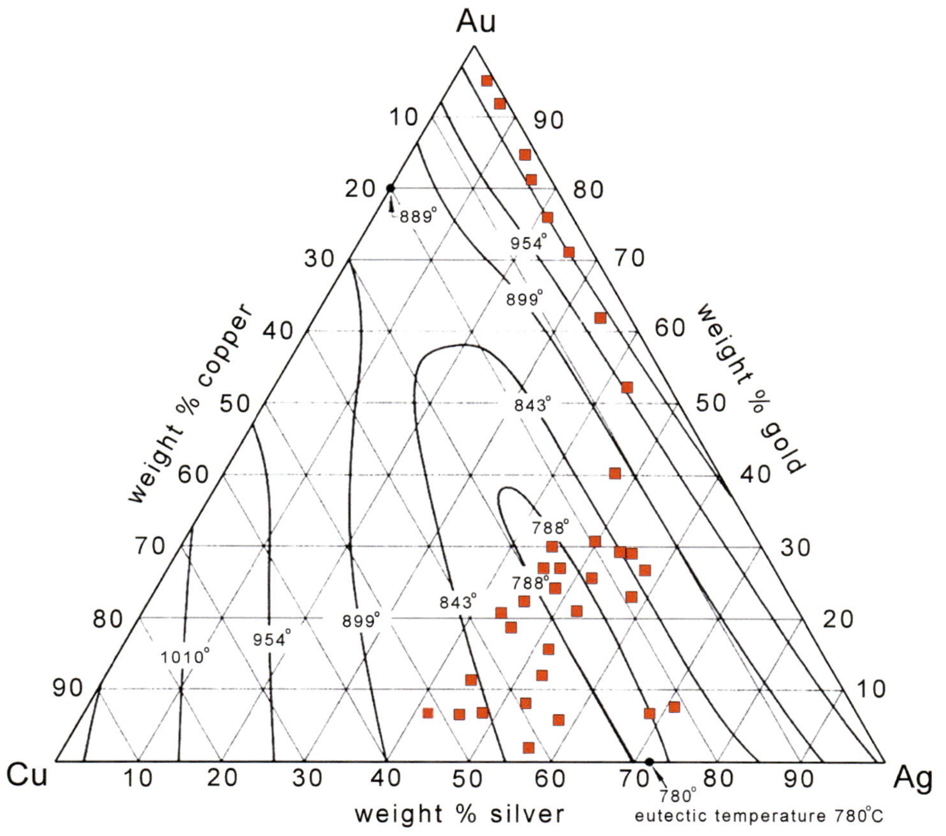

a

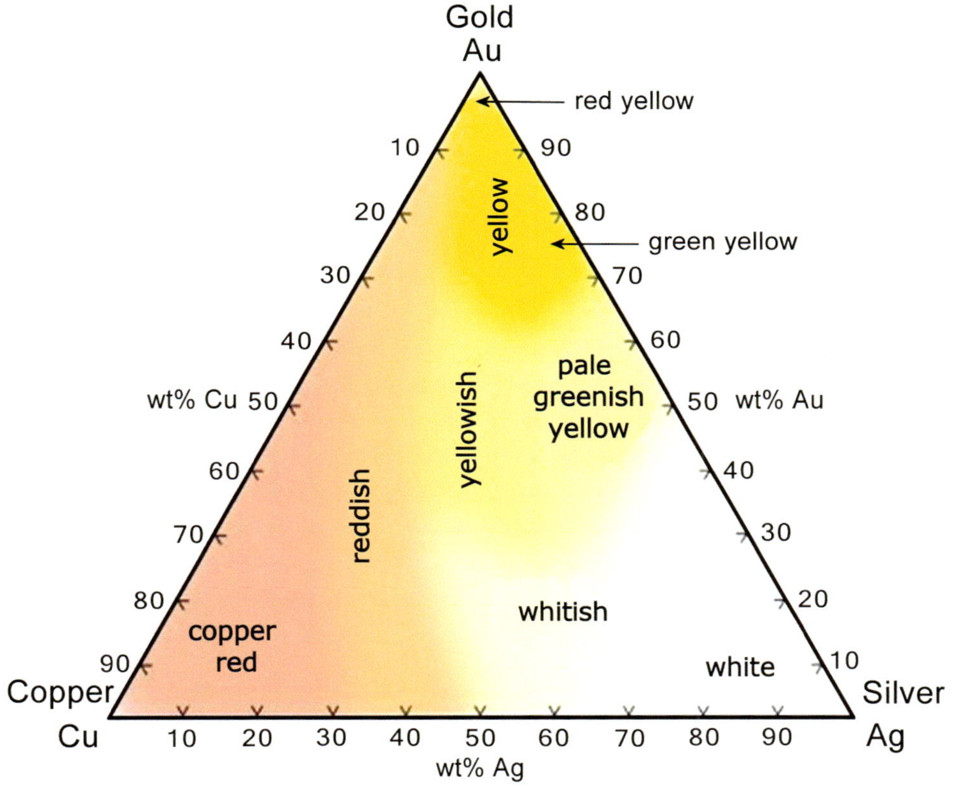

b

Figure 17.47a–b a) Plot of all the sampled core alloy compositions on the Au/Ag/Cu ternary diagram with isothermal contours of melting temperatures at 55 °C intervals for ternary gold, silver, copper alloys over the full range of temperatures from the lowest melting point at 780 °C (silver-copper eutectic) to that of solid gold (1064.4 °C), silver (961.9 °C) and copper (1084.5 °C) (Lyman 1973). Note the general clustering of the copper-rich wire alloys around the lowest melting temperature region (lower centre), in sharp contrast with the high-gold and low-copper sheet alloys, which all plot between the 1010 °C isotherm and upper gold/silver axis (upper right); b) Au/Ag/Cu ternary diagram indicating general colour zones of the alloys (modified after Cretu and Van der Lingen 1999) to compare with the plotted data from Snettisham in a). Note that the sheet core alloys are mostly in the yellow region, while the wire core alloys are in the paler yellowish/whitish regions, knowing that most are surface enriched and therefore moving towards the white/pale greenish yellow/yellow colour range (see Fig. 17.46)

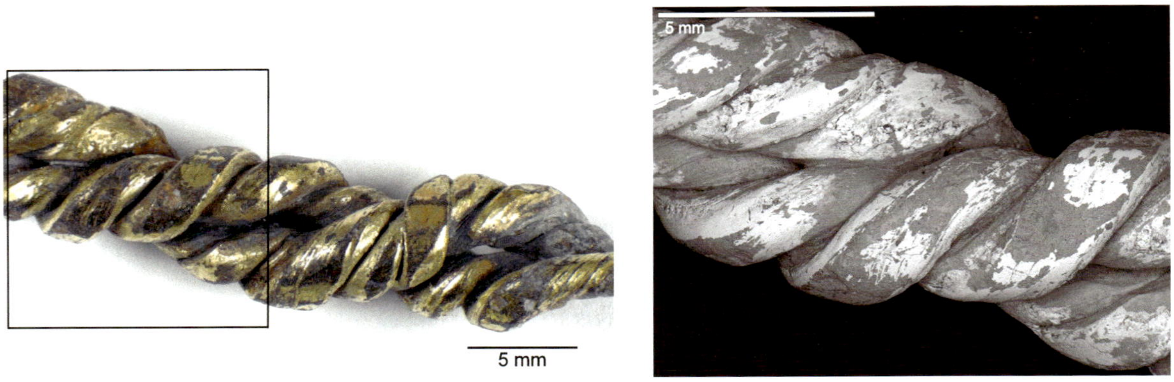

a b

Figure 17.48a–b a) Torc/bracelet F.182, with tightly plied pairs of gilded bronze wire; b) SEM BSE image of the outlined area in the optical image a). The mercury-gilded surface areas appear bright

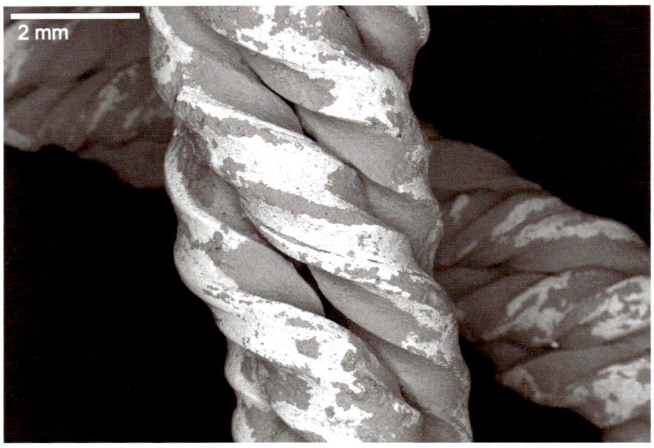

Figure 17.49 SEM BSE image of bronze torc/bracelet fragment F.15a, plied from gilded square-section individually twisted bronze wires. There is heavy wear between the adjacent wires from use of the torc

These latter alloys are quite suitable for wire making. The processes of hammering with frequent annealing and pickling that are necessary to make wires also leads to surface enrichment in gold and silver. The low-melting characteristics of these alloys make them easier to melt and cast.

Surface enrichment in gold and silver on the wires

Most low-gold alloy wires and many sheet fragments show some degree of surface enrichment of gold and silver, and in many cases substantial thickness in the compacted enriched surface layer has been found in the sectioned samples. Given the improvements in colour and corrosion resistance that surface enrichment bestows on the alloys, it is most likely that the effects of enrichment that occurs during wire making were not just noticed, but exploited by the metalsmiths. Many cultures see the colours of gold and silver as significant in their cultural expressions and were sought after. For example, many South American cultures used copper-rich alloys, not dissimilar to some of those found in the Snettisham objects, and certainly exploited the enrichment processes that they enhanced technologically to produce their desired golden colours (La Niece and Meeks 2000) (see section 17.4).

There are three major effects of the surface-enrichment process:

1. Significant saving in 'precious metals' used in the bulk starting alloys compared to the visual appearance of the finished torcs. The relative perceived values of different materials and alloys are discussed in more detail in Chapters 22 and 23.

2. The colour of the surface becomes more golden/silvery, which would be a desirable outcome. This occurs almost by default during wire production with the higher copper alloys, although the significant depletion in silver at the surface in some high-gold alloy objects would imply a deliberate and separate technological process along the lines of 'parting'. In both cases, the colour shift may have been part of an intended and controlled effect, since goldsmiths would have been well aware of the visual results of these processes and used them accordingly for the enhanced colour of these high-status objects. Colour is considered in more detail below (p. 452).

3. By removing copper from the surface, the metal is made more resistant to daily exposure to perspiration and staining during use. This is a very useful outcome, to preserve the quality and appearance of a torc, as anyone who has worn 'cheap' thin gold-plated jewellery and has had their skin stained green by copper corrosion will know.

Mercury-gilded wires

There are also some bronze wires with golden surfaces that have been deliberately gilded, probably by mercury gilding (also called fire gilding) based on the presence of low levels of mercury in the surface metal (**Figs 17.48–9**). Three different types of wires have been mercury gilded and are illustrated here. The gilding has in most cases been partly worn away during use or has been lost due to underlying corrosion of the bronze. The SEM images of the surface of the wires show the residual gilding as light areas while darker areas show the exposed bronze, where the gilding has worn away. Surface analysis by EDX shows the presence of significant low levels of mercury in the gold areas.

At higher magnification, the cross-section of torc/bracelet F.182 shows the typical structure associated with mercury gilding: a burnished and slightly porous gold layer of variable thickness. This layer contains a little, and variable, residual mercury (in this case it is around 12 wt% Hg), with a corroded layer in the bronze directly under the gilding, which also varies in thickness. The gilding follows the exact form of the wire surface, but it varies in thickness between 2 and 10 microns (**Fig. 17.50**).

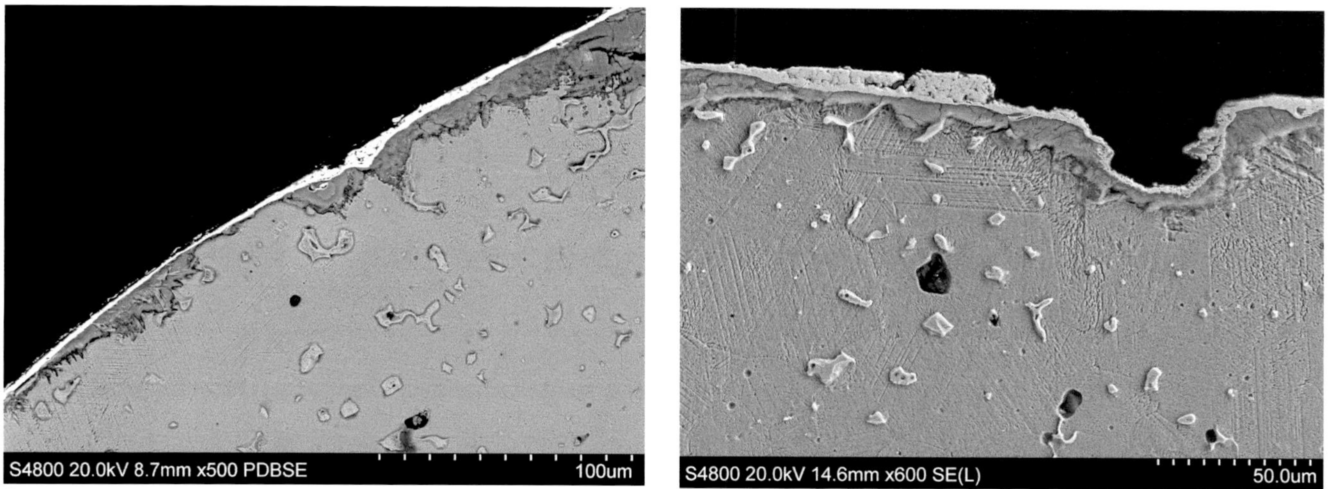

a b

Figure 17.50a–b a) SEM BSE and b) SE images of the etched cross-section of mercury-gilded bronze wire from F.182, showing the continuous and thin mercury-gilded surface layer of variable thickness, following the contours of the underlying wire, with some corrosion of the bronze beneath. The particles in the bronze core are α+δ eutectoid intermetallic compound phase (Meeks 1993)

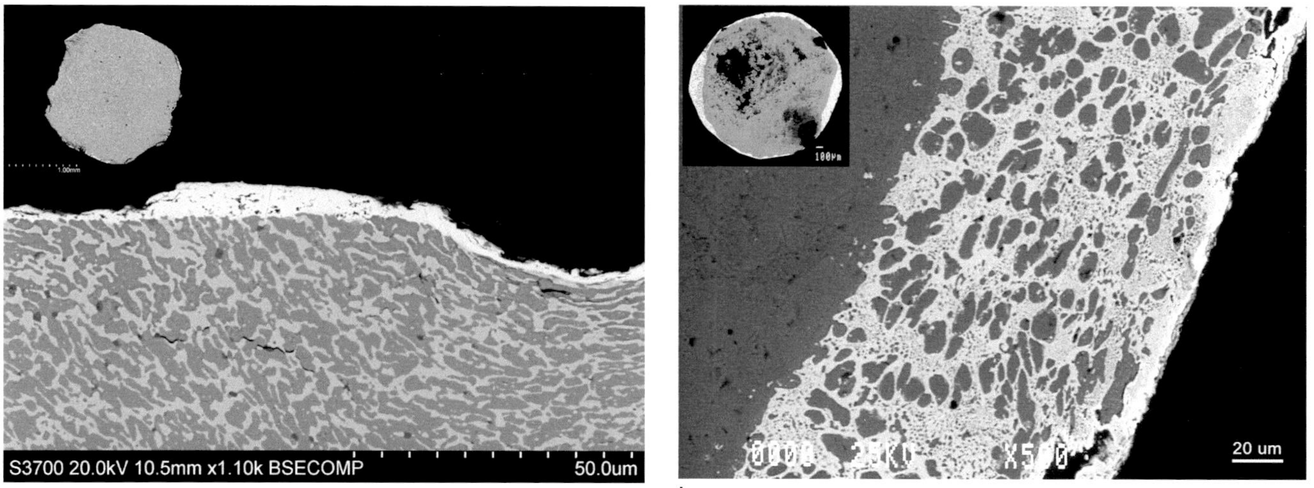

a b

Figure 17.51a–b a) SEM BSE image of a high-copper with low-gold silver alloy wire with mercury gilding (wire 2mm diameter, insert) (F.17b); b) SEM BSE image of a bronze wire from torc G.6 with a thick eutectic silver-copper layer underneath the thin surface gilding (wire 2mm diameter, insert)

It is hypothesised that gilding was achieved by rubbing a mercury amalgam (a paste-like mixture of liquid mercury with dissolved gold) onto the clean bronze surface (Lins and Oddy 1975). The complete object was then heated to above 357 °C to boil off the mercury leaving a porous gold layer on the surface. This porous layer would have then been compressed and given a shiny appearance by burnishing it. The thicker areas of gilding that are preserved still have the characteristic porosity, which resulted from the vaporisation of mercury (**Fig. 17.50b**). The gilding is closely bonded to the surface, which is now the underlying corrosion layer on the bronze that has been propagating down to a depth of around 10 microns during burial. In this case the gilding has largely protected the bronze from corrosion.

Two other types of metal from Snettisham in addition to bronze wire have been identified as having been mercury gilded: a high-copper with low-gold silver alloy wire (F.17b) and a bronze wire with an unusual complex multiple layer surface (G.6). The first is a typical example of mercury/fire gilding on a silver-copper alloy wire (42 wt% Ag, 51 wt% Cu, 7 wt% Au) (**Fig. 17.51a**) of a composition representative of alloys in **Table 17.6**. The gold layer varies in thickness and is burnished, but is still slightly porous, and its microstructure is very similar to that seen on the bronze wire from F.182. The gilding is very well bonded to the underlying uncorroded silver-copper alloy. EDX analysis detected up to 26 wt% residual mercury in the gilding with 39 wt% gold while the silver content of the gilding is around 30 wt% and is derived by interdiffusion from the silver-rich phase of the underlying wire alloy during the gilding process. Such high residual mercury implies that heating to remove the mercury during the gilding process was perhaps at a lower temperature or for less time than ideal. The gold layer has formed a perfect solid solution diffusion bond with the silver phase in the two-phase silver-copper core alloy and this produced a corrosion resistant join, which did not suffer the interface corrosion seen under the gilding of the bronze example above (**Fig. 17.50b**).

The other example of gilded bronze wire from torc G.6 is unusual, as it has been silvered before being mercury gilded, so it is a double-plated layer. The cross-section of this wire clearly shows a thick layer (*c.* 130 microns) of silver-copper eutectic underneath the thin surface gilding layer (**Fig. 17.51b**). It is difficult to explain the reasons for the choice of silvering the bronze wire in this case as it is the only piece found so far and silvering bronze is indeed itself unusual (Oddy 1993, La Niece 1990). However, from a metallurgical viewpoint, the copper-rich phase of the eutectic silvering layer would bond very easily to the copper-rich bronze core, and the applied gold layer would bond easily to the silver-rich phase of the intermediate silvered layer by diffusion, better than it would directly to the bronze. The gilding layer was compacted by burnishing to remove the porosity left by the vaporised mercury and produce a shiny surface.

The identification of mercury gilding on several artefacts from Snettisham is significant and is the earliest evidence known for this technique in Britain (Northover and Anheuser 2000). This is a sophisticated metallurgical process showing a knowledgeable understanding of the behaviour of different metals by the ancient craftworkers. The knowledge of mercury gilding had to be gained, as well as a supply of mercury, and it would seem most likely that this represents a transfer of knowledge from the continent. Mercury is not indigenous to the British Isles in any significant deposits, and noted only as a rarity in a few locations in northern England (e.g. Greenland and Braithwaite 2012; The Hudson Institute of Mineralogy database https://www.mindat.org/min-2647.html) Therefore mercury must have also been sourced from the continent. A possible archaeological source for mercury used in the British Isles is Almadén, Castile-La Mancha, Spain (Higueras *et al.* 2011; Saupe 1990). Research by Perea *et al.* (2008) notes that '[...] the hypothesis of a local origin for fire gilding in Iberian times around 4th century BC [...] has emerged'. This implies the knowledge of the technique had already been established in Iberia before the period in which the Snettisham torcs were made and deposited.

Mercury occurs in limited mineral forms in nature but principally the bright scarlet/reddish-brown mineral cinnabar, mercuric sulphide, which itself was historically used as a red pigment. Mercury can also be found in its native, liquid metallic form as droplets associated with crevices and pores in its host mineral (e.g. https://www.minerals.net/mineral/mercury.aspx) and is formed by the natural oxidation of the sulphide ore (https://geology.com/minerals/cinnabar.shtml). It may be assumed that native liquid mercury was available at the continental source exploited by Iron Age metalsmiths. Aristotle in the 4th century BC described mercury as being like 'liquid silver' or 'water silver', while his student Theophrastus of Eresos (*c.* 371–*c.* 287 BC) wrote the earliest surviving scientific book on minerals, *De lapidibus (On Stones)*, and describes cinnabar of Spanish origin, and he states that quicksilver '... is made by pounding cinnabar with vinegar in a copper mortar with a copper pestle'. This can be reproduced experimentally. Further support for the Almadén region being the possible ancient source of mercury for the Snettisham material is its association with later Roman settlements and remains of cinnabar mines (Higueras *et al.* 2011). Pliny the Elder in Book XXXIII of his *Natural History* notes cinnabar with the presence of natural liquid mercury was also found in silver mines: 'There is also a mineral found in these veins of silver which contains a humour, in round drops, that is always liquid, and is called quicksilver.' Furthermore, Pliny also describes a distillation and condensation technology to collect vaporised mercury from heating cinnabar:

> ... getting hydrargyrum or artificial quicksilver ... it [presumably cinnabar] is put in an iron shell in flat earthenware pans, and covered with a convex lid smeared on with clay, and then a fire is lit under the pans and kept constantly burning by means of bellows, and so the surface moisture (with the colour of silver and the fluidity of water) which forms on the lid is wiped off it. This moisture is also easily divided into drops and rains down freely with slippery fluidity. (Pliny the Elder 1952, XXXIII, 123)

It is very unlikely for mercury to have been transported to Snettisham in its heavy liquid form. It was probably traded as a pasty-solid amalgam of gold made at source by mixing gold with liquid mercury, in the proportions of around Au 1: Hg 6. It is a simple task, as mercury dissolves gold very rapidly at room temperature forming the pasty material. Pre-amalgamating gold at the source would have had benefits both for ease of transport and ease of use: the pasty/solid amalgam could have been easily rubbed directly onto bronze at a metal workshop and then heated to drive off the mercury, leaving the gold on the surface for burnishing to finish the gilding process.

Surface treatments and colour

Much has been written on colour in relation to Iron Age metalwork, and the role of colour and alloy composition in the structure and ordering of the Snettisham hoards are considered in detail in Chapter 24. Whilst there is some apparent grouping and ordering of torcs by colour and metal content, it does not appear to have been the main structuring principle behind the nested torc hoards (G, H, J, K and L). As demonstrated here, objects in the fragmentary hoards (B, C and F) represent a broad spectrum of colours, from the palest silver to rich yellow-golds, and everything in between. When objects were deliberately grouped and interlinked in the hoards, there appears to have been an emphasis on diversity of colours and alloys, rather than attempt to group like with like, or express a clear preference for one colour over another.

Three types of surface treatments are seen on torcs at Snettisham: surface enrichment of gold and silver taking place as a natural result of wire production processes, more interventive surface enrichment similar to the chemical treatments used in gold refining and gilding of bronze and silver alloys. All of these had an impact on the colour of the finished object. The application of parting-like processes to gold alloys would have emphasised the yellow-gold colour of the metal, and the gilding of bronze and silver alloy torcs would likewise have given these a yellowish gold outer surface colour. The surface enrichment of lower-gold wire alloys had the effect of shifting the colour from whitish and yellowish gold areas of the ternary diagram towards whiter alloy colours and pale greenish yellow (see **Figs 17.46–7**). In many cases, however, these would have been very subtle colour shifts, and it is difficult to ascertain how important the colour of the finished object was in terms of influencing alloy selection. As argued above, the lower-gold ternary alloys selected for use in many of the wires at Snettisham may have been chosen as much for their metallurgical properties as for their colour. They are optimal in terms of

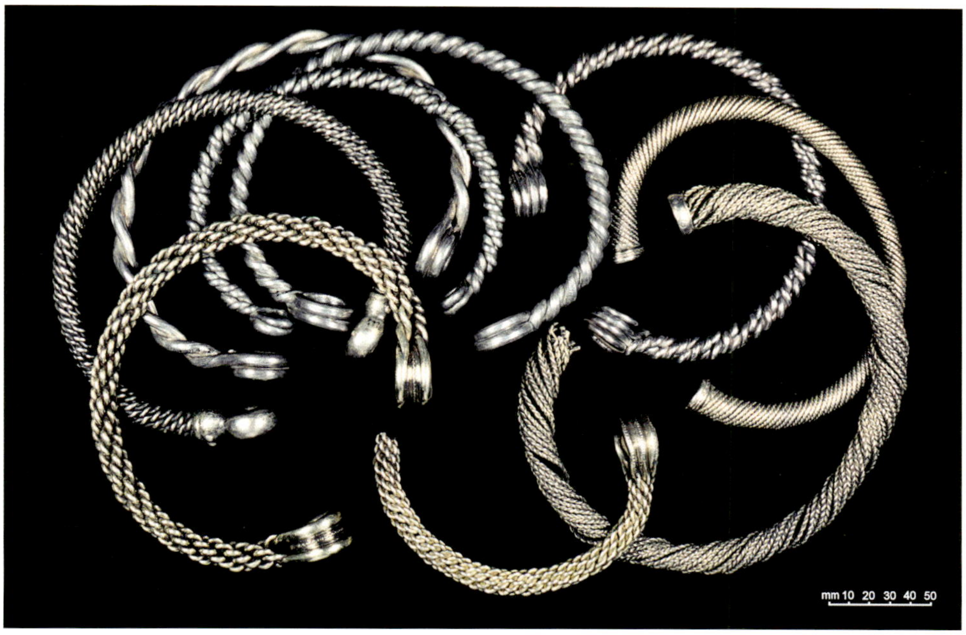

Figure 17.52 Group of thick and thin wire multi-strand torcs with ring, loop and buffer terminals (scale 50mm)

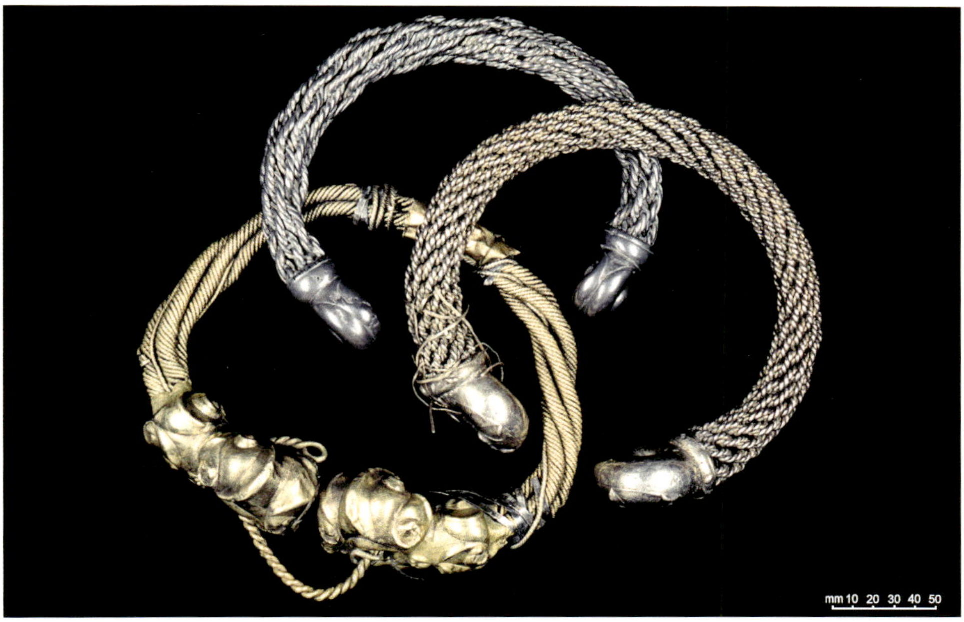

Figure 17.53 Three of the larger, heavier, more intricate multi-strand torcs, with torus terminals (scale 50mm)

providing the lowest possible melting temperatures and must have been easier to manipulate and work than many other combinations. However, there does seem to be a distinct preference at Snettisham for a range of colours on the right-hand side of the colour diagram shown in **Figure 17.47**, from whitish alloys to pale greenish gold and bright yellow gold. These colours may well have been conceptually related and, perhaps, preferred over the reddish colour of more copper-rich alloys. The most clearly intentional surface treatment, gilding, appears to have been applied most often to bronze objects, which would otherwise have tended towards this redder colour (Radivojevic *et al.* 2018).

17.6 Aspects of multi-strand torc manufacture and design

The majority of torcs from Snettisham are multi-strand types with neck-rings (and sometimes terminals) formed from wires of a variety of types and thicknesses, as discussed above. The colours of the torcs range from golden, through paler golds, to silver. These reflect the surface-enrichment techniques already discussed. A full typology of neck-rings and terminal types is given in Chapter 13, and the sheer variety can be appreciated through the range of torcs seen in **Figures 17.52–3**. Wires were combined in a variety of ways to make torc neck-rings, being either coiled around a core or plied directly together. The simplest wire neck-rings consist of just two wires plied together, while some, such as torc F.119–20, discussed in detail on p. 443, have neck-rings made from multiple stages of wire plying and coiling. The one common feature to all of these designs is that generally only one type and size of wire is used on each torc.

The range of terminal types is very wide (see **Fig. 13.3**). Some are formed from the thin or thick neck-ring wires/rods, ranging from simple loop terminals to more complicated 'cage' terminals (e.g. F.95, F.98, L.15). In some cases, loop terminals were thickened into closed-ring terminals by the overlapping and hammering of the wires or the addition of further material. Other types of terminals

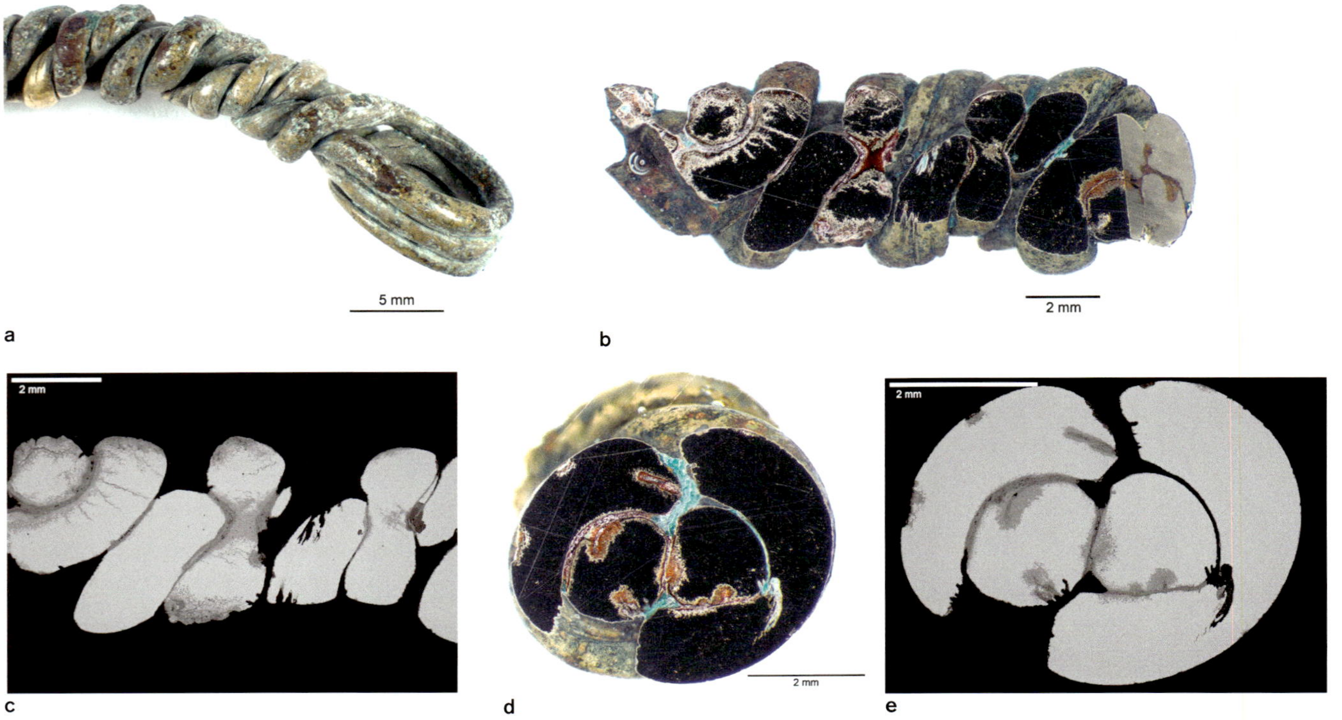

Figure 17.54a–e a) Bronze wire torc/bracelet F.361; photomicrographs (dark field illumination) of polished b) longitudinal and d) transverse cross-sections of tightly twisted ropes, each consisting of a pair of wires plied together S-twist. Note the green-blue corrosion products and red cuprite; c) and e) SEM BSE images of the same longitudinal and transverse cross-sections, showing the deep corrosion at grain boundaries and along folded grooves. Note the now corroded folded grooves leading from the surface into the wire, which result from the folding over of the corners of the original square-section rod used to make the wire during hammering

(buffer, torus or, in one case, reel form) were either cast or soldered onto the ends of the neck-ring wires. Soldered-on terminals could be formed from sheet or a combination of cast and sheet components, as found on the Great Torc. Presumably, these various types of terminals were being manufactured in parallel, if a relatively close dating of the hoard contents is suspected (see Chs 22 and 23).

Many cast and sheet terminals display a wide range of decoration from very simple to highly intricate and three-dimensional relief, including enhancements by engraving, punching and repoussé combined with chasing (see Ch. 21 for a full discussion of the decoration on the torcs). As explained above (see p. 425), repoussé/chasing and punching involve deforming the metal to create the motifs without removing any of the material being worked; in contrast, engraving requires cutting through the metal by hammering a sharp tool, such as a chisel, into the surface, to create decorative designs.

The range of torc terminal types seen at Snettisham surpasses those from any other single site in the UK, though a few precious metal torc terminal types known from other sites and thought to be contemporary do not appear in the Snettisham hoard (see Gazetteer in Ch. 22). These include the unusual wire torc from the Stirling Hoard, the sheet torc terminal from Clevedon, Somerset, the 'cushion'-terminal torc from Needwood Forest, Staffordshire and the torcs from the Ipswich Hoard in Suffolk. Five of the latter have neck-rings made from thick rods with ring terminals onto which (in four cases) thick additional relief decoration was cast, and in some cases further delineated (e.g. BM reg. no. 1969,0103.5 (Brailsford and Stapley 1972)), while one has a more complicated multi-strand neck-ring with unusual torus terminals (1971,0203.1).

This section on the construction of multi-strand torcs is divided into four parts. The first (p. 454) discusses neck-ring construction, while the latter three cover terminal manufacture. Loop and ring terminals made from the neck-ring wires are addressed on p. 457, cast-on terminals on p. 458 and other forms of terminal manufacture (including sheet and composite terminals) on p. 464. The discussion is primarily restricted to torcs from Snettisham, but in some instances similar torcs from other sites are mentioned for comparison, including the finds from Sedgeford (Norfolk), Newark (Nottinghamshire) and Netherurd (Peeblesshire).

Neck-ring construction

The typology developed for the study of the Snettisham torcs (Ch. 13) distinguishes between plied and coiled elements in multi-strand neck-rings. 'Plied' applies to pairs or groups of wires twisted directly and tightly together (e.g. see **Fig. 13.8**), while 'coiled' is used in cases where the wires (usually four or more) are wrapped or twisted around some supporting medium, which was subsequently removed, so that the wires form a hollow tube (see **Fig. 13.9**). The simplest multi-strand torc neck-rings (Stage II examples) consist of just two wires plied directly together (see **Fig. 13.11a**) or a single coil (see **Fig. 13.11b**). In some cases, two or more such elements are coiled or plied together (see **Fig. 13.11c–e**) (Stage III constructions) and in a rare handful of cases there is a fourth stage of plying or coiling, giving the most complicated (Stage IV) neck-rings, as seen in torcs F.119–20, H.7, L.1 and L.21 (see **Fig. 13.11f**).

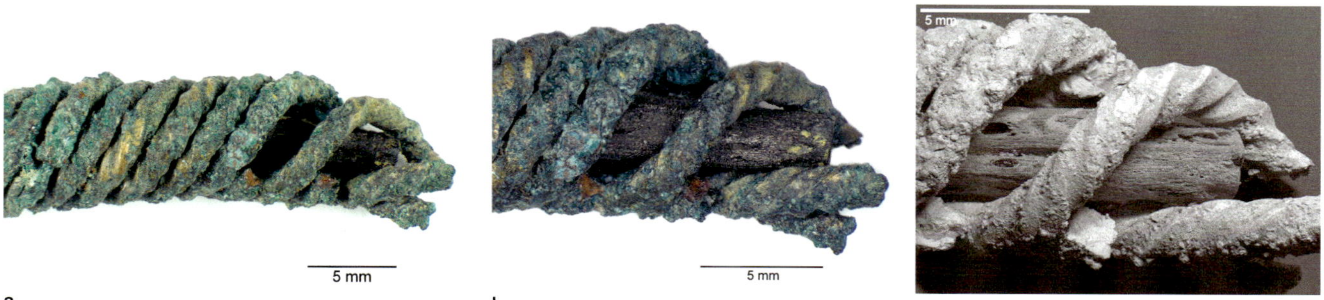

a b c

Figure 17.55a–c a) Corroded bronze torc fragment F.167; b) Photomicrograph and c) SEM BSE image of the corroded copper alloy wires and of the charred twig visible in the hollow centre of the torc

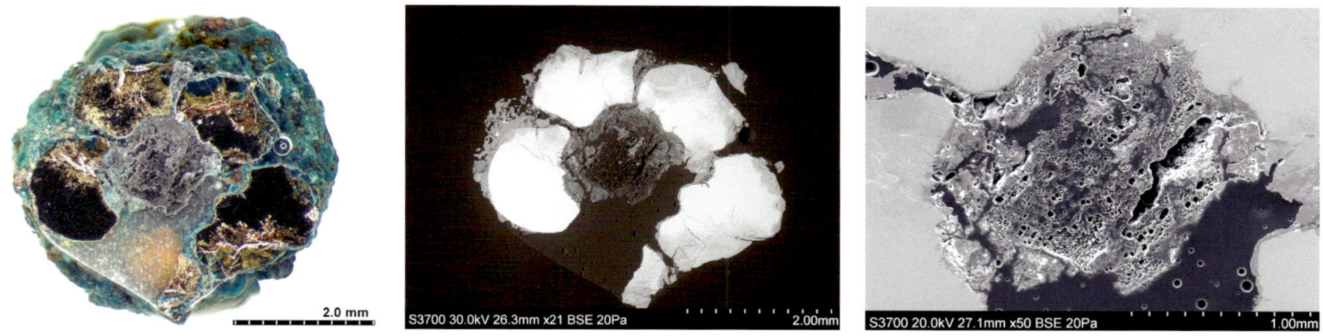

a b c

Figure 17.56a–c a) Photomicrograph and b, c) SEM BSE images of the polished cross-section of heavily corroded bronze torc/bracelet with five wires (F.250) surrounding a charred wooden support twig. Note how deeply the corrosion has penetrated the grain boundaries in the metal and deposited thick green corrosion on the outside of the wires; c) Note the cellular structure of the charred wooden core

Complex multi-stage plied neck-rings often combine different twist directions (S- and Z-twist – see Ch. 13 and especially **Fig. 13.10**), giving the appearance of a braid (see **Fig. 13.11c(ii)**), while in other cases a single twist direction (usually 'S') predominates (see **Fig. 13.11c(i)**). The latter case tends to result in a rather stiff neck-ring which appears tightly over-twisted, with a rather knobbly or knotted appearance (**Fig. 17.54**). This contrasts with the majority of symmetrically and uniformly twisted torcs.

Whilst plied neck-rings, with the wires twisted directly together, are relatively straightforward to manufacture, coiled neck-rings would have been more difficult to produce. As with plied neck-rings, some consist of a single Stage II coiled element (see **Fig. 13.9b**), whilst others combine Stage II plied or coiled elements to make a Stage III or IV neck-ring (see **Fig. 13.11d–f**).

Charred wooden cores in copper alloy torcs

The manufacture of coiled neck-rings raises the question of how to produce the perfect hollow form without it collapsing in on itself during twisting. The most likely solution would be to have a flexible or bendable core material present during bending (Cartwright *et al.* 2012; Ch. 19). Some of the small copper alloy torc fragments give a clue to the process. Caroline Cartwright (see Ch. 19) has studied and identified charred twigs found in the hollow centres of a number of fragmentary copper alloy (**Figs 17.55–6**).

The trapped charred twigs/stems must have been part of the manufacture of these small diameter torcs. The copper alloy wires appear to have been coiled tightly around a flexible twig to produce a uniform, hollow tubular torc shape. The twig cores prevented these coiled 'ropes' from collapsing onto themselves during the high mechanical torque while twisting wires and provided support during curvature to the final shape of the torc or bracelet. In this manner, it was possible to make elegant, uniformly spiralled wire torcs. The charring could have occurred during annealing, or potentially the casting-on of terminals, in cases where this technique was used. The charred material would then have been sealed in by the tightly coiled neck-rings and the terminals; the wooden cores only reveal themselves once a torc is broken.

In the case of the larger torcs and gold/silver alloy examples (e.g. **Figs 17.52–3**), there is no surviving evidence of support material for coiled wire ropes. Thicker flexible twigs may also have been used in these cases, but it could equally have been an annealed metal rod, either pre-bent to shape or possibly straight for the process of the coiling and then bent once the wires were coiled around it. Such a metal rod could be removed after bending and before affixing the terminals by casting or soldering. The advantage of a metal rod would be that during bending and manipulation of the large neck-ring, it would maintain its curved shape as an aid during complex construction, whereas a thick flexible twig, or similar, would spring open and be difficult to control.

Neck-ring construction case study: The 'Great Torc'

The manufacture of Stage III coiled torcs is typified by one of the most famous artefacts from the assemblage, the so-called Snettisham Great Torc (E.1a) (**Fig. 17.57**). This object is a supreme example of the tradition of goldsmithing of heavy gold torcs with multi-strand wire neck-rings and highly decorative terminals.

The design of the Great Torc neck-ring is based on eight 'ropes' coiled together in an S-twist direction, each rope being itself formed of eight circular-section wires of uniform

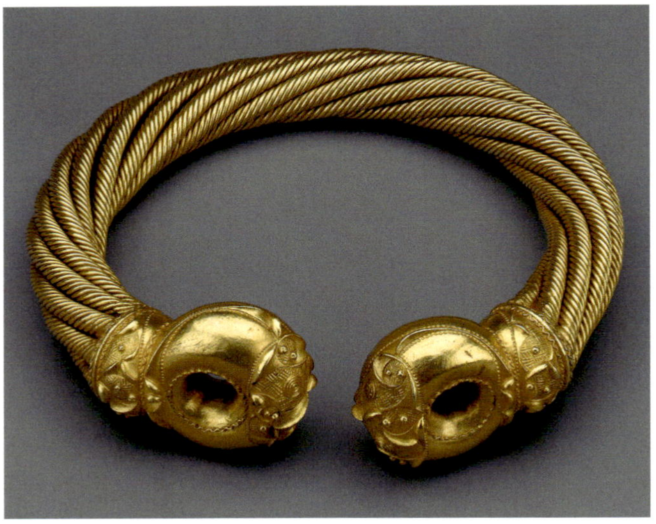

Figure 17.57 Snettisham Great Torc (E.1a), about 200mm in diameter

thickness, coiled tightly together S-twist. There is some evidence of linear faceting still remaining on the original wires, typical of the wire manufacture seen at Snettisham (see p. 429). A reconstruction of the torc made by the Department of Conservation at the British Museum (*c.* 1970) recreated many of the practical procedures necessary to create the heavy but flexible coiled wire neck-ring (**Fig. 17.58**).

The reconstruction was based on accurate measurements of the dimensions of the wires of the neck-ring. The methods used for making and subsequently coiling together the eight 'ropes' of the neck-ring are based on the practicalities of manual working of the heavy and springy metal construction (using brass wire in this case) and are thought to be broadly applicable to the original (**Fig. 17.58**). The replica terminals, being copper electroform copies made from silicone rubber moulds taken from the Great Torc, were made using a completely different process from the manufacturing method of the original artefact.

The first requirement was the production of wire of uniform thickness or diameter, which is illustrated by the experimental wire-making by John Fenn in this chapter (see p. 433). It proved challenging to produce large quantities of standardised wire, and this would have been an operation which required a great deal of skill. Fenn estimated that it would have taken at least 50 hours to produce the wire necessary for the Great Torc neck-ring.

Eight wires of the same length are brought together to make each of the coiled 'ropes' of the neck-ring. Coiling the wires requires the support of a solid central core, so that the very tight twisting does not collapse the wires together. For the reconstruction, a thick metal rod was used (**Fig. 17.58**). For the original, the core could have been a similar bronze or copper rod, but it could have also been a flexible twig, such as those preserved in some smaller bronze torcs (see below and Ch. 19). In the production of the replica, the coiled wires of each 'rope' were soldered together at one end so they could not untwist. Then, with the straight central rods still in place in each 'rope', the replica neck-ring was assembled around a straight, thick, round metal rod of a diameter such that it allowed the eight 'ropes' to just touch

Figure 17.58 Reconstruction components of the Great Torc by the British Museum Department of Conservation. Note the different stages in the wire construction: (from top to bottom) the eight individual wires, the supporting central wire/rod protruding from the eight wires before twisting into a 'rope', and the twisted wires with soldered ends to prevent untwisting; (left) the thick (now curved) metal core to support the 'ropes' during coiling and bending the neck-ring to shape and a cross-section of the neck-ring with the core support removed; (right) the clamped ends of the coiled neck-ring, needed to keep the twisted wires permanently in the curved position, showing the uneven extended 'ropes' from the bending operation; and some of the straight-cut ends of the neck-ring 'ropes' (as seen in the Great Torc X-radiographs, Figs 17.82–4). In this reconstruction, the completed terminal on the right-hand side is an electroform copy. There is also a complete replica of the Great Torc (not pictured)

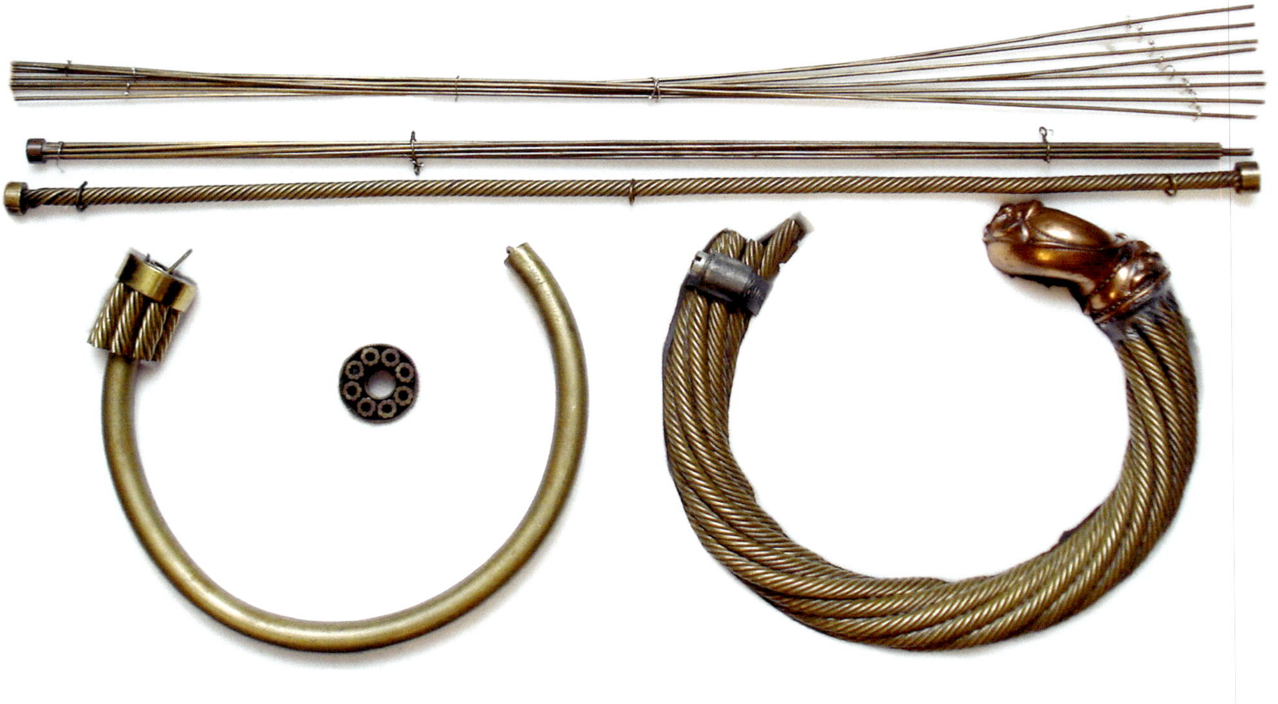

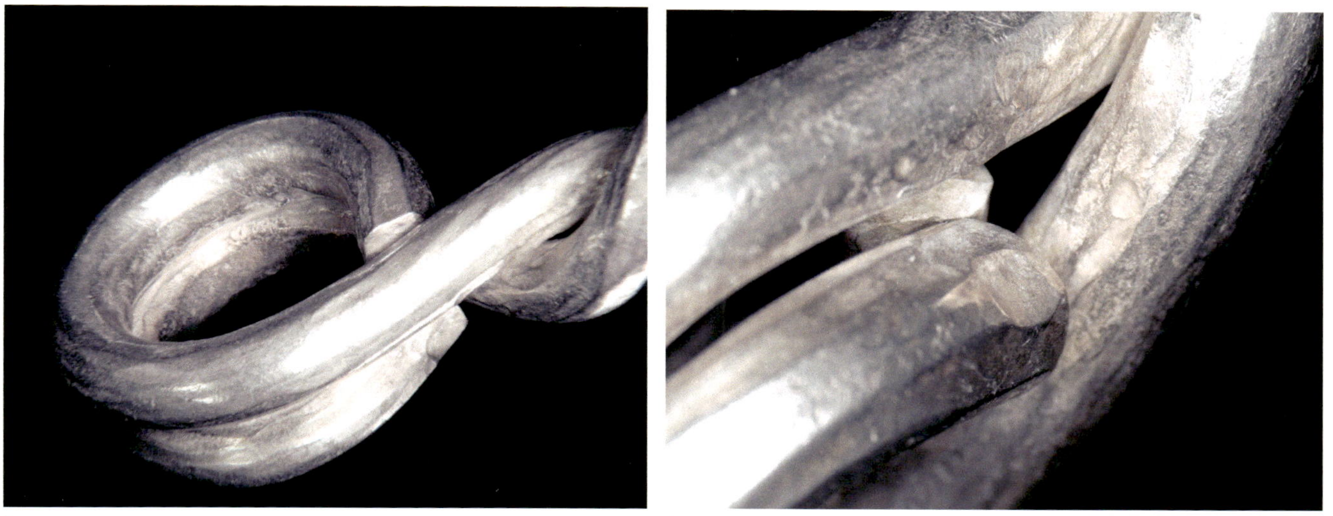

a b

Figure 17.59a–b Open-loop thick wire torc terminals (L.7)

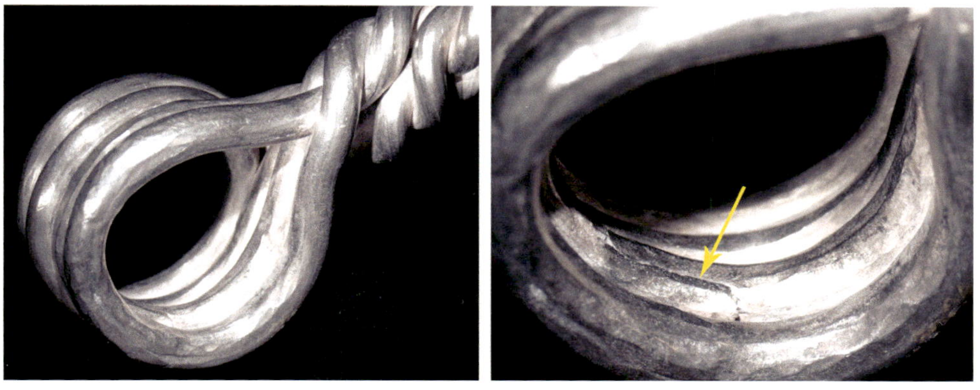

a b

Figure 17.60a–b Overlap joins seen in the interior of terminal loops on torc L.4 (arrow)

side-by-side around it. Measurements show that this core rod for the neck-ring had to be twice the diameter of an individual 'rope' to produce a tightly coiled neck-ring. This is indeed the case for the Great Torc.

The next step was to coil the ropes themselves around one another. At one end, the eight coiled 'ropes' were fixed with a collar and clamped or fixed (soldered) to allow twisting from the other end. The 'ropes' were then coiled together as tightly as possible around the core rod in a linear manner with some considerable torque force. As mentioned, the eight smaller core rods inside the individual 'ropes' prevented them from collapsing.

At this point, the replica neck-ring was still straight. The next stage, curving it into the final torc shape, is tricky, because the 'ropes' have to slip over one another while bending to take the final form. Simply trying to bend a straight multi-strand coiled neck-ring with two fixed ends could not work, because the outer curvature is considerably longer than the inner curvature and neither the outer could stretch nor the inner compress sufficiently to make or retain the curve. Once curvature was achieved, the free end had to be clamped or soldered like the first to hold the form without untwisting. This construction will now permanently maintain the correct curvature, as it cannot revert to a straight configuration. Indeed, it has an inherent springiness that allows the finished torc to flex and return to shape for putting on and taking off around the neck of the wearer.

At this point, the wire cores of the eight 'ropes' and the main core rod could be removed, leaving the springy final curved form of the torc body. The final stage would be to cut the wire ends square to the required length in preparation for the addition of the terminals (see p. 467). The straight-cut ends of the eight multiple-wire 'ropes' can clearly be seen in the X-radiographs of the Great Torc (see below, **Figs 17.82–4**).

Multi-strand torc terminal construction: Loop and ring terminals

The terminals of simple Stage II and III plied torcs are of two main types: loops (which may be open, with an end to the wire, or continuous loops made from a piece of wire that does not end within the area of the terminal) and thickened, closed rings (**Figs 17.59, 17.61** respectively). Most loop terminal torcs from Snettisham have between one and three loops on each side, generally formed from the ends of the neck-ring wires, as described in Chapter 13. A single example (L.4) (**Fig. 17.60**) has quadruple-loop terminals, as does a torc from Ulceby, Lincolnshire (see Gazetteer in Ch. 22). Torc L.7 shows the simplest kind of loop terminal construction (**Fig. 17.59**). Each terminal has two adjacent loops, one from each neck-ring wire, bent round a mandrel in opposite directions with gentle hammering of the square-cut ends to close each loop against itself to be a close fit.

It is likely, as seen in the experimental wire manufacture section (p. 433), that in simple cases such as L.7 the process of making the torc involved first making and cutting the wires to length, then pre-forming the wire loops and using these with the mandrel or a rod passed through the loops to

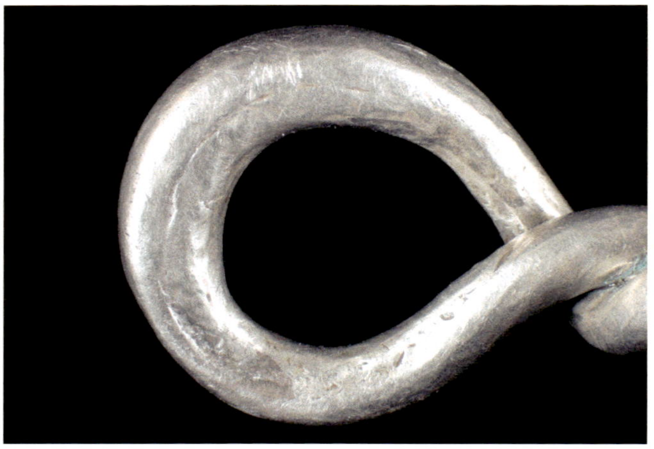

a

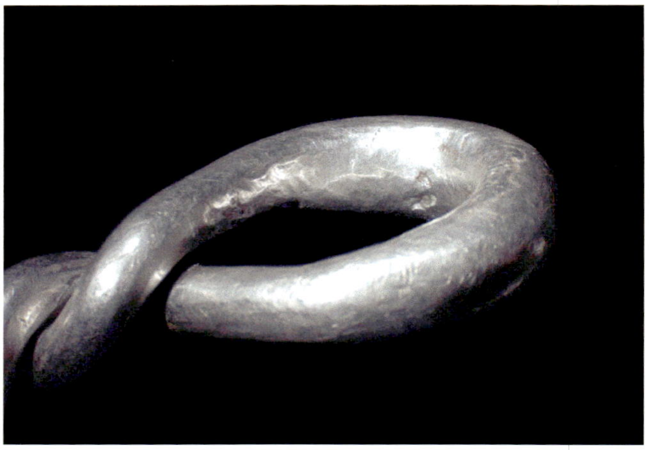

b

Figure 17.61a–b Silver alloy torc S.16, face and side views showing detail of round-section and closed-ring terminals with overlap joins

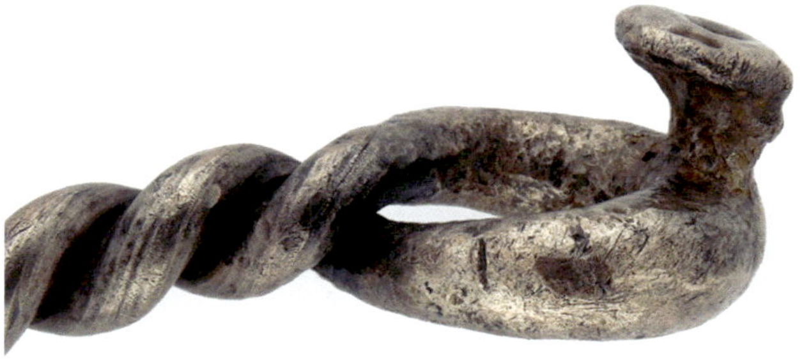

Figure 17.62 Terminal of torc S.17, which retains its sprues from the casting-on of additional metal to create the thickened ring terminals

provide leverage to twist the neck-ring wires tightly together. The amount of torque power needed to twist two thick, straight torc wires together is considerable and annealing the wires before twisting would have been likely. The loops would probably have needed reshaping somewhat after twisting. The completed straight twisted assembly would then have been bent into the familiar curved ring-shape of the finished torc.

Sometimes, rather than the neck-ring being formed of separate wires, as seen on L.7 (where each double terminal has two open loops), it appears to be made from a single wire folded over in the middle with a closed loop terminal at one end and an open loop at the other (e.g. bracelet F.121) or even gives the appearance of being formed from a single, continuous length (e.g. torcs H.5 and H.6). In the latter cases, the wire ends around the terminals have likely been soldered or hammered closed. Hammered overlap joins can be seen inside the loop terminals of L.4 (**Fig. 17.60**).

In some cases, this closing of the terminal loops has been taken further, with significant thickening of the loops to create tear-shaped closed rings which appear more bulbous and thicker than the main neck-ring wires. The closing mechanism for completing the ring terminals of these torcs appears to be shaping and overlapping the wire ends and soldering them along the long seam (**Fig. 17.61**). Another possibility could be casting-on more metal, in a similar way to the Ipswich torcs (e.g. BM 1969,0103.5 (Brailsford and Stapley 1972)), which have more refined ring terminals with cast-on decoration. On torc S.17 (**Fig. 17.62**), the two terminals retain their sprues from the casting-on of additional material to create the thickened rings.

In a small number of cases, multiple ring terminals are formed from the addition of sheet or cast elements to the original neck-ring loops. This is seen, for example, on torcs L.16 and L.18, and is described in detail in their catalogue entries in Chapter 14. It is notable in all cases where additional metal was added to complete the terminals, that care must have been taken to match the surface-enriched colour of the torc wires to the cast or sheet elements. This would have required a good deal of skill and careful consideration.

Multi-strand torc terminal construction: Cast buffer, torus and reel terminals

Cast and cast-on terminals are a major feature of many multi-strand torcs, from very small ones to the largest. We will look at the various torcs and see the similarities and differences in the cast terminals, but overall, the process of lost-wax casting is the same. The desired form of a terminal was sculpted in wax (probably a beeswax mixture) on a clay core, and an outer layer of clay applied to form the external part of the mould. Two main forms of terminals were cast: buffer terminals, which might be simple caps to the ends of a coiled wire neck-ring, and more complicated hollow torus terminals. There is also one example of an open reel terminal (F.119–20) (see Ch. 13, **Fig. 13.1**, for full terminal typology).

There are two methods used for cast terminals: some were cast as separate components for later attachment to neck-rings (by soldering or mechanical attachment, see Sedgeford Torc case study, below), and others were cast directly onto the neck-ring wires (see case study below on F.120, L.21 and S.19).

Hollow torus terminals cast directly onto the ends of the neck-ring wires each needed a 'doughnut-shaped' clay core, which was also used to plug the open ends of the wire torc body for the cast-on terminals to prevent molten gold flowing too far. The clay core would have been thoroughly dried out, before the wax model of the terminal was crafted over the clay. The core would otherwise have failed dramatically during heating to burn out the wax, as the retained water would create high steam pressure in the clay. A wax reservoir sprue and wax runners and risers, to provide channels for molten gold to run in and air to escape, would also have been attached to the wax model. The final procedure for finishing

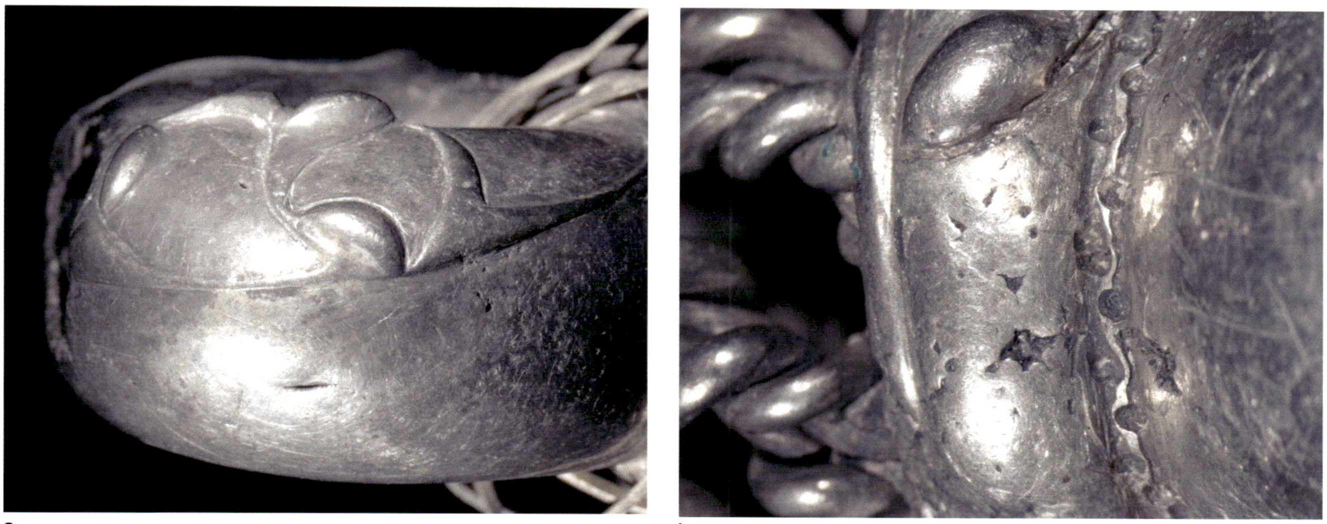

a b

Figure 17.63a–b a) Cast terminal of torc L.21 showing prominent decorative motifs with chased outlines, and b) dot-punched decoration along the thin wavy line where the torc terminal meets the collar. Note the small casting defects in the collar

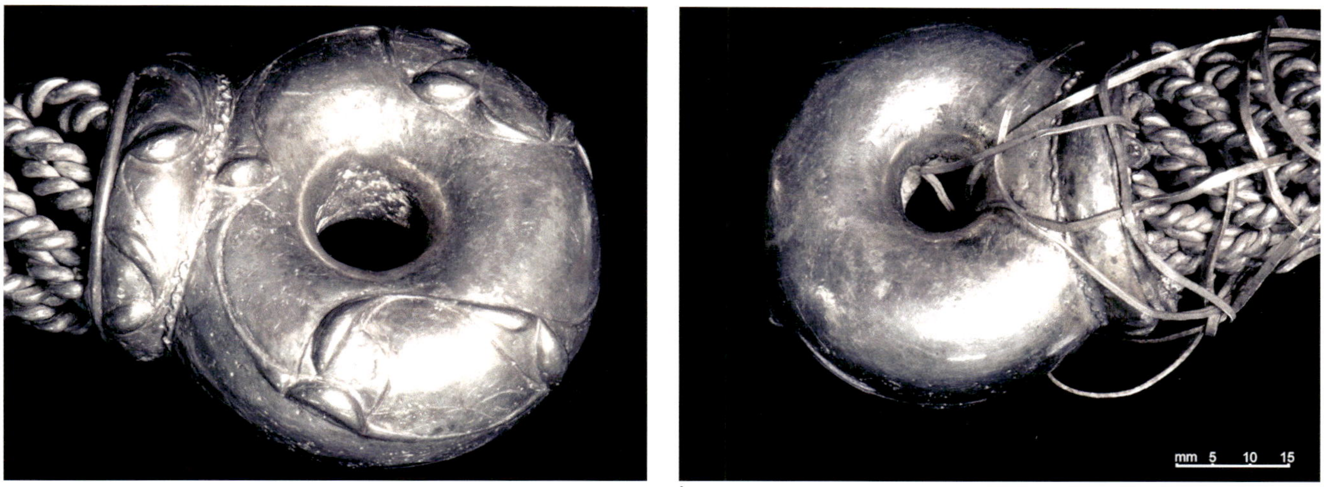

a b

Figure 17.64a–b a) Front and b) back of terminals of torc L.21, showing the oblique angle of entry of the wires into the cast-on terminals, and decoration on the front side (scale 15mm)

the mould would be to carefully cover the wax model with clay to mould exactly over the wax, probably using clay slip as the first layers to ensure accurate rendition of the wax design (Craddock 2014). The completed terminal mould would be thoroughly dried and then gently heated to several hundred degrees centigrade in a hearth to melt and burn out all the wax and harden the clay moulds. The mould needed to be maintained at high temperature prior to casting to facilitate good metal flow to all parts of the mould, preventing premature solidification, miscasts and cold-shuts from forming, such as those seen on torc L.21 (see below, **Fig. 17.68**). Gold alloys would be heated to around 1050–1100 °C before being poured into the mould. Given that there is generally a close visual match between the colour of the cast terminals and the colour of the neck-ring, care must have been taken to select an appropriate alloy that, when cast, would match the surface-enriched neck-ring wires. When cool, the clay mould was broken open, the cast terminal cleaned up and the clay core could potentially be removed through the neck of the terminal.

The practicalities of the casting process were probably similar to those of experimental procedures used for casting small bronze objects (Tulp *et al.* 2001; Meeks *et al.* 2001). In these experiments the clay lost-wax moulds were first placed carefully onto the outer edge of a pre-heating hearth to allow them to dry slowly for two hours and melt out the wax model leaving the hollow mould ready for the molten metal. The moulds were then moved further into the hotter regions of the hearth for several hours to fully dry them by driving out chemically bound water at about 400–500°C, and to bake and harden them, but not fire the clay (i.e. kept below around 800°C as the moulds have to be broken open to release the torc after casting). The molten metal would then have been poured into the terminal moulds. These preparatory conditions ensured that the clay mould performed correctly during the high-temperature thermal shock conditions of pouring in the molten metal at about 1050 °C. The temperature of these pre-heating and casting processes would easily char the support twigs that are found within some of the smaller multi-strand wire torcs (Ch. 19).

The majority of the decorative patterning on many terminals is cast, and so must have been modelled into the wax (e.g. **Fig. 17.63a**), but a fair amount of finishing work

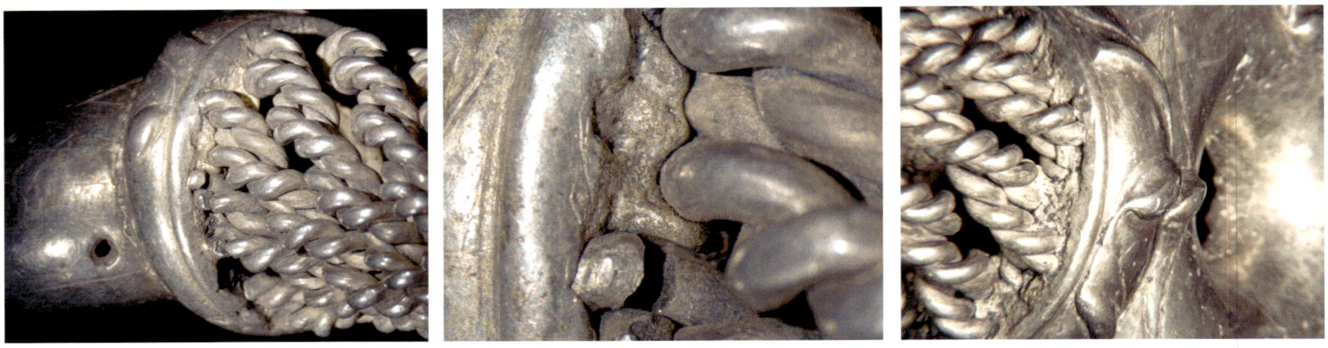

a b c

Figure 17.65a–c Torc L.21 with the wires mechanically trapped by the solidified casting metal

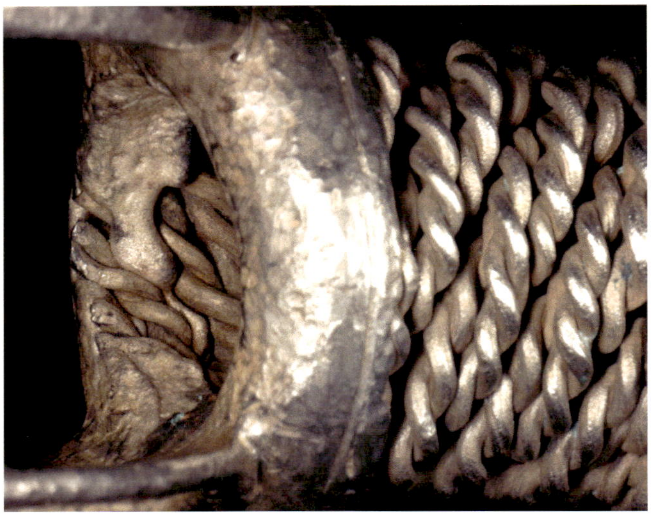

Figure 17.66 Torc F.120 (see also Fig. 17.40), cast reel terminal with open neck; note the cast terminal dribbles running over the wires (centre left)

was applied by hand to the cast terminals to add further details and sharpen up the designs by chasing lines around the larger prominent decorative motifs. A good example of punched dots and chased wavy decoration can be seen around the neck of the cast-on terminals of torc L.21 (**Fig. 17.63b**).

Most cast terminals appear to have been cast directly onto the neck-ring wires. It is clear from the oblique angle at which the wires enter the terminals that the neck-rings were twisted into their final form *before* the terminals were cast on, otherwise the wires would enter straight into the terminals (**Fig. 17.64**). Casting onto the pre-twisted neck-ring has the major advantage of permanently locking the twist into place, as there is no way that the neck-ring wires can untwist or uncoil themselves. Similarly, curving the neck-ring before casting-on the terminals allows all the wires to move over each other during shaping. Because the inner side of the curved neck-ring is shorter than the outer, casting-on the terminals fixes the curvature into place, preventing the torc from springing open.

Until fairly recently, it was assumed that casting-on was the method used for almost all torus, buffer and reel terminal torcs, with a handful of exceptions such as the metal terminals of the Grotesque Torc and F.72. Subsequent work has revealed alternative manufacturing routes in several cases (see: the sections on the Great Torc and Sedgeford Torc below, and Machling and Williamson, 2016, 2018).

Cast-on terminal case studies: Torcs F.120 (reel terminal), L.21 (torus terminal), S.19 and torc/bracelet F.179 (buffer terminals)

The evidence of casting-on is clearly seen on torc L.21, with the wires mechanically trapped by the solidified casting (**Fig. 17.65**). The terminals are hollow, so there must have been a clay core to the mould, and this would have also plugged the hollow end to the neck-ring, where the wires enter the terminals, to stop the molten metal running into the neck-ring. The wax model would have encapsulated the outer ends of the wires, being then encased with an outer layer of clay. Similar manufacturing evidence is seen on F.120 (**Fig. 17.66**) and S.19 (**Fig. 17.67**), where molten metal has flowed over and around wires. In the latter case, however, the cooler wires chilled this molten metal before it had a chance to fuse (self-solder) to them, but formed very secure and tight mechanical joints.

Figure 17.67a–c Cast buffer terminal on torc S.19: a) engraved pattern outlines with punched basket-weave infill (scale 5mm); b) and c) reverse side of the cast-on terminal: the terminal metal encases the neck-ring wires but is not fused to them

a b c

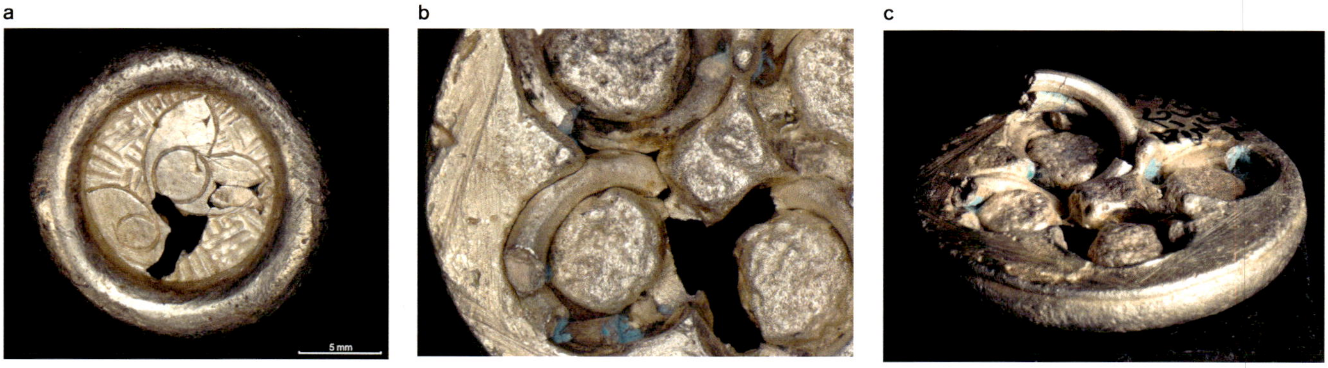

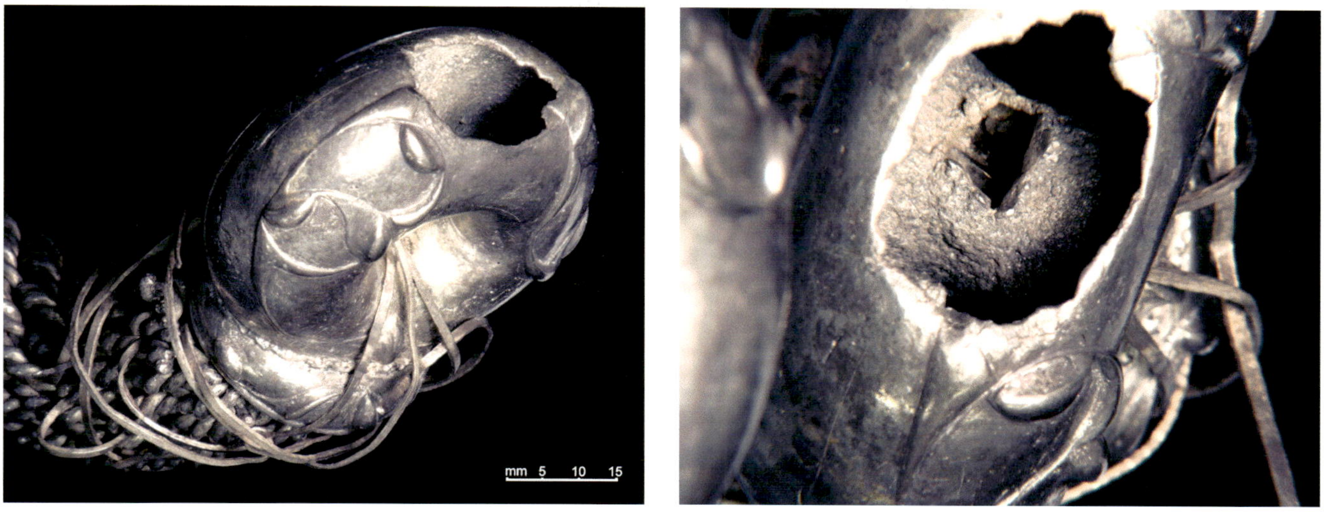

a b

Figure 17.68a–b Torc L.21 with a massive cold-shut casting defect in one terminal and no apparent attempt to repair it in antiquity

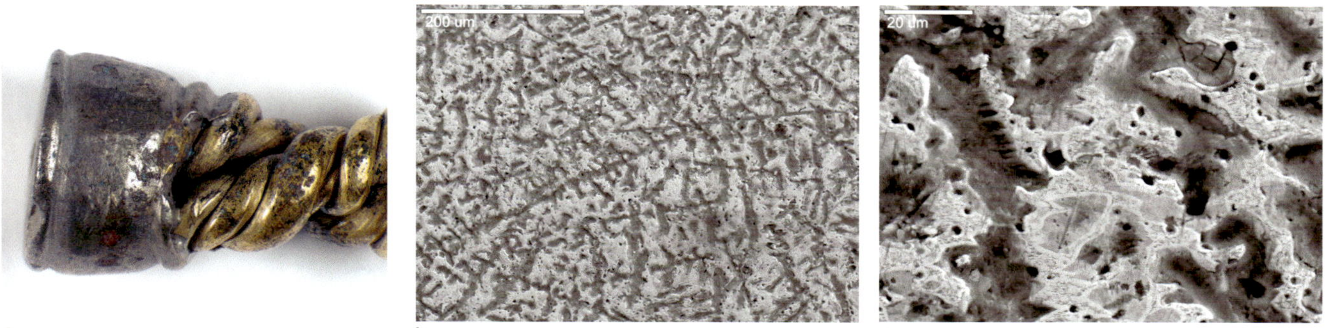

a b c

Figure 17.69a–c Bronze torc/bracelet F.179: a) silver-coloured terminal on a small bronze torc fragment; b) and c) SEM BSE images of the dendritic surface microstructure typical of the high-tin are α+δ eutectoid intermetallic compound (Meeks 1993) (image widths: b) *c*. 500 microns and c) *c*. 80 microns)

For practical reasons, one could suggest casting-on hollow terminals with the terminals pointing downwards to prevent inadvertent escape of molten metal along the wires, which could occur if the terminals were cast pointing upwards with the wires below. This is clearly demonstrated on one simple solid cast-on buffer terminal from torc S.19, where the ends of the wires are encapsulated by the cast metal (**Fig. 17.67**). The positioning of the terminals for casting may have depended on torc type; the simple ring terminals of multi-strand torc S.17 (**Fig. 17.62**) retain sprues, their position suggesting that the additional metal to thicken the terminal was cast on with the terminals lying on their sides.

Some terminals are imperfect and have various casting defects, such as the massive cold-shut defect in one terminal from torc L.21, which shows an area completely missing (**Fig. 17.68**). This casting defect is caused by either a trapped air pocket in the mould, around which the metal solidified, or by the metal having begun to solidify before fully filling the mould, due to chilling by a cold mould or low metal casting temperature (Hanson and Pell-Walpole 1951). The rounded edges of the hole are typical of the solidification front of the melt and not of subsequent physical damage. No attempt seems to have been made in antiquity to repair it. Looking right into the hollow terminal shows an oblong hole passing through the metal wall into the inner 'doughnut'. Its function is unclear, but is unlikely to be deliberately cut into the metal, so could be another cold-shut casting defect. The rough texture of the original mould surface is also seen inside the terminal (**Fig. 17.68b**).

Whilst most cast-on terminals used similar alloys to those seen in other torc components, one small bronze wire torc/bracelet fragment (F.179) has a silvery-coloured terminal which was made from an unusual alloy (**Fig. 17.69a**). SEM imaging and elemental analysis revealed that this terminal was made of high-tin bronze (*c*. 20 wt% Sn). The surface displays the characteristic cast dendritic eutectoid microstructure of the hard, high-tin delta compound (**Fig. 17.69b–c**). It has a polished colour that is very similar to

Figure 17.70 Sedgeford Torc terminals: detached terminal (left, BM 2005,1103.1) and terminal attached to the neck-ring wires (right, BM 1968,1004.1)

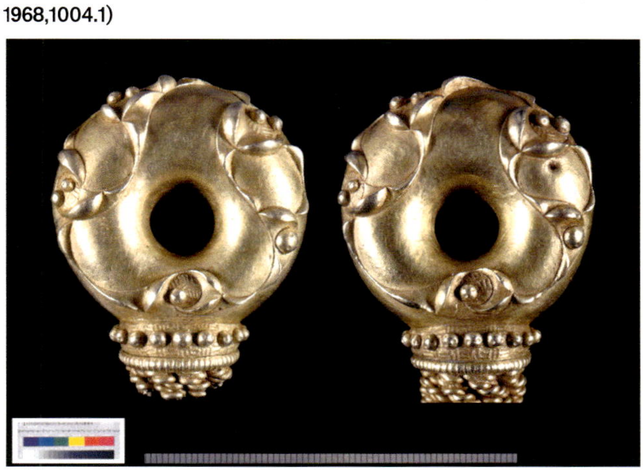

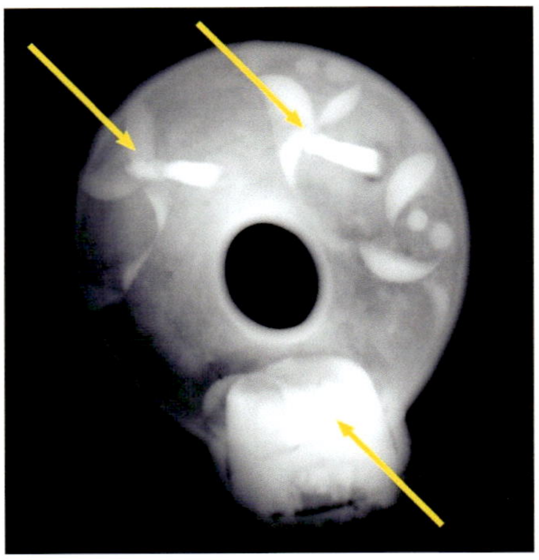

Figure 17.71 X-radiograph (DR) of the detached Sedgeford Torc terminal (see Appendix at the end of this chapter for terminology). The cylinder holding the broken-off neck-ring wires (Figure 17.70 left) can be seen at the base of the terminal. The yellow arrows point to the internal chaplets; the lower one is probably a rivet

silver. This peculiar artefact only adds to the interesting and varied mixture of materials seen across the assemblage, as silver-coloured high-tin bronze castings are a very special type of alloy and technology application not seen in the rest of the Snettisham hoards. Besides, high-tin bronze was generally deliberately used in the ancient world for specific and completely different types of artefact such as Roman and Chinese mirrors as well as some early medieval buckles and belt fittings (Meeks 1993).

Separately cast terminal case study: The Sedgeford Torc

It is instructive, when exploring the variety of terminal construction methods, to compare objects from Snettisham to similar artefacts from elsewhere in the UK. One gold/silver alloy torc with separately cast and mechanically attached terminals was found at the nearby site of Sedgeford, Norfolk (BM 1968,1004.1 and 2005,1103.1 **Fig. 17.70**; see Gazetteer in Ch. 22; Brailsford 1971; Jope 2000, 84, 254, pls 114–15; Hautenauve 2005, 238, no. 153). The main part of the torc, comprising a hollow torus terminal and most of the coiled neck-ring, was discovered in 1965. The missing broken-off terminal was subsequently found at the same location in 2004. The torc had apparently been struck during ploughing, which had severed one terminal and damaged the neck-ring wires (**Fig. 17.72a**). X-radiography of the torc was carried out at the British Museum (**Figs 17.71–3**), and the resulting images show that the torus terminals are fully cast.

The radiographs show the presence of chaplets used in the casting of these terminals. Chaplets are small metal supports that bridge the gap between the inner clay core and the clay mould surface. These would have provided structural stability for the clay core during the casting process, which would most likely be the lost-wax casting technique, widely used at the time and explained in detail above. A total of seven chaplets can be seen in the terminal still attached to the neck-ring, and three chaplets in the detached terminal (**Figs 17.71–3**). Photomicrographs of the detached terminal also show dendrites on the inner surface of the torus core (**Fig. 17.76a–c**), further confirming that these terminals were cast. Three of the features seen on the radiographs of the terminal still attached to the wires may be rivets, rather than chaplets, also visible externally on

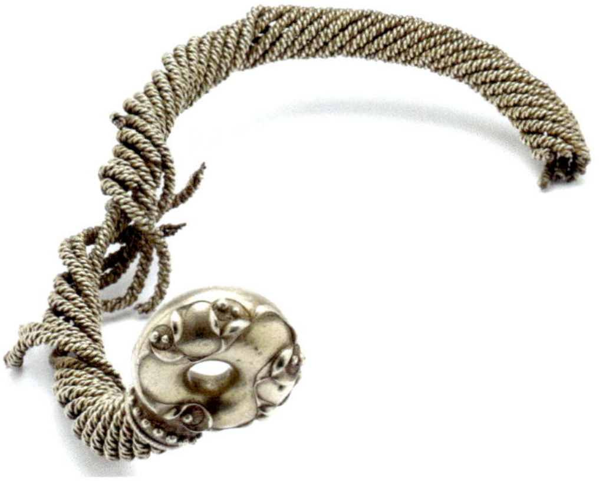

a

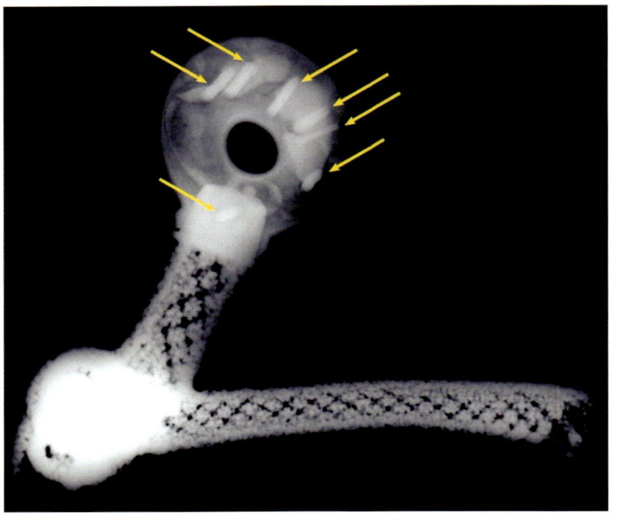

b

Figure 17.72a–b a) The larger fragment of the Sedgeford Torc, BM 1968,1004.1 with the attached neck-ring wires; (b) X-radiograph (DR) of the Sedgeford Torc terminal. The six yellow arrows within the torus of the terminal point to the chaplets inside the terminal, while the lower one at the collar points to a rivet

Figure 17.73 X-radiograph (DR) of the attached Sedgeford Torc terminal. The short internal cylindrical cap/tube holding the ends of the neck-ring wires is similar to that of the detached terminal and can be seen to be separate from the terminal neck in the close-up image

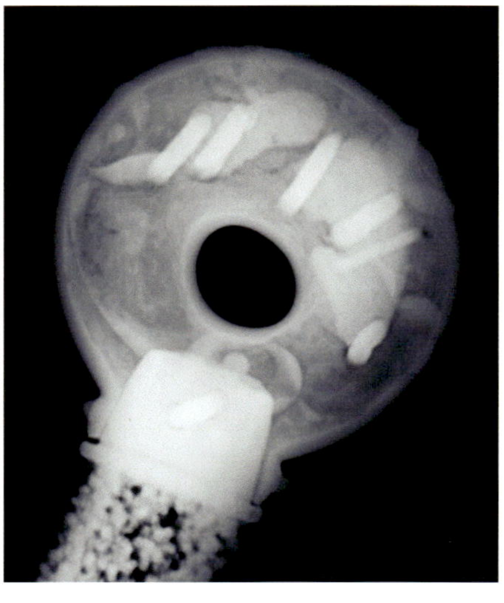

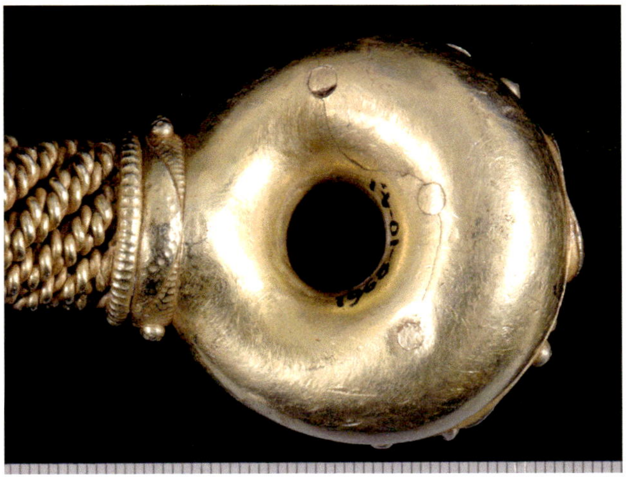

Figure 17.74 Rivets are seen along a crack line on the reverse side in the attached terminal of the Sedgeford Torc, and appear to have been repairs and concealment at the time of manufacture. Scale in mm

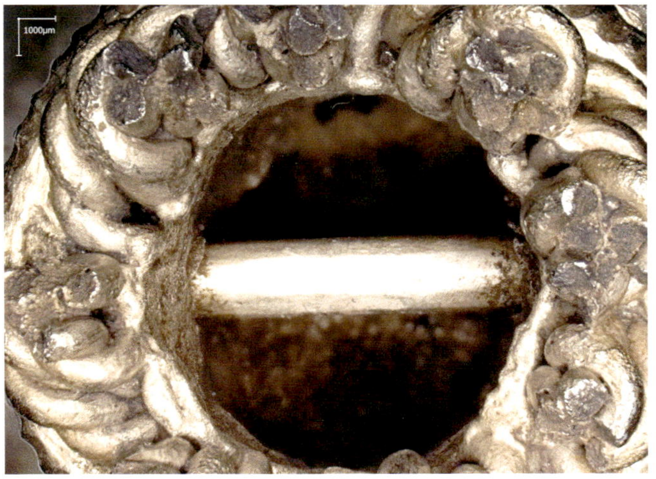

Figure 17.75 Detached Sedgeford Torc terminal: detail of the twisted and coiled wire ends fused to the tubular cap, and the thick rivet rod which secures this end tube or cap to the terminal (x20)

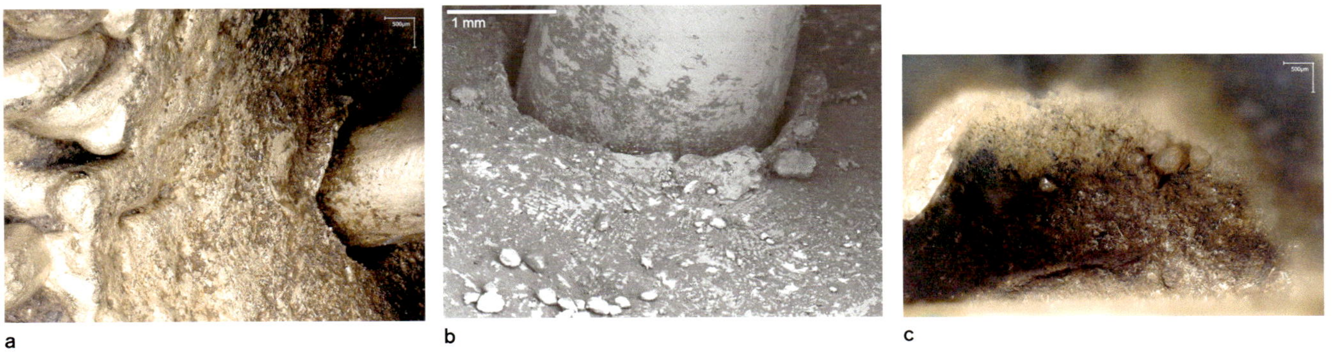

Figure 17.76a–c a) Photomicrographs of dendrites and characteristic surface textures from fusion on the inner surface of the end tube/cap, resulting from its soldering to the wires (left of image), within the detached Sedgeford Torc terminal (x50, width of image 7mm); b) SEM BSE detail of the dendrites within the dirty (darker grey) surface of the solder. Both a) and b) show the drilled hole for the rivet cuts through the dendrites; c) dendrites and characteristic surface textures from casting inside the detached terminal core beyond the rivet (bright horizontal bar at the bottom of the image) and end tube/cap (x50, width of image 7mm)

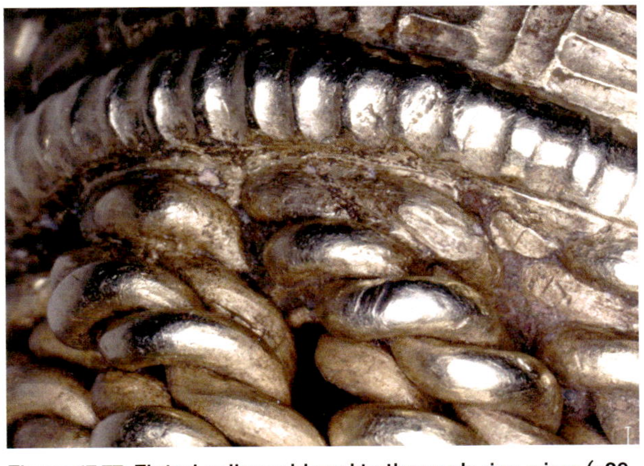

Figure 17.77 Fluted collar soldered to the neck-ring wires (x30, width of image 12mm) on the Sedgeford Torc. The fluting on the collar appears similar to that of the Netherurd terminal shown in Figure 17.81

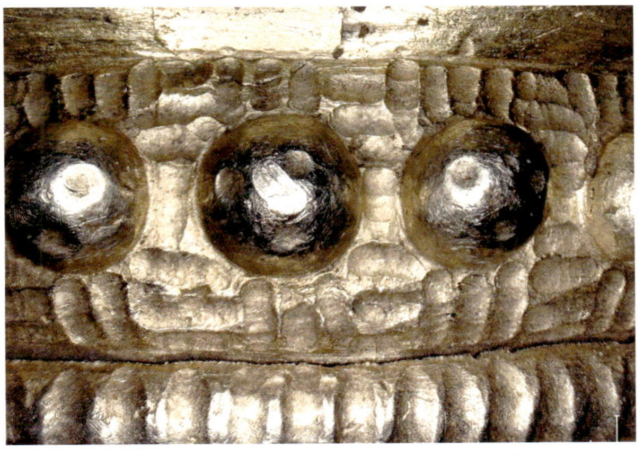

Figure 17.78 Detail of the decorated neck-flange of the detached terminal of the Sedgeford Torc, showing the flush rivet head outline (top centre of image) and fluted collar (bottom of image), the cast-in hemispherical beading and basket-weave punching. Note the gap running between the fluted collar and the neck-flange (x30, width of image 12mm)

either side of the terminal, with flat and round hammered heads. These three rivets run along a crack and suggest an ancient repair at the time of manufacture (**Fig. 17.74**).

The radiographs (**Figs 17.71–3**) also show that the ends of the neck-ring wires are fitted into a thick, short tube or cap, which encloses the multiple twisted wires for insertion into the hollow neck of the cast terminals. This cap has a fluted collar, seen externally, where it meets the neck-ring, giving the effect of beaded wire (**Fig. 17.75**) and is a separate component from the terminal torus. The detached terminal clearly displays solder dendrites on the inner surface of this

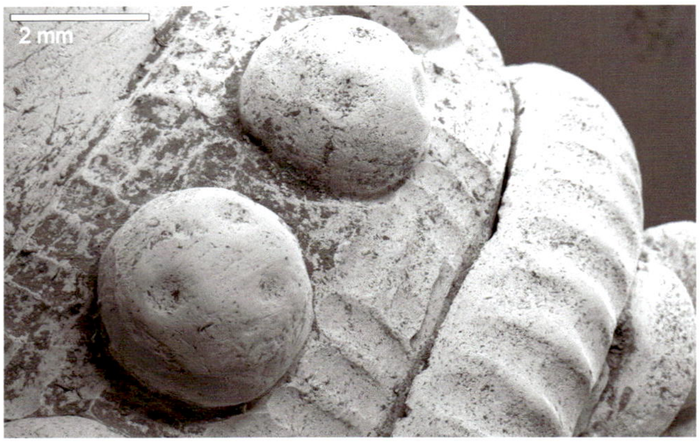

Figure 17.79 SEM BSE image of the Sedgeford Torc terminal still attached to its wires: detail of the gap between the fluted collar and the terminal, which extends completely around the neck (scale bar *c.* 2mm)

end tube/cap, where the neck-ring wires are firmly attached to it (**Figs 17.75–6**). The decorative fluted collar is also well soldered to the bottom of the end cap to disguise the join with the wires (**Fig. 17.77**). However, although the neck-ring wires are soldered to the cap, the cap itself is not soldered to the terminals, as shown by the gap between them in the X-radiographs (**Figs 17.71–3**). There is also a clear gap between the fluted collars and the terminals running all the way round, showing that the end tubes/caps are not directly soldered to the terminals (**Figs 17.78–9**). Instead, the attachment of the soldered neck-ring and tube assembly to the terminals was mechanical.

The completed neck-ring wires with soldered end tubes and decorative (fluted) collars were inserted into the cast terminals and each secured mechanically by a single thick rivet (*c.* 2.5mm diameter). This rivet passes fully through a

Figure 17.81 Torc terminal from Netherurd, Scotland. National Museums Scotland, X.FE 46. Image © National Museums Scotland

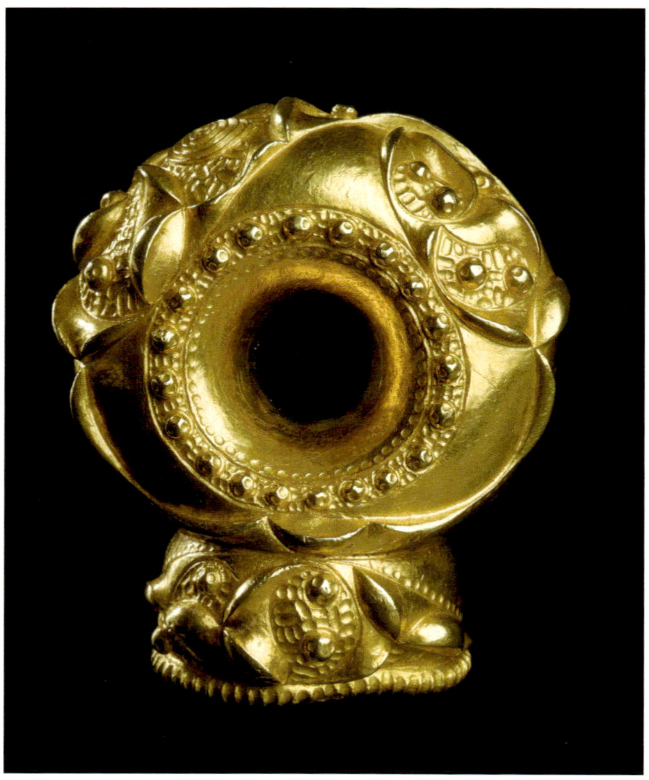

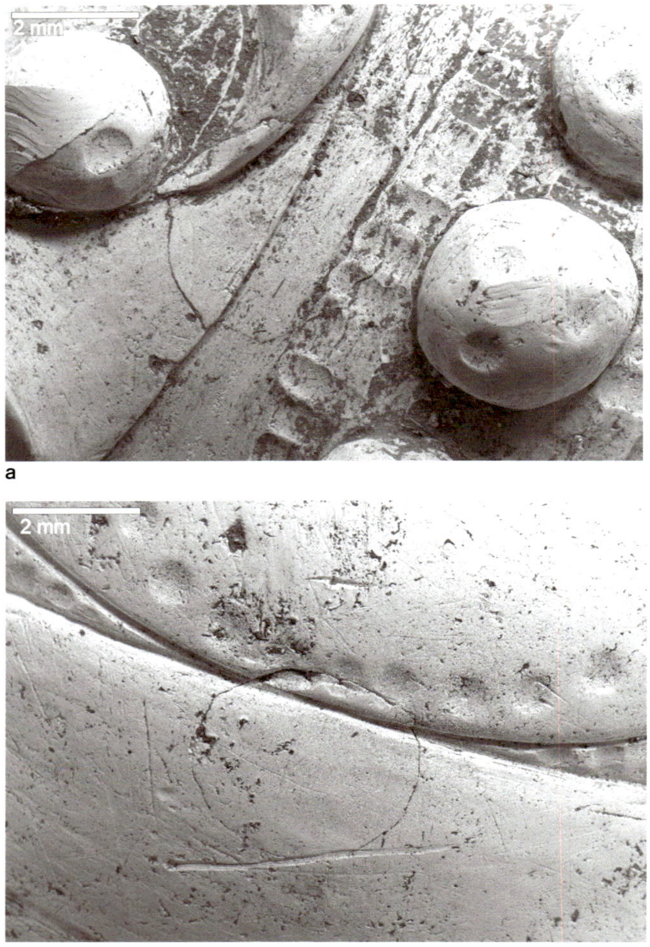

a

b

Figure 17.80a–b SEM BSE images of the rivet ends on the detached terminal of the Sedgeford Torc; this rivet is mechanically fixed and its ends are burnished and concealed within the punched and chased decoration, only the circular outline of the end of the rivet remains (scale bars *c.* 2mm)

pierced or drilled hole in the flange region of the terminals and in the internal tube wrapping the wires (**Figs 17.75–6**). The rivet holes cut through the solder dendrites, indicating that they were drilled after the end tube/cap was soldered to the wires. The ends of the rivet are concealed externally through burnishing and within the chased and punched decoration (**Fig. 17.80**).

Multi-strand torc terminal construction: Other forms of terminal manufacture

A small number of multi-strand torcs have unusual terminals formed from sheet or a combination of cast and sheet components. Two of these, the Great Torc and Grotesque Torc, are discussed in detail here.

Composite terminal manufacture case study: The Great Torc

The hollow terminals of the Great Torc (E.1a) have finely decorated, prominent design features that had always been thought to be formed by lost-wax casting directly onto the neck-ring terminals, as reported in Joy (2015), similar to other torcs from Snettisham and elsewhere. The Great Torc is complete, meaning direct internal examination of the terminals was not possible, unlike the fragmentary Sedgeford Torc, which has a detached terminal that could be viewed internally from the broken wire end to confirm

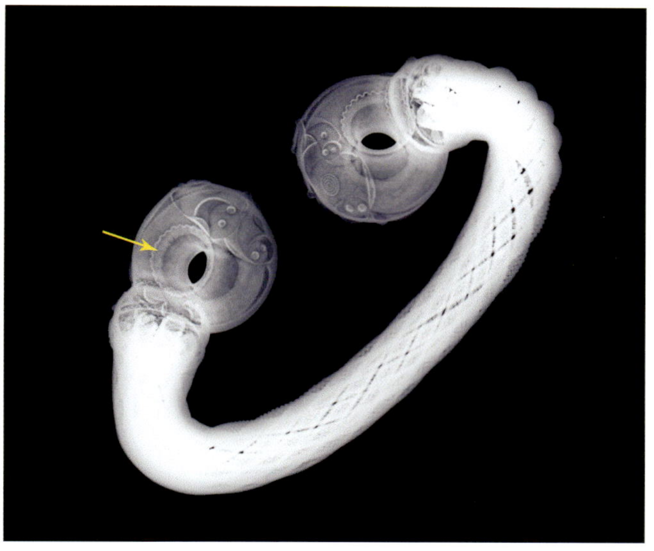

Figure 17.82 Oblique view X-radiograph (CR) of the Great Torc (corresponding colour image Fig. 17.57; see Appendix at end of this chapter for terminology). The arrow indicates the brighter, ring-shaped band that appears where the concave tubular sheet overlaps with the torus

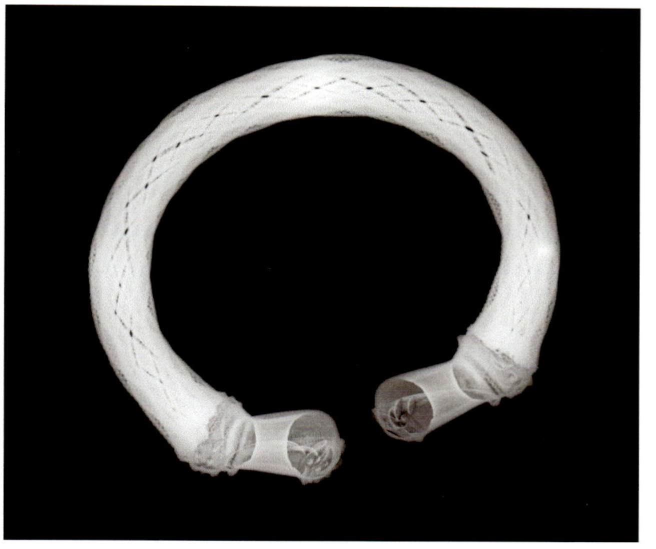

Figure 17.83 Axial view X-radiograph (CR) of the Great Torc. Note the brighter concave tubular-shaped sheet creating a hollow core within both terminals (see details in Fig. 17.85)

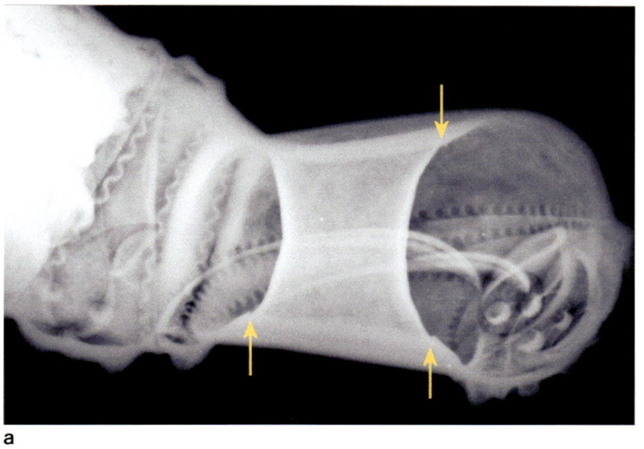

a

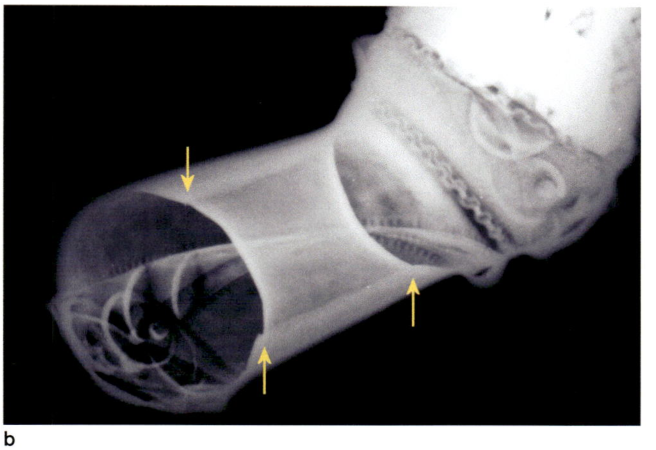

b

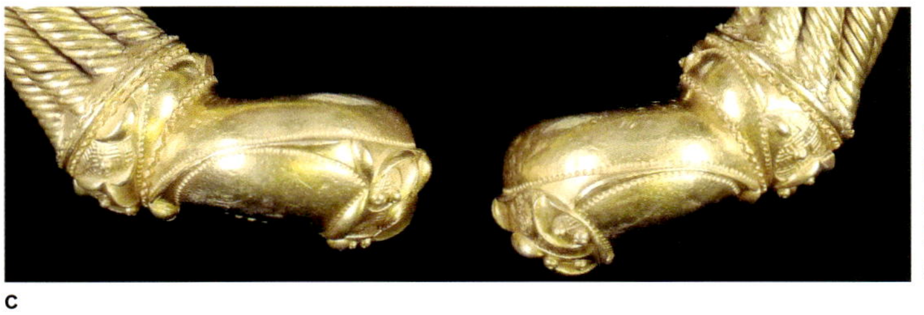

c

Figure 17.84a–c Close-ups of a) the left and b) the right terminals in Figure 17.83: the arrows indicate the overlap and discontinuity between the concave tubular sheet creating the hollow core and the main torus of the terminal; c) Photograph of the terminals for comparison

Figure 17.85a–c a–b) Enhanced X-radiograph (CR) detail of the two terminals showing the cuts (yellow arrows) along the edge of toroidal metal. Note the similar X-ray attenuation of the collars overlapping the wires of the neck-ring to the main torus; c) Optical detail of terminal in similar orientation to image (a)

a

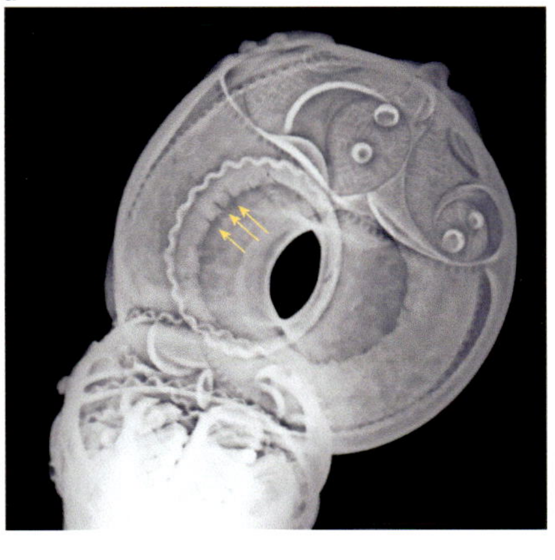

b

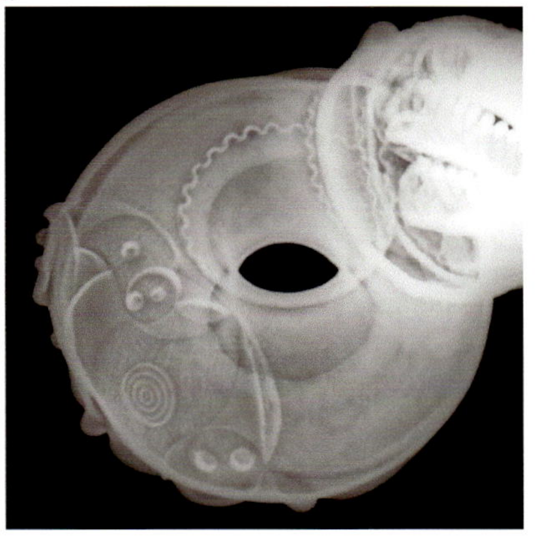

c

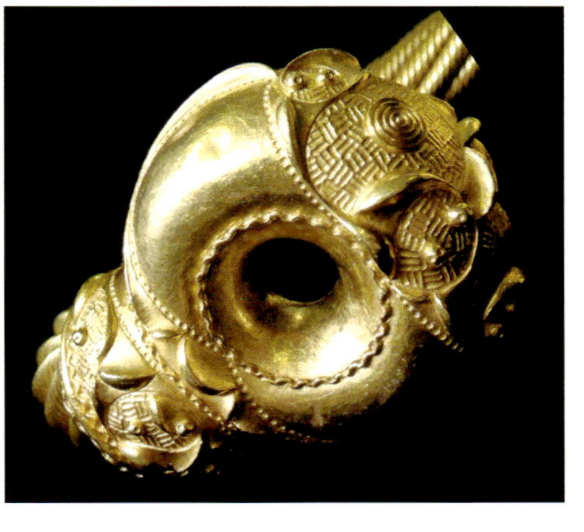

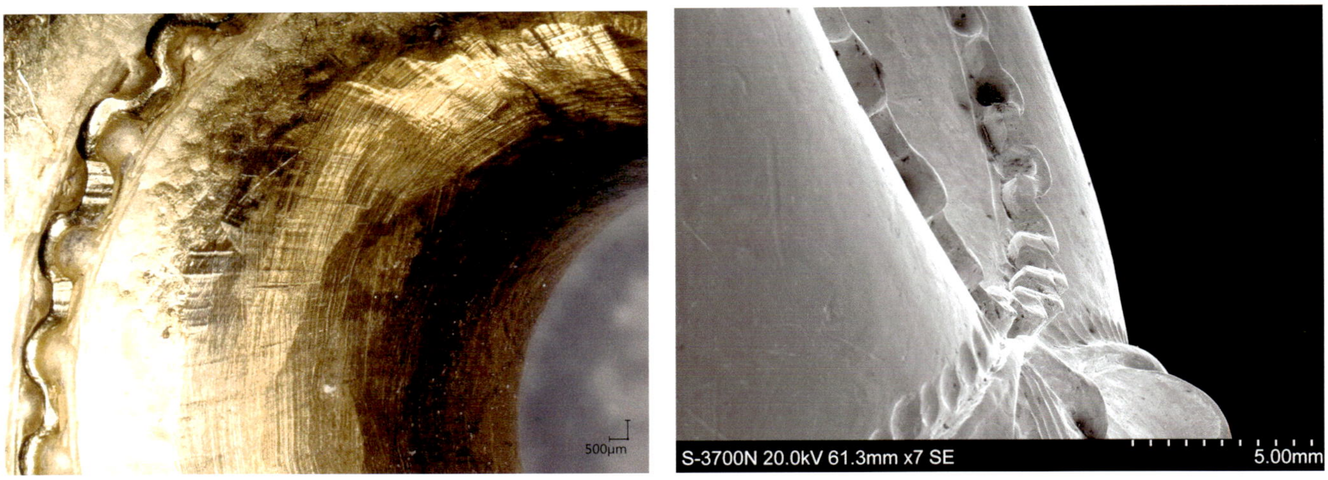

a b

Figure 17.86a–b a) Photomicrograph (width of view *c.* 17mm, x20) and b) SEM SE image of a Great Torc terminal showing fine hammer marks on the concave tubular core sheet of the terminal eye near the wavy decoration, where it overlaps with the toroidal component, and punched decoration enhancing the wavy strip that disguises the overlap join. Linear scraping is probably post-excavation

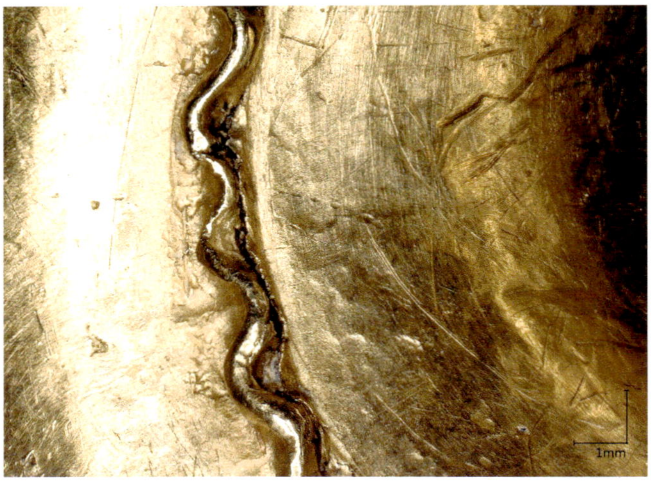

Figure 17.87 Edge of the tubular concave core sheet against the wavy decorative strip on a Great Torc terminal, which has partially detached, around the central hole (scale 1mm; x30, width of image 12mm)

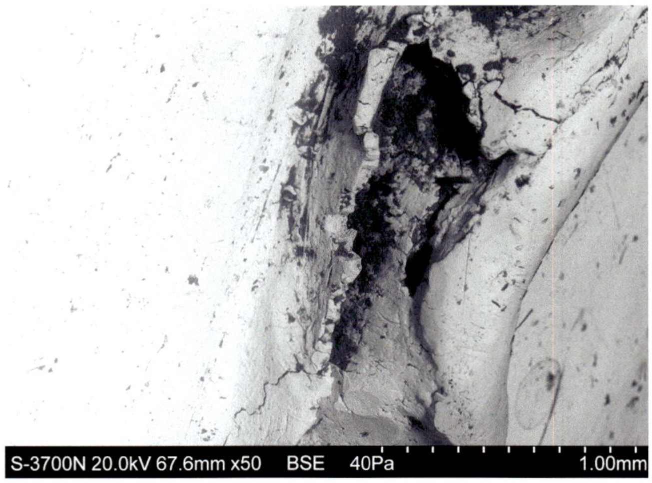

Figure 17.88 SEM BSE image of a damaged region of the Great Torc terminal core sheet edge (sheet from left and folded vertically, centre) adjacent to the wavy decoration (right) of the soldered overlap region shown in Figures 17.86–7

that the terminal component was cast (even if, in that case, not directly onto the neck-ring).

However, our understanding of the complexities of Iron Age goldsmithing is constantly evolving. Around 2016, work by Machling and Williamson suggested that another Iron Age torc component, the detached Netherurd terminal (National Museum of Scotland, **Fig. 17.81**) was formed from two separate pieces of gold alloy sheet: an internal hollow concave 'apple core'-shaped gold sheet and the main surrounding toroidal piece (Machling and Williamson 2016). Since the Great Torc (**Fig. 17.57**) shares some visual characteristics with the Netherurd terminal (**Fig. 17.81**), Machling and Williamson raised the possibility that the same might be true for the Great Torc.

A comprehensive study of the terminals of the Great Torc was subsequently carried out. This study combined new high-power X-radiography, to penetrate the thick gold terminals, and high-resolution imaging using optical microscopy and SEM to record technical details which had not previously been possible (Meeks *et al.* 2014). This enabled comparison of its construction with the Grotesque Torc (L.19), which has gold sheet terminals (see below), and the Sedgeford Torc (BM 1968,1004.1 and 2005,1103.1), which has cast terminals (discussed above). The results revealed that aspects of both theories (cast and sheet construction) were correct, with the Great Torc terminals being made separately from both cast and sheet components, before being soldered onto the neck-ring.

Gold has a high density and atomic number, and therefore strongly attenuates X-rays. Any thickness of gold or high-purity gold alloy from *c.* 0.3mm upwards presents a challenge for X-radiography due to heavy absorption (loss of signal) and scatter (poor edge definition). These effects were mitigated in this work by operating the X-ray tube up to the maximum power and with strong filtration of the incident X-ray beam. In light of this, the well-defined X-ray images of the Great Torc's terminals point to the metal being relatively thin (**Figs 17.82–5**), compared with the blurred edges seen on the images of the cast Sedgeford Torc terminals (**Figs 17.71–3**) caused by the thicker metal.

X-radiography of the Great Torc suggests that each terminal is made up of at least two separate components: a main toroidal element with its neck collar, and a central core that closes the central hole or 'eye' of the terminal.

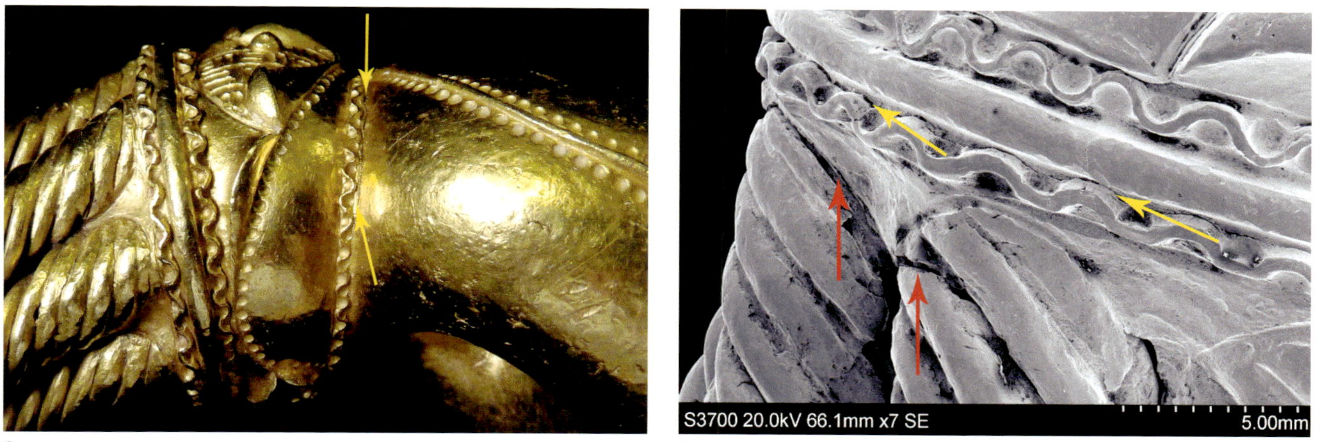

a b

Figure 17.89a–b Great Torc a) Macrograph (image width *c.* 65mm) showing start and end of shrinkage crack between the torus and neck, detailed in Figure 17.92, and the 'infill' between wire ropes and neck; b) SEM SE image of an 'infill' region between the neck-flange and wires with evidence of stress corrosion and fatigue cracking (red arrows) through some of the wires and thin gold infill. A thin gap can be seen along the top of the wavy decoration strip (yellow arrows); this might suggest an attached wavy strip, similar to those around the eye of the torus terminal (Figs 17.86–7)

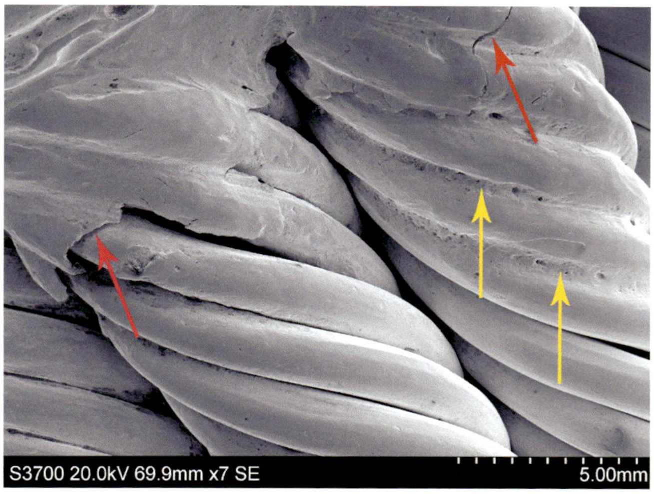

Figure 17.90 SEM SE image of the Great Torc terminal flange overlapping the wires, relatively thin metal at this point, and of the solder having run between some of the round-section wires (yellow arrows). Note how some wires have separated from the overlapping flange due to stress corrosion and fatigue cracking of the solder join and the wire (red arrows) similar to cracks in Figure 17.89

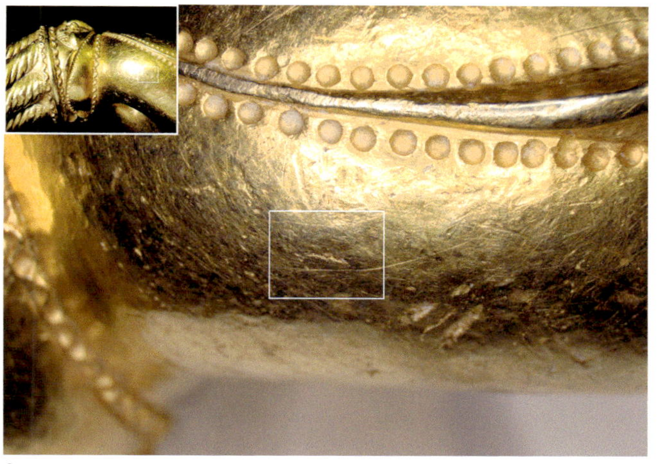

a

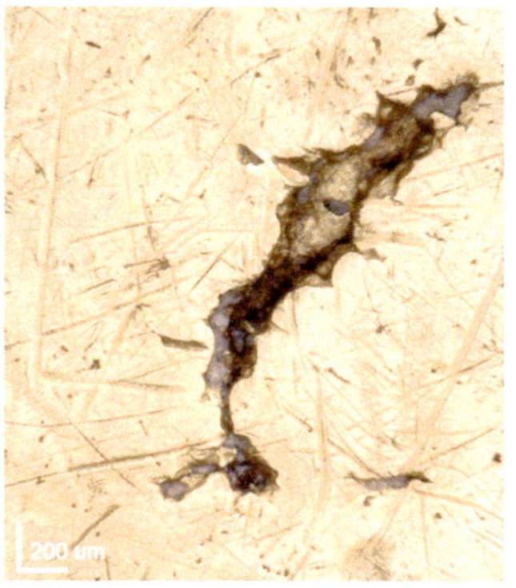

b

Figure 17.91a–b a) Great Torc terminal with the location of the casting defect on the side of the torus in the centre of the marked square (image width *c.* 35mm); b) Close-up of the same dendritic cold-shut casting defect. The solidity within the defect shows that it is not a crack from sheet-metalworking (x100. Note that the close-up image is rotated *c.* 90 degrees with respect to (a). Scale 200 µm (0.2mm), image width 2.5mm)

The oblique radiograph view of the Great Torc (**Figs 17.82, 17.85a–b**) shows a brighter, ring-shaped band at each end of the central eyes. The bands are brighter due to the X-rays having thicker metal to penetrate, indicating a region where gold alloy components are overlapping. The axial radiographs (**Figs 17.83–4**) clearly show the overlap between a concave tubular sheet core, which forms the terminal central hole, and the surrounding torus (cf. Machling and Williamson 2018 for the discussion on sheet core construction). The small sharp 'corners' (yellow arrows in **Figs 17.84**) indicate the edges of the underlying torus metal. Several small cuts on the edge of the toroidal terminal component are visible on an enhanced oblique view of this region of one terminal (yellow arrows in **Fig. 17.85a**); these would have allowed greater flexibility when inserting the core sheet for soldering into the torus to complete the terminal. The overlap has been disguised externally on the plainer reverse sides by burnishing the gold surface. On the more decorative front of the terminals, the join has also been hidden by adding a wavy strip of gold enhanced with a hemispherical punched design, presumably soldered on around the circumference of the hole (**Fig. 17.86**). Although largely hidden, some edges of the latter seam can be noticed on the magnified optical and SEM images (**Figs 17.87–8**).

The decorated collars of the terminals display a similar X-ray attenuation to the main toroidal metal and appear to be of similar thickness (**Fig. 17.85**). The 64 wires making up the neck-ring of the Great Torc appear to have flat ends, suggesting that they have been cut straight across after being twisted and curved into their final shape before the terminals were fitted (**Figs 17.82, 17.85**), as in the reconstruction of the Great Torc (p. 456; **Fig. 17.58**). The collar necks extend over these cut wires, forming a flange that is moulded and burnished over and between the 64

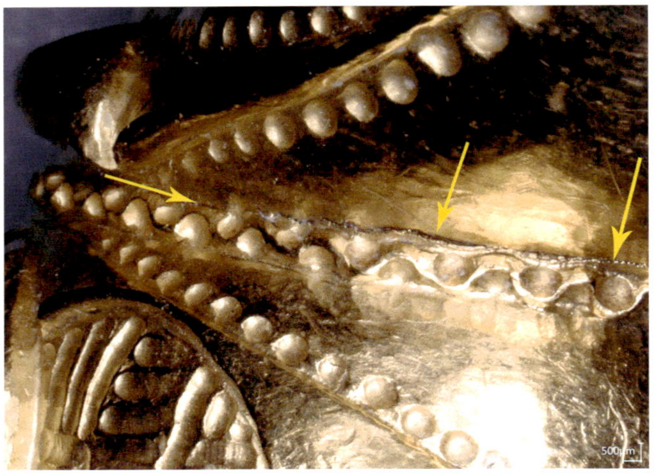

a

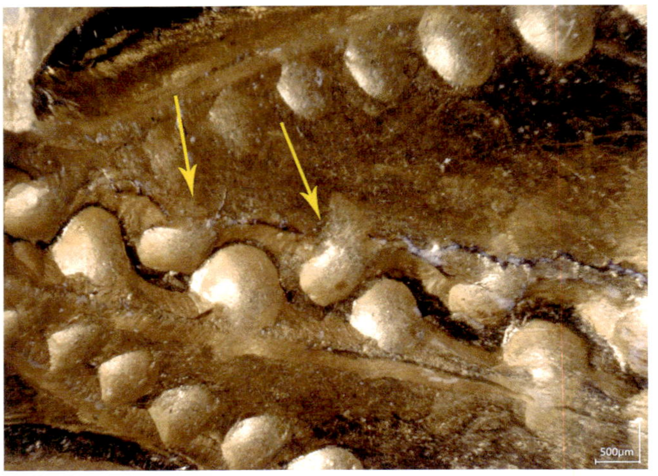

b

Figure 17.92a–b Great Torc terminal with a long shrinkage crack between the torus and neck showing the punched tool marks overlapping the shrinkage crack. b) Note the punched decorative hemispheres going over and closing the crack (yellow arrows) (a) x20, width of image 18mm, b) x50, width of image 7mm)

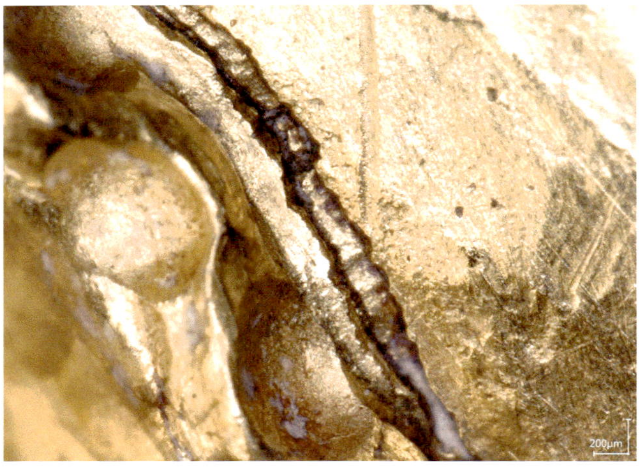

Figure 17.93 Detail of part of the long shrinkage crack in the Great Torc, showing depth and solidity of metal (x100, width of image 3.5mm)

wires of the neck-ring. This has created a solid-looking infill in some areas (**Fig. 17.89**), with associated dendritic microstructures in places, and more obvious overlapping thin metal in other areas (**Fig. 17.90**).

The appearance of once-molten metal around the join between the Great Torc terminal and neck-ring had been assumed to be evidence of casting-on (as reported in Joy 2015 and Meeks et al. 2014), but in fact further examination suggests that the appearance of the wire/terminal junctions on the Great Torc is very different to that of the cast-on terminals, on which the cooled metal appears globular (**Figs 17.64–6**). Instead, molten solder appears to have run between some of the wires and fused them together, suggesting in fact that the collar necks were soldered onto the neck-ring wires (**Figs 17.89–90**). Some wires and regions of thin neck metal have separated and cracked on one terminal, due to stress created by flexing and bending the torc during use. It is likely that, in these regions, the wire ends were originally probably not well supported or not fully soldered to the overlapping terminal flange (**Fig. 17.90**). The radiographs show no dense internal areas where the flange overlaps the wires, which suggests that there are no additional internal supporting metal components or rivets joining the terminals to the neck-ring.

While the radiographs show the internal structure of two overlapping components, the sheet core and the outer torus,

Figure 17.94a–b Grotesque Torc terminal with brittle cracks and missing metal/holes from work-hardened hammered sheet (x20, width of images 18mm). b) Note the thin metal and fracture along the bend line. These features are metallurgically very different from the cast defect seen on the Great Torc terminal torus in Figures 17.91–3

a

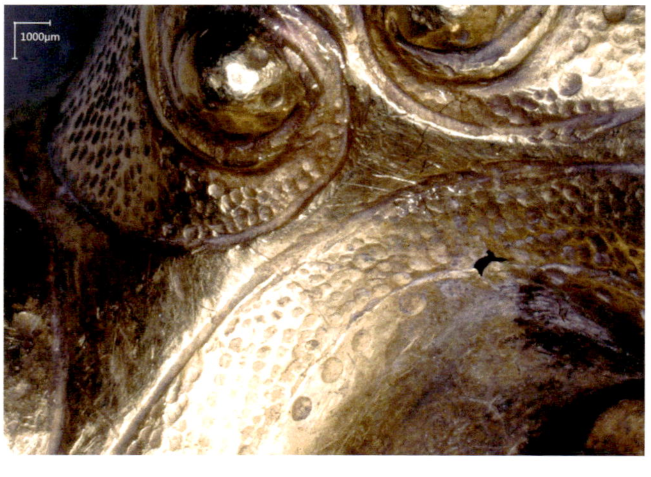

b

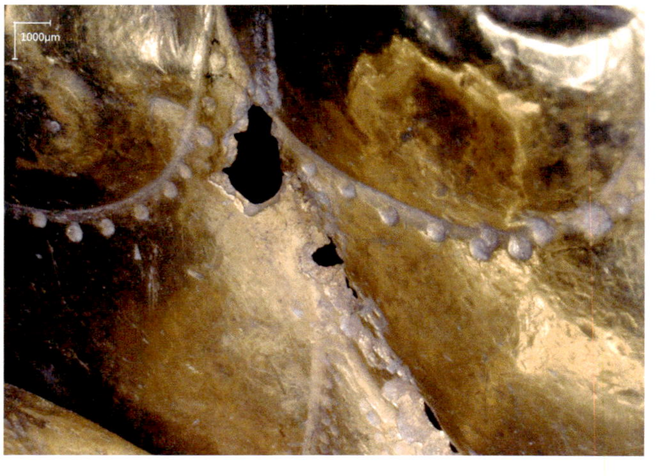

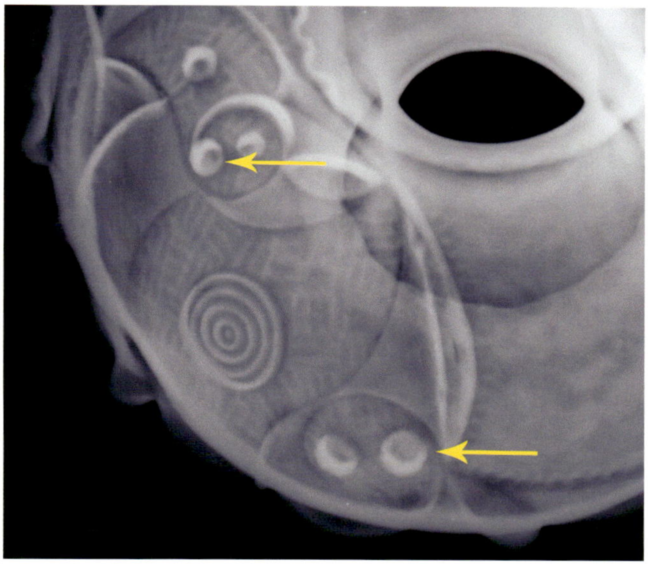

Figure 17.95 Enhanced X-radiograph (CR) detail of the Great Torc terminal showing the hollow spheres (yellow arrows) and apparently solid concentric rings

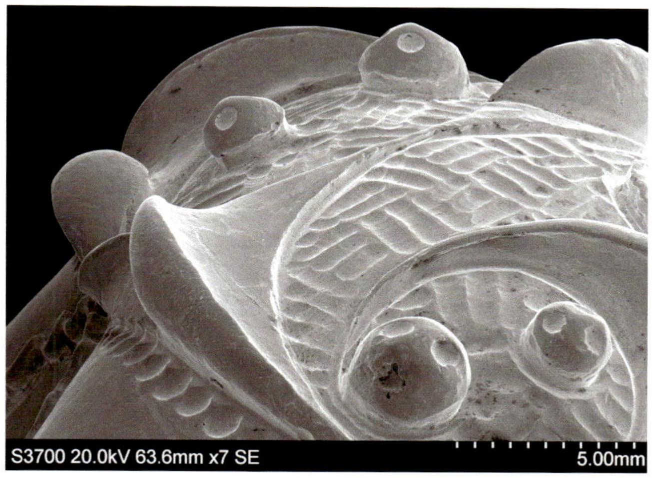

Figure 17.96 SEM SE image of the Great Torc terminal showing the highly three-dimensional decorative designs, engraving undercuts around features for emphasis, individual round punch-marks and the linear multiple-punch tracks forming the geometric hatched 'basket-weave' pattern

optical microscopy revealed a dendritic cold-shut casting defect on a smooth area of the outer surface of one terminal torus, away from the concave tubular core sheet (**Fig. 17.91**). Around this region are a few other similar defects, which confirm that the terminal torus was originally cast (Ott *et al.* 1985, 99: 'Figure 1 … typical crystallization voids of dendritic origin'). Additional evidence for casting is a long shrinkage crack found in the depression where the torus flares to become the collar (**Fig. 17.92**). The open collar would have been part of the original cast torus for the attachment and covering of the neck-ring wires. A close-up view of the deep crack shows the thickness of the gold at this point (**Fig. 17.93**). Clear punched hemispheres over the crack have sealed it (**Fig. 17.92b**, centre), indicating that the crack preceded the decorative punching and is not a post-depositional corrosion crack. These features are metallurgically different from hammered work-hardened cracking, which is often accompanied by loss of material and therefore holes in the gold sheet, as seen on the sheet terminals of the Grotesque Torc (see below and **Fig. 17.94**).

This evidence suggests that the toroidal terminals of the Great Torc were originally formed as open castings (e.g. see L.21; **Fig. 17.64**), with all the deep three-dimensional decorative design elements being cast to shape with the metal of the terminal. To facilitate the accurate positioning of the design elements, it is suggested that all the main design features could have been located on an accurately prepared clay core over which wax was then modelled to refine the decoration, such as the solid concentric circles, hollow waves and spheres (**Figs 17.95–7**), which were then cast in gold once the clay moulding process was completed. Despite the torus and collar being cast, no evidence of chaplets was found. However, these could have easily been removed before closing the torus. Alternatively, a very simple solution would be for the clay cores to simply extend up through what would become the open collar, where they could join directly with the applied external clay mould and become one complete moulded unit, and therefore be self-supporting.

The open torus and collar would have allowed easy access for finishing tools after casting, for example for carrying out repoussé of the hollow waves and spheres (*c.* 2.2–3.3mm diameter) (**Figs 17.95–7**). These highly three-dimensional hollow motifs may even have been additionally punched into moulds to fully define their shape. Internal support tools and materials could also have been inserted into the open casting for chasing and punching decoration from the front and for fine planishing (flattening of the surface with a smooth-faced hammer). Filling the terminals with a supporting material during final punching and chasing to refine the decoration would have avoided any

Figure 17.97a–c SEM a) BSE and b) SE images and c) photomicrograph (x20, width of view *c.* 10mm) of the concentric ring decoration on the Great Torc terminal. Note the height difference between the high three-dimensional features and the lower 'basket-weave' hatching

a b c

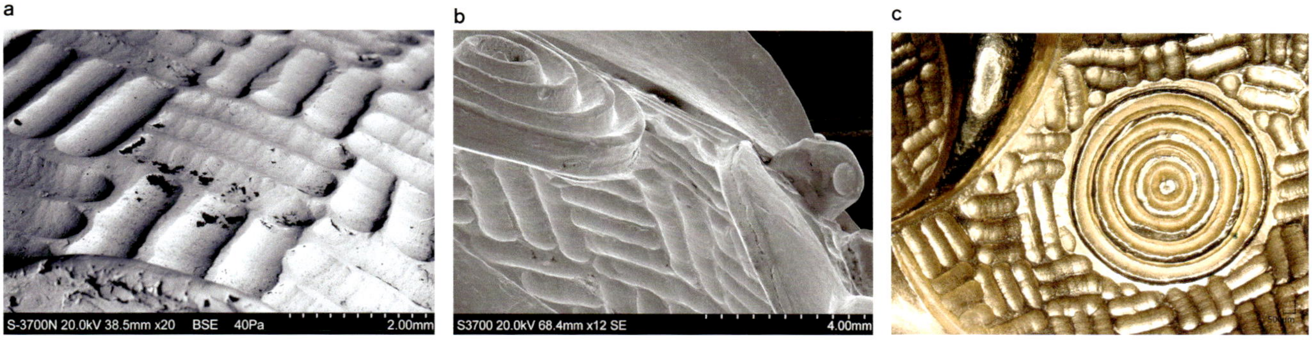

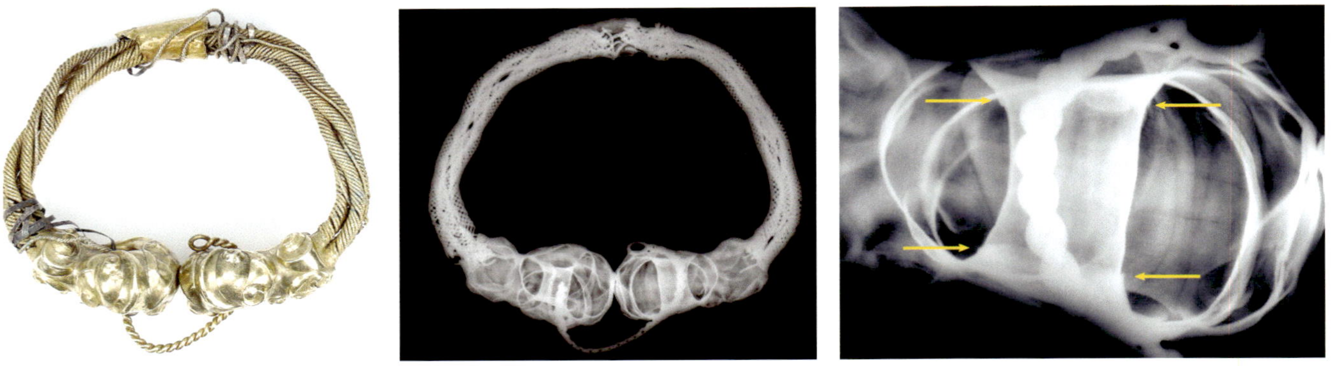

a b c

Figure 17.98a–c a) The Grotesque Torc (L.19) (210mm maximum external diameter); (b) X-radiograph (CR) showing the ancient repair of the broken wire neck-ring using sheet gold wrapping (radiograph: D. O'Flynn); (c) X-radiograph (CR) detail of the Grotesque Torc left terminal, with yellow arrows indicating the overlap and discontinuities between the concave tubular sheet creating the hollow core and the toroidal sheet of the terminal

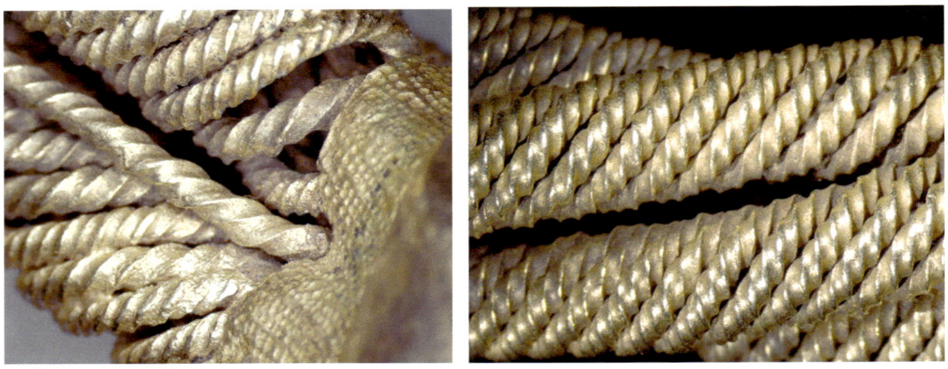

a b

Figure 17.99a–b a) Grotesque Torc terminal collar flange of thin sheet gold with dot-punched decoration, where it covers the twisted square section wires of the neck-ring. There is evidence of some solder on and between the wire ends (width of image *c.* 20mm); b) Uniformity of twisted square section wires (width of image *c.* 30mm)

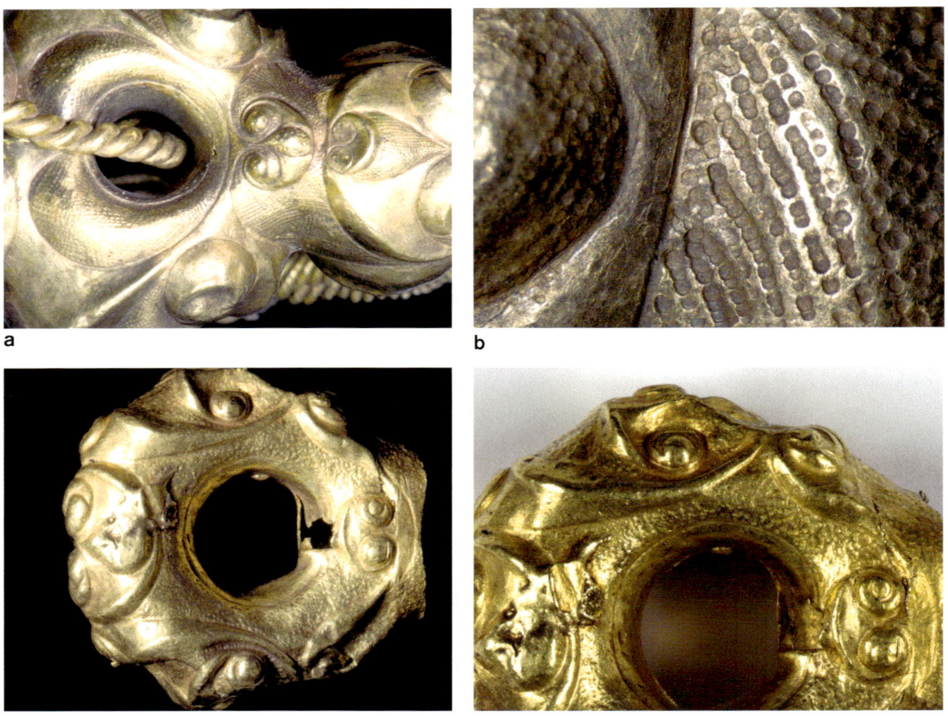

a b c d

Figure 17.100a–d Top (a–b): Grotesque Torc terminal, with deep, rounded decorative features shaped by repoussé, and outlined by chasing and areas infilled with closely spaced linear dot-punched decoration (left image width *c.* 70mm); Bottom (c–d): sheet torc terminal F.72 with areas between repoussé designs infilled with random multiple-punch stippling using a single round-ended tool

unwanted indentation or deformation of the thin metal around the tool marks. Engraved lines can be clearly seen at the base of most decoration in relief: they appear to be cut relatively deep into the metal (**Figs 17.96–7**). This suggests that the metal was significantly thicker at the base of these decorated areas to allow for the amount of engraving, undercutting and deep chasing observed on these terminals (**Figs 17.96–7**).

Once the decoration of the terminals had been completed, the eyes of the toroid components were closed by overlapping the concave tubular core sheet with the edges of the cast torus. The terminals were then soldered in place on the ends of the neck-ring, the resulting join being burnished and polished between and over the wires (**Figs 17.89a, 17.90**).

The complexity of the construction and attachment of the Great Torc terminals thus appears unique, combining elements of both sheet working (as theorised by Machling and Williamson, 2016 and 2018) and cast construction (as originally believed and reported in Joy 2015 and Meeks *et al.* 2014).

Sheet terminal manufacture case studies: The Grotesque Torc (L.19a) and F.72

Radiography of the so-called Grotesque Torc (L.19, **Fig. 17.98**) has shown evidence of an overlapped concave tubular core sheet on the terminals, similar to that seen on the Great Torc (Machling and Williamson 2018). In this case, however, there is no evidence that any of the components were cast, and the terminals seem to be constructed entirely from hand-worked gold sheet. The terminal flanges are moulded over the composite wires and appear to be soldered to them, but not very securely (**Fig. 17.99**). The relief designs have a 'softer', more rounded and less angular decoration (**Fig. 17.100**), as would be expected from a design created by repoussé and not necessarily punched into dies. This torc and another similar sheet terminal torc (F.72) also have a completely different punched stippling infill decoration within the design elements (Ch. 21; **Fig. 17.100**).

Comparing different forms of multi-strand torc construction

It is instructive to use X-radiography to compare the construction routes of four of the most impressive and well-known Iron Age gold alloy torcs: the Great and Grotesque Torcs from Snettisham, the Sedgeford Torc (discussed extensively above) and a similar example discovered at Newark, Nottinghamshire, in 2005, and subsequently subject to a Treasure Inquest. There are a number of similarities between these pieces, but close analysis suggests a wide range of terminal production routes.

Figure 17.101 compares the X-radiographs of three terminals with different construction routes (a separately cast and mechanically attached terminal from the

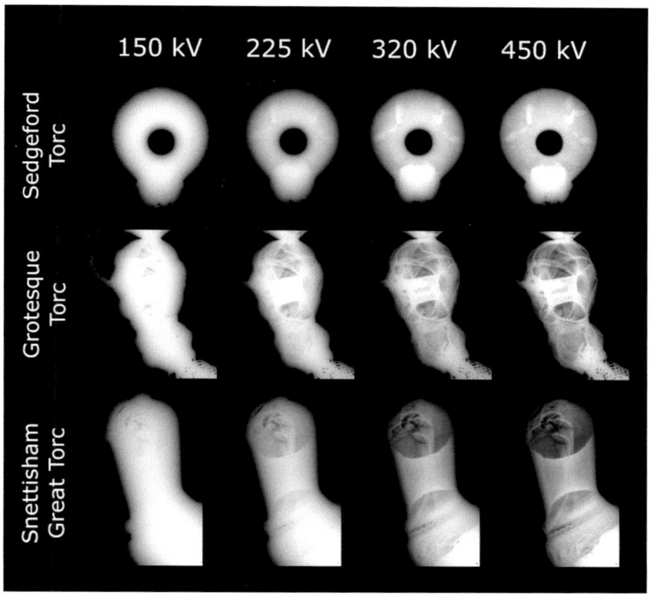

Figure 17.101 X-radiographs (CR) comparing terminals of the Sedgeford Torc (BM 2005,1103.1), the Grotesque Torc (L.19) and the Great Torc (E.1a) and showing the effects of increasing the voltage, which results in increased penetration of the X-rays in the gold

Sedgeford Torc, a sheet terminal of the Grotesque Torc, and a composite Great Torc terminal with both cast and sheet elements; see pp. 464–6). Moving from left to right, each row of images shows the effects of increasing the tube voltage (and so, the mean and maximum X-ray energies), resulting in increased penetration of the X-rays. Internal structures appear much better defined at the highest voltage, and the relative gold thicknesses of the different terminals can be distinguished. The sheet gold terminals of the Grotesque Torc show the most detail at all voltage settings, indicating that it is made of the thinnest gold. In contrast, the terminals of the Sedgeford Torc (**Fig. 17.70**) appear less well defined on radiographs acquired under the same exposure conditions (**Figs 17.71–3, 17.101**). They show blurred edges due to the thicker metal contributing more towards X-ray scatter (**Figs 17.71–3**).

Table 17.8 Construction summary for the Great Torc and Grotesque Torc from Snettisham, and the torcs from Newark (Nottinghamshire) and Sedgeford (Norfolk). MSCC: Multi-strand Construction Code, see typology in Chapter 13

Torc	Terminal construction method	Terminal attachment to neck-ring	MSCC	Neck-ring description
Great	Composite: cast and sheet elements	Soldering	(8C(8C))R	Stage III neck-ring formed from eight ropes coiled together around a hollow core, each rope made up of eight coiled circular-section wires
Grotesque	Sheet	Soldering	(4C(4C))T	Stage III neck-ring formed from four ropes coiled together around a hollow core, ropes made up of four coiled strands of square-section twisted wire
Newark	Cast(?)	?	(8C(4P))R	Stage III neck-ring formed from eight ropes coiled together around a hollow core, each rope made up of four circular-section wires plied together
Sedgeford	Cast	Mechanical. Rivets secure the internal tubular cap (containing the soldered ends of the neck-ring wires) to the terminal	(8C(3P))R	Stage III neck-ring formed from eight ropes coiled together around a hollow core, each rope made up of three circular-section wires plied together

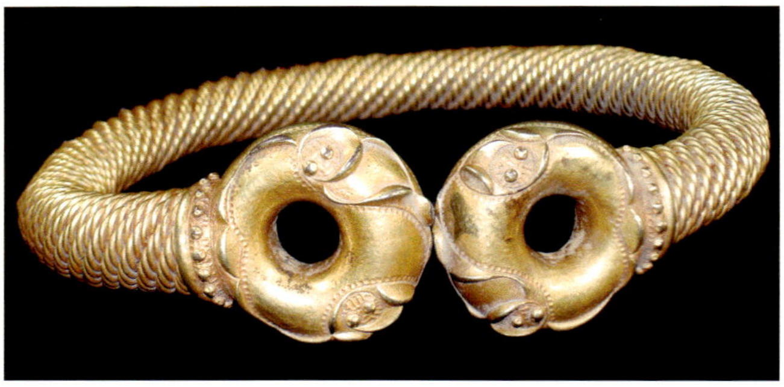

Figure 17.102 Iron Age gold torc from Newark, Nottinghamshire

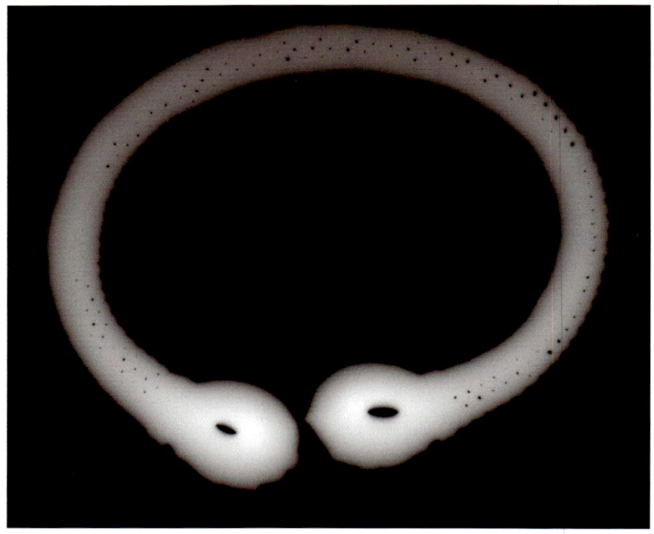

Figure 17.103 Film X-radiograph from archive material of the Newark Torc, acquired in 2008 during an earlier examination of this Treasure find at 150 kV, 5 mA and 5 minutes exposure time (radiograph: J. Ambers)

The use of a range of X-ray tube voltages (**Fig. 17.101**) also enabled comparison with an existing X-radiograph of the Newark Torc from Nottinghamshire (**Fig. 17.102**), which was taken as part of an earlier Treasure investigation (Hill in Hitchcock 2006, 55) (**Fig. 17.103**). The density of the Newark Torc terminals suggests a thickness more similar to the cast Sedgeford Torc terminals, than the sheet terminals of the Grotesque Torc (**Fig. 17.101**).

The three torc terminals shown in **Figure 17.101** were produced in very different ways, although connections can also be charted between them (see summaries in **Table 17.8**). The Sedgeford Torc terminals are closed-torus hollow castings with chaplets and what appears to be thicker metal on the radiographs. The Grotesque Torc and Great Torc terminals were both made from two main components: a relatively thin gold open torus (thinner for the Grotesque Torc and thicker for the deeply embossed Great Torc) and a concave tubular sheet core, which was soldered in place to close the eye of the terminal, burnished and the joins concealed. This core feature appears similar to that of the Netherurd terminal from Peeblesshire (described by Machling and Williamson 2016; 2018), which also shares the concentric circular decorative elements seen on the Great Torc (**Figs 17.81, 17.97**). Whilst the Grotesque Torc terminal components all appear to be made from sheet, a casting defect on one of the Great Torc terminals and shrinkage cracks in high-stress regions of the neck-flange confirm that the open torus elements of the Great Torc terminals were cast.

Evidence provided by the manufacturing techniques of the Great and Sedgeford torcs suggests that casting high-profile decorative terminals was a well-established metalsmithing technique. While successful in some cases, many castings suffered cold-shut surface defects. This could be due to the metal cooling prematurely or an air lock preventing full metal flow within the mould (e.g. L.21, **Fig. 17.68**). The Great Torc shows a similar small dendritic casting defect on the surface of one terminal (**Fig. 17.91**). The Sedgeford Torc terminals are excellent examples of cast terminals with perfectly formed three-dimensional motifs and largely without defects, apart from a crack on the back of one terminal which appears to have been repaired with rivets and concealed at the time of manufacture (**Fig. 17.74**).

All three sets of torc terminals seen in **Figure 17.101** were made as separate components from their wire neck-rings (**Table 17.8**). They have not been cast directly onto the wires, as previously hypothesised for the Great Torc and as is the case for most torus, reel and buffer terminal torcs from Snettisham. On the Great Torc and Grotesque Torc, the terminal collars were fitted over the completed wire neck-rings, the edges moulded over the wires, burnished and soldered in place. The cast terminals of the Sedgeford Torc were mechanically secured in place with rivets, fixed onto

Figure 17.104a–c a) Cast buffer terminal (24mm diameter) from Snettisham (L.13) showing linear post-casting punch tool mark 'basket-weave' hatched decoration similar to the Great Torc (see Figs 17.96–7); b) Engraved outlines of the design elements. c) Note that some of the wire ends passing into the edge of the cast-on terminal are square – presumably unfinished ends of the original hammered wire. Note the decorative edge dot decoration

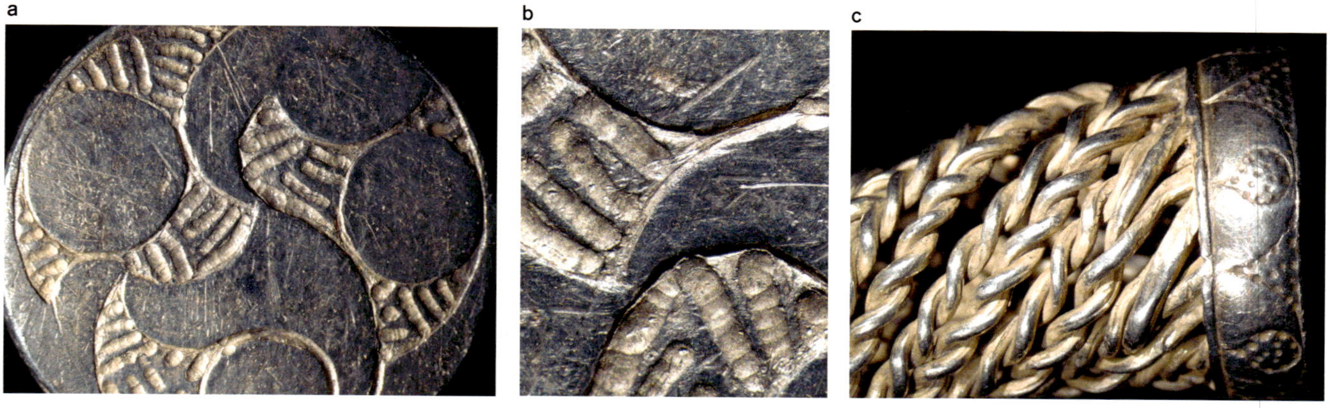

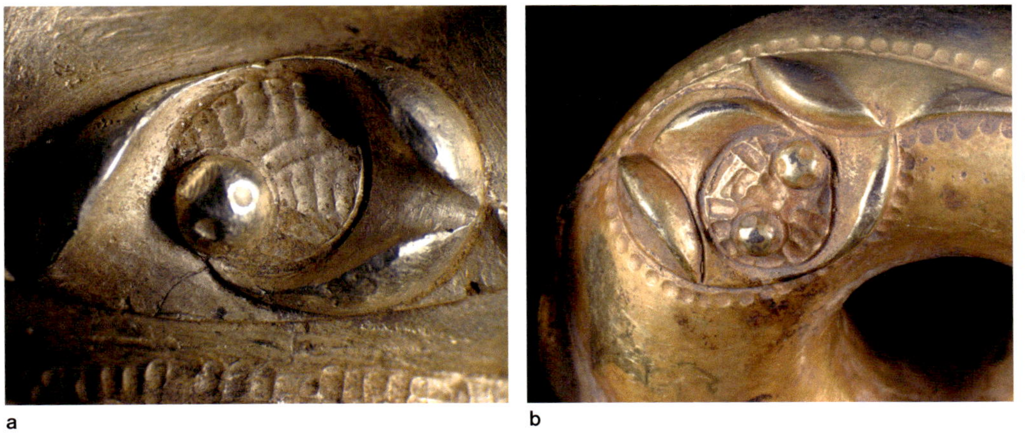

Figure 17.105a–b Cast a) Sedgeford, and b) Newark terminals with geometric, basket-weave pattern similar to that on the Great Torc and the cast buffer terminal torc L.13 (Fig. 17.104). This decoration on the Sedgeford and Newark terminals is less well defined than on the latter two torcs

metal tubes which had been soldered onto the ends of the neck-ring wires.

The Great Torc terminals appear to be the most elaborately decorated large terminals from the Snettisham hoards with very well-defined and highly three-dimensional decorative designs and detailed finishing. These decorative motifs are similar to those on the terminals of the Sedgeford Torc as well as Snettisham torcs with cast-on terminals (e.g. **Figs 17.67–8**). Both the Great and Sedgeford torcs also have detailed external tooling to define their decoration. The strong stylistic association between the Great Torc terminals and other cast terminals suggests a probable metalsmithing connection.

Despite sharing one common technological feature (the presence of a tubular sheet core in the centre of their terminals), the Great Torc and Grotesque Torc contrast stylistically: their decoration is very different, as are the type and arrangement of neck-ring wires: the highly twisted square-section wires of the Grotesque Torc (**Fig. 17.99**) contrast with the smooth circular-section wires of the Great (**Fig. 17.90**), Sedgeford (**Figs 17.74–5**) and Newark torcs (**Fig. 17.102**). The latter three all have Stage III coiled constructions comprising eight coiled or plied ropes made from circular section, while the Grotesque Torc has a neck-ring consisting of just four ropes made up of twisted wires (**Table 17.8**).

In addition to similarities in their neck-ring structures, the Great Torc also has far more in common in the design and shape of its three-dimensional decorative motifs with the torcs from Sedgeford (**Fig. 17.70**), Newark (**Fig. 17.102**), and Netherurd (**Fig. 17.81**). The punched infill decoration of the Grotesque Torc contrasts with the punched geometric, basket weave textured pattern of the Great Torc (**Figs 17.96–7**), which is very similar to that of a cast buffer terminal torc from Snettisham (L.13; **Fig. 17.104**). The tool marks on the Great Torc and L.13 suggest the use of a gently hammered chasing tool with a rounded tip used to create the hatched 'basket-weave' patterns, instead of using a single textured punch, and with the design elements outlined by engraved lines. This pattern is also seen on both the Sedgeford and Newark torcs, which display areas of similar design, although smaller and less well defined (**Fig. 17.105**).

Some of the differences between the Grotesque Torc and the Great, Sedgeford and Newark torcs are most likely due to chronology. On stylistic grounds, the Grotesque Torc, with its 'Plastic Style' decoration (see Ch. 21), is considered to have been manufactured earlier, and may be one of the oldest objects from Snettisham (Chs 20, 21). The similar sheet terminal, F.72, may be of similar date. The 'Style V' designs and hatched 'basket-weave' infill seen on many of the Snettisham torcs (including the Great Torc and L.13) as well as Sedgeford and Newark are likely later, although they cannot be closely dated (Ch. 21). The likely difference in age between the Great and Grotesque torcs suggests that the technology of closing a torus terminal with a sheet core (noted here and by Machling and Williamson e.g. 2016; 2018) was a long-lived and perhaps widespread technique, even though today it is preserved in only a relatively few objects.

Although bearing similar decorative styles, surface finishing and tool marks, the terminals of the Sedgeford Torc and the Great Torc have been produced using two different but complementary technologies, respectively lost-wax casting only for the former and casting with additional sheet working for the latter. The sheer range of construction techniques seen across the pieces discussed here shows the incredible creativity and diversity at play in goldsmithing traditions evident across Britain at the close of the Iron Age.

17.7 Discussion and conclusions

The technological study of the surfaces and structures of components and alloys of the Snettisham hoard objects has identified and recorded the wide range of metalsmithing skills and production processes used to manufacture the components for the torcs and their assembly, as well as the highly skilled decorative and finishing techniques used to embellish the finished products.

The archaeometric study of this unique assemblage has provided many new insights into Iron Age metalworking technologies. At least four groups of alloys have been identified:

- High gold-silver with low copper alloys (used in both wires and sheet objects)
- Silver-gold-copper alloys (wires)
- High-copper and low-gold silver alloys (wires)
- Bronzes (wires)

The selection of alloys for particular purposes may have been based on their metallurgical properties as much as, or perhaps more than, other criteria such as colour. The analytical data show the use of purer gold for sheet components; these high-gold alloys may have been selected for their malleability and ductility, as it is easier to hammer sheet from high-gold alloys. Many torc wires, in contrast, are made of high-copper / low-gold silver alloys which cluster in the area of the gold-silver-copper ternary diagram with the lowest melting points. Their low melting temperature ranges may have been of more importance to the metalsmiths than the primary alloy colour by way of making the production of the metal easier and more energy efficient. It must have been known to the metalsmiths that mixtures of gold, silver and copper in this range of proportions needed less heat and likely less fuel to melt. This was perhaps a more important practical consideration in the production process than colour, since they knew that the final colour of the torcs would change to a more gold/silvery colour during manufacture and also that the final objects would also be more resistant to corrosive effects in general, and be less susceptible to cause copper-colour skin staining when wearing. In addition, the initial alloy being richer in copper would save on the overall quantity of gold used without impacting on the final surface colour of the surface-enriched torcs.

Wires and sheets of a wide range of gold-silver-copper alloys were hand worked by hammering, quenching and annealing/pickling in mildly acidic medium. Experimental reconstruction of wires by practising metalsmith John Fenn has suggested a likely route for the production of the range of types and diameters seen at Snettisham, based on the hammering out of a square-section ingot or rod. Whilst it was relatively quick to produce wire in this way, the experimental work emphasised the great skill needed to produce wire of a uniform diameter.

A wide range of alloy colours are present at Snettisham, spanning from a pale whitish silver to yellow-gold. At least three different processes revealed through analytical work on the Snettisham material affected the final surface composition (and hence colour) of the objects:

- Surface enrichment of gold/silver through the cycles of hammering, annealing and pickling that were used to shape both wires and sheet elements
- The use of a salt parting-like process perhaps related to gold-refining techniques
- Mercury gilding

In the case of surface enrichment due to hammering and pickling, especially notable in the lower-gold alloys used for many wires, the alloy composition at the surface was modified by depleting the copper content and thus enriching the proportions of gold and/or silver. The resulting shift to a whiter colour may have been an expected but largely unintentional or at least unavoidable, yet a beneficial and exploitable result of the wire-making processes. However, some of the objects studied (especially high-gold alloy sheet objects) also showed variable but significantly reduced silver concentrations at the surface with, in some cases, losses of at least one third of the silver. While the removal of copper from the surface of a gold-silver-copper alloy could be achieved by oxidation and pickling, this would have only a minor effect on the silver content, suggesting that in some cases the goldsmiths making the gold sheet objects used technologies more akin to gold-refining processes. The colour shift here would, however, have been subtle, all taking place within the yellow-gold range, and thus it is possible that, if surface enrichment was an intended outcome, it was concerned as much with the durability and corrosion-resistance of the finished product as with the colour. The clearest evidence for deliberate control of surface colour and texture comes in the form of gilding. Several silver-copper and bronze wires have been shown to be mercury gilded, the earliest use of this technique in Britain so far documented. Overall, the techniques observed suggest a preference for colours ranging from white, through pale greenish gold to yellow-gold, with perhaps some avoidance of more reddish/copper-coloured ternary alloys, though of course bronze objects appear in most of the hoards. The presence of gilded objects, however, does suggest that yellow-gold was highly valued amongst the available range of colours.

The question of sources of gold for these artefacts remains difficult to answer with any certainty, but Northover (1995a) makes the interesting observation about Britain that 'gold disappears from the archaeological record at or about the end of the 8th century B.C. and does not reappear until the arrival of the first imported Celtic gold coins in the late 3rd or 2nd century B.C.'. There is a probable link to continental goldsmiths producing tubular torcs and if there was paucity of native gold in Britain (or the knowledge of where and how to access it), it could be suggested that the gold for the main bulk of the Snettisham torcs and fragments might also have come from the continent, possibly in the form of coinage which was recycled to make torcs (see Ch. 23; discussion in Sharples 2010, 146–59; La Niece *et al.* 2018). Ancient European sources of gold are many and widespread and are reviewed by Lehrberger (1995).

Both wire and sheet elements were employed in the manufacture of multi-strand and tubular torcs. The range of objects and techniques at the site is extraordinary, with an incredible degree of variation on certain standard elements of torc construction. Tubular torcs were generally constructed from high-gold alloy sheets, and most are composite objects constructed from multiple components soldered or mechanically attached together. The large (Type 6) tubular torcs from Hoard A are very complex, with sheet gold elements combined with iron cores, stabilised by a sandy filler. In most cases the terminals are separate components, often with decorative elements, some comprising beaded wire and filigree, with tooled decoration including both simple punch-marks and high-relief repoussé designs. Other tubular torcs also exhibit multi-component construction and relief decoration embellished with punching and chasing.

Multi-strand torcs from the site also exhibit great diversity, with wire neck-rings in a range of alloys, types and sizes. Simple wires in a variety of thicknesses were combined in inventive ways to create complicated neck-rings. Sometimes wires were plied/twisted directly together, and in other cases they were coiled around a core made of flexible wood or another material to facilitate accurate bending and prevent collapse of the coiled 'ropes'. These core supports were probably removed before the terminals were cast on, having served their purpose, except for the small bronze torcs where charred wooden core remains are found (see Ch. 19). The simplest multi-strand neck-rings are made from a pair of wires plied together or a single coiled 'rope', but many torcs combined these elements in multiple stages to produce effects resembling cables or braids. Terminals are just as diverse, ranging from simple loops made from the ends of the neck-ring wires, to solid cast-on buffer and torus terminals, right through to complex composite terminals with both cast and sheet elements. Some cast terminals had high-relief motifs incorporated into their designs, and surface decoration such as repoussé/chasing, punching and engraving were used to embellish the most ornate examples.

Neck-ring and terminal types were combined in a remarkable and exceptional number of variations, with many torcs from the site being unique, or at least having some small detail which marked them out from others, whether in terms of neck-ring construction, a terminal design choice, or some unusual combination of the two elements. The range of techniques used suggests a rich and varied metalworking tradition in the region, even if the precise location of manufacture remains unknown, with long-lived techniques perhaps persisting over centuries. The variety of colours, designs and styles of torcs speaks to the incredible skill of their makers, and hints at the desire to make these objects highly recognisable to those who wore and encountered them.

17.8 Appendix on scientific methods

The Department of Scientific Research at The British Museum has a comprehensive range of scientific equipment that was used to study the Snettisham Hoards. The techniques used are listed below with details of their operating parameters.

From the wide range of torcs, wire components and fragments of gold/silver and bronze alloys and organic materials in the Snettisham collection, representative examples of most types were examined and analysed by a comprehensive range of scientific instrumentation to provide visual, analytical and technological evidence of the sophisticated metalworking traditions and practices, alloy compositions and surface enrichment processes used by the Iron Age metalsmiths.

Scientific instrumentation:

- Microscopy: Optical microscopy (OM) – three types: binocular, digital and inverted stage metallographic microscopy
- Scanning Electron Microscopy with Energy Dispersive X-ray microanalysis (SEM-EDX)
- X-radiography
- X-ray fluorescence analysis (XRF)

Microscopy

In order to fully characterise the range of objects and fragments from Snettisham, from the largest torcs to the smallest wire, complementary microscopy techniques were used, as well as macro-photography of the objects, therefore covering the full range of visualisation of the objects and their components and structures. A combination of optical microscopy techniques (OM) (with a range of magnifications - 6x to 200x), and analytical scanning electron microscopy imaging (SEM-EDX) across a wide magnification range -10x to 3000x for routine examination, and up to 20,000x for specialised examination - were used. OM and SEM imaging of samples provided microstructural information about the mechanical working and thermal treatment of the metal, while the elemental analysis allowed the investigation of surface treatments by identifying variation in compositions between core metal and surface.

Scale measurements on micrographs have the notation of '**µ**m' ('micrometre' sometimes referred to as 'micron'). 1000 µm = 1 mm (millimetre).

Optical microscopy (OM)

Conventional binocular optical microscopy was used extensively to examine the whole objects at low magnification to study the physical form of the torcs, their components, construction methods, tool marks, decoration and wear patterns as well as allowing comparison of their relative colours. The stereo vision that this gives is essential for fully understanding the objects' form and intricacies (Leica MZ stereo zoom binocular microscope, 6 – 60x magnification).

Digital optical microscopy

Digital optical microscopy is a variation of zoom optical microscopy but the object image is displayed on a high resolution screen. A new fully digital optical microscopy system was introduced to record images digitally and at very high resolution (maximum resolution 4800 x 3600 pixels). The instrument used was a Keyence digital microscope VHX-5000 with a VH-Z 20R lens, a range of magnification between 20 and 200x, an automated stage VHX-S 550E and LED reflected illumination). The digital optical microscope has no conventional eyepiece lenses for observing the objects in detail, but instead it has a high-resolution camera on the microscope body with its objective zoom lens and mounted on a stable platform with a motorised X-Y stage movement to accurately track across the object. The images are displayed on a high-resolution monitor. The digital system allows multiple users to examine the object at the same time.

Metallographic optical microscopy

For optical microscopy of polished resin mounted samples of wires etc. an inverted stage metallographic microscope with dark field illumination was used to examine the metallography of prepared polished samples (see p. 424). Dark field illumination is a combination of a low angle raking light and a specific type of lens system which highlights grain boundaries and displays regions of corrosion from burial in bright colours without specular light reflection. This allowed observation of the etched metal microstructures that retain evidence of the last mechanical and heating processes applied to the metal during fabrication, by highlighting the grain structure, size and deformation, and the compositional distribution within grains and dendrites (coring), showing the extent of working. Information about whether the metal is cast, mechanically worked (hammered), annealed and deformed after annealing is thereby revealed, giving the technological history of the object. Surface-enriched layers are seen in their different colours relative to the core metals. The instrument used was a Zeiss Axiovert 100 Inverted Microscope connected to a digital camera for image capture at magnification of 25x to above 1000x.

Scanning Electron Microscopy with energy dispersive X-ray microanalysis (SEM-EDX)

SEM examination was carried out in three different instruments. A high vacuum analytical SEM (JEOL JSM840), a large chamber Variable Pressure (VP) SEM (Hitachi S-3700N), and an ultra-high-resolution Field Emission SEM (Hitachi S-4800 FESEM). All were equipped with energy dispersive X-ray microanalysis (SEM-EDX): Oxford Instruments ISIS™ analyser on the former and Oxford Instruments NanoAnalysis INCA™ and AZtec™ analytical systems on the latter two. These were used for detailed study directly on the object surfaces and of polished cross-sections prepared from representative metal samples taken from damaged fragments. Imaging techniques used low energy secondary electron (SE) and high energy backscattered electron (BSE) detectors. The different detectors give complementary information about the surface topography and composition of the objects and samples respectively. SE imaging gives a more 'naturalistic' view similar to a black and white photograph of an object under idealised illumination. BSE images provide two types of information: first, a very clinical view of 3D object surfaces, due to the directionality of the electrons creating high contrast and shadowing; and second, very important chemical information. The latter is due to the different relative reflectivity of the focused electron beam from areas of different alloy compositions or other material phases within the polished sample surface. This creates different shades of grey, caused by the mean atomic number (mass) distribution within the sample material and is very effective in promoting microstructural observation of different alloy phases, as well as alloy diffusion and homogeneity. Therefore, as well as high contrast structural images that are essential when observing and interpreting the polished cross-sections of wires, they show the complex interaction zones and changes in composition at the surfaces of the wires that are key to understanding the manufacturing processes involved in surface enrichment.

SEM Variable Pressure operating conditions were typically 30 Pa pressure and 20 kV accelerating voltage. The sample stage for the Hitachi SEM allowed an area of 200mm diameter to be covered and was just large enough to accommodate large torcs, including The Great Torc. Working distances varied according to the types of images required, object sizes and heights, but for EDX analysis of polished cross-sections, the working distance was the standard 10mm.

Analysis of the elemental X-ray spectra, produced by the irradiation of the incident electron beam on the object or sample, is a fundamental technique for obtaining quantitative and qualitative compositional analyses and elemental distribution maps across polished samples. The EDX analytical conditions were 20 kV, a high-count rate of *c.* 10,000 counts per second (cps) at 30–35% dead time and acquisition time of 200 seconds. This gave the most efficient count rates and good counting statistics with consistent reproducibility. All elemental concentrations are given in weight percent (wt%). Precision and accuracy were assessed, and standardisation of this instrument carried out using a standard alloy of composition 50 wt% gold, 30 wt% silver and 20 wt% copper. The detection limits vary between elements and are determined by the physics of X-ray generation; they are typically 0.1–0.3 wt%. Measured standard errors of analysed elements (Au, Ag, Cu) of individual spectra are typically within +/- 0.18 wt% for major and minor elements in the alloys.

For the purpose of SEM-EDX microscopy and quantitative microanalysis, the polished samples were coated with a very thin layer of evaporated carbon to make the resin mounts conductive in the electron beam during observation in the SEM at high vacuum. VP mode was not used in the case of quantitative microanalysis, because the very low-pressure air used in this mode could cause a little scatter of the electron beam (skirting) around the targeted area of the sample and cause a small contribution from the surrounding area to be incorporated into the area being analysed.

Macro photography

Macro photography was also essential to record the physical structures, intricate designs and goldsmithing techniques and the condition of the metalwork prior to binocular microscopy examination and then high-resolution detailed study and analysis by SEM.

X-radiography

In 2017, the Department of Scientific Research at the British Museum acquired a high-power X-ray imaging installation (YXLON Access Y.100, equipped with a Y.TU450-D11 X-ray tube) that was used to investigate some of the larger hollow Snettisham and other torc terminals (see pp. 462–72). The high density of gold alloys and thickness of some terminals required the use of high energy X-rays to successfully penetrate the metal and obtain a clear image of the internal structure.

Two radiographic techniques were used to image the torcs: digital radiography (DR) and computed radiography (CR).

With DR, radiographs are recorded on a pixellated digital detector (in this case, a PerkinElmer XRD 1621 AN15 ES flat panel detector), giving images in real-time. A key advantage of DR is the ability to instantaneously see the effects of adjustments to the imaging parameters (e.g. X-ray tube voltage and current) on the image contrast, such that the maximum information can be extracted from particularly dense or thick objects. DR also provides the ability to quickly acquire a series of images of an object whilst it is rotated in sequential steps on a motorised turntable. This method allows the separation and identification of constructional and decorative features of the object, both external and internal which may otherwise be obscured or difficult to interpret in a single radiograph: for example, overlapping features at different object depths, including decoration at the front and back of the object, which may become foreshortened due to object orientation. In addition, these sequential images can also be run as a 'movie' that is a valuable aid to the interpretation of complex 3D objects.

With CR the radiograph is recorded on a plate (typically with a layer of photostimulable phosphor) which is subsequently digitised by scanning with laser light. Two archival X-radiographs recorded on film are also included in this chapter and are referred to as 'film X-radiographs'.

DR and CR were carried out on selected objects, notably the so-called 'Great Torc' (E.1a), and 'Grotesque Torc' (L.19). In addition, the torc from Sedgeford, Norfolk (1968,1004.1; 2005,1103.1), which is broadly contemporary with the items from Snettisham, was also examined using this technique as a useful comparison in terms of manufacturing technology. Radiography was conducted up to the maximum X-ray tube voltage of 450 kV and beam current of 1.55 mA, with a focal spot selection of 0.4mm. Images were integrated over 75 frames of 500 ms each (total exposure time of 37.5 seconds). The X-ray beam was pre-filtered with 3.3mm brass in order to remove the lower energy photons from the spectrum; low energy X-rays would not penetrate the torcs, but are likely to be scattered by them, affecting image quality. The Great Torc was mounted at an angle inside a foam mount for an optimum viewing orientation given its structure. The Sedgeford Torc and its detached terminal were mounted such that the terminals were upright.

X-ray fluorescence (XRF)

With the large number of objects in the Snettisham treasure, one of the first objectives was to identify the range of metal alloys in the collection and to focus on the more complete torcs. The preferred technique for such initial surveys is non-invasive analysis using X-ray fluorescence (XRF) in which a fine X-ray beam is directed at the surface of the metal to reflect back the signature spectrum of the elements, allowing identification of the surface metal alloys. The initial results obtained from these non-invasive analyses were useful although limited: a wide range of gold/silver/copper alloys and bronze were identified, but due to potential surface effects, such as deliberate treatment during manufacture and corrosion, surface analysis may not fully reflect the core metal. However, XRF pointed the way for sample selection for microscopy and SEM-EDX to fully characterise the alloys. XRF also identified the presence of mercury gilding on some fragmentary small bronze bracelets/torcs.

Chapter 18
Compositional Analysis of Objects from Snettisham Hoards A, B and C in the Collections of Norwich Castle Museum

Peter Northover

This chapter describes the metallurgy of the copper-based alloys at Snettisham and their metallurgical context in Late Iron Age Britain. The work presented here draws on a programme of analytical work carried out on Hoards A, B, C, and assorted stray finds from the 1960s and 70s which are held at Norwich Castle Museum. This work was begun in 1986–7, at the instigation of the then curator, Ms E.B. Green, with the aim of sampling every identifiable object but, not, of course, every single fragment. Approximately 165 samples from the collections of Norwich Castle Museum were examined by electron probe microanalysis and optical metallography by Ms E.C. Stone for her thesis for Part II of the degree of BA in Metallurgy and Science of Materials in the University of Oxford (Stone 1987). A summary of the methods used is given below; electron probe microanalysis of archaeological metalwork has been discussed in more detail elsewhere, especially in comparison with other methods of analysis (Northover and Rychner 1998).

This chapter focuses on copper alloys. The compositional analyses of the gold and silver alloy objects from Hoards A, B and C and stray finds S.16–18 and S.31 are shown in **Figures 18.1–3** and tabulated in Appendix 5, and a comparison of these alloys with those of Iron Age coins has also been published (Northover 1992). A short summary of the gold and silver alloys is given below, but in this volume the composition of precious metal objects is primarily discussed in Chapter 17.

Methods

Samples were either drilled or cut: complete pieces were generally drilled but where a fragment presented easy access for the saw a cut was made. For drilling, drill bits of 1mm diameter or less were used in a hand-held modelmaker's electric drill, while cut samples were taken with a jeweller's saw with 100 teeth/inch. The samples were hot-mounted in a copper-filled acrylic resin, ground and polished to a 1μm diamond finish.

Analysis was by electron probe microanalysis with wavelength dispersive spectrometry. Eleven elements were analysed over three 50μm squares on all samples, as listed in the tables. For the copper alloys arsenic was also quantified by three-point analyses on the bronze matrix remote from any possible lead inclusions, avoiding the well-known interference between the arsenic and lead X-ray spectra. As it transpired, almost all the bronze was unleaded. The data were combined to produce a composition in weight %, normalised to 100%. Where the metal was heavily corroded the uncorrected data are presented in italics with no concentration given for copper (**Table 18.1**).

After analysis the cut samples were examined with a metallographic microscope in both as-polished and etched states; the etch used was an acidified aqueous solution of ferric chloride, further diluted with ethanol.

Alloy definitions

In an assemblage which combines gold-, silver- and copper-based alloys with every evidence of recycling, alloy definitions can be rather fluid. To obtain a working definition of copper-based alloys, the compositions of all analysed objects from Hoards A, B and C were first sorted in

Cat. no.	Sample batch	Sample no.	Clarke hoard no.	Clarke inv. no.	Object type	Component tested	Sn	As	Sb	Pb	Co	Ni	Fe	Ag	Au	Zn	Bi	Cu
B.1d	SHMA	5	Hd. B No. 12	R1	Ring (small)		14.01	0.04	0.04	0.07	0.01	0.27	0.03	0.75	0.00	0.01	0.01	84.77
B.1d	SHMB	12	Hd. B No. 12	R1	Ring (small)		12.99	0.11	0.01	0.09	0.01	0.10	0.01	0.03	0.00	0.00	0.02	86.73
B.1d	SHMB	70	Hd. B No. 12	R6	Ring (small)		9.14	0.01	0.01	0.04	0.02	0.21	0.15	0.03	0.00	0.00	0.00	90.40
B.15, B.17	SHMB	P	Hd. B No. 24	LT20	Torc/bracelet (multi-strand, ?loop terminal)		14.88	0.09	0.05	0.07	0.02	0.27	0.02	0.01	0.01	0.01	0.02	84.55
B.16	SHMB	U	Hd. B No. 25	LT21	Wire/?torc/?bracelet		*17.61*	*0.00*	*0.04*	*0.30*	*0.04*	*0.07*	*0.07*	*0.24*	*0.05*	*0.06*	*0.00*	
B.28	SHMB	47	Hd. B No. 8	M1	Miscellaneous (staple/clamp)		14.13	0.32	0.31	1.03	0.08	0.13	0.11	0.06	0.00	0.01	0.03	83.79
C.22, C.26	SHMB	V	Hd. C No. 17	BT1	Torc/bracelet (multi-strand, buffer terminal)	Wire	12.60		0.01	0.04	0.01	0.10	0.01	0.01	0.00	0.01	0.01	87.23
C.23–4, C.28–30	SHMB	20	Hd. C No. 19	LT22	Torc/bracelet (multi-strand)		12.98	0.23	0.19	0.31	0.01	0.18	0.01	0.14	0.00	0.02	0.00	85.93
C.23–4, C.28–30	SHMA	8	Hd. C No. 19	LT22	Torc/bracelet (multi-strand)		11.18	0.21	0.04	0.07	0.18	0.07	0.17	0.01	0.01	0.00	0.02	88.05
C.25	SHMB	7	Hd. C No. 18	BT2	Torc/bracelet (multi-strand, buffer terminal)	Wire	9.26	0.10	0.94	0.18	0.01	0.11	0.01	0.09	0.00	0.00	0.03	89.27
C.27, C.31	SHMB	16	Hd. C No. 20	BT3	Torc/bracelet (multi-strand, buffer terminal)	Wire	13.19	0.11	0.68	0.05	0.00	0.35	0.08	0.03	0.03	0.00	0.01	85.47
C.27, C.31	SHMB	79	Hd. C No. 20	BT3	Torc/bracelet (multi-strand, buffer terminal)	Terminal	12.99	0.15	0.18	0.28	0.01	0.17	0.01	0.04	0.01	0.03	0.02	86.11
C.49	SHMB	68	Hd. C No. 5	R3	Ring (small)		10.32	0.22	0.13	0.71	0.02	0.08	0.03	0.28	0.02	0.01	0.00	88.18
C.49	SHMB	69	Hd. C No. 5	R3	Ring (small)		9.22	0.19	0.20	0.53	0.05	0.07	0.08	0.04	0.00	0.00	0.04	89.58
C.54	SHMA	9	Hd. C No. 7	SB2	Sheet (binding strip/fitting)		10.94	0.29	0.11	0.14	0.09	0.05	0.07	0.04	0.00	0.01	0.02	88.25
B/C.9	SHMB	84	Hd. B/C No. 39	LT33	Torc (multi-strand, loop terminal)		10.89	0.31	0.09	0.26	0.16	0.06	0.09	0.50	0.01	0.00	0.01	87.62
B/C.10	SHMB	81	Hd. B/C No. 37	LT31	Torc (multi-strand, loop terminal)		10.43	0.38	0.24	0.46	0.05	0.10	0.11	0.11	0.03	0.00	0.06	88.03
B/C.11	SHMB	82	Hd. B/C No. 38	LT32	Torc (multi-strand, loop terminal)		11.33	0.28	0.21	0.25	0.05	0.11	0.14	0.00	0.04	0.01	0.02	87.56
B/C.12	SHMB	83	Hd. B/C No. 36	LT30	Bracelet (multi-strand, loop terminal)		10.39	0.46	0.08	0.39	0.06	0.09	0.03	0.13	0.01	0.00	0.00	88.36
B/C.13	SHMB	30	Hd. B/C No. 47	LT41	Torc/bracelet (multi-strand, loop terminal)		10.94	0.24	0.10	0.41	0.06	0.07	1.55	0.04	0.00	0.00	0.03	86.97
B/C.14	SHMA	22	Hd. B/C No. 51	LT45	Torc/bracelet (multi-strand, loop terminal)		11.46	0.45	0.29	0.09	0.04	0.11	0.04	0.08	0.08	0.01	0.03	87.33
B/C.15	SHMB	W	Hd. B/C No. 54	LT48	Torc/bracelet (multi-strand, loop terminal)		13.53		0.12	0.62	0.04	0.05	0.06	0.03	0.00	0.00	0.01	85.55

Table 18.1 Analysis of copper alloy objects from Snettisham Hoards B and C

In the table the sample numbers have two components: 'Batch' (SHMA and SHMB), which groups the samples taken in a given museum visit, and 'No.' is the number within a batch. The Clarke (1954) hoard numbers and inventory numbers are both given, as well as the catalogue numbers from this volume. Due to the complexities of cross-referencing with Clarke's system (see Concordance, Appendix 3a), it has not always been possible to create a one-to-one concordance with the catalogue numbers used in this volume, and thus sometimes a range is given. Two objects were highly corroded; their compositions are given in italics with copper omitted; a blank in the column for arsenic means that the analysis was not made.

Cat. no.	Sample batch	Sample no.	Clarke hoard no.	Clarke inv. no.	Object type	Component tested	Sn	As	Sb	Pb	Co	Ni	Fe	Ag	Au	Zn	Bi	Cu
B/C.16	SHMB	51	Hd. B/C No. 44	LT38	Torc/bracelet (multi-strand, loop terminal)		12.87	0.04	0.05	0.09	0.00	0.27	0.02	0.07	0.00	0.03	0.00	86.56
B/C.17–8, B/C.21–2, B/C.26–34, B/C.38–40	SHMB	28	Hd. B/C No. 46	LT40	Torc/bracelet (multi-strand, loop terminal)		7.86	0.12	1.44	0.11	0.01	0.43	0.18	0.05	0.02	0.00	0.00	89.78
B/C.17–8, B/C.21–2, B/C.26–34, B/C.38–40	SHMB	49	Hd. B/C No. 46	LT40	Torc/bracelet (multi-strand, loop terminal)		12.19	0.28	0.11	0.91	0.12	0.07	0.24	0.17	0.05	0.00	0.02	85.84
B/C.17–8, B/C.21–2, B/C.26–34, B/C.38–40	SHMB	58	Hd. B/C No. 46	LT40	Torc/bracelet (multi-strand, loop terminal)		12.80	0.08	0.07	0.20	0..01	0.25	0.07	0.18	0.04	0.00	0.00	86.32
B/C.17–8, B/C.21–2, B/C.26–34, B/C.38–40	SHMB	54	Hd. B/C No. 46	LT40	Torc/bracelet (multi-strand, loop terminal)		11.58	0.30	0.06	1.54	0.07	0.06	0.01	0.50	0.00	0.03	0.00	85.85
B/C.17–8, B/C.21–2, B/C.26–34, B/C.38–40	SHMB	55	Hd. B/C No. 46	LT40	Torc/bracelet (multi-strand, loop terminal)		12.83	0.19	0.04	0.30	0.02	0.06	0.03	0.33	0.00	0.01	0.00	86.19
B/C.17–8, B/C.21–2, B/C.26–34, B/C.38–40	SHMB	53	Hd. B/C No. 46	LT40	Torc/bracelet (multi-strand, loop terminal)		11.79	0.15	0.03	0.22	0.04	0.06	0.09	0.65	0.18	0.04	0.05	86.70
B/C.17–8, B/C.21–2, B/C.26–34, B/C.38–40	SHMA	1	Hd. B/C No. 46	LT40	Torc/bracelet (multi-strand, loop terminal)		11.52	0.11	0.59	0.03	0.01	0.30	0.07	0.02	0.00	0.00	0.04	87.31
B/C.17–8, B/C.21–2, B/C.26–34, B/C.38–40	SHMA	2	Hd. B/C No. 46	LT40	Torc/bracelet (multi-strand, loop terminal)		11.67	0.11	0.61	0.03	0.01	0.29	0.06	0.04	0.01	0.00	0.03	87.15
B/C.19	SHMB	27	Hd. B/C No. 41	LT35	Torc/bracelet (multi-strand, loop terminal)		11.72	0.23	0.05	0.31	0.02	0.05	0.01	0.26	0.02	0.01	0.00	87.32
B/C.20	SHMB	50	Hd. B/C No. 45	LT39	Torc/bracelet (multi-strand, loop terminal)		13.10	0.03	0.05	0.06	0.00	0.25	0.04	0.02	0.19	0.00	0.00	86.26
B/C.24	SHMB	35	Hd. B/C No. 49	LT43	Torc/bracelet (multi-strand, loop terminal)		11.38	0.43	0.10	0.67	0.06	0.07	0.07	0.10	0.00	0.00	0.01	87.11
B/C.24	SHMB	37	Hd. B/C No. 49	LT43	Torc/bracelet (multi-strand, loop terminal)		12.63	0.58	0.12	0.48	0.07	0.08	0.08	0.08	0.00	0.02	0.02	86.39
B/C.24	SHMB	34	Hd. B/C No. 49	LT43	Torc/bracelet (multi-strand, loop terminal)		12.33	0.27	0.09	0.42	0.01	0.05	0.06	0.03	0.02	0.00	0.00	86.72
B/C.25	SHMB	X	Hd. B/C No. 43	LT37	Torc/bracelet (multi-strand, loop terminal)		13.11		0.11	0.32	0.11	0.05	0.17	0.15	0.04	0.00	0.08	85.86

Table 18.1 continued

Cat. no.	Sample batch	Sample no.	Clarke hoard no.	Clarke inv. no.	Object type	Component tested	Sn	As	Sb	Pb	Co	Ni	Fe	Ag	Au	Zn	Bi	Cu
B/C.35	SHMB	38	Hd. B/C No. 48	LT42	Torc/bracelet (multi-strand, loop terminal)		11.55	0.45	0.29	0.09	0.04	0.11	0.07	0.02	0.02	0.00	0.00	87.36
B/C.36	SHMB	29	Hd. B/C No. 52	LT46	Torc/bracelet (multi-strand, loop terminal)		9.20	0.39	0.24	0.19	0.04	0.11	0.07	0.02	0.00	0.00	0.00	89.74
B/C.37	SHMB	52	Hd. B/C No. 40	LT34	Torc/bracelet (multi-strand, loop terminal)		10.36	0.24	0.02	0.47	0.08	0.09	0.06	0.13	0.03	0.00	0.00	88.52
B/C.41	SHMB	Y	Hd. B/C No. 35	LT29	Wire/?torc/?bracelet		12.29		0.55	0.08	0.01	0.30	0.00	0.09	0.04	0.02	0.01	86.62
B/C.41	SHMB	Z	Hd. B/C No. 35	LT29	Wire/?torc/?bracelet		12.37		0.55	0.07	0.01	0.33	0.01	0.07	0.00	0.00	0.02	86.58
B/C.42–5	SHMB	32	Hd. B/C No. 32	LT26	Torc/bracelet (multi-strand)		12.31	0.22	0.13	0.58	0.07	0.09	0.32	0.05	0.00	0.00	0.00	86.23
B/C.42–5	SHMB	19	Hd. B/C No. 32	LT26	Torc/bracelet (multi-strand)		12.04	0.31	0.13	0.47	0.10	0.07	0.19	0.03	0.00	0.00	0.00	86.66
B/C.47–8	SHMB	11	Hd. B/C No. 29	LT23	Small Torc (multi-strand)		10.26	0.04	0.19	0.11	0.01	0.35	0.01	0.01	0.00	0.00	0.02	89.00
B/C.47–8	SHMB	3	Hd. B/C No. 29	LT23	Small Torc (multi-strand)		10.57	0.31	0.18	0.21	0.01	0.35	0.01	0.02	0.00	0.00	0.01	88.34
B/C.49, B/C.51–3, B/C.56, B/C.60–2	SHMA	10	Hd. B/C No. 31	LT25	Torc/bracelet (multi-strand, ?loop terminal)		11.99	0.07	0.66	0.00	0.00	0.35	0.09	0.02	0.01	0.01	0.02	86.79
B/C.49, B/C.51–3, B/C.56, B/C.60–2	SHMA	15	Hd. B/C No. 31	LT25	Torc/bracelet (multi-strand, ?loop terminal)		11.32	0.40	0.14	0.31	0.09	0.09	0.21	0.02	0.00	0.00	0.00	87.42
B/C.50	SHMB	15	Hd. B/C No. 30	LT24	Torc/bracelet (multi-strand, loop terminal)		12.03	0.06	0.61	0.03	0.01	0.29	0.03	0.03	0.01	0.01	0.01	86.88
B/C.54–5	SHMB	13	Hd. B/C No. 33	LT27	Torc/bracelet (multi-strand, loop terminal)		11.17	0.04	0.30	0.82	0.01	0.10	0.12	0.06	0.00	0.01	0.01	87.37
B/C. 57–9	SHMB	1	Hd. B/C No. 34	LT28	Torc/bracelet (multi-strand)		12.02	0.11	0.02	0.16	0.19	0.06	0.18	0.03	0.04	0.02	0.03	87.14
B/C.65	SHMB	73	Hd. B/C No. 1	RL2	Ring (large)		8.95	0.16	0.18	0.19	0.02	0.15	0.04	0.06	0.04	0.00	0.01	90.20
B/C.66	SHMA	26	Hd. B/C No. 3	RL4	Ring (large)		9.81	0.28	0.08	1.00	0.07	0.07	0.14	0.14	0.01	0.03	0.03	88.35
B/C.66	SHMB	71	Hd. B/C No. 3	RL4	Ring (large)		10.16	0.23	0.08	0.32	0.07	0.06	0.07	0.17	0.00	0.00	0.04	88.80
B/C.67	SHMB	74	Hd. B/C No. 2	RL3	Ring (large)		9.57	0.16	0.20	0.16	0.00	0.14	0.05	0.08	0.01	0.01	0.02	89.60
B/C.68	SHMB	75	Hd. B/C No. 4	RL5	Ring (large)		9.63	0.26	0.10	0.40	0.09	0.05	0.03	0.89	0.03	0.00	0.00	88.52
B/C.69	SHMB	72	Hd. B/C No. 5	RL6	Ring (large)		12.67	0.16	0.21	0.16	0.03	0.16	0.04	0.12	0.00	0.00	0.01	86.44
B/C.70	SHMB	67	Hd. B/C No. 8	RL9	Ring (large)		13.19	0.03	0.05	0.02	0.01	0.26	0.06	0.54	0.02	0.01	0.02	85.80

Table 18.1 continued

Cat. no.	Sample batch	Sample no.	Clarke hoard no.	Clarke inv. no.	Object type	Component tested	Sn	As	Sb	Pb	Co	Ni	Fe	Ag	Au	Zn	Bi	Cu
B/C.71	SHMB	59	Hd. B/C No. 6	RL7	Ring (large)		10.69	0.19	0.21	0.20	0.01	0.16	0.05	0.10	0.00	0.00	0.00	88.39
B/C.72	SHMB	D	Hd. B/C No. 7	RL8	Ring (large)		16.11	0.26	0.08	0.50	0.05	0.06	0.71	0.11	0.09	0.00	0.01	82.02
B/C.72	SHMA	4	Hd. B/C No. 7	RL8	Ring (large)		14.43	0.04	0.07	0.05	0.01	0.30	0.03	0.56	0.01	0.00	0.02	84.48
B/C.73–6	SHMB	64	Hd. B/C No. 9	RL10	Ring (large)		12.37	0.18	0.15	0.30	0.06	0.11	0.05	0.05	0.00	0.00	0.01	86.72
B/C.73–6	SHMA	25	Hd. B/C No. 9	RL10	Ring (large)		13.11	0.04	0.04	0.03	0.01	0.27	0.07	0.67	0.00	0.00	0.01	85.76
B/C.73–6	SHMB	31	Hd. B/C No. 9	RL10	Ring (large)		13.87	0.04	0.03	0.01	0.01	0.25	0.03	0.48	0.00	0.00	0.00	85.28
B/C.77	SHMB	78	Hd. B/C No. 11	R5	Ring (small)		9.83	0.20	0.06	2.59	0.06	0.04	0.01	0.45	0.05	0.01	0.00	86.70
B/C.79	SHMB	76	Hd. B/C No. 14	R8	Ring (small)		11.64	0.23	0.02	0.25	0.03	0.05	0.05	0.38	0.03	0.01	0.00	87.31
B/C.80	SHMB	65	Hd. B/C No. 16	R10	Ring (small)		8.89	0.15	0.11	0.45	0.03	0.07	0.01	0.04	0.03	0.00	0.00	90.22
B/C.81	SHMB	R	Hd. B/C No. 17	R13	Ring (small)		22.32		*0.11*	*1.42*	*0.05*	*0.06*	*0.22*	*0.01*	*0.00*	*0.00*	*0.03.*	
B/C.82	SHMB	80	Hd. B/C No. 13	R7	Ring (small)		11.88	0.36	0.14	1.02	0.11	0.06	0.07	0.04	0.00	0.00	0.01	86.31
B/C.83	SHMB	96	Hd. B/C No. 15	R9	Ring (small)		11.36	0.25	0.21	0.26	0.05	0.11	0.02	0.00	0.04	0.00	0.02	87.68
B/C.88	SHMB	44	Hd. B/C No. 22	SB4	Sheet (scale pan)		11.03	0.45	0.06	0.38	0.07	0.07	0.10	0.05	0.02	0.02	0.01	87.74
B/C.89	SHMA	6	Hd. B/C No. 23	SB1	Sheet (shield binding)		4.97	0.17	0.40	0.15	0.08	0.14	0.01	0.17	0.00	0.03	0.00	93.88
B/C.89	SHMA	14	Hd. B/C No. 23	SB1	Sheet (shield binding)		4.75	0.17	0.39	0.07	0.10	0.14	0.01	0.14	0.01	0.02	0.03	94.18
B/C.90	SHMB	41	Hd. B/C No. 25	M2	Sheet (fitting)		11.03	0.36	0.18	0.49	0.03	0.05	0.02	0.20	0.05	0.00	0.02	87.58
B/C.91–5	SHMA	12	Hd. B/C No. 24	SB7	Sheet		10.65	0.22	0.20	0.27	0.26	0.14	0.10	0.03	0.01	0.00	0.00	88.13
B/C.91–5	SHMA	13	Hd. B/C No. 24	SB7	Sheet		15.73	0.51	0.05	0.14	0.13	0.07	0.19	0.04	0.02	0.02	0.00	83.10
B/C.91–5	SHMB	39	Hd. B/C No. 24	SB7	Sheet		13.02	0.41	0.04	0.29	0.13	0.05	0.16	0.00	0.00	0.02	0.00	85.88
B/C.91–5	SHMB	45	Hd. B/C No. 24	SB7	Sheet		12.87	0.46	0.04	0.42	0.13	0.05	0.16	0.03	0.02	0.00	0.00	85.82
B/C.91–5	SHMB	33	Hd. B/C No. 24	SB7	Sheet		11.94	0.41	0.03	0.28	0.13	0.05	0.64	0.03	0.03	0.04	0.01	86.41
B/C.91–5	SHMA	3	Hd. B/C No. 24	SB7	Sheet		13.26	0.22	0.03	0.09	0.11	0.03	0.20	0.01	0.03	0.06	0.02	85.95
B/C.91–5	SHMB	40	Hd. B/C No. 24	M7	Sheet		12.81	0.40	0.09	0.42	0.13	0.06	0.15	0.01	0.00	0.00	0.00	85.93

Table 18.1 continued

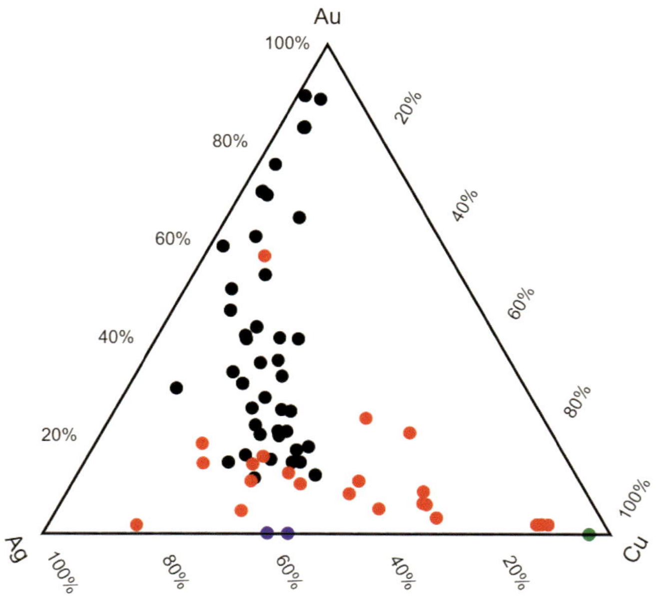

Figure 18.1 Alloy compositions of objects from Snettisham Hoards A, B and C containing more than impurity levels of gold or silver (see Appendix 5). Black indicates objects with over 1.78% gold and no tin, or only trace levels. These are ternary alloys of gold, silver and copper. Objects with over 1.78% gold and higher than trace levels of tin are shown in red. These are a mixture of a gold-silver-copper alloy and bronze. The two objects shown in blue are silver-copper alloys. The sample shown in green contained very little gold but 6.57% tin, suggesting bronze alloyed with a small percentage of a gold-silver-copper alloy (© Peter Northover)

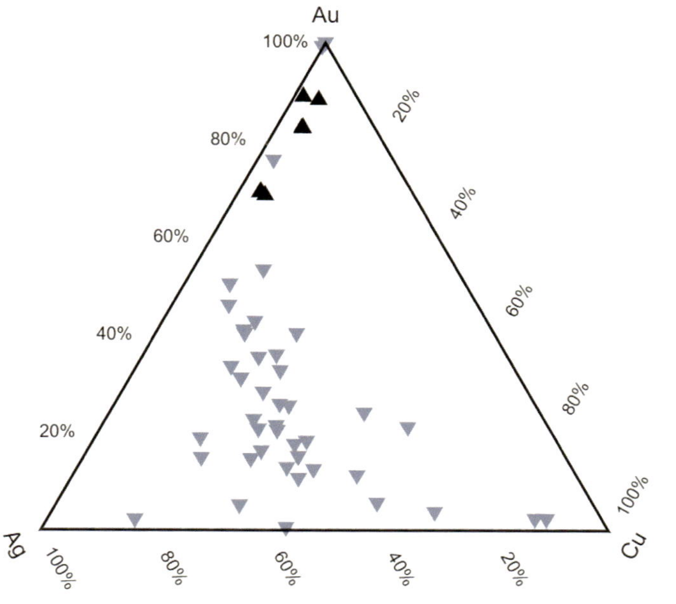

Figure 18.2 Alloy compositions of torcs from Snettisham Hoards A, B and C containing more than impurity levels of gold or silver (see Figure 18.1 and Appendix 5). Black triangles are samples from tubular torcs. Grey inverted triangles are samples from multi-strand torcs (© Peter Northover)

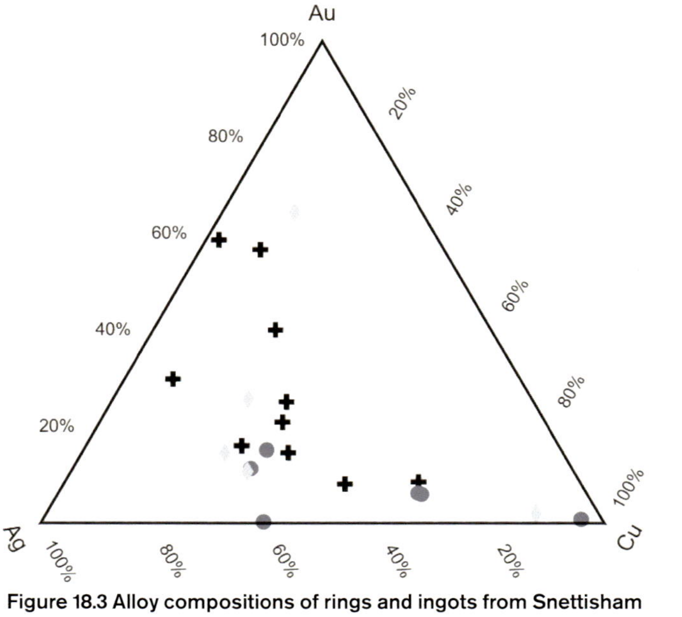

Figure 18.3 Alloy compositions of rings and ingots from Snettisham Hoards A, B and C containing more than impurity levels of gold or silver (see Fig. 18.1 and Appendix 5). Black crosses are samples from ingots. Grey circles are samples from large rings, and light-grey diamonds are samples from small rings (© Peter Northover)

descending order of gold content. An abrupt break at 1.78% gold was observed. Objects with below 1.78% gold were then sorted by silver content, which revealed two silver-copper alloys (large ring B.20 and torc S.18, shown in blue in **Fig. 18.1**, see Appendix 5) and one object (large ring C.46, shown in green in **Fig. 18.1**, see Appendix 5) made from bronze alloyed with a small percentage of a gold-silver-copper alloy, the mixed alloy containing 3.67% silver. The alloys containing levels of gold and silver above these limits are tabulated in Appendix 5, and summarised in **Figures 18.1–3**.

The remaining 82 compositions contained very little gold or silver, and can all realistically be described as copper-based alloys. They are listed in **Table 18.1**. A short summary of the precious metal alloys follows, whilst the remainder of this chapter focuses on the copper alloy objects. Two are so corroded that a valid analysis could not be made, and they are excluded from the following discussion: for these two the element concentrations are given in italics in **Table 18.1**.

Gold/silver alloy objects

The compositions of the gold and silver alloy objects are summarised in **Figures 18.1–3** with the data presented in Appendix 5. This includes the analysed objects from Hoards B and C, as well as a small number of torc stray finds from the 1960s–70s: S.16, S.17, S.18 and S.31. Most of the objects with at least 1.78% gold were ternary alloys of gold, silver, and copper, clustered in the whitish to yellow colour zones of the ternary diagram (Northover 1992, see black dots in **Fig. 18.1**, and Appendix 5). Other objects with over 1.78% gold, including all of those with the lowest gold levels, contain levels of tin sufficient to suggest that they are clearly a mixture of a gold-silver-copper alloy and bronze. From the 1987 analyses there are 26 samples from gold-silver-copper alloys where tin is detected at more than a low trace level contents (shown in red in **Fig. 18.1**, see Appendix 5); all but two have >10% silver, and tin contents vary from 0.2% to 6.9%. At one extreme, three examples (samples from B.7–8, B.9 and C.46) have 80% or more copper and could realistically be described as bronzes. These would probably have had the appearance, when wrought and polished, of medium to high-tin bronzes. At the other extreme is an alloy

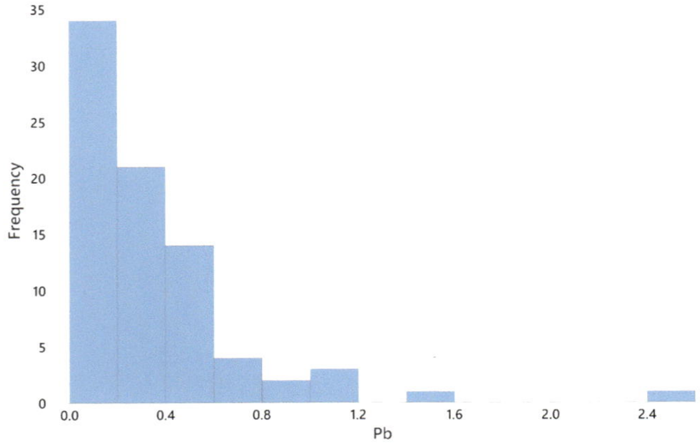

Figure 18.4 Histogram of lead (Pb) content for the copper alloy objects in Hoards A, B and C (see Table 18.1) (© Peter Northover)

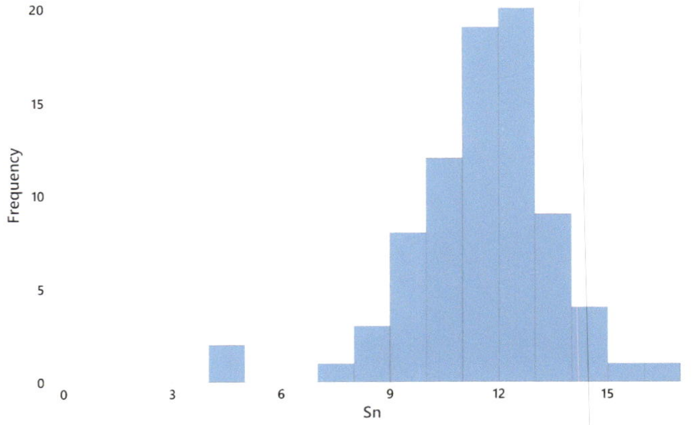

Figure 18.5 Histogram of tin (Sn) content in Hoards A, B and C (see Table 18.1) (© Peter Northover)

with 56.3% gold in which the proportions of copper (10.51%) and tin (0.73%) suggest that bronze rather than copper was used in making up the alloy (sample from B.26). The remaining alloys are very varied but the maximum gold content is 23.1% so that there would be limits to how much the surface could be manipulated to achieve a gold colour, while others would certainly have a silvery finish. Without experiment it is difficult to predict the original appearance of many of these objects.

Figures 18.2 and **18.3** show the same composition data as **Figure 18.1**, broken down by object type. **Figure 18.2** shows a small group of high-gold (over 65%), low-copper torcs, clustered in the top left of the ternary diagram. This group includes all the tubular torc samples and three multi-strand torcs. Most of the multi-strand torc samples were lower in gold, below 55%, including both ternary gold-silver-copper alloys and the lower-gold group of gold-silver-copper alloys mixed with bronze (shown in red in **Fig. 18.1**). Ingots and rings also showed a similarly broad range of alloy compositions (**Fig. 18.3**), with no clear grouping by object type, suggesting that similar alloys were used in precious metal ingots, rings, and multi-strand torcs, with only tubular torcs consistently showing a distinctive, high-gold composition.

Copper alloys

Within the ambit of copper-based alloys in the Late Iron Age there are four possibilities: copper, bronze, leaded bronze, and copper-zinc alloys. Inspection of **Table 18.1** shows that there is no unalloyed copper at Snettisham, and zinc is barely detected. In fact, the earliest copper-zinc alloy so far identified in England is in the Trinovantian coinage in approximately the last decade of the 1st century BC (Northover 1992). To identify possible instances of the use of leaded bronze, a histogram of lead contents was constructed (**Fig. 18.4**). There are only two lead contents above 1%, at 1.5% and 2.6%: these are both wrought products (small ring B/C.77 and a torc fragment from the group with Clarke ref. B/C46, which includes the following catalogue numbers in this volume: B/C.17–B/C.18, B/C.21–B/C.22, B/C.26–B/C.34, B/C.38–B/C.40) so the lead offers very little useful contribution to the properties of the bronze. It is most probable that some leaded bronze was included in a melt; such bronze could have been acquired either through trade, however indirect, with the Roman world, or through the accidental recovery of Late Bronze Age metalwork, something very possible in Norfolk. This is consistent with the results from Iron Age bronze so far analysed in England as a whole although these are mainly concentrated in a small number of major excavations such as Danebury (Northover 1984; 1987; 1991a; 1991b; 2004a; Barnes 2023).

For understanding the variety of tin contents a histogram was constructed (**Fig. 18.5**). This shows a near normal distribution of medium-tin bronzes with an observed mean of 11.5 ± 1.9% tin. There will be some bias to higher tin contents because of the effects of corrosion penetrating the samples; the true mean and standard deviation will be slightly smaller. There is also an outlier of two low-tin bronze compositions which in fact come from the same set of bindings from a hide-shaped shield (B/C.89); this is just an anomaly as other samples of sheet, for example from B/C.88 or B/C.91–5, fall in the centre of the main distribution.

The use of a bronze with 11–12% tin would serve the makers of bronze torcs very well because of its combination of strength, hardenability, wear resistance, and colour. Comparison with other sites such as Maiden Castle (Northover 1991a) and Danebury (1991b) shows the importance of this type of bronze by the 1st century BC, although in earlier phases of the Iron Age tin contents might be rather lower. Further, there appears to be no significant difference between wrought and cast products for the period during which it is proposed that most of the copper alloy objects from Snettisham were produced, in the final centuries BC.

Impurity patterns

As the metallurgical study of Iron Age bronze developed during the 1980s and 1990s (e.g. Northover 1991a; 1991b) an attempt was made to classify impurity patterns in the same way as had been done for the Bronze Age (Northover 1980). The Bronze Age classification itself could not be used because patterns were found which did not exist in the Bronze Age. The results were not completely satisfactory save for the definition of what is known as 'Group 1', which was characterised by Co>Ni and Sb<0.10%. It was felt that the use of the patterns in the present context would be too confusing, especially where there was a strong probability that much of the metal was recycled, and for clarity a

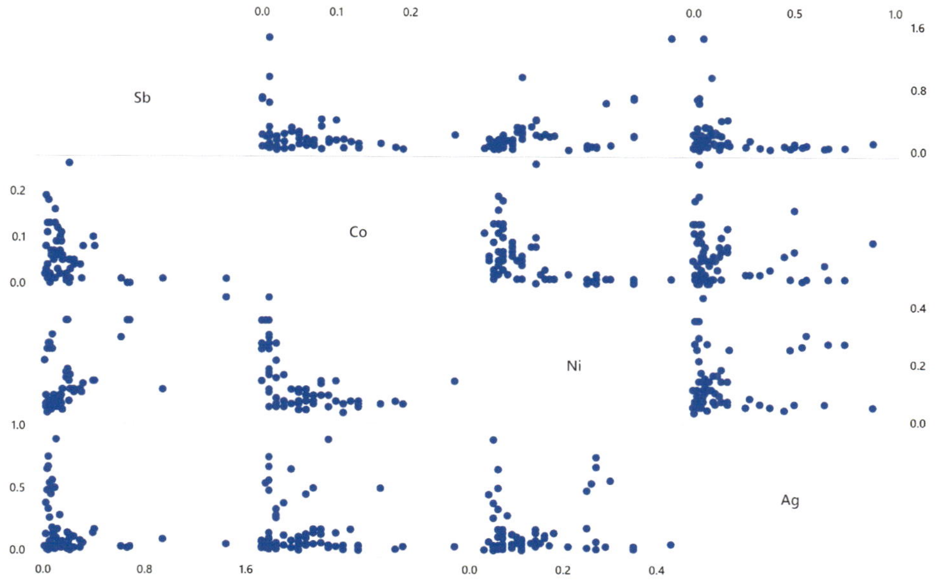

Figure 18.6 Matrix plot of antimony (Sb), cobalt (Co), nickel (Ni) and silver (Ag) in Hoards A, B and C (see Table 18.1) (© Peter Northover)

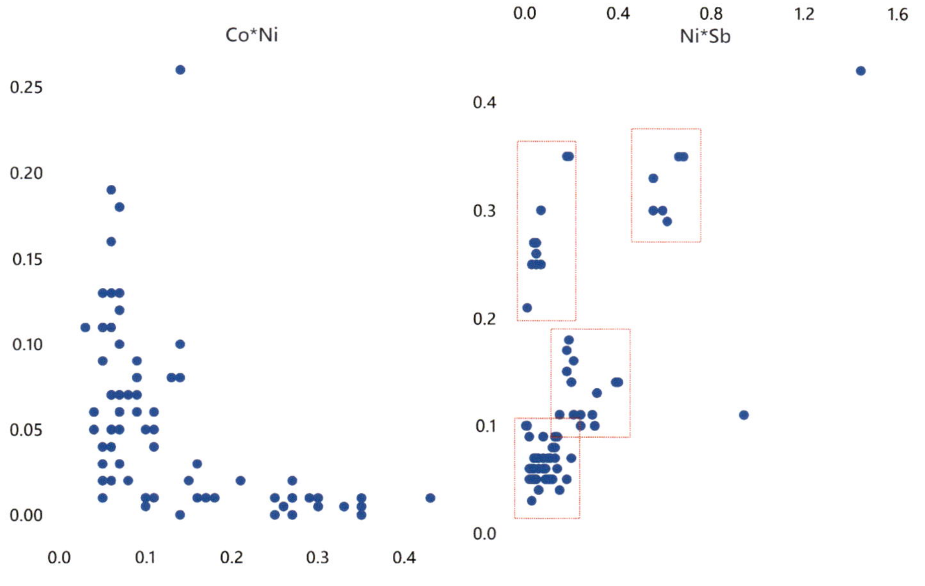

Figure 18.7 Scatterplots of cobalt vs. nickel, and nickel vs. antimony in Hoards A, B and C (see Table 18.1) (© Peter Northover)

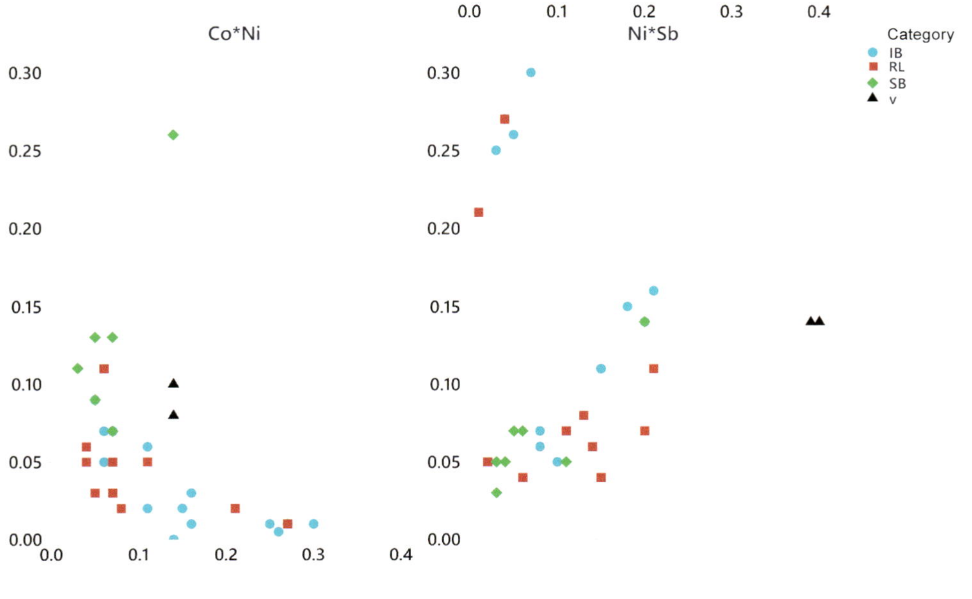

Figure 18.8 Scatterplots of cobalt vs. nickel, and nickel vs. antimony for copper alloy rings and sheet objects in Hoards A, B and C (see Table 18.2 for object type abbreviations) (© Peter Northover)

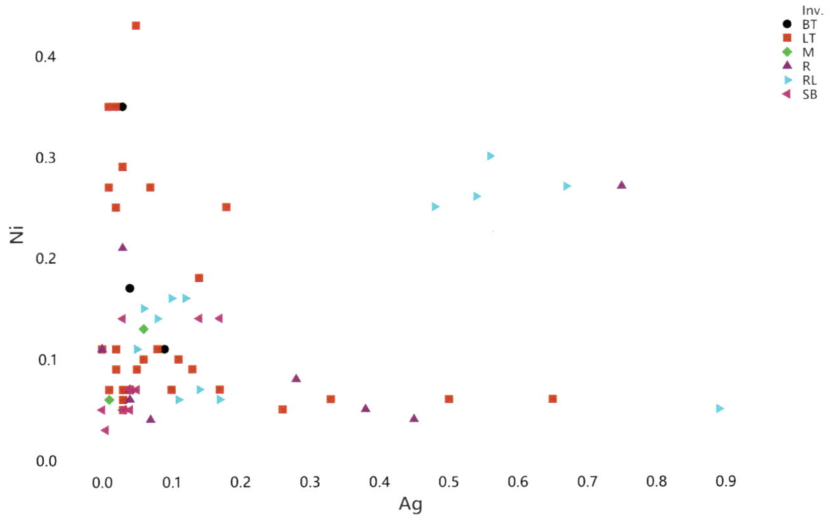

Figure 18.9 Scatterplot of nickel vs. silver for copper alloy objects in Hoards A, B and C (see Table 18.2 for object type abbreviations) (© Peter Northover)

graphical approach to identifying significant groupings amongst the Snettisham material was adopted.

As a first step a matrix plot was constructed for the four most diagnostic impurities: antimony, cobalt, nickel, and silver (**Fig. 18.6**). The plot is designed to give an overview of impurity patterns by presenting scatterplots of all possible element pairs of the selected impurities. Very visibly there is considerable diversity among the impurity patterns, and there are groupings where one element or another is important in some way, for example the Group 1 metal already mentioned with Co>Ni, and the higher cobalt contents are associated with low antimony. Another grouping has nickel strongly correlated with antimony, a feature which, on the basis of comparison with Late Bronze Age material, is of Alpine or Central European origin. Also worthy of note is a small cluster with relatively high silver and nickel.

The next step was to examine one or two element pairs at a larger scale and begin to make a better definition of possible groupings. The plots of cobalt against nickel and nickel against antimony in **Figure 18.7** demonstrate the influence of Group 1 metal with Co>Ni, and also a degree of separation into clusters based on nickel and antimony. There is a caveat to be made here in that some of the groups may contain multiple samples from the same object; inevitable given the fragmentary nature of many objects, the loop terminal and buffer terminal torcs in particular. Even so, it is clear that the bronze represented in the Snettisham hoards has a variety of ultimate origins but, with such small parcels of bronze, the results will be descriptive of the connections of individual craftspeople rather than providing a picture of the circulation of metal on a regional or even larger scale.

A first step in exploring these connections is to determine whether any of the impurity patterns correlate with specific object types. For the sake of clarity in this endeavour the torcs and other types are treated separately. **Figure 18.8** picks out from the data in **Figure 18.7** for just the rings and sheet bronze, with the V-shaped shield bindings identified separately. There is, plainly, a correlation between object type and impurity pattern. One cluster comprises sheet bronze pieces with Co>Ni and Sb<0.10%, i.e. Group 1. At both Maiden Castle and Danebury this bronze is very much associated with the working, reworking, or recycling of sheet and the copper was associated with an origin in the south-west of England. In the Snettisham collection this metal could have come to the area as scrap or have come from an object, be it a shield or a scabbard, dismantled locally. There are three outliers among the sheet samples: the two samples from the V-shaped shield binding and one other piece of sheet. These have what can be best described as an As/Sb/Co/Ni/Ag impurity pattern (Group 2), the antimony contents suggesting a continental origin for the copper. The best parallels so far, especially for the example with the high cobalt content of 0.26% (a sample from B/C.91–5), lie in Switzerland in the Late Bronze Age (Northover 2004b).

The rings are wrought products that can be regarded as either finished, for use as we see them, or semi-finished, a stage in the manufacture of another product. Overall, it is perhaps possible to see some differentiation in composition between the smaller and larger rings, but this may just be the effect of analysing a small sample from what was once a larger population. Overall, the rings fall into two clusters, one trending to higher nickel contents and low antimony, and the other with nickel and antimony correlated. While the latter group certainly reflects the incorporation of some continental metal, not surprising in Norfolk, the former certainly poses a puzzle in that in a small number of objects, the nickel is associated with a high silver content, as seen in **Figure 18.9**. This Ni/Ag pattern has only been observed at Snettisham and, in that context, it is quite possible that some silver metal or alloy has been incorporated in the alloy. This is certainly true of three objects with a sufficiently high silver content that they are included in Appendix 5, rather than in

Table 18.2 The object type codes used in Figures 18.8–11

Object type	Category code
Multi-strand torc (loop terminal)	LT
Multi-strand torc (buffer terminal)	BT
Ring (small)	R
Ring (large)	RL
Sheet or binding fragment	SB
V-shaped binding from hide-shaped shield	V
Miscellaneous	M

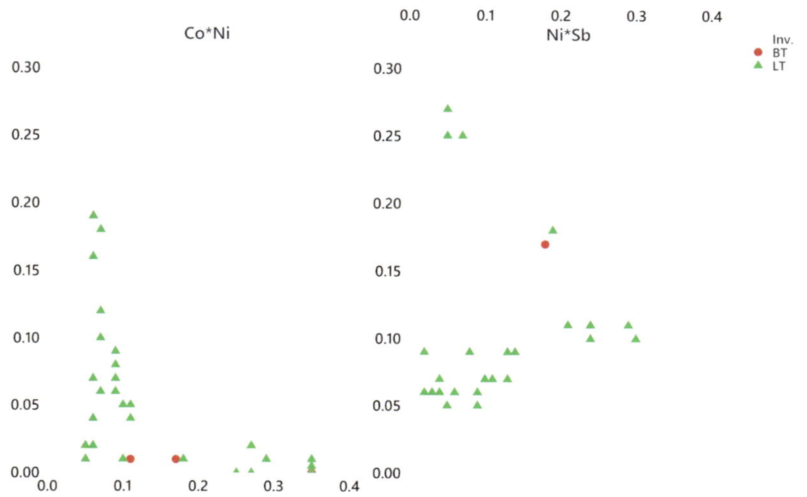

Figure 18.10 Scatterplots of cobalt vs. nickel, and nickel vs. antimony for loop terminal (LT) and buffer terminal (BT) torcs (© Peter Northover)

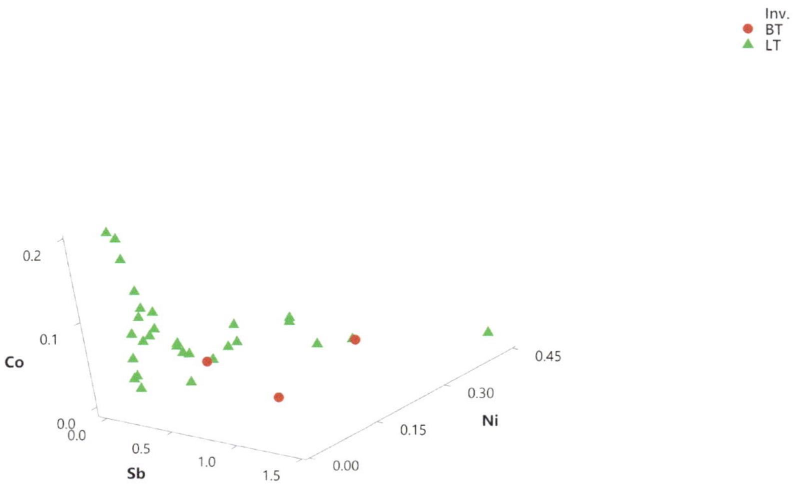

Figure 18.11 3D scatterplot of cobalt vs. nickel vs. antimony for loop terminal (LT) and buffer terminal (BT) torcs (© Peter Northover)

Table 18.1 among the copper alloys. These are large ring C.46 which contains 6.6% tin, 3.7% silver, and 0.8% gold, but has a more normal 0.11% nickel, and the two straight silver-copper alloys (large ring B.20 and torc S.18). Another series of increasing silver contents is associated with very low nickel contents mainly in loop terminal torcs, but there are no objects with nickel contents intermediate between these two groups. A general conclusion is that only certain bronze types were processed where silver was present, but it can also be argued that the Ni/Ag pattern is an addition to the diversity of copper sources represented at Snettisham.

The graphical treatment of the impurities in the rings and sheet is repeated for the bronze wire torcs in **Figure 18.10**. Because the axes have been truncated to match those in **Figure 18.8**, a 3D scatterplot of cobalt, nickel, and antimony is presented in **Figure 18.11** to show the full dataset, the excluded values being increased percentages of nickel, up to 0.43%, and antimony, up to 1.44%. These two elements are quite strongly correlated, a trait of bronze imported into East Anglia from the continent at various times in the later Bronze Age (Northover 1982; 1983), but not one associated with British ores. Overlaps between the distributions in **Figures 18.8** and **18.10** are only partial; for example, some high Co, low Ni and low Co Ni appearing in both, and the simplest explanation is that the metal in the bracelets and rings is the result of recycling and mixing the metal in the torcs, the broken fragments of wire making an ideal crucible charge.

The impurity patterns also offer some chronological clues when they are compared with the sequences from excavations such as Danebury and Maiden Castle. One of the main conclusions from these was that Group 1 metal was disappearing from circulation during the second half of the 1st century BC, if not a little earlier; it is absent from demonstrably later sites in eastern England such as ACS Stansted (Northover 2004a) and the Lexden tumulus (Northover unpublished). Therefore, any such metal at Snettisham is not going to be any later than mid-1st century BC. This chronological marker is also consistent with the absence of alloys with zinc and the almost complete absence of leaded bronze from the Snettisham assemblages.

Metallography

Many of the bronze samples were cut rather than drilled and so were available for metallography. The results were simple and rather uniform, with the wrought bronze typically having a recrystallised grain size of around 30μm, and almost all showed substantial cold work. In the case of the bracelets and rings this could be the stage at which they were left before further work while with the wire torcs the wire would have been annealed, cleaned, and polished, and then twisted, no further heat treatment then taking place. See Chapter 17 for more on manufacturing techniques.

Conclusion

This analysis has shown that the bronze at Snettisham, or at least the copper in it, had diverse origins, that with Co>Ni undoubtedly British, and that with nickel and antimony as characteristic impurities having a continental origin. Local recycling which produced products such as the rings could mix these two together. The form in which metal arrived in the workshops could be sheet or wire scrap, or finished objects which were then dismantled, or possibly just re-used. Bronze also contributed to some of the precious metal alloys, notably those that were silver-rich: as copper metal is not represented in the hoards, one can envisage ternary alloys such as those in the contemporary British and Gallic gold coinages being further debased with bronze and with silver-copper alloys. Impurity patterns support a date of manufacture for many of the bronze objects tested as no later than the first half of the 1st century BC.

Chapter 19
Seeing the Wood for the Trees: Evaluating the Woody Resources of Snettisham

Caroline Cartwright

Introduction

Scanning electron microscopy examination of four small coiled multi-strand wire copper alloy torcs from Snettisham in the BM and four examples from NCM (see **Table 19.1**) revealed that each had an organic core, around which the torc wires had been wound. Although these cores are now preserved in the form of charred wood, originally they were slender coppiced fresh wood wands from alder, hazel, dogwood, field maple, willow, hawthorn and elder trees, which were sufficiently flexible to provide the appropriate support for these torcs during the wire-coiling process.

In 2011, Cartwright undertook a series of charring experiments of coppiced alder wood, documenting the resultant anatomical changes as a case study for comparison with the alder cores of torcs F.166 and C.22, C.26. The principle behind such charring experiments rests in the fact that wood retains most of its anatomical characteristics when charred, but the charring temperature determines the appearance of the qualitative cellular features necessary for identification, with each species reacting differently (Gasson *et al.* 2017). These laboratory experiments on modern alder wood, coupled with anatomical comparisons with the alder cores of the torcs, suggest that the temperature at which charring occurred was around 360°C. The extent and nature of the charring is similar in both the terminals and body of all of the torcs examined (Cartwright *et al.* 2012). Importantly, this suggests that the coiled wire copper alloy torcs were substantially complete (with the terminals attached) before charring of the organic cores occurred. The heating appears regular and controlled, and thus a consequence of an intentional manufacturing process.

This work was published by Cartwright *et al.* (2012) in a paper that focused on characterising the organic cores through optical microscopy (OM) and scanning electron microscopy (SEM), and evaluating the technological advantages provided by the use of such material during manufacture. This chapter presents a summary of that research, and also explores the woody resources available at Snettisham, aiming to understand in more detail why specific trees were selected for torc core wood.

Identifying the organic cores of coiled wire copper alloy torcs through scanning electron microscopy

The first examination of the organic cores was carried out using a JEOL JSM840 scanning electron microscope (SEM) in high vacuum (HV) mode. Imaging of the composite objects comprising copper alloy and charred wood cores was achieved using a scintillator backscattered electron (BSE) detector (K.E. Centaurus®), offset from the electron beam axis to give topographic images that were uncompromised by charging effects. Selected areas were also documented by secondary electron (SE) imaging to show details of cell structures, carefully avoiding any areas with surface charging. Subsequent examination was undertaken using a variable pressure (VP) Hitachi S-3700N SEM for additional imaging of the torcs, for the examination of the uncoated experimentally charred alder specimens (Cartwright *et al.* 2012), and also for the charcoal fragments from the later enclosure ditch (see Chapter 9). VP SEM operating

Accession number	Description	Identification of wood
Snettisham F.168 (BM)	Coiled wire copper alloy torc neck-ring fragment, including terminal	*Acer campestre*, field maple
Snettisham F.167 (BM)	Coiled wire copper alloy torc neck-ring fragment	*Corylus avellana*, hazel
Snettisham F.166 (BM)	Coiled wire copper alloy torc neck-ring fragment	*Alnus glutinosa*, alder
Snettisham F.199 (BM)	Coiled copper alloy torc neck-ring fragment	*Cornus sanguinea*, dogwood
C.27 (NCM)	Coiled wire copper alloy torc terminal fragment	*Salix* sp., willow
C.31 (NCM)	Coiled wire copper alloy torc terminal fragment	*Sambucus nigra*, elder
C.22, C26 (NCM)	Coiled wire copper alloy torc neck-ring fragments, including terminals	*Alnus glutinosa*, alder
C.1–5 (NCM)	Coiled wire copper alloy torc neck-ring fragments	*Corylus avellana*, hazel

Table 19.1 Identification of woody taxa used in Snettisham copper alloy torcs with organic cores

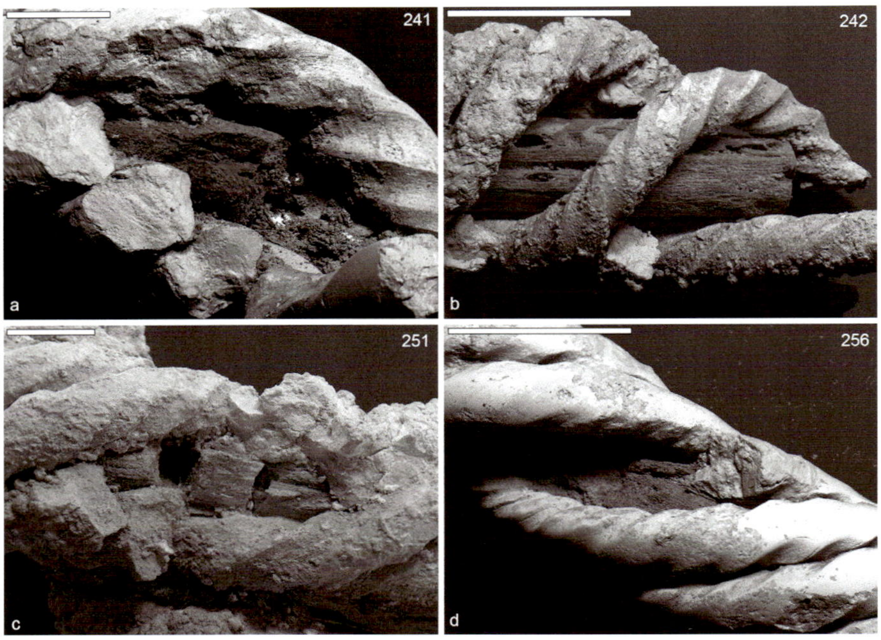

Figure 19.1a–d Four small coiled wire copper alloy torcs in the BM were examined in the scanning electron microscope where the charred wood cores were exposed at fractured ends or by corroded breaks in the metal: a) F.168 (scale bar 2mm); b) F.167 (scale bar 5mm); c) F.166 (scale bar 2mm); d) F.199 (scale bar 5mm)

conditions varied according to the specimen: 15kV or 20kV; working distance from 12.2mm to 21.4mm; magnifications from x70 to x1500 and a chamber pressure of 30Pa. The highly sensitive, five-segment BSE detector on the model of VP SEM used enabled detailed interrogation and imaging of the topography of the charred woods. The 3D mode, rather than Compositional, produced maximum surface topography information in most instances although Compositional was used (with 20kV) for the transverse section of the experimentally charred alder samples.

Figure 19.2 Optical microscope image of *Tilia* sp. lime bast (inner bark) fibres used as string bound round Snettisham torc G.16

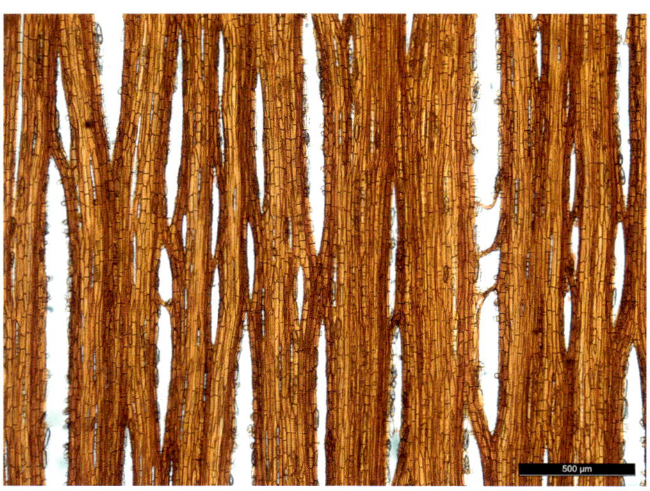

Standard techniques of wood identification and terminology determined by the International Association of Wood Anatomists (IAWA) were adopted in a modified form suitable for archaeological wood, in order to accommodate the effects of charring (Cartwright 2015). Standard protocol requires transverse, radial longitudinal and tangential longitudinal sections/surfaces (TS, RLS and TLS) to be available for species identification using the SEM through fine resolution and high magnification of crucial diagnostic features. However, because the charred wood cores of some of the torcs could only be examined in the SEM in locations where the charred wood cores were exposed at fractured ends or by corroded breaks in the metal (**Fig. 19.1a–d**), certain restrictions to standard identification procedures were present when not all of the three requisite sections (TS, RLS and TLS) were visible. Nonetheless, because of good cellular preservation, sufficient diagnostic features (as described in **Table 19.2**) could be distinguished in each case and secure identifications of the six woody taxa were achieved (**Table 19.1**).

Two of the BM charred wood cores (F.168 and F.167) were sampled for radiocarbon dating carried out as part of the 'Technologies of Enchantment' project (Garrow *et al.* 2009, see **Table 5.2**) thus permitting access to TS, RLS and TLS.

Key diagnostic features	*Acer campestre*, field maple	*Alnus glutinosa*, alder	*Cornus sanguinea*, dogwood	*Corylus avellana*, hazel	*Salix* sp., willow	*Sambucus nigra*, elder
growth ring boundaries	distinct; a few rows of radially-flattened fibres occur at growth ring boundaries	distinct; growth ring boundaries undulate near aggregate rays	sometimes distinct; growth ring boundaries may undulate	distinct; growth ring boundaries may undulate	distinct	usually distinct because of a clear difference in size of earlywood and latewood vessels or of marginal bands of thin-walled vascular tracheids in latewood
diffuse-porous / ring-porous / semi ring-porous	diffuse-porous	diffuse-porous to semi ring-porous	diffuse-porous to semi ring-porous	semi ring-porous to diffuse-porous	semi ring-porous to diffuse-porous	semi ring-porous to diffuse-porous
vessel arrange-ment	widely spaced, solitary, often in short (2 to 4) radial multiples	radial multiples of 4 or more vessels common; clusters in earlywood	generally solitary; mostly similar in size; relatively widely distributed across growth ring	in diagonal (dendritic) and/or radial arrangement, in multiples, radial rows or clusters	solitary or in short radial files with 2 to 3 vessels, occasionally in clusters	thin-walled vessels grouped in oblique / radial / tangential bands or clusters; sometimes dendritic
vessel shape (other than round or oval)		angular solitary vessel outline				angular solitary vessel outline
perforation plates	simple	scalariform	scalariform	Scalariform	simple	simple and scalariform
intervessel pit arrangement	alternate	opposite or alternate	scalariform or opposite	alternate; shape of pits polygonal	alternate; shape of pits polygonal	alternate; shape of pits polygonal
vessel-ray pits	with distinct borders, similar to intervessel pits	with distinct borders, similar to intervessel pits	with distinct borders, similar to intervessel pits	with distinct borders, similar to intervessel pits	large, rounded or angular pits with much reduced borders or apparently simple	with much reduced borders to apparently simple: pits rounded or angular
helical (spiral) thickenings in vessels	present			present		
tyloses in vessels					occasional thin-walled tyloses present	occasional thin-walled tyloses present
fibres	non-septate; thin- to thick-walled	non-septate; thin-walled; fibre-tracheids rare	non-septate; thin- to thick-walled	non-septate; thin- to thick-walled	non-septate; fibres very thin-walled but also some that are thin- to thick-walled	septate and non-septate; thin- to thick-walled;
fibre pitting		with simple to minutely bordered pits or distinctly bordered	with distinctly bordered pits; common in both radial and tangential walls	simple to minutely bordered pits or distinctly bordered; mainly restricted to radial walls	simple to minute-ly bordered pits	simple to minutely bordered pits
axial parenchyma	absent or extremely rare apotracheal diffuse or marginal; scanty paratracheal;	apotracheal axial parenchyma diffuse, or diffuse-in-aggre-gates	apotracheal axial parenchyma diffuse; scanty paratracheal parenchyma	diffuse apotracheal axial parenchyma	sparse apotracheal parenchyma, occasionally terminal / marginal parenchyma in discontinuous uniseriate bands	axial parenchyma absent or extremely rare; scanty paratracheal, diffuse or in marginal bands
rays	mostly 2–4 seriate; homocellular; all ray cells procumbent	exclusively uniseriate; homocellular; all ray cells procumbent	heterocellular; multiseriate rays; mostly 3–5 cells wide; larger rays commonly 4–10 seriate; with 1 to over 4 rows of upright / square marginal cells	1–3 cells wide; heterocellular rays; square and upright cells restricted to marginal rows	uniseriate; heterocellular with square and upright marginal cells	heterocellular; larger rays commonly 4–10 seriate, mostly with 1–4 rows of square and upright marginal cells
sheath cells			present			Present
aggregate rays		present, with bi- to triseriate rays common		present		
calcium oxalate crystals	prismatic crystals in chambered axial parenchyma cells	not observed	not observed	Present	not observed	not observed

Table 19.2 Key anatomical features of the six woody taxa identified in the organic cores of some Snettisham coiled wire torcs

Taxon	Notes
***Acer campestre*, field maple**	**Organic torc core wood.** Makes good charcoal
Acer pseudoplatanus, sycamore	Not a native species; introduced from Central Europe, possibly in Roman period
Aesculus hippocastanum, horse chestnut	Not a native species; introduced from south-east Europe in late 16th century
***Alnus glutinosa*, alder**	**Organic torc core wood; charcoal in Hoard M ingots.** Makes excellent charcoal
Betula pendula, silver birch	Makes high-quality charcoal
Betula pubescens, downy birch	Makes high-quality charcoal
Calluna vulgaris, heather	Can be used for charcoal
Carpinus betulus, hornbeam	Makes exceptionally good charcoal. Hornbeam charcoal present in enclosure ditch
Castanea sativa, sweet chestnut	Charcoal provided good fuel for iron smelting. Chestnut charcoal present in enclosure ditch
***Cornus sanguinea*, dogwood**	**Organic torc core wood.** Makes good charcoal
***Corylus avellana*, hazel**	**Organic torc core wood.** Makes good charcoal. Hazel charcoal present in enclosure ditch
Crataegus monogyna, hawthorn	Makes good charcoal
Euonymus europaeus, spindle	Makes high-quality charcoal
Fagus sylvatica, beech	Makes good charcoal
Frangula alnus, alder buckthorn	Makes high-quality charcoal
Fraxinus excelsior, ash	Makes good charcoal
Hedera helix, ivy	Found as charcoal through secondary usage/burning
Hippophae rhamnoides, sea buckthorn	Can be used for charcoal
Ilex aquifolium, holly	Found as charcoal through secondary usage/burning
Ligustrum vulgare, wild privet	Can be used for charcoal
Lonicera spp., honeysuckle	Found as charcoal through secondary usage/burning
Malus sylvestris, crab apple	Can be used for charcoal
Pinus sylvestris, Scot's pine	Native species, but plantation created to west of site. Can be used for charcoal
Populus alba, white poplar	Not a native species; introduced and planted
Populus nigra, black poplar	Can be used for charcoal
Populus tremula, aspen	Makes good charcoal
Prunus avium, wild cherry	Can be used for charcoal
Prunus padus, bird cherry	Can be used for charcoal
Prunus spinosa, blackthorn	Makes good charcoal
Quercus ilex, holm oak	Makes good charcoal
Quercus robur, pedunculate oak	Makes good charcoal
Rubus fruticosus, bramble	Found as charcoal through secondary usage/burning
Salix alba, white willow	Makes good charcoal
***Salix* sp., willow**	**Organic torc core wood.** Makes good charcoal. Willow charcoal present in enclosure ditch
***Sambucus nigra*, elder**	**Organic torc core wood**
Sorbus aucuparia, rowan	Can be used for charcoal
Taxus baccata, yew	Can be used for charcoal
Tilia cordata, small-leaved lime	Makes good charcoal
Tilia platyphyllos, large-leaved lime	Makes good charcoal
Tilia sp., lime	Makes good charcoal. Lime charcoal present in enclosure ditch
***Tilia* sp., lime**	**String used to wrap around torcs**
Ulex europaeus, gorse	Makes good charcoal, giving off much heat
Ulmus glabra, wych elm	Can be used for charcoal
Ulmus minor, elm	Can be used for charcoal
Viburnum opulus, guelder-rose	Found as charcoal through secondary usage/burning

Table 19.3 Selected woody taxa recorded in and around Snettisham in 1990
Bold: species found in association with torc manufacture and repair or Hoard M ingots
Underlined: species present in Late Roman charcoal deposits in the enclosure ditch (see Chapter 9)

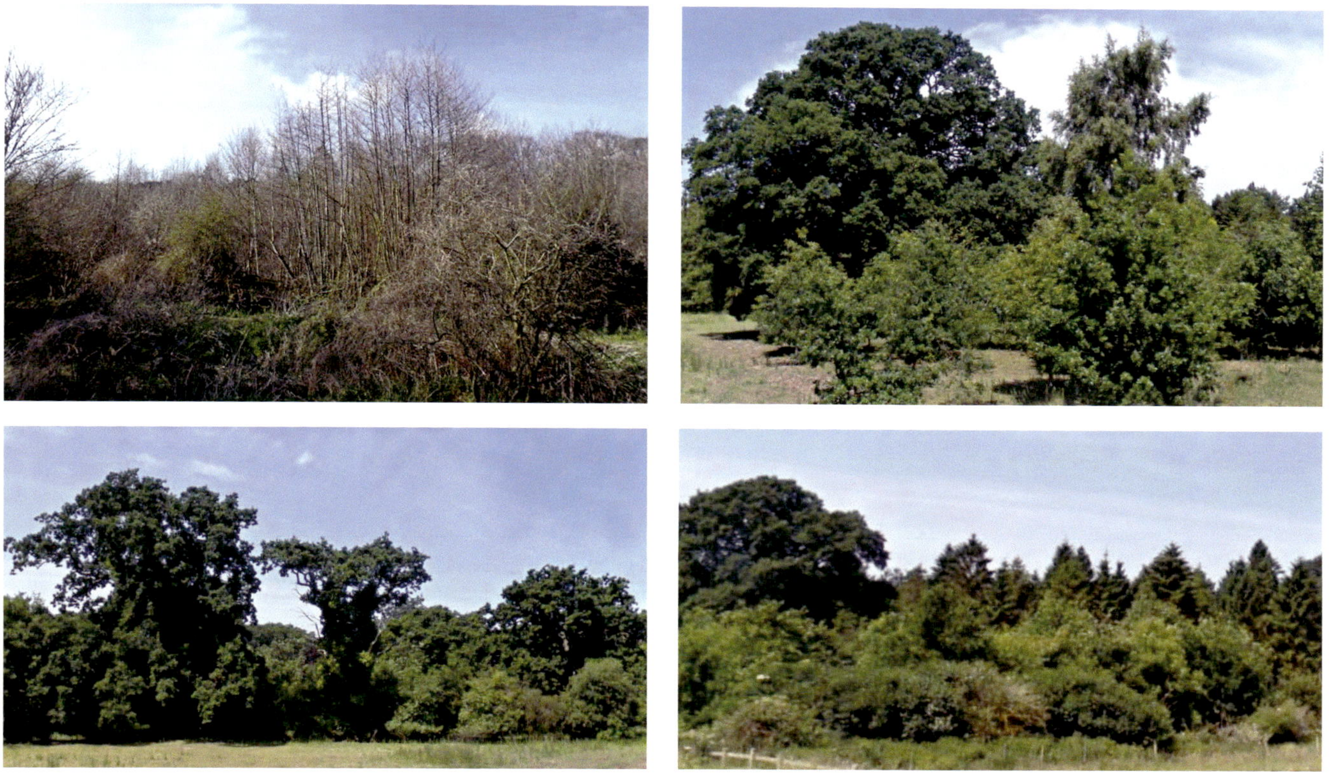

Figure 19.3a–d Vegetation near the Snettisham torc site, including pockets of woodland, hedgerow species, planted poplars and pines

In addition, tiny samples were permitted from the cores of four coiled wire copper alloy torc fragments from NCM, again allowing TS, RLS and TLS examination. For the same radiocarbon dating programme (Garrow *et al.* 2009), Cartwright also identified two instances of the presence of *Tilia* sp. lime bast (inner bark) fibres (**Fig. 19.2**) used as string bound round Snettisham torcs G.16 and L.6, as well as *Alnus glutinosa* (alder) charcoal found embedded in silver and copper alloy lumps/ingots from Hoard M (M.1–M.5). No evidence for torc metalworking activities has been revealed by archaeological excavations at Snettisham (to date), and the presence of metal ingots/lumps associated with alder charcoal does not conclusively testify to silversmithing on site either. It is worth recording on **Table 19.3**, nonetheless, those woods that make excellent charcoal, if only to indicate that excellent charcoal fuel resources were most likely readily available (and were utilised in later periods).

The woody resources of Snettisham

Whilst there is no evidence that the coiled wire copper alloy torcs with organic cores were actually made at Snettisham using local woods, there is no evidence to the contrary either. It follows, therefore, that it is important to understand the preferred habitats of the six taxa present – alder, hazel, dogwood, field maple, willow and elder – to establish whether or not it was possible for the local vegetation at Snettisham to provide sources of the organic cores and string wrappings.

In 1990, Cartwright undertook a survey of the local vegetation in the area of Ken Hill (**Fig. 19.3a–d**). In addition to land given over to farming, it was apparent that the areas of mixed oak deciduous woodland had been replaced to the west of the excavation site by a pine plantation, and to the south by a poplar plantation. Understorey vegetation of hawthorn (**Fig. 19.4**), hazel and bramble (amongst many other taxa) was present in the hedgerows.

The distribution maps and associated data from the Botanical Society of Britain & Ireland (2018) provide a wealth of information about the local woody vegetation in and around the Snettisham area recorded from 1930 to the present day. This is summarised in **Table 19.3**, with notes of uses of these materials seen in the archaeological evidence from the site, and recent introductions that would not have been available at the time of torc manufacture.

Many of these species are present as dominant trees or understorey in primary or secondary mixed oak woodland, largely deciduous in character. However, given the proximity of Snettisham to the coast, some heathland taxa

Figure 19.4 Hedgerow specimen of *Crataegus monogyna*, hawthorn bearing fruit

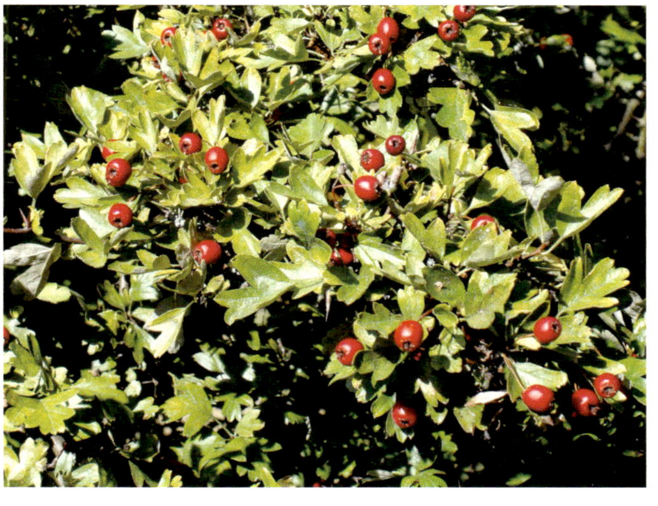

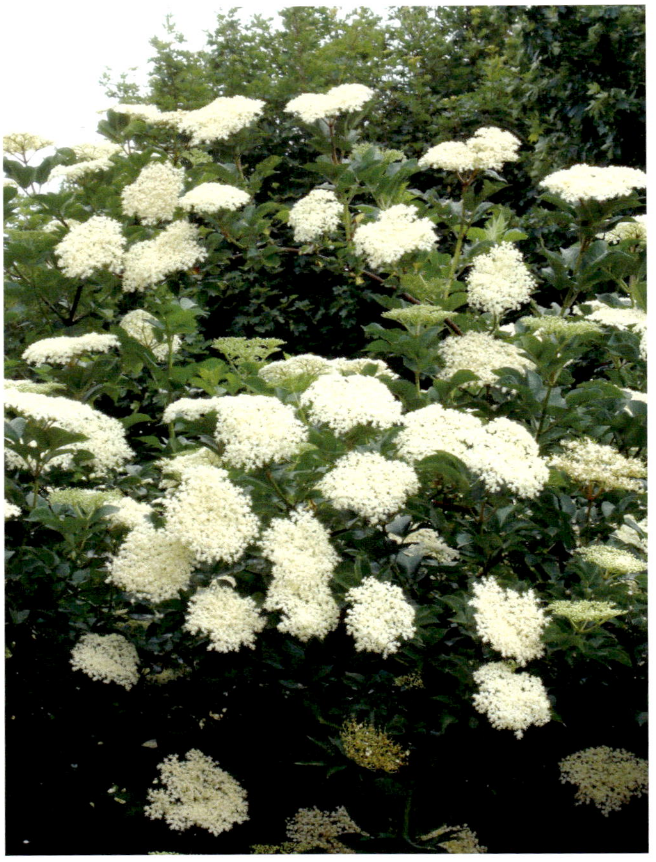

Figure 19.5 *Sambucus nigra*, elder tree, predominantly found in hedgerows, woodland margins and open areas. Elder tree wood was identified from the core of C.30b (NCM), a coiled wire copper alloy torc terminal fragment

are also present. Certain species, notably *Sambucus nigra* (elder) (**Fig. 19.5**) are predominantly found in hedgerows, woodland margins and open areas, often associated with eutrophic (nutrient-rich) or disturbed soil (Atkinson and Atkinson 2002). *Alnus glutinosa* (alder) prefers habitats near streams, often forming pure woods in succession to marshes or fens; it is tolerant of cutting and coppices well.

Although there may be no direct significance, it is interesting to note that four of the six woods used for torc cores were selected from useful fruit-bearing trees (**Figs 19.4–5**). If some form of woodland management had been present, both for coppicing young stems and for harvesting of fruits, this may (in part at least) explain the use of these species. However, the different wood properties of the selected species (frequently found in association with one another) are likely to have been the crucial determining factors.

Field maple (*Acer campestre*), a wood with good bending properties, was used for the core of torc F.168 (**Fig. 19.1a**). When coppiced, *Acer campestre* (**Fig. 19.6**) tends to remain as a shrub. The cores of torc F.167 (**Fig. 19.1b**) and C.1–5 were of hazel (*Corylus avellana*) wood, which has excellent flexibility and resists compression and fracturing well (Özden *et al.* 2017). Although for an entirely different function, it is informative to see a photograph showing the extent to which hazel wood can be twisted and bent back on itself in the formation of broches (or spars) used in thatching (Forestry Commission 1956, pl. 23). Alder (*Alnus glutinosa*) wood, whose properties include good elasticity, was selected for the cores

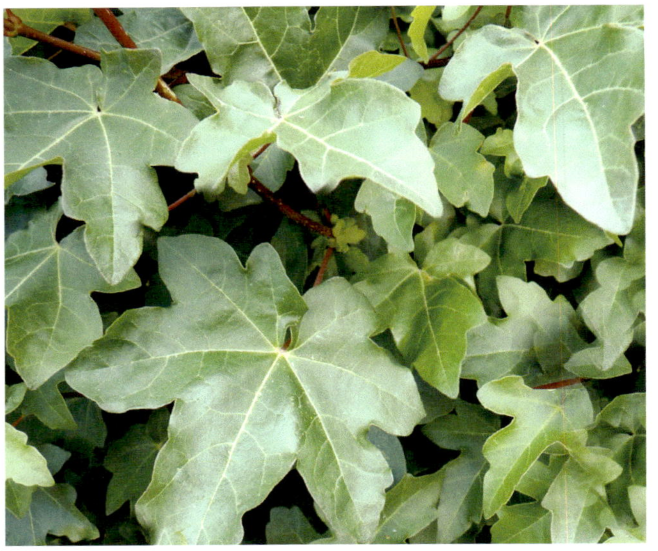

Figure 19.6 *Acer campestre*, field maple; this species of tree was used for the wooden core of torc F.168

of torc F.166 (**Fig. 19.1c**) and torc fragment C.22 and C.26. The core of torc/bracelet F.199 (**Fig. 19.1d**) is dogwood (*Cornus sanguinea*), another highly flexible wood (often used in basketry). If coppiced regularly dogwood will produce long straight stems after being cut back (**Fig. 19.7**). The two cores of C.27 and C.31 are samples from torc terminals rather than from coiled wire copper alloy bodies (C.27 and C.31 in **Table 19.1**). Their cores have been identified as consisting of willow (*Salix* sp.) (**Fig. 19.8**), and elder (*Sambucus nigra*) wood. Willow wood is light and, whilst it can be bent easily, it will ultimately buckle (Van Casteren *et al.* 2012). Like willow, elder wood is noted for its elasticity. Not only does coppicing promote growth of new, slender, flexible stems – ideal for use as organic cores in torc manufacture – it also contributes to the rotational harvesting, maintenance and management of healthy woodland and field hedgerows (Buckley 1992). Land management of woodland and hedgerow resources, in addition to meadows and heaths, has contributed to the rich diversity of Norfolk's vegetational communities over the centuries (Norfolk Biodiversity Partnership 2006), most likely over the millennia, in fact. There is clear survival of pockets of ancient woodland, which Barnes and Williamson (2015) define as consisting of long-established semi-natural woods, shaped by centuries of traditional management. Nowadays in Norfolk woodland distribution, structure and composition is threatened by overgrazing, agriculture, invasion by non-native species, creation of conifer plantations, trees disease and dieback, recession of traditional practices of woodland management, as well as urban, road and recreational developments and quarrying (Norfolk Biodiversity Partnership 2006), although there have been recent attempts to regenerate environments through rewilding (https://wildkenhill.co.uk).

The materials used for the torc cores and associated string are typically found in primary or secondary mixed oak woodland and field hedgerows. As seen in **Table 19.3**, these types of vegetation are characteristic of Snettisham and its environs today, and there is no evidence to suppose that such vegetation was markedly different in the Iron Age. Elsewhere in southern England, palynological studies and

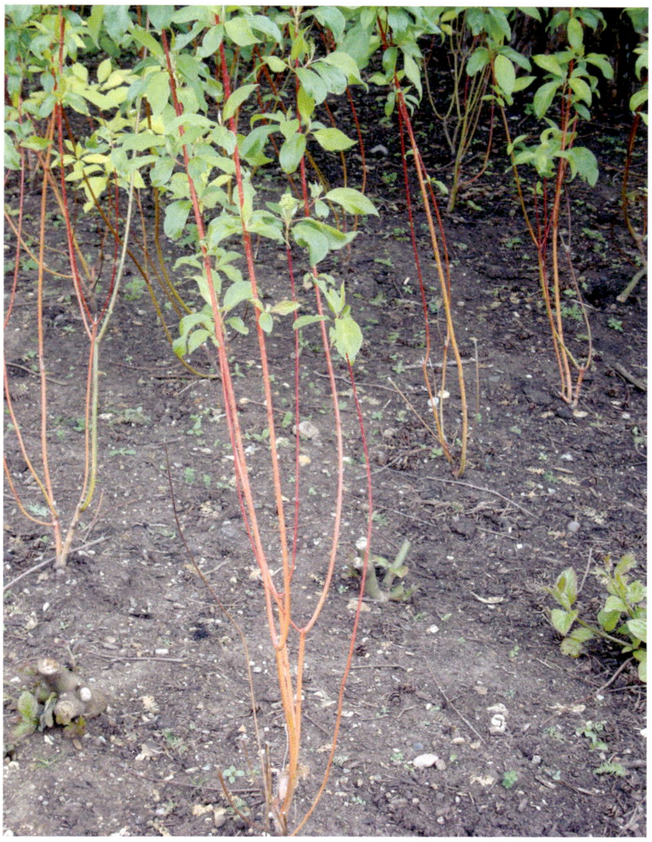

Figure 19.7 Young shoots of *Cornus sanguinea*, dogwood; this species of tree was used for the core of torc/bracelet F.199

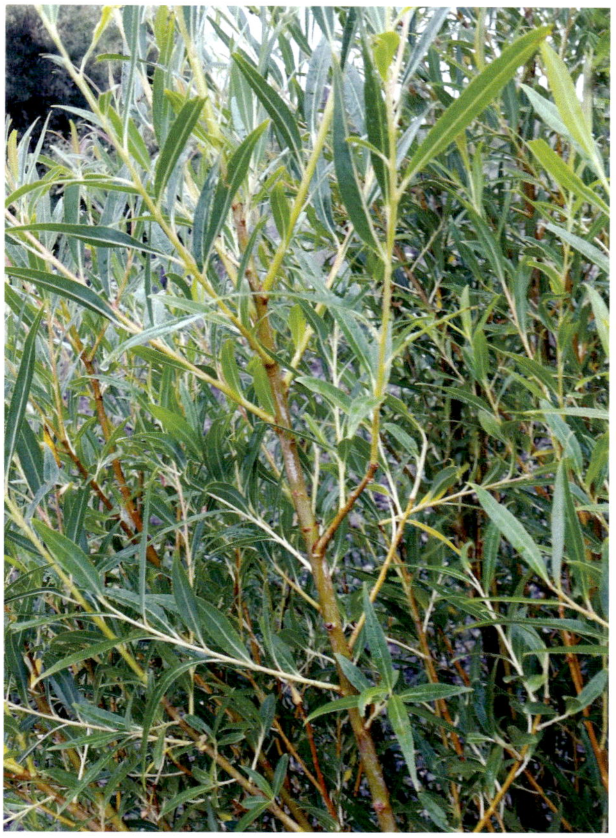

Figure 19.8 Young growth of *Salix alba*, white willow; *Salix* sp., willow wood was used for the core of C.30a (NCM), a coiled wire copper alloy torc terminal fragment

investigation of waterlogged remains have suggested the presence of well-established hedgerows as early as the Bronze Age (Allen and Robinson 1993; Evans and Hodder 2006; Greig 1992; Taylor 1996; Wiltshire 2003; Wright *et al.* 2009, 71–2). Locally available woody resources could therefore have been utilised. However, similar vegetational communities were probably common across much of Britain and western Europe, and so the use of these materials does not help to narrow down the possible manufacturing location for the torcs.

Using the woody resources for torc cores

The team of Snettisham colleagues at the BM has been endeavouring to understand the technological processes involved in using a central core of wood for some types of torc (Cartwright *et al.* 2012) and see Ch. 17). It seems that by using a central core of thin, flexible wood the metalsmiths could prevent multiple copper alloy wires from collapsing in on one another during coiling to form the composite 'hollow' body of the torc. Such a core would also have played an important part in avoiding wire collapse or distortion during the stage at which the torc was bent into its final curved shape. As a result of heating processes during the finishing of the torcs, the fresh wood became charred. Although not fully annealed, it is possible that the torcs were gently heated after the coiling and/or bending processes (Cartwright *et al.* 2012). There was no need to remove the cores once their primary support function had been fulfilled; in fact, it may not have been possible to remove them. These cores are only visible now due to the fragmentation of the copper alloy torcs. Although they now have the superficial appearance of being charcoal, they should be categorised as charred wood.

The scientific evidence provided by the wood identifications reinforces the importance of the material properties of alder, hazel, dogwood, field maple, willow and elder. It is clear that the use of organic cores was an integral part of the manufacturing process during the coiling of some of the copper alloy wire torcs (Cartwright *et al.* 2012). It is interesting to note that for making willow baskets, slender branches from the first year's growth are the most suitable as these are very supple and have not yet developed the hard woody bark of second year growth, which renders the branch much less supple. Moreover, first year willow branches have bark that peels easily in early spring, just after the sap starts to flow. No bark was visible on the torc cores; this either signifies (1) that the bark was peeled off prior to curving the slender branch in a circle to form a core, or (2) that the thin layer of bark charred through and disintegrated when heat was transferred to the wood from the coiled wires. The best willow rods for basket-making are long, thin and pliant, have small pith relative to xylem, and are of uniform diameter along their length. Some willow rods (osier wands) are used freshly cut ('green'), some are used in 'semi-green' state, and some are soaked before weaving into a basket (Basketry and Beyond 2012). There is no direct evidence of basket-making employing the same methods as used for torc cores, but the similarities of raw materials and their working properties are worth noting, nonetheless and could imply some cross-over or borrowing of craft techniques.

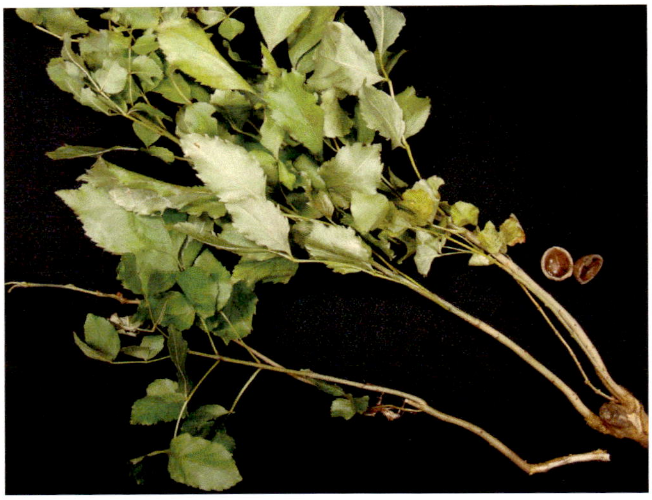

Figure 19.9 New-growth hazel shoots 2mm to 2.7mm in stem diameter for experimental bending

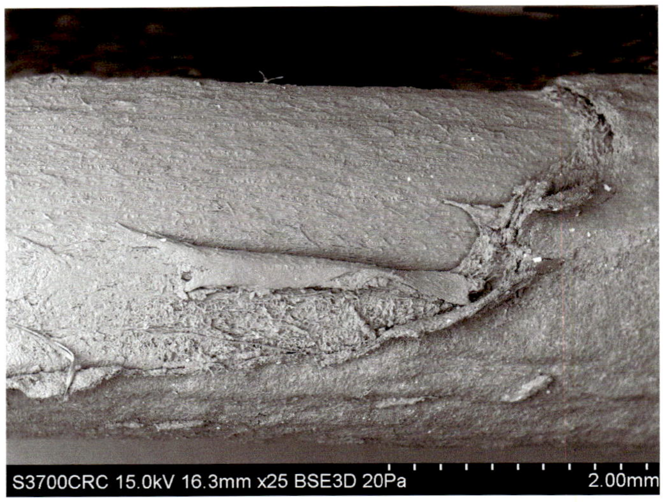

Figure 19.10 Variable pressure scanning electron microscope image of the freshly peeled surface of a 2.7mm-diameter hazel stem revealing the tangential longitudinal arrangement of cells

Experimental bending of new-growth hazel shoots 2mm to 2.7mm in diameter (**Fig. 19.9**) was carried out by Cartwright in August 2018, and VP SEM examination of a freshly peeled 2.7mm stem followed the day after cutting. These narrow stems were highly flexible and almost impossible to snap without much force being exerted in a twisting motion. As there was no woody bark present, peeling the freshly cut 2.7mm stem was easy, revealing the tangential longitudinal arrangement of cells in the VP SEM (**Fig. 19.10**). Whilst it is understandable that peeled willow osiers would slide more easily over one another during the process of weaving a basket, there seems no obvious reason for peeling any of the thin stems used for the torc cores. Three more hazel shoots formed part of the extended experiment. Cut early in the morning on 8 August 2018, the three stems, which measured 10mm, 7mm and 4mm in diameter, were bent and tied four hours later in a roughly circular 'torc-friendly' shape to compare with the 2.7mm stem diameter. One of the 4mm stem diameter shoots was so flexible that the ends could be roughly knotted together (temporarily) without the shoot breaking. All the examples displayed a decreasing stem diameter size towards the tip of each shoot. All the hazel shoots (of different stem dimensions) were extremely pliable, and could be bent into a torc-like shape with no difficulty, even the 10mm diameter hazel shoot, although this specimen was slightly less flexible and did require some effort to hold the ends together for crossover binding (for expedience, with a modern cotton tie instead of a lime bast fibre one). Aligning the cut shoot ends in a parallel formation enabled a tighter tying attachment than placing the shoot ends at right angles to one another – although both orientations worked successfully (**Fig. 19.11a–b**). However, for making a Snettisham coiled wire copper alloy torc, it is not clear whether the wood shoot needed to be curved into a semi-open or closed circular shape *before* the copper alloy wires were coiled around it, or whether the wires were coiled around a straight (but flexible) wood shoot and then the composite artefact (copper alloy wires coiled around wood) was curved into the requisite torc shape with a gap left between each terminal so that the torc could be used as a slightly 'adjustable' neck-ring. From these experiments, it is possible to suggest that it would be very simple and quick to create a suitable shape for the torc-making process by selecting a freshly cut hazel shoot with a uniform diameter, ideally between 3mm and 7mm in width. Having cut the shoot, no major preparation would be needed, just stripping off any leaf

Figure 19.11a–b New-growth hazel stems: aligning the cut shoot ends in a parallel formation (a) enabled a tighter tying attachment than placing the shoot ends at right angles to one another (b)

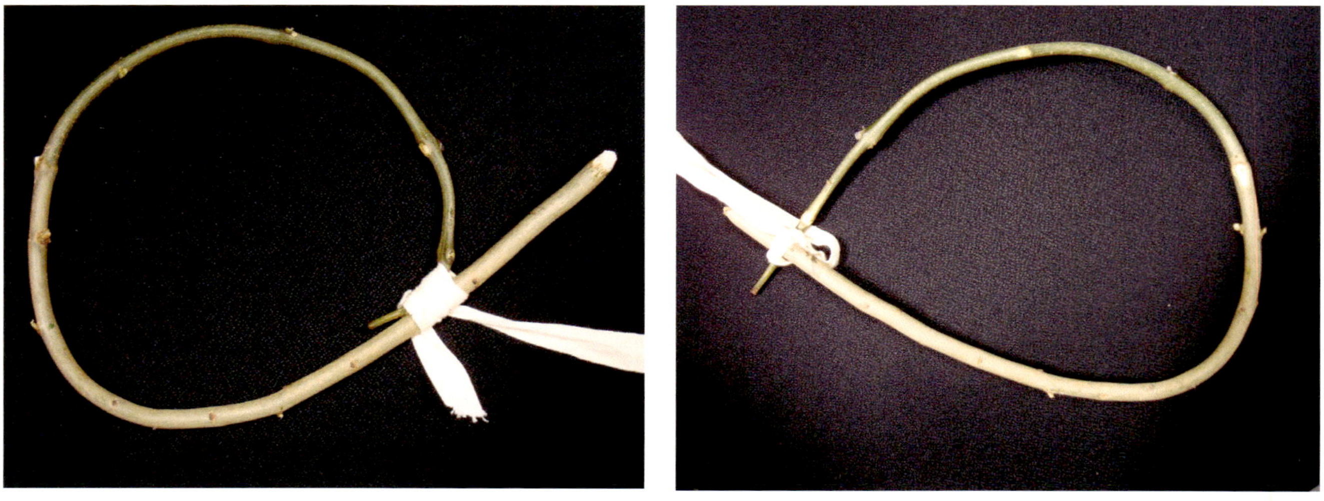

stalks present. These experiments were extended to the other species represented in the torcs – alder, dogwood, field maple, elder and willow in order to evaluate whether, given their similar wood properties (outlined above), they would produce comparable results, which they did.

Consideration must be given as to whether the use of organic cores represents a widespread technological innovation or the product of a single workshop (local or distant). This is difficult to evaluate given the fact that so few wooden (or other organic) cores have been preserved in the archaeological record. Evidence is emerging for wooden withies being used in Iron Age cauldron rims, so this manufacturing method may have been more widespread than thought hitherto (Baldwin and Joy 2017, 40, fig. 46, 89–91, table 12; see also Gerlof 1986). Preservation mostly occurs either through the object and its organic component(s) having been charred, or the wood core being in close association with metalwork and its corrosion products. Some other artefacts, such as Bronze Age gold lock-rings, also display wood cores (La Niece and Cartwright 2009). Although no wooden cores were observed in the Snettisham gold alloy wire torcs, these could have been removed before the terminals were affixed to the neck-ring. It seems no single hypothesis can cover all the metallurgical and technological complexities involved.

Conclusions

It is clear that although the torc cores are now preserved in charred condition, originally it is most likely they were slender wands of fresh (possibly coppiced) wood with sufficient flexibility to provide the appropriate support during construction of these torcs. Central to this evaluation has been the SEM identification of the woody taxa and consideration of their physical characteristics for their role as core material. Making comparisons with experimentally fired examples in an earlier study (Cartwright *et al.* 2012) allowed the charring temperatures of the archaeological material to be determined, at around 360°C. The charring seems to have occurred after the manufacture of the torc was largely complete, reflecting a regular and controlled heating process applied to both the neck-ring and terminals. Whilst it cannot be unequivocally concluded that the managed mixed oak woodland and hedgerows at or around Snettisham itself provided the resources needed, the evidence of these types of vegetational communities being the source of such materials is not in dispute.

Chapter 20
Torc Biographies

Jody Joy, Nigel Meeks and Julia Farley

In this chapter we examine torcs for details of how they were worn, as well as the intensity and duration of usage, such as patterns of polishing, wear and repair. Our aim is to piece together information written into the artefacts throughout their lives to help inform torc biographies (cf. Kopytoff 1986; Gosden and Marshall 1999; Joy 2009a). In addition, many torcs show signs of deliberate breakage prior to burial, as well as other forms of alteration such as heating and melting. Some were even broken and joined or linked together with other objects, creating new artefacts or assemblages. Detailed information listing evidence for wear, damage and repair appears in individual catalogue entries in Chapter 14. The following account summarises patterns and observations, before this information is drawn together to consider implications for the life trajectories of torcs: how long they were in circulation and the identification of potential life-paths.

Systematic study was made of all torcs and torc fragments, involving visual inspection as well as closer examination of areas of interest using optical as well as, in some cases, scanning electron microscopy. Evidence for wear included polished and smoothed surfaces where torcs had come into contact with skin or clothing, scratches, general wear and tear, breakage and repair.

Evidence of use wear, damage and repair

Most of the torcs showed some evidence of the characteristic features of wear, which is important because it demonstrates that they were not made especially for deposition: they had use-lives before they were deposited. In some instances, objects were probably very long-lived. A difference in wear patterns was also noted between tubular and multi-strand torcs. Many wire torcs of all sizes showed extensive evidence of wear from their use in antiquity. In contrast, some of the large tubular torcs show only limited evidence of wear. Perhaps, as these objects were manufactured from thin gold sheet, they would not have stood up to the mechanical wear, abrasion and knocks that would inevitably occur through daily usage. They may therefore have been reserved for special occasions.

Tubular torcs

Owing to the fact that many tubular torcs were found in a crushed state, which may be in part a product of post-depositional damage, finding extensive evidence for wear and repair on these objects proved to be quite difficult. Nevertheless, where they are relatively undamaged, such as the examples from Hoard A, it appears that tubular torcs were relatively lightly used when compared to multi-strand torcs.

Tubular torc A.1 has a repair patch soldered in place in antiquity, with decorative circles (see Ch. 21) punched over the repair (**Fig. 20.1**). This might imply that it was repaired at the time of manufacture, perhaps due to a thinning or tear in the metal. While the present state of the torc is a little dented, it does not seem to have much additional evidence of use wear.

Multi-strand torcs

Wear on multi-strand torcs can be seen on the exposed surfaces of the wires of the neck-rings and on the protruding design features of terminals that have been subject to rubbing on clothes, or the body, or possibly even during storage (**Fig. 20.2a–b**). Wear also resulted from general wear-and-tear such as putting torcs on and taking them off.

Tightly coiled ropes made from multiple wires often show a high level of wear, with grooves worn into adjacent wires at the points of contact and friction. This pattern of wear is indicative of prolonged usage. The flexing of putting torcs on and taking them off and movement from frequent wearing resulted in the characteristic wear patterns illustrated in **Figures 20.3–4**, which show the worn wires of comparatively stiff neck-rings. When new, the wires would have had prominent linear facets running all the way along their lengths (cf. Ch. 17, e.g. **Figure 17.14a–d**, showing torc fragments S.31–9; **Figure 17.20a–b**). While these facets have been preserved in certain protected areas, they have been polished smooth at the points where wires have rubbed together, or on the outer faces, where they would have rubbed against clothing or the body, or been susceptible to polishing.

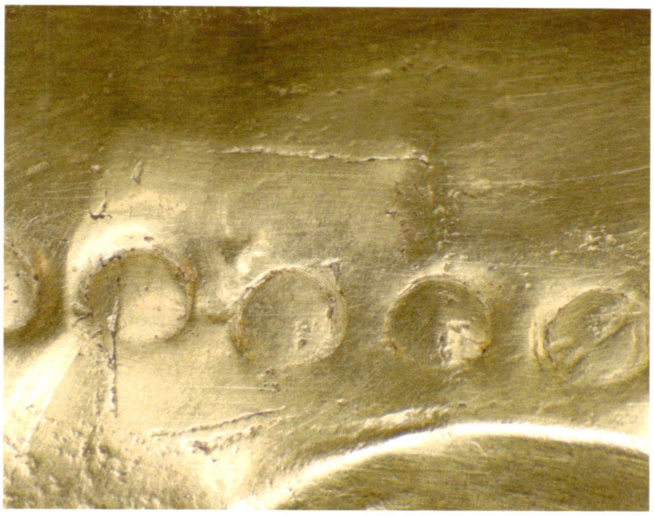

Figure 20.1 Repair patch soldered onto large tubular torc A.1

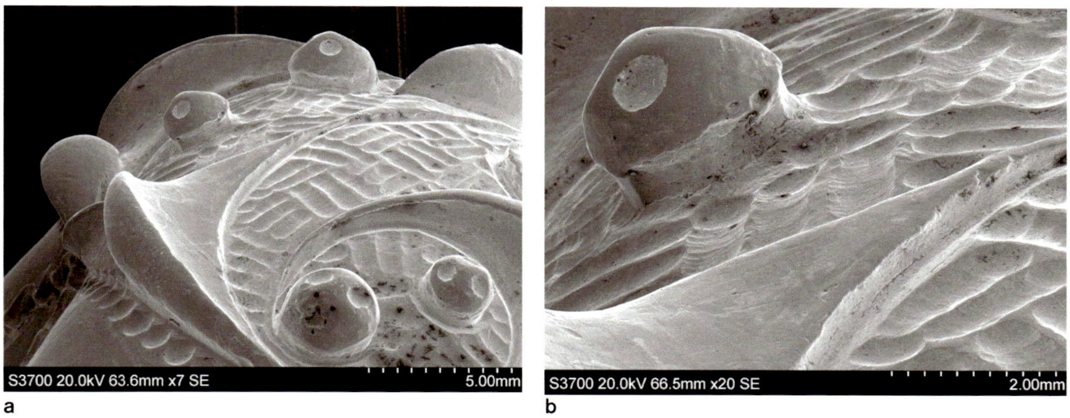

Figure 20.2a–b SEM details of one of the terminals of the 'Great Torc' (E.1a), showing rounded polish on prominent features

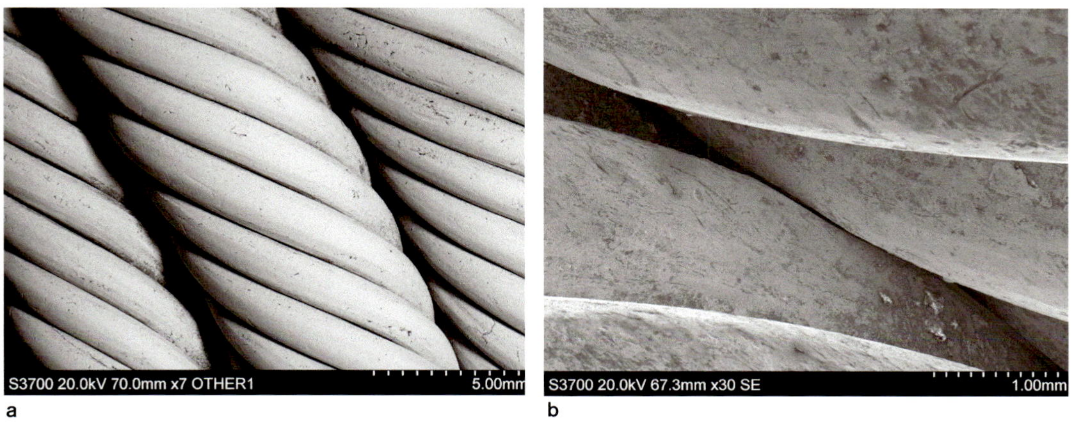

Figure 20.3a–b SEM images: left, wear and polish on the Great Torc neck-ring wires has worn away the linear facets on exposed outer surfaces, but not in protected regions between wires; right, detail of the friction zone between adjacent wires, with significant wear from one wire creating a curved groove in the adjacent wire (centre of image)

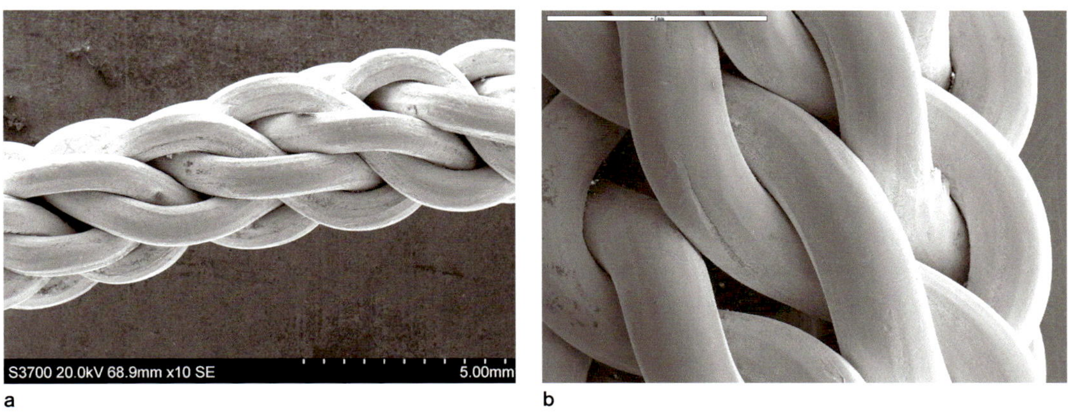

Figure 20.4a–b SEM images of a stiff multi-strand torc F.116 (left), and detail of similar torc L.16 (right), showing wear patterns between tightly fitting adjacent wires, and smoothed surfaces at prominent outer points. For F.116, contrast the worn areas with protected parts of the wire, where linear facets are still visible

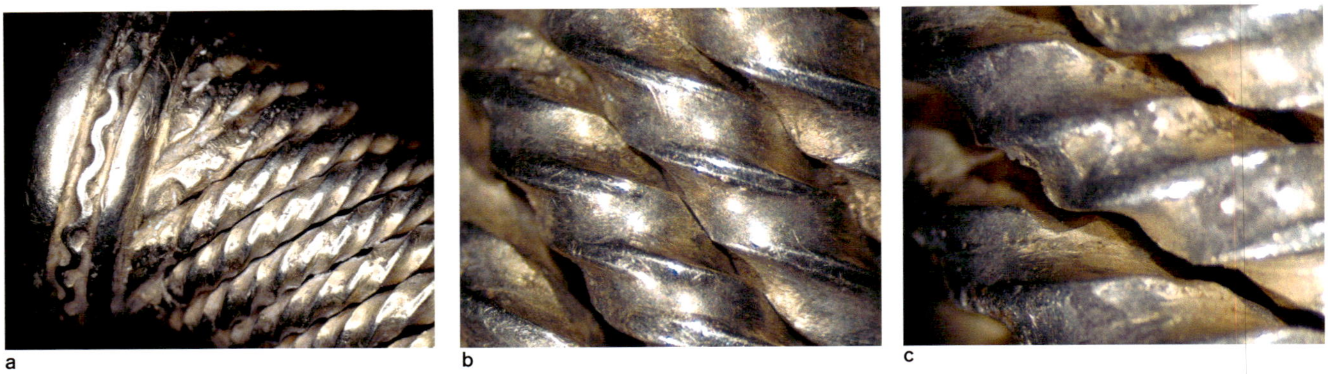

a b c

Figure 20.5a–c Extreme wear between the very flexible, springy wires of torc L.17. In some areas flat areas have been worn (centre), and in others the wires have created grooves (right)

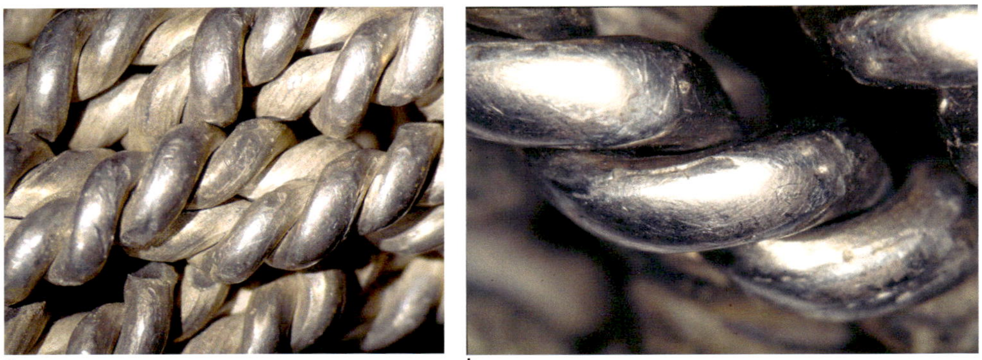

a b

Figure 20.6a–b Torc L.21a, with protected wires retaining their surface facets, while heavily worn surfaces reveal the coppery-coloured core metal (right)

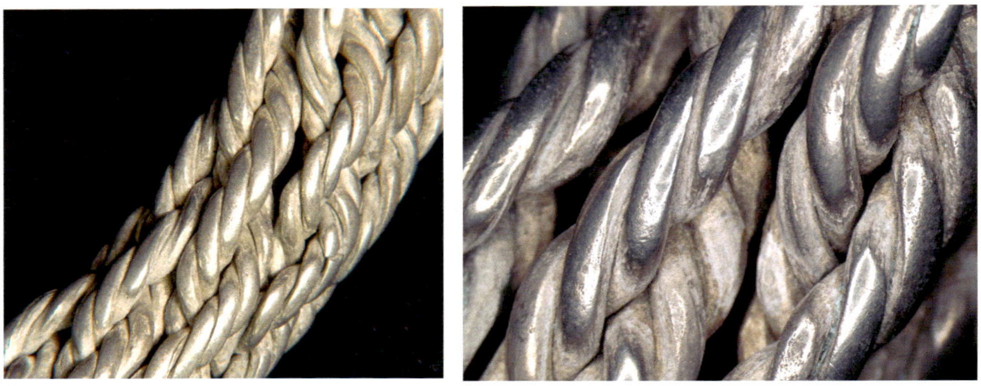

a b

Figure 20.7a–b Torc L.1, showing extensive wear on and between wires, giving a flattened appearance to the surface of the neck-ring ropes

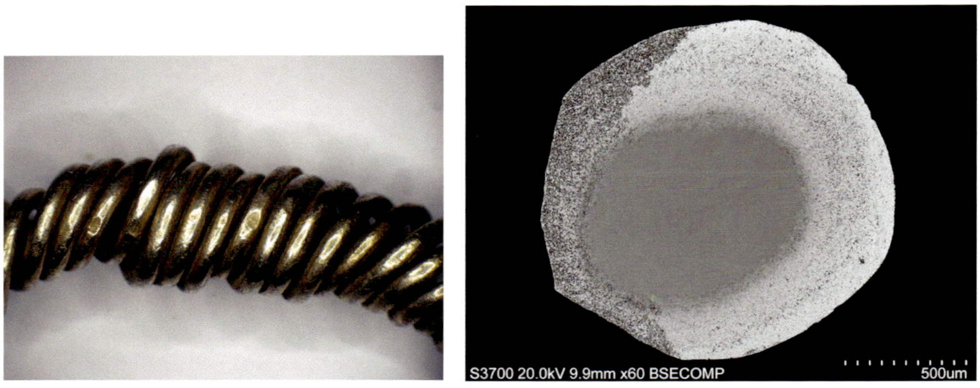

a b

Figure 20.8a–b Small torc F.88, a fragment of tightly coiled wire neck-ring. The SEM cross-section image (right) shows the heavy wear cutting through the original surface enrichment on the left side of the wire

The more flexible the torc, the more wear is seen between the wires. For example, **Figure 20.5a–c** shows how worn the wires are on the very springy and flexible multi-strand torc L.17. In some instances, adjacent wires have worn the corners of the square-section twisted wires completely flat (**Fig. 20.5b**), whereas in other areas deep grooves have been worn into the adjacent wires (**Fig. 20.5c**). Similarly, other multi-strand torcs such as torc L.21a (**Fig. 20.6a–b**) and L.1 (**Fig. 20.7**), which are also quite flexible, have extensive wear on the surfaces of the outer wires. On L.21a, polishing has even worn through the silvery-gold surface-enriched layer, exposing the coppery-coloured core.

The size of torc does not seem to have had a bearing on patterns of wear. Both large and small torcs are equally affected, although the effects of wear may have been more pronounced on examples where neck-ring wires were

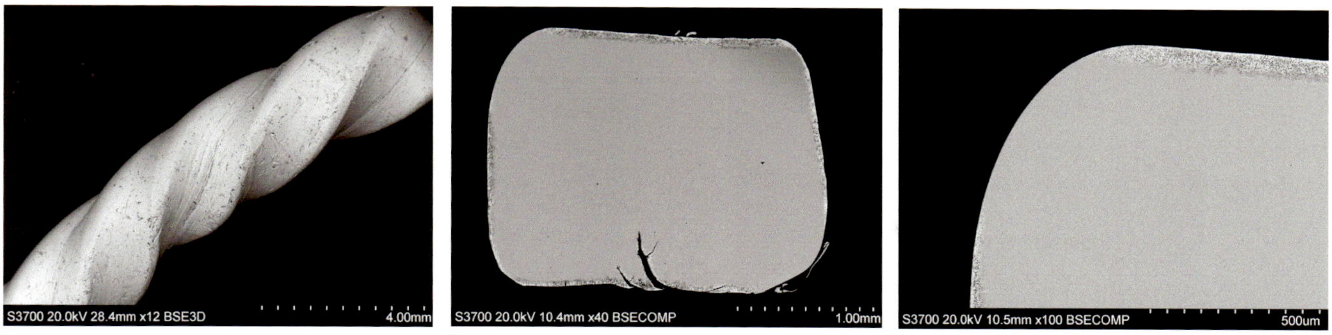

a b c

Figure 20.9a–c Twisted square-section wire F.429, with very worn exposed corners. Originally this wire would have been square in cross-section; the heavy wear on the corners has polished through the outer surface-enriched layer

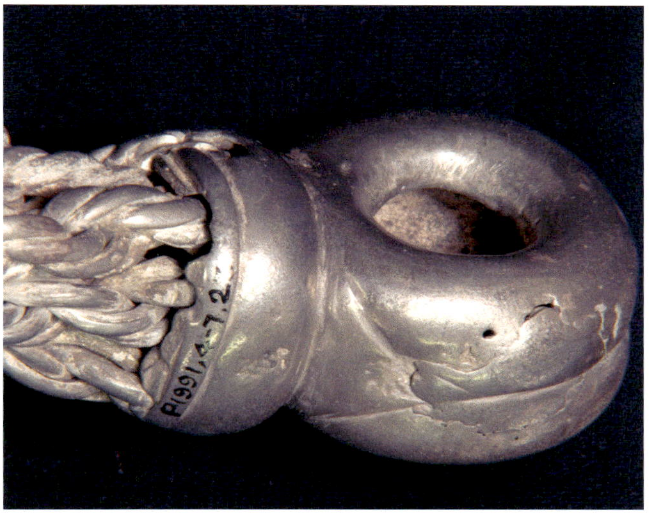

Figure 20.10 Torc L.1, showing an area of cast-on repair to a large cold-shut on the original terminal casting

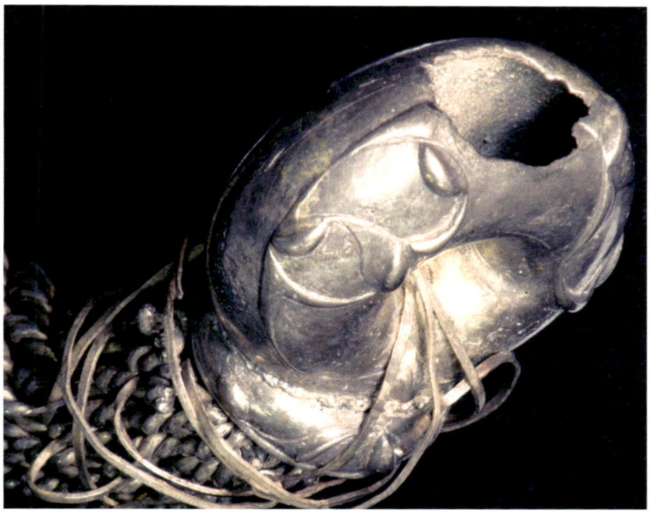

Figure 20.11 Terminal of torc L.21a, with a massive cold-shut casting defect

thinner. On larger objects, such as L.1, the exterior wires (originally circular in cross-section) are polished down to a flattened oval (see **Fig. 20.7a–b**). On some smaller torcs and bracelets such as F.88 (**Fig. 20.8a–b**), the original round wire has been so heavily worn that abrasion has cut deeply through the thick original surface-enriched layer. This has allowed corrosion to penetrate deep into the interior as the protective burnished gold-rich outer surface region has completely worn away.

Some individual wires also show heavy wear. The square-section twisted wire F.429 is typical, the exposed corners of the square wire having worn smooth, right through the original surface enrichment (**Fig. 20.9a–c**). Note also on this wire the longitudinal groove along the centre-line of the two faces. This groove is also seen in cross-section, where it cuts deeply into the wire's core. This would appear to be the result of a hammered fold where the two edges met but did not become hammer-welded together, demonstrating how vagaries of manufacture can affect patterns of wear. The difference between worn square-section wires with rounded corners and those which have been protected enough to keep their sharply squared ridges can be seen near the collar of the 'Grotesque Torc', L.19 (see **Fig. 17.99a–b**).

As seen with tubular torc A.1, repairs to rectify manufacturing errors are also present on some cast terminals. For example, a terminal of torc L.1 shows a cast-on repair where additional metal has been added to close a large cold-shut (mis-casting hole) (**Fig. 20.10**). The repair seems to have been successful and is firmly attached. The irregular outline suggests the repair may have been cast-on then polished before a decorative groove was finally added. But manufacturing errors were not always rectified. The cold-shut hole at the end of one of the terminals of L.21a was left unrepaired (**Fig. 20.11**).

Other torcs appear, to modern eyes, unfinished. For example, whilst in most cases cast-on terminals were cleaned, hammered and polished, and had the projecting sprues from the casting process removed, they remain present on torc S.17 (**Fig. 20.12**). The only torc with clear 'hook' terminals, H.3 (**Fig. 20.13**), has hammered wire terminals dis-similar to any other complete torc. These may have been being prepared for the casting-on of additional metal to create a thickened ring terminal.

Areas of wear, vulnerability and repair

Looking at the areas where wear occurs most often, it is possible to make inferences as to how torcs were taken on and off and also to estimate how often this happened. In effect it is a crude measure of usage as similar wear patterns could result on the one hand from a relatively short period of heavy use, or on the other from a much longer, less intense, use-life.

Many examples of complete torcs have raised or broken wires at the very back of the neck-ring. In a few cases, such damage has required repair. Copper alloy torcs G.16 and

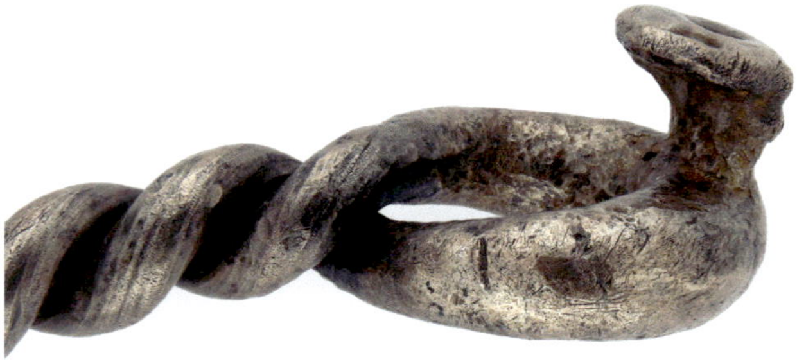

Figure 20.12 The sprues from casting-on the thickened ring terminals have been left in place on torc S.17

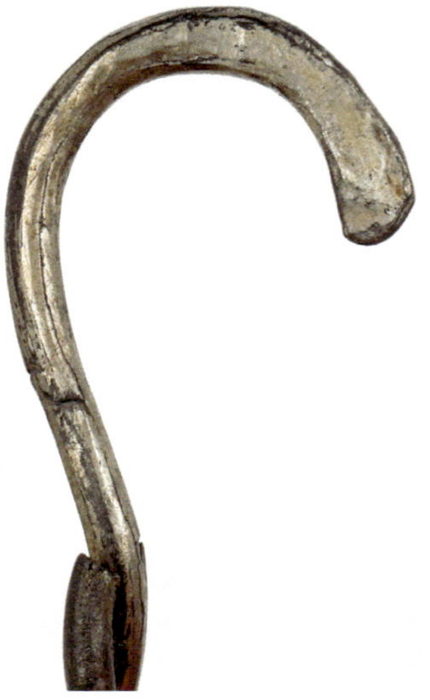

Figure 20.13 The hammered ends of hook terminal torc H.3 may represent unfinished terminals which had been prepared for the casting-on of additional material to create a thickened ring

L.6 have both been bound around with organic 'string' at the back of their neck-rings to reinforce the wires. Two more heavily worn torcs which broke entirely at the back (L.19 and L.20) are discussed in more detail below.

The join between the terminal and the neck-ring also seems to have been unreliable. Even among torcs which remain relatively undamaged, some, such as E.1a (Great Torc), show evidence for stress and cracking around the joins between terminal and neck-ring (**Fig. 20.14a–b**). In other cases, greater breakage has occurred. For example, attempts were made to fix the join on one of the ring terminals of L.21a, which has been secured to the neck-ring using strands of wire looped through the neck-ring at one end and the terminal loop at the other (**Fig. 20.11**). It is unclear whether the terminal was ever completely detached, but if this had happened, we might expect that the springy wires of the neck-ring would have unravelled somewhat more than appears to be the case. Torcs L.12 and L.13 are both missing buffer terminals which appear to have become detached during the life of the torc. On L.12 the break is very clean and it is possible that the terminal was cut off in antiquity, or perhaps the broken area was trimmed after breakage occurred. Similarly, on L.13 the wires also appear to have been cut, either to remove the missing terminal or in an attempt to tidy the break. On L.12, the wires of the neck-ring remain tightly coiled, but L.13 has begun to uncoil, the wires becoming more disorganised. Copper alloy torc G.13 has also lost a terminal, and in this case the open ends of the wires have been bound with an organic repair, perhaps to prevent uncoiling of the wires. On torc L.20, the three pieces of wire used to 'repair' the heavily broken neck-ring pass through holes in the terminals (as seen on L.21a) and may also function to reinforce the join between terminal and neck-ring.

Piecing all of this evidence together (and assuming damage has occurred on torcs where they have been most heavily strained during use) it appears that putting a torc on involved pressure on both the back of the neck-ring and the join between the terminals and the body of the torc. The most likely explanation is that the terminals were first pulled apart, with one terminal pulled forward and possibly slightly upwards to create a sufficient gap to allow it to be twisted on around the neck. They were likely removed in a similar fashion. This has left some torcs, including the 'Great Torc' (E.1a) permanently deformed, with one terminal pulled slightly higher than the other. Interestingly, when viewed from above it is the unrepaired terminal on L.21a which is furthest forwards, suggesting that whoever wore it was careful not to put unnecessary pressure on the opposite terminal where the join with the neck-ring had been reinforced.

Patterns of wear can also be seen on multi-strand torcs from other sites, though there appear to be some differences in the treatment of these objects. For example, the Newark, Nottinghamshire, Torc (see **Fig. 17.102**) has one terminal higher and further forward than the other (cf. Joy 2016), like many of the Snettisham torcs. In the case of Newark, polishing and wear on the terminals is more marked on one side, implying the torc was consistently worn the same way up. When oriented with the polished side down as the torc was worn, the terminal furthest forward is the right-hand terminal. This implies that the person/s who wore it were right-handed. This could indicate it was worn by just one person, or perhaps that there was a 'correct' way for the decoration on the terminals to be oriented. Wear patterns on other torcs, such as the largely undecorated examples from Leekfrith, Staffordshire (Farley *et al.* 2018), also seem to show a preferred orientation. In contrast, the decoration on the terminals of torcs from Snettisham appears equally worn on both sides, suggesting there was not one appropriate orientation in which their decoration should be viewed. Similarly, undecorated terminals from the site can also show polishing and wear on both sides.

The wear and repair on torc L.19 (**Fig. 20.15**) is probably the most obvious and striking on any of the torcs known from Britain. Certainly, the repairs are highly visible and seemingly rudimentary (cf. Joy 2019a), but patterns of wear also closely match those identified on the other torcs. At some point in its history, the join between one of the terminals and the neck-ring has been reinforced (similar to repairs seen on L.20 and L.21a). This was achieved using a length of crudely cut metal ribbon which has been wrapped several times around the neck-ring and looped through the hole at the centre of the doughnut-shaped terminal. A second piece of metal ribbon was coiled around the neck-ring at the back of the torc. It is so similar to the ribbon holding the terminal in place as to indicate that the two repairs may have been executed at the same time. It is difficult to be certain whether the terminal ever became

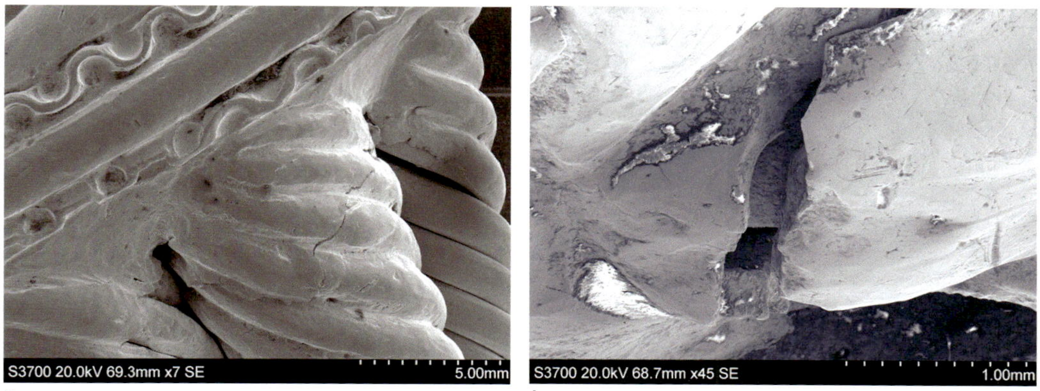

a
b

Figure 20.14a–b SEM images of the fatigue cracks across the thick gold flange covering wires on the terminal of the 'Great Torc', E.1a

fully detached but, unlike L.21a, the neck-ring is only very loosely twisted. This could have resulted through prolonged use but may also have been exaggerated if the terminal was at some point completely detached from the neck-ring. A further addition to torc L.19 is part of a multi-strand torc or bracelet which has been passed through the central hole of each terminal. This may have been looped through the terminals at or near the time of deposition, but it could also have served a practical function as a clasp to hold the terminals together when the torc was worn. The tension of the coiled neck-ring wires gives a torc its shape. As the neck-ring of L.19 has lost so much of this tension, perhaps looping the bracelet through the terminals helped hold them in place at the neck when the torc was worn.

As is dramatically shown in a radiograph of torc L.19 (**Fig. 20.16a–b**), at some point in its history the neck-ring broke completely in two. The break occurred at exactly the point of greatest tension when torcs were taken on and off, at the very back of the neck-ring. This implies the breakage could have occurred through the wear and tear of being repeatedly taken on and off rather than as a result of deliberate damage. Perhaps it was weakened in this area through heavy usage and finally broken by accident or through heavy handling, but it is impossible to be certain without disassembling the torc. There is certainly no evidence for the broken ends being neatly cut as a group, as seen on some undoubtedly deliberately fragmented torcs (see below). The neck-ring was repaired by taking a fragment of tubular torc and slotting the broken sections of the neck-ring into opposite ends of the tube. The join is secured rather loosely, without solder (**Fig. 20.16a–b**). It has been reinforced using lengths of twisted wire (perhaps sourced from the neck-rings of decommissioned multi-strand torcs) which were threaded through the cavity in the tubular torc and were then interwoven with the four ropes of the neck-ring. One of these wires also loops through the ring of a

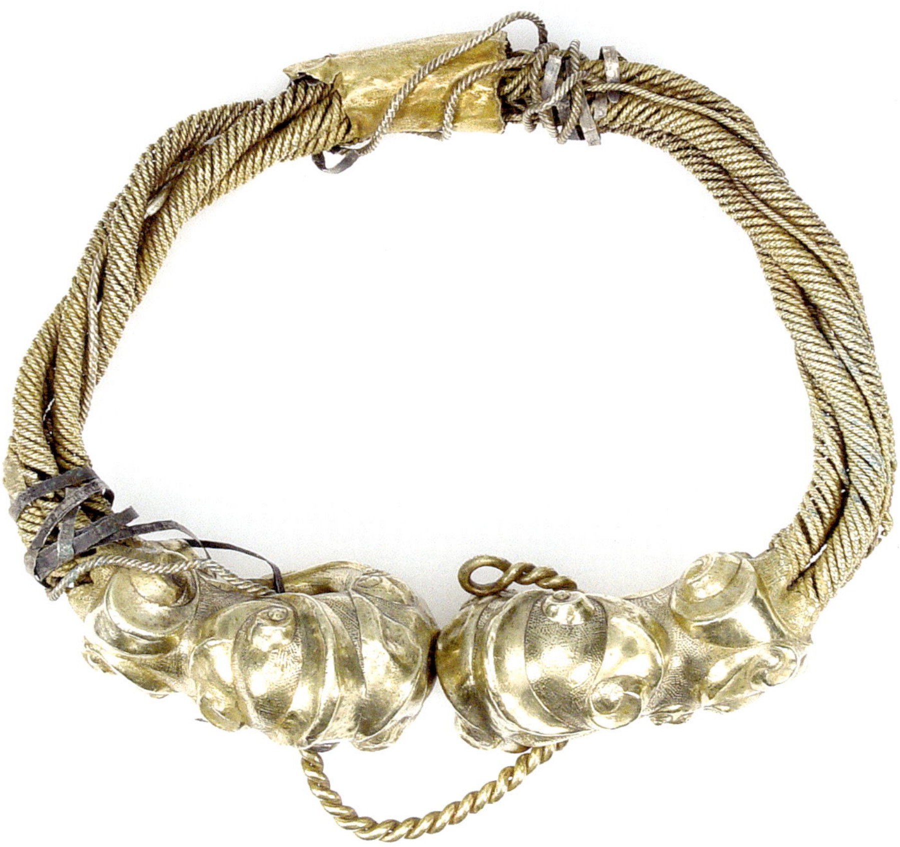

Figure 20.15 Torc L.19, the so-called 'Grotesque Torc'

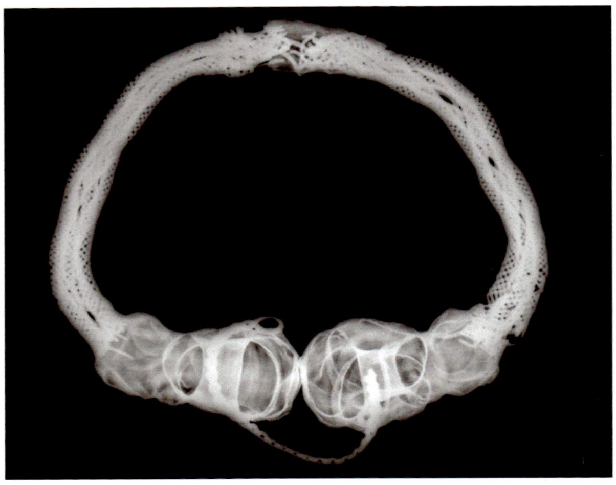

a

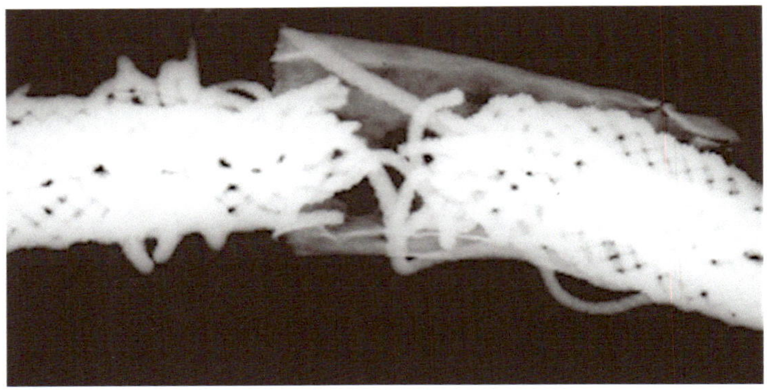

b

Figure 20.16a–b Radiograph of torc L.19 showing central break and wrapped sheet repair at the back of the neck-ring (Radiograph, Janet Ambers)

terminal, as already discussed, further securing it to the neck-ring. At least one of the gold alloy wires underlies the metal ribbon also used to secure the join between the terminal and neck-ring, whereas others are twisted around it.

In summary, L.19 was extensively repaired in antiquity. It was probably wearable, but the repairs are mechanically rather insecure. It is possible it was fixed in one episode using materials to hand at the time. The repairs certainly have an ad hoc appearance. If this were the case, the repairer must have had 'scrap' components readily available. Alternatively, it could have been repaired a number of times but, as the various wires and ribbons have been threaded through and wrapped around each other so extensively, it is impossible now to unravel the precise sequence of the repairs or when exactly they took place, presumably towards the end of the torc's life. Machling and Williamson (2020a) have argued that, rather than being functional, the extensive repairs to this torc were carried out at or near the time of deposition, with the intention to make the torc look as close to complete as possible when it was deposited in the ground. This is perfectly possible, although it is worth noting that the repairs to the torc also meant that it could still have been worn. If the intention was simply to deposit the torc, why use a fragment of tubular torc to join the two broken ends of the neck-ring when they could easily have been reunited through their close placement together in the ground as the two ends of the broken neck-ring of L.20 (see below) were in the same hoard?

Few torcs damaged this extensively were repaired. The only other 'complete' torc which shows a comparable degree of wear and breakage is L.20 (see **Pl. 14.59**), which is also broken at the back. It has similar additional wires running along the neck-ring; in this instance they pass through holes in the sides of the terminal collars and are then wrapped around the coiled wire cables of the neck-ring, probably reinforcing the terminal joins. The neck-ring itself is missing several cables and completely broken into two pieces, though (unlike L.19) it has not been repaired at the back. The added wires could perhaps have been used to join the two halves (one ends in a neat loop). But, even with these repairs, the torc is so broken that it is hard to imagine how it could have been worn. It was deposited in two halves. Looking at the broken ends, there is no evidence for deliberate cutting of the wires, so it is probably most likely that it was fractured through heavy use and/or by accident. Either way, a repair was theoretically possible, but for some reason was not attempted. Whenever the torc was broken, the halves were retained together, and the object was deposited 'whole'.

Cut and broken torcs

Many of the artefacts from the fragmentary hoards, particularly Hoard F, are damaged or broken. Close

Figure 20.17 Small multi-strand torc fragment F.96, showing the cut ends of the wires

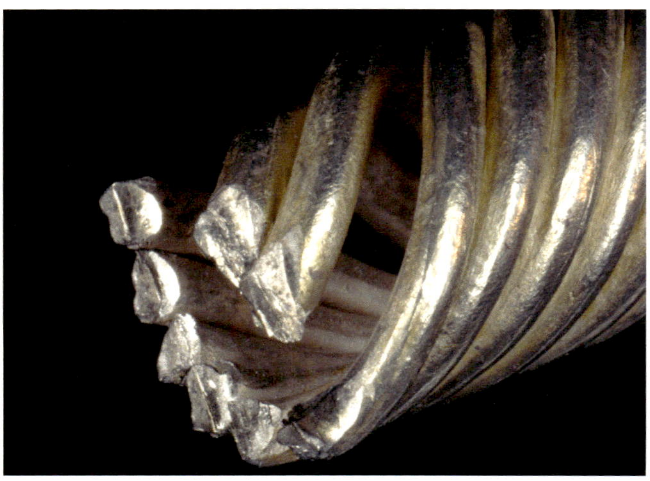

Figure 20.18 The ends of experimental wire (produced by John Fenn) cut using a double-bladed wire cutter (SEM image)

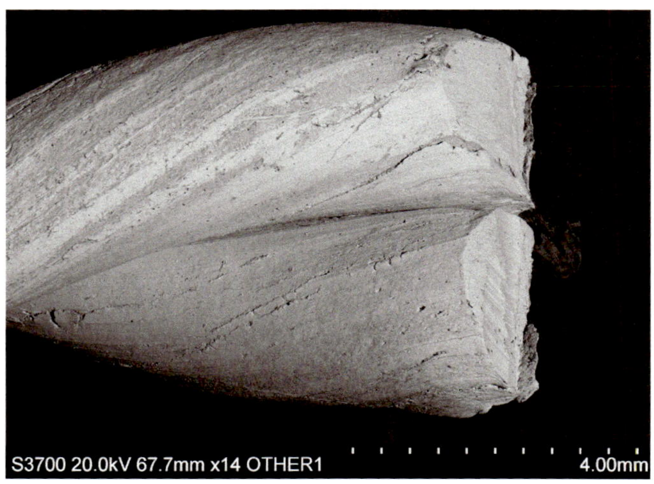

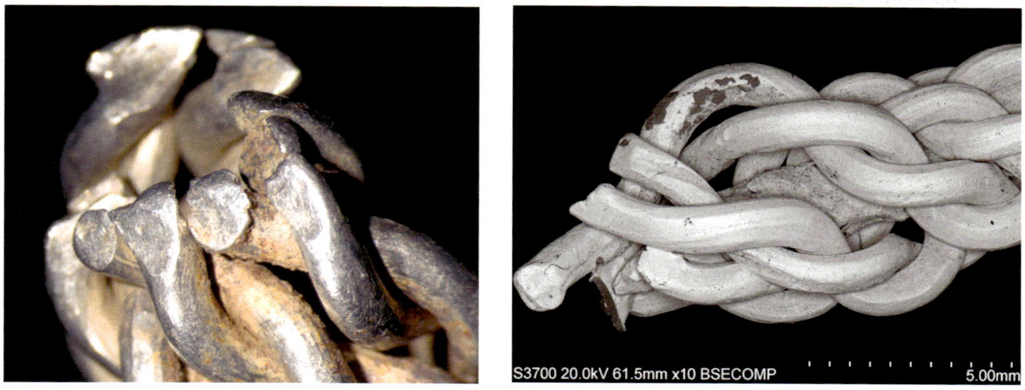

a b

Figure 20.19a–b Detail of cut end of half torc L.16 (left) and SEM detail (right) of similar cut wire ends on torc F.116

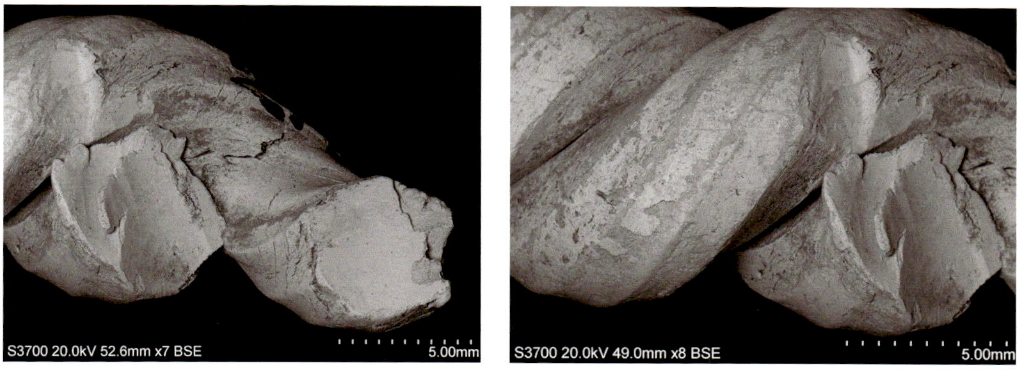

a b

Figure 20.20a–b SEM images of the ends of torc fragment F.77, whose thick wires were deliberately cut through by chisel blows

examination has revealed that much of this damage was deliberate and ancient and not accidental, as can occur when torcs are uncovered by ploughing for example (e.g. the Sedgeford Torc), or through burrowing (as seen on many of the Hoard G torcs). It is interesting that coins in the fragmentary hoards also seem to have been treated like objects in this sense, being cut (e.g. no. 174, from Hoard F) or hammered flat (nos 11–12, from Hoard B). The treatment of the coins from the hoards is discussed in detail in Chapter 15.

A number of damage patterns were identified amongst the hoard objects and stray finds. Torcs of various sizes, wire thicknesses and alloy colours were deliberately bent or cut. For example, **Figure 20.17** shows one end of a short length of multi-strand neck-ring (F.96); note the characteristic sloping, clean-cut ends. In this case, the wire metal is sound and in excellent condition, therefore an apparently serviceable torc has been deliberately rendered unusable. As a comparison with the cut wires of F.96, a test cut was made on one of the experimentally made copper wires of similar diameter (Ch. 17), using a double-bladed wire cutter. The cut ends (**Fig. 20.18**) show the same double-sided cut with a central ridge, suggesting that F.96 was most likely also cut with a double-bladed tool, such as a pair of shears.

Other torcs, such as L.16, have been cut in half (**Fig. 20.19a**). This is quite an elaborate object that seems to be otherwise undamaged and has been deliberately and cleanly cut through at the mid-point. Similarly, torc F.116 (**Fig. 20.19b**) has had its terminals cut away, leaving only the neck-ring.

Some of the thickest multi-strand torcs have been cut through by heavy blows from a chisel (**Fig. 20.20a–b**). Numerous short pieces (*c.* 20mm long) of similar thick rods from multi-strand torc neck-rings were found (e.g. **Fig. 20.21**). Their similar lengths suggest that cutting was intended to produce fragments of a uniform length or weight which might have had other uses beyond recycling. One piece was in the process of being cut into smaller sections with a deep cut half-way through the thick twisted wire, about one third of the way along, but the final blow to separate the pieces was not done (**Fig. 20.22**). As well as cutting the torcs with shears and chisels, there are numerous deliberately bent, kinked, and folded wires and torc fragments. Others have been twisted to destruction. There are also cut, flattened and crushed sheet pieces (e.g. **Fig. 20.23**), many of which are probably parts of dismantled and broken-up tubular torcs.

Fusing

Hoard F in particular not only contains numerous fragments of broken torcs, wires and sheet, but some are partly fused together or have droplets of solidified molten metal on their surfaces (e.g. F.32–F.44; see **Pls 14.22–3**). Either a molten alloy was splashed or poured onto these fragments, or very localised heating was applied (likely by blow pipe) that only melted the component with the lowest melting point and was stopped before the rest of the wires were fully melted. Machling and Williamson (2020a) have also theorised that these part-melted pieces could have been part of a failed melt or that spatters of molten droplets could have been caused by a failed casting in the vicinity of these objects. This is possible in some instances, although the frequency and nature of this phenomenon suggests that it very probably was not all accidental and other processes were involved.

One compact assemblage has cut gold wires with gold droplets partially melted and fused onto a shapeless copper-rich alloy lump (**Fig. 20.24**). Another example is the assemblage F.40 (**Fig. 20.25**) which is made up of a long, thick wire bent into a loop and folded back on itself with two

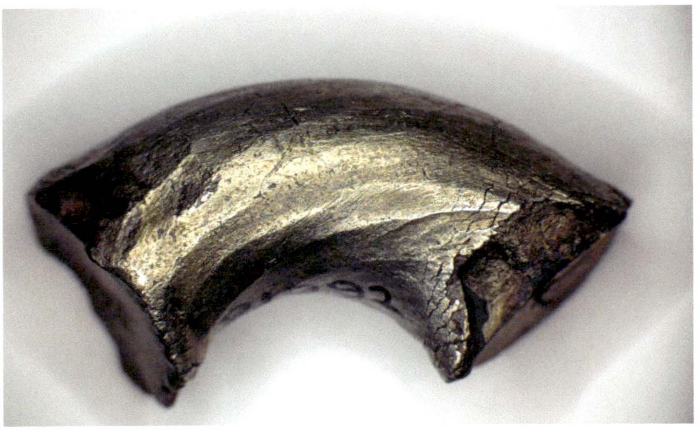

Figure 20.21 Chiselled torc wire (S.42), *c.* 9mm in diameter

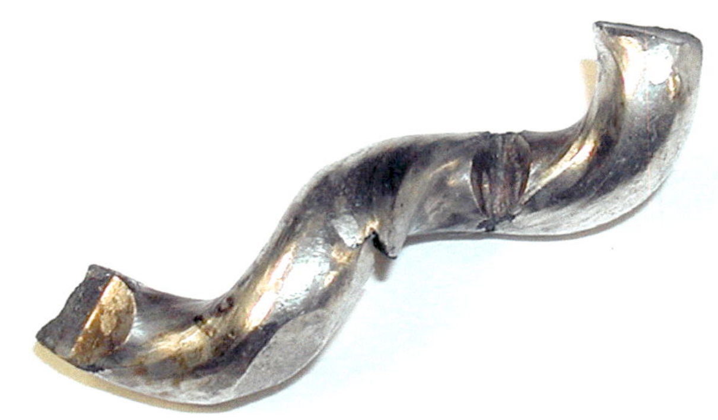

Figure 20.22 Thick torc wire fragment (F.75), with chiselled ends and deep incomplete cuts in the centre

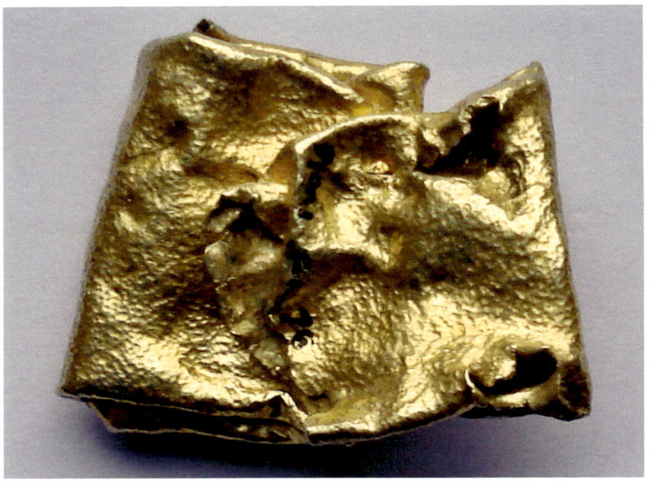

Figure 20.23 Cut, crushed and folded sheet fragment from dismantled tubular torc (F.52)

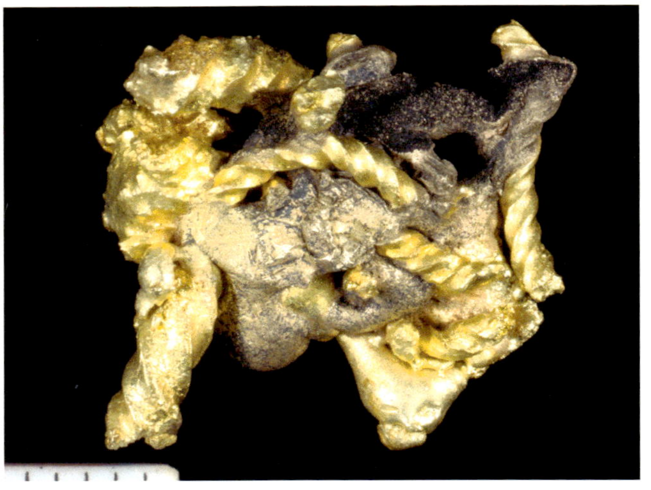

Figure 20.24 Conglomerate of part-fused wires and molten blobs of mixed alloys (S.134) (width of object 25mm)

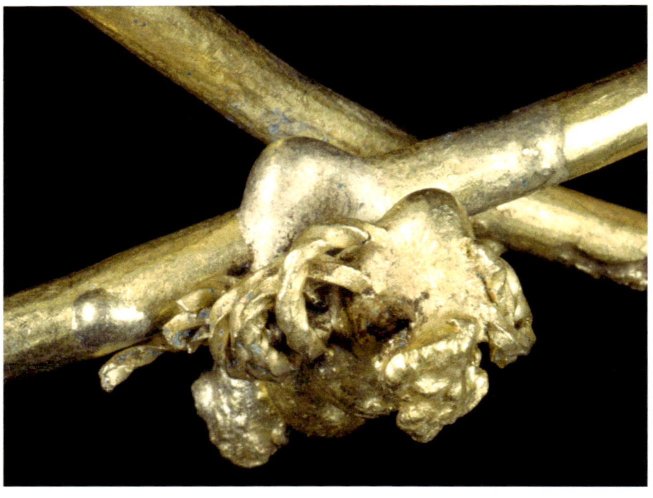

Figure 20.25 Fused wires and fragments on F.40

twists. At one end there is a part-fused blob containing square-section wire and dribbles of molten gold. The bent, thin tubular torc F.42 (**Fig. 20.26**) has a broken wire torc fragment lying across it; the join is well fused and there are also splashes of molten gold on the tube and wire. Torc fragment F.34 is formed of round-section wires which have been cut at one end, whereas on the opposing side there is a semi-fused mass made up of wires from the torc plus other square-section twisted wires melted onto it (**Fig. 20.27**). Hoard F (and stray finds e.g. S.11a–b, S.47, S.67, S.131–6, which are possibly associated with F) is not the only assemblage to show heating processes; the broken end of L.15 also shows melting (though not fused additions), and melted droplets are seen on the terminal of torc fragment E.1b. A group of plated coins from the wooded area of the site also seem to have been affected by heat, with metal droplets, perhaps from the plating or underlying metal, visible on their surface (see **Fig. 15.6**).

These fusions most likely result from some kind of deliberate activity rather than accidental heating, such as a fire, because of the unusual splattering of molten metal and fused cut fragments, and the lack of other general fire damage in the hoards. The compositions of these partly fused composite metal fragments and wires vary from high-gold to copper-rich alloys, with the gold alloys forming the main fusing component because of their lower melting point. In the case of F.40 the localised fusing-together of several small cut pieces of wire of different compositions points towards a desire to consolidate these small fragments into a single larger piece. Other examples appear to be fusing of fragments with no obvious connection, such as scraps of twisted wire onto a sheet-metal terminal (F.42).

Linking

There are several composite bundles of artefacts. These can include quite a mixture of objects in terms of their colour, and neck-ring and terminal types. Over 20 of these bundles are present in Hoard F (F.1–F.28). No two bundles are the same, perhaps implying they were collected by different

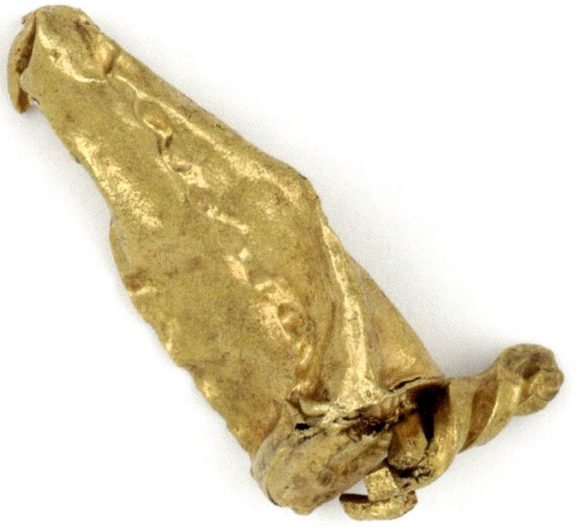

Figure 20.26 F.42: wires from a multi-strand torc or bracelet fused onto the face of a tubular torc terminal fragment

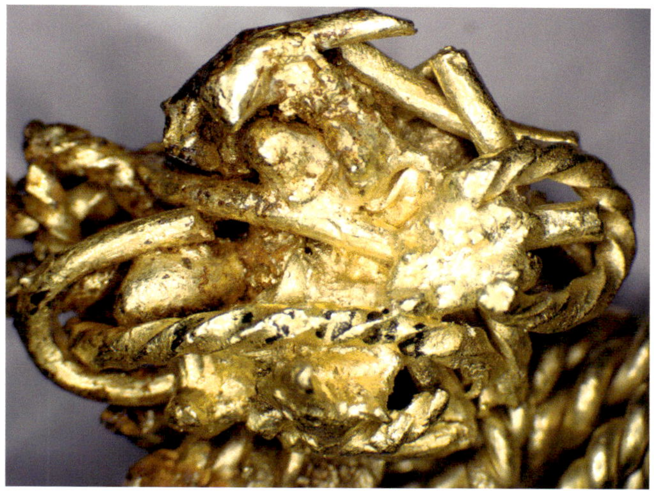

Figure 20.27 Fused mass on one end of cut multi-strand neck-ring fragment F.34, incorporating other types of wire

individuals or groups, or for a variety of purposes. Some artefacts were simply looped together, for example to create a chain of small rings (**Fig. 20.28**). In cases of bundles including torcs, as with the example shown in **Figure 20.29**, the terminal loops (or looped neck-ring sections) of broken torcs or bracelets were sometimes threaded onto a ring. Other groups were interlinked in more complicated ways, such as the six torc fragments that make up F.4a–f.

Whilst some of these composite groups are made up of similar objects (such as small rings, F.25–F.27) or possibly fragments of the same broken torc (F.11a–b, F.16a–b), most seem to emphasise variety. Note the range of alloys of varying colours in **Figure 20.29**: from deep gold to silver, and even including copper alloy fragments. The selection of fragments with a wide range of colours is seen in the majority of these bundles, and was surely intentional. There is also often variation in the types of objects represented in a single bundle. For example, group F.5a–g (**Fig. 20.30**) is a combination of a small silvery-gold-coloured ring formed from a wrought rectangular-section bar (F.5b), a large cut section of thick gold multi-strand torc neck-ring (F.5c), a large section of a multi-strand gold wire torc which has been folded into a tight loop (F.5d), a single length of tightly twisted square-section gold wire curled into a ring (F.5e), a piece of a simple, thin, silver-coloured pair of plied wires, likely from a torc or bracelet (F.5f), and part of a narrow tubular torc kinked twice where it has been folded over (F.5g). All of these are looped onto a second (silvery-coloured) small ring (F.5a), also formed from a wrought bar with rectangular cross-section. Even in groups where similar objects or fragments are brought together, they often come from different objects. For example, bundles F.1a–e and F.2a–i each include two very similar tubular torc terminals. But on close inspection these paired terminals are not identical, suggesting that they came from different torcs. The possible functions of these varied assemblages are discussed below.

In some instances, the collection or interlinking process was itself destructive, with, for example, rough perforations

Figure 20.28 Linked assemblage F.18e–h, j–l (drawing by Craig Williams)

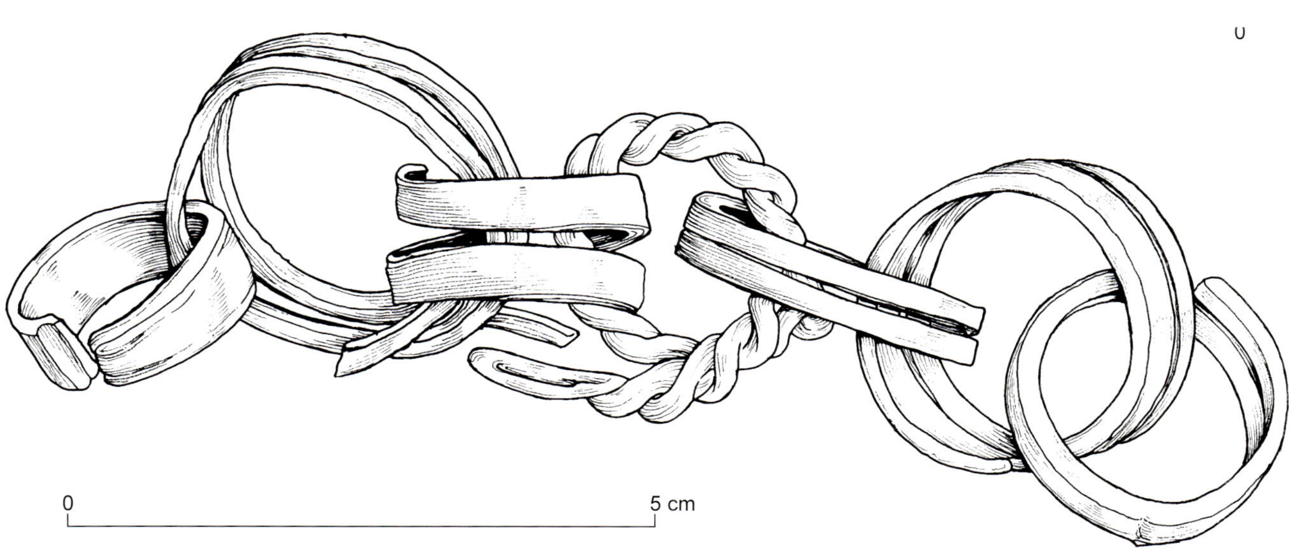

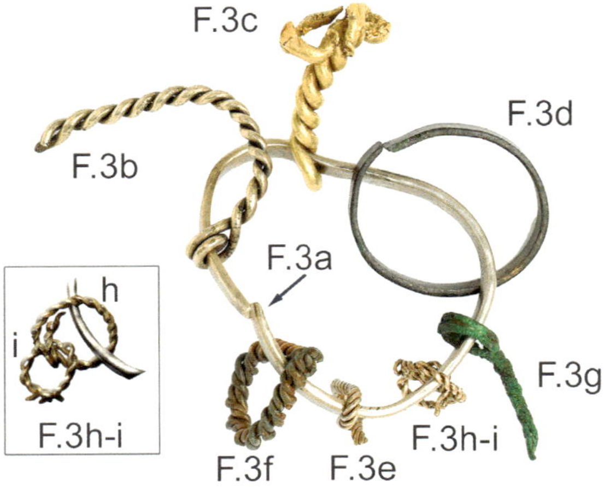

Figure 20.29 Bundle F.3a–i: An interlinked group of torc fragments and rings

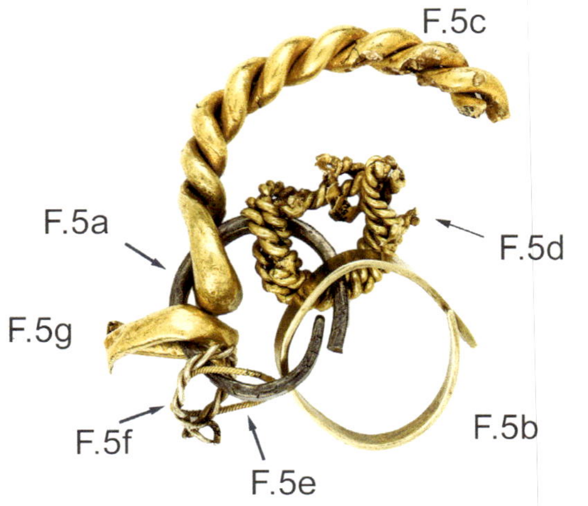

Figure 20.30 Bundle F.5a–g: An interlinked group of torc fragments and rings

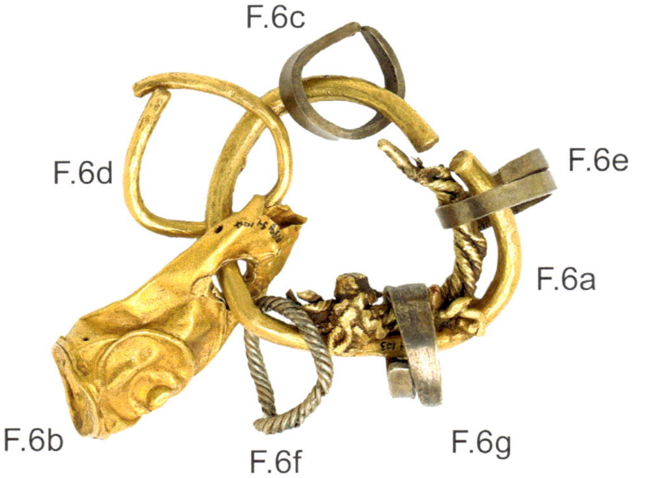

Figure 20.31 Bundle F.6a–g: An interlinked group of torc fragments and rings

made in tubular torc fragments to attach them to rings (**Fig. 20.31**). Tubular torc fragments were also flattened and folded (as on F.19). In Hoard F, a group of coins (nos 174–8) were deposited contained within a cut section of tubular torc (F.53), folded to create a sealed 'package'.

Hoard E (**Fig. 20.32**) could also be viewed as another form of bundle. A torc fragment (E.1b) and bracelet (E.1c) were both looped together, and the torc fragment was passed through the eyes of the terminals of the 'Great Torc' (E.1a), while a coin (no. 169) was found inside one of its terminals.

In addition, some 'individual' artefacts could also be viewed as bundles, especially those repaired using parts of other objects. The most obvious example is the 'Grotesque Torc', L.19, with a piece of gold sheet (possibly a fragment of tubular torc) used to repair the back of the neck-ring and a broken multi-strand torc or bracelet employed as a 'clasp' to hold the terminals together. In both instances little attempt was made to modify these additional components beyond what was necessary to execute the repair. They therefore remained recognisable artefacts, each with their own histories and biographies. By combining these objects with the torc, their biographies also became intertwined.

Torc biographies

We now turn to the question of how analysis of use and damage can tell us about the lives of torcs before they were buried. As we have seen, many of the torcs (especially multi-strand examples) were heavily worn and must have had long lives before they were collected and deposited in the Snettisham hoards. Few, if any, of the artefacts examined were new, meaning that they were not made especially for deposition and that torcs must have formed an important part of daily and/or ceremonial life. If not an everyday sight, they must have been familiar objects to people living in Norfolk in the 3rd, 2nd and early to mid-1st centuries BC. Examples such as L.19 and L.20 were extensively repaired and could easily have been well over a hundred years old when they were deposited (Ch. 21). This not only underlines the potential social significance of the artefacts but possibly also the value placed on the skill of their manufacture. The fact that such objects had long lives, perhaps regularly being passed down as heirlooms, is perhaps unsurprising given that many were made of gold/silver alloy, a material not extensively used in Britain since the end of the Bronze Age (La Niece *et al.* 2018) and which must have been relatively scarce, at least when torcs were first made in Iron Age Britain, probably sometime in the 3rd or 4th century BC (Chs 21, 22).

Based on this evidence, a number of different scenarios present themselves as the potential biography or itinerary for a torc (Kopytoff 1986; Gosden and Marshall 1999; Joy 2009a; Joyce and Gillespie 2015). The simplest possible narrative is that a torc was commissioned and made for a single person; they wore it intensively, possibly daily and certainly regularly. Torcs could have been given as gifts, to mark life stages and transitions, or in other specific systems of gift exchange (cf. Sharples 2010, 92–5). Through the repeated performance of wearing a torc it became a part of that person: torc and person combined in negotiations of status and identity. Based on the extensive wear on some of the torcs, it is likely that their lives extended beyond a single human lifespan. Perhaps some were therefore passed down to the next generation as a form of heirloom (Lillios 1999). Others may have been exchanged, building histories as they moved between people and places (Gosden and Marshall 1999).

It is difficult to establish whether extensive wear is the result of intensive usage over a relatively short period or less regular usage over an extended period, perhaps decades or even centuries. It is probable that examples from Snettisham represent both extremes and various points in between. Certainly, as evidenced by the way some torcs were decorated (Ch. 21) and through radiocarbon dating of organic components (see **Table 5.2**), some of the torcs were quite old when deposited. Radiocarbon dates were acquired for two torcs as part of the Oxford University 'Technologies of Enchantment' project (Garrow *et al.* 2009). The charcoal core inside fragment F.168 (roundwood less than 10 years old) gave a date of 370–120 cal BC at 95% probability, and 350–170 cal BC at 68% probability. This object was part of Hoard F, which also included Gallo-Belgic coins dating to the mid-1st century BC. This suggests a probable age of at least a hundred years for the torc fragment at the time of burial. Two samples of lime wood fibre string (less than five years old) bound around the back of torc L.6 as a repair to the neck-ring were also tested. One gave an unexpectedly early date of 780–510 cal BC (at 95% probability), most likely an error (Garrow *et al.* 2009, 95), while the other produced a date closely in line with the Hoard F fragment: 360–110 cal BC at 95% probability and 350–170 cal BC at 68% probability. Whilst an early date for the deposition of Hoard L cannot be ruled out, the close stylistic similarities between Hoard L and Hoard F support the likelihood they were deposited within a fairly narrow timeframe. This suggests that torc L.6 was probably of considerable antiquity when it was buried, and the same is probably true of some of the other very heavily worn and repaired torcs from Hoard L (L.19 and L.20 in particular). It is interesting that these demonstrably old and damaged objects were at the bases of their respective pits (L.19–L.21 were at the bottom of the main Hoard L pit, and L.6 was at the base of the upper deposit). These pieces (likely heirlooms, and in at least one case broken to the point of being unwearable), were placed into the ground first, before other (likely newer and certainly less worn) torcs were placed on top. The implications of the placement of torcs of different ages within the hoards are discussed further in Chapter 23.

A distinction must be drawn between the generally high levels of wear observed on multi-strand torcs versus the relatively light wear seen on tubular torcs. Whether this implies a short use-life for tubular torcs or low intensity usage over a longer period is difficult to determine. If the latter is the case, when not in use, the tubular torcs must have been carefully stored. Given the considerable evidence for the damage, both deliberate and accidental, of multi-strand torcs outlined above, it is perhaps likely that the tubular torcs were relatively new and therefore little-used when buried, especially when compared to the multi-strand torcs. This has implications in terms of the possible dating of tubular and multi-strand torcs. Depending on when the hoards were deposited, which is thought to be most likely sometime in the 2nd century BC through to *c.* 60 BC, it implies that tubular torcs could be a product of the 2nd and 1st centuries BC, whereas stylistic and radiocarbon dating demonstrates that multi-strand torcs date back at least to the 3rd century BC.

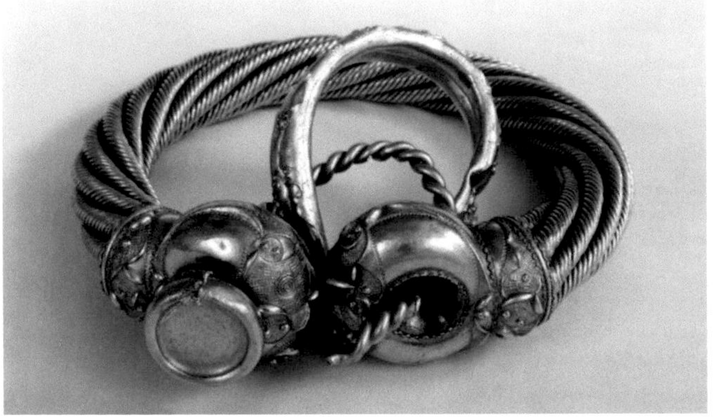

Figure 20.32 A reconstruction of the Great Torc assemblage (objects E.1a–c) as found

The broad-bodied tubular torcs in particular were made from very thin sheet gold and would have been damaged very easily. Their use was therefore most probably ceremonial, or at least restricted to very particular individuals or occasions. It is possible that some of the larger, more ostentatious multi-strand torcs were also reserved for ceremonial use, but this would have to have taken place over a very long period of time to achieve the extensive wear that has been observed. In this instance they could have been worn as expressions of status (or by holders of a particular office or role) but, given the archaeological record of Norfolk at the time that they were made and used, such a position is possibly more likely to have been acquired through actions and experience rather than through birth-right (cf. Hill 2006). Rather than sharing intertwined life trajectories with specific individuals, ceremonial torcs may have spent much of their lives unused. They perhaps built biographies through the performances and events at which they were worn. Joy (2010) suggested that this may also have been how some Iron Age mirrors were used: they remained covered and stored away for much of their lives.

Whatever their individual life trajectories, all of these artefacts were collected together and incorporated into special deposits at Snettisham. It is uncertain what proportion of the torcs in general circulation ended their Iron Age lives in this way, but other evidence suggests that many were probably recycled and made into something else. For example, both at Snettisham and elsewhere it is clear that a number of different processes were employed to break torcs up, including the use of double-bladed tools (such as shears) and chisels to cut wires (see above, and Gazetteer in Ch. 22). It is quite hard to determine exactly how long before deposition these destructive processes took place. But, given specialist tools were often employed, it is likely there was some degree of planning involved: it was not a spontaneous act. This raises the possibility that many more torcs were in circulation and that only a small proportion made their way into the archaeological record. The presence of many bits of torcs and/or bracelets which cannot be re-formed into a complete artefact also invites the question 'Where is the rest?' (cf. Chapman, J. 2000). Was a part of the artefact kept for special deposition and the remainder recycled, or were they buried in as-yet undiscovered places (cf. Garrow and Gosden 2012, 172–3)?

As noted by Garrow and Gosden (2012, 191, see also Chapman, J. 2000, 45–6), fragmentation of artefacts can take two forms: breaking up individual objects and separating items designed to be a part of a set. In the case of the Snettisham hoards, it is difficult to be certain if sets of artefacts were also broken up. For example, if a particular torc was intended to be worn with a specific bracelet or armlet. Nevertheless, as is demonstrated in Hoard E, where a torc and a bracelet with very similar decoration (see Ch. 21) and probably made as a set were linked together in the hoard, some sets were maintained. This does not necessarily mean that the life trajectories of these two artefacts followed the same path. They could have been worn by different people or reserved for different occasions, but certainly in deposition an attempt was made to maintain links between the two artefacts or even to reunite them.

Close examination of artefacts from the fragmentary hoards, particularly Hoard F, also shows how artefacts were not only deliberately broken up, but were also linked and fused together to create something new. As Garrow and Gosden observed, 'artefacts have been transformed from wholes to parts and then combined in new ways' (Garrow and Gosden 2012, 140). Groups of artefacts, whether looped, inserted or fused together, form distinct collections of objects within the hoards. Thinking of these as individual 'mini-collections' may help us to account for how the artefacts from large hoards like Hoard F were collected, highlighting a stage in the biographies of hoarded objects which is often neglected: collecting (Joy 2016). As has been suggested for Late Bronze Age hoards from the Carpathian Basin (Dietrich 2014, 479–80; Hansen 1996–8, 19–23), smaller groups of artefacts within a larger whole could have been intended to separate out contributions to the hoard made by individuals or groups. In this way, the grouping of objects may have been entangled with the relationships of the people who made, owned and wore them. That they are deliberately held together implies collection by an individual person for easy storing, holding or transporting, or as a unit of value, so the concept of ownership also comes into play for these bundles and their potential as exchange value. Joy raised some potential motivations behind gathering and depositing these smaller collections within a larger hoard: 'collections such as looped finger rings could have been gathered from various family members, or wider social groups, before being incorporated into the larger collection, explaining the variations in the diameter and form of these rings. In this instance, personal gifts towards the collection were linked together to represent broader social groupings and a collective effort' (Joy 2016, 247). The Snettisham fragmentary hoards are quite heterogeneous, which could imply that the objects were collected by different individuals and groups (Joy 2016, 247). It is difficult to tell exactly how long the collection phase prior to deposition lasted, which raises other questions such as 'Where were they kept?' and 'Were they displayed?'. The implications of these observations on the possible purposes and significance of the Snettisham hoards are further considered in Chapter 23.

It seems likely that some composite objects were not linked purely for deposition but were used or worn in this way. Wearing is unlikely (although not impossible) in the cases of the groups from Hoard F (often looped onto a ring), but highly plausible in other cases. L.19 (if worn at all in its broken state) must have been worn along with its 'clasp' formed from a torc or bracelet fragment, as otherwise the broken neck-ring would have rendered it unusable. Other complete torcs deposited in carefully nested hoards have rings or wires looped through their terminals (for example D.1, G.5 and L.10). Even the Great Torc (E.1a) was not found in the solitary state in which it is now displayed at the British Museum, but as an entanglement of objects more closely resembling the composite group that forms the 'Grotesque' Torc (L.19) (compare **Figs 20.15, 20.32**). Bundle H.2 is a particularly interesting case, being formed of two similar but distinct torcs wound around one another to form a single object. Were these additions functional repairs, extra decoration, or a means of keeping scrap together? Alternatively, did they represent an accumulation or layering of their wearers' life stages, relationships, or other kinds of connection?

Fragmentation and accumulation

A variety of explanations have been put forward for the presence of fragmentary object groups such as Hoards B, C and F. In past explanations of the Snettisham deposits, these have generally been interpreted as metalworkers' hoards (Clarke 1954). This potential use is certainly possible, but the patterns of breakage and linkage seem to be of a different nature than one would expect from a collection purely of scrap. For example, why create such elaborate collections of artefacts within the hoard? Whilst in a few cases, as noted above, these groups could have been worn as ornaments in their own right, most could not.

It is possible that the complex interlinked groups present in Hoards B and F represent scrap gathered together, but these mixed sets of artefacts are difficult to explain from a modern understanding of metal recycling in which different alloys would be first separated before melting. Within the bundles there is generally no selection by alloy colour (composition): gold-rich, silver-rich and copper alloy pieces are incorporated together. Whilst the sheet gold objects tend to be high in gold content, the precious metal rings and multi-strand torcs are varied ternary alloys of gold, silver and copper (Ch. 17). Indeed, in some cases such as bundle F.3a–i, it is almost as if the aim was to collect together examples of as many different colours as were produced. Machling and Williamson (2020) have suggested that some of these composite groups could represent a kind of 'pattern book' for torc makers, although this explanation works better for some bundles (such as F.3 and F.7) than others.

Whilst an intended use as batches of scrap for melting and recycling into other objects cannot be ruled out, it would have been extremely hard to control alloy composition when mixing objects in this way. Refining gold would have been a very time consuming, specialised and technical process (Ramage and Craddock 2000) that surely would have been largely avoided, if possible, by simply pre-sorting the metals. Such groups could in theory, however, have been used to make new rings, torcs or bracelets. Indeed, Northover (Ch. 18) has argued that the wrought large and small rings found at Snettisham were probably made from mixed recycled torc components. In this scenario, the careful grouping of such disparate elements into discrete bundles raises the question of whether the identities and biographies of the objects chosen to be recycled together were more important than their metal content.

Joy (2016, 247) argued that the deposition of the Snettisham torc hoards coincided with the period when coinage was first minted in Norfolk (Ch. 23; Chadburn 2006). Whilst the metal content of coinage was relatively carefully controlled and in many cases seems to have used standard alloys based on diluted bullion (Northover 1992; Creighton 2000; Farley 2012), there does seem to have been some addition of recycled metal. For example, Northover (1992) highlights the similar compositions of early gold coinage and torcs in Late Iron Age Gaul, and Northover (*ibid.*, 247) and Ponting (Appendix 4) have argued that high-tin copper alloy Kentish potin coinage may have been melted down and incorporated into some of the early insular precious metal issues. Mixed groups of objects (such as the composite interlinked groups) would probably only have been readily recyclable into coinage as a small component of a much larger batch of metal, but it is likely that at least in some instances high-gold torcs or refined gold and silver from other objects could have been re-used to make coins.

If indeed many torcs (or parts of torcs) were recycled into coinage or other objects, this raises the question of why so many were buried at Snettisham, thus removing their metal content from circulation. It is likely that to some degree there were social rules regulating such recycling behaviours, and it may have been considered necessary to employ a certain proportion of such objects in votive practices. If and when torcs were broken up to make coins, perhaps a fragment was kept, looped onto a ring and held aside for appropriate deposition. Offering a part of an object to represent a whole, or *pars pro toto*, is a practice which was followed at Greek sanctuaries. It has also been offered as an explanation for why some Bronze Age hoards contain fragments (Hansen 2013, 180) and is widely practised in cremation burial on the continent at this time. In Britain, a small fragment of gold foil, likely from a tubular torc, was also recovered from a cremation burial at Westhampnett, West Sussex (Fitzpatrick 1997, 97–9).

Alternatively, if as is suggested above, some of the bundles operated as a kind of 'pattern book' (Machling and Williamson 2020), it provides a different perspective on so-called 'scrap' hoards. Interpreted from this viewpoint, some of these bundles may have served important roles in the selection by consumers of what they wanted metalworkers to make. Their incorporation into hoards brought about a ceremonial closure to this process, perhaps signalling an end to the manufacture and consumption of torcs.

In other cases, particularly those of complete torcs, it is possible that these were potent or deeply personal objects in their own right, and that it may not have been considered appropriate to melt down these pieces. The value of coinage lies explicitly in its standardisation and multiplicity – the possibility of creating, distributing or keeping many similar, small, portable objects. Torcs are different. Every torc represented at Snettisham is unique. In some cases, there may have been a pressure or preference not to dissolve recognisable (and perhaps powerful) objects with individual histories into the more anonymous and standardised world of coinage, where it is essential that batches of similar issues hold like-for-like value (regardless of the previous forms of the metal).

Fragmentation could also be considered a form of decommissioning or symbolic 'killing' of the artefact in preparation for deposition, as is sometimes argued for the deliberate damage inflicted on weaponry in watery contexts and burials. The practice of deliberate damage to martial metalwork is seen in 1st-century BC grave goods from Britain including the warrior burial from Kelvedon, Essex (Sealey 2007), where the sword was removed from its scabbard and bent prior to burial, and an iron spearhead was also bent and its shaft possibly snapped.

J. Chapman's (2000; see also Chapman and Gaydarska 2007) well-known theories on fragmentation and accumulation are useful for thinking through the patterns of wear and re-forming observed at Snettisham (although it is noted that there are some problems with this theory (Fowler 2004; Jones 2005; Gamble 2007; Brittain and Harris 2010) and that it relates to a particular case study from Balkan prehistory). Chapman stated that, '…the notion that fragments of objects transmit not only the symbolism of their complete, once-intact form but also the enchained, or fractal, connotations of past makers and owners would account for a wide variety of fragmentation behaviour' (Chapman, J. 2000, 39). In other words, fragments were not just intended to stand for whole objects (*pars pro toto*); they enchained relationships between people and objects.

Returning to Snettisham, it is clear that in many instances, fragmentation of torcs was deliberate. Perhaps a part was kept for deposition, representative of the whole, but allowing the bulk of the object to be recycled. Their inclusion in the hoards might have embodied or made present particular individuals/groups and even the relationships between them. Following this line of thinking, other scenarios also present themselves. For example, as Gosden has suggested, bits of torc '…could have operated in small units like coins, and in some cases, like the highly decorated tubular torc fragment, they carried complex decorations' (Gosden 2013, 49). These bits of torc may have acted as 'extended' (cf. Gell 1998) versions of the whole object, only multiplied and transformed into smaller, more transferable units. Another more prosaic explanation could be that some forms of breakage, for example the division of thick wires into roughly equal sizes, was a part of the recycling process – a standard unit perhaps used in weighing out specific quantities of different alloys to make a batch of metal with a certain composition. The two explanations are of course not mutually exclusive as memories of previous artefacts could have been maintained in new artefact forms (Ch. 23).

J. Chapman's (2000) original work was focused on the Balkans, where he contended Neolithic people selected fragmentary objects for use in exchange and as a means of linking people, objects and places through what he called enchainment. A further aspect to his work, which has received less attention, is the related category of accumulation, whereby objects were gathered into sets which generate different types of relations. At first sight, this model seems to fit well with the objects from the Snettisham

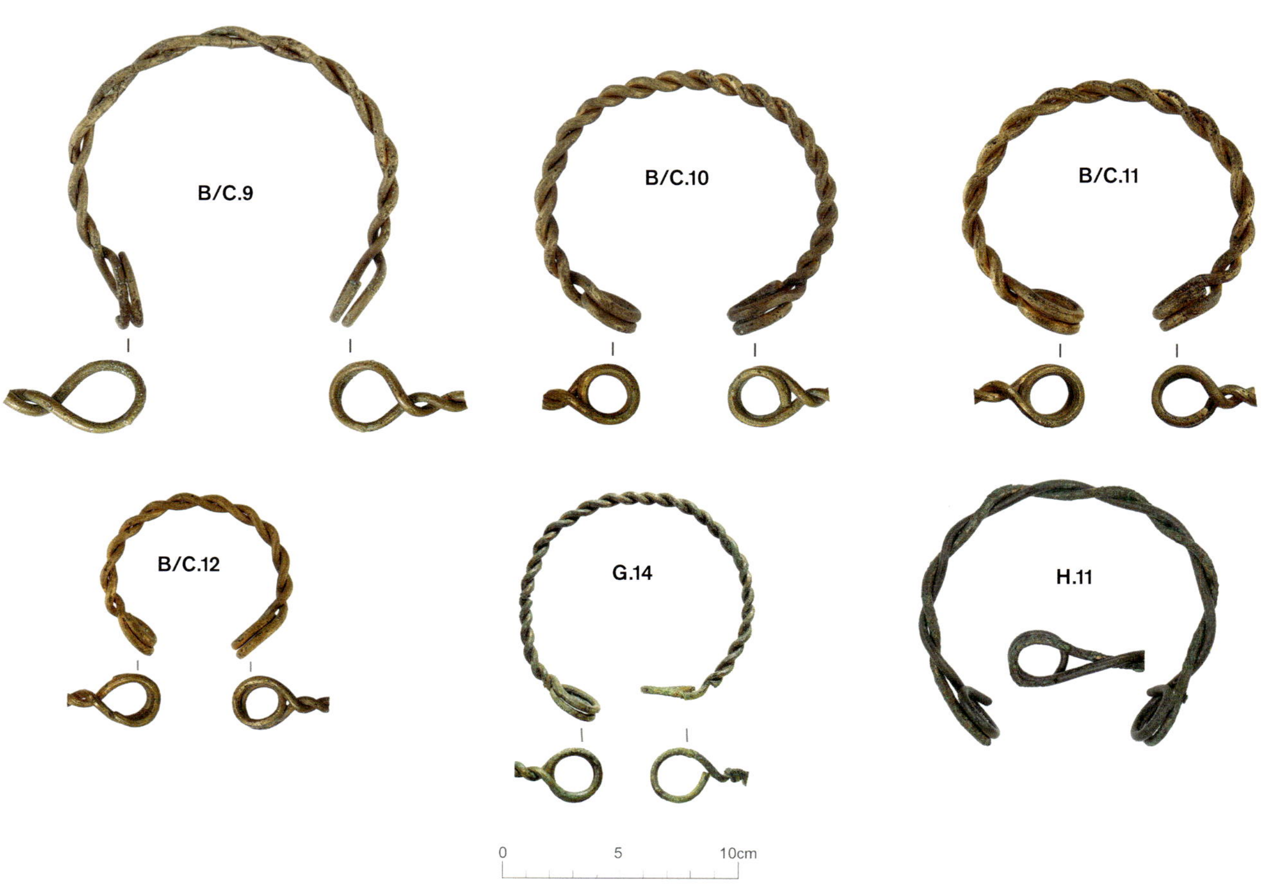

Figure 20.33 Torcs B/C.9, B/C.10, B/C.11, G.14, H.11 and bracelet B/C.12

hoards. There is abundant evidence for the deliberate fragmentation of objects as well as accumulation through the creation of sets or collections of artefacts as hoards, and also within hoards. Whilst Chapman's is a highly plausible explanation of material from the Balkans, following Brittain and Harris (2010), we are alert to the issues related to imprinting it onto Iron Age Norfolk. Rather, the fragmentation and accumulation of artefacts is viewed as transformational, whereby processes associated with recycling (such as breaking up and re-forming objects) were cited through the collection and manipulation of artefacts prior to their deposition.

Biography case study: twist direction, makers and selective treatment in deposition

Beyond interlinked groups, sealed hoard contexts or 'matched' sets such as E.1a and E.1c, it is generally hard to distinguish apparent groups or sets of objects at Snettisham, and any implications this may have for their makers, users and treatment in deposition. One case where this may be possible is an unusual group of simple torcs incorporating Z-twist in their manufacture.

Both S-twist and Z-twist directions are used in the Snettisham multi-strand torcs, though S-twist overwhelmingly predominates. Z-twist is used almost exclusively in complex multi-stage neck-rings where it is combined with S-twist to produced particular effects (see Ch. 13). Eight small objects/fragments in Hoard F (F.3e, F.3h-i, F.4d, F.8b, F.11a-b, F.44, F.141, F.142) have a primary Z-twist construction, i.e. represent simple Stage II objects with wires plied directly together Z-twist. Only two of these sets (F.4d, F.3.h-i) seem likely to represent the existence of Stage II Z-twist objects. The others are more likely re-twisted, unfinished or fragments from more complex torcs. There are only two other objects in the BM collection with a primary Z-twist construction: G.14 and K.5. Each of these is of (2PZ) construction, i.e. two wires plied directly together Z-twist.

Among the NCM material, Hoard 'B/C' (the mixed material deriving from Hoards B and C) has four complete torcs/bracelets with the same (2PZ) construction (B/C.9, B/C.10, B/C.11, B/C.12; **Fig. 20.33**) and fragments representing at least another five such objects (B/C.5, B/C.14–15, B/C.24, B/C.35, and B/C.36). There are also two fragments of neck-ring with (3PZ) construction (B/C.42–3), a design not shared by any other objects from the site. Together, this suggests a minimum number of ten objects from Hoard B/C objects with a simple Stage II Z-twist construction. These include more-or-less the only complete torcs/bracelets from Hoards B and C (the only other contenders being the two now-fragmentary torcs represented by B/C.47–53).

This is a significantly higher proportion of simple Z-twist torcs and bracelets in Hoards B and/or C than in other assemblages (around 16% of multi-strand objects/fragments with an identifiable construction across assemblages B, C and B/C, compared to just 2% in Hoard F). The complete Hoard B/C pieces (three small torcs – B/C.9, B/C.10, B/C.11, and a bracelet – B/C.12), are distinctive enough to appear to represent a group or set. All are very simple copper alloy pieces, made from either two wires, giving open loop terminals (B/C.9), or one wire doubled-back on itself to give one closed and one open loop (B/C.10-12). This is unusual across the site, where closed loops (soldered or hammered to give the effect of a single continuous wire) are the norm. Their alloys are similar in terms of bulk composition; impurity patterns suggest that the smaller objects, B/C.10–12, may have had a similar metal source, with comparable levels of Co, Ni and Ag, whilst B/C.9 is higher in both Co and Ag, and falls into Northover's 'Group 1' (Co>Ni and Sb<0.10%).

K.5 is very different (in a gold/silver alloy and with ring terminals), so does not seem to belong with the B/C group. Torc G.14, whilst made from wire with a finer gauge, is otherwise very similar to the B/C examples in terms of both external diameter and construction, and could be suggested as part of the same group (**Fig. 20.33**).

The small size of these simple Z-twist torcs is notable. Torc B/C.9 is small, but has had its terminals pulled open quite wide. By internal diameter, torcs B/C.10 and B.C/11, with G.14, are three of the five smallest torcs from the site. The others are H.9, a coiled torc with its terminals overlapping, reducing its diameter significantly, and H.11 (**Fig. 20.33**). The latter is made S-twist, but is otherwise virtually identical to B/C.9 (made from two wires to give open loop terminals, and having a loose neck-ring twist). Notably, Torcs H.11 and G.14 were both treated in a similar way, being placed at the base of the lower pits of nested hoard deposits (see Ch. 23). The B/C.9-12 group also seem to have received special treatment, being perhaps the only torcs and bracelets from Hoards B and C that were not broken up before deposition.

The small size, simple design and unusual Z-twist construction of bracelet B/C.12 and torcs B/C.9-11 and G.14 perhaps suggest the work of a single person. To the casual observer, there is little difference in the overall effect created by S and Z-twist, but the use of Z-direction twist on these five objects is unlikely to be accidental given its overall rarity across the assemblage and the close visual and technological similarity between the pieces. It is worth noting that Z-twist is the direction a left-handed maker would naturally tend to twist, while for a metalsmith who usually tended to twist wires in the S-direction, this would be a notable change from that habitual motion. Perhaps this was simple personal preference, or maybe Z-twist was considered more appropriate for some individuals, roles or circumstances? H.11, with its similar size and simple construction, may be a related or similar object, despite its opposing twist direction.

It is likely that decisions about collection, grouping, deposition and treatment such as fragmentation were often influenced by factors from the biography of a torc, such as its maker(s) and/or owner/wearer(s). Usually, these elements remain invisible to us, but it seems that in this case a group of torcs, potentially the work of a single maker or workshop, can be identified by their appearance and twist direction. These objects were disproportionately kept whole (rather than being fragmented), and chosen for deposition either in Hoard B/C or at the base of the lower pits of Hoards G and H. They may well have been in some way associated with particular individuals, roles or families/communities.

Summary

The very idea of a straightforward, individual 'object biography' from raw material to finished object to heavily worn heirloom is challenged by the assemblages from Snettisham. While many torcs certainly passed through these stages, some appear unfinished, such as S.17 which retains the casting sprues on its terminals. Others have been repaired, damaged, fragmented and (re)combined in a wide variety of ways. The precise meanings behind these processes are now lost, but it seems certain that they related in some way to referencing, transforming and reconfiguring the complex interrelationships between these objects and their owners, wearers and makers. Further implications of the relationships between fragmentary hoards, hoards of complete or near-complete objects, and other potential groupings among the Snettisham material are considered in Chapter 23.

Chapter 21
Decoration of the Snettisham Torcs and Other Objects

Jody Joy

Excluding coins, roughly 4% of the metalwork finds from Snettisham (over 40 objects) are decorated. This may seem quite a small proportion but, taken as a whole, this represents one of the greatest concentrations of so-called Celtic art from Britain. The decorated finds are summarised in **Table 21.1**. In this chapter the decoration is examined in detail. First the ornament on different artefacts is discussed, before an account is presented of the implications for our understanding of the Snettisham deposits and Celtic art in Britain. A final section questions what the art on torcs may have done. Although features such as the filigree found on two of the large tubular torcs in Hoard A are also considered decorative (see Ch. 17), here analysis is focused on raised, inscribed and punched ornament.

The following account of the decoration, which forms the first section, is broken down by artefact type, beginning with art on torcs.

Decoration on torcs

Most of the decorated objects from Snettisham are torcs, or fragments which might have belonged to either torcs or bracelets/armlets (**Table 21.1**; **Fig. 21.1**). This is also reflected in the dominance of decorated objects which are made of gold/silver alloys (**Fig. 21.2**). Owing to the large number of decorated artefacts, and as an attempt to create some order for the discussion, the art is broadly categorised following Garrow's (2008) distinction between 'swirly' and 'non-swirly', with the terminology altered slightly here to 'curvilinear' and 'non-curvilinear'. Unsurprisingly, objects with curvilinear decoration are considered to be 'artefacts adorned with curvilinear motifs' (Garrow 2008, 19). Other forms of decoration are included in the non-curvilinear group. Stead's (1985a; 1985b; 1996) art 'styles' or 'stages' (he uses both terms in various publications), which build on Jacobsthal's (1969 [1944]) and de Navarro's (1952) categorisations, have been critical to our understanding of Celtic art in Britain. They are drawn upon extensively here, forming the basis of discussion. Stead characterised his styles as 'stages', a sequence of styles replacing each other in a chronological order, albeit with some overlaps. As Stead (2009) himself has recognised, the sequential nature of these styles has been undermined by recent discoveries showing that there is actually considerable overlap, particularly during the 3rd century BC. In this chapter, styles are primarily used as a means of categorisation. Following Garrow and Gosden (2012), Celtic art styles are seen as overlapping and cumulative, not sequential and successive. Close consideration will also be given to the use of different styles on the same object, in particular the deployment of different styles to make potential connections and relations to the past, present and future.

Non-curvilinear

Discussion of non-curvilinear decoration in this section is restricted to torcs decorated exclusively with non-curvilinear patterns. Torcs decorated with a combination of curvilinear and non-curvilinear motifs are discussed in the section on mixtures of motifs.

Only a small number of torcs are decorated exclusively with geometric or other non-curvilinear designs, and the

Cat. no.	Object type	Material	Curvilinear decoration	Non-curvilinear decoration	Stead's 'Style'	Notes
A.1	torc (tubular)	gold/silver alloy	Y	Y	V	Mixes raised curvilinear and non-curvilinear (including punch-marks)
A.2	torc (tubular)	gold/silver alloy	-	Y	-	Punch-marks
A.3	torc (tubular)	gold/silver alloy	-	Y	-	Punch-marks
E.1a	torc (multi-strand)	gold/silver alloy	Y	-	V	Raised curvilinear
E.1c	bracelet	gold/silver alloy	Y	-	V	Raised curvilinear
F.2c	?torc (?tubular)	gold/silver alloy	-	Y	-	Non-curvilinear
F.6b	torc (tubular)	gold/silver alloy	Y	-	V	Raised curvilinear
F.31a	torc (tubular)	gold/silver alloy	Y	Y	II, V	Mixes non-curvilinear with a variety of 'curvilinear' art styles
F.31b	torc (tubular)	gold/silver alloy	-	Y	-	Non-curvilinear
F.32	torc (tubular)	gold/silver alloy	-	Y	-	Non-curvilinear
F.42	torc (tubular)	gold/silver alloy	-	Y	-	Non-curvilinear
F.43	torc (tubular)	gold/silver alloy	Y	-	IV, V	Mixes a variety of 'curvilinear' art styles
F.46	torc (tubular)	gold/silver alloy	Y	Y	V	Mixes raised curvilinear and non-curvilinear
F.53	torc (tubular)	gold/silver alloy	-	Y	-	Non-curvilinear
F.54	torc (tubular)	gold/silver alloy	-	Y	-	Non-curvilinear
F.55	torc (tubular)	gold/silver alloy	-	Y	-	Non-curvilinear
F.57	torc (tubular)	gold/silver alloy	Y	-	V	Raised curvilinear
F.72	torc (multi-strand)	gold/silver alloy	Y	-	III	Plastic Style
F.92	torc (multi-strand)	gold/silver alloy	Y	-	V	Inscribed curvilinear
F.106	torc (multi-strand)	gold/silver alloy	Y	-	V	Mixes raised curvilinear (terminal face) and inscribed curvilinear (terminal edges)
F.115	torc (multi-strand)	gold/silver alloy	Y	-	V	Raised curvilinear
F.119–20	torc (multi-strand)	gold/silver alloy	Y	-	V	Raised curvilinear
F.146	torc (multi-strand)	gold/silver alloy	-	Y	-	Non-curvilinear
F.185	torc (multi-strand)	copper alloy	Y	-	V	Raised curvilinear
F.445	helmet	copper alloy	Y	-	V	Raised curvilinear (decorated patches)
H.7	torc (multi-strand)	gold/silver alloy	-	Y	-	Non-curvilinear
K.7	torc (multi-strand)	gold/silver alloy	-	Y	-	Non-curvilinear
L.10a	torc (multi-strand)	gold/silver alloy	Y	-	V	Inscribed curvilinear
L.11	torc (multi-strand)	gold/silver alloy	Y	-	V	Raised curvilinear
L.12	torc (multi-strand)	gold/silver alloy	Y	-	V	Raised curvilinear
L.13	torc (multi-strand)	gold/silver alloy	Y	-	V	Inscribed curvilinear
L.14	torc (multi-strand)	gold/silver alloy	-	Y	-	Non-curvilinear
L.16	torc (multi-strand)	gold/silver alloy	-	Y	-	Non-curvilinear
L.17	torc (multi-strand)	gold/silver alloy	-	Y	-	Non-curvilinear
L.18	torc (multi-strand)	gold/silver alloy	-	Y	-	Non-curvilinear
L.19a	torc (multi-strand)	gold/silver alloy	Y	-	III	Plastic Style
L.20a	torc (multi-strand)	gold/silver alloy	Y	-	V	Inscribed curvilinear
L.21a	torc (multi-strand)	gold/silver alloy	Y	-	V	Raised curvilinear
S.11a	torc (tubular)	gold/silver alloy	-	Y	-	Non-curvilinear
S.13	torc (tubular)	gold/silver alloy	Y	-	?III, ?V	Anthropomorphic
S.48	torc (multi-strand)	gold/silver alloy	Y	-	V	Raised curvilinear
S.19	torc (multi-strand)	gold/silver alloy	Y	-	V	Inscribed curvilinear
S.83	torc/bracelet	copper alloy	Y	-	?III	Zoomorphic
S.253	horn terminal	copper alloy	Y	-	?IV	Zoomorphic
S.254	horn terminal	copper alloy	Y	-	?IV	Zoomorphic

Table 21.1 Decorated objects from Snettisham

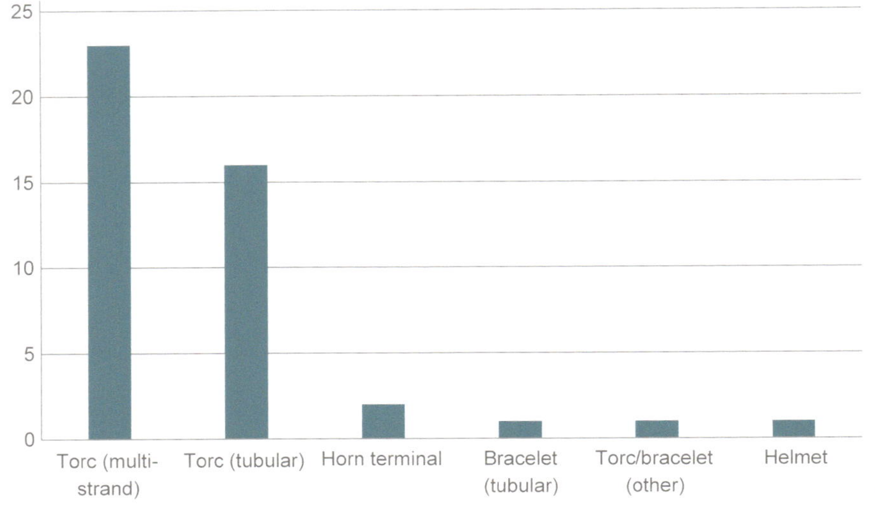

Figure 21.1 Numbers of decorated items by object type (n=44)

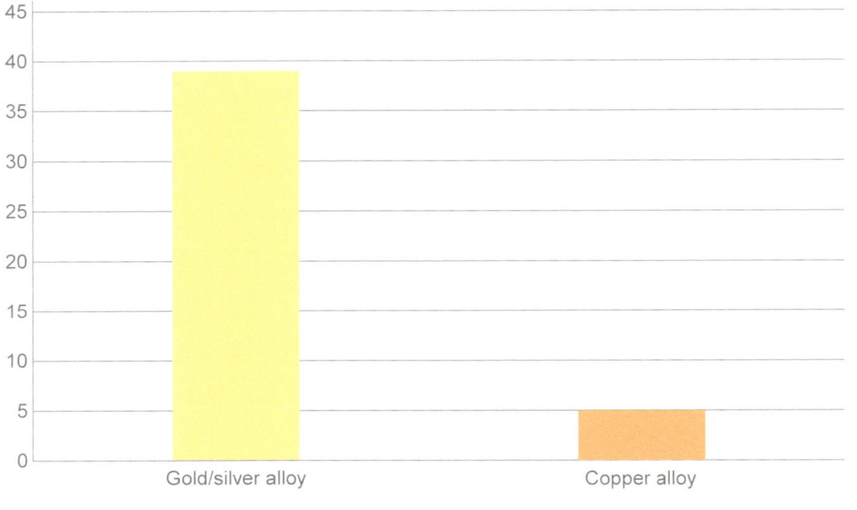

Figure 21.2 Numbers of decorated items by material (n=44)

majority of these are tubular torcs (especially the narrower-bodied neck-rings of Type 4–5 tubular torcs, see Ch. 13). Tubular torcs are also decorated with curvilinear motifs, but these are most often broader-bodied Type 6 torcs, the buffer terminals of Type 1 examples, or the large, flaring terminals of Type 5 torcs (e.g. F.31a, see Ch. 13 for typology). F.54 is a fragment of gold/silver alloy Type 4/5 tubular torc neck-ring, broken at both ends. It is decorated with impressed lines, both angular and spiralled, and a zone of punch-texture/stippling (**Fig. 21.3**). Similarly, F.55 is also a fragment of gold/silver alloy Type 4/5 tubular torc, comprising a short section of neck-ring, broken at both ends. It is decorated with impressed lines, creating a spiral design or mock-twist, with alternating plain and punch-textured zones. The surface of the Type 4–5 tubular torc neck-ring fragment F.53 (**Fig. 21.4**) is elaborately decorated with punched and chased designs. Zones are separated by simple double-grooved lines. One zone is quite simple, with punch-texture/stippling and a line of small, untextured triangles. Another is divided into diamond and triangular-shaped panels within which decorative motifs include concentric circles, crescents and punch-texturing. Terminal F.42 is made of a gold/silver alloy but unlike the examples already mentioned, it is a Type 5 tubular torc fragment with a flat buffer terminal and a lightly tapering neck-ring. The neck-ring has three crimped 'pie-crust' seams and a punch-textured or stippled surface (**Fig. 21.5**). The expanded terminal has a round end-plate with a raised circular 'segmented wreath' motif. F.31b is a short length of narrow Type 1 tubular torc neck-ring (discovered inside Type 5 tubular torc terminal F.31a), with simple decoration consisting of zig-zagging lines of punched dots which divide the surface into lozenge shapes. Similar decoration is also seen on F.32, a Type 4–5 tubular torc neck-ring fragment (**Fig. 21.6**) and the fragment S.11a. S.11a is a gold/silver alloy Type 4 or 5 tubular torc fragment which has been torn at both ends and bent into a tight V-shape. It is decorated with lines of punched dots creating a line of elongated diamond shapes along the surface of the torc (see **Pl. 14.63**).

Small gold alloy sheet fragment F.2c has a raised area of decoration comprising a series of concentric circles, set in a plain field, and may also derive from a tubular torc or torus terminal (**Fig. 21.7**).

As these descriptions indicate, non-curvilinear decoration is largely made up of zones, often bordered by double-grooved lines and chevrons. Zones are triangular, rectangular or diamond-shaped and can be textured by stippling and light punching or left untextured. Areas containing concentric circles and crescents are primarily untextured.

It is of note that non-curvilinear patterns occur only rarely on multi-strand torcs. Here, non-curvilinear designs are generally very simple. They take various different forms, ranging from zig-zag or 'pie-crust' lines or mouldings (seen on F.146, L.17 and L.18), to lines of inscribed dots (K.7, L.16) or raised dots (such as the line of five knobs on the outside of L.14, which may be the heads of rivets which serve a mechanical function, or the decorative raised dots on H.7).

There are few parallels for non-curvilinear decoration on Iron Age metalwork, which is dominated by curvilinear patterns (cf. Garrow 2008). Some swords and scabbards are decorated with concentric circles, such as the raised concentric circles at the bottom of the scabbard from Bugthorpe, Yorkshire. In addition, harness pieces dating to the 1st century AD are decorated with geometric patterns (Davis and Gwilt 2008). But, geometric shapes and non-curvilinear patterns are more common on pottery and antler and bone artefacts than metalwork, with ring and dot motifs but also triangles and diamond patterns often found on objects like long-handled combs made of antler and bone (Tuohy 1999). It is argued elsewhere (Joy 2011) that two parallel decorative traditions can be identified in the later Iron Age in Britain: curvilinear motifs primarily on metalwork, and non-curvilinear motifs on bone and antler artefacts and pots. Of course, there are notable exceptions, such as the curvilinear decoration found on Glastonbury ware (e.g. Cunliffe 2005, A.22–3) and also pottery from some parts of eastern England (e.g. Cunliffe 2005, A.26, A.28–9) but in the main the identified pattern holds true. The decoration on tubular torcs represents another exception.

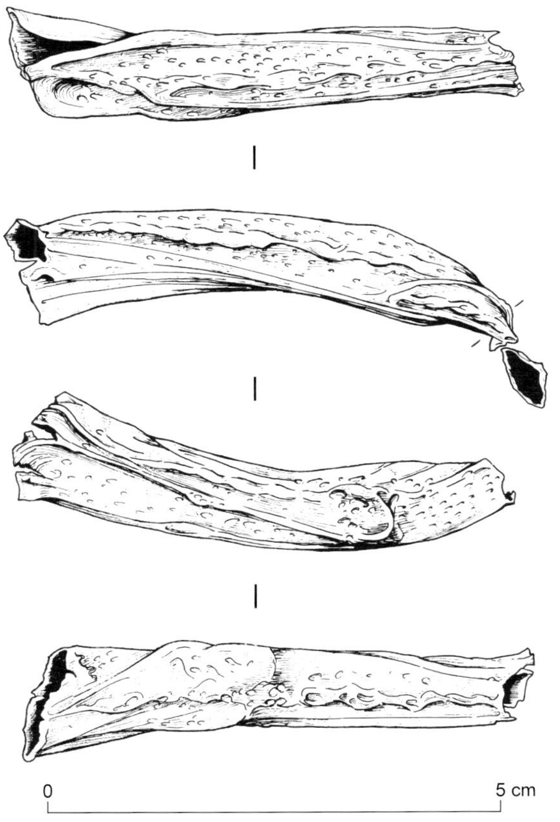

Figure 21.3 Illustration of torc F.54 (drawing by Craig Williams)

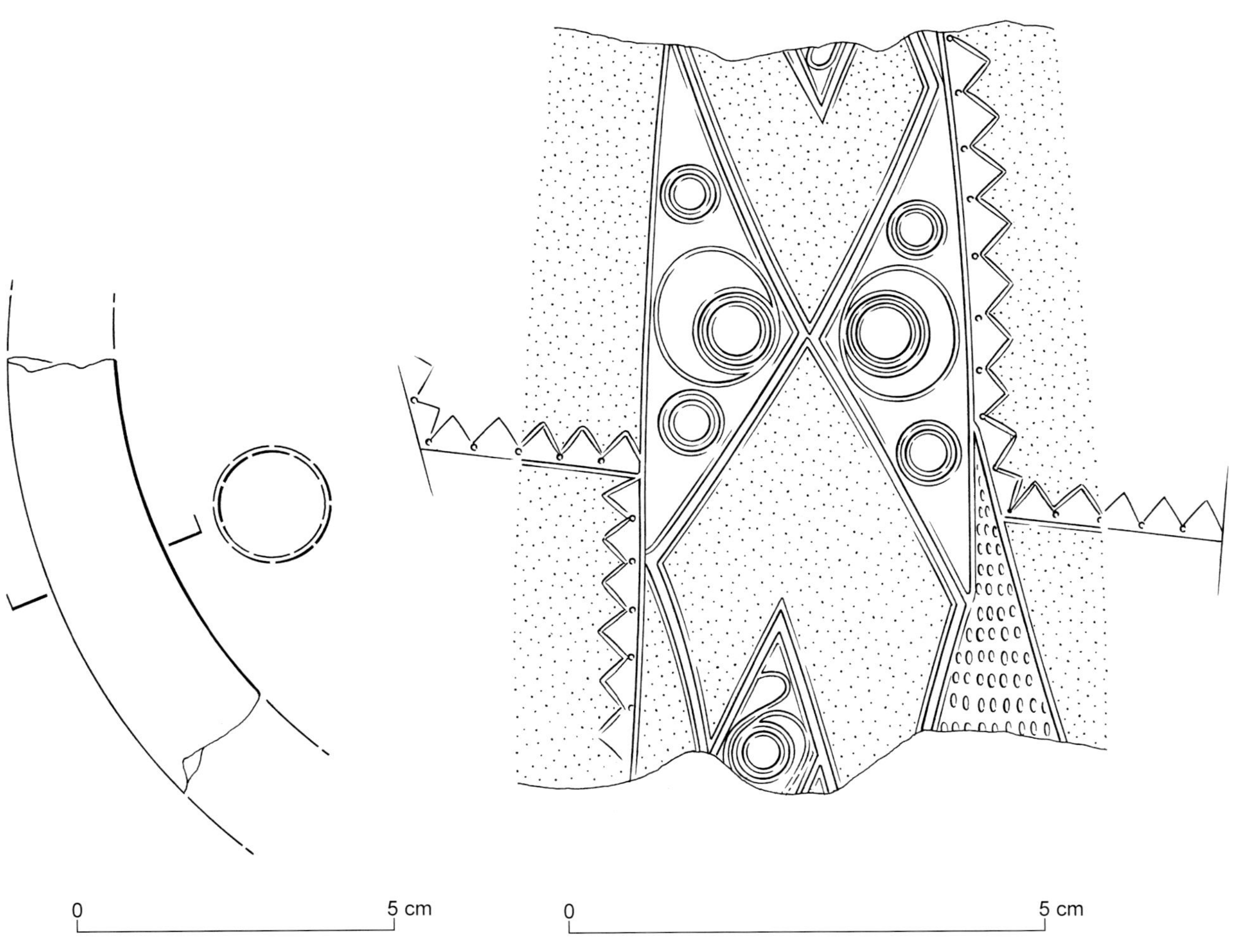

Figure 21.4 Illustration of torc F.53 (drawing by Jim Farrant)

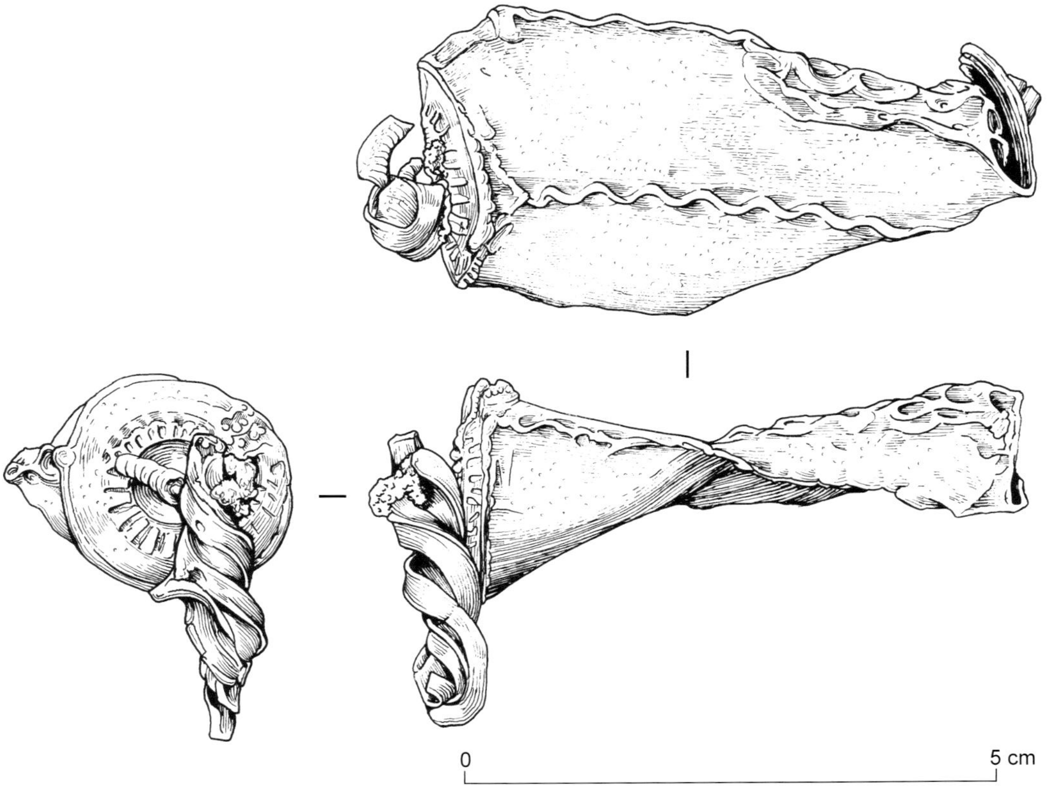

Figure 21.5 Illustration of torc F.42 (drawing by Craig Williams)

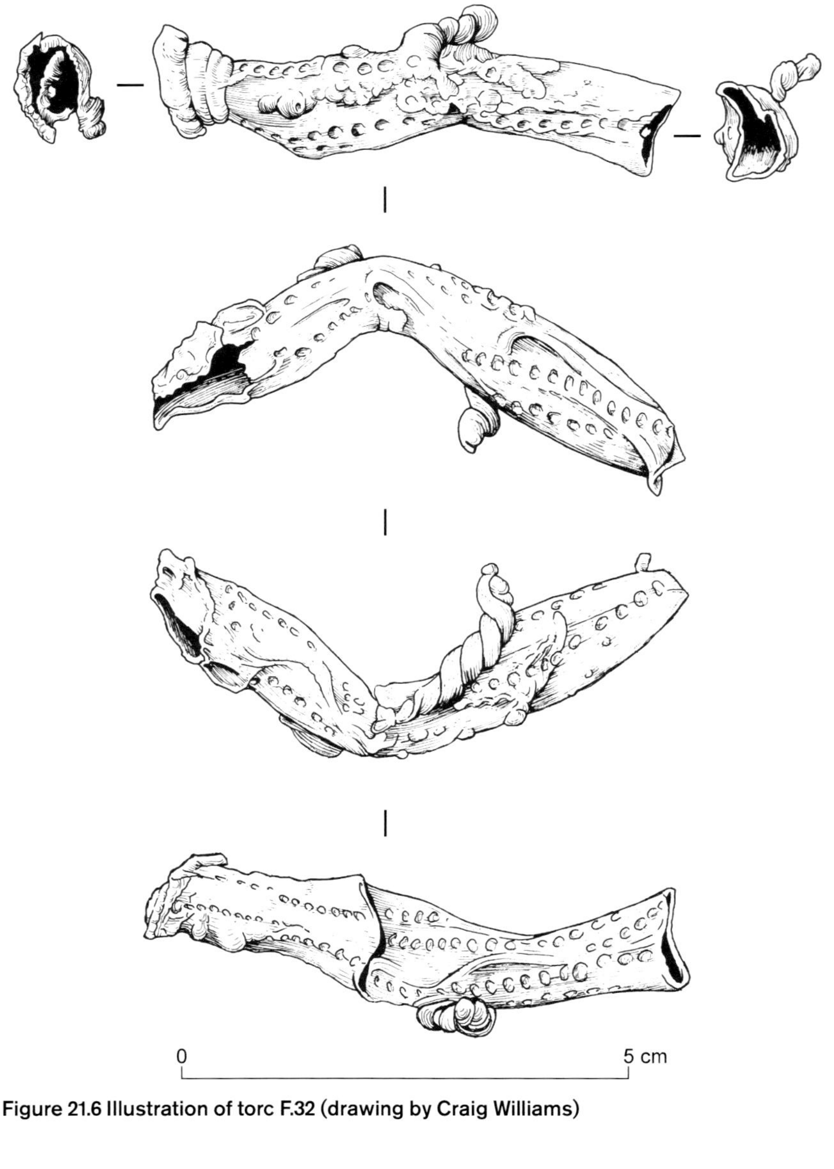

Figure 21.6 Illustration of torc F.32 (drawing by Craig Williams)

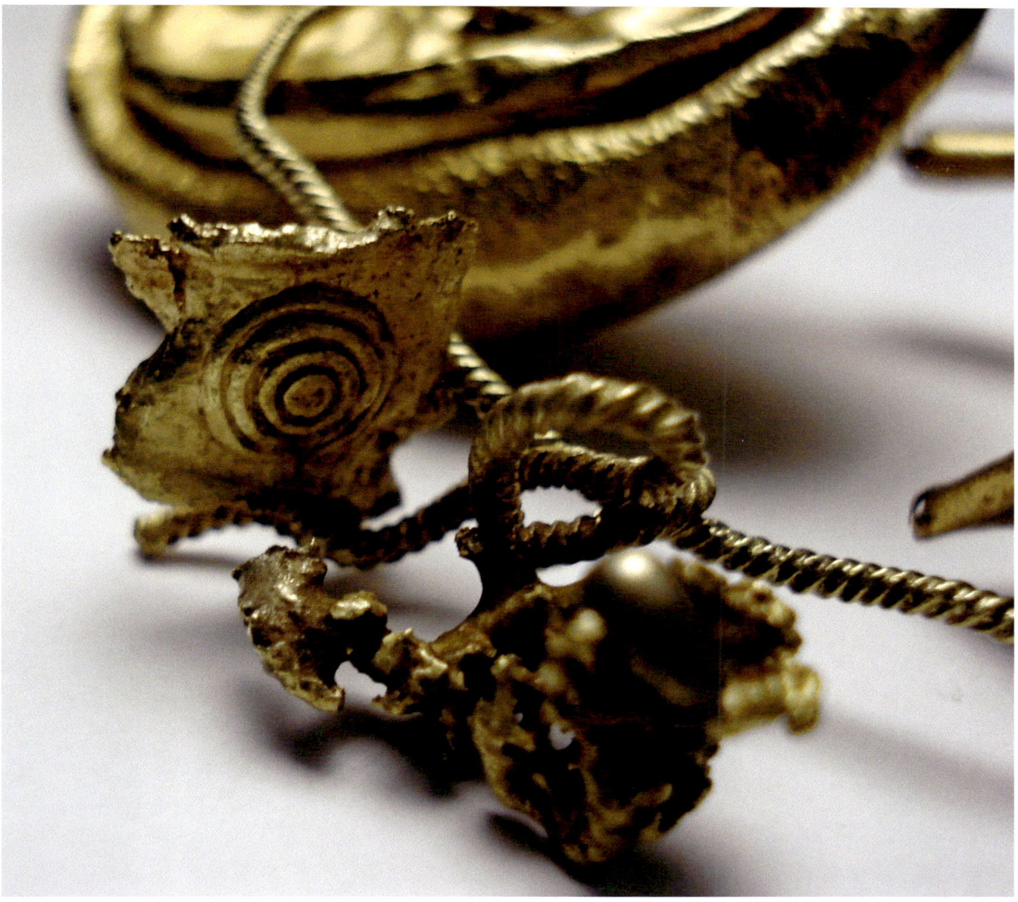

Figure 21.7 Detail of fragment F.2c, a piece of gold alloy sheet with concentric circle decoration. There are similar concentric circle motifs on both tubular torcs such as S.13 and the torus terminals of the 'Great Torc', E.1a. It is likely that F.2c ultimately derives from a similar object

Overall, there is less consistency to tubular torc ornament than the decoration on multi-strand torcs. For example, complete Type 6 tubular torc A.1 (**Fig. 21.8**) sports a raised curvilinear design on its rear decorative band, but the decoration also includes non-curvilinear elements, such as punch-marks, a chevron pattern created by inset wires (Ch. 17), and the swastika motifs within the raised domes of the curvilinear pattern. It is easy to read too much into these inconsistencies, but one possibility is that the Snettisham tubular torcs originated from various suppliers, including some on the continent, whereas sources for multi-strand torcs were restricted to a smaller region and therefore they were more consistent in the motifs employed. But, as we will see, there is also variation in terms of the decoration on multi-strand torcs. Another likely explanation is that different decoration rules applied to tubular torcs.

Punch-marks

One particular 'non-curvilinear' feature appears on the neck-rings of some of the tubular torcs from Hoard A: circular punch-marks in various arrangements. The inner curve of the tube of A.1 (**Fig. 21.8**) has three rows of offset circular punch-marks. Each of these is around 3mm in diameter and they are arranged so that the central row has 33 punch-marks whereas the upper and lower rows are each made up of 10. Similarly, on the inside of the tube of torc A.2 (**Fig. 21.9**) there are also punch-marks; in this instance they are around 2.5mm in diameter and are arranged into a row of seven on one tube and 14 punch-marks in a line on the other. Finally, on the inside of the tube of torc A.3 (**Fig. 21.10**) there is a centrally positioned row of 13 groups of four punch-marks, each arranged in a square, and a line of three such groups above and below this main run. Similar punch-marks have been noted on large tubular torcs of the same type from elsewhere. For example, one of the torcs from the hoard found at Frasnes-lez-Buissenal in southern Belgium also has a row of punch-marks each arranged into four dots forming squares, just like torc A.3 (Clarke 1954, 44).

The role of these punch-marks is unclear. They appear on the inside surface of tubes so would not have been visible when the torc was worn. Although there are multiple punch-marks, owing to the consistency of their diameters they were most probably applied at the same time or, less likely, on several occasions using the same tool. This appears to rule out the possibility that punch-marks recorded events in the life of the object. More probably, they were applied at the time of manufacture. It is therefore possible that they represent some form of maker's mark, but this seems unlikely given their number and often complicated arrangement as surely one unique mark would suffice for this purpose. The fact that similar (although varied) sets of markings appear on all known complete tubular torcs of this type, led Hautenauve (2005, 85–6) to suggest that the addition of these marks was part of a widely shared ritual practice. It is notable that the tubular torc from Mailly-le-Camp, France (NE, Aube) (Hautenauve 2005, no. 113, 85–6), in the same area as its punch-marks, is inscribed with a series of symbols, some seemingly constituting personal names and one perhaps related to the tribe of the Nitiobroges. Lejeune (1969, 76) argued that these were the names of dedicants associated with the hoard of which the torc formed part.

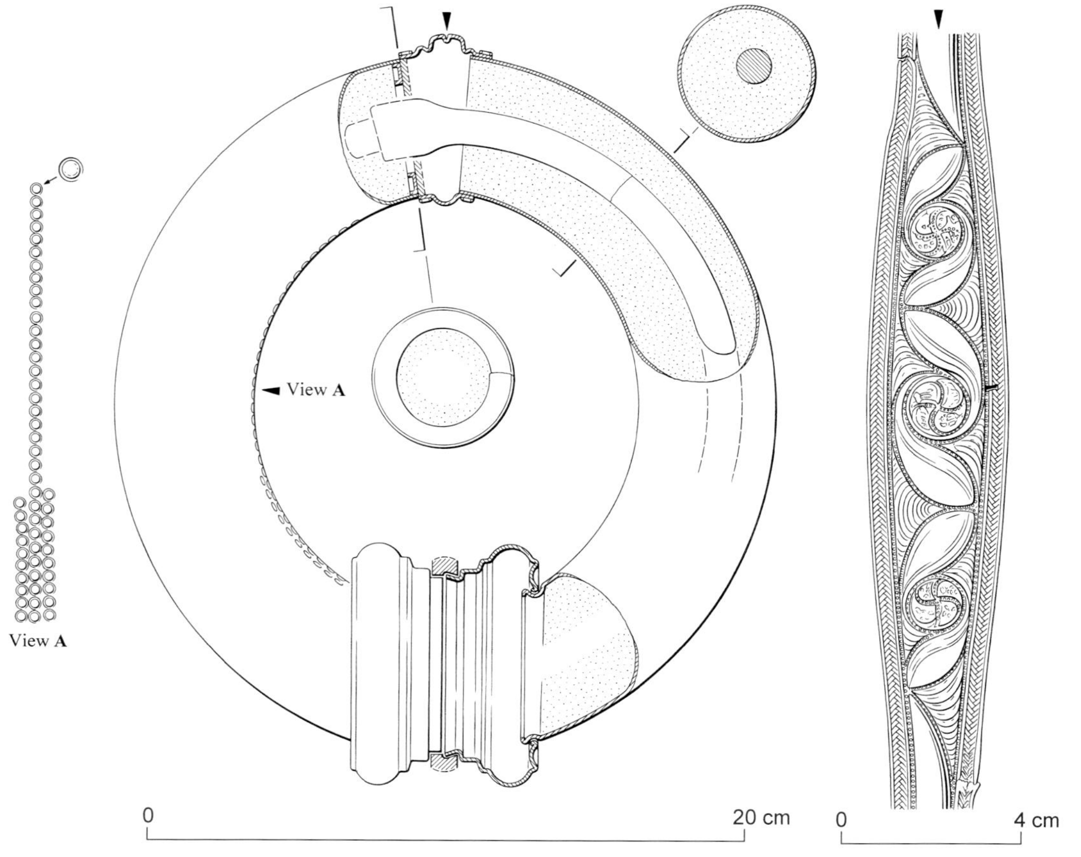

Figure 21.8 Illustration of torc A.1 (drawing by Jim Farrant)

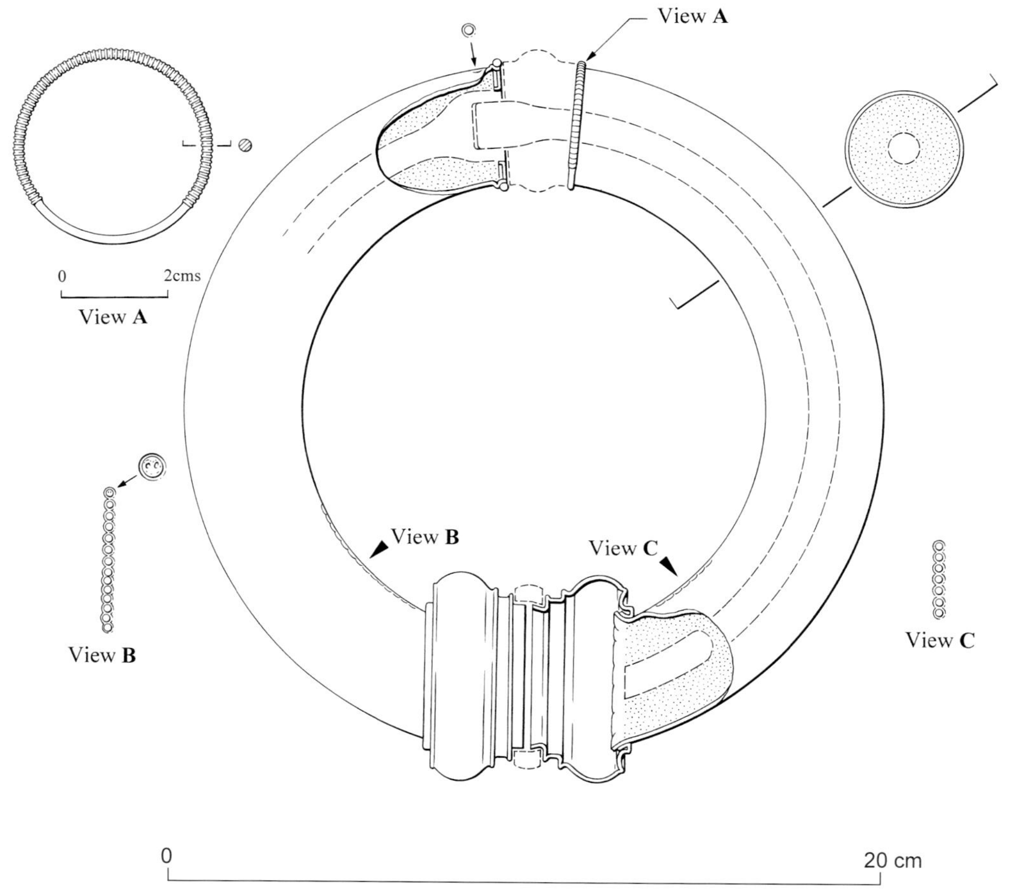

Figure 21.9 Illustration of torc A.2 (drawing by Jim Farrant)

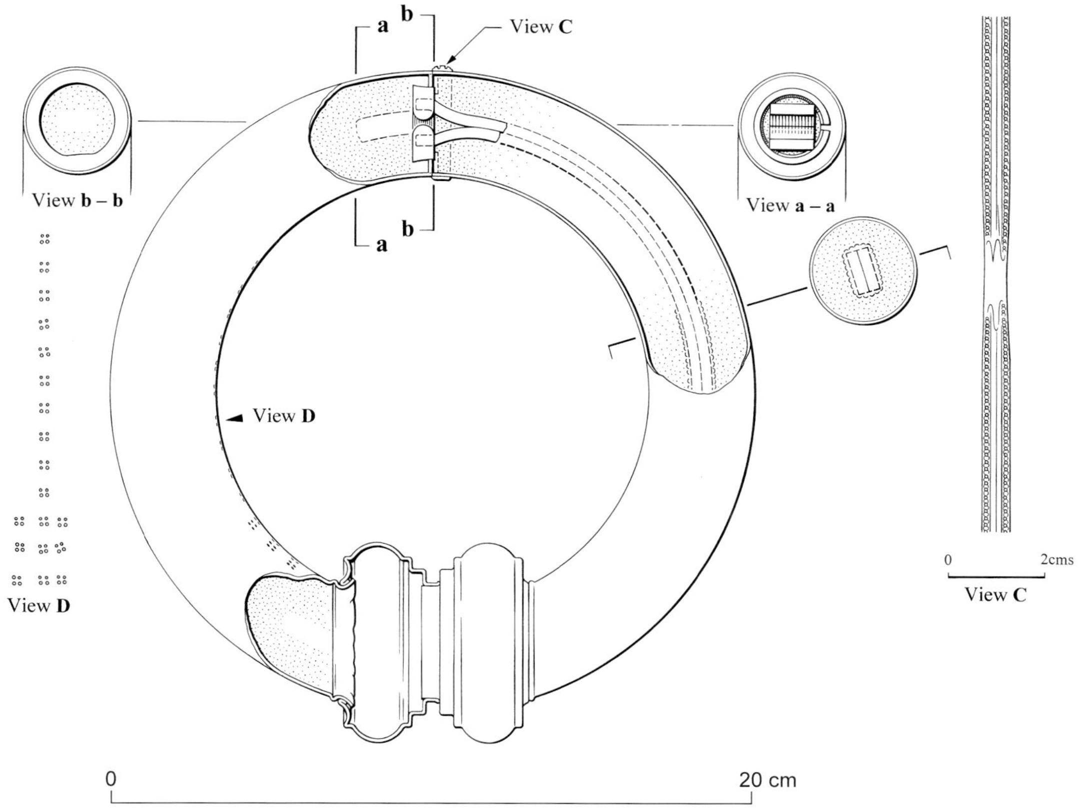

Figure 21.10 Illustration of torc A.3 (drawing by Jim Farrant)

Curvilinear

Curvilinear decoration on torcs can be broadly divided into inscribed curvilinear designs and raised curvilinear designs. Both frequently employ 'basket-weave' hatching and define the same distinctive motifs, particularly trumpets, fins, and cusp shapes, but they use different techniques. Raised decoration is most commonly fashioned through lost-wax casting (or very occasionally repoussé), whereas inscribed decoration is often engraved/chased directly onto the metal.

These two categories compare well with identified patterns in Style V art (Stead 2009). For example, many parallels can be found for raised curvilinear decoration on other contemporary objects, such as the ornament on the plaque from Llyn Cerrig Bach, Anglesey, with its

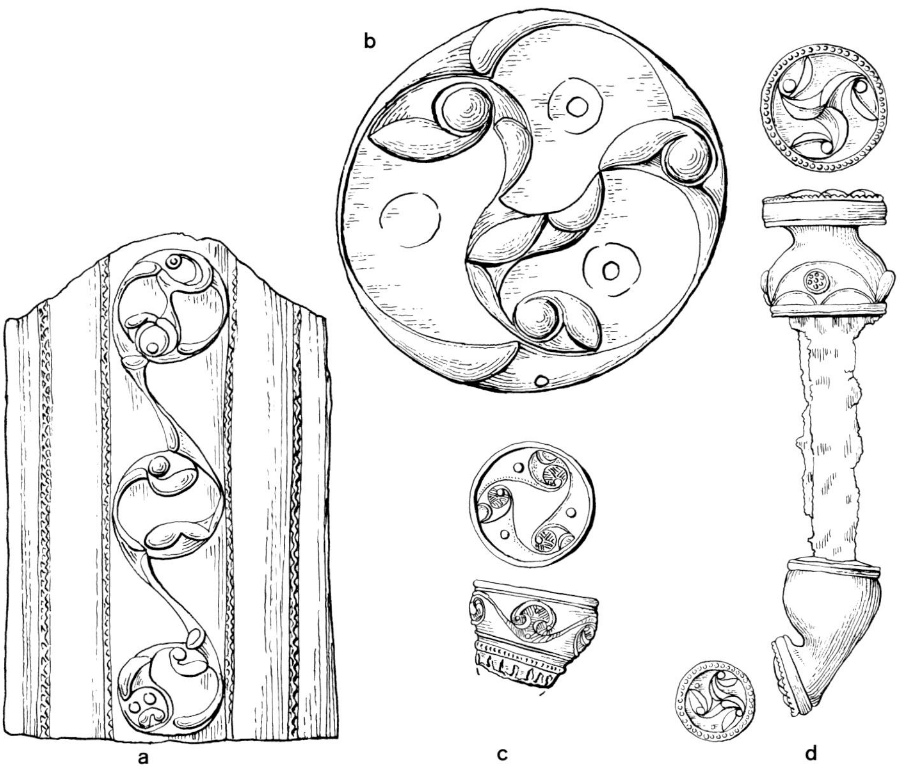

Figure 21.11 Raised curvilinear decoration on a scabbard from a) Deal, b) a plaque from Llyn Cerrig Bach, c) a torc terminal from Clevedon and d) a linch-pin from Kirkburn (drawings by Craig Williams)

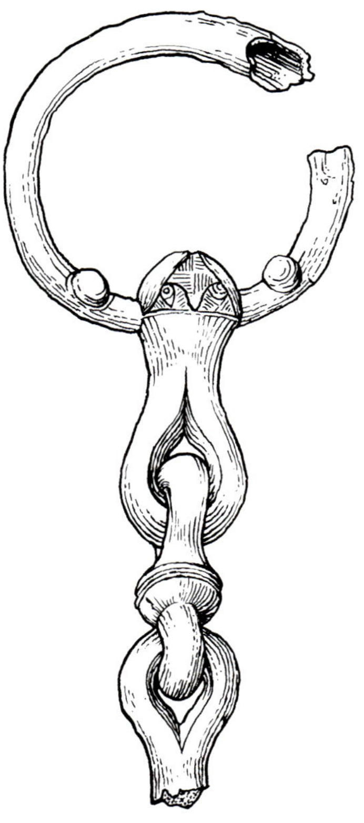

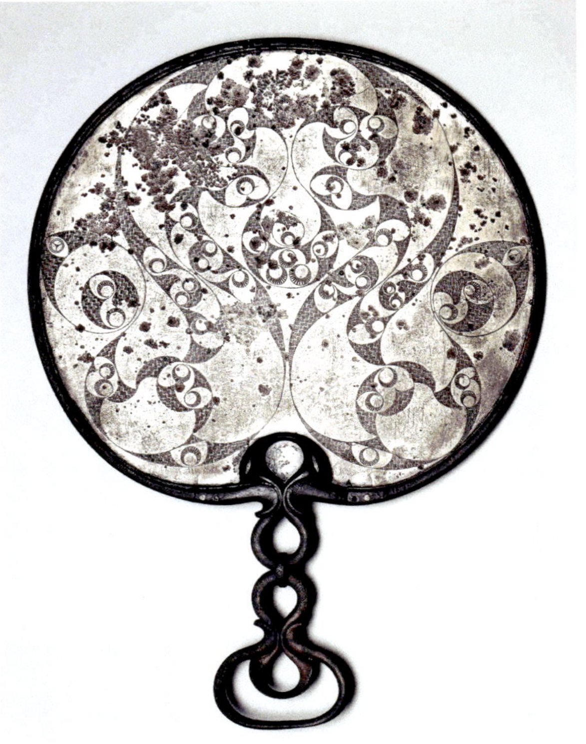

Figure 21.12 (far left) Raised curvilinear decoration on a bridle bit from Ulceby (drawing by Craig Williams after May 1976)

Figure 21.13 (left) The Desborough mirror decorated in characteristic inscribed patterns, *c.* 50 BC–AD 50. British Museum, 1924,0109.1

characteristic trumpet voids (Macdonald 2007b, no. 47, fig. 24; **Fig. 21.11b**), the Clevedon Torc from North Somerset (**Fig. 21.11c**), a sword scabbard from Deal, Kent (Stead 1995b; **Fig. 21.11a**), the linch-pins from Kirkburn, East Yorkshire (Stead 1991b; **Fig. 21.11d**), and a bridle bit from Ulceby, Lincolnshire (May 1976; **Fig. 21.12**). In terms of inscribed decoration, by far the best parallel is the decoration on mirror backs (**Fig. 21.13**) and other artefacts such as sword scabbards (see compendium in Joy 2010, app. C). An important difference here is that, in the case of torc terminals, inscribed decoration is sometimes three- rather than two-dimensional (e.g. F.43, L.13, L.20a–b).

Raised curvilinear decoration on multi-strand torcs

Possibly the best-known example of the decoration which I term 'raised curvilinear' appears on the torus terminals and collars of the so-called 'Great Torc' (E.1a), which comprises embossed ridges contrasting with areas filled by chased 'basket-weave' hatching (**Fig. 21.14**). As is the case with the inscribed decoration on torc L.20 (described below), the major areas of decoration appear towards the front of each terminal, within an oval-shaped panel with tapering wings on either side. The decoration on each terminal is different, but the patterns of both are made up of raised lobes framing hatched trumpet and circle motifs. Within two circles are two raised knobs, both with three punched dots. Within two of the trumpets are raised concentric circle motifs. The decoration on each collar is also slightly different, but the ornament on both is similar to that on the terminals, with raised lobes, raised knobs with punched dots and hatched trumpet motifs positioned on the outside face (when worn) of the torc. Overall, the pattern forms an elongated lyre with this design at its centre.

One other torus torc shows similar raised curvilinear designs, though in this case without hatching. The torus terminals and collars of torc L.21 (**Fig. 21.15**) have a deceptively simple design, made up solely of raised lobes framing plain trumpet and fin motifs. The designs on both terminals are almost identical. The collars are wider on the terminal side, and each has a plain cordon on the neck-ring side and a crimped cordon where the collar meets the head of the terminal.

Another example is a broken ring terminal, F.185 (**Fig. 21.16**). Its design is now indistinct owing to corrosion products, but the decoration on the outer edge is made up of raised lobes and knobs in an elongated lyre pattern. At the centre is a raised keeled roundel, with the relief decoration also framing trumpet motifs in the negative. These are both elements familiar from the designs on the 'Great Torc' (E.1a), and L.21.

The multi-strand torc types which most commonly exhibit raised curvilinear motifs are reel and buffer terminal torcs. The two reel terminals F.119 and F.120 (**Fig. 21.17**), a pair deriving from a single torc, are decorated on both faces in relief. Lobes, tendrils and bosses in a tripartite design are repeated on each face. A simple indented line marks the rim. The inside of the reel is undecorated, and there is a plain collar where it meets the neck-ring. Face-on, the design forms a triskele pattern with the void of the ring forming a part of the overall design.

S.48 (**Fig. 21.18**) is a cast gold/silver alloy buffer terminal, probably originally from a multi-strand torc. The face is decorated with a raised rim around the circumference, and a simple tripartite relief design forming a recessed triangular motif in the negative space in the centre. In all other cases of multi-strand buffer terminal torcs with raised curvilinear designs, the decoration is exclusively on the outside edges of the buffer terminals. On torc L.11 (**Fig. 21.19**) these are decorated on the front (as worn) in high relief (rising to a maximum of about 2.5mm

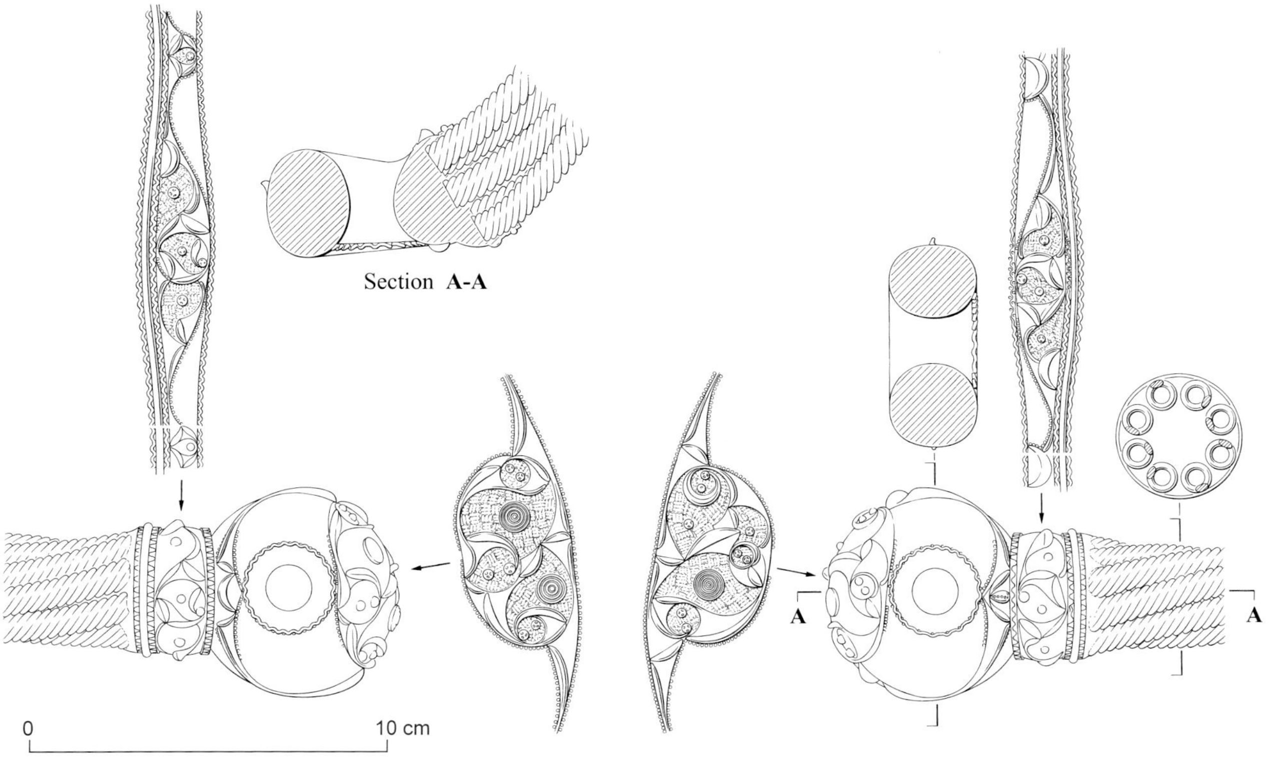

Figure 21.14 Illustration of torc E.1a (the 'Great Torc') (drawing by Jim Farrant)

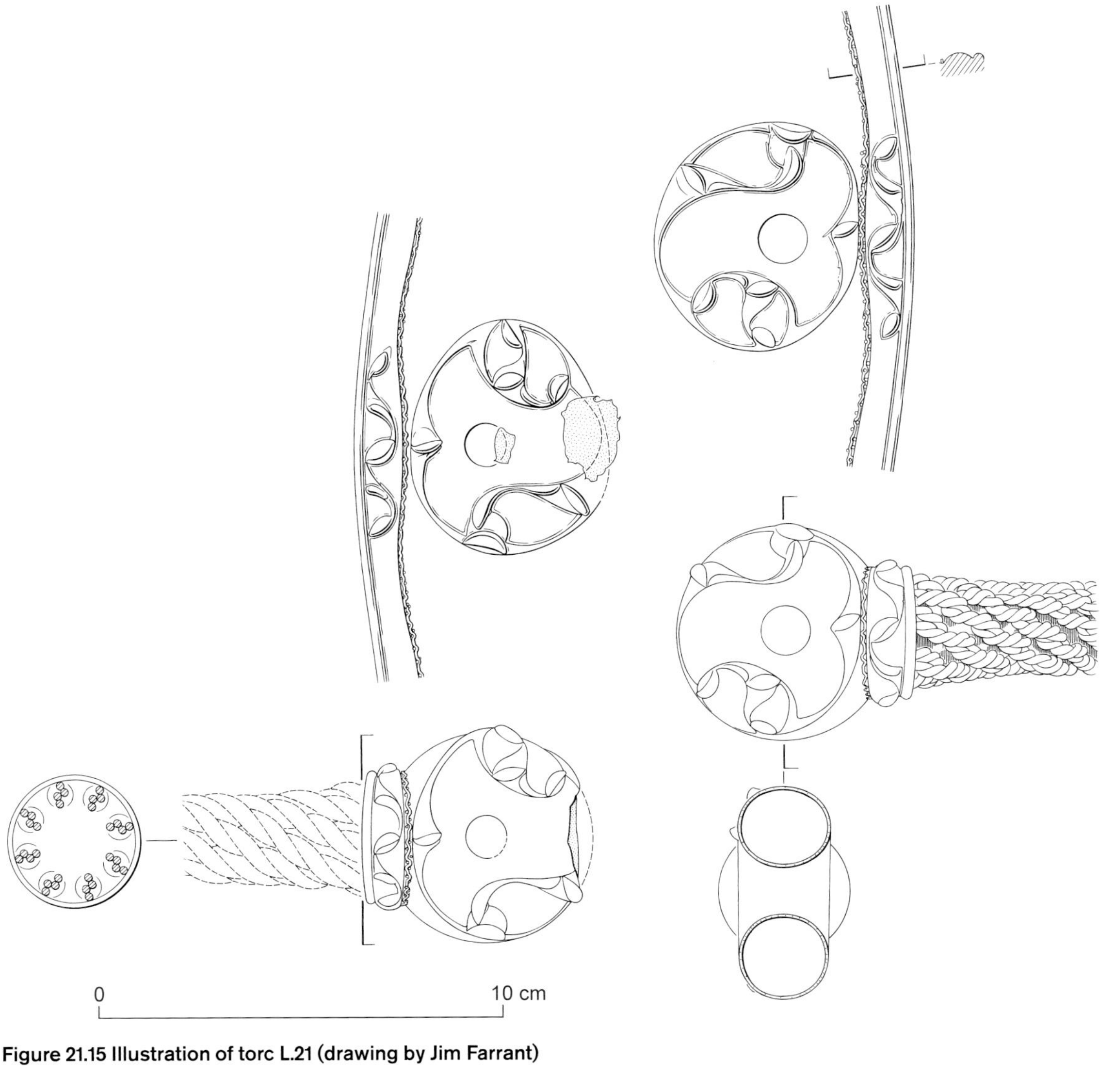

Figure 21.15 Illustration of torc L.21 (drawing by Jim Farrant)

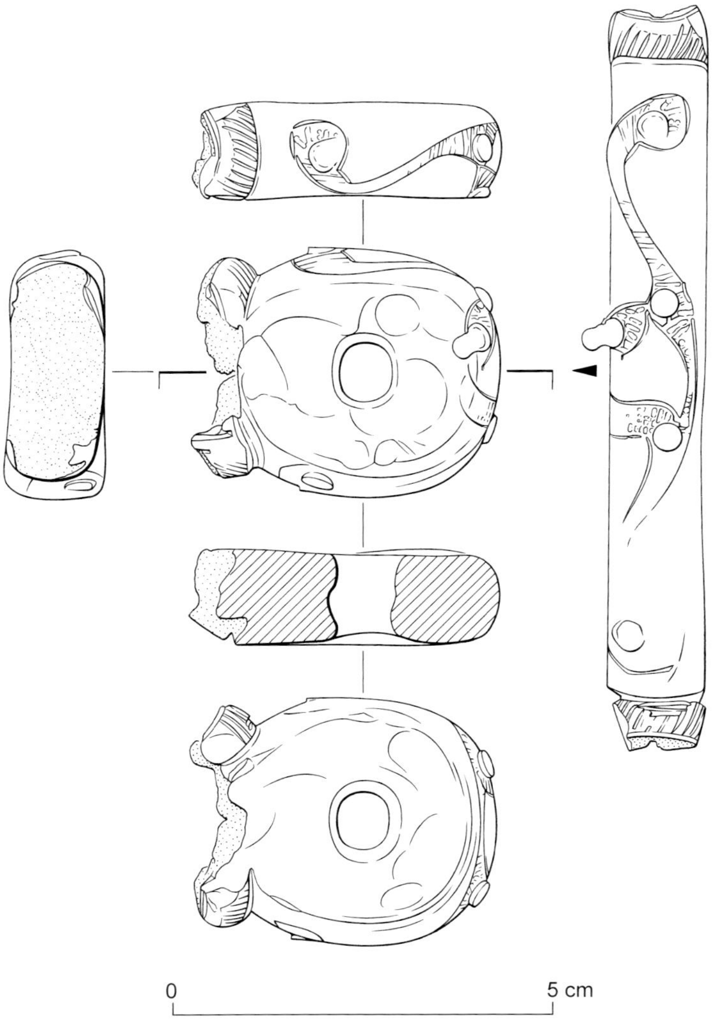

Figure 21.16 Illustration of torc F.185 (drawing by Jim Farrant)

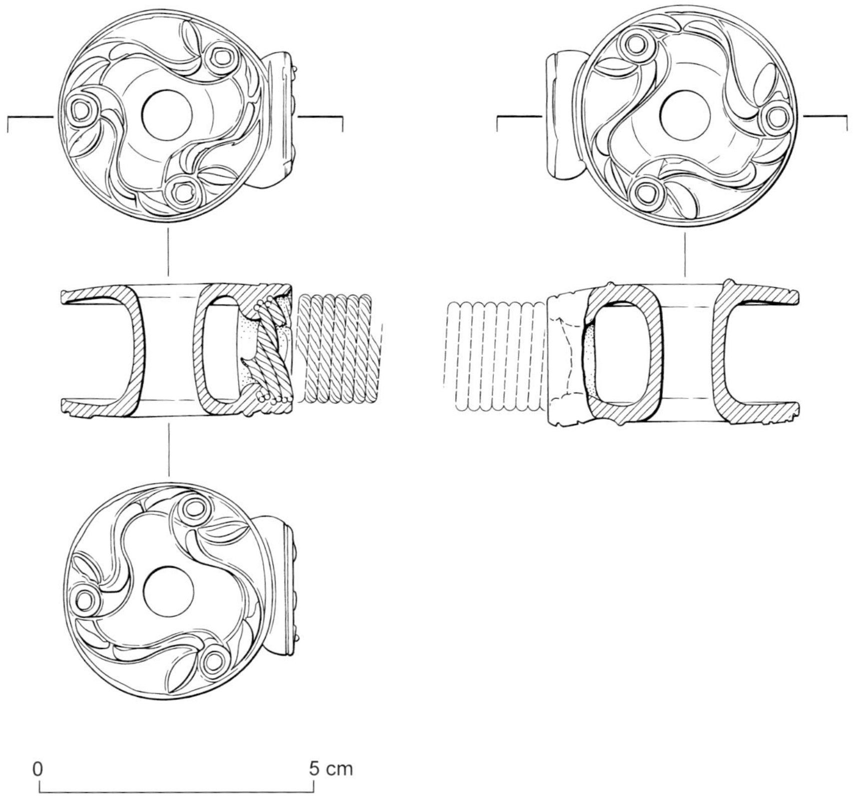

Figure 21.17 Illustration of torc F.119–120 (drawing by Jim Farrant)

above the surface) with a three-part design: a central lobe and dot set between two swags with semi-circular terminals. The orientation of the lobe and dot motif differs from one terminal to the other. The outside edge of L.12 (**Fig. 21.20**) is ornamented with raised curvilinear zig-zagging hatched petal and fin-shaped motifs. The flat face has a raised outer rim and a raised central button with a slight depression in the middle but is otherwise undecorated. In the central band around the edge of the buffer terminal of F.115 (**Fig. 21.21**), on the front (as worn) only, are six raised circled triangular motifs. There is also a simple grooved moulding around the circumference of the terminal end and a beaded moulding at the neck-ring end. The flat face of the terminal is plain.

Raised curvilinear decoration on tubular torcs

Raised curvilinear decoration occurs primarily on the terminals of multi-strand torcs, but also on a small number of tubular torcs. F.6b (**Fig. 21.22**) is a gold/silver alloy fragment of Type 4 tubular torc, comprising the terminal and a section of neck-ring. The face of the terminal is decorated by concentric circles with the inside of one delineated by punch-marks. The decoration around the outside of the neck-ring, starting near the edge of the terminal, is formed of raised and chased ornament. Overall, the pattern is in the form of an elongated lyre. The background is stippled, but the raised motifs are predominantly plain, although some of the motifs, particularly the raised sections delineating the lyre, are laddered. Laddering such as this is also found on the decoration of other artefacts such as the mirror from Chilham Castle, Kent (cf. Joy 2010).

The terminal of narrow Type 1 tubular torc F.57 (**Fig. 21.23**) has a raised central triskele design which is set against

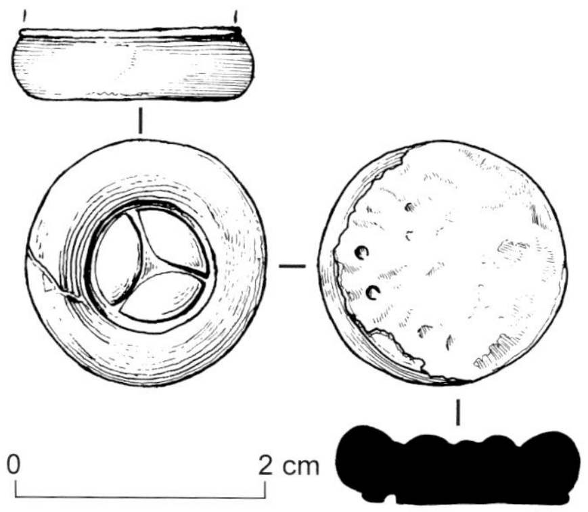

Figure 21.18 Illustration of torc S.48 (drawing by Craig Williams)

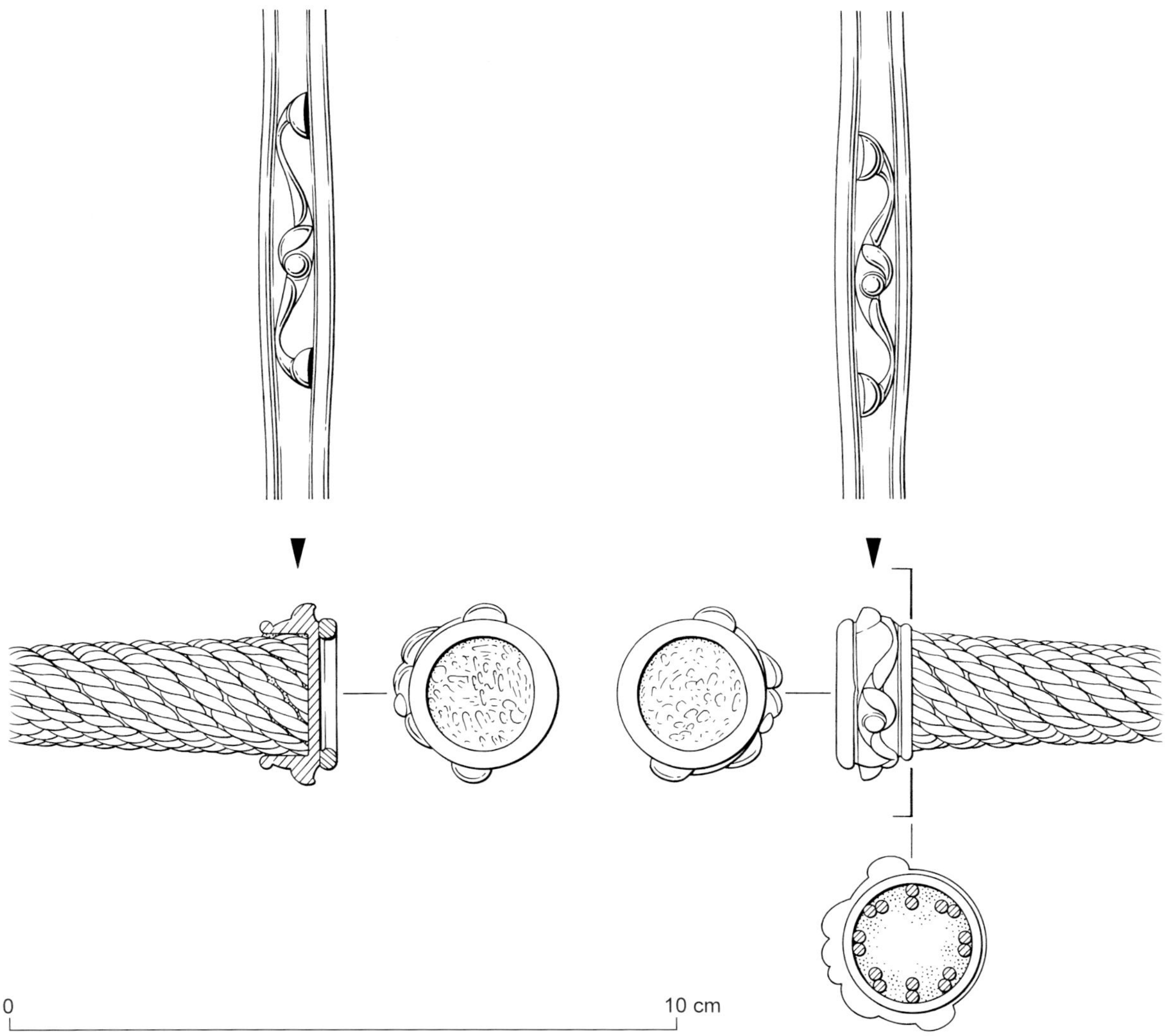

Figure 21.19 Illustration of torc L.11 (drawing by Jim Farrant)

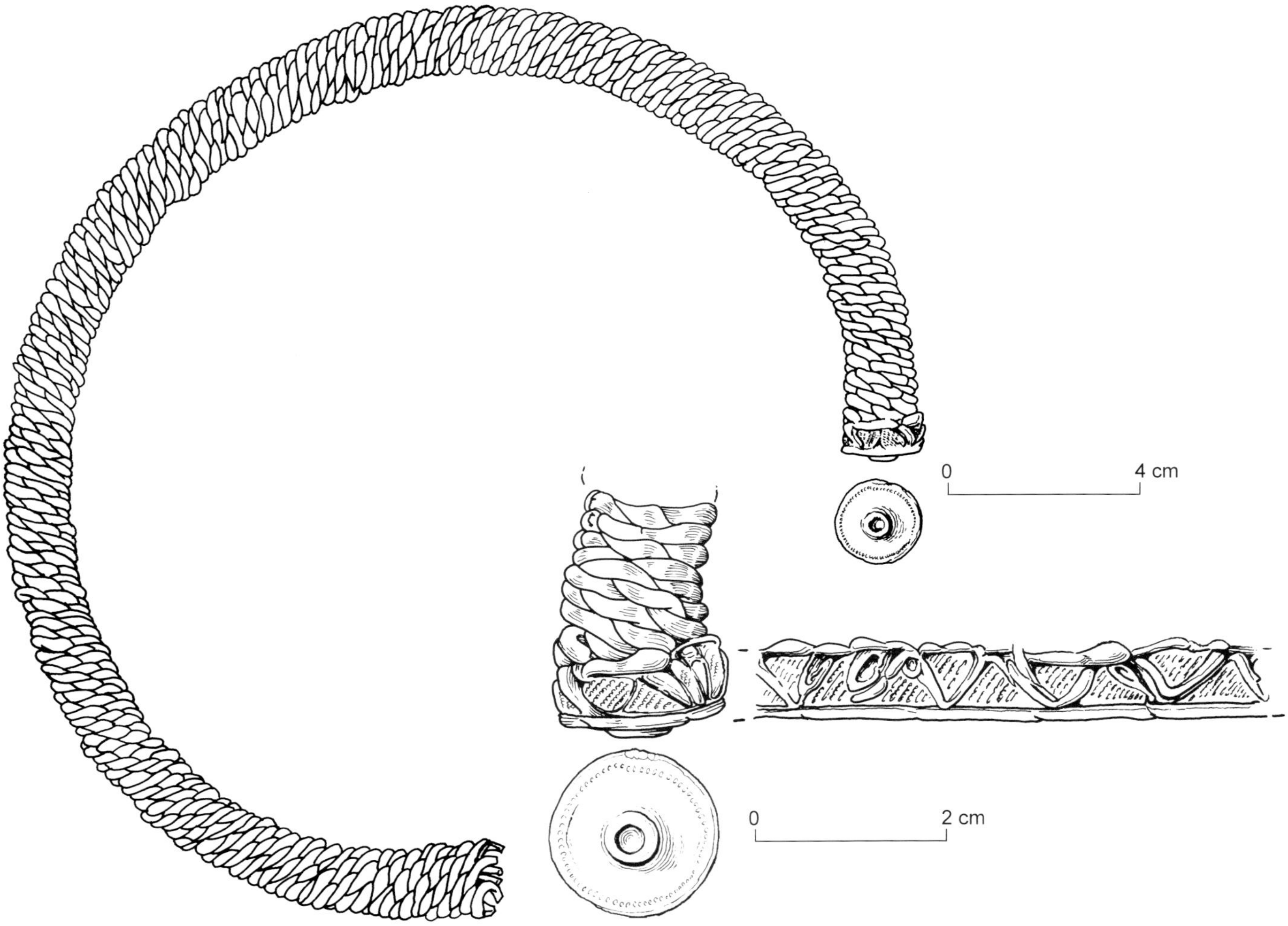

Figure 21.20 Illustration of torc L.12 (drawing by Craig Williams)

a stippled/punch-textured background. The neck-ring of Type 4 tubular torc F.46 (**Fig. 21.24**) expands towards a flat trefoil-shaped buffer terminal, the end-plate of which is decorated with a raised circular 'segmented wreath' motif. Within the wreath is a four-armed star with simple dot-punched stippled decoration.

The raised decoration on a muff positioned at the back of tubular torc A.1 (**Fig. 21.8**) is the most extensive and impressive area of raised curvilinear decoration on a tubular torc. Bordered by narrow bands arranged in a chevron pattern is a sinuous, high-relief design of repeated circles linked by two opposing lobes. Unusually, the raised circles are partitioned into quarters by a four-winged swastika motif, defined by punch-marks. The decoration on torc A.1 has a slightly different feel from the other artefacts ornamented by raised curvilinear patterns. This may be related to the fact that the raised decorative elements on this torc were produced by hammering rather than casting, though the same is also true of some sheet metal terminals (see below).

Seeking parallels elsewhere, at least two other Type 6 tubular torcs have raised decoration, though of a very different character. The tube of the tubular torc from the Broighter Hoard, County Londonderry, is intricately decorated with raised motifs, but its design is entirely in

Figure 21.21 Illustration of torc F.115 (drawing by Craig Williams)

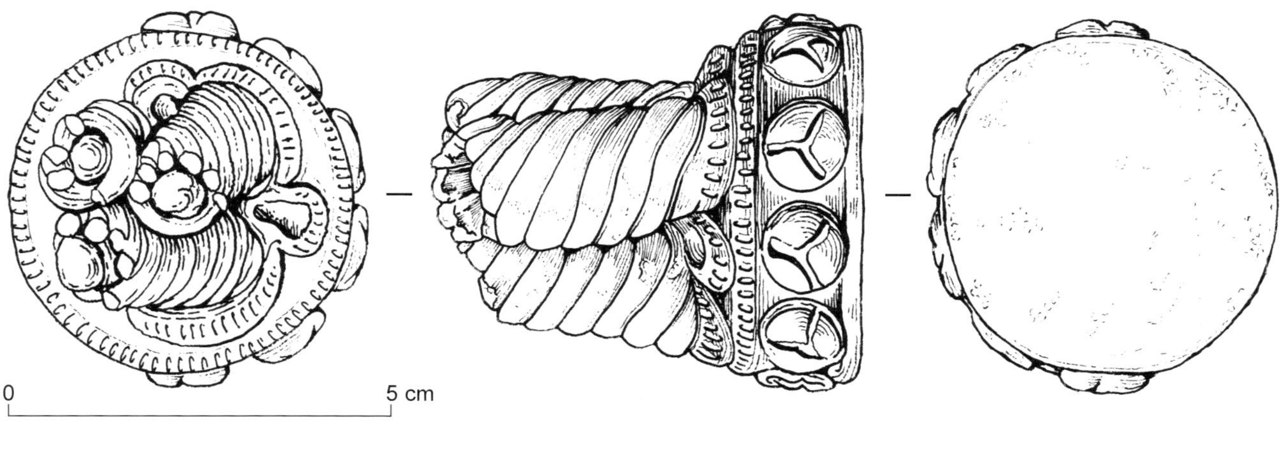

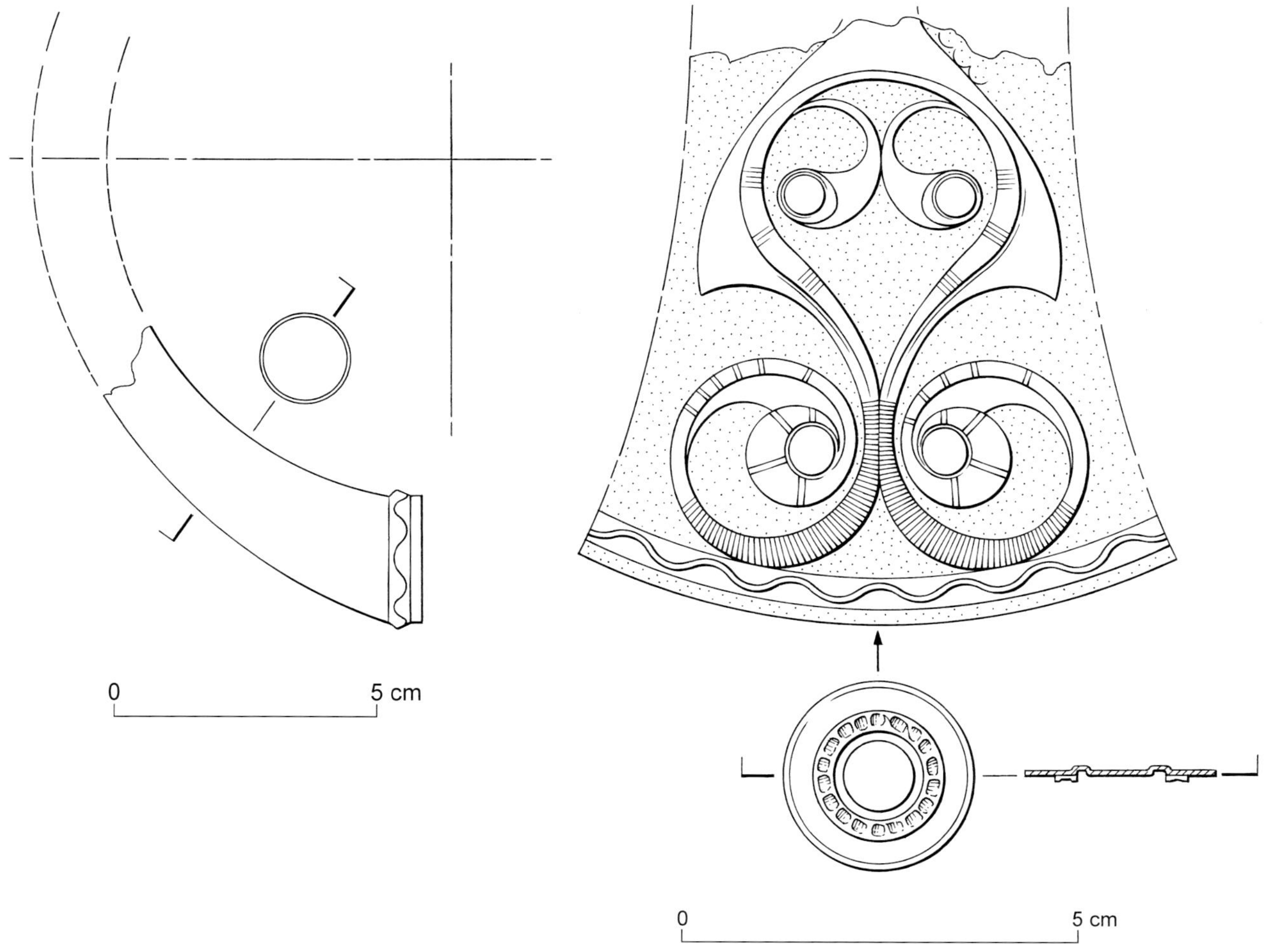

Figure 21.22 Illustration of torc F.6b (drawing by Jim Farrant)

keeping with other decorated Irish artefacts. One of the tubular torcs from the Frasnes-lez-Buissenal Hoard, Belgium (Hautenauve 2005, 194, no. 14), also has raised decoration positioned both towards the front buffers and at the back, as is the case with A.1. But here the decoration includes zoomorphic designs as well as interlinking raised reverse-S shapes; Jacobsthal (1969 [1944], 135) placed it within his Plastic Style. Piecing all of this evidence together, it seems there are precedents for decorating broad-bodied Type 6 tubular torcs with a wide variety of raised ornament and A.1 neatly fits this, particularly with its decoration being positioned at the back of the neck-ring, as is some of the decoration on the torc from Frasnes.

Beyond Britain and Ireland, Type 6 tubular torcs very similar to those from Snettisham have also been found in northern France and Belgium (Hautenauve 2005, 82–4, carte 9), e.g. Frasnes-lez-Buissenal, Belgium (*ibid.*, nos 14–15), Mailly-le-Camp, France (Joffroy 1969; Lejeune 1969), and Saint-Louis, France (Furger-Gunti 1982). However, the decoration of the Snettisham objects speaks of local rather than continental connections. Although different, the decoration on A.1 shares more similarities with British

Figure 21.23 Illustration of torc F.57 (drawing by Craig Williams)

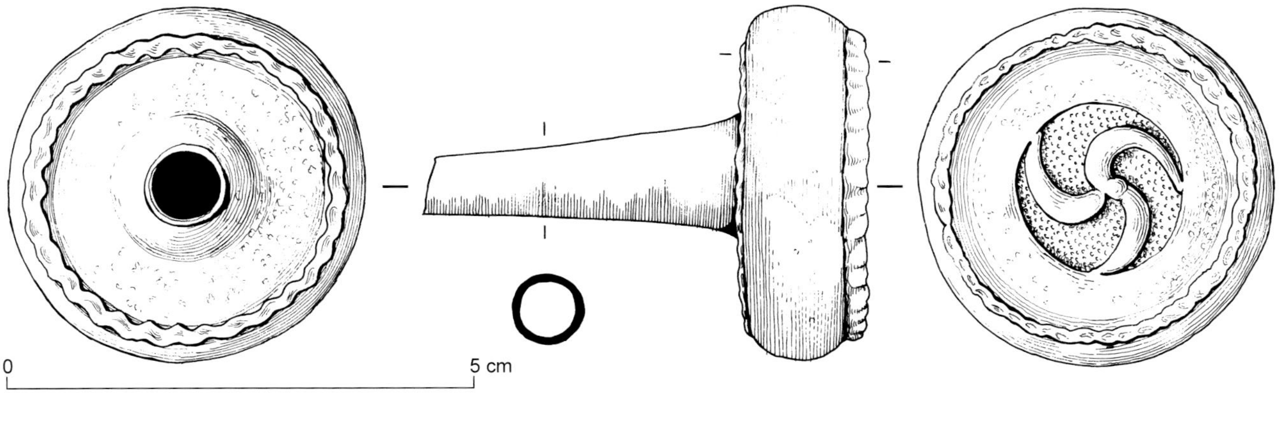

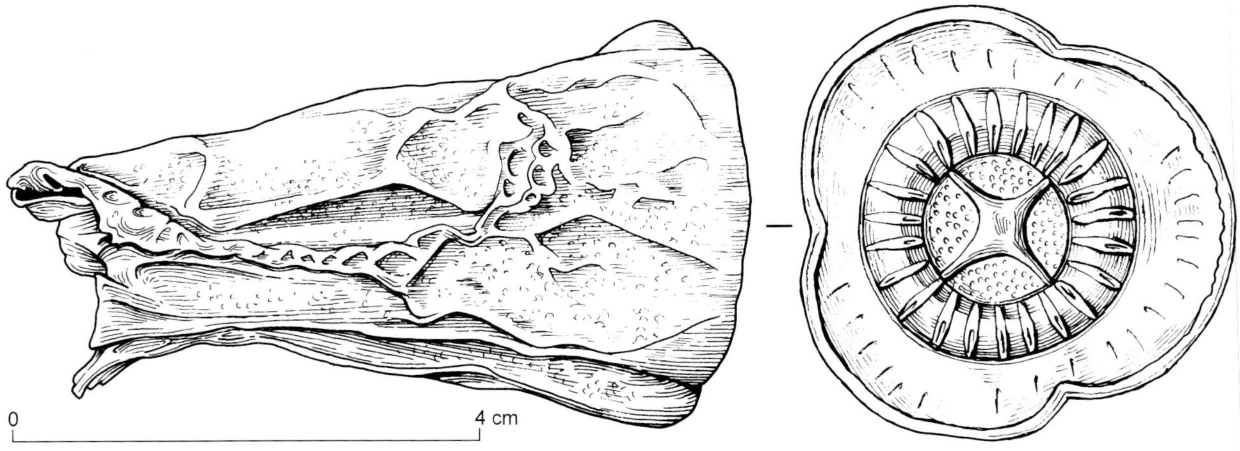

Figure 21.24 Illustration of torc F.46 (drawing by Craig Williams)

artefacts than tubular torcs found elsewhere, as is the case with the Broighter torc with its Irish-style decoration (Clarke 1954, 44). It therefore seems as though on each of these large, broad tubular torcs with raised curvilinear designs, the decoration is peculiar to the region in which the torcs were found, perhaps indicating that this is where they were also manufactured. Certainly, tubular torcs show similarities and continuities of design over a wide area, but this could be accounted for by wide contacts between groups (Joy 2015) and the production of locally produced versions rather than necessarily implying common manufacture by metalworkers based somewhere in continental Europe.

Inscribed curvilinear decoration on multi-strand torcs

A smaller number of objects exhibit two-dimensional curvilinear decoration, etched or chased directly into the surface of the metal. These include both torus and buffer terminal multi-strand torcs. Positive shapes are generally defined using hatching.

Two torus-terminal torcs (L.10a and L.20) are decorated with such inscribed curvilinear decoration. The decoration on the torus terminals of torc L.10a (**Fig. 21.25**) is very faint and heavily worn. The designs of each terminal differ slightly. The patterns of both form a wave and are delineated by an inscribed edge with most of the space infilled with hatching. At the ends of each wave are triangular shapes with unfilled circles placed off-centre in each. At the centre of one terminal is a triangular-shaped panel with an unfilled circle in the middle. In the centre of the other is a circular design formed by two linked hatched fin-motifs forming a circle, a lentoid shape and a trumpet motif in the negative.

Both torus terminals of L.20 (**Fig. 21.26**) are decorated with different inscribed designs and motifs are filled with

Figure 21.25 Illustration of torc L.10a (drawing by Jim Farrant)

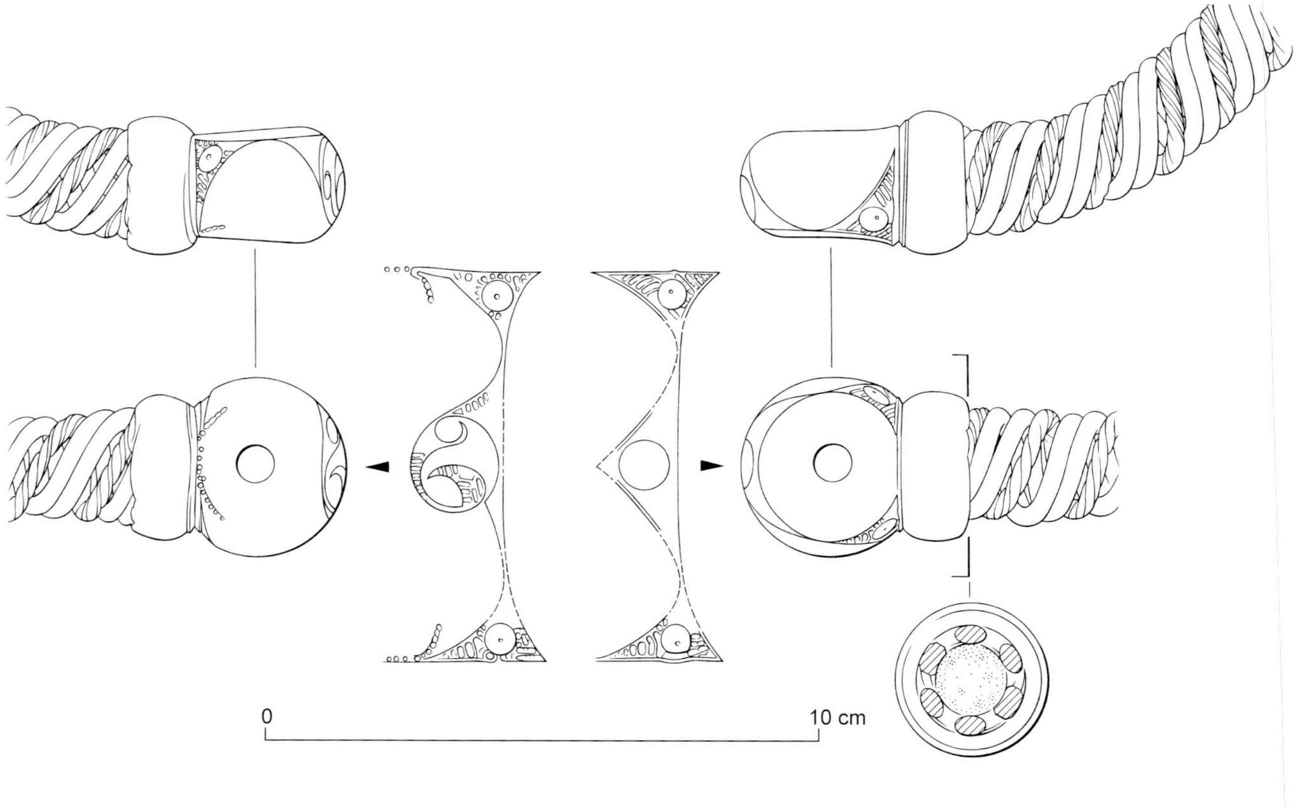

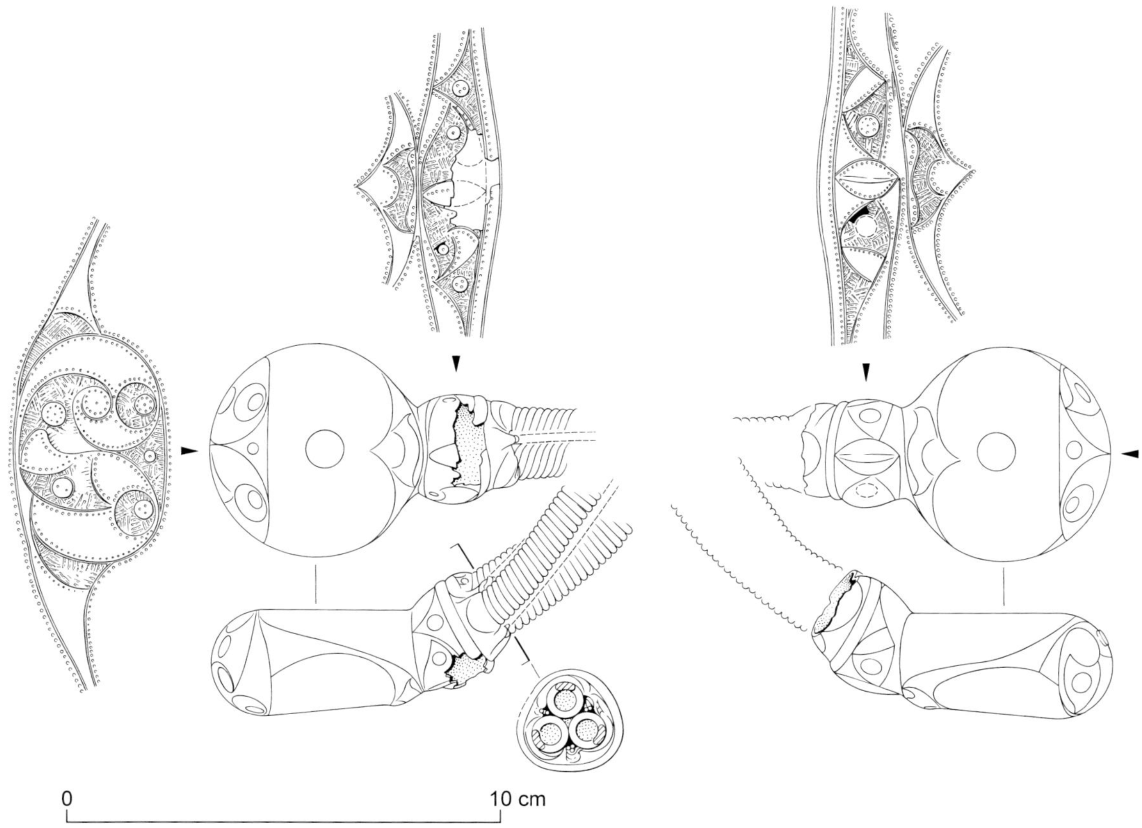

Figure 21.26 Illustration of torc L.20 (drawing by Craig Williams)

hatching set against a plain background. The designs on both terminals are split into two parts, with a zone of decoration at the front of each terminal and a second area of ornament at the other end of the ring and on the collar. The designs at the end of the terminals are oval in shape with fin-shaped 'wings' on either side (when the decoration is flattened out). The pattern and motifs are formed of inscribed lines but unusually there are also lines of punched dots on the outside of these lines. There are fin and crescent-shaped motifs, with unfilled areas forming primarily circles, fin and trumpet shapes. This decoration is also unusual for the punched dots within circular voids. They range in number from two or three to thirteen. The decoration at the collar end of the terminal and on the collar is similarly formed with the same range of motifs, but the pattern is more elongated and arranged within stretched oval and cusp-shaped zones.

Three buffer terminals from gold/silver alloy multi-strand torcs also exclusively exhibit inscribed curvilinear decoration. In two cases (S.19 and F.92), this is limited to the flat face of the terminal. S.19 (**Fig. 21.27**) is decorated with keeled-roundel and circle motifs, surrounded by three fin-shaped motifs filled with basket-hatching. F.92 (**Fig. 21.28**) is decorated on the end with a simple incised design of interlocking circles and hatched crescents. A simple raised bead runs around the edge on the outside of the terminal. In the case of L.13 (**Fig. 21.29**), the final buffer terminal torc with only inscribed decoration, the decoration includes not

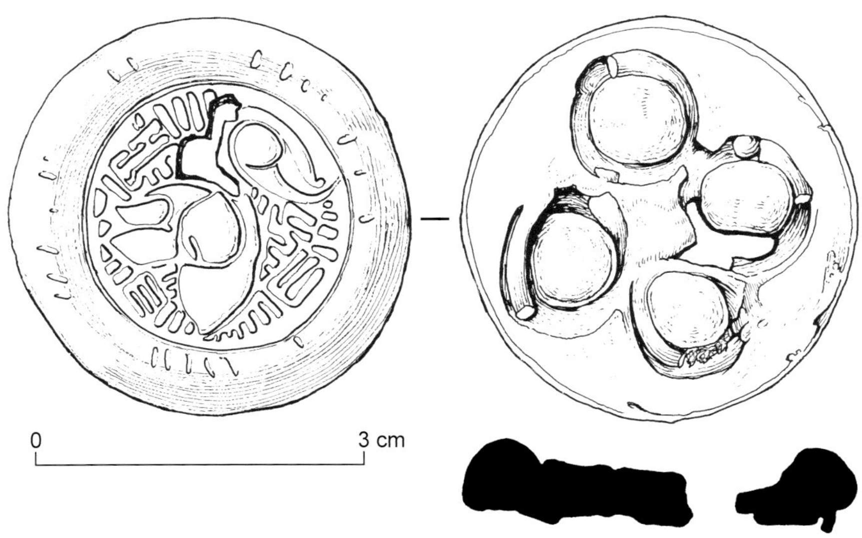

Figure 21.27 Illustration of torc S.19 (drawing by Craig Williams)

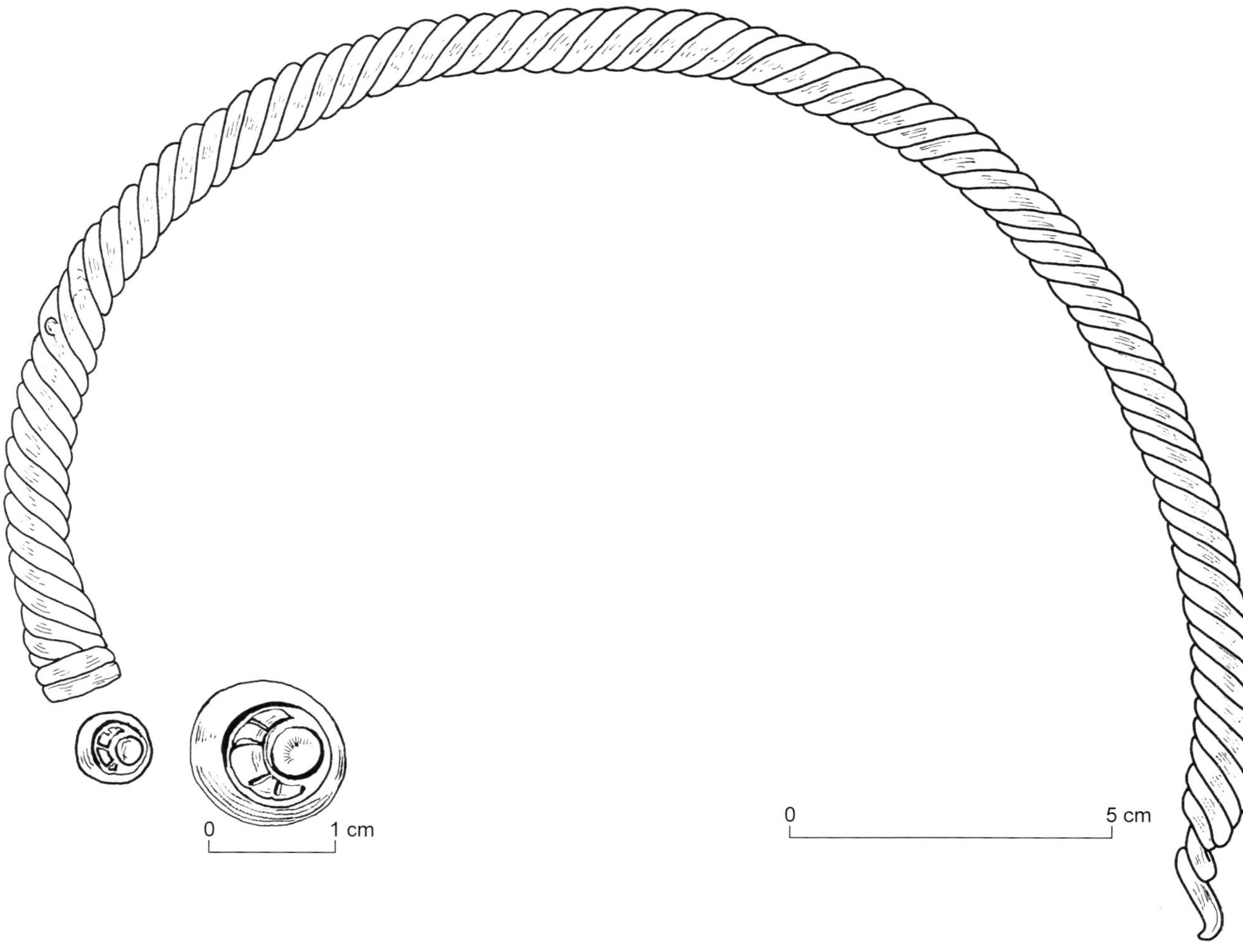

Figure 21.28 Illustration of torc F.92 (drawing by Craig Williams)

only the front face but also the curved outer rim. The face has chased/engraved decoration in the form of mirror-style motifs filled by hatching. Around the edge on the outside, there is inscribed dot-punched ornament outlining alternate teardrop and triangular shapes.

Plastic, anthropomorphic and zoomorphic decoration

Although the designs on most torcs fit relatively easily into the defined categories of raised or inscribed curvilinear (broadly speaking correlating with Stead's Style V) and non-curvilinear designs, a few torcs exhibit other types of decoration. Two appear to be influenced by Plastic Style (Stead's Style III), and two have distinctive anthropomorphic or zoomorphic designs. Others show clear mixtures of styles and are considered in the following section.

Plastic Style

Stead (1996, 26) suggested that the ornament on the Grotesque Torc (L.19a; **Fig. 21.30**) was 'strongly influenced' by the Plastic Style. Here it is also argued that the decoration on torc terminal F.72 (**Fig. 21.31**) which also stands proud (albeit not to the same extent as L.19a) could similarly be viewed as influenced by the Plastic Style. The pattern is also similar to L.19a and is made up of raised pelta and keeled roundels, creating a shape similar to a snail shell. It is interesting that both examples are also made from sheet metal. Based on evidence for high amounts of use wear, these torcs could be some of the oldest from the Snettisham hoards (Chs 20, 22). Perhaps they represent examples of an early and/or separate form of torc making (before the majority of terminals were cast) and when torc makers were more heavily influenced by designs from the continent – objects decorated in the Plastic Style are relatively scarce in Britain. Sheet-metalworking may also have lent itself to this style of decoration.

The Plastic Style is characterised by three-dimensional decoration formed in high relief and is a product of the 3rd century BC. It is certainly more prevalent on the continent than in Britain with examples identified by Jacobsthal (1969 [1944]) and others, but discoveries made in recent decades (Joy 2015) indicate that the style was by no means unknown on these islands, albeit that examples may have been quite scarce. For example, **Figure 21.32** shows three UK finds decorated with Plastic Style ornament. One is a copper alloy linch-pin from Cambridgeshire. This is similar to some examples on the continent and may represent an import or a local copy. A pin from Ropley, Hampshire, has a head decorated with similar high-relief ornament. Part of another pin decorated in the same style has since been discovered at Wield, also in Hampshire.

It is difficult to draw conclusions from such a small number of discoveries, but it is possible the two pins might represent a local tradition of the use of Plastic Style art in Hampshire, and/or the work of a particular workshop. Similarly, the two examples from Snettisham (L.19a and

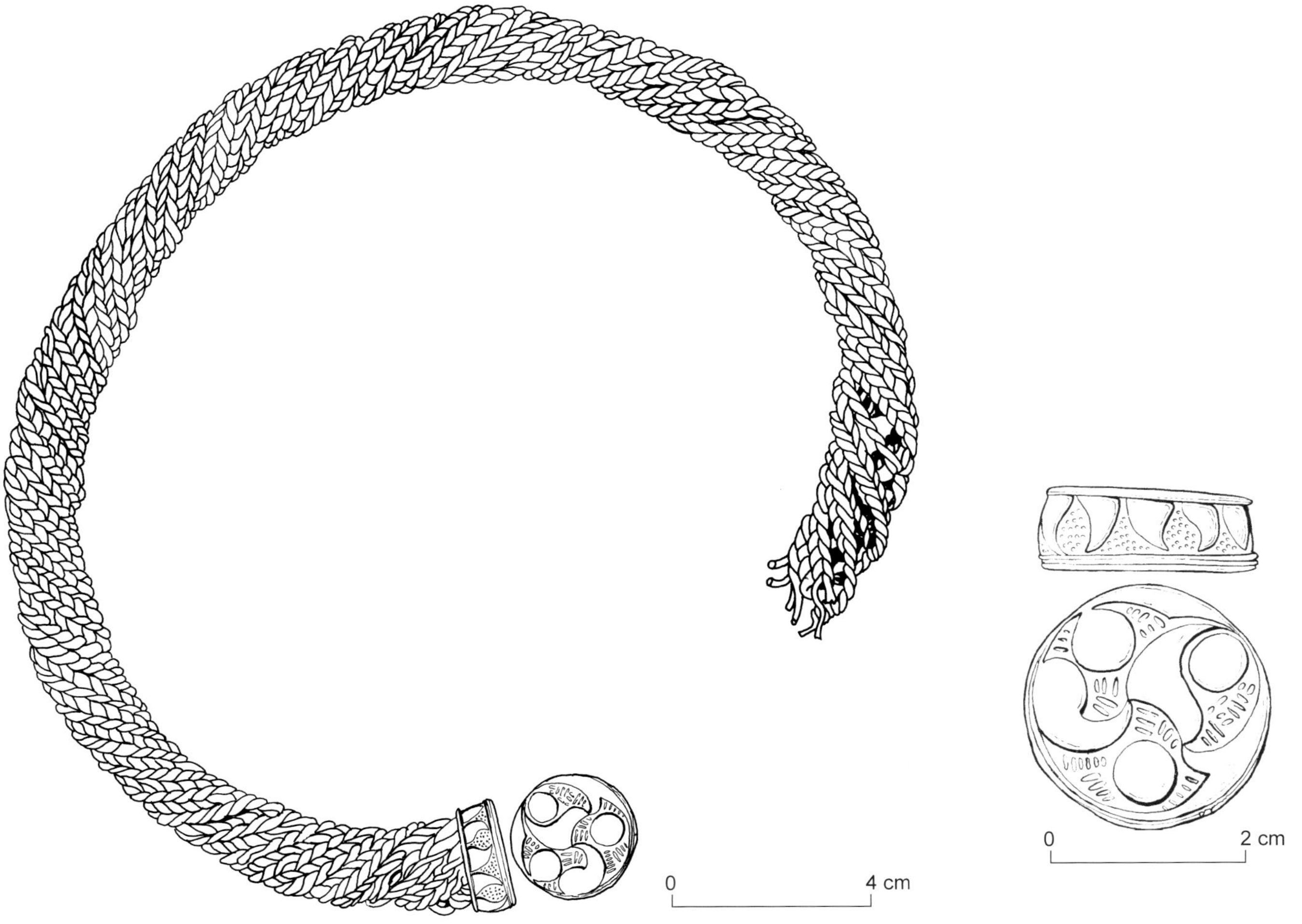

Figure 21.29 Illustration of torc L.13 (drawing by Craig Williams)

F.72) may characterise a specific phase or local tradition of torc making which is probably older than that represented by most of the objects from the Snettisham hoards.

Anthropomorphic

Interpretation of art is always subjective. Some patterns (such as those appearing on the muffs of the Grotesque Torc, L.19a, **Fig. 21.30**) can be interpreted as faces. But here we restrict our categorisation to clearer representations of the human form with defined features (two eyes, a nose and a mouth), as we do below for animal forms. According to this criterion, only one of the Snettisham torcs, S.13, is decorated with a design which could be described as anthropomorphic. It is also an example of mixed decorative styles, as the torc also has non-curvilinear decoration.

S.13 (**Fig. 21.33**) is a fragment of gold/silver alloy narrow-bodied Type 4 tubular torc. The terminal survives but the neck-ring is broken at the opposite end, and the whole fragment is bent into a tight V-shape. It is decorated with raised and inscribed decoration with a raised sinuous band surrounded by a series of concentric circles, wavy lines and areas of stippling. Near the terminal is a humanoid face with raised, lentoid-shaped eyes, concentric circles for irises and pupils, and even eyelashes. The image is abstract, but it is unmistakably a human face. Above the eyes, a cusp-shaped motif could be seen to form the forehead or hairline.

Some other Late Iron Age anthropomorphic images, like the bucket escutcheons from Aylesford, Kent (**Fig. 21.34**), appear to be wearing a hat or headdress. The same cusp motif seen on torc S.13 here provides the impression of a horned helmet. Citing other similar examples, such as the bucket escutcheons from Baldock, Hertfordshire, and a silver coin of Tasciovanus, Fitzpatrick (2007, 303–5) suggested these images could depict a religious practitioner or authority. They may also represent deities. It is unclear why this image appears on a torc. Perhaps this particular example was meant for a religious practitioner or for a specific type of event.

It is also important to consider what this decoration did. The face on S.13 is less obvious than, for example, related images on the Aylesford and Baldock buckets. This is achieved by portraying minimal yet unmistakable elements of the human face. The image on S.13 draws the viewer in, with playful details such as the eyelashes and angular nose acting to hold their attention.

Zoomorphic

S.83 (**Fig. 21.35**) is a curved section of copper alloy rod, broken at both ends, with relief zoomorphic decoration in the form of a stylised animal head with flaring nostrils. The surfaces have been partially hammered flat to give a squarish cross-section, suggesting that the object was deliberately broken up and damaged in antiquity. It is most likely part of a torc or bracelet. The closest parallels are from north-eastern France, dated between *c.* 350–250 BC (cf. Stead and Rigby 1999, 70–1; BM ML.1709). The lack of

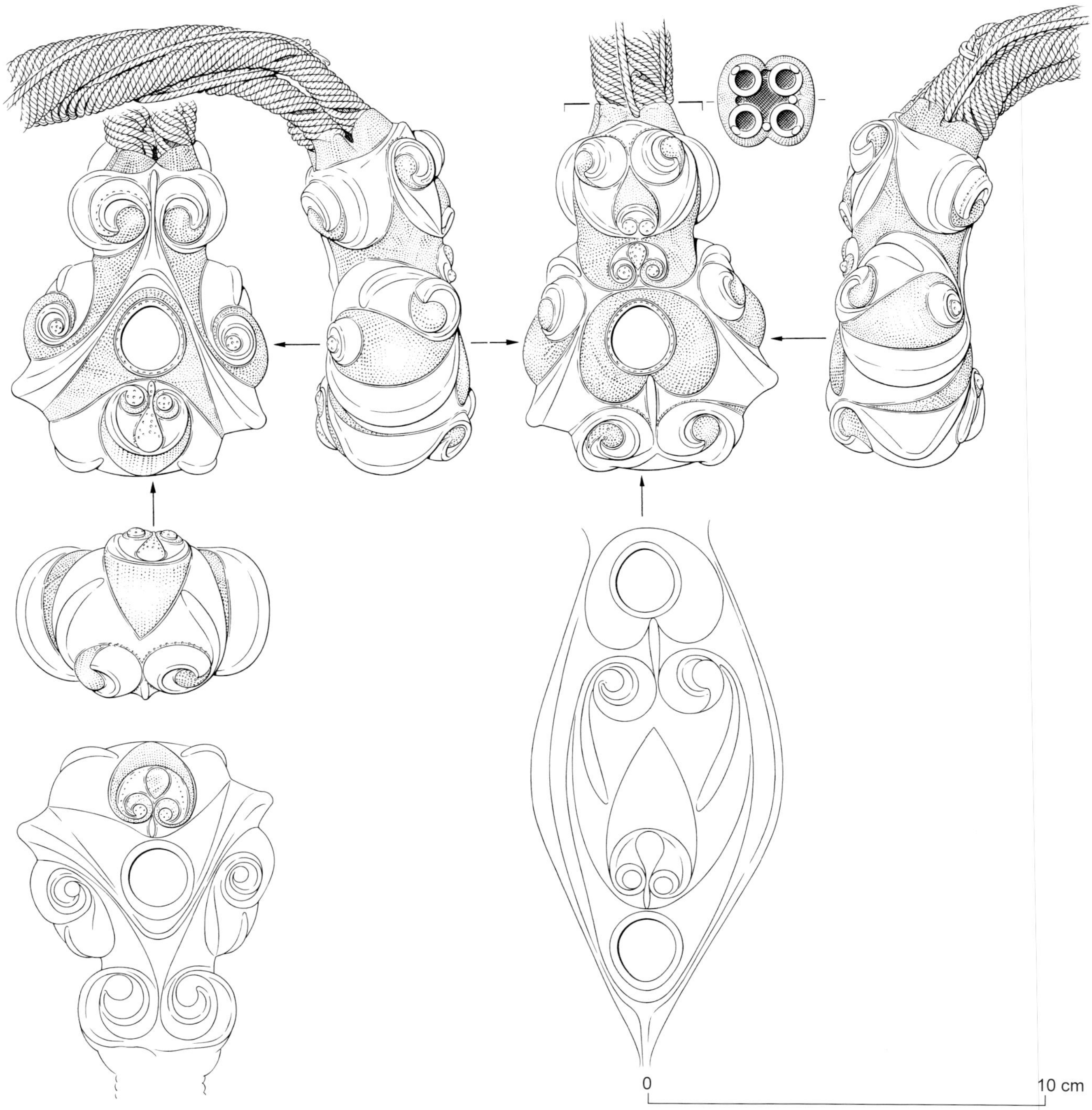

Figure 21.30 Illustration of torc L.19a (the so-called 'Grotesque Torc') (drawing by Jim Farrant)

close equivalents at Snettisham or elsewhere in Britain may suggest that this was an imported continental object.

Mixtures of styles

The mixing of styles on torcs takes three broad forms: mixing of curvilinear and more geometric motifs ('curvilinear and non-curvilinear'), mixing 'raised curvilinear' and 'inscribed curvilinear' decoration, and mixing motifs from different styles of Celtic art.

Mixing curvilinear and non-curvilinear decoration

Relatively few torcs mix both curvilinear and geometric decoration. Complete tubular torc A.1 (**Fig. 21.8**) has a raised curvilinear pattern, but much of the rest of the ornament is made up of non-curvilinear patterns, in particular circular punch-marks, chevrons created by inset wire, and perhaps the reoccurring swastika motifs seen within the raised domes of the curvilinear design. F.46 (**Fig. 21.24**) combines a very similar segmented wreath to that seen on (non-curvilinear) F.42 with a curvilinear four-armed star pattern. F.31a (**Fig. 21.36**) is a gold alloy terminal and neck-ring fragment of Type 5 tubular torc. Although heavily distorted, it is possible to make out much of the pattern, partly thanks to extensive conservation work (Ch. 16). The neck-ring is ornamented with non-curvilinear designs similar to those outlined above for torcs decorated exclusively in this style. Rectangular, triangular and diamond-shaped zones are defined by parallel lines and chevrons. Various zones contain inscribed motifs, including concentric circles and curvilinear fin motifs.

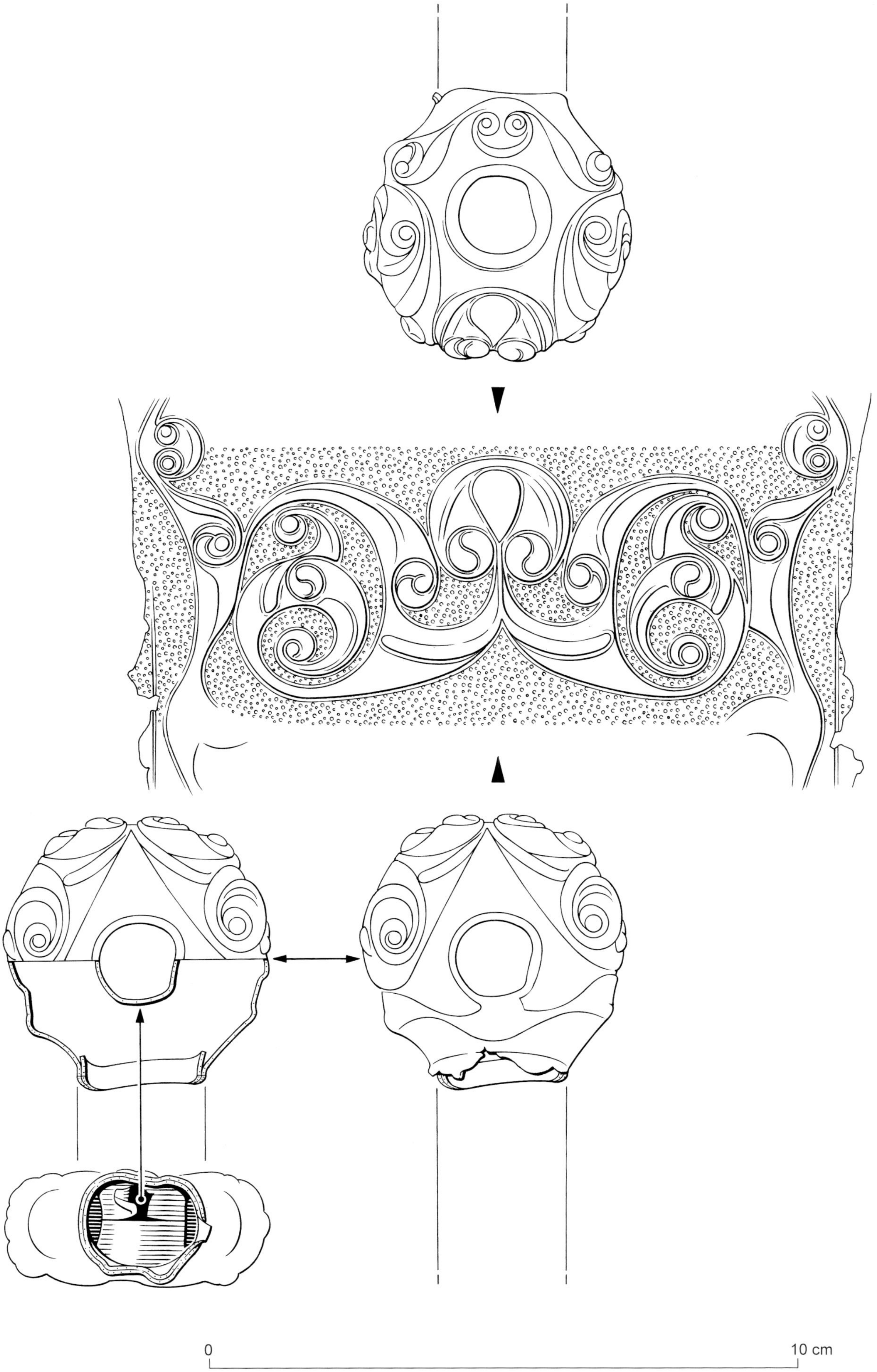

Figure 21.31 Illustration of torc F.72 (drawing by Jim Farrant)

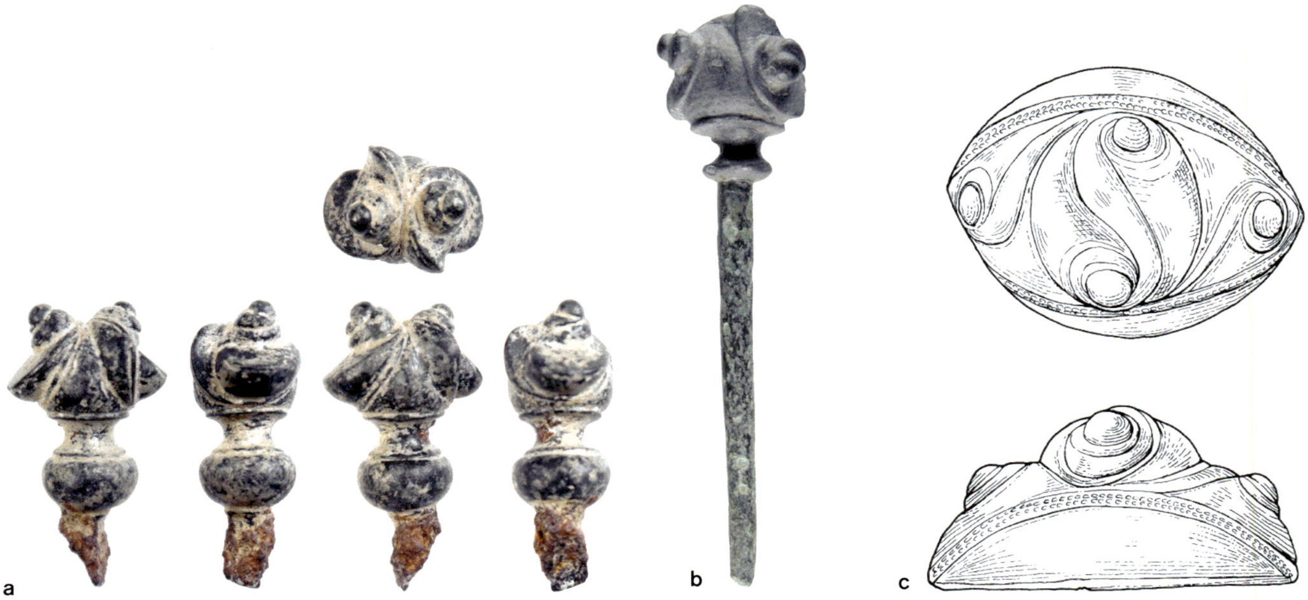

Figure 21.32 Other artefacts from Britain decorated in the Plastic Style: a) pin from Wield, Hampshire (PAS ID: HAMP-A63ECB); b) pin from Ropley, Hampshire (PAS ID: HAMP-C319B7); c) possible linch-pin head from Cambridgeshire (British Museum, 2013,8044.1; drawing by Craig Williams)

Backgrounds also differ and include dimples, regular dots, and plain areas. The flat(ish) terminal is decorated in a different style. The overall pattern forms a rough lyre-shape with an opposing pair of swirls flanked by an arrangement of fin motifs and tendrils. The motifs are plain, and the background is stippled. Of note are the tendrils at each end of the pattern. Whilst the overall design is of a similar style to the decoration on many of the other torcs (fitting broadly into Stead's Style V), the tendrils clearly reference the so-called Vegetal Style (Style II of Stead's classification).

Mixing different styles of Celtic art

In addition to F.31a (**Fig. 21.36**), described above, which mixes Style II and Style V, perhaps the most individual design on any of the torcs appears on F.43 (**Fig. 21.37**), another piece reshaped as part of the conservation programme (Ch. 16). A fragment of gold alloy Type 5

Figure 21.33 Illustration of torc S.13 (drawing by Craig Williams)

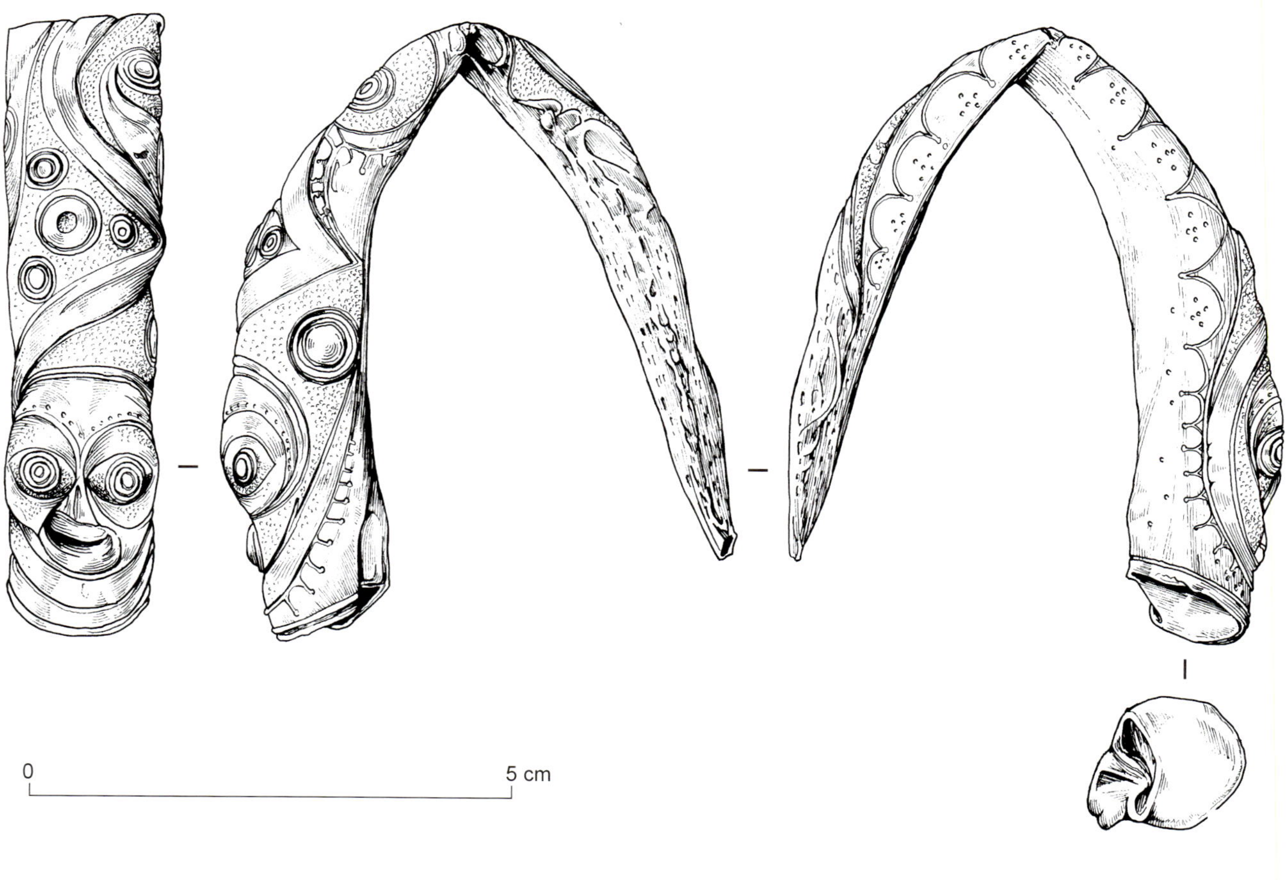

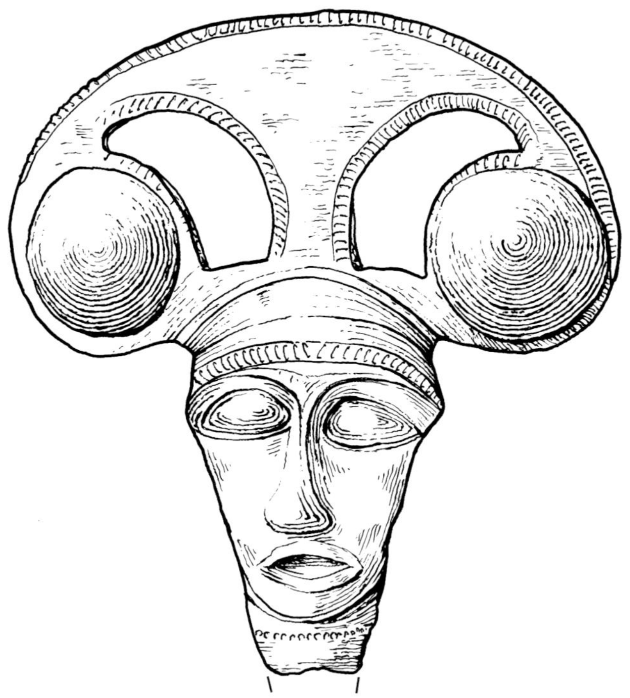

Figure 21.34 Escutcheon from the Aylesford bucket (drawing by Craig Williams after Brailsford 1975a, fig. 131). British Museum, 1886,1112.3

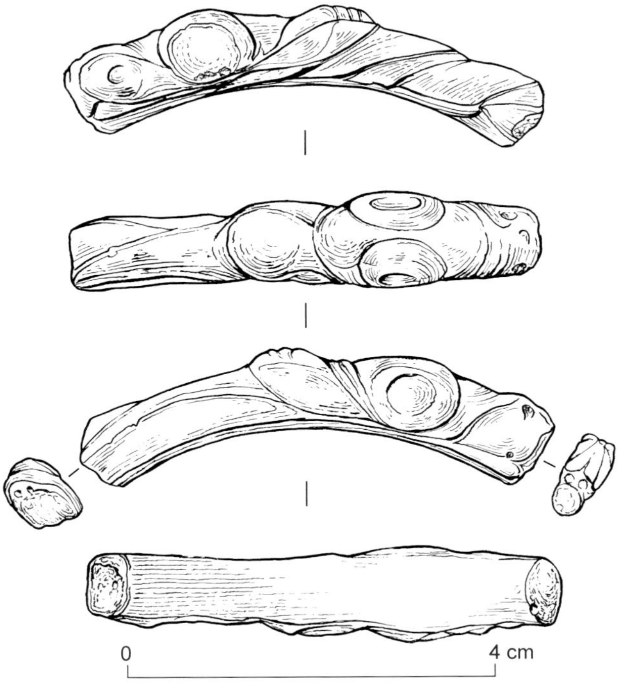

Figure 21.35 Illustration of torc S.83 (drawing by Craig Williams)

tubular torc, the decoration extends across the terminal and much of the neck-ring, comprising embossed curvilinear motifs on a punch-textured background. The overall pattern is broadly formed of two lyres, one sitting on top of the other. Much of the composition is formed of cusp and crescent shapes filled by small punch-marks and larger dots. Five decorated panels are also framed within the composition, each filled with an individual motif. Located immediately below the main decoration is a pelta shape.

Of great interest here is that the design mixes elements from at least two of Stead's Celtic art styles. Without the panels, the design would fit easily into Style V, whereas the decoration within the panels more closely corresponds to other styles. Stead (2009, 327, fig. 1) linked them to La Tène I motifs, and other connections are also apparent. For example, parallels to the motif labelled 'E' in **Figure 21.37** can easily be identified on the inscribed design on the central section of the Wandsworth shield boss, SW London (**Fig. 21.38a**) and the sword scabbards from Wetwang Slack, East Yorkshire (Stead 2006, nos 173–4). The way in which individual motifs are framed inside discrete panels also recalls the Wandsworth shield boss (**Fig. 21.38b**), on which areas of incised decoration are sectioned-off by raised ornament. These artefacts belong to Stead's Style IV, within the so-called 'Witham-Wandsworth Style' (Stead 1996, 31).

Mixing inscribed and raised curvilinear decoration

Just one torc could be seen to mix flat, 'inscribed curvilinear' decoration with relief or 'raised curvilinear' decoration. F.106 (**Fig. 21.39**) is the buffer terminal of a multi-strand gold/silver alloy torc. On its face there is a roughly engraved circular design comprising basket-hatch-filled trumpet motifs and a surrounding ring of punched dots. The outside, however, is decorated in relief with nine small dot-punched domes set in a basket-hatched field. This relief decoration is not in itself curvilinear, but it echoes the knobs with punched dots seen on torcs with 'raised curvilinear' designs, such as E.1a.

The rarity of combining 'inscribed curvilinear' and 'raised curvilinear' motifs on torcs is likely due to the different manufacturing processes involved. Inscribed curvilinear designs are generally chased or engraved onto otherwise finished terminals after casting, whereas raised curvilinear designs are either lost-wax cast or (in rare instances) sheet-worked (Ch. 17; Machling and Williamson 2018). On sheet-worked pieces, inscribed texturing is also often added, but the form of the curvilinear motifs themselves is defined three-dimensionally rather than two-dimensionally. For cast terminals, it seems that there were two production routes. Makers might choose to cast relatively plain terminals and decorate these with inscribed curvilinear designs at a final stage in manufacturing, or even later in the life of the object. Alternatively, they might mould more complex three-dimensional curvilinear designs which then formed part of the casting. These were occasionally augmented with chased or engraved texturing (such as hatching), but generally not with inscribed curvilinear motifs. These could represent preferences of individual makers or workshops, or different object biographies.

Other decorated objects

Bracelet from Hoard E (E.1c)

The sections above discussed the decoration on torcs, but other decorated object types are also present at Snettisham. The gold/silver alloy bracelet from Hoard E (**Fig. 21.40**) is hollow, being formed from sheet metal. The outside edge is decorated and there is a join running around the inside. The

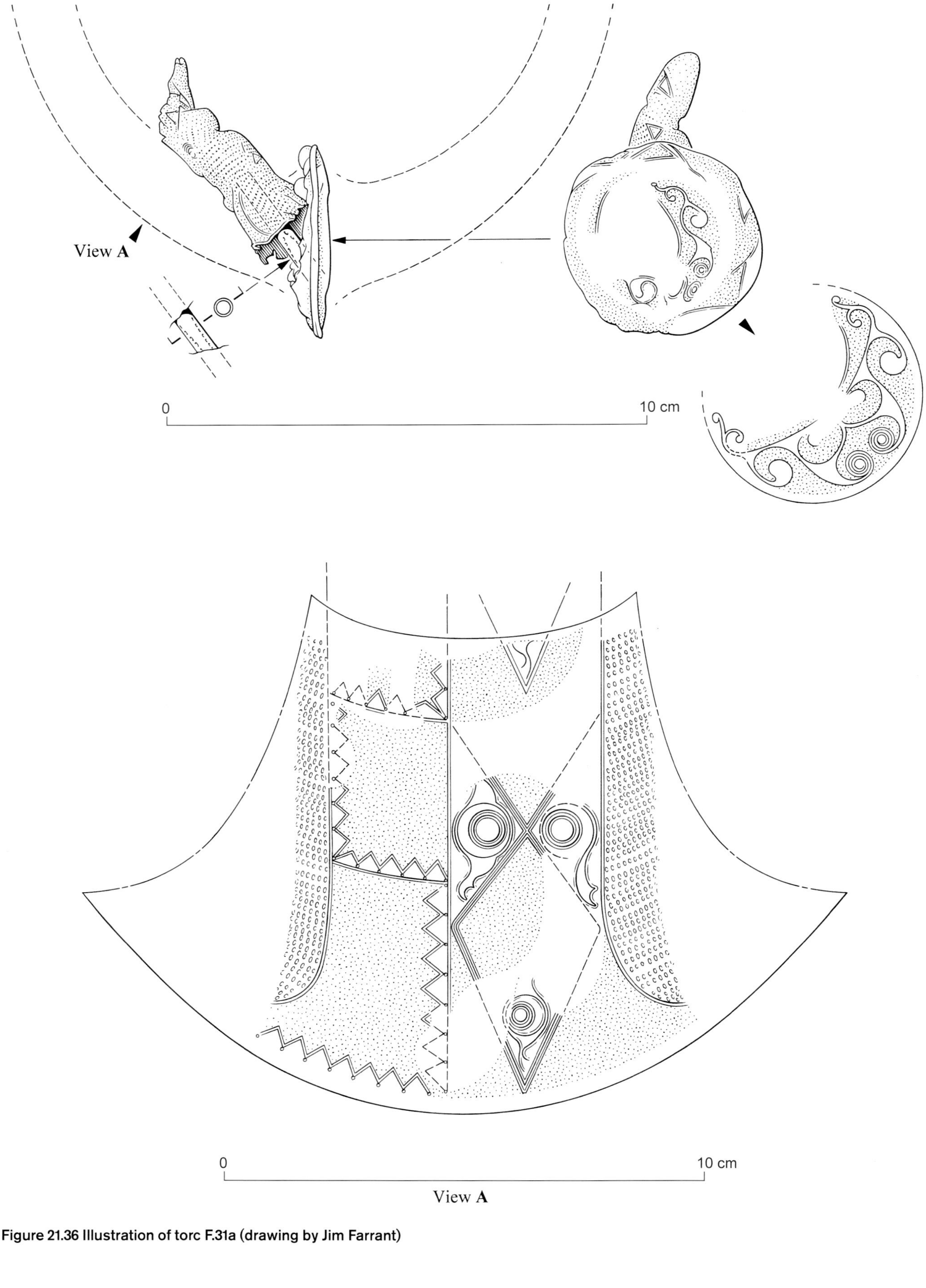

Figure 21.36 Illustration of torc F.31a (drawing by Jim Farrant)

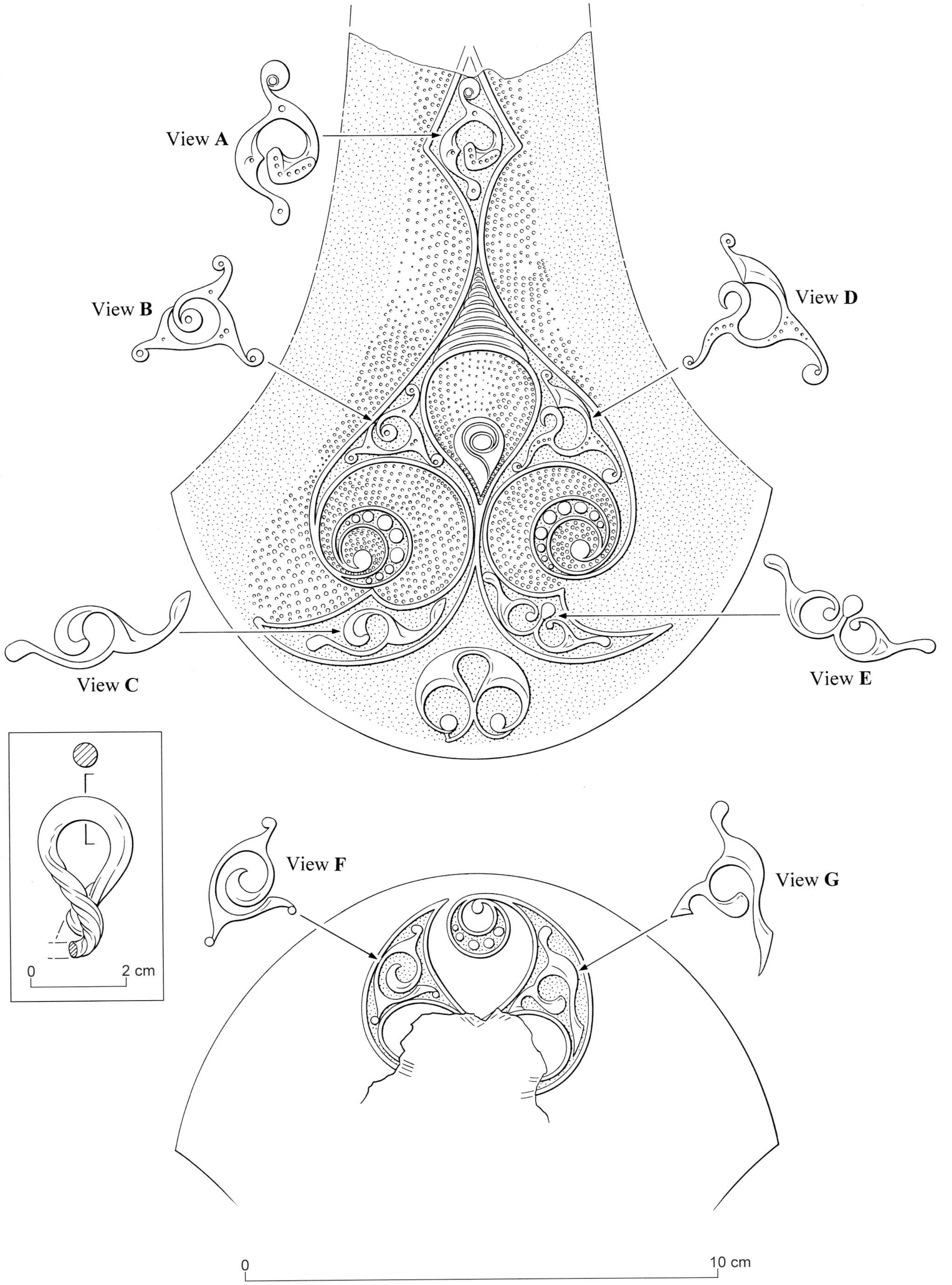

Figure 21.37 Illustration of torc F.43 (drawing by Jim Farrant)

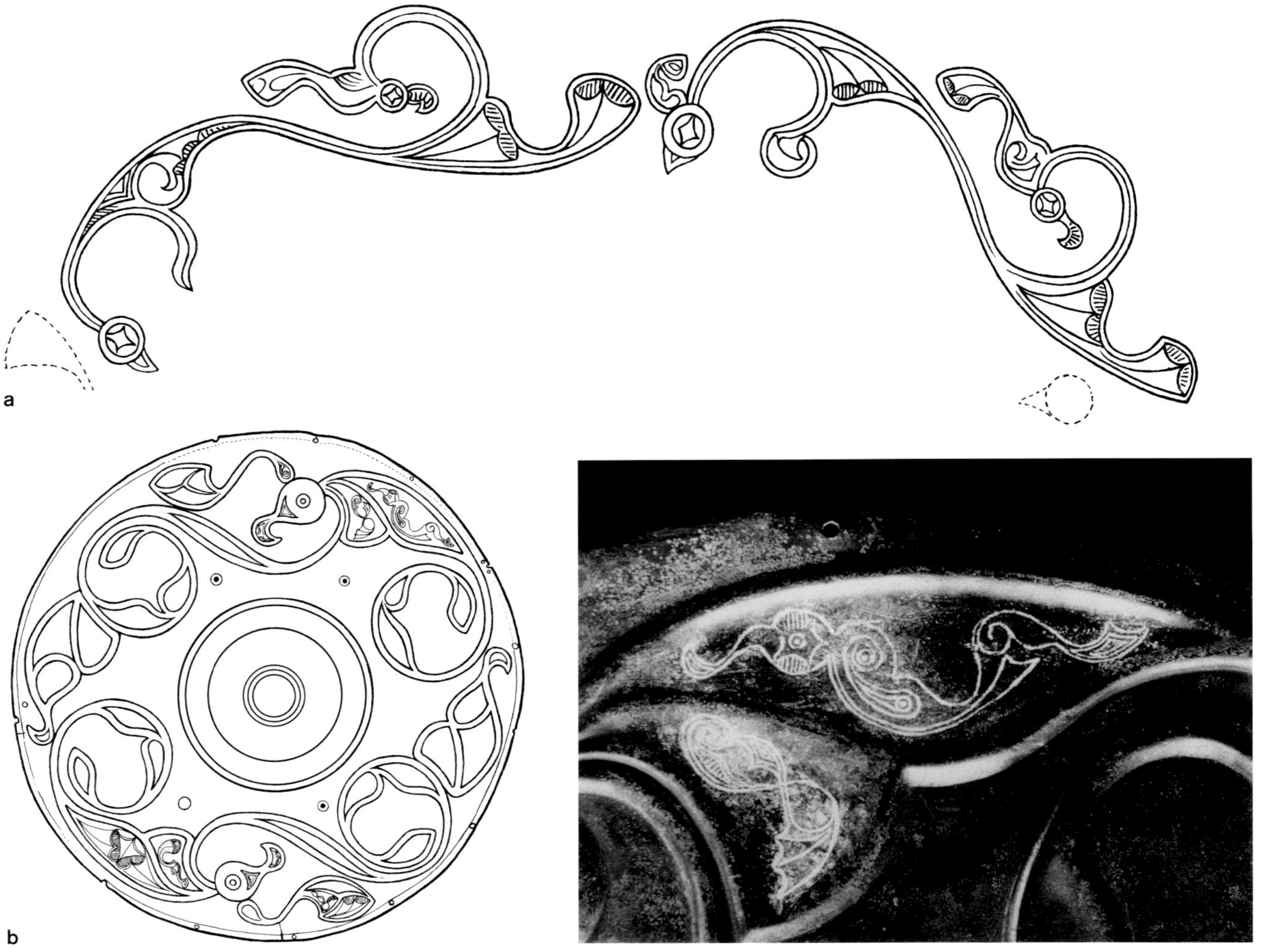

Figure 21.38 Decoration on the Wandsworth shield boss (British Museum, 1858,1116.2). (A) is a two-dimensional reconstruction of the inscribed decoration on the raised central section of the boss. (B) shows the overall raised design, including a detail of inscribed motifs which have been sectioned off within discrete panels (drawings by Craig Williams)

exterior ornament is in the same style as the terminals of the torc it was linked to when discovered (E.1a, the so-called 'Great Torc'), with two opposing scrolls comprising hatched motifs linked by flowing raised lobe motifs. A line runs along the middle, separating the two scrolls. The raised decoration is bordered on both sides by an inscribed pattern of joining semi-circles set within two parallel lines. Correspondences for this type of decoration are discussed above in relation to Torc E.1a. But it is notable that the closest parallels for the ornamentation on these two objects are each other, particularly in the case of the circular button-like motif, with hatched background and the holes of the 'button' formed by raised knobs. Given their contextual association in addition to these similarities in design, the two items may have been made as a pair, intended to be worn together as a set.

Copper alloy helmet (F.445)

Owing to the condition of the metal, the decoration on the helmet (F.445; see **Figs 14.23–31**) is difficult to make out. It is clearer on the X-rays (**Fig. 21.41a–b**). One area of raised decoration (**Fig. 21.41a**) forms a reverse-S pattern parallel to an original straight edge. On the left, as it is seen in **Figure 21.41a**, is a keeled roundel with the motif delineated by raised lobes in the form of what MacGregor (1976, grammar of ornament) described as trumpet coils and Fox (1958, fig. 82) listed as sub-triangular, curvilinear forms. The circle within the keeled roundel is formed of a raised dome. The roundel is linked by a sweeping S pattern to a similar but slightly larger raised dome on the far right of the composition. A curving chased or inscribed line extends from the bottom of the central raised lobe up to the right-hand side of this dome forming a fin-shaped motif in the negative. The other decorated area (**Fig. 21.41b**) appears to be a patch to repair a defect in the metal sheet (whether applied at the time of manufacture or later is difficult to ascertain). The irregular-shaped patch also has so-called basket-hatching. (See the catalogue entry for F.445 in Chapter 14 for further discussion of these fragments and their relationship to the helmet.)

As is the case for much of the 'raised curvilinear' decoration at Snettisham, parallels for the raised decoration on the helmet can be seen on the shield boss and spine cover from South Cadbury, Somerset (Jope 2000, pl. 91a–d), the pony-cap from Torrs, Dumfries and Galloway (ibid., pls 100–1), the crescentic plaque from Llyn Cerrig Bach (**Fig. 21.11b**; Fox 1946, no. 75; 1958, fig. 18) and the linch-pins from a vehicle burial at Kirkburn (**Fig. 21.11d**; Stead 1996, 13). The plaque from Llyn Cerrig Bach in particular is

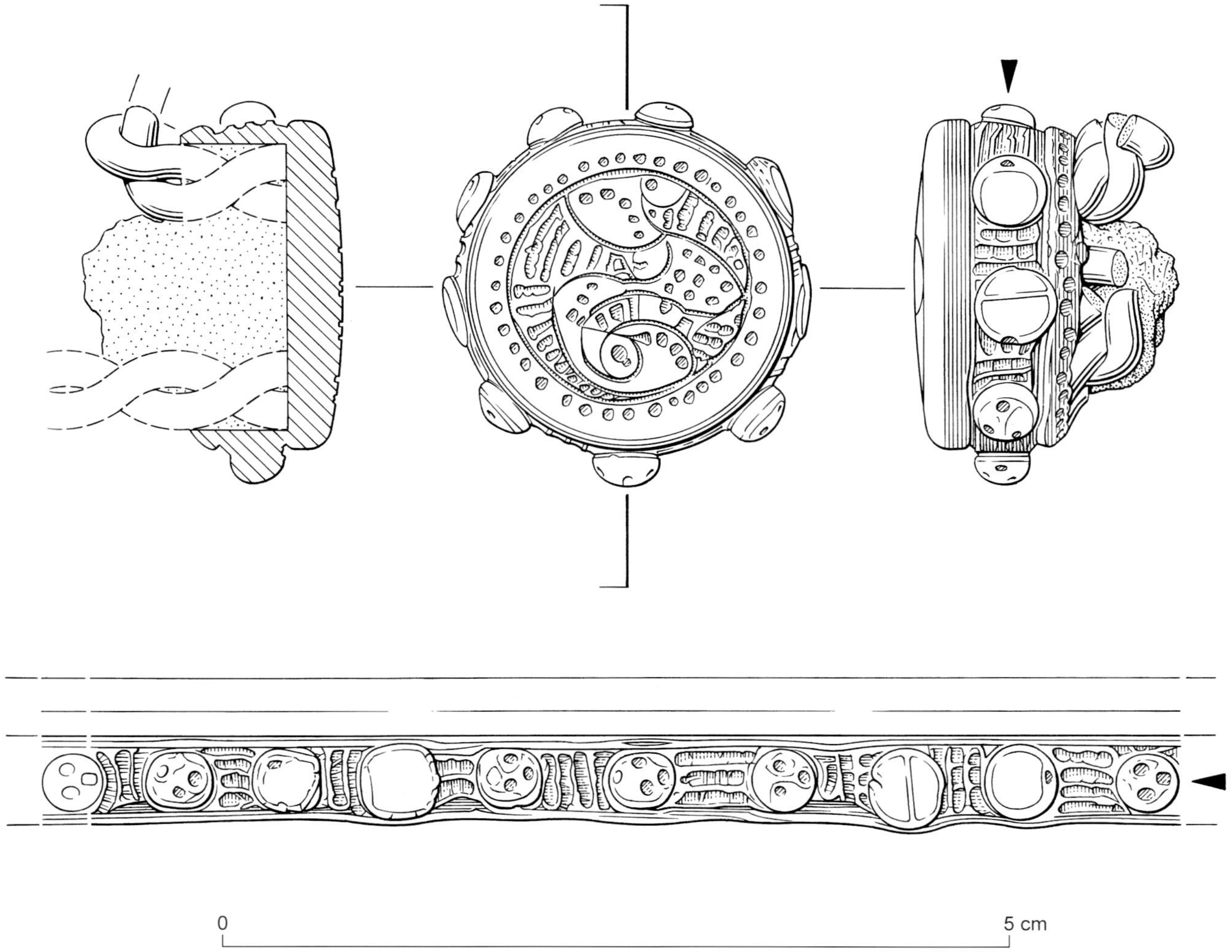

Figure 21.39 Illustration of torc F.106 (drawing by Jim Farrant)

Figure 21.40 Raised decoration on sheet gold bracelet E.1c (drawing by Craig Williams)

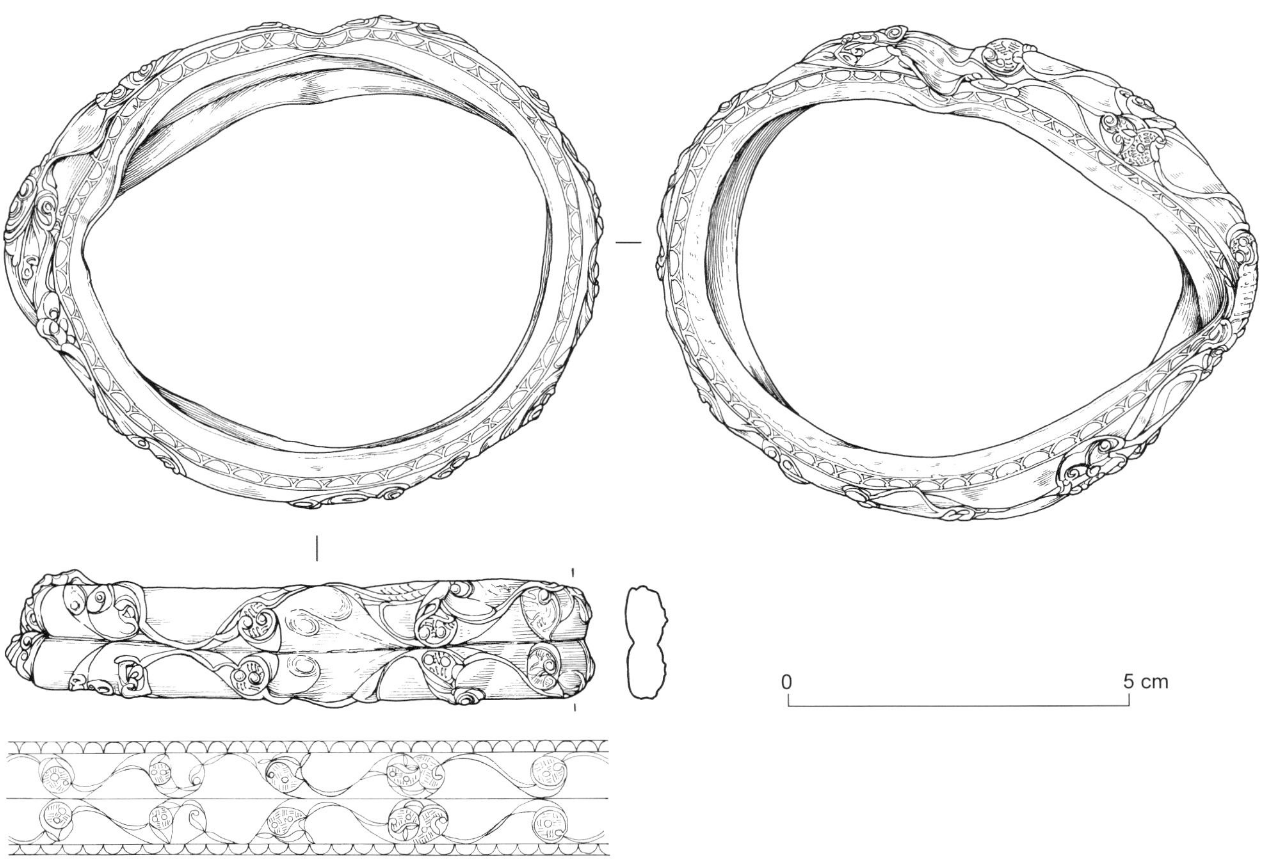

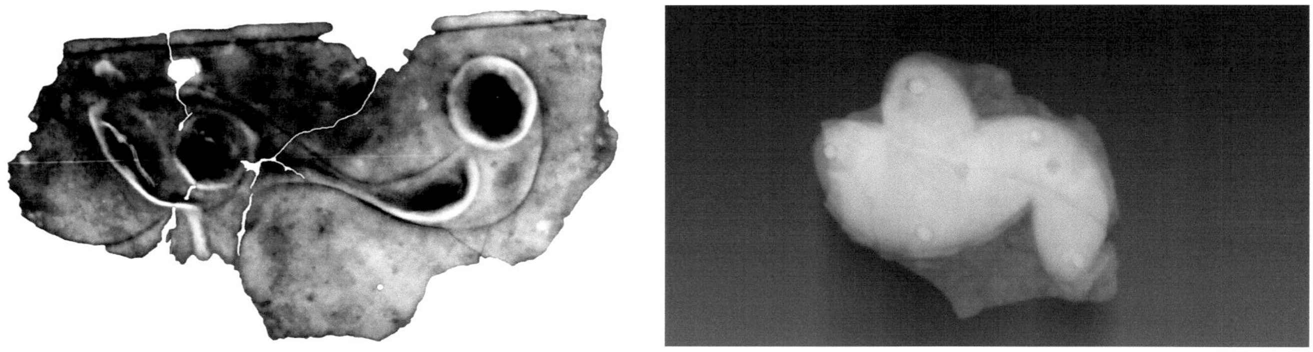

Figure 21.41a–b X-ray views of fragments from the copper alloy helmet, showing the decoration

identified by Stead (1996, 32–5) as a defining example of Style V Celtic art. The helmet decoration does not have the trumpet voids identified by Stead as a primary distinguishing feature of the style, but it does have the raised lobes and characteristic curvilinear pattern. In addition, the keeled-roundel shape which is prominent in the helmet plaque's decoration is found on many examples of Style V art. This motif has been much discussed and has been read as possibly depicting the head of a bird (Megaw and Megaw 2001, Ill. 338), perhaps even a puffin (Jope 2000, pls 184–5a and 248 a–f), whereas Spratling (2008, 195) suggested it could have depicted a horse's head, with the overall composition showing a horse on the move. Stead dated Style V decoration to the 2nd and 1st centuries BC (Stead 1996, 34). But owing to the general lack of contextual information for many of the artefacts decorated in Style V (other than mirrors (Joy 2010)), Macdonald (2007a; 2007b, 157–62) argued that this date range should be extended back to the 3rd century BC. This style of decoration can also be seen on artefacts found in 1st-century AD contexts, such as the mirrors from Portesham, Dorset, and Holcombe, Devon (Joy 2010, ch. 8).

In summary, on stylistic grounds, the decoration on the helmet is not out of place with the rest of the assemblage. But we cannot be more specific than restating the point that this type of decoration is found on objects dating from the 3rd century BC to the 1st century AD.

Terminals (S.253 and S.254)

Two cast copper alloy terminals (S.253, S.254; **Fig. 21.42**) each in the form of a bird's head, possibly a duck or a swan, were found to the east of the main focus of activity at Ken Hill (NHER 25249; Ch. 5, Trench SA15). The animal heads are sharply modelled in the round and were cast by the lost-wax method. Their precise function is unknown, but their conical shape suggests that they may be terminals from drinking horns. Drinking horns are rarely encountered in British Iron Age contexts. On the continent they are known from rich graves such as the nine iron examples from the 6th-century BC Hochdorf grave, SW Germany (Biel 1985), or the pair of gold drinking horns with rams' head terminals from the 5th-century BC Kleinaspergle barrow, SW Germany (Kimmig 1988). These items were probably used for alcoholic drinks. In the case of the Hochdorf burial, the drinking horns were possibly intended for the grave occupant and his guests (Fitzpatrick 2009). In Britain, the curved horns of the Torrs pony-cap were thought to have originally been drinking horn terminals (Piggott and Daniel 1951, 18), but this theory has now been questioned (Briggs 2014, 345). A number of fairly recent finds from Norfolk, reported to the Portable Antiquities Scheme, from Ashwellthorpe (PAS ID: NMS-003D82), Needham (PAS ID: SF-882904) (see also Davies 2011, 63–4) and Scarning (PAS ID: NMS-178AE0) could all derive from drinking horns, but this attribution is not certain. In these three cases, the terminals are bovine in form with two (Needham and Scarning) complete with protruding horns.

Mounts and terminals decorated with bovine heads are a reasonably common feature of the later Iron Age and Early Roman period (cf. Jope 2000, pls 166, 182–3; Ellis 2020) and are thought to have served as decoration on different types of vessel, appearing as escutcheons on buckets, and more rarely on tankard handles and cauldrons (Joy in Baldwin and Joy 2017, 61–2). Ducks and other water birds are less frequent. Probably best known are the ducks appearing to swim along a river of wine mounted on the spouts of the flagons from Basse-Yutz, NE France (Megaw and Megaw 1990), but these are much earlier than the Snettisham terminals. The handle of the copper alloy bowl from Keshcarrigan, County Leitrim, Ireland, has a cast handle in the almost cartoonish form of a duck's head. Jope (2000, pls 194–5) also illustrated a less ornate example of a duck-headed vessel handle from Somerset, County Galway, Ireland, alongside the Keshcarrigan bowl. In Britain, as discussed above, it has been argued that the keeled roundel could represent the head of a water bird. The raised decoration on the Wandsworth shield boss also defines two birds, possibly swans, flying around the rim (Joy 2015, fig. 31). One end of a small hooked copper alloy blade found near St Albans, Hertfordshire, could also represent the eyes and beak of a water bird (Stead 1996, fig. 4).

In sum, the decoration on the terminals is unusual and they can be dated no more closely than 300 BC–AD 50, possibly later. The discovery of other possible drinking horn terminals in the region, but with bovine decoration, could indicate a Norfolk tradition of their use. Such drinking horns would probably have been used to consume alcoholic drinks. Their deposition close to Ken Hill could be related to ceremonies or rituals accompanying depositional activity at the site.

Discussion

Owing to the extraordinary nature of the Snettisham deposits, it is difficult to assess whether there is a higher

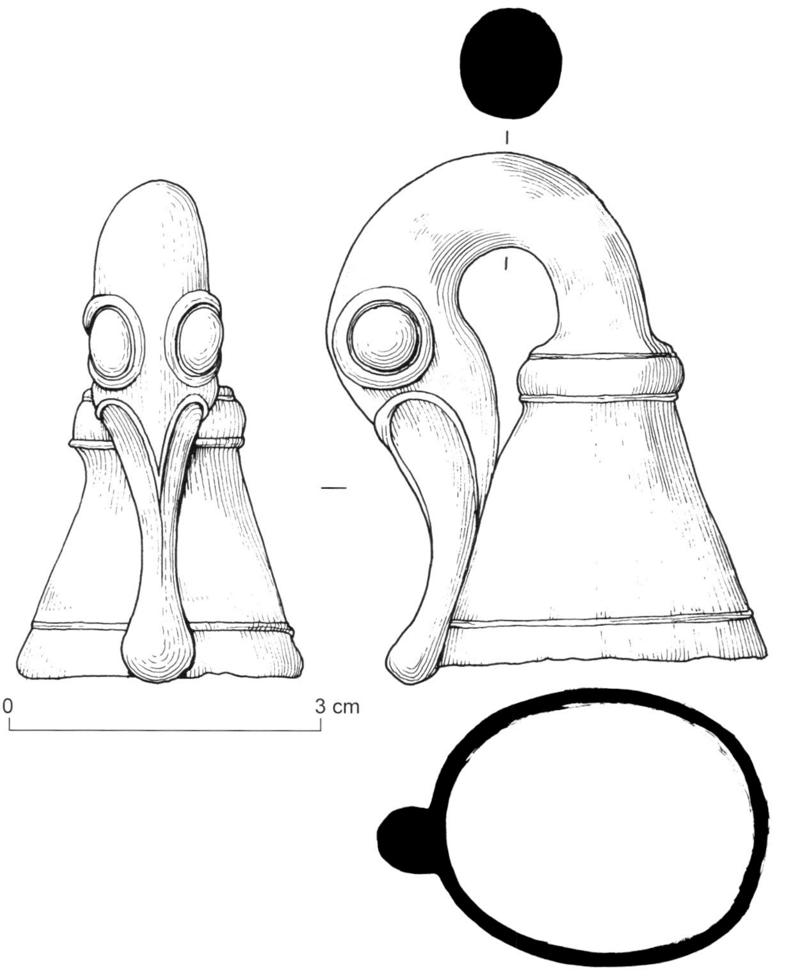

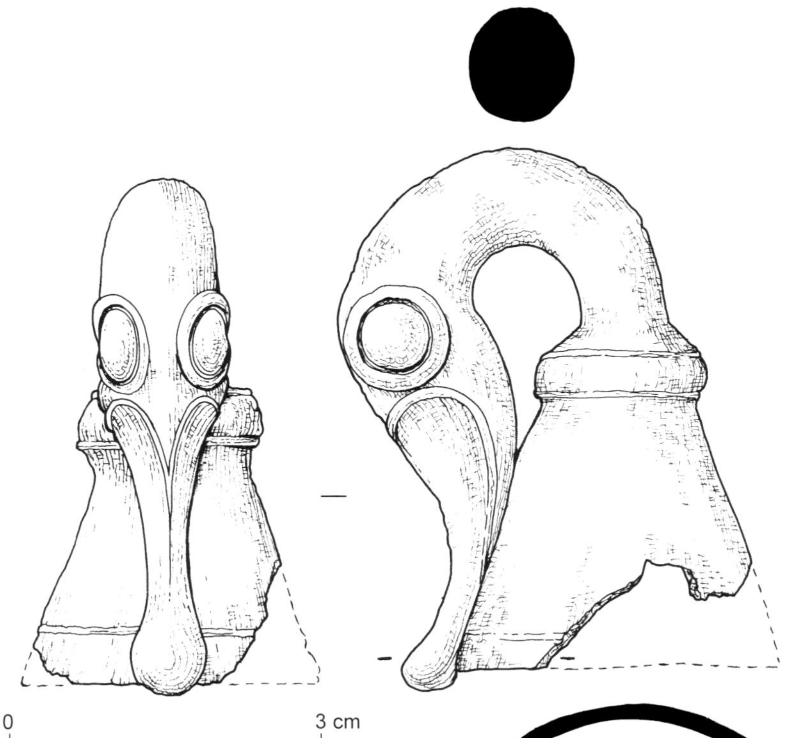

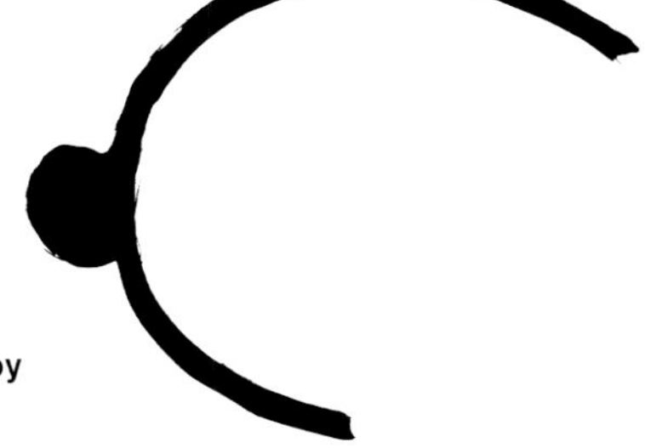

Figure 21.42 Terminals S.253 (top) and S.254 (bottom) (drawings by Craig Williams)

proportion of decorated versus undecorated artefacts than seen at other sites. As a broad comparison, four out of the six torcs from the Ipswich Hoard, Suffolk, are decorated, and one out of four objects in both hoards from near Stirling in Scotland and Leekfrith, Staffordshire. On these terms, the Snettisham hoards appear a little light on decoration, with only around 4% of objects being ornamented in this way, but there are many fragments present and also relatively plain objects such as ingots, and rings formed from flat metal strips. Also, we may not be comparing like with like, as the total assemblage is made up of many hoards. It is clear that some of the nested hoards which are most similar to torc hoards from elsewhere, such as E and L, contained a higher proportion of decorated artefacts (over 50%). Hoards with a higher proportion of fragmentary objects, most notably F, have fewer decorated items as a proportion of the total number of artefacts (although it should be noted that Hoard F contained at least 20 decorated objects, 12 with curvilinear designs: a large number compared to most known deposits from Britain containing Celtic art).

The art on the objects from Snettisham is more varied than is sometimes apparent when flicking through Celtic art compendiums, which tend to focus on the raised curvilinear ornament of the 'Great Torc' and its accompanying bracelet. Looking at the overall proportion of decorated torcs, roughly 40% of the ornamented examples are actually tubular torcs, with around 60% being multi-strand torcs with wire neck-rings (**Fig. 21.43**). Decoration appears to have been more common on particular types of multi-strand torc (**Fig. 21.44**), with buffer and torus terminal torcs comprising around 80% of the corpus of decorated multi-strand torcs, despite representing only around 30% of multi-strand torcs with an identifiable terminal type (see Ch. 13, **Fig. 13.4**). A possible explanation is that these terminal forms provide the best 'canvass' for decoration, over ring and loop terminals.

It is interesting to note the relatively high number of artefacts from Snettisham decorated with non-curvilinear motifs. In Garrow's broad-ranging survey (2008, fig. 2.3), the proportion of, as he termed it, 'swirly' versus 'non-swirly' decoration, on objects he categorised as torcs or collars was roughly 40:60. It must be stressed that within this category other object types such as beaded torcs and Wraxall-type collars were also included. The ratio for the Snettisham torcs is probably 80:20 in favour of curvilinear decoration, but non-curvilinear decoration still forms a reasonably high proportion. Those which are ornamented by exclusively non-curvilinear designs tend to be narrower-bodied tubular torcs. Perhaps there were special design rules or conventions which dictated the type of decoration appropriate for such objects, or alternatively they may have been manufactured by different producers. Some artefacts, especially broader-bodied Type 5 and Type 6 tubular torcs, are also ornamented by both curvilinear and non-curvilinear motifs, indicating that there may have been crossover of producers, or perhaps that different rules were applied to the decoration of these objects compared to multi-strand torcs.

In terms of the curvilinear decoration, most of the decorated artefacts from Snettisham are ornamented in a manner conforming to Stead's Style V. The raised peltas and berries and (in many instances) hatching which occur on torcs are all distinctive features of art in southern Britain dating to the last three centuries BC and the 1st century AD. Such designs also adorn other types of artefact, including mirrors, sword scabbards, and horse trappings.

Like much of this art, it has also been possible to group artefacts further into categories (Stead 1996, 34–5). In this instance it is suggested that a distinction could be made between 'raised curvilinear' and 'inscribed curvilinear' designs. Raised curvilinear decoration occurs most often on the terminals and collars of multi-strand torcs. Sometimes motifs in the negative, defined by lobes in relief, are hatched, as is the case on the so-called 'Great Torc'. As has already been highlighted, this is the style most often encountered in Celtic art compendiums. In part this is likely due to the popularity of the 'Great Torc', but also because gold alloy torcs from elsewhere are decorated in a similar style (e.g. the Newark, Sedgeford, and Ipswich torcs and the terminals from Netherurd, Clevedon, Hengistbury Head and North Creake, see Gazetteer in Ch. 22). Inscribed curvilinear designs, often defining positive and negative motifs through selective hatching, are also found on torc terminals, especially those with multi-strand neck-rings. As both these styles of decoration overlap chronologically and geographically, it is not possible to draw many other distinctions between raised and inscribed ornament. For example, when designs are extrapolated in two dimensions, the outlines used to form both raised and inscribed patterns are the same, and in at least one case the two styles are found together on one object (F.106).

Outside of the main decorative scheme is anthropomorphic and zoomorphic art. Only one torc (S.13) is clearly anthropomorphic, though torc L.19a with its enigmatic face can be fitted into a scarce but widespread tradition of 'hidden' faces in Celtic art (cf. Jacobsthal 1969 [1944], ch. 1). Other examples include a face encompassed within a curvilinear design on a copper alloy mount on an iron helmet from Umbria (*ibid.*, no. 144), a number of linch-pin heads from Europe (*ibid.*, nos 161–3), as well as other torcs, such as the copper alloy example from Nancy, France (*ibid.*, no. 208). In all of these cases, the head alone is depicted and it is not so much 'hidden', more 'hidden in plain sight'. Similarly, there is a tradition of depicting animal forms on torcs, such as the beasts on one of the torcs from Frasnes and the huge silver torc from Trichtingen, south-west Germany, with its bull's head terminals. In terms of numbers of objects, the traces of anthropomorphic and zoomorphic decoration within the Snettisham hoards are probably present in the same proportions as they occur elsewhere in Britain.

As shown in **Table 21.2**, Hoards A, F and L contain objects decorated with both curvilinear and non-curvilinear decoration. This sometimes occurs on the same object. Hoards F and L also contain objects decorated in different Celtic art styles. The decoration on a number of torcs, such as F.43, crosses Stead's Celtic art styles. F.31a is another good example of this. Some motifs can clearly be assigned to Style V (which Stead (1996, 35) originally argued was a product of the 2nd and 1st centuries BC), whereas others resemble the Vegetal Style (Style II), commonly thought to date to the 4th century BC. Interestingly, the decoration on non-hoard finds

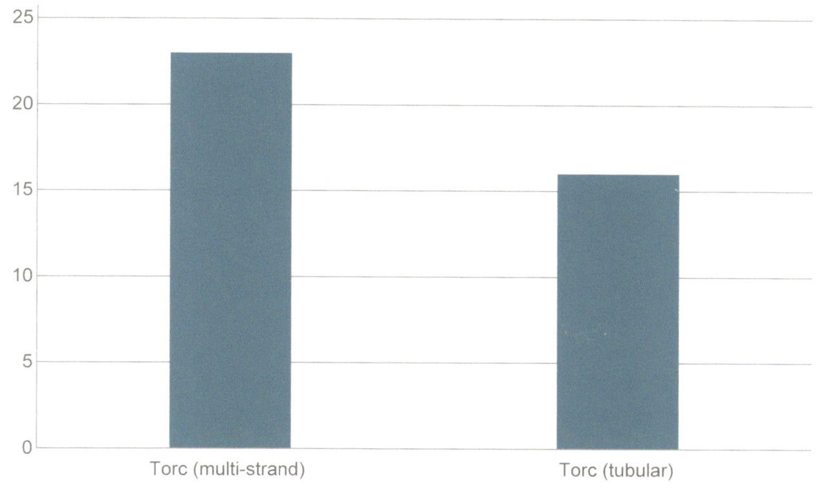

Figure 21.43 Numbers of decorated torcs by type of neck-ring (n=39)

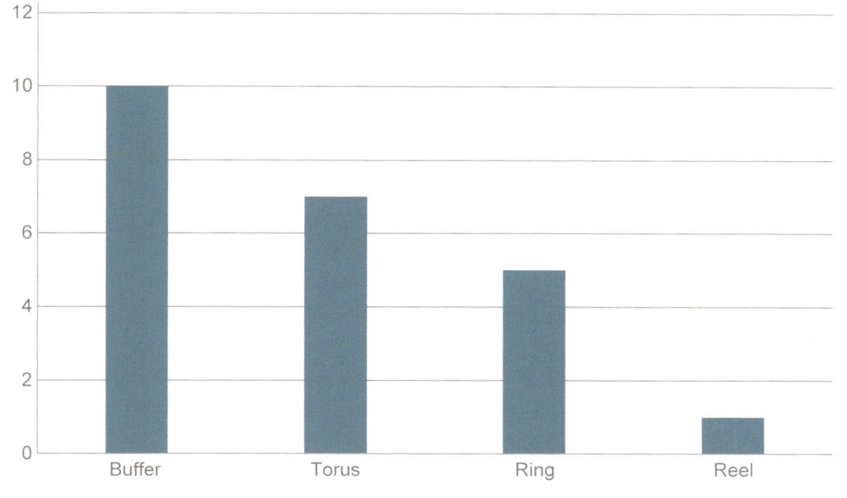

Figure 21.44 Number of decorated multi-strand torcs by terminal type (n=23)

is quite varied (**Table 21.3**) with anthropomorphic and zoomorphic decoration in addition to curvilinear and non-curvilinear. The number of artefacts is small so it is difficult to tell if this is a 'real' phenomenon, particularly as it includes other types of artefacts, not just torcs, such as terminals, which may conform to different decoration rules and traditions.

As was suggested in the introduction, the chronological significance of these style categories, or stages as Stead termed them, in Britain has been called into question (Macdonald 2007a; Garrow *et al.* 2009; Garrow and Gosden 2012). Macdonald (2007a, 332) identified individual objects decorated in different styles, such as the terminal of the torc from Clevedon (on which the face is decorated with Style V art whereas the collar is decorated in Style II or possibly even Style I art). A growing number of artefacts decorated in Style V art from well-excavated contexts, such as the artefacts from the Deal grave (Parfitt 1995), also show that the style can be pushed back in date to at least the 3rd century BC (Macdonald 2007a, 332–3). Taking account of these findings, Stead modified his categorisation and concluded that Styles II, III, IV and V overlapped in the 3rd century BC (Stead 2009, 331). These assertions support the notion put forward by Garrow and Gosden (2012, 80) that Celtic art styles were accumulative rather than successive in character (see also Garrow *et al.* 2009). Rather than a wholesale replacement, new styles were added to the available decorative repertoire. Garrow and Gosden (2012, 80) described the lifecycle of motifs as a battleship curve with a long tail. Older styles were referenced in later works, meaning that the art became more complicated over time. Perhaps we can see this with the design on torc F.31a, with its curvilinear Style V design ending in Style II (or so-called Vegetal Style) tendrils. This is supported by radiocarbon dating of organic components of, and material associated with, Celtic art objects (Garrow *et al.* 2009; Hamilton *et al.* 2015). Garrow *et al.* (2009) conducted a wide-ranging survey, obtaining multiple dates for decorated metalwork from Britain. Bayesian modelling of these dates indicated that Styles I to V were in use in Britain between the 4th and 1st centuries BC, but it was particularly hard to separate Styles III to V chronologically. Using the term 'Stage' rather than 'Style', Garrow *et al.* concluded '… decorated metalwork in Britain between the 4th and early 1st centuries BC did not follow a recognisable progression of styles. While Stage II probably did first appear at an earlier date than Stage III, for example, and Stage IV seems to have appeared earlier than Stage V, they were not strictly successive – i.e. Stage IV did not replace Stage III and so on. Rather, we would suggest that there was a gradual accumulation of motifs, and while some were earlier and others later, both could be combined on later pieces' (Garrow *et al.* 2009). The results of a second Bayesian statistical analysis of radiocarbon dates conducted by Hamilton *et al.* (2015) produced similar results,

Hoard	Curvilinear decoration	Non-curvilinear decoration	Stead's 'Style'	Notes
A	Y	Y	V	Raised curvilinear, non-curvilinear, punch-marks
E	Y	-	V	Raised curvilinear
F	Y	Y	II, III, IV, V	Raised curvilinear, non-curvilinear, inscribed curvilinear, Plastic Style
H	-	Y	-	Non-curvilinear
K	-	Y	-	Non-curvilinear
L	Y	Y	III, V	Raised curvilinear, non-curvilinear, inscribed curvilinear, Plastic Style

Table 21.2 Different decorative styles in each hoard

Cat. no.	Curvilinear decoration	Non-curvilinear decoration	Stead's 'Style'	Notes
S.13	Y	-	?III, ?V	Anthropomorphic
S.19	Y	-	V	Inscribed curvilinear
S.48	Y	-	V	Raised curvilinear
S.83	Y	-	?III	Zoomorphic
S.253	Y	-	?IV	Zoomorphic
S.254	Y	-	?IV	Zoomorphic

Table 21.3 Decorative styles on non-hoard finds

concluding that Style V was in use possibly as early as 380–320 cal BC (13% probability), but more probably from 275–200 cal BC (82 % probability), and ending sometime in the 2nd century AD (Hamilton *et al.* 2015, 652) and therefore overlapped with other styles.

As we have seen, using stylistic analysis as a means of dating Celtic art is fraught with problems, especially with so many styles seemingly coalescing in the 3rd century BC. But in some instances, such as the 'Grotesque Torc' (L.19a), if we combine evidence from use wear analysis with the use of a style which is otherwise rare in Britain, it is possible to infer that it was probably made some time in the 3rd century BC, when the Plastic Style was most prevalent on the continent, and that therefore the torc must have been old by the time it was deposited (Ch. 20; Joy 2016). With other examples which include a mixture of styles without evidence for wear (such as F.31a or F.43), dating is more difficult. They could have been made in the 3rd, 2nd or 1st centuries BC, some possibly even the 1st century AD if they are assessed purely on stylistic grounds.

In sum, the decorated artefacts from Snettisham are extremely varied. Given the different styles employed, and by correlating stylistic dating with radiocarbon dating and evidence for wear and repair (see Ch. 20), it is likely that the objects span two to three centuries. The decorated objects may be representative of those in circulation at the time of deposition, or could be a specially selected sample. Potentially, the majority of artefacts were manufactured within two generations or so of their dates of deposition (most likely concentrated in the mid-1st century BC, see Chs 8, 20, 22–3), but a small proportion were far older. These older artefacts provide clues as to how previous generations of torcs may have looked.

What does art on torcs do?

Many debates on torc decoration in particular have focused on stylistic dating and fitting patterns into wider stylistic schemes. The great majority of this chapter can be viewed as a further contribution, influenced by works such as Bradley 2009; Chittock 2014, 314; Gosden and Hill 2008, 9; Joy 2011, 206. In this last section, we ask a different question: 'What did the art do?' focusing on torcs. In order to answer this question, we first consider the character of the decoration and its position on the objects before then thinking through its potential effects on the wearer and viewer.

First, as we have seen, the decoration on torcs varies greatly but (with the exception of the punch-marks seen on some of the tubular torcs) decoration most often occurs on the most visible areas of the object: the terminals and collars and, occasionally, the back of the neck-ring. We can conclude from this that the decoration was intended to be seen when torcs were worn. Second, much of the decoration was outlined through texture, with raised motifs and hatching, as well as different forms of punching and stippling. This bestows the decoration with a number of properties which might affect how it works on other actors. For example, most of the decorated torcs are made of gold/silver alloy and would therefore have had a shiny surface. Raised and textured surfaces would have acted to break up light and reflections, making the decoration stand out more clearly, especially from a distance. Another outcome of a textured surface is that it makes an object more tactile. It is difficult to quantify, but intense wear on the decoration of some torc terminals (seen for example on L.10a and L.20a) is unlikely to be purely the result of normal use, and may have been caused by torc wearers touching the terminals, tracing their hatched surfaces. Here, we can see how decoration afforded interaction at different distances and removes of access. Those with the right and access to handle torcs could examine the decoration in detail, tracing its often sinuous pathways with their fingertips. People who only encountered the objects from a distance, perhaps as they were worn on a special occasion, would have seen the decoration in glimpses as the textured surfaces glinted in the sunlight or flickering firelight.

The complexity of patterns could also have affected the viewer. Looking at examples of Celtic art from elsewhere, and influenced by the work of the social anthropologist Alfred Gell (1992; 1998), some researchers have suggested that complicated designs could have acted like a kind of mind trap, drawing the viewer in by leading the eye in different directions and holding the viewer's attention (Giles 2008, 66; Joy 2011, 206). If we think of the example of the human figure depicted on torc S.13, or the more enigmatic faces suggested on L.19a, they are not so much hidden, but rather concealed or obscurred despite being in full view. The human brain is adept at recognising specific arrangements of patterns or marks (Malafouris 2013, ch. 8), and the faces on these torcs would have grabbed the viewer's attention. A casual glance may have revealed a possible human figure, requiring a second look and turning a fleeting glance into a closer engagement. In terms of the meanings of certain motifs (such as whether keeled roundels represent animals or birds), this is unfortunately now unknowable.

Also inspired by the work of Gell, some Celtic art has been interpreted as a kind of 'technology of enchantment'. According to this model, artefacts are seen to be so skilfully made that viewers are awed by their complexity. The skill of their manufacture appears impossible to explain, except by some form of divine or magical intervention (Giles 2008, 60; Macdonald 2007a, 336). Certainly, as is exemplified by discussion in Chapter 17, the exact skills employed to manufacture some of the torcs are difficult to fathom even today.

In sum, decoration on torcs was not only there to make them look nice. It acted to enhance particular effects and characteristics as the object and the torc wearer moved and interacted with one another and others. Raised surfaces and varying textures made decoration visible from a distance, but the full complexity of designs was only visible to those with intimate access, creating different arenas of interaction and knowledge.

A final possible means by which the decoration on torcs could be seen to act is explored in more detail elsewhere (Joy 2019b), but it is worth restating some of these ideas here. Focusing on the retention of relict motifs in the various torc designs discussed above, it is argued that the incorporation of these designs was deliberate and not accidental and that these motifs would have stood out just as obviously to an Iron Age audience as they do to a specialist in Celtic art. One reason why these motifs might have been retained is as a means of manifesting relations across time. The discovery of artefacts from Snettisham such as torc F.43 decorated in different styles has significance beyond Macdonald's (2007a, 332–3) observation that the presence of different styles on the same artefact undermines the security of stylistic dating. The complicated mixing of different decorative styles on the same object provides a powerful new interpretative tool to interrogate Celtic art from Britain: the relationships between styles and motifs, new and old, manifested by their presence on the same object. Art styles were not simply cast aside, following the latest fashion. Knowledge of past styles was retained (perhaps in part through the continuing circulation of long-lived artefacts) and elements of old styles were incorporated into new designs. These 'retentions' would have been readily evident to makers and consumers and this deployment of earlier styles alongside newer styles created connections between the past, present and future. The inclusion of already old objects decorated in different styles, such as the Grotesque Torc in Hoard L, extends this notion further to stylistic relationships between different objects selected for deposition in the same context.

Chapter 22
Torcs in Iron Age Britain

Jody Joy and Julia Farley

The purpose of the next two chapters is to bring together the evidence compiled in this volume to assess the significance of Snettisham with a focus on torcs and hoards. As the most commonly represented object type at Snettisham, and perhaps the best studied group of Iron Age objects, torcs warrant an in-depth analysis. This chapter considers how they were worn in life, who might have worn them and what effects they had on the human body. It is concluded that torcs played an important role in negotiations of identity and social standing. The following chapter (Ch. 23) examines what hoards do. It is argued that by repeatedly depositing artefacts at Snettisham, but with subtle differences in the composition and make-up of the hoards, social change was enacted in inferences, facilitating the replacement of a 'world of torcs' with a 'world of coins' (Gosden 2013).

Torcs from Britain and beyond

What is a torc?

The word 'torc' or 'torque' comes from the Latin *torques*, ultimately from torquere, meaning 'to twist', and is defined by the *Oxford English Dictionary* (*OED*) as: 'a collar, necklace, bracelet, or similar ornament, consisting of a narrow band or strip, usually of precious metal, worn especially by the ancient Gauls and Britons' (Anon. 1973, 2330). Torc is used here to describe all ornaments formed of a neck-ring with prominent terminals (cf. Eluère 1987, 22) and is not restricted to those formed of twisted wires. Iron Age torcs may be made of precious metals, copper alloy or iron and date from the 6th century BC to the 1st century AD. They are found across a wide area from the Czech Republic, to Germany and France, and as far west as Ireland, Britain and the Iberian Peninsula (**Fig. 22.1**). There is significant regional variation and torc terminals can often be highly decorative. This decoration has attracted much attention and debate in terms of seeking stylistic parallels (e.g. Stead 2009).

It is of note that even in the *OED* definition, torcs are specifically related to the Gauls and Britons: ancient peoples and identities. This association can be attributed to the influence of classical authors on modern-day understandings of Iron Age society as they described some of the people of north-western Europe wearing torcs. For example, writing about the battle of Telamon in 225 BC, the Greek historian Polybius described the warriors facing the Roman troops: 'Very terrifying too were the gestures of the naked warriors in front, all in the prime of life and finely built men, and all in the leading companies richly adorned with gold torcs and armlets' (quoted in Cunliffe 1995, 87). Similarly, Dio Cassius described Boudica as wearing a golden torc: 'She had a mass of very fair hair which she grew down to her hips and she wore a great gold torque and a multi-coloured tunic folded round her, over which was a thick cloak fastened with a brooch. This is how she always dressed' (Dio Cassius, *Hist. rom*. 62.2, quoted in Aldhouse-Green 2006, 130–1). These associations are of relevance here because they have influenced past interpretations of British torcs; for example, describing the torcs from Ipswich, Brailsford suggested they '… obviously belonged to chieftains of the tribal nobility, if they belonged to individuals at all. Dio Cassius (LXII) recorded that Boudicca, queen of the Iceni, habitually wore

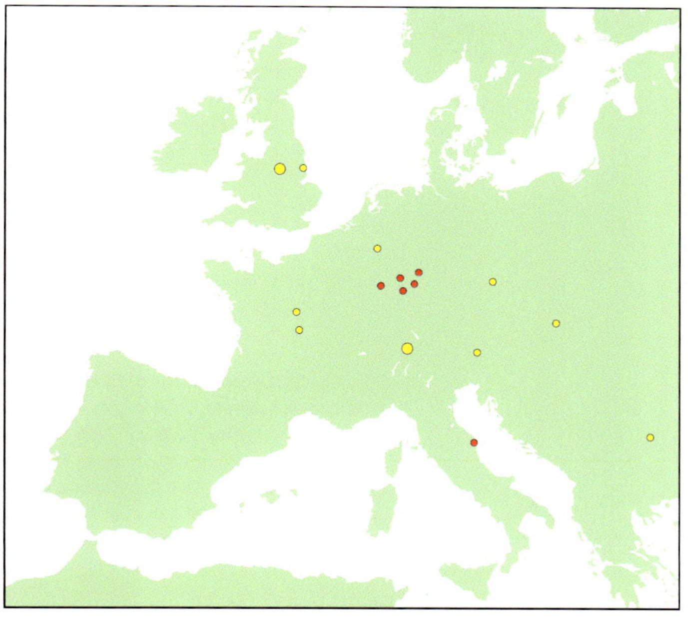

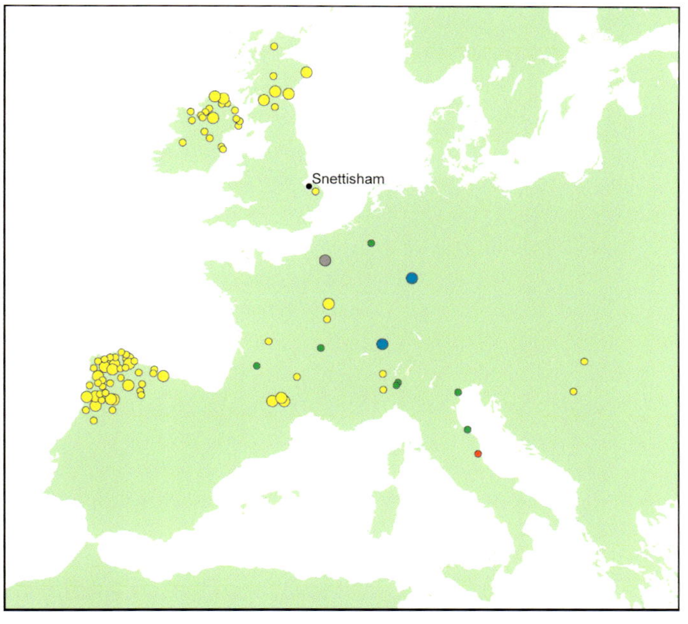

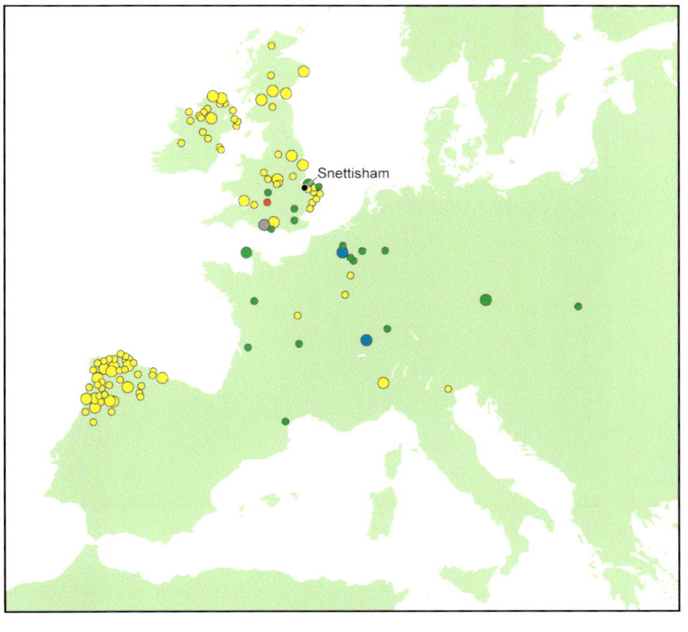

Figure 22.1 Gold Iron Age torc finds from Europe, grouped by period. Ribbon torcs are shown in both the latter two chronological stages, as they cannot be clearly assigned to one or other. Snettisham is also shown in both latter maps, as it is possible that some of the torc hoards (those not containing coins, such as A, D, G, H, K and L) could have been deposited before 150 BC. Sources for the continental finds include Hautenauve (2005) and Fitzpatrick (2005)

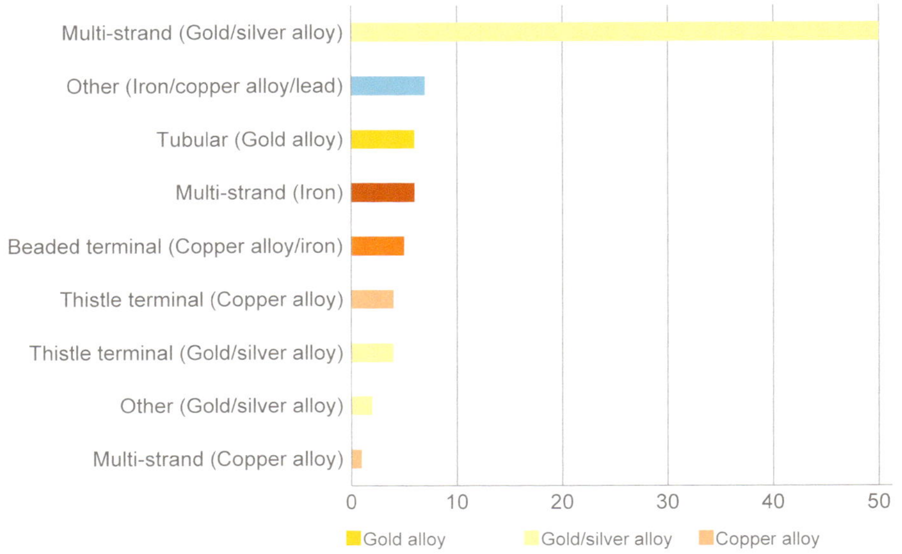

Figure 22.2 Proportions of torc types from other sites across Britain (n= 85; see Table 22.2), by type and material. This excludes the two torcs of unknown type, and the two ribbon torcs from the Stirling Hoard as well as later copper alloy torcs (beaded, Wraxall and Baldock types, see below)

a large golden necklace which was no doubt a torc' (Brailsford and Stapley 1972, 227). The idea of a link to hierarchy and even nobility will be discussed further below, but it should be questioned exactly how representative these classical texts were intended to be, or whether their authors were more concerned with the expectations of their intended audience, for whom torcs were clearly tied to the identity of the peoples, or barbarians, who lived north of the Alps (Hutton 1991; 2007, 3–6; Wells 2001, 82). This notion has perhaps also proved attractive because in Western society excessive adornment is often viewed as superfluous, unimportant and vain (Entwistle 2000, 53), and perhaps this is also one of the reasons why the trope of the 'vain Celt' continues to be propagated (see e.g. Cunliffe 1995).

Beyond Snettisham: other torcs and neck-rings from Britain and their European context

Before questioning the possible importance of the Snettisham torcs, it is first necessary to set them in their wider context. Torcs show a great variety, especially considering that they are not common objects. Hautenauve (2005) only recorded 276 complete gold alloy torcs from continental Europe (Garrow and Gosden 2012, 134–8). Many more copper alloy torcs are known, being common finds in grave assemblages in certain regions, particularly in France (cf. Stead *et al.* 2006).

Figure 22.1 shows the distribution of Middle to Late Iron Age gold alloy torcs across Europe. Early finds are rare and predominantly appear as grave goods, such as the beautifully decorated examples from Reinheim (Echt 1999) and Waldalgesheim, or as single finds, though small hoards are known including the wonderful torcs and bracelets from Erstfeld, Switzerland (Guggisberg 2000). Later torcs are found in larger hoards and (especially after *c.* 150 BC) often appear in mixed hoards including both torcs and coins (Fitzpatrick 2005).

The significance and meaning of these artefacts clearly differed over time, and also regionally. Depending on the region, torcs are found in association with both sexes and different age groups. For example, in eastern France torcs are found primarily with middle-aged women, but are also found in the graves of children and older individuals (Pope and Ralston 2011, 380). In western Germany, gold torcs from the 5th and 4th centuries BC are found in both female (Besseringen, Reinheim, Waldalgesheim) and male (Glauberg) graves. But these German examples are stylistically distinct, with complicated Celtic art decoration of hidden faces and beasts on the examples from the female graves and a simple three-lobed pendant form in the case of the male warrior grave at Glauberg. Thus, it is likely that more complex rules governed these elements of dress than simply a binary gender distinction as to whether torcs were (or were not) appropriate in each case.

Later, from the 1st century AD onwards, the form of the torc was also adapted by the Romans where it took on military associations (Maxfield 1981). Roman torcs or *maniakions* are thought to have been introduced into the Roman army from Gaul. Over time they became progressively more important, worn on armour (over the chest, rather than at the neck) as military decorations and later as a mark of office (Goldberg 2015, 165–6). They were also awarded for bravery (Mráv 2015, 287).

In terms of discoveries made from elsewhere in Britain, discussion here is mainly limited to the main torc types found at Snettisham (multi-strand torcs in copper alloys and precious metals, and gold alloy tubular torcs). **Table 22.1** provides a summary, with full details outlined in the Gazetteer which appears at the end of this chapter. In addition to multi-strand and tubular torcs, unusual torc finds and comparable bracelets are included, as well as thistle-terminal and beaded-terminal rod torcs in both precious metal and copper alloys (although only one possible fragment of a copper alloy rod torc has been recovered from Snettisham, S.83, and its terminal form is unknown). The ring from Knaresborough (PAS ID BM-CDF17E) is not included here given its current form, though Machling and Williamson (2024) have argued that it might have been made from a fragment of an Iron Age torus torc.

Distinct torc traditions that are discussed in detail elsewhere are omitted from **Table 22.1** and the Gazetteer. Gold (and, in rare cases, silver) ribbon torcs are concentrated in Ireland and Scotland, probably dating from 300–50 BC (Warner 2004; Eogan 1983; Hunter 2018). With the exception of the hoard from near Stirling, which also

No.	Site/location	County	Torc types	No. torcs	Material	Deposit type	Coins?	Frag.?
1	Stirling area	Central Scotland	MS; OTH	4	Gold/silver alloy	Hoard	N	Y
2	Hengistbury Head	Dorset	MS; MS (B)	3	Gold/silver alloy	?Hoard; ?Multiple deposits	Y	Y
3	Maiden Castle	Dorset	BT	1	Copper alloy	Single find	N	Y
4	Spetisbury	Dorset	MS	1	Iron	Single find	N	N
5	Dungyle Camp	Dumfries & Galloway	OTH	1	Iron/copper alloy	Single find	N	N
6	Colchester (i)	Essex	BT	1	Copper alloy	Single find	N	Y
7	Colchester (ii)	Essex	?TUB	1	Gold/silver alloy	Single find	N	Y
8	West Tilbury, Thurrock	Essex	TT	1	Gold/silver alloy	Single find	N	Y
9	Merthyr Mawr	Glamorgan	MS	1	Gold/silver alloy	Single find	N	Y
10	Walbrook	Greater London	TT	1	Copper alloy	?Watery deposit	N	N
11	Danebury	Hampshire	MS	1	Iron	Single find	N	N
12	Whitchurch	Hampshire	MS	1	Silver alloy	Hoard	N	Y
13	Essendon	Hertfordshire	TUB	1	Gold/silver alloy	?Multiple deposits	Y	N
14	Wendy	Hertfordshire	OTH	1	Copper alloy	Single find	N	Y
15	Auldearn	Highland	MS	1	Copper alloy	Hoard	N	N
16	Aylesford (River Medway)	Kent	TT	1	Copper alloy	?Watery deposit	N	N
17	Shepherdswell with Coldred	Kent	MS	1	Gold/silver alloy	Single find	N	Y
18	Upchurch	Kent	OTH; BT	2	Iron/copper alloy	Hoard	Y	Y
19	Burnley	Lancashire	MS	1	Gold/silver alloy	Single find	N	N
20	Caistor	Lincolnshire	TT	1	Gold/silver alloy	Single find	N	Y
21	Bawsey	Norfolk	MS	*c.* 4	Gold/silver alloy	?Hoard/ ?Multiple deposits	N	Y
22	Blackborough End	Norfolk	MS	1	Gold/silver alloy	Single find	N	N
23	Diss (near)	Norfolk	MS	1	Gold/silver alloy	Single find	N	N
24	Forncett	Norfolk	MS	1	Gold/silver alloy	Single find	N	Y
25	Gayton	Norfolk	MS	1	Gold/silver alloy	Single find	N	Y
26	North Creake	Norfolk	MS	1	Gold/silver alloy	Single find	N	Y
27	Norwich	Norfolk	TUB	1	Gold/silver alloy	Single find	N	Y
28	Sedgeford	Norfolk	MS	1	Gold/silver alloy	Single find	N	N
29	South-west Norfolk	Norfolk	MS	1	Gold/silver alloy	Single find	N	N
30	Weybourne	Norfolk	?TUB	1	Gold/silver alloy	Hoard	Y	Y
31	Ulceby (*some finds lost)	North Lincolnshire	MS	3	Gold/silver alloy	Hoard	N	N
32	Fremington Hagg	North Yorkshire	BT	1	Copper alloy	?Hoard	N	Y
33	Towton	North Yorkshire	MS (B)	2	Gold/silver alloy	?Hoard	?N	N
34	Great Houghton	Northamptonshire	OTH	1	Lead alloy	Burial	N	N
35	Newark	Nottinghamshire	MS	1	Gold/silver alloy	Single find	N	N
36	Ellesmere	Shropshire	MS	1	Gold/silver alloy	Single find	N	Y
37	Telford	Shropshire	MS	1	Gold/silver alloy	Single find	N	Y
38	Cadbury Castle	Somerset	OTH	3	Iron	?Single finds	N	Y
39	Camerton	Somerset	MS	1	Iron	Single find	N	N
40	Clevedon	Somerset	MS	1	Gold/silver alloy	Single find	N	Y
41	Ham Hill	Somerset	MS; OTH	4	Iron	Burial (1); Single find (1); ?Hoard (2)	N	N
42	Polden Hills	Somerset	MS	1	Iron/copper alloy	Hoard	N	N

Table 22.1 Multi-strand, tubular and thistle-terminal type torcs from Britain (for full details see Gazetteer). Finds marked * are lost. Abbreviations of torc types: BT: beaded-terminal rod torc; MS: multi-strand; OTH: other; TT: thistle-terminal rod torc; TUB: tubular; (B): bracelet; frag.: fragmented

No.	Site/location	County	Torc types	No. torcs	Material	Deposit type	Coins?	Frag.?
43.	Alrewas	Staffordshire	MS	*c.* 3	Gold/silver alloy	Hoard	N	Y
44.	Glascote	Staffordshire	MS	1	Gold/silver alloy	Single find	N	N
45.	Leekfrith	Staffordshire	MS; TT; TT (B)	4	Gold/silver alloy	Hoard	N	N
46.	Needwood Forest	Staffordshire	MS	1	Gold/silver alloy	Single find	N	N
47.	Shenstone	Staffordshire	TT	1	Copper alloy	Single find	N	?Y
48.	Great Finborough	Suffolk	MS	1	Gold/silver alloy	Single find	N	Y
49.	Ipswich	Suffolk	MS	6	Gold/silver alloy	Hoard	N	N
50.	Shepherd's Fen	Suffolk	TT (B)	1	Copper alloy	Single find	N	N
51.	Netherurd (*some finds lost)	Tweeddale	MS; MS (B); OTH (B)	?4	Gold/silver alloy	Hoard	Y	Y
52.	Middleton Hall	Warwickshire	MS	1	Gold/silver alloy	Single find	N	Y
53.	Westhampnett	West Sussex	TUB	1	Gold/silver alloy	Burial	N	Y
54.	Pershore	Worcestershire	?MS; ?TUB	?2	Gold/silver alloy	Hoard	Y	Y
55.	Dorchester*	Dorset	?MS	1	Iron	?Single find	N	N
56.	Arras*	East Riding of Yorkshire	?	1	Copper alloy	Burial	N	N
57.	Birdlip*	Gloucestershire	MS	1	Gold/silver alloy	?Burial	N	Y
58.	Marham*	Norfolk	?MS	1	Gold/silver alloy	Single find	N	N
59.	Narford*	Norfolk	MS	?3	Gold/silver alloy	Hoard	N	Y
60.	Pattington*	Staffordshire	?	1	?	?	?	?
61.	Mildenhall*	Suffolk	?	1	Gold/silver alloy	Burial	N	N
62.	Wallingford	Suffolk	?	5	Gold/silver alloy	?Hoard	N	?
63.	Rawden Billing*	West Yorkshire	?	1	?	?	?	?

Table 22.1 continued

included other torc types, they will not be discussed further. Three distinct groups of copper alloy torcs dating to the 1st century AD and beyond represent separate traditions, and will likewise not be considered further here. These are 'Wraxall'-type collars, largely found in the south-west of Britain (Megaw 1971; Beswick *et al.* 1990; Nowakowski *et al.* 2009), 'Baldock tradition' strip and rod torcs from the south-east (Marshall 2023), and beaded torcs, which are generally restricted to northern and western Britain (MacGregor 1976, 97–9, 113–15, nos 198–208; Beswick *et al.* 1990; Hunter 2018).

Torc types present in different finds are given in the Gazetteer and summarised in **Table 22.1** and **Figure 22.2**. The vast majority are multi-strand torcs similar to those seen at Snettisham, whilst a handful are tubular torcs (Essendon), tubular torc components (Norwich) or small sheet fragments which may represent tubular torcs (Pershore, Westhampnett, Weybourne). There are a handful of unique or highly unusual torcs classified simply as 'other' in **Table 22.1**, such as the lead alloy torc from Great Houghton, or the jointed iron torcs from Cadbury Castle. Others fall into groups. Two finds of gold alloy thistle terminal torcs (from Leekfrith and Caistor) and a possible third poorly recorded similar find from Thurrock, Essex, can most likely be stylistically dated to the 3rd or 4th centuries BC, with their closest parallels on the continent (see e.g. Farley *et al.* 2018). Finds of copper alloy torcs or bracelets in a similar form (Aylesford, Shenstone, Shepherd's Fen, Walbrook) may date to a similar early period or, especially given an apparent association with 1st to 2nd-century Romano-British finds at the River Walbrook in London (Marshall 2023, fig. 7), be either long-lived forms or examples of another type of 1st and 2nd-century AD copper alloy torc tradition comparable to the Baldock type, beaded torcs and Wraxall-type collars. The latter is perhaps particularly likely in the case of copper alloy rod torcs with beaded terminals: Colchester (i), Fremington Hagg, and Upchurch (the latter two associated or potentially associated with Early Roman material). The unusual iron and copper alloy torcs from 1st and 2nd-century AD hoards at Polden Hills and Upchurch are probably also part of such later traditions, and the same may be true of some of the other iron torc finds. Fitzpatrick (1999) noted that iron multi-strand torcs (with finds from Camerton, Danebury, Ham Hill, and Spetisbury) appear to have a south-western distribution similar to those of the Wraxall-type collars (**Fig. 22.4a**), and thus might represent a distinctive local tradition. Although, whilst the Camerton and Spetisbury finds were found alongside Early Roman material, the Danebury and Ham Hill finds appear to be Late Iron Age in date. Several of these distinctive iron torcs have clasps which close the gap between the ring terminals, and Sellwood (1984, 371) suggested they might have functioned as slave chains similar to the gang chains from Llyn Cerrig Bach and Bigbury, although the twisted iron rods and ring terminals are certainly more decorative than those examples. The copper alloy multi-strand torc from Auldearn, dated stylistically and by its possible association with the nearby find of a large trumpet brooch, most likely also dates to the 1st or 2nd century AD.

The Snettisham finds comprise two main types of torc: tubular and multi-strand (see Typology in Ch. 13). In terms of deposition at least, the two types are contemporary. For example, tubular and multi-strand torcs were both recovered from Hoard F. But, it is difficult to be certain exactly how old artefacts were before they were put in the ground and therefore to determine precisely the relative duration of circulation for each type (below and Chs 20 and 21). Whilst the multi-strand torcs that form the majority of finds at Snettisham and elsewhere across the UK have traditionally been stylistically dated to the 1st century BC, dating evidence from Snettisham and beyond suggests a much longer period of production and circulation of these objects, perhaps dating as far back as the 3rd or 4th centuries BC (see below).

History of discoveries

The history of discoveries at Snettisham is outlined in detail in Chapter 4. The purpose of this subsection is to summarise the information presented in the Gazetteer and provide some background to the sequence of finds of similar torcs from the rest of Britain. Three major periods of discovery can be identified. A series of chance finds were made during the 19th century, such as at Burnley (1802), Netherurd (1806), Ulceby (1847), Needwood Forest (1848) and Clevedon (acquired by the British Museum in 1897). A second cluster of discoveries was made in a period of agricultural and commercial intensification between the 1940s and 1970s. In addition to the Snettisham finds made at this time, torcs were unearthed in Norfolk at Bawsey (1941 and 1944) and North Creake (1947). The Glascote torc was found in 1943, although it was not identified until 1970 (Painter 1970; 1971). Similarly, a torc was discovered near Diss sometime in 1942/3 but only came to light in 2010. From *c.* 1914 to the late 1960s up to 60 coins as well as a tubular torc fragment were eroded out of the cliffs at Weybourne near Sheringham. A broken torc was ploughed up in 1965 at Sedgeford (the missing terminal not being found until 2004) and building work in 1968 just outside Ipswich revealed five torcs, with a sixth being discovered in 1970 (Brailsford 1968; Brailsford and Stapley 1972; Owles 1969; 1970). A torc fragment was also discovered during farming activities at Middleton Hall in 1968 but was not identified by archaeologists until 1976. A small number of unusual torcs were also discovered during archaeological excavations between the 1930s and 1990s (see below), but, since the beginning of the 1980s most new discoveries have been made by metal-detector users (the exception being a torc unearthed during quarrying at Blackborough End, Middleton, Norfolk, in 1984). The first known metal-detected find was at Bawsey in 1984, followed by Hodder's discoveries at Snettisham in 1989. Since then, further discoveries have been made by metal detector at Bawsey (1987–90, 1996 and 2006) and Sedgeford (2004), and new finds made at Essendon (1992), Alrewas (1994), Colchester (1996), south-west Norfolk (2003), Newark (2005), Stirling (2009) and Caistor (2013). A more recent find was made in 2016 at Leekfrith (Farley *et al.* 2018). These latest two finds (at Caistor and Leekfrith) are also, by coincidence, stylistically the earliest known gold torcs from Britain, potentially pushing back the date of such objects into the early 4th century BC. This shows how quickly new discoveries can (and may again in future) change the archaeological narrative. See, for example, Adams *et al.* (2024), which discusses the recent find of the Pulborough torc (not included in the table and gazeteer here).

History of research

Considering some torcs were discovered as long ago as the early 19th century, it is surprising that torcs from Britain did not feature more prominently in the literature until at least the 1950s. Birch's (1846) 'On the torc of the Celts' examined the evidence for torcs in classical literature and iconography, including Late Iron Age coinage from Britain, but the artefacts he considers are now known to be Bronze Age in date. The Clevedon Torc terminal was illustrated in Smith's British Museum *Guide to the Antiquities of the Early Iron Age* (Smith 1905, fig. 126), but overall discussion of torcs only made up a single page of text (*ibid.*, 137–8) and the wording was not significantly updated for the 1925 edition (Smith 1925, 149–50). In his short note on the 'Torcs of the Early Iron Age in Britain' Leeds (1933, 467) identified the torcs from Ulceby, Lincolnshire as Iron Age, based on the bridle bits found with them. He also drew a distinction between the Ulceby torcs and the collars of the 'Wraxall' type discussed above, placing the torc from Needwood Forest and the Clevedon Torc alongside the Ulceby examples within his torc catalogue. The discovery of a torc terminal at North Creake prompted Clarke (1939, 60) to re-categorise published artefacts previously identified as something else. For example, prior to Clarke's study, the terminal from Netherurd was thought to be a 'sceptre head' and the terminal excavated by Bushe-Fox at Hengistbury Head was identified as the head of a linch-pin (Bushe-Fox 1915). The discovery of Hoards A–E at Snettisham and then further finds made during the 1960s and 1970s elevated the status of torcs to the level of an important artefact type worthy of extended discussion (cf. Sealey 1979). Following Stead's excavations in the early 1990s it became clear that a good proportion of all the Iron Age torcs ever recovered originate from Britain, particularly East Anglia (cf. Hautenauve 2005).

Aside from Leeds' distinction between torcs and collars, torcs were first categorised by Clarke in his publication of the initial hoards found at Snettisham (Clarke 1954). He drew a distinction between the tubular bodies of torcs from Hoard A and the multi-strand torcs found in many of the other hoards. Multi-strand torcs were further subdivided based on their terminals: in particular Clarke identified loop and buffer terminals. He also compiled a full catalogue of other British finds known at the time, setting British torcs in their wider European context. In his publication of the Snettisham excavations, Stead (1991a, 451–5, figs 2–10)

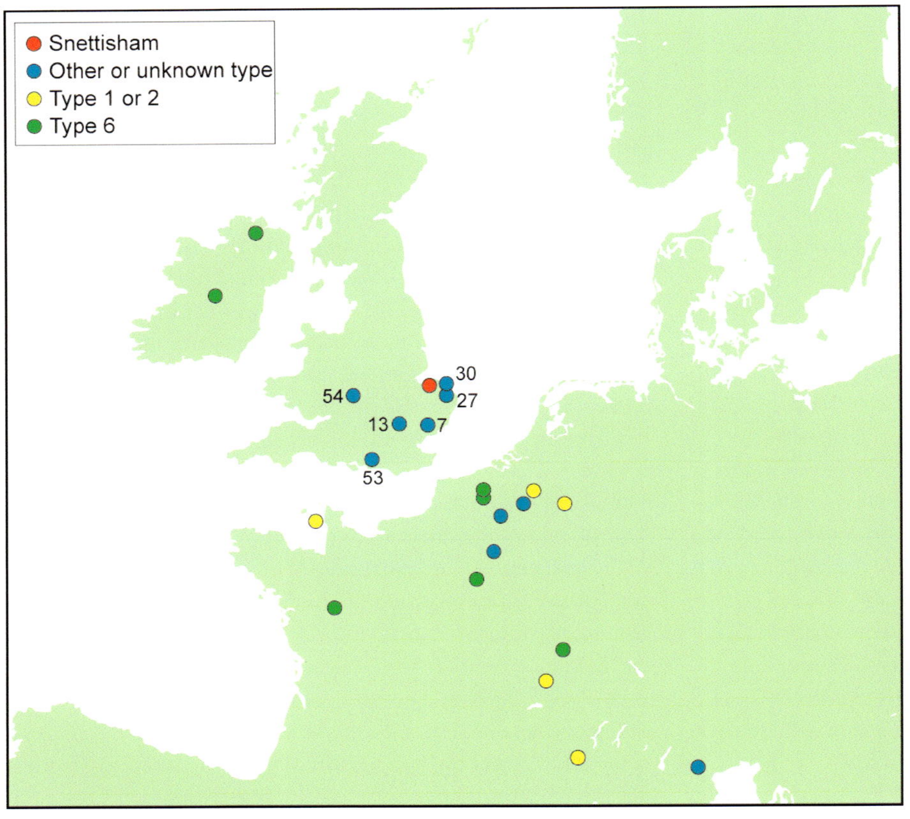

Figure 22.3 Distribution of gold tubular torcs of the types found at Snettisham, drawing on data from Fitzpatrick (2005), Hautenauve (2005), Roymans *et al.* (2012) and de Jersey (2021). Note that all types are represented at Snettisham. The 'knobbly' sheet gold torcs and arm rings of the types found at Aurillac, Fenouillet, and Lasgraïsses (France) and Stirling (Scotland) have been omitted, as has an unusual segmented tubular torc from Hungary (Hautenauve 2005, no. 229). Numbers are those from the Gazetteer and Table 22.1

defined six types based on his new discoveries (tubular torcs; and twisted wire torcs with loop, buffer, ring, cage and reel terminals), but overall Clarke's method of categorisation was not changed. Hautenauve's (2005) thesis on European gold alloy torcs included detailed discussion of British examples and her catalogue covers discoveries made up to the 1990s, including some of the finds from the Snettisham excavations (Hautenauve 2005, 232–56). She also constructed a 'typologie des torques des îles britanniques' (*ibid.*, 88–118), in addition to separate typologies for continental and Iberian examples. Like Clarke and Stead, she distinguished two broad types based on the construction of torc neck-rings: tubular and twisted. Within her category of 'les torques au corps torsadé' ('torcs with twisted bodies'), she identified two subsets: 'les torques à torsade simple' and 'les torques à torsades multiples'. The bodies or neck-rings of her 'simple twist' torcs comprise individual wires twisted/plied or coiled together (here referred to as Stage II construction), whereas the bodies of 'multiple twisted' torcs are made up of ropes, each comprising many wires together (here referred to as Stage III and IV construction, see Ch. 13). Simple-twist torcs were further divided into 14 subsets based on the type and number of terminal loops. Multiple twisted torcs were similarly subdivided, this time into 19 groups. Tubular torcs were split into five categories (globular buffer terminals, cylindrical tubes, trumpet ends, truncated and double buckle). In addition to torcs with tubular and twisted bodies, Hautenauve defined a third type: filiform. She identified six torcs of this type, most from Hoard F at Snettisham (F.1c, F.1d, F.57, F.58. F.59), but additionally an example of unknown provenance with a knot in the neck-ring acquired by the British Museum sometime before 1848 (see unprovenanced torcs in Gazetteer; Birch 1846; James and Rigby 1997, 46). Here, these finds from Hoard F are treated as a subset of tubular torcs (Type 1), since in all cases where a terminal is present, the neck-rings are hollow types.

Hautenauve's typology is considered too unwieldy and complicated for use in this volume, and the typology which is presented here is based on Clarke's original distinction between tubular and twisted with Stead's additional terminal types (see Ch. 13). Tubular torcs are divided into six groups. Multi-strand torcs are described as having Stage II, III or IV neck-rings (based on the number of stages of wire twisting/coiling/plying) and terminals are grouped as buffer, loop (either single or multiple), hook, ring, reel, torus or cage.

Distribution

Tubular torcs similar to those recovered from Hoard A (Type 6 in this volume, see Ch. 13) have been found in Ireland and parts of the continent in addition to Britain (Fitzpatrick 2005; Hautenauve 2005), and a similar although distinct torc was also found as part of the Broighter Hoard from Northern Ireland (**Fig. 22.3**). In contrast, the well-documented distribution of multi-strand torcs (e.g. Brailsford and Stapley 1972; Davies 1996, 72; 2008, fig. 66; Hutcheson 2004, ch. 6; 2007, 359–62) shows they are confined to Britain, with a concentration of finds in East Anglia (**Fig. 22.4a**).

By far the greatest number of torcs from a single site have been recovered from Snettisham, but a high proportion have also been found from elsewhere in Norfolk, most from the north-west of the county. In addition, six torcs were discovered at Ipswich, Suffolk (Brailsford 1971; Brailsford and Stapley 1972; Owles 1969; 1970). A smaller cluster of finds can also be observed in the West Midlands (**Fig. 22.4a**). Like the East Anglian finds, many have been recovered from a relatively confined area. For example,

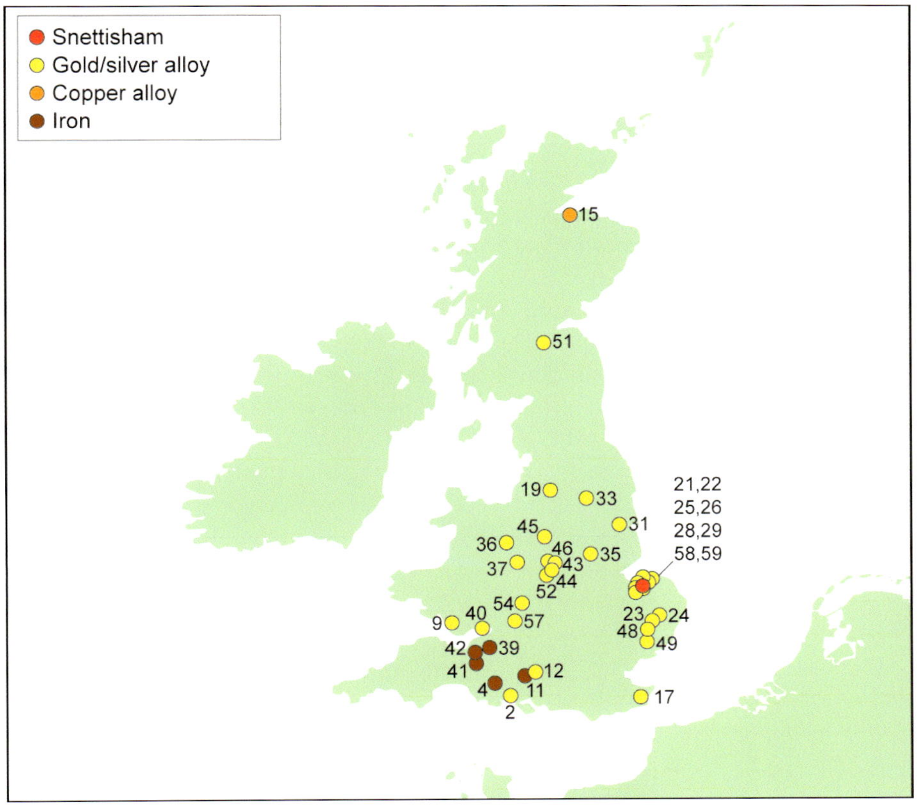

Figure 22.4a UK distribution of multi-strand torcs of the type found at Snettisham. These finds are generally restricted to Britain, though a similar torc is also known from Beringen, Belgium (Hautenauve 2005, no. 13). The wire torcs from Winchester and Stirling, which are rather different in construction, are omitted here. Numbers are those from the Gazetteer and Table 22.1

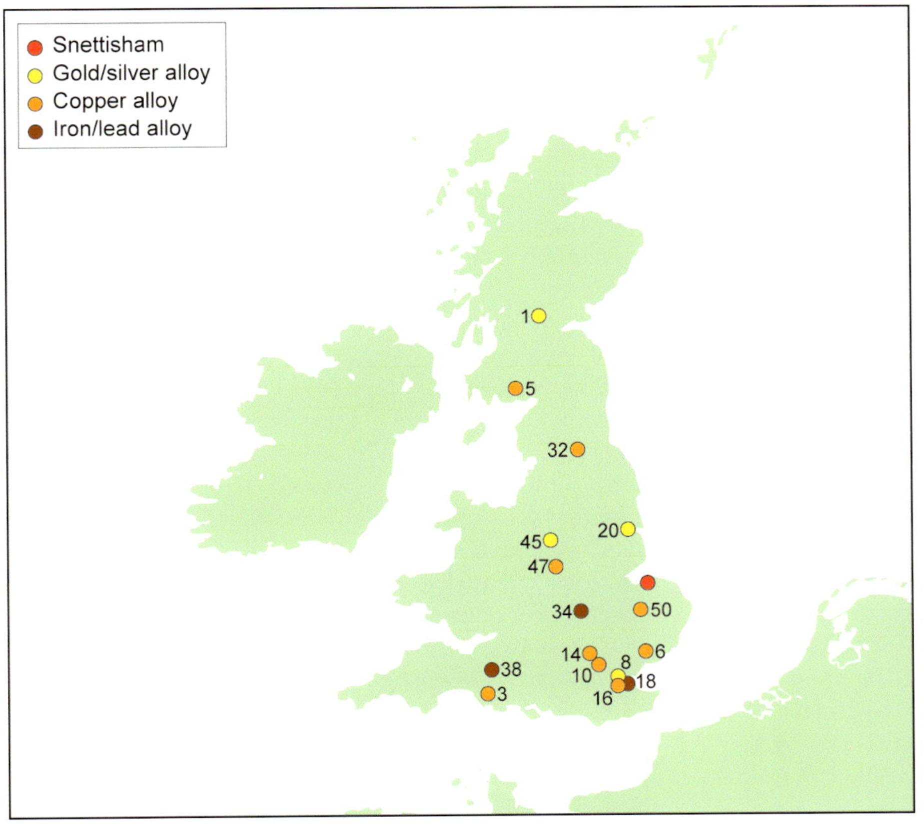

Figure 22.4b UK distribution of other torc types, including buffer terminal and thistle terminal torcs. Note that well-known later torc types such as beaded, ribbon, Baldock-type and Wraxall-type torcs are omitted, as these are more fully discussed elsewhere. Numbers are those from the Gazetteer and Table 22.1. Gazetteer entries 55–6 and 60–3 have been omitted as insufficient reliable information about these finds exists

Middleton Hall and Needwood Forest are only 16 miles apart, with Alrewas and Glascote located between the two in a zone roughly located between present-day Birmingham and Derby. The West Midland torcs are an extremely varied group, and some are quite visually distinct from most East Anglian examples. The wire and ring terminal fragments from Alrewas resemble finds from Snettisham, but Middleton Hall is the only multi-strand torc to have a braided (rather than simply twisted/plied) neck-ring (its terminals do not survive). The complete torcs from both Glascote and Needwood Forest have been described as having 'cushion' terminals. On the Needwood Forest example, these are quite distinctive, though Glascote is equally similar to some of the ring terminal torcs from Snettisham. This varied group from the West Midlands, centred on Staffordshire, may well represent a separate manufacturing tradition from the East Anglian torcs. The discovery of an early torc hoard from Leekfrith, Staffordshire, most likely dating to the 3rd or 4th century BC (Farley *et al.* 2018) is a tantalising suggestion of possible independent early origins for the West Midlands torcs.

A small number of multi-strand torcs have been found outside of these two regions. These are thinly spread across Britain, ranging from the south coast to as far north as Scotland. More recent discoveries near Newark, Nottinghamshire and at Stirling, central Scotland, have strengthened this northerly distribution. Many of these 'outliers' appear more similar to East Anglian examples than those from the West Midlands. It is possible some could have originated from East Anglia, moving through trade and exchange (Joy 2015). Alternatively, they may represent locally made versions or interpretations of multi-strand torcs (Machling and Williamson 2018). The latter certainly seems to be true in the case of the unusual copper alloy torc from Auldearn (Hunter 2014a), although this more clearly fits in with local forms and styles, closely resembling aspects of the Scottish massive metalwork tradition. Either way, knowledge and use of torcs must have been widespread to account for the wide geographical distribution of these 'outliers'.

As with all distribution maps, the vagaries of discovery and patterns of deposition mean it is unclear exactly how representative a picture of torc usage is painted. For example, we only see artefacts that have entered the archaeological record, not those that were recycled to make something else. This is a particular issue for precious metal torcs because the materials are so readily recycled, and an alternative gold artefact form, coinage, was prevalent throughout the later Iron Age. The possibility therefore remains that torcs were far more common and geographically widespread than is now apparent, but in most cases were recycled rather than being disposed of in archaeologically visible ways. For example, commenting on the uneven distribution of gold torcs Colin Haselgrove (2015) stated, '…it seems likely that many powerful or significant individuals possessed torcs in Late Iron Age Britain and they regularly exchanged them, but outside the East Anglia "hotspot" we typically see glimpses of this only when they were incorporated in deposits that break with normal ritual traditions in an area…' (Haselgrove 2015, 34). This is perhaps supported by the fact that finds outside the main torc distribution areas are more likely to be small pieces of broken-up torcs, sometimes incorporated into coin hoards. Nevertheless, the two regional concentrations of finds are unambiguous. Certain absences are also notable; in East Yorkshire, an area with a strong burial tradition during the early period of torc manufacture (*c.* 250–150 BC), torcs are virtually absent (with only one possible bronze example from Arras, now lost), suggesting that they were not a normal part of local dress. Overall, the evidence seems to imply that torcs were distributed, in small numbers at least, across much of Britain but that they took on particular importance in East Anglia and the West Midlands. Such local importance would most likely have been reflected in increased numbers in circulation, as well as contributing to their relatively frequent selection for deposition.

Context of discovery

The Hengistbury Head torcs were the first British examples to be recovered during modern archaeological excavation (Bushe-Fox 1915; Cunliffe 1987). Since then, the only excavations which have uncovered precious metal torcs are those at Snettisham, although other unusual copper alloy and iron torcs (see **Table 22.1** and Gazetteer) have been excavated at Maiden Castle (1934–7), Cadbury Castle (1966–70), Danebury (1969–78), and Great Houghton (1996). The findspots of the Newark Torc, and hoards from Stirling (Hunter 2018), Leekfrith (Farley *et al.* 2018) and Essendon (unpublished) were also investigated subsequent to discovery.

A few patterns can be discerned in the findspot types of torcs from Britain. Iron torcs (such as the finds from Cadbury Castle, Camerton, Danebury, Ham Hill and Spetisbury) seem to be more common on settlement sites, often as part of wider deposits of material. Maiden Castle has also produced a small copper alloy rod torc or bracelet. Unusual torc types of probable 1st or 2nd-century AD date are most commonly found in the mixed hoards seen in this period (e.g. Upchurch, Fremington Hagg, Polden Hills).

Watery deposition of torcs is highly unusual, but two stylistically early copper alloy rod torcs with thistle terminals have been recovered from watery contexts in the River Medway (Fox 1959, 66) and River Walbrook, London (Marshall 2023). The Essendon hoards are also thought to have been deposited in a shallow pool in a bog (Stead 2006, 51). These hoards also contained weapons (though not in direct association with the torcs and coins). Since the Bronze Age, there had been a long-running tradition of depositing weaponry in rivers and watery places (Fitzpatrick 1984), and it is possible that at Essendon deposition rules governing weapons superseded conventions regarding torcs (the latter formed only a small proportion of the assemblages). The bracelets from Towton were reportedly found in a streambed, but there is considerable uncertainty about the accuracy of their reported findspot (see Gazetteer).

On the continent, many torcs have been recovered from graves, but this is rare in Britain where there are only five reports (of varying quality) of torcs found in inhumations, and one small probable torc fragment from a cremation burial at Westhampnett (**Table 22.1**; Gazetteer). The lead alloy torc from Great Houghton, Northamptonshire, was found in an unusual female burial (Chapman 2000–1). The skeleton lay face down and the hands may have been bound. The torc is also exceptional: it is crudely fashioned, and its two halves were originally bound with organic material. The possibility that its purpose was not the same as other torcs remains likely. Four other burials in Britain have supposedly produced torcs (though none were subject to controlled excavation, and three are now lost). A simple iron torc was found in a burial at Ham Hill, Somerset, apparently worn around the neck; other grave goods included an iron chisel and adze (Anon. 1886; Whimster 1981, 239). A gold alloy multi-strand torc recovered from Birdlip, Gloucestershire, may have been a grave good from one of the nearby burials, but there is no clear account of its discovery and it is now lost (Green 1949, 188, fig. 1a; Staelens 1982). A torc is also said to have been discovered in burial A5 at the Arras cemetery, East Yorkshire, although unfortunately this too is now lost (Stead

1979, 80). According to an account in a letter by a Dr Hull (noted by Greenwell 1906, 275), the torc was found worn around the neck. The burial also contained nine small jet beads and a copper alloy wheel ornament (Greenwell 1906, 301). A gold torc was apparently found at Mildenhall, Suffolk, in 1812 in an extended inhumation burial also containing two horses, an iron sword and a 'celt'; it was later melted down (Bunbury 1834, 610).

Most of the precious metal torc discoveries from Britain originate from hoards, or as single finds in the landscape such as the torcs from Newark and Sedgeford. Like Snettisham, most are dryland deposits positioned on higher ground, many overlooking river systems or, as at Snettisham, marine inlets or the sea. There are no obvious parallels to the great number of separate deposits and the sheer quantity of torcs from Snettisham, although in terms of the quantity of precious metals the Snettisham finds pale into insignificance to the massive hoard of 70,000 coins and at least 11 gold torcs from Le Câtillon I and II, Jersey, which weighed almost a ton when lifted (Miles and Mead 2015). Only three other UK sites (Bawsey, Essendon and Hengistbury Head) have possible multiple hoards including torcs, and in most cases the evidence is ambiguous (**Table 22.1**; Gazetteer). The discoveries at Bawsey were made over a number of years no more than 80m apart. They could represent the remains of a single scattered hoard, or several separate deposits. The hoard containing a tubular torc from Essendon, Hertfordshire, is thought to have been one of three hoards deposited in the same location (though the other groups did not contain torcs). The torc and bracelet fragments from the Late Iron Age settlement at Hengistbury Head were found alongside many Late Iron Age coins and in the vicinity of metalworking debris, including evidence for hearths and large lumps of copper and silver alloys (Bushe-Fox 1915, 24–6, 72–4). The excavator, Bushe-Fox, noted distinct clusters of finds. He proposed that the area, 'Site 33', might have been a structure, though the evidence for this is slight. Cunliffe interpreted it as an area of metallurgical activity dating to *c.* 50 BC–AD 50.

With this general absence of contextual information in mind, the best we can say at present is that most British precious metal torcs are from hoards, but because many were found by chance we have little information concerning exactly how the hoards were arranged in the ground (see Gazetteer). For deposits where torcs are the main or only objects present, there are, broadly speaking, two hoard types. Some (Bawsey, Hengistbury Head, Alrewas, Narford) consist of groups or bundles of fragments which show evidence of being deliberately broken up and sometimes interlinked (Hengistbury Head, Alrewas), or melted (Narford). A number resemble the bundles or collections noted at Snettisham, especially from Hoard F. For example, prior to deposition the Alrewas torcs were cut up, bent out of shape, bundled together and looped through a gold alloy ring. A torc fragment with a buffer terminal and a gold alloy torc/bracelet from Hengistbury Head were also found bound together with pieces of wire (Cunliffe 1978, fig. 18). The other type of hoard is the 'nested' arrangement of torcs, seen or suspected at Ipswich, Leekfrith and the Stirling area Hoard. From the account made of their discovery, it is possible that some of the Ipswich torcs were linked before they were placed in the ground (Owles 1969, 208). But as with a number of the Snettisham hoards where 'nests' of torcs were tightly packed in the ground, this linking could have resulted from torcs being packed together in close proximity. In sum, we can only speculate as to the arrangements of most other torc hoards. But it is possible that as at Snettisham, torcs were deposited arranged in nests, or collected in bundles (Joy 2016).

Associated finds

Mixed hoards including torcs again fall broadly into two types. In some, one or more complete torcs are included alongside other complete (or largely complete) objects: a 'matching' brooch at Auldearn, harness fittings at Ulceby and Polden Hills. But the most frequent type of mixed hoard combines torcs (often fragmentary) with coins and/or ingots. Mixed torc and coin hoards are also relatively common on the continent (Fitzpatrick 2005). Torcs may be either a major component of the deposit or appear only as smaller fragments incorporated in amongst the coins. The gold tubular torc from Essendon was discovered at the same time as 253 Iron Age gold coins and four ingots (probably representing at least two hoards, Stead 2006, 51), with at least some of the coins found inside part of the tubular torc. The Hengistbury Head torc and bracelet fragments were found alongside many coins and pot sherds. It is difficult to date the torcs based on the associated material because the coins have a wide chronological range, spanning from around 100 BC to the 2nd century AD and the pottery from the area spans 'all periods', though Cunliffe suggested the Site 33 deposits most likely fall in the period *c.* 50 BC–AD 50 (Cunliffe 1987, 75, 136–41). The Netherurd torcs were found with 'upwards of 40 gold coins' (Feachem 1958, 112). Two other coin hoards include only very small torc fragments: a piece of tubular torc was discovered alongside around 200 gold coins (predominantly thought to be Gallo-Belgic E types) at Weybourne (Chadburn 2006, no. 14), and two small torc fragments were mixed in with a mid-1st-century AD coin hoard at Pershore.

Torc hoards B, C, E and F at Snettisham also included coins and, in some cases, ingots. Coins are discussed further below, but the ingots from Snettisham come in three main forms. Most are linear 'bar' ingots, or metal lumps (some resembling coin blanks), and there are at least two triangular ingots (B/C.84 and S.105). No crucible or mould fragments have been recovered from Snettisham, but the size and form of the ingots conform well with the evidence for crucibles and moulds found elsewhere (cf. Webley *et al.* 2020). For example, the crucible and furnace debris from Weelsby Avenue, Grimsby, included fired clay triangular crucibles and a bar-shaped mould (Foster 1995, figs 32–3). Similarly, several triangular crucibles, in addition to a small bar-shaped investment mould and two fragments of copper alloy rod, were recovered from Fison Way, Thetford (Gregory 1991, 138–41). Arguably the most common crucible type, the triangular shape, is relatively widespread with examples recovered from Wales and much of southern England (Musson *et al.* 1991, 272–4; Webley *et al.* 2020).

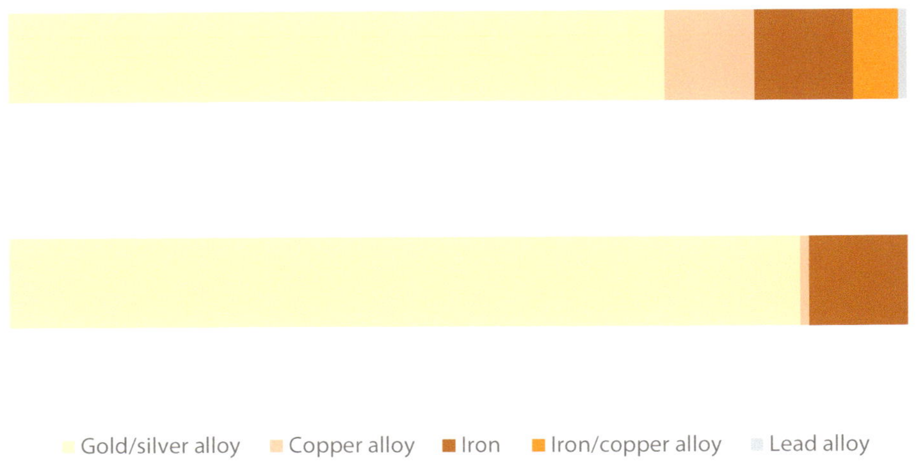

Figure 22.5 Relative proportions of metal types for all torcs and torc fragments from other UK sites (above, n=89, finds as listed in Table 22.2) and multi-strand and tubular torcs only (below, n=65). Compare the values for Snettisham complete torcs and fragments in Figure 13.14

Materials

Most of the torcs from Britain found outside of Snettisham are made from gold or gold/silver alloy (**Fig. 22.5**), with small numbers of copper alloy and iron torcs and a single example of an unusual lead alloy torc from Great Houghton. However, note that later copper alloy torc traditions (e.g. beaded torcs, 'Wraxall' collars and Baldock-type torcs) are not considered here. There are six examples of iron multi-strand torcs from elsewhere in the UK, but none from Snettisham.

The predominance of precious metal torcs in non-Snettisham UK torc finds is particularly pronounced when only multi-strand and tubular torcs (the types present at Snettisham) are included (**Fig. 22.5**, lower). Outside of Snettisham, there is only one find of a multi-strand copper alloy torc, the example from Auldearn in Scotland, which is most likely a later object, dating to the 1st or 2nd century AD (see Gazetteer). At Snettisham, in contrast, copper alloy multi-strand torcs make up over 30% of complete torcs and bracelets, and almost 50% of fragments (see **Fig. 13.14**), showing that here local traditions of torc manufacture and deposition included both gold/silver alloy and copper alloy objects. Elsewhere, precious metals appear to have been preferred, though this may reflect depositional practices rather than the use and wearing of torcs. It is tempting to suggest that the extensive depositional practices evident at Snettisham caught up and incorporated a wider variety of torcs than was usual practice in the region, including copper alloy examples which might otherwise have been recycled rather than deposited. The fact that copper alloy torcs from Snettisham appear more likely to be fragmented than their precious metal counterparts is most likely due, at least in part, to corrosion and post-deposition processes (there are many extremely small wire fragments from Hoard F). However, there is a slight suggestion that gilded copper alloy torcs were less likely to be fragmented than non-gilded examples (see Ch. 13). This could be because of the difficulty in recycling such objects, or they may have been treated differently owing to their colour and appearance.

Origins and importance of gold

Many of the most complicated and heavily decorated objects from Snettisham are made from alloys of gold (**Fig. 22.5**, see also Chs 17, 18 and 21). There is a widely signalled hiatus in the use and production of gold items in southern Britain from around 800 BC to the 3rd or 4th centuries BC (Northover 1995a; La Niece *et al.* 2018). This stands in stark contrast to the widespread earlier presence of Bronze Age gold ornaments, particularly those from graves and hoards, many of which are thought to have been made from British and Irish sources of gold (Northover 1995a; Needham 2012; Standish *et al.* 2015). The archaeological record in this respect also differs from the continent where gold objects are found in Late Hallstatt and early La Tène burials (e.g. Biel 1985).

Gold objects begin to reappear in the archaeological record of southern Britain from around 400–300 BC, with the earliest objects (all stylistically dated) being gold V-shaped finger-rings and early torcs such as the examples from Leekfrith and Caistor (Joy 2015; La Niece *et al.* 2018). These objects resemble continental types and at least some are likely to be imports, though the alloy composition of the Leekfrith torcs raises the possibility that they may more likely be of local manufacture (Farley *et al.* 2018). In northern Britain and Ireland there was also a separate gold ribbon torc tradition, dating from *c.* 300 to 50 BC (Hunter 2018, 432). Stylistically early torcs from Snettisham such as L.19 and F.72 (see Ch. 21) may also represent some of the earliest known gold objects from Iron Age Britain.

The interruption in gold production is difficult to explain and it may be that a small number of gold items continued to be made but simply do not appear in the archaeological record. Perhaps links to gold sources broke down at the end of the Bronze Age, or gold was no longer socially desirable, with bronze becoming the preferred material to manufacture prestige items. Provenancing gold is notoriously difficult (cf. La Niece *et al.* 2018). It is possible that native gold sources were used to make torcs, for example if there was pre-Roman mining at the gold mine at Dolaucothi in South Wales, but there is no direct evidence for the exploitation of insular gold deposits in the mid- to Late Iron Age (Bayley *et al.* 2008, 41). Given its prior absence from the archaeological record, perhaps the impetus to use gold again derived from contacts with the continent. Certainly, the earliest known Iron Age gold objects from Britain, include likely imports (Joy 2015; La Niece *et al.* 2018). This suggests the likelihood that precious metal artefacts and coins may well have found their way to Britain from the continent, albeit probably in small quantities. It is likely that at least some of this imported material was used to make torcs (Joy 2015; La Niece *et al.* 2018), and probably also the first insular British coinage. The source of the gold might well have been known and understood by the makers and wearers of torcs, carrying additional layers of meaning that are now hard to unpick.

In archaeology we deal almost exclusively with those objects that endure, but metals in particular are easily recycled. Unless they are intentionally removed from circulation, they can be transformed again and again rather than being fixed in a particular form. Gold is a substance which retains its identity no matter what form it takes (Oakley 2013, 64). It is heavy, highly resistant to corrosion, has a reflective, shiny surface and a distinctive colour. It can be hammered to form fine wires and very thin sheet, or quickly melted down and cast into new forms. Like silver, it can be combined and recombined, meaning, as Oakley has argued, that it holds the '…potential for an infinite number and range of future amalgamations that undermines the stability of any current object: any existing gold or silver object can all too easily be perceived as a mass of raw material for the manufacture of a future object-in-waiting' (Oakley 2013, 64). Oakley's focus was artefacts with hallmarks, where the value placed on gold was similar to the importance we place on gold today. Gold is so obviously valuable in many modern societies that it can seem only logical that people in the past ascribed it similar worth. But any or all of the qualities of gold we have highlighted above could have been important in an Iron Age context, and it is possible that varying qualities and facets were drawn on at different points in the life of an object. The same may be true for objects which are not entirely made of gold but appear to be gold because of their surfaces. It certainly seems that the alloys and materials used in the objects from Snettisham were deliberately manipulated to affect their surface colour (Ch. 17). Elsewhere, there is much evidence for societies valuing substances for their material properties such as colour or shininess (Saunders 1999). There has been extensive discussion of the role and importance of colour in Iron Age Britain. Creighton (2000, 38–40) argued that the distinctive yellowish colour of early gold Iron Age coinage might have been associated with high status or even kingship, and Hutcheson (2007, 361–2) has argued that colour may have been an important factor in the ordering of the Snettisham hoards (this is discussed further in Ch. 23). The incorruptibility of gold can also lead to links or associations with the divine (Oakley 2015, 160). Gold's durability, combined with its relative scarcity but wide availability, is important for its role in many societies as a store of wealth or medium of exchange (Oakley 2015, 160–1). Its potential to be easily re-formed into something else also means that gold objects are relatively unstable: social effort and will is required for it not to be re-formed into something else (Oakley 2013, 64).

The 'vitality of materials' has a growing currency in the social sciences (e.g. Bennett 2010; Drazin and Küchler 2015). In social terms, the materials used to make torcs were not 'raw' (cf. Drazin 2015, xviii). As is particularly the case with metal artefacts, but also potentially those made of any material which has been re-used or reworked to form something else, traces of previous forms remain in the material or substance of the new object. The concept of 'informed material' provides a means by which we can think about these material traces. According to Bensaude-Vincent and Stengers (1996), whilst researching and developing chemicals, 'instead of imposing a shape on the mass of material, one develops an "informed material" in the sense that the material structure becomes richer and richer in information' (Bensaude-Vincent and Stengers 1996, 206). Andrew Barry (2005) further developed this idea. Discussing how we can understand the notion that materials can be informed he stated, 'one way of understanding the idea that a material entity (such as a potential drug molecule) could be informed or "rich in information" would be to say that the material *embodies* information' (Barry 2005, 57, his emphasis). Drawing on theories developed by Whitehead (1978; 1985), Barry argued that rather than viewing material objects as concrete manifestations to which meanings are added, we should view them instead as 'historical' forms (Barry 2005, 64). Things endure but their lives do eventually end, whereas the materials they are made from do not. When objects are recycled, although the atoms and molecules they are made from are not the same as they were before, previous traces endure. In other words, as materials flow from form to form, they become more and more 'informed', containing information about previous material forms.

One of the outcomes of research into informed materials has been to challenge the notion of the social life or 'biography' of things. The biography metaphor does not fit materials, it is argued, as they are not born and do not die, instead materials flow and transform. Hence, according to Drazin, 'the "life" of materials concerns questions about how materials are "vitalist", what they do and how they have effects, how they have meaning, how they are known and what social and cultural forms happen through and around them' (Drazin 2015, 14). The concept of 'informed' material is useful in a number of respects when considering the Snettisham remains. First, the material an object is made from is socially significant. Second, traces of past material forms are preserved in the materials objects are made from. This has long been recognised in terms of scientific examination of trace elements, but if knowledge of past forms and the 'origins' of materials is preserved in the social memory and viewed as significant, then this is an important observation. In short, the concept of informed material provides a means by which to conceptualise and approach the flow and transformation of materials as they change form. The enduring objects we encounter in archaeology contain information and traces of these past material forms and their flow (Needham 2001).

Wear and use

As at Snettisham, most British torcs appear to have been used, with many damaged and/or showing signs of wear, implying they were not made especially for deposition. For example, the torc from Middleton Hall, Warwickshire was missing both its terminals, and the torcs from Leekfrith show clear wear patterns (Farley *et al.* 2018). Many torcs also

Torc	Type	Date	Method	Source
Great Houghton	Other	545–203 cal BC (95% probability)	Radiocarbon (human bone from burial)	Chapman, A. 2000, table 6
Westhampnett	Fragment: ?Tubular	200–80 cal BC (95% probability)	Radiocarbon (cremated human bone from burial)	Haselgrove *et al.* 2018, table 1
Ulceby	Multi-strand	300 BC–AD 100	Stylistic: associated bridle bits	Macdonald 2007b
Essendon	Tubular	80–60 BC or *c.* 20 BC–AD 40	Associated coinage	Fitzpatrick 2005; Stead 2006
Netherurd	Multi-strand	120–80 BC	Associated coinage	Haselgrove 2009
Pershore	Fragments: ?Multi-strand; ?Tubular	40 BC–AD 50	Associated coinage	Unpublished
Weybourne	Fragment: ?Tubular	*c.* 60–50 BC	Associated coinage	Haselgrove 1987, 328
Upchurch	Other	*c.* AD 180	Associated coinage	Payne 1893, 75–6
Polden Hills	Multi-strand	AD 40–70	Stylistic: associated horse-gear	Brailsford 1975b

Table 22.2 Dating of torcs and torc deposition from other sites in Britain, based on associated finds

appear to have been deliberately fragmented. One of the torcs from Hengistbury Head comprised a single buffer terminal and neck-ring section, and fragments from Forncett, Gayton, Great Finborough, Pershore and Shepherdswell with Coldred all show evidence for being cut up. This fits with the impression gained from careful examination of the Snettisham torcs (Ch. 20) and wider patterns noted for other artefact types, particularly decorated artefacts (Joy 2010; 2011; 2014).

In contrast, the torcs from Alrewas, Staffordshire are unusual as, in his unpublished Treasure report on the artefacts, Ian Stead implied they were unfinished. The complete gold bracelet from Hengistbury Head (Cunliffe 1987, 156–7) has mismatched terminals – one simply formed from loops of the neck-ring, and the other hammered and worked, with the possible addition of more metal, to form a ring terminal. It is possible the loop terminal is therefore unfinished, not yet having received such treatment. The ring terminal from Netherurd may also never have been joined to a neck-ring (Machling and Williamson 2018). At least one torc from Snettisham (S.17) shows clear signs of being possibly unfinished, with casting sprues remaining on its terminals, and H.3 may similarly be incomplete (Ch. 20). This indicates that torcs could be deposited at various different stages in their biographies or itineraries, although, as suggested in Chapter 20, it may also imply that simplistic modern notions of a simple passage from work in progress, to finished object, to worn and potentially repaired object-in-use, to scrap, are anachronistic in relation to Iron Age torcs; the reality may have been more complicated.

Chronology

Although Smith (1905, 137; 1925, 149) attributed torcs to the Iron Age, he was understandably reluctant to define a chronological sequence until further examples had been uncovered. With more discoveries to work with, Leeds (1933, 466) suggested they belonged to the 2nd or 1st centuries BC based on his dating of the bridle bits found with the Ulceby torcs. Working on the first discoveries from Snettisham and drawing on continental evidence, Clarke (1954, 44 and 52) dated the tubular torcs from Hoard A to the 2nd or 1st centuries BC and suggested that multi-strand torcs belonged to the 1st century BC and early 1st century AD. Brailsford (in Brailsford and Stapley 1972, 226) favoured a mid-1st-century BC date for the Ipswich torcs and tentatively recommended a typological sequence moving towards larger terminals, although he later contradicted himself by also pointing out that the chronological significance of typological features is doubtful because it could also result from regional variation. Sealey (1979, 165) was the first to conduct a comprehensive dating audit and cited the absence of torcs from Early Roman hoards in East Anglia to indicate that they were made before AD 43. He then closely examined the coins found in the Snettisham, Weybourne and Netherurd hoards to refine his dating. Largely following the coin dating of Allen and Scheers, he concluded that the three hoards were all deposited in the mid-1st century BC, around the time of the Gallic Wars (Sealey 1979, 167).

Clarke, Brailsford and Sealey were all limited in their discussions because of a lack of good contextual information. As we have seen, many torcs were chance discoveries from the 19th and early 20th centuries. Of the more recent finds, most were made by metal-detector users in disturbed plough soil. This means that we are largely reliant on associated dating of other artefacts deposited with torcs, such as coins and horse-gear, as well as European parallels for those torc types, such as tubular torcs, also found on the continent. Dating of these artefacts, particularly Gallo-Belgic coinage, has changed since Sealey's analysis (cf. Haselgrove 1993, table 1; 1999, 164–8). Later discoveries and analyses, including radiocarbon dating of organic remains found inside neck-rings and adhering to torcs have also significantly improved our understanding of torc chronology (Garrow *et al.* 2009; **Table 5.2**).

Table 22.2 summarises the torc finds from Britain which can be more directly dated through associated finds, coins, or organic material. Beyond Snettisham only two torcs have radiocarbon dates: the lead alloy torc from Great Houghton, Northants (Chapman 2000–1), and a small fragment of gold foil from a cremation burial at Westhampnett, West Sussex, which is likely from a tubular torc (Fitzpatrick 1997, 97–9; Haselgrove *et al.* 2018). The lead torc from Great Houghton is the earliest datable torc find from Britain by some margin, but it is also highly unusual, and it is unclear how it fits within the wider group, if indeed it is related at all. The tubular torc fragment from Westhampnett has been dated by association with cremated human remains from the burial in which it was found to the 2nd or early 1st century BC.

Torcs are also found in association with a range of artefact types. Probably the most useful for dating purposes are coins. Dates for torcs found with coins (beyond Snettisham) are summarised in **Table 22.2** and follow Haselgrove's chronology (1993, table 1; 1999, 164–8). The finds from the Polden Hills hoard and Upchurch represent a very different style of torc (an iron core wrapped around with copper alloy wire) and are most likely a later tradition distinct from the types found at Snettisham. They are perhaps better situated alongside Wraxall-type collars and beaded torcs of a similar date and will not be considered further here. Tubular torc fragments, including two terminals, were discovered at the same time as coins and ingots at Essendon. The overall date range of these coins is quite wide, spanning more than a century. They cluster into two groups and it is possible they originate from two hoards containing coins: one dating from *c.* 80–60 BC, the other from *c.* 20 BC–AD 40. It is tempting to suggest that the tubular torc was associated with a hoard containing the earlier coins. Unfortunately, because the metal-detector users were unable to satisfactorily identify the coins found in the torc terminal, it is not possible to date the deposition of the Essendon torc fragments more closely than *c.* 80 BC–*c.* AD 40. Coins were found with the torc fragments at Hengistbury Head, but their association is not proven and they covered a very broad span of time (Cunliffe 1987). The Netherurd torcs were found with over 40 gold 'globules-à-la-croix' or 'bullet' coins (Hunter 1997, 515). The distribution of bullet coins is centred in Belgic Gaul, with a small number of finds in south-west England (Fitzpatrick 1992b, 10; Haselgrove 2009, fig. 1; Sills 2003). These coins date from the late 2nd century BC to the early decades of the 1st century BC, with those from Britain seen to belong to the later stages of the series (Haselgrove 2009, 184–5). Finally, very small torc fragments were found with coin hoards at Weybourne, Norfolk and Pershore, Worcestershire. At Weybourne, a small fragment of gold sheet, perhaps from a tubular torc, was found at the same time as coins on the beach. Haselgrove (1987, 328; see also Sealey 1979, 166) noted at least 63 coins, predominantly Gallo-Belgic E types, and speculated the finds originated from two hoards. Unfortunately, owing to the nature of the discoveries, the association between specific coins and the torc fragment is unclear. The Pershore hoard contains a small fragment of twisted wire alongside south-western Iron Age coins minted from 40 BC–AD 50.

Torcs have also been found in association with other types of artefact. Three fragmentary bridle bits and a bracelet were discovered alongside the torcs from Ulceby (May 1976, fig. 76). The bracelet is not closely datable, but the bridle bits belong to Palk's (1984, 7–8) 'double-jointed snaffle' class. These are also known as three-link bridle bits. The group was further subdivided by Palk and the example from Ulceby belongs to class A, described as possessing an 'iron core with sheet bronze casing'. Palk's subdivision is based on technology and seems to have little or no chronological significance. The double-jointed snaffle is one of Palk's largest groups including finds from across the country, appearing in East Yorkshire graves and at Llyn Cerrig Bach in Anglesey, as well as Meare Lake Village. Consequently, firm dating is difficult. In his analysis of the bronze work from Llyn Cerrig Bach, Philip Macdonald (2007b, 53–72) discussed the dating of three-link bridle bits in detail. According to Macdonald the earliest examples probably date from as early as the 4th or 3rd centuries BC, but the type may have continued in usage as late as the early 1st century AD (Macdonald 2007b, 72; see also Palk 1984, fig. 17). Unfortunately, the presence of 'pseudo-stitch' decoration on the Ulceby bridle bit does not help in this instance as pseudo-stitch decoration has a similar date range (Macdonald 2007b, 63). Macdonald's dating of three-link bridle bits is possibly a little conservative. For example, Bayesian modelling of radiocarbon dates obtained from East Yorkshire chariot burials has indicated that these probably clustered in the late 3rd and early 2nd centuries BC (Hamilton *et al.* 2015, 651). It is possible therefore that while some of these bridle bits could be as early as the 4th and early 3rd centuries BC, most probably dated from the later 3rd to the 1st centuries BC. In sum, while not definitive, the Ulceby deposit could be contemporary or possibly earlier than the deposition of the hoards at Snettisham.

For those torc types which have not been found in association with organics or other artefact types, we are reliant on stylistic dating. Of the torcs found in Britain, the copper alloy example with thistle-shaped buffer terminals from Aylesford, Kent is stylistically perhaps the earliest. It appears to belong to a type distributed from Central Europe to France and dating from the 6th to the 3rd centuries BC (Hautenauve 2005, 67–70). There is a possibility it could be an import as Jope (2000, 16, 234) has suggested, but the wide distribution of this type also does not exclude the possibility it was manufactured in Britain. However, the difficulty of stylistic dating for such objects is shown by the fact that a similar torc from the River Walbrook in London appears to have been discovered in association with 1st and 2nd-century AD Romano-British material (Marshall 2023), and thus may represent a long-lived object type.

As was outlined above (**Fig. 22.3**), tubular torcs are also found on the continent. In Hautenauve's catalogue of torcs, she argued that the large-bodied tubular torcs, like the (Type 6) examples from Snettisham Hoard A, date to the first half of the 1st century BC (Hautenauve 2005, 87), and narrower tubular torc types (1 and 2) to the first half of the 2nd century BC (2005, 77). Similar torc finds appear in the Le Câtillon II hoard, Jersey, alongside around 70,000 coins Late Iron Age coins. Fitzpatrick (forthcoming) suggested a date for the deposition of this hoard in the mid-1st century BC. Evidence from Chapter 20, where it was shown that the tubular torcs from Snettisham were far less worn than the multi-strand examples, might support the idea that at least at Snettisham these objects were relatively new when they were deposited, perhaps decades old or less, whereas some of the multi-strand torcs from Snettisham could have been over 100 years old at the time they were taken out of circulation.

Table 22.3 summarises the dating evidence available for each of the Snettisham torc hoards, ranging from

Snettisham torc hoard	Torc type(s)	Art styles present	Radiocarbon dates	Terminal date from associated coinage	Source
A	Tubular	V	-	-	See Ch. 21
B	Multi-strand	-	-	60 BC	See Ch. 15
C	Multi-strand	-	-	60 BC	See Ch. 15
D	Multi-strand	-	-	-	-
E	Multi-strand	V	-	60 BC	See Ch. 15; Ch. 21
F	Multi-strand; Tubular	II, III, V	F.168: 370–120 cal BC (95.4%); carbonised roundwood < 10 years old	80–60 BC	See Ch. 15; Ch. 21; **Table 5.2**; Garrow *et al.* 2009
G	Multi-strand	-	-	-	-
H	Multi-strand	-	-	-	-
J	Multi-strand	-	-	-	-
K	Multi-strand	-	-	-	-
L	Multi-strand	III, V	L.6: 360–110 cal BC (93.8%); lime wood fibre string <5 years old	-	See Ch. 21; **Table 5.2**; Garrow *et al.* 2009

Table 22.3 Dating of torc hoards from Snettisham

radiocarbon dates (for Hoards F and L), to associated coinage (Hoards B, C, E and F) and the art styles present on the torcs themselves (Hoards A, E, F and L).

As discussed in Chapter 21, it is difficult to use art styles to closely date the manufacture of the torcs, since many styles seem to have remained in use over a long period of time. For example, a single object in Hoard F (tubular torc fragment F.31a) mixes the supposedly earlier 'Vegetal' style (Stead's Style II) with Stead's Style V. Thus, for the vast majority of the torcs, the decoration cannot be more closely dated than the 3rd century BC to 1st century AD. It is likely, however, that the small number of 'Plastic Style' torcs (Style III) present in Hoards F and L (F.72 and L.19a) may be some of the earlier objects from the hoards. Torc L.19a (the so-called 'Grotesque Torc'), in particular, shows extremely heavy levels of wear, and has been extensively repaired (see Ch. 20).

The two radiocarbon dates taken from the Snettisham torcs (**Tables 5.2**, **22.3**) were both from material under 10 years old. We cannot be sure when the lime wood fibre was wrapped around torc L.6, but the small piece of carbonised wood from F.168 was inside the neck-ring and was used as part of the manufacturing process (Chs 17, 19; Cartwright *et al.* 2012). This date therefore provides an indication of when the object was manufactured, not when it was deposited. Given the terminal dates obtained for the deposition of the Snettisham hoards based on associated coinage (see below), F.168 at the very least was most likely in circulation for a long time before it was deposited, and may well have been an heirloom well over a century old (Joy 2016). The same is also possible in the case of L.6.

The coins from Snettisham Hoards B, C, E and F are discussed in Chapter 15. Stead (1991a, 165–6), argued that the mixture of coins from the hoards suggested they were deposited before Caesar's incursions into Britain. Haselgrove (1993, note 37; 1999, 182) stressed the significance of the absence of Gallo-Belgic E coins (the predominant gold coinage in circulation *c.* 60–50 BC), which he argued indicate that Hoards B, C, E and F were deposited sometime before *c.* 60 BC. Whilst dating of some of the types present at Snettisham has been revised since Haselgrove was writing, the broad picture remains similar, and the dating of the coins from Hoards B, C, E, and F support the idea that these hoards were more or less contemporary (Ch. 15). The latest coins in Hoard C are potins dated by Holman (2016, Ch. 15) to *c.* 75/70–60/55 BC, with the composition of the assemblage suggesting that the hoard was deposited around 60 BC or shortly thereafter. The Gallo-Belgic gold coins from Hoard F terminate with issues minted *c.* 80–60 BC, while Hoards B and E each contain a singular insular gold issue which may have been minted in the period *c.* 60–50 BC (based on Sills' revised dating, see Ch. 15).

Thus, the coin evidence suggests that Hoards B, C, E and F were likely deposited around the mid-1st century BC, and probably around or before 60 BC, pre-dating Caesar's expeditions to Britain. As the range of torcs found in Hoards B to L are so similar, it seems likely that the other torc hoards from Snettisham were deposited around the same time, although strictly speaking Hoards A, D, G, H, J and K are dated only stylistically, and the radiocarbon date from Hoard L is earlier (comparable to that from Hoard F).

It is entirely possible (and perhaps likely) that the torc hoards were all deposited over a fairly short period. However, this cannot be conclusively demonstrated. Given the early radiocarbon dates from Hoard F and Hoard L (at least compared to the coin finds from the site) it is apparent that multi-strand torcs were in circulation by the 2nd century BC at the latest and most probably during the 3rd or even 4th century BC. Thus, some of the torc hoards which do not have a *terminus post quem* provided by coinage could have been assembled and deposited much earlier. While the editors of this volume tend to prefer a shorter chronology for the deposition of the hoards, a conservative date range of *c.* 350–60 BC is given here for Phase 3 (the period which saw the deposition of the torc hoards, see Ch. 8), allowing for the possibility of a longer tradition of deposition at the site.

In summary, other datable torc hoards, such as Essendon, share similar chronologies to Snettisham. The general absence of torcs deposited with Gallo-Belgic E coins (except the fragment from Weybourne) indicates that torcs continued in circulation until the mid-1st century BC, but may have been much more scarce or absent after this, by which time torcs had been largely replaced by coins in precious metal deposits (Hutcheson 2007). Both hoards containing multi-strand torcs and those with tubular torcs have produced similar deposition dates. In addition, hoards such as Hoard F contained fragments of both types, suggesting that in deposition, and therefore probably use, the two groups overlap. With so few known examples, and the great challenges posed by the lack of good contextual evidence, it is impossible to determine which (if either) came first, although the evidence amassed in Chapter 20 could indicate that multi-strand torcs were possibly made first and probably, on average, had longer use-lives than the more fragile tubular torcs, particularly those with large bodies. As is indicated by the radiocarbon dates from Snettisham, many of the multi-strand torcs could have been in circulation for centuries prior to deposition and patterns of wear suggest that some were already quite old when they were put in the ground. Stylistic dating of the decorated terminals of the 'Grotesque Torc' L.19a places its manufacture sometime in the 3rd century BC (Ch. 21). Along with the early radiocarbon dates from Hoards F and L, this implies a fairly long duration for the production of East Anglian multi-strand torcs, probably running from at least the 3rd to 1st centuries BC. At least some torcs apparently remained in use and circulation for long periods of time, perhaps even hundreds of years. Owing to a lack of good contextual information for the West Midlands group of torcs, it is not possible at present to comment definitively on how the two regional groups interrelated: whether they were contemporary, overlapped one another, or one followed the other. The discovery of a torc hoard at Leekfrith, Staffordshire, containing a torc closely resembling an example from the well-known 3rd-century continental grave at Waldalgesheim (Farley *et al.* 2018), suggests the West Midlands tradition is at least as old as that in East Anglia, if not older.

Iron and copper alloy torcs are known from 1st-century AD contexts (Polden Hills, Upchurch), and copper alloy Wraxall-type collars and beaded types also date to this period. This (as well as continued references in texts such as Dio Cassius's description of Boudica) suggests that the idea of the metal neck-ring as ornament probably persisted, at least in some regions and contexts, but that after the 1st century BC both styles and materials changed. In particular, no gold or silver alloy torcs can be securely ascribed a 1st-century AD or later date.

Interpreting torcs

As we have seen, much is known about torcs in terms of their chronology and distribution, but there has been less work examining how they were worn, how they felt and what effects they had on the wearer and social relations (cf. Entwistle 2000, 10). In this section we will consider these aspects in detail. Also, following comments made by Elizabeth Foulds in her examination of glass beads, we will also examine how torcs related to the socially constructed body, and how they were used to build dress and identity (Foulds 2017, 20).

How torcs have been interpreted

Personal adornment has for some time been a focus in Iron Age studies (e.g. Hill 1997; Jundi and Hill 1998; Giles 2012; Adams 2014; Foulds 2017). For example, J.D. Hill (1997) cited the presence of cosmetic sets in Late Iron Age contexts in southern Britain as evidence for increasing concerns over personal appearance and individual identity. Melanie Giles (2012, 121) also highlighted the effects of wearing objects such as brooches. But for the most part, many items of adornment have simply been viewed as passively representing the status of their wearer or other forms of identity. There are also issues with the 'common-sense' attribution of material culture types to gender, particularly the uncritical dismissal of some dress items simply as 'female costume' or 'jewellery', with no thought as to what these artefacts can tell us about identity and how it was performed (cf. Pope and Ralston 2011; Giles 2012).

For the most part, the interpretation of torcs mirrors these general patterns in Iron Age studies. In many previous and current interpretations, both the torc and the human body are passive. The torc is seen to be representational of the status of its wearer but the body is also inscriptive: a skin for public display of the identity or status of the individual within (cf. Joyce 2005). An example of this can be seen in an illustration in Simon James's (1993) book *Exploring the World of the Celts*, which shows a 'generalised structure of a Celtic community' (**Fig. 22.6**). It neatly exemplifies the traditional view of how Iron Age or 'Celtic' societies were structured, headed by a chief with his retinue of warriors. Just below this 'aristocracy' are the craftsmen, bards, and Druids with everyone else at the bottom. The chief is shown wearing a large torc. Behind him, bards, warriors, and Druids are depicted wearing less ostentatious examples. The people at the back – the rest of society – do not wear torcs. James's illustration neatly summarises how torcs and other valuables have traditionally been interpreted: as the preserve of power and nobility, the object passively denoting chiefly authority, or other high social status and position. The individuals shown wearing torcs are also exclusively male. As noted by Pope and Ralston (2011, 376), when women are associated with torcs (for example when the connection cannot be ignored because they are found in a female grave), until relatively recently they were rarely interpreted as symbols of power, but rather as items of jewellery or costume perhaps denoting marital or maternal status.

Hill has questioned whether a torc necessarily represented the status of an elite individual: 'a gold torc may not have been an "elite" object (i.e. an object whose ownership and use defined the wearer as a member of an elite status group) in terms of showing off the individual's wealth and power. Rather it may have symbolised the status and power of the larger group that the wearer represented – a symbol of office not a personal status item' (Hill 2011, 256). Similarly, Creighton (2000) viewed torcs as 'insignias of office'. This reinterpretation fits better with our understanding of society in Iron Age Norfolk at the time torcs were in circulation, whereby it is likely that status was achieved rather than hereditary (Ch. 23), and power structures may well have been fluid and heterarchical, rather than fixed hierarchies (see Joy in Baldwin and Joy 2017). This does not mean torcs were not active in negotiations of status between individuals and groups, rather that they played a dynamic role in these negotiations depending on where and how they were worn, exchanged and handled.

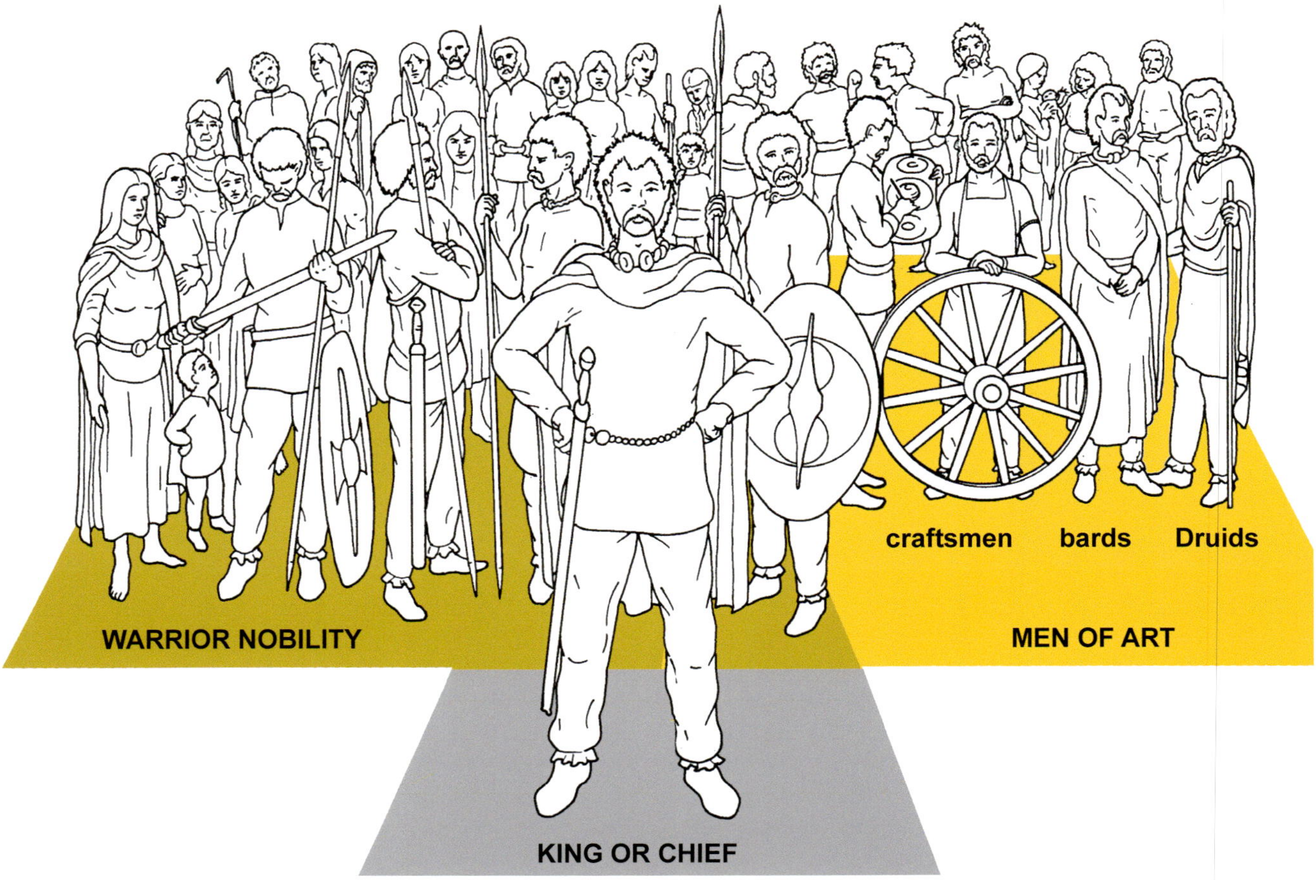

Figure 22.6 Simon James's (1993) depiction of the traditional model of Celtic society, a conception which has since been widely debated, not least by James himself (image © Simon James)

Sharples (2007; 2010) has highlighted the role objects play in 'creating a community'. He argued that they achieve this 'by establishing relationships between individuals and mediating relationships between groups' (Sharples 2010, 92). This can be accomplished, for example, by gift giving, which can act to construct or cement relationships as well as creating social obligations. Objects continue to build relationships throughout their lives until they are eventually disposed of. As already outlined, Hunter (2006) speculated that so-called massive armlets may have been exchanged as gifts, whether diplomatic, a form of bride wealth, or to pay other social debts and obligations. Torcs similarly would have made spectacular gifts. Indeed, two torcs which show close similarities, both to each other (Machling and Williamson 2018) and finds from East Anglia, were found much further north, suggesting they may have travelled through trade and exchange to their eventual sites of deposition. The Newark Torc was found in Nottinghamshire, some distance from Norfolk and located on the other side of the Wash, while the Netherurd torus terminal was recovered in eastern Scotland. As well as its close similarities to finds from further south, the Netherurd terminal is decorated with 'basket-weave' hatching, a stylistic element otherwise confined to southern Britain. Whilst Machling and Williamson (2018) have argued for a northern origin for the Newark and Netherurd torcs, both could just as easily be interpreted as objects made in or around eastern England which changed hands to move north as gifts or through trade.

Owing to the fact that many torcs are highly decorated, they have also been valued in academic discourse as art objects (e.g. Jope 2000). This could be seen to transform them into a fetish: discussions debate in exquisite detail the date and techniques of manufacture, as well as stylistic parallels, but they do not tell us how the objects were worn, how they felt and moved on the body (cf. Entwistle 2000, 10). What is missing from these interpretations of torcs is a consideration of their 'lived' performance: a view of the person and the body as a whole. How did the body and torc interact? How did one affect the other when they were worn as opposed to being handled? Visual qualities are often given preference (Joyce 2005, 148), but what did it feel like to wear a torc? The neck-ring and terminal decoration are highly tactile. How did torcs affect memory? Could their decorations have wider significance, perhaps related to 'special' knowledge? What about their links to people who had worn them in the past? How were they worn? Over clothing or directly on the skin? What about the temperature of the object or its weight? Were they noticeable when worn or did this change over time as the body became accustomed to wearing one? What about their effect on the body? How did they affect posture and movement?

Rethinking torcs

Who wore torcs?

As is illustrated in **Figure 22.7** (see also **Fig. 13.1**), the torcs from Snettisham vary a great deal in size, although the vast majority would comfortably fit an adult neck. The massive silver-coloured torc from Hoard G (G.11) weighs over 2kg and has an internal circumference of around 544mm. It is

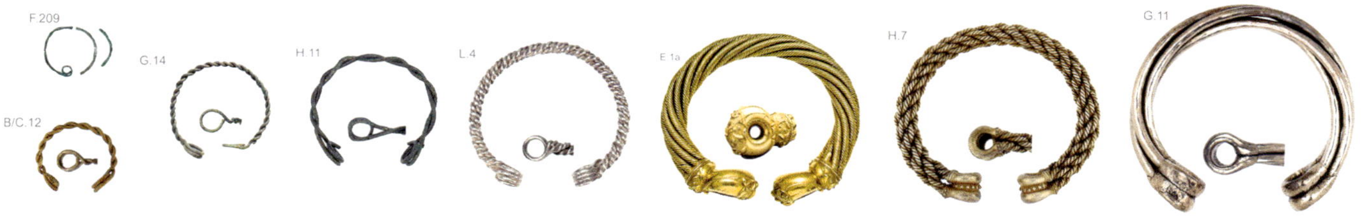

Figure 22.7 Image showing a range of objects of different sizes, from small bracelets to the largest torcs, reproduced at the same scale for comparison (compare with Figure 13.1)

difficult to equate the size of people in the past to those today, but this circumference is larger than most available male shirt collar sizes today (a size 4X fits a neck circumference of *c.* 500mm, *c.* 19.5 inches). The torc with the largest internal circumference is D.1a, at 568mm. These large sizes may be misleading, as torcs often have their terminals pulled apart. Most could of course have been squeezed more tightly closed to fit a smaller neck, though G.11 is too robust to bend in this way, and so would also have required its wide neck opening to take it on and off.

At the other end of the scale, of those items classified as 'torcs' in the catalogue (so excluding the smaller objects which have been classified as 'bracelets', see Ch. 13), the three smallest torcs (B/C.47–8, F.116 and G.14) have internal circumferences of around 280mm (11 inches), which would be on the small side for an adult. These could have been worn at the neck by an adolescent or child, although if this is the case, this evidence works against the argument that torcs were markers of achieved or ascribed rather than hereditary status. Alternatively, these small torcs could conceivably have been worn elsewhere on the body, such as the upper arm.

Aside from these small torcs and the four clear examples of multi-strand bracelets, 54 torcs are complete enough to allow measurement of their internal circumference. When looking at the overall distribution of measurements (see **Fig. 13.1**), the greatest frequency of circumferences (30 examples, or around 56% of the torcs) cluster between 400 and 500mm (15.5 to 19.5 inches). This range falls within modern-day men's collar sizes. Thirteen torcs (24%) have internal circumferences under 400mm (*c.* 15.5 inches). Many of those fall into the range of roughly 340–390mm (13.9 to 15.5 inches), in keeping with modern women's collar sizes. Some caution should be exercised here as people today are probably bigger and on average heavier than in the past, and of course it may have been desirable for a torc to sit differently on the neck, perhaps much lower than a modern shirt collar. Nevertheless, these measurements do provide some indication that the Snettisham torcs could have been worn by both women and men and possibly even (in rare cases) by children and adolescents. This conclusion is supported by evidence from continental Europe where, as we have seen, torcs are found in the graves, chiefly of women, but also children and the elderly. Hoard G contains torcs running from almost the smallest (G.14) to the largest sizes (G.11), and other large hoards such as L also show wide variation. This emphasises that these groups of objects collected together for deposition had probably been made for and worn by a wide variety of individuals or roles.

Ornaments and the body: Wider scholarship

> Some of the key generative structuring principles of identity, or the repeated, habitual actions from which identity emerges, lie in how people choose to wear garments or ornaments, how this material culture shapes and gives meaning to the body and how clothing influences or inspires particular movements and gestures (Martin 2014, 28).

The focus on bodily adornment and dress in Iron Age studies reflect wider discussions of the body and personhood in archaeological discourse (e.g. Borić and Robb 2008a; Thomas 2002; Harris and Robb 2013a; Fowler 2004; Sofaer 2006; Stig Sørensen and Rebay-Salisbury 2013; Rebay-Salisbury 2016; Martin and Weetch 2017). This is in part a reaction to discussions of the human body focusing on bodily symbolism and metaphors (Hamilakis 2002a, 99; Hamilakis *et al.* 2002a, 11–12), where dress is viewed as a symbolic means of non-verbal communication, denoting specific categories such as status, age, ethnicity and gender (Joyce 2005, 142–3). 'Archaeologies of the body' have been informed by a number of different thinkers (see Borić and Robb 2008b, 2–5), from Giddens (1979) and Bourdieu (1977), who highlighted the difference between modern and pre-modern societies, to work in ethnography and anthropology where different ideas of the self are presented, such as 'fractal', 'dividual' and 'extended' personhood (e.g. Strathern 1990; Wagner 1991; Busby 1997; Gell 1998; LiPuma 1998). Foucault's (1988) ideas of the body as a means of social control and appropriate conduct in terms of 'techniques of the self', as well as Mauss's (1973 [1934]) notion of 'techniques of the body' have been influential (e.g. Treherne 1995; Hill 1997). There has also been a focus on embodiment (Csordas 1994; Hamilakis 2002b) motivated in part by phenomenology, but also the performative and gender theory of Judith Butler (1990; 1993) and Elizabeth Grosz (1994). Finally, the 'Perspectivism' of Amazonian ethnographers such as Viveiros de Castro (1992; 1998), which highlights the instability of bodies through varying relations between humans and non-humans, has become increasingly prevalent.

Overall, one of the main outcomes of all this work has been an acceptance that the body is not a biological universal, but rather, it is a culturally variable entity. In other words, culture is not spread over the surface of a biological body which exists outside of it (Turner 1980, 112; Csordas 1994, 1; Thomas 2002, 31) and there is no template like the individual which transcends human experience (Fowler 2002, 63). Even within individual societies, several contradictory ways of looking at the body can simultaneously be held (Harris and Robb 2013b, 20).

Personhood is something which one does rather than something one has (Thomas 2002, 36). Of particular relevance to this discussion is a focus on the relationships between the body and the rest of the material world (Morris and Peatfield 2002). Prehistorians like Fowler (2002) have convincingly argued that bodies in the past were not necessarily like us, in particular that the body and the material world were not always separated in the same way (Fowler 2002, 47; Hamilakis 2002b, 125). Similarly, Thomas stated, 'I argue that people's bodies in some prehistoric contexts may have involved non-human elements…' (Thomas 2002, 50). The social body therefore may extend outside of the biological body through relationships with others and with objects (Fowler 2008, 47).

In the following account, two components of these discussions are particularly influential. First, we advocate a 'flatter' ontology between humans and non-humans and reject the unquestioned projection of the Western autonomous individual into narratives of the past. For example, when an Awá man from Amazonia makes arrows, this is not only done so that he can hunt (González-Ruibal *et al.* 2011). Making an arrow is part of what it means to be a man in Awá society. If you do not make arrows you are not an 'Awá man'. This rejection of Western individualism does not imply that people in the past were 'faceless' and 'unthinking', or that everyone was equal. As Thomas (2002) expressed it, 'instead, it means that we recognise that people are different by virtue of their differential positioning within the networks of power and knowledge. We are not free to be what we will, but we realise our potentials differently because of our opportunities, experiences, access to knowledge… and because we may have been excluded, dominated or oppressed by others' (Thomas 2002, 38).

Secondly, Strathern's (1990) notion of the socially constituted body, viewed as the sum of the relations in which it participates, is seen as especially important. As Harris and Robb (2013b) neatly expressed it discussing bodily ornamentation in New Guinea, 'colourful body ornaments, often including traded or gifted items such as arm shells, are a way of displaying the sum of relationships making up the body' (Harris and Robb 2013b). How closely objects were 'linked' to the human body is dependent on the strength of both physical and relational attachments. As Harris *et al.* (2013, 81–2) noted, some types of prehistoric bracelets and anklets have no obvious attachment and may have been put on at a young age and 'grown into', becoming a part of the body. Others were put on and removed depending on occasion and context.

Ornaments also have their own biographies, comprising the sum of the relationships they have been a part of throughout their lifetimes (Joy 2009a). For example, Turner (1980, 118) identified cylindrical lip-plugs made from ground and polished rock crystal as being particularly important in Kayapo groups living in the Amazon Basin. Much time and labour were invested in their manufacture and they were passed down the generations, acting as family heirlooms. Their milky white colour was also associated with age and they were particularly worn by elderly men. In essence, bodies and ornaments were bound through relationships both physical and historical. Physical qualities such as material, colour and age embodied specific cultural qualities. As stated by Alfred Gell when discussing Kula valuables, 'an important arm-shell or necklace does not "stand for" someone important, in a symbolic way; to all intents and purposes it is an important person in that age, influence and something like "wisdom" inheres in its physical substance, in its smooth and patinated surfaces, just as they do in the mind and body of the man of renown to whom it was attached' (Gell 1998, 231). Object histories of exchange and gift-giving actively linked wearers to relations, creating connections with the past, present and future. Wearing an heirloom also can be seen as a form of 'inscribed' history (cf. Joyce 1998, 160). Objects of adornment therefore can, as Melanie Giles memorably expressed it, crystallise a 'social geography of relations' (Giles 2012, 154).

Turner (1980) has discussed the concept of a 'social skin'. According to Turner, as the skin is on the outside of the body, it is a part of the body that is presented to other people in relations. Since people in Melanesia are constituted by their relations with others (Strathern 1990) the person is his or her skin (Gell 1993, 24). Entwistle (2000) has also argued that '…dress is both an intimate experience of the body and a public presentation of it. Operating on the boundary between self and other is the interface between the individual and the social world, the meeting place of the private and the public' (Entwistle 2000, 7). Similarly, Borić *et al.* (2013, 37) viewed ornaments and clothing as a 'second skin' between the body and the outside world. These perspectives go some way to blurring the boundaries between the person and the outside, but they still maintain something of the Western autonomous individual as the exterior social skin creates an artificial distinction between what is on the surface and what lies beneath (Joyce 2005, 145). Alfred Gell's (1993, 38) notion of 'artefactual skin' comes closer to what we want to argue for here. Describing tattooing in Polynesia he explained, 'one can understand this as a process of involution, the creation of an extra layer by folding the skin over upon itself, making an inside of an outside and an outside of an inside' (Gell 1993, 39). This 'folding over' encompasses or wraps up many different relations in the presentation of the social person but is also transformative. Viveiros de Castro (1998, 482) also demonstrated the transformative qualities of animal masks in Amerindian societies. The purpose of animal masks was not to conceal the human identity of its wearer. Rather, through the performance of wearing a mask in the appropriate context, it possessed the power to transform its wearer.

From this brief examination of the wider literature, it is clear that objects of adornment are not straightforward reflections of identity; they are active in creating it (Fisher and Di Paolo Loren 2003, 226). Identity is performed and is dependent on context and the perceptions of the viewer. Performance is therefore of particular significance (e.g. Inomata and Coben 2006a) and will also form a focus of our discussion. Objects of adornment are more than a costume or a prop, rather they are a part of an embodied person (Meskell and Joyce 2003, 10). In the words of Malafouris (2008, 116), they transform and extend the boundaries of our 'body schema'. People and dress interact through use and movement, creating different effects, both on the wearer and observers. For example, Jones (2007, 11) has used the idea of 'body memory' to describe a process by which memory is 'sedimented' through bodily movement.

Here we also take inspiration from the evocative descriptions of Iron Age dress described by Melanie Giles (2012) in her book *A Forged Glamour*. For example, describing an amber bead and several rings made of jet and copper alloy found at the neck of a woman buried in the Kirkburn cemetery, East Yorkshire, Giles stated, 'in life, as someone moved, these ear-pendants, hair loops or necklace charms may have clanked softly together: impressive flashes of light reflecting off their polished surfaces in contrasting warm and dark colours' (Giles 2012, 121).

How torcs were worn

Torcs were worn at the neck with the terminals facing forwards. Evidence from wear and repair (Ch. 20) suggests that torcs were put on by widening the gap between the terminals sufficiently to fit around the wearer's neck. This was achieved by lifting and pulling one terminal slightly, creating tension at the back of the neck-ring and pulling one terminal further forward than the other. Some torcs would have sprung back into shape once fitted around the neck, others with stiffer neck-rings would have needed to be squeezed closed, or those too thick and inflexible to bend (e.g. G.11) would have been worn with a wider opening at the front. Tubular torcs were probably secured around the neck by some form of locking device positioned at the back.

Over time, as torcs were worn, contact with skin or clothing caused polishing on the terminals. Some torcs (such as the examples from Newark and Leekfrith) have polishing on one side only, suggesting they were worn one preferred way up. This could have been related to how decoration was designed to be viewed, or perhaps each of these torcs was worn by just one person over an extended period of time. Other examples, including those from Snettisham, do not show this consistency of polishing on the terminals, implying that there was not a 'correct' way up to wear them.

The necessary movements required to manipulate the torc around the neck would have required some practice but would have soon become second nature. It is difficult to determine whether torcs were worn directly on the skin or over clothing. If they were in contact with the body, then the metal may initially have felt cold to the skin until it was sufficiently warmed by body heat. Much like wearing a heavy watch, it might have taken some time to become accustomed to the weight of a torc. The notion of an item of dress becoming so familiar it almost forms a part of the body is interesting in the case of torcs as it is likely that even though it took a while to adjust to wearing one, it would eventually have become second nature. In addition to the weight, how the torc sat on the neck would also affect comfort. The position of the terminals in relation to the collar bone, for example, could cause pain or irritation, especially if the terminals lay directly over the bone.

In addition to the objects themselves, evidence for how torcs were worn can be gleaned from depictions on Iron Age artwork and classical representations of Iron Age peoples (Eluère 1987). Well-known examples include: the stone statue dating to the second half of the 6th century BC from Hirschlanden, Baden-Württemberg, Germany; the 5th-century BC sandstone figure of a warrior from the Glauberg, Hesse, Germany; the Ragstone head from Mšecké Žehrovice, near Prague, Czech Republic, dating to the 2nd century BC, depicting a moustachioed male wearing a buffer terminal torc; the 'Dying Gaul', a Roman marble copy of a late 3rd-century BC statue from the sanctuary of Athena Nikephoros, Pergamon, western Turkey; the cast sheet bronze statue with one surviving blue and white glass eye from Bouray, France dating to the 1st centuries BC/AD; the wooden carving of a woman wearing a buffer terminal neck-ring from Sources des Roches, France; and, perhaps best known, the cross-legged, horned figure wearing a torc and holding another in his right hand depicted on the silver cauldron from Gundestrup, Denmark. People only rarely appear in Iron Age art (Joy 2011). Where they do, often only the head or face is shown, and it is also debatable whether they are depictions of individuals or, rather, heroes and deities. We should probably not view these images as 'windows on the past' as they create an ideal of bodily adornment and identity rather than a precise representation of day-to-day dress (cf. Fisher and Di Paolo Loren 2003, 227). They may have served as 'citations' for lived performances (Bachand *et al.* 2003, 238–9), but unlike societies where human sculpture was pervasive, unless there were images made of perishable materials such as wood which no longer survive, few people in the Iron Age would have had the opportunity to compare themselves to these idealised images. Rather, people learned through experience the appropriate ways and contexts in which items of adornment were worn and by whom. Nevertheless, in all of these representations the torc is worn at the neck with the terminals positioned facing forwards, sitting on the clavicle. This detail is corroborated by evidence for the wear and repair discussed elsewhere (Ch. 20).

The individuals wearing a torc in classical images such as the Dying Gaul are naked, but this is likely associated with classical notions of beauty, and the idea of the 'noble' barbarian (e.g. Williams 2001, 90). The association between torcs and people from temperate Europe in the minds of people from the classical world can be described as a stereotype, in that it must have simplified reality (otherwise we would likely find many more torcs). It also allowed classical people to make sense of the 'other'. As Bailey (2008, 12) observed, 'stereotypes are especially potent for understanding the relationships among different groups of people'. In the classical world in particular, it was taken for granted that the northern barbarians wore torcs and this perspective was widely held. It is a particularly powerful stereotype because torcs transform the body (cf. Bailey 2008, 13), promoting the difference between 'us' and 'them'.

It is not certain how uncomfortable torcs, especially heavy examples, were to wear for long periods. Anecdotal evidence from people today who wear replica torcs suggests they are perfectly comfortable (Durman pers. comm. 2016). Similarly, some people wear replicas over clothing whereas others prefer to wear them underneath their clothes directly touching the skin. Owing to the fact that many Iron Age depictions show only the head and torc, it is hard to determine what sort of clothing, if any, was worn on the upper body.

Modern Western ideas of comfort may also not be wholly relevant when considering Iron Age torcs. Considerable discomfort is often endured through bodily adornment in other cultures, through practices such as tattooing, scarification and dental modification (cf. Joyce 1998, 159). In her survey of the significance of copper in Africa, Eugenia Herbert (1984) made several interesting observations concerning copper ornaments. She argued that they were almost universal in African societies and 'copper adorned the human body from head to foot and laterally to the tips of the fingers: hair ornaments, earrings, collars and necklaces, pendants, girdles and cache-sexes, bracelets, anklets, rings, bells, amulets, crowns' (Herbert 1984, 210). Surveying notes from ethnographers and travellers, one aspect of these ornaments that was particularly striking was their size (*ibid.*, 213–14). For example, late in the 16th century Paludanus noted that the women at Cape Lopez, Gabon wore metal rings weighing 'three or four pounds'. Similarly, in modern-day Zambia during the 19th century Du Chaillu claimed Mpongwe women wore ornaments weighing up to 25 to 30 pounds on each ankle. But these heavy ornaments were not confined to the legs and ankles. In the middle Congo, Bentley and Johnston observed Bobangi people wearing collars weighing from 20 to 30 pounds. Coquilhat claimed that collars he found at Wangata weighed an eye-watering 15 to 25 kilograms, remarking '…the well-turned woman of the world wears day and night a weight equal to the pack of a Belgian infantryman in the field' (quoted in Herbert 1984, 214). And neither could some collars be easily put on and taken off. They were fitted by blacksmiths and the wearer had to lie on the floor, with one end of the collar resting on an anvil. To remove it, the ends had to be forced apart using a metal wedge (*ibid.*). Herbert (1984, 214–16) also noted just how great the variety of ornaments could be even within a single group. For example, she cited Gutersohn's observations of the Mongo who noted that a single local smith produced eight different types of bracelets, collars and leglets. These ranged from a 10kg neck-ring to spiral-shaped leg rings covering all of the lower leg. Even where individual items were not as big, many smaller artefacts could be worn together with equally staggering combined weights. For example, in Burundi bracelets each weighing 5½ pounds were worn three or four to an arm (*ibid.*, 216).

A further factor to consider is how wearing a torc potentially affected the movement of the wearer. Although torcs are heavy, because they are not fixed tightly around the neck they may have moved around. This would not be a problem when the person was walking, but if worn when running, the terminals would have bounced up and down, potentially hitting the face of the wearer and also bruising the skin around the collar bone if it was worn directly over the body. This could have been mitigated by tucking the terminals under clothing but then the visual impact of the object would have been severely affected.

In terms of deportment, wearing a torc could have also influenced posture. This at first seems strange, but even today objects restrict movement and affect posture. An obvious example is the stiletto shoe, which changes how a person walks and can be painful to wear. To prevent a torc from moving, or perhaps to display it to its best effect (cf. Martin 2014), its wearer may have subconsciously adjusted their gait and straightened their backs. Given that, as Melanie Giles (2012) has shown, many Iron Age artefacts were brought to life through movement, the particular qualities of the torc combined, transforming the body by promoting an erect posture and slowing movements. Torc wearers therefore may have possessed a certain bearing which was ascribed social significance.

In terms of the viewer, a large gold torc with decorated terminals would clearly have been more obvious to the casual observer than a small copper alloy example. Either way, their position on the neck makes them particularly conspicuous. When people interact, often the first thing they do is look at each other's faces. The torc acts to frame the face. The prominent terminals accentuate this effect, drawing the eye away from the face to the chest and back again. It is thought that the head held a special significance to Iron Age people. As the most recognisable part of the human body, it provided a focus for ritual practice (Armit 2012, 224).

Interacting with torcs could also be a sensory experience for the viewer. Raised decoration, the complex twists of wire neck-rings, and the shiny golden or silvery colour of most examples would have created different experiences depending on levels of closeness and access. Viewed from afar, a torc may have only been glimpsed at the neck as a golden band, or a facet of the raised decoration on a terminal might be seen when it caught the sun or flickering firelight. Close-up, details of the decoration could be deciphered, holding the eye and leading it in different directions. The attention of the viewer may also have been captured (cf. Giles 2008), attempting to unravel in their minds the intricacies of the twists of the neck-ring. Touching the raised decoration and textured hatching of the terminals and the uneven but smooth surfaces of the ropes and wires of the neck-ring would have provided an additional sensory experience. Just as Giles (2012, 121) posited the soft clanking of metal pendants and earrings, so some composite objects from Snettisham (such as D.1, G.5, and the 'Grotesque Torc', L.19) would have carried a particular soundscape with them as the wearer moved: the soft chink of metal against metal and the scrape of shifting wires.

Harris and Robb (2013a, 3) introduced the concept of the 'body world', and suggested examining the bodily experiences and representations of a specific place and time. They cited for example the Mesolithic period, where dogs were buried like people and sculptures were carved showing humans transforming into fish (Harris and Robb 2013a, 3). Torcs existed in a particular body world. There are many clues in the archaeological record that Iron Age people did not conceive of the relationships between humans, animals and objects in the same ways we do today. For example, bits of bodies were placed in pits alongside objects and animal bones, suggesting that, in deposition at least, all three could become potent and symbolically charged (Hill 1995). Similarly, the full human form was rarely depicted in art, being rejected in favour of deities, or half-human, half-animal forms. Heads were favoured, some shown wearing torcs. The seemingly abstract, ambiguous art styles also make allusions to faces and animals, but they often remain concealed or half glimpsed (Megaw 1970). This 'body world' is transformative, with no hard and fast distinctions or fixed relationships between people, animals, and objects.

A final consideration concerns not only how torcs were worn on the body but also how they were combined with other items such as bracelets and rings as a costume. One of the ways archaeologists have studied bodies and their relationships with objects of adornment has been through analysis of their position in relation to the human body in graves (e.g. Stig Sørensen 1997; Treherne 1995; Giles 2012). Unfortunately, very few torcs have been discovered in graves in Britain (see above) and Iron Age human remains are relatively rare in Norfolk (Hill 2007, 28; Tremlett 2011, 34). Davies (2008, 92–3) recorded only 14 instances from the county in which human remains had been discovered, including a single inhumation from Shouldham and four cremations from Thetford, Weeting, Heacham and Stiffkey. The inhumation at Shouldham is reported to have contained an iron sword with an anthropoid hilt (Clarke and Hawkes 1956) but otherwise associations between human remains and objects are rare. Data collected under the Norfolk National Mapping Programme, and in excavations, indicate the presence of around 30 sites across the region where a possible funerary or mortuary function could be attributed to ditched enclosures, both square and circular (Davies 2008, 93; Tremlett 2011, 34–7). Although many are likely not to be funerary, this evidence possibly indicates the presence of a widespread but sparse burial tradition, at least for a small proportion of the population (Tremlett 2011, 36). The rest of the people were disposed of in a manner which left little archaeological trace. Individual bones or bits of bodies, including skulls, have been recovered in addition to burials (Davies 2008, 92–3) leading to speculation that secondary burial rites incorporating processes such as exposure and excarnation were the dominant practices (Hill 2007, 28), although this is by no means proven. There is also the possibility that the dead were placed in rivers.

Other types of necklace

Other than torcs, most Iron Age necklaces took the form of pendants or strings of beads. Glass beads, for example, were sometimes strung as necklaces (Foulds 2017).

Where their position in the grave is well recorded, glass beads from East Yorkshire burials were found at the neck, in patterns suggesting they were probably strung on a single strand (Giles 2012, 145). These would have been obvious and dramatic items of dress. By combining beads of various colours, designs and sizes, they could also be customised. Beads could easily have been added to or removed from strings, meaning they may also have acted as adaptable and useful exchange items (*ibid.*, 149). This could have allowed beaded necklaces to change as their owner aged and took on different roles – adolescent, mother, leader, religious specialist, grandmother, elder, etc. Removing and adding beads could also facilitate and enact extended relationships.

No glass beads were recovered from Snettisham, and only two shale objects which may represent beads (SA/HC and SA/HW, see Ch. 9). The dating of these finds is uncertain, though they could in theory be Iron Age or, more likely, Romano-British or later. Both were stray finds. Nevertheless, how glass beads were worn, and how bead necklaces possibly changed over time as new beads were added and others were removed, could provide clues as to how torcs such as the Grotesque torc and other composite groups of artefacts from the Snettisham hoards could have worked in performing various changing identities.

Performing identity

As discussed above, another factor to consider is the potential transformative effect of wearing a torc. When reading ethnographies, it is hard to conceive that anyone truly believed that a person donning a mask could become an animal. When read through a Western cultural lens they can only ever be a person acting like an animal. But other societies have different ways of understanding the world, with different relations to animals and things (Harris and Robb 2013b, 12–13). Both perspectives of the masks are valid from the standpoint of different ontologies but we need to bear different possible understandings of the world in mind when examining prehistoric objects like torcs. The transformative effects of wearing a torc should not be dismissed.

Melanie Giles put this succinctly when she stated '… that identity is not something you simply "have" or "are," but is constituted through what you do in the world' (Giles 2012, 31). The same is true for objects. They are defined not by their physical attributes, but by what they do. Just as people age and their roles in society change, so too do objects. They accumulate but sometimes 'lose' biographies; their lives evolve and change as they move from context to context and gather time. The potential accumulation of biographies for torcs and composite objects at Snettisham is considered in detail in Chapter 20.

We do not know the social arenas in which torcs were worn and experienced. But, ritual performance is probably one of the contexts in which it was appropriate to wear torcs. Rituals provide an idealised version of reality which can be interpreted in different ways in different situations, mirroring but also creating social change. They can also act as a means of establishing and manipulating power relations across society (Inomata and Coben 2006a, 18–19). Objects can form important components of ritual performances, serving as containers of knowledge associated with the narrative of ritual practice and acting to physically manifest specific events or occasions (Inomata and Coben 2006a, 31; Triadan 2006, 162). As outlined above, Hill (2011) argued that torcs were not high-status objects owned by particular individuals, but communal possessions deployed in certain contexts to represent a specific social or ritual office. Given the large number of examples, it is unlikely that this interpretation could apply to all of the Snettisham torcs and many are likely to have been personal objects. But if some were communal possessions, perhaps the larger more ornate examples, this is another example of the transformative power of the torc: changing the wearer by allowing them to step into a special role, which they perhaps then laid aside when the torc was removed. If such a role could be played by different people, then it may be that as much of the ritual power was bound up in the torc as in the practitioner. Ritual or sacred objects are rarely found at the location of these performances, but through archaeological research we can at least gain some insight concerning the final performance they were a part of, for instance the burial and placement of torcs in hoards. The acts that led up to and constituted the creation of the torc hoards are discussed in detail in Chapter 23, taking Hoard L as a case study, including an exploration of how the field systems revealed by geophysical survey (see Ch. 8) may have helped structure ritual activity and movement around the site. Whilst we do not know for certain, some of the torcs could have been old enough to have been present for earlier midden-generating activity at the site (see Ch. 7) long before they were eventually deposited.

Even if the torcs were worn in less formal contexts, wearing a large, decorated, golden-coloured torc probably generated a certain amount of attention given their likely scarcity and the investment placed in their manufacture. Ian Hodder (2006, 83) has argued that spectacle, which he defined as 'showing and looking', is a component of all societies. There is plenty of evidence for large public events in the Iron Age such as the feasting sites at Chiseldon (Baldwin and Joy 2017) and Hallaton (Score 2011), and some of the pottery evidence from Snettisham suggests that this place may also have been the site of feasts earlier in the Iron Age. Spectacle can also take place in domestic contexts (Hodder 2006, 98). According to Houston (2006, 135–6), emotions and reactions are generated through spectacle, ranging from awe and wonder to fear and revulsion. Such events also act to unify groups as well as delineate social differences. Spectacle requires an audience. Audiences judge whether a performance is conducted correctly. Each participant brings their own level of knowledge and understanding to a performance. Describing the Katsina society of south-west North America, Daniela Triadan (2006, 165) described how, because masks are never removed in public, uninitiated children do not realise that some of the mask wearers are their fathers and uncles. Each of the ceremonies undertaken by the Katsina required distinct ritual paraphernalia, which was kept in their clan houses (*ibid.*, 168). Individuals charged with specific responsibilities were annually appointed. Checks and balances meant that power stayed principally within groups, rather than being in the possession of individuals (*ibid.*, 170).

The concept of 'beautification', put forward by Nancy Munn (1977, 47) to describe social practices in Gawa, and also developed by Rosemary Joyce (2000, 11) in her work on Mesoamerican performance, provides a different notion of what torcs may have 'done'. Beautification involves the deliberate increase of the sensory attraction of the body through the addition of skilfully worked artefacts. These 'draw attention' to individuals during performances resulting in what Joyce (2000, 11) termed a 'quality of renown'. In small-scale societies this can result in these individuals being perceived as more 'persuasive' or 'potent' (*ibid.*). Perhaps wearing torcs had a similar affect. In addition, could someone wearing a torc have taken on a different identity? Not just in terms of a sign of status or an insignia of office, but a transferal from a known individual to a hybrid 'torc/person', where the torc and the person become something different, able to transcend the limitations of 'normal' human interaction. This could be particularly advantageous in a world like 4th to 1st-century BC Norfolk, where most people were likely of a similar status, and many would have been known to one another.

Torcs and status

The question seems to be not 'Were torcs involved in negotiations of status and identity?', but rather, 'How?'. As we have seen, torcs were heavily used and they were objects that altered the human body when worn, not only the appearance of the wearer, but also probably their movement and posture. Torcs were therefore not passive reflections of the social standing of their wearer, they were active in negotiations of identity and status through how they were worn.

A further question is 'What kind of status are we referring to?'. Cunliffe's chiefly model of Iron Age society (see e.g. Cunliffe 1984, 559–62; 2005, 588–94) provides one possibility, with large, ostentatious torcs being the ultimate sign of chiefly authority. If this was the case, then torcs would have been active agents in creating the authority of leadership, not just a sign of authority or badge of office. Worn at special occasions, most people could only have glimpsed them from afar. Only those privileged with intimate access could fully appreciate the intricate decoration. Wearing a torc could also have affected the body, changing posture and slowing down movement. These effects might have been viewed in a positive way in terms of emphasising the authority of the wearer and their difference from others.

However, this is only one model for the organisation of Iron Age society. Ethnographic studies have shown that chiefdoms are inherently unstable and often last only a few generations (see e.g. Earle 2011). The archaeological record for the Iron Age also suggests a great chronological and geographical variety in forms of social organisation (Gwilt and Haselgrove 1997; Moore 2011; Hill 2006). This evidence combined implies that if chiefdom-like hierarchies were present during the Iron Age in Britain, which they probably were in some form or other, particularly towards the end of the period, this was not the only type of society present, and was probably not the norm. We therefore also need to look towards other forms of social organisation and means by which objects like torcs could have been made and used. As we have seen, Hill (2006; 2007) has suggested 'flatter' social hierarchies were probably present in much of Britain, with a greater emphasis on 'achieved' rather than ascribed or inherited status. Here we could see the commissioning and wearing of torcs as a form of competition between individuals and social groups such as households, worn as symbols of wealth, used in exchange and gifts, or in negotiations with the gods through their collection and deposition. Some of the more ostentatious torcs could have been reserved for community roles and positions bestowed on individuals who have attained a particular status perhaps through their actions in the community. In terms of the organisation of metalworkers, the patronage of an elite supporting specialist metalworkers is not the only means by which complicated and ostentatious objects such as torcs could be manufactured. As has been suggested for the manufacture of cauldrons in the Middle Iron Age (Baldwin and Joy 2017), a 'ritual' mode of production is also possible. Competition between households could also support a group or groups of specialist metalworkers.

Just as modes of social organisation varied widely across time and space in Iron Age Europe so, most likely, did the role of torcs in negotiating status and identity. In some regions and periods, for example in the 5th to 4th centuries BC in western Germany, precious metal torcs are largely restricted to small numbers of richly furnished graves. In these cases, the torcs may well have been possessions of the deceased, associated with the personal power and rank of particular high-status individuals. In other regions, such as eastern France, bronze torcs appear to have been worn by a wider range of individuals, at least in death (Pope and Ralston 2011, 380), and may have been associated with performing and constructing particular aspects of identity around gender and life stage.

The evidence from Britain is very different. Whilst it is highly likely that torcs were active in the creation of status, authority, gender roles, and community identities, it is difficult to reconstruct details of such significance when precious metal torcs are found almost exclusively in hoards, and very few torcs of any kind are known from burials. Both hierarchical and more fluid or heterarchical models of social organisation could conceivably result in the evidence seen at Snettisham. Looking more broadly, Iron Age Norfolk, with its lack of burials or other signs of a distinct and fixed social hierarchy, suggests that the latter is more likely. There are few indications to support the idea of torcs as personal symbols of individual power, and indeed many objects seem to have had long lives before being deposited, suggesting that they must have been owned, used and worn by more than one person. Of course, if a richly equipped grave with the grave-occupant interred wearing a large gold torc was ever discovered it might push interpretation in another direction.

Conclusions

Lacking other sources of evidence, we must rely on the artefacts themselves. The sheer range of torcs at Snettisham hints at the importance of uniqueness in these objects, and perhaps gradations in importance or subtle variation in social cues. Spectacular objects such as the 'Great Torc' and 'Grotesque Torc' stand out in terms of their material, colour, decoration, and the technological skill inherent in their manufacture. Were these connected to the power of a particular family line, kin group or other collective entity? Could they be passed from one person or group to another, whether as gifts or social payments, by succession, the achievement of some form of ascribed status, or the taking of a particular role or office? Were torcs themselves the active agents, the possession and wearing of which brought status and rank, but only for the duration for which they were held before being passed on to another? The details may never be possible to disentangle, but wearing torcs clearly influenced the status and identity of individuals. The main argument presented here, through a detailed consideration of the artefacts themselves, is that torcs played a crucial and active role in these negotiations, rather than being passive symbols of power. The materials they were made from, their decorations, their weight and form, all influenced the ways their wearers moved and held themselves. The different surfaces of the neck-ring ropes and raised and inscribed decoration on the terminals created varying ways in which they could be experienced from near and far. All of these different attributes meant that the person wearing a torc was not quite the same person without it. These objects effected 'spectacle' and 'beautification' and we cannot understand them fully without taking this perspective into account.

Of course, torcs without people become something different again. Perhaps, memory of the people who wore them and the ceremonies and events of which they were a part were preserved and this is why they were selected for deposition at Snettisham. In the next chapter we consider the hoards themselves, with a focus on the idea of a shift in Late Iron Age Norfolk from a 'world of torcs' to a 'world of coins'.

Gazetteer of other Torcs from Britain

The following list is largely limited to torcs and bracelets of the types found at Snettisham (multi-strand and tubular), though it also includes unusual copper alloy and iron torcs, and those with beaded and thistle terminals. Distinct groups which are discussed in detail elsewhere in the literature are not included here, including ribbon torcs, Wraxall-type collars, Baldock-tradition torcs and beaded torcs (see above). The Winchester necklaces (Hill *et al.* 2004), which are very different in construction, have also been omitted.

This Gazetteer is a significantly expanded version of a preliminary list compiled by Ian Stead. It uses the same typology as devised for the Snettisham finds; see Chapter 13 for a full discussion. Direction of twist for multi-strand torcs, where known, is only given for pieces which have a Z-twist element; otherwise the direction should be assumed to be S. The Gazetteer is divided into three parts:

- Well-recorded torcs of known type and known location
- Torcs of unknown type and/or location
- Unprovenanced torcs, possibly from Britain.

To aid finding objects from specific regions, each section is ordered alphabetically by county and then by findspot name where there is more than one discovery from a single county. Torcs falling into the first category, and the better recorded finds from the second category, are summarised in **Table 22.1**, where they appear in the same order that they are listed here.

Well-recorded torcs of known type

1. Stirling area Hoard, central Scotland

Location: National Museum of Scotland

Discovered by a metal-detector user on 28 September 2009, the hoard was formed of five fragments originating from four torcs:

1. Gold/silver alloy multi-strand torc of highly unusual construction. The core of the neck-ring is formed of a bar with square cross-section. Numerous twisted wires are wrapped and coiled around the bar. The terminals are solid loops or rings adorned with decorative wirework and granulation. A chain and hook links the terminals.
2. Two joining fragments making up roughly half of a tubular hinged annular torc of a type known from south-west France. The fragments are formed of multiple lobes of folded sheet arranged in three rows.
3. Ribbon torc with disc terminals.
4. Ribbon torc with knobbed terminals.

Subsequent excavation of the findspot revealed a small pit. No traces of any container were found. Like the hoard from Netherurd, Peeblesshire, the composition of this one is unusual and mixes artefact types from a number of different regions or at least with diverse influences, even if they are of local manufacture. The ribbon torcs are local to the region. Hinged annular torcs are known from south-west France. The looped terminal torc shares similarities with examples from Snettisham but the employment of unusual decorative techniques such as granulation perhaps also hints at Mediterranean influence (Hunter 2010; Joy 2015, 153–4), as with the torcs from near Winchester, Hampshire (cf. Hill *et al.* 2004). The hoard likely dates from 300–50 BC (Hunter 2010).

2. Hengistbury Head, Dorset

Location: Hinton Admiral; No. 1 on loan to the British Museum from the Society of Antiquaries

Fragments of at least three gold/silver alloy multi-strand torcs/bracelets were found alongside a large number of coins at 'Site 33' at Hengistbury Head during excavations carried out in 1911–12 (Bushe-Fox 1915, 24–6; Cunliffe 1987, 156–7). The area also produced metalworking debris, including evidence for hearths and large lumps of copper and silver alloys (Bushe-Fox 1915, 24–6, 72–4). Bushe-Fox proposed that Site 33 might have been a structure, though the evidence for this is slight. Cunliffe (1987, 75) interpreted it as an area of metallurgical activity. It is difficult to date precisely because the coins have a wide chronological range, spanning from around 100 BC to the 2nd century AD (Cunliffe 1987, 136–41), but Cunliffe (*ibid.*, 75) preferred a date range of *c.* 50 BC–AD 50 for the activity at Site 33. The coins were spread over a large area, mainly to the south of the site and may have been disturbed by rabbits. Despite this, Bushe-Fox (1915, 24–6) uncovered evidence for distinct concentrations of coins (hoards?), which may have been wrapped before they were deposited. For example, 734 coins were found 'lying on a stone with two stones either side'. A 'cylindrical mass of 281 coins' was also uncovered. In addition to the coins, a large block of copper/silver alloy metal was also discovered (Gowland in Bushe-Fox 1915, 73). The torc and related fragments include the cast terminal from multi-strand gold/silver/copper alloy torc (1), a complete gold/silver alloy multi-strand bracelet (2), and fragments from a gold/silver alloy multi-strand torc with buffer terminal (3–4). Nos 2–4 were found wrapped together as a composite group (Bushe-Fox 1915, pl. IX.3). A fragment of gold ribbon/strip now kept with the two torc fragments (Cunliffe 1987, 156, no. 95, ill. 113), possibly represents the objects described by Bushe-Fox as 'pieces of gold wire' found at location 'M' at Site 33, 25ft (7.6m) north of the other torc fragments (Bushe-Fox 1915, 26, fig. 17).

1. Cast torus torc terminal found by Bushe-Fox at Site 33 (Bushe-Fox 1915, 26, pl. XXX; Clarke 1951a, 60; 1954, pl. XVII.7–8; Cunliffe 1987, 153, pl. 111, no. 49; Hautenauve 2005, 235, no. 140). The terminal was originally described as a 'silvered linchpin head' by Bushe-Fox (1915, 26) but was re-identified as a torc terminal by Clarke (1951a, 60). The metal is described by Northover (in Cunliffe 1987, 186) as silver/gold plate over a probable leaded copper alloy core. The terminal is decorated with nine raised pellets and incised lines that follow the form of the terminal. Clarke (1951a, 60) examined the socket of the terminal and found the remains of 18 wires arranged in a circle cast onto the inside edge of the socket. These wires had been sheared off, but suggest an original coiled multi-strand neck-ring construction.
2. Gold/silver alloy multi-strand bracelet, found at Site 33 (Bushe-Fox 1915, 26, pl. IX; Cunliffe 1987, 156, no. 95; pl. 113). The torc/bracelet was originally twisted around 3 and 4 but this arrangement was subsequently unravelled (Bushe-Fox 1915, pl. IX). The neck-ring was described by Cunliffe (1987, 156) as being 'composed of three plaited rods'. From the photographs, however, it looks to be a Stage III construction of two ropes plied together Z-twist, each rope formed of two circular section wires plied together S-twist: (2PZ(2P))R. It is the mix of twist directions which creates the impression of a braided structure. One of the terminals is a simple double loop formed from the body of the bracelet looped around on itself. Unusually, the ply twist of the wires continues into the terminal itself. The other is a ring terminal, described by Cunliffe as '… a rough solid disc created by beating the loose ends of the rods into a single mass' (Cunliffe 1987, 156), although it appears that additional metal may also have been added to thicken the ring and cover the wires, as seen on many of the ring terminal torcs at Snettisham. There are several broken wires in the body of the bracelet. The unusual and mismatched terminals suggest that either the bracelet was unfinished, or perhaps it had been repaired and what remains is an attempt to make a smaller object out of one which was originally larger.
3. Fragment of gold/silver alloy multi-strand torc, comprising a single buffer terminal and a fragment of the neck-ring (Cunliffe 1987, 156–7, no. 94; Hautenauve 2005, 235, no. 141). The neck-ring is formed of six twisted wires, formed into a spiral and hollow in the centre: (6C)T. Three of the twisted wires have become detached since discovery (see Cunliffe 1987, pl. 113). Cunliffe (1987, 156) stated that the ends of the neck-ring wires had been roughly cut, providing probable evidence for deliberate breakage prior to deposition.
4. Comprising a twisted wire bent over to form a loop (Bushe-Fox 1915, pl. IX), this wire probably originally formed part of the neck-ring of 3. It was found wrapped together in a mass with 2 and 3.

3. Maiden Castle, Dorset

Location: Dorset County Museum

A simple one-piece copper alloy torc found at Wheeler's 'Site F', just inside the main western hillfort entrance at Maiden Castle (Wheeler 1943, 276–7, fig. 90, no. 11). Found with Early Roman material, though Wheeler interpreted it as belonging to the latest pre-Roman phase. Slightly expanded circular-section buffer terminals and narrow neck-ring made from twisted square-section wire. See similar finds from Colchester (i), Fremington Hagg, and Upchurch.

4. Spetisbury, Dorset

Location: British Museum (1862,0627.13)

Iron multi-strand torc with single-loop terminals formed from the ends of the two plied circular-section neck-ring wires: (2P)R. From the hillfort at Spetisbury Rings, Dorset. Found during the cutting of a ditch by Central Dorset Railway in 1857 and given to the British Museum by J.Y. Akerman in June 1862 (Hawkes 1940). See similar finds from Camerton, Danebury, and Ham Hill.

5. Dungyle Camp, Dumfries & Galloway

Location: National Museum of Scotland (FA96)

A small copper alloy and iron torc found before 1829 (MacGregor 1976, no. 195). Formed from two circular-section cast copper alloy rods, joined by iron pins/tenons on one section fitting into corresponding mortices/tubes on the other. One joint is at the slightly expanded buffer terminals and the other towards the back of the neck-ring.

6. Colchester, Essex (i) (before 1870)

Location: British Museum (1870,0402.124)

Two copper alloy torc terminals of 'Gaulish type' were recorded by Smith (1905, 137, continental parallel illustrated, fig. 51, no. 10). These were acquired by the British Museum in 1870 from the Pollexfen Collection, and are reported to have been discovered at Beverley Road in Colchester. They are plain buffer terminals (each with two beaded 'collars' behind the terminal, and incised or moulded decoration between the beads). The hollow neck-ring is circular in cross-section. The closest parallels, as noted by Smith, are on the continent, but see similar finds from Britain made at: Fremington Hagg, Maiden Castle and Upchurch.

7. Colchester, Essex (ii) (1996)

Location: Colchester Museum (2021.10)

Gold alloy torc terminal discovered on 24 January 1996 by a metal detectorist, Mr Ken Kirtley, on the eastern outskirts of Colchester, at Crockleford Heath (Anon. 1996, 18). In a report written 13 February 1996 (quoted in *Treasure Hunting*, May 1996), Peter Berridge, Curator of Archaeology for Colchester Museums, described the object as a 'buffer type' terminal with 'a rectangular slot on the flat end of the terminal… which is capable of being slotted into an aperture on the other terminal'. Paul Sealey (pers. comm.) has examined the terminal and suggests that it is an unusual Gallic type, likely dating to *c.* 200–50 BC, appearing to be unfinished and unused.

8. West Tilbury, Thurrock, Essex

Location: Unknown

Supposedly discovered in or before 2000 by a farmworker 'while tractoring' (Bingley 2015, 71). The find was not officially reported and few details are known other than poor quality photographs. The neck-ring consists of three ropes and there is a repair at the back. The vase-shaped buffer terminals are decorated with raised ornament. The find has features usually seen on different styles of torc.

9. Merthyr Mawr Warren, Glamorgan

Location: National Museum Wales (29.447)

Possible fragment of gold/silver alloy multi-strand torc or bracelet (Hautenauve 2005, 237, no. 148), found at the Iron Age settlement site of Merthyr Mawr Warren. Described by Savory (1976, 67, no. 67) as a 'twisted silver wire bracelet', the fragment comprises two silver-coloured wires loosely plied together Z-twist, broken at both ends and part melted.

10. Walbrook, Greater London

Location: Museum of London (18661)

A complete one-piece penannular copper alloy torc with thistle terminals found in the River Walbrook, possibly in association with late 1st to mid-2nd-century AD Romano-British brooches (Marshall 2023). The neck-ring rod is lozenge-shaped in cross-section. Similar finds have been made in Britain at the River Medway near Aylesford and at Shenstone.

11. Danebury, Hampshire

Location: Museum of the Iron Age, Andover, Hampshire

Iron multi-strand torc with single-loop terminals and neck-ring formed from two wires or rods plied together (Sellwood 1984, 371, 2.202, fig. 7.25). Found in a cp7 context at the hillfort (this period dated by Cunliffe to *c.* 300–100/50 BC). The two terminals are joined by a linking bar of similar construction to the torc itself: an iron rod doubled back on itself to give a loop at one end (passing through one of the torc terminals), and the two strands plied together in the central section. The other end of the linking bar is broken, but would probably originally have been hooked to link into the opposite torc terminal. See similar finds from Camerton, Ham Hill and Spetisbury.

12. Whitchurch, Hampshire

Location: Unknown

A silver-alloy torc fragment consisting of two short pieces of wire forming a single strand. The fragment was snipped at both ends. The torc fragment was part of a hoard discovered by a metal-detector user in 2011 found 3–4 inches below the ground, which also included 15 other artefacts from various periods (2011T152; HAMP-8A11A7; Bliss 2020, 6, fig. 3). The manufacture of three of the objects can be dated to the Middle–Late Bronze Age: a gold lock-ring (*c.* 1000–800 BC), a gold composite ring (*c.* 1300–1100 BC) and a copper-alloy spear tip (*c.* 1500–800 BC). The remaining 13 objects including the torc fragment, a silver-alloy lump, two sections of copper-alloy binding strip probably from a shield or possibly a tankard, and a possible copper-alloy brooch fragment, all probably date to the later Iron Age (2nd or 1st centuries BC). The date of the five copper-alloy miniature axes is unclear. They could date to the Late Bronze Age or Early Iron Age or indeed be later (Bliss 2020, 11).

13. Essendon, Hertfordshire

Location: British Museum (1994,0401.1–52)

The fragmentary remains of a gold alloy tubular torc were discovered by metal detectorists in 1992 and the findspot was subsequently investigated by Ian Stead of the British Museum in 1992–4 (Stead 2006, 51; Hautenauve 2005, 234, no. 137). Tubular torc fragments, including two terminals, were discovered alongside a total of 66 coins and four ingots. It is thought the torc originated from a hoard as some of the coins were found in a terminal (unfortunately the metal detectorists did not recall which coins).

Although yet to be fully published, Stead gave a short account of the Essendon excavations in his book *British Iron Age Swords and Scabbards*:

> The remains of a gold tubular torc, one brass and three gold ingots, fragments of copper-alloy bowl and 253 British gold coins were found. Although there were distinct concentrations in the distribution of coins, indicating at least two hoards (A and B), no nucleus had survived ploughing. Another hoard (C) did have a nucleus, but instead of coins it was composed mainly of weapons … The hoard had been deposited in a shallow pool in a bog (Stead 2006, 51).

The tubular torc is plain, with a simple, hollow neck-ring and large, undecorated, bulbous terminals. Whilst the terminals are heavily damaged, what survives suggests that the torc was probably penannular, rather than fastening to form a continuous circuit as seen in the Type 1 tubular torcs from Snettisham Hoard A. The Essendon torc does not fit neatly into the typology created for the Snettisham tubular torcs (Ch. 13), but is likely closest to Type 5.

14. Wendy, nr. Royston, Herts

Location: Royston Museum (2016.2039)

Copper alloy torc fragment comprising a section of round-sectioned neck-ring and a single beaded terminal. Found in a field wall at Wendy, Cambridgeshire. No date was recorded for the discovery. Probably 1st century AD.

15. Auldearn, Highland

Location: National Museums Scotland

Two copper alloy objects, a torus terminal multi-strand torc and a large Romano-British-style brooch, were recovered by a metal detectorist in 2014 and have since been acquired by National Museums Scotland through the Treasure Process (TT 86/14, 87/14; Hunter 2014a). The torc has a neck-ring formed from coiled copper alloy circular-section wires, alternating broad and narrow wires, and torus terminals with worn decoration including trumpet motifs. The terminals resemble triple-loop terminals, with broad outer loops and a narrow central loop, echoing the construction of the neck-ring. The style of decoration on both the torc and brooch suggest a date in the 1st or 2nd century AD. Hunter (2014a) proposed that although the closest parallels for the torc are in southern Britain, the decorative motifs suggest a local origin.

16. Aylesford, Kent

Location: Maidstone Museum

A complete penannular copper alloy torc with thistle terminals was found in the River Medway near Aylesford, Kent (Fox 1958, 66, pl. 26b; Jope 2000, 16, 234, pl. 32). The neck-ring rod is unusual in being square rather than round in cross-section. The torc belongs to Hautenauve's Type IIIa ('torque au corps massif à tampons sans fermoir') distributed from Central Europe to France with bronze examples dating from the end of the 6th century BC to the beginning of the 3rd century BC (Hautenauve 2005, 67–70). Jope (2000, 16 and 234) suggested it may have been an import but given the wide distribution of the type it is also possible that it was manufactured in Britain. Similar finds have been made in Britain at Shenstone and the River Walbrook.

17. Shepherdswell with Coldred, Kent

Location: Unknown

Short length of gold/silver alloy multi-strand torc neck-ring or bracelet body formed from two circular-section strands of wire plied together (KENT-0E7EAB, 2015 T287). The curvature of the piece strongly suggests that it was originally part of a larger Stage III plied construction: (?P(2P))R. Both ends show signs of having been chiselled, suggesting that the original object was deliberately broken up.

Non-destructive XRF analysis carried out as part of the Treasure process indicated a surface composition of approximately 56–57% gold, 35–40% silver, the rest being copper.

18. Upchurch, Kent

Location: British Museum (1894,0803.54–55)

Two torcs were found at Slay Hill Saltings on the Medway near Upchurch, Kent, now in the collections of the British Museum (Smith 1905, 138). According to the British Museum register for 1894, the four accessioned objects from Slay Hill Saltings were all discovered in an urn found in about 1864 on the Saltings west of Greenborough Marshes. These objects are an Iron Age gilded copper alloy and iron torc (1894,0803.54), the decorated buffer-shaped terminals of another (1894,0803.55), and two Roman silver finger-rings set with engraved stones (1894,0803.56–7). Coins were also found with the hoard, although these are now lost. The BM register states that the find included 'coins down to Aurelius'. The only other contemporary reference to the hoard is from Payne (1893, 75–6). He states that the jewellery was found together with silver coins of Nero (1), Vespasian (2), Domitian (1), Trajan (3), Hadrian (2), Antoninus Pius (2), Marcus Aurelius (2), Faustina Junior (2), 'and a Greek coin', and bronze coins of Pius and Crispina. The coin of Crispina is actually likely to be the latest in the hoard, fixing the date of the deposit after about AD 180. The rings are of late 2nd-century type; the intaglios represent (i) Perseus holding up the Gorgon's head, and (ii) a cock upon an ear of corn.

1. Iron rod torc, hinged at the back of the neck-ring, with copper alloy wire coiled around part of the body of the torc. Slightly expanded, undecorated copper alloy buffer terminals. Similar to the example from the Polden Hills, although the latter is not hinged.
2. Beaded buffer terminals from a gilded copper alloy torc, with hollow circular-section neck-ring. These (as noted by Smith 1905, 138) are most similar to examples from the continent, although see similar finds from Britain at: Colchester (i), Fremington Hagg, and Maiden Castle.

19. Burnley, Lancashire

Location: Manchester Museum (O.9194)

A complete gold/silver alloy multi-strand torc with double-loop terminals. Said to have been discovered at Cliviger, near Burnley in 1802, it was in the possession of the Whitaker family from 1824, and was acquired by the Manchester Museum at a sale at Sotheby's on 11 April 1960 (Anon. 1980, no. M24; Hautenauve 2005, 233, no. 132; Lamb 2020). The neck-ring is formed from two faceted wires plied together (Stage II construction: (2P)F). Each double-loop terminal is continuous with the neck-ring wires, implying that on at least one side the ends of the wire have been closed by hammering or soldering. Metallurgical analysis carried out at Manchester Museum (Lamb 2020) revealed a surface composition of around 68% gold, 30% silver, and 0.5% copper.

20. Caistor, Lincolnshire

Location: The Collection Museum Lincoln

Gold alloy torc fragment with one surviving trumpet-headed buffer terminal, with a bead behind the flared trumpet, giving a thistle-shaped head. It was discovered by a metal detector user in 2013 (2013 T130; NLM-605352; Joy 2015, 151, fig. 9.6). The neck-ring is a solid bar with circular cross-section. The broken end of the neck-ring is an old break, but not particularly abraded. The neck-ring has been bent out of shape, with two distinct 'kinks'. The torc belongs to Eluère's (1987) 'Torcs with Buffer Terminals and Intermediate Collars' group and to Hautenauve's (2005) Type IIIa ('Torcs with a Large Body and Terminals without a Clasp'). These torcs have a distribution centred on north-eastern France and western Germany, with one from as far away as Bulgaria (see Jacobsthal 1969 [1944], nos 43–8). Well-known examples of this type include the torcs from the Waldalgesheim grave (Joachim 1995, 61–3). Torcs of this type are dated by Eluère (1987, 28) to the end of the 5th century to the late 4th century BC and by Hautenauve (2005, 67–70) to the second half of the 4th and the beginning of the 3rd centuries BC.

Surface XRF analysis carried out as part of the Treasure process showed a composition of: 71–73% gold; 24–26% silver; 3% copper.

21. Bawsey, Norfolk

Location: British Museum and Norwich Castle Museum

Discoveries of complete or fragmentary torcs have been made over many years no more than 80m apart in a field located to the west of the church at Bawsey, near King's Lynn (NHER 5326). At least four torcs are represented. They may all come from a scattered hoard, although they could also originate from separate deposits. The first discovery of a complete gold/silver alloy loop terminal multi-strand torc (1) was made by a farmworker in 1941 (Wake 1942; Maryon 1944). In 1944 a loop terminal from another multi-strand gold/silver-alloy torc (2) was discovered, close to the site of the first find (Clarke 1950, 157). A few sherds of Iron Age pottery were also recovered (NHER 5326). Both torcs are now held at Norwich Castle Museum. In 1984, two decorated gold alloy buffer terminals (3) were discovered by a metal detectorist, Geoffrey Peach. Initially unreported, the findspot of Bawsey was eventually established (Stead 1998, 135–7, pl. 19).

There are many additional gold/silver alloy wire fragments (4) that probably derive from torc (3). In 1987 and 1988 metal-detector user S. Brown discovered further twisted wire strands (Stead 1998, 135–7): a gold/silver alloy wire was found in 1987 and two silver-plated wires in 1988. The metal was examined by Peter Northover but his report is unpublished (Stead 1998, 137) (NHER 5326). Further metal-detector finds of multiple twisted wire fragments were made by Brown in 1989, 1990, 1996 and 2006 (Hill in Barton and Hitchcock 2008, 54). The strands were broken rather than cut. Based on the colour of the metal and similarities between strands they probably all derive from the same torc broken up by agricultural machinery.

Two additional gold/silver alloy buffer terminals from a multi-strand torc (5) were recovered in 2005–7.

1. A complete gold/silver alloy multi-strand torc with thickened ring terminals and Stage II neck-ring formed from two thick wires plied together: (2P)R. Discovered in 1941 (Hautenauve 2005, 232, no. 128; Wake 1942, 26, fig. 4). Surface XRF metal analysis for the Treasure Trove inquiry revealed the following results:
   - Terminal A: 44.4% gold, 49.6% silver
   - Terminal B: 44.4% gold, 50.3% silver
   - Middle: 42.3% gold, 50.8% silver

   Norwich Castle Museum (1942.126)
2. Fragment of gold/silver alloy multi-strand torc comprising one thickened ring terminal and a section of neck-ring. formed from two thick wires plied together (Stage II construction: (2P)R). Found in 1944 (Clarke 1950, 157; 1954, 50–1, pl. xi, lower left; Hautenauve 2005, 232, no. 129).
   Norwich Castle Museum (1944.106)
3. Two decorated gold/silver alloy buffer terminals from a multi-strand torc. Found by metal detectorist Geoffrey Peach in 1984 who originally claimed they were from 'Fincham' (Hautenauve 2005, 232–3, no. 131). The flat faces of the cast terminals are decorated with curvilinear decoration in relief, including lobes, pellets, fin motifs, possible stylised bird heads, and trumpet voids. Only small lengths of the wire neck-ring remain, showing a Stage III construction of an unknown number of ropes coiled around a hollow core, with each rope formed from two circular-section wires plied together: (?C(2P))R.
   British Museum (1985,1204.1–2)
4. A large number of wire fragments from the same site are believed to have originally been part of Bawsey torc 3 (above); each consists of a short length of the Stage II 'rope', broken at both ends, formed from two circular-section wires plied together (Hautenauve 2005, 232, no. 130). Two such fragments were found by a second metal detectorist, S. Brown, in 1987 (Stead 1998, 135–7, pl. 19; Jope 2000, 255, pl. 121, l; unpublished metal analyses of the strands by Peter Northover). Further discoveries were made by Brown in June–November 1989, November 1990, November 1996 and March 2006. All are thought to derive from torc 3 (Hill in Barton and Hitchcock 2008, 54). The four fragments discovered in 2006 were analysed at the British Museum research lab. The report prepared for the Treasure report stated: 'Non-destructive X-ray fluorescence analysis has shown that the surface of each contained 26–38% gold and 54–66% copper, the remainder being copper. In all cases, there was a lower percentage of precious metal at the core than at the surface of the wires. Three of the four have wires of almost identical diameter (1.8mm), the fourth is slightly thinner. There is no analytical reason to suspect that the four fragments did not come from the same object.'
   British Museum (1989,1201.1–2, 1990,0304.1–135, 1991,0602.1–7, 1997,0901.1–3)
5. Another pair of decorated gold/silver alloy buffer terminals from a multi-strand torc were discovered by metal-detecting in 2005–7 (2006 T13; 2005/6 TAR no. 81; 2007 T104; 2007 TAR no. 68; NMS-D3BF38). Each has short stubs of neck-ring wires protruding on the reverse, though the precise construction of the neck-ring cannot be determined. The flat front faces of the terminals are decorated with engraved curvilinear designs based around a triskele, areas of which are infilled with finely punched dots. On one terminal these dots are arranged in lines to create the impression of 'basket-weave' hatching, whilst on the other the arrangement is apparently random. The edges of the terminals are decorated with a cable design. Surface analysis carried out as part of the Treasure process revealed similar metal

contents for both terminals: 33–36% gold, 58–61% silver, with the remainder being copper.
Norwich Castle Museum 2007.229 and 2008.226

22. Blackborough End Quarry pits, Middleton, Norfolk
Location: British Museum (1985,0303.1)
A complete gold/silver-alloy multi-strand torc with triple-loop/ring terminals was found in June 1984 at a carrstone quarry called Mill Drove Quarry at Blackborough End, East Winch, Norfolk (Hautenauve 2005, 237, no. 149). An account of its discovery is provided by Natasha Hutcheson: 'This torc … was recovered after it had been through the Quarry's stone crusher (SMR 12559); miraculously it survived' (Hutcheson 2004, 43). The torc was declared Treasure Trove at an inquest on 25 October 1984 and acquired by the British Museum. The neck-ring is a Stage III construction of two ropes plied together Z-twist, each of which is formed from two circular-section wires plied together S-twist: (2PZ(2P))R. The combination of different twist directions gives the effect of a braid, but the neck-ring is formed purely by twisting. Each triple terminal consists of, at the front, a double loop continuing into one of the neck-ring ropes and, at the back, a thickened ring formed from the ends of the wires of the other neck-ring rope, with additional metal added to create a closed ring from the open ends of the wire.

23. Near Diss, Norfolk
Location: Unknown
Gold/silver alloy multi-strand torc with double-loop terminals. The torc was rediscovered in 2004–5, during the disposal of the estate of Mr Walter Banks by his widow Mrs Doris Banks. It was given by Mrs Banks to Diana Birch who sent it to Mr John Haywood of Spink for valuation. Mr Haywood recognised the artefact as possibly ancient and contacted the British Museum in March 2010, who confirmed it could be Iron Age. The torc is thought to have been found 'near Diss' sometime in 1942/3 and had remained in a safe deposit box until Mr Banks' death. As it was found before 1996 it came under the Treasure Trove legislation. It was subsequently declared not Treasure Trove (2010 T194) on the grounds it was probably not buried with the intention of retrieval. The Stage II neck-ring comprises two circular-section wires plied together. Rather than being made from a continuous length of wire doubled back on itself at one of the terminals, the torc is formed from two wires. Each terminates in an open loop at each end, giving the two double-loop terminals. Non-destructive XRF analysis conducted in the Department of Conservation and Science, the British Museum, revealed the metal was 81–85% gold, 14–16% silver, the remainder being copper.

24. Forncett, Norfolk
Location: Norwich Castle Museum
Metal-detected find made in 2015 and subsequently acquired by Norwich Castle Museum (NMS-7ACEC5; 2015 T863). Short length of gold/silver alloy multi-strand torc neck-ring or bracelet body formed from two circular-section strands of wire plied together. Stage II construction: (2P)R. Cut at both ends. The slight S-shaped curvature of the piece may suggest that it was originally part of a larger Stage III construction, but this is now impossible to determine with certainty.

25. Gayton, Norfolk
Location: Unknown
A metal-detected find made in 2005, comprising a short length of gold/silver alloy multi-strand torc neck-ring or bracelet body (2005 T544; 2005/6 TAR no. 83; NMS-35C242). What remains is a Stage II construction formed of four circular-section wires plied together. The slightly coiled shape of the piece strongly suggests that it was originally part of a larger Stage III plied or coiled construction: (?C/P(2P))R. The fragment has been deliberately cut at one end, although the other end appears to be a break. Surface XRF carried out as part of the Treasure process shows the wires are over 80% gold.

26. North Creake, Norfolk
Location: Norwich Castle Museum (1949.97)
Gold/silver alloy hollow cast torus terminal from a multi-strand torc. Discovered during ploughing in 1947, about half a mile north-west of Shammer House, North Creake, on high ground five miles from the north Norfolk coast (Clarke 1951a, 59; Hautenauve 2005, 238, no. 152). The terminal is decorated with raised lobes, pellets and inscribed fin motifs. Broken-off wires cast onto the interior still survive at the mouth of the terminal. The original neck-ring was probably a Stage III construction with six ropes coiled around a hollow core, each made from a number of circular-section wires: (6C(?P))R.

27. Norwich, Norfolk
Location: Norwich Castle Museum
Gold/silver alloy rotating dorsal muff from a small tubular torc, a metal-detected find made in 2007 and since acquired by Norwich Castle Museum (2007 T119; 2007 TAR no. 69; NMS-C6DFC1). A composite ring formed from an inner sheet tube, around the outside of which are two broad semi-circular-section concentric hollow ribs (or tubes), decorated in between and on each outer face with rings of narrow, twisted square-section wire. Surface XRF carried out as part of the Treasure process shows a composition of 84–87% gold and 10–12% silver, the remainder being copper.

28. Sedgeford, Norfolk
Location: British Museum (1968,1004.1 and 2005,1103.1)
A gold/silver alloy multi-strand torc in two parts, one, discovered in 1965, comprised a hollow torus terminal and most of the neck-ring (Brailsford 1971; Jope 2000, 84, 254, pls 114–15; Hautenauve 2005, 238, no. 153); the missing terminal was found in 2004. The Stage III neck-ring is formed of eight ropes coiled together around a hollow core, each rope made up of three circular-section wires plied together: (8C(3P))R. The terminals are decorated with relief curvilinear decoration including lobes, trumpet voids, and raised pellets with triple dots set in circular fields of 'basket-hatching'. The collars are also decorated with raised pellets set in a 'basket-hatched' background. The larger torc fragment was discovered on 6 May 1965 during mechanised

harrowing of a field called Polar Brek at West Hall Farm, Sedgeford, in Norfolk (Brailsford 1971, 16). In 1993 a British Museum project which aimed to locate the second part of the torc was abandoned when the landowner withdrew permission because he wanted to benefit financially from any potential new discoveries. The missing terminal was subsequently located at the site in April 2004 by Dr Hammond whilst metal-detecting as part of a survey conducted by SHARP (Sedgeford Historical and Archaeological Research Project) in a long-running study of the history and archaeology of the parish of Sedgeford (Dennis and Faulkner 2004). As Hill suggested in his Treasure report on the find, 'this discovery is almost certainly the missing terminal, as it is identical in size and design to the earlier discovery' (Hill in Hitchcock 2006, 48–9). There is no sign that the terminal was deliberately separated from the rest of the torc in the past. It is more likely damage was caused by modern agricultural activity.

29. South-west Norfolk

Location: Norwich Castle Museum (2005.218)

Gold/silver alloy multi-strand torc with torus terminals (Hill in Gannon *et al.* 2004; Davies 2008, fig. 67), discovered by two metal-detector users, Mr Leach and Mr Carter, sometime before May 2003. It was declared Treasure in November 2003 and acquired by Norwich Castle Museum.

The terminals are crude torus, open in the interior of the eye, similar in form to Snettisham torc L.1. Each terminal has a groove running down the centre of the torus, as if dividing it into two adjacent rings; this dividing line is decorated with raised scallop or zig-zag mouldings. The collar is decorated with raised pellets with triple dots, set in a 'basket-hatched' field. The Stage III neck-ring comprises four ropes plied together, each rope formed of six circular-section wires coiled together around a hollow core: (4P(6C))R. The torc was damaged by recent agricultural activity. One rope is 'buckled' close to one of the terminals and the ropes are less tightly coiled on one half of the neck-ring.

30. Weybourne, near Sheringham, Norfolk

Location: Unknown

A hoard of gold coins was eroded out of the cliffs at Weybourne and discoveries of coins were made there from *c.* 1914 to the late 1960s (Allen 1971, 140–1; Haselgrove 1987, 327–8). Haselgrove (1987, 328) noted at least 63 coins as well as a possible fragment of a gold alloy tubular torc and speculated the finds originated from two hoards, perhaps held in a pottery container due to the presence of small quantities of Iron Age pottery at the site.

31. Ulceby, North Lincolnshire

Location: Ashmolean Museum (torcs) and Liverpool Museum (bridle bit); other finds lost

Three multi-strand torcs and a simple bar bracelet were discovered sometime around 1847 during excavations for a railway cutting (Cuming 1859; Leeds 1933; May 1976, 156–62). They were found alongside three horse bit fragments, all constructed of copper alloy around an iron core. It is thought that the bridle bits were damaged in antiquity (May 1976, 159). Two of the bits are now lost, while one ring with the decorated end of a link is now in Liverpool Museum (Leeds 1933, 466).

1. Gold/silver alloy multi-strand torc with double-loop/ring terminals (Hautenauve 2005, 256, no. 225). The neck-ring is formed of four circular-section wires plied together: (4P)R. The front part of each terminal is a thickened ring, continuous with two of the neck-ring wires; the back part is a simple continuous loop formed from the other two neck-ring wires. Ashmolean Museum (1927.6659)
2. Gold/silver alloy multi-strand torc with quadruple-loop terminals (Hautenauve 2005, 256, no. 226). The Stage III neck-ring is formed of three ropes plied together S-twist, each made up of two circular-section wires plied together Z-twist: (3P(2PZ))R. The mixture of twist directions creates the effect of a braid. At each terminal, the two wires of each neck-ring rope form a continuous loop: two single and one double, creating quadruple-loop terminals. Ashmolean Museum (1927.6660)
3. Fragment of gold/silver alloy multi-strand torc, comprising a single-loop terminal and a section of neck-ring (Hautenauve 2005, 256, no. 227). The neck-ring was originally formed of two thick wires plied together. The torc is said to have been complete when it was found but was broken up by a lady '... who snapped it in pieces for distribution among her friends' (Cuming 1859, 226). Lost.
4. Gold/silver alloy bracelet. It was complete when found but like torc 3 it was broken up following its discovery (Cuming 1859, 227). Judging by the illustration in Cuming (1859), it was formed from a bar with rectangular cross-section, like some of the examples from Snettisham (May 1976, 159). Lost.

32. Fremington Hagg, North Yorkshire

Location: Yorkshire Museums Trust (H 141 105)

Fragment of copper alloy beaded-terminal rod torc or bracelet, found before 1833, possibly in association with a large hoard of Early Roman copper alloy fittings (MacGregor 1976, no. 196). The fragment comprises one of the terminals, a slightly dished buffer terminal with three bead mouldings behind it along the short surviving length of circular-section neck-ring or body. See similar finds from Colchester (i), Maiden Castle and Upchurch.

33. Towton, North Yorkshire

Location: York Museums Trust

Two Iron Age gold/silver alloy multi-strand bracelets were reportedly discovered in a streambed in the Towton area, though there are uncertainties about the accuracy of this findspot information.

1. Gold/silver alloy multi-strand bracelet with loop terminals (2010 T350: SWYOR-CFE7F7). The body of the bracelet is made up of two circular-section wires plied together: (2P)R. Each terminal is a continuous loop formed from the neck-ring wires. Surface XRF carried out as part of the Treasure process shows a composition of 80–84% gold; 12–14% silver; and at least 4% copper.
2. Gold/silver alloy multi-strand bracelet with ring terminals (2011 T326: SWYOR-681CE4). The Stage III body is formed from two ropes plied together Z-twist, each of which is formed from two circular-section wires

plied together S-twist: (2PZ(2P))R. The mixture of twist directions creates a braided effect. Each terminal was originally formed from two loops, each loop continuous with the two wires of one of the neck-ring ropes. The outside surface of the terminals has been filled with a lower melting point gold/silver/copper alloy, containing approximately 16% more copper than the rest of the bracelet. The overall effect is to transform double-loop terminals into single-ring terminals. Surface XRF carried out as part of the Treasure process shows a composition of 55% gold, 38% silver, and at least 7% copper.

34. Great Houghton (Brackmills), Northants

Location: Northampton Museums

A female skeleton wearing a neck-ring was discovered during archaeological excavation at Great Houghton, Northamptonshire (Chapman, A. 1998; 2000–1). The skeleton lay face down in a large circular pit. It was crouched laying on its right side and the excavator thought the hands may have been bound (Chapman, A. 2000, 9). The woman was 30–40 years old when she died and 1.56m tall. Radiocarbon dates were obtained which dated the skeleton as Iron Age, specifically to 2320 ± 60 BP (405–370 cal BC at 68 % probability, 505–205 cal BC at 95.4% probability) (*ibid.*, table 6).

The torc comprises two curved rods, each terminating at one end in a slightly flared, flat buffer terminal. These terminals are circular in cross-section, while the rest of the neck-ring is broadly square in section and slightly twisted. The opposite ends of each rod seem to articulate: one is notched and the other perforated, suggesting the halves were originally bound together with an organic material which no longer survives. The torc was found around the neck of the deceased, with the circular terminals overlapping at the nape, suggesting the torc was being worn 'backwards' compared to the position that might be expected (see discussion above on how torcs were worn).

Metal analysis revealed the torc is made from an alloy of lead with a high tin content, also containing traces of zinc, copper and iron (*ibid.*, 24).

35. Newark, Nottinghamshire

Location: Acquired by Newark and Sherwood Museums Service, Millgate Museum, Newark

A gold/silver alloy multi-strand torc with hollow torus terminals, found by Mr M. Richardson while metal-detecting in February 2005 (Hill in Barton and Hitchcock 2008, 55, see also Machling and Williamson 2018). The terminals are decorated with a raised curvilinear design of ovals, trumpets and peltas, and have narrow collars decorated with raised pellets with triple dots. The Stage III neck-ring comprises eight ropes coiled around a hollow core; each rope is formed of four circular-section wires plied together: (8C(4P))R. There is evidence of wear: black silver oxide deposits can be seen on the raised parts of the decoration of both terminals and in an ancient cut on one of the terminals. Some ropes on the back of the neck-ring are also raised, indicating stresses where the torc has been put on and taken off. Both terminals are also polished or worn on one side (presumably the underside when worn), showing the torc was consistently worn the same way up. Surface analysis of the terminal and neck-ring indicated a metal content of around 67% gold and 32% silver.

36. Ellesmere, Shropshire

Location: British Museum (2015,8032.1)

A metal-detected find from 2012 comprising a short length of gold/silver alloy multi-strand torc neck-ring or bracelet body, cut or broken at both ends (HESH-D6AEA; 2013 T38). What remains is a Stage II component of two circular-section wires plied together: (2P)R. As part of the Treasure process, non-destructive XRF analysis of the surface on each of the wire strands was carried out by Teresa Gilmore and staff of the Conservation Department of Birmingham Museum and Art Gallery/Birmingham Museums Trust. The results were:

- Strand 1: 58.74% +/- 0.38 gold; 36.27% +/- 0.31 silver; 4.55% +/- 0.10 copper
- Strand 2: 59.58% +/- 0.37 gold; 31.66% +/- 0.28 silver; 8.76% +/- 0.13 copper

37. Telford, Shropshire

Location: Acquired by Shropshire County Museum Service

Part of a gold/silver alloy multi-strand torc (in two pieces), comprising a single-loop terminal, a continuous loop formed from the end of the two remaining neck-ring wires, and a second fragment of the neck-ring wire, cut at one end (2008 T557; 2008 TAR no. 72; WMID-C53CB8). What remains of the neck-ring rope is a Stage II component of two circular-section wires twisted together. It is coiled in such a way as to suggest that it originally formed part of a Stage III construction, e.g. (?P(2P))R, probably with at least one other similar rope, perhaps forming a double-loop terminal torc.

Surface XRF carried out as part of the Treasure process shows a composition of gold 55–60%, silver 39–43%, the remainder being copper.

38. Cadbury Castle, Somerset

Location: Museum of Somerset, Taunton

Five components of jointed iron neck-rings, representing at least three objects, were found in the mid-1st-century AD deposits in the south-west gateway complex at Cadbury Castle (MacDonald in Barrett *et al.* 2000, 123–5, 130–1, fig. 59, nos 19–20, fig. 63, nos 64, 72, 73). These are simple ornaments formed from circular-section iron rods. Each neck-ring comprised two separate components, one rod forming around two thirds of the circumference, and another to complete the final third, the two coming together with mortice and tenon joints.

39. Camerton, Somerset

Location: British Museum (1982,0103.274)

Iron multi-strand torc with single-loop terminals and neck-ring formed from two wires or rods plied together Z-twist: (2PZ)R (Jackson 1990, 63–4, pl. 28, no. 274). Found with a large assemblage of bronze and iron finds unearthed by deep ploughing in 1980 in fields north of a Romano-British settlement at Camerton, likely dating to the 1st century AD. The two terminals are joined by a linking bar of similar construction to the torc itself: an iron rod doubled back on itself to give a loop at one end (passing through one of the torc terminals) and a hook at the other (to hook into the other terminal); in the central section of the linking bar the doubled rod is plied Z-twist, as for the torc. See similar finds from Spetisbury, Ham Hill and Danebury.

40. Clevedon, Somerset

Location: British Museum (AF.412: Part of the Franks bequest acquired in 1897)

Gold/silver alloy buffer terminal and neck-ring fragment (Smith 1905, 138, fig. 126; Hautenauve 2005, 234, no. 136). According to S.J. Percival, the torc was 'found near Walton Castle, Clevedon, Somerset: about 20oz [567g] was found but it was mostly melted by Parson & Son, Bristol' (Franks catalogue held by the Department of Britain, Europe and Prehistory, British Museum).

The buffer terminal is hollow and is ornamented in relief on the flat face and around the edges (**Fig. 21.11c**). The decoration on the face is arranged in a triangular pattern with raised detail and three motifs filled with basket-hatching. The side is decorated with a series of adjoined cusp motifs also filled with basket-hatching and linked by a raised sinuous line. The neck-ring fragment is a Stage III construction: (3PZ(2P))R. Three ropes are plied together Z-twist; each rope is formed of two circular-section wires plied together S-twist.

Both Clarke (1954, 64, note 6) and Jope (2000, 85, 254, pl. 120) argued the neck-ring does not belong to the terminal. Jope even suggested the terminal belongs to a tubular torc. Based on the description of the discovery from the Franks catalogue this seems unlikely. Although the surviving strand is not thick enough to form the neck-ring, the original neck-ring could have been formed of multiple ropes (perhaps three or four) of this type, the substantial remains of which were lamentably melted down by Parson & Son. Machling and Williamson (2019) have suggested that parts of the terminal might be from a reworked torus terminal similar to that seen on the Snettisham 'Great Torc'.

41. Ham Hill, Somerset

Location: Museum of Somerset, Taunton

At least three multi-strand iron torcs with loop terminals and a plain iron neck-ring have been recovered from Ham Hill Hillfort, the latter in a burial. See similar multi-strand iron torcs from Camerton, Danebury and Spetisbury.

1. Plain iron ring found in an inhumation burial excavated within the hillfort, worn around the neck. Other grave goods with the individual included an iron chisel and adze (Anon. 1886, 82, pl. III.2; Whimster 1981, 239; Smith 1905, 138; Fitzpatrick 1999, 114).
2. Iron multi-strand torc with single-loop terminals and neck-ring formed from two wires or rods plied together Z-twist: (2PZ)R. Found during quarrying on the site in 1930 (Thomas 1965, pl. 270; Fitzpatrick 1999, 114).
3. Iron multi-strand torc with single-loop terminals and neck-ring formed from two wires or rods plied together, with a linking bar through the terminals. Found at the foot of a quarry face, probably eroded out of pits on the site (Fitzpatrick 1999, 113–15).
4. As no. 3 and found interlinked with no. 3 at the terminals (Fitzpatrick 1999, 113–15).

42. Polden Hills, Somerset

Location: British Museum (1846,0322.117 and 118)

A simple buffer terminal torc formed of an iron core with six copper alloy wires coiled around it (Brailsford 1975b, 230, pl. XXi, e). The torc was found in a hoard mostly comprising horse harness gear and trappings, first reported in 1803, from the Polden Hills, Somerset. The material from the hoard dates from *c.* AD 43–70 (Davis and Gwilt 2008, 164).

43. Alrewas, Staffordshire

Location: Potteries Museum and Art Gallery, Stoke-on-Trent

The hoard was discovered in July 1994 by a metal detectorist, Mrs Emma Gray, at Overley Farm, Alrewas, Staffordshire (Hautenauve 2005, 255–6, no. 224, fig. 349). It contained a group of three gold/silver alloy multi-strand torcs or torc fragments (1–3), a circular-section penannular gold/silver alloy ring (4) and a length of narrow, circular-section gold alloy wire (5). The torcs were bent out of shape in antiquity, bundled together and passed through the ring. The wire fragment (5), which is coiled into a spiral, was also looped through the ring (4). A separate fragment (6, one of the buffer terminals of torc 1) probably became detached from the bundle of artefacts during recent agricultural activity. The hoard was declared Treasure Trove (TT 336) on 3 May 1996 and was later acquired by the Potteries Museum and Art Gallery, Stoke-on-Trent. Further investigation of the site was attempted by Dr Ian Stead of the British Museum, but plans were abandoned when the landowner insisted on financial reward for any potential further finds.

1. Fragment of gold/silver alloy multi-strand torc neck-ring, broken at both ends. Formed from six wires (three circular-section, three twisted), coiled around a hollow core. Stage II construction: (6C)[3R+3T].
2. Gold/silver alloy multi-strand torc with loop terminals and neck-ring formed from three circular-section wires plied together. Stage II construction: (3P)R. The whole torc is formed from a single wire: each terminal comprises one continuous loop where the wire is doubled back on itself, and one open loop. At one terminal this open loop is incomplete, and the wire hammered partly flat around the continuous loop; this terminal may be unfinished. The whole torc is distorted, pulled open, bent near the centre, and slightly untwisted.
3. Gold/silver alloy multi-strand torc with loop terminals and neck-ring formed from three twisted wires plied together. Stage II construction: (3P)T. The whole torc is formed from a single wire: each terminal comprises one continuous loop of twisted wire where it is doubled back on itself, and one open loop formed from the circular-section end of the wire. The whole torc is distorted into a T-shape, with the folded body of the torc forming the double-thickness stem of the 'T' and the terminal ends crossed and bent to form the two halves of the cross-bar. The ring (4) passes through the centre of the cross-bar of the T.
4. A gold/silver alloy penannular ring of thick circular-section wire.

5. A length of gold/silver alloy wire bent to form a spiral ring. A droplet of melted gold is also visible on the wire.
6. Fragment of gold/silver alloy multi-strand torc comprising a short length of neck-ring and one simple buffer terminal. The neck-ring construction is as for fragment 1, (6C)[3R+3T], and this most likely represents one of the missing pieces of this torc. The simple cap terminal was not cast on; instead it is formed from sheet metal hammered onto the neck-ring wires.

The artefacts were analysed using non-destructive surface XRF for the Treasure Trove report. The semi-quantitative results were as follows:

- Torc 1: 78% gold, 20% silver, 1.3% copper
- Torc 2: 71% gold, 26% silver, 2.4% copper
- Torc 3: 67% gold, 29% silver, 4.1% copper
- Ring 4: 72% gold, 27% silver, 1.5% copper
- Ring 5: 71% gold, 26% silver, 2.4% copper
- Torc 6: 78% gold, 20% silver, 1.6% copper

44. Glascote, Tamworth, Staffordshire

Location: Birmingham Museum

A complete gold/silver alloy multi-strand torc with triple-ring terminals (Painter 1970; 1971; details of metal analysis by M.J. Hughes in Painter 1971; Jope 2000, 84, 254, pl. 119; Hautenauve 2005, 234, no. 138). The torc was found around 1943 by two workers while digging a trench at a boat building yard situated by the Coventry Canal, between Glascote and Amington, near Tamworth, Staffordshire. It was identified and declared Treasure Trove in 1970.

The Stage III neck-ring comprises six ropes coiled together Z-twist around a hollow core, each rope made up of two circular-section wires plied together S-twist: (6CZ(2P))R. The mixed twist directions created a braided effect. One wire is broken near the back of the torc. The ring terminal is a merged triple loop, with significant additional metal added onto the neck-ring wires, decorated with two punched lines of zig-zag decoration between the three loops. The ring terminals are continuous with the neck-ring wires, each of the three ring elements extending into two of the ropes.

Whilst unusual, the torc exhibits strong similarities to finds from Snettisham. The neck-ring construction and general form of the triple terminal is very similar to torc L.16, and the zig-zag decoration between the loops of the merged ring terminal is similar to that seen on L.18.

Metal analysis for the Treasure Trove report revealed the metal content at the surface:

- Wire: 29.8% gold; 41.9% silver; 27.2% copper
- Terminal: 53.9% gold; 36.6% silver; 9.9% copper

45. Leekfrith, Staffordshire

Location: Potteries Museum and Art Gallery, Stoke-on-Trent

Metal-detected find made in 2016, acquired by the Potteries Museum. The hoard comprises four objects. Although disturbed by ploughing, it appears that they were placed into the ground as a single nested deposit, near the top of a low hill. The two thistle terminal torcs and the bracelet have their closest parallels on the continent, dating from the 4th to 3rd centuries BC (see also the find from Caistor, above). Imports from this period are rare in Britain (Joy 2015). The torcs were tested using non-destructive XRF at Birmingham Museums Conservation Laboratory by Pieta Greaves (Drakon Heritage and Conservation), assisted by Teresa Gilmore (Birmingham Museums). The results showed a relatively consistent surface composition across all four objects of 74–78% gold, 18–22% silver, 2–3% copper, with small amounts of iron (0.3–1.5%), which may be from the soil. The lower gold purity of the torcs compared to continental pieces leaves open the possibility that these objects could have been made in Britain, even if undoubtedly based on continental types (Farley *et al.* 2018).

1. Gold alloy torc with a plain, circular-section neck-ring which expands towards thistle-shaped buffer terminals. Each terminal consists of a circular 'bead', narrowing towards a slimmer waist and then flaring out to a trumpet-shaped head with slightly concave circular face. Each terminal is decorated with concentric lines around either side of the 'bead' and the wide external edge of the 'trumpet'. It also has stamped decoration in the form of small triple-circle motifs where each end of the neck-ring meets its terminal. The torc has been bent out of shape but is otherwise in very good condition.
2. Gold alloy torc with a plain, circular-section neck-ring which expands towards thistle-shaped buffer terminals. Similar to no. 1, but slimmer and less ornate in form. The circular inner face of each 'trumpet' head has an irregular polygonal indentation, but the surface is otherwise undecorated. The torc is broken into two pieces, probably plough damage along an existing stress line in the metal, and its shape is distorted.
3. Gold alloy torc formed from a pair of circular-section gold wires plied around one another. At either end, the two wires are hammered and soldered together to form a single rod, which is bent back on itself in a hair-pin bend. The two ends are hooked together to form a simple clasp. Each clasp terminates in a small trumpet-shaped knob with concave circular face. The torc has been bent into an irregular shape as if it has been 'folded'; this was probably caused by plough damage.
4. Gold alloy bracelet with flared trumpet-shaped terminals, a variant of the thistle type, with smaller and simpler circular buffer ends, though with the same concave circular face. The outside of each terminal is decorated with three pelta-shaped loops of gold wire creating a fan-like motif. The surface of the bracelet is decorated with chased or engraved lines which fan out from the centre of the motif towards the sides. The overall effect creates an unusual design which may be connected to Early Style traditions of Celtic art, referencing Mediterranean motifs such as the Greek palmette. The body of the bracelet is made from four 'wires' twisted around one another Z-twist. Two are thick strips extending from the terminals, each flattened into a U-shape. The other pair, which spiral around the central join between the larger two, are thin lengths of square-section wire which have been tightly twisted on themselves to give a rope-like effect.

46. Needwood Forest, Staffordshire

Location: Property of the Crown (Duchy of Lancaster), on loan to the British Museum (DR.40)

A gold/silver alloy multi-strand torc found at the mouth of a fox hole in Needwood Forest in 1848 (Ellis 1849; Hawkes 1936; Jope 2000, 84, 254, pl. 118; metal analysis by M. J. Hughes in Painter 1971, 309; Hautenauve 2005, 237, no. 151). The ring terminals are cast onto the ends of the neck-ring wires, and give the impression of two merged loops. The outside edge of each terminal is decorated with nine raised pellets. Each is further ornamented with incised decoration positioned between the two loops, including zig-zag lines. The Stage IV neck-ring comprises four cables loosely plied together Z-twist. Each cable is formed from two ropes plied together S-twist and each rope is formed from four circular-section wires coiled together S-twist: (4PZ(2P(4P)))R. The mixture of twist directions creates a complex visual effect.

Surface metal analysis for the Treasure Trove inquiry showed:

- Wire: 65.9% gold; 29.4% silver; 5.63% copper
- Terminal: 50.0% gold; 30.6% silver; 17.2% copper

47. Shenstone, Staffordshire

Location: Unknown

Metal-detecting in 2019 uncovered a fragment comprising around half of a copper alloy torc with thistle-headed buffer terminals and solid circular-section neck-ring (WMID-62A518). The break appears to be in an area of natural weakness in the metal and may be due to plough damage rather than deliberate fragmentation. The torc most likely dates to the 4th to 2nd centuries BC and is most widely paralleled on the continent. Similar finds have been made in Britain in the River Medway near Aylesford and the River Walbrook, in London.

48. Great Finborough, near Stowmarket, Suffolk

Location: Unknown

A fragment of folded gold sheet with decoration similar to that seen on the terminals of the Snettisham 'Great Torc' was discovered by a metal detectorist in 1996 (Anon. 1997, 86, fig. 17.G). As the find was made before the Treasure Act (1996) came into place in July 1996, it was processed under Treasure Trove (TT 384) and returned to the finder. The fragment has been deliberately cut and folded, but was probably originally part of the torus terminal of a multi-strand torc.

49. Ipswich, Suffolk

Location: British Museum (1969,0103.1–5 and 1971,0203.1)

A hoard of six gold/silver alloy multi-strand torcs (Brailsford 1968; Brailsford and Stapley 1972; Owles 1969; 1970; Jope 2000, pls 116–17; Hautenauve 2005, 235–6, nos 142–7). The findspot is on higher land (30.5m OD), 3.2km east of Ipswich town centre, overlooking a tributary of the Belstead Brook (Owles 1969, 208). The first five torcs were discovered on 26 October 1968 by Mr Malcolm Tricker while operating a mechanical digger. The sixth torc was found on 18 October 1970 by Mr P.J. Gorham whilst digging in his garden at 50 Holcombe Crescent. The findspot of the sixth torc was around 65m from the original hoard. It is thought all six torcs originated from the same hoard but the sixth torc was separated during earth-moving at the site (Owles 1970, 294; Brailsford and Stapley 1972, 219) which involved cutting back a part of the hillside to enlarge the gardens on Holcombe Crescent (Owles 1969, 208).

The first two torcs uncovered in 1968 were hooked together. Mr Tricker uncovered three more also linked (Owles 1969, 208; Brailsford and Stapley 1972, 219). In a letter to John Brailsford dated 12 November 1968 and located in the correspondence archive held by the Department of Britain, Europe and Prehistory at the British Museum, the finder is quoted as saying: 'I should think they were in the soil at an angle of 45 degrees, about six feet [1.8m] down. Having pulled out the first, I discovered a second attached to it. Laying close by, at the same angle, I found another one, and this time two were entangled with it. One of these being the plain one, and the rest all patterned.' On later inspection of the findspot Owles concluded: '… there was no trace of a pit, either at the level at which the torcs were found or in the area above it. The top soil had already slipped down the slope and it seems likely that the torcs were lying fairly close to the surface and that they too had fallen from a higher level. There was no evidence of a burial' (Owles 1969, 208).

1. Gold/silver alloy multi-strand torc with thickened ring terminals and Stage II neck-ring of two faceted wires plied together Z-twist: (2PZ)F. (1969,0103.1)
2. to 5. Gold/silver alloy multi-strand torcs with ring terminals. The terminals are elaborately decorated with curvilinear designs in relief and were formed using the lost-wax technique (Stapley in Brailsford and Stapley 1972). The neck-rings each comprise two thick faceted wires plied together. On three of the torcs this is S-twist, while on one (1969,0103.2) it is Z-twist. Brailsford (in Brailsford and Stapley 1972, 220–1) suggested the decoration on torcs 2–5 is unfinished due to its rough appearance. This argument was challenged by Spratling (in Wainwright and Spratling 1973, 123–4), following his work on the moulds from Gussage All Saints. (1969,0103.2–5)
6. Gold/silver alloy multi-strand torc with torus terminals cast or soldered onto the neck-ring. The Stage III neck-ring is formed of two ropes plied together S-twist, each of which is made up of two thick, faceted wires plied together Z-twist: (2P(2PZ))F. The mixture of twist directions creates the impression of a braid. The terminals resemble triple-ring terminals, with zig-zag decoration around the outside of the eye of the ring, and lines of simple beaded decoration running around the circumference of the joins between the rings. The narrow collar is decorated with a herringbone pattern, suggesting a braid. (1971,0203.1)

Metal analysis for the Treasure Trove inquest revealed the following surface compositions::

- Torc 1 terminal: 80.2% gold; 12.4% silver; 4.4% copper
  neck-ring: 81.3% gold; 16.7% silver; 2.0% copper
- Torc 2 terminal: 78.1% gold; 10.1% silver; 11.8% copper
  neck-ring: 65.9% gold; 27.8% silver; 6.3% copper
- Torc 3 terminal: 85.5% gold; 10.7% silver; 1.3% copper
  neck-ring: 80.6% gold; 18.8% silver; 0.4% copper
- Torc 4 terminal: 88.7% gold; 11.3% silver; 1.8% copper
  neck-ring: 85.2% gold; 11.0% silver; 0.7% copper

- Torc 5 terminal: 82.0% gold; 16.9% silver; 1.6% copper neck-ring: 77.3% gold; 16.9% silver; 1.4% copper
- Torc 6 neck-ring: 84.0% gold; 15.0% silver; 0.3% copper

50. Shepherd's Fen, Suffolk

Location: Museum of Archaeology and Anthropology, Cambridge (1929.186)

Penannular copper alloy bracelet found in Shepherd's Fen near Mildenhall around 1930 (Lethbridge and O'Reilly 1931, 152, pl. VI, fig. 1). A simple one-piece ornament with body formed from circular-section rod and expanded buffer terminals with stylised curvilinear zoomorphic decoration. Closest in form to the thistle terminal torcs seen in the UK at Aylesford, Shenstone and Walbrook.

51. Netherurd, Kirkurd, Tweeddale (also known as 'Cairnmuir' or 'New Cairnmuir')

Location: National Museum of Scotland (FE46–48) (some finds lost)

Found in March 1806 in a hollow on the side of Shaw Hill, near New Cairnmuir house, Kirkurd, Peeblesshire (Lawson 1858; Feachem 1958; MacGregor 1976, nos 191–4; Jope 2000, 81–4, 253, pl. 110.). Confusion over the name given to the hoard derives from changes to the name of the nearby house which gives the hoard its title.

Three bracelets and a torc fragment were found with 'upwards of 40 gold coins' of which only two survive (Feachem 1958, 112). The remaining coins are both Gallo-Belgic XB. The distribution of this type of coin is focused in an area north-east of Paris (Hunter 1997, 515). The only other known examples from Britain are all from Dorset and the type dates from the late 2nd century BC–mid-1st century BC (Fitzpatrick 1992b, 10; Haselgrove 2009).

Of the torcs, only the terminal (4) remains; the others were sold/and or destroyed. Fortunately, illustrations of the torcs were published (Lawson 1858 1833; Feachem 1958).

1. and 2. Two gold/silver alloy multi-strand bracelets with double-loop terminals and Stage II bodies formed from two circular-section wires plied together Z-twist: (2PZ)R (Hautenauve 2005, 233, no. 134).
3. Gold/silver alloy bracelet formed from a single, twisted square-section wire. The terminals are solid, flattened and point outwards (Hautenauve 2005, 233, no. 135).
4. Gold/silver alloy hollow torus terminal, probably originally from a multi-strand torc (identified by Clarke 1951a, 60; Hautenauve 2005, 233, no. 133). The terminal is decorated with raised lobes, petals and cusps, defined by hatching. See also Machling and Williamson (2018).

52. Middleton Hall, Middleton, Warwickshire (near Tamworth, Staffordshire)

Location: British Museum (1977,0401.1)

Gold/silver alloy multi-strand torc fragment comprising a neck-ring of six braided ropes (Hautenauve 2005, 237, no. 150). Each rope is formed of two circular-section wires twisted together. Both terminals are missing. The torc was found by Mrs G.M. Sadler while working land at Middleton Hall, Warwickshire in October 1968. It was identified in 1976, declared Treasure Trove in 1977 and acquired by the British Museum. Metal analysis conducted for the Treasure Trove inquiry showed the surface metal content was 74% silver, 25% gold and 1% copper.

53. Westhampnett, West Sussex

Location: Chichester and District Museum

A small fragment of gold alloy sheet found in burial 20095 at the Late Iron Age cremation cemetery at Westhampnett is believed to be from a tubular torc (Fitzpatrick 1997, 97–9, 149). The burial contained the cremated remains of an infant or young juvenile and an older sub-adult. The remains have been radiocarbon dated to 200–80 cal BC (95% probability; Haselgrove *et al.* 2018, table 1). Metallurgical analysis of the surface of the fragment showed a composition of around 89% gold, 10% silver and 1% copper.

54. Pershore, Worcestershire

Location: British Museum (2014,8003.1–2)

Two gold/silver alloy fragments associated with a coin hoard found in 1993 near Pershore in Worcestershire are likely torc fragments. The discovery comprised 1,494 Iron Age gold and silver coins, mostly of the Western regional series, struck *c.* 40 BC–AD 50 (Hurst and Leins 2013).

1. Short length of thick, coiled, gold/silver alloy wire, cut at both ends. Probably originally part of a multi-strand torc neck-ring. Surface XRF carried out as part of the Treasure process indicated a composition of 67% gold, 32% silver and 1% copper.
2. Fragment of gold/silver alloy sheet, possibly from a tubular torc. The sheet takes the form of a rectangular strip which tapers and is pierced at both ends.

Torcs of unknown type and/or location

55. Dorchester, Dorset

Smith recorded an iron torc from Dorchester but its whereabouts are unknown and we have no detailed description of the artefact (Smith 1905, 138). It is possible this is a mistaken reference to the iron torc from Spetisbury, Dorset (see above).

56. Arras, East Riding of Yorkshire

A copper alloy torc said to have been five and a half inches (140mm) in diameter (Greenwell 1906, 275) was discovered in burial A5 at the Arras cemetery (Stead 1979, 80 and 98). The burial also contained nine small jet beads and a copper alloy wheel ornament (Greenwell 1906, 301). According to an account in a letter by a Dr Hull (noted by Greenwell 1906, 275), the torc was found around the neck of the individual it was buried with. The torc was not illustrated and is now lost. Unfortunately, there is no detailed description of the torc.

57. Birdlip, Gloucestershire

A gold alloy multi-strand torc fragment recovered from Birdlip in 1947 may have been a grave good from one of the nearby burials (Staelens 1982, 21). There is no clear account of its discovery and it is now lost, but an illustration survives (Green 1949, 188, fig. 1a). This appears to show part of the neck-ring of a multi-strand torc formed from three wires plied together. There are wire knots or similar forms of ornamentation equally spaced along the remaining length. One end is broken, whilst the other appears to have the surviving remains of a solid wire loop terminal.

58. Marham, Norfolk

An account of the discovery and a brief description of a torc found at Marham, Norfolk, thought to have been discarded, was recorded by Natasha Hutcheson (2004, 43): 'The example from Marham, which unfortunately was thrown away (SMR 0855) ... was described as being similar to the North Creake and Sedgeford examples and the "best Snettisham" torc. Given that the reference to the Marham torc was made in 1966, it is likely that the torc referred to is the Great Torc from hoard E.' The location of the find is a low-lying valley within a gently undulating landscape (Hutcheson 2007, 360).

59. Narford, Norfolk (TT 132)

Natasha Hutcheson (2004, 43) reported the find of several gold/silver alloy multi-strand torcs at Narford: '... part of a buffer terminal torc, which was partly melted and had fragments of twisted bar and loop terminal torcs fused to it, was recovered by metal detector in 1980–81. A complete elongated loop terminal torc was subsequently recovered from Narford, as were a number of wire fragments (SMR 3974). Unfortunately, none of the material from this site went to the local museum, it was recovered at night and then sold to an antiquities dealer, consequently there is no illustration, photograph or full report on these artefacts' (Hutcheson 2004, 43). The Narford torcs were found within 200m of the River Nar (Hutcheson 2007, 361).

60. Pattington, Staffordshire

Found in 1700, no further details known (Ellis 1849, 176).

61. Mildenhall, Suffolk

A gold torc was reportedly found in 1812 in an extended inhumation burial also containing two horses. The torc is said to have been melted down by a silversmith at Bury St Edmunds. Other grave goods included an iron sword and a 'celt' (Bunbury 1834, 610; Fox 1923, 81, 86; 1958, 10–11, 20; Clarke 1939, 43; Stead 1965, 9; Sealey 1979, 175).

62. Wallingford, Suffolk

Location: Unknown

Five gold torcs are reported to have been ploughed up on the Henham estate (grid ref. TM4478) perhaps in the 1930s. Thought to have been made of brass, they were slung in a ditch. The discovery is recorded by the Suffolk HER and was reported by an old man to M.J. Hardy of Metfield in 1984 (HAM 036, https://heritage.suffolk.gov.uk/Monument/MSF458). Apparently, a boy had kept one and put it on his bicycle, but he later sold it to a scrap metal merchant.

63. Rawden Billing, Yeadon, West Yorkshire

Found in 1781 (Whitaker 1816). Few details known, although from the description of the torc as 'consisting of two rods not quite cylindrical but growing thinner towards the extremities and twisted together', the object is perhaps more likely to be Viking period in date.

Unprovenanced torcs, possibly from Britain

64. Location: British Museum (OA.10883)

Gold alloy tubular torc with buffer terminals. The neck-ring is knotted on one side (James and Rigby 1997, 46, fig. 54). It was in the British Museum collections as early as 1846 but no provenance is known (Birch 1846, 31). Smith (1905, 56) originally suggested the torc was probably from France but later amended this to 'without locality' (Smith 1925, 62). Nonetheless, the torc is often viewed as continental, as is evidenced by its inclusion in Jacobsthal's catalogue of European Celtic art objects (1969 [1944], 169, no. 40, pl. 33). Hautenauve (2005, 256, no. 228) included it in her catalogue of British torcs, citing similarities with some of the tubular torc fragments found in Hoard F at Snettisham.

65. Location: Unknown

Gold/silver alloy multi-strand torc or bracelet with single-loop terminals, sold at Christie's, London, 7 December 1994, lot 172 (Anon. 1994, 91). The neck-ring or body is formed of two thick, circular-section wires plied together, and the terminals form continuous loops with these wires. The torc/bracelet is distorted into a loose spiral, with one of the loops overlapping the other. The auction catalogue states that the gold content of the object is '97% pure'.

Chapter 23
Interpreting Snettisham: What do Hoards 'do'?

Jody Joy and Julia Farley

This chapter focuses on the Snettisham hoards asking what hoards do and exploring their potentially transformative effects. Above all it is concluded that, although the deposits are clearly related, it is not productive to view the Snettisham hoards as a whole, as a single 'treasure'. Each hoard is different, with different collection and depositional histories. Individual hoards 'did' something different. They are of course related: they were all deposited in an appropriate place of importance. We argue that when interpreting hoards in archaeology we should approach them as a related and useful category, but from the perspective of individual depositional events with their own distinctive identity and narrative.

The chapter is divided into two main parts. The first examines the phenomenon of hoarding more broadly, it explores previous interpretations of the deposits at Snettisham, and gives a detailed examination of the structure of the individual hoards. The second presents a model for understanding the social role of hoarding at Snettisham in terms of a shift from a 'world of torcs' to a 'world of coins'.

Interpreting Snettisham: what do hoards 'do'?

Approaching hoards

Bradley defined hoards as 'collections of buried objects that were apparently deposited together on the same occasion' (Bradley 2013, 122). Hoards are found throughout many parts of the world, and across broad expanses of time. In Europe, it is possible to trace a continual sequence of hoarding lasting 5,000 years (Bradley 1996, 306). Despite its longevity and variety, general explanations of hoarding have remained oddly consistent in the 150 or so years since the phenomenon was first identified and discussed (Fontijn 2002, 15–19, table 2.3). Debates have primarily centred on motivations and intentions. For example, were hoards deposited for safekeeping, with the purpose of later retrieval as is so famously exemplified in Samuel Pepys's diaries? If so, why did so many hoards go unrecovered (Fontijn 2002, 14)? And why are there identifiable patterns in the location and contents of deposits?

In recent decades, long-standing assumptions about hoards have seen significant challenge and revision. For example, the division between hoards and single finds has been questioned (Bradley 2013), as have the distinctions often made between dryland and watery deposits (Yates and Bradley 2010a; 2010b). As Strang (2005) cautioned, there are many 'different kinds of water'; with artefacts deposited in rivers, lakes, meres and bogs, distinctions between dry and wet are sometimes difficult to reconcile. More broadly, much discussion has taken place over the use of 'ritual' to describe practices perceived as above and beyond functional necessity and that defy explanation from a modern-day perspective. As Brück (1999) and Bradley (2005) have both argued, this creates an opposition between ritual and everyday activities which might be artificial, or at least anachronistic. The dominance of metalwork in discussions of hoards has also been noted. For example, a class of ceramic hoards has been identified in Central Europe consisting of deposits of fine vessels (Bradley 2013, 121), and in faunal studies there has been much discussion of 'Articulated/Associated Bone Groups' as often representing intentional deposits (Hill 1995; Morris 2010). Finally, Joy (2016) argued that owing to the concentration of discussion on questions of motivation and intentionality, too much attention has been paid to the moment of deposition as opposed to the collection and accumulation of artefacts (exceptions cited by Joy include: Dietrich 2014; Garrow and Gosden 2012, ch. 5; Hansen 1996–8).

Iron Age hoarding

As Joy has highlighted (in Baldwin and Joy 2017, 107), with the notable exception of Haselgrove (2015) and Wilkinson (2019), the examination of hoarding practices has occupied a marginal position in Iron Age studies compared to the extensive literature on Bronze Age hoards. Discussion has tended to focus on deposition at individual sites, on regional surveys (e.g. Hunter 1997; Hutcheson 2004) or on specific artefact types and materials (e.g. Haselgrove and Hingley 2006; Hingley 1990; 1997; 2005; 2006; Joy 2014). Mirroring the trends identified above, interpretations of Iron Age hoards have shifted over time from deposits intended for safekeeping and later retrieval to examples of votive deposition. Few though have considered further what votive deposition might entail. A notable exception is Sharples (2010, 96–7) who, following Godelier's (1999, 155) account of potlatches undertaken by the people of the north-west coast of North America, argued that hoarding created relationships between people and gods through the conspicuous consumption and mass destruction of objects. Fitzpatrick (2005) also discussed the idea that damage to objects could enable the transfer of metaphysical essence.

Owing to the identification of deliberate deposition in varied domestic contexts, particularly pits (e.g. Hill's ground-breaking (1995) study centred on Wessex, see also Cunliffe 1993; Sharples 2010), hoards have tended to be subsumed into a wider category of deliberate or special deposit. As Garrow and Gosden (2012, 157) argued, this has created significant 'blurring of the boundaries' between different types of deposition. Haselgrove (2015) also suggested that no rigid distinction should be made between hoards and other types of deposit. Related to these ideas are wider concerns already identified with the potentially artificial distinctions made by prehistorians between ritual and the everyday (Brück 1999; Bradley 2005).

In sum, the term 'hoard' is clearly problematic and encompasses a huge range of different motivations and behaviours. Nevertheless, the practice was long-lasting and widespread, and the idea of the hoard remains a useful category as long as each one is treated as a discrete deposit with a unique collection and depositional history, rather than attributing universal motivations and explanations. The perspective adopted here is that, as Garrow and Gosden (2012) neatly expressed it, hoards '…brought groups of artefacts together and might in the process also have brought groups of people together, in some cases at least' (*ibid.*, 191). Whatever the intentions and motivations behind their deposition, hoards also provide 'snap shots' or 'time traps' of networks of people, places and things. They provide a window on past relationships, a rare instance in which these survive into the present, albeit in a stage-managed manner (Garrow and Gosden 2012, 156; Joy 2016, 242; see also Wingfield 2013, 80).

A history of interpretations of Snettisham

Before presenting a more detailed examination of the Snettisham hoards, it is first necessary to briefly discuss how they have been interpreted in the literature. In his publication of the earlier finds and excavations at Snettisham (including Hoards A–E), Rainbird Clarke (1954, 70) interpreted the discoveries as smiths' or founders' hoards. As justification, he cited the valuable and portable nature of the material, as well as the hammering, working and dismemberment of the objects, which he related to the activities of metalworkers. According to Clarke, 'the Snettisham treasure, then, may represent the culmination of a successful business career, the banking in the ground of the accumulated acquisitions of a lifetime' (*ibid.*, 70). Two other possibilities were also put forward by Clarke (*ibid.*, 71): that the material was the possession of 'aristocratic refugees' from south-east England; or loot accumulated through raiding. All three of his interpretations were based on the opinion that many of the objects from Snettisham were manufactured outside of Norfolk because at the time the only other torcs found nearby for Clarke to consider were those from Bawsey and North Creake (see Gazetteer in Ch. 22). He therefore had to account for how the material got there, either via mobile craftspeople, refugees, or through tribal raiding. The idea that some of the objects reached Norfolk in the form of gifts was also considered (Clarke 1954, 70). Whilst it is undoubtedly true that many of the finds from Snettisham (including the potin coins, and the Gallo-Belgic coinage) came from outside Norfolk, subsequent discoveries have revealed a high concentration of torcs and related finds in north-west Norfolk, rendering much of Clarke's considered argument obsolete for the bulk of the objects represented at the site, many of which may well in fact have been locally made.

Thirty-five years later, in his interim report on the British Museum excavations at Snettisham, Stead (1991a, 463) maintained Clarke's position that the hoards were deposited for safekeeping. He suggested that: 'perhaps they should be seen as a gradual accumulation of wealth – a veritable treasury. The quantity of the treasure was the possession of more than one individual – perhaps a family, or even a tribe.' Elsewhere Stead reiterated his position: 'the entire treasure, some 20kg of silver and 15kg of gold, is surely more than the savings of an individual and must represent the wealth of a community. Perhaps it was a tribal treasury' (Stead 1996, 49).

Much of the popular literature has followed Stead's interpretation (e.g. Hobbs 2003, 137–43). Others have suggested the hoards were buried for safekeeping ahead of Caesar's invasions (e.g. Rodwell 1976, 198–203; Cunliffe 1991, 120), or they have drawn on the potential significance of the choice of location for deposition, situated on a conspicuous promontory overlooking the Wash (e.g. Hutcheson 2011, 44).

As Stead's interpretation has been so influential, it is worth detailed consideration here. Stead did consider the possibility of a votive interpretation, noting accepted Iron Age votive deposits from watery contexts and sanctuary sites. However, he correctly pointed out that watery deposits, 'only very rarely … include a torque' and that in Britain 'votive deposits in Iron Age sanctuaries at Hayling Island, Hampshire, and Harlow, Essex, do not seem to have included a torque, nor do they feature collections of other artefacts buried in small pits' (Stead 1991a, 462). He does not dismiss the possibility of offerings in the case of other, smaller torc hoards found elsewhere: 'None … was found at a known temple site, and none was associated with undoubted votive deposits, but it is still possible that they had been offerings' (*ibid.*, 459). Despite this, he came down in favour of a 'treasury' or savings hoards at Snettisham for a number of reasons (*ibid.*, 459–63). These included the restricted range of artefacts (especially when compared to the broad range of finds from some contemporary sanctuaries and temple sites such as Hayling Island), the inclusion of objects at a range of different stages, from apparently unfinished pieces to 'scrap from the metalsmith's workshop', which he suggested 'seems unparalleled in an Iron Age votive deposit' (*ibid.*, 463), and the fact that the hoards were hidden, with the pit deposits structured according to metal content: 'The disposition of Hoard L suggests that some of the more precious [gold-rich alloy] items were given greater protection, with a less valuable [copper and silver-rich] "decoy" hoard nearer the surface' (*ibid.*, 463). In sum, he argued that, 'although the suggestion that the Snettisham hoards belonged to a treasury leaves some questions unanswered, it is more satisfactory than the votive explanation … The hoards were surely hidden, and the presumption must be that whoever hid them intended to retrieve them' (*ibid.*, 463).

Although he acknowledged that it was possible the Snettisham hoards were offerings, Stead's core argument was somewhat circular: votive offerings are deposited in water or at sanctuaries and because the hoards (and indeed other torc finds) were not discovered in these contexts they are unlikely to have been votive. Emerging literature at the time advocated votive interpretations of dryland hoards, including so-called 'founders' hoards' (see especially Bradley 1990). Although he did refer to other torcs found nearby, Stead's (1991a) article understandably focused on the site of Snettisham itself, rather than considering its place in wider regional depositional practices. Subsequent scholarship (see Hutcheson 2003, 94) has emphasised that Snettisham fits into a pattern of 2nd and 1st-century BC dryland metalwork hoards across Norfolk, particularly at high points in the landscape overlooking rivers or the sea.

In a response to Stead's interim report, Fitzpatrick (1992a) promptly raised many of these issues. First and foremost, he suggested '… it is possible to make a stronger case for the Snettisham hoards being votive than Stead allows' (*ibid.*, 398). He went on to explain that the divisions between sacred and profane may not have been as distinct in the Iron Age as they are today. For Fitzpatrick, the interpretation that the Snettisham hoards represent a treasury therefore may not exclude the fact that their deposition was votive (*ibid.*, 396). He also questioned the influence of the primary concerns of the Treasure Trove law on Stead's interpretation, as the focus of Treasure Trove at the time was to distinguish between burial with the intention of retrieval and other types of deposition (Longworth 1992, 337). These perspectives, he argued, have no relevance to the actions and intentions of people in the past (Fitzpatrick 1992a, 398).

Subsequent discoveries have also changed the picture at Snettisham: Stead's initial interpretation was made before his subsequent seasons of excavation revealed the large enclosure ditch around the 'gold field'. Writing on the subject of Celtic art, Stead later stated: 'It is likely that the ditch was constructed sometime after about AD 100, more than a century and a half after the torques had been deposited. It is tempting to relate the enclosure to the torques that were found near its centre; the ditch was not an impressive defensive work but might have defined an area that had had more formidable defenders, such as ghosts or gods. Whatever its function, the Snettisham site lost its significance in the 1st century AD and the Britons never recovered their treasure' (Stead 1996, 49–50; see also Stead 1995a, 110). It is notable that in this later interpretation there is also consideration of ancient beliefs or superstition. In a similar vein and considering Norfolk torc hoards more generally, Cunliffe stated: 'the strong probability is that these depositions were made within ritual contexts, but only at Snettisham is it possible to begin to define something of the ritual nature of the larger site where the hoards were found' (Cunliffe 2005, 197).

More recent interpretations of Snettisham, which we follow here, have sought to place the discoveries within their wider regional, spatial and temporal context (Chadburn 2006; Davies 1996, 87; 2008, 100–6; Hutcheson 2003; 2004; 2007; 2011). For example, John Davies (1996, 87; 2008, 100–6) saw west and north-west Norfolk as a focus of political power in the early decades of the 1st century BC. In addition to a concentration of elaborate metalwork hoards, he viewed the presence of earthworks and other sites as evidence that this part of Norfolk was probably a focus of maritime trade, with Snettisham as a centre of religious activity of importance to his 'north-west zone' of Norfolk. Joy (2015, 155) also argued that Snettisham's location and aspect were possibly propitious to Iron Age beliefs, citing Steven Willis (2007, 120–1), who noted that a number of Late Iron Age sites interpreted as shrines were located on higher ground overlooking the point where freshwater meets the sea. Joy suggested that siting an important religious site close to the coast may have referenced contacts across the sea: presumably the sources of some of the precious metals used to make torcs, in the form of scrap and coins, and possibly the origin of some of the torcs from the hoards. Interestingly, the Snettisham hoards were not positioned facing the sea, but rather oriented towards the surrounding landscape (Ch. 3): the location was meant to be seen, but with the promontory of Ken Hill and the coastline in the background.

Hutcheson (2003; 2004, ch. 6; 2007) also placed the Snettisham finds within their regional context. Like Davies, Snettisham was not her primary focus. She argued that during the later Iron Age, metalwork was deposited in high places in north-west Norfolk, isolated from settlement. In contrast, where present, human remains and settlements were located on land below 30m OD. Hutcheson also noted patterns in deposition, in particular the inclusion of fragments or 'scrap' in many hoards. In essence, she identified 'rules' of deposition, specific manners in which it was appropriate to deposit particular artefacts. Put succinctly, Hutcheson argued that 'the landscape was structured' (Hutcheson 2003, 95). Like Davies (1996; 2008), Hutcheson (2003; 2007) observed a number of chronological changes in the archaeological record. Towards the end of the 2nd century and ending sometime around 60 BC, north-west Norfolk was the focus of torc deposition, particularly in locations overlooking rivers and adjacent to the Wash. The first coin hoards in the region contained Gallo-Belgic gold coins, but after *c.* 50 BC coin hoards became dominated by local gold issues. After *c.* 20 BC, silver coin hoards were most prevalent, and these were distributed more broadly throughout Norfolk. Davies (1996; 2008) also recorded this shift in the nucleus of activity away from the north-west of the county, not just visible through the deposition of metalwork, but also the location and distribution of settlements. We see this shift away from a focus on north-west Norfolk as important for the changes in deposition that occurred at Snettisham. The 1st-century BC deposits from the site are unique in scale, but later hoards are far more restricted in number and fit into the wider pattern of deposition across Norfolk rather than representing an exceptional regional focus.

Another distinction discussed by Hutcheson (2007, 361) was that between hoards of torcs and single deposits. She noted a correlation between findspots that have been further investigated and those that have not: sites that are excavated often turn up more finds. Most single finds are therefore from sites which have not subsequently been investigated by archaeologists, meaning that single finds may reflect patterns of recovery rather than deposition. The only notable exception to Hutcheson's observation is the Newark Torc, found in Nottinghamshire, where archaeological investigation of the findspot revealed no further finds. But, whilst this torc is of a similar type to Norfolk finds and could have originated in East Anglia, its location is outside of both Hutcheson's study area and the main distributions of such torcs, and thus its making, acquisition, use and deposition may have followed a different trajectory. It is also unclear, as already discussed, if any distinction was drawn between single and multiple deposits in ancient times (Bradley 2013): both involved selecting a location, digging a hole and placing something in the ground. The only major difference is the accumulation of material required before deposition. Contrast, for example, the deposition of a single torc versus the vast collection of artefacts contained in Hoard F.

In sum, although Stead's carefully reasoned account of Snettisham is still popular, many others view it as a religious site or interpret the deposits as votive, though often without much further explanation. Only Davies and Hutcheson offer further thoughts as to what was happening at Snettisham, and where it is located within a broader context of artefact deposition and society. In short, Snettisham is viewed as a centre for ritual activity (Davies 1996, 87) and the concentration of depositional activity in north-west Norfolk between the late 2nd and early 1st centuries BC is seen as reflecting the prominence of a single group, whose success was supported through trade and the acquisition of notable quantities of gold (Hutcheson 2004, 94). As both Davies and Hutcheson examined Norfolk in general, they inferred changes in society from broad trends in the archaeological record rather than closely examining the differences and variation between individual deposits. Here we are able to focus more closely on the different acts of collection and deposition evidenced at a single site. In addition, we will further explore the question of what hoards do, and the potential roles of hoarding in emphasising and consolidating power in the region. This is an aspect that, as Garrow and Gosden (2012, 184) observed, has not been extensively discussed by Davies or Hutcheson.

The nature of the Snettisham hoards

The Snettisham hoards are quite diverse, ranging from only two objects in Hoard D to over 500 in Hoard F. In the following analysis, the Snettisham hoards are viewed as a set of individual (but related) deposits rather than a collective treasure. Nevertheless, it is possible to identify patterns and draw similarities between the hoards. Of those hoards containing torcs, two main types can be identified: tightly packed groups or nests of torcs and hoards made up primarily of fragments (Stead 1991a, 455; Joy 2016, 243). Hoards A, G, H, J, K and L belong to the former and Hoards B, C and F to the latter. Hoards D and E each consist of a single complete torc with (an)other item(s) interlinked through the terminals, and other individual complete torcs were also found in 1964, 1968 and 1973 (Cat. Nos). It is harder to ascribe these finds to either group, but Stead (1991a, 450) suggested that they might have been from 'similar hoards [to G, H, J, K and L], some perhaps from the hoards now discovered'.

Fragmentary hoards

Of the fragmentary hoards, it is now impossible to separate out exactly the contents of Hoards B and C because the objects have become intermixed (Clarke 1954, see Ch. 14). Similarly, because Hoard F was recovered by a metal-detector user, the exact arrangement of the objects in the ground was not recorded, although we know that at least some of the artefacts were contained in a copper alloy helmet (see Chs 8 and 12, and entry for F.445 in Ch. 14). Some relationships between objects can, however, still be inferred, either because they are still linked or where there is a record that they were formerly associated.

As is outlined in Chapter 20, many of the artefacts from all three fragmentary hoards were subjected to a number of different destructive processes before deposition. Broken objects include fragments of torcs and bracelets, and Hoards B and C in particular include broken-up ingots and numerous fragments from simple rectangular-section rings. Examination of broken and deformed edges has revealed evidence for deliberate cutting, bending, squashing and twisting (Ch. 20). Thicker wires or strips were often struck with a sharp-edged tool, possibly a chisel. Some thinner wires have triangular-shaped edges, implying they were cut from both sides, probably by a pair of snips. Other thin

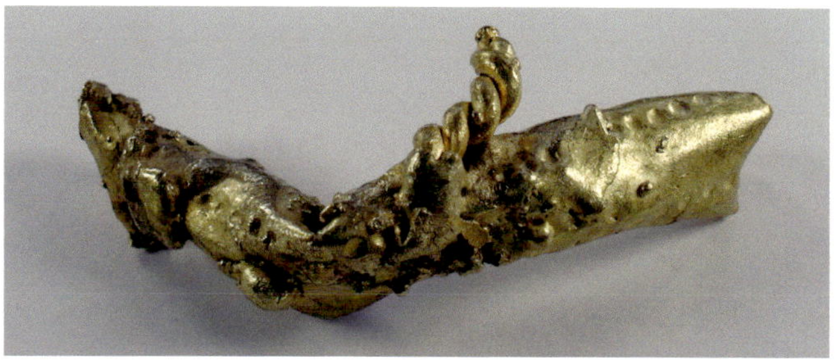

Figure 23.1 Tubular torc fragment F.32 with twisted wire fused onto it

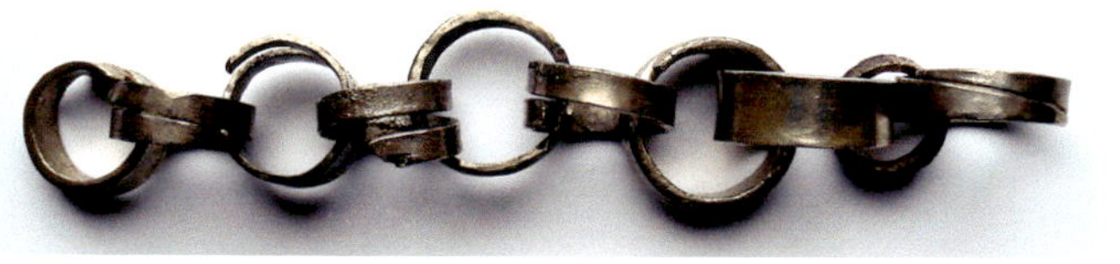

Figure 23.2 F.25a–j: Linked group of small rings

wires, and potentially some of the rectangular-section metal strips, were repeatedly twisted and bent until they snapped.

In contrast to breakage, some fragments, particularly from Hoard F, were fused together into lumps or onto the ends of different objects by partial melting, in effect creating new artefacts or combinations. In many instances a contrast seems to have been sought, for example by fusing simple twisted wires onto a decorated tubular torc fragment (**Fig. 23.1**).

Interlinking is another quality of fragmentary hoards, whereby objects form small but distinct collections or assemblages within the larger whole of the hoard. In its simplest form objects such as groups of rings were linked together by looping (**Fig. 23.2**). Sometimes one object was inserted into another: wires were inserted into tubular torc fragments in groups F.29 and F.30, and five coins were carefully sealed inside tubular torc fragment F.53. Attaching various broken artefacts, particularly torc terminal fragments, onto a large ring was another method employed to create such a group or collection (**Fig. 23.3**). Exact methods of attachment vary, but include looping the ring through the terminal of a torc, through a bent loop of wire, or through rough perforations (especially in the case of tubular torc fragments). There are more than 20 of these collections in Hoard F, and the number of objects in each group ranges from two to the low teens. Their nature varies quite widely but often they are made up of heterogeneous objects with different alloy compositions and a range of colours (**Fig. 23.3**). Whilst the general tendency is towards diversity, there are a handful of cases of very similar interlinked rings (F.25–F.28; **Fig. 23.2**) and sometimes similar fragments are grouped together, even when they are from different torcs, such as the pair of slightly mismatched tubular torc terminals in groups F.1 and F.2 (**Fig. 23.4**). There is also limited but tantalising evidence in the fragmentary hoards for the production and processing of metals, such as the scale pan folded into quarters from Hoard B/C (B/C.23) and the possible wire-sizing stone from Hoard A (A.8). These hoards also contain ingots and small amorphous metal lumps that seem to have solidified from a molten state without being further processed.

Gosden (2013, 46) described Hoard F as a 'nested set of relationships'. One way in which these relationships were manifested is through the selection and arrangement of objects included in the hoard. Examining Hoard F from the perspective of collecting and accumulating objects, Joy (2016) speculated that some of the interlinking occurred as part of the process of gathering artefacts for inclusion in the hoard, physically creating connections between them. He also suggested that these linked artefacts and collections might provide clues as to how a large assemblage like Hoard F was gathered. Citing Late Bronze Age hoards from the Carpathian Basin which contain groupings of artefacts within a larger hoard (Dietrich 2014, 479–80; Hansen 1996–8, 19–23), Joy (2016, 247) suggested that these collections could have been gathered by individuals or groups before being incorporated into the larger

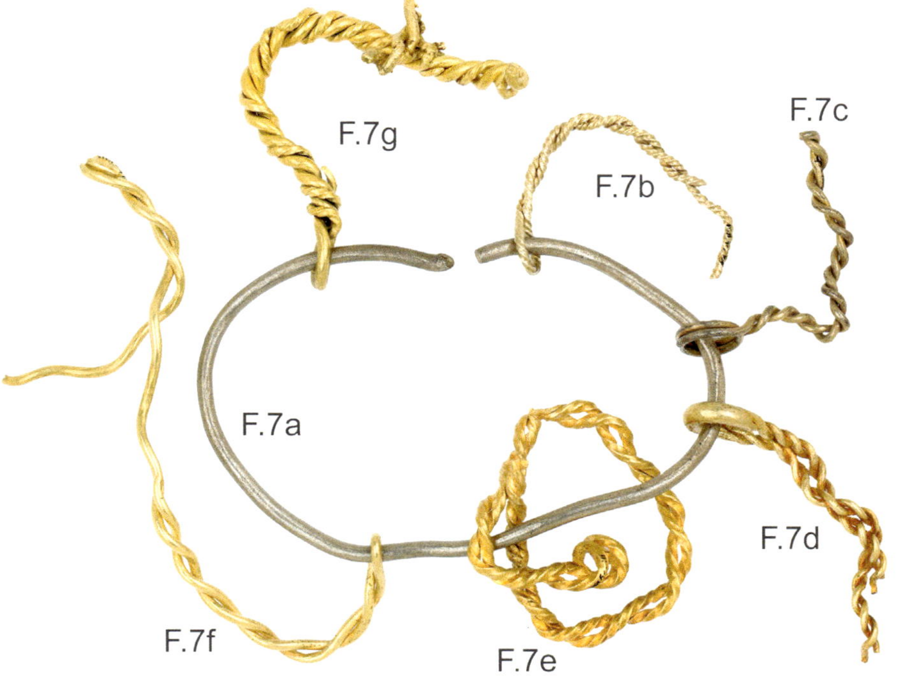

Figure 23.3 F.7a–g: Group of torc/bracelet fragments looped onto a large ring

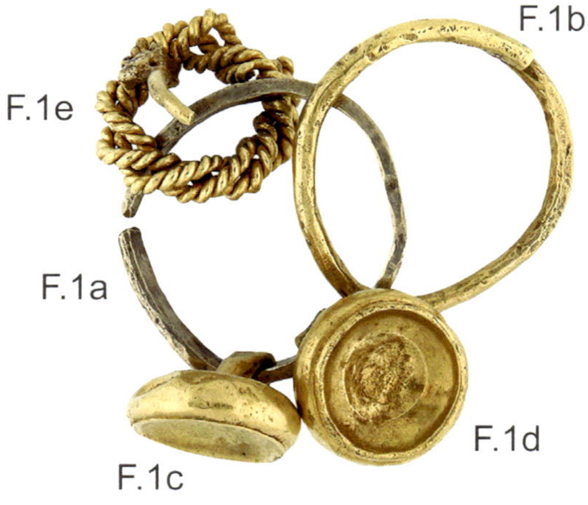

Figure 23.4 F.1a–e: Group of artefacts looped around a large ring

assemblage, representing contributions to a greater whole. Joy speculated that the sets of small rings (potentially finger or toe-rings) present in some of the fragmentary hoards (e.g. F.25–F.28), '… could have been gathered from various family members, or wider social groups, before being incorporated into the larger collection, explaining the variations in the diameter and form of these rings… personal gifts towards the collection were linked together to represent broader social groupings and a collective effort' (Joy 2016, 247). Loops of rings could also represent how they were worn or displayed, collected and linked together rather like glass beads on a string. Like a bead necklace, these could be added to or objects taken away (Giles 2012). Similarly, the hoards were not static and artefacts could have been added or taken away at any point up until the moment of deposition. But, importantly, as suggested by Garrow and Gosden (2012, 193, 312), we can view hoards as a group or communal endeavour, much as Sharples (2010, 116–24) has argued for the construction of hillforts. Stead's notion of the Snettisham deposits as a 'tribal treasury' can be debated on two counts: the existence of 'tribal' societies at that time in north-west Norfolk and the idea that the Snettisham hoards represented a 'treasury' ready for later retrieval. But, Stead's argument that the Snettisham hoards represent too much material to be the result of the activities of a single individual is fully endorsed here. The hoards must have represented some form of communal enterprise in terms of the gathering and collecting of resources to acquire material for deposition. Indeed, it is possible that one of the reasons why so many hoards were deposited at the same site is because of competition, as different households and groups attempted to outdo each other through the material that was collected and deposited in individual hoards. But, the fact that they returned to the same location to do this also suggests some kind of overall goal or motivation, and lying behind this, the site at Ken Hill must have been significant for people to gather there, or to keep returning.

It is likely that, over the long period that torcs were being made, worn and used, from at least the 3rd to 1st centuries BC (see Ch. 22), torcs were sometimes broken up and recycled into other torcs. Thus, in theory, the type of assemblage represented by Hoards B, C and F could have been part of the standard materials in the care of a metalworker or workshop, ready to be converted into new objects. This is certainly possible but, were this the primary mechanism through which such assemblages had been gathered, we might expect to see multiple parts of the same broken object in different interlinked groups. In fact, whilst the fragmentary hoards do contain some objects clearly broken into multiple sections (as indeed does Hoard K, see K.3), there have been no joins established between hoards or between interlinked groups. Thus, it appears that when part of a torc or bracelet was assigned to a hoard or an interlinked group, something else happened to the rest of the object (whether it was immediately recycled, gifted or exchanged, or separated out for storage or deposition elsewhere). This seems to support the idea that there was a particular end in mind for these interlinked groups, most likely storage, display or deposition, which differed from the fate of the rest of the object.

This connects to a final aspect of the fragmentary hoards, also highlighted by Fitzpatrick (1992a, 396; 2005) and Joy (2016, 247): their potential transformative effect. As the Snettisham torc hoards were likely deposited in the mid-1st century BC, a time when many torcs were probably being broken up and recycled into coins (see below), perhaps the fragments were given as a part which was taken for a whole, or *pars pro toto*, freeing up the rest of the physical object to be reworked or recycled. This is a practice known from Archaic Greece and has been suggested for Bronze Age hoards (Hansen 2013, 180). Rather than passively reflecting the activities and products of metalworkers as the terms founders' or metalworkers' hoard implies, it is possible that some of the accumulations of objects deposited in fragmentary hoards were intended to represent the transformative activities of metalworkers. As is suggested in Chapter 20, the variety of fragments included in many of the bundles in Hoard F (e.g. **Fig. 23.3**) showcase the breadth of torc production traditions. The deposition of these objects may have signalled a closure to these activities.

In Chapman's work on the Neolithic Balkans (2001; see also Chapman and Gaydarska 2007), he contended that people selected fragmentary objects for use in exchange and as a means of linking people, objects and places through what he called enchainment. A further aspect to his work, which has received less attention in archaeology, is his related category of accumulation, whereby other objects were gathered into sets which generated different types of relations. At first sight, Chapman's model seems to fit well with the objects from the Snettisham hoards. There is abundant evidence for the deliberate fragmentation of objects, as well as accumulation through the creation of sets or collections of artefacts as hoards, and also within hoards. We would not argue with Chapman's theory as a plausible explanation of material from the Balkan Neolithic, but following Brittain and Harris (2010), we do express caution in terms of mapping his model onto Iron Age Norfolk. Whilst being influenced by Chapman's work, the following analysis will therefore examine what fragments do, especially their transformative qualities (Brittain and Harris 2010, 589). As we have seen, collections of fragmentary material have historically primarily been interpreted as metalworker's hoards (e.g. Clarke 1954). But looked at from the perspective of gathering and transforming, they can also be interpreted as a form of offering connected with making, processing and recycling artefacts (Joy 2016, 247), as they contain objects at a variety of life stages, ranging from incomplete or unfinished torcs to broken-up fragments, all potentially representing the activities of metalworkers. A representative sample of bits of objects collected and curated for final deposition could act as offerings whilst also referencing re-processing and re-purposing. This form of deposition may have acted to validate the replacement of torcs by coins (see below). Both parts of recycling are cited: the breaking up of artefacts and the re-forming of material.

Hoards of 'nested' torcs

'Nested' torc hoards are more frequent at Snettisham (though they account for a much smaller total number of objects). They include Hoards A, G, H, J, K and L. Fortunately, most of these were excavated by Ian Stead and his team, so we have a good understanding of the arrangement of the objects in the ground (see Ch. 12).

These deposits are distinct from Hoards B, C and F in that they consist primarily of complete or near-complete objects which, at the time of burial, could still have been worn. The distinction is not entirely clear-cut; almost all of the nested hoards also contain objects which were deliberately broken, and only part selected for deposition, or (especially in Hoard L) so heavily damaged that they would have been difficult to wear. It is difficult to ascertain for certain in some instances, especially the disturbed hoards where burrowing has displaced many fragments, but it appears that torcs G.2, G.15 and G.16 were incomplete at the time of burial. Hoard H seemingly consisted only of complete objects (though one, H.3 is either unfinished or damaged, with only simple 'hook' terminals, hammered flat). In Hoard J, group J.5 (laid over two complete torcs, J.6–J.7) comprised two half-torcs, each deliberately cut at the back of the neck-ring. A length of broken copper alloy torc had been threaded through their remaining loop terminals. Hoard K contains at least one torc which had been deliberately cut up into small pieces (K.3). Hoard L is discussed in more detail below, but the lower deposit included a torc/bracelet where the terminals had been partially untwisted (L.8), half of a broken gilded copper alloy torc (L.9), and two gold alloy torcs that had been deliberately broken and only around half of each deposited (in one case, L.15, partially melted at the end, and in the other, L.16, showing a clear cut across the back of the neck-ring). The 'Grotesque Torc' L.19, with its extensive repairs incorporating fragments of other objects, could be considered a composite group, and L.10 also had two lengths of cut gold alloy wire inserted through one of its terminals. Torcs L.20 and L.21 were damaged or fragile and would have been difficult or (in the case of L.20) impossible to wear in their current state.

In most instances of nested hoards, torcs were placed one on top of the other, tightly packed into relatively small holes. Torc H.7 had even been compressed to fit into the hoard pit, but sprang back into shape once it was removed (Stead 1991a, 450; Ch. 12). Stead (1991a) noted that many of the nested hoards were arranged according to material, with gold alloy objects at the bottom and silver artefacts towards the top (*ibid.*, table 1). He argued that, 'the disposition of Hoard L suggests that some of the more precious [gold alloy] items were given greater protection, with a less valuable [silver alloy] "decoy" hoard nearer the surface' (*ibid.*, 463). As is argued above, we cannot be certain how Iron Age people valued different materials and whether gold was more highly esteemed than silver, as it is today. Taking this into account, Hutcheson (2007, 362) suggested that rather than material properties, this arrangement could equally have been based on colour, with, 'the more silvery near the top, the more golden near the bottom (gold and bronze)'. The significance of colour and metal content are likely, of course, to be closely interlinked, and the placing of golden-coloured and/or gold-rich objects closest to the base of the hoards could have been connected to the symbolic associations of this colour as well as pragmatic concerns about safekeeping.

Nevertheless, as is often the case at Snettisham, the reality is complicated and varied. **Figure 23.5** shows a simplified schematic representation of the hoards ordered by colour, which is closely related to surface metal content (note that, as described in Ch. 17, surface enrichment means that the metal content at the surface is not representative of the ancient alloys used to make the torcs). There are slight differences in the ordering presented here compared to Stead's interim report (1991a). These are due to the fact that in **Figure 23.5** interlinked groups have been dealt with as a unit, and torcs are shown in order of deposition (as far as can be reconstructed, see Ch. 12), rather than reverse order of recovery. In a small number of cases, subsequent conservation work slightly altered the number of torcs identified in each hoard, or scientific analysis identified additional examples of gilding.

Broadly speaking, some ordering by metal content can be observed, especially in the placement of the gold-rich alloy torcs towards the base of Hoards J, K and L, as noted by Stead (1991a). As Hutcheson (2007, 362) suggested, golden-coloured copper alloy and gilded copper alloy torcs are perhaps slightly more likely to be grouped with the gold alloy examples, but this varies by hoard. In Hoards J, K, and the lower pit of L, metal content appears most significant, with copper alloy and gilded torcs appearing immediately above silver-rich alloy (in the case of K and the lower pit of L) and gold-rich alloy torcs, with the highest-gold alloys towards the base of the pits. The upper pits of Hoards G, H and L, in contrast, contain a mixture of silver-rich and copper alloy torcs, some gilded, with no hard and fast divisions based on colour or metal content. In the lower pits of Hoards G and H, colour appears more significant than metal content, with each containing a single silver/gold alloy torc as the uppermost piece (in each case silvery-gold in colour, but the most impressive and gold-rich torc from either hoard), above a group of (originally more golden-coloured) copper alloy and gilded copper alloy torcs, with a mix of alloys in the rings present at the base of Hoard G.

Overall, the picture is more complicated than previously suggested, and (particularly outside of Hoard L) it seems likely that neither colour nor metal content was the strongest guiding principle behind the structuring of the hoards. If

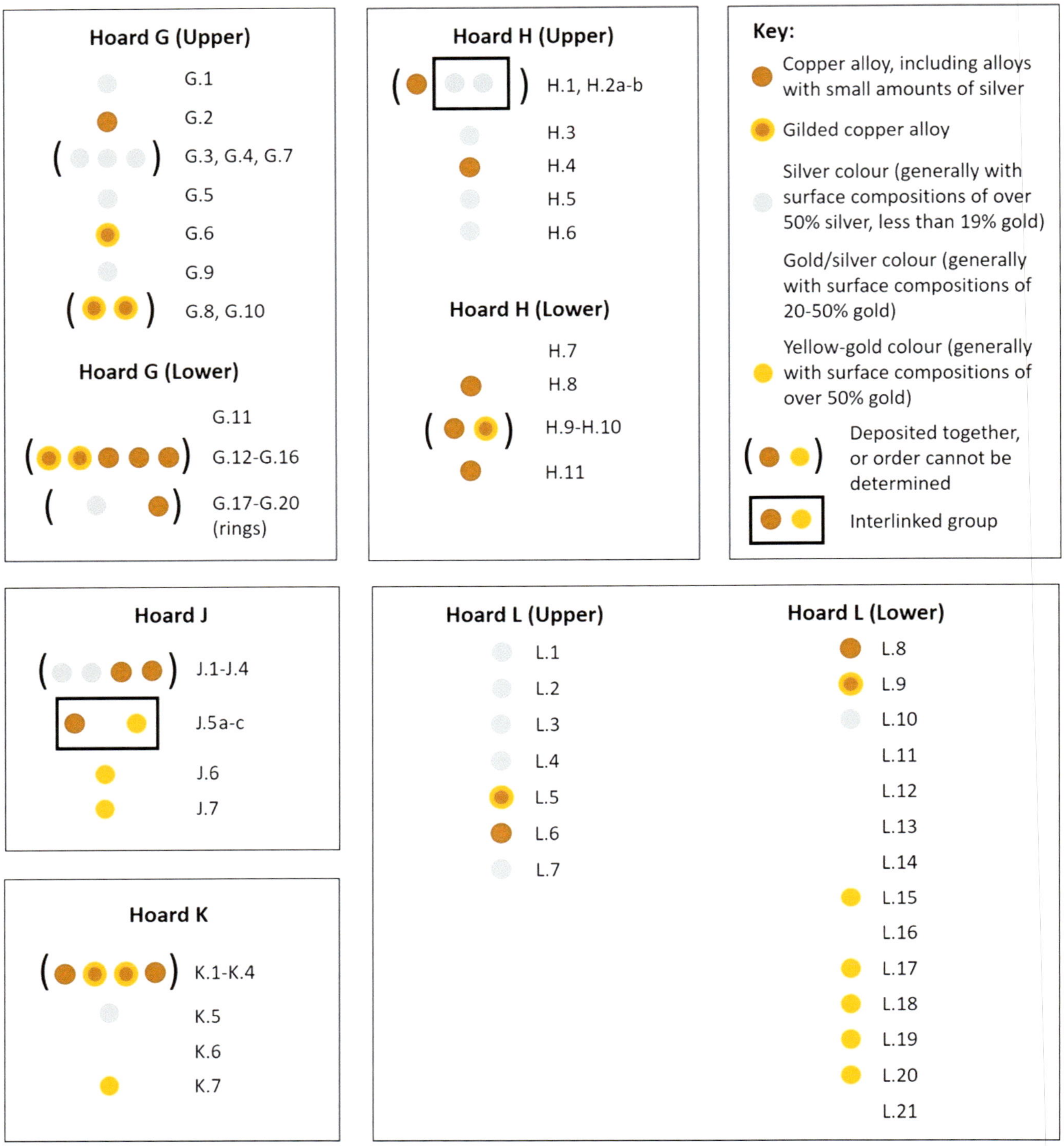

Figure 23.5 Schematic representation of the hoards in order of deposition, coded by colour. All objects are multi-strand torcs, bracelets or fragments, except the four large rings noted in Hoard G (G.17–G.20). Generally, the colour assigned is based on surface metal content according to XRF analyses carried out by Duncan Hook (see Stead 1991a, table 1). This was updated where new information was available, or (in the case of L.11) where this differed significantly from the visual appearance of the torc

anything, there seems to have been an attempt to represent a broad range of colours and alloys in each hoard, a concern also reflected in the collections of artefacts found within fragmentary hoards, many of which similarly cover a broad range of hues, from silver to golden yellow.

In order to more fully understand the hoards, they need to be considered in detail, and as separate individual deposits. Two hoards, G and H, are quite similar, and their structures could be seen to reference one another. The excavation images of these hoards are included in Chapter 12 (for G see **Figs 12.5–17**, and for H see **Figs 12.18–31**). In each case, a pit was dug, and the simplest, least complicated objects were placed into the bottom. In Hoard G this was a group of large rings (possibly bracelets) in a variety of alloys, likely followed by G.14, a very simple two-strand ring terminal torc. G.14 is one of the smallest torc from the hoards, possibly sized to fit an adolescent (see Chs 13 and 22, internal circumference approx. 282mm), and is unusual in being twisted Z-twist (the opposite direction to almost all other Stage I torcs at the site, apart from K.5 and a group from Hoards B and C, see Ch. 20). In Hoard H the first object placed was H.11, a simple torc very similar to G.14, and also with a small internal circumference (around 338mm, again one of the smallest from the hoards, see **Fig. 13.1**). In each case, above this were placed a small number of buffer terminal copper alloy torcs with coiled neck-rings (H.8–H.10, all apparently complete, and G.12, G.13, G.15 and G.16, some of them possibly damaged or incomplete). Next was placed the largest and most unusual torc in each hoard. In G this was G.11, a massive, silvery/gold-coloured torc with one of the largest internal circumferences of any from Snettisham (544mm). In H it was H.7, a slightly more golden-coloured but still silver-rich gold alloy torc with complex (Stage IV) multi-strand neck-ring and decorated ring terminals (internal diameter 509mm). It was so large it had to be compressed to fit into the pit. These deposits closed the lower pits of the hoards, and soil was backfilled over them.

Above the soil which closed the lower pit, an upper deposit was now carefully placed. In Hoard G, this upper component of the hoard took the form of ten torcs. First, two gilded copper alloy buffer terminal torcs (G.8 and G.10) were deposited together, then three silver-rich or silver/copper alloy ring or loop terminal torcs, one gilded and silvered (G.9, G.6 and G.5) were placed in turn, then three more similar torcs (G.3, G.4 and G.7) together, intertwined, and finally copper alloy buffer terminal torc G.2 and silver alloy ring terminal torc G.1. In Hoard H, the six torcs in the upper pit also consisted primarily of silver and copper alloy torcs. The lower four, all fairly simple loop or ring terminal torcs, were seemingly placed one by one (H.6, H.5, H.4 and then H.3). Closing the deposit, torcs H.1 and H.2 were placed together. H.1 is a simple buffer terminal copper alloy torc with coiled neck-ring, but H.2 is a more unusual example, consisting of two silver-rich alloy loop terminal torcs twisted together to make a single neck-ring. After the second deposits were made, the pits were closed.

It is difficult to make precise deductions from these patterns of deposition in Hoards G and H, but it certainly seems that these were carefully structured acts, and most likely performances designed to reinforce kinship ties, social networks or power structures. It is tempting to see the first deposits as representing a wide range of individuals. Whilst it is impossible to be certain, it seems highly unlikely that the small, simple copper alloy torcs placed at the bottom of each lower pit (G.14 and H.11) were worn by the same people as the large, elaborate gold alloy torcs that closed these lower deposits (G.11 and H.7). They might have represented different roles within a family or community. Or, if they were worn by the same person, they might be associated with different life stages. The fact that these objects seem to have been placed one by one conjures an image of a small group of five to six people standing around the pit, taking turns to step forward and place a torc (their own?) into the ground. Any larger audience would have struggled to see the moment of placement, but the order in which the deposits were made seems choreographed to echo and reinforce a social order, perhaps of authority or seniority. The act of covering up these deposits might have marked the end stage of this first event. The second act has a different feel, with a much narrower range of torcs represented: all plain, undecorated torcs with simple loop, ring or buffer terminals and either coiled or simple plied neck-rings. The precious metal torcs are all silverish rather than golden in colour and are mixed in with copper alloy examples. The variation in internal neck-ring diameter is less in the upper pits (380–498mm in Hoard G, 393–469mm in Hoard H), but still enough to suggest that a range of individuals must have been represented. If the order of deposition here was also calculated to reflect social hierarchies or different roles, then this is now hard to interpret. Whatever the case, the similarities between Hoards G and H emphasise that these nested torc hoards were not rushed or casual deposits, but planned events which surely held wider meanings for their participants.

Another, perhaps related, form of patterning is also apparent in Hoard L. Joy (2016, 247–50) noted that artefacts which appeared to be old at the time of deposition were found at the bottom of both the lower and upper pits in this hoard. This could indicate that ordering of the hoard was also based on the age and also perhaps the seniority of the artefact, with some of the oldest and/or most used objects deposited first.

We can imagine the sequence of events for Hoard L in the same way as for Hoards G and H, above. First, a pit was dug, larger than those required for the other hoards. Hoard L was one of the largest nested torc deposits, and there may also have been a desire to arrange the torcs openly in the ground, rather than having them in a tight stack as in Hoards G, H, K and J. In the stacked hoards, each torc when placed would have obscured the one below it at least partially, meaning that only one torc was ever fully visible. The alternative approach taken with Hoard L would have given viewers a spectacular visual impression of the torcs in the ground – an array of some of the finest examples from Snettisham, each one unique. Indeed, the image of the lower hoard *in situ* in the base of the pit (**Fig. 23.6**, bottom left) has become an iconic photograph, reproduced in almost every publication which mentions Snettisham.

Once the pit was dug, the torcs began to be placed into the ground. First was repaired torc L.21, its terminal reattached with a metal strip. Then came L.20, so broken it could probably no longer be worn, with its separated ends carefully overlapped to leave it looking almost complete again. Next was the heavily repaired, much worn 'Grotesque Torc', L.19. As Joy (2016, 247–50) has noted, these three were quite likely the oldest torcs in the lower pit. Torc L.19 is decorated in a style of art that was in vogue in the 2nd and 3rd centuries BC (see also Stead 2009, 329) meaning that (if Hoard L was deposited at the same time as the hoards dated by coinage to the mid-1st century BC, including B, C, E and F) it could have been more than a century old at the time of burial. In this case, it would have long outlived those who made and first wore it. Another nine gold alloy torcs (L.18–L.10) were then placed into the ground one by one, all but two of them (L.15 and L.16) complete. Whilst each torc was generally placed on top of the previous one, they were arranged so as not to obscure the others, especially the terminals. Gradually, the assemblage spread out to cover the entire base of the pit. Of the twelve torcs so far deposited, almost all were decorated: seven with Celtic art (a quarter of all objects at Snettisham with curvilinear art) and four with

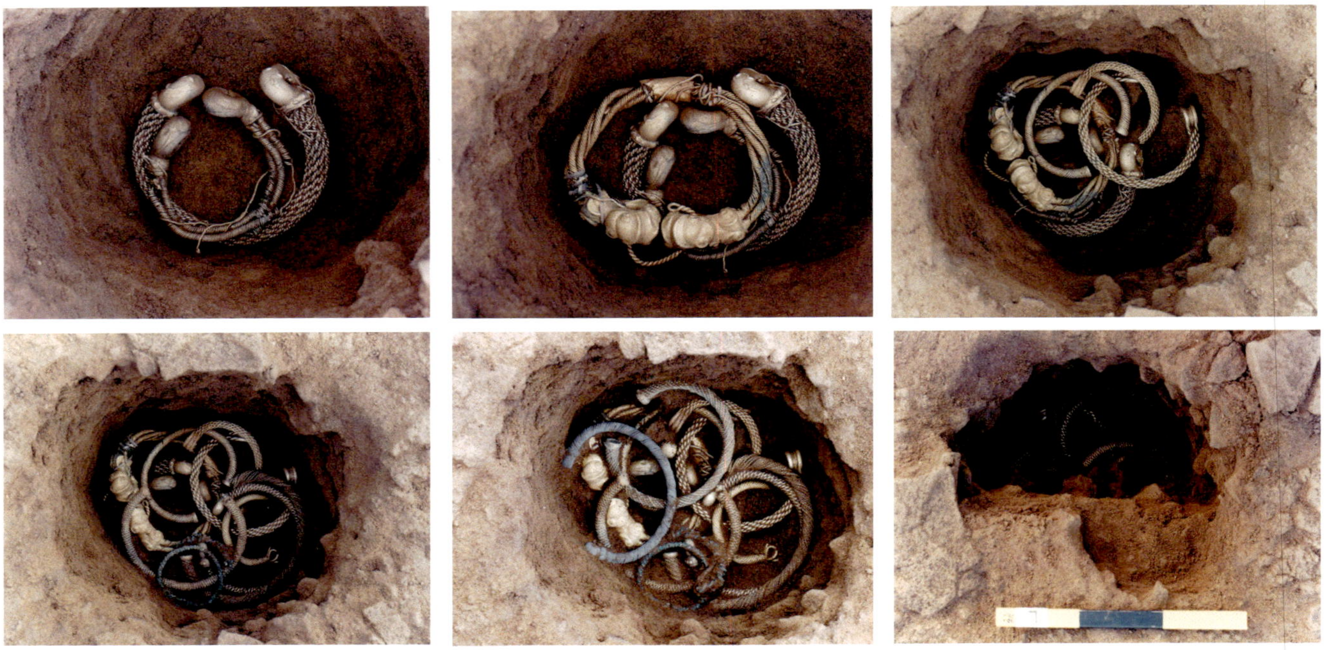

Figure 23.6 The lower pit in Hoard L (photographs in reverse order of excavation sequence, to give an impression of the act of depositing the torcs)

simpler ornament (representing most of the multi-strand torcs from Snettisham decorated with non-curvilinear motifs, see Ch. 21). All the complete torcs in the lower pit have quite large internal circumferences (424–540mm), but it is difficult to know how much weight to give this, especially given that many have their terminals open quite wide, meaning they would not in any case have fitted closely around the neck.

There can be no doubt that this assemblage was special, and it has a very different flavour from the other nested hoards. Whilst assigning relative importance to objects is fraught with difficulty, in terms of their complexity, level of decoration, precious metal content and size, the group which form the main component of the Hoard L lower pit are all comparable to the two exceptional torcs which capped the lower stacks in Hoards G and H. Those assemblages each contained only one such torc, whereas Hoard L has 12. It is also notable that whereas overall only around 4% of items from the Snettisham hoards were decorated (Ch. 21), there was additional ornament on all but one of the first 12 items placed into Hoard L. The final two objects placed into the lower pit are slightly different. L.9 is a broken fragment comprising around half of a gilded copper alloy multi-strand torc, and L.8 a broken copper alloy multi-strand object large enough to have been worn at either the upper arm or the neck, depending on the individual. The resulting hoard (**Fig. 23.6** bottom middle) is so visually arresting that it is hard not to wonder if it was designed to be viewed by a larger audience before the pit was backfilled: seeing these objects nested in the ground would have been spectacular, probably a greater density of such incredible metalwork would almost never have been seen in any other context. Given the long lives some of these objects had, the meanings and associations they could have accumulated, the sight of them in the ground together would surely have made a strong impression on anyone who had seen them worn in life, whether by powerful individuals for whom the torc was a part of their identity, or by varied people as an insignia which denoted a time-and-place-specific role. Finally, these torcs were covered with soil, and would not be revealed again for over 2,000 years.

But the deposition of Hoard L was not yet complete. Either immediately afterwards, or perhaps some time later (there is no surviving evidence of a marker for the hoard, but one could have been placed temporarily), another, much smaller, pit was opened up in the top of the first. This upper part of Hoard L consisted of just six torcs, and much more closely resembles the upper pits in Hoards G and H, perhaps suggesting that these deposits date to the same event or period of activity at the site. The first torc placed was L.7, a very simple two-strand silver-coloured loop terminal torc (**Fig. 23.7** top left). Then came two buffer terminal copper alloy torcs with coiled neck-rings, one of them (L.6) repaired at the back where the wires had begun to fail from repeated opening and closing of the torc (**Fig. 23.7** top right). As Joy (2016) has noted, this repair suggests that this may be one of the older torcs in the deposit, perhaps mirroring the placing of older, heavily repaired torcs at the base of the lower Hoard L pit. Organic remains found on L.6 were radiocarbon dated by Garrow *et al.* (2009; **Table 5.2**) to the 4th to late 2nd centuries BC, supporting the idea that it could have been at least 50–100 years old at the time of deposition. Three simple silver-coloured loop terminal torcs followed (L.4–L.2) (**Fig. 23.7** bottom row). The final torc, L.1, is interesting. It is more complicated than any of the other torcs in the upper pit, and the only one which is in any way decorated (albeit only with the suggestion of a fin motif in the negative space between arcs on its terminals, see **Fig. 23.8**, hence this piece is not discussed in Ch. 21). It is one of only five torcs (out of perhaps 500) from the site to have a Stage IV neck-ring (the most complicated multi-strand construction). The others are a fragmented reel terminal torc from Hoard F (F.119–20), the torc which capped the lower pit in Hoard H (H.7), a possible Stage IV fragment from Hoard B/C

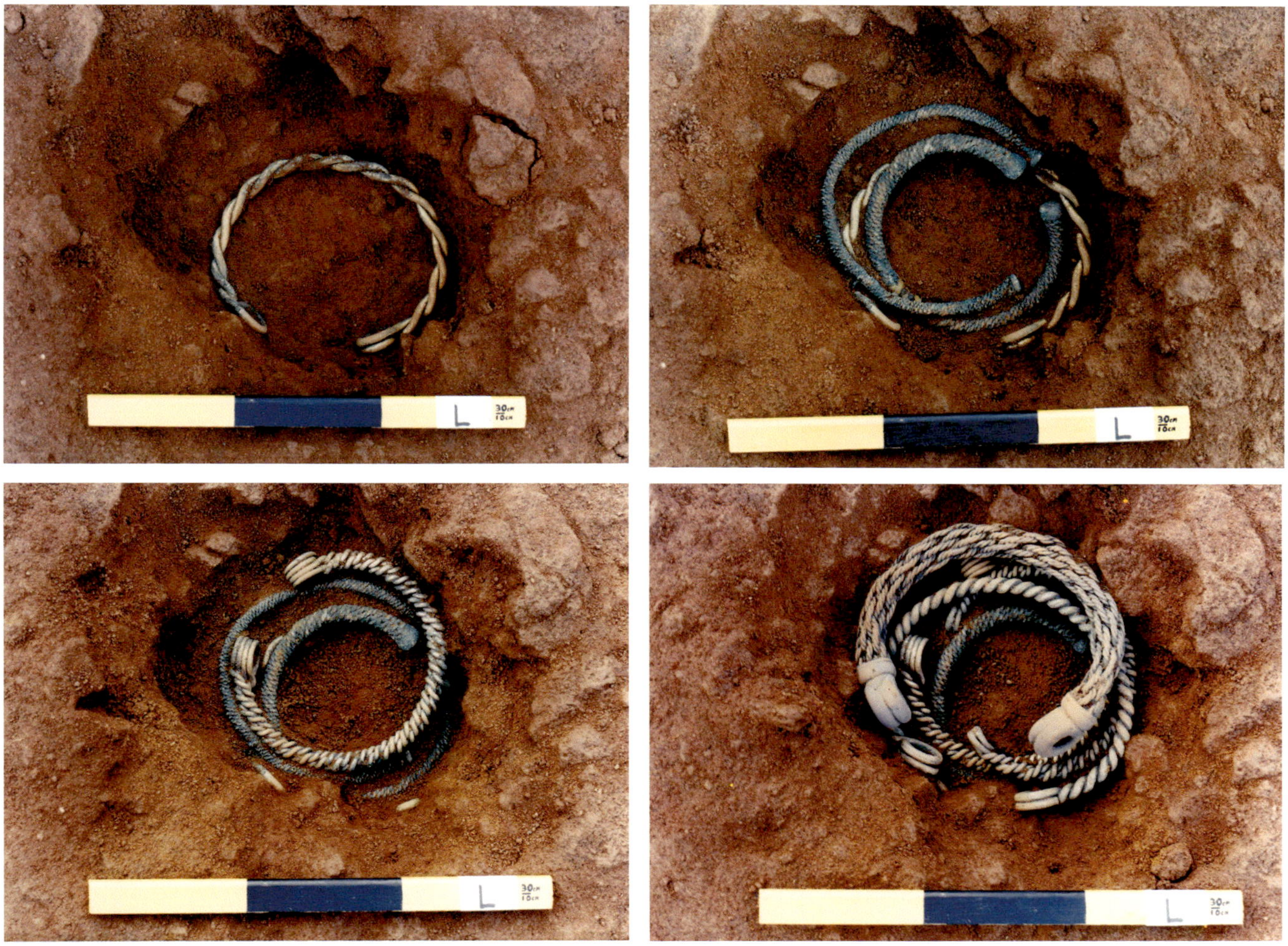

Figure 23.7 The upper pit in Hoard L (photographs in reverse order of excavation sequence, to give an impression of the act of depositing the torcs)

(B/C.62) and the torc which began the deposition of Hoard L: L.21. Torcs L.21 and L.1 are far from identical (L.1 is slightly smaller, and its terminals simpler), but they do resemble one another (**Fig. 23.8**), and differ from the other torcs in the deposits. It is hard not to wonder if the closing object was chosen as a deliberate reference to the torc which began the hoard.

Overall, within the nested torc hoards at least three or four groups of deposits can be identified: the spectacular lower deposit of Hoard L is without parallel, though the bases of Hoards J and K (their upper layers heavily disturbed by ploughing) may be smaller, less ornate, more tightly stacked versions of similar assemblages. The lower pits of Hoard G and H are similar to one another, with simple, largely copper alloy objects towards the base and each capped with a single silvery/gold-coloured torc, between them representing a wide range of sizes. The upper deposits of Hoards G, H and L form the final group, each a tightly stacked set of silver-rich and copper alloy torcs, including coiled buffer terminal examples, and representing a narrower range of diameters.

None of these assemblages can be closely dated, and it is theoretically possible (as discussed in Chapter 22) that their deposition spanned over a century. However, the close interrelationship of their structures argues for a shorter timeframe. The similarities between the upper pits of G, H and L are such that it seems likely that their depositors were aware of one another, and were perhaps present for all three occasions. Likewise for the lower deposits of G and H, which are too similar for this to be mere coincidence. And if the capping of the upper pit of Hoard L with a torc which echoed the first placed in the lower pit was indeed intentional, then it suggests that those who made these upper deposits were closely aware of the earlier ones. Hoards J and K, severely truncated by ploughing, are hardest to tie into this picture, but are most similar, if anything, to the lower part of Hoard L.

It is also possible to suggest connections between the nested hoards and the fragmentary ones, though these are more circumstantial (and no joins have been found). Overall, as noted in Chapter 22, the range of material represented in almost all the torc hoards (B, C, D, E, F, G, H, J, K and L) is certainly similar, with only Hoard A being noticeably distinct. It was argued in Chapter 20 that the simple Z-twist torc from the base of Hoard G (G.14) may have been made by the same individual as the very similar groups from Hoards B and C. Machling and Williamson (2020) have called attention to the similarities between the wire strips used as repairs in Hoard L and similar fragments from Hoard F. They also note that the small droplet on torc fragment E.1b (passed through the terminals of the 'Great Torc') resembles the splashes of molten metal seen on pieces on Hoard F, perhaps suggesting that E.1b was drawn from the same pool or collection of material.

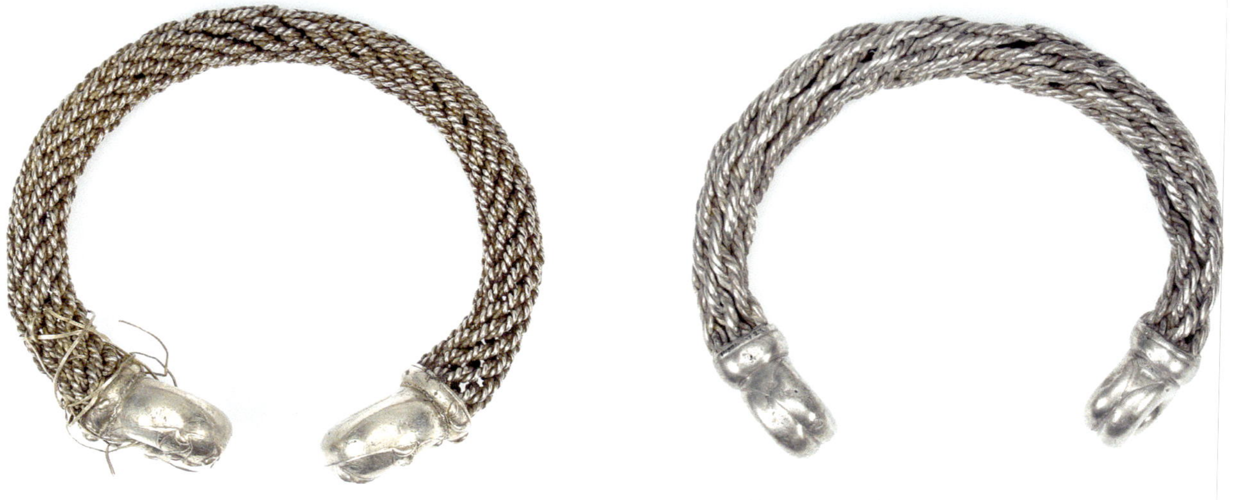

Figure 23.8 Torcs L.21 (left) and L.1 (right), the first and last torcs deposited in Hoard L, respectively

The spatial organisation of hoards across the site may also reflect some of these relationships. Hoards G, H, J and K are all in a tight cluster around 30m across, in an area which also contained B, C, D and E. G and H themselves, overall the most similar hoards, are only around 10m apart. The more unusual and, perhaps, most impressive hoards are spatially separated from the main group: Hoard L is approximately 40m to the south, just down the slope, while Hoard A (including the only complete tubular torcs from the site) and Hoard F (with by far the largest number of objects represented) lie slightly to the east (see **Fig. 1.3**).

The discovery of the field system (see Ch. 8) allows us to translate this spatial arrangement into an understanding of potential movement across the site. Entering the hoard field from the south-west (as suggested by the location of the entrance to the later enclosure ditch) would lead straight to what appears to be a narrow entrance way in the field system, opening out into an open area where Hoard F was buried, hundreds of fragments placed into the ground in an upturned helmet. Just to the right was a small square enclosure, approximately 20m by 20m. The exceptional Hoard L and coin-hoard N were each buried in one corner of this space. Turning instead to the left of the open area would take one to a larger enclosed space, perhaps a sanctuary of some kind. Hoard J and Hoard E were buried on either side of the entrance, while within were placed a cluster of hoards, including B, C, D, G, H and K. Hoard A is buried some 50m to the east, in another defined area.

These close connections between the torc hoards, in terms of both their contents and structure, suggest a relatively compressed timeframe for their deposition. Hoards B, C, E and F all contain coins with terminal dates around 80–60 BC (see Ch. 22, **Table 22.3**), and it seems most likely that the majority of the torc hoards at the site were buried around this time, in the mid-1st century BC. Some of these objects had long biographies, while others seem unfinished or only lightly worn (Ch. 20), but they were most likely taken out of circulation at around the same time. The only assemblage that cannot be closely tied into this series is Hoard A, also the most spatially separated, making it the strongest contender for an earlier or later deposit.

Why were the torcs buried?

The decisions leading up to the burial of the torc hoards at Snettisham are far harder to reconstruct than the depositional sequences. Were these objects still in regular use, perhaps worn by particular individuals, or representative of an office or other more fluid roles? Or had they been retired some time previously, and either displayed in a public place, or hidden away? If the latter, did this happen when their owner died, when a particular office or social role was no longer required, or when new ways of displaying power and authority had rendered them obsolete? Most of the torcs in the nested hoards were complete and could still have functioned as ornaments. But some of these, and the majority of torcs represented across the site, were fragments, or so broken they could no longer be worn. The fact that many fragments (both in Hoard F and elsewhere, e.g. E.1b and L.15) show evidence of melting suggests that this breaking up did not happen at the moment of deposition, but sometime previously, in another context. Had a decision been made to re-use or recycle parts of these objects, and to retain the remainder for later recycling, display, or planned future deposition? No joins have been found between hoards or composite groups. This suggests that the fragmentary objects were only partially represented in depositional acts at the site. The other sections of these objects must have been treated differently. Most likely they were eventually recycled; if they were deposited elsewhere, then none have been found.

In his paper exploring the possible processes of collecting the artefacts represented in the Snettisham hoards, Joy (2016, 248–9) speculated that perhaps individuals were encouraged to give up their torcs, or, once the wearer died, instead of being passed on to someone else they were collected for eventual deposition. This raises the intriguing question of where and how they were kept. Perhaps the torcs were displayed for a time prior to deposition, as he (Joy in Baldwin and Joy 2017, 116) has speculated in the case of a large deposit of Middle Iron Age cauldrons at Chiseldon. In his paper on the Snettisham hoards, Joy (2016, 249) referred to the Anglo-Saxon story of the Deeds of Hereward, who, as Gilchrist (2012, 18–19) outlined, met a Flanders girl called Turfrida who was responsible for treasured family possessions. These included artefacts belonging to her mother, father, grandfather and great-grandfather, with Turfrida acting as a custodian of both the objects and the knowledge which accompanied them. This is of course a story originating from a different time and context, but it does highlight one mechanism by which objects and knowledge could be gathered. Other potential processes include the gathering of artefacts through gift exchange and alliances, as some Bronze Age deposits have been interpreted (Needham 2007, 280). We can also only guess how the torcs were carried to the site. Were the complete objects perhaps borne around the necks of their owners, or chosen individuals? What about the fragments? Were some hoarding events accompanied by a public procession, or were torcs carried to the site more discreetly, in a box or bag? Were the deposits public affairs, or quieter occasions?

We do not know precisely how the site at Snettisham was approached, but it was seemingly set apart from the nearest settlement, which lay across an inlet from the Wash, if not further afield (Ch. 3). When the site was unenclosed, as it most likely was when the torc hoards were buried, it could have been approached from any direction: across the water and upslope from the southern side of the site, or on foot on the way out towards the promontory at Ken Hill. As noted above, the enclosure system may have served to structure movement across the hoard field. Nestled at the foot of the hill, gently sloping down inland towards the inlet and settled landscape of field systems to the south and east (see **Fig. 3.7**), the site would likely have been visible to anyone watching from the landward side of the inlet. Looking out north and west, the 'gold field' would have lain at the edge of the water on the right, with the long narrow promontory of Ken Hill rising up to the left, pointing towards the Wash and the mouth of the inlet. When the site was enclosed, the southern side of the field was left open, sloping down towards marshy ground and the water. The main entrance entrance to the later Romano-British polygonal enclosure was put on the far western side of the hoards, opening out onto the upward slope of Ken Hill, rather than on the inland side that might have connected more directly with settled areas to the south and east. This suggests that perhaps the journey to and from the site did not take the most direct route, but may have included other areas and paths, perhaps continuing out along the promontory. Nevertheless, despite the clear importance of the coastal topography of the site, depositional activity appears closely focused in the delimited, enclosed area of the hoard field rather than at the wetland margins around Ken Hill. The digging of the enclosure ditch, probably sometime in the 2nd century AD, hints at a broader theatre of ritual or religious performance, perhaps formalising existing paths, spaces, and practices evidenced through the field system discussed above and in Chapter 8.

The precise nature of the rituals and performance around the deposition of the hoards will never be recovered, but a crucial question which we have more hope of answering is, 'Why were the torcs not all recycled?'. Metal is readily transformed into new forms, and the broken and part-melted appearance of many of the objects (especially from Hoards B, C and F) strongly suggests that some torcs, or at least fragments, were indeed melted down. So why not all of them? As already discussed above, torcs are intimately associated with the human body. It is likely that connections with, or memories of, the people who had worn them were maintained at the time of deposition. Andrew Jones has highlighted how objects can act as 'physical traces' of events in the past, their persistence over time acting to call up past events, evoking the senses (Jones 2007, 19–25). Memories are not fixed and do not create themselves. They are created and recreated, narrated and re-narrated (Meskell and Joyce 2003, 160). Objects act as anchors. Memories can be maintained and created through the persistence of objects across generations, as well as by reading physical signs of damage and age (Jones 2007, 57). Rosemary Joyce (2000, 13) highlighted the tradition across much of Mesoamerica, in Indonesia, Oceania and the north-west coast of North America of incorporating 'heirloom objects' into costumes, particularly those intended for younger members of social groups. These were passed through generations along with knowledge of their histories. Some of the long-lived torcs may have acted in this way. Heirloom has also been used to describe prehistoric objects thought to have been curated for multiple generations of the same family (Lillios 1999), some of which might have been linked to named individuals and had known histories and genealogies (cf. Hinton 2005). These associations may not have been exclusive to families as is implied by describing torcs as heirlooms. Whitley (2013, 406) noted a group of artefacts from the Mediterranean Bronze Age retained in circulation for many years because they embodied and sustained important relations between people across a wide geographical expanse. Discussing the role of Roman material culture in the Augustan period, Haug (2001) also drew a useful distinction between what she referred to as the recent and distant pasts. The recent past is restricted to the experiences of still living people, spanning three to four generations (*ibid.*, 112). The distant past on the other hand can only be accessed through collective memory and is semi-fictive or mythical (*ibid.*, 113). Caple (2010, 315) labelled artefacts related to the distant past as venerable objects which, according to him, are valued for their great age and links to or associations with a mythical past. It is possible that many of the torcs deposited in Hoard L were regarded as heirlooms, or Whitley's somewhat broader group; some may even have fitted into Caple's venerable object category. As already highlighted, there is a distinct generational element to the deposit (Joy 2016, 249). The individual torcs could represent the people depositing the hoard, or perhaps the generation immediately preceding them and the older adults present. The radiocarbon dated torc L.6, probably at least around 50 years old at deposition, could represent two to three generations past, and the 'Grotesque Torc', L.19, might have reached back four to five generations or more. Depending on the preservation of knowledge, the individuals who wore these torcs and the events they were worn at could have been remembered in the form of a genealogy or history of ownership. The 'Grotesque Torc' was so old its origins and early history may have been largely forgotten and it could instead have been venerated for its great age.

The manufacture of torcs from an exotic material – precious metal, some or most of which was probably ultimately sourced from the continent – could have bestowed certain qualities on the objects, perhaps associated with an ancestral place or stories about people from far away (Helms 1988). Describing the 10th-century will of a woman named Wynflaed, Hinton (2005) explained how Wynflaed's grandson was bequeathed a gold cup so that he could add it to his arm-ring to make it bigger (Hinton 2005, 310). But as Caple (2010, 310) speculated, it is unclear whether in the grandson's mind the reformed arm-ring became associated with his grandmother or was valued simply because it was even larger. Nevertheless, the details of Wynflaed's will point to another mechanism by which material from a past object was incorporated into a new one and also how that newly formed artefact might be valued. This need not be restricted to manufacture. For example, the repairs to the 'Grotesque Torc' include fragmentary artefacts such as the gold sheet (probably a section of tubular torc) used to repair the back of the neck-ring, and the multi-strand torc or bracelet used as a clasp. They could have been selected at random from available material at any time up to the point of deposition, but equally, memories of the histories of these objects and the people to whom they related may have been preserved, with these objects deliberately chosen to bind together the different histories of multiple artefacts, people, or families.

One of the necessary processes of enacting change is to break down or alter the existing state of affairs. The first East Anglian torcs were probably made from gold alloys ultimately sourced from the continent – possibly in the form of coins, torcs, or other ornaments. In this case, the recycled artefacts were seemingly valued primarily as a usable material, albeit an exotic one. Certainly, the value placed on the origins and pasts of these objects was less than that placed on their properties as re-usable material. But, as we have argued, when it came to recycling torcs of the types seen at Snettisham (later most likely for making coins), this was not always the case. Perhaps the artefacts deposited in nested hoards were so intimately tied to their wearer(s), and/or the roles, events and performances of which they were a part, that they were deemed unsuitable for recycling. They may have become in Weiner's (1985; 1992) terms, inalienable: 'imbued with intrinsic and ineffable identities of their owners which are not easy to give away. Ideally, these inalienable possessions are kept by their owners from one generation to the next' (Weiner 1992, 6). They could even be viewed as a kind of absent body, disrupting the normal flow or transition of objects into new types (Needham 2001). Hoard E, which we have speculated might represent a discrete jewellery set (with matching torc and bracelet), could be cited as an example of what we mean by an absent body. As already mentioned, burials are rarely found in the region. This may be as a result of poor preservation or, more likely, burial practices leaving little archaeological trace. But we could also be missing a vital perspective in Iron Age practice, whereby deposited objects could also have stood for people. Just as bits of bodies appear in other contexts, particularly settlements, we may see a blurring of the boundaries between objects and people. The relationships and events of which these objects were a part, their histories, who owned and used them, where and when, were also interred, bringing lives and biographies to an end. Through the process of hoarding, these social facts were transformed into something different. Memories were no doubt preserved about the hoards and what was buried at Ken Hill, but the artefacts were removed from the living world. Perhaps, by consigning objects to a hoard they entered what Appadurai (1986) termed the 'ex-community state', whereby torcs became exclusive to the god, goddess, spirit, or place they were offered to, physically, conceptually and permanently removing them from the social sphere (Aarts 2005, 22). This could have created social space for coins as a new symbol of wealth, power and political allegiances (see below). Appadurai (1986, 21) also proposed the term 'tournaments of value': recurring events in which status and identity are redefined (Aarts 2005, 24). Hoarding provided a stage setting whereby artefacts were reformulated and given new significance, communicating specific concepts for the articulation and re-articulation of society (Arwill-Nordbladh 2002, 201; Jones 2007, 45). Some of this 'stage-managed' creation/communication/reinforcement of relationships, rules, or hierarchies is perhaps seen in the careful ordering of Hoards G and H.

Most of the torc hoards buried at Snettisham seem to have been deposited around or sometime before *c.* 60 BC. Certainly, there is no evidence from either radiocarbon dates or associated coinage that any of the torc hoards were deposited significantly later and, as argued above, most may well have been deposited over a relatively short frame of time. The site did remain in use, but the major later deposits were restricted to 1st-century AD coinage (Hoard P) or unformed lumps of metal (Hoard M). The mid-1st century BC seems to have been a time where, throughout Norfolk, torcs were being replaced by coins as key objects in social networks, particularly in as far as the use of precious metals was concerned. Could repeated deposition at Snettisham mark major social events which facilitated the transformation from a world of torcs to a world of coins (Gosden 2013; see below)?

The performance of wearing torcs must have been a significant aspect of life in north-west Norfolk before the mid-1st century BC. Therefore, in order for a world of torcs to be replaced by a world of coins, torcs had to be taken out of circulation. Gathering them together and placing them in the ground at an important site, possibly as an offering, was a socially acceptable means of removing these objects from the living world of Iron Age communities. Repeated depositions at Snettisham performed this social change, reinforcing and sometimes subtly manipulating exactly what was being communicated.

The processes of fragmentation and accumulation represented by the two types of hoard (nested, fragmentary) worked in tandem. Sufficient artefacts had to be accumulated in order to emphasise the significance of the change. Fragmentation, melting and combining of selected artefacts represented the transformation of materials, and possibly the creation of new social and political ties, or the breaking down of others. Deposition of both types of hoard therefore enabled and enacted a shift in society. These activities and the relationships they embodied all coalesced at Snettisham, an important location in the landscape. If we view the hoards as collections, we can imagine these collections as a way of being (Moutu 2007, 108). By this we mean, as Moutu (2007) stated, collections, through the interaction of people and things, bring about '…a combined effect that is greater than individual persons or things could effect on their own accord' (*ibid.*, 108).

Treasure, or a related set of deposits?

In his survey of Iron Age hoards, Haselgrove (2015, 27) drew a distinction between closed groups of objects deposited in a single act (hoards) and other collections of artefacts which have accumulated over a period of time or have subsequently become associated through good fortune. Examples of this might include the material found at Hallaton, Leicestershire, where the artefacts appear to have resulted from a series of related but distinct episodes of activity (Score 2011). As an example of association through good fortune, many of the Celtic art objects now on public display at the British Museum were found during dredging of the Thames, most likely becoming an assemblage through the vagaries of tides and currents, and location of bridge building and dredging on the river, rather than the ancient activities which led to their deposition.

In terms of the Snettisham hoards, as already outlined, Stead (1991a) suggested the artefacts should be interpreted as a single treasure, although he acknowledged the complexity of the division into separate groups, writing, 'although the hoards could have been contemporary with one another, it was not a matter of one huge treasure being divided into a series of equal instalments. Hoards B/C and F, with coins and scrap metal, are quite different from the "nests" of torques, and the only complete tubular torques were set apart from the others, in Hoard A' (*ibid.*, 455). Most of the hoards were discrete deposits. Some (Hoards G, H, L) had at least two phases or levels, but these seem to reference one another and seem unlikely to have taken place over anything other than a fairly short period of time. If they were separated by a longer interval, there must have been an attempt to mark the location of the original pits (albeit temporarily, since no markers now survive), and keep alive the memories of the earlier deposits. None of the hoards containing only torcs can be closely dated, since there is evidence that objects sometimes circulated for a long time, and in the absence of additional material for radiocarbon dating or more closely datable associated objects, it is difficult to narrow down the timeframe. Nonetheless, the range of objects contained in the torc-only hoards map closely onto those found in hoards such as E and F which can also be dated through associated coinage, suggesting a date before *c.* 60 BC for their deposition (see above and Ch. 22). Unfortunately, we cannot establish the period of time that elapsed between each deposit, so they may all have taken place within a few days, a number of years, or even over decades. Either way, on Haselgrove's terms, these are discrete hoards or collections that have accumulated in the same location over a period of time. They are a series of separate but related deposits, buried at Snettisham sometime between the late 2nd century and *c.* 60 BC, with the site being chosen because it was simply a special place and/or because its location on a coastal promontory reaching out into the Wash was significant (**Fig. 3.1**). Each of these hoards share similarities but are sufficiently different to indicate assorted collection histories. Perhaps individual hoards served related but subtly different purposes. For example, the wide variety of bronze and silver-coloured torcs deposited in a very specific order in stacked Hoards G and H suggests a different type of event to the more visually similar (though each unique) gold alloy torcs laid out in the base of Hoard L. Each new deposit would have referenced those made previously and possibly looked to future hoards: this was not a static process, but rather one of transformation. While hoard deposition was probably not an everyday experience, as Farley (2012) noted, '…in periods of dramatic social change it [hoarding] appears to have become a field of discourse through which political allegiances and new systems of value were negotiated and reinforced' (*ibid.*, 46–7).

Hoards M and P, which were deposited up to a century later, fall more easily into Haselgrove's second category: objects which have subsequently become associated. It is unlikely that they directly followed the practices that took place in the 2nd to 1st centuries BC, but knowledge of these earlier hoards as well as of the significance of the site must have contributed to the decision to deposit material at Snettisham again. Indeed, the evidence from coinage (including a possible scattered hoard of Norfolk Wolf B staters, dating to the late 1st century BC, see Ch. 15) supports the idea that the 'gold field' at Ken Hill may have remained in use over subsequent generations as a place for more infrequent acts of deposition, in line with wider phases of intensive deposition across Norfolk (Talbot 2017, 110). This continued usage was very probably the main motivation behind digging an enclosure ditch around the site and possibly building a temple there sometime after AD 100 (see Ch. 9). As with Hoards M and P, the site's importance and the motivations behind the activities there are likely to have shifted over time.

On transformation: from 'torc world' to 'coin world'

> From as early as the third century BC, torcs are joined by coins of gold (and later silver), with which they seem to have a close relationship (Gosden 2013, 47).

The purpose of this section is to consider the social processes leading to the deposition of the Snettisham hoards, particularly the burial of hundreds of torcs, an artefact type otherwise rarely represented by more than half a dozen examples in any single deposit (see Ch. 22 and Gazetteer). In particular, we argue that the decision to bury such an unprecedentedly large number of torcs at Snettisham was closely entangled with the shift from a 'world of torcs', where bodily ornament, predominantly of precious metal and bronze neck-rings, was a central element of creating, signalling and embodying social roles and structures, to a 'world of coins' where precious metals were deployed in a very different manner.

Before exploring this further, it is necessary to very briefly outline the chronology of coinage in Late Iron Age Britain, and specifically in East Anglia, in which we follow the excellent discussion by Talbot (2017). The chronology of Iron Age coinage is also covered in Chapter 15, where coins from the site are discussed in detail. Coinage first appears in southern Britain in the mid- to late 2nd century BC. Types circulating at this time include imported Gallo-Belgic A and B gold, probably originating from the area of present-day north-eastern France and Belgium (though Sills (2017) has argued that some were made in Britain). The earliest British coin production, cast bronze potins made in the south-east, began in the late 2nd century BC. Gallo-Belgic C issues appear in southern Britain by the early 1st century BC, and the period *c.* 80–60 BC sees the production of the first insular gold issues in the south (British A, B, C, D, F, G), as well as the continued production of potin coinage. Gallo-Belgic E coinage appears in Britain from *c.* 60–50 BC, with its main phase of manufacture conventionally being associated with the Gallic Wars.

At first, coins must have been quite scarce. Exactly how coins came to Britain is unclear, but it is unlikely to have been via a single process or to serve just one particular role. Perhaps they arrived as the result of cross-Channel trade, gift exchange or were even payments to mercenaries (Leins 2012). Their presence likely emerged through long-established contacts and relationships with people living on the continent (*ibid.*). Whatever the exact mechanisms, they were rapidly incorporated into local contexts.

Early gold coinage is rare in East Anglia. The first type to have been found in any quantity is Gallo-Belgic E. Potins are also found in the region, though, as Talbot (2017, 141) has argued, 'little is known about the use of this early coinage, and whilst it adds to the general picture of familiarity with coinage, it has little in common with Icenian coinage and seems unlikely to have been a major factor in the commencement of local production'. The first coinage issued specifically for the region was most likely the Ingoldisthorpe stater and quarter stater, which were probably minted in the North Thames area around 58–55 BC (*ibid.*, 11–13, 141). Local production of coinage begins in East Anglia in around 55 BC (*ibid.*, 8, 13–18), when the Ingoldisthorpe coinage was superseded by the earliest East Anglian gold issues, Norfolk Wolf A staters and quarter staters, which Talbot argued began to be produced during or shortly after the Gallic War, and were most likely predominantly made in a single location (*ibid.*, 14–15). This was followed shortly after by Norfolk Wolf B gold staters, a complicated and long-lived coinage which Talbot argued was produced across at least three locations (*ibid.*, 15–18). Production of the first local East Anglian silver coinage (Bury A, Bury C and Bury H types) may have begun within a few years of the gold coin production (*ibid.*, 19). Talbot (*ibid.*, 141) described the first 40 or so years of East Anglian coin production as the 'early local period', spanning *c.* 55–15 BC. Coins from this period have stylistic imagery including wolves, horses and heavily abstracted faces (see below). Talbot noted that at this time coinage was 'generally more local than in later periods… [with different types] not uniform in their production and distribution characteristics; different coinages were produced in parallel' (*ibid.*, 141).

The metal sources for these early local coinages have been much debated. Talbot (2017, 15, 73) speculated that the first local gold coins, Norfolk Wolf A, were produced using metal from recycled Gallo-Belgic E coins. But the metal composition does not match exactly, with varied proportions of gold, silver and copper among the coins tested by Talbot (40–55% gold, 35–44% silver, the rest being copper), and a slightly higher proportion of tin than seen in Gallo-Belgic E (*ibid.*, 72–4, table 4.16). The Norfolk Wolf B staters tested by Talbot are substantially more debased and varied in their compositions (14–31% gold, 28–46% silver, and most of the rest copper). We argue that the discrepancies highlighted by Talbot could possibly be accounted for by the use of additional metal from recycled torcs. The earliest local gold coinage was therefore probably made from recycled Gallo-Belgic E coins *and* melted down torcs. This cannot be ascertained with certainty, especially since torcs comprise such varied alloys (see Chs 17 and 18), and the degree of sorting and processing of the material would have strongly affected the result. But while it is unlikely, based on composition, that torcs were melted down non-selectively en masse as the primary component of alloys intended for coinage, some inclusion of torc fragments would explain the varied and debased gold alloys seen especially in Norfolk Wolf B types. However, torcs (or at least precious metal examples) probably did not form a major component of East Anglian *silver* coinage, since the bullion content of early silver issues is generally extremely high (Dennis 2005; Talbot 2017, 74–7, table 4.17), and they appear to have been made from imported Roman silver bullion debased with small amounts of copper alloy (Dennis 2005, 2.2). The small amounts of gold present in early East Anglian silver coinage (*c.* 0.45%) can be accounted for in the naturally occurring levels of gold in silver bullion (Talbot 2017, 75).

The end of this 'early local period' of coinage production in East Anglia (*c.* 20–10 BC) was a time of major change. The Norfolk Wolf B coin series had become increasingly debased, and the end of the period sees the largest incidence of Icenian gold coin hoarding (Talbot 2017, 142). A possible scattered coin hoard of Norfolk Wolf B staters at Snettisham may date to this time (*ibid.*, 110, and see Ch. 15). After *c.* 15 BC came a period of more organised and restricted production of gold and silver 'denominational' coinage in East Anglia, based at two to three mint sites. Inscribed coinage began *c.* AD 25. The next major peak in coin evidence comes at the end of the main period of local production, during the Boudican revolt, *c.* AD 60/61. Hoard P at Snettisham can be linked to this horizon.

Torcs at Snettisham have been found in association with early potins (Hoard C), Gallo-Belgic A and C staters and quarter staters (Hoards B, C and F) as well as very early insular issues minted in southern Britain (British Cf gold quarter staters) (Hoards B, E). Most of these coins were most likely produced before *c.* 60 BC.

All of these types are rare finds in Norfolk, imported from the continent or southern Britain, and pre-date or coincide closely with the first local coin production in East Anglia. The absence of Gallo-Belgic D and E or any subsequent coin issues from closed deposits supports the hypothesis that the torc hoards at Snettisham all most likely pre-date *c.* 60 BC. We have argued for a relatively short chronology of deposition at around this time. After *c.* 55 BC, the majority of precious metal objects circulating in Iron Age Norfolk were probably locally produced gold and silver coins rather than torcs. The burial of the Snettisham hoards therefore coincides with a period of major transformation: the transition from a 'world of torcs' to a 'world of coins'. This is important in a number of respects, not least that the Snettisham hoards were not solely about closure, a socially acceptable means of disposing of objects: they were also transformative, enabling a major social shift. But what is it about coins (and torcs) that might have driven these changes? What can coins do that torcs cannot? Also, thinking from the opposite direction, what do torcs do that may no longer have been desirable?

One factor which makes this question difficult to answer is that, owing to the intellectual traditions which separate the study of coins from other types of artefact, coins have not always been studied in the same way as other types of archaeological object (Kemmers and Myrberg 2011, 88). As is exemplified by discussions of coins so far in this monograph, certain qualities of coins are useful to archaeologists, such as their helpfulness for dating (Lockyear 2012, 191). These aspects often form the focus of discussion, whereas the potential qualities of coinage in social interaction are often ignored (Creighton 2000 and 2006, Leins 2012 and Talbot 2017 are notable exceptions). Owing to the fact they are in use today, coins are also often interpreted from our Western capitalist understanding of what coins are and do. Yet, as is exemplified by their inclusion in votive hoards, coins have many other characteristics rather than as tokens of value, stores of wealth, or chronological markers. Unlike other Iron Age artefacts, many later examples also combine image and text with their material form (Kemmers and Myrberg 2011, 89). Coins are small and portable. They can travel through multiple hands, carrying messages and forming diverse relationships across space and time. Similar to torcs, colour was also an important aspect of Late Iron Age coinage, first with clear attempts to maintain a consistent yellow-gold colour, and later (after a transitional period *c.* 50–20 BC) a preference, or necessity, for redder hues (Creighton 2000; Farley 2012; La Niece *et al.* 2018). Many accounts of coins also rely on it being issued by a 'competent authority'. But as Haselgrove (1987, 22) stated: '…a "competent authority" could be *any* individual with the necessary resources and technical skills'.

Just as individual coins can have their own lifecycles, so too can we chart a general lifecycle of coin use during the Norfolk Iron Age. Initially, coins and other precious metal objects came from southern Britain or the continent and many were probably melted down to make local-style torcs, production of which seems to have begun, at the latest, in the 3rd century BC. Indeed, one Gallo-Belgic A coin (no. 174, found in Hoard F in a 'package' formed from broken tubular torc fragment F.53) had been cut in half, and a stater in Hoard B (no. 11) had been hammered out, suggesting a willingness to break up and rework these imported objects. In the initial phase of torc making, continental items used as a source of material could be described as 'scrap', but as discussed above, they probably also carried other associations linked to their distant origins and their role as gifts and items of exchange. Drawing on the idea of 'informed' material discussed in Chapter 22, these associations could have been preserved in the new artefacts. Gold alloys could have been originally preferred as the raw material for torcs because of their exotic origins (cf. Helms 1988), one of the inherent qualities, alongside shininess and colour, that dictated the symbolic importance of both gold and the objects it was used to create. Later, it became established and 'traditional' for torcs to be made from precious metals.

As argued above, it is likely that in north-west Norfolk many torcs which were not deposited in the mid-1st century BC were melted down to make coins. Here we can see the 'cycle of materials' exemplified by Needham (2007), but also a transformation of roles from coins → torcs, to torcs → coins. It is also possible to interpret this link between torcs and coins as a form of 'biographical entanglement' (Rainbird 1999; Joy 2002), whereby aspects of the biographies of one item could have been maintained in another of a different material form. If this were the case, it could imply a level of maintenance and stability in contrast to the abrupt change from coins → torcs → coins that we see in the archaeological record.

Looking more broadly, it is interesting to note that, on the continent, mixed hoards of torcs and coins are found from the 3rd century BC onwards (Fitzpatrick 2005), although torcs were in circulation long before the appearance of coins (Aarts 2005, 23; Hautenauve 2005). Indeed, by the mid-1st century BC, when torcs were seemingly most widespread in Britain, torcs, neck-rings and collars no longer appear in such frequency in graves on the continent as they had done in previous generations (cf. Stead *et al.* 2006), but rather in hoards (Fitzpatrick 2005). The combining of coins and torcs in hoards on the continent over such a long period of time suggests that here there was no dramatic shift from a 'world of torcs' to a 'world of coins' but a longer and more gradual change, with the two forms of precious metal object co-existing for many decades or even centuries. For example, the Frasnes-lez-Buissenal torc and coin hoard from Belgium contains Gallo-Belgic E and other contemporary coin issues from the mid-1st century BC (Hautenauve 2005, 194–5), but is located in the heart of the distribution of earlier Gallo-Belgic A and B issues, suggesting that, in this region at least, coins and torcs had co-existed for at least 75 years (Fitzpatrick pers. comm.). In East Anglia, the shift is much sharper.

The decision to strike coins locally in Britain, rather than just to utilise and adapt imports into local contexts, was an important one. Not only did it increase the frequency of coins, resulting in them being more widely available, but as Ian Leins has expressed, 'the decision to strike coins also reveals a fundamental change in function, reflecting the transition from coinage as a passively absorbed object to a desirable or *necessary* [original emphasis] object within local society' (Leins 2012, 291). This suggests that coinage and, perhaps more importantly, the authority to mint an issue of coins, had become important in local politics and society.

The uses of money have been much debated in archaeological and anthropological discourse (e.g. Bohannan 1959; Bloch and Parry 1989; Maurer 2006).

Money is often seen to inspire radical social change (Bloch and Parry 1989, 3), such as a shift from a gift-based to a commodity-based economy, and this idea has been influential in some discussions about the Iron Age. From a Western capitalist perspective, it is hard to argue with this statement. The adoption of coinage is seemingly an inevitable step towards capitalism. But this reasoning is teleological. As we have seen, it is not at all clear that the initial usage of coinage in Britain was regarded as anything other than the adoption of another kind of valuable. Ethnographic examples show money means many different things, even in different contexts within the same society (Bloch and Parry 1989, 22). For example, it is not obvious that the introduction of coins always simplifies transactions (Haselgrove 1987). Often when coinage is newly adopted it is absorbed into a specific social context creating new relations that can be just as complicated as the ones they replace (Maurer 2006, 21). In an Iron Age context, it often seems that the predominance of coins is predestined: once a society adopts coins, their unique qualities will inevitably result in a monetary economy. As was discussed in detail above, in terms of gold coins (and torcs), another complication is the value we place on gold today. Gold is so obviously precious to us, it seems only logical that people in the past ascribed it similar value.

In an account of the potential uses of coins in the British Iron Age, Ian Leins (2012) argued British Iron Age numismatics has undergone a series of 'stages' of interpretation. Early studies such as the early work of Allen (1960), Mack's *The Coinage of Ancient Britain* (1953), but also later work by Van Arsdell (1989), were undertaken from a 'modernist' perspective, viewing the primary function of coins as fulfilling a function as a unit of account, a medium of exchange and a store of value (Leins 2012, 27). Haselgrove (1987, 17) termed this the 'formalist approach'. Dominant throughout much European Iron Age scholarship, gold coins are viewed as representing the 'natural' first stage in the development of a full commercial economy where goods and services can be bought and sold freely through monetary exchange. Largely following Polanyi's (1944) treatise on reciprocity and redistribution, whereby coins were seen as a means of payment for gift exchange, tributes, fines, compensations, ritual offerings and bride wealth, later 'substantavist' approaches allowed for the fact that coins could take on socially specific purposes or functions (Leins 2012, 27). For example, through examining the different contexts in which coins made from different metals were found, Haselgrove (1987) concluded that gold, silver and bronze coinage did not necessarily denote different denominations of value, but rather each coin type served a different function. A further critique of the modern or formalist approach was forwarded by structural Marxists who insisted on the historical specificity of different modes of production, but worked always in relation to capitalism (Haselgrove 1987, 18). More recently, 'cultural-economic' approaches to coinage have viewed the meaning of money as culturally specific (Leins 2012, 28). For example, Haselgrove and Wigg-Wolf (2005) have stressed the role of coinage in Iron Age ritual practices. But as Leins (2012, 29) argued, ritual functions are often inferred from the final archaeological context of the artefacts, often when coins were deposited as hoards. Coins may have served a number of different purposes throughout their lifecycles. Leins also stressed how function can be 'dynamic', as coins were adopted in new regions and by different parts of society (Leins 2012, 290).

Examining the denominations and distribution of early gold coins, Leins (2012, 294) concluded that they were 'stores of value' and were incorporated, with other artefacts of worth such as torcs, into existing social networks. This is supported by the widely distributed group of largely continental torc/coin hoards hoards considered by Fitzpatrick (2005), spanning the 3rd to 1st centuries BC. At some point, coins took on other significances beyond traditional social networks. Talbot's (2017) four phases of East Anglian coinage takes account of this, with his initial phase of early local coinage which was later replaced by denominational forms. The latter display more features associated with money (such as linked denominations, standardised weights, centralised control of minting, and stable imagery), and Talbot argued that 'over the hundred years or so of coin production, Icenian society became increasingly monetised' (Talbot 2017, 145).

When considering trade and exchange, particularly between Britain and the continent, much of the discourse has concentrated on what items were given in exchange for imports. These ideas, as Fitzpatrick (1985; 1993) has demonstrated through his analysis of imported wine amphorae, are based on our own concepts of the forms trade and exchange should take. As a result, much has been made, for example, of the quote from Strabo that the ancient Britons traded cereals, slaves and war dogs in exchange for wine – handily these were commodities leaving little archaeological trace, which explains why so few exports from Britain are found in Europe (Joy 2015). An alternative viewpoint could be that items such as gold staters were exchanged to help maintain long-distance relationships, and that these social and, perhaps, kinship networks were more important than maintaining a 'balance of trade' (Webley 2015, 130; Fitzpatrick 2001). Therefore, not only did the people of East Anglia gain from the availability of a new 'exotic' material, but the continental issuers of the coins, through exchange over the sea, extended their sphere of influence (Leins 2012, 295). If one subscribes to the presence of something like Gell's (1998) notion of distributed agency, in the eyes of the issuer, something of their 'selves' was also transported across the sea. Following this line of thinking, the 'exchange' may not be as asymmetric as it first appears and there is no need for items always to travel in the opposite direction.

Turning to the question of 'Why coins and not torcs?', one interpretation we could adopt for the demise of torcs would be to follow Simmel's (1957 [1904]) theory of fashion as emulation, where styles start at the top of a social hierarchy and are gradually adopted by the classes below until they are abandoned by the elite (presumably because their role as symbols of authority had been undermined or something else has developed to take their place) once they are taken up by the lower classes. This theory has been applied to Late Iron Age cremation burials accompanied by Roman imports which began on the continent and were soon copied in Britain (Stead and Rigby 1989). One could therefore view the switch from torcs to coins from this perspective, but the theory of fashion as emulation has been criticised as being too mechanistic and simplistic (Entwistle 2000, 62–3). In this case it also does not explain the seemingly rapid transition from torcs to coins, at least in East Anglia (on the continent, the two forms of value seem to have co-existed for much longer).

Creighton (2000, 31) suggested torcs acted as insignias of kingship, while because of their portability, coins were a transferable system of the authority of kings. But this interpretation does not take adequate account of the active role of material culture in relations. What possibilities did coins create that torcs could not? Or what did torcs do that was no longer desirable around the mid-1st century BC? Focusing on the early local phase of coin production, something about coins afforded new kinds of relationship not previously possible and/or necessary. Here we see the adoption of coinage not necessarily as a revolutionary driver of change, but rather, the acceptance of a novel form of material culture initially assimilated into pre-existing social relationships. This was not predestined. Over time, the function and significance of coinage adapted and changed with Iron Age societies drawing on the affordances of coins, facilitating and enabling social change from within.

Talbot (2017, ch. 5) viewed the early local phase of coinage in East Anglia not as the death of a local art form with the demise of torcs, but rather as 'a massive burst of creativity' (*ibid.*, 85). In one of the best analyses of images on Iron Age coins, Talbot underlines the properties of these early local coins as examples of art, containing hidden images which require close scrutiny to uncover such as hidden faces, or certain qualities of images that can only be viewed from certain angles (**Fig. 23.9**). These images are just as rich and complex as those examined in Chapter 21 on torcs. Coins in this sense are therefore not so very different from torcs, but with the advantage that images were more easily reproducible. Just as torcs are unique artefacts, the nature of the dies used to strike early coinage which were 150–200% bigger than the surface area of the coin, also means that no two coins were exactly identical. Coin imagery did, however, tend to be more representative than the Celtic art on torcs. Whilst only a small proportion of torcs have recognisable faces in their decoration (Ch. 21), most early East Anglian gold coins clearly depicted stylised wolves on the reverse, and some silver coinage showed more naturalistic human faces and horses, alongside more stylised 'hidden face' imagery (Talbot 2017, 86–96).

The material forms of coins and torcs are clearly different. A torc is a form of visible wealth worn on the body. Experiences of torcs are shared with everyone who encounters the torc/person. Coins on the other hand are small and portable. Close scrutiny is encouraged by their small size and is restricted to the individual scrutineer. But experience of coins can be shared by others who also possess similar coins. Perhaps there was no longer a social need to display wealth on the body (Csordas 1994, 2); wealth may have been displayed through other means such as wearing gold and silver brooches, or possibly coins just proved more flexible in terms

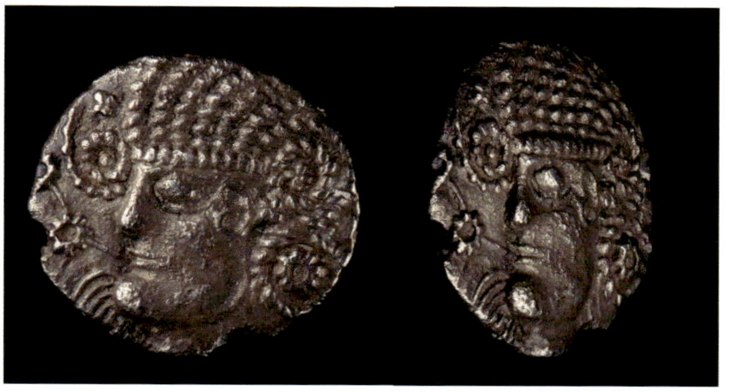

Figure 23.9 A Bury F type early East Anglian silver coin, showing how the face depicted in two dimensions (left) takes on a three-dimensional aspect when viewed from an angle. Ashmolean Museum, Oxford, HCR121002. Accepted under the Cultural Gifts Scheme by HM Government from John Talbot and allocated to the Ashmolean, 2021. Image © Ashmolean Museum, University of Oxford

of their potential roles in relations. In particular, their qualities of reproducibility and transferability, as well as their ability to act as 'distributed persons' and carry messages through images may have made them irresistible.

The issuing of coins demonstrated control over and access to a number of different factors: raw materials, knowledge, labour and resources (Farley 2012, 184–92; Farley 2021). These could be brought together and deployed to create a physical manifestation of authority, a batch of coins, which could then be distributed as a symbol of social and political ties and allegiances. A key element in the production of an issue of coins is the idea of standardisation; the value of coins is tied up with their multiplicity and reproducibility. One coin may not precisely resemble another, but two coins of the same type should, broadly speaking, be interchangeable. With torcs, the opposite aspect – variety and uniqueness – seems to be emphasised, both in terms of the sheer range of neck-ring and terminal forms and combinations, and the way that disparate objects are brought together in hoards and interlinked groups. This probably meant that individual torcs were highly recognisable and, perhaps, personal objects. The concepts of informed material (Bensaude-Vincent and Stengers 1996) and biographical entanglement (Rainbird 1999; Joy 2002) discussed above suggest that, when one item is recycled into another, aspects of the biographies and associations of the original artefact may be extended to the new material form. It may be that some torcs held such potent histories and identities that it was not considered appropriate to subsume them into the world of coinage.

Burying torcs at Snettisham and other sites did not necessarily represent an ending, but, rather, was an act of transformation. Instead of destroying these objects, they were deployed in another social sphere, that of deposition. An object which had perhaps become problematic through association with an older form of social authority could be converted into a new form of potential. The collection, fragmentation, recombination and deposition of torcs were carefully structured acts, most likely performances designed to challenge or reinforce social structures such as hierarchical relationships or kinship ties. We argue that taking these potent older objects out of circulation in a socially sanctioned way also created space for a new kind of object, local coinage, and with it, new ways of negotiating power and authority. In these terms, the non-local Gallo-Belgic A–C coins and potins imported into Norfolk may have occupied a kind of intermediate position in a shifting social world, paving the way for the first locally produced coinage.

Conclusions: a site of transformation

Although the precise meanings of the Snettisham hoards are probably now lost to us, it is likely that the site had a deep and long-standing significance and that at least one aspect of deposition concerned making an offering of some kind. But, as is relevant more widely in terms of the interpretation of prehistoric hoards, these deposits are not just about ending or closing some event or ceremony: they were also transformational.

Ken Hill is conspicuous in the landscape and was an important place to which people kept returning. Its social and symbolic significance altered over time, but in many instances with reference to past human activities. Its aspect, a prominent hill overlooking the Wash and located near the fen edge, was probably a powerful factor in it being deemed an appropriate place for Neolithic settlement, and for the deposition of hoards (Lawson 2018) and perhaps feasting or other midden-generating activities in the Late Bronze Age to Earlier Iron Age (Chs 6–8; cf. Yates and Bradley 2010a; 2010b). Indeed, its conspicuous topographic position almost certainly contributed to its importance in the later Iron Age, as perhaps did social memories of past events and their significance. Perhaps some of the older torcs buried at the site had once been worn at feasts that took place there centuries before they were finally deposited. Whatever attracted people there, the activities carried out at Ken Hill in the later Iron Age were on a much larger scale than those from the Neolithic and Bronze Age. Over a period (whether decades or a very short timeframe) preceding *c.* 60 BC, unprecedented quantities of precious metal artefacts were buried in a series of separate deposits.

How such places are viewed can vary over time. In some instances, they were places of value and attraction. At other times, they may have been places to avoid or fear (Caple 2010, 307). For whatever reason, there was then most likely a brief hiatus in depositional activities at Ken Hill until a second, smaller series of deposits were made. The earliest that can be suggested is a possible small scattered hoard of Norfolk Wolf B coins dating to the late 1st century BC (Talbot 2017, 110; Ch. 15). In the 1st century AD, two hoards were buried: one of large part-melted silver alloy lumps (Hoard M), and a revolt-period coin hoard consisting primarily of local silver issues (Hoard P). The hiatus may be more illusory than real, or at least reflect wider social shifts rather than changing site use exclusive to Snettisham. Talbot (2017, 110) has suggested that coinage evidence at Ken Hill from the later 1st century BC and 1st century AD fits in well with wider periods of intense depositional activity across Norfolk, suggesting that Snettisham was never abandoned, but perhaps ceased to be such an exceptional site. Finally, sometime after AD 100, an area of the hilltop covering around 8 hectares was demarcated by a large polygonal enclosure ditch. Perhaps this marked the sacred space surrounding a Roman temple (Hutcheson 2011). It may also have been an attempt to keep people out, or even a means of containing whatever was thought to be present on the hill. Even in the early 20th century, local folklore warned children to beware the woods on the hill (NHER 1437).

As we have seen, dating evidence for the Snettisham hoards supports the hypothesis that the torc hoards were deposited within a relatively short space of time. The widest possible date range is from the 4th to 1st centuries BC, though we favour a much tighter chronology, focused just before or around 60 BC. A lack of chronological precision means it is impossible to determine for certain if they represent a short period of intense hoarding, or if the hoards were spread out over a period of 50 years or so, with deposits occurring on average every five years. Either is possible, but the likely period of time and effort required to collect the material, particularly for larger hoards, might imply individual deposits were separated by at least a few years (Joy 2016).

Chapter 24 Summary and Conclusions

Julia Farley and Jody Joy

The site

The 'gold field', near the village of Snettisham in Norfolk, has a long history both in terms of its ancient use and the 70-year span of archaeological discoveries, beginning in 1948. The site is situated on the lower slopes of Ken Hill, a prominent feature along the north-west Norfolk coast. Looked at on a map, this long, thin promontory resembles a finger pointing down from north to south, with its highest point at the southern 'fingertip' (up to 42m OD) and the hoard field nestled on the sheltered lower slope towards the base of the 'finger' (around 35m OD). Although very close to the coast, the site itself is on the inland side of the hill, overlooking the Ingol valley and the contemporary village of Snettisham.

Currently located slightly inland, during the Late Iron Age Ken Hill would have stood as a headland reaching out into the Wash. The hill was surrounded by saltmarsh leading down to open water on three sides and was probably accessible by boat at high tide. The southern, unenclosed, side of the hoard field sloped down towards an inlet from the Wash.

History of discoveries and investigations

The finds from Snettisham were recovered in a series of three main interventions. Early discoveries were made during ploughing in the 1940s–60s, followed by excavations led by Clarke (1954). These included torc hoards A (with its complete tubular torcs), B, C, D and E (the latter includes the so-called 'Great Torc').

Metal-detecting at the site in 1989–90 led to the discovery of Hoard F, and the subsequent British Museum excavations in 1990–2 which uncovered torc hoards G, H, J, K and L, scattered coin hoard N and the large amorphous silver-copper alloy lumps which form Hoard M. These excavations also revealed a large polygonal enclosure ditch partially surrounding the site. During this period, a large coin hoard, P, was stolen from the site by illicit metal detectorists working without permission of the landowner.

The final main period of discoveries came in 2003–9, when a metal-detecting survey of the wooded western half of the hoard field produced a large number of metalwork and coin finds, as well as revealing the stone footings of the square Roman structure excavated by Hutcheson (2011).

The finds are now cared for by Norwich Castle Museum and the British Museum, and have been brought together here in a single publication for the first time.

Phases of activity

In this volume, activity at the site has been divided into six phases. The evidence from each is summarised below.

Phase 1: Early Neolithic (c. 3650–3400 BC)

The main evidence for Early Neolithic occupation at Ken Hill takes the form of a cluster of seven pits in the vicinity of the hoards, another outlying pit, and areas of burning and/or flint concentrations which are more widely distributed across the site. The pits contained quantities of pottery, likely domestic debris from pre-pit or midden material. The ceramic assemblage is overwhelmingly Early Neolithic, and the lithic assemblage is predominantly Early to Middle

Neolithic. Lithic finds also suggest activity stretching back as far as the Mesolithic period, a possibility supported by earlier stray finds of Mesolithic flakes and points from the immediate vicinity (NHER 1487).

The Early Neolithic pit cluster at Snettisham fits into a wider pattern of similar sites across Norfolk, with well-studied examples at Spong Hill (33km from Snettisham; Healy 1988; 2013) and Kilverstone (55km from Snettisham; Garrow 2006, 40–58). Evidence varies, but generally suggests persistent use of these sites in the form of intermittent occupation events, rather than long periods of continuous settlement. A small pit cluster such as that seen at Snettisham could have developed over a relatively short period. Many activities are attested at these sites; with Garrow (2006, 57) suggesting that they were places where: 'flint was knapped, pots used and broken, fires lit; cereals were processed and wild resources eaten, and we can probably assume that domestic animals were kept.'

It was not possible to carry out radiocarbon dating for this phase, due to an absence of organic material. However, the pit clusters at Kilverstone, which has produced a very similar ceramic assemblage, have been dated to *c.* 3650–3400 BC (Garrow *et al.* 2006, 72), and it is likely that the activity at Snettisham dates to around the same time.

There is very little evidence for later Neolithic activity at the site, although some of the flint may date from this period.

Phase 2: Bronze Age to Earlier Iron Age (c. 2500–350 BC)

There is little evidence for earlier Bronze Age activity at Snettisham, despite the presence of a small number of Beaker sherds, but the site seems to have taken on a special significance in the Late Bronze Age to Earlier Iron Age. There was clearly substantial wider Late Bronze Age depositional activity in the vicinity, with at least five known Late Bronze Age hoards from the surrounding area of Snettisham and Shernborne parishes, one from the site itself (Lawson 2018; NHER 1504, 1670, 1671, 1672, 1679, 17665, 25920, 28136; Treasure case 2006 T441).

Only a small number of surviving features dating to this phase were excavated in 1990–2. Phase 2 ceramics were concentrated in two areas: Trenches 7 and 12 on the southern side of the site, and pit SN25 to the east. Most of the Phase 2 pottery from the southern trenches was found in disturbed deposits. These finds span the Late Bronze Age to Earlier Iron Age, and appear to represent midden material. The broad date range suggests that activity may have taken place over an extended period of time. However, the majority of ceramics from Phase 2 were recovered from pit SN25 (to the east of the metalwork hoards), which contained a large quantity of Earlier Iron Age pottery. This material was probably deposited in a single episode, or derived from a single source, and it may represent a midden deposit from an event associated with food consumption.

The nature of the activity which generated these deposits cannot be ascertained with certainty, but it is possible that they represent communal gatherings or feasting. Although the evidence from Snettisham is on a smaller scale, Percival (this volume) draws parallels with large midden sites in south-central England (Waddington *et al.* 2019). Such long-lived Late Bronze Age to Earlier Iron Age midden sites are rare in eastern England, but Grandcourt Farm, Norfolk (Malone 2010) may represent comparable activity in the vicinity of Snettisham. This unusual site has a large number of pits with extensive evidence for Middle Iron Age structured deposits of pottery, brooches, amber, glass and shale, and lies around 18km to the south of Ken Hill.

The small number of non-ceramic finds from Ken Hill that can be securely dated to Phase 2 are from the wooded area to the west, suggesting that activity in this period may have been concentrated away from the hoard field. The high levels of phosphate in the woods (see **Fig. 5.15**) indicate an area of intensive activity or occupation over about 4,000m^2. This may be related to the Phase 2 midden-generating activity, although it is equally possible that it could be associated with the Phase 3 hoarding activity or the nearby Phase 4 Romano-Celtic temple.

Phase 3: Later Iron Age (c. 350–60 BC)

The most spectacular finds from the site date to the Later Iron Age, Phase 3 (*c.* 350–60 BC), the period which saw the deposition of the torc and coin hoards A, B, C, D, E, F, G, H, J, K, L and N. It is notable that some of these objects were ancient when they were deposited, their use perhaps even stretching back as far as the activities which led to the generation of midden material at the site during Phase 2.

Aside from the hoard pits, no other features can be securely assigned to Phase 3, though it is likely that the enclosure or field system identified through geophysical survey (see Ch. 8, **Fig. 8.2a–b**) was contemporary with the hoards, and may have served to structure movement and activity across the site. The majority of the hoards are located around the entrance into an enclosure which may have defined a shrine or sacred precinct. This enclosure seems to have extended west into what is now the wooded area, and shows high phosphate levels, as discussed above. We have argued in this volume that the torc hoards were buried over quite a short period, ending around *c.* 60 BC. The stray finds of metalwork and coins which date to this period probably predominantly derive from hoard material dispersed by ploughing, other agricultural activity, or animal burrowing. The small quantities of Late Iron Age ceramics from the site are not sufficient to suggest any significant settlement or domestic activity; the main role of the site at this time appears to have been as a place of deposition.

Phase 4: Latest Iron Age/Early Roman (c. AD 1–200)

Snettisham seems to have retained its importance into the earlier Roman period. Two hoards most likely date to the 1st and 2nd centuries AD: the large silver alloy lumps of Hoard M and the night-hawked silver coin hoard, P.

The site was also partially enclosed during this period by a series of deep V-shaped ditches (2.3–2.8m wide at the base of the plough soil, and 1.5–1.8m below the present ground surface). These delimit an area of around 8 hectares, centred on the Phase 3 torc hoards, presumably demarcating an area which was still held to be sacred, or at least considered worthy of recognition. The south side was probably unenclosed, sloping down towards boggy ground and an inlet from the Wash. Based on pottery analysis and radiocarbon dating, the enclosure ditch seems to have been dug sometime shortly after around AD 100, and began silting from at least the early to mid-2nd century AD.

It was also most likely during Phase 4 that the square stone structure (identified by Hutcheson (2011) as a possible Romano-Celtic temple) uncovered in the wooded area was constructed. It lay directly opposite the entrance to the enclosure on the south-west side. Though there is no evidence that the structure itself was a focus for deposition of any kind, it would have stood between the entrance to the enclosure and the area which produced the hoards. The high levels of phosphate in the wooded area are concentrated just north-west of the temple structure. Romano-British pottery was found in the same area, suggesting that this may have been contemporary with the temple, although it is equally possible that it might be associated with the midden-generating activity from Phase 2 or the Phase 3 depositional activity.

Hutcheson (2011; 2004, 90–2) has argued that in Early Roman Norfolk the building of Roman temples at sites which saw Late Iron Age deposition (such as Snettisham, North Creake and Fring) was a way of formalising a previously more fluid depositional landscape. The transformation of the site at Ken Hill in the Early Roman period would certainly have redefined and perhaps overtly controlled the way in which the site was used and accessed.

The importance of the site may have begun to wane in the 2nd century AD. The Snettisham jeweller's hoard of Roman coins and jewellery was likely buried in the mid-2nd century (with closing coin issues dating to AD 155). It includes small wire fragments that may derive from an Iron Age torc (Johns 1997, 46), suggesting the possibility that some hoards were disturbed around this time.

Phase 5: Late Roman (c. AD 350–400)

There seems to have been a change in the use of the site in the Late Roman period, and perhaps even deliberate abandonment. At the beginning of this phase, it appears that the enclosure ditch was only partially infilled, but there may have been a deliberate attempt to level the inner bank in at least some areas during Phase 5. At the centre of the north side, the enclosure ditch was completely infilled for a length of around 20m with slag and furnace debris, probably to create a causeway across the ditch, suggesting a re-organisation of the layout and use of the site. Pottery finds and radiocarbon dates suggest this occurred in the mid-4th century AD. In the Late Roman period, it is evident that there were a range of industrial processes taking place in the immediate vicinity of Snettisham (see e.g. Lyons 2004), and it is likely that the ironworking which produced the furnace debris filling the north side of the enclosure ditch probably occurred nearby. The square stone structure in the woods was also probably demolished at around this time, with a Roman coin dated AD 350–360 securely lodged under the rubble of the north wall (Hutcheson 2011, 44).

There is little evidence for early medieval activity at Ken Hill, and so it may be that this was the final decommissioning of a site that had seen exceptional objects deposited for a period of at least a century from the Late Iron Age to the Early Roman period.

Phase 6: Medieval and post-medieval (c. AD 1100 onwards)

Ceramic evidence suggests 12th to 14th-century occupation in the vicinity, although no excavated features could be securely dated to this period. The evidence from the 1990–2 excavations suggests that Phase 6 interventions at the site mainly consisted of post-medieval agricultural and drainage activity.

The disturbed state of many of the archaeological features across the site was due to animal burrowing (especially rabbits), and deep ploughing across the hoard field. From at least the 16th century, an area of common land just south of Ken Hill was used as a rabbit warren, and there are numerous historical accounts of the problems caused on adjacent agricultural land around Snettisham by escaping rabbits (Whyte 2009, 91–124; Bailey 1988). Extensive disturbance was also noted in the wooded area to the west of the 'gold field' by Hutcheson during her 2004 excavations (2011). She suggested that this could be due to deliberate destruction of the site and structure, but it is possible that it simply results from later agricultural, drainage, landscaping and animal activity.

The Late Iron Age finds

The Phase 3 hoards and most of the Late Iron Age stray finds from Snettisham represent almost exclusively a small number of artefact types, mostly associated with personal ornament. The majority are torcs, bracelets, small and large rings, and coins. There is also evidence for highly fragmented sheet objects, and categories of find seemingly associated with metalworking such as a scale pan, perforated pebble (perhaps for working with wire), and ingots. There are hints of possible martial associations in hoards B/C and F, with the inclusion of a shield binding in B/C and F being contained within an unusual form of bronze helmet.

The stray finds likely associated with the same period of activity generally represent material comparable to that contained within the hoards: a small number of complete or near-complete gold/silver alloy multi-strand torcs, fragments of both tubular and multi-strand torcs in a range of alloys (some deliberately broken up or exposed to heat), ingots and rings, as well as amorphous copper alloy lumps, sprues from casting, bronze sheet fragments and small bronze rivets and rivet heads.

Additionally, a handful of (mostly copper alloy) stray finds represent object types likely dating to Phase 3, but not seen in the hoards: a terret, a linch-pin head, two brooch fragments, an unusual mount, a small pair of tweezers, and one possible loop from a button and loop fastener or strap fitting. There are also a small number of fragments of mail armour, most likely of a Late Iron Age to Early Roman date. The under-representation of strap fittings, brooches, fasteners, and toiletry items related to personal grooming is notable compared to most contemporary Late Iron Age sites. There are also no finds of animal bone, human remains, or tools from the site that can be dated to Phase 3, and very little pottery.

The torcs

The most spectacular objects from Snettisham, and those which make the site exceptional, are undoubtedly the torcs and related ornaments. There are over 60 complete or near-complete torcs from the site, with hundreds more represented by fragments. This compares to around 85 complete and fragmented Iron Age torcs in total from the rest of the UK.

There is huge variety in the materials and manufacturing techniques used in the production of these objects. Tubular torcs in a wide range of forms were made in gold sheet, while bronze and gold/silver alloy multi-strand torcs instead use wire as the primary material for their neck-rings. On the multi-strand neck-rings, prominent terminals were either formed from the ends of the neck-ring wires, cast directly onto the wires, cast separately and soldered/riveted on, or made in sheet and soldered or mechanically attached to the neck-rings. Both wire neck-ring construction and terminal form are hugely varied, making almost every torc unique. Colour was evidently important in the selection of alloys and surface treatments, with precious metal torcs being made in a wide range of ternary alloys of gold, silver and copper, often showing surface enrichment of their precious metal content to give colours from yellow gold to very pale, whitish silver. Some copper alloy torcs had even been mercury gilded to give them a golden surface appearance, the earliest known example of this technology in Britain. The manufacture of torcs used a wide variety of materials, including organic components such as wooden cores which enabled the construction of coiled wire neck-rings.

Many of the torcs were decorated, making the finds from Snettisham one of the densest known concentrations of Celtic art. It is no surprise that these finds have featured prominently in almost every account of Celtic art since their discovery. The decoration is highly varied, also including geometric motifs only rarely otherwise found on Iron Age metalwork. Several objects show motifs generally ascribed to different phases or stages of Celtic art, adding to an emerging understanding that later styles of Celtic art were more an accumulation of designs and motifs than a wholesale replacement of earlier styles. The anachronistic nature of some of the designs might have been deliberate, creating connections between past, present and even the future for the communities that made and used these objects (Joy 2016; 2019a; 2020). The wide variety of textures and patterning hints at the fact that torcs were designed to be seen from a range of viewpoints. Some elements could be appreciated from a distance, but others would only have been visible to those who had personal access to the objects, close enough to see and even touch the intricate designs. Today, it is only possible to appreciate some of these objects because of meticulous conservation work undertaken at the British Museum.

Location or even region of manufacture of the torcs is hard to determine with any certainty. Most of the torcs and fragments from Snettisham, especially the multi-strand examples, are in styles best paralleled in Britain. They are probably insular products, if not more locally made, given the preponderance of these types in East Anglia (see **Fig. 22.4a**). Many of the tubular torcs are so unusual that it is impossible to be certain about their origins, but the art styles on the more ornate pieces (e.g. A.1, F.43, see **Tables 21.2–3**) are most commonly seen on objects from Britain (see Ch. 21). This suggests that while objects such as the Type 6 tubular torcs from Hoard A are part of a wider distribution of such types across north-west Europe (see **Fig. 22.3**) the majority of the tubular torcs from Snettisham may well have been made in Britain, even though in some cases they are local versions of a widespread style. The undecorated Type 1 and 2 tubular torcs are harder to place, and objects such as F.59 and F.63–6 are perhaps the most likely examples of imported objects in the hoards, along with stray finds such as S.83, a small zoomorphic rod torc fragment with its closest parallels on the continent (Ch. 21).

Evidence from both stylistic analysis, studies of wear and repair, and radiocarbon dating suggests that at least some torcs were over a century old before they were deposited. Thus, their lives extended beyond any single human lifespan. Whether they were passed down the generations as heirlooms, stood for a specific role potentially held by a number of individuals, or were held in a communal treasury, by the time they were placed into the ground they must have accumulated their own rich histories and networks of relationships. Many of these objects are highly distinctive, and it is hard not to imagine that they would have been known and recognised entities in their communities.

There has been much discussion over the social role of torcs and other ornaments in Late Iron Age societies. Who wore these objects? Were these high-status, prestige objects accessible only to a small number of powerful individuals, perhaps local leaders? Or were they communal possessions associated with roles, rites or offices which could be held by different people at different times? With very little evidence available from contemporary burials, some of these questions may remain impossible to answer, but close analysis of the objects themselves provides some clues. The range of neck-ring sizes present at Snettisham suggests that they were most likely worn by a wide range of people, including young people and adult men and women. The smallest torcs (suitable in size for an adolescent or, possibly, worn on the upper arm) tend to be simpler in design and construction, but more decorative torcs come in a wide range of adult neck sizes. Many torcs were heavily worn and repaired, suggesting wear over a very long period, most likely by more than one individual. There is also the clear suggestion from damage to neck-rings and terminal attachments that torcs were taken on and off continually over their lifetimes. This could be as simple as one careful owner removing the object at night but may also suggest wear by different people or for specific events. Torcs from other sites in Britain often show preferential wear on one side, showing that they were generally worn one particular way up. This does not tend to be the case at Snettisham. This is not definitive, but might suggest different wearers, or at least gaps between periods of wear.

Here, we have argued that torcs were active objects which played a part in the construction of identities. Putting on a torc transformed the wearer and may have allowed them to step into roles or positions of power that they did not occupy on a daily basis. Other forms of archaeological evidence from Late Iron Age Norfolk, such as settlement pattern data, are often ephemeral, but there is little evidence for a rigidly structured hierarchical society, or an extensive single political entity. Power structures may have been relatively fluid, local, and perhaps heterarchical. Torcs, and who had the right to wear them, would have played a role in the creation, negotiation and maintenance of these relationships.

The structure and dating of the hoards

The torc hoards from Snettisham are very varied in form. Broadly speaking they can be divided into two groups: the fragmentary hoards B, C and F (which contain cut up torcs, very few complete objects, and potin or gold alloy coinage), and the complete torc hoards A, G, H, J, K and L. In the latter, where they have been recovered under excavation conditions, torcs were placed into the ground in nested groups, either in tight stacks (G, H, J, K) or more widely spaced in a larger pit (L, which is also the most spectacular of the hoards). Three hoards show clear evidence of multiple stages of deposition: G, H and L all have clear upper and lower pits.

The Phase 3 hoards are summarised here:

Hoard A: At least four tubular torcs, and a perforated pebble possibly associated with wire manufacture or finishing.

Hoards B and C: A small number of complete, simple multi-strand bronze torcs and a similar bracelet. Fragmentary multi-strand torcs/bracelets in a range of gold/silver alloys as well as bronze, accompanied by other objects including both large and small rings, ingots, fragments of shield binding, other unidentifiable sheet fragments, and a folded scale pan used for weighing out small quantities of material. Hoard B included at least one composite group of multi-strand torc fragments and rings looped onto a larger ring. Hoard B also contained gold Gallo-Belgic coins and one insular quarter stater, while Hoard C included over 150 potin coins.

Hoards D and E: Each comprises one composite group based around a complete multi-strand torc. In the case of Hoard E (the 'Great Torc') a single gold insular quarter stater had been inserted into one of the terminals.

Hoard F: The largest hoard from the site, consisting almost exclusively of fragmentary multi-strand torcs/ bracelets in a range of gold/silver and bronze alloys, as well as fragments of gold alloy tubular torcs in a variety of types. Many of these were interlinked to form composite groups, and some show evidence of melting or exposure to molten metal. The assemblage also included rings, ingots and Gallo-Belgic gold coins and was contained within an upturned copper alloy helmet.

Hoards G, H, J, K, L: Nested hoards primarily of complete multi-strand torcs in a range of gold, silver and bronze alloys. Also includes some fragmentary torcs, and interlinked groups. Hoard G included four large rings at the base of the pit, and one of its upper torcs had small rings inserted through its terminals. Hoards G, H and L have evidence for two pits, upper and lower, while Hoards J and K had been truncated by ploughing.

Hoard N: Dispersed hoard of nine Gallo-Belgic gold coins.

Dating of the hoards is not straightforward. The majority of the Phase 3 hoards (A, D, G, H, J, K and L) contained only torcs and other ornaments/metalwork such as wrought rings of various sizes. Hoards B, C, E and F were torc hoards (mostly fragmentary, except for E) which also included coinage, and Hoard N was a dispersed coin hoard. The dating of the coins from hoards B, C, E, F and N support the idea that these hoards were more or less contemporary. The Hoard B, E, F and N coins are Gallo-Belgic gold (with two possible insular gold issues), while those from Hoard C are potins. The latest potins in Hoard C are dated by Holman (Ch. 15) to *c.* 75/70–60/55 BC, with the composition of the assemblage suggesting that the hoard was deposited around 60 BC or shortly thereafter. The Gallo-Belgic gold coins from Hoards B, E, F and N terminate with issues minted *c.* 80–60 BC (see Ch. 15 for a full discussion of coin dating). Gallo-Belgic E coins (the predominant gold coinage in circulation *c.* 60–50 BC) are, notably, absent from the hoards. As no objects from the torc hoards can be securely dated to after *c.* 60 BC, this is taken as a likely terminal date for their deposition. Stray finds suggest the possibility that there were continued (albeit apparently much smaller) deposits of coinage at the site in the later 1st century BC, but none of these were found in a closed context.

It is more difficult to establish a date for the beginning of hoarding at Snettisham. In terms of the types and styles of torcs represented, it is not possible to order the hoards chronologically. Aside from Hoard A, which contained exclusively large tubular torcs, the range of torcs contained within each hoard is broadly similar, and it is clear that many torcs were in circulation for a long time, perhaps generations, before deposition. Organic material from two torcs (one from Hoard F and one from Hoard L) was used to provide radiocarbon dates (see **Table 5.2**; Garrow *et al.* 2009), giving results of *c.* 370–110 cal BC at 95% probability, and 350–170 cal BC at 68% probability. Given the associated coinage from Hoard F, some of the objects in the hoard were most likely over a century old at the time of burial.

The clustering of the latest dates for hoard coins in the early to mid-1st century BC (Hoards B, C, E, F and N) strongly suggests at the very least a peak of deposition at this time, but the nested torc hoards could in theory have been buried en masse over a relatively short length of time, or gradually over a much longer period. There could even have been decades between some of these deposits. Here, a date of *c.* 350–250 BC is cautiously offered as an indication of the earliest possible date of deposition for the hoards which cannot be given a *terminus post quem* through coinage (A, D, G, H, J, K and L). However, the editors of this volume favour a significantly tighter chronology focused around *c.* 60 BC.

Whilst none of the assemblages which do not contain coins can be closely dated, the close relationship between both the objects and the structuring of the deposits seems to argue for a relatively compressed timeframe for their burial. Within the nested torc hoards, at least three or four groups of deposit can be identified: the spectacular lower deposit of Hoard L is without parallel, although the bases of Hoards J and K (their upper layers heavily disturbed by ploughing) may be smaller, less ornate, more tightly stacked versions of similar assemblages. The lower pits of Hoard G and H are very similar to one another, with simple, largely copper alloy

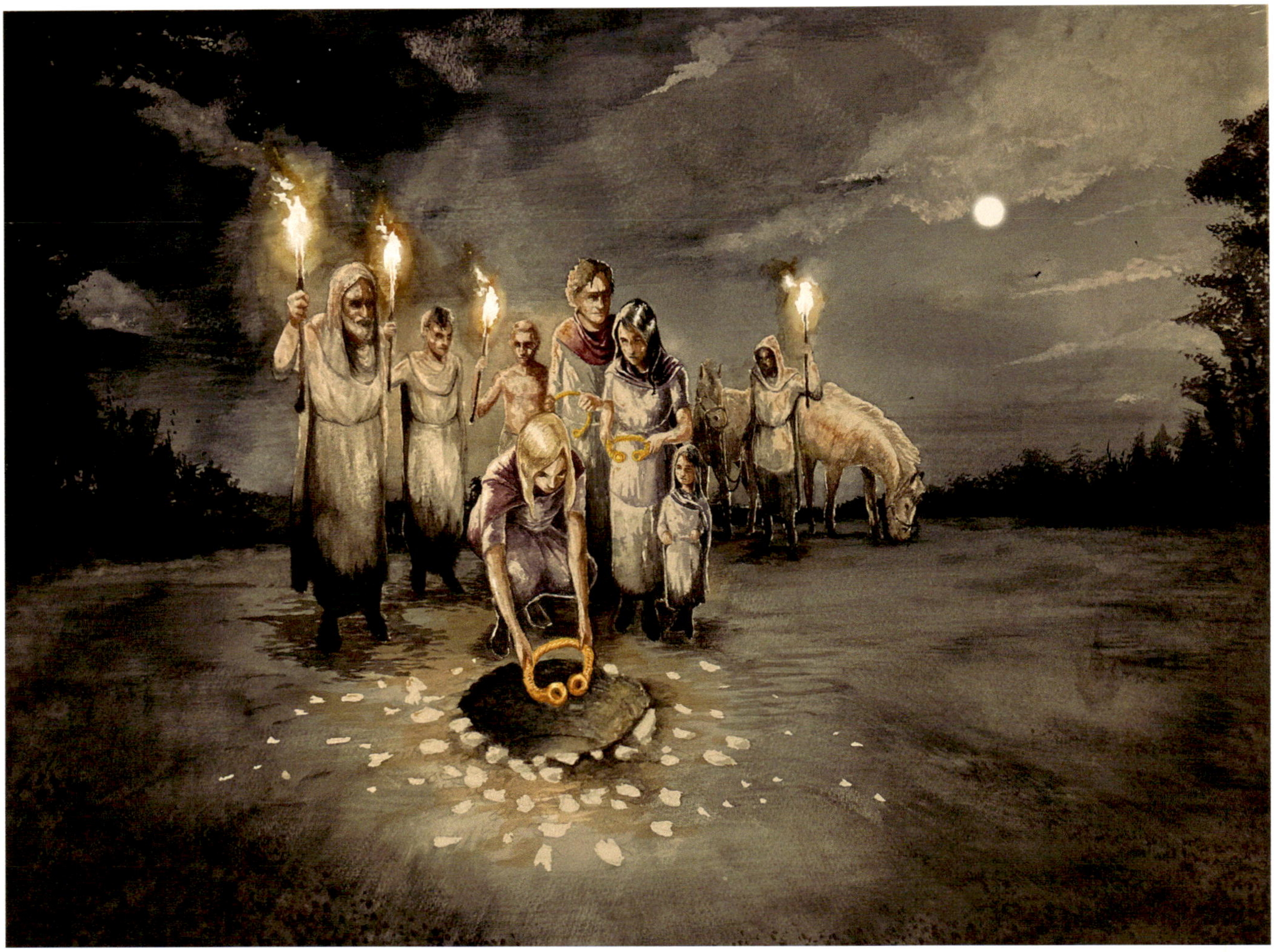

Figure 24.1 Imaginative reconstruction of the deposition of one of the torc hoards at Snettisham (drawing by Craig Williams)

objects towards the base and each capped with a single silvery-gold-coloured torc, between them representing a wide range of sizes. The upper deposits of Hoards G, H and L form the final group, each a tightly stacked set of silver-rich and copper alloy torcs, including coiled buffer terminal examples, and representing a narrower range of diameters.

The similarities between the upper pits of G, H and L are such that it seems likely that their depositors were aware of one another, and were perhaps present for all three occasions. Likewise for the lower deposits of G and H, which are too similar for this to be mere coincidence. And if the capping of the upper pit of Hoard L with a torc which echoed the first placed in the lower pit was intentional, then it suggests that those who made these upper deposits were closely aware of the earlier ones. It is also possible to suggest connections between the nested hoards and the fragmentary ones (though no joins have been identified). The only assemblage that cannot be tied into this series is Hoard A, also the most spatially separated, making it the strongest contender for an earlier or later deposit.

Why were the hoards buried?

Previous interpretations of the site (e.g. Clarke 1954; Stead 1991a) have tended to view the hoards as a communal treasury, buried in a time of stress (perhaps related to Caesar's incursions into southern Britain), with the intention of recovery. Here we follow Fitzpatrick (1992a) in arguing that the clear division between founders' or savings hoards (intended for recovery) and votive hoards (intended to be left undisturbed) is perhaps anachronistic when applied to Iron Age Britain. Nonetheless, the Snettisham hoards, whilst exceptional, fit into a clear wider pattern of unrecovered coin, torc, vessel and harness fitting hoards across Late Iron Age Norfolk (Hutcheson 2005; Davies 2008). Many of these deposits, including the excavated hoards at Snettisham, show structure and patterning which strongly suggests that selecting, collecting and depositing material was not a hurried act but a carefully considered process and perhaps even a staged performance. Certainly, the strong relationships between Hoards G and H at Snettisham, and the echoes/connections between the upper and lower pits of Hoard L speak to the wider social significance of the act of placing these objects in the ground, a process imagined in **Figure 24.1**. We view these as curated individual deposits buried at a sacred site, and understand the creation of these hoards as a social process which actively established, negotiated and performed meaning and networks of relationships between people and objects.

The sense of torcs as active objects in the negotiation and display of power may go some way to suggesting why these objects were taken out of circulation in the late Iron Age. The number of torcs buried at Snettisham is unprecedented, and there must have been a powerful motivation behind the interment of so many objects at a single site, perhaps over a relatively short period of time in the years or decades leading up to *c.* 60 BC. Other coin evidence from the site supports the idea that deposition continued to take place over the following century (culminating in the burial of large revolt-period coin hoard, P, around AD 60/61) but none of these later deposits contain torcs.

Mixed hoards of torcs and coins are widespread across much of Europe in the 1st century BC (Fitzpatrick 2005). Often, torcs and coins are present in similar quantities by weight of metal, or torcs (often fragmented) are just a small proportion of a larger coin hoard. In these cases, torcs and coins seem to be treated more or less equally, with an equivalence perhaps drawn between the two. In some cases, the torcs (and even the coins) may represent a source of scrap metal. The pattern is different at Snettisham, where torcs and coins are not treated interchangeably. In a small number of cases torcs and coins are directly associated (with a gold quarter stater inside one of the terminals of the Great Torc in Hoard E, and Gallo-Belgic gold coins found sealed inside a broken fragment of tubular torc in Hoard F). However, none of the nested hoards of complete torcs contained coins, and coins only ever represent a small proportion of the fragmentary hoards.

The precious metal which formed the raw material of many of the Snettisham torcs is eminently recyclable. Indeed, it is most likely that these objects were themselves made from recycled imported Gallic gold, arriving in Britain as ornaments or coins. No direct connections have been discovered between fragmentary objects in different hoards, or composite groups within hoards, and so there is the clear implication that only parts of some objects were being deposited. The rest of these objects could have been deposited somewhere else or (more likely given the vast number of partial objects at Snettisham and the fact that no associated fragments have been discovered elsewhere) recycled into a new form. Northover (this volume) argues that the composition of the small and large rings from the site suggests they may have been made from melted down torcs. Aside from these rings, the most likely contender for the fate of recycled torc metal is coinage. The period around *c.* 60 BC which seems to have seen the bulk of torc deposition at Snettisham coincides with the beginnings of local gold coin production in East Anglia. The precise source of the metal used for early East Anglian gold coins is unknown, but their composition is consistent with a production route that included the recycling of imported continental Gallo-Belgic E issues and some incorporation of recycled metal from torcs.

Following Gosden (2013), we argue that the shift from a 'world of torcs' to a 'world of coins' is fundamental to understanding the deposits at Snettisham. Torcs are powerful objects, worn on the body, perhaps associated with individual people, families or communities. They may have been worn at particular events, ceremonies or celebrations, perhaps even denoting a specific role or office held by the wearer (at least while they wore the torc). The huge range of torcs at Snettisham strongly suggests that their value lay in their singularity: almost every torc from the site is unique and many are highly recognisable, even from a distance. These may well have been objects with rich histories and layers of meaning, even their own names and stories which not only connected but also reached beyond the people who wore them.

Coins are a different matter altogether. Coinage was a new way of demonstrating wealth, status and connections, arriving in southern Britain in the 2nd century BC (a time when torcs were possibly already widespread, although few from this early period seem to have been deposited). Coins became more common in the early to mid-1st century BC. The coins found in torc hoards at Snettisham represent some of the earliest types from East Anglia. Coinage would not become widespread here until the 50s BC, when Gallo-Belgic E was introduced, and local production began. Coins are portable, and easily distributed among many people. Their value lies in their multiplicity, standardisation and reproducibility. Issuing a batch of coinage was a physical manifestation of a very particular (and possibly new) form of authority. An individual or group had to gather the raw materials and resources, as well as needing access to the required labour and knowledge. What was created was not a single ornament that could only be worn by one person at a time, and only seen by those present nearby, but a mass of standardised discs literally stamped with images denoting the authority of the issuer(s). Distributing coinage was a way to mark and create alliances, political affiliations and connections; coins were physical symbols of a system of power and allegiance that could be carried by and shared among many people. In this new 'world of coins', torcs, or at least the social relations and power networks they represented, may have seemed outdated.

The shift from torcs to coins as symbols and mechanisms of negotiating power and status may have been slow, perhaps taking place over decades, with objects such as early non-local coinage and simple wrought rings taking on an intermediate role. However, the mid-1st-century BC expansion of local coin production coincides with a tide mark in the hoard evidence: many torcs were seemingly buried at this time. But why were they buried, rather than being recycled into new symbols of power? The long histories of many of the objects from Snettisham suggests an answer: were these objects simply too potent to be absorbed into the standardised world of coinage, where one batch must, by definition, be equal to another? The torcs from Snettisham were powerful objects in their own right, entangled (perhaps problematically so) with people, power structures, and relationships.

In this sense, burying these objects can be seen not as ending their lives, but as transforming potent objects into a different kind of potential. The careful structuring of hoards such as G, H and L, and the large and diverse collection(s) represented by Hoard F hint that the very act of collecting and depositing these objects was a sphere in which power and relations could be created, negotiated and enacted anew: the hoards were transformational. Taking these objects out of circulation created space for a new kind of object, coinage, and with it new forms of authority and new kinds of interaction between people, objects and materials.

These new systems of power may have been referenced through the later (Phase 4) hoards from the site. Hoard M consisted of a group of large, amorphous lumps of silver-copper alloy, with embedded lumps of charcoal. The incorporation of these objects within the enclosed area of the hoard field seems to suggest a deliberate connection to the transformative potential of metalworking processes. Hoard P was a large assemblage of (mostly silver) 1st-century AD coinage, likely deposited around AD 60/61 or shortly thereafter. This fits into wider patterns of deposition across Norfolk at this time, when coinage became the favoured material for inclusion in hoards.

Why Snettisham?

If torcs were being taken out of circulation to make way for coinage, the question remains as to why so many were deposited at a single site, and why Snettisham was chosen. The finds from the 'gold field' are unprecedented, but they do fit into wider patterns of torc deposition around this time across southern Britain. East Anglia, and especially Norfolk, has the largest number of finds, and it is clear that torcs (or at least torc deposition) were particularly important in this region. Late Iron Age hoards are well attested across Norfolk, often being located at high points with views across rivers or the sea (Hutcheson 2005; Davies 2008).

Ken Hill meets all these criteria and more. It is located in north-west Norfolk, one of the densest areas for Late Iron Age hoarding (even taking Snettisham out of the equation), and is not just a high point but a very significant landmark: a distinctively shaped hilltop promontory reaching out into the Wash. It is an unusual and conspicuous feature, visible from some way in either direction along the coast in a landscape that otherwise consists mainly of flat, low-lying, marshy ground. In the Late Iron Age, it would have been surrounded by water on three sides, commanding views across the North Sea to the north and east, falling away to the Wash in the west, curling around an inlet so that the southern side of the hoard field sloped away down to the water. This was also a place where freshwater running down from the chalk ridge near Shernbourne met the saltwater of the Wash. Whilst today north-west Norfolk is a relatively rural area, this was a well-populated region in the Iron Age, with productive agricultural land and rich in fenland resources such as wildfowl, salt and reeds for thatch and other crafts. Its inhabitants were well connected to other regions of Iron Age southern Britain via the Icknield Way, across the Wash to Lincolnshire, and via the North Sea to the continent, perhaps accessed via the Rhineland Delta. Many of the objects from Snettisham speak of these connections, including the beautifully decorated tubular torcs from Hoard A which find their closest parallels in the Low Countries.

By the Late Iron Age, Snettisham had a history as a special site, with evidence of possible feasting activity going back at least as far as the Earlier Iron Age, and perhaps even prior periods. It was well suited for torc deposition in terms of location and setting. It may be that such practices were in some ways self-reinforcing: that torcs were not just buried at Ken Hill because it was an important place, but that Ken Hill in part drew its increasing importance from the fact that it became a socially sanctioned place to bury torcs. These were potent objects which people were motivated to take out of circulation, and there must have been a need for appropriate places and events at which to do so.

The resulting hoards are exceptional archaeological assemblages today, and the scale of deposition at the site must surely have been exceptional even at the time. Neighbouring sites such as Sedgeford, perhaps part of an interconnected landscape of settlement and deposition, are nowhere near approaching the richness of the Snettisham finds, and there is nothing like them from elsewhere in the UK or Europe.

Who gathered here to make these deposits? Given the hundreds of torcs represented at the site, these must surely have been drawn from the possessions or collections of many people and probably several communities. It seems likely that the site drew visitors from across much of north-west Norfolk at the very least. Was it also an inter-regional centre drawing together people from across Britain and perhaps even beyond? Certainly the people who owned and used the objects found at the site were well-connected. The coins assemblage suggests wide regional networks reaching to the south and east. The types of torcs found at Snettisham would not be out of place elsewhere in southern and western Britain (in the case of multi-strand torcs) or the near continent (for tubular torc types), but the very nature of these widespread styles makes it hard to narrow down their origins. There are close connections between many of the objects in terms of the metalsmithing techniques used, but these are nonetheless varied enough to make it highly plausible that several different workshops, and certainly many individuals given the long potential timeframes, were involved in their production.

Bringing these objects together in carefully structured deposits at a site with a long history of importance and a distinctive topographic location was likely a way of recognising and building new relationships and allegiances, as well as marking the end of an older system of social authority. The torcs themselves were laid to rest, but the stories they embodied may not have been forgotten. Over a century after the main period of deposition at the site, it was demarcated by a large-scale ditched enclosure, with the area of the hoards at its centre, suggesting that the significance of the site continued for generations after the hoards were buried.

Appendix 3
Concordance of Finds

Over the years, a large number of different cataloguing systems have been used to order and understand the material from Snettisham. This volume represents the first attempt at a unified metalwork catalogue, and so a new numbering and ordering system has been introduced, covering all finds.

Previous numbering and codes are included in individual catalogue entires, but to allow for easier cross-referencing with previous publications, full concordances with all known previous cataloguing systems are given here.

The main concordance, ordered by the catalogue numbers used in this volume, includes information about the museum where the object is held, registration number, published references in previous catalogues (Clarke 1954 and Burns 1971), the four-letter site codes assigned to material excavated in 1990–2 ('Stead code'), the numbers given by Ralph Jackson to finds recovered by Hodder in 1990 when they were brought into the BM ('Jackson no.'), as well as 'Ticket nos' assigned to NCM material by Farley in 2021 (see Ch. 1 for a full discussion of all these systems and codes).

For each object, a summary is also given of key information such as findspot, context details, object name, multi-strand torc/bracelet construction code (MSCC, see Ch. 13) or tubular torc type, terminal type, material, and any known joining or related fragments. The intention is to assist the reader, and future researchers, in navigating these complicated assemblages. To this end, the summary of hoards in Chapter 11, and **Table 11.1** which orders the material by find type rather than hoard, will also be useful.

Whilst a concordance with the two simultaneous cataloguing systems used by Clarke (1954) is included in the main concordance for the material he published (Hoards A–E), the correspondence with these is complicated. Thus, for those who wish to make a more detailed referencing between these publications, a final more detailed concordance with Clarke (1954) is also included, with two tables, ordered according to Clarke's own systems, one numbering the finds by hoard, and one ordering them by object type.

Cat no.	Museum	Reg. no.	Ticket no.	Published ref.	Stead code	Ralph no.	Ex. year	Findspot	Context details	Object name	MSCC or TUB torc type	Torc terminal type	Material	Joining / related fragments?
A.1	NCM	1949.74.2		Clarke 1954, 37; pls i, ii; Tubular Torc 1			1948	Area 8	Hoard A; found during ploughing	Torc	TUBULAR (Type 6)	BUFFER	Gold alloy; iron	
A.2	NCM	1949.74.1		Clarke 1954, 38; pls i, ii; Tubular Torc 2			1948	Area 8	Hoard A; found during ploughing	Torc	TUBULAR (Type 6)	BUFFER	Gold alloy	
A.3	NCM	1949.74.3		Clarke 1954, 38–9; pls i, ii; Tubular Torc 3			1948	Area 8	Hoard A; found during ploughing	Torc	TUBULAR (Type 6)	BUFFER	Gold alloy	
A.4	NCM	1949.74.6		Clarke 1954, 39; Tubular Torc 4			1948	Area 8	Hoard A; found during ploughing and Rainbird Clarke excavations	Torc	TUBULAR (Type 6)	BUFFER	Gold alloy; iron	A.4–A.7 may be from the same torc
A.5	NCM	1949.74.4		Clarke 1954, 39; pl. i; Tubular Torc 4			1948	Area 8	Hoard A; found during ploughing	Torc	TUBULAR (Type 6)	BUFFER	Gold alloy	A.4–A.7 may be from the same torc
A.6	NCM	1949.74.5		Clarke 1954, 39, pl. i; Tubular Torc 4			1948	Area 8	Hoard A; found during ploughing	Torc	TUBULAR (Type 6)	BUFFER	Gold alloy	A.4–A.7 may be from the same torc
A.7	NCM	1949.74.		Clarke 1954, 39, pl. i; Tubular Torc 4			1948	Area 8	Hoard A; found during ploughing	Torc	TUBULAR (Type 6)	BUFFER	Gold alloy	A.4–A.7 may be from the same torc
A.8	NCM	1949.74.7		Clarke 1954, p. 39; fig. 6			1948	Area 8	Hoard A; found during ploughing	Gritstone pebble			Stone	
B.1a	NCM	1949.75.24	BLUE.14	Clarke 1954, 54, no. 14; pl xii, in group; Hd. B no. 7			1948	Area 1	Hoard B; found during Rainbird Clarke excavations, Trench 2	Large ring			Gold/silver alloy	
B.1b	NCM	1949.75.17	BLUE.16	Clarke 1954, 54, no. 13; pl. xii, in group; Hd. B no. 6			1948	Area 1	Hoard B; found during Rainbird Clarke excavations, Trench 2	Large ring			Gold/silver alloy	
B.1c	NCM	1949.75.9	BLUE.19	Clarke 1954, 56, no. 12; pl. xii, in group; Hd. B no. 10			1948	Area 1	Hoard B; found during Rainbird Clarke excavations, Trench 2	Small ring			Gold/silver alloy	
B.1d	NCM	1949.75	BLUE.21	Clarke 1954, 55, no. 1; pl xii, bottom right of group; Hd. B no. 12			1948	Area 1	Hoard B; found during Rainbird Clarke excavations, Trench 2	Small ring			Copper alloy	
B.1e	NCM	1949.75.72	BLUE.22	Clarke 1954, 46, no. 1; pl. xii, top left of group; Hd. B no. 13			1948	Area 1	Hoard B; found during Rainbird Clarke excavations, Trench 2	Torc/bracelet		LOOP	Gold/silver alloy	
B.1f	NCM	1949.75.37	BLUE.24	Clarke 1954, 46, no. 3; pl. xii, no. 3 and in group, centre right; Hd. B no. 15			1948	Area 1	Hoard B; found during Rainbird Clarke excavations, Trench 2	Torc/bracelet	(5C)R		Gold/silver alloy	
B.1g	NCM	1949.75.40	BLUE.25	Clarke 1954, 46, no. 4; pl. xii, no. 4; Hd. B no. 16			1948	Area 1	Hoard B; found during Rainbird Clarke excavations, Trench 2	Torc/bracelet	(4C)Q		Gold/silver alloy	
B.1h	NCM	1949.75	BLUE.126	Clarke 1954, 56, no. 14; pl xii, bottom left of group; Hd. B no. 11			1948	Area 1	Hoard B; found during Rainbird Clarke excavations, Trench 2	Small ring			Gold/silver alloy	
B.2	NCM	1949.75.38	BLUE.23	Clarke 1954, 46, no. 2; pl. xii, no. 2; Hd. B no. 14			1948	Area 1	Hoard B; found during ploughing	Torc/bracelet	(2P)R		Gold/silver alloy	
B.3	NCM	1949.75.48	BLUE.29	Clarke 1954, 47, no. 8; pl. ix; Hd. B no. 20			1948	Area 1	Hoard B; found during ploughing	Torc/bracelet	(2P)R		Gold/silver alloy	
B.4	NCM	1949.75.41	BLUE.28	Clarke 1954, 47, no. 7; pl. xii; Hd. B no. 19			1948	Area 1	Hoard B; found during ploughing	Torc/bracelet	(?2P)R		Gold/silver alloy	
B.5	NCM	1949.75.15	BLUE.30	Clarke 1954, 47, no. 14; pl. ix; Hd. B no. 21			1948	Area 1	Hoard B; found during ploughing	Torc/bracelet	(2P)T	LOOP	Gold/silver alloy	
B.6	NCM	1949.75	BLUE.46	Clarke 1954, 47, no. 15; pl. ix; Hd. B no. 22			1948	Area 1	Hoard B; found during Rainbird Clarke excavations, Trench 2	Wire/?torc/ ?bracelet	(?P)F		Gold/silver alloy	
B.7	NCM	1949.75.39	BLUE.44	Clarke 1954, 46, no. 5; Hd. B no. 17			1948	Area 1	Hoard B; found during ploughing	Torc/bracelet	(?3C)R		Gold/silver alloy	
B.8	NCM	1949.75.16	BLUE.27	Clarke 1954, 46, no. 6; pl. ix; Hd. B no. 18			1948	Area 1	Hoard B; found during ploughing	Bracelet	(?3P)R		Gold/silver alloy	
B.9	NCM	1949.75	GREY.96	Clarke 1954, 47, no. 20; Hd. B no. 24			1948	Area 1	Hoard B; found during ploughing	Torc/bracelet		?LOOP	Gold/silver alloy	
B.10	NCM	1949.75	GREY.74	Not in Clarke 1954			1948	Area 1	Hoard B; found during ploughing	Wire/?torc/ ?bracelet			Gold/silver alloy	
B.11	NCM	1949.75.30	BLUE.32	Clarke 1954, 47, no. 19; pl. ix; Hd. B no. 23			1948	Area 1	Hoard B; found during ploughing	Torc/bracelet	(2P)R	LOOP	Copper alloy	
B.12	NCM	1949.75	GREY.81	Not in Clarke 1954			1948	Area 1	Hoard B; found during ploughing	Wire/?bracelet			Gold/silver alloy	B.12 and B.13 may be part of the same object.
B.13	NCM	1949.75	GREY.80	Not in Clarke 1954			1948	Area 1	Hoard B; found during ploughing	Wire/?bracelet		?LOOP	Gold/silver alloy	B.12 and B.13 may be part o the same object.
B.14	NCM	1949.75	BLUE.48	Not in Clarke 1954			1948	Area 1	Hoard B; found during ploughing	Torc/bracelet	(?3P)R		Copper alloy	

Cat no.	Museum	Reg. no.	Ticket no.	Published ref.	Stead code	Ralph no.	Ex. year	Findspot	Context details	Object name	MSCC or TUB torc type	Torc terminal type	Material	Joining / related fragments?
B.15	NCM	1949.75	GREY.48	Clarke 1954, 47, no. 20; Hd. B no. 24			1948	Area 1	Hoard B; found during ploughing	Wire/?torc / ?bracelet			Copper alloy	
B.16	NCM	1949.75	GREY.100	Clarke 1954, 47, no. 21; Hd. B no. 25			1948	Area 1	Hoard B; found during ploughing	Wire/?torc / ?bracelet			Copper alloy	
B.17	NCM	1949.75	GREY.88	Clarke 1954, 47, no. 20; Hd. B no. 24			1948	Area 1	Hoard B; found during Rainbird Clarke excavations, Trench 2	Torc/bracelet		?LOOP	Copper alloy	
B.18	NCM	1949.75	GREY.83	Not in Clarke 1954			1948	Area 1	Hoard B; found during ploughing	Wire/?torc/ ?bracelet			Copper alloy	
B.19	NCM	1949.75	GREY.82	Not in Clarke 1954			1948	Area 1	Hoard B; found during ploughing	Wire/?torc/ ?bracelet			Copper alloy	
B.20	NCM	1949.75.13	BLUE.127	Clarke 1954, 54, no. 12; Hd. B no. 5			1948	Area 1	Hoard B; found during ploughing	Large ring			Gold/silver alloy	
B.21	NCM	1949.75; 1949.75.26	BLUE.6-8	Clarke 1954, 54, no. 11; Hd. B no. 3			1948	Area 1	Hoard B; found during ploughing	Large ring			Gold/silver alloy	
B.22	NCM	1949.75	BLUE.9-10	Clarke 1954, 54, no. 11; Hd. B no. 3			1948	Area 1	Hoard B; found during ploughing	Large ring			Gold/silver alloy	
B.23	NCM	1949.75	BLUE.11-12	Clarke 1954, 54, no. 11; Hd. B no. 3			1948	Area 1	Hoard B; found during ploughing	Large ring			Gold/silver alloy	
B.24	NCM	1949.75; 1949.75.84	BLUE.3-5	Clarke 1954, 54, no. 15; Hd. B no. 4			1948	Area 1	Hoard B; found during ploughing	Large ring			Gold/silver alloy	
B.25	NCM	1949.75.46	BLUE.20	Clarke 1954, 56, no. 11; pl xii; Hd. B no. 9			1948	Area 1	Hoard B; found during Rainbird Clarke excavations, Trench 2	Small ring			Gold/silver alloy	
B.26	NCM	1949.75.51	BLUE.2	Clarke 1954, 58 (cake), no. 2; pl. xiii, upper; Hd. B no. 2			1948	Area 1	Hoard B; found during Rainbird Clarke excavations, Trench 2	Ingot			Gold/silver alloy	
B.27	NCM	1949.75	BLUE.1	Clarke 1954, 58 (cake), no. 1; pl. xiii, upper; Hd. B no. 1			1948	Area 1	Hoard B; found during Rainbird Clarke excavations, Trench 2	Lump ingot			Gold/silver alloy	
B.28	NCM	1949.75.41	BLUE.17	Clarke 1954, 58 (Misc.), no. 1; pl xiii, lower, Misc. 1; Hd. B no. 8			1948	Area 1	Hoard B; found during Rainbird Clarke excavations, Trench 2	Clamp			Copper alloy	
B.29	NCM	1949.75	BLUE.121	Clarke 1954, 58 (Misc.), no. 3; Hd. B no. 26			1948	Area 1	Hoard B; found during Rainbird Clarke excavations	Nail			Iron	
B.30	NCM	1949.75	BLUE.122	Clarke 1954, 58 (Misc.), no. 3; Hd. B no. 26			1948	Area 1	Hoard B; found during Rainbird Clarke excavations	Nail			Iron	
B.31	NCM	1949.75	BLUE.123	Clarke 1954, 58 (Misc.), no. 3; Hd. B no. 26			1948	Area 1	Hoard B; found during Rainbird Clarke excavations	Nail			Iron	
B.32	NCM	1949.75	BLUE.124	Clarke 1954, 58 (Misc.), no. 3; Hd. B no. 26			1948	Area 1	Hoard B; found during Rainbird Clarke excavations	Nail			Iron	
B.33	NCM	1949.75	BLUE.125	Clarke 1954, 58 (Misc.), no. 3; Hd. B no. 26			1948	Area 1	Hoard B; found during Rainbird Clarke excavations	Nail			Iron	
C.1	NCM	1949.75	BLUE.43	Clarke 1954, 47, no. 12; Hd. C no. 16			1948	Area 1	Hoard C; found during ploughing	Torc/bracelet	(4C)R		Gold/silver alloy	C.1–5 may be from the same torc
C.2	NCM	1949.75	BLUE.41	Clarke 1954, 47, no. 12; Hd. C no. 16			1948	Area 1	Hoard C; found during ploughing	Torc/bracelet	(4C)R		Gold/silver alloy	C.1–5 may be from the same torc
C.3	NCM	1949.75	BLUE.39	Clarke 1954, 47, no. 12; Hd. C no. 16			1948	Area 1	Hoard C; found during ploughing	Torc/bracelet	(4C)R		Gold/silver alloy	C.1–5 may be from the same torc
C.4	NCM	1949.75	BLUE.40	Clarke 1954, 47, no. 12; Hd. C no. 16			1948	Area 1	Hoard C; found during ploughing	Torc/bracelet	(4C)R		Gold/silver alloy	C.1–5 may be from the same torc
C.5	NCM	1949.75	BLUE.42	Clarke 1954, 47, no. 12; Hd. C no. 16			1948	Area 1	Hoard C; found during ploughing	Torc/bracelet	(4C)R		Gold/silver alloy	C.1–5 may be from the same torc
C.6	NCM	1949.75.50	GREY.78	Clarke 1954, 47, no. 9; pl. ix; Hd. C no. 12			1948	Area 1	Hoard C; found during ploughing	Rod/?torc/ ?bracelet			Gold/silver alloy	
C.7	NCM	1949.75	WHITE.14	Clarke 1954, 47, no. 9; pl. ix; Hd. C no. 12			1948	Area 1	Hoard C; found during ploughing	Wire/?torc/ ?bracelet			Gold/silver alloy	C.7–18 may be from the same torc
C.8	NCM	1949.75	WHITE.13	Clarke 1954, 47, no. 9; pl. ix; Hd. C no. 12			1948	Area 1	Hoard C; found during ploughing	Wire/?torc/ ?bracelet			Gold/silver alloy	C.7–18 may be from the same torc
C.9	NCM	1949.75	WHITE.50	Clarke 1954, 47, no. 9; pl. ix; Hd. C no. 12			1948	Area 1	Hoard C; found during Rainbird Clarke excavations, Trench 20	Wire/?torc/ ?bracelet	(?P)F		Gold/silver alloy	C.7–18 may be from the same torc
C.10	NCM	1949.75	WHITE.10	Clarke 1954, 47, no. 9; pl. ix; Hd. C no. 12			1948	Area 1	Hoard C; found during ploughing	Wire/?torc/ ?bracelet	(?P)R		Gold/silver alloy	C.7–18 may be from the same torc
C.11	NCM	1949.75	WHITE.12	Clarke 1954, 47, no. 9; pl. ix; Hd. C no. 12			1948	Area 1	Hoard C; found during ploughing	Wire/?torc/ ?bracelet			Gold/silver alloy	C.7–18 may be from the same torc
C.12	NCM	1949.75	BLUE.31	Clarke 1954, 47, no. 9; pl. ix; Hd. C no. 12			1948	Area 1	Hoard C; found during ploughing	Wire/?torc/ ?bracelet	(?P)F		Gold/silver alloy	C.7–18 may be from the same torc

Cat no.	Museum	Reg. no.	Ticket no.	Published ref.	Stead code	Ralph no.	Ex. year	Findspot	Context details	Object name	MSCC or TUB torc type	Torc terminal type	Material	Joining / related fragments?
C.13	NCM	1949.75	WHITE.11	Clarke 1954, 47, no. 11; pl. ix; Hd. C no. 12			1948	Area 1	Hoard C; found during ploughing	Wire/?torc/ ?bracelet	(?P)F		Gold/silver alloy	C.7–18 may be from the same torc
C.14	NCM	1949.75	WHITE.31	Clarke 1954, 47, no. 10; Hd. C no. 13			1948	Area 1	Hoard C; found during ploughing	Wire/?torc/ ?bracelet		?LOOP	Gold/silver alloy	C.7–18 may be from the same torc
C.15	NCM	1949.75	WHITE.17	Clarke 1954, 47, no. 9; pl. ix; Hd. C no. 12			1948	Area 1	Hoard C; found during ploughing	Wire/?torc/ ?bracelet			Gold/silver alloy	C.7–18 may be from the same torc
C.16	NCM	1949.75	WHITE.16	Clarke 1954, 47, no. 9; pl. ix; Hd. C no. 12			1948	Area 1	Hoard C; found during ploughing	Wire/?torc/ ?bracelet			Gold/silver alloy	C.7–18 may be from the same torc
C.17	NCM	1949.75	GREY.27	Clarke 1954, 58 (cake), no. 5; Hd. C no. 15			1948	Area 1	Hoard C; found during ploughing	Wire/?torc/ ?bracelet		?LOOP	Gold/silver alloy	C.7–18 may be from the same torc
C.18	NCM	1949.75	WHITE.15	Clarke 1954, 47, no. 9; pl. ix; Hd. C no. 12			1948	Area 1	Hoard C; found during ploughing	Wire/?torc/ ?bracelet			Gold/silver alloy	C.7–18 may be from the same torc
C.19	NCM	1949.75.36	WHITE.18	Clarke 1954, 47, no. 11; pl. ix; Hd. C no. 14			1948	Area 1	Hoard C; found during ploughing	Wire/?torc/ ?bracelet	(?C/P)R	?LOOP	Gold/silver alloy	
C.20	NCM	1949.75	GREY.72	Clarke 1954, 47, no. 11; pl. ix (this fragment not pictured); Hd. C no. 14			1948	Area 1	Hoard C; found during ploughing	Torc/bracelet		?LOOP	Gold/silver alloy	
C.21	NCM	1949.75	GREY.76	Clarke 1954, 47, no. 12; Hd. C no. 16			1948	Area 1	Hoard C; found during ploughing	Torc/bracelet	(??(4C))R		Gold/silver alloy	
C.22	NCM	1949.75	WHITE.23	Clarke 1954, 52, no. 1; pl xi, right; Hd. C no. 17			1948	Area 1	Hoard C; found during ploughing	Torc/bracelet	(7C)T	BUFFER	Copper alloy	
C.23	NCM	1949.75	BLUE.35	Clarke 1954, 47, no. 22; Hd. C no. 19			1948	Area 1	Hoard C; found during ploughing	Torc/bracelet	(6C)[3T,3R, alternating]		Copper alloy	
C.24	NCM	1949.75	BLUE.45	Clarke 1954, 47, no. 22; Hd. C no. 19			1948	Area 1	Hoard C; found during ploughing	Torc/bracelet	(6C)T		Copper alloy	
C.25	NCM	1949.75.12	WHITE.38	Clarke 1954, 52, no. 2; pl xi, right; Hd. C no. 18			1948	Area 1	Hoard C; found during ploughing	Torc/bracelet	(5C)T		Copper alloy	C.25–7 may be from the same torc
C.26	NCM	1949.75.54	WHITE.24	Clarke 1954, 52, no. 1; pl xi, right; Hd. C no. 17			1948	Area 1	Hoard C; found during ploughing	Torc/bracelet	(5C)T	BUFFER	Copper alloy	C.25–7 may be from the same torc
C.27	NCM	1949.75	WHITE.30	Clarke 1954, 52, no. 3 (left); pl xi, right; Hd. C no. 20			1948	Area 1	Hoard C; found during ploughing	Torc/bracelet	(5C)T	BUFFER	Copper alloy	C.25–7 may be from the same torc
C.28	NCM	1949.75	BLUE.37	Clarke 1954, 47, no. 22; Hd. C no. 19			1948	Area 1	Hoard C; found during ploughing	Torc/bracelet	(5C)T		Copper alloy	C.28–30 may be from the same torc
C.29	NCM	1949.75	BLUE.38	Clarke 1954, 47, no. 22; Hd. C no. 19			1948	Area 1	Hoard C; found during ploughing	Torc/bracelet	(5C)T		Copper alloy	C.28–30 may be from the same torc
C.30	NCM	1949.75	BLUE.36	Clarke 1954, 47, no. 22; Hd. C no. 19			1948	Area 1	Hoard C; found during ploughing	Torc/bracelet	(5C)T		Copper alloy	C.28–30 may be from the same torc
C.31	NCM	1949.75.53	WHITE.39	Clarke 1954, 52, no. 3 (right); pl xi, right; Hd. C no. 20			1948	Area 1	Hoard C; found during ploughing	Torc/bracelet	(3P(2P))Q	BUFFER	Copper alloy	
C.32	NCM	1949.75	WHITE.43	Not in Clarke 1954			1948	Area 1	Hoard C; found during ploughing	Wire/?torc/ ?bracelet	(?C)T		Copper alloy	
C.33	NCM	1949.75	BLUE.80	Not in Clarke 1954			1948	Area 1	Hoard C; found during ploughing	Wire/?torc/ ?bracelet	(?P/C)T		Copper alloy	
C.34	NCM	1949.75	WHITE.40	Not in Clarke 1954			1948	Area 1	Hoard C; found during ploughing	Torc/bracelet	(?C)T		Copper alloy	
C.35	NCM	1949.75	WHITE.41	Not in Clarke 1954			1948	Area 1	Hoard C; found during ploughing	Torc/bracelet	(?C)T		Copper alloy	
C.36	NCM	1949.75	WHITE.42	Not in Clarke 1954			1948	Area 1	Hoard C; found during ploughing	Torc/bracelet	(?C)T		Copper alloy	
C.37	NCM	1949.75	WHITE.47	Not in Clarke 1954			1948	Area 1	Hoard C; found during ploughing	Wire/?torc/ ?bracelet	(?C)T		Copper alloy	
C.38	NCM	1949.75	BLUE.79	Not in Clarke 1954			1948	Area 1	Hoard C; found during ploughing	Wire/?torc/ ?bracelet	(?P/C)Q		Copper alloy	
C.39	NCM	1949.75	WHITE.48	Not in Clarke 1954			1948	Area 1	Hoard C; found during ploughing	Wire/?torc/ ?bracelet			Copper alloy	
C.40	NCM	1949.75	BLUE.82	Not in Clarke 1954			1948	Area 1	Hoard C; found during ploughing	Wire/?torc/ ?bracelet	(?P/C)R		Copper alloy	
C.41	NCM	1949.75	BLUE.81	Not in Clarke 1954			1948	Area 1	Hoard C; found during ploughing	Wire/?torc/ ?bracelet	(?P/C)R		Copper alloy	
C.42	NCM	1949.75	WHITE.46	Not in Clarke 1954			1948	Area 1	Hoard C; found during ploughing	Wire/?torc/ ?bracelet	(?P/C)R		Copper alloy	

Cat no.	Museum	Reg. no.	Ticket no.	Published ref.	Stead code	Ralph no.	Ex. year	Findspot	Context details	Object name	MSCC or TUB torc type	Torc terminal type	Material	Joining / related fragments?
C.43	NCM	1949.75	BLUE.83-120	Not in Clarke 1954			1948	Area 1	Hoard C; found during ploughing	Torc/bracelet	(?C)R		Copper alloy	
C.44	NCM	1949.75	BLUE.78	Not in Clarke 1954			1948	Area 1	Hoard C; found during ploughing	Wire/?torc/ ?bracelet			Copper alloy	
C.45	NCM	1949.75.51	WHITE.1	Clarke 1954, 58 (cake), no. 4; pl xiii, upper; Hd. C no. 2			1948	Area 1	Hoard C; found during ploughing	Large ring			Gold/silver alloy	
C.46	NCM	1949.75.41	WHITE.2	Clarke 1954, 54, no. 1; Hd. C no. 3			1948	Area 1	Hoard C; found during ploughing	Large ring			Gold/silver alloy	
C.47	NCM	1949.75.6	WHITE.37	Clarke 1954, 56, no. 15; pl. xii; Hd. C no. 6			1948	Area 1	Hoard C; found during ploughing	Small ring			Gold/silver alloy	
C.48	NCM	1949.75	WHITE.3	Clarke 1954, 55, no. 2; Hd. C no. 4			1948	Area 1	Hoard C; found during ploughing	Small ring			Copper alloy	
C.49	NCM	1949.75	WHITE.4	Clarke 1954, 55, no. 3; Hd. C no. 5			1948	Area 1	Hoard C; found during ploughing	Small ring			Copper alloy	
C.50	NCM	1949.75	WHITE.51	Clarke 1954, 58 (cake), no. 3; pl. xiii, upper, 3; Hd. C no. 11			1948	Area 1	Hoard C; found during ploughing	Sheet			Gold/silver alloy	
C.51	NCM	1949.75.57	WHITE.7	Clarke 1954, 57, no. 5; pl xiii, lower; Hd. C no. 8			1948	Area 1	Hoard C; found during ploughing	Rivet head			Copper alloy	
C.52	NCM	1949.75.58	WHITE.8	Clarke 1954, 57, no. 3; pl xiii, lower; Hd. C no. 9			1948	Area 1	Hoard C; found during ploughing	Rivet head			Copper alloy	
C.53	NCM	1949.75.58	WHITE.9	Clarke 1954, 57, no. 3; pl xiii, lower; Hd. C no. 9			1948	Area 1	Hoard C; found during ploughing	Rivet head			Copper alloy	
C.54	NCM	1949.75.45	WHITE.6	Clarke 1954, 57, no. 2; pl xiii, lower; Hd. C no. 7			1948	Area 1	Hoard C; found during ploughing	Binding strip / fitting			Copper alloy	
C.55	NCM	1949.75	GREY.56	Clarke 1954, 57, no. 6; Hd. C no. 10			1948	Area 1	Hoard C; found during ploughing	Sheet			Copper alloy	
C.56	NCM	1949.75	WHITE.49	Clarke 1954, 57, no. 6; Hd. C no. 10			1948	Area 1	Hoard C; found during Rainbird Clarke excavations, Trench 20	Sheet			Copper alloy	
C.57	NCM	1949.75	WHITE.32	Clarke 1954, 58 (Misc.), no. 4; fig. 9; Hd. C no. 1			1948	Area 1	Hoard C; found during Rainbird Clarke excavations	Nail			Iron	
C.58	NCM	1949.75	WHITE.33	Clarke 1954, 58 (Misc.), no. 4; fig. 9; Hd. C no. 1			1948	Area 1	Hoard C; found during Rainbird Clarke excavations	Nail			Iron	
C.59	NCM	1949.75	WHITE.34	Clarke 1954, 58 (Misc.), no. 4; fig. 9; Hd. C no. 1			1948	Area 1	Hoard C; found during Rainbird Clarke excavations	Nail			Iron	
C.60	NCM	1949.75	WHITE.35	Clarke 1954, 58 (Misc.), no. 4; fig. 9; Hd. C no. 1			1948	Area 1	Hoard C; found during Rainbird Clarke excavations	Nail			Iron	
C.61	NCM	1949.75	WHITE.36	Clarke 1954, 58 (Misc.), no. 4; fig. 9; Hd. C no. 1			1948	Area 1	Hoard C; found during Rainbird Clarke excavations	Nail			Iron	
B/C.1	NCM	1949.75.49	GREY.26	Clarke 1954, 47, no. 16; pl. ix; Hd. B/C no. 26			1948	Area 1	Hoard B/C; found during ploughing	Torc/bracelet	(?2P(2P))R	LOOP	Gold/silver alloy	
B/C.2	NCM	1949.75	GREY.28	Clarke 1954, 47, no. 18; pl. ix; Hd. B/C no. 28			1948	Area 1	Hoard B/C; found during ploughing	Torc/bracelet	(?2P(2P))R	LOOP	Gold/silver alloy	
B/C.3	NCM	1949.75	GREY.70	Clarke 1954, 48, no. 47; pl ix; Hd. B/C no. 53			1948	Area 1	Hoard B/C; found during ploughing	Torc/bracelet	(2P)R		Gold/silver alloy	B/C.3 and B/C.4 join
B/C.4	NCM	1949.75	GREY.69	Clarke 1954, 48, no. 47; pl ix; Hd. B/C no. 53			1948	Area 1	Hoard B/C; found during ploughing	Torc/bracelet	(2P)R		Gold/silver alloy	B/C.3 and B/C.4 join
B/C.5	NCM	1949.75.29	GREY.66	Clarke 1954, 48, no. 44; pl ix; Hd. B/C no. 50			1948	Area 1	Hoard B/C; found during ploughing	Torc/bracelet	(2PZ)Q	LOOP	Gold/silver alloy	
B/C.6	NCM	1949.75	GREY.73	Clarke 1954, 47, no. 17; pl. ix; Hd. B/C no. 27			1948	Area 1	Hoard B/C; found during ploughing	Wire/?torc/ ?bracelet		?LOOP	Gold/silver alloy	
B/C.7	NCM	1949.75	GREY.91	Clarke 1954, 48, no. 36; pl. ix; Hd. B/C no. 42			1948	Area 1	Hoard B/C; found during ploughing	Torc/bracelet		?LOOP	Gold/silver alloy	B/C.7 and B/C.8 may be from the same loop terminal
B/C.8	NCM	1949.75	GREY.97	Clarke 1954, 48, no. 36; pl. ix; Hd. B/C no. 42			1948	Area 1	Hoard B/C; found during ploughing	Torc/bracelet		?LOOP	Gold/silver alloy	B/C.7 and B/C.8 may be from the same loop terminal
B/C.9	NCM	1949.75.9	GREY.101	Clarke 1954, 48, no. 33; pl. viii; Hd. B/C no. 39			1948	Area 1	Hoard B/C; found during ploughing	Torc	(2PZ)R	LOOP	Copper alloy	
B/C.10	NCM	1949.75.3	GREY.38	Clarke 1954, 47, no. 31; pl viii; Hd. B/C no. 37			1948	Area 1	Hoard B/C; found during ploughing	Torc	(2PZ)R	LOOP	Copper alloy	
B/C.11	NCM	1949.75.7	GREY.102	Clarke 1954, 48, no. 32; pl. viii; Hd. B/C no. 38			1948	Area 1	Hoard B/C; found during ploughing	Torc	(2PZ)F	LOOP	Copper alloy	
B/C.12	NCM	1949.75.4	GREY.37	Clarke 1954, 47, no. 30; pl. viii; Hd. B/C no. 36			1948	Area 1	Hoard B/C; found during ploughing	Bracelet	(2PZ)F	LOOP	Copper alloy	

Cat no.	Museum	Reg. no.	Ticket no.	Published ref.	Stead code	Ralph no.	Ex. year	Findspot	Context details	Object name	MSCC or TUB torc type	Torc terminal type	Material	Joining / related fragments?
B/C.13	NCM	1949.75	GREY.62	Clarke 1954, 48, no. 41; pl ix; Hd. B/C no. 47			1948	Area 1	Hoard B/C; found during ploughing	Torc/bracelet	(2P)Q	LOOP	Copper alloy	
B/C.14	NCM	1949.75	GREY.67	Clarke 1954, 48, no. 45; pl ix; Hd. B/C no. 51			1948	Area 1	Hoard B/C; found during ploughing	Torc/bracelet	(2PZ)Q	LOOP	Copper alloy	B/C.14 and B/C.15 may be from the same torc
B/C.15	NCM	1949.75	GREY.71	Clarke 1954, 48, no. 48; pl ix; Hd. B/C no. 54			1948	Area 1	Hoard B/C; found during ploughing	Torc/bracelet	(2PZ)Q		Copper alloy	B/C.14 and B/C.15 may be from the same torc
B/C.16	NCM	1949.75.20	WHITE.5	Clarke 1954, 48, no. 38; pl ix; Hd. B/C no. 44			1948	Area 1	Hoard B/C; found during ploughing	Torc/bracelet		LOOP	Copper alloy	
B/C.17	NCM	1949.75	GREY.89	Clarke 1954, 48, no. 40; pl ix; Hd. B/C no. 46			1948	Area 1	Hoard B/C; found during ploughing	Wire/?torc/ ?bracelet	(?2P)R		Copper alloy	
B/C.18	NCM	1949.75	GREY.79	Clarke 1954, 48, no. 40; pl ix; Hd. B/C no. 46			1948	Area 1	Hoard B/C; found during ploughing	Wire/?torc/ ?bracelet		?LOOP	Copper alloy	
B/C.19	NCM	1949.75	GREY.41	Clarke 1954, 48, no. 35; pl ix; Hd. B/C no. 41			1948	Area 1	Hoard B/C; found during ploughing	Torc/bracelet		LOOP	Copper alloy	B/C.19-B/C.22 may be part of the same torc or bracelet
B/C.20	NCM	1949.75	GREY.45	Clarke 1954, 48, no. 39; pl ix; Hd. B/C no. 45			1948	Area 1	Hoard B/C; found during ploughing	Wire/?torc/ ?bracelet		?LOOP	Copper alloy	B/C.19-B/C.22 may be part of the same torc or bracelet
B/C.21	NCM	1949.75	GREY.64	Clarke 1954, 48, no. 40; pl ix (top left, mis-labelled in the plate as no. 42); Hd. B/C no. 46			1948	Area 1	Hoard B/C; found during ploughing	Wire/?torc/ ?bracelet		?LOOP	Copper alloy	B/C.19-B/C.22 may be part of the same torc or bracelet
B/C.22	NCM	1949.75.20	GREY.44	Clarke 1954, 48, no. 40; pl ix; Hd. B/C no. 46			1948	Area 1	Hoard B/C; found during ploughing	Wire/?torc/ ?bracelet		LOOP	Copper alloy	B/C.19-B/C.22 may be part of the same torc or bracelet
B/C.23	NCM	1949.75.47	GREY.33	Not in Clarke 1954			1948	Area 1	Hoard B/C; found during ploughing	Torc/bracelet	(2P)R		Copper alloy	
B/C.24	NCM	1949.75.27	GREY.65	Clarke 1954, 48, no. 43; pl viii; Hd. B/C no. 49			1948	Area 1	Hoard B/C; found during ploughing	Torc/bracelet	(2PZ)Q	LOOP	Copper alloy	
B/C.25	NCM	1949.75.25	GREY.43	Clarke 1954, 48, no. 37; pl ix; Hd. B/C no. 43			1948	Area 1	Hoard B/C; found during ploughing	Torc/bracelet		LOOP	Copper alloy	
B/C.26	NCM	1949.75	GREY.46	Clarke 1954, 48, no. 40; pl ix; Hd. B/C no. 46			1948	Area 1	Hoard B/C; found during ploughing	Torc/bracelet		?LOOP	Copper alloy	B/C.26–31 may be from the same torc or bracelet
B/C.27	NCM	1949.75	GREY.47	Clarke 1954, 48, no. 40; pl ix; Hd. B/C no. 46			1948	Area 1	Hoard B/C; found during ploughing	Wire/?torc/ ?bracelet			Copper alloy	B/C.26–31 may be from the same torc or bracelet
B/C.28	NCM	1949.75	GREY.49	Clarke 1954, 48, no. 40; pl ix; Hd. B/C no. 46			1948	Area 1	Hoard B/C; found during ploughing	Wire/?torc/ ?bracelet			Copper alloy	B/C.26-30 may be from the same torc or bracelet
B/C.29	NCM	1949.75	GREY.50	Clarke 1954, 48, no. 40; pl ix; Hd. B/C no. 46			1948	Area 1	Hoard B/C; found during ploughing	Wire/?torc/ ?bracelet			Copper alloy	B/C.26–31 may be from the same torc or bracelet
B/C.30	NCM	1949.75	GREY.51	Clarke 1954, 48, no. 40; pl ix; Hd. B/C no. 46			1948	Area 1	Hoard B/C; found during ploughing	Wire/?torc/ ?bracelet			Copper alloy	B/C.26–31 may be from the same torc or bracelet
B/C.31	NCM	1949.75	GREY.52	Clarke 1954, 48, no. 40; pl ix; Hd. B/C no. 46			1948	Area 1	Hoard B/C; found during ploughing	Wire/?torc/ ?bracelet			Copper alloy	B/C.26–31 may be from the same torc or bracelet
B/C.32	NCM	1949.75	GREY.92	Clarke 1954, 48, no. 40; pl ix; Hd. B/C no. 46			1948	Area 1	Hoard B/C; found during ploughing	Wire/?torc/ ?bracelet			Copper alloy	
B/C.33	NCM	1949.75	GREY.93	Clarke 1954, 48, no. 40; pl ix; Hd. B/C no. 46			1948	Area 1	Hoard B/C; found during ploughing	Wire/?torc/ ?bracelet			Copper alloy	
B/C.34	NCM	1949.75	GREY.95	Clarke 1954, 48, no. 40; pl ix; Hd. B/C no. 46			1948	Area 1	Hoard B/C; found during ploughing	Wire/?torc/ ?bracelet			Copper alloy	
B/C.35	NCM	1949.75.28	GREY.63	Clarke 1954, 48, no. 42; pl ix; Hd. B/C no. 48			1948	Area 1	Hoard B/C; found during ploughing	Torc/bracelet	(2PZ)R	LOOP	Copper alloy	
B/C.36	NCM	1949.75	GREY.68	Clarke 1954, 48, no. 46; pl ix; Hd. B/C no. 52			1948	Area 1	Hoard B/C; found during ploughing	Torc/bracelet	(2PZ)F	LOOP	Copper alloy	

Cat no.	Museum	Reg. no.	Ticket no.	Published ref.	Stead code	Ralph no.	Ex. year	Findspot	Context details	Object name	MSCC or TUB torc type	Torc terminal type	Material	Joining / related fragments?
B/C.37	NCM	1949.75.22	GREY.104	Clarke 1954, 48, no. 34; pl. ix; Hd. B/C no. 40			1948	Area 1	Hoard B/C; found during ploughing	Torc/bracelet		LOOP	Copper alloy	
B/C.38	NCM	1949.75	GREY.94	Clarke 1954, 48, no. 40; pl ix; Hd. B/C no. 46			1948	Area 1	Hoard B/C; found during ploughing	Wire/?torc/ ?bracelet			Copper alloy	
B/C.39	NCM	1949.75	GREY.98	Clarke 1954, 48, no. 40; pl ix; Hd. B/C no. 46			1948	Area 1	Hoard B/C; found during ploughing	Wire/?torc/ ?bracelet			Copper alloy	
B/C.40	NCM	1949.75	GREY.99	Clarke 1954, 48, no. 40; pl ix; Hd. B/C no. 46			1948	Area 1	Hoard B/C; found during ploughing	Wire/?torc/ ?bracelet			Copper alloy	
B/C.41	NCM	1949.75	WHITE.19-22; WHITE.25-29	Clarke 1954, 47, no. 29; pl. ix, upper right; Hd. B/C no. 35			1948	Area 1	Hoard B/C; found during ploughing	Wire/?torc/ ?bracelet	(?C)T		Copper alloy	
B/C.42	NCM	1949.75.37	BLUE.33	Clarke 1954, 47, no. 26; Hd. B/C no. 32			1948	Area 1	Hoard B/C; found during ploughing	Torc/bracelet	(3PZ)R		Copper alloy	B/C.42–3 may be from the same torc
B/C.43	NCM	1949.75	GREY.31	Clarke 1954, 47, no. 26; Hd. B/C no. 32			1948	Area 1	Hoard B/C; found during ploughing	Torc/bracelet	(3PZ)R		Copper alloy	B/C.42–3 may be from the same torc
B/C.44	NCM	1949.75.37	BLUE.34	Clarke 1954, 47, no. 26; Hd. B/C no. 32			1948	Area 1	Hoard B/C; found during ploughing	Torc/bracelet	(3P)R		Copper alloy	B/C.44–5 may be from the same torc
B/C.45	NCM	1949.75	GREY.32	Clarke 1954, 47, no. 26; Hd. B/C no. 32			1948	Area 1	Hoard B/C; found during ploughing	Torc/bracelet	(3P)R		Copper alloy	B/C.44–5 may be from the same torc
B/C.46	NCM	1949.75	BLUE.60-77	Not in Clarke 1954			1948	Area 1	Hoard B/C; found during ploughing	Wire/?torc/ ?bracelet	(?P/C)R		Copper alloy	
B/C.47	NCM	1949.75.11	GREY.103	Clarke 1954, 47, no. 23; pl. viii; pl. ix; Hd. B/C no. 29			1948	Area 1	Hoard B/C; found during ploughing	Torc	(2P(2P))R	RING	Copper alloy	B/C.47–8 are from the same torc
B/C.48	NCM	1949.75.11	GREY.29	Clarke 1954, 47, no. 23; pl. viii; pl. ix; Hd. B/C no. 29			1948	Area 1	Hoard B/C; found during ploughing	Torc	(2P(2P))R	RING	Copper alloy	B/C.47–8 are from the same torc
B/C.49	NCM	1949.75	GREY.35	Clarke 1954, 47, no. 25; Hd. B/C no. 31			1948	Area 1	Hoard B/C; found during ploughing	Torc	(2P(2P))R		Copper alloy	B/C.49 may be from the same torc as B/C.47-8
B/C.50	NCM	1949.75.14	GREY.30	Clarke 1954, 47, no. 24; pl. viii; Hd. B/C no. 30			1948	Area 1	Hoard B/C; found during ploughing	Torc/bracelet	(2P(2P))R	LOOP	Copper alloy	B/C. 50–3 may be from the same torc
B/C.51	NCM	1949.75	GREY.34	Clarke 1954, 47, no. 25; Hd. B/C no. 31			1948	Area 1	Hoard B/C; found during ploughing	Torc/bracelet	(2P(2P))R	LOOP	Copper alloy	B/C. 50–3 may be from the same torc
B/C.52	NCM	1949.75.31	GREY.54	Clarke 1954, 47, no. 25; Hd. B/C no. 31			1948	Area 1	Hoard B/C; found during ploughing	Torc/bracelet	(2P(2P))R		Copper alloy	B/C. 50–3 may be from the same torc
B/C.53	NCM	1949.75	BLUE.57-9	Clarke 1954, 47, no. 25; Hd. B/C no. 31			1948	Area 1	Hoard B/C; found during ploughing	Torc/bracelet	((?P)2P)R		Copper alloy	B/C. 50–3 may be from the same torc
B/C.54	NCM	1949.75.12	GREY.36	Clarke 1954, 47, no. 27; pl. ix, lower left (erroneously labelled as 'no. 29'); Hd. B/C no. 33			1948	Area 1	Hoard B/C; found during ploughing	Torc/bracelet	(?3C(2P))R	LOOP	Copper alloy	B/C.54–5 join
B/C.55	NCM	1949.75	GREY.77	Clarke 1954, 47, no. 27; pl. ix, lower left (erroneously labelled as 'no. 29'); Hd. B/C no. 33			1948	Area 1	Hoard B/C; found during ploughing	Torc/bracelet	(?3C(2P))R	LOOP	Copper alloy	B/C.54–5 join
B/C.56	NCM	1949.75	BLUE.50-56	Clarke 1954, 47, no. 25; Hd. B/C no. 31			1948	Area 1	Hoard B/C; found during ploughing	Torc/bracelet	(?C(2P))R		Copper alloy	
B/C.57	NCM	1949.75	BLUE.47	Clarke 1954, 47, no. 28; Hd. B/C no. 34			1948	Area 1	Hoard B/C; found during ploughing	Torc/bracelet	(2P)R		Copper alloy	
B/C.58	NCM	1949.75	WHITE.44	Clarke 1954, 47, no. 28; Hd. B/C no. 34			1948	Area 1	Hoard B/C; found during ploughing	Torc/bracelet	(?P(2P))R		Copper alloy	
B/C.59	NCM	1949.75	WHITE.45	Clarke 1954, 47, no. 28; Hd. B/C no. 34			1948	Area 1	Hoard B/C; found during ploughing	Torc/bracelet	(?C([1+1x2P]P))R		Copper alloy	
B/C.60	NCM	1949.75.24	GREY.55	Clarke 1954, 47, no. 25; Hd. B/C no. 31			1948	Area 1	Hoard B/C; found during ploughing	Torc/bracelet	(?C(2P))R		Copper alloy	
B/C.61	NCM	1949.75	BLUE.49	Clarke 1954, 47, no. 25; Hd. B/C no. 31			1948	Area 1	Hoard B/C; found during ploughing	Wire/?torc/ ?bracelet		?LOOP	Copper alloy	
B/C.62	NCM	1949.75	BLUE.26	Clarke 1954, 47, no. 25; Hd. B/C no. 31			1948	Area 1	Hoard B/C; found during ploughing	Torc/bracelet	(?C(3P(2P)))R		Copper alloy	
B/C.63	NCM	1949.75	GREY.53	Not in Clarke 1954			1948	Area 1	Hoard B/C; found during ploughing	Wire/?torc/ ?bracelet	(?C)T		Copper alloy	
B/C.64	NCM	1949.75	GREY.11	Clarke 1954, 55, no. 4; Hd. B/C no. 10			1948	Area 1	Hoard B/C; found during ploughing	Small ring			Gold/silver alloy	

Cat no.	Museum	Reg. no.	Ticket no.	Published ref.	Stead code	Ralph no.	Ex. year	Findspot	Context details	Object name	MSCC or TUB torc type	Torc terminal type	Material	Joining / related fragments?
B/C.65	NCM	1949.75.23	GREY.1	Clarke 1954, 54, no. 2; fig. 7; Hd. B/C no. 1			1948	Area 1	Hoard B/C; found during ploughing	Large ring			Copper alloy	
B/C.66	NCM	1949.75.17	GREY.4	Clarke 1954, 54, no. 4; fig. 7; Hd. B/C no. 3			1948	Area 1	Hoard B/C; found during ploughing	Large ring			Copper alloy	
B/C.67	NCM	1949.75.21	GREY.3	Clarke 1954, 54, no. 3; Hd. B/C no. 2			1948	Area 1	Hoard B/C; found during ploughing	Large ring			Copper alloy	
B/C.68	NCM	1949.75.10	GREY.39	Clarke 1954, 54, no. 5; fig. 7; Hd. B/C no. 4			1948	Area 1	Hoard B/C; found during ploughing	Large ring			Copper alloy	
B/C.69	NCM	1949.75.19	GREY.2	Clarke 1954, 54, no. 6; Hd. B/C no. 5			1948	Area 1	Hoard B/C; found during ploughing	Large ring			Copper alloy	
B/C.70	NCM	1949.75.48	GREY.8	Clarke 1954, 54, no. 9; Hd. B/C no. 8			1948	Area 1	Hoard B/C; found during ploughing	Large ring			Copper alloy	
B/C.71	NCM	1949.75.8	GREY.5	Clarke 1954, 54, no. 7; fig. 7; Hd. B/C no. 6			1948	Area 1	Hoard B/C; found during ploughing	Large ring			Copper alloy	
B/C.72	NCM	1949.75	GREY.7	Clarke 1954, 54, no. 8; Hd. B/C no. 7			1948	Area 1	Hoard B/C; found during ploughing	Large ring			Copper alloy	
B/C.73	NCM	1949.75	GREY.75	Clarke 1954, 54, no. 10; Hd. B/C no. 9			1948	Area 1	Hoard B/C; found during ploughing	Large ring			Copper alloy	
B/C.74	NCM	1949.75	GREY.87	Clarke 1954, 54, no. 10; Hd. B/C no. 9			1948	Area 1	Hoard B/C; found during ploughing	Large ring			Copper alloy	
B/C.75	NCM	1949.75	GREY.10	Clarke 1954, 54, no. 10; Hd. B/C no. 9			1948	Area 1	Hoard B/C; found during ploughing	Large ring			Copper alloy	
B/C.76	NCM	1949.75	GREY.9	Clarke 1954, 54, no. 10; Hd. B/C no. 9			1948	Area 1	Hoard B/C; found during ploughing	Large ring			Copper alloy	
B/C.77	NCM	1949.75.11	GREY.12	Clarke 1954, 55, no. 5; Hd. B/C no. 11			1948	Area 1	Hoard B/C; found during ploughing	Small ring			Copper alloy	
B/C.78	NCM	1949.75.12	GREY.13	Clarke 1954, 55, no. 6; Hd. B/C no. 12			1948	Area 1	Hoard B/C; found during ploughing	Small ring			Copper alloy	
B/C.79	NCM	1949.75.14	GREY.15	Clarke 1954, 55, no. 8; Hd. B/C no. 14			1948	Area 1	Hoard B/C; found during ploughing	Small ring			Copper alloy	
B/C.80	NCM	1949.75.16	GREY.17	Clarke 1954, 55, no. 10; Hd. B/C no. 16			1948	Area 1	Hoard B/C; found during ploughing	Small ring			Copper alloy	
B/C.81	NCM	1949.75.17	GREY.18	Clarke 1954, 56, no. 13; Hd. B/C no. 17			1948	Area 1	Hoard B/C; found during ploughing	Small ring			Copper alloy	
B/C.82	NCM	1949.75.13	GREY.14	Clarke 1954, 55, no. 7; Hd. B/C no. 13			1948	Area 1	Hoard B/C; found during ploughing	Small ring			Copper alloy	
B/C.83	NCM	1949.75.15	GREY.16	Clarke 1954, 55, no. 9 (pl. xii); Hd. B/C no. 15			1948	Area 1	Hoard B/C; found during ploughing	Small ring			Copper alloy	
B/C.84	NCM	1949.75.193	GREY.20	Clarke 1954, 58 (cake), no. 7; pl xiii, upper; Hd. B/C no. 19			1948	Area 1	Hoard B/C; found during ploughing	Triangular ingot			Gold/silver alloy	
B/C.85	NCM	1949.75.52	GREY.19	Clarke 1954, 58 (cake), no. 6; pl xiii, upper; Hd. B/C no. 18			1948	Area 1	Hoard B/C; found during ploughing	Linear ingot			Gold/silver alloy	
B/C.86	NCM	1949.75	GREY.21	Clarke 1954, 58 (cake), no. 8; pl xiii, upper; Hd. B/C no. 20			1948	Area 1	Hoard B/C; found during ploughing	Linear ingot			Gold/silver alloy	
B/C.87	NCM	1949.75.49	GREY.22	Clarke 1954, 58 (cake), no. 9; pl xiii, upper; Hd. B/C no. 21			1948	Area 1	Hoard B/C; found during ploughing	Amorphous lump			Gold/silver alloy	
B/C.88	NCM	1949.75.45	GREY.23	Clarke 1954, 57, no. 4; pl. xiii, lower; fig. 8; Hd. B/C no. 22.			1948	Area 1	Hoard B/C; found during ploughing	Scale pan			Copper alloy	
B/C.89	NCM	1949.75.56	GREY.24	Clarke 1954, 57, no. 1; pl xiii, lower; Hd. B/C no. 23. Stead (1991c, 24, 30, Type E no. 10)			1948	Area 1	Hoard B/C; found during ploughing	Binding strip			Copper alloy	
B/C.90	NCM	1949.75.44	GREY.25	Clarke 1954, 58 (Misc.), no.2; pl xiii, lower, Misc.2; Hd. B/C no. 25			1948	Area 1	Hoard B/C; found during ploughing	Fitting			Copper alloy	
B/C.91	NCM	1949.75	GREY.61	Clarke 1954, 57, no. 7; Hd. B/C no. 24			1948	Area 1	Hoard B/C; found during ploughing	Sheet			Copper alloy	
B/C.92	NCM	1949.75	GREY.57	Clarke 1954, 57, no. 7; Hd. B/C no. 24			1948	Area 1	Hoard B/C; found during ploughing	Sheet			Copper alloy	
B/C.93	NCM	1949.75	GREY.58	Clarke 1954, 57, no. 7; Hd. B/C no. 24			1948	Area 1	Hoard B/C; found during ploughing	Sheet			Copper alloy	
B/C.94	NCM	1949.75	GREY.59	Clarke 1954, 57, no. 7; Hd. B/C no. 24			1948	Area 1	Hoard B/C; found during ploughing	Sheet			Copper alloy	

Cat no.	Museum	Reg. no.	Ticket no.	Published ref.	Stead code	Ralph no.	Ex. year	Findspot	Context details	Object name	MSCC or TUB torc type	Torc terminal type	Material	Joining / related fragments?
B/C.95	NCM	1949.75	GREY.60	Clarke 1954, 57, no. 7; Hd. B/C no. 24			1948	Area 1	Hoard B/C; found during ploughing	Binding strip			Copper alloy	
B/C.96	NCM	1949.75	GREY.105	Not in Clarke 1954			1948	Area 1	Hoard B/C; found during ploughing	Metalworking waste			Slag	
D.1a	BM	1951,0402.1		Clarke 1954, 47, no. 13; pl. x			1950	Area 1	Hoard D; found during ploughing in 1950	Torc	(2P)R	LOOP	Gold/silver alloy	
D.1b	BM	1951,0402.1		Clarke 1954, 56, no. 16; pl. x			1950	Area 1	Hoard D; found during ploughing in 1950	Large ring			Gold/silver alloy	
E.1a	BM	1951,0402.2					1950	Area 4	Hoard E; found during ploughing in 1950	Torc	(8C(8C))R	TORUS	Gold/silver alloy	
E.1b	BM	1951,0402.3					1950	Area 4	Hoard E; found during ploughing in 1950	Torc	(2P)R	BUFFER	Gold/silver alloy	
E.1c	BM	1951,0402.4					1950	Area 4	Hoard E; found during ploughing in 1950	bracelet			Gold/silver alloy	
F.1a	BM	1991,0501.1				1a	1990	Area 4	Hoard F pit; metal-detected find August 1990	Large ring			Gold/silver alloy	
F.1b	BM	1991,0501.2				1b	1990	Area 4	Hoard F pit; metal-detected find August 1990	Large ring			Gold/silver alloy	
F.1c	BM	1991,0501.5				1c	1990	Area 4	Hoard F pit; metal-detected find August 1990	Torc	TUBULAR (TYPE 1)	BUFFER	Gold/silver alloy	
F.1d	BM	1991,0501.3				1e	1990	Area 4	Hoard F pit; metal-detected find August 1990	Torc	TUBULAR (TYPE 1)	BUFFER	Gold/silver alloy	
F.1e	BM	1991,0501.4				1d	1990	Area 4	Hoard F pit; metal-detected find August 1990	Torc/bracelet	(2P)R/ 3P(2P))R		Gold/silver alloy	
F.2a	BM	1991,0501.6				2a	1990	Area 4	Hoard F pit; metal-detected find August 1990	Torc	TUBULAR (TYPE 1)		Gold/silver alloy	
F.2b	BM	1991,0501.6				2a	1990	Area 4	Hoard F pit; metal-detected find August 1990	Wire			Gold/silver alloy	
F.2c	BM	1991,0501.7				2b	1990	Area 4	Hoard F pit; metal-detected find August 1990	Torc	?TUBULAR		Gold/silver alloy	
F.2d	BM	1991,0501.8				2c	1990	Area 4	Hoard F pit; metal-detected find August 1990	Torc/bracelet	(3P)R		Gold/silver alloy	
F.2e	BM	1991,0501.9				2d	1990	Area 4	Hoard F pit; metal-detected find August 1990	Torc	TUBULAR (TYPE 4/5)		Gold/silver alloy	
F.2f	BM	1991,0501.10				2e	1990	Area 4	Hoard F pit; metal-detected find August 1990	Torc/bracelet	(2P)R	LOOP	Gold/silver alloy	
F.2g	BM	1991,0501.11				2f	1990	Area 4	Hoard F pit; metal-detected find August 1990	Torc	TUBULAR (TYPE 3)	BUFFER	Gold/silver alloy	
F.2h	BM	1991,0501.13				2g	1990	Area 4	Hoard F pit; metal-detected find August 1990	Torc	TUBULAR (TYPE 3)	BUFFER	Gold/silver alloy	
F.2i	BM	1991,0501.12				2h	1990	Area 4	Hoard F pit; metal-detected find August 1990	Wire			Gold/silver alloy	
F.3a	BM	1991,0501.120				3a	1990	Area 4	Hoard F pit; metal-detected find August 1990	Large ring			Gold/silver alloy	
F.3b	BM	1991,0501.121				3b	1990	Area 4	Hoard F pit; metal-detected find August 1990	Torc/bracelet	(2P)R	LOOP	Gold/silver alloy	
F.3c	BM	1991,0501.122				3c	1990	Area 4	Hoard F pit; metal-detected find August 1990	Torc/bracelet	(2P)R	RING	Gold/silver alloy	
F.3d	BM	1991,0702.10				3d	1990	Area 4	Hoard F pit; metal-detected find August 1990	Large ring			Copper alloy	
F.3e	BM	1991,0501.123				3e	1990	Area 4	Hoard F pit; metal-detected find August 1990	Torc/bracelet	(4PZ)R		Gold/silver alloy	
F.3f	BM	1991,0702.11				3f	1990	Area 4	Hoard F pit; metal-detected find August 1990	Torc/bracelet	(2P(2P))R		Copper alloy	
F.3g	BM	1991,0702.12				3g	1990	Area 4	Hoard F pit; metal-detected find August 1990	Torc/bracelet	(4P)?Q	LOOP	Copper alloy	
F.3h	BM	1991,0501.124				3h	1990	Area 4	Hoard F pit; metal-detected find August 1990	Torc/bracelet	(2PZ)Q	LOOP	Gold/silver alloy	Probably part of the same object as F.3i, with which it is interlinked.

Cat no.	Museum	Reg. no.	Ticket no.	Published ref.	Stead code	Ralph no.	Ex. year	Findspot	Context details	Object name	MSCC or TUB torc type	Torc terminal type	Material	Joining / related fragments?
F.3i	BM	1991,0501.124				3h	1990	Area 4	Hoard F pit; metal-detected find August 1990	Torc/bracelet	(2PZ)Q		Gold/silver alloy	Probably part of the same object as F.3h, with which it is interlinked.
F.4a	BM	1991,0501.46				53a	1990	Area 4	Hoard F pit; metal-detected find August 1990	Torc	(6C)T	CAGE	Gold/silver alloy	
F.4b	BM	1991,0501.47				53b	1990	Area 4	Hoard F pit; metal-detected find August 1990	Torc	(4C)T	RING	Gold/silver alloy	
F.4c	BM	1991,0501.48				53c	1990	Area 4	Hoard F pit; metal-detected find August 1990	Torc/bracelet	(2P)R	LOOP/RING	Gold/silver alloy	
F.4d	BM	1991,0501.49				53d	1990	Area 4	Hoard F pit; metal-detected find August 1990	Torc/bracelet	(2PZ)R	LOOP	Gold/silver alloy	
F.4e	BM	1991,0501.50				53e	1990	Area 4	Hoard F pit; metal-detected find August 1990	Torc/bracelet	(3P(2P))R	LOOP	Gold/silver alloy	
F.4f	BM	1991,0501.51				53f	1990	Area 4	Hoard F pit; metal-detected find August 1990	Torc	TUBULAR (TYPE 1)		Gold/silver alloy	
F.5a	BM	1991,0501.53				55a	1990	Area 4	Hoard F pit; metal-detected find August 1990	Large ring			Gold/silver alloy	
F.5b	BM	1991,0501.54				55b	1990	Area 4	Hoard F pit; metal-detected find August 1990	Large ring			Gold/silver alloy	
F.5c	BM	1991,0501.55				55c	1990	Area 4	Hoard F pit; metal-detected find August 1990	Torc	(2P)R	RING	Gold/silver alloy	
F.5d	BM	1991,0501.56				55d	1990	Area 4	Hoard F pit; metal-detected find August 1990	Torc/bracelet	(4P(2P))R		Gold/silver alloy	
F.5e	BM	1991,0501.57				55e	1990	Area 4	Hoard F pit; metal-detected find August 1990	Wire			Gold/silver alloy	
F.5f	BM	1991,0501.58				55f	1990	Area 4	Hoard F pit; metal-detected find August 1990	Torc/bracelet	(2P)R		Gold/silver alloy	
F.5g	BM	1991,0501.59				55g	1990	Area 4	Hoard F pit; metal-detected find August 1990	Torc	TUBULAR (TYPE 1)		Gold/silver alloy	
F.6a	BM	1991,0501.103				116a	1990	Area 4	Hoard F pit; metal-detected find August 1990	Large ring; torc	(4C)T		Gold/silver alloy	
F.6b	BM	1991,0501.104				116b	1990	Area 4	Hoard F pit; metal-detected find August 1990	Torc	TUBULAR (TYPE 4)	BUFFER	Gold/silver alloy	
F.6c	BM	1991,0501.105				116c	1990	Area 4	Hoard F pit; metal-detected find August 1990	Small ring			Gold/silver alloy	
F.6d	BM	1991,0501.106				116d	1990	Area 4	Hoard F pit; metal-detected find August 1990	Large ring			Gold/silver alloy	
F.6e	BM	1991,0501.107				116e	1990	Area 4	Hoard F pit; metal-detected find August 1990	Small ring			Gold/silver alloy	
F.6f	BM	1991,0702.2				116f	1990	Area 4	Hoard F pit; metal-detected find August 1990	Torc/bracelet	(5C)R		Gold/silver alloy	
F.6g	BM	1991,0501.108				116g	1990	Area 4	Hoard F pit; metal-detected find August 1990	Small ring			Gold/silver alloy	
F.7a	BM	1991,0702.3				117a	1990	Area 4	Hoard F pit; metal-detected find August 1990	Large ring			Gold/silver alloy	
F.7b	BM	1991,0501.109				117b	1990	Area 4	Hoard F pit; metal-detected find August 1990	Wire/?torc/ ?bracelet	?(2P)T	?LOOP	Gold/silver alloy	
F.7c	BM	1991,0702.4				117c	1990	Area 4	Hoard F pit; metal-detected find August 1990	Torc/bracelet	(2P)R	LOOP	Gold/silver alloy	
F.7d	BM	1991,0501.110				117d	1990	Area 4	Hoard F pit; metal-detected find August 1990	Torc/bracelet	(2P(2PZ))R	RING	Gold/silver alloy	
F.7e	BM	1991,0501.111				117e	1990	Area 4	Hoard F pit; metal-detected find August 1990	Torc/bracelet	(2P)T	?CAGE	Gold/silver alloy	
F.7f	BM	1991,0501.112				117f	1990	Area 4	Hoard F pit; metal-detected find August 1990	Bracelet	(2P)R	HOOK/LOOP	Gold/silver alloy	
F.7g	BM	1991,0501.113				117g	1990	Area 4	Hoard F pit; metal-detected find August 1990	Torc/bracelet	(3P)2R+1T	RING	Gold/silver alloy	
F.8a	BM	1991,0702.62				262a	1990	Area 4	Hoard F pit; metal-detected find August 1990	Torc	(2P(3P))R	RING	Gold/silver alloy	

Cat no.	Museum	Reg. no.	Ticket no.	Published ref.	Stead code	Ralph no.	Ex. year	Findspot	Context details	Object name	MSCC or TUB torc type	Torc terminal type	Material	Joining / related fragments?
F.8b	BM	1991,0702.63				262b	1990	Area 4	Hoard F pit; metal-detected find August 1990	Torc/bracelet	(2PZ)R	LOOP	Copper alloy	
F.8c	BM	1991,0702.64				262c	1990	Area 4	Hoard F pit; metal-detected find August 1990	Wire/strip			Copper alloy	
F.8d	BM	1991,0702.65				262c	1990	Area 4	Hoard F pit; metal-detected find August 1990	Wire/strip			Copper alloy	
F.8e	BM	1991,0702.66				262c	1990	Area 4	Hoard F pit; metal-detected find August 1990	Wire/strip			Copper alloy	
F.9a	BM	1991,0501.125				4a	1990	Area 4	Hoard F pit; metal-detected find August 1990	Torc/bracelet	(4P)T	RING	Gold/silver alloy	
F.9b	BM	1991,0501.126				4b	1990	Area 4	Hoard F pit; metal-detected find August 1990	Torc/bracelet	(2P)R	LOOP	Gold/silver alloy	
F.9c	BM	1991,0501.127				4c	1990	Area 4	Hoard F pit; metal-detected find August 1990	Torc/bracelet	(2P)T		Gold/silver alloy	
F.9d	BM	1991,0501.128				4d	1990	Area 4	Hoard F pit; metal-detected find August 1990	Torc/bracelet	(2P)R		Gold/silver alloy	
F.10a	BM	1991,0501.40				46a	1990	Area 4	Hoard F pit; metal-detected find August 1990	Torc/bracelet	(4P)T	RING/CAGE	Gold/silver alloy	
F.10b	BM	1991,0501.41				46b	1990	Area 4	Hoard F pit; metal-detected find August 1990	Wire			Gold/silver alloy	
F.11a	BM	1991,0501.133				22a	1990	Area 4	Hoard F pit; metal-detected find August 1990	Torc/bracelet	(2PZ)R		Gold/silver alloy	Probably from the same object as interlinked strand F.11b
F.11b	BM	1991,0501.133				22b	1990	Area 4	Hoard F pit; metal-detected find August 1990	Torc/bracelet	(2PZ)R		Gold/silver alloy	Probably from the same object as interlinked strand F.11a
F.12a	BM	1991,0702.51				205a	1990	Area 4	Hoard F pit; metal-detected find August 1990	Wire			Gold/silver alloy	
F.12b	BM	1991,0702.50				205b	1990	Area 4	Hoard F pit; metal-detected find August 1990	Wire			Gold/silver alloy	
F.13a	BM	1991,0501.182				155a/b	1990	Area 4	Hoard F pit; metal-detected find August 1990	Torc/bracelet	(4P)T		Copper alloy	
F.13b	BM	1991,0501.182				155c	1990	Area 4	Hoard F pit; metal-detected find August 1990	Torc/bracelet	(2P)R		Gold/silver alloy	
F.14a	BM	1991,0501.209				214a	1990	Area 4	Hoard F pit; metal-detected find August 1990	Torc/bracelet	(2P)R	LOOP	Gold/silver alloy	
F.14b	BM	1991,0702.9				214b	1990	Area 4	Hoard F pit; metal-detected find August 1990	Wire			Copper alloy	
F.15a	BM	1991,0702.137				257a	1990	Area 4	Hoard F pit; metal-detected find August 1990	Torc/bracelet	(4P)T	RING	Copper alloy	
F.15b	BM	1991,0702.138				257b	1990	Area 4	Hoard F pit; metal-detected find August 1990	Torc/bracelet	(5C)T		Copper alloy	
F.16a	BM	1991,0702.226				450a	1990	Area 4	Hoard F pit; metal-detected find August 1990	Torc/bracelet	(2P)R	LOOP	Copper alloy	Probably from the same object as F.16b, with which it is interlinked
F.16b	BM	1991,0702.227				450b	1990	Area 4	Hoard F pit; metal-detected find August 1990	Torc/bracelet	(2P)R		Copper alloy	Probably from the same object as F.16a, with which it is interlinked
F.17a	BM	1991,0501.216				286a	1990	Area 4	Hoard F pit; metal-detected find August 1990	Torc/bracelet	(2P)Q		Gold/silver alloy	
F.17b	BM	1991,0702.8				286b	1990	Area 4	Hoard F pit; metal-detected find August 1990	Wire			Gold/silver alloy	
F.17c	BM	1991,0501.217				286c	1990	Area 4	Hoard F pit; metal-detected find August 1990	Torc/bracelet		LOOP	Gold/silver alloy	
F.18a	BM	1991,0501.62				59a	1990	Area 4	Hoard F pit; metal-detected find August 1990	Wire			Gold/silver alloy	
F.18b	BM	1991,0501.63				59b	1990	Area 4	Hoard F pit; metal-detected find August 1990	Small ring			Gold/silver alloy	
F.18c	BM	1991,0501.64				59c	1990	Area 4	Hoard F pit; metal-detected find August 1990	Small ring			Gold/silver alloy	

Cat no.	Museum	Reg. no.	Ticket no.	Published ref.	Stead code	Ralph no.	Ex. year	Findspot	Context details	Object name	MSCC or TUB torc type	Torc terminal type	Material	Joining / related fragments?
F.18d	BM	1991,0501.65				59d	1990	Area 4	Hoard F pit; metal-detected find August 1990	Small ring			Gold/silver alloy	
F.18e	BM	1991,0501.66				59e	1990	Area 4	Hoard F pit; metal-detected find August 1990	Small ring			Gold/silver alloy	
F.18f	BM	1991,0501.67				59f	1990	Area 4	Hoard F pit; metal-detected find August 1990	Small ring			Gold/silver alloy	
F.18g	BM	1991,0501.68				59g	1990	Area 4	Hoard F pit; metal-detected find August 1990	Small ring			Gold/silver alloy	
F.18h	BM	1991,0501.69				59h	1990	Area 4	Hoard F pit; metal-detected find August 1990	Torc/bracelet	(2P)R	LOOP	Gold/silver alloy	
F.18i	BM	1991,0501.69.a				59h	1990	Area 4	Hoard F pit; metal-detected find August 1990	Strip			Gold/silver alloy	
F.18j	BM	1991,0501.70				59i	1990	Area 4	Hoard F pit; metal-detected find August 1990	Small ring			Gold/silver alloy	
F.18k	BM	1991,0501.71				59j	1990	Area 4	Hoard F pit; metal-detected find August 1990	Small ring			Gold/silver alloy	
F.18l	BM	1991,0501.72				59k	1990	Area 4	Hoard F pit; metal-detected find August 1990	Small ring			Gold/silver alloy	
F.19a	BM	1991,0501.160				96a	1990	Area 4	Hoard F pit; metal-detected find August 1990	Large ring			Gold/silver alloy	
F.19b	BM	1991,0501.161				96b	1990	Area 4	Hoard F pit; metal-detected find August 1990	Torc	TUBULAR (TYPE 4/5)		Gold/silver alloy	
F.20a	BM	1991,0702.29				128a	1990	Area 4	Hoard F pit; metal-detected find August 1990	Large ring			Gold/silver alloy	
F.20b	BM	1991,0702.30				128b	1990	Area 4	Hoard F pit; metal-detected find August 1990	Torc/bracelet	(2P)R		Gold/silver alloy	
F.21a	BM	1991,0501.206				204a	1990	Area 4	Hoard F pit; metal-detected find August 1990	Small ring			Gold/silver alloy	
F.21b	BM	1991,0501.207				204b	1990	Area 4	Hoard F pit; metal-detected find August 1990	Torc/bracelet	(2P(2P))R		Gold/silver alloy	
F.22a	BM	1991,0501.148				82a	1990	Area 4	Hoard F pit; metal-detected find August 1990	Torc/bracelet	(2P)R		Gold/silver alloy	
F.22b	BM	1991,0501.149				82b	1990	Area 4	Hoard F pit; metal-detected find August 1990	Small ring/?torc		?LOOP	Gold/silver alloy	
F.23a	BM	1991,0702.42				207a	1990	Area 4	Hoard F pit; metal-detected find August 1990	Small ring			Gold/silver alloy	
F.23b	BM	1991,0702.43				207b	1990	Area 4	Hoard F pit; metal-detected find August 1990	Torc/bracelet	(2P(2P))R		Copper alloy	
F.24a	BM	1991,0501.130				20b	1990	Area 4	Hoard F pit; metal-detected find August 1990	Torc/bracelet	(2P)R	LOOP	Gold/silver alloy	
F.24b	BM	1991,0501.131				20a	1990	Area 4	Hoard F pit; metal-detected find August 1990	Small ring			Gold/silver alloy	
F.25a	BM	1991,0501.14.a				5a	1990	Area 4	Hoard F pit; metal-detected find August 1990	Small ring			Gold/silver alloy	
F.25b	BM	1991,0501.14.b				5b	1990	Area 4	Hoard F pit; metal-detected find August 1990	Small ring			Gold/silver alloy	
F.25c	BM	1991,0501.14.c				5c	1990	Area 4	Hoard F pit; metal-detected find August 1990	Small ring			Gold/silver alloy	
F.25d	BM	1991,0501.14.d				5d	1990	Area 4	Hoard F pit; metal-detected find August 1990	Small ring			Gold/silver alloy	
F.25e	BM	1991,0501.14.e				5e	1990	Area 4	Hoard F pit; metal-detected find August 1990	Small ring			Gold/silver alloy	
F.25f	BM	1991,0501.14.f				5f	1990	Area 4	Hoard F pit; metal-detected find August 1990	Small ring			Gold/silver alloy	
F.25g	BM	1991,0501.14.g				5g	1990	Area 4	Hoard F pit; metal-detected find August 1990	Small ring			Gold/silver alloy	
F.25h	BM	1991,0501.14.h				5h	1990	Area 4	Hoard F pit; metal-detected find August 1990	Small ring			Gold/silver alloy	
F.25i	BM	1991,0501.14.i				5i	1990	Area 4	Hoard F pit; metal-detected find August 1990	Small ring			Gold/silver alloy	

Cat no.	Museum	Reg. no.	Ticket no.	Published ref.	Stead code	Ralph no.	Ex. year	Findspot	Context details	Object name	MSCC or TUB torc type	Torc terminal type	Material	Joining / related fragments?
F.25j	BM	1991,0501.14.j				5j	1990	Area 4	Hoard F pit; metal-detected find August 1990	Small ring			Gold/silver alloy	
F.26a	BM	1991,0501.140				58a	1990	Area 4	Hoard F pit; metal-detected find August 1990	Large ring			Gold/silver alloy	
F.26b	BM	1991,0501.141				58b	1990	Area 4	Hoard F pit; metal-detected find August 1990	Small ring			Gold/silver alloy	
F.26c	BM	1991,0501.142				58c	1990	Area 4	Hoard F pit; metal-detected find August 1990	Small ring			Gold/silver alloy	
F.26d	BM	1991,0501.143				58d	1990	Area 4	Hoard F pit; metal-detected find August 1990	Small ring			Gold/silver alloy	
F.26e	BM	1991,0702.7				58e	1990	Area 4	Hoard F pit; metal-detected find August 1990	Small ring			Gold/silver alloy	
F.27a	BM	1991,0501.139				51a	1990	Area 4	Hoard F pit; metal-detected find August 1990	Small ring			Gold/silver alloy	
F.27b	BM	1991,0702.22				51b	1990	Area 4	Hoard F pit; metal-detected find August 1990	Small ring			Gold/silver alloy	
F.28a	BM	1991,0501.167				129a	1990	Area 4	Hoard F pit; metal-detected find August 1990	Small ring			Gold/silver alloy	
F.28b	BM	1991,0501.168				129b	1990	Area 4	Hoard F pit; metal-detected find August 1990	Large ring			Gold/silver alloy	
F.29a	BM	1991,0501.135				25	1990	Area 4	Hoard F pit; metal-detected find August 1990	Torc	TUBULAR (TYPE 4/5)		Gold/silver alloy	Perhaps from the same torc as F.56
F.29b	BM	1991,0501.135				25	1990	Area 4	Hoard F pit; metal-detected find August 1990	Torc/bracelet	(2P)R		Gold/silver alloy	
F.29c	BM	1991,0501.135				25	1990	Area 4	Hoard F pit; metal-detected find August 1990	Wire			Gold/silver alloy	
F.30a	BM	1991,0501.90				101	1990	Area 4	Hoard F pit; metal-detected find August 1990	Torc	TUBULAR (TYPE 4)	BUFFER	Gold/silver alloy	
F.30b	BM	1991,0501.90				101	1990	Area 4	Hoard F pit; metal-detected find August 1990	Wire/?torc			Gold/silver alloy	
F.31a	BM	1991,0501.28				33	1990	Area 4	Hoard F pit; metal-detected find August 1990	Torc	TUBULAR (TYPE 5)	BUFFER	Gold/silver alloy	
F.31b	BM	1991,0501.28.a					1990	Area 4	Hoard F pit; metal-detected find August 1990	Torc	TUBULAR (TYPE 1)		Gold/silver alloy	
F.32	BM	1991,0501.136				26	1990	Area 4	Hoard F pit; metal-detected find August 1990	Torc; torc / bracelet	TUBULAR (TYPE 4/5); (2P)R		Gold/silver alloy	
F.33	BM	1991,0501.165				102	1990	Area 4	Hoard F pit; metal-detected find August 1990	Torc; strip/?small/ large ring; wire	TUBULAR (TYPE 1)		Gold/silver alloy	
F.34	BM	1991,0501.16				7	1990	Area 4	Hoard F pit; metal-detected find August 1990	Torc/bracelet; wire; sheet	(6C(2P))R		Gold/silver alloy	
F.35	BM	1991,0501.21				13	1990	Area 4	Hoard F pit; metal-detected find August 1990	Torc; wire	TUBULAR (TYPE 3)	BUFFER	Gold/silver alloy	
F.36	BM	1991,0501.23				18	1990	Area 4	Hoard F pit; metal-detected find August 1990	Torc/bracelet; ?wire	(2P)TZ	RING	Gold/silver alloy	
F.37	BM	1991,0501.24				19	1990	Area 4	Hoard F pit; metal-detected find August 1990	Torc/bracelet; sheet	(2P)R		Gold/silver alloy	
F.38	BM	1991,0501.43				48	1990	Area 4	Hoard F pit; metal-detected find August 1990	Torc/bracelet; ?wire	(4C)T	CAGE	Gold/silver alloy	
F.39	BM	1991,0501.44				50	1990	Area 4	Hoard F pit; metal-detected find August 1990	Torc; wire	(3P)T	LOOP	Gold/silver alloy	
F.40	BM	1991,0501.52				54	1990	Area 4	Hoard F pit; metal-detected find August 1990	Torc/bracelet; wire	(2P)R	RING	Gold/silver alloy	
F.41	BM	1991,0501.78				66	1990	Area 4	Hoard F pit; metal-detected find August 1990	Torc	(3P)R	?BUFFER	Gold/silver alloy	
F.42	BM	1991,0501.96				108	1990	Area 4	Hoard F pit; metal-detected find August 1990	Torc	TUBULAR (TYPE 4); (2P)Q	BUFFER	Gold/silver alloy	
F.43	BM	1991,0501.29				34	1990	Area 4	Hoard F pit; metal-detected find August 1990	Torc/bracelet; wire; sheet	TUBULAR (TYPE 5); (2P)T	BUFFER; RING	Gold/silver alloy	
F.44	BM	1991,0407.46			SN/AJ		1990	Area 4	Hoard F pit; excavated find, at edge of hoard pit.	Torc/bracelet	(2PZ)R		Copper alloy	
F.45	BM	1991,0501.91				103	1990	Area 4	Hoard F pit; metal-detected find August 1990	Torc	TUBULAR (TYPE 4)	BUFFER	Gold/silver alloy	

Cat no.	Museum	Reg. no.	Ticket no.	Published ref.	Stead code	Ralph no.	Ex. year	Findspot	Context details	Object name	MSCC or TUB torc type	Torc terminal type	Material	Joining / related fragments?
F.46	BM	1991,0501.98				110	1990	Area 4	Hoard F pit; metal-detected find August 1990	Torc	TUBULAR (TYPE 4)	BUFFER	Gold/silver alloy	
F.47	BM	1991,0501.20				12	1990	Area 4	Hoard F pit; metal-detected find August 1990	Torc	TUBULAR (TYPE 3)	BUFFER	Gold/silver alloy	Possibly the pair to F.48
F.48	BM	1991,0501.27				32	1990	Area 4	Hoard F pit; metal-detected find August 1990	Torc	TUBULAR (TYPE 3)	BUFFER	Gold/silver alloy	Possibly the pair to F.47
F.49	BM	1991,0501.138				35	1990	Area 4	Hoard F pit; metal-detected find August 1990	Torc	TUBULAR	?BUFFER	Gold/silver alloy	
F.50	BM	1991,0501.208				209	1990	Area 4	Hoard F pit; metal-detected find August 1990	Torc	TUBULAR (TYPE 4/5)		Gold/silver alloy	
F.51	BM	1991,0501.34				40	1990	Area 4	Hoard F pit; metal-detected find August 1990	Torc	TUBULAR (TYPE 4/5)		Gold/silver alloy	
F.52	BM	1991,0501.76				64	1990	Area 4	Hoard F pit; metal-detected find August 1990	Torc	TUBULAR (TYPE 4/5)		Gold/silver alloy	
F.53	BM	1991,0501.118				307	1990	Area 4	Hoard F pit; metal-detected find August 1990	Torc	TUBULAR (TYPE 4/5)		Gold/silver alloy	Coins cat nos 174–8 found inside
F.54	BM	1991,0501.31				37	1990	Area 4	Hoard F pit; metal-detected find August 1990	Torc	TUBULAR (TYPE 4/5)		Gold/silver alloy	Similar to F.55, though not a joining piece
F.55	BM	1991,0501.32				38	1990	Area 4	Hoard F pit; metal-detected find August 1990	Torc	TUBULAR (TYPE 4/5)		Gold/silver alloy	Similar to F.54, though not a joining piece
F.56	BM	1991,0501.97				109	1990	Area 4	Hoard F pit; metal-detected find August 1990	Torc	TUBULAR (TYPE 4/5)		Gold/silver alloy	Perhaps part of the same object as F.29a
F.57	BM	1991,0501.119				30	1990	Area 4	Hoard F pit; metal-detected find August 1990	Torc	TUBULAR (TYPE 1)	BUFFER	Gold/silver alloy	
F.58	BM	1991,0501.25				29	1990	Area 4	Hoard F pit; metal-detected find August 1990	Torc	TUBULAR (TYPE 1)	BUFFER	Gold/silver alloy	
F.59	BM	1991,0501.77				65	1990	Area 4	Hoard F pit; metal-detected find August 1990	Torc	TUBULAR (TYPE 1)	BUFFER	Gold/silver alloy	
F.60	BM	1991,0501.26				31	1990	Area 4	Hoard F pit; metal-detected find August 1990	Torc	TUBULAR (TYPE 3)	BUFFER	Gold/silver alloy	
F.61	BM	1991,0501.164				100	1990	Area 4	Hoard F pit; metal-detected find August 1990	Torc	TUBULAR (TYPE 4)	BUFFER	Gold/silver alloy	
F.62	BM	1991,0501.30				36	1990	Area 4	Hoard F pit; metal-detected find August 1990	Torc; wire	TUBULAR (?TYPE 3)	?BUFFER	Gold/silver alloy	
F.63	BM	1991,0501.33				39	1990	Area 4	Hoard F pit; metal-detected find August 1990	Torc	TUBULAR (TYPE 2)	BUFFER	Gold/silver alloy	F.63–6 may be from the same torc
F.64	BM	1991,0501.35				41	1990	Area 4	Hoard F pit; metal-detected find August 1990	Torc	TUBULAR (TYPE 2)	?BUFFER	Gold/silver alloy; iron	F.63–6 may be from the same torc
F.65	BM	1991,0501.36				42	1990	Area 4	Hoard F pit; metal-detected find August 1990	Torc	TUBULAR (TYPE 2)	?BUFFER	Gold/silver alloy; iron	F.63–6 may be from the same torc
F.66	BM	1991,0501.134				24	1990	Area 4	Hoard F pit; metal-detected find August 1990	Torc	TUBULAR (TYPE 2)		Gold/silver alloy; iron	F.63–6 may be from the same torc
F.67	BM	1991,0501.132				21	1990	Area 4	Hoard F pit; metal-detected find August 1990	Strip/?torc			Gold/silver alloy	
F.68	BM	1991,0702.46				208	1990	Area 4	Hoard F pit; metal-detected find August 1990	Torc		RING	Gold/silver alloy	
F.69	BM	1991,0702.47				308	1990	Area 4	Hoard F pit; metal-detected find August 1990	Wire/?torc/ ?bracelet		?LOOP	Gold/silver alloy	
F.70	BM	1991,0501.212				218	1990	Area 4	Hoard F pit; metal-detected find August 1990	Torc/bracelet		LOOP	Gold/silver alloy	
F.71	BM	1991,0501.183				156	1990	Area 4	Hoard F pit; metal-detected find August 1990	Torc		BUFFER	Gold/silver alloy	
F.72	BM	1991,0501.45				52	1990	Area 4	Hoard F pit; metal-detected find August 1990	Torc		TORUS	Gold/silver alloy	
F.73	BM	1991,0501.89				77	1990	Area 4	Hoard F pit; metal-detected find August 1990	Torc/bracelet	(2P)R	LOOP	Gold/silver alloy	
F.74	BM	1991,0501.151				84	1990	Area 4	Hoard F pit; metal-detected find August 1990	Torc	?(2P)R		Gold/silver alloy	
F.75	BM	1991,0501.173				134	1990	Area 4	Hoard F pit; metal-detected find August 1990	Torc	(2P)F		Gold/silver alloy	F.75 and F.76 may be part of the same torc

Cat no.	Museum	Reg. no.	Ticket no.	Published ref.	Stead code	Ralph no.	Ex. year	Findspot	Context details	Object name	MSCC or TUB torc type	Torc terminal type	Material	Joining / related fragments?
F.76	BM	1991,0501.174				135	1990	Area 4	Hoard F pit; metal-detected find August 1990	Torc	(2P)F		Gold/silver alloy	F.75 and F.76 may be part of the same torc
F.77	BM	1991,0501.210				215	1990	Area 4	Hoard F pit; metal-detected find August 1990	Torc	(2P)F		Gold/silver alloy	
F.78	BM	1991,0501.37				43	1990	Area 4	Hoard F pit; metal-detected find August 1990	Torc	(2P)F	LOOP	Gold/silver alloy	
F.79	BM	1991,0501.152				85	1990	Area 4	Hoard F pit; metal-detected find August 1990	Torc	(?P(2P))R		Gold/silver alloy	
F.80	BM	1991,0501.38				44	1990	Area 4	Hoard F pit; metal-detected find August 1990	Torc	(2P)R	LOOP	Gold/silver alloy	
F.81	BM	1991,0501.147				81	1990	Area 4	Hoard F pit; metal-detected find August 1990	Torc/bracelet	(2P)R		Gold/silver alloy	
F.82	BM	1991,0501.155				88	1990	Area 4	Hoard F pit; metal-detected find August 1990	Torc/bracelet	(2P)R	RING	Gold/silver alloy	
F.83	BM	1991,0501.159				95	1990	Area 4	Hoard F pit; metal-detected find August 1990	Torc/bracelet	(2P)R		Gold/silver alloy	
F.84	BM	1991,0501.158				94	1990	Area 4	Hoard F pit; metal-detected find August 1990	Torc/bracelet	(2P)R		Gold/silver alloy	
F.85	BM	1991,0501.95				107	1990	Area 4	Hoard F pit; metal-detected find August 1990	Torc/bracelet	(3P)R	?CAGE	Gold/silver alloy	
F.86	BM	1991,0501.42				47	1990	Area 4	Hoard F pit; metal-detected find August 1990	Torc/bracelet	(4C)T	CAGE	Gold/silver alloy	
F.87	BM	1991,0501.93				105	1990	Area 4	Hoard F pit; metal-detected find August 1990	Torc/bracelet	(3P)R	LOOP	Gold/silver alloy	
F.88	BM	1991,0501.22				17	1990	Area 4	Hoard F pit; metal-detected find August 1990	Torc/bracelet	(4C)R		Gold/silver alloy	
F.89	BM	1991,0501.101				113	1990	Area 4	Hoard F pit; metal-detected find August 1990	Torc/bracelet	(4P)R	LOOP	Gold/silver alloy	
F.90	BM	1991,0501.157				91	1990	Area 4	Hoard F pit; metal-detected find August 1990	Torc/bracelet	(4P)T	LOOP	Gold/silver alloy	
F.91	BM	1991,0501.100				112	1990	Area 4	Hoard F pit; metal-detected find August 1990	Torc/bracelet	(4P)T	LOOP	Gold/silver alloy	
F.92	BM	1991,0501.82				70	1990	Area 4	Hoard F pit; metal-detected find August 1990	Torc	(5C)R		Gold/silver alloy	F.92 and F.93 join
F.93	BM	1991,0501.83				71	1990	Area 4	Hoard F pit; metal-detected find August 1990	Torc	(5C)R		Gold/silver alloy	F.92 and F.93 join
F.94	BM	1991,0501.17				8	1990	Area 4	Hoard F pit; metal-detected find August 1990	Torc/bracelet	(5C)T		Gold/silver alloy	
F.95	BM	1991,0501.18				9	1990	Area 4	Hoard F pit; metal-detected find August 1990	Torc/bracelet	(6C)T	CAGE	Gold/silver alloy	
F.96	BM	1991,0501.84				72	1990	Area 4	Hoard F pit; metal-detected find August 1990	Torc	(8C)R		Gold/silver alloy	F.96 and F.97 may be part of the same torc
F.97	BM	1991,0501.85				73	1990	Area 4	Hoard F pit; metal-detected find August 1990	Torc	(8C)R		Gold/silver alloy	F.96 and F.97 may be part of the same torc
F.98	BM	1991,0501.15				6	1990	Area 4	Hoard F pit; metal-detected find August 1990	Torc	(8C)T	CAGE	Gold/silver alloy	
F.99	BM	1991,0501.137				27	1990	Area 4	Hoard F pit; metal-detected find August 1990	Torc	(9C)R		Gold/silver alloy	F.99–104 may be part of the same torc
F.100	BM	1991,0501.185				164	1990	Area 4	Hoard F pit; metal-detected find August 1990	Torc	(9C)R		Gold/silver alloy	F.99–104 may be part of the same torc
F.101	BM	1991,0501.186				165	1990	Area 4	Hoard F pit; metal-detected find August 1990	Torc	(9C)R		Gold/silver alloy	F.99–104 may be part of the same torc
F.102	BM	1991,0501.187				166	1990	Area 4	Hoard F pit; metal-detected find August 1990	Torc	(9C)R		Gold/silver alloy	F.99–104 may be part of the same torc
F.103	BM	1991,0501.215				275	1990	Area 4	Hoard F pit; metal-detected find August 1990	Torc	(9C)R		Gold/silver alloy	F.99–104 may be part of the same torc
F.104	BM	1991,0702.182				360	1990	Area 4	Hoard F pit; metal-detected find August 1990	Torc/bracelet	(9C)R		Gold/silver alloy	F.99–104 may be part of the same torc
F.105	BM	1991,0501.211				217	1990	Area 4	Hoard F pit; metal-detected find August 1990	Torc/bracelet	(?P(3PZ))R	RING	Gold/silver alloy	

Cat no.	Museum	Reg. no.	Ticket no.	Published ref.	Stead code	Ralph no.	Ex. year	Findspot	Context details	Object name	MSCC or TUB torc type	Torc terminal type	Material	Joining / related fragments?
F.106	BM	1991,0501.19				10	1990	Area 4	Hoard F pit; metal-detected find August 1990	Torc	(?C(2P))R	BUFFER	Gold/silver alloy	
F.107	BM	1991,0501.92				104	1990	Area 4	Hoard F pit; metal-detected find August 1990	Torc/bracelet	(2P(2P))R	RING	Gold/silver alloy	
F.108	BM	1991,0501.154				87	1990	Area 4	Hoard F pit; metal-detected find August 1990	Torc/bracelet	(2P(2P))R		Gold/silver alloy	
F.109	BM	1991,0702.48				324	1990	Area 4	Hoard F pit; metal-detected find August 1990	Torc	(2PZ(2P))R		Gold/silver alloy	F.109–11 may be part of the same torc
F.110	BM	1991,0501.175				136	1990	Area 4	Hoard F pit; metal-detected find August 1990	Torc	(2PZ(2P))R		Gold/silver alloy	F.109–11 may be part of the same torc
F.111	BM	1991,0501.176				137	1990	Area 4	Hoard F pit; metal-detected find August 1990	Torc	(2PZ(2P))R		Gold/silver alloy	F.109–11 may be part of the same torc
F.112	BM	1991,0702.59				267	1990	Area 4	Hoard F pit; metal-detected find August 1990	Torc	(2PZ(4P))R		Gold/silver alloy	F.112 and F.113 may be part of the same torc
F.113	BM	1991,0501.184				157	1990	Area 4	Hoard F pit; metal-detected find August 1990	Torc	(2PZ(4P))R		Gold/silver alloy	F.112 and F.113 may be part of the same torc
F.114	BM	1991,0501.39				45	1990	Area 4	Hoard F pit; metal-detected find August 1990	Torc/bracelet	(3C(2P))R		Gold/silver alloy	
F.115	BM	1991,0501.163				98	1990	Area 4	Hoard F pit; metal-detected find August 1990	Torc	(3P(6C))R	BUFFER	Gold/silver alloy	
F.116	BM	1991,0501.145				79	1990	Area 4	Hoard F pit; metal-detected find August 1990	Torc	(4CZ(2P))R		Gold/silver alloy	
F.117	BM	1991,0501.94				106	1990	Area 4	Hoard F pit; metal-detected find August 1990	Torc	(4P(2P))R	RING	Gold/silver alloy	
F.118	BM	1991,0501.129				16	1990	Area 4	Hoard F pit; metal-detected find August 1990	Torc	(6C(2PZ))R	BUFFER	Gold/silver alloy	
F.119	BM	1991,0501.81				69	1990	Area 4	Hoard F pit; metal-detected find August 1990	Torc	(5C(3P(2P)))R	REEL	Gold/silver alloy	F.119 and F.120 join
F.120	BM	1991,0501.80				68	1990	Area 4	Hoard F pit; metal-detected find August 1990	Torc	(5C(3P(2P)))R	REEL	Gold/silver alloy	F.119 and F.120 join
F.121	BM	1991,0501.146				80	1990	Area 4	Hoard F pit; metal-detected find August 1990	Bracelet	(2P)R	LOOP	Gold/silver alloy	
F.122	BM	1991,0501.153				86	1990	Area 4	Hoard F pit; metal-detected find August 1990	Wire/?torc/ ?bracelet	(?3P)T		Gold/silver alloy	
F.123	BM	1991,0501.79				67	1990	Area 4	Hoard F pit; metal-detected find August 1990	Torc/bracelet	(2P)R		Gold/silver alloy	
F.124	BM	1991,0501.194				176	1990	Area 4	Hoard F pit; metal-detected find August 1990	Torc/bracelet	(2P)R		Gold/silver alloy	
F.125	BM	1991,0702.70				269, 416, 417, 418, 420, 421	1990	Area 4	Hoard F pit; metal-detected find August 1990	Torc/bracelet	(2P)R		Gold/silver alloy	
F.126	BM	1991,0702.72				427	1990	Area 4	Hoard F pit; metal-detected find August 1990	Torc/bracelet	(2P)R		Gold/silver alloy	
F.127	BM	1991,0702.69				260	1990	Area 4	Hoard F pit; metal-detected find August 1990	Torc/bracelet	(2P)R		Gold/silver alloy	
F.128	BM	1991,0702.204				383	1990	Area 4	Hoard F pit; metal-detected find August 1990	Torc/bracelet	(2P)R		Gold/silver alloy	
F.129	BM	1991,0702.221				407	1990	Area 4	Hoard F pit; metal-detected find August 1990	Torc/bracelet	(2P)R		Gold/silver alloy	
F.130	BM	1991,0702.68				259	1990	Area 4	Hoard F pit; metal-detected find August 1990	Torc/bracelet	(2P)R		Gold/silver alloy	
F.131	BM	1991,0702.219				399	1990	Area 4	Hoard F pit; metal-detected find August 1990	Torc/bracelet	(2P)R		Gold/silver alloy	
F.132	BM	1991,0501.180				146	1990	Area 4	Hoard F pit; metal-detected find August 1990	Torc/bracelet	(2P)R		Gold/silver alloy	May be part of the same object as F.133

Cat no.	Museum	Reg. no.	Ticket no.	Published ref.	Stead code	Ralph no.	Ex. year	Findspot	Context details	Object name	MSCC or TUB torc type	Torc terminal type	Material	Joining / related fragments?
F.133	BM	1991,0501.181				147	1990	Area 4	Hoard F pit; metal-detected find August 1990	Torc/bracelet	(2P)R		Gold/silver alloy	May be part of the same object as F.132
F.134	BM	1991,0702.205				384	1990	Area 4	Hoard F pit; metal-detected find August 1990	Torc/bracelet	(2P)R		Gold/silver alloy	
F.135	BM	1991,0501.222				380	1990	Area 4	Hoard F pit; metal-detected find August 1990	Torc/bracelet	(?P(2P))R		Gold/silver alloy	
F.136	BM	1991,0702.220				400	1990	Area 4	Hoard F pit; metal-detected find August 1990	Torc/bracelet	(2P)R	LOOP	Gold/silver alloy	
F.137	BM	1991,0702.212				392	1990	Area 4	Hoard F pit; metal-detected find August 1990	Torc/bracelet	(2P)R		Gold/silver alloy	
F.138	BM	1991,0501.177				138	1990	Area 4	Hoard F pit; metal-detected find August 1990	Torc/bracelet	(?C(2P))R		Gold/silver alloy	
F.139	BM	1991,0501.178				139	1990	Area 4	Hoard F pit; metal-detected find August 1990	Torc/bracelet	(2P)R		Gold/silver alloy	
F.140	BM	1991,0501.102				115	1990	Area 4	Hoard F pit; metal-detected find August 1990	Torc/bracelet	(2P)R	?CAGE/ ?LOOP	Gold/silver alloy	
F.141	BM	1991,0702.71				419	1990	Area 4	Hoard F pit; metal-detected find August 1990	Torc/bracelet	(2PZ)R		Gold/silver alloy	
F.142	BM	1991,0501.179				141	1990	Area 4	Hoard F pit; metal-detected find August 1990	Torc/bracelet	(?P(2PZ))R		Gold/silver alloy	
F.143	BM	1991,0702.67				266, 271	1990	Area 4	Hoard F pit; metal-detected find August 1990	Torc/bracelet	(?C(3P))R		Gold/silver alloy	
F.144	BM	1991,0501.188				168	1990	Area 4	Hoard F pit; metal-detected find August 1990	Torc/bracelet	(3P)2T+1R		Gold/silver alloy	
F.145	BM	1991,0501.190				170	1990	Area 4	Hoard F pit; metal-detected find August 1990	Torc/bracelet	(4P)T		Gold/silver alloy	
F.146	BM	1991,0501.214				240	1990	Area 4	Hoard F pit; metal-detected find August 1990	Torc/bracelet	(6C)3R+3T	BUFFER	Gold/silver alloy	
F.147	BM	1991,0501.221				353	1990	Area 4	Hoard F pit; metal-detected find August 1990	Torc/bracelet	(6C)R		Gold/silver alloy	F.147 and F.148 may be part of the same object
F.148	BM	1991,0501.86				74	1990	Area 4	Hoard F pit; metal-detected find August 1990	Torc/bracelet	(6C)R		Gold/silver alloy	F.147 and F.148 may be part of the same object
F.149	BM	1991,0702.95				167	1990	Area 4	Hoard F pit; metal-detected find August 1990	Wire/?torc/ ?bracelet	(?C)R		Gold/silver alloy	
F.150	BM	1991,0702.96				175	1990	Area 4	Hoard F pit; metal-detected find August 1990	Wire/?torc/ ?bracelet	(?C)T		Gold/silver alloy	
F.151	BM	1991,0702.228.b				451	1990	Area 4	Hoard F pit; metal-detected find August 1990	Torc/bracelet	(?C)R		Gold/silver alloy	
F.152	BM	1991,0702.228.a				451	1990	Area 4	Hoard F pit; metal-detected find August 1990	Torc/bracelet	(?C)R		Gold/silver alloy	
F.153	BM	1991,0407.44.a			SN/AD		1990	Area 4	Hoard F pit; excavated find, surface trowelling	Torc/bracelet	(2P(2P))R		Gold/silver alloy	
F.154	BM	1991,0501.144				78	1990	Area 4	Hoard F pit; metal-detected find August 1990	Torc/bracelet	(2P(3P))R		Gold/silver alloy	F.154–7 may be part of the same torc
F.155	BM	1991,0702.17				23	1990	Area 4	Hoard F pit; metal-detected find August 1990	Torc/bracelet	(2P(3P))R		Gold/silver alloy	F.154–7 may be part of the same torc
F.156	BM	1991,0501.87				75	1990	Area 4	Hoard F pit; metal-detected find August 1990	Torc/bracelet	(2P(3P))R		Gold/silver alloy	F.154–7 may be part of the same torc
F.157	BM	1991,0501.88				76	1990	Area 4	Hoard F pit; metal-detected find August 1990	Torc/bracelet	(2P(3P))R		Gold/silver alloy	F.154–7 may be part of the same torc
F.158	BM	1991,0501.191				172	1990	Area 4	Hoard F pit; metal-detected find August 1990	Torc/bracelet	(2P(3P))R		Gold/silver alloy	
F.159	BM	1991,0501.193				174	1990	Area 4	Hoard F pit; metal-detected find August 1990	Torc/bracelet	(3P(2P))R		Gold/silver alloy	
F.160	BM	1991,0501.192				173	1990	Area 4	Hoard F pit; metal-detected find August 1990	Torc/bracelet	(?C(2P))R		Gold/silver alloy	
F.161	BM	1991,0501.189				169	1990	Area 4	Hoard F pit; metal-detected find August 1990	Torc/bracelet	(?C(4P))T		Gold/silver alloy	
F.162	BM	1991,0702.92				161	1990	Area 4	Hoard F pit; metal-detected find August 1990	Torc	(5C)3Q+2T	BUFFER	Copper alloy	F.162–5 may be part of the same torc

Cat no.	Museum	Reg. no.	Ticket no.	Published ref.	Stead code	Ralph no.	Ex. year	Findspot	Context details	Object name	MSCC or TUB torc type	Torc terminal type	Material	Joining / related fragments?
F.163	BM	1991,0702.94				163	1990	Area 4	Hoard F pit; metal-detected find August 1990	Torc	(5C)3Q+2T		Copper alloy	F.162–5 may be part of the same torc
F.164	BM	1991,0702.123				243	1990	Area 4	Hoard F pit; metal-detected find August 1990	Torc	(5C)3Q+2T	BUFFER	Copper alloy	F.162–5 may be part of the same torc
F.165	BM	1991,0702.135				255	1990	Area 4	Hoard F pit; metal-detected find August 1990	Torc	(5C)3Q+2T		Copper alloy	F.162–5 may be part of the same torc
F.166	BM	1991,0702.132				251	1990	Area 4	Hoard F pit; metal-detected find August 1990	Torc	(5C)T		Copper alloy	
F.167	BM	1991,0702.122				242	1990	Area 4	Hoard F pit; metal-detected find August 1990	Torc	(6C)T		Copper alloy	
F.168	BM	1991,0702.121				241	1990	Area 4	Hoard F pit; metal-detected find August 1990	Torc	(6C)T	BUFFER	Copper alloy	
F.169	BM	1991,0702.61				302, 303	1990	Area 4	Hoard F pit; metal-detected find August 1990	Torc	(6CZ(2PZ))R	BUFFER	Copper alloy	
F.170	BM	1991,0702.274				501c	1990	Area 4	Hoard F pit; metal-detected find August 1990	Wire/?torc/ ?bracelet	(?C)T		Copper alloy	
F.171	BM	1991,0702.88				154	1990	Area 4	Hoard F pit; metal-detected find August 1990	Torc/bracelet	(4P)T		Copper alloy	
F.172	BM	1991,0702.14				92, 93	1990	Area 4	Hoard F pit; metal-detected find August 1990	Torc/bracelet	(6C)T		Copper alloy	
F.173	BM	1991,0702.140				263	1990	Area 4	Hoard F pit; metal-detected find August 1990	Torc/bracelet	(?C(2P))R		Copper alloy	
F.174	BM	1991,0501.213				235	1990	Area 4	Hoard F pit; metal-detected find August 1990	Torc/bracelet	(2P(3P))R		Copper alloy	
F.175	BM	1991,0702.169				336	1990	Area 4	Hoard F pit; metal-detected find August 1990	Torc/bracelet	(2P(2P))R		Copper alloy	F.175–8 may be from the same torc
F.176	BM	1991,0702.161				328	1990	Area 4	Hoard F pit; metal-detected find August 1990	Torc/bracelet	(2P(2P))R		Copper alloy	F.175–8 may be from the same torc
F.177	BM	1991,0702.156				322	1990	Area 4	Hoard F pit; metal-detected find August 1990	Torc/bracelet	(2P(2P))R		Copper alloy	F.175–8 may be from the same torc
F.178	BM	1991,0702.158				325	1990	Area 4	Hoard F pit; metal-detected find August 1990	Torc/bracelet	(2P(2P))R		Copper alloy	F.175–8 may be from the same torc
F.179	BM	1991,0702.117				236	1990	Area 4	Hoard F pit; metal-detected find August 1990	Torc/bracelet	(2P(2P+ 3P))R	BUFFER	Copper alloy	
F.180	BM	1991,0702.164				331	1990	Area 4	Hoard F pit; metal-detected find August 1990	Torc/bracelet	(2P(2P))R		Copper alloy	F.180–4 may be part of the same object
F.181	BM	1991,0702.172				339	1990	Area 4	Hoard F pit; metal-detected find August 1990	Torc/bracelet	(2P(2P))R		Copper alloy	F.180–4 may be part of the same object
F.182	BM	1991,0702.111				229	1990	Area 4	Hoard F pit; metal-detected find August 1990	Torc/bracelet	(2P(2P))R		Copper alloy	F.180–4 may be part of the same object
F.183	BM	1991,0702.112				230	1990	Area 4	Hoard F pit; metal-detected find August 1990	Torc/bracelet	(2P(2P))R		Copper alloy	F.180–4 may be part of the same object
F.184	BM	1991,0702.116				234	1990	Area 4	Hoard F pit; metal-detected find August 1990	Torc/bracelet	(2P(2P))R		Copper alloy	F.180–4 may be part of the same object
F.185	BM	1991,0702.49				210, 211, 212, 213	1990	Area 4	Hoard F pit; metal-detected find August 1990	Torc		RING/ TORUS	Copper alloy	
F.186	BM	1991,0702.54				391, 402, 404, 405, 408, 409	1990	Area 4	Hoard F pit; metal-detected find August 1990	Torc	(4P)R	LOOP	Copper alloy	
F.187	BM	1991,0702.16				15	1990	Area 4	Hoard F pit; metal-detected find August 1990	Torc	(8C)T	BUFFER	Copper alloy	
F.188	BM	1991,0702.139				258	1990	Area 4	Hoard F pit; metal-detected find August 1990	Torc	(7C)T	BUFFER	Copper alloy	
F.189	BM	1991,0702.120				239	1990	Area 4	Hoard F pit; metal-detected find August 1990	Torc	(6C)3R+3T		Copper alloy	

Cat no.	Museum	Reg. no.	Ticket no.	Published ref.	Stead code	Ralph no.	Ex. year	Findspot	Context details	Object name	MSCC or TUB torc type	Torc terminal type	Material	Joining / related fragments?
F.190	BM	1991,0702.124				244	1990	Area 4	Hoard F pit; metal-detected find August 1990	Torc	(6C)T		Copper alloy	F.190–6 may be part of the same torc
F.191	BM	1991,0702.125				244	1990	Area 4	Hoard F pit; metal-detected find August 1990	Torc	(6C)T		Copper alloy	F.190–6 may be part of the same torc
F.192	BM	1991,0702.126				245	1990	Area 4	Hoard F pit; metal-detected find August 1990	Torc	(6C)T		Copper alloy	F.190–6 may be part of the same torc
F.193	BM	1991,0702.128				247	1990	Area 4	Hoard F pit; metal-detected find August 1990	Torc	(6C)T		Copper alloy	F.190–6 may be part of the same torc
F.194	BM	1991,0702.129				248	1990	Area 4	Hoard F pit; metal-detected find August 1990	Torc	(?6C)T		Copper alloy	F.190–6 may be part of the same torc
F.195	BM	1991,0702.131				250	1990	Area 4	Hoard F pit; metal-detected find August 1990	Torc	(6C)T		Copper alloy	F.190–6 may be part of the same torc
F.196	BM	1991,0702.134				253	1990	Area 4	Hoard F pit; metal-detected find August 1990	Torc	(?C)T		Copper alloy	F.190–6 may be part of the same torc
F.197	BM	1991,0702.127				246	1990	Area 4	Hoard F pit; metal-detected find August 1990	Torc	(5C)T		Copper alloy	F.197–8 may be part of the same torc
F.198	BM	1991,0702.130				249	1990	Area 4	Hoard F pit; metal-detected find August 1990	Torc	(5C)T		Copper alloy	F.197–8 may be part of the same torc
F.199	BM	1991,0702.136				256	1990	Area 4	Hoard F pit; metal-detected find August 1990	Torc/bracelet	(4C)T		Copper alloy	
F.200	BM	1991,0702.133				252	1990	Area 4	Hoard F pit; metal-detected find August 1990	Torc/bracelet	(5C)T		Copper alloy	
F.201	BM	1991,0702.18				28, 89, 171, 265	1990	Area 4	Hoard F pit; metal-detected find August 1990	Torc	(4C)R		Copper alloy	
F.202	BM	1991,0702.1				11	1990	Area 4	Hoard F pit; metal-detected find August 1990	Torc	(4P(6C))T	BUFFER	Copper alloy	Almost certainly the pair to F.203
F.203	BM	1991,0702.13				99	1990	Area 4	Hoard F pit; metal-detected find August 1990	Torc	(4P(6C))T	BUFFER	Copper alloy	Almost certainly the pair to F.202
F.204	BM	1991,0702.76				410	1990	Area 4	Hoard F pit; metal-detected find August 1990	Torc/bracelet	(?3C(2P))R	LOOP	Copper alloy	May be part of the same object as F.205
F.205	BM	1991,0702.74				411, 412, 423, 425, 428, 431, 436, 438, 439, 442, 443, 447, 471	1990	Area 4	Hoard F pit; metal-detected find August 1990	Torc/bracelet	(?3C(2P))R		Copper alloy	May be part of the same object as F.204
F.206	BM	1991,0702.20				49	1990	Area 4	Hoard F pit; metal-detected find August 1990	Torc	(2P(2P))R	LOOP	Copper alloy	
F.207	BM	1991,0702.15				14	1990	Area 4	Hoard F pit; metal-detected find August 1990	Torc	(7C(2P))R	TORUS	Copper alloy	
F.208	BM	1991,0702.52				342, 403	1990	Area 4	Hoard F pit; metal-detected find August 1990	Bracelet	(2P)T	LOOP/HOOK	Copper alloy	
F.209	BM	1991,0702.53				272, 273, 274, 340, 341, 343, 344, 345	1990	Area 4	Hoard F pit; metal-detected find August 1990	Bracelet	(2P)T	LOOP	Copper alloy	
F.210	BM	1991,0702.224				448	1990	Area 4	Hoard F pit; metal-detected find August 1990	Torc/bracelet		LOOP	Copper alloy	

Cat no.	Museum	Reg. no.	Ticket no.	Published ref.	Stead code	Ralph no.	Ex. year	Findspot	Context details	Object name	MSCC or TUB torc type	Torc terminal type	Material	Joining / related fragments?
F.211	BM	1991,0702.81				145	1990	Area 4	Hoard F pit; metal-detected find August 1990	Torc/bracelet	(2P)R		Copper alloy	
F.212	BM	1991,0407.44.b			SN/AD		1990	Area 4	Hoard F pit; excavated find, surface trowelling	Torc/bracelet	(2P)R		Copper alloy	
F.213	BM	1991,0407.45.f			SN/AE; SN/AF		1990	Area 4	Hoard F pit; excavated find, surface trowelling/within hoard pit, down to 25cm	Torc/bracelet	(2P)R		Copper alloy	
F.214	BM	1991,0407.65.d			SN/AG		1990	Area 4	Hoard F pit; excavated find, within hoard pit, down to bottom	Torc/bracelet	(2P)R		Copper alloy	
F.215	BM	1991,0702.73				268, 415, 422, 424, 426, 429, 430, 432, 433, 434, 435, 437, 440, 441, 445, 446, 469, 470	1990	Area 4	Hoard F pit; metal-detected find August 1990	Torc/bracelet	(?C(2P))R		Copper alloy	
F.216	BM	1991,0702.213				393	1990	Area 4	Hoard F pit; metal-detected find August 1990	Torc/bracelet	(2P)R		Copper alloy	
F.217	BM	1991,0702.276			SN/AC		1990	Area 4	Hoard F pit; excavated find, surface trowelling	Torc/bracelet	(?C)T		Copper alloy	
F.218	BM	1991,0702.209				388	1990	Area 4	Hoard F pit; metal-detected find August 1990	Torc/bracelet	(2P)R		Copper alloy	F.218–40 may be part of the same object
F.219	BM	1991,0702.210				389	1990	Area 4	Hoard F pit; metal-detected find August 1990	Torc/bracelet	(2P)R		Copper alloy	F.218–40 may be part of the same object
F.220	BM	1991,0702.217				397	1990	Area 4	Hoard F pit; metal-detected find August 1990	Torc/bracelet	(2P)R		Copper alloy	F.218–40 may be part of the same object
F.221	BM	1991,0702.193				371	1990	Area 4	Hoard F pit; metal-detected find August 1990	Torc/bracelet	(2P)R		Copper alloy	F.218–40 may be part of the same object
F.222	BM	1991,0702.195				373	1990	Area 4	Hoard F pit; metal-detected find August 1990	Torc/bracelet	(2P)R		Copper alloy	F.218–40 may be part of the same object
F.223	BM	1991,0702.211				390	1990	Area 4	Hoard F pit; metal-detected find August 1990	Torc/bracelet	(2P)R		Copper alloy	F.218–40 may be part of the same object
F.224	BM	1991,0702.216				396	1990	Area 4	Hoard F pit; metal-detected find August 1990	Torc/bracelet	(2P)R		Copper alloy	F.218–40 may be part of the same object
F.225	BM	1991,0702.273				501b	1990	Area 4	Hoard F pit; metal-detected find August 1990	Torc/bracelet	(2P)R		Copper alloy	F.218–40 may be part of the same object
F.226	BM	1991,0702.275			SN/AC		1990	Area 4	Hoard F pit; excavated find, surface trowelling	Torc/bracelet	(2P)R		Copper alloy	F.218–40 may be part of the same object
F.227	BM	1991,0702.78				142	1990	Area 4	Hoard F pit; metal-detected find August 1990	Torc/bracelet	(2P)R		Copper alloy	F.218–40 may be part of the same object
F.228	BM	1991,0702.77				140	1990	Area 4	Hoard F pit; metal-detected find August 1990	Torc/bracelet	(2P)R		Copper alloy	F.218–40 may be part of the same object
F.229	BM	1991,0702.190				368	1990	Area 4	Hoard F pit; metal-detected find August 1990	Torc/bracelet	(2P)R		Copper alloy	F.218–40 may be part of the same object
F.230	BM	1991,0702.79				143	1990	Area 4	Hoard F pit; metal-detected find August 1990	Torc/bracelet	(2P)R		Copper alloy	F.218–40 may be part of the same object
F.231	BM	1991,0702.185				363	1990	Area 4	Hoard F pit; metal-detected find August 1990	Torc/bracelet	(2P)R		Copper alloy	F.218–40 may be part of the same object
F.232	BM	1991,0702.186				364	1990	Area 4	Hoard F pit; metal-detected find August 1990	Torc/bracelet	(2P)R		Copper alloy	F.218–40 may be part of the same object

Cat no.	Museum	Reg. no.	Ticket no.	Published ref.	Stead code	Ralph no.	Ex. year	Findspot	Context details	Object name	MSCC or TUB torc type	Torc terminal type	Material	Joining / related fragments?
F.233	BM	1991,0702.196				374	1990	Area 4	Hoard F pit; metal-detected find August 1990	Torc/bracelet	(2P)R		Copper alloy	F.218–40 may be part of the same object
F.234	BM	1991,0702.189				367	1990	Area 4	Hoard F pit; metal-detected find August 1990	Torc/bracelet	(2P)R		Copper alloy	F.218–40 may be part of the same object
F.235	BM	1991,0702.192				370	1990	Area 4	Hoard F pit; metal-detected find August 1990	Torc/bracelet	(2P)R		Copper alloy	F.218–40 may be part of the same object
F.236	BM	1991,0702.201				379	1990	Area 4	Hoard F pit; metal-detected find August 1990	Torc/bracelet	(2P)R		Copper alloy	F.218–40 may be part of the same object
F.237	BM	1991,0702.187				365	1990	Area 4	Hoard F pit; metal-detected find August 1990	Torc/bracelet	(2P)R		Copper alloy	F.218–40 may be part of the same object
F.238	BM	1991,0702.191				369	1990	Area 4	Hoard F pit; metal-detected find August 1990	Torc/bracelet	(2P)R		Copper alloy	F.218–40 may be part of the same object
F.239	BM	1991,0702.197				375	1990	Area 4	Hoard F pit; metal-detected find August 1990	Torc/bracelet	(2P)R		Copper alloy	F.218–40 may be part of the same object
F.240	BM	1991,0702.188				366	1990	Area 4	Hoard F pit; metal-detected find August 1990	Torc/bracelet	(2P)R		Copper alloy	F.218–40 may be part of the same object
F.241	BM	1991,0702.19					1990	Area 4	Found inside F.43 during conservation	Torc/bracelet	(?P(2P))R		Copper alloy	
F.242	BM	1991,0702.223				444	1990	Area 4	Hoard F pit; metal-detected find August 1990	Wire/?torc/ ?bracelet	(?2P)R		Copper alloy	
F.243	BM	1991,0702.142				270	1990	Area 4	Hoard F pit; metal-detected find August 1990	Torc/bracelet	(3P)R		Copper alloy	
F.244	BM	1991,0702.194				372	1990	Area 4	Hoard F pit; metal-detected find August 1990	Torc/bracelet	(?C(3P))R		Copper alloy	
F.245	BM	1991,0702.57				261	1990	Area 4	Hoard F pit; metal-detected find August 1990	Torc/bracelet	(3P)R		Copper alloy	
F.246	BM	1991,0702.180				358	1990	Area 4	Hoard F pit; metal-detected find August 1990	Torc/bracelet	(4P)T		Copper alloy	
F.247	BM	1991,0702.60				401, 406, 413	1990	Area 4	Hoard F pit; metal-detected find August 1990	Torc/bracelet	(4P)R		Copper alloy	
F.248	BM	1991,0702.175				352	1990	Area 4	Hoard F pit; metal-detected find August 1990	Torc/bracelet	(5C)3P+2T		Copper alloy	
F.249	BM	1991,0702.141				264	1990	Area 4	Hoard F pit; metal-detected find August 1990	Torc/bracelet	(5C)T	BUFFER	Copper alloy	
F.250	BM	1991,0702.181				359	1990	Area 4	Hoard F pit; metal-detected find August 1990	Torc/bracelet	(5C)T		Copper alloy	
F.251	BM	1991,0702.173				350	1990	Area 4	Hoard F pit; metal-detected find August 1990	Torc/bracelet	(5C)T		Copper alloy	
F.252	BM	1991,0702.174				351	1990	Area 4	Hoard F pit; metal-detected find August 1990	Torc/bracelet	(?5C)T		Copper alloy	
F.253	BM	1991,0702.183				361	1990	Area 4	Hoard F pit; metal-detected find August 1990	Torc/bracelet	(?5C)T		Copper alloy	
F.254	BM	1991,0702.176				354	1990	Area 4	Hoard F pit; metal-detected find August 1990	Torc/bracelet	(?5C)T		Copper alloy	
F.255	BM	1991,0702.58				254	1990	Area 4	Hoard F pit; metal-detected find August 1990	Torc/bracelet	(6C)R		Copper alloy	
F.256	BM	1991,0702.184				362	1990	Area 4	Hoard F pit; metal-detected find August 1990	Torc/bracelet	(6C)T	LOOP	Copper alloy	F.256–61 may be part of the same object
F.257	BM	1991,0702.178				356	1990	Area 4	Hoard F pit; metal-detected find August 1990	Torc/bracelet	(6C)T		Copper alloy	F.256–61 may be part of the same object
F.258	BM	1991,0702.179				357	1990	Area 4	Hoard F pit; metal-detected find August 1990	Torc/bracelet	(6C)T		Copper alloy	F.256–61 may be part of the same object
F.259	BM	1991,0702.23				114	1990	Area 4	Hoard F pit; metal-detected find August 1990	Torc/bracelet	(6C)T		Copper alloy	F.256–61 may be part of the same object
F.260	BM	1991,0702.93				162	1990	Area 4	Hoard F pit; metal-detected find August 1990	Torc/bracelet	(6C)T		Copper alloy	F.256–61 may be part of the same object
F.261	BM	1991,0702.177				355	1990	Area 4	Hoard F pit; metal-detected find August 1990	Torc/bracelet	(6C)T		Copper alloy	F.256–61 may be part of the same object
F.262	BM	1991,0702.154				301	1990	Area 4	Hoard F pit; metal-detected find August 1990	Torc/bracelet	(??)R		Copper alloy	

Cat no.	Museum	Reg. no.	Ticket no.	Published ref.	Stead code	Ralph no.	Ex. year	Findspot	Context details	Object name	MSCC or TUB torc type	Torc terminal type	Material	Joining / related fragments?
F.263	BM	1991,0702.153				300	1990	Area 4	Hoard F pit; metal-detected find August 1990	Wire/torc / bracelet	(??)R		Copper alloy	
F.264	BM	1991,0702.248				474	1990	Area 4	Hoard F pit; metal-detected find August 1990	Wire/?torc/ ?bracelet	(??)R		Copper alloy	
F.265	BM	1991,0702.151				298	1990	Area 4	Hoard F pit; metal-detected find August 1990	Wire/?torc/ ?bracelet	(??)Q		Copper alloy	F.265–6 may be part of the same object
F.266	BM	1991,0702.152				299	1990	Area 4	Hoard F pit; metal-detected find August 1990	Wire/?torc/ ?bracelet	(??)Q		Copper alloy	F.265–6 may be part of the same object
F.267	BM	1991,0702.233				456	1990	Area 4	Hoard F pit; metal-detected find August 1990	Wire/?torc/ ?bracelet	(??)R		Copper alloy	
F.268	BM	1991,0702.263				489	1990	Area 4	Hoard F pit; metal-detected find August 1990	Wire/?torc/ ?bracelet	(??)R		Copper alloy	
F.269	BM	1991,0702.232				455	1990	Area 4	Hoard F pit; metal-detected find August 1990	Wire/?torc/ ?bracelet	(??)R		Copper alloy	
F.270	BM	1991,0702.231				454	1990	Area 4	Hoard F pit; metal-detected find August 1990	Wire/?torc/ ?bracelet	(??)R		Copper alloy	
F.271	BM	1991,0702.253				479	1990	Area 4	Hoard F pit; metal-detected find August 1990	Wire/?torc/ ?bracelet	(??)T		Copper alloy	F.271–80 may be part of the same object
F.272	BM	1991,0702.238				461	1990	Area 4	Hoard F pit; metal-detected find August 1990	Wire/?torc/ ?bracelet	(??)T		Copper alloy	F.271–80 may be part of the same object
F.273	BM	1991,0702.235				458	1990	Area 4	Hoard F pit; metal-detected find August 1990	Wire/?torc/ ?bracelet	(??)T		Copper alloy	F.271–80 may be part of the same object
F.274	BM	1991,0702.237				460	1990	Area 4	Hoard F pit; metal-detected find August 1990	Wire/?torc/ ?bracelet	(??)T		Copper alloy	F.271–80 may be part of the same object
F.275	BM	1991,0702.234				457	1990	Area 4	Hoard F pit; metal-detected find August 1990	Wire/?torc/ ?bracelet	(??)T		Copper alloy	F.271–80 may be part of the same object
F.276	BM	1991,0702.236				459	1990	Area 4	Hoard F pit; metal-detected find August 1990	Wire/?torc/ ?bracelet	(??)T		Copper alloy	F.271–80 may be part of the same object
F.277	BM	1991,0702.242				465	1990	Area 4	Hoard F pit; metal-detected find August 1990	Wire/?torc/ ?bracelet	(??)T		Copper alloy	F.271–80 may be part of the same object
F.278	BM	1991,0702.230				453	1990	Area 4	Hoard F pit; metal-detected find August 1990	Wire/?torc/ ?bracelet	(??)T		Copper alloy	F.271–80 may be part of the same object
F.279	BM	1991,0702.241				464	1990	Area 4	Hoard F pit; metal-detected find August 1990	Wire/?torc/ ?bracelet	(??)T		Copper alloy	F.271–80 may be part of the same object
F.280	BM	1991,0702.240				463	1990	Area 4	Hoard F pit; metal-detected find August 1990	Wire/?torc/ ?bracelet	(??)T		Copper alloy	F.271–80 may be part of the same object
F.281	BM	1991,0702.266				492	1990	Area 4	Hoard F pit; metal-detected find August 1990	Wire/?torc/ ?bracelet	(?C)R		Copper alloy	
F.282	BM	1991,0407.45.g			SN/AE; SN/ AF		1990	Area 4	Hoard F pit; excavated find, surface trowelling/within hoard pit, down to 25cm	Wire/?torc/ ?bracelet	(?C)R		Copper alloy	
F.283	BM	1991,0702.256				482	1990	Area 4	Hoard F pit; metal-detected find August 1990	Wire/?torc/ ?bracelet	(?C)R	?LOOP	Copper alloy	F.283–8 may be part of the same object
F.284	BM	1991,0702.264				490	1990	Area 4	Hoard F pit; metal-detected find August 1990	Wire/?torc/ ?bracelet	(?C)R	?LOOP	Copper alloy	F.283–8 may be part of the same object
F.285	BM	1991,0702.268				494	1990	Area 4	Hoard F pit; metal-detected find August 1990	Wire/?torc/ ?bracelet	(?C)R	?LOOP	Copper alloy	F.283–8 may be part of the same object
F.286	BM	1991,0702.270				496	1990	Area 4	Hoard F pit; metal-detected find August 1990	Wire/?torc/ ?bracelet	(?C)R	?LOOP	Copper alloy	F.283–8 may be part of the same object
F.287	BM	1991,0702.267				493	1990	Area 4	Hoard F pit; metal-detected find August 1990	Wire/?torc/ ?bracelet	(?C)R	?LOOP	Copper alloy	F.283–8 may be part of the same object
F.288	BM	1991,0702.269				495	1990	Area 4	Hoard F pit; metal-detected find August 1990	Wire/?torc/ ?bracelet	(?C)R	?LOOP	Copper alloy	F.283–8 may be part of the same object
F.289	BM	1991,0702.258				484	1990	Area 4	Hoard F pit; metal-detected find August 1990	Wire/?torc/ ?bracelet	(?C)R		Copper alloy	F.289–90 may be part of the same object
F.290	BM	1991,0702.250				476	1990	Area 4	Hoard F pit; metal-detected find August 1990	Wire/?torc/ ?bracelet	(?C)R		Copper alloy	F.289–90 may be part of the same object
F.291	BM	1991,0702.265				491	1990	Area 4	Hoard F pit; metal-detected find August 1990	Wire/?torc/ ?bracelet	(?C)R		Copper alloy	

Cat no.	Museum	Reg. no.	Ticket no.	Published ref.	Stead code	Ralph no.	Ex. year	Findspot	Context details	Object name	MSCC or TUB torc type	Torc terminal type	Material	Joining / related fragments?
F.292	BM	1991,0702.247				473	1990	Area 4	Hoard F pit; metal-detected find August 1990	Wire/torc / bracelet	(?C)T		Copper alloy	F.292–309 may be part of the same object
F.293	BM	1991,0702.254				480	1990	Area 4	Hoard F pit; metal-detected find August 1990	Wire/torc / bracelet	(?C)T		Copper alloy	F.292–309 may be part of the same object
F.294	BM	1991,0702.260				486	1990	Area 4	Hoard F pit; metal-detected find August 1990	Wire/torc / bracelet	(?C)T		Copper alloy	F.292–309 may be part of the same object
F.295	BM	1991,0702.244				467	1990	Area 4	Hoard F pit; metal-detected find August 1990	Wire/torc / bracelet	(?C)T		Copper alloy	F.292–309 may be part of the same object
F.296	BM	1991,0702.251				477	1990	Area 4	Hoard F pit; metal-detected find August 1990	Wire/torc / bracelet	(?C)T		Copper alloy	F.292–309 may be part of the same object
F.297	BM	1991,0702.259				485	1990	Area 4	Hoard F pit; metal-detected find August 1990	Wire/?torc/ ?bracelet	(?C)T		Copper alloy	F.292–309 may be part of the same object
F.298	BM	1991,0702.243				466	1990	Area 4	Hoard F pit; metal-detected find August 1990	Wire/?torc/ ?bracelet	(?C)T		Copper alloy	F.292–309 may be part of the same object
F.299	BM	1991,0702.252				478	1990	Area 4	Hoard F pit; metal-detected find August 1990	Wire/?torc/ ?bracelet	(?C)T		Copper alloy	F.292–309 may be part of the same object
F.300	BM	1991,0702.245				468	1990	Area 4	Hoard F pit; metal-detected find August 1990	Wire/?torc/ ?bracelet	(?C)T		Copper alloy	F.292–309 may be part of the same object
F.301	BM	1991,0702.257				483	1990	Area 4	Hoard F pit; metal-detected find August 1990	Wire/?torc/ ?bracelet	(?C)T		Copper alloy	F.292–309 may be part of the same object
F.302	BM	1991,0702.261				487	1990	Area 4	Hoard F pit; metal-detected find August 1990	Wire/?torc/ ?bracelet	(?C)T		Copper alloy	F.292–309 may be part of the same object
F.303	BM	1991,0702.262				488	1990	Area 4	Hoard F pit; metal-detected find August 1990	Wire/?torc/ ?bracelet	(?C)T		Copper alloy	F.292–309 may be part of the same object
F.304	BM	1991,0702.249				475	1990	Area 4	Hoard F pit; metal-detected find August 1990	Wire/?torc/ ?bracelet	(?C)T		Copper alloy	F.292–309 may be part of the same object
F.305	BM	1991,0702.255				481	1990	Area 4	Hoard F pit; metal-detected find August 1990	Wire/?torc/ ?bracelet	(?C)T		Copper alloy	F.292–309 may be part of the same object
F.306	BM	1991,0407.45.d			SN/AE; SN/ AF		1990	Area 4	Hoard F pit; excavated find, surface trowelling/within hoard pit, down to 25cm	Wire/?torc/ ?bracelet	(?C)T		Copper alloy	F.292–309 may be part of the same object
F.307	BM	1991,0407.65.c			SN/AG		1990	Area 4	Hoard F pit; excavated find, surface trowelling/within hoard pit, down to bottom	Wire/?torc/ ?bracelet	(?C)T		Copper alloy	F.292–309 may be part of the same object
F.308	BM	1991,0702.246				472	1990	Area 4	Hoard F pit; metal-detected find August 1990	Wire/?torc/ ?bracelet	(?C)T		Copper alloy	F.292–309 may be part of the same object
F.309	BM	1991,0702.239				462	1990	Area 4	Hoard F pit; metal-detected find August 1990	Wire/?torc/ ?bracelet	(?C)T		Copper alloy	F.292–309 may be part of the same object
F.310	BM	1991,0702.90				159	1990	Area 4	Hoard F pit; metal-detected find August 1990	Wire/?torc/ ?bracelet	(?C)T		Copper alloy	F.310–23 may be part of the same object
F.311	BM	1991,0702.91				160	1990	Area 4	Hoard F pit; metal-detected find August 1990	Wire/?torc/ ?bracelet	(?C)T		Copper alloy	F.310–23 may be part of the same object
F.312	BM	1991,0702.89				158	1990	Area 4	Hoard F pit; metal-detected find August 1990	Wire/?torc/ ?bracelet	(?C)T		Copper alloy	F.310–23 may be part of the same object
F.313	BM	1991,0702.150				283	1990	Area 4	Hoard F pit; metal-detected find August 1990	Wire/?torc/ ?bracelet	(?C)T		Copper alloy	F.310–23 may be part of the same object
F.314	BM	1991,0702.147				280	1990	Area 4	Hoard F pit; metal-detected find August 1990	Wire/?torc/ ?bracelet	(?C)T		Copper alloy	F.310–23 may be part of the same object
F.315	BM	1991,0702.148				281	1990	Area 4	Hoard F pit; metal-detected find August 1990	Wire/?torc/ ?bracelet	(?C)T		Copper alloy	F.310–23 may be part of the same object
F.316	BM	1991,0407.45.c			SN/AE; SN/ AF		1990	Area 4	Hoard F pit; excavated find, surface trowelling/within hoard pit, down to 25cm	Wire/?torc/ ?bracelet	(?C)T		Copper alloy	F.310–23 may be part of the same object
F.317	BM	1991,0702.145				278	1990	Area 4	Hoard F pit; metal-detected find August 1990	Wire/?torc/ ?bracelet	(?C)T		Copper alloy	F.310–23 may be part of the same object
F.318	BM	1991,0702.146				279	1990	Area 4	Hoard F pit; metal-detected find August 1990	Wire/?torc/ ?bracelet	(?C)T		Copper alloy	F.310–23 may be part of the same object
F.319	BM	1991,0702.149				282	1990	Area 4	Hoard F pit; metal-detected find August 1990	Wire/?torc/ ?bracelet	(?C)T		Copper alloy	F.310–23 may be part of the same object

Cat no.	Museum	Reg. no.	Ticket no.	Published ref.	Stead code	Ralph no.	Ex. year	Findspot	Context details	Object name	MSCC or TUB torc type	Torc terminal type	Material	Joining / related fragments?
F.320	BM	1991,0702.143				276	1990	Area 4	Hoard F pit; metal-detected find August 1990	Wire/?torc/ ?bracelet	(?C)T		Copper alloy	F.310–23 may be part of the same object
F.321	BM	1991,0702.229				452	1990	Area 4	Hoard F pit; metal-detected find August 1990	Wire/?torc/ ?bracelet	(?C)T		Copper alloy	F.310–23 may be part of the same object
F.322	BM	1991,0407.44.c			SN/AD		1990	Area 4	Hoard F pit; excavated find from surface trowelling	Wire/?torc/ ?bracelet	(?C)T		Copper alloy	F.310–23 may be part of the same object
F.323	BM	1991,0702.144				277	1990	Area 4	Hoard F pit; metal-detected find August 1990	Wire/?torc/ ?bracelet	(?C)T		Copper alloy	F.310–23 may be part of the same object
F.324	BM	1991,0407.45.i			SN/AE; SN/ AF		1990	Area 4	Hoard F pit; excavated find, surface trowelling/within hoard pit, down to 25cm	Wire/?torc/ ?bracelet	(?C)R		Copper alloy	
F.325	BM	1991,0702.198				376	1990	Area 4	Hoard F pit; metal-detected find August 1990	Wire/?torc/ ?bracelet	(?P)R		Copper alloy	
F.326	BM	1991,0702.202				381	1990	Area 4	Hoard F pit; metal-detected find August 1990	Torc/bracelet	(?2P(2P))R	LOOP	Copper alloy	F.326 and F.327 join
F.327	BM	1991,0702.203				382	1990	Area 4	Hoard F pit; metal-detected find August 1990	Torc/bracelet	(?2P(2P))R		Copper alloy	F.326 and F.327 join
F.328	BM	1991,0702.105				223	1990	Area 4	Hoard F pit; metal-detected find August 1990	Wire/torc / bracelet	(?C(2P))R		Copper alloy	F.328–35 may be part of the same object
F.329	BM	1991,0702.101				219	1990	Area 4	Hoard F pit; metal-detected find August 1990	Wire/torc	(?C(2P))R		Copper alloy	F.328–35 may be part of the same object
F.330	BM	1991,0702.102				220	1990	Area 4	Hoard F pit; metal-detected find August 1990	Wire/torc	(?C(2P))R		Copper alloy	F.328–35 may be part of the same object
F.331	BM	1991,0702.106				224	1990	Area 4	Hoard F pit; metal-detected find August 1990	Wire/torc / bracelet	(?C(2P))R		Copper alloy	F.328–35 may be part of the same object
F.332	BM	1991,0702.107				225	1990	Area 4	Hoard F pit; metal-detected find August 1990	Wire/torc/bracelet	(?C(2P))R		Copper alloy	F.328–35 may be part of the same object
F.333	BM	1991,0702.104				222	1990	Area 4	Hoard F pit; metal-detected find August 1990	Wire/torc / bracelet	(?C(2P))R		Copper alloy	F.328–35 may be part of the same object
F.334	BM	1991,0702.100				216	1990	Area 4	Hoard F pit; metal-detected find August 1990	Wire/torc/bracelet	(?C(2P))R		Copper alloy	F.328–35 may be part of the same object
F.335	BM	1991,0702.103				221	1990	Area 4	Hoard F pit; metal-detected find August 1990	Wire/torc/bracelet	(?C(2P))R		Copper alloy	F.328–35 may be part of the same object
F.336	BM	1991,0702.86				152	1990	Area 4	Hoard F pit; metal-detected find August 1990	Torc/bracelet	(?C(2P))R		Copper alloy	F.336 and 337 may be part of the same object
F.337	BM	1991,0702.85				151	1990	Area 4	Hoard F pit; metal-detected find August 1990	Torc/bracelet	(?C(2P))R		Copper alloy	F.336 and 337 may be part of the same object
F.338	BM	1991,0407.45.e			SN/AE; SN/ AF		1990	Area 4	Hoard F pit; excavated find, surface trowelling/within hoard pit, down to 25cm	Torc/bracelet	(?C(2P))R		Copper alloy	
F.339	BM	1991,0702.200				378	1990	Area 4	Hoard F pit; metal-detected find August 1990	Torc/bracelet	(?C(2P))R		Copper alloy	
F.340	BM	1991,0407.65.b			SN/AG		1990	Area 4	Hoard F pit; excavated find, within hoard pit, down to bottom	Torc/bracelet	(?C(2P))R		Copper alloy	
F.341	BM	1991,0702.207				386	1990	Area 4	Hoard F pit; metal-detected find August 1990	Torc/bracelet	(?C(2P))R		Copper alloy	
F.342	BM	1991,0702.218				398	1990	Area 4	Hoard F pit; metal-detected find August 1990	Torc/bracelet	(?C(2P))R		Copper alloy	
F.343	BM	1991,0702.206				385	1990	Area 4	Hoard F pit; metal-detected find August 1990	Torc/bracelet	(?C(2P))R		Copper alloy	
F.344	BM	1991,0407.45.b			SN/AE; SN/ AF		1990	Area 4	Hoard F pit; excavated find, surface trowelling/within hoard pit, down to 25cm	Torc/bracelet	(?C(2P))R		Copper alloy	
F.345	BM	1991,0702.214				394	1990	Area 4	Hoard F pit; metal-detected find August 1990	Torc/bracelet	(?C(2P))R		Copper alloy	F.345–6 may be part of the same object
F.346	BM	1991,0702.208				387	1990	Area 4	Hoard F pit; metal-detected find August 1990	Torc/bracelet	(?C(2P))R		Copper alloy	F.345–6 may be part of the same object
F.347	BM	1991,0702.199				377	1990	Area 4	Hoard F pit; metal-detected find August 1990	Torc/bracelet	(?C(2P))R		Copper alloy	

Cat no.	Museum	Reg. no.	Ticket no.	Published ref.	Stead code	Ralph no.	Ex. year	Findspot	Context details	Object name	MSCC or TUB torc type	Torc terminal type	Material	Joining / related fragments?
F.348	BM	1991,0702.222				414	1990	Area 4	Hoard F pit; metal-detected find August 1990	Torc/bracelet	(?C(3P))R		Copper alloy	
F.349	BM	1991,0702.80				144	1990	Area 4	Hoard F pit; metal-detected find August 1990	Torc/bracelet	(?P(2P))R		Copper alloy	
F.350	BM	1991,0702.215				395	1990	Area 4	Hoard F pit; metal-detected find August 1990	Torc/bracelet	(?P(2P))R		Copper alloy	
F.351	BM	1991,0702.87				153	1990	Area 4	Hoard F pit; metal-detected find August 1990	Torc/bracelet	(4C(2P))R	TORUS	Copper alloy	May be part of the same object as F.336–7
F.352	BM	1991,0407.45.a			SN/AE; SN/AF		1990	Area 4	Hoard F pit; excavated find, surface trowelling/within hoard pit, down to 25cm	Torc	(2P(2P))R		Copper alloy	F.352–60 may be part of the same torc
F.353	BM	1991,0702.109				227	1990	Area 4	Hoard F pit; metal-detected find August 1990	Torc	(2P(2P))R	LOOP	Copper alloy	F.352–60 may be part of the same torc
F.354	BM	1991,0702.110				228	1990	Area 4	Hoard F pit; metal-detected find August 1990	Torc	(2P(2P))R	LOOP	Copper alloy	F.352–60 may be part of the same torc
F.355	BM	1991,0702.108				226	1990	Area 4	Hoard F pit; metal-detected find August 1990	Torc	(2P(2P))R		Copper alloy	F.352–60 may be part of the same torc
F.356	BM	1991,0702.113				231	1990	Area 4	Hoard F pit; metal-detected find August 1990	Torc	(2P(2P))R		Copper alloy	F.352–60 may be part of the same torc
F.357	BM	1991,0702.114				232	1990	Area 4	Hoard F pit; metal-detected find August 1990	Torc	(2P(2P))R		Copper alloy	F.352–60 may be part of the same torc
F.358	BM	1991,0702.115				233	1990	Area 4	Hoard F pit; metal-detected find August 1990	Torc	(2P(2P))R		Copper alloy	F.352–60 may be part of the same torc
F.359	BM	1991,0702.118				237	1990	Area 4	Hoard F pit; metal-detected find August 1990	Torc	(2P(2P))R		Copper alloy	F.352–60 may be part of the same torc
F.360	BM	1991,0702.119				238	1990	Area 4	Hoard F pit; metal-detected find August 1990	Torc	(2P(2P))R		Copper alloy	F.352–60 may be part of the same torc
F.361	BM	1991,0702.84				150	1990	Area 4	Hoard F pit; metal-detected find August 1990	Torc/bracelet	(2P(2P))R	LOOP	Copper alloy	
F.362	BM	1991,0702.160				327	1990	Area 4	Hoard F pit; metal-detected find August 1990	Torc/bracelet	(2P(2P))R	LOOP	Copper alloy	F.362–3 may be part of the same object
F.363	BM	1991,0702.82				148	1990	Area 4	Hoard F pit; metal-detected find August 1990	Torc/bracelet	(2P(2P))R	LOOP	Copper alloy	F.362–3 may be part of the same object
F.364	BM	1991,0702.162				329	1990	Area 4	Hoard F pit; metal-detected find August 1990	Torc/bracelet	(2P(2P))R		Copper alloy	F.364–74 may be part of the same object
F.365	BM	1991,0702.163				330	1990	Area 4	Hoard F pit; metal-detected find August 1990	Torc/bracelet	(2P(2P))R		Copper alloy	F.364–74 may be part of the same object
F.366	BM	1991,0702.83				149	1990	Area 4	Hoard F pit; metal-detected find August 1990	Torc/bracelet	(2P(2P))R		Copper alloy	F.364–74 may be part of the same object
F.367	BM	1991,0702.155				321	1990	Area 4	Hoard F pit; metal-detected find August 1990	Torc/bracelet	(2P(2P))R		Copper alloy	F.364–74 may be part of the same object
F.368	BM	1991,0702.159				326	1990	Area 4	Hoard F pit; metal-detected find August 1990	Torc/bracelet	(2P(2P))R		Copper alloy	F.364–74 may be part of the same object
F.369	BM	1991,0702.165				332	1990	Area 4	Hoard F pit; metal-detected find August 1990	Torc/bracelet	(2P(2P))R		Copper alloy	F.364–74 may be part of the same object
F.370	BM	1991,0702.166				333	1990	Area 4	Hoard F pit; metal-detected find August 1990	Torc/bracelet	(2P(2P))R		Copper alloy	F.364–74 may be part of the same object
F.371	BM	1991,0702.170				337	1990	Area 4	Hoard F pit; metal-detected find August 1990	Torc/bracelet	(2P(2P))R		Copper alloy	F.364–74 may be part of the same object
F.372	BM	1991,0702.167				334	1990	Area 4	Hoard F pit; metal-detected find August 1990	Torc/bracelet	(2P(2P))R		Copper alloy	F.364–74 may be part of the same object
F.373	BM	1991,0702.171				338	1990	Area 4	Hoard F pit; metal-detected find August 1990	Torc/bracelet	(2P(2P))R		Copper alloy	F.364–74 may be part of the same object
F.374	BM	1991,0702.168				335	1990	Area 4	Hoard F pit; metal-detected find August 1990	Torc/bracelet	(2P(2P))R		Copper alloy	F.364–74 may be part of the same object
F.375	BM	1991,0702.75				346, 347, 348, 349	1990	Area 4	Hoard F pit; metal-detected find August 1990	Torc/bracelet	(?C(3P(2P)))R		Copper alloy	

Cat no.	Museum	Reg. no.	Ticket no.	Published ref.	Stead code	Ralph no.	Ex. year	Findspot	Context details	Object name	MSCC or TUB torc type	Torc terminal type	Material	Joining / related fragments?
F.376	BM	1991,0702.157				323	1990	Area 4	Hoard F pit; metal-detected find August 1990	Torc/bracelet	(3P(2P))R		Copper alloy	
F.377	BM	1991,0501.195				179	1990	Area 4	Hoard F pit; metal-detected find August 1990	Strip			Gold/silver alloy	
F.378	BM	1991,0501.196				181	1990	Area 4	Hoard F pit; metal-detected find August 1990	Strip			Gold/silver alloy	
F.379	BM	1991,0501.197				182	1990	Area 4	Hoard F pit; metal-detected find August 1990	Strip			Gold/silver alloy	
F.380	BM	1991,0501.218				287	1990	Area 4	Hoard F pit; metal-detected find August 1990	Strip			Gold/silver alloy	
F.381	BM	1991,0702.97				177	1990	Area 4	Hoard F pit; metal-detected find August 1990	Strip			Gold/silver alloy	
F.382	BM	1991,0407.45.j			SN/AE; SN/AF		1990	Area 4	Hoard F pit; excavated find, surface trowelling/within hoard pit, down to 25cm	Strip			Copper alloy	
F.383	BM	1991,0702.98				178	1990	Area 4	Hoard F pit; metal-detected find August 1990	Strip			Copper alloy	
F.384	BM	1991,0702.55				285	1990	Area 4	Hoard F pit; metal-detected find August 1990	Strip			Copper alloy	
F.385	BM	1991,0702.56				284, 288, 289, 290, 291, 292, 293, 294, 295, 296, 297, 497, 498, 500	1990	Area 4	Hoard F pit; metal-detected find August 1990	Strip			Copper alloy	
F.386	BM	1991,0501.162				97	1990	Area 4	Hoard F pit; metal-detected find August 1990	Small ring			Gold/silver alloy	
F.387	BM	1991,0501.166				125	1990	Area 4	Hoard F pit; metal-detected find August 1990	Small ring			Gold/silver alloy	
F.388	BM	1991,0501.171				132	1990	Area 4	Hoard F pit; metal-detected find August 1990	Small ring			Gold/silver alloy	
F.389	BM	1991,0501.172				133	1990	Area 4	Hoard F pit; metal-detected find August 1990	Small ring			Gold/silver alloy	
F.390	BM	1991,0501.202				194	1990	Area 4	Hoard F pit; metal-detected find August 1990	Small ring			Gold/silver alloy	
F.391	BM	1991,0501.203				200	1990	Area 4	Hoard F pit; metal-detected find August 1990	Small ring			Gold/silver alloy	
F.392	BM	1991,0702.28				127	1990	Area 4	Hoard F pit; metal-detected find August 1990	Small ring			Gold/silver alloy	
F.393	BM	1991,0702.36				311	1990	Area 4	Hoard F pit; metal-detected find August 1990	Small ring			Gold/silver alloy	
F.394	BM	1991,0702.38				313	1990	Area 4	Hoard F pit; metal-detected find August 1990	Small ring			Gold/silver alloy	
F.395	BM	1991,0702.39				314	1990	Area 4	Hoard F pit; metal-detected find August 1990	Small ring			Gold/silver alloy	
F.396	BM	1991,0702.32				191, 197	1990	Area 4	Hoard F pit; metal-detected find August 1990	Small ring			Gold/silver alloy	
F.397	BM	1991,0702.33				193	1990	Area 4	Hoard F pit; metal-detected find August 1990	Small ring			Gold/silver alloy	
F.398	BM	1991,0501.205				203	1990	Area 4	Hoard F pit; metal-detected find August 1990	Large/small ring			Gold/silver alloy	
F.399	BM	1991,0702.34				198, 199	1990	Area 4	Hoard F pit; metal-detected find August 1990	Small ring			Gold/silver alloy	
F.400	BM	1991,0501.204				201	1990	Area 4	Hoard F pit; metal-detected find August 1990	Small ring			Gold/silver alloy	

Cat no.	Museum	Reg. no.	Ticket no.	Published ref.	Stead code	Ralph no.	Ex. year	Findspot	Context details	Object name	MSCC or TUB torc type	Torc terminal type	Material	Joining / related fragments?
F.401	BM	1991,0501.169				130	1990	Area 4	Hoard F pit; metal-detected find August 1990	Small ring			Gold/silver alloy	
F.402	BM	1991,0501.170				131	1990	Area 4	Hoard F pit; metal-detected find August 1990	Large/small ring			Gold/silver alloy	
F.403	BM	1991,0501.73				61	1990	Area 4	Hoard F pit; metal-detected find August 1990	Small ring			Gold/silver alloy	
F.404	BM	1991,0702.26				124, 195, 196	1990	Area 4	Hoard F pit; metal-detected find August 1990	Small ring			Copper alloy	
F.405	BM	1991,0702.27				126	1990	Area 4	Hoard F pit; metal-detected find August 1990	Small ring			Copper alloy	
F.406	BM	1991,0702.37				312, 315, 319	1990	Area 4	Hoard F pit; metal-detected find August 1990	Small ring			Copper alloy	
F.407	BM	1991,0702.40				316, 318, 320	1990	Area 4	Hoard F pit; metal-detected find August 1990	Small ring			Copper alloy	
F.408	BM	1991,0702.41				317	1990	Area 4	Hoard F pit; metal-detected find August 1990	Small ring			Copper alloy	
F.409	BM	1991,0702.44				202	1990	Area 4	Hoard F pit; metal-detected find August 1990	Large ring			Copper alloy	
F.410	BM	1991,0702.35				310	1990	Area 4	Hoard F pit; metal-detected find August 1990	Small ring			Copper alloy	
F.411	BM	1991,0702.277			SN/AC		1990	Area 4	Hoard F pit; excavated find, surface trowelling	Small ring			Copper alloy	
F.412	BM	1991,0501.150				83	1990	Area 4	Hoard F pit; metal-detected find August 1990	Large ring			Gold/silver alloy	
F.413	BM	1991,0501.199				187	1990	Area 4	Hoard F pit; metal-detected find August 1990	?Large ring			Gold/silver alloy	
F.414	BM	1991,0501.200				188	1990	Area 4	Hoard F pit; metal-detected find August 1990	?Large ring			Gold/silver alloy	
F.415	BM	1991,0501.201				190	1990	Area 4	Hoard F pit; metal-detected find August 1990	?Large ring			Gold/silver alloy	
F.416	BM	1991,0702.24				122	1990	Area 4	Hoard F pit; metal-detected find August 1990	Large ring			Gold/silver alloy	
F.417	BM	1991,0702.25.a-c				123, 185, 186	1990	Area 4	Hoard F pit; metal-detected find August 1990	Large ring			Gold/silver alloy	
F.418	BM	1991,0702.31				189	1990	Area 4	Hoard F pit; metal-detected find August 1990	Large ring			Gold/silver alloy	
F.419	BM	1991,0501.219				304, 305, 306	1990	Area 4	Hoard F pit; metal-detected find August 1990	Large ring			Gold/silver alloy	
F.420	BM	1991,0501.220				309	1990	Area 4	Hoard F pit; metal-detected find August 1990	?Large ring			Gold/silver alloy	
F.421	BM	1991,0407.65.a			SN/AG		1990	Area 4	Hoard F pit; excavated find, within hoard pit, down to bottom	Large ring			Gold/silver alloy	
F.422	BM	1991,0501.61				57	1990	Area 4	Hoard F pit; metal-detected find August 1990	Large ring			Gold/silver alloy	
F.423	BM	1991,0501.117				192	1990	Area 4	Hoard F pit; metal-detected find August 1990	Large ring			Gold/silver alloy	
F.424	BM	1991,0501.60				56	1990	Area 4	Hoard F pit; metal-detected find August 1990	Large ring			Gold/silver alloy	
F.425	BM	1991,0501.99				111	1990	Area 4	Hoard F pit; metal-detected find August 1990	Large ring			Gold/silver alloy	
F.426	BM	1991,0501.115				121	1990	Area 4	Hoard F pit; metal-detected find August 1990	Large ring			Gold/silver alloy	
F.427	BM	1991,0501.116				184	1990	Area 4	Hoard F pit; metal-detected find August 1990	Large ring			Gold/silver alloy	
F.428	BM	1991,0702.21				60	1990	Area 4	Hoard F pit; metal-detected find August 1990	Large ring			Copper alloy	

Cat no.	Museum	Reg. no.	Ticket no.	Published ref.	Stead code	Ralph no.	Ex. year	Findspot	Context details	Object name	MSCC or TUB torc type	Torc terminal type	Material	Joining / related fragments?
F.429	BM	1991,0501.156				90	1990	Area 4	Hoard F pit; metal-detected find August 1990	Wire			Gold/silver alloy	
F.430	BM	1991,0702.45				206	1990	Area 4	Hoard F pit; metal-detected find August 1990	Wire			Copper alloy	
F.431	BM	1991,0702.99				180	1990	Area 4	Hoard F pit; metal-detected find August 1990	Wire			Copper alloy	
F.432	BM	1991,0407.45.h			SN/AE; SN/AF		1990	Area 4	Hoard F pit; excavated find, surface trowelling/within hoard pit, down to 25cm	Wire			Copper alloy	
F.433	BM	1991,0702.271				499	1990	Area 4	Hoard F pit; metal-detected find August 1990	Wire			Copper alloy	
F.434	BM	1991,0702.225				449	1990	Area 4	Hoard F pit; metal-detected find August 1990	Wire			Copper alloy	
F.435	BM	1991,0702.5				118	1990	Area 4	Hoard F pit; metal-detected find August 1990	Large ring/?ingot/?bracelet			Copper alloy	
F.436	BM	1991,0501.74				62	1990	Area 4	Hoard F pit; metal-detected find August 1990	Amorphous lump			Gold/silver alloy	F.436 and F.437 join
F.437	BM	1991,0501.75				63	1990	Area 4	Hoard F pit; metal-detected find August 1990	Amorphous lump			Gold/silver alloy	F.436 and F.437 join
F.438	BM	1991,0501.114				120	1990	Area 4	Hoard F pit; metal-detected find August 1990	Linear ingot			Gold/silver alloy	
F.439	BM	1991,0501.198				183	1990	Area 4	Hoard F pit; metal-detected find August 1990	Linear ingot			Gold/silver alloy	
F.440	BM	1991,0702.6				119	1990	Area 4	Hoard F pit; metal-detected find August 1990	Linear ingot			Copper alloy	
F.441	BM	1991,0407.45.k			SN/AE; SN/AF		1990	Area 4	Hoard F pit; excavated find, surface trowelling/within hoard pit, down to 25cm	Sheet			Copper alloy	
F.442	BM	1991,0407.45.l			SN/AE; SN/AF		1990	Area 4	Hoard F pit; excavated find, surface trowelling/within hoard pit, down to 25cm	Amorphous lump			Copper alloy	
F.443	BM	1991,0407.65.e			SN/AG		1990	Area 4	Hoard F pit; excavated find, within hoard pit, down to bottom	Sheet/lump			Copper alloy	
F.444	BM	1991,0407.43			SN/AH		1990	Area 4	Excavated find. Near Hoard F	Torc	(2P)R	LOOP	Gold/silver alloy	
F.445	BM	1991,0702.272			SN/AC; SN/AE; SN/AJ	501a	1990	Area 4	Hoard F pit; reconstructed from fragments.	Helmet			Copper alloy	
G.1	BM	1991,0407.1			SN/AQ		1990	Area 1	Excavated find: Hoard G upper pit	Torc	(4P)R	RING	Gold/silver alloy	
G.2	BM	1990,1101.23			SN/BP; SN/CD; SN/CE;SN/CF; SN/CG		1990	Area 1	Excavated find: Hoard G upper pit	Torc	(6C)T	BUFFER	Copper alloy	
G.?2	BM	1990,1101.24			SN/BO; SN/BQ; SN/CW; SN/DB; SN/DD; SN/DF; SN/DL; SN/DQ; SN/DT(ii); SN/FC; SN/FG; SN/GE; SN/GG; SN/JG		1990	Area 1	Excavated find: found loose around top level of Hoard G, and in Hoard G upper pit	Torc	?(6C)T	?BUFFER	Copper alloy	Most likely from torc G.2
G.3	BM	1991,0407.2			SN/CH		1990	Area 1	Excavated find: Hoard G upper pit	Torc	(2P)R	LOOP	Gold/silver alloy	
G.4	BM	1991,0407.3			SN/CI		1990	Area 1	Excavated find: Hoard G upper pit	Torc	(2P(2P))R	LOOP	Gold/silver alloy	
G.5a	BM	1991,0407.4			SN/CK		1990	Area 1	Excavated find: Hoard G upper pit	Torc	(2PZ(2P))R	LOOP	Gold/silver alloy	

Cat no.	Museum	Reg. no.	Ticket no.	Published ref.	Stead code	Ralph no.	Ex. year	Findspot	Context details	Object name	MSCC or TUB torc type	Torc terminal type	Material	Joining / related fragments?
G.5b	BM	1991,0407.4			SN/CK		1990	Area 1	Excavated find: Hoard G upper pit	Small ring			Gold/silver alloy	
G.5c	BM	1991,0407.4			SN/CK		1990	Area 1	Excavated find: Hoard G upper pit	Small ring			Gold/silver alloy	
G.5d	BM	1991,0407.4			SN/CK		1990	Area 1	Excavated find: Hoard G upper pit	Small ring			Gold/silver alloy	
G.6	BM	1990,1101.12; 1990,1101.14			SN/CL; SN/BR		1990	Area 1	Excavated find: Hoard G upper pit	Torc	(3P(2P))R	LOOP	Copper alloy	
G.7	BM	1991,0407.5			SN/CM		1990	Area 1	Excavated find: Hoard G upper pit	Torc	(2P)R	LOOP	Gold/silver alloy	
G.8	BM	1990,1101.16			SN/CN		1990	Area 1	Excavated find: Hoard G upper pit	Torc	(4C)2T+2R	BUFFER	Copper alloy	
G.9	BM	1991,0407.6			SN/CO		1990	Area 1	Excavated find: Hoard G upper pit	Torc	(2P)R	RING	Gold/silver alloy	
G.10	BM	1990,1101.17			SN/CP		1990	Area 1	Excavated find: Hoard G upper pit	Torc	(3C)R	BUFFER	Copper alloy	
G.11	BM	1991,0407.7			SN/EA		1990	Area 1	Excavated find: Hoard G lower pit	Torc	(4P)R	RING	Gold/silver alloy	
G.12	BM	1990,1101.19			SN/DW; SN/DY; SN/DZ; SN/FD; SN/FL; SN/FT; SN/GF		1990	Area 1	Excavated find: Hoard G lower pit	Torc	(6C)T	BUFFER	Copper alloy	
G.13	BM	1990,1101.1			SN/FO		1990	Area 1	Excavated find: Hoard G lower pit	Torc	(7C)Q	BUFFER	Copper alloy	
G.14	BM	1990,1101.25			SN/DX; SN/GH		1990	Area 1	Excavated find: Hoard G lower pit	Torc	(2PZ)F	LOOP	Copper alloy	
G.?14	BM	1990,1101.26			SN/FO (ii)		1990	Area 1	Excavated find: Hoard G lower pit	Torc			Copper alloy	Possibly part of the missing terminal from torc G.14, or one of the more heavily corroded torcs from the upper pit of Hoard G
G.15	BM	1990,1101.27			SN/FU; SN/FW(i)		1990	Area 1	Excavated find: Hoard G lower pit	Torc	(8C)4T+4Q	BUFFER	Copper alloy	
G.?12/ 15	BM	1990,1101.28			SN/BS; SN/BT; SN/BV; SN/CD(ii); SN/CJ; SN/CX; SN/CY; SN/CZ; SN/DG; SN/DJ; SN/DK; SN/DN; SN/DP; SN/DU(i); SN/DV(i); SN/FB; SN/FH; SN/FI; SN/FM; SN/FN; SN/FV; SN/FW(ii); SN/GB; SN/GC; SN/HF		1990	Area 1	Excavated find: found loose around and within Hoard G pit	Torc		?BUFFER	Copper alloy	Most likely part of either torc G.12 or G.15
G.16	BM	1990,1101.29			SN/DA; SN/FX; SN/GU; SN/HB; SN/HC		1990	Area 1	Excavated find: Hoard G lower pit	Torc	(5C(2P))R	BUFFER	Copper alloy	

Cat no.	Museum	Reg. no.	Ticket no.	Published ref.	Stead code	Ralph no.	Ex. year	Findspot	Context details	Object name	MSCC or TUB torc type	Torc terminal type	Material	Joining / related fragments?
G.?16	BM	1990,1101.13			SN/BU; SN/CL; SN/DI; SN/DS; SN/DT(i); SN/DU(ii); SN/DV(ii); SN/GI		1990	Area 1	Excavated find: found loose around and within Hoard G pit	Torc	(?5C(2P))R	?BUFFER	Copper alloy	Very likely from torc G.16
G.17	BM	1991,0407.8			SN/GQ		1990	Area 1	Excavated find: Hoard G lower pit	Large ring			Gold/silver alloy	
G.18	BM	1991,0407.9			SN/GR		1990	Area 1	Excavated find: Hoard G lower pit	Large ring			Gold/silver alloy	
G.19	BM	1991,0407.10			SN/GS		1990	Area 1	Excavated find: Hoard G lower pit	Large ring			Gold/silver alloy	
G.20	BM	1990,1101.2			SN/GT		1990	Area 1	Excavated find: Hoard G lower pit	Large ring			Copper alloy	
H.1	BM	1990,1101.18			SN/AW; SN/CR		1990	Area 1	Excavated find: Hoard H upper pit	Torc	(6C)?R	BUFFER	Copper alloy	
H.2a	BM	1991,0407.11			SN/CS		1990	Area 1	Excavated find: Hoard H upper pit	Torc	(2PZ(2P))R	LOOP	Gold/silver alloy	
H.2b	BM	1991,0407.11			SN/CS		1990	Area 1	Excavated find: Hoard H upper pit	Torc	(2P)R	RING	Gold/silver alloy	
H.3	BM	1991,0407.12			SN/CT		1990	Area 1	Excavated find: Hoard H upper pit	Torc	(2P)R	HOOK	Gold/silver alloy	
H.4	BM	1990,1101.3			SN/CU		1990	Area 1	Excavated find: Hoard H upper pit	Torc	(3P(2P))R	RING	Copper alloy	
H.5	BM	1991,0407.13			SN/CV		1990	Area 1	Excavated find: Hoard H upper pit	Torc	(4C)R	LOOP	Gold/silver alloy	
H.6	BM	1991,0407.14			SN/DR		1990	Area 1	Excavated find: Hoard H upper pit	Torc	(2P(2PZ))R	LOOP	Gold/silver alloy	
H.7	BM	1991,0407.15			SN/FJ		1990	Area 1	Excavated find: Hoard H lower pit	Torc	(4CZ(3P(3P)))R	RING	Gold/silver alloy	
H.8	BM	1990,1101.4			SN/FK; SN/FZ		1990	Area 1	Excavated find: Hoard H lower pit	Torc	(6C)?Q	BUFFER	Copper alloy	
H.9	BM	1990,1101.8			SN/FY; SN/GK; SN/GL		1990	Area 1	Excavated find: Hoard H lower pit	Torc	(4C)R	BUFFER	Copper alloy	
H.10	BM	1990,1101.5			SN/GO		1990	Area 1	Excavated find: Hoard H lower pit	Torc	(4C(2P))R	BUFFER	Copper alloy	
H.11	BM	1990,1101.6			SN/GP		1990	Area 1	Excavated find: Hoard H lower pit	Torc	(2P)R	LOOP	Copper alloy	
J.1	BM	1991,0407.42			SN/GV; SN/GW; SN/GX; SN/GZ; SN/HG; SN/JX		1990	Area 2	Found in plough scatter around Hoard J	Torc		LOOP	Gold/silver alloy	J.1 and S.54 may be part of the same torc
J.2	BM	1991,0407.41; 1991,0407.55			SN/HA; SN/KZ		1990	Area 2	Found in plough scatter around Hoard J	Torc	(3P(2PZ))R	LOOP	Gold/silver alloy	J.2 may be part of the same torc as S.20
J.3	BM	1990,1101.30			SN/EV; SN/GY; SN/HD; SN/HL; SN/HR; SN/JC; SN/HE; SN/HH; SN/HJ; SN/HK; SN/HM		1990	Area 2	Excavated find: Hoard J pit	Torc	(?CT)	BUFFER	Copper alloy	
J.4	BM	1990,1101.32			SN/HO; SN/JF; SN/JY		1990	Area 2	Excavated find: Hoard J pit	Torc	(3P(2P))R		Copper alloy	
J.5a	BM	1990,1101.31			SN/JD; SN/JL; SN/JM; SN/JN; SN/JE; SN/JK		1990	Area 2	Excavated find: Hoard J pit	Torc	(6C)T	BUFFER	Copper alloy	
J.5b	BM	1991,0407.18			SN/JQ		1990	Area 2	Excavated find: Hoard J pit	Torc	(4CZ(2P))R	RING	Gold/silver alloy	
J.5c	BM	1991,0407.17			SN/JP		1990	Area 2	Excavated find: Hoard J pit	Torc	(2P)R	LOOP	Gold/silver alloy	

Cat no.	Museum	Reg. no.	Ticket no.	Published ref.	Stead code	Ralph no.	Ex. year	Findspot	Context details	Object name	MSCC or TUB torc type	Torc terminal type	Material	Joining / related fragments?
J.6	BM	1991,0407.16			SN/JO		1990	Area 2	Excavated find: Hoard J pit	Torc	(2CZ(2P))R	RING	Gold/silver alloy	
J.7	BM	1991,0407.19			SN/JR		1990	Area 2	Excavated find: Hoard J pit	Torc	(2P(2P))R	RING	Gold/silver alloy	
J.?	BM	1990,1101.33			SN/HN		1990	Area 2	Excavated find: Hoard J pit	Torc			Copper alloy	
K.1	BM	1990,1101.34			SN/LA; SN/LB; SN/LC; SN/LD; SN/MC; SN/MD; SN/MF; SN/MH; ?ST/AC; ?ST/AJ		1990	Area 5	Excavated find: Hoard K pit	Torc	(2P)R	RING	Copper alloy	
K.2	BM	1990,1101.35			SN/LE; SN/LG; SN/LJ; SN/LM; SN/LO; SN/LP; SN/LQ; SN/LR; SN/LS; SN/LT; SN/MA; SN/MB; SN/MG		1990	Area 5	Excavated find: Hoard K pit	Torc	(?C)T+Q		Copper alloy	
K.3	BM	1990,1101.36			SN/LF; SN/LK; SN/LN		1990	Area 5	Excavated find: Hoard K pit	Torc	(6C)T		Copper alloy	
K.4	BM	1990,1101.37			SN/LL; SN/ME		1990	Area 5	Excavated find: Hoard K pit	Torc	(3P(2P))R	LOOP	Copper alloy	
K.5	BM	1991,0407.20			SN/LV		1990	Area 5	Excavated find: Hoard K pit	Torc	(2PZ)R	RING	Gold/silver alloy	
K.6	BM	1991,0407.21			SN/LX		1990	Area 5	Excavated find: Hoard K pit	Torc	(2P)R	RING	Gold/silver alloy	
K.7	BM	1991,0407.22			SN/LY		1990	Area 5	Excavated find: Hoard K pit	Torc	(8C)R	RING	Gold/silver alloy	
L.1	BM	1991,0407.23			SN/NM		1990	Area 9	Excavated find: Hoard L upper pit	Torc	(6C(2PZ(3P)))R	TORUS	Gold/silver alloy	
L.2	BM	1991,0407.24			SN/NO		1990	Area 9	Excavated find: Hoard L upper pit	Torc	(2P)F	LOOP	Gold/silver alloy	
L.3	BM	1991,0407.25			SN/NR		1990	Area 9	Excavated find: Hoard L upper pit	Torc	(2P(2P))R	RING	Gold/silver alloy	
L.4	BM	1991,0407.26			SN/NW		1990	Area 9	Excavated find: Hoard L upper pit	Torc	(3P(2P))R	LOOP	Gold/silver alloy	
L.5	BM	1990,1101.10			SN/NY		1990	Area 9	Excavated find: Hoard L upper pit	Torc	(5C(2P))R	BUFFER	Copper alloy	
L.6	BM	1990,1101.7			SN/NZ		1990	Area 9	Excavated find: Hoard L upper pit	Torc	(7C(2P))R	BUFFER	Copper alloy	
L.7	BM	1991,0407.27			SN/OA		1990	Area 9	Excavated find: Hoard L upper pit	Torc	(2P)R	LOOP	Gold/silver alloy	
L.8	BM	1990,1101.9			SN/OS; SN/OT		1990	Area 9	Excavated find: Hoard L lower pit	Torc/bracelet	(2P(2P))R	LOOP	Copper alloy	
L.9	BM	1990,1101.11			SN/OL; SN/OL; SN/OU		1990	Area 9	Excavated find: Hoard L lower pit	Torc	(2P(2P))R	LOOP	Copper alloy	
L.10a	BM	1991,0407.28			SN/OF		1990	Area 9	Excavated find: Hoard L lower pit	Torc	(6C)2T+4Q	TORUS	Gold/silver alloy	
L.10b	BM	1991,0407.28			SN/OG		1990	Area 9	Excavated find: Hoard L lower pit	Torc/wire	(?2P)T		Gold/silver alloy	
L.11	BM	1991,0407.29			SN/OH		1990	Area 9	Excavated find: Hoard L lower pit	Torc	(8CZ(2P))R	BUFFER	Gold/silver alloy	
L.12	BM	1991,0407.30			SN/OW		1990	Area 9	Excavated find: Hoard L lower pit	Torc	(8C(2P))R	BUFFER	Gold/silver alloy	
L.13	BM	1991,0407.31			SN/OY		1990	Area 9	Excavated find: Hoard L lower pit	Torc	(14C(2P(Z)))R	BUFFER	Gold/silver alloy	

Cat no.	Museum	Reg. no.	Ticket no.	Published ref.	Stead code	Ralph no.	Ex. year	Findspot	Context details	Object name	MSCC or TUB torc type	Torc terminal type	Material	Joining / related fragments?
L.14	BM	1991,0407.32			SN/PA		1990	Area 9	Excavated find: Hoard L lower pit	Torc	(6C(2P))R	TORUS	Gold/silver alloy	
L.15	BM	1991,0407.33			SN/PC		1990	Area 9	Excavated find: Hoard L lower pit	Torc	(8C)T	CAGE	Gold/silver alloy	
L.16	BM	1991,0407.34			SN/PE		1990	Area 9	Excavated find: Hoard L lower pit	Torc	(6C(2PZ))R	RING	Gold/silver alloy	
L.17	BM	1991,0407.35			SN/PG		1990	Area 9	Excavated find: Hoard L lower pit	Torc	(8C)T	BUFFER	Gold/silver alloy	
L.18	BM	1991,0407.36			SN/PJ		1990	Area 9	Excavated find: Hoard L lower pit	Torc	(4CZ(2P))R	RING	Gold/silver alloy	
L.19a	BM	1991,0407.37			SN/PL		1990	Area 9	Excavated find: Hoard L lower pit	Torc	(4C(4C))T	TORUS	Gold/silver alloy	
L.19b	BM	1991,0407.37			SN/PL		1990	Area 9	Excavated find: Hoard L lower pit	Wire			Gold/silver alloy	
L.19c	BM	1991,0407.37			SN/PL		1990	Area 9	Excavated find: Hoard L lower pit	Torc/bracelet	(2P)R	LOOP	Gold/silver alloy	
L.19d	BM	1991,0407.37			SN/PL		1990	Area 9	Excavated find: Hoard L lower pit	Torc/sheet	?TUBULAR (?TYPE 4/5/6)		Gold/silver alloy	
L.19e	BM	1991,0407.37			SN/PL		1990	Area 9	Excavated find: Hoard L lower pit	Strip			Gold/silver alloy	
L.19f	BM	1991,0407.37			SN/PL		1990	Area 9	Excavated find: Hoard L lower pit	Strip			Gold/silver alloy	
L.20a	BM	1991,0407.38			SN/PN		1990	Area 9	Excavated find: Hoard L lower pit	Torc	(6C([2Px3]+[4Cx3]))R	TORUS	Gold/silver alloy	
L.20b	BM	1991,0407.38			SN/PN		1990	Area 9	Excavated find: Hoard L lower pit	Wire			Gold/silver alloy	
L.21a	BM	1991,0407.39			SN/PO		1990	Area 9	Excavated find: Hoard L lower pit	Torc	(8C(2P(2P)))R	TORUS	Gold/silver alloy	
L.21b	BM	1991,0407.39			SN/PO		1990	Area 9	Excavated find: Hoard L lower pit	Strip			Gold/silver alloy	
M.1	BM	1992,1203.7					1990–1	Wood	Hoard M; Metal detected find made Dec. 1990–April 1991	Amorphous lump			Silver-copper alloy	
M.2	BM	1992,1203.8					1990–1	Wood	Hoard M; Metal detected find made Dec. 1990–April 1991	Amorphous lump			Silver-copper alloy	
M.3	BM	1992,1203.9					1990–1	Wood	Hoard M; Metal detected find made Dec. 1990–April 1991	Amorphous lump			Silver-copper alloy	
M.4	BM	1992,1203.10					1990–1	Wood	Hoard M; Metal detected find made Dec. 1990–April 1991	Amorphous lump			Silver-copper alloy	
M.5	BM	1992,1203.11					1990–1	Wood	Hoard M; Metal detected find made Dec. 1990–April 1991	Amorphous lump			Silver-copper alloy	
M.6	BM	1991,0409.1					1990–1		Hoard M; Metal detected find made Dec. 1990–April 1991	Amorphous lump			Copper alloy	
P.1	BM	1992,1202.7			ST/GT		1991	Area 21	Metal-detected stray find from 1991 excavation	Vessel			Silver alloy	P.1–7 may be from the same silver vessel
P.2	BM	1992,1202.4			ST/GQ		1991	Area 21	Metal-detected stray find from 1991 excavation	Vessel			Silver alloy	P.1–7 may be from the same silver vessel
P.3	BM	1992,1202.9			ST/GW		1991	Area 21	Metal-detected stray find from 1991 excavation	Vessel			Silver alloy	P.1–7 may be from the same silver vessel
P.4	BM	1992,1202.8			ST/GV		1991	Area 21	Metal-detected stray find from 1991 excavation	Vessel			Silver alloy	P.1–7 may be from the same silver vessel
P.5	BM	1992,1202.6			ST/GS		1991	Area 21	Metal-detected stray find from 1991 excavation	Vessel			Silver alloy	P.1–7 may be from the same silver vessel
P.6	BM	1992,1202.5			ST/GQ		1991	Area 21	Metal-detected stray find from 1991 excavation	Vessel			Silver alloy	P.1–7 may be from the same silver vessel
P.7	BM	1992,0210.2			SM/AC		1992	Wood	Metal-detected stray find March 1992	Vessel			Silver alloy	P.1–7 may be from the same silver vessel
S.1	BM	1990,1101.42			SN/JZ		1990	Area 21	Metal-detected stray find from 1990 excavation	Socketed axe			Copper alloy	
S.2	BM	1991,0409.27					1990–1	Not recorded	Metal-detected stray find Dec. 1990–April 1991	Sword chape			Copper alloy	
S.3	NCM		YELLOW.3				2003–9	Wood	Metal-detected stray find 2003–9	Razor			Copper alloy	

Cat no.	Museum	Reg. no.	Ticket no.	Published ref.	Stead code	Ralph no.	Ex. year	Findspot	Context details	Object name	MSCC or TUB torc type	Torc terminal type	Material	Joining / related fragments?
S.4	NCM		YELLOW.251				2003–9	Wood	Metal-detected stray find 2003–9	Arrowhead			Copper alloy	
S.5	NCM		YELLOW.249				2003–9	Wood	Metal-detected stray find 2003–9	Spearhead			Copper alloy	
S.6	NCM		YELLOW.250				2003–9	Wood	Metal-detected stray find 2003–9	Blade fragment; ?spearhead			Copper alloy	
S.7	NCM		YELLOW.248				2003–9	Wood	Metal-detected stray find 2003–9	?Blade fragment			Copper alloy	
S.8	NCM		YELLOW.89				2003–9	Wood	Metal-detected stray find 2003–9	Unidentified object fragment			Copper alloy	
S.9	NCM		YELLOW.2				2003–9	Wood	Metal-detected stray find 2003–9	Miniature axe			Copper alloy	
S.10	NCM		YELLOW.10				2003–9	Wood	Metal-detected stray find 2003–9	Moustache mount			Copper alloy	
S.11a	BM	1991,0407.57			SN/KD		1990	Area 3	Metal-detected stray find from 1990 excavation	Torc	TUBULAR (TYPE 4/5)		Gold/silver alloy	
S.11b	BM	1991,0407.47			SN/KD		1990	Area 3	Metal-detected stray find from 1990 excavation	Torc/bracelet	(2P)R	LOOP	Gold/silver alloy	
S.12	NCM	1999.44					?1999	Not recorded	Metal-detected stray find 1999.	Torc	TUBULAR (Type 6)		Iron	
S.13	BM	1991,0407.40			SN/RO		1990	Area 15	Metal-detected stray find from 1990 excavation	Torc	TUBULAR (TYPE 4)	BUFFER	Gold/silver alloy	
S.14	NCM		YELLOW.34				2003–9	Wood	Metal-detected stray find 2003–9	Torc	TUBULAR (TYPE 1)		Gold/silver alloy	
S.15	BM	1992,1203.6					1990–1	Not recorded	Metal-detected stray find Dec. 1990–April 1991	?Torc	?TUBULAR (?Type 2/Type 6)		Gold/silver alloy	
S.16	NCM	1969.55.3		Burns 1971, 228–9			1968	South-west corner of the 'gold field'	Found during ploughing in 1968	Torc	(2P)R	RING	Gold/silver alloy	
S.17	NCM	1965.30.1		Burns 1971, 228–9			1964	Area 2	Found during ploughing in 1964.	Torc	(2P)R	RING	Gold/silver alloy	
S.18	NCM	1977.307					1973	To northwest of 'gold field'	Found during ploughing in 1973	Torc	(2P)R	LOOP	Gold/silver alloy	
S.19	BM	1992,1203.4					1990–1	Not recorded	Metal-detected stray find Dec. 1990–April 1991	Torc	(4P(?5C))R	BUFFER	Gold/silver alloy	
S.20	BM	1991,0501.228				507	1990	Not recorded	Metal-detected stray find August 1990	Torc	(3P(2PZ))R		Gold/silver alloy	S.20 may be part of the same torc as J.2
S.21	BM	1992,1203.3					1990–1	Not recorded	Metal-detected stray find Dec. 1990–April 1991	Torc	(?2P(2P))R	LOOP	Gold/silver alloy	
S.22	BM	1992,1203.2					1990–1	Not recorded	Metal-detected stray find Dec. 1990–April 1991	Torc	(2PZ(2P))R		Gold/silver alloy	
S.23	BM	1991,0501.231				510	1990	Not recorded	Metal-detected stray find August 1990	Torc	(4P)R		Gold/silver alloy	Fragments S.23–9 may be part of the same torc
S.24	BM	1991,0501.232				511	1990	Not recorded	Metal-detected stray find August 1990	Torc	(4P)R		Gold/silver alloy	Fragments S.23–9 may be part of the same torc
S.25	NCM	1990204					1989	Area 20	Metal-detected stray find 1989	Torc	(4P)R		Gold/silver alloy	Fragments S.23–9 may be part of the same torc
S.26	BM	1991,0501.230				509	1990	Not recorded	Metal-detected stray find August 1990	Torc		LOOP	Gold/silver alloy	Fragments S.23–9 may be part of the same torc
S.27	NCM	1990203b					1989	Area 20	Metal-detected stray find 1989.	Torc			Gold/silver alloy	Fragments S.23–9 may be part of the same torc
S.28	NCM	1990203a					1989	Area 20	Metal-detected stray find 1989	Torc			Gold/silver alloy	Fragments S.23–9 may be part of the same torc

Cat no.	Museum	Reg. no.	Ticket no.	Published ref.	Stead code	Ralph no.	Ex. year	Findspot	Context details	Object name	MSCC or TUB torc type	Torc terminal type	Material	Joining / related fragments?
S.29	BM	1991,0501.229				508	1990	Not recorded	Metal-detected stray find August 1990	Torc	(?P)R		Gold/silver alloy	Fragments S.23–9 may be part of the same torc
S.30	NCM		YELLOW.93				2003–9	Wood	Metal-detected stray find 2003–9	Torc/bracelet	(3P)R		Gold/silver alloy	
S.31	NCM	1965.30.2.1		Burns 1971, 228-29			1964	Area 3	Found during ploughing in 1964	Torc	(2P)F	LOOP	Gold/silver alloy	Fragments S.31–9 may be part of the same torc
S.32	BM	1991,0407.50			SN/AO		1990	Area 1	Metal-detected stray find from 1990 excavation	Torc		LOOP	Gold/silver alloy	Fragments S.31–9 may be part of the same torc
S.33	BM	1991,0501.224				503	1990–1	Not recorded	Metal-detected stray find Dec. 1990–April 1991	Torc		LOOP	Gold/silver alloy	Fragments S.31–9 may be part of the same torc
S.34	BM	1991,0501.226				505	1990–1	Not recorded	Metal-detected stray find Dec. 1990–April 1991	Torc		LOOP	Gold/silver alloy	Fragments S.31–9 may be part of the same torc
S.35	BM	1991,0407.51			SN/KM		1990	Area 5	Metal-detected stray find from 1990 excavation	Torc	(2P)F		Gold/silver alloy	Fragments S.31–9 may be part of the same torc
S.36	BM	1991,0407.49			SN/AU		1990	Area 1	Metal-detected stray find from 1990 excavation	Torc	(2P)F		Gold/silver alloy	Fragments S.31–9 may be part of the same torc
S.37	BM	1992,1203.1					1990–1	Not recorded	Metal-detected stray find Dec. 1990–April 1991	Torc	(2P)F		Gold/silver alloy	Fragments S.31–9 may be part of the same torc
S.38	BM	1991,0501.223				502	1990–1	Not recorded	Metal-detected stray find Dec. 1990–April 1991	Torc	(2P)F		Gold/silver alloy	Fragments S.31–9 may be part of the same torc
S.39	BM	1991,0501.225				504	1990–1	Not recorded	Metal-detected stray find Dec. 1990–April 1991	Torc	(2P)F		Gold/silver alloy	Fragments S.31–9 may be part of the same torc
S.40	BM	1991,0407.66			SN/KE		1990	Area 3	Metal-detected stray find from 1990 excavation	Torc		LOOP	Gold/silver alloy	S.40 may be part of the same torc as fragments S.31–9
S.41	BM	1991,0407.59			SN/KH		1990	Area 4	Metal-detected stray find from 1990 excavation	Rod/?torc	(?2P)R		Gold/silver alloy	S.41–4 may be from the same torc
S.42	BM	1992,1203.5					1990–1	Not recorded	Metal-detected stray find Dec. 1990–April 1991	Rod/?torc	(?2P)R		Gold/silver alloy	S.41–4 may be from the same torc
S.43	BM	1992,1202.2			ST/BM		1991	Area 19	Metal-detected stray find from 1991 excavation	Rod/?torc	(?2P)R		Gold/silver alloy	S.41–4 may be from the same torc
S.44	BM	1991,0501.233			SN/NJ		1990	Not recorded	Metal-detected stray find from 1990 excavation	Rod/?torc	(?2P)R		Gold/silver alloy	S.41–4 may be from the same torc
S.45	BM	1991,0407.48			SN/RC		1990	Area 12	Metal-detected stray find from 1990 excavation	Torc/bracelet	(2P)R		Gold/silver alloy	
S.46	NCM		YELLOW.81				2003–9	Wood	Metal-detected stray find 2003–9	Amorphous lump; wire; ?torc / ?bracelet			Gold/silver alloy	
S.47	NCM		YELLOW.73				2003–9	Wood	Metal-detected stray find 2003–9	Wire; ?torc / ?bracelet			Gold/silver alloy	
S.48	BM	1991,0407.60			SN/MY		1990	Area 9	Metal-detected stray find from 1990 excavation	Torc		BUFFER	Gold/silver alloy	
S.49	NCM		YELLOW.30				2003–9	Wood	Metal-detected stray find 2003–9	Rod/?large ring/?torc		?LOOP	Gold/silver alloy	
S.50	NCM		YELLOW.129B				2003–9	Wood	Metal-detected stray find 2003–9	Rod/?torc/ ?bracelet			Gold/silver alloy	
S.51	BM	1991,0407.53			SN/AX		1990	Area 1	Metal-detected stray find from 1990 excavation	Wire/?torc/ ?bracelet	(?2P)R		Gold/silver alloy	

Cat no.	Museum	Reg. no.	Ticket no.	Published ref.	Stead code	Ralph no.	Ex. year	Findspot	Context details	Object name	MSCC or TUB torc type	Torc terminal type	Material	Joining / related fragments?
S.52	BM	1992,1202.1			ST/BP		1991	Area 20	Metal-detected stray find from 1991 excavation	Wire/?torc/ ?bracelet	(?P)R		Gold/silver alloy	
S.53	BM	1991,0407.52			SN/KF		1990	Area 4	Metal-detected stray find from 1990 excavation	Wire/?torc/ ?bracelet	(?P)R		Gold/silver alloy	
S.54	BM	1991,0407.56			SN/EE		1990	Area 2	Metal-detected stray find from 1990 excavation	Wire/?torc/ ?bracelet	(?P)R		Gold/silver alloy	S.54 and J.1 may be part of the same torc
S.55	NCM		YELLOW.78				2003–9	Wood	Metal-detected stray find 2003–9	Wire; ?torc / bracelet			Gold/silver alloy	
S.56	NCM		YELLOW.142				2003–9	Wood	Metal-detected stray find 2003–9	Wire; ?torc /bracelet			Gold/silver alloy	
S.57	NCM		YELLOW.103				2003–9	Wood	Metal-detected stray find 2003–9	Wire; ?torc/ ?bracelet			Gold/silver alloy	
S.58	NCM		YELLOW.91				2003–9	Wood	Metal-detected stray find 2003–9	Wire; ?torc/ ?bracelet			Gold/silver alloy	
S.59	NCM		YELLOW.95				2003–9	Wood	Metal-detected stray find 2003–9	Wire; ?torc/ ?bracelet			Gold/silver alloy	
S.60	NCM		YELLOW.122				2003–9	Wood	Metal-detected stray find 2003–9	Wire; ?torc/ ?bracelet			Gold/silver alloy	
S.61	NCM		YELLOW.70				2003–9	Wood	Metal-detected stray find 2003–9	Torc/bracelet			Gold/silver alloy	
S.62	NCM		YELLOW.50				2003–9	Wood	Metal-detected stray find 2003–9	Torc/bracelet / wire			Gold/silver alloy	
S.63	NCM		YELLOW.112				2003–9	Wood	Metal-detected stray find 2003–9	Wire; ?torc / ?bracelet			Gold/silver alloy	
S.64	NCM		YELLOW.28				2003–9	Wood	Metal-detected stray find 2003–9	Wire; ?torc/ ?bracelet			Gold/silver alloy	
S.65	NCM		YELLOW.144				2003–9	Wood	Metal-detected stray find 2003–9	Wire; ?torc / bracelet			Gold/silver alloy	
S.66	NCM		YELLOW.68				2003–9	Wood	Metal-detected stray find 2003–9	Wire; amorphous lump			Gold/silver alloy	
S.67	BM	1991,0407.58			SN/AP		1990	Area 1	Metal-detected stray find from 1990 excavation	Wire; ?torc/ ?bracelet			Gold/silver alloy	
S.68	BM	1991,0407.54			SN/JJ		1990	Area 2	Metal-detected stray find from 1990 excavation	Wire/?torc/ ?bracelet			Gold/silver alloy	
S.69	NCM		YELLOW.69				2003–9	Wood	Metal-detected stray find 2003–9	Ring/?torc/ ?bracelet			Gold/silver alloy	
S.70	NCM		YELLOW.60				2003–9	Wood	Metal-detected stray find 2003–9	Sheet/?torc			Gold/silver alloy	
S.71	NCM		YELLOW.36				2003–9	Wood	Metal-detected stray find 2003–9	Sheet/?torc			Gold/silver alloy	
S.72	NCM		YELLOW.138				2003–9	Wood	Metal-detected stray find 2003–9	Sheet/?torc			Gold/silver alloy	
S.73	NCM		YELLOW.64				2003–9	Wood	Metal-detected stray find 2003–9	Sheet/?torc			Gold/silver alloy	
S.74	NCM		YELLOW.67				2003–9	Wood	Metal-detected stray find 2003–9	Sheet/?torc			Gold/silver alloy	
S.75	NCM		YELLOW.158				2003–9	Wood	Metal-detected stray find 2003–9	Sheet/?torc			Gold/silver alloy	
S.76	NCM		YELLOW.66				2003–9	Wood	Metal-detected stray find 2003–9	Strip/?torc			Gold/silver alloy	
S.77	BM	1990,1101.21			SN/KP		1990	Area 5	Metal-detected stray find from 1990 excavation	Torc	(?6C)R	TORUS	Copper alloy	
S.78	BM	1992,0210.1			SM/AA		1992	Wood	Metal-detected stray find March 1992. Redeposited.	Torc		TORUS	Copper alloy	
S.79	BM	1990,1101.22			SN/EG		1990	Area 2	Metal-detected stray find from 1990 excavation	Torc	(7C)T	BUFFER	Copper alloy	
S.80	BM	1990,1101.20			SN/AV		1990	Area 1	Metal-detected stray find from 1990 excavation	Torc	(2P)R		Copper alloy	
S.81	BM	1991,0409.22			ST/HD		1991	Area 21	Metal-detected stray find from 1991 excavation, most likely from 1990 backfill.	Wire/?torc/ ?bracelet	?(?P)R		Copper alloy	

Cat no.	Museum	Reg. no.	Ticket no.	Published ref.	Stead code	Ralph no.	Ex. year	Findspot	Context details	Object name	MSCC or TUB torc type	Torc terminal type	Material	Joining / related fragments?
S.82	BM	1990,1101.43			SN/MT		1990	Area 7	Metal-detected stray find from 1990 excavation	Wire/?torc/ ?bracelet		?LOOP	Copper alloy	
S.83	BM	1990,1101.48			SN/RF		1990	Area 14	Metal-detected stray find from 1990 excavation	Rod/?torc / ?bracelet			Copper alloy	
S.84	BM	1991,0407.62			SN/CQ		1990	Area 1	Metal-detected stray find from 1990 excavation	Large ring			Gold/silver alloy	
S.85	BM	1991,0501.227				506	1990	Not recorded	Metal-detected stray find August 1990	Large ring			Gold/silver alloy	
S.86	BM	1992,1202.3			ST/FS		1991	Area 21	Metal-detected stray find from 1991 excavation, most likely from 1990 backfill	Strip; ?large/small ring			Gold/silver alloy	
S.87	NCM		YELLOW.31				2003–9	Wood	Metal-detected stray find 2003–9	Strip; ?large /small ring			Gold/silver alloy	
S.88	NCM		YELLOW.124				2003–9	Wood	Metal-detected stray find 2003–9	Strip; ?large /?small ring			Gold/silver alloy	
S.89	NCM		YELLOW.32				2003–9	Wood	Metal-detected stray find 2003–9	Strip; ?large /?small ring			Gold/silver alloy	
S.90	NCM		YELLOW.52				2003–9	Wood	Metal-detected stray find 2003–9	Strip; ?large /?small ring			Gold/silver alloy	
S.91	NCM		YELLOW.38				2003–9	Wood	Metal-detected stray find 2003–9	Strip; ?large /?small ring			Gold/silver alloy	
S.92	NCM		YELLOW.106				2003–9	Wood	Metal-detected stray find 2003–9	Strip; ?large /?small ring			Gold/silver alloy	
S.93	NCM		YELLOW.99				2003–9	Wood	Metal-detected stray find 2003–9	Strip; ?large /?small ring			Gold/silver alloy	
S.94	NCM		YELLOW.94				2003–9	Wood	Metal-detected stray find 2003–9	Strip; ?large /?small ring			Gold/silver alloy	
S.95	NCM		YELLOW.97				2003–9	Wood	Metal-detected stray find 2003–9	Strip; ?large /?small ring			Gold/silver alloy	
S.96	NCM		YELLOW.77				2003–9	Wood	Metal-detected stray find 2003–9	Strip; ?large /?small ring			Gold/silver alloy	
S.97	NCM		YELLOW.131				2003–9	Wood	Metal-detected stray find 2003–9	Strip; ?large /?small ring			Gold/silver alloy	
S.98	NCM		YELLOW.98				2003–9	Wood	Metal-detected stray find 2003–9	Strip; ?large /?small ring			Gold/silver alloy	
S.99	NCM		YELLOW.192				2003–9	Wood	Metal-detected stray find 2003–9	Strip; ?large /?small ring			Copper alloy	
S.100	NCM		YELLOW.42				2003–9	Wood	Metal-detected stray find 2003–9	Strip; ?large/?small ring			Copper alloy	
S.101	BM	2009,4213.20			SN/PY		1990	Area 10	Metal-detected stray find from 1990 excavation	Lump ingot			Gold/silver alloy	
S.102	BM	2009,4213.21			SN/QA		1990	Area 11	Metal-detected stray find from 1990 excavation	Lump ingot			Gold/silver alloy	
S.103	NCM		YELLOW.135				2003–9	Wood	Metal-detected stray find 2003–9	Lump ingot			Gold/silver alloy	
S.104	BM	1991,0409.28					1990–1	Not recorded	Metal-detected stray find Dec. 1990–April 1991	Lump ingot			?Tin/copper alloy	
S.105	NCM		YELLOW.245				2003–9	Wood	Metal-detected stray find 2003–9	Triangular ingot			Copper alloy; ?gold/silver alloy	
S.106	BM	1991,0409.4			ST/AK		1991	Area 17	Metal-detected stray find from 1991 excavation	Lump ingot			Copper alloy/?Silver alloy/?Lead alloy	
S.107	NCM		YELLOW.47				2003–9	Wood	Metal-detected stray find 2003–9	Lump ingot			Copper alloy	
S.108	NCM		YELLOW.195				2003–9	Wood	Metal-detected stray find 2003–9	Lump ingot			Copper alloy/lead alloy	
S.109	NCM		YELLOW.143				2003–9	Wood	Metal-detected stray find 2003–9	Lump ingot			Copper alloy	

Cat no.	Museum	Reg. no.	Ticket no.	Published ref.	Stead code	Ralph no.	Ex. year	Findspot	Context details	Object name	MSCC or TUB torc type	Torc terminal type	Material	Joining / related fragments?
S.110	NCM		YELLOW.118				2003–9	Wood	Metal-detected stray find 2003–9	Lump ingot			Copper alloy	
S.111	NCM		YELLOW.116				2003–9	Wood	Metal-detected stray find 2003–9	Lump ingot			Copper alloy	
S.112	NCM		YELLOW.141				2003–9	Wood	Metal-detected stray find 2003–9	Linear ingot			Gold/silver alloy	
S.113	NCM		YELLOW.140				2003–9	Wood	Metal-detected stray find 2003–9	Linear ingot			Gold/silver alloy	
S.114	NCM		YELLOW.110				2003–9	Wood	Metal-detected stray find 2003–9	Linear ingot			Gold/silver alloy	
S.115	NCM		YELLOW.129A				2003–9	Wood	Metal-detected stray find 2003–9	Linear ingot			Gold/silver alloy	
S.116	NCM		YELLOW.134				2003–9	Wood	Metal-detected stray find 2003–9	Linear ingot			Gold/silver alloy	
S.117	BM	1990,1101.38			SN/AL		1990	Not recorded	Metal-detected stray find from 1990 excavation	Linear ingot			Copper alloy	
S.118	BM	1991,0409.12			ST/DC		1991	Area 23	Metal-detected stray find from 1991 excavation	Linear ingot			Copper alloy	
S.119	NCM		YELLOW.173				2003–9	Wood	Metal-detected stray find 2003–9	Linear ingot			Copper alloy	
S.120	BM	1991,0409.18			ST/EG		1991	Area 25	Metal-detected stray find from 1991 excavation	Linear ingot/?wire			Copper alloy	
S.121	NCM		YELLOW.155				2003–9	Wood	Metal-detected stray find 2003–9	Linear ingot			Copper alloy	
S.122	NCM		YELLOW.153				2003–9	Wood	Metal-detected stray find 2003–9	Linear ingot			Copper alloy	
S.123	BM	1991,0409.13			ST/DE		1991	Area 23	Metal-detected stray find from 1991 excavation	?Ingot/?fitting			Copper alloy	
S.124	BM	1991,0409.6			ST/BG		1991	Area 18	Metal-detected stray find from 1991 excavation	?Ingot/?fitting			Copper alloy	
S.125	NCM		YELLOW.61				2003–9	Wood	Metal-detected stray find 2003–9	Wire			Gold/silver alloy	
S.126	NCM		YELLOW.62				2003–9	Wood	Metal-detected stray find 2003–9	Wire/?tool			Gold/silver alloy	
S.127	NCM		YELLOW.198				2003–9	Wood	Metal-detected stray find 2003–9	Rod			Copper alloy	
S.128	NCM		YELLOW.175				2003–9	Wood	Metal-detected stray find 2003–9	Wire			Copper alloy	
S.129	NCM		YELLOW.29				2003–9	Wood	Metal-detected stray find 2003–9	Wire/strip			Copper alloy	
S.130	BM	1990,1101.49			SN/RR		1990	Not recorded	Metal-detected stray find from 1990 excavation, found during backfilling.	Casting sprue			Copper alloy	
S.131	NCM		YELLOW.247				2003–9	Wood	Metal-detected stray find 2003–9	Casting sprue			Copper alloy	
S.132	NCM		YELLOW.63				2003–9	Wood	Metal-detected stray find 2003–9	Amorphous lump; wire			Gold/silver alloy	
S.133	BM	1992,1203.12					1990–1	Not recorded	Metal-detected stray find Dec. 1990–April 1991	Amorphous lump; wire			Gold/silver alloy	
S.134	BM	1991,0407.61			SN/JW		1990	Area 2; SN21	Metal-detected stray find from 1990 excavation	Amorphous lump; wire			Gold/silver alloy	
S.135	NCM		YELLOW.72				2003–9	Wood	Metal-detected stray find 2003–9	Amorphous lump; wire			Gold/silver alloy	
S.136	NCM		YELLOW.71				2003–9	Wood	Metal-detected stray find 2003–9	Amorphous lump; wire			Gold/silver alloy	
S.137	NCM		YELLOW.128				2003–9	Wood	Metal-detected stray find 2003–9	Amorphous lump (worked)			Gold/silver alloy	
S.138	NCM		YELLOW.85				2003–9	Wood	Metal-detected stray find 2003–9	Amorphous lump (worked)			Gold/silver alloy	
S.139	NCM		YELLOW.74				2003–9	Wood	Metal-detected stray find 2003–9	Amorphous lump; ?disc			Gold/silver alloy; copper alloy	

Cat no.	Museum	Reg. no.	Ticket no.	Published ref.	Stead code	Ralph no.	Ex. year	Findspot	Context details	Object name	MSCC or TUB torc type	Torc terminal type	Material	Joining / related fragments?
S.140	NCM		YELLOW.130				2003–9	Wood	Metal-detected stray find 2003–9	Amorphous lump; sheet; wire			Copper alloy; Gold/silver alloy	
S.141	NCM		YELLOW.113				2003–9	Wood	Metal-detected stray find 2003–9	Amorphous lump			Gold/silver alloy	
S.142	NCM		YELLOW.136				2003–9	Wood	Metal-detected stray find 2003–9	Amorphous lump			Gold/silver alloy	
S.143	NCM		YELLOW.82				2003–9	Wood	Metal-detected stray find 2003–9	Amorphous lump			Gold/silver alloy	
S.144	NCM		YELLOW.148				2003–9	Wood	Metal-detected stray find 2003–9	Amorphous lump			Gold/silver alloy	
S.145	NCM		YELLOW.108				2003–9	Wood	Metal-detected stray find 2003–9	Amorphous lump			Gold/silver alloy	
S.146	NCM		YELLOW.261				2003–9	Wood	Metal-detected stray find 2003–9	Amorphous lump			Gold/silver alloy	
S.147	NCM		YELLOW.92				2003–9	Wood	Metal-detected stray find 2003–9	Amorphous lump			Gold/silver alloy	
S.148	NCM		YELLOW.120				2003–9	Wood	Metal-detected stray find 2003–9	Amorphous lump			Gold/silver alloy	
S.149	NCM		YELLOW.125				2003–9	Wood	Metal-detected stray find 2003–9	Amorphous lump			Gold/silver alloy	
S.150	NCM		YELLOW.126				2003–9	Wood	Metal-detected stray find 2003–9	Amorphous lump			Gold/silver alloy	
S.151	NCM		YELLOW.149				2003–9	Wood	Metal-detected stray find 2003–9	Amorphous lump			Gold/silver alloy	
S.152	NCM		YELLOW.51				2003–9	Wood	Metal-detected stray find 2003–9	Amorphous lump			Gold/silver alloy	
S.153	NCM		YELLOW.35				2003–9	Wood	Metal-detected stray find 2003–9	Amorphous lump			Gold/silver alloy	
S.154	NCM		YELLOW.37				2003–9	Wood	Metal-detected stray find 2003–9	Amorphous lump			Gold/silver alloy	
S.155	NCM		YELLOW.65				2003–9	Wood	Metal-detected stray find 2003–9	Amorphous lump			Gold/silver alloy	
S.156	NCM		YELLOW.90				2003–9	Wood	Metal-detected stray find 2003–9	Amorphous lump			Gold/silver alloy	
S.157	NCM		YELLOW.100				2003–9	Wood	Metal-detected stray find 2003–9	Amorphous lump			Gold/silver alloy	
S.158	NCM		YELLOW.109				2003–9	Wood	Metal-detected stray find 2003–9	Amorphous lump			Gold/silver alloy	
S.159	NCM		YELLOW.150				2003–9	Wood	Metal-detected stray find 2003–9	Amorphous lump			Gold/silver alloy	
S.160	NCM		YELLOW.104				2003–9	Wood	Metal-detected stray find 2003–9	Amorphous lump			Gold/silver alloy	
S.161	NCM		YELLOW.121				2003–9	Wood	Metal-detected stray find 2003–9	Amorphous lump			Gold/silver alloy	
S.162	NCM		YELLOW.152				2003–9	Wood	Metal-detected stray find 2003–9	Amorphous lump			Gold/silver alloy	
S.163	NCM		YELLOW.56				2003–9	Wood	Metal-detected stray find 2003–9	Amorphous lump			Gold/silver alloy	
S.164	NCM		YELLOW.87				2003–9	Wood	Metal-detected stray find 2003–9	Amorphous lump			Gold/silver alloy	
S.165	NCM		YELLOW.115				2003–9	Wood	Metal-detected stray find 2003–9	Amorphous lump			Gold/silver alloy	
S.166	NCM		YELLOW.123				2003–9	Wood	Metal-detected stray find 2003–9	Amorphous lump			Gold/silver alloy	
S.167	NCM		YELLOW.154				2003–9	Wood	Metal-detected stray find 2003–9	Amorphous lump			Gold/silver alloy	
S.168	NCM		YELLOW.80				2003–9	Wood	Metal-detected stray find 2003–9	Amorphous lump			Gold/silver alloy	

Cat no.	Museum	Reg. no.	Ticket no.	Published ref.	Stead code	Ralph no.	Ex. year	Findspot	Context details	Object name	MSCC or TUB torc type	Torc terminal type	Material	Joining / related fragments?
S.169	NCM		YELLOW.79				2003–9	Wood	Metal-detected stray find 2003–9	Amorphous lump			Gold/silver alloy	
S.170	NCM		YELLOW.114				2003–9	Wood	Metal-detected stray find 2003–9	Amorphous lump			Gold/silver alloy	
S.171	NCM		YELLOW.137				2003–9	Wood	Metal-detected stray find 2003–9	Amorphous lump			Gold/silver alloy	
S.172	NCM		YELLOW.101				2003–9	Wood	Metal-detected stray find 2003–9	Amorphous lump			Gold/silver alloy	
S.173	NCM		YELLOW.105				2003–9	Wood	Metal-detected stray find 2003–9	Amorphous lump			Gold/silver alloy	
S.174	NCM		YELLOW.151				2003–9	Wood	Metal-detected stray find 2003–9	Amorphous lump			Gold/silver alloy	
S.175	NCM		YELLOW.83				2003–9	Wood	Metal-detected stray find 2003–9	Amorphous lump			Gold/silver alloy	
S.176	NCM		YELLOW.107				2003–9	Wood	Metal-detected stray find 2003–9	Amorphous lump			Gold/silver alloy	
S.177	NCM		YELLOW.88				2003–9	Wood	Metal-detected stray find 2003–9	Amorphous lump			Gold/silver alloy	
S.178	NCM		YELLOW.117				2003–9	Wood	Metal-detected stray find 2003–9	Amorphous lump			Gold/silver alloy	
S.179	BM	1991,0409.16			ST/DT		1991	Area 24	Metal-detected stray find from 1991 excavation	Amorphous lump			Lead alloy	
S.180	NCM		YELLOW.246				2003–9	Wood	Metal-detected stray find 2003–9	Amorphous lump			Copper alloy	
S.181	BM	1991,0409.21			ST/GZ		1991	Area 21	Metal-detected stray find from 1991 excavation	Amorphous lump			Copper alloy	
S.182	NCM		YELLOW.266				2003–9	Wood	Metal-detected stray find 2003–9	Amorphous lump			Copper alloy	
S.183	NCM		YELLOW.200				2003–9	Wood	Metal-detected stray find 2003–9	Amorphous lump			Copper alloy	
S.184	NCM		YELLOW.265				2003–9	Wood	Metal-detected stray find 2003–9	Amorphous lump			Copper alloy; ?lead alloy	
S.185	BM	1990,1101.46			SN/OE		1990	Area 9	Metal-detected stray find from 1990 excavation	Amorphous lump			Copper alloy	
S.186	NCM		YELLOW.193				2003–9	Wood	Metal-detected stray find 2003–9	Amorphous lump			Copper alloy	
S.187	BM	1990,1101.44			SN/MX		1990	Area 9	Metal-detected stray find from 1990 excavation	Amorphous lump			Copper alloy	
S.188	NCM		YELLOW.252				2003–9	Wood	Metal-detected stray find 2003–9	Amorphous lump			Copper alloy	
S.189	BM	1991,0409.9			ST/CA		1991	Area 20	Metal-detected stray find from 1991 excavation	Amorphous lump			?Lead; ?silver alloy	
S.190	BM	1991,0409.2			ST/AA		1991	Area 20	Metal-detected stray find from 1991 excavation	Amorphous lump			Copper alloy	
S.191	BM	1991,0409.10			ST/CC		1991	Area 20	Metal-detected stray find from 1991 excavation	Amorphous lump			?Lead; ?silver alloy	
S.192	NCM		YELLOW.264				2003–9	Wood	Metal-detected stray find 2003–9	Amorphous lump			Copper alloy	
S.193	NCM		YELLOW.197				2003–9	Wood	Metal-detected stray find 2003–9	Amorphous lump			Lead alloy	
S.194	BM	1991,0409.7			ST/BL		1991	Area 19	Metal-detected stray find from 1991 excavation	Amorphous lump			Copper alloy	
S.195	BM	1990,1101.39			SN/BD		1990	Area 1	Metal-detected stray find from 1990 excavation	Amorphous lump			Copper alloy	
S.196	BM	1990,1101.45			SN/MZ		1990	Area 9	Metal-detected stray find from 1990 excavation	Amorphous lump			Copper alloy	
S.197	BM	1991,0409.17			ST/DV		1991	Area 24	Metal-detected stray find from 1991 excavation	Amorphous lump			Copper alloy	
S.198	NCM		YELLOW.190				2003–9	Wood	Metal-detected stray find 2003–9	Amorphous lump			Copper alloy	

Cat no.	Museum	Reg. no.	Ticket no.	Published ref.	Stead code	Ralph no.	Ex. year	Findspot	Context details	Object name	MSCC or TUB torc type	Torc terminal type	Material	Joining / related fragments?
S.199	BM	1991,0409.26					1990–1	Not recorded	Metal-detected stray find Dec. 1990–April 1991	Amorphous lump			Copper alloy	
S.200	NCM		YELLOW.182				2003–9	Wood	Metal-detected stray find 2003–9	Amorphous lump			Copper alloy	
S.201	NCM		YELLOW.161				2003–9	Wood	Metal-detected stray find 2003–9	Amorphous lump			Copper alloy	
S.202	NCM		YELLOW.162				2003–9	Wood	Metal-detected stray find 2003–9	Amorphous lump			Copper alloy	
S.203	NCM		YELLOW.132				2003–9	Wood	Metal-detected stray find 2003–9	Amorphous lump			Copper alloy	
S.204	NCM		YELLOW.263				2003–9	Wood	Metal-detected stray find 2003–9	Amorphous lump			Copper alloy; ?lead alloy	
S.205	NCM		YELLOW.181				2003–9	Wood	Metal-detected stray find 2003–9	Amorphous lump			Copper alloy	
S.206	BM	1990,1101.41			SN/EN		1990	Area 2	Metal-detected stray find from 1990 excavation	Amorphous lump			Copper alloy	
S.207	NCM		YELLOW.86				2003–9	Wood	Metal-detected stray find 2003–9	Amorphous lump			Copper alloy	
S.208	NCM		YELLOW.84				2003–9	Wood	Metal-detected stray find 2003–9	Amorphous lump			Copper alloy	
S.209	BM	1991,0409.3			ST/AE		1991	Area 16	Metal-detected stray find from 1991 excavation	Amorphous lump			Copper alloy	
S.210	NCM		YELLOW.53				2003–9	Wood	Metal-detected stray find 2003–9	Amorphous lump			Copper alloy	
S.211	NCM		YELLOW.159				2003–9	Wood	Metal-detected stray find 2003–9	Amorphous lump			Copper alloy	
S.212	BM	1991,0409.14			ST/DF		1991	Not recorded	Metal-detected stray find from 1991 excavation, most likely from 1990 backfill.	Amorphous lump			Copper alloy	
S.213	NCM		YELLOW.46				2003–9	Wood	Metal-detected stray find 2003–9	Amorphous lump			Copper alloy; ?lead alloy	
S.214	NCM		YELLOW.48				2003–9	Wood	Metal-detected stray find 2003–9	Amorphous lump			Copper alloy	
S.215	NCM		YELLOW.163				2003–9	Wood	Metal-detected stray find 2003–9	Amorphous lump			Copper alloy	
S.216	NCM		YELLOW.170				2003–9	Wood	Metal-detected stray find 2003–9	Amorphous lump			Copper alloy	
S.217	NCM		YELLOW.165				2003–9	Wood	Metal-detected stray find 2003–9	Amorphous lump			Copper alloy	
S.218	NCM		YELLOW.185				2003–9	Wood	Metal-detected stray find 2003–9	Amorphous lump			Copper alloy	
S.219	NCM		YELLOW.58				2003–9	Wood	Metal-detected stray find 2003–9	Amorphous lump			Copper alloy	
S.220	NCM		YELLOW.260				2003–9	Wood	Metal-detected stray find 2003–9	Amorphous lump			Copper alloy	
S.221	NCM		YELLOW.147				2003–9	Wood	Metal-detected stray find 2003–9	Amorphous lump			Copper alloy	
S.222	NCM		YELLOW.262				2003–9	Wood	Metal-detected stray find 2003–9	Amorphous lump			Copper alloy	
S.223	NCM		YELLOW.55				2003–9	Wood	Metal-detected stray find 2003–9	Amorphous lump			Copper alloy	
S.224	NCM		YELLOW.160				2003–9	Wood	Metal-detected stray find 2003–9	Amorphous lump			Copper alloy	
S.225	NCM		YELLOW.96				2003–9	Wood	Metal-detected stray find 2003–9	Amorphous lump			Copper alloy	
S.226	NCM		YELLOW.176				2003–9	Wood	Metal-detected stray find 2003–9	Amorphous lump			Copper alloy	
S.227	NCM		YELLOW.54				2003–9	Wood	Metal-detected stray find 2003–9	Amorphous lump			Copper alloy	
S.228	NCM		YELLOW.146				2003–9	Wood	Metal-detected stray find 2003–9	Amorphous lump			Copper alloy	
S.229	NCM		YELLOW.111				2003–9	Wood	Metal-detected stray find 2003–9	Amorphous lump			Copper alloy	

Cat no.	Museum	Reg. no.	Ticket no.	Published ref.	Stead code	Ralph no.	Ex. year	Findspot	Context details	Object name	MSCC or TUB torc type	Torc terminal type	Material	Joining / related fragments?
S.230	NCM		YELLOW.102				2003–9	Wood	Metal-detected stray find 2003–9	Amorphous lump			Copper alloy	
S.231	NCM		YELLOW.57				2003–9	Wood	Metal-detected stray find 2003–9	Amorphous lump			Copper alloy	
S.232	NCM		YELLOW.59				2003–9	Wood	Metal-detected stray find 2003–9	Amorphous lump			Copper alloy	
S.233	NCM		YELLOW.177				2003–9	Wood	Metal-detected stray find 2003–9	Amorphous lump			Copper alloy	
S.234	NCM		YELLOW.49				2003–9	Wood	Metal-detected stray find 2003–9	Amorphous lump			Iron	
S.235	NCM		YELLOW.4				2003–9	Wood	Metal-detected stray find 2003–9	Bead/?torc/ ?bracelet			Copper alloy; iron	Pair to S.236
S.236	NCM		YELLOW.258				2003–9	Wood	Metal-detected stray find 2003–9	Bead/?torc/ ?bracelet			Iron; copper alloy	Pair to S.235
S.237	NCM		YELLOW.6				2003–9	Wood	Metal-detected stray find 2003–9	Bead/?torc/ ?bracelet			Copper alloy	S.237–9 may be from the same beaded torc or bracelet
S.238	NCM		YELLOW.7				2003–9	Wood	Metal-detected stray find 2003–9	Bead/?torc/ ?bracelet			Copper alloy; Iron	S.237–9 may be from the same beaded torc or bracelet
S.239	NCM		YELLOW.9				2003–9	Wood	Metal-detected stray find 2003–9	Bead/?torc/ ?bracelet			Copper alloy	S.237–9 may be from the same beaded torc or bracelet
S.240	NCM		YELLOW.8				2003–9	Wood	Metal-detected stray find 2003–9	Bead/?torc/ ?bracelet			Iron	
S.241	NCM		YELLOW.5				2003–9	Wood	Metal-detected stray find 2003–9	?Bead/?torc/ ?bracelet			Copper alloy	
S.242	NCM		YELLOW.157				2003–9	Wood	Metal-detected stray find 2003–9	Brooch spring			?Silver alloy	
S.243	NCM		YELLOW.11				2003–9	Wood	Metal-detected stray find 2003–9	Brooch			Copper alloy	
S.244	BM	1992,0210.4			SA/BL		1992	Trench 6	Excavated find: Enclosure ditch: SA6/2, section C, Layer 1	Brooch			Copper alloy	
S.245	NCM		YELLOW.267				2003–9	Wood	Metal-detected stray find 2003–9	Brooch			Copper alloy (tinned)	
S.246	BM	1992,0210.5			SA/DV		1992	Trench 6	Excavated find: Ditch: SA6/7	Strip/?brooch			Copper alloy	
S.247	BM	1991,0409.15			ST/DG		1991	Not recorded	Metal-detected stray find from 1991 excavation, most likely from 1990 backfill	Finger ring			Copper alloy	
S.248	BM	1991,0409.19			ST/FO		1991	Area 26	Metal-detected stray find from 1991 excavation	?Finger ring			Copper alloy, ?glass	
S.249	NCM		YELLOW.17				2003–9	Wood	Metal-detected stray find 2003–9	Button/fastener			Copper alloy	S.249–52 may be from the same object
S.250	NCM		YELLOW.16				2003–9	Wood	Metal-detected stray find 2003–9	Button/fastener			Copper alloy	S.249–52 may be from the same object
S.251	NCM		YELLOW.18				2003–9	Wood	Metal-detected stray find 2003–9	Button/fastener			Copper alloy	S.249–52 may be from the same object
S.252	NCM		YELLOW.19				2003–9	Wood	Metal-detected stray find 2003–9	Button/fastener			Copper alloy	S.249–52 may be from the same object
S.253	BM	1993,0201.1					1989	Trench 15	Metal-detected stray find 1989.	Terminal			Copper alloy	Pair to S.254
S.254	BM	1993,0201.2					1989	Trench 15	Metal-detected stray find 1989.	Terminal			Copper alloy	Pair to S.253
S.255	BM	1991,0409.24			ST/HX		1991	Not recorded	Metal-detected stray find from 1991 excavation	Linch-pin / fitting			Copper alloy	
S.256	BM	1991,0409.8			ST/BR		1991	Area 20	Metal-detected stray find from 1991 excavation	Terret			Copper alloy	
S.257	BM	1991,0409.8			ST/BS		1991	Area 20	Metal-detected stray find from 1991 excavation	Terret			Copper alloy	
S.258	BM	1991,0409.11			ST/CE		1991	Not recorded	Metal-detected stray find from 1991 excavation	Fitting			Copper alloy; iron	

Cat no.	Museum	Reg. no.	Ticket no.	Published ref.	Stead code	Ralph no.	Ex. year	Findspot	Context details	Object name	MSCC or TUB torc type	Torc terminal type	Material	Joining / related fragments?
S.259	BM	1990,1101.47			SN/PZ		1990	Area 11	Metal-detected stray find from 1990 excavation	Fitting			Copper alloy	
S.260	NCM		YELLOW.139				2003–9	Wood	Metal-detected stray find 2003–9	Fitting			Copper alloy	
S.261	NCM		YELLOW.254				2003–9	Wood	Metal-detected stray find 2003–9	Rod /?strap fitting			Copper alloy	
S.262	NCM		YELLOW.188				2003–9	Wood	Metal-detected stray find 2003–9	?Strap fitting			Copper alloy	
S.263	NCM		YELLOW.240				2003–9	Wood	Metal-detected stray find 2003–9	Strip/?strap fitting			Copper alloy	
S.264	NCM		YELLOW.39				2003–9	Wood	Metal-detected stray find 2003–9	Strap fitting			Copper alloy; iron	
S.265	NCM		YELLOW.26				2003–9	Wood	Metal-detected stray find 2003–9	Strap fitting			Copper alloy; iron	
S.266	NCM		YELLOW.241				2003–9	Wood	Metal-detected stray find 2003–9	Sheet/?ring; rivet			Copper alloy; iron	
S.267	NCM		YELLOW.168				2003–9	Wood	Metal-detected stray find 2003–9	Mount/rivet			Copper alloy	
S.268	NCM		YELLOW.20				2003–9	Wood	Metal-detected stray find 2003–9	Rivet			Copper alloy	
S.269	NCM		YELLOW.43				2003–9	Wood	Metal-detected stray find 2003–9	Rivet head			Copper alloy	
S.270	NCM		YELLOW.24				2003–9	Wood	Metal-detected stray find 2003–9	Rivet head			Copper alloy	
S.271	NCM		YELLOW.201				2003–9	Wood	Metal-detected stray find 2003–9	Rivet			Copper alloy	
S.272	NCM		YELLOW.23				2003–9	Wood	Metal-detected stray find 2003–9	Rivet head			Copper alloy	
S.273	NCM		YELLOW.22				2003–9	Wood	Metal-detected stray find 2003–9	Rivet head			Copper alloy	
S.274	NCM		YELLOW.25				2003–9	Wood	Metal-detected stray find 2003–9	Rivet head			Copper alloy	
S.275	NCM		YELLOW.257				2003–9	Wood	Metal-detected stray find 2003–9	Rivet head			Copper alloy	
S.276	NCM		YELLOW.33				2003–9	Wood	Metal-detected stray find 2003–9	Binding strip; ?shield			Copper alloy	Similar to the hide-shaped shield binding B/C.89
S.277	NCM		YELLOW.244				2003–9	Wood	Metal-detected stray find 2003–9	Binding clamp			Copper alloy	
S.278	NCM		YELLOW.27				2003–9	Wood	Metal-detected stray find 2003–9	?Binding clamp			Copper alloy	
S.279	NCM		YELLOW.40				2003–9	Wood	Metal-detected stray find 2003–9	?Binding clamp			Copper alloy	
S.280	NCM		YELLOW.186				2003–9	Wood	Metal-detected stray find 2003–9	Binding strip			Copper alloy	
S.281	NCM		YELLOW.169				2003–9	Wood	Metal-detected stray find 2003–9	Binding strip			Copper alloy	
S.282	NCM		YELLOW.178				2003–9	Wood	Metal-detected stray find 2003–9	Binding strip			Copper alloy	
S.283	NCM		YELLOW.256				2003–9	Wood	Metal-detected stray find 2003–9	Binding strip			Copper alloy	
S.284	NCM		YELLOW.127				2003–9	Wood	Metal-detected stray find 2003–9	Binding strip			Copper alloy	
S.285	NCM		YELLOW.189				2003–9	Wood	Metal-detected stray find 2003–9	?Binding strip			Copper alloy	
S.286	BM	1992,0210.6			SA/GM		1992	Trench 7	Excavated find: Ditch: SA7/5, section D	?Binding strip			Copper alloy	
S.287	BM	1991,0409.20			ST/GM		1991	Area 27	Metal-detected stray find from 1991 excavation	Strip (sheet) (decorative)			Copper alloy	
S.288	NCM		YELLOW.218				2003–9	Wood	Metal-detected stray find 2003–9	Strip; ?wire; ?rivet			Copper alloy	
S.289	NCM		YELLOW.255				2003–9	Wood	Metal-detected stray find 2003–9	Strip; rivet			Copper alloy	

Cat no.	Museum	Reg. no.	Ticket no.	Published ref.	Stead code	Ralph no.	Ex. year	Findspot	Context details	Object name	MSCC or TUB torc type	Torc terminal type	Material	Joining / related fragments?
S.290	NCM		YELLOW.212				2003–9	Wood	Metal-detected stray find 2003–9	Strip; rivet			Copper alloy	
S.291	NCM		YELLOW.213				2003–9	Wood	Metal-detected stray find 2003–9	Strip; rivet			Copper alloy	
S.292	NCM		YELLOW.217				2003–9	Wood	Metal-detected stray find 2003–9	Strip; rivet			Copper alloy	
S.293	NCM		YELLOW.205				2003–9	Wood	Metal-detected stray find 2003–9	Strip			Copper alloy	
S.294	NCM		YELLOW.208				2003–9	Wood	Metal-detected stray find 2003–9	Strip			Copper alloy	
S.295	NCM		YELLOW.167B				2003–9	Wood	Metal-detected stray find 2003–9	Strip			Copper alloy	
S.296	NCM		YELLOW.235				2003–9	Wood	Metal-detected stray find 2003–9	Strip			Copper alloy	
S.297	NCM		YELLOW.209				2003–9	Wood	Metal-detected stray find 2003–9	Strip			Copper alloy	
S.298	NCM		YELLOW.184				2003–9	Wood	Metal-detected stray find 2003–9	Strip			Copper alloy	
S.299	NCM		YELLOW.214				2003–9	Wood	Metal-detected stray find 2003–9	Strip			Copper alloy	
S.300	NCM		YELLOW.219				2003–9	Wood	Metal-detected stray find 2003–9	Strip			Copper alloy	
S.301	NCM		YELLOW.233				2003–9	Wood	Metal-detected stray find 2003–9	Strip			Copper alloy	
S.302	NCM		YELLOW.167A				2003–9	Wood	Metal-detected stray find 2003–9	Strip			Copper alloy	
S.303	NCM		YELLOW.222				2003–9	Wood	Metal-detected stray find 2003–9	Strip			Copper alloy	
S.304	NCM		YELLOW.236				2003–9	Wood	Metal-detected stray find 2003–9	Strip			Copper alloy	
S.305	NCM		YELLOW.239				2003–9	Wood	Metal-detected stray find 2003–9	Strip			Copper alloy; ?Lead alloy	
S.306	NCM		YELLOW.187				2003–9	Wood	Metal-detected stray find 2003–9	Strip			Copper alloy	
S.307	NCM		YELLOW.45				2003–9	Wood	Metal-detected stray find 2003–9	Strip			Iron	
S.308	NCM		YELLOW.207				2003–9	Wood	Metal-detected stray find 2003–9	Sheet; rivet			Copper alloy	
S.309	NCM		YELLOW.215				2003–9	Wood	Metal-detected stray find 2003–9	Sheet; rivet			Copper alloy	
S.310	NCM		YELLOW.206				2003–9	Wood	Metal-detected stray find 2003–9	Sheet; rivet			Copper alloy	
S.311	NCM		YELLOW.228				2003–9	Wood	Metal-detected stray find 2003–9	Sheet; rivet			Copper alloy	
S.312	NCM		YELLOW.210				2003–9	Wood	Metal-detected stray find 2003–9	Sheet; rivet			Copper alloy	
S.313	NCM		YELLOW.221				2003–9	Wood	Metal-detected stray find 2003–9	Sheet; rivet			Copper alloy	
S.314	NCM		YELLOW.230				2003–9	Wood	Metal-detected stray find 2003–9	Sheet; rivet			Copper alloy	
S.315	NCM		YELLOW.216				2003–9	Wood	Metal-detected stray find 2003–9	Sheet; rivet			Copper alloy	
S.316	NCM		YELLOW.224				2003–9	Wood	Metal-detected stray find 2003–9	Sheet; rivet			Copper alloy; ?iron	

Cat no.	Museum	Reg. no.	Ticket no.	Published ref.	Stead code	Ralph no.	Ex. year	Findspot	Context details	Object name	MSCC or TUB torc type	Torc terminal type	Material	Joining / related fragments?
S.317	NCM		YELLOW.202				2003–9	Wood	Metal-detected stray find 2003–9	Thick sheet			Copper alloy	
S.318	NCM		YELLOW.204				2003–9	Wood	Metal-detected stray find 2003–9	Sheet			Copper alloy	
S.319	NCM		YELLOW.133				2003–9	Wood	Metal-detected stray find 2003–9	Sheet			Copper alloy	
S.320	NCM		YELLOW.253				2003–9	Wood	Metal-detected stray find 2003–9	Sheet			Copper alloy	
S.321	NCM		YELLOW.259				2003–9	Wood	Metal-detected stray find 2003–9	Sheet			Copper alloy	
S.322	NCM		YELLOW.171				2003–9	Wood	Metal-detected stray find 2003–9	Sheet			Copper alloy	
S.323	NCM		YELLOW.203				2003–9	Wood	Metal-detected stray find 2003–9	Sheet			Copper alloy	
S.324	NCM		YELLOW.242				2003–9	Wood	Metal-detected stray find 2003–9	Sheet			Copper alloy	
S.325	NCM		YELLOW.237				2003–9	Wood	Metal-detected stray find 2003–9	Sheet			Copper alloy	
S.326	NCM		YELLOW.231				2003–9	Wood	Metal-detected stray find 2003–9	Sheet			Copper alloy	
S.327	NCM		YELLOW.164B				2003–9	Wood	Metal-detected stray find 2003–9	Sheet			Copper alloy	
S.328	NCM		YELLOW.220				2003–9	Wood	Metal-detected stray find 2003–9	Sheet			Copper alloy	
S.329	NCM		YELLOW.223				2003–9	Wood	Metal-detected stray find 2003–9	Sheet			Copper alloy	
S.330	NCM		YELLOW.179				2003–9	Wood	Metal-detected stray find 2003–9	Sheet			Copper alloy	
S.331	NCM		YELLOW.211				2003–9	Wood	Metal-detected stray find 2003–9	Sheet			Copper alloy	
S.332	NCM		YELLOW.227				2003–9	Wood	Metal-detected stray find 2003–9	Sheet			Copper alloy	
S.333	NCM		YELLOW.229				2003–9	Wood	Metal-detected stray find 2003–9	Sheet			Copper alloy	
S.334	NCM		YELLOW.232				2003–9	Wood	Metal-detected stray find 2003–9	Sheet			Copper alloy	
S.335	NCM		YELLOW.225				2003–9	Wood	Metal-detected stray find 2003–9	Sheet			Copper alloy	
S.336	NCM		YELLOW.234				2003–9	Wood	Metal-detected stray find 2003–9	Sheet			Copper alloy	
S.337	NCM		YELLOW.238				2003–9	Wood	Metal-detected stray find 2003–9	Sheet			Copper alloy	
S.338	NCM		YELLOW.174				2003–9	Wood	Metal-detected stray find 2003–9	Sheet			Copper alloy	
S.339	NCM		YELLOW.226				2003–9	Wood	Metal-detected stray find 2003–9	Sheet			Copper alloy	
S.340	NCM		YELLOW.166				2003–9	Wood	Metal-detected stray find 2003–9	Sheet			Copper alloy	
S.341	NCM		YELLOW.199				2003–9	Wood	Metal-detected stray find 2003–9	Sheet			Copper alloy	
S.342	NCM		YELLOW.194				2003–9	Wood	Metal-detected stray find 2003–9	Sheet			Copper alloy	
S.343	NCM		YELLOW.196				2003–9	Wood	Metal-detected stray find 2003–9	Sheet			Copper alloy	

Cat no.	Museum	Reg. no.	Ticket no.	Published ref.	Stead code	Ralph no.	Ex. year	Findspot	Context details	Object name	MSCC or TUB torc type	Torc terminal type	Material	Joining / related fragments?
S.344	NCM		YELLOW.164A				2003–9	Wood	Metal-detected stray find 2003–9	Sheet			Copper alloy	
S.345	BM	1990,1101.40			SN/EF		1990	Area 2	Metal-detected stray find from 1990 excavation	Sheet			Copper alloy	
S.346	NCM		YELLOW.172				2003–9	Wood	Metal-detected stray find 2003–9	Sheet			Copper alloy	
S.347	NCM		YELLOW.180				2003–9	Wood	Metal-detected stray find 2003–9	Sheet			Copper alloy	
S.348	BM	1991,0409.25					1991	Area 21	Metal-detected stray find from 1991 excavation	Sheet			Copper alloy	
S.349	NCM		YELLOW.119				2003–9	Wood	Metal-detected stray find 2003–9	Sheet			Copper alloy	
S.350	NCM		YELLOW.76				2003–9	Wood	Metal-detected stray find 2003–9	Sheet			Copper alloy	
S.351	NCM		YELLOW.191				2003–9	Wood	Metal-detected stray find 2003–9	Sheet			Copper alloy	
S.352	BM	1991,0409.23			ST/HV		1991	Area 21	Metal-detected stray find from 1991 excavation	Knife			Iron	
S.353	BM	1992,0210.3			SA/BH		1992	Trench 5	Excavated find: Pit: SA5/3. From top 2–3cm of pit	Knife			Iron	
S.354	BM	1991,0409.5			ST/AV		1991	Area 18	Metal-detected stray find from 1991 excavation	Tweezers			Copper alloy	
S.355	BM	1990,1101.50					1990	Not recorded	Metal-detected stray find from 1990 excavation	Mail armour			Copper alloy	
S.356	NCM		YELLOW.12				2003–9	Wood	Metal-detected stray find 2003–9	Mail armour			Iron	S.356–9 may be from the same set of mail armour
S.357	NCM		YELLOW.13				2003–9	Wood	Metal-detected stray find 2003–9	Mail armour			Iron	S.356–9 may be from the same set of mail armour
S.358	NCM		YELLOW.14				2003–9	Wood	Metal-detected stray find 2003–9	Mail armour			Iron	S.356–9 may be from the same set of mail armour
S.359	NCM		YELLOW.15				2003–9	Wood	Metal-detected stray find 2003–9	Mail armour			Iron	S.356–9 may be from the same set of mail armour
S.360	NCM		YELLOW.183				2003–9	Wood	Metal-detected stray find 2003–9	Unidentified object fragment			Copper alloy	
S.361	NCM		YELLOW.75				2003–9	Wood	Metal-detected stray find 2003–9	Unidentified object fragment			Copper alloy; iron	
S.362	NCM		YELLOW.44				2003–9	Wood	Metal-detected stray find 2003–9	Unidentified object fragment			Copper alloy	
S.363	NCM		YELLOW.243				2003–9	Wood	Metal-detected stray find 2003–9	Unidentified object fragment			Copper alloy	
S.364	NCM		YELLOW.41				2003–9	Wood	Metal-detected stray find 2003–9	Unidentified object fragment			Copper alloy	
S.365	NCM		YELLOW.145				2003–9	Wood	Metal-detected stray find 2003–9	Unidentified object fragment			Copper alloy	

Concordance with Clarke (1954)

Clarke (1954) published Snettisham Hoards A–E. He used two separate, simultaneous cataloguing systems to organise finds from Hoards A–D by both hoard and type. He assigned each find a number within the hoard (e.g. 'Hd. B No. 1') but the actual listing of finds was done not by hoard but by object type. For this purpose, Clarke divided the finds into seven groups, giving an 'inventory' of each. These find types are listed here along with the abbreviations used for these Clarke groups in this volume:

- Tubular torcs (TT)
- Loop terminal torcs (LT)
- Buffer terminal torcs (BT)
- Ingot bracelets (here corresponding to large rings, and given abbreviation RL)
- Ingot rings (here corresponding to small rings, and given abbreviation R)
- Sheet bronze (SB)
- Metal 'cake' (MC)
- Miscellaneous objects (M)

While Clarke's division of object types is not followed closely in this volume, these categories were used in earlier studies, such as Northover's compositional analyses of the NCM material, and thus these 'inventory numbers' (e.g. BT1, LT20) are referred to in Chapter 18 and Appendix 5.

In this volume, objects have been treated by hoard, and within hoard by material and then by object type (see explanation of cataloguing ordering in Chapter 14). New numbering has been introduced for the Hoard A–D material for four reasons: to ensure comparable numbering between both BM and NCM material (e.g. the grouping of interlinked objects); to reflect the fact that cataloguing carried out for this volume identified new connections/distinctions between object fragments (see below); because some fragments not illustrated in Clarke (1954) could not be securely assigned to their Clarke catalogue entries; and since not all objects from Hoards A, B and C were included in Clarke's publication. In the full catalogue entries for Hoards A–D in Chapter 14, the Clarke references are given, or a note included that the object was not published by Clarke. In the cases of objects which were not illustrated in Clarke's publication, photocopies taken by Peter Northover in the 1980s (now held in the BM archive) were used for cross-referencing purposes to ensure correct IDs.

Since Clarke's catalogue has been the main point of reference for the Hoard A–D Snettisham material for many decades, a complete concordance is also included here to assist the reader in cross-referencing between these publications. Two tables are given below. The first lists the objects in order of their Clarke hoard number. The format used by Clarke (e.g. 'Hd. B No. 1'), is kept here to avoid confusion with the catalogue numbers used in this volume (e.g. B.27). The second table below lists the objects in order of their Clarke inventory number, i.e. grouped by object type, in the order they are presented in Clarke's publication. For a summary of Clarke references ordered by the catalogue numbers used in this volume, see the main concordance table for all objects.

The objects from Hoards A–D not published by Clarke are: B.10, B.12, B.13, B.14, B.18, B.19, C.32, C.33, C.34, C.35, C.36, C.37, C.38, C.39, C.40, C.41, C.42, C.43, C.44, B/C.23, B/C.46, B/C.63, B/C.96.

Table of Hoard A–D material by Clarke (1954) hoard number

Clarke hoard no.	Cat. no. (this volume)	Clarke inv. no.	Full Clarke (1954) reference
Hd. A No. 1	A.1	TT1	Clarke 1954, 37; pls i, ii; Tubular Torc 1
Hd. A No. 2	A.2	TT2	Clarke 1954, 38; pls i, ii; Tubular Torc 2
Hd. A No. 3	A.3	TT3	Clarke 1954, 38–9; pls i, ii; Tubular Torc 3
Hd. A No. 4	A.4	TT4	Clarke 1954, 39; Tubular Torc 4
Hd. A No. 4	A.5	TT4	Clarke 1954, 39, pl. i; Tubular Torc 4
Hd. A No. 4	A.6	TT4	Clarke 1954, 39; pl. i; Tubular Torc 4
Hd. A No. 4	A.7	TT4	Clarke 1954, 39; pl. i; Tubular Torc 4
N/A	A.8	N/A	Clarke 1954, 39; fig. 6
Hd. B No. 1	B.27	MC1	Clarke 1954, 58 (cake), no. 1; pl. xiii, upper
Hd. B No. 2	B.26	MC2	Clarke 1954, 58 (cake), no. 2; pl. xiii, upper
Hd. B No. 3	B.21–B.23	RL11	Clarke 1954, 54, no. 11
Hd. B No. 4	B.24	RL15	Clarke 1954, 54, no. 15
Hd. B No. 5	B.20	RL12	Clarke 1954, 54, no. 12
Hd. B No. 6	B.1b	RL13	Clarke 1954, 54, no. 13; pl. xii, in group
Hd. B No. 7	B.1a	RL14	Clarke 1954, 54, no. 14; pl. xii, in group
Hd. B No. 8	B.28	M1	Clarke 1954, 58 (Misc.), no. 1; pl. xiii, lower
Hd. B No. 9	B.25	R11	Clarke 1954, 56, no. 11; pl. xii
Hd. B No. 10	B.1c	R12	Clarke 1954, 56, no. 12; pl. xii, in group
Hd. B No. 11	B.1h	R14	Clarke 1954, 56, no. 14; pl. xii, bottom left of group
Hd. B No. 12	B.1d	R1	Clarke 1954, 55, no. 1; pl. xii, bottom right of group
Hd. B No. 13	B.1e	LT1	Clarke 1954, 46, no. 1; pl. xii, top left of group
Hd. B No. 14	B.2	LT2	Clarke 1954, 46, no. 2; pl. xii, no. 2
Hd. B No. 15	B.1f	LT3	Clarke 1954, 46, no. 3; pl. xii, no. 3 and in group, centre right
Hd. B No. 16	B.1g	LT4	Clarke 1954, 46, no. 4; pl. xii, no. 4
Hd. B No. 17	B.7	LT5	Clarke 1954, 46, no. 5
Hd. B No. 18	B.8	LT6	Clarke 1954, 46, no. 6; pl. ix
Hd. B No. 19	B.4	LT7	Clarke 1954, 47, no. 7; pl. xii
Hd. B No. 20	B.3	LT8	Clarke 1954, 47, no. 8; pl. ix
Hd. B No. 21	B.5	LT14	Clarke 1954, 47, no. 14; pl. ix
Hd. B No. 22	B.6	LT15	Clarke 1954, 47, no. 15; pl. ix
Hd. B No. 23	B.11	LT19	Clarke 1954, 47, no. 19; pl. ix
Hd. B No. 24	B.9, B.15, B.17	LT20	Clarke 1954, 47, no. 20
Hd. B No. 25	B.16	LT21	Clarke 1954, 47, no. 21
Hd. B No. 26	B.29–33	M3	Clarke 1954, 58 (Misc.), no. 3
Hd. C No. 1	C.57–61	M4	Clarke 1954, 58 (Misc.), no. 4; fig. 9
Hd. C No. 2	C.45	MC4	Clarke 1954, 58 (cake), no. 4; pl. xiii, upper
Hd. C No. 3	C.46	RL1	Clarke 1954, 54, no. 1
Hd. C No. 4	C.48	R2	Clarke 1954, 55, no. 2
Hd. C No. 5	C.49	R3	Clarke 1954, 55, no. 3
Hd. C No. 6	C.47	R15	Clarke 1954, 56, no. 15; pl. xii
Hd. C No. 7	C.54	SB2	Clarke 1954, 57, no. 2; pl. xiii, lower
Hd. C No. 8	C.51	SB5	Clarke 1954, 57, no. 5; pl. xiii, lower
Hd. C No. 9	C.52–C.53	SB3	Clarke 1954, 57, no. 3; pl. xiii, lower
Hd. C No. 10	C.55–C.56	SB6	Clarke 1954, 57, no. 6
Hd. C No. 11	C.50	MC3	Clarke 1954, 58 (cake), no. 3; pl. xiii, upper, 3

Hd. C No. 12	C.6–C.12, C.15–16, C.18	LT9	Clarke 1954, 47, no. 9; pl. ix
Hd. C No. 13	C.14	LT10	Clarke 1954, 47, no. 10
Hd. C No. 14	C.13, C.19–C.20	LT11	Clarke 1954, 47, no. 11; pl. ix (C.20 not pictured)
Hd. C No. 15	C.17	MC5	Clarke 1954, 58 (cake), no. 5
Hd. C No. 16	C.1–5, C.21	LT12	Clarke 1954, 47, no. 12
Hd. C No. 17	C.22, C.26	BT1	Clarke 1954, 52, no. 1; pl. xi, right
Hd. C No. 18	C.25	BT2	Clarke 1954, 52, no. 2; pl. xi, right
Hd. C No. 19	C.23–C.24, C.28–30	LT22	Clarke 1954, 47, no. 22
Hd. C No. 20	C.27, C.31	BT3	Clarke 1954, 52, no. 3; pl. xi, right
Hd. B/C No. 1	B/C.65	RL2	Clarke 1954, 54, no. 2; fig. 7
Hd. B/C No. 2	B/C.67	RL3	Clarke 1954, 54, no. 3
Hd. B/C No. 3	B/C.66	RL4	Clarke 1954, 54, no. 4; fig. 7
Hd. B/C No. 4	B/C.68	RL5	Clarke 1954, 54, no. 5; fig. 7
Hd. B/C No. 5	B/C.69	RL6	Clarke 1954, 54, no. 6
Hd. B/C No. 6	B/C.71	RL7	Clarke 1954, 54, no. 7; fig. 7
Hd. B/C No. 7	B/C.72	RL8	Clarke 1954, 54, no. 8
Hd. B/C No. 8	B/C.70	RL9	Clarke 1954, 54, no. 9
Hd. B/C No. 9	B/C.73–B/C.76	RL10	Clarke 1954, 54, no. 10
Hd. B/C No. 10 (Listed as 'Hd. C No. 10' in Clarke 1954, in error)	B/C.64	R4	Clarke 1954, 55, no. 4
Hd. B/C No. 11	B/C.77	R5	Clarke 1954, 55, no. 5
Hd. B/C No. 12	B/C.78	R6	Clarke 1954, 55, no. 6
Hd. B/C No. 13	B/C.82	R7	Clarke 1954, 55, no. 7
Hd. B/C No. 14	B/C.79	R8	Clarke 1954, 55, no. 8
Hd. B/C No. 15	B/C.83	R9	Clarke 1954, 55, no. 9; pl. xii
Hd. B/C No. 16	B/C.80	R10	Clarke 1954, 55, no. 10
Hd. B/C No. 17	B/C.81	R13	Clarke 1954, 56, no. 13
Hd. B/C No. 18	B/C.85	MC6	Clarke 1954, 58 (cake), no. 6; pl. xiii, upper
Hd. B/C No. 19	B/C.84	MC7	Clarke 1954, 58 (cake), no. 7; pl. xiii, upper
Hd. B/C No. 20	B/C.86	MC8	Clarke 1954, 58 (cake), no. 8; pl. xiii, upper
Hd. B/C No. 21	B/C.87	MC9	Clarke 1954, 58 (cake), no. 9; pl. xiii, upper
Hd. B/C No. 22	B/C.88	SB4	Clarke 1954, 57, no. 4; pl. xiii, lower; fig. 8
Hd. B/C No. 23	B/C.89	SB1	Clarke 1954, 57, no. 1; pl. xiii, lower
Hd. B/C No. 24	B/C.91–B/C.95	SB7	Clarke 1954, 57, no. 7
Hd. B/C No. 25	B/C.90	M2	Clarke 1954, 58 (Misc.), no. 2; pl. xiii, lower
Hd. B/C No. 26	B/C.1	LT16	Clarke 1954, 47, no. 16; pl. ix
Hd. B/C No. 27	B/C.6	LT17	Clarke 1954, 47, no. 17; pl. ix
Hd. B/C No. 28	B/C.2	LT18	Clarke 1954, 47, no. 18; pl. ix
Hd. B/C No. 29	B/C.47–8	LT23	Clarke 1954, 47, no. 23; pl. viii; pl. ix
Hd. B/C No. 30	B/C.50	LT24	Clarke 1954, 47, no. 24; pl. viii
Hd. B/C No. 31	B/C.49, B/C.51–3, B/C.56, B/C.60–2	LT25	Clarke 1954, 47, no. 25

Hd. B/C No. 32	B/C.42–B/C.45	LT26	Clarke 1954, 47, no. 26
Hd. B/C No. 33	B/C.54–5	LT27	Clarke 1954, 47, no. 27; pl. ix, lower left (erroneously labelled as 'no. 29')
Hd. B/C No. 34	B/C.57–B/C.59	LT28	Clarke 1954, 47, no. 28
Hd. B/C No. 35	B/C.41	LT29	Clarke 1954, 47, no. 29; pl. ix, upper right
Hd. B/C No. 36	B/C.12	LT30	Clarke 1954, 47, no. 30; pl. viii
Hd. B/C No. 37	B/C.10	LT31	Clarke 1954, 47, no. 31; pl. viii
Hd. B/C No. 38	B/C.11	LT32	Clarke 1954, 48, no. 32; pl. viii
Hd. B/C No. 39	B/C.9	LT33	Clarke 1954, 48, no. 33; pl. viii
Hd. B/C No. 40	B/C.37	LT34	Clarke 1954, 48, no. 34; pl. ix
Hd. B/C No. 41	B/C.19	LT35	Clarke 1954, 48, no. 35; pl. ix
Hd. B/C No. 42	B/C.7–8	LT36	Clarke 1954, 48, no. 36; pl. ix
Hd. B/C No. 43	B/C.25	LT37	Clarke 1954, 48, no. 37; pl. ix
Hd. B/C No. 44	B/C.16	LT38	Clarke 1954, 48, no. 38; pl. ix
Hd. B/C No. 45	B/C.20	LT39	Clarke 1954, 48, no. 39; pl. ix
Hd. B/C No. 46	B/C.17–B/C.18, B/C.21–B/C.22, B/C.26–B/C.34, B/C.38–B/C.40	LT40	Clarke 1954, 48, no. 40; pl. ix (B/C.21 is top left, mis-labelled in the plate as no. 42)
Hd. B/C No. 47	B/C.13	LT41	Clarke 1954, 48, no. 41; pl. ix
Hd. B/C No. 48	B/C.35	LT42	Clarke 1954, 48, no. 42; pl. ix
Hd. B/C No. 49	B/C.24	LT43	Clarke 1954, 48, no. 43; pl. viii
Hd. B/C No. 50	B/C.5	LT44	Clarke 1954, 48, no. 44; pl. ix
Hd. B/C No. 51	B/C.14	LT45	Clarke 1954, 48, no. 45; pl. ix
Hd. B/C No. 52	B/C.36	LT46	Clarke 1954, 48, no. 46; pl. ix
Hd. B/C No. 53	B/C.3–4	LT47	Clarke 1954, 48, no. 47; pl. ix
Hd. B/C No. 54	B/C.15	LT48	Clarke 1954, 48, no. 48; pl. ix
Hd. D No. 1	D.1a	LT13	Clarke 1954, 47, no. 13; pl. x
Hd. D No. 2	D.1b	R16	Clarke 1954, 56, no. 16; pl. x

Table of Hoard A–D material by Clarke (1954) inventory number

Clarke inv. no.	Cat. no. (this volume)	Clarke hoard no.	Full Clarke (1954) reference
TT1	A.1	Hd. A No. 1	Clarke 1954, 37; pls i, ii; Tubular Torc 1
TT2	A.2	Hd. A No. 2	Clarke 1954, 38; pls i, ii; Tubular Torc 2
TT3	A.3	Hd. A No. 3	Clarke 1954, 38–9; pls i, ii; Tubular Torc 3
TT4	A.4	Hd. A No. 4	Clarke 1954, 39, pl. i; Tubular Torc 4
TT4	A.5	Hd. A No. 4	Clarke 1954, 39, pl. i; Tubular Torc 4
TT4	A.6	Hd. A No. 4	Clarke 1954, 39; pl. i; Tubular Torc 4
TT4	A.7	Hd. A No. 4	Clarke 1954, 39; Tubular Torc 4
N/A	A.8	N/A	Clarke 1954, 39; fig. 6
LT1	B.1e	Hd. B No. 13	Clarke 1954, 46, no. 1; pl. xii, top left of group
LT2	B.2	Hd. B No. 14	Clarke 1954, 46, no. 2; pl. xii, no. 2
LT3	B.1f	Hd. B No. 15	Clarke 1954, 46, no. 3; pl. xii, no. 3 and in group, centre right
LT4	B.1g	Hd. B No. 16	Clarke 1954, 46, no. 4; pl. xii, no. 4
LT5	B.7	Hd. B No. 17	Clarke 1954, 46, no. 5
LT6	B.8	Hd. B No. 18	Clarke 1954, 46, no. 6; pl. ix
LT7	B.4	Hd. B No. 19	Clarke 1954, 47, no. 7; pl. xii
LT8	B.3	Hd. B No. 20	Clarke 1954, 47, no. 8; pl. ix
LT9	C.6–C.12, C.15–16, C.18	Hd. C No. 12	Clarke 1954, 47, no. 9; pl. ix
LT10	C.14	Hd. C No. 13	Clarke 1954, 47, no. 10
LT11	C.13, C.19–C.20	Hd. C No. 14	Clarke 1954, 47, no. 11; pl. ix (C.20 not pictured)
LT12	C.1–5, C.21	Hd. C No. 16	Clarke 1954, 47, no. 12
LT13	D.1a	Hd. D No. 1	Clarke 1954, 47, no. 13; pl. x
LT14	B.5	Hd. B No. 21	Clarke 1954, 47, no. 14; pl. ix
LT15	B.6	Hd. B No. 22	Clarke 1954, 47, no. 15; pl. ix
LT16	B/C.1	Hd. B/C No. 26	Clarke 1954, 47, no. 16; pl. ix
LT17	B/C.6	Hd. B/C No. 27	Clarke 1954, 47, no. 17; pl. ix
LT18	B/C.2	Hd. B/C No. 28	Clarke 1954, 47, no. 18; pl. ix
LT19	B.11	Hd. B No. 23	Clarke 1954, 47, no. 19; pl. ix
LT20	B.9, B.15, B.17	Hd. B No. 24	Clarke 1954, 47, no. 20
LT21	B.16	Hd. B No. 25	Clarke 1954, 47, no. 21
LT22	C.23–C.24, C.28–30	Hd. C No. 19	Clarke 1954, 47, no. 22
LT23	B/C.47–8	Hd. B/C No. 29	Clarke 1954, 47, no. 23; pl. viii; pl. ix
LT24	B/C.50	Hd. B/C No. 30	Clarke 1954, 47, no. 24; pl. viii
LT25	B/C.49, B/C.51–3, B/C.56, B/C.60–2	Hd. B/C No. 31	Clarke 1954, 47, no. 25
LT26	B/C.42–B/C.45	Hd. B/C No. 32	Clarke 1954, 47, no. 26
LT27	B/C.54–5	Hd. B/C No. 33	Clarke 1954, 47, no. 27; pl. ix, lower left (erroneously labelled as 'no. 29')
LT28	B/C.57–B/C.59	Hd. B/C No. 34	Clarke 1954, 47, no. 28
LT29	B/C.41	Hd. B/C No. 35	Clarke 1954, 47, no. 29; pl. ix, upper right

LT30	B/C.12	Hd. B/C No. 36	Clarke 1954, 47, no. 30; pl. viii
LT31	B/C.10	Hd. B/C No. 37	Clarke 1954, 47, no. 31; pl. viii
LT32	B/C.11	Hd. B/C No. 38	Clarke 1954, 48, no. 32; pl. viii
LT33	B/C.9	Hd. B/C No. 39	Clarke 1954, 48, no. 33; pl. viii
LT34	B/C.37	Hd. B/C No. 40	Clarke 1954, 48, no. 34; pl. ix
LT35	B/C.19	Hd. B/C No. 41	Clarke 1954, 48, no. 35; pl. ix
LT36	B/C.7–8	Hd. B/C No. 42	Clarke 1954, 48, no. 36; pl. ix
LT37	B/C.25	Hd. B/C No. 43	Clarke 1954, 48, no. 37; pl. ix
LT38	B/C.16	Hd. B/C No. 44	Clarke 1954, 48, no. 38; pl. ix
LT39	B/C.20	Hd. B/C No. 45	Clarke 1954, 48, no. 39; pl. ix
LT40	B/C.17–B/C.18, B/C.21–B/C.22, B/C.26–B/C.34, B/C.38–B/C.40	Hd. B/C No. 46	Clarke 1954, 48, no. 40; pl. ix (B/C.21 is top left, mis-labelled in the plate as no. 42)
LT41	B/C.13	Hd. B/C No. 47	Clarke 1954, 48, no. 41; pl. ix
LT42	B/C.35	Hd. B/C No. 48	Clarke 1954, 48, no. 42; pl. ix
LT43	B/C.24	Hd. B/C No. 49	Clarke 1954, 48, no. 43; pl. viii
LT44	B/C.5	Hd. B/C No. 50	Clarke 1954, 48, no. 44; pl. ix
LT45	B/C.14	Hd. B/C No. 51	Clarke 1954, 48, no. 45; pl. ix
LT46	B/C.36	Hd. B/C No. 52	Clarke 1954, 48, no. 46; pl. ix
LT47	B/C.3–4	Hd. B/C No. 53	Clarke 1954, 48, no. 47; pl. ix
LT48	B/C.15	Hd. B/C No. 54	Clarke 1954, 48, no. 48; pl. ix
BT1	C.22, C.26	Hd. C No. 17	Clarke 1954, 52, no. 1; pl. xi, right
BT2	C.25	Hd. C No. 18	Clarke 1954, 52, no. 2; pl. xi, right
BT3	C.27, C.31	Hd. C No. 20	Clarke 1954, 52, no. 3; pl. xi, right
RL1	C.46	Hd. C No. 3	Clarke 1954, 54, no. 1
RL2	B/C.65	Hd. B/C No. 1	Clarke 1954, 54, no. 2; fig. 7
RL3	B/C.67	Hd. B/C No. 2	Clarke 1954, 54, no. 3
RL4	B/C.66	Hd. B/C No. 3	Clarke 1954, 54, no. 4; fig. 7
RL5	B/C.68	Hd. B/C No. 4	Clarke 1954, 54, no. 5; fig. 7
RL6	B/C.69	Hd. B/C No. 5	Clarke 1954, 54, no. 6
RL7	B/C.71	Hd. B/C No. 6	Clarke 1954, 54, no. 7; fig. 7
RL8	B/C.72	Hd. B/C No. 7	Clarke 1954, 54, no. 8
RL9	B/C.70	Hd. B/C No. 8	Clarke 1954, 54, no. 9
RL10	B/C.73–B/C.76	Hd. B/C No. 9	Clarke 1954, 54, no. 10
RL11	B.21–B.23	Hd. B No. 3	Clarke 1954, 54, no. 11
RL12	B.20	Hd. B No. 5	Clarke 1954, 54, no. 12
RL13	B.1b	Hd. B No. 6	Clarke 1954, 54, no. 13; pl. xii, in group
RL14	B.1a	Hd. B No. 7	Clarke 1954, 54, no. 14; pl. xii, in group
RL15	B.24	Hd. B No. 4	Clarke 1954, 54, no. 15
R1	B.1d	Hd. B No. 12	Clarke 1954, 55, no. 1; pl. xii, bottom right of group
R2	C.48	Hd. C No. 4	Clarke 1954, 55, no. 2
R3	C.49	Hd. C No. 5	Clarke 1954, 55, no. 3
R4	B/C.64	Hd. B/C No. 10 (Listed as 'Hd. C No. 10' in Clarke 1954, in error)	Clarke 1954, 55, no. 4
R5	B/C.77	Hd. B/C No. 11	Clarke 1954, 55, no. 5
R6	B/C.78	Hd. B/C No. 12	Clarke 1954, 55, no. 6
R7	B/C.82	Hd. B/C No. 13	Clarke 1954, 55, no. 7
R8	B/C.79	Hd. B/C No. 14	Clarke 1954, 55, no. 8
R9	B/C.83	Hd. B/C No. 15	Clarke 1954, 55, no. 9 (pl. xii)
R10	B/C.80	Hd. B/C No. 16	Clarke 1954, 55, no. 10

R11	B.25	Hd. B No. 9	Clarke 1954, 56, no. 11; pl. xii
R12	B.1c	Hd. B No. 10	Clarke 1954, 56, no. 12; pl. xii, in group
R13	B/C.81	Hd. B/C No. 17	Clarke 1954, 56, no. 13
R14	B.1h	Hd. B No. 11	Clarke 1954, 56, no. 14; pl. xii, bottom left of group
R15	C.47	Hd. C No. 6	Clarke 1954, 56, no. 15; pl. xii
R16	D.1b	Hd. D No. 2	Clarke 1954, 56, no. 16; pl. x
SB1	B/C.89	Hd. B/C No. 23	Clarke 1954, 57, no. 1; pl. xiii, lower
SB2	C.54	Hd. C No. 7	Clarke 1954, 57, no. 2; pl. xiii, lower
SB3	C.52–C.53	Hd. C No. 9	Clarke 1954, 57, no. 3; pl. xiii, lower
SB4	B/C.88	Hd. B/C No. 22	Clarke 1954, 57, no. 4; pl. xiii, lower; fig. 8
SB5	C.51	Hd. C No. 8	Clarke 1954, 57, no. 5; pl. xiii, lower
SB6	C.55–C.56	Hd. C No. 10	Clarke 1954, 57, no. 6
SB7	B/C.91–B/C.95	Hd. B/C No. 24	Clarke 1954, 57, no. 7
MC1	B.27	Hd. B No. 1	Clarke 1954, 58 (cake), no. 1; pl. xiii, upper
MC2	B.26	Hd. B No. 2	Clarke 1954, 58 (cake), no. 2; pl. xiii, upper
MC3	C.50	Hd. C No. 11	Clarke 1954, 58 (cake), no. 3; pl. xiii, upper, 3
MC4	C.45	Hd. C No. 2	Clarke 1954, 58 (cake), no. 4; pl. xiii, upper
MC5	C.17	Hd. C No. 15	Clarke 1954, 58 (cake), no. 5
MC6	B/C.85	Hd. B/C No. 18	Clarke 1954, 58 (cake), no. 6; pl. xiii, upper
MC7	B/C.84	Hd. B/C No. 19	Clarke 1954, 58 (cake), no. 7; pl. xiii, upper
MC8	B/C.86	Hd. B/C No. 20	Clarke 1954, 58 (cake), no. 8; pl. xiii, upper
MC9	B/C.87	Hd. B/C No. 21	Clarke 1954, 58 (cake), no. 9; pl. xiii, upper
M1	B.28	Hd. B No. 8	Clarke 1954, 58 (Misc.), no. 1; pl. xiii, lower
M2	B/C.90	Hd. B/C No. 25	Clarke 1954, 58 (Misc.), no. 2; pl. xiii, lower
M3	B.29–33	Hd. B No. 26	Clarke 1954, 58 (Misc.), no. 3
M4	C.57–61	Hd. C No. 1	Clarke 1954, 58 (Misc.), no. 4; fig. 9

Key differences from Clarke's catalogue

In general, although numbers have been standardised and updated, there is a one-to-one concordance between entries in Clarke's catalogue and that in this volume. In certain cases, objects or fragments grouped together by Clarke have been subdivided here, to reflect the fact that they represent separate individual objects. For example, Clarke grouped the nails he believed to be from Hoards B and C under single numbers (Clarke's Hd. B No. 26, Hd. C No. 1), whilst we separate them. In several cases a large number of wire fragments were grouped, which can now be identified as coming from different torcs, based on diameter or construction (e.g. Clarke's Hd. B/C No. 32, where the fragments exhibit different twist directions, or the wires from Hd. B/C No. 46 or Hd. C No. 12, which are of varying diameter). We have also been more cautious than Clarke in grouping fragments of ring or torc wire which may have been deliberately fragmented (e.g. Hd. B No. 3, Hd. C No. 16), or similar/related fragments which may or may not be from the same object (e.g. Clarke's Tubular torc number 4, or Hd. B/C No. 9). This subdivision means that, in some cases, Northover's compositional analyses of the NCM material (which were labelled according to Clarke's listings) can only be assigned to a group of objects falling under a range of catalogue numbers in this volume, not to precise fragments (see Chapter 18 and Appendix 5 for this analytical work).

In a few cases, objects have been grouped differently here from Clarke's catalogue in more significant ways. This is most notable in the case of the buffer terminal torcs from Hoard C, and certain loop and ring terminal torcs from the mixed B/C assemblage.

Clarke identified three buffer terminal torcs (Hd. C Nos 17, 18 and 20) from a number of fragments in Hoard C (four buffer terminals – our C.22, C.26, C.27, C.31 – and one section of neck-ring – our C.25), whilst identifying similar neck-ring fragments without terminals as being from a loop terminal torc (his Hd. C no. 19, our catalogue numbers C.23–C.24, C.28–30). Clarke groups buffer terminals C.22 and C.26 as a pair (his Hd. C No. 17), but these cannot have come from the same torc: C.26 has five wires in its coiled neck-ring, while C.22 has seven. Likewise, Clarke groups buffer terminals C.27 with C.31, but these also have different neck-ring structures. In fact, C.26 and C.27 are a better match, being similar in terms of size, wire diameter and structure. Clarke groups neck-ring fragments C.23–C.24 with C.28–30 (as his loop terminal torc Hd. C no. 19), but C.23–C.24 have different structures both from each other and from C.28–30, bearing a closer relationship to the buffer terminal fragments in some cases.

We group these various fragments differently based on their structures and sizes, and suggest that they come from at least six torcs/bracelets (rather than Clarke's four):

Cat. no. (this volume)	Clarke hoard no.	Structure	Wire diameter/ mm (approx.)	Neck-ring diameter/mm (approx.)	Element(s) present
C.22	Hd. C No. 17	(7C)T	0.8	7.0	Buffer terminal fragment
C.23	Hd. C No. 19	(6C)[3T,3R, alternating]	1.5	5.0	Neck-ring/body fragment
C.24	Hd. C No. 19	(6C)T	1.4	6.0	Neck-ring/body fragment
C.25–7	Hd. C Nos 17, 18, 20	(5C)T	1.2	6.0	Neck-ring/body fragment (C.25), two buffer terminals (C.26–7)
C.28–30	Hd. C No. 19	(5C)T	1.1	4.0	Three neck-ring/body fragments
C.31	Hd. C No. 20	(3P(2P))Q	1.0	6.0	Buffer terminal fragment

Similarly, Clarke grouped a large number of fragments under Hd. B/C No. 31 (his torc LT25), but these can now be demonstrated to be part of a number of different objects, which can more sensibly be grouped in different ways, also incorporating Clarke's Hd. B/C No. 29 (his torc LT23), and Hd. B/C No. 30 (his torc LT24):

Cat. no. (this volume)	Clarke hoard no.	Structure	Wire diameter/ mm (approx.)	Neck-ring diameter/mm (approx.)	Element(s) present
B/C.47–9	Hd. B/C No. 29, 31	(2P(2P))R	1.4	5.5	Neck-ring/body fragment (B/C.49), two ring terminals (B/C.47–8). Corroded, matt surface.
B/C.50–3	Hd. B/C No. 30, 31	(2P(2P))R	1.2	5.0	Two large fragments incorporating loop terminals (B/C.50–1), many additional small neck-ring/body fragments (B/C.52–3). Polished bronze surface, highly worn.
B/C.56	Hd. B/C No. 31	(?C(2P))R	1.0	N/A	Small neck-ring/body fragments, tight coil
B/C.60	Hd. B/C No. 31	(?C(2P))R	1.0	N/A	Small neck-ring/body fragments, loose coil
B/C.61	Hd. B/C No. 31	N/A	1.3	N/A	Possible loop terminal fragment
B/C.62	Hd. B/C No. 31	(?C(3P(2P)))R	1.0	N/A	Small neck-ring/body fragment

The evident challenges in dealing with such complex material emphasise the virtual impossibility of coming up with a firm estimate for the number of objects represented at Snettisham. The close study undertaken for this volume, organising fragments by a wide variety of nested criteria (including material, construction, wire diameter, overall size and form, colour and patina), has allowed us to discern connections and possible joins with more clarity than previously possible. No doubt, further study will continue to find new associations, or suggest different groupings.

Appendix 4
Compositional Analysis of Iron Age Gold Alloy Coins from Snettisham Parish

Matthew Ponting

Introduction

Analysis of 35 gold alloy coins from Snettisham parish was requested by Andrew Burnett, then Keeper of the Coins and Medals Department at the BM, in 1994. The aim of this work was to establish the levels of fineness of the coins, and to determine if any of the pieces were plated.

The report is reproduced here largely in its original form, with the exception of updates to relate the coin typologies used with more recent publications, and the addition of a concordance to this end (**Table A4.2**). The coins analysed are from the BM collection and are predominantly taken from two separate assemblages. Four of the coins are from the BM excavations at Snettisham (cat. nos 235, 239, 247 and 250), and most of the remainder are from a dispersed coin hoard discovered over a number of years a few km to the east (de Jersey 2014, 'Shernborne I and II', 308–10, no. 195, see also Ch. 15). All are local, East Anglian types, likely produced in the second half of the 1st century BC.

The analysis of these gold alloy coins by XRF and EDX-SEM revealed differences in fineness between stylistic groups. Trends in the precious metal components between issues within groups were also found. The base metal component was found to be added as a bronze alloy and similarities are noted between this alloy and that of contemporary potin coinage.

Analytical technique and results

Two analytical techniques were applied to the coins: X-ray fluorescence (XRF) and the energy dispersive analysing facility on a scanning electron microscope (EDX-SEM). For both techniques it was necessary to abrade and then carefully polish a small area on each coin's edge. First silicon carbide paper was used to remove the corrosion products and enriched/depleted layers. The exposed 'heart-metal' of the coin was then polished using successively finer grades of diamond paste down to lμm. The XRF spectrometer used was a Link Systems Model 290 with a molybdenum target X-ray tube operated at 45Kv. This was used to analyse an approximately 1mm^2 area of the polished interior of each coin. The elements sought were gold, silver, copper, tin and lead. The EDX-SEM used was a Jeol JSM-840 with a Link Systems 860 analyser. This was used to image the polished area at a magnification of x350 in order to enable an examination of the metal structure and the selection of sound matrix metal for analysis. Only the three major elements were quantified by this method: gold, silver and copper. Detection limits for the minor elements, lead and tin, are significantly improved on the XRF spectrometer, being in the order of 0.4% for tin and 0.07 % for lead. However, detection limits are not so important for major components whereas problems of heterogeneity and corrosion are. Consequently, the EDX-SEM values for gold, silver and copper were used here, together with the XRF values for lead and tin. The full results are shown in **Table A4.1**. The precision of the EDX-SEM values are approximately ± 1–2% for the major components and ± 10–20% for the XRF values for the minor components. Where an element was not detected in a particular coin a value of less than the detection limit for that analysis has been indicated.

BMRL no.	BM reg. no.	Cat. no. (this volume)	Gold	Silver	Copper	Tin	Lead	Classification
47912t	1991,1017.10	235	16.3	42.4	40.3	<0.4	0.61	Wolf B
47913r	1988,0403.22		12.3	37.2	46.6	3.3	0.65	Wolf C
47914p	1988,0403.23		17.0	42.9	37.0	2.5	0.58	Wolf C
47915y	1988,0403.14		16.7	26.6	52.4	4.0	0.30	Wolf D
47916w	1989,0422.12		13.6	40.6	43.6	1.7	0.48	Wolf D
47917u	1988,0403.24		14.1	37.8	45.0	2.5	0.57	Wolf D
47918s	1991,1018.1	239	20.7	38.8	38.5	1.6	0.29	Wolf D var
47919q	1989,0422.16		12.6	39.2	44.9	2.7	0.66	Wolf E
47920t	1989,0422.5		10.3	35.7	51.5	1.8	0.79	Wolf E
47921r	1989,0422.8		12.8	24.2	57.1	4.3	1.60	Wolf F
47922p	1988,0403.21		15.3	27.8	50.8	5.5	0.65	Wolf F
47923y	1989,0422.11		11.4	29.9	53.4	4.7	0.52	Wolf G
47924w	1988,0403.17		19.6	31.0	40.8	7.8	0.89	Wolf F/G
47925u	1991,1018.5	247	10.0	8.5	75.9	4.5	0.76	Wolf F/G
47926s	1988,0403.19		10.2	27.6	57.0	4.6	0.68	Wolf H
47927q	1991,1018.3	250	13.0	28.8	52.2	5.2	0.95	Wolf H
47928z	1988,0403.30		35.6	38.8	20.5	4.9	0.28	Snettisham A
47929x	1989,0422.25		34.8	35.0	28.2	1.7	0.25	Snettisham A
47930p	1988,0403.33		36.2	33.0	28.2	2.3	0.32	Snettisham B
47931y	1989,0422.26		38.8	30.2	27.0	3.6	0.42	Snettisham B
47932w	1988,0403.39		38.9	34.9	23.9	1.9	0.35	Snettisham C
47933u	1989,0422.30		38.5	31.3	29.1	0.9	0.15	Snettisham C
47934s	1988,0403.41		39.1	33.2	27.1	<0.3	0.25	Snettisham D
47935q	1989,0422.36		38.1	26.6	34.3	0.8	0.18	Snettisham D
47936z	1988,0403.36		31.2	23.7	42.9	1.8	0.38	Snettisham E
47937x	1989,0422.31		39.0	35.3	24.3	1.0	0.32	Snettisham E
47938v	1989,0422.38		37.1	23.8	38.7	<0.3	<0.07	Snettisham F
47939t	1988,0403.28		38.5	36.2	21.7	3.3	0.27	Snettisham A quarter stater
47940w	1989,0422.18		39.7	34.3	23.9	2.0	0.22	Snettisham A quarter stater
47941u	1988,0403.27		36.6	31.0	31.6	0.7	0.13	Snettisham B quarter stater
47942s	1989,0422.24		37.4	31.9	29.7	0.8	0.22	Snettisham B quarter stater
47943q	1989,1120.4		36.8	36.5	23.8	2.6	0.32	Snettisham C quarter stater
47944z	1989,1120.6		37.9	31.3	28.1	2.4	0.28	Snettisham C quarter stater
47945x	1991,1110.33		28.8	22.4	44.8	3.6	0.35	Snettisham C quarter stater
47946v	1989,1120.3		40.0	38.4	19.1	2.4	0.18	Snettisham D quarter stater

Table A4.1 Analytical results from EDX-SEM (gold, silver and copper) and XRF (lead and tin) for gold alloy coins from Snettisham parish. The precision of these analyses is approximately ± 1–2% for the major components and ± 10–20% for the XRF values for the minor components

Discussion

The coins fall into three main groups stylistically: the Snettisham-type staters (*ABC* 1402, 1405, 1408 and 1411), their quarters (*ABC* 1462 and 1465; the latter is Talbot's Early Snettisham-type quarter stater) and the Norfolk Wolf-type staters (*ABC* 1399). The sub-types discussed in this article relate to the groupings published in Hobbs 1996. The Snettisham types are similar to the Whaddon Chase types and can be compared to Allen's British La and Lb types. The Norfolk Wolf types correspond broadly to Allen's British Jb type. Talbot (2017, 8) suggests that Norfolk Wolf coins (part of the series of early local coinage) were minted in 55–15 BC, while the Snettisham types were minted around 15 BC–AD 5.

Compositionally, the Snettisham staters and their quarters are identical, being composed of a ternary alloy of 30–40% gold, 30–40% silver and the remainder predominantly copper. The Norfolk Wolf types are composed of a significantly baser ternary alloy of 10–20% gold, 30–40% silver and the remainder predominantly copper. Both types also contain small but significant amounts of tin and lead. The strong correlation of the tin with the copper suggests that a significant part of the base component of the alloy was added as a premixed bronze alloy. This is particularly apparent with the more debased Norfolk Wolf coins (see **Fig. A4.1**). By running a regression analysis after removing the two aberrant coins (both type F/G (*BMC* 262–7)) we can quantify this apparent association

Terminology used in this appendix	Hobbs (*BMC*)	*ABC*	Talbot (2017)
Wolf B	274–8	1399	Norfolk Wolf B
Wolf C	221–6	1399	
Wolf D	227–49	1399	
Wolf E	253–7	1399	
Wolf F	258–9	1399	
Wolf G	260–1	1399	
Wolf F/G	262–7	1399	
Wolf H	268–73	1399	
Snettisham A	3353–5	1402	Snettisham type
Snettisham B	3356–9	1405	
Snettisham C	3360–4	1408	
Snettisham D	3365–74	1411	
Snettisham E	3375–82	1411	
Snettisham F	3383	1411	
Snettisham quarter A	3420–1	1462	N/A
Snettisham quarter B	3422–6	1462	Snettisham-type quarter stater
Snettisham quarter C	3427–34	1462	
Snettisham quarter D	3435	1465	Early Snettisham-type quarter stater

Table A4.2 Concordance of coin typologies with the terminology used in this appendix (Hobbs (*BMC*) = Hobbs 1996; *ABC* = Cottam *et al.* 2010)

(R^2 value of 60% significant at above the 1% level) and confirm that this is a valid relationship (see regression line in **Fig. A4.1**). Furthermore, the later types (F, G, F/G and H (*BMC* 258–9, 260–1, 262–7 and 268–73 respectively) are noticeably richer in tin and copper (corresponding to an approximately 12–14% tin-bronze) and would therefore agree with the stylistic chronology and a gradual debasement over time. The F/G type coins were excluded from the calculations because their compositions differ obviously from the remainder of the series. However, it is interesting to note that both coins are also stylistically 'odd'. The very base coin (1991,1018.5; cat. no. 247) was initially thought to be a contemporary forgery, and the coin with a high tin content (1988,0403.17) is catalogued as an 'uncertain sub-type' (as Hobbs 1996, 59). Certainly these two coins are different; however, a larger sample would be needed before any firm idea can be gained as to the 'normal' compositional parameters of this series.

The Snettisham-type coins cluster tightly in the ternary plot (**Fig. A4.2**) but there is a suggestion of a chronological debasement through types D, E and F (*ABC* 1411). One type C quarter stater (*BMC* 3433; *ABC* 1462) is particularly base containing nearly twice as much base metal (44.8% copper) as the other two. This coin (1991,1110.33) was an unprovenanced metal-detector find from the Mossop collection purchased in 1991. It is likely that the coin was found in the Snettisham region and there is no reason to doubt its authenticity. However, its composition and light weight (0.98g compared to about 1.1g for others of the series) do mark it out as an inferior coin.

Comparison of the composition of the Snettisham-type staters with that of the Whaddon Chase coins (Allen's British La and Lb types) analysed by similar techniques (Cowell 1992) proved interesting (**Fig. A4.3**). The earlier British La types (*ABC* 2433, 2436, 2439) are markedly finer than either the British Lb type (*ABC* 2338 to 2347, 2442, 2445) or the Snettisham coins, with the gold being diluted primarily with silver rather than copper. In the Lb type both the silver and gold contents are reduced and replaced by copper with the copper content almost matching the silver. The Snettisham types are further debased although the silver and copper contents are not greatly increased. It is the additions of tin and lead which mark the Snettisham coins out as different from the British Lb type. However, two coins analysed by Cowell and listed as 'late' types (1919,0213.90 and 1919,0213.541; *BMC* 346, now classified as *ABC* 2344, and *BMC* 3375, now reclassified as *ABC* 1411, a Snettisham type), have a tin content of 3.7% and 1.8% respectively. These values are consistent with the Snettisham-type coins. This may suggest that the Snettisham types are related to the very latest Lb types, where a significant proportion of the base metal was added as bronze whereas only 'pure' copper had been used previously. If, as is suggested (Cowell 1992, 220), the British L type was produced directly from recycled British A2 type coins (*ABC* 482) plus base metal, we can see a distinct change in alloying practice with the use of a tin bronze. On the basis of the figures presented here, a 12% tin-bronze containing about 2% lead is suggested, which was then added to the gold-silver-copper alloy of the A2-type coinage.

A further interesting relationship is also apparent in the plot of lead against tin for the coins analysed in this study (**Fig. A4.4**). The regression line plotted indicates a significant correlation between these metals (R^2 value of 33% significant at the 1% level) although the relationship becomes more diffuse at high concentrations. It is, however, interesting that there is a higher correlation between the lead and tin than between the lead and silver (R^2 value of 0.2%). This would indicate that the bulk of the lead in these coins is

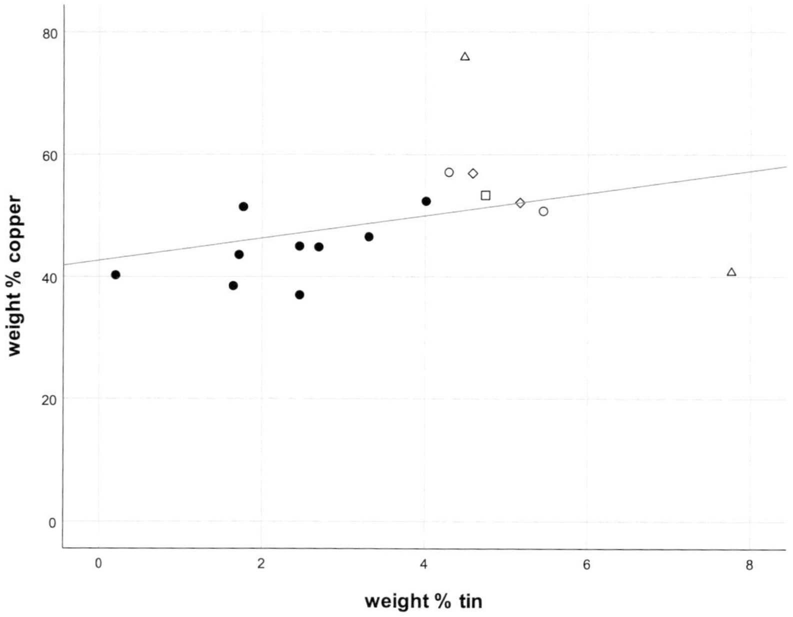

Figure A4.1 Norfolk Wolf-type coins: plot of tin against copper values

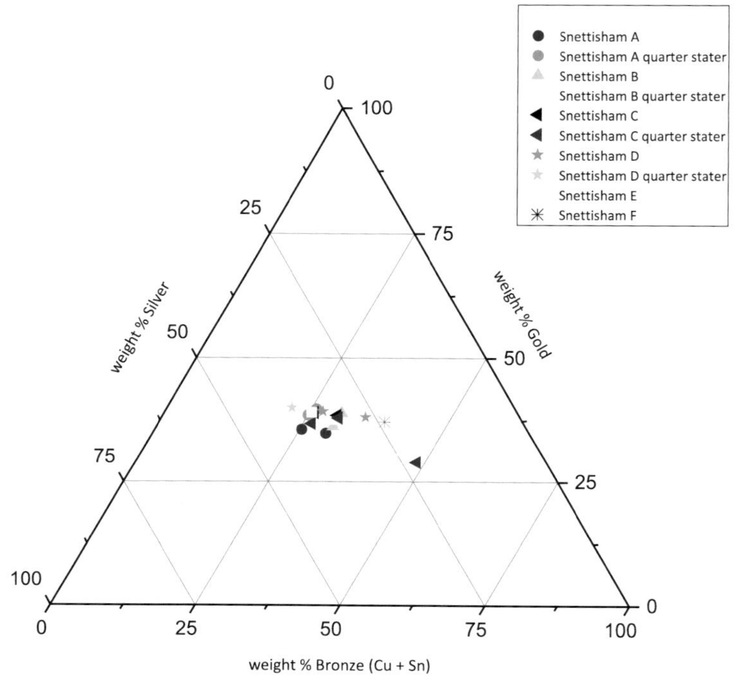

Figure A4.2 Snettisham-type staters and quarter staters by issue: ternary plot of gold, silver and copper/tin

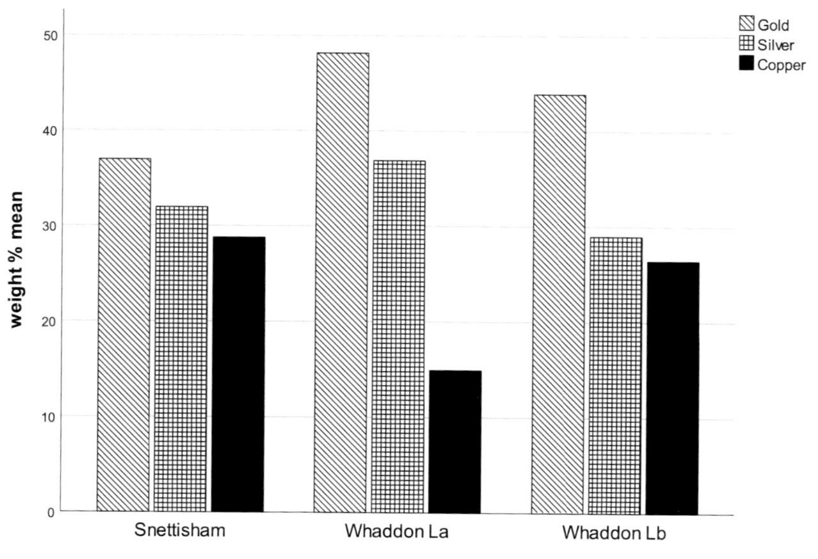

Figure A4.3 Comparison of the metal contents of Snettisham-type coins and British La and Lb types (the latter analysed by Cowell 1992)

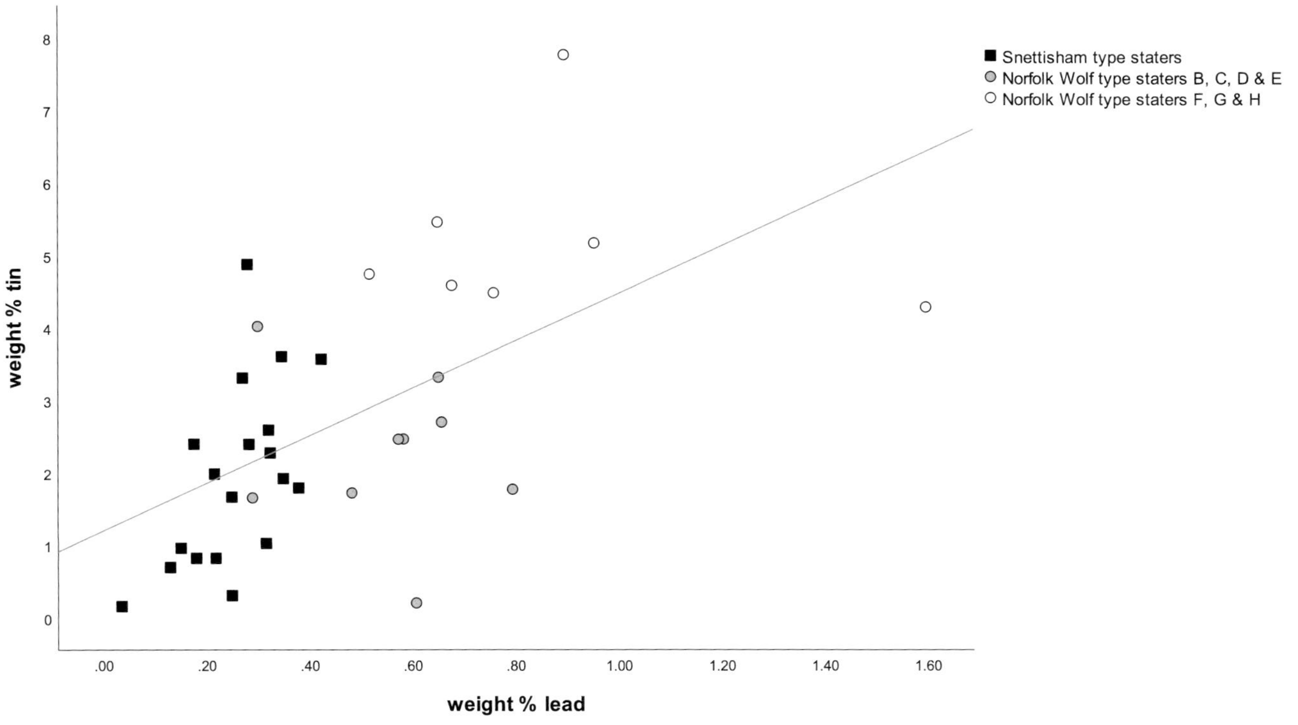

Figure A4.4 Plot of tin against lead values for the coins analysed in this report

associated with the tin rather than with the silver. This is unusual at such low levels, lead being an inevitable by-product of the cupellation process used to refine silver in antiquity. At these levels it seems reasonable to suggest that very little lead was coming from the silver, indicating a very efficient refining technology. The ratio of lead to tin is in the order of 1:5/1:7 for both the Snettisham and Norfolk Wolf types, and it is perhaps interesting to note that this is the same ratio found in the cast potin coins from the Snettisham area. Northover (1992, 247) suggests that a similar alloy to that of this base metal coinage was being used to produce the British Lb and Lc (*ABC* 2240) types and we may be seeing a similar phenomenon here.

Appendix 5
Analysis of Selected Gold and Silver Alloy Objects from Hoards A, B and C and Comparative Material

Peter Northover

In the tables that follow, the sample numbers have two components: 'Batch' (SHMA and SHMB), which groups the samples taken in a given museum visit, and 'No.', which is the number within a batch. NB: Arsenic (As) not analysed in Ag/Au-based alloys.

The Clarke (1954) hoard numbers and inventory numbers are both given, as well as the catalogue numbers from this volume. Due to the complexities of cross-referencing with Clarke's system (see Concordance, Appendix 3a), it has not always been possible to create a one-to-one concordance with the catalogue numbers used in this volume, and thus sometimes a range is given. Two samples were highly corroded; their compositions are given in italics with copper omitted.

Table A5.1 Analysis of gold and silver alloy objects from Snettisham Hoards A, B and C (See Chapter 18 for methods and Figs 18.1–3)

Cat. no.	Sample batch	Sample no.	Clarke cat. no.	Clarke inv. no.	Object type	Component tested	Sn	Sb	Pb	Co	Ni	Fe	Ag	Au	Zn	Bi	Cu
A.2	SHMB	22	Hd. A No. 2	TT2	Torc (tubular)	Torc terminal	0.00	0.00	0.02	0.00	0.00	0.05	12.62	83.01	0.00	0.00	4.30
A.3	SHMB	25	Hd. A No. 3	TT3	Torc (tubular)	Torc terminal	0.00	0.02	0 02	0.00	0.02	0.05	9.13	89.45	0.00	0.00	1.33
A.3	SHMB	23	Hd. A No. 3	TT3	Torc (tubular)	Sheet	0.00	0.00	0.00	0.01	0.01	0.07	12.43	83.00	0.00	0.00	4.49
?A.3	SHMA	7	Hd. A No. 3?	?TT3	Torc (tubular)	Sheet fragment	0.00	0.01	0.00	0.00	0.01	0.07	12.37	83.10	0.00	0.00	4.45
A.4	SHMB	A	Hd. A No. 4	TT4	Torc (tubular)	Gold band on core	0.00	0.00	0.02	0.01	0.01	0.09	6.74	88.76	0.00	0.00	4.38
A.4	SHMB	43	Hd. A No. 4	TT4	Torc (tubular)	Small section of tube	0.00	0.00	0.02	0.01	0.02	0.06	26.55	69.81	0.00	0.00	3.54
A.4	SHMB	42	Hd. A No. 4	TT4	Torc (tubular)	Large section of tube	0.00	0.01	0.01	0.01	0.01	0.05	25.97	69.18	0.00	0.00	4.76
A.5/A.6	SHMB	24	Hd. A No. 4	TT4	Torc (tubular)	Loose terminal	0.00	0.01	0.00	0.01	0.01	0.05	26.35	69.95	0.00	0.00	3.63
B.1a	SHMB	92	Hd. B No. 7	RL14	Ring (large)		0.00	0.00	0.04	0.005	0.01	0.02	52.25	15.22	0.01	0.00	32.45
B.1b	SHMA	27	Hd. B No. 6	RL13	Ring (large)		0.00	0.08	0.07	0.005	0.03	0.02	56.94	11.38	0.00	0.03	31.45
B.1c	SHMB	G	Hd. B No. 10	R1	Ring (small)		0.00	0.00	0.11	0.01	0.01	0.03	59.91	14.61	0.02	0.00	25.31
B.1e	SHMB	63	Hd. B No. 13	LT1	Torc/bracelet (multi-strand, loop terminal)		0.00	0.01	0.00	0.01	0.01	0.03	41.78	49.97	0.00	0.00	8.19
B.1f	SHMA	17	Hd. B No. 15	LT3	Torc/bracelet (multi-strand)		0.00	0.02	0.05	0.01	0.01	0.01	41.18	42.27	0.01	0.01	16.45
B.1g	SHMB	6	Hd. B No. 16	LT4	Torc/bracelet (multi-strand)		0.00	0.00	0.04	0.00	0.00	0.02	44.14	45.61	0.00	0.00	10.19
B.1h	SHMB	94	Hd. B No. 11	R14	Ring (small)		0.00	0.00	0.11	0.00	0.01	0.01	50.26	25.70	0.00	0.00	23.92
B.2	SHMB	10	Hd. B No. 14	LT2	Torc/bracelet (multi-strand)		0.00	0.01	0.02	0.01	0.01	0.12	34.39	52.83	0.01	0.00	12.61
B.3	SHMB	21	Hd. B No. 20	LT8	Torc/bracelet (multi-strand)		0.00	0.01	0.00	0.01	0.01	0.01	21.38	75.51	0.00	0.00	3.08
B.4	SHMB	2	Hd. B No. 19	LT7	Torc/bracelet (multi-strand)		0.00	0.01	0.06	0.01	0.01	0.02	44.20	39.84	0.00	0.00	15.86
B.5	SHMB	9	Hd. B No. 21	LT14	Torc/bracelet (multi-strand, loop terminal)		0.21	0.23	0.24	0.01	0.01	0.01	62.25	4.71	0.00	0.02	32.32
B.6	SHMB	90	Hd. B No. 22	LT15	Wire/?torc/?bracelet		2.68	0.16	0.18	0.01	0.03	0.02	37.77	10.46	0.00	0.00	48.70
B.7	SHMB	5	Hd. B No. 17	LT5	Torc/bracelet (multi-strand)		0.00	0.02	0.16	0.01	0.02	0.01	43.71	25.05	0.00	0.00	31.03
B.8	SHMA	21	Hd. B No. 18	LT6	Bracelet (multi-strand, loop terminal)		0.00	0.00	0.03	0.02	0.02	0.01	44.03	40.54	0.00	0.00	15.36
B.9	SHMB	L	Hd. B No. 24	LT20	Torc/bracelet (multi-strand, loop terminal)		4.92	0.03	0.17	0.02	0.05	0.13	11.39	1.85	0.01	0.00	81.43
B.20	SHMB	H	Hd. B No. 5	RL12	Ring (large)		0.00	0.12	0.05	0.01	0.06	0.01	60.12	0.27	0.01	0.16	39.19
B.24	SHMA	29	Hd. B No. 4	RL15	Ring (large)		0.22	0.03	0.07	0.01	0.03	0.01	29.79	6.24	0.00	0.01	63.61

Cat. no.	Sample batch	Sample no.	Clarke cat. no.	Clarke inv. no.	Object type	Component tested	Sn	Sb	Pb	Co	Ni	Fe	Ag	Au	Zn	Bi	Cu
B.24	SHMA	28	Hd. B No. 4	RL15	Ring (large)		0.23	0.04	0.1	0.01	0.01	0.00	29.30	6.01	0.01	0.00	64.31
B.25	SHMB	95	Hd. B No. 9	R11	Ring (small)		0.41	0.03	0.10	0.00	0.01	0.01	57.64	10.74	0.02	0.00	31.04
B.26	SHMA	32	Hd. B No. 2	MC2	Ingot		0.73	0.02	0.08	0.00	0.01	0.02	32.37	56.26	0.00	0.00	10.51
B.27	SHMB	61	Hd. B No. 1	MC1	Ingot		0.00	0.02	0.02	0.00	0.01	0.01	56.23	16.12	0.00	0.00	27.59
C.1–5, C.21	SHMB	18	Hd. C No. 16	LT12	Torc/bracelet (multi-strand)		0.37	0.04	0.19	0.01	0.01	0.05	62.28	18.33	0.01	0.00	18.72
C.1–5, C.21	SHMB	14	Hd. C No. 16	LT12	Torc/bracelet (multi-strand)		0.94	0.06	0.03	0.00	0.02	0.01	55.36	14.07	0.00	0.02	29.49
C.1–5, C.21	SHMB	O	Hd. C No. 16	LT12	Torc/bracelet (multi-strand)		0.51	0.03	0.23	0.01	0.01	0.01	50.09	12.33	0.00	0.00	36.79
C.6–12, C.15–6, C.18	SHMB	4	Hd. C No. 12	LT9	Rod/wire/?torc/?bracelet		0.00	0.00	0.00	0.01	0.01	0.01	49.95	33.14	0.01	0.00	16.88
C.6–12, C.15–6, C.18	SHMB	8	Hd. C No. 12	LT9	Rod/wire/?torc/?bracelet		0.00	0.00	0.14	0.01	0.02	0.02	49.34	30.73	0.00	0.00	19.74
C.6–12, C.15–6, C.18	SHMB	88	Hd. C No. 12	LT9	Rod/wire/?torc/?bracelet		0.00	0.00	0.14	0.02	0.02	0.02	49.34	30.73	0.00	0.00	19.73
C.6–12, C.15–6, C.18	SHMB	I	Hd. C No. 12	LT9	Rod/wire/?torc/?bracelet		0.00	0.01	0.08	0.01	0.01	0.01	51.40	22.25	0.03	0.00	26.24
C.6–12, C.15–6, C.18	SHMB	J	Hd. C No. 12	LT9	Rod/wire/?torc/?bracelet		0.00	0.01	0.07	0.00	0.01	0.01	51.54	20.31	0.00	0.00	28.06
C.6–12, C.15–6, C.18	SHMB	93	Hd. C No. 12	LT9	Rod/wire/?torc/?bracelet		0.00	0.02	0.07	0.01	0.02	0.01	48.35	20.03	0.00	0.00	31.50
C.6–12, C.15–6, C.18	SHMB	89	Hd. C No. 12	LT9	Rod/wire/?torc/?bracelet		0.03	0.02	0.03	0.01	0.01	0.01	44.26	17.79	0.01	0.00	37.83
C.6–12, C.15–6, C.18	SHMB	91	Hd. C No. 12	LT9	Rod/wire/?torc/?bracelet		0.00	0.01	0.08	0.01	0.02	0.01	46.68	17.14	0.01	0.00	36.04
C.6–12, C.15–6, C.18	SHMB	K	Hd. C No. 12	LT9	Rod/wire/?torc/?bracelet		0.00	0.04	0.08	0.01	0.01	0.02	47.27	14.64	0.01	0.00	37.93
C.13, C.19–20	SHMA	20b	Hd. C No. 14	LT11	Wire/?Torc/?bracelet (multi-strand, ?loop terminal)		0.00	0.03	0.00	0.01	0.02	0.01	35.04	39.85	0.00	0.00	25.04
C.13, C.19–20	SHMA	20a	Hd. C No. 14	LT11	Wire/?Torc/?bracelet (multi-strand, ?loop terminal)		0.00	0.02	0.08	0.01	0.01	0.01	40.77	35.47	0.00	0.00	23.64

Cat. no.	Sample batch	Sample no.	Clarke cat. no.	Clarke inv. no.	Object type	Component tested	Sn	Sb	Pb	Co	Ni	Fe	Ag	Au	Zn	Bi	Cu
C.13, C.19–20	SHMB	C	Hd. C No. 14	LT11	Wire/?Torc/?bracelet (multi-strand, ?loop terminal)		0.00	0.01	0.02	0.00	0.00	0.03	44.18	34.99	0.00	0.00	20.77
C.13, C.19–20	SHMB	87	Hd. C No. 14	LT11	Wire/?Torc/?bracelet (multi-strand, ?loop terminal)		0.01	0.02	0.02	0.00	0.01	0.01	41.72	32.27	0.00	0.00	25.94
C.13, C.19–20	SHMA	19	Hd. C No. 14	LT11	Wire/?Torc/?bracelet (multi-strand, ?loop terminal)		0.00	0.01	0.07	0.00	0.01	0.01	48.04	21.02	0.00	0.00	30.85
C.13, C.19–20	SHMB	88	Hd. C No. 14	LT11	Wire/?Torc/?bracelet (multi-strand, ?loop terminal)		0.00	0.01	0.14	0.00	0.02	0.01	45.90	12.01	0.01	0.00	41.90
C.14	SHMB	F	Hd. C No. 13	LT10	Wire/?torc/?bracelet		1.13	0.04	0.14	0.01	0.02	0.02	52.60	15.64	0.00	0.00	30.41
C.17	SHMB	S	Hd. C No. 15	MC5	Wire/?torc/?bracelet		0.00	0.11	0.02	0.00	0.01	0.02	61.47	29.75	0.00	0.00	8.62
C.17	SHMB	8	Hd. C No. 15	MC5	Wire/?torc/?bracelet		0.00	0.02	0.16	0.01	0.02	0.01	43.71	25.05	0.00	0.00	31.03
C.45	SHMA	31	Hd. C No. 2	MC4	Ring (large)		1.57	0.10	0.23	0.01	0.02	0.02	41.11	8.04	0.00	0.01	48.90
C.46	SHMB	77	Hd. C No. 3	RL1	Ring (large)		6.57	0.15	0.75	0.02	0.11	0.18	3.67	0.81	0.02	0.03	94.26
C.47	SHMB	B	Hd. C No. 6	R15	Ring (small)		0.00	0.00	0.03	0.00	0.01	0.06	22.55	64.57	0.00	0.00	12.78
C.50	SHMB	46	Hd. C No. 11	MC3	Sheet		0.00	0.00	0.02	0.01	0.01	0.02	38.95	58.73	0.00	0.00	2.27
B/C.1	SHMA	23	Hd. B/C No. 26	LT16	Torc/bracelet (multi-strand, loop terminal)		0.55	0.07	0.08	0.01	0.02	0.01	49.18	10.12	0.01	0.00	39.96
B/C.2	SHMA	24	Hd. B/C No. 28	LT18	Torc/bracelet (multi-strand, loop terminal)		1.21	0.04	0.25	0.00	0.01	0.01	81.27	1.78	0.02	0.06	15.36
B/C.3–4	SHMA	30	Hd. B/C No. 53	LT47	Torc/bracelet (multi-strand)		9.34	0.20	0.07	0.30	0.01	0.01	0.22	18.41	3.53	0.00	
B/C.3–4	SHMB	56	Hd. B/C No. 53	LT47	Torc/bracelet (multi-strand)		6.46	0.17	0.04	0.20	0.01	0.01	0.03	13.01	2.23	0.00	
B/C.5	SHMB	36	Hd. B/C No. 50	LT44	Torc/bracelet (multi-strand, loop terminal)		0.00	0.03	0.05	0.01	0.01	0.01	45.22	25.40	0.00	0.00	29.27
B/C.6	SHMA	18	Hd. B/C No. 27	LT17	Wire/torc/bracelet (multi-strand, ?loop terminal)		2.06	0.03	0.27	0.01	0.03	0.03	37.32	5.02	0.00	0.01	55.23
B/C.6	SHMB	59	Hd. B/C No. 27	LT17	Wire/torc/bracelet (multi-strand, ?loop terminal)		1.60	0.04	0.23	0.01	0.02	0.03	28.41	3.26	0.00	0.01	66.39
B/C.7–8	SHMB	T	Hd. B/C No. 42	LT36	Torc/bracelet (multi-strand, loop terminal)		6.90	0.02	0.07	0.02	0.01	0.06	9.31	1.80	0.01	0.00	81.81
B/C.64	SHMB	Q	Hd. B/C No. 10	R4	Ring (small)		5.41	0.04	0.21	0.04	0.03	0.01	10.15	1.81	0.01	0.00	78.97
B/C.84	SHMB	60	Hd. B/C No. 19	MC7	Ingot		0.00	0.01	0.02	0.00	0.01	0.01	46.54	20.94	0.01	0.00	32.47
B/C.85	SHMB	62	Hd. B/C No. 18	MC6	Ingot		0.00	0.03	0.10	0.01	0.02	0.02	48.64	14.64	0.01	0.00	36.54

Cat. no.	Sample batch	Sample no.	Clarke cat. no.	Clarke inv. no.	Object type	Component tested	Sn	Sb	Pb	Co	Ni	Fe	Ag	Au	Zn	Bi	Cu
B/C.86	SHMA	33	Hd. B/C No. 20	MC8	Ingot		2.24	0.11	0.08	0.01	0.09	0.11	27.87	8.41	0.01	0.00	61.08
B/C.87	SHMA	34	Hd. B/C No. 21	MC9	Lump		0.00	0.01	0.01	0.00	0.01	0.01	38.25	40.08	0.00	0.00	21.65
S.16	SHMB	E	N/A	N/A	Torc (multi-strand, ring terminal)		0.76	0.00	0.52	0.06	0.02	0.01	63.69	14.21	0.00	0.00	20.73
S.17	SHMB	86	N/A	N/A	Torc (multi-strand, ring terminal)		2.26	0.07	0.16	0.01	0.04	0.04	30.46	23.05	0.00	0.00	43.91
S.17	SHMB	85	N/A	N/A	Torc (multi-strand, ring terminal)		2.10	0.04	0.13	0.00	0.03	0.01	24.47	20.22	0.00	0.00	53.00
S.18	SHMB	17	N/A	N/A	Torc (multi-strand, loop terminal)		1.07	0.02	0.59	0.01	0.00.	0.02	55.74	0.14	0.01	0.09	42.32
S.31	SHMA	16	N/A	N/A	Torc (multi-strand, loop terminal)		0.00	0.02	0.02	0.01	0.01	0.01	46.92	27.90	0.00	0.01	25.11

Table A5.2 Analysis of comparative gold/silver alloy torcs from other sites

Site	Sample batch	Sample no.	Object type	Component tested	Sn	Sb	Pb	Co	Ni	Fe	Ag	Au	Zn	Bi	Cu
Bawsey, Norfolk, UK (NCM reg. no. 1942.126)	SHME	3	Torc (multi-strand, loop terminal)		0	0	0	0.01	0	0.01	50.78	38.32	0	0	10.88
Bawsey, Norfolk, UK (NCM reg. no. 1944.106)	SHMC	3	Torc (multi-strand, loop terminal)		0.01	0.01	0.09	0.01	0.01	0.02	47.04	21.87	0.01	0	30.93
Hengistbury Head, Dorset, UK	HH	A	Bracelet (multi-strand, loop terminal)	wire	0	0.01	0.01	0.01	0.01	0.01	18.92	78.42	0	0	2.64
Hengistbury Head, Dorset, UK	HH	B	Torc (multi-strand, buffer terminal)	wire	0	0	0	0.01	0.01	0.01	46.31	44.32	0	0	9.38
Mailly-le-Camp, France	MAN	23	Torc (tubular)	tube	0	0	0.04	0.01	0	0.08	4.25	93.92	0	0	1.71
Netherurd, Tweeddale, UK (National Museums Scotland)	SHME	4	Torc (torus terminal)	terminal	0	0.01	0	0.01	0	0.03	25.21	70.03	0	0	4.72
North Creake, Norfolk, UK (NCM reg. no. 1949.97)	SHMC	1	Torc (torus terminal)	terminal, interior	1.85	0.02	0.18	0	0.02	0.04	31.76	14.17	0	0	51.96
North Creake, Norfolk, UK (NCM reg. no. 1949.97)	SHMC	2	Torc (torus terminal)	terminal, exterior	0.17	0.02	0.08	0.01	0.01	0.02	43.95	19.32	0.01	0	36.42
Ulceby, Lincolnshire, UK (Ashmolean Museum Reg. No. 1927.6659)	SHMR	2	Torc (multi-strand, loop terminal)		0	0	0	0.01	0.01	0.01	41.77	30.37	0	0	27.84
Ulceby, Lincolnshire, UK (Ashmolean Museum Reg. No. 1927.6660)	SHME	1	Torc (multi-strand, loop terminal)		0	0.01	0.07	0	0.01	0.04	49.48	28.95	0.01	0	21.44

Bibliography

Note that web references where given were correct and accessible in May 2024.

Aarts, J. 2005. 'Coins, money and exchange in the Roman world. A cultural-economic perspective', *Archaeological Dialogues* 12(1): 1–28.

ACBMG 2002. *Ceramic Building Material. Minimum Standards for Recovery, Curation, Analysis and Publication* (http://www.archaeologicalceramics.com/uploads/1/1/9/3/11935072/ceramic_building_material_guidelines.pdf).

Adams, S. 2014. 'The first brooches in Britain: from manufacture to deposition in the Early and Middle Iron Age', unpublished PhD thesis, University of Leicester.

Adams, S. 2020. 'The brooches', in T. Moore (ed.), *A Biography of Power. Research and Excavations at the Iron Age 'oppidum' of Bagendon, Gloucestershire (1979–2017)*, Oxford, 245–61.

Adams, S. Craddock, P., Hook, D., La Niece, S., Meeks, N., O'Flynn, D. and Perucchetti, L. 2024. 'The Pulborough torc: a fourth to third century BCE artefact of European significance', *Internet Archaeology* 67.

Aines, E. 2019. 'The memory of a forgotten landscape: a socio-topographical inquiry into the remains of Later Prehistoric Norfolk', unpublished PhD thesis, University of Cambridge (https://doi.org/10.17863/CAM.56773).

Albone, J., Massey, S. and Tremlett, S. 2007. *The Archaeology of Norfolk's Coastal Zone. Results of the National Mapping Programme* (https://research.historicengland.org.uk/Report.aspx?i=15700&ru=%2fResults.aspx%3fp%3d1%26n%3d10%26a%3d4914%26ns%3d1).

Aldhouse-Green, M. 2006. *Boudica Britannia*, London.

Alexandropoulos, J. 2007. *Les monnaies de l'Afrique antique 400 av. J.-C. – 40 ap. J.-C.* Toulouse.

Allason-Jones, L. and Roger, M. 1984. *The Catalogue of Small Finds from South Shields Roman Fort*, Newcastle upon Tyne.

Allen, D.F. 1938. 'British tin coinage of the Iron Age', in J. Allan, H. Mattingly and E. Robinson (eds), *Transactions of the International Numismatic Congress, 1936* (London), 351–7.

Allen, D. 1958. 'Belgic coins as illustrations of life in the late pre-Roman Iron Age of Britain', *Proceedings of the Prehistoric Society* 24: 43–63.

Allen, D.F. 1960. 'The origins of coinage in Britain: a reappraisal', in S.S. Frere (ed.), *Problems of the Iron Age in Southern Britain*, London, 97–308.

Allen, D.F. 1971. 'British potin coins; a review', in M. Jesson and D. Hill (eds), *The Iron Age and its Hill-Forts*, Southampton, 127–54.

Allen, T.G. and Robinson, M.A. 1993. *The Prehistoric and Iron Age Enclosed Settlement at Mingies Ditch; Hardwick-with-Yelford, Oxfordshire*, Thames Valley Landscapes: The Windrush Valley vol. 2, Oxford.

Andrews, G. 1985. 'The coarse wares', in J. Hinchliffe with C. Sparey Green, *Excavations at Brancaster 1974 and 1977*, East Anglian Archaeology 23, Dereham, 82–116.

Andrews, P., Biddulph, E., Hardy, A. and Brown, R. 2011. *Settling the Ebbsfleet Valley: High Speed 1 Excavations at Springhead and Northfleet, Kent. The Late Iron Age, Roman, Saxon and Medieval Landscape. Vol 1: The Sites*, Oxford Wessex Archaeology Monograph, Oxford and Salisbury.

Anon. 1886. 'Description of plates illustrating Hamdon Hill relics', *Proceedings of the Somerset Archaeological and Natural History Society* 32: 81–3.

Anon. 1960. *Sotheby Sales Catalogue Monday 11th April 1960*, London.

Anon. 1973. *Oxford English Dictionary* (2nd edn), Oxford.

Anon. 1980. *Treasures of the University of Manchester*, Manchester.

Anon. 1994. *Christie's Fine Antiquities Sale Catalogue, Wednesday 7th December 1990*, London.

Anon. 1996. 'Celtic gold terminal makes history', *Treasure Hunting* (May 1996): 18.

Anon. 1997. 'Archaeology in Suffolk 1996', *Proceedings of the Suffolk Institute of Archaeology and History* 39(1): 77–104.

Appadurai, A. 1986. 'Introduction: commodities and the politics of value', in A. Appadurai (ed.), *The Social Life of Things: Commodities in Cultural Perspective*, Cambridge, 3–63.

Armit, I. 2012. *Headhunting and the Body in Iron Age Europe*, Cambridge.

Armstrong, E.C.R. 1920. *Catalogue of Irish Gold Ornaments in the Collection of the Royal Irish Academy*, Dublin.

Arwill-Nordbladh, E. 2002. 'Re-arranging history: the contested bones of the Osberg Grave', in Hamilakis *et al.* 2002b, 201–16.

Ashwin, T. and Bates, S. 2000. *Excavations on the Norwich Southern By-pass, 1989–91*, East Anglian Archaeology 91, Gressenhall.

Ashwin, T. and Flitcroft, M. 1999. 'The Launditch and its setting', *Norfolk Archaeology* 43 Part II: 217–57.

Atkinson, M.D. and Atkinson, E. 2002. '*Sambucus nigra* L', *Journal of Ecology* 90: 895–923.

Bachand, H., Joyce, R.A. and Hendon, J.A. 2003. 'Bodies moving in space: ancient Mesoamerican human sculpture and embodiment', *Cambridge Archaeological Journal* 13(2): 238–47.

Bailey, D. 2008. 'The corporeal politics of being in the Neolithic', in Borić and Robb 2008a, 9–18.

Bailey, M. 1988. 'The rabbit and the medieval East Anglian economy', *The Agricultural History Review* 36(1): 1–20.

Baldwin, A. and Joy, J. 2017. *A Celtic Feast: The Iron Age Cauldrons from Chiseldon, Wiltshire*, British Museum Research Publication 203, London.

Ball, P. 2015. 'Flowing rivers of mercury', *Chemistry World*, 7 January 2015.

Barclay, A., Knight, D., Booth, P., Evans, J., Brown, D.H. and Wood, I. 2016. *A Standard for Pottery Studies in Archaeology*, London.

Barnes, G. and Williamson, T. 2015. *Rethinking Ancient Woodland. The Archaeology and History of Woods in Norfolk*, Studies in Regional and Local History vol. 13, Hatfield.

Barnes, I. 2023. 'Hunsbury Hillfort, Northampton: a typological and metallurgical stidy of the non-ferrous metalwork', *Northamptonshire Archaeology* 42: 7–54.

Barrett, J., Woodward, A. and Freeman, P. 2000. *Cadbury Castle Somerset: The Later Prehistoric and Early Historic Archaeology*, London.

Barry, A. 2005. 'Pharmaceutical matters: the invention of informed materials', *Theory, Culture and Society* 22(1): 51–69.

Barton, C. and Hitchcock, F. 2008. *Treasure Annual Report 2005/6*, London.

Basketry and Beyond 2012. *Heritage of Basketry in the South West of England. Willow for Basket Making and Structures* (http://www.basketryandbeyond.org.uk/willow-basketmaking-structures/).

Bass, G.F. 2005. 'Cargo from the age of bronze: Cape Gelidonya, Turkey', in G.F. Bass (ed.), *Beneath the Seven Seas*, New York and London, 48–55.

Bayley J., Crossley, D. and Ponting, M. 2008. *Metals and Metalworking: A Research Framework for Archaeometallurgy*, London.

Becker, K. 2008. 'Iron Age ring-headed pins in Ireland and Britain and on the Continent', *Archaeologisches Korrespondenzblatt* 38(4): 513–20.

Bennett, J. 2010. *Vibrant Matter: A Political Ecology of Things*, Durham, NC.

Bensaude-Vincent, B. and Stengers, I. 1996. *A History of Chemistry*, Cambridge, MA.

Besly, E.M. and Bland, R.F. 1983. *The Cunetio Treasure: Roman Coinage of the Third Century*, London.

Beswick, P., Megaw, M.R., Megaw, J.V.S. and Northover, P. 1990. 'A decorated Late Iron Age torc from Dinnington, South Yorkshire', *The Antiquaries Journal* 70: 16–33.

Biel, J. 1985. *Der Keltenfürst von Hochdorf: Katalog zur Ausstellung Stuttgart, Kunstgebäude vom 14 August bis 13 Oktober 1985*, Stuttgart.

Bingley, R. 2015. 'The West Tilbury torc: a confirmatory note', *Panorama: The Journal of the Thurrock Local History Society* 53: 70–6.

Birch, S. 1846. 'On the torc of the Celts', *Archaeological Journal* 2: 27–38.

Bishop, M.C. and Coulston, J.C.N. 1993. *Roman Military Equipment: From The Punic War To The Fall Of Rome*, London.

Blakelock, E.S. 2016. 'Never judge a gold object by its surface analysis: a study of surface phenomena in a selection of gold objects from the Staffordshire Hoard', *Archaeometry* 58 (6): 912–29.

Bland, R., Chadwick, A., Ghey, E., Haselgrove, C. and Mattingly, D.J. 2020. *Iron Age and Roman Coin Hoards in Britain*, Oxford.

Bloch, M. and Parry, J. 1989. 'Introduction: money and the morality of exchange', in J. Parry and M. Bloch (eds), *Money and the Morality of Exchange*, Cambridge, 1–32.

Bliss, A. 2020. 'Re-appraising and re-classifying: a new look at the corpus of miniature socketed axes from Britain', *Hampshire Studies 2020: Proceedings of the Hampshire Field Club & Archaeology Society* 75(1): 1–28.

Bohannan, P. 1959. 'The impact of money on an African subsistence economy', *Journal of Economic History* 19: 491–503.

Bonanno, A. 1976. *Roman Relief Portraiture to Septimus Severus*, British Archaeological Reports Suppl. Series 6.

Boon, G.C. 1988. 'Counterfeit coins in Roman Britain', in P.J. Casey and R. Reece (eds.) *Coins and the Archaeologist*, London, 102–88.

Borić, D. and Robb, J. 2008a. *Past Bodies: Body-Centred Research in Archaeology*, Oxford.

Borić, D. and Robb, J. 2008b. 'Body theory in archaeology', in Borić and Robb 2008a, 1–7.

Borić, D., Harris, O.J.T., Miracle, P. and Robb, J. 2013. 'The limits of the body', in Robb and Harris 2013, 32–63.

Botanical Society of Britain & Ireland [accessed 2018]. *Mapping the Flora of the British Isles* (https://bsbi.org/maps-and-data).

Bottini, A. 1988. *Antike Helme: Sammlung Lipperheide und andere Bestände des Antikenmuseums Berlin*, Mainz.

Bourdieu, P. 1977. *Outline of a Theory of Practice*, Cambridge.

Bozzolo, N. and Bernacki, M. 2020. 'Viewpoint on the formation and evolution of annealing twins during thermomechanical processing of FCC metals and alloys', *Metallurgical and Materials Transactions* 51: 2665–84.

Bradley, R. 1990. *The Passage of Arms. An Archaeological Analysis of Prehistoric Hoards and Votive Deposits*, Cambridge.

Bradley, R. 1996. 'Hoards and hoarding', in B.M. Fagan (ed.), *The Oxford Companion to Archaeology*, Oxford, 305–7.

Bradley, R. 2005. *Ritual and Domestic Life in Prehistoric Europe*, London.

Bradley, R. 2009. *Image and Audience: Rethinking Prehistoric Art*, Oxford.

Bradley, R. 2013. 'Hoards and the deposition of metalwork', in H. Fokkens and A. Harding (eds), *The Oxford Handbook of the European Bronze Age*, Oxford, 121–39.

Brailsford, J.W. 1951. 'The Snettisham Treasure', *The British Museum Quarterly* 16(3): 79–80.

Brailsford, J.W. 1962. 'Antiquities from Hod Hill in the Durden Collection', London.

Brailsford, J.W. 1968. 'A hoard of early Iron Age gold torcs from Ipswich', *Proceedings of the Suffolk Institute of Archaeology* 31(2): 158–9.

Brailsford, J.W. 1971. 'The Sedgeford Torc', *The British Museum Quarterly* 35(1): 16–19.

Brailsford J.W. 1975a. *Early Celtic Masterpieces from Britain in the British Museum*, London.

Brailsford, J.W. 1975b. 'The Polden Hill Hoard, Somerset', *Proceedings of the Prehistoric Society* 41: 222–34.

Brailsford, J. and Stapley, J.E. 1972. 'The Ipswich torcs', *Proceedings of the Prehistoric Society* 38: 219–34.

Brennand, M. 2004. 'Archaeological background and aerial photography', in A. Lyons (ed.), *Romano-British Industrial Activity at Snettisham, Norfolk*, East Anglian Archaeology Occasional Paper 18, 2–5.

Briggs, S. 2014. 'The Torrs *Chamfrain* of Hear-piece: restoring "A very curious relic of antiquity"', in C. Gosden, S. Crawford and K. Ulmschneider (eds), *Celtic Art in Europe: Making Connections*, Oxford, 341–55.

Britnell, W. 1976. 'Antler cheekpieces of the British Late Bronze Age', *The Antiquaries Journal* 56(1): 24–34.

Brittain, M. and Harris, O. 2010. 'Enchaining arguments and fragmenting assumptions: reconsidering the fragmentation debate in archaeology', *World Archaeology* 42(4): 581–94.

Bronk Ramsey, C. 2009. 'Bayesian analysis of radiocarbon dates', *Radiocarbon* 51(1): 337–60.

Brück, J. 1999. 'Ritual and rationality: some problems of interpretation in European archaeology', *European Journal of Archaeology* 2(3): 313–44.

Brudenell, M., 2012. 'Pots, practice and society: an investigation of pattern and variability in the post-Deverel Rimbury ceramic tradition of East Anglia', unpublished PhD thesis, York University.

Brudenell, M. and Cooper, A. 2008. 'Post-middenism: depositional histories on later Bronze Age settlements at Broom, Bedfordshire', *Oxford Journal of Archaeology* 27(1): 15–36.

Buckley, G.P. (ed.) 1992. *Ecology and Management of Coppice Woodlands*, London.

Bullen, R.A. 1912. *Harlyn Bay and the Discovery of its Prehistoric Remains* (3rd edn), Harlyn Bay.

Bulleid, A. and Gray, H. 1911. *The Glastonbury Lake Village, vol. 1*, Glastonbury.

Bulleid, A. and Gray, H. 1917. *The Glastonbury Lake Village, vol. 2*, Glastonbury.

Bunbury, H. 1834. 'Roman and British antiquities discovered at Mildenhall, in Suffolk', *Archaeologia* 31: 609–12.

Burleigh, G. R. 1982. 'Excavations at Baldock 1980–81: an interim report', *Hertfordshire Past* 12, 3–18.

Burnett, A.M. 1986. 'Scole, Norfolk, Treasure Trove', in *Coin Hoards from Roman Britain*, VI (British Museum Occasional Paper 58), 7–12.

Burns, J.E. 1971. 'Additional torcs from Snettisham, Norfolk', *Proceedings of the Prehistoric Society* 37: 228–9.

Busby, C. 1997. 'Permeable and partible person: a comparative analysis of gender and body in South India and Melanesia', *The Journal of the Royal Anthropological Institute* 3(2): 261–78.

Bushe-Fox, J.P. 1915. *Excavations at Hengistbury Head, Hampshire in 1911–12*, London.

Butler, J. 1990. *Gender Trouble: Feminism and the Subversion of Identity*, London.

Butler, J. 1993. *Bodies that Matter: On the Discursive Limits of 'Sex'*, London.

Caldwell, D.H., Ewart, G., Triscott, J., Cullen, I.S., Franklin, J.A. Hunter, F. and Paterson, L. 1998. 'Auldhill, Portencross', *Archaeological Journal* 155(1): 22–81.

Camurçuoglu, D., Hockey, M. and Shearman, F. 2013. 'The Hallaton Helmet: excavation and reconstruction of a unique assemblage', in *Proceedings of the ICOM Committee for Conservation Metals Working Group*, Edinburgh.

Caple, C. 2010. 'Ancestor artefacts – ancestor materials', *Oxford Journal of Archaeology* 29(3): 305–18.

Carroll, M. and Lang, A. 2008. 'The Iron Age', in R. Adkins, L. Adkins and V. Leitch (eds), *The Handbook of British Archaeology*, London, 94–133.

Carson, R.A.G. 1950. 'A hoard of British "tin" coins from Sunbury-on-Thames', *Numismatic Chronicle* (Series 6) 10, 148–9.

Cartwright, C.R. 2015. 'The principles, procedures and pitfalls in identifying archaeological and historical wood samples', *Annals of Botany* 116(1): 1–13.

Cartwright, C.R., Meeks, N.D., Hook, D.R., Mongiatti, A. and Joy, J. 2012. 'Organic cores from the Iron Age Snettisham torc hoard: technological insights revealed by scanning electron microscopy', in N.D. Meeks, C.R. Cartwright, A. Meek and A. Mongiatti (eds), *SEM and Microanalysis in the Study of Historical Technology, Materials and Conservation*, London, 21–9.

Chadburn, A. 1990. 'A hoard of Iron Age silver coins from Fring, Norfolk, and some observations on the Icenian coin series', *British Numismatic Journal* 60: 1–12.

Chadburn, A. 2006. 'Aspects of the Iron Age coinages of northern East Anglia with especial reference to hoards', unpublished PhD dissertation, University of Nottingham.

Changsun Moon and Naksoo Kim 2012. 'Analysis of wire-drawing process with friction and thermal conditions obtained by inverse engineering', *Journal of Mechanical Science and Technology* 26 (9): 2903–911.

Chapman, A. 1998. 'Blackmills, Northampton: an early Iron Age torc', *Current Archaeology* 159: 92–5.

Chapman, A. 2000. 'Excavation of an Iron Age settlement and a middle Saxon cemetery at Great Houghton, Northampton, 1996', *Northampton Archaeology* 29: 6–41.

Chapman, J. 2000. *Fragmentation in Archaeology: People, Places and Broken Objects in the Prehistory of South Eastern Europe*, London.

Chapman, A. 2000–1. 'Excavation of an Iron Age Settlement and a Middle Saxon Cemetery at Great Houghton, Northampton, 1996', *Northamptonshire Archaeology* 29: 1–41.

Chapman, J. and Gaydarska, B. 2007. *Parts and Wholes: Fragmentation in Prehistoric Context*, Oxford.

Chirikure, S. and Painter, S. 2002. *A Metallurgical Investigation of Metalworking Remains from Snettisham, Norfolk*, English Heritage report 50/2002, London.

Chittock, H. 2014. 'Arts and crafts in Iron Age Britain: reconsidering the aesthetic effects of weaving combs', *Oxford Journal of Archaeology* 33(3): 313–26.

Chowne, P., Cleal, R.M.J. and Fitzpatrick, A.P. 2001. *Excavations at Billingborough, Lincolnshire, 1975–8: A Bronze-Iron Age Settlement and Salt-working Site*, East Anglian Archaeology 94, Salisbury.

Clark, J.G.D. 1934. 'Derivative forms of the Petit Tranchet in Britain', *Archaeological Journal* 91: 32–58.

Clark, J.G.D, Higgs, E.S. and Longworth, I.H. 1960. 'Excavations at the Neolithic site at Hurst Fen, Mildenhall, Suffolk (1954, 1957 and 1958)', *Proceedings of the Prehistoric Society* 26: 202–45.

Clark, J.G.D. and Fell, C.I. 1953. 'The Early Iron Age site of

Micklemoor Hill, West Harling, Norfolk, and its pottery', *Proceedings of the Prehistoric Society* 29: 1–40.
Clarke, D.V. 1971. 'Small finds in the Atlantic province: problems of approach', *Scottish Archaeological Forum* 3: 22–54.
Clarke, R.R. 1939. 'The Iron Age in Norfolk and Suffolk', *Archaeological Journal* 96: 1–113.
Clarke, R.R. 1950. 'Note on recent archaeological discoveries in Norfolk (1943–8)', *Norfolk Archaeology* 30: 156–9.
Clarke, R.R. 1951a. 'A Celtic torc-terminal from North Creake, Norfolk', *Archaeological Journal* 106: 59–61.
Clarke, R.R. 1951b. 'A hoard of metalwork of the early Iron Age from Ringstead, Norfolk', *Proceedings of the Prehistoric Society* 17: 214–25.
Clarke, R.R. 1951c. 'Notes on recent archaeological discoveries in Norfolk 1943–8', *Norfolk Archaeology* 30: 56–9.
Clarke, R.R. 1954. 'The early Iron Age treasure from Snettisham, Norfolk', *Proceedings of the Prehistoric Society* 20: 27–86.
Clark, J.G.D. and Fell, C.I. 1953. 'The Early Iron Age Site at Micklemoor Hill, West Harling, Norfolk', *Proceedings of the Prehistoric Society* 19, 1–40.
Clarke, R.R. and Hawkes, C.F.C. 1956. 'An iron anthropoid sword from Shouldham, Norfolk with related continental and British weapons', *Proceedings of the Prehistoric Society* 21: 198–227.
Cottam, E., de Jersey, P., Rudd, C. and Sills, J. 2010. *Ancient British Coins*, Aylsham, Norfolk.
Cowell, M.R. 1992. 'An analytical survey of the British Celtic gold coinage', in M. May (ed.), *Celtic Coinage: Britain and Beyond*, BAR British Series 222, Oxford, 207–33.
Craddock, P.T. 2014. 'Refractories with a purpose II: ceramics for casting', *The Old Potter's Almanack* 19(1): 2–17.
Craddock, P.T., Cowell, M. and Stead, I. 2004. 'Britain's first brass', *Antiquaries Journal* 84: 339–46.
Craddock, P.T., Gurney, D., Pryor, F. and Hughes, M.J. 1985. 'The application of phosphate analysis to the location and interpretation of archaeological sites', *Archaeological Journal* 142: 361–76.
Crawford, M.H. 1974. *Roman Republican Coinage*, Cambridge.
Creighton, J. 2000. *Coins and Power in Late Iron Age Britain*, Cambridge.
Creighton, J. 2006. *Britannia: The Creation of a Roman Province*, London.
Cretu, C. and Van der Lingen, E. 1999. 'Coloured gold alloys', *Gold Bulletin* 32 (4): 115–26.
Cronyn, J.M. 1990. *The Elements of Archaeological Conservation*, London.
Crummy, N. 1983. *The Roman Small Finds from Excavations in Colchester, 1971–9*, Colchester Archaeology Report 2, Colchester.
Crummy, N. and Eckardt, H. 2008. *Styling the Body in Late Iron Age and Roman Britain: A Contextual Approach to Toilet Instruments*, Instrumentum Monograph no. 36, Montagnac.
Csordas, T.J. 1994. 'Introduction: the body as representation and being-in-the-world', in T.J. Csordas (ed.), *Embodiment and Experience: The Existential Ground of Culture and Self*, Cambridge, 1–24.
Cuming, H.S. 1859. 'On Celtic antiquities exhumed in Lincolnshire and Dorsetshire', *Journal of the British Archaeological Association* 25: 225–30.
Cunliffe, B. 1978. *Hengistbury Head*, London.
Cunliffe, B. 1984. *Danebury and Iron Age Hillfort in Hampshire. Volume 2: The Excavations 1969–1978: The Finds*, Council for British Archaeology Research Report No. 52, London.
Cunliffe, B. 1987. *Hengistbury Head, Dorset. Volume 1: The Prehistoric and Roman Settlement, 3500 BC – AD 500*, Oxford University Committee for Archaeology Monograph no. 13, Oxford.
Cunliffe, B. 1988. *Mountbatten, Plymouth: A Prehistoric and Roman Port*, Oxford.
Cunliffe, B. 1991. *Iron Age Communities in Britain* (3rd edn), London.
Cunliffe, B. 1993. 'Pits, preconceptions and propitiation in the British Iron Age', *Oxford Journal of Archaeology* 11(1): 69–83.
Cunliffe, B. 1995. *Iron Age Britain*, London.
Cunliffe, B. 2005. *Iron Age Communities in Britain* (4th edn), London.
Davey, J. 2020. 'Initial findings on unidentified moustache objects using PAS data', *Later Prehistoric Finds Group Newsletter* no. 16 (Winter 2020): 12–17.
Davies, D., Dennis, M. and Thirkettle, R. 2004. 'A hoard of Iron Age coins discovered at Sedgeford, 2003', *Norfolk Archaeology* 44(3): 538–40.
Davies, J. 1996. 'Where eagles dare: the Iron Age of Norfolk', *Proceedings of the Prehistoric Society* 62: 63–92.
Davies, J. 1999. 'Patterns, power and political progress in Iron Age Norfolk', in Davies and Williamson 1999, 14–43.
Davies, J. 2008. *The Land of Boudica: Prehistoric and Roman Norfolk*, Oxford.
Davies, J. 2011. 'Boars, bulls, and Norfolk's Celtic menagerie', in J. Davies (ed.), *The Iron Age in Northern East Anglia: New Work in the Land of the Iceni*, Oxford, 59–68.
Davies, J. and Williamson, T. (eds) 1999. *Land of the Iceni: The Iron Age in Northern East Anglia*, Norwich.
Davis, M. and Gwilt, A. 2008. 'Material, style and identity in first century AD metalwork, with particular reference to the Severn Sisters hoard', in D. Garrow, C. Gosden and J.D. Hill (eds), *Rethinking Celtic Art*, Oxford, 146–84.
Davis, S.J.M. 1987. *The Archaeology of Animals*, London.
de Bootman, M. and Lyons, A. 2021. 'Mortaria production at Pentney, in the Lower Nar Valley, West Norfolk', *Journal of Roman Pottery Studies* 18.
de Jersey, P. 2014. *Coin Hoards in Iron Age Britain*, London.
de Jersey, P.J. 2014. *Coin Hoards from Iron Age Britain*, British Numismatic Society Special Publication 12, London.
de Navarro, J.M. 1952. 'The Celts in Britain and their art', in M. Charlesworth and M. Knowles (eds), *The Heritage of Early Britain*, London, 56–82.
Delestrée, L.-P. and Tache, M. 2002–8. *Nouvel Atlas des Monnaies Gauloises* (4 vols), St Germain-en-Laye.
Dennis, M. 2005. 'Silver in Late Iron Age and Early Roman East Anglia', unpublished doctoral thesis, Oxford University.
Dennis, M. and Faulkner, N. 2004. *The Sedgeford Hoard*, Stroud.
Dietrich, O. 2014. 'Learning from "scrap" about Late Bronze Age hoarding practices: a biographical approach to individual acts of dedication in large metal hoards of the Carpathian Basin', *European Journal of Archaeology* 17(3): 468–86.
Dixon, K.A. 1957. 'Systematic cordage structure analysis', *American Anthropologist* 59(1): 134–6.
Dolley, R.H.M. 1954. 'Appendix: the speculum ('tin') coins in Hoard C', in R.R. Clarke, 'The early Iron Age treasure from Snettisham, Norfolk', *Proceedings of the Prehistoric Society* 20: 72–84.
Drazin, A. 2015. 'Preface: materials transformations', in Drazin and Küchler 2015, xvi–xxviii.
Drazin, A. and Küchler, S. (eds) 2015. *The Social Life of Materials: Studies in Material and Society*, London.
Drewett, P. 1982. 'Later Bronze Age downlands economy and excavations at Black Patch, East Sussex', *Proceedings of the Prehistoric Society* 48: 321–400.
Driesch, A. von den 1976. 'A guide to the measurement of animal bones from archaeological sites', *Harvard University Peabody Museum Bulletin 1*, Cambridge, MA.

Driesch, A. von den and Boessneck, J. 1974. 'Kritsche Anmerkungen zue Widerristhohenberechnung aus langenmassen vor-und fruhgeschtlicher Tierknochen', *Saugetierkundliche Mitteilungen* 22: 325–48.

Drury, P.J. 1978. *Excavations at Little Waltham 1970–71*, Chelmsford Excavation Committee Report 1, Chelmsford.

Dugmore, M.M. and DesForges, C.D. 1979. 'Stress corrosion in gold alloys', *Gold Bulletin*, 12(4): 140–4.

Dunbar, E., Cook, G.T., Naysmith, P., Tripney, B.G. and Xu, S. 2016. 'AMS ^{14}C dating at the Scottish Universities Environmental Research Centre (SUERC) Radiocarbon Dating Laboratory', *Radiocarbon* 58(01), 9–23.

Earle, T. 2011. 'Chiefs, chieftaincies, chiefdoms, and chiefly confederacies: power in the evolution of political systems', *Social Evolution and History* 10: 27–54.

Echt, R. 1999. *Das Furstinnengrab von Reinheim: Studien zur Kulturgeschichte der Fruh-La-Tene-Zeit (Saarbrucker Beitrage zur Altertumskunde)*, Bonn.

Ellis, H. 1849. 'Account of a gold torquois found in Needwood Forest in Staffordshire', *Archaeologia* 33: 175–6.

Ellis, R.L. 2020. 'Seen but not "herd": animals in La Tène art in England and Wales', in K. Kearcher *et al.* (eds), *New Frontiers in Archaeology: Proceedings of the Cambridge Annual Student Archaeology Conference 2019*, Oxford, 179–94.

Eluère, C. 1987. 'Celtic gold torcs', *Gold Bulletin* 20: 22–37.

Entwistle, J. 2000. *The Fashioned Body: Fashion, Dress and Modern Social Theory*, Cambridge.

Eogan, G. 1983. 'Ribbon torcs in Britain and Ireland', in A. O'Connor and D. Clarke (eds), *From the Stone Age to the Forty-five*, Edinburgh, 87–126.

Evans, C. and Hodder, I. 2006. *Marshland Communities and Cultural Landscapes: The Haddenham Project. Volume 2*, Cambridge.

Farley, J. 2011. 'The deposition of miniature weaponry in Iron Age Lincolnshire', *Pallas* 86: 97–121.

Farley, J. 2012. 'At the edge of empire: Iron Age and Early Roman metalwork in the East Midlands', unpublished PhD thesis, University of Leicester (https://hdl.handle.net/2381/10840).

Farley, J. 2021. 'The Hallaton Ingot: silver in Iron Age Britain', *Oxford Journal of Archaeology* 40(1): 87–104.

Farley, J. and Hunter, F. (eds) 2015. *Celts: Art and Identity*, London.

Farley, J. and Parfitt, K. 2014. 'A late Iron Age helmet burial from Bridge, near Canterbury, Kent', *Proceedings of the Prehistoric Society* 80: 379–88.

Farley, J., Gilmore, T., Sutherland, Z. and Nicholls, A. 2018. 'The Leekfrith torcs', *Transactions of the Staffordshire Archaeological and Historical Society* 50: 110–14.

Farwell, D.E. and Molleson, T.I. 1993. *Excavations at Poundbury 1966–80. II: The Cemeteries*, Dorchester.

Feachem, R.W. 1958. 'The "Cairnmuir" hoard from Netherurd, Peeblesshire', *Proceedings of the Society of Antiquaries of Scotland* 91 (1957–58): 112–16.

Feugère, M. 1994. *Casques Antiques. Visages de la guerre de Mycènes à l'Antiquité tardive*, Paris.

Feugère, M. and Py, M. 2011. *Dictionnaire des monnaies découvertes en Gaule Méditerréenne (530–27 av. notre ère)*, Paris.

Fisher, G. and Di Paolo Loren, D. 2003. 'Embodying identity in archaeology: introduction', *Cambridge Archaeological Journal* 13(2): 225–30.

Fitton, J.L. 2009. *The Aigina Treasure. Aegean Bronze Age Jewellery and a Mystery Revisited*, London.

Fitzpatrick, A.P. 1984. 'The deposition of La Tène metalwork in watery contexts in southern England', in B. Cunliffe and D. Miles (eds), *Aspects of the Iron Age in Central Southern Britain*, Oxford, 178–90.

Fitzpatrick, A.P. 1985. 'The distribution of Dressel 1 amphorae in northwest Europe', *Oxford Journal of Archaeology* 4(3): 305–40.

Fitzpatrick, A.P. 1992a. 'The Snettisham, Norfolk, hoards of Iron Age torques: sacred or profane?', *Antiquity* 66: 395–8.

Fitzpatrick, A.P. 1992b. 'The roles of Celtic coinage in south-east England', in M. Mays (ed.), *Celtic Coinage: Britain and Beyond*, BAR British Series 222, Oxford, 1–32.

Fitzpatrick, A.P. 1993. 'Ethnicity and exchange: Celts, Germans and Romans in the late (pre-Roman) Iron Age', in F.M.A. Healy and C.J. Scarre (eds), *Trade and Exchange in European Prehistory*, Oxbow Monograph 33, Oxford, 233–44.

Fitzpatrick, A.P. 1997. *Archaeological Excavations on the Route of the A27 Westhampnett Bypass, West Sussex, 1992. Volume 2: The Cemeteries*, Wessex Archaeology Report 12, Salisbury.

Fitzpatrick, A.P. 1999. 'Iron objects', in J.I. McKinley, 'Excavations at Ham Hill, Montacute, Somerset 1994 and 1998', *Somerset Archaeology and Natural History* 142: 111–15.

Fitzpatrick, A.P. 2001, 'Cross-Channel exchange, Hengistbury Head and the end of Hillforts', in J.R. Collis (ed.), *Society and Settlement in Iron Age Europe. Actes du XVIIIe colloque de l'Association Française pour l'Étude de l'Age du Fer, Winchester, (April 1994)* Sheffield Archaeological Monograph 11, Sheffield, 82–97.

Fitzpatrick, A.P. 2005. 'Gifts for the golden gods: Iron Age hoards of torques and coins', in C. Haselgrove and D. Wigg-Wolf (eds), *Iron Age Coinage and Ritual Practices*, Mainz am Rhein, 157–82.

Fitzpatrick, A.P. 2007. 'Druids: towards an archaeology', in C. Gosden, H. Hamerow, P. De Jersey and G. Lock (eds), *Communities and Connections: Essays in Honour of Barry Cunliffe*, Oxford, 287–315.

Fitzpatrick, A.P. 2009. 'The champion's portion: feasting in the Celtic pre-Roman Iron Age', in G. Cooney, K. Becker, J. Coles, M. Ryan and S. Sievers (eds), *Relics of Old Decency: Archaeological Studies in Later Prehistory, Festschrift for Barry Raftery*, Dublin, 389–404.

Fitzpatrick, A.P. forthcoming. 'The objects other than coins', in P. de Jersey (ed.), 'Le Câtillon II: an interim report', *Bulletin Société Jersiaise*.

Fletcher, P. 2017. 'X-ray computed tomography of the boxwood bead', in P. Shirley and D. Thornton (eds), *A Rothschild Renaissance: A New Look at the Waddesdon Bequest in the British Museum*, British Museum Research Publication 212, London.

Flitcroft, M. 2001. *Excavation of a Romano-British Settlement on the A149 Snettisham Bypass, 1989*, East Anglian Archaeology 93, Dereham.

Fontijn, D. 2002. *Sacrificial Landscapes: Cultural Biographies of Persons, Objects and 'Natural' Places in the Bronze Age of the Southern Netherlands, c. 2300–600 BC*, Leiden.

Forestry Commission 1956. *Utilisation of Hazel Coppice*, Forestry Commission Bulletin No. 27, Her Majesty's Stationery Office, London.

Foster, J.A.A. 1986. *The Lexden Tumulus. A Re-appraisal of an Iron Age Burial from Colchester, Essex*, BAR British Series 156, Oxford.

Foster, J. 1995. 'Metalworking in the British Iron Age: the evidence from Weelsby Avenue, Grimsby', in B. Raftery, V. Megaw and V. Rigby (eds), *Sites and Sights of the Iron Age: Essays on Fieldwork and Museum Research Presented to Ian Mathieson Stead*, Oxbow Monographs in Archaeology 56, Oxford, 49–61.

Foucault, M. 1988. 'The ethic of care for the self as a practice of freedom: an interview with Michel Foucault on January 20, 1984', in J. Bernauer and D. Rasmussen (eds), *The Final Foucault*, Cambridge, MA, 1–20.

Foulds, E.M. 2017. *Dress and Identity in Iron Age Britain: A Study of Glass Beads and other Objects of Personal Adornment*, Oxford.
Fowler, C. 2002. 'Body parts: personhood and materiality in the earlier Manx Neolithic', in Hamilakis *et al.* 2002b, 47–69.
Fowler, C. 2004. *The Archaeology of Personhood: An Anthropological Approach*, London.
Fowler, C. 2008. 'Fractal bodies in the past and present', in Borić and Robb 2008a, 47–57.
Fox, C. 1923. *The Archaeology of the Cambridge Region*, Cambridge.
Fox, C. 1946. *A Find of the Early Iron Age from Llyn Cerrig Bach, Anglesey*, Cardiff.
Fox, C. 1958. *Pattern and Purpose: A Survey of Early Celtic Art in Britain*, Cardiff.
Furger, A. 2015. *Der Goldfund von Saint-Louis bei Basel: Keltische Hortfunde mit Münzen und Ringschmuck im Kontext* (https://www.academia.edu/10286133/Der_Goldfund_von_Saint-Louis_bei_Basel_-_Keltische_Hortfunde_mit_Münzen_und_Ringschmuck_im_Kontext).
Furger-Gunti, A. 1982. 'Der "Goldfund von Saint-Louis" bei Basel und ähnliche keltische Schatzfunde', *Zeitschrift für Schweizerische Archäologie und Kunstgeschichte* 39: 1–47.
Gamble, C. 2007. *Origins and Revolutions: Human Identity in Earliest Prehistory*. Cambridge.
Gannon, A., Voden-Decker, L. and Bland, R. 2004. *Treasure Annual Report 2003*, London.
Garrow, D. 2006. *Pits, Settlement and Deposition during the Neolithic and Early Bronze Age in East Anglia*, BAR British Series 414, Oxford.
Garrow, D. 2008. 'The space and time of Celtic Art: interrogating the 'Technologies of Enchantment' database', in D. Garrow, C. Gosden and J.D. Hill (eds), *Rethinking Celtic Art*, Oxford, 15–39.
Garrow, D. and Gosden, C. 2012. *Technologies of Enchantment? Exploring Celtic Art: 400 BC to AD 100*, Oxford.
Garrow, D., Gosden, C., Hill, J.D. and Bronk Ramsey, C. 2009. 'Dating Celtic Art: a major radiocarbon dating programme of Iron Age and early Roman metalwork in Britain', *Archaeological Journal* 166: 79–123.
Garrow, D., Lucy, S. and Gibson, D. 2006. *Excavations at Kilverstone, Norfolk: An Episodic Landscape History. Neolithic pits, Later Prehistoric, Roman and Anglo-Saxon Occupation, and Later Activity*, East Anglian Archaeology 113, Dereham.
Gasson, P., Cartwright, C.R. and Leme, C.L.D. 2017. 'Anatomical changes to the wood of *Croton sonderianus* (Euphorbiaceae) when charred at different temperatures', *IAWA Journal* 38: 117–23.
Gell, A. 1992. 'The technology of enchantment and the enchantment of technology', in J. Coote and A. Shelton (eds), *Anthropology, Art and Aesthetics*, Oxford, 40–63.
Gell, A. 1993. *Wrapping in Images: Tattooing in Polynesia*, Oxford.
Gell, A. 1998. *Art and Agency: An Anthropological Theory*, Oxford.
Gibson, A.M. 1982. *Beaker Domestic Sites, A Study of the Domestic Pottery of the Late Third and Early Second Millennium BC in the British Isles*, British Archaeological Report 107, Oxford.
Giddens, A. 1979. *Central Problems in Social Theory: Action, Structure and Contradiction in Social Analysis*, London.
Gilchrist, R. 2012. *Medieval Life: Archaeology and the Life Course*, Woodbridge.
Giles, M. 2008. 'Seeing red: the aesthetics of martial objects in the British and Irish Iron Age', in D. Garrow, C. Gosden and J.D. Hill (eds), *Rethinking Celtic Art*, Oxford, 59–77.
Giles, M. 2012. *A Forged Glamour: Landscape, Identity and Material Culture in the Iron Age*, Oxford.
Godelier, M. 1999. *The Enigma of the Gift*, Chicago.
Goldberg, M. 2015. 'Out of a Roman world, *c.* AD 250–650', in J. Farley and F. Hunter (eds), *Celts: Art and Identity*, London, 155–72.
González-Ruibal, A., Hernando, A. and Polotis, G. 2011. 'Ontology of the self and material culture: arrow-making among the Awá hunter-gatherers (Brazil)', *Journal of Anthropological Archaeology* 30: 1–16.
Gosden, C. 2013. 'Technologies of routine and of enchantment', in L. Chua and M. Elliott (eds), *Distributed Objects: Meaning and Mattering after Alfred Gell*, Oxford, 39–57.
Gosden, C. and Hill, J.D. 2008. 'Introduction: re-integrating "Celtic art"', in D. Garrow, C. Gosden and J.D. Hill (eds), *Rethinking Celtic Art*, Oxford, 1–14.
Gosden, C. and Marshall, Y. 1999. 'The cultural biography of objects', *World Archaeology* 31(2): 169–78.
Graham, D. and Graham, A. 2017. 'An early ritual site on Frensham Common', *Surrey Archaeological Collections* 100: 187–211.
Gray, G. and Bulleid, A. 1953. *The Meare Lake Village, vol. II*, Taunton.
Green, C. 1949. 'The Birdlip Early Iron Age burials: a review', *Proceedings of the Prehistoric Society* 15: 188–90.
Green, H.S. 1980. *The Flint Arrowheads of the British Isles*, BAR British Series 75 i–ii, Oxford.
Greenland, T.B. and Braithwaite, R.S.W. 2012. 'Native mercury from Derbyshire', *Journal of the Russel Society* 15: 75–6.
Greenwell, W. 1906. 'Early Iron Age burials in Yorkshire', *Archaeologia* 60: 251–324.
Gregory, T. 1991. *Excavations in Thetford, 1980–1982, Fison Way*, East Anglian Archaeology 53, Gressenhall.
Gregory, T. 1992. 'Snettisham and Bury: some new light on the earliest Icenian coinage', in M. Mays (ed.), *Celtic Coinage: Britain and Beyond*. BAR British Series 222, 47–70.
Greig, J.R.A. 1992. 'An Iron Age hedgerow flora form Alcester', English Heritage, Ancient Monuments Laboratory Report 11/92.
Grosz, E. 1994. *Volatile Bodies: Toward a Corporeal Feminism (Theories of Representation and Difference)*, Bloomington, IN.
Guggisberg, M.A. 2000. *Der Goldschatz von Erstfeld: Ein keltischer Bilderzyklus zwischen Mitteleuropa und der Mittelmeerwelt*, Basel.
Gurney, D. (ed.) 1990 'Archaeological finds in Norfolk', *Norfolk Archaeology* 41(1): 96–106.
Gurney, D. and Chadburn, A. 1991. 'The Fring Coin Hoard', *Norfolk Archaeology* 42(2): 218–25.
Gwilt, A. and Haselgrove, C. (eds) 1997. *Reconstructing Iron Age Societies: New Approaches to the British Iron Age*, Oxbow Monographs in Archaeology 71, Oxford.
Gwilt, A., Lodwick, M. and Deacon, J. 2006. 'Excavation at Llanmaes, Vale of Glamorgan, 2006', *Archaeology in Wales* 46, 15–24.
Gwilt, A., Lodwick, M., Deacon, J. and Madgwick, R. 2016. 'The gathering place: pork cauldrons and feasting in Iron Age Wales', *British Archaeology* 149: 30–7.
Hamilakis, T. 2002a. 'Experience and corporeality: introduction', in Hamilakis *et al.* 2002b, 99–103.
Hamilakis, T. 2002b. 'The past as oral history: towards and archaeology of the senses', in Hamilakis *et al.* 2002b, 121–36.
Hamilakis, Y., Pluciennik, M. and Tarlow, S. 2002a. 'Introduction: thinking through the body', in Hamilakis *et al.* 2002b, New York, 1–21.
Hamilakis, Y., Pluciennik, M. and Tarlow, S. (eds) 2002b. *Thinking through the Body: Archaeologies of Corporeality*, New York.
Hamilton, W.D, Bayliss, A., Bronk Ramsey, C., Meadows, J. and van

der Plicht, H. 2007. 'Radiocarbon dating', in M. Germany (ed.), *Neolithic and Bronze Age Monuments and Middle Iron Age Settlement at Lodge Farm, St Osyth, Essex*, East Anglian Archaeology 117, Braintree, 95–102.

Hamilton, W.D., Haselgrove, C. and Gosden, C. 2015. 'The impact of Bayesian chronologies on the British Iron Age', *World Archaeology* 47(4): 642–60.

Hansen, S. 1996–8. 'Migration und Kommunikation während der späten Bronzezeit. Die Depots als Quelle für ihren Nachweis', *Dacia* (New Series) 40–2: 5–28.

Hansen, S. 2013. 'Bronze Age hoards and their role in social structure: a case study from South-West Zealand', in S. Bergerbrant and S. Sabatini (eds), *Counterpoint: Essays in Archaeology and Heritage Studies in Honour of Professor Kristian Kristiansen*, BAR International Series S2508, Oxford, 179–91.

Hanson, D. and Pell-Walpole, W.T. 1951. *Chill-Cast Tin Bronzes*, London.

Hargrave, F. 2018. 'Ritual and religious sites in Later Iron Age Britain with particular reference to Eastern England', unpublished PhD thesis, University of Leicester (https://hdl.handle.net/2381/42793).

Harris, O.J.T., Rebay-Salisbury, K., Robb, J. and Stig Sørensen, M.-L. 2013. 'The body in its social context', in Robb and Harris 2013, 64–97.

Harris, O.J.T. and Robb, J. 2013a. 'O brave new world, that has such people in it', in Robb and Harris 2013, 1–6.

Harris, O.J.T. and Robb, J. 2013b. 'Body worlds and their history: some working concepts', in Robb and Harris 2013, 7–31.

Haselgrove, C. 1987. *Iron Age Coinage in South-East England: The Archaeological Context*, BAR British Series 174, Oxford.

Haselgrove, C. 1993. 'The development of British Iron Age coinage', *The Numismatic Chronicle* 153: 31–63.

Haselgrove, C. 1995. 'Potin coinage in Iron Age Britain: archaeology and chronology', *Gallia* 52, 117–27.

Haselgrove, C. 1999. 'The development of Iron Age coinage in Belgic Gaul', *The Numismatic Chronicle* 159: 111–68.

Haselgrove, C. 2005. 'A trio of temples: a reassessment of Iron Age coin deposition at Hayling Island, Harlow and Wanborough', in C. Haselgrove and D. Wigg-Wolf (eds), *Iron Age Coinage and Ritual Practices*, Studien zu Fundmünzen der Antike 20, Mainz am Rhein, 381–417.

Haselgrove, C. 2006. 'Early potin coinage in Britain: an update', in P. de Jersey (ed.), *Celtic Coinage: New Discoveries, New Discussions*, BAR International Series 1532, Oxford, 17–27.

Haselgrove, C. 2009. 'Noughts and crosses: the archaeology of "globules-à-la-croix"', in J. van Heesch and I. Heeren (eds), *Coinage in the Iron Age: Essays in Honour of Simone Scheers*, London, 173–86.

Haselgrove, C. 2015. 'Hoarding and other forms of metalwork deposition in Iron Age Britain', in J. Naylor and R. Bland (eds), *Hoarding and Deposition of Metalwork from the Bronze Age to the 20th Century: A British Perspective*, Oxford, BAR British Series 615, 24–37.

Haselgrove, C. 2019. 'The Gallic War in the chronology of Iron Age coinage', in A.P. Fitzpatrick and C. Haselgrove (eds), *Julius Caesar's Battle for Gaul: New Archaeological Perspectives*, Oxford and Philadelphia, 241–66.

Haselgrove, C. and Hingley, R. 2006. 'Iron deposition and its significance in pre-Roman Britain', in G. Bataille and J.-P. Guillaumet (eds), *Les depots metalliques au second age du Fer en Europe temperee*, Bibracte, 147–62.

Haselgrove, C. and Moore, T. (eds) 2007. *The Later Iron Age in Britain and Beyond*, Oxford.

Haselgrove, C. and Wigg-Wolf, D. (eds) 2005. *Iron Age Coinage and Ritual Practices*, Studien zu Fundmünzen der Antike Band 20, Mainz.

Haselgrove, C., Fitzpatrick, A. and Hamilton, D. 2018. 'Radiocarbon dating and Bayesian modelling of the Late Iron Age cremation burial cemetery at Westhampnett (West Sussex/GB)', *Archaologisches Korrespondenzblatt* 47: 359–81.

Haug, A. 2001. 'Constituting the past – forming the present: the role of material culture in the Augustan period', *Journal of the History of Collections* 13(2): 111–23.

Hautenauve, H. 2005. 'Les torques d'or du second âge du fer en Europe: techniques, typologies et symbolique', *Travaux du Laboratoire anthropologie, préhistoire, protohistoire, quaternaire armoricains*: 7–340.

Hawkes, C.F.C. 1936. 'The Needwood Forest Torc', *The British Museum Quarterly* 11(1): 3–4.

Hawkes, C.F.C. 1940. 'An iron torc from Spettisbury Rings, Dorset', *Archaeological Journal* 97: 112–14.

Hayward, P., Nelson-Smith, A. and Shields, C. 1996. *Seashore of Britain and Europe*, London.

Healy, F. 1988. *Spong Hill Part VI: 7th to 2nd Millennia BC*, East Anglian Archaeology 39, Gressenhall.

Healy, F. 1996. *The Fenland Project, Number 11: The Wissey Embayment: Evidence for pre-Iron Age Occupation*, East Anglian Archaeology 78, Gressenhall.

Healy, F. 2012. 'Chronology, corpses ceramics, copper and lithics' in Allen, M.J., Gardiner, J. and Sheridan, A. (eds), *Is there a British Chalcolithic? People, Place and Polity in the Late 3rd Millennium*, Prehistoric Society Research Paper 4, Oxford: 144–64.

Healy, F. 2013. 'In the shadow of hindsight: pre-Iron Age Spong Hill viewed from 2010', in C. Hills and S. Lucy (eds), *Spong Hill. Part IX: Chronology and Synthesis*, Cambridge, 12–21.

Helms, M. 1988. *Ulysses' Sail: An Ethnographic Odyssey of Power, Knowledge and Geographical Distance*, Princeton, NJ.

Herbert, E.W. 1984. *Red Gold of Africa: Copper in Precolonial History and Culture*, Madison, WI.

Higueras, P.L., Mansilla Plaza, L., Lorenzo Alvarez, S. and Esbri Víctor, J.M. 2011. 'The Almadén mercury mining district', in E. Ortiz, O. Puche, I. Rábano and L. F. Mazadiego (eds), *History of Research in Mineral Resources, Cuadernos del Museo Geominero* 13, Madrid: 75–88.

Hill, J.D. 1995. *Ritual and Rubbish in the Iron Age of Wessex: A Study of Formation of a Specific Archaeological Record*, BAR British Series 242, Oxford.

Hill, J.D. 1997. 'The end of one kind of body and the beginning of another kind of body? Toilet instruments and "Romanisation"', in Gwilt and Haselgrove 1997, 96–107.

Hill, J.D. 1999. 'Settlement, landscape and regionality: Norfolk and Suffolk in the pre-Roman Iron Age of Britain and beyond', in Davies and Williamson 1999, 185–207.

Hill, J.D. 2006. 'Are we any closer to understanding how later Iron Age societies worked (or did not work)?', in C. Haselgrove (ed.), *Celtes et Gaulous l'Archéologie face à l'Histoire: Les mutations de la fin de l'âge du Fer*, Collection Bibracte 12/4, Glux-en-Glenne, 167–79.

Hill, J.D. 2007. 'The dynamics of social change in Later Iron Age eastern and south-eastern England *c.* 300 BC–AD 43', in Haselgrove and Moore 2007, 16–40.

Hill, J.D. 2011. 'How did British Middle and late pre-Roman Iron Age societies work (if they did)?', in T. Moore and X.-L. Armada (eds), *Atlantic Europe in the First Millennium BC: Crossing the Divide*, Oxford, 242–63.

Hill, J.D., Spence, A.J., La Niece, S. and Worrell, S. 2004. 'The Winchester hoard: a find of unique Iron Age gold jewellery from southern England', *The Antiquaries Journal* 84: 1–22.
Hingley, R. 1990. 'Iron Age "currency bars": the archaeological and social context', *Archaeological Journal* 147: 91–117.
Hingley, R. 1997. 'Iron, ironworking and regeneration: a study of the symbolic meaning of metalwork in Iron Age Britain', in Gwilt and Haselgrove 1997, 9–18.
Hingley, R. 2005. 'Iron Age "currency bars" in Britain: items of exchange in liminal contexts?', in C. Haselgrove and D. Wigg-Wolf (eds), *Iron Age Coinage and Ritual Practice*, Mainz am Rhein, 183–205.
Hingley, R. 2006. 'The deposition of iron objects in Britain during the later Prehistoric and Roman periods: contextual analysis and the significance of iron', *Britannia* 37: 213–57.
Hinton, D. 2005. *Gold and Gilt, Pots and Pins: Possessions and People in Medieval Britain*, Oxford.
Historic England 2018. *Shrines (Roman and Post-Roman): Introductions to Heritage Assets*, Swindon.
Hitchcock, F. (ed.) 2006. *Treasure Annual Report 2004*, London.
Hobbs, R. 1996. *British Iron Age Coinage in the British Museum*, London.
Hobbs, R. 2003. *Treasure: Finding our Past*, London.
Hockey, M. 1989. 'The composition and structure of a Byzantine torc', *Jewellery Studies* 3: 33–9.
Hockey, M. 1993. 'Report on the examination of four pieces of Late Bronze Age gold at the National Museum of Ireland', Department of Metals Conservation, British Museum, unpublished report no. 93/6/M/1.
Hockey, M. 1999. 'Report on the conservation of gold artefacts from Mapungubwe', Department of Metals Conservation, British Museum, unpublished report no. 99/19/M6.
Hockey, M. 2001. 'Approaches to the conservation of gold at the British Museum', in I. Macleod, J. Thiele and C. Degrigny (eds), *Metal 2001. Proceedings of the International Conference of Metals Conservation*, 263–9.
Hockey, M. and Shearman, F. 2006. 'Aspects of the conservation and restoration of archaeological arms and armour', in R. Douglas Smith (ed.), *Make All Sure. The Conservation and Restoration of Arms and Armour*, Leeds, 31–7.
Hockey, M., Shearman, F. and Çamurcuoğlu, D. 2013. 'The Hallaton Helmet: excavation and reconstruction of a unique assemblage', *ICOM-CC Metals 2013 Conference Proceedings*, Edinburgh, 13–17.
Hockey, M., Shearman, F., La Niece, S., Meek, A. and Cartwright, C. 2018. 'The Ashwell Hoard: conservation and scientific study', in R. Jackson and G. Burleigh (eds), *Dea Senuna: Cult and Ritual at Ashwell, Hertfordshire*, British Museum Research Publication 194, London, 6–17.
Hodder, I. 2006. 'The spectacle of daily performance at Çatalhöyük', in Inomata and Coben 2006b, 81–102.
Hogg, A.H.A. 1962. 'Carn Noduan and Tre'r Ceiri, excavations at two Caernarvonshire hill-forts', *Archaeological Journal* 117: 1–39.
Holman, D.J. 2005. 'Iron Age coinage and settlement in East Kent', *Britannia* 36: 1–54.
Holman, D.J. 2016. 'A new classification system for the Flat Linear potin coinage', *British Numismatic Journal* 86: 1–67.
Holman, D.J. 2020. 'The Flat Linear potin hoards from Birchington and North Foreland, Kent', *British Numismatic Journal* 90: 17–51.
Holman, D.J. 2022. 'The Takeley Iron Age potin coin hoard reconsidered', in T*ransactions of the Essex Society for Archaeology & History* 11: 50–7.
Houston, S.D. 2006. 'Impersonation, dance and the problem of spectacle among the Classic Maya', in Inomata and Coben 2006b, 135–55.
Hughes, M.J., Craddock, P.T. and Cowell, M.R. 2012. 'The phosphate survey', in I. Longworth, G. Varndell and J. Lech (eds), *Excavations at Grimes Graves, Norfolk, 1972–1976. Fascicule 6: Exploration and Excavation beyond the Deep Mines*, London, 30–41.
Hull, M.R. and Hawkes, C.F.C. 1987. *Corpus of Ancient Brooches in Britain; Pre-Roman Bow Brooches*, BAR British Series 168, Oxford.
Hunter, F. 1997. 'Iron Age coins in Scotland', *Proceedings of the Society of Antiquaries of Scotland* 127: 513–25.
Hunter, F. 2006. 'New light on Iron Age massive armlets', *Proceedings of the Society of Antiquaries Scotland* 136: 135–60.
Hunter, F. 2014a. 'Highland, Auldearn, Metal detector find', *Discovery and Excavation in Scotland* (New Series) 15 (2014): 97.
Hunter, F. 2018. 'The Blair Drummond (UK) gold torc hoard: regional styles and international connections in the Later Iron Age', in R. Schwab, P.-Y. Milcent, B. Armbruster and E. Pernicka (eds), *Early Iron Age Gold in Celtic Europe: Society, Technology and Archaeometry*, Rahden/Westf, 431–40.
Hurcombe, L.M. 2014. *Perishable Material Culture in Prehistory: Investigating the Missing Majority*, London.
Hurst, D. and Leins, I. 2013. 'The Pershore Hoards and votive deposition in the Iron Age', *Proceedings of the Prehistoric Society* 79: 297–325.
Hutcheson, N. 2003. 'Material culture in the landscape: a new approach to the Snettisham hoards', in J. Humphrey (ed.), *Researching the Iron Age*, Leicester Archaeology Monograph 11, Leicester, 87–97.
Hutcheson, N. 2004. *Later Iron Age Norfolk: Metalwork, Landscape and Society*, BAR British Series 361, Oxford.
Hutcheson, N. 2007. 'An archaeological investigation of later Iron Age Norfolk: analysing hoarding patterns across the landscape', in Haselgrove and Moore 2007, 358–70.
Hutcheson, N. 2011. 'Excavations at Snettisham, Norfolk, 2004: re-investigating the past', in J.A. Davies (ed.), *The Iron Age in Northern East Anglia: New Work in the Land of the Iceni*, BAR British Series 549, Oxford, 41–8.
Hutton, R. 1991. *The Pagan Religions of the Ancient British Isles: Their Nature and Legacy*, Oxford.
Hutton, R. 2007. *The Druids*, London.
Inomata, T. and Coben, L.S. 2006a. 'Overture: an invitation to the archaeological theatre', in Inomata and Coben 2006b, 11–44.
Inomata, T. and Coben, L.S. (eds) 2006b. *Archaeology of Performance: Theatres of Power, Community and Politics*, Lanham.
Jackson, R. 1990. *Camerton: A Catalogue of Late Iron Age and Early Roman Metalwork*, London.
Jackson, R. and Burleigh, G. 2018. *Dea Senuna: Treasure, Cult and Ritual at Ashwell, Hertfordshire*, British Museum Research Publication 194, London.
Jacobsthal, P. 1969 [1944]. *Early Celtic Art*, Oxford.
James, S. 1993. *Exploring the World of the Celts*, London.
James, S. and Rigby, V. 1997. *Britain and the Celtic Iron Age*, London.
Joachim, H.-E. 1995. *Waldalgesheim. Das Grab einer keltischen Fürstin. Kataloge des Rheinischen Landesmuseums Bonn*, Cologne.
Jockenhövel, A. 1980. 'Die Rasiermesser in Westeuropa', *Prähistorische Bronzefunde, Abteilung VIII*, Munich.
Joffroy, R. 1969. 'Le Torc de Mailly-le-Camp (Aube)', *Monuments et Mémoires, Fondation E. Piot* 56: 45–59.
Johns, C. 1996. *The Jewellery of Roman Britain: Celtic and Classical Traditions*, London.

Johns, C. 1997. *The Snettisham Roman Jeweller's Hoard*, London.
Johns, C. 2006. 'An Iron Age sword and mirror cist burial from Bryher, Isles of Scilly', *Cornish Archaeology* 41–2: 1–79.
Jones, A. 2005. 'Lives in fragments? Personhood and the European Neolithic', *Journal of Social Archaeology* 5: 193–224.
Jones, A. 2007. *Memory and Material Culture*, Cambridge.
Jope, E.M. 2000. *Early Celtic Art in the British Isles*, Oxford.
Jope, E.M. and Wilson, B.C.S. 1957. 'A burial group of the first century AD near Donaghadee, Co. Down', *Ulster Journal of Archaeology* 20: 73–95.
Joy, J. 2002. 'Biography of a medal: people and the things they value', in J. Schofield, W. Gray Johnson and C.M. Beck (eds), *Matériel Culture: The Archaeology of Twentieth Century Conflict*, London, 132–42.
Joy, J. 2008. 'Reflections on Celtic art: a re-examination of mirror decoration', in D. Garrow, C. Gosden and J.D. Hill (eds), *Rethinking Celtic Art*, Oxford, 78–99.
Joy, J. 2009a. 'Reinvigorating object biography: reproducing the drama of object lives', *World Archaeology* 41(4): 540–56.
Joy, J. 2009b. *Lindow Man*, London.
Joy, J. 2010. *Iron Age Mirrors: A Biographical Approach*, BAR British Series 518, Oxford.
Joy, J. 2011. '"Fancy objects" in the British Iron Age: why decorate?', *Proceedings of the Prehistoric Society* 77: 205–99.
Joy, J. 2014. 'Brit-art: Celtic art in Roman Britain and on its frontiers', in C. Gosden, S. Crawford and K. Ulmschneider (eds), *Celtic Art in Europe: Making Connections*, Oxford, 315–24.
Joy, J. 2015. 'Connections and separation? Narratives of Iron Age art in Britain and its relationships with the Continent', in H. Anderson-Whymark, D. Garrow and F. Sturt (eds), *Continental Connections: Exploring Cross-Channel Relationships from the Mesolithic to the Iron Age*, Oxford, 145–65.
Joy, J. 2016. 'Hoards as collections: re-examining the Snettisham Iron Age hoards from the perspective of collecting practice', *World Archaeology* 48(2), 239–53.
Joy, J. 2019a. 'A power to intrigue? Exploring the "timeless" qualities of the so-called "grotesque" Iron Age torc from Snettisham, Norfolk', *Oxford Journal of Archaeology* 38(4): 464–75.
Joy, J. 2019b. 'How can Celtic art styles and motifs act? A case study from later Iron Age Norfolk', in C. Nimura, H. Chittock, P. Hommel and C. Gosden (eds), *Art in the Eurasian Iron Age: Context, Connections and Scale*, Oxford, 111–26.
Joyce, R.A. 1998. 'Performing the body in pre-Hispanic Central America', *RES: Anthropology and Aesthetics* 33: 147–65.
Joyce, R.A. 2000. *Gender and Power in Prehispanic Mesoamerica*, Austin, TX.
Joyce, R.A. 2005. 'Archaeology of the body', *Annual Review of Anthropology* 34: 139–58.
Joyce, R.A. and Gillespie, S.D. 2015. 'Making things out of objects that move', in R.A. Joyce and S.D. Gillespie (eds), *Things in Motion: Object Itineraries in Anthropological Practice*, Santa Fe, NM, 3–20.
Jundi, S. and Hill, J.D. 1998. 'Brooches and identity in first century AD Britain: more than meets the eye?', in C. Forcey, J. Hawthorne and R. Witcher (eds), *TRAC 97: Proceedings of the Seventh Annual Theoretical Roman Archaeology Conference, Nottingham 1997*, Oxford, 125–37.
Karl, R. 2005. 'Master and apprentice, knight and squire. Education in the "Celtic" Iron Age', *Oxford Journal of Archaeology* 24(3): 225–71.
Kemmers, F. and Myrberg, N. 2011. 'Rethinking numismatics. The archaeology of coins', *Archaeological Dialogues* 18(1): 87–108.
Kent, J.P.C. and Burnett, A.M. 1984. 'The Eriswell, Suffolk, Treasure Trove' in *Coin Hoards from Roman Britain IV*, British Museum Occasional Paper 43, 6–13.
Kimmig, W. 1988. *Das Kleinaspergle: Studien zu einem* Fürstengrabhügel der *frühen Latènezeit bei Stuttgart*, Stuttgart.
King, A.C., Soffe, G. and Downey, R.R. 1979. *The Hayling Island Temple. Third Interim Report on the Excavations of the Iron Age and Roman Temple 1976–1978*, London.
King, A. and Soffe, G. 2001. 'Internal organisation and deposition at the Iron age temple on Hayling Island', in J.R. Collis (ed.), *Society and Settlement in Iron Age Europe*, Sheffield Archaeological Monograph 11, Sheffield, 111–24.
King, A.C. and Soffe, G. 2007. 'Hayling Island: a Gallo-Roman temple in Britain', in D. Rudling (ed.), *Ritual Landscapes of Roman South-East England*, Oxford, 139–51.
Kopytoff, I. 1986. 'The cultural biography of things: commoditization as process', in A. Appadurai (ed.), *The Social Life of Things: Commodities in Cultural Perspective*, Cambridge, 3–63.
Lamb, A.W. 2020. 'An Iron Age torc from Burnley, Lancashire', *Transactions of the Lancashire and Cheshire Antiquarian Society* 112: 182–201.
Lambrick, G. and Allen, T. 2004. *Gravelly Guy, Santon Harcourt, Oxfordshire: The Development of a Prehistoric and Romano-British Community*, Oxford Archaeology Thames Valley Landscapes Monograph No. 21, Oxford.
Lang, J. Craddock, P.T., Farley, J., Stead, I. and Perucchetti, L. 2019. 'An unusual iron find from Snettisham', *The Crucible* 101: 8–10.
La Niece, S. 1995. 'Depletion gilding from third millennium BC Ur', *Iraq* 57: 41–7.
La Niece, S. 1990. 'Silver plating on copper, bronze and brass', *The Antiquaries Journal* 70 (1): 102–14.
La Niece, S. and Cartwright, C.R. 2009. 'Bronze Age gold lock-rings with cores of wax and wood', in T.L. Kienlin and B.W. Roberts (eds), *Metals and Societies. Studies in Honour of Barbara S. Ottaway*, Universitätsforchungen zur Prähistorischen Archäologie Aus dem Institut für Archäologische Wissenschaften der Universität Bochum Fach Ur- und Frügeschichte, Band 169, Bonn, 307–12.
La Niece, S., Farley, J., Meeks, N. and Joy, J. 2018. 'Gold in Iron Age Britain', in R. Schwab, P.-Y. Milcent, B. Armbruster and E. Pernicka (eds), *Early Iron Age Gold in Celtic Europe: Society, Technology and Archaeometry*, Rahden/Westf, 407–30.
La Niece, S. and Meeks, N.D. 2000. 'Diversity of goldsmithing traditions in the Americas and the Old World', in C. McEwan (ed.), *Precolombian Gold: Technology Style and Iconography*, London, 220–39.
Laver, P.G. 1927. 'The excavation of a tumulus at Lexden, Colchester', *Archaeologia* 76: 241–54.
Lawson, A.J. 2018. *Late Bronze Age Hoards: New Light on Old Norfolk Finds*, East Anglian Archaeology 166, Dereham.
Lawson, J. 1858. 'Letter from John Lawson of Cairnmuir, Esq., to Sir Walter Scott, Baronet, describing some Golden Ornaments found in March 1806, near the house of New Cairnmuir, Peeblesshire', *Archaeologia Scotica: Transactions of the Society of Antiquaries of Scotland* 4: 217–19.
Leeds, E.T. 1933. 'Torcs of the Early Iron Age in Britain', *The Antiquaries Journal* 13: 466–8.
Lehrberger, G. 1995. 'The gold deposits of Europe: an overview of the possible metal sources for Prehistoric gold objects', in G. Morteani and J.P. Northover (eds), *Prehistoric Gold in Europe, Mines, Metallurgy and Manufacture*, Dordrecht, 115–44.
Leins, I. 2007. 'Coins in context: coinage and votive deposition in Iron Age southeast Leicestershire', *British Numismatic Journal* 77: 22–48.

Leins, I. 2011. 'The coins', in V. Score (ed.), *Hoards, Hounds and Helmets: A conquest-period ritual site at Hallaton, Leicestershire*, Leicester Archaeology Monograph 21, 39–60.
Leins, I. 2012. 'Numismatic data reconsidered: coin distributions and interpretation in studies of late Iron Age Britain', unpublished PhD thesis, Newcastle University.
Lejeune, M. 1969. 'Les graffities gallo-grecs du torc de Mailly-le-Camp', *Monuments et Mémoires, Fondation E. Piot* 56: 60–76.
Lethbridge, T.C. 1954. 'Burial of an Iron Age Warrior at Snailwell', *Proceedings of the Cambridge Antiquarian Society* 47: 25–37.
Lethbridge, T.C. and O'Reilly, M.M. 1931. 'Archaeological notes', *Proceedings of the Cambridge Antiquarian Society* 31: 150–5.
Lewis, M. 1966. *Temples in Roman Britain*, Cambridge.
Lewis, A. 2015. 'Iron Age and Roman-era vehicle terrets from western and central Britain: an interpretive study', unpublished PhD thesis, University of Leicester.
Lillios, K.T. 1999. 'Objects of memory: the ethnography and archaeology of heirlooms', *Journal of Archaeological Method and Theory* 6(3): 235–62.
Lins, P.A. and Oddy, W.A. 1975. 'The origins of mercury gilding', *Journal of Archaeological Science* 2(4): 365–73.
LiPuma, E. 1998. 'Modernity and forms of personhood in Melanesia', in M. Lambek and A. Strathern (eds), *Bodies and Persons: Comparative Perspectives from Africa and Melanesia*, Cambridge, 53–79.
Lockyear, K. 2012. 'Dating coins, dating with coins', *Oxford Journal of Archaeology* 31(2): 191–211.
Longley, D. 1980. *Runnymede Bridge 1976: Excavations on the Site of a Late Bronze Age Settlement, with a Report on the Bronze Finds by Stuart Needham*, Surrey Archaeological Society Research Volumes 6, 1–85.
Longworth, I. 1960 'Pottery' in Clark, J.G.D., 'Excavations at the Neolithic site at Hurst Fen, Mildenhall, Suffolk', *Proceedings of the Prehistoric Society* 26: 228–40.
Longworth, I.H. 1992. 'Snettisham revisited', *Cultural Property* 2(1): 333–41.
Lyman, R.L. 1994. *Vertebrate Taphonomy*, Cambridge.
Lyman, T. (ed.). 1973. *Metals Handbook, Vol. 8, Metallography, Structures and Phase Diagrams* (8th edn), Metals Park, OH.
Lyons, A. 2004. *Romano-British Activity at Snettisham, Norfolk. Archaeological Investigations at Strickland Avenue and Station Road*, East Anglian Archaeology Occasional Paper 18, Dereham.
Lyons, A. and Tester, C. 2014. 'Roman pottery fabrics', in T. Ashwin and A. Tester (eds), *A Romano-British Settlement in the Waveney Valley: Excavations at Scole, 1993–4*, East Anglian Archaeology 152, Dereham, 256–61.
Macdonald, P. 2007a. 'Perspectives on insular La Tène art', in Haselgrove and Moore 2007, 329–38.
Macdonald, P. 2007b. *Llyn Cerrig Bach: A Study of the Copper-alloy Artefacts from the Insular La Tène Assemblage*, Cardiff.
MacGregor, M. 1962. 'The early Iron Age metalwork hoard from Stanwick, N.R. Yorks', *Proceedings of the Prehistoric Society* 28: 17–57.
MacGregor, M. 1976. *Early Celtic Art in North Britain: A Study of Decorative Metalwork from the Third Century BC to the Third Century AD*, Leicester.
Machling, T. and Williamson, R. 2016. 'The Netherurd torc terminal – insights into torc technology', *PAST: The Newsletter of the Prehistoric Society* 84: 3–5.
Machling, T. and Williamson, R. 2018. 'Up close and personal': The later Iron Age torcs from Newark, Nottinghamshire and Netherurd, Peebleshire', *Proceedings of the Prehistoric Society* 84: 387–403.
Machling, T. and Williamson, R. 2019. '"Cut and shuts": the reworking of Iron Age gold torus torcs', *Later Prehistoric Finds Group Newsletter* 13: 4–7.
Machling, T. and Williamson, R. 2020a. 'Thoughts on the Grotesque torc and the Snettisham (Ken Hill) hoards in the light of new research' (https://bigbookoftorcs.com/2020/09/22/thoughts-on-the-grotesque-torc).
Machling, T. and Williamson, R. 2020b. 'A rediscovered Iron Age torus torc terminal fragment from "Near Stowmarket", Suffolk' (https://bigbookoftorcs.com/2020/02/02/near-stowmarket-torc/).
Machling, T. and Williamson, R. 2024. 'Nicked and "nicked": the Knaresborough gold ring and a possible Viking-redeposited Iron Age hoard from eastern England' (https://bigbookoftorcs.com/2024/04/16/nicked-and-nicked-the-knaresborough-gold-ring-and-a-possible-viking-redeposited-iron-age-hoard-from-eastern-england/).
Mack, R.P. 1953. *The Coinage of Ancient Britain*, Spink.
Mackreth, D.F. 2011. *Brooches in Late Iron Age and Roman Britain*, 2 vols, Oxford.
Malafouris, L. 2008. 'Is it "me" or is it "mine"? The Mycenaean sword as a body-part', in Borić and Robb 2008a, 115–23.
Malafouris, L. 2013. *How Things Shape the Mind*, London.
Malone, S. 2010. *Assessment of the Archaeological Remains and an Updated Project Design for Excavations at Grandcourt Quarry East Winch Norfolk*, Archaeological Project Services Report No. 17/10.
Manby, T.G. 1974. *Grooved Ware Sites in the North of England*, BAR British Series 9, Oxford.
Manning, W.H. 1985. *Catalogue of the Romano-British Iron Tools, Fittings and Weapons in the British Museum*, London.
Marcellesi, M.-C. 2004. *Milet des Hécatomnides à la domination romaine*, Mainz.
Marsden, A. 2011. 'Iron Age coins from Snettisham', in J.A. Davies (ed.), *The Iron Age in North East Anglia: New Work in the Land of the Iceni*, BAR British Series 549, Oxford, 49–58.
Marshall, M. 2023. 'Baldock torcs: penannular neck rings from south-eastern Roman Britain and their significance for the development of provincial identities', *Acta ad archaeologiam et artium historia pertinentia* 33: 321–55.
Martin, T.F. 2014. '(Ad)Dressing the Anglo-Saxon body: corporeal meanings and artefacts in early England', in P. Blinkhorn and C. Cumberpatch (eds), *The Chiming of Crack'd Bells: Recent Approaches to the Study of Artefacts in Archaeology*, BAR International Series S2677, Oxford, 27–38.
Martin, T. and Weetch, R. 2017. *Dress and Society: Contributions from Archaeology*, Oxford.
Maryon, H. 1944. 'The Bawsey torc', *The Antiquaries Journal* 24: 149–51.
Maryon, H. 2011. *Metalwork and Enamelling* (5th rev. edn), New York.
Massey, S., Brennand, M. and Clare, H. 2003. 'The national mapping programme in Norfolk, 2001–3', *Norfolk Archaeology* 44(2): 335–44.
Maurer, B. 2006. 'The anthropology of money', *Annual Review of Anthropology* 35: 15–36.
Mauss, M. 1973 [1934]. 'Techniques of the body', *Economy and Society* 2(1): 70–88.
Maxfield, V. A. 1981. *The Military Decorations of the Roman Army*, Berkeley and Los Angeles.
May, J. 1976. *Prehistoric Lincolnshire*, Lincoln.
May, J. 1996. *Dragonby: Report on Excavations at an Iron Age and Romano-British Settlement in North Lincolnshire*, Oxbow Monograph 61, Oxford.
Meeks, N.D. 1993. 'Surface characterisation of tinned bronze, high-tin

bronze, tinned iron and arsenical bronze', in S. La Niece and P.T Craddock (eds), *Metal Plating and Patination*, Oxford, 247–75.

Meeks, N.D. and Tite, M.S. 1980. 'The analysis of platinum-group element inclusions in gold antiquities', *Journal of Archaeological Science* 7(3): 267–75.

Meeks, N., Mongiatti, A. and Joy, J. 2014. 'Precious metal torcs from the Iron Age Snettisham Treasure: metallurgy and analysis', in E. Pernicka and R. Schwab (eds), *Under the Volcano: Proceedings of the International Symposium on the Metallurgy of the European Iron Age (SMEIA) held in Mannheim, Germany, 20–22 April 2010*, Rahden, 135–55.

Meeks, N.D., Tulp, C. and Söderberg, A. 2001. 'Precision lost-wax casting', in C. Tulp, N.D. Meeks and R. Paardekooper (eds), *Proceedings of the 1st International Workshop on Experimental and Educational Aspects of Bronze Metallurgy, Wilhelminaoord, October 1999*, Leiden, 56–78 (http://journal.exarc.net/issue-2012-3/ea/precision-lost-wax-casting).

Megaw, J.V.S. 1970. 'Cheshire Cat and Mickey Mouse: analysis, interpretation and the art of the La Tène Iron Age', *Proceedings of the Prehistoric Society* 36: 261–79.

Megaw, J.V.S. 1971. 'A group of later Iron Age collars or neck-rings from western Britain', *The British Museum Quarterly* 35(1): 145–56.

Megaw, J.V.S. and Megaw, M.R. 1990. *The Base-Yutz Find. Masterpieces of Celtic Art*, London.

Megaw, R. and Megaw, V. 2001. *Celtic Art: From its Beginnings to the Book of Kells* (2nd edn), London.

Megaw, R. and Megaw, V. 2005. *Early Celtic Art in Britain and Ireland* (2nd edn), London.

Meskell, L.M. and Joyce, R.A. 2003. *Embodied Lives: Figuring Ancient Maya and Egyptian Experience*, London.

Miles, R. and Mead, R. 2015. *The Jersey Hoard: Le Catillon II*, St. Mary.

Millett, M. and Russell, D. 1982. 'An Iron Age burial from Viables Farm', *The Archaeological Journal* 139: 69–90.

Montero-Ruis, I. and Perea, A. 2007. 'Brasses in the early metallurgy of the Iberian Peninsula', in S. La Niece, D. Hook and P.T. Craddock (eds), *Metals and Mines: Studies in Archaeometallurgy*, London, 136–40.

Moore, T. 2011. 'Detribalizing the later prehistoric past: concepts of tribes in Iron Age and Roman studies', *Journal of Social Archaeology* 11(3): 334–60.

Morris, J. 2010. 'Associated bone groups: beyond the Iron Age', in J. Morris and M. Maltby (eds), *Integrating Social and Environmental Archaeologies; Reconsidering Deposition*, British Archaeological Reports, International Series no. 2077, Oxford, 12–23.

Morris, C. and Peatfield, A. 2002. 'Feeling through the body: gesture in Cretan Bronze Age religion', in Hamilakis *et al.* 2002b, 105–20.

Moscati, S., Andreose, M. and Ellis, A. 1991. *The Celts*, London.

Moshenska, G. (ed.) 2004. *Sedgeford Historical and Archaeological Research Project Annual Report 2004*, Sedgeford.

Moshenska, G. 2005. 'Sedgeford historical and archaeological research project: interim report 2004', *Norfolk Archaeology* 44(4): 727–8.

Moutu, A. 2007. 'Collecting as a way of being', in A. Henare, M. Holbraad and S. Wastell (eds), *Thinking Through Things: Theorising Artefacts Ethnographically*, London, 93–112.

Mráv, Z. 2015. 'Maniakion – the golden torc in the Late Roman and early Byzantine army: preliminary research report', in T. Vida (ed.), *The Frontier World: Romans, Barbarians and Military Culture*, Budapest, 287–303.

Mulhall, I. and Briggs, E.K. 2007. 'Presenting a past society to a present day audience: bog bodies in Iron Age Ireland', *Museum Ireland* 17: 71–81.

Munn, N.D. 1977. 'The spatiotemporal transformations of Gawa canoes', *Journal de la Société des Océanistes* 33: 39–53.

Munsell Rock-Color Chart 1991. *Munsell Rock-Color Chart*, The Geological Society of America, Boulder, CO.

Murillo-Barroso, M., Martinón-Torres, M., Hunt Ortiz, M., Forteza González, M., Hernández Arnedo, M.J., García Sanjuán, L. and Wheatley, D. 2015. 'New objects in old structures. The Iron Age hoard of the Palacio III megalithic funerary complex (Almadén de la Plata, Seville, Spain)', *Journal of Archaeological Science* 57: 322–34.

Musson, C.R., with Britnell, W.J. and Smith, A.G. 1991. *The Beiddin Hillfort: A Later Prehistoric Settlement in the Welsh Marches*', Council for British Archaeology Report 76, London.

Naylor, J. and Bland, R. (eds) 2015. *Hoarding and Deposition of Metalwork from the Bronze Age to the 20th Century: A British Perspective*, BAR British Series 615, Oxford.

Needham, S. 2001. 'When expediency broaches ritual intention: the flow of metal between systemic and buried domains', *Journal of the Royal Anthropological Institute* 7(2): 275–98.

Needham, S. 2007. 'Bronze makes a Bronze Age? Considering the systematics of Bronze Age metal use and the implications of selective deposition', in C. Burgess, P. Topping and F. Lynch (eds), *Beyond Stonehenge: Essays on the Bronze Age in Honour of Colin Burgess*, Oxford, 278–87.

Needham, S. 2012. 'Case and place for the British Chalcolithic', in M. Allen, J. Gardiner and J.A. Sheridan (eds), *Is there a British Chalcolithic? People, Place and Polity in the Late Third Millennium*, Oxford, 1–26.

Needham, S.P., Bronk Ramsey, C., Coombs, D., Cartwright, C. and Petitt, P. 1997. 'An independent chronology for British Bronze Age metalwork: the results of the Oxford Radiocarbon Accelerator Programme', *Archaeological Journal* 154: 55–107.

Niblett, R. 1992. 'A Catuvellaunian chieftain's burial from St. Albans', *Antiquity* 66: 917–29.

Norfolk Biodiversity Partnership. 2006. *Lowland Mixed Deciduous Woodland* (http://www.norfolkbiodiversity.org/assets/Uploads/Lowland-mixed-deciduous-woodland-HAP2.pdf) [accessed 2021].

Northover, J.P. 1980. 'The analysis of Welsh Bronze Age metalwork', appendix to H.N. Savory, *Guide Catalogue to the Bronze Age collections*, Cardiff.

Northover, J.P. 1982: 'The metallurgy of the Wilburton hoards', *Oxford Journal of Archaeology* 1(1): 69–109.

Northover, J.P. 1983. 'The exploration of the long-distance movement of bronze in Bronze and early Iron Age Europe', *Bulletin of the Institute of Archaeology, University of London* 19: 45–72.

Northover, J.P. 1984. 'Analysis of the bronze metalwork', in B.W. Cunliffe (ed.), *Danebury, an Iron Age Hillfort in Hampshire*, Vol. 2, *The Excavations 1969–78: The Finds*, CBA Research Report 52, London, 430–3.

Northover, J.P. 1987. 'Non-ferrous metallurgy', in B.W. Cunliffe, *Hengistbury Head, Dorset*, Vol. 1, *The Prehistoric and Roman Settlement, 3500 BC–AD 500*, OUCA Monograph 13, Oxford, 186–96, Fiche 7: A3–12, B1–4.

Northover, J.P. 1991a. 'Non-ferrous metalwork and metallurgy', in N. Sharples, *The excavations at Maiden Castle, 1985–6*, London, 159–65 and microfiche.

Northover, J.P. 1991b. 'Non-ferrous metalwork and metallurgy', in B.W. Cunliffe, *Danebury: an Iron Age hillfort in Hampshire*, vol. 5, *The excavations 1979–1988: the finds*, London, CBA Research Report 73, 407–12.

Northover, J.P. 1992. 'Materials issues in the Celtic coinage', in M. Mays (ed.), *Celtic Coinage: Britain and Beyond*, Eleventh Oxford Symposium on Coinage and Monetary history, BAR British Series 222, Oxford, 235–300.

Northover, J.P. 1995a. 'Bronze Age gold in Britain', in G. Morteani and J.P. Northover (eds), *Prehistoric Gold in Europe, Mines, Metallurgy and Manufacture*, Dordrecht, 515–31.

Northover, J.P. 1995b. 'Late Bronze Age drawplates in the Isleham hoard', in B. Schmid-Sikimić and P. della Casa (eds), *Trans Europam: Beiträge zur Bronze- und Eisenzeit zwischen Atlantik und Altai – Festschrift für Margarita Primas*, Bonn, 15–22.

Northover, J.P. 2004a. 'Analyses of copper alloy metalwork from ACS', in R. Havis and Howard Brooks, *Excavations at Stansted Airport, 1986–91, Vol. I, Prehistoric and Romano-British*, Chelmsford: Heritage Conservation, Essex County Council, East Anglian Archaeology Report 107, 128–30.

Northover, J.P. 2004b. 'Analyse der Metallfunde aus Zug-Sumpf, (tr. S. Hämmerle)', in I. Bauer, B. Rückstuhl and J. Speck, *Der Funde der Grabungen 1923–37: Zug Sumpf*, (Zug: Kantonales Museum für Urgeschichte Zug), Bd 3/1, 102–43 and Bd 3/2 A1.

Northover, P. and Anheuser, K. 2000. 'Gilding in Britain: Celtic, Roman and Saxon', in T. Drayman-Wesisser (ed.), *Gilded Metals: History, Technology and Conservation*, London, 109–21.

Northover, J.P. and Rychner, V. 1998. 'Bronze analysis, experience of a comparative programme', in C. Mordant, M. Pernot and V. Rychner (eds), *L'Atelier du bronzier en Europe du XXe au VIIIe siècle avant Notre* Ère, *I (Session de Neuchâtel)*, Paris, 19–40.

Nowakowski, J.A. 1991. 'Trethellan Farm, Newquay: the excavation of a lowland Bronze Age settlement and Iron Age cemetery', *Cornish Archaeology* 30: 5–242.

Nowakowski, J., Gwilt, A. Megaw, V. and La Niece, S. 2009. 'A late Iron Age neck-ring from Pentire, Newquay, Cornwall, with a note on the find from Boverton, Vale of Glamorgan', *The Antiquaries Journal* 89: 35–52.

Oakley, P. 2013. 'Containing precious metals: hallmarking, minting and the materiality of gold and silver in medieval and modern England', in H.P. Hahn and H. Weiss (eds), *Mobility, Meaning and Transformations of Things: Shifting Contexts of Material Culture through Time and Space*, Oxford, 63–77.

Oakley, P. 2015. 'Introducing fairtrade and fairmined gold: an attempt to reconfigure the social identity of a substance', in A. Drazin and S. Küchler (eds), *The Social Life of Materials: Studies in Materials and Society*, London, 155–74.

O'Connor, B. 1980. *Cross-Channel Relations in the Later Bronze Age: Relations between Britain, NE France and the Low Countries during the Later Bronze Age and the Early Iron Age, with Particular Reference to the Metalwork*, BAR International Series S91(i–ii), Oxford.

O'Connor, B. 2007. 'Llyn Fawr metalwork in Britain: a review', in C. Haselgrove and R. Pope (eds), *The Earlier Iron Age in Britain and the Near Continent*, Oxford, 64–79.

Oddy, W.A. 1977. 'The production of gold wire in antiquity: hand-making methods before the introduction of the draw-plate', *Gold Bulletin* 10: 79–87.

Oddy, A. 1992. *The Art of the Restorer*, London.

Oddy, A. 1993. 'The gilding of metals in the Old World', in S. La Niece and P.T. Craddock (eds), *Metal Plating and Patination*, Oxford, 161–70.

Ogden, J. 1977. 'Platinum group metal inclusions in Ancient Gold Artifacts', *Journal of Historical Metallurgical Society* 11(2): 53–70.

Olsen, B. 2007. 'Keeping things at arm's length: a genealogy of asymmetry', *World Archaeology* 39(4): 579–88.

Ott, D., Raub, C.J. and Rapson, W.S. 1985. 'Investment casting of gold jewellery: porosity in castings, its causes and prevention', *Gold Bulletin* 18 (3): 98–108.

Owles, E. 1969. 'The Ipswich gold torcs', *Antiquity* 43: 208–12.

Owles, E. 1970. 'The sixth Ipswich torc', *Antiquity* 45: 294–6.

Özden, S., Slater, D. and Ennos, R. 2017. 'Fracture properties of green wood formed within the forks of hazel (*Corylus avellana* L.)', *Trees* 31: 903–17.

Özşen, I. and Willer, F. 2016. 'Gezogener antiker Draht? Zur Drahtproduktion des Kettenpanzers aus Zemplín', *Restaurierung und Archäologie* 9: 85–102.

Painter, K. 1970. 'An Iron Age gold-alloy torc from Glascote, Tamworth, Staffordshire', *Staffordshire Archaeological and Historical Society* 11: 1–6.

Painter, K.S. 1971. 'An Iron Age gold-alloy torc from Glascote, Tamworth, Staffordshire', *The Antiquaries Journal* 50: 307–11.

Palk, N.A. 1984. *Iron Age bridle-bits from Britain*, University of Edinburgh Department of Archaeology Occasional Paper No. 10, Edinburgh.

Palk, N. 1992. 'Metal horse harness of the British and Irish Iron Ages', unpublished PhD thesis, University of Oxford.

Parfitt, K. 1995. *Iron Age Burials from Mill Hill, Deal*, London.

Payne, G. 1893. *Collectanea Cantiana: Or, Archaeological Researches in the Neighbourhood of Sittingbourne, and Other Parts of Kent*, London.

PCRG (Prehistoric Ceramics Research Group) 2010. *The Study of Later Prehistoric Pottery: General Policies and Guidelines for Analysis and Publication*, PCRG Occasional Papers 1 and 2 (3rd edn).

Pendergast, D.M. 1982. 'Ancient Maya mercury', *Science* 217, issue 4559: 533–5.

Penn, K. 2006. 'Excavation and survey at the Iron Age fort at Bloodgate Hill, South Creake, 2003', *Norfolk Archaeology* 45(1): 1–27.

Percival, S., 2000. 'The pottery' in Ashwin, T. and Bates, S. (eds), *Excavations on the Norwich Southern Bypass, 1989–91. Part I: Excavations at Bixley, Caistor St Edmund and Trowse*. East Anglian Archaeology 91, Gressenhall: Part 1.

Perea, A., Montero, I., Gutiérrez, P.C. and Climent-Fo, A. 2008. 'Origen y trayectoria de una técnica esquiva: el dorado sobre metal. Rise and course of an elusive technology: metal gilding', *Trabajos de Prehistoria* 65 (2): 117–30.

Pernet, L. 2010. *Armement et auxilaires gaulois (IIe a et Ier siècles avant notre ère)*, Éditions Monique Mergoil Protohistoire Européenne 12, Montagne.

Perrin, J.R. 1999. 'Roman pottery from excavations at and near to the Roman small town of Durobrivae, Water Newton, Cambridgeshire, 1956–58', *Journal of Pottery Studies* 8: 1–139.

Piggott, S. and Daniel, G.E. 1951. *A Picture Book of Ancient British Art*, Cambridge.

Plenderleith, H.J. and Wernher, A.E.A. 1971 [1956]. *The Conservation of Antiquities and Works of Art, Treatment, Repair and Restoration*, London.

Pliny the Elder, 1952 edn. *Natural History*, Volume IX: Books 33–35, translated by H. Rackham, Loeb Classical Library 394, Cambridge, MA.

Pluciennik, M. 2002. 'Art, artefact, metaphor', in Hamilakis *et al.* 2002b, 217–32.

Polanyi, K. 1944. *The Great Transformation: The Political and Economic Origins of Our Time*, Boston.

Pope, R. and Ralston, I. 2011. 'Approaching sex and status in Iron Age Britain with reference to the nearer continent', in T. Moore and

X.-L. Armada (eds), *Atlantic Europe in the First Millennium BC: Crossing the Divide*, Oxford, 375–414.
Pryor, F. 2001. *The Flag Fen Basin: Archaeology and Environment of a Fenland Landscape*, English Heritage Archaeological Reports, London.
Raftery, J. 1940. 'A decorated bronze disc from the River Bann', *Ulster Journal of Archaeology* 3: 27–30.
Rainbird, P. 1999. 'Entangled biographies: Western Pacific ceramics and the tombs of Pohnpei', *World Archaeology* 31(2): 214–24.
Ramage, A. and Craddock, P. 2000. *King Croesus' Gold. Excavations at Sardis and the History of Gold Refining*, London.
Rebay-Salisbury, K. 2016. *The Human Body in Early Iron Age Central Europe: Burial Practices and Images of the Hallstatt World*, London.
Radivojevic, M., Pendić, J., Srejić, A., Korać, M., Daveye, C., Benzonelli, A., Martinón-Torres, M., Jovanović, N. and Kamberović, Ž. 2018. 'Experimental design of the Cu-As-Sn ternary colour diagram', *Journal of Archaeological Science* 90: 106–19.
Reece, R. 1968. 'Summary of the Roman coins from Richborough', in B. Cunliffe, *Fifth report on the Excavations of the Roman Fort at Richborough, Kent*, Reports of the Research Committee of the Society of Antiquaries of London 23, 200–17.
Reid, P. (ed.). 2003. *Sedgeford Historical and Archaeological Research Project Annual Report 2003*, Sedgeford.
Reimer, P.J., Baillie, M.G.L., Bard, E., Bayliss, A., Beck, J.W., Blackwell, P.G., Bronk Ramsey, C., Buck, C.E., Burr, G.S., Edwards, R.L., Friedrich, M., Grootes, P.M., Guilderson, T.P., Hajdas, I., Heaton, T.J., Hogg, A.G., Hughen, K.A., Kaiser, K.F., Kromer, B., McCormac, F.G., Manning, S.W., Reimer, R.W., Richards, D.A., Southon, J.R., Talamo, S., Turney, C.S.M., van der Plicht, J. and Weyhenmeyer, C.E. 2009. 'IntCal09 and Marine09 radiocarbon age calibration curves, 0–50,000 years cal BP', *Radiocarbon* 51(4), 1111–50.
Reimer, P.J., Bard, E., Bayliss, A., Beck, J.W., Blackwell, P.G., Bronk Ramsey, C., Grootes, P.M., Guilderson, T.P., Haflidason, H., Hajdas, I., Hatt'e, C., Heaton, T.J., Hoffmann, D.L., Hogg, A.G., Hughen, K.A., Kaiser, K.F., Kromer, B., Manning, S.W., Niu, M., Reimer, R.W., Richards, D.A., Scott, E.M., Southon, J.R., Staff, R.A., Turney, C.S.M. and van der Plicht, J. 2013. 'IntCal13 and Marine13 Radiocarbon Age Calibration Curves 0–50,000 Years cal BP', *Radiocarbon* 55(4): 1869–87.
Reynolds, P.J. 1979. *Life in the Iron Age*, Minneapolis, MN.
Rigby, V. 2004. *Pots in Pits: The British Museum Yorkshire Settlements Project 1988–92*, East Riding Archaeologist vol. 11, Hull.
Robb, M.H. 2017. *Teotihuacan: City of Water, City of Fire*, San Francisco.
Robb, J. and Harris, O.J.T. (eds) 2013. *The Body in History: Europe from the Palaeolithic to the Future*, Cambridge.
Roberts, B.W. 2007. 'Adorning the living but not the dead: a reassessment of Middle Bronze Age ornaments in Britain', *Proceedings of the Prehistoric Society* 73: 135–67.
Robinson, P. 1995. 'Miniature socketed bronze axes from Wiltshire', *The Wiltshire Archaeological and Natural History Magazine* 88: 60–8.
Rodwell, W. 1976. 'Coinage, oppida and the rise of Belgic power in south-eastern Britain', in B. Cunliffe and T. Rowley (eds), *Oppida: The Beginnings of Urbanisation in Barbaric Europe, Papers Presented to a Conference at Oxford, October 1975*, BAR Supplementary Series 11, Oxford, 181–367.
Russell, M., Smith, M., Cheetham, P., Evans, D. and Manley, H. 2019. 'The girl with the chariot medallion: a well-furnished, Late Iron Age Durotrigian burial from Langton Herring, Dorset', *Archaeological Journal* 176(2): 196–230 (doi: 10.1080/00665983.2019.1573551).
Saunders, N.J. 1999. 'Biographies of brilliance: pearls, transformations of matter and being, c. AD 1492', *World Archaeology* 31(2): 243–57.
Saupe, F. 1990. 'Geology of the Almadén mercury deposit, province of Ciudad Real, Spain', *Economic Geology* 85(3): 482–510.
Savory, H. N. 1976. *Guide Catalogue of the Early Iron Age Collections*, Cardiff.
Scheers, S. 1977. *Traité de Numismatique Celtique II: La Gaule Belgique*, Paris (2nd ed. Leuven, 1983).
Score, V. 2011. *Hoards, Hounds and Helmets. A Conquest-period Ritual Site at Hallaton, Leicestershire*, Leicester Archaeology Monograph 21, Leicester.
Scott, D.A. 2002. *Copper and Bronze in Art, Corrosion, Colorants, Conservation*, Los Angeles.
Seager Smith, R. 2000. 'Worked bone and antler, in A.J. Lawson (ed.), *Potterne 1982–5: Animal Husbandry in Later Prehistoric Wiltshire*, Wessex Archaeological Report 16, Salisbury, 222–40.
Sealey, P.R. 1979. 'The later history of Icenian electrum torcs', *Proceedings of the Prehistoric Society* 45: 165–78.
Sealey, P.R. 1999. 'Finds from the cauldron pit. The spouted strainer bowls', in N.R. Brown (ed.), *The Archaeology of Ardleigh, Essex: Excavations 1955–1980*, East Anglian Archaeology 90, Chelmsford, 117–24.
Sealey, P. 2007. *A Late Iron Age Warrior Burial from Kelvedon, Essex*, East Anglian Archaeology 118, Colchester.
Sellwood, L. 1984. 'Objects of iron', in B. Cunliffe, *Danebury: An Iron Age Hillfort in Hampshire. Volume 2. The Excavations, 1969–1978: The Finds*, Council for British Archaeology Research Report 52, London, 346–71.
Shalev, S. 1993. 'The earliest gold artifacts in the Southern Levant. Reconstruction of the manufacturing process', in C. Éluère (ed.), *Outils et ateliers d'orfèvres des temps anciens*, Saint Germain en Laye, 9–12.
Shanks, M. 2007. 'Symmetrical archaeology', *World Archaeology* 39(4): 589–96.
SHARP 2014. *Digging Sedgeford, A People's Archaeology*, Cromer.
Sharples, N.M. 1991. *Maiden Castle: Excavations and Field Survey 1985–6*, English Heritage Archaeological Report No. 19, London.
Sharples, N. 2007. 'Building communities and creating identities in the first millennium BC', in C. Haselgrove and R. Pope (eds), *The Earlier Iron Age in Britain and the Near Continent*, Oxford, 174–84.
Sharples, N. 2010. *Social Relations in Later Prehistory: Wessex in the First Millennium BC*, Oxford.
Shearman, F. and Dove, S. 1997. 'Applications of radiography in conservation', in J. Lang and A. Middleton (eds), *Radiography of Cultural Material*, London (repr. 2005).
Sills, J. 2003. *Gaulish and Early British Gold Coinage*, London.
Sills, J. 2017. *Divided Kingdoms: The Iron Age Gold Coinage of Southern England*, Aylsham, Norfolk.
Simmel, G. 1957 [1904]. 'Fashion', *The American Journal of Sociology* 62: 541–58.
Smith, R.A. 1905. *A Guide to the Antiquities of the Early Iron Age of Central and Western Europe*, London.
Smith, R.A. 1925. *A Guide to the Antiquities of the Early Iron Age of Central and Western Europe* (2nd edn), London.
Sofaer, J.R. 2006. *The Body as Material Culture: A Theoretical Osteoarchaeology*, Cambridge.
Splitstoser, J.C. 2012. 'The parenthetical notation method for recording yarn structure', *Textile Society of America Symposium*

Proceedings (2012): paper 745 (http://digitalcommons.unl.edu/tsaconf/745).
Spratling, M.G. 1972. 'Southern British decorated bronzes of the late pre-Roman Iron Age', unpublished PhD thesis, University of London.
Spratling, M.G. 1973. 'The Iron Age settlement of Gussage All Saints. Part II: the bronze foundry', *Antiquity* 47: 117–30.
Spratling, M. 2008. 'On the aesthetics of the Ancient Britons', in D. Garrow, C. Gosden and J.D. Hill (eds), *Rethinking Celtic Art*, Oxford, 185–202.
Staelens, Y.J.E. 1982. 'The Birdlip Cemetery', *Transactions of the Bristol and Gloucestershire Archaeological Society* 100: 19–31.
Standish, C.D., Dhuime, B., Hawkesworth, C.J. and Pike, A.W.G. 2015. 'A non-local source of Irish Chalcolithic and Early Bronze Age gold', *Proceedings of the Prehistoric Society* 81: 149–77.
Stead, I.M. 1965. *The La Tène Cultures of Eastern Yorkshire*, York.
Stead, I.M. 1967. 'A La Tène burial at Welwyn Garden City', *Archaeologia* 101: 1–62.
Stead, I.M. 1976. *Excavations at Winterton Roman Villa and other Roman sites in North Lincolnshire, 1958–1967*, Department of the Environment archaeological reports, London.
Stead, I.M. 1979. *The Arras Culture*, York.
Stead, I.M. 1985a. *Celtic Art: In Britain Before the Roman Conquest*, London.
Stead, I.M. 1985b. *The Battersea Shield*, London.
Stead, I.M. 1991a. 'The Snettisham treasure: excavations in 1990', *Antiquity* 65: 447–65.
Stead, I.M. 1991b. *Iron Age Cemeteries in East Yorkshire*, London.
Stead, I. 1991c. 'Many more Iron Age shields from Britain', *The Antiquaries Journal* 71: 1–35 (doi:10.1017/S0003581500086807).
Stead, I.M. 1995a. 'Die Schatzfunde von Snettisham', *Archäologie in Deutschland*: 100–10.
Stead, I.M. 1995b. 'The metalwork', in K. Parfitt (ed.), *Iron Age Burials from Mill Hill, Deal*, London, 59–111.
Stead, I.M. 1996. *Celtic Art* (2nd edn), London.
Stead, I.M. 1998. *The Salisbury Hoard*, Stroud.
Stead, I.M. 2006. *British Iron Age Swords and Scabbards*, London.
Stead, I.M. 2009. 'The chronology of La Tène art in Britain', in G. Cooney, K. Becker, J. Coles, M. Ryan and S. Sievers (eds), *Relics of Old Decency: Archaeological Studies in Later Prehistory, Festschrift for Barry Raftery*, Dublin, 323–32.
Stead, I.M. 2014. 'A Snettisham swan song', in C. Gosden, S. Crawford and K. Ulmschneider (eds), *Celtic Art in Europe: Making Connections*, Oxford, 297–303.
Stead, I.M. and Jackson, R. (unpublished). *Snettisham Draft Catalogue*, London.
Stead, I.M. and Rigby, V. 1989. *Verulamium: The King Harry Lane Site*, English Heritage Report No. 12, London.
Stead, I.M. and Rigby, V. 1999. *The Morel Collection: Iron Age Antiquities from Champagne in the British Museum*, London.
Stead, I.M., Bourke, J.B. and Brothwell, D. 1985. *Lindow Man: The Body in the Bog*, London.
Stead, I.M., Flouest, J.-L. and Rigby, V. (eds) 2006. *Iron Age and Roman Burials in Champagne*, Oxford.
Stig Sørensen, M.-L. 1997. 'Reading dress: the construction of social categories and identities in Bronze Age Europe', *Journal of European Archaeology* 5(1): 93–114.
Stig Sørensen, M.-L. and Rebay-Salisbury, K. (eds) 2013. *Embodied Knowledge: Historical Perspectives on Belief and Technology*, Oxford.
Stone, E.C. 1987. 'Iron Age metalcraft in southern Britain', unpublished BA dissertation, Department of Metallurgy and Science of Materials, University of Oxford.
Strang, V. 2005. 'Common senses: water, sensory experience and the generation of meaning', *Journal of Material Culture* 10(1): 92–120.
Strathern, M. 1990. *The Gender of the Gift: Problems with Women and Problems with Society in Melanesia*, Oakland, CA.
Swift, E. 2017. *Roman Artefacts and Society: Design, Behaviour and Experience*. Oxford, Oxford University Press.
Talbot, J. 2017. *Made for Trade: A New View of Icenian Coinage*, Oxford.
TAR 2004. *Treasure Annual Report 2004* (published 2007), Department for Culture, Media & Sport, London.
Taylor, A., Weale, A. and Ford, S. 2014. *Bronze Age, Iron Age and Roman Landscapes of the Coastal Plain, and a Late Iron Age Warrior Burial at North Bersted, Bognor Regis, West Sussex*, Thames Valley Archaeological Services Monograph 23, Reading.
Taylor, M. 1996. 'Worked wood', in J. Pollard, 'Iron Age riverside pit alignments at St Ives, Cambridgeshire', *Proceedings of the Prehistoric Society* 62: 93–115.
Thomas, J. 2002. 'Archaeology's humanism and the materiality of the body', in Hamilakis *et al.* 2002b, 29–45.
Thomas, N. 2005. *Conderton Camp, Worcestershire: A Small Middle Iron Age Hillfort on Bredon Hill*, Council for British Archaeology Report 143, London.
Thomas, S. 1965. *Pre-Roman Britain*, London.
Tomber, R. and Dore, J. 1998. *The National Roman Fabric Reference Collection: A Handbook*, MoLAS Monograph 2, London.
Treherne, P. 1995. 'The warrior's beauty: the masculine body and self-identity in Bronze-Age Europe', *Journal of European Archaeology* 3(1): 105–44.
Tremlett, S. 2011. 'Iron Age landscapes from the air: results from the Norfolk national mapping programme', in J.A. Davies (ed.), *The Iron Age in Northern East Anglia: New Work in the Land of the Iceni*, BAR British Series 549, Oxford, 25–40.
Triadan, D. 2006. 'Dancing gods: ritual, performance, and political organisation in the prehistoric Southwest', in Inomata and Coben 2006b, 159–86.
Tulp, C., Meeks, N.D. and Paardekooper, R.P. (eds) 2001. *Proceedings of the 1st International Workshop on Experimental and Educational Aspects of Bronze Metallurgy, Wilhelminaoord, October 1999*, Leiden.
Tuohy, T. 1999. *Prehistoric Combs of Antler and Bone*, BAR British Series 285, Oxford.
Turner, T.S. 1980. 'The social skin', in J. Cherfas and R. Lewin (eds), *Not Work Alone: A Cross-Cultural View of Activities Superfluous to Survival*, London, 112–40.
Tyers, P. 1996. *Roman Pottery in Britain*, London.
Tylecote, R.F. 1967. 'The bloomery site at West Rundton', *Norfolk Archaeology* 34(2): 187–214.
Tyrrell, R. and Major, H. 2015. 'Jet and shale beads', in M. Atkinson and S.J. Preston (eds), Heybridge: A Late Iron Age and Roman Settlement, Excavations at Elms Farm 1993–5, *Internet Archaeology* 40 (http://dx.doi.org/10.11141/ia.40.1.major3).
Untracht, O. 1969. *Metal Techniques for Craftsmen. A Basic Manual on the Methods of Forming and Decorating metals*, London.
Untracht, O. 1982. *Jewelry Concepts and Technology*, London.
Van Arsdell, R.D. 1989. *Celtic Coinage of Britain*, London.
Van Arsdell, R.D. 1993. 'Coin scales in late pre-Roman Iron Age Britain', *Oxford Journal of Archaeology* 12: 361–5.
Van Arsdell, R.D. and Northover, J.P. 2004. 'Ancient British coins', in R. Havis and H. Brooks (eds), *Excavations at Stansted Airport, 1986–91*,

Vol I: Prehistoric and Romano-British, East Anglian Archaeology Report 107 (Chelmsford), 115–20.

Van Casteren, A., Sellers, W.I., Thorpe, S.K.S., Coward, S., Crompton, R.H. and Ennos, A.R. 2012. 'Why don't branches snap? The mechanics of bending failure in three temperate angiosperm trees', *Trees – Structure and Function* 26: 789–97.

Van de Noort, R., Chapman, H.P. and Collis, J. 2007. *Sutton Common: The Excavation of an Iron Age 'Marsh Fort'*, London.

Viveiros de Castro, E. 1992. *From the Enemy's Point of View: Humanity and Divinity in an Amazonian Society*, Chicago.

Viveiros de Castro, E. 1998. 'Cosmological deixis and Amerindian perspectivism', *The Journal of the Royal Anthropological Institute* 4(3): 469–88.

Viveiros de Castro, E. 2004. 'Exchanging perspectives: the transformation of objects into subjects in Amerindian ontologies', *Common Knowledge* 10(3): 463–84.

Waddington, K. and Sharples, N. 2011. *The Excavation at Whitchurch 2006–2009: An Interim Report*, Oxford.

Waddington, K., Bayliss, A., Higham, T., Madgwick, R. and Sharples, N. 2019. 'Histories of deposition: creating chronologies for the Late Bronze Age-Early Iron Age transition in southern Britain', *Archaeological Journal* 176(1): 84–133.

Wagner, R. 1991. 'The fractal person', in M. Strathern and M. Godelier (eds), *Big Men and Great Men: Personifications of Power in Melanesia*, Cambridge, 159–73.

Wainwright, G.J. 1972. 'The excavation of a Neolithic settlement on Broome Heath, Ditchingham, Norfolk, England', *Proceedings of the Prehistoric Society* 38: 1–107.

Wainwright, G.J. 1973. 'The excavation of prehistoric and Romano-British settlements at Eaton Heath, Norwich', *Archaeological Journal* 130(1): 1–43.

Wainwright, G. and Spratling, M. 1973. 'The Iron Age settlement of Gussage All Saints', *Antiquity* 47: 109–30.

Wake, T. 1942. 'Some recent archaeological discoveries in Norfolk', *Norfolk Archaeology* 28: 26–7.

Waller, M. 1994. *The Fenland Project, Number 9: Flandrian Environmental Change in Fenland*, East Anglian Monograph no. 70, Cambridge.

Warner, R. 2004. 'Irish gold artefacts: observations from Hartmann's analytical data', in H. Roche, E. Grogan, J. Bradley, J. Coles and B. Raftery (eds), *From Megaliths to Metal: Essays in Honour of George Eogan*, Oxford, 72–82.

Webley, L. 2015. 'Rethinking Iron Age connections across the Channel and North Sea', in H. Anderson-Whymark, D. Garrow and F. Sturt (eds), *Continental Connections: Exploring Cross-Channel Relationships from the Mesolithic to the Iron Age*, Oxford, 122–44.

Webley, L., Timby, J. and Wilson, M. 2007. *Fairfield Park: Later Prehistoric Settlement in the Eastern Chilterns*, Bedfordshire Archaeology Monograph 7, Bedford.

Webley, L., Adams, S. and Brück, J. 2020. *The Social Context of Technology: Non-ferrous Metalworking in Later Prehistoric Britain and Ireland*, Havertown (doi:10.2307/j.ctv12pntnj).

Webmoor, T. 2007. 'What about "one more turn after the social" in archaeological reasoning? Taking things seriously', *World Archaeology* 39(4): 563–78.

Webmoor, T. and Witmore, C.L. 2008. 'Things are us! A commentary on human/thing relations under the banner of a "social" archaeology', *Norwegian Archaeological Review* 41(1): 53–70.

Weiner, A.B. 1985. 'Inalienable wealth', *American Ethnologist* 12: 210–27.

Weiner, A.B. 1992. *Inalienable Possessions: The Paradox of Keeping-While-Giving*, Berkeley, CA.

Wells, P.S. 2001. *The Barbarians Speak: How the Conquered Peoples Shaped the Roman Empire*, Princeton.

Wheeler, R.E.M. 1943. *Maiden Castle, Dorset*, Oxford.

Wheeler, R.E.M. and Wheeler, T.V. 1936. *Verulamium: A Belgic and Two Roman Cities. Reports of the Research Committee of the Society of Antiquaries* 11, Oxford.

Whimster, R. 1977. 'Harlyn Bay reconsidered: the excavations of 1900–1905 in the light of recent work', *Cornish Archaeology* 16: 61–88.

Whimster, R. 1981. *Burial Practices in Iron Age Britain: A Discussion and Gazetteer of the Evidence c. 700 BC–AD 43*, BAR British Series 90, Oxford.

Whitaker, T.D. 1816. *Loidis and Elmete*, Leeds.

Whitehead, A.N. 1978. *Process and Reality*, New York.

Whitehead, A.N. 1985. *Science and the Modern World*, London.

Whitfield, N. 1990. 'Round wire in the early Middle Ages', *Jewellery Studies* 4: 13–28.

Whitfield, N. 1998. 'The manufacture of ancient beaded wire: experiments and observations', *Jewellery Studies* 8: 57–86.

Whitfield, N. 2004. 'The manufacture of beaded wire in the post-Roman period', in A. Perea, I. Montero and Ó. García-Vuelta (eds), *Tecnología del Oro Antiguo: Europa y América, Ancient Gold Technology: America and Europe*, Madrid, 127–37.

Whitley, J. 2013. 'Homer's entangled objects: narrative, agency and personhood in and out of Iron Age texts', *Cambridge Journal of Archaeology* 23(3): 395–416.

Whitmore, D. 2004. 'Excavations at a Neolithic Site at the John Innes Centre, Colney 2000', *Norfolk Archaeology* XLIV (III): 422–26.

Whittle, A., Healy, F. and Bayliss A. 2011. *Gathering Time. Dating the Early Neolithic Enclosures of Southern Britain and Ireland*, Oxford.

Whyte, N. 2009. *Inhabiting the Landscape: Place, Custom and Memory, 1500–1800*, Oxford.

Wijnhoven, M.A. 2022. *European Mail Armour: Ringed Battle Shirts from the Iron Age, Roman Period and Early Middle Ages*, Amsterdam.

Wild, J. 1970. 'Button-and-loop fasteners in the Roman provinces', *Britannia* 1: 137–55.

Willkinson, R. 2019. 'Iron Age metalwork object hoards of Britain, 800 BC–AD 100', unpublished PhD dissertation, University of Leicester.

Williams, C.E. and McArdle, P. 1978. 'Ireland', in S.H.U. Bowie, A. Kvalheim and H.W. Haslam (eds), *Mineral Deposits of Europe, vol. 1: Northwest Europe*, London, 319–45.

Williams, D. 2007. 'Green Lane Wanborough: excavations at the Roman religious site 1999', *Surrey Archaeological Collections* 93: 149–265.

Williams, D. and Ogden, J. 1994. *Greek Gold. Jewellery of the Classical World*, London.

Williams, J.H.C. 2001. *Beyond the Rubicon: Romans and Gauls in Republican Italy*, Oxford.

Willis, S. 2007. 'Sea, coast, estuary, land, and culture in Iron Age Britain', in Haselgrove and Moore 2007, 107–29.

Wiltshire, P. 2003. 'Palynology', in C. Evans (ed.), *Power and Island Communities: Excavations at the Wardy Hill Ringwork, Coveney, Ely*, East Anglian Archaeology 103, Cambridge, 71–84.

Wiltshire, P. E. J. and Murphy, P. L. 1999. 'Current knowledge of the Iron Age environment and agrarian economy of Norfolk and adjacent areas', in J. Davies and T. Williamson (eds), *Land of the Iceni: The Iron Age in Northern East Anglia*, Norwich, 132–61.

Wingfield, C. 2011. 'Donors, loaners and swappers: the relationships behind the English collections at the Pitt Rivers Museum', in S. Byrne, A. Clarke, R. Harrison and R. Torrence (eds), *Unpacking the*

Collection: Networks of Material and Social Agency in the Museum, New York, 119–40.
Wingfield, C. 2013. 'Reassembling the London Missionary Society collection: experiments with symmetrical anthropology and the archaeological sensibility', in S. Byrne, A. Clarke and R. Harrison (eds), *Reassembling the Collection*, SAR Seminar Series, Santa Fe, NM, 61–87.
Witmore, C.L. 2007. 'Symmetrical archaeology: excerpts of a manifesto', *World Archaeology* 39(4): 546–62.
Woodward, A. 2002. Beads and beakers: heirlooms and relics in the British Early Bronze Age', *Antiquity* 76: 1040–7.
Wright, J., Leivers, M. Seager Smith, R. and Stevens, C. 2009. *Cambourne New Settlement: Iron Age and Romano-British Settlement on the Clay Uplands of West Cambridgeshire*, Wessex Archaeology Report No. 23, Salisbury.
Yates, D. and Bradley, R. 2010a. 'Still water, hidden depths: the deposition of Bronze Age metalwork in the English Fenland', *Antiquity* 84: 405–15.
Yates, D. and Bradley, R. 2010b. 'The sting of metalwork hoards in the Bronze Age of southeast England', *The Antiquaries Journal* 90: 41–72.
Young, C.J. 1977. *The Roman Pottery Industry of the Oxford Region*, BAR British Series 43, Oxford.

Contributors

Julia Farley is a curator at the British Museum. She was responsible for the European Iron Age collections from 2014 to 2021, and now works as the Lead Curator on the Reimagining the British Museum project. She has curated a number of exhibitions, including *Celts: art and identity* (2015–16), organised in partnership between the British Museum and National Museums Scotland. Julia also held a Leverhulme Early Career Fellowship at the University of Leicester, looking at the circulation of gold and silver. Her work explores craft, making and materials, and the colonial encounter between communities in Iron Age Britain and the Roman world.

Jody Joy is a Senior Curator at the Museum of Archaeology and Anthropology, University of Cambridge, where he is responsible for the European Archaeology collections. Prior to that, he was Curator of the European Iron Age at the British Museum. He has curated numerous exhibitions over the past 20 years on subjects as varied as the Archaeology of Childhood and the Mesolithic site of Star Carr. He has published widely on numerous topics including, the archaeology and art of the European Iron Age and the ethics of displaying human remains in museums.

Sophia Adams is Curator of the First Millennium European and Roman Conquest period collections at the British Museum. Her post-doctoral research has focused on metalworking evidence from artefacts to sites and artefact chronologies. In her current role she draws on experience gained through a variety of heritage-based roles including development-led and community archaeology projects and higher and further education teaching and research.

Caroline Cartwright is a Senior Scientist in the Department of Scientific Research at the British Museum. Her primary areas of scientific expertise cover the identification and interpretation of organic materials, including wood, charcoal, fibres, macro-plant remains, bone, ivory and shell. Reconstructing past environments, charting vegetation and climate changes, and investigating bioarchaeological evidence from sites and data form important aspects of her research, with 310 publications (to date).

Mike Cowell has applied a range of scientific methodologies investigating archaeological contexts and, more often, artefacts of all types and materials, but particularly metalwork, during his career at the British Museum, Department of Scientific Research.

Paul Craddock graduated in chemistry from the University of Birmingham in 1966 and joined the British Museum where he remained for the rest of his career. He worked first as an analyst, but latterly he has researched all aspects of early mining, extractive metallurgy and metalworking. This has included excavating early mines and smelting sites around the world as well as the scientific and technical study of archaeological and historical artefacts.

John Davies was Chief Curator for Norfolk Museums Service (NMS) and Keeper of Archaeology until December 2018. He was also Project Director (at NMS) for the major redevelopment of the historic Norman keep at Norwich Castle between 2013–18. He previously led the Interreg European project 'Norman Connections', linking historic sites in Normandy and southern England. He has worked as an archaeologist in Norfolk since 1984. Joining NMS in 1991, he has specialised in the Roman and later prehistoric periods. He is also a numismatist and has published widely on the subject of coinage from British archaeological sites.

Michael de Bootman has been interested in Roman pottery since finding a Roman kiln site on his father's farm at Pentney, Norfolk aged 8. On leaving school, he worked on the Raunds project in Northamptonshire fieldwalking and then joined the army before setting up a specialist book selling and publishing company in the late 1990s. Working with Alice Lyons, he is currently involved in bringing to publication a corpus of the Nar Valley Roman pottery industry.

Philip de Jersey has been the Archaeology Officer for the States of Guernsey since 2008. After reading Geography at Hertford College, Oxford, he completed a DPhil in the archaeology of north-west France, published as *Coinage in Iron Age Armorica* in 1994. Between 1992 and 2007 he worked at the Celtic Coin Index, held at the Institute of Archaeology in Oxford. He has published widely on the archaeology and numismatics of Iron Age Britain and France, with a particular focus in recent years on the huge Iron Age hoard of coins and metalwork found at Le Câtillon, Jersey in 2012.

John Fenn is a silver/goldsmith specialising in little used hand-working methods, for example deep surface embossing, and hammer graving that allows duplication of the cross-hatching of many British Iron Age bronze mirrors. Techniques of lap grinding and polishing bronze demonstrate the remarkable clarity and reflectivity of British mirrors. Experience with these processes and materials has made the authenticity of finds of particular interest, as well as highlighting problems of manufacture and function that are not always certain, for example demonstrating economical production of Snettisham torc wire.

Eleanor Ghey is a curator in the Department of Money and Medals at the British Museum with responsibility for coin hoards reported as potential Treasure under the Treasure Act 1996. This role includes reporting and advising on new discoveries and she has researched and published Iron Age and Roman hoards and site assemblages from the British Isles. Her previous publications include *Hoards: Hidden History* (2015) and has recently edited *Recent Discoveries of Tetrarchic Hoards from Roman Britain and their Wider Context* (2024).

Marilyn Hockey joined the British Museum's Department of Conservation in 1976 and worked on the conservation of historical and archaeological metalwork of all periods. In the course of her career she developed a particular specialism in the investigative re-shaping and repair of precious metals. She retired in 2015, having served for ten years as Head of the Ceramics, Glass and Metals Section.

David Holman is an independent numismatist with a particular interest in Iron Age coinage made and found in Kent. He has been recording Iron Age coins found by metal detector users and on archaeological excavations across the county since the early 1990s, and has contributed significant numbers of records to the Celtic Coin Index. More recently, the opportunity to record the Flat Linear potin hoards from Thanet led to the development of an entirely new classification of the series, making it possible to improve identifications and gain new insights into the hoards.

Duncan Hook is a research scientist specialising in the examination and analysis of museum and archaeological artefacts. He has applied analytical techniques such as X-ray fluorescence, atomic absorption spectrophotometry and ICP-AES to a wide range of materials, but especially to gold, silver and copper alloys, dating from the inception of metallurgy to the present day. These studies have enabled objects to be characterised accurately for purposes such as authenticity issues and aspects of conservation. He is a Visiting Academic in the Department of Scientific Research at the British Museum.

Susan La Niece publishes extensively on the metal technology of many periods and cultures. For the Treasure process she has reported the results of examination and XRF analysis of hundreds of metal finds from all over England. These have included a number of important Iron Age pieces, for example the Winchester Hoard. Amongst her research interests at the British Museum are Bronze Age and Iron Age Britain, gold alloys, gilding, silver plating, patination and inlays. She is the editor of the online journal *Jewellery Studies*.

Janet Lang is Visiting Academic at the British Museum and a former member of staff in the Department of Scientific Research at the British Museum, specialising in research into the metallurgy and metallography of ancient silver, iron and steel. She has published extensively on the manufacture of silver in the Classical world and is currently working on an edited volume about silver in Late Antiquity.

Alice Lyons first studied archaeology as an undergraduate at York University, before undertaking a 'Ceramics and Lithics' master's degree at Southampton University, finally completing a doctorate in Archaeological Ceramics at the University of East Anglia (2022). Working at Norfolk Archaeological Unit, Oxford Archaeology East and Pre-Construct Archaeology has led to a diverse career evolving from an excavator to a Roman pottery specialist, to an author and post-excavation manager. Currently Alice is the President for the Study Group of Roman Pottery, and the Managing Editor of *East Anglian Archaeology*.

Peter Makey is a freelance flint specialist and archaeologist based in East Yorkshire. He studied archaeology and prehistory at the University of Sheffield and practical archaeology and conservation crafts in Dorset. He has worked in the field for the British Museum on numerous occasions and was one of the principal members of the Snettisham excavation team.

Nigel Meeks is a former member of staff and a Visiting Academic in the Department of Scientific Research at the British Museum. He specialises in metallurgy, materials science and microscopy applied to technological studies and research into metalsmithing techniques used in antiquity – in particular, studies of Greek gold jewellery, South American goldwork, Iron Age goldwork and a variety of gold antiquities. He has applied analytical scanning electron microscopy (SEM-EDX) to a wide range of gold jewellery and other materials, objects and polished samples including ceramics, high-tin bronzes, metalworking debris and toolmarks on objects.

Aude Mongiatti is a scientist in the Department of Scientific Research at the British Museum, specialising in the study of metallurgical remains and metalwork. Her research includes contemporary silversmithing in Oman, the Oxus Treasure and related Achaemenid gold and technical ceramics and metallurgical remains from ancient Nubia. She has more recently been involved in projects on the analysis of Sasanian copper alloys, the study of West African copper metalwork and Eurasian and Chinese gold and copper alloy artefacts from the first two millennia BC.

Peter Northover read Metallurgy at Oxford where he also completed a DPhil. Since then he has been pursuing the characterisation of non-ferrous and precious metals in archaeology up to and beyond the Industrial Revolution. Particular projects include developing a quantitative approach to metallography for correlation with compositional analysis, with projects ranging from the metallography of fire-damaged bronze and silver to the metallurgy of early railways. In retirement he is pursuing a PhD in landscape archaeology at the University of Exeter.

Daniel O'Flynn is X-ray Imaging Scientist in the Department of Scientific Research at the British Museum, where he applies advanced X-ray and neutron imaging techniques across the collection. His publications include research into animal mummification, ancient cancer and the manufacture of metal and ceramic objects. He holds a PhD in Physics from the University of Warwick.

Sarah Percival is a highly experienced prehistoric pottery specialist working on Neolithic, Bronze Age and Iron Age assemblages from across East Anglia and the East Midlands. She first studied archaeology and prehistory as an undergraduate at Sheffield University (1986–9), before undertaking a 'Ceramics and Lithics' master's degree at Southampton University (2004–5), and has worked at Norfolk Archaeological Unit, Oxford Archaeology East and Cambridge Archaeology Unit, though she is primarily a freelance specialist. She is the incoming Chair of the PCRG.

Alan Pipe graduated in 1974 from Royal Holloway College with a Zoology B.Sc. He worked in vertebrate palaeontology at University College London, before undertaking a marine biology research fellowship at the University of Strathclyde. In 1985, he began working on archaeological animal bone at the Ancient Monuments Laboratory, and the Passmore Edwards Museum, before his appointment as archaeozoologist at the Museum of London (1990). He is now senior archaeozoologist at the Museum of London Archaeology (MOLA).

Matthew Ponting is Reader in Archaeological Materials at the University of Liverpool. He graduated with a BA in Archaeological Studies from the University of Leicester in 1990 and a PhD in Archaeometallurgy from University College London (Institute of Archaeology) in 1994. He subsequently held positions as Scientific Officer in the British Museum, Post-Doctoral Fellow at the Hebrew University of Jerusalem and Chemistry Fellow at The British School at Athens. In 2000 Matthew was appointed Research Officer in the Department of Archaeology at Nottingham University and this was followed by a period as an Archaeological Scientist for English Heritage.

Fleur Shearman worked at the British Museum as a conservator-restorer from 1980–2020. She specialised in the investigative conservation of archaeological grave goods and their associated organic remains; Egyptian polychrome bronze; the Museum's historic collections and the X-radiography of metals, ceramics and Renaissance enamel. She has supported training and research initiatives for the Museum and the wider conservation profession. External collaborations have included the Hallaton Roman militaria and Anglo-Saxon horse burials.

Tony Spence graduated in Archaeology from University College, Cardiff in 1983 and joined the British Museum the following year. In the next 15 years he combined fieldwork and collection management, working on a variety of Iron Age and Medieval research excavations and post-excavations, and collections documentation at the Museum. From 2006 he undertook a variety of roles around collections storage and consultancy on museum architectural schemes, alongside a continued interest in reconstructing Iron Age chariots. He retired as Head of Collection Services in the BM in 2019.

Ian Stead was an Assistant Inspector (1962–4) then Inspector (1964–74) of Ancient Monuments, Ministry of Works (Department of the Environment); subsequently he was in charge of Iron Age antiquities in the Department of Prehistoric and Romano-British Antiquities, British Museum, as Assistant Keeper (1974–7) and then Deputy Keeper (1977–96). He is a Fellow of the British Academy.

Index

Page numbers in *italic* indicate illustrations, those in **bold**, tables

Collins

CW01639462

Livemocha ACTIVE GERMAN

HarperCollins Publishers
77–85 Fulham Palace Road
London W6 8JB
Great Britain

www.collinslanguage.com

First edition 2011

Reprint 10 9 8 7 6 5 4 3 2 1 0

ISBN (UK edition) 978-0-00-737354-3
ISBN (export edition) 978-0-00-741978-4
ISBN (US edition) 978-0-87779-556-8

A catalogue record for this book is available from the British Library

Typeset by Macmillan Publishing Services

Audio material recorded and produced by Networks SRL, Milan

Printed and Bound in China by Leo Paper Products Ltd.
Series Editor: Rob Scriven

INTRODUCTION

Welcome to your Livemocha Active German experience! This new course goes above and beyond what a traditional book-based course can offer. With its focus on online learning, Active German provides the opportunity not just to study but to experience the language for yourself by interacting with native speakers online.

Why go online?
Studying a language online allows you to learn in a more natural atmosphere – watching people interact in a **video** is far more lifelike than listening to conversations on a CD. After watching a video dialog, you will be walked through an explanation of some of the **grammar** and **vocabulary** items that were introduced in the new dialog. Then, by completing a variety of **interactive quizzes**, the system will instantly be able to tell you how well you are doing. You can then **talk online** with native German speakers to practice what you've learned.

Who else is online?
Livemocha boasts over 7 million members and is growing every day. These members are online for the same reason as you – to learn and experience a new language. Native German-speaking members will be happy to read through your written and spoken submissions and to give you feedback on how you're doing. You can also connect with people who want to chat in any given language – interaction on an informal, nonacademic basis is an ideal way for you to perfect your language skills.

What do the books do?
The four accompanying books are designed to complement the online course – the dialogs for all of the videos that you can watch online are available here for you to study whenever you don't have access to the Internet. You will also find all of the Grammar and Vocabulary sections explained in the books, plus the culture notes to teach you a little about Germany.

LEVEL 1

This book is the first of four. It corresponds with Level 1 of the online course.

Level 1 is ideal for students who are newcomers to the language or for those who need to start from the basics.

What you will learn

- How to talk about yourself and where you are from
- How to use articles, ask questions and form negative and plural statements
- How to talk about possession
- How to form the present tense
- Vocabulary for numbers, the alphabet, jobs, the weather, rooms of the house, furniture and household objects, telling the time, days of the week and months of the year

Every time you see this coffee cup symbol in these books, it indicates the presence of a pathway – a guide to exactly where you can find that particular piece of content online. Log on at www.livemocha.com and follow the path to find the online version of what you are studying in the book.

Video Dialog

A warm welcome for Matthias as he gets to know his new colleagues a little better.

Active German: Level 1 > *Unit 2* > *Lesson 1* > *Video dialog*

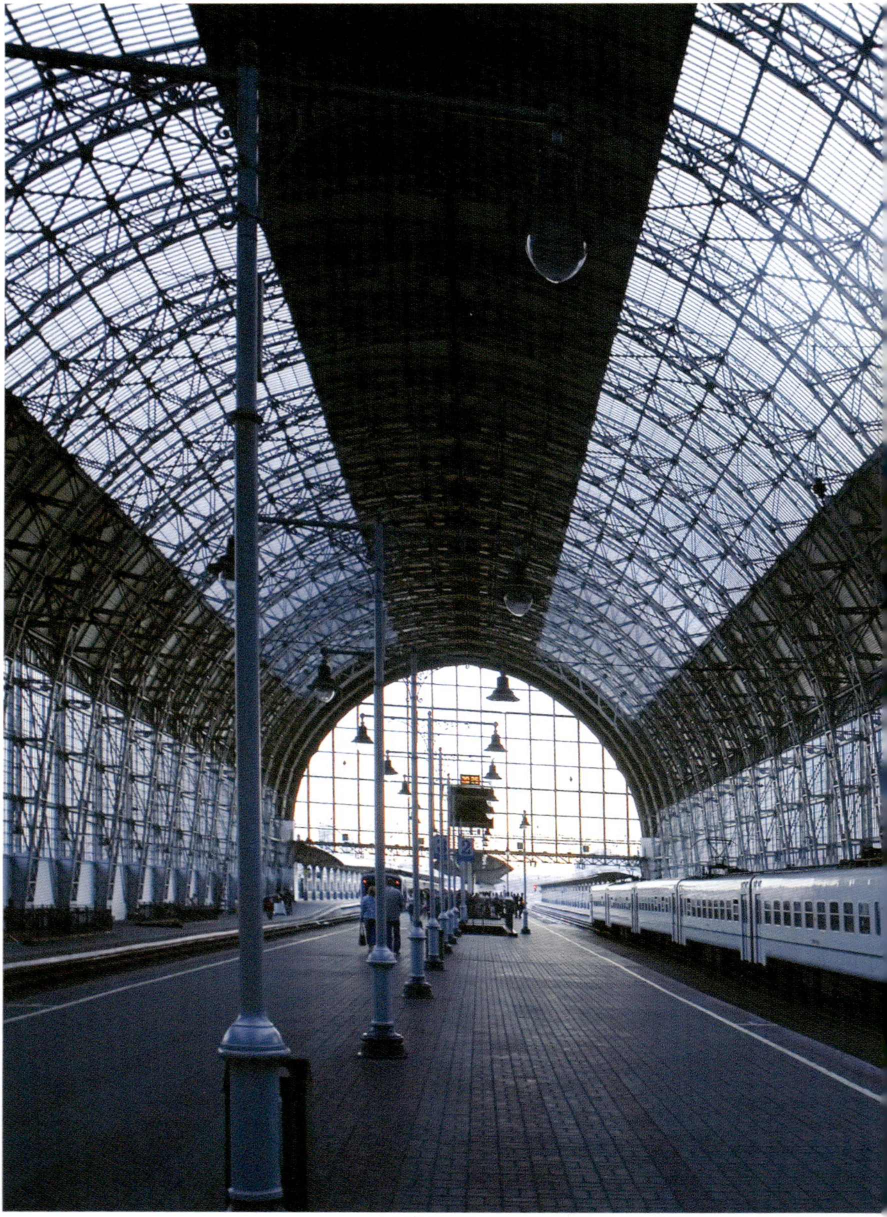
2

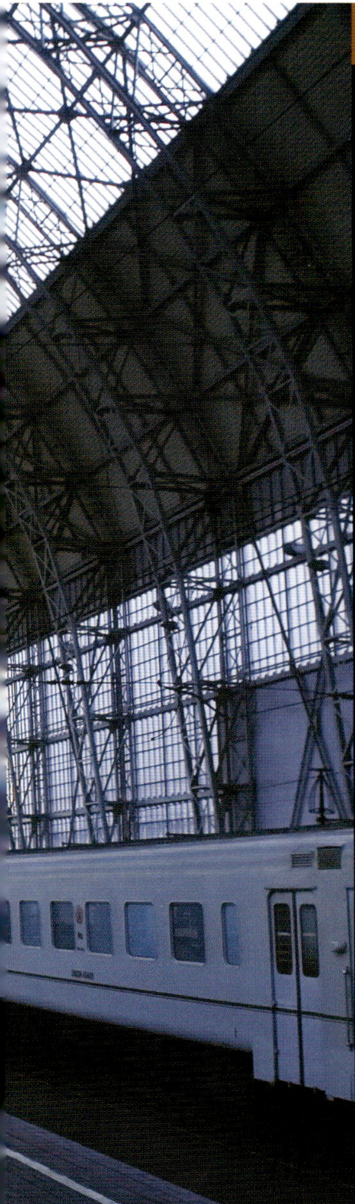

1

Lesson 1: Arrival – At the train station 1

- How to introduce yourself: ***Ich heiße...***
- How to greet someone and say how you are: ***Guten Tag, wie geht es Ihnen?***
- How to form verbs: ***Ich heiße, er heißt ..., Ich komme, er kommt.***
- Vocabulary for titles: ***Herr/Frau.***
- Vocabulary for nationalities.

Lesson 2: Arrival – At the train station 2

- How to give information about yourself.
- How to spell out words in German.
- How verbs work: ***Ich trinke.***
- How to form questions: ***Was trinken Sie?***

Collins | Livemocha™

UNIT 1 › LESSON 1

Arrival – At the train station 1

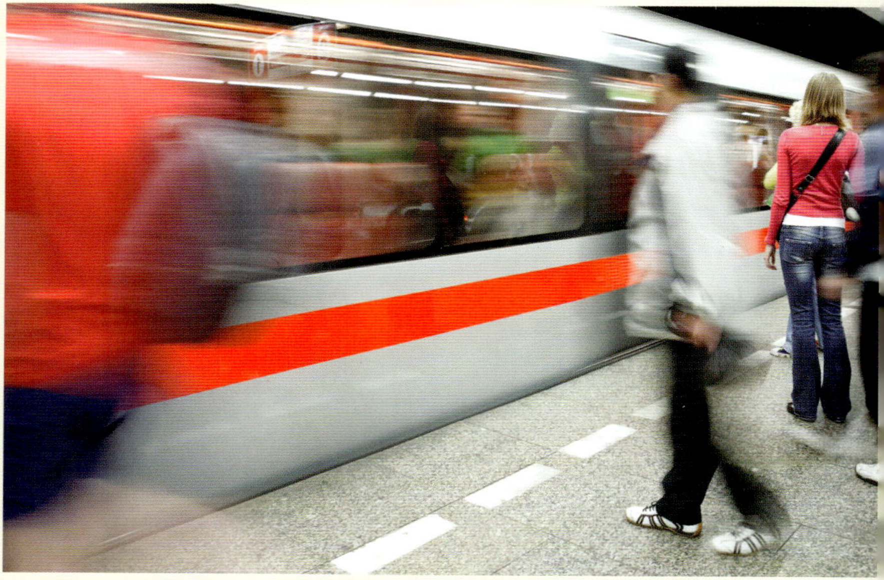

Culture note

German is not only spoken in Germany. Today it has over 100 million speakers and it is the official language in Germany and Austria. It is one of the official languages of Switzerland and is also used in parts of Belgium, Luxembourg, Liechtenstein, and northern Italy. Over 80 million people speak German as a foreign language.

Video Dialog

Mr. Buschel is at the train station, waiting to collect Matthias. When Matthias arrives they introduce themselves.

Watch the video dialog online at
Active German: Level 1 > Unit 1 > Lesson 1 > Video dialog

Herr Buschel:	*Herr Meisinger?*
Matthias:	*Ja.*
Herr Buschel:	*Guten Tag. Ich heiße Philip Buschel. Ich bin Ihr Kollege. Willkommen in Pulheim bei Köln und willkommen bei Waterfront & Co.*
Matthias:	*Guten Tag. Matthias Meisinger.*
Herr Buschel:	*Wie geht es Ihnen?*
Matthias:	*Danke gut. Und Ihnen?*
Herr Buschel:	*Gut.*
Matthias:	*Woher kommen Sie, Herr Buschel?*
Herr Buschel:	*Ich komme aus Österreich. Und Sie?*
Matthias:	*Ich komme aus München.*

Mr. Buschel:	Mr. Meisinger?
Matthias:	Yes.
Mr. Buschel:	Hello, my name is Philip Buschel. I'm your colleague. Welcome to Pulheim in Cologne and welcome to Waterfront & Co.
Matthias:	Hello. Matthias Meisinger.

Mr. Buschel:	How are you?
Matthias:	Good, thank you. And you?
Mr. Buschel:	Good.
Matthias:	Where do you come from, Mr. Buschel?
Mr. Buschel:	I come from Austria. And you?
Matthias:	I come from Munich.

Grammar

In this section we go over some of the grammar points introduced in the dialog.

Go to Active German: Level 1 > Unit 1 > Lesson 1 > Grammar to listen to these explanations and to access some interactive practice activities.

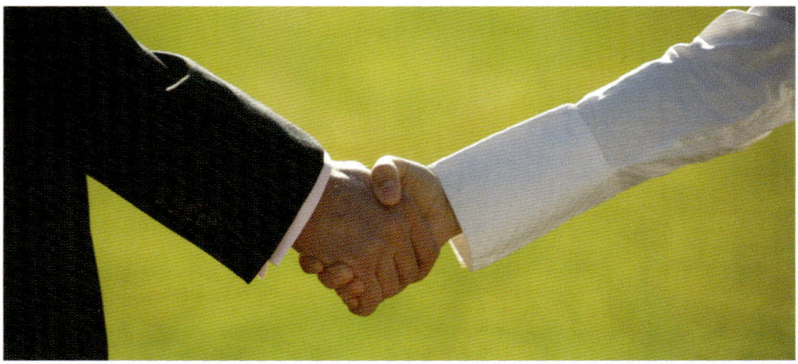

1 › How are you?

To ask somebody how he or she is, there are two different ways in German:

Formally: *Wie geht es Ihnen?*	How are you?
Informally: *Wie geht es dir?*	How are you?

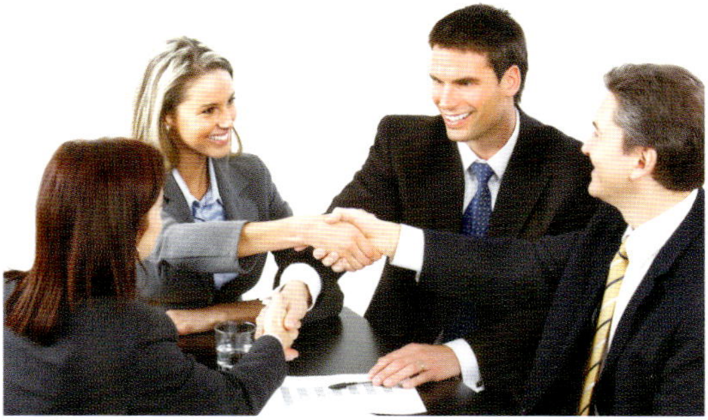

2 › **How are you? I am fine, thank you.**

To answer and then ask the question in return, you use:

Formally: *Danke. Gut. Und Ihnen?*	I am fine, thank you. And you?
Informally: *Danke. Gut. Und dir?*	I am fine, thank you. And you?

Culture note

Cologne, with almost one million inhabitants, is Germany's fourth-largest city (after Berlin, Hamburg, and Munich). It is one of the oldest cities in Germany. Cologne lies on the River Rhine. It is very close to Belgium and France and is very well connected to Brussels and Paris. Many tourists visit Cologne to look at the famous *Kölner Dom* (Cologne Cathedral), the first construction of which dates back to the 9th century. Cologne is well known for its beer, called *Kölsch*, which is a very light beer served in small glasses.

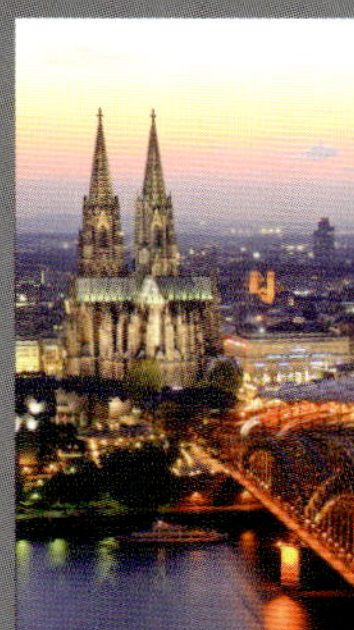

3 › What is your name? The verb *heißen*

In many languages the verb ending changes according to who is doing the action. The patterns of the verb have to be learned.

Let's look at the verb *heißen*:

ich heiße	my name is (literally: I am called)
du heißt	your name is (*informal*)
Sie heißen	your name is (*formal*)

Note that in *heißen* we have the letter *ß* (called *Eszett*) which represents a special form of the letters *ss*. It is pronounced the same way as an *s*.

Ich heiße Matthias Meisinger.
My name is Matthias Meisinger.

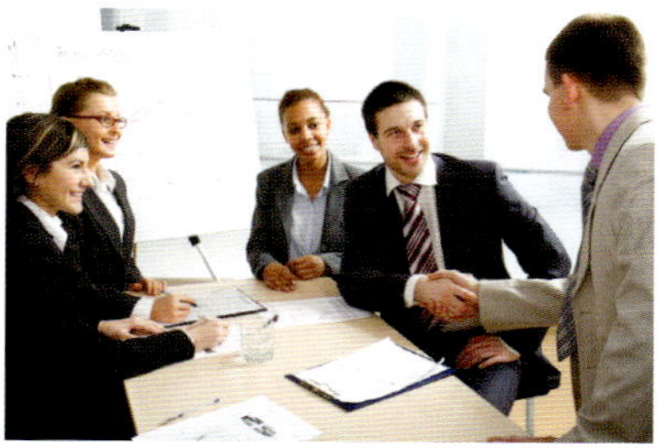

4 › What is your name?

er heißt	his name is
sie heißt	her name is
Wie heißt du?	What's your name? (*informal*)
Wie heißen Sie?	What's your name? (*formal*)

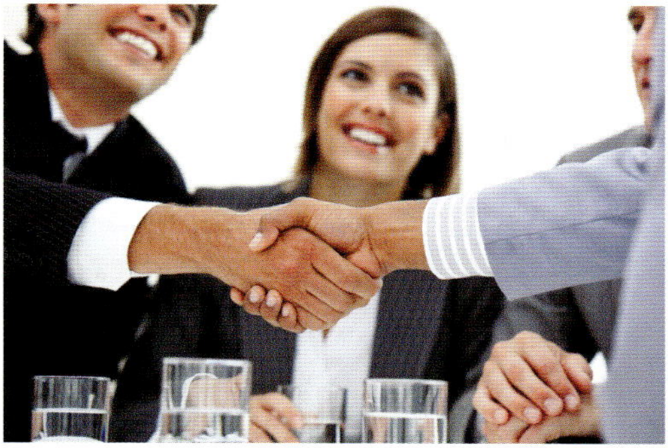

5 › The verb *kommen*

Let's look at the verb *kommen* (to come):

kommen to come

ich komme	I come
du kommst	you come (*informal*)
Sie kommen	you come (*formal*)
er kommt	he comes
sie kommt	she comes

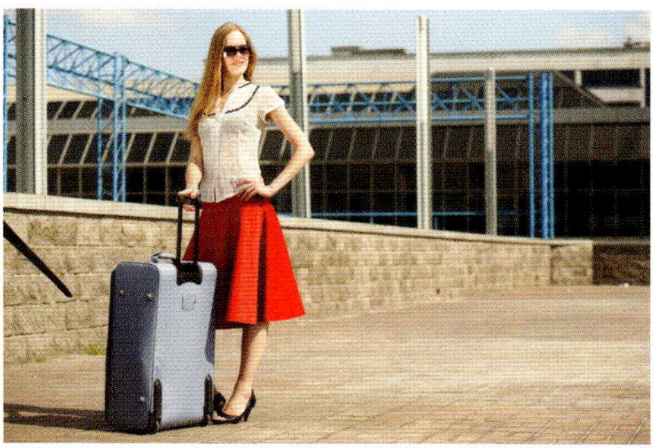

6 › Different forms of "you"

There are different ways of saying "you." If you're talking to a relative or good friend, use the familiar form *du*. If you're talking to an adult whom you don't know well (e.g. your boss) you use the formal *Sie*.

Compare:

Formal: *Wie heißen Sie?*	What's your name?
Informal: *Wie heißt du?*	What's your name?

Note that the formal *Sie* is written with a capital letter.

Mr. Meisinger and Mr. Buschel have just met for the first time. They are using *Sie*.

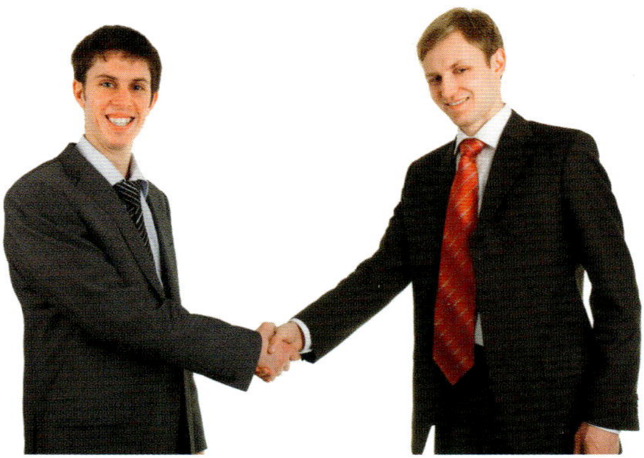

7 › Where from? A question word

In order to ask where somebody is from you would say:

woher?	where from?
Woher kommen Sie?	Where do you come from?

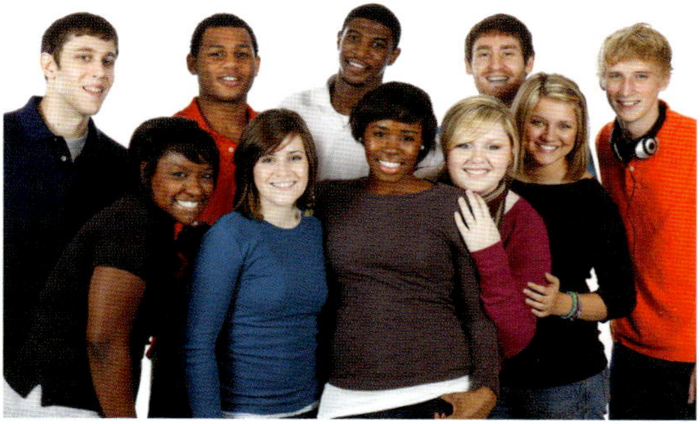

For the answer you use the word *aus* (from).

Ich komme aus Deutschland.

I'm from Germany.

Note that in order to say "from the USA" you say *aus den USA*. Similarly, for Turkey, Switzerland, and the Netherlands, you say *aus der Türkei*, *aus der Schweiz*, *aus den Niederlanden*.

8 › Hello! Greetings

In order to greet other people you use the following phrases: Until about 10:00 a.m. you say:

Guten Morgen!

Good morning!

After 10:00 a.m. you say:

Guten Tag!

Hello! (literally: Good day!)

After 5:00 p.m. you say:

Guten Abend!

Good evening!

It is also very common just to say:

Hallo!	Hi!
Guten Morgen Herr Meisinger!	Good morning, Mr. Meisinger.
Guten Tag Frau Müller!	Hello, Mrs. Müller.
Guten Abend alle zusammen!	Good evening, everyone.

9 › Goodbye!

There are different ways to say "goodbye" in German. Which expression you use depends on the region.

The most common ones are:

Formal: *Auf Wiedersehen*	Goodbye
Informal: *Tschüss*	Bye

These two expressions can be used everywhere.

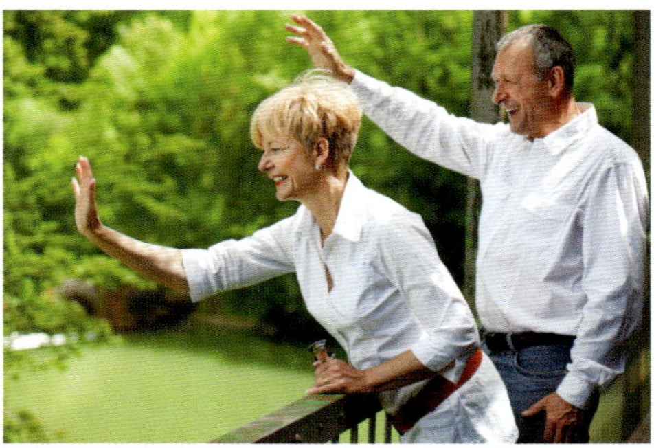

Vocabulary

In this section you will learn some useful words and expressions from the dialog.

Go to Active German: Level 1 > Unit 1 > Lesson 1 > Vocabulary to listen to each of the words being pronounced and to access some interactive practice activities.

Titles and nationalities

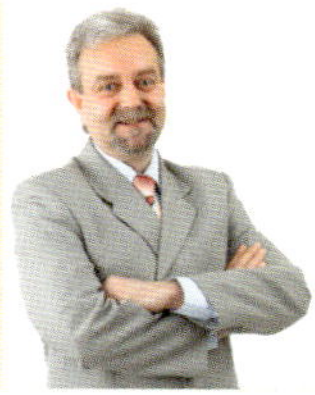

Herr
Mr.

Herr Buschel kommt aus Österreich.
Mr. Buschel is from Austria.

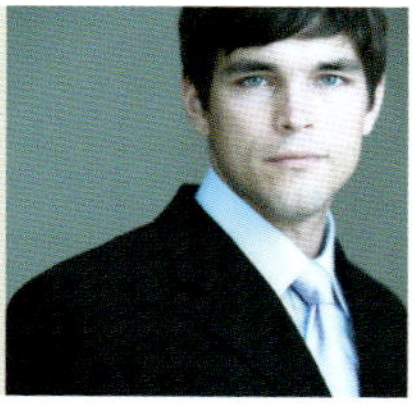

Mann
man/husband

Das ist Frau Müllers Mann.
That is Mrs. Müller's husband.

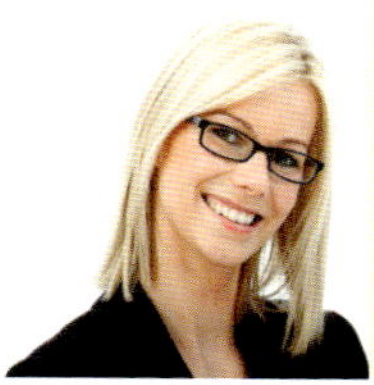

Frau
woman/wife

Das ist Frau Müller.
That is Mrs. Müller.

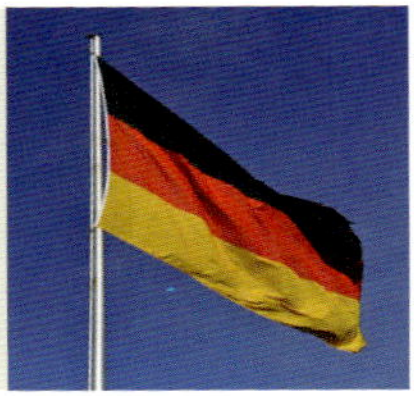

Deutschland
Germany

Deutschland ist in Europa.
Germany is in Europe.

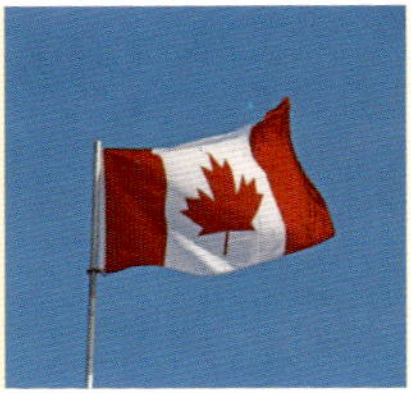

Kanada
Canada

Kanada ist ein Nachbarland von den USA.
Canada is a neighboring country of the USA.

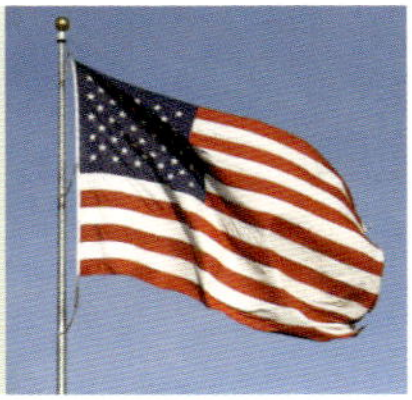

USA
United States

Die USA sind sehr groß.
The USA is very big.

Culture note

The German language offers two ways of addressing people, depending on the situation and the relationship between the speakers. One form – *Sie* (you) – is used with people you don't know and can also be used to maintain a certain level of formality, professional distance, and respect, while the other – *du* (you) – is used with family, friends, and even in informal situations where the speaker wishes to create a sense of familiarity, informality, or complicity.

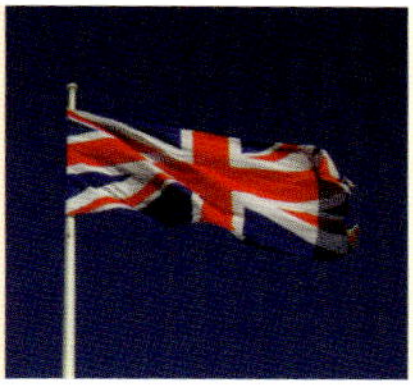

England/Großbritannien
England/Great Britain

Großbritannien besteht aus Wales, England und Schottland.
Great Britain consists of Wales, England, and Scotland.

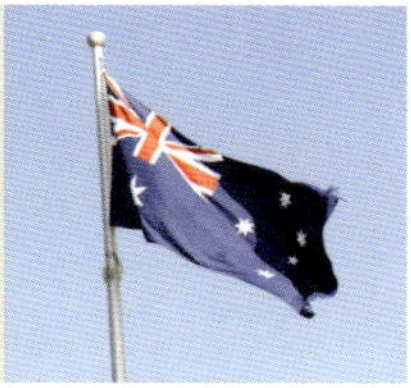

Australien
Australia

Australien ist ein Kontinent.
Australia is a continent.

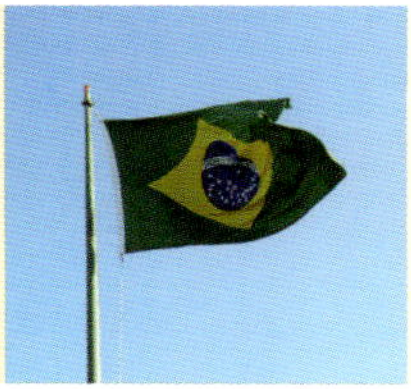

Brasilien
Brazil

Brasilien liegt in Südamerika.
Brazil is in South America.

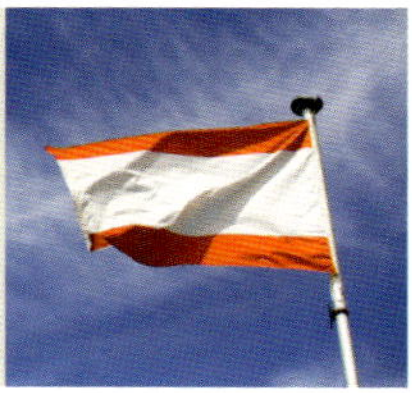

Österreich
Austria

In Österreich spricht man Deutsch.
In Austria they speak German.

UNIT 1 › LESSON 2

Arrival – At the train station 2

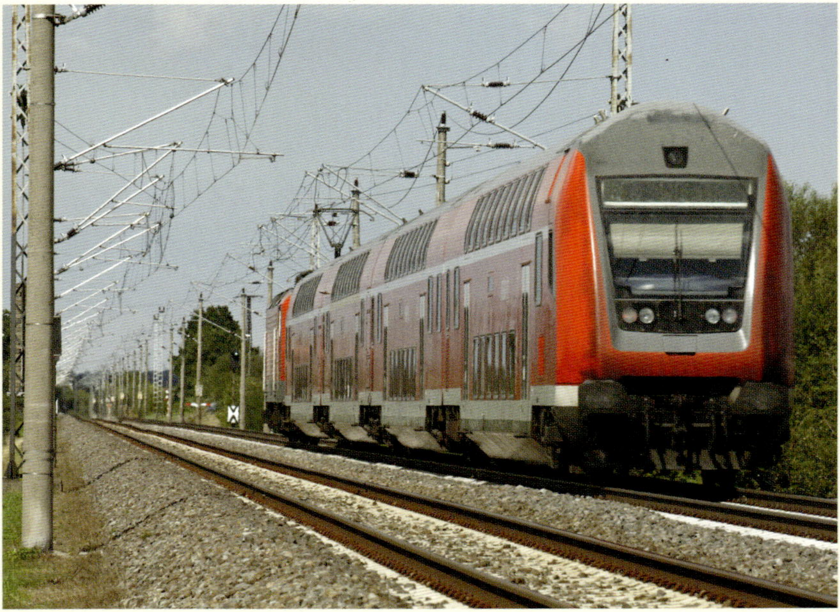

Culture note

To greet somebody you normally shake hands. Closer friends and young people may hug each other or even give each other a little kiss. However, if you don't know the person or if it is a professional relationship you should just shake hands.

Video Dialog

Lara Roellinger introduces herself to Matthias.

Active German: Level 1 > *Unit 1* > *Lesson 2* > *Video dialog*

Herr Buschel:	*Ah, Frau Roellinger.*
Lara:	*Hallo. Guten Tag. Ah, der neue Kollege. Ich heiße Lara Roellinger.*
Matthias:	*La . . . Wie heißen Sie?*
Lara:	*Mein Vorname ist Lara. Lara Roellinger. L-A-R-A R-O-E-L-L-I-N-G-E-R.*
Matthias:	*Ich heiße Matthias Meisinger. Matthias mit -t-t- und -h- und der Nachname ist Meisinger.*
Herr Buschel:	*Ah, hier ist das Auto. Kommen Sie!*

Mr. Buschel:	Ah, Mrs. Roellinger.
Lara:	Hello. Ah, our new colleague. My name is Lara Roellinger.
Matthias:	Lara... What is your name?
Lara:	Lara is my first name, Lara Roellinger. L-A-R-A R-O-E-L-L-I-N-G-E-R.
Matthias:	My name is Matthias Meisinger. Matthias with *t-t* and *h*, and my last name is Meisinger.
Mr. Buschel:	Ah, here is the car. Let's go!

Grammar

Active German: Level 1 > *Unit 1* > *Lesson 2* > *Grammar*

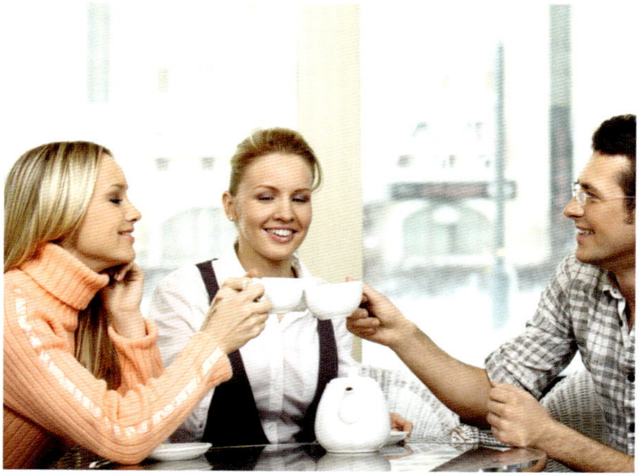

1 › **How to form verbs**

In lesson 1 you learned about the verb *kommen* (to come). Most verbs follow this same pattern. Here are some examples: *trinken* (to drink), *gehen* (to go, to walk), *spielen* (to play), *singen* (to sing), *fragen* (to ask), *machen* (to do, to make)

Ich trinke Kaffee.	I drink coffee.
Du trinkst Kaffee.	You drink coffee.
Er trinkt Kaffee.	He drinks coffee.
Sie trinkt Kaffee.	She drinks coffee.

2 › **Some question words**

wie?	how?
Wie heißen Sie?	What is your name?
Wie geht es Ihnen?	How are you?
Wie geht es dir?	How are you?

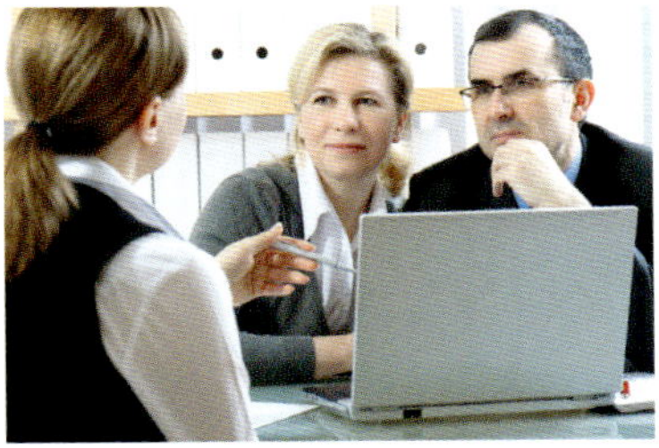

3 › **Some question words**

was?	what?
Was trinken Sie?	What are you drinking?
wo?	where?
Wo spielt er?	Where is he playing?

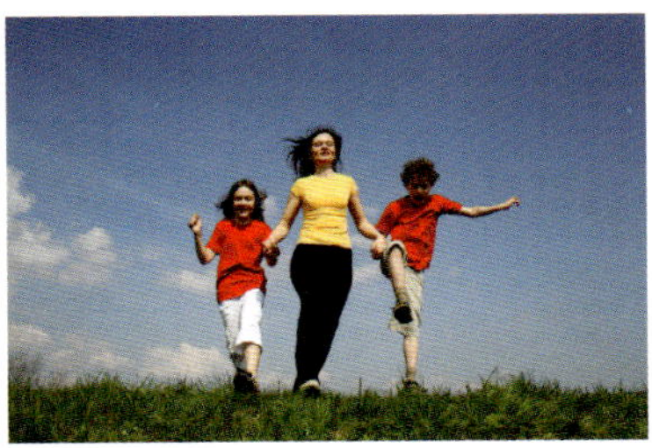

4 › I, you, he, and she

The subject of a sentence is usually a person or a thing performing the action shown by the verb.

***Ich** fliege nach Deutschland.*

I am flying to Germany.

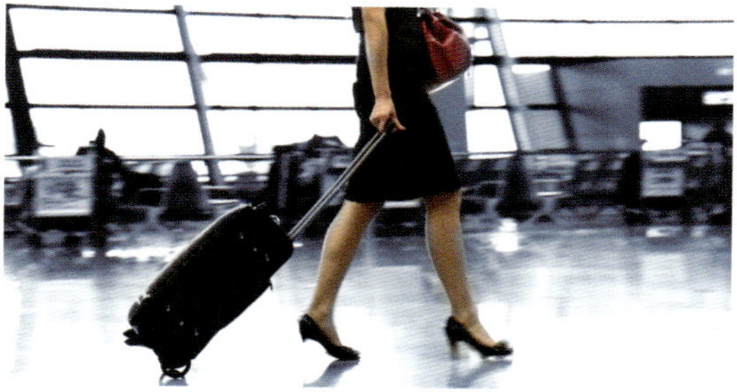

5 › I, you, he, and she

The following words are called pronouns and are used as the subject of a sentence. They represent a person or a thing. The singular pronouns are:

ich	I
du	you (*informal*)
Sie	you (*formal*)
er	he, it
es	it
sie	she, it

6 › Capital letters

Note that German nouns are always written with a capital letter.

*Lara ist mein **V**orname.*

Lara is my first name.

*Hier ist das **A**uto.*

Here is the car.

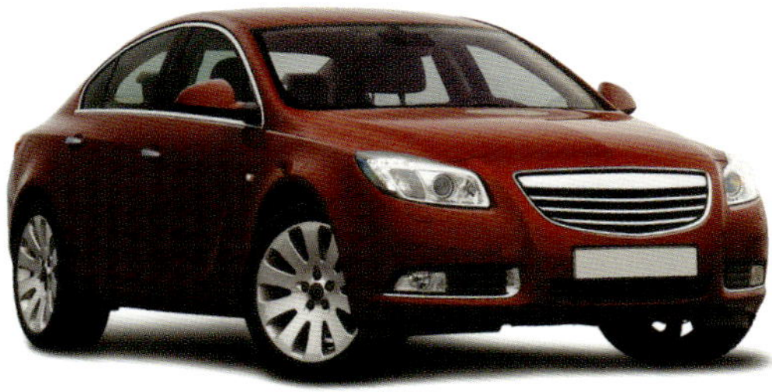

Vocabulary

Active German: Level 1 > *Unit 1* > *Lesson 2* > *Vocabulary*

The alphabet

The name of almost every letter in German contains the sound ordinarily represented by that letter. The German alphabet is based on the Latin alphabet but has four additional letters.

a b c
d e f g

a – *ah*	b – *beh*	c – *tseh*
d – *deh*	e – *eh*	f – *eff*
g – *geh*		

h i j k
l m

h – *hah* i – *ih* j – *jott*
k – *kah* l – *ell* m – *emm*

n o p
q r

n – *enn* o – *oh* p – *peh*
q – *kuh* r – *err*

s t u
v w

s – *ess* t – *teh* u – *uh*
v – *fau* w – *weh*

x y z ß
ä ö ü

x – *iks* y – *üppsilon*
z – *tsett* ß – *ess-tsett*
ä ö ü

ä, *ö* and *ü* are extra letters in the German alphabet. The pair of dots on each letter is called an umlaut and it changes the sound quality.

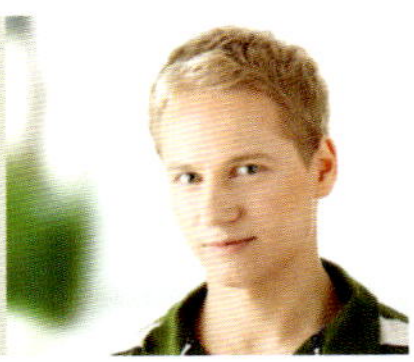

Vorname
first name

Mein Vorname ist Matthias.
My first name is Matthias.

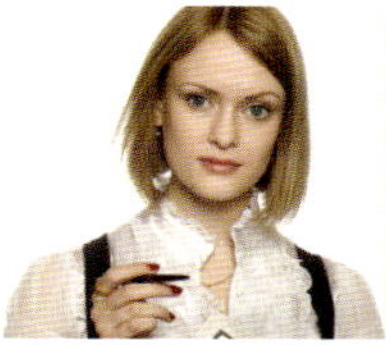

Familienname / Nachname
last name

Mein Familienname ist Roellinger.
My last name is Roellinger.

Culture note

Germans tend to keep private and professional lives quite separate. However, colleagues of the same age, especially younger people without their own families, like to go for after-work drinks or meals.

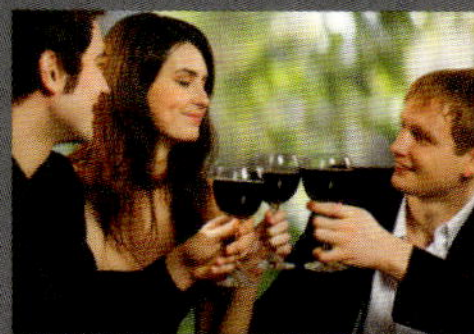

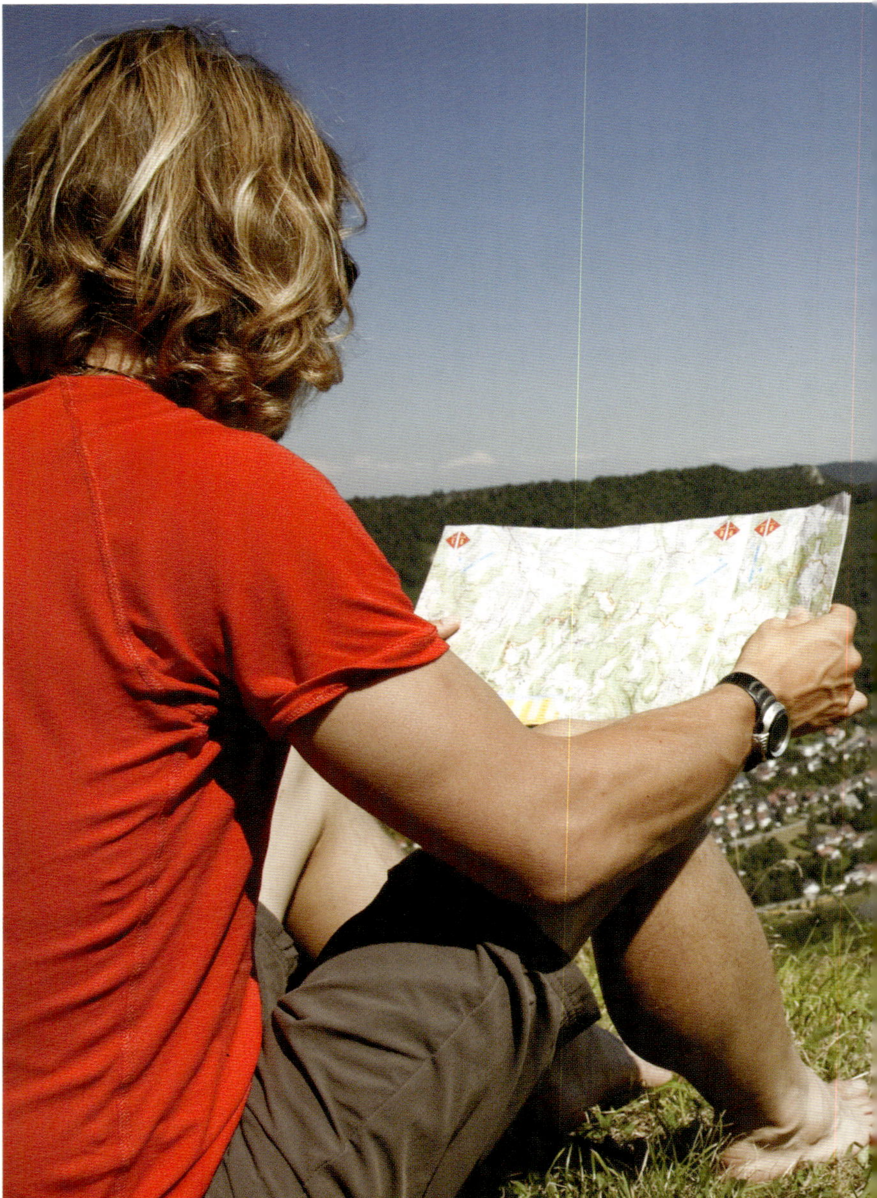

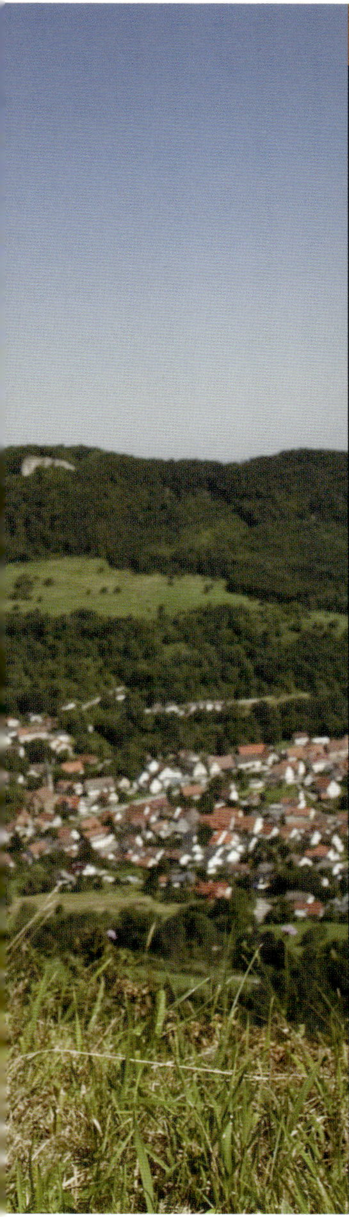

2

Lesson 1: Welcome!

- » How to form verbs in plural.
- » How to form the verb ***sein*** (to be).
- » How to say where you work: ***Ich arbeite bei Waterfront & Co.***
- » Vocabulary about jobs and companies.
- » How to understand a small brochure about a company.

Lesson 2: The sun is shining!

- » How to ask questions.
- » How to talk about the weather.
- » Vocabulary about the weather.
- » How to write a short letter about the weather and your job.

Collins | Livemocha™

UNIT 2 › LESSON 1

Welcome!

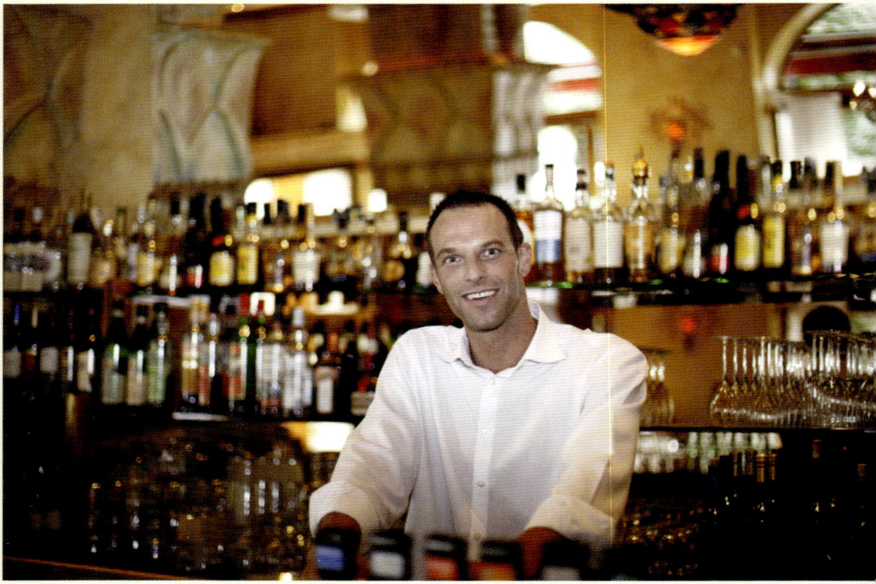

Culture note

Do the Germans live to work? This old saying describes the reputation of the German attitude towards work. Even though it is true, the Germans have learned how to relax as well and the leisure industry is quite advanced. Nevertheless, the work ethic is very strong, and the Germans rank very high among the most hard-working countries (around 41 hours a week) in Europe. But, it's not all work and no play – Germans are able to enjoy up to 30 days off in a year.

Video Dialog

A warm welcome for Matthias as he gets to know his new colleagues a little better.

Active German: Level 1 > *Unit 2* > *Lesson 1* > *Video dialog*

Matthias:	*Arbeiten Sie auch im Marketing?*
Herr Buschel:	*Nein, ich arbeite im Controlling.*
Lara:	*Ich arbeite im Marketing.*
Matthias:	*Ah schön, dann arbeiten wir ja zusammen.*
Herr Buschel:	*Die Firma hat viele Mitarbeiter und ist sehr groß. Herr Baumann, unser Chef, ist sehr nett.*
Lara:	*Alle Kollegen bei Waterfront & Co. sind sehr nett.*
Herr Buschel:	*Wir sind sehr international. Wir arbeiten mit den USA, Japan, China und Mexiko.*
Lara:	*Hier sind wir. Das ist die Firma.*

Matthias:	Do you work in marketing as well?
Mr. Buschel:	No, I work as a controller.
Lara:	I work in the marketing department.
Matthias:	Ah, good, we will be working together then.
Mr. Buschel:	The company has many members of staff and is very big. Mr. Baumann, our boss, is very nice.
Lara:	All colleagues working for Waterfront & Co. are very nice.

Mr. Buschel:	We are very international. We work with the USA, Japan, China, and Mexico.
Lara:	Here we are. This is the company.

Grammar

Active German: Level 1 > *Unit 2* > *Lesson 1* > *Grammar*

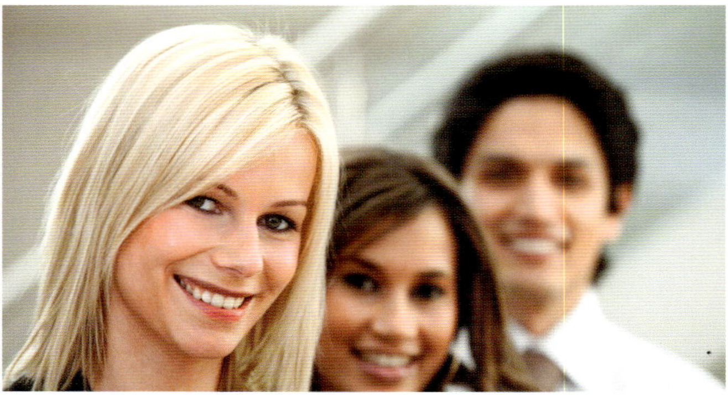

1 › **Plural pronouns**

So far we have covered the singular pronouns: *Ich, du, er / sie*. Here are the plural pronouns:

wir	we
ihr	you (*informal*)
Sie	you (*formal*)
sie	they

2 › Lara – she!

Note:

Herr Meisinger und Frau Roellinger → sie arbeiten im Marketing.

Mr. Meisinger and Mrs. Roellinger → they work in marketing.

Frau Roellinger → sie arbeitet

she works

Herr Meisinger → er arbeitet

he works

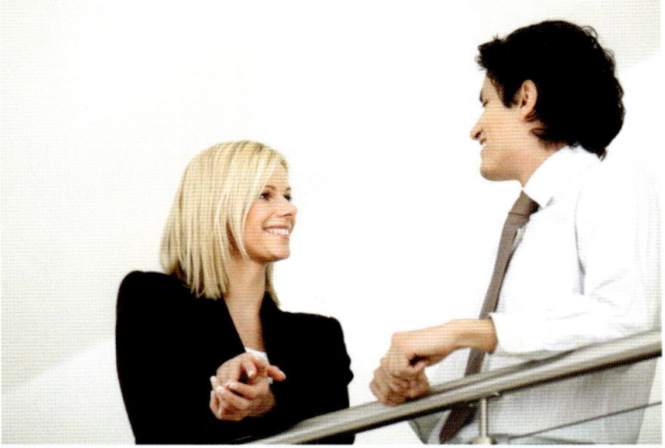

3 › Verbs in plural

So far we have covered the verb endings in the singular: *ich komme, du kommst, er / sie kommt.*

The plural endings take the following pattern:

wir kommen	we come
ihr kommt	you come (*informal*)
Sie kommen	you come (*formal*)
sie kommen	they come

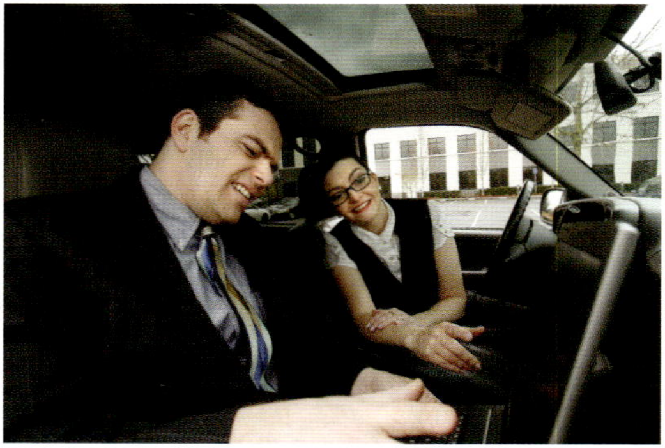

4 › The verb "to work" (1)

arbeiten	to work
ich arbeite	I work
du arbeitest	you work
er / sie / es arbeitet	he / she / it works

Ich arbeite im Controlling. Herr Meisinger arbeitet im Marketing.

I work as a controller. Mr. Meisinger works in the marketing department.

Arbeiten has slightly different endings in the *du* and *er / sie* forms than regular verbs.

Compare:

*du komm**st***	*er / sie komm**t***
*du arbeit**est***	*er / sie arbeit**et***

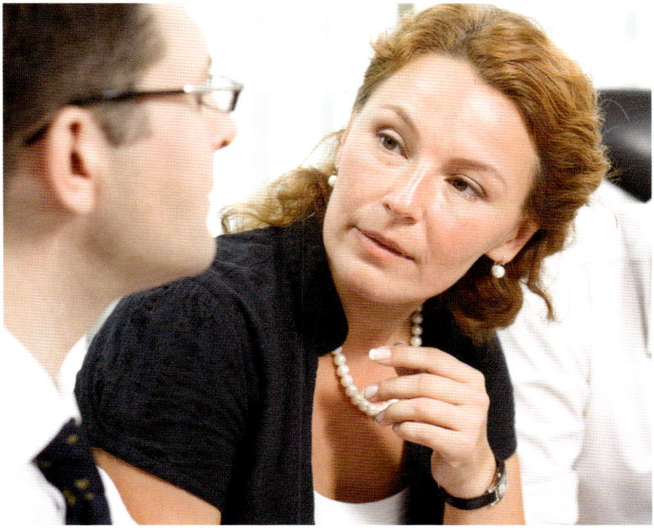

5 › The verb "to work" (2)

wir arbeiten	we work
ihr arbeitet	you work (*informal*)
Sie arbeiten	you work (*formal*)
sie arbeiten	they work

Arbeiten has a slightly different ending in the *ihr* form than regular verbs.

Compare:

ihr kommt
ihr arbeitet

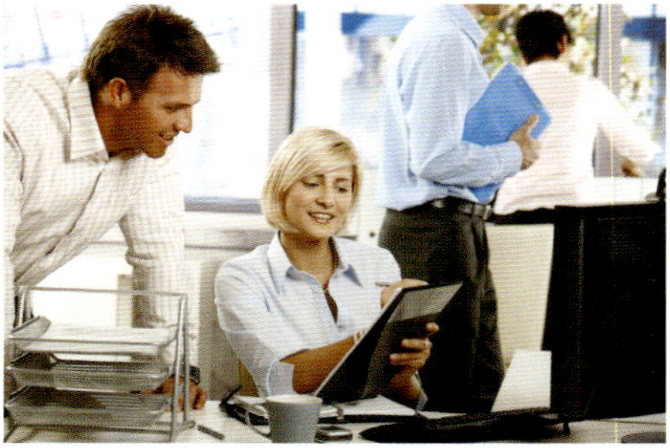

6 › I work at Siemens

To say where you work, you use the prepositions *bei* or *für*.

Ich arbeite bei Siemens.
I work at Siemens.

Ich arbeite für BMW.
I work for BMW.

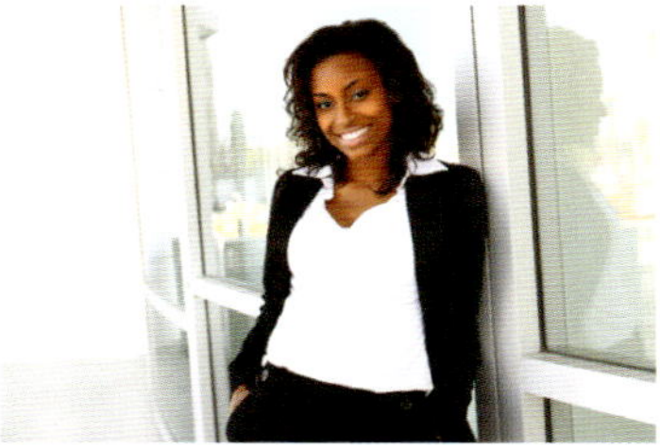

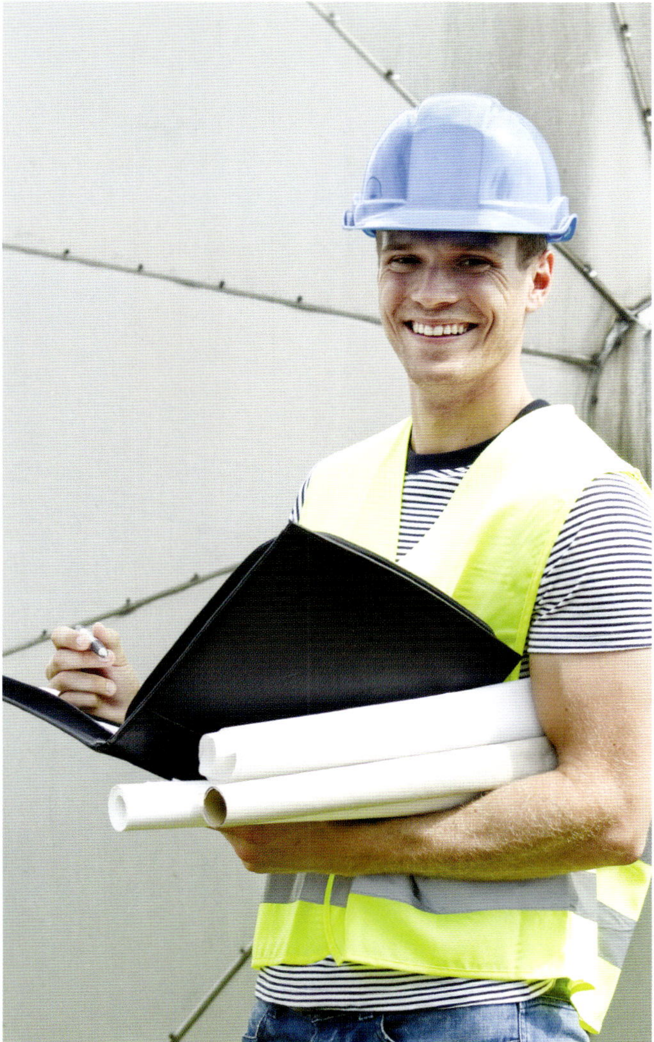

7 › Female forms

In German you use the ending *-in* for female forms of nouns:

*Kollege – Kolleg**in***	female colleague
*Lehrer – Lehrer**in***	female teacher

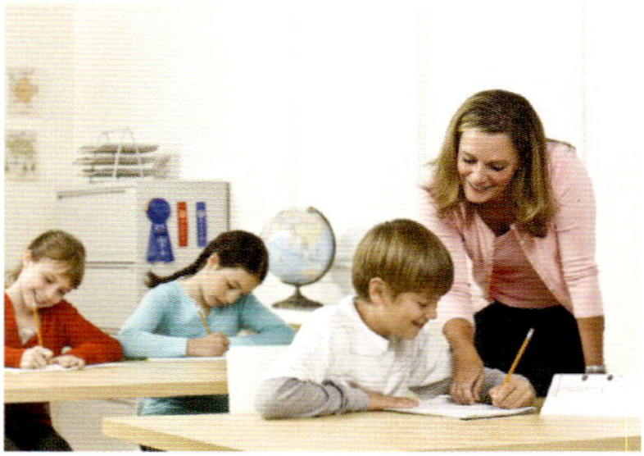

8 › I am

The verb *sein* (to be) is irregular. Take some time to memorize its forms.

Singular:

ich bin	I am
du bist	you are
er / sie / es ist	he / she / it is

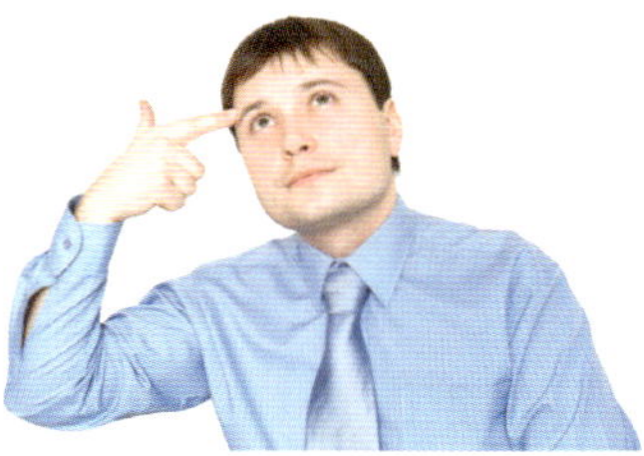

9 › We are

Plural:

wir sind	we are
ihr seid	you are
sie / Sie sind	they / you are

Tip: In German you don't translate the "a" when you talk about your job. *Ich bin Ingenieur.* "I'm an engineer."

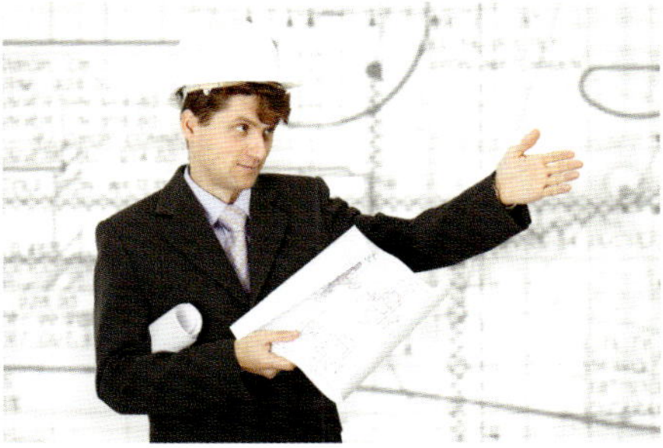

Vocabulary

Active German: Level 1 > Unit 2 > Lesson 1 > Vocabulary

Jobs and the company

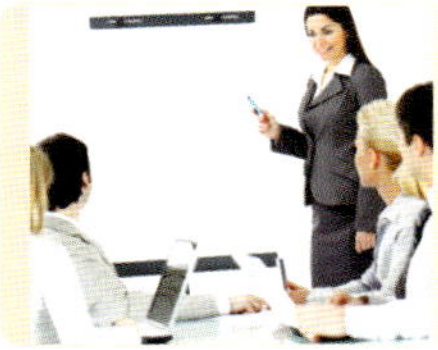

Chef
boss

Herr Baumann ist der Chef.
Mr. Baumann is the boss.

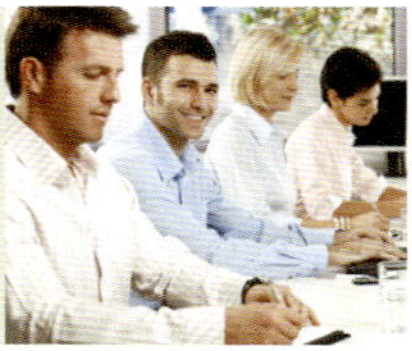

Kollege
colleague

Das ist mein Kollege.
This is my colleague.

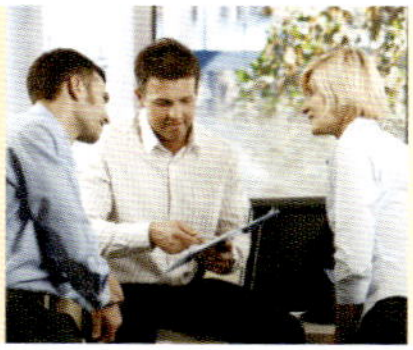

Mitarbeiter
employees

Herr Baumann hat viele Mitarbeiter.
Mr. Baumann has many employees.

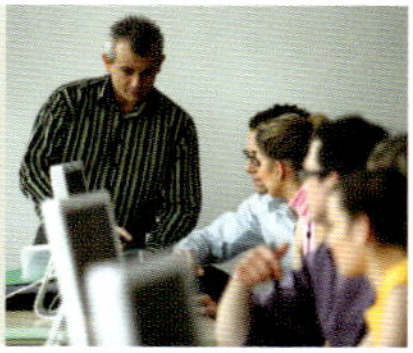

Lehrer
teacher

Ich bin Lehrer.
I'm a teacher.

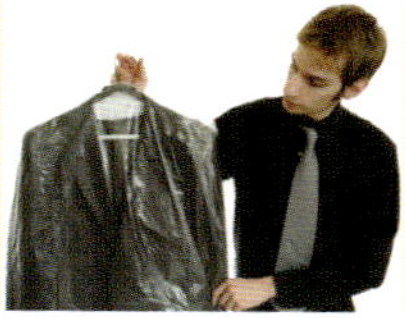

Verkäufer
salesclerk

Er ist Verkäufer.
He is a salesclerk.

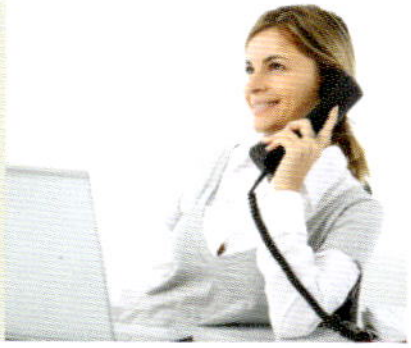

Sekretärin
(female) secretary

Herr Baumann hat eine Sekretärin.
Mr. Baumann has a secretary.

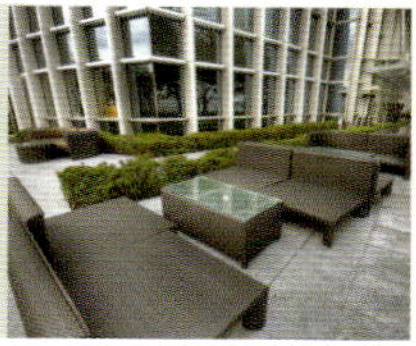

Firma
company

Waterfront & Co. ist eine große Firma.
Waterfront & Co. is a big company.

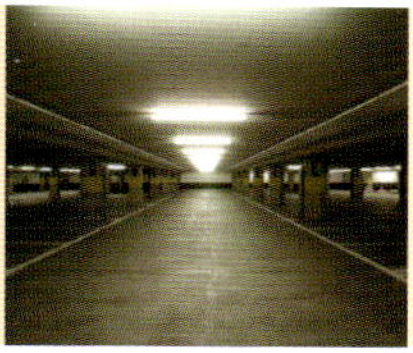

parken
to park

Hier parken wir.
We'll park here.

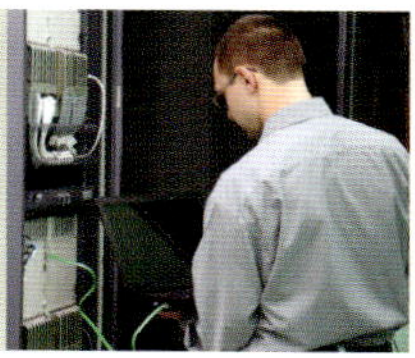

*der Beruf / Berufe**
job, profession

Was sind Sie von Beruf?
What is your profession?

*The plural form of all German nouns has been included next to the singular form. In some cases both forms are identical.

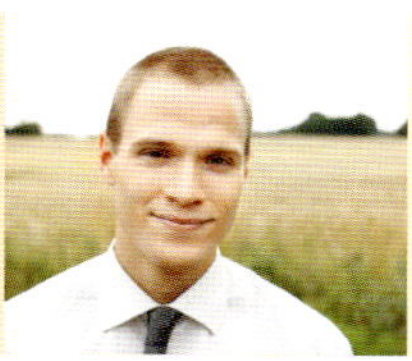

nett
nice

Matthias ist sehr nett.
Matthias is very nice.

UNIT 2 › LESSON 2

The sun is shining!

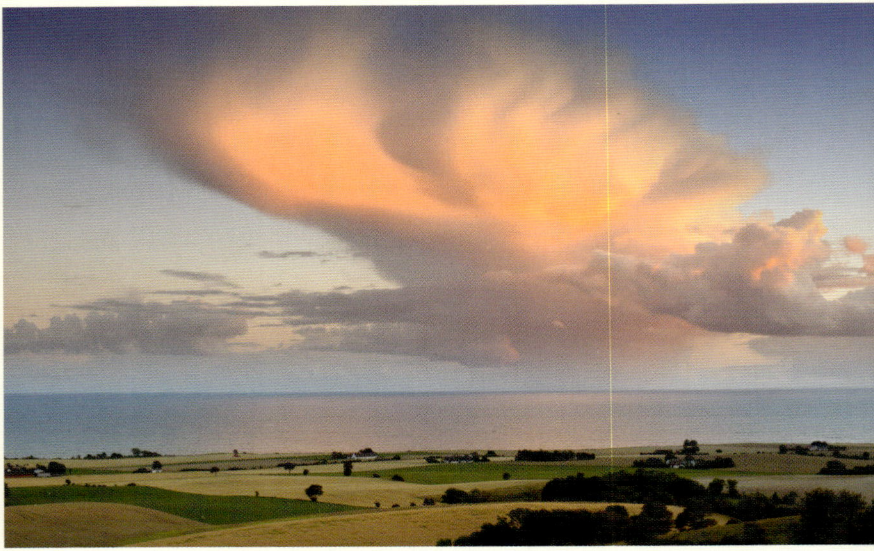

Culture note

The climate in Germany is mainly moderate. Large fluctuations in temperature are rare, even though in some summers the temperature might rise to 95°F (35°C) and in some winters fall to 5°F (–15°C). Rain falls throughout the year. Temperatures vary from east to west and from north to south. The south of Germany is slightly warmer than the north. The north is influenced by the Baltic and North Seas, and a breeze is present most of the time. Summer temperatures are typically between 64° and 86°F (18° and 30°C), and a nice summer might keep beer gardens open through October.

Video Dialog

Matthias gets to know the company before they all go for a morning coffee.

Active German: Level 1 > *Unit 2* > *Lesson 2* > *Video dialog*

Herr Buschel:	*Wir sind da. Willkommen bei Waterfront & Co. in Pulheim.*
Lara:	*Leider ist es heute nicht so schön. Es ist ein bisschen kalt.*
Matthias:	*Regnet es oft in Pulheim?*
Herr Buschel:	*Ja, leider. In Pulheim ist es aber oft warm.*
Matthias:	*Das Haus ist aber groß!*
Lara:	*Ja, und es ist sehr modern.*
Herr Buschel:	*Und sehr schön. Waterfront & Co. – freundlich und kompetent. Das ist unser Motto.*
Lara:	*Gehen wir erst in ein Café?*
Matthias:	*Ja, gerne.*

Mr. Buschel:	Here we are. Welcome to Waterfront & Co. in Pulheim.
Lara:	Unfortunately the weather's not so nice today. It's a bit cold.
Matthias:	Does it often rain in Pulheim?
Mr. Buschel:	Yes, unfortunately. But it is often warm in Pulheim.
Matthias:	What a big building!
Lara:	Yes, and it is very modern.

Mr. Buschel:	And very beautiful. Waterfront & Co. – friendly and competent. That is our motto.
Lara:	Shall we go to a café first?
Matthias:	Yes, with pleasure.

Grammar

Active German: Level 1 > *Unit 2* > *Lesson 2* > *Grammar*

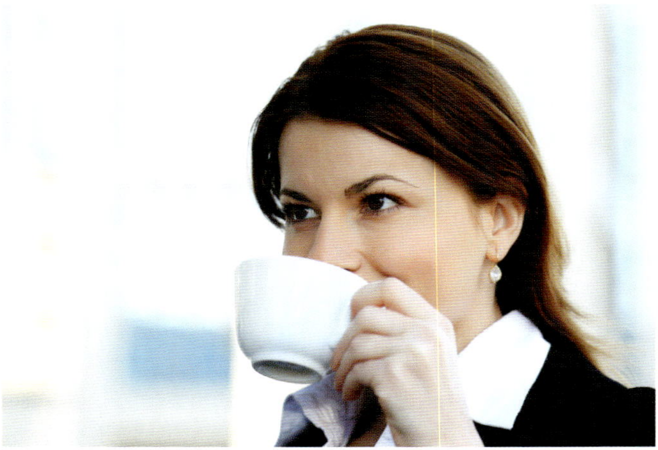

1 › **Word order**

In a sentence the verb is normally in position two. This is a very strict word-order rule in German.

*Ich **arbeite** hier.*	I work here.
*Du **trinkst** Kaffee.*	You drink coffee.

2 › Question words

In unit 1 you saw how to form a question with a question word:

Wo arbeiten Sie?	Where do you work?
Wo sind Sie?	Where are you?
Was trinken Sie?	What do you drink?

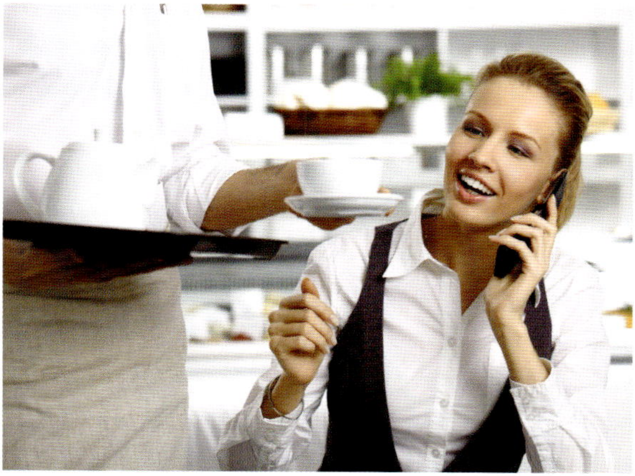

3 › Questions

Now you will see how to form a question with a verb. The verb goes at the beginning of the question:

***Arbeiten** Sie bei Waterfront & Co?*	Do you work at Waterfront & Co.?
***Sind** Sie neu hier?*	Are you new here?
***Geht** es Ihnen gut?*	Is everything good with you?

4 › Answers

Arbeiten Sie hier?
The answer is *ja* (yes) or *nein* (no).

Arbeiten Sie bei Waterfront & Co?	Do you work at Waterfront & Co.?
Ja, ich arbeite hier.	Yes, I work here.
Nein, ich arbeite bei BMW.	No, I work at BMW.

5 › The weather

In order to talk about the weather, very often the word *es* (it) is used along with the form *ist* (is) of the verb *sein* (to be).

Es ist schön.	It is beautiful.
Es ist warm.	It is warm.
Es ist kalt.	It is cold.

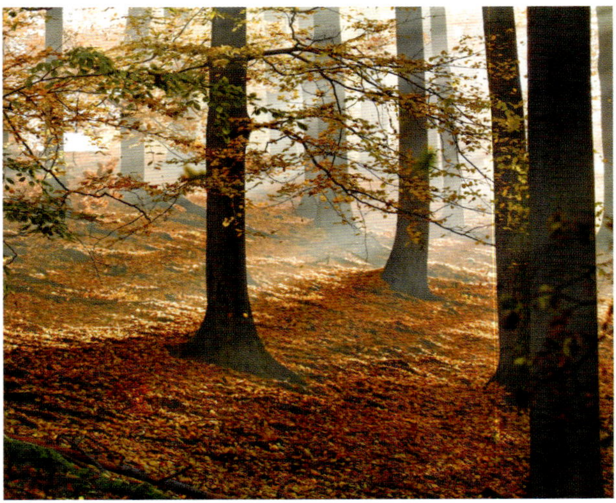

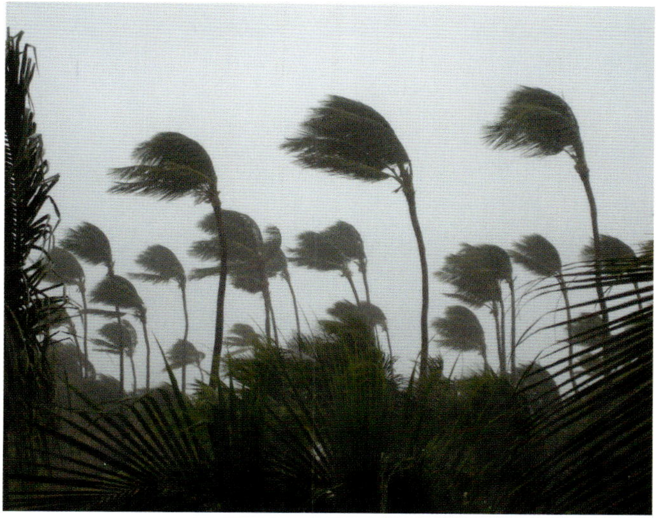

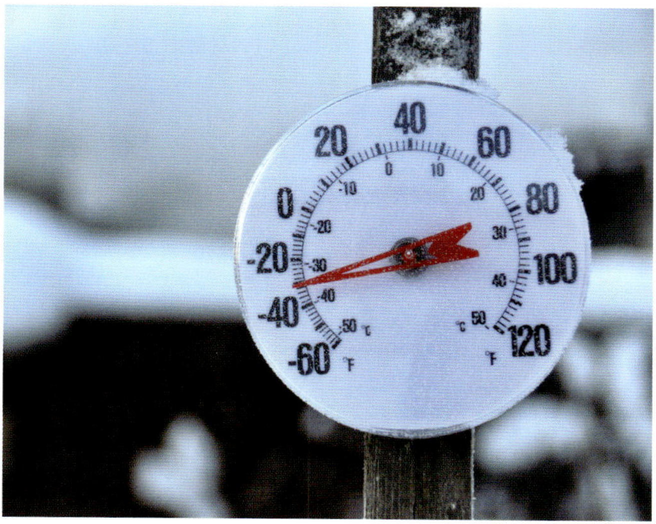
40
20
60
0
80
-20
100
-40
120
-60
°F
°F
°C
°C
0
10
-10
20
-20
30
-30
40
-40
50
-50

6 › The weather

When talking about the rain, the verb *regnen* is used.

Es regnet.

It is raining.

When talking about the sun (*die Sonne*) shining, the verb *scheinen* is used.

Die Sonne scheint.

The sun is shining.

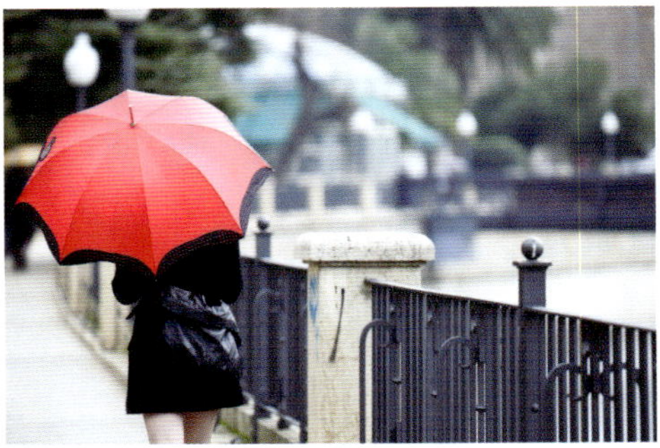

Culture note

Pulheim is in the northwest of Cologne. With 53,000 inhabitants it is a rather small town. In 1981, however, it was granted city status. It is a fairly typical German *Mittelstadt* (medium-sized town) with a market place, a town hall, and all the necessary stores. Pulheim's beautiful surroundings are perfect for cycling and walking tours.

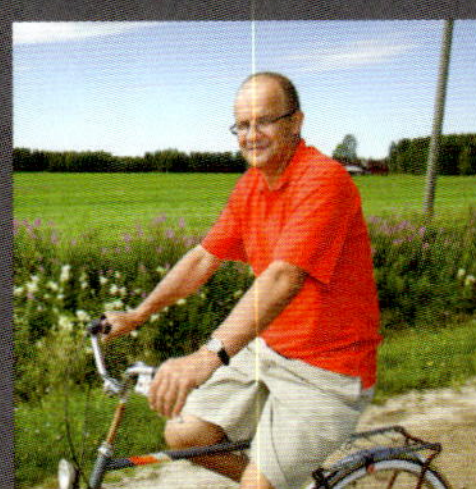

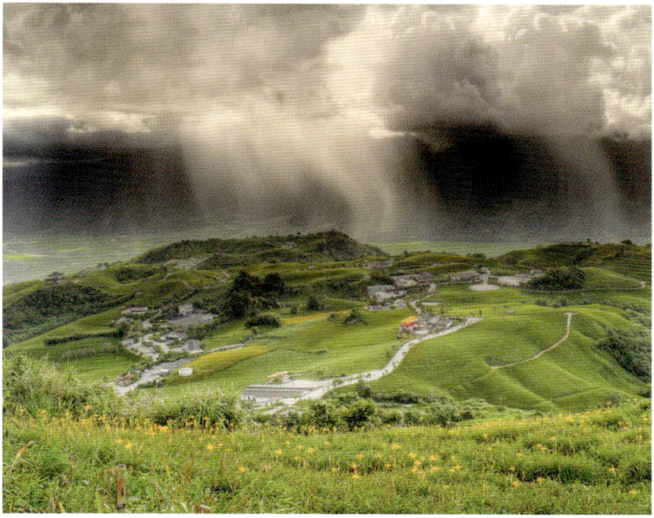

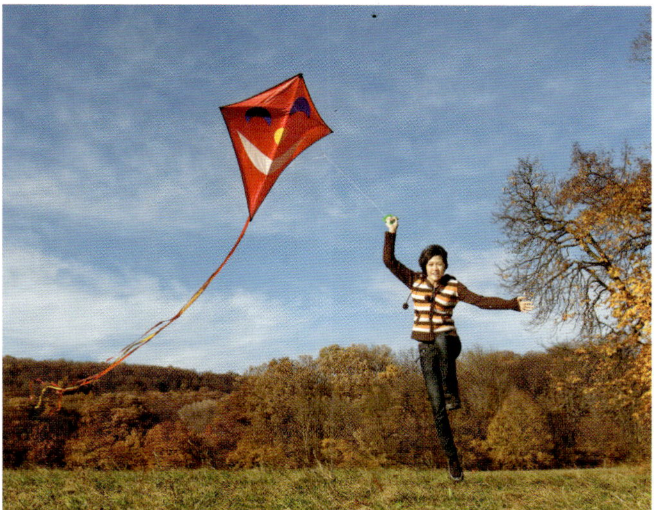

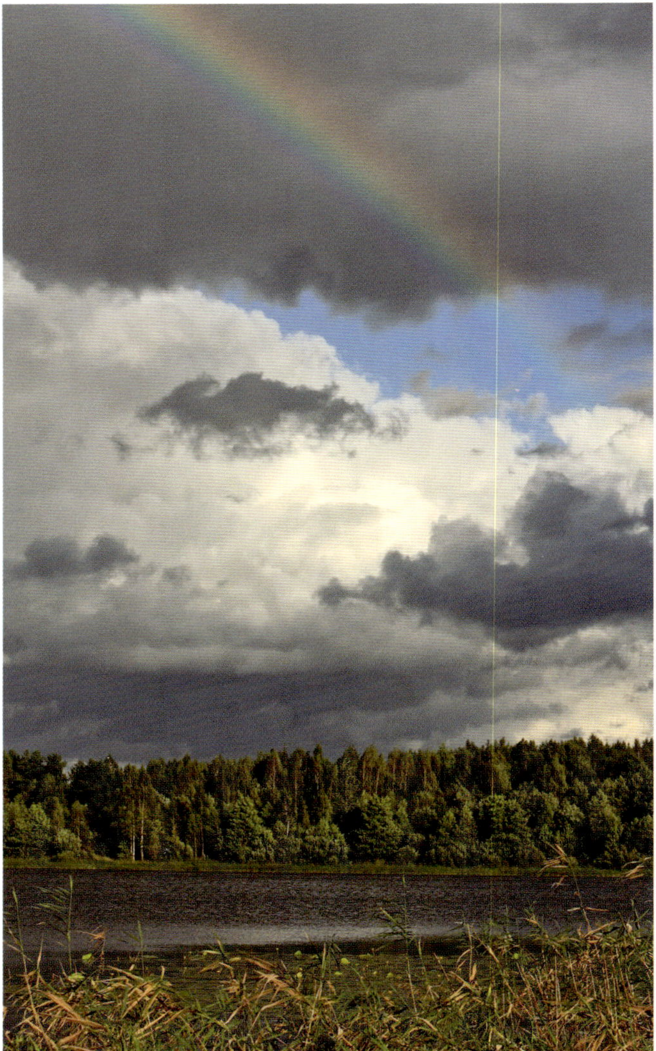

Vocabulary

Active German: Level 1 > Unit 2 > Lesson 2 > Vocabulary

The weather

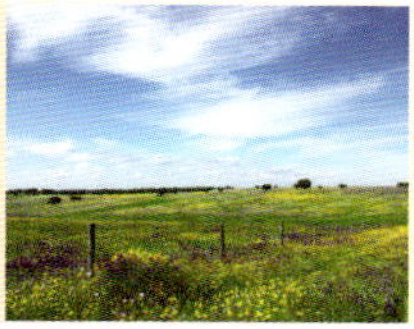

schön
beautiful

Heute ist es schön.
Today it is nice.

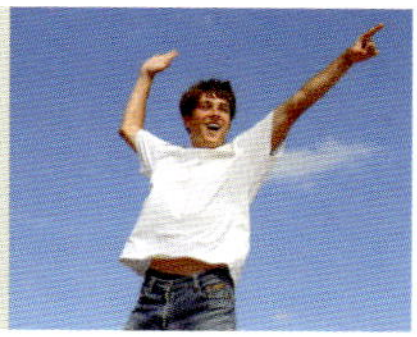

warm
warm

In München ist es warm.
It is warm in Munich.

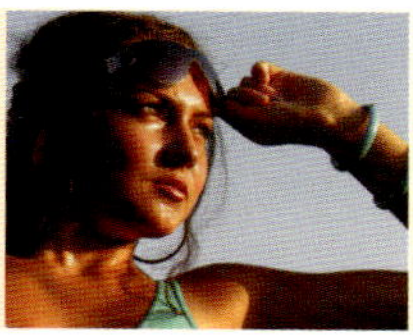

heiß
hot

Heute ist es heiß.
It is hot today.

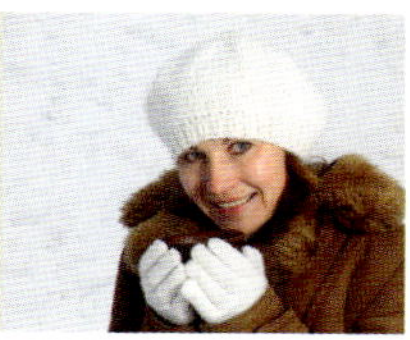

kalt
cold

Es ist kalt.
It is cold.

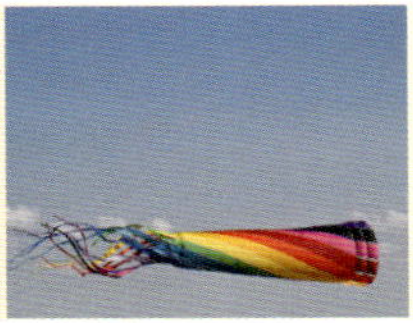

windig
windy

Am Meer ist es sehr windig.
At the seaside it is very windy.

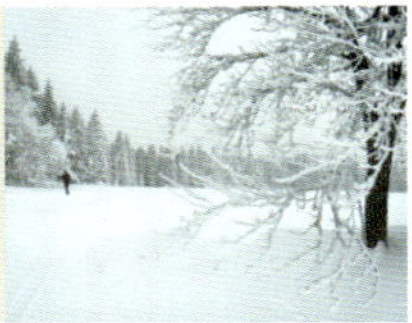

schneien
to snow

Im Winter schneit es oft.
In winter it snows very often.

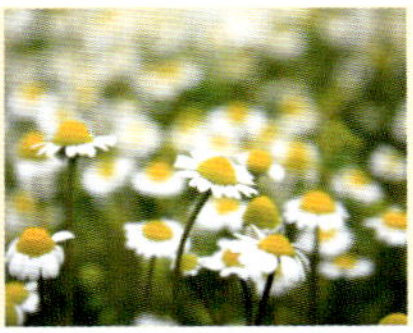

Frühling
spring

Im Frühling scheint die Sonne.
In spring the sun shines.

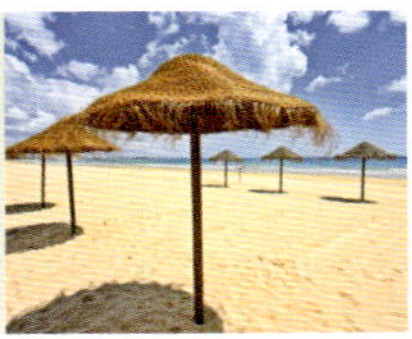

Sommer
summer

Im Sommer ist es heiß.
It is hot in summer.

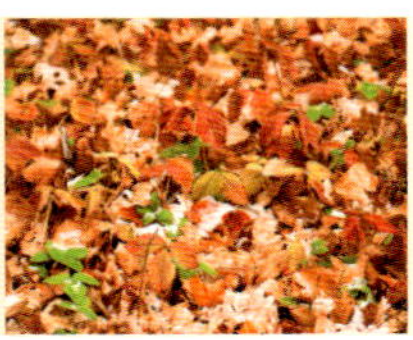

Herbst
fall

Im Herbst ist es oft windig.
It is very windy in fall.

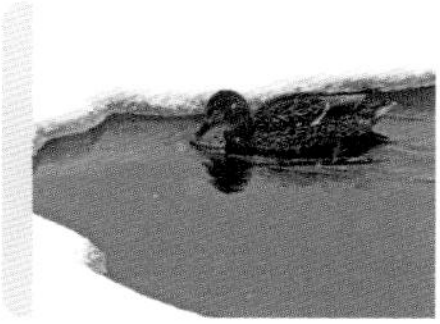

Winter
winter

Im Winter ist es kalt.
In winter it is cold.

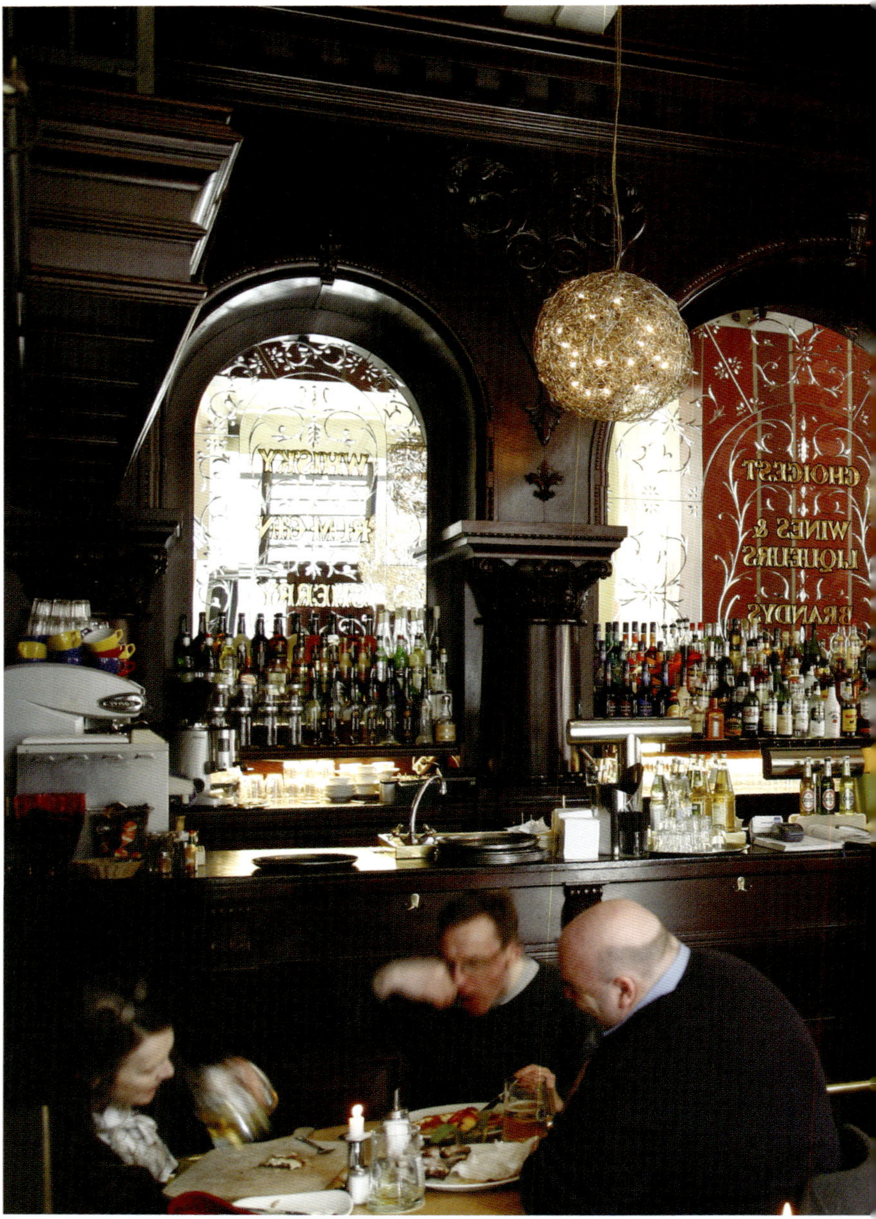
CHOICEST
WINES &
LIQUEURS
BRANDYS

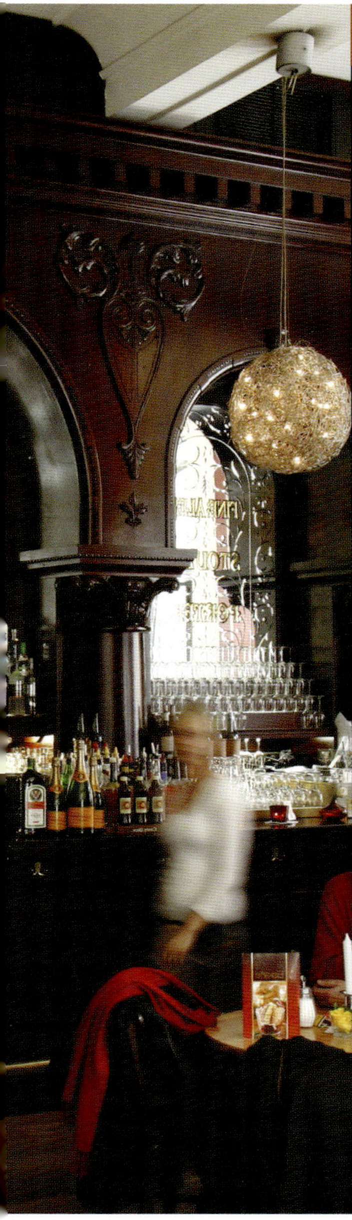

3

Lesson 1: In a café 1

- How to get information about drinks and food: ***Ist die Suppe gut?***
- About articles: ***der Kaffee, die Frau, das Auto.***
- About the verb ***kosten.***
- Vocabulary in a café.

Lesson 2: In a café 2

- How to ask for prices: ***Was kostet …?***
- How to count from 0–20.
- About the plural form: e.g. ***Hotels, Männer.***
- About a menu in a café.

Collins | Livemocha™

UNIT 3 › LESSON 1

In a café 1

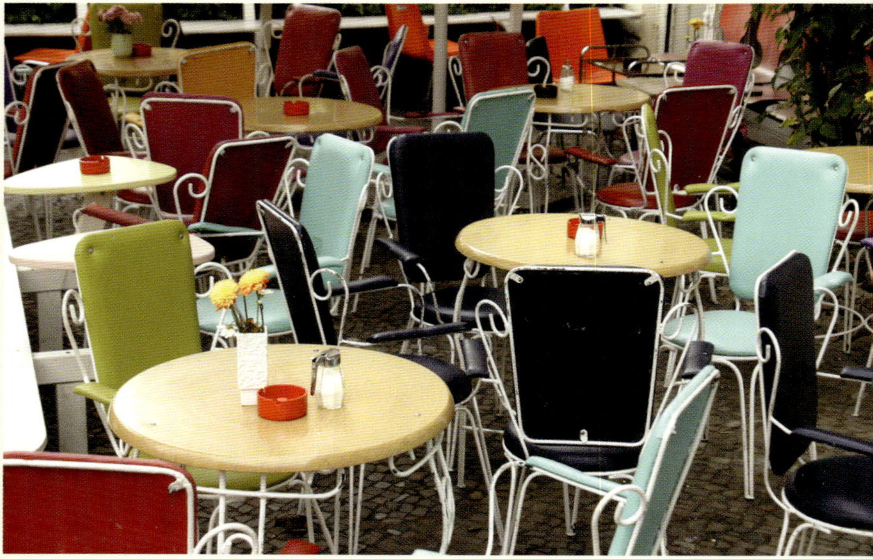

Culture note

Germany is the second largest market for coffee. At home people normally drink filtered coffee. They drink it either black, with milk (hot or cold) and/or with sugar. Coffee is often enjoyed as an accompaniment to cake (*Kuchen*). In fact, a favorite snack is the afternoon *Kaffee und Kuchen*, a tradition which is enjoyed as part of a social gathering either at home or in a café. Germany has also seen an upsurge in a new coffee culture, and you can select from a wide range of different coffee drinks: café latte, cappuccino, latte macchiato, etc. *Milchkaffee* is the German version of the French *café au lait*.

Video Dialog

In the café, Matthias, Lara, and Mr. Buschel order food and drinks.

Active German: Level 1 > *Unit 3* > *Lesson 1* > *Video dialog*

Lara:	*Ah, der Stuhl ist noch frei.*
Herr Buschel:	*Haben Sie Durst oder Hunger?*
Matthias:	*Ich habe Durst und ein bisschen Hunger.*
Herr Buschel:	*Was trinken Sie?*
Matthias:	*Ich trinke Kaffee und ein Glas Wasser, bitte. Ist die Suppe gut?*
Lara:	*Ja, ja die Suppe ist sehr lecker. Essen Sie Suppe?*
Matthias:	*Ja, gerne.*
Lara:	*Zwei Suppen, bitte.*
Herr Buschel:	*Zwei Suppen, ein Kaffee, ein Glas Wasser und...?*
Lara:	*Ich trinke eine Cola.*

Lara:	Ah, this chair is free.
Mr. Buschel:	Are you thirsty or hungry?
Matthias:	I am thirsty and a little bit hungry.
Mr. Buschel:	What are you having to drink?
Matthias:	I'll have a coffee and a glass of water, please. Is the soup good?

Lara:	Yes, the soup is really good. Are you going to have some?
Matthias:	Yes, please.
Lara:	Two soups, please.
Mr. Buschel:	Two soups, a coffee, a glass of water and...?
Lara:	I'll have a soda.

Grammar

Active German: Level 1 > Unit 3 > Lesson 1 > Grammar

1 › Articles (1)

In German, as in most languages, nouns are not normally used on their own, but are very often preceded by an article (*Artikel*). In German, we have three different articles for "the": *der - die - das*.

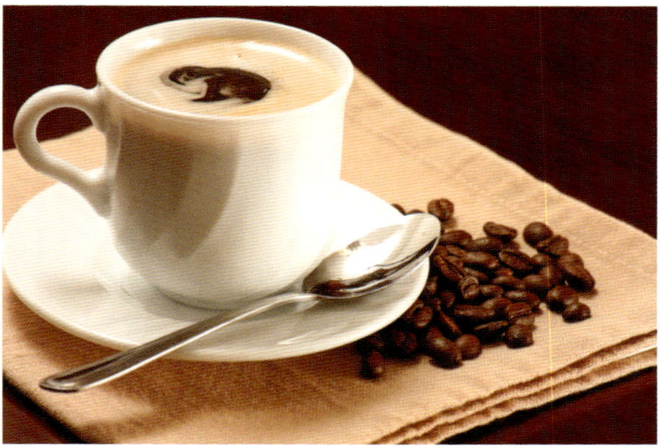

2 › Articles (2)

This article is used if there is only one object or person or if something is new or unknown. It normally refers to something particular or something we already know.

Der Stuhl ist da.

The chair is over there.

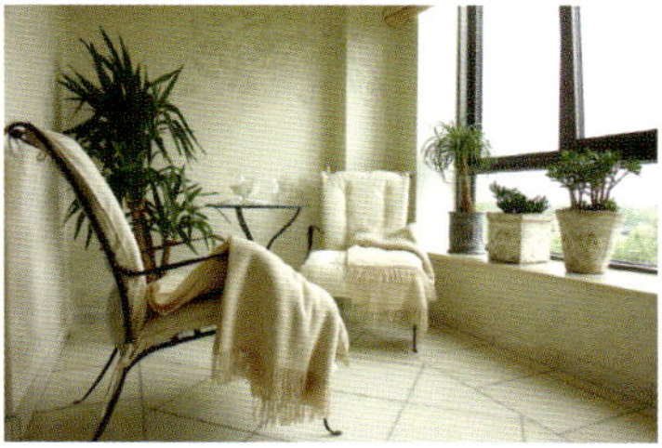

3 › *der – die – das* (1)

All German nouns are either masculine (*der*), feminine (*die*), or neuter (*das*):

der Stuhl: Ist der Stuhl frei?	Is the chair free?
die Suppe: Ist die Suppe gut?	Is the soup good?
das Haus: Das Haus ist groß.	The house is big.

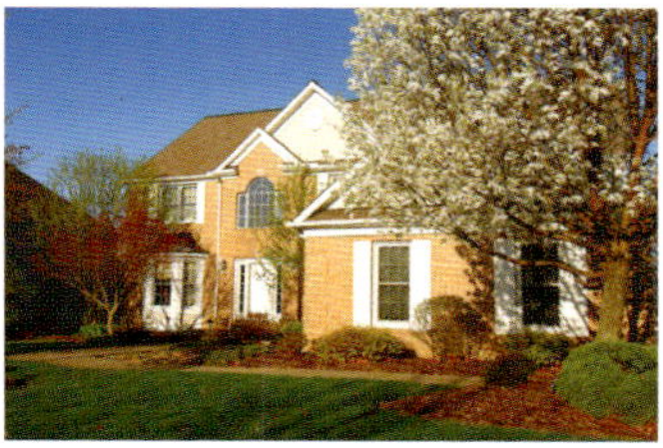

4 › *der – die – das* (2)

There is often no logic as to whether a noun is masculine, feminine, or neuter.

One important rule is that grammatical gender usually reflects real gender for words denoting people: *die Frau* (the woman), *der Mann* (the man), *der Kollege* (the male colleague), *die Kollegin* (the female colleague).

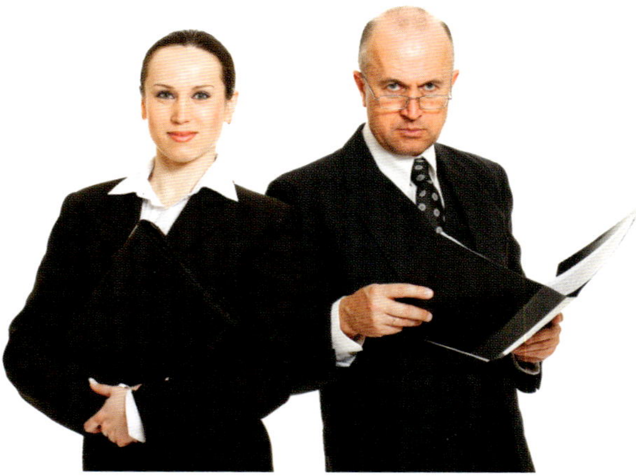

5 › Learning tip

It's a good idea to learn the article with the noun when you come across a word for the first time, so that you know whether it is masculine, feminine, or neuter. Some learners like to try to remember the noun by using colors when writing them down, e.g.,

der	blue
die	red
das	yellow

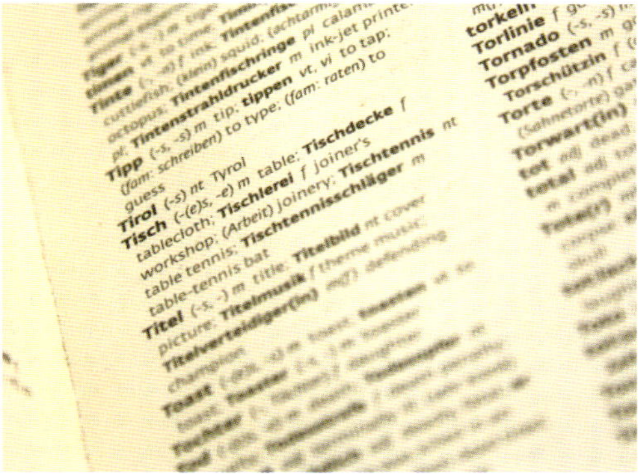

6 › Articles (3)

We use a different article – *ein* (meaning "a") – to refer to any item that is not a specific one.

There are three different forms:

ein	masculine
eine	feminine
ein	neuter

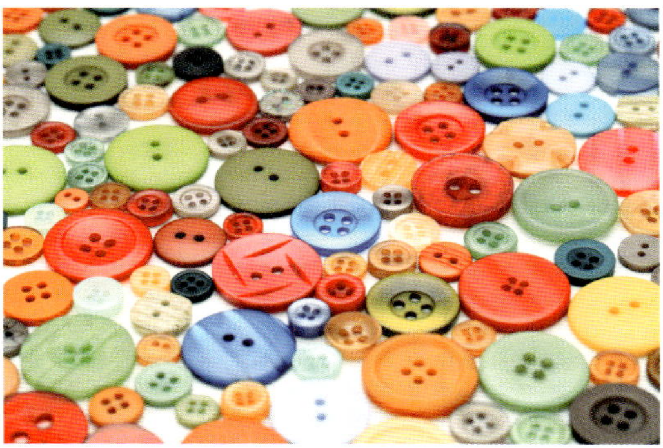

7 › "A" or "the"?

Was kostet ***der*** *Kaffee?*

How much is **the** coffee?

The speaker is referring to a particular coffee.

Ein *Kaffee kostet €2,20.*

A coffee costs €2.20.

This is general information and you are not referring to a particular coffee.

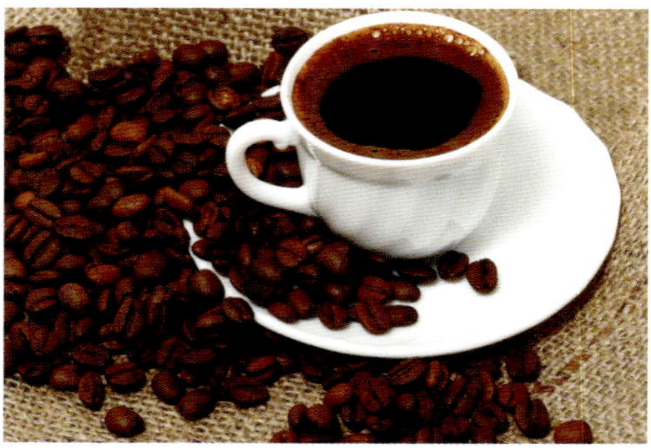

8 › The verb *kosten*

You use the verb *kosten* (to cost) to state prices.

Singular: *Was kost****et*** *der Kaffee?*
How much is the coffee?

Plural: *Was kost****en*** *die Suppen?*
How much are the soups?

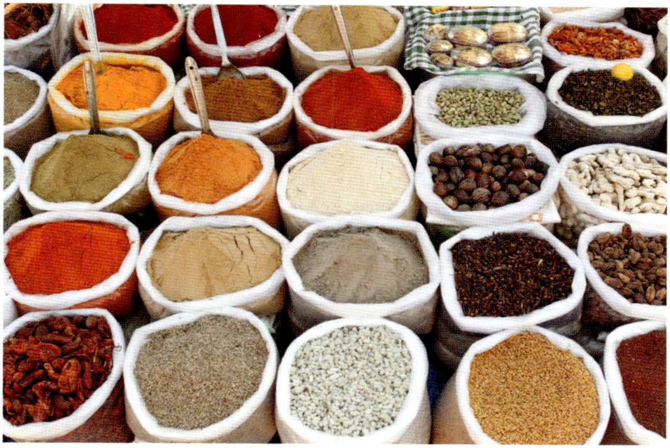

9 › **How to read out prices**

The word *Euro* is added between the whole number and the cents:

So for €3.20 say: 3 *Euro* 20.

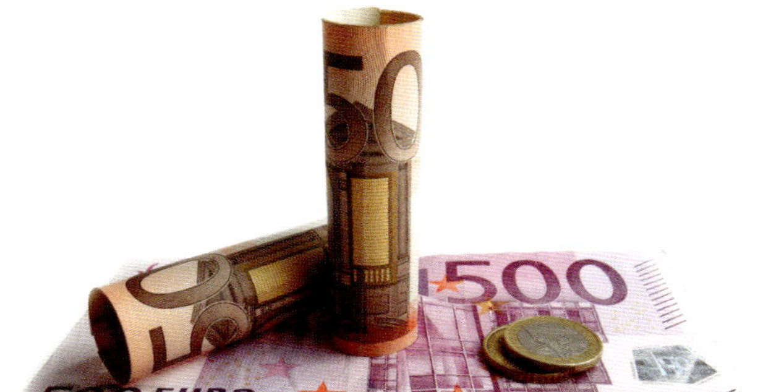

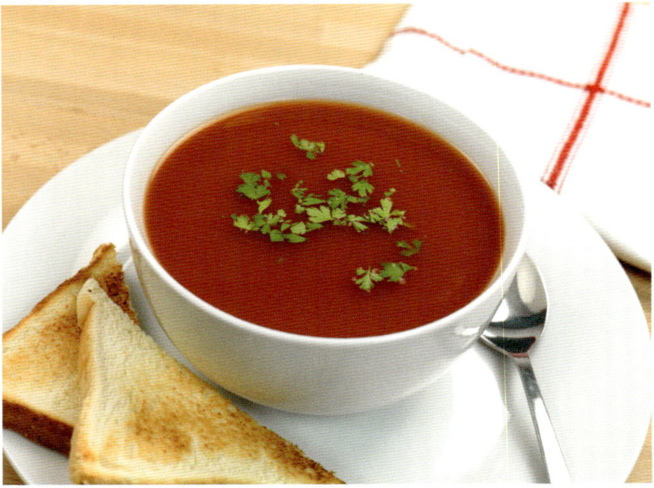

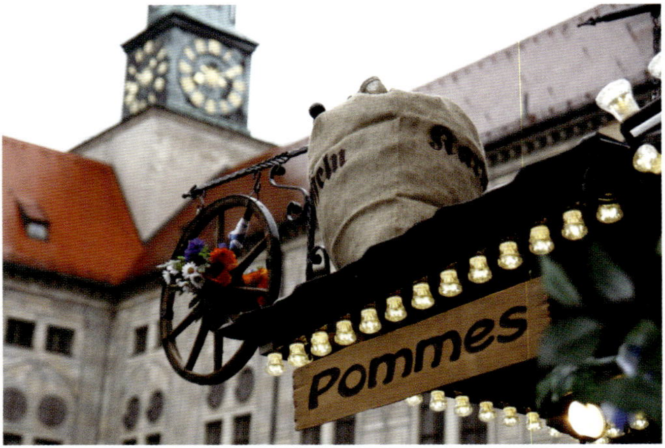
Pommes

Vocabulary

Active German: Level 1 > Unit 3 > Lesson 1 > Vocabulary

In a café

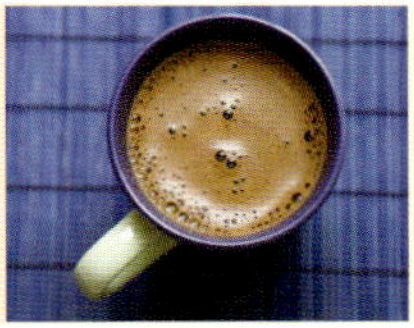

der Kaffee / Kaffees
coffee

Der Kaffee kostet 2 Euro.
The coffee costs 2 Euros.

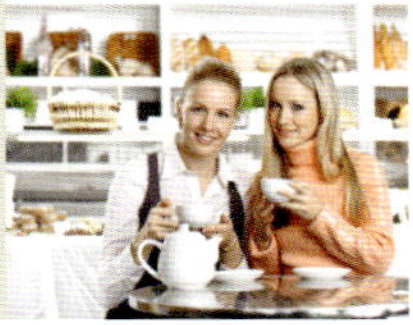

das Café / Cafés
café

Das Café ist sehr nett.
The café is very nice.

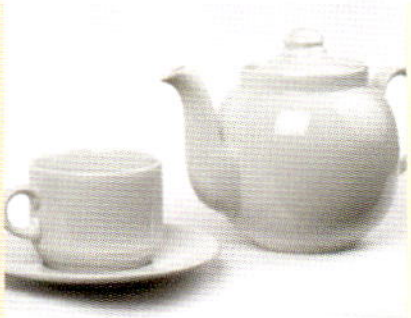

der Tee / Tees
tea

Ich trinke gern Tee.
I like drinking tea.

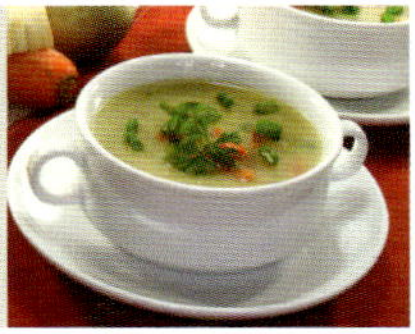

die Suppe / Suppen
soup

Ist die Suppe gut?
Is the soup good?

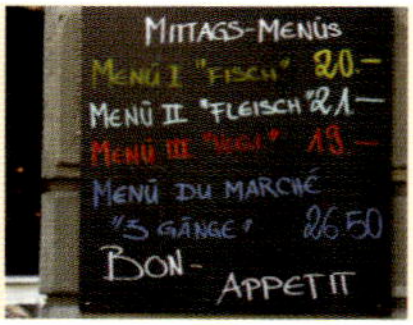

die Speisekarte/Speisekarten
menu

Ist das die Speisekarte?
Is that the menu?

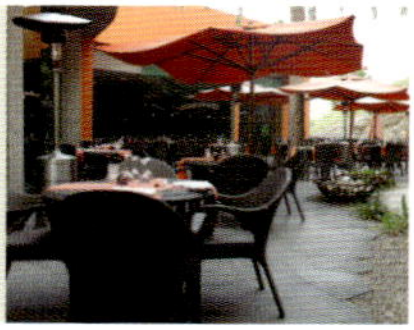

der Stuhl / Stühle
chair

Ist der Stuhl frei?
Is the chair free?

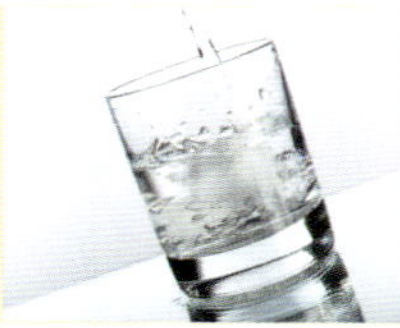

das Glas / Gläser
glass

Ich trinke ein Glas Wasser.
I'll have a glass of water.

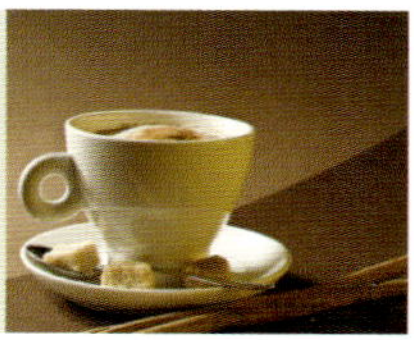

die Tasse / Tassen
cup

Eine Tasse Kaffee, bitte.
A cup of coffee, please.

der Teller / Teller
plate

Hier ist ein Teller mit Kuchen.
Here is a plate of cake.

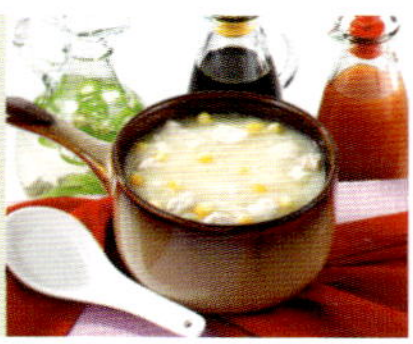

der Löffel / Löffel
spoon

Wo ist der Löffel für die Suppe?
Where is the spoon for the soup?

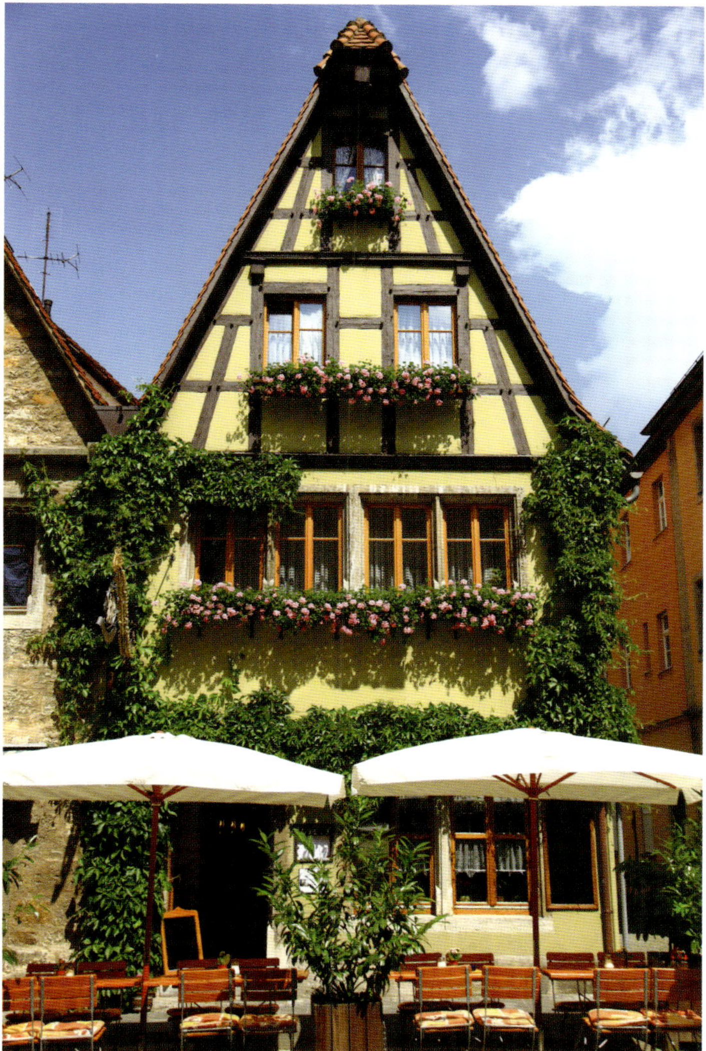

UNIT 3 › LESSON 2

In a café 2

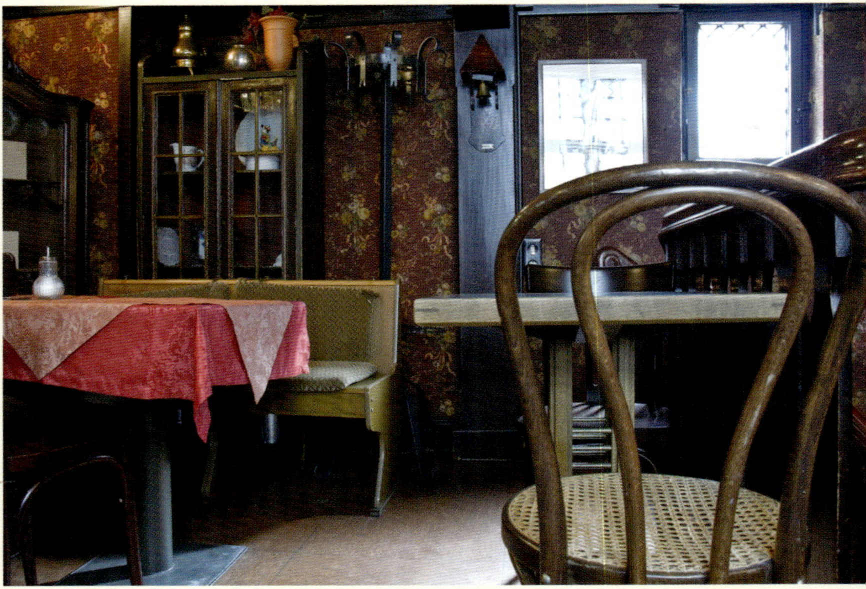

Culture note

In Germany there are several possibilities for the midday meal at work. It is not unusual to bring your own lunch with you. Bigger companies have their own cafeterias with a variety of hot and cold dishes. It is common to have lunch with your colleagues. In restaurants or cafés there is often a *Mittagstisch* (lunch special).

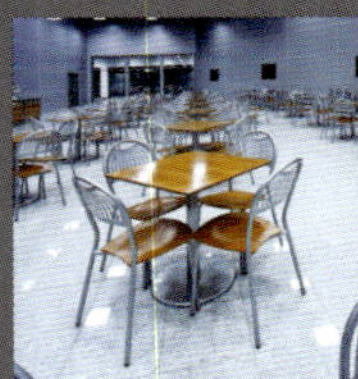

Video Dialog

Having finished their meals, it's time to ask for the check.

Active German: Level 1 > *Unit 3* > *Lesson 2* > *Video dialog*

Herr Buschel:	*Hier ist die Suppe.*
Lara:	*Danke.*
Matthias:	*Danke.*
Herr Buschel:	*Eine Cola?*
Lara:	*Ja.*
Matthias:	*Was kostet die Suppe?*
Herr Buschel:	*Mmh, die zwei Suppen kosten €6,20, also kostet eine €3,10.*
Matthias:	*Und was kostet der Kaffee?*
Herr Buschel:	*Der Kaffee kostet €2,15.*
Matthias:	*Und das Wasser?*
Herr Buschel:	*Ach, das Wasser kostet nichts.*
Matthias:	*Hier sind 6 Euro.*
Herr Buschel:	*Nein, nein ich bezahle heute.*
Matthias:	*Danke schön.*

Mr. Buschel:	Here is the soup.
Lara:	Thanks.
Matthias:	Thanks.
Mr. Buschel:	A soda?

Lara:	Yes.
Matthias:	How much does the soup cost?
Mr. Buschel:	Hmm, two soups cost €6.20, so one costs €3.10.
Matthias:	And how much does the coffee cost?
Mr. Buschel:	The coffee costs €2.15.
Matthias:	And the water?
Mr. Buschel:	Oh, the water doesn't cost anything.
Matthias:	Here are 6 euros.
Mr. Buschel:	No, no, I'll pay today.
Matthias:	Thank you.

Grammar

Active German: Level 1 > *Unit 3* > *Lesson 2* > *Grammar*

1 › Plurals (1)

Nouns normally have a singular and a plural form. The article indicates this. Fortunately, the plural article is always the same – *die*. It doesn't matter whether the noun is masculine, feminine, or neuter. In German, there are several different ways of making nouns plural.

Singular: *Eine Suppe kostet €3,10.*
A soup costs €3.10.

Plural: *Zwei Suppen kosten €6,20.*
Two soups cost €6.20.

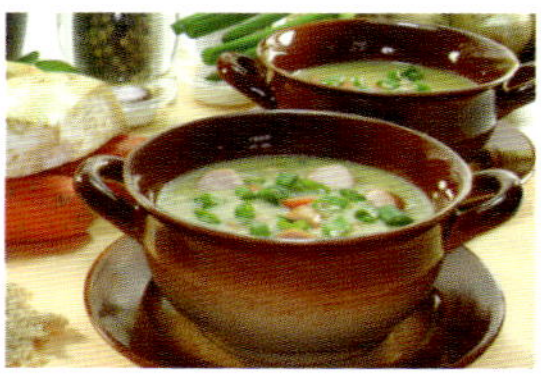

2 › Plurals (2)

Here are some examples:

Most feminine nouns form their plural by adding -n, -en or -nen to their singular form:

*die Information – die Information**en***	(information / information)
*die Frau – die Frau**en***	(woman / women)
*die Lehrerin – die Lehrerin**nen***	(teacher / teachers)
*die Speisekarte – die Speisekarte**n***	(menu / menus)
*die Suppe – die Suppe**n***	(soup / soups)

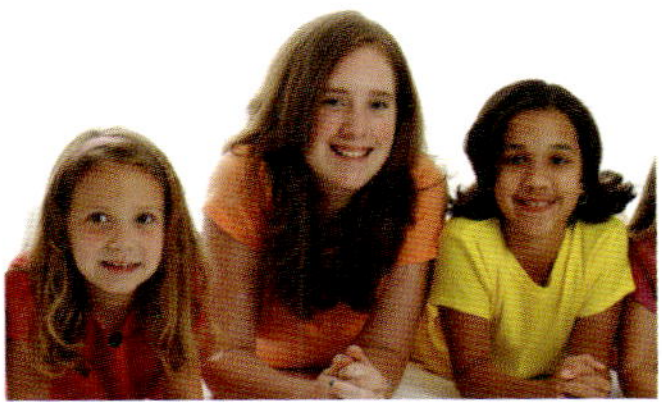

3 › Plurals (3)

Some masculine or neuter nouns add -e, -er or umlaut and -er to form their plural:

*der Mann – die M**ä**nn**er***	(man / men)
*das Haus – die H**ä**us**er***	(house / houses)

Some masculine nouns add an umlaut (¨) above the first vowel a, o or u and an -e ending to form the plural:

*der Stuhl – die St**ü**hl**e***

(chair / chairs)

4 › Plurals (4)

Many nouns have no plural ending. They are mostly masculine or neuter nouns ending in -en, -er or -el.

der Mitarbeiter – die Mitarbeiter	(employee / employees)
der Computer – die Computer	(computer / computers)
der Lehrer – die Lehrer	(teacher / teachers)

Some of these nouns also have an umlaut added to the first vowel a, o or u in the plural:

*der Vater – die **Vä**ter*
(father / fathers)

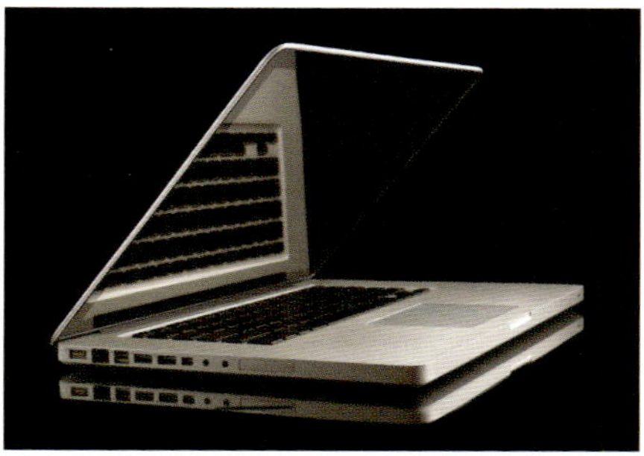

5 › Plurals (5)

There is another group of German nouns (very often words from other languages) which don't follow the rules that have just been mentioned. It is common for such words to form their plural by adding -s.

das Hotel - die Hotels	(hotel / hotels)
der Chef - die Chefs	(boss / bosses)

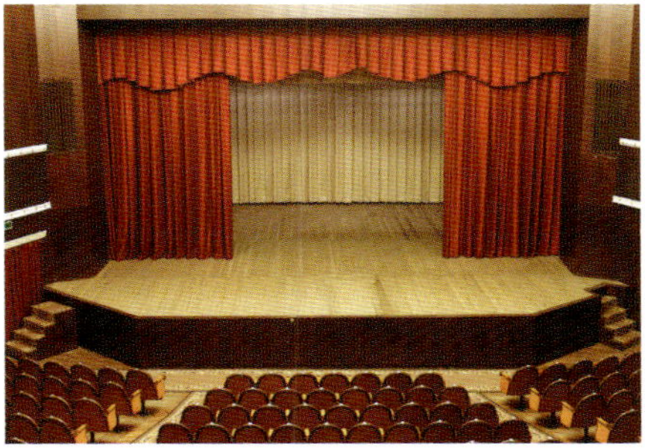

All nouns ending in -o and many ending in -a add an -s as well.

das Kino - die Kinos	(movie theater / movie theaters)
das Auto - die Autos	(car / cars)

6 › Plurals (6)

Note that plural verb forms must be used with plural nouns:

*Das Hotel **ist** gut. - Die Hotels **sind** gut.*

The hotel is good. – The hotels are good.

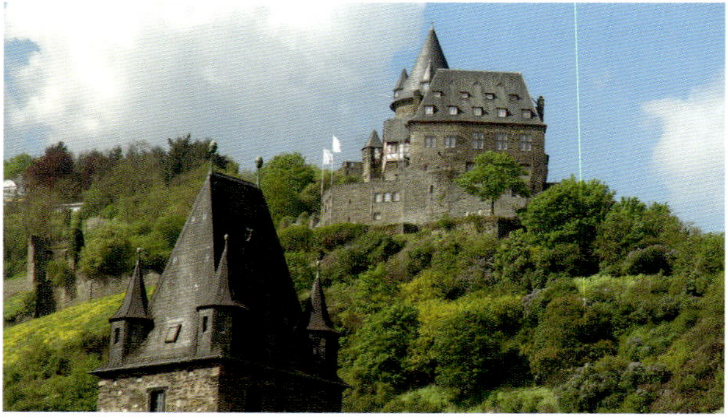

Vocabulary

Active German: Level 1 > *Unit 3* > *Lesson 2* > *Vocabulary*

Numbers and prices

0 1 2 3 4	*0 – null* *1 – eins* *2 – zwei* *3 – drei* *4 – vier*
5 6 7 8 9	*5 – fünf* *6 – sechs* *7 – sieben* *8 – acht* *9 – neun*

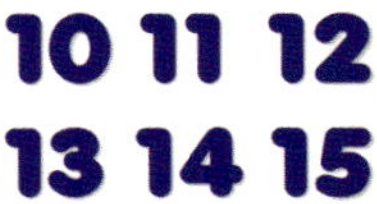

10 – zehn
11 – elf
12 – zwölf
13 – dreizehn
14 – vierzehn
15 – fünfzehn

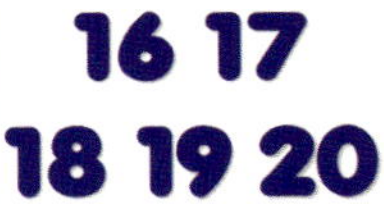

16 – sechzehn
17 – siebzehn
18 – achtzehn
19 – neunzehn
20 – zwanzig

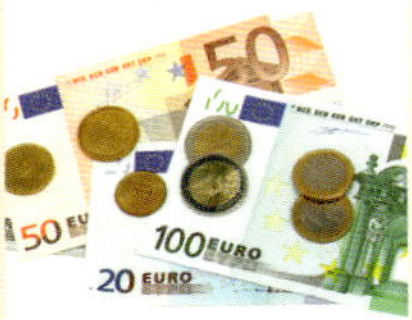

der Euro
euro

In Deutschland bezahlt man mit Euro.
In Germany you pay in euros.

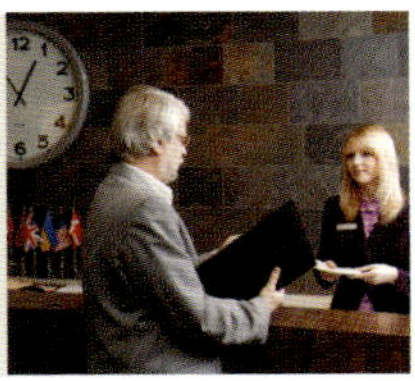

der Cent
cent

Das kostet 3 Euro und 20 Cent.
That costs 3 euros 20 cents.

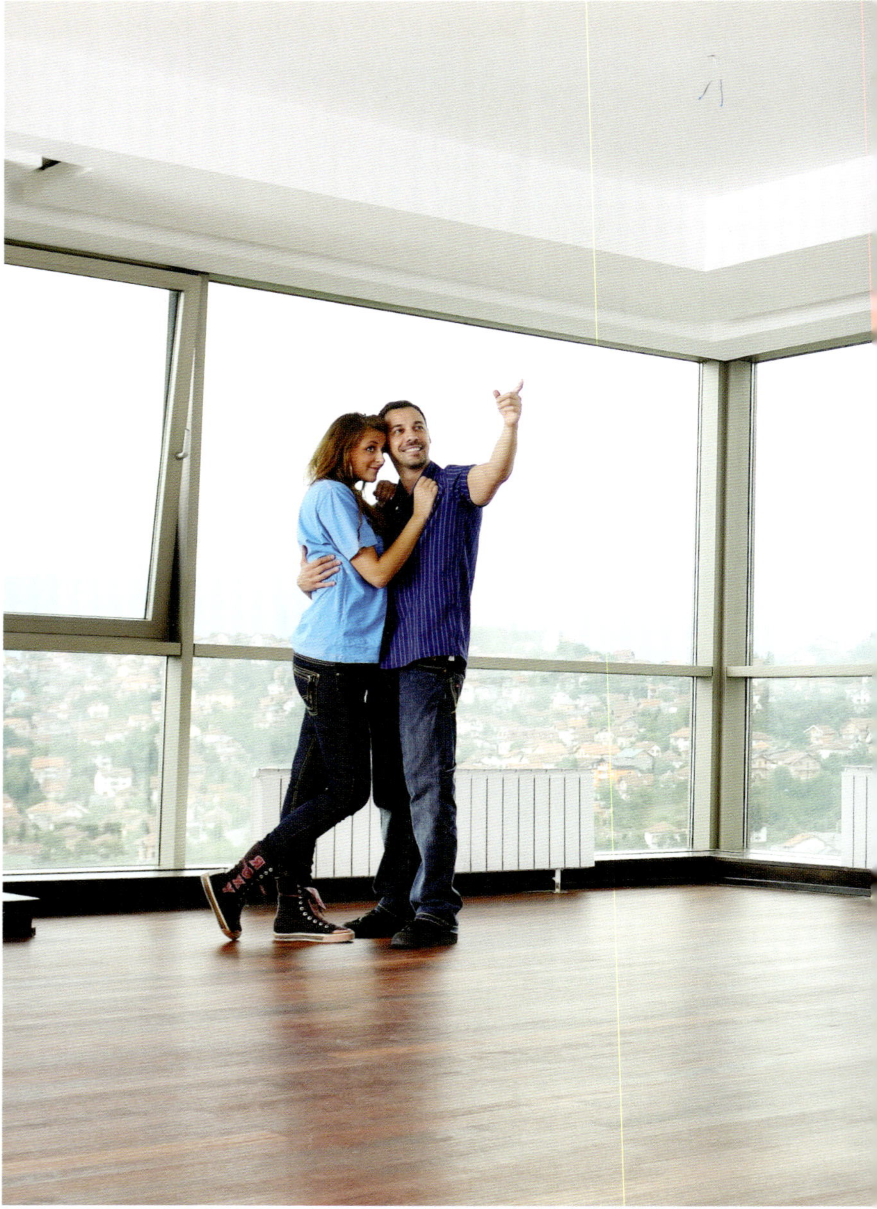

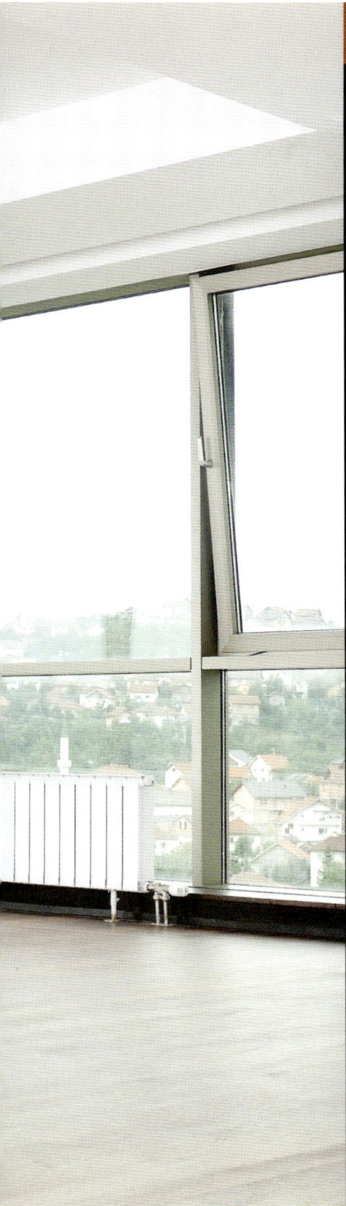

4

Lesson 1: The new home

- How to form sentences such as "I have an apartment."
- Vocabulary about the different rooms in an apartment or house.
- How to talk about your apartment.
- How to express whether you like your apartment or not.
- About the verb ***haben*** (to have).

Lesson 2: In the apartment

- How to talk about an apartment and say what you have and what you need: ***Ich habe einen Schrank, Ich brauche die Telefonnummer***.
- How to use the verbs ***brauchen*** (to need) and ***kaufen*** (to buy).
- Vocabulary about your apartment and objects in daily life.

Collins | Livemocha™

UNIT 4 › LESSON 1

The new home

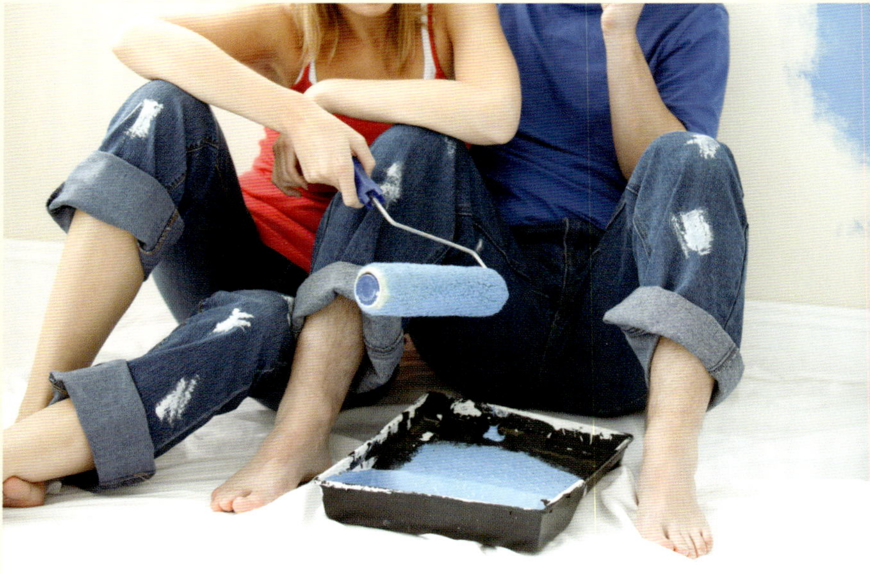

Culture note

Gemütlichkeit (coziness) is a very important concept in German. This term describes more than just a warm and nicely furnished place; it conveys the notion of quality and satisfaction. Finding this cozy place to live is not always easy, and finding good accommodation can be hard, especially in large cities. It is very common for people under 40 in Germany to rent an apartment. Young people like to share apartments and live in so called WGs (*Wohngemeinschaften* – shared housing).

Video Dialog

When Lara asks Matthias about his new apartment, he invites her to come and see what it's like for herself.

Active German: Level 1 > *Unit 4* > *Lesson 1* > *Video dialog*

Matthias: *Danke schön.*

Lara: *Wo wohnen Sie eigentlich?*

Matthias: *Ich habe eine Wohnung in Brauweiler.*

Lara: *Ist das im Osten, bei einem Park?*

Matthias: *Ja, ich wohne in der Bebelstraße.*

Lara: *Ist die Wohnung schön?*

Matthias: *Ja, ich finde meine Wohnung schön. Ich habe zwei Zimmer – ein Wohnzimmer und ein Schlafzimmer – ein Badezimmer und natürlich eine Küche.*

Lara: *Gut. Haben Sie einen Balkon oder einen Garten?*

Matthias: *Ich habe einen Balkon.*

Lara: *Ist die Wohnung teuer?*

Matthias: *Na ja, die Wohnung ist nicht teuer und nicht billig. Die Miete ist OK. Und die Lage ist ganz wunderbar. Ein Supermarkt ist direkt um die Ecke. Besuchen Sie mich doch mal!*

Matthias:	Thank you.
Lara:	Tell me, where do you live?
Matthias:	I have an apartment in Brauweiler.
Lara:	Is that in the east, near a park?
Matthias:	Yes, I live in Bebelstraße.
Lara:	Is it a nice apartment?
Matthias:	Yes, I think my apartment is very nice. I have two rooms – a living room and a bedroom – a bathroom and a kitchen, of course.
Lara:	Good. Do you have a balcony or a garden?
Matthias:	I have a balcony.
Lara:	Is the apartment expensive?
Matthias:	Well, it's not expensive and not cheap. The rent is OK. And the location is great. A supermarket is just around the corner. Come and visit me!

Grammar

Active German: Level 1 > *Unit 4* > *Lesson 1* > *Grammar*

1 › **The nominative case (1)**

A case shows you the function or role of a noun in a sentence. So far you have learned the forms and functions of the nominative case. The nominative case is used for the subject (a person, animal or thing) which is *doing* the action:

***Der Mann** arbeitet.*

The man is working.

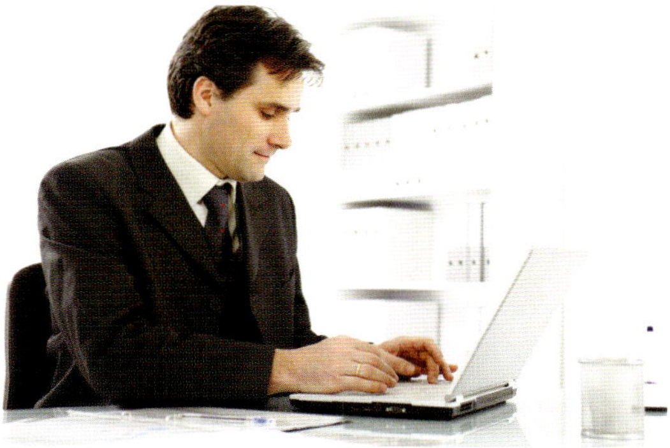

2 › The nominative case (2)

The nominative case is always used after *sein* (to be), *werden* (to become), and *bleiben* (to stay, to remain).

Herr Beier ist der Chef.

Mr. Beier is the boss.

Der, die, das and *ein, eine, ein* are the articles in the nominative case.

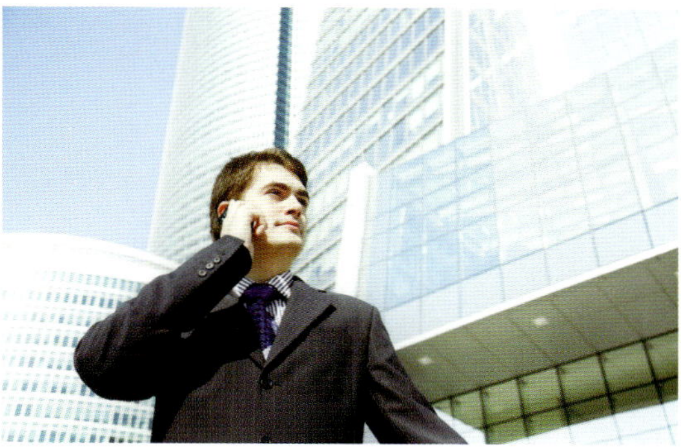

3 › The accusative case

Matthias trinkt einen Kaffee.

Matthias drinks a coffee.

In this sentence the doer of the action "drink" is Matthias and the person or thing affected by the action is the coffee. Matthias is the subject of the sentence and the coffee is the object.

Matthias hat eine Wohnung.

Matthias has an apartment.

In the second example again Matthias is the subject – the doer – and this time the apartment is the object.

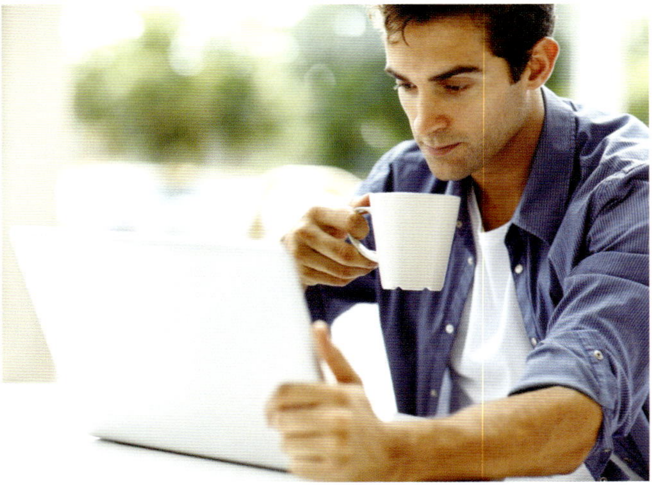

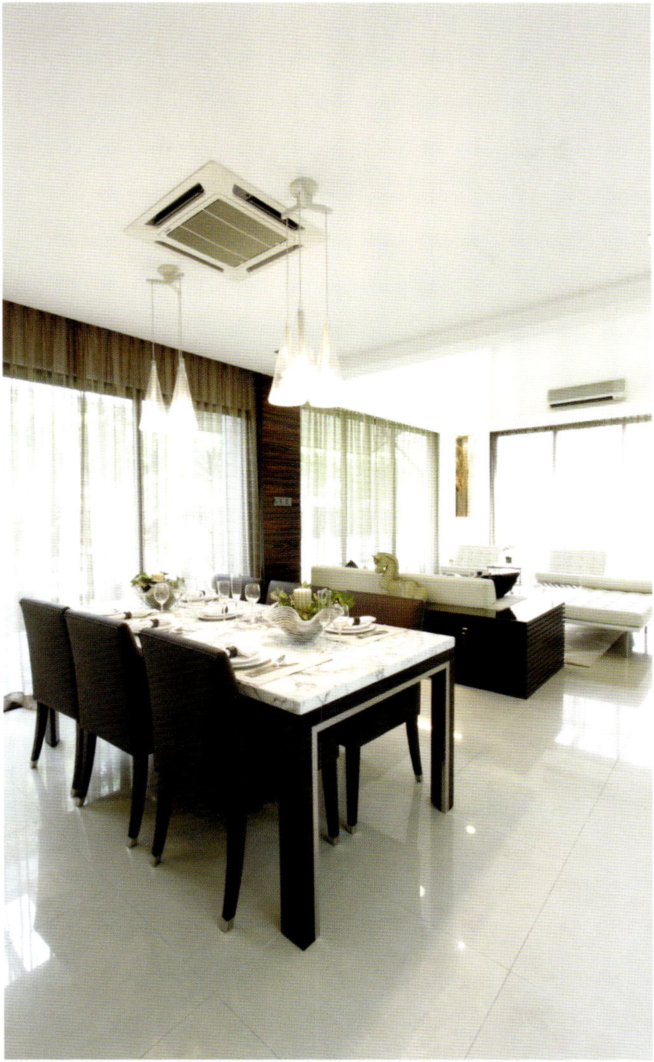

4 › "I have an apartment." The accusative case

The case of the object in a sentence is the accusative case. The articles in the accusative case are identical to the nominative, with the exception of their masculine forms.

*Das ist **eine** Wohnung. - Ich habe **eine** Wohnung.*

This is an apartment. – I have an apartment.

*Das ist **ein** Zimmer. - Ich habe **ein** Zimmer.*

This is a room. – I have a room.

*Das ist **ein** Balkon. - Ich habe **einen** Balkon.*

This is a balcony. – I have a balcony.

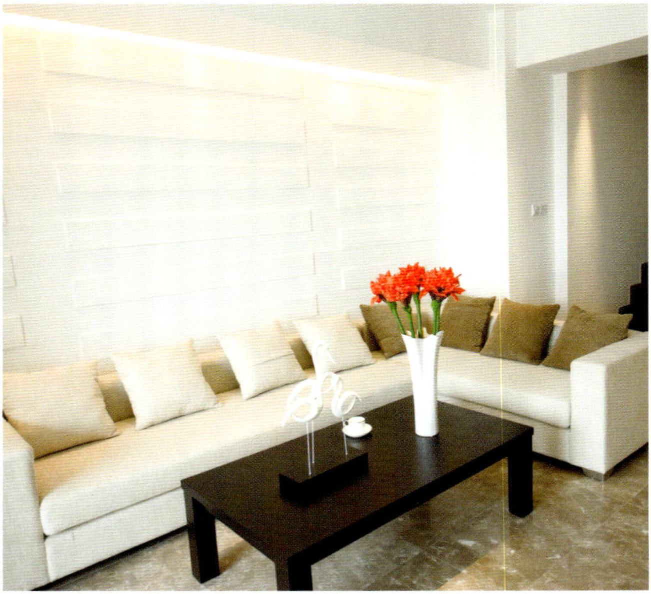

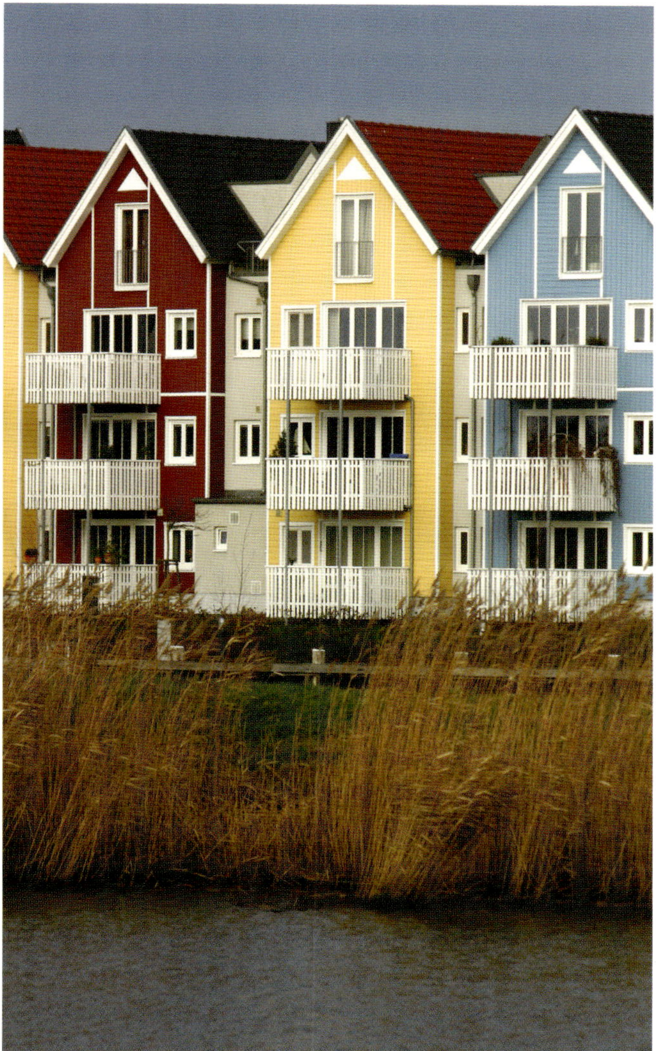

5 › The verb *haben*

Haben (to have) is a very frequently used verb in German. The forms are slightly irregular.

haben

ich habe	I have
du hast	you have
er, sie, es hat	he, she, it has
wir haben	we have
ihr habt	you have
sie, Sie haben	they, you have

6 › The verb *haben*

Haben requires an object that is in the accusative case. It is a verb expressing that someone has something. The sentence must have a second noun to complete the meaning.

masculine:	*Ich habe ein**en** Balkon.* I have a balcony.
feminine:	*Ich habe eine Küche.* I have a kitchen.
neuter:	*Ich habe ein Badezimmer.* I have a bathroom.

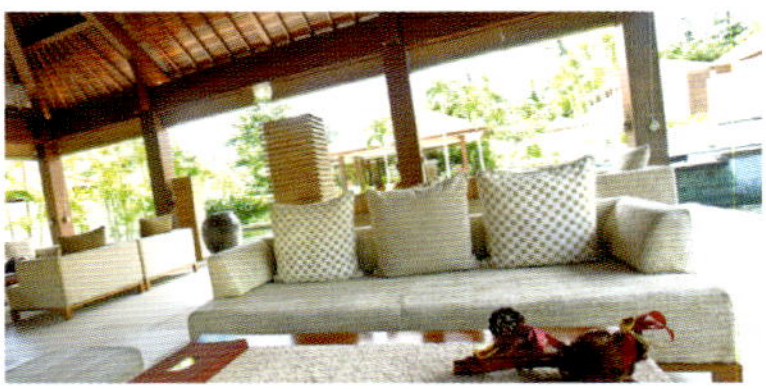

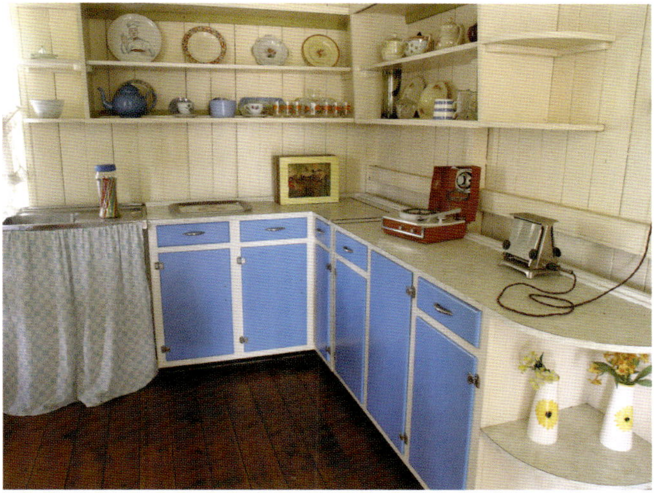

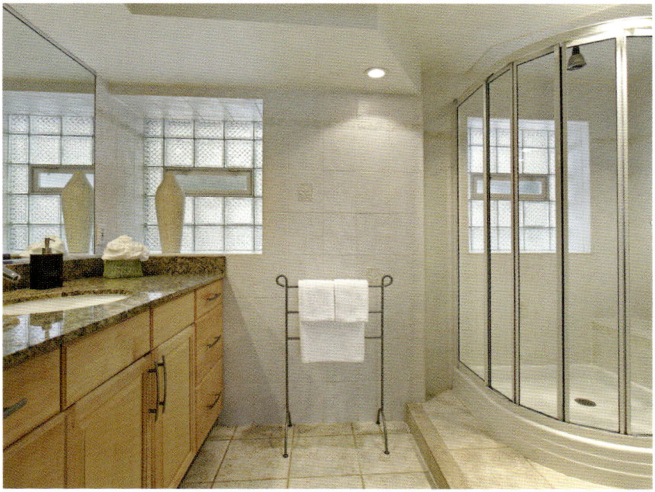

Another example of a verb with an object in the accusative is *trinken*:

Ich trinke einen Tee.

I drink a cup of tea.

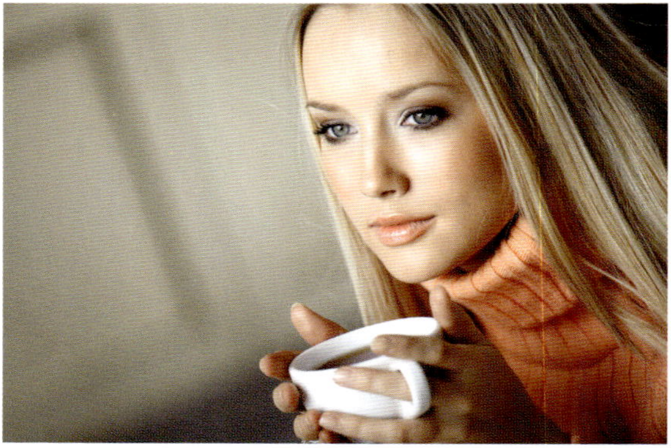

Vocabulary

Active German: Level 1 > Unit 4 > Lesson 1 > Vocabulary

Living

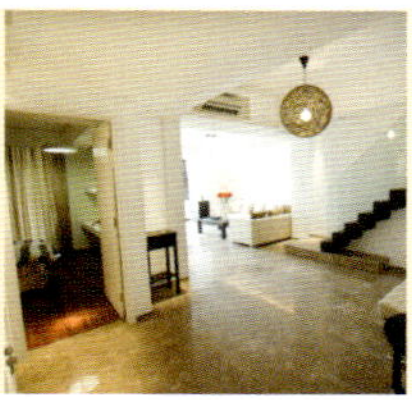

die Wohnung / Wohnungen
apartment

Ich habe eine Wohnung in Berlin.
I have an apartment in Berlin.

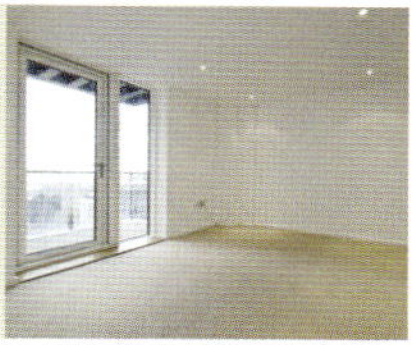

das Zimmer / Zimmer
room

Meine Wohnung hat 3 Zimmer.
My apartment has 3 rooms.

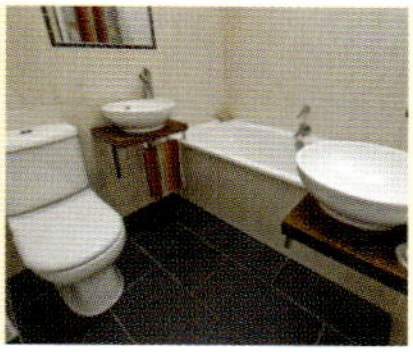

das Badezimmer / Badezimmer
bathroom

Hast du ein Badezimmer und eine Toilette?
Do you have a bathroom and a toilet?

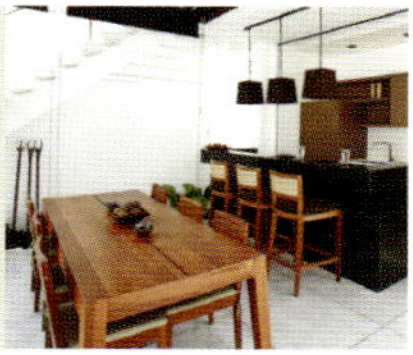

die Küche / Küchen
kitchen

Wo ist die Küche?
Where is the kitchen?

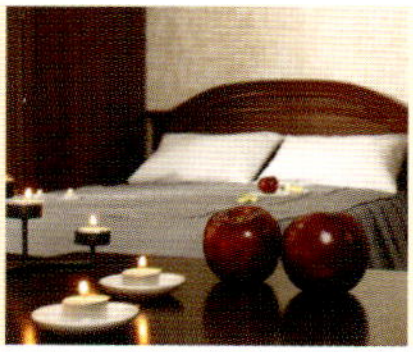

das Schlafzimmer / Schlafzimmer
bedroom

Das Schlafzimmer ist gemütlich.
The bedroom is cozy.

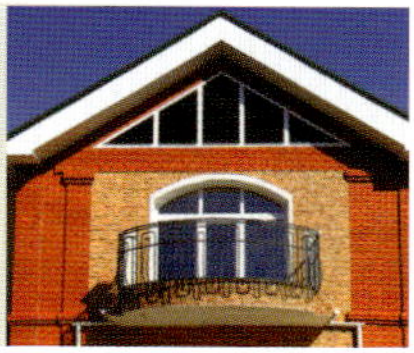

der Balkon / Balkone
balcony

Wir haben einen Balkon und einen Garten.
We have a balcony and a garden.

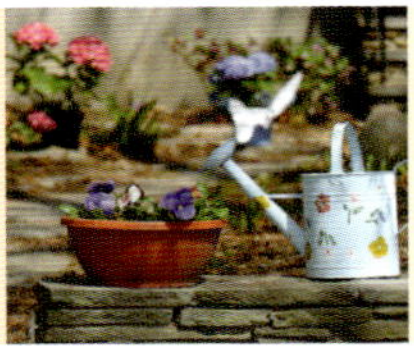

der Garten / Gärten
garden

Der Garten ist schön!
The garden is beautiful.

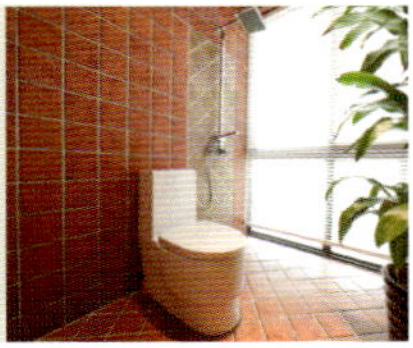

die Toilette / Toiletten
toilet

Entschuldigung, wo sind die Toiletten?
Excuse me, where are the toilets?

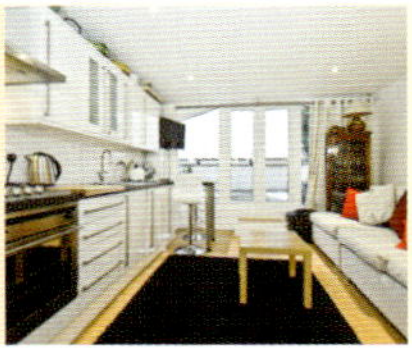

klein
small

Die Wohnung ist klein, aber gemütlich.
The apartment is small, but cozy.

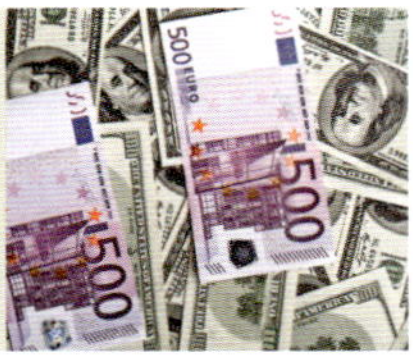

teuer
expensive

Die Wohnung ist teuer.
The apartment is expensive.

Culture note

Nearly 82 million people live in Germany. Germany has the largest population of all the countries in the European Union and is one of the most densely populated countries in Europe.

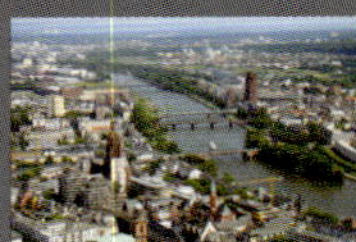

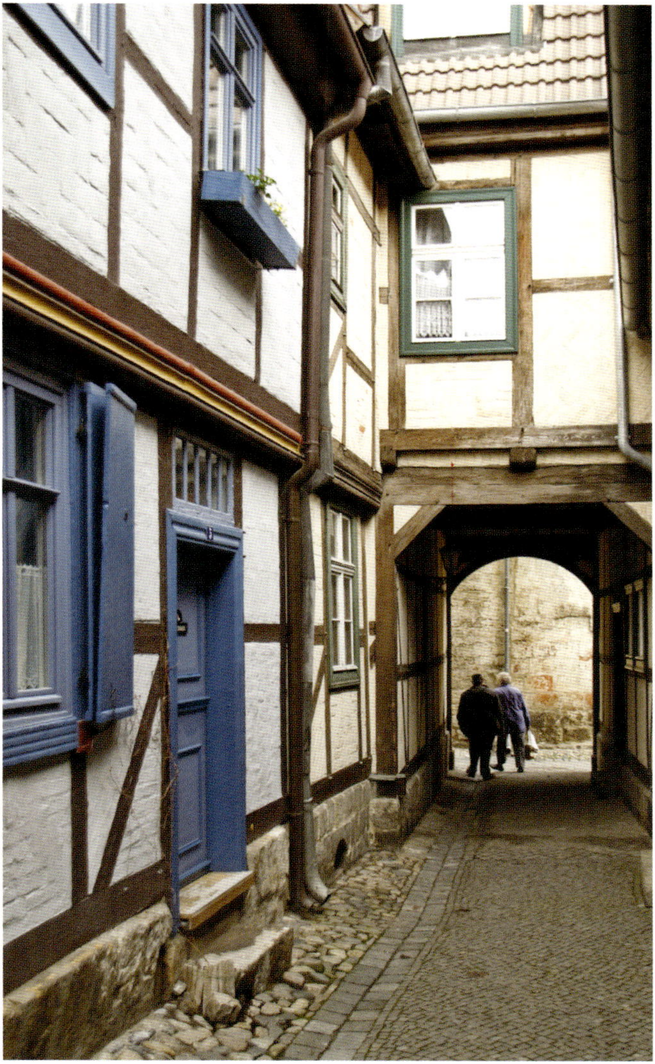

UNIT 4 › LESSON 2

In the apartment

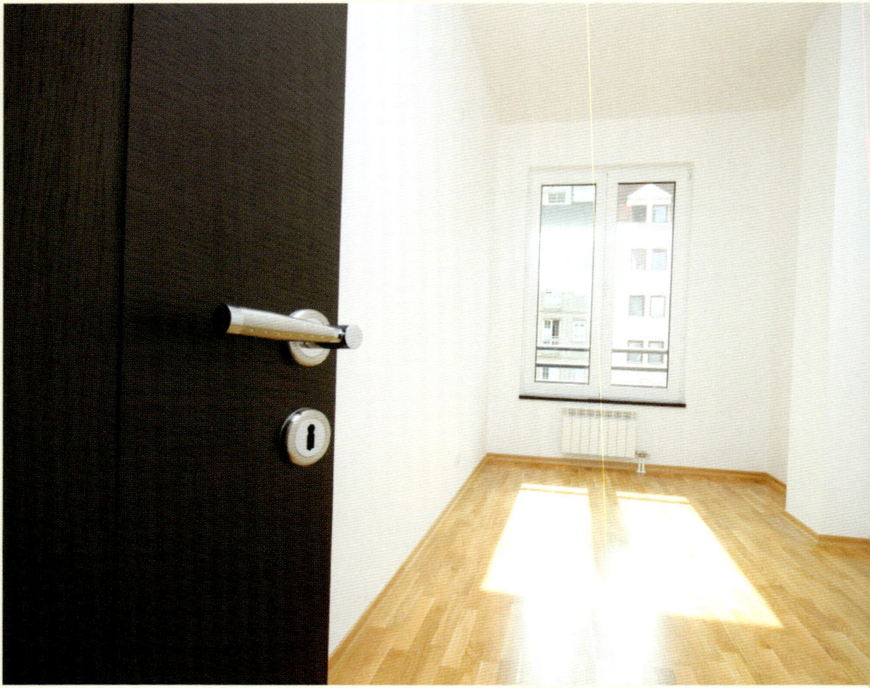

Culture note

In Germany it is common to rent an empty apartment, without any furniture at all. Apart from a stove and a washing machine the tenants have to bring their own furniture and electrical appliances.

Video Dialog

Matthias shows Lara around his apartment. Lara asks what furniture Matthias still needs and the two exchange phone numbers.

Active German: Level 1 > *Unit 4* > *Lesson 2* > *Video dialog*

Matthias:	*Und das ist die Küche.*
Lara:	*Ah, einen Kühlschrank und einen Herd haben Sie. Haben Sie schon alle Möbel?*
Matthias:	*Nein, ich brauche noch einen Schrank für das Schlafzimmer. Den Schrank kaufe ich morgen.*
Lara:	*Haben Sie eine Toilette und ein Badezimmer?*
Matthias:	*Ja.*
Lara:	*Ich brauche Ihre Telefonnummer noch.*
Matthias:	*Haben Sie einen Stift?*
Lara:	*Moment. Wo habe ich den Stift? Ja.*
Matthias:	*Meine Telefonnummer ist: 032*
Lara:	*032*
Matthias:	*57*
Lara:	*57*
Matthias:	*88*

Lara:	*88*
Matthias:	*70*
Lara:	*70. Danke.*
Matthias:	*Gerne.*

Matthias:	And this is the kitchen.
Lara:	Ah, you have a fridge and a stove. Do you already have all your furniture?
Matthias:	No, I still need a closet for the bedroom. I am going to buy one tomorrow.
Lara:	Do you have a toilet and a bathroom?
Matthias:	Yes.
Lara:	I need your phone number.
Matthias:	Do you have a pen?
Lara:	Hold on. Where is my pen? Yes.
Matthias:	My number is: 032
Lara:	032
Matthias:	57
Lara:	57
Matthias:	88
Lara:	88
Matthias:	70
Lara:	70. Thank you.
Matthias:	You're welcome.

Culture note

German is famous for its long words. The language allows you to add as many words as you want to a noun. One of the most famous ones is: *Donaudampfschifffahrtsgesellschaftskapitän*, which in English is: "Danube steamship company captain." This German word has 42 letters, while some others are even longer.

Grammar

Active German: Level 1 > Unit 4 > Lesson 2 > Grammar

1 › The accusative case

In lesson 1 we learned about the noun as an object with the article "a" (*einen, eine, ein* – indefinite article). Let's have a look now at the noun as object with "the" (definite article). The article in the accusative case is very similar to the nominative case. The only difference is the masculine form.

Nominative	Accusative
Masculine: *Hier ist der Kaffee.* Here is the coffee.	*Der Mann trinkt* ***den Kaffee.*** The man drinks the coffee.
Feminine: *Hier ist die Cola.* Here is the soda.	*Frau Roellinger trinkt* ***die Cola.*** Mrs. Roellinger drinks the soda.
Neuter: *Hier ist das Wasser.* Here is the water.	*Die Frau trinkt* ***das Wasser.*** The woman drinks the water.
Plural: *Hier sind die Stühle.* Here are the chairs.	*Wir haben* ***die Stühle.*** We have the chairs.

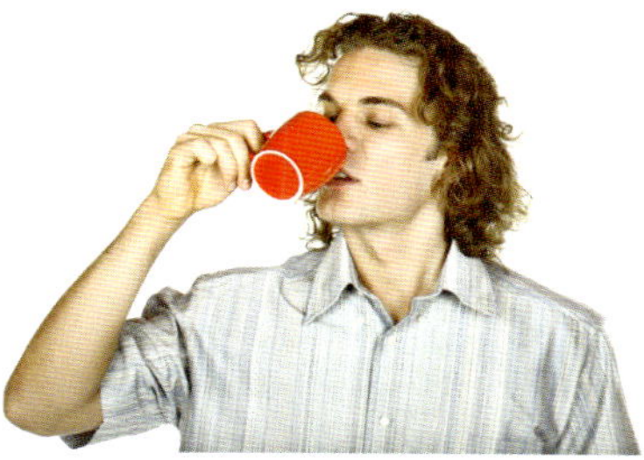

2 › Whom?

The question word *wer* or *was* (who or what) in the nominative case is used for the person or thing that is doing something. The accusative form of the question word *wer* is *wen* (whom). *Was* (what) remains the same in both nominative and accusative cases.

Wer ist das?	Who is that?
Das ist der Mann von Frau Schulz.	That is the husband of Mrs. Schulz.
Wen kennst du?	Whom do you know?
Ich kenne den Mann von Frau Schulz.	I know the husband of Mrs. Schulz.

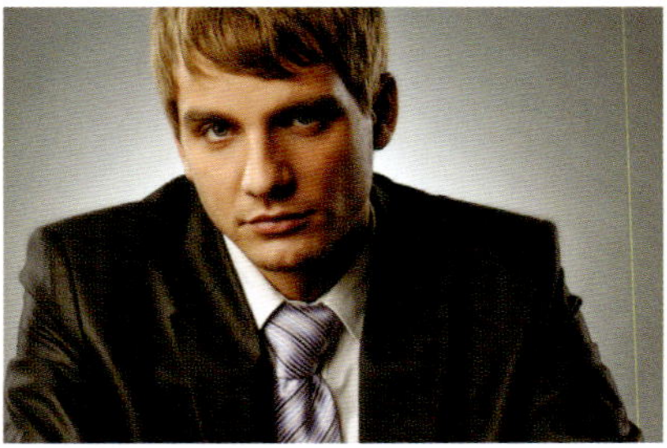

3 › The verb *brauchen*

Ich brauche einen Schrank.

I need a closet.

The verb *brauchen* requires the accusative case as well. In the sentence *Ich brauche einen Schrank* – *Ich* is the subject and *einen Schrank* the object.

4 › The verb *kaufen*

The verb *kaufen* (to buy) and many other verbs require an object in the accusative:

Ich kaufe eine Flasche Wein.

I buy a bottle of wine. (*eine* is in the accusative case)

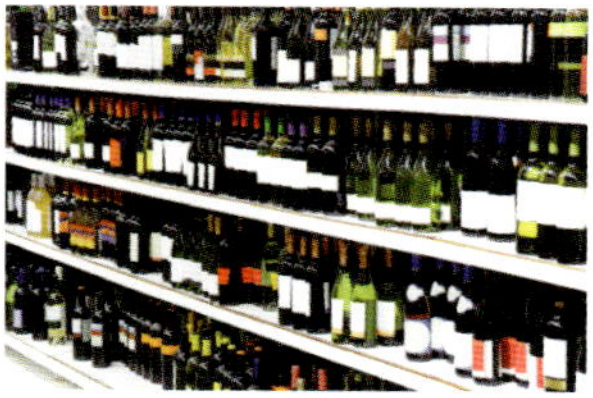

5 › Verbs with accusative

So far we have seen four verbs with the accusative: *trinken* (to drink), *haben* (to have), *kaufen* (to buy), and *brauchen* (to need).

Let's look at another example – *suchen* (to look for, to search).

Wen suchst du?	Who (Whom) are you looking for?
Den Chef.	The boss.
Wer sucht den Chef?	Who is looking for the boss?
Ich.	I am.

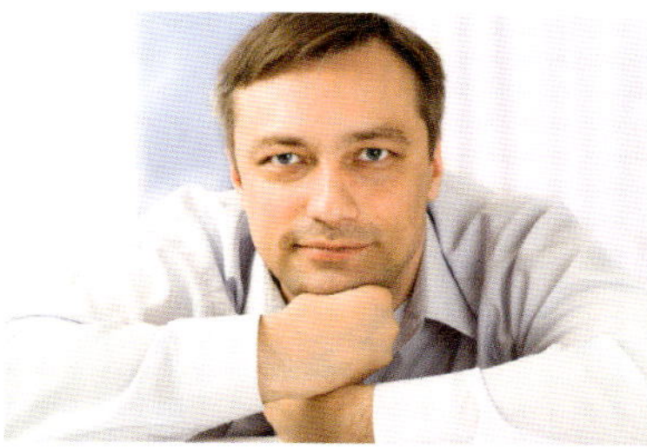

Vocabulary

Active German: Level 1 > Unit 4 > Lesson 2 > Vocabulary

Furniture and useful objects

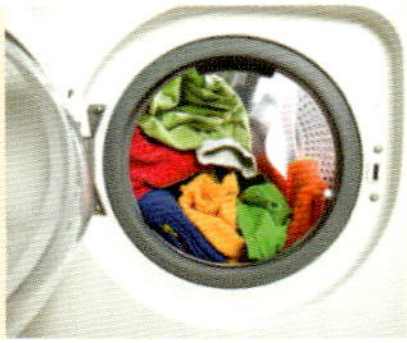

die Waschmaschine / Waschmaschinen
washing machine

Die Waschmaschine ist kaputt.
The washing machine is broken.

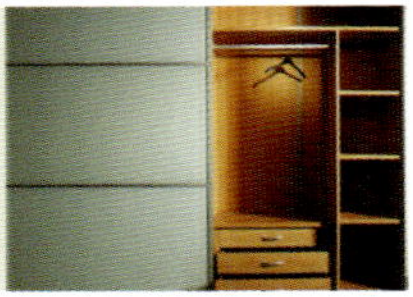

der Schrank / Schränke
closet

Heute kaufe ich einen Schrank.
Today I'm going to buy a closet.

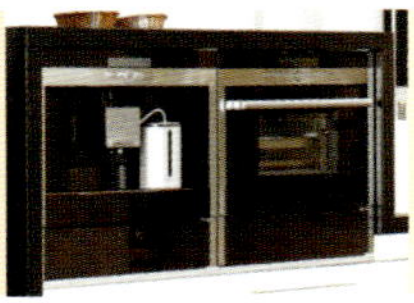

der Herd / Herde
stove

Der Herd ist in der Küche.
The stove is in the kitchen.

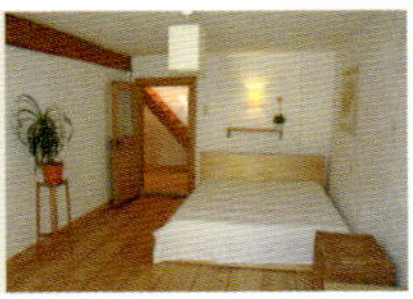

die Möbel
furniture

Ich kaufe meine Möbel bei IKEA.
I buy my furniture in IKEA.

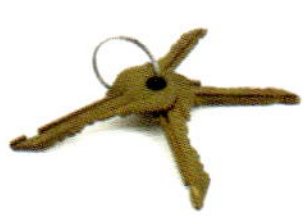

der Schlüssel / Schlüssel
key

Wo sind meine Schlüssel?
Where are my keys?

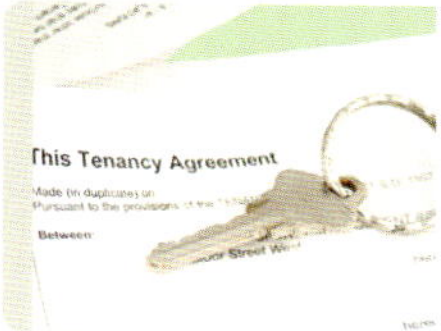

der Vertrag / Verträge
contract

Ich unterschreibe den Vertrag.
I sign the contract.

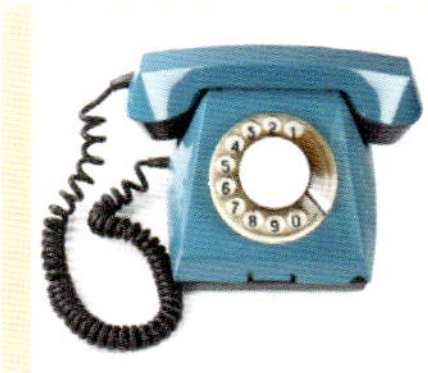

die Telefonnummer / Telefonnummern
phone number

Meine Telefonnummer ist 040/348827.
My phone number is 040/348827

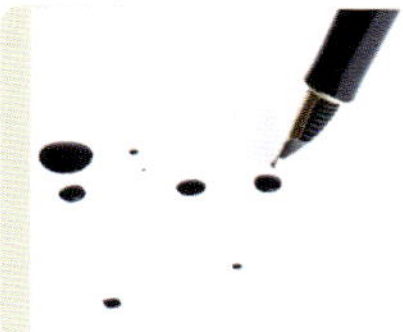

der Stift / Stifte
pen

Hast du einen Stift?
Do you have a pen?

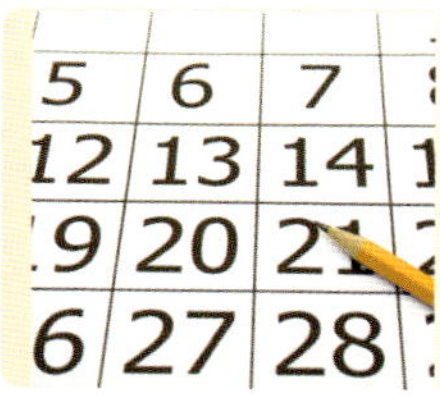

die Miete / Mieten
rent

Ich bezahle 500 Euro Miete im Monat.
I pay rent of 500 euros a month.

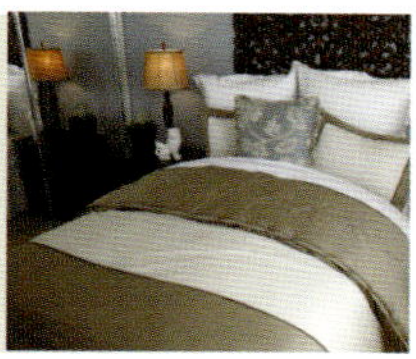

das Bett / Betten
bed

Mein Schlafzimmer ist klein, aber mein Bett ist groß.
My bedroom is small, but my bed is big.

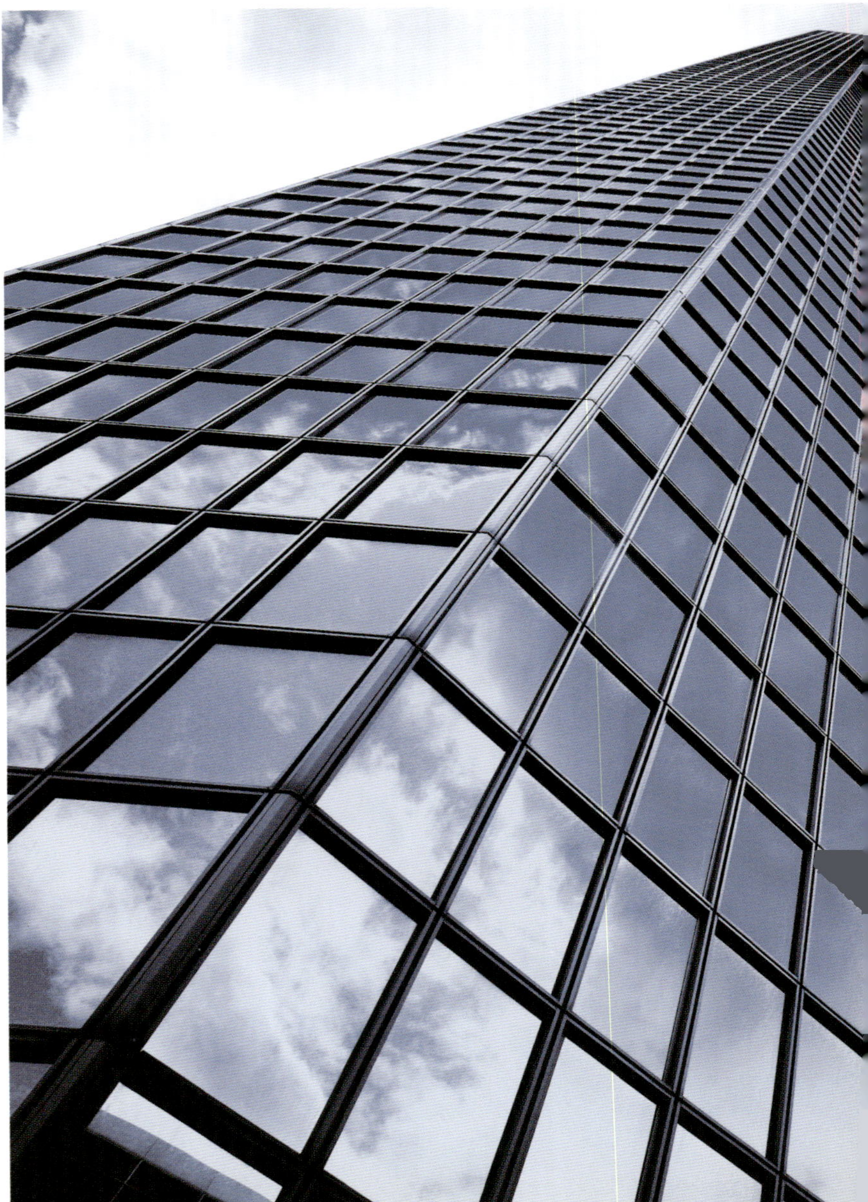

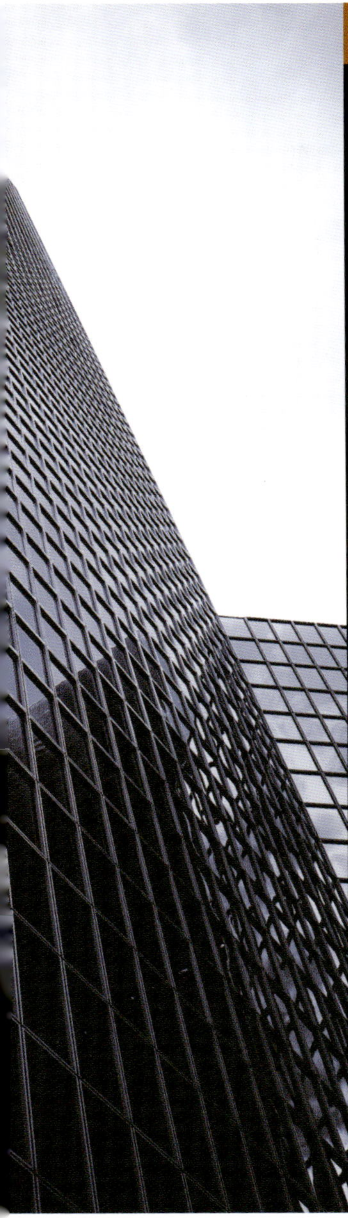

Active German *Level 1*

5

Lesson 1: My new office

- » How to say what belongs to you and others: ***Das ist mein Buch, Ist das Ihre Tasse?***
- » Vocabulary for the office and the working world.
- » Eliciting information from advertisements.

Lesson 2: At work

- » How to give basic personal information about yourself.
- » How to say that you don't do something: ***Ich arbeite nicht, ich habe keine Kinder.***
- » Vocabulary for personal details: ***Meine Adresse, meine Handynummer.***
- » How to fill out a simple form.

Collins | Livemocha™

UNIT 5 › LESSON 1

My new office

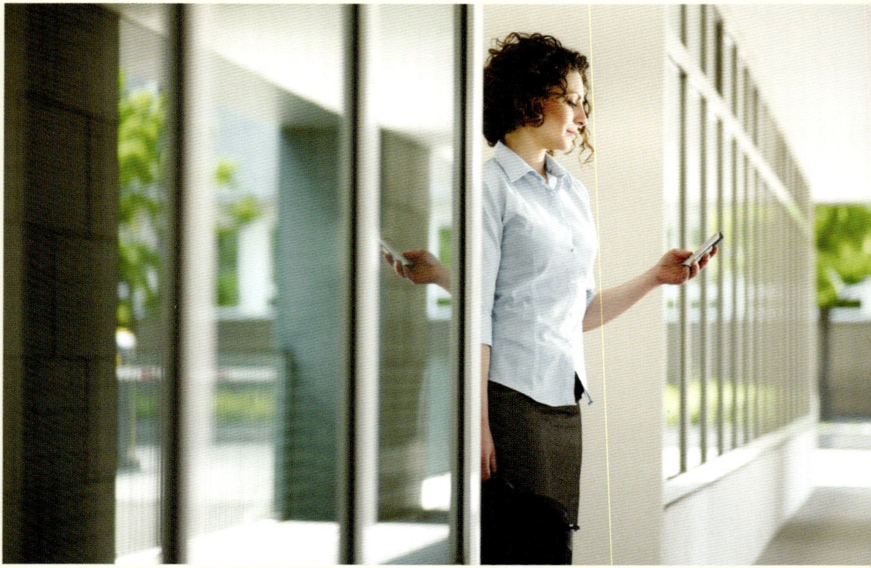

Culture note

You'll find many English words in a German office. Most of the time these words are related to technology, and English words have been adopted in the language when there has been the need to name new inventions, e.g., *der Computer*, *der Scanner*, *die Email* or new verbs such as *downloaden*. In addition, German has often taken English words and given them a completely different meaning e.g. *das Handy* for cell phone or *der Beamer* for data projector. Some Germans don't even know that these words are not the same in English!

Video Dialog

Back at work, Matthias meets Mr. Baumann and settles into his new office.

Active German: Level 1 > *Unit 5* > *Lesson 1* > *Video dialog*

Matthias:	*Guten Morgen, Herr Baumann. Wie geht es Ihnen?*
Herr Baumann:	*Sehr gut. Und Ihnen?*
Matthias:	*Gut, alles ist neu. Das ist sehr interessant.*
Herr Baumann:	*Ja, ja, Sie sind noch jung, da ist alles neu. Schauen Sie, das ist Ihr Büro. Das ist Ihr Schreibtisch und alles, was Sie brauchen. Unser Drucker ist dort.*
Matthias:	*Ist das Ihr Büro rechts?*
Herr Baumann:	*Nein, mein Büro ist oben. Viel Glück und viel Spaß!*
Matthias:	*Gut, danke. Mmh. Mein Schreibtisch, mein Computer und mein Telefon.*

Matthias:	Good morning, Mr. Baumann. How are you?
Mr. Baumann:	Very good. And you?
Matthias:	Good, everything is new. It is very interesting.
Mr. Baumann:	Yes, yes, you are still young. Everything is new then. Have a look. This is your office. This is your desk and everything else that you'll need. Our printer is over there.

Matthias:	Is that your office on the right?
Mr. Baumann:	No, my office is upstairs. Good luck and enjoy!
Matthias:	Good, thank you. Hmm. My desk, my computer and my phone.

Grammar

Active German: Level 1 > *Unit 5* > *Lesson 1* > *Grammar*

1 › **My office**

*Das ist **Ihr** Schreibtisch.*

This is your desk.

*Das ist **mein** Büro.*

This is my office.

Mein (my), *unser* (our), *Ihr* (your) and *sein* (his) are adjectives to indicate possession. They tell us what belongs to whom.

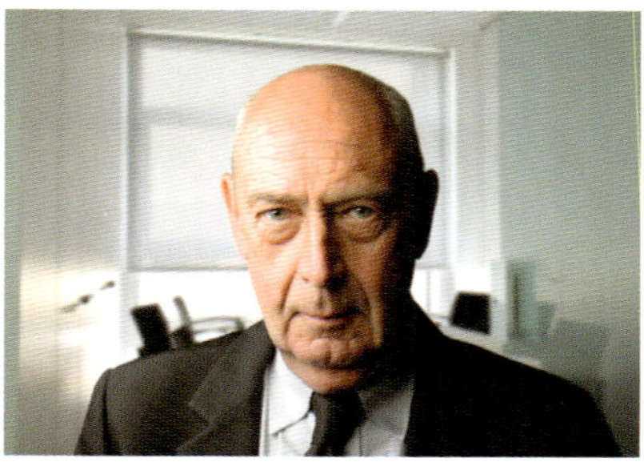

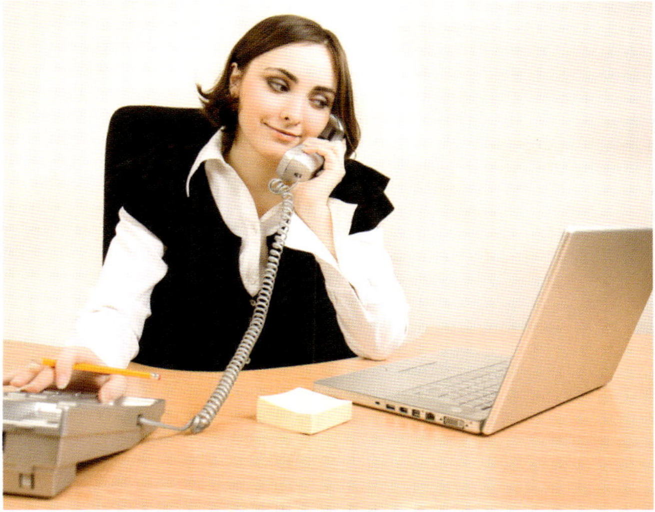

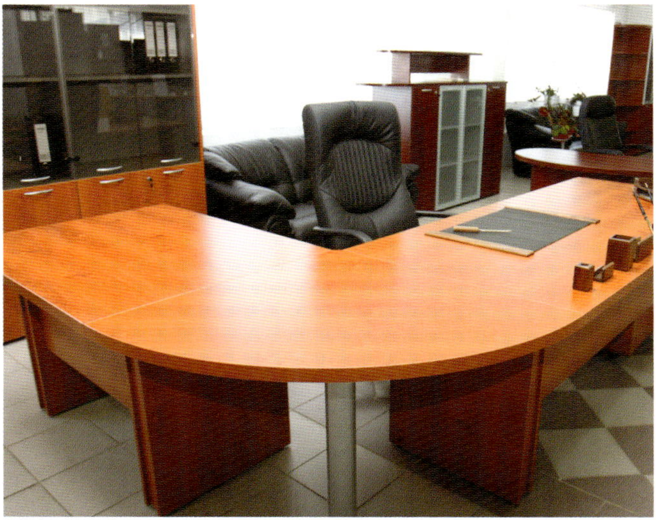

2 › My office

In German these adjectives change according to the gender of the noun.

Masculine	*ein Mann → mein Mann*	my husband
Feminine	*eine Frau → meine Frau*	my wife
Neuter	*ein Büro → mein Büro*	my office
Plural	*Stifte → meine Stifte*	my pens

3 › Your office

The form of the German for "my," "your," "his," "her," and "our" depends on the gender of the noun.

my

mein Chef	my boss
meine Wohnung	my apartment
mein Büro	my office
meine Stifte	my pens (*plural*)

your

dein Chef	your boss
deine Wohnung	your apartment
dein Büro	your office
deine Stifte	your pens
Ist das dein Chef?	Is that your boss?

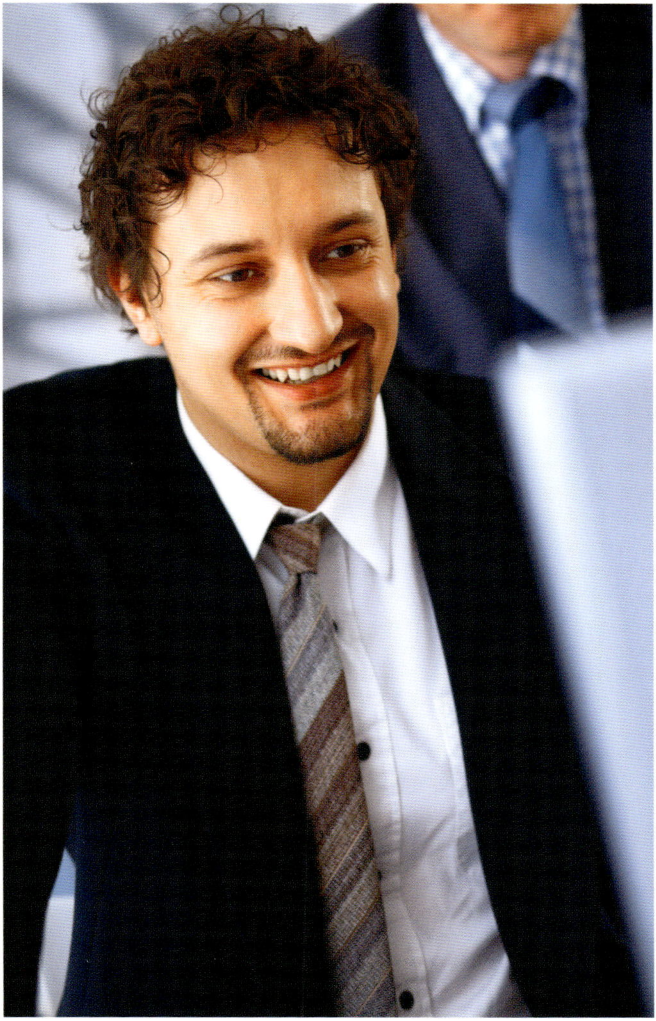

4 › Her office

These are the words for "his" and "her":

his

sein Chef	his boss
seine Wohnung	his apartment
sein Büro	his office
seine Stifte	his pens
Das ist seine Telefonnummer.	That is his phone number.

her

ihr Chef	her boss
ihre Wohnung	her apartment
ihr Büro	her office
ihre Stifte	her pens
Das ist ihr Mann.	That is her husband.

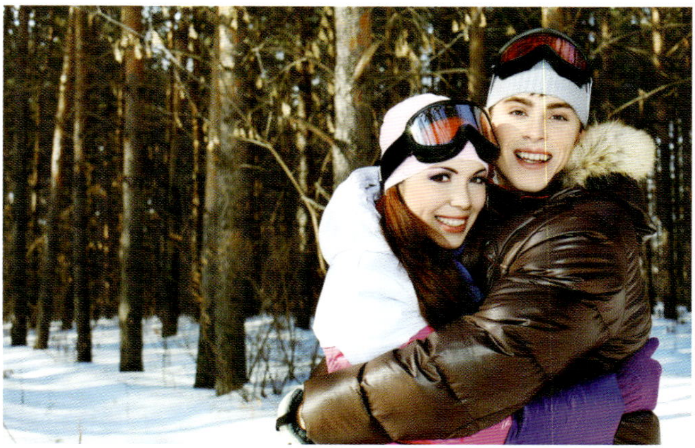

5 › Our office

our

unser Chef	our boss
unsere Wohnung	our apartment
unser Büro	our office
Unser Chef ist sehr nett.	Our boss is very nice.

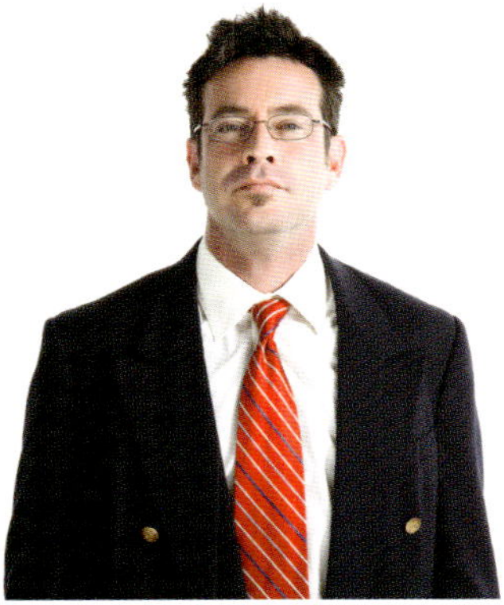

6 › Your office

When you address someone formally you use the following form:

your (formal)

Ihr Chef	your boss
Ihre Wohnung	your apartment
Ihr Büro	your office
Ist das Ihr Kaffee, Herr Meisinger?	Is that your coffee, Mr. Meisinger?

7 › Note the difference

Das ist ***ihr*** *Haus.*
It is her house.

Das ist ***Ihr*** *Haus.*
It is your house. This could be singular or plural. In this case *Ihr* has a capital letter.

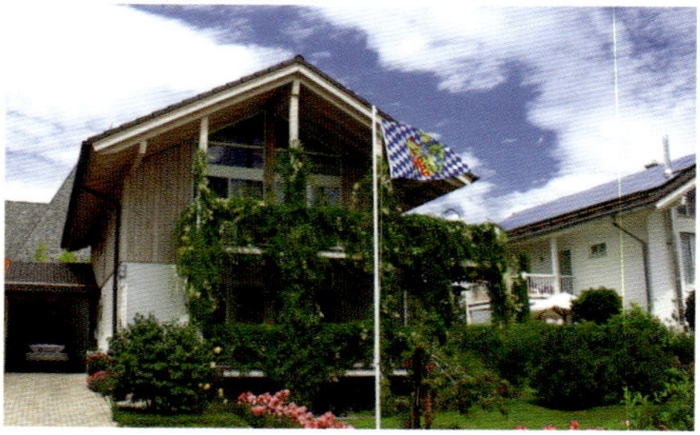

Vocabulary

Active German: Level 1 > *Unit 5* > *Lesson 1* > *Vocabulary*

Office and personal information

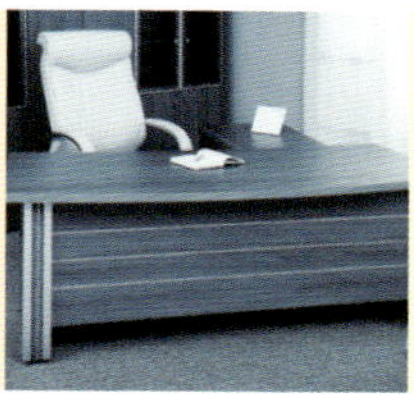

der Schreibtisch / Schreibtische
desk

Mein Schreibtisch ist sehr groß.
My desk is very big.

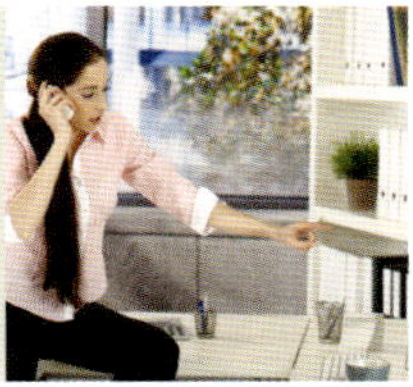

das Büro / Büros
office

Wo ist Ihr Büro?
Where is your office?

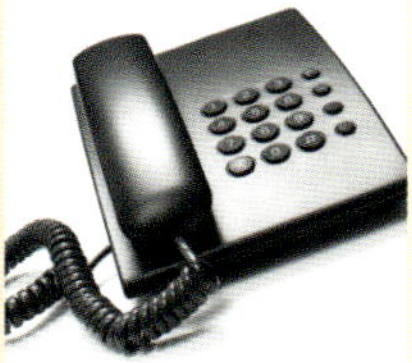

das Telefon / Telefone
phone

Mein Telefon ist kaputt.
My phone is broken.

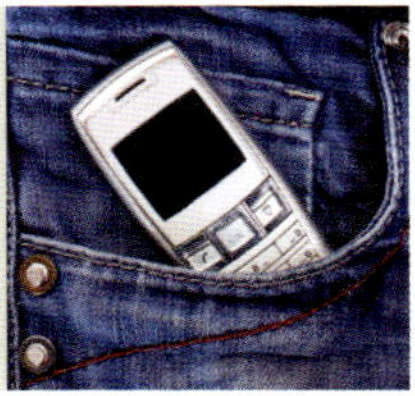

das Handy / Handys
cell phone

Heute kaufe ich ein Handy.
Today I'm buying a cell phone.

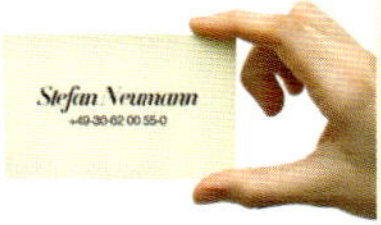

die Telefonnummer / Telefonnummern
phone number

Entschuldigung, wie ist Ihre Telefonnummer?
Excuse me, what is your phone number?

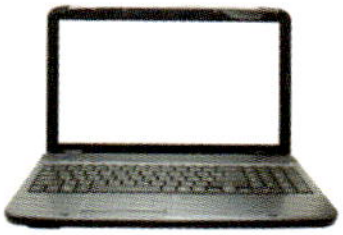

der Computer / Computer
computer

Ich brauche einen Computer.
I need a computer.

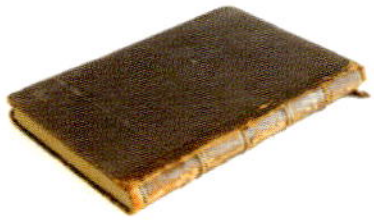

das Buch / Bücher
book

Das sind alle Bücher von Goethe.
These are all books by Goethe.

die Post
mail

Ist das meine Post?
Is that my mail?

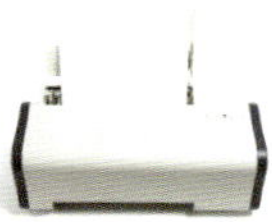

der Drucker / Drucker
printer

Ist der Drucker neu?
Is the printer new?

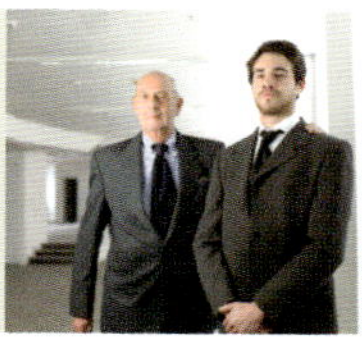

jung
young

Matthias ist noch jung.
Matthias is still young.

UNIT 5 › LESSON 2

At work

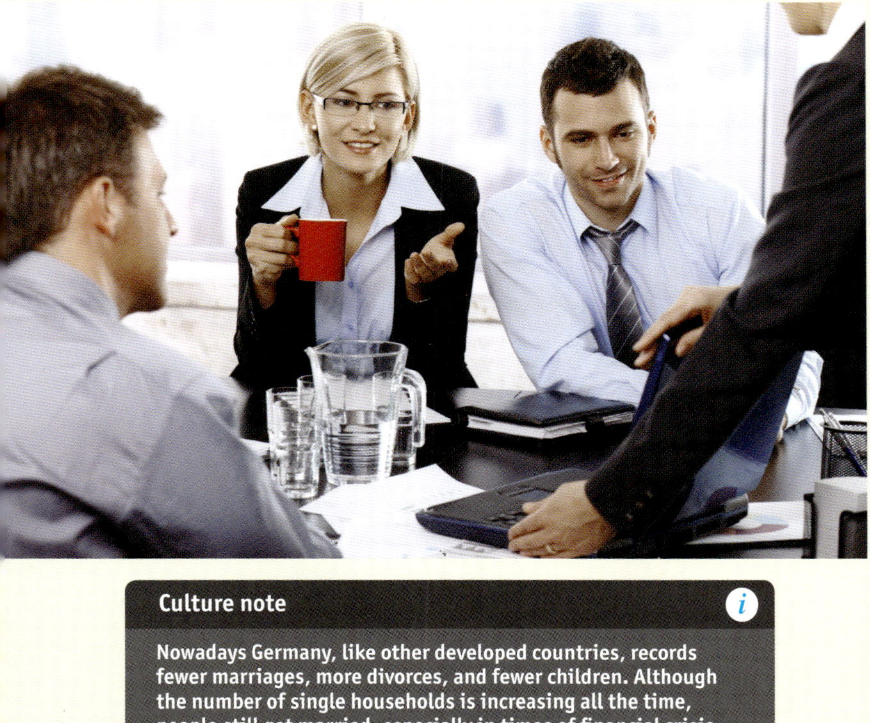

Culture note

Nowadays Germany, like other developed countries, records fewer marriages, more divorces, and fewer children. Although the number of single households is increasing all the time, people still get married, especially in times of financial crisis. Interestingly, educational achievement is a crucial factor for determining the age at which people get married: the higher the education, the older couples are when they get married. Yearlong engagements used to be common, but nowadays many couples who get married do so without getting officially engaged beforehand.

Video Dialog

Matthias has some forms to fill out at work.

Active German: Level 1 > *Unit 5* > *Lesson 2* > *Video dialog*

Lara: *Hallo.*

Matthias: *Hallo.*

Lara: *Wir brauchen ein paar Informationen von Ihnen. Das ist für die Personalabteilung. Brauchen Sie Hilfe?*

Matthias: *Nein, ich brauche keine Hilfe. Ah, ich habe meine Postleitzahl nicht im Kopf.*

Lara: *Kein Problem. Das machen wir später.*

Matthias: *Danke. Also, männlich, weiblich. Ok, das ist einfach. Mein Familienname ist Meisinger, mein Vorname ist Matthias. Familienstand: Nein, ich bin nicht verheiratet, ich bin ledig. Kinder, nein ich habe keine Kinder. Meine Adresse: Bebelstraße 33. Meine Telefonnummer ist: 032 578870. Meine Handynummer ist 0173 452345. Alter: Ich bin 31 Jahre alt. Das ist alles.*

Lara: Hello.
Matthias: Hello.
Lara: We need some information from you. It is for Human Resources. Do you need help?

Matthias:	No, I don't need help. Ah, I can't remember my zip code.
Lara:	No problem. We'll do it later.
Matthias:	Thank you. Well, male, female. OK, that's easy. My family name is Meisinger, my first name is Matthias. Family status: no, I am not married, I am single. Children: no, I don't have children. My address is: Bebelstraße 33. My phone number is: 032 578870. My cell number is: 0173 452345. Age: I am 31 years old. That's it.

Grammar

Active German: Level 1 > *Unit 5* > *Lesson 2* > *Grammar*

1 › How to say no! (1)

To say that you don't do something, you use the word *nicht*. *Nicht* is used with verbs and makes the sentence negative.

Ich arbeite ***nicht.***

I'm not working.

2 › I'm not Mr. Müller!

Nicht can follow the verb:

Er ist ***nicht*** *mein Chef.*	He is not my boss.
Ich bin ***nicht*** *verheiratet.*	I am not married.
Es regnet ***nicht.***	It is not raining.
Ich bin ***nicht*** *Herr Müller.*	I am not Mr. Müller.

3 › **How to say no! (2)**

Nicht can follow the object:

Ich benutze den Drucker ***nicht.***

I don't use the printer.

or the subject:

Arbeitest du ***nicht****?*

Don't you work?

4 › **How to say no! (3)**

The word *nicht* applies to verbs. When you want to make a negative statement about a noun, you must use *kein*.

Compare:

Ich arbeite nicht.	I don't work.
Ich habe keine Kinder.	I don't have children.

5 › **How to say no! (4)**

Kein is the negative form of *ein*. It takes the same endings as *ein* in the nominative case:

Das ist ein Herd.	*Das ist kein Herd.*	That is not a stove.
Das ist eine Lösung.	*Das ist keine Lösung.*	That is not a solution.
Das ist ein Problem.	*Das ist kein Problem.*	That is not a problem.

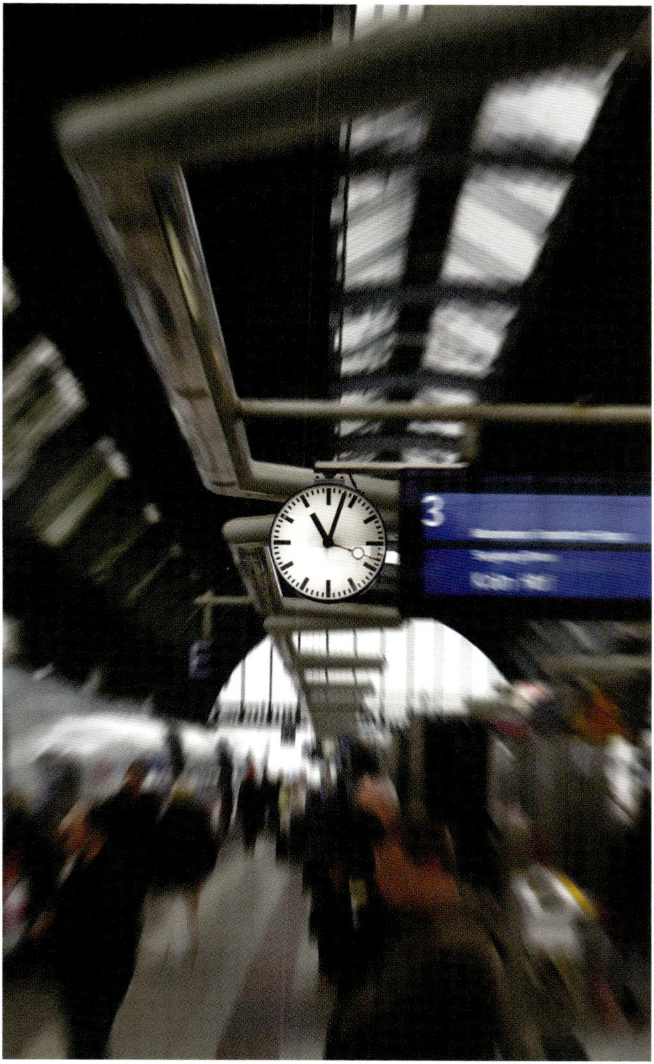
3

6 › How to say no!

How to make the object of a sentence negative:

Ich habe einen Computer.	*Ich habe keinen Computer.*	I don't have a computer.
Ich habe eine Mikrowelle.	*Ich habe keine Mikrowelle.*	I don't have a microwave.
Ich habe ein Haus.	*Ich habe kein Haus.*	I don't have a house.

Note that there is a plural form of *kein* (no):

Ich habe keine Kinder.

I don't have children.

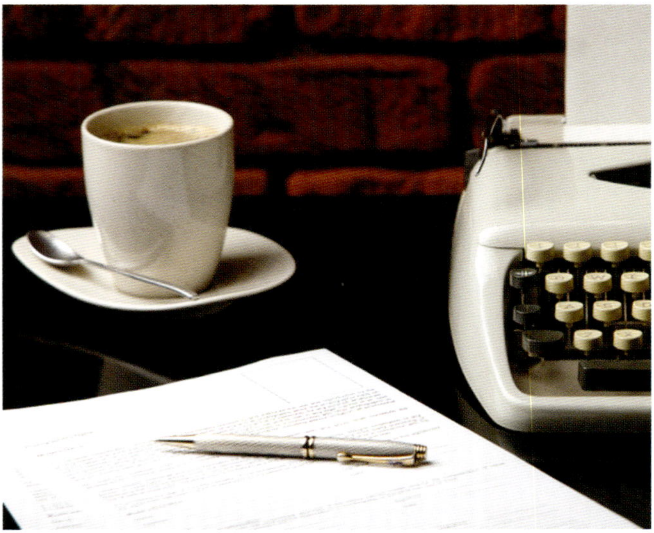

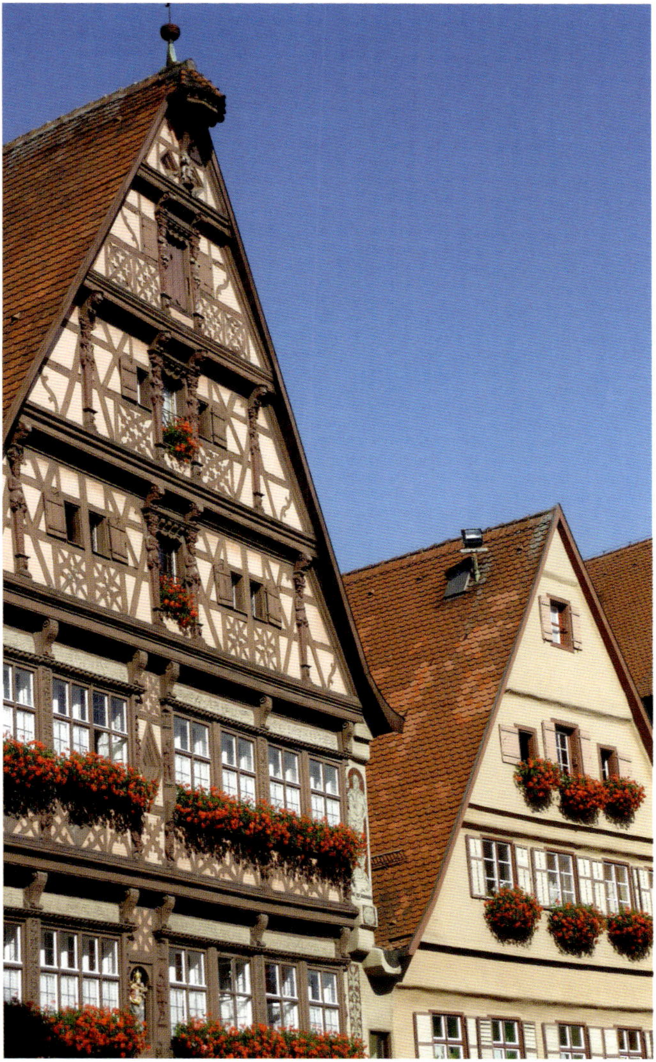

Vocabulary

Active German: Level 1 > Unit 5 > Lesson 2 > Vocabulary

Personal information

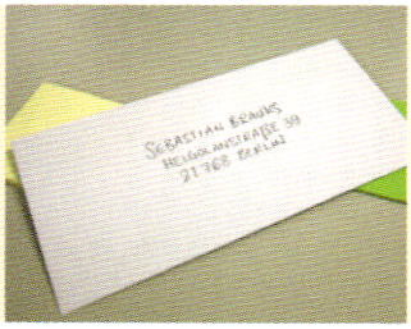

die Postleitzahl / Postleitzahlen
zip code, postal code

Meine Postleitzahl ist 21 768.
My zip code is 21 768.

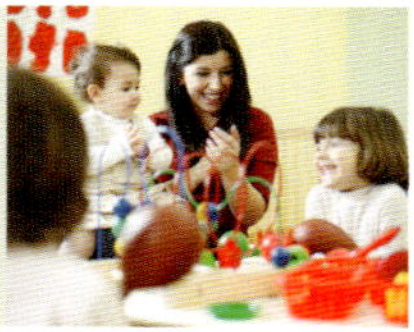

das Kind / Kinder
child

Ich habe drei Kinder.
I have three children.

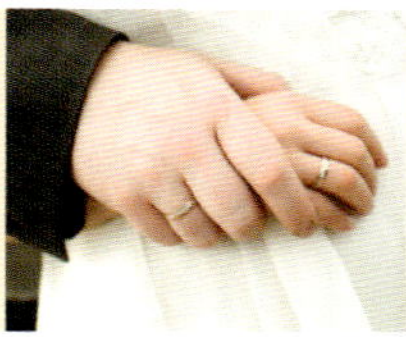

verheiratet
married

Sind Sie verheiratet?
Are you married?

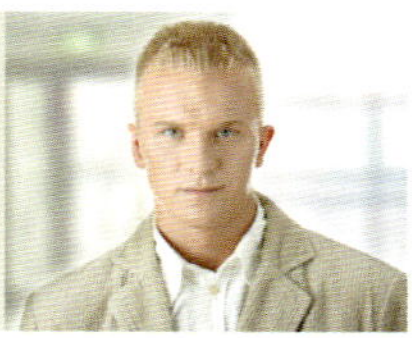

ledig
single

Ich bin ledig.
I'm single.

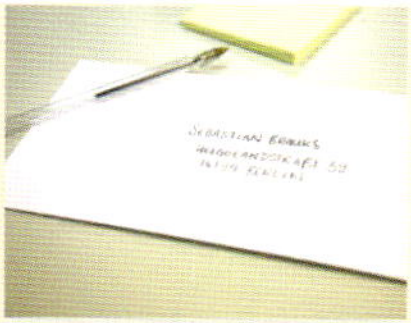

die Adresse / Adressen
address

Wie ist Ihre Adresse?
What is your address?

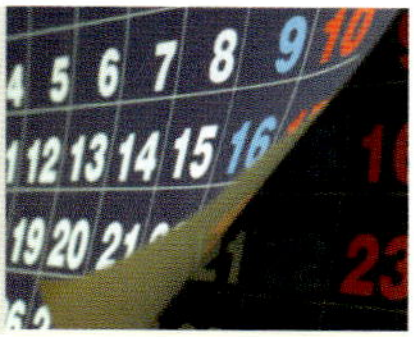

das Jahr / Jahre
year

Ich bin 32 Jahre alt.
I'm 32 years old.

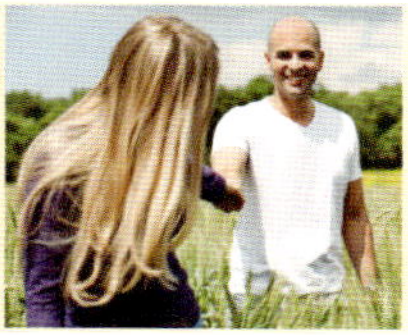

das Problem / Probleme
problem

Ich brauche Ihre Hilfe. Ich habe ein Problem.
I need your help. I have a problem.

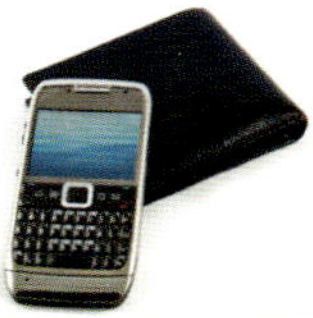

die Handynummer / Handynummern
cell phone number

Wie ist Ihre Handynummer?
What is your cell phone number?

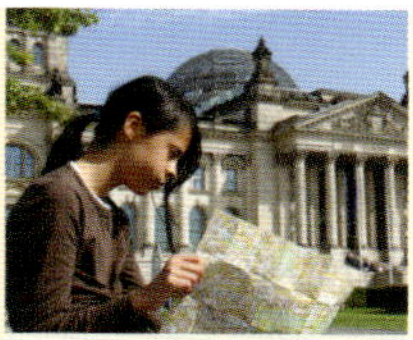

die Straße / Straßen
street / road

Entschuldigung, wo ist die Bebelstraße?
Excuse me, where is Bebelstraße?

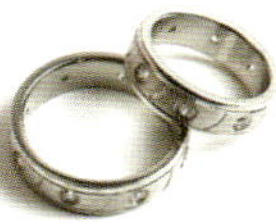

der Familienstand
marital status

Wie ist Ihr Familienstand?
What is your marital status?

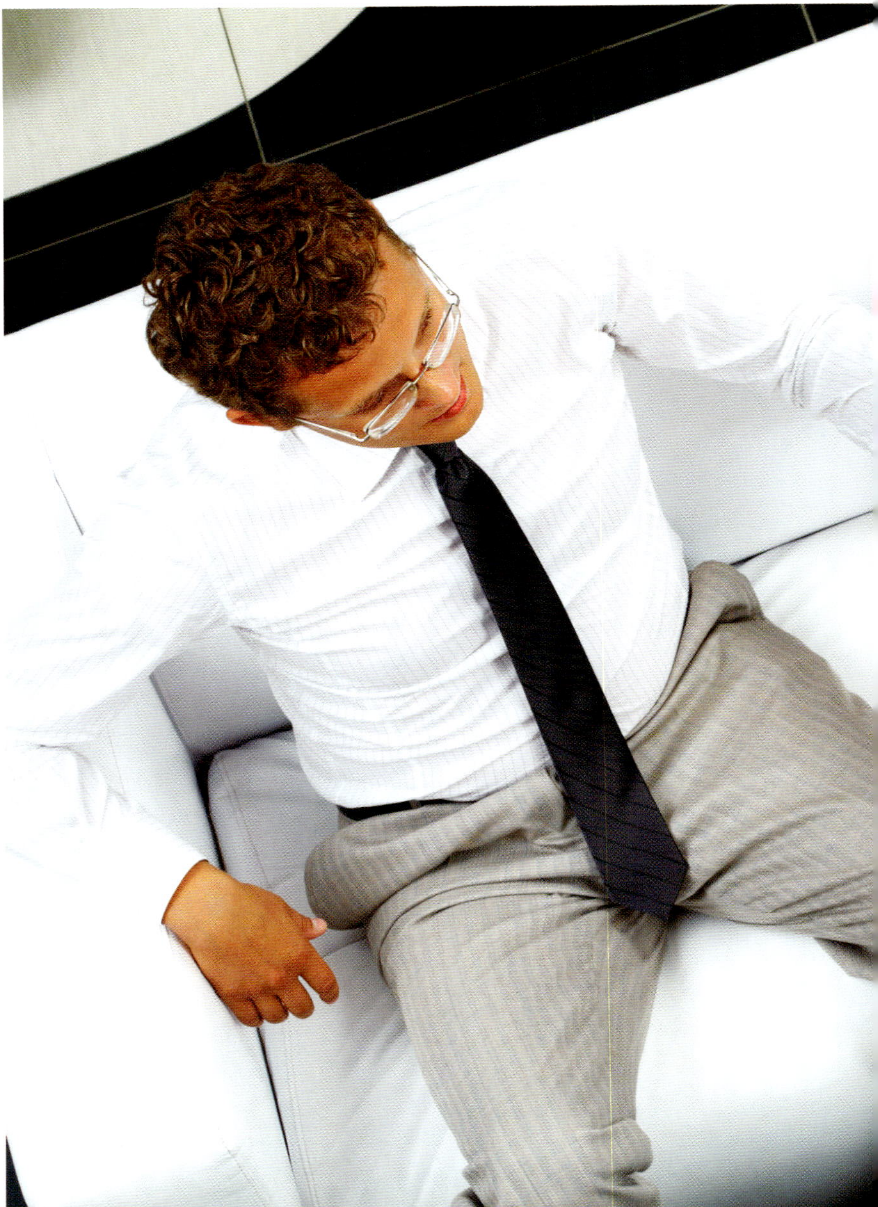

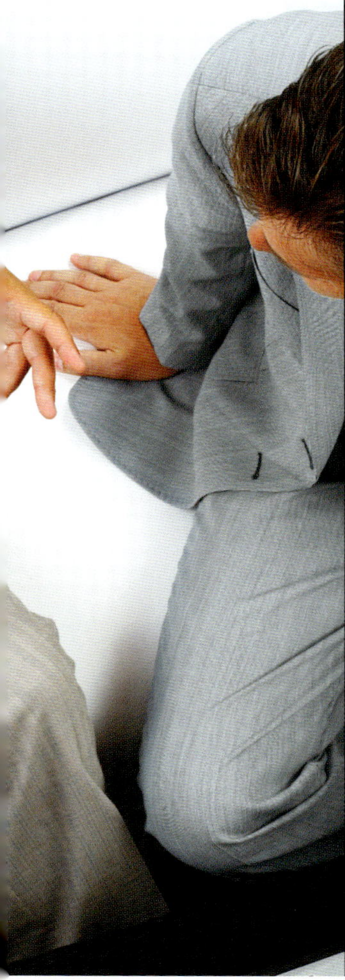

6

Lesson 1: An appointment

- How to ask the time.
- How to say what time it is.
- How to count above 20.
- Vocabulary for dates and times.
- How to extract information from a calendar.

Lesson 2: A dinner

- How to form the verbs ***lesen, essen, sehen***, and ***sprechen***.
- How to say what you like and what you don't like.
- Vocabulary for dining with friends.

Collins | Livemocha™

UNIT 6 › LESSON 1

An appointment

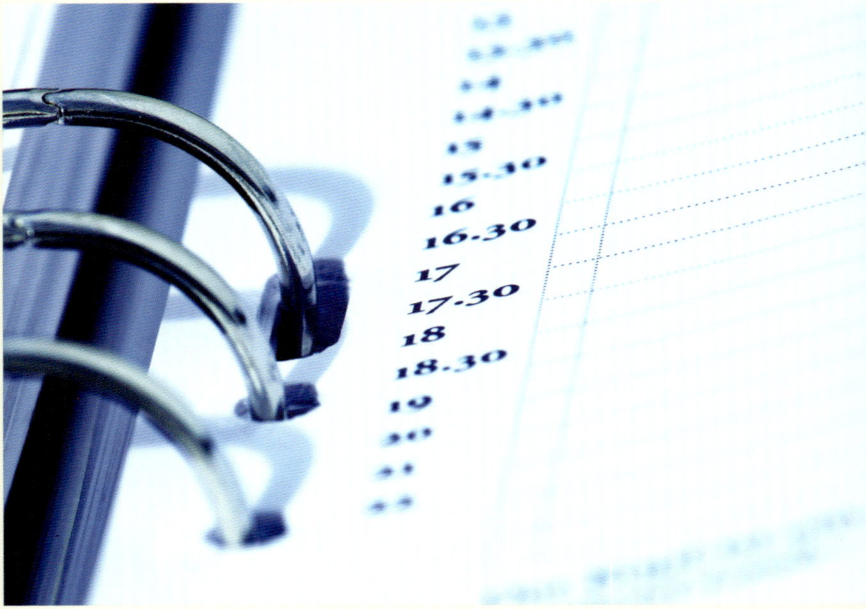

Culture note

Germany is part of the Central European time (CET) zone. That means that clocks are ticking 6 hours ahead of Eastern Standard Time (EST) in the United States and 1 hour ahead of Greenwich Mean Time (GMT).

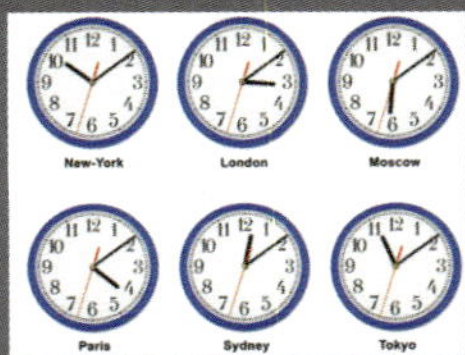

Video Dialog

Matthias tries to find a free space in his datebook for an appointment with Mr. Baumann.

Active German: Level 1 > *Unit 6* > *Lesson 1* > *Video dialog*

Herr Baumann:	*Wir brauchen einen Termin für das neue Projekt. Haben Sie am Montag Zeit?*
Matthias:	*Am Montag passt es nicht so gut. Am Morgen habe ich einen Termin mit der Firma Baulitz und am Nachmittag habe ich einen Termin von 15:00 bis 16:00 Uhr.*
Herr Baumann:	*Um 16:00 Uhr habe ich einen Termin. Mmh. Danach fliege ich nach London.*
Matthias:	*Von wann bis wann sind Sie in London?*
Herr Baumann:	*Von Dienstag bis Donnerstag.*
Matthias:	*Um wie viel Uhr kommen Sie zurück?*
Herr Baumann:	*Am Morgen, um 10:30 Uhr.*
Matthias:	*Geht es um 12:00 Uhr?*
Herr Baumann:	*12.00 Uhr ist wunderbar. Oh, es ist schon 18:15. Das Kino beginnt in 30 Minuten. Also bis Donnerstag.*
Matthias:	*Tschüss.*

Mr. Baumann:	We need a meeting for our new project. Are you free on Monday?

Matthias:	Monday's not so good. In the morning I have a meeting with the Baulitz company and in the afternoon I have a meeting from 3 p.m. to 4 p.m.
Mr. Baumann:	At 4 o'clock I have a meeting. Afterwards I'm flying to London.
Matthias:	How long are you going to be in London?
Mr. Baumann:	From Tuesday through Thursday.
Matthias:	What time do you get back?
Mr. Baumann:	In the morning, at 10:30.
Matthias:	Does 12 o'clock work for you?
Mr. Baumann:	12 o'clock is great. Oh, it's already 6:15. The movie starts in 30 minutes. See you Thursday.
Matthias:	Bye.

Grammar

Active German: Level 1 > *Unit 6* > *Lesson 1* > *Grammar*

1 › **What time is it? Telling the time (1)**

In everyday speech the 12-hour clock is used, whereas in official contexts the 24-hour clock is used.

Es ist ein Uhr / Es ist eins.	It is one (o'clock).
Es ist 13 Uhr.	It is one p.m.
Es ist drei Uhr.	It is three (o'clock).
Es ist 15 Uhr.	It is three p.m.

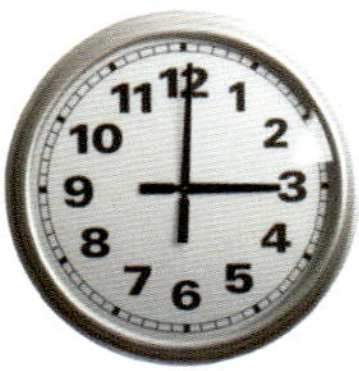

2 › What time is it? Telling the time (2)

Es ist zehn nach drei.	It is ten past three.
Es ist 15 Uhr 10.	It is 3:10 p.m.
Es ist Viertel nach drei.	It is quarter past three.
Es ist 15 Uhr 15.	It is 3:15 p.m.
Es ist halb vier.	It is half past three
Es ist 15 Uhr 30.	It is 3:30 p.m.

Take note:
halb vier in German means "half of the 4th hour," i.e. 3:30.

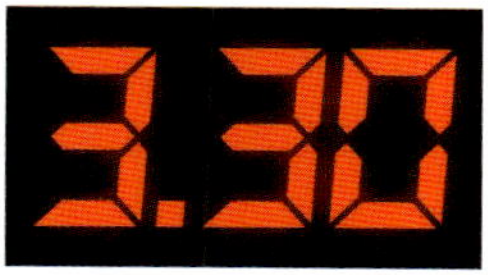

3 › What time is it? Telling the time (3)

Es ist zwanzig vor vier.	It is twenty to four.
Es ist 15 Uhr 40.	It is 3:40 p.m.
Es ist Viertel vor vier.	It is quarter to four.
Es ist 15 Uhr 45.	It is 3:45 p.m.
Es ist zehn vor vier.	It is ten to four.
Es ist 15 Uhr 50.	It is 3:50 p.m.

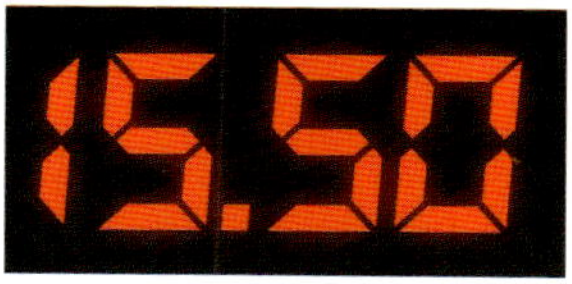

4 › What time is it? Telling the time (4)

If you want to ask the time you can use the following phrases.

Wie spät ist es?	What time is it? (literally: How late is it?)
Wie viel Uhr ist es?	What time is it? (literally: How many hours is it?)
Es ist 13 Uhr.	It is 1 o'clock.

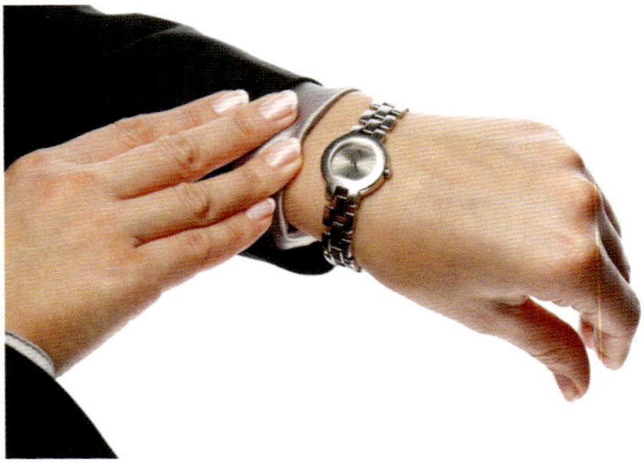

5 › When? (1)

You use the question word *wann* (meaning "when") to ask about a specific moment in time.

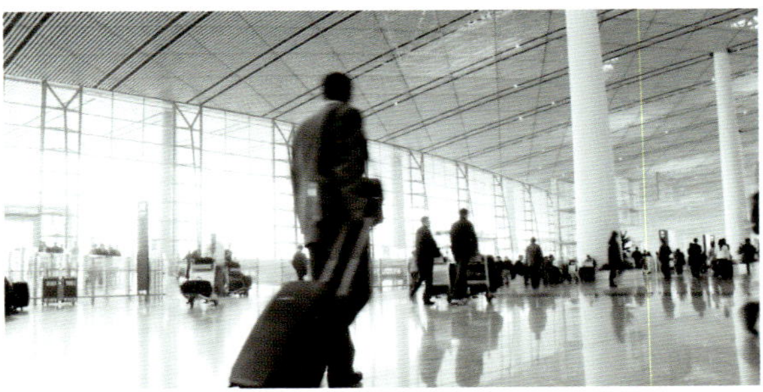

Wann fliegen Sie nach London?	When do you fly to London?
Ich fliege am Montag.	I'm flying on Monday.

6 › When? (2)

You use the preposition *am* for days and parts of the day and the preposition *im* for months.

am Morgen	in the morning
am Montag	on Monday
im Oktober	in October

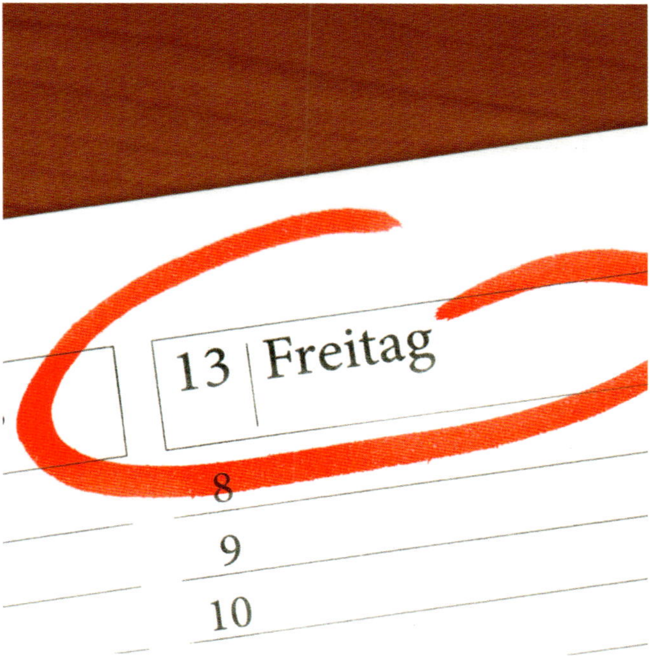

7 › When? (3)

You use the preposition *um* to refer to a specific time.

Wann kommst du?	When are you coming?
*Ich komme **um** 13 Uhr.*	I'm coming at 1 o'clock.

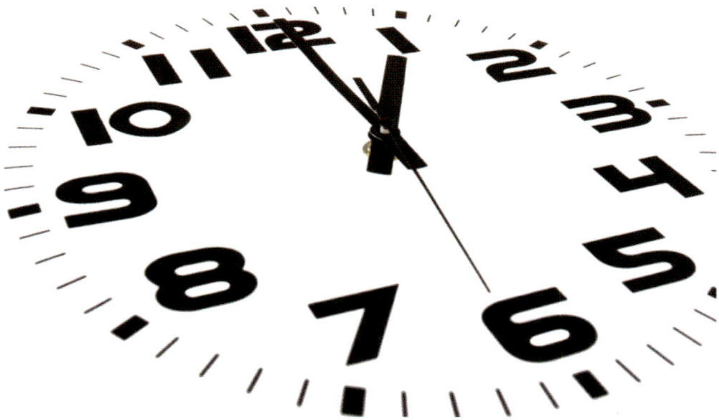

8 › How to express a time period

You use *von wann* to ask for the beginning of the time period and *bis wann* for the end of the time period.

Von wann bis wann sind Sie in London?	How long are you going to be in London? (literally "from when until when")
Von Dienstag bis Donnerstag.	From Tuesday till Thursday.
Von wann bis wann ist unser Termin?	From when until when is our appointment?
Von 9 bis 13 Uhr.	From 9 to 1 o'clock.

9 › Numbers between 20 and 30

To read numbers above 20 you start with the second number and follow with the first number.

So: 21 is *ein-und-zwanzig*

21	*einundzwanzig*
22	*zweiundzwanzig*
23	*dreiundzwanzig*
24	*vierundzwanzig*
25	*fünfundzwanzig*
26	*sechsundzwanzig*
27	*siebenundzwanzig*
28	*achtundzwanzig*
29	*neunundzwanzig*

10 › Numbers between 30 and 200

The numbers above 30 are formed the same way.

These are the numbers up to 200:

30	*dreißig*
40	*vierzig*
50	*fünfzig*
60	*sechzig*
70	*siebzig*
80	*achtzig*
90	*neunzig*
100	*hundert*
200	*zweihundert*

Vocabulary

Active German: Level 1 > Unit 6 > Lesson 1 > Vocabulary

Days and months

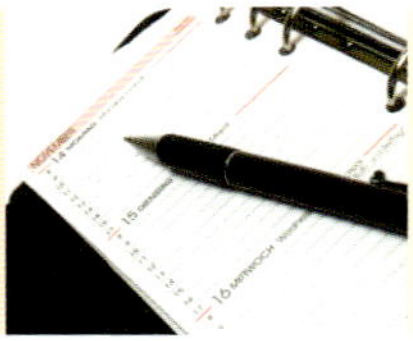

Montag
Monday

Am Montag habe ich einen Termin.
I have an appointment on Monday.

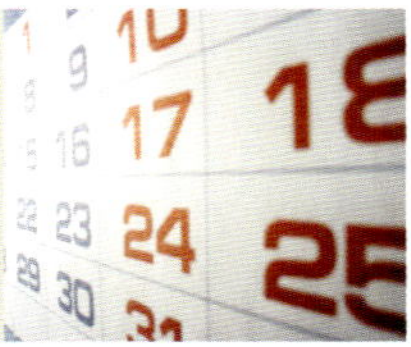

Dienstag
Tuesday

Morgen ist Dienstag.
Tomorrow is Tuesday.

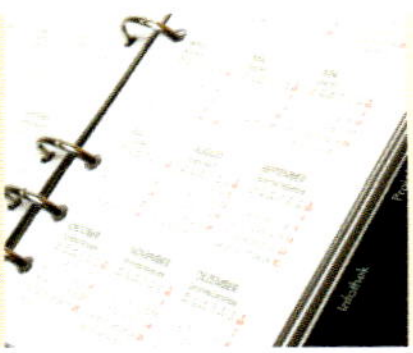

Mittwoch
Wednesday

Herr Mayer kommt am Mittwoch.
Mr. Mayer is coming on Wednesday.

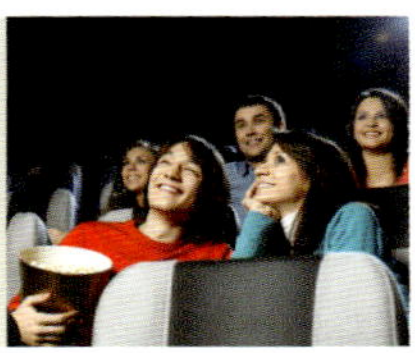

Donnerstag
Thursday

Am Donnerstag gehe ich ins Kino.
On Thursday I'm going to the movies.

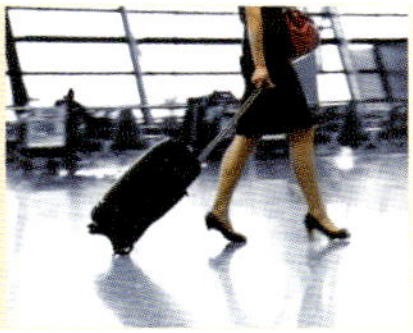

Freitag
Friday

Kommt sie am Freitag?
Is she coming on Friday?

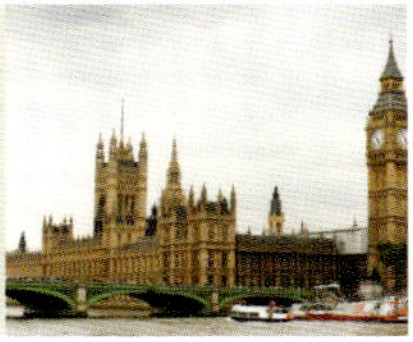

Samstag
Saturday

Am Samstag fliege ich nach London.
On Saturday I'm flying to London.

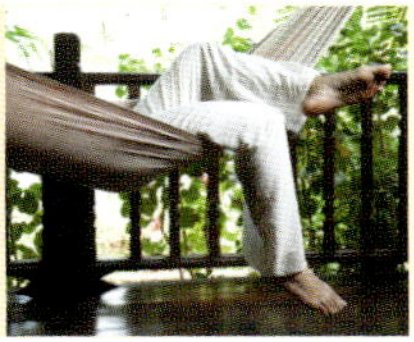

Sonntag
Sunday

Am Sonntag arbeite ich nicht.
On Sunday I'm not working.

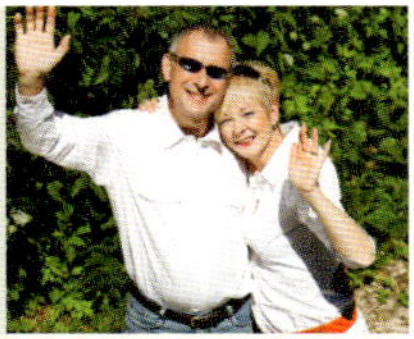

das Wochenende / Wochenenden
weekend

Am Wochenende kommt meine Frau.
My wife is coming this weekend.

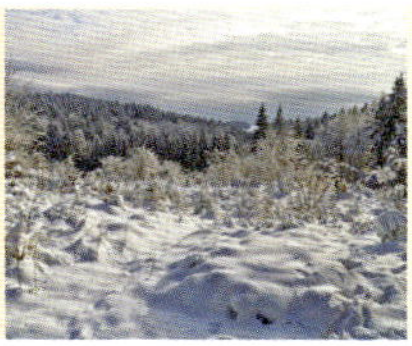

Januar
January

Im Januar schneit es manchmal.
In January it sometimes snows.

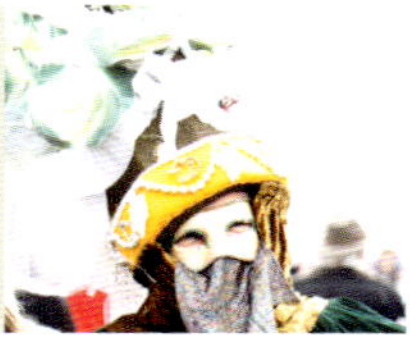

Februar
February

Im Februar ist Karneval.
Carnival takes place in February.

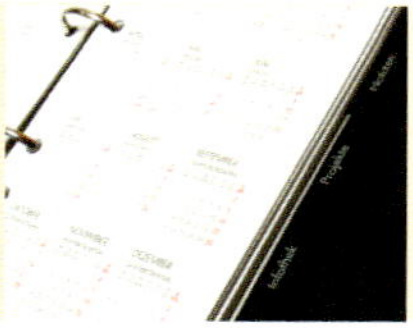

März
March

Kommen Sie im März zurück?
Are you coming back in March?

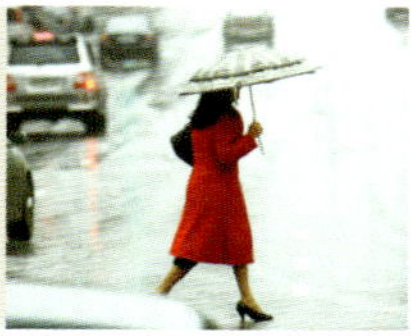

April
April

Regnet es oft im April?
Does it often rain in April?

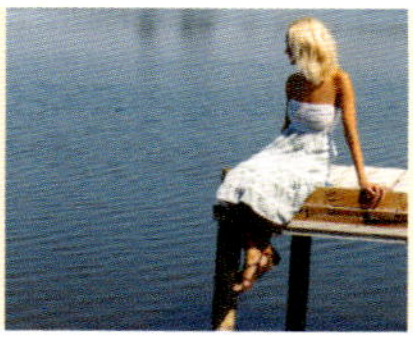

Mai
May

Der Mai ist sehr schön.
May is very nice.

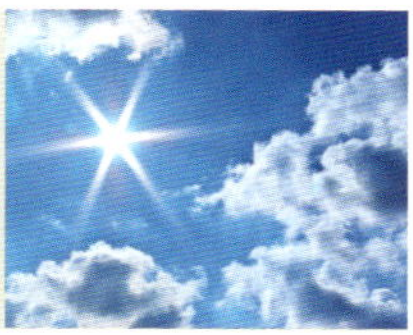

Juni
June

Im Juni beginnt der Sommer.
In June summer begins.

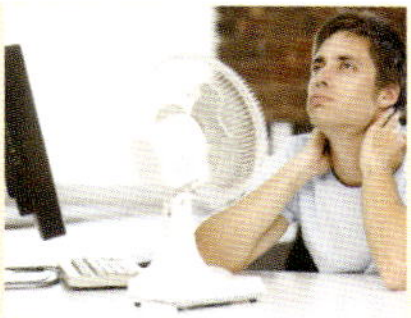

Juli
July

Im Juli ist es heiß.
It is hot in July.

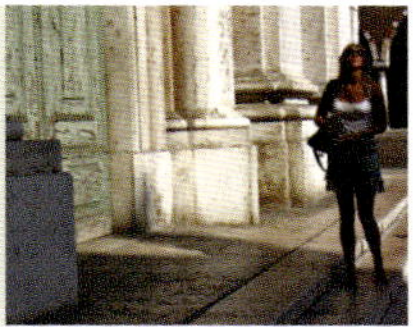

August
August

Im August fliege ich nach Italien.
In August I'm flying to Italy.

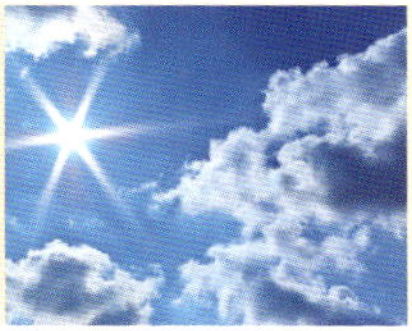

September
September

Ist es im September noch sonnig?
Is it still sunny in September?

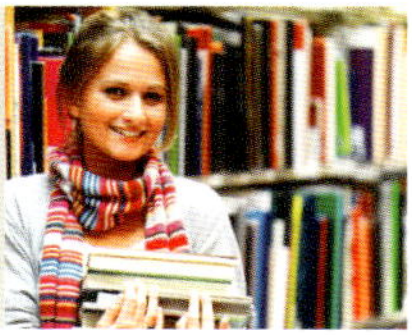

Oktober
October

Ich habe den Test im Oktober.
I have the test in October.

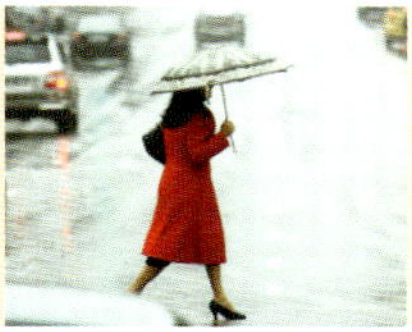

November
November

Im November regnet es oft.
In November it often rains.

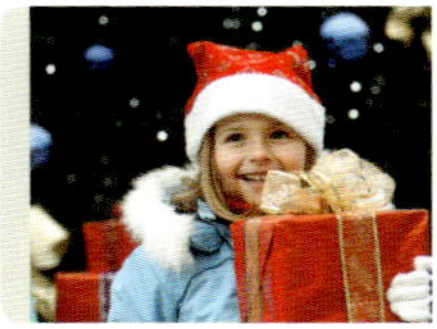

Dezember
December

Weihnachten ist im Dezember.
Christmas is in December.

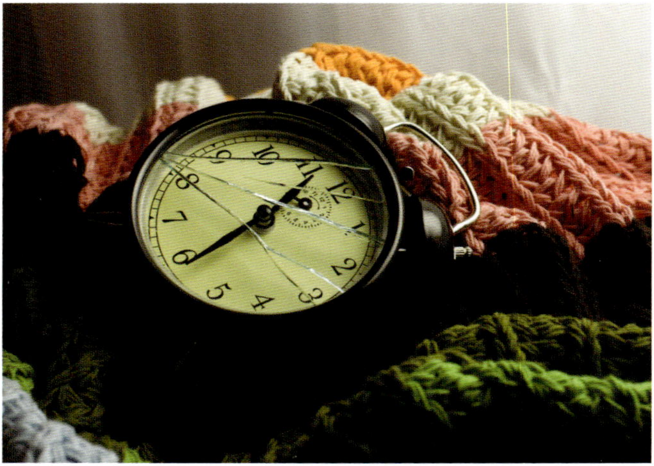

Culture note

The world sometimes laughs at the Germans for their punctuality and their constant clock-watching. But are modern Germans really so punctual? According to a recent study only 18% of Germans still believe in strict timekeeping. Even trains are well-known for being late nowadays. Nevertheless, punctuality is very much appreciated, especially for official meetings. If you realize you are not going to arrive somewhere at the appointed time, you should call and advise that you will be late.

UNIT 6 › LESSON 2

A dinner

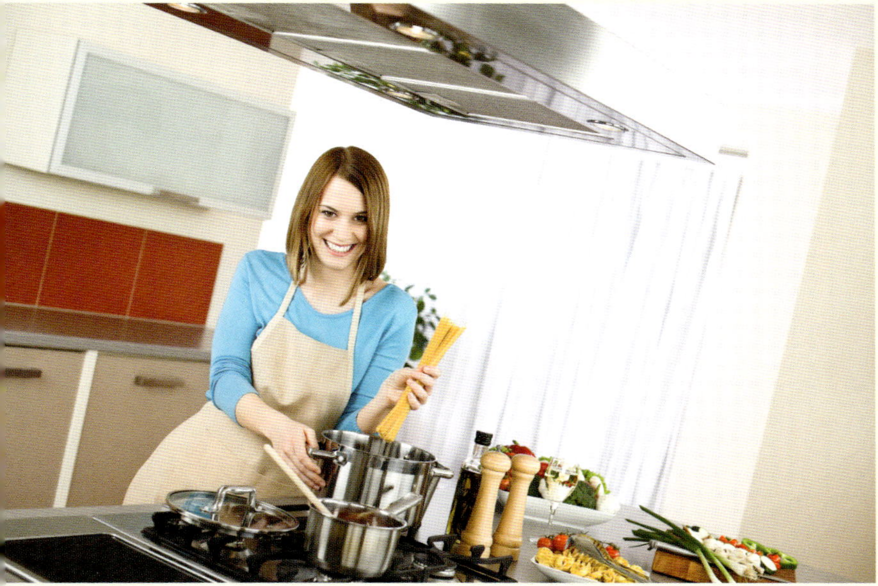

Culture note

Germans like to have little dinner parties. But before they invite you to their home for a private dinner, they prefer meeting in a pub or restaurant first. If you are invited to a German person's house, you should bring a gift such as chocolates, wine, or flowers.

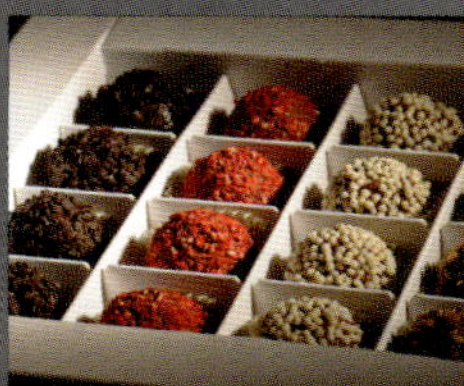

Video Dialog

Lara visits Matthias again and brings a welcome gift before the two get to know one another a little better.

Active German: Level 1 > *Unit 6* > *Lesson 2* > *Video dialog*

Lara:	*Entschuldigung, ich bin ein bisschen spät.*
Matthias:	*Kein Problem.*
Lara:	*Die Pralinen sind für Sie.*
Matthias:	*Oh, wie nett, danke schön. Bitte. Trinken Sie Wein?*
Lara:	*Ja, gerne.*
Matthias:	*Warum sagen wir nicht „du“ zueinander?*
Lara:	*Gerne.*
Matthias:	*Zum Wohl.*
Lara:	*Zum Wohl. Sie, ich meine du, liest gerne?*
Matthias:	*Ja, sehr gerne.*
Lara:	*Ich lese auch sehr gerne.*
Matthias:	*Isst du gerne Reis?*
Lara:	*Ja, sehr gerne.*
Matthias:	*Es gibt Reis mit Huhn und Salat.*

Lara:	Sorry, I'm a bit late.
Matthias:	No problem.
Lara:	The chocolates are for you.

Matthias:	Oh, how nice of you, thank you. Please. Would you like wine?
Lara:	Yes, please.
Matthias:	Why don't we say "du" to each other?
Lara:	With pleasure.
Matthias:	Cheers.
Lara:	Cheers. Do you like reading?
Matthias:	Yes, very much.
Lara:	I like reading as well.
Matthias:	Do you like rice?
Lara:	Yes, very much.
Matthias:	We're having rice with chicken and salad.

Grammar

Active German: Level 1 > *Unit 6* > *Lesson 2* > *Grammar*

1 › More on verbs

Some German verbs are irregular and they have a different pattern of endings.

In the case of *lesen* (to read) the vowel -e is replaced by -ie in the *du* and *er / sie / es* form.

lesen

to read

singular:

ich lese	I read
*du **lie**st*	you read
*er / sie / es **lie**st*	he / she / it reads

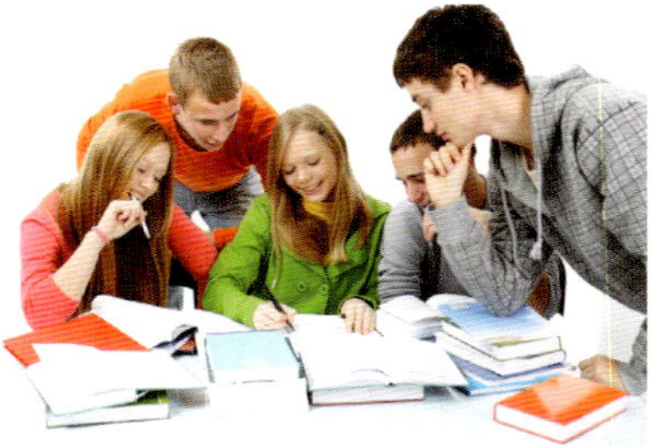

2 › The verb *lesen*

The plural follows the normal pattern.

wir lesen	we read
ihr lest	you read
sie, Sie lesen	they read, you read
Lara liest gerne.	Lara likes reading.

3 › More on verbs

The verbs *sehen* (to see) and *essen* (to eat) follow the same pattern as the verb *lesen*.

Wen siehst du?	Whom do you see?
Er isst gerne Reis.	He likes eating rice.

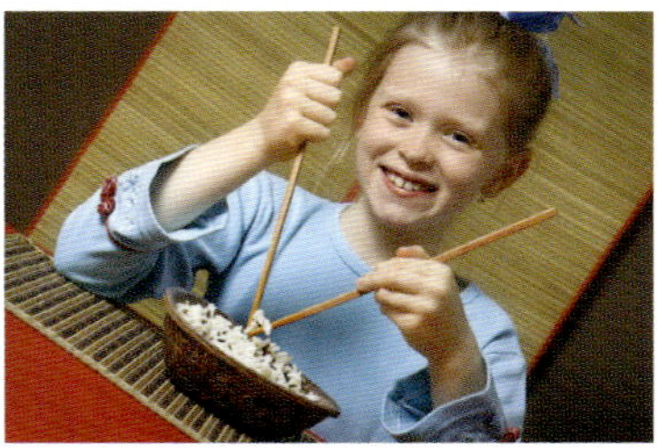

4 › The verb *sprechen*

The verb *sprechen* (to speak) has a change of vowel as well.

sprechen
to speak

singular:

ich spreche	I speak
du sprichst	you speak
er / sie / es spricht	he / she / it speaks
Katja spricht Spanisch	Katja speaks Spanish.

5 › The verb *sprechen*

plural:

wir sprechen	we speak
ihr sprecht	you speak
sie, Sie sprechen	they speak, you speak

6 › What do you like?

In German, in order to express that you like to do something you use the verb + *gern* or *gerne*

Ich lese gern.	I like reading.
Essen Sie gern Fisch?	Do you like eating fish?

To make *gern* negative say *nicht gern* (I don't like doing).

Ich arbeite nicht gern.
I don't like working.

Vocabulary

Active German: Level 1 > Unit 6 > Lesson 2 > Vocabulary

Dinner and food

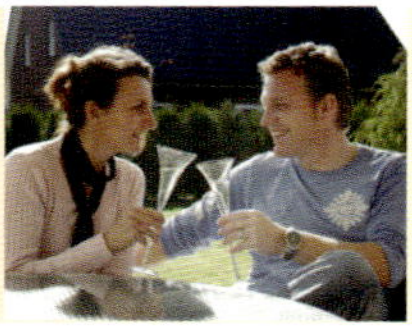

zum Wohl or *Prost*
Cheers

In Deutschland sagt man „Zum Wohl" oder „Prost".
In Germany you say "Cheers."

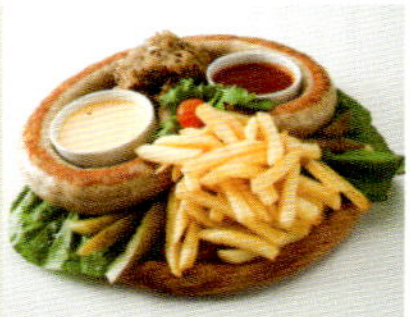

das Essen
food

Ist das Essen fertig?
Is the food ready?

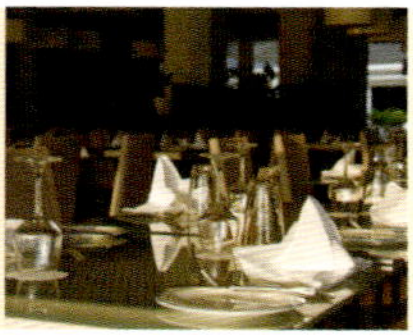

das Abendessen / Abendessen
dinner

Ich gehe heute zum Abendessen ins Restaurant.
I'm going to a restaurant for dinner tonight.

Culture note

You already know that there are two ways of addressing people. After you have known someone for a while, the person might suggest you use the informal du. Matthias suggests this to Lara in the video. To use the informal "you" is called duzen. To use the formal "you" is called siezen.

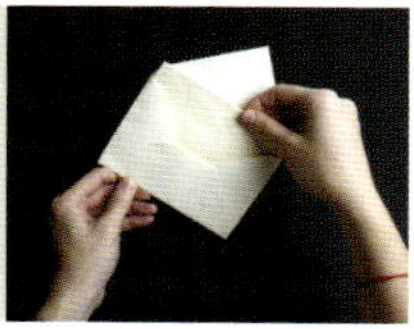

die Einladung / Einladungen
invitation

Vielen Dank für die Einladung.
Thank you for the invitation.

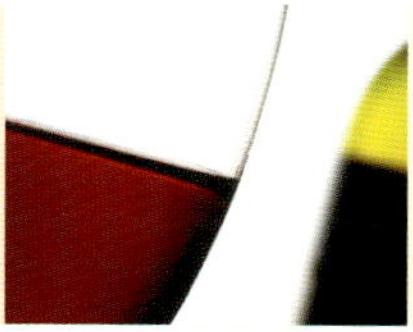

der Wein / Weine
wine

Trinkst du gerne Wein?
Do you like drinking wine?

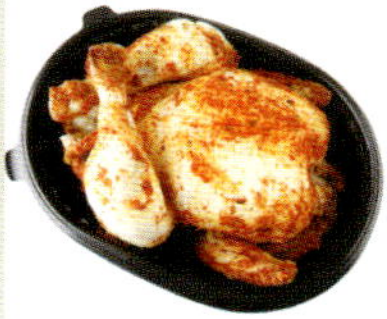

das Huhn / Hühner
chicken

Ich esse gerne Huhn.
I like eating chicken.

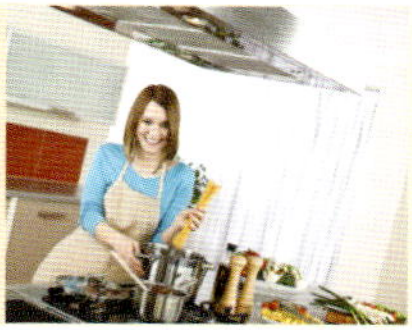

kochen
to cook

Matthias kocht nicht gerne.
Matthias doesn't like cooking.

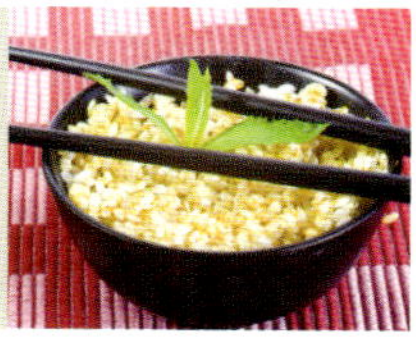

der Reis
rice

Heute gibt es Huhn mit Reis.
Today we have chicken with rice.

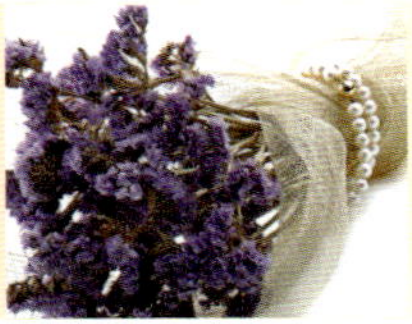

die Blume / Blumen
flower

Danke für die Blumen.
Thank you for the flowers.

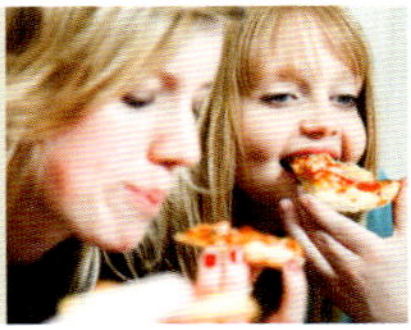

lecker
tasty

Das Essen ist sehr lecker.
The food is really tasty.

Collins

Livemocha ACTIVE GERMAN

HarperCollins Publishers
77–85 Fulham Palace Road
London W6 8JB
Great Britain

www.collinslanguage.com

First edition 2011

Reprint 10 9 8 7 6 5 4 3 2 1 0

ISBN (UK edition) 978-0-00-737354-3
ISBN (export edition) 978-0-00-741978-4
ISBN (US edition) 978-0-87779-556-8

A catalogue record for this book is available from the British Library

Typeset by Macmillan Publishing Services

Audio material recorded and produced by Networks SRL, Milan

Printed and Bound in China by Leo Paper Products Ltd.
Series Editor: Rob Scriven

INTRODUCTION

Welcome to your Livemocha Active German experience! This new course goes above and beyond what a traditional book-based course can offer. With its focus on online learning, Active German provides the opportunity not just to study but to experience the language for yourself by interacting with native speakers online.

Why go online?
Studying a language online allows you to learn in a more natural atmosphere – watching people interact in a **video** is far more lifelike than listening to conversations on a CD. After watching a video dialog, you will be walked through an explanation of some of the **grammar** and **vocabulary** items that were introduced in the new dialog. Then, by completing a variety of **interactive quizzes**, the system will instantly be able to tell you how well you are doing. You can then **talk online** with native German speakers to practice what you've learned.

Who else is online?
Livemocha boasts over 7 million members and is growing every day. These members are online for the same reason as you – to learn and experience a new language. Native German-speaking members will be happy to read through your written and spoken submissions and to give you feedback on how you're doing. You can also connect with people who want to chat in any given language – interaction on an informal, nonacademic basis is an ideal way for you to perfect your language skills.

What do the books do?
The four accompanying books are designed to complement the online course – the dialogs for all of the videos that you can watch online are available here for you to study whenever you don't have access to the Internet. You will also find all of the Grammar and Vocabulary sections explained in the books, plus the culture notes to teach you a little about Germany.

LEVEL 2

This book is the second of four. It corresponds with Level 2 of the online course.

Level 2 is ideal for students who can understand a simple conversation but who may still have difficulty taking part.

What you will learn

- How to order food and ask for things in restaurants
- How to talk about things you have to do or would like to do
- How to address people formally and informally
- How to talk about your daily activities and routines
- How to use expressions of time
- How to say where things are
- How to make requests and suggestions and ask for help
- How to use words such as "me," "him," "her"
- How to say that things happened in the past
- Vocabulary for food and restaurants, emails and letters, family, health, transportation, daily life, cities, buildings and shopping

Every time you see this coffee cup symbol in these books, it indicates the presence of a pathway – a guide to exactly where you can find that particular piece of content online. Log on at www.livemocha.com and follow the path to find the online version of what you are studying in the book.

Video Dialog

A warm welcome for Matthias as he gets to know his new colleagues a little better.

Active German: Level 1 > *Unit 2* > *Lesson 1* > *Video dialog*

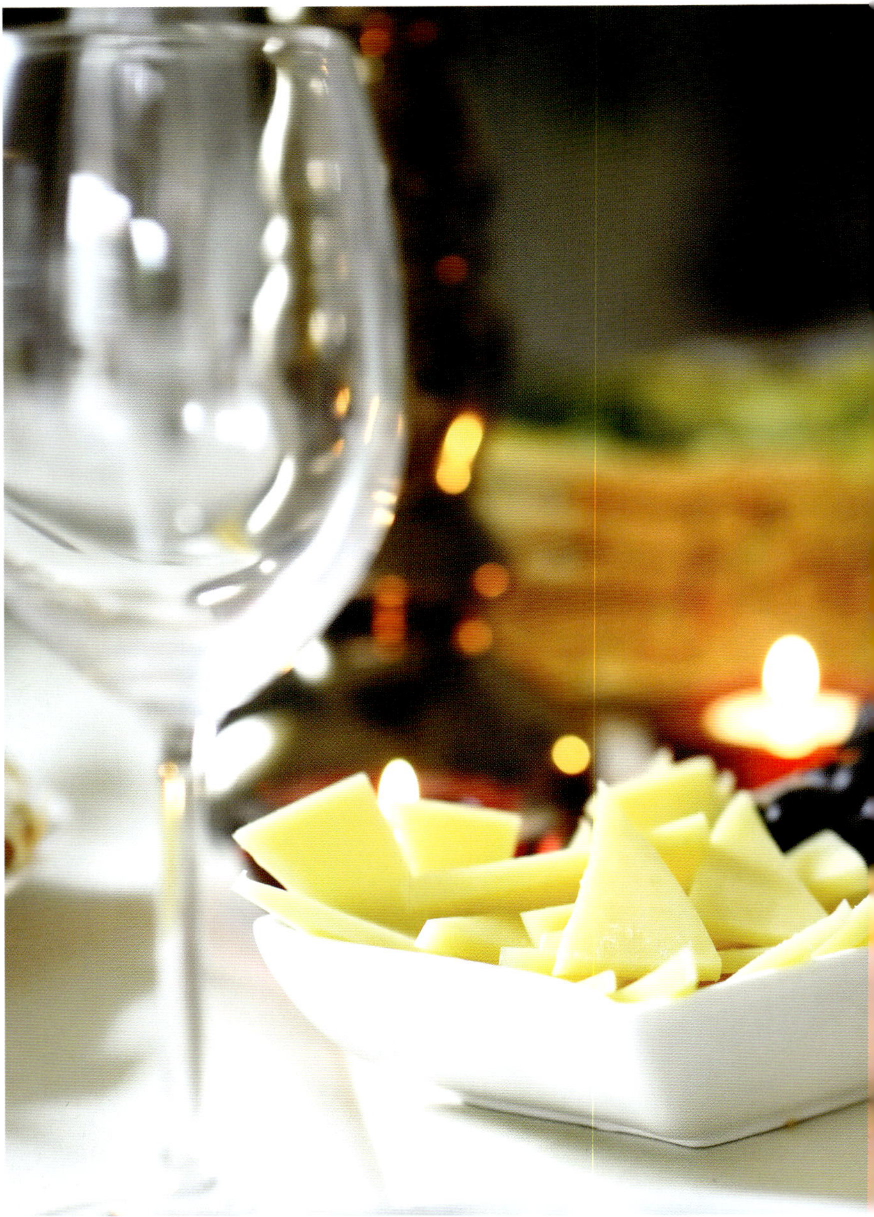

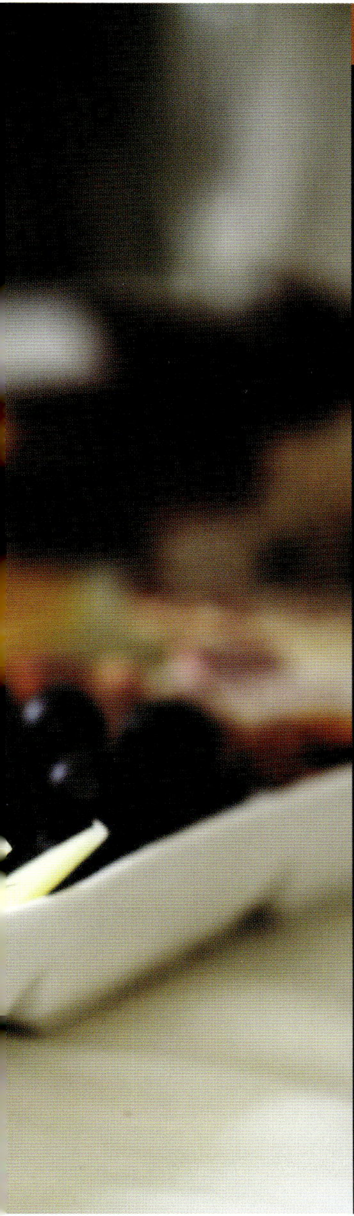

1

Lesson 1: In a restaurant 1

- » How to understand a menu.
- » How to make small talk in a restaurant.
- » How to use ***können*** (can / be able to do).
- » How to use the verb ***nehmen*** (to take).
- » Vocabulary for food and restaurants.

Lesson 2: In a restaurant 2

- » How to ask for the bill.
- » How to use the verb ***müssen*** (to have to, must) and how to say "I would like to."
- » How to use the verb ***sein*** (to be) in the past.
- » Vocabulary for payments.

Collins | Livemocha™

UNIT 1 › LESSON 1

In a restaurant 1

Culture note

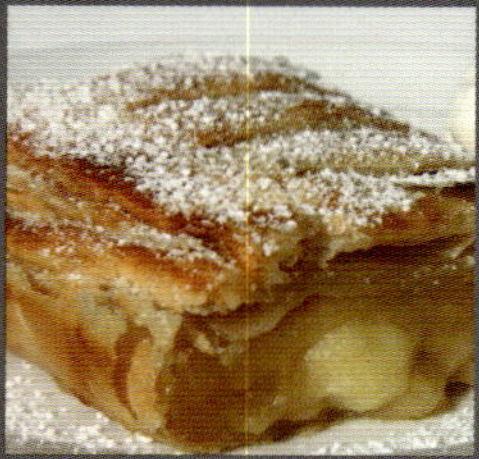

German restaurants offer a great number of traditional dishes as well as international ones. Some of these traditional dishes are regional specialties.

Here is a list of some of the most popular German national dishes:

Schweinebraten
A pork roast in a rich brown gravy. It is served with boiled potatoes, *Knödel* (dumplings), or *Spätzle* (egg noodles) in Swabia. It is often cooked as a Sunday lunch.

Wiener Schnitzel
A thin veal fillet, coated in breadcrumbs and fried. Served with fries/potatoes and salad.

Sauerkraut
Pickled cabbage with a sour flavor. It is a side dish mainly served with meat (e.g. *Kassler* cured pork chops).

Apfelstrudel
A famous dessert. It is originally from Vienna, but is now available everywhere. It is a type of sweet layered pastry with an apple filling.

Video Dialog

Matthias and Mr Baumann dine together in a local restaurant. Over dinner, Mr. Baumann makes a good recommendation.

Watch the video dialog online at
Active German: Level 2 > *Unit 1* > *Lesson 1* > *Video dialog*

Matthias:	*Waren Sie schon oft hier?*
Herr Baumann:	*Ja, ich war schon oft hier. Ich kann das Rumpsteak empfehlen.*
Matthias:	*Danke. Was nehmen Sie?*
Herr Baumann:	*Ich nehme die Tomatensuppe als Vorspeise. Dann ein Wiener Schnitzel mit Pommes Frites. Und Sie?*
Matthias:	*Ich nehme die Minestrone. Dann das Rumpsteak mit Bratkartoffeln und einen Salat.*
Herr Baumann:	*Wie möchten Sie das Rumpsteak?*
Matthias:	*Medium.*
Herr Baumann:	*Kann ich die Weinkarte haben, bitte?*

Matthias:	Do you come to this place very often?
Mr. Baumann:	Yes, I come here very often. I can recommend the sirloin steak.
Matthias:	Thank you. What are you having?
Mr. Baumann:	I'll have the tomato soup as a starter. Then I'll have a Wiener schnitzel with french fries. And you?
Matthias:	I'll have the minestrone. Then the sirloin steak with roast potatoes and a salad.

Mr. Baumann:	How do you want your sirloin steak?
Matthias:	Medium.
Mr. Baumann:	Could I have the wine list, please?

Grammar

In this section we go over some of the grammar points introduced in the dialog.

Go to Active German: Level 2 > Unit 1 > Lesson 1 > Grammar to listen to these explanations and to access some interactive practice activities.

1 › Some modal verbs

Können is a modal verb. Modal verbs are used to express such things as ability, permission, or necessity. For example:

May I order?
Can you speak German?

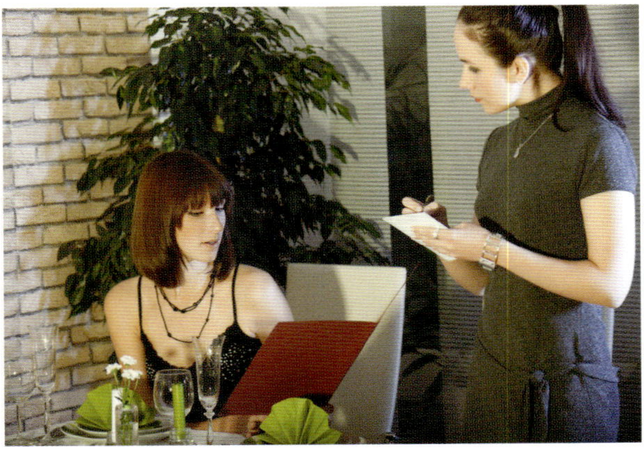

2 › The modal verb *können*

Here are the main uses of *können*:

Können means "can/to be able to," and "to be allowed to." It expresses ability or a friendly request.

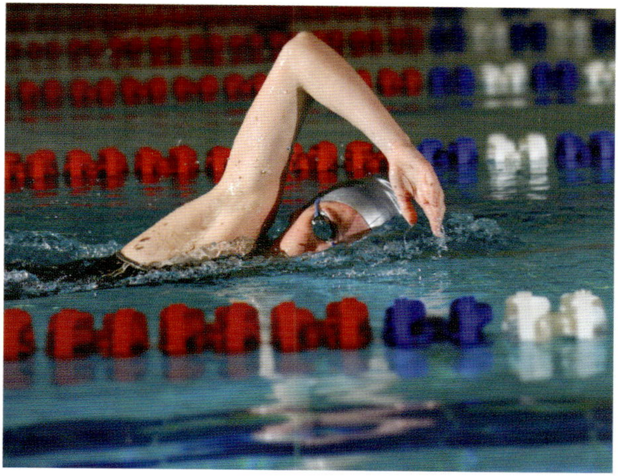

These are the forms of *können*:

ich kann	I can
du kannst	you can
er / sie / es kann	he / she / it can
wir können	we can
ihr könnt	you can
sie / Sie können	they / you can

Kannst du schwimmen?
Can you swim?

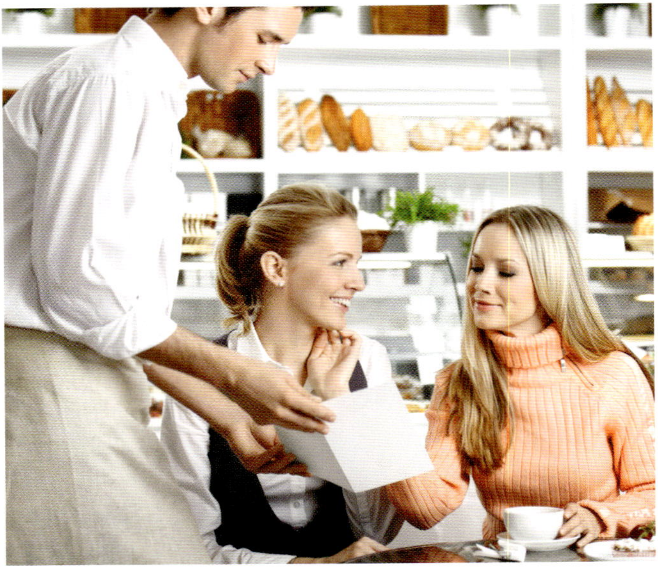

Kann ich bitte den Fisch mit Reis in Weißweinsoße haben?
May I have the fish with rice in white wine sauce?

3 › How to use modal verbs

Note that the second verb used with the modal verb comes in its basic form at the end of the sentence.

Können *wir bitte* ***bestellen****?*
May we order, please?

Ich ***kann*** *gut* ***schwimmen.***
I can swim well.

4 › Some examples with *können*

Kannst du bitte kommen?
Could you please come?

Können Sie singen?
Can you sing?

5 › The verb *nehmen*

The verb *nehmen* means "to take" and has the following pattern:

ich nehme	I take
du nimmst	you take
er / sie / es nimmt	he / she / it takes
wir nehmen	we take
ihr nehmt	you take
sie / Sie nehmen	they / you take

Nehmen is also used to express "I'll have."

Ich nehme das Steak. I'll have the steak.

Note that with *nehmen* we need to use the accusative case. You might remember it from previous units. It has the forms *den*, *die* and *das* or *einen*, *eine*, *ein*.

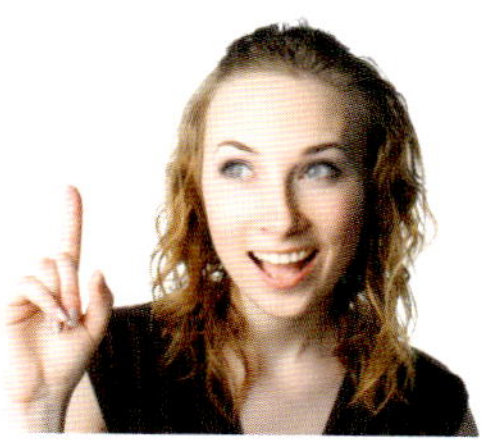

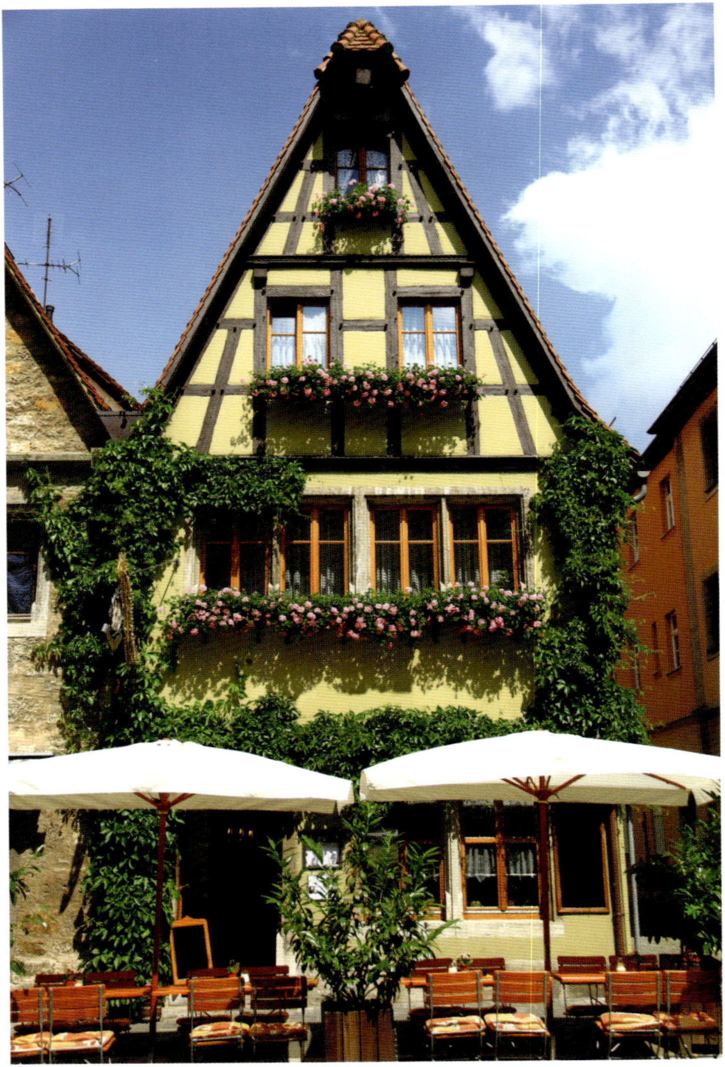

Vocabulary

In this section you will learn some useful words and expressions from the dialog.

Go to Active German: Level 2 > Unit 1 > Lesson 1 > Vocabulary to listen to each of the words being pronounced and to access some interactive practice activities.

In a restaurant

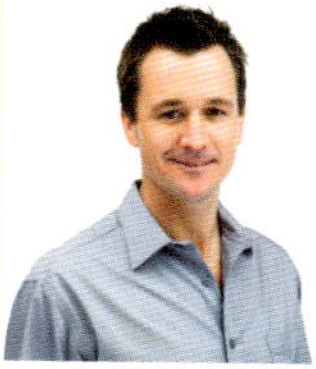

bestellen
to order

Herr Baumann möchte bestellen.
Mr. Baumann wants to order.

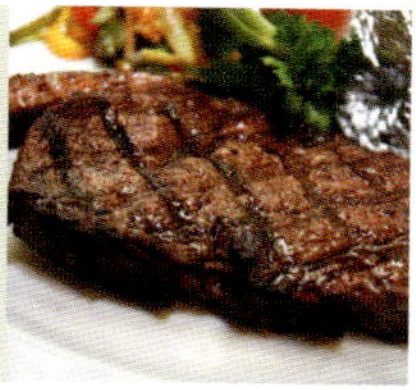

*das Hauptgericht / Hauptgerichte**
entrée

Als Hauptgericht nehme ich das Steak.
As an entrée I'll have the steak.

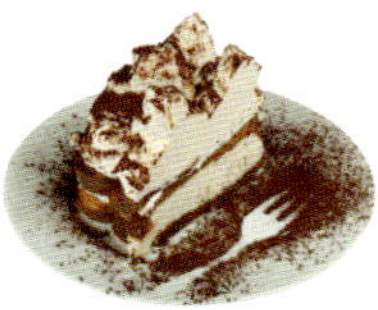

der Nachtisch / Nachtische
dessert

Ich nehme Tiramisu als Nachtisch.
I'll have the tiramisu as a dessert.

*The plural form of all German nouns has been included next to the singular form. In some cases both forms are identical.

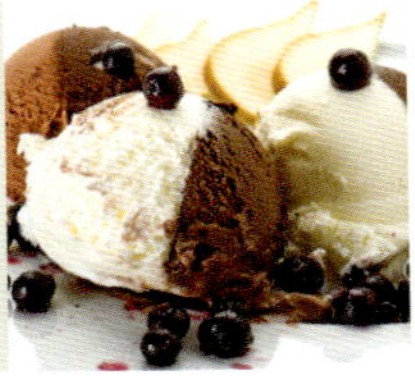

das Eis
ice cream

Alle Kinder lieben Eis.
All children love ice cream.

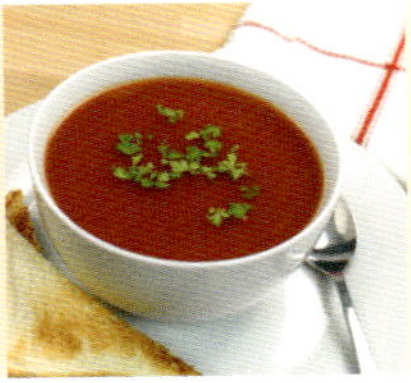

die Vorspeise / Vorspeisen
starter, appetizer

Kann ich bitte die Suppe als Vorspeise haben?
May I have the soup as a starter, please?

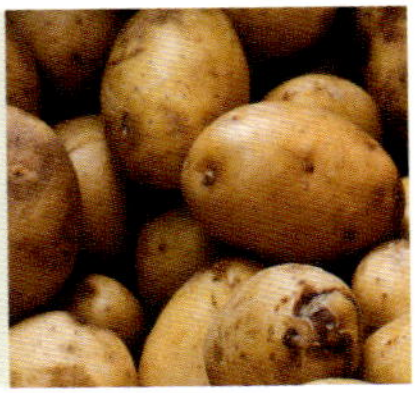

die Kartoffel / Kartoffeln
potato

In Deutschand isst man oft Kartoffeln.
In Germany, people often eat potatoes.

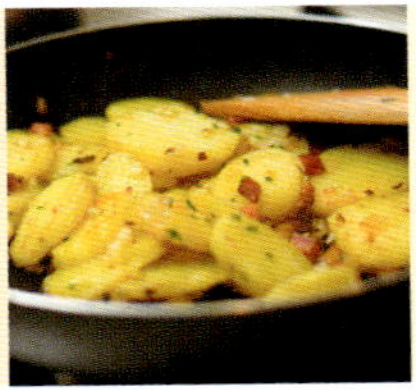

die Bratkartoffeln
home fries

Bratkartoffeln sind lecker.
Home fries are yummy.

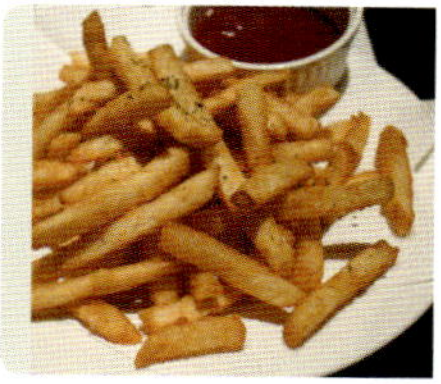

die Pommes frites
french fries

Ich esse Pommes frites gerne mit Ketchup.
I like eating french fries with ketchup.

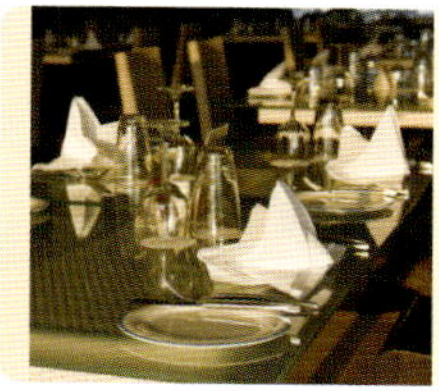

das Restaurant / Restaurants
restaurant

Das Restaurant „Bella" ist sehr gut.
The restaurant Bella is very good.

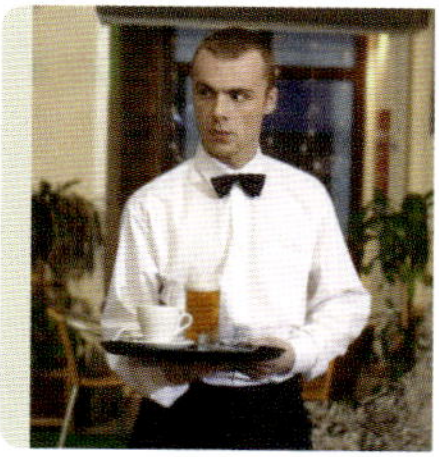

der Kellner / Kellner
waiter

Herr Schmidt arbeitet im Restaurant „Bella". Er ist der Kellner.
Mr. Schmidt works in the restaurant Bella. He is the waiter.

UNIT 1 › LESSON 2

In a restaurant 2

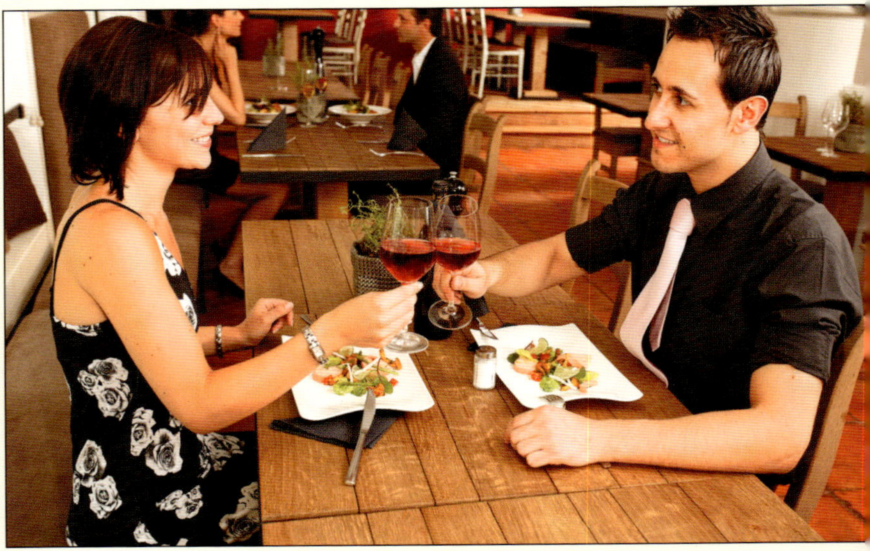

Culture note

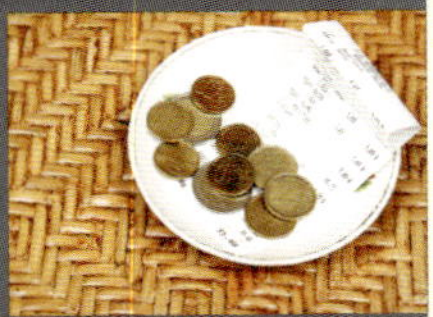

In restaurants and bars service and VAT are included in the menu price. It is, however, common to round up the amount. In German a tip is called *Trinkgeld*. You normally don't claim small change between 1 and 30 cents. A general rule is to add 5–10%, depending on your satisfaction with the service. If you pay for more than one person, you tend to go even higher.

Video Dialog

Having both enjoyed their food, Mr. Baumann kindly offers to pay for his new colleague's meal.

Active German: Level 2 > *Unit 1* > *Lesson 2* > *Video dialog*

Matthias:	*Das Essen war sehr gut.*
Herr Baumann:	*Können wir bitte bezahlen?*
Kellnerin:	*Hier ist die Rechnung. Möchten Sie zusammen oder getrennt bezahlen?*
Herr Baumann:	*Zusammen bitte. Kann ich mit Kreditkarte bezahlen?*
Kellnerin:	*Entschuldigen Sie, aber das Gerät ist kaputt.*
Herr Baumann:	*Kein Problem. Stimmt so.*
Kellnerin:	*Vielen Dank und einen schönen Abend noch.*
Herr Baumann:	*Ihnen auch. Auf Wiedersehen.*
Matthias:	*Vielen Dank. Das ist sehr nett.*

Matthias:	The food was very good.
Mr. Baumann:	Can we pay please?
Waitress:	Here is the bill. Would you like to pay together or separately?
Mr. Baumann:	Together please. Can I pay by credit card?
Waitress:	I am sorry, but the machine is broken.
Mr. Baumann:	No problem. Keep the change.

Waitress:	Thank you very much and have a nice evening.
Mr. Baumann:	The same to you. Goodbye.
Matthias:	Thank you very much. That is very kind of you.

Grammar

Active German: Level 2 > Unit 1 > Lesson 2 > Grammar

1 › **The modal verb *müssen***

In lesson 1 we saw the modal verb *können*. *Müssen* is another modal verb. *Müssen* means "to have to" or "must." Here are the main uses of *müssen*.

Ich muss arbeiten.
I have to work.

Man muss essen.
One must eat.

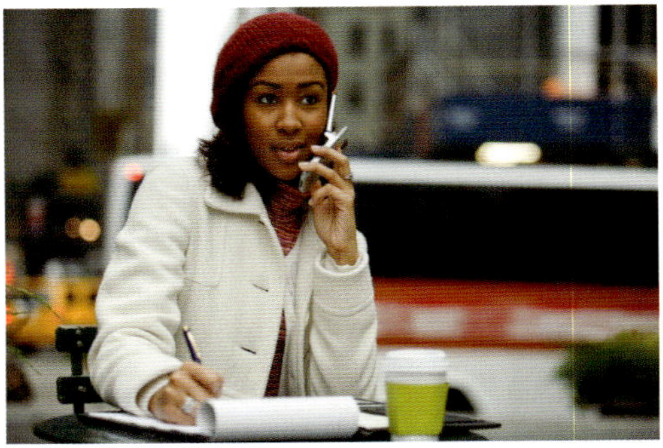

The pattern is as follows:

ich muss	I must
du musst	you must
er / sie / es muss	he / she / it must
wir müssen	we must
ihr müsst	you must
sie / Sie müssen	they / you must

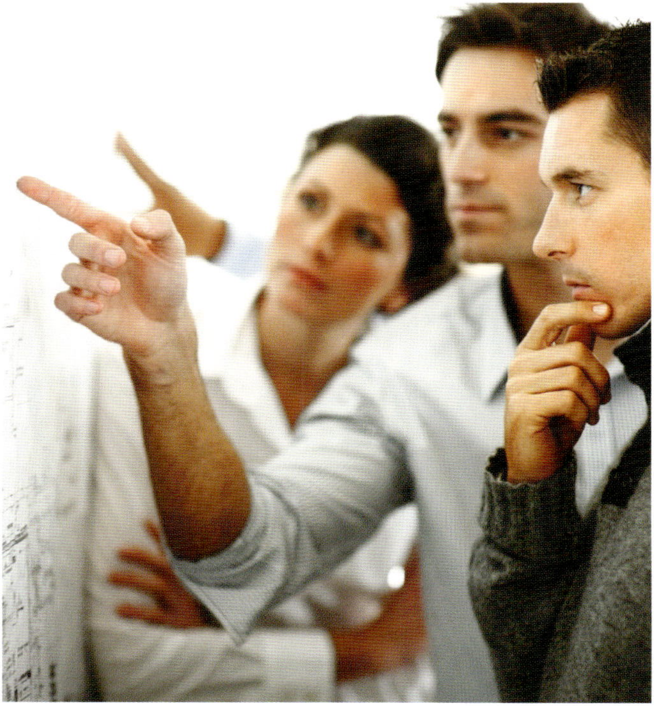

2 › The verb form *möchte*

To say "I would like to" you use *ich möchte*. *Möchte* and *möchten* are forms of the verb *mögen* which is a modal verb and must come before a second verb.

Ich möchte bitte bezahlen.
I would like to pay, please.

Ich möchte bitte bestellen.
I would like to order, please.

Here are the forms:

ich möchte	I would like
du möchtest	you would like
er / sie möchte	he / she would like
wir möchten	we would like
ihr möchtet	you would like
sie / Sie möchten	they / you would like

Culture note

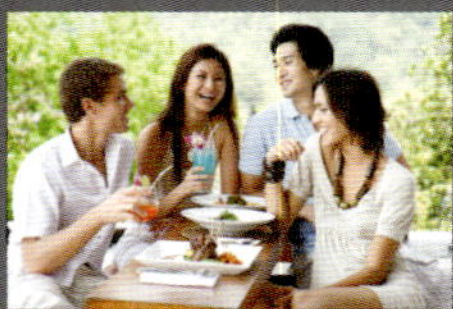

It is not uncommon to split a bill in a restaurant or a bar. The waiter is likely to ask you at the end of the meal: "All together?" (*Zusammen*?). You can ask the waiter for individual bills. In bigger groups you should, however, say so in advance. Nowadays it is more and more common to split the bill among all the guests, especially when friends are dining together.

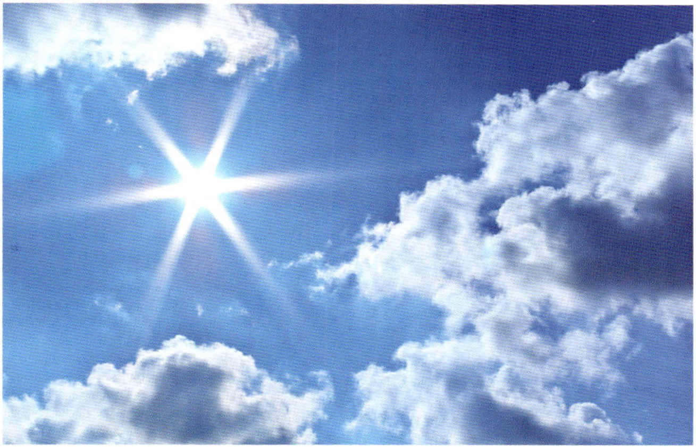

3 › **The imperfect tense of *sein***

The imperfect tense is a verb tense used to talk about the past, especially in descriptions, and to say what used to happen.

Es war sonnig.
It was sunny.

Ich war hier.
I was here.

Let's have a look at the imperfect of *sein* (to be).

ich war	I was
du warst	you were
er / sie / es war	he / she / it was
wir waren	we were
ihr wart	you were
sie / Sie waren	they / you were

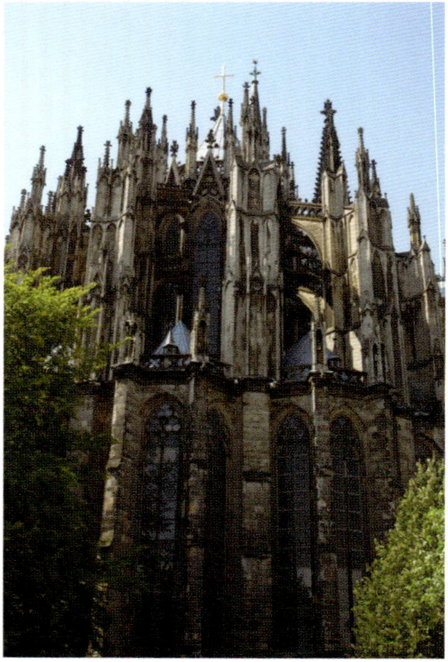

4 › Where were you?

Here are some examples with *war* (was).

Wo warst du gestern?	Where were you yesterday?
Wir waren gestern in Köln.	We were in Cologne yesterday.
Waren Sie gestern in München?	Were you in Munich yesterday?

5 › Keep the change!

You say *stimmt so* when you want to say to the waiter: "Keep the change."

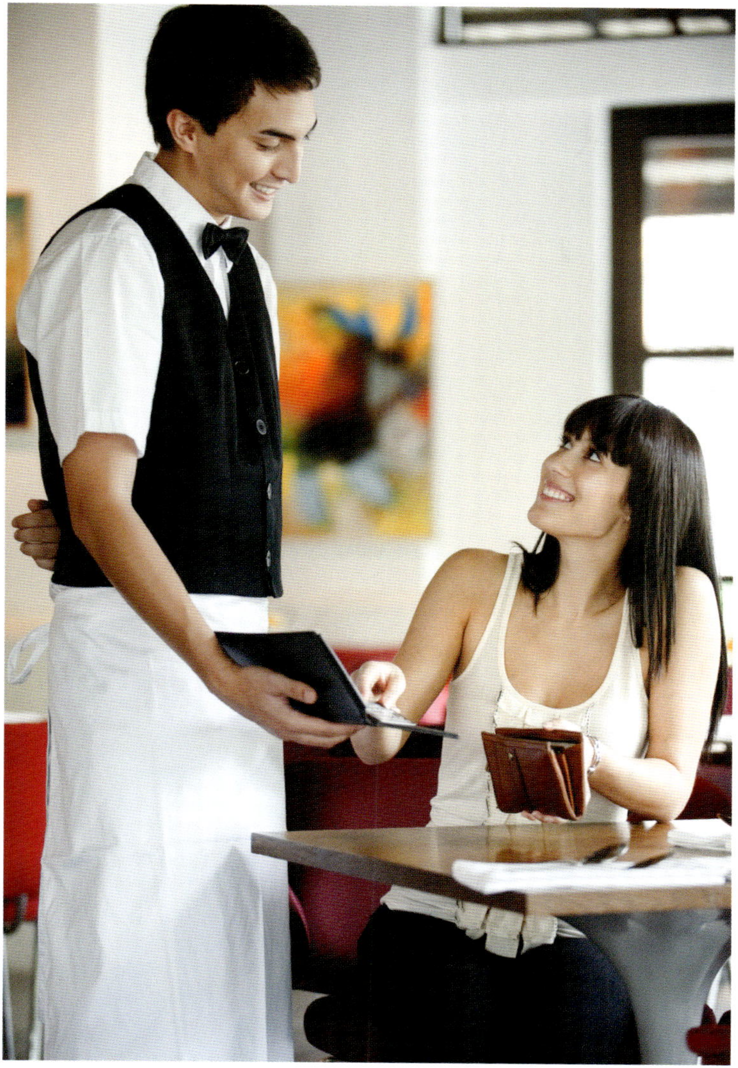

Vocabulary

Active German: Level 2 > Unit 1 > Lesson 2 > Vocabulary

Bills and payments

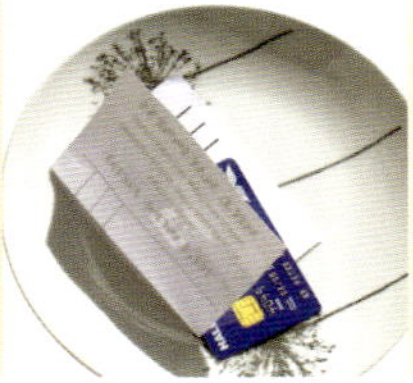

die Rechnung / Rechnungen
bill

Wer bezahlt die Rechnung?
Who pays the bill?

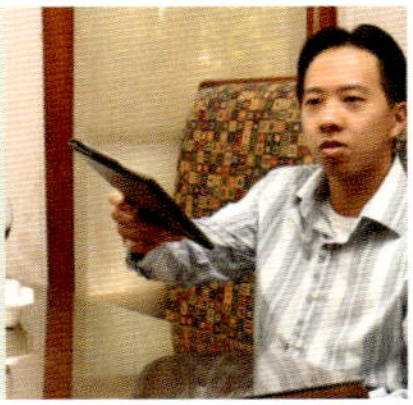

bezahlen
to pay

Ich bezahle heute.
I'll pay today.

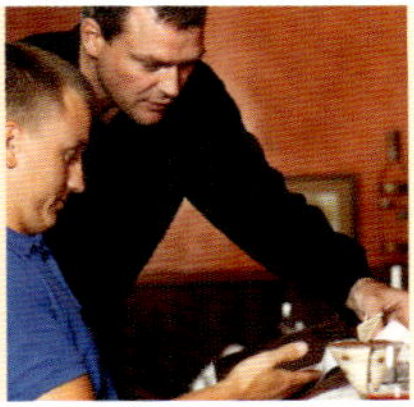

zusammen
together

Bezahlen Sie zusammen oder getrennt?
Are you paying together or separately?

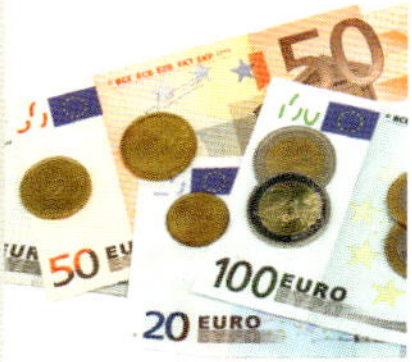

getrennt
separate

Ich bezahle mein Essen und Sie bezahlen Ihr Essen. Wir bezahlen getrennt.
I'm paying for my food and you're paying for your food. We're paying separately.

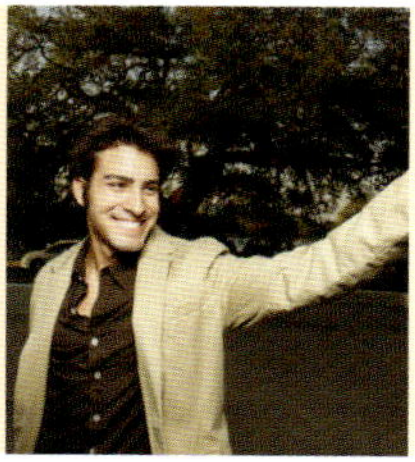

gleichfalls
same to you

Einen schönen Abend.
– Danke, gleichfalls.
Have a nice evening.
– Thanks, same to you.

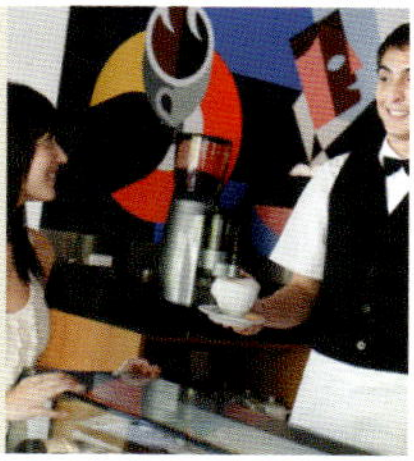

Vielen Dank.
Thank you very much.

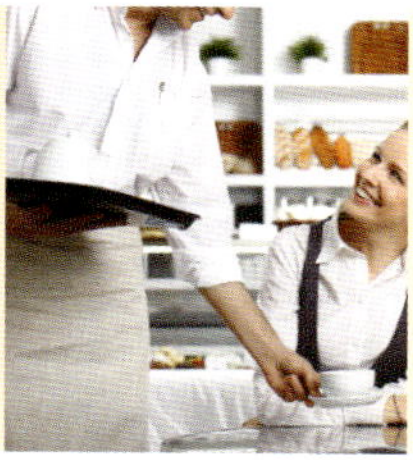

nett
nice, kind

Das ist sehr nett von Ihnen.
That is very kind of you.

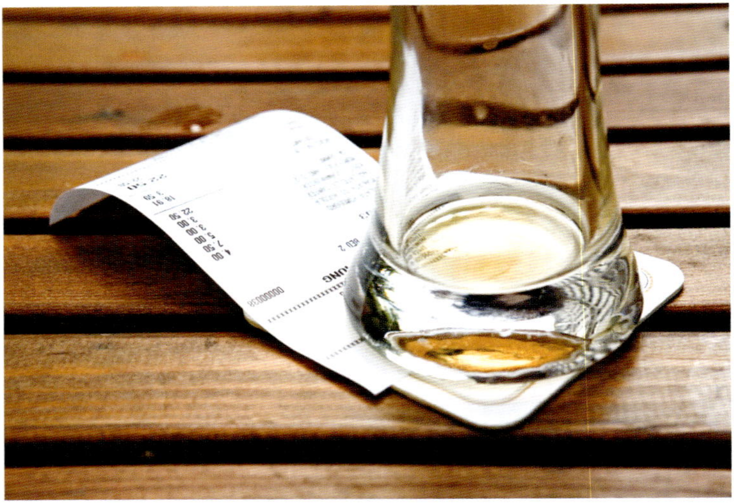

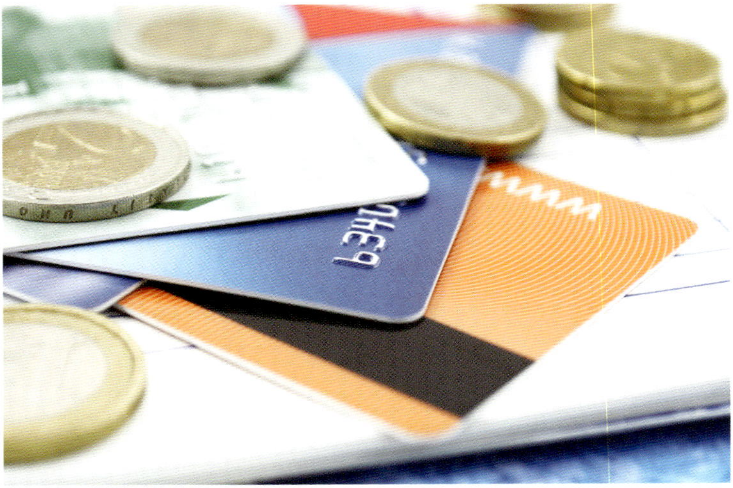

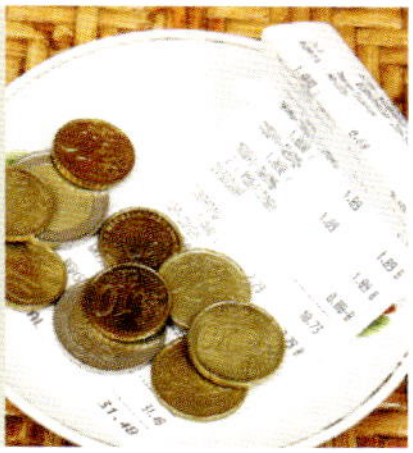

das Trinkgeld
tip

Das Trinkgeld ist sehr wichtig für einen Kellner.
The tip is very important for a waiter.

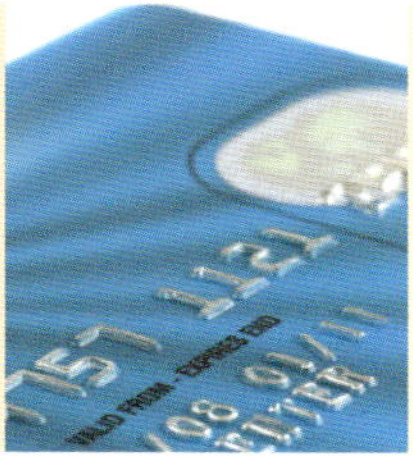

die Kreditkarte / Kreditkarten
credit card

Kann ich mit Kreditkarte bezahlen?
Can I pay by credit card?

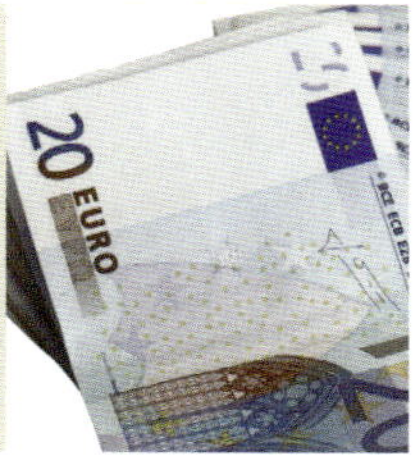

bar
cash

Zahlen Sie in bar oder mit Kreditkarte?
Are you paying in cash or by credit card?

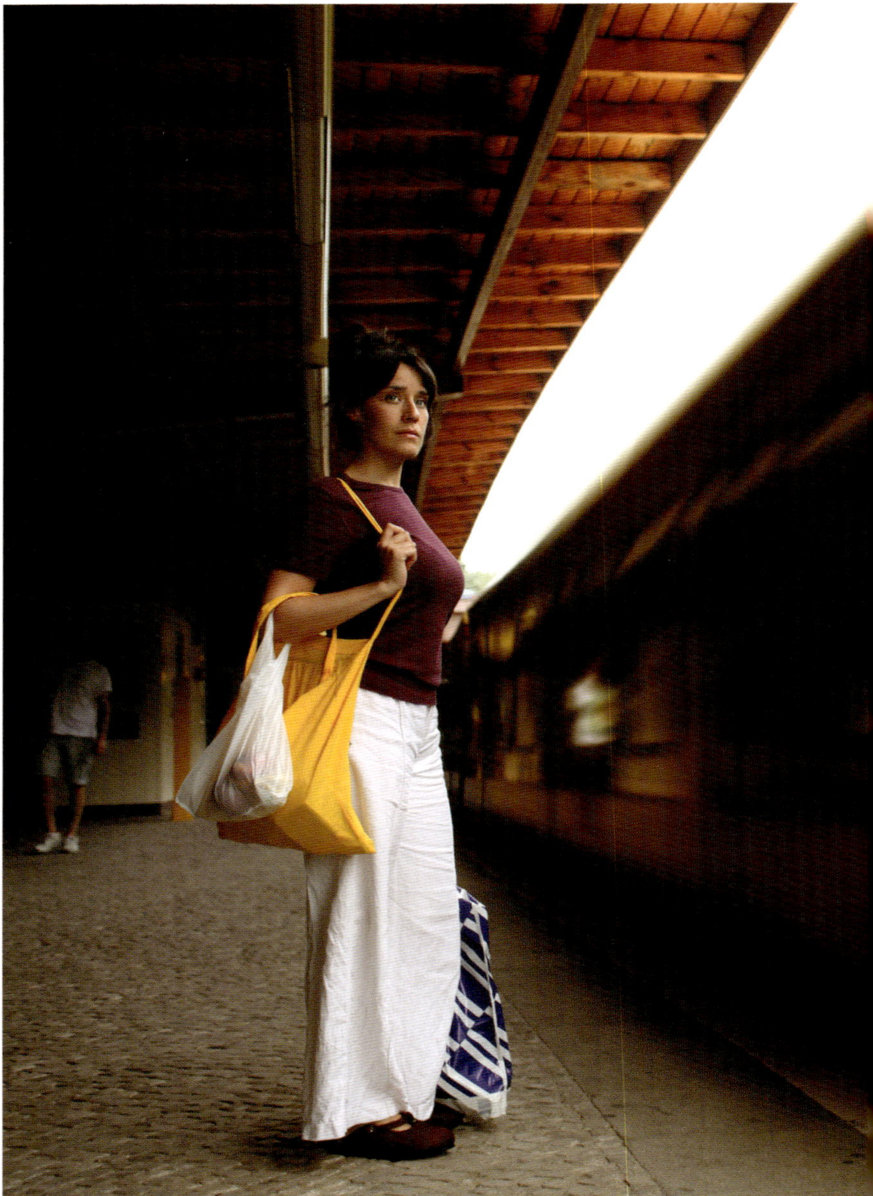

Active German *Level 2*

2

Lesson 1: A visitor – Nina is coming

- » How to say that you would like to visit somebody: ***Ich möchte dich gerne besuchen.***
- » How to address somebody informally and formally: ***Lieber Matthias, Sehr geehrter Herr Meisinger.***
- » Vocabulary for letters / emails and family.
- » How to say me, you, him, her, it, us, you, them.

Lesson 2: At the train station

- » How to talk about your health.
- » How to talk about public transportation.
- » How to say "Where to?": ***Wohin?***
- » How to say "We are going home / to the movies": ***Wir gehen nach Hause / ins Kino.***
- » How to use the verb ***fahren*** (to drive).
- » Vocabulary for health and public transportation.

Collins | Livemocha™

UNIT 2 › LESSON 1

A visitor – Nina is coming

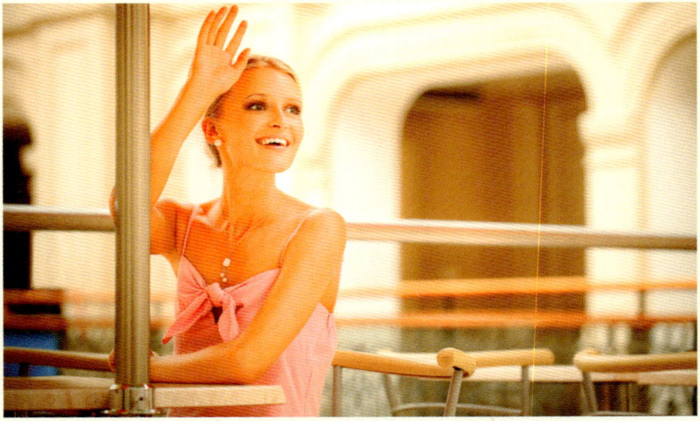

Culture note

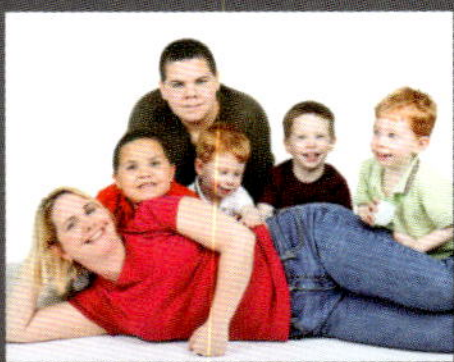

Even in the 21st century the family remains the most important center of social life. Even among young people family is highly regarded. What has changed are the ways people live together. Families are smaller nowadays and there are more so-called blended families. 64% of women work. The one-child family is also quite common. Statistics say that the birth rate is 1.3 children per woman in Germany today.

Video Dialog

Nina writes an email to her brother, Matthias. She plans to visit him in Pulheim soon.

Active German: Level 2 > *Unit 2* > *Lesson 1* > *Video dialog*

Nina: *Lieber Matthias, Wie geht es dir? Vielen Dank für deine Email. Ich möchte dich gerne besuchen. Ich war noch nie in Pulheim. In zwei Wochen habe ich Urlaub. Hast du Zeit? Kann ich meinen Freund Tom mitbringen? Kennst du ihn? Unsere Eltern lassen grüßen und auch unsere Großmutter. Ich habe ein Geschenk für dich. Liebe Grüße, deine Schwester Nina.*

Nina: Dear Matthias, How are you? Thank you very much for your email. I would really like to visit you. I've never been to Pulheim. In two weeks I'll be on vacation. Do you have time? Can I bring my boyfriend Tom with me? Do you know him? Our parents say "hello" and so does our grandmother. I have a present for you. Best wishes, your sister Nina.

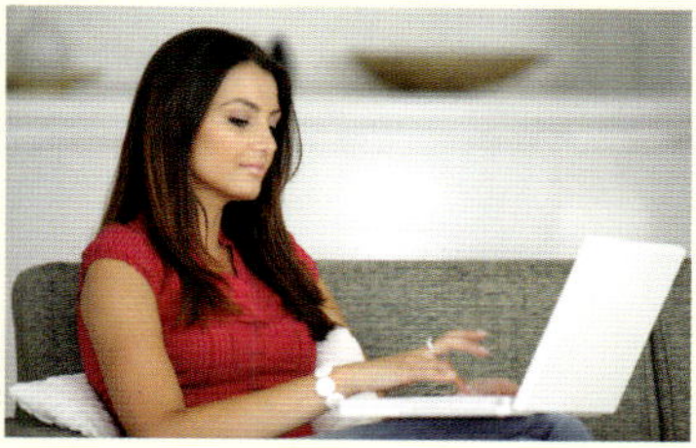

Grammar

Active German: Level 2 > *Unit 2* > *Lesson 1* > *Grammar*

1 › **Do you know him?**

Nina asks if Matthias knows her boyfriend. She asks:

Kennst du ihn?
Do you know him?

Ihn is a pronoun which replaces the object of the sentence (Tom). It is in the accusative case, the form needed for objects in a sentence. These pronouns are used when you want to replace the noun and it is clear who you are talking about.

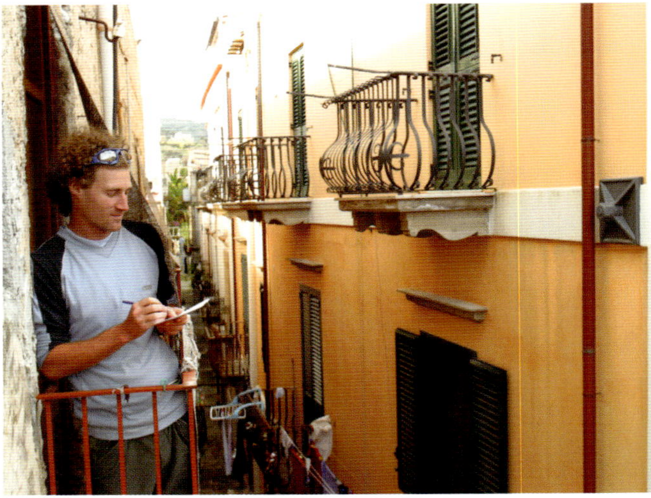

2 › Do you know him?

Kennst du meinen Freund? Ja, ich kenne ihn.
Do you know my boyfriend? Yes, I know him.
Kennst du die Frau? Ja, ich kenne sie.
Do you know the woman? Yes, I know her.
Sind die Hamburger für Sie? Ja, sie sind für uns.
Are the hamburgers for you? Yes, they are for us.

The pronouns in the accusative case in the singular are:

mich	me
dich	you
ihn	him
sie	her
es	it

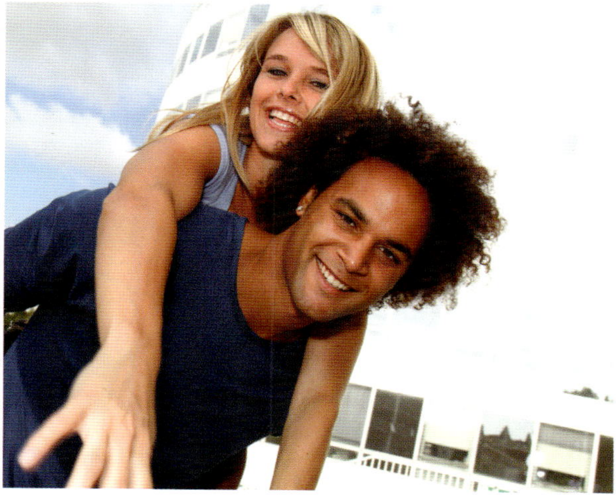

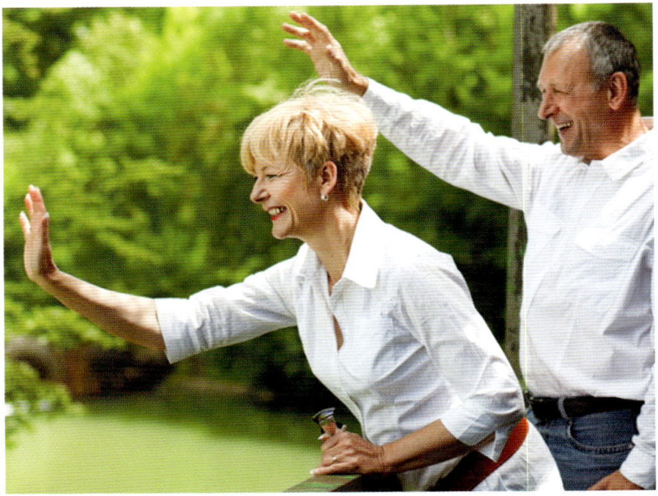

3 › Do you see us?

The accusative pronouns in the plural are:

uns	us
euch	you
sie	them
Sie	you

4 › The verb *kennen*

Note that in the dialog Nina says: *Kennst du meinen Freund?* The verb *kennen* means "to know someone" and requires an object in the accusative case. This was introduced in Level 1. You have to use the articles *den*, *die*, and *das* or *einen*, *eine*, and *ein*.

jemanden kennen – to know somebody, to be acquainted with somebody

Ich kenne den Mann.
I know the man.

Ich kenne dich.
I know you.

Kennst du meinen Freund?
Do you know my boyfriend?

Ja, ich kenne deinen Freund. Ja, ich kenne ihn.
Yes, I know your boyfriend. Yes, I know him.

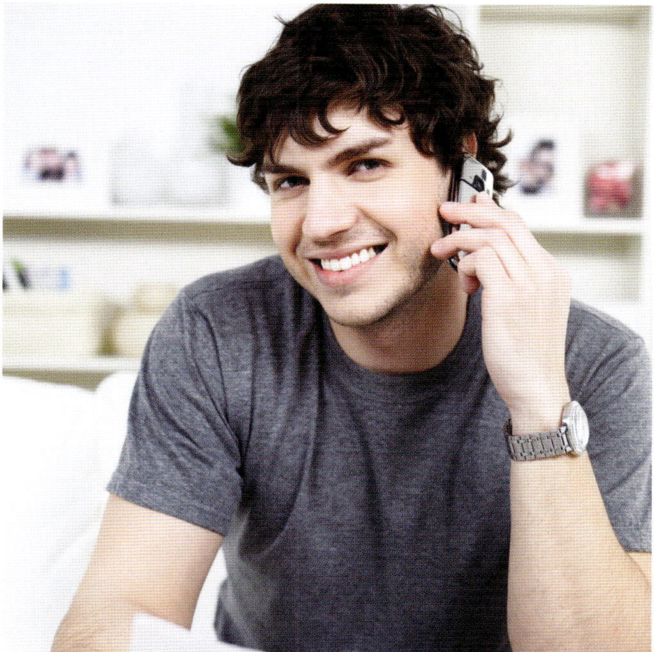

5 › For you!

The preposition *für* (for) takes the accusative case.

Ich habe ein Geschenk für dich.
I have a present for you.
Für mich?
For me?

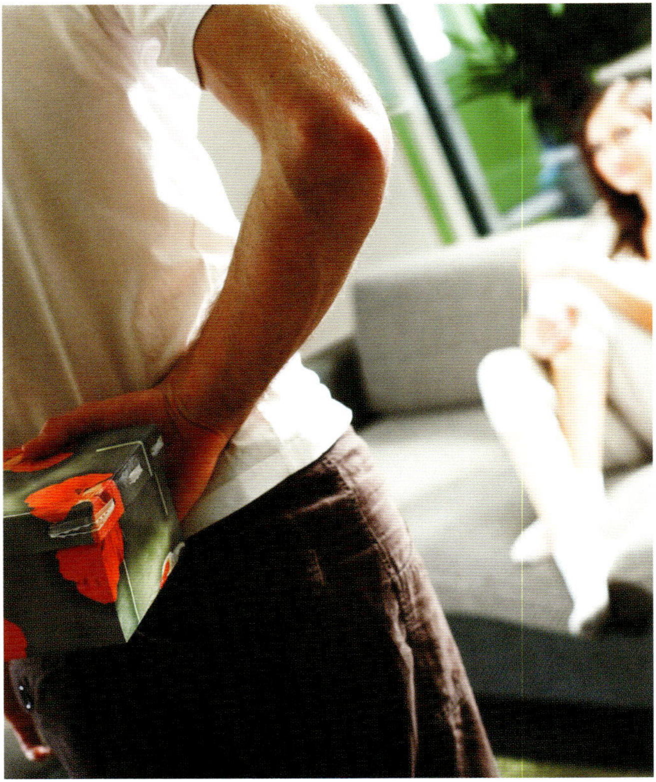

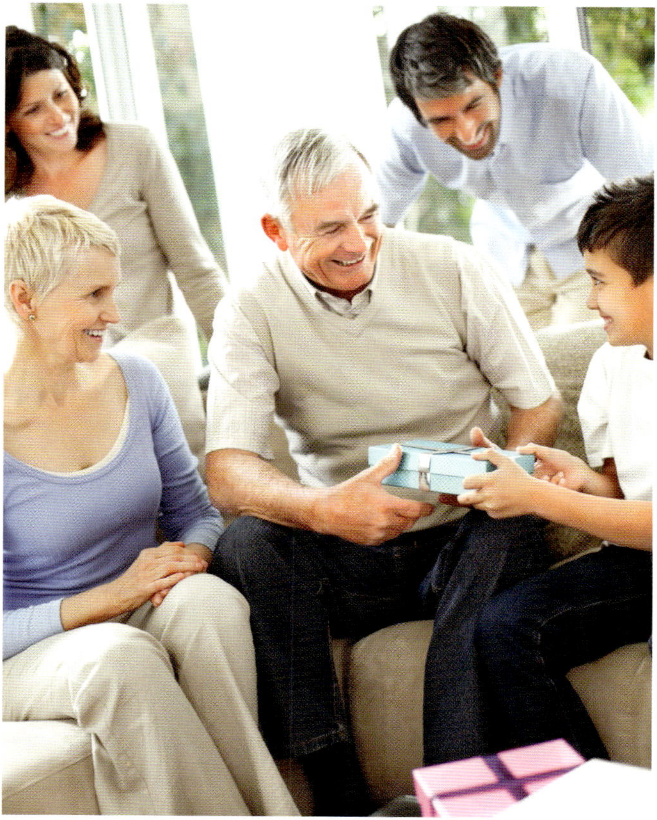

6 › Dear Matthias

To address somebody you know quite well in a letter or email, you use *Lieber* + name for masculine and *Liebe* + name for feminine.

Lieber Matthias	Dear Matthias
Liebe Nina	Dear Nina

To address somebody formally in a letter or email, you use:

masculine: *Sehr geehrter Herr Baumann*
Dear Mr. Baumann

feminine: *Sehr geehrte Frau Roellinger*
Dear Mrs. Roellinger

7 › How to finish an email

To finish an email or letter to somebody you know very well you use *dein* + name for masculine and *deine* + name for feminine.

dein Matthias yours, Matthias
deine Nina yours, Nina

In an informal letter or email to a friend you use *Liebe Grüße* to say "with love." A more formal way to finish is:

Mit freundlichen Grüßen Kind regards

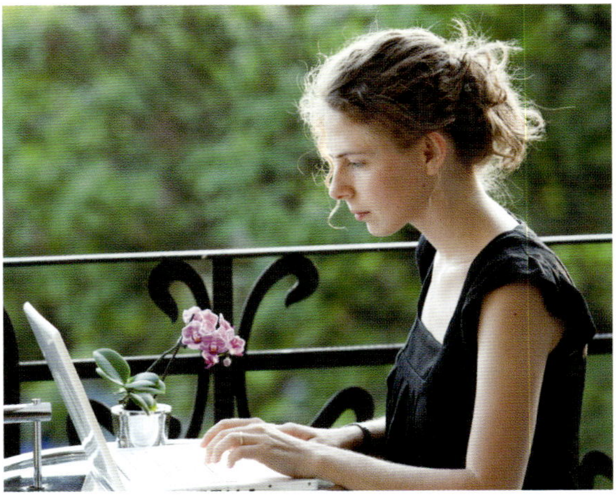

Vocabulary

Active German: Level 2 > *Unit 2* > *Lesson 1* > *Vocabulary*

Family

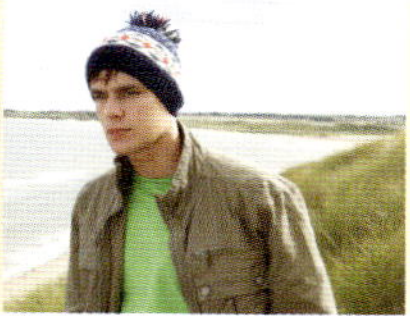

der Bruder / Brüder
brother

Mein Bruder heißt Stefan.
My brother's name is Stefan.

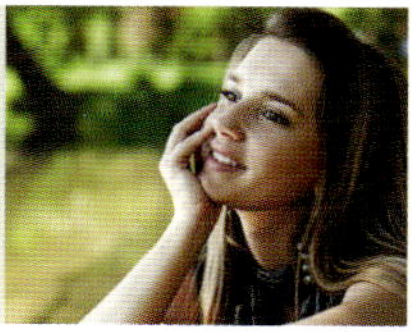

die Schwester / Schwestern
sister

Ich habe drei Schwestern.
I have three sisters.

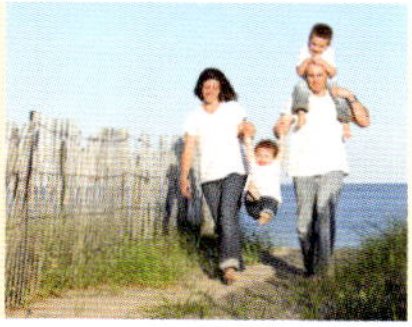

die Familie / Familien
family

Meine Familie ist sehr klein.
My family is very small.

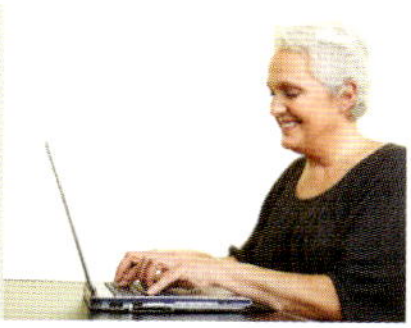

die Mutter / Mütter
mother

Meine Mutter ist 60 Jahre alt.
My mother is 60 years old.

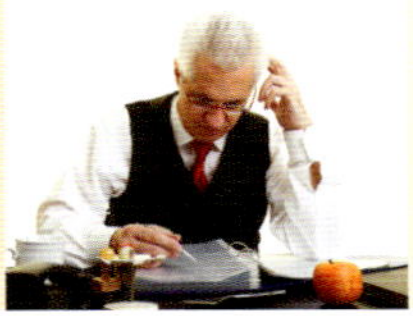

der Vater / Väter
father

Kennst du meinen Vater?
Do you know my father?

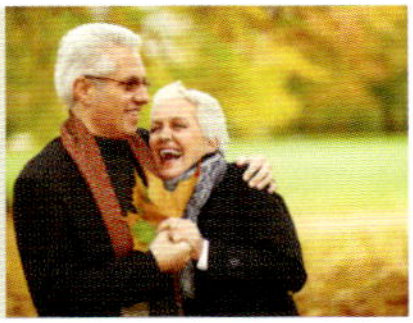

die Eltern
parents

Das sind meine Eltern.
These are my parents.

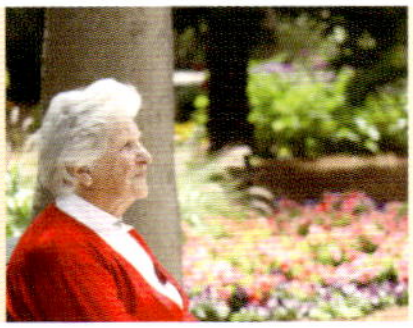

die Großmutter / Großmütter
grandmother

Lebt deine Großmutter noch?
Is your grandmother still alive?

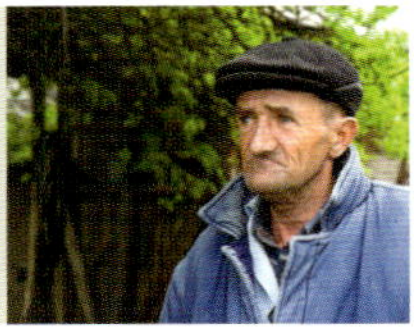

der Großvater / Großväter
grandfather

Mein Großvater ist schon sehr alt.
My grandfather is very old.

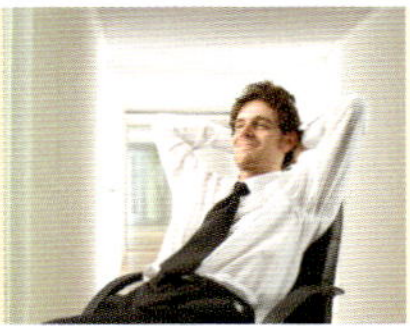

der Freund / Freunde
friend (male) / boyfriend

Hast du einen Freund?
Do you have a boyfriend?

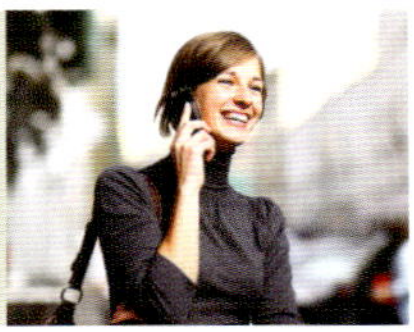

die Freundin / Freundinnen
friend (female) / girlfriend

Meine Freundin wohnt in Stuttgart.
My friend / girlfriend lives in Stuttgart.

UNIT 2 › LESSON 2

At the train station

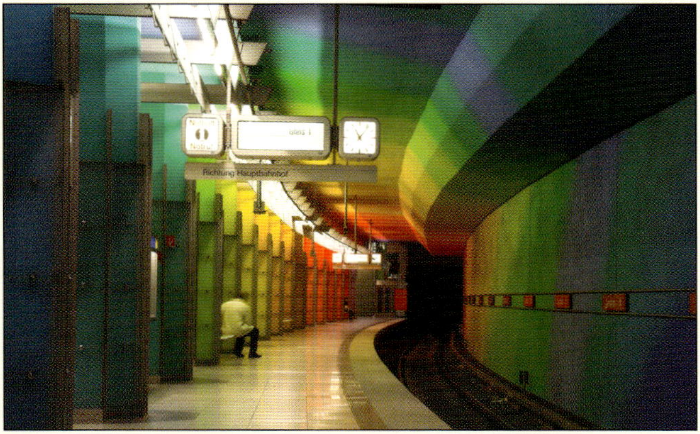

Culture note

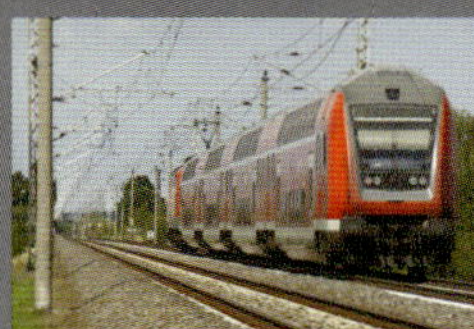

The first German train was on the tracks in 1835. Over the years a nationwide network developed. Nowadays, the German railway cooperative is the *Deutsche Bahn*. Depending on the size and the structure of a city there are different means of transportation. In some cities you still find streetcars. Subways are found in bigger cities. German trains are very comfortable and the service has improved over time.

Video Dialog

Matthias is surprised to see that Nina has come alone but the siblings are happy to be together again.

Active German: Level 2 > *Unit 2* > *Lesson 2* > *Video dialog*

Matthias:	*Hallo, da bist du ja schon. Schön dich zu sehen.*
Nina:	*Hallo Matthias.*
Matthias:	*Wo ist dein Freund?*
Nina:	*Oh, er ist krank. Er hat Kopfschmerzen und eine Erkältung.*
Matthias:	*Oh, wie schade.*
Nina:	*Ja, aber ich bin ja da. Wohin fahren wir jetzt?*
Matthias:	*Möchtest du nach Hause oder lieber in ein Café?*
Nina:	*Lieber nach Hause. Ich bin ein bisschen müde.*
Matthias:	*Wir fahren mit dem Bus, zu Fuß dauert es 40 Minuten.*
Nina:	*Gehen wir zur Bushaltestelle?*
Matthias:	*Ja, die Bushaltestelle ist dort.*
Nina:	*OK.*

Matthias:	Hello, there you are already. Good to see you.
Nina:	Hello, Matthias.
Matthias:	Where is your boyfriend?

Nina:	Oh, he is ill. He has a headache and a cold.
Matthias:	Oh, what a shame.
Nina:	Yes, but I'm here. Where shall we go now?
Matthias:	Do you want to go home or to a café?
Nina:	I'd rather go home. I'm a bit tired.
Matthias:	We'll take the bus. It takes 40 minutes to walk.
Nina:	Shall we walk to the bus stop?
Matthias:	Yes, the bus stop is over there.
Nina:	OK.

Grammar

Active German: Level 2 > *Unit 2* > *Lesson 2* > *Grammar*

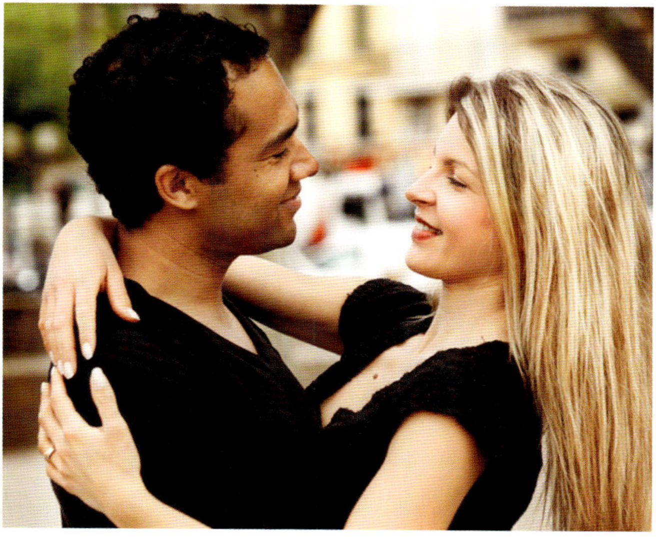

1 › Where to? The question word *wohin*

To ask where you are going you use *Wohin?* Where to?

Nina asks in the video dialog: *Wohin fahren wir jetzt?* Where are we going (to) now?

There are different ways to answer that question.

Use *nach* for cities, states, and most countries.

nach Hause	home
nach Deutschland	to Germany
nach Frankfurt	to Frankfurt
nach Europa	to Europe

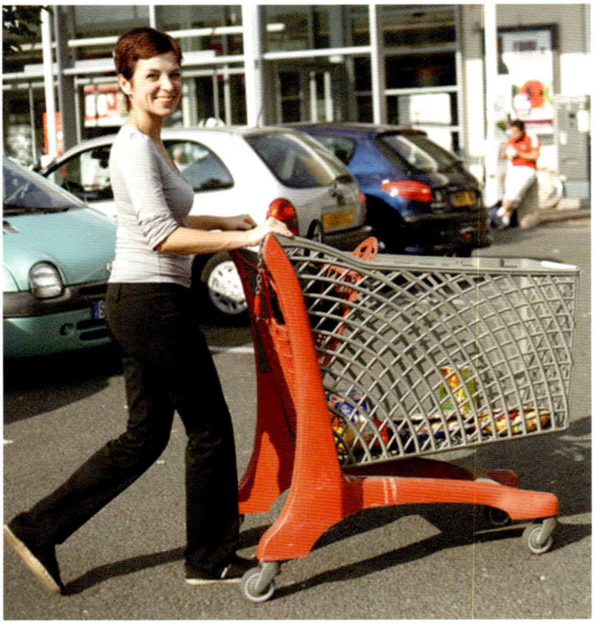

2 › I'm going to a café

When you want to say "I'm going to a café," in German you use *in*. Look at the articles you use after *in*.

Ich gehe in ein Café.

You use *in* with destinations where you will spend a relatively long time.

Wohin gehst du?

in einen Supermarkt	to a supermarket
in eine Oper	to an opera house
in ein Café	to a café
in den Supermarkt	to the supermarket
in die Kneipe	to the bar
in das Kino	to the movies

Note that you normally combine *in das* and say *ins: Ich gehe ins Kino.*

3 › I'm going to the bus station

You use *zum* or *zur* with destinations involving a short visit.

masculine and neuter:

zum Bahnhof
to the train station

feminine:

zur Bushaltestelle
to the bus stop

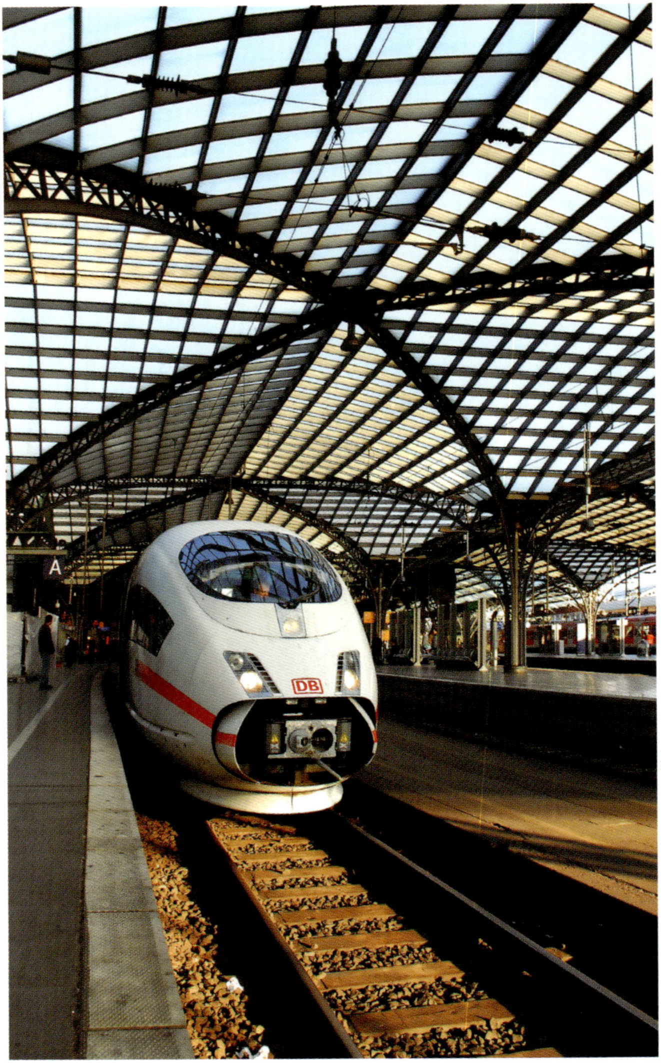
A
DB

4 › The verb *fahren*

The verb *fahren* means “to go,” “to travel,” or “to drive.”

Wohin fährst du?

Where are you driving to?

The verb *fahren* has an *Umlaut* (ä) in the *du* and *er / sie / es* forms. The rest follows the normal pattern.

ich fahre	I drive
du fährst	you drive
er / sie / es fährt	he / she / it drives
wir fahren	we drive
ihr fahrt	you drive
Sie / sie fahren	you / they drive

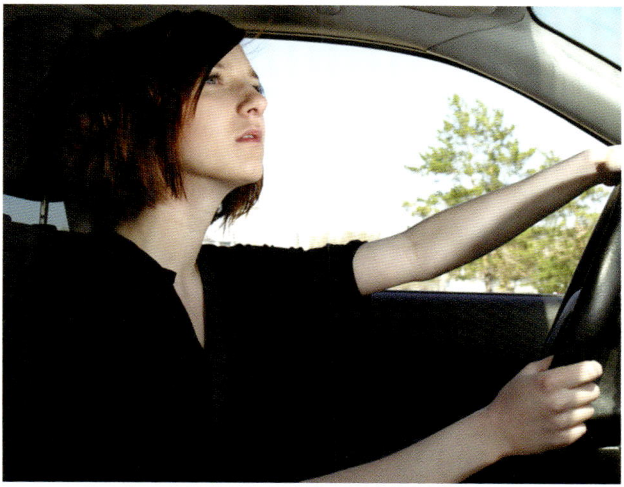

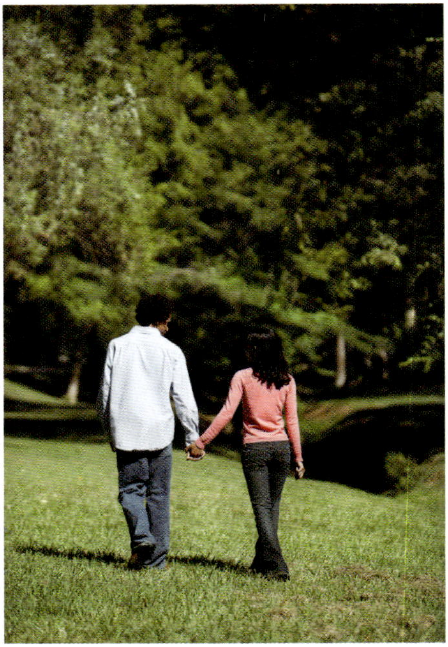

5 › The verb *gehen*

Gehen means “to go,” “to walk.”

Note that in German you use *gehen* in order to refer to the actual walking action.

Wohin fährst du am Wochenende?
Where are you going this weekend?

Ich fahre / fliege nach London.
I'm going / flying to London.

Gehen wir oder fahren wir?
Shall we walk or drive?

Vocabulary

Active German: Level 2 > Unit 2 > Lesson 2 > Vocabulary

Health and transport

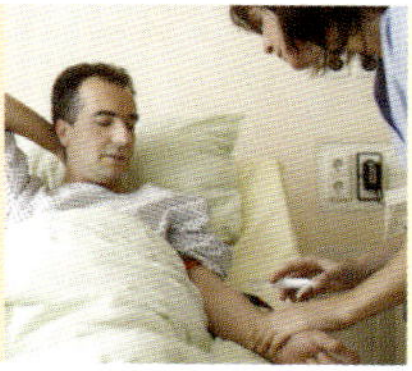

krank
ill

Sind Sie krank?
Are you ill?

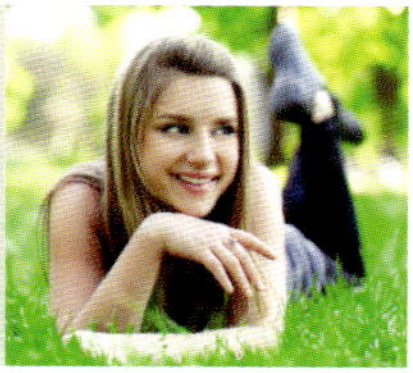

gesund
healthy, well

Ich bin wieder gesund.
I am well again.

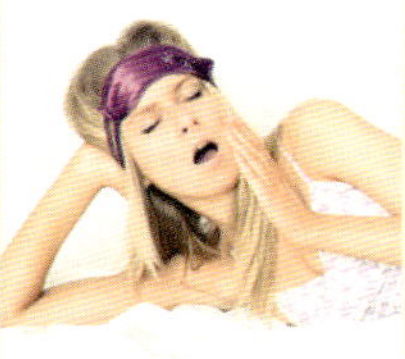

müde
tired

Ich bin so müde.
I'm so tired.

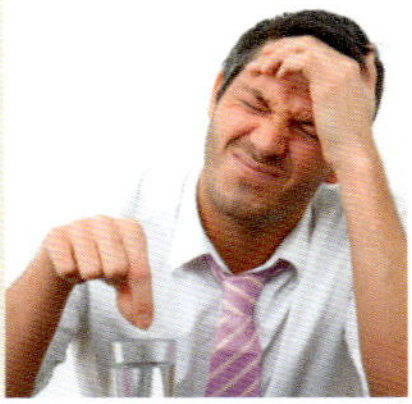

die Kopfschmerzen
headache

Ich habe Kopfschmerzen. Haben Sie eine Kopfschmerztablette für mich?
I have a headache. Do you have a headache pill for me?

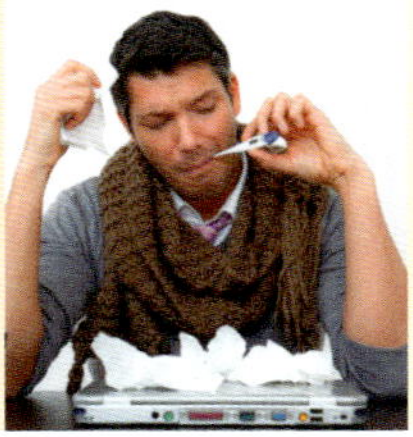

die Erkältung
cold

Im Januar hat jeder eine Erkältung.
In January everybody has a cold.

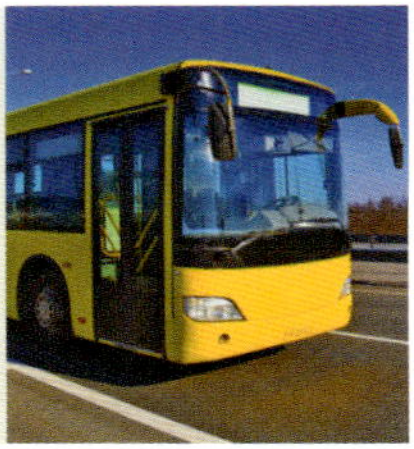

der Bus / Busse
bus

Nehmen wir den Bus?
Are we going to take the bus?

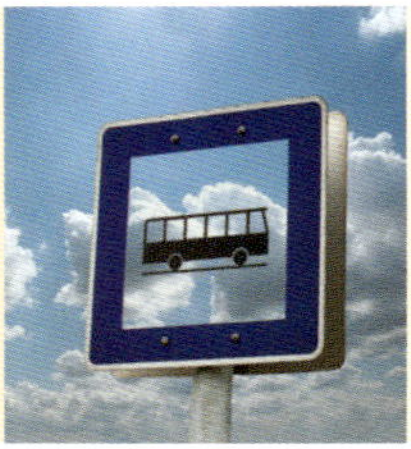

die Bushaltestelle / Bushaltestellen
bus stop

Entschuldigen Sie, wo ist die Bushaltestelle?
Excuse me, where is the bus stop?

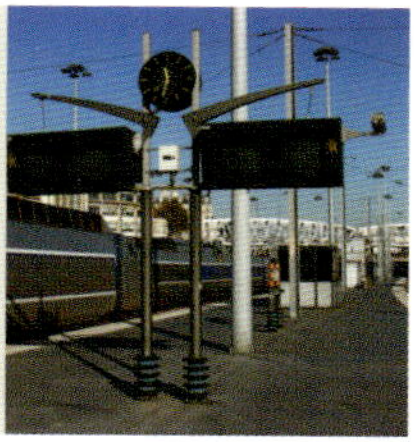

der Bahnhof / Bahnhöfe
train station
Ist das der Bahnhof?
Is that the train station?

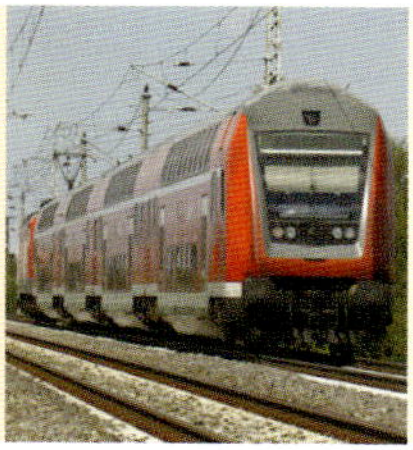

der Zug / Züge
train
Ich fahre gerne mit dem Zug.
I like going by train.

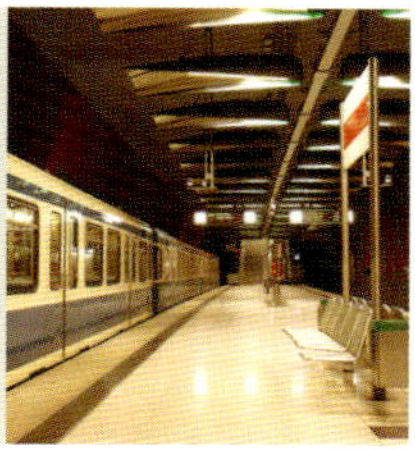

die U-Bahn / U-Bahnen
metro / subway
Gibt es hier eine U-Bahn?
Is there a subway here?

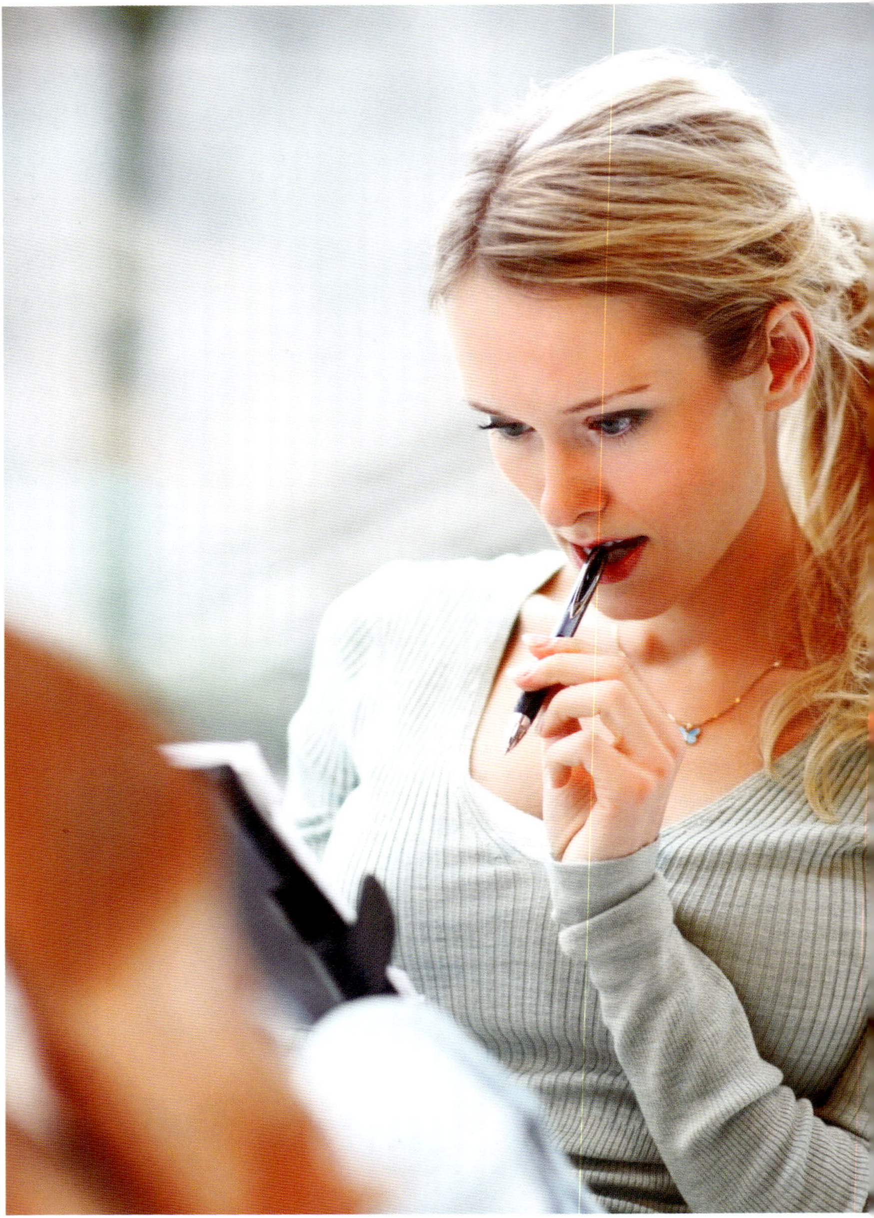

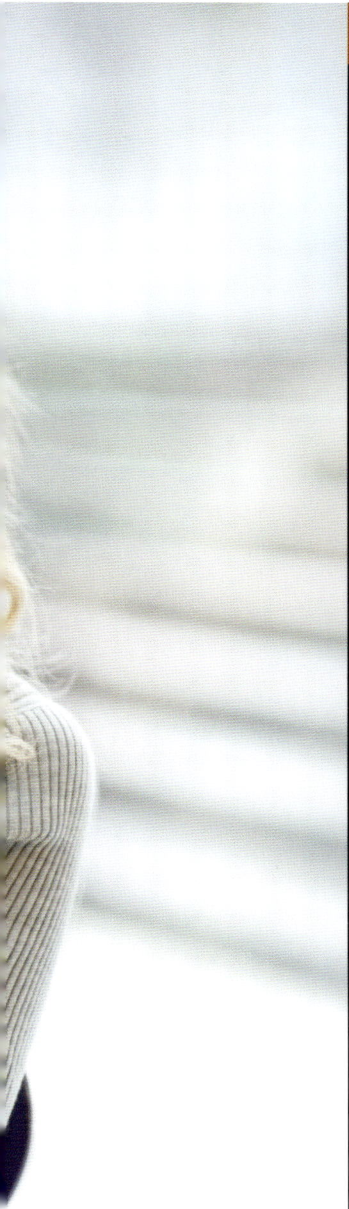

Active German *Level 2*

3

Lesson 1: My daily life 1

- How to say what you do every day.
- Vocabulary for daily life.
- How to say "to get up," "to start the day," "to go shopping," and "to call somebody."

Lesson 2: My daily life 2

- How to talk about your life and daily routines.
- Vocabulary for everyday life.
- How to say how often you do things.
- How to form sentences with time and frequency expressions such as: today, tonight, on the weekend, never.
- Some new verbs.

Collins | Livemocha™

UNIT 3 › LESSON 1

My daily life 1

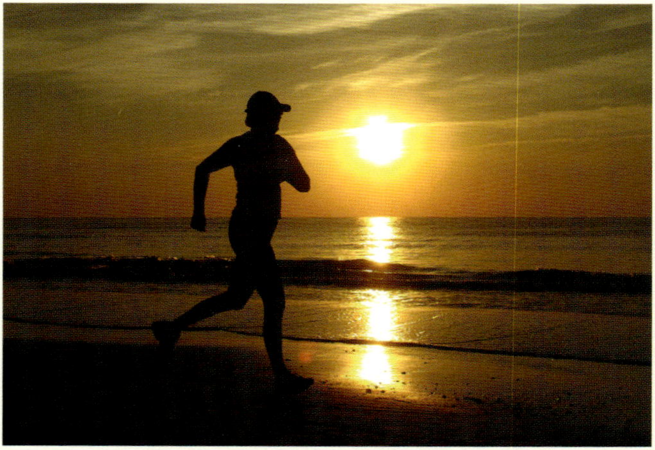

Culture note

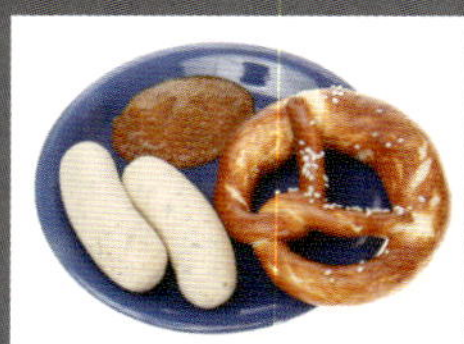

A day can't begin without a good breakfast. A typical German breakfast *(Frühstück)* consists of various things. Cold meats – sliced cured ham, dry-cured ham – and cheeses are served alongside a variety of rye breads and sweet toppings like jam, marmalade, and honey. Soft-boiled eggs, cereal or muesli, and fruit would round off a large breakfast. Of course, a full breakfast is not possible every day. But if you can't enjoy it during the week, you definitely will have an ample breakfast on the weekend. Sometimes friends even meet up to enjoy their brunch together.

Video Dialog

Happy to see her brother, Nina asks Matthias all sorts of questions about his new life in Pulheim.

Active German: Level 2 > Unit 3 > Lesson 1 > Video dialog

Nina:	*Wie ist dein Leben hier in Pulheim?*
Matthias:	*Wunderbar.*
Nina:	*Musst du viel arbeiten?*
Matthias:	*Manchmal ja, aber es ist OK.*
Nina:	*Wann stehst du morgens auf?*
Matthias:	*Meine Arbeit fängt um 9 Uhr an. Ich stehe meistens um 7:30 Uhr auf. Mein Kollege holt mich oft ab.*
Nina:	*Und wann kaufst du ein?*
Matthias:	*Am Wochenende.*
Nina:	*Wie oft machst du Sport?*
Matthias:	*Manchmal, meistens abends.*
Nina:	*Und, rufst du unsere Eltern jede Woche an?*
Matthias:	*Nina, so viele Fragen. Ja, ich rufe unsere Eltern jede Woche an.*

Nina:	How is your life in Pulheim?
Matthias:	Very good.
Nina:	Do you have to work a lot?
Matthias:	Sometimes, yes, but it's OK.

Nina:	When do you get up in the morning?
Matthias:	Work starts at 9 o'clock. Most of the time, I get up at 7:30. A colleague often picks me up.
Nina:	And when do you go shopping?
Matthias:	On the weekend.
Nina:	How often do you do sports?
Matthias:	From time to time, usually in the evening.
Nina:	And, do you call our parents every week?
Matthias:	Nina, so many questions. Yes, I call our parents every week.

Grammar

Active German: Level 2 > *Unit 3* > *Lesson 1* > *Grammar*

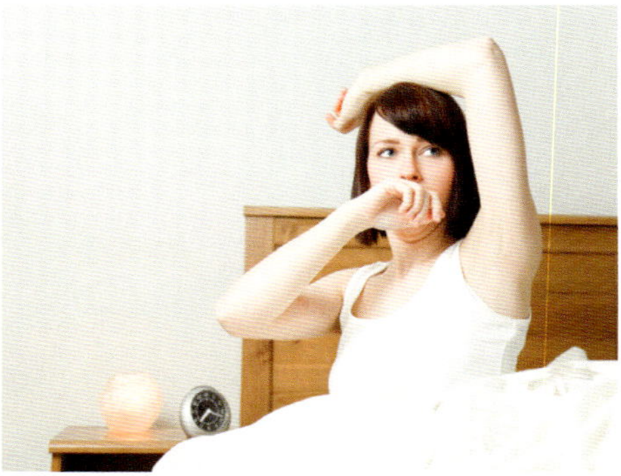

1 › I get up. Separable verbs

Nina asks her brother when he gets up:

Wann stehst du morgens auf?
When do you get up in the morning?

The verb in the sentence is *aufstehen* to get up.

Aufstehen is a separable verb which means it is made up of two parts: *auf* and *stehen*. To form a sentence you have to cut off the *auf* in *aufstehen* and put it at the end of the sentence.

Wann stehst du auf?
When do you get up?
Ich stehe um 7 Uhr auf.
I get up at 7 a.m.

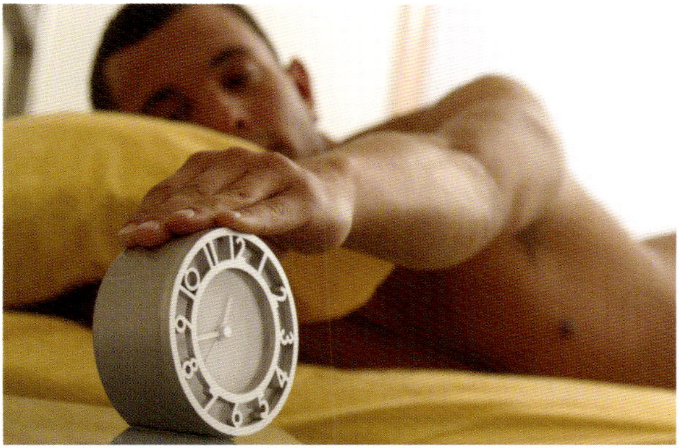

2 › I go shopping

Some of the important verbs you use to describe your daily life are separable:

einkaufen to go shopping
Wann kaufst du ein?
When do you go shopping?
Ich kaufe um 16 Uhr ein.
I go shopping at 4 p.m.

anrufen to call somebody

Ich <u>rufe</u> dich <u>an</u>.

I call you.

abholen to pick somebody up

Ich <u>hole</u> Sie <u>ab</u>.

I pick you up.

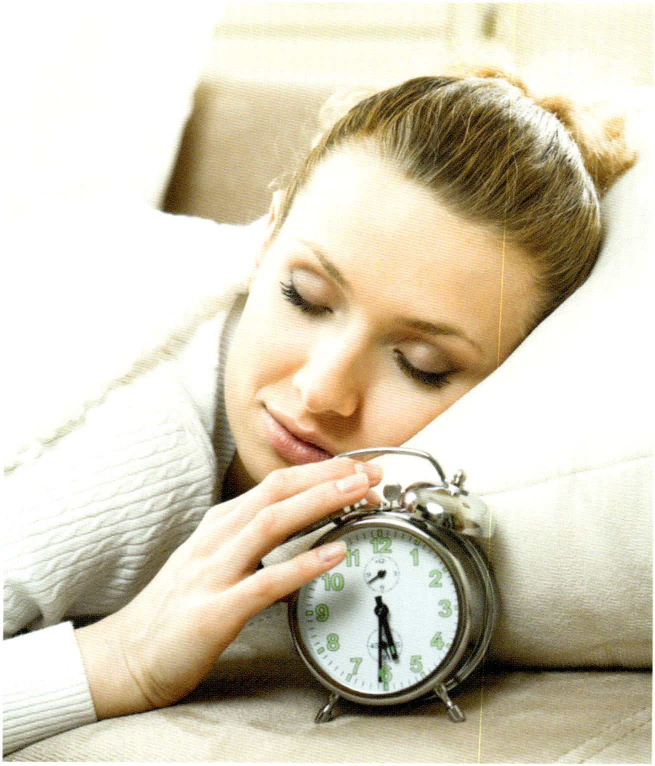

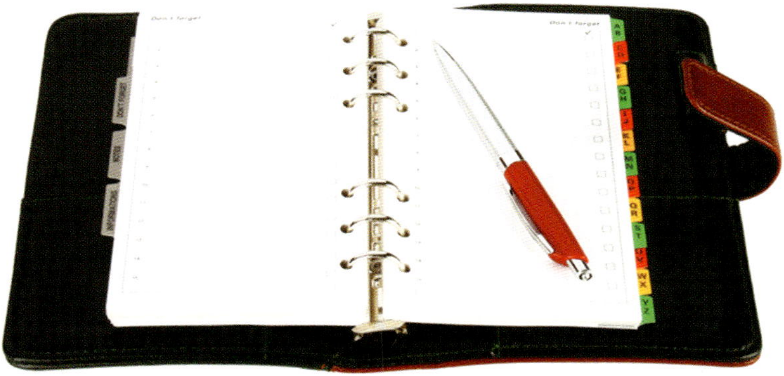

Another separable verb is *umziehen* (to move from one house to another).

Ich ziehe um.
I move.

3 › It starts at 6

The verb *anfangen* (to start) is a separable verb as well. It is not regular and has a vowel change. Note the *du* and the *er* forms.

ich fange an	I start
du fängst an	you start
er / sie / es fängt an	he / she / it starts
wir fangen an	we start
ihr fangt an	you start
sie / Sie fangen an	they / you start

4 › Daily activities

To talk about your daily activities you sometimes need to use time expressions:

heute
today
Was machst du heute?
What are you doing today?

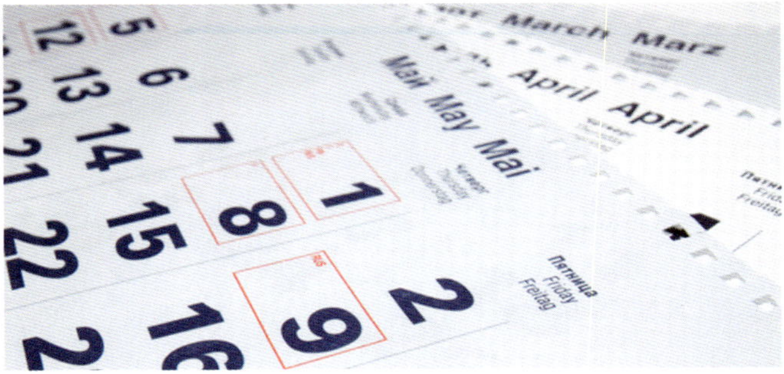

morgen
tomorrow
Was machst du morgen?
What are you doing tomorrow?

heute Abend
tonight
Was machst du heute Abend?
What are you doing tonight?

or you need to say in which part of the day:

morgens	in the morning
mittags	at noon
abends	in the evening

5 › How often?

To indicate frequency you use the questionphrase *wie oft* (how often).

> *Wie oft machst du Sport?*
> How often do you do sports?

To answer, you can say

jede Woche	every week
jeden Tag	every day
einmal pro Woche	once a week
zweimal im Monat	twice a month

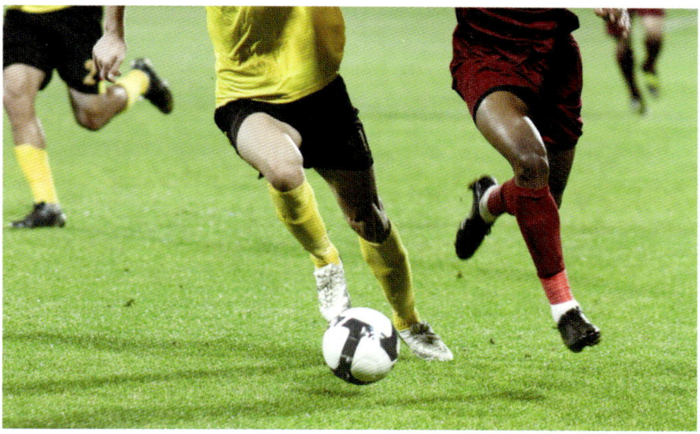

abc

Vocabulary

Active German: Level 2 > Unit 3 > Lesson 1 > Vocabulary

Daily life

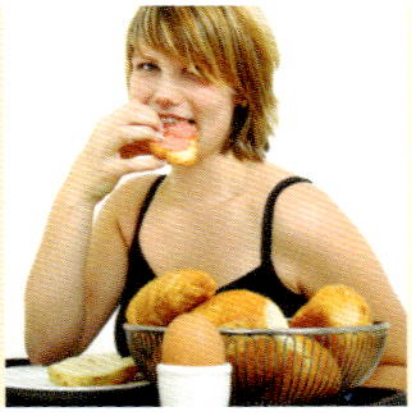

frühstücken
to have breakfast

Ich trinke morgens nur einen Kaffee. Ich frühstücke nicht.
In the morning I just have a coffee. I don't have breakfast.

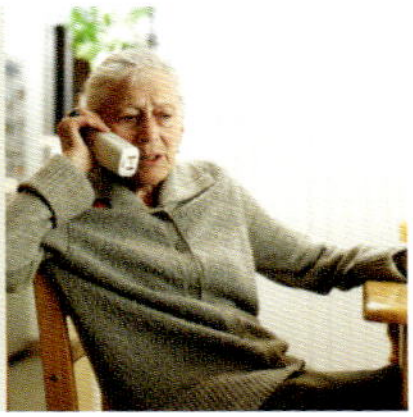

telefonieren
to call somebody / talk on the phone

Wir telefonieren heute Abend.
We are going to talk on the phone tonight.

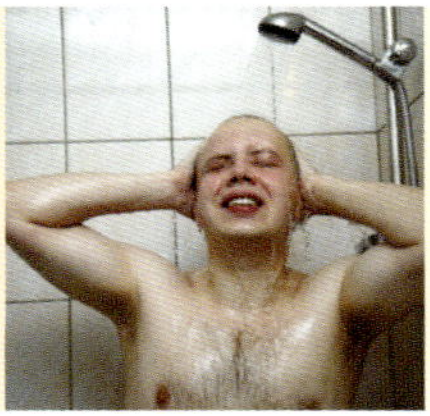

duschen
to shower

Ich dusche jeden Morgen.
I shower every morning.

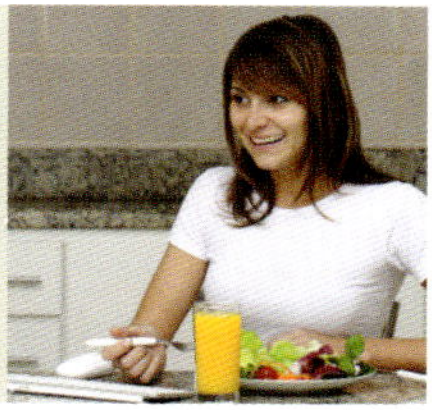

zu Mittag essen
to eat lunch

Wann isst du zu Mittag?
When are you having lunch?

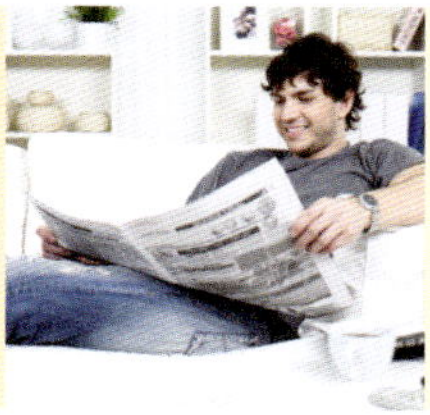

die Zeitung lesen
to read the newspaper

Morgens lese ich die Zeitung.
In the morning I read the newspaper.

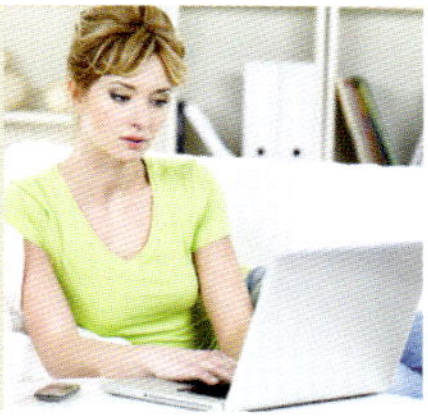

Emails schreiben
to write emails

Ich muss noch einige Emails schreiben.
I still have to write some emails.

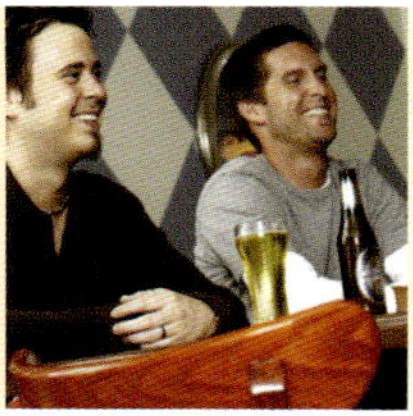

in die Kneipe gehen
to go to the bar

Wir gehen heute Abend in die Kneipe. Kommen Sie mit?
We are going to the bar tonight. Do you want to come along?

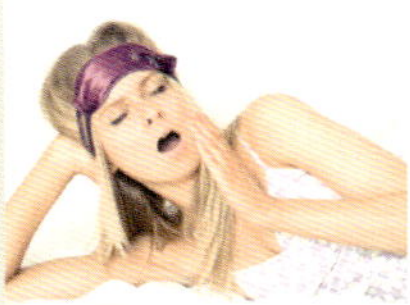

ins Bett gehen
to go to bed

Wann gehst du ins Bett?
When do you go to bed?

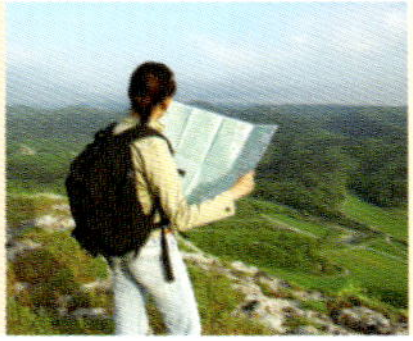

spazieren gehen
to go for a walk

Am Wochenende gehe ich gerne spazieren.
On weekends I like to go for a walk.

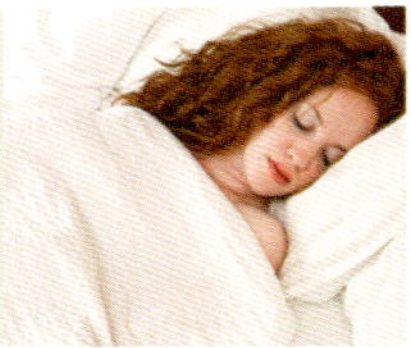

schlafen
to sleep

Schläfst du schon?
Are you already asleep?

UNIT 3 › LESSON 2

My daily life 2

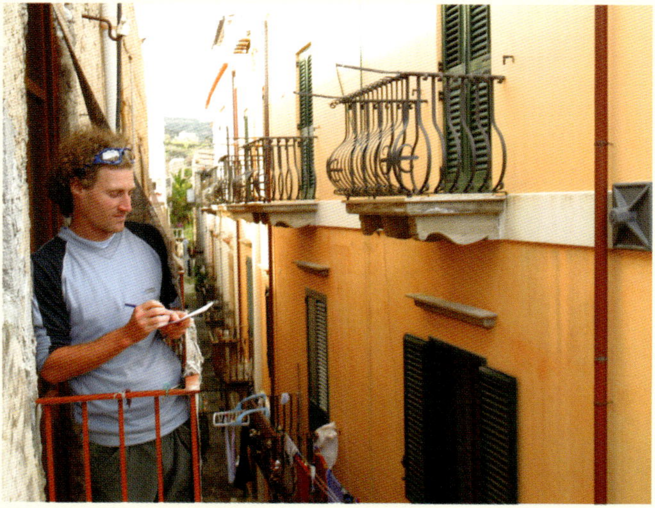

Culture note

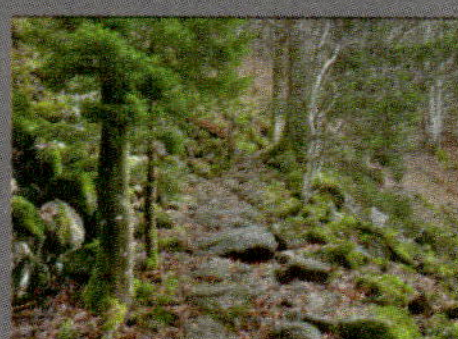

Fresh air and going for walks are important in German daily life. Parks and forests are highly valued. The Black Forest (*Schwarzwald*) is probably the most famous one. It is in the southwest corner of the southern state *Baden-Württemberg*. It has borders with France and Switzerland. The name might be misleading since it is a beautiful spot. The high concentration of pine trees and the nearby mountains make it look dark. That is how the forest got its name.

Video Dialog

Matthias and Nina plan their time together.

Active German: Level 2 > *Unit 3* > *Lesson 2* > *Video dialog*

Nina:	*Morgen kann ich einkaufen und später kann ich kochen.*
Matthias:	*Super. Ich muss morgen früh aufstehen. Ich habe um 8:30 einen Termin.*
Nina:	*Ok, ich kann ausschlafen! Ich habe Urlaub.*
Matthias:	*Bist du immer noch müde?*
Nina:	*Nein, jetzt geht es mir gut.*
Matthias:	*Möchtest du spazieren gehen?*
Nina:	*Gerne. Kann ich erst Tom anrufen?*
Matthias:	*Natürlich.*

Nina:	I could go shopping tomorrow, and later on I could cook.
Matthias:	Great. I have to get up early tomorrow. I have an appointment at 8:30 a.m.
Nina:	OK, I can sleep in! I'm on vacation.
Matthias:	Are you still tired?
Nina:	No, I'm fine now.
Matthias:	Would you like to go for a walk?
Nina:	I would love to. Can I call Tom first?
Matthias:	Of course.

Grammar

Active German: Level 2 > *Unit 3* > *Lesson 2* > *Grammar*

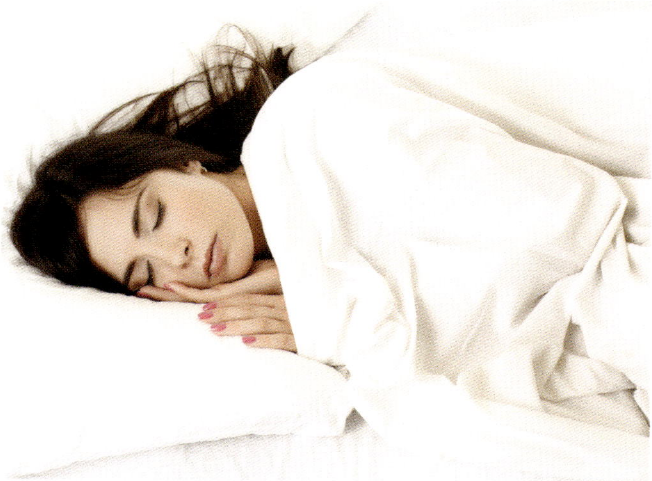

1 › I have to get up

In the last unit we looked at some modal verbs like *müssen* and *können*.

You can combine these verbs with separable verbs. But then you don't cut off the *-ein*, *-an*, *-aus* prefixes.

> *Ich kann einkaufen.*
> I can go shopping.
> *Ich muss morgen früh aufstehen.*
> I have to get up early tomorrow.

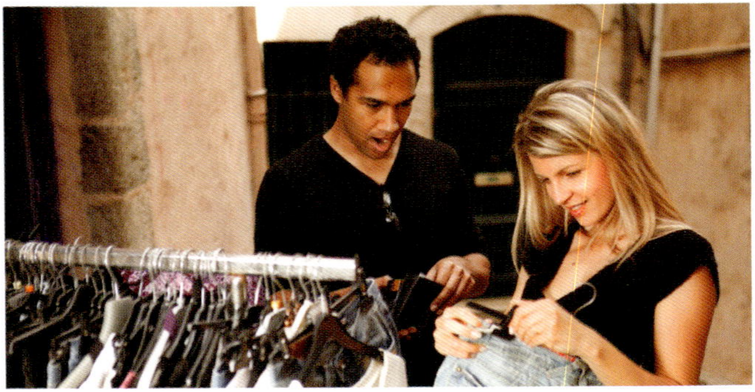

Compare:

Ich kaufe ein.
I go shopping.
Ich muss einkaufen.
I have to go shopping.

2 › I go for a walk

Nina and Matthias are going to go for a walk. Look at how this is expressed.

spazieren gehen
to go for a walk
Ich gehe spazieren.
I go for a walk / I'm going for a walk.

3 › The verb *schlafen*

The verb *schlafen* means to sleep.

It follows the same pattern as some other verbs we have seen already.

ich schlafe	I sleep
du schläfst	you sleep
er / sie / es schläft	he / she / it sleeps
wir schlafen	we sleep
ihr schlaft	you sleep
sie / Sie schlafen	they / you sleep

Note the *Umlaut!*

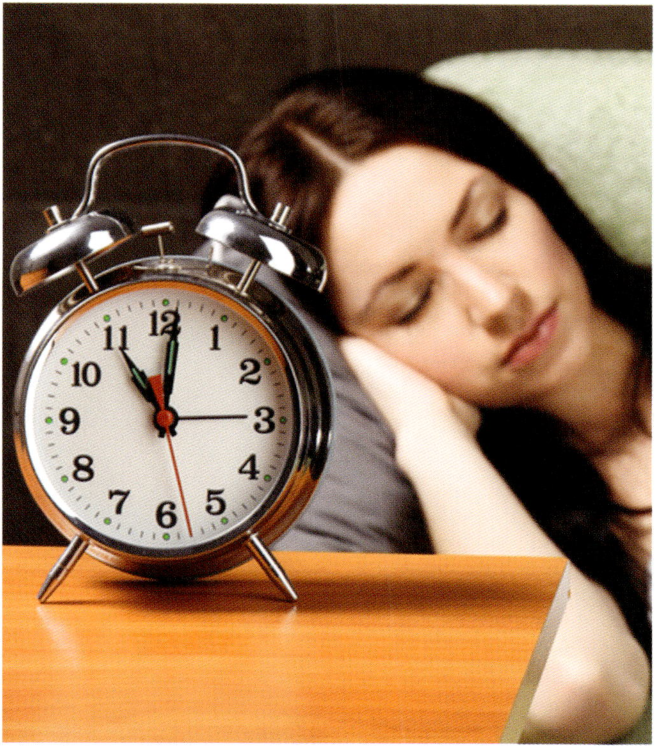

4 › **More on verbs**

The verb *ausschlafen* means "to sleep in." It is a separable verb.

It has a vowel change in the *du* and *er* forms as well.

ich schlafe aus	I sleep in
du schläfst aus	you sleep in
er / sie / es schläft aus	he / she / it sleeps in

5 › **How often?**

To express how often you do something you use the following words.

nie	never
manchmal	sometimes
oft	often
meistens	mostly
immer	always

6 › **Word order**

Expressions of time and frequency are placed between the two parts of the verb or at the beginning.

Ich gehe am Wochenende einkaufen / Am Wochenende gehe ich einkaufen.
I go shopping on weekends.

Ich gehe nie spazieren.
I never go for a walk.

7 › Word order

When you talk about your daily life you might want to use the word *dann* (then).

Ich frühstücke. Dann <u>dusche</u> ich.
I have breakfast. Then I take a shower.

Note the position of the words. The verb stays in the second position. This is a very important rule in German.

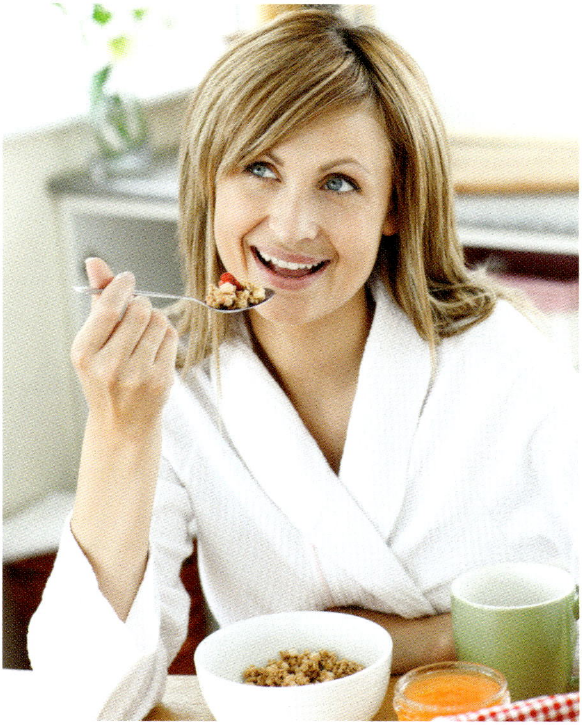

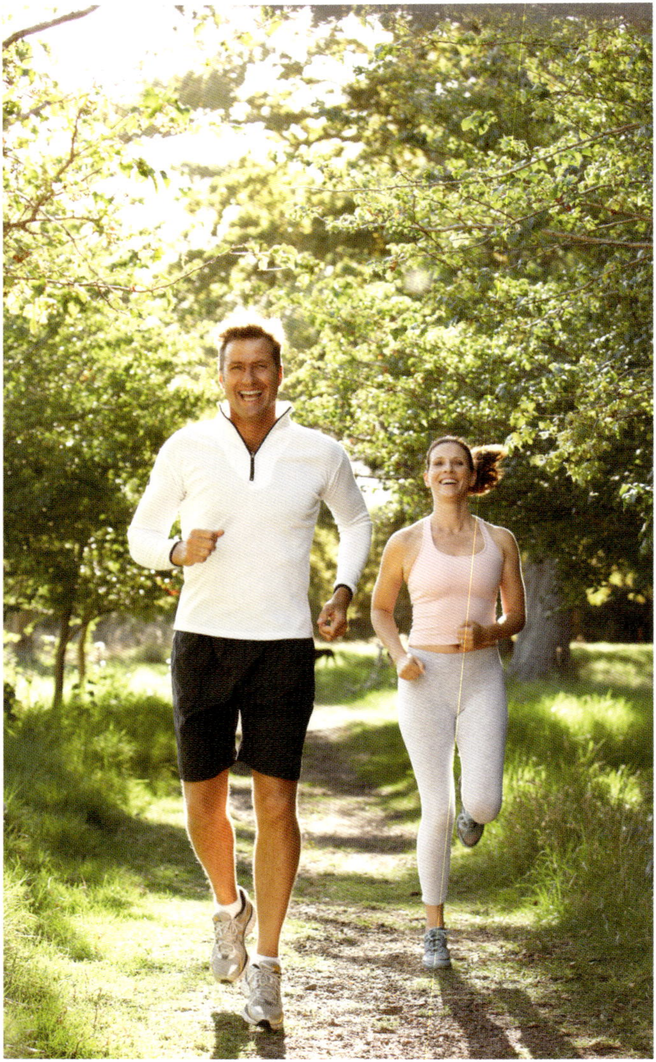

Vocabulary

Active German: Level 2 > Unit 3 > Lesson 2 > Vocabulary

Daily life

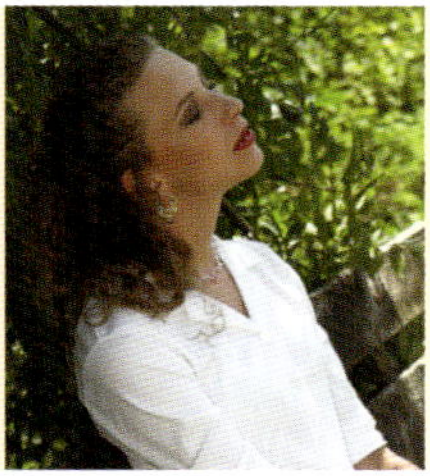

die Mittagspause / Mittagspausen
lunch break

Von 13 Uhr bis 14 Uhr habe ich eine Mittagspause.
From 1 p.m. to 2 p.m. I have a lunch break.

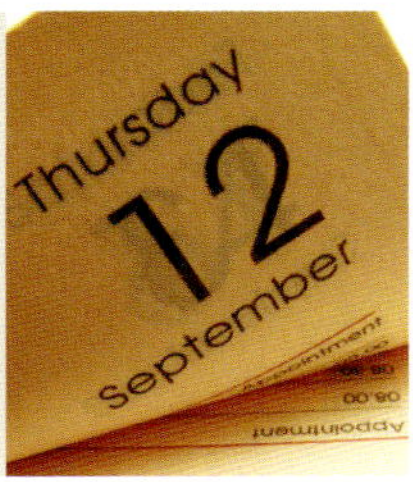

die Arbeitszeit / Arbeitszeiten
workday

Meine Arbeitszeit ist von 9 Uhr bis 18 Uhr.
My workday is from 9 a.m. to 6 p.m.

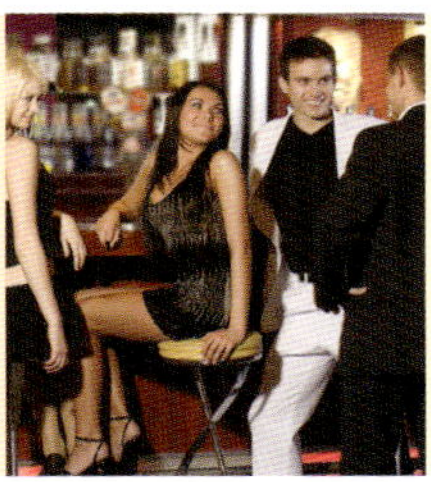

Leute treffen
to meet people

Am Wochenende treffe ich gerne Freunde.
On weekends I like to meet friends.

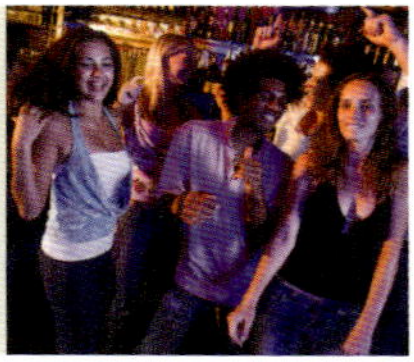

ausgehen
to go out

Manchmal gehe ich am Samstag aus.
Sometimes I go out on Saturdays.

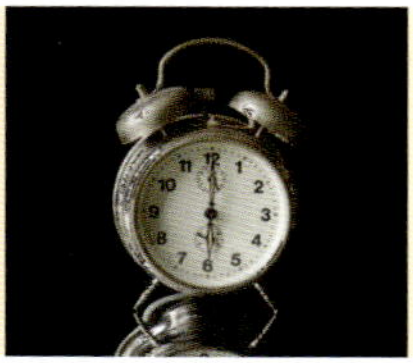

früh
early

Morgen muss ich früh aufstehen.
Tomorrow I have to get up early.

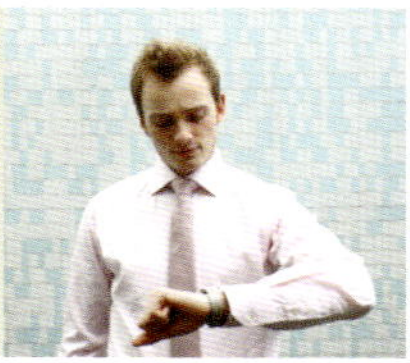

spät
late

Oh, es ist schon spät. Ich muss nach Hause gehen.
Oh, it is already late. I have to go home.

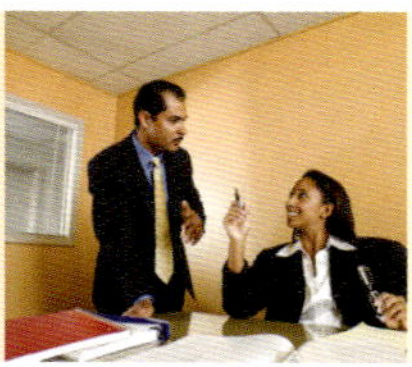

fragen
to ask

Ich frage meinen Chef.
I'll ask my boss.

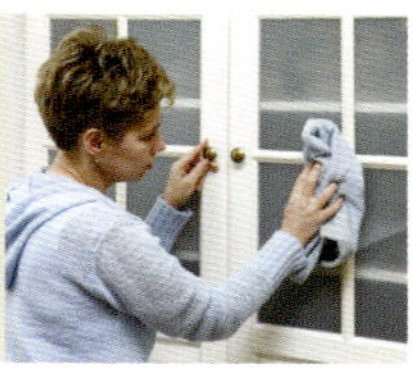

putzen
to clean

I putze nicht gerne.
I don't like cleaning.

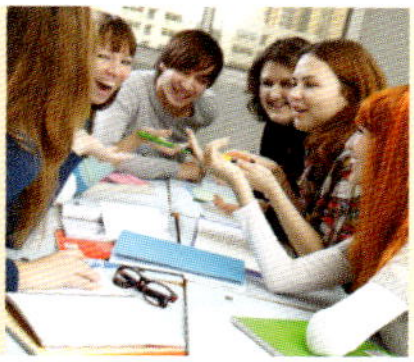

diskutieren
to discuss

Wir diskutieren oft über Politik.
We discuss politics very often.

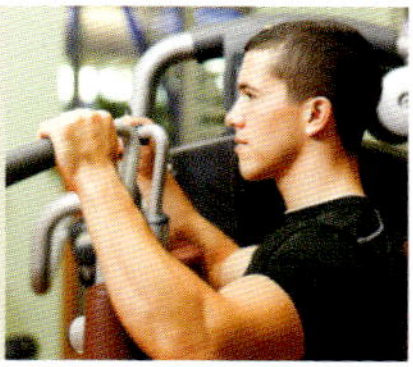

regelmäßig
on a regular basis, regularly

Ich mache regelmäßig Sport.
I play sports on a regular basis.

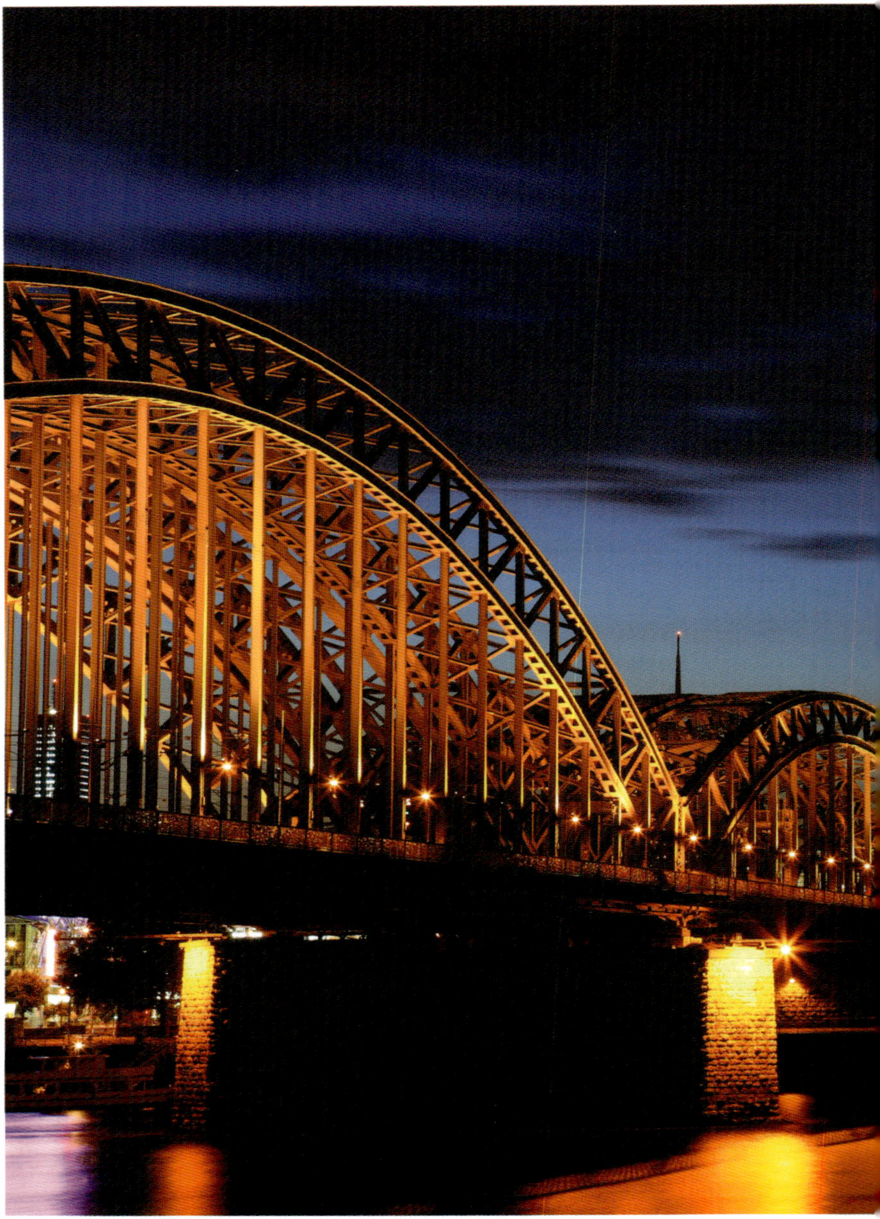

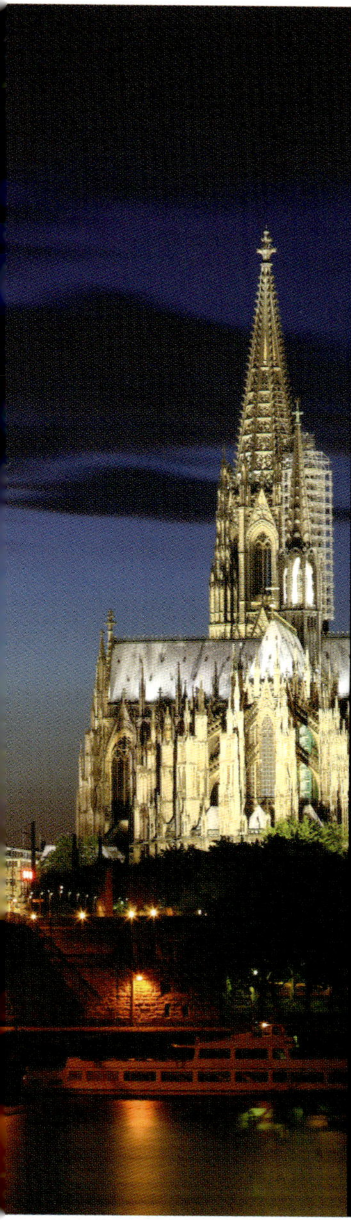

4

Lesson 1: Sightseeing

- » How to say "next to," "behind," "in front of," and "in."
- » How to say where a building is: ***Das Rathaus ist neben dem Bahnhof*.**
- » How to ask the way.
- » Vocabulary for important sights / buildings in a city.

Lesson 2: At the bus stop

- » How to say "I give the book to the man."
- » How to say me, you, him, her, etc.
- » More vocabulary for a city.
- » How to talk about bus schedules / tickets.

Collins | Livemocha™

UNIT 4 › LESSON 1

Sightseeing

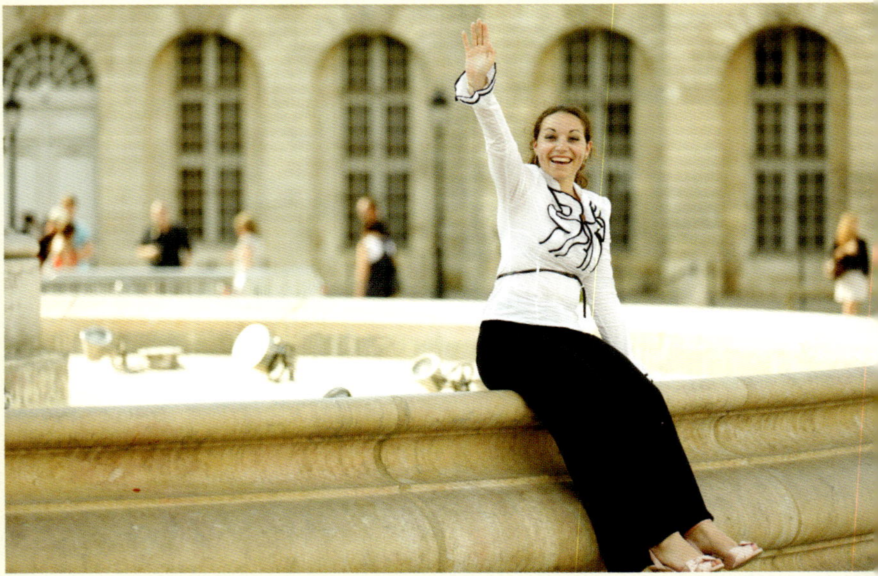

Culture note

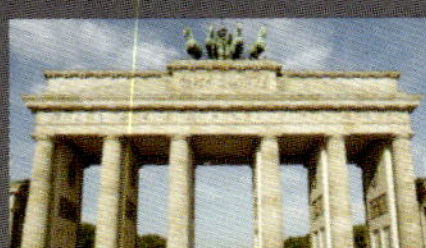

What is the most famous sight in Germany? There are many historic castles and cities worth seeing. But the Brandenburg Gate is Germany's national symbol. When Berlin was divided in two, the Brandenburg Gate stood between East and West Berlin. It was built in 1791 and was a symbol of peace. After the wall fell in 1989, the gate became the symbol of Germany's reunification.

Video Dialog

Matthias suggests to Nina that they go on a sightseeing tour in the town center: there is a lot to see!

Active German: Level 2 > *Unit 4* > *Lesson 1* > *Video dialog*

Matthias: *Möchtest du eine Stadttour machen?*

Nina: *Mit dem Bus?*

Matthias: *Nein, wir können zu Fuß gehen.*

Nina: *OK, gerne. Also, wo beginnt die Stadttour?*

Matthias: *Im Zentrum, gleich hinter dem Rathaus. Wir können erst zum Marktplatz gehen.*

Nina: *Wo ist das?*

Matthias: *Das ist neben dem Bahnhof.*

Nina: *Aha. Und was gibt es noch für Sehenswürdigkeiten in Pulheim?*

Matthias: *Neben dem Marktplatz ist auch gleich der Stadtgarten. Wir können viel besichtigen!*

Nina: *Gibt es auch nette Cafés?*

Matthias: *Ja, auf dem Marktplatz ist ein Café.*

Matthias: Would you like to go on a sightseeing tour?
Nina: By bus?
Matthias: No, we can walk.
Nina: Sure. So, where does the tour start?

Matthias:	Downtown, right behind the city hall. We can go to the market square first.
Nina:	Where is that?
Matthias:	That's next to the train station.
Nina:	I see. And what other sights are there in Pulheim?
Matthias:	Next to the market square there is also a park. There is a lot to see!
Nina:	Are there nice cafés, too?
Matthias:	Yes, there's a café in the market square.

Grammar

Active German: Level 2 > *Unit 4* > *Lesson 1* > *Grammar*

1 › Where is it?

In order to describe where something is, you need prepositions. A preposition links the words of a sentence and shows the relationships between those words. The relationships include direction, place, and time.

In the video Matthias says:

> *Der Marktplatz ist hinter dem Bahnhof.*
> The market square is behind the train station.

hinter (behind) is one of these prepositions.

> *Mein Büro ist hinter dem Supermarkt.*
> My office is behind the supermarket.

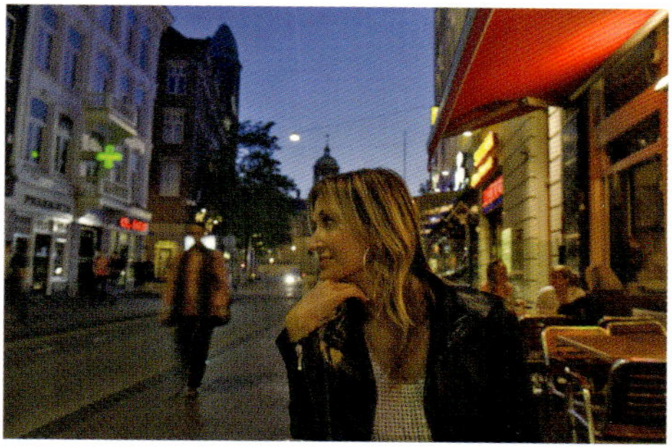

Some other important prepositions are:

neben next to

Der Mann steht neben dem Auto.
The man is standing next to the car.

auf on

Die Zeitung liegt auf dem Tisch.
The newspaper is lying on the table.

vor in front of

Ich bin vor dem Cafè.
I'm in front of the cafè.

2 › Some prepositions

In our example we use these prepositions (*hinter*, *neben*, *auf*, and *vor*) to indicate location and to answer the question of where (*wo?*) something is. The nouns which follow the prepositions require a special article. These are articles in the dative. The dative is a case which plays different roles in the German language. Here we use the dative to designate a location.

Wo ist der Supermarkt? Der Supermarkt ist neben dem Bahnhof.
Where is the supermarket? The supermarket is next to the train station.

3 › **Some prepositions**

Let's have a look at the articles in the dative case:

masculine:

der in the dative case is *dem*

der Bahnhof → neben dem Bahnhof
next to the train station

feminine:

die in the dative case is *der*

die Kathedrale → hinter der Kathedrale
behind the cathedral

neuter:

das in the dative case is *dem*

das Auto → neben dem Auto
next to the car

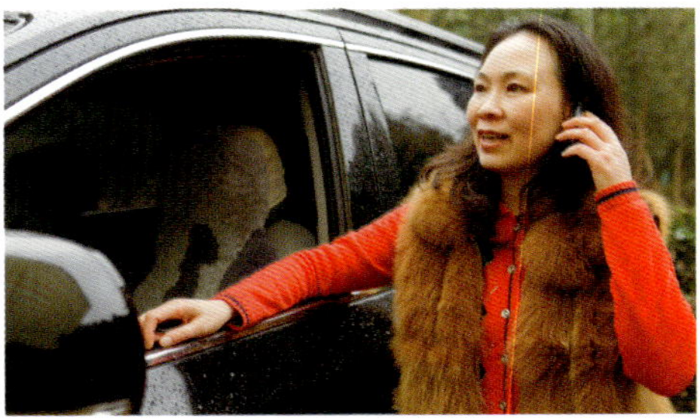

4 › Some prepositions

As you can see the dative article follows the preposition.

Let's consider possible answers to the question:

Wo ist das Glas? Where is the glass?

masculine: *Das Glas ist neben dem Computer.*
The glass is next to the computer.

feminine: *Das Glas ist neben der Mikrowelle.*
The glass is next to the microwave.

neuter: *Das Glas ist neben dem Buch.*
The glass is next to the book.

Note that the article which follows the preposition *neben* is in the dative.

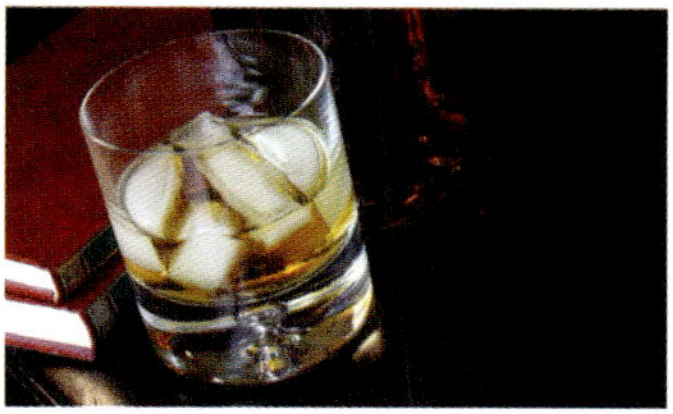

5 › In the center

Let's have a look at how the preposition *in* works to indicate location. When used like this it is followed by the dative case.

In merges with the masculine and neuter article *dem* to become *im*.

masculine: *Wo ist die Tasse? Die Tasse ist im Schrank.*
Where is the cup? The cup is in the cupboard.

neuter: *Wo ist das Büro? Es ist im Zentrum.*
Where is the office? It is downtown.

The feminine article is different.

feminine: ***Wo ist Matthias? Er ist in der Küche.***
Where is Matthias? He is in the kitchen.

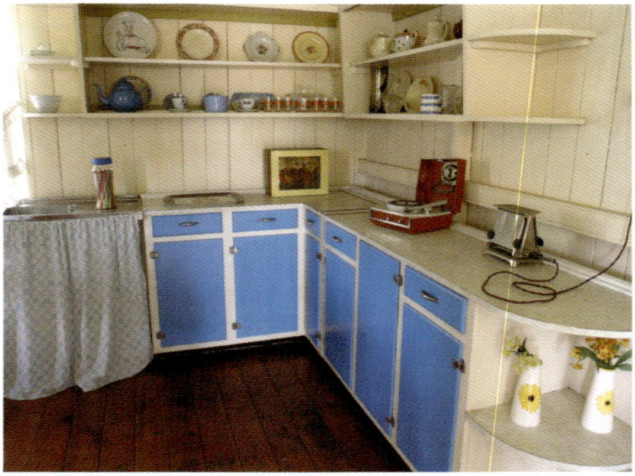

6 › ## Where to?

It is very important to note that in German there is a difference between saying **where** and **where to.**

We have already had a look at the questions:

Wohin gehst du? Ich gehe ins Kino.
Where are you going to? I'm going to the movies.
Wohin gehst du? Ich gehe in die Küche.
Where are you going to? I'm going to the kitchen.
Wohin gehst du? Ich gehe in den Supermarkt.
Where are you going to? I'm going to the supermarket.

In these sentences the articles work in a different way, using the accusative case.

The difference is between movement and location:

Wohin gehst du? Ich gehe in den Supermarkt.
Where are you going to? I'm going to the supermarket.
(This expresses movement.)

Wo bist du? Ich bin im Supermarkt.
Where are you? I'm in the supermarket.
(This expresses location.)

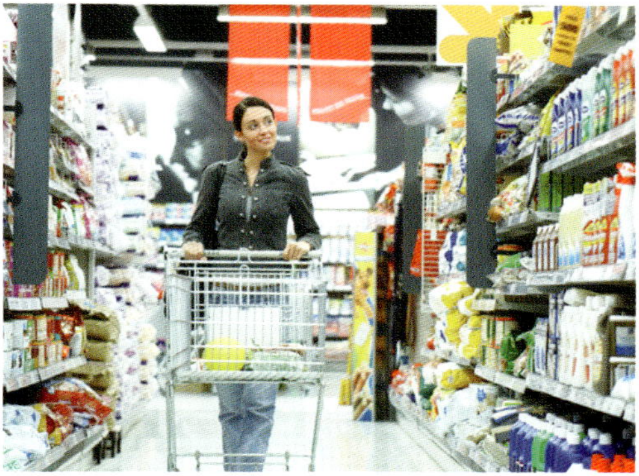

Culture note

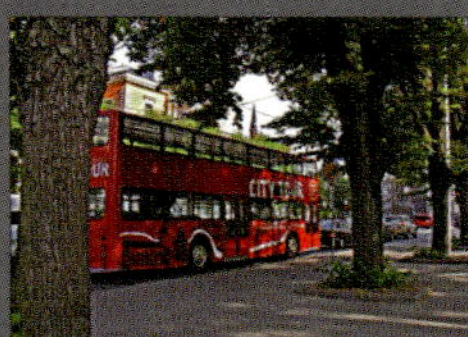

In many cities you can take a sightseeing tour in a double-decker bus. They look different in every city. The guide is always multilingual. In some cities individual tours are possible. Nowadays, it is more and more common to have pedicabs as well. This is actually quite popular since Germans love their bikes. It's possible to rent bikes for a day as well, pick them up at a train station, and leave them at any of a number of designated areas in the city.

Vocabulary

Active German: Level 2 > Unit 4 > Lesson 1 > Vocabulary

Sightseeing

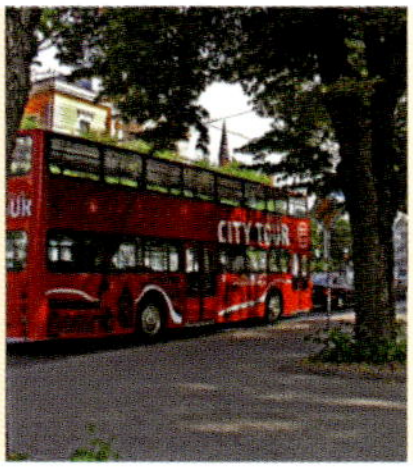

die Stadttour / Stadttouren
sightseeing tour

Morgen machen wir eine Stadttour.
Tomorrow we are going on a sightseeing tour.

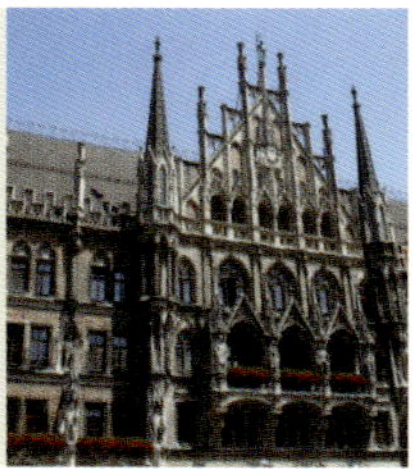

das Rathaus / Rathäuser
city hall, town hall

Das Rathaus ist im Zentrum.
The city hall is in the center (of town).

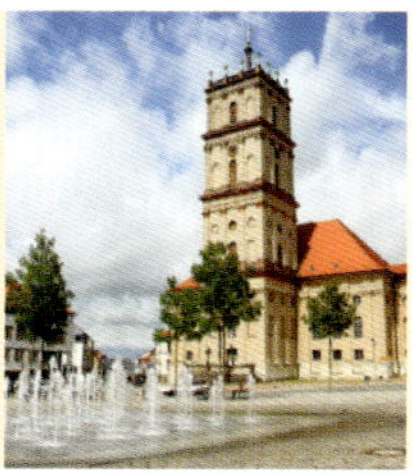

der Marktplatz / Marktplätze
market square

Der Marktplatz ist das Zentrum von Pulheim.
The market square is the center of Pulheim.

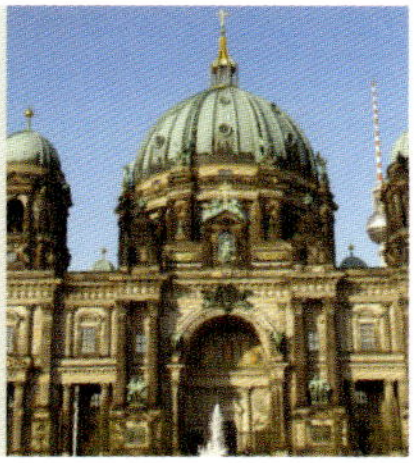

die Sehenswürdigkeit / Sehenswürdigkeiten
sight

Es gibt viele Sehenswürdigkeiten in Berlin.
There are many sights in Berlin.

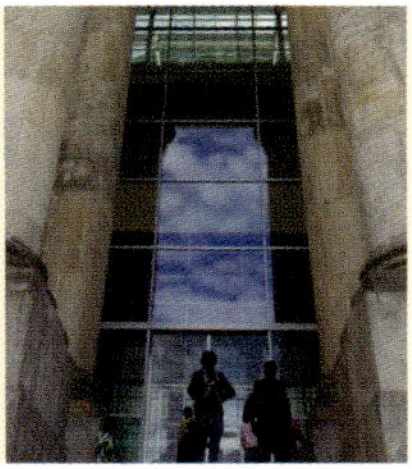

besichtigen
to see / to visit

Möchten Sie die Stadt besichtigen?
Do you want to see the city?

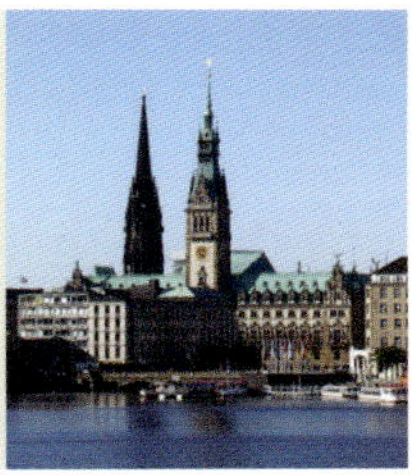

das Zentrum / Zentren
center

Das Zentrum von Hamburg ist sehr groß.
The center of Hamburg is very big.

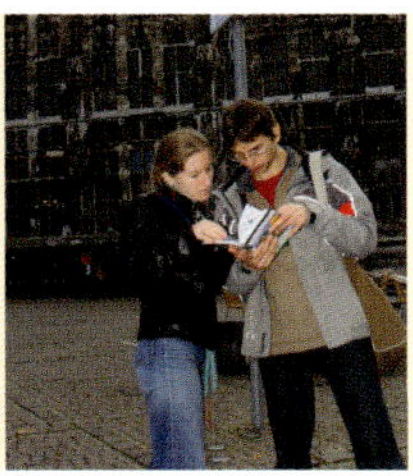

der Reiseführer / Reiseführer
travel guide

Hast du einen Reiseführer für Deutschland?
Do you have a travel guide for Germany?

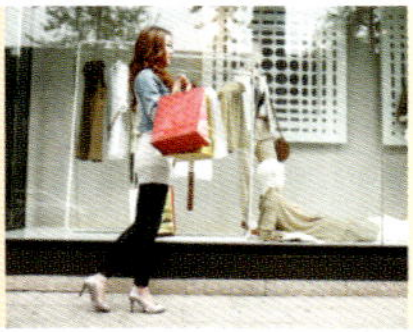

das Geschäft / Geschäfte
store

Hier gibt es schöne Geschäfte.
There are some nice stores here.

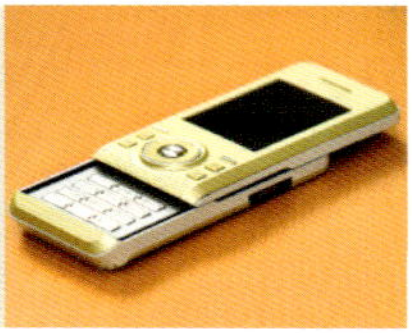

liegen
to lie, to be situated

Wo liegt das Handy?
Where is the cell phone?

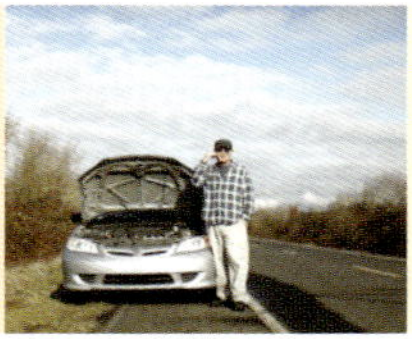

stehen
to stand

Der Mann steht vor dem Auto.
The man is standing in front of the car.

UNIT 4 › LESSON 2

At the bus stop

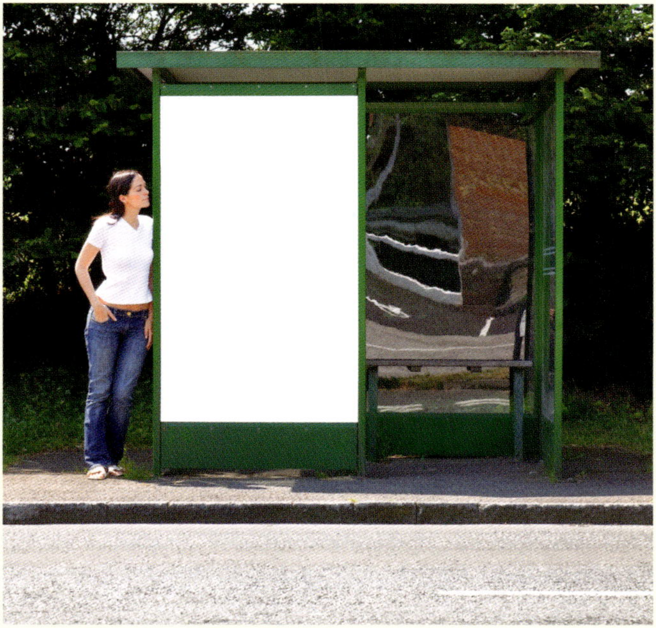

Culture note

The heritage of the Middle Ages is very well-preserved in many German cities. In Pulheim, you can see an abbey that was built in 1024. After a long and complex restoration, the abbey now displays Roman paintings alongside baroque architecture.

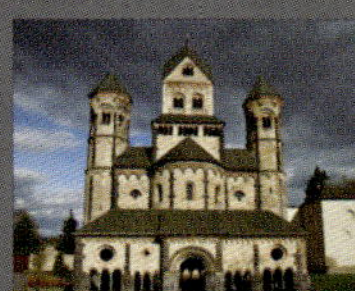

Video Dialog

Matthias and Nina set off on their sightseeing trip.

Active German: Level 2 > *Unit 4* > *Lesson 2* > *Video dialog*

Nina:	*Warst du schon in der Kirche?*
Matthias:	*Ja, die zeige ich dir morgen. Jetzt fahren wir zur Abtei.*
Nina:	*Hast du mein Ticket?*
Matthias:	*Ja, ich gebe es dir. Das ist ein Tagesticket.*
Nina:	*Welchen Bus nehmen wir?*
Matthias:	*Wir nehmen die Linie 980.*
Nina:	*Wann kommt denn der Bus?*
Matthias:	*In 5 oder 10 Minuten.*
Nina:	*Dann habe ich noch Zeit einen Kaffee zu holen. Möchtest du einen Kaffee? Ich bringe ihn dir.*
Matthias:	*Aber der Bus kommt gleich.*

Nina:	Have you been in the church yet?
Matthias:	Yes, I'll show you that tomorrow. Now we're going to the abbey.
Nina:	Have you got my ticket?
Matthias:	Yes, I'll give it to you. It's a day ticket.
Nina:	Which bus are we getting?
Matthias:	We're getting the 980.
Nina:	When's the bus coming?

Matthias:	In 5 or 10 minutes.
Nina:	Then I've still got time to get a coffee. Would you like a coffee? I'll bring it to you.
Matthias:	But the bus is coming right now.

Grammar

Active German: Level 2 > *Unit 4* > *Lesson 2* > *Grammar*

1 › I give it to him

Consider the following sentence.

Ich trinke einen Kaffee.
I drink a coffee.

What are the roles of the elements in this sentence? *Ich* is the subject and *einen Kaffee* is the object.

Ich gebe ***dem Mann*** *einen Kaffee.*
I give a coffee **to the man.**

The receiver of what happens in the sentence – giving coffee – is the man. This receiver role (indirect object) is expressed using the dative case in German. The receiver is normally a person. You have to ask yourself "for whom" or "to whom" the action happens.

In the video dialog Matthias has a ticket and gives it to Nina.

Ich gebe ***Nina*** *das Ticket.*
I give the ticket **to Nina**.

Nina is the receiver of the ticket.

2 › I give it to him

The verb determines what kind of object we need.

The verb *trinken* (to drink) requires one object: the thing that you are drinking (direct object).

Ich trinke einen Kaffee.
I drink a coffee.

The verb *geben* (to give) requires two objects: the thing you are giving (direct object) and the person you are giving that thing to (indirect object).

Ich gebe es ihm.
I give it to him.

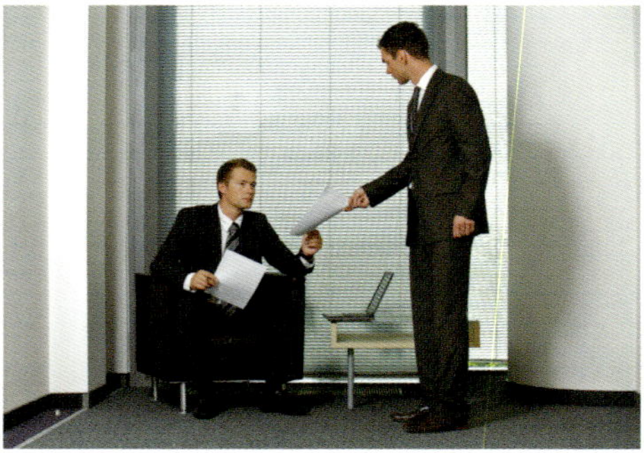

3 › Articles

A considerable number of verbs in German require the dative case. You already have seen in Lesson 1 how the dative case is used with certain prepositions.

Let's have a look now how it works for verbs. Note that the articles take the same form as they did with the prepositions.

masculine: *dem* and *einem*
feminine: *der* and *einer*
neuter: *dem* and *einem*

*Das Rathaus ist **neben dem** Bahnhof.*
The city hall is **next to** the train station.
*Ich gebe **dem Mann** den Kaffee.*
I give the coffee **to the man.**

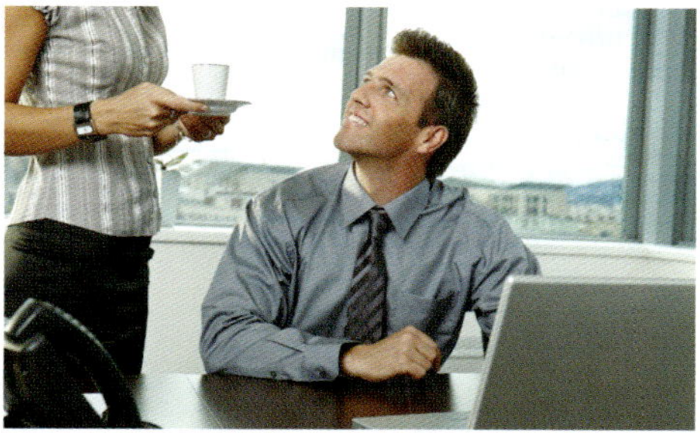

4 › I show it to her

Here are some more examples:

zeigen (to show something to someone) works the same way:

*Ich zeige **der Frau** das Rathaus.*
I show the town hall **to the woman**.
*Ich zeige **dem Mann** das Rathaus.*
I show the town hall **to the man**.

bringen (to bring)

Ich bringe ***der Frau*** *das Glas.*
I bring the glass **to the woman**.
Ich bringe ***dem Kind*** *die Schokolade.*
I bring the chocolate **to the child**.

Other verbs which follow the same pattern are *schicken* (to send) and *erklären* (to explain).

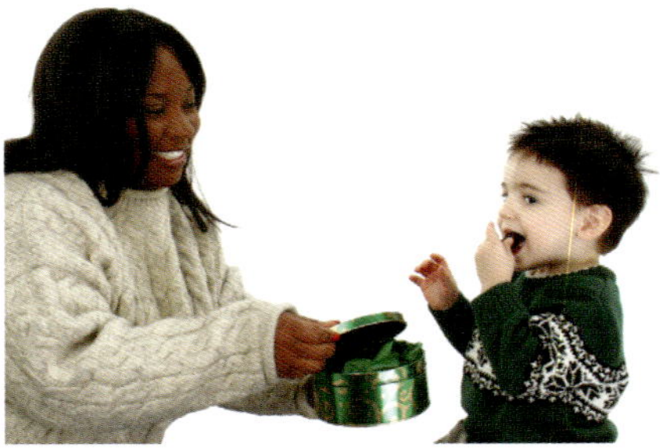

5 › Me, you, and him

In many cases you don't actually use the nouns for the receiver, but instead you use pronouns such as "me," "you," and "him," etc. These are the pronouns in the dative case:

ich (I)	*mir* (to me)
du (you)	*dir* (to you)
er (he)	*ihm* (to him)
sie (she)	*ihr* (to her)
wir (we)	*uns* (to us)
ihr (you)	*euch* (to you)
sie (they)	*ihnen* (to them)
Sie (you)	*Ihnen* (to you) (formal)

6 › I give it to her

Here are some examples:

*Ich gebe **der Frau** den Kaffee.*
I give **the woman** the coffee.

*Ich gebe **ihr** den Kaffee.*
I give **her** the coffee.

*Ich zeige **dem Mann** das Rathaus.*
I show **the man** the city hall.

*Ich zeige **ihm** das Rathaus.*
I show **him** the town hall.

*Ich bringe **Herrn Buschel** einen Kaffee.*
I bring **Mr. Buschel** a coffee.

*Ich bringe **Ihnen** einen Kaffee.*
I bring **you** a coffee.

*Ich kann **dir** einen Kaffee bringen.*
I can bring **you** a coffee.

abc Vocabulary

Active German: Level 2 > *Unit 4* > *Lesson 2* > *Vocabulary*

About the city

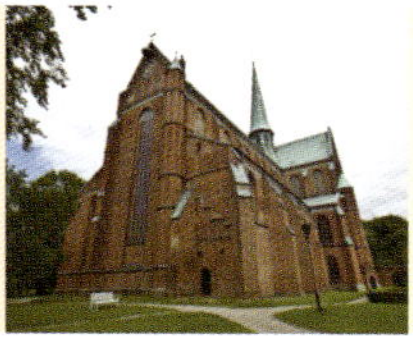

die Kirche / Kirchen
church

Die Kirche ist sehr alt.
The church is very old.

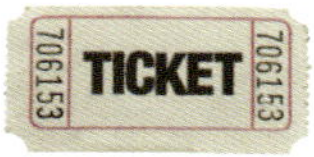

das Ticket / Tickets
ticket

Entschuldigung, wo kann ich hier Tickets kaufen?
Excuse me, where can I buy tickets around here?

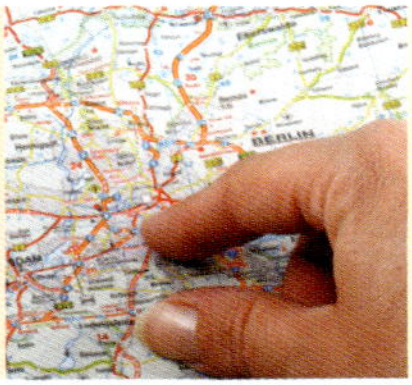

die Linie / Linien
line / route

Mit der Linie 101 kann man durch Berlin fahren.
On route 101 you can ride through Berlin.

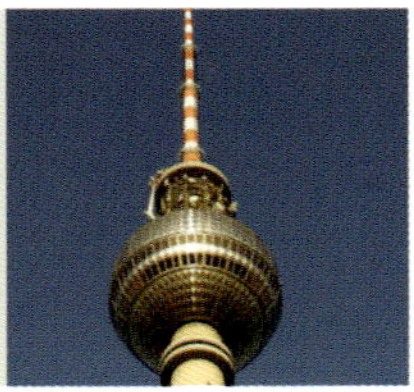

berühmt
famous

Der Alexanderplatz ist sehr berühmt.
The Alexanderplatz is very famous.

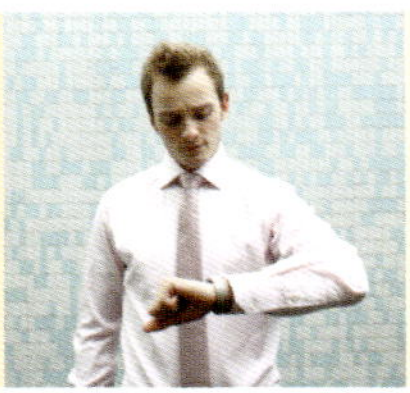

gleich
shortly / in a moment

Der Bus kommt gleich.
The bus is coming in a moment.

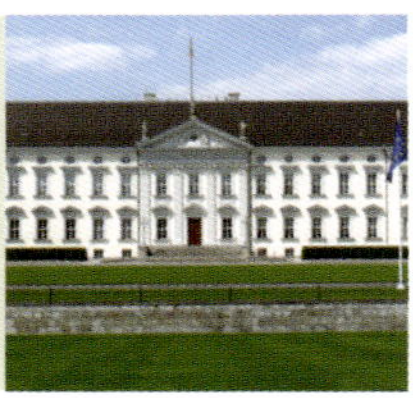

das Schloss / Schlösser
castle

Im Schloss „Bellevue" wohnt der Präsident.
The president lives in Bellevue castle.

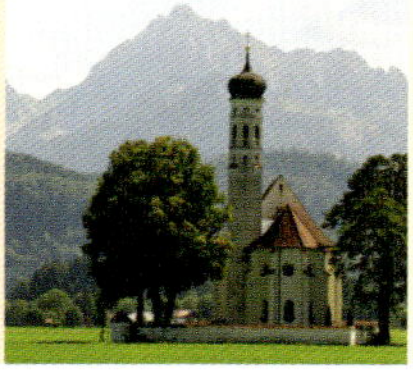

rechts
right

Die Kirche ist rechts.
The church is to the right.

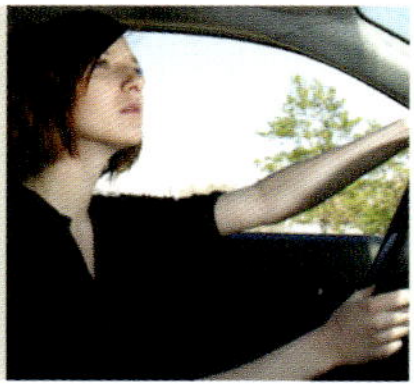

links
left

Muss ich rechts oder links fahren?
Do I have to drive on the right or left?

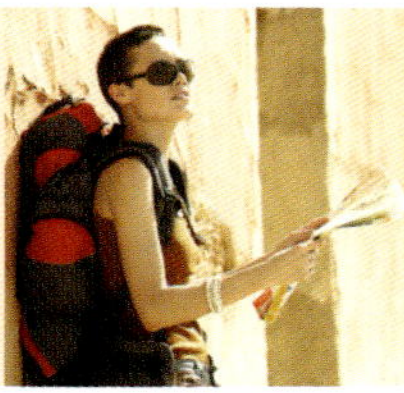

der Tourist / Touristen
tourist

Ich bin Tourist hier.
I'm a tourist here.

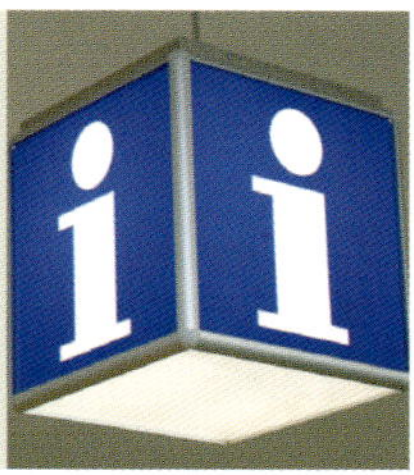

die Touristeninformation / Touristeninformationen
tourist information office

Entschuldigung, wo ist die Touristeninformation hier?
Excuse me, where is the tourist information office here?

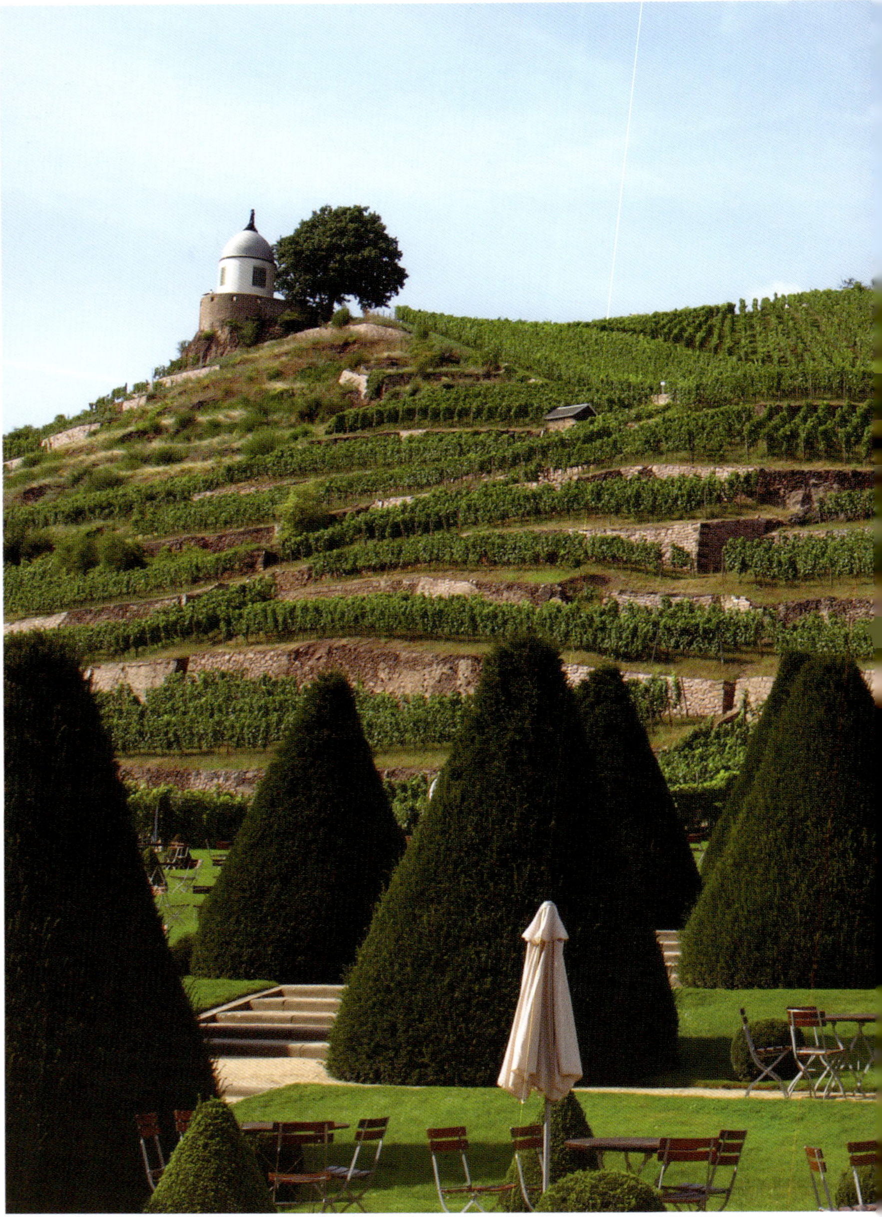

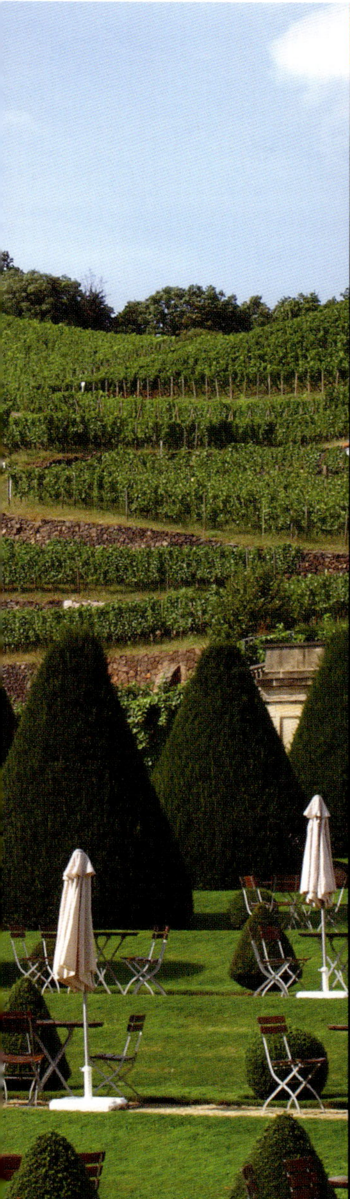

5

Lesson 1: In a park 1

- How to talk about past events, saying what you have done or what happened.
- How to use verbs such as "make," "buy," "see," etc. in the past.
- How to refer to the past.
- Vocabulary for past events and leisure time activities.

Lesson 2: In a park 2

- How to form important verbs in the past.
- How to say sentences such as "I have gone home": ***Ich bin nach Hause gegangen.***
- Some useful words for the city and leisure time.

Collins | Livemocha™

UNIT 5 › LESSON 1

In a park 1

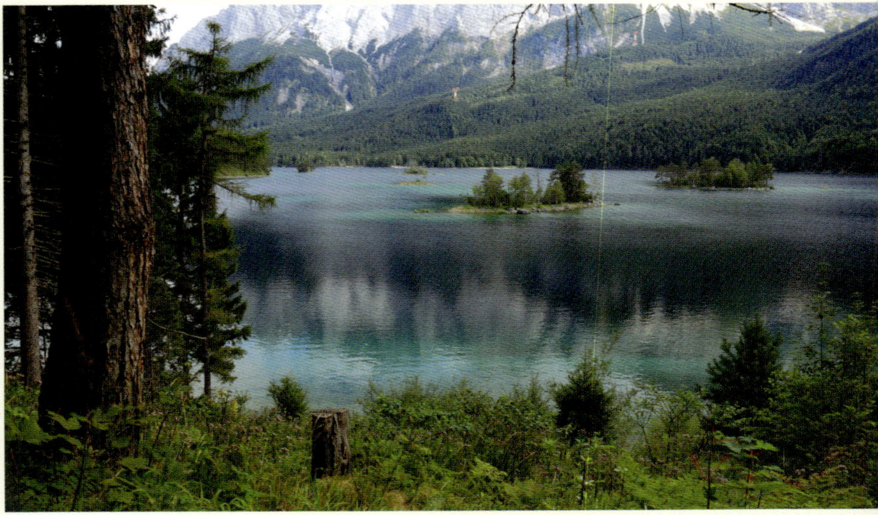

Culture note

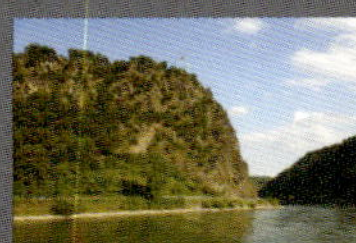

The River Rhine (*Rhein*) is the longest river in Germany and one of the longest in Europe. It runs for over 1,320 kilometers (820 miles) and flows through six countries. From its source in the Swiss Alps it flows through Switzerland, Liechtenstein, Austria, Germany, France, and the Netherlands. In Rotterdam it flows into the North Sea. The river is not just famous for its length and importance but also for its legends. According to one legend, the Lorelei, a beautiful maiden, used to sit on a rock by the river and lure sailors to their deaths with her hypnotic singing.

Video Dialog

Back in Matthias' apartment, Lara, Nina, and Matthias tell each other about their last few weeks.

Active German: Level 2 > *Unit 5* > *Lesson 1* > *Video dialog*

Matthias:	*Was hast du in den letzten Wochen gemacht?*
Nina:	*Ich habe viel gearbeitet.*
Matthias:	*Du hast nur gearbeitet?*
Nina:	*Nein, am Wochenende habe ich mit Tom einen Ausflug gemacht.*
Lara:	*Oh, wie schön. Ich war am Wochenende am Rhein und habe den ganzen Tag gelesen.*
Matthias:	*Ich habe neue Möbel bei Ikea gekauft und …*
Lara:	*Und wir haben zusammen zu Abend gegessen. Italienisch. Das Restaurant war toll.*
Matthias:	*Stimmt. Nina und ich haben gestern zusammen die ganze Stadt besichtigt.*
Lara:	*Das klingt gut.*

Matthias:	What have you been doing in the last few weeks?
Nina:	I've been working a lot.
Matthias:	You've only been working?
Nina:	No, this weekend I went on an outing with Tom.
Lara:	Oh, how nice. I was by the Rhine this weekend and read all day long.

Matthias: I bought new furniture at Ikea and...
Lara: And we had dinner together. Italian. The restaurant was great.
Matthias: True. Nina and I went on a sightseeing trip together yesterday.
Lara: That sounds good.

Grammar

Active German: Level 2 > Unit 5 > Lesson 1 > Grammar

1 › Past events

In the video dialog Matthias, Lara, and Nina are telling each other what they have been doing over the last weeks. They are talking about past events.

Ich habe viel gearbeitet.
I have been working a lot.

You use the past tense to say what you have done or what has happened.

With most verbs, spoken German uses the perfect tense (e.g. "I have been working") to talk about events in the past. You use it to say what you have done or what has happened.

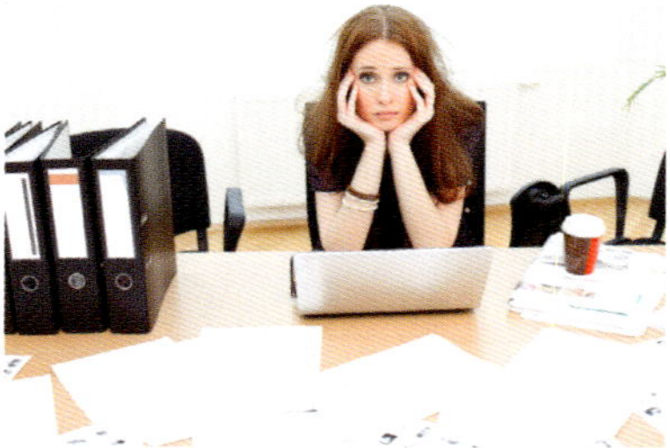

2 › The perfect tense

The perfect tense is always made up of two words.

Ich habe Kaffee gemacht. I have made coffee.

You can see that we need the verb *haben* in order to make this form. When making the perfect tense, you will always use either *haben* or *sein*. We will cover *sein* in Lesson 2.

Haben follows its normal pattern according to the person speaking.

Ich habe nichts gemacht.	I haven't done anything.
Du hast Kaffee gemacht.	You have made coffee.
Er / sie hat Suppe gemacht.	He / she has made soup.
Wir haben einen Ausflug gemacht.	We went on an outing.
Ihr habt Tee gemacht.	You have made tea.
Sie / sie haben eine Stadttour gemacht.	You / they went on a sightseeing tour.

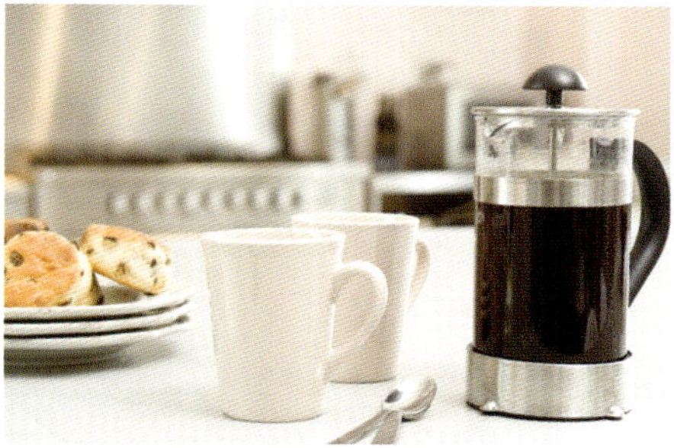

3 › The perfect tense

Let's have a look at the second part of the perfect tense, in the previous example: *Ich habe Kaffee gemacht.*

The verb *machen*:
1. Cut off the ending *-en*: *mach-*
2. Add *ge-* at the beginning and *-t* at the end: ***ge**mach**t***

Ich habe gemacht.
I have made.

Other verbs that work the same are:

kaufen → gekauft
spielen → gespielt

and with a small difference *arbeiten* → ***ge**arbeit**et***

The second part of the verb almost always starts with *ge-*.

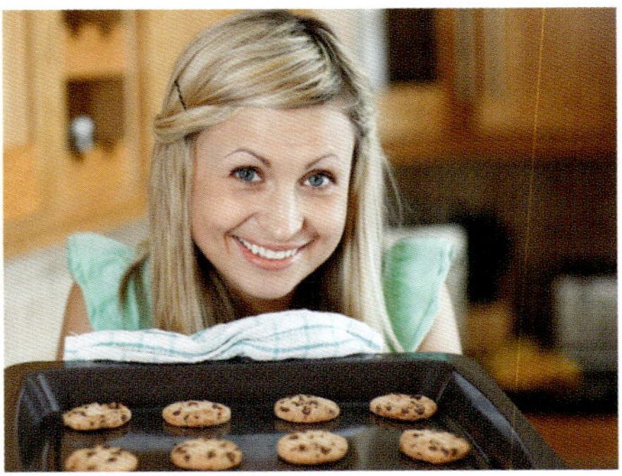

4 › Have you bought it?

Let's have a look at how we construct sentences with the perfect tense.

The verb *haben* is in the second position in the sentence and comes after the subject (*Ich* or *Du*). The second part of the form always goes to the end of a sentence.

Ich habe Möbel gekauft.
I've bought furniture.

Du hast Fußball gespielt.
You've played soccer.

When the sentence is a question, *haben* precedes the subject (*du*):

Wo hast du die Möbel gekauft?
Where did you buy the furniture?

Hast du Fußball gespielt?
Did you play soccer?

You can add a time indication as well. Again, *haben* comes before the subject (*ich*).

Gestern habe ich Fußball gespielt.
Yesterday I played soccer.

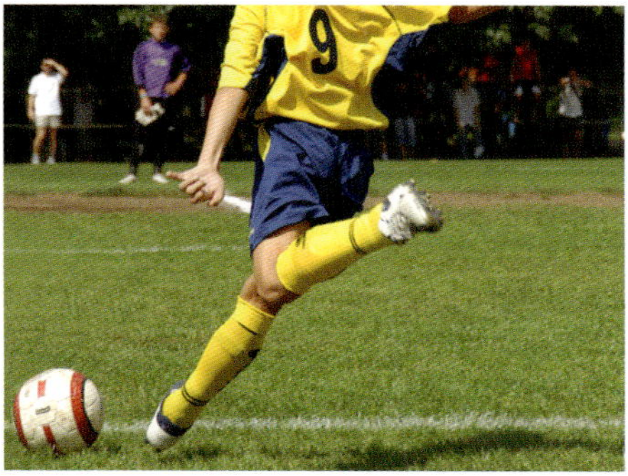

5 › I've seen it!

The second part of the perfect tense form of *machen*, *kaufen*, and *spielen* ends in *-t* (*gemacht*, *gekauft*, *gespielt*). Many verbs work the same way.

Some verbs such as *sehen* (to see) have a perfect tense form that ends in *-n* (*gesehen*).

> *Ich habe einen Film gesehen.*
> I've seen a movie / I've watched a movie.
>
> *Ich habe viel gelesen.*
> I have read a lot.

We will learn more forms in this unit.

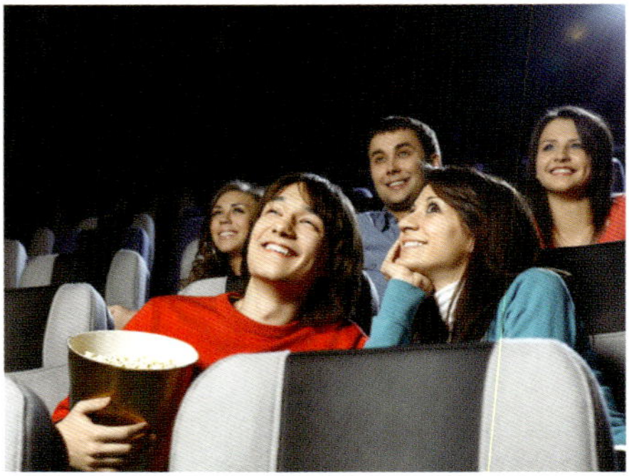

6 › I was

In an earlier unit we had a look at *sein*. Note that we can always use *Ich war* (I was) to express past events.

> *Ich war in Berlin.* I was in Berlin.

Culture note

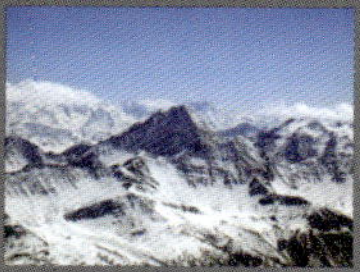

The Alps are the highest mountain range in the middle of Europe. They run from France in the west to Austria and Slovenia in the east. Standing on Mont Blanc (4,810 m, 15,781 ft), the highest point in the Alps, Goethe said, *"Es sind keine Worte für die Größe und Schöne dieses Anblicks."* (There are no words for the size and the beauty of this view). The Alps offer a wide range of winter sports and are also a challenge for climbers.

Vocabulary

Active German: Level 2 > Unit 5 > Lesson 1 > Vocabulary

Time and times

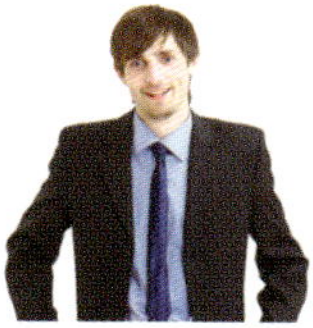

letzte Woche
last week

Letzte Woche habe ich Herrn Buschel gesehen.
Last week I saw Mr. Buschel.

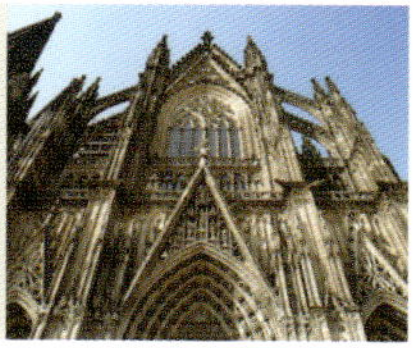

nächste Woche
next week

Nächste Woche fahre ich nach Köln.
Next week I go to Cologne.

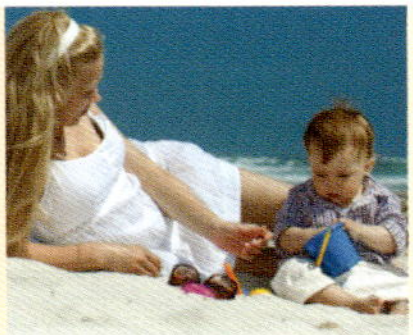

der Urlaub
vacation

Nächste Woche habe ich Urlaub.
Next week I have a vacation.

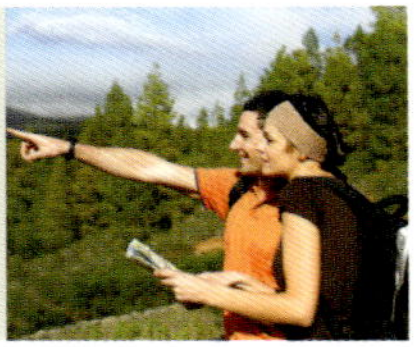

der Ausflug / Ausflüge
outing, excursion

Wir haben einen Ausflug nach Dresden gemacht.
We went on an outing to Dresden.

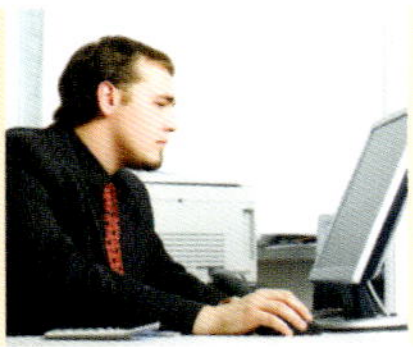

antworten
to reply, to answer

Hast du ihm schon geantwortet?
Have you answered him?

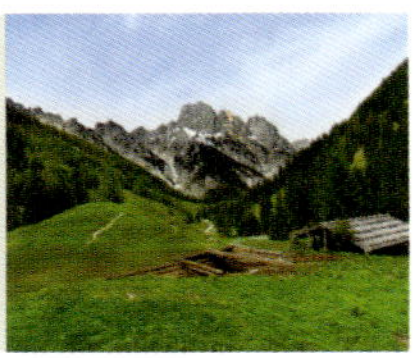

der Berg / Berge
mountain

Ich liebe die Berge.
I love the mountains.

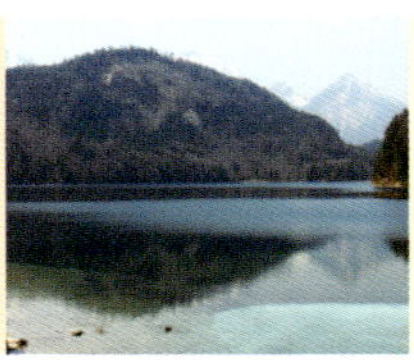

der See / Seen
lake

Ich schwimme im See.
I swim in the lake.

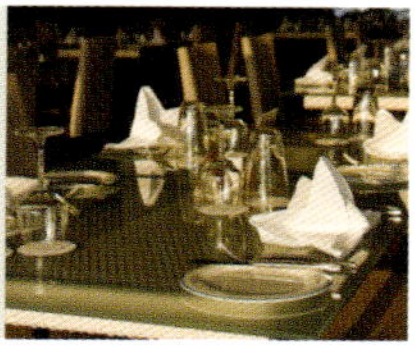

bekannt
well-known

Das Restaurant ist sehr bekannt.
The restaurant is well-known.

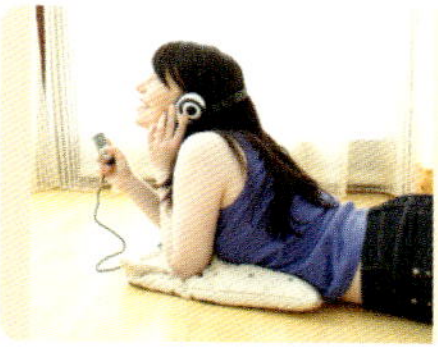

hören
to hear, to listen to

Ich habe viel Musik gehört.
I've listened to a lot of music.

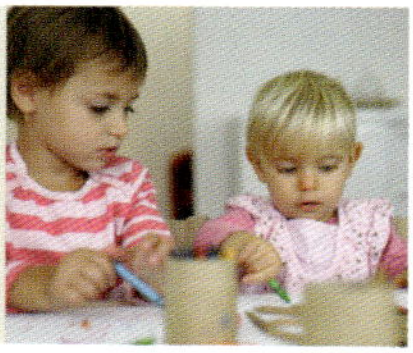

nur
only

Ich habe nur eine Schwester.
I have only one sister.

UNIT 5 › LESSON 2

In a park 2

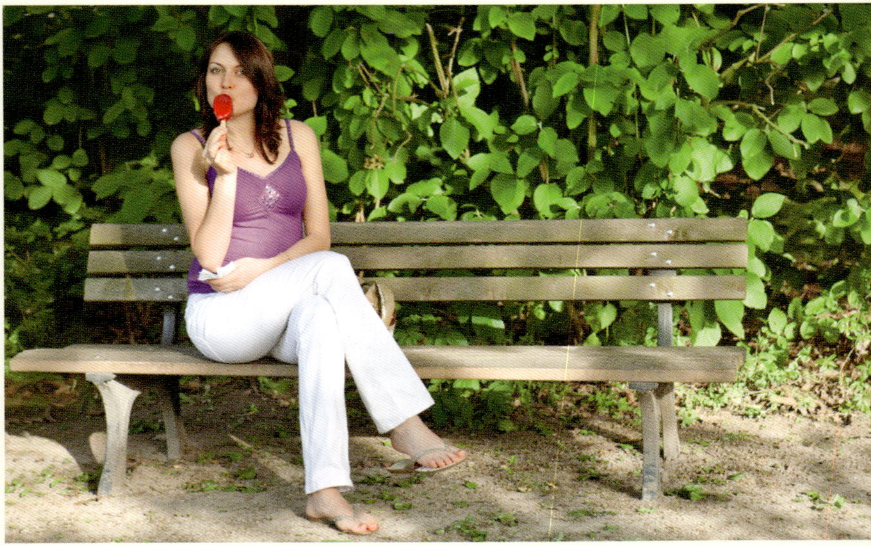

Culture note

Germans, like people of many other nations, love ice cream. Ice cream shops are very common (in German: *Eiscafé* or *Eisdiele*). The ice cream tradition is largely influenced by the Italian ice cream style. A German specialty, invented by an Italian in Germany, is the so-called "*Spaghettieis*" (spaghetti ice cream). Vanilla ice cream is squeezed out into a bowl in long spaghetti-like threads. The strawberry sauce looks like tomato sauce and coconut or white chocolate replaces the Parmesan cheese.

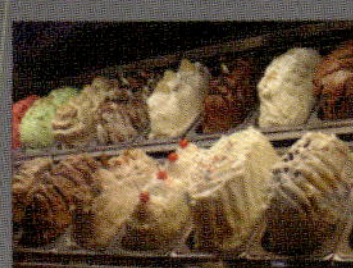

Video Dialog

Lara makes some suggestions to Nina on how to spend her time in Pulheim.

Active German: Level 2 > *Unit 5* > *Lesson 2* > *Video dialog*

Lara:	*Seid ihr schon nach Köln gefahren?*
Matthias:	*Nein, noch nicht. Morgen fahren wir nach Köln.*
Lara:	*Köln ist eine tolle Stadt. Mit meiner Familie war ich beim Kölner Dom. Das lohnt sich!*
Nina:	*Oh ja, das machen wir.*
Lara:	*Hast du schon unseren Chef getroffen?*
Nina:	*Ja, Herrn Baumann. Wir sind mit ihm in ein Café gegangen.*
Lara:	*Dann habt ihr ja schon viel gemacht.*
Nina:	*Ja, ich kenne Pulheim jetzt gut!*
Matthias:	*Aber es gibt noch viel mehr. Kommt, wir gehen Eis essen.*

Lara:	Have you already been to Cologne?
Matthias:	No, not yet. We're going to Cologne tomorrow.
Lara:	Cologne is a great city. I visited the cathedral with my family. It's worth doing!
Nina:	Oh, yes, we'll do that.
Lara:	Have you met our boss already?
Nina:	Yes, Mr. Baumann. We went to a café with him.

Lara:	Then you've already done a lot.
Nina:	Yes, I now know Pulheim well!
Matthias:	But there's still much more. Come on, let's have ice cream.

Grammar

Active German: Level 2 > *Unit 5* > *Lesson 2* > *Grammar*

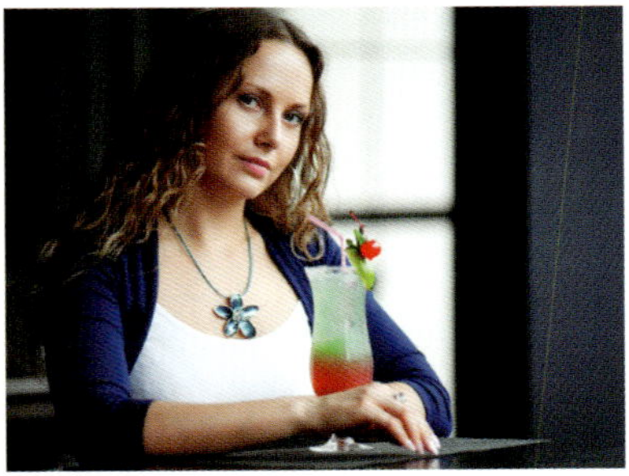

1 › More on verbs in the past

In Lesson 1 we learned how to form the perfect tense with *ge-* and *-t* or *-n*. Some other verbs form the perfect tense by making slight changes to their original spelling. These are some of the important ones:

treffen (to meet) ⟶ *getroffen*

Ich habe meinen Chef getroffen.
I have met my boss.

sprechen (to speak) ⟶ *gesprochen*

Ich habe mit Lara gesprochen.
I have spoken to Lara.

2 › **More on verbs in the past**

Some other useful verbs are:

schreiben (to write) ⟶ *geschrieben*

> *Ich habe ihr eine Email geschrieben.*
> I wrote her an email.

essen (to eat) ⟶ *gegessen*

> *Ich habe im Hotel gegessen.*
> I ate in the hotel.

Add *nicht* to make these sentences negative.

> *Ich habe nicht zu Hause gegessen.*
> I haven't eaten at home.
> *Ich habe ihm nicht geschrieben.*
> I haven't written to him.

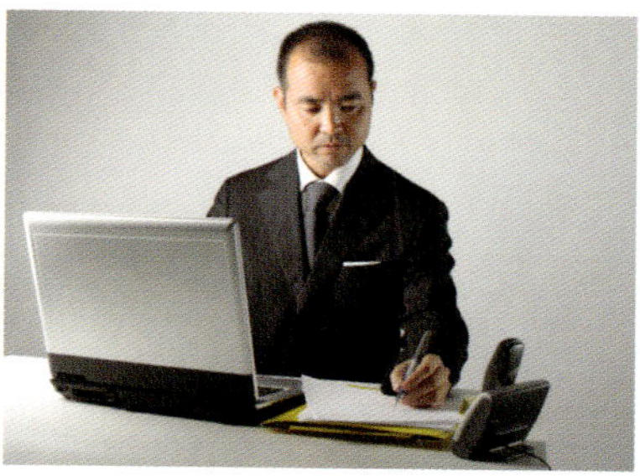

3 › **More on verbs in the past**

Most verbs take *haben* in the perfect tense. However, there are some verbs that use *sein* instead of *haben*. These verbs normally indicate a change or movement of some kind.

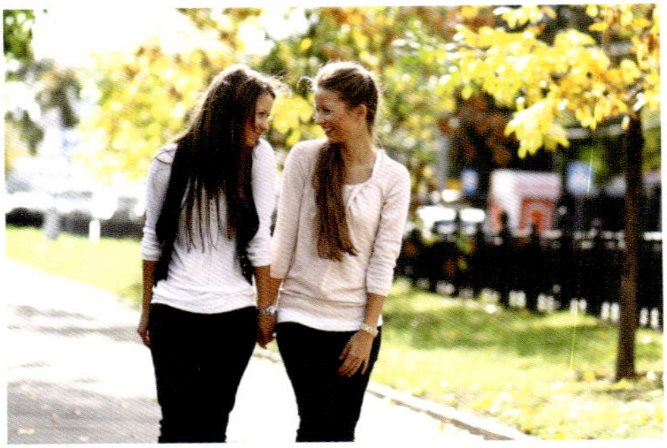

In the video dialog Matthias says: *Wir sind durch die Stadt gelaufen.* We walked around town.

Laufen means "to walk" or "to walk around."

Other examples of verbs that take *sein* in the perfect tense are:

fahren → *gefahren* to drive
gehen → *gegangen* to go / to walk
fliegen → *geflogen* to fly
kommen → *gekommen* to come

4 › I have come, I came

Ich bin gegangen.	I have gone. / I went.
Du bist geflogen.	You have flown. / You flew.
Er / sie ist gefahren.	He / she has driven. / He / she drove.
Wir sind gekommen.	We have come. / We came.
Ihr seid gelaufen.	You have run. / You ran.
Sie / sie sind gegangen.	You / they have gone. / You / they went.

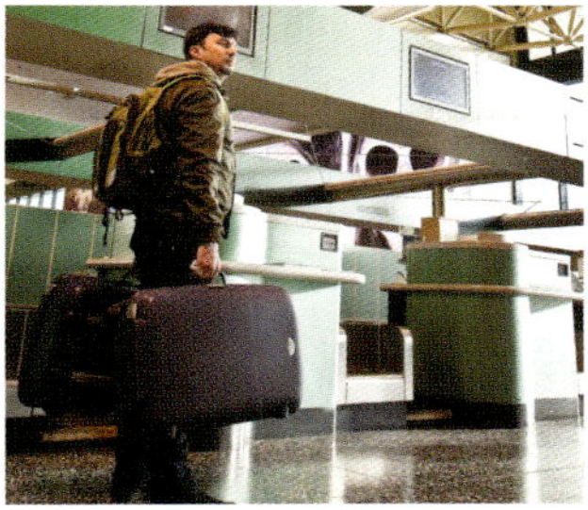

5 › I called you

In an earlier unit we had a look at separable verbs (*Ich kaufe ein*). They maintain their specific characteristics in the present perfect as well.

einkaufen → eingekauft
anrufen → angerufen

Ich habe Sie angerufen.
I called you.

Vocabulary

Active German: Level 2 > Unit 5 > Lesson 2 > Vocabulary

In the city and other useful words

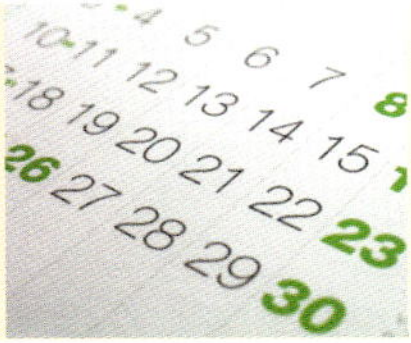

der Plan / Pläne
plan

Hast du einen Plan für das Wochenende?
Do you have a plan for the weekend?

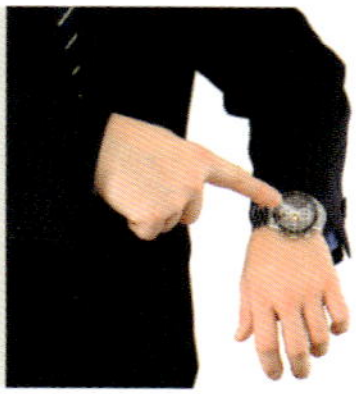

jetzt
now

Wir müssen jetzt gehen.
We have to go now.

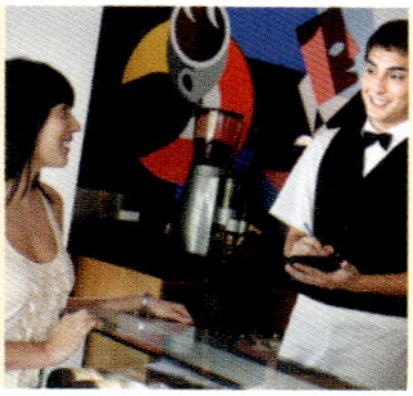

mehr
more

Möchten Sie noch mehr?
Do you want to have more?

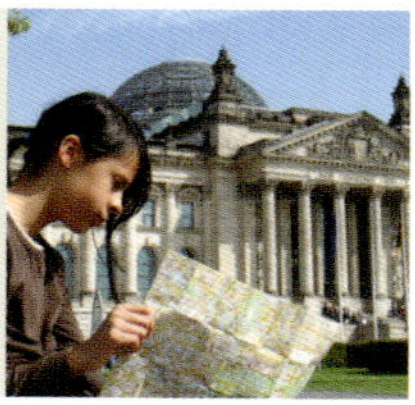

durch die Stadt
around town

Wir sind durch die Stadt gelaufen.
We walked around town.

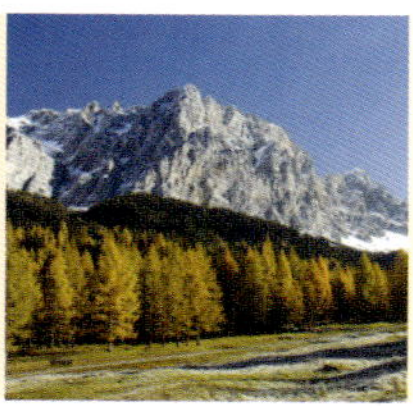

das lohnt sich
it is worth doing

Der Blick von der Zugspitze ist wunderschön. Das lohnt sich.
The view from the Zugspitze is beautiful. It is worth doing.

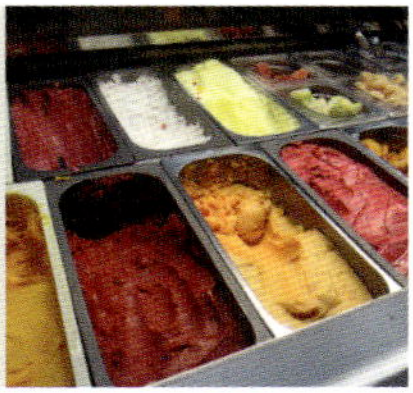

das Eiscafé / Eiscafés
ice cream parlor

Im Eiscafé „Lindner" ist das Eis so lecker.
In the Lindner ice cream parlor the ice cream is really yummy.

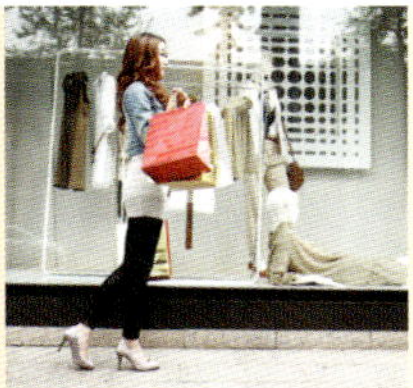

bummeln
to stroll

Wir sind den ganzen Tag durch die Stadt gebummelt.
We strolled around town the whole day.

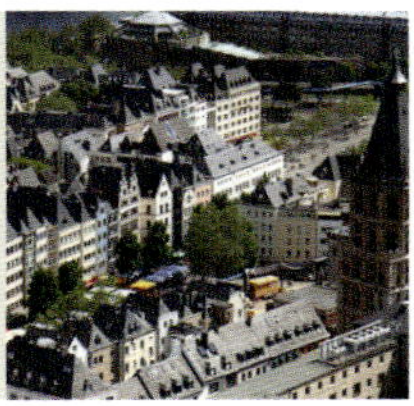

genießen
to enjoy

Ich genieße den Ausblick über die Stadt.
I enjoy the view over the city.

6

Lesson 1: Healthy food 1

- How to make polite requests: ***Würden Sie mir bitte 1 Kilo Kartoffeln geben?***
- How to say what you would like to have: ***Ich hätte gerne ein Stück Kuchen.***
- How to say what else you need or that you don't need anything else.
- Vocabulary for shopping and food.
- How to express weights and measures (liter, kilo etc.).

Lesson 2: Healthy food 2

- How to express suggestions and commands: ***Fahren Sie doch nach Berlin!***
- More on weights and measurements.
- Food shopping vocabulary.
- Useful phrases such as "not at all" or "have fun."

Collins | Livemocha™

UNIT 6 › LESSON 1

Healthy food 1

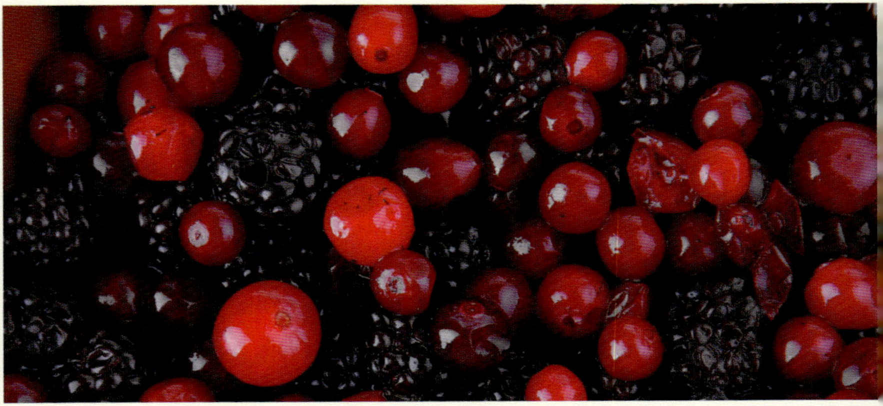

Culture note

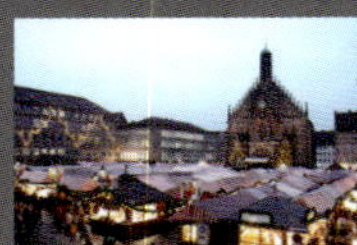

Even though nowadays more and more supermarket chains are established in Germany, many Germans still love their little shops and retail stores. In every town and city you will find open air markets. Normally they are held twice a week and offer a great choice of fresh food. These markets might be a bit more expensive, but it is worth having a look for the variety that is offered. In Hamburg, every Sunday morning there is the so-called *Fischmarkt*. You can buy nearly everything there – from live animals to flowers, vegetables, and fish of course. It starts very early, at 5 a.m., and some people go there to enjoy the atmosphere after a night out. Some early birds will definitely grab a bargain. Later on you will see bananas flying through the air when the people try to get rid of their goods for give-away prices.

Video Dialog

Matthias visits the local grocery store to buy some ingredients for dinner.

Active German: Level 2 > Unit 6 > Lesson 1 > Video dialog

Matthias:	*Guten Tag. Ich hätte gern ein paar Tomaten.*
Verkäuferin:	*Wie viele denn?*
Matthias:	*Ein halbes Kilo, bitte.*
Verkäuferin:	*500 Gramm Tomaten.*
Matthias:	*Würden Sie mir noch einen Salat geben?*
Verkäuferin:	*Natürlich. Einen Salat. Möchten Sie noch etwas?*
Matthias:	*Ah ja, ich hätte gerne noch 100g grüne Oliven, 10 Eier und etwas Käse.*
Verkäuferin:	*Wie viel Käse möchten Sie denn?*
Matthias:	*300 Gramm bitte.*

Matthias:	Hello. I'd like some tomatoes, please.
Salesclerk:	How many?
Matthias:	Half a kilo, please.
Salesclerk:	500 grams of tomatoes.
Matthias:	Could you also give me one head of lettuce?
Salesclerk:	Of course. One head of lettuce. Would you like anything else?
Matthias:	Oh yes, I'd also like 100 grams of green olives, 10 eggs, and some cheese, please.
Salesclerk:	How much cheese would you like?
Matthias:	300 grams, please.

Grammar

Active German: Level 2 > *Unit 6* > *Lesson 1* > *Grammar*

1 › I would like to

In some situations you want to express requests politely. In the video dialog Matthias talks to a salesclerk.

Würden Sie mir noch einen Salat geben?
Would you give me one head of lettuce?

You use *würden* and the basic form of any other verb in combination to express polite requests.

Have a look at the pattern:

ich würde	I would
du würdest	you would
er / sie würde	he / she would
wir würden	we would
ihr würdet	you would
sie / Sie würden	they / you would

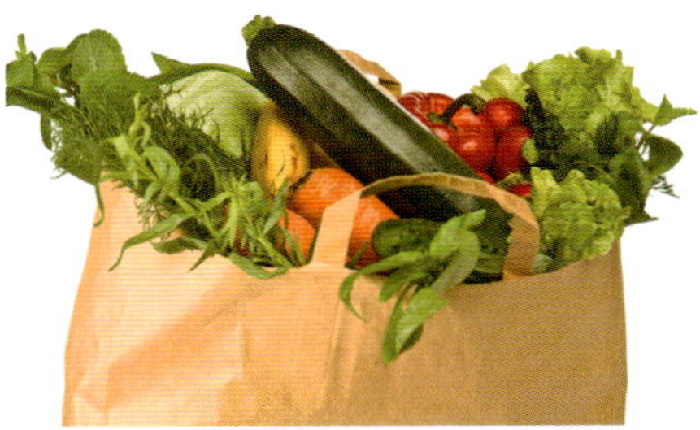

2 › Would you give it to me?

The second part of this form goes at the end of the sentence.

Würdest du bitte kommen?
Would you please come?
Würden Sie mir bitte das Dokument geben?
Would you please give me the document?

You use this form not only to talk to the person serving you in stores and businesses, but also among colleagues.

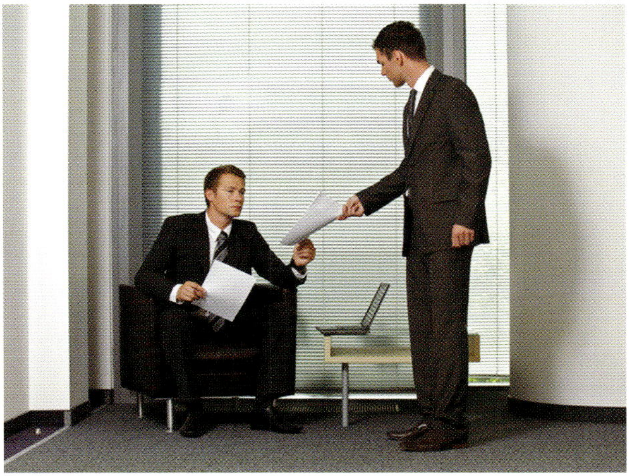

3 › I would like to have

There is another way of expressing polite requests.
Matthias says in the video dialog:

Ich hätte gerne ein paar Tomaten.
I would like to have some tomatoes.

Hätten (would like to have) follows the normal verb pattern.

ich hätte
du hättest
er / sie hätte
wir hätten
ihr hättet
Sie / sie hätten

4 › What can I do for you?

A salesclerk may address you with the following sentences:

Sie wünschen, bitte?
What would you like?
Was kann ich für Sie tun?
What can I do for you?

or:

Was hätten Sie gerne?
What would you like?
Ich hätte gerne 1 Kilo Tomaten.
I would like 1 kilo of tomatoes please.

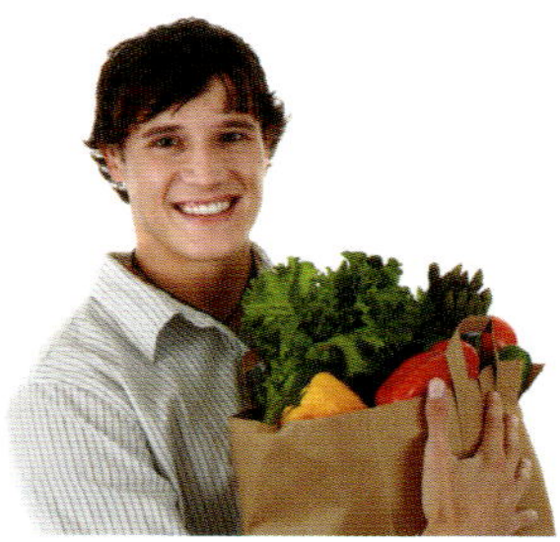

Hätten is usually accompanied by *gerne* which expresses a preference or liking.

5 › Could you do this for me?

You can apply the polite form to the verb *können* as well. Instead of *können*, you use *könnten*.

Könnten Sie mir bitte helfen?
Could you please help me?
Könnten Sie bitte Frau Claudius anrufen?
Could you please call Mrs. Claudius?

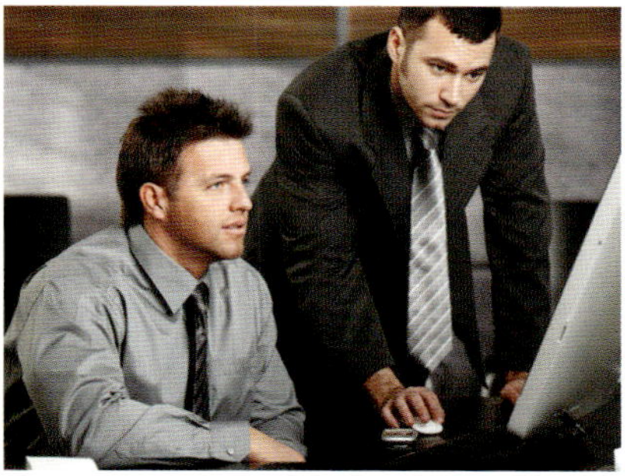

6 › How many? How much?

The salesclerk asks Matthias how many tomatoes he wants.

Wie viele Tomaten möchten Sie?
How many tomatoes would you like?

You use *wie viele* (how many) for things that are countable.

Wie viele Kollegen hast du?
How many colleagues do you have?

You use *wie viel* (how much) for things that are not countable.

Wie viel Zeit hast du?
How much time do you have?

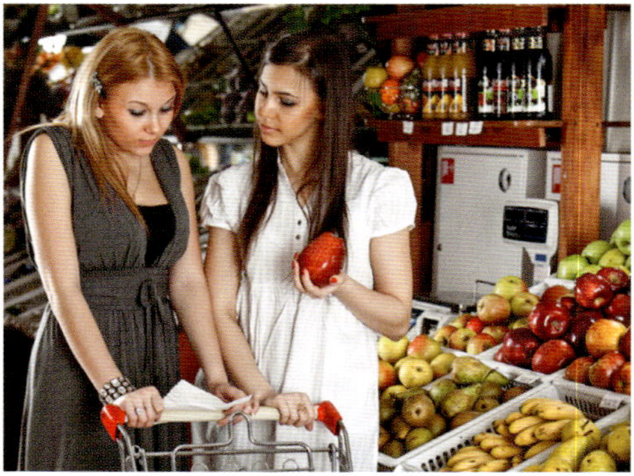

7 › Anything else?

The salesclerk asks if Matthias wants anything else.

Möchten Sie noch etwas?
Do you want anything else?

The positive answer is:

Ja, ich möchte noch etwas.
Yes, I want some more *or* something else.

The negative answer is:

Nein, ich möchte nichts mehr.
No, I don't want anything else.

Vocabulary

Active German: Level 2 > Unit 6 > Lesson 1 > Vocabulary

Food shopping and quantities

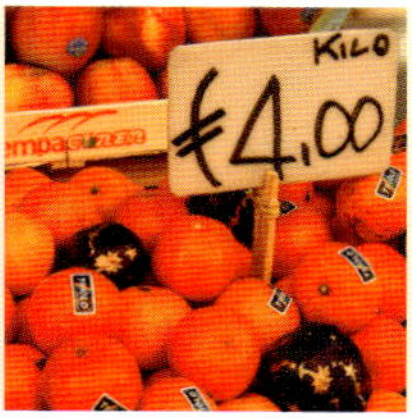

das Kilo / Kilos
kilogram

Ich hätte gern ein Kilo Orangen, bitte.
I would like a kilogram of oranges.

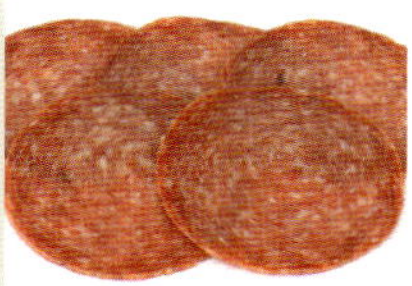

das Gramm
gram

Könnten Sie mir bitte 300 Gramm Salami geben?
Could you please give me 300 grams of salami?

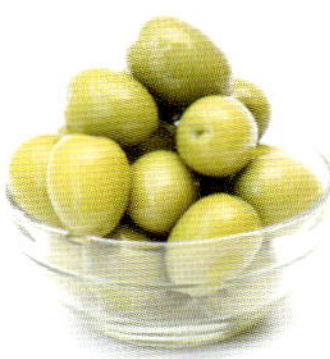

ein paar
a few / a couple / some

Ich möchte bitte ein paar Oliven.
I would like some olives please.

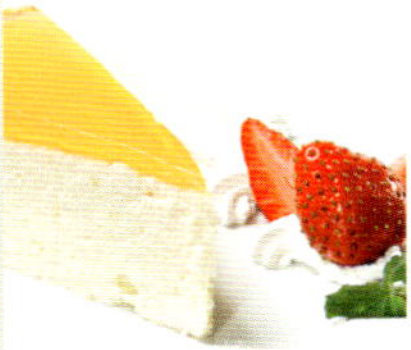

das Stück / Stücke
piece

Kann ich bitte zwei Stück Käsekuchen haben?
Could I please have two pieces of cheesecake?

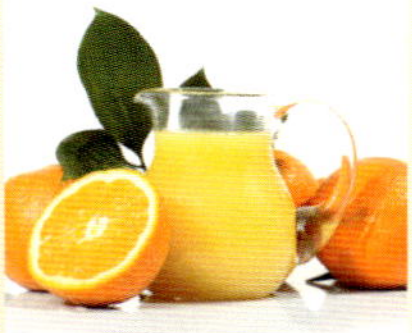

der Liter / Liter
liter

Ich brauche noch zwei Liter Orangensaft.
I need two liters of orange juice.

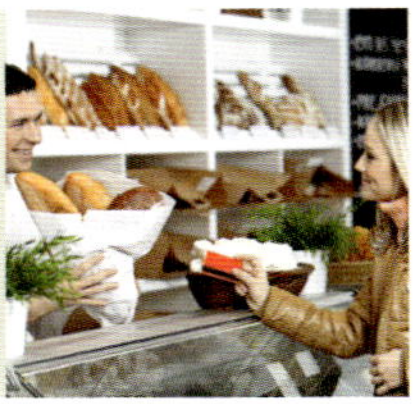

der Kunde / Kunden
customer

Wir haben einen neuen Kunden.
We have a new customer.

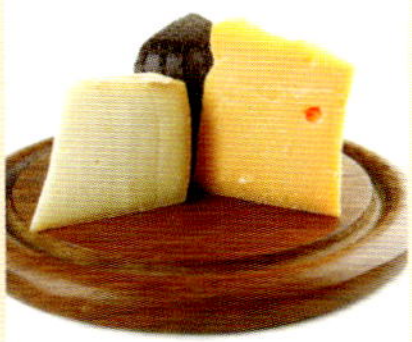

der Käse
cheese

Isst du gerne Käse?
Do you like eating cheese?

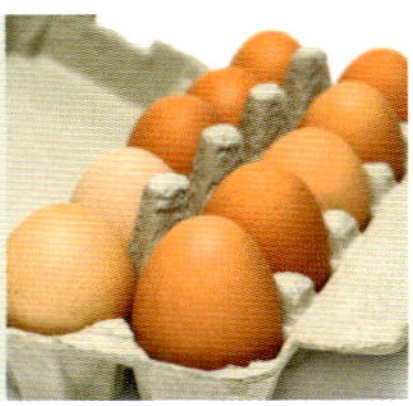

das Ei / Eier
egg

Brauchst du noch Eier?
Do you need eggs?

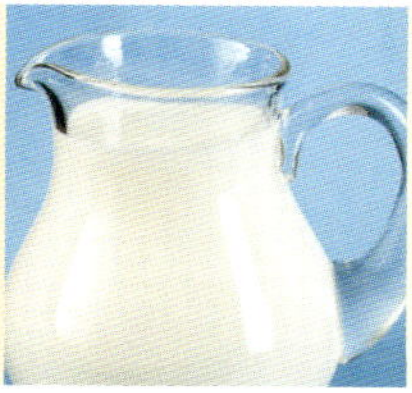

die Milch
milk

Trinken Sie den Kaffee mit Milch?
Do you take milk in your coffee?

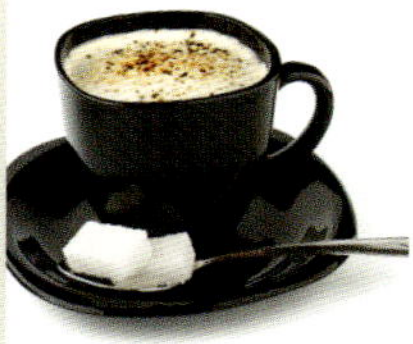

der Zucker
sugar

Ich trinke meinen Kaffee ohne Milch, aber mit Zucker.
I take my coffee without milk, but with sugar.

UNIT 6 › LESSON 2

Healthy food 2

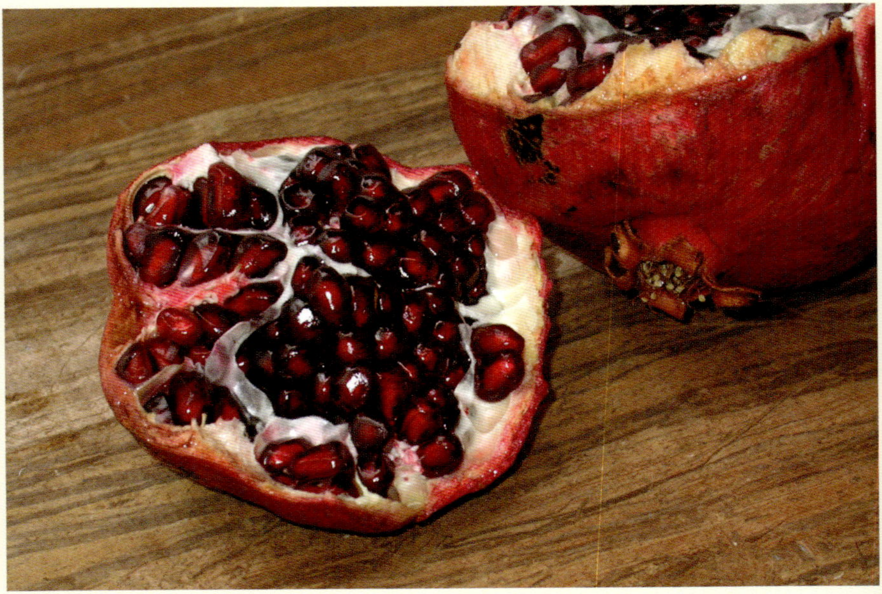

Culture note

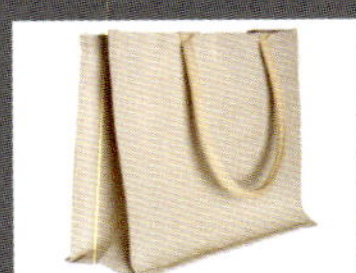

In Germany, it is quite common to bring your own bags to the supermarket. Of course, you can get bags in supermarkets, but you sometimes have to pay for them. Germans are famous for using linen bags in different designs – it's part of their environmentally-friendly attitude. Bag-packing service is not common in Germany.

Video Dialog

The helpful salesclerk suggests a nice surprise for dessert.

Active German: Level 2 > *Unit 6* > *Lesson 2* > *Video dialog*

Verkäuferin:	*Sie leben aber gesund!*
Matthias:	*Nicht immer. Heute koche ich für meine Schwester.*
Verkäuferin:	*Ah, was gibt es denn?*
Matthias:	*Zuerst einen Salat. Und dann Lachs und Gemüse.*
Verkäuferin:	*Nehmen Sie doch ein paar Erdbeeren und kaufen Sie Vanilleeis! Fertig ist der Nachtisch.*
Matthias:	*OK, dann nehme ich noch ein halbes Kilo Erdbeeren.*
Verkäuferin:	*Bitte sehr. Brauchen Sie eine Tüte?*
Matthias:	*Ich habe eine Tasche. Danke. Vielen Dank für den Tipp.*
Verkäuferin:	*Nichts zu danken. Viel Spaß.*

Salesclerk:	You live healthily!
Matthias:	Not always. Today I'm cooking for my sister.
Salesclerk:	Oh, what are you making?
Matthias:	First a salad. Then salmon and vegetables.
Salesclerk:	You should get some strawberries and buy some vanilla ice cream! Then the dessert is ready.

Matthias: OK, I'll also take half a kilo of strawberries then.
Salesclerk: Here you are. Do you need a bag?
Matthias: I've got a bag. Thank you. Thank you very much for your help.
Salesclerk: Not at all. Have fun.

Grammar

Active German: Level 2 > Unit 6 > Lesson 2 > Grammar

1 › **Get some ice cream!**

Let's take a look at how to express orders and suggestions.

We use the imperative form which is the structure for making orders and commands.

When addressing someone as *Sie* you would form the imperative as follows:

Sie nehmen	You take
Nehmen Sie!	Take!
Sie schreiben	You write
Schreiben Sie!	Write!

Just swap the position of the words in the sentence.

To make an order more polite you can insert the word *bitte* (please).

Kommen Sie bitte.
Come, please.

Note that German uses an exclamation mark to add emphasis to commands.

2 › Why don't you?

In the video the salesclerk suggests Matthias should buy some ice cream:

> *Kaufen Sie doch etwas Eis.*
> Why don't you buy some ice cream?

In order to soften a command to just a suggestion you add *doch*.

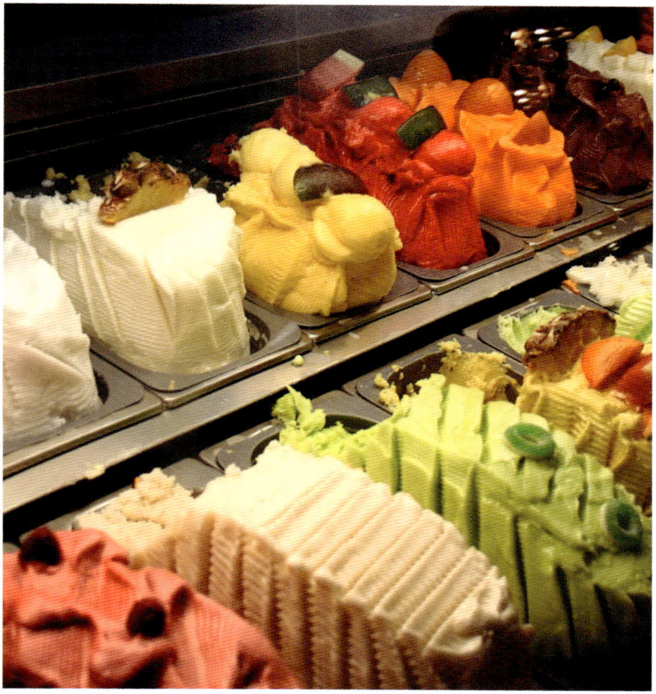

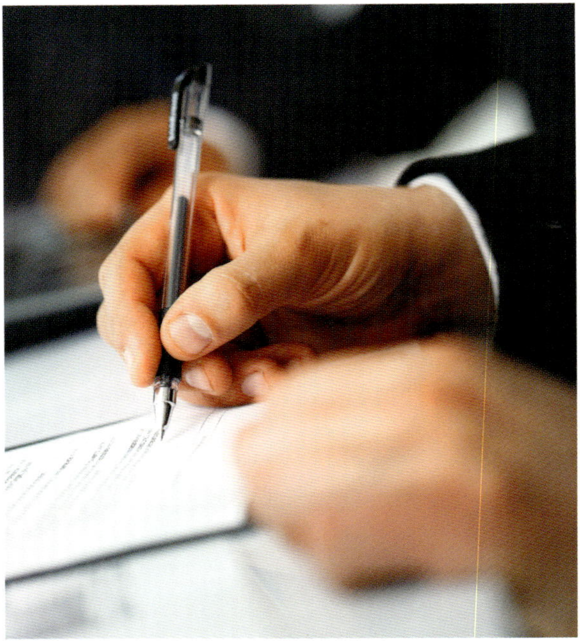

Kommen Sie doch um 16 Uhr.
Why don't you come at 4 p.m.?

3 › **Be on time!**

The structure we have mentioned works basically with every verb. There is just one exception: the verb *sein* (to be).

Seien Sie is the imperative form of *sein*.

Seien Sie pünktlich!
Be on time!

4 › Measures

In Lesson 1 you learned vocabulary about quantities.

Let's have a look at it again.

In German, you combine the measurement directly with the noun. There is no translation for "of."

ein Glas Bier	a glass of beer
eine Tasse Tee	a cup of tea
ein Liter Milch	a liter of milk
eine Portion Pommes frites	a serving of french fries

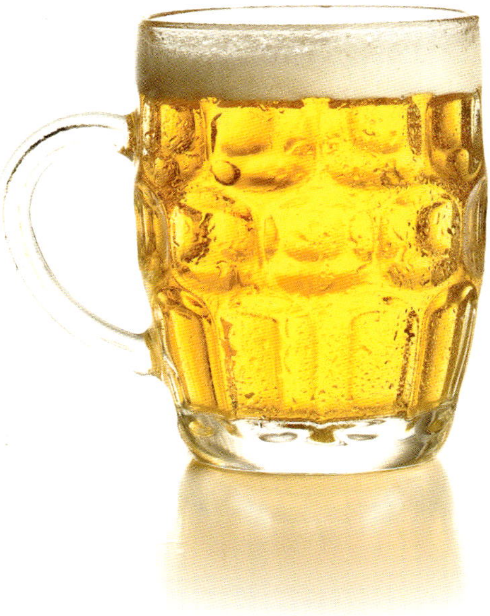

5 › Measures

Some measurements don't change in the plural:

*drei **Glas** Milch*	three glasses of milk
*zwei **Stück** Brot*	two pieces of bread
*2 **Kilo** Kartoffeln*	2 kilos of potatoes

Some measurements do change form in the plural:

*zwei Tass**en** Kaffee*	two cups of coffee
*drei Flasch**en** Wein*	three bottles of wine

6 › You have to do that

We are going to have a look now at a very common German word: *man*.

Für den Nachtisch braucht man Erdbeeren.
For the dessert you need strawberries.

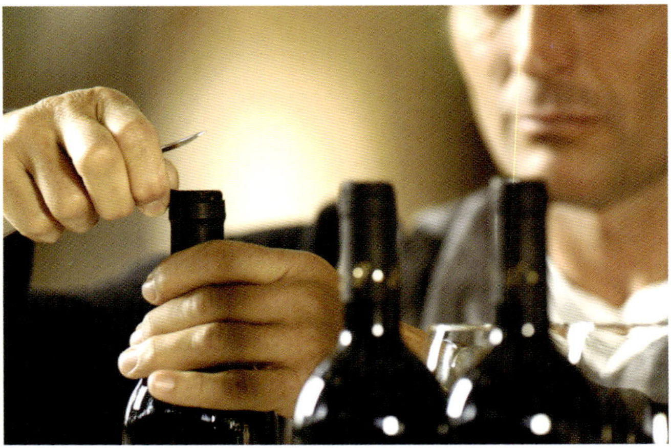

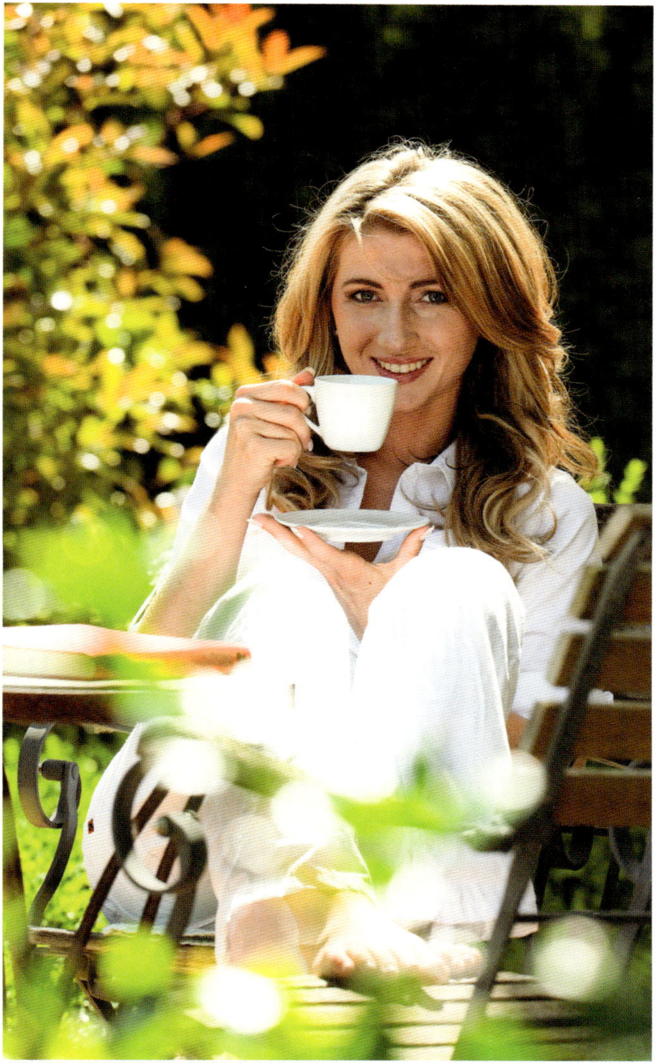

Man (not *der Mann* which means "the man"!) refers to people in general. It is used very often in both colloquial and formal language.

It is the subject of a sentence.

Man muss das machen.
You have to do that. / One has to do that.

After *man* you use the same verb form as you do for he and she.

Er trinkt Bier.	He drinks beer.
Man trinkt Bier.	People drink beer.

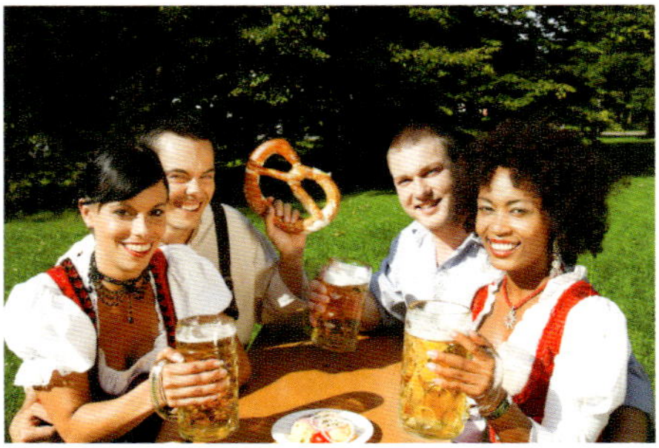

Culture note

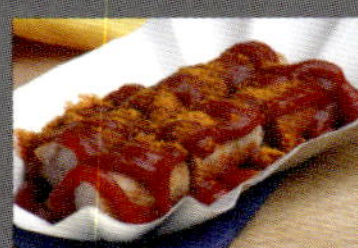

On German shopping streets you will see two things at nearly every corner: Snack bars for *Currywurst* and *Döner*. The *Currywurst* was invented after the Second World War. It is a hot pork sausage cut into slices and then seasoned with curry sauce, which is basically tomato ketchup with a good amount of curry powder. The *Döner*, a Turkish dish, is traditionally made out of lamb (nowadays you can have it made of chicken as well). The meat is served in bread with a yogurt sauce, lettuce, tomato, and cabbage.

Vocabulary

Active German: Level 2 > *Unit 6* > *Lesson 2* > *Vocabulary*

Food shopping

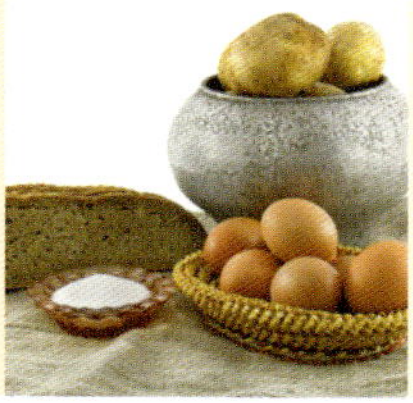

die Lebensmittel
food, groceries

Wichtige Lebensmittel sind Brot, Kartoffeln und Eier.
Important groceries are bread, potatoes, and eggs.

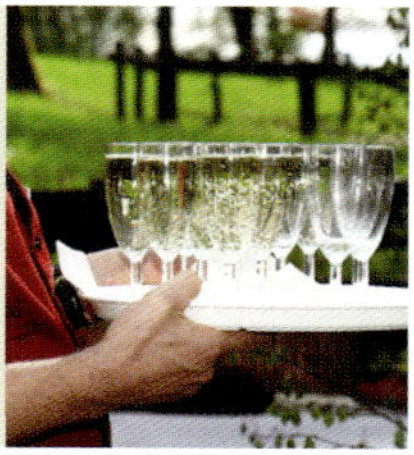

das Getränk / Getränke
drink

Wer kauft die Getränke?
Who's buying the drinks?

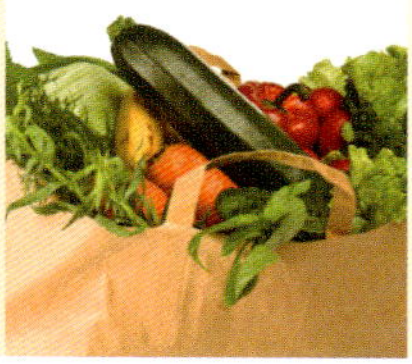

das Gemüse
vegetable

Ich muss noch Gemüse kaufen
I have to buy vegetables.

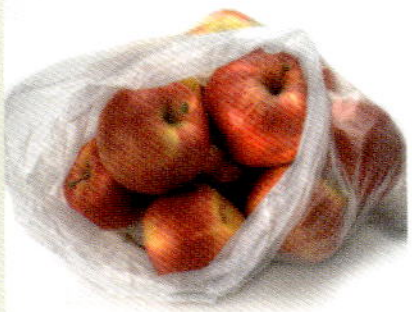

das Obst
fruit

Obst ist sehr gesund.
Fruit is very healthy.

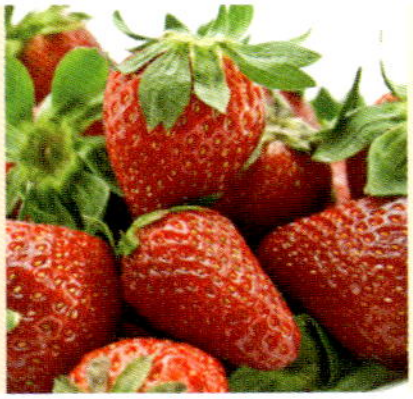

die Erdbeere / Erdbeeren
strawberry

Im Mai kann man wieder Erdbeeren kaufen.
In May you can buy strawberries again.

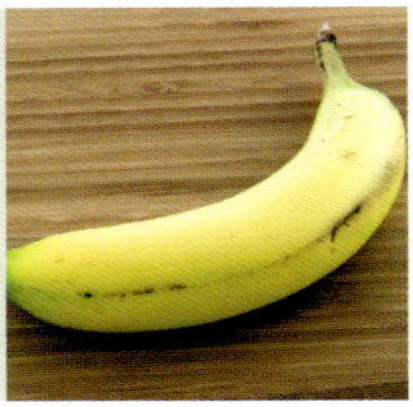

die Banane / Bananen
banana

Zum Frühstück esse ich immer eine Banane.
For breakfast I always have a banana.

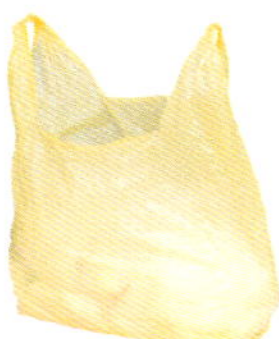

die Tüte / Tüten
(disposable) plastic bag

Nein danke, ich brauche keine Tüte.
No thanks, I don't need a plastic bag.

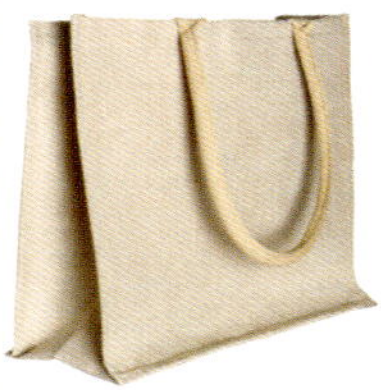

die Tasche / Taschen
(shopping) bag

Ich brauche keine Tüte. Ich habe eine Tasche.
I don't need a plastic bag. I have a bag.

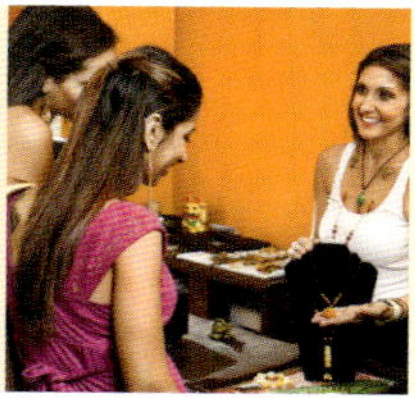

Nichts zu danken.
Not at all.

Nichts zu danken. Das mache ich gerne.
Not at all. I like doing it.

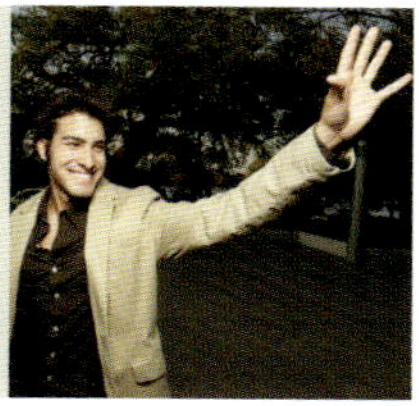

Viel Spaß.
Have fun.

Viel Spaß heute Abend im Kino.
Have fun at the movies tonight.

Collins

Livemocha ACTIVE GERMAN

HarperCollins Publishers
77–85 Fulham Palace Road
London W6 8JB
Great Britain

www.collinslanguage.com

First edition 2011

Reprint 10 9 8 7 6 5 4 3 2 1 0

ISBN (UK edition) 978-0-00-737354-3
ISBN (export edition) 978-0-00-741978-4
ISBN (US edition) 978-0-87779-556-8

A catalogue record for this book is available from the British Library

Typeset by Macmillan Publishing Services

Audio material recorded and produced by Networks SRL, Milan

Printed and Bound in China by Leo Paper Products Ltd.
Series Editor: Rob Scriven

INTRODUCTION

Welcome to your Livemocha Active German experience! This new course goes above and beyond what a traditional book-based course can offer. With its focus on online learning, Active German provides the opportunity not just to study but to experience the language for yourself by interacting with native speakers online.

Why go online?
Studying a language online allows you to learn in a more natural atmosphere – watching people interact in a **video** is far more lifelike than listening to conversations on a CD. After watching a video dialog, you will be walked through an explanation of some of the **grammar** and **vocabulary** items that were introduced in the new dialog. Then, by completing a variety of **interactive quizzes**, the system will instantly be able to tell you how well you are doing. You can then **talk online** with native German speakers to practice what you've learned.

Who else is online?
Livemocha boasts over 7 million members and is growing every day. These members are online for the same reason as you – to learn and experience a new language. Native German-speaking members will be happy to read through your written and spoken submissions and to give you feedback on how you're doing. You can also connect with people who want to chat in any given language – interaction on an informal, nonacademic basis is an ideal way for you to perfect your language skills.

What do the books do?
The four accompanying books are designed to complement the online course – the dialogs for all of the videos that you can watch online are available here for you to study whenever you don't have access to the Internet. You will also find all of the Grammar and Vocabulary sections explained in the books, plus the culture notes to teach you a little about Germany.

LEVEL 3

This book is the third of four. It corresponds with Level 3 of the online course.

Level 3 is ideal for students who can hold a simple conversation and are looking to start to cope in slightly more complex situations.

What you will learn

- How to express an interest in things
- How to say what you like and what fits you
- How to make suggestions, commands and invitations
- How to use prepositions and say where things are
- How to talk about things that happened in the past
- How you say you were able to do something or had to do something
- How to say what you should do, are allowed to do and can do
- How to make comparisons between things
- Vocabulary for sports, clothes and sizes, colors, health, medicine and parts of

Every time you see this coffee cup symbol in these books, it indicates the presence of a pathway – a guide to exactly where you can find that particular piece of content online. Log on at www.livemocha.com and follow the path to find the online version of what you are studying in the book.

Video Dialog

A warm welcome for Matthias as he gets to know his new colleagues a little better.

Active German: Level 1 > *Unit 2* > *Lesson 1* > *Video dialog*

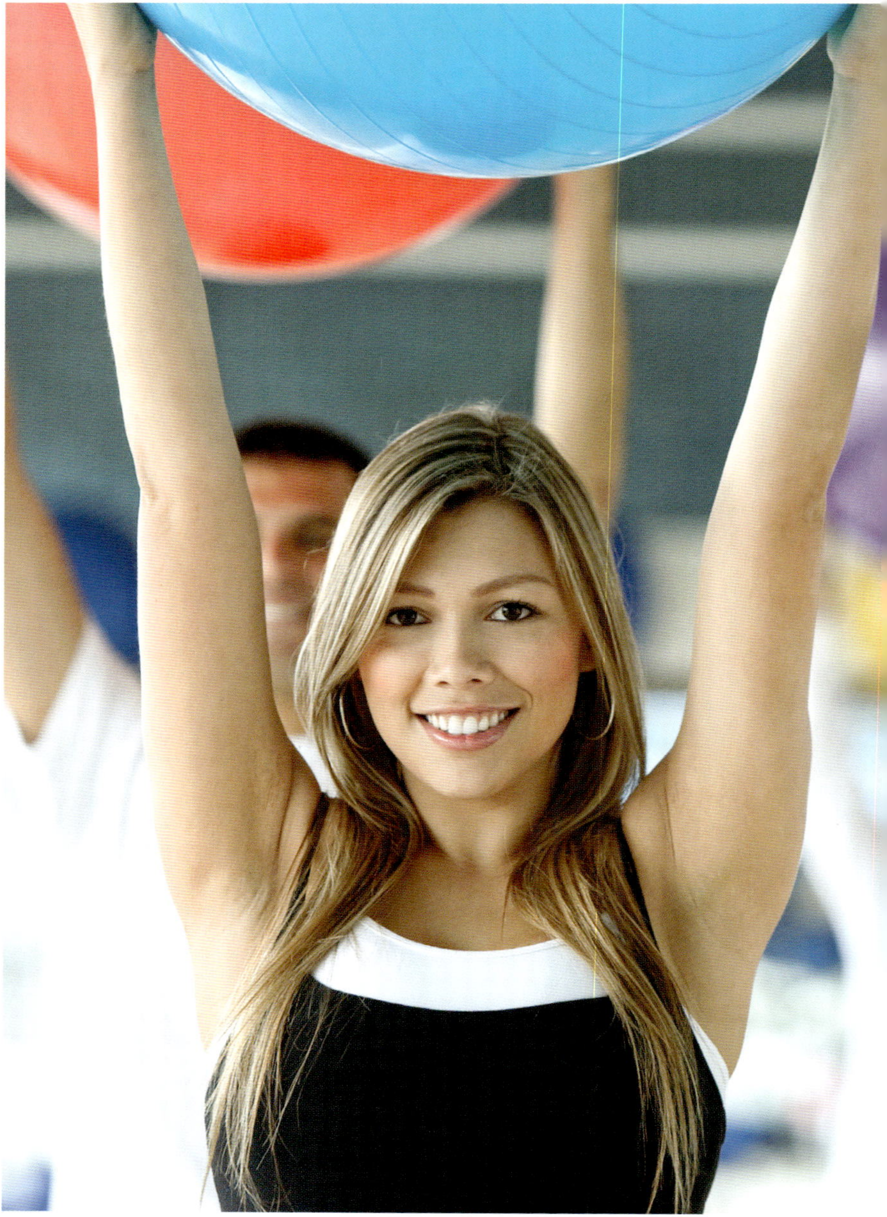

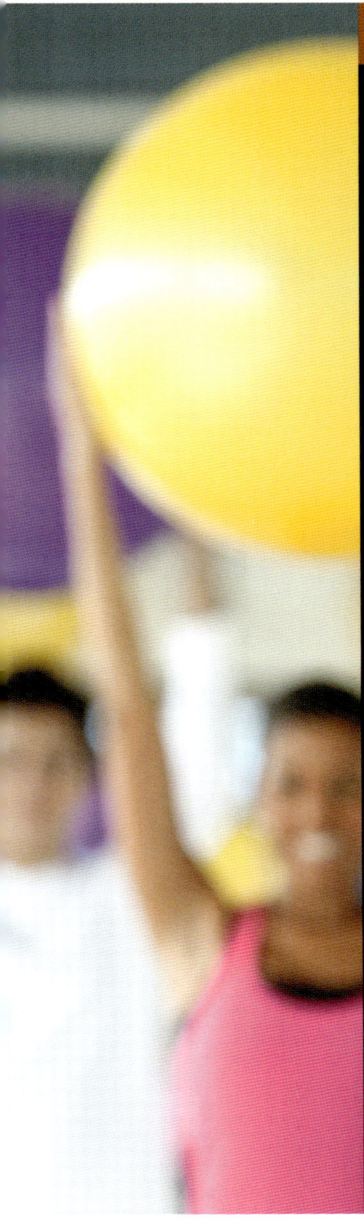

1

Lesson 1: In a gym

- How to sign up / to register: ***Ich möchte mich anmelden.***
- How to become a member: ***Ich möchte ein Mitglied werden.***
- How to say "I'm interested in ...": ***Ich interessiere mich für ...***
- How to talk about paying conditions.
- Vocabulary for registrations, sports, and fitness centers.

Lesson 2: Sports

- How to talk about sports, the gym, and soccer.
- How to express "I do a lot of sports," "I work out," etc.
- Vocabulary for sports and clubs.

Collins | Livemocha™

UNIT 1 › LESSON 1

In a gym

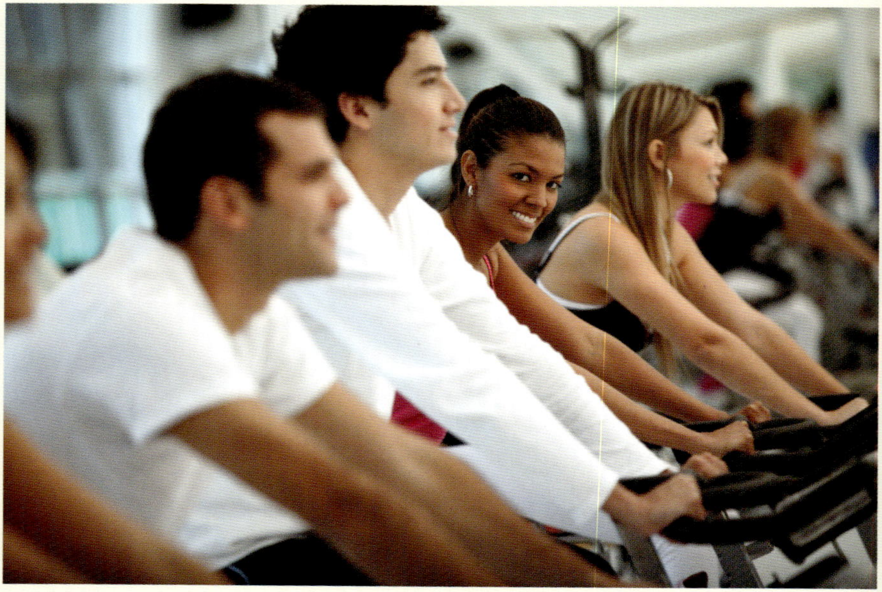

Culture note

Fitness, relaxation, and wellness are common leisure activities in Germany. Germans tend to see wellness as a way to improve their health. Health resorts are often located in an ancient spa town or by the sea with access to springs or sea water. Some treatments are even prescribed by your doctor and taken very seriously. A well-known treatment is the *Kneippkur* – a special water therapy.

Video Dialog

Lara helps Matthias sort out membership to the local gym.

Watch the video dialog online at
Active German: Level 3 > *Unit 1* > *Lesson 1* > *Video dialog*

Lara:	*Na, interessierst du dich für Fitness?*
Matthias:	*Ja, ich interessiere mich für eine Mitgliedschaft bei Fit & Fun.*
Lara:	*Hattest du schon eine Probestunde?*
Matthias:	*Ja, ich möchte mich gerne anmelden. Möchtest du dich nicht setzen?*
Lara:	*Gern. Hast du das Formular?*
Matthias:	*Ja, ich muss es nur noch ausfüllen.*
Lara:	*Wie hoch ist der Beitrag?*
Matthias:	*Hier siehst du die Preise.*
Lara:	*Möchtest du monatlich oder jährlich bezahlen?*
Matthias:	*Monatlich. Am Anfang möchte ich gerne einen Trainer haben.*
Lara:	*Gute Idee.*

Lara:	Oh, are you interested in fitness?
Matthias:	Yes, I'm interested in becoming a member of Fit & Fun.
Lara:	Have you had a trial session?
Matthias:	Yes, I'd like to join. Don't you want to sit down?
Lara:	Yes. Do you have the form?
Matthias:	Yes, I just have to fill it out.

Lara:	How much is the membership fee?
Matthias:	Here are the prices.
Lara:	Would you like to pay monthly or annually?
Matthias:	Monthly. I'd like a personal trainer to start with.
Lara:	That's a good idea.

Grammar

In this section we go over some of the grammar points introduced in the dialog.

Go to Active German: Level 3 > Unit 1 > Lesson 1 > Grammar to listen to these explanations and to access some interactive practice activities.

1 › **Reflexive verbs (1)**

A reflexive verb is one where the action reflects back on the subject. For example: I introduce myself.

Reflexive verbs are used with myself, yourself, himself etc.

Darf ich mich vorstellen?

May I introduce myself?

In German, reflexive verbs are very common and occur in everyday language. They consist of two parts: the verb and the reflexive pronoun. In this case the reflexive pronoun is *sich* and the verb is *vorstellen: sich vorstellen*.

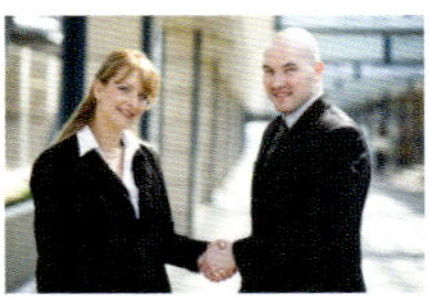

2 › Reflexive verbs (2)

In the video dialog Matthias asked Lara:

Möchtest du dich nicht setzen?
Don't you want to sit down?

The verb is *sich setzen* (have a seat / sit down).

The present tense forms of a reflexive verb work in just the same way as an ordinary verb.

Let's have a look at the pronouns. Take the verb *sich setzen* as an example:

ich setze ***mich***	I sit down
du setzt ***dich***	you sit down
er / sie / es setzt ***sich***	he / she / it sits down
wir setzen ***uns***	we sit down
ihr setzt ***euch***	you sit down
Sie / sie setzen ***sich***	you / they sit down

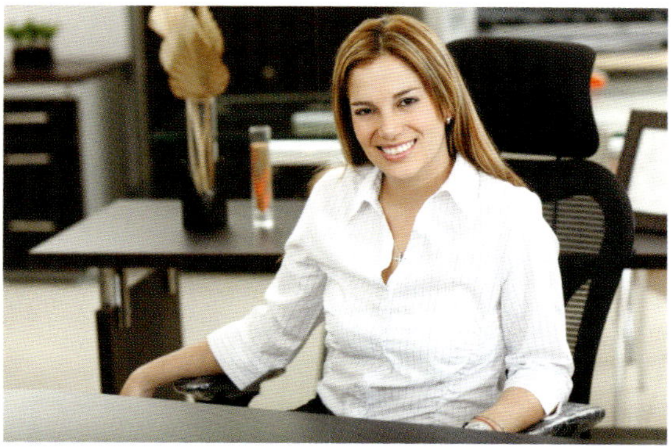

3 › Reflexive verbs (3)

In the present tense the reflexive pronoun usually comes after the verb.

Ich setze mich auf den Stuhl.
I sit down (on the chair).

4 › Reflexive verbs (4)

Here is a list of some important reflexive verbs:

sich anmelden	to sign up for, to enroll
sich anziehen	to get dressed
sich rasieren	to shave
sich beeilen	to hurry up
sich informieren	to find out, to inform yourself
sich bedanken	to say thank you
sich freuen	to look forward to

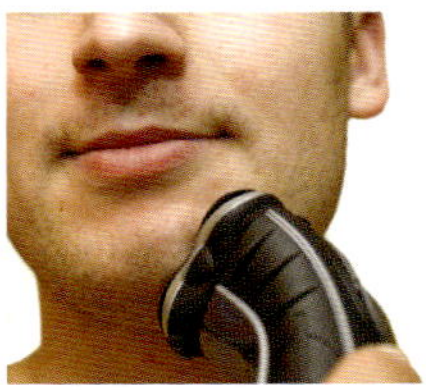

Note that *sich anmelden* and *sich anziehen* are separable verbs and the *an-* prefix is cut off. We had a look at separable verbs in earlier lessons.

Ich ziehe mich an.	I get dressed.
Ich melde mich an.	I sign up.

5 › Reflexive verbs (5)

Some reflexive verbs take a preposition as well.
In the video dialog Matthias says:

Ich interessiere mich für eine Mitgliedschaft.

I'm interested in becoming a member.

The whole verb is: *sich interessieren für* (to be interested in).

Ich interessiere mich für Sport.

I'm interested in sports.

Ich interessiere mich für Autos.

I'm interested in cars.

Another example is: to look forward to

Ich freue mich auf Sie.

I look forward to meeting you.

We will have a look at more reflexive verbs later on.

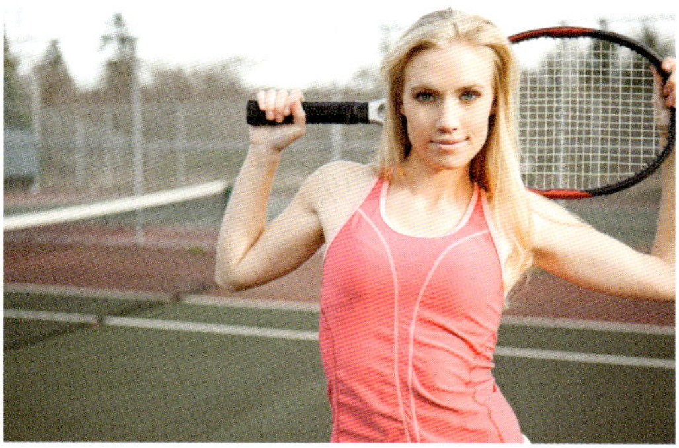

6 › How to register

Two expressions are important if you want to become a member of a club or similar institution.

In order to say "to become" you need to use the verb *werden*. It is an irregular verb.

ich werde	I become
du wirst	you become
er / sie / es wird	he / she / it becomes
wir werden	we become
ihr werdet	you become
Sie / sie werden	you / they become

"To become a member" in German is *Mitglied werden*.
To say "to fill out" use the verb *ausfüllen*. It is separable.

Ich fülle das Formular aus.
I fill out the form.

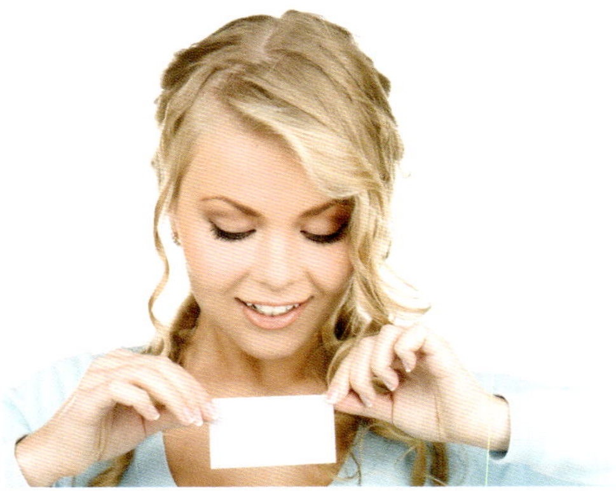

7 › Gender

We have learned that the gender of German nouns is very often arbitrary. Nevertheless, there are some endings which tell you the gender of a noun:

Feminine endings:

-ung: Wohnung	apartment
-heit: Gesundheit	health
-keit: Kleinigkeit	something small
-schaft: Mitgliedschaft	membership

Nouns with the ending *-e* as in *Stunde* (hour) are mostly feminine.

Masculine endings:

-mus: Kommunismus	communism
-ent: Student	student
-er: Lehrer	teacher
-ist: Pianist	pianist

Neuter endings:

-o: Kino *Büro*	movie theater office
-chen: Mädchen	girl

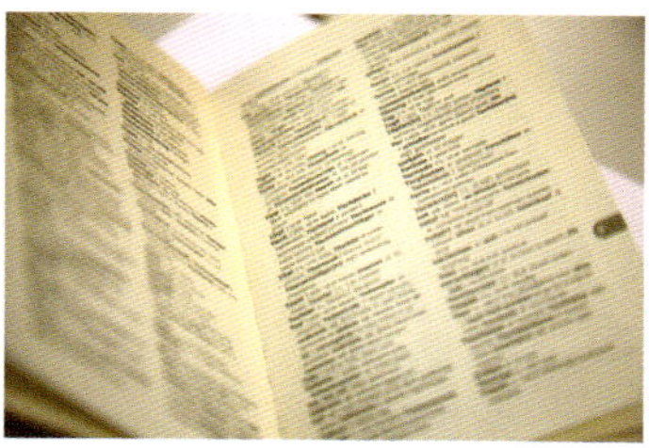

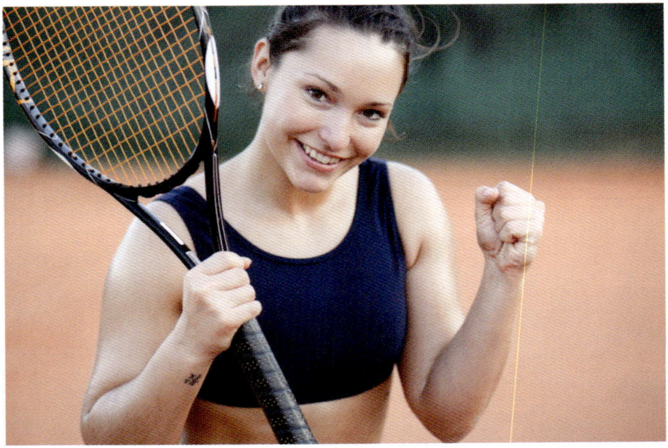

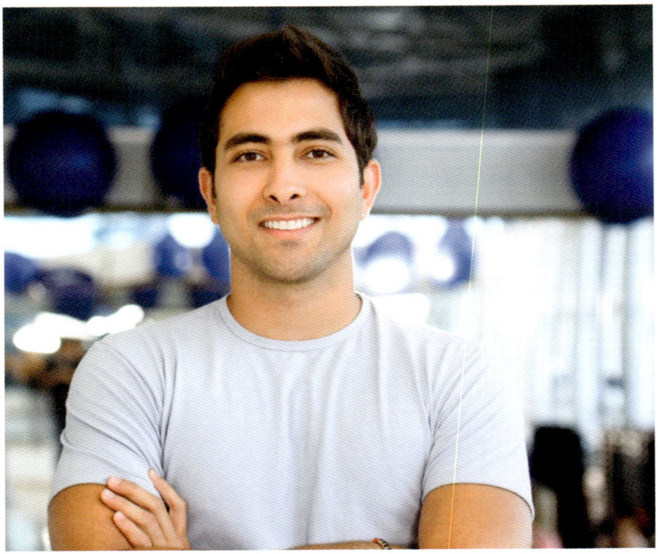

Vocabulary

In this section you will learn some useful words and expressions from the dialog.

Go to Active German: Level 3 > Unit 1 > Lesson 1 > Vocabulary to listen to each of the words being pronounced and to access some interactive practice activities.

Registration and membership

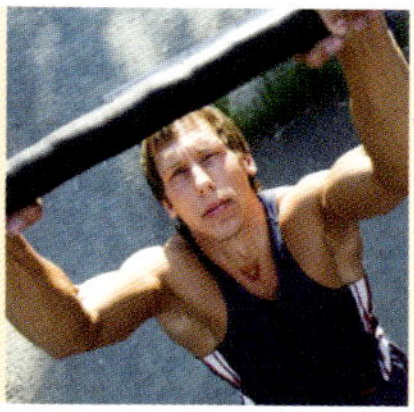

der Trainer / Trainer
trainer

Mein Trainer hilft mir immer.
My trainer always helps me.

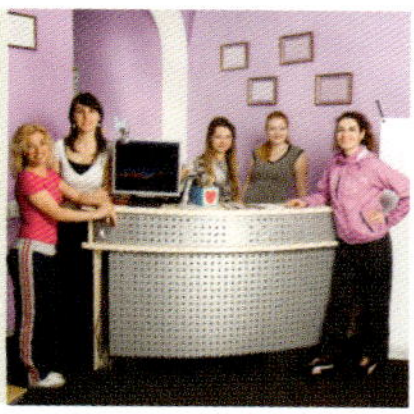

der Beitrag / Beiträge
fee, contribution

Ist der Beitrag für das Fitnessstudio hoch?
Is the fee for the fitness center high?

das Mitglied / Mitglieder
member

Ich möchte gerne Mitglied werden.
I want to become a member.

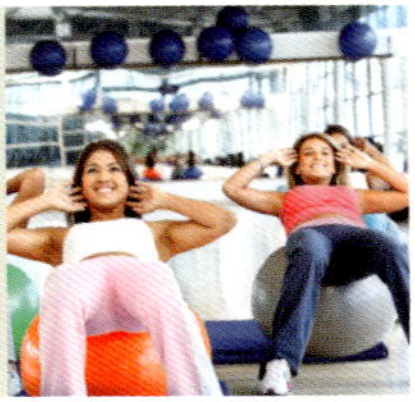

das Fitnessstudio / Fitnessstudios
fitness center

Gehst du oft ins Fitnessstudio?
Do you often go to the fitness center?

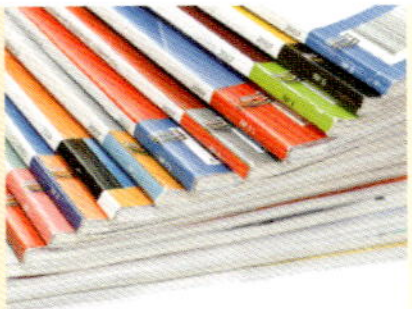

monatlich
monthly

Diese Zeitschrift erscheint monatlich.
This magazine comes out monthly.

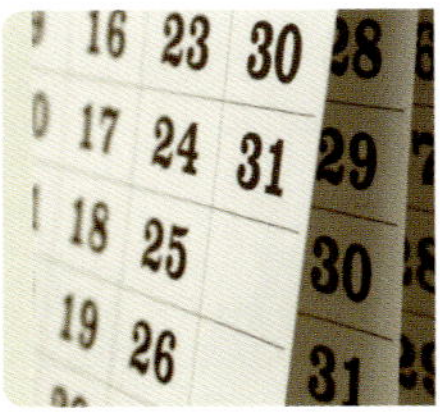

jährlich
annual, annually

Möchten Sie lieber monatlich oder jährlich bezahlen?
Would you prefer to pay monthly or annually?

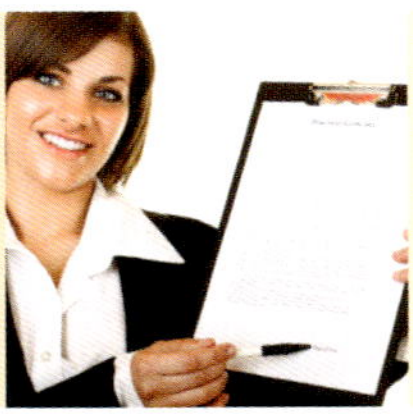

das Formular / Formulare
form

Füllen Sie bitte das Formular aus.
Fill out the form, please.

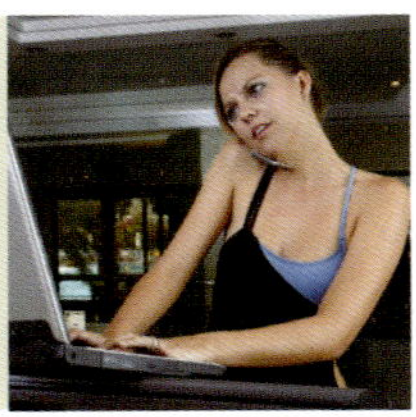

buchen
to reserve, to book

Ich möchte bitte einen Kurs bei Ihnen buchen.
I would like to sign up for a course.

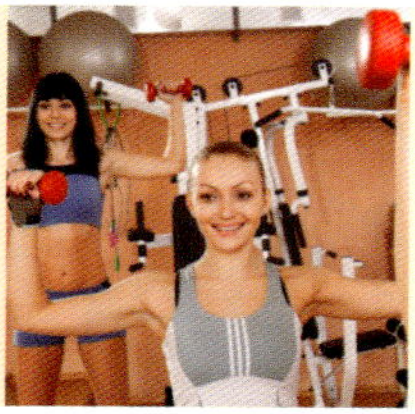

die Probestunde / Probestunden
trial session

Sie müssen sich nicht jetzt entscheiden. Sie können erst mal eine Probestunde nehmen.
You don't have to decide right now. You can take a trial session.

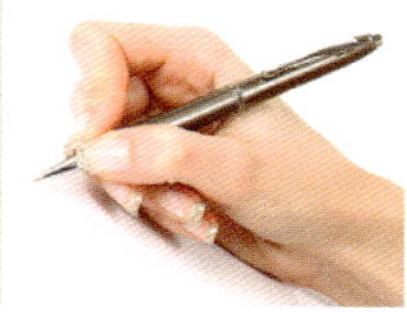

unterschreiben
to sign

Können Sie bitte hier unterschreiben?
Could you please sign here?

UNIT 1 › LESSON 2

Sports

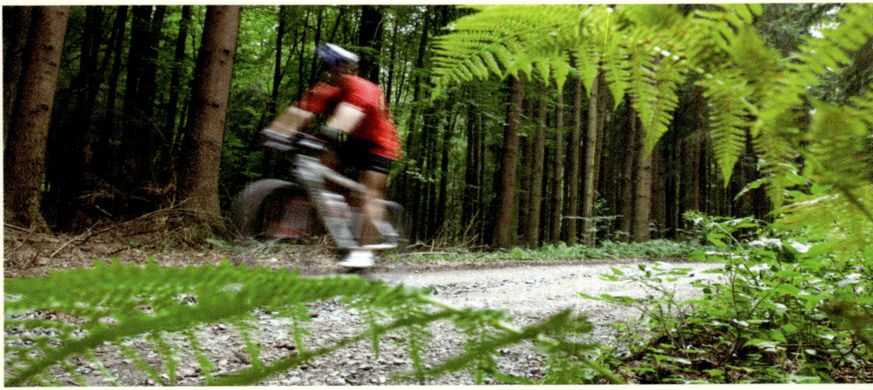

Culture note

Sports play an important role in German society. The sports leagues in Germany are well organized and widely spread.

Men's soccer, *Fußball*, is probably the most famous one. During the 2006 World Cup in Germany, the country developed an unprecedented feeling of national unity – soccer became the national craze.

Nevertheless, there are also leagues and organizations for women's soccer, basketball, ice hockey, and handball as well as a number of other sports.

Handball (team handball) is a German invention and is probably more popular in Germany than in most other countries. *Handball* teams are located everywhere, especially in the north of Germany. It is played by two teams of seven players each. The aim of the game is to pass a ball to throw it into the goal of the other team. It is usually played indoors.

Video Dialog

Matthias and Mr. Buschel discuss what sports they play.

Active German: Level 3 > Unit 1 > Lesson 2 > Video dialog

Matthias:	*Ich habe mich gestern bei einem Fitnessstudio angemeldet.*
Herr Buschel:	*Ah, gut. Treibst du viel Sport?*
Matthias:	*Na ja, ich gehe einmal pro Woche joggen und ich gehe einmal pro Woche ins Fitnessstudio. Und du? Treibst du viel Sport?*
Herr Buschel:	*Nein, nicht wirklich. Ich gehe manchmal schwimmen und am Wochenende spiele ich manchmal Fußball.*
Matthias:	*Ich spiele sehr gerne Fußball. Hast du ein Team?*
Herr Buschel:	*Ja, wir treffen uns immer um 17 Uhr am Sonntag auf dem Sportplatz.*
Matthias:	*Kann ich mal mitkommen?*
Herr Buschel:	*Na klar.*
Matthias:	*Super.*

Matthias:	I joined a gym yesterday.
Mr. Buschel:	That's great. Do you do a lot of sports?
Matthias:	Well, I run once a week and I go to the gym once a week. And you, do you do a lot of sports?

Mr. Buschel:	No, not really. Sometimes I go for a swim and on weekends I sometimes play soccer.
Matthias:	I love playing soccer. Do you have a team?
Mr. Buschel:	Yes, we always meet at 5 o'clock on Sundays at the sports ground.
Matthias:	Can I join you some day?
Mr. Buschel:	Yeah, sure.
Matthias:	Great.

Grammar

Active German: Level 3 > *Unit 1* > *Lesson 2* > *Grammar*

1 › Expressions in sports (1)

In German, you use the expression *Sport treiben* generally to say "to do sports / to get exercise."

Matthias asks:

Treibst du viel Sport?

Do you do a lot of sports?

When referring to a fitness center you can either say

Ich trainiere im Fitnessstudio.

I work out in a fitness center.

or

Ich gehe manchmal ins Fitnessstudio.

Sometimes I go to a fitness center.

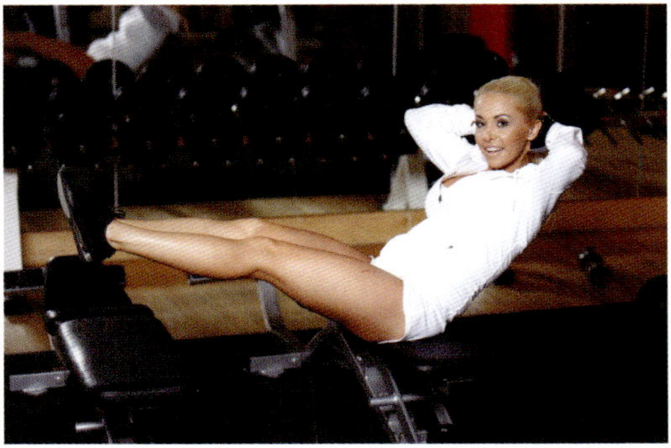

2 › Expressions in sports (2)

Another important expression is *sich fit halten* – to keep in shape

Wie hältst du dich fit?	How do you keep in shape?
Ich gehe zweimal pro Woche laufen.	I go for a run twice a week.

Note that it is a reflexive verb and that *halten* is irregular and has an umlaut in the 2nd and 3rd person.

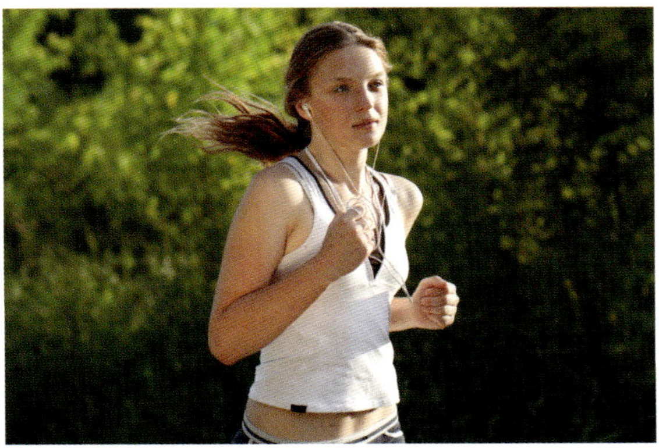

3 › Expressions in sports (3)

There are some expressions in which you use the verb *gehen* + infinitive.

Ich gehe laufen.	I go for a run.
Ich gehe schwimmen.	I go swimming.

Look what happens in combination with a modal verb:

Wollen wir schwimmen gehen?

Do you want to go swimming?

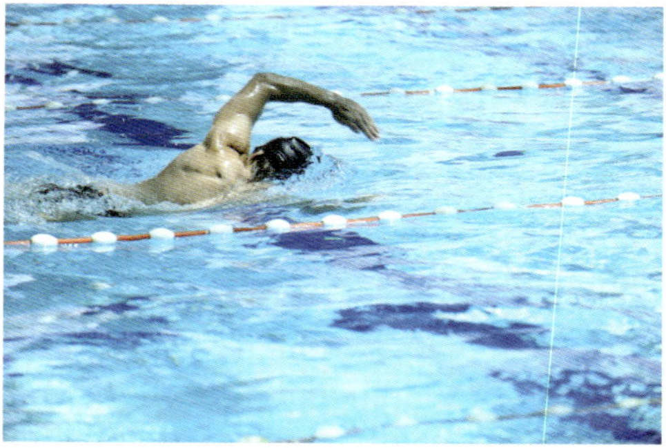

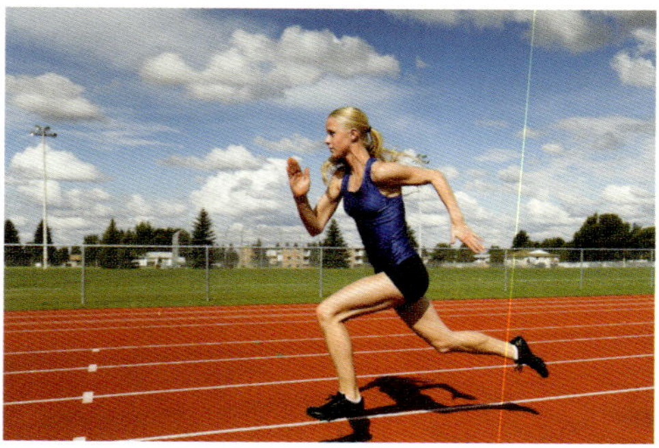

4 › Expressions in sports (4)

Here are some other popular sports:

Rad fahren	to cycle
Ich fahre Rad.	I cycle.
Ski fahren	to ski
Ich fahre Ski.	I ski.
Tennis spielen	to play tennis
Ich spiele Tennis.	I play tennis.
Fußball spielen	to play soccer
Ich spiele gerne Fußball.	I like to play soccer.

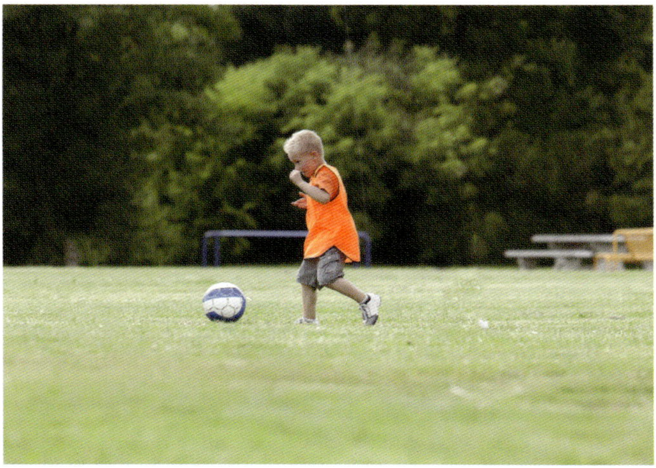

5 › ## Word order

Now let's look at some sentences which contain time or frequency expressions as well.

Am Wochenende fahre ich manchmal Rad.
On weekends I sometimes cycle.

Note that the expression *Rad fahren* is split.

Ich spiele nie Tennis.	I never play tennis.
Einmal pro Woche gehe ich ins Fitnessstudio.	Once a week I go to a fitness center.
Fährst du gerne Ski?	Do you like to ski?

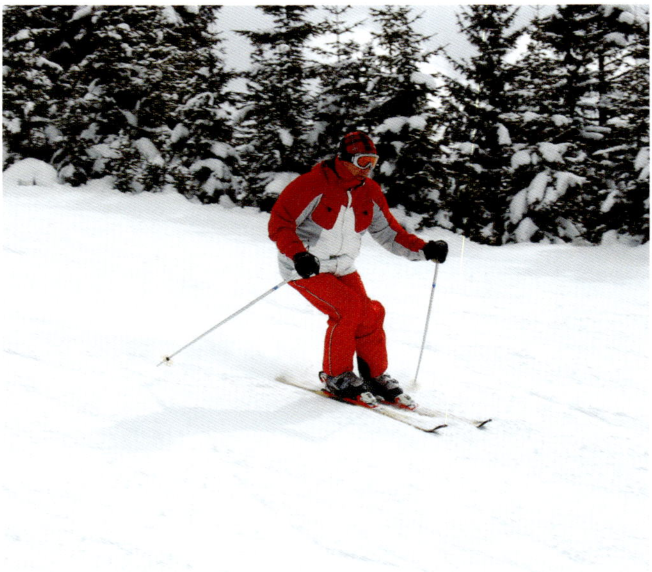

Vocabulary

Active German: Level 3 > *Unit 1* > *Lesson 2* > *Vocabulary*

Sports

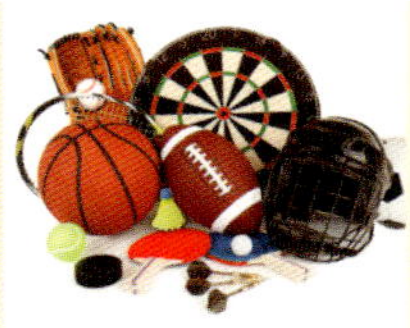

die Sportart / Sportarten
(type of) sport

Welche Sportart magst du gern?
Which sport do you like?

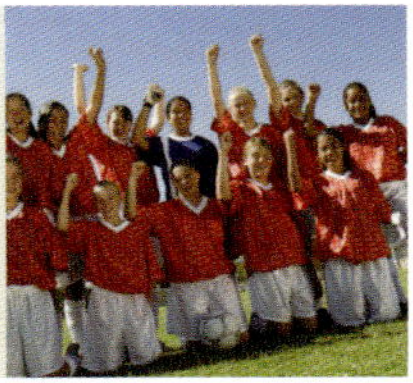

die Mannschaft / Mannschaften
team

Die Mannschaft hat heute schlecht gespielt.
The team played badly today.

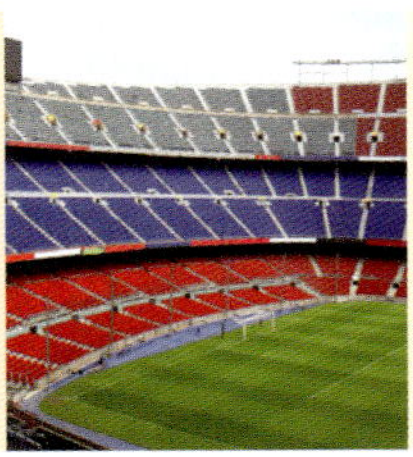

das Stadion / Stadien
stadium

30.000 Menschen waren gestern im Stadion.
30,000 people were in the stadium yesterday.

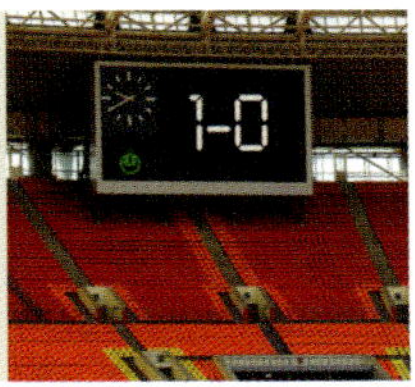

das Ergebnis / Ergebnisse
result

2:1 für Köln, das Ergebnis ist gut.
2–1 to Cologne, the result is good.

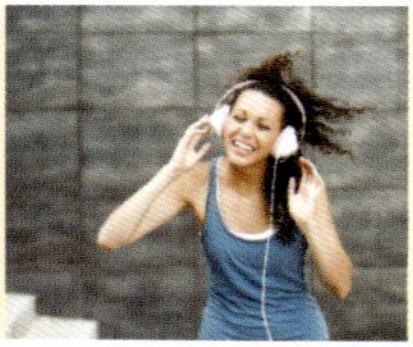

tanzen
to dance

Tanzt du mit mir?
Are you going to dance with me?

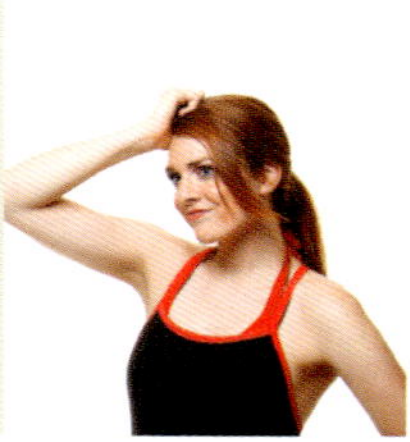

sportlich
athletic

Mike ist sehr sportlich; er trainiert dreimal pro Woche im Fitnessstudio.
Mike is very athletic; he works out three times a week.

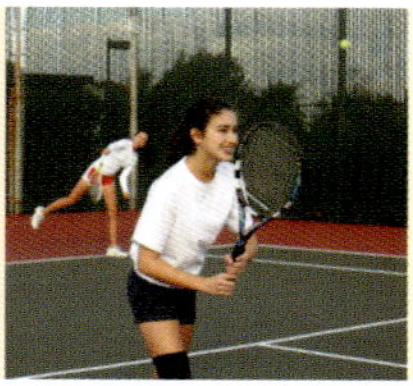

der Verein / Vereine
association, club

Katrin ist Mitglied in einem Tennisverein.
Katrin is a member of a tennis club.

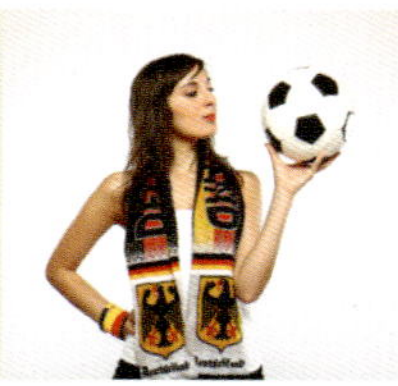

der Fan / Fans
fan / supporter

Dies sind alles Fans von Bayern München.
These are all fans of Bayern Munich.

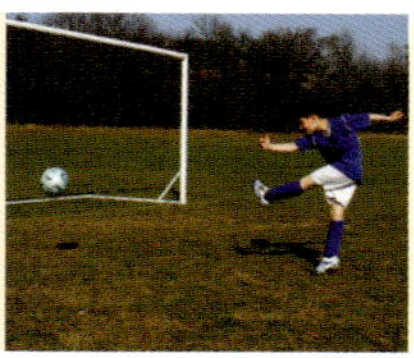

gewinnen
to win

Wer gewinnt heute?
Who is going to win today?

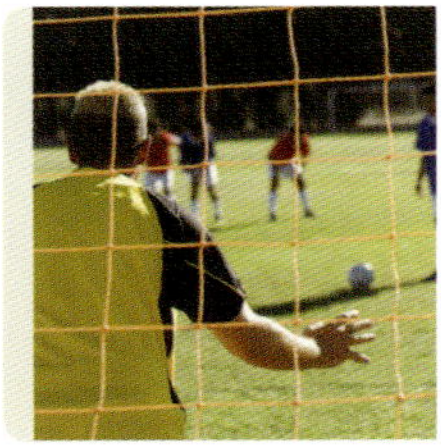

verlieren
to lose

Verlieren oder gewinnen, der Spaß ist wichtig.
Whether you lose or win, having fun is important.

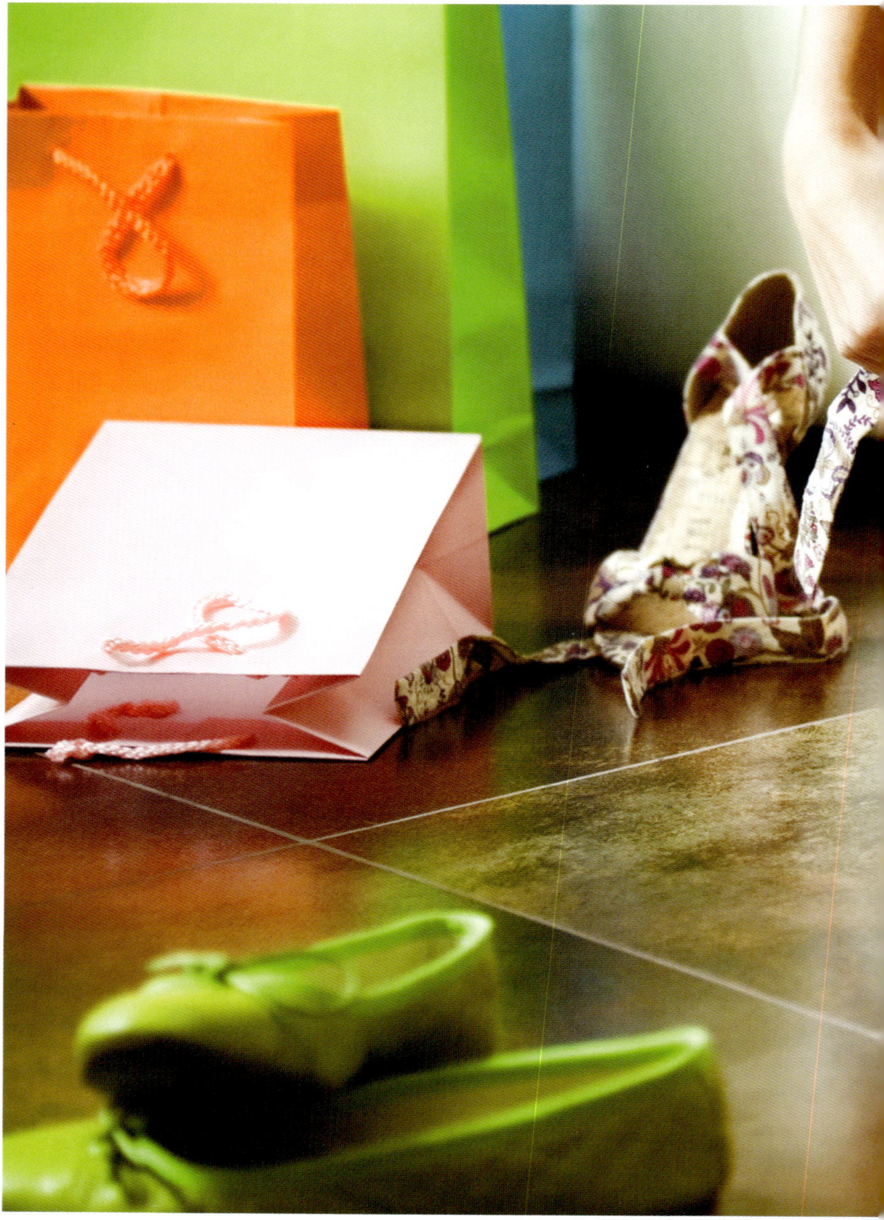

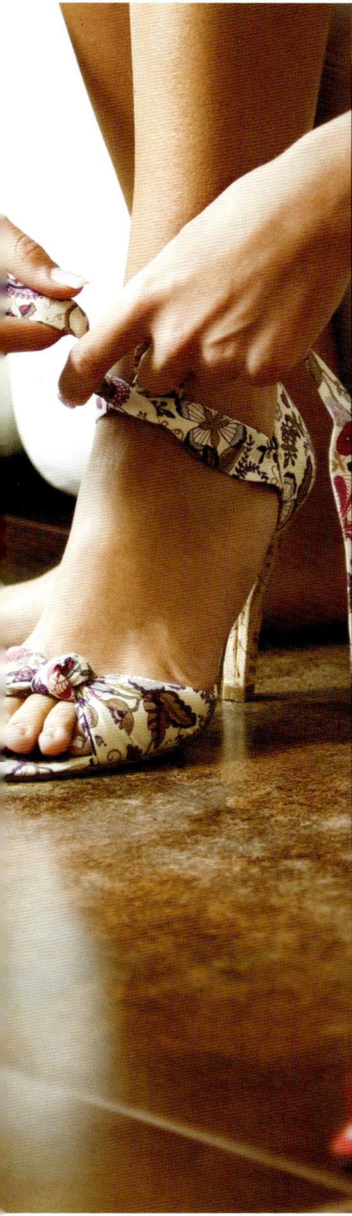

2

Lesson 1: New clothes 1

- About clothes and sizes
- How to express what you like and what fits you: ***Mir gefällt das Hemd.***
- How to express whether something belongs to you: ***Das gehört mir.***
- How to say "Which one? – This one!"

Lesson 2: New clothes 2

- How to express your opinion on clothes and situations.
- Vocabulary for clothing and colors.
- How to say what you are wearing.
- How to express that something is not quite right.

Collins | Livemocha™

UNIT 2 › LESSON 1

New clothes 1

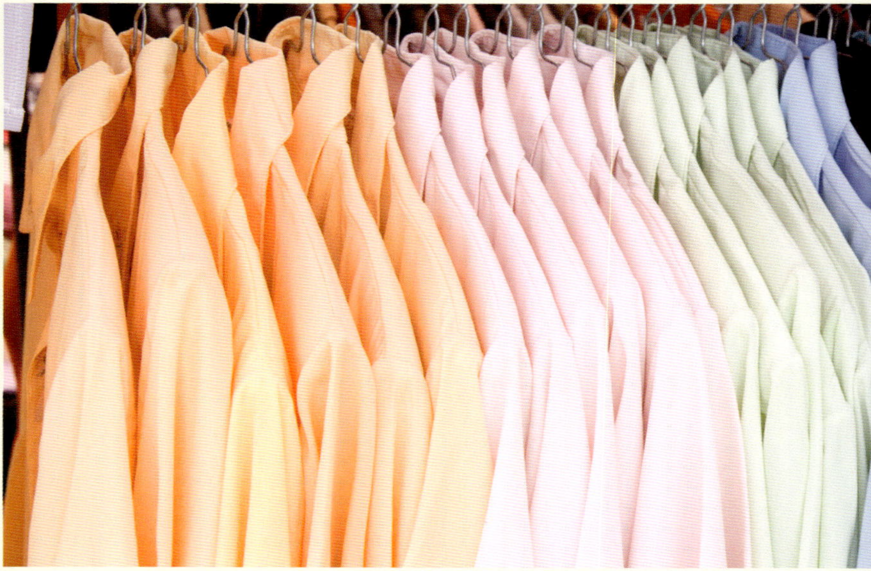

Culture note

In Germany clothing and shoe sizes are different than other countries in Europe.

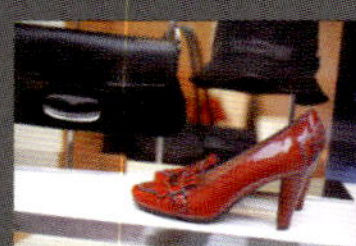

For women the smallest size for a dress is a 34 (US 4 / UK 6). For shoes a size 36 (US 6 / UK 4) is the smallest.

In the men's world sizes in S, M, L, XL, XXL, and XXXL are widely used. In numbers the sizes range from 46 / 48 to 62. Shoe sizes for men range from 39 (US 8) to 47 (US 13).

Video Dialog

Lara helps Matthias with his hunt for new clothes.

Active German: Level 3 > *Unit 2* > *Lesson 1* > *Video dialog*

Lara:	*Was brauchst du denn?*
Matthias:	*Ich suche eine Hose und ein Hemd.*
Lara:	*Welche Farbe? Welche Größe hast du denn?*
Matthias:	*Die Farbe ist mir egal. Ich habe Größe 48.*
Lara:	*Was ist mit dem Hemd?*
Matthias:	*Oh, das gefällt mir ganz gut. Hoffentlich passt es mir.*
Lara:	*Schau mal, hier sind noch ein paar Hosen und Hemden.*
Matthias:	*Ich probiere alles an.*

Lara:	What do you actually need?
Matthias:	I need some pants and a shirt.
Lara:	What color? And what size are you?
Matthias:	I don't care which color. I'm a size 48.
Lara:	What about this shirt?
Matthias:	Oh, I like that! Hopefully it will fit me.
Lara:	Look, there are some more pants and shirts here.
Matthias:	I'll try everything on.

Grammar

Active German: Level 3 > *Unit 2* > *Lesson 1* > *Grammar*

1 › I like it!(1)

In the video dialog Lara asks Matthias if he likes the shirt:

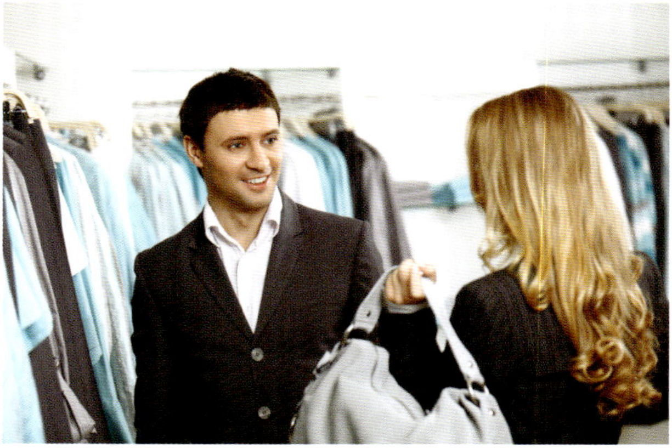

Was ist mit dem Hemd?

What about this shirt?

He answers:

Das (Hemd) gefällt mir ganz gut.

I really like the shirt.

You use the verb *gefallen* to say you like something. The literal translation is: "The shirt pleases me." The person expressing the preference is in the dative case.

Do you remember the dative case? Here are the forms:

ich → mir	me
du → dir	you
er → ihm	him
sie → ihr	her
wir → uns	us
ihr → euch	you
Sie → Ihnen	you
sie → ihnen	them

2 › I like it! (2)

Let's have a look at some examples:

Das Haus gefällt mir.

I like the house.
Or literally: The house pleases me.

Was gefällt dir?	What do you like?
Die Hose gefällt ihm.	He likes the pants.
Der Film gefällt ihr.	She likes the movie.

Note that *gefallen* takes an umlaut in the 3rd person singular. Here is the plural:

Die Hemden gefallen mir.

I like the shirts.

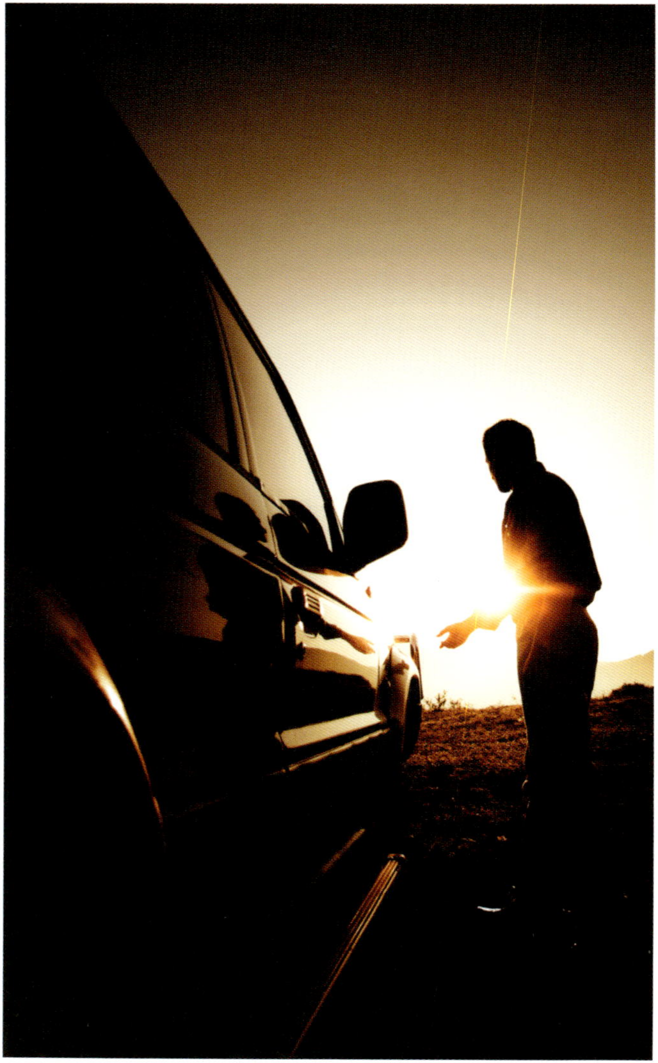

3 › **Does it belong to you?**

There are some other verbs that work in the same way:

passen
to fit

Matthias says:

Hoffentlich passt mir das Hemd.
Hopefully the shirt will fit me.

The shirt rather than Matthias is the subject of the sentence.

gehören	to belong to
Das Auto gehört mir.	The car belongs to me.
Gehört Ihnen das Handy?	Does the cell phone belong to you?

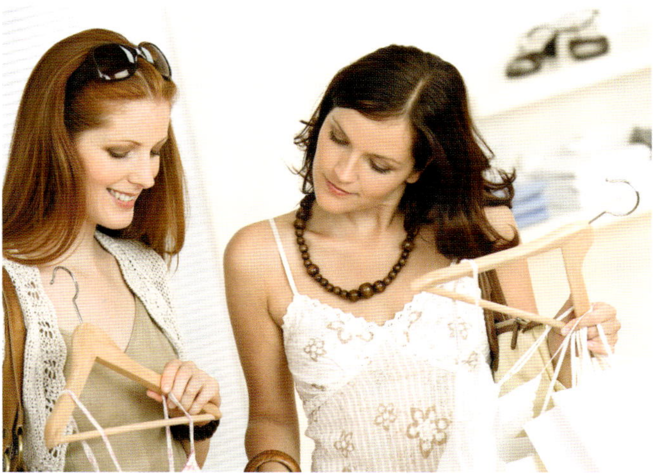

4 › Which one?

In the video dialog Lara asks which color Matthias wants and what size he is:

Welche Farbe möchtest du?	What color would you like?
Welche Größe hast du?	What size are you?

We use the article *welch-* to ask for specific information. Note that it agrees with the noun:

masculine	*Welcher Pullover?*	Which sweater?
feminine	*Welche Hose?*	Which pair of pants?
neuter	*Welches Hemd?*	Which shirt?
plural	*Welche T-Shirts?*	Which t-shirts?

5 › This one!

To refer to a specific object you use:

Welcher Pullover?	*dieser Pullover*	this sweater
Welche Hose?	*diese Hose*	this pair of pants
Welches Hemd?	*dieses Hemd*	this shirt
Welche T-Shirts?	*diese T-Shirts*	these t-shirts

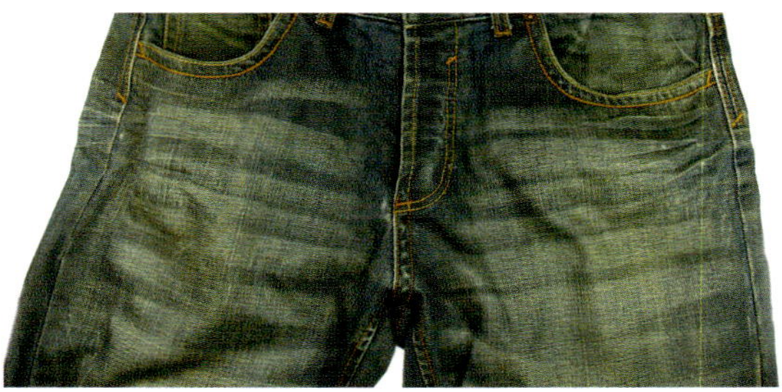

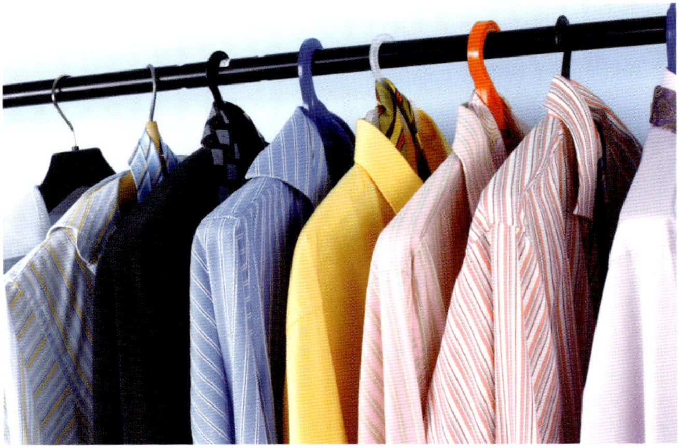

Vocabulary

Active German: Level 3 > *Unit 2* > *Lesson 1* > *Vocabulary*

Clothes

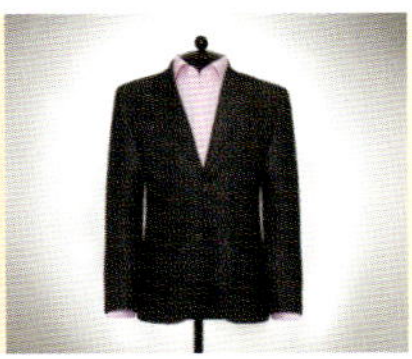

der Anzug / Anzüge
suit

Haben Sie einen neuen Anzug?
Do you have a new suit?

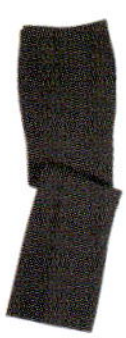

die Hose / Hosen
(pair of) pants

Ist die Hose neu?
Are these pants new?

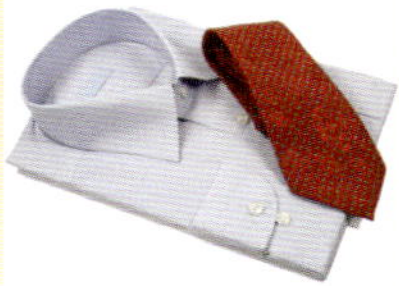

das Hemd / Hemden
shirt

Gefällt dir das Hemd?
Do you like the shirt?

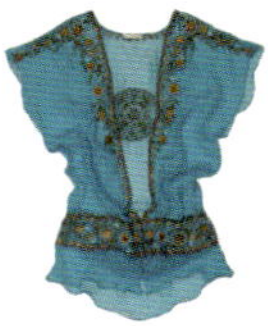

die Bluse / Blusen
blouse

Das ist aber eine schöne Bluse.
This is a really nice blouse.

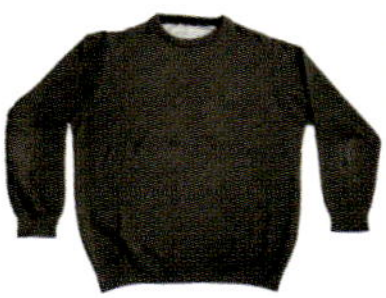

der Pullover / Pullover
sweater

Es ist ein bisschen kalt. Hast du einen Pullover für mich?
It is a bit cold. Do you have a sweater for me?

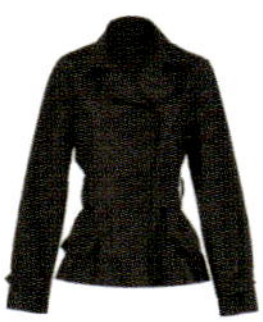

das Jackett / Jacketts
jacket / coat

Passt dir das Jackett noch?
Does this jacket still fit you?

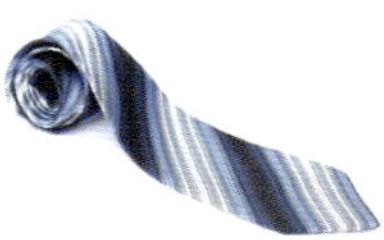

die Krawatte / Krawatten
tie

Brauche ich eine Krawatte?
Do I need a tie?

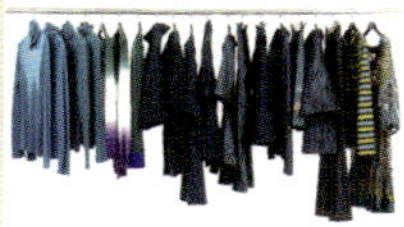

die Kleidung
clothes

Wo kann man hier gut Kleidung kaufen?
Where is a good place to buy clothes?

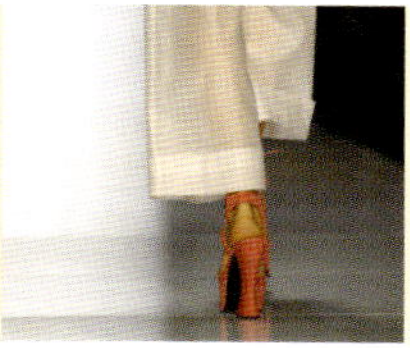

die Mode / Moden
fashion

Interessierst du dich für Mode?
Are you interested in fashion?

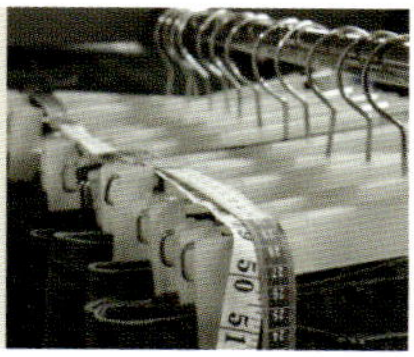

die Größe / Größen
size

Welche Größe haben Sie?
What size are you?

UNIT 2 › LESSON 2

New clothes 2

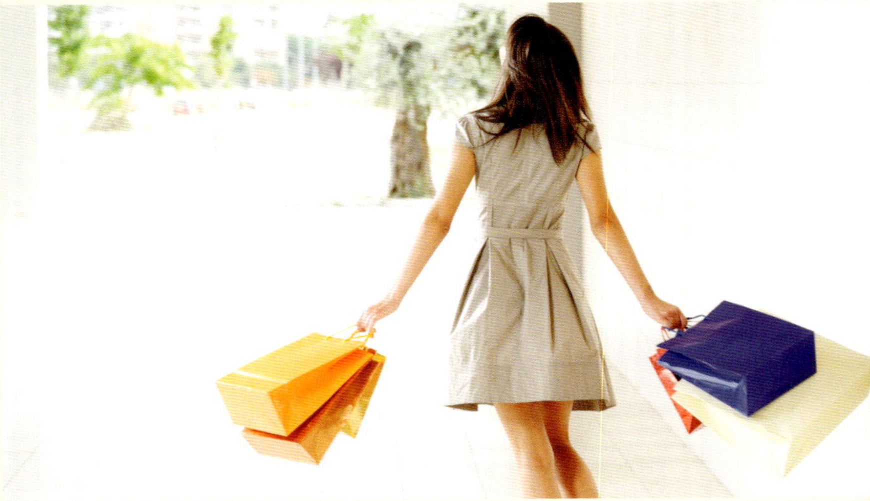

Culture note

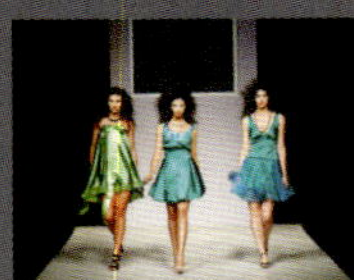

Nowadays, "Fashion made in Germany" appears quite regularly on international catwalks and in famous fashion houses. Well-known designers from Hamburg, Düsseldorf, and Munich are creating a new image. Berlin is the stronghold of the young German fashion scene. The most famous German fashion designer abroad is undoubtedly Karl Lagerfeld, who is Creative Director of Chanel. Labels like *Wunderkind* by Wolfgang Joop, Escada, Strenesse Gabriele Strehle, and René Lezard are established names on the world market. In the sportswear segment, Boss, Bogner, and Adidas should also be mentioned.

Video Dialog

In the fitting rooms Matthias tries on different sizes while Lara tries to convince him to choose something for the summertime.

Active German: Level 3 > *Unit 2* > *Lesson 2* > *Video dialog*

Lara:	*Und?*
Matthias:	*Die Hose passt mir nicht, aber die Hose ist gut und die Hemden auch.*
Lara:	*Ist dir die Farbe nicht zu dunkel?*
Matthias:	*Nein, das ist mir egal. Gefällt es dir nicht?*
Lara:	*Doch, aber wir brauchen etwas Farbe für den Sommer. Was ist mit diesem Hemd?*
Matthias:	*Das ist viel zu groß.*
Lara:	*Und das?*
Matthias:	*Das ist zu teuer.*
Lara:	*Schade.*

Lara:	Well?
Matthias:	These pants don't fit, but these pants are good and the shirts as well.
Lara:	Don't you think the color is too dark?
Matthias:	No, I don't care. Don't you like it?
Lara:	Yes, but we need a bit of color for summer. What about this shirt?
Matthias:	That's far too big.
Lara:	And that?
Matthias:	That's too expensive.
Lara:	What a shame.

Grammar

Active German: Level 3 > Unit 2 > Lesson 2 > Grammar

1 › I don't care

Matthias says that he doesn't care about the color of his shirt. He says:

Das ist mir egal.

I don't care.

He uses *mir* (to me) to refer to himself. In Lesson 1 we saw that in some expressions the person speaking is not the subject of the sentence and therefore is in the dative case.

2 › I'm fine

Let's have a look at some other important expressions which follow the same pattern.

Mir ist schlecht.	I feel sick.
Mir geht es gut.	I'm fine.
Das tut mir leid.	I'm sorry about that.

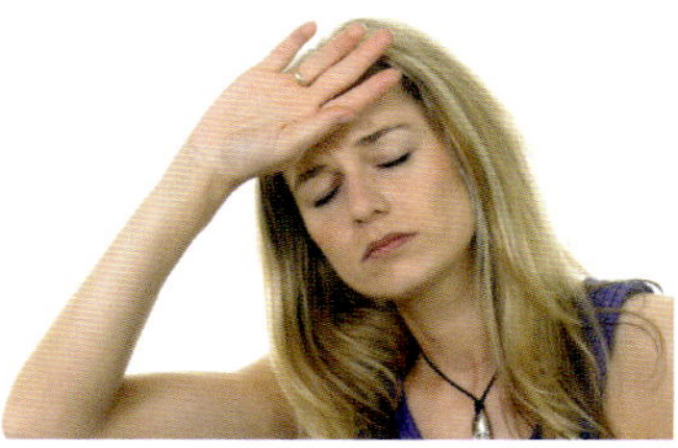

3 › **That is too big**

To express that something is not quite what you want, you can say: *zu* (too)+ adjective

Die Hose ist mir zu groß.	The pants are too big for me.
Das Hemd ist mir zu teuer.	The shirt is too expensive for me.

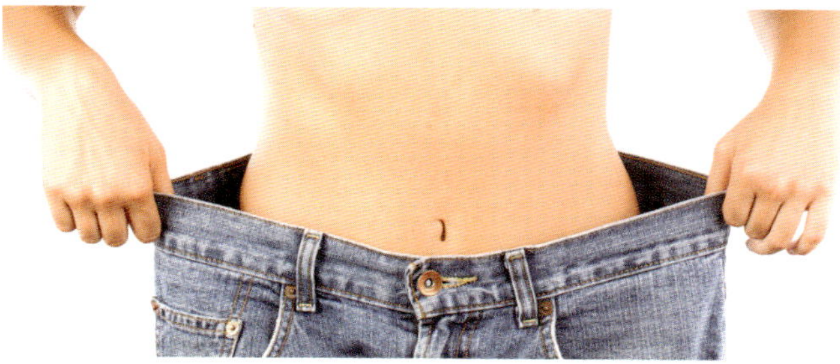

Note again that you are referring to yourself using the dative case.

This construction works with basically every adjective.

Das ist mir zu heiß / zu kalt.

I'm too hot / too cold.

4 › **I'll try it on**

We are now going to have a look at some useful verbs for talking about clothing.

Matthias wants to try on some shirts and pants. He says:

Ich probiere alles an.

I'll try everything on.

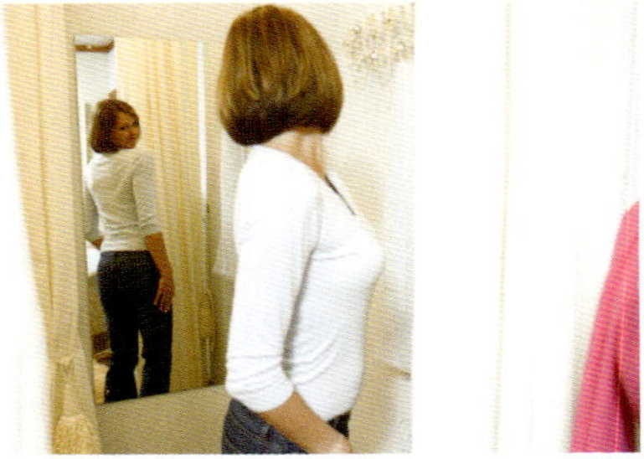

Note that *anprobieren* is a separable verb.

Anziehen means to put something on / to dress.

> *Was ziehst du an?*
> What are you going to put on?

It is a separable verb as well.

5 › The verb *tragen*

The verb *tragen* means "to wear" or "to carry."

Have a look at its forms:

Ich trage einen Pullover.	I wear a sweater.
Trägst du gerne Blusen?	Do you like wearing blouses?
Trägt er eine Krawatte?	Does he wear a tie?
Wir tragen gerne Jeans.	We like wearing jeans.
Was tragt ihr bei der Arbeit?	What do you wear at work?
Tragen Sie gerne einen Anzug?	Do you like wearing a suit?
Was tragen sie heute?	What are they wearing today?

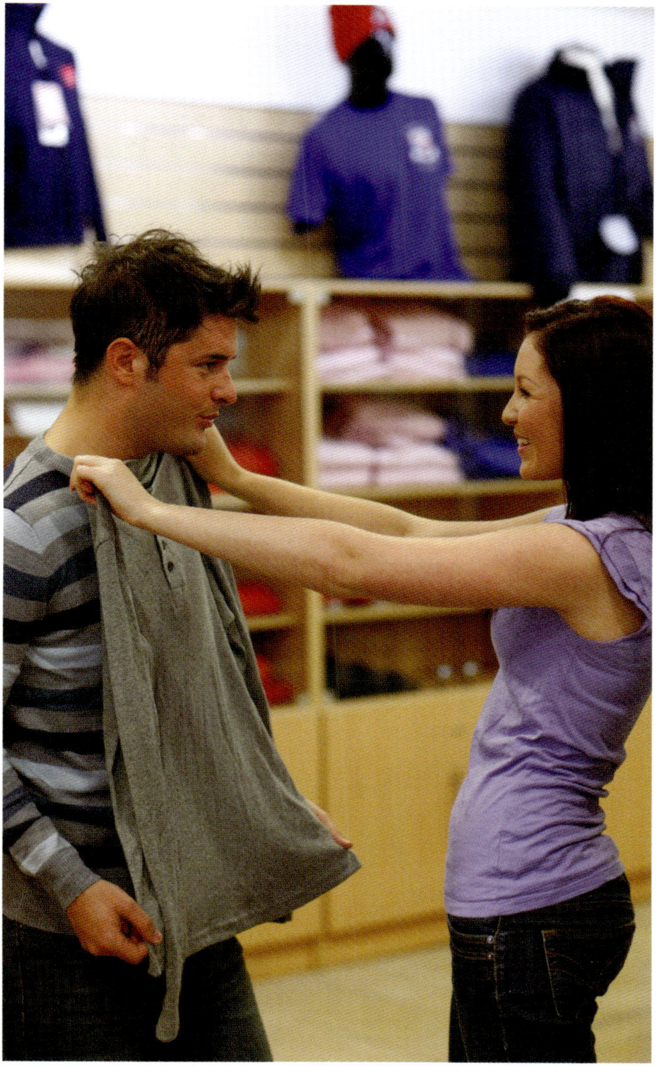

Vocabulary

Active German: Level 3 > Unit 2 > Lesson 2 > Vocabulary

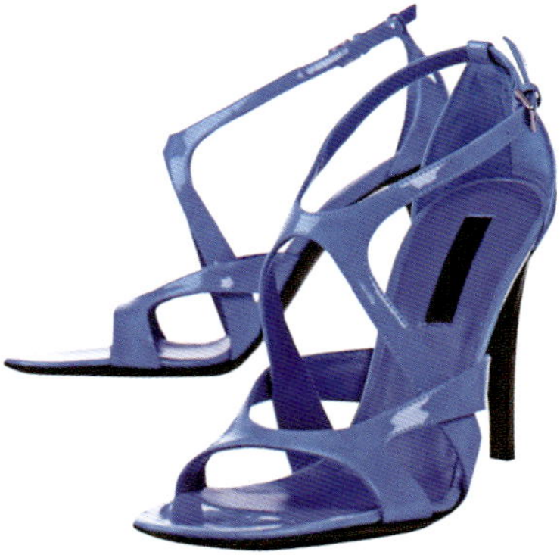

Colors

die Farbe / Farben
color

Wir brauchen mehr Farbe.
We need more color.

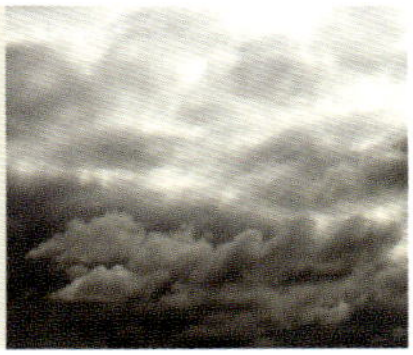

dunkel
dark

Es ist sehr dunkel. Es regnet gleich.
It's very dark. It is going to rain soon.

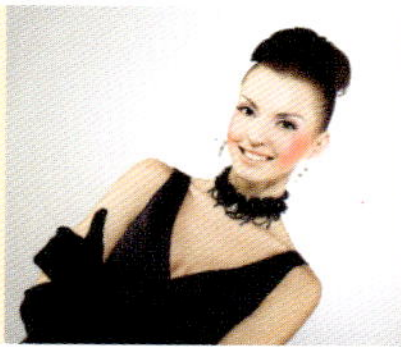

schwarz
black

Ich trage gerne schwarz.
I like to wear black.

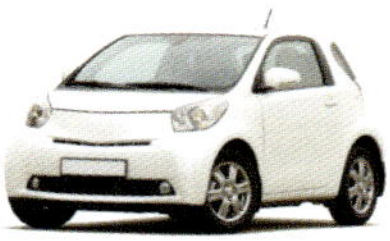

weiß
white

Ihr Auto ist weiß.
Her car is white.

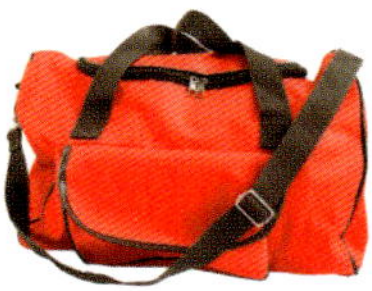

rot
red

Sie hat eine rote Tasche.
She has a red bag.

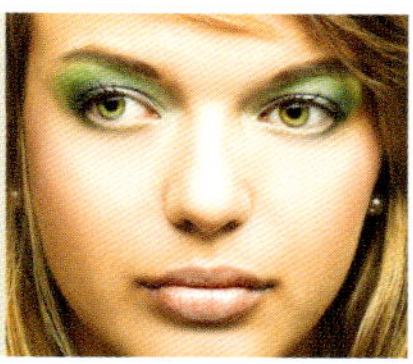

grün
green

Ihre Augen sind grün.
Her eyes are green.

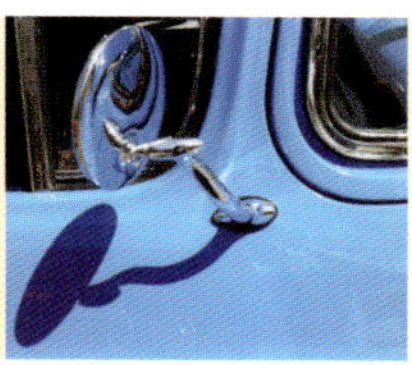

blau
blue

Ich liebe die Farbe blau.
I love the color blue.

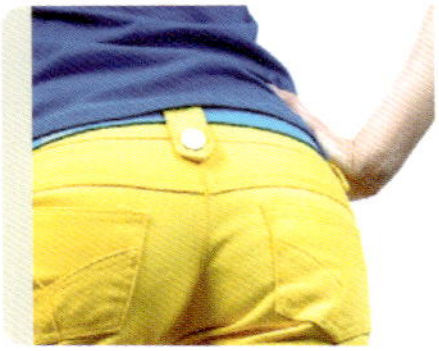

gelb
yellow

Sie trägt eine gelbe Hose.
She wears yellow pants.

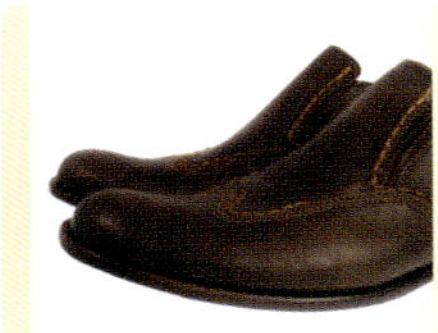

der Schuh / Schuhe
shoe

Ich habe Schuhgröße 42.
I take shoe size 42.

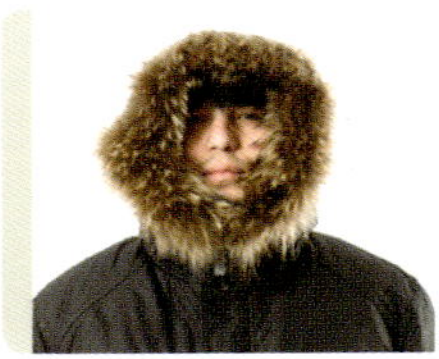

der Mantel / Mäntel
coat

Ich brauche einen dicken Mantel für den Winter.
I need a warm coat for the winter.

Culture note

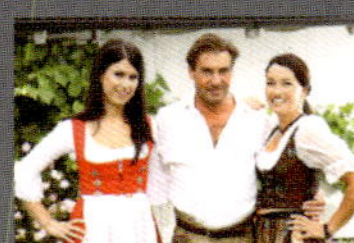

Everybody associates *Dirndl* (traditional women's attire) and *Lederhosen* with the Germans. The *Dirndl* consists of close-fitting bodice and a wide skirt with an apron which has different patterns and colors according to the region. The *Lederhose* – knee-length pants – is made from leather. Men wear it with knee high socks. Traditional dress (*Tracht*) varies from region to region. It is common to wear this on official occasions, especially in Southern Germany, Bavaria, and Austria.

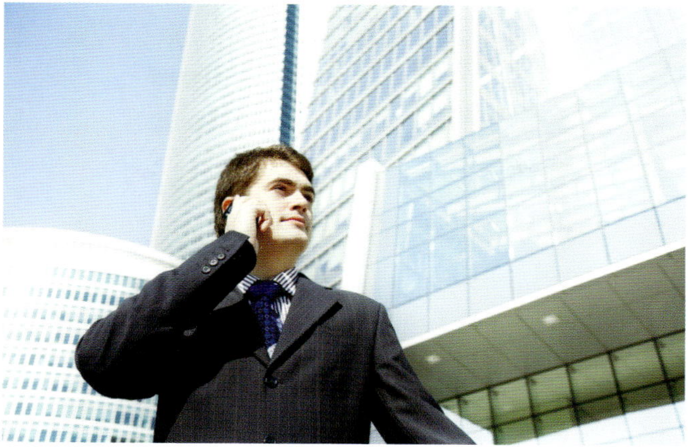

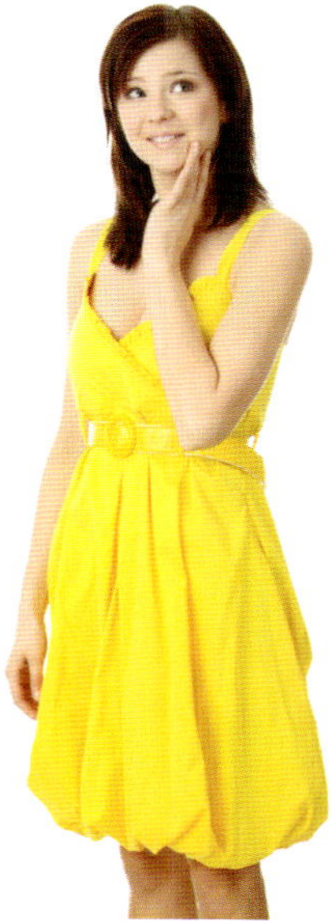

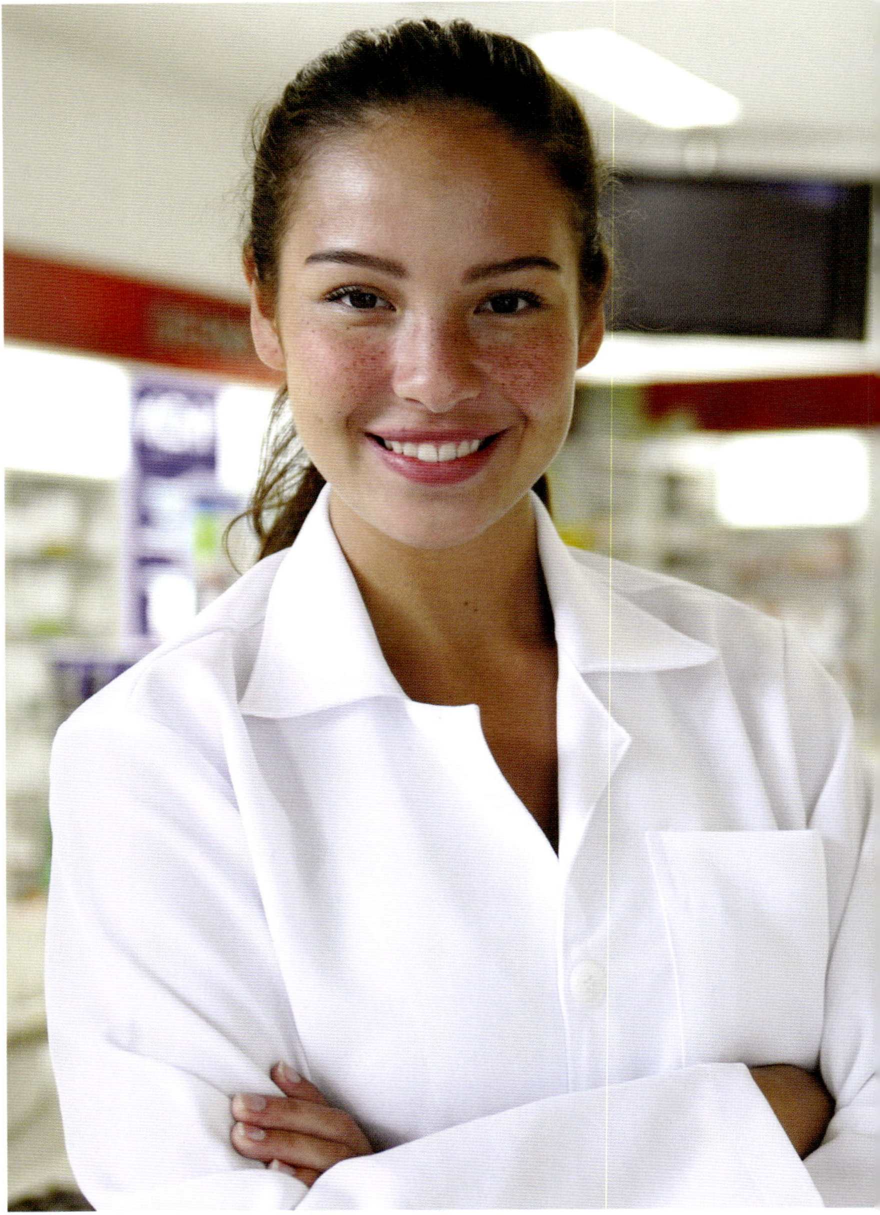

Active German *Level 3*

3

Lesson 1: Excuse me

- How to ask for directions: ***Entschuldigung, wie komme ich zum Bahnhof?***
- How to ask if something is nearby: ***Ist eine Apotheke in der Nähe?***
- How to express suggestion and commands for ***du***.
- Vocabulary for important places in a city.

Lesson 2: In a pharmacy

- How to say where you put things.
- How to say where things are.
- Important phrases for medicine and pharmacies.
- How to use ***nach*** (after), ***seit*** (since, for), ***mit*** (with) und ***zu*** (to).
- Vocabulary for health and parts of the body.

Collins | Livemocha™

UNIT 3 › LESSON 1

Excuse me

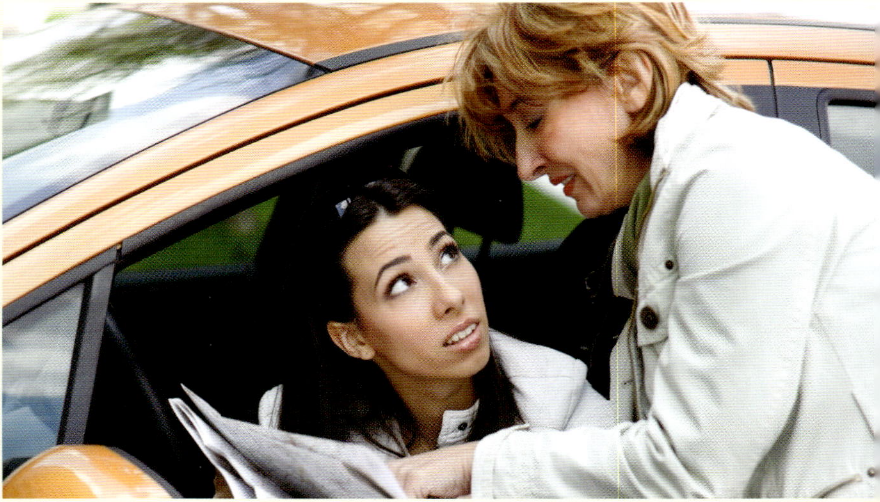

Culture note

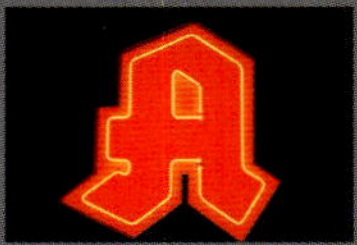

What English speakers refer to as a pharmacy or a chemist's is known as an *Apotheke* in Germany. They are denoted by a large red A. You shouldn't confuse them with *Drogerie* (like a drugstore) where you can buy toiletries. In an *Apotheke* there are two types of medication: over-the-counter drugs and prescription – only medicines. For the latter you need a *Rezept* (prescription) from a doctor. The prescription is taken to the pharmacy by the patient and the pharmacist dispenses or sells the medicines. The law on prescription is very strict. Many medicines, such as antibiotics, must be prescribed by a doctor.

Video Dialog

Lara gives Matthias directions to the pharmacy.

Active German: Level 3 > *Unit 3* > *Lesson 1* > *Video dialog*

Matthias:	*Lara? Wo ist denn hier eine Apotheke in der Nähe?*
Lara:	*Eine Apotheke. Also, geh geradeaus bis zum Marktplatz, geh über den Marktplatz am Rathaus entlang.*
Matthias:	*Oh, ok. Nicht so schnell bitte.*
Lara:	*Kennst du den Marktplatz?*
Matthias:	*Ja, natürlich.*
Lara:	*Geh über den Marktplatz. Am Ende siehst du eine Bank. Geh an der Bank vorbei. Geh rechts in die Konradstraße.*
Matthias:	*Ok, vielen Dank.*
Lara:	*Geht es dir nicht gut? Warte, ich komme mit.*

Matthias:	Lara? Where is there a pharmacy around here?
Lara:	A pharmacy. OK, you go straight on until you get to the market square, cross the market square alongside the town hall.
Matthias:	Oh, OK. Not so fast, please.
Lara:	Do you know the market square?
Matthias:	Yes, of course.

Lara:	Cross the market square. At the end you'll see a bank. Go past the bank. Then turn right onto Conrad Street.
Matthias:	OK, thanks a lot.
Lara:	Aren't you feeling well? Wait, I'll come with you.

Grammar

Active German: Level 3 > Unit 3 > Lesson 1 > Grammar

1 › How to ask for directions

If you are not familiar with a place you have to ask for directions. The most typical sentences to introduce your question are:

Entschuldigung, wie komme ich ...

Excuse me, how do I get ...

... zum Bahnhof?

... to the train station?

... zur Post?

... to the post office?

or:

Entschuldigung, wo finde ich das Rathaus?

Excuse me, where do I find the town hall?

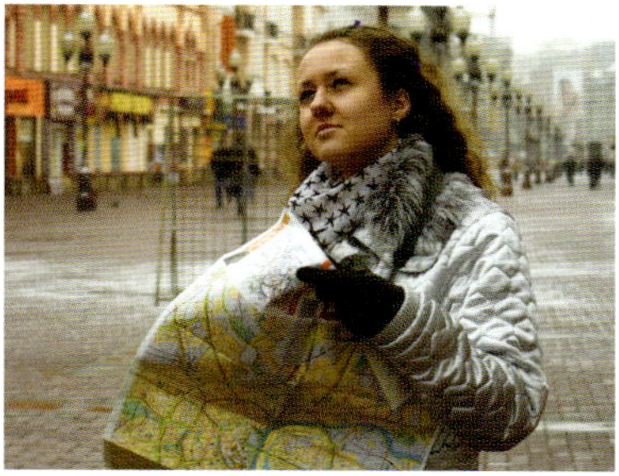

2 › **How to ask for directions**

The person you are asking might reply with the following:

Das Rathaus ist gleich in der Nähe.	The town hall is very close by.
Das Rathaus ist weit von hier. / Das Rathaus ist nicht weit von hier.	The town hall is far away from here. / The town hall is not far away from here.

Here are some useful phrases that occur very often:

Gehen Sie geradeaus bis zum Marktplatz / zur Kirche.	Go straight ahead until you get to the market square / the church.
Gehen Sie nach links / rechts.	Turn left / right.
Gehen Sie links / rechts in die Konradstraße.	Turn left / right onto Conrad Street.
Gehen Sie an der Bank vorbei.	Go past the bank.
Gehen Sie über den Marktplatz.	Go across the market square.
Gehen Sie am Fluss entlang.	Go alongside the river.

3 › Go!

In some earlier lessons we had a look at the imperative for *Sie* (you):

As a suggestion:

> *Kaufen Sie doch Vanilleeis.*
> Why don't you buy vanilla ice cream?

As a command:

> *Seien Sie pünktlich!*
> Be punctual!

We can express the same intention in the *du* form as well.

In the video dialog Lara gives Matthias directions to the pharmacy. In order to do so she uses the imperative form:

> *Geh geradeaus bis zum Marktplatz.*

Geh is a form of the verb *gehen*.

4 › Wait!

Let's have a look at how to express suggestions and commands in the *du* form.

gehen to go, to walk

du gehst (you go or walk) becomes *Geh* (Go)

You leave out the person and cut off the *-st*.

In the *Sie* form: *Sie gehen* becomes *Gehen Sie* (Go)

Simply reverse the verb and the person.

Lara wants to go with Matthias and says:

Warte, ich komme mit.

Wait, I'll come with you.

Warte derives from *warten* (to wait).

By leaving out the person and cutting off the *-st*, *du wartest* (you wait) becomes *Warte* (Wait).

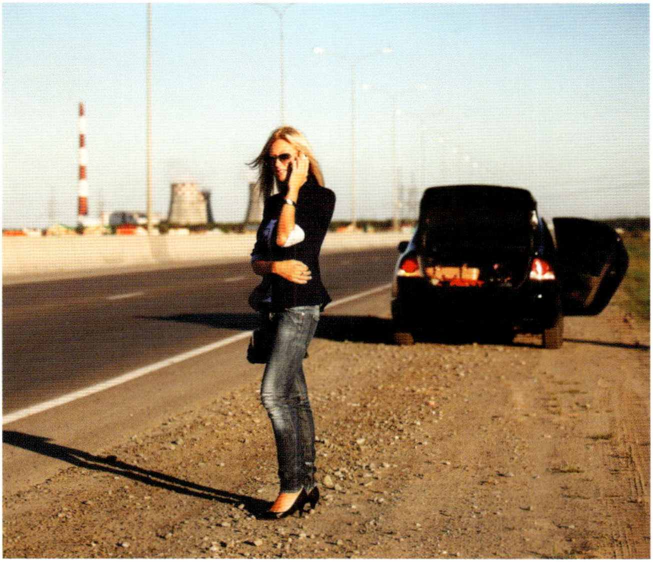

5 › Why don't you?

Let's consider some other examples:

kommen

in the *du* form	*Komm doch bitte.*	Come, please.
in the *Sie* form	*Kommen Sie bitte.*	Come, please.

If you want to suggest that somebody should call somebody else using *anrufen* you say:

in the *du* form	*Ruf ihn doch an.*	Why don't you call him?
in the *Sie* form	*Rufen Sie ihn doch an.*	Why don't you call him?

Separable verbs preserve their characteristics so you cut off *an-* as well.

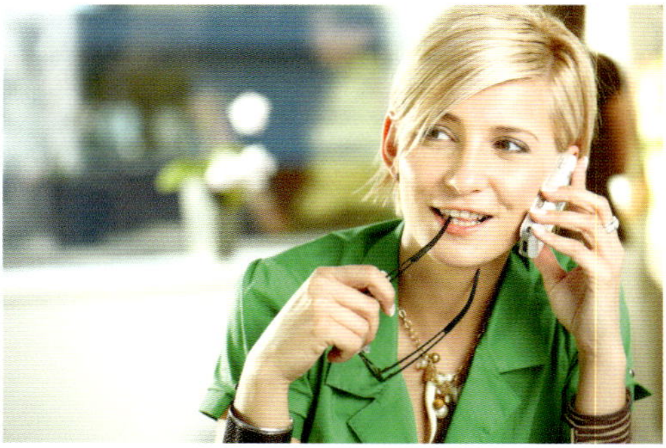

6 › Be nice!

You might remember that *sein* (to be) has a special form for the imperative.

Seien Sie pünktlich.

Be on time.

The form for *du* is very similar.

Sei pünktlich.	Be on time.
Sei nett.	Be nice.

Vocabulary

Active German: Level 3 > Unit 3 > Lesson 1 > Vocabulary

In a city

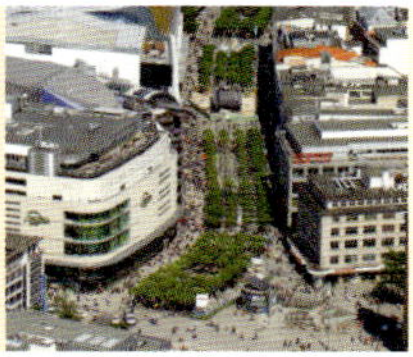

die Hauptstraße / Hauptstraßen
main road

Ich wohne neben der Hauptstraße.
I live next to the main road.

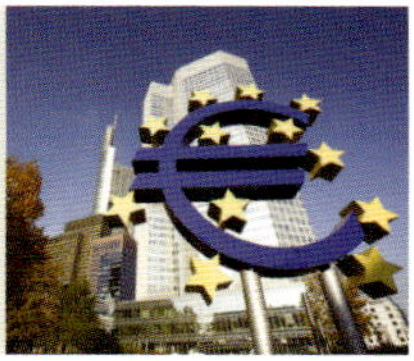

die Bank / Banken
bank

Entschuldigen Sie, ich suche eine Bank.
Excuse me, I'm looking for a bank.

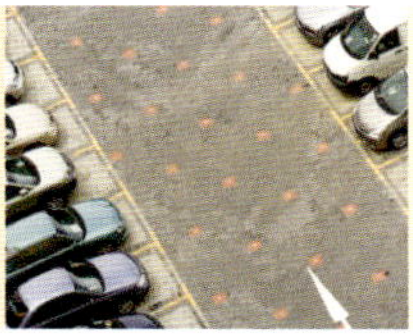

der Parkplatz / Parkplätze
parking lot

Gibt es hier einen Parkplatz?
Is there a parking lot around here?

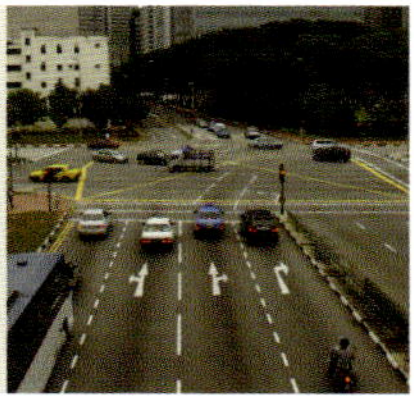

die Kreuzung / Kreuzungen
intersection / junction

Fahren Sie geradeaus bis zur Kreuzung.
Go straight on to the intersection.

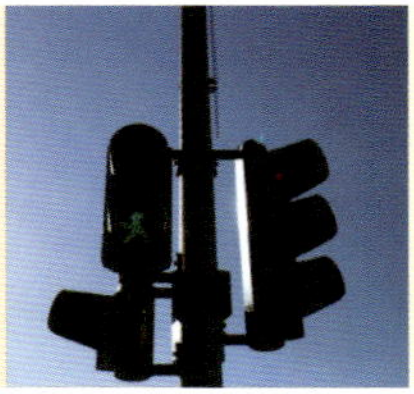

die Ampel / Ampeln
traffic light

In Ostberlin waren die Ampeln sehr schön.
In East Berlin the traffic lights were really nice.

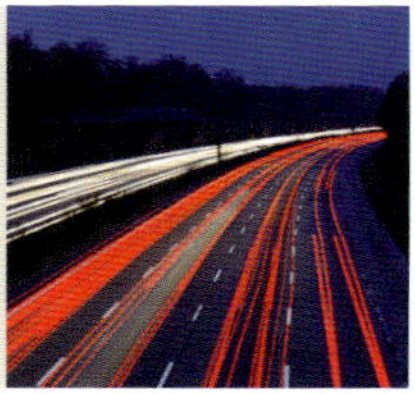

schnell
fast / quick

Fahren Sie bitte nicht so schnell.
Please don't drive so fast.

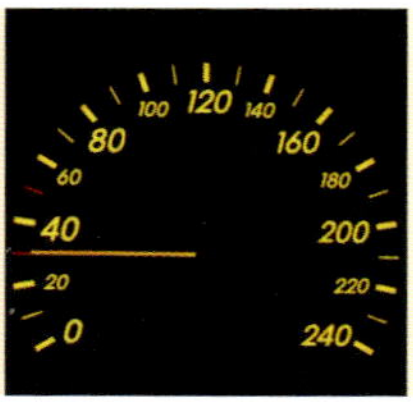

langsam
slow

Du bist heute so langsam.
You are so slow today.

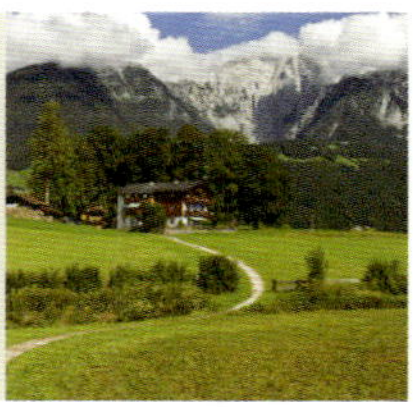

der Weg / Wege
path, way

Kennst du den Weg nach Hause?
Do you know the way home?

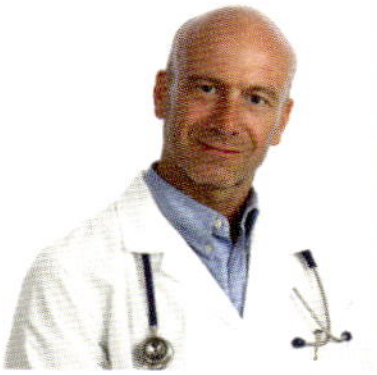

der Arzt / Ärzte
doctor

Hilfe, wir brauchen einen Arzt.
Help, we need a doctor.

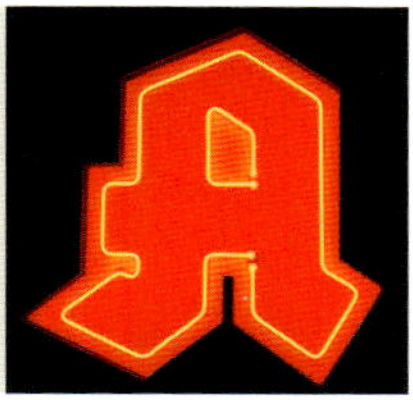

die Apotheke / Apotheken
pharmacy

Ist hier eine Apotheke in der Nähe?
Is there a pharmacy around here?

Culture note

The word *Bank* has actually two meanings. On the one hand it refers to the credit institution. On the other hand *eine Bank* is a bench. The words have a different plural form:

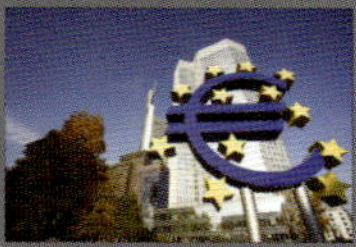

Credit institution: *die Bank / Banken*
Bench: *die Bank / Bänke*

UNIT 3 › LESSON 2

In a pharmacy

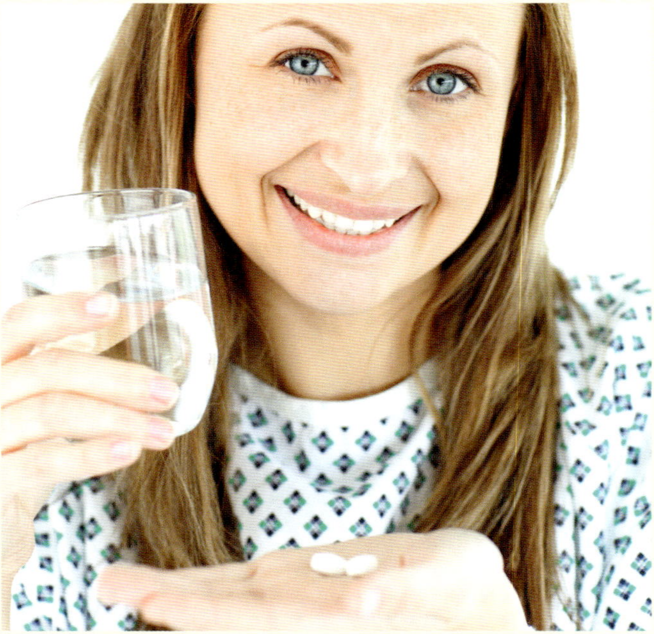

Culture note

Everybody knows the wonder drug aspirin. But where does it come from? The effects of aspirin-like substances had already been recorded in ancient Greece but aspirin as we know it today is mostly based on the version developed by Bayer, the pharmaceutical company founded in Germany in 1863. Felix Hoffmann, a Bayer scientist, was searching for a way to treat his father's arthritis and is now credited with the invention of the modern form of the drug.

Video Dialog

At the pharmacy, Matthias buys some medication.

Active German: Level 3 > *Unit 3* > *Lesson 2* > *Video dialog*

Matthias:	*Vielen Dank.*
Verkäufer:	*Bitte schön. Gute Besserung.*
Matthias:	*Danke schön.*
Lara:	*Wie lange hast du schon Halsschmerzen und Husten?*
Matthias:	*Seit drei Tagen.*
Lara:	*Was für Medikamente hast du gekauft?*
Matthias:	*Das hier ist gegen die Halsschmerzen und das ist ... Wohin habe ich denn jetzt die Tabletten gelegt?*
Lara:	*Ah hier. Neben die Kasse.*
Matthias:	*Und das ist gegen den Husten.*
Lara:	*Wie oft sollst du die Tabletten nehmen?*
Matthias:	*Ich soll dreimal täglich eine Tablette nach dem Essen nehmen.*

Matthias:	Thank you very much.
Salesclerk:	Here you go. Get well soon.
Matthias:	Thank you.
Lara:	How long have you had a sore throat and a cough?
Matthias:	For three days.

Lara:	What kind of medicine did you buy?
Matthias:	This is something for a sore throat and this is ... Where did I put the tablets?
Lara:	Ah, here, next to the checkout.
Matthias:	And this is for the cough.
Lara:	How often should you take the tablets?
Matthias:	I should take one tablet after a meal three times a day.

Grammar

Active German: Level 3 > *Unit 3* > *Lesson 2* > *Grammar*

1 › Since when?

In the video dialog Lara asks Matthias how long he has been suffering from his cold.

He answers:

Seit drei Tagen.

For three days.

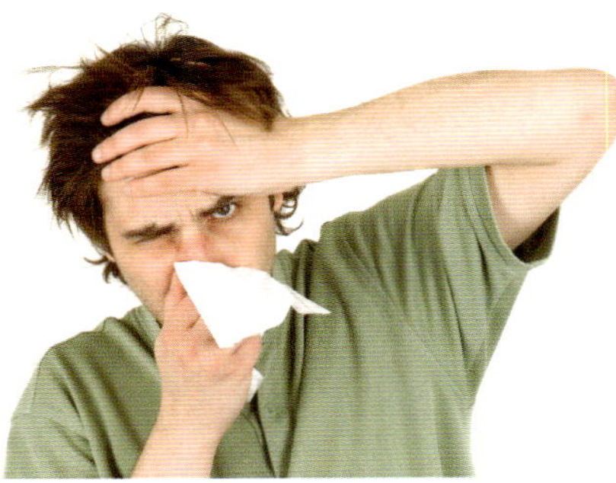

You use *seit* (since or for) to indicate the starting point of a period of time.

Seit wann wohnst du in Köln?

Since when / How long have you been living in Cologne?

Seit is a preposition. It is always followed by the dative case. We had a look at the dative case before.

Ich wohne seit einem Monat hier.

I have been living here for one month.

Note that you use the present tense after *seit*!

2 › After a meal

Matthias has to take his medicine after a meal. He says:

Ich soll die Tabletten ***nach dem*** *Essen nehmen.*

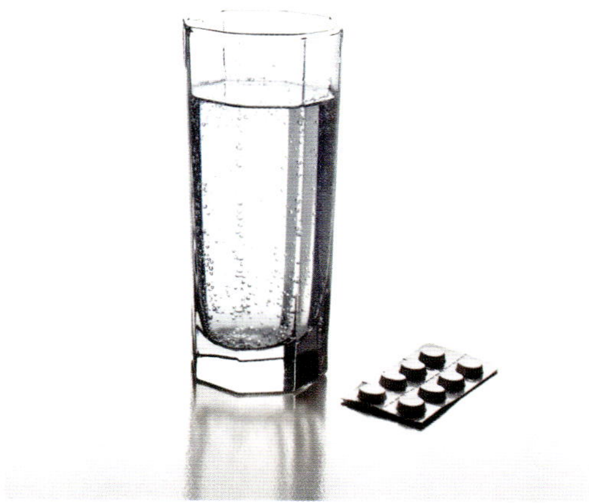

Note that *nach* (after) is another preposition that requires the dative case.

Nach der Arbeit treffe ich meine Freunde.

After work I meet my friends.

Mit (with, by) is another preposition that requires the dative case.

Fährst du mit dem Auto oder mit der U-Bahn zur Arbeit?

Do you go by car to work or do you take the subway?

So far we have met the following dative prepositions: *zu* (*zum* or *zur*), *seit*, *nach*, and *mit*.

3 › I put it next to the checkout

Matthias doesn't know where he put the tablets.

Lara says:

neben die Kasse

next to the checkout

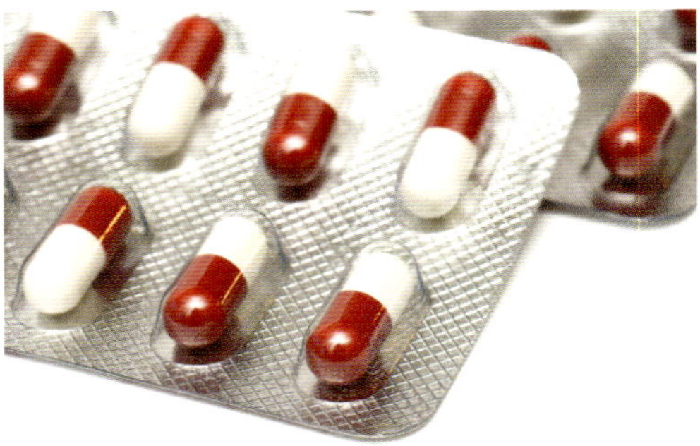

Do you remember the preposition *neben*? So far we have used it in combination with a location, asking where something is:

Wo ist das Handy? Neben dem Computer.

In this case, the use of the verb "to put" means that movement is involved (the act of putting the tablets somewhere) and so the accusative case must be used and not the dative case (which is used to indicate location and not movement).

Wohin hast du die Tabletten gelegt?	Where did you put the tablets?
Ich habe sie neben die Kasse gelegt.	I put them next to the checkout.

4 › Where are the tablets? Where did you put them? (1)

This concept works for some of the prepositions you have already seen:

hinter	behind
auf	on / onto
vor	in front of
in	in / into

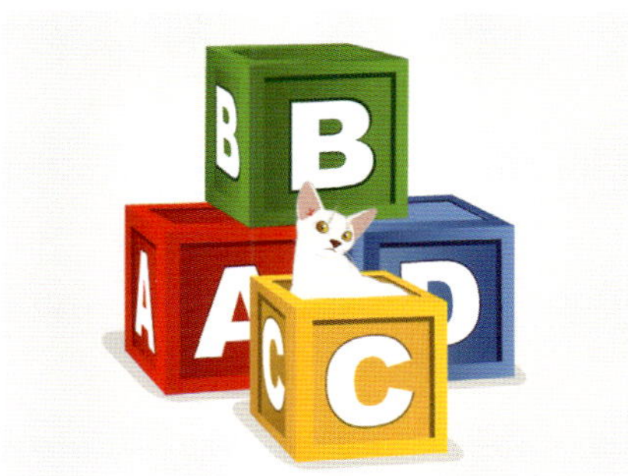

5 › Where are the tablets? Where did you put them? (2)

Compare:

movement – accusative	*Ich lege das Buch auf den Tisch.*	I put the book onto the table.
location – dative	*Das Buch liegt auf dem Tisch.*	The book is on the table.
movement – accusative	*Ich stelle das Glas vor die Mikrowelle.*	I put the glass in front of the microwave.
location – dative	*Das Glas steht vor der Mikrowelle.*	The glass is in front of the microwave.

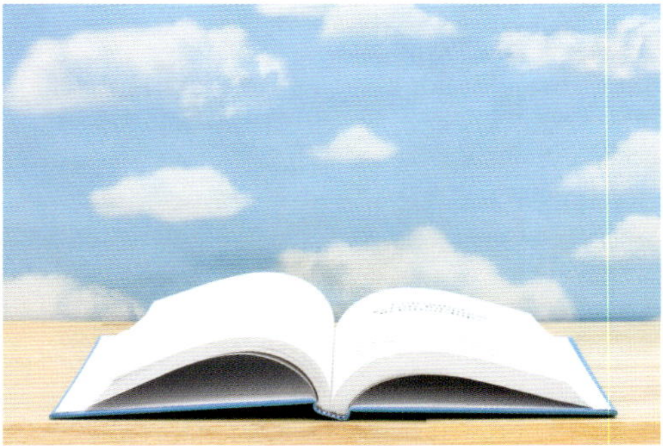

6 › I put it there!

Let's have a look at the verbs involved:

Stellen (to put) and *legen* (to put) are used when movement is involved.

Stehen (to be / to stand) and *liegen* (to be / to lie) are used when location is involved.

You use *stellen* and *stehen* for a vertical movement / location and *legen* and *liegen* for a horizontal movement / location.

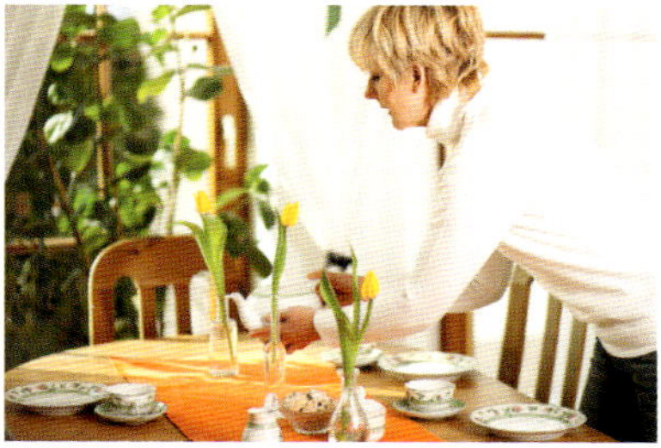

7 › For a sore throat

Matthias gets medicine for his cold.

Have a look at how this is expressed.

Das ist gegen die Halsschmerzen.
This is for a sore throat.

Gegen literally means "against." The medicine is a remedy against his pain.

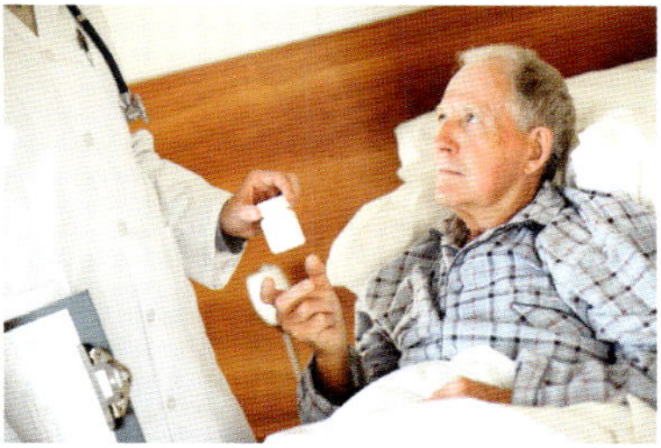

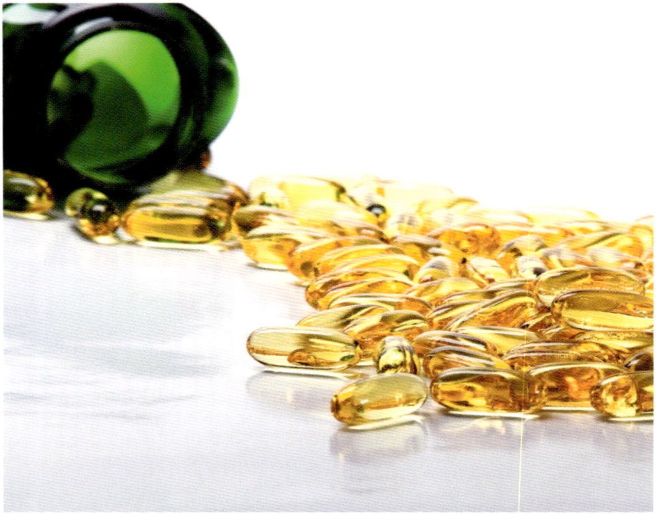

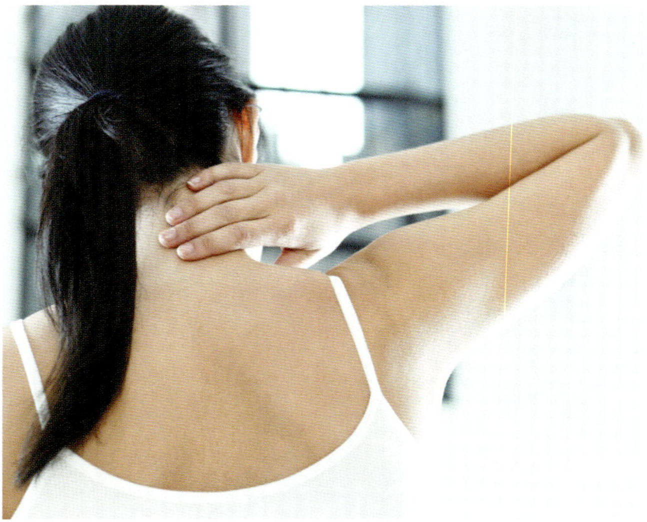

Vocabulary

Active German: Level 3 > Unit 3 > Lesson 2 > Vocabulary

Health, medicine, and parts of the body

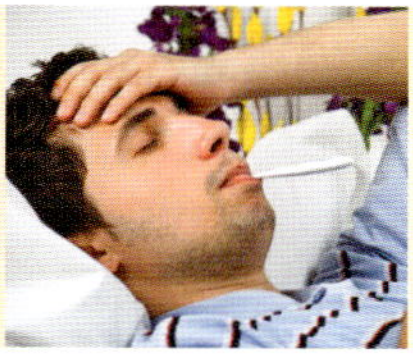

das Fieber
fever

Hast du Fieber?
Are you feverish?

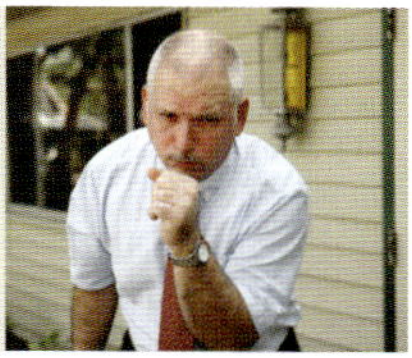

der Husten
cough

Ich habe seit fünf Tagen Husten.
I have had a cough for five days.

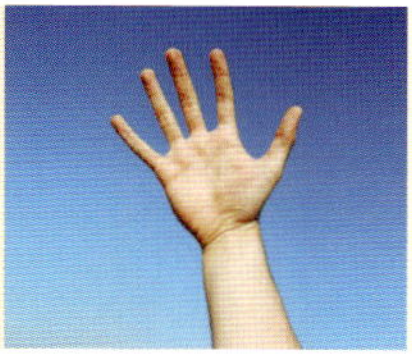

die Hand / Hände
hand

Wir haben alle Hände voll zu tun.
We've got our hands full.

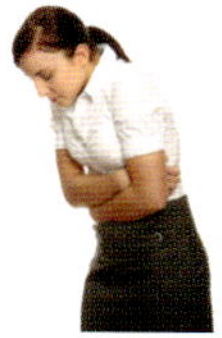

der Schmerz / Schmerzen
pain

Haben Sie noch Schmerzen?
Are you still in pain?

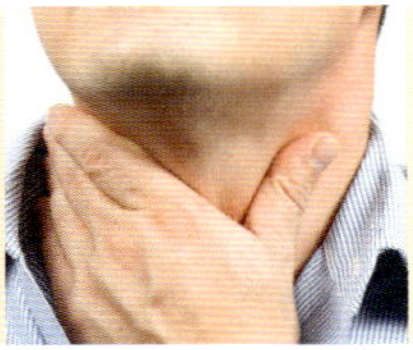

der Hals / Hälse
throat

Ich habe Halsschmerzen.
I have a sore thoat.

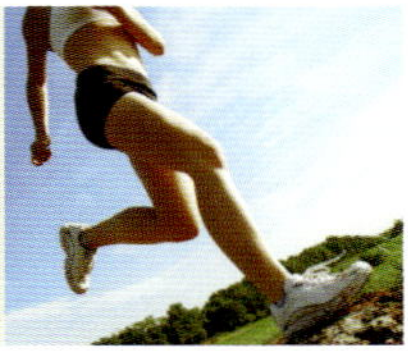

das Bein / Beine
leg

Sie hat aber schöne Beine.
She has really beautiful legs.

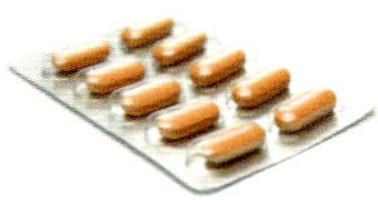

die Tablette / Tabletten
tablet

Nehmen Sie die Tabletten nach dem Essen.
Take the tablets after a meal.

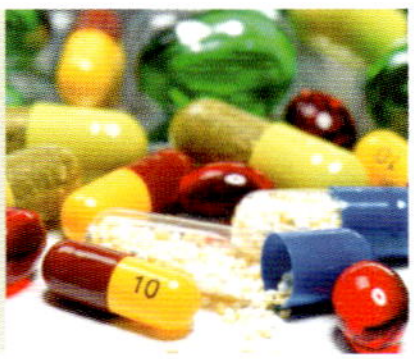

das Medikament / Medikamente
medicine

Kaufen Sie dieses Medikament in der Apotheke.
Buy this medicine in a pharmacy.

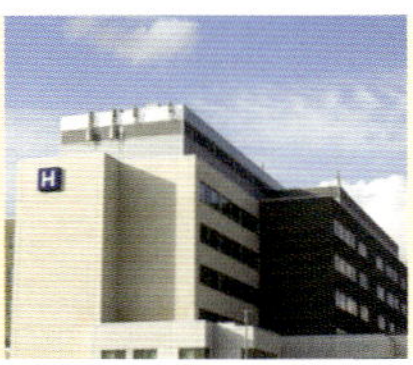

das Krankenhaus / Krankenhäuser
hospital

Arbeitet er in einem Krankenhaus?
Does he work in a hospital?

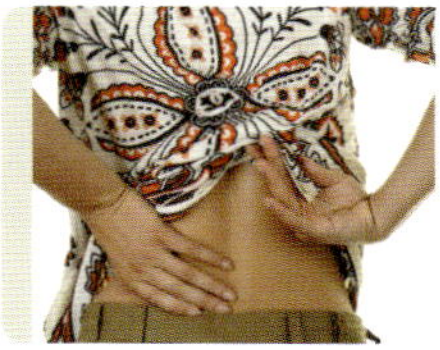

der Rücken / Rücken
back

Ich habe Rückenschmerzen.
I have a back pain.

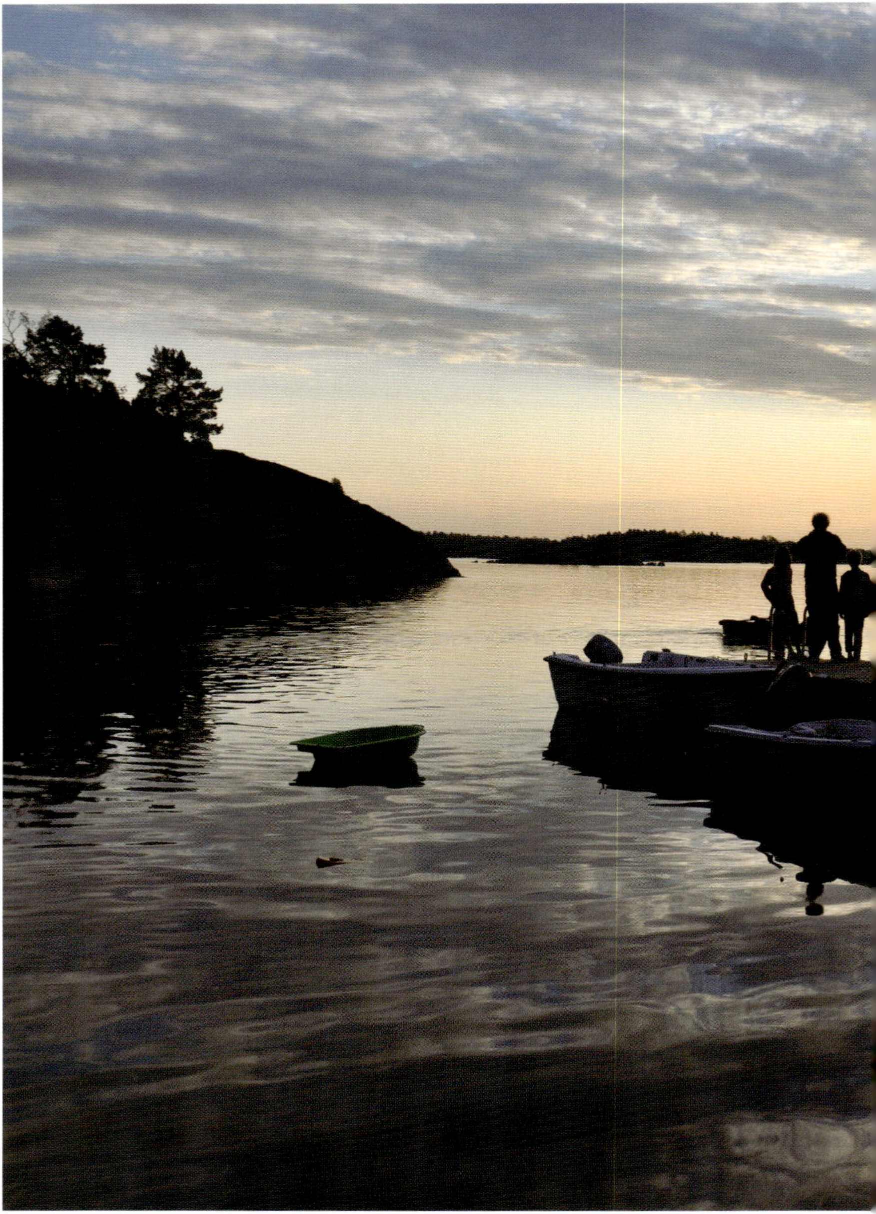

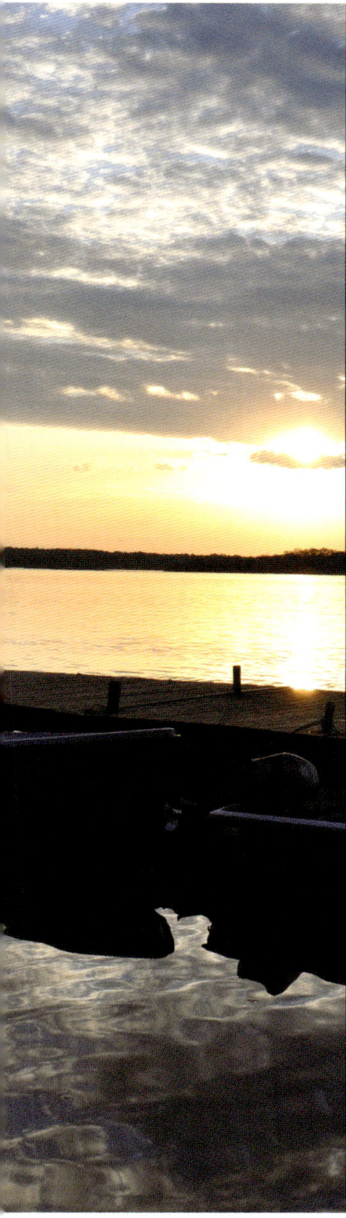

4

Lesson 1: People

- How to talk about past events.
- How to say where you were born and where you grew up.
- How to talk about important steps in your life, such as moving or getting married, etc.
- Vocabulary for events and periods in your life.
- How to say “I was able to, I had, I had to”: ***Ich konnte***, ***ich hatte***, ***ich musste***.

Lesson 2: Résumés

- How to talk about your education.
- How to say what subjects you studied.
- How to talk about your skills.
- Vocabulary for your résumé.
- Vocabulary for your education.
- How to use the verbs ***wissen*** and ***kennen*** (to know).

Collins | Livemocha™

UNIT 4 › LESSON 1

People

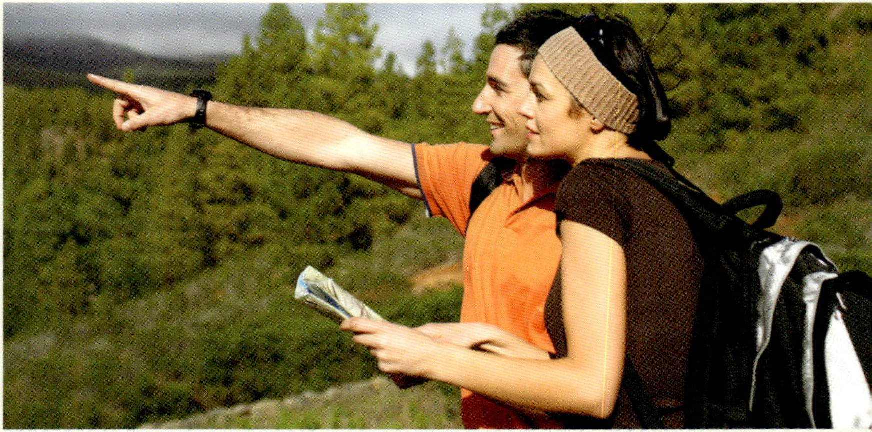

Culture note

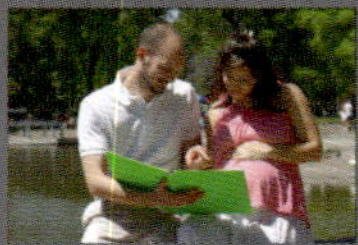

Over the last few years a fashion for short first names has developed. Also, names are now sounding more international, reflecting travel among the younger generation. Another trend is the resurgence of traditional baby names such as Paul.

The most popular German names over recent years:

for girls:

1. Hannah, 2. Leonie, 3. Lea, 4. Lena, 5. Mia, 6. Anna, 7. Emily, 8. Lara, 9. Laura, 10. Sarah.

for boys:

1. Leon, 2. Lukas, 3. Luca, 4. Tim, 5. Finn, 6. Luis, 7. Jonas, 8. Felix, 9. Paul, 10. Maximilian.

Video Dialog

Lara tells Mr. Buschel about her family.

Active German: Level 3 > *Unit 4* > *Lesson 1* > *Video dialog*

Herr Buschel:	*Was hast du denn da?*
Lara:	*Das ist ein Foto von meiner Familie. Meine Schwester hat ein Baby bekommen. Es ist vor einer Woche geboren.*
Herr Buschel:	*Oh, wie süß!*
Lara:	*Das ist meine Großmutter. Sie lebt nicht mehr. Sie hatte ein Restaurant in München. Sie musste viel arbeiten. In den Ferien konnte ich sie immer besuchen.*
Herr Buschel:	*Und dein Großvater?*
Lara:	*Mein Großvater hat schon viel erlebt. Er ist schon 85 Jahre alt.*

Mr. Buschel:	What do you have there, then?
Lara:	It's a picture of my family. My sister has had a baby. He was born one week ago.
Mr. Buschel:	How lovely!
Lara:	That's my grandmother. She's no longer with us. She had a restaurant in Munich. She had to work a lot. During vacations I used to visit her.
Mr. Buschel:	And your grandfather?
Lara:	My grandfather has experienced a lot. He's already 85 years old.

Grammar

Active German: Level 3 > Unit 4 > Lesson 1 > Grammar

1 › **I was there**

In earlier units we had a look at the verb *sein* (to be) in the past tense:

Ich war im Büro.
I was in the office.

This form is called the simple past. It is a form that is mostly used in written language. However, the verbs *sein* and *haben* and also *müssen* (must, to have to) and *können* (can, to be able to) are an exception. In these cases you use the simple past form quite regularly.

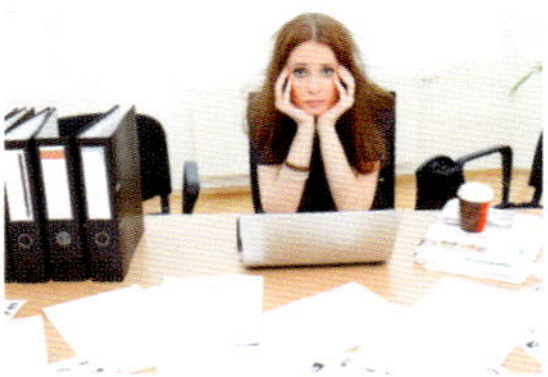

2 › **I had**

Let's have a look at the verb *haben* in the simple past.

ich hatte	I had
du hattest	you had
er / sie / es hatte	he / she / it had
wir hatten	we had
ihr hattet	you had
sie / Sie hatten	they / you had

In the video dialog Lara says:

Sie hatte ein Restaurant.
She had a restaurant.

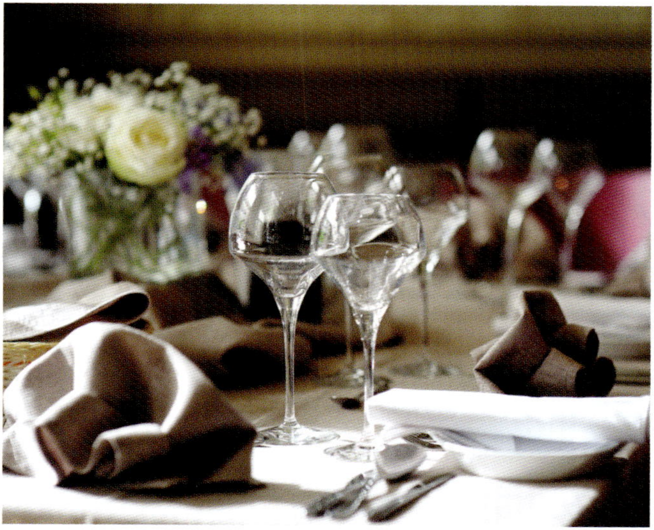

3 › I had to work a lot

Müssen follows a similar pattern:

ich musste	I had to
du musstest	you had to
er / sie / es musste	he / she / it had to
wir mussten	we had to
ihr musstet	you had to
sie / Sie mussten	they / you had to

Note that the umlaut is dropped in this form.

Lara says:

Sie musste viel arbeiten.
She had to work a lot.

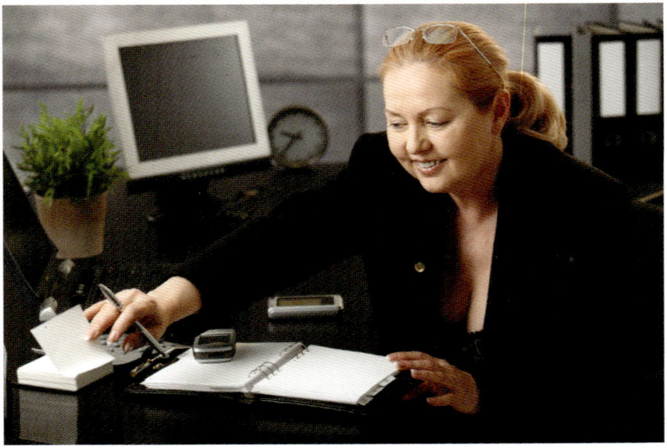

4 › I was able to

This is the verb *können* in the simple past:

ich konnte	I was able to / could
du konntest	you were able to / could
er / sie / es konnte	he / she / it was able to / could
wir konnten	we were able to / could
ihr konntet	you were able to / could
sie / Sie konnten	they / you were able to / could

Konnten Sie ihm helfen?

Were you able to help him?

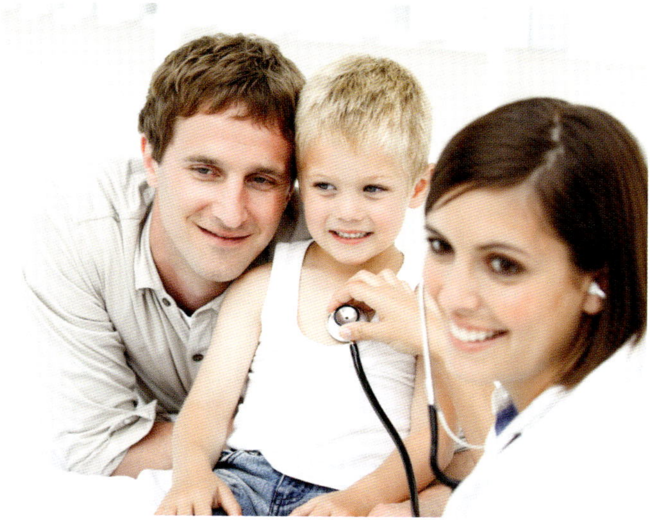

5 › **Where do you live?**

In German you use two different words to say "to live":

In earlier units you learned the verb *wohnen* which means "to live" or "to dwell."

Leben, on the other hand, means "to live" in the sense of existing.

Compare:

Wo wohnst du?

Where do you live?

Lara says:

Meine Großmutter lebt nicht mehr.

My grandmother doesn't live anymore (or is no longer alive).

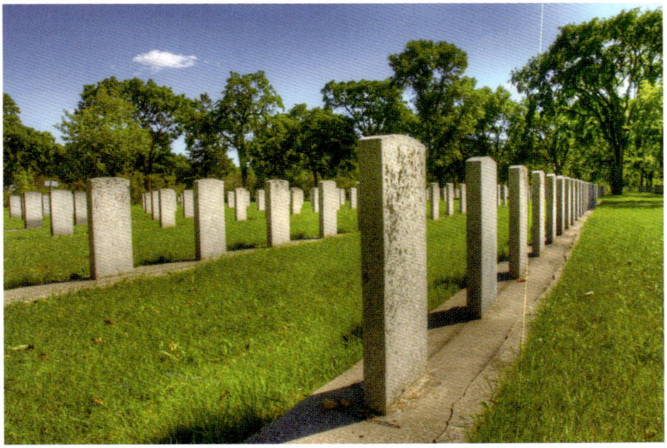

6 › **Some important expressions**

When you want to talk about your life you might need the following expressions:

Lara says:

Meine Schwester hat ein Baby bekommen. Es ist vor einer Woche geboren.

My sister has had a baby. It was born one week ago.

Wann sind Sie geboren?

When were you born?

Aufwachsen means “to grow up.” It is a separable verb so you cut off the *auf-*.

Look at the form:

Ich bin in Bonn aufgewachsen.

I grew up in Bonn.

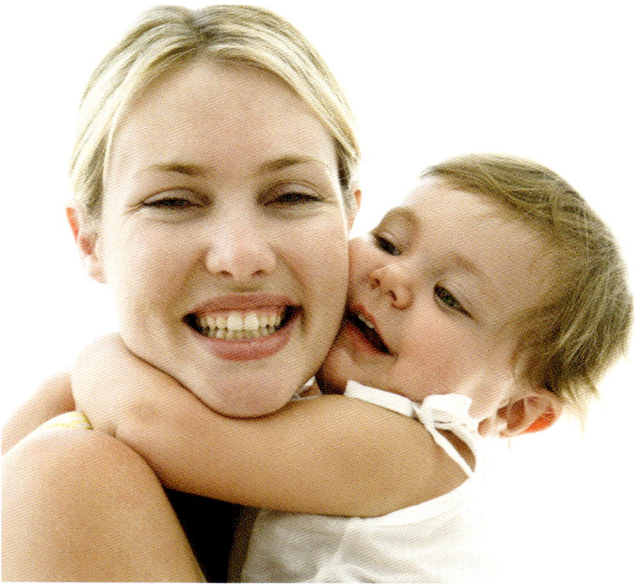

Umziehen means “to move” or “to change clothes.” *Umziehen* is separable as well.

Ich habe in Bonn gewohnt. Dann bin ich umgezogen.

I lived in Bonn. Then I moved.

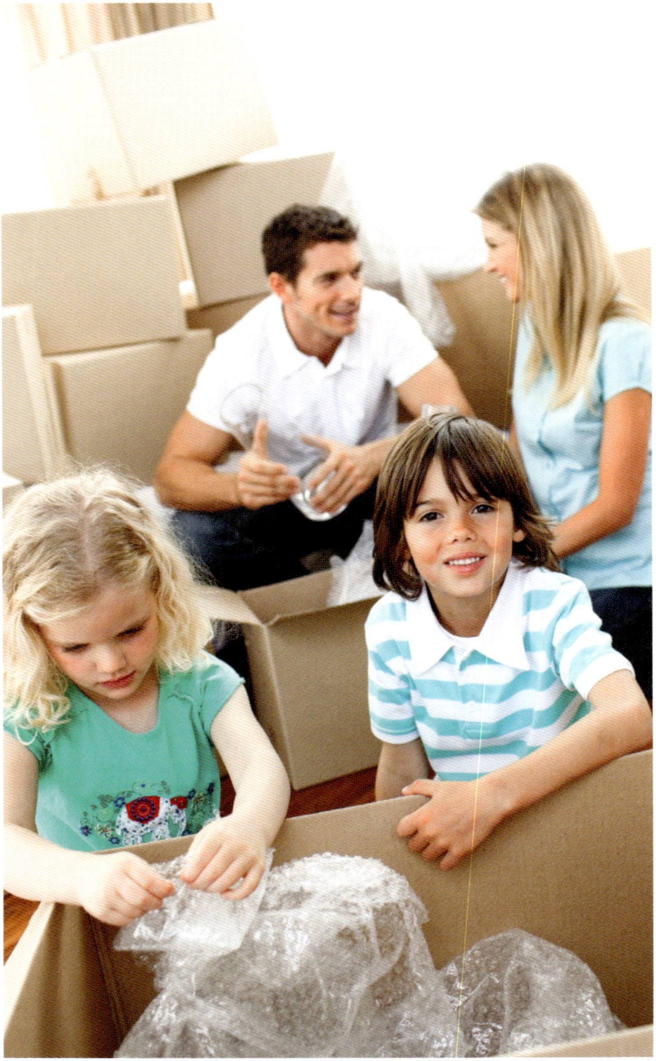

Vocabulary

Active German: Level 3 > *Unit 4* > *Lesson 1* > *Vocabulary*

Events and periods in your life

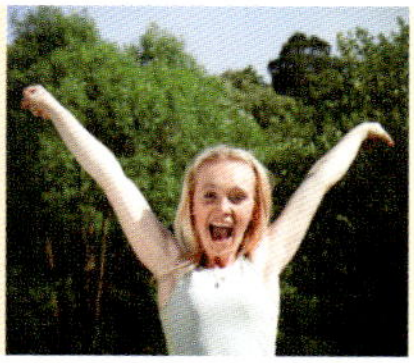

das Leben / Leben
life

Ich genieße mein Leben.
I enjoy life.

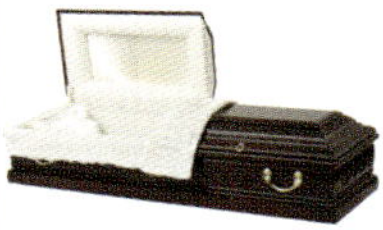

sterben
to die

Frau Glauter ist letzte Woche gestorben.
Mrs Glauter died last week.

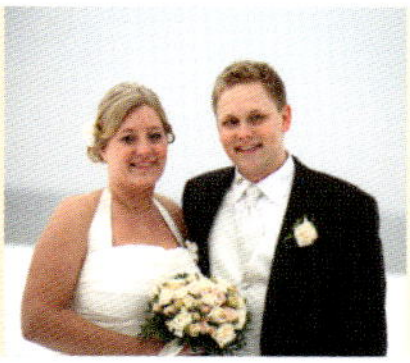

heiraten
to marry

Wann haben Sie geheiratet?
When did you get married?

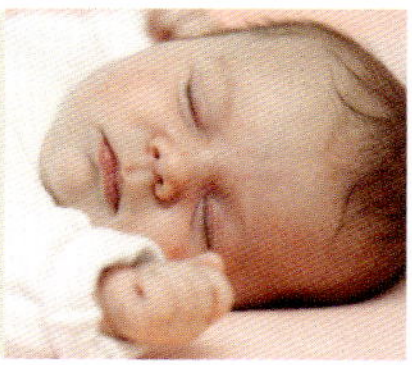

der Geburtsort / Geburtsorte
place of birth

Wo liegt dein Geburtsort?
Where is your place of birth?

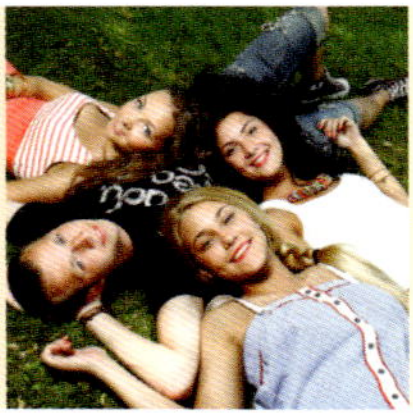

die Jugend
youth

Die heutige Jugend hat ein anderes Leben.
The youth of today has a different lifestyle.

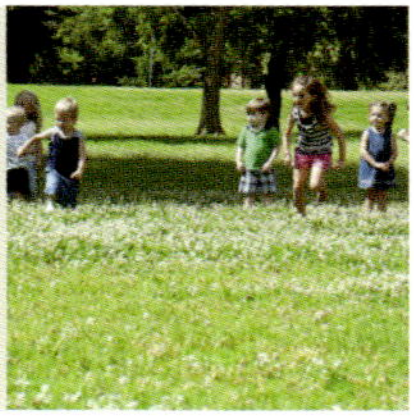

die Kindheit
childhood

Ich hatte eine schöne Kindheit.
I had a nice childhood.

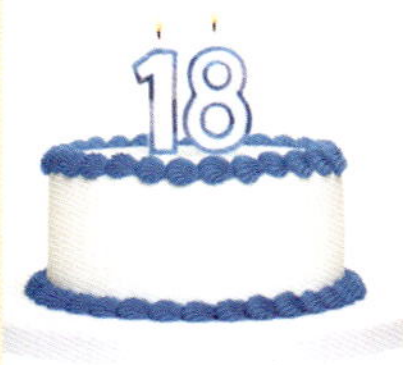

erwachsen
adult

Mit 18 Jahren ist man erwachsen.
At 18 years old you are an adult.

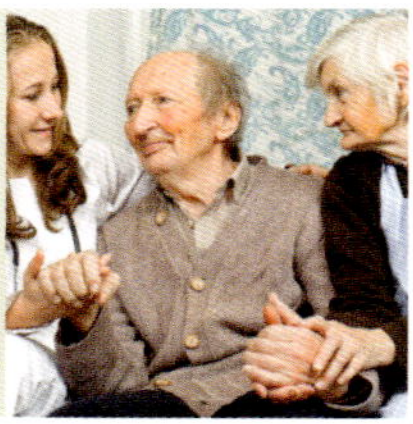

das Alter
age

In welchem Alter hast du geheiratet?
At what age did you get married?

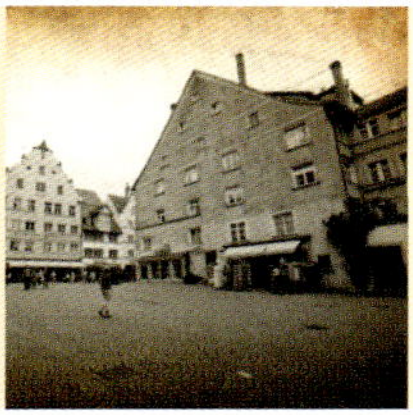

früher
in the past

Früher konnte ich alles machen.
In the past I was able to do everything.

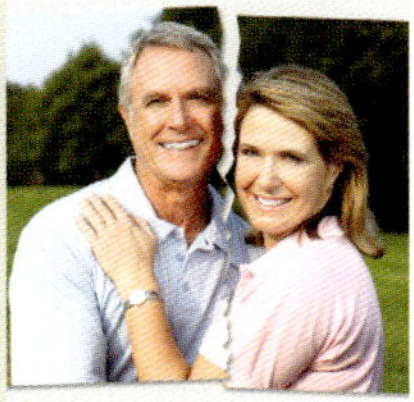

geschieden
divorced

Ich bin geschieden.
I'm divorced.

UNIT 4 › LESSON 2

Résumés

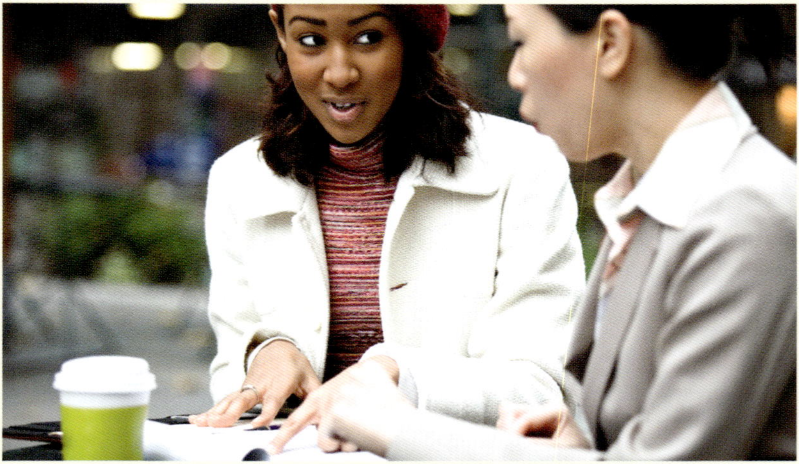

Culture note

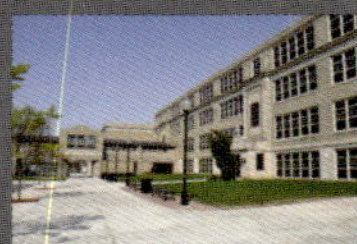

How does the education system work in Germany? Children aged three to six may attend kindergarten. After that, school is compulsory for nine or ten years at one of three different kinds of schools: *Hauptschule*, *Realschule* or *Gymnasium*. After graduation from school between the ages of 15 and 19, students start an apprenticeship (mostly at 15 or 16) in their chosen professions or go to university (mostly at 18–20). In Germany, an apprenticeship is a very important part of the educational system. There are hundreds of recognized trades (*Ausbildungsberufe*) where an apprenticeship can be completed, including for example, doctor's assistant, banker, optician, plumber or builder. It is a dual system which means that apprentices spend about 50–70% of their time at the work place and the rest in formal education.

Video Dialog

Lara shows Matthias her résumé and asks his advice. He is obviously impressed!

Active German: Level 3 > *Unit 4* > *Lesson 2* > *Video dialog*

Lara:	*Matthias, wie findest du meinen Lebenslauf?*
Matthias:	*Schule. 1998 Abitur. Ausbildung und Studium. Du hast in Göttingen studiert?*
Lara:	*Ja, ich habe erst eine Ausbildung zur Kauffrau gemacht und dann habe ich Wirtschaft studiert.*
Matthias:	*Berufserfahrung. Sieht gut aus. Du hast ein Praktikum bei Siemens gemacht. Schön! Sprachkenntnisse und Computerkenntnisse. Gut.*

Lara:	Matthias, what do you think of my résumé?
Matthias:	School. 1998, high school graduation. Education and college. You went to college in Göttingen?
Lara:	Yes, I first trained as a saleswoman and then I studied economics.
Matthias:	Professional experience. It looks good. You did an internship with Siemens. Well done! Language skills and IT skills. Good.

Grammar

Active German: Level 3 > Unit 4 > Lesson 2 > Grammar

1 › University and school

In German you use the verb *studieren* (to study) exclusively in relation to universities and subjects there.

Ich studiere in Köln.

I study in Cologne.

In the context of schools or any other learning experience you use the verb *lernen* (to learn).

Ich habe Physik studiert.	I studied physics.
Ich habe für das Physikexamen gelernt.	I studied for my exam in physics.

Note that the past tense form of *studieren* is slightly different from the regular form. There is no *ge-*.

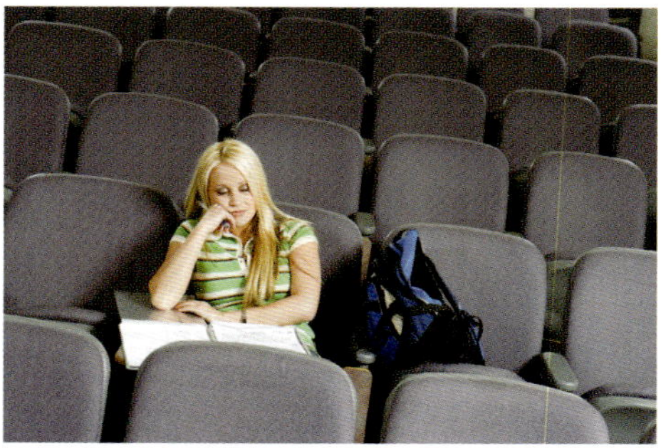

2 › Education

To talk about your education you might need the following expressions:

To refer to your time in school you say:

Ich bin von 1986 bis 1998 zur Schule gegangen.
From 1986 to 1998 I went to school.

To refer to your time at a university you say:

Ich habe an der Universität Heidelberg studiert.
I studied at the University of Heidelberg.

To refer to an apprenticeship you say:

Ich habe eine Ausbildung zum Kaufmann gemacht.	I trained as a salesman.
Ich habe eine Ausbildung zum Fotografen gemacht.	I trained as a photographer.
Ich habe eine Ausbildung zur Verkäuferin gemacht.	I trained as a salesclerk.
Ich habe eine Ausbildung zur Medienkauffrau gemacht.	I trained as a media assistant.

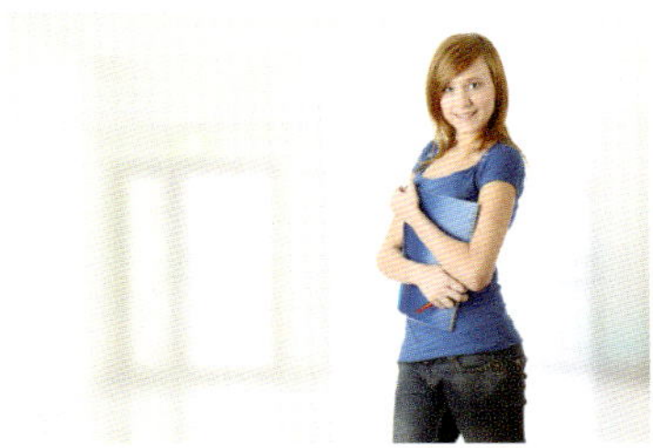

3 › Experiences

In the working world the following expressions might be very useful:

The word *Erfahrung* (experience) mostly occurs with the verb *sammeln* (here: to gain).

Bei meinem Praktikum habe ich viele Erfahrungen gesammelt.

During my internship I gained a lot of experiences.

To say that you are computer-literate use the following expression:

Ich kann gut mit dem Computer umgehen.

I'm good at dealing with computers.

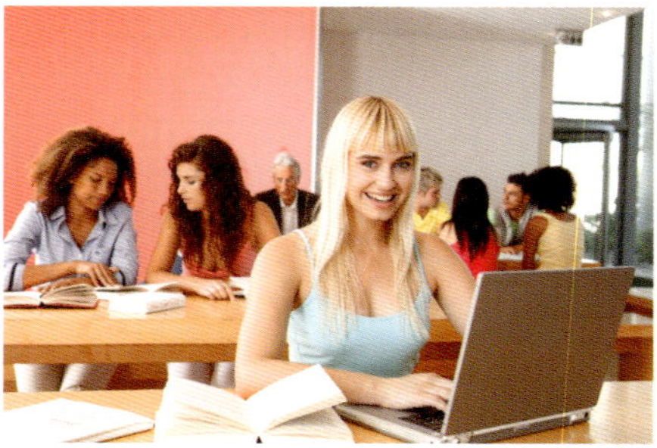

4 › How many languages do you speak?

Use the noun *Kenntnisse* to refer to your skills:

Was für Sprachkenntnisse haben Sie?	What language skills do you have?
Was für Computerkenntnisse haben Sie?	What computer skills do you have?

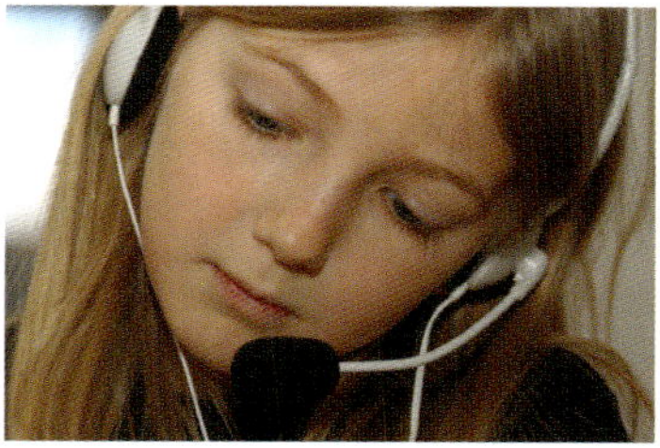

Concerning your language skills you could answer:

Ich spreche ein bisschen Deutsch.	I speak a little German.
Ich spreche gut Deutsch.	I speak German well.
Ich spreche sehr gut Deutsch.	I speak German very well.
Ich spreche fließend Deutsch.	I'm fluent in German.

5 › To know something or someone

In German there is an important difference between the words *kennen* and *wissen*.

Wissen means to know a fact:

Wissen Sie, wie spät es ist?

Do you know what time it is?

Kennen means to be familiar with, acquainted with:

Kennst du sie?

Do you know her?

The verb *wissen* is an irregular verb:

ich weiß	I know
du weißt	you know
er / sie / es weiß	he / she / it knows
wir wissen	we know
ihr wisst	you know
sie / Sie wissen	they / you know

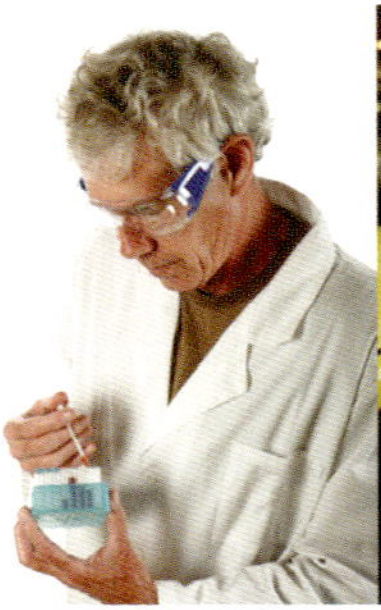

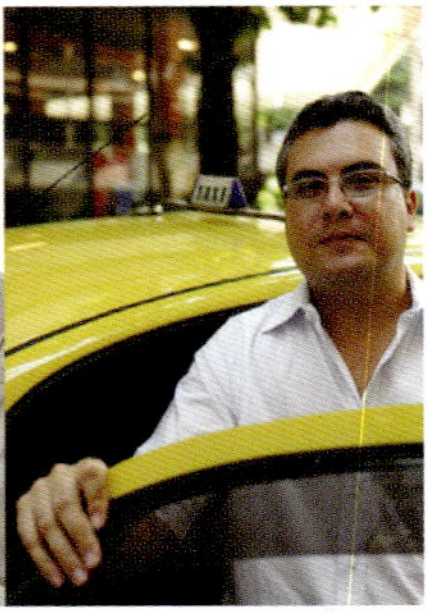

Culture note

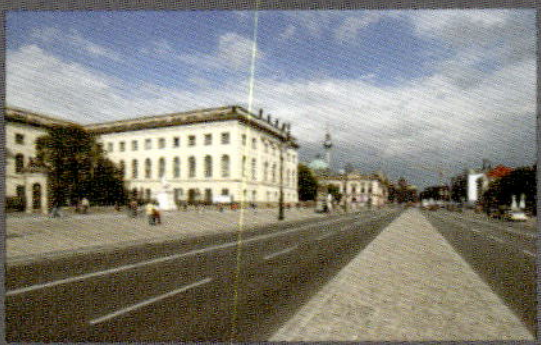

In most cases German school education is free and available to everybody. Recently there has been much discussion about fees in higher education. Until 2005 German students just had to pay for their students union and for living costs. Thousands of students at all universities tried to fight for the old system, but couldn't prevent most federal states introducing a new system. Many universities now charge fees which are around 500 Euros per semester.

Vocabulary

Active German: Level 3 > Unit 4 > Lesson 2 > Vocabulary

Education

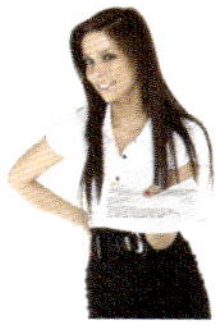

der Lebenslauf / Lebensläufe
résumé

Ich muss heute meinen Lebenslauf schreiben.
I have to write my résumé today.

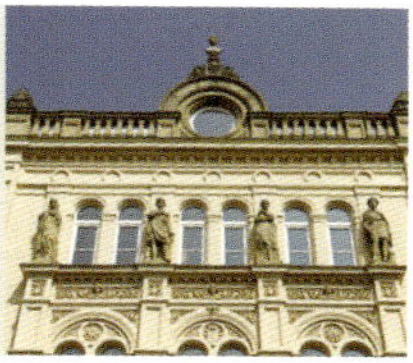

die Schule / Schulen
school

Ich bin von 1986 bis 1998 zur Schule gegangen.
I went to school from 1986 to 1998.

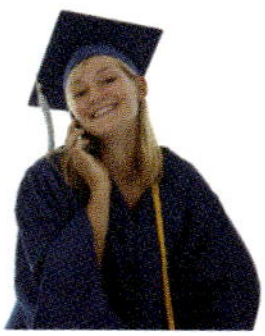

das Abitur
high school graduation

1998 habe ich mein Abitur gemacht.
I graduated from high school in 1998.

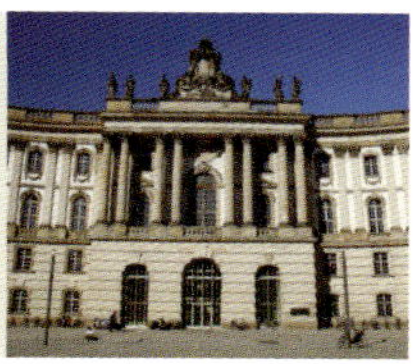

die Universität / Universitäten
university, college

An der Universität habe ich Physik studiert.
In college I studied physics.

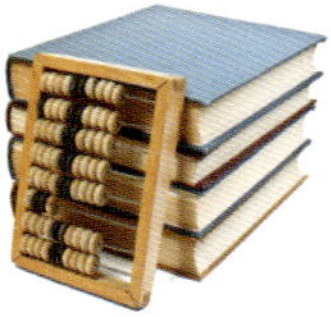

die Wirtschaft
economics

Ich habe 5 Jahre Wirtschaft studiert.
I studied economics for 5 years.

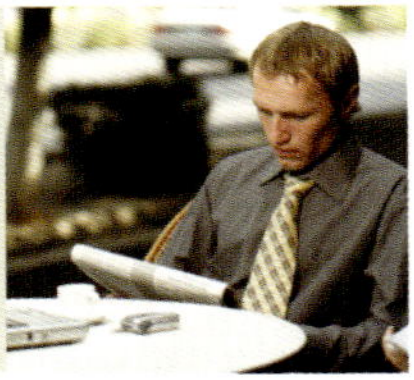

die Politik
politics

Interessieren Sie sich für Politik?
Are you interested in politics?

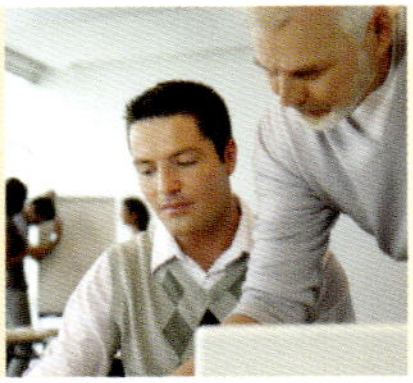

das Praktikum / Praktika
internship

Ich habe ein Praktikum bei VW gemacht.
I did an internship with VW.

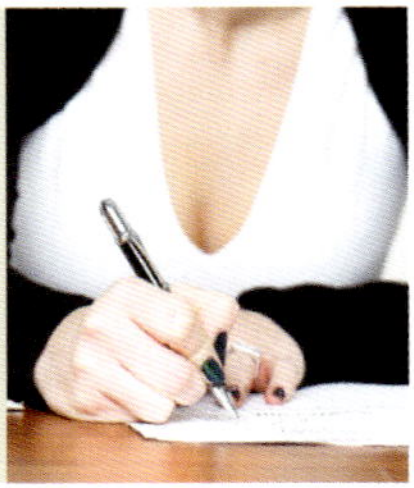

sich bewerben um
to apply for

Ich bewerbe mich um die Stelle als Verkäuferin.
I'm applying for the position of salesclerk.

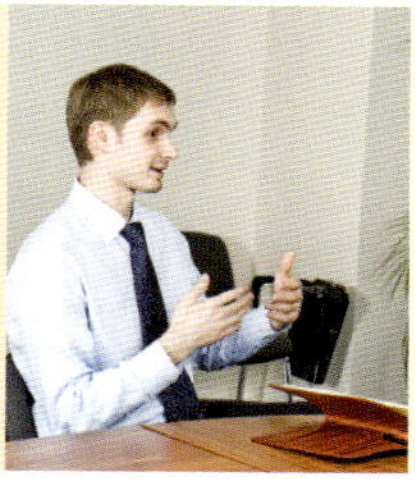

das Vorstellungsgespräch / Vorstellungsgespräche
interview

Ich habe ein Vorstellungsgespräch bei Beiersdorf.
I have an interview at Beiersdorf.

das Fach / Fächer
subject

Welche Fächer hast du studiert?
Which subjects did you study?

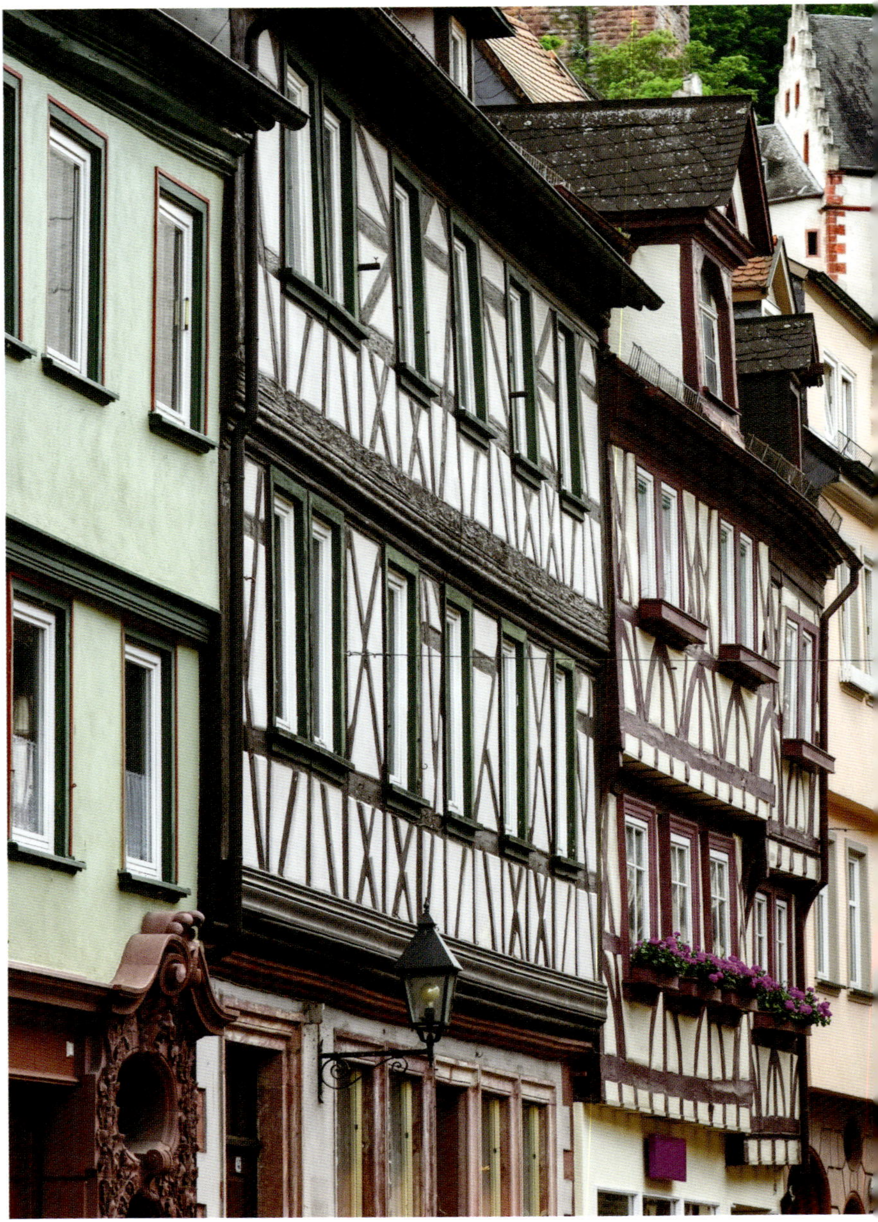

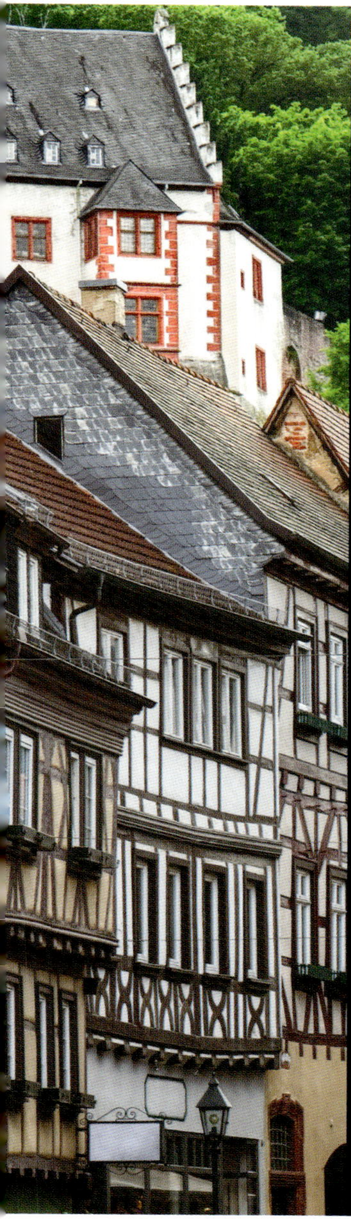

Active German *Level 3*

5

Lesson 1: About Germany

» How to compare things and say what is bigger, better, and more beautiful.
» How to talk, write, and read about the landscape in a country.
» Vocabulary for geography and landscape.
» How to say "I like the city."

Lesson 2: A new television – Made in Germany

» How to say what is the best, the most beautiful, and the biggest.
» How to use the verb *fernsehen* (to watch TV).
» How to say that something has the same qualities as something else.
» Vocabulary for electrical appliances.
» How to compare products.

Collins | Livemocha™

UNIT 5 › LESSON 1

About Germany

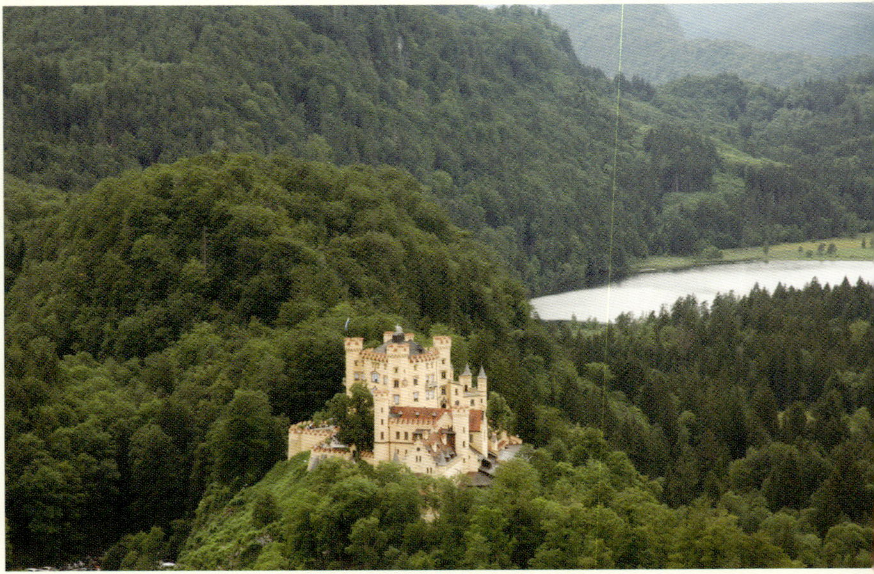

Culture note

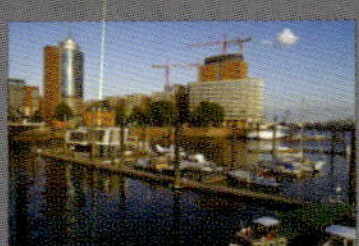

The port of Hamburg is situated on the river Elbe. After Rotterdam and Antwerp it is the third-largest port in Europe. It is called "*Das Tor zur Welt*" (the gateway to the world). The area around the port is very lively and over the last few decades land development has led to new housing opportunities. There is a huge variety of museums, theaters, bars, and restaurants. The port is just a stone's throw from the *Reeperbahn* – Hamburg's famous nightlife center and the city's red light district.

Video Dialog

Mr. Baumann helps Lara with her crossword, which leads to a discussion about Germany.

Active German: Level 3 > *Unit 5* > *Lesson 1* > *Video dialog*

Herr Baumann:	*Na Frau Roellinger, machen Sie ein Kreuzworträtsel?*
Lara:	*Ja, setzen Sie sich. Ein Fluss mit fünf Buchstaben länger als der Rhein.*
Herr Baumann:	*Die Donau.*
Lara:	*Die Donau. Ist der Rhein länger als die Elbe?*
Herr Baumann:	*Ja, aber die Elbe ist schöner.*
Lara:	*Ja, meinen Sie?*
Herr Baumann:	*Welche Stadt mögen Sie lieber: Hamburg oder München?*
Lara:	*München!*
Herr Baumann:	*Aber Hamburg ist schöner.*

Mr. Baumann:	So, Mrs. Roellinger, are you doing the crossword?
Lara:	Yes, take a seat. A river with five letters which is longer than the Rhine.
Mr. Baumann:	The Danube.
Lara:	The Danube. Is the Rhine longer than the Elbe?
Mr. Baumann:	Yes, but the Elbe is more beautiful.
Lara:	Do you think so?

Mr. Baumann:	Which city do you prefer: Hamburg or Munich?
Lara:	Munich!
Mr. Baumann:	But Hamburg is more beautiful.

Grammar

Active German: Level 3 > Unit 5 > Lesson 1 > Grammar

1 › **This is more beautiful!**

In the video dialog Mr. Baumann and Lara compare different things. You use the comparative for this. In German, you form the comparative by adding *-er* to the adjective.

Mr. Baumann compares Hamburg to Munich.

München ist schön.	Munich is beautiful.
Hamburg ist schöner.	Hamburg is more beautiful.

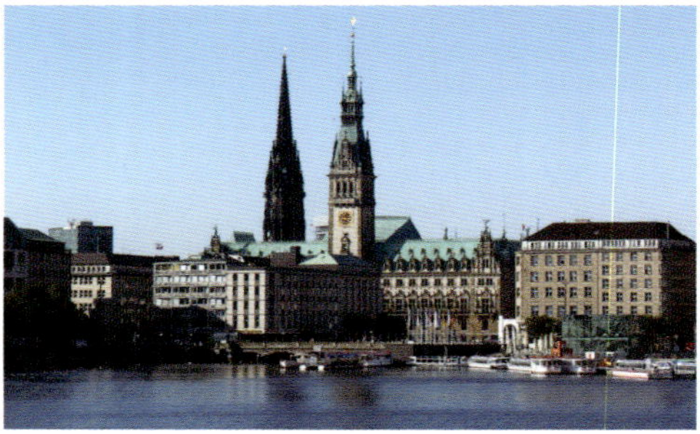

2 › **How to compare**

The *-er* form works for almost all adjectives. In some cases you add an umlaut to the main vowel.

kurz – kürzer	short – shorter
lang – länger	long – longer
groß – größer	big / tall – bigger / taller
klein – kleiner	small / short – smaller / shorter
jung – jünger	young – younger
alt – älter	old – older
schnell – schneller	fast – faster
langsam – langsamer	slow – slower

Welches Auto ist schneller? Ferrari oder Porsche?	Which car is faster? Ferrari or Porsche?

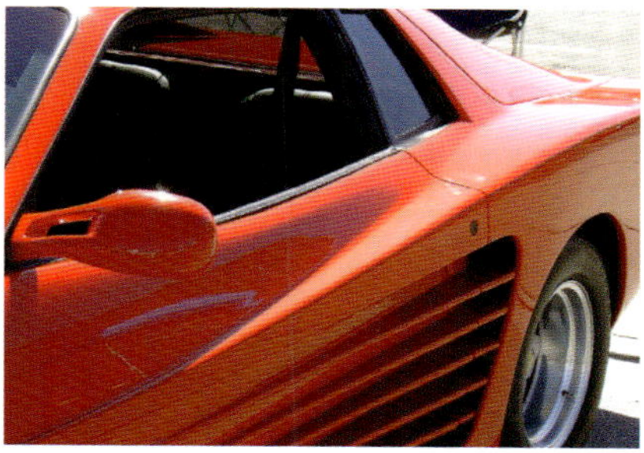

3 › I like it more

Some forms, but not many, have a different comparative form. Here are some important ones.

gerne (like to)	*lieber* (prefer to)
viel (much)	*mehr* (more)
gut (good)	*besser* (better)

Trinkst du lieber Wein oder Bier?	Do you prefer drinking wine or beer?
Du hast mehr Studenten.	You have more students.
Sprichst du besser Englisch oder Spanisch?	Is your English or your Spanish better?

4 › More than yours

To compare two different things you need the word *als* (than) as well.

Mein Auto ist schneller als dein Auto.	My car is faster than your car.
Der Kaffee hier schmeckt besser als im Café „Mai".	The coffee here tastes nicer than in the café Mai.

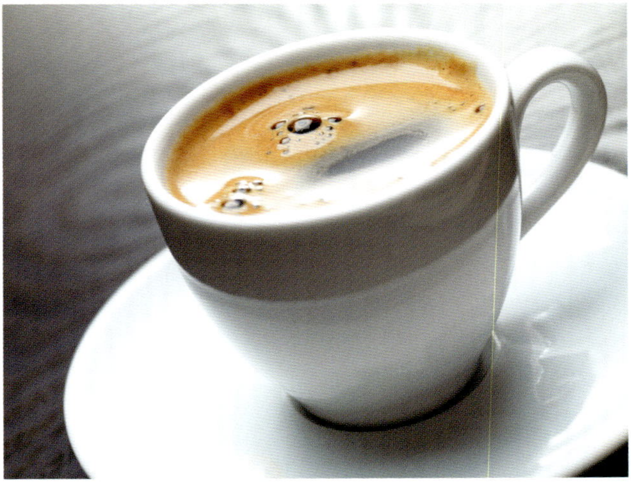

5 › I like that more

In earlier units we have seen how to use the word *gerne*.

Ich lese gerne.
I like reading.

You use it in combination with a verb.

There is another way to express "to like." You use the verb *mögen* with a noun:

Wir mögen Hamburg.	We like Hamburg.
Wir mögen unsere Kollegin.	We like our colleague.

Compare:

Wir leben gerne in Hamburg.	We like living in Hamburg.
Wir mögen Hamburg.	We like Hamburg.

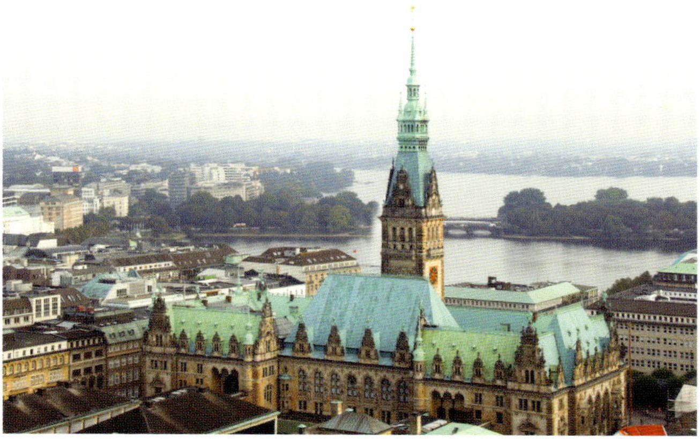

6 › **I like it**

Look at how the verb *mögen* works.

ich mag	I like
du magst	you like
er / sie / es mag	he / she / it likes
wir mögen	we like
ihr mögt	you like
sie / Sie mögen	they / you like

Ich mag Pizza.

I like Pizza.

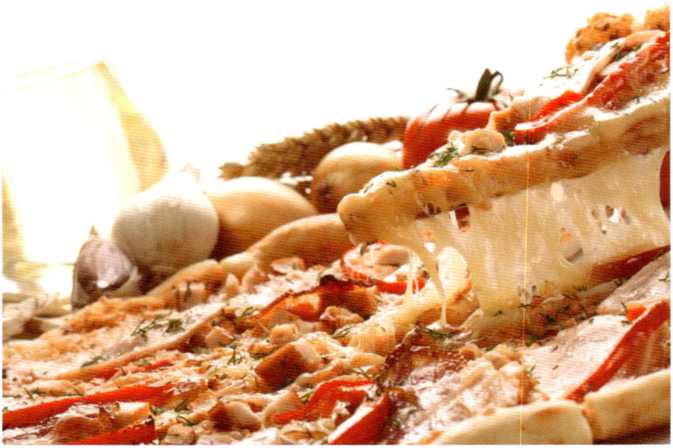

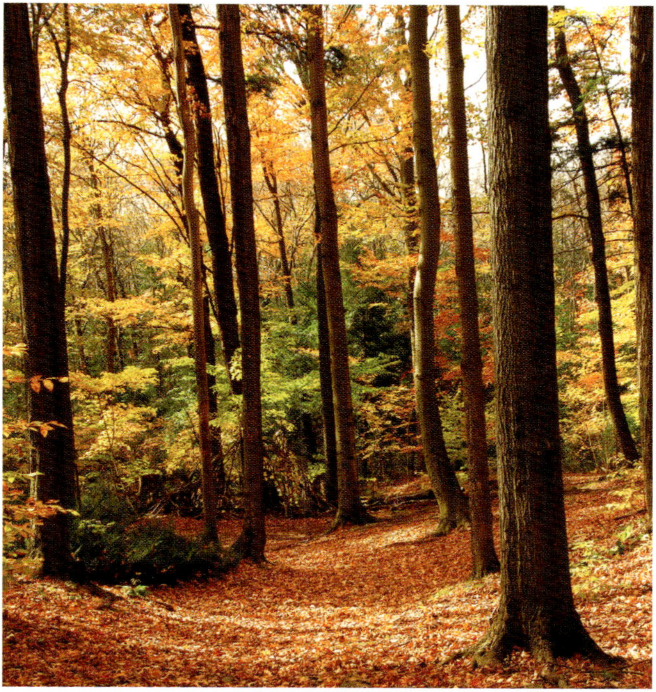

Culture note

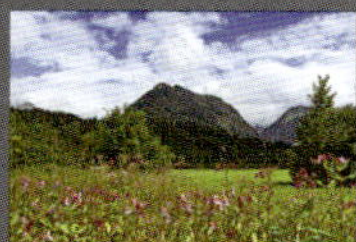

Many jokes and prejudices characterize the rivalry between the north and the south of the country. Northern and southern Germans don't trust each other's food, dialects or mentality. Whereas the people from the south are considered to be warm, easygoing, earthy, but rural and backward, the northerners are seen as liberal, intellectual, reserved, and snobby. Some of this probably has to do with the landscape and the climate, but also religion has an influence. Much of southern Germany is Catholic while the northern Germans are almost exclusively Protestant.

Vocabulary

Active German: Level 3 > Unit 5 > Lesson 1 > Vocabulary

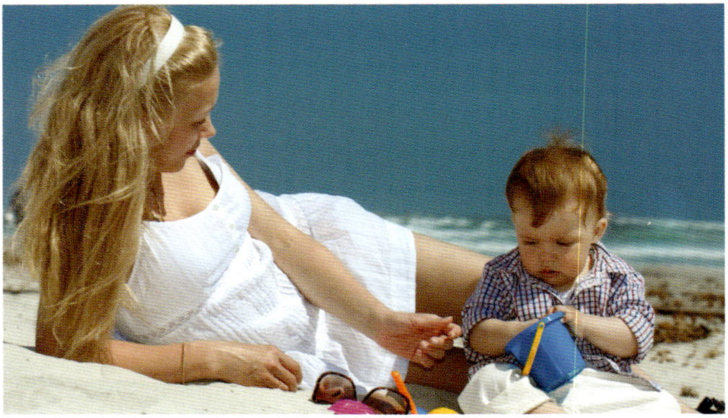

Geography and landscape

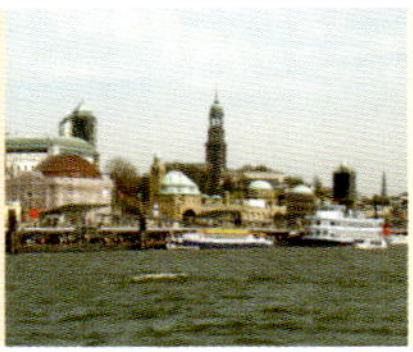

der Fluss / Flüsse
river

Ein Fluss fließt durch Hamburg.
A river flows through Hamburg.

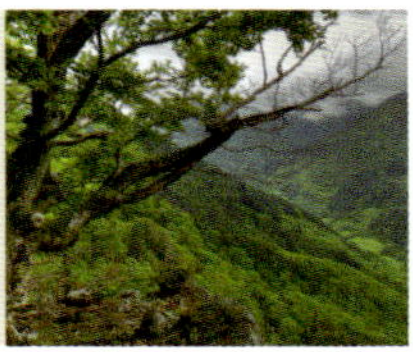

der Wald / Wälder
forest

Die Deutschen lieben den Wald.
Germans love forests.

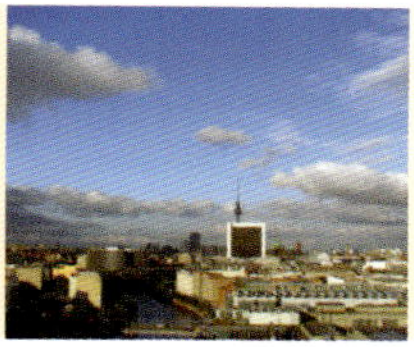

die Landschaft / Landschaften
landscape

Wie ist die Landschaft in Ihrem Land?
What is the landscape like in your country?

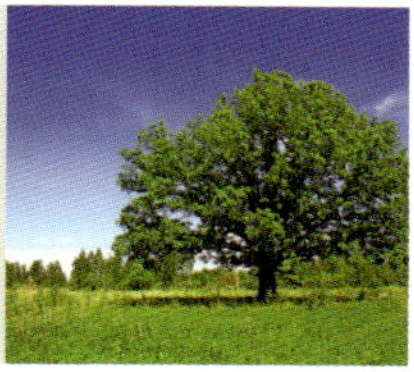

der Baum / Bäume
tree

Die Eiche ist der Nationalbaum von Deutschland.
The oak tree is the national tree of Germany.

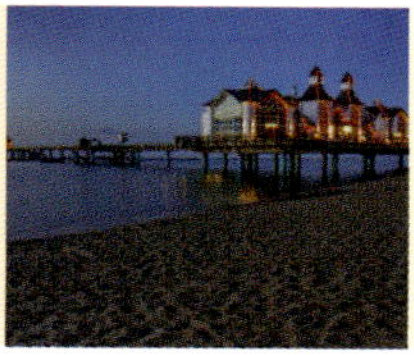

der Strand / Strände
beach

Möchten Sie an den Strand fahren?
Do you want to go to the beach?

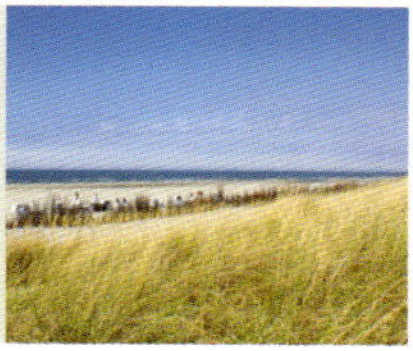

das Meer / Meere
sea

Wir sind am Meer.
We are at the seaside / by the sea.

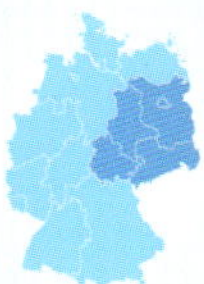

der Osten
east

Dresden liegt im Osten von Deutschland.
Dresden is in eastern Germany.

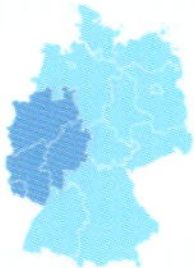

der Westen
west

Köln ist im Westen von Deutschland.
Cologne is in western Germany.

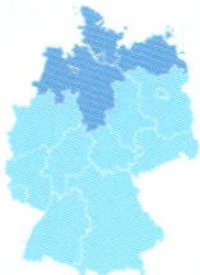

der Norden
north

Hamburg ist im Norden von Deutschland.
Hamburg is in the north of Germany.

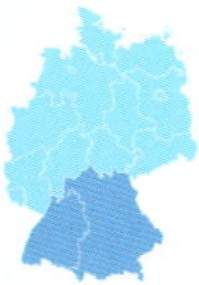

der Süden
south

Stuttgart ist im Süden von Deutschland.
Stuttgart is in the south of Germany.

UNIT 5 › LESSON 2

A new television – Made in Germany

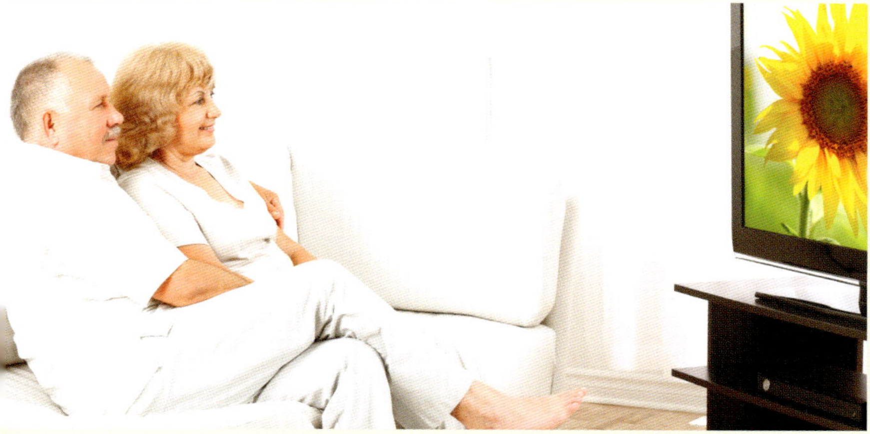

Culture note

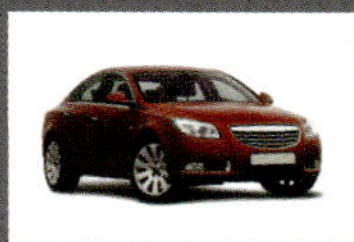

The label "Made in Germany" has a world-wide reputation. Germany is known for products of high quality, standards, and value. Germany's global significance extends to great inventions, including the harmonica, the coffee filter, and the thermos flask. Special mention should be also made of the little gold bear (*Gummibärchen*) that is the symbol of the Haribo candy range. The slogan "*Haribo macht Kinder froh und Erwachsene ebenso*" (Kids and grown-ups love it so – the happy world of Haribo) is well-known in Germany.

Video Dialog

At Matthias' apartment, Lara and Matthias discuss their television preferences.

Active German: Level 3 > *Unit 5* > *Lesson 2* > *Video dialog*

Lara:	*Hattest du schon immer einen Fernseher?*
Matthias:	*Nein, ich habe ihn letzte Woche gekauft.*
Lara:	*Von welcher Marke ist er?*
Matthias:	*„Philips". Die finde ich am besten.*
Lara:	*Findest du? Ich finde „Grundig" besser. Wo hast du ihn gekauft?*
Matthias:	*Bei „Schuberts". Die sind am billigsten.*
Lara:	*Bei Schuberts sind die Möbel aber nicht schön, die sind bei „Mira" am schönsten und auch die Qualität ist besser.*
Matthias:	*Ja, wenn du meinst, dann gehe ich das nächste Mal dorthin.*

Lara:	Did you already have a TV?
Matthias:	No, I bought it last week.
Lara:	Which brand is it?
Matthias:	Philips. It's the best.
Lara:	Do you think so? I prefer Grundig. Where did you buy it?
Matthias:	At Schubert's. They're the cheapest.
Lara:	But at Schubert's the furniture isn't nice; it's nicest at Mira's, and the quality is better, too.
Matthias:	If you think so, then I'll go there next time.

Grammar

Active German: Level 3 > *Unit 5* > *Lesson 2* > *Grammar*

1 › They are the cheapest

In Lesson 1 we compared two things saying what is bigger, better, or more beautiful. In the video dialog Lara and Matthias compare the quality and prices of different manufacturers. They are not just saying what is better, but what is the best. This form is the superlative and it expresses the end of the scale.

Let's have a look at the different degrees:

klein (small)	*kleiner* (smaller)	*am kleinsten* (the smallest)

To form the superlative you add *-sten* to the adjective and you use the word *am*.

schön (beautiful)	*schöner* (more beautiful)	*am schönsten* (the most beautiful)
billig (cheap)	*billiger* (cheaper)	*am billigsten* (the cheapest)

Robert ist klein. Nina ist kleiner. Marion ist am kleinsten.

Robert is small. Nina is smaller. Marion is the smallest.

2 › That is the best

In Lesson 1 you learned the comparative of *gut, viel, gerne*. Here are the forms in the superlative.

gut (good)	*besser* (better)	*am besten* (the best)
viel (much)	*mehr* (more)	*am meisten* (the most)
gerne (like to)	*lieber* (prefer to)	*am liebsten* (most of all like to)

Ich esse gerne Pizza. Ich esse Salat lieber. Am liebsten esse ich Fisch.

I like eating pizza. I prefer eating salad. Most of all I like eating fish.

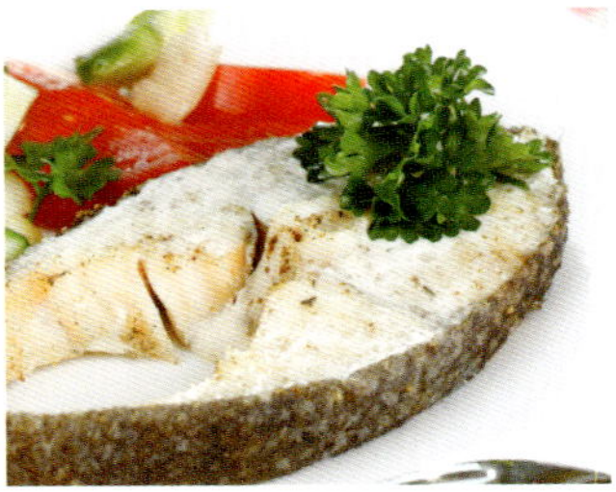

3 › That is the most expensive

Let's have a look at some other adjectives. These have some spelling modifications.

teuer (expensive)	*teurer* (more expensive)	*am teuersten* (the most expensive)

→ in the comparative form you drop the second *-e*

groß (tall, big)	*größer* (taller, bigger)	*am größten* (the tallest, the biggest)

→ in the superlative form you drop the *-s* and an umlaut is added in both the comparative and the superlative.

alt (old)	*älter* (older)	*am ältesten* (the oldest / the eldest)

→ in the superlative form you add an *-e* and again add an umlaut in both the comparative and the superlative.

Ich bin groß. Mein Bruder ist größer. Mein Vater ist am größten.

I am tall. My brother is taller. My father is the tallest.

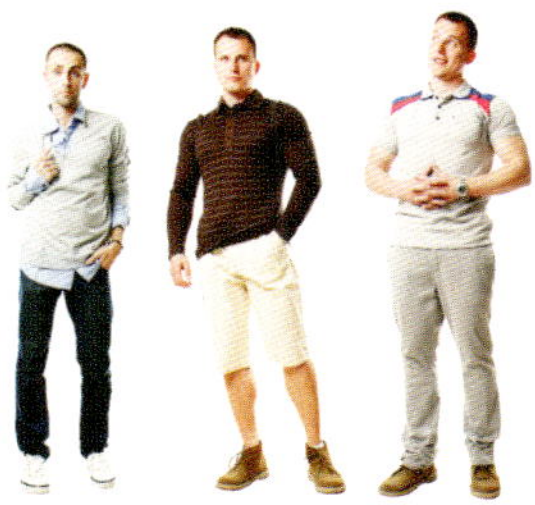

4 › As tall as you

If the two things you compare have the *same* quality you use a different form.

Daniel ist genauso groß wie sein Vater.

Daniel is just as tall as his father.

You use *genauso* + adjective + *wie* to say that something is the same:

Das Auto ist genauso schnell wie der Zug.

The car is just as fast as the train.

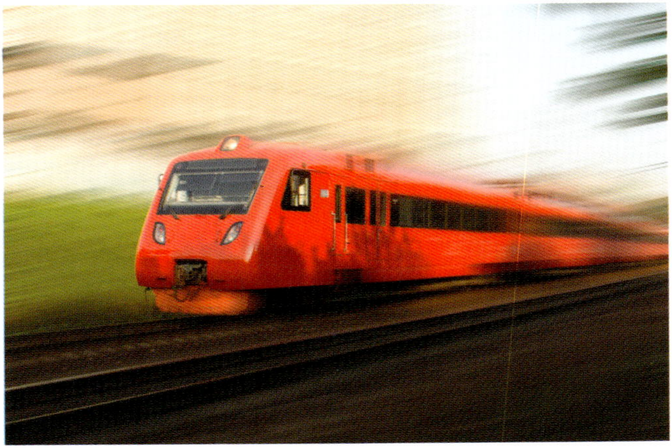

5 › To watch television

Matthias has just bought a new television. The verb you use is *fernsehen*.

It is a separable verb.

Ich sehe fern.	I watch TV.
Siehst du fern?	Do you watch TV?
Hast du gestern ferngesehen?	Did you watch TV yesterday?

Vocabulary

Active German: Level 3 > Unit 5 > Lesson 2 > Vocabulary

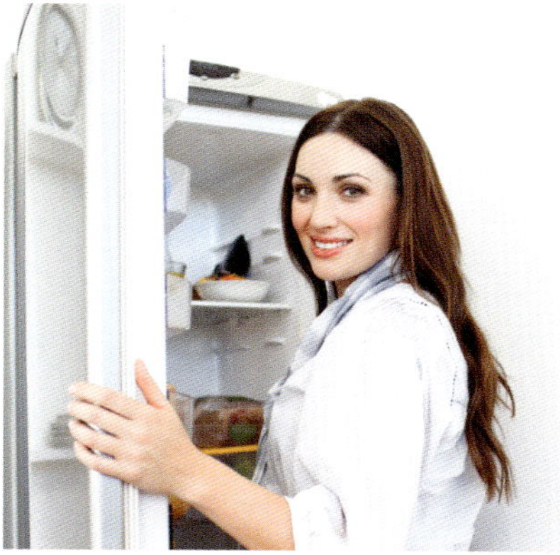

Electrical devices

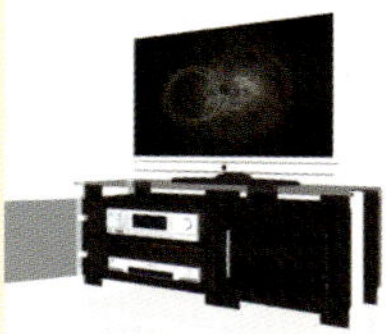

die Qualität / Qualitäten
quality

Diese Produkte haben eine gute Qualität.
These products are of good quality.

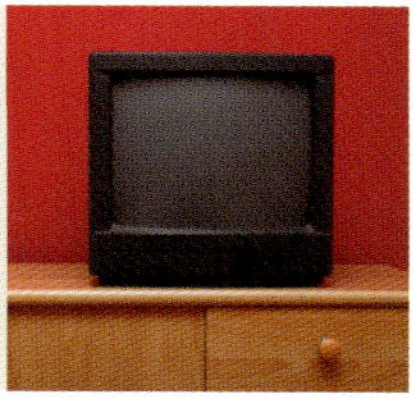

der Fernseher / Fernseher
television set

Ist der Fernseher neu?
Is the television set new?

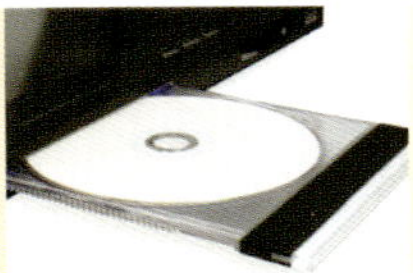

der DVD-Spieler / DVD-Spieler
DVD player
Hast du einen DVD-Spieler?
Do you have a DVD player?

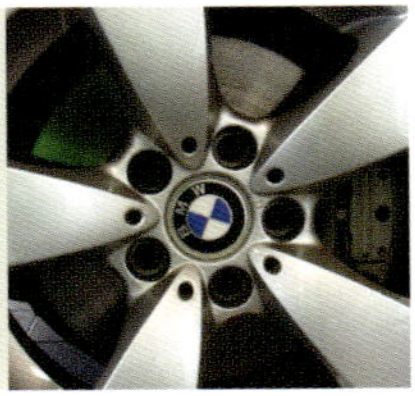

die Marke / Marken
brand
Von welcher Marke ist dieser Fernseher?
Which brand is this television?

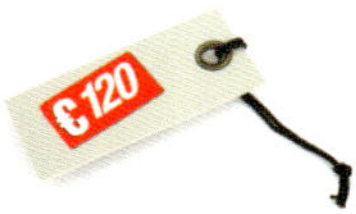

der Preis / Preise
price
Der Preis ist in Ordnung.
The price is alright.

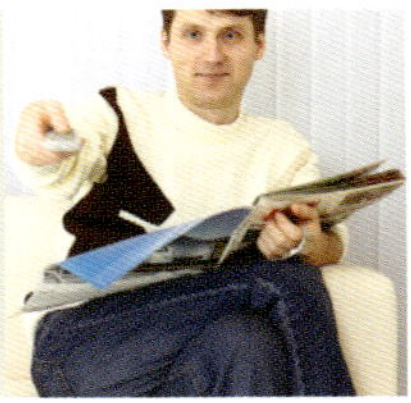

das Programm / Programme
schedule, program
Kennen Sie das Programm für nächste Woche?
Do you know the schedule for next week?

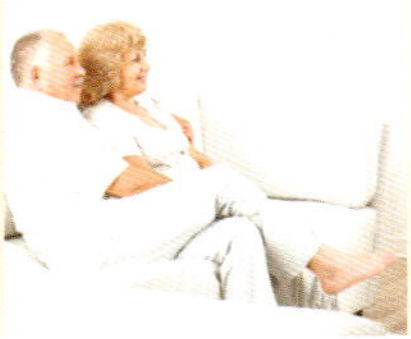

die Sendung / Sendungen
program, broadcast
Magst du diese Sendung?
Do you like this program?

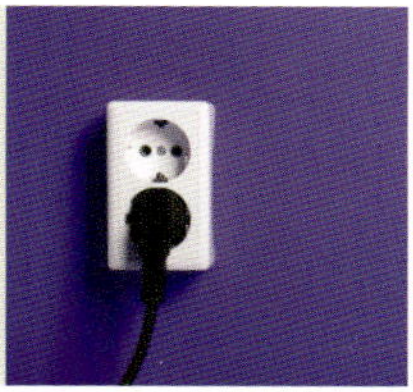

elektrisch
electrical

Schalten Sie alle elektrischen Geräte bitte aus.
Please switch off all electrical devices.

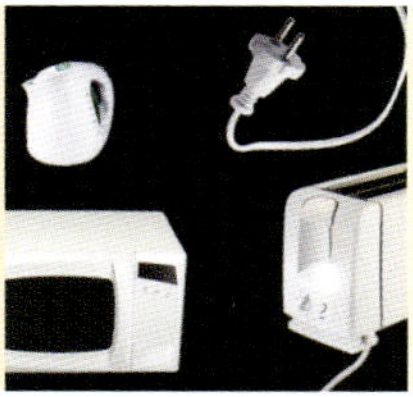

das Gerät / Geräte
device / appliance

Wo kann man gut elektrische Geräte kaufen?
Where is a good place to buy electrical appliances?

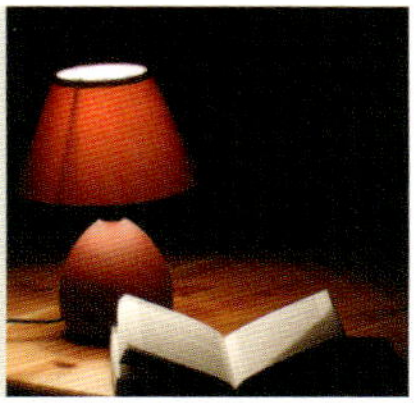

das Licht / Lichter
light

Können Sie bitte das Licht anmachen?
Could you please switch on the light?

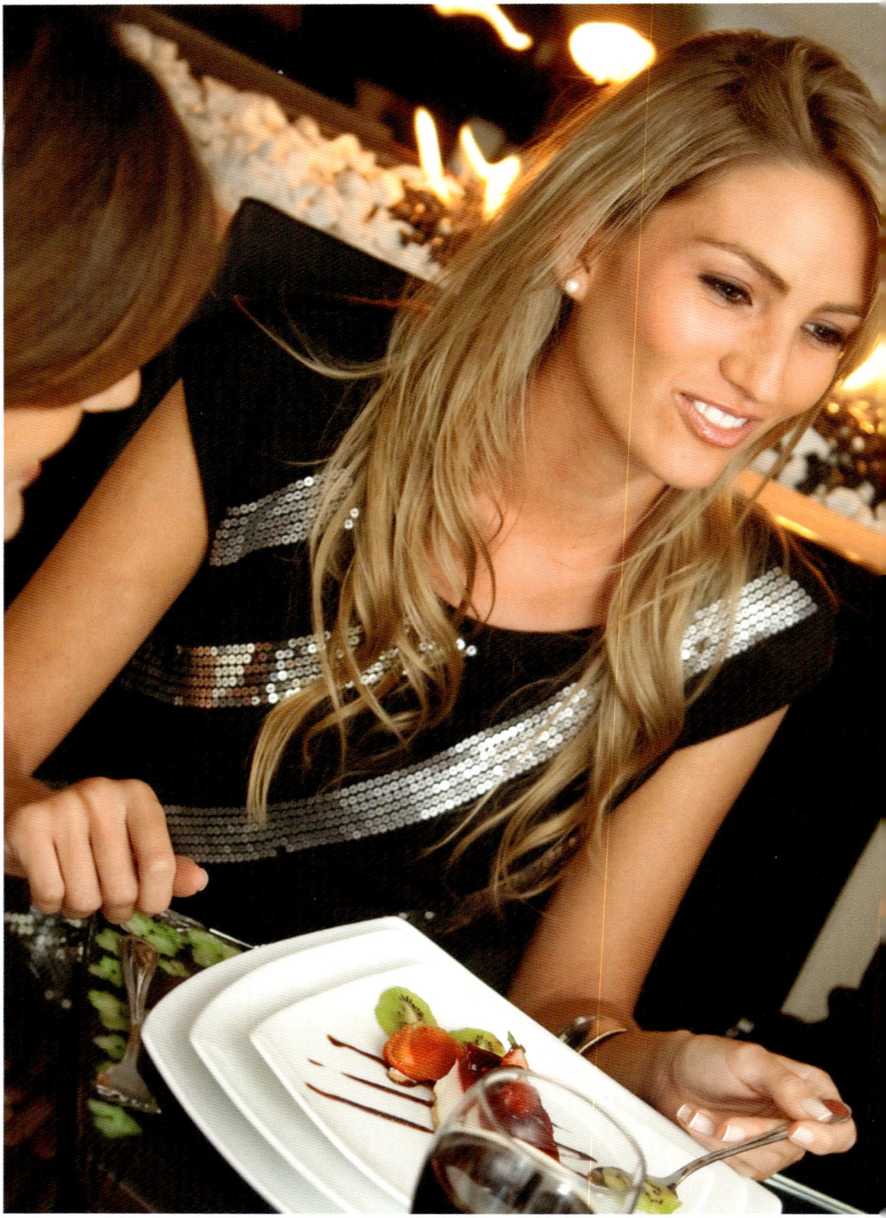

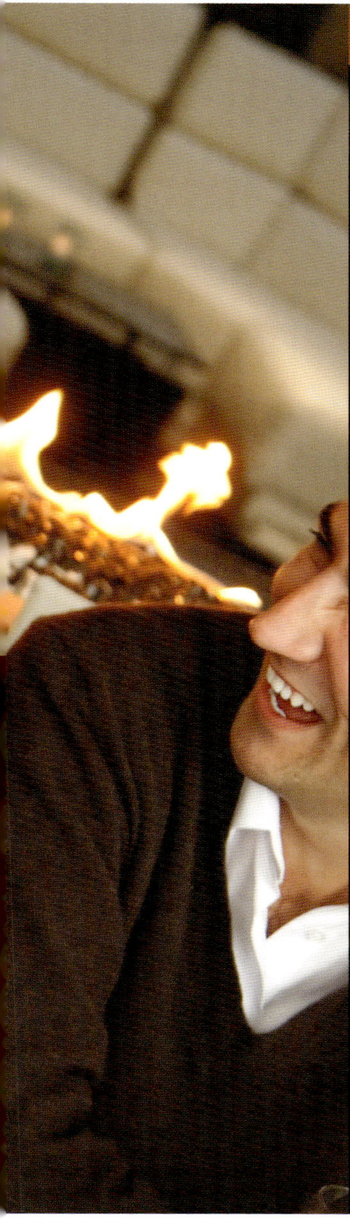

6

Lesson 1: An invitation

» How to say what you should do (***Ich soll***), what you are allowed to do (***Ich darf***), and what you want to do (***Ich will***).

» How to say: to bring along (***mitbringen***), to come along (***mitkommen***), and to take along (***mitnehmen***).

» Vocabulary for invitations and celebrations / parties.

» How to invite somebody and to say what the occasion is.

Lesson 2: An enjoyable evening

» How to say what is yours.

» How to say: "That is my brother's wife." ***Das ist die Frau von meinem Bruder.***

» Vocabulary for events and celebrations.

» Important phrases for hosting a party, small talk.

Collins | Livemocha™

UNIT 6 › LESSON 1

An invitation

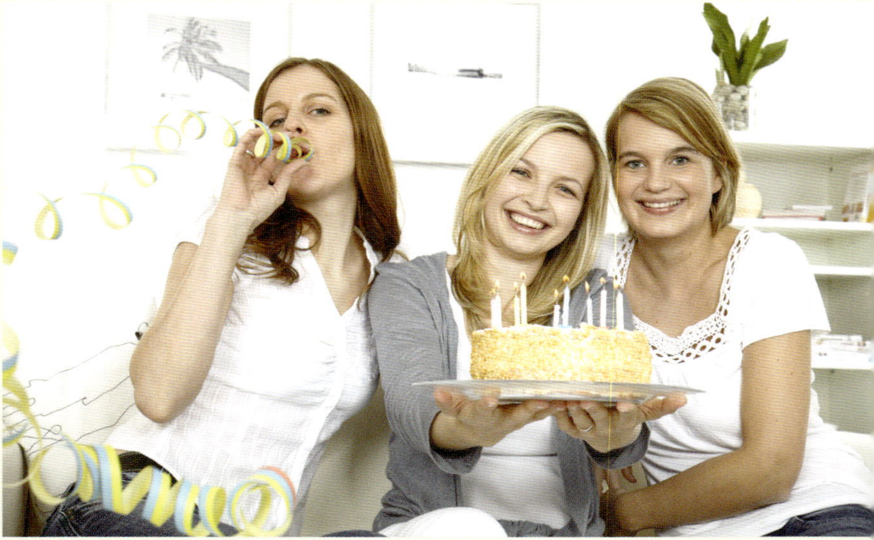

Culture note

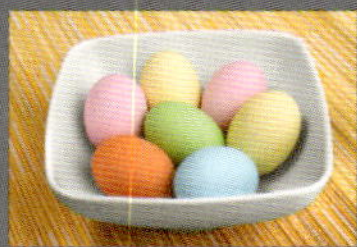

There is always a reason for people to come together and to celebrate. As well as many Christian celebrations there are many local festivities in Germany. The most important holidays are undoubtedly Christmas and Easter which are accompanied by various traditions. Their importance is underlined by the fact that the government, schools, and most businesses close on those days. Famous festivals are the Munich *Oktoberfest* and Carnival. On the Germany's national day, October 3rd, the country celebrates its reunification, which occurred in 1990.

Video Dialog

Matthias is planning a housewarming party.

Active German: Level 3 > *Unit 6* > *Lesson 1* > *Video dialog*

Matthias:	*Herr Buschel, ich mache eine Party am Freitag. Möchten Sie auch kommen?*
Herr Buschel:	*Gerne. Was ist der Anlass?*
Matthias:	*Ich mache eine Einweihungsparty. Ich wohne schon seit drei Monaten hier.*
Herr Buschel:	*Oh, schön.*
Matthias:	*Ich habe auch Lara eingeladen.*
Herr Buschel:	*Ja, vielen Dank für die Einladung. Was soll ich mitbringen?*
Matthias:	*Sie müssen nichts mitbringen. Ich habe alles.*
Herr Buschel:	*Und wann gehts los?*
Matthias:	*So gegen 20 Uhr.*
Herr Buschel:	*Schön. Ich komme.*
Matthias:	*Prima.*

Matthias:	Mr. Buschel, I'm having a party on Friday. Would you like to come?
Mr. Buschel:	Yes, I would. What's the occasion?
Matthias:	I'm going to have a housewarming party. I've been living here for three months.
Mr. Buschel:	How nice.

Matthias:	I've invited Lara as well.
Mr. Buschel:	OK, thank you very much for the invitation. What should I bring along?
Matthias:	You don't have to bring anything. I have everything.
Mr. Buschel:	And when does it start?
Matthias:	Around 8 o'clock.
Mr. Buschel:	Good. I'll be there.
Matthias:	Great.

Grammar

Active German: Level 3 > *Unit 6* > *Lesson 1* > *Grammar*

1 › **Should I?**

In previous units we had a look at modal verbs. You might remember *müssen, können, und möchten*. You are going to learn three more. These are the last ones.

Mr. Buschel in the video dialog asks whether he should bring something along to the party:

> *Soll ich etwas mitbringen?*
> Should I bring anything along?

The verb *sollen* expresses an obligation or a suggestion. It means should, shall, or to be supposed to.

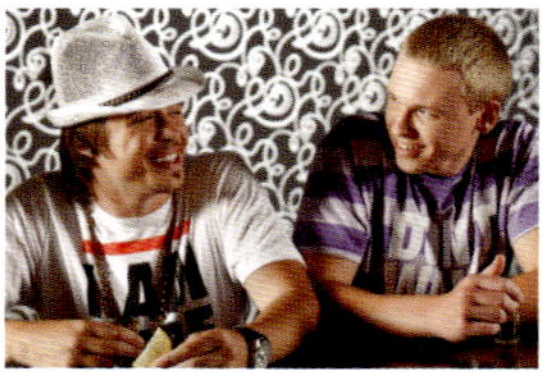

Here are the forms of *sollen*:

ich soll	I should
du sollst	you should
er / sie / es soll	he / she / it should
wir sollen	we should
ihr sollt	you should
sie / Sie sollen	they / you should

2 › Shall I?

Here are some examples:

Soll ich Ihnen helfen?	Shall I help you?
Wo sollen wir uns treffen?	Where shall we meet?
Ich soll nicht so viel essen.	I'm not supposed to eat that much.

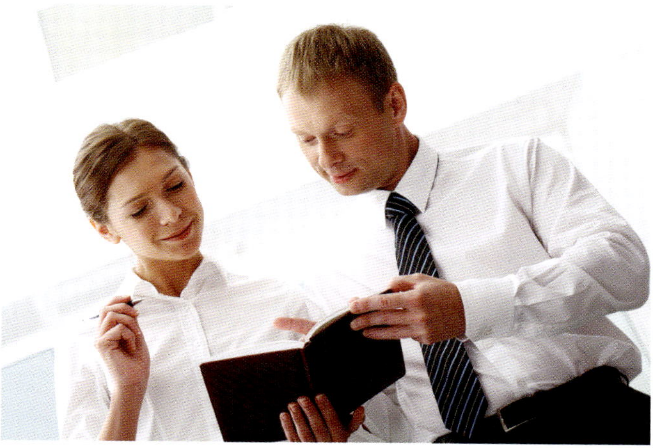

3 › I'm allowed to do that

The verb *dürfen* indicates permission. It means to be allowed to, or may.

That is how the verb works:

ich darf	I may
du darfst	you may
er / sie / es darf	he / she / it may
wir dürfen	we may
ihr dürft	you may
sie / Sie dürfen	they / you may

Ich darf das machen.
I'm allowed to do that.

Darf ich bitte telefonieren?
May I make a phone call?

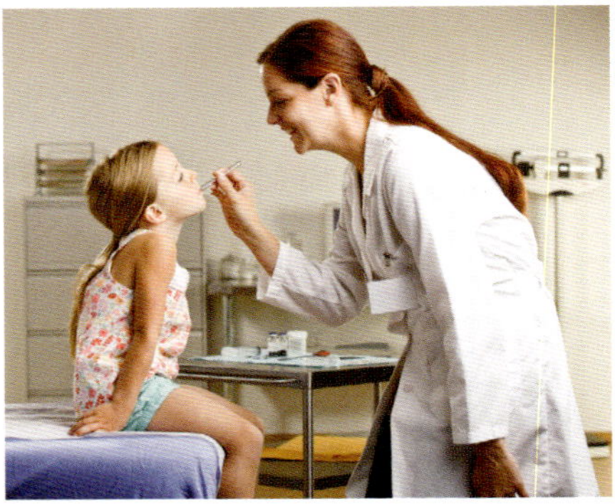

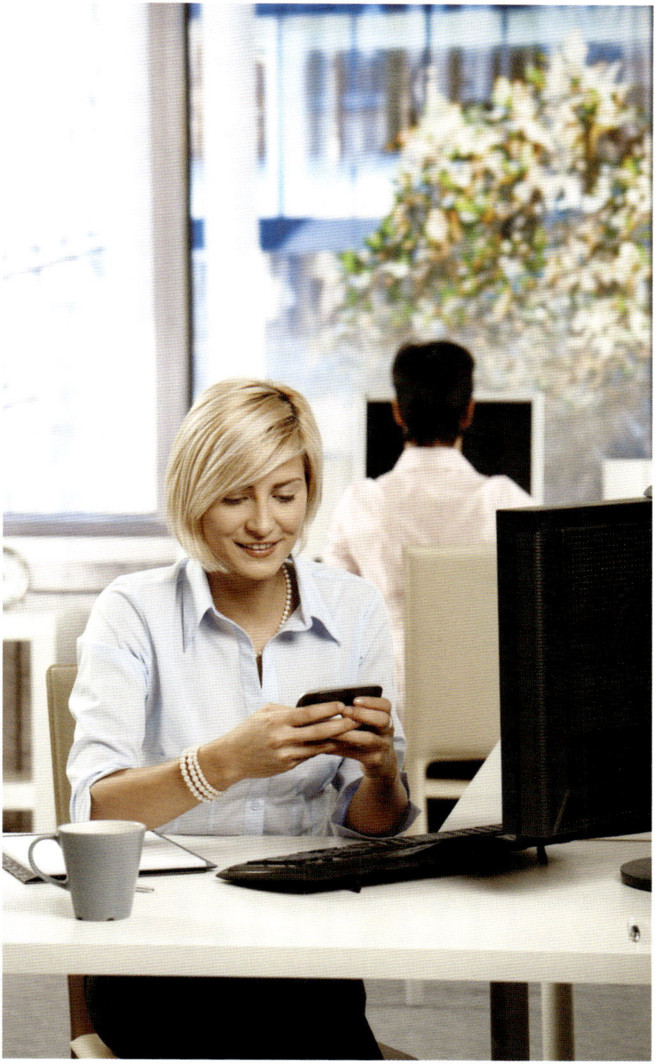

4 › I want it

The verb *wollen* is the last modal verb. *Wollen* is used to express a desire or an intention. It means to want to or to intend to.

Möchten expresses a desire as well. Compared to *wollen* the verb *möchten* is more polite. *Wollen* focuses more on an actual wish.

ich will	I want
du willst	you want
er / sie / es will	he / she / it wants
wir wollen	we want
ihr wollt	you want
sie / Sie wollen	they / you want

Wohin wollt ihr gehen?	Where do you want to go?
Willst du jetzt essen?	Do you want to eat now?

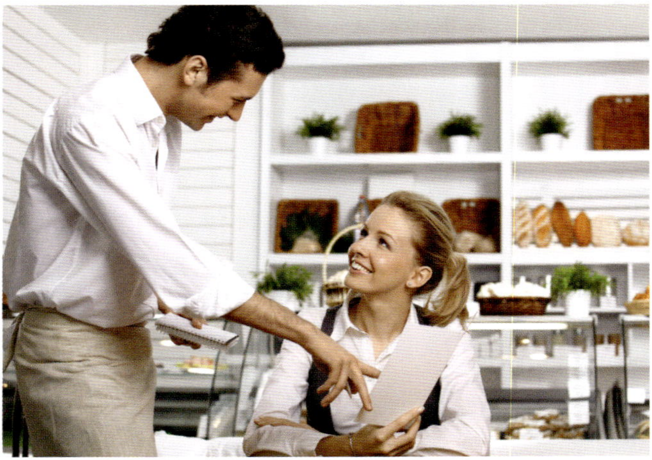

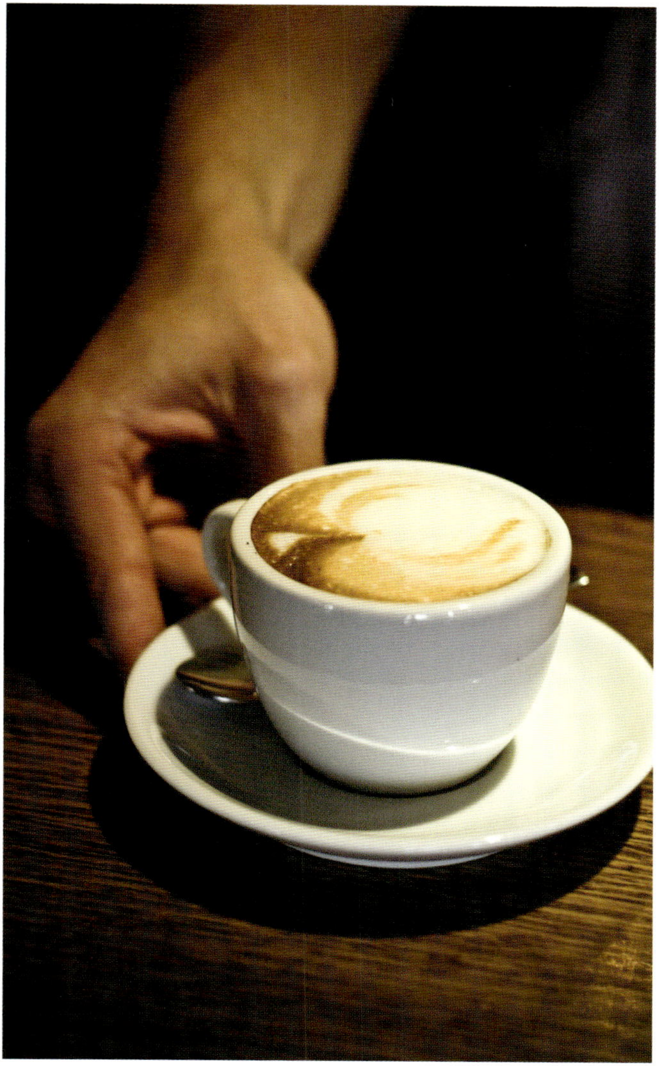

5 › What should I bring along?

Let's have a look at three other important verbs.

mitbringen	to bring along
mitnehmen	to take along
mitkommen	to come along

All three verbs are separable. Here are some example sentences:

Kann ich diese Broschüre mitnehmen?	Can I take along that flyer?
Warum ist deine Frau nicht mitgekommen?	Why didn't your wife come along?
Was soll ich mitbringen?	What should I bring along?
Ich nehme meine Kamera mit.	I'm taking along my camera.

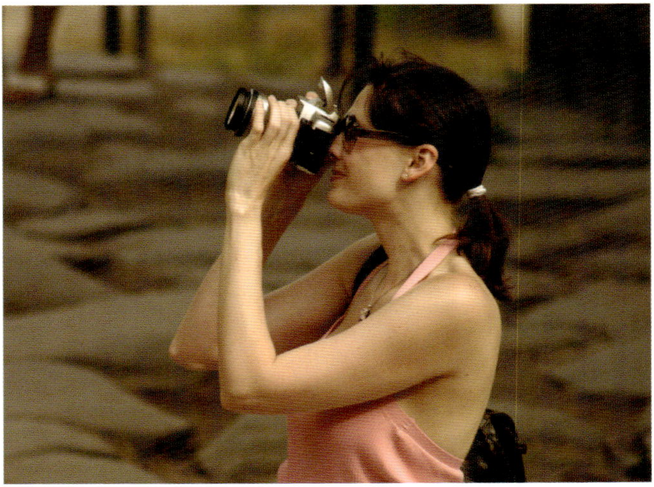

Vocabulary

Active German: Level 3 > Unit 6 > Lesson 1 > Vocabulary

Invitations and parties

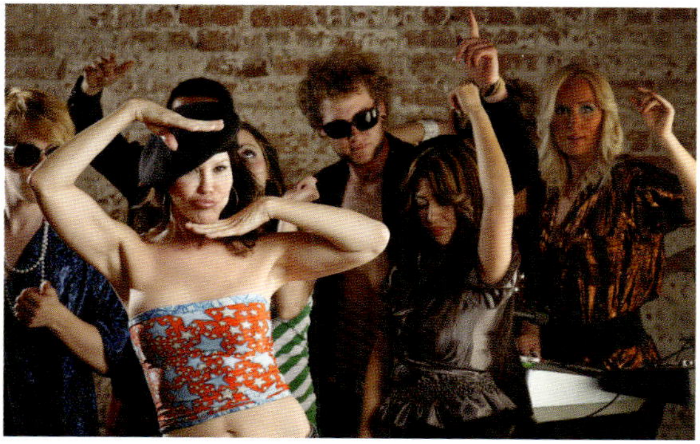

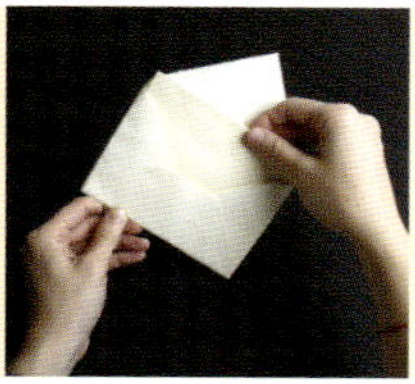

jemanden einladen
to invite somebody

Ich möchte dich zu meiner Party einladen.
I want to invite you to my party.

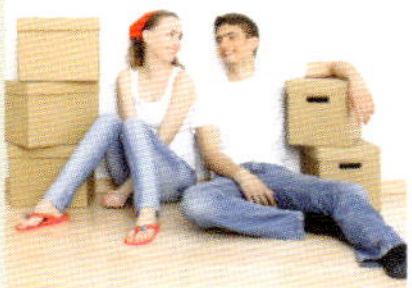

die Einweihungsparty / Einweihungspartys
housewarming party

Am Freitag mache ich eine Einweihungsparty.
On Friday I'm having a housewarming party.

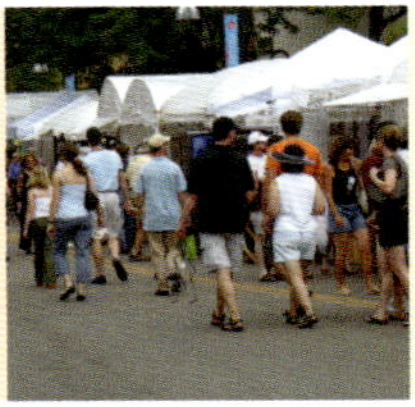

das Fest / Feste
celebration

Am Wochenende ist das Stadtfest in Pulheim.
This weekend there's the village fair in Pulheim.

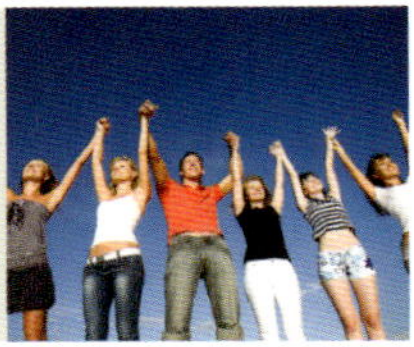

feiern
to celebrate

Wollen wir am Wochenende feiern?
Shall we celebrate this weekend?

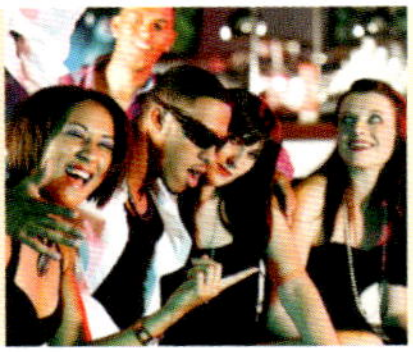

die Party / Partys
party

Wann ist die Party?
When is the party?

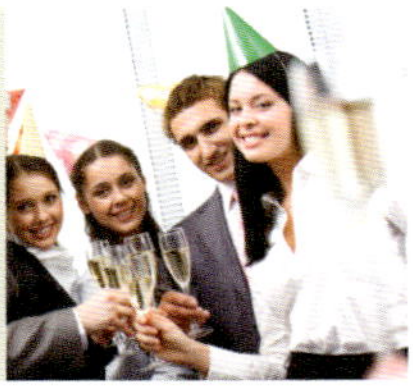

der Anlass / Anlässe
occasion

Was ist der Anlass für die Party?
What is the occasion for the party?

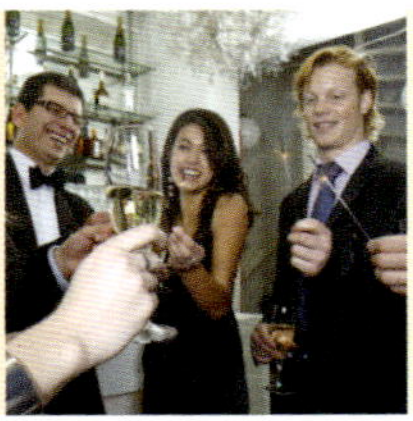

der Gast / Gäste
guest

Wie viele Gäste kommen zu der Party?
How many guests are going to be at the party?

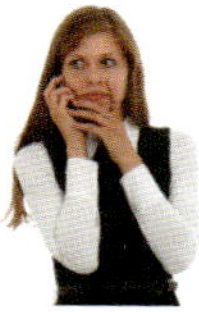

absagen
to cancel

Ich muss den Termin absagen.
I have to cancel the meeting.

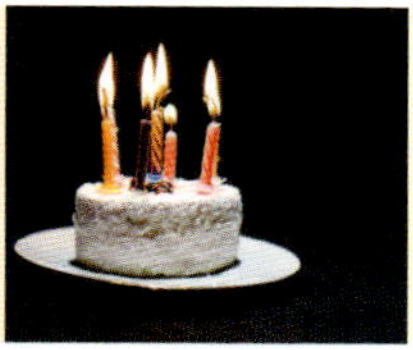

der Geburtstag / Geburtstage
birthday

Wann ist Ihr Geburtstag?
When is your birthday?

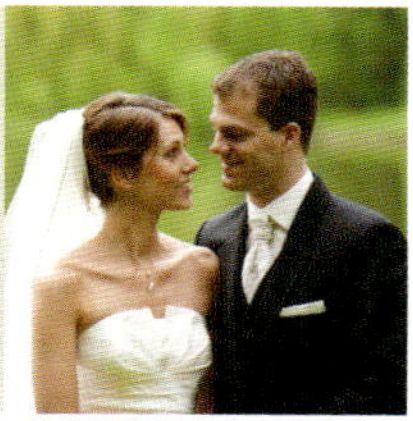

die Hochzeit / Hochzeiten
wedding

Ich lade euch hiermit zu unserer Hochzeit ein.
I hereby invite you to our wedding.

Culture note

The Munich *Oktoberfest* paradoxically begins in mid September. The 16-day party attracts over 6 million people every year who, in giant tents, consume 1.5 million gallons of beer, 200,000 pairs of pork sausage, and 480,000 spit-roasted chickens.

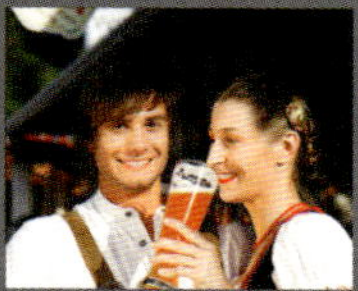

UNIT 6 › LESSON 2

An enjoyable evening

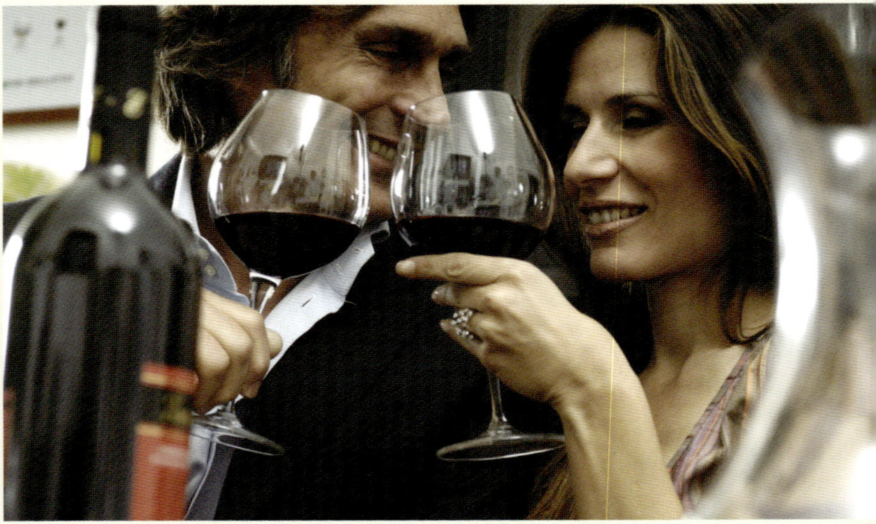

Culture note

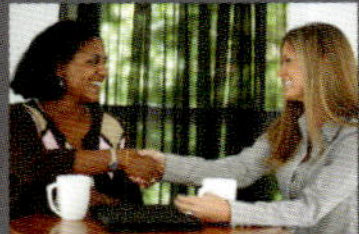

How does small talk work in Germany? Standard topics like the weather and food are common. Nevertheless, Germans are considered to be more direct, and serious topics such as politics or religion might come up during a party conversation. If there are not too many people in the room, it is quite common to greet everybody individually with a handshake.

Video Dialog

At the party, Lara tells Mr. Buschel who the guests are while they enjoy some snacks.

Active German: Level 3 > *Unit 6* > *Lesson 2* > *Video dialog*

Matthias:	*Was wollt ihr trinken?*
Lara:	*Wein bitte.*
Herr Buschel:	*Ich trinke lieber Bier.*
Lara:	*Mmh, das sieht aber gut aus.*
Matthias:	*Ach, das sind nur Kleinigkeiten. Bedient euch. Ich hole noch mehr Gläser.*
Herr Buschel:	*Weißt du, wer das ist?*
Lara:	*Das ist Matthias' Schwester Nina. Kennst du sie nicht?*
Herr Buschel:	*Nein, du weißt immer alles. Und das?*
Lara:	*Das ist Ninas Freund.*

Matthias:	What do you want to drink?
Lara:	Wine please.
Mr. Buschel:	I prefer beer.
Lara:	Mm, that looks delicious.
Matthias:	It's only a few snacks. Help yourselves. I'll get some more glasses.
Mr. Buschel:	Do you know who she is?
Lara:	That's Matthias' sister Nina. Don't you know her?
Mr. Buschel:	No, you always know everything. And who is that?
Lara:	That's Nina's boyfriend.

Grammar

Active German: Level 3 > Unit 6 > Lesson 2 > Grammar

1 › **Nina's boyfriend**

In the video dialog Lara and Mr. Buschel talk about Matthias' sister and her boyfriend. They are talking about relationships between people.

Das ist Ninas Freund.

That is Nina's boyfriend.

Note that in German you don't separate the *s* by an apostrophe. Instead you add it directly to the noun.

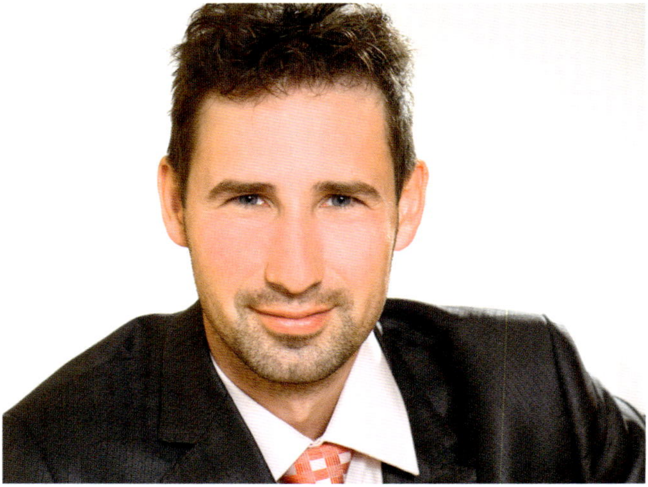

2 › Whose?

To express "whose" in German you use: *wessen*.

Wessen Auto ist das?	Whose car is that?
Das ist Frau Müllers Auto.	This is Mrs. Müller's car.
Wessen Kamera ist das?	Whose camera is it?
Das ist Peters Kamera.	It is Peter's camera.

3 › Possession

Another way of saying what is yours is to use the verb *gehören* (to belong to). We had a look at this verb in earlier lessons. Let's repeat it briefly.

Wem gehört das Handy? Das gehört mir.

Whose cell phone is that? (To whom does it belong?)
It belongs to me.

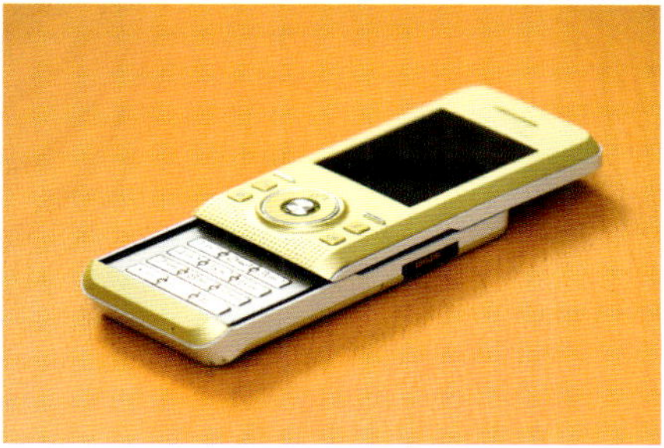

Note that the verb *gehören* needs the dative case. Let's have a look at some examples:

Gehört dir die Schokolade?

Is that your chocolate? (Does the chocolate belong to you?)

Die Bluse gehört meiner Mutter.

The blouse belongs to my mother.

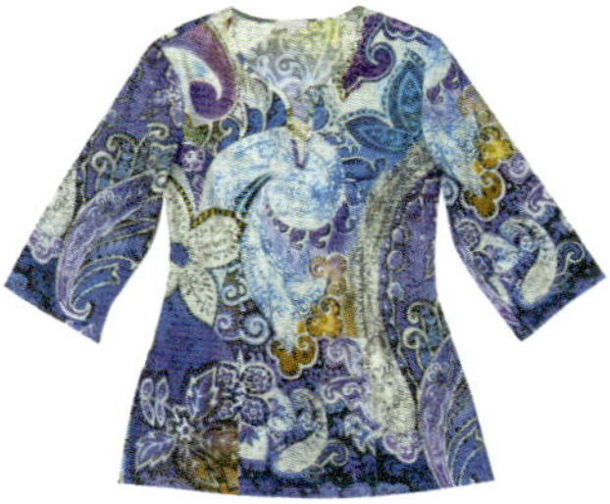

4 › Possession

There are other ways to express possession. You can use the preposition *von* as well.

Das ist das Auto von meiner Mutter.

That is my mother's car. (That is the car of my mother.)

You use this form if you are not using names.

Das ist das Büro von meinem Kollegen.

That is my colleague's office.

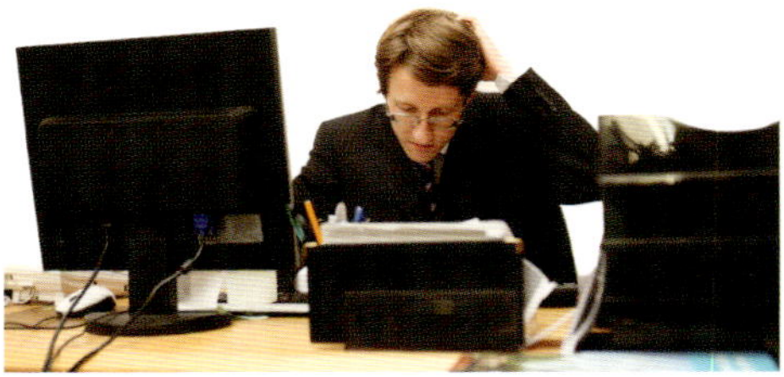

5 › Possession

The preposition *von* requires the dative case. Let's have a look at it again.

masculine	*Das ist das Auto von meinem Vater.*	That is my father's car.
feminine	*Das ist der Computer von deiner Mutter.*	That is your mother's computer.
neuter	*Das ist der Preis von dem Buch.*	That is the price of the book.

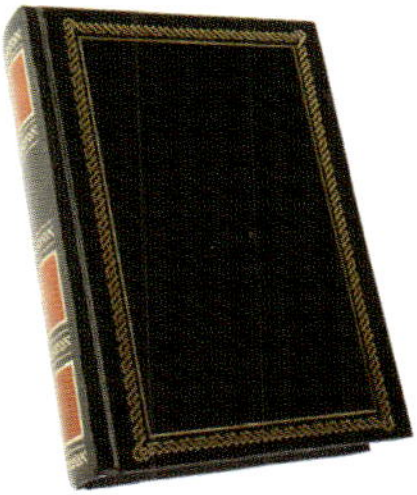

Vocabulary

Active German: Level 3 > Unit 6 > Lesson 2 > Vocabulary

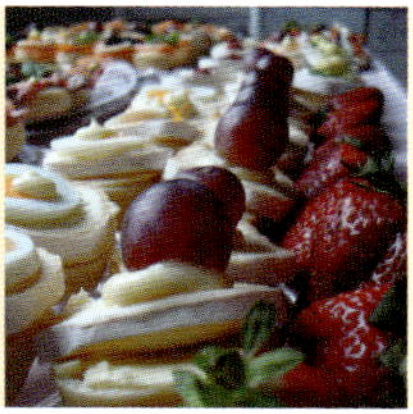

das Buffet / Buffets
buffet

Auf der Party gibt es ein Buffet.
There is a buffet at the party.

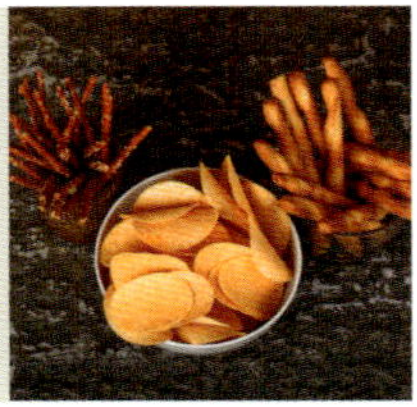

die Kleinigkeit / Kleinigkeiten
a bit

Ich habe nicht viel Hunger. Ich möchte nur eine Kleinigkeit.
I'm not very hungry. I just want a little bit to eat.

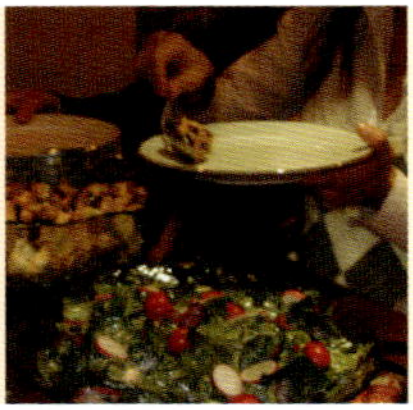

sich bedienen
to help oneself

Können wir uns bedienen?
Can we help ourselves?

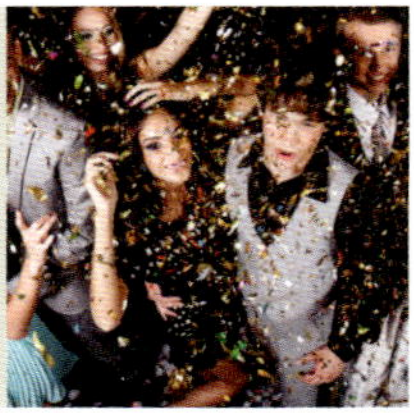

die Stimmung
mood, atmosphere

Die Stimmung hier ist gut.
The atmosphere here is good.

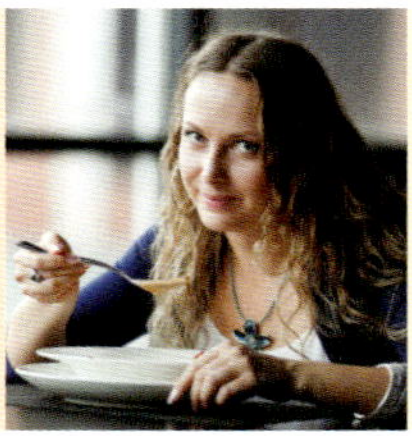

schmecken
to taste

Das schmeckt sehr gut.
This really tastes delicious.

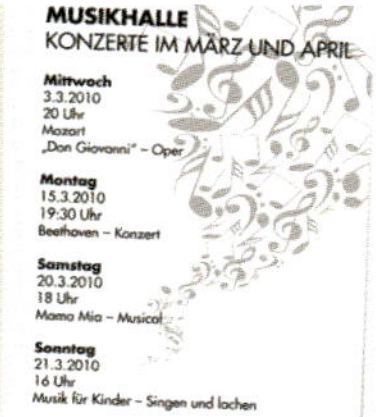

stattfinden
to take place

Wann und wo findet das Konzert statt?
When and where does the concert take place?

das Geschenk / Geschenke
present, gift

Hast du ein Geschenk für ihn?
Do you have a present for him?

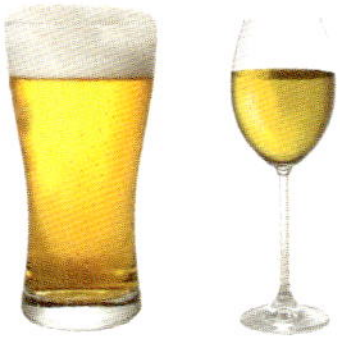

holen
to get

Ich muss ein paar Gläser holen.
I have to get a few glasses.

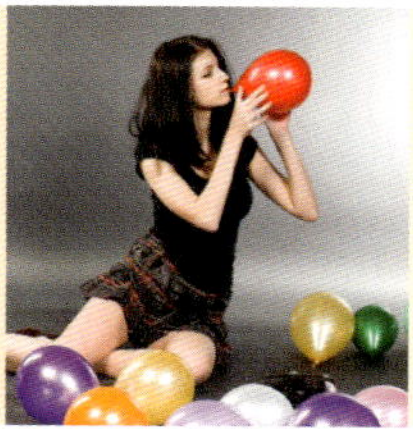

die Veranstaltung / Veranstaltungen
event

Kommst du morgen zu der Veranstaltung?
Are you going to the event tomorrow?

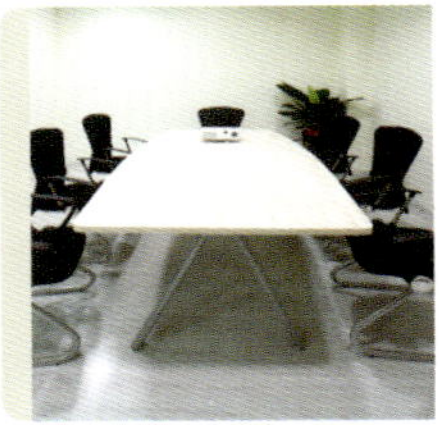

der Raum / Räume
room / space

In welchem Raum findet die Veranstaltung statt?
In which room is the event going to take place?

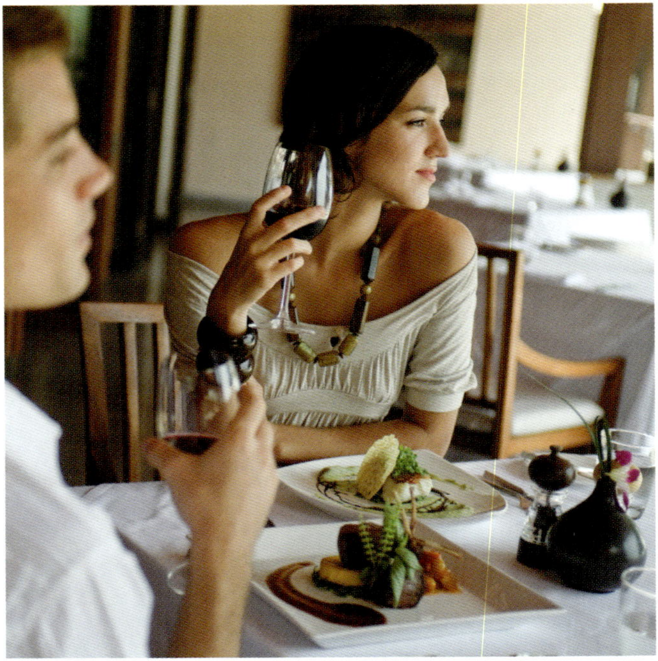

Collins

Livemocha ACTIVE GERMAN

HarperCollins Publishers
77–85 Fulham Palace Road
London W6 8JB
Great Britain

www.collinslanguage.com

First edition 2011

Reprint 10 9 8 7 6 5 4 3 2 1 0

ISBN (UK edition) 978-0-00-737354-3
ISBN (export edition) 978-0-00-741978-4
ISBN (US edition) 978-0-87779-556-8

A catalogue record for this book is available from the British Library

Typeset by Macmillan Publishing Services

Audio material recorded and produced by Networks SRL, Milan

Printed and Bound in China by Leo Paper Products Ltd.
Series Editor: Rob Scriven

INTRODUCTION

Welcome to your Livemocha Active German experience! This new course goes above and beyond what a traditional book-based course can offer. With its focus on online learning, Active German provides the opportunity not just to study but to experience the language for yourself by interacting with native speakers online.

Why go online?
Studying a language online allows you to learn in a more natural atmosphere – watching people interact in a **video** is far more lifelike than listening to conversations on a CD. After watching a video dialog, you will be walked through an explanation of some of the **grammar** and **vocabulary** items that were introduced in the new dialog. Then, by completing a variety of **interactive quizzes**, the system will instantly be able to tell you how well you are doing. You can then **talk online** with native German speakers to practice what you've learned.

Who else is online?
Livemocha boasts over 7 million members and is growing every day. These members are online for the same reason as you – to learn and experience a new language. Native German-speaking members will be happy to read through your written and spoken submissions and to give you feedback on how you're doing. You can also connect with people who want to chat in any given language – interaction on an informal, nonacademic basis is an ideal way for you to perfect your language skills.

What do the books do?
The four accompanying books are designed to complement the online course – the dialogs for all of the videos that you can watch online are available here for you to study whenever you don't have access to the Internet. You will also find all of the Grammar and Vocabulary sections explained in the books, plus the culture notes to teach you a little about Germany.

LEVEL 4

This book is the fourth of four. It corresponds with Level 4 of the online course.

Level 4 is ideal for those who feel at ease making general conversation in French and who are looking for further practice of more complex topics and grammar.

What you will learn

- How to make suggestions and recommendations
- How to express your opinion and ask for information
- How to join sentences together
- How to say "yet," "not yet," "never," "not any more," etc.
- How to use the different words for "when"
- How to give dates
- How to use business vocabulary to talk about the working world
- Vocabulary for shopping, cultural activities, traveling, birthdays and celebrations, and relaxing and socializing

Every time you see this coffee cup symbol in these books, it indicates the presence of a pathway – a guide to exactly where you can find that particular piece of content online. Log on at www.livemocha.com and follow the path to find the online version of what you are studying in the book.

Video Dialog

A warm welcome for Matthias as he gets to know his new colleagues a little better.

Active German: Level 1 > *Unit 2* > *Lesson 1* > *Video dialog*

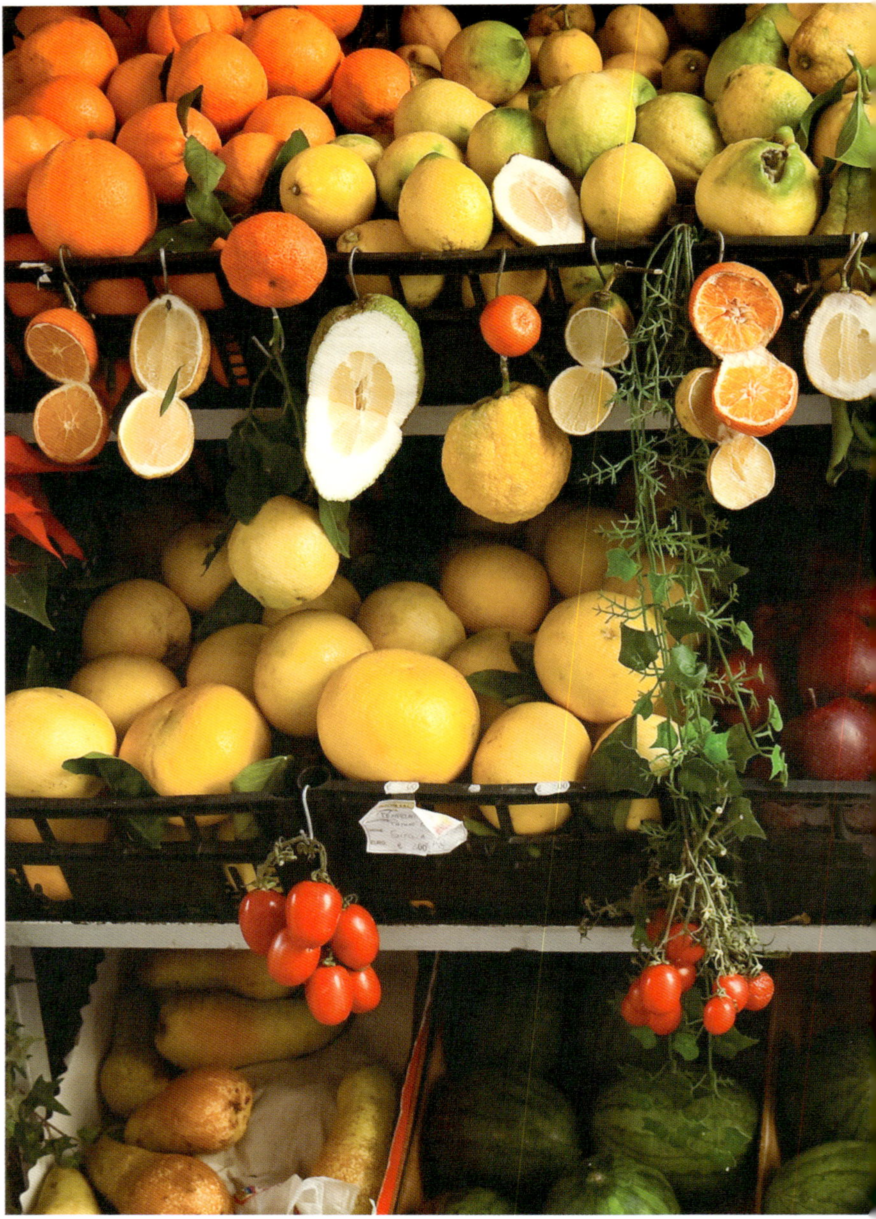

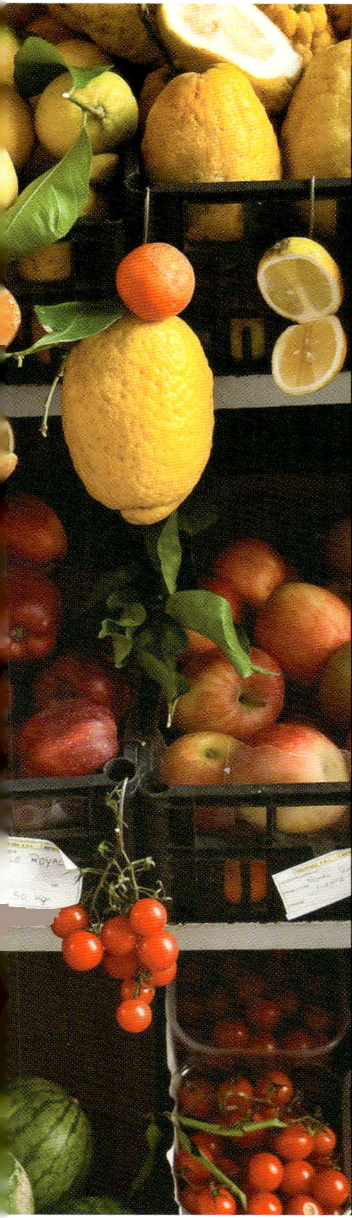

1

Lesson 1: In the supermarket 1

- How to describe products.
- Some adjectives for tastes, sizes, and people: ***süß***, ***trocken***, ***dünn***.
- How to use adjectives.

Lesson 2: In the supermarket 2

- How to describe nouns.
- How to ask for product information.
- New vocabulary relating to shopping: ***das Angebot***, ***geschlossen***.

Collins | Livemocha™

UNIT 1 › LESSON 1

In the supermarket 1

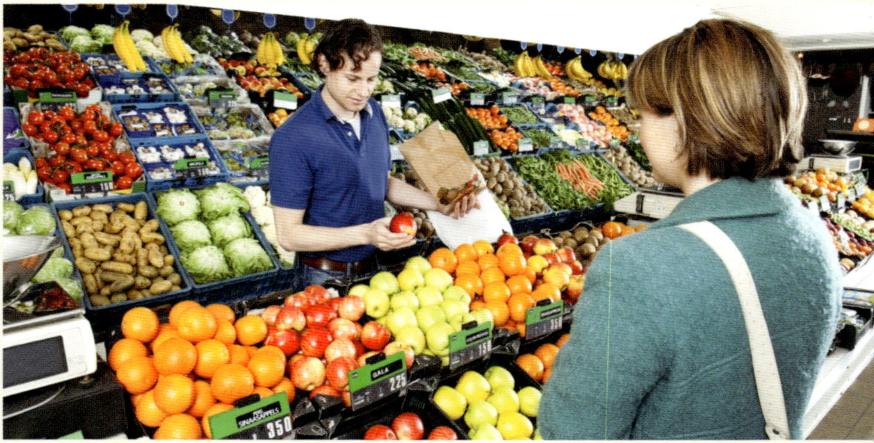

Culture note

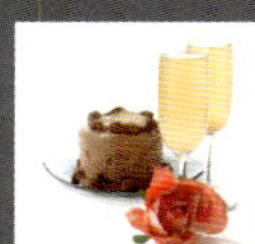

Although Germany is famous for its beers, Germans also enjoy a good glass of wine. It is primarily produced in the southwest of Germany, along the river Rhine and its tributaries.

Germany's reputation is mainly based on white wines made from the *Riesling* grape variety.

***Dornfelder* and *Spätburgunder* (the German name for pinot noir) are darker, richer wines.**

Hot red wine with spices (*Glühwein*) is especially popular during the cold season.

Video Dialog

Matthias pays a visit to the local food store.

Watch the video dialog online at
Active German: Level 4 > *Unit 1* > *Lesson 1* > *Video dialog*

Matthias:	*Ich suche einen guten Wein.*
Lena:	*Möchten Sie einen süßen oder einen trockenen?*
Matthias:	*Einen trockenen.*
Lena:	*Hier habe ich eine gute Flasche.*
Matthias:	*Dornfelder. Ein deutscher Wein?*
Lena:	*Ja, es gibt gute deutsche Weine.*
Matthias:	*Ok. Und dann brauche ich noch eine gute Tafel Schokolade.*
Lena:	*Hier habe ich eine sehr leckere Tafel.*
Matthias:	*Dann brauche ich noch ein kleines Brot.*

Matthias:	I'm looking for a good bottle of wine.
Lena:	Would you like a sweet or dry one?
Matthias:	A dry one.
Lena:	Here's a good bottle.
Matthias:	Dornfelder. A German wine?
Lena:	Yes, there are some good German wines.
Matthias:	OK. And I also need a good bar of chocolate.
Lena:	Here's some very tasty chocolate.
Matthias:	Then I just need a small loaf of bread.

Grammar

In this section we go over some of the grammar points introduced in the dialog.

Go to Active German: Level 4 > Unit 1 > Lesson 1 > Grammar to listen to these explanations and to access some interactive practice activities.

1 › Adjective endings

Adjectives can be used in two different ways.

1. They can be after the verb.

*Der Wein ist **gut**.*

The wine is good.

*Die Schokolade ist **süß**.*

The chocolate is sweet.

These adjectives do not change.

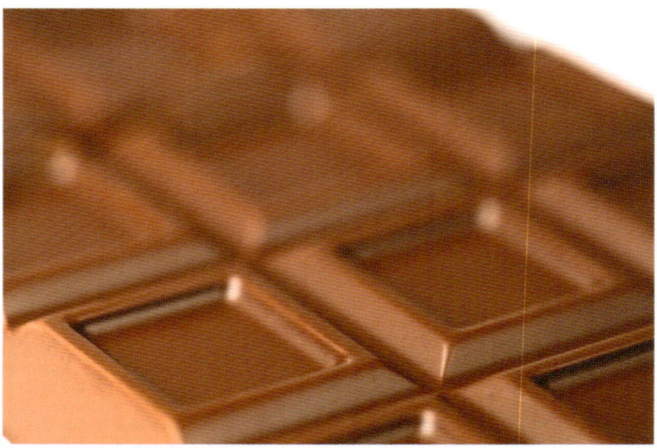

2. Adjectives may come before the noun they are describing.

Ich trinke einen ***guten*** *Wein.*

I'm drinking a good (glass of) wine.

Ich esse gerne ***süße*** *Schokolade.*

I like sweet chocolate.

These adjectives take different endings. They must agree with the noun.

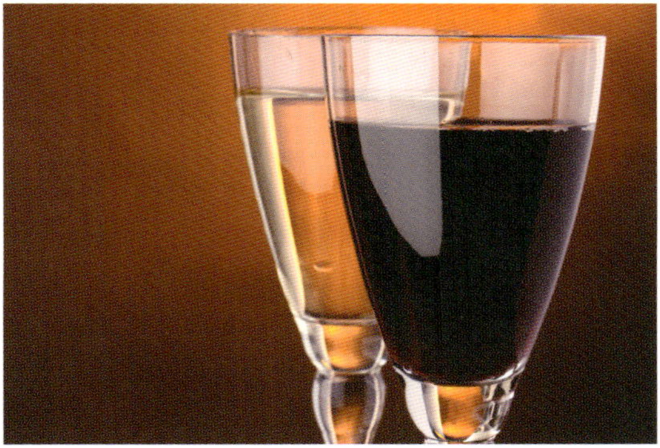

2 › Adjective endings

First we are going to look at adjectives describing the subject of a sentence (the acting part) with the article - *ein*.

Masculine:

der *Wein – ein Wein*

Das ist ***ein*** *trocken****er*** *Wein.*

That is a dry wine.

Feminine:

*di**e** Tafel Schokolade – eine Tafel*

*Das ist **eine** gut**e** Tafel Schokolade.*

That is a good bar of chocolate.

Neuter:

*da**s** Brot – ein Brot*

*Das ist **ein** klein**es** Brot.*

That is a small loaf of bread.

There is no article in the plural equivalent. This is how the adjective works:

*di**e** Orangen – Orangen*
*Das sind süß**e** Orangen.*

These are sweet oranges.

In summary: You use *-er* for masculine, *-e* for feminine, *-es* for neuter, and *-e* for plural.

3 › Adjective endings

Now we are going to have a look at adjectives describing the person or thing to which the action is done (the direct object of a sentence, which is in the accusative case).

Masculine:

*Ich möchte ein**en** Schrank. Ich möchte ein**en** groß**en** Schrank.*

I would like a wardrobe. I would like a big wardrobe.

Feminine:

*Ich kaufe ein**e** Flasche. Ich kaufe ein**e** groß**e** Flasche.*

I buy a bottle. I buy a big bottle.

Neuter:

*Ich nehme ein Glas. Ich nehme ein groß**es** Glas.*

I take a glass. I take a big glass.

Plural:

*Ich kaufe Bücher. Ich kaufe interessant**e** Bücher.*

I buy books. I buy interesting books.

In summary: masculine takes *-en*, feminine takes *-e*, neuter takes *-es*, and plural takes an *-e*.

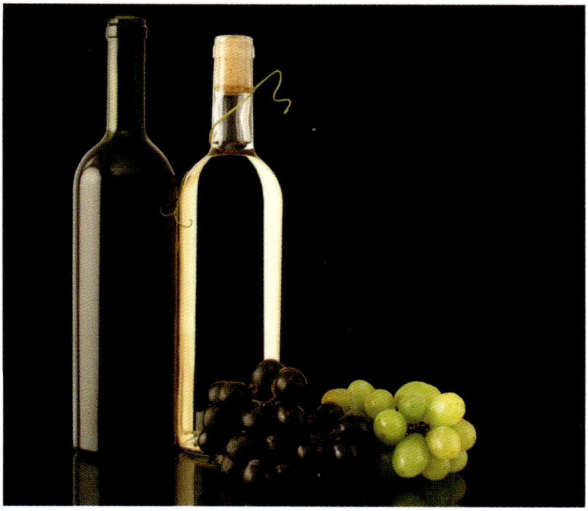

4 › **Adjective endings**

In order to find out which ending you need there are three important steps to consider:

1. The gender of the noun (*der, die, das*)
2. The case of the noun (nominative or accusative) – Is it the subject or the direct object of a sentence?
3. Is there an article? What kind of article is it?

The adjective endings are a bit tricky in German and it takes a while to get them right. Depending on your learning style you might want to draw a table or just work with examples. It is entirely up to you.

5 › ***Kein* and adjective endings**

The adjective endings after the article *kein* (no / not / not a / not any) are the same as those for *ein* (a).

*Ich trinke keinen trocken**en** Wein.*	I don't drink dry wine.
*Ich mag keine klassisch**e** Musik.*	I don't like classical music.
*Ich habe kein neu**es** Handy.*	I don't have a new cell phone.
*Ich habe keine schön**en** Fotos.*	I don't have any nice photos.

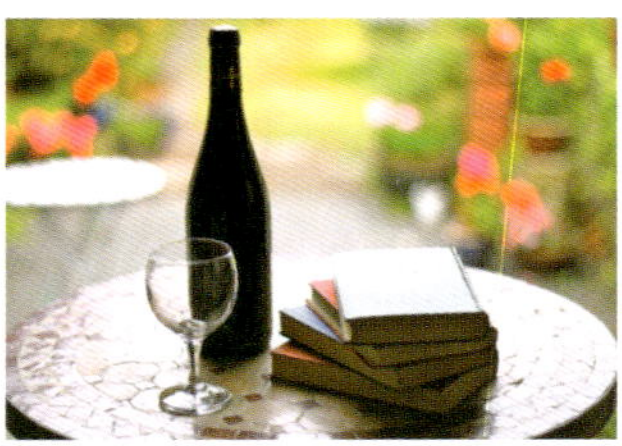

6 › Possessive adjectives and adjective endings

The possessive adjectives – *mein* (my), *dein* (your), *sein* (his), *ihr* (her), *unser* (our), *euer* (your), *Ihr* (your), *ihr* (your) – follow the same pattern.

Ist das Ihr schwarzer Mantel?	Is that your black coat?
Das ist unsere kleine Katze.	That is our little cat.
Ist das sein neues Handy?	Is that his new cell phone?
Das sind meine gelben Schuhe.	These are my yellow shoes.

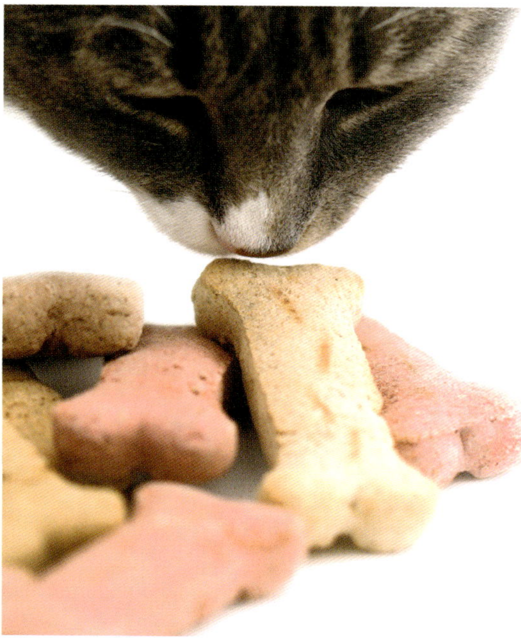

Vocabulary

In this section you will learn some useful words and expressions from the dialog.

Go to Active German: Level 4 > Unit 1 > Lesson 1 > Vocabulary to listen to each of the words being pronounced and to access some interactive practice activities.

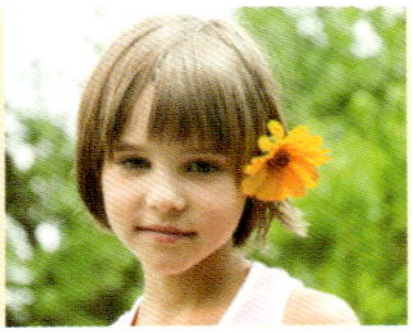

süß
sweet, cute

Ist sie nicht süß?
Isn't she sweet?

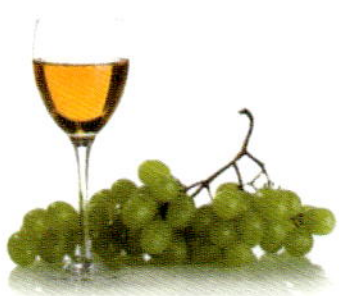

trocken
dry

Der Wein ist sehr trocken.
The wine is very dry.

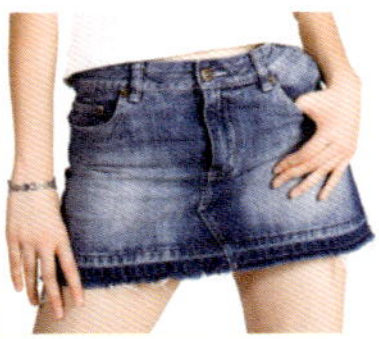

kurz
short

Sie trägt einen kurzen Rock.
She is wearing a short skirt.

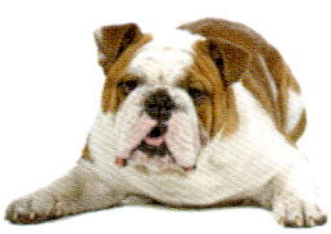

dick
thick, fat

Der Hund ist ein bisschen dick.
The dog is a bit fat.

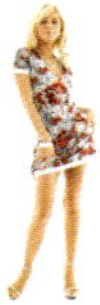

dünn
thin, slim

Steffi ist so dünn. Sie isst nur Salat.
Steffi is so thin. She just eats salad.

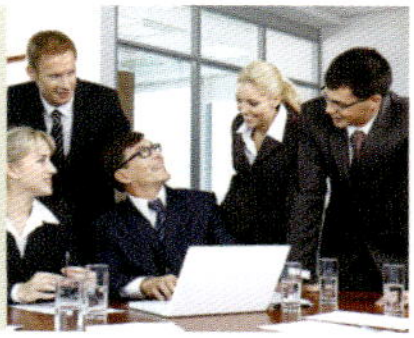

sympathisch
nice, friendly

Meine Kollegen sind sehr sympathisch.
My colleagues are very friendly.

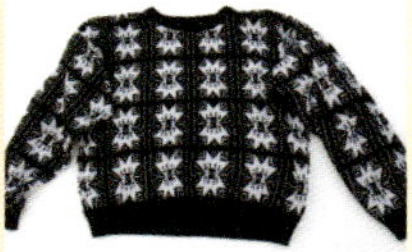

hässlich
ugly

Das ist aber ein hässlicher Pullover.
This is a really ugly sweater.

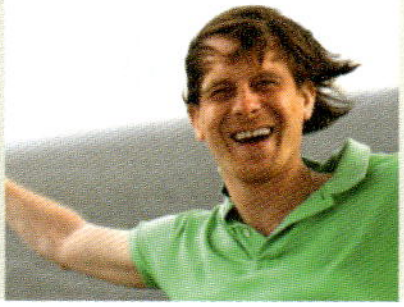

lustig
funny

Er ist lustig. Ich muss die ganze Zeit lachen.
He is so funny. I have to laugh the whole time.

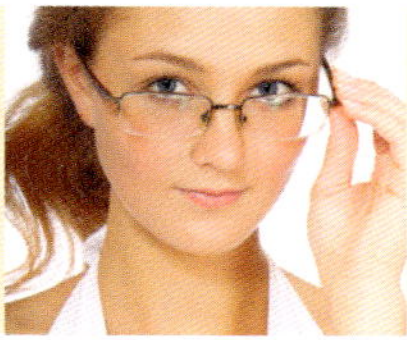

intelligent
intelligent

Sie ist ein intelligentes Mädchen.
She is an intelligent girl.

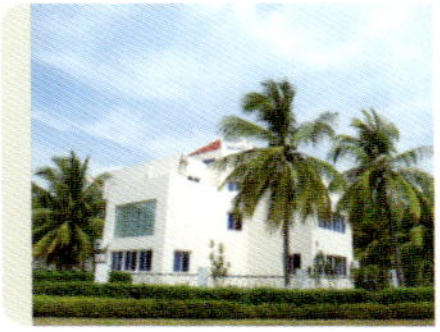

hoch
high, tall

Dieses Haus ist sehr hoch.
This house is very tall.

Culture note

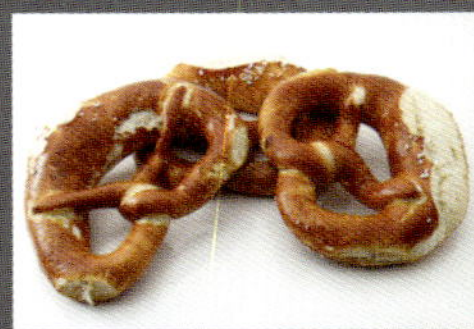

Bread is Germany's staple food. In a German supermarket or bakery you will find a huge range of different types of bread, with more than 300 different sorts produced. In general, Germans prefer wholemeal or coarse rye bread, rather than white. On a Sunday morning it is not uncommon to see a long line of people outside their favorite bakery waiting to buy their Sunday breakfast bread rolls (*Brötchen*).

UNIT 1 › LESSON 2

In the supermarket 2

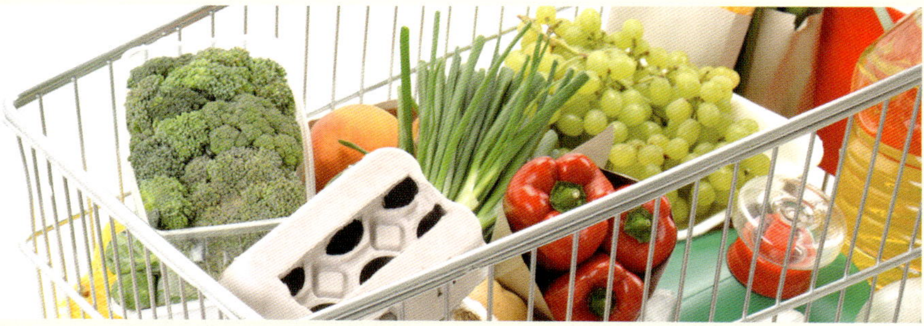

Culture note

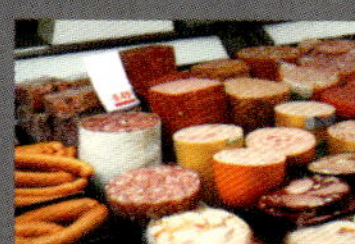

Most supermarkets in Germany are rather small, especially in the more central areas of the city. They generally fall into two categories: the cheaper discounters and slightly more upscale ones, which have a greater selection, though you might not find the same brands you are used to from other countries.

Opening hours are regulated by law. Shops are officially allowed to open on weekdays and Saturdays from 6 a.m. to 8 p.m. or sometimes 10 p.m. However, many small stores (especially in the countryside and suburban areas) close at 6 p.m. during the week and as early as 1 p.m. or 2 p.m. on Saturdays. Some close during lunchtime. Shops must remain closed on Sundays. This law is widely debated in Germany and may change in the future. With very few exceptions, there is no such thing as round-the-clock shopping. Among the exceptions are gas stations on main roads, newsstands, and stores in major train stations and airports.

Video Dialog

Matthias also needs to buy coffee but things are less straight-forward than he expected.

Active German: Level 4 > *Unit 1* > *Lesson 2* > *Video dialog*

Matthias:	*Ist der Kaffee im Angebot?*
Lara:	*Die große Packung ist im Angebot, die kleine nicht.*
Matthias:	*Danke.*
Lara:	*Sehen Sie das rote Schild? Da steht es.*
Matthias:	*Oh ja, ich bin ein bisschen blind.*
Lara:	*Haben Sie schon den Kaffee gesehen?*
Matthias:	*Den grünen?*
Lara:	*Ja, der ist auch im Angebot.*
Matthias:	*Danke schön.*

Matthias:	Is the coffee on sale?
Lara:	The big pack is on sale, but not the small one.
Matthias:	Thank you.
Lara:	Do you see the red sign? It says it there.
Matthias:	Oh, yes. I'm a bit blind.
Lara:	Have you seen this coffee yet?
Matthias:	The green one?
Lara:	Yes, that one's also on sale.
Matthias:	Many thanks.

Grammar

Active German: Level 4 > *Unit 1* > *Lesson 2* > *Grammar*

1 › More on adjective endings

In the first lesson we had a look at adjective endings after *ein* (a). Now let's have a look at the articles *der*, *die*, and *das* (the). This is even easier!

In the nominative case (subject) we have the following pattern:

Masculine:

*der groß**e** Mann*

the tall man

Feminine:

*die grün**e** Flasche*

the green bottle

Neuter:

*das klein**e** Kind*

the small child

Plural:

*die groß**en** Flaschen*

the big bottles

Note that, apart from in the plural, the ending in the nominative case is always *-e*!

2 › More on adjective endings

In the accusative case (object) the pattern is as follows:

Masculine:

*Siehst du den klein**en** Mann?*

Do you see the small man?

Feminine:

*Kennst du die blond**e** Frau?*

Do you know the blonde woman?

Neuter:

*Siehst du das rot**e** Schild?*

Do you see the red sign?

Plural without article:

*Ich habe schön**e** Blumen.*

I have (some) beautiful flowers.

Plural with article:

*Wo hast du die schön**en** Blumen gekauft?*

Where did you buy the beautiful flowers?

In summary: masculine takes *-en*, feminine takes *-e*, neuter takes *-e*, plural without article takes *-e* and plural with article takes *-en*.

3 › Do you see the green one?

Matthias says in the video: *Den grünen?* (The green one?) without saying the noun. If it is obvious what you are referring to you can leave out the noun.

Sehen Sie das Auto?	Do you see the car?
Das rote?	The red one?

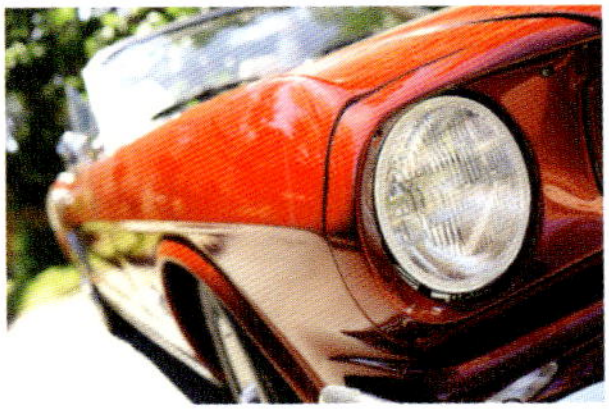

4 › On offer

If you want to say that something is on sale, you use *im Angebot*:

Der Kaffee ist im Angebot.
The coffee is on sale.

If you want to make an offer to somebody, you say:

Ich mache Ihnen ein Angebot.
I'll make you an offer.

The verb “to offer” is *anbieten*.

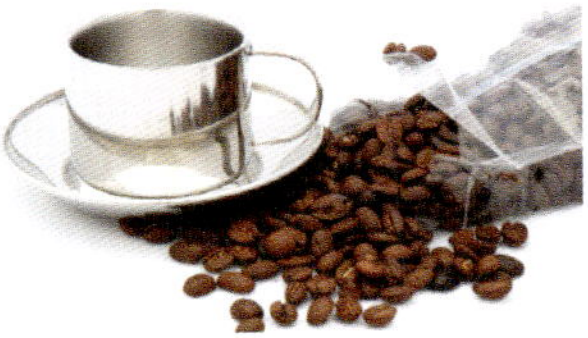

Note that it is separable and takes the dative.

Sie bietet ihm einen Kaffee an.	She offers him a coffee.
Darf ich Ihnen etwas anbieten.	May I offer you something?

5 › *Da!* Adverbs of place

To talk about directions you might want to use the following adverbs: *Hier* refers to a place close to the speaker.

Hier ist dein Handy.

Here is your cell phone.

To show where something is and to say that it is "over there" you use *da* or *dort*. *Dort* refers to a place away from the speaker.

Dort steht das Auto.

The car is over there.

Da means there as well, but is used more frequently than *dort*. It is used to refer to the presence of a person or thing.

Er ist da.	He is here.
Ist Matthias da?	Is Matthias there?

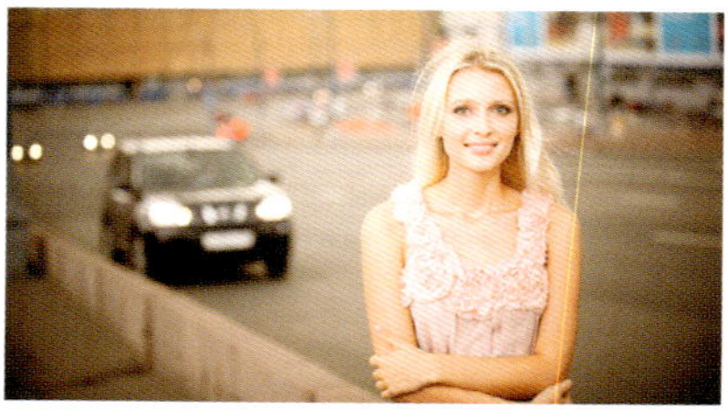

Vocabulary

Active German: Level 4 > *Unit 1* > *Lesson 2* > *Vocabulary*

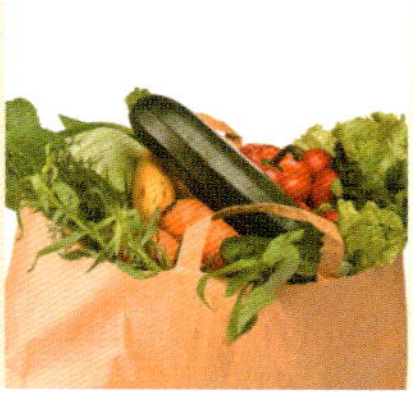

die Packung / Packungen
pack

Kannst du mir bitte die große Packung geben?
Could you please give me the large pack?

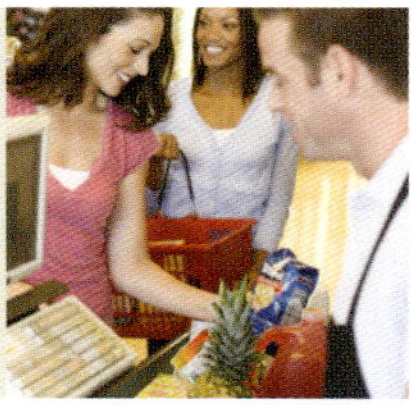

die Kasse / Kassen
cashier, checkout

Entschuldigung, wo ist denn die Kasse?
Excuse me, where is the checkout please?

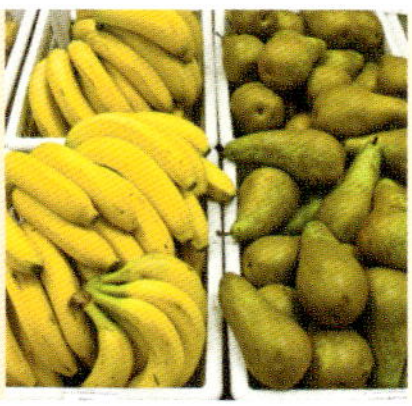

das Angebot / Angebote
sale

Diese Woche sind die Bananen im Angebot.
This week, bananas are on sale.

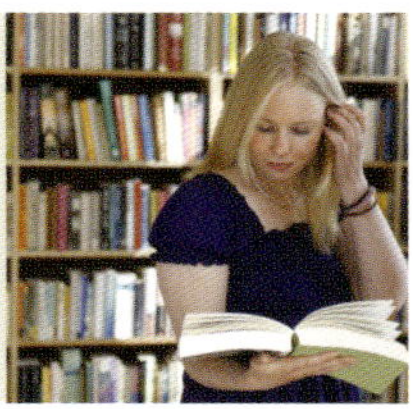

das Regal / Regale
shelf

Stehen die Bücher im Regal?
Are the books on the shelf?

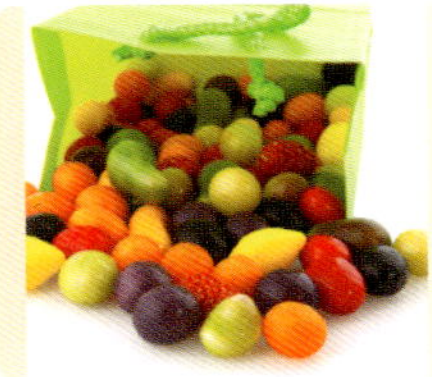

die Süßigkeit / Süßigkeiten
candy

Kinder lieben Süßigkeiten.
Children love candy.

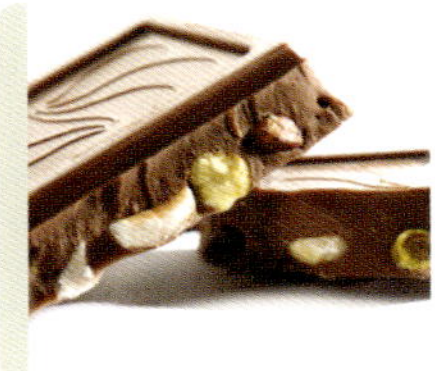

die Schokolade
chocolate

Gute Schokolade kommt aus der Schweiz.
Good chocolate comes from Switzerland.

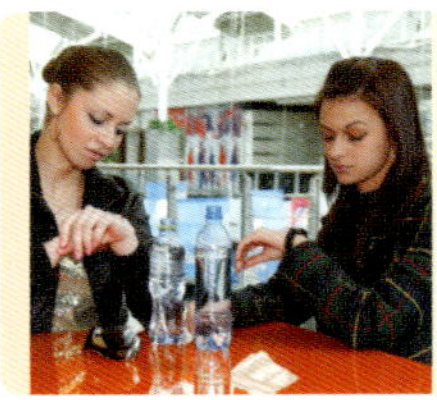

die Öffungszeiten
business hours

Kennen Sie die Öffnungszeiten von diesem Supermarkt?
Do you know the business hours of this supermarket?

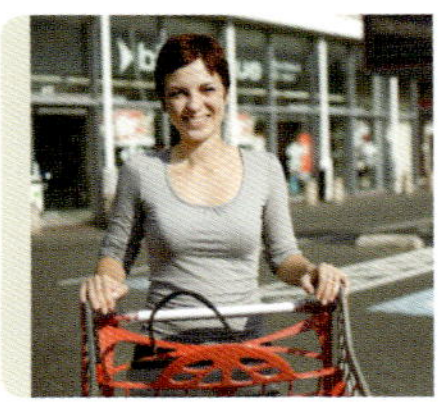

geöffnet
open

Ist der Supermarkt geöffnet?
Is the supermarket open?

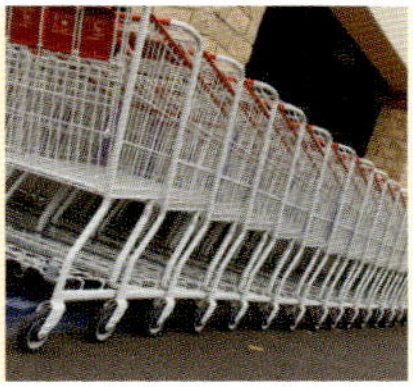

geschlossen
closed

Nein, der Supermarkt ist geschlossen.
No, the supermarket is closed.

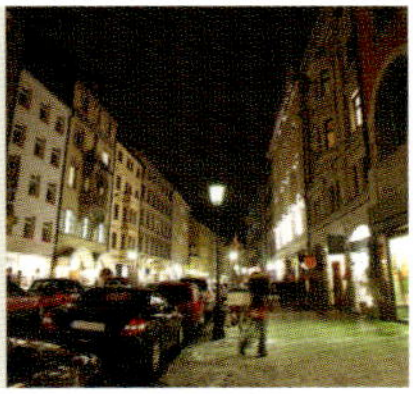

der Laden / Läden
store

Gibt es hier schöne Läden?
Are there any nice stores here?

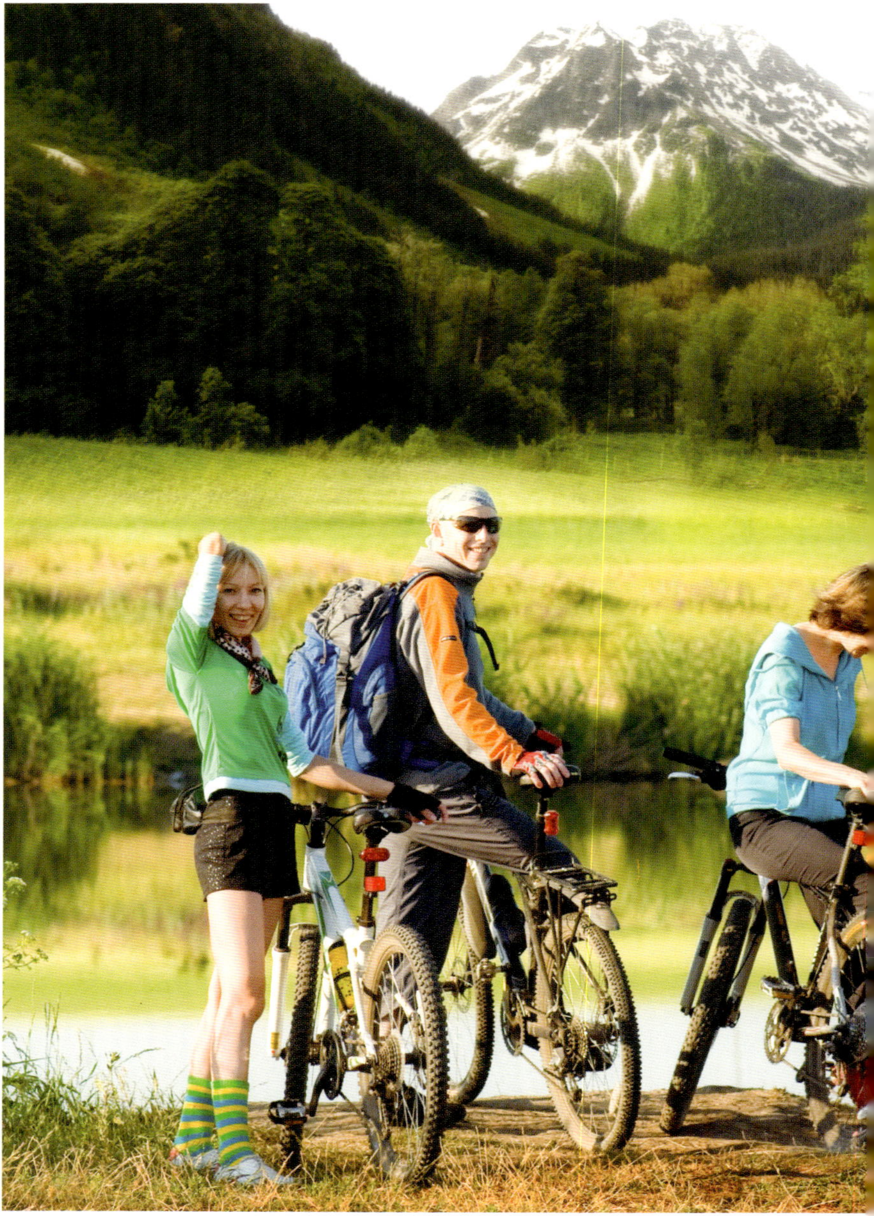

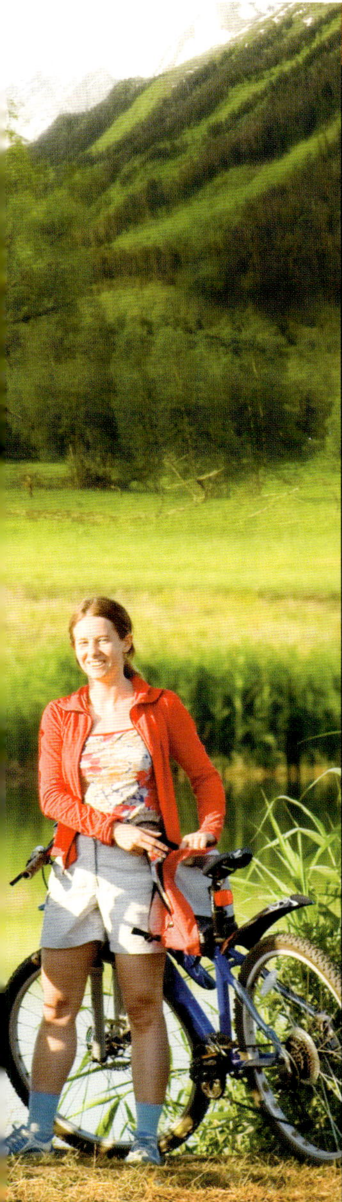

2

Lesson 1: What shall we do?

- How to talk about evening / weekend plans.
- How to say what you would like to do.
- How to suggest something.
- How to use the verb ***lassen*** (to let, leave).
- Vocabulary for cultural activities.

Lesson 2: A concert

- How to express your opinion and comment on other people's ideas.
- How to contradict.
- Vocabulary for music, thoughts, and opinions.

Collins | Livemocha™

UNIT 2 › LESSON 1

What shall we do?

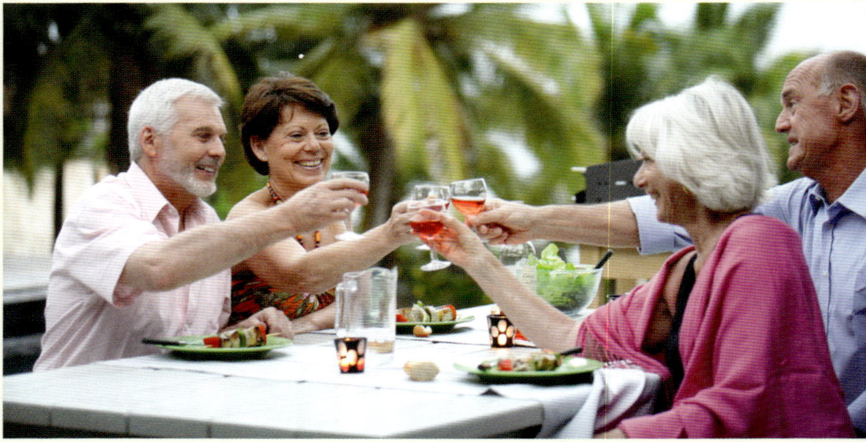

Culture note

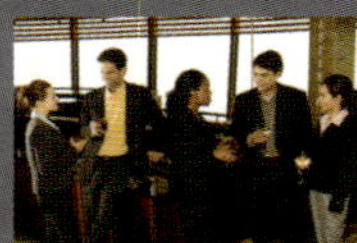

Schönen Feierabend! The German word *Feierabend* means the end of a working day. You use it to say good bye to colleagues when it is time to go home. In earlier times the word *Feierabend* was used the day before a public holiday to wish everybody a nice day off. Nowadays *Feierabend* marks the end of the working day. Some might go home; others go for a beer after work (*Feierabendbier*). Afterwork life is not necessarily quiet. Socializing among colleagues is quite common and nowadays so-called After-Work clubs are often seen.

There are some common expressions using the word *Feierabend: Jetzt machen wir Feierabend* (Let's finish for today. We've done enough); *Einen schönen Feierabend* (Have a nice evening); *Für mich ist jetzt Feierabend* (I'm done for today).

Video Dialog

Lara and Matthias come to a compromise.

Active German: Level 4 > *Unit 2* > *Lesson 1* > *Video dialog*

Matthias:	*Oh, guck mal. Am Wochenende spielen die „Buffalos“.*
Lara:	*Die „Buffalos“? Popmusik? Lass uns doch zu einem klassischen Konzert gehen.*
Matthias:	*Klassisch, ich weiß nicht.*
Lara:	*Magst du keine klassische Musik?*
Matthias:	*Doch, aber ich höre lieber Popmusik und Jazz.*
Lara:	*Jazz mag ich auch.*
Matthias:	*Ok, ein Kompromiss: Am Samstag gehen wir zu deinem Konzert und am Sonntag zu meinem.*
Lara:	*Einverstanden!*

Matthias:	Oh, look. The Buffalos are playing this weekend.
Lara:	The Buffalos? Pop music? Why don't we go to a classical concert?
Matthias:	Classical ... I don't know.
Lara:	Don't you like classical music?
Matthias:	Yes, I do, but I prefer pop music and jazz.
Lara:	I like jazz as well.
Matthias:	OK, a compromise: on Saturday we'll go to your concert and on Sunday to mine.
Lara:	OK!

Grammar

Active German: Level 4 > Unit 2 > Lesson 1 > Grammar

1 › Let's get something to drink

In earlier units we had a look at how to form suggestions:

Gehen wir doch ins Kino.	Why don't we go to the movies?
Geh doch nach Hause.	Why don't you go home?

Another way of suggesting something is to use the verb *lassen* (to let).

Lass uns doch ins Kino gehen.

Let's go to the movies.

Do you remember how to build the imperative form?

Sie gehen ⊠ Gehen Sie.	Go.
Du gehst ⊠ Geh.	Go.

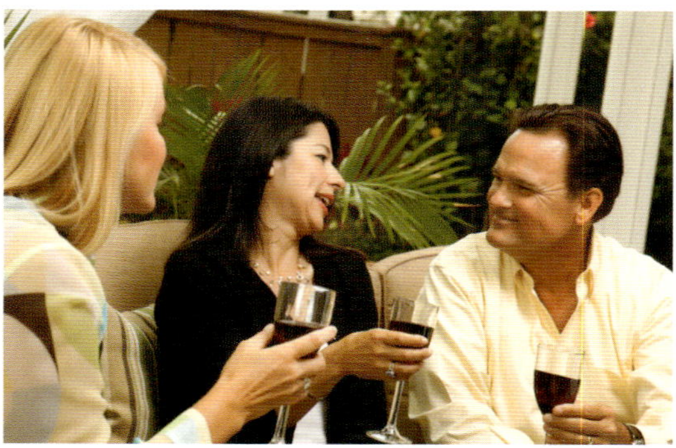

The verb *lassen* (to let) when used to suggest something works the same way.

Lassen Sie uns noch etwas trinken gehen.	Shall we go for a drink? / Let's go for a drink.
Lass uns doch etwas essen gehen.	Shall we get some food? / Let's get some food.

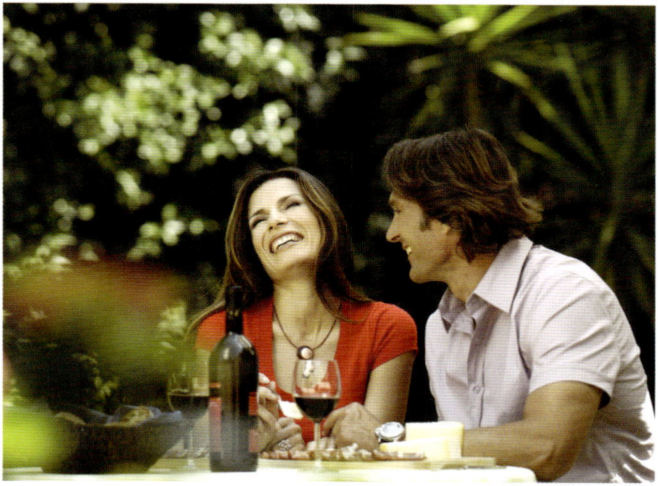

2 › Let's go

The verb *lassen* has other meanings. Let's have a look at the common ones.

lassen	to get / have done
Ich lasse mein Auto reparieren.	I get my car repaired.
Ich habe mein Auto reparieren lassen.	I got my car repaired.

lassen	to allow / to let
Lass uns gehen.	Let's go.
Lassen Sie ihn gehen.	Let him go.

lassen	to leave behind
Ich lasse meinen Laptop im Büro.	I leave my laptop in the office.
Ich habe mein Handy im Auto gelassen.	I left my cell phone in the car.

Have a look at how the verb works:

ich lasse	I let
du lässt	you let
er / sie / es lässt	he / she / it lets
wir lassen	we let
ihr lasst	you let
sie / Sie lassen	they / you let

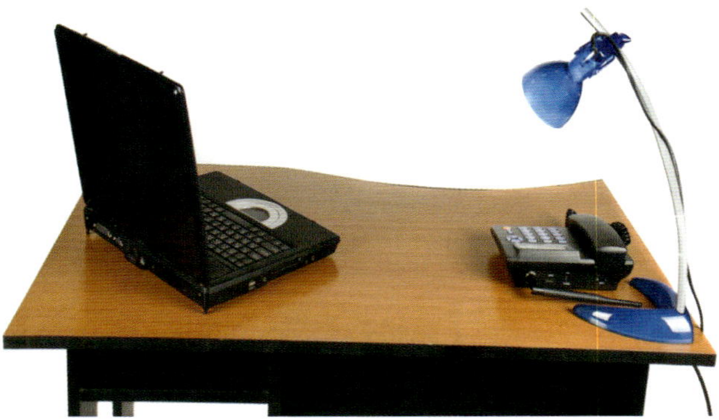

3 › Let's go dancing

Some activities are expressed with the verb *gehen*.

essen gehen	to go for food / to eat out
tanzen gehen	to go dancing
etwas trinken gehen	to go for a drink

Wollen wir etwas trinken gehen?
Shall we go for a drink?

Lass uns tanzen gehen.
Let's go dancing.

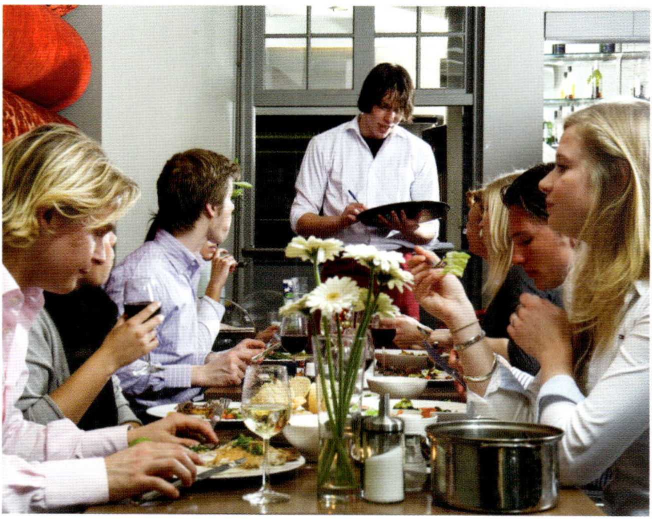

4 › Shall we go for a drink?

Let's consider some different ways of saying what you like to do and what you would like to do.

Ich gehe gerne Griechisch essen.	I like to go for Greek food.
Ich habe Lust auf Kino.	I feel like going to the movies.
Wie wäre es mit Kino?	How about a movie?
Ich würde gerne spazieren gehen.	I would like to go for a walk.
Was möchtest du gerne machen?	What would you like to do?
Was sollen wir machen?	What shall we do?
Gehen wir ein Bierchen trinken?	Do you want to go for a beer?

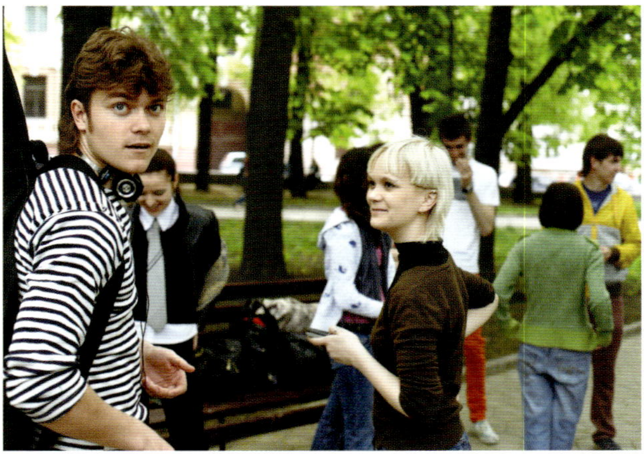

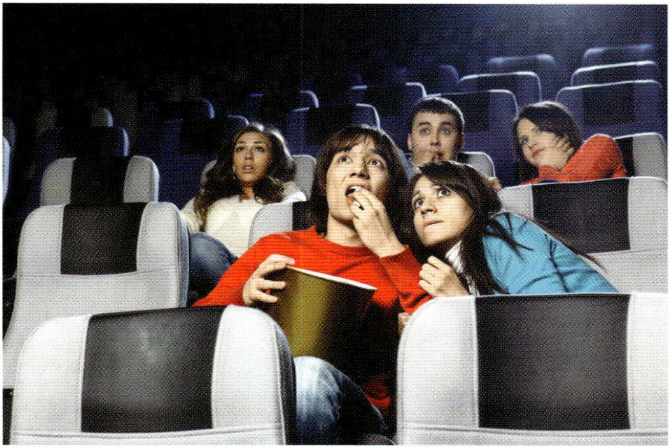

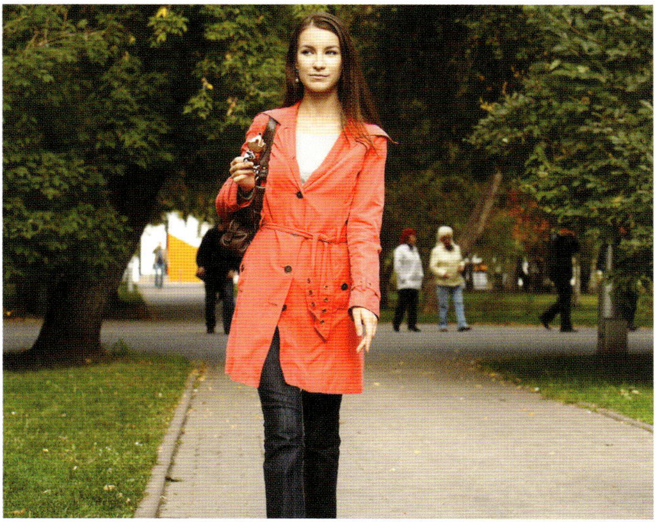

5 › Who are you?

In earlier lessons we had a look at how prepositions work. Let's look at them again with examples related to (evening) activities.

Wohin gehst du?	Where are you going?
Ich gehe in ein Konzert / auf ein Konzert.	I'm going to a concert.
Ich gehe auf eine Party.	I'm going to a party.
Ich gehe ins Kino.	I'm going to the movies.

Wo warst du?	Where were you?
Ich war in einem Konzert / auf einem Konzert.	I was at a concert.
Ich war auf einer Party.	I was at a party.
Ich war im Kino.	I was at the movies.

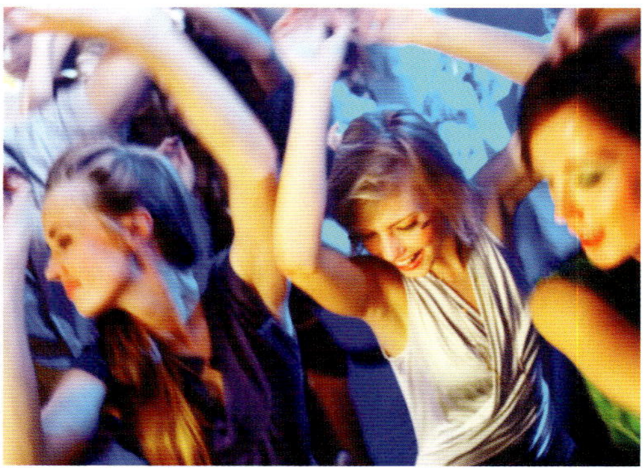

Remember that the article case depends on whether there is movement (*wohin?* where to?) involved or not (*wo?* where?).

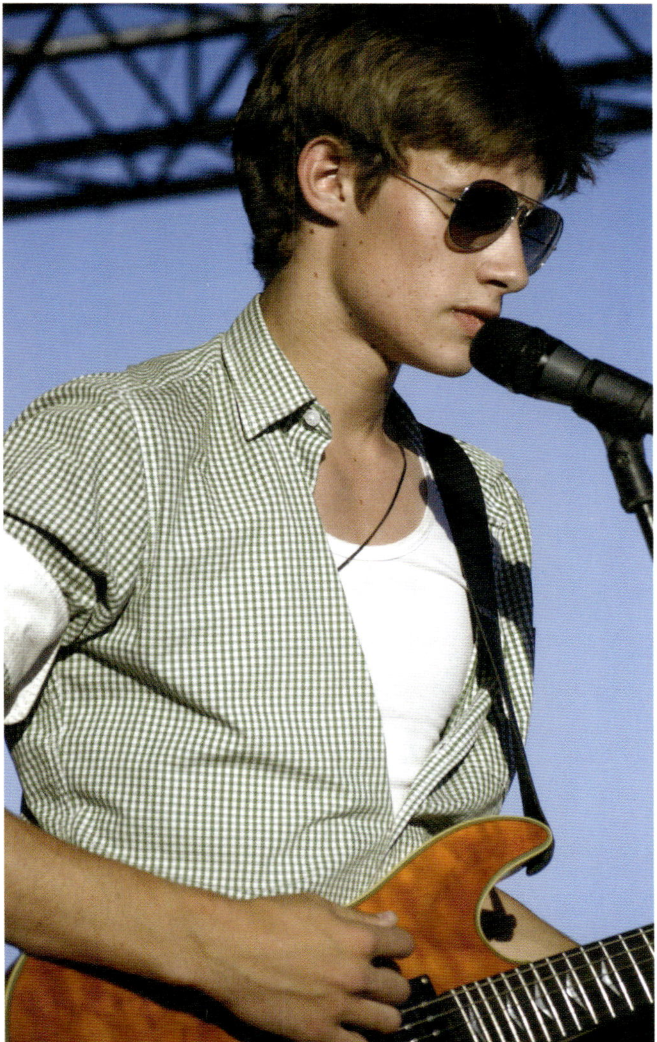

Vocabulary

Active German: Level 4 > *Unit 2* > *Lesson 1* > *Vocabulary*

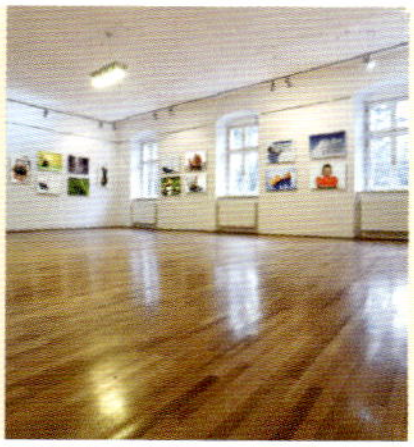

die Kultur / Kulturen
culture

Wenn Sie sich für Kultur interessieren, müssen Sie nach Weimar reisen.
If you are interested in culture you have to travel to Weimar.

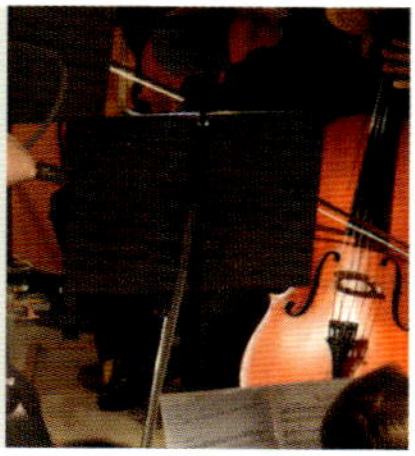

das Konzert / Konzerte
concert

Am Wochenende gehe ich auf ein Konzert.
This weekend I'm going to a concert.

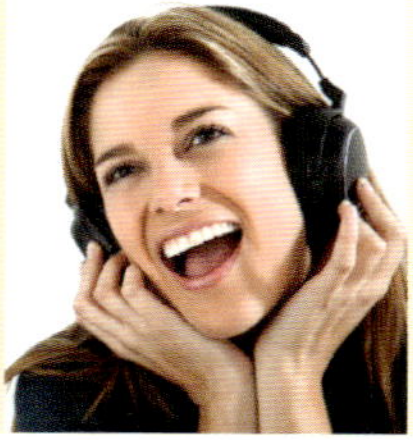

die Musik
music

Welche Musik hörst du am liebsten?
Which music do you like best?

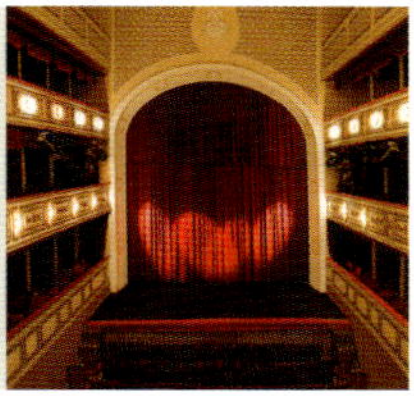

das Theater / Theater
theater

Ich gehe sehr gerne ins Theater.
I like to go to the theater.

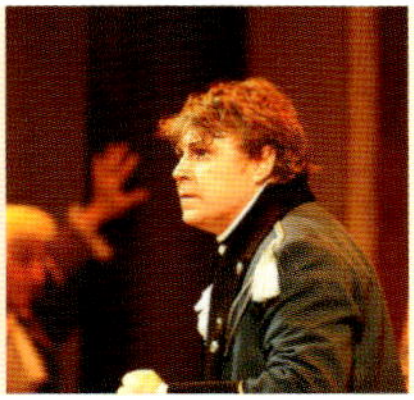

die Oper / Opern
opera

Magst du Opern?
Do you like operas?

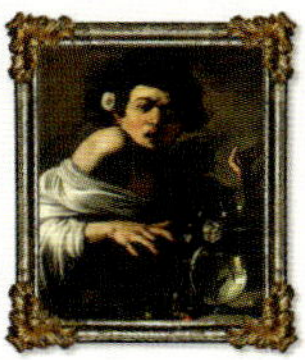

die Kunst
art

Interessieren Sie sich für Kunst?
Are you interested in art?

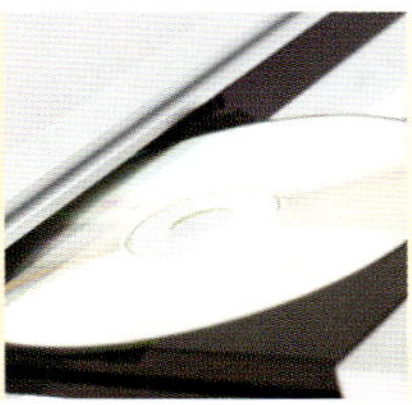

der Film / Filme
movie, film

Kennst du einen guten Film?
Do you know a good movie?

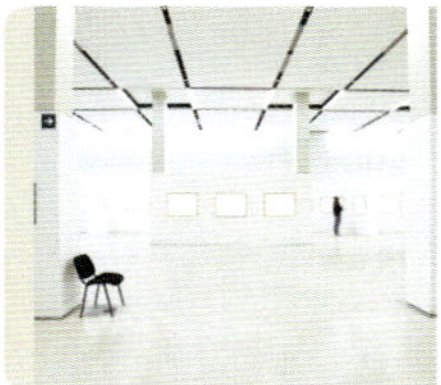

die Ausstellung / Ausstellungen
exhibition

Möchtest du in eine Ausstellung gehen?
Do you want to go to an exhibition?

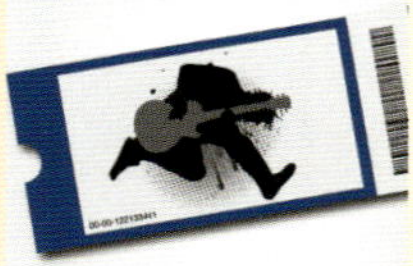

die Karte / Karten
card, ticket

Gibt es noch Karten für das Konzert?
Are there still tickets for the concert left?

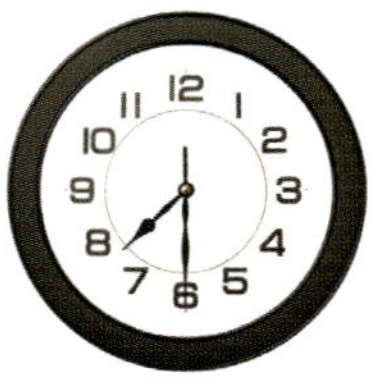

losgehen
to start, to go off

Wann geht es los?
When does it start?

UNIT 2 › LESSON 2

A concert

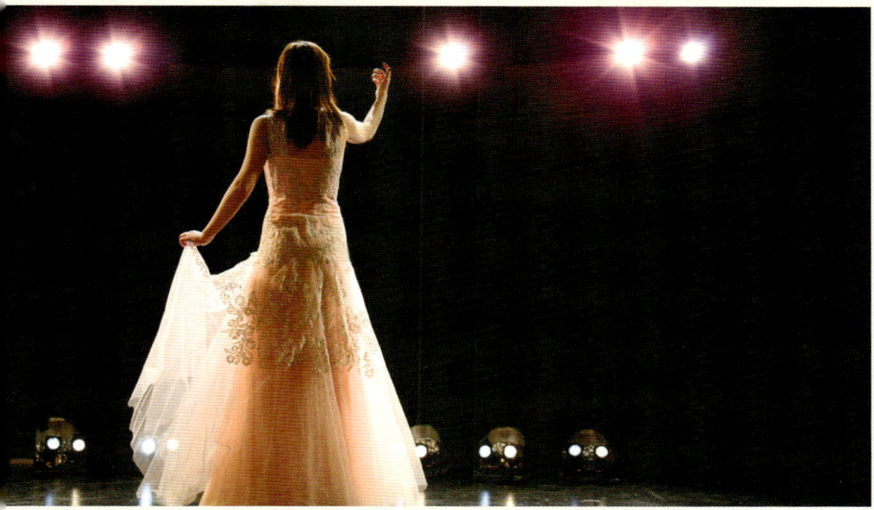

Culture note

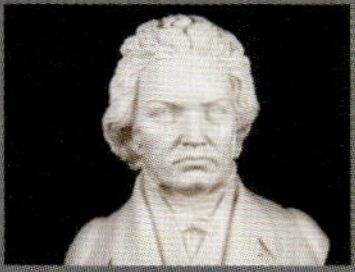

In Germany and all over the world one important name is undoubtedly associated with classical music: Ludwig van Beethoven. Beethoven is one of the world's most famous and influential composers of classical music. He wrote nine symphonies and 32 piano sonatas, several of which are very well-known, such as *Pathétique*, *Appassionata*, and the *Moonlight Sonata*. He was born in Bonn in 1770 but moved to Vienna in his early twenties and settled there, studying with Joseph Haydn and quickly gaining a reputation as a virtuoso pianist. Around 1796, Beethoven began to lose his hearing and was almost totally deaf by 1816.

Video Dialog

Matthias and Lara share their different opinions of the concert.

Active German: Level 4 > *Unit 2* > *Lesson 2* > *Video dialog*

Matthias:	*Das war aber ein langes Konzert.*
Lara:	*Hat es dir gefallen? Was denkst du?*
Matthias:	*Ja, aber ich finde klassische Konzerte immer ein bisschen langweilig.*
Lara:	*Langweilig? Ich fand, es war super! Findest du nicht?*
Matthias:	*Doch, ich meine, es war nur sehr lang und manchmal ein bisschen langsam.*
Lara:	*Du hast keine Ahnung. Hast du das Klavier gehört?*
Matthias:	*Der Pianist war gut.*
Lara:	*Gut? Der Pianist war einfach brillant.*

Matthias:	What a long concert.
Lara:	Did you like it? What do you think?
Matthias:	Yes, but I always find classical concerts a bit boring.
Lara:	Boring? I thought it was great! Don't you think?
Matthias:	Yes, I did. I mean, it was very long and sometimes a bit slow.
Lara:	You have no idea. Did you hear the piano?
Matthias:	The pianist was good.
Lara:	Good? The pianist was just brilliant.

Grammar

Active German: Level 4 > Unit 2 > Lesson 2 > Grammar

1 › How to express your opinion

There are many different ways to ask for another person's opinion. Let's have a look at the most common ones.

meinen – to think (from the word *Meinung* – opinion):

Was meinst du?

What do you think?

You can use the word *finden* (to find / think) as well:

Wie findest du den Film?

How do you find the movie?

What do you think of the movie?

Denken also means "to think."

Was denkst du?

What do you think?

You can use the verb *halten* as well.

Was halten Sie davon?

What do you think of that?

2 › I find it interesting

Let's look at some other ways to express your opinion:

Ich finde den Film spannend.	I find the movie exciting.
Ich denke, der Film ist spannend.	I think the movie is exciting.

Here are some other useful adjectives:

interessant	interesting
langweilig	boring
fantastisch	fantastic
traurig	sad

Another verb used to express an opinion is *glauben* (to think, to believe).

Wir glauben, die Qualität ist besser.
We think the quality is better.

A common phrase used to agree with something is:

Das hört sich gut an.
That sounds good to me.

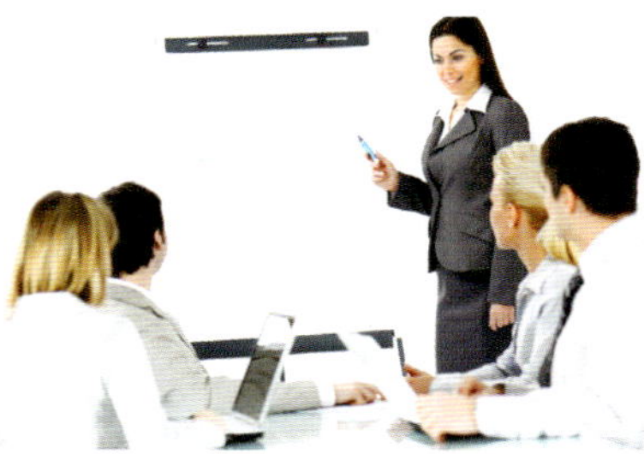

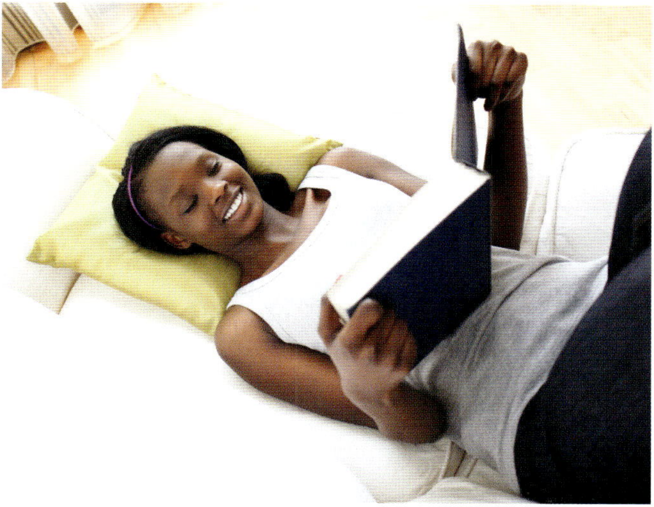

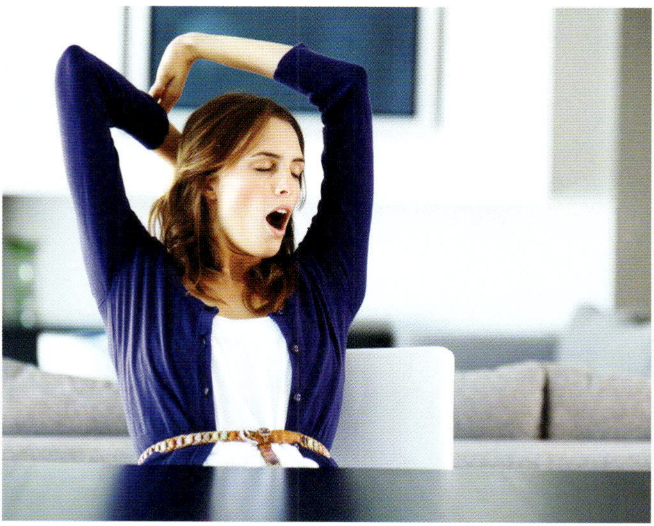

3 › **I don't like it**

If you want to say that you don't like something, you can use the following expressions.

Ich mag es nicht so sehr.	I don't really like it, I don't like it so much.
Ich finde ihn nicht gut.	I don't think it's good.
Das ist nicht mein Geschmack.	It's not to my taste.

4 › **In my opinion**

The phrase *meiner Meinung nach* means "in my opinion."

Meiner Meinung nach ist die Idee gut.

In my opinion it's a good idea.

If you want to balance one reason against another you can use the two words *einerseits* (on the one hand) and *andererseits* (on the other hand).

Einerseits ist das eine gute Idee. Andererseits ist es ein bisschen teuer.

On the one hand, it's a good idea. On the other hand, it's a bit expensive.

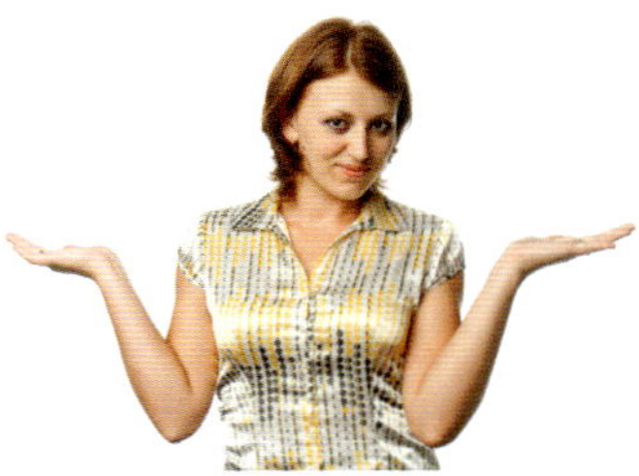

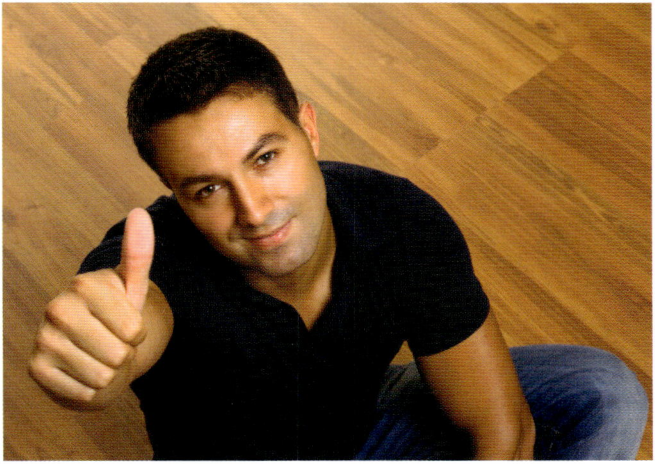

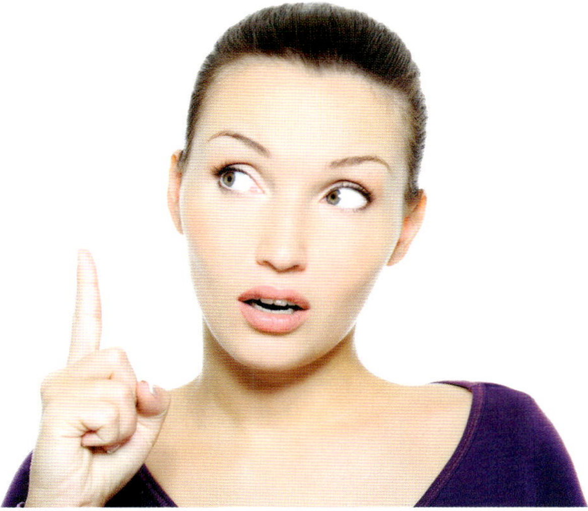

5 › **I have no idea**

Sometimes you might not know what to say or you might not agree:

Ich habe keine Ahnung.	I have no idea.
Ich weiß es nicht.	I don't know.
Ich habe eine andere Meinung.	I have a different point of view.

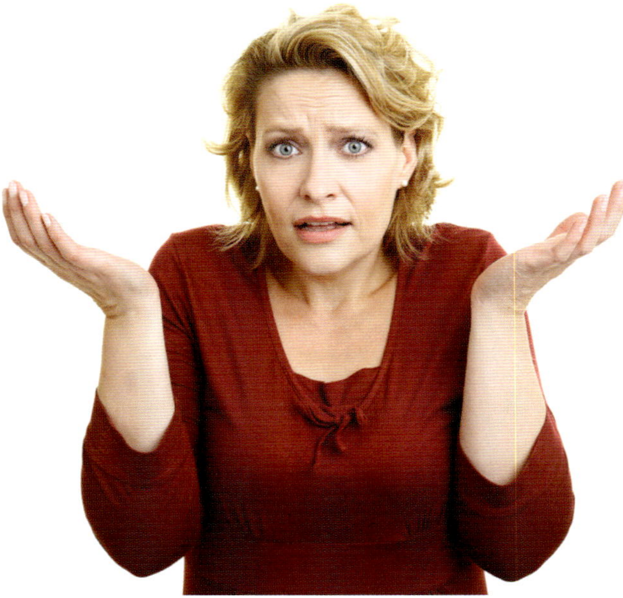

Vocabulary

Active German: Level 4 > Unit 2 > Lesson 2 > Vocabulary

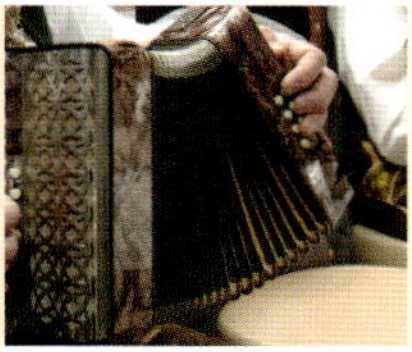

das Instrument / Instrumente
instrument

Spielst du ein Instrument?
Do you play an instrument?

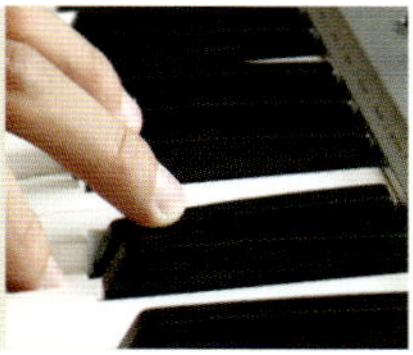

das Klavier / Klaviere
piano

Das Klavier ist ein schönes Instrument.
The piano is a beautiful instrument.

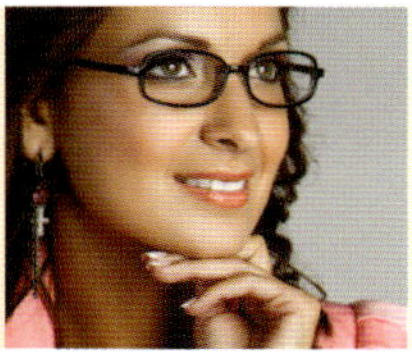

der Gedanke / Gedanken
thought

Das ist ein guter Gedanke.
That is a good thought.

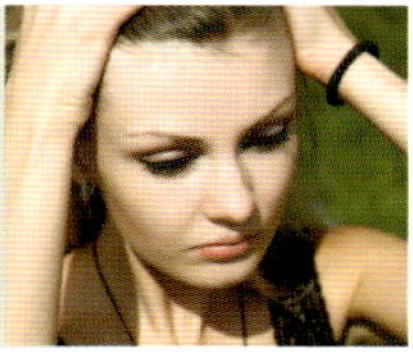

das Gefühl / Gefühle
feeling

Ich habe ein schlechtes Gefühl.
I have a bad feeling.

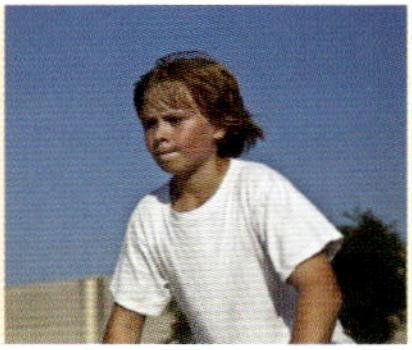

begeistert
enthusiastic

Ich bin sehr begeisert von dieser Idee.
I am very enthusiastic about this idea.

bedeuten
to signify, to mean

Was bedeutet das?
What does it mean?

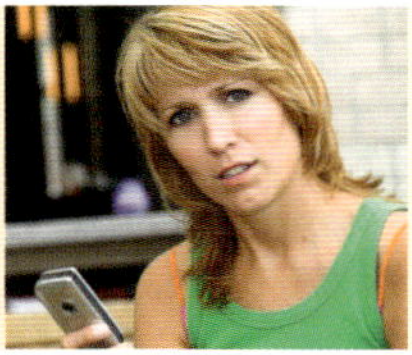

verstehen
to understand

Ich verstehe das nicht.
I don't understand that.

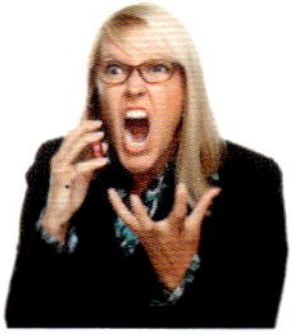

wütend
furious

Warum bist du so wütend?
Why are you so furious?

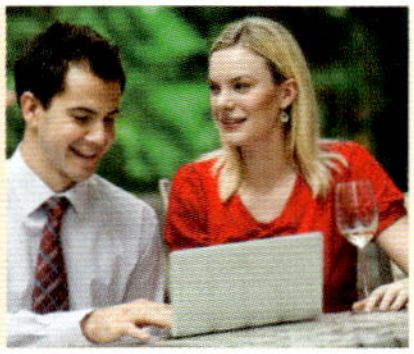

das Gespräch / Gespräche
conversation

Vielen Dank für das nette Gespräch.
Thank you very much for the pleasant conversation.

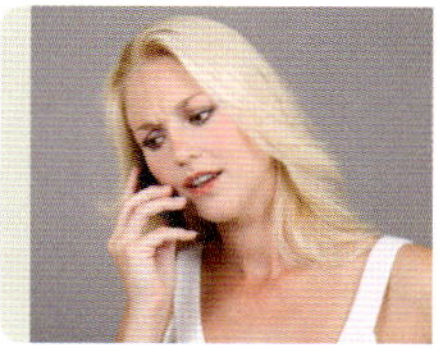

sich ärgern
to be annoyed

Warum ärgerst du dich?
Why are you annoyed?

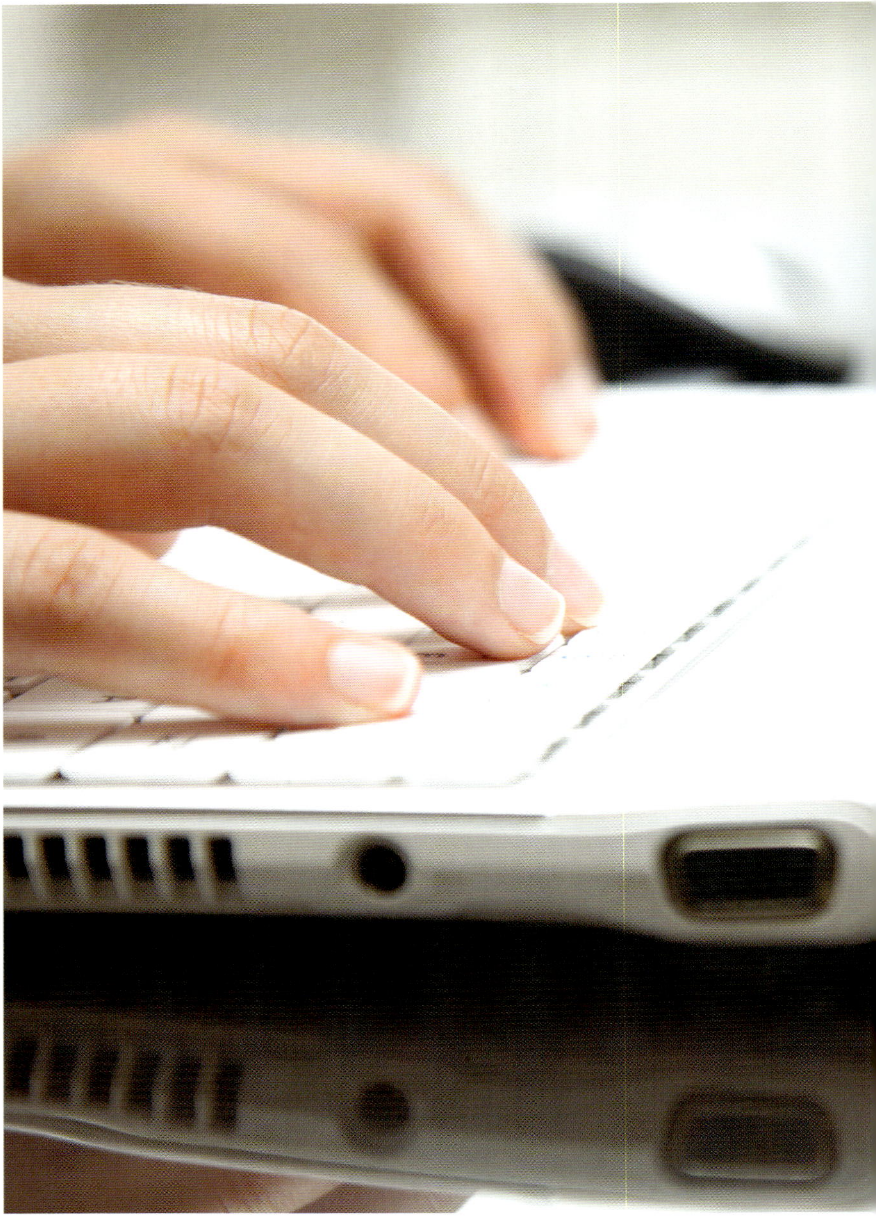

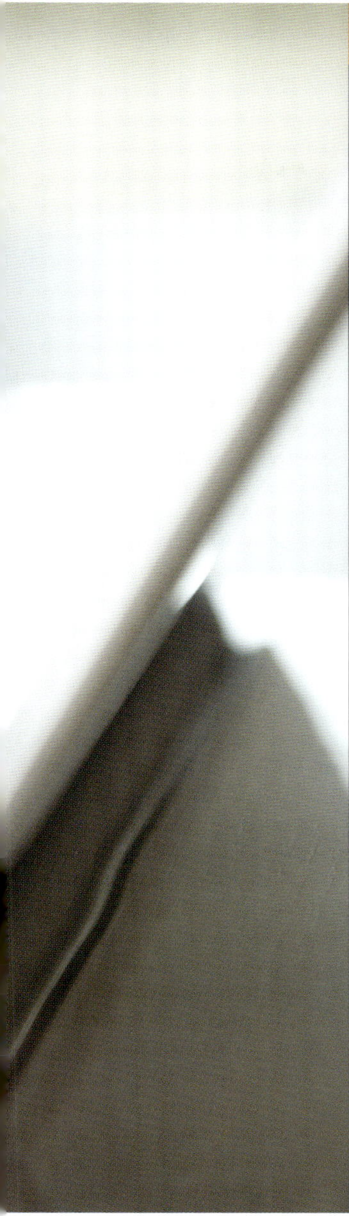

Active German *Level 4*

3

Lesson 1: The working world

- » How to join sentences by using “and,” “or,” “because,” and “but.”
- » Important phrases for business communication.
- » Vocabulary for the working world.

Lesson 2: My computer – media and communication

- » How to say “because,” “although,” “whether,” and “that.”
- » How to join sentences together.
- » Useful phrases for business communication.
- » Vocabulary for media and communication.

Collins | Livemocha™

UNIT 3 › LESSON 1

The working world

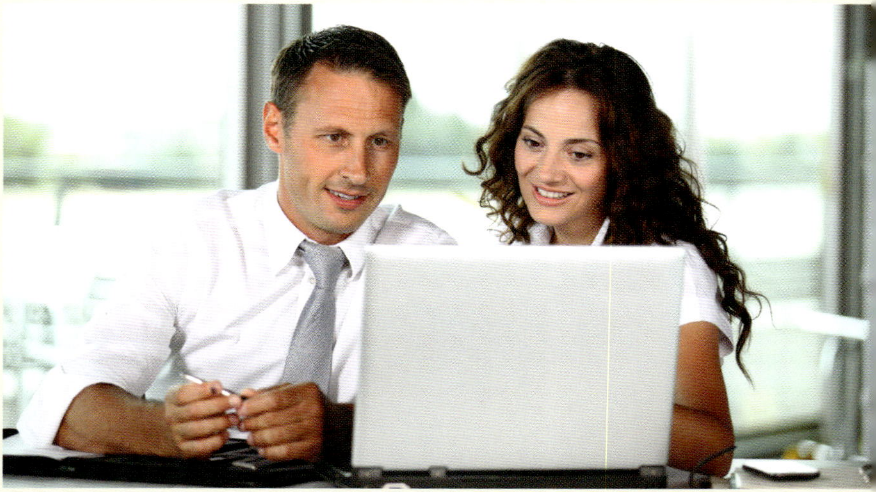

Culture note

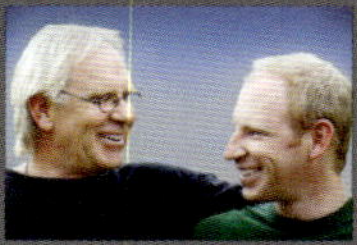

When doing business in Germany or with Germans you will notice careful planning and consideration. The Germans – and not only in the business world – may be perceived as direct, curt and to the point; facts are what matters. It is important to know that directness is a sign of respect and is considered essential in the search for the correct answer to a particular problem. Humor is another important cultural characteristic. It is certainly not the case that Germans lack a sense of humor; the difference lies in context and style. It is considered that there is a time and a place for humor and that its place is not during serious business negotiations.

Video Dialog

Mr. Baumann sets Matthias a new challenge in the office.

Active German: Level 4 > *Unit 3* > *Lesson 1* > *Video dialog*

Herr Baumann:	*Wir müssen sehr genau arbeiten, denn der Kunde ist sehr wichtig.*
Matthias:	*Ist es ein neuer oder ein alter Kunde?*
Herr Baumann:	*Es ist ein neuer Kunde, aber ich kenne den Chef schon länger.*
Matthias:	*In Ordnung.*
Herr Baumann:	*Ihre Aufgabe, Herr Meisinger, ist die Kundenbetreuung.*
Matthias:	*Haben Sie alle Daten?*
Herr Baumann:	*Die sind alle in diesem Ordner.*
Matthias:	*Danke.*
Herr Baumann:	*Alles Weitere müssen wir noch besprechen. Wir bleiben in Kontakt.*
Matthias:	*Gut.*

Mr. Baumann:	We must work really carefully because the client is very important.
Matthias:	Is it a new or an old client?
Mr. Baumann:	It is a new client, but I've known the CEO for some time.
Matthias:	Fine.
Mr. Baumann:	Your task, Mr. Meisinger, is customer service.
Matthias:	Have you got all the data?

Mr. Baumann:	It's all in this file.
Matthias:	Thank you.
Mr. Baumann:	We still need to discuss everything else. We'll keep in touch.
Matthias:	OK.

Grammar

Active German: Level 4 > *Unit 3* > *Lesson 1* > *Grammar*

1 › The conjunction *denn*

In the video dialog Mr. Baumann and Matthias talk about a new client. Mr. Baumann gives the reason why they have to work carefully:

> *Wir müssen sehr genau arbeiten, denn der Kunde ist sehr wichtig.*
>
> We must work really carefully because the client is very important.

The word *denn* (for, because) links the two sentences and is called a conjunction.

Have a look at the two separate sentences:

> *Wir müssen genau arbeiten. Der Kunde ist sehr wichtig.*
>
> We must work really carefully. The client is very important.

The word *denn* gives us the possibility to join the two sentences together.

Let's have a look at another example.

Ich gehe einkaufen, denn ich brauche noch Milch.

I'm going shopping because I need milk.

Note that there is a comma between the linked sentences.

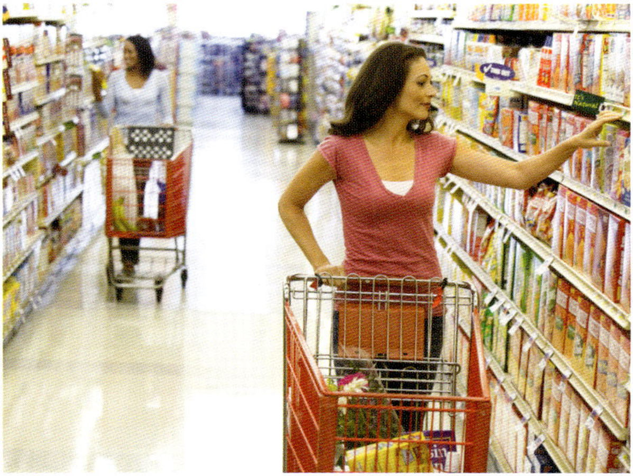

2 › The conjunction *und*

You can use other words to link phrases or sentences:

You can combine two sentences with *und* (and).

If the subject in the two sentences is the same you don't have to repeat it:

Ich lese die Zeitung und mein Mann arbeitet im Garten.

I'm reading the newspaper and my husband is working in the garden. (*different subject*)

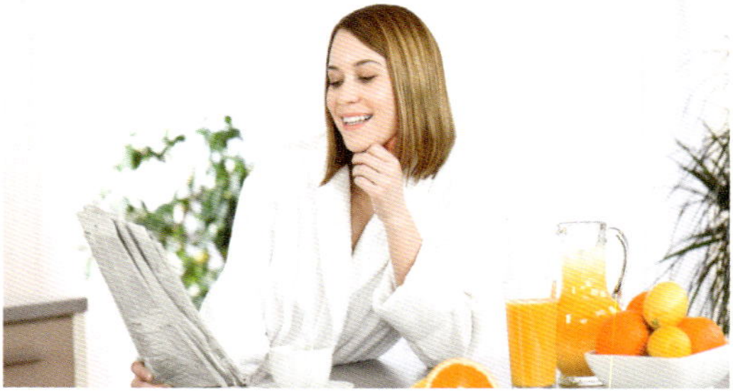

Er war krank und (er) konnte nicht arbeiten.

He was ill and couldn't work. (*same subject*)

You can leave out both subject and verb if they are the same.

Er hat drei Brüder und (er hat) eine Schwester.

He has three brothers and a sister.

3 › The conjunction *oder*

Oder (or) basically follows the same rules as *und* (and):
You can combine two whole sentences.

Morgen können wir hier essen, oder wir können ins Kino gehen.

Tomorrow we can eat here or we can go to the movies.

If the verbs are the same you can omit them.

Ist es ein alter Kunde oder ein neuer Kunde?

Is it an old client or a new client?

Isst du Fisch oder Fleisch?

Do you eat fish or meat?

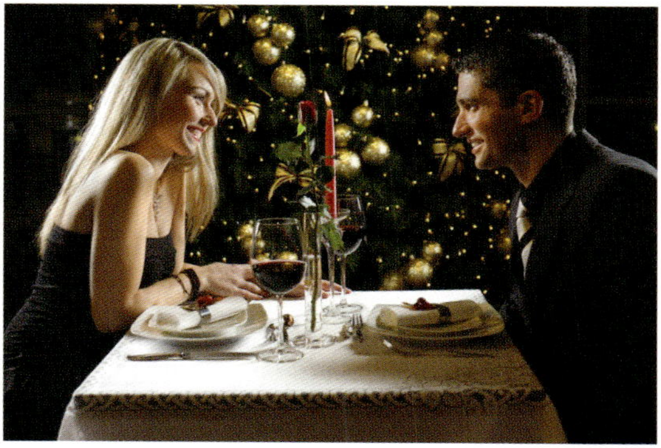

4 › The conjunctions *aber* and *sondern*

The conjunction *aber* means "but."

Sie hat ihn angerufen, aber er war nicht zu Hause.

She called him, but he wasn't at home.

Es ist ein neuer Kunde, aber ich kenne den Chef schon länger.

It is a new client, but I've known the CEO for some time.

In contrast to *aber* (but), *sondern* (but rather) is used in a negative sentence to contradict a preceding negative statement.

*Wir sind **nicht** ins Kino gegangen, **sondern** wir haben ferngesehen.*

We didn't go to the movies; we watched TV instead.

*Ich esse **kein** Fleisch, **sondern** nur Fisch.*

I don't eat meat, only fish.

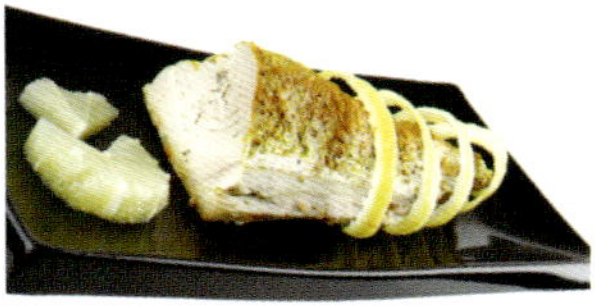

5 › We'd love to help you

You might find the following phrases useful in the working world.

To offer your help you can use the following:

Wir stehen Ihnen jederzeit zur Verfügung.

Please don't hesitate to contact us., Please feel free to contact us.

Wir helfen Ihnen gerne.

We are more than happy to help.

To say thank you:

Herzlichen Dank für Ihre Email.

Many thanks for your email.

Ich habe mich sehr über Ihre Email gefreut.

I was very pleased to receive your email.

Ich danke Ihnen für Ihr Verständnis.

Thank you for your understanding.

6 › We'll stay in contact

To arrange further meetings:

Wir bleiben in Kontakt / Verbindung.
We'll keep in touch.

Ich melde mich bei Ihnen.
I'll contact you.

Ihre Ansprechperson ist Herr Meisinger.
Your contact is Mr. Meisinger.

Wäre ein Treffen am Dienstag möglich?
Would a meeting on Tuesday suit you?

Ich freue mich sehr darauf von Ihnen zu hören.
I'm looking forward to hearing from you.

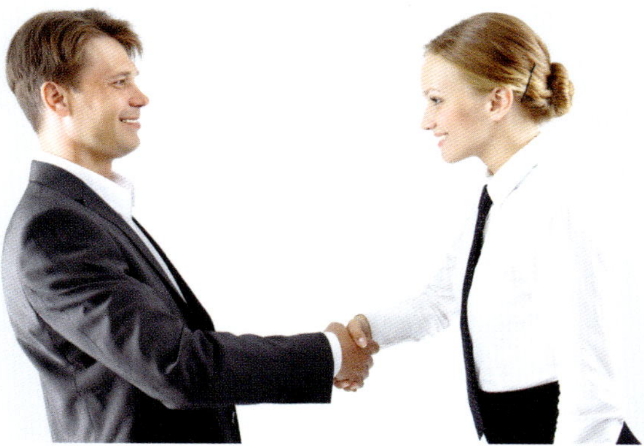

Vocabulary

Active German: Level 4 > Unit 3 > Lesson 1 > Vocabulary

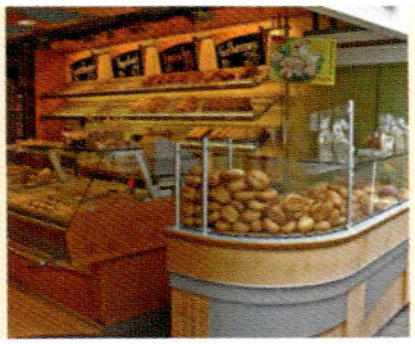

das Geschäft / Geschäfte
business, shop

Wie gehen die Geschäfte?
How is business?

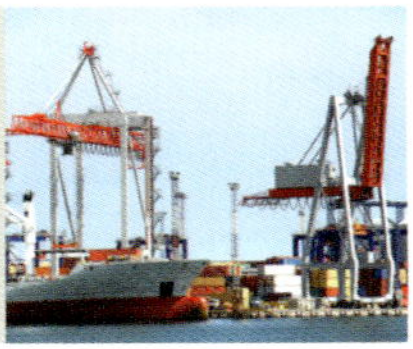

der Hand
trade

Wir treiben Handel mit internationalen Firmen.
We do business with international companies.

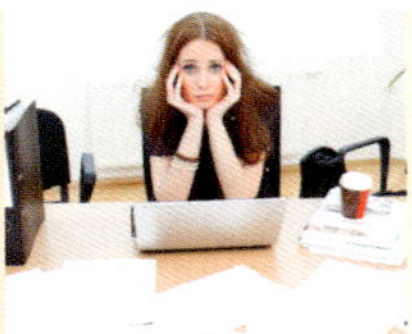

die Aufgabe / Aufgaben
task, duty

Das ist meine Aufgabe.
That is my duty.

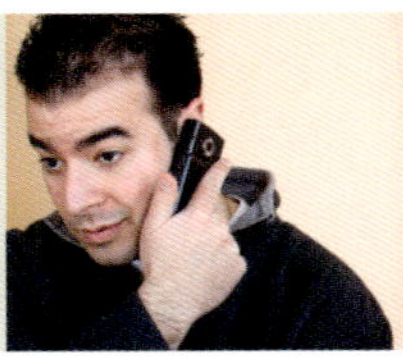

der Auftrag / Aufträge
order

Wir bearbeiten Ihre Auftrag sofort.
We'll deal with your order immediately.

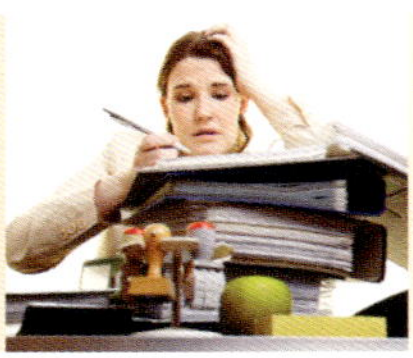

der Ordner / Ordner
folder, file

Wo ist der Ordner für das neue Projekt?
Where is the folder for the new project?

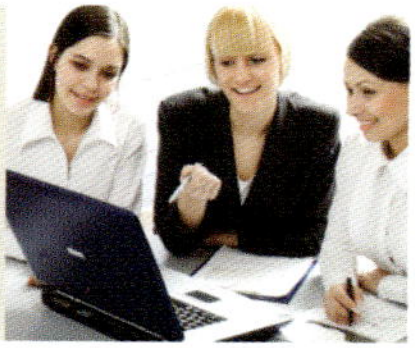

besprechen
to discuss, to talk over

Wir müssen das noch besprechen.
We still have to talk it over.

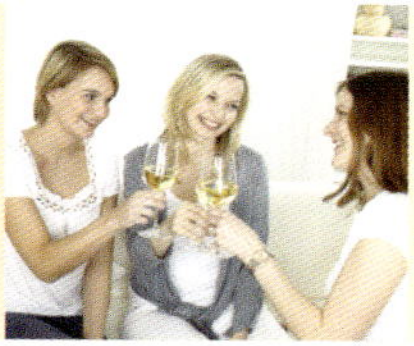

bleiben
to stay, to remain

Wir bleiben zu Hause.
We're staying at home.

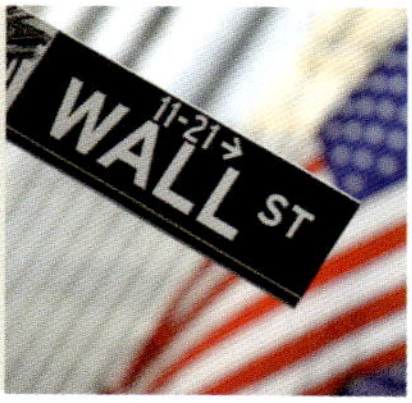

die Wirtschaft
economy

Wenn Kunden mehr einkaufen, geht es der Wirtschaft besser.
If customers buy more, the economy improves.

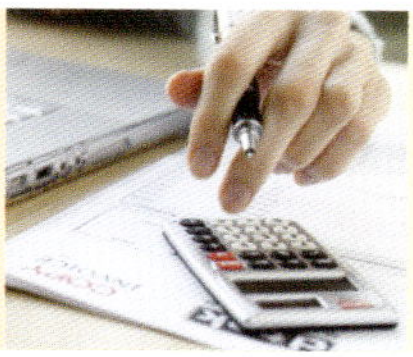

die Kosten
costs

Die Kosten sind sehr hoch.
The costs are very high.

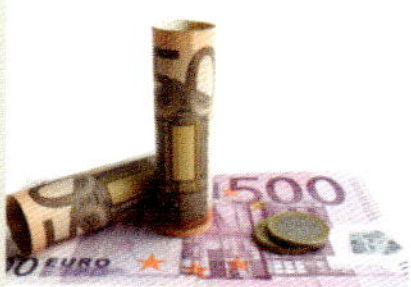

das Gehalt / Gehälter
salary, earnings

Ich habe ein gutes Gehalt.
I have a good salary.

UNIT 3 › LESSON 2

My computer – media and communication

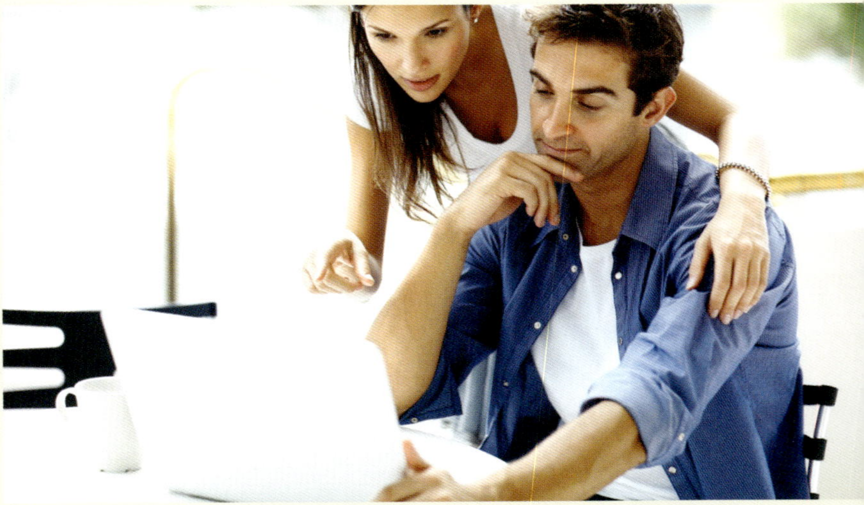

Culture note

The *CeBit* is the world's largest computer trade fair and takes place each spring in Hannover, northern Germany. It provides a showcase for up-to-date developments in information technology. Every year the most modern and recent developments are exhibited.

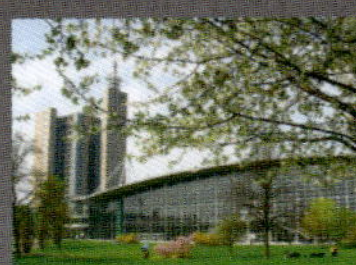

Video Dialog

Matthias gets a phone call from Nina who needs his help.

Active German: Level 4 > *Unit 3* > *Lesson 2* > *Video dialog*

Matthias: *Was ist denn passiert, Nina? Du hast einen neuen Computer, weil dein alter kaputt war, aber nichts funktioniert. Hast du alles installiert? Du kannst nicht drucken, nicht scannen und du hast keinen Internetzugang. Nein, dein Computer ist nicht kaputt. Du hast wahrscheinlich die Software nicht richtig installiert, deshalb funktioniert nichts. Also, fangen wir ganz von vorne an ...*

Matthias: What's happened, Nina? You've got a new computer, because your old one was broken, but nothing's working. Have you installed everything? You can't print, you can't scan, and you don't have Internet access. No, your computer isn't broken. You probably didn't install the software correctly, that's why nothing's working. OK, let's start from the beginning...

Grammar

Active German: Level 4 > Unit 3 > Lesson 2 > Grammar

1 › Because it's broken

In the video Matthias says why Nina has bought a new computer.

Du hast einen neuen Computer, weil dein alter kaputt war

You've got a new computer because your old one was broken.

You use the word *weil* (because) to introduce a reason (*warum?* why?). *Weil* is therefore a conjunction that links two sentences in a logical way. Note that the word order is affected.

Ich esse, ***weil*** *ich Hunger* ***habe.***

I eat because I'm hungry.

The verb in the second part of the sentence (the subordinate clause) is at the end.

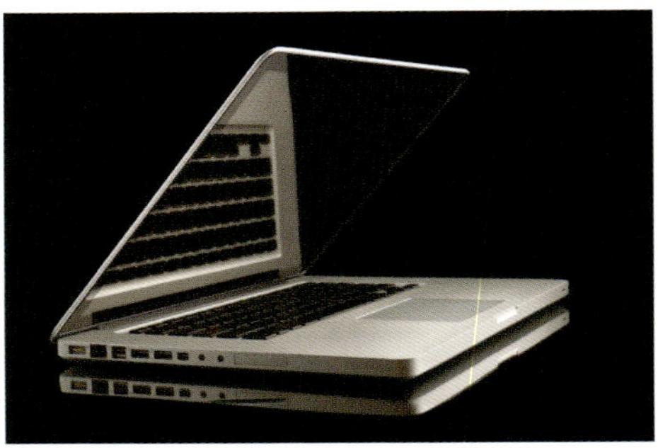

2 › Because I'm tired

Both *denn* (for, because) and *weil* (because) are used in the same context and have the same meaning, but *weil* is used more frequently.

The important difference between the two words is their effect on word order. Compare the following two sentences:

*Ich gehe nach Hause, **weil** ich müde **bin**.*
*Ich gehe nach Hause, **denn** ich **bin** müde.*

I'm going home because I'm tired.

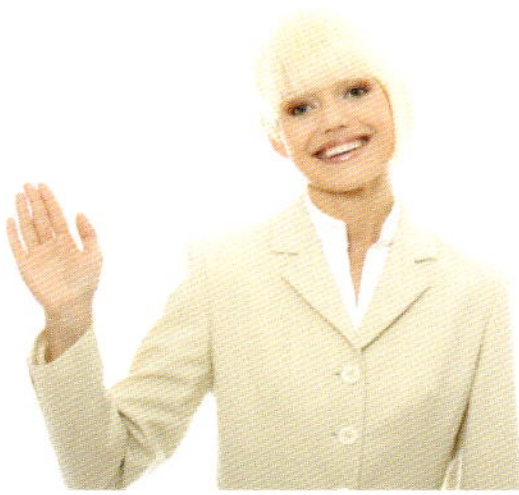

3 › How to use *dass* and *ob*

There are other conjunctions that work the same way as *weil*; we are now going to focus on two very important ones.

The conjunction *dass* means "that."

*Ich denke, **dass** die Idee gut **ist**.*	I think that the idea is good.
*Ich glaube, **dass** er zu Hause **ist**.*	I think that he's at home.

Watch out for the word order. The verb is placed at the end of the subordinate clause.

The conjunction *ob* means "whether" or "if" and is used to express uncertainty.

*Ich weiß nicht, **ob** sie **kommt.***

I don't know whether she is coming.

*Weißt du, **ob** Herrn Baumann in seinem Büro **ist**?*

Do you know whether Mr. Baumann is in his office?

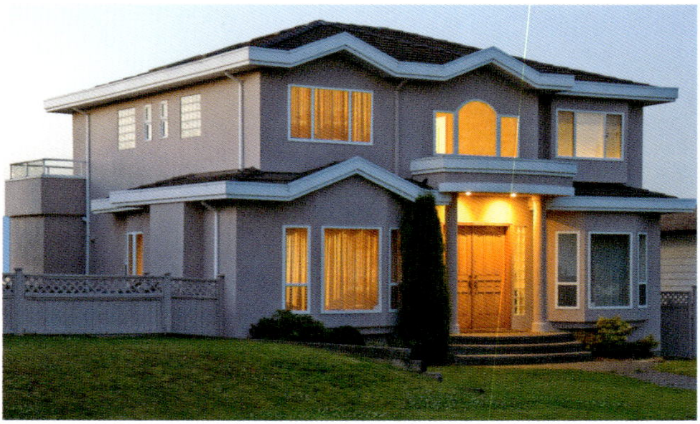

4 › Although

The conjunction *obwohl* means "although."

*Ich helfe dir, **obwohl** ich keine Zeit **habe.***

I'll help you although I don't have time.

In general terms, you use *obwohl* in sentences that follow the pattern "I think / do X although Y is true."

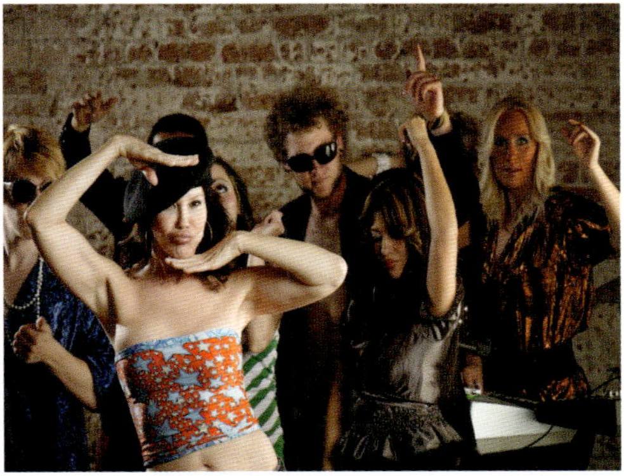

Ich gehe auf die Party, ***obwohl*** *ich müde* ***bin****.*

I'll go to the party although I'm tired.

5 › **Sentence structure**

All the sentences we have just analyzed contain a subordinate clause that depends on or relates to the main clause. In a subordinate clause separable verbs are not split.

Ich denke, dass er dich ***anruft****.*

I think that he'll call you.

The verb *anrufen* is at the end of the sentence and the *an-* is not cut off.

If the second clause of the sentence is in the past tense, the part of the verb *haben* or *sein* is placed at the very end.

Ich weiß nicht, ob er ***angerufen hat****.*

I don't know whether he has called.

Note that if a modal verb like *müssen* (to have to) is used, it is also placed at the end of a sentence.

Ich denke, dass er ***anrufen muss.***

I think that he has to call.

6 › **Could you please...?**

There are some useful expressions which you may use while talking to people on the phone. Here is a list of some of them. It might be useful to learn them as whole sentences.

Können Sie das bitte wiederholen?

Could you please repeat that?

Können Sie bitte lauter sprechen?

Could you please speak up / talk louder?

Möchten Sie eine Nachricht hinterlassen.

Would you like to leave a message?

Culture note i

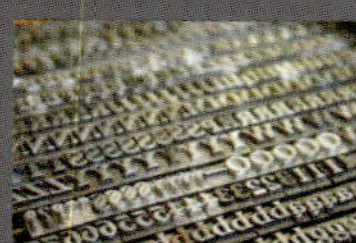

Where would we be in the 21st century without Johannes Gutenberg's invention of the printing press in 1439? He invented a press with movable wooden and metal letters – a technique that changed the world. The first text printed was a German poem. The most famous print is undoubtedly the Gutenberg Bible, which was published in 1455.

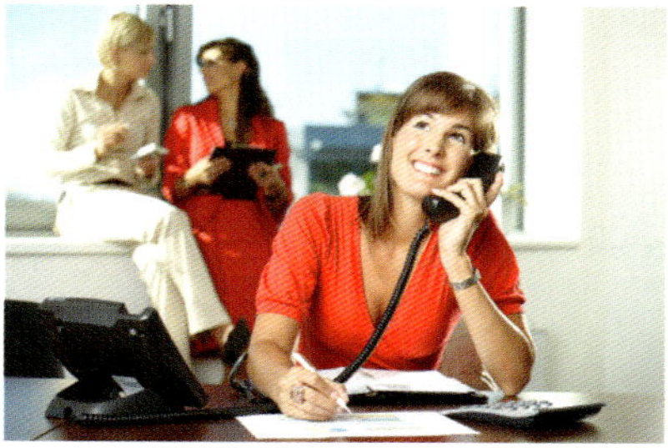

Vielen Dank für die Auskunft.

Many thanks for the information.

Können Sie mich bitte mit Herrn Meyer verbinden.

Could you put me through to Mr. Meyer, please?

Vocabulary

Active German: Level 4 > Unit 3 > Lesson 2 > Vocabulary

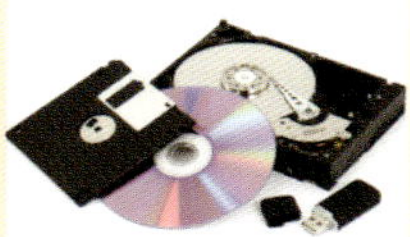

die Medien
media

Heutzutage sind die Medien sehr wichtig.
Nowadays the media is very important.

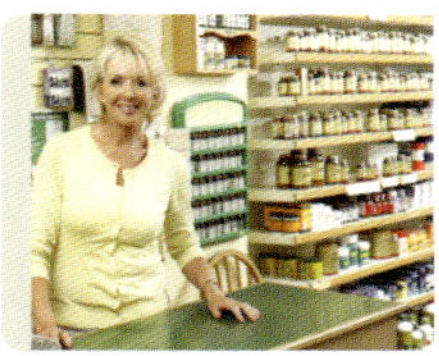

verkaufen
to sell

Möchten Sie das alte Auto verkaufen?
Do you want to sell the old car?

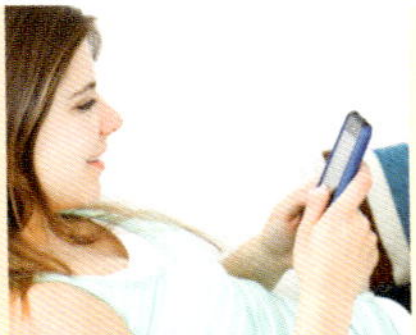

die SMS
text message

Ich schicke dir eine SMS.
I'll send you a text message.

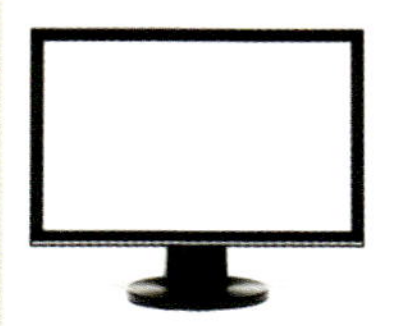

der Bildschirm / Bildschirme
screen

Ihr Bildschrim ist schön groß.
Your screen is pretty big.

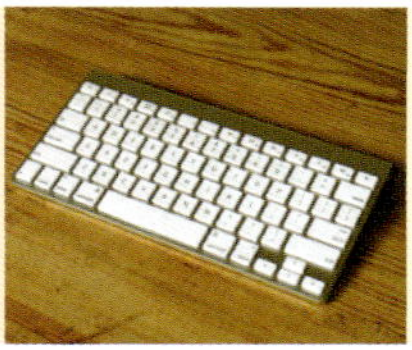

die Tastatur / Tastaturen
keyboard

Ich glaube, dass meine Tastatur kaputt ist.
I think that my keyboard is broken.

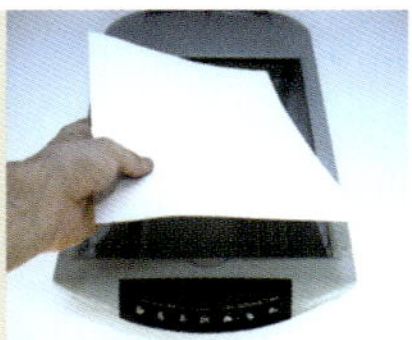

scannen
to scan

Kannst du das bitte für mich scannen?
Could you please scan that for me?

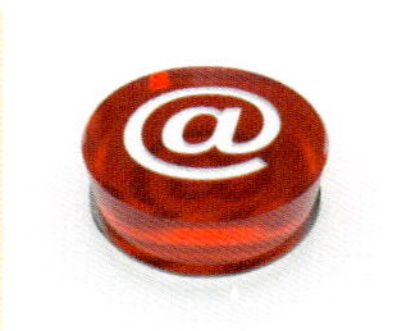

das Internet
Internet

Ich brauche Zugang zum Internet.
I need access to the Internet.

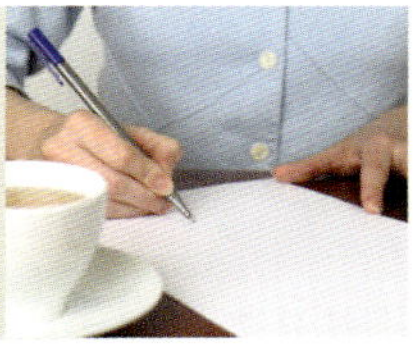

beantworten
to answer

Ich muss die Email beantworten.
I have to answer the email.

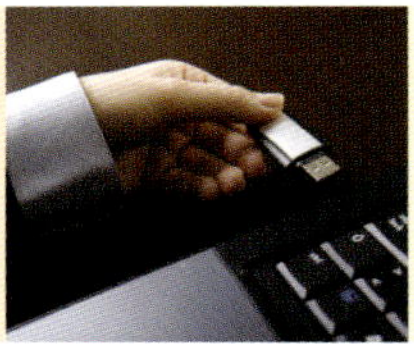

speichern
to save

Haben Sie das Dokument gespeichert?
Did you save the document?

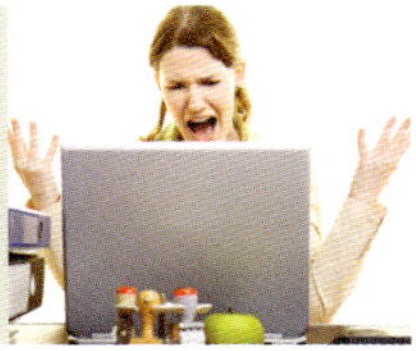

funktionieren
to work, to function

Heute funktioniert nichts.
Today nothing is working.

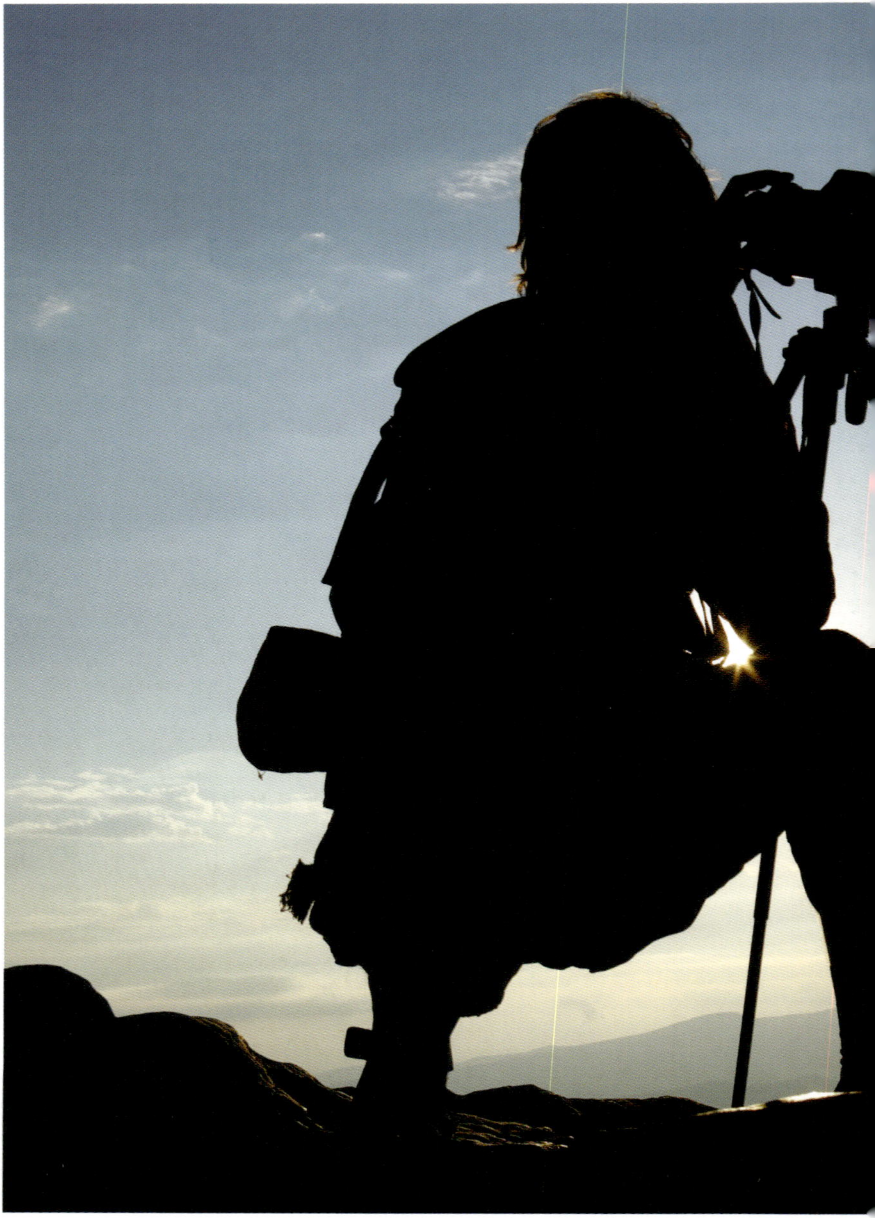

Active German *Level 4*

4

Lesson 1: Interests

» How to use ***wenn*** and ***wann***.

» How to say what your favorite thing is.

» Vocabulary for literature, print media, and the arts.

» How to talk about relaxing.

Lesson 2: Social life

» How to use the verbs "to talk to," "to meet up," and "to wait for."

» How to say whom or what you are waiting for, getting used to etc.

» Vocabulary for communication and socializing.

Collins | Livemocha™

UNIT 4 › LESSON 1

Interests

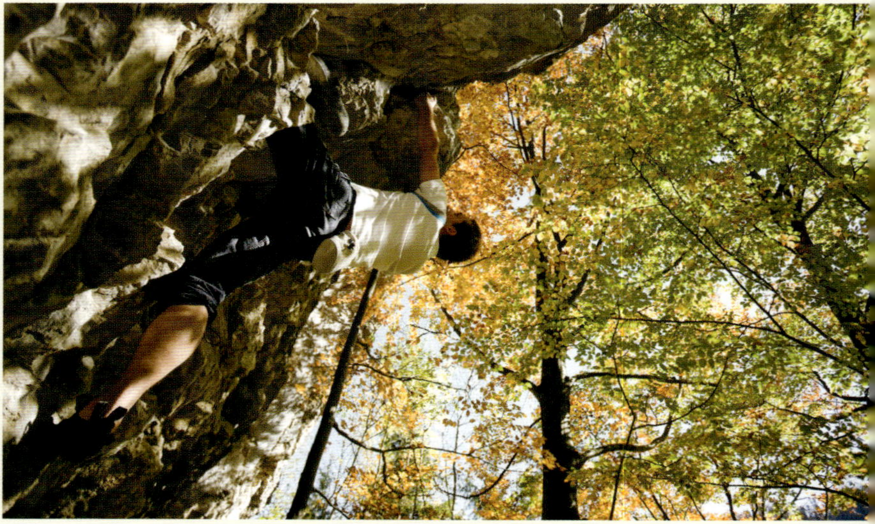

Culture note

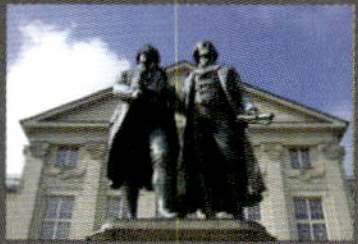

Germany is a country of poets and thinkers (*Land der Dichter und Denker*). This expression has its root in the 18th and 19th centuries. The German nation was a cradle of philosophy and literature, with names such as Nietzsche, Kant, Goethe, and Schiller associated with that time. There were also some very important authors in the 20th century. Thomas Mann, Hermann Hesse and Günther Grass, to name a few, won the Nobel Prize for literature. Nowadays more and more literature is translated into English, for example, *Perfume* by Patrick Süsskind, *The Reader* by Bernhard Schlink and *Measuring the World* by Daniel Kehlmann.

Video Dialog

Lara and Matthias get to know each other more while chatting about culture.

Active German: Level 4 > *Unit 4* > *Lesson 1* > *Video dialog*

Lara:	*Gestern haben meine Malstunden angefangen.*
Matthias:	*Du malst?*
Lara:	*Ja, dabei kann ich mich richtig entspannen.*
Matthias:	*Welcher Maler ist denn dein Lieblingsmaler?*
Lara:	*Ich glaube, Paul Klee ist mein Lieblingsmaler.*
Matthias:	*Lieblingsmaler habe ich keinen.*
Lara:	*Welchen Schriftsteller magst du am liebsten?*
Matthias:	*Bernhard Schlink.*
Lara:	*Den mag ich auch.*
Matthias:	*Ich erhole mich am besten, wenn ich mich bewege.*

Lara:	My painting lessons started yesterday.
Matthias:	You paint?
Lara:	Yes, I can really relax while doing it.
Matthias:	Who is your favorite painter?
Lara:	I think Paul Klee is my favorite painter.
Matthias:	I don't have a favorite painter.
Lara:	Which author do you like the most?
Matthias:	Bernhard Schlink.
Lara:	I like him, too.
Matthias:	I relax best when I exercise.

Grammar

Active German: Level 4 > *Unit 4* > *Lesson 1* > *Grammar*

1 › When I'm ready

Wenn is a very common word. It means "if," "when," and "whenever."

Matthias says that he relaxes best when he is exercising.

*Ich erhole mich am besten, **wenn** ich mich **bewege**.*

I relax best when I exercise.

*Ich komme, **wenn** ich fertig **bin**.*

I'll come when I'm ready.

*Rufen Sie mich an, **wenn** Sie Hilfe **brauchen**.*

Call me if you need help.

Note that *wenn* is a conjunction like *weil* (because), *ob* (whether), *dass* (that), and *obwohl* (although) and that is why the verb is at the end of the sentence.

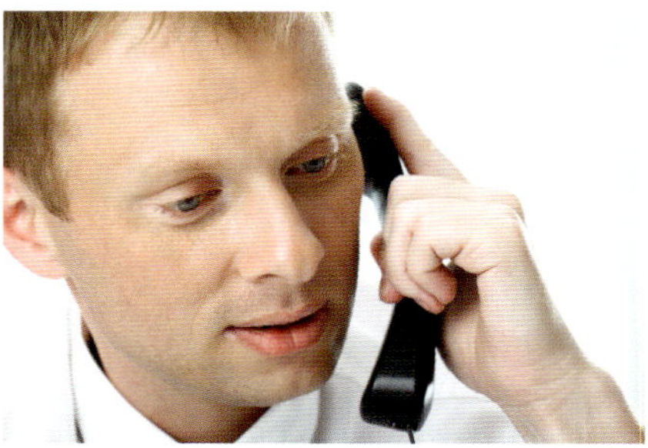

2 › If it rains

It is quite common to start a sentence with *wenn*.

*Wenn du morgen **kommst, koche** ich für dich.*

If you come tomorrow, I'll cook for you.

Look at the word order. In the *wenn* clause the verb is at the end and the other clause starts with the verb.

*Wenn es **regnet, fahre** ich mit dem Bus.*

If it rains, I'll take the bus.

In this example you are naming the condition first and then the consequence of it.

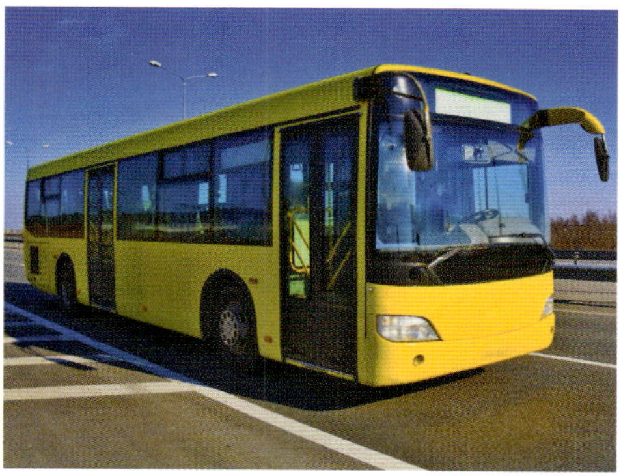

3 › When

Let's consider some other examples:

***Wann** kommst du?*

When are you coming?

Er weißt nicht, ***wann*** *sie kommt.*

He doesn't know when she's coming.

Ich bin morgen da, ***wenn*** *du kommst.*

I'll be there tomorrow when you come.

Wann is used to mean "when" either when asking questions or if the question "when?" is implied in the sentence. For example, in the second sentence above, the question *Wann kommt sie?* is implied.

Wenn (when) is used in statements to refer to a point in time or a period of time, when there is no notion of a direct question about the time being asked.

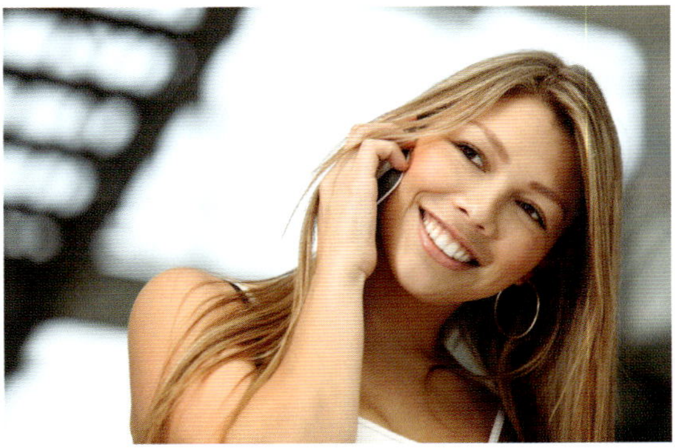

4 › Relax

In earlier units we had a look at reflexive verbs. Reflexive verbs refer back to the speaker.

Ich setze mich.	I sit down.
Du ziehst dich an.	You put your clothes on.
Er beeilt sich.	He hurries up. / He is in a hurry.

In the video dialog Lara and Matthias are talking about different ways to relax.

Ich entspanne ich mich, wenn ich male.	I relax while painting.
Ich erhole mich, wenn ich mich bewege.	I relax while exercising.

Ausruhen is another way to say relax.

Ruht euch aus.

Relax.

Note that *sich entspannen*, *sich erholen*, *sich ausruhen*, and *sich bewegen* are all reflexive verbs. In lesson 2 we are going to work more on these constructions.

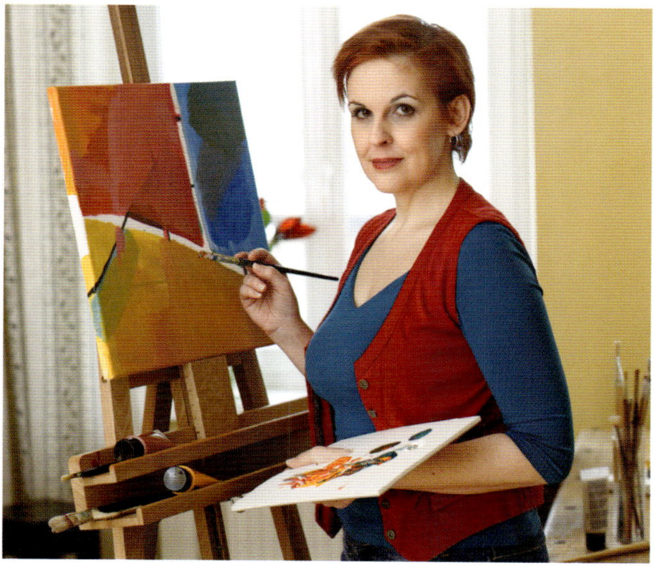

5 › My favorite

In order to express who her favorite painter is, Lara uses the prefix *Lieblings* ...

Paul Klee ist mein Lieblingsmaler.
Paul Klee is my favorite painter.

Lieblings ... can be combined with any other noun:

Lieblingsbuch	favorite book
Lieblingessen	favorite food
Lieblingsrestaurant	favorite restaurant

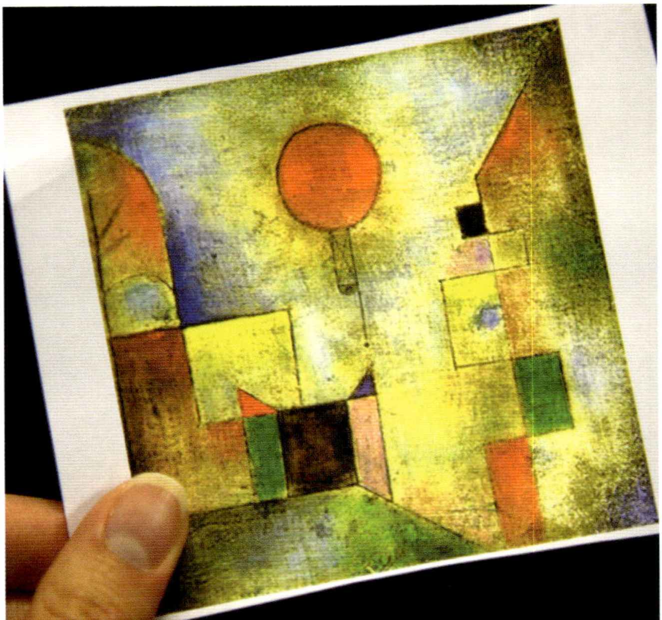

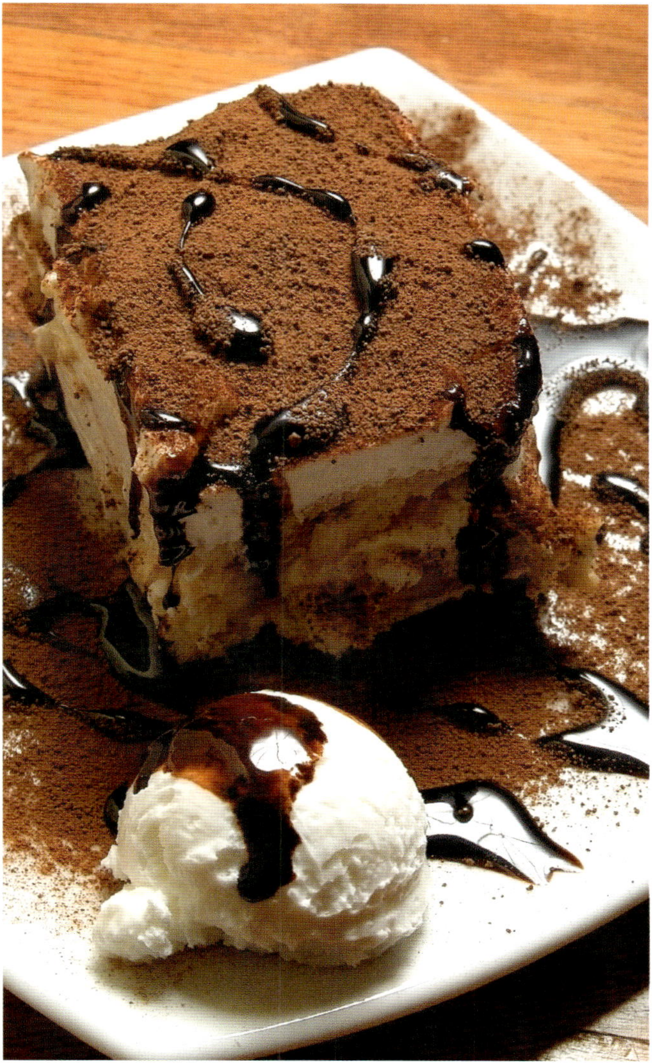

Vocabulary

Active German: Level 4 > *Unit 4* > *Lesson 1* > *Vocabulary*

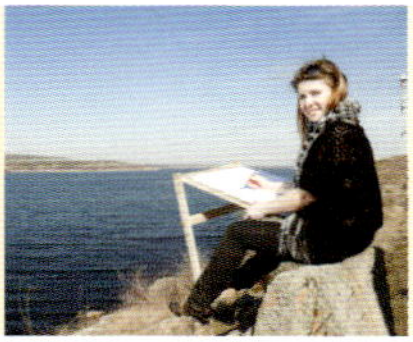

malen
to paint

Am Wochenende male ich gerne.
On weekends I like to paint.

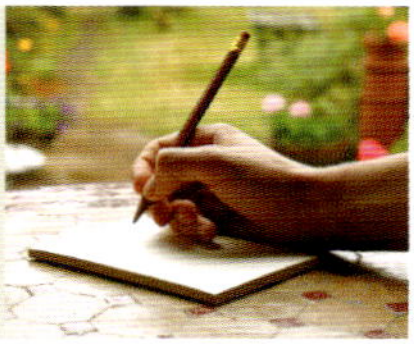

zeichnen
to draw

Kannst du zeichnen?
Can you draw?

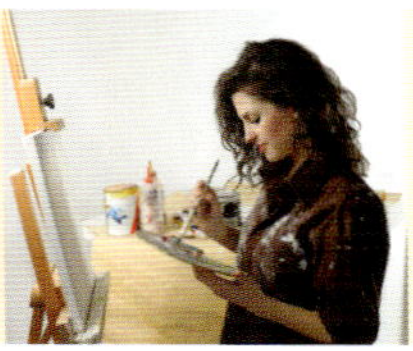

der Maler / Maler
painter

Wer ist dein Lieblingsmaler?
Who is your favorite painter?

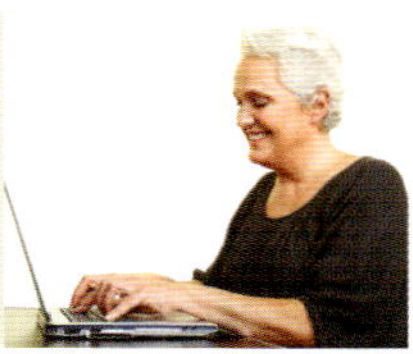

der Schriftsteller / Schriftsteller
author

Kennst du den Schriftsteller?
Do you know that author?

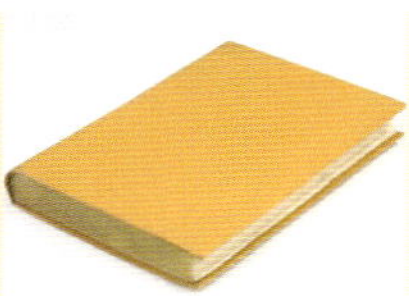

der Roman / Romane
novel

Wie viele Romane hat er geschrieben?
How many novels has he written?

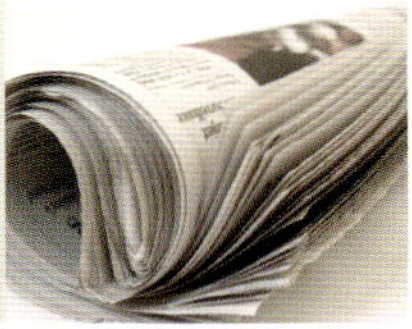

der Artikel / Artikel
article

Haben Sie den Artikel über Brasilien gelesen?
Have you read the article about Brazil?

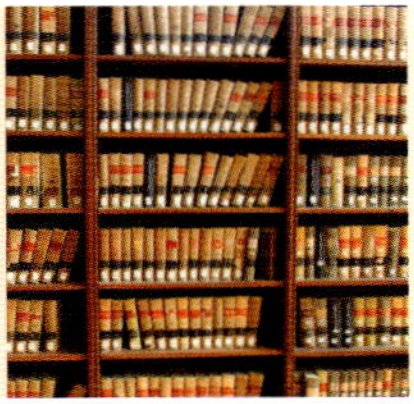

die Bibliothek / Bibliotheken
library

Entschuldigung, wo ist denn die Bibliothek?
Excuse me, where can I find the library?

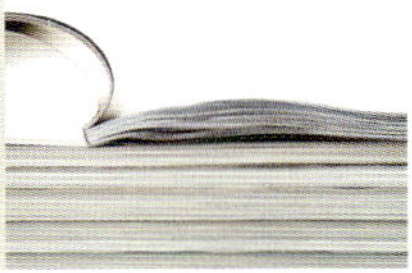

die Zeitschrift / Zeitschriften
magazine

Welche Zeitschrift lesen Sie gerne?
Which magazine do you like to read?

die Seite / Seiten
page

Auf welcher Seite ist das?
Which page is it on?

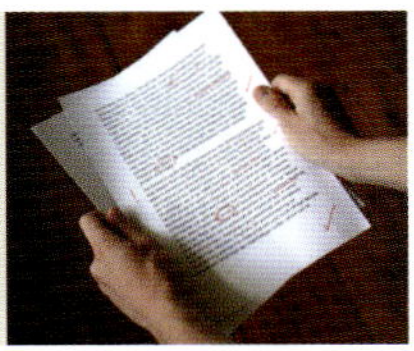

korrigieren
to correct

Können Sie mich bitte korrigieren?
Could you please correct me?

UNIT 4 › LESSON 2

Social life

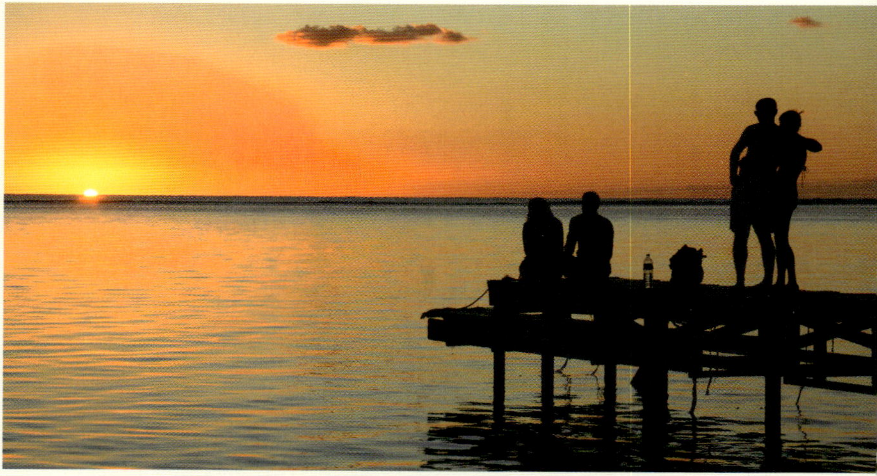

Culture note

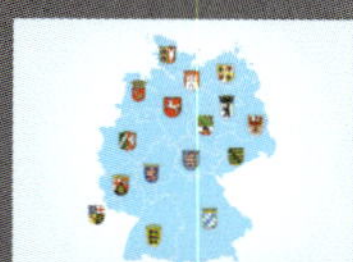

In Germany you'll hear a wide range of different dialects. In theory, all 82 million Germans speak the same language. However, just as in many other languages, there are many considerable regional differences. The word bread roll (*Brötchen*), for example, is *Semmel* in the south of Germany and *Schrippen* in the north. Someone from Hamburg could greet you with a *Moin Moin* instead of *Guten Tag*. People from Bavaria might say *Servus* (good bye) to you when departing, whereas in other dialects this could be *Tschüss*. Germany is basically defined by its regional linguistic varieties as almost every region in Germany has its dialectal coloring. In the southwest you use the word *schwätzen* for to talk or to speak, where someone from the north uses the word *klönen*.

Video Dialog

Matthias invites Lara to join him and some friends for the evening.

Active German: Level 4 > *Unit 4* > *Lesson 2* > *Video dialog*

Matthias:	*Am liebsten treffe ich mich eigentlich mit Freunden.*
Lara:	*Ja, ich kann mich auch den ganzen Tag mit Freunden unterhalten.*
Matthias:	*Heute Abend kommen ein paar Freunde zu mir. Hast du Lust?*
Lara:	*Wann denn?*
Matthias:	*Wir haben uns für 20 Uhr verabredet. Interessierst du dich für Fußball?*
Lara:	*Ja und nein. Warum?*
Matthias:	*Heute Abend ist ein wichtiges Spiel.*
Lara:	*Na gut. Ich bin ja kein Spielverderber.*
Matthias:	*Gut, ich freue mich auf heute Abend.*

Matthias:	Most of all I like meeting up with friends.
Lara:	Yes, I can talk to friends all day long as well.
Matthias:	A couple of friends are coming to my place tonight. Are you up for it?
Lara:	When?
Matthias:	We arranged to meet at 8 o'clock. Are you interested in football?
Lara:	Yes and no. Why?

Matthias: Tonight, an important game is on.
Lara: OK. I'm not a party pooper.
Matthias: Good, I'm looking forward to tonight.

Grammar

Active German: Level 4 > *Unit 4* > *Lesson 2* > *Grammar*

1 › Are you looking forward to it?

In earlier units we had a look at reflexive verbs with prepositions:

*Ich interessiere mich **für** Sport.*

I'm interested in sports.

You use the preposition *für* to indicate what you are interested in.

Another example we had was the verb *sich freuen auf*:

*Ich freue mich **auf** dich.*

I'm looking forward **to** meeting you.

With the preposition *auf* you indicate what you are looking forward to.

It is very common to attach a preposition to a verb to expand its meaning. Try to learn the verb and the preposition used with it together as this will make it easier to remember.

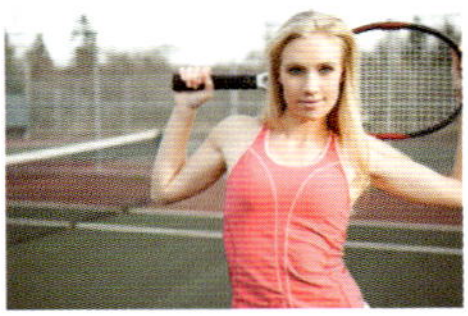

2 › I talk to her

We are now going to focus on some very common verbs used with prepositions.

sich treffen mit	to meet up with
*Wir treffen uns **mit** Herr Baumann.*	We're meeting up with Mr. Baumann.
sich unterhalten mit	to talk to
*Ich unterhalte mich **mit** Claudia.*	I'm talking to Claudia.
sich verabreden mit	to arrange a meeting with
*Sie hat sich **mit** Matthias verabredet.*	She arranged a meeting with Matthias.
sich erinnern an	to remember
*Erinnerst du dich **an** sie?*	Do you remember her?
sich bedanken für	to say thank you for
*Habt ihr euch **für** die Süßigkeiten bedankt?*	Did you say thank you for the candy?

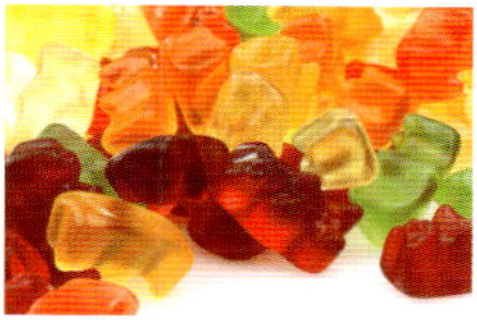

sich gewöhnen an	to get used to
*Haben Sie sich **an** Deutschland gewöhnt?*	Have you gotten used to Germany?

3 › I'm looking forward to seeing you

Let's have a closer look at some of the prepositions.

Ich erinnere mich ***an*** *ihn.*

I remember him.

Er bedankt sich ***für*** *den schönen Tag.*

He says thank you for the lovely day.

Ich freue mich ***auf*** *ihn.*

I'm looking forward to seeing him.

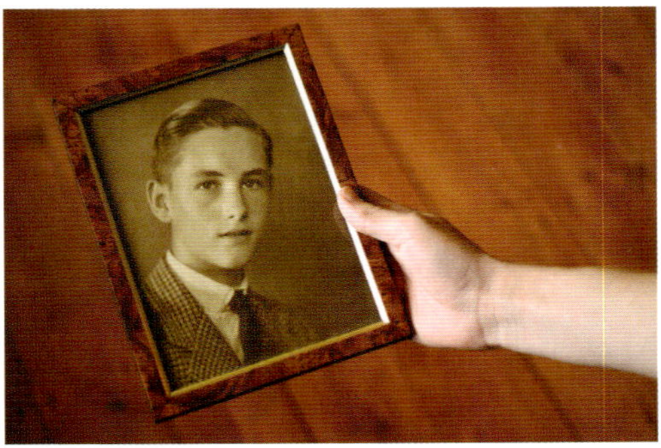

Note that the prepositions *an*, *für*, and *auf* are followed by the accusative.

As a quick reminder:

"the" in the accusative: *den*, *die*, *das*
"a" in the accusative: *einen*, *eine*, *ein*.

Possessive articles in the accusative: *mich* (me), *dich* (you), *ihn* (him), *sie* (her), *uns* (us), *euch* (you), *Sie* / *sie* (you / they)

4 › I talk to him

The verbs using the preposition *mit* take the dative:

Ich unterhalte mich ***mit*** *ihm.*	I talk to him.
Ich verabrede mich ***mit*** *ihm.*	I arrange a meeting with him.
Ich treffe mich ***mit*** *ihm.*	I meet up with him.

Do you remember the dative forms?

"the" in the dative: *dem*, *der*, *dem*
"a" in the dative: *einem*, *einer*, *einem*.

Possessive articles in the dative: *mir* (me), *dir* (you), *ihm* (him), *ihr* (her), *uns* (us), *euch* (you), *Ihnen / ihnen* (you / them).

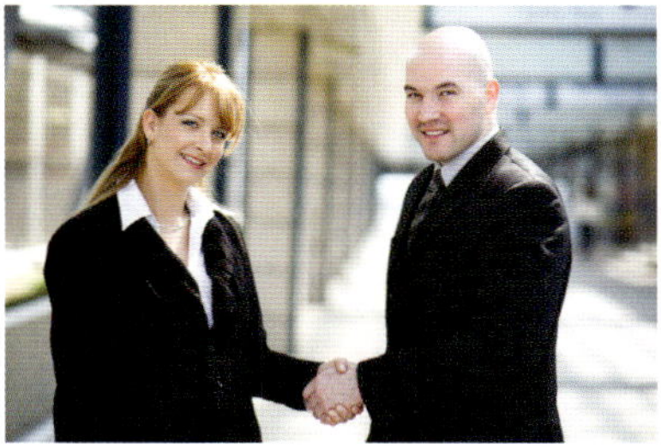

5 › I think of you

Some verbs have a fixed preposition but aren't reflexive:

Ich denke ***an*** *dich.*

I'm thinking of you.

Ich spreche ***mit*** *ihm.*

I'm speaking to him.

*Wir sprechen **über** das Projekt.*
We're speaking about the project.

*Ich warte **auf** dich.*
I'll wait for you.

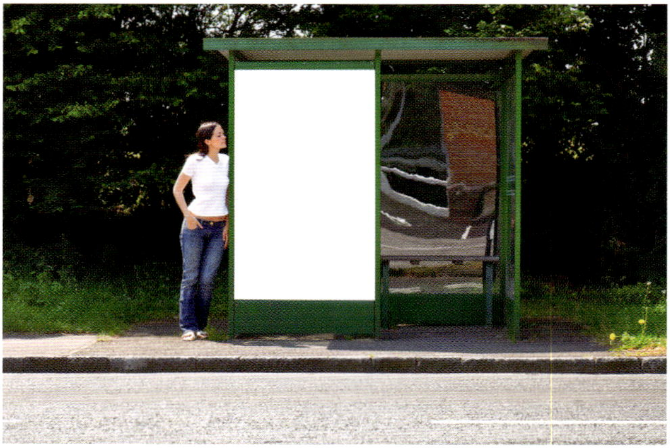

Vocabulary

Active German: Level 4 > *Unit 4* > *Lesson 2* > *Vocabulary*

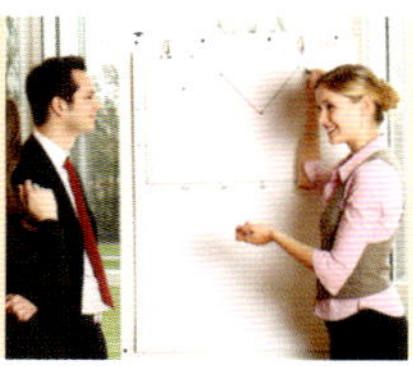

beschreiben
to describe
Kannst du das Gefühl beschreiben?
Can you describe that feeling?

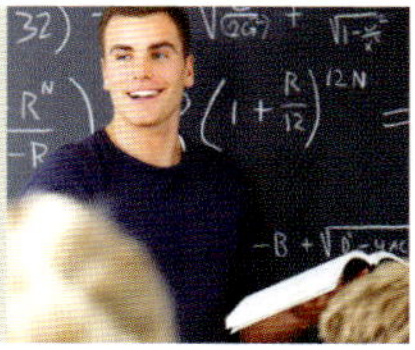

erklären
to explain

Ich verstehe das nicht. Können Sie das erklären?
I don't understand. Could you explain it?

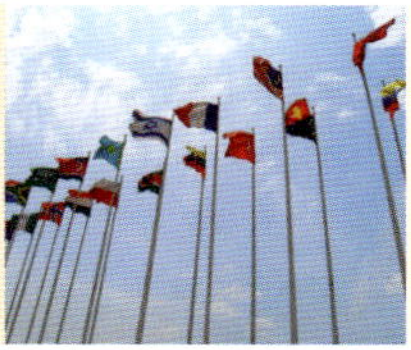

die Fremdsprache / Fremdsprachen
foreign language

Sprechen Sie eine Fremdsprache?
Do you speak a foreign language?

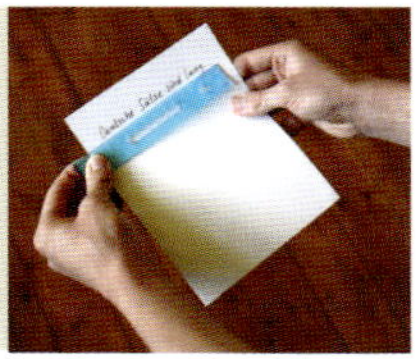

der Satz / Sätze
sentence

Deutsche Sätze sind lang.
German sentences are long.

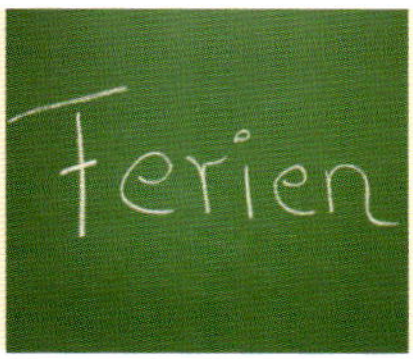

das Wort / Wörter
word

Was bedeutet das Wort?
What does this word mean?

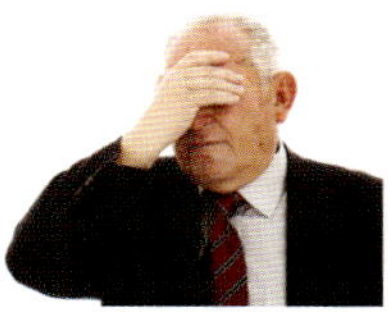

vergessen
to forget

Ich habe seine Telefonnummer vergessen.
I've forgotten his phone number.

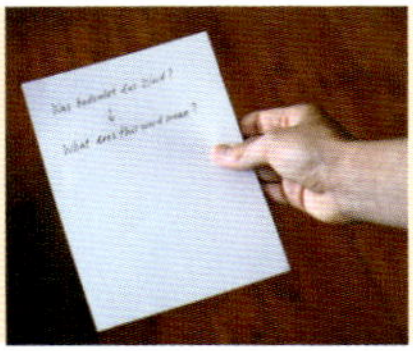

übersetzen
to translate

Kannst du diesen Satz übersetzen?
Can you translate this sentence?

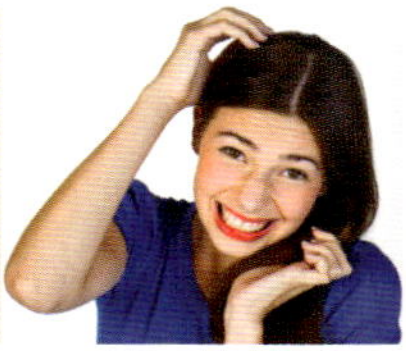

sich entschuldigen
to apologize

Ich möchte mich bei Ihnen entschuldigen.
I would like to apologize to you.

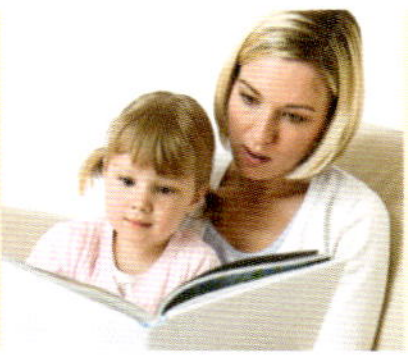

erzählen
to tell

Was hast du gestern gemacht? Erzähl.
What did you do yesterday? Tell me.

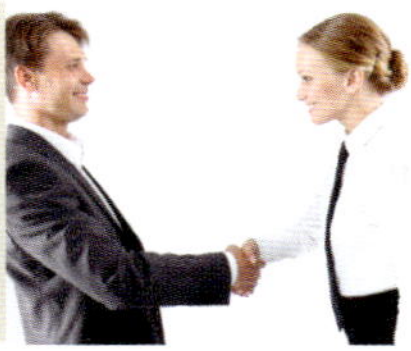

kennenlernen
to get to know, to get acquainted with

Ich habe gestern einen netten Mann kennengelernt.
Yesterday I got acquainted with a nice man.

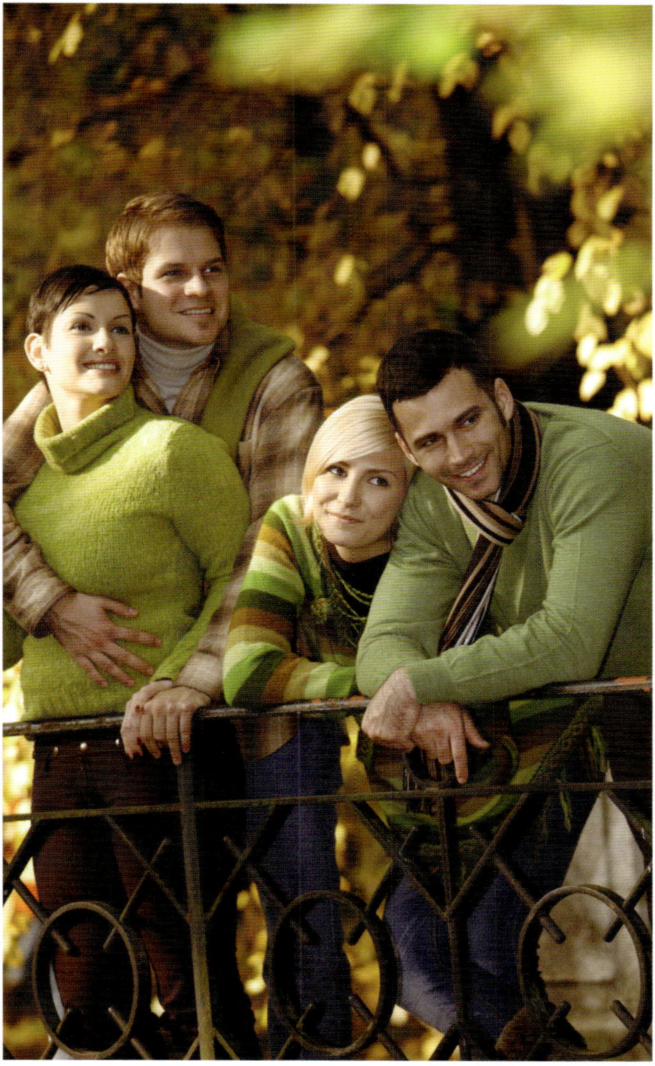

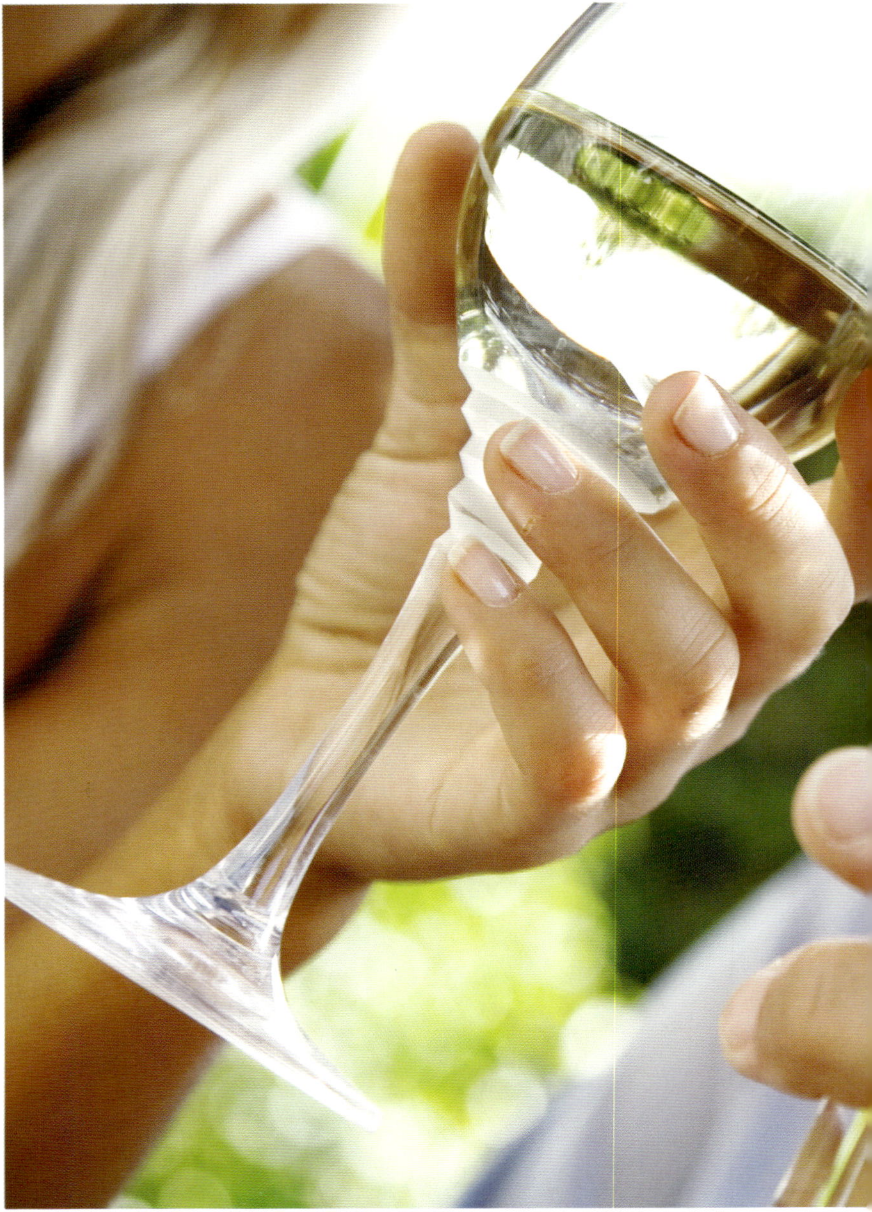

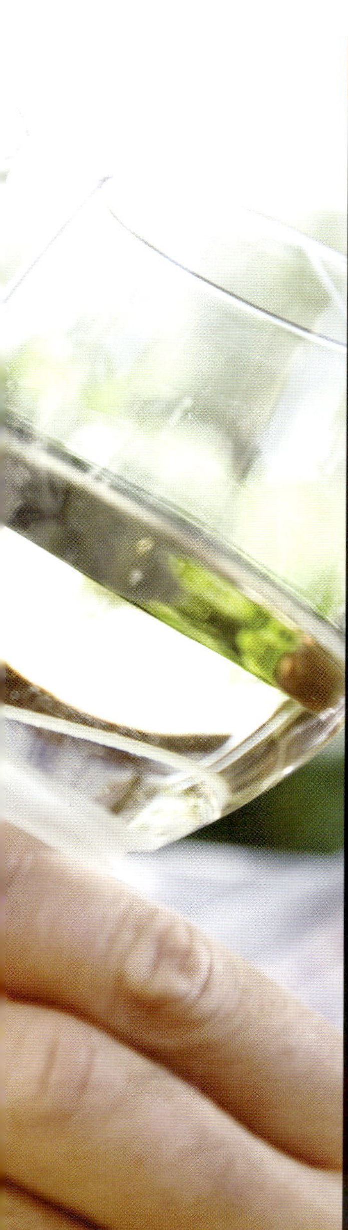

Active German *Level 4*

5

Lesson 1: Celebrations 1

- How to say "to become," "to get," and "to turn."
- How to talk about congratulating someone, helping someone, and thanking someone.
- Vocabulary for birthdays and congratulations.
- More on celebrations.

Lesson 2: Celebrations 2

- How to use ***wenn***, ***wann***, and ***als***.
- How to say "every," "all," "some," and "few."
- How the verbs "to help" and "to meet" work.
- Vocabulary for customs and emotional states.

Collins | Livemocha™

UNIT 5 › LESSON 1

Celebrations 1

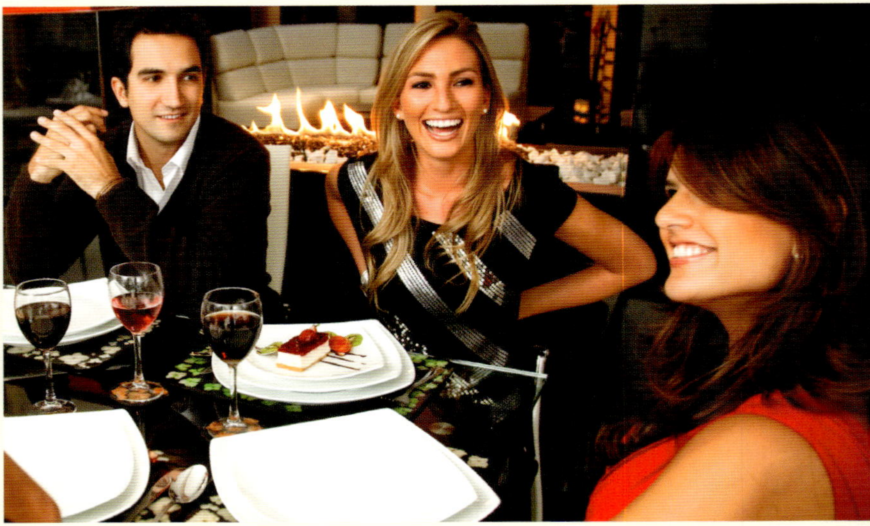

Culture note

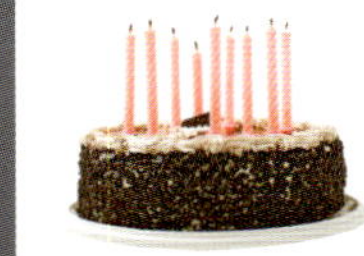

Germans have some special rules about birthdays. One of them is particularly important: Never congratulate the birthday boy or girl before the actual day. The Germans consider this bad luck. It is customary for Germans to throw their own birthday parties and to pay for all food, drink, and entertainment. At the office, it is common that the person whose birthday it is brings cake or pastries for everyone. Often someone within the department will collect money for a birthday present. You may even find that your colleagues bring in home-baked cakes.

Video Dialog

The team celebrates Mr. Baumann's birthday.

Active German: Level 4 > *Unit 5* > *Lesson 1* > *Video dialog*

Herr Buschel:	*Alles Gute zum Geburtstag. Herzlichen Glückwunsch.*
Herr Baumann:	*Meine lieben Kollegen, Herzlichen Dank für diese nette Überraschung.*
Herr Buschel:	*Zum Wohl.*
Herr Baumann:	*Zum Wohl.*
Lara:	*Zum Wohl.*
Matthias:	*Zum Wohl.*
Herr Baumann:	*Zum Wohl.*
Lara:	*Wie alt wird Herr Baumann denn?*
Matthias:	*Ich weiß es nicht. Was glaubst du?*
Lara:	*45?*
Matthias:	*Ja, 45 ungefähr.*
Lara:	*Ich werde bald 33.*
Matthias:	*33, das ist doch noch jung. Feierst du dann?*
Lara:	*Na, klar. Ich liebe Partys.*

Mr. Buschel:	Happy birthday. Congratulations.
Mr. Baumann:	My dear colleagues, thank you for this lovely surprise.
Mr. Buschel:	Cheers.
Mr. Baumann:	Cheers.
Lara:	Cheers.
Matthias:	Cheers.
Mr. Baumann:	Cheers.
Lara:	How old is Mr. Baumann now?
Matthias:	I don't know. What do you think?
Lara:	45?
Matthias:	Yes, about 45.
Lara:	I'm turning 33 soon.
Matthias:	33, that's still young. Are you celebrating?
Lara:	Of course! I love parties.

Grammar

Active German: Level 4 > *Unit 5* > *Lesson 1* > *Grammar*

1 › The verb *werden*

In an earlier unit we learned about the verb *werden*:

Ich möchte Mitglied werden.

I want to become a member.

The verb *werden* means to become or to get.
Let's have a closer look at how it is used.

It is used to describe a change:

Es wird kalt.	It's getting cold.
Meine Haare werden grau.	My hair is getting gray.
Er wird nervös.	He gets nervous.

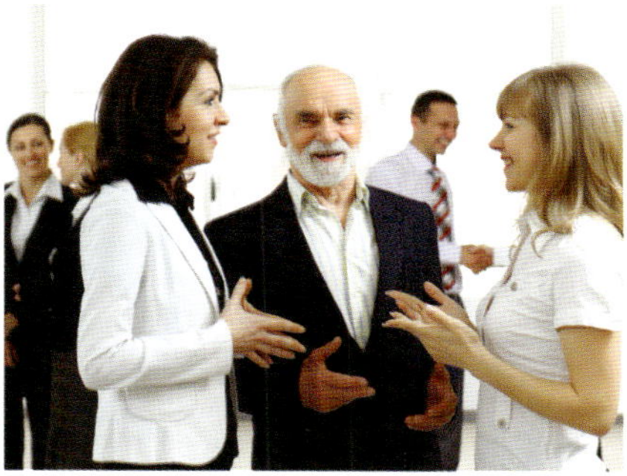

It is also used to express what you want to become professionally.

Ich will Schriftstellerin werden.	I want to become an author.
Katja möchte Malerin werden.	Katja wants to become a painter.

Note that you don't use an article ("a" or "an") when you state your profession.

2 › I'm turning 33

The people in the video dialog are talking about birthdays and age. In order to express a future age you use *werden* as well.

Wie alt wird Herr Baumann?	How old will Mr. Baumann be?
Ich werde bald 33.	I'm turning 33 soon.

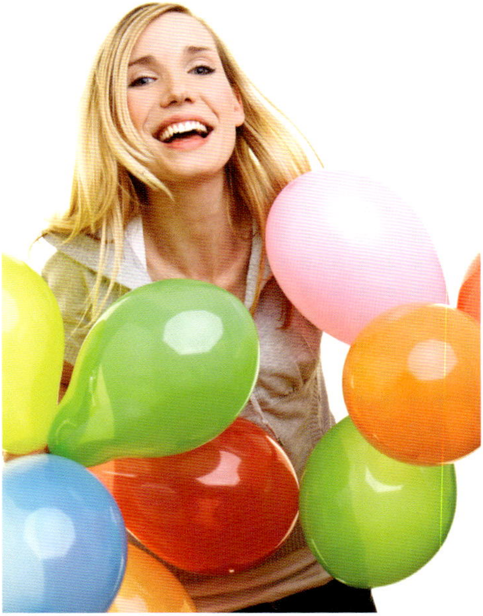

We've had a look at the different verb forms of *werden* before. Let's review them.

*Ich **werde** nächsten Monat 38.*	I'll be 38 next month.
***Wirst** du Lehrerin?*	Will you become a teacher?
*Er **wird** immer nervös, wenn er eine Präsentation gibt.*	He always gets nervous when he has to give a presentation.
*Sie **wird** groß.*	She is getting tall.
*Wir **werden** berühmt.*	We're becoming famous.
***Werdet** ihr 30?*	Are you turning 30?

3 › The verb *werden*

Do you remember the past tense forms we have covered so far?

We had the simple past (used especially for written language and some frequent verbs):

ich war (I was), *er hatte* (he had), *sie musste* (she had to), and *wir konnten* (we could)

The simple past forms of *werden* are:

ich wurde	I became
du wurdest	you became
er / sie / es wurde	he / she / it became
wir wurden	we became
ihr wurdet	you became
sie / Sie wurden	they / you became

In the present perfect (the tense you almost always use when talking about the past) the construction is:

*Ich **bin** Lehrerin **geworden**.*	I have become a teacher.
*Er **ist** nervös **geworden**.*	He got nervous.

Note that the present perfect of *werden* is built with *sein* and not with *haben*.

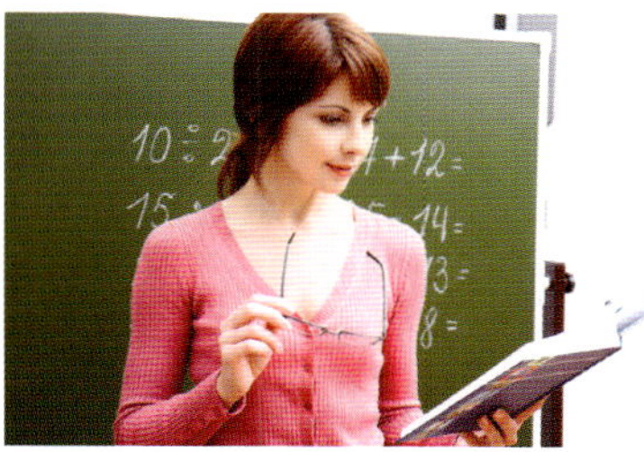

4 › Verbs with dative objects

So far we have seen three different functions of the dative:

with prepositions and location:

Das Glas steht neben dem Computer.

The glass is next to the computer.

with two objects:

Ich zeige dir dein Zimmer.

I'll show you your room. / I'll show the room to you.

with some verbs such as *gefallen* (to like), *gehören* (to belong to) and *passen* (to fit).

Mir gefällt das T-Shirt.

I like the T-shirt.

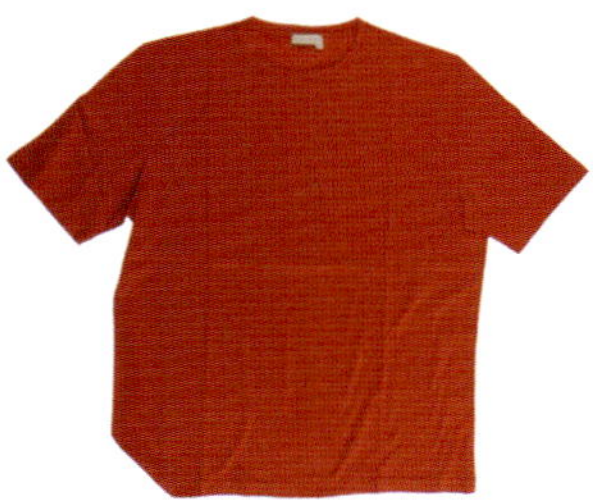

In German some other verbs take the dative as well.

*Ich danke **Ihnen** für diese nette Überraschung.*	Thank you for this lovely surprise.
*Ich danke **dem** Mann.*	I thank the man. (literally, to the man)

5 › More verbs with the dative

Some important verbs which follow the same pattern are:

jemandem helfen	to help someone
jemandem antworten	to answer someone
jemandem gratulieren	to congratulate someone
jemandem glauben	to believe someone

Kann ich Ihnen helfen?	May I help you?
Hast du ihm geantwortet?	Have you answered him?
Wir gratulieren dir.	We congratulate you.
Glaubst du mir?	Do you believe me?

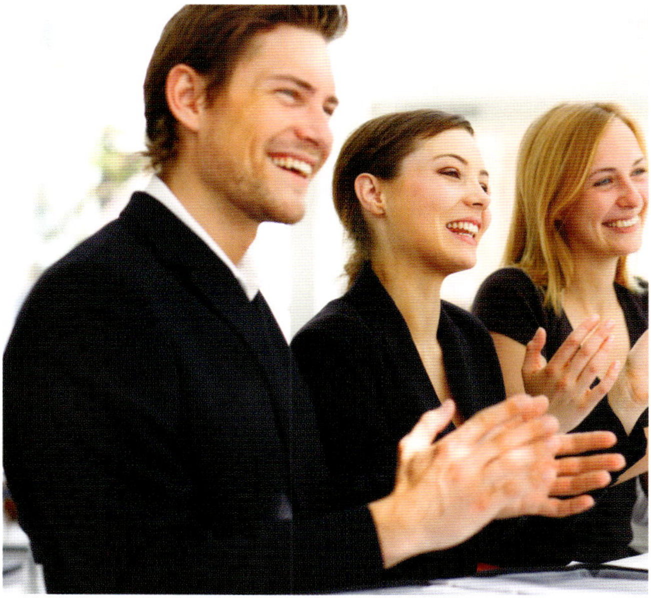

Vocabulary

Active German: Level 4 > Unit 5 > Lesson 1 > Vocabulary

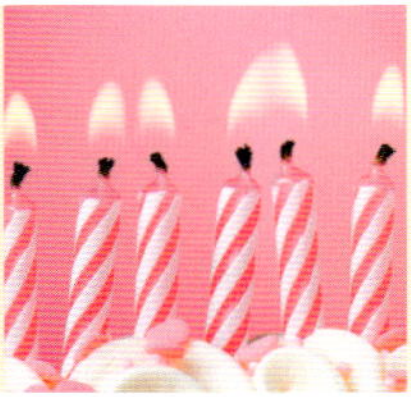

Herzlichen Glückwunsch
congratulations

Herzlichen Glückwunsch zum Geburtstag.
Congratulations on your birthday.

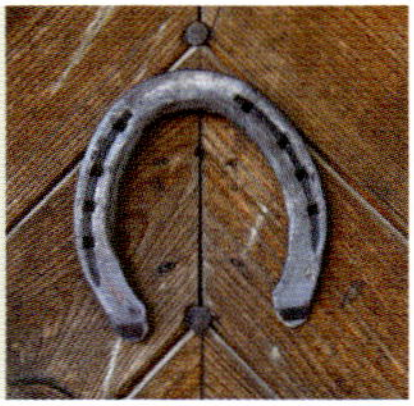

alles Gute
all the best, best wishes

Alles Gute zum Geburtstag.
Happy birthday. / All the best for your birthday.

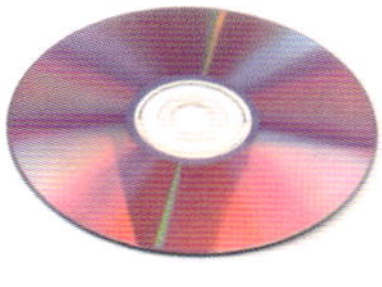

schenken
to give (as a present)

Er hat mir eine CD geschenkt.
He gave me a CD.

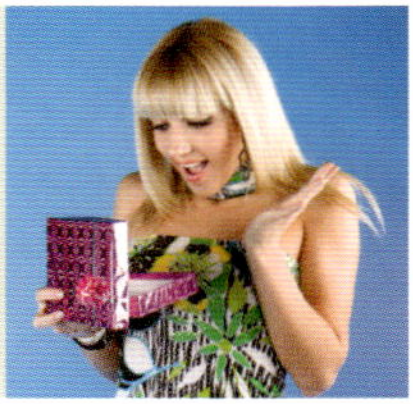

die Überraschung / Überraschungen
surprise

Das ist aber eine schöne Überraschung.
This is a really nice surprise.

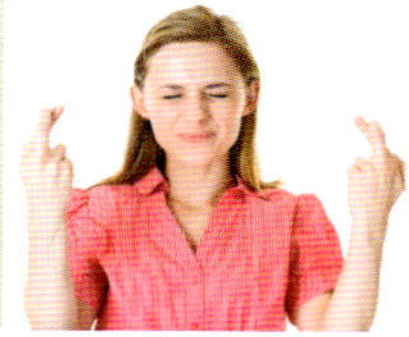

wünschen
to wish

Ich wünsche dir alles Gute.
I wish you all the best.

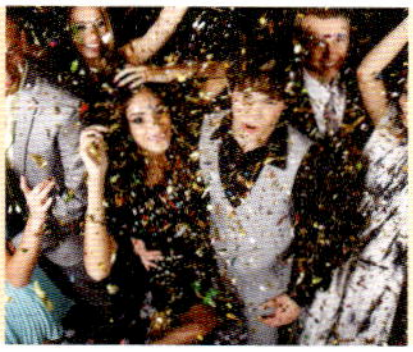

das Vergnügen / Vergnügen
pleasure, enjoyment

Ich wünsche Ihnen viel Vergnügen.
Have a good time

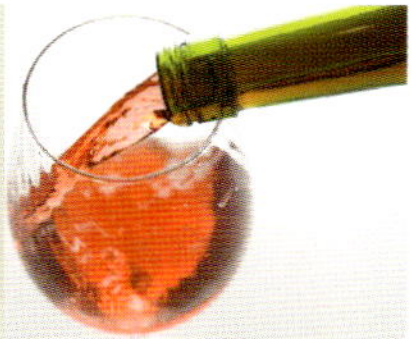

der Sekt
sparkling wine

Möchten Sie ein Glas Sekt?
Would you like a glass of sparkling wine?

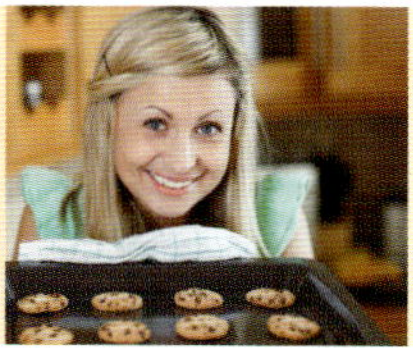

backen
to bake

Ich kann nicht gut backen.
I'm not good at baking.

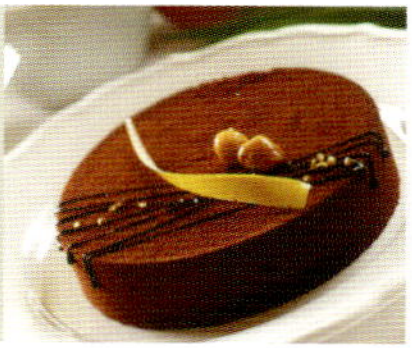

der Kuchen / Kuchen
cake

Hast du den Kuchen gebacken?
Did you bake the cake?

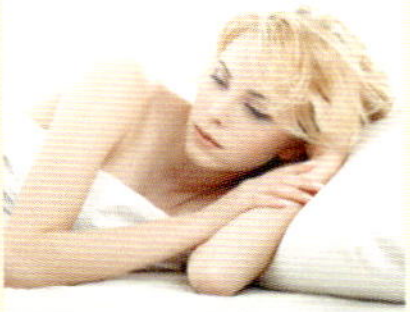

träumen
to dream

Träum schön.
Sweet dreams.

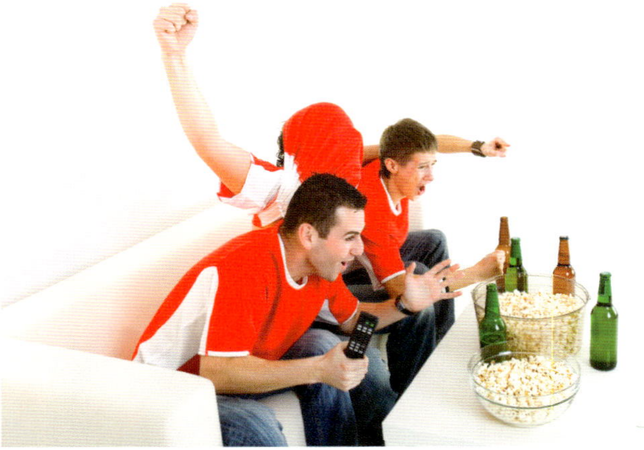

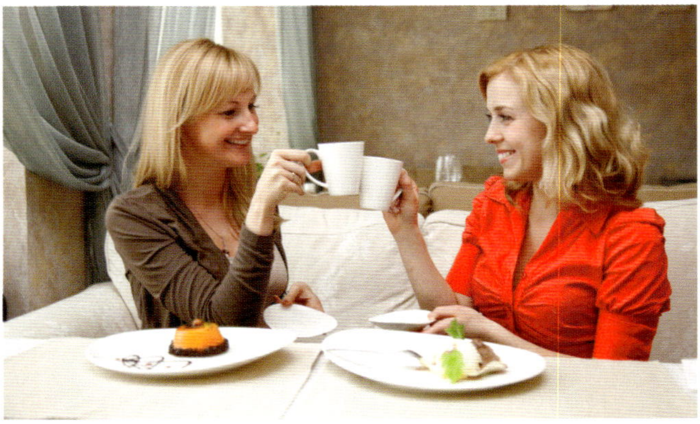

UNIT 5 › LESSON 2

Celebrations 2

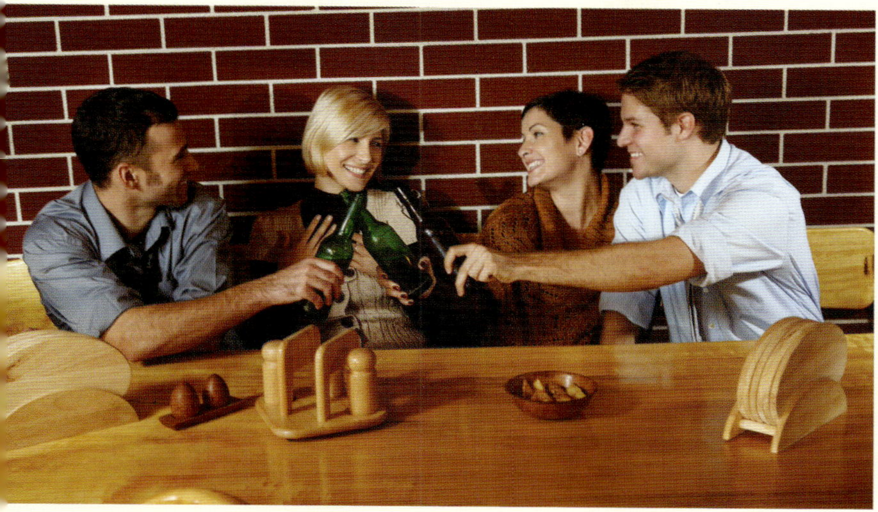

Culture note

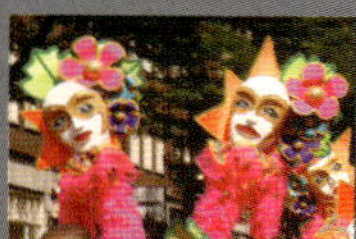

The Cologne Carnival takes place every year. It is called the "fifth season" (carnival season) and begins on November 11th at 11 minutes past 11. But the real "crazy days" do not start until the Thursday before Lent. The carnival is celebrated with parties on the street, in public squares, and in bars. The highlight of the crazy days is the *Rosenmontag* (Rose Monday). All through Cologne everybody wears costumes. The typical greeting during the festival is *Kölle Alaaf* (Cologne alive). There is a famous parade on Rose Monday that is around 6.5 kilometers long and in which around 10,000 people participate. It is a tradition to throw candy (*Kamelle*) from the floats into the crowd.

Video Dialog

Lara and Matthias share fond childhood memories.

Active German: Level 4 > *Unit 5* > *Lesson 2* > *Video dialog*

Matthias: *Gehst du gerne zum Karneval?*

Lara: *Oh ja. Als ich klein war, sind wir jedes Jahr nach Köln gefahren.*

Matthias: *Als ich Kind war, hat meine Mutter mich auch jedes Jahr verkleidet.*

Lara: *Wenn ich Geburtstag hatte, hatten wir immer eine kleine Party.*

Matthias: *Schön.*

Lara: *Alle Feste – Weihnachten, Ostern – sind wichtig bei uns.*

Matthias: *Nächstes Mal fahren wir zusammen zum Karneval.*

Lara: *Aber nur, wenn du dich verkleidest.*

Matthias: Do you like going to the carnival?
Lara: Oh, yes. When I was a child we went to Cologne every year.
Matthias: When I was a child my mother dressed me up every year in a costume as well.
Lara: Whenever it was my birthday we always had a small party.
Matthias: Nice.

Lara:	Every holiday – Christmas, Easter – is important for us.
Matthias:	Next time we'll go to the carnival together.
Lara:	But only if you go in costume.

Grammar

Active German: Level 4 > *Unit 5* > *Lesson 2* > *Grammar*

1 › **When I was a child**

In the video dialog Lara says that when she was a child she went to Cologne every year.

> ***Als ich klein war, sind wir jedes Jahr nach Köln gefahren.***
> When I was a child we went to Cologne every year.

Als (when) in this case refers to an event or state (being a child) in the past.

Compare the following sentences:

Als er das sagte, wurde sie rot.	When he said that, she turned red.
Wenn sie das sagte, wurde sie (immer) rot.	Whenever he said that, she (always) turned red.
Wenn ich Geburtstag hatte, hatten wir immer eine kleine Party.	Whenever it was my birthday we always had a small party.

The difference between the sentences is that in the first one we are talking about a single event and in the subsequent sentences we are talking about an event that happened regularly.

In German you use *als* to talk about a single event or state in the past and *wenn* to talk about an event that happened more often.

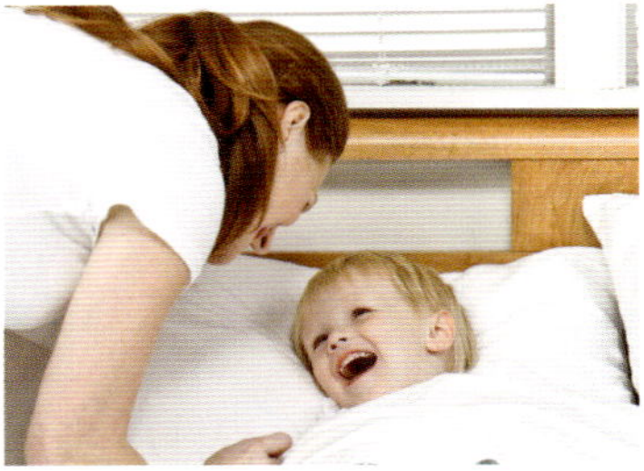

2 › **The conjunction "when"**

Als is a conjunction like *weil* and *dass*.

Note the word order:

> *Mein Freund hat mich gestern angerufen,* ***als*** *ich zu Hause war.*
>
> My friend called me yesterday while I was at home.

Wenn can refer to the past, present or future. *Als* only refers to the past.

> *Wenn er anruft, freue ich mich.*
>
> When he calls, I'm very happy.

The third important conjunction in this context is *wann* (when), which you saw in an earlier unit. Remember that *wann* is used when there is a question, either asked directly or implied.

> *Ich weiß nicht, wann er kommt.*
>
> I don't know when he is going to come.

Here, the implied question is "When will he come?"

In summary:

Use:

- *als* for singular events / states in the past
- *wenn* for regular events in the past or the present
- *wann* to answer the question "at what time?"

3 › Every year

In the video dialog Matthias says that his mother dressed him up every year.

Meine Mutter hat mich ***jedes*** *Jahr verkleidet.*

My mother dressed me in a costume every year.

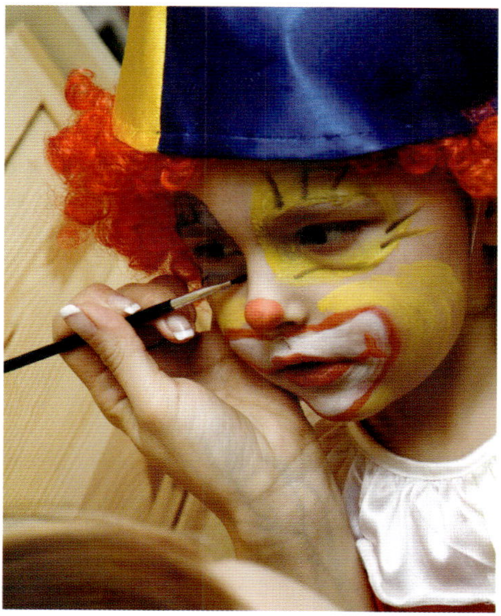

He uses the word *jed* to refer to the noun *Jahr* (year).

The word *jed-* has different endings according to the gender of the noun.

masculine	*jeder Tag*	every year
feminine	*jede Woche*	every week
neuter	*jedes Jahr*	every year

Jed- works the same way as *welch-* and *dies-*.

Welches Hemd gefällt dir?	Which shirt do you like?
Dieses Hemd gefällt mir.	I like this shirt.

4 › All, several and few

Here are some other words that determine which noun is being referred to:

viele	many
alle	all
mehrere	several
einige	some
wenige	few

They are all used in the plural and therefore all end in *-e*. Let's consider some examples:

Alle Menschen haben die gleichen Rechte.
All people have the same rights.

Viele Menschen leben in Berlin.
Many people live in Berlin.

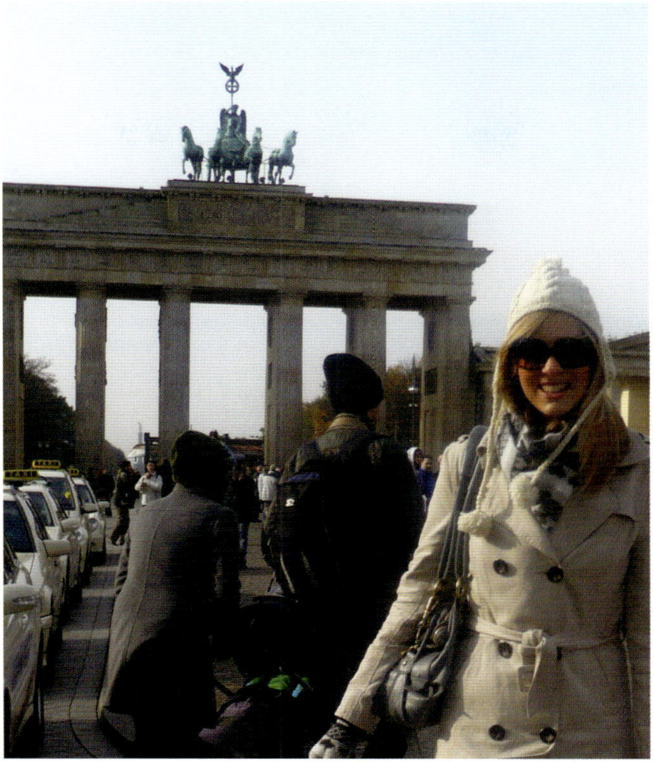

Einige Leute mögen kein Fußball.

Some people don't like soccer.

Wenige Menschen in Deutschland sprechen Chinesisch.

Few people in Germany speak Chinese.

5 ›

Some new verbs and their forms

Let's take a closer look at some more irregular new verbs:

helfen to help	
ich helfe	I help
du hilfst	you help
er / sie hilft	he / she helps
wir helfen	we help
ihr helft	you help
sie / Sie helfen	they / you help
Er hilft seiner Mutter.	He helps his mother.

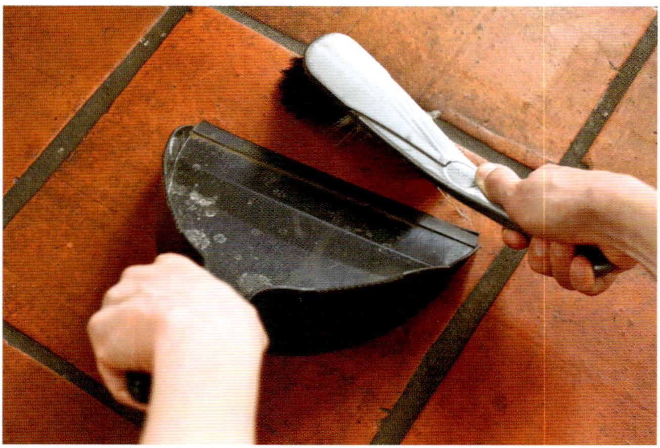

And in the present perfect the form of *helfen* is *geholfen*:

Er hat seiner Mutter geholfen.
He (has) helped his mother.

treffen	to meet
ich treffe	I meet
du triffst	you meet
er / sie trifft	he / she meets
wir treffen	we meet
ihr trefft	you meet
sie / Sie treffen	they / you meet

And in the present perfect:

Ich habe ihn getroffen.
I (have) met him.

Vocabulary

Active German: Level 4 > Unit 5 > Lesson 2 > Vocabulary

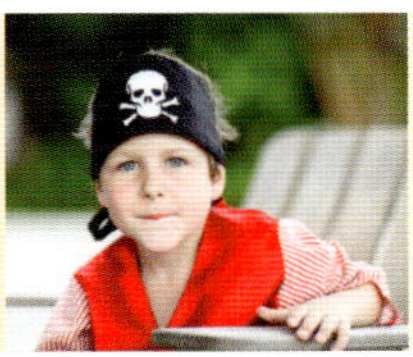

sich verkleiden
to dress up

Er hat sich als Pirat verkleidet.
He got dressed up as a pirate.

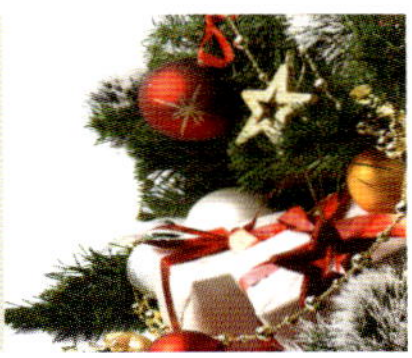

der Brauch / Bräuche
custom

Welche Bräuche gibt es in deinem Land?
Which customs do you have in your country?

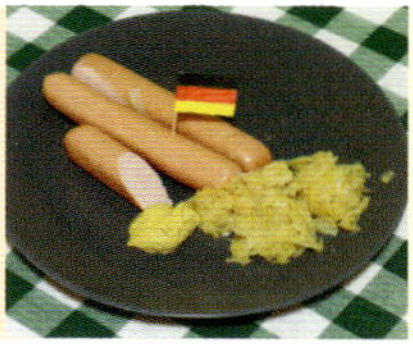

typisch
typical

Das ist typisch für ihn.
That's typical of him.

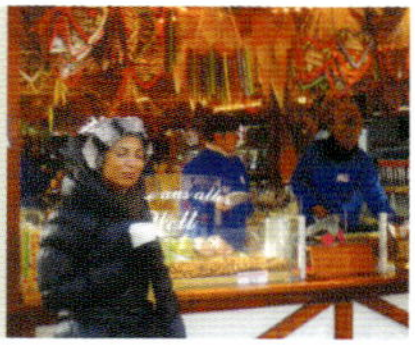

frohe Weihnachten
Merry Christmas

Ich wünsche Ihnen frohe Weihnachten.
I wish you a Merry Christmas.

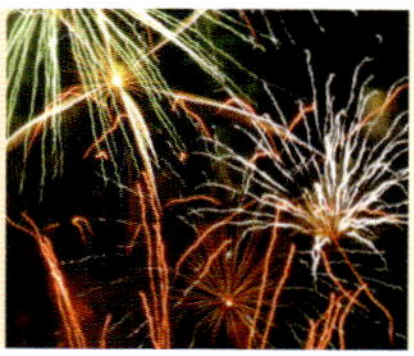

frohes neues Jahr
Happy New Year

Ich wünsche Ihnen eines frohes neues Jahr.
I wish you a Happy New Year.

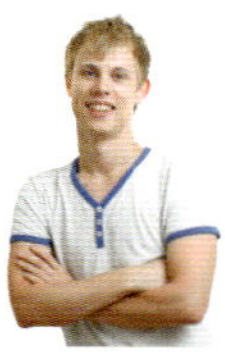

glücklich
happy

Er ist immer glücklich.
He is always happy.

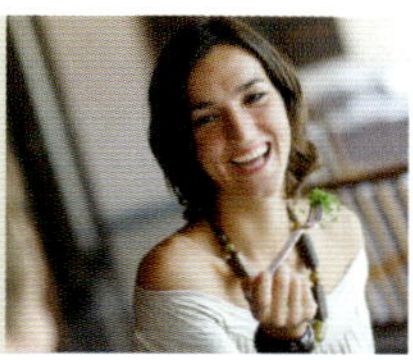

lachen
to laugh

Warum lachst du?
Why are you laughing?

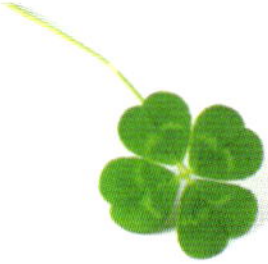

Glück haben
to be lucky
Da haben wir Glück gehabt.
We were lucky.

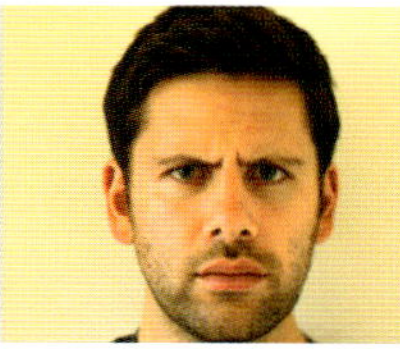

die Laune / Launen
mood
Max hat heute schlechte Laune.
Max is in a bad mood today.

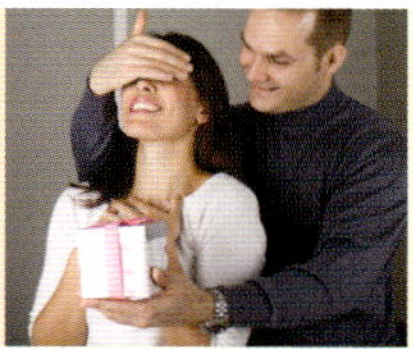

die Freude / Freuden
joy
Es war mir eine Freude.
It was a pleasure for me.

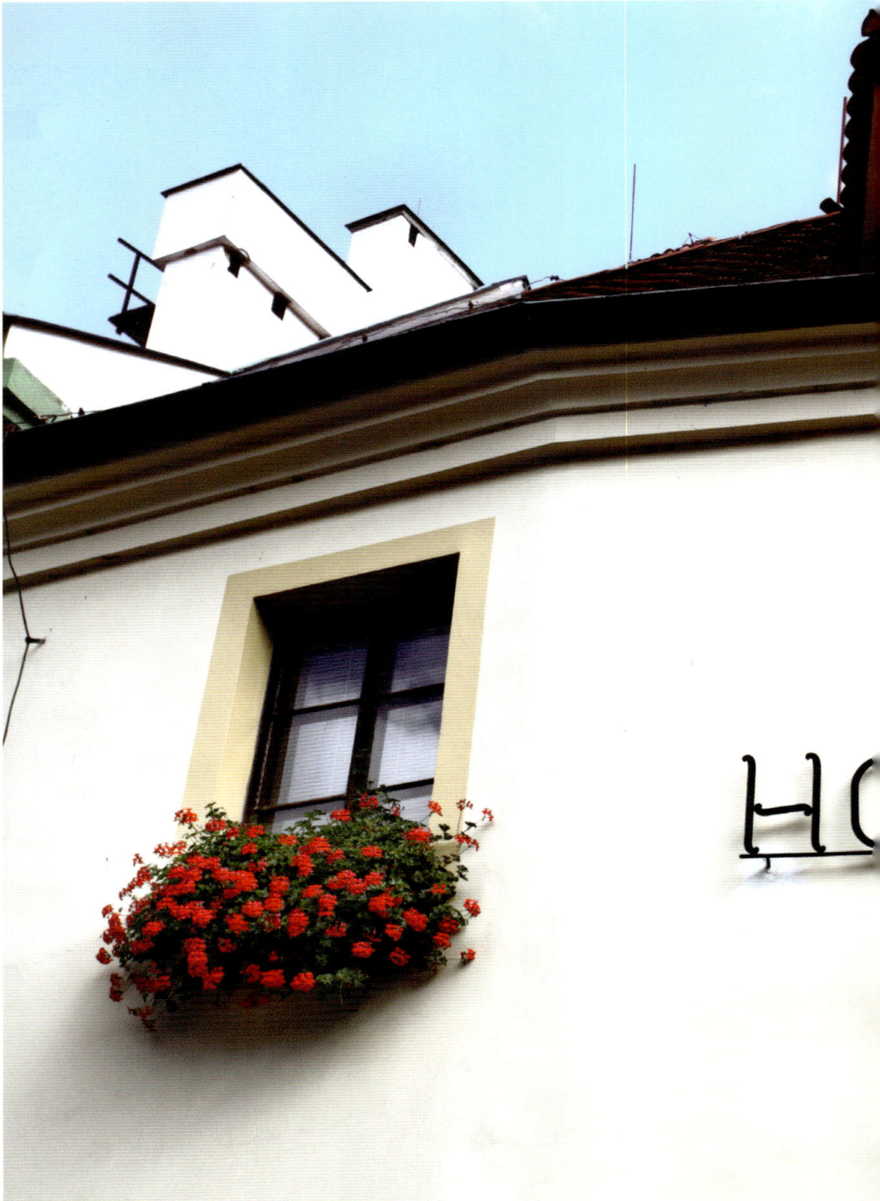

Active German *Level 4*

6

Lesson 1: A nice place to stay

- How to suggest something and recommend something.
- How to talk about trips.
- How to say: "I have no time to do ...," "I don't want to do ...," "It is important to do ..." etc.
- Vocabulary for planning and booking trips.

Lesson 2: A trip to Pulheim

- How to say "yet," "not yet," "never," "not any more," etc.
- How to say the 1st, the 2nd, the 3rd, etc.
- How to give dates.
- Vocabulary for traveling and travel information.

Collins | Livemocha™

UNIT 6 › LESSON 1

A nice place to stay

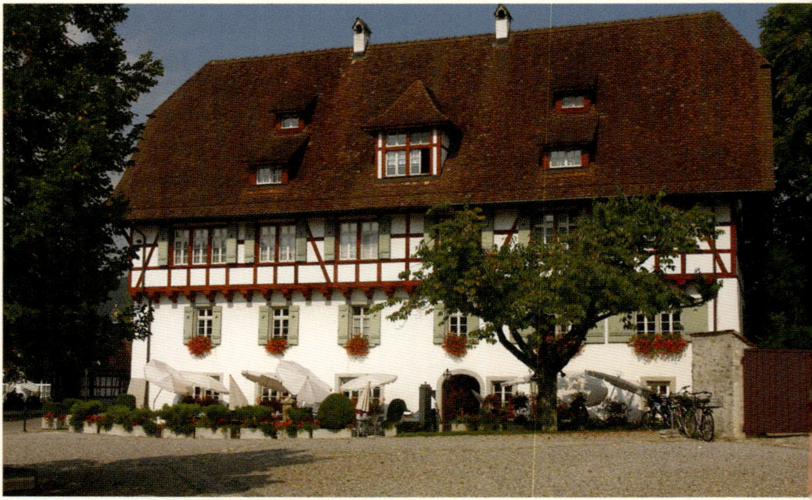

Culture note

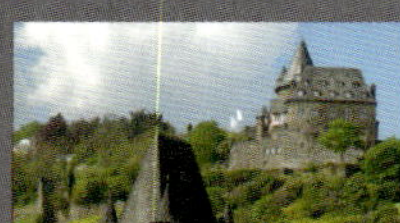

Germany has hotel rooms in every price range, ranging from very inexpensive accommodations in small hotels to rooms in mid-range hotels to luxury suites. Many hotels offer facilities such as a swimming pool, a sauna,and a gym. Hotels are classified using a system that ranges from one star (*ein Sterne-Hotel* – accommodations for modest requirements) to five stars (*5-Sterne-Hotel* – accommodations for top-level requirements).

Video Dialog

Lara helps Matthias with some local hotel research.

Active German: Level 4 > *Unit 6* > *Lesson 1* > *Video dialog*

Matthias:	*Lara, meine Eltern kommen mich besuchen. Kannst du mir ein gutes Hotel empfehlen?*
Lara:	*Was suchst du denn genau?*
Matthias:	*Ich suche ein Zimmer für zwei Nächte. Ein Doppelzimmer mit Bad.*
Lara:	*Mmh, dann kann ich dir das Hotel „Am Stadtpark“ empfehlen. Und wenn das ausgebucht ist, kann ich dir noch etwas anderes vorschlagen. Wie wäre es mit dem Hotel „Zur Post“?*
Matthias:	*Oh ja, das ist ein sehr schönes Hotel. Das liegt am See?*
Lara:	*Genau. Komm, wir schauen im Internet.*

Matthias:	Lara, my parents are coming to visit me. Can you recommend a good hotel?
Lara:	What exactly are you looking for?
Matthias:	I'm looking for a room for two nights. A double room with bathroom.
Lara:	Then I can recommend the Am Stadtpark Hotel. And if that one is full, I can suggest something else. How about the Hotel Zur Post?
Matthias:	Yes, that is a really nice hotel. It's next to the lake?
Lara:	Yes. Come on, let's have a look online.

Grammar

Active German: Level 4 > *Unit 6* > *Lesson 1* > *Grammar*

1 › What can you recommend?

Matthias asks Lara for a recommendation for a hotel:

Kannst du mir ein gutes Hotel empfehlen?

Can you recommend a good hotel?

The verb *empfehlen* works the same way as the verbs *zeigen* (to show), *bringen* (to bring), and *geben* (to give). It requires two objects – one in the dative and the other in the accusative:

jemandem (to somebody – dative)
etwas (something – accusative) *empfehlen*

Ich empfehle dir ein Hotel.

I recommend you a hotel.

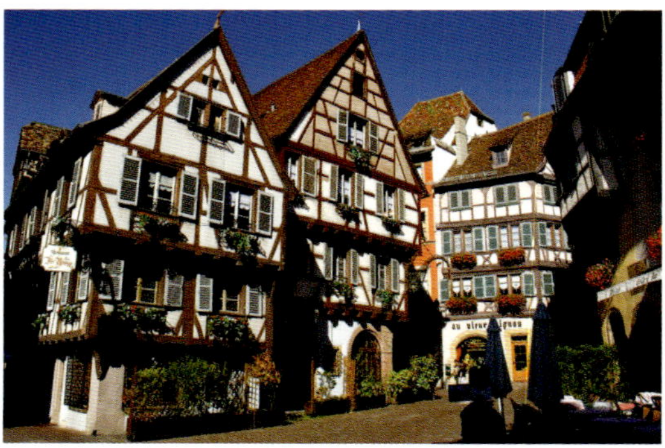

Lara uses the verb *vorschlagen* (to suggest).

Ich kann dir noch etwas anderes vorschlagen.
I can suggest something else.

This verb works the same way:

jemandem etwas vorschlagen	to suggest something to somebody
Ich schlage dir das Hotel „Zur Post" vor.	I suggest the Hotel Zur Post.

Note that *vorschlagen* is separable.

2 › The verb "to suggest"

You can use the verb *vorschlagen* in a different way.

*Ich schlage dir vor, das Hotel „Zur Post" **zu nehmen**.*
I suggest you take the Hotel Zur Post.

The second part, after the comma, is an action introduced by the verb *vorschlagen* rather than just a thing.

*Ich schlage dir vor, etwas **zu tun**.*
I suggest you do something.

Note that the verb in the second part is in its basic form and is always at the end of the clause.

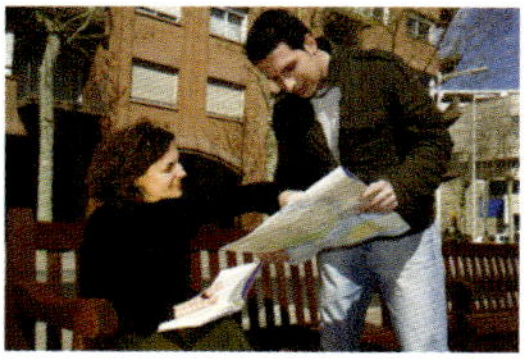

3 › I'll try to come earlier

There are many other verbs which work the same way. Let's look at some important ones.

versuchen	to try
Ich versuche, früher zu kommen.	I'll try to come earlier.
planen	to plan
Ich plane, nach Spanien zu fliegen.	I plan to fly to Spain.
vergessen	to forget
Ich habe vergessen, das Dokument zu speichern.	I forgot to save the document.
anfangen	to start
Ich fange an, die Email zu schreiben.	I'll start to write the email.

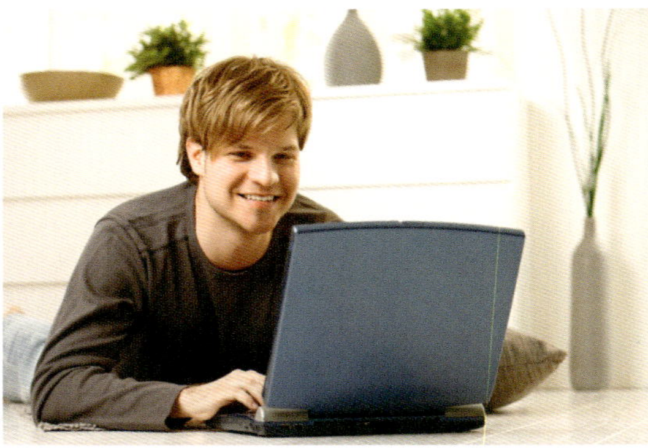

4 › It is time to go

There are some other expressions that follow the same pattern.

Ich habe keine Zeit, die Zeitung zu lesen.	I don't have time to read the newspaper.
Ich habe keine Lust zu arbeiten.	I don't want to work.
Hast du Lust, ins Kino zu gehen?	Would you like to go to the movies?
Es ist schön / traurig / wichtig etwas zu machen.	It is nice / sad / important to do something.
Es ist schön am Sonntag auszuschlafen.	It is nice to sleep in on Sundays.

Note that you put the *zu* between the two parts of the verb *ausschlafen*.

5 › A trip

Let's have a look at some useful expressions for planning trips.

To travel:

reisen	to travel
verreisen	to travel, to be away
eine Reise machen	to go on a trip

To book or reserve something:

eine Reise buchen	to book a trip
ein Zimmer reservieren	to reserve a room

For tickets:

hin und zurück	round-trip ticket
einfache Fahrt	one-way ticket

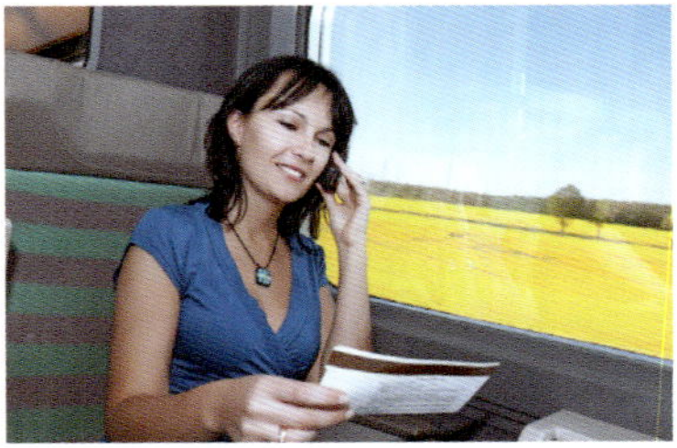

6 › **Departure**

The following verbs are very common when you talk about trips and traveling. Note that they are all separable:

abfahren	to depart
Wann fährt der Zug ab?	When does the train leave?
ankommen	to arrive
Wann kommt der Zug an?	When does the train arrive?
einsteigen	to board, to get in
Bitte, steigen Sie ein.	Please board the train.
aussteigen	to get off
Wann muss ich aussteigen?	When do I have to get off?
umsteigen	to change
Wo muss ich umsteigen?	Where do I have to change?

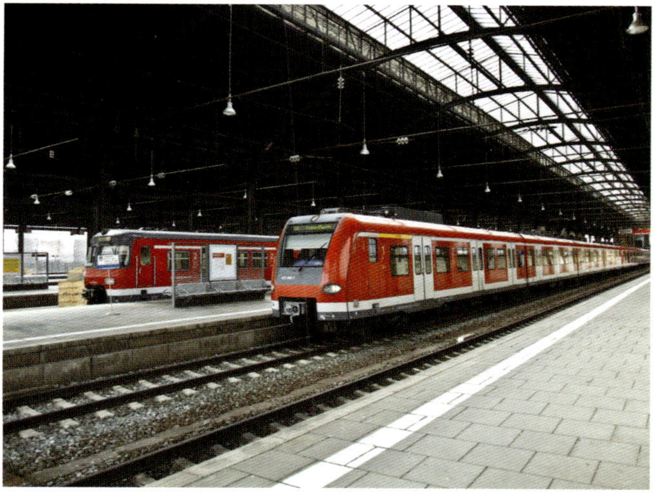

Vocabulary

Active German: Level 4 > Unit 6 > Lesson 1 > Vocabulary

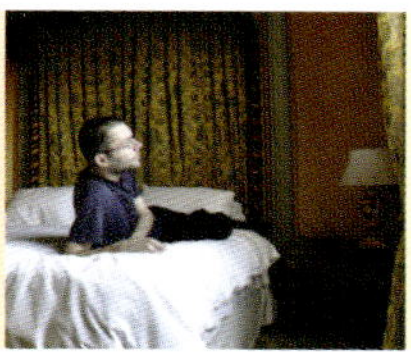

das Doppelzimmer / Doppelzimmer
double room

Ich hätte gerne ein Doppelzimmer.
I would rather have a double room.

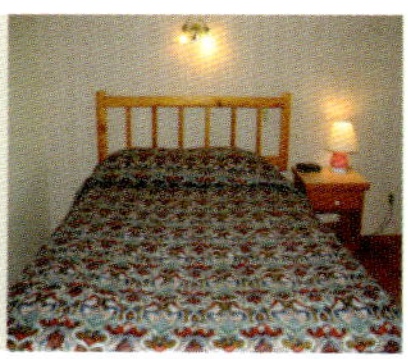

das Einzelzimmer / Einzelzimmer
single room

Möchten Sie ein Einzelzimmer oder ein Doppelzimmer?
Would you like a single room or a double room?

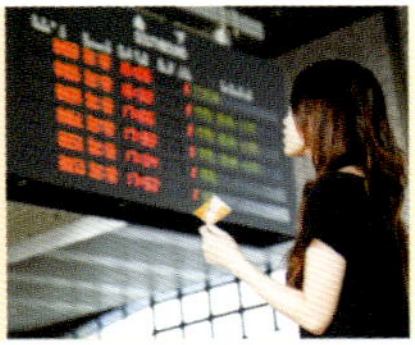

die Abfahrt / Abfahrten
departure

Wo stehen die Abfahrtzeiten?
Where are the departure times?

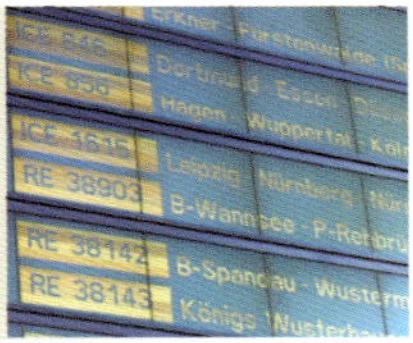

die Ankunft / Ankünfte
arrival

Folgen Sie bitte den Ankunftsschildern.
Please follow the arrival signs.

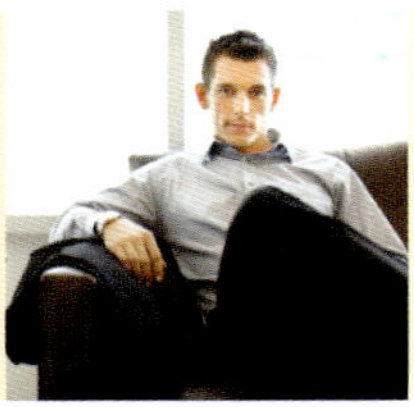

die Geschäftsreise / Geschäftsreisen
business trip

Reisen Sie privat oder ist dies eine Geschäftsreise?
Are you traveling privately or is this a business trip?

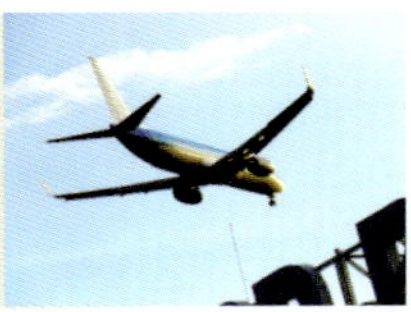

der Flug / Flüge
flight

Wann ist Ihr Flug?
When is your flight?

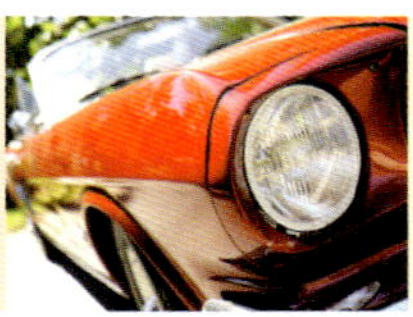

die Fahrt / Fahrten
drive, tour

Wie lange dauert die Fahrt?
How long is the drive?

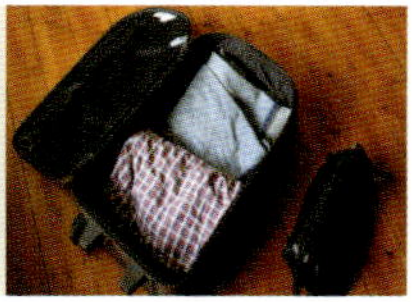

packen
to pack

Hast du schon gepackt?
Have you packed already?

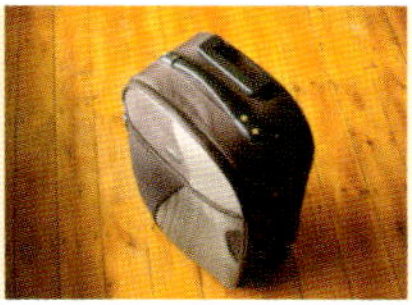

der Koffer / Koffer
suitcase

Wie viele Koffer haben Sie?
How many suitcases do you have?

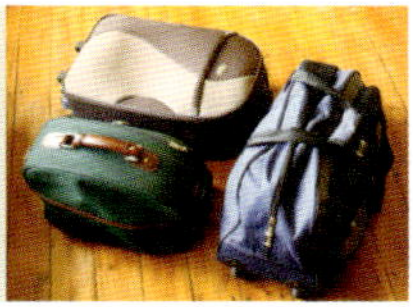

das Gepäck
luggage

Wo ist Ihr Gepäck?
Where is your luggage?

Culture note

Guesthouses (*Pensionen*) provide good-value accommodations in a friendly, informal atmosphere. They cost less than hotels and their furnishings are more basic. The service is limited to room cleaning. *Pensionen* do not generally have a hotel-style kitchen, so the only meal they provide is breakfast. Vacant rooms are often advertised with a *Zimmer frei* (vacancies) sign on the edge of the road or in a window of the house itself.

UNIT 6 › LESSON 2

A trip to Pulheim

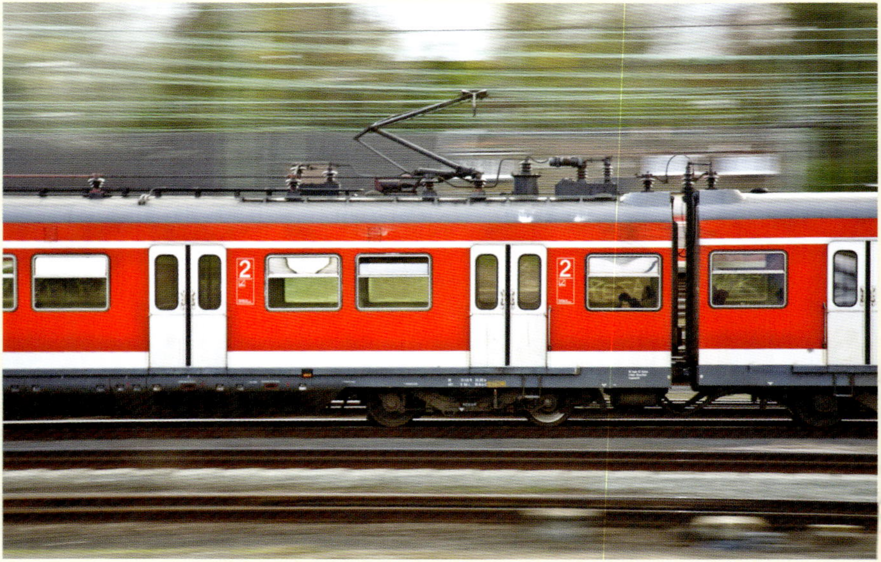

Culture note

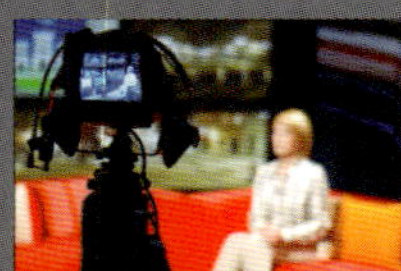

If you are planning a trip to Germany and you are looking for some tips, the travel magazine program *Deutsche Welle (DW) Discover Germany* might be helpful. It guides you to the best locations around the country. Every week DW-TV visits the most interesting German towns and cities and uncovers their hidden charms. *Deutsche Welle* broadcasts online, on TV, and on radio. The international broadcaster's services are targeted at people around the world who are interested in Germany and Europe.

Video Dialog

Having found just the right hotel, Matthias makes the reservation.

Active German: Level 4 > *Unit 6* > *Lesson 2* > *Video dialog*

Lara:	*Waren deine Eltern schon mal in Pulheim?*
Matthias:	*Mein Vater war schon einmal hier, meine Mutter noch nicht.*
Lara:	*Wann genau kommen sie?*
Matthias:	*Mitte Juli, vom 15. bis zum 18.*
Lara:	*Das Zimmer kostet 70 Euro pro Nacht.*
Matthias:	*Ist das Frühstück inklusive?*
Lara:	*Ja.*
Matthias:	*Dann buche ich es gleich. Muss ich jetzt schon bezahlen?*
Lara:	*Nein, noch nicht. Das können deine Eltern machen, wenn sie abreisen.*

Lara:	Have your parents been to Pulheim before?
Matthias:	My father has been here before. My mother hasn't yet.
Lara:	When are they coming exactly?
Matthias:	Mid July, from the 15th to the 18th.
Lara:	A room is 70 euros per night.
Matthias:	Is breakfast included?
Lara:	Yes.
Matthias:	Then I'll book it right now. Do I have to pay now?
Lara:	No, not yet. Your parents can pay when they leave.

Grammar

Active German: Level 4 > Unit 6 > Lesson 2 > Grammar

1 › I haven't been here before

Lara asks Matthias whether his parents have been to Pulheim before.

Waren deine Eltern schon mal in Pulheim?	Have your parents been to Pulheim before?
Mein Vater war schon hier, meine Mutter noch nicht.	My father has been here before. My mother hasn't yet.

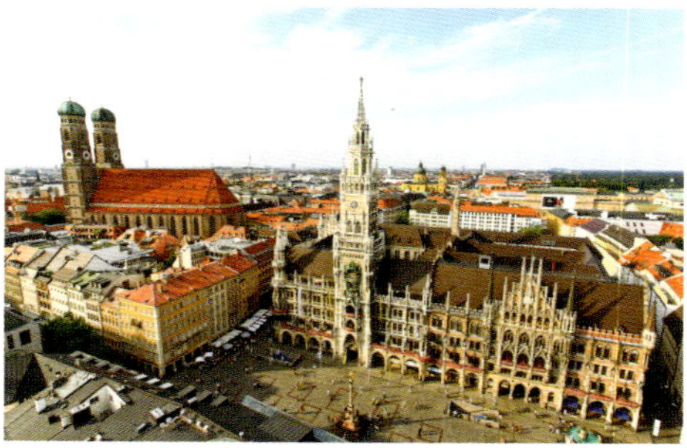

Let's have a closer look at words like *schon* (already) and *noch nicht* (not yet).

In a negative statement:

noch nie (or *noch nicht / nichts*) expresses that something has not yet occurred or does not yet exist.

nicht (or *kein*) *mehr* expresses that something did exist or occur, but that it no longer does.

noch nicht	not yet
Es ist noch nicht zu spät.	It is not yet too late.
noch nie	never before
Ich war noch nie in München.	I have never been to Munich.
nicht mehr	no longer, not anymore
Das Wetter ist nicht mehr schön.	The weather is no longer nice / is not nice anymore.
kein ... mehr	no more ...
Ich habe keine Zeit mehr.	I have no more time.
nichts mehr	anything else, nothing else
Ich möchte nichts mehr.	I don't want anything else.

In a positive statement:

*Warst du **schon** hier? Ja, ich war **schon** hier.*

Have you been here before? Yes, I have been here before.

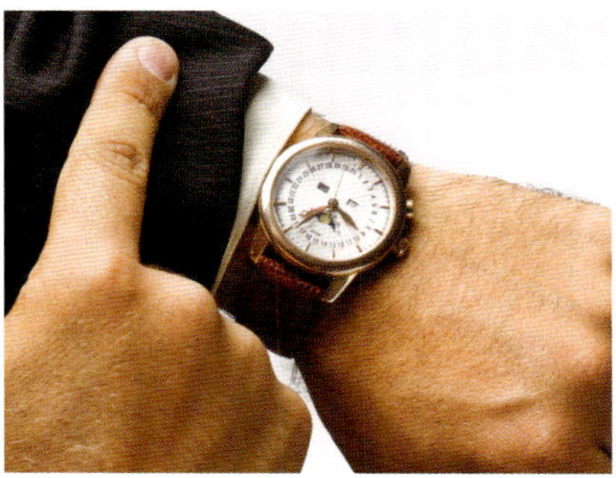

2 › **Nobody**

Jemand (somebody / someone) and *niemand* (nobody / no one) are used to replace nouns. They only have singular forms.

The pronoun *jemand* refers to an indefinite person of either sex.

The pronoun *niemand* is the negation of *jemand*. Its meaning is *kein Mensch* (no one).

Kann mir jemand helfen?
Could somebody help me?

Niemand weiß, wie der Scanner funktioniert.
Nobody knows how the scanner works.

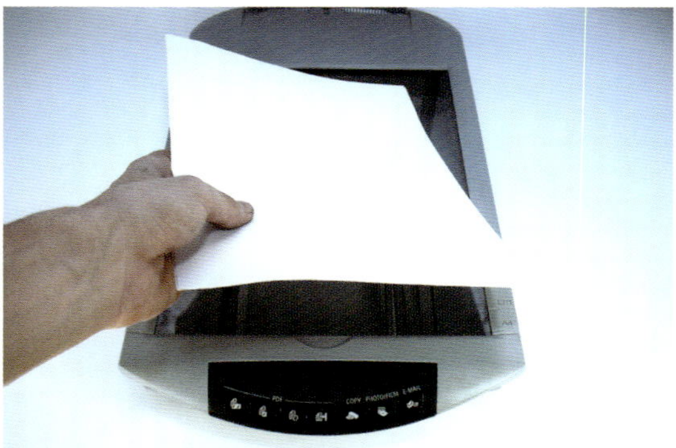

3 › **Ordinal numbers**

In the video dialog Lara and Matthias are talking about dates. In order to do so you use ordinal numbers (first, second, third, etc.). You form them by taking the number itself and adding *-te* to the end.

fünf	*5*	*fünfte*	fifth	*der 5.*	5th
elf	*11*	*elfte*	eleventh	*der 11.*	11th

There some irregular forms:

eins	*1*	*erste*	first	*der 1.*	1st
drei	*3*	*dritte*	third	*der 3.*	3rd
sieben	*7*	*siebte*	seventh	*der 7.*	7th

For the numbers over 20 *-ste* is added:

zwanzig	20	*zwanzigste*	twentieth	*der 20.*	20th
achtundzwanzig	28	*achtundzwanzigste*	twenty-eighth	*der 28.*	28th

Note that the ordinal numbers are indicated by a period in writing.

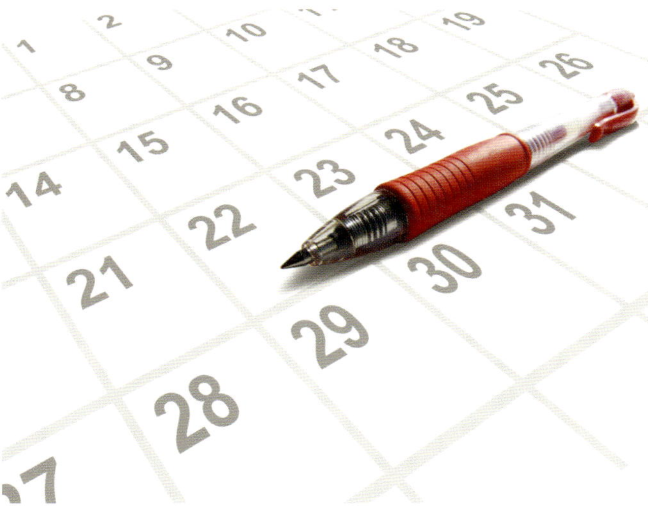

4 › Dates

In German, the full date is given in order: day, month, and year.

den 1.3.2015

March 1st, 2015

Here is how to say on what date something happens or happened:

*Ich bin am 18. (achtzehnt**en**) Januar nach Berlin geflogen.*	I flew to Berlin on January 18th.
*Meine Eltern kommen am 15. (fünfzehnt**en**) Juli an.*	My parents arrive on July 15th.

The ordinal numbers follow the same pattern as the adjective endings which we learned some units ago. But only two endings are used here.

Welches Datum ist heute?

What's the date today?

*Heute ist der 5. (fünft**e**) April.* or
*Heute haben wir den 5. (fünft**en**) April.*

Today is the April 5th.

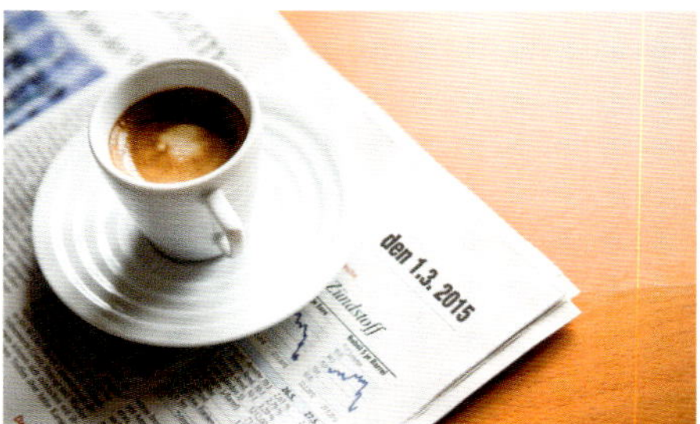

Wann sind Sie geboren?

When were you born?

*Am 5. (fünft**en**) April.*

On April 5th.

Note that there is no "in" before the year:

Ich bin 1970 geboren.

I was born in 1970.

5 › Ordinal numbers

Let's have a look at some other common expressions using ordinal numbers:

das dritte Mal	the third time
die zweite Tür	the second door
die erste Email	the first email
zum ersten Mal	for the first time
zum zweiten Mal	for the second time

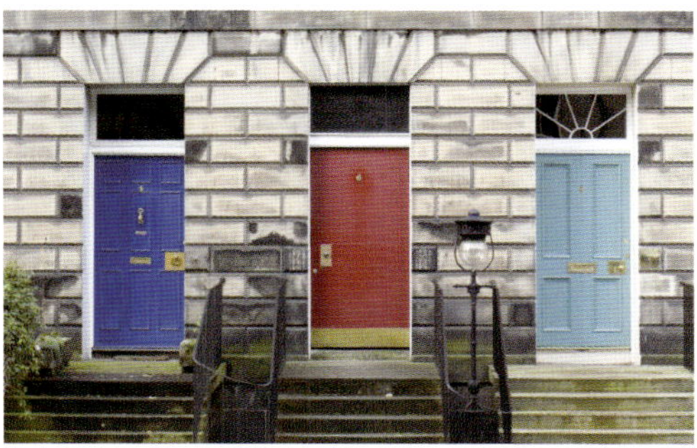

Vocabulary

Active German: Level 4 > *Unit 6* > *Lesson 2* > *Vocabulary*

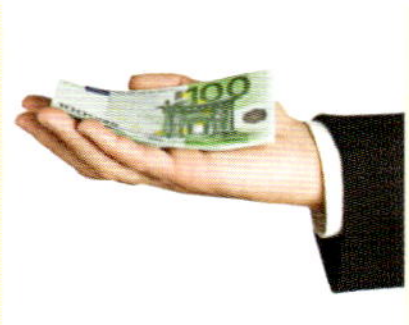

die Währung / Währungen
currency

In Deutschland ist der Euro die Währung.
In Germany the euro is the currency.

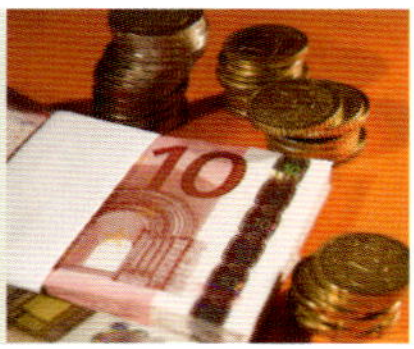

das Geld
money

Hast du noch genug Geld?
Do you still have enough money?

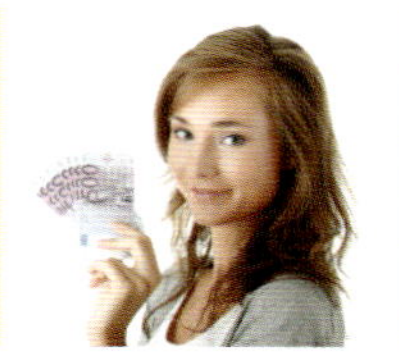

anzahlen
to pay in advance

Man muss 15% anzahlen.
You have to pay 15 percent in advance.

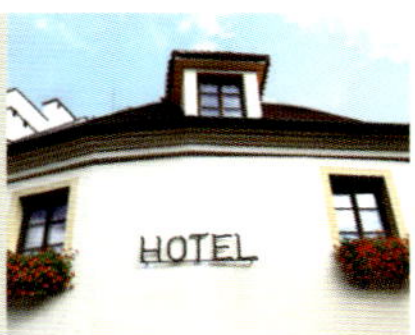

die Unterkunft / Unterkünfte
accommodations

Wir brauchen noch eine Unterkunft in Würzburg.
We still need accommodations in Würzburg.

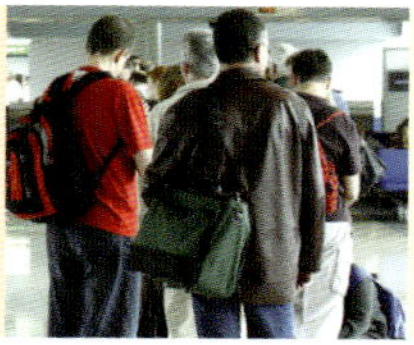

ausgebucht
sold out

Es tut mir leid, aber wir sind ausgebucht.
I'm sorry, but we are sold out.

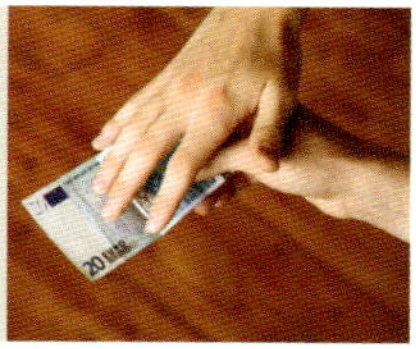

kostenlos
free of charge

Bei uns können Sie kostenlos telefonieren.
You can make free phone calls here.

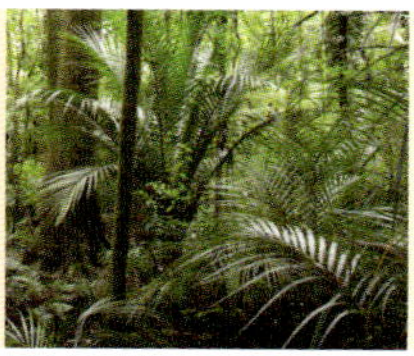

das Abenteuer / Abenteuer
adventure

Ich mache gerne Abenteuerurlaub.
I like to go on adventure trips.

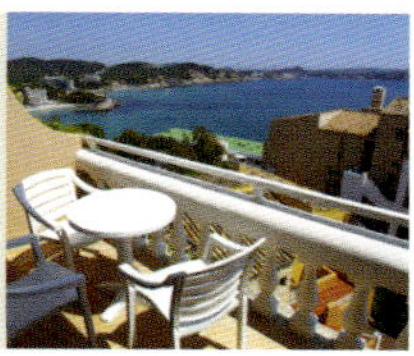

die Aussicht / Aussichten
view

Ich hätte gerne ein Zimmer mit Aussicht aufs Meer.
I would like to a have a room with an ocean view.

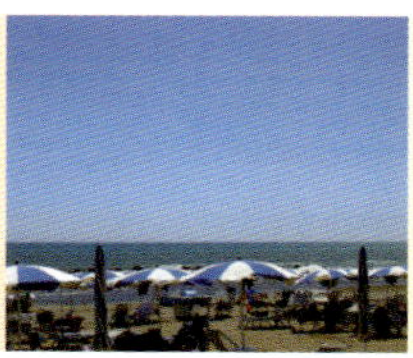

die Saison / Saisons
season

Unsere Hauptsaison ist von März bis Oktober.
Our main season is from March until October.

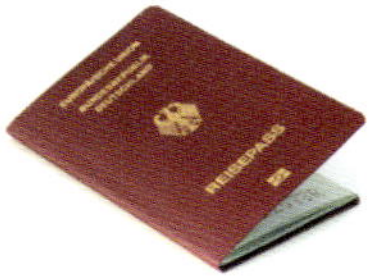

der Reisepass / Reisepässe
passport

Ich brauche Ihren Reisepass.
I need your passport.

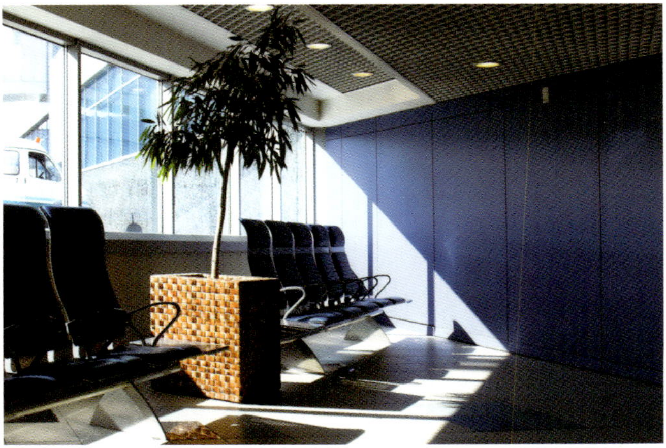

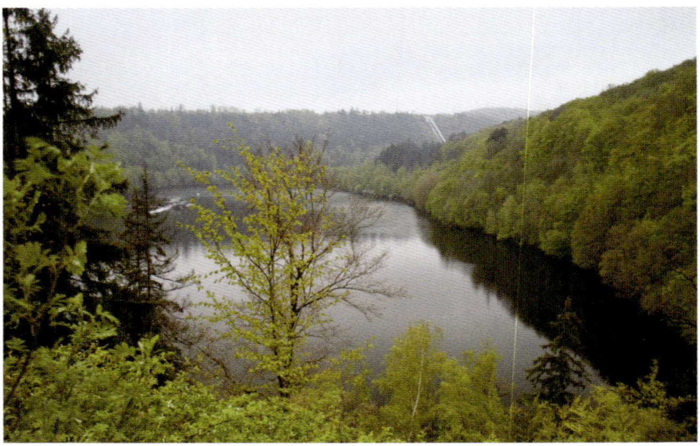